PRECIOUS™
MOMENTS
ILLUSTRATED
FAMILY-TIME
B I B L E

_____

THIS BIBLE BELONGS TO

_____

PRESENTED BY

_____

_____

_____

DATE

Family History

Children In Our Family

NAME _____

BIRTHDAY _____ BIRTHPLACE _____

NAME _____

BIRTHDAY _____ BIRTHPLACE _____

NAME _____

BIRTHDAY _____ BIRTHPLACE _____

NAME _____

BIRTHDAY _____ BIRTHPLACE _____

Mother

NAME _____

BIRTHDAY _____ BIRTHPLACE _____

Father

NAME _____

BIRTHDAY _____ BIRTHPLACE _____

Mother's Family

GRANDMOTHER _____

HER MOM _____

GRANDFATHER _____

GRANDMOTHER _____

HER DAD _____

GRANDFATHER _____

HER BROTHERS _____

HER SISTERS _____

Father's Family

GRANDMOTHER _____

HIS MOM _____

GRANDFATHER _____

GRANDMOTHER _____

HIS DAD _____

GRANDFATHER _____

HIS BROTHERS _____

HIS SISTERS _____

Interesting Family History

_____

_____

_____

_____

_____

Special Family Memories

EVENT _____

_____

_____ DATE _____

EVENT _____

_____

_____ DATE _____

EVENT _____

_____

_____ DATE _____

EVENT _____

_____

_____ DATE _____

EVENT _____

_____

_____ DATE _____

EVENT _____

_____

_____ DATE _____

EVENT _____

_____

_____ DATE _____

EVENT _____

_____

_____ DATE _____

EVENT _____

_____

_____ DATE _____

EVENT _____

_____

_____ DATE _____

EVENT _____

_____

_____ DATE _____

The Ten Commandments

EXODUS 20:3–17

One
You shall have no other gods before Me.

Two
You shall not make for yourself
a carved image.

Three
You shall not take the name of the LORD
your God in vain.

Four
Remember the Sabbath day, to keep it holy.

Five
Honor your father and your mother.

Six
You shall not murder.

Seven
You shall not commit adultery.

Eight
You shall not steal.

Nine
You shall not bear false witness.

Ten
You shall not covet.

The Beatitudes

MATTHEW 5:3–10

Blessed *are* the poor in spirit,
　For theirs is the kingdom of heaven.
Blessed *are* those who mourn,
　For they shall be comforted.
Blessed *are* the meek,
　For they shall inherit the earth.
Blessed *are* those who hunger and
　　thirst for righteousness,
　For they shall be filled.
Blessed *are* the merciful,
　For they shall obtain mercy.
Blessed *are* the pure in heart,
　For they shall see God.
Blessed *are* the peacemakers,
　For they shall be called sons of God.
Blessed *are* those who are persecuted
　　for righteousness' sake,
　For theirs is the kingdom of heaven.

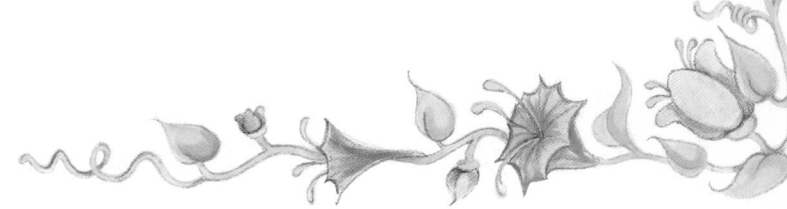

The Lord's Prayer

MATTHEW 6:9–13

Our Father in heaven,
Hallowed be Your name.
Your kingdom come.
Your will be done
On earth as *it is* in heaven.
Give us this day our daily bread.
And forgive us our debts,
As we forgive our debtors.
And do not lead us into temptation,
But deliver us from the evil one.
For Yours is the kingdom and the
    power and the glory forever. Amen.

PRECIOUS™ MOMENTS
ILLUSTRATED
FAMILY-TIME
B I B L E

The New King James Version

with Bible Stories, Family-Time Devotionals,
and Praise, Promise, Prayer Features
written by
V. Gilbert Beers and Ronald A. Beers.

Illustrated by Samuel J. Butcher

THOMAS NELSON PUBLISHERS

Nashville · Atlanta · London · Vancouver

Precious Moments™ Illustrated Family-Time Bible
Copyright © 1994 by Thomas Nelson, Inc.

The Holy Bible, New King James Version
Copyright © 1982 by Thomas Nelson, Inc.

The New King James Bible, New Testament
Copyright © 1979 by Thomas Nelson, Inc.
The New King James Bible, New Testament and Psalms
Copyright © 1980 by Thomas Nelson, Inc.

Bible Stories, Family-Time Devotionals, Praises/Promises/Prayers
Copyright © 1994 by V. Gilbert Beers and Ronald A. Beers

Artwork © 1994 by Samuel J. Butcher

Title page logo: The triquetra (from a Latin word meaning "three-cornered") is an ancient symbol for the Trinity. It comprises three interwoven arcs, distinct yet equal and inseparable, symbolizing that the Father, Son, and Holy Spirit are three distinct yet equal Persons and indivisibly One God.

Table of Contents

A Word to Wise Parents from Gil and Ron Beers

The Illustrated Family-Time Bible is more than a Bible. It is a Bible *plus*—God's Word with a special treasury of delightful devotionals for your child, and for all the family. This special book will help your child fall in love with the Bible. A love for the Word encourages learning from the Word. You don't have to force your child to learn from a book he or she loves. So the key to this special book is to make the Word of God delightful, and to make learning from it a joy. Bible learning then leads to life building.

We're talking about more than raising a child. We are talking about building a life. We are talking about building heritage, enriching and enhancing your child's future, and the future of all whom your child will influence through the years ahead.

You are a wise parent. How do we know? You have acquired this special book because you are concerned for your child's future and want to do something special about it now.

Your child may not recognize all you are trying to do today, but wait a few years. Wait until your child reflects on the wonderful experiences you will have together in this special edition of the Bible. He or she will then "rise up to call you blessed." That may be next year, or twenty years from now. But it will happen.

Parents we have met are deeply interested in helping their children develop strong character. Most of them realize that character comes from strong belief, and that the truths of God's Word are the building blocks of that strong belief. What these parents want is a simple, easy-to-use, yet delightful and forceful program that helps them build that belief and character in their children. This book offers exactly what they say they want. Together, families can have fun, enjoy the Bible, and learn its life-changing truths.

Above all else, help your child to enjoy family times with the Bible. That keeps her coming back again and again. That assures a lifetime of Bible learning for him.

Family-Time Devotionals

"On location," right in the Bible text, we have built 280 family devotional times, Bible-learning and life-building times. Seven different titles indicate some of the key learning approaches you will find.

What Should I Do?

The Bible is God's answer book to life's little, and not-so-little, problems. What should I do when I face a problem? The answer: seek God's advice. We make it easy and enjoyable to deal with mistakes, learn to say "I'm sorry," get a handle on sharing, cope with loneliness, and dozens of other problems. This

is the stuff where God's wonderful truths come down to "Main Street" to meet us where we have needs.

What the Bible Says

Does doctrine sound too heavy for your child, even your little child? It can be. But it doesn't need to be. We can make doctrine complicated, but it really is as simple as "Jesus loves me." That's a key doctrine. In this special family Bible, we make doctrine super simple and right to the point for even a young child. You and your child will learn almost 40 key doctrines for families and children, but that learning will be an experience of delight. "Doctrine" is simply truth about God, life-changing truth. It's the stuff from which He builds godly lives, isn't it?

Values

Values has been much in the news lately. That's because the absence of values makes news—dysfunctional behavior, broken families, broken lives, ungodly conduct. Values are the building blocks of character—truthfulness, generosity, sharing, thankfulness, obedience, and others. If someone asks, "What do you want your child to become?" you will soon get on the subject of character, and that leads to a list of values. We could call them character values. Ultimately each of these flows from Bible truth. Truthfulness comes from the Bible truth that "God is truth." Thankfulness comes from the Bible teaching about gratitude. Loving others flows from "God is love." Many of the special devotionals in this Bible focus on values.

Family Memories

Heritage is woven from family memories. We remember those special experiences we shared as a family and this is a bonding force for our family. Bible truth is learned with joy in the context of joyful family experiences, and these form the fabric of memories, good memories, memories we want to tuck into our memory bank and keep for a lifetime. These features are family memory builders with the Word.

Family Friends

Some of our friends reflect Bible characters. As we observe them, we learn about Bible people. And as we observe Bible people, we learn more about our friends. This is a friend-enhancing feature through which we learn Bible and bond with friends at the same time.

Favorite Bible Words

Some words are special Bible words—resurrection, crucifixion, salvation, Good News. They are not the stuff from which newspapers and magazines are made, but they are powerful little bullets which pack great truth. They are words that your child should learn in the context of special family Bible

times. How can we think about Jesus, for example, without thinking of crucifixion and resurrection? And how can we think of living for Jesus without capturing the vital truth of Jesus' crucifixion and resurrection? These favorite Bible words are powerful points of Bible light.

Favorite Family Verses

Scattered throughout the Bible are special verses, so important that we want to memorize them or focus our lives on their special truths. How can we focus on Jesus without reflecting on John 3:16? Many of us have memorized special verses which keep coming to our mind again and again throughout our lives, giving us special answers when we wrestle with special problems.

These seven titles give you a choice of seven different approaches to family devotions. In addition, the devotionals discuss family-life topics, such as "Choices," "Facing Trials," "Forgiveness" (see p. xvi). Chain references at the bottom of each page will help you locate more devotionals on the same *topic,* or by the same *title.* So your family can choose to read all the devotionals on a particular *title* (for example, "What the Bible Says" or "Family Memories"). Or you can follow a particular *topic* (such as "Sharing" or "Thankfulness").

Praises, Promises, Prayers

Yet another approach to family devotions focuses on the place of praise, promise, and prayer in our relationship with God. Throughout the Bible text 90 important Bible praises, promises, and prayers are shaded and accompanied by devotional thoughts for enriching our spiritual experiences.

Bible Praises

Are there times when God does something special for you? Praise Him. Our talks with God should be much more than just asking Him for things. Praise means telling God how wonderful He is and how much you love Him. Inside the Bible 30 praise features walk you and your child into the presence of God to praise Him.

Bible Promises

When God promises something, you know it will happen. The power of a promise is wrapped up in the person of promise. As you read 30 of God's great promises, a key truth for children, and parents, will emerge: God *always* keeps His promises. Seeing how God keeps promises will impress upon us the importance of keeping our promises, as well.

Bible Prayers

Prayer is a powerful connection between us and God. It is so much more than "saying prayers"; prayer is communicating with the Creator. Bible prayers are key learning centers that help us discover the power of God.

Throughout the Bible 30 features highlight some of the most important prayers.

Bible Stories

How many of the great Bible Stories could you name? In this special Bible we highlight *the 100 greatest stories* where each appears in the Bible. With each you will find an interesting introduction to "get you into the story" and a short interesting quiz to capture what you and your child learned. When a story occurs more than once in the Bible, cross-references guide you to the location of the story introduction and quiz (see Matt. 4:22, p. 1451).

Illustrations

Visuals To Reinforce Learning

Powerful visuals, 200 in all, reinforce the truths you learn. We learn through the eye gate as well as through the ear gate. This special Bible is rich in visuals to make learning not only powerful, but delightful.

Family Time Together

Start today on this wonderful family-building program. As you watch God's footprints and fingerprints on your child's life, you will be so very grateful for those little family times with the Word. Keep family Bible times short. Send children away a little hungry and they will want to come back. Send them away force-fed and they will be reluctant to return to the family Bible circle. Keep family Bible times delightful, fun-filled times. Be there yourself, for your part is intimately tied to the power of your presence. You will discover that this wonderful time that you spend with your child and God's Word is the greatest investment you will ever make.

Bible Stories

Praises

Promises

Prayers

What the Bible Says

What Should I Do?

What Should I Do? *continued*

What Should I Do? *continued*

Values

Values *continued*

Family Memories

Family Memories *continued*

Family Friends

Favorite Bible Words

Favorite Family Verses

Devotional Topics

The devotionals of *The Illustrated Family-Time Bible* discuss topics that affect family life today. To read all of the devotionals on a particular topic, turn to the page number listed below. That page is the *first page* of a chain of devotionals on the listed topic. Then follow the chain references at the bottom of each page to find more devotionals on that topic.

Your Child and the New King James Version

You will be happy to know that the text of *The Illustrated Family-Time Bible,* which is called the New King James Version, is especially suitable for the young.

It is not a brand new version, but the traditional King James Version that has been beloved for centuries, but where necessary, brought up to date in language. One hundred and thirty scholars and laymen from all the English-speaking countries spent seven years to insure the accuracy, readability, and beauty of this Bible.

If you went to Sunday school and had to memorize verses, you probably remember that, while it was not necessarily difficult to memorize obsolete words, unusual word order or strange verb endings, they were a hindrance to *understanding*. This Bible overcomes those problems for your children very nicely. For example, the *thee's, thou's, ye's, thy's,* and *thine's* (and other similar archaic pronouns) have been replaced by today's *you* and *your*. Long sentences have been broken into two, without leaving anything out or changing the meaning. No doctrine has been changed and not a single verse has been eliminated, which is by no means true of all modern Bibles.

Probably the three most beloved and memorized Bible texts are the Lord's Prayer, the Twenty-third Psalm, and John 3:16. If you have learned any or all of these in years gone by you will see how similar the NKJV is to the King James Version.

Yet the small changes add up to increased understanding, especially for children.

Look at the Lord's Prayer, for example (Matt. 6:9–13, p. 1457). The main differences are that *thee* and *thy* have changed to *You* and *Your*. Notice that they have been capitalized to show honor for deity. This is a standard practice. Also observe that the ending of the Lord's Prayer, "for Yours is the kingdom and the power and the glory forever" is not eliminated, as in many Bibles. While some manuscripts do lack this ending, most have it, and there is nothing to be gained by deleting this beautiful portion of the prayer.

Psalm 23 (p. 829) is another passage that many children learn by heart. The changes in this lovely Psalm consist almost entirely of changing the pronouns and especially the obsolete ending *-eth* to *-es* in the old forms *maketh, leadeth, restoreth,* and so forth. Even the somewhat old-fashioned "Yea" is retained in verse four because it is so very famous.

In John 3:16 (p. 1617) the only change from the old King James is that "whosoever believeth" is updated to "whoever believes."

Children and young people have been tested regarding the readability and understandability of the NKJV text. Children can understand the language of the NKJV four grade levels sooner than they can understand the old King James. This certainly makes a sound Christian education more accessible at an earlier age.

47 "And if you greet your brethren*a* only, what do you do more *than others?* Do not even the tax collectors*b* do so?

As you read, you will often see a raised letter in the biblical text. Each raised letter designates a New King James footnote, to be found at the foot of the right-hand column of text. Each footnote is designated by the chapter and verse in which its raised letter is contained. Then you will see the raised letter, followed by the footnote. (The letter *a* is used for the first footnote connected to each verse. If a verse has more than one footnote connected to it, then the second footnote receives the letter *b*. The chapter and verse are not repeated in such cases.)

New King James footnotes contain helpful information about significant textual variations and alternate translations, as well as some explanations and references to other passages of Scripture.

Footnotes concerning textual variations make no evaluation of readings, but do clearly indicate the manuscript sources of readings. They objectively present the facts without such remarks as "the best manuscripts omit" or "the most reliable manuscripts read," which are value judgments that differ according to varying viewpoints on the text.

Where significant variations occur in the New Testament Greek manuscripts, textual notes are classified as follows:

1. NU-Text

These variations from the traditional text represent the text as published in the twenty-seventh edition of the Nestle-Aland Greek New Testament (N) and in the United Bible Societies' fourth edition (U), hence the abbreviation, "NU-Text."

heard for their many words.

6:4 *a*NU-Text omits *openly.* 6:6 *a*NU-Text omits *openly.*

2. M-Text

These variations from the traditional text represent the Majority Text, which is based on the majority of surviving manuscripts. It should be noted that M stands for whatever reading is printed in the published *The Greek New Testament According to the Majority Text,* whether supported by overwhelming, strong, or only a divided majority textual tradition.

4   But He answered and said, "It is

3:11 *a*M-Text omits *and fire.* 3:16 *a*Or *he*

The textual notes reflect the scholarship of the past 150 years and will assist the reader to observe the variations between the different manuscript traditions of the New Testament. Such information is generally not available in English translations of the New Testament.

The
Old Testament

The
Old Testament

GENESIS

THE HISTORY OF CREATION

Once there was only God, and nothing else. Then He decided to make the world. This is how He did it.

IN the beginning God created the heavens and the earth.

2 The earth was without form, and void; and darkness *was*ᵃ on the face of the deep. And the Spirit of God was hovering over the face of the waters.

3 Then God said, "Let there be light"; and there was light.

4 And God saw the light, that *it was* good; and God divided the light from the darkness.

5 God called the light Day, and the darkness He called Night. So the evening and the morning were the first day.

6 Then God said, "Let there be a firmament in the midst of the waters, and let it divide the waters from the waters."

7 Thus God made the firmament, and divided the waters which *were* under the firmament from the waters which *were* above the firmament; and it was so.

8 And God called the firmament Heaven. So the evening and the morning were the second day.

9 Then God said, "Let the waters under the heavens be gathered together into one place, and let the dry *land* appear"; and it was so.

10 And God called the dry *land* Earth, and the gathering together of the waters He called Seas. And God saw that *it was* good.

11 Then God said, "Let the earth bring forth grass, the herb *that* yields seed, *and* the fruit tree *that* yields fruit according to its kind, whose seed *is* in itself, on the earth"; and it was so.

12 And the earth brought forth grass, the herb *that* yields seed according to its kind, and the tree *that* yields fruit, whose seed *is* in itself according to its kind. And God saw that *it was* good.

13 So the evening and the morning were the third day.

14 Then God said, "Let there be lights in the firmament of the heavens to divide the day from the night; and let them be for signs and seasons, and for days and years;

15 "and let them be for lights in the firmament of the heavens to give light on the earth"; and it was so.

16 Then God made two great lights: the greater light to rule the day, and the lesser light to rule the night. *He made* the stars also.

17 God set them in the firmament of the heavens to give light on the earth,

18 and to rule over the day and over the night, and to divide the light from the darkness. And God saw that *it was* good.

19 So the evening and the morning were the fourth day.

20 Then God said, "Let the waters abound with an abundance of living creatures, and let birds fly above the earth across the face of the firmament of the heavens."

21 So God created great sea creatures and every living thing that moves, with which the waters abounded, according to their kind, and every winged bird according to its kind. And God saw that *it was* good.

22 And God blessed them, saying,

1:2 ᵃWords in italic type have been added for clarity. They are not found in the original Hebrew or Aramaic.

ABOUT GOD'S PROVISION Genesis 1:6–10

God Gives Us Water

Suppose every drop of water in the world disappeared tomorrow morning. How long would the world survive? What would you drink? What would water crops and gardens? What would animals drink? How long would it be before everything on earth died? Do you think water is important? Does God think it is important?

1. Who gives us water? Read Genesis 1:6–10. Would you like to have seen God do this?
2. Think of all the ways you use water. How many can you name? Have you thanked God today for giving you water? Remember to thank Him each day.

For more on *What the Bible Says* turn to page 3
For more on *God's Care* turn to page 3

What the Bible Says

ABOUT GOD'S PROVISION Genesis 1:29

Who Gives Us Food to Eat?
Where do you get most of your food? Does your mother or father go to a grocery store? But what if there were no grocery stores? Where would you get your food? People sometimes must fish for food, or gather berries or fruit or grain. Bible-time people had no grocery stores, but God still gave them food to eat. Thank You, God. You provide!

1. Who gives us food to eat? Read Genesis 1:29. Thank You, God.
2. Who gives us cows for milk, animals for meat, bushes and vines for berries, trees for fruit and a sea full of fish? Thank You, God.
3. Can you think of any food that does not come from God? There is none. God gives us every kind of food. But He gives it in different ways.
4. Ask mother and father to tell you about some things that make your favorite foods—such as pancakes, ice cream, or birthday cake. What kinds of food do they use to make each of these?

For more on *What the Bible Says* turn to page 16
For more on *God's Care* turn to page 14

"Be fruitful and multiply, and fill the waters in the seas, and let birds multiply on the earth."

23 So the evening and the morning were the fifth day.

24 Then God said, "Let the earth bring forth the living creature according to its kind: cattle and creeping thing and beast of the earth, *each* according to its kind"; and it was so.

25 And God made the beast of the earth according to its kind, cattle according to its kind, and everything that creeps on the earth according to its kind. And God saw that *it was* good.

26 Then God said, "Let Us make man in Our image, according to Our likeness; let them have dominion over the fish of the sea, over the birds of the air, and over the cattle, over all*a* the earth and over every creeping thing that creeps on the earth."

27 So God created man in His *own* image; in the image of God He created him; male and female He created them.

28 Then God blessed them, and God said to them, "Be fruitful and multiply; fill the earth and subdue it; have dominion over the fish of the sea, over the birds of the air, and over every living thing that moves on the earth."

29 And God said, "See, I have given you every herb *that* yields seed which *is* on the face of all the earth, and every tree whose fruit yields seed; to you it shall be for food.

30 "Also, to every beast of the earth, to every bird of the air, and to everything that creeps on the earth, in which *there is* life, *I have given* every green herb for food"; and it was so.

1:26 *a*Syriac reads *all the wild animals of.*

31 Then God saw everything that He had made, and indeed *it was* very good. So the evening and the morning were the sixth day.

2 Thus the heavens and the earth, and all the host of them, were finished.

2 And on the seventh day God ended His work which He had done, and He rested on the seventh day from all His work which He had done.

3 Then God blessed the seventh day and sanctified it, because in it He rested from all His work which God had created and made.

4 This *is* the history*a* of the heavens and the earth when they were created, in the day that the LORD God made the earth and the heavens,

5 before any plant of the field was in the earth and before any herb of the field had grown. For the LORD God had not caused it to rain on the earth, and *there was* no man to till the ground;

6 but a mist went up from the earth and watered the whole face of the ground.

7 And the LORD God formed man *of* the dust of the ground, and breathed into his nostrils the breath of life; and man became a living being.

LIFE IN GOD'S GARDEN

8 The LORD God planted a garden eastward in Eden, and there He put the man whom He had formed.

9 And out of the ground the LORD God made every tree grow that is pleasant to the sight and good for food. The tree of life *was* also in the midst of the garden, and the tree of the knowledge of good and evil.

10 Now a river went out of Eden to water the garden, and from there it parted and became four riverheads.

11 The name of the first *is* Pī'shon; it *is* the one which skirts the whole land of Hav'i·lah, where *there is* gold.

12 And the gold of that land *is* good. Bdellium and the onyx stone *are* there.

13 The name of the second river *is* Gī'hon; it *is* the one which goes around the whole land of Cush.

14 The name of the third river *is* Hid'de·kel;*a* it *is* the one which goes toward the east of Assyria. The fourth river *is* the Eū·phrā'tēs.

15 Then the LORD God took the man and put him in the garden of Eden to tend and keep it.

16 And the LORD God commanded the man, saying, "Of every tree of the garden you may freely eat;

17 "but of the tree of the knowledge of good and evil you shall not eat, for in the day that you eat of it you shall surely die."

18 And the LORD God said, "*It is* not good that man should be alone; I will make him a helper comparable to him."

19 Out of the ground the LORD God formed every beast of the field and every bird of the air, and brought *them* to Adam to see what he would call them. And whatever Adam called each living creature, that *was* its name.

20 So Adam gave names to all cattle, to the birds of the air, and to every beast of the field. But for Adam there was not found a helper comparable to him.

21 And the LORD God caused a deep sleep to fall on Adam, and he slept; and He took one of his ribs, and closed up the flesh in its place.

22 Then the rib which the LORD God had taken from man He made into a woman, and He brought her to the man.

2:4 *a*Hebrew *toledoth*, literally *generations*
2:14 *a*Or *Tigris*

23 And Adam said:

"This *is* now bone of my bones
And flesh of my flesh;
She shall be called Woman,
Because she was taken out of
　Man."

24 Therefore a man shall leave his father and mother and be joined to his wife, and they shall become one flesh.
25 And they were both naked, the man and his wife, and were not ashamed.

☑ *Bible Quiz*

Genesis 1; 2 **God Makes the World**

1. What did God make first? What did He make second?
2. How did God feel about what He made?
3. How many days did it take God to make the world?
4. What can you make?
5. Can you make something from nothing? Can God? What does this say about God?

THE TEMPTATION AND FALL OF MAN

It didn't seem wrong. Just one bite of that delicious fruit. What harm could it do? But God had told Adam and Eve not to eat that fruit. Would they really disobey God? Would they take a bite and change the world forever?

3 Now the serpent was more cunning than any beast of the field which the LORD God had made. And he said to the woman, "Has God indeed said, 'You shall not eat of every tree of the garden'?"
2 And the woman said to the serpent, "We may eat the fruit of the trees of the garden;
3 "but of the fruit of the tree which *is* in the midst of the garden, God has said, 'You shall not eat it, nor shall you touch it, lest you die.' "
4 Then the serpent said to the woman, "You will not surely die.
5 "For God knows that in the day you eat of it your eyes will be opened, and you will be like God, knowing good and evil."
6 So when the woman saw that the tree *was* good for food, that it *was* pleasant to the eyes, and a tree desirable to make *one* wise, she took of its fruit and ate. She also gave to her husband with her, and he ate.
7 Then the eyes of both of them were opened, and they knew that they *were* naked; and they sewed fig leaves together and made themselves coverings.
8 And they heard the sound of the LORD God walking in the garden in the cool of the day, and Adam and his wife hid themselves from the presence of the LORD God among the trees of the garden.
9 Then the LORD God called to Adam and said to him, "Where *are* you?"
10 So he said, "I heard Your voice in the garden, and I was afraid because I was naked; and I hid myself."
11 And He said, "Who told you that you *were* naked? Have you eaten from the tree of which I commanded you that you should not eat?"
12 Then the man said, "The woman whom You gave *to be* with me, she gave me of the tree, and I ate."
13 And the LORD God said to the woman, "What *is* this you have

What Should I Do?

SOMETHING FREE ISN'T ALWAYS FREE Genesis 3:1–6

Little bear wanted some honey. It looked free. All he had to do was take it. But you can see that it wasn't quite free. Little bear paid a price. What was it?

1. Little bear's price for the honey was a bee sting. He will feel that for a long time. The honey seemed free. But he did pay a price.
2. A little sin may seem free, like it wouldn't cost you anything. But it may hurt you. It may cost you a lot of hurt for a long, long time. Is it worth it?

For more on *What Should I Do?* turn to page 44
For more on *Sin* turn to page 255

done?" The woman said, "The serpent deceived me, and I ate."

14 So the LORD God said to the serpent:

"Because you have done this,
  You *are* cursed more than all
    cattle,
  And more than every beast of the
    field;
  On your belly you shall go,
  And you shall eat dust
  All the days of your life.
15 And I will put enmity
  Between you and the woman,
  And between your seed and her
    Seed;
  He shall bruise your head,
  And you shall bruise His heel."

16 To the woman He said:

"I will greatly multiply your
    sorrow and your conception;
  In pain you shall bring forth
    children;
  Your desire *shall be* for your
    husband,
  And he shall rule over you."

17 Then to Adam He said, "Because you have heeded the voice of your wife, and have eaten from the tree of which I commanded you, saying, 'You shall not eat of it':

"Cursed *is* the ground for your
    sake;
  In toil you shall eat *of* it
  All the days of your life.
18 Both thorns and thistles it shall
    bring forth for you,
  And you shall eat the herb of the
    field.
19 In the sweat of your face you shall
    eat bread

Till you return to the ground,
For out of it you were taken;
For dust you *are*,
And to dust you shall return."

20 And Adam called his wife's name Eve, because she was the mother of all living.
21 Also for Adam and his wife the LORD God made tunics of skin, and clothed them.
22 Then the LORD God said, "Behold, the man has become like one of Us, to know good and evil. And now, lest he put out his hand and take also of the tree of life, and eat, and live forever"—
23 therefore the LORD God sent him out of the garden of Eden to till the ground from which he was taken.
24 So He drove out the man; and He placed cherubim at the east of the garden of Eden, and a flaming sword which turned every way, to guard the way to the tree of life.

☑ *Bible Quiz*

Genesis 3 **Adam and Eve Are Tempted**

1. Who was the serpent?
2. What did He want Eve to do?
3. Why do you think Adam and Eve ate the fruit?
4. What happened after they ate the fruit?
5. In what ways are you tempted to do wrong?
6. How can you keep from doing wrong and do what is right?

CAIN MURDERS ABEL

*Have you ever been so angry
with someone that you felt like
hitting him? Be careful!
Something terrible happened
when a brother let his anger
get the best of him.*

4 Now Adam knew Eve his wife,
and she conceived and bore Cain, and
said, "I have acquired a man from the
LORD."
2   Then she bore again, this time his
brother Abel. Now Abel was a keeper
of sheep, but Cain was a tiller of the
ground.
3   And in the process of time it came
to pass that Cain brought an offering
of the fruit of the ground to the
LORD.
4   Abel also brought of the firstborn
of his flock and of their fat. And the
LORD respected Abel and his offering,
5   but He did not respect Cain and
his offering. And Cain was very angry, and his countenance fell.
6   So the LORD said to Cain, "Why
are you angry? And why has your
countenance fallen?
7   "If you do well, will you not be accepted? And if you do not do well, sin
lies at the door. And its desire *is* for
you, but you should rule over it."
8   Now Cain talked with Abel his
brother;*a* and it came to pass, when
they were in the field, that Cain rose
up against Abel his brother and
killed him.
9   Then the LORD said to Cain,
"Where *is* Abel your brother?" He
said, "I do not know. *Am* I my
brother's keeper?"
10   And He said, "What have you
done? The voice of your brother's
blood cries out to Me from the
ground.
11   "So now you *are* cursed from the
earth, which has opened its mouth to

receive your brother's blood from
your hand.
12   "When you till the ground, it shall
no longer yield its strength to you. A
fugitive and a vagabond you shall be
on the earth."
13   And Cain said to the LORD, "My
punishment *is* greater than I can bear!
14   "Surely You have driven me out
this day from the face of the ground;
I shall be hidden from Your face; I
shall be a fugitive and a vagabond on
the earth, and it will happen *that*
anyone who finds me will kill me."
15   And the LORD said to him, "Therefore,*a* whoever kills Cain, vengeance
shall be taken on him sevenfold."
And the LORD set a mark on Cain, lest
anyone finding him should kill him.

☑   *Bible Quiz*

Genesis 4:1–15   **Cain Kills Abel**

1.   What offering did Cain
     bring to God? What did Abel
     bring?
2.   How did Cain feel when God
     didn't accept his offering?
3.   What did God tell Cain he
     should do to get rid of his
     anger? What did Cain do
     instead?
4.   What makes you angry?
5.   When you get angry at
     friends, brothers, or sisters,
     do you feel like hurting
     them or saying something
     unkind to them? Why?
6.   What would God want us to
     do when we are angry with
     someone? How does God say
     we can get rid of our anger?

4:8 *a*Samaritan Pentateuch, Septuagint, Syriac,
and Vulgate add *"Let us go out to the field."*
4:15 *a*Following Masoretic Text and Targum; Septuagint, Syriac, and Vulgate read *Not so.*

THE FAMILY OF CAIN

16 Then Cain went out from the presence of the LORD and dwelt in the land of Nod on the east of Eden.

17 And Cain knew his wife, and she conceived and bore Ē'noch. And he built a city, and called the name of the city after the name of his son—Ē'noch.

18 To Ē'noch was born Ī'rad; and Ī'rad begot Me·hū'ja·el, and Me·hū'ja·el begot Me·thū'sha·el, and Me·thū'sha·el begot Lā'mech.

19 Then Lā'mech took for himself two wives: the name of one *was* Ā'dah, and the name of the second *was* Zil'lah.

20 And Ā'dah bore Jā'bal. He was the father of those who dwell in tents and have livestock.

21 His brother's name *was* Jū'bal. He was the father of all those who play the harp and flute.

22 And as for Zil'lah, she also bore Tū'bal-Cāin, an instructor of every craftsman in bronze and iron. And the sister of Tū'bal-Cāin *was* Nā'amah.

23 Then Lā'mech said to his wives:

"Ā'dah and Zil'lah, hear my voice;
Wives of Lā'mech, listen to my speech!
For I have killed a man for wounding me,
Even a young man for hurting me.
24 If Cain shall be avenged sevenfold,
Then Lā'mech seventy-sevenfold."

A NEW SON

25 And Adam knew his wife again, and she bore a son and named him Seth, "For God has appointed another seed for me instead of Abel, whom Cain killed."

26 And as for Seth, to him also a son was born; and he named him Ē'nosh.*a* Then *men* began to call on the name of the LORD.

THE FAMILY OF ADAM

5 This is the book of the genealogy of Adam. In the day that God created man, He made him in the likeness of God.

2 He created them male and female, and blessed them and called them Mankind in the day they were created.

3 And Adam lived one hundred and thirty years, and begot *a son* in his own likeness, after his image, and named him Seth.

4 After he begot Seth, the days of Adam were eight hundred years; and he had sons and daughters.

5 So all the days that Adam lived were nine hundred and thirty years; and he died.

6 Seth lived one hundred and five years, and begot Ē'nosh.

7 After he begot Ē'nosh, Seth lived eight hundred and seven years, and had sons and daughters.

8 So all the days of Seth were nine hundred and twelve years; and he died.

9 Ē'nosh lived ninety years, and begot Cā·ī'nan.*a*

10 After he begot Cā·ī'nan, Ē'nosh lived eight hundred and fifteen years, and had sons and daughters.

11 So all the days of Ē'nosh were nine hundred and five years; and he died.

12 Cā·ī'nan lived seventy years, and begot Ma·hal'a·lel.

13 After he begot Ma·hal'a·lel, Cā·ī'nan lived eight hundred and forty years, and had sons and daughters.

4:26 *a*Greek *Enos*   5:9 *a*Hebrew *Qenan*

14 So all the days of Cā·ī'nan were nine hundred and ten years; and he died.

15 Ma·hal'a·lel lived sixty-five years, and begot Jar'ed.

16 After he begot Jar'ed, Ma·hal'a·lel lived eight hundred and thirty years, and had sons and daughters.

17 So all the days of Ma·hal'a·lel were eight hundred and ninety-five years; and he died.

18 Jar'ed lived one hundred and sixty-two years, and begot Ē'noch.

19 After he begot Ē'noch, Jar'ed lived eight hundred years, and had sons and daughters.

20 So all the days of Jar'ed were nine hundred and sixty-two years; and he died.

21 Ē'noch lived sixty-five years, and begot Me·thū'se·lah.

22 After he begot Me·thū'se·lah, Ē'noch walked with God three hundred years, and had sons and daughters.

23 So all the days of Ē'noch were three hundred and sixty-five years.

24 And Ē'noch walked with God; and he *was* not, for God took him.

25 Me·thū'se·lah lived one hundred and eighty-seven years, and begot Lā'mech.

26 After he begot Lā'mech, Me·thū'se·lah lived seven hundred and eighty-two years, and had sons and daughters.

27 So all the days of Me·thū'se·lah were nine hundred and sixty-nine years; and he died.

28 Lā'mech lived one hundred and eighty-two years, and had a son.

29 And he called his name Noah, saying, "This *one* will comfort us concerning our work and the toil of our hands, because of the ground which the LORD has cursed."

30 After he begot Noah, Lā'mech lived five hundred and ninety-five years, and had sons and daughters.

31 So all the days of Lā'mech were seven hundred and seventy-seven years; and he died.

32 And Noah was five hundred years old, and Noah begot Shem, Ham, and Jā'pheth.

THE WICKEDNESS AND JUDGMENT OF MAN

6 Now it came to pass, when men began to multiply on the face of the earth, and daughters were born to them,

2 that the sons of God saw the daughters of men, that they *were* beautiful; and they took wives for themselves of all whom they chose.

3 And the LORD said, "My Spirit shall not strive*a* with man forever, for he *is* indeed flesh; yet his days shall be one hundred and twenty years."

4 There were giants on the earth in those days, and also afterward, when the sons of God came in to the daughters of men and they bore *children* to them. Those *were* the mighty men who *were* of old, men of renown.

What if God asked you to do something that seemed very strange? Would you still do it? Here's one man who did.

5 Then the LORD*a* saw that the wickedness of man *was* great in the earth, and *that* every intent of the thoughts of his heart *was* only evil continually.

6 And the LORD was sorry that He had made man on the earth, and He was grieved in His heart.

7 So the LORD said, "I will destroy

6:3 *a*Septuagint, Syriac, Targum, and Vulgate read *abide.*   6:5 *a*Following Masoretic Text and Targum; Vulgate reads *God;* Septuagint reads LORD *God.*

man whom I have created from the face of the earth, both man and beast, creeping thing and birds of the air, for I am sorry that I have made them."

8   But Noah found grace in the eyes of the LORD.

NOAH PLEASES GOD

9   This is the genealogy of Noah. Noah was a just man, perfect in his generations. Noah walked with God.

10 And Noah begot three sons: Shem, Ham, and Jā′pheth.

11 The earth also was corrupt before God, and the earth was filled with violence.

12 So God looked upon the earth, and indeed it was corrupt; for all flesh had corrupted their way on the earth.

THE ARK PREPARED

13 And God said to Noah, "The end of all flesh has come before Me, for the earth is filled with violence through them; and behold, I will destroy them with the earth.

14 "Make yourself an ark of gopherwood; make rooms in the ark, and cover it inside and outside with pitch.

15 "And this is how you shall make it: The length of the ark *shall be* three hundred cubits, its width fifty cubits, and its height thirty cubits.

16 "You shall make a window for the ark, and you shall finish it to a cubit from above; and set the door of the ark in its side. You shall make it *with* lower, second, and third *decks.*

17 "And behold, I Myself am bringing floodwaters on the earth, to destroy from under heaven all flesh in which *is* the breath of life; everything that *is* on the earth shall die.

18 "But I will establish My covenant with you; and you shall go into the ark—you, your sons, your wife, and your sons' wives with you.

19 "And of every living thing of all flesh you shall bring two of every *sort* into the ark, to keep *them* alive with you; they shall be male and female.

20 "Of the birds after their kind, of animals after their kind, and of every creeping thing of the earth after its kind, two of every *kind* will come to you to keep *them* alive.

21 "And you shall take for yourself of all food that is eaten, and you shall gather *it* to yourself; and it shall be food for you and for them."

22 Thus Noah did; according to all that God commanded him, so he did.

✓	*Bible Quiz*

Genesis 6:5–22 **Noah Builds the Ark**

1. Why did God tell Noah to build the boat? What was going to happen?

2. What must the world have been like if Noah and his family were the only good people left on the earth? Do you think God would have let you on the boat?

3. How many of each animal could Noah bring into the boat?

4. Read verse 22. Noah's obedience is what pleased God so much. Would God be pleased with the way you obey Him? How can we obey Him even better?

THE GREAT FLOOD

This is a story about the biggest rainstorm ever. Read on to see how it ended.

7 Then the LORD said to Noah, "Come into the ark, you and all your household, because I have seen *that* you *are* righteous before Me in this generation.

2 "You shall take with you seven each of every clean animal, a male and his female; two each of animals that *are* unclean, a male and his female;

3 "also seven each of birds of the air, male and female, to keep the species alive on the face of all the earth.

4 "For after seven more days I will cause it to rain on the earth forty days and forty nights, and I will destroy from the face of the earth all living things that I have made."

5 And Noah did according to all that the LORD commanded him.

6 Noah *was* six hundred years old when the floodwaters were on the earth.

7 So Noah, with his sons, his wife, and his sons' wives, went into the ark because of the waters of the flood.

8 Of clean animals, of animals that *are* unclean, of birds, and of everything that creeps on the earth,

9 two by two they went into the ark to Noah, male and female, as God had commanded Noah.

10 And it came to pass after seven days that the waters of the flood were on the earth.

11 In the six hundredth year of Noah's life, in the second month, the seventeenth day of the month, on that day all the fountains of the great deep were broken up, and the windows of heaven were opened.

12 And the rain was on the earth forty days and forty nights.

13 On the very same day Noah and Noah's sons, Shem, Ham, and Jā′pheth, and Noah's wife and the three wives of his sons with them, entered the ark—

14 they and every beast after its kind, all cattle after their kind, every creeping thing that creeps on the earth after its kind, and every bird after its kind, every bird of every sort.

15 And they went into the ark to Noah, two by two, of all flesh in which *is* the breath of life.

16 So those that entered, male and female of all flesh, went in as God had commanded him; and the LORD shut him in.

17 Now the flood was on the earth forty days. The waters increased and lifted up the ark, and it rose high above the earth.

18 The waters prevailed and greatly increased on the earth, and the ark moved about on the surface of the waters.

19 And the waters prevailed exceedingly on the earth, and all the high hills under the whole heaven were covered.

20 The waters prevailed fifteen cubits upward, and the mountains were covered.

21 And all flesh died that moved on the earth: birds and cattle and beasts and every creeping thing that creeps on the earth, and every man.

22 All in whose nostrils *was* the breath of the spirit[a] of life, all that *was* on the dry *land,* died.

23 So He destroyed all living things which were on the face of the ground: both man and cattle, creeping thing and bird of the air. They were destroyed from the earth. Only Noah

7:22 aSeptuagint and Vulgate omit *of the spirit*.

and those who *were* with him in the ark remained *alive.*

24 And the waters prevailed on the earth one hundred and fifty days.

NOAH'S DELIVERANCE

8 Then God remembered Noah, and every living thing, and all the animals that *were* with him in the ark. And God made a wind to pass over the earth, and the waters subsided.

2   The fountains of the deep and the windows of heaven were also stopped, and the rain from heaven was restrained.

3   And the waters receded continually from the earth. At the end of the hundred and fifty days the waters decreased.

4   Then the ark rested in the seventh month, the seventeenth day of the month, on the mountains of Ar′a·rat.

5   And the waters decreased continually until the tenth month. In the tenth *month,* on the first *day* of the month, the tops of the mountains were seen.

6   So it came to pass, at the end of forty days, that Noah opened the window of the ark which he had made.

7   Then he sent out a raven, which kept going to and fro until the waters had dried up from the earth.

8   He also sent out from himself a dove, to see if the waters had receded from the face of the ground.

9   But the dove found no resting place for the sole of her foot, and she returned into the ark to him, for the waters *were* on the face of the whole earth. So he put out his hand and took her, and drew her into the ark to himself.

10 And he waited yet another seven days, and again he sent the dove out from the ark.

11 Then the dove came to him in the evening, and behold, a freshly plucked olive leaf *was* in her mouth; and Noah knew that the waters had receded from the earth.

12 So he waited yet another seven days and sent out the dove, which did not return again to him anymore.

13 And it came to pass in the six hundred and first year, in the first *month,* the first *day* of the month, that the waters were dried up from the earth; and Noah removed the covering of the ark and looked, and indeed the surface of the ground was dry.

14 And in the second month, on the twenty-seventh day of the month, the earth was dried.

15 Then God spoke to Noah, saying,

16 "Go out of the ark, you and your wife, and your sons and your sons' wives with you.

17 "Bring out with you every living thing of all flesh that *is* with you: birds and cattle and every creeping thing that creeps on the earth, so that they may abound on the earth, and be fruitful and multiply on the earth."

18 So Noah went out, and his sons and his wife and his sons' wives with him.

19 Every animal, every creeping thing, every bird, *and* whatever creeps on the earth, according to their families, went out of the ark.

GOD'S COVENANT WITH CREATION

20 Then Noah built an altar to the LORD, and took of every clean animal and of every clean bird, and offered burnt offerings on the altar.

21 And the LORD smelled a soothing aroma. Then the LORD said in His heart, "I will never again curse the

Favorite Family Verses

WHILE THE EARTH REMAINS, / SEEDTIME AND HARVEST, / COLD AND HEAT, / WINTER AND SUMMER, / AND DAY AND NIGHT / SHALL NOT CEASE. Genesis 8:22

Who Makes Seeds Grow?

Jonathan has just planted some seeds. He dug up the dirt. He put the seeds in the dirt. Then he covered them. But can Jonathan make the seeds grow?

1. Who makes the seeds grow?
2. What does God send to water the seeds?
3. What does He send to warm the seeds?
4. Why is Jonathan praying?
5. How is Jonathan's friend Jenny helping?

For more on *Favorite Family Verses* turn to page 255
For more on *God's Care* turn to page 462

ground for man's sake, although the imagination of man's heart *is* evil from his youth; nor will I again destroy every living thing as I have done.

22 "While the earth remains,
Seedtime and harvest,
Cold and heat,
Winter and summer,
And day and night
Shall not cease."

9 So God blessed Noah and his sons, and said to them: "Be fruitful and multiply, and fill the earth.*a*
2 "And the fear of you and the dread of you shall be on every beast of the earth, on every bird of the air, on all that move *on* the earth, and on all the fish of the sea. They are given into your hand.
3 "Every moving thing that lives shall be food for you. I have given you all things, even as the green herbs.
4 "But you shall not eat flesh with its life, *that is,* its blood.
5 "Surely for your lifeblood I will demand *a reckoning;* from the hand of every beast I will require it, and from the hand of man. From the hand of every man's brother I will require the life of man.

6 "Whoever sheds man's blood,
By man his blood shall be shed;
For in the image of God
He made man.
7 And as for you, be fruitful and multiply;
Bring forth abundantly in the earth
And multiply in it."

8 Then God spoke to Noah and to his sons with him, saying:
9 "And as for Me, behold, I establish My covenant with you and with your descendants*a* after you,

10 "and with every living creature that *is* with you: the birds, the cattle, and every beast of the earth with you, of all that go out of the ark, every beast of the earth.
11 "Thus I establish My covenant with you: Never again shall all flesh be cut off by the waters of the flood; never again shall there be a flood to destroy the earth."
12 And God said: "This *is* the sign of the covenant which I make between Me and you, and every living creature that *is* with you, for perpetual generations:
13 "I set My rainbow in the cloud, and it shall be for the sign of the covenant between Me and the earth.
14 "It shall be, when I bring a cloud over the earth, that the rainbow shall be seen in the cloud;
15 "and I will remember My covenant which *is* between Me and you and every living creature of all flesh; the waters shall never again become a flood to destroy all flesh.
16 "The rainbow shall be in the cloud, and I will look on it to remember the everlasting covenant between God and every living creature of all flesh that *is* on the earth."
17 And God said to Noah, "This *is* the sign of the covenant which I have established between Me and all flesh that *is* on the earth."

NOAH AND HIS SONS

18 Now the sons of Noah who went out of the ark were Shem, Ham, and Jā′pheth. And Ham *was* the father of Cā′naan.
19 These three *were* the sons of Noah, and from these the whole earth was populated.
20 And Noah began *to be* a farmer, and he planted a vineyard.

9:1 *a*Compare Genesis 1:28   9:9 *a*Literally *seed*

What the Bible Says

ABOUT GOD'S PROMISES   Genesis 9:16, 17

Does God Keep His Promises?

Have you seen a rainbow? Rainbows remind us of God's promises (Genesis 9:16, 17). But does God keep His promises? Can you trust Him to do what He says?

1. Why is it important to know that God keeps His promises? What if He didn't? What would that mean to you?
2. Why is it important to know that parents keep their promises? What if they didn't? What would that mean to you?
3. Why is it important for others to know that you keep your promises? What if you didn't? What would that mean to you?

For more on *What the Bible Says* turn to page 138
For more on *God's Promises* turn to page 354

✓ Bible Quiz

Genesis 7:1—9:17   **The Great Flood**

1. How long did it rain? How high did the water get?
2. How long did the water cover even the highest mountains?
3. What do you suppose Noah and his family talked about as they floated safely inside the boat?
4. What was the first thing Noah did when he got out of the boat?
5. After the flood, what promise did God make to Noah? What did God put in the sky to remind Noah of that promise? What do you think of when you see a rainbow in the sky?

21 Then he drank of the wine and was drunk, and became uncovered in his tent.
22 And Ham, the father of Cā′naan, saw the nakedness of his father, and told his two brothers outside.
23 But Shem and Jā′pheth took a garment, laid *it* on both their shoulders, and went backward and covered the nakedness of their father. Their faces *were* turned away, and they did not see their father's nakedness.
24 So Noah awoke from his wine, and knew what his younger son had done to him.
25 Then he said:

"Cursed *be* Cā′naan;
A servant of servants
He shall be to his brethren."

26 And he said:

"Blessed *be* the LORD,
The God of Shem,
And may Cā′naan be his servant.
27 May God enlarge Jā′pheth,
And may he dwell in the tents of
   Shem;

And may Cā'naan be his
servant."

28 And Noah lived after the flood
three hundred and fifty years.
29 So all the days of Noah were nine
hundred and fifty years; and he
died.

NATIONS DESCENDED FROM NOAH

10 Now this *is* the genealogy of
the sons of Noah: Shem, Ham, and
Jā'pheth. And sons were born to
them after the flood.
2 The sons of Jā'pheth *were* Gō'-
mer, Mā'gog, Mā'dai, Jā'van, Tū'bal,
Mē'shech, and Tī'ras.
3 The sons of Gō'mer *were* Ash'ke-
naz, Rī'phath,*a* and Tō·gar'mah.
4 The sons of Jā'van *were* E·li'shah,
Tar'shish, Kit'tim, and Dō'da·nim.*a*
5 From these the coastland *peoples*
of the Gentiles were separated into
their lands, everyone according to his
language, according to their families,
into their nations.
6 The sons of Ham *were* Cush,
Miz'ra·im, Put,*a* and Cā'naan.
7 The sons of Cush *were* Sē'ba,
Hav'i·lah, Sab'tah, Rā'a·mah, and
Sab'te·chah; and the sons of Rā'a-
mah *were* Shē'ba and Dē'dan.
8 Cush begot Nim'rod; he began to
be a mighty one on the earth.
9 He was a mighty hunter before
the LORD; therefore it is said, "Like
Nim'rod the mighty hunter before
the LORD."
10 And the beginning of his kingdom
was Bā'bel, Ē'rech, Ac'cad, and
Cal'neh, in the land of Shī'nar.
11 From that land he went to Assyria and built Nin'e·veh, Re·hō'both
Ir, Cā'lah,
12 and Rē'sen between Nin'e·veh
and Cā'lah (that *is* the principal
city).

13 Miz'ra·im begot Lū'dim, An'a-
mim, Le·hā'bim, Naph'tū·him,
14 Path·rū'sim, and Cas·lū'him
(from whom came the Phi·lis'tines
and Caph'to·rim).
15 Cā'naan begot Sī'don his firstborn, and Heth;
16 the Jeb'ū·site, the Am'o·rīte, and
the Gir'ga·shīte;
17 the Hī'vīte, the Ar'kīte, and the
Sī'nīte;
18 the Ar'vad·īte, the Zem'a·rīte, and
the Hā'math·īte. Afterward the families of the Cā'naan·ītes were dispersed.
19 And the border of the Cā'naan-
ītes was from Sī'don as you go toward Gē'rar, as far as Gā'za; then as
you go toward Sod'om, Go·mor'rah,
Ad'mah, and Ze·boi'im, as far as
Lā'sha.
20 These *were* the sons of Ham, according to their families, according to
their languages, in their lands *and* in
their nations.
21 And *children* were born also to
Shem, the father of all the children of
Ē'ber, the brother of Jā'pheth the elder.
22 The sons of Shem *were* Ē'lam,
As'shur, Ar·phā'xad, Lud, and Ar'am.
23 The sons of Ar'am *were* Uz, Hul,
Gē'ther, and Mash.*a*
24 Ar·phā'xad begot Sā'lah,*a* and
Sā'lah begot Ē'ber.
25 To Ē'ber were born two sons: the
name of one *was* Pē'leg, for in his
days the earth was divided; and his
brother's name *was* Jok'tan.
26 Jok'tan begot Al·mō'dad, Shē-
leph, Hā·zar·mā'veth, Jē'rah,
27 Ha·dor'am, Ū'zal, Dik'lah,

10:3 *a*Spelled *Diphath* in 1 Chronicles 1:6
10:4 *a*Spelled *Rodanim* in Samaritan Pentateuch
and 1 Chronicles 1:7   10:6 *a*Or *Phut*
10:23 *a*Called *Meshech* in Septuagint and 1 Chronicles 1:17   10:24 *a*Following Masoretic Text, Vulgate, and Targum; Septuagint reads *Arphaxad begot Cainan, and Cainan begot Salah* (compare
Luke 3:35, 36).

28 Ō'bal,*a* A·bim'a·el, Shē'ba,
29 Ō'phir, Hav'i·lah, and Jō'bab. All these *were* the sons of Jok'tan.
30 And their dwelling place was from Mē'sha as you go toward Sē'phar, the mountain of the east.
31 These *were* the sons of Shem, according to their families, according to their languages, in their lands, according to their nations.
32 These *were* the families of the sons of Noah, according to their generations, in their nations; and from these the nations were divided on the earth after the flood.

THE TOWER OF BABEL

This is a story about the world's tallest building. But something went wrong and God wouldn't let the people finish it. Why not?

11 Now the whole earth had one language and one speech.
2 And it came to pass, as they journeyed from the east, that they found a plain in the land of Shī'nar, and they dwelt there.
3 Then they said to one another, "Come, let us make bricks and bake *them* thoroughly." They had brick for stone, and they had asphalt for mortar.
4 And they said, "Come, let us build ourselves a city, and a tower whose top *is* in the heavens; let us make a name for ourselves, lest we be scattered abroad over the face of the whole earth."
5 But the LORD came down to see the city and the tower which the sons of men had built.
6 And the LORD said, "Indeed the people *are* one and they all have one language, and this is what they begin to do; now nothing that they propose to do will be withheld from them.

7 "Come, let Us go down and there confuse their language, that they may not understand one another's speech."
8 So the LORD scattered them abroad from there over the face of all the earth, and they ceased building the city.
9 Therefore its name is called Bā'bel, because there the LORD confused the language of all the earth; and from there the LORD scattered them abroad over the face of all the earth.

☑ *Bible Quiz*

Genesis 11:1–9 **The Tower of Babel**

1. Where was the tower to be built? What was it made from?
2. What makes you think God wasn't happy with the tower?
3. These people didn't think they needed God's help. They thought they could do everything without Him. How did God stop the building and show that He is really in control of everything?
4. Do you take all the credit when you do something well? Why should God get some of the credit?

SHEM'S DESCENDANTS

10 This *is* the genealogy of Shem: Shem *was* one hundred years old, and begot Ar·phā'xad two years after the flood.

10:28 *a*Spelled *Ebal* in 1 Chronicles 1:22

11 After he begot Ar·pha'xad, Shem lived five hundred years, and begot sons and daughters.
12 Ar·pha'xad lived thirty-five years, and begot Sā'lah.
13 After he begot Sā'lah, Ar·pha'xad lived four hundred and three years, and begot sons and daughters.
14 Sā'lah lived thirty years, and begot Ē'ber.
15 After he begot Ē'ber, Sā'lah lived four hundred and three years, and begot sons and daughters.
16 Ē'ber lived thirty-four years, and begot Pē'leg.
17 After he begot Pē'leg, Ē'ber lived four hundred and thirty years, and begot sons and daughters.
18 Pē'leg lived thirty years, and begot Rē'ū.
19 After he begot Rē'ū, Pē'leg lived two hundred and nine years, and begot sons and daughters.
20 Rē'ū lived thirty-two years, and begot Sē'rug.
21 After he begot Sē'rug, Rē'ū lived two hundred and seven years, and begot sons and daughters.
22 Sē'rug lived thirty years, and begot Nā'hor.
23 After he begot Nā'hor, Sē'rug lived two hundred years, and begot sons and daughters.
24 Nā'hor lived twenty-nine years, and begot Tē'rah.
25 After he begot Tē'rah, Nā'hor lived one hundred and nineteen years, and begot sons and daughters.
26 Now Tē'rah lived seventy years, and begot Abram, Nā'hor, and Har'an.

TERAH'S DESCENDANTS

27 This is the genealogy of Tē'rah: Tē'rah begot Abram, Nā'hor, and Har'an. Har'an begot Lot.
28 And Har'an died before his father Tē'rah in his native land, in Ūr of the Chal·dē'ans.
29 Then Abram and Nā'hor took wives: the name of Abram's wife was Sar'aī, and the name of Nā'hor's wife, Mil'cah, the daughter of Har'an the father of Mil'cah and the father of Is'cah.
30 But Sar'aī was barren; she had no child.
31 And Tē'rah took his son Abram and his grandson Lot, the son of Har'an, and his daughter-in-law Sar'aī, his son Abram's wife, and they went out with them from Ūr of the Chal·dē'ans to go to the land of Cā'naan; and they came to Har'an and dwelt there.
32 So the days of Tē'rah were two hundred and five years, and Tē'rah died in Har'an.

PROMISES TO ABRAM

12 Now the LORD had said to Abram:

"Get out of your country,
From your family
And from your father's house,
To a land that I will show you.
2 I will make you a great nation;
I will bless you
And make your name great;
And you shall be a blessing.
3 I will bless those who bless you,
And I will curse him who curses you;
And in you all the families of the earth shall be blessed."

4 So Abram departed as the LORD had spoken to him, and Lot went with him. And Abram was seventy-five years old when he departed from Har'an.
5 Then Abram took Sar'aī his wife and Lot his brother's son, and all

their possessions that they had gathered, and the people whom they had acquired in Har′an, and they departed to go to the land of Cā′naan. So they came to the land of Cā′naan.

6 Abram passed through the land to the place of Shē′chem, as far as the terebinth tree of Mō′reh.*a* And the Cā′naan·ites *were* then in the land.

7 Then the LORD appeared to Abram and said, "To your descendants I will give this land." And there he built an altar to the LORD, who had appeared to him.

8 And he moved from there to the mountain east of Beth′el, and he pitched his tent *with* Beth′el on the west and Aī on the east; there he built an altar to the LORD and called on the name of the LORD.

9 So Abram journeyed, going on still toward the South.*a*

ABRAM IN EGYPT

10 Now there was a famine in the land, and Abram went down to Egypt to dwell there, for the famine *was* severe in the land.

11 And it came to pass, when he was close to entering Egypt, that he said to Sar′aī his wife, "Indeed I know that you *are* a woman of beautiful countenance.

12 "Therefore it will happen, when the Egyptians see you, that they will say, 'This *is* his wife'; and they will kill me, but they will let you live.

13 "Please say you *are* my sister, that it may be well with me for your sake, and that I*a* may live because of you."

14 So it was, when Abram came into Egypt, that the Egyptians saw the woman, that she *was* very beautiful.

15 The princes of Pharaoh also saw her and commended her to Pharaoh.

And the woman was taken to Pharaoh's house.

16 He treated Abram well for her sake. He had sheep, oxen, male donkeys, male and female servants, female donkeys, and camels.

17 But the LORD plagued Pharaoh and his house with great plagues because of Sar′aī, Abram's wife.

18 And Pharaoh called Abram and said, "What *is* this you have done to me? Why did you not tell me that she *was* your wife?

19 "Why did you say, 'She *is* my sister'? I might have taken her as my wife. Now therefore, here is your wife; take *her* and go your way."

20 So Pharaoh commanded *his* men concerning him; and they sent him away, with his wife and all that he had.

ABRAM INHERITS CANAAN

Do you know what a selfish person is like? You will after reading this story.

13 Then Abram went up from Egypt, he and his wife and all that he had, and Lot with him, to the South.*a*

2 Abram *was* very rich in livestock, in silver, and in gold.

3 And he went on his journey from the South as far as Beth′el, to the place where his tent had been at the beginning, between Beth′el and Aī,

4 to the place of the altar which he had made there at first. And there Abram called on the name of the LORD.

5 Lot also, who went with Abram, had flocks and herds and tents.

6 Now the land was not able to support them, that they might dwell together, for their possessions were so

12:6 *a*Hebrew *Alon Moreh*   12:9 *a*Hebrew *Negev*
12:13 *a*Literally *my soul*   13:1 *a*Hebrew *Negev*

great that they could not dwell together.

7 And there was strife between the herdsmen of Abram's livestock and the herdsmen of Lot's livestock. The Cā′naan·ītes and the Per′iz·zītes then dwelt in the land.

8 So Abram said to Lot, "Please let there be no strife between you and me, and between my herdsmen and your herdsmen; for we are brethren.

9 "Is not the whole land before you? Please separate from me. If you take the left, then I will go to the right; or, if you go to the right, then I will go to the left."

10 And Lot lifted his eyes and saw all the plain of Jordan, that it was well watered everywhere (before the LORD destroyed Sod′om and Gomor′rah) like the garden of the LORD, like the land of Egypt as you go toward Zō′ar.

11 Then Lot chose for himself all the plain of Jordan, and Lot journeyed east. And they separated from each other.

12 Abram dwelt in the land of Cā′naan, and Lot dwelt in the cities of the plain and pitched his tent even as far as Sod′om.

13 But the men of Sod′om were exceedingly wicked and sinful against the LORD.

14 And the LORD said to Abram, after Lot had separated from him: "Lift your eyes now and look from the place where you are—northward, southward, eastward, and westward;

15 "for all the land which you see I give to you and your descendants[a] forever.

16 "And I will make your descendants as the dust of the earth; so that if a man could number the dust of the earth, then your descendants also could be numbered.

17 "Arise, walk in the land through its length and its width, for I give it to you."

18 Then Abram moved his tent, and went and dwelt by the terebinth trees of Mam′re,[a] which are in Hē′bron, and built an altar there to the LORD.

☑ *Bible Quiz*

Genesis 13 **Lot Takes the Best for Himself**

1. Who was traveling with Abram?
2. What did Abram and Lot do for a living?
3. Why did the shepherds of Abram and Lot fight?
4. What did Abram suggest to stop the fighting? Was this selfish?
5. When Abram offered Lot first pick, what did Lot take? Was this selfish?
6. In what ways are we selfish? What can we do to be more like Abram?

LOT'S CAPTIVITY AND RESCUE

14 And it came to pass in the days of Am′ra·phel king of Shī′nar, Ar′i·och king of El·lā′sar, Ched·or·la·ō′mer king of Ē′lam, and Tidal king of nations,[a]

2 that they made war with Bē′ra king of Sod′om, Bir′sha king of Gomor′rah, Shī′nab king of Ad′mah, Shem·ē′ber king of Ze·boi′im, and the king of Bē′la (that is, Zō′ar).

3 All these joined together in the Valley of Sid′dim (that is, the Salt Sea).

13:15 aLiterally seed, and so throughout the book
13:18 aHebrew Alon Mamre   14:1 aHebrew goyim

4 Twelve years they served Ched·or·la·ō′mer, and in the thirteenth year they rebelled.

5 In the fourteenth year Ched·or·la·ō′mer and the kings that *were* with him came and attacked the Reph′a·im in Ash′te·roth Kar·nā′im, the Zū′zim in Ham, the Ē′mim in Shā′-veh Kir·i·a·thā′im,

6 and the Hor′ītes in their mountain of Sē′ir, as far as El Par′an, which *is* by the wilderness.

7 Then they turned back and came to En Mish′pat (that *is*, Kā′desh), and attacked all the country of the A·mal′e·kītes, and also the Am′o·rītes who dwelt in Ha·zē′zon Tā′mar.

8 And the king of Sod′om, the king of Go·mor′rah, the king of Ad′mah, the king of Ze·boi′im, and the king of Bē′la (that *is*, Zō′ar) went out and joined together in battle in the Valley of Sid′dim

9 against Ched·or·la·ō′mer king of Ē′lam, Tidal king of nations,a Am·ra·phel king of Shī′nar, and Ar′i·och king of El·lā′sar—four kings against five.

10 Now the Valley of Sid′dim *was full of* asphalt pits; and the kings of Sod′om and Go·mor′rah fled; *some* fell there, and the remainder fled to the mountains.

11 Then they took all the goods of Sod′om and Go·mor′rah, and all their provisions, and went their way.

12 They also took Lot, Abram′s brother′s son who dwelt in Sod′om, and his goods, and departed.

13 Then one who had escaped came and told Abram the Hebrew, for he dwelt by the terebinth trees of Mam′rea the Am′o·rīte, brother of Esh′col and brother of Ā′ner; and they *were* allies with Abram.

14 Now when Abram heard that his brother was taken captive, he armed his three hundred and eighteen trained *servants* who were born in his own house, and went in pursuit as far as Dan.

15 He divided his forces against them by night, and he and his servants attacked them and pursued them as far as Hō′bah, which *is* north of Damascus.

16 So he brought back all the goods, and also brought back his brother Lot and his goods, as well as the women and the people.

17 And the king of Sod′om went out to meet him at the Valley of Shā′veh (that *is*, the King′s Valley), after his return from the defeat of Ched·or·la·ō′mer and the kings who *were* with him.

ABRAM AND MELCHIZEDEK

18 Then Mel·chiz′e·dek king of Sā′lem brought out bread and wine; he *was* the priest of God Most High.

19 And he blessed him and said:

"Blessed be Abram of God Most
   High,
Possessor of heaven and earth;
20 And blessed be God Most High,
Who has delivered your enemies
   into your hand."

And he gave him a tithe of all.

21 Now the king of Sod′om said to Abram, "Give me the persons, and take the goods for yourself."

22 But Abram said to the king of Sod′om, "I have raised my hand to the LORD, God Most High, the Possessor of heaven and earth,

23 "that I *will take* nothing, from a thread to a sandal strap, and that I will not take anything that *is* yours, lest you should say, 'I have made Abram rich'—

24 "except only what the young men have eaten, and the portion of the

14:9 aHebrew *goyim*   14:13 aHebrew *Alon Mamre*

men who went with me: Ā′ner,
Esh′col, and Mam′re; let them take
their portion.”

GOD'S COVENANT WITH ABRAM

15 After these things the word of
the LORD came to Abram in a vision,
saying, “Do not be afraid, Abram. I
am your shield, your exceedingly
great reward.”
2 But Abram said, “Lord GOD, what
will You give me, seeing I go childless, and the heir of my house *is*
El·i·ē′zer of Damascus?”
3 Then Abram said, “Look, You
have given me no offspring; indeed
one born in my house is my heir!”
4 And behold, the word of the LORD
came to him, saying, “This one shall
not be your heir, but one who will
come from your own body shall be
your heir.”
5 Then He brought him outside
and said, “Look now toward heaven,
and count the stars if you are able
to number them.” And He said
to him, “So shall your descendants
be.”
6 And he believed in the LORD, and
He accounted it to him for righteousness.
7 Then He said to him, “I *am* the
LORD, who brought you out of Ūr of
the Chal·dē′ans, to give you this land
to inherit it.”
8 And he said, “Lord GOD, how shall
I know that I will inherit it?”
9 So He said to him, “Bring Me a
three-year-old heifer, a three-year-old
female goat, a three-year-old ram, a
turtledove, and a young pigeon.”
10 Then he brought all these to Him
and cut them in two, down the middle, and placed each piece opposite
the other; but he did not cut the birds
in two.
11 And when the vultures came

down on the carcasses, Abram drove
them away.
12 Now when the sun was going
down, a deep sleep fell upon Abram;
and behold, horror *and* great darkness fell upon him.
13 Then He said to Abram: “Know
certainly that your descendants will
be strangers in a land *that is* not
theirs, and will serve them, and they
will afflict them four hundred
years.
14 “And also the nation whom they
serve I will judge; afterward they
shall come out with great possessions.
15 “Now as for you, you shall go to
your fathers in peace; you shall be
buried at a good old age.
16 “But in the fourth generation they
shall return here, for the iniquity of
the Am′o·rītes *is* not yet complete.”
17 And it came to pass, when the
sun went down and it was dark, that
behold, there appeared a smoking
oven and a burning torch that passed
between those pieces.
18 On the same day the LORD made
a covenant with Abram, saying:
“To your descendants I have given
this land, from the river of Egypt to
the great river, the River Eū·phrā′-
tēs—
19 “the Ken′ītes, the Kē′nez·zītes,
the Kad′mon·ītes,
20 “the Hit′tītes, the Per′iz·zītes, the
Reph′a·im,
21 “the Am′o·rītes, the Cā′naan·ites,
the Gir′ga·shītes, and the Jeb′ū-
sītes.”

HAGAR AND ISHMAEL

16 Now Sar′aī, Abram’s wife, had
borne him no *children*. And she had
an Egyptian maidservant whose
name was Hā′gar.
2 So Sar′aī said to Abram, “See

now, the LORD has restrained me from bearing *children*. Please, go in to my maid; perhaps I shall obtain children by her." And Abram heeded the voice of Sar´aī.

3 Then Sar´aī, Abram's wife, took Hā´gar her maid, the Egyptian, and gave her to her husband Abram to be his wife, after Abram had dwelt ten years in the land of Cā´naan.

4 So he went in to Hā´gar, and she conceived. And when she saw that she had conceived, her mistress became despised in her eyes.

5 Then Sar´aī said to Abram, "My wrong *be* upon you! I gave my maid into your embrace; and when she saw that she had conceived, I became despised in her eyes. The LORD judge between you and me."

6 So Abram said to Sar´aī, "Indeed your maid *is* in your hand; do to her as you please." And when Sar´aī dealt harshly with her, she fled from her presence.

7 Now the Angel of the LORD found her by a spring of water in the wilderness, by the spring on the way to Shūr.

8 And He said, "Hā´gar, Sar´aī's maid, where have you come from, and where are you going?" She said, "I am fleeing from the presence of my mistress Sar´aī."

9 The Angel of the LORD said to her, "Return to your mistress, and submit yourself under her hand."

10 Then the Angel of the LORD said to her, "I will multiply your descendants exceedingly, so that they shall not be counted for multitude."

11 And the Angel of the LORD said to her:

"Behold, you *are* with child,
And you shall bear a son.
You shall call his name Ish´ma·el,
Because the LORD has heard your
affliction.

12 He shall be a wild man;
His hand *shall be* against every
man,
And every man's hand against
him.
And he shall dwell in the
presence of all his brethren."

13 Then she called the name of the LORD who spoke to her, You-Are-the-God-Who-Sees; for she said, "Have I also here seen Him who sees me?"

14 Therefore the well was called Bē´er La·haī´ Roi;*a* observe, *it is* between Kā´desh and Bē´red.

15 So Hā´gar bore Abram a son; and Abram named his son, whom Hā´gar bore, Ish´ma·el.

16 Abram *was* eighty-six years old when Hā´gar bore Ish´ma·el to Abram.

THE SIGN OF THE COVENANT

17 When Abram was ninety-nine years old, the LORD appeared to Abram and said to him, "I *am* Almighty God; walk before Me and be blameless.

2 "And I will make My covenant between Me and you, and will multiply you exceedingly."

3 Then Abram fell on his face, and God talked with him, saying:

4 "As for Me, behold, My covenant is with you, and you shall be a father of many nations.

5 "No longer shall your name be called Abram, but your name shall be Abraham; for I have made you a father of many nations.

6 "I will make you exceedingly fruitful; and I will make nations of you, and kings shall come from you.

16:14 *a*Literally *Well of the One Who Lives and Sees Me*

7 "And I will establish My covenant between Me and you and your descendants after you in their generations, for an everlasting covenant, to be God to you and your descendants after you.

8 "Also I give to you and your descendants after you the land in which you are a stranger, all the land of Cā′naan, as an everlasting possession; and I will be their God."

9 And God said to Abraham: "As for you, you shall keep My covenant, you and your descendants after you throughout their generations.

10 "This *is* My covenant which you shall keep, between Me and you and your descendants after you: Every male child among you shall be circumcised;

11 "and you shall be circumcised in the flesh of your foreskins, and it shall be a sign of the covenant between Me and you.

12 "He who is eight days old among you shall be circumcised, every male child in your generations, he who is born in your house or bought with money from any foreigner who is not your descendant.

13 "He who is born in your house and he who is bought with your money must be circumcised, and My covenant shall be in your flesh for an everlasting covenant.

14 "And the uncircumcised male child, who is not circumcised in the flesh of his foreskin, that person shall be cut off from his people; he has broken My covenant."

15 Then God said to Abraham, "As for Sar′aī your wife, you shall not call her name Sar′aī, but Sarah *shall be* her name.

16 "And I will bless her and also give you a son by her; then I will bless her, and she shall be *a mother* of nations; kings of peoples shall be from her."

17 Then Abraham fell on his face and laughed, and said in his heart, "Shall *a child* be born to a man who is one hundred years old? And shall Sarah, who is ninety years old, bear *a child?*"

18 And Abraham said to God, "Oh, that Ish′ma·el might live before You!"

19 Then God said: "No, Sarah your wife shall bear you a son, and you shall call his name Isaac; I will establish My covenant with him for an everlasting covenant, *and* with his descendants after him.

20 "And as for Ish′ma·el, I have heard you. Behold, I have blessed him, and will make him fruitful, and will multiply him exceedingly. He shall beget twelve princes, and I will make him a great nation.

21 "But My covenant I will establish with Isaac, whom Sarah shall bear to you at this set time next year."

22 Then He finished talking with him, and God went up from Abraham.

23 So Abraham took Ish′ma·el his son, all who were born in his house and all who were bought with his money, every male among the men of Abraham's house, and circumcised the flesh of their foreskins that very same day, as God had said to him.

24 Abraham *was* ninety-nine years old when he was circumcised in the flesh of his foreskin.

25 And Ish′ma·el his son *was* thirteen years old when he was circumcised in the flesh of his foreskin.

26 That very same day Abraham was circumcised, and his son Ish′-ma·el;

27 and all the men of his house, born in the house or bought with money from a foreigner, were circumcised with him.

THE SON OF PROMISE

18 Then the LORD appeared to him by the terebinth trees of Mam'-re,*a* as he was sitting in the tent door in the heat of the day.
2   So he lifted his eyes and looked, and behold, three men were standing by him; and when he saw *them,* he ran from the tent door to meet them, and bowed himself to the ground,
3   and said, "My Lord, if I have now found favor in Your sight, do not pass on by Your servant.
4   "Please let a little water be brought, and wash your feet, and rest yourselves under the tree.
5   "And I will bring a morsel of bread, that you may refresh your hearts. After that you may pass by, inasmuch as you have come to your servant." They said, "Do as you have said."
6   So Abraham hurried into the tent to Sarah and said, "Quickly, make ready three measures of fine meal; knead *it* and make cakes."
7   And Abraham ran to the herd, took a tender and good calf, gave *it* to a young man, and he hastened to prepare it.
8   So he took butter and milk and the calf which he had prepared, and set *it* before them; and he stood by them under the tree as they ate.
9   Then they said to him, "Where *is* Sarah your wife?" So he said, "Here, in the tent."
10   And He said, "I will certainly return to you according to the time of life, and behold, Sarah your wife shall have a son." (Sarah was listening in the tent door which *was* behind him.)
11   Now Abraham and Sarah were old, well advanced in age; *and* Sarah had passed the age of childbearing.*a*
12   Therefore Sarah laughed within herself, saying, "After I have grown old, shall I have pleasure, my lord being old also?"
13   And the LORD said to Abraham, "Why did Sarah laugh, saying, 'Shall I surely bear *a child,* since I am old?'
14   "Is anything too hard for the LORD? At the appointed time I will return to you, according to the time of life, and Sarah shall have a son."
15   But Sarah denied *it,* saying, "I did not laugh," for she was afraid. And He said, "No, but you did laugh!"

ABRAHAM INTERCEDES FOR SODOM

16   Then the men rose from there and looked toward Sod'om, and Abraham went with them to send them on the way.
17   And the LORD said, "Shall I hide from Abraham what I am doing,
18   "since Abraham shall surely become a great and mighty nation, and all the nations of the earth shall be blessed in him?
19   "For I have known him, in order that he may command his children and his household after him, that they keep the way of the LORD, to do righteousness and justice, that the LORD may bring to Abraham what He has spoken to him."
20   And the LORD said, "Because the outcry against Sod'om and Go·mor'-rah is great, and because their sin is very grave,
21   "I will go down now and see whether they have done altogether according to the outcry against it that has come to Me; and if not, I will know."
22   Then the men turned away from there and went toward Sod'om, but Abraham still stood before the LORD.
23   And Abraham came near and

18:1 *a*Hebrew *Alon Mamre*   18:11 *a*Literally *the manner of women had ceased to be with Sarah*

said, "Would You also destroy the righteous with the wicked?

24 "Suppose there were fifty righteous within the city; would You also destroy the place and not spare *it* for the fifty righteous that were in it?

25 "Far be it from You to do such a thing as this, to slay the righteous with the wicked, so that the righteous should be as the wicked; far be it from You! Shall not the Judge of all the earth do right?"

26 So the LORD said, "If I find in Sod'om fifty righteous within the city, then I will spare all the place for their sakes."

27 Then Abraham answered and said, "Indeed now, I who *am but* dust and ashes have taken it upon myself to speak to the Lord:

28 "Suppose there were five less than the fifty righteous; would You destroy all of the city for *lack of* five?" So He said, "If I find there forty-five, I will not destroy *it*."

29 And he spoke to Him yet again and said, "Suppose there should be forty found there?" So He said, "I will not do *it* for the sake of forty."

30 Then he said, "Let not the Lord be angry, and I will speak: Suppose thirty should be found there?" So He said, "I will not do *it* if I find thirty there."

31 And he said, "Indeed now, I have taken it upon myself to speak to the Lord: Suppose twenty should be found there?" So He said, "I will not destroy *it* for the sake of twenty."

32 Then he said, "Let not the Lord be angry, and I will speak but once more: Suppose ten should be found there?" And He said, "I will not destroy *it* for the sake of ten."

33 So the LORD went His way as soon as He had finished speaking with Abraham; and Abraham returned to his place.

SODOM'S DEPRAVITY

19 Now the two angels came to Sod'om in the evening, and Lot was sitting in the gate of Sod'om. When Lot saw *them,* he rose to meet them, and he bowed himself with his face toward the ground.

2 And he said, "Here now, my lords, please turn in to your servant's house and spend the night, and wash your feet; then you may rise early and go on your way." And they said, "No, but we will spend the night in the open square."

3 But he insisted strongly; so they turned in to him and entered his house. Then he made them a feast, and baked unleavened bread, and they ate.

4 Now before they lay down, the men of the city, the men of Sod'om, both old and young, all the people from every quarter, surrounded the house.

5 And they called to Lot and said to him, "Where are the men who came to you tonight? Bring them out to us that we may know them *carnally.*"

6 So Lot went out to them through the doorway, shut the door behind him,

7 and said, "Please, my brethren, do not do so wickedly!

8 "See now, I have two daughters who have not known a man; please, let me bring them out to you, and you may do to them as you wish; only do nothing to these men, since this is the reason they have come under the shadow of my roof."

9 And they said, "Stand back!" Then they said, "This one came in to stay *here,* and he keeps acting as a judge; now we will deal worse with you than with them." So they pressed hard against the man Lot, and came near to break down the door.

10 But the men reached out their hands and pulled Lot into the house with them, and shut the door.

11 And they struck the men who *were* at the doorway of the house with blindness, both small and great, so that they became weary *trying* to find the door.

SODOM AND GOMORRAH DESTROYED

12 Then the men said to Lot, "Have you anyone else here? Son-in-law, your sons, your daughters, and whomever you have in the city—take *them* out of this place!

13 "For we will destroy this place, because the outcry against them has grown great before the face of the LORD, and the LORD has sent us to destroy it."

14 So Lot went out and spoke to his sons-in-law, who had married his daughters, and said, "Get up, get out of this place; for the LORD will destroy this city!" But to his sons-in-law he seemed to be joking.

15 When the morning dawned, the angels urged Lot to hurry, saying, "Arise, take your wife and your two daughters who are here, lest you be consumed in the punishment of the city."

16 And while he lingered, the men took hold of his hand, his wife's hand, and the hands of his two daughters, the LORD being merciful to him, and they brought him out and set him outside the city.

17 So it came to pass, when they had brought them outside, that he*ᵃ* said, "Escape for your life! Do not look behind you nor stay anywhere in the plain. Escape to the mountains, lest you be destroyed."

18 Then Lot said to them, "Please, no, my lords!

19 "Indeed now, your servant has found favor in your sight, and you have increased your mercy which you have shown me by saving my life; but I cannot escape to the mountains, lest some evil overtake me and I die.

20 "See now, this city *is* near *enough* to flee to, and it *is* a little one; please let me escape there (*is* it not a little one?) and my soul shall live."

21 And he said to him, "See, I have favored you concerning this thing also, in that I will not overthrow this city for which you have spoken.

22 "Hurry, escape there. For I cannot do anything until you arrive there." Therefore the name of the city was called Zō'ar.

23 The sun had risen upon the earth when Lot entered Zō'ar.

24 Then the LORD rained brimstone and fire on Sod'om and Go·mor'rah, from the LORD out of the heavens.

25 So He overthrew those cities, all the plain, all the inhabitants of the cities, and what grew on the ground.

26 But his wife looked back behind him, and she became a pillar of salt.

27 And Abraham went early in the morning to the place where he had stood before the LORD.

28 Then he looked toward Sod'om and Go·mor'rah, and toward all the land of the plain; and he saw, and behold, the smoke of the land which went up like the smoke of a furnace.

29 And it came to pass, when God destroyed the cities of the plain, that God remembered Abraham, and sent Lot out of the midst of the overthrow, when He overthrew the cities in which Lot had dwelt.

THE DESCENDANTS OF LOT

30 Then Lot went up out of Zō'ar and dwelt in the mountains, and his two daughters were with him; for he was afraid to dwell in Zō'ar. And he

---

19:17 ᵃSeptuagint, Syriac, and Vulgate read *they*.

and his two daughters dwelt in a cave.

31 Now the firstborn said to the younger, "Our father *is* old, and *there is* no man on the earth to come in to us as is the custom of all the earth.

32 "Come, let us make our father drink wine, and we will lie with him, that we may preserve the lineage of our father."

33 So they made their father drink wine that night. And the firstborn went in and lay with her father, and he did not know when she lay down or when she arose.

34 It happened on the next day that the firstborn said to the younger, "Indeed I lay with my father last night; let us make him drink wine tonight also, and you go in *and* lie with him, that we may preserve the lineage of our father."

35 Then they made their father drink wine that night also. And the younger arose and lay with him, and he did not know when she lay down or when she arose.

36 Thus both the daughters of Lot were with child by their father.

37 The firstborn bore a son and called his name Mō'ab; he *is* the father of the Mō'ab-ītes to this day.

38 And the younger, she also bore a son and called his name Ben-Am'mī; he *is* the father of the people of Am'mon to this day.

ABRAHAM AND ABIMELECH

20 And Abraham journeyed from there to the South, and dwelt between Kā'desh and Shūr, and stayed in Gē'rar.

2 Now Abraham said of Sarah his wife, "She *is* my sister." And A·bim'-e·lech king of Gē'rar sent and took Sarah.

3 But God came to A·bim'e·lech in a dream by night, and said to him, "Indeed you *are* a dead man because of the woman whom you have taken, for she *is* a man's wife."

4 But A·bim'e·lech had not come near her; and he said, "Lord, will You slay a righteous nation also?

5 "Did he not say to me, 'She *is* my sister'? And she, even she herself said, 'He *is* my brother.' In the integrity of my heart and innocence of my hands I have done this."

6 And God said to him in a dream, "Yes, I know that you did this in the integrity of your heart. For I also withheld you from sinning against Me; therefore I did not let you touch her.

7 "Now therefore, restore the man's wife; for he *is* a prophet, and he will pray for you and you shall live. But if you do not restore *her,* know that you shall surely die, you and all who *are* yours."

8 So A·bim'e·lech rose early in the morning, called all his servants, and told all these things in their hearing; and the men were very much afraid.

9 And A·bim'e·lech called Abraham and said to him, "What have you done to us? How have I offended you, that you have brought on me and on my kingdom a great sin? You have done deeds to me that ought not to be done."

10 Then A·bim'e·lech said to Abraham, "What did you have in view, that you have done this thing?"

11 And Abraham said, "Because I thought, surely the fear of God *is* not in this place; and they will kill me on account of my wife.

12 "But indeed *she is* truly my sister. She *is* the daughter of my father, but not the daughter of my mother; and she became my wife.

13 "And it came to pass, when God caused me to wander from my father's house, that I said to her, 'This

is your kindness that you should do for me: in every place, wherever we go, say of me, "He *is* my brother." ' "

14 Then A·bim′e·lech took sheep, oxen, and male and female servants, and gave *them* to Abraham; and he restored Sarah his wife to him.

15 And A·bim′e·lech said, "See, my land *is* before you; dwell where it pleases you."

16 Then to Sarah he said, "Behold, I have given your brother a thousand *pieces* of silver; indeed this vindicates you[a] before all who *are* with you and before everybody." Thus she was rebuked.

17 So Abraham prayed to God; and God healed A·bim′e·lech, his wife, and his female servants. Then they bore *children;*

18 for the LORD had closed up all the wombs of the house of A·bim′e·lech because of Sarah, Abraham's wife.

ISAAC IS BORN

21 And the LORD visited Sarah as He had said, and the LORD did for Sarah as He had spoken.

2 For Sarah conceived and bore Abraham a son in his old age, at the set time of which God had spoken to him.

3 And Abraham called the name of his son who was born to him—whom Sarah bore to him—Isaac.

4 Then Abraham circumcised his son Isaac when he was eight days old, as God had commanded him.

5 Now Abraham was one hundred years old when his son Isaac was born to him.

6 And Sarah said, "God has made me laugh, *and* all who hear will laugh with me."

7 She also said, "Who would have said to Abraham that Sarah would nurse children? For I have borne *him* a son in his old age."

HAGAR AND ISHMAEL DEPART

8 So the child grew and was weaned. And Abraham made a great feast on the same day that Isaac was weaned.

9 And Sarah saw the son of Hā′gar the Egyptian, whom she had borne to Abraham, scoffing.

10 Therefore she said to Abraham, "Cast out this bondwoman and her son; for the son of this bondwoman shall not be heir with my son, *namely* with Isaac."

11 And the matter was very displeasing in Abraham's sight because of his son.

12 But God said to Abraham, "Do not let it be displeasing in your sight because of the lad or because of your bondwoman. Whatever Sarah has said to you, listen to her voice; for in Isaac your seed shall be called.

13 "Yet I will also make a nation of the son of the bondwoman, because he *is* your seed."

14 So Abraham rose early in the morning, and took bread and a skin of water; and putting *it* on her shoulder, he gave *it* and the boy to Hā′gar, and sent her away. Then she departed and wandered in the Wilderness of Bē·er·shē′ba.

15 And the water in the skin was used up, and she placed the boy under one of the shrubs.

16 Then she went and sat down across from *him* at a distance of about a bowshot; for she said to herself, "Let me not see the death of the boy." So she sat opposite *him,* and lifted her voice and wept.

17 And God heard the voice of the

20:16 aLiterally *it is a covering of the eyes for you*

lad. Then the angel of God called to Hā′gar out of heaven, and said to her, "What ails you, Hā′gar? Fear not, for God has heard the voice of the lad where he *is*.

18 "Arise, lift up the lad and hold him with your hand, for I will make him a great nation."

19 Then God opened her eyes, and she saw a well of water. And she went and filled the skin with water, and gave the lad a drink.

20 So God was with the lad; and he grew and dwelt in the wilderness, and became an archer.

21 He dwelt in the Wilderness of Par′an; and his mother took a wife for him from the land of Egypt.

A COVENANT WITH ABIMELECH

22 And it came to pass at that time that A·bim′e·lech and Phī′chol, the commander of his army, spoke to Abraham, saying, "God *is* with you in all that you do.

23 "Now therefore, swear to me by God that you will not deal falsely with me, with my offspring, or with my posterity; but that according to the kindness that I have done to you, you will do to me and to the land in which you have dwelt."

24 And Abraham said, "I will swear."

25 Then Abraham rebuked A·bim′-e·lech because of a well of water which A·bim′e·lech's servants had seized.

26 And A·bim′e·lech said, "I do not know who has done this thing; you did not tell me, nor had I heard *of it* until today."

27 So Abraham took sheep and oxen and gave them to A·bim′e·lech, and the two of them made a covenant.

28 And Abraham set seven ewe lambs of the flock by themselves.

29 Then A·bim′e·lech asked Abraham, "What *is the meaning of* these seven ewe lambs which you have set by themselves?"

30 And he said, "You will take *these* seven ewe lambs from my hand, that they may be my witness that I have dug this well."

31 Therefore he called that place Bē·er·shē′ba,*a* because the two of them swore an oath there.

32 Thus they made a covenant at Bē·er·shē′ba. So A·bim′e·lech rose with Phī′chol, the commander of his army, and they returned to the land of the Phi·lis′tines.

33 Then *Abraham* planted a tamarisk tree in Bē·er·shē′ba, and there called on the name of the LORD, the Everlasting God.

34 And Abraham stayed in the land of the Phi·lis′tines many days.

ABRAHAM'S FAITH CONFIRMED

God has changed Abram's name to Abraham. Now God has asked Abraham to do something. It would be the hardest thing Abraham has ever done. Will he do it?

22 Now it came to pass after these things that God tested Abraham, and said to him, "Abraham!" And he said, "Here I am."

2 Then He said, "Take now your son, your only *son* Isaac, whom you love, and go to the land of Mō·rī′ah, and offer him there as a burnt offering on one of the mountains of which I shall tell you."

3 So Abraham rose early in the morning and saddled his donkey, and took two of his young men with him, and Isaac his son; and he split the wood for the burnt offering, and

21:31 *a*Literally *Well of the Oath* or *Well of the Seven*

arose and went to the place of which God had told him.

4   Then on the third day Abraham lifted his eyes and saw the place afar off.

5   And Abraham said to his young men, "Stay here with the donkey; the lad*a* and I will go yonder and worship, and we will come back to you."

6   So Abraham took the wood of the burnt offering and laid *it* on Isaac his son; and he took the fire in his hand, and a knife, and the two of them went together.

7   But Isaac spoke to Abraham his father and said, "My father!" And he said, "Here I am, my son." Then he said, "Look, the fire and the wood, but where *is* the lamb for a burnt offering?"

8   And Abraham said, "My son, God will provide for Himself the lamb for a burnt offering." So the two of them went together.

9   Then they came to the place of which God had told him. And Abraham built an altar there and placed the wood in order; and he bound Isaac his son and laid him on the altar, upon the wood.

10 And Abraham stretched out his hand and took the knife to slay his son.

11 But the Angel of the LORD called to him from heaven and said, "Abraham, Abraham!" So he said, "Here I am."

12 And He said, "Do not lay your hand on the lad, or do anything to him; for now I know that you fear God, since you have not withheld your son, your only *son,* from Me."

13 Then Abraham lifted his eyes and looked, and there behind *him was* a ram caught in a thicket by its horns. So Abraham went and took the ram, and offered it up for a burnt offering instead of his son.

14 And Abraham called the name of the place, The-LORD-Will-Provide;*a* as it is said *to* this day, "In the Mount of the LORD it shall be provided."

15 Then the Angel of the LORD called to Abraham a second time out of heaven,

16 and said: "By Myself I have sworn, says the LORD, because you have done this thing, and have not withheld your son, your only *son*—

17 "blessing I will bless you, and multiplying I will multiply your descendants as the stars of the heaven and as the sand which *is* on the seashore; and your descendants shall possess the gate of their enemies.

18 "In your seed all the nations of the earth shall be blessed, because you have obeyed My voice."

19 So Abraham returned to his young men, and they rose and went together to Bē·er·shē′ba; and Abraham dwelt at Bē·er·shē′ba.

☑ *Bible Quiz*

Genesis 22:1–19 **Abraham Offers Isaac**

1. What was the hard thing God asked Abraham to do?
2. Why do you think Abraham obeyed so willingly?
3. How did God reward Abraham for his obedience?
4. Do you trust God so much that you would do anything for Him? How can you learn to trust God even more?

THE FAMILY OF NAHOR

20 Now it came to pass after these things that it was told Abraham, say-

---

22:5 *a*Or *young man*   22:14 *a*Hebrew *YHWH Yireh*

ing, "Indeed Mil′cah also has borne children to your brother Nā′hor:

21 "Huz his firstborn, Buz his brother, Ke·mū′el the father of Ar′am,

22 "Chē′sed, Hā′zō, Pil′dash, Jid′laph, and Be·thū′el."

23 And Be·thū′el begot Rebekah.ᵃ These eight Mil′cah bore to Nā′hor, Abraham's brother.

24 His concubine, whose name was Re·ū′mah, also bore Tē′bah, Gā′ham, Thā′hash, and Mā′a·chah.

SARAH'S DEATH AND BURIAL

23 Sarah lived one hundred and twenty-seven years; *these were* the years of the life of Sarah.

2 So Sarah died in Kir′jath Ar′ba (that *is,* Hē′bron) in the land of Cā′naan, and Abraham came to mourn for Sarah and to weep for her.

3 Then Abraham stood up from before his dead, and spoke to the sons of Heth, saying,

4 "I *am* a foreigner and a visitor among you. Give me property for a burial place among you, that I may bury my dead out of my sight."

5 And the sons of Heth answered Abraham, saying to him,

6 "Hear us, my lord: You *are* a mighty prince among us; bury your dead in the choicest of our burial places. None of us will withhold from you his burial place, that you may bury your dead."

7 Then Abraham stood up and bowed himself to the people of the land, the sons of Heth.

8 And he spoke with them, saying, "If it is your wish that I bury my dead out of my sight, hear me, and meet with Ē′phron the son of Zō′har for me,

9 "that he may give me the cave of Mach·pē′lah which he has, which *is* at the end of his field. Let him give it

to me at the full price, as property for a burial place among you."

10 Now Ē′phron dwelt among the sons of Heth; and Ē′phron the Hit′tīte answered Abraham in the presence of the sons of Heth, all who entered at the gate of his city, saying,

11 "No, my lord, hear me: I give you the field and the cave that *is* in it; I give it to you in the presence of the sons of my people. I give it to you. Bury your dead!"

12 Then Abraham bowed himself down before the people of the land;

13 and he spoke to Ē′phron in the hearing of the people of the land, saying, "If you *will give it,* please hear me. I will give you money for the field; take *it* from me and I will bury my dead there."

14 And Ē′phron answered Abraham, saying to him,

15 "My lord, listen to me; the land *is worth* four hundred shekels of silver. What *is* that between you and me? So bury your dead."

16 And Abraham listened to Ē′phron; and Abraham weighed out the silver for Ē′phron which he had named in the hearing of the sons of Heth, four hundred shekels of silver, currency of the merchants.

17 So the field of Ē′phron which *was* in Mach·pē′lah, which *was* before Mam′re, the field and the cave which *was* in it, and all the trees that *were* in the field, which *were* within all the surrounding borders, were deeded

18 to Abraham as a possession in the presence of the sons of Heth, before all who went in at the gate of his city.

19 And after this, Abraham buried Sarah his wife in the cave of the field of Mach·pē′lah, before Mam′re (that *is,* Hē′bron) in the land of Cā′naan.

20 So the field and the cave that *is* in

22:23 ᵃSpelled *Rebecca* in Romans 9:10

it were deeded to Abraham by the sons of Heth as property for a burial place.

A BRIDE FOR ISAAC

24 Now Abraham was old, well advanced in age; and the LORD had blessed Abraham in all things.

2 So Abraham said to the oldest servant of his house, who ruled over all that he had, "Please, put your hand under my thigh,

3 "and I will make you swear by the LORD, the God of heaven and the God of the earth, that you will not take a wife for my son from the daughters of the Cā′naan·ītes, among whom I dwell;

4 "but you shall go to my country and to my family, and take a wife for my son Isaac."

5 And the servant said to him, "Perhaps the woman will not be willing to follow me to this land. Must I take your son back to the land from which you came?"

6 But Abraham said to him, "Beware that you do not take my son back there.

7 "The LORD God of heaven, who took me from my father's house and from the land of my family, and who spoke to me and swore to me, saying, 'To your descendants*a* I give this land,' He will send His angel before you, and you shall take a wife for my son from there.

8 "And if the woman is not willing to follow you, then you will be released from this oath; only do not take my son back there."

9 So the servant put his hand under the thigh of Abraham his master, and swore to him concerning this matter.

10 Then the servant took ten of his master's camels and departed, for all his master's goods *were in* his hand. And he arose and went to Mes·o·po·tā′mi·a, to the city of Nā′hor.

11 And he made his camels kneel down outside the city by a well of water at evening time, the time when women go out to draw *water.*

Prayers

Genesis 24:12–27

Eliezer needed help. He had a job to do and he needed more wisdom than he had. He must find a wife for Abraham's son Isaac, the next chief of the tribe. But how would he find her? "Please give me success," Eliezer prayed. Do you ever pray for success? Do you ever pray for God to show you how to do something, or when, or where? When you think God knows more than you, ask for His wisdom.

---

12 Then he said, "O LORD God of my master Abraham, please give me success this day, and show kindness to my master Abraham.

13 "Behold, *here* I stand by the well of water, and the daughters of the men of the city are coming out to draw water.

14 "Now let it be that the young woman to whom I say, 'Please let down your pitcher that I may drink,' and she says, 'Drink, and I will also give your camels a drink'—*let* her *be the one* You have appointed for Your servant Isaac. And by this I will know that You have shown kindness to my master."

15 And it happened, before he had finished speaking, that behold, Rebekah, who was born to Be·thū′el, son of Mil′cah, the wife of Nā′hor,

24:7 *a*Literally *seed*

SERVING Genesis 24:15–20

What May I Do to Serve You?

Do you like others to do things for you? Are you glad when mother makes dinner for you or makes your bed? Are you glad when she washes and irons your clothes? Are you glad when father helps you fix something or takes you to a ball game? Are you really glad when others do special things for you? But are you just as glad to do special things for others?

1. What will this boy do to help someone? Why do you think he will do this?

2. What would you like to say to this boy? Read Genesis 24:18, 20. How did Rebekah serve?

3. What can you do today to make someone happy? What can you do to serve a friend or family member? Will you?

For more on *Values* turn to page 62
For more on *Serving* turn to page 467

Abraham's brother, came out with her pitcher on her shoulder.

16 Now the young woman *was* very beautiful to behold, a virgin; no man had known her. And she went down to the well, filled her pitcher, and came up.

17 And the servant ran to meet her and said, "Please let me drink a little water from your pitcher."

18 So she said, "Drink, my lord." Then she quickly let her pitcher down to her hand, and gave him a drink.

19 And when she had finished giving him a drink, she said, "I will draw *water* for your camels also, until they have finished drinking."

20 Then she quickly emptied her pitcher into the trough, ran back to the well to draw *water,* and drew for all his camels.

21 And the man, wondering at her, remained silent so as to know whether the LORD had made his journey prosperous or not.

22 So it was, when the camels had finished drinking, that the man took a golden nose ring weighing half a shekel, and two bracelets for her wrists weighing ten *shekels* of gold,

23 and said, "Whose daughter *are* you? Tell me, please, is there room *in* your father's house for us to lodge?"

24 So she said to him, "I *am* the daughter of Be·thu'el, Mil'cah's son, whom she bore to Na'hor."

25 Moreover she said to him, "We have both straw and feed enough, and room to lodge."

26 Then the man bowed down his head and worshiped the LORD.

27 And he said, "Blessed *be* the LORD God of my master Abraham, who has not forsaken His mercy and His truth toward my master. As for me, being on the way, the LORD led me to the house of my master's brethren."

28 So the young woman ran and told her mother's household these things.

29 Now Rebekah had a brother whose name *was* La'ban, and La'ban ran out to the man by the well.

30 So it came to pass, when he saw the nose ring, and the bracelets on his sister's wrists, and when he heard the words of his sister Rebekah, saying, "Thus the man spoke to me," that he went to the man. And there he stood by the camels at the well.

31 And he said, "Come in, O blessed of the LORD! Why do you stand outside? For I have prepared the house, and a place for the camels."

32 Then the man came to the house. And he unloaded the camels, and provided straw and feed for the camels, and water to wash his feet and the feet of the men who *were* with him.

33 *Food* was set before him to eat, but he said, "I will not eat until I have told about my errand." And he said, "Speak on."

34 So he said, "I *am* Abraham's servant.

35 "The LORD has blessed my master greatly, and he has become great; and He has given him flocks and herds, silver and gold, male and female servants, and camels and donkeys.

36 "And Sarah my master's wife bore a son to my master when she was old; and to him he has given all that he has.

37 "Now my master made me swear, saying, 'You shall not take a wife for my son from the daughters of the Ca'naan·ites, in whose land I dwell;

38 'but you shall go to my father's house and to my family, and take a wife for my son.'

39 "And I said to my master, 'Perhaps the woman will not follow me.'

40 "But he said to me, 'The LORD, before whom I walk, will send His angel

with you and prosper your way; and you shall take a wife for my son from my family and from my father's house.

41 'You will be clear from this oath when you arrive among my family; for if they will not give *her* to you, then you will be released from my oath.'

42 "And this day I came to the well and said, 'O LORD God of my master Abraham, if You will now prosper the way in which I go,

43 'behold, I stand by the well of water; and it shall come to pass that when the virgin comes out to draw *water,* and I say to her, "Please give me a little water from your pitcher to drink,"

44 'and she says to me, "Drink, and I will draw for your camels also,"—*let* her *be* the woman whom the LORD has appointed for my master's son.'

45 "But before I had finished speaking in my heart, there was Rebekah, coming out with her pitcher on her shoulder; and she went down to the well and drew *water.* And I said to her, 'Please let me drink.'

46 "And she made haste and let her pitcher down from her *shoulder,* and said, 'Drink, and I will give your camels a drink also.' So I drank, and she gave the camels a drink also.

47 "Then I asked her, and said, 'Whose daughter *are* you?' And she said, 'The daughter of Be·thū'-el, Nā'hor's son, whom Mil'cah bore to him.' So I put the nose ring on her nose and the bracelets on her wrists.

48 "And I bowed my head and worshiped the LORD, and blessed the LORD God of my master Abraham, who had led me in the way of truth to take the daughter of my master's brother for his son.

49 "Now if you will deal kindly and truly with my master, tell me. And if not, tell me, that I may turn to the right hand or to the left."

50 Then Lā'ban and Be·thū'el answered and said, "The thing comes from the LORD; we cannot speak to you either bad or good.

51 "Here *is* Rebekah before you; take *her* and go, and let her be your master's son's wife, as the LORD has spoken."

52 And it came to pass, when Abraham's servant heard their words, that he worshiped the LORD, *bowing himself* to the earth.

53 Then the servant brought out jewelry of silver, jewelry of gold, and clothing, and gave *them* to Rebekah. He also gave precious things to her brother and to her mother.

54 And he and the men who *were* with him ate and drank and stayed all night. Then they arose in the morning, and he said, "Send me away to my master."

55 But her brother and her mother said, "Let the young woman stay with us *a few* days, at least ten; after that she may go."

56 And he said to them, "Do not hinder me, since the LORD has prospered my way; send me away so that I may go to my master."

57 So they said, "We will call the young woman and ask her personally."

58 Then they called Rebekah and said to her, "Will you go with this man?" And she said, "I will go."

59 So they sent away Rebekah their sister and her nurse, and Abraham's servant and his men.

60 And they blessed Rebekah and said to her:

"Our sister, *may* you *become
 The mother of* thousands of ten
     thousands;
 And may your descendants
     possess

The gates of those who hate
    them.''

61 Then Rebekah and her maids
arose, and they rode on the camels
and followed the man. So the servant
took Rebekah and departed.

62 Now Isaac came from the way of
Bē′er La·haī′ Roi, for he dwelt in the
South.

63 And Isaac went out to meditate in
the field in the evening; and he lifted
his eyes and looked, and there, the
camels *were* coming.

64 Then Rebekah lifted her eyes, and
when she saw Isaac she dismounted
from her camel;

65 for she had said to the servant,
''Who *is* this man walking in the field
to meet us?'' The servant said, ''It *is*
my master.'' So she took a veil and
covered herself.

66 And the servant told Isaac all the
things that he had done.

67 Then Isaac brought her into his
mother Sarah's tent; and he took Rebekah and she became his wife, and
he loved her. So Isaac was comforted
after his mother's *death.*

ABRAHAM AND KETURAH

25 Abraham again took a wife,
and her name *was* Ke·tū′rah.

2 And she bore him Zim′ran,
Jok′shan, Mē′dan, Mid′i·an, Ish′bak,
and Shū′ah.

3 Jok′shan begot Shē′ba and
Dē′dan. And the sons of Dē′dan were
As·shū′rim, Le·tū′shim, and Le·um′-
mim.

4 And the sons of Mid′i·an *were*
Ē′phah, Ē′pher, Hā′noch, A·bī′dah,
and El·dā′ah. All these *were* the children of Ke·tū′rah.

5 And Abraham gave all that he
had to Isaac.

6 But Abraham gave gifts to the

sons of the concubines which Abraham had; and while he was still living he sent them eastward, away
from Isaac his son, to the country of
the east.

ABRAHAM'S DEATH AND BURIAL

7 This *is* the sum of the years of
Abraham's life which he lived: one
hundred and seventy-five years.

8 Then Abraham breathed his last
and died in a good old age, an old
man and full *of years,* and was gathered to his people.

9 And his sons Isaac and Ish′ma·el
buried him in the cave of Mach-
pē′lah, which *is* before Mam′re, in
the field of Ē′phron the son of Zō′har
the Hit′tīte,

10 the field which Abraham purchased from the sons of Heth. There
Abraham was buried, and Sarah his
wife.

11 And it came to pass, after the
death of Abraham, that God blessed
his son Isaac. And Isaac dwelt at
Bē′er La·haī′ Roi.

THE FAMILIES OF ISHMAEL
AND ISAAC

12 Now this *is* the genealogy of
Ish′ma·el, Abraham's son, whom
Hā′gar the Egyptian, Sarah's
maidservant, bore to Abraham.

13 And these *were* the names of the
sons of Ish′ma·el, by their names, according to their generations: The
firstborn of Ish′ma·el, Ne·bā′joth;
then Kē′dar, Ad′bē·el, Mib′sam,

14 Mish′ma, Dū′mah, Mas′sa,

15 Hā′dar,[a] Tē′ma, Jē′tur, Nā′phish,
and Ked′e·mah.

16 These *were* the sons of Ish′ma·el
and these *were* their names, by their

25:15 [a]Masoretic Text reads *Hadad.*

towns and their settlements, twelve princes according to their nations.

17 These *were* the years of the life of Ish′ma·el: one hundred and thirty-seven years; and he breathed his last and died, and was gathered to his people.

18 (They dwelt from Hav′i·lah as far as Shūr, which *is* east of Egypt as you go toward Assyria.) He died in the presence of all his brethren.

> *This is a story about two brothers who could never get along. If they could have learned to be kind to one another, how much better things would have turned out!*

19 This *is* the genealogy of Isaac, Abraham's son. Abraham begot Isaac.

20 Isaac was forty years old when he took Rebekah as wife, the daughter of Be·thū′el the Syrian of Pad′an Ar′am, the sister of Lā′ban the Syrian.

21 Now Isaac pleaded with the LORD for his wife, because she *was* barren; and the LORD granted his plea, and Rebekah his wife conceived.

22 But the children struggled together within her; and she said, "If *all is* well, why *am I like* this?" So she went to inquire of the LORD.

23 And the LORD said to her:

"Two nations *are* in your womb,
Two peoples shall be separated
    from your body;
One people shall be stronger than
    the other,
And the older shall serve the
    younger."

24 So when her days were fulfilled *for her* to give birth, indeed *there were* twins in her womb.

25 And the first came out red. *He was* like a hairy garment all over; so they called his name Esau.*a*

26 Afterward his brother came out, and his hand took hold of Esau's heel; so his name was called Jacob.*a* Isaac *was* sixty years old when she bore them.

27 So the boys grew. And Esau was a skillful hunter, a man of the field; but Jacob was a mild man, dwelling in tents.

28 And Isaac loved Esau because he ate *of his* game, but Rebekah loved Jacob.

ESAU SELLS HIS BIRTHRIGHT

29 Now Jacob cooked a stew; and Esau came in from the field, and he *was* weary.

30 And Esau said to Jacob, "Please feed me with that same red *stew,* for I *am* weary." Therefore his name was called Ē′dom.*a*

31 But Jacob said, "Sell me your birthright as of this day."

32 And Esau said, "Look, I *am* about to die; so what *is* this birthright to me?"

33 Then Jacob said, "Swear to me as of this day." So he swore to him, and sold his birthright to Jacob.

34 And Jacob gave Esau bread and stew of lentils; then he ate and drank, arose, and went his way. Thus Esau despised *his* birthright.

ISAAC AND ABIMELECH

26 There was a famine in the land, besides the first famine that was in the days of Abraham. And Isaac went to A·bim′e·lech king of the Phi·lis′tines, in Gē′rar.

25:25 *a*Literally *Hairy*   25:26 *a*Literally *Supplanter*   25:30 *a*Literally *Red*

☑ *Bible Quiz*

Genesis 25:19–34 **Jacob and Esau Fight**

1. Who was the older brother? What did he look like?
2. What was the name of the younger brother?
3. In what ways were Jacob and Esau different?
4. How did Jacob deceive Esau? Why do you think Esau gave away his birthright so easily?
5. If you were their parents, what would you have told Jacob and Esau about getting along better?

---

2 Then the LORD appeared to him and said: "Do not go down to Egypt; live in the land of which I shall tell you.

3 "Dwell in this land, and I will be with you and bless you; for to you and your descendants I give all these lands, and I will perform the oath which I swore to Abraham your father.

4 "And I will make your descendants multiply as the stars of heaven; I will give to your descendants all these lands; and in your seed all the nations of the earth shall be blessed;

5 "because Abraham obeyed My voice and kept My charge, My commandments, My statutes, and My laws."

6 So Isaac dwelt in Gē′rar.

7 And the men of the place asked about his wife. And he said, "She *is* my sister"; for he was afraid to say, "*She is* my wife," *because he thought,* "lest the men of the place kill me for Rebekah, because she *is* beautiful to behold."

8 Now it came to pass, when he had been there a long time, that A·bim′e·lech king of the Phi·lis′tines looked through a window, and saw, and there was Isaac, showing endearment to Rebekah his wife.

9 Then A·bim′e·lech called Isaac and said, "Quite obviously she *is* your wife; so how could you say, 'She *is* my sister'?" Isaac said to him, "Because I said, 'Lest I die on account of her.' "

10 And A·bim′e·lech said, "What *is* this you have done to us? One of the people might soon have lain with your wife, and you would have brought guilt on us."

11 So A·bim′e·lech charged all *his* people, saying, "He who touches this man or his wife shall surely be put to death."

12 Then Isaac sowed in that land, and reaped in the same year a hundredfold; and the LORD blessed him.

13 The man began to prosper, and continued prospering until he became very prosperous;

14 for he had possessions of flocks and possessions of herds and a great number of servants. So the Phi·lis′tines envied him.

15 Now the Phi·lis′tines had stopped up all the wells which his father's servants had dug in the days of Abraham his father, and they had filled them with earth.

16 And A·bim′e·lech said to Isaac, "Go away from us, for you are much mightier than we."

17 Then Isaac departed from there and pitched his tent in the Valley of Gē′rar, and dwelt there.

18 And Isaac dug again the wells of water which they had dug in the days of Abraham his father, for the Phi·lis′tines had stopped them up after the death of Abraham. He called

them by the names which his father had called them.

19 Also Isaac's servants dug in the valley, and found a well of running water there.

20 But the herdsmen of Gē′rar quarreled with Isaac's herdsmen, saying, "The water is ours." So he called the name of the well Ē′sek,a because they quarreled with him.

21 Then they dug another well, and they quarreled over that one also. So he called its name Sit′nah.a

22 And he moved from there and dug another well, and they did not quarrel over it. So he called its name Re·hō′both,a because he said, "For now the LORD has made room for us, and we shall be fruitful in the land."

23 Then he went up from there to Bē·er·shē′ba.

24 And the LORD appeared to him the same night and said, "I am the God of your father Abraham; do not fear, for I am with you. I will bless you and multiply your descendants for My servant Abraham's sake."

25 So he built an altar there and called on the name of the LORD, and he pitched his tent there; and there Isaac's servants dug a well.

26 Then A·bim′e·lech came to him from Gē′rar with A·huz′zath, one of his friends, and Phī′chol the commander of his army.

27 And Isaac said to them, "Why have you come to me, since you hate me and have sent me away from you?"

28 But they said, "We have certainly seen that the LORD is with you. So we said, 'Let there now be an oath between us, between you and us; and let us make a covenant with you,

29 'that you will do us no harm, since we have not touched you, and since we have done nothing to you but good and have sent you away in peace. You are now the blessed of the LORD.' "

30 So he made them a feast, and they ate and drank.

31 Then they arose early in the morning and swore an oath with one another; and Isaac sent them away, and they departed from him in peace.

32 It came to pass the same day that Isaac's servants came and told him about the well which they had dug, and said to him, "We have found water."

33 So he called it Shē′bah.a Therefore the name of the city is Bē·er·shē′bab to this day.

34 When Esau was forty years old, he took as wives Judith the daughter of Be·ē′rī the Hit′tīte, and Bas′e·math the daughter of Ē′lon the Hit′tīte.

35 And they were a grief of mind to Isaac and Rebekah.

ISAAC BLESSES JACOB

Jacob wanted something very much, but he couldn't have it. So he made a plan to get it anyway. The plan even included tricking his own father. Would Jacob really do that?

27 Now it came to pass, when Isaac was old and his eyes were so dim that he could not see, that he called Esau his older son and said to him, "My son." And he answered him, "Here I am."

2 Then he said, "Behold now, I am old. I do not know the day of my death.

3 "Now therefore, please take your weapons, your quiver and your bow,

26:20 aLiterally *Quarrel*   26:21 aLiterally *Enmity*   26:22 aLiterally *Spaciousness*
26:33 aLiterally *Oath* or *Seven*   bLiterally *Well of the Oath* or *Well of the Seven*

and go out to the field and hunt game for me.

4 "And make me savory food, such as I love, and bring *it* to me that I may eat, that my soul may bless you before I die."

5 Now Rebekah was listening when Isaac spoke to Esau his son. And Esau went to the field to hunt game and to bring *it*.

6 So Rebekah spoke to Jacob her son, saying, "Indeed I heard your father speak to Esau your brother, saying,

7 'Bring me game and make savory food for me, that I may eat it and bless you in the presence of the LORD before my death.'

8 "Now therefore, my son, obey my voice according to what I command you.

9 "Go now to the flock and bring me from there two choice kids of the goats, and I will make savory food from them for your father, such as he loves.

10 "Then you shall take *it* to your father, that he may eat *it,* and that he may bless you before his death."

11 And Jacob said to Rebekah his mother, "Look, Esau my brother *is* a hairy man, and I *am* a smooth-*skinned* man.

12 "Perhaps my father will feel me, and I shall seem to be a deceiver to him; and I shall bring a curse on myself and not a blessing."

13 But his mother said to him, "*Let* your curse *be* on me, my son; only obey my voice, and go, get *them* for me."

14 And he went and got *them* and brought *them* to his mother, and his mother made savory food, such as his father loved.

15 Then Rebekah took the choice clothes of her elder son Esau, which *were* with her in the house, and put them on Jacob her younger son.

16 And she put the skins of the kids of the goats on his hands and on the smooth part of his neck.

17 Then she gave the savory food and the bread, which she had prepared, into the hand of her son Jacob.

18 So he went to his father and said, "My father." And he said, "Here I am. Who *are* you, my son?"

19 Jacob said to his father, "I *am* Esau your firstborn; I have done just as you told me; please arise, sit and eat of my game, that your soul may bless me."

20 But Isaac said to his son, "How *is* it that you have found *it* so quickly, my son?" And he said, "Because the LORD your God brought *it* to me."

21 Then Isaac said to Jacob, "Please come near, that I may feel you, my son, whether you *are* really my son Esau or not."

22 So Jacob went near to Isaac his father, and he felt him and said, "The voice *is* Jacob's voice, but the hands *are* the hands of Esau."

23 And he did not recognize him, because his hands were hairy like his brother Esau's hands; so he blessed him.

24 Then he said, "*Are* you really my son Esau?" He said, "I *am.*"

25 He said, "Bring *it* near to me, and I will eat of my son's game, so that my soul may bless you." So he brought *it* near to him, and he ate; and he brought him wine, and he drank.

26 Then his father Isaac said to him, "Come near now and kiss me, my son."

27 And he came near and kissed him; and he smelled the smell of his clothing, and blessed him and said:

"Surely, the smell of my son
  Is like the smell of a field
  Which the LORD has blessed.

28 Therefore may God give you
   Of the dew of heaven,
   Of the fatness of the earth,
   And plenty of grain and wine.
29 Let peoples serve you,
   And nations bow down to you.
   Be master over your brethren,
   And let your mother's sons bow
     down to you.
   Cursed *be* everyone who curses
     you,
   And blessed *be* those who bless
     you!"

Esau's Lost Hope

30 Now it happened, as soon as Isaac had finished blessing Jacob, and Jacob had scarcely gone out from the presence of Isaac his father, that Esau his brother came in from his hunting.
31 He also had made savory food, and brought it to his father, and said to his father, "Let my father arise and eat of his son's game, that your soul may bless me."
32 And his father Isaac said to him, "Who *are* you?" So he said, "I *am* your son, your firstborn, Esau."
33 Then Isaac trembled exceedingly, and said, "Who? Where *is* the one who hunted game and brought *it* to me? I ate all *of it* before you came, and I have blessed him—*and* indeed he shall be blessed."
34 When Esau heard the words of his father, he cried with an exceedingly great and bitter cry, and said to his father, "Bless me—me also, O my father!"
35 But he said, "Your brother came with deceit and has taken away your blessing."
36 And *Esau* said, "Is he not rightly named Jacob? For he has supplanted me these two times. He took away my birthright, and now look, he has taken away my blessing!" And he

said, "Have you not reserved a blessing for me?"
37 Then Isaac answered and said to Esau, "Indeed I have made him your master, and all his brethren I have given to him as servants; with grain and wine I have sustained him. What shall I do now for you, my son?"
38 And Esau said to his father, "Have you only one blessing, my father? Bless me—me also, O my father!" And Esau lifted up his voice and wept.
39 Then Isaac his father answered and said to him:

  "Behold, your dwelling shall be of
    the fatness of the earth,
   And of the dew of heaven from
    above.
40 By your sword you shall live,
   And you shall serve your brother;
   And it shall come to pass, when
    you become restless,
   That you shall break his yoke
    from your neck."

Jacob Escapes from Esau

41 So Esau hated Jacob because of the blessing with which his father blessed him, and Esau said in his heart, "The days of mourning for my father are at hand; then I will kill my brother Jacob."
42 And the words of Esau her older son were told to Rebekah. So she sent and called Jacob her younger son, and said to him, "Surely your brother Esau comforts himself concerning you *by intending* to kill you.
43 "Now therefore, my son, obey my voice: arise, flee to my brother Lā′ban in Har′an.
44 "And stay with him a few days, until your brother's fury turns away,
45 "until your brother's anger turns away from you, and he forgets what you have done to him; then I will

What Should I Do?

WOULD YOU LIKE TO SEND YOUR BROTHER OR SISTER TO THE MOON?
Genesis 27:35, 36, 41

There are times when you might like to send your sister or brother to the moon. Because his sister has done something special, this brother is jealous. He would like to send her to the moon. Sometimes your brother or sister says something you don't like, or has something better than you have, or makes fun of you. You'd like to send him or her to the moon. What should you do instead?

1. Have you been angry at your brother or sister lately? Why? What did you want to do?
2. What would Jesus want you to do when you are angry at your brother or sister, or are jealous of something?
3. What will you do next time this happens?

For more on *What Should I Do?* turn to page 55
For more on *Temptation* turn to page 631

send and bring you from there. Why should I be bereaved also of you both in one day?"

46 And Rebekah said to Isaac, "I am weary of my life because of the daughters of Heth; if Jacob takes a wife of the daughters of Heth, like these *who are* the daughters of the land, what good will my life be to me?"

28 Then Isaac called Jacob and blessed him, and charged him, and said to him: "You shall not take a wife from the daughters of Cā′naan.
2 "Arise, go to Pad′an Ar′am, to the house of Be·thū′el your mother's father; and take yourself a wife from there of the daughters of Lā′ban your mother's brother.

3 "May God Almighty bless you,
   And make you fruitful and
      multiply you,
   That you may be an assembly of
      peoples;
4 And give you the blessing of
      Abraham,
   To you and your descendants with
      you,
   That you may inherit the land
   In which you are a stranger,
   Which God gave to Abraham."

5 So Isaac sent Jacob away, and he went to Pad′an Ar′am, to Lā′ban the son of Be·thū′el the Syrian, the brother of Rebekah, the mother of Jacob and Esau.

ESAU MARRIES MAHALATH

6 Esau saw that Isaac had blessed Jacob and sent him away to Pad′an Ar′am to take himself a wife from there, *and that* as he blessed him he gave him a charge, saying, "You shall not take a wife from the daughters of Cā′naan,"

7 and that Jacob had obeyed his father and his mother and had gone to Pad′an Ar′am.
8 Also Esau saw that the daughters of Cā′naan did not please his father Isaac.
9 So Esau went to Ish′ma·el and took Mā′ha·lath the daughter of Ish′ma·el, Abraham's son, the sister of Ne·bā′joth, to be his wife in addition to the wives he had.

JACOB'S VOW AT BETHEL

10 Now Jacob went out from Bē·er-shē′ba and went toward Har′an.
11 So he came to a certain place and stayed there all night, because the sun had set. And he took one of the stones of that place and put it at his head, and he lay down in that place to sleep.
12 Then he dreamed, and behold, a ladder *was* set up on the earth, and its top reached to heaven; and there the angels of God were ascending and descending on it.
13 And behold, the LORD stood above it and said: "I *am* the LORD God of Abraham your father and the God of Isaac; the land on which you lie I will give to you and your descendants.
14 "Also your descendants shall be as the dust of the earth; you shall spread abroad to the west and the east, to the north and the south; and in you and in your seed all the families of the earth shall be blessed.
15 "Behold, I *am* with you and will keep you wherever you go, and will bring you back to this land; for I will not leave you until I have done what I have spoken to you."
16 Then Jacob awoke from his sleep and said, "Surely the LORD is in this place, and I did not know *it.*"
17 And he was afraid and said, "How awesome *is* this place! This *is* none

other than the house of God, and this *is* the gate of heaven!"

18 Then Jacob rose early in the morning, and took the stone that he had put at his head, set it up as a pillar, and poured oil on top of it.
19 And he called the name of that place Beth'el;*a* but the name of that city had been Luz previously.
20 Then Jacob made a vow, saying, "If God will be with me, and keep me in this way that I am going, and give me bread to eat and clothing to put on,
21 "so that I come back to my father's house in peace, then the Lord shall be my God.
22 "And this stone which I have set as a pillar shall be God's house, and of all that You give me I will surely give a tenth to You."

JACOB MEETS RACHEL

Here is a story about how God helped Jacob when he moved to a new place. But it is also a story about how Jacob, the person who deceived others, was about to be deceived himself.

29 So Jacob went on his journey and came to the land of the people of the East.
2 And he looked, and saw a well in the field; and behold, there *were* three flocks of sheep lying by it; for out of that well they watered the flocks. A large stone *was* on the well's mouth.
3 Now all the flocks would be gathered there; and they would roll the stone from the well's mouth, water the sheep, and put the stone back in its place on the well's mouth.
4 And Jacob said to them, "My brethren, where *are* you from?" And they said, "We *are* from Har'an."

☑ *Bible Quiz*

Genesis 27; 28 **Jacob Tricks His Father**

1. What did Jacob want so much? Why do you think this was so important to him?
2. How did Jacob try to get the blessing?
3. Why was it easy for Jacob to deceive his father?
4. What did Esau do when he found out he also had been deceived?
5. Where did Jacob go when he had to leave home? What strange dream did he have along the way?
6. Now the two brothers would be enemies for a long time. Was it worth it for Jacob to break up the family in order to get what he wanted? What will you do the next time you really want something you can't have?

---

5 Then he said to them, "Do you know La'ban the son of Na'hor?" And they said, "We know him."
6 So he said to them, "Is he well?" And they said, "*He is* well. And look, his daughter Rachel is coming with the sheep."
7 Then he said, "Look, *it is* still high day; *it is* not time for the cattle to be gathered together. Water the sheep, and go and feed *them.*"
8 But they said, "We cannot until all the flocks are gathered together, and they have rolled the stone from

28:19 aLiterally *House of God*

the well's mouth; then we water the sheep."

9 Now while he was still speaking with them, Rachel came with her father's sheep, for she was a shepherdess.

10 And it came to pass, when Jacob saw Rachel the daughter of Lā′ban his mother's brother, and the sheep of Lā′ban his mother's brother, that Jacob went near and rolled the stone from the well's mouth, and watered the flock of Lā′ban his mother's brother.

11 Then Jacob kissed Rachel, and lifted up his voice and wept.

12 And Jacob told Rachel that he *was* her father's relative and that he *was* Rebekah's son. So she ran and told her father.

13 Then it came to pass, when Lā′ban heard the report about Jacob his sister's son, that he ran to meet him, and embraced him and kissed him, and brought him to his house. So he told Lā′ban all these things.

14 And Lā′ban said to him, "Surely you *are* my bone and my flesh." And he stayed with him for a month.

Jacob Marries Leah and Rachel

15 Then Lā′ban said to Jacob, "Because you *are* my relative, should you therefore serve me for nothing? Tell me, what *should* your wages *be?*"

16 Now Lā′ban had two daughters: the name of the elder *was* Leah, and the name of the younger *was* Rachel.

17 Leah's eyes *were* delicate, but Rachel was beautiful of form and appearance.

18 Now Jacob loved Rachel; so he said, "I will serve you seven years for Rachel your younger daughter."

19 And Lā′ban said, "*It is* better that I give her to you than that I should give her to another man. Stay with me."

20 So Jacob served seven years for Rachel, and they seemed *only* a few days to him because of the love he had for her.

21 Then Jacob said to Lā′ban, "Give *me* my wife, for my days are fulfilled, that I may go in to her."

22 And Lā′ban gathered together all the men of the place and made a feast.

23 Now it came to pass in the evening, that he took Leah his daughter and brought her to Jacob; and he went in to her.

24 And Lā′ban gave his maid Zil′pah to his daughter Leah *as* a maid.

25 So it came to pass in the morning, that behold, it *was* Leah. And he said to Lā′ban, "What is this you have done to me? Was it not for Rachel that I served you? Why then have you deceived me?"

26 And Lā′ban said, "It must not be done so in our country, to give the younger before the firstborn.

27 "Fulfill her week, and we will give you this one also for the service which you will serve with me still another seven years."

28 Then Jacob did so and fulfilled her week. So he gave him his daughter Rachel as wife also.

29 And Lā′ban gave his maid Bil′hah to his daughter Rachel as a maid.

30 Then *Jacob* also went in to Rachel, and he also loved Rachel more than Leah. And he served with Lā′ban still another seven years.

The Children of Jacob

31 When the LORD saw that Leah *was* unloved, He opened her womb; but Rachel *was* barren.

32 So Leah conceived and bore a son, and she called his name Reuben;*a* for

29:32 *a*Literally *See, a Son*

☑ Bible Quiz

Genesis 29:1–30 **Jacob Meets Rachel**

1. Who was the woman Jacob met at the well? What did she do for a living?
2. Who was Rachel's father?
3. How did Jacob feel about Rachel? How long did he have to work to marry her?
4. How was Jacob deceived on his wedding day?
5. Do you remember when Jacob deceived his father and brother (Genesis 25:27–34 and Genesis 27)? Now Jacob was the one being deceived! The bad things Jacob had done to others were now being done to him. How can you keep that from happening to you?

---

she said, "The LORD has surely looked on my affliction. Now therefore, my husband will love me."

33 Then she conceived again and bore a son, and said, "Because the LORD has heard that I *am* unloved, He has therefore given me this *son* also." And she called his name Sim'-ē·on.*a*

34 She conceived again and bore a son, and said, "Now this time my husband will become attached to me, because I have borne him three sons." Therefore his name was called Levi.*a*

35 And she conceived again and bore a son, and said, "Now I will praise the LORD." Therefore she called his name Judah.*a* Then she stopped bearing.

30 Now when Rachel saw that she bore Jacob no children, Rachel envied her sister, and said to Jacob, "Give me children, or else I die!"

2 And Jacob's anger was aroused against Rachel, and he said, "*Am* I in the place of God, who has withheld from you the fruit of the womb?"

3 So she said, "Here is my maid Bil'hah; go in to her, and she will bear *a child* on my knees, that I also may have children by her."

4 Then she gave him Bil'hah her maid as wife, and Jacob went in to her.

5 And Bil'hah conceived and bore Jacob a son.

6 Then Rachel said, "God has judged my case; and He has also heard my voice and given me a son." Therefore she called his name Dan.*a*

7 And Rachel's maid Bil'hah conceived again and bore Jacob a second son.

8 Then Rachel said, "With great wrestlings I have wrestled with my sister, *and* indeed I have prevailed." So she called his name Naph'ta·li.*a*

9 When Leah saw that she had stopped bearing, she took Zil'pah her maid and gave her to Jacob as wife.

10 And Leah's maid Zil'pah bore Jacob a son.

11 Then Leah said, "A troop comes!"*a* So she called his name Gad.*b*

12 And Leah's maid Zil'pah bore Jacob a second son.

13 Then Leah said, "I am happy, for the daughters will call me blessed." So she called his name Ash'er.*a*

14 Now Reuben went in the days of wheat harvest and found mandrakes

---

29:33 *a*Literally *Heard*   29:34 *a*Literally *Attached*   29:35 *a*Literally *Praise*   30:6 *a*Literally *Judge*   30:8 *a*Literally *My Wrestling*   30:11 *a*Following Qere, Syriac, and Targum; Kethib, Septuagint, and Vulgate read *in fortune.* *b*Literally *Troop* or *Fortune*   30:13 *a*Literally *Happy*

in the field, and brought them to his mother Leah. Then Rachel said to Leah, "Please give me *some* of your son's mandrakes."

15 But she said to her, "*Is it* a small matter that you have taken away my husband? Would you take away my son's mandrakes also?" And Rachel said, "Therefore he will lie with you tonight for your son's mandrakes."

16 When Jacob came out of the field in the evening, Leah went out to meet him and said, "You must come in to me, for I have surely hired you with my son's mandrakes." And he lay with her that night.

17 And God listened to Leah, and she conceived and bore Jacob a fifth son.

18 Leah said, "God has given me my wages, because I have given my maid to my husband." So she called his name Is′sa·char.*a*

19 Then Leah conceived again and bore Jacob a sixth son.

20 And Leah said, "God has endowed me *with* a good endowment; now my husband will dwell with me, because I have borne him six sons." So she called his name Zeb′ū·lun.*a*

21 Afterward she bore a daughter, and called her name Dī′nah.

22 Then God remembered Rachel, and God listened to her and opened her womb.

23 And she conceived and bore a son, and said, "God has taken away my reproach."

24 So she called his name Joseph,*a* and said, "The LORD shall add to me another son."

JACOB'S AGREEMENT WITH LABAN

25 And it came to pass, when Rachel had borne Joseph, that Jacob said to Lā′ban, "Send me away, that I may go to my own place and to my country.

26 "Give *me* my wives and my children for whom I have served you, and let me go; for you know my service which I have done for you."

27 And Lā′ban said to him, "Please *stay,* if I have found favor in your eyes, *for* I have learned by experience that the LORD has blessed me for your sake."

28 Then he said, "Name me your wages, and I will give *it.*"

29 So *Jacob* said to him, "You know how I have served you and how your livestock has been with me.

30 "For what you had before I *came was* little, and it has increased to a great amount; the LORD has blessed you since my coming. And now, when shall I also provide for my own house?"

31 So he said, "What shall I give you?" And Jacob said, "You shall not give me anything. If you will do this thing for me, I will again feed and keep your flocks:

32 "Let me pass through all your flock today, removing from there all the speckled and spotted sheep, and all the brown ones among the lambs, and the spotted and speckled among the goats; and *these* shall be my wages.

33 "So my righteousness will answer for me in time to come, when the subject of my wages comes before you: every one that *is* not speckled and spotted among the goats, and brown among the lambs, will be considered stolen, if *it is* with me."

34 And Lā′ban said, "Oh, that it were according to your word!"

35 So he removed that day the male goats that were speckled and spotted, all the female goats that were speckled and spotted, every one that had *some* white in it, and all the brown

30:18 *a*Literally *Wages*   30:20 *a*Literally *Dwelling*   30:24 *a*Literally *He Will Add*

ones among the lambs, and gave *them* into the hand of his sons.

36 Then he put three days' journey between himself and Jacob, and Jacob fed the rest of Lā′ban's flocks.

37 Now Jacob took for himself rods of green poplar and of the almond and chestnut trees, peeled white strips in them, and exposed the white which *was* in the rods.

38 And the rods which he had peeled, he set before the flocks in the gutters, in the watering troughs where the flocks came to drink, so that they should conceive when they came to drink.

39 So the flocks conceived before the rods, and the flocks brought forth streaked, speckled, and spotted.

40 Then Jacob separated the lambs, and made the flocks face toward the streaked and all the brown in the flock of Lā′ban; but he put his own flocks by themselves and did not put them with Lā′ban's flock.

41 And it came to pass, whenever the stronger livestock conceived, that Jacob placed the rods before the eyes of the livestock in the gutters, that they might conceive among the rods.

42 But when the flocks were feeble, he did not put *them* in; so the feebler were Lā′ban's and the stronger Jacob's.

43 Thus the man became exceedingly prosperous, and had large flocks, female and male servants, and camels and donkeys.

JACOB FLEES FROM LABAN

31 Now *Jacob* heard the words of Lā′ban's sons, saying, "Jacob has taken away all that was our father's, and from what was our father's he has acquired all this wealth."

2 And Jacob saw the countenance of Lā′ban, and indeed it *was* not *favorable* toward him as before.

3 Then the LORD said to Jacob, "Return to the land of your fathers and to your family, and I will be with you."

4 So Jacob sent and called Rachel and Leah to the field, to his flock,

5 and said to them, "I see your father's countenance, that it *is* not *favorable* toward me as before; but the God of my father has been with me.

6 "And you know that with all my might I have served your father.

7 "Yet your father has deceived me and changed my wages ten times, but God did not allow him to hurt me.

8 "If he said thus: 'The speckled shall be your wages,' then all the flocks bore speckled. And if he said thus: 'The streaked shall be your wages,' then all the flocks bore streaked.

9 "So God has taken away the livestock of your father and given *them* to me.

10 "And it happened, at the time when the flocks conceived, that I lifted my eyes and saw in a dream, and behold, the rams which leaped upon the flocks *were* streaked, speckled, and gray-spotted.

11 "Then the Angel of God spoke to me in a dream, saying, 'Jacob.' And I said, 'Here I am.'

12 "And He said, 'Lift your eyes now and see, all the rams which leap on the flocks *are* streaked, speckled, and gray-spotted; for I have seen all that Lā′ban is doing to you.

13 'I *am* the God of Beth′el, where you anointed the pillar *and* where you made a vow to Me. Now arise, get out of this land, and return to the land of your family.' "

14 Then Rachel and Leah answered and said to him, "Is there still any portion or inheritance for us in our father's house?

15 "Are we not considered strangers by him? For he has sold us, and also completely consumed our money.
16 "For all these riches which God has taken from our father are *really* ours and our children's; now then, whatever God has said to you, do it."
17 Then Jacob rose and set his sons and his wives on camels.
18 And he carried away all his livestock and all his possessions which he had gained, his acquired livestock which he had gained in Pad′an Ar′am, to go to his father Isaac in the land of Cā′naan.
19 Now Lā′ban had gone to shear his sheep, and Rachel had stolen the household idols that were her father's.
20 And Jacob stole away, unknown to Lā′ban the Syrian, in that he did not tell him that he intended to flee.
21 So he fled with all that he had. He arose and crossed the river, and headed toward the mountains of Gil′ē·ad.

LABAN PURSUES JACOB

22 And Lā′ban was told on the third day that Jacob had fled.
23 Then he took his brethren with him and pursued him for seven days' journey, and he overtook him in the mountains of Gil′ē·ad.
24 But God had come to Lā′ban the Syrian in a dream by night, and said to him, "Be careful that you speak to Jacob neither good nor bad."
25 So Lā′ban overtook Jacob. Now Jacob had pitched his tent in the mountains, and Lā′ban with his brethren pitched in the mountains of Gil′ē·ad.
26 And Lā′ban said to Jacob: "What have you done, that you have stolen away unknown to me, and carried away my daughters like captives *taken* with the sword?

27 "Why did you flee away secretly, and steal away from me, and not tell me; for I might have sent you away with joy and songs, with timbrel and harp?
28 "And you did not allow me to kiss my sons and my daughters. Now you have done foolishly in *so* doing.
29 "It is in my power to do you harm, but the God of your father spoke to me last night, saying, 'Be careful that you speak to Jacob neither good nor bad.'
30 "And now you have surely gone because you greatly long for your father's house, *but* why did you steal my gods?"
31 Then Jacob answered and said to Lā′ban, "Because I was afraid, for I said, 'Perhaps you would take your daughters from me by force.'
32 "With whomever you find your gods, do not let him live. In the presence of our brethren, identify what I have of yours and take *it* with you." For Jacob did not know that Rachel had stolen them.
33 And Lā′ban went into Jacob's tent, into Leah's tent, and into the two maids' tents, but he did not find *them*. Then he went out of Leah's tent and entered Rachel's tent.
34 Now Rachel had taken the household idols, put them in the camel's saddle, and sat on them. And Lā′ban searched all about the tent but did not find *them*.
35 And she said to her father, "Let it not displease my lord that I cannot rise before you, for the manner of women *is* with me." And he searched but did not find the household idols.
36 Then Jacob was angry and rebuked Lā′ban, and Jacob answered and said to Lā′ban: "What *is* my trespass? What *is* my sin, that you have so hotly pursued me?
37 "Although you have searched all my things, what part of your house-

hold things have you found? Set *it* here before my brethren and your brethren, that they may judge between us both!

38 "These twenty years I *have been* with you; your ewes and your female goats have not miscarried their young, and I have not eaten the rams of your flock.

39 "That which was torn *by beasts* I did not bring to you; I bore the loss of it. You required it from my hand, *whether* stolen by day or stolen by night.

40 "*There* I was! In the day the drought consumed me, and the frost by night, and my sleep departed from my eyes.

41 "Thus I have been in your house twenty years; I served you fourteen years for your two daughters, and six years for your flock, and you have changed my wages ten times.

42 "Unless the God of my father, the God of Abraham and the Fear of Isaac, had been with me, surely now you would have sent me away emptyhanded. God has seen my affliction and the labor of my hands, and rebuked *you* last night."

LABAN'S COVENANT WITH JACOB

43 And Lā'ban answered and said to Jacob, "*These* daughters *are* my daughters, and *these* children *are* my children, and *this* flock *is* my flock; all that you see *is* mine. But what can I do this day to these my daughters or to their children whom they have borne?

44 "Now therefore, come, let us make a covenant, you and I, and let it be a witness between you and me."

45 So Jacob took a stone and set it up *as* a pillar.

46 Then Jacob said to his brethren, "Gather stones." And they took stones and made a heap, and they ate there on the heap.

47 Lā'ban called it Jē'gar Sā·ha·dū'tha,*a* but Jacob called it Gal'e·ed.*b*

48 And Lā'ban said, "This heap *is* a witness between you and me this day." Therefore its name was called Gal'e·ed,

49 also Miz'pah,*a* because he said, "May the LORD watch between you and me when we are absent one from another.

50 "If you afflict my daughters, or if you take *other* wives besides my daughters, *although* no man *is* with us—see, God *is* witness between you and me!"

51 Then Lā'ban said to Jacob, "Here is this heap and here is *this* pillar, which I have placed between you and me.

52 "This heap *is* a witness, and *this* pillar *is* a witness, that I will not pass beyond this heap to you, and you will not pass beyond this heap and this pillar to me, for harm.

53 "The God of Abraham, the God of Nā'hor, and the God of their father judge between us." And Jacob swore by the Fear of his father Isaac.

54 Then Jacob offered a sacrifice on the mountain, and called his brethren to eat bread. And they ate bread and stayed all night on the mountain.

55 And early in the morning Lā'ban arose, and kissed his sons and daughters and blessed them. Then Lā'ban departed and returned to his place.

ESAU COMES TO MEET JACOB

32 So Jacob went on his way, and the angels of God met him.

2 When Jacob saw them, he said,

31:47 *a*Literally, in Aramaic, *Heap of Witness* *b*Literally, in Hebrew, *Heap of Witness*
31:49 *a*Literally *Watch*

"This *is* God's camp." And he called the name of that place Mā·ha·na'im.*a*

3 Then Jacob sent messengers before him to Esau his brother in the land of Sē'ir, the country of Ē'dom.

4 And he commanded them, saying, "Speak thus to my lord Esau, 'Thus your servant Jacob says: "I have dwelt with Lā'ban and stayed there until now.

5 "I have oxen, donkeys, flocks, and male and female servants; and I have sent to tell my lord, that I may find favor in your sight." ' "

6 Then the messengers returned to Jacob, saying, "We came to your brother Esau, and he also is coming to meet you, and four hundred men *are* with him."

7 So Jacob was greatly afraid and distressed; and he divided the people that *were* with him, and the flocks and herds and camels, into two companies.

8 And he said, "If Esau comes to the one company and attacks it, then the other company which is left will escape."

Prayers

Genesis 32:9–12

Have you ever been afraid that you will get hurt? Jacob was afraid that Esau would hurt him. Esau might even kill him. What do you do in a time like that? Where do you turn? Who do you ask for help? Jacob prayed. "Deliver me," Jacob begged. Have you ever said to God, "Help me" or "Save me" or "Protect me?" He will. He helped Jacob. He will also help you. He protected Jacob. He will also protect you. Ask Him.

---

9 Then Jacob said, "O God of my father Abraham and God of my father Isaac, the LORD who said to me, 'Return to your country and to your family, and I will deal well with you':

10 "I am not worthy of the least of all the mercies and of all the truth which You have shown Your servant; for I crossed over this Jordan with my staff, and now I have become two companies.

11 "Deliver me, I pray, from the hand of my brother, from the hand of Esau; for I fear him, lest he come and attack me *and* the mother with the children.

12 "For You said, 'I will surely treat you well, and make your descendants as the sand of the sea, which cannot be numbered for multitude.' "

13 So he lodged there that same night, and took what came to his hand as a present for Esau his brother:

14 two hundred female goats and twenty male goats, two hundred ewes and twenty rams,

15 thirty milk camels with their colts, forty cows and ten bulls, twenty female donkeys and ten foals.

16 Then he delivered *them* to the hand of his servants, every drove by itself, and said to his servants, "Pass over before me, and put some distance between successive droves."

17 And he commanded the first one, saying, "When Esau my brother meets you and asks you, saying, 'To whom do you belong, and where are you going? Whose *are* these in front of you?'

18 "then you shall say, 'They *are* your servant Jacob's. It *is* a present sent to my lord Esau; and behold, he also *is* behind us.' "

19 So he commanded the second, the third, and all who followed the

32:2 *a*Literally *Double Camp*

droves, saying, "In this manner you shall speak to Esau when you find him;

20 "and also say, 'Behold, your servant Jacob is behind us.' " For he said, "I will appease him with the present that goes before me, and afterward I will see his face; perhaps he will accept me."

21 So the present went on over before him, but he himself lodged that night in the camp.

WRESTLING WITH GOD

22 And he arose that night and took his two wives, his two female servants, and his eleven sons, and crossed over the ford of Jab'bok.

23 He took them, sent them over the brook, and sent over what he had.

24 Then Jacob was left alone; and a Man wrestled with him until the breaking of day.

25 Now when He saw that He did not prevail against him, He touched the socket of his hip; and the socket of Jacob's hip was out of joint as He wrestled with him.

26 And He said, "Let Me go, for the day breaks." But he said, "I will not let You go unless You bless me!"

27 So He said to him, "What is your name?" He said, "Jacob."

28 And He said, "Your name shall no longer be called Jacob, but Israel;a for you have struggled with God and with men, and have prevailed."

29 Then Jacob asked, saying, "Tell me Your name, I pray." And He said, "Why is it that you ask about My name?" And He blessed him there.

30 So Jacob called the name of the place Pe·ni′el:a "For I have seen God face to face, and my life is preserved."

31 Just as he crossed over Pe·nu′ela the sun rose on him, and he limped on his hip.

32 Therefore to this day the children

of Israel do not eat the muscle that shrank, which is on the hip socket, because He touched the socket of Jacob's hip in the muscle that shrank.

JACOB AND ESAU MEET

33 Now Jacob lifted his eyes and looked, and there, Esau was coming, and with him were four hundred men. So he divided the children among Leah, Rachel, and the two maidservants.

2 And he put the maidservants and their children in front, Leah and her children behind, and Rachel and Joseph last.

3 Then he crossed over before them and bowed himself to the ground seven times, until he came near to his brother.

4 But Esau ran to meet him, and embraced him, and fell on his neck and kissed him, and they wept.

5 And he lifted his eyes and saw the women and children, and said, "Who are these with you?" So he said, "The children whom God has graciously given your servant."

6 Then the maidservants came near, they and their children, and bowed down.

7 And Leah also came near with her children, and they bowed down. Afterward Joseph and Rachel came near, and they bowed down.

8 Then Esau said, "What do you mean by all this company which I met?" And he said, "These are to find favor in the sight of my lord."

9 But Esau said, "I have enough, my brother; keep what you have for yourself."

10 And Jacob said, "No, please, if I have now found favor in your sight,

32:28 aLiterally Prince with God   32:30 aLiterally Face of God   32:31 aSame as Peniel, verse 30

DON'T YELL AT ME Genesis 32:6, 7; 33:1, 4

Connie and Craig are pounding nails. But Connie hit Craig's fingernail, not the other nail. It was an accident, of course. But Connie could have been more careful. What do you think Craig will say to Connie?

1. Has someone hurt you accidentally? What did you say? What should you have said?
2. Have you hurt someone accidentally? What did that person say to you? What should that person have said to you?
3. Should we yell at our friends or family? Why not? Should we forgive friends and family when they do something wrong and hurt us? Why?

For more on *What Should I Do?* turn to page 84
For more on *Forgiveness* turn to page 84

then receive my present from my hand, inasmuch as I have seen your face as though I had seen the face of God, and you were pleased with me.

11 "Please, take my blessing that is brought to you, because God has dealt graciously with me, and because I have enough." So he urged him, and he took *it.*

12 Then Esau said, "Let us take our journey; let us go, and I will go before you."

13 But Jacob said to him, "My lord knows that the children *are* weak, and the flocks and herds which are nursing *are* with me. And if the men should drive them hard one day, all the flock will die.

14 "Please let my lord go on ahead before his servant. I will lead on slowly at a pace which the livestock that go before me, and the children, are able to endure, until I come to my lord in Sē′ir."

15 And Esau said, "Now let me leave with you *some* of the people who *are* with me." But he said, "What need is there? Let me find favor in the sight of my lord."

16 So Esau returned that day on his way to Sē′ir.

17 And Jacob journeyed to Suc′coth, built himself a house, and made booths for his livestock. Therefore the name of the place is called Suc′coth.*a*

JACOB COMES TO CANAAN

18 Then Jacob came safely to the city of Shē′chem, which *is* in the land of Cā′naan, when he came from Pad′an Ar′am; and he pitched his tent before the city.

19 And he bought the parcel of land, where he had pitched his tent, from the children of Hā′mor, Shē′chem's father, for one hundred pieces of money.

20 Then he erected an altar there and called it El Ē·lō′he Israel.*a*

THE DINAH INCIDENT

34 Now Dī′nah the daughter of Leah, whom she had borne to Jacob, went out to see the daughters of the land.

2 And when Shē′chem the son of Hā′mor the Hī′vīte, prince of the country, saw her, he took her and lay with her, and violated her.

3 His soul was strongly attracted to Dī′nah the daughter of Jacob, and he loved the young woman and spoke kindly to the young woman.

4 So Shē′chem spoke to his father Hā′mor, saying, "Get me this young woman as a wife."

5 And Jacob heard that he had defiled Dī′nah his daughter. Now his sons were with his livestock in the field; so Jacob held his peace until they came.

6 Then Hā′mor the father of Shē′chem went out to Jacob to speak with him.

7 And the sons of Jacob came in from the field when they heard *it;* and the men were grieved and very angry, because he had done a disgraceful thing in Israel by lying with Jacob's daughter, a thing which ought not to be done.

8 But Hā′mor spoke with them, saying, "The soul of my son Shē′chem longs for your daughter. Please give her to him as a wife.

9 "And make marriages with us; give your daughters to us, and take our daughters to yourselves.

10 "So you shall dwell with us, and the land shall be before you. Dwell and trade in it, and acquire possessions for yourselves in it."

33:17 *a*Literally *Booths*   33:20 *a*Literally *God, the God of Israel*

11 Then Shē′chem said to her father and her brothers, "Let me find favor in your eyes, and whatever you say to me I will give.
12 "Ask me ever so much dowry and gift, and I will give according to what you say to me; but give me the young woman as a wife."
13 But the sons of Jacob answered Shē′chem and Hā′mor his father, and spoke deceitfully, because he had defiled Dī′nah their sister.
14 And they said to them, "We cannot do this thing, to give our sister to one who is uncircumcised, for that *would be* a reproach to us.
15 "But on this *condition* we will consent to you: If you will become as we *are*, if every male of you is circumcised,
16 "then we will give our daughters to you, and we will take your daughters to us; and we will dwell with you, and we will become one people.
17 "But if you will not heed us and be circumcised, then we will take our daughter and be gone."
18 And their words pleased Hā′mor and Shē′chem, Hā′mor's son.
19 So the young man did not delay to do the thing, because he delighted in Jacob's daughter. He *was* more honorable than all the household of his father.
20 And Hā′mor and Shē′chem his son came to the gate of their city, and spoke with the men of their city, saying:
21 "These men *are* at peace with us. Therefore let them dwell in the land and trade in it. For indeed the land *is* large enough for them. Let us take their daughters to us as wives, and let us give them our daughters.
22 "Only on this *condition* will the men consent to dwell with us, to be one people: if every male among us is circumcised as they *are* circumcised.
23 "*Will* not their livestock, their property, and every animal of theirs *be* ours? Only let us consent to them, and they will dwell with us."
24 And all who went out of the gate of his city heeded Hā′mor and Shē′chem his son; every male was circumcised, all who went out of the gate of his city.
25 Now it came to pass on the third day, when they were in pain, that two of the sons of Jacob, Sim′ē·on and Levi, Dī′nah's brothers, each took his sword and came boldly upon the city and killed all the males.
26 And they killed Hā′mor and Shē′chem his son with the edge of the sword, and took Dī′nah from Shē′chem's house, and went out.
27 The sons of Jacob came upon the slain, and plundered the city, because their sister had been defiled.
28 They took their sheep, their oxen, and their donkeys, what *was* in the city and what *was* in the field,
29 and all their wealth. All their little ones and their wives they took captive; and they plundered even all that *was* in the houses.
30 Then Jacob said to Sim′ē·on and Levi, "You have troubled me by making me obnoxious among the inhabitants of the land, among the Cā′naan·ītes and the Per′iz·zītes; and since I *am* few in number, they will gather themselves together against me and kill me. I shall be destroyed, my household and I."
31 But they said, "Should he treat our sister like a harlot?"

JACOB'S RETURN TO BETHEL

35 Then God said to Jacob, "Arise, go up to Beth′el and dwell there; and make an altar there to God, who appeared to you when you fled from the face of Esau your brother."

2 And Jacob said to his household and to all who *were* with him, "Put away the foreign gods that *are* among you, purify yourselves, and change your garments.

3 "Then let us arise and go up to Beth'el; and I will make an altar there to God, who answered me in the day of my distress and has been with me in the way which I have gone."

4 So they gave Jacob all the foreign gods which *were* in their hands, and the earrings which *were* in their ears; and Jacob hid them under the terebinth tree which *was* by Shē'-chem.

5 And they journeyed, and the terror of God was upon the cities that *were* all around them, and they did not pursue the sons of Jacob.

6 So Jacob came to Luz (that *is,* Beth'el), which *is* in the land of Cā'naan, he and all the people who *were* with him.

7 And he built an altar there and called the place El Beth'el,*a* because there God appeared to him when he fled from the face of his brother.

8 Now Deb'or·ah, Rebekah's nurse, died, and she was buried below Beth'el under the terebinth tree. So the name of it was called Al'lon Bach'uth.*a*

9 Then God appeared to Jacob again, when he came from Pad'an Ar'am, and blessed him.

10 And God said to him, "Your name *is* Jacob; your name shall not be called Jacob anymore, but Israel shall be your name." So He called his name Israel.

11 Also God said to him: "I *am* God Almighty. Be fruitful and multiply; a nation and a company of nations shall proceed from you, and kings shall come from your body.

12 "The land which I gave Abraham and Isaac I give to you; and to your descendants after you I give this land."

13 Then God went up from him in the place where He talked with him.

14 So Jacob set up a pillar in the place where He talked with him, a pillar of stone; and he poured a drink offering on it, and he poured oil on it.

15 And Jacob called the name of the place where God spoke with him, Beth'el.

DEATH OF RACHEL

16 Then they journeyed from Beth'el. And when there was but a little distance to go to Eph'rath, Rachel labored *in childbirth,* and she had hard labor.

17 Now it came to pass, when she was in hard labor, that the midwife said to her, "Do not fear; you will have this son also."

18 And so it was, as her soul was departing (for she died), that she called his name Ben-Ō'ni;*a* but his father called him Benjamin.*b*

19 So Rachel died and was buried on the way to Eph'rath (that *is,* Bethlehem).

20 And Jacob set a pillar on her grave, which *is* the pillar of Rachel's grave to this day.

21 Then Israel journeyed and pitched his tent beyond the tower of Ē'der.

22 And it happened, when Israel dwelt in that land, that Reuben went and lay with Bil'hah his father's concubine; and Israel heard *about it.*

JACOB'S TWELVE SONS

Now the sons of Jacob were twelve:

23 the sons of Leah *were* Reuben, Ja-

35:7 *a*Literally *God of the House of God*
35:8 *a*Literally *Terebinth of Weeping*
35:18 *a*Literally *Son of My Sorrow* *b*Literally *Son of the Right Hand*

cob's firstborn, and Sim'e·on, Levi, Judah, Is'sa·char, and Zeb'u·lun;
24 the sons of Rachel *were* Joseph and Benjamin;
25 the sons of Bil'hah, Rachel's maidservant, *were* Dan and Naph'ta·li;
26 and the sons of Zil'pah, Leah's maidservant, *were* Gad and Ash'er. These *were* the sons of Jacob who were born to him in Pad'an Ar'am.

DEATH OF ISAAC

27 Then Jacob came to his father Isaac at Mam're, or Kir'jath Ar'ba*a* (that *is,* He'bron), where Abraham and Isaac had dwelt.
28 Now the days of Isaac were one hundred and eighty years.
29 So Isaac breathed his last and died, and was gathered to his people, *being* old and full of days. And his sons Esau and Jacob buried him.

THE FAMILY OF ESAU

36 Now this *is* the genealogy of Esau, who is E'dom.
2 Esau took his wives from the daughters of Ca'naan: A'dah the daughter of E'lon the Hit'tite; A·hol·i·ba'mah the daughter of An'ah, the daughter of Zib'e·on the Hi'vite;
3 and Bas'e·math, Ish'ma·el's daughter, sister of Ne·ba'joth.
4 Now A'dah bore E·li'phaz to Esau, and Bas'e·math bore Reu'el.
5 And A·hol·i·ba'mah bore Je'ush, Ja'a·lam, and Ko'rah. These *were* the sons of Esau who were born to him in the land of Ca'naan.
6 Then Esau took his wives, his sons, his daughters, and all the persons of his household, his cattle and all his animals, and all his goods which he had gained in the land of Ca'naan, and went to a country away from the presence of his brother Jacob.
7 For their possessions were too great for them to dwell together, and the land where they were strangers could not support them because of their livestock.
8 So Esau dwelt in Mount Se'ir. Esau *is* E'dom.
9 And this *is* the genealogy of Esau the father of the E'dom·ites in Mount Se'ir.
10 These *were* the names of Esau's sons: E·li'phaz the son of A'dah the wife of Esau, and Reu'el the son of Bas'e·math the wife of Esau.
11 And the sons of E·li'phaz were Te'man, O'mar, Ze'pho,*a* Ga'tam, and Ke'naz.
12 Now Tim'na was the concubine of E·li'phaz, Esau's son, and she bore Am'a·lek to E·li'phaz. These *were* the sons of A'dah, Esau's wife.
13 These *were* the sons of Reu'el: Na'hath, Ze'rah, Sham'mah, and Miz'zah. These were the sons of Bas'e·math, Esau's wife.
14 These were the sons of A·hol·i·ba'mah, Esau's wife, the daughter of An'ah, the daughter of Zib'e·on. And she bore to Esau: Je'ush, Ja'a·lam, and Ko'rah.

THE CHIEFS OF EDOM

15 These *were* the chiefs of the sons of Esau. The sons of E·li'phaz, the firstborn *son* of Esau, were Chief Te'man, Chief O'mar, Chief Ze'pho, Chief Ke'naz,
16 Chief Ko'rah,*a* Chief Ga'tam, *and* Chief Am'a·lek. These *were* the chiefs of E·li'phaz in the land of E'dom. They *were* the sons of A'dah.

35:27 *a*Literally *Town of Arba*   36:11 *a*Spelled *Zephi* in 1 Chronicles 1:36   36:16 *a*Samaritan Pentateuch omits *Chief Korah.*

17 These *were* the sons of Reū′el, Esau's son: Chief Nā′hath, Chief Zē′rah, Chief Sham′mah, and Chief Miz′zah. These *were* the chiefs of Reū′el in the land of Ē′dom. These *were* the sons of Bas′e·math, Esau's wife.

18 And these *were* the sons of A·hol·i·bā′mah, Esau's wife: Chief Jē′ush, Chief Jā′a·lam, and Chief Kō′rah. These *were* the chiefs *who descended* from A·hol·i·bā′mah, Esau's wife, the daughter of An′ah.

19 These *were* the sons of Esau, who is Ē′dom, and these *were* their chiefs.

The Sons of Seir

20 These *were* the sons of Sē′ir the Hor′īte who inhabited the land: Lō′tan, Shō′bal, Zib′e·on, An′ah,

21 Dī′shon, Ē′zer, and Dī′shan. These *were* the chiefs of the Hor′ītes, the sons of Sē′ir, in the land of Ē′dom.

22 And the sons of Lō′tan were Hō′rī and Hē′mam.*a* Lō′tan's sister *was* Tim′na.

23 These *were* the sons of Shō′bal: Al′van,*a* Man′a·hath, Ē′bal, Shē′-phō,*b* and Ō′nam.

24 These *were* the sons of Zib′e·on: both Ā′jah and An′ah. This *was the* An′ah who found the water*a* in the wilderness as he pastured the donkeys of his father Zib′e·on.

25 These *were* the children of An′ah: Dī′shon and A·hol·i·bā′mah the daughter of An′ah.

26 These *were* the sons of Dī′shon:*a* Hem′dan,*b* Esh′ban, Ith′ran, and Chē′ran.

27 These *were* the sons of Ē′zer: Bil′han, Zā′a·van, and Ā′kan.*a*

28 These *were* the sons of Dī′shan: Uz and Ar′an.

29 These *were* the chiefs of the Hor′ītes: Chief Lō′tan, Chief Shō′bal, Chief Zib′e·on, Chief An′ah,

30 Chief Dī′shon, Chief Ē′zer, and Chief Dī′shan. These *were* the chiefs of the Hor′ītes, according to their chiefs in the land of Sē′ir.

The Kings of Edom

31 Now these *were* the kings who reigned in the land of Ē′dom before any king reigned over the children of Israel:

32 Bē′la the son of Bē′or reigned in Ē′dom, and the name of his city *was* Din′ha·bah.

33 And when Bē′la died, Jō′bab the son of Zē′rah of Boz′rah reigned in his place.

34 When Jō′bab died, Hū′sham of the land of the Tē′man·ītes reigned in his place.

35 And when Hū′sham died, Hā′dad the son of Bē′dad, who attacked Mid′i·an in the field of Mō′ab, reigned in his place. And the name of his city *was* Ā′vith.

36 When Hā′dad died, Sam′lah of Mas·rē′kah reigned in his place.

37 And when Sam′lah died, Saul of Re·hō′both-*by*-the-River reigned in his place.

38 When Saul died, Bā′al-Hā′nan the son of Ach′bor reigned in his place.

39 And when Bā′al-Hā′nan the son of Ach′bor died, Hā′dar*a* reigned in his place; and the name of his city *was* Pā′ū.*b* His wife's name *was* Me·het′a·bel, the daughter of Mā′-tred, the daughter of Mez′a·hab.

36:22 *a*Spelled *Homam* in 1 Chronicles 1:39
36:23 *a*Spelled *Alian* in 1 Chronicles 1:40 *b*Spelled *Shephi* in 1 Chronicles 1:40
36:24 *a*Following Masoretic Text and Vulgate (*hot springs*); Septuagint reads *Jamin;* Targum reads *mighty men;* Talmud interprets as *mules.*
36:26 *a*Hebrew *Dishan* *b*Spelled *Hamran* in 1 Chronicles 1:41   36:27 *a*Spelled *Jaakan* in 1 Chronicles 1:42   36:39 *a*Spelled *Hadad* in Samaritan Pentateuch, Syriac, and 1 Chronicles 1:50 *b*Spelled *Pai* in 1 Chronicles 1:50

THE CHIEFS OF ESAU

40 And these *were* the names of the chiefs of Esau, according to their families and their places, by their names: Chief Tim′nah, Chief Al′vah,*a* Chief Jē′theth,
41 Chief A·hol·i·bā′mah, Chief Ē′lah, Chief Pī′non,
42 Chief Kē′naz, Chief Tē′man, Chief Mib′zar,
43 Chief Mag′di·el, and Chief Ī′ram. These *were* the chiefs of Ē′dom, according to their dwelling places in the land of their possession. Esau *was* the father of the Ē′dom·ītes.

JOSEPH DREAMS OF GREATNESS

Have you ever been jealous of a friend because everything seemed to go right for him or her? This story tells what will happen when you let jealousy get the best of you.

37 Now Jacob dwelt in the land where his father was a stranger, in the land of Cā′naan.
2 This *is* the history of Jacob. Joseph, *being* seventeen years old, was feeding the flock with his brothers. And the lad *was* with the sons of Bil′hah and the sons of Zil′pah, his father's wives; and Joseph brought a bad report of them to his father.
3 Now Israel loved Joseph more than all his children, because he *was* the son of his old age. Also he made him a tunic of *many* colors.
4 But when his brothers saw that their father loved him more than all his brothers, they hated him and could not speak peaceably to him.
5 Now Joseph had a dream, and he told *it* to his brothers; and they hated him even more.
6 So he said to them, "Please hear this dream which I have dreamed:

7 "There we were, binding sheaves in the field. Then behold, my sheaf arose and also stood upright; and indeed your sheaves stood all around and bowed down to my sheaf."
8 And his brothers said to him, "Shall you indeed reign over us? Or shall you indeed have dominion over us?" So they hated him even more for his dreams and for his words.
9 Then he dreamed still another dream and told it to his brothers, and said, "Look, I have dreamed another dream. And this time, the sun, the moon, and the eleven stars bowed down to me."
10 So he told *it* to his father and his brothers; and his father rebuked him and said to him, "What *is* this dream that you have dreamed? Shall your mother and I and your brothers indeed come to bow down to the earth before you?"
11 And his brothers envied him, but his father kept the matter *in mind.*

JOSEPH SOLD BY HIS BROTHERS

12 Then his brothers went to feed their father's flock in Shē′chem.
13 And Israel said to Joseph, "Are not your brothers feeding *the flock* in Shē′chem? Come, I will send you to them." So he said to him, "Here I am."
14 Then he said to him, "Please go and see if it is well with your brothers and well with the flocks, and bring back word to me." So he sent him out of the Valley of Hē′bron, and he went to Shē′chem.
15 Now a certain man found him, and there he was, wandering in the field. And the man asked him, saying, "What are you seeking?"
16 So he said, "I am seeking my

36:40 *a*Spelled *Aliah* in 1 Chronicles 1:51

HELPFULNESS Genesis 37:13, 14

Someone to Help Me

What if each family member said, "I won't help anyone else in the family?" How would all of the family work get done? Where would you get your food? How would you have clean clothes? How would you have a house to live in? But what if each family member said, "I *will* help everyone else in the family?" How would things be different?

1. What is this lady doing? What are some other chores that you think she does?
2. What chores can you do to help the family? Will you? Will you today?

For more on *Values* turn to page 117
For more on *Helpfulness* turn to page 401

brothers. Please tell me where they are feeding *their flocks*."

17 And the man said, "They have departed from here, for I heard them say, 'Let us go to Dō'than.'" So Joseph went after his brothers and found them in Dō'than.

18 Now when they saw him afar off, even before he came near them, they conspired against him to kill him.

19 Then they said to one another, "Look, this dreamer is coming!

20 "Come therefore, let us now kill him and cast him into some pit; and we shall say, 'Some wild beast has devoured him.' We shall see what will become of his dreams!"

21 But Reuben heard *it*, and he delivered him out of their hands, and said, "Let us not kill him."

22 And Reuben said to them, "Shed no blood, *but* cast him into this pit which *is* in the wilderness, and do not lay a hand on him"—that he might deliver him out of their hands, and bring him back to his father.

23 So it came to pass, when Joseph had come to his brothers, that they stripped Joseph *of* his tunic, the tunic of *many* colors that *was* on him.

24 Then they took him and cast him into a pit. And the pit *was* empty; *there was* no water in it.

25 And they sat down to eat a meal. Then they lifted their eyes and looked, and there was a company of Ish'ma·el·ītes, coming from Gil'ē·ad with their camels, bearing spices, balm, and myrrh, on their way to carry *them* down to Egypt.

26 So Judah said to his brothers, "What profit *is there* if we kill our brother and conceal his blood?

27 "Come and let us sell him to the Ish'ma·el·ītes, and let not our hand be upon him, for he *is* our brother *and* our flesh." And his brothers listened.

28 Then Mid'i·an·īte traders passed by; so *the brothers* pulled Joseph up and lifted him out of the pit, and sold him to the Ish'ma·el·ītes for twenty *shekels* of silver. And they took Joseph to Egypt.

29 Then Reuben returned to the pit, and indeed Joseph *was* not in the pit; and he tore his clothes.

30 And he returned to his brothers and said, "The lad *is* no *more;* and I, where shall I go?"

31 So they took Joseph's tunic, killed a kid of the goats, and dipped the tunic in the blood.

32 Then they sent the tunic of *many* colors, and they brought *it* to their father and said, "We have found this. Do you know whether it *is* your son's tunic or not?"

33 And he recognized it and said, "*It is* my son's tunic. A wild beast has devoured him. Without doubt Joseph is torn to pieces."

34 Then Jacob tore his clothes, put sackcloth on his waist, and mourned for his son many days.

35 And all his sons and all his daughters arose to comfort him; but he refused to be comforted, and he said, "For I shall go down into the grave to my son in mourning." Thus his father wept for him.

36 Now the Mid'i·an·ītes[a] had sold him in Egypt to Pot'i·phar, an officer of Pharaoh *and* captain of the guard.

JUDAH AND TAMAR

38 It came to pass at that time that Judah departed from his brothers, and visited a certain A·dul'lam·īte whose name *was* Hī'rah.

2 And Judah saw there a daughter of a certain Cā'naan·īte whose name *was* Shū'a, and he married her and went in to her.

37:36 a Masoretic Text reads *Medanites*.

Genesis 37 **Joseph Sold Into Slavery**

1. Jacob had many sons. Which was his favorite? How did this make the other brothers feel?
2. What beautiful gift did Jacob give Joseph? How did this make his brothers feel?
3. Describe one of Joseph's dreams. How did this make his brothers feel?
4. Everything seemed to be going right for Joseph. How did this make his brothers feel? What did the brothers do about it?
5. Do you have any friends like Joseph, where everything seems to go right for them? How does this make you feel? If you are angry, watch out! When jealousy turns to anger you have taken the first step toward hurting your own friend.
6. What could Joseph's brothers have done to keep their jealousy from turning to anger? What can you do?

3 So she conceived and bore a son, and he called his name Er.
4 She conceived again and bore a son, and she called his name Ō′nan.
5 And she conceived yet again and bore a son, and called his name Shē′lah. He was at Chē′zib when she bore him.
6 Then Judah took a wife for Er his firstborn, and her name *was* Tā′mar.
7 But Er, Judah's firstborn, was wicked in the sight of the LORD, and the LORD killed him.
8 And Judah said to Ō′nan, "Go in to your brother's wife and marry her, and raise up an heir to your brother."
9 But Ō′nan knew that the heir would not be his; and it came to pass, when he went in to his brother's wife, that he emitted on the ground, lest he should give an heir to his brother.
10 And the thing which he did displeased the LORD; therefore He killed him also.
11 Then Judah said to Tā′mar his daughter-in-law, "Remain a widow in your father's house till my son Shē′lah is grown." For he said, "Lest he also die like his brothers." And Tā′mar went and dwelt in her father's house.
12 Now in the process of time the daughter of Shū′a, Judah's wife, died; and Judah was comforted, and went up to his sheepshearers at Tim′nah, he and his friend Hī′rah the A·dul′-lam·īte.
13 And it was told Tā′mar, saying, "Look, your father-in-law is going up to Tim′nah to shear his sheep."
14 So she took off her widow's garments, covered *herself* with a veil and wrapped herself, and sat in an open place which *was* on the way to Tim′nah; for she saw that Shē′lah was grown, and she was not given to him as a wife.
15 When Judah saw her, he thought she *was* a harlot, because she had covered her face.
16 Then he turned to her by the way, and said, "Please let me come in to you"; for he did not know that she *was* his daughter-in-law. So she said, "What will you give me, that you may come in to me?"
17 And he said, "I will send a young goat from the flock." So she said, "Will you give *me* a pledge till you send *it?*"

18 Then he said, "What pledge shall I give you?" So she said, "Your signet and cord, and your staff that *is* in your hand." Then he gave *them* to her, and went in to her, and she conceived by him.

19 So she arose and went away, and laid aside her veil and put on the garments of her widowhood.

20 And Judah sent the young goat by the hand of his friend the A·dul′lam-īte, to receive *his* pledge from the woman's hand, but he did not find her.

21 Then he asked the men of that place, saying, "Where is the harlot who *was* openly by the roadside?" And they said, "There was no harlot in this *place*."

22 So he returned to Judah and said, "I cannot find her. Also, the men of the place said there was no harlot in this *place*."

23 Then Judah said, "Let her take *them* for herself, lest we be shamed; for I sent this young goat and you have not found her."

24 And it came to pass, about three months after, that Judah was told, saying, "Tā′mar your daughter-in-law has played the harlot; furthermore she *is* with child by harlotry." So Judah said, "Bring her out and let her be burned!"

25 When she *was* brought out, she sent to her father-in-law, saying, "By the man to whom these belong, I *am* with child." And she said, "Please determine whose these *are*—the signet and cord, and staff."

26 So Judah acknowledged *them* and said, "She has been more righteous than I, because I did not give her to Shē′lah my son." And he never knew her again.

27 Now it came to pass, at the time for giving birth, that behold, twins *were* in her womb.

28 And so it was, when she was giv-ing birth, that *the one* put out *his* hand; and the midwife took a scarlet *thread* and bound it on his hand, saying, "This one came out first."

29 Then it happened, as he drew back his hand, that his brother came out unexpectedly; and she said, "How did you break through? *This* breach *be* upon you!" Therefore his name was called Per′ez.*a*

30 Afterward his brother came out who had the scarlet *thread* on his hand. And his name was called Zē′rah.

JOSEPH A SLAVE IN EGYPT

39 Now Joseph had been taken down to Egypt. And Pot′i·phar, an officer of Pharaoh, captain of the guard, an Egyptian, bought him from the Ish′ma·el·ītes who had taken him down there.

2 The LORD was with Joseph, and he was a successful man; and he was in the house of his master the Egyptian.

3 And his master saw that the LORD *was* with him and that the LORD made all he did to prosper in his hand.

4 So Joseph found favor in his sight, and served him. Then he made him overseer of his house, and all *that* he had he put under his authority.

5 So it was, from the time *that* he had made him overseer of his house and all that he had, that the LORD blessed the Egyptian's house for Joseph's sake; and the blessing of the LORD was on all that he had in the house and in the field.

6 Thus he left all that he had in Joseph's hand, and he did not know what he had except for the bread

38:29 *a*Literally *Breach* or *Breakthrough*

which he ate. Now Joseph was handsome in form and appearance.

7 And it came to pass after these things that his master's wife cast longing eyes on Joseph, and she said, "Lie with me."

8 But he refused and said to his master's wife, "Look, my master does not know what *is* with me in the house, and he has committed all that he has to my hand.

9 "*There is* no one greater in this house than I, nor has he kept back anything from me but you, because you *are* his wife. How then can I do this great wickedness, and sin against God?"

10 So it was, as she spoke to Joseph day by day, that he did not heed her, to lie with her *or* to be with her.

11 But it happened about this time, when Joseph went into the house to do his work, and none of the men of the house *was* inside,

12 that she caught him by his garment, saying, "Lie with me." But he left his garment in her hand, and fled and ran outside.

13 And so it was, when she saw that he had left his garment in her hand and fled outside,

14 that she called to the men of her house and spoke to them, saying, "See, he has brought in to us a Hebrew to mock us. He came in to me to lie with me, and I cried out with a loud voice.

15 "And it happened, when he heard that I lifted my voice and cried out, that he left his garment with me, and fled and went outside."

16 So she kept his garment with her until his master came home.

17 Then she spoke to him with words like these, saying, "The Hebrew servant whom you brought to us came in to me to mock me;

18 "so it happened, as I lifted my voice and cried out, that he left his garment with me and fled outside."

19 So it was, when his master heard the words which his wife spoke to him, saying, "Your servant did to me after this manner," that his anger was aroused.

20 Then Joseph's master took him and put him into the prison, a place where the king's prisoners *were* confined. And he was there in the prison.

21 But the LORD was with Joseph and showed him mercy, and He gave him favor in the sight of the keeper of the prison.

22 And the keeper of the prison committed to Joseph's hand all the prisoners who *were* in the prison; whatever they did there, it was his doing.

23 The keeper of the prison did not look into anything *that was* under Joseph's authority,[a] because the LORD was with him; and whatever he did, the LORD made *it* prosper.

THE PRISONERS' DREAMS

Joseph, the boy sold into slavery, is about to become governor of Egypt. Read on to find out how this happened.

40 It came to pass after these things *that* the butler and the baker of the king of Egypt offended their lord, the king of Egypt.

2 And Pharaoh was angry with his two officers, the chief butler and the chief baker.

3 So he put them in custody in the house of the captain of the guard, in the prison, the place where Joseph *was* confined.

4 And the captain of the guard charged Joseph with them, and he served them; so they were in custody for a while.

39:23 ªLiterally *his hand*

5 Then the butler and the baker of the king of Egypt, who *were* confined in the prison, had a dream, both of them, each man's dream in one night *and* each man's dream with its *own* interpretation.

6 And Joseph came in to them in the morning and looked at them, and saw that they *were* sad.

7 So he asked Pharaoh's officers who *were* with him in the custody of his lord's house, saying, "Why do you look *so* sad today?"

8 And they said to him, "We each have had a dream, and *there is* no interpreter of it." So Joseph said to them, "Do not interpretations belong to God? Tell *them* to me, please."

9 Then the chief butler told his dream to Joseph, and said to him, "Behold, in my dream a vine *was* before me,

10 "and in the vine *were* three branches; it *was* as though it budded, its blossoms shot forth, and its clusters brought forth ripe grapes.

11 "Then Pharaoh's cup *was* in my hand; and I took the grapes and pressed them into Pharaoh's cup, and placed the cup in Pharaoh's hand."

12 And Joseph said to him, "This *is* the interpretation of it: The three branches *are* three days.

13 "Now within three days Pharaoh will lift up your head and restore you to your place, and you will put Pharaoh's cup in his hand according to the former manner, when you were his butler.

14 "But remember me when it is well with you, and please show kindness to me; make mention of me to Pharaoh, and get me out of this house.

15 "For indeed I was stolen away from the land of the Hebrews; and also I have done nothing here that they should put me into the dungeon."

16 When the chief baker saw that the interpretation was good, he said to Joseph, "I also *was* in my dream, and there *were* three white baskets on my head.

17 "In the uppermost basket *were* all kinds of baked goods for Pharaoh, and the birds ate them out of the basket on my head."

18 So Joseph answered and said, "This *is* the interpretation of it: The three baskets *are* three days.

19 "Within three days Pharaoh will lift off your head from you and hang you on a tree; and the birds will eat your flesh from you."

20 Now it came to pass on the third day, *which was* Pharaoh's birthday, that he made a feast for all his servants; and he lifted up the head of the chief butler and of the chief baker among his servants.

21 Then he restored the chief butler to his butlership again, and he placed the cup in Pharaoh's hand.

22 But he hanged the chief baker, as Joseph had interpreted to them.

23 Yet the chief butler did not remember Joseph, but forgot him.

PHARAOH'S DREAMS

41 Then it came to pass, at the end of two full years, that Pharaoh had a dream; and behold, he stood by the river.

2 Suddenly there came up out of the river seven cows, fine looking and fat; and they fed in the meadow.

3 Then behold, seven other cows came up after them out of the river, ugly and gaunt, and stood by the *other* cows on the bank of the river.

4 And the ugly and gaunt cows ate up the seven fine looking and fat cows. So Pharaoh awoke.

5 He slept and dreamed a second time; and suddenly seven heads of

grain came up on one stalk, plump and good.

6 Then behold, seven thin heads, blighted by the east wind, sprang up after them.

7 And the seven thin heads devoured the seven plump and full heads. So Pharaoh awoke, and indeed, *it was* a dream.

8 Now it came to pass in the morning that his spirit was troubled, and he sent and called for all the magicians of Egypt and all its wise men. And Pharaoh told them his dreams, but *there was* no one who could interpret them for Pharaoh.

9 Then the chief butler spoke to Pharaoh, saying: "I remember my faults this day.

10 "When Pharaoh was angry with his servants, and put me in custody in the house of the captain of the guard, *both* me and the chief baker,

11 "we each had a dream in one night, he and I. Each of us dreamed according to the interpretation of his *own* dream.

12 "Now there *was* a young Hebrew man with us there, a servant of the captain of the guard. And we told him, and he interpreted our dreams for us; to each man he interpreted according to his *own* dream.

13 "And it came to pass, just as he interpreted for us, so it happened. He restored me to my office, and he hanged him."

14 Then Pharaoh sent and called Joseph, and they brought him quickly out of the dungeon; and he shaved, changed his clothing, and came to Pharaoh.

15 And Pharaoh said to Joseph, "I have had a dream, and *there is* no one who can interpret it. But I have heard it said of you *that* you can understand a dream, to interpret it."

16 So Joseph answered Pharaoh, saying, "*It is* not in me; God will give Pharaoh an answer of peace."

17 Then Pharaoh said to Joseph: "Behold, in my dream I stood on the bank of the river.

18 "Suddenly seven cows came up out of the river, fine looking and fat; and they fed in the meadow.

19 "Then behold, seven other cows came up after them, poor and very ugly and gaunt, such ugliness as I have never seen in all the land of Egypt.

20 "And the gaunt and ugly cows ate up the first seven, the fat cows.

21 "When they had eaten them up, no one would have known that they had eaten them, for they *were* just as ugly as at the beginning. So I awoke.

22 "Also I saw in my dream, and suddenly seven heads came up on one stalk, full and good.

23 "Then behold, seven heads, withered, thin, *and* blighted by the east wind, sprang up after them.

24 "And the thin heads devoured the seven good heads. So I told *this* to the magicians, but *there was* no one who could explain *it* to me."

25 Then Joseph said to Pharaoh, "The dreams of Pharaoh *are* one; God has shown Pharaoh what He *is* about to do:

26 "The seven good cows *are* seven years, and the seven good heads *are* seven years; the dreams *are* one.

27 "And the seven thin and ugly cows which came up after them *are* seven years, and the seven empty heads blighted by the east wind are seven years of famine.

28 "This *is* the thing which I have spoken to Pharaoh. God has shown Pharaoh what He *is* about to do.

29 "Indeed seven years of great plenty will come throughout all the land of Egypt;

30 "but after them seven years of famine will arise, and all the plenty

will be forgotten in the land of Egypt; and the famine will deplete the land.

31 "So the plenty will not be known in the land because of the famine following, for it *will be* very severe.

32 "And the dream was repeated to Pharaoh twice because the thing *is* established by God, and God will shortly bring it to pass.

33 "Now therefore, let Pharaoh select a discerning and wise man, and set him over the land of Egypt.

34 "Let Pharaoh do *this,* and let him appoint officers over the land, to collect one-fifth *of the produce* of the land of Egypt in the seven plentiful years.

35 "And let them gather all the food of those good years that are coming, and store up grain under the authority of Pharaoh, and let them keep food in the cities.

36 "Then that food shall be as a reserve for the land for the seven years of famine which shall be in the land of Egypt, that the land may not perish during the famine."

JOSEPH'S RISE TO POWER

37 So the advice was good in the eyes of Pharaoh and in the eyes of all his servants.

38 And Pharaoh said to his servants, "Can we find *such a one* as this, a man in whom *is* the Spirit of God?"

39 Then Pharaoh said to Joseph, "Inasmuch as God has shown you all this, *there is* no one as discerning and wise as you.

40 "You shall be over my house, and all my people shall be ruled according to your word; only in regard to the throne will I be greater than you."

41 And Pharaoh said to Joseph, "See, I have set you over all the land of Egypt."

42 Then Pharaoh took his signet ring off his hand and put it on Joseph's hand; and he clothed him in garments of fine linen and put a gold chain around his neck.

43 And he had him ride in the second chariot which he had; and they cried out before him, "Bow the knee!" So he set him over all the land of Egypt.

44 Pharaoh also said to Joseph, "I *am* Pharaoh, and without your consent no man may lift his hand or foot in all the land of Egypt."

45 And Pharaoh called Joseph's name Zaph′nath-Pā·a·nē′ah. And he gave him as a wife As′e·nath, the daughter of Pō·ti′-Phe·rah′ priest of On. So Joseph went out over *all* the land of Egypt.

46 Joseph was thirty years old when he stood before Pharaoh king of Egypt. And Joseph went out from the presence of Pharaoh, and went throughout all the land of Egypt.

47 Now in the seven plentiful years the ground brought forth abundantly.

48 So he gathered up all the food of the seven years which were in the land of Egypt, and laid up the food in the cities; he laid up in every city the food of the fields which surrounded them.

49 Joseph gathered very much grain, as the sand of the sea, until he stopped counting, for *it was* immeasurable.

50 And to Joseph were born two sons before the years of famine came, whom As′e·nath, the daughter of Pō·ti′-Phe·rah′ priest of On, bore to him.

51 Joseph called the name of the firstborn Ma·nas′seh:*a* "For God has made me forget all my toil and all my father's house."

52 And the name of the second he called Ē′phra·im:*a* "For God has

41:51 *a*Literally *Making Forgetful*   41:52 *a*Literally *Fruitfulness*

caused me to be fruitful in the land of my affliction."

53 Then the seven years of plenty which were in the land of Egypt ended,

54 and the seven years of famine began to come, as Joseph had said. The famine was in all lands, but in all the land of Egypt there was bread.

55 So when all the land of Egypt was famished, the people cried to Pharaoh for bread. Then Pharaoh said to all the Egyptians, "Go to Joseph; whatever he says to you, do."

56 The famine was over all the face of the earth, and Joseph opened all the storehouses*a* and sold to the Egyptians. And the famine became severe in the land of Egypt.

57 So all countries came to Joseph in Egypt to buy *grain,* because the famine was severe in all lands.

☑	*Bible Quiz*

Genesis 40; 41 **From Prison to the Palace**

1. Who were Joseph's two friends in prison? What strange thing happened to both of them?
2. Who else had a strange dream in this story? Who told Pharaoh what the dream meant?
3. What happened to Joseph then?
4. What did Joseph tell Pharaoh about God?
5. How can you tell your friends about what God has done for you?

JOSEPH'S BROTHERS GO TO EGYPT

Joseph's brothers are about to go on a trip. They have no idea what surprises await them.

42 When Jacob saw that there was grain in Egypt, Jacob said to his sons, "Why do you look at one another?"

2 And he said, "Indeed I have heard that there is grain in Egypt; go down to that place and buy for us there, that we may live and not die."

3 So Joseph's ten brothers went down to buy grain in Egypt.

4 But Jacob did not send Joseph's brother Benjamin with his brothers, for he said, "Lest some calamity befall him."

5 And the sons of Israel went to buy *grain* among those who journeyed, for the famine was in the land of Cā′naan.

6 Now Joseph *was* governor over the land; and it was he who sold to all the people of the land. And Joseph's brothers came and bowed down before him with *their* faces to the earth.

7 Joseph saw his brothers and recognized them, but he acted as a stranger to them and spoke roughly to them. Then he said to them, "Where do you come from?" And they said, "From the land of Cā′naan to buy food."

8 So Joseph recognized his brothers, but they did not recognize him.

9 Then Joseph remembered the dreams which he had dreamed about them, and said to them, "You *are* spies! You have come to see the nakedness of the land!"

10 And they said to him, "No, my lord, but your servants have come to buy food.

11 "We *are* all one man's sons; we *are*

41:56 *a*Literally *all that was in them*

honest *men;* your servants are not spies."

12 But he said to them, "No, but you have come to see the nakedness of the land."

13 And they said, "Your servants *are* twelve brothers, the sons of one man in the land of Cā′naan; and in fact, the youngest *is* with our father today, and one *is* no more."

14 But Joseph said to them, "It *is* as I spoke to you, saying, 'You *are* spies!'

15 "In this *manner* you shall be tested: By the life of Pharaoh, you shall not leave this place unless your youngest brother comes here.

16 "Send one of you, and let him bring your brother; and you shall be kept in prison, that your words may be tested to see whether *there is* any truth in you; or else, by the life of Pharaoh, surely you *are* spies!"

17 So he put them all together in prison three days.

18 Then Joseph said to them the third day, "Do this and live, *for* I fear God:

19 "If you *are* honest *men,* let one of your brothers be confined to your prison house; but you, go and carry grain for the famine of your houses.

20 "And bring your youngest brother to me; so your words will be verified, and you shall not die." And they did so.

21 Then they said to one another, "We *are* truly guilty concerning our brother, for we saw the anguish of his soul when he pleaded with us, and we would not hear; therefore this distress has come upon us."

22 And Reuben answered them, saying, "Did I not speak to you, saying, 'Do not sin against the boy'; and you would not listen? Therefore behold, his blood is now required of us."

23 But they did not know that Joseph understood *them,* for he spoke to them through an interpreter.

24 And he turned himself away from them and wept. Then he returned to them again, and talked with them. And he took Sim′ē·on from them and bound him before their eyes.

THE BROTHERS RETURN TO CANAAN

25 Then Joseph gave a command to fill their sacks with grain, to restore every man's money to his sack, and to give them provisions for the journey. Thus he did for them.

26 So they loaded their donkeys with the grain and departed from there.

27 But as one *of them* opened his sack to give his donkey feed at the encampment, he saw his money; and there it was, in the mouth of his sack.

28 So he said to his brothers, "My money has been restored, and there it is, in my sack!" Then their hearts failed *them* and they were afraid, saying to one another, "What *is* this *that* God has done to us?"

29 Then they went to Jacob their father in the land of Cā′naan and told him all that had happened to them, saying:

30 "The man *who is* lord of the land spoke roughly to us, and took us for spies of the country.

31 "But we said to him, 'We *are* honest *men;* we are not spies.

32 'We *are* twelve brothers, sons of our father; one *is* no *more,* and the youngest *is* with our father this day in the land of Cā′naan.'

33 "Then the man, the lord of the country, said to us, 'By this I will know that you *are* honest *men:* Leave one of your brothers *here* with me, take *food for* the famine of your households, and be gone.

34 'And bring your youngest brother to me; so I shall know that you *are* not spies, but *that* you *are* honest *men.* I will grant your brother to you, and you may trade in the land.' "

35 Then it happened as they emptied their sacks, that surprisingly each man's bundle of money *was* in his

sack; and when they and their father saw the bundles of money, they were afraid.

36 And Jacob their father said to them, "You have bereaved me: Joseph is no *more,* Sim′ĕ·on is no *more,* and you want to take Benjamin. All these things are against me."

37 Then Reuben spoke to his father, saying, "Kill my two sons if I do not bring him *back* to you; put him in my hands, and I will bring him back to you."

38 But he said, "My son shall not go down with you, for his brother is dead, and he is left alone. If any calamity should befall him along the way in which you go, then you would bring down my gray hair with sorrow to the grave."

Joseph's Brothers Return with Benjamin

43 Now the famine *was* severe in the land.

2 And it came to pass, when they had eaten up the grain which they had brought from Egypt, that their father said to them, "Go back, buy us a little food."

3 But Judah spoke to him, saying, "The man solemnly warned us, saying, 'You shall not see my face unless your brother *is* with you.'

4 "If you send our brother with us, we will go down and buy you food.

5 "But if you will not send *him,* we will not go down; for the man said to us, 'You shall not see my face unless your brother *is* with you.' "

6 And Israel said, "Why did you deal *so* wrongfully with me *as* to tell the man whether you had still *another* brother?"

7 But they said, "The man asked us pointedly about ourselves and our family, saying, '*Is* your father still alive? Have you *another* brother?' And we told him according to these words. Could we possibly have known that he would say, 'Bring your brother down'?"

8 Then Judah said to Israel his father, "Send the lad with me, and we will arise and go, that we may live and not die, both we and you *and* also our little ones.

9 "I myself will be surety for him; from my hand you shall require him. If I do not bring him *back* to you and set him before you, then let me bear the blame forever.

10 "For if we had not lingered, surely by now we would have returned this second time."

11 And their father Israel said to them, "If *it must be* so, then do this: Take some of the best fruits of the land in your vessels and carry down a present for the man—a little balm and a little honey, spices and myrrh, pistachio nuts and almonds.

12 "Take double money in your hand, and take back in your hand the money that was returned in the mouth of your sacks; perhaps it was an oversight.

13 "Take your brother also, and arise, go back to the man.

14 "And may God Almighty give you mercy before the man, that he may release your other brother and Benjamin. If I am bereaved, I am bereaved!"

15 So the men took that present and Benjamin, and they took double money in their hand, and arose and went down to Egypt; and they stood before Joseph.

16 When Joseph saw Benjamin with them, he said to the steward of his house, "Take *these* men to my home, and slaughter an animal and make ready; for *these* men will dine with me at noon."

17 Then the man did as Joseph ordered, and the man brought the men into Joseph's house.

18 Now the men were afraid because they were brought into Joseph's house; and they said, "*It is* because of the money, which was returned in our sacks the first time, that we are brought in, so that he may make a case against us and seize us, to take us as slaves with our donkeys."

19 When they drew near to the steward of Joseph's house, they talked with him at the door of the house,

20 and said, "O sir, we indeed came down the first time to buy food;

21 "but it happened, when we came to the encampment, that we opened our sacks, and there, *each* man's money *was* in the mouth of his sack, our money in full weight; so we have brought it back in our hand.

22 "And we have brought down other money in our hands to buy food. We do not know who put our money in our sacks."

23 But he said, "Peace *be* with you, do not be afraid. Your God and the God of your father has given you treasure in your sacks; I had your money." Then he brought Sim′ē·on out to them.

24 So the man brought the men into Joseph's house and gave *them* water, and they washed their feet; and he gave their donkeys feed.

25 Then they made the present ready for Joseph's coming at noon, for they heard that they would eat bread there.

26 And when Joseph came home, they brought him the present which *was* in their hand into the house, and bowed down before him to the earth.

27 Then he asked them about *their* well-being, and said, "*Is* your father well, the old man of whom you spoke? *Is* he still alive?"

28 And they answered, "Your servant our father *is* in good health; he *is* still alive." And they bowed their heads down and prostrated themselves.

29 Then he lifted his eyes and saw his brother Benjamin, his mother's son, and said, "*Is* this your younger brother of whom you spoke to me?" And he said, "God be gracious to you, my son."

30 Now his heart yearned for his brother; so Joseph made haste and sought *somewhere* to weep. And he went into *his* chamber and wept there.

31 Then he washed his face and came out; and he restrained himself, and said, "Serve the bread."

32 So they set him a place by himself, and them by themselves, and the Egyptians who ate with him by themselves; because the Egyptians could not eat food with the Hebrews, for that *is* an abomination to the Egyptians.

33 And they sat before him, the firstborn according to his birthright and the youngest according to his youth; and the men looked in astonishment at one another.

34 Then he took servings to them from before him, but Benjamin's serving was five times as much as any of theirs. So they drank and were merry with him.

☑ Bible Quiz

Genesis 42; 43 **Joseph's Brothers Go to Egypt**

1. Why did Joseph's brothers have to go to Egypt?
2. To get food, who did they have to talk to?
3. Why do you think Joseph acted the way he did?
4. What surprise did Joseph send back with his brothers?
5. What do you think the brothers were talking about on the way home?

JOSEPH'S CUP

*Joseph was sold into slavery
by his own brothers. Now he
can get even. What will he do?*

44 And he commanded the steward of his house, saying, "Fill the men's sacks with food, as much as they can carry, and put each man's money in the mouth of his sack.

2 "Also put my cup, the silver cup, in the mouth of the sack of the youngest, and his grain money." So he did according to the word that Joseph had spoken.

3 As soon as the morning dawned, the men were sent away, they and their donkeys.

4 When they had gone out of the city, *and* were not *yet* far off, Joseph said to his steward, "Get up, follow the men; and when you overtake them, say to them, 'Why have you repaid evil for good?

5 '*Is* not this *the one* from which my lord drinks, and with which he indeed practices divination? You have done evil in so doing.' "

6 So he overtook them, and he spoke to them these same words.

7 And they said to him, "Why does my lord say these words? Far be it from us that your servants should do such a thing.

8 "Look, we brought back to you from the land of Cā'naan the money which we found in the mouth of our sacks. How then could we steal silver or gold from your lord's house?

9 "With whomever of your servants it is found, let him die, and we also will be my lord's slaves."

10 And he said, "Now also *let* it *be* according to your words; he with whom it is found shall be my slave, and you shall be blameless."

11 Then each man speedily let down his sack to the ground, and each opened his sack.

12 So he searched. He began with the oldest and left off with the youngest; and the cup was found in Benjamin's sack.

13 Then they tore their clothes, and each man loaded his donkey and returned to the city.

14 So Judah and his brothers came to Joseph's house, and he *was* still there; and they fell before him on the ground.

15 And Joseph said to them, "What deed *is* this you have done? Did you not know that such a man as I can certainly practice divination?"

16 Then Judah said, "What shall we say to my lord? What shall we speak? Or how shall we clear ourselves? God has found out the iniquity of your servants; here we are, my lord's slaves, both we and *he* also with whom the cup was found."

17 But he said, "Far be it from me that I should do so; the man in whose hand the cup was found, he shall be my slave. And as for you, go up in peace to your father."

JUDAH INTERCEDES FOR BENJAMIN

18 Then Judah came near to him and said: "O my lord, please let your servant speak a word in my lord's hearing, and do not let your anger burn against your servant; for you *are* even like Pharaoh.

19 "My lord asked his servants, saying, 'Have you a father or a brother?'

20 "And we said to my lord, 'We have a father, an old man, and a child of *his* old age, *who is* young; his brother is dead, and he alone is left of his mother's children, and his father loves him.'

21 "Then you said to your servants, 'Bring him down to me, that I may set my eyes on him.'

22 "And we said to my lord, 'The lad cannot leave his father, for *if* he should leave his father, *his father* would die.'
23 "But you said to your servants, 'Unless your youngest brother comes down with you, you shall see my face no more.'
24 "So it was, when we went up to your servant my father, that we told him the words of my lord.
25 "And our father said, 'Go back *and* buy us a little food.'
26 "But we said, 'We cannot go down; if our youngest brother is with us, then we will go down; for we may not see the man's face unless our youngest brother *is* with us.'
27 "Then your servant my father said to us, 'You know that my wife bore me two sons;
28 'and the one went out from me, and I said, "Surely he is torn to pieces"; and I have not seen him since.
29 'But if you take this one also from me, and calamity befalls him, you shall bring down my gray hair with sorrow to the grave.'
30 "Now therefore, when I come to your servant my father, and the lad *is* not with us, since his life is bound up in the lad's life,
31 "it will happen, when he sees that the lad *is* not *with us,* that he will die. So your servants will bring down the gray hair of your servant our father with sorrow to the grave.
32 "For your servant became surety for the lad to my father, saying, 'If I do not bring him *back* to you, then I shall bear the blame before my father forever.'
33 "Now therefore, please let your servant remain instead of the lad as a slave to my lord, and let the lad go up with his brothers.
34 "For how shall I go up to my father if the lad *is* not with me, lest

perhaps I see the evil that would come upon my father?"

JOSEPH REVEALED TO HIS BROTHERS

45 Then Joseph could not restrain himself before all those who stood by him, and he cried out, "Make everyone go out from me!" So no one stood with him while Joseph made himself known to his brothers.
2 And he wept aloud, and the Egyptians and the house of Pharaoh heard *it.*
3 Then Joseph said to his brothers, "I *am* Joseph; does my father still live?" But his brothers could not answer him, for they were dismayed in his presence.
4 And Joseph said to his brothers, "Please come near to me." So they came near. Then he said: "I *am* Joseph your brother, whom you sold into Egypt.
5 "But now, do not therefore be grieved or angry with yourselves because you sold me here; for God sent me before you to preserve life.
6 "For these two years the famine *has been* in the land, and *there are* still five years in which *there will be* neither plowing nor harvesting.
7 "And God sent me before you to preserve a posterity for you in the earth, and to save your lives by a great deliverance.
8 "So now *it was* not you *who* sent me here, but God; and He has made me a father to Pharaoh, and lord of all his house, and a ruler throughout all the land of Egypt.
9 "Hurry and go up to my father, and say to him, 'Thus says your son Joseph: "God has made me lord of all Egypt; come down to me, do not tarry.
10 "You shall dwell in the land of Gō'shen, and you shall be near to me,

you and your children, your children's children, your flocks and your herds, and all that you have.

11 "There I will provide for you, lest you and your household, and all that you have, come to poverty; for *there are* still five years of famine." '

12 "And behold, your eyes and the eyes of my brother Benjamin see that *it is* my mouth that speaks to you.

13 "So you shall tell my father of all my glory in Egypt, and of all that you have seen; and you shall hurry and bring my father down here."

14 Then he fell on his brother Benjamin's neck and wept, and Benjamin wept on his neck.

15 Moreover he kissed all his brothers and wept over them, and after that his brothers talked with him.

16 Now the report of it was heard in Pharaoh's house, saying, "Joseph's brothers have come." So it pleased Pharaoh and his servants well.

17 And Pharaoh said to Joseph, "Say to your brothers, 'Do this: Load your animals and depart; go to the land of Cā′naan.

18 'Bring your father and your households and come to me; I will give you the best of the land of Egypt, and you will eat the fat of the land.

19 'Now you are commanded—do this: Take carts out of the land of Egypt for your little ones and your wives; bring your father and come.

20 'Also do not be concerned about your goods, for the best of all the land of Egypt *is* yours.' "

21 Then the sons of Israel did so; and Joseph gave them carts, according to the command of Pharaoh, and he gave them provisions for the journey.

22 He gave to all of them, to each man, changes of garments; but to Benjamin he gave three hundred *pieces* of silver and five changes of garments.

23 And he sent to his father these

things: ten donkeys loaded with the good things of Egypt, and ten female donkeys loaded with grain, bread, and food for his father for the journey.

24 So he sent his brothers away, and they departed; and he said to them, "See that you do not become troubled along the way."

25 Then they went up out of Egypt, and came to the land of Cā′naan to Jacob their father.

26 And they told him, saying, "Joseph *is* still alive, and he *is* governor over all the land of Egypt." And Jacob's heart stood still, because he did not believe them.

27 But when they told him all the words which Joseph had said to them, and when he saw the carts which Joseph had sent to carry him, the spirit of Jacob their father revived.

28 Then Israel said, "*It is* enough. Joseph my son *is* still alive. I will go and see him before I die."

✓ *Bible Quiz*

Genesis 44; 45 **Joseph Reveals Himself to His Brothers**

1. What surprise did Joseph put into Benjamin's grain sack?

2. What did Joseph want to do to Benjamin?

3. Who spoke up for Benjamin? What did he say?

4. What did Joseph do then? Could you have forgiven your brothers or sisters if they had sold you as a slave?

5. Do you need to forgive someone now? How can you do that?

JACOB'S JOURNEY TO EGYPT

46 So Israel took his journey with all that he had, and came to Bē·er-shē'ba, and offered sacrifices to the God of his father Isaac.

2   Then God spoke to Israel in the visions of the night, and said, "Jacob, Jacob!" And he said, "Here I am."

3   So He said, "I *am* God, the God of your father; do not fear to go down to Egypt, for I will make of you a great nation there.

4   "I will go down with you to Egypt, and I will also surely bring you up *again;* and Joseph will put his hand on your eyes."

5   Then Jacob arose from Bē·er-shē'ba; and the sons of Israel carried their father Jacob, their little ones, and their wives, in the carts which Pharaoh had sent to carry him.

6   So they took their livestock and their goods, which they had acquired in the land of Cā'naan, and went to Egypt, Jacob and all his descendants with him.

7   His sons and his sons' sons, his daughters and his sons' daughters, and all his descendants he brought with him to Egypt.

8   Now these *were* the names of the children of Israel, Jacob and his sons, who went to Egypt: Reuben *was* Jacob's firstborn.

9   The sons of Reuben *were* Hā'noch, Pal'lū, Hez'ron, and Car'mi.

10   The sons of Sim'ē·on *were* Je-mū'el,*a* Jā'min, Ō'had, Jā'chin,*b* Zō'har,*c* and Shā'ūl, the son of a Cā'naan·ite woman.

11   The sons of Levi *were* Ger'shon, Kō'hath, and Me·rar'ī.

12   The sons of Judah *were* Er, Ō'nan, Shē'lah, Per'ez, and Zē'rah (but Er and Ō'nan died in the land of Cā'naan). The sons of Per'ez were Hez'ron and Hā'mul.

13   The sons of Is'sa·char *were* Tō'la, Pū'vah,*a* Job,*b* and Shim'ron.

14   The sons of Zeb'ū·lun *were* Sē'red, Ē'lon, and Jah'lē·el.

15   These *were* the sons of Leah, whom she bore to Jacob in Pad'an Ar'am, with his daughter Dī'nah. All the persons, his sons and his daughters, *were* thirty-three.

16   The sons of Gad *were* Ziph'i·on,*a* Hag'gī, Shū'nī, Ez'bon,*b* Ē'rī, A·rō'dī,*c* and A·rē'lī.

17   The sons of Ash'er *were* Jim'nah, Ish'ū·ah, Is'ū·ī, Bē·rī'ah, and Sē'rah, their sister. And the sons of Bē·rī'ah *were* Hē'ber and Mal'chi·el.

18   These *were* the sons of Zil'pah, whom Lā'ban gave to Leah his daughter; and these she bore to Jacob: sixteen persons.

19   The sons of Rachel, Jacob's wife, *were* Joseph and Benjamin.

20   And to Joseph in the land of Egypt were born Ma·nas'seh and Ē'phra·im, whom As'e·nath, the daughter of Pō·ti'-Phe·rah' priest of On, bore to him.

21   The sons of Benjamin *were* Bē'lah, Bē'cher, Ash'bel, Gē'ra, Nā'-a·man, Ē'hī, Rosh, Mup'pim, Hup'-pim,*a* and Ard.

22   These *were* the sons of Rachel, who were born to Jacob: fourteen persons in all.

23   The son of Dan *was* Hū'shim.*a*

24   The sons of Naph'ta·lī *were* Jah'-zē·el,*a* Gū'nī, Jē'zer, and Shil'lem.*b*

25   These *were* the sons of Bil'hah, whom Lā'ban gave to Rachel his

---

46:10 *a*Spelled *Nemuel* in 1 Chronicles 4:24 *b*Called *Jarib* in 1 Chronicles 4:24 *c*Called *Zerah* in 1 Chronicles 4:24   46:13 *a*Spelled *Puah* in 1 Chronicles 7:1 *b*Same as *Jashub* in Numbers 26:24 and 1 Chronicles 7:1 46:16 *a*Spelled *Zephon* in Samaritan Pentateuch, Septuagint, and Numbers 26:15 *b*Called *Ozni* in Numbers 26:16 *c*Spelled *Arod* in Numbers 26:17   46:21 *a*Called *Hupham* in Numbers 26:39   46:23 *a*Called *Shuham* in Numbers 26:42   46:24 *a*Spelled *Jahziel* in 1 Chronicles 7:13 *b*Spelled *Shallum* in 1 Chronicles 7:13

daughter, and she bore these to Jacob: seven persons in all.
26 All the persons who went with Jacob to Egypt, who came from his
body, besides Jacob's sons' wives,
were sixty-six persons in all.
27 And the sons of Joseph who were
born to him in Egypt *were* two persons. All the persons of the house of
Jacob who went to Egypt were seventy.

JACOB SETTLES IN GOSHEN

28 Then he sent Judah before him to
Joseph, to point out before him *the
way* to Gō'shen. And they came to
the land of Gō'shen.
29 So Joseph made ready his chariot
and went up to Gō'shen to meet
his father Israel; and he presented
himself to him, and fell on his
neck and wept on his neck a good
while.
30 And Israel said to Joseph, "Now
let me die, since I have seen your
face, because you *are* still alive."
31 Then Joseph said to his brothers
and to his father's household, "I
will go up and tell Pharaoh, and
say to him, 'My brothers and those
of my father's house, who *were* in
the land of Cā'naan, have come to
me.
32 'And the men *are* shepherds, for
their occupation has been to feed
livestock; and they have brought
their flocks, their herds, and all that
they have.'
33 "So it shall be, when Pharaoh
calls you and says, 'What is your occupation?'
34 "that you shall say, 'Your servants' occupation has been with livestock from our youth even till now,
both we *and* also our fathers,' that
you may dwell in the land of Gō'shen;
for every shepherd *is* an abomination
to the Egyptians."

47 Then Joseph went and told
Pharaoh, and said, "My father and
my brothers, their flocks and their
herds and all that they possess, have
come from the land of Cā'naan; and
indeed they *are* in the land of Gō'-
shen."
2 And he took five men from among
his brothers and presented them to
Pharaoh.
3 Then Pharaoh said to his brothers, "What *is* your occupation?" And
they said to Pharaoh, "Your servants
are shepherds, both we *and* also our
fathers."
4 And they said to Pharaoh, "We
have come to dwell in the land, because your servants have no pasture
for their flocks, for the famine *is* severe in the land of Cā'naan. Now
therefore, please let your servants
dwell in the land of Gō'shen."
5 Then Pharaoh spoke to Joseph,
saying, "Your father and your brothers have come to you.
6 "The land of Egypt *is* before you.
Have your father and brothers dwell
in the best of the land; let them dwell
in the land of Gō'shen. And if you
know *any* competent men among
them, then make them chief herdsmen over my livestock."
7 Then Joseph brought in his father
Jacob and set him before Pharaoh;
and Jacob blessed Pharaoh.
8 Pharaoh said to Jacob, "How old
are you?"
9 And Jacob said to Pharaoh, "The
days of the years of my pilgrimage
are one hundred and thirty years;
few and evil have been the days of
the years of my life, and they have
not attained to the days of the years
of the life of my fathers in the days of
their pilgrimage."
10 So Jacob blessed Pharaoh, and
went out from before Pharaoh.
11 And Joseph situated his father

and his brothers, and gave them a possession in the land of Egypt, in the best of the land, in the land of Ram′e·sēs, as Pharaoh had commanded.

12 Then Joseph provided his father, his brothers, and all his father's household with bread, according to the number in *their* families.

JOSEPH DEALS WITH THE FAMINE

13 Now *there was* no bread in all the land; for the famine *was* very severe, so that the land of Egypt and the land of Cā′naan languished because of the famine.

14 And Joseph gathered up all the money that was found in the land of Egypt and in the land of Cā′naan, for the grain which they bought; and Joseph brought the money into Pharaoh's house.

15 So when the money failed in the land of Egypt and in the land of Cā′naan, all the Egyptians came to Joseph and said, "Give us bread, for why should we die in your presence? For the money has failed."

16 Then Joseph said, "Give your livestock, and I will give you *bread* for your livestock, if the money is gone."

17 So they brought their livestock to Joseph, and Joseph gave them bread *in exchange* for the horses, the flocks, the cattle of the herds, and for the donkeys. Thus he fed them with bread *in exchange* for all their livestock that year.

18 When that year had ended, they came to him the next year and said to him, "We will not hide from my lord that our money is gone; my lord also has our herds of livestock. There is nothing left in the sight of my lord but our bodies and our lands.

19 "Why should we die before your eyes, both we and our land? Buy us and our land for bread, and we and our land will be servants of Pharaoh; give *us* seed, that we may live and not die, that the land may not be desolate."

20 Then Joseph bought all the land of Egypt for Pharaoh; for every man of the Egyptians sold his field, because the famine was severe upon them. So the land became Pharaoh's.

21 And as for the people, he moved them into the cities,*a* from *one* end of the borders of Egypt to the *other* end.

22 Only the land of the priests he did not buy; for the priests had rations *allotted to them* by Pharaoh, and they ate their rations which Pharaoh gave them; therefore they did not sell their lands.

23 Then Joseph said to the people, "Indeed I have bought you and your land this day for Pharaoh. Look, *here is* seed for you, and you shall sow the land.

24 "And it shall come to pass in the harvest that you shall give one-fifth to Pharaoh. Four-fifths shall be your own, as seed for the field and for your food, for those of your households and as food for your little ones."

25 So they said, "You have saved our lives; let us find favor in the sight of my lord, and we will be Pharaoh's servants."

26 And Joseph made it a law over the land of Egypt to this day, *that* Pharaoh should have one-fifth, except for the land of the priests only, *which* did not become Pharaoh's.

JOSEPH'S VOW TO JACOB

27 So Israel dwelt in the land of Egypt, in the country of Gō′shen; and they had possessions there and grew and multiplied exceedingly.

28 And Jacob lived in the land of

47:21 *a*Following Masoretic Text and Targum; Samaritan Pentateuch, Septuagint, and Vulgate read *made the people virtual slaves.*

Egypt seventeen years. So the length of Jacob's life was one hundred and forty-seven years.

29 When the time drew near that Israel must die, he called his son Joseph and said to him, "Now if I have found favor in your sight, please put your hand under my thigh, and deal kindly and truly with me. Please do not bury me in Egypt,

30 "but let me lie with my fathers; you shall carry me out of Egypt and bury me in their burial place." And he said, "I will do as you have said."

31 Then he said, "Swear to me." And he swore to him. So Israel bowed himself on the head of the bed.

JACOB BLESSES JOSEPH'S SONS

48 Now it came to pass after these things that Joseph was told, "Indeed your father is sick"; and he took with him his two sons, Ma·nas'-seh and Ē'phra·im.

2 And Jacob was told, "Look, your son Joseph is coming to you"; and Israel strengthened himself and sat up on the bed.

3 Then Jacob said to Joseph: "God Almighty appeared to me at Luz in the land of Cā'naan and blessed me,

4 "and said to me, 'Behold, I will make you fruitful and multiply you, and I will make of you a multitude of people, and give this land to your descendants after you as an everlasting possession.'

5 "And now your two sons, Ē'phraim and Ma·nas'seh, who were born to you in the land of Egypt before I came to you in Egypt, are mine; as Reuben and Sim'ē·on, they shall be mine.

6 "Your offspring whom you beget after them shall be yours; they will be called by the name of their brothers in their inheritance.

7 "But as for me, when I came from Pad'an, Rachel died beside me in the land of Cā'naan on the way, when there was but a little distance to go to Eph'rath; and I buried her there on the way to Eph'rath (that is, Bethlehem)."

8 Then Israel saw Joseph's sons, and said, "Who are these?"

9 And Joseph said to his father, "They are my sons, whom God has given me in this place." And he said, "Please bring them to me, and I will bless them."

10 Now the eyes of Israel were dim with age, so that he could not see. Then Joseph brought them near him, and he kissed them and embraced them.

11 And Israel said to Joseph, "I had not thought to see your face; but in fact, God has also shown me your offspring!"

12 So Joseph brought them from beside his knees, and he bowed down with his face to the earth.

13 And Joseph took them both, Ē'phra·im with his right hand toward Israel's left hand, and Ma·nas'seh with his left hand toward Israel's right hand, and brought them near him.

14 Then Israel stretched out his right hand and laid it on Ē'phra·im's head, who was the younger, and his left hand on Ma·nas'seh's head, guiding his hands knowingly, for Ma·nas'seh was the firstborn.

15 And he blessed Joseph, and said:

"God, before whom my fathers
   Abraham and Isaac walked,
The God who has fed me all my
   life long to this day,
16 The Angel who has redeemed me
   from all evil,
Bless the lads;
Let my name be named upon
   them,

And the name of my fathers
    Abraham and Isaac;
And let them grow into a
    multitude in the midst of the
    earth."

17 Now when Joseph saw that his father laid his right hand on the head of Ē′phra·im, it displeased him; so he took hold of his father's hand to remove it from Ē′phra·im's head to Ma·nas′seh's head.
18 And Joseph said to his father, "Not so, my father, for this *one is* the firstborn; put your right hand on his head."
19 But his father refused and said, "I know, my son, I know. He also shall become a people, and he also shall be great; but truly his younger brother shall be greater than he, and his descendants shall become a multitude of nations."
20 So he blessed them that day, saying, "By you Israel will bless, saying, 'May God make you as Ē′phra·im and as Ma·nas′seh!' " And thus he set Ē′phra·im before Ma·nas′seh.
21 Then Israel said to Joseph, "Behold, I am dying, but God will be with you and bring you back to the land of your fathers.
22 "Moreover I have given to you one portion above your brothers, which I took from the hand of the Am′o·rīte with my sword and my bow."

JACOB'S LAST WORDS TO HIS SONS

49 And Jacob called his sons and said, "Gather together, that I may tell you what shall befall you in the last days:

2 "Gather together and hear, you
    sons of Jacob,
And listen to Israel your father.

3 "Reuben, you are my firstborn,
    My might and the beginning of
      my strength,
    The excellency of dignity and the
      excellency of power.
4 Unstable as water, you shall not
    excel,
    Because you went up to your
      father's bed;
    Then you defiled *it*—
    He went up to my couch.

5 "Sim′ē·on and Levi *are* brothers;
    Instruments of cruelty *are in*
      their dwelling place.
6 Let not my soul enter their
    council;
    Let not my honor be united to
      their assembly;
    For in their anger they slew a
      man,
    And in their self-will they
      hamstrung an ox.
7 Cursed *be* their anger, for *it is*
    fierce;
    And their wrath, for it is cruel!
    I will divide them in Jacob
    And scatter them in Israel.

8 "Judah, you *are he* whom your
    brothers shall praise;
    Your hand *shall be* on the neck of
      your enemies;
    Your father's children shall bow
      down before you.
9 Judah *is* a lion's whelp;
    From the prey, my son, you have
      gone up.
    He bows down, he lies down as a
      lion;
    And as a lion, who shall rouse
      him?
10 The scepter shall not depart from
    Judah,
    Nor a lawgiver from between his
      feet,
    Until Shī′lōh comes;
    And to Him *shall be* the obedience
      of the people.

11 Binding his donkey to the vine,
   And his donkey's colt to the choice
      vine,
   He washed his garments in wine,
   And his clothes in the blood of
      grapes.
12 His eyes *are* darker than wine,
   And his teeth whiter than milk.

13 "Zeb'ū·lun shall dwell by the
      haven of the sea;
   He *shall become* a haven for
      ships,
   And his border shall adjoin
      Sī'don.

14 "Is'sa·char is a strong donkey,
   Lying down between two burdens;
15 He saw that rest *was* good,
   And that the land *was* pleasant;
   He bowed his shoulder to bear *a*
      burden,
   And became a band of slaves.

16 "Dan shall judge his people
   As one of the tribes of Israel.
17 Dan shall be a serpent by the
      way,
   A viper by the path,
   That bites the horse's heels
   So that its rider shall fall
      backward.
18 I have waited for your salvation,
   O LORD!

19 "Gad, a troop shall tramp upon
      him,
   But he shall triumph at last.

20 "Bread from Ash'er *shall be* rich,
   And he shall yield royal dainties.

21 "Naph'ta·lī *is* a deer let loose;
   He uses beautiful words.

22 "Joseph *is* a fruitful bough,
   A fruitful bough by a well;
   His branches run over the wall.
23 The archers have bitterly grieved
      him,

Shot *at him* and hated him.
24 But his bow remained in
      strength,
   And the arms of his hands were
      made strong
   By the hands of the Mighty *God*
      of Jacob
   (From there *is* the Shepherd, the
      Stone of Israel),
25 By the God of your father who
      will help you,
   And by the Almighty who will
      bless you
   With blessings of heaven above,
   Blessings of the deep that lies
      beneath,
   Blessings of the breasts and of
      the womb.
26 The blessings of your father
   Have excelled the blessings of my
      ancestors,
   Up to the utmost bound of the
      everlasting hills.
   They shall be on the head of
      Joseph,
   And on the crown of the head of
      him who was separate from his
      brothers.

27 "Benjamin is a ravenous wolf;
   In the morning he shall devour
      the prey,
   And at night he shall divide the
      spoil."

28 All these *are* the twelve tribes of
Israel, and this *is* what their father
spoke to them. And he blessed them;
he blessed each one according to his
own blessing.

JACOB'S DEATH AND BURIAL

29 Then he charged them and said to
them: "I am to be gathered to my people; bury me with my fathers in the
cave that *is* in the field of Ē'phron
the Hit'tīte,
30 "in the cave that *is* in the field of

Mach·pē′lah, which *is* before Mam′re in the land of Cā′naan, which Abraham bought with the field of Ē′phron the Hit′tīte as a possession for a burial place.

31 "There they buried Abraham and Sarah his wife, there they buried Isaac and Rebekah his wife, and there I buried Leah.

32 "The field and the cave that *is* there *were* purchased from the sons of Heth."

33 And when Jacob had finished commanding his sons, he drew his feet up into the bed and breathed his last, and was gathered to his people.

50

Then Joseph fell on his father's face, and wept over him, and kissed him.

2 And Joseph commanded his servants the physicians to embalm his father. So the physicians embalmed Israel.

3 Forty days were required for him, for such are the days required for those who are embalmed; and the Egyptians mourned for him seventy days.

4 Now when the days of his mourning were past, Joseph spoke to the household of Pharaoh, saying, "If now I have found favor in your eyes, please speak in the hearing of Pharaoh, saying,

5 'My father made me swear, saying, "Behold, I am dying; in my grave which I dug for myself in the land of Cā′naan, there you shall bury me." Now therefore, please let me go up and bury my father, and I will come back.' "

6 And Pharaoh said, "Go up and bury your father, as he made you swear."

7 So Joseph went up to bury his father; and with him went up all the servants of Pharaoh, the elders of his house, and all the elders of the land of Egypt,

8 as well as all the house of Joseph, his brothers, and his father's house. Only their little ones, their flocks, and their herds they left in the land of Gō′shen.

9 And there went up with him both chariots and horsemen, and it was a very great gathering.

10 Then they came to the threshing floor of Ā′tad, which *is* beyond the Jordan, and they mourned there with a great and very solemn lamentation. He observed seven days of mourning for his father.

11 And when the inhabitants of the land, the Cā′naan·ītes, saw the mourning at the threshing floor of Ā′tad, they said, "This *is* a deep mourning of the Egyptians." Therefore its name was called Abel Miz′ra·im,*a* which *is* beyond the Jordan.

12 So his sons did for him just as he had commanded them.

13 For his sons carried him to the land of Cā′naan, and buried him in the cave of the field of Mach·pē′lah, before Mam′re, which Abraham bought with the field from Ē′phron the Hit′tīte as property for a burial place.

14 And after he had buried his father, Joseph returned to Egypt, he and his brothers and all who went up with him to bury his father.

JOSEPH REASSURES HIS BROTHERS

15 When Joseph's brothers saw that their father was dead, they said, "Perhaps Joseph will hate us, and may actually repay us for all the evil which we did to him."

16 So they sent *messengers* to Joseph,

50:11 *a*Literally *Mourning of Egypt*

What Should I Do?

WHEN A FRIEND GETS ME INTO TROUBLE Genesis 50:15–21

Rick and Rita are playing a duet. They need each other. How can you play a duet without the other person? They even need to be friends. That's when a duet sounds best. Rick and Rita want to be friends. They want to help each other. But Rick is getting Rita into trouble. Do you see how? Or is Rita getting Rick into trouble?

1. Does a friend ever get you into trouble? How?
2. What should you say to a friend who does that?
3. What should you say when you get a friend into trouble?
4. What would Jesus want you to do?

For more on *What Should I Do?* turn to page 157
For more on *Forgiveness* turn to page 275

saying, "Before your father died he commanded, saying,

17 'Thus you shall say to Joseph: "I beg you, please forgive the trespass of your brothers and their sin; for they did evil to you." ' Now, please, forgive the trespass of the servants of the God of your father." And Joseph wept when they spoke to him.

18 Then his brothers also went and fell down before his face, and they said, "Behold, we *are* your servants."

19 Joseph said to them, "Do not be afraid, for *am* I in the place of God?

20 "But as for you, you meant evil against me; *but* God meant it for good, in order to bring it about as *it is* this day, to save many people alive.

21 "Now therefore, do not be afraid; I will provide for you and your little ones." And he comforted them and spoke kindly to them.

DEATH OF JOSEPH

22 So Joseph dwelt in Egypt, he and his father's household. And Joseph lived one hundred and ten years.

23 Joseph saw Ē′phra·im's children to the third *generation.* The children of Mā′chir, the son of Ma·nas′seh, were also brought up on Joseph's knees.

24 And Joseph said to his brethren, "I am dying; but God will surely visit you, and bring you out of this land to the land of which He swore to Abraham, to Isaac, and to Jacob."

25 Then Joseph took an oath from the children of Israel, saying, "God will surely visit you, and you shall carry up my bones from here."

26 So Joseph died, *being* one hundred and ten years old; and they embalmed him, and he was put in a coffin in Egypt.

EXODUS

ISRAEL'S SUFFERING IN EGYPT

Joseph moved his family to Egypt when he became governor there. Over the years his family grew into a nation of people. The Book of Exodus begins 400 years after Joseph. Joseph's descendants were called Hebrews. But the new king of Egypt didn't like them. He made them slaves. This is how it happened.

NOW these *are* the names of the children of Israel who came to Egypt; each man and his household came with Jacob:

2 Reuben, Sim′ē·on, Levi, and Judah;

3 Is′sa·char, Zeb′ū·lun, and Benjamin;

4 Dan, Naph′ta·lī, Gad, and Ash′er.

5 All those who were descendants*a* of Jacob were seventy*b* persons (for Joseph was in Egypt *already*).

6 And Joseph died, all his brothers, and all that generation.

7 But the children of Israel were fruitful and increased abundantly, multiplied and grew exceedingly mighty; and the land was filled with them.

8 Now there arose a new king over Egypt, who did not know Joseph.

9 And he said to his people, "Look, the people of the children of Israel *are* more and mightier than we;

10 "come, let us deal shrewdly with them, lest they multiply, and it happen, in the event of war, that they also join our enemies and fight against us, and *so* go up out of the land."

11 Therefore they set taskmasters over them to afflict them with their burdens. And they built for Pharaoh supply cities, Pī′thom and Rā·am′sēs.

12 But the more they afflicted them, the more they multiplied and grew. And they were in dread of the children of Israel.

13 So the Egyptians made the children of Israel serve with rigor.

14 And they made their lives bitter with hard bondage—in mortar, in brick, and in all manner of service in the field. All their service in which they made them serve *was* with rigor.

15 Then the king of Egypt spoke to the Hebrew midwives, of whom the

1:5 *a*Literally *who came from the loins of* *b*Dead Sea Scrolls and Septuagint read *seventy-five* (compare Acts 7:14).

☑ *Bible Quiz*

Exodus 1:1–21 **The Hebrews Become Slaves**

1. Why didn't the new king of Egypt care about Joseph? What was he afraid of?

2. What did he do to the Hebrews?

3. How did the king treat the Hebrews? Did this keep the Hebrews from growing in number?

4. What happened to the Hebrew boys? Who helped them? How did God bless them for helping?

5. What if you became a slave today? Could you keep trusting God like the Hebrew midwives did? How would you do that?

name of one *was* Shiph′rah and the name of the other Pū′ah;

16 and he said, "When you do the duties of a midwife for the Hebrew women, and see *them* on the birthstools, if it *is* a son, then you shall kill him; but if it *is* a daughter, then she shall live."

17 But the midwives feared God, and did not do as the king of Egypt commanded them, but saved the male children alive.

18 So the king of Egypt called for the midwives and said to them, "Why have you done this thing, and saved the male children alive?"

19 And the midwives said to Pharaoh, "Because the Hebrew women *are* not like the Egyptian women; for they *are* lively and give birth before the midwives come to them."

20 Therefore God dealt well with the midwives, and the people multiplied and grew very mighty.

21 And so it was, because the midwives feared God, that He provided households for them.

> *The Hebrews were slaves in Egypt. But no matter how badly they were treated, they kept growing in number. Finally, the king ordered his soldiers to throw all the Hebrew baby boys into the river and drown them. But his soldiers missed one very special baby.*

22 So Pharaoh commanded all his people, saying, "Every son who is born*a* you shall cast into the river, and every daughter you shall save alive."

MOSES IS BORN

2 And a man of the house of Levi went and took *as wife* a daughter of Levi.

2 So the woman conceived and bore a son. And when she saw that he *was* a beautiful *child,* she hid him three months.

3 But when she could no longer hide him, she took an ark of bulrushes for him, daubed it with asphalt and pitch, put the child in it, and laid *it* in the reeds by the river's bank.

4 And his sister stood afar off, to know what would be done to him.

5 Then the daughter of Pharaoh came down to bathe at the river. And her maidens walked along the riverside; and when she saw the ark among the reeds, she sent her maid to get it.

6 And when she opened *it,* she saw the child, and behold, the baby wept. So she had compassion on him, and said, "This is one of the Hebrews' children."

7 Then his sister said to Pharaoh's daughter, "Shall I go and call a nurse for you from the Hebrew women, that she may nurse the child for you?"

8 And Pharaoh's daughter said to her, "Go." So the maiden went and called the child's mother.

9 Then Pharaoh's daughter said to her, "Take this child away and nurse him for me, and I will give *you* your wages." So the woman took the child and nursed him.

10 And the child grew, and she brought him to Pharaoh's daughter, and he became her son. So she called his name Moses,*a* saying, "Because I drew him out of the water."

MOSES FLEES TO MIDIAN

11 Now it came to pass in those days, when Moses was grown, that he

---

1:22 *a*Samaritan Pentateuch, Septuagint, and Targum add *to the Hebrews.*   2:10 *a*Literally *Drawn Out*

☑	*Bible Quiz*

Exodus 1:22—2:10 **Moses Is Born**

1. How did the baby's mother hide him?
2. Who found the baby? What did the princess do? Whom did the princess ask to take care of her baby?
3. What was the baby's name?
4. What do you think the king would have said if he knew a Hebrew baby boy was being raised by the princess?
5. When something bad happens, watch for the good things God will bring from it. Is something bad happening to you or someone you know? What good things might God bring from it?

---

went out to his brethren and looked at their burdens. And he saw an Egyptian beating a Hebrew, one of his brethren.

12 So he looked this way and that way, and when he saw no one, he killed the Egyptian and hid him in the sand.

13 And when he went out the second day, behold, two Hebrew men were fighting, and he said to the one who did the wrong, "Why are you striking your companion?"

14 Then he said, "Who made you a prince and a judge over us? Do you intend to kill me as you killed the Egyptian?" So Moses feared and said, "Surely this thing is known!"

15 When Pharaoh heard of this matter, he sought to kill Moses. But Moses fled from the face of Pharaoh and dwelt in the land of Mid′i·an; and he sat down by a well.

16 Now the priest of Mid′i·an had seven daughters. And they came and drew water, and they filled the troughs to water their father's flock.

17 Then the shepherds came and drove them away; but Moses stood up and helped them, and watered their flock.

18 When they came to Reū′el their father, he said, "How *is it that* you have come so soon today?"

19 And they said, "An Egyptian delivered us from the hand of the shepherds, and he also drew enough water for us and watered the flock."

20 So he said to his daughters, "And where *is* he? Why *is* it *that* you have left the man? Call him, that he may eat bread."

21 Then Moses was content to live with the man, and he gave Zip·pō′rah his daughter to Moses.

22 And she bore *him* a son. He called his name Ger′shom,*a* for he said, "I have been a stranger in a foreign land."

23 Now it happened in the process of time that the king of Egypt died. Then the children of Israel groaned because of the bondage, and they cried out; and their cry came up to God because of the bondage.

24 So God heard their groaning, and God remembered His covenant with Abraham, with Isaac, and with Jacob.

25 And God looked upon the children of Israel, and God acknowledged *them.*

2:22 *a*Literally *Stranger There*

MOSES AT THE BURNING BUSH

*Moses had to escape from
Egypt. Now he was a shepherd
living in the desert. One day,
as he was watching his sheep,
he saw a bush on fire that
never burned up. This is what
he found when he took a closer
look.*

3 Now Moses was tending the flock
of Jeth′rō his father-in-law, the priest
of Mid′i·an. And he led the flock to
the back of the desert, and came to
Hō′reb, the mountain of God.
2   And the Angel of the LORD appeared to him in a flame of fire from
the midst of a bush. So he looked,
and behold, the bush was burning
with fire, but the bush *was* not consumed.
3   Then Moses said, "I will now turn
aside and see this great sight, why
the bush does not burn."
4   So when the LORD saw that he
turned aside to look, God called to
him from the midst of the bush and
said, "Moses, Moses!" And he said,
"Here I am."
5   Then He said, "Do not draw near
this place. Take your sandals off your
feet, for the place where you stand *is*
holy ground."
6   Moreover He said, "I *am* the God
of your father—the God of Abraham,
the God of Isaac, and the God of Jacob." And Moses hid his face, for he
was afraid to look upon God.
7   And the LORD said: "I have surely
seen the oppression of My people who
are in Egypt, and have heard their
cry because of their taskmasters, for
I know their sorrows.
8   "So I have come down to deliver
them out of the hand of the Egyptians, and to bring them up from that
land to a good and large land, to a
land flowing with milk and honey, to

the place of the Cā′naan·ītes and the
Hit′tītes and the Am′o·rītes and the
Per′iz·zītes and the Hī′vītes and the
Jeb′ū·sītes.
9   "Now therefore, behold, the cry of
the children of Israel has come to Me,
and I have also seen the oppression
with which the Egyptians oppress
them.
10   "Come now, therefore, and I will
send you to Pharaoh that you may
bring My people, the children of Israel, out of Egypt."
11   But Moses said to God, "Who *am* I
that I should go to Pharaoh, and that
I should bring the children of Israel
out of Egypt?"
12   So He said, "I will certainly be
with you. And this *shall be* a sign to
you that I have sent you: When you
have brought the people out of Egypt,
you shall serve God on this mountain."
13   Then Moses said to God, "Indeed,
when I come to the children of Israel
and say to them, 'The God of your fathers has sent me to you,' and they
say to me, 'What *is* His name?' what
shall I say to them?"
14   And God said to Moses, "I AM
WHO I AM." And He said, "Thus you
shall say to the children of Israel, 'I
AM has sent me to you.' "
15   Moreover God said to Moses,
"Thus you shall say to the children of
Israel: 'The LORD God of your fathers,
the God of Abraham, the God of
Isaac, and the God of Jacob, has sent
me to you. This *is* My name forever,
and this *is* My memorial to all generations.'
16   "Go and gather the elders of Israel together, and say to them, 'The
LORD God of your fathers, the God of
Abraham, of Isaac, and of Jacob, appeared to me, saying, "I have surely
visited you and *seen* what is done to
you in Egypt;
17   "and I have said I will bring you

up out of the affliction of Egypt to the land of the Cā′naan·ītes and the Hit′tītes and the Am′o·rītes and the Per′iz·zītes and the Hī′vītes and the Jeb′ū·sītes, to a land flowing with milk and honey." '

18 "Then they will heed your voice; and you shall come, you and the elders of Israel, to the king of Egypt; and you shall say to him, 'The LORD God of the Hebrews has met with us; and now, please, let us go three days' journey into the wilderness, that we may sacrifice to the LORD our God.'

19 "But I am sure that the king of Egypt will not let you go, no, not even by a mighty hand.

20 "So I will stretch out My hand and strike Egypt with all My wonders which I will do in its midst; and after that he will let you go.

21 "And I will give this people favor in the sight of the Egyptians; and it shall be, when you go, that you shall not go empty-handed.

22 "But every woman shall ask of her neighbor, namely, of her who dwells near her house, articles of silver, articles of gold, and clothing; and you shall put *them* on your sons and on your daughters. So you shall plunder the Egyptians."

MIRACULOUS SIGNS FOR PHARAOH

4 Then Moses answered and said, "But suppose they will not believe me or listen to my voice; suppose they say, 'The LORD has not appeared to you.' "

2 So the LORD said to him, "What *is* that in your hand?" He said, "A rod."

3 And He said, "Cast it on the ground." So he cast it on the ground, and it became a serpent; and Moses fled from it.

4 Then the LORD said to Moses, "Reach out your hand and take *it* by the tail" (and he reached out his hand and caught it, and it became a rod in his hand),

5 "that they may believe that the LORD God of their fathers, the God of Abraham, the God of Isaac, and the God of Jacob, has appeared to you."

6 Furthermore the LORD said to him, "Now put your hand in your bosom." And he put his hand in his bosom, and when he took it out, behold, his hand *was* leprous, like snow.

7 And He said, "Put your hand in your bosom again." So he put his hand in his bosom again, and drew it out of his bosom, and behold, it was restored like his *other* flesh.

8 "Then it will be, if they do not believe you, nor heed the message of the first sign, that they may believe the message of the latter sign.

9 "And it shall be, if they do not believe even these two signs, or listen to your voice, that you shall take water from the river*a* and pour *it* on the dry *land*. The water which you take from the river will become blood on the dry *land*."

10 Then Moses said to the LORD, "O my Lord, I *am* not eloquent, neither before nor since You have spoken to Your servant; but I *am* slow of speech and slow of tongue."

11 So the LORD said to him, "Who has made man's mouth? Or who makes the mute, the deaf, the seeing, or the blind? *Have* not I, the LORD?

12 "Now therefore, go, and I will be with your mouth and teach you what you shall say."

13 But he said, "O my Lord, please send by the hand of whomever *else* You may send."

14 So the anger of the LORD was kindled against Moses, and He said: "Is not Aaron the Lē′vīte your brother? I know that he can speak well. And

4:9 *a*That is, the Nile

look, he is also coming out to meet you. When he sees you, he will be glad in his heart.

15 "Now you shall speak to him and put the words in his mouth. And I will be with your mouth and with his mouth, and I will teach you what you shall do.

16 "So he shall be your spokesman to the people. And he himself shall be as a mouth for you, and you shall be to him as God.

17 "And you shall take this rod in your hand, with which you shall do the signs."

MOSES GOES TO EGYPT

18 So Moses went and returned to Jeth′rō his father-in-law, and said to him, "Please let me go and return to my brethren who *are* in Egypt, and see whether they are still alive." And Jeth′rō said to Moses, "Go in peace."

19 Now the LORD said to Moses in Mid′i·an, "Go, return to Egypt; for all the men who sought your life are dead."

20 Then Moses took his wife and his sons and set them on a donkey, and he returned to the land of Egypt. And Moses took the rod of God in his hand.

21 And the LORD said to Moses, "When you go back to Egypt, see that you do all those wonders before Pharaoh which I have put in your hand. But I will harden his heart, so that he will not let the people go.

22 "Then you shall say to Pharaoh, 'Thus says the LORD: "Israel *is* My son, My firstborn.

23 "So I say to you, let My son go that he may serve Me. But if you refuse to let him go, indeed I will kill your son, your firstborn." ' "

24 And it came to pass on the way, at the encampment, that the LORD met him and sought to kill him.

☑ *Bible Quiz*

Exodus 3:1—4:20 **The Burning Bush**

1. When Moses went over to the burning bush, who called out to him?
2. What was the first thing Moses had to do at the burning bush?
3. What job did God ask of Moses?
4. Did Moses want to do what God asked? What were some of his excuses?
5. Name three things God did to help Moses.
6. God might ask you to do something special. Think of some things God might ask you to do. How can you be ready to do what God wants?

---

25 Then Zip·pō′rah took a sharp stone and cut off the foreskin of her son and cast *it* at *Moses*'[a] feet, and said, "Surely you *are* a husband of blood to me!"

26 So He let him go. Then she said, "*You are* a husband of blood!"—because of the circumcision.

27 And the LORD said to Aaron, "Go into the wilderness to meet Moses." So he went and met him on the mountain of God, and kissed him.

28 So Moses told Aaron all the words of the LORD who had sent him, and all the signs which He had commanded him.

29 Then Moses and Aaron went and gathered together all the elders of the children of Israel.

30 And Aaron spoke all the words

4:25 [a]Literally *his*

which the LORD had spoken to Moses. Then he did the signs in the sight of the people.

31 So the people believed; and when they heard that the LORD had visited the children of Israel and that He had looked on their affliction, then they bowed their heads and worshiped.

FIRST ENCOUNTER WITH PHARAOH

5 Afterward Moses and Aaron went in and told Pharaoh, "Thus says the LORD God of Israel: 'Let My people go, that they may hold a feast to Me in the wilderness.'"

2 And Pharaoh said, "Who *is* the LORD, that I should obey His voice to let Israel go? I do not know the LORD, nor will I let Israel go."

3 So they said, "The God of the Hebrews has met with us. Please, let us go three days' journey into the desert and sacrifice to the LORD our God, lest He fall upon us with pestilence or with the sword."

4 Then the king of Egypt said to them, "Moses and Aaron, why do you take the people from their work? Get *back* to your labor."

5 And Pharaoh said, "Look, the people of the land *are* many now, and you make them rest from their labor!"

6 So the same day Pharaoh commanded the taskmasters of the people and their officers, saying,

7 "You shall no longer give the people straw to make brick as before. Let them go and gather straw for themselves.

8 "And you shall lay on them the quota of bricks which they made before. You shall not reduce it. For they are idle; therefore they cry out, saying, 'Let us go *and* sacrifice to our God.'

9 "Let more work be laid on the men, that they may labor in it, and let them not regard false words."

10 And the taskmasters of the people and their officers went out and spoke to the people, saying, "Thus says Pharaoh: 'I will not give you straw.

11 'Go, get yourselves straw where you can find it; yet none of your work will be reduced.'"

12 So the people were scattered abroad throughout all the land of Egypt to gather stubble instead of straw.

13 And the taskmasters forced *them* to hurry, saying, "Fulfill your work, *your* daily quota, as when there was straw."

14 Also the officers of the children of Israel, whom Pharaoh's taskmasters had set over them, were beaten *and* were asked, "Why have you not fulfilled your task in making brick both yesterday and today, as before?"

15 Then the officers of the children of Israel came and cried out to Pharaoh, saying, "Why are you dealing thus with your servants?

16 "There is no straw given to your servants, and they say to us, 'Make brick!' And indeed your servants *are* beaten, but the fault *is* in your *own* people."

17 But he said, "You *are* idle! Idle! Therefore you say, 'Let us go *and* sacrifice to the LORD.'

18 "Therefore go now *and* work; for no straw shall be given you, yet you shall deliver the quota of bricks."

19 And the officers of the children of Israel saw *that* they *were* in trouble after it was said, "You shall not reduce *any* bricks from your daily quota."

20 Then, as they came out from Pharaoh, they met Moses and Aaron who stood there to meet them.

21 And they said to them, "Let the LORD look on you and judge, because you have made us abhorrent in the

sight of Pharaoh and in the sight of his servants, to put a sword in their hand to kill us."

ISRAEL'S DELIVERANCE ASSURED

22 So Moses returned to the LORD and said, "Lord, why have You brought trouble on this people? Why *is* it You have sent me?
23 "For since I came to Pharaoh to speak in Your name, he has done evil to this people; neither have You delivered Your people at all."

6 Then the LORD said to Moses, "Now you shall see what I will do to Pharaoh. For with a strong hand he will let them go, and with a strong hand he will drive them out of his land."
2 And God spoke to Moses and said to him: "I *am* the LORD.
3 "I appeared to Abraham, to Isaac, and to Jacob, as God Almighty, but *by* My name LORD*a* I was not known to them.
4 "I have also established My covenant with them, to give them the land of Cā′naan, the land of their pilgrimage, in which they were strangers.
5 "And I have also heard the groaning of the children of Israel whom the Egyptians keep in bondage, and I have remembered My covenant.
6 "Therefore say to the children of Israel: 'I *am* the LORD; I will bring you out from under the burdens of the Egyptians, I will rescue you from their bondage, and I will redeem you with an outstretched arm and with great judgments.
7 'I will take you as My people, and I will be your God. Then you shall know that I *am* the LORD your God who brings you out from under the burdens of the Egyptians.
8 'And I will bring you into the land which I swore to give to Abraham, Isaac, and Jacob; and I will give it to you *as* a heritage: I *am* the LORD.' "
9 So Moses spoke thus to the children of Israel; but they did not heed Moses, because of anguish of spirit and cruel bondage.
10 And the LORD spoke to Moses, saying,
11 "Go in, tell Pharaoh king of Egypt to let the children of Israel go out of his land."
12 And Moses spoke before the LORD, saying, "The children of Israel have not heeded me. How then shall Pharaoh heed me, for I *am* of uncircumcised lips?"
13 Then the LORD spoke to Moses and Aaron, and gave them a command for the children of Israel and for Pharaoh king of Egypt, to bring the children of Israel out of the land of Egypt.

THE FAMILY OF MOSES AND AARON

14 These *are* the heads of their fathers' houses: The sons of Reuben, the firstborn of Israel, *were* Hā′noch, Pal′lū, Hez′ron, and Car′mī. These are the families of Reuben.
15 And the sons of Sim′ē·on *were* Je·mū′el,*a* Jā′min, Ō′had, Jā′chin, Zō′har, and Shā′ūl the son of a Cā′naan·ite woman. These *are* the families of Sim′ē·on.
16 These *are* the names of the sons of Levi according to their generations: Ger′shon, Kō′hath, and Me-rar′ī. And the years of the life of Levi *were* one hundred and thirty-seven.
17 The sons of Ger′shon *were* Lib′nī and Shim′ī according to their families.
18 And the sons of Kō′hath *were* Am′-ram, Iz′har, Hē′bron, and Uz′zi·el.

6:3 *a*Hebrew *YHWH,* traditionally *Jehovah*
6:15 *a*Spelled *Nemuel* in Numbers 26:12

And the years of the life of Kō'hath *were* one hundred and thirty-three.

19 The sons of Me·rar'ī *were* Mah'lī and Mū'shī. These *are* the families of Levi according to their generations.

20 Now Am'ram took for himself Joch'e·bed, his father's sister, as wife; and she bore him Aaron and Moses. And the years of the life of Am'ram *were* one hundred and thirty-seven.

21 The sons of Iz'har *were* Kō'rah, Nē'pheg, and Zich'rī.

22 And the sons of Uz'zi·el *were* Mish'a·el, El'za·phan, and Zith'rī.

23 Aaron took to himself E·lish'e·ba, daughter of Am·min'a·dab, sister of Nah'shon, as wife; and she bore him Nā'dab, A·bī'hū, El·e·ā'zar, and Ith'a·mar.

24 And the sons of Kō'rah *were* As'-sir, El·kā'nah, and A·bī'a·saph. These are the families of the Kō'ra·hītes.

25 El·e·ā'zar, Aaron's son, took for himself one of the daughters of Pū'-ti·el as wife; and she bore him Phin'-e·has. These *are* the heads of the fathers' houses of the Lē'vītes according to their families.

26 These *are the same* Aaron and Moses to whom the LORD said, "Bring out the children of Israel from the land of Egypt according to their armies."

27 These *are* the ones who spoke to Pharaoh king of Egypt, to bring out the children of Israel from Egypt. These *are the same* Moses and Aaron.

AARON IS MOSES' SPOKESMAN

28 And it came to pass, on the day the LORD spoke to Moses in the land of Egypt,

29 that the LORD spoke to Moses, saying, "I *am* the LORD. Speak to Pharaoh king of Egypt all that I say to you."

30 But Moses said before the LORD,

"Behold, I *am* of uncircumcised lips, and how shall Pharaoh heed me?"

7 So the LORD said to Moses: "See, I have made you *as* God to Pharaoh, and Aaron your brother shall be your prophet.

2 "You shall speak all that I command you. And Aaron your brother shall tell Pharaoh to send the children of Israel out of his land.

3 "And I will harden Pharaoh's heart, and multiply My signs and My wonders in the land of Egypt.

4 "But Pharaoh will not heed you, so that I may lay My hand on Egypt and bring My armies *and* My people, the children of Israel, out of the land of Egypt by great judgments.

5 "And the Egyptians shall know that I *am* the LORD, when I stretch out My hand on Egypt and bring out the children of Israel from among them."

6 Then Moses and Aaron did *so;* just as the LORD commanded them, so they did.

7 And Moses *was* eighty years old and Aaron eighty-three years old when they spoke to Pharaoh.

AARON'S MIRACULOUS ROD

Moses and his brother Aaron were now in Egypt. They went before Pharaoh to ask him to let the Hebrew slaves go free. But Pharaoh made the slaves work harder. He didn't believe in God. But he soon would! This is how God got Pharaoh's attention.

8 Then the LORD spoke to Moses and Aaron, saying,

9 "When Pharaoh speaks to you, saying, 'Show a miracle for yourselves,' then you shall say to Aaron, 'Take your rod and cast *it* before

Pharaoh, *and* let it become a serpent.' "

10 So Moses and Aaron went in to Pharaoh, and they did so, just as the LORD commanded. And Aaron cast down his rod before Pharaoh and before his servants, and it became a serpent.

11 But Pharaoh also called the wise men and the sorcerers; so the magicians of Egypt, they also did in like manner with their enchantments.

12 For every man threw down his rod, and they became serpents. But Aaron's rod swallowed up their rods.

13 And Pharaoh's heart grew hard, and he did not heed them, as the LORD had said.

THE FIRST PLAGUE: WATERS BECOME BLOOD

14 So the LORD said to Moses: "Pharaoh's heart *is* hard; he refuses to let the people go.

15 "Go to Pharaoh in the morning, when he goes out to the water, and you shall stand by the river's bank to meet him; and the rod which was turned to a serpent you shall take in your hand.

16 "And you shall say to him, 'The LORD God of the Hebrews has sent me to you, saying, "Let My people go, that they may serve Me in the wilderness"; but indeed, until now you would not hear!

17 'Thus says the LORD: "By this you shall know that I *am* the LORD. Behold, I will strike the waters which *are* in the river with the rod that *is* in my hand, and they shall be turned to blood.

18 "And the fish that *are* in the river shall die, the river shall stink, and the Egyptians will loathe to drink the water of the river." ' "

19 Then the LORD spoke to Moses, "Say to Aaron, 'Take your rod and stretch out your hand over the waters of Egypt, over their streams, over their rivers, over their ponds, and over all their pools of water, that they may become blood. And there shall be blood throughout all the land of Egypt, both in *buckets of* wood and *pitchers of* stone.' "

20 And Moses and Aaron did so, just as the LORD commanded. So he lifted up the rod and struck the waters that *were* in the river, in the sight of Pharaoh and in the sight of his servants. And all the waters that *were* in the river were turned to blood.

21 The fish that *were* in the river died, the river stank, and the Egyptians could not drink the water of the river. So there was blood throughout all the land of Egypt.

22 Then the magicians of Egypt did so with their enchantments; and Pharaoh's heart grew hard, and he did not heed them, as the LORD had said.

23 And Pharaoh turned and went into his house. Neither was his heart moved by this.

24 So all the Egyptians dug all around the river for water to drink, because they could not drink the water of the river.

25 And seven days passed after the LORD had struck the river.

THE SECOND PLAGUE: FROGS

8 And the LORD spoke to Moses, "Go to Pharaoh and say to him, 'Thus says the LORD: "Let My people go, that they may serve Me.

2 "But if you refuse to let *them* go, behold, I will smite all your territory with frogs.

3 "So the river shall bring forth frogs abundantly, which shall go up and come into your house, into your bedroom, on your bed, into the

houses of your servants, on your people, into your ovens, and into your kneading bowls.

4 "And the frogs shall come up on you, on your people, and on all your servants." ' "

5 Then the LORD spoke to Moses, "Say to Aaron, 'Stretch out your hand with your rod over the streams, over the rivers, and over the ponds, and cause frogs to come up on the land of Egypt.' "

6 So Aaron stretched out his hand over the waters of Egypt, and the frogs came up and covered the land of Egypt.

7 And the magicians did so with their enchantments, and brought up frogs on the land of Egypt.

8 Then Pharaoh called for Moses and Aaron, and said, "Entreat the LORD that He may take away the frogs from me and from my people; and I will let the people go, that they may sacrifice to the LORD."

9 And Moses said to Pharaoh, "Accept the honor of saying when I shall intercede for you, for your servants, and for your people, to destroy the frogs from you and your houses, *that* they may remain in the river only."

10 So he said, "Tomorrow." And he said, "*Let it be* according to your word, that you may know that *there is* no one like the LORD our God.

11 "And the frogs shall depart from you, from your houses, from your servants, and from your people. They shall remain in the river only."

12 Then Moses and Aaron went out from Pharaoh. And Moses cried out to the LORD concerning the frogs which He had brought against Pharaoh.

13 So the LORD did according to the word of Moses. And the frogs died out of the houses, out of the courtyards, and out of the fields.

14 They gathered them together in heaps, and the land stank.

15 But when Pharaoh saw that there was relief, he hardened his heart and did not heed them, as the LORD had said.

THE THIRD PLAGUE: LICE

16 So the LORD said to Moses, "Say to Aaron, 'Stretch out your rod, and strike the dust of the land, so that it may become lice throughout all the land of Egypt.' "

17 And they did so. For Aaron stretched out his hand with his rod and struck the dust of the earth, and it became lice on man and beast. All the dust of the land became lice throughout all the land of Egypt.

18 Now the magicians so worked with their enchantments to bring forth lice, but they could not. So there were lice on man and beast.

19 Then the magicians said to Pharaoh, "This *is* the finger of God." But Pharaoh's heart grew hard, and he did not heed them, just as the LORD had said.

THE FOURTH PLAGUE: FLIES

20 And the LORD said to Moses, "Rise early in the morning and stand before Pharaoh as he comes out to the water. Then say to him, 'Thus says the LORD: "Let My people go, that they may serve Me.

21 "Or else, if you will not let My people go, behold, I will send swarms *of flies* on you and your servants, on your people and into your houses. The houses of the Egyptians shall be full of swarms *of flies,* and also the ground on which they *stand.*

22 "And in that day I will set apart the land of Gō'shen, in which My people dwell, that no swarms *of flies* shall be there, in order that you may

know that I *am* the LORD in the midst of the land.

23 "I will make a difference^a between My people and your people. Tomorrow this sign shall be." ' "

24 And the LORD did so. Thick swarms *of flies* came into the house of Pharaoh, *into* his servants' houses, and into all the land of Egypt. The land was corrupted because of the swarms *of flies.*

25 Then Pharaoh called for Moses and Aaron, and said, "Go, sacrifice to your God in the land."

26 And Moses said, "It is not right to do so, for we would be sacrificing the abomination of the Egyptians to the LORD our God. If we sacrifice the abomination of the Egyptians before their eyes, then will they not stone us?

27 "We will go three days' journey into the wilderness and sacrifice to the LORD our God as He will command us."

28 So Pharaoh said, "I will let you go, that you may sacrifice to the LORD your God in the wilderness; only you shall not go very far away. Intercede for me."

29 Then Moses said, "Indeed I am going out from you, and I will entreat the LORD, that the swarms *of flies* may depart tomorrow from Pharaoh, from his servants, and from his people. But let Pharaoh not deal deceitfully anymore in not letting the people go to sacrifice to the LORD."

30 So Moses went out from Pharaoh and entreated the LORD.

31 And the LORD did according to the word of Moses; He removed the swarms *of flies* from Pharaoh, from his servants, and from his people. Not one remained.

32 But Pharaoh hardened his heart at this time also; neither would he let the people go.

Bible Quiz

Exodus 7:8—8:32 **God Begins the Ten Plagues**

1. What happened when Aaron threw his rod on the ground? What did Pharaoh think?
2. What was the first plague God sent to Egypt? Did it persuade Pharaoh to let the slaves go?
3. What was the second plague? What did Pharaoh do this time?
4. What was the third plague? The fourth?
5. How does the Bible describe Pharaoh's heart? What do you think this means? How do you think Pharaoh got this way?
6. What can you do to keep your heart open to God?

THE FIFTH PLAGUE: LIVESTOCK DISEASED

God had already sent four plagues upon Egypt to convince Pharaoh to let the Hebrew slaves go. But Pharaoh wouldn't listen. Now Pharaoh was about to see more of the mighty power of God.

9 Then the LORD said to Moses, "Go in to Pharaoh and tell him, 'Thus says the LORD God of the Hebrews: "Let My people go, that they may serve Me.

8:23 ^aLiterally *set a ransom* (compare Exodus 9:4 and 11:7)

2 "For if you refuse to let *them* go, and still hold them,

3 "behold, the hand of the LORD will be on your cattle in the field, on the horses, on the donkeys, on the camels, on the oxen, and on the sheep—a very severe pestilence.

4 "And the LORD will make a difference between the livestock of Israel and the livestock of Egypt. So nothing shall die of all *that* belongs to the children of Israel." ' "

5 Then the LORD appointed a set time, saying, "Tomorrow the LORD will do this thing in the land."

6 So the LORD did this thing on the next day, and all the livestock of Egypt died; but of the livestock of the children of Israel, not one died.

7 Then Pharaoh sent, and indeed, not even one of the livestock of the Israelites was dead. But the heart of Pharaoh became hard, and he did not let the people go.

THE SIXTH PLAGUE: BOILS

8 So the LORD said to Moses and Aaron, "Take for yourselves handfuls of ashes from a furnace, and let Moses scatter it toward the heavens in the sight of Pharaoh.

9 "And it will become fine dust in all the land of Egypt, and it will cause boils that break out in sores on man and beast throughout all the land of Egypt."

10 Then they took ashes from the furnace and stood before Pharaoh, and Moses scattered *them* toward heaven. And *they* caused boils that break out in sores on man and beast.

11 And the magicians could not stand before Moses because of the boils, for the boils were on the magicians and on all the Egyptians.

12 But the LORD hardened the heart of Pharaoh; and he did not heed them, just as the LORD had spoken to Moses.

THE SEVENTH PLAGUE: HAIL

13 Then the LORD said to Moses, "Rise early in the morning and stand before Pharaoh, and say to him, 'Thus says the LORD God of the Hebrews: "Let My people go, that they may serve Me,

14 "for at this time I will send all My plagues to your very heart, and on your servants and on your people, that you may know that *there is* none like Me in all the earth.

15 "Now if I had stretched out My hand and struck you and your people with pestilence, then you would have been cut off from the earth.

16 "But indeed for this *purpose* I have raised you up, that I may show My power *in* you, and that My name may be declared in all the earth.

17 "As yet you exalt yourself against My people in that you will not let them go.

18 "Behold, tomorrow about this time I will cause very heavy hail to rain down, such as has not been in Egypt since its founding until now.

19 "Therefore send now *and* gather your livestock and all that you have in the field, for the hail shall come down on every man and every animal which is found in the field and is not brought home; and they shall die." ' "

20 He who feared the word of the LORD among the servants of Pharaoh made his servants and his livestock flee to the houses.

21 But he who did not regard the word of the LORD left his servants and his livestock in the field.

22 Then the LORD said to Moses, "Stretch out your hand toward heaven, that there may be hail in all the land of Egypt—on man, on beast,

and on every herb of the field, throughout the land of Egypt."

23 And Moses stretched out his rod toward heaven; and the LORD sent thunder and hail, and fire darted to the ground. And the LORD rained hail on the land of Egypt.

24 So there was hail, and fire mingled with the hail, so very heavy that there was none like it in all the land of Egypt since it became a nation.

25 And the hail struck throughout the whole land of Egypt, all that *was* in the field, both man and beast; and the hail struck every herb of the field and broke every tree of the field.

26 Only in the land of Gō′shen, where the children of Israel *were,* there was no hail.

27 And Pharaoh sent and called for Moses and Aaron, and said to them, "I have sinned this time. The LORD *is* righteous, and my people and I *are* wicked.

28 "Entreat the LORD, that there may be no *more* mighty thundering and hail, for *it is* enough. I will let you go, and you shall stay no longer."

29 So Moses said to him, "As soon as I have gone out of the city, I will spread out my hands to the LORD; the thunder will cease, and there will be no more hail, that you may know that the earth *is* the LORD's.

30 "But as for you and your servants, I know that you will not yet fear the LORD God."

31 Now the flax and the barley were struck, for the barley *was* in the head and the flax *was* in bud.

32 But the wheat and the spelt were not struck, for they *are* late crops.

33 So Moses went out of the city from Pharaoh and spread out his hands to the LORD; then the thunder and the hail ceased, and the rain was not poured on the earth.

34 And when Pharaoh saw that the rain, the hail, and the thunder had ceased, he sinned yet more; and he hardened his heart, he and his servants.

35 So the heart of Pharaoh was hard; neither would he let the children of Israel go, as the LORD had spoken by Moses.

THE EIGHTH PLAGUE: LOCUSTS

10 Now the LORD said to Moses, "Go in to Pharaoh; for I have hardened his heart and the hearts of his servants, that I may show these signs of Mine before him,

2 "and that you may tell in the hearing of your son and your son's son the mighty things I have done in Egypt, and My signs which I have done among them, that you may know that I *am* the LORD."

3 So Moses and Aaron came in to Pharaoh and said to him, "Thus says the LORD God of the Hebrews: 'How long will you refuse to humble yourself before Me? Let My people go, that they may serve Me.

4 'Or else, if you refuse to let My people go, behold, tomorrow I will bring locusts into your territory.

5 'And they shall cover the face of the earth, so that no one will be able to see the earth; and they shall eat the residue of what is left, which remains to you from the hail, and they shall eat every tree which grows up for you out of the field.

6 'They shall fill your houses, the houses of all your servants, and the houses of all the Egyptians—which neither your fathers nor your fathers' fathers have seen, since the day that they were on the earth to this day.' " And he turned and went out from Pharaoh.

7 Then Pharaoh's servants said to him, "How long shall this man be a snare to us? Let the men go, that

they may serve the LORD their God. Do you not yet know that Egypt is destroyed?"

8 So Moses and Aaron were brought again to Pharaoh, and he said to them, "Go, serve the LORD your God. Who *are* the ones that are going?"

9 And Moses said, "We will go with our young and our old; with our sons and our daughters, with our flocks and our herds we will go, for we must hold a feast to the LORD."

10 Then he said to them, "The LORD had better be with you when I let you and your little ones go! Beware, for evil is ahead of you.

11 "Not so! Go now, you *who are* men, and serve the LORD, for that is what you desired." And they were driven out from Pharaoh's presence.

12 Then the LORD said to Moses, "Stretch out your hand over the land of Egypt for the locusts, that they may come upon the land of Egypt, and eat every herb of the land—all that the hail has left."

13 So Moses stretched out his rod over the land of Egypt, and the LORD brought an east wind on the land all that day and all *that* night. When it was morning, the east wind brought the locusts.

14 And the locusts went up over all the land of Egypt and rested on all the territory of Egypt. *They were* very severe; previously there had been no such locusts as they, nor shall there be such after them.

15 For they covered the face of the whole earth, so that the land was darkened; and they ate every herb of the land and all the fruit of the trees which the hail had left. So there remained nothing green on the trees or on the plants of the field throughout all the land of Egypt.

16 Then Pharaoh called for Moses and Aaron in haste, and said, "I have sinned against the LORD your God and against you.

17 "Now therefore, please forgive my sin only this once, and entreat the LORD your God, that He may take away from me this death only."

18 So he went out from Pharaoh and entreated the LORD.

19 And the LORD turned a very strong west wind, which took the locusts away and blew them into the Red Sea. There remained not one locust in all the territory of Egypt.

20 But the LORD hardened Pharaoh's heart, and he did not let the children of Israel go.

THE NINTH PLAGUE: DARKNESS

21 Then the LORD said to Moses, "Stretch out your hand toward heaven, that there may be darkness over the land of Egypt, darkness *which* may even be felt."

22 So Moses stretched out his hand toward heaven, and there was thick darkness in all the land of Egypt three days.

23 They did not see one another; nor did anyone rise from his place for three days. But all the children of Israel had light in their dwellings.

24 Then Pharaoh called to Moses and said, "Go, serve the LORD; only let your flocks and your herds be kept back. Let your little ones also go with you."

25 But Moses said, "You must also give us sacrifices and burnt offerings, that we may sacrifice to the LORD our God.

26 "Our livestock also shall go with us; not a hoof shall be left behind. For we must take some of them to serve the LORD our God, and even we do not know with what we must serve the LORD until we arrive there."

27 But the LORD hardened Pharaoh's heart, and he would not let them go.
28 Then Pharaoh said to him, "Get away from me! Take heed to yourself and see my face no more! For in the day you see my face you shall die!"
29 So Moses said, "You have spoken well. I will never see your face again."

☑ *Bible Quiz*

Exodus 9; 10   **The Plagues Keep Coming**

1. Can you name the five plagues in this story? Now can you name them in order?
2. What was happening to the land of Egypt?
3. How could Pharaoh watch his own land and people get hurt so much?
4. What were Pharaoh's last words to Moses?
5. Pharaoh had become so stubborn and angry that he sent away the only person who could help him. What do you think will happen to him now?
6. Sometimes when we are doing something wrong, God tries to get our attention. What will you do then? Will you send away the people God has sent to help you? Or will you listen?

DEATH OF THE FIRSTBORN
ANNOUNCED

11 And the LORD said to Moses, "I will bring one more plague on Pharaoh and on Egypt. Afterward he will let you go from here. When he lets *you* go, he will surely drive you out of here altogether.
2 "Speak now in the hearing of the people, and let every man ask from his neighbor and every woman from her neighbor, articles of silver and articles of gold."
3 And the LORD gave the people favor in the sight of the Egyptians. Moreover the man Moses *was* very great in the land of Egypt, in the sight of Pharaoh's servants and in the sight of the people.
4 Then Moses said, "Thus says the LORD: 'About midnight I will go out into the midst of Egypt;
5 'and all the firstborn in the land of Egypt shall die, from the firstborn of Pharaoh who sits on his throne, even to the firstborn of the female servant who *is* behind the handmill, and all the firstborn of the animals.
6 'Then there shall be a great cry throughout all the land of Egypt, such as was not like it *before,* nor shall be like it again.
7 'But against none of the children of Israel shall a dog move its tongue, against man or beast, that you may know that the LORD does make a difference between the Egyptians and Israel.'
8 "And all these your servants shall come down to me and bow down to me, saying, 'Get out, and all the people who follow you!' After that I will go out." Then he went out from Pharaoh in great anger.
9 But the LORD said to Moses, "Pharaoh will not heed you, so that My wonders may be multiplied in the land of Egypt."
10 So Moses and Aaron did all these wonders before Pharaoh; and the LORD hardened Pharaoh's heart, and he did not let the children of Israel go out of his land.

THE PASSOVER INSTITUTED

God would send just one more plague to Egypt. This time Pharaoh would listen. But what a terrible price he had to pay. Soon the Hebrew slaves would be free.

12 Now the LORD spoke to Moses and Aaron in the land of Egypt, saying,

2 "This month *shall be* your beginning of months; it *shall be* the first month of the year to you.

3 "Speak to all the congregation of Israel, saying: 'On the tenth of this month every man shall take for himself a lamb, according to the house of *his* father, a lamb for a household.

4 'And if the household is too small for the lamb, let him and his neighbor next to his house take *it* according to the number of the persons; according to each man's need you shall make your count for the lamb.

5 'Your lamb shall be without blemish, a male of the first year. You may take *it* from the sheep or from the goats.

6 'Now you shall keep it until the fourteenth day of the same month. Then the whole assembly of the congregation of Israel shall kill it at twilight.

7 'And they shall take *some* of the blood and put *it* on the two doorposts and on the lintel of the houses where they eat it.

8 'Then they shall eat the flesh on that night; roasted in fire, with unleavened bread *and* with bitter *herbs* they shall eat it.

9 'Do not eat it raw, nor boiled at all with water, but roasted in fire—its head with its legs and its entrails.

10 'You shall let none of it remain until morning, and what remains of it until morning you shall burn with fire.

11 'And thus you shall eat it: *with* a belt on your waist, your sandals on your feet, and your staff in your hand. So you shall eat it in haste. It *is* the LORD's Passover.

12 'For I will pass through the land of Egypt on that night, and will strike all the firstborn in the land of Egypt, both man and beast; and against all the gods of Egypt I will execute judgment: I *am* the LORD.

13 'Now the blood shall be a sign for you on the houses where you *are*. And when I see the blood, I will pass over you; and the plague shall not be on you to destroy *you* when I strike the land of Egypt.

14 'So this day shall be to you a memorial; and you shall keep it as a feast to the LORD throughout your generations. You shall keep it as a feast by an everlasting ordinance.

15 'Seven days you shall eat unleavened bread. On the first day you shall remove leaven from your houses. For whoever eats leavened bread from the first day until the seventh day, that person shall be cut off from Israel.

16 'On the first day *there shall be* a holy convocation, and on the seventh day there shall be a holy convocation for you. No manner of work shall be done on them; but *that* which everyone must eat—that only may be prepared by you.

17 'So you shall observe *the Feast of* Unleavened Bread, for on this same day I will have brought your armies out of the land of Egypt. Therefore you shall observe this day throughout your generations as an everlasting ordinance.

18 'In the first *month,* on the fourteenth day of the month at evening, you shall eat unleavened bread, until the twenty-first day of the month at evening.

19 'For seven days no leaven shall be found in your houses, since whoever eats what is leavened, that same person shall be cut off from the congregation of Israel, whether *he is* a stranger or a native of the land.

20 'You shall eat nothing leavened; in all your dwellings you shall eat unleavened bread.'"

21 Then Moses called for all the elders of Israel and said to them, "Pick out and take lambs for yourselves according to your families, and kill the Passover *lamb.*

22 "And you shall take a bunch of hyssop, dip *it* in the blood that *is* in the basin, and strike the lintel and the two doorposts with the blood that *is* in the basin. And none of you shall go out of the door of his house until morning.

23 "For the LORD will pass through to strike the Egyptians; and when He sees the blood on the lintel and on the two doorposts, the LORD will pass over the door and not allow the destroyer to come into your houses to strike *you.*

24 "And you shall observe this thing as an ordinance for you and your sons forever.

25 "It will come to pass when you come to the land which the LORD will give you, just as He promised, that you shall keep this service.

26 "And it shall be, when your children say to you, 'What do you mean by this service?'

27 "that you shall say, 'It *is* the Passover sacrifice of the LORD, who passed over the houses of the children of Israel in Egypt when He struck the Egyptians and delivered our households.' " So the people bowed their heads and worshiped.

28 Then the children of Israel went away and did *so;* just as the LORD had commanded Moses and Aaron, so they did.

THE TENTH PLAGUE: DEATH OF THE FIRSTBORN

29 And it came to pass at midnight that the LORD struck all the firstborn in the land of Egypt, from the firstborn of Pharaoh who sat on his throne to the firstborn of the captive who *was* in the dungeon, and all the firstborn of livestock.

30 So Pharaoh rose in the night, he, all his servants, and all the Egyptians; and there was a great cry in Egypt, for *there was* not a house where *there was* not one dead.

THE EXODUS

31 Then he called for Moses and Aaron by night, and said, "Rise, go out from among my people, both you and the children of Israel. And go, serve the LORD as you have said.

32 "Also take your flocks and your herds, as you have said, and be gone; and bless me also."

33 And the Egyptians urged the people, that they might send them out of the land in haste. For they said, "We *shall* all *be* dead."

34 So the people took their dough before it was leavened, having their kneading bowls bound up in their clothes on their shoulders.

35 Now the children of Israel had done according to the word of Moses, and they had asked from the Egyptians articles of silver, articles of gold, and clothing.

36 And the LORD had given the people favor in the sight of the Egyptians, so that they granted them *what they requested.* Thus they plundered the Egyptians.

37 Then the children of Israel journeyed from Ram′e·sēs to Suc′coth, about six hundred thousand men on foot, besides children.

38 A mixed multitude went up with them also, and flocks and herds—a great deal of livestock.

39 And they baked unleavened cakes of the dough which they had brought out of Egypt; for it was not leavened, because they were driven out of Egypt and could not wait, nor had they prepared provisions for themselves.

40 Now the sojourn of the children of Israel who lived in Egypt*a was* four hundred and thirty years.

41 And it came to pass at the end of the four hundred and thirty years—on that very same day—it came to pass that all the armies of the LORD went out from the land of Egypt.

42 It *is* a night of solemn observance to the LORD for bringing them out of the land of Egypt. This *is* that night of the LORD, a solemn observance for all the children of Israel throughout their generations.

✓	*Bible Quiz*

Exodus 12:1–42 **The Last Plague**

1. The Hebrew slaves ate a strange meal on their last night in Egypt. What was it called? Why was it called that? What were some of the things they ate?
2. What was the last plague?
3. What did the Hebrews do to keep the plague from entering their homes?
4. What was Pharaoh's heart like now? What did he say to Moses?
5. What do you think the slaves must have talked about as they packed up to leave Egypt forever?

PASSOVER REGULATIONS

43 And the LORD said to Moses and Aaron, "This *is* the ordinance of the Passover: No foreigner shall eat it.

44 "But every man's servant who is bought for money, when you have circumcised him, then he may eat it.

45 "A sojourner and a hired servant shall not eat it.

46 "In one house it shall be eaten; you shall not carry any of the flesh outside the house, nor shall you break one of its bones.

47 "All the congregation of Israel shall keep it.

48 "And when a stranger dwells with you *and wants* to keep the Passover to the LORD, let all his males be circumcised, and then let him come near and keep it; and he shall be as a native of the land. For no uncircumcised person shall eat it.

49 "One law shall be for the native-born and for the stranger who dwells among you."

50 Thus all the children of Israel did; as the LORD commanded Moses and Aaron, so they did.

51 And it came to pass, on that very same day, that the LORD brought the children of Israel out of the land of Egypt according to their armies.

THE FIRSTBORN CONSECRATED

13 Then the LORD spoke to Moses, saying,

2 "Consecrate to Me all the firstborn, whatever opens the womb among the children of Israel, *both* of man and beast; it is Mine."

THE FEAST OF UNLEAVENED BREAD

3 And Moses said to the people: "Remember this day in which you

---

12:40 *a*Samaritan Pentateuch and Septuagint read *Egypt and Canaan.*

went out of Egypt, out of the house of bondage; for by strength of hand the LORD brought you out of this *place.* No leavened bread shall be eaten.

4 "On this day you are going out, in the month Ā′bib.

5 "And it shall be, when the LORD brings you into the land of the Cā′naan·ītes and the Hit′tītes and the Am′o·rītes and the Hī′vītes and the Jeb′ū·sītes, which He swore to your fathers to give you, a land flowing with milk and honey, that you shall keep this service in this month.

6 "Seven days you shall eat unleavened bread, and on the seventh day *there shall be* a feast to the LORD.

7 "Unleavened bread shall be eaten seven days. And no leavened bread shall be seen among you, nor shall leaven be seen among you in all your quarters.

8 "And you shall tell your son in that day, saying, *'This is done* because of what the LORD did for me when I came up from Egypt.'

9 "It shall be as a sign to you on your hand and as a memorial between your eyes, that the LORD's law may be in your mouth; for with a strong hand the LORD has brought you out of Egypt.

10 "You shall therefore keep this ordinance in its season from year to year.

THE LAW OF THE FIRSTBORN

11 "And it shall be, when the LORD brings you into the land of the Cā′naan·ītes, as He swore to you and your fathers, and gives it to you,

12 "that you shall set apart to the LORD all that open the womb, that is, every firstborn that comes from an animal which you have; the males *shall be* the LORD's.

13 "But every firstborn of a donkey you shall redeem with a lamb; and if you will not redeem *it,* then you shall break its neck. And all the firstborn of man among your sons you shall redeem.

14 "So it shall be, when your son asks you in time to come, saying, 'What *is* this?' that you shall say to him, 'By strength of hand the LORD brought us out of Egypt, out of the house of bondage.

15 'And it came to pass, when Pharaoh was stubborn about letting us go, that the LORD killed all the firstborn in the land of Egypt, both the firstborn of man and the firstborn of beast. Therefore I sacrifice to the LORD all males that open the womb, but all the firstborn of my sons I redeem.'

16 "It shall be as a sign on your hand and as frontlets between your eyes, for by strength of hand the LORD brought us out of Egypt."

THE WILDERNESS WAY

17 Then it came to pass, when Pharaoh had let the people go, that God did not lead them *by* way of the land of the Phi·lis′tines, although that *was* near; for God said, "Lest perhaps the people change their minds when they see war, and return to Egypt."

18 So God led the people around *by* way of the wilderness of the Red Sea. And the children of Israel went up in orderly ranks out of the land of Egypt.

19 And Moses took the bones of Joseph with him, for he had placed the children of Israel under solemn oath, saying, "God will surely visit you, and you shall carry up my bones from here with you."[a]

20 So they took their journey from

13:19 [a]Genesis 50:25

Suc'coth and camped in Ē'tham at the edge of the wilderness.

21 And the LORD went before them by day in a pillar of cloud to lead the way, and by night in a pillar of fire to give them light, so as to go by day and night.

22 He did not take away the pillar of cloud by day or the pillar of fire by night *from* before the people.

THE RED SEA CROSSING

Some people never learn. Ten plagues forced Pharaoh to let the Hebrew slaves go. He could not fight God. But as soon as the slaves left, Pharaoh thought he could make them come back. Did he think God would stop taking care of them? God was about to teach Pharaoh one last lesson. When you read this story notice that the Hebrews are no longer called slaves, but the children of Israel. They are now God's special people.

14 Now the LORD spoke to Moses, saying:

2 "Speak to the children of Israel, that they turn and camp before Pī Ha·hī'roth, between Mig'dōl and the sea, opposite Bā'al Zē'phon; you shall camp before it by the sea.

3 "For Pharaoh will say of the children of Israel, 'They *are* bewildered by the land; the wilderness has closed them in.'

4 "Then I will harden Pharaoh's heart, so that he will pursue them; and I will gain honor over Pharaoh and over all his army, that the Egyptians may know that I *am* the LORD." And they did so.

5 Now it was told the king of Egypt that the people had fled, and the heart of Pharaoh and his servants was turned against the people; and they said, "Why have we done this, that we have let Israel go from serving us?"

6 So he made ready his chariot and took his people with him.

7 Also, he took six hundred choice chariots, and all the chariots of Egypt with captains over every one of them.

8 And the LORD hardened the heart of Pharaoh king of Egypt, and he pursued the children of Israel; and the children of Israel went out with boldness.

9 So the Egyptians pursued them, all the horses *and* chariots of Pharaoh, his horsemen and his army, and overtook them camping by the sea beside Pī Ha·hī'roth, before Bā'al Zē'phon.

10 And when Pharaoh drew near, the children of Israel lifted their eyes, and behold, the Egyptians marched after them. So they were very afraid, and the children of Israel cried out to the LORD.

11 Then they said to Moses, "Because *there were* no graves in Egypt, have you taken us away to die in the wilderness? Why have you so dealt with us, to bring us up out of Egypt?

12 "*Is* this not the word that we told you in Egypt, saying, 'Let us alone that we may serve the Egyptians'? For *it would have been* better for us to serve the Egyptians than that we should die in the wilderness."

13 And Moses said to the people, "Do not be afraid. Stand still, and see the salvation of the LORD, which He will accomplish for you today. For the Egyptians whom you see today, you shall see again no more forever.

14 "The LORD will fight for you, and you shall hold your peace."

15 And the LORD said to Moses, "Why do you cry to Me? Tell the children of Israel to go forward.

16 "But lift up your rod, and stretch out your hand over the sea and divide it. And the children of Israel shall go on dry *ground* through the midst of the sea.
17 "And I indeed will harden the hearts of the Egyptians, and they shall follow them. So I will gain honor over Pharaoh and over all his army, his chariots, and his horsemen.
18 "Then the Egyptians shall know that I *am* the LORD, when I have gained honor for Myself over Pharaoh, his chariots, and his horsemen."
19 And the Angel of God, who went before the camp of Israel, moved and went behind them; and the pillar of cloud went from before them and stood behind them.
20 So it came between the camp of the Egyptians and the camp of Israel. Thus it was a cloud and darkness *to the one,* and it gave light by night *to the other,* so that the one did not come near the other all that night.
21 Then Moses stretched out his hand over the sea; and the LORD caused the sea to go *back* by a strong east wind all that night, and made the sea into dry *land,* and the waters were divided.
22 So the children of Israel went into the midst of the sea on the dry *ground,* and the waters *were* a wall to them on their right hand and on their left.
23 And the Egyptians pursued and went after them into the midst of the sea, all Pharaoh's horses, his chariots, and his horsemen.
24 Now it came to pass, in the morning watch, that the LORD looked down upon the army of the Egyptians through the pillar of fire and cloud, and He troubled the army of the Egyptians.
25 And He took off[a] their chariot wheels, so that they drove them with difficulty; and the Egyptians said, "Let us flee from the face of Israel, for the LORD fights for them against the Egyptians."
26 Then the LORD said to Moses, "Stretch out your hand over the sea, that the waters may come back upon the Egyptians, on their chariots, and on their horsemen."
27 And Moses stretched out his hand over the sea; and when the morning appeared, the sea returned to its full

14:25 [a]Samaritan Pentateuch, Septuagint, and Syriac read *bound.*

☑ *Bible Quiz*

Exodus 14 **A Dry Path Through the Sea**

1. Why do you think Pharaoh changed his mind and chased after the children of Israel?
2. Where did Pharaoh find the people?
3. What did the children of Israel do when they saw the Egyptian army racing toward them? How could they have forgotten God so quickly?
4. What did God do to save them? What did God do to the Egyptian army?
5. When you are in trouble, do you start blaming God? Remember that God is the only one who knows the way out of your troubles.
6. The next time things are going badly, what can you do to stay close to God? How can you trust God to help you get out of trouble?

depth, while the Egyptians were fleeing into it. So the LORD overthrew the
Egyptians in the midst of the sea.
28 Then the waters returned and
covered the chariots, the horsemen,
and all the army of Pharaoh that
came into the sea after them. Not so
much as one of them remained.
29 But the children of Israel had
walked on dry *land* in the midst of
the sea, and the waters *were* a wall to
them on their right hand and on
their left.
30 So the LORD saved Israel that day
out of the hand of the Egyptians, and
Israel saw the Egyptians dead on the
seashore.
31 Thus Israel saw the great work
which the LORD had done in Egypt; so
the people feared the LORD, and believed the LORD and His servant Moses.

THE SONG OF MOSES

15 Then Moses and the children
of Israel sang this song to the LORD,
and spoke, saying:

   "I will sing to the LORD,
   For He has triumphed gloriously!
   The horse and its rider
   He has thrown into the sea!
2 The LORD *is* my strength and
      song,
   And He has become my salvation;
   He *is* my God, and I will praise
      Him;
   My father's God, and I will exalt
      Him.
3 The LORD *is* a man of war;
   The LORD *is* His name.
4 Pharaoh's chariots and his army
      He has cast into the sea;
   His chosen captains also are
      drowned in the Red Sea.
5 The depths have covered them;
   They sank to the bottom like a
      stone.

6 "Your right hand, O LORD, has
      become glorious in power;
   Your right hand, O LORD, has
      dashed the enemy in pieces.
7 And in the greatness of Your
      excellence
   You have overthrown those who
      rose against You;
   You sent forth Your wrath;
   It consumed them like stubble.
8 And with the blast of Your
      nostrils
   The waters were gathered
      together;
   The floods stood upright like a
      heap;
   The depths congealed in the heart
      of the sea.
9 The enemy said, 'I will pursue,
   I will overtake,
   I will divide the spoil;
   My desire shall be satisfied on
      them.
   I will draw my sword,
   My hand shall destroy them.'
10 You blew with Your wind,
   The sea covered them;
   They sank like lead in the mighty
      waters.

11 "Who *is* like You, O LORD, among
      the gods?
   Who *is* like You, glorious in
      holiness,
   Fearful in praises, doing
      wonders?
12 You stretched out Your right
      hand;
   The earth swallowed them.
13 You in Your mercy have led forth
   The people whom You have
      redeemed;
   You have guided *them* in Your
      strength
   To Your holy habitation.

14 "The people will hear *and* be
      afraid;

Family Friends

SINGING A BIG THANK YOU TO GOD Exodus 15:1–21

Sometimes it is fun to say "thank you" when someone does something special for us. At other times it's fun to *sing* a big "thank you." When God led Moses and his people through the sea, they wanted to say a big "thank you" to God (read Exodus 15). But saying it didn't seem big enough. It seemed an even bigger "thank you" when they sang it.

1. What special thing did God do for the Israelites? How did they say "thank you?"
2. What special thing has God done for you lately? Did you thank Him? Did you *say* it or *sing* it?
3. Would you like to say or sing a big "thank you" to God now? He's listening.

For more on *Family Friends* turn to page 435
For more on *Thankfulness* turn to page 624

Sorrow will take hold of the
  inhabitants of Phi·lis′ti·a.
15 Then the chiefs of Ē′dom will be
    dismayed;
  The mighty men of Mō′ab,
  Trembling will take hold of them;
  All the inhabitants of Cā′naan
    will melt away.
16 Fear and dread will fall on
    them;
  By the greatness of Your arm
  They will be *as* still as a stone,
  Till Your people pass over,
    O LORD,
  Till the people pass over
  Whom You have purchased.
17 You will bring them in and plant
    them
  In the mountain of Your
    inheritance,
  In the place, O LORD, *which* You
    have made
  For Your own dwelling,
  The sanctuary, O LORD, *which*
    Your hands have established.

18 "The LORD shall reign forever and
    ever."

19 For the horses of Pharaoh went
with his chariots and his horsemen
into the sea, and the LORD brought
back the waters of the sea upon
them. But the children of Israel went
on dry *land* in the midst of the sea.

THE SONG OF MIRIAM

20 Then Miriam the prophetess, the
sister of Aaron, took the timbrel in
her hand; and all the women went
out after her with timbrels and with
dances.
21 And Miriam answered them:

  "Sing to the LORD,
  For He has triumphed gloriously!
  The horse and its rider
  He has thrown into the sea!"

BITTER WATERS MADE SWEET

22 So Moses brought Israel from the
Red Sea; then they went out into the
Wilderness of Shūr. And they went
three days in the wilderness and
found no water.
23 Now when they came to Mar′ah,
they could not drink the waters of
Mar′ah, for they *were* bitter. Therefore the name of it was called
Mar′ah.*a*
24 And the people complained
against Moses, saying, "What shall
we drink?"
25 So he cried out to the LORD, and
the LORD showed him a tree. When
he cast *it* into the waters, the waters
were made sweet. There He made a
statute and an ordinance for them,
and there He tested them,
26 and said, "If you diligently heed
the voice of the LORD your God and
do what is right in His sight, give ear
to His commandments and keep all
His statutes, I will put none of the
diseases on you which I have brought
on the Egyptians. For I *am* the LORD
who heals you."
27 Then they came to Ē′lim, where
there *were* twelve wells of water and
seventy palm trees; so they camped
there by the waters.

BREAD FROM HEAVEN

*God saved the children of
Israel from Pharaoh's army.
Now, in the middle of the
wilderness, they ran out of
food and water. Would God
take care of them again?*

16 And they journeyed from
Ē′lim, and all the congregation of the
children of Israel came to the Wilderness of Sin, which is between Ē′lim

15:23 *a*Literally *Bitter*

and Sinai, on the fifteenth day of the second month after they departed from the land of Egypt.

2   Then the whole congregation of the children of Israel complained against Moses and Aaron in the wilderness.

3   And the children of Israel said to them, "Oh, that we had died by the hand of the LORD in the land of Egypt, when we sat by the pots of meat *and* when we ate bread to the full! For you have brought us out into this wilderness to kill this whole assembly with hunger."

4   Then the LORD said to Moses, "Behold, I will rain bread from heaven for you. And the people shall go out and gather a certain quota every day, that I may test them, whether they will walk in My law or not.

5   "And it shall be on the sixth day that they shall prepare what they bring in, and it shall be twice as much as they gather daily."

6   Then Moses and Aaron said to all the children of Israel, "At evening you shall know that the LORD has brought you out of the land of Egypt.

7   "And in the morning you shall see the glory of the LORD; for He hears your complaints against the LORD. But what *are* we, that you complain against us?"

8   Also Moses said, *"This shall be seen* when the LORD gives you meat to eat in the evening, and in the morning bread to the full; for the LORD hears your complaints which you make against Him. And what *are* we? Your complaints *are* not against us but against the LORD."

9   Then Moses spoke to Aaron, "Say to all the congregation of the children of Israel, 'Come near before the LORD, for He has heard your complaints.' "

10   Now it came to pass, as Aaron spoke to the whole congregation of the children of Israel, that they looked toward the wilderness, and behold, the glory of the LORD appeared in the cloud.

11   And the LORD spoke to Moses, saying,

12   "I have heard the complaints of the children of Israel. Speak to them, saying, 'At twilight you shall eat meat, and in the morning you shall be filled with bread. And you shall know that I *am* the LORD your God.' "

13   So it was that quails came up at evening and covered the camp, and in the morning the dew lay all around the camp.

14   And when the layer of dew lifted, there, on the surface of the wilderness, was a small round substance, *as* fine as frost on the ground.

15   So when the children of Israel saw *it,* they said to one another, "What is it?" For they did not know what it *was.* And Moses said to them, "This *is* the bread which the LORD has given you to eat.

16   "This is the thing which the LORD has commanded: 'Let every man gather it according to each one's need, one omer for each person, *according to the* number of persons; let every man take for *those* who *are* in his tent.' "

17   Then the children of Israel did so and gathered, some more, some less.

18   So when they measured *it* by omers, he who gathered much had nothing left over, and he who gathered little had no lack. Every man had gathered according to each one's need.

19   And Moses said, "Let no one leave any of it till morning."

20   Notwithstanding they did not heed Moses. But some of them left part of it until morning, and it bred worms and stank. And Moses was angry with them.

21   So they gathered it every morning, every man according to his need.

And when the sun became hot, it melted.

22 And so it was, on the sixth day, *that* they gathered twice as much bread, two omers for each one. And all the rulers of the congregation came and told Moses.

23 Then he said to them, "This *is* what the LORD has said: 'Tomorrow *is* a Sabbath rest, a holy Sabbath to the LORD. Bake what you will bake *today,* and boil what you will boil; and lay up for yourselves all that remains, to be kept until morning.'"

24 So they laid it up till morning, as Moses commanded; and it did not stink, nor were there any worms in it.

25 Then Moses said, "Eat that today, for today *is* a Sabbath to the LORD; today you will not find it in the field.

26 "Six days you shall gather it, but on the seventh day, the Sabbath, there will be none."

27 Now it happened *that some* of the people went out on the seventh day to gather, but they found none.

28 And the LORD said to Moses, "How long do you refuse to keep My commandments and My laws?

29 "See! For the LORD has given you the Sabbath; therefore He gives you on the sixth day bread for two days. Let every man remain in his place; let no man go out of his place on the seventh day."

30 So the people rested on the seventh day.

31 And the house of Israel called its name Manna.*a* And it *was* like white coriander seed, and the taste of it *was* like wafers *made* with honey.

32 Then Moses said, "This *is* the thing which the LORD has commanded: 'Fill an omer with it, to be kept for your generations, that they may see the bread with which I fed you in the wilderness, when I brought you out of the land of Egypt.'"

33 And Moses said to Aaron, "Take a pot and put an omer of manna in it, and lay it up before the LORD, to be kept for your generations."

34 As the LORD commanded Moses, so Aaron laid it up before the Testimony, to be kept.

35 And the children of Israel ate manna forty years, until they came to an inhabited land; they ate manna until they came to the border of the land of Cā'naan.

36 Now an omer *is* one-tenth of an ephah.

WATER FROM THE ROCK

17 Then all the congregation of the children of Israel set out on their journey from the Wilderness of Sin, according to the commandment of the LORD, and camped in Reph'i·dim; but *there was* no water for the people to drink.

2 Therefore the people contended with Moses, and said, "Give us water, that we may drink." So Moses said to them, "Why do you contend with me? Why do you tempt the LORD?"

3 And the people thirsted there for water, and the people complained against Moses, and said, "Why *is* it you have brought us up out of Egypt, to kill us and our children and our livestock with thirst?"

4 So Moses cried out to the LORD, saying, "What shall I do with this people? They are almost ready to stone me!"

5 And the LORD said to Moses, "Go on before the people, and take with you some of the elders of Israel. Also take in your hand your rod with which you struck the river, and go.

16:31 *a*Literally *What?* (compare Exodus 16:15)

6 "Behold, I will stand before you there on the rock in Hō′reb; and you shall strike the rock, and water will come out of it, that the people may drink." And Moses did so in the sight of the elders of Israel.

7 So he called the name of the place Mas′sah*a* and Mer′i·bah,*b* because of the contention of the children of Israel, and because they tempted the LORD, saying, "Is the LORD among us or not?"

☑   *Bible Quiz*

Exodus 16:1—17:7 **Bread from Heaven; Water from a Rock**

1. When the children of Israel ran out of food, what was the first thing they did?
2. After all God had done for them, what would have been a better way to act?
3. What did God provide for the people to eat?
4. When the children of Israel ran out of water, what did they do first?
5. God had been so good to the children of Israel. How do you think He felt about all the complaining?
6. The next time you need something, how will you ask?

VICTORY OVER THE AMALEKITES

8 Now Am′a·lek came and fought with Israel in Reph′i·dim.

9 And Moses said to Joshua, "Choose us some men and go out,

fight with Am′a·lek. Tomorrow I will stand on the top of the hill with the rod of God in my hand."

10 So Joshua did as Moses said to him, and fought with Am′a·lek. And Moses, Aaron, and Hur went up to the top of the hill.

11 And so it was, when Moses held up his hand, that Israel prevailed; and when he let down his hand, Am′a·lek prevailed.

12 But Moses' hands *became* heavy; so they took a stone and put *it* under him, and he sat on it. And Aaron and Hur supported his hands, one on one side, and the other on the other side; and his hands were steady until the going down of the sun.

13 So Joshua defeated Am′a·lek and his people with the edge of the sword.

14 Then the LORD said to Moses, "Write this *for* a memorial in the book and recount *it* in the hearing of Joshua, that I will utterly blot out the remembrance of Am′a·lek from under heaven."

15 And Moses built an altar and called its name, The-LORD-Is-My-Banner;*a*

16 for he said, "Because the LORD has sworn: the LORD *will have* war with Am′a·lek from generation to generation."

JETHRO'S ADVICE

18 And Jeth′rō, the priest of Mid′i·an, Moses' father-in-law, heard of all that God had done for Moses and for Israel His people—that the LORD had brought Israel out of Egypt.

2 Then Jeth′rō, Moses' father-in-law, took Zip·pō′rah, Moses' wife, after he had sent her back,

---

17:7 *a*Literally *Tempted*   *b*Literally *Contention*
17:15 *a*Hebrew *YHWH Nissi*

3 with her two sons, of whom the name of one *was* Ger'shom (for he said, "I have been a stranger in a foreign land")a

4 and the name of the other *was* El·i·ē'zera (for *he said,* "The God of my father *was* my help, and delivered me from the sword of Pharaoh");

5 and Jeth'rō, Moses' father-in-law, came with his sons and his wife to Moses in the wilderness, where he was encamped at the mountain of God.

6 Now he had said to Moses, "I, your father-in-law Jeth'rō, am coming to you with your wife and her two sons with her."

7 So Moses went out to meet his father-in-law, bowed down, and kissed him. And they asked each other about *their* well-being, and they went into the tent.

8 And Moses told his father-in-law all that the LORD had done to Pharaoh and to the Egyptians for Israel's sake, all the hardship that had come upon them on the way, and *how* the LORD had delivered them.

9 Then Jeth'rō rejoiced for all the good which the LORD had done for Israel, whom He had delivered out of the hand of the Egyptians.

10 And Jeth'rō said, "Blessed *be* the LORD, who has delivered you out of the hand of the Egyptians and out of the hand of Pharaoh, *and* who has delivered the people from under the hand of the Egyptians.

11 "Now I know that the LORD *is* greater than all the gods; for in the very thing in which they behaved proudly, *He was* above them."

12 Then Jeth'rō, Moses' father-in-law, tooka a burnt offering and *other* sacrifices *to offer* to God. And Aaron came with all the elders of Israel to eat bread with Moses' father-in-law before God.

13 And so it was, on the next day, that Moses sat to judge the people; and the people stood before Moses from morning until evening.

14 So when Moses' father-in-law saw all that he did for the people, he said, "What *is* this thing that you are doing for the people? Why do you alone sit, and all the people stand before you from morning until evening?"

15 And Moses said to his father-in-law, "Because the people come to me to inquire of God.

16 "When they have a difficulty, they come to me, and I judge between one and another; and I make known the statutes of God and His laws."

17 So Moses' father-in-law said to him, "The thing that you do *is* not good.

18 "Both you and these people who *are* with you will surely wear yourselves out. For this thing *is* too much for you; you are not able to perform it by yourself.

19 "Listen now to my voice; I will give you counsel, and God will be with you: Stand before God for the people, so that you may bring the difficulties to God.

20 "And you shall teach them the statutes and the laws, and show them the way in which they must walk and the work they must do.

21 "Moreover you shall select from all the people able men, such as fear God, men of truth, hating covetousness; and place *such* over them *to be* rulers of thousands, rulers of hundreds, rulers of fifties, and rulers of tens.

22 "And let them judge the people at all times. Then it will be *that* every

---

18:3 aCompare Exodus 2:22   18:4 aLiterally *My God Is Help*   18:12 aFollowing Masoretic Text and Septuagint; Syriac, Targum, and Vulgate read *offered.*

great matter they shall bring to you, but every small matter they themselves shall judge. So it will be easier for you, for they will bear *the burden* with you.

23 "If you do this thing, and God *so* commands you, then you will be able to endure, and all this people will also go to their place in peace."

24 So Moses heeded the voice of his father-in-law and did all that he had said.

25 And Moses chose able men out of all Israel, and made them heads over the people: rulers of thousands, rulers of hundreds, rulers of fifties, and rulers of tens.

26 So they judged the people at all times; the hard cases they brought to Moses, but they judged every small case themselves.

27 Then Moses let his father-in-law depart, and he went his way to his own land.

ISRAEL AT MOUNT SINAI

19 In the third month after the children of Israel had gone out of the land of Egypt, on the same day, they came *to* the Wilderness of Sinai.

2 For they had departed from Reph'i·dim, had come *to* the Wilderness of Sinai, and camped in the wilderness. So Israel camped there before the mountain.

3 And Moses went up to God, and the LORD called to him from the mountain, saying, "Thus you shall say to the house of Jacob, and tell the children of Israel:

4 'You have seen what I did to the Egyptians, and *how* I bore you on eagles' wings and brought you to Myself.

5 'Now therefore, if you will indeed obey My voice and keep My covenant, then you shall be a special treasure to Me above all people; for all the earth *is* Mine.

6 'And you shall be to Me a kingdom of priests and a holy nation.' These *are* the words which you shall speak to the children of Israel."

7 So Moses came and called for the elders of the people, and laid before them all these words which the LORD commanded him.

8 Then all the people answered together and said, "All that the LORD has spoken we will do." So Moses brought back the words of the people to the LORD.

9 And the LORD said to Moses, "Behold, I come to you in the thick cloud, that the people may hear when I speak with you, and believe you forever." So Moses told the words of the people to the LORD.

10 Then the LORD said to Moses, "Go to the people and consecrate them today and tomorrow, and let them wash their clothes.

11 "And let them be ready for the third day. For on the third day the LORD will come down upon Mount Sinai in the sight of all the people.

12 "You shall set bounds for the people all around, saying, 'Take heed to yourselves *that* you do *not* go up to the mountain or touch its base. Whoever touches the mountain shall surely be put to death.

13 'Not a hand shall touch him, but he shall surely be stoned or shot *with an arrow;* whether man or beast, he shall not live.' When the trumpet sounds long, they shall come near the mountain."

14 So Moses went down from the mountain to the people and sanctified the people, and they washed their clothes.

15 And he said to the people, "Be

ready for the third day; do not come near *your* wives.″

16 Then it came to pass on the third day, in the morning, that there were thunderings and lightnings, and a thick cloud on the mountain; and the sound of the trumpet was very loud, so that all the people who *were* in the camp trembled.

17 And Moses brought the people out of the camp to meet with God, and they stood at the foot of the mountain.

18 Now Mount Sinai *was* completely in smoke, because the LORD descended upon it in fire. Its smoke ascended like the smoke of a furnace, and the whole mountain*a* quaked greatly.

19 And when the blast of the trumpet sounded long and became louder and louder, Moses spoke, and God answered him by voice.

20 Then the LORD came down upon Mount Sinai, on the top of the mountain. And the LORD called Moses to the top of the mountain, and Moses went up.

21 And the LORD said to Moses, ″Go down and warn the people, lest they break through to gaze at the LORD, and many of them perish.

22 ″Also let the priests who come near the LORD consecrate themselves, lest the LORD break out against them.″

23 But Moses said to the LORD, ″The people cannot come up to Mount Sinai; for You warned us, saying, 'Set bounds around the mountain and consecrate it.'″

24 Then the LORD said to him, ″Away! Get down and then come up, you and Aaron with you. But do not let the priests and the people break through to come up to the LORD, lest He break out against them.″

25 So Moses went down to the people and spoke to them.

THE TEN COMMANDMENTS

After three months of traveling in the wilderness, the children of Israel came to Mount Sinai. Here God would teach them ten things they must never forget.

20 And God spoke all these words, saying:

2 ″I *am* the LORD your God, who brought you out of the land of Egypt, out of the house of bondage.

3 ″You shall have no other gods before Me.

4 ″You shall not make for yourself a carved image—any likeness *of anything* that *is* in heaven above, or that *is* in the earth beneath, or that *is* in the water under the earth;

5 you shall not bow down to them nor serve them. For I, the LORD your God, *am* a jealous God, visiting the iniquity of the fathers upon the children to the third and fourth *generations* of those who hate Me,

6 but showing mercy to thousands, to those who love Me and keep My commandments.

7 ″You shall not take the name of the LORD your God in vain, for the LORD will not hold *him* guiltless who takes His name in vain.

8 ″Remember the Sabbath day, to keep it holy.

9 Six days you shall labor and do all your work,

10 but the seventh day *is* the Sabbath of the LORD your God.

19:18 *a*Septuagint reads *all the people.*

HONESTY Exodus 20:15

You Don't Really Want to Be a Pirate, Do You?

You don't really want to be a pirate, do you? Pirates steal from other people. That's why they are called pirates. Pirate stories are fun to read. But you really wouldn't want to *be* a pirate, would you?

1. Look up Exodus 20:15. What does it say? Does God want you to be a pirate? Why not?
2. Look up Ephesians 4:28. What does it say? Why is it better to work for things than steal them?
3. Do you want others to steal from you? Why not? Do others want you to steal from them? Why not? What would you say to a friend if you see that person steal something?

For more on *Values* turn to page 179
For more on *Honesty* turn to page 179

In it you shall do no work: you, nor your son, nor your daughter, nor your male servant, nor your female servant, nor your cattle, nor your stranger who *is* within your gates.

11 For *in* six days the LORD made the heavens and the earth, the sea, and all that *is* in them, and rested the seventh day. Therefore the LORD blessed the Sabbath day and hallowed it.

12 "Honor your father and your mother, that your days may be long upon the land which the LORD your God is giving you.

13 "You shall not murder.

14 "You shall not commit adultery.

15 "You shall not steal.

16 "You shall not bear false witness against your neighbor.

17 "You shall not covet your neighbor's house; you shall not covet your neighbor's wife, nor his male servant, nor his female servant, nor his ox, nor his donkey, nor anything that *is* your neighbor's."

☑ Bible Quiz

Exodus 20:1–17 **The Ten Commandments**

1. Can you name five of the ten commandments God gave the children of Israel?

2. Now take a few minutes to memorize all ten. These are the rules God wants His people to live by. How can we follow them if we do not know them?

3. Recite them each day until you know them by heart.

THE PEOPLE AFRAID OF GOD'S PRESENCE

18 Now all the people witnessed the thunderings, the lightning flashes, the sound of the trumpet, and the mountain smoking; and when the people saw *it,* they trembled and stood afar off.

19 Then they said to Moses, "You speak with us, and we will hear; but let not God speak with us, lest we die."

20 And Moses said to the people, "Do not fear; for God has come to test you, and that His fear may be before you, so that you may not sin."

21 So the people stood afar off, but Moses drew near the thick darkness where God *was.*

THE LAW OF THE ALTAR

22 Then the LORD said to Moses, "Thus you shall say to the children of Israel: 'You have seen that I have talked with you from heaven.

23 'You shall not make *anything to be* with Me—gods of silver or gods of gold you shall not make for yourselves.

24 'An altar of earth you shall make for Me, and you shall sacrifice on it your burnt offerings and your peace offerings, your sheep and your oxen. In every place where I record My name I will come to you, and I will bless you.

25 'And if you make Me an altar of stone, you shall not build it of hewn stone; for if you use your tool on it, you have profaned it.

26 'Nor shall you go up by steps to My altar, that your nakedness may not be exposed on it.'

THE LAW CONCERNING SERVANTS

21 "Now these *are* the judgments which you shall set before them:

2 "If you buy a Hebrew servant, he shall serve six years; and in the seventh he shall go out free and pay nothing.

3 "If he comes in by himself, he shall go out by himself; if he *comes in* married, then his wife shall go out with him.

4 "If his master has given him a wife, and she has borne him sons or daughters, the wife and her children shall be her master's, and he shall go out by himself.

5 "But if the servant plainly says, 'I love my master, my wife, and my children; I will not go out free,'

6 "then his master shall bring him to the judges. He shall also bring him to the door, or to the doorpost, and his master shall pierce his ear with an awl; and he shall serve him forever.

7 "And if a man sells his daughter to be a female slave, she shall not go out as the male slaves do.

8 "If she does not please her master, who has betrothed her to himself, then he shall let her be redeemed. He shall have no right to sell her to a foreign people, since he has dealt deceitfully with her.

9 "And if he has betrothed her to his son, he shall deal with her according to the custom of daughters.

10 "If he takes another *wife,* he shall not diminish her food, her clothing, and her marriage rights.

11 "And if he does not do these three for her, then she shall go out free, without *paying* money.

THE LAW CONCERNING VIOLENCE

12 "He who strikes a man so that he dies shall surely be put to death.

13 "However, if he did not lie in wait, but God delivered *him* into his hand, then I will appoint for you a place where he may flee.

14 "But if a man acts with premeditation against his neighbor, to kill him by treachery, you shall take him from My altar, that he may die.

15 "And he who strikes his father or his mother shall surely be put to death.

16 "He who kidnaps a man and sells him, or if he is found in his hand, shall surely be put to death.

17 "And he who curses his father or his mother shall surely be put to death.

18 "If men contend with each other, and one strikes the other with a stone or with *his* fist, and he does not die but is confined to *his* bed,

19 "if he rises again and walks about outside with his staff, then he who struck *him* shall be acquitted. He shall only pay *for* the loss of his time, and shall provide *for him* to be thoroughly healed.

20 "And if a man beats his male or female servant with a rod, so that he dies under his hand, he shall surely be punished.

21 "Notwithstanding, if he remains alive a day or two, he shall not be punished; for he *is* his property.

22 "If men fight, and hurt a woman with child, so that she gives birth prematurely, yet no harm follows, he shall surely be punished accordingly as the woman's husband imposes on him; and he shall pay as the judges *determine.*

23 "But if *any* harm follows, then you shall give life for life,

24 "eye for eye, tooth for tooth, hand for hand, foot for foot,

25 "burn for burn, wound for wound, stripe for stripe.

26 "If a man strikes the eye of his male or female servant, and destroys it, he shall let him go free for the sake of his eye.

27 "And if he knocks out the tooth of his male or female servant, he shall

let him go free for the sake of his tooth.

ANIMAL CONTROL LAWS

28 "If an ox gores a man or a woman to death, then the ox shall surely be stoned, and its flesh shall not be eaten; but the owner of the ox *shall be* acquitted.

29 "But if the ox tended to thrust with its horn in times past, and it has been made known to his owner, and he has not kept it confined, so that it has killed a man or a woman, the ox shall be stoned and its owner also shall be put to death.

30 "If there is imposed on him a sum of money, then he shall pay to redeem his life, whatever is imposed on him.

31 "Whether it has gored a son or gored a daughter, according to this judgment it shall be done to him.

32 "If the ox gores a male or female servant, he shall give to their master thirty shekels of silver, and the ox shall be stoned.

33 "And if a man opens a pit, or if a man digs a pit and does not cover it, and an ox or a donkey falls in it,

34 "the owner of the pit shall make *it* good; he shall give money to their owner, but the dead *animal* shall be his.

35 "If one man's ox hurts another's, so that it dies, then they shall sell the live ox and divide the money from it; and the dead *ox* they shall also divide.

36 "Or if it was known that the ox tended to thrust in time past, and its owner has not kept it confined, he shall surely pay ox for ox, and the dead animal shall be his own.

RESPONSIBILITY FOR PROPERTY

22 "If a man steals an ox or a sheep, and slaughters it or sells it, he shall restore five oxen for an ox and four sheep for a sheep.

2 "If the thief is found breaking in, and he is struck so that he dies, *there shall be* no guilt for his bloodshed.

3 "If the sun has risen on him, *there shall be* guilt for his bloodshed. He should make full restitution; if he has nothing, then he shall be sold for his theft.

4 "If the theft is certainly found alive in his hand, whether it is an ox or donkey or sheep, he shall restore double.

5 "If a man causes a field or vineyard to be grazed, and lets loose his animal, and it feeds in another man's field, he shall make restitution from the best of his own field and the best of his own vineyard.

6 "If fire breaks out and catches in thorns, so that stacked grain, standing grain, or the field is consumed, he who kindled the fire shall surely make restitution.

7 "If a man delivers to his neighbor money or articles to keep, and it is stolen out of the man's house, if the thief is found, he shall pay double.

8 "If the thief is not found, then the master of the house shall be brought to the judges *to see* whether he has put his hand into his neighbor's goods.

9 "For any kind of trespass, *whether it concerns* an ox, a donkey, a sheep, or clothing, *or* for any kind of lost thing which *another* claims to be his, the cause of both parties shall come before the judges; *and* whomever the judges condemn shall pay double to his neighbor.

10 "If a man delivers to his neighbor a donkey, an ox, a sheep, or any animal to keep, and it dies, is hurt, or driven away, no one seeing *it,*

11 "*then* an oath of the LORD shall be between them both, that he has not put his hand into his neighbor's

goods; and the owner of it shall accept *that,* and he shall not make *it* good.

12 "But if, in fact, it is stolen from him, he shall make restitution to the owner of it.

13 "If it is torn to pieces *by a beast, then* he shall bring it as evidence, *and* he shall not make good what was torn.

14 "And if a man borrows *anything* from his neighbor, and it becomes injured or dies, the owner of it not *being* with it, he shall surely make *it* good.

15 "If its owner *was* with it, he shall not make *it* good; if it *was* hired, it came for its hire.

MORAL AND CEREMONIAL PRINCIPLES

16 "If a man entices a virgin who is not betrothed, and lies with her, he shall surely pay the bride-price for her *to be* his wife.

17 "If her father utterly refuses to give her to him, he shall pay money according to the bride-price of virgins.

18 "You shall not permit a sorceress to live.

19 "Whoever lies with an animal shall surely be put to death.

20 "He who sacrifices to *any* god, except to the LORD only, he shall be utterly destroyed.

21 "You shall neither mistreat a stranger nor oppress him, for you were strangers in the land of Egypt.

22 "You shall not afflict any widow or fatherless child.

23 "If you afflict them in any way, *and* they cry at all to Me, I will surely hear their cry;

24 "and My wrath will become hot, and I will kill you with the sword; your wives shall be widows, and your children fatherless.

25 "If you lend money to *any of* My people *who are* poor among you, you shall not be like a moneylender to him; you shall not charge him interest.

26 "If you ever take your neighbor's garment as a pledge, you shall return it to him before the sun goes down.

27 "For that *is* his only covering, it *is* his garment for his skin. What will he sleep in? And it will be that when he cries to Me, I will hear, for I *am* gracious.

28 "You shall not revile God, nor curse a ruler of your people.

29 "You shall not delay *to offer* the first of your ripe produce and your juices. The firstborn of your sons you shall give to Me.

30 "Likewise you shall do with your oxen *and* your sheep. It shall be with its mother seven days; on the eighth day you shall give it to Me.

31 "And you shall be holy men to Me: you shall not eat meat torn *by beasts* in the field; you shall throw it to the dogs.

JUSTICE FOR ALL

23 "You shall not circulate a false report. Do not put your hand with the wicked to be an unrighteous witness.

2 "You shall not follow a crowd to do evil; nor shall you testify in a dispute so as to turn aside after many to pervert *justice.*

3 "You shall not show partiality to a poor man in his dispute.

4 "If you meet your enemy's ox or his donkey going astray, you shall surely bring it back to him again.

5 "If you see the donkey of one who hates you lying under its burden, and you would refrain from helping it, you shall surely help him with it.

6 "You shall not pervert the judgment of your poor in his dispute.

7 "Keep yourself far from a false matter; do not kill the innocent and righteous. For I will not justify the wicked.

8 "And you shall take no bribe, for a bribe blinds the discerning and perverts the words of the righteous.

9 "Also you shall not oppress a stranger, for you know the heart of a stranger, because you were strangers in the land of Egypt.

THE LAW OF SABBATHS

10 "Six years you shall sow your land and gather in its produce,

11 "but the seventh *year* you shall let it rest and lie fallow, that the poor of your people may eat; and what they leave, the beasts of the field may eat. In like manner you shall do with your vineyard *and* your olive grove.

12 "Six days you shall do your work, and on the seventh day you shall rest, that your ox and your donkey may rest, and the son of your female servant and the stranger may be refreshed.

13 "And in all that I have said to you, be circumspect and make no mention of the name of other gods, nor let it be heard from your mouth.

THREE ANNUAL FEASTS

14 "Three times you shall keep a feast to Me in the year:

15 "You shall keep the Feast of Unleavened Bread (you shall eat unleavened bread seven days, as I commanded you, at the time appointed in the month of Ā'bib, for in it you came out of Egypt; none shall appear before Me empty);

16 "and the Feast of Harvest, the firstfruits of your labors which you have sown in the field; and the Feast of Ingathering at the end of the year, when you have gathered in *the fruit of* your labors from the field.

17 "Three times in the year all your males shall appear before the Lord GOD.*a*

18 "You shall not offer the blood of My sacrifice with leavened bread; nor shall the fat of My sacrifice remain until morning.

19 "The first of the firstfruits of your land you shall bring into the house of the LORD your God. You shall not boil a young goat in its mother's milk.

THE ANGEL AND THE PROMISES

20 "Behold, I send an Angel before you to keep you in the way and to bring you into the place which I have prepared.

21 "Beware of Him and obey His voice; do not provoke Him, for He will not pardon your transgressions; for My name *is* in Him.

22 "But if you indeed obey His voice and do all that I speak, then I will be an enemy to your enemies and an adversary to your adversaries.

23 "For My Angel will go before you and bring you in to the Am'o·rītes and the Hit'tītes and the Per'iz·zītes and the Cā'naan·ītes and the Hī'vītes and the Jeb'ū·sītes; and I will cut them off.

24 "You shall not bow down to their gods, nor serve them, nor do according to their works; but you shall utterly overthrow them and completely break down their *sacred* pillars.

25 "So you shall serve the LORD your God, and He will bless your bread and your water. And I will take sickness away from the midst of you.

26 "No one shall suffer miscarriage or be barren in your land; I will fulfill the number of your days.

27 "I will send My fear before you, I

23:17 *a*Hebrew YHWH, usually translated LORD

will cause confusion among all the people to whom you come, and will make all your enemies turn *their* backs to you.

28 "And I will send hornets before you, which shall drive out the Hī'-vīte, the Cā'naan·īte, and the Hit'tīte from before you.

29 "I will not drive them out from before you in one year, lest the land become desolate and the beasts of the field become too numerous for you.

30 "Little by little I will drive them out from before you, until you have increased, and you inherit the land.

31 "And I will set your bounds from the Red Sea to the sea, Phi·lis'ti·a, and from the desert to the River.*a* For I will deliver the inhabitants of the land into your hand, and you shall drive them out before you.

32 "You shall make no covenant with them, nor with their gods.

33 "They shall not dwell in your land, lest they make you sin against Me. For *if* you serve their gods, it will surely be a snare to you."

ISRAEL AFFIRMS THE COVENANT

24 Now He said to Moses, "Come up to the LORD, you and Aaron, Nā'-dab and A·bī'hū, and seventy of the elders of Israel, and worship from afar.

2 "And Moses alone shall come near the LORD, but they shall not come near; nor shall the people go up with him."

3 So Moses came and told the people all the words of the LORD and all the judgments. And all the people answered with one voice and said, "All the words which the LORD has said we will do."

4 And Moses wrote all the words of the LORD. And he rose early in the morning, and built an altar at the foot of the mountain, and twelve pillars according to the twelve tribes of Israel.

5 Then he sent young men of the children of Israel, who offered burnt offerings and sacrificed peace offerings of oxen to the LORD.

6 And Moses took half the blood and put *it* in basins, and half the blood he sprinkled on the altar.

7 Then he took the Book of the Covenant and read in the hearing of the people. And they said, "All that the LORD has said we will do, and be obedient."

8 And Moses took the blood, sprinkled *it* on the people, and said, "This is the blood of the covenant which the LORD has made with you according to all these words."

ON THE MOUNTAIN WITH GOD

9 Then Moses went up, also Aaron, Nā'dab, and A·bī'hū, and seventy of the elders of Israel,

10 and they saw the God of Israel. And *there was* under His feet as it were a paved work of sapphire stone, and it was like the very heavens in *its* clarity.

11 But on the nobles of the children of Israel He did not lay His hand. So they saw God, and they ate and drank.

12 Then the LORD said to Moses, "Come up to Me on the mountain and be there; and I will give you tablets of stone, and the law and commandments which I have written, that you may teach them."

13 So Moses arose with his assistant Joshua, and Moses went up to the mountain of God.

14 And he said to the elders, "Wait here for us until we come back to you. Indeed, Aaron and Hur *are* with you.

23:31 *a*Hebrew *Nahar,* the Euphrates

If any man has a difficulty, let him go to them."

15 Then Moses went up into the mountain, and a cloud covered the mountain.

16 Now the glory of the LORD rested on Mount Sinai, and the cloud covered it six days. And on the seventh day He called to Moses out of the midst of the cloud.

17 The sight of the glory of the LORD *was* like a consuming fire on the top of the mountain in the eyes of the children of Israel.

18 So Moses went into the midst of the cloud and went up into the mountain. And Moses was on the mountain forty days and forty nights.

OFFERINGS FOR THE SANCTUARY

25 Then the LORD spoke to Moses, saying:

2 "Speak to the children of Israel, that they bring Me an offering. From everyone who gives it willingly with his heart you shall take My offering.

3 "And this *is* the offering which you shall take from them: gold, silver, and bronze;

4 "blue, purple, and scarlet *thread,* fine linen, and goats' *hair;*

5 "ram skins dyed red, badger skins, and acacia wood;

6 "oil for the light, and spices for the anointing oil and for the sweet incense;

7 "onyx stones, and stones to be set in the ephod and in the breastplate.

8 "And let them make Me a sanctuary, that I may dwell among them.

9 "According to all that I show you, *that is,* the pattern of the tabernacle and the pattern of all its furnishings, just so you shall make *it.*

THE ARK OF THE TESTIMONY

10 "And they shall make an ark of acacia wood; two and a half cubits

shall be its length, a cubit and a half its width, and a cubit and a half its height.

11 "And you shall overlay it with pure gold, inside and out you shall overlay it, and shall make on it a molding of gold all around.

12 "You shall cast four rings of gold for it, and put *them* in its four corners; two rings *shall be* on one side, and two rings on the other side.

13 "And you shall make poles *of* acacia wood, and overlay them with gold.

14 "You shall put the poles into the rings on the sides of the ark, that the ark may be carried by them.

15 "The poles shall be in the rings of the ark; they shall not be taken from it.

16 "And you shall put into the ark the Testimony which I will give you.

17 "You shall make a mercy seat of pure gold; two and a half cubits *shall be* its length and a cubit and a half its width.

18 "And you shall make two cherubim of gold; of hammered work you shall make them at the two ends of the mercy seat.

19 "Make one cherub at one end, and the other cherub at the other end; you shall make the cherubim at the two ends of it *of one piece* with the mercy seat.

20 "And the cherubim shall stretch out *their* wings above, covering the mercy seat with their wings, and they shall face one another; the faces of the cherubim *shall be* toward the mercy seat.

21 "You shall put the mercy seat on top of the ark, and in the ark you shall put the Testimony that I will give you.

22 "And there I will meet with you, and I will speak with you from above the mercy seat, from between the two cherubim which *are* on the ark of the Testimony, about everything which I

will give you in commandment to the children of Israel.

The Table for the Showbread

23 "You shall also make a table of acacia wood; two cubits *shall be* its length, a cubit its width, and a cubit and a half its height.

24 "And you shall overlay it with pure gold, and make a molding of gold all around.

25 "You shall make for it a frame of a handbreadth all around, and you shall make a gold molding for the frame all around.

26 "And you shall make for it four rings of gold, and put the rings on the four corners that *are* at its four legs.

27 "The rings shall be close to the frame, as holders for the poles to bear the table.

28 "And you shall make the poles of acacia wood, and overlay them with gold, that the table may be carried with them.

29 "You shall make its dishes, its pans, its pitchers, and its bowls for pouring. You shall make them of pure gold.

30 "And you shall set the showbread on the table before Me always.

The Gold Lampstand

31 "You shall also make a lampstand of pure gold; the lampstand shall be of hammered work. Its shaft, its branches, its bowls, its *ornamental* knobs, and flowers shall be *of one piece.*

32 "And six branches shall come out of its sides: three branches of the lampstand out of one side, and three branches of the lampstand out of the other side.

33 "Three bowls *shall be* made like almond *blossoms* on one branch, *with* an *ornamental* knob and a flower,

and three bowls made like almond *blossoms* on the other branch, *with* an *ornamental* knob and a flower— and so for the six branches that come out of the lampstand.

34 "On the lampstand itself four bowls *shall be* made like almond *blossoms, each with* its *ornamental* knob and flower.

35 "And *there shall be* a knob under the *first* two branches of the same, a knob under the *second* two branches of the same, and a knob under the *third* two branches of the same, according to the six branches that extend from the lampstand.

36 "Their knobs and their branches *shall be of one piece;* all of it *shall be* one hammered piece of pure gold.

37 "You shall make seven lamps for it, and they shall arrange its lamps so that they give light in front of it.

38 "And its wick-trimmers and their trays *shall be* of pure gold.

39 "It shall be made of a talent of pure gold, with all these utensils.

40 "And see to it that you make *them* according to the pattern which was shown you on the mountain.

The Tabernacle

26 "Moreover you shall make the tabernacle *with* ten curtains *of* fine woven linen, and blue, purple, and scarlet *thread;* with artistic designs of cherubim you shall weave them.

2 "The length of each curtain *shall be* twenty-eight cubits, and the width of each curtain four cubits. And every one of the curtains shall have the same measurements.

3 "Five curtains shall be coupled to one another, and *the other* five curtains *shall be* coupled to one another.

4 "And you shall make loops of blue *yarn* on the edge of the curtain on the selvedge of *one* set, and likewise you

shall do on the outer edge of *the other* curtain of the second set.

5 "Fifty loops you shall make in the one curtain, and fifty loops you shall make on the edge of the curtain that *is* on the end of the second set, that the loops may be clasped to one another.

6 "And you shall make fifty clasps of gold, and couple the curtains together with the clasps, so that it may be one tabernacle.

7 "You shall also make curtains of goats' *hair,* to be a tent over the tabernacle. You shall make eleven curtains.

8 "The length of each curtain *shall be* thirty cubits, and the width of each curtain four cubits; and the eleven curtains shall all have the same measurements.

9 "And you shall couple five curtains by themselves and six curtains by themselves, and you shall double over the sixth curtain at the forefront of the tent.

10 "You shall make fifty loops on the edge of the curtain that is outermost in *one* set, and fifty loops on the edge of the curtain of the second set.

11 "And you shall make fifty bronze clasps, put the clasps into the loops, and couple the tent together, that it may be one.

12 "The remnant that remains of the curtains of the tent, the half curtain that remains, shall hang over the back of the tabernacle.

13 "And a cubit on one side and a cubit on the other side, of what remains of the length of the curtains of the tent, shall hang over the sides of the tabernacle, on this side and on that side, to cover it.

14 "You shall also make a covering of ram skins dyed red for the tent, and a covering of badger skins above that.

15 "And for the tabernacle you shall make the boards of acacia wood, standing upright.

16 "Ten cubits *shall be* the length of a board, and a cubit and a half *shall be* the width of each board.

17 "Two tenons *shall be* in each board for binding one to another. Thus you shall make for all the boards of the tabernacle.

18 "And you shall make the boards for the tabernacle, twenty boards for the south side.

19 "You shall make forty sockets of silver under the twenty boards: two sockets under each of the boards for its two tenons.

20 "And for the second side of the tabernacle, the north side, *there shall be* twenty boards

21 "and their forty sockets of silver: two sockets under each of the boards.

22 "For the far side of the tabernacle, westward, you shall make six boards.

23 "And you shall also make two boards for the two back corners of the tabernacle.

24 "They shall be coupled together at the bottom and they shall be coupled together at the top by one ring. Thus it shall be for both of them. They shall be for the two corners.

25 "So there shall be eight boards with their sockets of silver—sixteen sockets—two sockets under each of the boards.

26 "And you shall make bars of acacia wood: five for the boards on one side of the tabernacle,

27 "five bars for the boards on the other side of the tabernacle, and five bars for the boards of the side of the tabernacle, for the far side westward.

28 "The middle bar shall pass through the midst of the boards from end to end.

29 "You shall overlay the boards with gold, make their rings of gold *as* hold-

ers for the bars, and overlay the bars with gold.

30 "And you shall raise up the tabernacle according to its pattern which you were shown on the mountain.

31 "You shall make a veil woven of blue, purple, and scarlet *thread,* and fine woven linen. It shall be woven with an artistic design of cherubim.

32 "You shall hang it upon the four pillars of acacia *wood* overlaid with gold. Their hooks *shall be* gold, upon four sockets of silver.

33 "And you shall hang the veil from the clasps. Then you shall bring the ark of the Testimony in there, behind the veil. The veil shall be a divider for you between the holy *place* and the Most Holy.

34 "You shall put the mercy seat upon the ark of the Testimony in the Most Holy.

35 "You shall set the table outside the veil, and the lampstand across from the table on the side of the tabernacle toward the south; and you shall put the table on the north side.

36 "You shall make a screen for the door of the tabernacle, *woven of* blue, purple, and scarlet *thread,* and fine woven linen, made by a weaver.

37 "And you shall make for the screen five pillars of acacia *wood,* and overlay them with gold; their hooks *shall be* gold, and you shall cast five sockets of bronze for them.

The Altar of Burnt Offering

27 "You shall make an altar of acacia wood, five cubits long and five cubits wide—the altar shall be square—and its height *shall be* three cubits.

2 "You shall make its horns on its four corners; its horns shall be of one piece with it. And you shall overlay it with bronze.

3 "Also you shall make its pans to receive its ashes, and its shovels and its basins and its forks and its firepans; you shall make all its utensils of bronze.

4 "You shall make a grate for it, a network of bronze; and on the network you shall make four bronze rings at its four corners.

5 "You shall put it under the rim of the altar beneath, that the network may be midway up the altar.

6 "And you shall make poles for the altar, poles of acacia wood, and overlay them with bronze.

7 "The poles shall be put in the rings, and the poles shall be on the two sides of the altar to bear it.

8 "You shall make it hollow with boards; as it was shown you on the mountain, so shall they make *it.*

The Court of the Tabernacle

9 "You shall also make the court of the tabernacle. For the south side *there shall be* hangings for the court *made of* fine woven linen, one hundred cubits long for one side.

10 "And its twenty pillars and their twenty sockets *shall be* bronze. The hooks of the pillars and their bands *shall be* silver.

11 "Likewise along the length of the north side *there shall be* hangings one hundred *cubits* long, with its twenty pillars and their twenty sockets of bronze, and the hooks of the pillars and their bands of silver.

12 "And along the width of the court on the west side *shall be* hangings of fifty cubits, with their ten pillars and their ten sockets.

13 "The width of the court on the east side *shall be* fifty cubits.

14 "The hangings on *one* side *of the gate shall be* fifteen cubits, *with* their three pillars and their three sockets.

15 "And on the other side *shall be*

hangings of fifteen *cubits, with* their three pillars and their three sockets.

16 "For the gate of the court *there shall be* a screen twenty cubits long, *woven of* blue, purple, and scarlet *thread,* and fine woven linen, made by a weaver. It *shall have* four pillars and four sockets.

17 "All the pillars around the court shall have bands of silver; their hooks *shall be* of silver and their sockets of bronze.

18 "The length of the court *shall be* one hundred cubits, the width fifty throughout, and the height five cubits, *made of* fine woven linen, and its sockets of bronze.

19 "All the utensils of the tabernacle for all its service, all its pegs, and all the pegs of the court, *shall be* of bronze.

THE CARE OF THE LAMPSTAND

20 "And you shall command the children of Israel that they bring you pure oil of pressed olives for the light, to cause the lamp to burn continually. 21 "In the tabernacle of meeting, outside the veil which *is* before the Testimony, Aaron and his sons shall tend it from evening until morning before the LORD. *It shall be* a statute forever to their generations on behalf of the children of Israel.

GARMENTS FOR THE PRIESTHOOD

28 "Now take Aaron your brother, and his sons with him, from among the children of Israel, that he may minister to Me as priest, Aaron *and* Aaron's sons: Nā′dab, A·bī′hū, El·ē·ā′zar, and Ith′a·mar.

2 "And you shall make holy garments for Aaron your brother, for glory and for beauty.

3 "So you shall speak to all *who are* gifted artisans, whom I have filled with the spirit of wisdom, that they may make Aaron's garments, to consecrate him, that he may minister to Me as priest.

4 "And these *are* the garments which they shall make: a breastplate, an ephod,*a* a robe, a skillfully woven tunic, a turban, and a sash. So they shall make holy garments for Aaron your brother and his sons, that he may minister to Me as priest.

THE EPHOD

5 "They shall take the gold, blue, purple, and scarlet *thread,* and the fine linen,

6 "and they shall make the ephod of gold, blue, purple, *and* scarlet *thread,* and fine woven linen, artistically worked.

7 "It shall have two shoulder straps joined at its two edges, and *so* it shall be joined together.

8 "And the intricately woven band of the ephod, which *is* on it, shall be of the same workmanship, *made of* gold, blue, purple, and scarlet *thread,* and fine woven linen.

9 "Then you shall take two onyx stones and engrave on them the names of the sons of Israel:

10 "six of their names on one stone and six names on the other stone, in order of their birth.

11 "With the work of an engraver in stone, *like* the engravings of a signet, you shall engrave the two stones with the names of the sons of Israel. You shall set them in settings of gold.

12 "And you shall put the two stones on the shoulders of the ephod *as* memorial stones for the sons of Israel. So Aaron shall bear their names before the LORD on his two shoulders as a memorial.

28:4 *a*That is, an ornamented vest

13 "You shall also make settings of gold,

14 "and you shall make two chains of pure gold like braided cords, and fasten the braided chains to the settings.

THE BREASTPLATE

15 "You shall make the breastplate of judgment. Artistically woven according to the workmanship of the ephod you shall make it: of gold, blue, purple, and scarlet *thread,* and fine woven linen, you shall make it.

16 "It shall be doubled into a square: a span *shall be* its length, and a span *shall be* its width.

17 "And you shall put settings of stones in it, four rows of stones: *The first* row *shall be* a sardius, a topaz, and an emerald; *this shall be* the first row;

18 "the second row *shall be* a turquoise, a sapphire, and a diamond;

19 "the third row, a jacinth, an agate, and an amethyst;

20 "and the fourth row, a beryl, an onyx, and a jasper. They shall be set in gold settings.

21 "And the stones shall have the names of the sons of Israel, twelve according to their names, *like* the engravings of a signet, each one with its own name; they shall be according to the twelve tribes.

22 "You shall make chains for the breastplate at the end, like braided cords of pure gold.

23 "And you shall make two rings of gold for the breastplate, and put the two rings on the two ends of the breastplate.

24 "Then you shall put the two braided *chains* of gold in the two rings which are on the ends of the breastplate;

25 "and the *other* two ends of the two braided *chains* you shall fasten to the two settings, and put them on the shoulder straps of the ephod in the front.

26 "You shall make two rings of gold, and put them on the two ends of the breastplate, on the edge of it, which is on the inner side of the ephod.

27 "And two *other* rings of gold you shall make, and put them on the two shoulder straps, underneath the ephod toward its front, right at the seam above the intricately woven band of the ephod.

28 "They shall bind the breastplate by means of its rings to the rings of the ephod, using a blue cord, so that it is above the intricately woven band of the ephod, and so that the breastplate does not come loose from the ephod.

29 "So Aaron shall bear the names of the sons of Israel on the breastplate of judgment over his heart, when he goes into the holy *place,* as a memorial before the LORD continually.

30 "And you shall put in the breastplate of judgment the Ū'rim and the Thum'mim,[a] and they shall be over Aaron's heart when he goes in before the LORD. So Aaron shall bear the judgment of the children of Israel over his heart before the LORD continually.

OTHER PRIESTLY GARMENTS

31 "You shall make the robe of the ephod all of blue.

32 "There shall be an opening for his head in the middle of it; it shall have a woven binding all around its opening, like the opening in a coat of mail, so that it does not tear.

33 "And upon its hem you shall make pomegranates of blue, purple, and scarlet, all around its hem, and

28:30 [a]Literally *the Lights and the Perfections* (compare Leviticus 8:8)

bells of gold between them all around:

34 "a golden bell and a pomegranate, a golden bell and a pomegranate, upon the hem of the robe all around.

35 "And it shall be upon Aaron when he ministers, and its sound will be heard when he goes into the holy *place* before the LORD and when he comes out, that he may not die.

36 "You shall also make a plate of pure gold and engrave on it, *like* the engraving of a signet:

HOLINESS TO THE LORD.

37 "And you shall put it on a blue cord, that it may be on the turban; it shall be on the front of the turban.

38 "So it shall be on Aaron's forehead, that Aaron may bear the iniquity of the holy things which the children of Israel hallow in all their holy gifts; and it shall always be on his forehead, that they may be accepted before the LORD.

39 "You shall skillfully weave the tunic of fine linen *thread,* you shall make the turban of fine linen, and you shall make the sash of woven work.

40 "For Aaron's sons you shall make tunics, and you shall make sashes for them. And you shall make hats for them, for glory and beauty.

41 "So you shall put them on Aaron your brother and on his sons with him. You shall anoint them, consecrate them, and sanctify them, that they may minister to Me as priests.

42 "And you shall make for them linen trousers to cover their nakedness; they shall reach from the waist to the thighs.

43 "They shall be on Aaron and on his sons when they come into the tabernacle of meeting, or when they come near the altar to minister in the holy *place,* that they do not incur iniquity and die. *It shall be* a statute forever to him and his descendants after him.

AARON AND HIS SONS CONSECRATED

29 "And this is what you shall do to them to hallow them for ministering to Me as priests: Take one young bull and two rams without blemish,

2 "and unleavened bread, unleavened cakes mixed with oil, and unleavened wafers anointed with oil (you shall make them of wheat flour).

3 "You shall put them in one basket and bring them in the basket, with the bull and the two rams.

4 "And Aaron and his sons you shall bring to the door of the tabernacle of meeting, and you shall wash them with water.

5 "Then you shall take the garments, put the tunic on Aaron, and the robe of the ephod, the ephod, and the breastplate, and gird him with the intricately woven band of the ephod.

6 "You shall put the turban on his head, and put the holy crown on the turban.

7 "And you shall take the anointing oil, pour *it* on his head, and anoint him.

8 "Then you shall bring his sons and put tunics on them.

9 "And you shall gird them with sashes, Aaron and his sons, and put the hats on them. The priesthood shall be theirs for a perpetual statute. So you shall consecrate Aaron and his sons.

10 "You shall also have the bull brought before the tabernacle of meeting, and Aaron and his sons shall put their hands on the head of the bull.

11 "Then you shall kill the bull before the LORD, *by* the door of the tabernacle of meeting.

12 "You shall take *some* of the blood of the bull and put *it* on the horns of the altar with your finger, and pour all the blood beside the base of the altar.

13 "And you shall take all the fat that covers the entrails, the fatty lobe *attached* to the liver, and the two kidneys and the fat that *is* on them, and burn *them* on the altar.

14 "But the flesh of the bull, with its skin and its offal, you shall burn with fire outside the camp. It *is* a sin offering.

15 "You shall also take one ram, and Aaron and his sons shall put their hands on the head of the ram;

16 "and you shall kill the ram, and you shall take its blood and sprinkle *it* all around on the altar.

17 "Then you shall cut the ram in pieces, wash its entrails and its legs, and put *them* with its pieces and with its head.

18 "And you shall burn the whole ram on the altar. It *is* a burnt offering to the LORD; it *is* a sweet aroma, an offering made by fire to the LORD.

19 "You shall also take the other ram, and Aaron and his sons shall put their hands on the head of the ram.

20 "Then you shall kill the ram, and take some of its blood and put *it* on the tip of the right ear of Aaron and on the tip of the right ear of his sons, on the thumb of their right hand and on the big toe of their right foot, and sprinkle the blood all around on the altar.

21 "And you shall take some of the blood that is on the altar, and some of the anointing oil, and sprinkle *it* on Aaron and on his garments, on his sons and on the garments of his sons with him; and he and his garments shall be hallowed, and his sons and his sons' garments with him.

22 "Also you shall take the fat of the ram, the fat tail, the fat that covers the entrails, the fatty lobe *attached to* the liver, the two kidneys and the fat on them, the right thigh (for it *is* a ram of consecration),

23 "one loaf of bread, one cake *made with* oil, and one wafer from the basket of the unleavened bread that *is* before the LORD;

24 "and you shall put all these in the hands of Aaron and in the hands of his sons, and you shall wave them *as* a wave offering before the LORD.

25 "You shall receive them back from their hands and burn *them* on the altar as a burnt offering, as a sweet aroma before the LORD. It *is* an offering made by fire to the LORD.

26 "Then you shall take the breast of the ram of Aaron's consecration and wave it *as* a wave offering before the LORD; and it shall be your portion.

27 "And from the ram of the consecration you shall consecrate the breast of the wave offering which is waved, and the thigh of the heave offering which is raised, of *that* which *is* for Aaron and of *that* which is for his sons.

28 "It shall be from the children of Israel *for* Aaron and his sons by a statute forever. For it is a heave offering; it shall be a heave offering from the children of Israel from the sacrifices of their peace offerings, *that is,* their heave offering to the LORD.

29 "And the holy garments of Aaron shall be his sons' after him, to be anointed in them and to be consecrated in them.

30 "That son who becomes priest in his place shall put them on for seven days, when he enters the tabernacle of meeting to minister in the holy *place.*

31 "And you shall take the ram of the consecration and boil its flesh in the holy place.

32 "Then Aaron and his sons shall eat the flesh of the ram, and the bread that *is* in the basket, *by* the door of the tabernacle of meeting.

33 "They shall eat those things with which the atonement was made, to consecrate *and* to sanctify them; but an outsider shall not eat *them,* because they *are* holy.

34 "And if any of the flesh of the consecration offerings, or of the bread, remains until the morning, then you shall burn the remainder with fire. It shall not be eaten, because it *is* holy.

35 "Thus you shall do to Aaron and his sons, according to all that I have commanded you. Seven days you shall consecrate them.

36 "And you shall offer a bull every day *as* a sin offering for atonement. You shall cleanse the altar when you make atonement for it, and you shall anoint it to sanctify it.

37 "Seven days you shall make atonement for the altar and sanctify it. And the altar shall be most holy. Whatever touches the altar must be holy.*a*

THE DAILY OFFERINGS

38 "Now this *is* what you shall offer on the altar: two lambs of the first year, day by day continually.

39 "One lamb you shall offer in the morning, and the other lamb you shall offer at twilight.

40 "With the one lamb shall be one-tenth *of an ephah* of flour mixed with one-fourth of a hin of pressed oil, and one-fourth of a hin of wine *as* a drink offering.

41 "And the other lamb you shall offer at twilight; and you shall offer with it the grain offering and the drink offering, as in the morning, for a sweet aroma, an offering made by fire to the LORD.

42 "*This shall be* a continual burnt offering throughout your generations *at* the door of the tabernacle of meeting before the LORD, where I will meet you to speak with you.

43 "And there I will meet with the children of Israel, and *the tabernacle* shall be sanctified by My glory.

44 "So I will consecrate the tabernacle of meeting and the altar. I will also consecrate both Aaron and his sons to minister to Me as priests.

45 "I will dwell among the children of Israel and will be their God.

46 "And they shall know that I *am* the LORD their God, who brought them up out of the land of Egypt, that I may dwell among them. I *am* the LORD their God.

THE ALTAR OF INCENSE

30 "You shall make an altar to burn incense on; you shall make it of acacia wood.

2 "A cubit *shall be* its length and a cubit its width—it shall be square—and two cubits *shall be* its height. Its horns *shall be* of one piece with it.

3 "And you shall overlay its top, its sides all around, and its horns with pure gold; and you shall make for it a molding of gold all around.

4 "Two gold rings you shall make for it, under the molding on both its sides. You shall place *them* on its two sides, and they will be holders for the poles with which to bear it.

5 "You shall make the poles of acacia wood, and overlay them with gold.

6 "And you shall put it before the veil that *is* before the ark of the Testimony, before the mercy seat that *is* over the Testimony, where I will meet with you.

7 "Aaron shall burn on it sweet incense every morning; when he tends

29:37 *a*Compare Numbers 4:15 and Haggai 2:11–13

the lamps, he shall burn incense on it.

8 "And when Aaron lights the lamps at twilight, he shall burn incense on it, a perpetual incense before the LORD throughout your generations.

9 "You shall not offer strange incense on it, or a burnt offering, or a grain offering; nor shall you pour a drink offering on it.

10 "And Aaron shall make atonement upon its horns once a year with the blood of the sin offering of atonement; once a year he shall make atonement upon it throughout your generations. It *is* most holy to the LORD."

THE RANSOM MONEY

11 Then the LORD spoke to Moses, saying:

12 "When you take the census of the children of Israel for their number, then every man shall give a ransom for himself to the LORD, when you number them, that there may be no plague among them when *you* number them.

13 "This is what everyone among those who are numbered shall give: half a shekel according to the shekel of the sanctuary (a shekel *is* twenty gerahs). The half-shekel *shall be* an offering to the LORD.

14 "Everyone included among those who are numbered, from twenty years old and above, shall give an offering to the LORD.

15 "The rich shall not give more and the poor shall not give less than half a shekel, when *you* give an offering to the LORD, to make atonement for yourselves.

16 "And you shall take the atonement money of the children of Israel, and shall appoint it for the service of the tabernacle of meeting, that it may be a memorial for the children of Israel before the LORD, to make atonement for yourselves."

THE BRONZE LAVER

17 Then the LORD spoke to Moses, saying:

18 "You shall also make a laver of bronze, with its base also of bronze, for washing. You shall put it between the tabernacle of meeting and the altar. And you shall put water in it,

19 "for Aaron and his sons shall wash their hands and their feet in water from it.

20 "When they go into the tabernacle of meeting, or when they come near the altar to minister, to burn an offering made by fire to the LORD, they shall wash with water, lest they die.

21 "So they shall wash their hands and their feet, lest they die. And it shall be a statute forever to them—to him and his descendants throughout their generations."

THE HOLY ANOINTING OIL

22 Moreover the LORD spoke to Moses, saying:

23 "Also take for yourself quality spices—five hundred *shekels* of liquid myrrh, half as much sweet-smelling cinnamon (two hundred and fifty *shekels*), two hundred and fifty *shekels* of sweet-smelling cane,

24 "five hundred *shekels* of cassia, according to the shekel of the sanctuary, and a hin of olive oil.

25 "And you shall make from these a holy anointing oil, an ointment compounded according to the art of the perfumer. It shall be a holy anointing oil.

26 "With it you shall anoint the tabernacle of meeting and the ark of the Testimony;

27 "the table and all its utensils, the

lampstand and its utensils, and the altar of incense;

28 "the altar of burnt offering with all its utensils, and the laver and its base.

29 "You shall consecrate them, that they may be most holy; whatever touches them must be holy.*a*

30 "And you shall anoint Aaron and his sons, and consecrate them, that *they* may minister to Me as priests.

31 "And you shall speak to the children of Israel, saying: 'This shall be a holy anointing oil to Me throughout your generations.

32 'It shall not be poured on man's flesh; nor shall you make *any other* like it, according to its composition. It *is* holy, *and* it shall be holy to you.

33 'Whoever compounds *any* like it, or whoever puts *any* of it on an outsider, shall be cut off from his people.'"

THE INCENSE

34 And the LORD said to Moses: "Take sweet spices, stacte and onycha and galbanum, and pure frankincense with *these* sweet spices; there shall be equal amounts of each.

35 "You shall make of these an incense, a compound according to the art of the perfumer, salted, pure, *and* holy.

36 "And you shall beat *some* of it very fine, and put some of it before the Testimony in the tabernacle of meeting where I will meet with you. It shall be most holy to you.

37 "But *as for* the incense which you shall make, you shall not make any for yourselves, according to its composition. It shall be to you holy for the LORD.

38 "Whoever makes *any* like it, to smell it, he shall be cut off from his people."

ARTISANS FOR BUILDING THE TABERNACLE

31 Then the LORD spoke to Moses, saying:

2 "See, I have called by name Bez'a·lel the son of Ū′rī, the son of Hur, of the tribe of Judah.

3 "And I have filled him with the Spirit of God, in wisdom, in understanding, in knowledge, and in all *manner of* workmanship,

4 "to design artistic works, to work in gold, in silver, in bronze,

5 "in cutting jewels for setting, in carving wood, and to work in all *manner of* workmanship.

6 "And I, indeed I, have appointed with him A·hō′li·ab the son of A·his′a·mach, of the tribe of Dan; and I have put wisdom in the hearts of all the gifted artisans, that they may make all that I have commanded you:

7 "the tabernacle of meeting, the ark of the Testimony and the mercy seat that *is* on it, and all the furniture of the tabernacle—

8 "the table and its utensils, the pure *gold* lampstand with all its utensils, the altar of incense,

9 "the altar of burnt offering with all its utensils, and the laver and its base—

10 "the garments of ministry,*a* the holy garments for Aaron the priest and the garments of his sons, to minister as priests,

11 "and the anointing oil and sweet incense for the holy *place*. According to all that I have commanded you they shall do."

THE SABBATH LAW

12 And the LORD spoke to Moses, saying,

30:29 *a*Compare Numbers 4:15 and Haggai 2:11–13
31:10 *a*Or *woven garments*

13 "Speak also to the children of Israel, saying: 'Surely My Sabbaths you shall keep, for it *is* a sign between Me and you throughout your generations, that *you* may know that I *am* the LORD who sanctifies you.

14 'You shall keep the Sabbath, therefore, for *it is* holy to you. Everyone who profanes it shall surely be put to death; for whoever does *any* work on it, that person shall be cut off from among his people.

15 'Work shall be done for six days, but the seventh *is* the Sabbath of rest, holy to the LORD. Whoever does *any* work on the Sabbath day, he shall surely be put to death.

16 'Therefore the children of Israel shall keep the Sabbath, to observe the Sabbath throughout their generations *as* a perpetual covenant.

17 'It *is* a sign between Me and the children of Israel forever; for *in* six days the LORD made the heavens and the earth, and on the seventh day He rested and was refreshed.' "

18 And when He had made an end of speaking with him on Mount Sinai, He gave Moses two tablets of the Testimony, tablets of stone, written with the finger of God.

THE GOLD CALF

Moses had been up on Mount Sinai for many days. He was there talking with God, and receiving all God's laws for the people. But the people thought Moses would not return, so they made up their own laws. They were not laws that pleased God. Here is what Moses did when he found out what the people were doing.

32 Now when the people saw that Moses delayed coming down from the mountain, the people gathered together to Aaron, and said to him, "Come, make us gods that shall go before us; for *as for* this Moses, the man who brought us up out of the land of Egypt, we do not know what has become of him."

2 And Aaron said to them, "Break off the golden earrings which *are* in the ears of your wives, your sons, and your daughters, and bring *them* to me."

3 So all the people broke off the golden earrings which *were* in their ears, and brought *them* to Aaron.

4 And he received *the gold* from their hand, and he fashioned it with an engraving tool, and made a molded calf. Then they said, "This *is* your god, O Israel, that brought you out of the land of Egypt!"

5 So when Aaron saw *it,* he built an altar before it. And Aaron made a proclamation and said, "Tomorrow *is* a feast to the LORD."

6 Then they rose early on the next day, offered burnt offerings, and brought peace offerings; and the people sat down to eat and drink, and rose up to play.

7 And the LORD said to Moses, "Go, get down! For your people whom you brought out of the land of Egypt have corrupted *themselves.*

8 "They have turned aside quickly out of the way which I commanded them. They have made themselves a molded calf, and worshiped it and sacrificed to it, and said, 'This *is* your god, O Israel, that brought you out of the land of Egypt!' "

9 And the LORD said to Moses, "I have seen this people, and indeed it *is* a stiff-necked people!

10 "Now therefore, let Me alone, that My wrath may burn hot against them and I may consume them. And I will make of you a great nation."

11 Then Moses pleaded with the

Lord his God, and said: "Lord, why does Your wrath burn hot against Your people whom You have brought out of the land of Egypt with great power and with a mighty hand?

12 "Why should the Egyptians speak, and say, 'He brought them out to harm them, to kill them in the mountains, and to consume them from the face of the earth'? Turn from Your fierce wrath, and relent from this harm to Your people.

13 "Remember Abraham, Isaac, and Israel, Your servants, to whom You swore by Your own self, and said to them, 'I will multiply your descendants as the stars of heaven; and all this land that I have spoken of I give to your descendants, and they shall inherit *it* forever.' "*a*

14 So the Lord relented from the harm which He said He would do to His people.

15 And Moses turned and went down from the mountain, and the two tablets of the Testimony *were* in his hand. The tablets *were* written on both sides; on the one *side* and on the other they were written.

16 Now the tablets *were* the work of God, and the writing *was* the writing of God engraved on the tablets.

17 And when Joshua heard the noise of the people as they shouted, he said to Moses, "*There is* a noise of war in the camp."

18 But he said:

"*It is* not the noise of the shout of
     victory,
Nor the noise of the cry of defeat,
But the sound of singing I hear."

19 So it was, as soon as he came near the camp, that he saw the calf *and* the dancing. So Moses' anger became hot, and he cast the tablets out of his hands and broke them at the foot of the mountain.

20 Then he took the calf which they had made, burned *it* in the fire, and ground *it* to powder; and he scattered *it* on the water and made the children of Israel drink *it*.

21 And Moses said to Aaron, "What did this people do to you that you have brought *so* great a sin upon them?"

22 So Aaron said, "Do not let the anger of my lord become hot. You know the people, that they *are set* on evil.

23 "For they said to me, 'Make us gods that shall go before us; *as for* this Moses, the man who brought us out of the land of Egypt, we do not know what has become of him.'

24 "And I said to them, 'Whoever has any gold, let them break *it* off.' So they gave *it* to me, and I cast it into the fire, and this calf came out."

25 Now when Moses saw that the people *were* unrestrained (for Aaron had not restrained them, to *their* shame among their enemies),

26 then Moses stood in the entrance of the camp, and said, "Whoever *is* on the Lord's side—*come* to me!" And all the sons of Levi gathered themselves together to him.

27 And he said to them, "Thus says the Lord God of Israel: 'Let every man put his sword on his side, and go in and out from entrance to entrance throughout the camp, and let every man kill his brother, every man his companion, and every man his neighbor.' "

28 So the sons of Levi did according to the word of Moses. And about three thousand men of the people fell that day.

29 Then Moses said, "Consecrate yourselves today to the Lord, that He may bestow on you a blessing this

32:13 *a*Genesis 13:15 and 22:17

day, for every man has opposed his son and his brother."

30 Now it came to pass on the next day that Moses said to the people, "You have committed a great sin. So now I will go up to the LORD; perhaps I can make atonement for your sin."

31 Then Moses returned to the LORD and said, "Oh, these people have committed a great sin, and have made for themselves a god of gold!

32 "Yet now, if You will forgive their sin—but if not, I pray, blot me out of Your book which You have written."

33 And the LORD said to Moses, "Whoever has sinned against Me, I will blot him out of My book.

34 "Now therefore, go, lead the people to *the place* of which I have spoken to you. Behold, My Angel shall go before you. Nevertheless, in the day when I visit for punishment, I will visit punishment upon them for their sin."

35 So the LORD plagued the people because of what they did with the calf which Aaron made.

Bible Quiz

Exodus 32 **The Gold Calf**

1. When Moses didn't come down the mountain, what did the people ask Aaron to do?
2. What did Aaron make?
3. Name three things Moses did when he saw the people sinning.
4. How did Aaron try to excuse his part in the wrongdoing?
5. When you do something wrong, do you ask God to forgive you, or do you try to make excuses? Which is the better thing to do?

THE COMMAND TO LEAVE SINAI

33 Then the LORD said to Moses, "Depart *and* go up from here, you and the people whom you have brought out of the land of Egypt, to the land of which I swore to Abraham, Isaac, and Jacob, saying, 'To your descendants I will give it.'

2 "And I will send *My* Angel before you, and I will drive out the Cā´-naan·īte and the Am´o·rīte and the Hit´tīte and the Per´iz·zīte and the Hī´vīte and the Jeb´ū·sīte.

3 "*Go up* to a land flowing with milk and honey; for I will not go up in your midst, lest I consume you on the way, for you *are* a stiff-necked people."

4 And when the people heard this bad news, they mourned, and no one put on his ornaments.

5 For the LORD had said to Moses, "Say to the children of Israel, 'You *are* a stiff-necked people. I could come up into your midst in one moment and consume you. Now therefore, take off your ornaments, that I may know what to do to you.' "

6 So the children of Israel stripped themselves of their ornaments by Mount Hō´reb.

MOSES MEETS WITH THE LORD

7 Moses took his tent and pitched it outside the camp, far from the camp, and called it the tabernacle of meeting. And it came to pass *that* everyone who sought the LORD went out to the tabernacle of meeting which *was* outside the camp.

8 So it was, whenever Moses went out to the tabernacle, *that* all the people rose, and each man stood *at* his tent door and watched Moses until he had gone into the tabernacle.

9 And it came to pass, when Moses entered the tabernacle, that the

ABOUT GOD'S WILL Exodus 33:13

How Can We Know What God Wants?

Some have asked, "Is it harder to know God's will or to do God's will when we know it?" Is it harder to know God's ways or to walk in them? Is it harder to know what God wants or to do what God wants? Which is harder? But first, how *do* you know what God wants? How do we know the mind of God?

1. In Moses' prayer, in Exodus 33:13, he asked for God to show him His way. There's one way to know God and what He wants—ask Him to help you. We know God and what He wants by talking with Him day by day.
2. Read Psalm 119:105. There's another way to know God and what He wants—by reading His Word.
3. Remember to read your Bible and pray daily. Ask God to show you what He wants.

For more on *What the Bible Says* turn to page 354
For more on *Obeying* turn to page 183

pillar of cloud descended and stood *at* the door of the tabernacle, and *the* LORD talked with Moses.

10 All the people saw the pillar of cloud standing *at* the tabernacle door, and all the people rose and worshiped, each man *in* his tent door.

11 So the LORD spoke to Moses face to face, as a man speaks to his friend. And he would return to the camp, but his servant Joshua the son of Nun, a young man, did not depart from the tabernacle.

THE PROMISE OF GOD'S PRESENCE

12 Then Moses said to the LORD, "See, You say to me, 'Bring up this people.' But You have not let me know whom You will send with me. Yet You have said, 'I know you by name, and you have also found grace in My sight.'

13 "Now therefore, I pray, if I have found grace in Your sight, show me now Your way, that I may know You and that I may find grace in Your sight. And consider that this nation *is* Your people."

14 And He said, "My Presence will go *with you,* and I will give you rest."

15 Then he said to Him, "If Your Presence does not go *with us,* do not bring us up from here.

16 "For how then will it be known that Your people and I have found grace in Your sight, except You go with us? So we shall be separate, Your people and I, from all the people who *are* upon the face of the earth."

17 So the LORD said to Moses, "I will also do this thing that you have spoken; for you have found grace in My sight, and I know you by name."

18 And he said, "Please, show me Your glory."

19 Then He said, "I will make all My goodness pass before you, and I will proclaim the name of the LORD before you. I will be gracious to whom I will be gracious, and I will have compassion on whom I will have compassion."

20 But He said, "You cannot see My face; for no man shall see Me, and live."

21 And the LORD said, "Here is a place by Me, and you shall stand on the rock.

22 "So it shall be, while My glory passes by, that I will put you in the cleft of the rock, and will cover you with My hand while I pass by.

23 "Then I will take away My hand, and you shall see My back; but My face shall not be seen."

MOSES MAKES NEW TABLETS

34 And the LORD said to Moses, "Cut two tablets of stone like the first *ones,* and I will write on *these* tablets the words that were on the first tablets which you broke.

2 "So be ready in the morning, and come up in the morning to Mount Sinai, and present yourself to Me there on the top of the mountain.

3 "And no man shall come up with you, and let no man be seen throughout all the mountain; let neither flocks nor herds feed before that mountain."

4 So he cut two tablets of stone like the first *ones.* Then Moses rose early in the morning and went up Mount Sinai, as the LORD had commanded him; and he took in his hand the two tablets of stone.

5 Now the LORD descended in the cloud and stood with him there, and proclaimed the name of the LORD.

6 And the LORD passed before him and proclaimed, "The LORD, the LORD God, merciful and gracious, long-suffering, and abounding in goodness and truth,

7 "keeping mercy for thousands, forgiving iniquity and transgression and sin, by no means clearing *the guilty,* visiting the iniquity of the fathers upon the children and the children's children to the third and the fourth generation."

8 So Moses made haste and bowed his head toward the earth, and worshiped.

9 Then he said, "If now I have found grace in Your sight, O Lord, let my Lord, I pray, go among us, even though we *are* a stiff-necked people; and pardon our iniquity and our sin, and take us as Your inheritance."

THE COVENANT RENEWED

10 And He said: "Behold, I make a covenant. Before all your people I will do marvels such as have not been done in all the earth, nor in any nation; and all the people among whom you *are* shall see the work of the LORD. For it *is* an awesome thing that I will do with you.

11 "Observe what I command you this day. Behold, I am driving out from before you the Am′o·rīte and the Cā′naan·īte and the Hit′tīte and the Per′iz·zīte and the Hī′vīte and the Jeb′ū·sīte.

12 "Take heed to yourself, lest you make a covenant with the inhabitants of the land where you are going, lest it be a snare in your midst.

13 "But you shall destroy their altars, break their *sacred* pillars, and cut down their wooden images

14 "(for you shall worship no other god, for the LORD, whose name *is* Jealous, *is* a jealous God),

15 "lest you make a covenant with the inhabitants of the land, and they play the harlot with their gods and make sacrifice to their gods, and *one of them* invites you and you eat of his sacrifice,

16 "and you take of his daughters for your sons, and his daughters play the harlot with their gods and make your sons play the harlot with their gods.

17 "You shall make no molded gods for yourselves.

18 "The Feast of Unleavened Bread you shall keep. Seven days you shall eat unleavened bread, as I commanded you, in the appointed time of the month of Ā′bib; for in the month of Ā′bib you came out from Egypt.

19 "All that open the womb *are* Mine, and every male firstborn among your livestock, *whether* ox or sheep.

20 "But the firstborn of a donkey you shall redeem with a lamb. And if you will not redeem *him,* then you shall break his neck. All the firstborn of your sons you shall redeem. And none shall appear before Me empty-handed.

21 "Six days you shall work, but on the seventh day you shall rest; in plowing time and in harvest you shall rest.

22 "And you shall observe the Feast of Weeks, of the firstfruits of wheat harvest, and the Feast of Ingathering at the year's end.

23 "Three times in the year all your men shall appear before the Lord, the LORD God of Israel.

24 "For I will cast out the nations before you and enlarge your borders; neither will any man covet your land when you go up to appear before the LORD your God three times in the year.

25 "You shall not offer the blood of My sacrifice with leaven, nor shall the sacrifice of the Feast of the Passover be left until morning.

26 "The first of the firstfruits of your land you shall bring to the house of the LORD your God. You shall not boil a young goat in its mother's milk."

27 Then the LORD said to Moses,

"Write these words, for according to the tenor of these words I have made a covenant with you and with Israel." 28 So he was there with the LORD forty days and forty nights; he neither ate bread nor drank water. And He wrote on the tablets the words of the covenant, the Ten Commandments.*a*

THE SHINING FACE OF MOSES

29 Now it was so, when Moses came down from Mount Sinai (and the two tablets of the Testimony *were* in Moses' hand when he came down from the mountain), that Moses did not know that the skin of his face shone while he talked with Him. 30 So when Aaron and all the children of Israel saw Moses, behold, the skin of his face shone, and they were afraid to come near him. 31 Then Moses called to them, and Aaron and all the rulers of the congregation returned to him; and Moses talked with them. 32 Afterward all the children of Israel came near, and he gave them as commandments all that the LORD had spoken with him on Mount Sinai. 33 And when Moses had finished speaking with them, he put a veil on his face. 34 But whenever Moses went in before the LORD to speak with Him, he would take the veil off until he came out; and he would come out and speak to the children of Israel whatever he had been commanded. 35 And whenever the children of Israel saw the face of Moses, that the skin of Moses' face shone, then Moses would put the veil on his face again, until he went in to speak with Him.

SABBATH REGULATIONS

35 Then Moses gathered all the congregation of the children of Israel together, and said to them, "These *are* the words which the LORD has commanded *you* to do: 2 "Work shall be done for six days, but the seventh day shall be a holy day for you, a Sabbath of rest to the LORD. Whoever does any work on it shall be put to death. 3 "You shall kindle no fire throughout your dwellings on the Sabbath day."

OFFERINGS FOR THE TABERNACLE

4 And Moses spoke to all the congregation of the children of Israel, saying, "This *is* the thing which the LORD commanded, saying: 5 'Take from among you an offering to the LORD. Whoever *is* of a willing heart, let him bring it as an offering to the LORD: gold, silver, and bronze; 6 'blue, purple, and scarlet *thread,* fine linen, and goats' *hair;* 7 'ram skins dyed red, badger skins, and acacia wood; 8 'oil for the light, and spices for the anointing oil and for the sweet incense; 9 'onyx stones, and stones to be set in the ephod and in the breastplate.

ARTICLES OF THE TABERNACLE

10 'All *who are* gifted artisans among you shall come and make all that the LORD has commanded: 11 'the tabernacle, its tent, its covering, its clasps, its boards, its bars, its pillars, and its sockets; 12 'the ark and its poles, *with* the mercy seat, and the veil of the covering; 13 'the table and its poles, all its utensils, and the showbread; 14 'also the lampstand for the light,

34:28 *a*Literally *Ten Words*

its utensils, its lamps, and the oil for the light;

15 'the incense altar, its poles, the anointing oil, the sweet incense, and the screen for the door at the entrance of the tabernacle;

16 'the altar of burnt offering with its bronze grating, its poles, all its utensils, *and* the laver and its base;

17 'the hangings of the court, its pillars, their sockets, and the screen for the gate of the court;

18 'the pegs of the tabernacle, the pegs of the court, and their cords;

19 'the garments of ministry,*a* for ministering in the holy *place*—the holy garments for Aaron the priest and the garments of his sons, to minister as priests.' "

THE TABERNACLE OFFERINGS PRESENTED

20 And all the congregation of the children of Israel departed from the presence of Moses.

21 Then everyone came whose heart was stirred, and everyone whose spirit was willing, *and* they brought the LORD's offering for the work of the tabernacle of meeting, for all its service, and for the holy garments.

22 They came, both men and women, as many as had a willing heart, *and* brought earrings and nose rings, rings and necklaces, all jewelry of gold, that is, every man who *made* an offering of gold to the LORD.

23 And every man, with whom was found blue, purple, and scarlet *thread,* fine linen, and goats' *hair,* red skins of rams, and badger skins, brought *them.*

24 Everyone who offered an offering of silver or bronze brought the LORD's offering. And everyone with whom was found acacia wood for any work of the service, brought *it.*

25 All the women *who were* gifted artisans spun yarn with their hands, and brought what they had spun, of blue, purple, *and* scarlet, and fine linen.

26 And all the women whose hearts stirred with wisdom spun yarn of goats' *hair.*

27 The rulers brought onyx stones, and the stones to be set in the ephod and in the breastplate,

28 and spices and oil for the light, for the anointing oil, and for the sweet incense.

29 The children of Israel brought a freewill offering to the LORD, all the men and women whose hearts were willing to bring *material* for all kinds of work which the LORD, by the hand of Moses, had commanded to be done.

THE ARTISANS CALLED BY GOD

30 And Moses said to the children of Israel, "See, the LORD has called by name Bez'a·lel the son of Ū'rī, the son of Hur, of the tribe of Judah;

31 "and He has filled him with the Spirit of God, in wisdom and understanding, in knowledge and all manner of workmanship,

32 "to design artistic works, to work in gold and silver and bronze,

33 "in cutting jewels for setting, in carving wood, and to work in all manner of artistic workmanship.

34 "And He has put in his heart the ability to teach, *in* him and A·hō'li·ab the son of A·his'a·mach, of the tribe of Dan.

35 "He has filled them with skill to do all manner of work of the engraver and the designer and the tapestry maker, in blue, purple, and scarlet *thread,* and fine linen, and of the weaver—those who do every work and those who design artistic works.

35:19 *a*Or *woven garments*

36 "And Bez′a·lel and A·hō′li·ab, and every gifted artisan in whom the LORD has put wisdom and understanding, to know how to do all manner of work for the service of the sanctuary, shall do according to all that the LORD has commanded."

THE PEOPLE GIVE MORE THAN ENOUGH

2 Then Moses called Bez′a·lel and A·hō′li·ab, and every gifted artisan in whose heart the LORD had put wisdom, everyone whose heart was stirred, to come and do the work.

3 And they received from Moses all the offering which the children of Israel had brought for the work of the service of making the sanctuary. So they continued bringing to him freewill offerings every morning.

4 Then all the craftsmen who were doing all the work of the sanctuary came, each from the work he was doing,

5 and they spoke to Moses, saying, "The people bring much more than enough for the service of the work which the LORD commanded us to do."

6 So Moses gave a commandment, and they caused it to be proclaimed throughout the camp, saying, "Let neither man nor woman do any more work for the offering of the sanctuary." And the people were restrained from bringing,

7 for the material they had was sufficient for all the work to be done—indeed too much.

BUILDING THE TABERNACLE

8 Then all the gifted artisans among them who worked on the tabernacle made ten curtains woven of fine linen, and of blue, purple, and scarlet *thread; with* artistic designs of cherubim they made them.

9 The length of each curtain *was* twenty-eight cubits, and the width of each curtain four cubits; the curtains *were* all the same size.

10 And he coupled five curtains to one another, and *the other* five curtains he coupled to one another.

11 He made loops of blue *yarn* on the edge of the curtain on the selvedge of one set; likewise he did on the outer edge of *the other* curtain of the second set.

12 Fifty loops he made on one curtain, and fifty loops he made on the edge of the curtain on the end of the second set; the loops held one *curtain* to another.

13 And he made fifty clasps of gold, and coupled the curtains to one another with the clasps, that it might be one tabernacle.

14 He made curtains of goats' *hair* for the tent over the tabernacle; he made eleven curtains.

15 The length of each curtain *was* thirty cubits, and the width of each curtain four cubits; the eleven curtains *were* the same size.

16 He coupled five curtains by themselves and six curtains by themselves.

17 And he made fifty loops on the edge of the curtain that is outermost in one set, and fifty loops he made on the edge of the curtain of the second set.

18 He also made fifty bronze clasps to couple the tent together, that it might be one.

19 Then he made a covering for the tent of ram skins dyed red, and a covering of badger skins above *that.*

20 For the tabernacle he made boards of acacia wood, standing upright.

21 The length of each board *was* ten

cubits, and the width of each board a cubit and a half.

22 Each board had two tenons for binding one to another. Thus he made for all the boards of the tabernacle.

23 And he made boards for the tabernacle, twenty boards for the south side.

24 Forty sockets of silver he made to go under the twenty boards: two sockets under each of the boards for its two tenons.

25 And for the other side of the tabernacle, the north side, he made twenty boards

26 and their forty sockets of silver: two sockets under each of the boards.

27 For the west side of the tabernacle he made six boards.

28 He also made two boards for the two back corners of the tabernacle.

29 And they were coupled at the bottom and coupled together at the top by one ring. Thus he made both of them for the two corners.

30 So there were eight boards and their sockets—sixteen sockets of silver—two sockets under each of the boards.

31 And he made bars of acacia wood: five for the boards on one side of the tabernacle,

32 five bars for the boards on the other side of the tabernacle, and five bars for the boards of the tabernacle on the far side westward.

33 And he made the middle bar to pass through the boards from one end to the other.

34 He overlaid the boards with gold, made their rings of gold to be holders for the bars, and overlaid the bars with gold.

35 And he made a veil of blue, purple, and scarlet thread, and fine woven linen; it was worked with an artistic design of cherubim.

36 He made for it four pillars of aca-cia wood, and overlaid them with gold, with their hooks of gold; and he cast four sockets of silver for them.

37 He also made a screen for the tabernacle door, of blue, purple, and scarlet thread, and fine woven linen, made by a weaver,

38 and its five pillars with their hooks. And he overlaid their capitals and their rings with gold, but their five sockets were bronze.

MAKING THE ARK OF THE TESTIMONY

37 Then Bez′a·lel made the ark of acacia wood; two and a half cubits was its length, a cubit and a half its width, and a cubit and a half its height.

2 He overlaid it with pure gold inside and outside, and made a molding of gold all around it.

3 And he cast for it four rings of gold to be set in its four corners: two rings on one side, and two rings on the other side of it.

4 He made poles of acacia wood, and overlaid them with gold.

5 And he put the poles into the rings at the sides of the ark, to bear the ark.

6 He also made the mercy seat of pure gold; two and a half cubits was its length and a cubit and a half its width.

7 He made two cherubim of beaten gold; he made them of one piece at the two ends of the mercy seat:

8 one cherub at one end on this side, and the other cherub at the other end on that side. He made the cherubim at the two ends of one piece with the mercy seat.

9 The cherubim spread out their wings above, and covered the mercy seat with their wings. They faced one

another; the faces of the cherubim were toward the mercy seat.

MAKING THE TABLE FOR THE SHOWBREAD

10 He made the table of acacia wood; two cubits *was* its length, a cubit its width, and a cubit and a half its height.

11 And he overlaid it with pure gold, and made a molding of gold all around it.

12 Also he made a frame of a hand-breadth all around it, and made a molding of gold for the frame all around it.

13 And he cast for it four rings of gold, and put the rings on the four corners that *were* at its four legs.

14 The rings were close to the frame, as holders for the poles to bear the table.

15 And he made the poles of acacia wood to bear the table, and overlaid them with gold.

16 He made of pure gold the utensils which were on the table: its dishes, its cups, its bowls, and its pitchers for pouring.

MAKING THE GOLD LAMPSTAND

17 He also made the lampstand of pure gold; of hammered work he made the lampstand. Its shaft, its branches, its bowls, its *ornamental* knobs, and its flowers were of the same piece.

18 And six branches came out of its sides: three branches of the lampstand out of one side, and three branches of the lampstand out of the other side.

19 There were three bowls made like almond *blossoms* on one branch, with an *ornamental* knob and a flower, and three bowls made like almond *blossoms* on the other branch, with

an *ornamental* knob and a flower— and so for the six branches coming out of the lampstand.

20 And on the lampstand itself *were* four bowls made like almond *blossoms, each with* its *ornamental* knob and flower.

21 *There was* a knob under the *first* two branches of the same, a knob under the *second* two branches of the same, and a knob under the *third* two branches of the same, according to the six branches extending from it.

22 Their knobs and their branches were of one piece; all of it *was* one hammered piece of pure gold.

23 And he made its seven lamps, its wick-trimmers, and its trays of pure gold.

24 Of a talent of pure gold he made it, with all its utensils.

MAKING THE ALTAR OF INCENSE

25 He made the incense altar of acacia wood. Its length *was* a cubit and its width a cubit—*it was* square—and two cubits *was* its height. Its horns were *of one piece* with it.

26 And he overlaid it with pure gold: its top, its sides all around, and its horns. He also made for it a molding of gold all around it.

27 He made two rings of gold for it under its molding, by its two corners on both sides, as holders for the poles with which to bear it.

28 And he made the poles of acacia wood, and overlaid them with gold.

MAKING THE ANOINTING OIL AND THE INCENSE

29 He also made the holy anointing oil and the pure incense of sweet spices, according to the work of the perfumer.

MAKING THE ALTAR OF BURNT OFFERING

38 He made the altar of burnt offering of acacia wood; five cubits *was* its length and five cubits its width—*it was* square—and its height *was* three cubits.

2 He made its horns on its four corners; the horns were *of one piece* with it. And he overlaid it with bronze.

3 He made all the utensils for the altar: the pans, the shovels, the basins, the forks, and the firepans; all its utensils he made of bronze.

4 And he made a grate of bronze network for the altar, under its rim, midway from the bottom.

5 He cast four rings for the four corners of the bronze grating, *as* holders for the poles.

6 And he made the poles of acacia wood, and overlaid them with bronze.

7 Then he put the poles into the rings on the sides of the altar, with which to bear it. He made the altar hollow with boards.

MAKING THE BRONZE LAVER

8 He made the laver of bronze and its base of bronze, from the bronze mirrors of the serving women who assembled at the door of the tabernacle of meeting.

MAKING THE COURT OF THE TABERNACLE

9 Then he made the court on the south side; the hangings of the court *were of* fine woven linen, one hundred cubits long.

10 There *were* twenty pillars for them, with twenty bronze sockets. The hooks of the pillars and their bands *were* silver.

11 On the north side *the hangings were* one hundred cubits *long,* with twenty pillars and their twenty bronze sockets. The hooks of the pillars and their bands *were* silver.

12 And on the west side *there were* hangings of fifty cubits, with ten pillars and their ten sockets. The hooks of the pillars and their bands *were* silver.

13 For the east side *the hangings were* fifty cubits.

14 The hangings of one side *of the gate were* fifteen cubits *long, with* their three pillars and their three sockets,

15 and the same for the other side of the court gate; on this side and that *were* hangings of fifteen cubits, *with* their three pillars and their three sockets.

16 All the hangings of the court all around *were of* fine woven linen.

17 The sockets for the pillars *were* bronze, the hooks of the pillars and their bands *were* silver, and the overlay of their capitals *was* silver; and all the pillars of the court had bands of silver.

18 The screen for the gate of the court *was* woven of blue, purple, and scarlet *thread,* and of fine woven linen. The length *was* twenty cubits, and the height along its width *was* five cubits, corresponding to the hangings of the court.

19 And *there were* four pillars *with* their four sockets of bronze; their hooks *were* silver, and the overlay of their capitals and their bands *was* silver.

20 All the pegs of the tabernacle, and of the court all around, *were* bronze.

MATERIALS OF THE TABERNACLE

21 This is the inventory of the tabernacle, the tabernacle of the Testimony, which was counted according to the commandment of Moses, for the service of the Lē′vītes, by the

hand of Ith′a·mar, son of Aaron the priest.

22 Bez′a·lel the son of Ū′rī, the son of Hur, of the tribe of Judah, made all that the LORD had commanded Moses.

23 And with him *was* A·hō′li·ab the son of A·his′a·mach, of the tribe of Dan, an engraver and designer, a weaver of blue, purple, and scarlet *thread,* and of fine linen.

24 All the gold that was used in all the work of the holy *place,* that is, the gold of the offering, was twenty-nine talents and seven hundred and thirty shekels, according to the shekel of the sanctuary.

25 And the silver from those who were numbered of the congregation *was* one hundred talents and one thousand seven hundred and seventy-five shekels, according to the shekel of the sanctuary:

26 a bekah for each man (*that is,* half a shekel, according to the shekel of the sanctuary), for everyone included in the numbering from twenty years old and above, for six hundred and three thousand, five hundred and fifty *men.*

27 And from the hundred talents of silver were cast the sockets of the sanctuary and the bases of the veil: one hundred sockets from the hundred talents, one talent for each socket.

28 Then from the one thousand seven hundred and seventy-five *shekels* he made hooks for the pillars, overlaid their capitals, and made bands for them.

29 The offering of bronze *was* seventy talents and two thousand four hundred shekels.

30 And with it he made the sockets for the door of the tabernacle of meeting, the bronze altar, the bronze grating for it, and all the utensils for the altar,

31 the sockets for the court all around, the bases for the court gate, all the pegs for the tabernacle, and all the pegs for the court all around.

MAKING THE GARMENTS OF THE PRIESTHOOD

39 Of the blue, purple, and scarlet *thread* they made garments of ministry,*a* for ministering in the holy *place,* and made the holy garments for Aaron, as the LORD had commanded Moses.

MAKING THE EPHOD

2 He made the ephod of gold, blue, purple, and scarlet *thread,* and of fine woven linen.

3 And they beat the gold into thin sheets and cut *it into* threads, to work *it* in *with* the blue, purple, and scarlet *thread,* and the fine linen, *into* artistic designs.

4 They made shoulder straps for it to couple *it* together; it was coupled together at its two edges.

5 And the intricately woven band of his ephod that *was* on it *was* of the same workmanship, *woven of* gold, blue, purple, and scarlet *thread,* and *of* fine woven linen, as the LORD had commanded Moses.

6 And they set onyx stones, enclosed in settings of gold; they were engraved, as signets are engraved, with the names of the sons of Israel.

7 He put them on the shoulders of the ephod *as* memorial stones for the sons of Israel, as the LORD had commanded Moses.

MAKING THE BREASTPLATE

8 And he made the breastplate, artistically woven like the workman-

39:1 *a*Or *woven garments*

ship of the ephod, of gold, blue, purple, and scarlet *thread,* and of fine woven linen.

9 They made the breastplate square by doubling it; a span *was* its length and a span its width when doubled.

10 And they set in it four rows of stones: a row with a sardius, a topaz, and an emerald was the first row;

11 the second row, a turquoise, a sapphire, and a diamond;

12 the third row, a jacinth, an agate, and an amethyst;

13 the fourth row, a beryl, an onyx, and a jasper. *They were* enclosed in settings of gold in their mountings.

14 *There were* twelve stones according to the names of the sons of Israel: according to their names, *engraved like* a signet, each one with its own name according to the twelve tribes.

15 And they made chains for the breastplate at the ends, like braided cords of pure gold.

16 They also made two settings of gold and two gold rings, and put the two rings on the two ends of the breastplate.

17 And they put the two braided *chains* of gold in the two rings on the ends of the breastplate.

18 The two ends of the two braided *chains* they fastened in the two settings, and put them on the shoulder straps of the ephod in the front.

19 And they made two rings of gold and put *them* on the two ends of the breastplate, on the edge of it, which *was* on the inward side of the ephod.

20 They made two *other* gold rings and put them on the two shoulder straps, underneath the ephod toward its front, right at the seam above the intricately woven band of the ephod.

21 And they bound the breastplate by means of its rings to the rings of the ephod with a blue cord, so that it would be above the intricately woven band of the ephod, and that the breastplate would not come loose from the ephod, as the LORD had commanded Moses.

MAKING THE OTHER PRIESTLY GARMENTS

22 He made the robe of the ephod of woven work, all of blue.

23 And *there was* an opening in the middle of the robe, like the opening in a coat of mail, *with* a woven binding all around the opening, so that it would not tear.

24 They made on the hem of the robe pomegranates of blue, purple, and scarlet, and of fine woven *linen.*

25 And they made bells of pure gold, and put the bells between the pomegranates on the hem of the robe all around between the pomegranates:

26 a bell and a pomegranate, a bell and a pomegranate, all around the hem of the robe to minister in, as the LORD had commanded Moses.

27 They made tunics, artistically woven of fine linen, for Aaron and his sons,

28 a turban of fine linen, exquisite hats of fine linen, short trousers of fine woven linen,

29 and a sash of fine woven linen with blue, purple, and scarlet *thread,* made by a weaver, as the LORD had commanded Moses.

30 Then they made the plate of the holy crown of pure gold, and wrote on it an inscription *like* the engraving of a signet:

HOLINESS TO THE LORD.

31 And they tied to it a blue cord, to fasten *it* above on the turban, as the LORD had commanded Moses.

THE WORK COMPLETED

32 Thus all the work of the tabernacle of the tent of meeting was fin-

ished. And the children of Israel did according to all that the LORD had commanded Moses; so they did.

33 And they brought the tabernacle to Moses, the tent and all its furnishings: its clasps, its boards, its bars, its pillars, and its sockets;

34 the covering of ram skins dyed red, the covering of badger skins, and the veil of the covering;

35 the ark of the Testimony with its poles, and the mercy seat;

36 the table, all its utensils, and the showbread;

37 the pure *gold* lampstand with its lamps (the lamps set in order), all its utensils, and the oil for light;

38 the gold altar, the anointing oil, and the sweet incense; the screen for the tabernacle door;

39 the bronze altar, its grate of bronze, its poles, and all its utensils; the laver with its base;

40 the hangings of the court, its pillars and its sockets, the screen for the court gate, its cords, and its pegs; all the utensils for the service of the tabernacle, for the tent of meeting;

41 and the garments of ministry,*a* to minister in the holy *place:* the holy garments for Aaron the priest, and his sons' garments, to minister as priests.

42 According to all that the LORD had commanded Moses, so the children of Israel did all the work.

43 Then Moses looked over all the work, and indeed they had done it; as the LORD had commanded, just so they had done it. And Moses blessed them.

THE TABERNACLE ERECTED AND ARRANGED

40 Then the LORD spoke to Moses, saying:

2 "On the first day of the first month you shall set up the tabernacle of the tent of meeting.

3 "You shall put in it the ark of the Testimony, and partition off the ark with the veil.

4 "You shall bring in the table and arrange the things that are to be set in order on it; and you shall bring in the lampstand and light its lamps.

5 "You shall also set the altar of gold for the incense before the ark of the Testimony, and put up the screen for the door of the tabernacle.

6 "Then you shall set the altar of the burnt offering before the door of the tabernacle of the tent of meeting.

7 "And you shall set the laver between the tabernacle of meeting and the altar, and put water in it.

8 "You shall set up the court all around, and hang up the screen at the court gate.

9 "And you shall take the anointing oil, and anoint the tabernacle and all that *is* in it; and you shall hallow it and all its utensils, and it shall be holy.

10 "You shall anoint the altar of the burnt offering and all its utensils, and consecrate the altar. The altar shall be most holy.

11 "And you shall anoint the laver and its base, and consecrate it.

12 "Then you shall bring Aaron and his sons to the door of the tabernacle of meeting and wash them with water.

13 "You shall put the holy garments on Aaron, and anoint him and consecrate him, that he may minister to Me as priest.

14 "And you shall bring his sons and clothe them with tunics.

15 "You shall anoint them, as you anointed their father, that they may minister to Me as priests; for their anointing shall surely be an everlast-

39:41 *a*Or *woven garments*

ing priesthood throughout their generations."

16 Thus Moses did; according to all that the LORD had commanded him, so he did.

17 And it came to pass in the first month of the second year, on the first *day* of the month, *that* the tabernacle was raised up.

18 So Moses raised up the tabernacle, fastened its sockets, set up its boards, put in its bars, and raised up its pillars.

19 And he spread out the tent over the tabernacle and put the covering of the tent on top of it, as the LORD had commanded Moses.

20 He took the Testimony and put *it* into the ark, inserted the poles through the rings of the ark, and put the mercy seat on top of the ark.

21 And he brought the ark into the tabernacle, hung up the veil of the covering, and partitioned off the ark of the Testimony, as the LORD had commanded Moses.

22 He put the table in the tabernacle of meeting, on the north side of the tabernacle, outside the veil;

23 and he set the bread in order upon it before the LORD, as the LORD had commanded Moses.

24 He put the lampstand in the tabernacle of meeting, across from the table, on the south side of the tabernacle;

25 and he lit the lamps before the LORD, as the LORD had commanded Moses.

26 He put the gold altar in the tabernacle of meeting in front of the veil;

27 and he burned sweet incense on it, as the LORD had commanded Moses.

28 He hung up the screen *at* the door of the tabernacle.

29 And he put the altar of burnt offering *before* the door of the tabernacle of the tent of meeting, and offered upon it the burnt offering and the grain offering, as the LORD had commanded Moses.

30 He set the laver between the tabernacle of meeting and the altar, and put water there for washing;

31 and Moses, Aaron, and his sons would wash their hands and their feet *with water* from it.

32 Whenever they went into the tabernacle of meeting, and when they came near the altar, they washed, as the LORD had commanded Moses.

33 And he raised up the court all around the tabernacle and the altar, and hung up the screen of the court gate. So Moses finished the work.

THE CLOUD AND THE GLORY

34 Then the cloud covered the tabernacle of meeting, and the glory of the LORD filled the tabernacle.

35 And Moses was not able to enter the tabernacle of meeting, because the cloud rested above it, and the glory of the LORD filled the tabernacle.

36 Whenever the cloud was taken up from above the tabernacle, the children of Israel would go onward in all their journeys.

37 But if the cloud was not taken up, then they did not journey till the day that it was taken up.

38 For the cloud of the LORD *was* above the tabernacle by day, and fire was over it by night, in the sight of all the house of Israel, throughout all their journeys.

LEVITICUS

THE BURNT OFFERING

NOW the LORD called to Moses, and spoke to him from the tabernacle of meeting, saying,

2 "Speak to the children of Israel, and say to them: 'When any one of you brings an offering to the LORD, you shall bring your offering of the livestock—of the herd and of the flock.

3 'If his offering is a burnt sacrifice of the herd, let him offer a male without blemish; he shall offer it of his own free will at the door of the tabernacle of meeting before the LORD.

4 'Then he shall put his hand on the head of the burnt offering, and it will be accepted on his behalf to make atonement for him.

5 'He shall kill the bull before the LORD; and the priests, Aaron's sons, shall bring the blood and sprinkle the blood all around on the altar that is by the door of the tabernacle of meeting.

6 'And he shall skin the burnt offering and cut it into its pieces.

7 'The sons of Aaron the priest shall put fire on the altar, and lay the wood in order on the fire.

8 'Then the priests, Aaron's sons, shall lay the parts, the head, and the fat in order on the wood that is on the fire upon the altar;

9 'but he shall wash its entrails and its legs with water. And the priest shall burn all on the altar as a burnt sacrifice, an offering made by fire, a sweet aroma to the LORD.

10 'If his offering is of the flocks—of the sheep or of the goats—as a burnt sacrifice, he shall bring a male without blemish.

11 'He shall kill it on the north side of the altar before the LORD; and the priests, Aaron's sons, shall sprinkle its blood all around on the altar.

12 'And he shall cut it into its pieces, with its head and its fat; and the priest shall lay them in order on the wood that is on the fire upon the altar;

13 'but he shall wash the entrails and the legs with water. Then the priest shall bring it all and burn it on the altar; it is a burnt sacrifice, an offering made by fire, a sweet aroma to the LORD.

14 'And if the burnt sacrifice of his offering to the LORD is of birds, then he shall bring his offering of turtledoves or young pigeons.

15 'The priest shall bring it to the altar, wring off its head, and burn it on the altar; its blood shall be drained out at the side of the altar.

16 'And he shall remove its crop with its feathers and cast it beside the altar on the east side, into the place for ashes.

17 'Then he shall split it at its wings, but shall not divide it completely; and the priest shall burn it on the altar, on the wood that is on the fire. It is a burnt sacrifice, an offering made by fire, a sweet aroma to the LORD.

THE GRAIN OFFERING

2 'When anyone offers a grain offering to the LORD, his offering shall be of fine flour. And he shall pour oil on it, and put frankincense on it.

2 'He shall bring it to Aaron's sons, the priests, one of whom shall take from it his handful of fine flour and oil with all the frankincense. And the priest shall burn it as a memorial on the altar, an offering made by fire, a sweet aroma to the LORD.

3 'The rest of the grain offering *shall be* Aaron's and his sons'. *It is* most holy of the offerings to the LORD made by fire.

4 'And if you bring as an offering a grain offering baked in the oven, *it shall be* unleavened cakes of fine flour mixed with oil, or unleavened wafers anointed with oil.

5 'But if your offering *is* a grain offering *baked* in a pan, *it shall be of* fine flour, unleavened, mixed with oil.

6 'You shall break it in pieces and pour oil on it; it *is* a grain offering.

7 'If your offering *is* a grain offering *baked* in a covered pan, it shall be made *of* fine flour with oil.

8 'You shall bring the grain offering that is made of these things to the LORD. And when it is presented to the priest, he shall bring it to the altar.

9 'Then the priest shall take from the grain offering a memorial portion, and burn *it* on the altar. *It is* an offering made by fire, a sweet aroma to the LORD.

10 'And what is left of the grain offering *shall be* Aaron's and his sons'. *It is* most holy of the offerings to the LORD made by fire.

11 'No grain offering which you bring to the LORD shall be made with leaven, for you shall burn no leaven nor any honey in any offering to the LORD made by fire.

12 'As for the offering of the first-fruits, you shall offer them to the LORD, but they shall not be burned on the altar for a sweet aroma.

13 'And every offering of your grain offering you shall season with salt; you shall not allow the salt of the covenant of your God to be lacking from your grain offering. With all your offerings you shall offer salt.

14 'If you offer a grain offering of your firstfruits to the LORD, you shall offer for the grain offering of your firstfruits green heads of grain roasted on the fire, grain beaten from full heads.

15 'And you shall put oil on it, and lay frankincense on it. It *is* a grain offering.

16 'Then the priest shall burn the memorial portion: *part* of its beaten grain and *part* of its oil, with all the frankincense, as an offering made by fire to the LORD.

THE PEACE OFFERING

3 'When his offering *is* a sacrifice of a peace offering, if he offers *it* of the herd, whether male or female, he shall offer it without blemish before the LORD.

2 'And he shall lay his hand on the head of his offering, and kill it *at* the door of the tabernacle of meeting; and Aaron's sons, the priests, shall sprinkle the blood all around on the altar.

3 'Then he shall offer from the sacrifice of the peace offering an offering made by fire to the LORD. The fat that covers the entrails and all the fat that *is* on the entrails,

4 'the two kidneys and the fat that *is* on them by the flanks, and the fatty lobe *attached* to the liver above the kidneys, he shall remove;

5 'and Aaron's sons shall burn it on the altar upon the burnt sacrifice, which *is* on the wood that *is* on the fire, *as* an offering made by fire, a sweet aroma to the LORD.

6 'If his offering as a sacrifice of a peace offering to the LORD *is* of the flock, *whether* male or female, he shall offer it without blemish.

7 'If he offers a lamb as his offering, then he shall offer it before the LORD.

8 'And he shall lay his hand on the head of his offering, and kill it before the tabernacle of meeting; and Aaron's sons shall sprinkle its blood all around on the altar.

9 'Then he shall offer from the sacrifice of the peace offering, as an offering made by fire to the LORD, its fat *and* the whole fat tail which he shall remove close to the backbone. And the fat that covers the entrails and all the fat that *is* on the entrails,

10 'the two kidneys and the fat that *is* on them by the flanks, and the fatty lobe *attached* to the liver above the kidneys, he shall remove;

11 'and the priest shall burn *them* on the altar *as* food, an offering made by fire to the LORD.

12 'And if his offering *is* a goat, then he shall offer it before the LORD.

13 'He shall lay his hand on its head and kill it before the tabernacle of meeting; and the sons of Aaron shall sprinkle its blood all around on the altar.

14 'Then he shall offer from it his offering, as an offering made by fire to the LORD. The fat that covers the entrails and all the fat that *is* on the entrails,

15 'the two kidneys and the fat that *is* on them by the flanks, and the fatty lobe *attached* to the liver above the kidneys, he shall remove;

16 'and the priest shall burn them on the altar *as* food, an offering made by fire for a sweet aroma; all the fat *is* the LORD's.

17 *'This shall be* a perpetual statute throughout your generations in all your dwellings: you shall eat neither fat nor blood.' "

THE SIN OFFERING

4 Now the LORD spoke to Moses, saying,

2 "Speak to the children of Israel, saying: 'If a person sins unintentionally against any of the commandments of the LORD *in anything* which ought not to be done, and does any of them,

3 'if the anointed priest sins, bringing guilt on the people, then let him offer to the LORD for his sin which he has sinned a young bull without blemish as a sin offering.

4 'He shall bring the bull to the door of the tabernacle of meeting before the LORD, lay his hand on the bull's head, and kill the bull before the LORD.

5 'Then the anointed priest shall take some of the bull's blood and bring it to the tabernacle of meeting.

6 'The priest shall dip his finger in the blood and sprinkle some of the blood seven times before the LORD, in front of the veil of the sanctuary.

7 'And the priest shall put some of the blood on the horns of the altar of sweet incense before the LORD, which is in the tabernacle of meeting; and he shall pour the remaining blood of the bull at the base of the altar of the burnt offering, which is at the door of the tabernacle of meeting.

8 'He shall take from it all the fat of the bull as the sin offering. The fat that covers the entrails and all the fat which *is* on the entrails,

9 'the two kidneys and the fat that *is* on them by the flanks, and the fatty lobe *attached* to the liver above the kidneys, he shall remove,

10 'as it was taken from the bull of the sacrifice of the peace offering; and the priest shall burn them on the altar of the burnt offering.

11 'But the bull's hide and all its flesh, with its head and legs, its entrails and offal—

12 'the whole bull he shall carry outside the camp to a clean place, where the ashes are poured out, and burn it on wood with fire; where the ashes are poured out it shall be burned.

13 'Now if the whole congregation of Israel sins unintentionally, and the thing is hidden from the eyes of the assembly, and they have done some-

thing against any of the command-ments of the LORD *in anything* which should not be done, and are guilty;

14 'when the sin which they have committed becomes known, then the assembly shall offer a young bull for the sin, and bring it before the taber-nacle of meeting.

15 'And the elders of the congrega-tion shall lay their hands on the head of the bull before the LORD. Then the bull shall be killed before the LORD.

16 'The anointed priest shall bring some of the bull's blood to the taber-nacle of meeting.

17 'Then the priest shall dip his fin-ger in the blood and sprinkle *it* seven times before the LORD, in front of the veil.

18 'And he shall put *some* of the blood on the horns of the altar which *is* before the LORD, which *is* in the tabernacle of meeting; and he shall pour the remaining blood at the base of the altar of burnt offering, which is at the door of the tabernacle of meet-ing.

19 'He shall take all the fat from it and burn *it* on the altar.

20 'And he shall do with the bull as he did with the bull as a sin offering; thus he shall do with it. So the priest shall make atonement for them, and it shall be forgiven them.

21 'Then he shall carry the bull out-side the camp, and burn it as he burned the first bull. It *is* a sin offer-ing for the assembly.

22 'When a ruler has sinned, and done *something* unintentionally *against* any of the commandments of the LORD his God *in anything* which should not be done, and is guilty,

23 'or if his sin which he has commit-ted comes to his knowledge, he shall bring as his offering a kid of the goats, a male without blemish.

24 'And he shall lay his hand on the head of the goat, and kill it at the place where they kill the burnt offering before the LORD. It *is* a sin offering.

25 'The priest shall take some of the blood of the sin offering with his fin-ger, put *it* on the horns of the altar of burnt offering, and pour its blood at the base of the altar of burnt offering.

26 'And he shall burn all its fat on the altar, like the fat of the sacrifice of the peace offering. So the priest shall make atonement for him con-cerning his sin, and it shall be for-given him.

27 'If anyone of the common people sins unintentionally by doing *some-thing against* any of the command-ments of the LORD *in anything* which ought not to be done, and is guilty,

28 'or if his sin which he has commit-ted comes to his knowledge, then he shall bring as his offering a kid of the goats, a female without blemish, for his sin which he has committed.

29 'And he shall lay his hand on the head of the sin offering, and kill the sin offering at the place of the burnt offering.

30 'Then the priest shall take *some* of its blood with his finger, put *it* on the horns of the altar of burnt offer-ing, and pour all *the remaining* blood at the base of the altar.

31 'He shall remove all its fat, as fat is removed from the sacrifice of the peace offering; and the priest shall burn it on the altar for a sweet aroma to the LORD. So the priest shall make atonement for him, and it shall be forgiven him.

32 'If he brings a lamb as his sin of-fering, he shall bring a female with-out blemish.

33 'Then he shall lay his hand on the head of the sin offering, and kill it as a sin offering at the place where they kill the burnt offering.

34 'The priest shall take *some* of the blood of the sin offering with his fin-

ger, put *it* on the horns of the altar of burnt offering, and pour all *the remaining* blood at the base of the altar.

35 'He shall remove all its fat, as the fat of the lamb is removed from the sacrifice of the peace offering. Then the priest shall burn it on the altar, according to the offerings made by fire to the LORD. So the priest shall make atonement for his sin that he has committed, and it shall be forgiven him.

THE TRESPASS OFFERING

5 'If a person sins in hearing the utterance of an oath, and *is* a witness, whether he has seen or known *of the matter*—if he does not tell *it,* he bears guilt.

2 'Or if a person touches any unclean thing, whether *it is* the carcass of an unclean beast, or the carcass of unclean livestock, or the carcass of unclean creeping things, and he is unaware of it, he also shall be unclean and guilty.

3 'Or if he touches human uncleanness—whatever uncleanness with which a man may be defiled, and he is unaware of it—when he realizes *it,* then he shall be guilty.

4 'Or if a person swears, speaking thoughtlessly with *his* lips to do evil or to do good, whatever *it is* that a man may pronounce by an oath, and he is unaware of it—when he realizes *it,* then he shall be guilty in any of these *matters.*

5 'And it shall be, when he is guilty in any of these *matters,* that he shall confess that he has sinned in that *thing;*

6 'and he shall bring his trespass offering to the LORD for his sin which he has committed, a female from the flock, a lamb or a kid of the goats as a sin offering. So the priest shall make atonement for him concerning his sin.

7 'If he is not able to bring a lamb, then he shall bring to the LORD, for his trespass which he has committed, two turtledoves or two young pigeons: one as a sin offering and the other as a burnt offering.

8 'And he shall bring them to the priest, who shall offer *that* which *is* for the sin offering first, and wring off its head from its neck, but shall not divide *it* completely.

9 'Then he shall sprinkle *some* of the blood of the sin offering on the side of the altar, and the rest of the blood shall be drained out at the base of the altar. It *is* a sin offering.

10 'And he shall offer the second *as* a burnt offering according to the prescribed manner. So the priest shall make atonement on his behalf for his sin which he has committed, and it shall be forgiven him.

11 'But if he is not able to bring two turtledoves or two young pigeons, then he who sinned shall bring for his offering one-tenth of an ephah of fine flour as a sin offering. He shall put no oil on it, nor shall he put frankincense on it, for it *is* a sin offering.

12 'Then he shall bring it to the priest, and the priest shall take his handful of it as a memorial portion, and burn *it* on the altar according to the offerings made by fire to the LORD. It *is* a sin offering.

13 'The priest shall make atonement for him, for his sin that he has committed in any of these matters; and it shall be forgiven him. *The rest* shall be the priest's as a grain offering.' "

OFFERINGS WITH RESTITUTION

14 Then the LORD spoke to Moses, saying:

15 "If a person commits a trespass, and sins unintentionally in regard to the holy things of the LORD, then he shall bring to the LORD as his trespass offering a ram without blemish from the flocks, with your valuation in shekels of silver according to the shekel of the sanctuary, as a trespass offering.

16 "And he shall make restitution for the harm that he has done in regard to the holy thing, and shall add one-fifth to it and give it to the priest. So the priest shall make atonement for him with the ram of the trespass offering, and it shall be forgiven him.

17 "If a person sins, and commits any of these things which are forbidden to be done by the commandments of the LORD, though he does not know *it,* yet he is guilty and shall bear his iniquity.

18 "And he shall bring to the priest a ram without blemish from the flock, with your valuation, as a trespass offering. So the priest shall make atonement for him regarding his ignorance in which he erred and did not know *it,* and it shall be forgiven him.

19 "It is a trespass offering; he has certainly trespassed against the LORD."

6

And the LORD spoke to Moses, saying:

2 "If a person sins and commits a trespass against the LORD by lying to his neighbor about what was delivered to him for safekeeping, or about a pledge, or about a robbery, or if he has extorted from his neighbor,

3 "or if he has found what was lost and lies concerning it, and swears falsely—in any one of these things that a man may do in which he sins:

4 "then it shall be, because he has sinned and is guilty, that he shall restore what he has stolen, or the thing which he has extorted, or what was delivered to him for safekeeping, or the lost thing which he found,

5 "or all that about which he has sworn falsely. He shall restore its full value, add one-fifth more to it, *and* give it to whomever it belongs, on the day of his trespass offering.

6 "And he shall bring his trespass offering to the LORD, a ram without blemish from the flock, with your valuation, as a trespass offering, to the priest.

7 "So the priest shall make atonement for him before the LORD, and he shall be forgiven for any one of these things that he may have done in which he trespasses."

THE LAW OF THE BURNT OFFERING

8 Then the LORD spoke to Moses, saying,

9 "Command Aaron and his sons, saying, 'This *is* the law of the burnt offering: The burnt offering *shall be* on the hearth upon the altar all night until morning, and the fire of the altar shall be kept burning on it.

10 'And the priest shall put on his linen garment, and his linen trousers he shall put on his body, and take up the ashes of the burnt offering which the fire has consumed on the altar, and he shall put them beside the altar.

11 'Then he shall take off his garments, put on other garments, and carry the ashes outside the camp to a clean place.

12 'And the fire on the altar shall be kept burning on it; it shall not be put out. And the priest shall burn wood on it every morning, and lay the burnt offering in order on it; and he shall burn on it the fat of the peace offerings.

13 'A fire shall always be burning on the altar; it shall never go out.

What Should I Do?

WHO CLEANS UP THE MESS? Leviticus 6:8–11

Mother wants to polish and wax the table. Kitty and Puppy want to play. But look what they did while they were playing. Now who will clean up the mess? Do you think Kitty and Puppy will do it?

1. When mother makes a mess, who cleans it up? Does she? Should she?
2. When you make a mess, who cleans it up? Do you? Should you?
3. When mother cleans up your mess, what do you say to her? What should you say? Why?

For more on *What Should I Do?* turn to page 180
For more on *Responsibility* turn to page 1753

THE LAW OF THE GRAIN OFFERING

14 'This *is* the law of the grain offering: The sons of Aaron shall offer it on the altar before the LORD.

15 'He shall take from it his handful of the fine flour of the grain offering, with its oil, and all the frankincense which *is* on the grain offering, and shall burn *it* on the altar *for* a sweet aroma, as a memorial to the LORD.

16 'And the remainder of it Aaron and his sons shall eat; with unleavened bread it shall be eaten in a holy place; in the court of the tabernacle of meeting they shall eat it.

17 'It shall not be baked with leaven. I have given it *as* their portion of My offerings made by fire; it *is* most holy, like the sin offering and the trespass offering.

18 'All the males among the children of Aaron may eat it. *It shall be* a statute forever in your generations concerning the offerings made by fire to the LORD. Everyone who touches them must be holy.' "*a*

19 And the LORD spoke to Moses, saying,

20 "This *is* the offering of Aaron and his sons, which they shall offer to the LORD, *beginning* on the day when he is anointed: one-tenth of an ephah of fine flour as a daily grain offering, half of it in the morning and half of it at night.

21 "It shall be made in a pan with oil. *When it is* mixed, you shall bring it in. The baked pieces of the grain offering you shall offer *for* a sweet aroma to the LORD.

22 "The priest from among his sons, who is anointed in his place, shall offer it. *It is* a statute forever to the LORD. It shall be wholly burned.

23 "For every grain offering for the priest shall be wholly burned. It shall not be eaten."

THE LAW OF THE SIN OFFERING

24 Also the LORD spoke to Moses, saying,

25 "Speak to Aaron and to his sons, saying, 'This *is* the law of the sin offering: In the place where the burnt offering is killed, the sin offering shall be killed before the LORD. It *is* most holy.

26 'The priest who offers it for sin shall eat it. In a holy place it shall be eaten, in the court of the tabernacle of meeting.

27 'Everyone who touches its flesh must be holy.*a* And when its blood is sprinkled on any garment, you shall wash that on which it was sprinkled, in a holy place.

28 'But the earthen vessel in which it is boiled shall be broken. And if it is boiled in a bronze pot, it shall be both scoured and rinsed in water.

29 'All the males among the priests may eat it. It *is* most holy.

30 'But no sin offering from which *any* of the blood is brought into the tabernacle of meeting, to make atonement in the holy *place,a* shall be eaten. It shall be burned in the fire.

THE LAW OF THE TRESPASS OFFERING

7 'Likewise this *is* the law of the trespass offering (it *is* most holy):

2 'In the place where they kill the burnt offering they shall kill the trespass offering. And its blood he shall sprinkle all around on the altar.

3 'And he shall offer from it all its fat. The fat tail and the fat that covers the entrails,

4 'the two kidneys and the fat that *is* on them by the flanks, and the

6:18 *a*Compare Numbers 4:15 and Haggai 2:11–13
6:27 *a*Compare Numbers 4:15 and Haggai 2:11–13
6:30 *a*The Most Holy Place when capitalized

fatty lobe *attached* to the liver above the kidneys, he shall remove;

5 'and the priest shall burn them on the altar *as* an offering made by fire to the LORD. It *is* a trespass offering.

6 'Every male among the priests may eat it. It shall be eaten in a holy place. It *is* most holy.

7 'The trespass offering *is* like the sin offering; *there is* one law for them both: the priest who makes atonement with it shall have *it*.

8 'And the priest who offers anyone's burnt offering, that priest shall have for himself the skin of the burnt offering which he has offered.

9 'Also every grain offering that is baked in the oven and all that is prepared in the covered pan, or in a pan, shall be the priest's who offers it.

10 'Every grain offering, *whether* mixed with oil or dry, shall belong to all the sons of Aaron, to one *as much* as the other.

THE LAW OF PEACE OFFERINGS

11 'This *is* the law of the sacrifice of peace offerings which he shall offer to the LORD:

12 'If he offers it for a thanksgiving, then he shall offer, with the sacrifice of thanksgiving, unleavened cakes mixed with oil, unleavened wafers anointed with oil, or cakes of blended flour mixed with oil.

13 'Besides the cakes, *as* his offering he shall offer leavened bread with the sacrifice of thanksgiving of his peace offering.

14 'And from it he shall offer one cake from each offering *as* a heave offering to the LORD. It shall belong to the priest who sprinkles the blood of the peace offering.

15 'The flesh of the sacrifice of his peace offering for thanksgiving shall be eaten the same day it is offered.

He shall not leave any of it until morning.

16 'But if the sacrifice of his offering *is* a vow or a voluntary offering, it shall be eaten the same day that he offers his sacrifice; but on the next day the remainder of it also may be eaten;

17 'the remainder of the flesh of the sacrifice on the third day must be burned with fire.

18 'And if *any* of the flesh of the sacrifice of his peace offering is eaten at all on the third day, it shall not be accepted, nor shall it be imputed to him; it shall be an abomination *to* him who offers it, and the person who eats of it shall bear guilt.

19 'The flesh that touches any unclean thing shall not be eaten. It shall be burned with fire. And as for the *clean* flesh, all who are clean may eat of it.

20 'But the person who eats the flesh of the sacrifice of the peace offering that *belongs* to the LORD, while he is unclean, that person shall be cut off from his people.

21 'Moreover the person who touches any unclean thing, *such as* human uncleanness, *an* unclean animal, or any abominable unclean thing,*a* and who eats the flesh of the sacrifice of the peace offering that *belongs* to the LORD, that person shall be cut off from his people.' "

FAT AND BLOOD MAY NOT BE EATEN

22 And the LORD spoke to Moses, saying,

23 "Speak to the children of Israel, saying: 'You shall not eat any fat, of ox or sheep or goat.

24 'And the fat of an animal that

7:21 *a*Following Masoretic Text, Septuagint, and Vulgate; Samaritan Pentateuch, Syriac, and Targum read *swarming thing* (compare 5:2).

dies *naturally,* and the fat of what is torn by wild beasts, may be used in any other way; but you shall by no means eat it.

25 'For whoever eats the fat of the animal of which men offer an offering made by fire to the LORD, the person who eats *it* shall be cut off from his people.

26 'Moreover you shall not eat any blood in any of your dwellings, *whether* of bird or beast.

27 'Whoever eats any blood, that person shall be cut off from his people.' "

THE PORTION OF AARON AND HIS SONS

28 Then the LORD spoke to Moses, saying,

29 "Speak to the children of Israel, saying: 'He who offers the sacrifice of his peace offering to the LORD shall bring his offering to the LORD from the sacrifice of his peace offering.

30 'His own hands shall bring the offerings made by fire to the LORD. The fat with the breast he shall bring, that the breast may be waved *as a* wave offering before the LORD.

31 'And the priest shall burn the fat on the altar, but the breast shall be Aaron's and his sons'.

32 'Also the right thigh you shall give to the priest *as* a heave offering from the sacrifices of your peace offerings.

33 'He among the sons of Aaron, who offers the blood of the peace offering and the fat, shall have the right thigh for *his* part.

34 'For the breast of the wave offering and the thigh of the heave offering I have taken from the children of Israel, from the sacrifices of their peace offerings, and I have given them to Aaron the priest and to his sons from the children of Israel by a statute forever.' "

35 This *is* the consecrated portion for Aaron and his sons, from the offerings made by fire to the LORD, on the day when *Moses* presented them to minister to the LORD as priests.

36 The LORD commanded this to be given to them by the children of Israel, on the day that He anointed them, *by* a statute forever throughout their generations.

37 This *is* the law of the burnt offering, the grain offering, the sin offering, the trespass offering, the consecrations, and the sacrifice of the peace offering,

38 which the LORD commanded Moses on Mount Sinai, on the day when He commanded the children of Israel to offer their offerings to the LORD in the Wilderness of Sinai.

AARON AND HIS SONS CONSECRATED

8 And the LORD spoke to Moses, saying:

2 "Take Aaron and his sons with him, and the garments, the anointing oil, a bull as the sin offering, two rams, and a basket of unleavened bread;

3 "and gather all the congregation together at the door of the tabernacle of meeting."

4 So Moses did as the LORD commanded him. And the congregation was gathered together at the door of the tabernacle of meeting.

5 And Moses said to the congregation, "This *is* what the LORD commanded to be done."

6 Then Moses brought Aaron and his sons and washed them with water.

7 And he put the tunic on him, girded him with the sash, clothed him with the robe, and put the ephod on him; and he girded him with the intricately woven band of the ephod, and with it tied *the ephod* on him.

8 Then he put the breastplate on him, and he put the Ū′rim and the Thum′mim*a* in the breastplate.

9 And he put the turban on his head. Also on the turban, on its front, he put the golden plate, the holy crown, as the LORD had commanded Moses.

10 Also Moses took the anointing oil, and anointed the tabernacle and all that *was* in it, and consecrated them.

11 He sprinkled some of it on the altar seven times, anointed the altar and all its utensils, and the laver and its base, to consecrate them.

12 And he poured some of the anointing oil on Aaron's head and anointed him, to consecrate him.

13 Then Moses brought Aaron's sons and put tunics on them, girded them with sashes, and put hats on them, as the LORD had commanded Moses.

14 And he brought the bull for the sin offering. Then Aaron and his sons laid their hands on the head of the bull for the sin offering,

15 and Moses killed *it*. Then he took the blood, and put *some* on the horns of the altar all around with his finger, and purified the altar. And he poured the blood at the base of the altar, and consecrated it, to make atonement for it.

16 Then he took all the fat that *was* on the entrails, the fatty lobe *attached to* the liver, and the two kidneys with their fat, and Moses burned *them* on the altar.

17 But the bull, its hide, its flesh, and its offal, he burned with fire outside the camp, as the LORD had commanded Moses.

18 Then he brought the ram as the burnt offering. And Aaron and his sons laid their hands on the head of the ram,

19 and Moses killed *it*. Then he sprinkled the blood all around on the altar.

20 And he cut the ram into pieces; and Moses burned the head, the pieces, and the fat.

21 Then he washed the entrails and the legs in water. And Moses burned the whole ram on the altar. It *was* a burnt sacrifice for a sweet aroma, an offering made by fire to the LORD, as the LORD had commanded Moses.

22 And he brought the second ram, the ram of consecration. Then Aaron and his sons laid their hands on the head of the ram,

23 and Moses killed *it*. Also he took *some* of its blood and put it on the tip of Aaron's right ear, on the thumb of his right hand, and on the big toe of his right foot.

24 Then he brought Aaron's sons. And Moses put *some* of the blood on the tips of their right ears, on the thumbs of their right hands, and on the big toes of their right feet. And Moses sprinkled the blood all around on the altar.

25 Then he took the fat and the fat tail, all the fat that *was* on the entrails, the fatty lobe *attached to* the liver, the two kidneys and their fat, and the right thigh;

26 and from the basket of unleavened bread that was before the LORD he took one unleavened cake, a cake of bread *anointed with* oil, and one wafer, and put *them* on the fat and on the right thigh;

27 and he put all *these* in Aaron's hands and in his sons' hands, and waved them *as* a wave offering before the LORD.

28 Then Moses took them from their hands and burned *them* on the altar, on the burnt offering. They *were* consecration offerings for a sweet aroma. That *was* an offering made by fire to the LORD.

8:8 *a*Literally *the Lights and the Perfections* (compare Exodus 28:30)

29 And Moses took the breast and waved it *as* a wave offering before the LORD. It was Moses' part of the ram of consecration, as the LORD had commanded Moses.

30 Then Moses took some of the anointing oil and some of the blood which *was* on the altar, and sprinkled *it* on Aaron, on his garments, on his sons, and on the garments of his sons with him; and he consecrated Aaron, his garments, his sons, and the garments of his sons with him.

31 And Moses said to Aaron and his sons, "Boil the flesh *at* the door of the tabernacle of meeting, and eat it there with the bread that *is* in the basket of consecration offerings, as I commanded, saying, 'Aaron and his sons shall eat it.'

32 "What remains of the flesh and of the bread you shall burn with fire.

33 "And you shall not go outside the door of the tabernacle of meeting *for* seven days, until the days of your consecration are ended. For seven days he shall consecrate you.

34 "As he has done this day, *so* the LORD has commanded to do, to make atonement for you.

35 "Therefore you shall stay *at* the door of the tabernacle of meeting day and night for seven days, and keep the charge of the LORD, so that you may not die; for so I have been commanded."

36 So Aaron and his sons did all the things that the LORD had commanded by the hand of Moses.

THE PRIESTLY MINISTRY BEGINS

9 It came to pass on the eighth day that Moses called Aaron and his sons and the elders of Israel.

2 And he said to Aaron, "Take for yourself a young bull as a sin offering and a ram as a burnt offering, without blemish, and offer *them* before the LORD.

3 "And to the children of Israel you shall speak, saying, 'Take a kid of the goats as a sin offering, and a calf and a lamb, *both* of the first year, without blemish, as a burnt offering,

4 'also a bull and a ram as peace offerings, to sacrifice before the LORD, and a grain offering mixed with oil; for today the LORD will appear to you.' "

5 So they brought what Moses commanded before the tabernacle of meeting. And all the congregation drew near and stood before the LORD.

6 Then Moses said, "This *is* the thing which the LORD commanded you to do, and the glory of the LORD will appear to you."

7 And Moses said to Aaron, "Go to the altar, offer your sin offering and your burnt offering, and make atonement for yourself and for the people. Offer the offering of the people, and make atonement for them, as the LORD commanded."

8 Aaron therefore went to the altar and killed the calf of the sin offering, which *was* for himself.

9 Then the sons of Aaron brought the blood to him. And he dipped his finger in the blood, put *it* on the horns of the altar, and poured the blood at the base of the altar.

10 But the fat, the kidneys, and the fatty lobe from the liver of the sin offering he burned on the altar, as the LORD had commanded Moses.

11 The flesh and the hide he burned with fire outside the camp.

12 And he killed the burnt offering; and Aaron's sons presented to him the blood, which he sprinkled all around on the altar.

13 Then they presented the burnt offering to him, with its pieces and

head, and he burned *them* on the altar.

14 And he washed the entrails and the legs, and burned *them* with the burnt offering on the altar.

15 Then he brought the people's offering, and took the goat, which *was* the sin offering for the people, and killed it and offered it for sin, like the first one.

16 And he brought the burnt offering and offered it according to the prescribed manner.

17 Then he brought the grain offering, took a handful of it, and burned *it* on the altar, besides the burnt sacrifice of the morning.

18 He also killed the bull and the ram *as* sacrifices of peace offerings, which *were* for the people. And Aaron's sons presented to him the blood, which he sprinkled all around on the altar,

19 and the fat from the bull and the ram—the fatty tail, what covers *the entrails* and the kidneys, and the fatty lobe *attached to* the liver;

20 and they put the fat on the breasts. Then he burned the fat on the altar;

21 but the breasts and the right thigh Aaron waved *as* a wave offering before the LORD, as Moses had commanded.

22 Then Aaron lifted his hand toward the people, blessed them, and came down from offering the sin offering, the burnt offering, and peace offerings.

23 And Moses and Aaron went into the tabernacle of meeting, and came out and blessed the people. Then the glory of the LORD appeared to all the people,

24 and fire came out from before the LORD and consumed the burnt offering and the fat on the altar. When all the people saw *it,* they shouted and fell on their faces.

THE PROFANE FIRE OF NADAB AND ABIHU

10 Then Nā′dab and A·bī′hū, the sons of Aaron, each took his censer and put fire in it, put incense on it, and offered profane fire before the LORD, which He had not commanded them.

2 So fire went out from the LORD and devoured them, and they died before the LORD.

3 And Moses said to Aaron, "This is what the LORD spoke, saying:

'By those who come near Me
I must be regarded as holy;
And before all the people
I must be glorified.' "

So Aaron held his peace.

4 Then Moses called Mish′a·el and El′za·phan, the sons of Uz′zi·el the uncle of Aaron, and said to them, "Come near, carry your brethren from before the sanctuary out of the camp."

5 So they went near and carried them by their tunics out of the camp, as Moses had said.

6 And Moses said to Aaron, and to El·ē·ā′zar and Ith′a·mar, his sons, "Do not uncover your heads nor tear your clothes, lest you die, and wrath come upon all the people. But let your brethren, the whole house of Israel, bewail the burning which the LORD has kindled.

7 "You shall not go out from the door of the tabernacle of meeting, lest you die, for the anointing oil of the LORD *is* upon you." And they did according to the word of Moses.

CONDUCT PRESCRIBED FOR PRIESTS

8 Then the LORD spoke to Aaron, saying:

9 "Do not drink wine or intoxicating

drink, you, nor your sons with you, when you go into the tabernacle of meeting, lest you die. *It shall be* a statute forever throughout your generations,

10 "that you may distinguish between holy and unholy, and between unclean and clean,

11 "and that you may teach the children of Israel all the statutes which the LORD has spoken to them by the hand of Moses."

12 And Moses spoke to Aaron, and to El·ē·ā′zar and Ith′a·mar, his sons who were left: "Take the grain offering that remains of the offerings made by fire to the LORD, and eat it without leaven beside the altar; for it *is* most holy.

13 "You shall eat it in a holy place, because it *is* your due and your sons' due, of the sacrifices made by fire to the LORD; for so I have been commanded.

14 "The breast of the wave offering and the thigh of the heave offering you shall eat in a clean place, you, your sons, and your daughters with you; for *they are* your due and your sons' due, *which* are given from the sacrifices of peace offerings of the children of Israel.

15 "The thigh of the heave offering and the breast of the wave offering they shall bring with the offerings of fat made by fire, to offer *as* a wave offering before the LORD. And it shall be yours and your sons' with you, by a statute forever, as the LORD has commanded."

16 Then Moses made careful inquiry about the goat of the sin offering, and there it was—burned up. And he was angry with El·ē·ā′zar and Ith′a·mar, the sons of Aaron *who were* left, saying,

17 "Why have you not eaten the sin offering in a holy place, since it *is* most holy, and *God* has given it to

you to bear the guilt of the congregation, to make atonement for them before the LORD?

18 "See! Its blood was not brought inside the holy *place;*[a] indeed you should have eaten it in a holy *place*, as I commanded."

19 And Aaron said to Moses, "Look, this day they have offered their sin offering and their burnt offering before the LORD, and such things have befallen me! *If* I had eaten the sin offering today, would it have been accepted in the sight of the LORD?"

20 So when Moses heard *that,* he was content.

FOODS PERMITTED AND FORBIDDEN

11 Now the LORD spoke to Moses and Aaron, saying to them,

2 "Speak to the children of Israel, saying, 'These *are* the animals which you may eat among all the animals that *are* on the earth:

3 'Among the animals, whatever divides the hoof, having cloven hooves *and* chewing the cud—that you may eat.

4 'Nevertheless these you shall not eat among those that chew the cud or those that have cloven hooves: the camel, because it chews the cud but does not have cloven hooves, is unclean to you;

5 'the rock hyrax, because it chews the cud but does not have cloven hooves, *is* unclean to you;

6 'the hare, because it chews the cud but does not have cloven hooves, *is* unclean to you;

7 'and the swine, though it divides the hoof, having cloven hooves, yet does not chew the cud, *is* unclean to you.

8 'Their flesh you shall not eat, and

10:18 *a*The Most Holy Place when capitalized

their carcasses you shall not touch. They *are* unclean to you.

9 'These you may eat of all that *are* in the water: whatever in the water has fins and scales, whether in the seas or in the rivers—that you may eat.

10 'But all in the seas or in the rivers that do not have fins and scales, all that move in the water or any living thing which *is* in the water, they *are* an abomination to you.

11 'They shall be an abomination to you; you shall not eat their flesh, but you shall regard their carcasses as an abomination.

12 'Whatever in the water does not have fins or scales—that *shall be* an abomination to you.

13 'And these you shall regard as an abomination among the birds; they shall not be eaten, they *are* an abomination: the eagle, the vulture, the buzzard,

14 'the kite, and the falcon after its kind;

15 'every raven after its kind,

16 'the ostrich, the short-eared owl, the sea gull, and the hawk after its kind;

17 'the little owl, the fisher owl, and the screech owl;

18 'the white owl, the jackdaw, and the carrion vulture;

19 'the stork, the heron after its kind, the hoopoe, and the bat.

20 'All flying insects that creep on *all* fours *shall be* an abomination to you.

21 'Yet these you may eat of every flying insect that creeps on *all* fours: those which have jointed legs above their feet with which to leap on the earth.

22 'These you may eat: the locust after its kind, the destroying locust after its kind, the cricket after its kind, and the grasshopper after its kind.

23 'But all *other* flying insects which

have four feet *shall be* an abomination to you.

UNCLEAN ANIMALS

24 'By these you shall become unclean; whoever touches the carcass of any of them shall be unclean until evening;

25 'whoever carries part of the carcass of any of them shall wash his clothes and be unclean until evening:

26 '*The carcass* of any animal which divides the foot, but is not cloven-hoofed or does not chew the cud, *is* unclean to you. Everyone who touches it shall be unclean.

27 'And whatever goes on its paws, among all kinds of animals that go on *all* fours, those *are* unclean to you. Whoever touches any such carcass shall be unclean until evening.

28 'Whoever carries *any such* carcass shall wash his clothes and be unclean until evening. It *is* unclean to you.

29 'These also *shall be* unclean to you among the creeping things that creep on the earth: the mole, the mouse, and the large lizard after its kind;

30 'the gecko, the monitor lizard, the sand reptile, the sand lizard, and the chameleon.

31 'These *are* unclean to you among all that creep. Whoever touches them when they are dead shall be unclean until evening.

32 'Anything on which *any* of them falls, when they are dead shall be unclean, whether *it is* any item of wood or clothing or skin or sack, whatever item *it is,* in which *any* work is done, it must be put in water. And it shall be unclean until evening; then it shall be clean.

33 'Any earthen vessel into which *any* of them falls you shall break; and whatever *is* in it shall be unclean:

34 'in such a vessel, any edible food

upon which water falls becomes unclean, and any drink that may be drunk from it becomes unclean.

35 'And everything on which *a part* of *any such* carcass falls shall be unclean; *whether it is* an oven or cooking stove, it shall be broken down; *for* they *are* unclean, and shall be unclean to you.

36 'Nevertheless a spring or a cistern, *in which there is* plenty of water, shall be clean, but whatever touches any such carcass becomes unclean.

37 'And if a part of *any such* carcass falls on any planting seed which is to be sown, it *remains* clean.

38 'But if water is put on the seed, and if *a part* of *any such* carcass falls on it, it *becomes* unclean to you.

39 'And if any animal which you may eat dies, he who touches its carcass shall be unclean until evening.

40 'He who eats of its carcass shall wash his clothes and be unclean until evening. He also who carries its carcass shall wash his clothes and be unclean until evening.

41 'And every creeping thing that creeps on the earth *shall be* an abomination. It shall not be eaten.

42 'Whatever crawls on its belly, whatever goes on *all* fours, or whatever has many feet among all creeping things that creep on the earth— these you shall not eat, for they *are* an abomination.

43 'You shall not make yourselves abominable with any creeping thing that creeps; nor shall you make yourselves unclean with them, lest you be defiled by them.

44 'For I *am* the LORD your God. You shall therefore consecrate yourselves, and you shall be holy; for I *am* holy. Neither shall you defile yourselves with any creeping thing that creeps on the earth.

45 'For I *am* the LORD who brings you up out of the land of Egypt, to be your God. You shall therefore be holy, for I *am* holy.

46 'This *is* the law of the animals and the birds and every living creature that moves in the waters, and of every creature that creeps on the earth,

47 'to distinguish between the unclean and the clean, and between the animal that may be eaten and the animal that may not be eaten.' "

THE RITUAL AFTER CHILDBIRTH

12 Then the LORD spoke to Moses, saying,

2 "Speak to the children of Israel, saying: 'If a woman has conceived, and borne a male child, then she shall be unclean seven days; as in the days of her customary impurity she shall be unclean.

3 'And on the eighth day the flesh of his foreskin shall be circumcised.

4 'She shall then continue in the blood of *her* purification thirty-three days. She shall not touch any hallowed thing, nor come into the sanctuary until the days of her purification are fulfilled.

5 'But if she bears a female child, then she shall be unclean two weeks, as in her customary impurity, and she shall continue in the blood of *her* purification sixty-six days.

6 'When the days of her purification are fulfilled, whether for a son or a daughter, she shall bring to the priest a lamb of the first year as a burnt offering, and a young pigeon or a turtledove as a sin offering, to the door of the tabernacle of meeting.

7 'Then he shall offer it before the LORD, and make atonement for her. And she shall be clean from the flow of her blood. This *is* the law for her who has borne a male or a female.

8 'And if she is not able to bring a lamb, then she may bring two turtle-doves or two young pigeons—one as a burnt offering and the other as a sin offering. So the priest shall make atonement for her, and she will be clean.' "

THE LAW CONCERNING LEPROSY

13 And the LORD spoke to Moses and Aaron, saying:

2 "When a man has on the skin of his body a swelling, a scab, or a bright spot, and it becomes on the skin of his body *like* a leprous*a* sore, then he shall be brought to Aaron the priest or to one of his sons the priests.

3 "The priest shall examine the sore on the skin of the body; and if the hair on the sore has turned white, and the sore appears *to be* deeper than the skin of his body, it *is* a leprous sore. Then the priest shall examine him, and pronounce him unclean.

4 "But if the bright spot *is* white on the skin of his body, and does not appear *to be* deeper than the skin, and its hair has not turned white, then the priest shall isolate *the one who has* the sore seven days.

5 "And the priest shall examine him on the seventh day; and indeed *if* the sore appears to be as it was, *and* the sore has not spread on the skin, then the priest shall isolate him another seven days.

6 "Then the priest shall examine him again on the seventh day; and indeed *if* the sore has faded, *and* the sore has not spread on the skin, then the priest shall pronounce him clean; it *is only* a scab, and he shall wash his clothes and be clean.

7 "But if the scab should at all spread over the skin, after he has been seen by the priest for his cleansing, he shall be seen by the priest again.

8 "And *if* the priest sees that the scab has indeed spread on the skin, then the priest shall pronounce him unclean. It *is* leprosy.

9 "When the leprous sore is on a person, then he shall be brought to the priest.

10 "And the priest shall examine *him;* and indeed *if* the swelling on the skin *is* white, and it has turned the hair white, and *there is* a spot of raw flesh in the swelling,

11 "it *is* an old leprosy on the skin of his body. The priest shall pronounce him unclean, and shall not isolate him, for he *is* unclean.

12 "And if leprosy breaks out all over the skin, and the leprosy covers all the skin of *the one who has* the sore, from his head to his foot, wherever the priest looks,

13 "then the priest shall consider; and indeed *if* the leprosy has covered all his body, he shall pronounce *him* clean *who has* the sore. It has all turned white. He *is* clean.

14 "But when raw flesh appears on him, he shall be unclean.

15 "And the priest shall examine the raw flesh and pronounce him to be unclean; *for* the raw flesh *is* unclean. It *is* leprosy.

16 "Or if the raw flesh changes and turns white again, he shall come to the priest.

17 "And the priest shall examine him; and indeed *if* the sore has turned white, then the priest shall pronounce *him* clean *who has* the sore. He *is* clean.

18 "If the body develops a boil in the skin, and it is healed,

13:2 *a*Hebrew *saraath,* disfiguring skin diseases, including leprosy, and so in verses 2–46 and 14:1–32

19 "and in the place of the boil there comes a white swelling or a bright spot, reddish-white, then it shall be shown to the priest;

20 "and if, when the priest sees it, it indeed *appears* deeper than the skin, and its hair has turned white, the priest shall pronounce him unclean. It *is* a leprous sore which has broken out of the boil.

21 "But if the priest examines it, and indeed *there are* no white hairs in it, and it *is* not deeper than the skin, but has faded, then the priest shall isolate him seven days;

22 "and if it should at all spread over the skin, then the priest shall pronounce him unclean. It *is* a leprous sore.

23 "But if the bright spot stays in one place, *and* has not spread, it *is* the scar of the boil; and the priest shall pronounce him clean.

24 "Or if the body receives a burn on its skin by fire, and the raw *flesh* of the burn becomes a bright spot, reddish-white or white,

25 "then the priest shall examine it; and indeed *if* the hair of the bright spot has turned white, and it appears deeper than the skin, it *is* leprosy broken out in the burn. Therefore the priest shall pronounce him unclean. It *is* a leprous sore.

26 "But if the priest examines it, and indeed *there are* no white hairs in the bright spot, and it *is* not deeper than the skin, but has faded, then the priest shall isolate him seven days.

27 "And the priest shall examine him on the seventh day. If it has at all spread over the skin, then the priest shall pronounce him unclean. It *is* a leprous sore.

28 "But if the bright spot stays in one place, *and* has not spread on the skin, but has faded, it *is* a swelling from the burn. The priest shall pro-nounce him clean, for it *is* the scar from the burn.

29 "If a man or woman has a sore on the head or the beard,

30 "then the priest shall examine the sore; and indeed if it appears deeper than the skin, *and there is* in it thin yellow hair, then the priest shall pronounce him unclean. It *is* a scaly leprosy of the head or beard.

31 "But if the priest examines the scaly sore, and indeed it does not appear deeper than the skin, and *there is* no black hair in it, then the priest shall isolate *the one who has* the scale seven days.

32 "And on the seventh day the priest shall examine the sore; and indeed *if* the scale has not spread, and there is no yellow hair in it, and the scale does not appear deeper than the skin,

33 "he shall shave himself, but the scale he shall not shave. And the priest shall isolate *the one who has* the scale another seven days.

34 "On the seventh day the priest shall examine the scale; and indeed *if* the scale has not spread over the skin, and does not appear deeper than the skin, then the priest shall pronounce him clean. He shall wash his clothes and be clean.

35 "But if the scale should at all spread over the skin after his cleansing,

36 "then the priest shall examine him; and indeed *if* the scale has spread over the skin, the priest need not seek for yellow hair. He *is* unclean.

37 "But if the scale appears to be at a standstill, and there is black hair grown up in it, the scale has healed. He *is* clean, and the priest shall pronounce him clean.

38 "If a man or a woman has bright spots on the skin of the body, *specifically* white bright spots,

39 "then the priest shall look; and indeed *if* the bright spots on the skin of the body *are* dull white, it *is* a white spot *that* grows on the skin. He *is* clean.

40 "As for the man whose hair has fallen from his head, he *is* bald, *but* he *is* clean.

41 "He whose hair has fallen from his forehead, he *is* bald on the forehead, *but* he *is* clean.

42 "And if there is on the bald head or bald forehead a reddish-white sore, it *is* leprosy breaking out on his bald head or his bald forehead.

43 "Then the priest shall examine it; and indeed *if* the swelling of the sore *is* reddish-white on his bald head or on his bald forehead, as the appearance of leprosy on the skin of the body,

44 "he is a leprous man. He *is* unclean. The priest shall surely pronounce him unclean; his sore *is* on his head.

45 "Now the leper on whom the sore *is,* his clothes shall be torn and his head bare; and he shall cover his mustache, and cry, 'Unclean! Unclean!'

46 "He shall be unclean. All the days he has the sore he shall be unclean. He *is* unclean, and he shall dwell alone; his dwelling *shall be* outside the camp.

The Law Concerning Leprous Garments

47 "Also, if a garment has a leprous plague*a* in it, *whether it is* a woolen garment or a linen garment,

48 "whether *it is* in the warp or woof of linen or wool, whether in leather or in anything made of leather,

49 "and if the plague is greenish or reddish in the garment or in the leather, whether in the warp or in the woof, or in anything made of leather, it *is* a leprous plague and shall be shown to the priest.

50 "The priest shall examine the plague and isolate *that which has* the plague seven days.

51 "And he shall examine the plague on the seventh day. If the plague has spread in the garment, either in the warp or in the woof, in the leather *or* in anything made of leather, the plague *is* an active leprosy. It *is* unclean.

52 "He shall therefore burn that garment in which is the plague, whether warp or woof, in wool or in linen, or anything of leather, for it *is* an active leprosy; *the garment* shall be burned in the fire.

53 "But if the priest examines *it,* and indeed the plague has not spread in the garment, either in the warp or in the woof, or in anything made of leather,

54 "then the priest shall command that they wash *the thing* in which *is* the plague; and he shall isolate it another seven days.

55 "Then the priest shall examine the plague after it has been washed; and indeed *if* the plague has not changed its color, though the plague has not spread, it *is* unclean, and you shall burn it in the fire; it continues eating away, *whether* the damage *is* outside or inside.

56 "If the priest examines *it,* and indeed the plague has faded after washing it, then he shall tear it out of the garment, whether out of the warp or out of the woof, or out of the leather.

57 "But if it appears again in the garment, either in the warp or in the woof, or in anything made of leather, it *is* a spreading *plague;* you shall

13:47 *a*A mold, fungus, or similar infestation, and so in verses 47–59

burn with fire that in which is the plague.

58 "And if you wash the garment, either warp or woof, or whatever is made of leather, if the plague has disappeared from it, then it shall be washed a second time, and shall be clean.

59 "This *is* the law of the leprous plague in a garment of wool or linen, either in the warp or woof, or in anything made of leather, to pronounce it clean or to pronounce it unclean."

THE RITUAL FOR CLEANSING HEALED LEPERS

14 Then the LORD spoke to Moses, saying,

2 "This shall be the law of the leper for the day of his cleansing: He shall be brought to the priest.

3 "And the priest shall go out of the camp, and the priest shall examine *him;* and indeed, *if* the leprosy is healed in the leper,

4 "then the priest shall command to take for him who is to be cleansed two living *and* clean birds, cedar wood, scarlet, and hyssop.

5 "And the priest shall command that one of the birds be killed in an earthen vessel over running water.

6 "As for the living bird, he shall take it, the cedar wood and the scarlet and the hyssop, and dip them and the living bird in the blood of the bird *that was* killed over the running water.

7 "And he shall sprinkle it seven times on him who is to be cleansed from the leprosy, and shall pronounce him clean, and shall let the living bird loose in the open field.

8 "He who is to be cleansed shall wash his clothes, shave off all his hair, and wash himself in water, that he may be clean. After that he shall come into the camp, and shall stay outside his tent seven days.

9 "But on the seventh day he shall shave all the hair off his head and his beard and his eyebrows—all his hair he shall shave off. He shall wash his clothes and wash his body in water, and he shall be clean.

10 "And on the eighth day he shall take two male lambs without blemish, one ewe lamb of the first year without blemish, three-tenths *of an ephah* of fine flour mixed with oil as a grain offering, and one log of oil.

11 "Then the priest who makes *him* clean shall present the man who is to be made clean, and those things, before the LORD, *at* the door of the tabernacle of meeting.

12 "And the priest shall take one male lamb and offer it as a trespass offering, and the log of oil, and wave them *as* a wave offering before the LORD.

13 "Then he shall kill the lamb in the place where he kills the sin offering and the burnt offering, in a holy place; for as the sin offering *is* the priest's, so *is* the trespass offering. It *is* most holy.

14 "The priest shall take *some* of the blood of the trespass offering, and the priest shall put *it* on the tip of the right ear of him who is to be cleansed, on the thumb of his right hand, and on the big toe of his right foot.

15 "And the priest shall take *some* of the log of oil, and pour *it* into the palm of his own left hand.

16 "Then the priest shall dip his right finger in the oil that *is* in his left hand, and shall sprinkle some of the oil with his finger seven times before the LORD.

17 "And of the rest of the oil in his hand, the priest shall put *some* on the tip of the right ear of him who is to be cleansed, on the thumb of his

right hand, and on the big toe of his right foot, on the blood of the trespass offering.

18 "The rest of the oil that *is* in the priest's hand he shall put on the head of him who is to be cleansed. So the priest shall make atonement for him before the LORD.

19 "Then the priest shall offer the sin offering, and make atonement for him who is to be cleansed from his uncleanness. Afterward he shall kill the burnt offering.

20 "And the priest shall offer the burnt offering and the grain offering on the altar. So the priest shall make atonement for him, and he shall be clean.

21 "But if he *is* poor and cannot afford it, then he shall take one male lamb *as* a trespass offering to be waved, to make atonement for him, one-tenth *of an ephah* of fine flour mixed with oil as a grain offering, a log of oil,

22 "and two turtledoves or two young pigeons, such as he is able to afford: one shall be a sin offering and the other a burnt offering.

23 "He shall bring them to the priest on the eighth day for his cleansing, to the door of the tabernacle of meeting, before the LORD.

24 "And the priest shall take the lamb of the trespass offering and the log of oil, and the priest shall wave them *as* a wave offering before the LORD.

25 "Then he shall kill the lamb of the trespass offering, and the priest shall take *some* of the blood of the trespass offering and put *it* on the tip of the right ear of him who is to be cleansed, on the thumb of his right hand, and on the big toe of his right foot.

26 "And the priest shall pour some of the oil into the palm of his own left hand.

27 "Then the priest shall sprinkle with his right finger *some* of the oil that *is* in his left hand seven times before the LORD.

28 "And the priest shall put *some* of the oil that *is* in his hand on the tip of the right ear of him who is to be cleansed, on the thumb of the right hand, and on the big toe of his right foot, on the place of the blood of the trespass offering.

29 "The rest of the oil that *is* in the priest's hand he shall put on the head of him who is to be cleansed, to make atonement for him before the LORD.

30 "And he shall offer one of the turtledoves or young pigeons, such as he can afford—

31 "such as he is able to afford, the one *as* a sin offering and the other *as* a burnt offering, with the grain offering. So the priest shall make atonement for him who is to be cleansed before the LORD.

32 "This *is* the law *for one* who had a leprous sore, who cannot afford the usual cleansing."

THE LAW CONCERNING LEPROUS HOUSES

33 And the LORD spoke to Moses and Aaron, saying:

34 "When you have come into the land of Cā'naan, which I give you as a possession, and I put the leprous plague*a* in a house in the land of your possession,

35 "and he who owns the house comes and tells the priest, saying, 'It seems to me that *there is* some plague in the house,'

36 "then the priest shall command that they empty the house, before the priest goes *into it* to examine the plague, that all that *is* in the house

14:34 *a*Decomposition by mildew, mold, dry rot, etc., and so in verses 34–53

may not be made unclean; and afterward the priest shall go in to examine the house.

37 "And he shall examine the plague; and indeed *if* the plague *is* on the walls of the house with ingrained streaks, greenish or reddish, which appear to be deep in the wall,

38 "then the priest shall go out of the house, to the door of the house, and shut up the house seven days.

39 "And the priest shall come again on the seventh day and look; and indeed *if* the plague has spread on the walls of the house,

40 "then the priest shall command that they take away the stones in which *is* the plague, and they shall cast them into an unclean place outside the city.

41 "And he shall cause the house to be scraped inside, all around, and the dust that they scrape off they shall pour out in an unclean place outside the city.

42 "Then they shall take other stones and put *them* in the place of *those* stones, and he shall take other mortar and plaster the house.

43 "Now if the plague comes back and breaks out in the house, after he has taken away the stones, after he has scraped the house, and after it is plastered,

44 "then the priest shall come and look; and indeed *if* the plague has spread in the house, it *is* an active leprosy in the house. It *is* unclean.

45 "And he shall break down the house, its stones, its timber, and all the plaster of the house, and he shall carry *them* outside the city to an unclean place.

46 "Moreover he who goes into the house at all while it is shut up shall be unclean until evening.

47 "And he who lies down in the house shall wash his clothes, and he who eats in the house shall wash his clothes.

48 "But if the priest comes in and examines *it,* and indeed the plague has not spread in the house after the house was plastered, then the priest shall pronounce the house clean, because the plague is healed.

49 "And he shall take, to cleanse the house, two birds, cedar wood, scarlet, and hyssop.

50 "Then he shall kill one of the birds in an earthen vessel over running water;

51 "and he shall take the cedar wood, the hyssop, the scarlet, and the living bird, and dip them in the blood of the slain bird and in the running water, and sprinkle the house seven times.

52 "And he shall cleanse the house with the blood of the bird and the running water and the living bird, with the cedar wood, the hyssop, and the scarlet.

53 "Then he shall let the living bird loose outside the city in the open field, and make atonement for the house, and it shall be clean.

54 "This *is* the law for any leprous sore and scale,

55 "for the leprosy of a garment and of a house,

56 "for a swelling and a scab and a bright spot,

57 "to teach when *it is* unclean and when *it is* clean. This *is* the law of leprosy."

THE LAW CONCERNING BODILY DISCHARGES

15 And the LORD spoke to Moses and Aaron, saying,

2 "Speak to the children of Israel, and say to them: 'When any man has a discharge from his body, his discharge *is* unclean.

3 'And this shall be his uncleanness in regard to his discharge—whether his body runs with his discharge, or his body is stopped up by his discharge, it *is* his uncleanness.

4 'Every bed is unclean on which he who has the discharge lies, and everything on which he sits shall be unclean.

5 'And whoever touches his bed shall wash his clothes and bathe in water, and be unclean until evening.

6 'He who sits on anything on which he who has the discharge sat shall wash his clothes and bathe in water, and be unclean until evening.

7 'And he who touches the body of him who has the discharge shall wash his clothes and bathe in water, and be unclean until evening.

8 'If he who has the discharge spits on him who is clean, then he shall wash his clothes and bathe in water, and be unclean until evening.

9 'Any saddle on which he who has the discharge rides shall be unclean.

10 'Whoever touches anything that was under him shall be unclean until evening. He who carries *any of* those things shall wash his clothes and bathe in water, and be unclean until evening.

11 'And whomever the one who has the discharge touches, and has not rinsed his hands in water, he shall wash his clothes and bathe in water, and be unclean until evening.

12 'The vessel of earth that he who has the discharge touches shall be broken, and every vessel of wood shall be rinsed in water.

13 'And when he who has a discharge is cleansed of his discharge, then he shall count for himself seven days for his cleansing, wash his clothes, and bathe his body in running water; then he shall be clean.

14 'On the eighth day he shall take for himself two turtledoves or two young pigeons, and come before the LORD, to the door of the tabernacle of meeting, and give them to the priest.

15 'Then the priest shall offer them, the one *as* a sin offering and the other *as* a burnt offering. So the priest shall make atonement for him before the LORD because of his discharge.

16 'If any man has an emission of semen, then he shall wash all his body in water, and be unclean until evening.

17 'And any garment and any leather on which there is semen, it shall be washed with water, and be unclean until evening.

18 'Also, when a woman lies with a man, and *there is* an emission of semen, they shall bathe in water, and be unclean until evening.

19 'If a woman has a discharge, *and* the discharge from her body is blood, she shall be set apart seven days; and whoever touches her shall be unclean until evening.

20 'Everything that she lies on during her impurity shall be unclean; also everything that she sits on shall be unclean.

21 'Whoever touches her bed shall wash his clothes and bathe in water, and be unclean until evening.

22 'And whoever touches anything that she sat on shall wash his clothes and bathe in water, and be unclean until evening.

23 'If *anything* is on *her* bed or on anything on which she sits, when he touches it, he shall be unclean until evening.

24 'And if any man lies with her at all, so that her impurity is on him, he shall be unclean seven days; and every bed on which he lies shall be unclean.

25 'If a woman has a discharge of blood for many days, other than at the time of her *customary* impurity,

or if it runs beyond her *usual time of* impurity, all the days of her unclean discharge shall be as the days of her *customary* impurity. She *shall be* unclean.

26 'Every bed on which she lies all the days of her discharge shall be to her as the bed of her impurity; and whatever she sits on shall be unclean, as the uncleanness of her impurity.

27 'Whoever touches those things shall be unclean; he shall wash his clothes and bathe in water, and be unclean until evening.

28 'But if she is cleansed of her discharge, then she shall count for herself seven days, and after that she shall be clean.

29 'And on the eighth day she shall take for herself two turtledoves or two young pigeons, and bring them to the priest, to the door of the tabernacle of meeting.

30 'Then the priest shall offer the one *as* a sin offering and the other *as* a burnt offering, and the priest shall make atonement for her before the LORD for the discharge of her uncleanness.

31 'Thus you shall separate the children of Israel from their uncleanness, lest they die in their uncleanness when they defile My tabernacle that *is* among them.

32 'This *is* the law for one who has a discharge, and *for him* who emits semen and is unclean thereby,

33 'and for her who is indisposed because of her *customary* impurity, and for one who has a discharge, either man or woman, and for him who lies with her who is unclean.' "

THE DAY OF ATONEMENT

16 Now the LORD spoke to Moses after the death of the two sons of Aaron, when they offered *profane fire* before the LORD, and died;

2 and the LORD said to Moses: "Tell Aaron your brother not to come at *just* any time into the Holy *Place* inside the veil, before the mercy seat which *is* on the ark, lest he die; for I will appear in the cloud above the mercy seat.

3 "Thus Aaron shall come into the Holy *Place:* with *the blood of* a young bull as a sin offering, and *of* a ram as a burnt offering.

4 "He shall put the holy linen tunic and the linen trousers on his body; he shall be girded with a linen sash, and with the linen turban he shall be attired. These *are* holy garments. Therefore he shall wash his body in water, and put them on.

5 "And he shall take from the congregation of the children of Israel two kids of the goats as a sin offering, and one ram as a burnt offering.

6 "Aaron shall offer the bull as a sin offering, which *is* for himself, and make atonement for himself and for his house.

7 "He shall take the two goats and present them before the LORD *at* the door of the tabernacle of meeting.

8 "Then Aaron shall cast lots for the two goats: one lot for the LORD and the other lot for the scapegoat.

9 "And Aaron shall bring the goat on which the LORD's lot fell, and offer it *as* a sin offering.

10 "But the goat on which the lot fell to be the scapegoat shall be presented alive before the LORD, to make atonement upon it, *and* to let it go as the scapegoat into the wilderness.

11 "And Aaron shall bring the bull of the sin offering, which is for himself, and make atonement for himself and for his house, and shall kill the bull as the sin offering which *is* for himself.

12 "Then he shall take a censer full

of burning coals of fire from the altar before the LORD, with his hands full of sweet incense beaten fine, and bring *it* inside the veil.

13 "And he shall put the incense on the fire before the LORD, that the cloud of incense may cover the mercy seat that *is* on the Testimony, lest he die.

14 "He shall take some of the blood of the bull and sprinkle *it* with his finger on the mercy seat on the east *side;* and before the mercy seat he shall sprinkle some of the blood with his finger seven times.

15 "Then he shall kill the goat of the sin offering, which *is* for the people, bring its blood inside the veil, do with that blood as he did with the blood of the bull, and sprinkle it on the mercy seat and before the mercy seat.

16 "So he shall make atonement for the Holy *Place,* because of the uncleanness of the children of Israel, and because of their transgressions, for all their sins; and so he shall do for the tabernacle of meeting which remains among them in the midst of their uncleanness.

17 "There shall be no man in the tabernacle of meeting when he goes in to make atonement in the Holy *Place,* until he comes out, that he may make atonement for himself, for his household, and for all the assembly of Israel.

18 "And he shall go out to the altar that *is* before the LORD, and make atonement for it, and shall take some of the blood of the bull and some of the blood of the goat, and put it on the horns of the altar all around.

19 "Then he shall sprinkle some of the blood on it with his finger seven times, cleanse it, and consecrate it from the uncleanness of the children of Israel.

20 "And when he has made an end of atoning for the Holy *Place,* the taber-nacle of meeting, and the altar, he shall bring the live goat.

21 "Aaron shall lay both his hands on the head of the live goat, confess over it all the iniquities of the children of Israel, and all their transgressions, concerning all their sins, putting them on the head of the goat, and shall send *it* away into the wilderness by the hand of a suitable man.

22 "The goat shall bear on itself all their iniquities to an uninhabited land; and he shall release the goat in the wilderness.

23 "Then Aaron shall come into the tabernacle of meeting, shall take off the linen garments which he put on when he went into the Holy *Place,* and shall leave them there.

24 "And he shall wash his body with water in a holy place, put on his garments, come out and offer his burnt offering and the burnt offering of the people, and make atonement for himself and for the people.

25 "The fat of the sin offering he shall burn on the altar.

26 "And he who released the goat as the scapegoat shall wash his clothes and bathe his body in water, and afterward he may come into the camp.

27 "The bull *for* the sin offering and the goat *for* the sin offering, whose blood was brought in to make atonement in the Holy *Place,* shall be carried outside the camp. And they shall burn in the fire their skins, their flesh, and their offal.

28 "Then he who burns them shall wash his clothes and bathe his body in water, and afterward he may come into the camp.

29 "*This* shall be a statute forever for you: In the seventh month, on the tenth *day* of the month, you shall afflict your souls, and do no work at all, *whether* a native of your own country or a stranger who dwells among you.

30 "For on that day *the priest* shall make atonement for you, to cleanse you, *that* you may be clean from all your sins before the LORD.

31 "It *is* a sabbath of solemn rest for you, and you shall afflict your souls. *It is* a statute forever.

32 "And the priest, who is anointed and consecrated to minister as priest in his father's place, shall make atonement, and put on the linen clothes, the holy garments;

33 "then he shall make atonement for the Holy Sanctuary,*a* and he shall make atonement for the tabernacle of meeting and for the altar, and he shall make atonement for the priests and for all the people of the assembly.

34 "This shall be an everlasting statute for you, to make atonement for the children of Israel, for all their sins, once a year." And he did as the LORD commanded Moses.

THE SANCTITY OF BLOOD

17 And the LORD spoke to Moses, saying,

2 "Speak to Aaron, to his sons, and to all the children of Israel, and say to them, 'This *is* the thing which the LORD has commanded, saying:

3 "Whatever man of the house of Israel who kills an ox or lamb or goat in the camp, or who kills *it* outside the camp,

4 "and does not bring it to the door of the tabernacle of meeting to offer an offering to the LORD before the tabernacle of the LORD, the guilt of bloodshed shall be imputed to that man. He has shed blood; and that man shall be cut off from among his people,

5 "to the end that the children of Israel may bring their sacrifices which they offer in the open field, that they may bring them to the LORD at the door of the tabernacle of meeting, to the priest, and offer them *as* peace offerings to the LORD.

6 "And the priest shall sprinkle the blood on the altar of the LORD *at* the door of the tabernacle of meeting, and burn the fat for a sweet aroma to the LORD.

7 "They shall no more offer their sacrifices to demons, after whom they have played the harlot. This shall be a statute forever for them throughout their generations." '

8 "Also you shall say to them: 'Whatever man of the house of Israel, or of the strangers who dwell among you, who offers a burnt offering or sacrifice,

9 'and does not bring it to the door of the tabernacle of meeting, to offer it to the LORD, that man shall be cut off from among his people.

10 'And whatever man of the house of Israel, or of the strangers who dwell among you, who eats any blood, I will set My face against that person who eats blood, and will cut him off from among his people.

11 'For the life of the flesh *is* in the blood, and I have given it to you upon the altar to make atonement for your souls; for it *is* the blood *that* makes atonement for the soul.'

12 "Therefore I said to the children of Israel, 'No one among you shall eat blood, nor shall any stranger who dwells among you eat blood.'

13 "Whatever man of the children of Israel, or of the strangers who dwell among you, who hunts and catches any animal or bird that may be eaten, he shall pour out its blood and cover it with dust;

14 "for *it is* the life of all flesh. Its blood sustains its life. Therefore I said to the children of Israel, 'You

16:33 *a*That is, the Most Holy Place

shall not eat the blood of any flesh, for the life of all flesh is its blood. Whoever eats it shall be cut off.'

15 "And every person who eats what died *naturally* or what was torn *by beasts, whether he is* a native of your own country or a stranger, he shall both wash his clothes and bathe in water, and be unclean until evening. Then he shall be clean.

16 "But if he does not wash *them* or bathe his body, then he shall bear his guilt."

LAWS OF SEXUAL MORALITY

18 Then the LORD spoke to Moses, saying,

2 "Speak to the children of Israel, and say to them: 'I am the LORD your God.

3 'According to the doings of the land of Egypt, where you dwelt, you shall not do; and according to the doings of the land of Cā′naan, where I am bringing you, you shall not do; nor shall you walk in their ordinances.

4 'You shall observe My judgments and keep My ordinances, to walk in them: I *am* the LORD your God.

5 'You shall therefore keep My statutes and My judgments, which if a man does, he shall live by them: I *am* the LORD.

6 'None of you shall approach anyone who is near of kin to him, to uncover his nakedness: I *am* the LORD.

7 'The nakedness of your father or the nakedness of your mother you shall not uncover. She *is* your mother; you shall not uncover her nakedness.

8 'The nakedness of your father's wife you shall not uncover; it *is* your father's nakedness.

9 'The nakedness of your sister, the daughter of your father, or the daughter of your mother, *whether* born at home or elsewhere, their nakedness you shall not uncover.

10 'The nakedness of your son's daughter or your daughter's daughter, their nakedness you shall not uncover; for theirs *is* your own nakedness.

11 'The nakedness of your father's wife's daughter, begotten by your father—she *is* your sister—you shall not uncover her nakedness.

12 'You shall not uncover the nakedness of your father's sister; she *is* near of kin to your father.

13 'You shall not uncover the nakedness of your mother's sister, for she *is* near of kin to your mother.

14 'You shall not uncover the nakedness of your father's brother. You shall not approach his wife; she *is* your aunt.

15 'You shall not uncover the nakedness of your daughter-in-law—she *is* your son's wife—you shall not uncover her nakedness.

16 'You shall not uncover the nakedness of your brother's wife; it *is* your brother's nakedness.

17 'You shall not uncover the nakedness of a woman and her daughter, nor shall you take her son's daughter or her daughter's daughter, to uncover her nakedness. They *are* near of kin to her. It *is* wickedness.

18 'Nor shall you take a woman as a rival to her sister, to uncover her nakedness while the other is alive.

19 'Also you shall not approach a woman to uncover her nakedness as long as she is in her *customary* impurity.

20 'Moreover you shall not lie carnally with your neighbor's wife, to defile yourself with her.

21 'And you shall not let any of your descendants pass through *the fire* to Mō′lech, nor shall you profane the name of your God: I *am* the LORD.

22 'You shall not lie with a male as with a woman. It *is* an abomination.

23 'Nor shall you mate with any animal, to defile yourself with it. Nor shall any woman stand before an animal to mate with it. It *is* perversion.

24 'Do not defile yourselves with any of these things; for by all these the nations are defiled, which I am casting out before you.

25 'For the land is defiled; therefore I visit the punishment of its iniquity upon it, and the land vomits out its inhabitants.

26 'You shall therefore keep My statutes and My judgments, and shall not commit *any* of these abominations, *either* any of your own nation or any stranger who dwells among you

27 '(for all these abominations the men of the land have done, who *were* before you, and thus the land is defiled),

28 'lest the land vomit you out also when you defile it, as it vomited out the nations that *were* before you.

29 'For whoever commits any of these abominations, the persons who commit *them* shall be cut off from among their people.

30 'Therefore you shall keep My ordinance, so that *you* do not commit *any* of these abominable customs which were committed before you, and that you do not defile yourselves by them: I *am* the LORD your God.' "

MORAL AND CEREMONIAL LAWS

19

And the LORD spoke to Moses, saying,

2 "Speak to all the congregation of the children of Israel, and say to them: 'You shall be holy, for I the LORD your God *am* holy.

3 'Every one of you shall revere his mother and his father, and keep My Sabbaths: I *am* the LORD your God.

4 'Do not turn to idols, nor make for yourselves molded gods: I *am* the LORD your God.

5 'And if you offer a sacrifice of a peace offering to the LORD, you shall offer it of your own free will.

6 'It shall be eaten the same day you offer *it,* and on the next day. And if any remains until the third day, it shall be burned in the fire.

7 'And if it is eaten at all on the third day, it *is* an abomination. It shall not be accepted.

8 'Therefore *everyone* who eats it shall bear his iniquity, because he has profaned the hallowed *offering* of the LORD; and that person shall be cut off from his people.

9 'When you reap the harvest of your land, you shall not wholly reap the corners of your field, nor shall you gather the gleanings of your harvest.

10 'And you shall not glean your vineyard, nor shall you gather *every* grape of your vineyard; you shall leave them for the poor and the stranger: I *am* the LORD your God.

11 'You shall not steal, nor deal falsely, nor lie to one another.

12 'And you shall not swear by My name falsely, nor shall you profane the name of your God: I *am* the LORD.

13 'You shall not cheat your neighbor, nor rob *him.* The wages of him who is hired shall not remain with you all night until morning.

14 'You shall not curse the deaf, nor put a stumbling block before the blind, but shall fear your God: I *am* the LORD.

15 'You shall do no injustice in judgment. You shall not be partial to the poor, nor honor the person of the mighty. In righteousness you shall judge your neighbor.

16 'You shall not go about *as* a

HONESTY   Leviticus 19:13

25 Gum Balls for a Penny!

The sign on the gum ball machine is clear. You get one gum ball for each penny. But when you put your penny in, out come 25 gum balls. What should you do?

1. If you stole 24 gum balls from a friend, would that be cheating? Why? If you stole 24 gum balls from a store, would that be cheating? Why?
2. If you broke into a gum ball machine and stole 24 gum balls, would that be cheating? Why?
3. If a gum ball machine accidentally gave you an extra 24 gum balls for your penny, should you keep them? Would that be cheating or stealing? Why?

For more on *Values* turn to page 220
For more on *Honesty* turn to page 301

AN EXTRA STITCH OF LOVE Leviticus 19:18

Alex has a problem. You can see what it is. He needs an extra stitch of love. Mary is helping him. She is giving Alex that extra stitch of love that he needs. What do you think he will say to Mary?

1. Do you ever need an extra little bit of love? Think of some times when you needed that.
2. Who helped you? Who gave you that extra stitch of love?
3. When you need an extra stitch of love, whom do you ask? A friend? Your parents? Jesus?
4. When a friend needs an extra stitch of love, does she ask you? Will you help a friend when a friend needs you? Read Leviticus 19:18. Will you show love to a neighbor?

For more on *What Should I Do?* turn to page 271
For more on *Love* turn to page 317

talebearer among your people; nor shall you take a stand against the life of your neighbor: I *am* the LORD.

17 'You shall not hate your brother in your heart. You shall surely rebuke your neighbor, and not bear sin because of him.

18 'You shall not take vengeance, nor bear any grudge against the children of your people, but you shall love your neighbor as yourself: I *am* the LORD.

19 'You shall keep My statutes. You shall not let your livestock breed with another kind. You shall not sow your field with mixed seed. Nor shall a garment of mixed linen and wool come upon you.

20 'Whoever lies carnally with a woman who *is* betrothed to a man as a concubine, and who has not at all been redeemed nor given her freedom, for this there shall be scourging; *but* they shall not be put to death, because she was not free.

21 'And he shall bring his trespass offering to the LORD, to the door of the tabernacle of meeting, a ram as a trespass offering.

22 'The priest shall make atonement for him with the ram of the trespass offering before the LORD for his sin which he has committed. And the sin which he has committed shall be forgiven him.

23 'When you come into the land, and have planted all kinds of trees for food, then you shall count their fruit as uncircumcised. Three years it shall be as uncircumcised to you. *It* shall not be eaten.

24 'But in the fourth year all its fruit shall be holy, a praise to the LORD.

25 'And in the fifth year you may eat its fruit, that it may yield to you its increase: I *am* the LORD your God.

26 'You shall not eat *anything* with the blood, nor shall you practice divination or soothsaying.

Praises

Leviticus 19:24

Have you ever thought of fruit as a praise to God? What about clouds or trees or bushes or flowers? Are birds a praise to God? What about sheep and puppies and kitties? All of the Creator's creation sings a song of praise to God. What about you?

---

27 'You shall not shave around the sides of your head, nor shall you disfigure the edges of your beard.

28 'You shall not make any cuttings in your flesh for the dead, nor tattoo any marks on you: I *am* the LORD.

29 'Do not prostitute your daughter, to cause her to be a harlot, lest the land fall into harlotry, and the land become full of wickedness.

30 'You shall keep My Sabbaths and reverence My sanctuary: I *am* the LORD.

31 'Give no regard to mediums and familiar spirits; do not seek after them, to be defiled by them: I *am* the LORD your God.

32 'You shall rise before the gray headed and honor the presence of an old man, and fear your God: I *am* the LORD.

33 'And if a stranger dwells with you in your land, you shall not mistreat him.

34 'The stranger who dwells among you shall be to you as one born among you, and you shall love him as yourself; for you were strangers in the land of Egypt: I *am* the LORD your God.

35 'You shall do no injustice in judgment, in measurement of length, weight, or volume.

36 'You shall have honest scales, honest weights, an honest ephah, and

an honest hin: I *am* the LORD your God, who brought you out of the land of Egypt.

37 'Therefore you shall observe all My statutes and all My judgments, and perform them: I *am* the LORD.' "

PENALTIES FOR BREAKING THE LAW

20 Then the LORD spoke to Moses, saying,

2 "Again, you shall say to the children of Israel: 'Whoever of the children of Israel, or of the strangers who dwell in Israel, who gives *any* of his descendants to Mō′lech, he shall surely be put to death. The people of the land shall stone him with stones.

3 'I will set My face against that man, and will cut him off from his people, because he has given *some* of his descendants to Mō′lech, to defile My sanctuary and profane My holy name.

4 'And if the people of the land should in any way hide their eyes from the man, when he gives *some* of his descendants to Mō′lech, and they do not kill him,

5 'then I will set My face against that man and against his family; and I will cut him off from his people, and all who prostitute themselves with him to commit harlotry with Mō′lech.

6 'And the person who turns to mediums and familiar spirits, to prostitute himself with them, I will set My face against that person and cut him off from his people.

7 'Consecrate yourselves therefore, and be holy, for I *am* the LORD your God.

8 'And you shall keep My statutes, and perform them: I *am* the LORD who sanctifies you.

9 'For everyone who curses his father or his mother shall surely be put to death. He has cursed his father or his mother. His blood *shall be* upon him.

10 'The man who commits adultery with *another* man's wife, *he* who commits adultery with his neighbor's wife, the adulterer and the adulteress, shall surely be put to death.

11 'The man who lies with his father's wife has uncovered his father's nakedness; both of them shall surely be put to death. Their blood *shall be* upon them.

12 'If a man lies with his daughter-in-law, both of them shall surely be put to death. They have committed perversion. Their blood *shall be* upon them.

13 'If a man lies with a male as he lies with a woman, both of them have committed an abomination. They shall surely be put to death. Their blood *shall be* upon them.

14 'If a man marries a woman and her mother, it *is* wickedness. They shall be burned with fire, both he and they, that there may be no wickedness among you.

15 'If a man mates with an animal, he shall surely be put to death, and you shall kill the animal.

16 'If a woman approaches any animal and mates with it, you shall kill the woman and the animal. They shall surely be put to death. Their blood *is* upon them.

17 'If a man takes his sister, his father's daughter or his mother's daughter, and sees her nakedness and she sees his nakedness, it *is* a wicked thing. And they shall be cut off in the sight of their people. He has uncovered his sister's nakedness. He shall bear his guilt.

18 'If a man lies with a woman during her sickness and uncovers her nakedness, he has exposed her flow, and she has uncovered the flow of her blood. Both of them shall be cut off from their people.

DEDICATE Leviticus 20:7, 8

Should I Stay Away from Bad Things?

In Old Testament times some sheep were set apart. They were given for the Lord's offering. They belonged to the Lord, dedicated to Him. The Lord said we should be like those sheep. We should be set apart for the Lord because we belong to Him. We are His people. He asks that we stay away from bad things. When we belong to the Lord, we would rather spend time with Jesus than with bad things. We would rather be with the Lord and His people than with bad people. When we accept Jesus as our Savior, we are different from others. We don't do all the things our playmates do. We don't say all the words they say. Read Leviticus 20:7, 8. What does it say? What does it mean?

1. Have you accepted Jesus as your Savior? Have you asked Him to take away your sin and make you clean? If you have, you are a Christian. Christians are different from others. They love Jesus and want to please Him.

2. Every Christian should try to stay away from bad things. Have you been tempted to do bad things or look at bad things this week? Don't! Read your Bible instead. Pray and spend time with Jesus instead.

3. Every Christian should try to please Jesus. He wants us to read our Bible and pray each day. He wants us to live the way the Bible says. He wants us to think good thoughts, say good words and do good things. That's because He is good. When we are Christians, we should be like Him.

For more on *Favorite Bible Words* turn to page 277
For more on *Obeying* turn to page 273

19 'You shall not uncover the nakedness of your mother's sister nor of your father's sister, for that would uncover his near of kin. They shall bear their guilt.

20 'If a man lies with his uncle's wife, he has uncovered his uncle's nakedness. They shall bear their sin; they shall die childless.

21 'If a man takes his brother's wife, it *is* an unclean thing. He has uncovered his brother's nakedness. They shall be childless.

22 'You shall therefore keep all My statutes and all My judgments, and perform them, that the land where I am bringing you to dwell may not vomit you out.

23 'And you shall not walk in the statutes of the nation which I am casting out before you; for they commit all these things, and therefore I abhor them.

24 'But I have said to you, "You shall inherit their land, and I will give it to you to possess, a land flowing with

milk and honey." I *am* the LORD your God, who has separated you from the peoples.

25 'You shall therefore distinguish between clean animals and unclean, between unclean birds and clean, and you shall not make yourselves abominable by beast or by bird, or by any kind of living thing that creeps on the ground, which I have separated from you as unclean.

■ *Promises* ■

Leviticus 20:26

Do you ever say dirty words? God doesn't want to hear dirty words, especially from His people. Do you ever think dirty thoughts? God is holy and pure. He is sad when we think dirty thoughts. God promised us that we who love Him will be His people. He has separated His people from dirty things. Remember that the next time you think a dirty thought or say a dirty word.

---

26 'And you shall be holy to Me, for I the LORD *am* holy, and have separated you from the peoples, that you should be Mine.

27 'A man or a woman who is a medium, or who has familiar spirits, shall surely be put to death; they shall stone them with stones. Their blood *shall be* upon them.' "

REGULATIONS FOR CONDUCT OF PRIESTS

21 And the LORD said to Moses, "Speak to the priests, the sons of Aaron, and say to them: 'None shall defile himself for the dead among his people,

2 'except for his relatives who are nearest to him: his mother, his father, his son, his daughter, and his brother;

3 'also his virgin sister who is near to him, who has had no husband, for her he may defile himself.

4 '*Otherwise* he shall not defile himself, *being* a chief man among his people, to profane himself.

5 'They shall not make any bald *place* on their heads, nor shall they shave the edges of their beards nor make any cuttings in their flesh.

6 'They shall be holy to their God and not profane the name of their God, for they offer the offerings of the LORD made by fire, *and* the bread of their God; therefore they shall be holy.

7 'They shall not take a wife *who is* a harlot or a defiled woman, nor shall they take a woman divorced from her husband; for *the priest*[a] is holy to his God.

8 'Therefore you shall consecrate him, for he offers the bread of your God. He shall be holy to you, for I the LORD, who sanctify you, *am* holy.

9 'The daughter of any priest, if she profanes herself by playing the harlot, she profanes her father. She shall be burned with fire.

10 '*He who is* the high priest among his brethren, on whose head the anointing oil was poured and who is consecrated to wear the garments, shall not uncover his head nor tear his clothes;

11 'nor shall he go near any dead body, nor defile himself for his father or his mother;

12 'nor shall he go out of the sanctuary, nor profane the sanctuary of his God; for the consecration of the

21:7 [a]Literally *he*

anointing oil of his God *is* upon him: I *am* the LORD.

13 'And he shall take a wife in her virginity.

14 'A widow or a divorced woman or a defiled woman *or* a harlot—these he shall not marry; but he shall take a virgin of his own people as wife.

15 'Nor shall he profane his posterity among his people, for I the LORD sanctify him.' "

16 And the LORD spoke to Moses, saying,

17 "Speak to Aaron, saying: 'No man of your descendants in *succeeding* generations, who has *any* defect, may approach to offer the bread of his God.

18 'For any man who has a defect shall not approach: a man blind or lame, who has a marred *face* or any *limb* too long,

19 'a man who has a broken foot or broken hand,

20 'or is a hunchback or a dwarf, or *a man* who has a defect in his eye, or eczema or scab, or is a eunuch.

21 'No man of the descendants of Aaron the priest, who has a defect, shall come near to offer the offerings made by fire to the LORD. He has a defect; he shall not come near to offer the bread of his God.

22 'He may eat the bread of his God, *both* the most holy and the holy;

23 'only he shall not go near the veil or approach the altar, because he has a defect, lest he profane My sanctuaries; for I the LORD sanctify them.' "

24 And Moses told *it* to Aaron and his sons, and to all the children of Israel.

22

Then the LORD spoke to Moses, saying,

2 "Speak to Aaron and his sons, that they separate themselves from the holy things of the children of Is-

rael, and that they do not profane My holy name *by* what they dedicate to Me: I *am* the LORD.

3 "Say to them: 'Whoever of all your descendants throughout your generations, who goes near the holy things which the children of Israel dedicate to the LORD, while he has uncleanness upon him, that person shall be cut off from My presence: I *am* the LORD.

4 'Whatever man of the descendants of Aaron, who *is* a leper or has a discharge, shall not eat the holy offerings until he is clean. And whoever touches anything made unclean *by* a corpse, or a man who has had an emission of semen,

5 'or whoever touches any creeping thing by which he would be made unclean, or any person by whom he would become unclean, whatever his uncleanness may be—

6 'the person who has touched any such thing shall be unclean until evening, and shall not eat the holy *offerings* unless he washes his body with water.

7 'And when the sun goes down he shall be clean; and afterward he may eat the holy *offerings,* because it *is* his food.

8 'Whatever dies *naturally* or is torn *by beasts* he shall not eat, to defile himself with it: I *am* the LORD.

9 'They shall therefore keep My ordinance, lest they bear sin for it and die thereby, if they profane it: I the LORD sanctify them.

10 'No outsider shall eat the holy *offering;* one who dwells with the priest, or a hired servant, shall not eat the holy thing.

11 'But if the priest buys a person with his money, he may eat it; and one who is born in his house may eat his food.

12 'If the priest's daughter is mar-

ried to an outsider, she may not eat of the holy offerings.

13 'But if the priest's daughter is a widow or divorced, and has no child, and has returned to her father's house as in her youth, she may eat her father's food; but no outsider shall eat it.

14 'And if a man eats the holy *offering* unintentionally, then he shall restore a holy *offering* to the priest, and add one-fifth to it.

15 'They shall not profane the holy *offerings* of the children of Israel, which they offer to the LORD,

16 'or allow them to bear the guilt of trespass when they eat their holy *offerings;* for I the LORD sanctify them.' "

OFFERINGS ACCEPTED AND NOT ACCEPTED

17 And the LORD spoke to Moses, saying,

18 "Speak to Aaron and his sons, and to all the children of Israel, and say to them: 'Whatever man of the house of Israel, or of the strangers in Israel, who offers his sacrifice for any of his vows or for any of his freewill offerings, which they offer to the LORD as a burnt offering—

19 'you shall offer of your own free will a male without blemish from the cattle, from the sheep, or from the goats.

20 'Whatever has a defect, you shall not offer, for it shall not be acceptable on your behalf.

21 'And whoever offers a sacrifice of a peace offering to the LORD, to fulfill *his* vow, or a freewill offering from the cattle or the sheep, it must be perfect to be accepted; there shall be no defect in it.

22 'Those *that are* blind or broken or maimed, or have an ulcer or eczema or scabs, you shall not offer to the LORD, nor make an offering by fire of them on the altar to the LORD.

23 'Either a bull or a lamb that has any limb too long or too short you may offer *as* a freewill offering, but for a vow it shall not be accepted.

24 'You shall not offer to the LORD what is bruised or crushed, or torn or cut; nor shall you make *any offering of them* in your land.

25 'Nor from a foreigner's hand shall you offer any of these as the bread of your God, because their corruption *is* in them, *and* defects *are* in them. They shall not be accepted on your behalf.' "

26 And the LORD spoke to Moses, saying:

27 "When a bull or a sheep or a goat is born, it shall be seven days with its mother; and from the eighth day and thereafter it shall be accepted as an offering made by fire to the LORD.

28 "*Whether it is* a cow or ewe, do not kill both her and her young on the same day.

29 "And when you offer a sacrifice of thanksgiving to the LORD, offer *it* of your own free will.

30 "On the same day it shall be eaten; you shall leave none of it until morning: I *am* the LORD.

31 "Therefore you shall keep My commandments, and perform them: I *am* the LORD.

32 "You shall not profane My holy name, but I will be hallowed among the children of Israel. I *am* the LORD who sanctifies you,

33 "who brought you out of the land of Egypt, to be your God: I *am* the LORD."

FEASTS OF THE LORD

23 And the LORD spoke to Moses, saying,

2 "Speak to the children of Israel, and say to them: 'The feasts of the LORD, which you shall proclaim *to be* holy convocations, these *are* My feasts.

THE SABBATH

3 'Six days shall work be done, but the seventh day *is* a Sabbath of solemn rest, a holy convocation. You shall do no work *on it;* it *is* the Sabbath of the LORD in all your dwellings.

THE PASSOVER AND UNLEAVENED BREAD

4 'These *are* the feasts of the LORD, holy convocations which you shall proclaim at their appointed times.
5 'On the fourteenth *day* of the first month at twilight *is* the LORD's Passover.
6 'And on the fifteenth day of the same month *is* the Feast of Unleavened Bread to the LORD; seven days you must eat unleavened bread.
7 'On the first day you shall have a holy convocation; you shall do no customary work on it.
8 'But you shall offer an offering made by fire to the LORD for seven days. The seventh day *shall be* a holy convocation; you shall do no customary work *on it.*' "

THE FEAST OF FIRSTFRUITS

9 And the LORD spoke to Moses, saying,
10 "Speak to the children of Israel, and say to them: 'When you come into the land which I give to you, and reap its harvest, then you shall bring a sheaf of the firstfruits of your harvest to the priest.
11 'He shall wave the sheaf before the LORD, to be accepted on your behalf; on the day after the Sabbath the priest shall wave it.
12 'And you shall offer on that day, when you wave the sheaf, a male lamb of the first year, without blemish, as a burnt offering to the LORD.
13 'Its grain offering *shall be* two-tenths *of an ephah* of fine flour mixed with oil, an offering made by fire to the LORD, for a sweet aroma; and its drink offering *shall be* of wine, one-fourth of a hin.
14 'You shall eat neither bread nor parched grain nor fresh grain until the same day that you have brought an offering to your God; *it shall be* a statute forever throughout your generations in all your dwellings.

THE FEAST OF WEEKS

15 'And you shall count for yourselves from the day after the Sabbath, from the day that you brought the sheaf of the wave offering: seven Sabbaths shall be completed.
16 'Count fifty days to the day after the seventh Sabbath; then you shall offer a new grain offering to the LORD.
17 'You shall bring from your dwellings two wave *loaves* of two-tenths *of an ephah*. They shall be of fine flour; they shall be baked with leaven. *They are* the firstfruits to the LORD.
18 'And you shall offer with the bread seven lambs of the first year, without blemish, one young bull, and two rams. They shall be *as* a burnt offering to the LORD, with their grain offering and their drink offerings, an offering made by fire for a sweet aroma to the LORD.
19 'Then you shall sacrifice one kid of the goats as a sin offering, and two male lambs of the first year as a sacrifice of a peace offering.

20 'The priest shall wave them with the bread of the firstfruits *as* a wave offering before the LORD, with the two lambs. They shall be holy to the LORD for the priest.

21 'And you shall proclaim on the same day *that* it is a holy convocation to you. You shall do no customary work *on it. It shall be* a statute forever in all your dwellings throughout your generations.

22 'When you reap the harvest of your land, you shall not wholly reap the corners of your field when you reap, nor shall you gather any gleaning from your harvest. You shall leave them for the poor and for the stranger: I *am* the LORD your God.' "

THE FEAST OF TRUMPETS

23 Then the LORD spoke to Moses, saying,

24 "Speak to the children of Israel, saying: 'In the seventh month, on the first *day* of the month, you shall have a sabbath-*rest,* a memorial of blowing of trumpets, a holy convocation.

25 'You shall do no customary work *on it;* and you shall offer an offering made by fire to the LORD.' "

THE DAY OF ATONEMENT

26 And the LORD spoke to Moses, saying:

27 "Also the tenth *day* of this seventh month *shall be* the Day of Atonement. It shall be a holy convocation for you; you shall afflict your souls, and offer an offering made by fire to the LORD.

28 "And you shall do no work on that same day, for it *is* the Day of Atonement, to make atonement for you before the LORD your God.

29 "For any person who is not afflicted *in soul* on that same day shall be cut off from his people.

30 "And any person who does any work on that same day, that person I will destroy from among his people.

31 "You shall do no manner of work; *it shall be* a statute forever throughout your generations in all your dwellings.

32 "It *shall be* to you a sabbath of *solemn* rest, and you shall afflict your souls; on the ninth *day* of the month at evening, from evening to evening, you shall celebrate your sabbath."

THE FEAST OF TABERNACLES

33 Then the LORD spoke to Moses, saying,

34 "Speak to the children of Israel, saying: 'The fifteenth day of this seventh month *shall be* the Feast of Tabernacles *for* seven days to the LORD.

35 'On the first day *there shall be* a holy convocation. You shall do no customary work *on it.*

36 'For seven days you shall offer an offering made by fire to the LORD. On the eighth day you shall have a holy convocation, and you shall offer an offering made by fire to the LORD. It *is* a sacred assembly, *and* you shall do no customary work *on it.*

37 'These *are* the feasts of the LORD which you shall proclaim *to be* holy convocations, to offer an offering made by fire to the LORD, a burnt offering and a grain offering, a sacrifice and drink offerings, everything on its day—

38 'besides the Sabbaths of the LORD, besides your gifts, besides all your vows, and besides all your freewill offerings which you give to the LORD.

39 'Also on the fifteenth day of the seventh month, when you have gathered in the fruit of the land, you shall keep the feast of the LORD *for* seven days; on the first day *there shall be* a

sabbath-*rest,* and on the eighth day a sabbath-*rest.*

40 'And you shall take for yourselves on the first day the fruit of beautiful trees, branches of palm trees, the boughs of leafy trees, and willows of the brook; and you shall rejoice before the LORD your God for seven days.

41 'You shall keep it as a feast to the LORD for seven days in the year. *It shall be* a statute forever in your generations. You shall celebrate it in the seventh month.

42 'You shall dwell in booths for seven days. All who are native Israelites shall dwell in booths,

43 'that your generations may know that I made the children of Israel dwell in booths when I brought them out of the land of Egypt: I *am* the LORD your God.'"

44 So Moses declared to the children of Israel the feasts of the LORD.

CARE OF THE TABERNACLE LAMPS

24 Then the LORD spoke to Moses, saying:

2 "Command the children of Israel that they bring to you pure oil of pressed olives for the light, to make the lamps burn continually.

3 "Outside the veil of the Testimony, in the tabernacle of meeting, Aaron shall be in charge of it from evening until morning before the LORD continually; *it shall be* a statute forever in your generations.

4 "He shall be in charge of the lamps on the pure *gold* lampstand before the LORD continually.

THE BREAD OF THE TABERNACLE

5 "And you shall take fine flour and bake twelve cakes with it. Two-tenths *of an ephah* shall be in each cake.

6 "You shall set them in two rows, six in a row, on the pure *gold* table before the LORD.

7 "And you shall put pure frankincense on *each* row, that it may be on the bread for a memorial, an offering made by fire to the LORD.

8 "Every Sabbath he shall set it in order before the LORD continually, *being taken* from the children of Israel by an everlasting covenant.

9 "And it shall be for Aaron and his sons, and they shall eat it in a holy place; for it *is* most holy to him from the offerings of the LORD made by fire, by a perpetual statute."

THE PENALTY FOR BLASPHEMY

10 Now the son of an Israelite woman, whose father *was* an Egyptian, went out among the children of Israel; and this Israelite *woman's* son and a man of Israel fought each other in the camp.

11 And the Israelite woman's son blasphemed the name *of the LORD* and cursed; and so they brought him to Moses. (His mother's name *was* She·lō′mith the daughter of Dib′rī, of the tribe of Dan.)

12 Then they put him in custody, that the mind of the LORD might be shown to them.

13 And the LORD spoke to Moses, saying,

14 "Take outside the camp him who has cursed; then let all who heard *him* lay their hands on his head, and let all the congregation stone him.

15 "Then you shall speak to the children of Israel, saying: 'Whoever curses his God shall bear his sin.

16 'And whoever blasphemes the name of the LORD shall surely be put to death. All the congregation shall certainly stone him, the stranger as well as him who is born in the land. When he blasphemes the

name *of the* LORD, he shall be put to death.

17 'Whoever kills any man shall surely be put to death.

18 'Whoever kills an animal shall make it good, animal for animal.

19 'If a man causes disfigurement of his neighbor, as he has done, so shall it be done to him—

20 'fracture for fracture, eye for eye, tooth for tooth; as he has caused disfigurement of a man, so shall it be done to him.

21 'And whoever kills an animal shall restore it; but whoever kills a man shall be put to death.

22 'You shall have the same law for the stranger and for one from your own country; for I *am* the LORD your God.' "

23 Then Moses spoke to the children of Israel; and they took outside the camp him who had cursed, and stoned him with stones. So the children of Israel did as the LORD commanded Moses.

THE SABBATH OF THE SEVENTH YEAR

25 And the LORD spoke to Moses on Mount Sinai, saying,

2 "Speak to the children of Israel, and say to them: 'When you come into the land which I give you, then the land shall keep a sabbath to the LORD.

3 'Six years you shall sow your field, and six years you shall prune your vineyard, and gather its fruit;

4 'but in the seventh year there shall be a sabbath of solemn rest for the land, a sabbath to the LORD. You shall neither sow your field nor prune your vineyard.

5 'What grows of its own accord of your harvest you shall not reap, nor gather the grapes of your untended

vine, *for* it is a year of rest for the land.

6 'And the sabbath *produce* of the land shall be food for you: for you, your male and female servants, your hired man, and the stranger who dwells with you,

7 'for your livestock and the beasts that *are* in your land—all its produce shall be for food.

THE YEAR OF JUBILEE

8 'And you shall count seven sabbaths of years for yourself, seven times seven years; and the time of the seven sabbaths of years shall be to you forty-nine years.

9 'Then you shall cause the trumpet of the Jubilee to sound on the tenth *day* of the seventh month; on the Day of Atonement you shall make the trumpet to sound throughout all your land.

10 'And you shall consecrate the fiftieth year, and proclaim liberty throughout *all* the land to all its inhabitants. It shall be a Jubilee for you; and each of you shall return to his possession, and each of you shall return to his family.

11 'That fiftieth year shall be a Jubilee to you; in it you shall neither sow nor reap what grows of its own accord, nor gather *the grapes* of your untended vine.

12 'For it *is* the Jubilee; it shall be holy to you; you shall eat its produce from the field.

13 'In this Year of Jubilee, each of you shall return to his possession.

14 'And if you sell anything to your neighbor or buy from your neighbor's hand, you shall not oppress one another.

15 'According to the number of years after the Jubilee you shall buy from your neighbor, and according to the

number of years of crops he shall sell to you.

16 'According to the multitude of years you shall increase its price, and according to the fewer number of years you shall diminish its price; for he sells to you *according* to the number *of the years* of the crops.

17 'Therefore you shall not oppress one another, but you shall fear your God; for I *am* the LORD your God.

PROVISIONS FOR THE SEVENTH YEAR

18 'So you shall observe My statutes and keep My judgments, and perform them; and you will dwell in the land in safety.

19 'Then the land will yield its fruit, and you will eat your fill, and dwell there in safety.

20 'And if you say, "What shall we eat in the seventh year, since we shall not sow nor gather in our produce?"

21 'Then I will command My blessing on you in the sixth year, and it will bring forth produce enough for three years.

22 'And you shall sow in the eighth year, and eat old produce until the ninth year; until its produce comes in, you shall eat *of* the old *harvest*.

REDEMPTION OF PROPERTY

23 'The land shall not be sold permanently, for the land *is* Mine; for you *are* strangers and sojourners with Me.

24 'And in all the land of your possession you shall grant redemption of the land.

25 'If one of your brethren becomes poor, and has sold *some* of his possession, and if his redeeming relative comes to redeem it, then he may redeem what his brother sold.

26 'Or if the man has no one to redeem it, but he himself becomes able to redeem it,

27 'then let him count the years since its sale, and restore the remainder to the man to whom he sold it, that he may return to his possession.

28 'But if he is not able to have *it* restored to himself, then what was sold shall remain in the hand of him who bought it until the Year of Jubilee; and in the Jubilee it shall be released, and he shall return to his possession.

29 'If a man sells a house in a walled city, then he may redeem it within a whole year after it is sold; *within* a full year he may redeem it.

30 'But if it is not redeemed within the space of a full year, then the house in the walled city shall belong permanently to him who bought it, throughout his generations. It shall not be released in the Jubilee.

31 'However the houses of villages which have no wall around them shall be counted as the fields of the country. They may be redeemed, and they shall be released in the Jubilee.

32 'Nevertheless the cities of the Lē′vītes, *and* the houses in the cities of their possession, the Lē′vītes may redeem at any time.

33 'And if a man purchases a house from the Lē′vītes, then the house that was sold in the city of his possession shall be released in the Jubilee; for the houses in the cities of the Lē′vītes *are* their possession among the children of Israel.

34 'But the field of the common-land of their cities may not be sold, for it *is* their perpetual possession.

LENDING TO THE POOR

35 'If one of your brethren becomes poor, and falls into poverty among

you, then you shall help him, like a stranger or a sojourner, that he may live with you.

36 'Take no usury or interest from him; but fear your God, that your brother may live with you.

37 'You shall not lend him your money for usury, nor lend him your food at a profit.

38 'I *am* the LORD your God, who brought you out of the land of Egypt, to give you the land of Cā′naan *and* to be your God.

THE LAW CONCERNING SLAVERY

39 'And if *one of* your brethren *who dwells* by you becomes poor, and sells himself to you, you shall not compel him to serve as a slave.

40 'As a hired servant *and* a sojourner he shall be with you, *and* shall serve you until the Year of Jubilee.

41 'And *then* he shall depart from you—he and his children with him—and shall return to his own family. He shall return to the possession of his fathers.

42 'For they *are* My servants, whom I brought out of the land of Egypt; they shall not be sold as slaves.

43 'You shall not rule over him with rigor, but you shall fear your God.

44 'And as for your male and female slaves whom you may have—from the nations that are around you, from them you may buy male and female slaves.

45 'Moreover you may buy the children of the strangers who dwell among you, and their families who are with you, which they beget in your land; and they shall become your property.

46 'And you may take them as an inheritance for your children after you, to inherit *them as* a possession; they shall be your permanent slaves. But regarding your brethren, the children of Israel, you shall not rule over one another with rigor.

47 'Now if a sojourner or stranger close to you becomes rich, and *one of* your brethren *who dwells* by him becomes poor, and sells himself to the stranger *or* sojourner close to you, or to a member of the stranger's family,

48 'after he is sold he may be redeemed again. One of his brothers may redeem him;

49 'or his uncle or his uncle's son may redeem him; or *anyone* who is near of kin to him in his family may redeem him; or if he is able he may redeem himself.

50 'Thus he shall reckon with him who bought him: The price of his release shall be according to the number of years, from the year that he was sold to him until the Year of Jubilee; *it shall be* according to the time of a hired servant for him.

51 'If *there are* still many years *remaining,* according to them he shall repay the price of his redemption from the money with which he was bought.

52 'And if there remain but a few years until the Year of Jubilee, then he shall reckon with him, *and* according to his years he shall repay him the price of his redemption.

53 'He shall be with him as a yearly hired servant, and he shall not rule with rigor over him in your sight.

54 'And if he is not redeemed in these *years,* then he shall be released in the Year of Jubilee—he and his children with him.

55 'For the children of Israel *are* servants to Me; they *are* My servants whom I brought out of the land of Egypt: I *am* the LORD your God.

PROMISE OF BLESSING AND RETRIBUTION

26 ¹You shall not make idols for yourselves;

neither a carved image nor a *sacred* pillar shall you rear up for yourselves;

nor shall you set up an engraved stone in your land, to bow down to it;

for I *am* the LORD your God.

2 You shall keep My Sabbaths and reverence My sanctuary:

I *am* the LORD.

3 'If you walk in My statutes and keep My commandments, and perform them,

4 then I will give you rain in its season, the land shall yield its produce, and the trees of the field shall yield their fruit.

5 Your threshing shall last till the time of vintage, and the vintage shall last till the time of sowing;

you shall eat your bread to the full, and dwell in your land safely.

6 I will give peace in the land, and you shall lie down, and none will make *you* afraid;

I will rid the land of evil beasts, and the sword will not go through your land.

7 You will chase your enemies, and they shall fall by the sword before you.

8 Five of you shall chase a hundred, and a hundred of you shall put ten thousand to flight;

your enemies shall fall by the sword before you.

9 'For I will look on you favorably and make you fruitful, multiply you and confirm My covenant with you.

Promises

Leviticus 26:12

Do you ever feel lonely or alone? Do you ever feel as if no one is there with you? Do you ever feel as if no one really understands you? Remember God's promise. He walks with us every day, all day. He is there when we think we are alone. He is with us when we think no one is around. He is our God. We are *never* alone. So we should never be lonely.

---

10 You shall eat the old harvest, and clear out the old because of the new.

11 I will set My tabernacle among you, and My soul shall not abhor you.

12 I will walk among you and be your God, and you shall be My people.

13 I *am* the LORD your God, who brought you out of the land of Egypt, that *you* should not be their slaves;

I have broken the bands of your yoke and made you walk upright.

14 'But if you do not obey Me, and do not observe all these commandments,

15 and if you despise My statutes, or if your soul abhors My judgments, so that you do not perform all My commandments, *but* break My covenant,

16 I also will do this to you:

I will even appoint terror over you, wasting disease and fever which shall consume the eyes and cause sorrow of heart.

And you shall sow your seed in vain, for your enemies shall eat it.

17 I will set My face against you, and you shall be defeated by your enemies.

Those who hate you shall reign over you, and you shall flee when no one pursues you.

18 'And after all this, if you do not obey Me, then I will punish you seven times more for your sins.

19 I will break the pride of your power;

I will make your heavens like iron and your earth like bronze.

20 And your strength shall be spent in vain;

for your land shall not yield its produce, nor shall the trees of the land yield their fruit.

21 'Then, if you walk contrary to Me, and are not willing to obey Me, I will bring on you seven times more plagues, according to your sins.

22 I will also send wild beasts among you, which shall rob you of your children, destroy your livestock, and make you few in number;

and your highways shall be desolate.

23 'And if by these things you are not reformed by Me, but walk contrary to Me,

24 then I also will walk contrary to you, and I will punish you yet seven times for your sins.

25 And I will bring a sword against you that will execute the vengeance of the covenant;

when you are gathered together within your cities I will send pestilence among you;

and you shall be delivered into the hand of the enemy.

26 When I have cut off your supply of bread, ten women shall bake your bread in one oven, and they shall bring back your bread by weight, and you shall eat and not be satisfied.

27 'And after all this, if you do not obey Me, but walk contrary to Me,

28 then I also will walk contrary to you in fury;

and I, even I, will chastise you seven times for your sins.

29 You shall eat the flesh of your sons, and you shall eat the flesh of your daughters.

30 I will destroy your high places, cut down your incense altars, and cast your carcasses on the lifeless forms of your idols;

and My soul shall abhor you.

31 I will lay your cities waste and bring your sanctuaries to desolation, and I will not smell the fragrance of your sweet aromas.

32 I will bring the land to desolation, and your enemies who dwell in it shall be astonished at it.

33 I will scatter you among the nations and draw out a sword after you;

your land shall be desolate and your cities waste.

34 Then the land shall enjoy its sabbaths as long as it lies desolate and you *are* in your enemies' land;

then the land shall rest and enjoy its sabbaths.

35 As long as *it* lies desolate it shall rest—

for the time it did not rest on your sabbaths when you dwelt in it.

36 'And as for those of you who are left, I will send faintness into their hearts in the lands of their enemies;

the sound of a shaken leaf shall cause them to flee;

they shall flee as though fleeing from a sword, and they shall fall when no one pursues.

37 They shall stumble over one another, as it were before a sword,
when no one pursues;
and you shall have no *power* to
stand before your enemies.
38 You shall perish among the nations, and the land of your enemies shall eat you up.
39 And those of you who are left
shall waste away in their iniquity in your enemies' lands;
also in their fathers' iniquities,
which are with them, they shall
waste away.

40 '*But* if they confess their iniquity
and the iniquity of their fathers, with their unfaithfulness
in which they were unfaithful
to Me, and that they also have
walked contrary to Me,
41 and *that* I also have walked contrary to them and have brought
them into the land of their enemies;
if their uncircumcised hearts are
humbled, and they accept their
guilt—
42 then I will remember My covenant
with Jacob, and My covenant
with Isaac and My cov-
enant with Abraham I will remember;
I will remember the land.
43 The land also shall be left empty
by them, and will enjoy its sabbaths while it lies desolate
without them;
they will accept their guilt, because they despised My judgments and because their soul
abhorred My statutes.
44 Yet for all that, when they are in
the land of their enemies, I will
not cast them away, nor shall I
abhor them, to utterly destroy
them and break My covenant
with them;
for I *am* the LORD their God.

45 But for their sake I will remember
the covenant of their ancestors,
whom I brought out of the land
of Egypt in the sight of the
nations, that I might be their
God:
I *am* the LORD.' "

46 These *are* the statutes and judgments and laws which the LORD
made between Himself and the children of Israel on Mount Sinai by the
hand of Moses.

REDEEMING PERSONS AND PROPERTY DEDICATED TO GOD

27 Now the LORD spoke to Moses,
saying,
2 "Speak to the children of Israel,
and say to them: 'When a man consecrates by a vow certain persons to the
LORD, according to your valuation,
3 'if your valuation is of a male
from twenty years old up to sixty
years old, then your valuation shall
be fifty shekels of silver, according to
the shekel of the sanctuary.
4 'If it *is* a female, then your valuation shall be thirty shekels;
5 'and if from five years old up to
twenty years old, then your valuation
for a male shall be twenty shekels,
and for a female ten shekels;
6 'and if from a month old up to five
years old, then your valuation for a
male shall be five shekels of silver,
and for a female your valuation shall
be three shekels of silver;
7 'and if from sixty years old and
above, if *it is* a male, then your valuation shall be fifteen shekels, and for
a female ten shekels.
8 'But if he is too poor to pay your
valuation, then he shall present himself before the priest, and the priest
shall set a value for him; according to
the ability of him who vowed, the
priest shall value him.

9 'If *it is* an animal that men may bring as an offering to the LORD, all that *anyone* gives to the LORD shall be holy.
10 'He shall not substitute it or exchange it, good for bad or bad for good; and if he at all exchanges animal for animal, then both it and the one exchanged for it shall be holy.
11 'If *it is* an unclean animal which they do not offer as a sacrifice to the LORD, then he shall present the animal before the priest;
12 'and the priest shall set a value for it, whether it is good or bad; as you, the priest, value it, so it shall be.
13 'But if he *wants* at all *to* redeem it, then he must add one-fifth to your valuation.
14 'And when a man dedicates his house *to be* holy to the LORD, then the priest shall set a value for it, whether it is good or bad; as the priest values it, so it shall stand.
15 'If he who dedicated it *wants to* redeem his house, then he must add one-fifth of the money of your valuation to it, and it shall be his.
16 'If a man dedicates to the LORD *part* of a field of his possession, then your valuation shall be according to the seed for it. A homer of barley seed *shall be valued* at fifty shekels of silver.
17 'If he dedicates his field from the Year of Jubilee, according to your valuation it shall stand.
18 'But if he dedicates his field after the Jubilee, then the priest shall reckon to him the money due according to the years that remain till the Year of Jubilee, and it shall be deducted from your valuation.
19 'And if he who dedicates the field ever wishes to redeem it, then he must add one-fifth of the money of your valuation to it, and it shall belong to him.
20 'But if he does not want to redeem the field, or if he has sold the field to another man, it shall not be redeemed anymore;
21 'but the field, when it is released in the Jubilee, shall be holy to the LORD, as a devoted field; it shall be the possession of the priest.
22 'And if a man dedicates to the LORD a field which he has bought, which is not the field of his possession,
23 'then the priest shall reckon to him the worth of your valuation, up to the Year of Jubilee, and he shall give your valuation on that day *as* a holy *offering* to the LORD.
24 'In the Year of Jubilee the field shall return to him from whom it was bought, to the one who *owned* the land as a possession.
25 'And all your valuations shall be according to the shekel of the sanctuary: twenty gerahs to the shekel.
26 'But the firstborn of the animals, which should be the LORD's firstborn, no man shall dedicate; whether *it is* an ox or sheep, it *is* the LORD's.
27 'And if *it is* an unclean animal, then he shall redeem *it* according to your valuation, and shall add one-fifth to it; or if it is not redeemed, then it shall be sold according to your valuation.
28 'Nevertheless no devoted *offering* that a man may devote to the LORD of all that he has, *both* man and beast, or the field of his possession, shall be sold or redeemed; every devoted *offering is* most holy to the LORD.
29 'No person under the ban, who may become doomed to destruction among men, shall be redeemed, *but* shall surely be put to death.
30 'And all the tithe of the land, *whether* of the seed of the land *or* of the fruit of the tree, *is* the LORD's. It *is* holy to the LORD.
31 'If a man wants at all to redeem

any of his tithes, he shall add one-fifth to it.

32 'And concerning the tithe of the herd or the flock, of whatever passes under the rod, the tenth one shall be holy to the LORD.

33 'He shall not inquire whether it is good or bad, nor shall he exchange it;

and if he exchanges it at all, then both it and the one exchanged for it shall be holy; it shall not be redeemed.'"

34 These *are* the commandments which the LORD commanded Moses for the children of Israel on Mount Sinai.

NUMBERS

THE FIRST CENSUS OF ISRAEL

NOW the LORD spoke to Moses in the Wilderness of Sinai, in the tabernacle of meeting, on the first *day* of the second month, in the second year after they had come out of the land of Egypt, saying:
2 "Take a census of all the congregation of the children of Israel, by their families, by their fathers' houses, according to the number of names, every male individually,
3 "from twenty years old and above—all who *are able to* go to war in Israel. You and Aaron shall number them by their armies.
4 "And with you there shall be a man from every tribe, each one the head of his father's house.
5 "These are the names of the men who shall stand with you: from Reuben, E·lī′zur the son of Shed′e·ur;
6 "from Sim′e·on, She·lū′mi·el the son of Zū·ri·shad′da̅ī;
7 "from Judah, Nah′shon the son of Am·min′a·dab;
8 "from Is′sa·char, Ne·than′el the son of Zū′ar;
9 "from Zeb′ū·lun, E·lī′ab the son of He̅′lon;
10 "from the sons of Joseph: from E̅′phra·im, E·lish′a·ma the son of Am·mī′hud; from Ma·nas′seh, Ga·mā′li·el the son of Pe·dah′zur;
11 "from Benjamin, A·bī′dan the son of Gid·e·ō′ni;
12 "from Dan, A̅·hi·e·ē′zer the son of Am·mi·shad′da̅ī;
13 "from Ash′er, Pā′gi·el the son of Oc′ran;
14 "from Gad, E·lī′a·saph the son of Deū′el;*a*
15 "from Naph′ta·lī, A·hī′ra the son of E̅′nan."
16 These *were* chosen from the con-gregation, leaders of their fathers' tribes, heads of the divisions in Israel.
17 Then Moses and Aaron took these men who had been mentioned by name,
18 and they assembled all the congregation together on the first *day* of the second month; and they recited their ancestry by families, by their fathers' houses, according to the number of names, from twenty years old and above, each one individually.
19 As the LORD commanded Moses, so he numbered them in the Wilderness of Sinai.
20 Now the children of Reuben, Israel's oldest son, their genealogies by their families, by their fathers' house, according to the number of names, every male individually, from twenty years old and above, all who *were able to* go to war:
21 those who were numbered of the tribe of Reuben *were* forty-six thousand five hundred.
22 From the children of Sim′e·on, their genealogies by their families, by their fathers' house, of those who were numbered, according to the number of names, every male individually, from twenty years old and above, all who *were able to* go to war:
23 those who were numbered of the tribe of Sim′e·on *were* fifty-nine thousand three hundred.
24 From the children of Gad, their genealogies by their families, by their fathers' house, according to the number of names, from twenty years old and above, all who *were able to* go to war:
25 those who were numbered of the

1:14 *a*Spelled *Reuel* in 2:14

tribe of Gad *were* forty-five thousand six hundred and fifty.

26 From the children of Judah, their genealogies by their families, by their fathers' house, according to the number of names, from twenty years old and above, all who *were able to* go to war:

27 those who were numbered of the tribe of Judah *were* seventy-four thousand six hundred.

28 From the children of Is'sa·char, their genealogies by their families, by their fathers' house, according to the number of names, from twenty years old and above, all who *were able to* go to war:

29 those who were numbered of the tribe of Is'sa·char *were* fifty-four thousand four hundred.

30 From the children of Zeb'ū·lun, their genealogies by their families, by their fathers' house, according to the number of names, from twenty years old and above, all who *were able to* go to war:

31 those who were numbered of the tribe of Zeb'ū·lun *were* fifty-seven thousand four hundred.

32 From the sons of Joseph, the children of Ē'phra·im, their genealogies by their families, by their fathers' house, according to the number of names, from twenty years old and above, all who *were able to* go to war:

33 those who were numbered of the tribe of Ē'phra·im *were* forty thousand five hundred.

34 From the children of Ma·nas'seh, their genealogies by their families, by their fathers' house, according to the number of names, from twenty years old and above, all who *were able to* go to war:

35 those who were numbered of the tribe of Ma·nas'seh *were* thirty-two thousand two hundred.

36 From the children of Benjamin, their genealogies by their families, by their fathers' house, according to the number of names, from twenty years old and above, all who *were able to* go to war:

37 those who were numbered of the tribe of Benjamin *were* thirty-five thousand four hundred.

38 From the children of Dan, their genealogies by their families, by their fathers' house, according to the number of names, from twenty years old and above, all who *were able to* go to war:

39 those who were numbered of the tribe of Dan *were* sixty-two thousand seven hundred.

40 From the children of Ash'er, their genealogies by their families, by their fathers' house, according to the number of names, from twenty years old and above, all who *were able to* go to war:

41 those who were numbered of the tribe of Ash'er *were* forty-one thousand five hundred.

42 From the children of Naph'ta·lī, their genealogies by their families, by their fathers' house, according to the number of names, from twenty years old and above, all who *were able to* go to war:

43 those who were numbered of the tribe of Naph'ta·lī *were* fifty-three thousand four hundred.

44 These are the ones who were numbered, whom Moses and Aaron numbered, with the leaders of Israel, twelve men, each one representing his father's house.

45 So all who were numbered of the children of Israel, by their fathers' houses, from twenty years old and above, all who *were able to* go to war in Israel—

46 all who were numbered were six hundred and three thousand five hundred and fifty.

47 But the Lē'vītes were not num-

bered among them by their fathers' tribe;

48 for the LORD had spoken to Moses, saying:

49 "Only the tribe of Levi you shall not number, nor take a census of them among the children of Israel;

50 "but you shall appoint the Lē′vītes over the tabernacle of the Testimony, over all its furnishings, and over all things that belong to it; they shall carry the tabernacle and all its furnishings; they shall attend to it and camp around the tabernacle.

51 "And when the tabernacle is to go forward, the Lē′vītes shall take it down; and when the tabernacle is to be set up, the Lē′vītes shall set it up. The outsider who comes near shall be put to death.

52 "The children of Israel shall pitch their tents, everyone by his own camp, everyone by his own standard, according to their armies;

53 "but the Lē′vītes shall camp around the tabernacle of the Testimony, that there may be no wrath on the congregation of the children of Israel; and the Lē′vītes shall keep charge of the tabernacle of the Testimony."

54 Thus the children of Israel did; according to all that the LORD commanded Moses, so they did.

THE TRIBES AND LEADERS BY ARMIES

2 And the LORD spoke to Moses and Aaron, saying:

2 "Everyone of the children of Israel shall camp by his own standard, beside the emblems of his father's house; they shall camp some distance from the tabernacle of meeting.

3 "On the east side, toward the rising of the sun, those of the standard of the forces with Judah shall camp according to their armies; and Nah′shon the son of Am·min′a·dab *shall be* the leader of the children of Judah."

4 And his army was numbered at seventy-four thousand six hundred.

5 "Those who camp next to him *shall be* the tribe of Is′sa·char, and Ne·than′el the son of Zū′ar *shall be* the leader of the children of Is′sa·char."

6 And his army was numbered at fifty-four thousand four hundred.

7 "Then *comes* the tribe of Zeb′-ū·lun, and E·lī′ab the son of Hē′lon *shall be* the leader of the children of Zeb′ū·lun."

8 And his army was numbered at fifty-seven thousand four hundred.

9 "All who were numbered according to their armies of the forces with Judah, one hundred and eighty-six thousand four hundred—these shall break camp first.

10 "On the south side *shall be* the standard of the forces with Reuben according to their armies, and the leader of the children of Reuben *shall be* E·lī′zur the son of Shed′ē·ur."

11 And his army was numbered at forty-six thousand five hundred.

12 "Those who camp next to him *shall be* the tribe of Sim′ē·on, and the leader of the children of Sim′ē·on *shall be* She·lū′mi·el the son of Zū·ri-shad′dai."

13 And his army was numbered at fifty-nine thousand three hundred.

14 "Then *comes* the tribe of Gad, and the leader of the children of Gad *shall be* E·lī′a·saph the son of Reū′el."a

15 And his army was numbered at forty-five thousand six hundred and fifty.

16 "All who were numbered according to their armies of the forces with

2:14 aSpelled *Deuel* in 1:14 and 7:42

Reuben, one hundred and fifty-one thousand four hundred and fifty—they shall be the second to break camp.

17 "And the tabernacle of meeting shall move out with the camp of the Lē'vītes in the middle of the camps; as they camp, so they shall move out, everyone in his place, by their standards.

18 "On the west side *shall be* the standard of the forces with Ē'phra·im according to their armies, and the leader of the children of Ē'phra·im *shall be* E·lish'a·ma the son of Am·mī'hud."

19 And his army was numbered at forty thousand five hundred.

20 "Next to him *comes* the tribe of Ma·nas'seh, and the leader of the children of Ma·nas'seh *shall be* Ga·mā'li·el the son of Pe·dah'zur."

21 And his army was numbered at thirty-two thousand two hundred.

22 "Then *comes* the tribe of Benjamin, and the leader of the children of Benjamin *shall be* A·bī'dan the son of Gid·ē·ō'ni."

23 And his army was numbered at thirty-five thousand four hundred.

24 "All who were numbered according to their armies of the forces with Ē'phra·im, one hundred and eight thousand one hundred—they shall be the third to break camp.

25 "The standard of the forces with Dan *shall be* on the north side according to their armies, and the leader of the children of Dan *shall be* Ā·hi·ē'zer the son of Am·mi·shad'daī."

26 And his army was numbered at sixty-two thousand seven hundred.

27 "Those who camp next to him *shall be* the tribe of Ash'er, and the leader of the children of Ash'er *shall be* Pā'gi·el the son of Oc'ran."

28 And his army was numbered at forty-one thousand five hundred.

29 "Then *comes* the tribe of Naph'-ta·lī, and the leader of the children of Naph'ta·lī *shall be* A·hī'ra the son of Ē'nan."

30 And his army was numbered at fifty-three thousand four hundred.

31 "All who were numbered of the forces with Dan, one hundred and fifty-seven thousand six hundred—they shall break camp last, with their standards."

32 These *are* the ones who were numbered of the children of Israel by their fathers' houses. All who were numbered according to their armies of the forces *were* six hundred and three thousand five hundred and fifty.

33 But the Lē'vītes were not numbered among the children of Israel, just as the LORD commanded Moses.

34 Thus the children of Israel did according to all that the LORD commanded Moses; so they camped by their standards and so they broke camp, each one by his family, according to their fathers' houses.

THE SONS OF AARON

3 Now these *are* the records of Aaron and Moses when the LORD spoke with Moses on Mount Sinai.

2 And these *are* the names of the sons of Aaron: Nā'dab, the firstborn, and A·bī'hū, El·ē·ā'zar, and Ith'a-mar.

3 These *are* the names of the sons of Aaron, the anointed priests, whom he consecrated to minister as priests.

4 Nā'dab and A·bī'hū had died before the LORD when they offered profane fire before the LORD in the Wilderness of Sinai; and they had no children. So El·ē·ā'zar and Ith'a·mar ministered as priests in the presence of Aaron their father.

THE LEVITES SERVE IN THE TABERNACLE

5 And the LORD spoke to Moses, saying:

6 "Bring the tribe of Levi near, and present them before Aaron the priest, that they may serve him.

7 "And they shall attend to his needs and the needs of the whole congregation before the tabernacle of meeting, to do the work of the tabernacle.

8 "Also they shall attend to all the furnishings of the tabernacle of meeting, and to the needs of the children of Israel, to do the work of the tabernacle.

9 "And you shall give the Lē'vītes to Aaron and his sons; they *are* given entirely to him*a* from among the children of Israel.

10 "So you shall appoint Aaron and his sons, and they shall attend to their priesthood; but the outsider who comes near shall be put to death."

11 Then the LORD spoke to Moses, saying:

12 "Now behold, I Myself have taken the Lē'vītes from among the children of Israel instead of every firstborn who opens the womb among the children of Israel. Therefore the Lē'vītes shall be Mine,

13 "because all the firstborn *are* Mine. On the day that I struck all the firstborn in the land of Egypt, I sanctified to Myself all the firstborn in Israel, both man and beast. They shall be Mine: I *am* the LORD."

CENSUS OF THE LEVITES COMMANDED

14 Then the LORD spoke to Moses in the Wilderness of Sinai, saying:

15 "Number the children of Levi by their fathers' houses, by their families; you shall number every male from a month old and above."

16 So Moses numbered them according to the word of the LORD, as he was commanded.

17 These were the sons of Levi by their names: Ger'shon, Kō'hath, and Me·rar'ī.

18 And these *are* the names of the sons of Ger'shon by their families: Lib'nī and Shim'ē·ī.

19 And the sons of Kō'hath by their families: Am'ram, Iz'e·har, Hē'bron, and Uz'zi·el.

20 And the sons of Me·rar'ī by their families: Mah'lī and Mū'shī. These *are* the families of the Lē'vītes by their fathers' houses.

21 From Ger'shon *came* the family of the Lib'nītes and the family of the Shim'ītes; these *were* the families of the Ger'shon·ītes.

22 Those who were numbered, according to the number of all the males from a month old and above— of those who were numbered *there were* seven thousand five hundred.

23 The families of the Ger'shon·ītes were to camp behind the tabernacle westward.

24 And the leader of the father's house of the Ger'shon·ītes *was* E·lī'a·saph the son of Lā'el.

25 The duties of the children of Ger'shon in the tabernacle of meeting *included* the tabernacle, the tent with its covering, the screen for the door of the tabernacle of meeting,

26 the screen for the door of the court, the hangings of the court which *are* around the tabernacle and the altar, and their cords, according to all the work relating to them.

27 From Kō'hath *came* the family of the Am'ram·ītes, the family of the Iz'har·ītes, the family of the Hē'-bron·ītes, and the family of the Uz'-

3:9 *a*Samaritan Pentateuch and Septuagint read *Me.*

zi·el·ites; these *were* the families of the Kō'hath·ites.

28 According to the number of all the males, from a month old and above, *there were* eight thousand six*a* hundred keeping charge of the sanctuary.

29 The families of the children of Kō'hath were to camp on the south side of the tabernacle.

30 And the leader of the fathers' house of the families of the Kō'-hath·ites *was* E·li·zā'phan the son of Uz'zi·el.

31 Their duty *included* the ark, the table, the lampstand, the altars, the utensils of the sanctuary with which they ministered, the screen, and all the work relating to them.

32 And El·e·ā'zar the son of Aaron the priest *was to be* chief over the leaders of the Lē'vites, *with* oversight of those who kept charge of the sanctuary.

33 From Me·rar'ī *came* the family of the Mah'lites and the family of the Mū'shites; these *were* the families of Me·rar'ī.

34 And those who were numbered, according to the number of all the males from a month old and above, *were* six thousand two hundred.

35 The leader of the fathers' house of the families of Me·rar'ī *was* Zū'ri·el the son of Ab·i·hā'il. These *were* to camp on the north side of the tabernacle.

36 And the appointed duty of the children of Me·rar'ī *included* the boards of the tabernacle, its bars, its pillars, its sockets, its utensils, all the work relating to them,

37 and the pillars of the court all around, with their sockets, their pegs, and their cords.

38 Moreover those who were to camp before the tabernacle on the east, before the tabernacle of meeting, *were* Moses, Aaron, and his sons, keeping charge of the sanctuary, to meet the needs of the children of Israel; but the outsider who came near was to be put to death.

39 All who were numbered of the Lē'vites, whom Moses and Aaron numbered at the commandment of the LORD, by their families, all the males from a month old and above, *were* twenty-two thousand.

LEVITES DEDICATED INSTEAD OF THE FIRSTBORN

40 Then the LORD said to Moses: "Number all the firstborn males of the children of Israel from a month old and above, and take the number of their names.

41 "And you shall take the Lē'vites for Me—I *am* the LORD—instead of all the firstborn among the children of Israel, and the livestock of the Lē'vites instead of all the firstborn among the livestock of the children of Israel."

42 So Moses numbered all the firstborn among the children of Israel, as the LORD commanded him.

43 And all the firstborn males, according to the number of names from a month old and above, of those who were numbered of them, were twenty-two thousand two hundred and seventy-three.

44 Then the LORD spoke to Moses, saying:

45 "Take the Lē'vites instead of all the firstborn among the children of Israel, and the livestock of the Lē'vites instead of their livestock. The Lē'vites shall be Mine: I *am* the LORD.

46 "And for the redemption of the two hundred and seventy-three of the firstborn of the children of Israel, who are more than the number of the Lē'vites,

3:28 *a*Some manuscripts of the Septuagint read *three.*

47 "you shall take five shekels for each one individually; you shall take *them* in the currency of the shekel of the sanctuary, the shekel of twenty gerahs.

48 "And you shall give the money, with which the excess number of them is redeemed, to Aaron and his sons."

49 So Moses took the redemption money from those who were over and above those who were redeemed by the Lē'vītes.

50 From the firstborn of the children of Israel he took the money, one thousand three hundred and sixty-five *shekels,* according to the shekel of the sanctuary.

51 And Moses gave their redemption money to Aaron and his sons, according to the word of the LORD, as the LORD commanded Moses.

DUTIES OF THE SONS OF KOHATH

4 Then the LORD spoke to Moses and Aaron, saying:

2 "Take a census of the sons of Kō'hath from among the children of Levi, by their families, by their fathers' house,

3 "from thirty years old and above, even to fifty years old, all who enter the service to do the work in the tabernacle of meeting.

4 "This *is* the service of the sons of Kō'hath in the tabernacle of meeting, *relating to* the most holy things:

5 "When the camp prepares to journey, Aaron and his sons shall come, and they shall take down the covering veil and cover the ark of the Testimony with it.

6 "Then they shall put on it a covering of badger skins, and spread over *that* a cloth entirely of blue; and they shall insert its poles.

7 "On the table of showbread they shall spread a blue cloth, and put on it the dishes, the pans, the bowls, and the pitchers for pouring; and the showbread[a] shall be on it.

8 "They shall spread over them a scarlet cloth, and cover the same with a covering of badger skins; and they shall insert its poles.

9 "And they shall take a blue cloth and cover the lampstand of the light, with its lamps, its wick-trimmers, its trays, and all its oil vessels, with which they service it.

10 "Then they shall put it with all its utensils in a covering of badger skins, and put *it* on a carrying beam.

11 "Over the golden altar they shall spread a blue cloth, and cover it with a covering of badger skins; and they shall insert its poles.

12 "Then they shall take all the utensils of service with which they minister in the sanctuary, put *them* in a blue cloth, cover them with a covering of badger skins, and put *them* on a carrying beam.

13 "Also they shall take away the ashes from the altar, and spread a purple cloth over it.

14 "They shall put on it all its implements with which they minister there—the firepans, the forks, the shovels, the basins, and all the utensils of the altar—and they shall spread on it a covering of badger skins, and insert its poles.

15 "And when Aaron and his sons have finished covering the sanctuary and all the furnishings of the sanctuary, when the camp is set to go, then the sons of Kō'hath shall come to carry *them;* but they shall not touch any holy thing, lest they die. These *are* the things in the tabernacle of meeting which the sons of Kō'hath are to carry.

16 "The appointed duty of El·e·ā'zar the son of Aaron the priest *is* the oil

4:7 [a]Literally *the continual bread*

for the light, the sweet incense, the daily grain offering, the anointing oil, the oversight of all the tabernacle, of all that *is* in it, with the sanctuary and its furnishings."

17 Then the LORD spoke to Moses and Aaron, saying:

18 "Do not cut off the tribe of the families of the Kō′hath·ites from among the Lē′vites;

19 "but do this in regard to them, that they may live and not die when they approach the most holy things: Aaron and his sons shall go in and appoint each of them to his service and his task.

20 "But they shall not go in to watch while the holy things are being covered, lest they die."

DUTIES OF THE SONS OF GERSHON

21 Then the LORD spoke to Moses, saying:

22 "Also take a census of the sons of Ger′shon, by their fathers' house, by their families.

23 "From thirty years old and above, even to fifty years old, you shall number them, all who enter to perform the service, to do the work in the tabernacle of meeting.

24 "This *is* the service of the families of the Ger′shon·ites, in serving and carrying:

25 "They shall carry the curtains of the tabernacle and the tabernacle of meeting *with* its covering, the covering of badger skins that *is* on it, the screen for the door of the tabernacle of meeting,

26 "the screen for the door of the gate of the court, the hangings of the court which *are* around the tabernacle and altar, and their cords, all the furnishings for their service and all that is made for these things: so shall they serve.

27 "Aaron and his sons shall assign

all the service of the sons of the Ger′shon·ites, all their tasks and all their service. And you shall appoint to them all their tasks as their duty.

28 "This *is* the service of the families of the sons of Ger′shon in the tabernacle of meeting. And their duties *shall be* under the authority[a] of Ith′a·mar the son of Aaron the priest.

DUTIES OF THE SONS OF MERARI

29 "*As for* the sons of Me·rar′i, you shall number them by their families and by their fathers' house.

30 "From thirty years old and above, even to fifty years old, you shall number them, everyone who enters the service to do the work of the tabernacle of meeting.

31 "And this *is* what they must carry as all their service for the tabernacle of meeting: the boards of the tabernacle, its bars, its pillars, its sockets,

32 "and the pillars around the court with their sockets, pegs, and cords, with all their furnishings and all their service; and you shall assign *to each man* by name the items he must carry.

33 "This *is* the service of the families of the sons of Me·rar′i, as all their service for the tabernacle of meeting, under the authority[a] of Ith′a·mar the son of Aaron the priest."

CENSUS OF THE LEVITES

34 And Moses, Aaron, and the leaders of the congregation numbered the sons of the Kō′hath·ites by their families and by their fathers' house,

35 from thirty years old and above, even to fifty years old, everyone who entered the service for work in the tabernacle of meeting;

36 and those who were numbered by

4:28 [a]Literally *hand*   4:33 [a]Literally *hand*

their families were two thousand seven hundred and fifty.

37 These *were* the ones who were numbered of the families of the Kō′hath·ītes, all who might serve in the tabernacle of meeting, whom Moses and Aaron numbered according to the commandment of the LORD by the hand of Moses.

38 And those who were numbered of the sons of Ger′shon, by their families and by their fathers' house,

39 from thirty years old and above, even to fifty years old, everyone who entered the service for work in the tabernacle of meeting—

40 those who were numbered by their families, by their fathers' house, were two thousand six hundred and thirty.

41 These *are* the ones who were numbered of the families of the sons of Ger′shon, of all who might serve in the tabernacle of meeting, whom Moses and Aaron numbered according to the commandment of the LORD.

42 Those of the families of the sons of Me·rar′ī who were numbered, by their families, by their fathers' house,

43 from thirty years old and above, even to fifty years old, everyone who entered the service for work in the tabernacle of meeting—

44 those who were numbered by their families were three thousand two hundred.

45 These *are* the ones who were numbered of the families of the sons of Me·rar′ī, whom Moses and Aaron numbered according to the word of the LORD by the hand of Moses.

46 All who were numbered of the Lē′vītes, whom Moses, Aaron, and the leaders of Israel numbered, by their families and by their fathers' houses,

47 from thirty years old and above, even to fifty years old, everyone who came to do the work of service and the work of bearing burdens in the tabernacle of meeting—

48 those who were numbered were eight thousand five hundred and eighty.

49 According to the commandment of the LORD they were numbered by the hand of Moses, each according to his service and according to his task; thus were they numbered by him, as the LORD commanded Moses.

CEREMONIALLY UNCLEAN PERSONS ISOLATED

5 And the LORD spoke to Moses, saying:
2 "Command the children of Israel that they put out of the camp every leper, everyone who has a discharge, and whoever becomes defiled by a corpse.
3 "You shall put out both male and female; you shall put them outside the camp, that they may not defile their camps in the midst of which I dwell."
4 And the children of Israel did so, and put them outside the camp; as the LORD spoke to Moses, so the children of Israel did.

CONFESSION AND RESTITUTION

5 Then the LORD spoke to Moses, saying,
6 "Speak to the children of Israel: 'When a man or woman commits any sin that men commit in unfaithfulness against the LORD, and that person is guilty,
7 'then he shall confess the sin which he has committed. He shall make restitution for his trespass in full, plus one-fifth of it, and give *it* to the one he has wronged.
8 'But if the man has no relative to whom restitution may be made for the wrong, the restitution for the

wrong *must go* to the LORD for the priest, in addition to the ram of the atonement with which atonement is made for him.

9 'Every offering of all the holy things of the children of Israel, which they bring to the priest, shall be his.

10 'And every man's holy things shall be his; whatever any man gives the priest shall be his.' "

CONCERNING UNFAITHFUL WIVES

11 And the LORD spoke to Moses, saying,

12 "Speak to the children of Israel, and say to them: 'If any man's wife goes astray and behaves unfaithfully toward him,

13 'and a man lies with her carnally, and it is hidden from the eyes of her husband, and it is concealed that she has defiled herself, and *there was* no witness against her, nor was she caught—

14 'if the spirit of jealousy comes upon him and he becomes jealous of his wife, who has defiled herself; or if the spirit of jealousy comes upon him and he becomes jealous of his wife, although she has not defiled herself—

15 'then the man shall bring his wife to the priest. He shall bring the offering required for her, one-tenth of an ephah of barley meal; he shall pour no oil on it and put no frankincense on it, because it *is* a grain offering of jealousy, an offering for remembering, for bringing iniquity to remembrance.

16 'And the priest shall bring her near, and set her before the LORD.

17 'The priest shall take holy water in an earthen vessel, and take some of the dust that is on the floor of the tabernacle and put *it* into the water.

18 'Then the priest shall stand the woman before the LORD, uncover the woman's head, and put the offering for remembering in her hands, which *is* the grain offering of jealousy. And the priest shall have in his hand the bitter water that brings a curse.

19 'And the priest shall put her under oath, and say to the woman, "If no man has lain with you, and if you have not gone astray to uncleanness *while* under your husband's *authority,* be free from this bitter water that brings a curse.

20 "But if you have gone astray *while* under your husband's *authority,* and if you have defiled yourself and some man other than your husband has lain with you"—

21 'then the priest shall put the woman under the oath of the curse, and he shall say to the woman—"the LORD make you a curse and an oath among your people, when the LORD makes your thigh rot and your belly swell;

22 "and may this water that causes the curse go into your stomach, and make *your* belly swell and *your* thigh rot." Then the woman shall say, "Amen, so be it."

23 'Then the priest shall write these curses in a book, and he shall scrape *them* off into the bitter water.

24 'And he shall make the woman drink the bitter water that brings a curse, and the water that brings the curse shall enter her *to become* bitter.

25 'Then the priest shall take the grain offering of jealousy from the woman's hand, shall wave the offering before the LORD, and bring it to the altar;

26 'and the priest shall take a handful of the offering, as its memorial portion, burn *it* on the altar, and afterward make the woman drink the water.

27 'When he has made her drink the water, then it shall be, if she has defiled herself and behaved unfaithfully

toward her husband, that the water that brings a curse will enter her *and become* bitter, and her belly will swell, her thigh will rot, and the woman will become a curse among her people.

28 'But if the woman has not defiled herself, and is clean, then she shall be free and may conceive children.

29 'This *is* the law of jealousy, when a wife, *while* under her husband's *authority,* goes astray and defiles herself,

30 'or when the spirit of jealousy comes upon a man, and he becomes jealous of his wife; then he shall stand the woman before the LORD, and the priest shall execute all this law upon her.

31 'Then the man shall be free from iniquity, but that woman shall bear her guilt.'"

THE LAW OF THE NAZIRITE

6 Then the LORD spoke to Moses, saying,

2 "Speak to the children of Israel, and say to them: 'When either a man or woman consecrates an offering to take the vow of a Naz'ir-īte, to separate himself to the LORD,

3 'he shall separate himself from wine and *similar* drink; he shall drink neither vinegar made from wine nor vinegar made from *similar* drink; neither shall he drink any grape juice, nor eat fresh grapes or raisins.

4 'All the days of his separation he shall eat nothing that is produced by the grapevine, from seed to skin.

5 'All the days of the vow of his separation no razor shall come upon his head; until the days are fulfilled for which he separated himself to the LORD, he shall be holy. *Then* he shall let the locks of the hair of his head grow.

6 'All the days that he separates himself to the LORD he shall not go near a dead body.

7 'He shall not make himself unclean even for his father or his mother, for his brother or his sister, when they die, because his separation to God *is* on his head.

8 'All the days of his separation he shall be holy to the LORD.

9 'And if anyone dies very suddenly beside him, and he defiles his consecrated head, then he shall shave his head on the day of his cleansing; on the seventh day he shall shave it.

10 'Then on the eighth day he shall bring two turtledoves or two young pigeons to the priest, to the door of the tabernacle of meeting;

11 'and the priest shall offer one as a sin offering and *the* other as a burnt offering, and make atonement for him, because he sinned in regard to the corpse; and he shall sanctify his head that same day.

12 'He shall consecrate to the LORD the days of his separation, and bring a male lamb in its first year as a trespass offering; but the former days shall be lost, because his separation was defiled.

13 'Now this *is* the law of the Naz'ir-īte: When the days of his separation are fulfilled, he shall be brought to the door of the tabernacle of meeting.

14 'And he shall present his offering to the LORD: one male lamb in its first year without blemish as a burnt offering, one ewe lamb in its first year without blemish as a sin offering, one ram without blemish as a peace offering,

15 'a basket of unleavened bread, cakes of fine flour mixed with oil, unleavened wafers anointed with oil, and their grain offering with their drink offerings.

16 'Then the priest shall bring *them*

before the Lord and offer his sin offering and his burnt offering;

17 'and he shall offer the ram as a
sacrifice of a peace offering to the
Lord, with the basket of unleavened
bread; the priest shall also offer its
grain offering and its drink offering.

18 'Then the Naz'ir·īte shall shave
his consecrated head *at* the door of
the tabernacle of meeting, and shall
take the hair from his consecrated
head and put *it* on the fire which is
under the sacrifice of the peace
offering.

19 'And the priest shall take the
boiled shoulder of the ram, one unleavened cake from the basket, and
one unleavened wafer, and put *them*
upon the hands of the Naz'ir·īte after
he has shaved his consecrated *hair,*

20 'and the priest shall wave them
as a wave offering before the Lord;
they *are* holy for the priest, together
with the breast of the wave offering
and the thigh of the heave offering.
After that the Naz'ir·īte may drink
wine.'

21 "This is the law of the Naz'ir·īte
who vows to the Lord the offering for
his separation, and besides that,
whatever else his hand is able to provide; according to the vow which he
takes, so he must do according to the
law of his separation."

THE PRIESTLY BLESSING

22 And the Lord spoke to Moses,
saying:

23 "Speak to Aaron and his sons, saying, 'This is the way you shall bless
the children of Israel. Say to them:

24 "The Lord bless you and keep you;

25 The Lord make His face shine
    upon you,
And be gracious to you;

26 The Lord lift up His countenance
    upon you,
And give you peace." '

27 "So they shall put My name on
the children of Israel, and I will bless
them."

OFFERINGS OF THE LEADERS

7 Now it came to pass, when Moses
had finished setting up the tabernacle, that he anointed it and consecrated it and all its furnishings, and
the altar and all its utensils; so he
anointed them and consecrated them.

2 Then the leaders of Israel, the
heads of their fathers' houses, who
were the leaders of the tribes and
over those who were numbered, made
an offering.

3 And they brought their offering
before the Lord, six covered carts
and twelve oxen, a cart for *every* two
of the leaders, and for each one an ox;
and they presented them before the
tabernacle.

4 Then the Lord spoke to Moses,
saying,

5 "Accept *these* from them, that
they may be used in doing the work
of the tabernacle of meeting; and you
shall give them to the Lē'vītes, *to*
every man according to his service."

6 So Moses took the carts and the
oxen, and gave them to the Lē'vītes.

7 Two carts and four oxen he gave
to the sons of Ger'shon, according to
their service;

8 and four carts and eight oxen he
gave to the sons of Me·rar'ī, according to their service, under the authority[a] of Ith'a·mar the son of Aaron the
priest.

9 But to the sons of Kō'hath he
gave none, because theirs *was* the
service of the holy things, *which* they
carried on their shoulders.

10 Now the leaders offered the dedication *offering* for the altar when it
was anointed; so the leaders offered
their offering before the altar.

7:8 [a]Literally *hand*

11 For the LORD said to Moses, "They shall offer their offering, one leader each day, for the dedication of the altar."

12 And the one who offered his offering on the first day *was* Nah'shon the son of Am·min'a·dab, from the tribe of Judah.

13 His offering *was* one silver platter, the weight of which *was* one hundred and thirty *shekels,* and one silver bowl of seventy shekels, according to the shekel of the sanctuary, both of them full of fine flour mixed with oil as a grain offering;

14 one gold pan of ten *shekels,* full of incense;

15 one young bull, one ram, and one male lamb in its first year, as a burnt offering;

16 one kid of the goats as a sin offering;

17 and for the sacrifice of peace offerings: two oxen, five rams, five male goats, and five male lambs in their first year. This *was* the offering of Nah'shon the son of Am·min'a·dab.

18 On the second day Ne·than'el the son of Zū'ar, leader of Is'sa·char, presented *an offering.*

19 *For* his offering he offered one silver platter, the weight of which *was* one hundred and thirty *shekels,* and one silver bowl of seventy shekels, according to the shekel of the sanctuary, both of them full of fine flour mixed with oil as a grain offering;

20 one gold pan of ten *shekels,* full of incense;

21 one young bull, one ram, and one male lamb in its first year, as a burnt offering;

22 one kid of the goats as a sin offering;

23 and as the sacrifice of peace offerings: two oxen, five rams, five male goats, and five male lambs in their first year. This *was* the offering of Ne·than'el the son of Zū'ar.

24 On the third day E·lī'ab the son of Hē'lon, leader of the children of Zeb'ū·lun, *presented an offering.*

25 His offering *was* one silver platter, the weight of which *was* one hundred and thirty *shekels,* and one silver bowl of seventy shekels, according to the shekel of the sanctuary, both of them full of fine flour mixed with oil as a grain offering;

26 one gold pan of ten *shekels,* full of incense;

27 one young bull, one ram, and one male lamb in its first year, as a burnt offering;

28 one kid of the goats as a sin offering;

29 and for the sacrifice of peace offerings: two oxen, five rams, five male goats, and five male lambs in their first year. This *was* the offering of E·lī'ab the son of Hē'lon.

30 On the fourth day E·lī'zur the son of Shed'ē·ur, leader of the children of Reuben, *presented an offering.*

31 His offering *was* one silver platter, the weight of which *was* one hundred and thirty *shekels,* and one silver bowl of seventy shekels, according to the shekel of the sanctuary, both of them full of fine flour mixed with oil as a grain offering;

32 one gold pan of ten *shekels,* full of incense;

33 one young bull, one ram, and one male lamb in its first year, as a burnt offering;

34 one kid of the goats as a sin offering;

35 and as the sacrifice of peace offerings: two oxen, five rams, five male goats, and five male lambs in their first year. This *was* the offering of E·lī'zur the son of Shed'ē·ur.

36 On the fifth day She·lū'mi·el the son of Zū·ri·shad'dai, leader of the children of Sim'ē·on, *presented an offering.*

37 His offering *was* one silver plat-

ter, the weight of which *was* one hundred and thirty *shekels,* and one silver bowl of seventy shekels, according to the shekel of the sanctuary, both of them full of fine flour mixed with oil as a grain offering;

38 one gold pan of ten *shekels,* full of incense;

39 one young bull, one ram, and one male lamb in its first year, as a burnt offering;

40 one kid of the goats as a sin offering;

41 and as the sacrifice of peace offerings: two oxen, five rams, five male goats, and five male lambs in their first year. This *was* the offering of She·lū′mi·el the son of Zū·ri·shad′daī.

42 On the sixth day E·lī′a·saph the son of Deū′el,*a* leader of the children of Gad, *presented an offering.*

43 His offering *was* one silver platter, the weight of which *was* one hundred and thirty *shekels,* and one silver bowl of seventy shekels, according to the shekel of the sanctuary, both of them full of fine flour mixed with oil as a grain offering;

44 one gold pan of ten *shekels,* full of incense;

45 one young bull, one ram, and one male lamb in its first year, as a burnt offering;

46 one kid of the goats as a sin offering;

47 and as the sacrifice of peace offerings: two oxen, five rams, five male goats, and five male lambs in their first year. This *was* the offering of E·lī′a·saph the son of Deū′el.

48 On the seventh day E·lish′a·ma the son of Am·mī′hud, leader of the children of Ē′phra·im, *presented an offering.*

49 His offering *was* one silver platter, the weight of which *was* one hundred and thirty *shekels,* and one silver bowl of seventy shekels, according to the shekel of the sanctu-

ary, both of them full of fine flour mixed with oil as a grain offering;

50 one gold pan of ten *shekels,* full of incense;

51 one young bull, one ram, and one male lamb in its first year, as a burnt offering;

52 one kid of the goats as a sin offering;

53 and as the sacrifice of peace offerings: two oxen, five rams, five male goats, and five male lambs in their first year. This *was* the offering of E·lish′a·ma the son of Am·mī′hud.

54 On the eighth day Ga·mā′li·el the son of Pe·dah′zur, leader of the children of Ma·nas′seh, *presented an offering.*

55 His offering *was* one silver platter, the weight of which *was* one hundred and thirty *shekels,* and one silver bowl of seventy shekels, according to the shekel of the sanctuary, both of them full of fine flour mixed with oil as a grain offering;

56 one gold pan of ten *shekels,* full of incense;

57 one young bull, one ram, and one male lamb in its first year, as a burnt offering;

58 one kid of the goats as a sin offering;

59 and as the sacrifice of peace offerings: two oxen, five rams, five male goats, and five male lambs in their first year. This *was* the offering of Ga·mā′li·el the son of Pe·dah′zur.

60 On the ninth day A·bī′dan the son of Gid·ē·ō′ni, leader of the children of Benjamin, *presented an offering.*

61 His offering *was* one silver platter, the weight of which *was* one hundred and thirty *shekels,* and one silver bowl of seventy shekels, according to the shekel of the sanctuary, both of them full of fine flour mixed with oil as a grain offering;

7:42 *a*Spelled *Reuel* in 2:14

62 one gold pan of ten *shekels,* full of incense;

63 one young bull, one ram, and one male lamb in its first year, as a burnt offering;

64 one kid of the goats as a sin offering;

65 and as the sacrifice of peace offerings: two oxen, five rams, five male goats, and five male lambs in their first year. This *was* the offering of A·bī′dan the son of Gid·ē·ō′ni.

66 On the tenth day A·hī·ē′zer the son of Am·mi·shad′daī, leader of the children of Dan, *presented an offering.*

67 His offering *was* one silver platter, the weight of which *was* one hundred and thirty *shekels,* and one silver bowl of seventy shekels, according to the shekel of the sanctuary, both of them full of fine flour mixed with oil as a grain offering;

68 one gold pan of ten *shekels,* full of incense;

69 one young bull, one ram, and one male lamb in its first year, as a burnt offering;

70 one kid of the goats as a sin offering;

71 and as the sacrifice of peace offerings: two oxen, five rams, five male goats, and five male lambs in their first year. This *was* the offering of Ā·hī·ē′zer the son of Am·mi·shad′daī.

72 On the eleventh day Pā′gi·el the son of Oc′ran, leader of the children of Ash′er, *presented an offering.*

73 His offering *was* one silver platter, the weight of which *was* one hundred and thirty *shekels,* and one silver bowl of seventy shekels, according to the shekel of the sanctuary, both of them full of fine flour mixed with oil as a grain offering;

74 one gold pan of ten *shekels,* full of incense;

75 one young bull, one ram, and one male lamb in its first year, as a burnt offering;

76 one kid of the goats as a sin offering;

77 and as the sacrifice of peace offerings: two oxen, five rams, five male goats, and five male lambs in their first year. This *was* the offering of Pā′gi·el the son of Oc′ran.

78 On the twelfth day A·hī′ra the son of Ē′nan, leader of the children of Naph′ta·lī, *presented an offering.*

79 His offering *was* one silver platter, the weight of which *was* one hundred and thirty *shekels,* and one silver bowl of seventy shekels, according to the shekel of the sanctuary, both of them full of fine flour mixed with oil as a grain offering;

80 one gold pan of ten *shekels,* full of incense;

81 one young bull, one ram, and one male lamb in its first year, as a burnt offering;

82 one kid of the goats as a sin offering;

83 and as the sacrifice of peace offerings: two oxen, five rams, five male goats, and five male lambs in their first year. This *was* the offering of A·hī′ra the son of Ē′nan.

84 This *was* the dedication *offering* for the altar from the leaders of Israel, when it was anointed: twelve silver platters, twelve silver bowls, and twelve gold pans.

85 Each silver platter *weighed* one hundred and thirty *shekels* and each bowl seventy *shekels.* All the silver of the vessels *weighed* two thousand four hundred *shekels,* according to the shekel of the sanctuary.

86 The twelve gold pans full of incense *weighed* ten *shekels* apiece, according to the shekel of the sanctuary; all the gold of the pans *weighed* one hundred and twenty *shekels.*

87 All the oxen for the burnt offering *were* twelve young bulls, the rams twelve, the male lambs in their first year twelve, with their grain offering,

and the kids of the goats as a sin offering twelve.

88 And all the oxen for the sacrifice of peace offerings were twenty-four bulls, the rams sixty, the male goats sixty, and the lambs in their first year sixty. This *was* the dedication *offering* for the altar after it was anointed.

89 Now when Moses went into the tabernacle of meeting to speak with Him, he heard the voice of One speaking to him from above the mercy seat that *was* on the ark of the Testimony, from between the two cherubim; thus He spoke to him.

ARRANGEMENT OF THE LAMPS

8 And the LORD spoke to Moses, saying:

2 "Speak to Aaron, and say to him, 'When you arrange the lamps, the seven lamps shall give light in front of the lampstand.'"

3 And Aaron did so; he arranged the lamps to face toward the front of the lampstand, as the LORD commanded Moses.

4 Now this workmanship of the lampstand *was* hammered gold; from its shaft to its flowers it *was* hammered work. According to the pattern which the LORD had shown Moses, so he made the lampstand.

CLEANSING AND DEDICATION OF THE LEVITES

5 Then the LORD spoke to Moses, saying:

6 "Take the Lē′vītes from among the children of Israel and cleanse them *ceremonially*.

7 "Thus you shall do to them to cleanse them: Sprinkle water of purification on them, and let them shave all their body, and let them wash their clothes, and *so* make themselves clean.

8 "Then let them take a young bull with its grain offering of fine flour mixed with oil, and you shall take another young bull as a sin offering.

9 "And you shall bring the Lē′vītes before the tabernacle of meeting, and you shall gather together the whole congregation of the children of Israel.

10 "So you shall bring the Lē′vītes before the LORD, and the children of Israel shall lay their hands on the Lē′vītes;

11 "and Aaron shall offer the Lē′vītes before the LORD, *like* a wave offering from the children of Israel, that they may perform the work of the LORD.

12 "Then the Lē′vītes shall lay their hands on the heads of the young bulls, and you shall offer one as a sin offering and the other as a burnt offering to the LORD, to make atonement for the Lē′vītes.

13 "And you shall stand the Lē′vītes before Aaron and his sons, and then offer them *like* a wave offering to the LORD.

14 "Thus you shall separate the Lē′vītes from among the children of Israel, and the Lē′vītes shall be Mine.

15 "After that the Lē′vītes shall go in to service the tabernacle of meeting. So you shall cleanse them and offer them, *like* a wave offering.

16 "For they *are* wholly given to Me from among the children of Israel; I have taken them for Myself instead of all who open the womb, the firstborn of all the children of Israel.

17 "For all the firstborn among the children of Israel *are* Mine, *both* man and beast; on the day that I struck all the firstborn in the land of Egypt I sanctified them to Myself.

18 "I have taken the Lē′vītes instead of all the firstborn of the children of Israel.

19 "And I have given the Lē′vītes as

a gift to Aaron and his sons from among the children of Israel, to do the work for the children of Israel in the tabernacle of meeting, and to make atonement for the children of Israel, that there be no plague among the children of Israel when the children of Israel come near the sanctuary."

20 Thus Moses and Aaron and all the congregation of the children of Israel did to the Lē'vītes; according to all that the LORD commanded Moses concerning the Lē'vītes, so the children of Israel did to them.

21 And the Lē'vītes purified themselves and washed their clothes; then Aaron presented them, *like* a wave offering before the LORD, and Aaron made atonement for them to cleanse them.

22 After that the Lē'vītes went in to do their work in the tabernacle of meeting before Aaron and his sons; as the LORD commanded Moses concerning the Lē'vītes, so they did to them.

23 Then the LORD spoke to Moses, saying,

24 "This *is* what *pertains* to the Lē'vītes: From twenty-five years old and above one may enter to perform service in the work of the tabernacle of meeting;

25 "and at the age of fifty years they must cease performing this work, and shall work no more.

26 "They may minister with their brethren in the tabernacle of meeting, to attend to needs, but they *themselves* shall do no work. Thus you shall do to the Lē'vītes regarding their duties."

The Second Passover

9 Now the LORD spoke to Moses in the Wilderness of Sinai, in the first month of the second year after they had come out of the land of Egypt, saying:

2 "Let the children of Israel keep the Passover at its appointed time.

3 "On the fourteenth day of this month, at twilight, you shall keep it at its appointed time. According to all its rites and ceremonies you shall keep it."

4 So Moses told the children of Israel that they should keep the Passover.

5 And they kept the Passover on the fourteenth day of the first month, at twilight, in the Wilderness of Sinai; according to all that the LORD commanded Moses, so the children of Israel did.

6 Now there were *certain* men who were defiled by a human corpse, so that they could not keep the Passover on that day; and they came before Moses and Aaron that day.

7 And those men said to him, "We *became* defiled by a human corpse. Why are we kept from presenting the offering of the LORD at its appointed time among the children of Israel?"

8 And Moses said to them, "Stand still, that I may hear what the LORD will command concerning you."

9 Then the LORD spoke to Moses, saying,

10 "Speak to the children of Israel, saying: 'If anyone of you or your posterity is unclean because of a corpse, or *is* far away on a journey, he may still keep the LORD's Passover.

11 'On the fourteenth day of the second month, at twilight, they may keep it. They shall eat it with unleavened bread and bitter herbs.

12 'They shall leave none of it until morning, nor break one of its bones. According to all the ordinances of the Passover they shall keep it.

13 'But the man who *is* clean and is not on a journey, and ceases to keep the Passover, that same person shall

be cut off from among his people, because he did not bring the offering of the LORD at its appointed time; that man shall bear his sin.

14 'And if a stranger dwells among you, and would keep the LORD's Passover, he must do so according to the rite of the Passover and according to its ceremony; you shall have one ordinance, both for the stranger and the native of the land.' "

THE CLOUD AND THE FIRE

It was almost time for the people of Israel to leave Mount Sinai and begin the long trip by foot to their new land. But how would they know the way? This is how God would lead them.

15 Now on the day that the tabernacle was raised up, the cloud covered the tabernacle, the tent of the Testimony; from evening until morning it was above the tabernacle like the appearance of fire.
16 So it was always: the cloud covered it *by day,* and the appearance of fire by night.
17 Whenever the cloud was taken up from above the tabernacle, after that the children of Israel would journey; and in the place where the cloud settled, there the children of Israel would pitch their tents.
18 At the command of the LORD the children of Israel would journey, and at the command of the LORD they would camp; as long as the cloud stayed above the tabernacle they remained encamped.
19 Even when the cloud continued long, many days above the tabernacle, the children of Israel kept the charge of the LORD and did not journey.

20 So it was, when the cloud was above the tabernacle a few days: according to the command of the LORD they would remain encamped, and according to the command of the LORD they would journey.
21 So it was, when the cloud remained only from evening until morning: when the cloud was taken up in the morning, then they would journey; whether by day or by night, whenever the cloud was taken up, they would journey.
22 *Whether it was* two days, a month, or a year that the cloud remained above the tabernacle, the children of Israel would remain encamped and not journey; but when it was taken up, they would journey.
23 At the command of the LORD they remained encamped, and at the command of the LORD they journeyed; they kept the charge of the LORD, at the command of the LORD by the hand of Moses.

✓ *Bible Quiz*

Numbers 9:15–23 **The Pillar of Cloud and Fire**

1. When would the people of Israel know it was time to go? When would they know it was time to stop?
2. The cloud and fire guided the people to their new land—the Promised Land. What are some of the ways God might guide you each day? How might the Bible help you understand what God wants you to do, or where He might want you to go someday?

TWO SILVER TRUMPETS

10 And the LORD spoke to Moses, saying:

2 "Make two silver trumpets for yourself; you shall make them of hammered work; you shall use them for calling the congregation and for directing the movement of the camps.

3 "When they blow both of them, all the congregation shall gather before you at the door of the tabernacle of meeting.

4 "But if they blow *only* one, then the leaders, the heads of the divisions of Israel, shall gather to you.

5 "When you sound the advance, the camps that lie on the east side shall then begin their journey.

6 "When you sound the advance the second time, then the camps that lie on the south side shall begin their journey; they shall sound the call for them to begin their journeys.

7 "And when the assembly is to be gathered together, you shall blow, but not sound the advance.

8 "The sons of Aaron, the priests, shall blow the trumpets; and these shall be to you as an ordinance forever throughout your generations.

9 "When you go to war in your land against the enemy who oppresses you, then you shall sound an alarm with the trumpets, and you will be remembered before the LORD your God, and you will be saved from your enemies.

10 "Also in the day of your gladness, in your appointed feasts, and at the beginning of your months, you shall blow the trumpets over your burnt offerings and over the sacrifices of your peace offerings; and they shall be a memorial for you before your God: I *am* the LORD your God."

DEPARTURE FROM SINAI

11 Now it came to pass on the twentieth *day* of the second month, in the second year, that the cloud was taken up from above the tabernacle of the Testimony.

12 And the children of Israel set out from the Wilderness of Sinai on their journeys; then the cloud settled down in the Wilderness of Par'an.

13 So they started out for the first time according to the command of the LORD by the hand of Moses.

14 The standard of the camp of the children of Judah set out first according to their armies; over their army was Nah'shon the son of Am·min'a·dab.

15 Over the army of the tribe of the children of Is'sa·char *was* Ne·than'el the son of Zū'ar.

16 And over the army of the tribe of the children of Zeb'ū·lun *was* E·lī'ab the son of Hē'lon.

17 Then the tabernacle was taken down; and the sons of Ger'shon and the sons of Me·rar'ī set out, carrying the tabernacle.

18 And the standard of the camp of Reuben set out according to their armies; over their army *was* E·lī'zur the son of Shed'ē·ur.

19 Over the army of the tribe of the children of Sim'ē·on *was* She·lū'mi·el the son of Zū·ri·shad'daī.

20 And over the army of the tribe of the children of Gad *was* E·lī'a·saph the son of Deū'el.

21 Then the Kō'hath·ites set out, carrying the holy things. (The tabernacle would be prepared for their arrival.)

22 And the standard of the camp of the children of Ē'phra·im set out according to their armies; over their army *was* E·lish'a·ma the son of Am·mī'hud.

23 Over the army of the tribe of the

children of Ma·nas′seh *was* Ga·mā′li·el the son of Pe·dah′zur.
24 And over the army of the tribe of the children of Benjamin *was* A·bī′dan the son of Gid·ē·ō′ni.
25 Then the standard of the camp of the children of Dan (the rear guard of all the camps) set out according to their armies; over their army *was* Ā·hī·ē′zer the son of Am·mi·shad′daī.
26 Over the army of the tribe of the children of Ash′er *was* Pā′gi·el the son of Oc′ran.
27 And over the army of the tribe of the children of Naph′ta·lī *was* A·hī′ra the son of Ē′nan.
28 Thus *was* the order of march of the children of Israel, according to their armies, when they began their journey.
29 Now Moses said to Hō′bab the son of Reū′el*a* the Mid′i·an·īte, Moses' father-in-law, "We are setting out for the place of which the LORD said, 'I will give it to you.' Come with us, and we will treat you well; for the LORD has promised good things to Israel."
30 And he said to him, "I will not go, but I will depart to my *own* land and to my relatives."
31 So *Moses* said, "Please do not leave, inasmuch as you know how we are to camp in the wilderness, and you can be our eyes.
32 "And it shall be, if you go with us—indeed it shall be—that whatever good the LORD will do to us, the same we will do to you."
33 So they departed from the mountain of the LORD on a journey of three days; and the ark of the covenant of the LORD went before them for the three days' journey, to search out a resting place for them.
34 And the cloud of the LORD *was* above them by day when they went out from the camp.
35 So it was, whenever the ark set out, that Moses said:

"Rise up, O LORD!
Let Your enemies be scattered,
And let those who hate You flee
    before You."

36 And when it rested, he said:

"Return, O LORD,
To the many thousands of Israel."

THE PEOPLE COMPLAIN

11 Now *when* the people complained, it displeased the LORD; for the LORD heard *it,* and His anger was aroused. So the fire of the LORD burned among them, and consumed *some* in the outskirts of the camp.
2 Then the people cried out to Moses, and when Moses prayed to the LORD, the fire was quenched.
3 So he called the name of the place Tab′e·rah,*a* because the fire of the LORD had burned among them.
4 Now the mixed multitude who were among them yielded to intense craving; so the children of Israel also wept again and said: "Who will give us meat to eat?
5 "We remember the fish which we ate freely in Egypt, the cucumbers, the melons, the leeks, the onions, and the garlic;
6 "but now our whole being *is* dried up; *there is* nothing at all except this manna *before* our eyes!"
7 Now the manna *was* like coriander seed, and its color like the color of bdellium.
8 The people went about and gathered *it,* ground *it* on millstones or beat *it* in the mortar, cooked *it* in pans, and made cakes of it; and its taste was like the taste of pastry prepared with oil.
9 And when the dew fell on the camp in the night, the manna fell on it.

10:29 *a*Septuagint reads *Raguel* (compare Exodus 2:18). 11:3 *a*Literally *Burning*

10 Then Moses heard the people weeping throughout their families, everyone at the door of his tent; and the anger of the LORD was greatly aroused; Moses also was displeased.

11 So Moses said to the LORD, "Why have You afflicted Your servant? And why have I not found favor in Your sight, that You have laid the burden of all these people on me?

12 "Did I conceive all these people? Did I beget them, that You should say to me, 'Carry them in your bosom, as a guardian carries a nursing child,' to the land which You swore to their fathers?

13 "Where am I to get meat to give to all these people? For they weep all over me, saying, 'Give us meat, that we may eat.'

14 "I am not able to bear all these people alone, because the burden *is* too heavy for me.

15 "If You treat me like this, please kill me here and now—if I have found favor in Your sight—and do not let me see my wretchedness!"

THE SEVENTY ELDERS

16 So the LORD said to Moses: "Gather to Me seventy men of the elders of Israel, whom you know to be the elders of the people and officers over them; bring them to the tabernacle of meeting, that they may stand there with you.

17 "Then I will come down and talk with you there. I will take of the Spirit that *is* upon you and will put *the same* upon them; and they shall bear the burden of the people with you, that you may not bear *it* yourself alone.

18 "Then you shall say to the people, 'Consecrate yourselves for tomorrow, and you shall eat meat; for you have wept in the hearing of the LORD, saying, "Who will give us meat to eat? For *it was* well with us in Egypt." Therefore the LORD will give you meat, and you shall eat.

19 'You shall eat, not one day, nor two days, nor five days, nor ten days, nor twenty days,

20 'but *for* a whole month, until it comes out of your nostrils and becomes loathsome to you, because you have despised the LORD who is among you, and have wept before Him, saying, "Why did we ever come up out of Egypt?" ' "

21 And Moses said, "The people whom I *am* among *are* six hundred thousand men on foot; yet You have said, 'I will give them meat, that they may eat *for* a whole month.'

22 "Shall flocks and herds be slaughtered for them, to provide enough for them? Or shall all the fish of the sea be gathered together for them, to provide enough for them?"

23 And the LORD said to Moses, "Has the LORD's arm been shortened? Now you shall see whether what I say will happen to you or not."

24 So Moses went out and told the people the words of the LORD, and he gathered the seventy men of the elders of the people and placed them around the tabernacle.

25 Then the LORD came down in the cloud, and spoke to him, and took of the Spirit that *was* upon him, and placed *the same* upon the seventy elders; and it happened, when the Spirit rested upon them, that they prophesied, although they never did *so* again.[a]

26 But two men had remained in the camp: the name of one *was* El'dad, and the name of the other Mē'dad.

11:25 [a]Targum and Vulgate read *did not cease.*

And the Spirit rested upon them. Now they *were* among those listed, but who had not gone out to the tabernacle; yet they prophesied in the camp.

27 And a young man ran and told Moses, and said, "El′dad and Mē′dad are prophesying in the camp."

28 So Joshua the son of Nun, Moses' assistant, *one* of his choice men, answered and said, "Moses my lord, forbid them!"

29 Then Moses said to him, "Are you zealous for my sake? Oh, that all the LORD's people were prophets *and* that the LORD would put His Spirit upon them!"

30 And Moses returned to the camp, *both* he and the elders of Israel.

THE LORD SENDS QUAIL

31 Now a wind went out from the LORD, and it brought quail from the sea and left *them* fluttering near the camp, about a day's journey on this side and about a day's journey on the other side, all around the camp, and about two cubits above the surface of the ground.

32 And the people stayed up all that day, all night, and all the next day, and gathered the quail (he who gathered least gathered ten homers); and they spread *them* out for themselves all around the camp.

33 But while the meat *was* still between their teeth, before it was chewed, the wrath of the LORD was aroused against the people, and the LORD struck the people with a very great plague.

34 So he called the name of that place Kib′roth Hat·tā′a·vah,*a* because there they buried the people who had yielded to craving.

35 From Kib′roth Hat·tā′a·vah the people moved to Ha·zē′roth, and camped at Ha·zē′roth.

DISSENSION OF AARON AND MIRIAM

12 Then Miriam and Aaron spoke against Moses because of the Ethiopian woman whom he had married; for he had married an Ethiopian woman.

2 So they said, "Has the LORD indeed spoken only through Moses? Has He not spoken through us also?" And the LORD heard *it*.

3 (Now the man Moses *was* very humble, more than all men who *were* on the face of the earth.)

4 Suddenly the LORD said to Moses, Aaron, and Miriam, "Come out, you three, to the tabernacle of meeting!" So the three came out.

5 Then the LORD came down in the pillar of cloud and stood *in* the door of the tabernacle, and called Aaron and Miriam. And they both went forward.

6 Then He said,

"Hear now My words:
If there is a prophet among you,
I, the LORD, make Myself known
    to him in a vision;
I speak to him in a dream.

7 Not so with My servant Moses;
He *is* faithful in all My house.

8 I speak with him face to face,
Even plainly, and not in dark
    sayings;
And he sees the form of the LORD.
Why then were you not afraid
To speak against My servant
    Moses?"

9 So the anger of the LORD was aroused against them, and He departed.

10 And when the cloud departed from above the tabernacle, suddenly Miriam *became* leprous, as *white as* snow. Then Aaron turned toward Miriam, and there she was, a leper.

11:34 *a*Literally *Graves of Craving*

HELPFULNESS Numbers 12:10–13

What Can I Do to Help?

Someone gets hurt. Or someone gets sick. Perhaps it's someone in your family. What can you do to help? What should you do to help?

1. What do you think happened here? How do you think the girl feels?
2. When a friend or family member gets hurt, how can you help most? Have you prayed? Sometimes we help most when we pray for God to help. He can do much more than we can do, can't He?

For more on *Values* turn to page 292
For more on *Prayer* turn to page 510

11 So Aaron said to Moses, "Oh, my lord! Please do not lay *this* sin on us, in which we have done foolishly and in which we have sinned.

12 "Please do not let her be as one dead, whose flesh is half consumed when he comes out of his mother's womb!"

13 So Moses cried out to the LORD, saying, "Please heal her, O God, I pray!"

14 Then the LORD said to Moses, "If her father had but spit in her face, would she not be shamed seven days? Let her be shut out of the camp seven days, and afterward she may be received *again.*"

15 So Miriam was shut out of the camp seven days, and the people did not journey till Miriam was brought in *again.*

16 And afterward the people moved from Ha·zē'roth and camped in the Wilderness of Par'an.

SPIES SENT INTO CANAAN

The people of Israel were on their way to Canaan. It was also called the Promised Land. God promised they could have this new land. That's how the land got its name. But before the people entered their new land, they had to check it out. Spies were sent into the land. This is what the spies found.

13 And the LORD spoke to Moses, saying,

2 "Send men to spy out the land of Cā'naan, which I am giving to the children of Israel; from each tribe of their fathers you shall send a man, every one a leader among them."

3 So Moses sent them from the Wilderness of Par'an according to the command of the LORD, all of them men who *were* heads of the children of Israel.

4 Now these *were* their names: from the tribe of Reuben, Sham'mū·a the son of Zac'cur;

5 from the tribe of Sim'e·on, Shā'phat the son of Hō'rī;

6 from the tribe of Judah, Caleb the son of Je·phūn'neh;

7 from the tribe of Is'sa·char, Ī'gal the son of Joseph;

8 from the tribe of Ē'phra·im, Hō·shē'a*a* the son of Nun;

9 from the tribe of Benjamin, Pal'tī the son of Rā'phū;

10 from the tribe of Zeb'ū·lun, Gad'di·el the son of Sō'dī;

11 from the tribe of Joseph, *that is,* from the tribe of Ma·nas'seh, Gad'dī the son of Sū'sī;

12 from the tribe of Dan, Am'mi·el the son of Ge·mal'lī;

13 from the tribe of Ash'er, Seth'ur the son of Michael;

14 from the tribe of Naph'ta·lī, Nah'bī the son of Voph'sī;

15 from the tribe of Gad, Ge·ū'el the son of Mā'chī.

16 These *are* the names of the men whom Moses sent to spy out the land. And Moses called Hō·shē'a*a* the son of Nun, Joshua.

17 Then Moses sent them to spy out the land of Cā'naan, and said to them, "Go up this *way* into the South, and go up to the mountains,

18 "and see what the land is like: whether the people who dwell in it *are* strong or weak, few or many;

19 "whether the land they dwell in *is* good or bad; whether the cities they inhabit *are* like camps or strongholds;

20 "whether the land *is* rich or poor; and whether there are forests there or not. Be of good courage. And bring

---

13:8 *a*Septuagint and Vulgate read *Oshea.*
13:16 *a*Septuagint and Vulgate read *Oshea.*

some of the fruit of the land." Now the time *was* the season of the first ripe grapes.

21 So they went up and spied out the land from the Wilderness of Zin as far as Rē′hob, near the entrance of Hā′math.

22 And they went up through the South and came to Hē′bron; A·hī′-man, Shē′shai, and Tal′mai, the descendants of Ā′nak, *were* there. (Now Hē′bron was built seven years before Zō′an in Egypt.)

23 Then they came to the Valley of Esh′col, and there cut down a branch with one cluster of grapes; they carried it between two of them on a pole. *They* also *brought* some of the pomegranates and figs.

24 The place was called the Valley of Esh′col,*a* because of the cluster which the men of Israel cut down there.

25 And they returned from spying out the land after forty days.

26 Now they departed and came back to Moses and Aaron and all the congregation of the children of Israel in the Wilderness of Par′an, at Kā′desh; they brought back word to them and to all the congregation, and showed them the fruit of the land.

27 Then they told him, and said: "We went to the land where you sent us. It truly flows with milk and honey, and this *is* its fruit.

28 "Nevertheless the people who dwell in the land *are* strong; the cities *are* fortified *and* very large; moreover we saw the descendants of Ā′nak there.

29 "The A·mal′e·kītes dwell in the land of the South; the Hit′tītes, the Jeb′ū·sītes, and the Am′o·rītes dwell in the mountains; and the Cā′naan-ītes dwell by the sea and along the banks of the Jordan."

30 Then Caleb quieted the people before Moses, and said, "Let us go up at once and take possession, for we are well able to overcome it."

31 But the men who had gone up with him said, "We are not able to go up against the people, for they *are* stronger than we."

32 And they gave the children of Israel a bad report of the land which they had spied out, saying, "The land through which we have gone as spies *is* a land that devours its inhabitants, and all the people whom we saw in it *are* men of *great* stature.

13:24 *a*Literally *Cluster*

☑ Bible Quiz

Numbers 13   Twelve Spies in Canaan

1. How many spies did Moses send into Canaan? Can you name one of them?

2. What were some of the things the spies saw?

3. When the spies got back, what did most of them say? Why do you think they were afraid?

4. Did anyone say something different? Who? Why weren't Joshua and Caleb afraid?

5. God promised the people He would give them this land. They didn't have to be afraid, because God always keeps His promises. God has made many promises to you in the Bible. Spend some time looking for them. How can you be sure God will keep them? Will that help you the next time you are afraid?

33 "There we saw the giants*a* (the descendants of Ā'nak came from the giants); and we were like grasshoppers in our own sight, and so we were in their sight."

ISRAEL REFUSES TO ENTER CANAAN

14 So all the congregation lifted up their voices and cried, and the people wept that night.

2   And all the children of Israel complained against Moses and Aaron, and the whole congregation said to them, "If only we had died in the land of Egypt! Or if only we had died in this wilderness!

3   "Why has the LORD brought us to this land to fall by the sword, that our wives and children should become victims? Would it not be better for us to return to Egypt?"

4   So they said to one another, "Let us select a leader and return to Egypt."

5   Then Moses and Aaron fell on their faces before all the assembly of the congregation of the children of Israel.

6   But Joshua the son of Nun and Caleb the son of Je·phūn'neh, *who were* among those who had spied out the land, tore their clothes;

7   and they spoke to all the congregation of the children of Israel, saying: "The land we passed through to spy out *is* an exceedingly good land.

8   "If the LORD delights in us, then He will bring us into this land and give it to us, 'a land which flows with milk and honey.'*a*

9   "Only do not rebel against the LORD, nor fear the people of the land, for they *are* our bread; their protection has departed from them, and the LORD *is* with us. Do not fear them."

10   And all the congregation said to stone them with stones. Now the glory of the LORD appeared in the tabernacle of meeting before all the children of Israel.

MOSES INTERCEDES FOR THE PEOPLE

11   Then the LORD said to Moses: "How long will these people reject Me? And how long will they not believe Me, with all the signs which I have performed among them?

12   "I will strike them with the pestilence and disinherit them, and I will make of you a nation greater and mightier than they."

13   And Moses said to the LORD: "Then the Egyptians will hear *it,* for by Your might You brought these people up from among them,

14   "and they will tell *it* to the inhabitants of this land. They have heard that You, LORD, *are* among these people; that You, LORD, are seen face to face and Your cloud stands above them, and You go before them in a pillar of cloud by day and in a pillar of fire by night.

15   "Now *if* You kill these people as one man, then the nations which have heard of Your fame will speak, saying,

16   'Because the LORD was not able to bring this people to the land which He swore to give them, therefore He killed them in the wilderness.'

17   "And now, I pray, let the power of my Lord be great, just as You have spoken, saying,

18   'The LORD is longsuffering and abundant in mercy, forgiving iniquity and transgression; but He by no means clears *the guilty,* visiting the iniquity of the fathers on the children to the third and fourth *generation.'a*

19   "Pardon the iniquity of this peo-

13:33 *a*Hebrew *nephilim*   14:8 *a*Exodus 3:8
14:18 *a*Exodus 34:6, 7

ple, I pray, according to the greatness of Your mercy, just as You have forgiven this people, from Egypt even until now."

20 Then the LORD said: "I have pardoned, according to your word;

21 "but truly, as I live, all the earth shall be filled with the glory of the LORD—

22 "because all these men who have seen My glory and the signs which I did in Egypt and in the wilderness, and have put Me to the test now these ten times, and have not heeded My voice,

23 "they certainly shall not see the land of which I swore to their fathers, nor shall any of those who rejected Me see it.

24 "But My servant Caleb, because he has a different spirit in him and has followed Me fully, I will bring into the land where he went, and his descendants shall inherit it.

25 "Now the A·mal'e·kītes and the Cā'naan·ītes dwell in the valley; tomorrow turn and move out into the wilderness by the Way of the Red Sea."

DEATH SENTENCE ON THE REBELS

26 And the LORD spoke to Moses and Aaron, saying,

27 "How long *shall I bear with* this evil congregation who complain against Me? I have heard the complaints which the children of Israel make against Me.

28 "Say to them, 'As I live,' says the LORD, 'just as you have spoken in My hearing, so I will do to you:

29 'The carcasses of you who have complained against Me shall fall in this wilderness, all of you who were numbered, according to your entire number, from twenty years old and above.

30 'Except for Caleb the son of Je·phūn'neh and Joshua the son of Nun, you shall by no means enter the land which I swore I would make you dwell in.

31 'But your little ones, whom you said would be victims, I will bring in, and they shall know the land which you have despised.

32 'But *as for* you, your carcasses shall fall in this wilderness.

33 'And your sons shall be shepherds in the wilderness forty years, and bear the brunt of your infidelity, until your carcasses are consumed in the wilderness.

34 'According to the number of the days in which you spied out the land, forty days, for each day you shall bear your guilt one year, *namely* forty years, and you shall know My rejection.

35 'I the LORD have spoken this. I will surely do so to all this evil congregation who are gathered together against Me. In this wilderness they shall be consumed, and there they shall die.' "

36 Now the men whom Moses sent to spy out the land, who returned and made all the congregation complain against him by bringing a bad report of the land,

37 those very men who brought the evil report about the land, died by the plague before the LORD.

38 But Joshua the son of Nun and Caleb the son of Je·phūn'neh remained alive, of the men who went to spy out the land.

A FUTILE INVASION ATTEMPT

39 Then Moses told these words to all the children of Israel, and the people mourned greatly.

40 And they rose early in the morning and went up to the top of the mountain, saying, "Here we are, and we will go up to the place which the

LORD has promised, for we have sinned!"

41 And Moses said, "Now why do you transgress the command of the LORD? For this will not succeed.

42 "Do not go up, lest you be defeated by your enemies, for the LORD *is* not among you.

43 "For the A·mal′e·kītes and the Cā′naan·ītes *are* there before you, and you shall fall by the sword; because you have turned away from the LORD, the LORD will not be with you."

44 But they presumed to go up to the mountaintop. Nevertheless, neither the ark of the covenant of the LORD nor Moses departed from the camp.

45 Then the A·mal′e·kītes and the Cā′naan·ītes who dwelt in that mountain came down and attacked them, and drove them back as far as Hor′mah.

LAWS OF GRAIN AND DRINK OFFERINGS

15 And the LORD spoke to Moses, saying,

2 "Speak to the children of Israel, and say to them: 'When you have come into the land you are to inhabit, which I am giving to you,

3 'and you make an offering by fire to the LORD, a burnt offering or a sacrifice, to fulfill a vow or as a freewill offering or in your appointed feasts, to make a sweet aroma to the LORD, from the herd or the flock,

4 'then he who presents his offering to the LORD shall bring a grain offering of one-tenth *of an ephah* of fine flour mixed with one-fourth of a hin of oil;

5 'and one-fourth of a hin of wine as a drink offering you shall prepare with the burnt offering or the sacrifice, for each lamb.

6 'Or for a ram you shall prepare as a grain offering two-tenths *of an*

ephah of fine flour mixed with one-third of a hin of oil;

7 'and as a drink offering you shall offer one-third of a hin of wine as a sweet aroma to the LORD.

8 'And when you prepare a young bull as a burnt offering, or as a sacrifice to fulfill a vow, or as a peace offering to the LORD,

9 'then shall be offered with the young bull a grain offering of three-tenths *of an ephah* of fine flour mixed with half a hin of oil;

10 'and you shall bring as the drink offering half a hin of wine as an offering made by fire, a sweet aroma to the LORD.

11 'Thus it shall be done for each young bull, for each ram, or for each lamb or young goat.

12 'According to the number that you prepare, so you shall do with everyone according to their number.

13 'All who are native-born shall do these things in this manner, in presenting an offering made by fire, a sweet aroma to the LORD.

14 'And if a stranger dwells with you, or whoever *is* among you throughout your generations, and would present an offering made by fire, a sweet aroma to the LORD, just as you do, so shall he do.

15 'One ordinance *shall be* for you of the assembly and for the stranger who dwells *with you,* an ordinance forever throughout your generations; as you are, so shall the stranger be before the LORD.

16 'One law and one custom shall be for you and for the stranger who dwells with you.' "[a]

17 Again the LORD spoke to Moses, saying,

18 "Speak to the children of Israel, and say to them: 'When you come into the land to which I bring you,

15:16 [a]Compare Exodus 12:49

19 'then it will be, when you eat of the bread of the land, that you shall offer up a heave offering to the LORD.

20 'You shall offer up a cake of the first of your ground meal *as* a heave offering; as a heave offering of the threshing floor, so shall you offer it up.

21 'Of the first of your ground meal you shall give to the LORD a heave offering throughout your generations.

LAWS CONCERNING UNINTENTIONAL SIN

22 'If you sin unintentionally, and do not observe all these commandments which the LORD has spoken to Moses—

23 'all that the LORD has commanded you by the hand of Moses, from the day the LORD gave commandment and onward throughout your generations—

24 'then it will be, if it is unintentionally committed, without the knowledge of the congregation, that the whole congregation shall offer one young bull as a burnt offering, as a sweet aroma to the LORD, with its grain offering and its drink offering, according to the ordinance, and one kid of the goats as a sin offering.

25 'So the priest shall make atonement for the whole congregation of the children of Israel, and it shall be forgiven them, for it was unintentional; they shall bring their offering, an offering made by fire to the LORD, and their sin offering before the LORD, for their unintended sin.

26 'It shall be forgiven the whole congregation of the children of Israel and the stranger who dwells among them, because all the people *did it* unintentionally.

27 'And if a person sins unintentionally, then he shall bring a fe-male goat in its first year as a sin offering.

28 'So the priest shall make atonement for the person who sins unintentionally, when he sins unintentionally before the LORD, to make atonement for him; and it shall be forgiven him.

29 'You shall have one law for him who sins unintentionally, *for* him who is native-born among the children of Israel and for the stranger who dwells among them.

LAW CONCERNING PRESUMPTUOUS SIN

30 'But the person who does *anything* presumptuously, *whether he is* native-born or a stranger, that one brings reproach on the LORD, and he shall be cut off from among his people.

31 'Because he has despised the word of the LORD, and has broken His commandment, that person shall be completely cut off; his guilt *shall be* upon him.' "

PENALTY FOR VIOLATING THE SABBATH

32 Now while the children of Israel were in the wilderness, they found a man gathering sticks on the Sabbath day.

33 And those who found him gathering sticks brought him to Moses and Aaron, and to all the congregation.

34 They put him under guard, because it had not been explained what should be done to him.

35 Then the LORD said to Moses, "The man must surely be put to death; all the congregation shall stone him with stones outside the camp."

36 So, as the LORD commanded Moses, all the congregation brought him

outside the camp and stoned him with stones, and he died.

TASSELS ON GARMENTS

37 Again the LORD spoke to Moses, saying,

38 "Speak to the children of Israel: Tell them to make tassels on the corners of their garments throughout their generations, and to put a blue thread in the tassels of the corners.

39 "And you shall have the tassel, that you may look upon it and remember all the commandments of the LORD and do them, and that you *may* not follow the harlotry to which your own heart and your own eyes are inclined,

40 "and that you may remember and do all My commandments, and be holy for your God.

41 "I *am* the LORD your God, who brought you out of the land of Egypt, to be your God: I *am* the LORD your God."

REBELLION AGAINST MOSES AND AARON

16 Now Kō'rah the son of Iz'har, the son of Kō'hath, the son of Levi, with Dā'than and A·bī'ram the sons of E·lī'ab, and On the son of Pē'leth, sons of Reuben, took *men;*

2 and they rose up before Moses with some of the children of Israel, two hundred and fifty leaders of the congregation, representatives of the congregation, men of renown.

3 They gathered together against Moses and Aaron, and said to them, "*You take* too much upon yourselves, for all the congregation *is* holy, every one of them, and the LORD *is* among them. Why then do you exalt yourselves above the assembly of the LORD?"

4 So when Moses heard *it,* he fell on his face;

5 and he spoke to Kō'rah and all his company, saying, "Tomorrow morning the LORD will show who *is* His and *who is* holy, and will cause *him* to come near to Him. That one whom He chooses He will cause to come near to Him.

6 "Do this: Take censers, Kō'rah and all your company;

7 "put fire in them and put incense in them before the LORD tomorrow, and it shall be *that* the man whom the LORD chooses *is* the holy one. *You take* too much upon yourselves, you sons of Levi!"

8 Then Moses said to Kō'rah, "Hear now, you sons of Levi:

9 "*Is it* a small thing to you that the God of Israel has separated you from the congregation of Israel, to bring you near to Himself, to do the work of the tabernacle of the LORD, and to stand before the congregation to serve them;

10 "and that He has brought you near *to Himself,* you and all your brethren, the sons of Levi, with you? And are you seeking the priesthood also?

11 "Therefore you and all your company *are* gathered together against the LORD. And what *is* Aaron that you complain against him?"

12 And Moses sent to call Dā'than and A·bī'ram the sons of E·lī'ab, but they said, "We will not come up!

13 "*Is it* a small thing that you have brought us up out of a land flowing with milk and honey, to kill us in the wilderness, that you should keep acting like a prince over us?

14 "Moreover you have not brought us into a land flowing with milk and honey, nor given us inheritance of fields and vineyards. Will you put out the eyes of these men? We will not come up!"

15 Then Moses was very angry, and said to the LORD, "Do not respect their offering. I have not taken one donkey from them, nor have I hurt one of them."

16 And Moses said to Kō′rah, "Tomorrow, you and all your company be present before the LORD—you and they, as well as Aaron.

17 "Let each take his censer and put incense in it, and each of you bring his censer before the LORD, two hundred and fifty censers; both you and Aaron, each *with* his censer."

18 So every man took his censer, put fire in it, laid incense on it, and stood at the door of the tabernacle of meeting with Moses and Aaron.

19 And Kō′rah gathered all the congregation against them at the door of the tabernacle of meeting. Then the glory of the LORD appeared to all the congregation.

20 And the LORD spoke to Moses and Aaron, saying,

21 "Separate yourselves from among this congregation, that I may consume them in a moment."

22 Then they fell on their faces, and said, "O God, the God of the spirits of all flesh, shall one man sin, and You be angry with all the congregation?"

23 So the LORD spoke to Moses, saying,

24 "Speak to the congregation, saying, 'Get away from the tents of Kō′rah, Dā′than, and A·bī′ram.' "

25 Then Moses rose and went to Dā′than and A·bī′ram, and the elders of Israel followed him.

26 And he spoke to the congregation, saying, "Depart now from the tents of these wicked men! Touch nothing of theirs, lest you be consumed in all their sins."

27 So they got away from around the tents of Kō′rah, Dā′than, and A·bī′ram; and Dā′than and A·bī′ram came out and stood at the door of their tents, with their wives, their sons, and their little children.

28 And Moses said: "By this you shall know that the LORD has sent me to do all these works, for *I have* not *done them* of my own will.

29 "If these men die naturally like all men, or if they are visited by the common fate of all men, *then* the LORD has not sent me.

30 "But if the LORD creates a new thing, and the earth opens its mouth and swallows them up with all that belongs to them, and they go down alive into the pit, then you will understand that these men have rejected the LORD."

31 Now it came to pass, as he finished speaking all these words, that the ground split apart under them,

32 and the earth opened its mouth and swallowed them up, with their households and all the men with Kō′rah, with all *their* goods.

33 So they and all those with them went down alive into the pit; the earth closed over them, and they perished from among the assembly.

34 Then all Israel who *were* around them fled at their cry, for they said, "Lest the earth swallow us up *also!*"

35 And a fire came out from the LORD and consumed the two hundred and fifty men who were offering incense.

36 Then the LORD spoke to Moses, saying:

37 "Tell El·ē·ā′zar, the son of Aaron the priest, to pick up the censers out of the blaze, for they are holy, and scatter the fire some distance away.

38 "The censers of these men who sinned against their own souls, let them be made into hammered plates as a covering for the altar. Because they presented them before the LORD, therefore they are holy; and they shall be a sign to the children of Israel."

39 So El·ē·ā′zar the priest took the bronze censers, which those who were burned up had presented, and they were hammered out as a covering on the altar,

40 *to be* a memorial to the children of Israel that no outsider, who *is* not a descendant of Aaron, should come near to offer incense before the LORD, that he might not become like Kō′rah and his companions, just as the LORD had said to him through Moses.

COMPLAINTS OF THE PEOPLE

41 On the next day all the congregation of the children of Israel complained against Moses and Aaron, saying, "You have killed the people of the LORD."

42 Now it happened, when the congregation had gathered against Moses and Aaron, that they turned toward the tabernacle of meeting; and suddenly the cloud covered it, and the glory of the LORD appeared.

43 Then Moses and Aaron came before the tabernacle of meeting.

44 And the LORD spoke to Moses, saying,

45 "Get away from among this congregation, that I may consume them in a moment." And they fell on their faces.

46 So Moses said to Aaron, "Take a censer and put fire in it from the altar, put incense *on it,* and take it quickly to the congregation and make atonement for them; for wrath has gone out from the LORD. The plague has begun."

47 Then Aaron took *it* as Moses commanded, and ran into the midst of the assembly; and already the plague had begun among the people. So he put in the incense and made atonement for the people.

48 And he stood between the dead and the living; so the plague was stopped.

49 Now those who died in the plague were fourteen thousand seven hundred, besides those who died in the Kō′rah incident.

50 So Aaron returned to Moses at the door of the tabernacle of meeting, for the plague had stopped.

THE BUDDING OF AARON'S ROD

17 And the LORD spoke to Moses, saying:

2 "Speak to the children of Israel, and get from them a rod from each father's house, all their leaders according to their fathers' houses—twelve rods. Write each man's name on his rod.

3 "And you shall write Aaron's name on the rod of Levi. For there shall be one rod for the head of *each* father's house.

4 "Then you shall place them in the tabernacle of meeting before the Testimony, where I meet with you.

5 "And it shall be *that* the rod of the man whom I choose will blossom; thus I will rid Myself of the complaints of the children of Israel, which they make against you."

6 So Moses spoke to the children of Israel, and each of their leaders gave him a rod apiece, for each leader according to their fathers' houses, twelve rods; and the rod of Aaron *was* among their rods.

7 And Moses placed the rods before the LORD in the tabernacle of witness.

8 Now it came to pass on the next day that Moses went into the tabernacle of witness, and behold, the rod of Aaron, of the house of Levi, had sprouted and put forth buds, had produced blossoms and yielded ripe almonds.

9 Then Moses brought out all the rods from before the LORD to all the children of Israel; and they looked, and each man took his rod.

10 And the LORD said to Moses, "Bring Aaron's rod back before the Testimony, to be kept as a sign against the rebels, that you may put their complaints away from Me, lest they die."

11 Thus did Moses; just as the LORD had commanded him, so he did.

12 So the children of Israel spoke to Moses, saying, "Surely we die, we perish, we all perish!

13 "Whoever even comes near the tabernacle of the LORD must die. Shall we all utterly die?"

DUTIES OF PRIESTS AND LEVITES

18 Then the LORD said to Aaron: "You and your sons and your father's house with you shall bear the iniquity *related to* the sanctuary, and you and your sons with you shall bear the iniquity *associated with* your priesthood.

2 "Also bring with you your brethren of the tribe of Levi, the tribe of your father, that they may be joined with you and serve you while you and your sons *are* with you before the tabernacle of witness.

3 "They shall attend to your needs and all the needs of the tabernacle; but they shall not come near the articles of the sanctuary and the altar, lest they die—they and you also.

4 "They shall be joined with you and attend to the needs of the tabernacle of meeting, for all the work of the tabernacle; but an outsider shall not come near you.

5 "And you shall attend to the duties of the sanctuary and the duties of the altar, that there *may* be no more wrath on the children of Israel.

6 "Behold, I Myself have taken your brethren the Lēʹvītes from among the children of Israel; *they are* a gift to you, given by the LORD, to do the work of the tabernacle of meeting.

7 "Therefore you and your sons with you shall attend to your priesthood for everything at the altar and behind the veil; and you shall serve. I give your priesthood *to you* as a gift for service, but the outsider who comes near shall be put to death."

OFFERINGS FOR SUPPORT OF THE PRIESTS

8 And the LORD spoke to Aaron: "Here, I Myself have also given you charge of My heave offerings, all the holy gifts of the children of Israel; I have given them as a portion to you and your sons, as an ordinance forever.

9 "This shall be yours of the most holy things *reserved* from the fire: every offering of theirs, every grain offering and every sin offering and every trespass offering which they render to Me, *shall be* most holy for you and your sons.

10 "In a most holy *place* you shall eat it; every male shall eat it. It shall be holy to you.

11 "This also *is* yours: the heave offering of their gift, with all the wave offerings of the children of Israel; I have given them to you, and your sons and daughters with you, as an ordinance forever. Everyone who is clean in your house may eat it.

12 "All the best of the oil, all the best of the new wine and the grain, their firstfruits which they offer to the LORD, I have given them to you.

13 "Whatever first ripe fruit is in their land, which they bring to the LORD, shall be yours. Everyone who is clean in your house may eat it.

14 "Every devoted thing in Israel shall be yours.

15 "Everything that first opens the womb of all flesh, which they bring to the LORD, whether man or beast, shall be yours; nevertheless the first-born of man you shall surely redeem, and the firstborn of unclean animals you shall redeem.

16 "And those redeemed of the devoted things you shall redeem when one month old, according to your valuation, for five shekels of silver, according to the shekel of the sanctuary, which *is* twenty gerahs.

17 "But the firstborn of a cow, the firstborn of a sheep, or the firstborn of a goat you shall not redeem; they *are* holy. You shall sprinkle their blood on the altar, and burn their fat *as* an offering made by fire for a sweet aroma to the LORD.

18 "And their flesh shall be yours, just as the wave breast and the right thigh are yours.

19 "All the heave offerings of the holy things, which the children of Israel offer to the LORD, I have given to you and your sons and daughters with you as an ordinance forever; it *is* a covenant of salt forever before the LORD with you and your descendants with you."

20 Then the LORD said to Aaron: "You shall have no inheritance in their land, nor shall you have any portion among them; I *am* your portion and your inheritance among the children of Israel.

TITHES FOR SUPPORT OF THE LEVITES

21 "Behold, I have given the children of Levi all the tithes in Israel as an inheritance in return for the work which they perform, the work of the tabernacle of meeting.

22 "Hereafter the children of Israel shall not come near the tabernacle of meeting, lest they bear sin and die.

23 "But the Lē'vītes shall perform the work of the tabernacle of meeting, and they shall bear their iniquity; *it shall be* a statute forever, throughout your generations, that among the children of Israel they shall have no inheritance.

24 "For the tithes of the children of Israel, which they offer up *as* a heave offering to the LORD, I have given to the Lē'vītes as an inheritance; therefore I have said to them, 'Among the children of Israel they shall have no inheritance.' "

THE TITHE OF THE LEVITES

25 Then the LORD spoke to Moses, saying,

26 "Speak thus to the Lē'vītes, and say to them: 'When you take from the children of Israel the tithes which I have given you from them as your inheritance, then you shall offer up a heave offering of it to the LORD, a tenth of the tithe.

27 'And your heave offering shall be reckoned to you as though *it were* the grain of the threshing floor and as the fullness of the winepress.

28 'Thus you shall also offer a heave offering to the LORD from all your tithes which you receive from the children of Israel, and you shall give the LORD's heave offering from it to Aaron the priest.

29 'Of all your gifts you shall offer up every heave offering due to the LORD, from all the best of them, the consecrated part of them.'

30 "Therefore you shall say to them: 'When you have lifted up the best of it, then *the rest* shall be accounted to the Lē'vītes as the produce of the threshing floor and as the produce of the winepress.

Family Memories

WRAPPING UP MY BEST GIFT Numbers 18:28–30

"I want to give my best gift to Jesus," said Jennifer. She won't really wrap herself as a gift for Jesus, will she? But wrapping and unwrapping gifts is a favorite family time. So Jennifer thinks of herself as a gift for Jesus to unwrap.

1. What do you think Jesus wants most, your money or you?
2. How can you give yourself to Jesus?
3. How does this remind you of Christmas or birthdays?

For more on *Family Memories* turn to page 270
For more on *Giving* turn to page 270

31 'You may eat it in any place, you and your households, for it *is* your reward for your work in the tabernacle of meeting.

32 'And you shall bear no sin because of it, when you have lifted up the best of it. But you shall not profane the holy gifts of the children of Israel, lest you die.' "

LAWS OF PURIFICATION

19 Now the LORD spoke to Moses and Aaron, saying,

2 "This *is* the ordinance of the law which the LORD has commanded, saying: 'Speak to the children of Israel, that they bring you a red heifer without blemish, in which there *is* no defect *and* on which a yoke has never come.

3 'You shall give it to El·e·ā′zar the priest, that he may take it outside the camp, and it shall be slaughtered before him;

4 'and El·e·ā′zar the priest shall take some of its blood with his finger, and sprinkle some of its blood seven times directly in front of the tabernacle of meeting.

5 'Then the heifer shall be burned in his sight: its hide, its flesh, its blood, and its offal shall be burned.

6 'And the priest shall take cedar wood and hyssop and scarlet, and cast *them* into the midst of the fire burning the heifer.

7 'Then the priest shall wash his clothes, he shall bathe in water, and afterward he shall come into the camp; the priest shall be unclean until evening.

8 'And the one who burns it shall wash his clothes in water, bathe in water, and shall be unclean until evening.

9 'Then a man *who is* clean shall gather up the ashes of the heifer, and store *them* outside the camp in a clean place; and they shall be kept for the congregation of the children of Israel for the water of purification;*a* it *is* for purifying from sin.

10 'And the one who gathers the ashes of the heifer shall wash his clothes, and be unclean until evening. It shall be a statute forever to the children of Israel and to the stranger who dwells among them.

11 'He who touches the dead body of anyone shall be unclean seven days.

12 'He shall purify himself with the water on the third day and on the seventh day; *then* he will be clean. But if he does not purify himself on the third day and on the seventh day, he will not be clean.

13 'Whoever touches the body of anyone who has died, and does not purify himself, defiles the tabernacle of the LORD. That person shall be cut off from Israel. He shall be unclean, because the water of purification was not sprinkled on him; his uncleanness *is* still on him.

14 'This *is* the law when a man dies in a tent: All who come into the tent and all who *are* in the tent shall be unclean seven days;

15 'and every open vessel, which has no cover fastened on it, *is* unclean.

16 'Whoever in the open field touches one who is slain by a sword or who has died, or a bone of a man, or a grave, shall be unclean seven days.

17 'And for an unclean *person* they shall take some of the ashes of the heifer burnt for purification from sin, and running water shall be put on them in a vessel.

18 'A clean person shall take hyssop and dip *it* in the water, sprinkle *it* on the tent, on all the vessels, on the persons who were there, or on the one who touched a bone, the slain, the dead, or a grave.

19:9 *a*Literally *impurity*

19 'The clean *person* shall sprinkle the unclean on the third day and on the seventh day; and on the seventh day he shall purify himself, wash his clothes, and bathe in water; and at evening he shall be clean.

20 'But the man who is unclean and does not purify himself, that person shall be cut off from among the assembly, because he has defiled the sanctuary of the LORD. The water of purification has not been sprinkled on him; he *is* unclean.

21 'It shall be a perpetual statute for them. He who sprinkles the water of purification shall wash his clothes; and he who touches the water of purification shall be unclean until evening.

22 'Whatever the unclean *person* touches shall be unclean; and the person who touches *it* shall be unclean until evening.' "

MOSES' ERROR AT KADESH

20 Then the children of Israel, the whole congregation, came into the Wilderness of Zin in the first month, and the people stayed in Kā′desh; and Miriam died there and was buried there.

2 Now there was no water for the congregation; so they gathered together against Moses and Aaron.

3 And the people contended with Moses and spoke, saying: "If only we had died when our brethren died before the LORD!

4 "Why have you brought up the assembly of the LORD into this wilderness, that we and our animals should die here?

5 "And why have you made us come up out of Egypt, to bring us to this evil place? It *is* not a place of grain or figs or vines or pomegranates; nor *is* there any water to drink."

6 So Moses and Aaron went from the presence of the assembly to the door of the tabernacle of meeting, and they fell on their faces. And the glory of the LORD appeared to them.

7 Then the LORD spoke to Moses, saying,

8 "Take the rod; you and your brother Aaron gather the congregation together. Speak to the rock before their eyes, and it will yield its water; thus you shall bring water for them out of the rock, and give drink to the congregation and their animals."

9 So Moses took the rod from before the LORD as He commanded him.

10 And Moses and Aaron gathered the assembly together before the rock; and he said to them, "Hear now, you rebels! Must we bring water for you out of this rock?"

11 Then Moses lifted his hand and struck the rock twice with his rod; and water came out abundantly, and the congregation and their animals drank.

12 Then the LORD spoke to Moses and Aaron, "Because you did not believe Me, to hallow Me in the eyes of the children of Israel, therefore you shall not bring this assembly into the land which I have given them."

13 This *was* the water of Mer′i·bah,ᵃ because the children of Israel contended with the LORD, and He was hallowed among them.

PASSAGE THROUGH EDOM REFUSED

14 Now Moses sent messengers from Kā′desh to the king of Ē′dom. "Thus says your brother Israel: 'You know all the hardship that has befallen us,

15 'how our fathers went down to Egypt, and we dwelt in Egypt a long

20:13 ᵃLiterally *Contention*

time, and the Egyptians afflicted us and our fathers.

16 'When we cried out to the LORD, He heard our voice and sent the Angel and brought us up out of Egypt; now here we are in Kā'desh, a city on the edge of your border.

17 'Please let us pass through your country. We will not pass through fields or vineyards, nor will we drink water from wells; we will go along the King's Highway; we will not turn aside to the right hand or to the left until we have passed through your territory.' "

18 Then Ē'dom said to him, "You shall not pass through my *land,* lest I come out against you with the sword."

19 So the children of Israel said to him, "We will go by the Highway, and if I or my livestock drink any of your water, then I will pay for it; let me only pass through on foot, nothing *more.*"

20 Then he said, "You shall not pass through." So Ē'dom came out against them with many men and with a strong hand.

21 Thus Ē'dom refused to give Israel passage through his territory; so Israel turned away from him.

DEATH OF AARON

22 Now the children of Israel, the whole congregation, journeyed from Kā'desh and came to Mount Hor.

23 And the LORD spoke to Moses and Aaron in Mount Hor by the border of the land of Ē'dom, saying:

24 "Aaron shall be gathered to his people, for he shall not enter the land which I have given to the children of Israel, because you rebelled against My word at the water of Mer'i·bah.

25 "Take Aaron and El·ē·ā'zar his son, and bring them up to Mount Hor;

26 "and strip Aaron of his garments and put them on El·ē·ā'zar his son; for Aaron shall be gathered *to his people* and die there."

27 So Moses did just as the LORD commanded, and they went up to Mount Hor in the sight of all the congregation.

28 Moses stripped Aaron of his garments and put them on El·ē·ā'zar his son; and Aaron died there on the top of the mountain. Then Moses and El·ē·ā'zar came down from the mountain.

29 Now when all the congregation saw that Aaron was dead, all the house of Israel mourned for Aaron thirty days.

CANAANITES DEFEATED AT HORMAH

21 The king of Ar'ad, the Cā'-naan·ite, who dwelt in the South, heard that Israel was coming on the road to Ath'a·rim. Then he fought against Israel and took *some* of them prisoners.

2 So Israel made a vow to the LORD, and said, "If You will indeed deliver this people into my hand, then I will utterly destroy their cities."

3 And the LORD listened to the voice of Israel and delivered up the Cā'naan·ites, and they utterly destroyed them and their cities. So the name of that place was called Hor'mah.*a*

THE BRONZE SERPENT

4 Then they journeyed from Mount Hor by the Way of the Red Sea, to go around the land of Ē'dom; and the soul of the people became very discouraged on the way.

21:3 *a*Literally *Utter Destruction*

5 And the people spoke against God and against Moses: "Why have you brought us up out of Egypt to die in the wilderness? For *there is* no food and no water, and our soul loathes this worthless bread."

6 So the LORD sent fiery serpents among the people, and they bit the people; and many of the people of Israel died.

7 Therefore the people came to Moses, and said, "We have sinned, for we have spoken against the LORD and against you; pray to the LORD that He take away the serpents from us." So Moses prayed for the people.

8 Then the LORD said to Moses, "Make a fiery *serpent,* and set it on a pole; and it shall be that everyone who is bitten, when he looks at it, shall live."

9 So Moses made a bronze serpent, and put it on a pole; and so it was, if a serpent had bitten anyone, when he looked at the bronze serpent, he lived.

FROM MOUNT HOR TO MOAB

10 Now the children of Israel moved on and camped in Ō'both.

11 And they journeyed from Ō'both and camped at Ī'jē Ab'a·rim, in the wilderness which *is* east of Mō'ab, toward the sunrise.

12 From there they moved and camped in the Valley of Zē'red.

13 From there they moved and camped on the other side of the Ar'non, which *is* in the wilderness that extends from the border of the Am'o·rītes; for the Ar'non *is* the border of Mō'ab, between Mō'ab and the Am'o·rītes.

14 Therefore it is said in the Book of the Wars of the LORD:

"Wa'heb in Sū'phah,*a*
The brooks of the Ar'non,

15 And the slope of the brooks
That reaches to the dwelling of Ar,
And lies on the border of Mō'ab."

16 From there *they went* to Bē'er, which *is* the well where the LORD said to Moses, "Gather the people together, and I will give them water."

17 Then Israel sang this song:

"Spring up, O well!
All of you sing to it—

18 The well the leaders sank,
Dug by the nation's nobles,
By the lawgiver, with their staves."

And from the wilderness *they went* to Mat'ta·nah,

19 from Mat'ta·nah to Na·hal'i·el, from Na·hal'i·el to Bā'moth,

20 and from Bā'moth, *in* the valley that *is* in the country of Mō'ab, to the top of Pis'gah which looks down on the wasteland.*a*

KING SIHON DEFEATED

21 Then Israel sent messengers to Sī'hon king of the Am'o·rītes, saying,

22 "Let me pass through your land. We will not turn aside into fields or vineyards; we will not drink water from wells. We will go by the King's Highway until we have passed through your territory."

23 But Sī'hon would not allow Israel to pass through his territory. So Sī'hon gathered all his people together and went out against Israel in the wilderness, and he came to Jā'haz and fought against Israel.

24 Then Israel defeated him with the edge of the sword, and took possession of his land from the Ar'non to

21:14 *a*Ancient unknown places; Vulgate reads *What He did in the Red Sea.* 21:20 *a*Hebrew *Jeshimon*

the Jab'bok, as far as the people of Am'mon; for the border of the people of Am'mon *was* fortified.

25 So Israel took all these cities, and Israel dwelt in all the cities of the Am'o·rītes, in Hesh'bon and in all its villages.

26 For Hesh'bon *was* the city of Sī'hon king of the Am'o·rītes, who had fought against the former king of Mō'ab, and had taken all his land from his hand as far as the Ar'non.

27 Therefore those who speak in proverbs say:

"Come to Hesh'bon, let it be built;
Let the city of Sī'hon be repaired.

28 "For fire went out from Hesh'bon,
A flame from the city of Sī'hon;
It consumed Ar of Mō'ab,
The lords of the heights of the
    Ar'non.

29 Woe to you, Mō'ab!
You have perished, O people of
    Chē'mosh!
He has given his sons as
    fugitives,
And his daughters into captivity,
To Sī'hon king of the Am'o·rītes.

30 "But we have shot at them;
Hesh'bon has perished as far as
    Dī'bon.
Then we laid waste as far as
    Nō'phah,
Which *reaches* to Med'e·ba."

31 Thus Israel dwelt in the land of the Am'o·rītes.

32 Then Moses sent to spy out Jā'zer; and they took its villages and drove out the Am'o·rītes who *were* there.

KING OG DEFEATED

33 And they turned and went up by the way to Bā'shan. So Og king of Bā'shan went out against them, he and all his people, to battle at Ed're·ī.

34 Then the LORD said to Moses, "Do not fear him, for I have delivered him into your hand, with all his people and his land; and you shall do to him as you did to Sī'hon king of the Am'o·rītes, who dwelt at Hesh'bon."

35 So they defeated him, his sons, and all his people, until there was no survivor left him; and they took possession of his land.

BALAK SENDS FOR BALAAM

22 Then the children of Israel moved, and camped in the plains of Mō'ab on the side of the Jordan *across from* Jericho.

2 Now Bā'lak the son of Zip'por saw all that Israel had done to the Am'o·rītes.

3 And Mō'ab was exceedingly afraid of the people because they *were* many, and Mō'ab was sick with dread because of the children of Israel.

4 So Mō'ab said to the elders of Mid'i·an, "Now this company will lick up everything around us, as an ox licks up the grass of the field." And Bā'lak the son of Zip'por *was* king of the Mō'ab·ītes at that time.

5 Then he sent messengers to Bā'laam the son of Bē'or at Pē'thor, which *is* near the River[a] in the land of the sons of his people,[b] to call him, saying: "Look, a people has come from Egypt. See, they cover the face of the earth, and are settling next to me!

6 "Therefore please come at once, curse this people for me, for they *are* too mighty for me. Perhaps I shall be able to defeat them and drive them out of the land, for I know that he

22:5 [a]That is, the Euphrates [b]Or *the people of Amau*

whom you bless *is* blessed, and he whom you curse is cursed."

7 So the elders of Mō'ab and the elders of Mid'i·an departed with the diviner's fee in their hand, and they came to Bā'laam and spoke to him the words of Bā'lak.

8 And he said to them, "Lodge here tonight, and I will bring back word to you, as the LORD speaks to me." So the princes of Mō'ab stayed with Bā'laam.

9 Then God came to Bā'laam and said, "Who *are* these men with you?"

10 So Bā'laam said to God, "Bā'lak the son of Zip'por, king of Mō'ab, has sent to me, *saying,*

11 'Look, a people has come out of Egypt, and they cover the face of the earth. Come now, curse them for me; perhaps I shall be able to overpower them and drive them out.' "

12 And God said to Bā'laam, "You shall not go with them; you shall not curse the people, for they *are* blessed."

13 So Bā'laam rose in the morning and said to the princes of Bā'lak, "Go back to your land, for the LORD has refused to give me permission to go with you."

14 And the princes of Mō'ab rose and went to Bā'lak, and said, "Bā'laam refuses to come with us."

15 Then Bā'lak again sent princes, more numerous and more honorable than they.

16 And they came to Bā'laam and said to him, "Thus says Bā'lak the son of Zip'por: 'Please let nothing hinder you from coming to me;

17 'for I will certainly honor you greatly, and I will do whatever you say to me. Therefore please come, curse this people for me.' "

18 Then Bā'laam answered and said to the servants of Bā'lak, "Though Bā'lak were to give me his house full of silver and gold, I could not go beyond the word of the LORD my God, to do less or more.

19 "Now therefore, please, you also stay here tonight, that I may know what more the LORD will say to me."

20 And God came to Bā'laam at night and said to him, "If the men come to call you, rise *and* go with them; but only the word which I speak to you—that you shall do."

21 So Bā'laam rose in the morning, saddled his donkey, and went with the princes of Mō'ab.

BALAAM, THE DONKEY, AND THE ANGEL

22 Then God's anger was aroused because he went, and the Angel of the LORD took His stand in the way as an adversary against him. And he was riding on his donkey, and his two servants *were* with him.

23 Now the donkey saw the Angel of the LORD standing in the way with His drawn sword in His hand, and the donkey turned aside out of the way and went into the field. So Bā'laam struck the donkey to turn her back onto the road.

24 Then the Angel of the LORD stood in a narrow path between the vineyards, *with* a wall on this side and a wall on that side.

25 And when the donkey saw the Angel of the LORD, she pushed herself against the wall and crushed Bā'laam's foot against the wall; so he struck her again.

26 Then the Angel of the LORD went further, and stood in a narrow place where there *was* no way to turn either to the right hand or to the left.

27 And when the donkey saw the Angel of the LORD, she lay down under Bā'laam; so Bā'laam's anger was aroused, and he struck the donkey with his staff.

28 Then the LORD opened the mouth of the donkey, and she said to Bā′laam, "What have I done to you, that you have struck me these three times?"

29 And Bā′laam said to the donkey, "Because you have abused me. I wish there were a sword in my hand, for now I would kill you!"

30 So the donkey said to Bā′laam, "*Am* I not your donkey on which you have ridden, ever since *I became* yours, to this day? Was I ever disposed to do this to you?" And he said, "No."

31 Then the LORD opened Bā′laam's eyes, and he saw the Angel of the LORD standing in the way with His drawn sword in His hand; and he bowed his head and fell flat on his face.

32 And the Angel of the LORD said to him, "Why have you struck your donkey these three times? Behold, I have come out to stand against you, because *your* way is perverse before Me.

33 "The donkey saw Me and turned aside from Me these three times. If she had not turned aside from Me, surely I would also have killed you by now, and let her live."

34 And Bā′laam said to the Angel of the LORD, "I have sinned, for I did not know You stood in the way against me. Now therefore, if it displeases You, I will turn back."

35 Then the Angel of the LORD said to Bā′laam, "Go with the men, but only the word that I speak to you, that you shall speak." So Bā′laam went with the princes of Bā′lak.

36 Now when Bā′lak heard that Bā′laam was coming, he went out to meet him at the city of Mō′ab, which *is* on the border at the Ar′non, the boundary of the territory.

37 Then Bā′lak said to Bā′laam, "Did I not earnestly send to you, call-ing for you? Why did you not come to me? Am I not able to honor you?"

38 And Bā′laam said to Bā′lak, "Look, I have come to you! Now, have I any power at all to say anything? The word that God puts in my mouth, that I must speak."

39 So Bā′laam went with Bā′lak, and they came to Kir′jath Hu′zoth.

40 Then Bā′lak offered oxen and sheep, and he sent *some* to Bā′laam and to the princes who *were* with him.

BALAAM'S FIRST PROPHECY

41 So it was, the next day, that Bā′lak took Bā′laam and brought him up to the high places of Bā′al, that from there he might observe the extent of the people.

23 Then Bā′laam said to Bā′lak, "Build seven altars for me here, and prepare for me here seven bulls and seven rams."

2 And Bā′lak did just as Bā′laam had spoken, and Bā′lak and Bā′laam offered a bull and a ram on *each* altar.

3 Then Bā′laam said to Bā′lak, "Stand by your burnt offering, and I will go; perhaps the LORD will come to meet me, and whatever He shows me I will tell you." So he went to a desolate height.

4 And God met Bā′laam, and he said to Him, "I have prepared the seven altars, and I have offered on *each* altar a bull and a ram."

5 Then the LORD put a word in Bā′laam's mouth, and said, "Return to Bā′lak, and thus you shall speak."

6 So he returned to him, and there he was, standing by his burnt offering, he and all the princes of Mō′ab.

7 And he took up his oracle and said:

"Bā′lak the king of Mō′ab has
brought me from Ar′am,
From the mountains of the east.
'Come, curse Jacob for me,
And come, denounce Israel!'

8 "How shall I curse whom God has
not cursed?
And how shall I denounce *whom*
the LORD has not denounced?
9 For from the top of the rocks I see
him,
And from the hills I behold him;
There! A people dwelling alone,
Not reckoning itself among the
nations.

10 "Who can count the dust*a* of Jacob,
Or number one-fourth of Israel?
Let me die the death of the
righteous,
And let my end be like his!"

11 Then Bā′lak said to Bā′laam,
"What have you done to me? I took
you to curse my enemies, and look,
you have blessed *them* bountifully!"
12 So he answered and said, "Must I
not take heed to speak what the LORD
has put in my mouth?"

BALAAM'S SECOND PROPHECY

13 Then Bā′lak said to him, "Please
come with me to another place from
which you may see them; you shall
see only the outer part of them, and
shall not see them all; curse them for
me from there."
14 So he brought him to the field of
Zō′phim, to the top of Pis′gah, and
built seven altars, and offered a bull
and a ram on *each* altar.
15 And he said to Bā′lak, "Stand
here by your burnt offering while I
meet*a* the LORD over there."
16 Then the LORD met Bā′laam, and
put a word in his mouth, and said,
"Go back to Bā′lak, and thus you
shall speak."

17 So he came to him, and there he
was, standing by his burnt offering,
and the princes of Mō′ab were with
him. And Bā′lak said to him, "What
has the LORD spoken?"
18 Then he took up his oracle and
said:

"Rise up, Bā′lak, and hear!
Listen to me, son of Zip′por!

19 "God *is* not a man, that He should
lie,
Nor a son of man, that He should
repent.
Has He said, and will He not do?
Or has He spoken, and will He
not make it good?
20 Behold, I have received *a
command* to bless;
He has blessed, and I cannot
reverse it.

21 "He has not observed iniquity in
Jacob,
Nor has He seen wickedness in
Israel.
The LORD his God *is* with him,
And the shout of a King *is* among
them.
22 God brings them out of Egypt;
He has strength like a wild ox.

23 "For *there is* no sorcery against
Jacob,
Nor any divination against Israel.
It now must be said of Jacob
And of Israel, 'Oh, what God has
done!'
24 Look, a people rises like a lioness,
And lifts itself up like a lion;
It shall not lie down until it
devours the prey,
And drinks the blood of the slain."

25 Then Bā′lak said to Bā′laam,

23:10 *a*Or *dust cloud*   23:15 *a*Following Masoretic Text, Targum, and Vulgate; Syriac reads *call;*
Septuagint reads *go and ask God.*

"Neither curse them at all, nor bless them at all!"

26 So Bā′laam answered and said to Bā′lak, "Did I not tell you, saying, 'All that the LORD speaks, that I must do'?"

BALAAM'S THIRD PROPHECY

27 Then Bā′lak said to Bā′laam, "Please come, I will take you to another place; perhaps it will please God that you may curse them for me from there."
28 So Bā′lak took Bā′laam to the top of Pē′or, that overlooks the wasteland.[a]
29 Then Bā′laam said to Bā′lak, "Build for me here seven altars, and prepare for me here seven bulls and seven rams."
30 And Bā′lak did as Bā′laam had said, and offered a bull and a ram on *every* altar.

24 Now when Bā′laam saw that it pleased the LORD to bless Israel, he did not go as at other times, to seek to use sorcery, but he set his face toward the wilderness.
2 And Bā′laam raised his eyes, and saw Israel encamped according to their tribes; and the Spirit of God came upon him.
3 Then he took up his oracle and said:

"The utterance of Bā′laam the son of Bē′or,
The utterance of the man whose eyes are opened,
4 The utterance of him who hears the words of God,
Who sees the vision of the Almighty,
Who falls down, with eyes wide open:

5 "How lovely are your tents, O Jacob!
Your dwellings, O Israel!
6 Like valleys that stretch out,
Like gardens by the riverside,
Like aloes planted by the LORD,
Like cedars beside the waters.
7 He shall pour water from his buckets,
And his seed *shall be* in many waters.

"His king shall be higher than Ā′gag,
And his kingdom shall be exalted.

8 "God brings him out of Egypt;
He has strength like a wild ox;
He shall consume the nations, his enemies;
He shall break their bones
And pierce *them* with his arrows.
9 'He bows down, he lies down as a lion;
And as a lion, who shall rouse him?'[a]

"Blessed *is* he who blesses you,
And cursed *is* he who curses you."

10 Then Bā′lak's anger was aroused against Bā′laam, and he struck his hands together; and Bā′lak said to Bā′laam, "I called you to curse my enemies, and look, you have bountifully blessed *them* these three times!
11 "Now therefore, flee to your place. I said I would greatly honor you, but in fact, the LORD has kept you back from honor."
12 So Bā′laam said to Bā′lak, "Did I not also speak to your messengers whom you sent to me, saying,
13 'If Bā′lak were to give me his house full of silver and gold, I could not go beyond the word of the LORD, to do good or bad of my own will. What the LORD says, that I must speak'?

23:28 ᵃHebrew *Jeshimon*   24:9 ᵃGenesis 49:9

14 "And now, indeed, I am going to my people. Come, I will advise you what this people will do to your people in the latter days."

BALAAM'S FOURTH PROPHECY

15 So he took up his oracle and said:

"The utterance of Bā′laam the son
   of Bē′or,
And the utterance of the man
   whose eyes are opened;
16 The utterance of him who hears
   the words of God,
And has the knowledge of the
   Most High,
Who sees the vision of the
   Almighty,
Who falls down, with eyes wide
   open:

17 "I see Him, but not now;
I behold Him, but not near;
A Star shall come out of Jacob;
A Scepter shall rise out of Israel,
And batter the brow of Mō′ab,
And destroy all the sons of
   tumult.*a*

18 "And Ē′dom shall be a possession;
Sē′ir also, his enemies, shall be a
   possession,
While Israel does valiantly.
19 Out of Jacob One shall have
   dominion,
And destroy the remains of the
   city."

20 Then he looked on Am′a·lek, and he took up his oracle and said:

"Am′a·lek *was* first among the
   nations,
But *shall be* last until he
   perishes."

21 Then he looked on the Ken′ītes, and he took up his oracle and said:

"Firm is your dwelling place,
And your nest is set in the rock;
22 Nevertheless Kāin shall be
   burned.
How long until As′shur carries
   you away captive?"

23 Then he took up his oracle and said:

"Alas! Who shall live when God
   does this?
24 But ships *shall come* from the
   coasts of Cyprus,*a*
And they shall afflict As′shur and
   afflict Ē′ber,
And so shall *Am′a·lek,b* until he
   perishes."

25 So Bā′laam rose and departed and returned to his place; Bā′lak also went his way.

ISRAEL'S HARLOTRY IN MOAB

25 Now Israel remained in Acacia Grove,*a* and the people began to commit harlotry with the women of Mō′ab.
2 They invited the people to the sacrifices of their gods, and the people ate and bowed down to their gods.
3 So Israel was joined to Bā′al of Pē′or, and the anger of the LORD was aroused against Israel.
4 Then the LORD said to Moses, "Take all the leaders of the people and hang the offenders before the LORD, out in the sun, that the fierce anger of the LORD may turn away from Israel."
5 So Moses said to the judges of Israel, "Every one of you kill his men who were joined to Bā′al of Pē′or."
6 And indeed, one of the children of Israel came and presented to his

24:17 *a*Hebrew *Sheth* (compare Jeremiah 48:45)
24:24 *a*Hebrew *Kittim*   *b*Literally *he* or *that one*
25:1 *a*Hebrew *Shittim*

brethren a Mid′i·an·ite woman in the sight of Moses and in the sight of all the congregation of the children of Israel, who *were* weeping at the door of the tabernacle of meeting.

7 Now when Phin′e·has the son of El·ē·ā′zar, the son of Aaron the priest, saw *it,* he rose from among the congregation and took a javelin in his hand;

8 and he went after the man of Israel into the tent and thrust both of them through, the man of Israel, and the woman through her body. So the plague was stopped among the children of Israel.

9 And those who died in the plague were twenty-four thousand.

10 Then the LORD spoke to Moses, saying:

11 "Phin′e·has the son of El·ē·ā′zar, the son of Aaron the priest, has turned back My wrath from the children of Israel, because he was zealous with My zeal among them, so that I did not consume the children of Israel in My zeal.

12 "Therefore say, 'Behold, I give to him My covenant of peace;

13 'and it shall be to him and his descendants after him a covenant of an everlasting priesthood, because he was zealous for his God, and made atonement for the children of Israel.' "

14 Now the name of the Israelite who was killed, who was killed with the Mid′i·an·ite woman, *was* Zim′ri the son of Sa′lu, a leader of a father's house among the Sim′e·on·ites.

15 And the name of the Mid′i·an·ite woman who was killed *was* Cōz′bi the daughter of Zūr; he *was* head of the people of a father's house in Mid′i·an.

16 Then the LORD spoke to Moses, saying:

17 "Harass the Mid′i·an·ites, and attack them;

18 "for they harassed you with their schemes by which they seduced you in the matter of Pē′or and in the matter of Cōz′bi, the daughter of a leader of Mid′i·an, their sister, who was killed in the day of the plague because of Pē′or."

THE SECOND CENSUS OF ISRAEL

26 And it came to pass, after the plague, that the LORD spoke to Moses and El·ē·ā′zar the son of Aaron the priest, saying:

2 "Take a census of all the congregation of the children of Israel from twenty years old and above, by their fathers' houses, all who are able to go to war in Israel."

3 So Moses and El·ē·ā′zar the priest spoke with them in the plains of Mō′ab by the Jordan, *across from* Jericho, saying:

4 "*Take a census of the people* from twenty years old and above, just as the LORD commanded Moses and the children of Israel who came out of the land of Egypt."

5 Reuben *was* the firstborn of Israel. The children of Reuben *were: of* Hā′noch, the family of the Hā′-noch·ites; *of* Pal′lu, the family of the Pal′lu·ites;

6 *of* Hez′ron, the family of the Hez′ron·ites; *of* Car′mi, the family of the Car′mites.

7 These *are* the families of the Reū′ben·ites: those who were numbered of them *were* forty-three thousand seven hundred and thirty.

8 And the son of Pal′lu *was* E·li′ab.

9 The sons of E·li′ab *were* Nem′u·el, Dā′than, and A·bi′ram. These *are* the Dā′than and A·bi′ram, representatives of the congregation, who contended against Moses and Aaron in the company of Kō′rah, when they contended against the LORD;

10 and the earth opened its mouth and swallowed them up together with Kō′rah when that company died, when the fire devoured two hundred and fifty men; and they became a sign.

11 Nevertheless the children of Kō′rah did not die.

12 The sons of Sim′e·on according to their families *were:* of Nem′ū·el,*a* the family of the Nem′ū·el·ites; *of* Jā′min, the family of the Jā′min·ites; *of* Jā′chin,*b* the family of the Jā′chin-ites;

13 *of* Zē′rah,*a* the family of the Zar′hites; *of* Shā′ul, the family of the Shā′u·lites.

14 These *are* the families of the Sim′e·on·ites: twenty-two thousand two hundred.

15 The sons of Gad according to their families *were:* of Zē′phon,*a* the family of the Zē′phon·ites; *of* Hag′gī, the family of the Hag′gites; *of* Shū′nī, the family of the Shū′nites;

16 *of* Oz′nī,*a* the family of the Oz′nites; *of* Ē′rī, the family of the Ē′rites;

17 *of* Ar′od,*a* the family of the Ar′od·ites; *of* A·rē′lī, the family of the A·rē′lites.

18 These *are* the families of the sons of Gad according to those who were numbered of them: forty thousand five hundred.

19 The sons of Judah *were* Er and Ō′nan; and Er and Ō′nan died in the land of Cā′naan.

20 And the sons of Judah according to their families were: *of* Shē′lah, the family of the Shē′la·nites; *of* Per′ez, the family of the Par′zites; *of* Zē′rah, the family of the Zar′hites.

21 And the sons of Per′ez were: *of* Hez′ron, the family of the Hez′ron-ites; *of* Hā′mul, the family of the Hā′-mul·ites.

22 These *are* the families of Judah according to those who were num-

bered of them: seventy-six thousand five hundred.

23 The sons of Is′sa·char according to their families *were:* of Tō′la, the family of the Tō′la·ites; of Pū′ah,*a* the family of the Pū′nites;*b*

24 of Jash′ub, the family of the Jash′ub·ites; of Shim′ron, the family of the Shim′ron·ites.

25 These *are* the families of Is′sa·char according to those who were numbered of them: sixty-four thousand three hundred.

26 The sons of Zeb′u·lun according to their families *were:* of Sē′red, the family of the Sar′dites; of Ē′lon, the family of the Ē′lon·ites; of Jah′le·el, the family of the Jah′le·el·ites.

27 These *are* the families of the Zeb′u·lun·ites according to those who were numbered of them: sixty thousand five hundred.

28 The sons of Joseph according to their families, by Ma·nas′seh and Ē′phra·im, *were:*

29 The sons of Ma·nas′seh: of Mā′-chir, the family of the Mā′chir·ites; and Mā′chir begot Gil′e·ad; of Gil′-e·ad, the family of the Gil′e·ad·ites.

30 These *are* the sons of Gil′e·ad: *of* Je·ē′zer,*a* the family of the Je·ē′zer-ites; of Hē′lek, the family of the Hē′-lek·ites;

31 *of* As′ri·el, the family of the As′-ri·el·ites; *of* Shē′chem, the family of the Shē′chem·ites;

32 *of* She·mī′da, the family of the She·mī′da·ites; *of* Hē′pher, the family of the Hē′pher·ites.

26:12 *a*Spelled *Jemuel* in Genesis 46:10 and Exodus 6:15   *b*Called *Jarib* in 1 Chronicles 4:24
26:13 *a*Called *Zohar* in Genesis 46:10
26:15 *a*Called *Ziphion* in Genesis 46:16
26:16 *a*Called *Ezbon* in Genesis 46:16
26:17 *a*Spelled *Arodi* in Samaritan Pentateuch, Syriac, and Genesis 46:16   26:23 *a*Hebrew *Puvah* (compare Genesis 46:13 and 1 Chronicles 7:1); Samaritan Pentateuch, Septuagint, Syriac, and Vulgate read *Puah.*   *b*Samaritan Pentateuch, Septuagint, Syriac, and Vulgate read *Puaites.*
26:30 *a*Called *Abiezer* in Joshua 17:2

33 Now Ze·loph'e·had the son of Hē'pher had no sons, but daughters; and the names of the daughters of Ze·loph'e·had *were* Mah'lah, Noah, Hog'lah, Mil'cah, and Tir'zah.

34 These *are* the families of Ma·nas'seh; and those who were numbered of them *were* fifty-two thousand seven hundred.

35 These *are* the sons of Ē'phra·im according to their families: of Shū'the·lah, the family of the Shū'thal·hītes; of Bē'cher,*a* the family of the Bach'rītes; of Tā'han, the family of the Tā'han·ītes.

36 And these *are* the sons of Shū'the·lah: of Ē'ran, the family of the Ē'ran·ītes.

37 These *are* the families of the sons of Ē'phra·im according to those who were numbered of them: thirty-two thousand five hundred. These *are* the sons of Joseph according to their families.

38 The sons of Benjamin according to their families were: of Bē'la, the family of the Bē'la·ītes; of Ash'bel, the family of the Ash'bel·ītes; of A·hī'ram, the family of the A·hī'ram·ītes;

39 of Shū'pham,*a* the family of the Shū'pham·ītes; of Hū'pham,*b* the family of the Hū'pham·ītes.

40 And the sons of Bē'la were Ard*a* and Nā'a·man: *of Ard,* the family of the Ard'ītes; of Nā'a·man, the family of the Nā'a·mītes.

41 These *are* the sons of Benjamin according to their families; and those who were numbered of them *were* forty-five thousand six hundred.

42 These *are* the sons of Dan according to their families: of Shū'ham,*a* the family of the Shū'ham·ītes. These *are* the families of Dan according to their families.

43 All the families of the Shū'ham·ītes, according to those who were numbered of them, *were* sixty-four thousand four hundred.

44 The sons of Ash'er according to their families *were:* of Jim'na, the family of the Jim'nītes; of Jes'ū·ī, the family of the Jes'ū·ītes; of Bē·rī'ah, the family of the Bē·rī'ītes.

45 Of the sons of Bē·rī'ah: of Hē'ber, the family of the Hē'ber·ītes; of Mal'chi·el, the family of the Mal'chi·el·ītes.

46 And the name of the daughter of Ash'er *was* Sē'rah.

47 These *are* the families of the sons of Ash'er according to those who were numbered of them: fifty-three thousand four hundred.

48 The sons of Naph'ta·lī according to their families *were:* of Jah'zē·el,*a* the family of the Jah'zē·el·ītes; of Gū'nī, the family of the Gū'nītes;

49 of Jē'zer, the family of the Jē'zer·ītes; of Shil'lem, the family of the Shil'lem·ītes.

50 These *are* the families of Naph'ta·lī according to their families; and those who were numbered of them *were* forty-five thousand four hundred.

51 These *are* those who were numbered of the children of Israel: six hundred and one thousand seven hundred and thirty.

52 Then the LORD spoke to Moses, saying:

53 "To these the land shall be divided as an inheritance, according to the number of names.

54 "To a large *tribe* you shall give a larger inheritance, and to a small *tribe* you shall give a smaller inheritance. Each shall be given its inheritance according to those who were numbered of them.

26:35 *a*Called *Bered* in 1 Chronicles 7:20
26:39 *a*Masoretic Text reads *Shephupham,* spelled *Shephuphan* in 1 Chronicles 8:5. *b*Called *Huppim* in Genesis 46:21   26:40 *a*Called *Addar* in 1 Chronicles 8:3   26:42 *a*Called *Hushim* in Genesis 46:23
26:48 *a*Spelled *Jahziel* in 1 Chronicles 7:13

55 "But the land shall be divided by lot; they shall inherit according to the names of the tribes of their fathers.

56 "According to the lot their inheritance shall be divided between the larger and the smaller."

57 And these *are* those who were numbered of the Lē′vītes according to their families: of Ger′shon, the family of the Ger′shon·ītes; of Kō′hath, the family of the Kō′hath·ītes; of Me·rar′ī, the family of the Me·rar′ītes.

58 These *are* the families of the Lē′vītes: the family of the Lib′nītes, the family of the Hē′bron·ītes, the family of the Mah′lītes, the family of the Mū′shītes, and the family of the Kō′ra·thītes. And Kō′hath begot Am′ram.

59 The name of Am′ram's wife *was* Joch′e·bed the daughter of Levi, who was born to Levi in Egypt; and to Am′ram she bore Aaron and Moses and their sister Miriam.

60 To Aaron were born Nā′dab and A·bī′hū, El·ē·ā′zar and Ith′a·mar.

61 And Nā′dab and A·bī′hū died when they offered profane fire before the LORD.

62 Now those who were numbered of them were twenty-three thousand, every male from a month old and above; for they were not numbered among the other children of Israel, because there was no inheritance given to them among the children of Israel.

63 These *are* those who were numbered by Moses and El·ē·ā′zar the priest, who numbered the children of Israel in the plains of Mō′ab by the Jordan, *across from* Jericho.

64 But among these there was not a man of those who were numbered by Moses and Aaron the priest when they numbered the children of Israel in the Wilderness of Sinai.

65 For the LORD had said of them, "They shall surely die in the wilderness." So there was not left a man of them, except Caleb the son of Je·phūn′neh and Joshua the son of Nun.

INHERITANCE LAWS

27 Then came the daughters of Ze·loph′e·had the son of Hē′pher, the son of Gil′ē·ad, the son of Mā′chir, the son of Ma·nas′seh, from the families of Ma·nas′seh the son of Joseph; and these *were* the names of his daughters: Mah′lah, Noah, Hog′lah, Mil′cah, and Tir′zah.

2 And they stood before Moses, before El·ē·ā′zar the priest, and before the leaders and all the congregation, *by* the doorway of the tabernacle of meeting, saying:

3 "Our father died in the wilderness; but he was not in the company of those who gathered together against the LORD, in company with Kō′rah, but he died in his own sin; and he had no sons.

4 "Why should the name of our father be removed from among his family because he had no son? Give us a possession among our father's brothers."

5 So Moses brought their case before the LORD.

6 And the LORD spoke to Moses, saying:

7 "The daughters of Ze·loph′e·had speak *what is* right; you shall surely give them a possession of inheritance among their father's brothers, and cause the inheritance of their father to pass to them.

8 "And you shall speak to the children of Israel, saying: 'If a man dies and has no son, then you shall cause his inheritance to pass to his daughter.

9 'If he has no daughter, then you shall give his inheritance to his brothers.

10 'If he has no brothers, then you shall give his inheritance to his father's brothers.

11 'And if his father has no brothers, then you shall give his inheritance to the relative closest to him in his family, and he shall possess it.' " And it shall be to the children of Israel a statute of judgment, just as the LORD commanded Moses.

JOSHUA THE NEXT LEADER OF ISRAEL

12 Now the LORD said to Moses: "Go up into this Mount Ab'a·rim, and see the land which I have given to the children of Israel.

13 "And when you have seen it, you also shall be gathered to your people, as Aaron your brother was gathered.

14 "For in the Wilderness of Zin, during the strife of the congregation, you rebelled against My command to hallow Me at the waters before their eyes." (These *are* the waters of Mer'i·bah, at Kā'desh in the Wilderness of Zin.)

15 Then Moses spoke to the LORD, saying:

16 "Let the LORD, the God of the spirits of all flesh, set a man over the congregation,

17 "who may go out before them and go in before them, who may lead them out and bring them in, that the congregation of the LORD may not be like sheep which have no shepherd."

18 And the LORD said to Moses: "Take Joshua the son of Nun with you, a man in whom *is* the Spirit, and lay your hand on him;

19 "set him before El·e·a'zar the priest and before all the congregation, and inaugurate him in their sight.

20 "And you shall give *some* of your authority to him, that all the congregation of the children of Israel may be obedient.

21 "He shall stand before El·e·a'zar the priest, who shall inquire before the LORD for him by the judgment of the Ū'rim. At his word they shall go out, and at his word they shall come in, he and all the children of Israel with him—all the congregation."

22 So Moses did as the LORD commanded him. He took Joshua and set him before El·e·a'zar the priest and before all the congregation.

23 And he laid his hands on him and inaugurated him, just as the LORD commanded by the hand of Moses.

DAILY OFFERINGS

28 Now the LORD spoke to Moses, saying,

2 "Command the children of Israel, and say to them, 'My offering, My food for My offerings made by fire as a sweet aroma to Me, you shall be careful to offer to Me at their appointed time.'

3 "And you shall say to them, 'This *is* the offering made by fire which you shall offer to the LORD: two male lambs in their first year without blemish, day by day, as a regular burnt offering.

4 'The one lamb you shall offer in the morning, the other lamb you shall offer in the evening,

5 'and one-tenth of an ephah of fine flour as a grain offering mixed with one-fourth of a hin of pressed oil.

6 '*It is* a regular burnt offering which was ordained at Mount Sinai for a sweet aroma, an offering made by fire to the LORD.

7 'And its drink offering *shall be* one-fourth of a hin for each lamb; in a holy *place* you shall pour out the drink to the LORD as an offering.

8 'The other lamb you shall offer in the evening; as the morning grain

offering and its drink offering, you shall offer *it* as an offering made by fire, a sweet aroma to the LORD.

SABBATH OFFERINGS

9 'And on the Sabbath day two lambs in their first year, without blemish, and two-tenths *of an ephah* of fine flour as a grain offering, mixed with oil, with its drink offering—
10 '*this is* the burnt offering for every Sabbath, besides the regular burnt offering with its drink offering.

MONTHLY OFFERINGS

11 'At the beginnings of your months you shall present a burnt offering to the LORD: two young bulls, one ram, and seven lambs in their first year, without blemish;
12 'three-tenths *of an ephah* of fine flour as a grain offering, mixed with oil, for each bull; two-tenths *of an ephah* of fine flour as a grain offering, mixed with oil, for the one ram;
13 'and one-tenth *of an ephah* of fine flour, mixed with oil, as a grain offering for each lamb, as a burnt offering of sweet aroma, an offering made by fire to the LORD.
14 'Their drink offering shall be half a hin of wine for a bull, one-third of a hin for a ram, and one-fourth of a hin for a lamb; this *is* the burnt offering for each month throughout the months of the year.
15 'Also one kid of the goats as a sin offering to the LORD shall be offered, besides the regular burnt offering and its drink offering.

OFFERINGS AT PASSOVER

16 'On the fourteenth day of the first month *is* the Passover of the LORD.
17 'And on the fifteenth day of this month *is* the feast; unleavened bread shall be eaten for seven days.
18 'On the first day *you shall have* a holy convocation. You shall do no customary work.
19 'And you shall present an offering made by fire as a burnt offering to the LORD: two young bulls, one ram, and seven lambs in their first year. Be sure they are without blemish.
20 'Their grain offering shall be of fine flour mixed with oil: three-tenths *of an ephah* you shall offer for a bull, and two-tenths for a ram;
21 'you shall offer one-tenth *of an ephah* for each of the seven lambs;
22 'also one goat *as* a sin offering, to make atonement for you.
23 'You shall offer these besides the burnt offering of the morning, which *is* for a regular burnt offering.
24 'In this manner you shall offer the food of the offering made by fire daily for seven days, as a sweet aroma to the LORD; it shall be offered besides the regular burnt offering and its drink offering.
25 'And on the seventh day you shall have a holy convocation. You shall do no customary work.

OFFERINGS AT THE FEAST OF WEEKS

26 'Also on the day of the firstfruits, when you bring a new grain offering to the LORD at your *Feast of Weeks*, you shall have a holy convocation. You shall do no customary work.
27 'You shall present a burnt offering as a sweet aroma to the LORD: two young bulls, one ram, and seven lambs in their first year,
28 'with their grain offering of fine flour mixed with oil: three-tenths *of an ephah* for each bull, two-tenths for the one ram,
29 'and one-tenth for each of the seven lambs;

30 'also one kid of the goats, to make atonement for you.

31 'Be sure they are without blemish. You shall present *them* with their drink offerings, besides the regular burnt offering with its grain offering.

OFFERINGS AT THE FEAST OF TRUMPETS

29 'And in the seventh month, on the first *day* of the month, you shall have a holy convocation. You shall do no customary work. For you it is a day of blowing the trumpets.

2 'You shall offer a burnt offering as a sweet aroma to the LORD: one young bull, one ram, *and* seven lambs in their first year, without blemish.

3 'Their grain offering *shall be* fine flour mixed with oil: three-tenths *of an ephah* for the bull, two-tenths for the ram,

4 'and one-tenth for each of the seven lambs;

5 'also one kid of the goats *as* a sin offering, to make atonement for you;

6 'besides the burnt offering with its grain offering for the New Moon, the regular burnt offering with its grain offering, and their drink offerings, according to their ordinance, as a sweet aroma, an offering made by fire to the LORD.

OFFERINGS ON THE DAY OF ATONEMENT

7 'On the tenth *day* of this seventh month you shall have a holy convocation. You shall afflict your souls; you shall not do any work.

8 'You shall present a burnt offering to the LORD *as* a sweet aroma: one young bull, one ram, *and* seven lambs in their first year. Be sure they are without blemish.

9 'Their grain offering *shall be of* fine flour mixed with oil: three-tenths *of an ephah* for the bull, two-tenths for the one ram,

10 'and one-tenth for each of the seven lambs;

11 'also one kid of the goats *as* a sin offering, besides the sin offering for atonement, the regular burnt offering with its grain offering, and their drink offerings.

OFFERINGS AT THE FEAST OF TABERNACLES

12 'On the fifteenth day of the seventh month you shall have a holy convocation. You shall do no customary work, and you shall keep a feast to the LORD seven days.

13 'You shall present a burnt offering, an offering made by fire as a sweet aroma to the LORD: thirteen young bulls, two rams, *and* fourteen lambs in their first year. They shall be without blemish.

14 'Their grain offering *shall be of* fine flour mixed with oil: three-tenths *of an ephah* for each of the thirteen bulls, two-tenths for each of the two rams,

15 'and one-tenth for each of the fourteen lambs;

16 'also one kid of the goats *as* a sin offering, besides the regular burnt offering, its grain offering, and its drink offering.

17 'On the second day *present* twelve young bulls, two rams, fourteen lambs in their first year without blemish,

18 'and their grain offering and their drink offerings for the bulls, for the rams, and for the lambs, by their number, according to the ordinance;

19 'also one kid of the goats *as* a sin offering, besides the regular burnt offering with its grain offering, and their drink offerings.

20 'On the third day *present* eleven bulls, two rams, fourteen lambs in their first year without blemish,

21 'and their grain offering and their drink offerings for the bulls, for the rams, and for the lambs, by their number, according to the ordinance;

22 'also one goat *as* a sin offering, besides the regular burnt offering, its grain offering, and its drink offering.

23 'On the fourth day *present* ten bulls, two rams, *and* fourteen lambs in their first year, without blemish,

24 'and their grain offering and their drink offerings for the bulls, for the rams, and for the lambs, by their number, according to the ordinance;

25 'also one kid of the goats *as* a sin offering, besides the regular burnt offering, its grain offering, and its drink offering.

26 'On the fifth day *present* nine bulls, two rams, *and* fourteen lambs in their first year without blemish,

27 'and their grain offering and their drink offerings for the bulls, for the rams, and for the lambs, by their number, according to the ordinance;

28 'also one goat *as* a sin offering, besides the regular burnt offering, its grain offering, and its drink offering.

29 'On the sixth day *present* eight bulls, two rams, *and* fourteen lambs in their first year without blemish,

30 'and their grain offering and their drink offerings for the bulls, for the rams, and for the lambs, by their number, according to the ordinance;

31 'also one goat *as* a sin offering, besides the regular burnt offering, its grain offering, and its drink offering.

32 'On the seventh day *present* seven bulls, two rams, *and* fourteen lambs in their first year without blemish,

33 'and their grain offering and their drink offerings for the bulls, for the rams, and for the lambs, by their number, according to the ordinance;

34 'also one goat *as* a sin offering, besides the regular burnt offering, its grain offering, and its drink offering.

35 'On the eighth day you shall have a sacred assembly. You shall do no customary work.

36 'You shall present a burnt offering, an offering made by fire as a sweet aroma to the LORD: one bull, one ram, seven lambs in their first year without blemish,

37 'and their grain offering and their drink offerings for the bull, for the ram, and for the lambs, by their number, according to the ordinance;

38 'also one goat *as* a sin offering, besides the regular burnt offering, its grain offering, and its drink offering.

39 'These you shall present to the LORD at your appointed feasts (besides your vowed offerings and your freewill offerings) as your burnt offerings and your grain offerings, as your drink offerings and your peace offerings.' "

40 So Moses told the children of Israel everything, just as the LORD commanded Moses.

THE LAW CONCERNING VOWS

30 Then Moses spoke to the heads of the tribes concerning the children of Israel, saying, "This *is* the thing which the LORD has commanded:

2 "If a man makes a vow to the LORD, or swears an oath to bind himself by some agreement, he shall not break his word; he shall do according to all that proceeds out of his mouth.

3 "Or if a woman makes a vow to the LORD, and binds *herself* by some agreement while in her father's house in her youth,

4 "and her father hears her vow and the agreement by which she has bound herself, and her father holds his peace, then all her vows shall stand, and every agreement with

which she has bound herself shall stand.

5 "But if her father overrules her on the day that he hears, then none of her vows nor her agreements by which she has bound herself shall stand; and the LORD will release her, because her father overruled her.

6 "If indeed she takes a husband, while bound by her vows or by a rash utterance from her lips by which she bound herself,

7 "and her husband hears *it,* and makes no response to her on the day that he hears, then her vows shall stand, and her agreements by which she bound herself shall stand.

8 "But if her husband overrules her on the day that he hears *it,* he shall make void her vow which she took and what she uttered with her lips, by which she bound herself, and the LORD will release her.

9 "Also any vow of a widow or a divorced woman, by which she has bound herself, shall stand against her.

10 "If she vowed in her husband's house, or bound herself by an agreement with an oath,

11 "and her husband heard *it,* and made no response to her *and* did not overrule her, then all her vows shall stand, and every agreement by which she bound herself shall stand.

12 "But if her husband truly made them void on the day he heard *them,* then whatever proceeded from her lips concerning her vows or concerning the agreement binding her, it shall not stand; her husband has made them void, and the LORD will release her.

13 "Every vow and every binding oath to afflict her soul, her husband may confirm it, or her husband may make it void.

14 "Now if her husband makes no response whatever to her from day to day, then he confirms all her vows or all the agreements that bind her; he confirms them, because he made no response to her on the day that he heard *them.*

15 "But if he does make them void after he has heard *them,* then he shall bear her guilt."

16 These *are* the statutes which the LORD commanded Moses, between a man and his wife, and between a father and his daughter in her youth in her father's house.

VENGEANCE ON THE MIDIANITES

31 And the LORD spoke to Moses, saying:

2 "Take vengeance on the Mid′i·an·ītes for the children of Israel. Afterward you shall be gathered to your people."

3 So Moses spoke to the people, saying, "Arm some of yourselves for war, and let them go against the Mid′i·an·ītes to take vengeance for the LORD on Mid′i·an.

4 "A thousand from each tribe of all the tribes of Israel you shall send to the war."

5 So there were recruited from the divisions of Israel one thousand from *each* tribe, twelve thousand armed for war.

6 Then Moses sent them to the war, one thousand from *each* tribe; he sent them to the war with Phin′e·has the son of El·ē·ā′zar the priest, with the holy articles and the signal trumpets in his hand.

7 And they warred against the Mid′i·an·ītes, just as the LORD commanded Moses, and they killed all the males.

8 They killed the kings of Mid′i·an with *the rest of* those who were killed—Ē′vī, Rē′kem, Zūr, Hur, and Rē′ba, the five kings of Mid′i·an.

Bā′laam the son of Bē′or they also killed with the sword.

9 And the children of Israel took the women of Mid′i·an captive, with their little ones, and took as spoil all their cattle, all their flocks, and all their goods.

10 They also burned with fire all the cities where they dwelt, and all their forts.

11 And they took all the spoil and all the booty—of man and beast.

RETURN FROM THE WAR

12 Then they brought the captives, the booty, and the spoil to Moses, to El·ē·ā′zar the priest, and to the congregation of the children of Israel, to the camp in the plains of Mō′ab by the Jordan, *across from* Jericho.

13 And Moses, El·ē·ā′zar the priest, and all the leaders of the congregation, went to meet them outside the camp.

14 But Moses was angry with the officers of the army, *with* the captains over thousands and captains over hundreds, who had come from the battle.

15 And Moses said to them: "Have you kept all the women alive?

16 "Look, these *women* caused the children of Israel, through the counsel of Bā′laam, to trespass against the LORD in the incident of Pē′or, and there was a plague among the congregation of the LORD.

17 "Now therefore, kill every male among the little ones, and kill every woman who has known a man intimately.

18 "But keep alive for yourselves all the young girls who have not known a man intimately.

19 "And as for you, remain outside the camp seven days; whoever has killed any person, and whoever has touched any slain, purify yourselves

and your captives on the third day and on the seventh day.

20 "Purify every garment, everything made of leather, everything woven of goats' *hair,* and everything made of wood."

21 Then El·ē·ā′zar the priest said to the men of war who had gone to the battle, "This *is* the ordinance of the law which the LORD commanded Moses:

22 "Only the gold, the silver, the bronze, the iron, the tin, and the lead,

23 "everything that can endure fire, you shall put through the fire, and it shall be clean; and it shall be purified with the water of purification. But all that cannot endure fire you shall put through water.

24 "And you shall wash your clothes on the seventh day and be clean, and afterward you may come into the camp."

DIVISION OF THE PLUNDER

25 Now the LORD spoke to Moses, saying:

26 "Count up the plunder that was taken—of man and beast—you and El·ē·ā′zar the priest and the chief fathers of the congregation;

27 "and divide the plunder into two parts, between those who took part in the war, who went out to battle, and all the congregation.

28 "And levy a tribute for the LORD on the men of war who went out to battle: one of every five hundred of the persons, the cattle, the donkeys, and the sheep;

29 "take *it* from their half, and give *it* to El·ē·ā′zar the priest as a heave offering to the LORD.

30 "And from the children of Israel's half you shall take one of every fifty, drawn from the persons, the cattle, the donkeys, and the sheep, from all

the livestock, and give them to the Lē'vītes who keep charge of the tabernacle of the LORD."

31 So Moses and El·ē·ā'zar the priest did as the LORD commanded Moses.

32 The booty remaining from the plunder, which the men of war had taken, was six hundred and seventy-five thousand sheep,

33 seventy-two thousand cattle,

34 sixty-one thousand donkeys,

35 and thirty-two thousand persons in all, of women who had not known a man intimately.

36 And the half, the portion for those who had gone out to war, was in number three hundred and thirty-seven thousand five hundred sheep;

37 and the LORD's tribute of the sheep was six hundred and seventy-five.

38 The cattle *were* thirty-six thousand, of which the LORD's tribute *was* seventy-two.

39 The donkeys *were* thirty thousand five hundred, of which the LORD's tribute *was* sixty-one.

40 The persons *were* sixteen thousand, of which the LORD's tribute *was* thirty-two persons.

41 So Moses gave the tribute *which was* the LORD's heave offering to El·ē·ā'zar the priest, as the LORD commanded Moses.

42 And from the children of Israel's half, which Moses separated from the men who fought—

43 now the half belonging to the congregation was three hundred and thirty-seven thousand five hundred sheep,

44 thirty-six thousand cattle,

45 thirty thousand five hundred donkeys,

46 and sixteen thousand persons—

47 and from the children of Israel's half Moses took one of every fifty, drawn from man and beast, and gave them to the Lē'vītes, who kept

charge of the tabernacle of the LORD, as the LORD commanded Moses.

48 Then the officers who *were* over thousands of the army, the captains of thousands and captains of hundreds, came near to Moses;

49 and they said to Moses, "Your servants have taken a count of the men of war who *are* under our command, and not a man of us is missing.

50 "Therefore we have brought an offering for the LORD, what every man found of ornaments of gold: armlets and bracelets and signet rings and earrings and necklaces, to make atonement for ourselves before the LORD."

51 So Moses and El·ē·ā'zar the priest received the gold from them, all the fashioned ornaments.

52 And all the gold of the offering that they offered to the LORD, from the captains of thousands and captains of hundreds, was sixteen thousand seven hundred and fifty shekels.

53 (The men of war had taken spoil, every man for himself.)

54 And Moses and El·ē·ā'zar the priest received the gold from the captains of thousands and of hundreds, and brought it into the tabernacle of meeting as a memorial for the children of Israel before the LORD.

THE TRIBES SETTLING EAST OF THE JORDAN

32 Now the children of Reuben and the children of Gad had a very great multitude of livestock; and when they saw the land of Jā'zer and the land of Gil'ē·ad, that indeed the region *was* a place for livestock,

2 the children of Gad and the children of Reuben came and spoke to Moses, to El·ē·ā'zar the priest, and to the leaders of the congregation, saying,

3 "At'a·roth, Dī'bon, Jā'zer, Nim'-rah, Hesh'bon, Ē·le·ā'leh, Shē'bam, Nē'bō, and Bē'on,

4 "the country which the LORD defeated before the congregation of Israel, *is* a land for livestock, and your servants have livestock."

5 Therefore they said, "If we have found favor in your sight, let this land be given to your servants as a possession. Do not take us over the Jordan."

6 And Moses said to the children of Gad and to the children of Reuben: "Shall your brethren go to war while you sit here?

7 "Now why will you discourage the heart of the children of Israel from going over into the land which the LORD has given them?

8 "Thus your fathers did when I sent them away from Kā'desh Bar-nē'a to see the land.

9 "For when they went up to the Valley of Esh'col and saw the land, they discouraged the heart of the children of Israel, so that they did not go into the land which the LORD had given them.

10 "So the LORD's anger was aroused on that day, and He swore an oath, saying,

11 'Surely none of the men who came up from Egypt, from twenty years old and above, shall see the land of which I swore to Abraham, Isaac, and Jacob, because they have not wholly followed Me,

12 'except Caleb the son of Je·phūn'-neh, the Kē'niz·zīte, and Joshua the son of Nun, for they have wholly followed the LORD.'

13 "So the LORD's anger was aroused against Israel, and He made them wander in the wilderness forty years, until all the generation that had done evil in the sight of the LORD was gone.

14 "And look! You have risen in your fathers' place, a brood of sinful men, to increase still more the fierce anger of the LORD against Israel.

15 "For if you turn away from following Him, He will once again leave them in the wilderness, and you will destroy all these people."

16 Then they came near to him and said: "We will build sheepfolds here for our livestock, and cities for our little ones,

17 "but we ourselves will be armed, ready *to go* before the children of Israel until we have brought them to their place; and our little ones will dwell in the fortified cities because of the inhabitants of the land.

18 "We will not return to our homes until every one of the children of Israel has received his inheritance.

19 "For we will not inherit with them on the other side of the Jordan and beyond, because our inheritance has fallen to us on this eastern side of the Jordan."

20 Then Moses said to them: "If you do this thing, if you arm yourselves before the LORD for the war,

21 "and all your armed men cross over the Jordan before the LORD until He has driven out His enemies from before Him,

22 "and the land is subdued before the LORD, then afterward you may return and be blameless before the LORD and before Israel; and this land shall be your possession before the LORD.

23 "But if you do not do so, then take note, you have sinned against the LORD; and be sure your sin will find you out.

24 "Build cities for your little ones and folds for your sheep, and do what has proceeded out of your mouth."

25 And the children of Gad and the children of Reuben spoke to Moses, saying: "Your servants will do as my lord commands.

BE SURE YOUR SIN WILL FIND YOU OUT. Numbers 32:23

Can You Sweep Your Sin Under a Rug?

A woman is cleaning her house. She has a little pile of dirt. She sweeps it under a rug. But does that really get rid of the dirt?

1. Can you get rid of dirt by sweeping it under a rug? Why not?
2. Can you get rid of sins by trying to hide them? Why not? What does the last part of Numbers 32:23 say? How will your sins "find you out?"
3. Can you hide sin from God? Does He know that it is there?

For more on *Favorite Family Verses* turn to page 761
For more on *Sin* turn to page 1786

26 "Our little ones, our wives, our flocks, and all our livestock will be there in the cities of Gil′ē·ad;

27 "but your servants will cross over, every man armed for war, before the LORD to battle, just as my lord says."

28 So Moses gave command concerning them to El·ē·ā′zar the priest, to Joshua the son of Nun, and to the chief fathers of the tribes of the children of Israel.

29 And Moses said to them: "If the children of Gad and the children of Reuben cross over the Jordan with you, every man armed for battle before the LORD, and the land is subdued before you, then you shall give them the land of Gil′ē·ad as a possession.

30 "But if they do not cross over armed with you, they shall have possessions among you in the land of Cā′naan."

31 Then the children of Gad and the children of Reuben answered, saying: "As the LORD has said to your servants, so we will do.

32 "We will cross over armed before the LORD into the land of Cā′naan, but the possession of our inheritance *shall remain* with us on this side of the Jordan."

33 So Moses gave to the children of Gad, to the children of Reuben, and to half the tribe of Ma·nas′seh the son of Joseph, the kingdom of Sī′hon king of the Am′o·rītes and the kingdom of Og king of Bā′shan, the land with its cities within the borders, the cities of the surrounding country.

34 And the children of Gad built Dī′bon and At′a·roth and A·rō′er,

35 At′roth and Shō′phan and Jā′zer and Jog′be·hah,

36 Beth Nim′rah and Beth Har′an, fortified cities, and folds for sheep.

37 And the children of Reuben built Hesh′bon and Ē·le·ā′leh and Kir·jath′-a·im,

38 Nē′bō and Bā′al Mē′on (*their* names being changed) and Shib′mah; and they gave *other* names to the cities which they built.

39 And the children of Mā′chir the son of Ma·nas′seh went to Gil′ē·ad and took it, and dispossessed the Am′o·rītes who *were* in it.

40 So Moses gave Gil′ē·ad to Mā′chir the son of Ma·nas′seh, and he dwelt in it.

41 Also Jā′ir the son of Ma·nas′seh went and took its small towns, and called them Hā′voth Jā′ir.[a]

42 Then Nō′bah went and took Kē′nath and its villages, and he called it Nō′bah, after his own name.

ISRAEL'S JOURNEY FROM EGYPT REVIEWED

33 These *are* the journeys of the children of Israel, who went out of the land of Egypt by their armies under the hand of Moses and Aaron.

2 Now Moses wrote down the starting points of their journeys at the command of the LORD. And these *are* their journeys according to their starting points:

3 They departed from Ram′e·sēs in the first month, on the fifteenth day of the first month; on the day after the Passover the children of Israel went out with boldness in the sight of all the Egyptians.

4 For the Egyptians were burying all *their* firstborn, whom the LORD had killed among them. Also on their gods the LORD had executed judgments.

5 Then the children of Israel moved from Ram′e·sēs and camped at Suc′coth.

6 They departed from Suc′coth and camped at Ē′tham, which *is* on the edge of the wilderness.

32:41 [a]Literally *Towns of Jair*

7 They moved from Ē'tham and turned back to Pī Ha·hī'roth, which *is* east of Bā'al Zē'phon; and they camped near Mig'dōl.

8 They departed from before Ha·hī'-roth*a* and passed through the midst of the sea into the wilderness, went three days' journey in the Wilderness of Ē'tham, and camped at Mar'ah.

9 They moved from Mar'ah and came to Ē'lim. At Ē'lim *were* twelve springs of water and seventy palm trees; so they camped there.

10 They moved from Ē'lim and camped by the Red Sea.

11 They moved from the Red Sea and camped in the Wilderness of Sin.

12 They journeyed from the Wilderness of Sin and camped at Doph'kah.

13 They departed from Doph'kah and camped at Ā'lush.

14 They moved from Ā'lush and camped at Reph'i·dim, where there was no water for the people to drink.

15 They departed from Reph'i·dim and camped in the Wilderness of Sinai.

16 They moved from the Wilderness of Sinai and camped at Kib'roth Hat·tā'a·vah.

17 They departed from Kib'roth Hat·tā'a·vah and camped at Ha·zē'roth.

18 They departed from Ha·zē'roth and camped at Rith'mah.

19 They departed from Rith'mah and camped at Rim'mon Per'ez.

20 They departed from Rim'mon Per'ez and camped at Lib'nah.

21 They moved from Lib'nah and camped at Ris'sah.

22 They journeyed from Ris'sah and camped at Kē·he·lā'thah.

23 They went from Kē·he·lā'thah and camped at Mount Shē'pher.

24 They moved from Mount Shē'-pher and camped at Ha·rā'dah.

25 They moved from Ha·rā'dah and camped at Mak·hē'loth.

26 They moved from Mak·hē'loth and camped at Tā'hath.

27 They departed from Tā'hath and camped at Tē'rah.

28 They moved from Tē'rah and camped at Mith'kah.

29 They went from Mith'kah and camped at Hash·mō'nah.

30 They departed from Hash·mō'nah and camped at Mō·sē'roth.

31 They departed from Mō·sē'roth and camped at Ben'ē Jā'a·kan.

32 They moved from Ben'ē Jā'a·kan and camped at Hor Ha·gid'gad.

33 They went from Hor Ha·gid'gad and camped at Jot'ba·thah.

34 They moved from Jot'ba·thah and camped at A·brō'nah.

35 They departed from A·brō'nah and camped at Ē'zi·on Gē'ber.

36 They moved from Ē'zi·on Gē'ber and camped in the Wilderness of Zin, which *is* Kā'desh.

37 They moved from Kā'desh and camped at Mount Hor, on the boundary of the land of Ē'dom.

38 Then Aaron the priest went up to Mount Hor at the command of the Lord, and died there in the fortieth year after the children of Israel had come out of the land of Egypt, on the first *day* of the fifth month.

39 Aaron *was* one hundred and twenty-three years old when he died on Mount Hor.

40 Now the king of Ar'ad, the Cā'-naan·īte, who dwelt in the South in the land of Cā'naan, heard of the coming of the children of Israel.

41 So they departed from Mount Hor and camped at Zal·mō'nah.

42 They departed from Zal·mō'nah and camped at Pū'non.

43 They departed from Pū'non and camped at Ō'both.

44 They departed from Ō'both and

33:8 *a*Many Hebrew manuscripts, Samaritan Pentateuch, Syriac, Targum, and Vulgate read *from Pi Hahiroth* (compare verse 7).

camped at Ī′jē Ab′a·rim, at the border of Mō′ab.

45 They departed from Ī′jim[a] and camped at Dī′bon Gad.

46 They moved from Dī′bon Gad and camped at Al′mon Dib·la·thā′im.

47 They moved from Al′mon Dib-la·thā′im and camped in the mountains of Ab′a·rim, before Nē′bo.

48 They departed from the mountains of Ab′a·rim and camped in the plains of Mō′ab by the Jordan, *across from* Jericho.

49 They camped by the Jordan, from Beth Jes′i·moth as far as the Abel Acacia Grove[a] in the plains of Mō′ab.

INSTRUCTIONS FOR THE CONQUEST OF CANAAN

50 Now the LORD spoke to Moses in the plains of Mō′ab by the Jordan, *across from* Jericho, saying,

51 "Speak to the children of Israel, and say to them: 'When you have crossed the Jordan into the land of Cā′naan,

52 'then you shall drive out all the inhabitants of the land from before you, destroy all their engraved stones, destroy all their molded images, and demolish all their high places;

53 'you shall dispossess *the inhabitants of* the land and dwell in it, for I have given you the land to possess.

54 'And you shall divide the land by lot as an inheritance among your families; to the larger you shall give a larger inheritance, and to the smaller you shall give a smaller inheritance; there everyone's *inheritance* shall be whatever falls to him by lot. You shall inherit according to the tribes of your fathers.

55 'But if you do not drive out the inhabitants of the land from before you, then it shall be that those whom you let remain *shall be* irritants in your

eyes and thorns in your sides, and they shall harass you in the land where you dwell.

56 'Moreover it shall be *that* I will do to you as I thought to do to them.' "

THE APPOINTED BOUNDARIES OF CANAAN

34 Then the LORD spoke to Moses, saying,

2 "Command the children of Israel, and say to them: 'When you come into the land of Cā′naan, this *is* the land that shall fall to you as an inheritance—the land of Cā′naan to its boundaries.

3 'Your southern border shall be from the Wilderness of Zin along the border of Ē′dom; then your southern border shall extend eastward to the end of the Salt Sea;

4 'your border shall turn from the southern side of the Ascent of Ak-rab′bim, continue to Zin, and be on the south of Kā′desh Bar·nē′a; then it shall go on to Hā′zar Ad′dar, and continue to Az′mon;

5 'the border shall turn from Az′-mon to the Brook of Egypt, and it shall end at the Sea.

6 'As for the western border, you shall have the Great Sea for a border; this shall be your western border.

7 'And this shall be your northern border: From the Great Sea you shall mark out your *border* line to Mount Hor;

8 'from Mount Hor you shall mark out *your border* to the entrance of Hā′math; then the direction of the border shall be toward Zē′dad;

9 'the border shall proceed to Ziph′ron, and it shall end at Hā′zar Ē′nan. This shall be your northern border.

33:45 *a*Same as *Ije Abarim,* verse 44
33:49 *a*Hebrew *Abel Shittim*

10 'You shall mark out your eastern border from Hā′zar Ē′nan to Shē′pham;

11 'the border shall go down from Shē′pham to Rib′lah on the east side of Ā′in; the border shall go down and reach to the eastern side of the Sea of Chin′ne·reth;

12 'the border shall go down along the Jordan, and it shall end at the Salt Sea. This shall be your land with its surrounding boundaries.' "

13 Then Moses commanded the children of Israel, saying: "This *is* the land which you shall inherit by lot, which the LORD has commanded to give to the nine tribes and to the half-tribe.

14 "For the tribe of the children of Reuben according to the house of their fathers, and the tribe of the children of Gad according to the house of their fathers, have received *their inheritance;* and the half-tribe of Ma·nas′seh has received its inheritance.

15 "The two tribes and the half-tribe have received their inheritance on this side of the Jordan, *across from* Jericho eastward, toward the sunrise."

THE LEADERS APPOINTED TO DIVIDE THE LAND

16 And the LORD spoke to Moses, saying,

17 "These *are* the names of the men who shall divide the land among you as an inheritance: El·e·ā′zar the priest and Joshua the son of Nun.

18 "And you shall take one leader of every tribe to divide the land for the inheritance.

19 "These *are* the names of the men: from the tribe of Judah, Caleb the son of Je·phūn′neh;

20 "from the tribe of the children of Sim′e·on, She·mū′el the son of Am·mī′hud;

21 "from the tribe of Benjamin, Ē·lī′dad the son of Chis′lon;

22 "a leader from the tribe of the children of Dan, Buk′kī the son of Jog′lī;

23 "from the sons of Joseph: a leader from the tribe of the children of Ma·nas′seh, Han′ni·el the son of Ē′phod,

24 "and a leader from the tribe of the children of Ē′phra·im, Ke·mū′el the son of Shiph′tan;

25 "a leader from the tribe of the children of Zeb′ū·lun, E·li·zā′phan the son of Par′nach;

26 "a leader from the tribe of the children of Is′sa·char, Pal′ti·el the son of Az′zan;

27 "a leader from the tribe of the children of Ash′er, A·hī′hud the son of She·lō′mī;

28 "and a leader from the tribe of the children of Naph′ta·lī, Ped′a·hel the son of Am·mī′hud."

29 These *are* the ones the LORD commanded to divide the inheritance among the children of Israel in the land of Cā′naan.

CITIES FOR THE LEVITES

35 And the LORD spoke to Moses in the plains of Mō′ab by the Jordan *across from* Jericho, saying:

2 "Command the children of Israel that they give the Lē′vītes cities to dwell in from the inheritance of their possession, and you shall *also* give the Lē′vītes common-land around the cities.

3 "They shall have the cities to dwell in; and their common-land shall be for their cattle, for their herds, and for all their animals.

4 "The common-land of the cities which you will give the Lē′vītes *shall extend* from the wall of the city outward a thousand cubits all around.

5 "And you shall measure outside the city on the east side two thousand cubits, on the south side two thousand cubits, on the west side two thousand cubits, and on the north side two thousand cubits. The city *shall be* in the middle. This shall belong to them as common-land for the cities.

6 "Now among the cities which you will give to the Lē′vītes *you shall appoint* six cities of refuge, to which a manslayer may flee. And to these you shall add forty-two cities.

7 "So all the cities you will give to the Lē′vītes *shall be* forty-eight; these *you shall give* with their common-land.

8 "And the cities which you will give *shall be* from the possession of the children of Israel; from the larger *tribe* you shall give many, from the smaller you shall give few. Each shall give some of its cities to the Lē′vītes, in proportion to the inheritance that each receives."

CITIES OF REFUGE

9 Then the LORD spoke to Moses, saying,

10 "Speak to the children of Israel, and say to them: 'When you cross the Jordan into the land of Cā′naan,

11 'then you shall appoint cities to be cities of refuge for you, that the manslayer who kills any person accidentally may flee there.

12 'They shall be cities of refuge for you from the avenger, that the manslayer may not die until he stands before the congregation in judgment.

13 'And of the cities which you give, you shall have six cities of refuge.

14 'You shall appoint three cities on this side of the Jordan, and three cities you shall appoint in the land of Cā′naan, *which* will be cities of refuge.

15 'These six cities shall be for refuge for the children of Israel, for the stranger, and for the sojourner among them, that anyone who kills a person accidentally may flee there.

16 'But if he strikes him with an iron implement, so that he dies, he *is* a murderer; the murderer shall surely be put to death.

17 'And if he strikes him with a stone in the hand, by which one could die, and he does die, he *is* a murderer; the murderer shall surely be put to death.

18 'Or *if* he strikes him with a wooden hand weapon, by which one could die, and he does die, he *is* a murderer; the murderer shall surely be put to death.

19 'The avenger of blood himself shall put the murderer to death; when he meets him, he shall put him to death.

20 'If he pushes him out of hatred or, while lying in wait, hurls something at him so that he dies,

21 'or in enmity he strikes him with his hand so that he dies, the one who struck *him* shall surely be put to death. He *is* a murderer. The avenger of blood shall put the murderer to death when he meets him.

22 'However, if he pushes him suddenly without enmity, or throws anything at him without lying in wait,

23 'or uses a stone, by which a man could die, throwing *it* at him without seeing *him,* so that he dies, while he was not his enemy or seeking his harm,

24 'then the congregation shall judge between the manslayer and the avenger of blood according to these judgments.

25 'So the congregation shall deliver the manslayer from the hand of the avenger of blood, and the congregation shall return him to the city of refuge where he had fled, and he

shall remain there until the death of the high priest who was anointed with the holy oil.

26 'But if the manslayer at any time goes outside the limits of the city of refuge where he fled,

27 'and the avenger of blood finds him outside the limits of his city of refuge, and the avenger of blood kills the manslayer, he shall not be guilty of blood,

28 'because he should have remained in his city of refuge until the death of the high priest. But after the death of the high priest the manslayer may return to the land of his possession.

29 'And these *things* shall be a statute of judgment to you throughout your generations in all your dwellings.

30 'Whoever kills a person, the murderer shall be put to death on the testimony of witnesses; but one witness is not *sufficient* testimony against a person for the death *penalty.*

31 'Moreover you shall take no ransom for the life of a murderer who *is* guilty of death, but he shall surely be put to death.

32 'And you shall take no ransom for him who has fled to his city of refuge, that he may return to dwell in the land before the death of the priest.

33 'So you shall not pollute the land where you *are;* for blood defiles the land, and no atonement can be made for the land, for the blood that is shed on it, except by the blood of him who shed it.

34 'Therefore do not defile the land which you inhabit, in the midst of which I dwell; for I the LORD dwell among the children of Israel.' "

MARRIAGE OF FEMALE HEIRS

36 Now the chief fathers of the families of the children of Gil′ē·ad the son of Mā′chir, the son of Ma·nas′seh, of the families of the sons of Joseph, came near and spoke before Moses and before the leaders, the chief fathers of the children of Israel.

2 And they said: "The LORD commanded my lord *Moses* to give the land as an inheritance by lot to the children of Israel, and my lord was commanded by the LORD to give the inheritance of our brother Ze·loph′e·had to his daughters.

3 "Now if they are married to any of the sons of the *other* tribes of the children of Israel, then their inheritance will be taken from the inheritance of our fathers, and it will be added to the inheritance of the tribe into which they marry; so it will be taken from the lot of our inheritance.

4 "And when the Jubilee of the children of Israel comes, then their inheritance will be added to the inheritance of the tribe into which they marry; so their inheritance will be taken away from the inheritance of the tribe of our fathers."

5 Then Moses commanded the children of Israel according to the word of the LORD, saying: "What the tribe of the sons of Joseph speaks is right.

6 "This *is* what the LORD commands concerning the daughters of Ze·loph′e·had, saying, 'Let them marry whom they think best, but they may marry only within the family of their father's tribe.'

7 "So the inheritance of the children of Israel shall not change hands from tribe to tribe, for every one of the children of Israel shall keep the inheritance of the tribe of his fathers.

8 "And every daughter who possesses an inheritance in any tribe of the children of Israel shall be the wife of one of the family of her father's tribe, so that the children of Israel each may possess the inheritance of his fathers.

9 "Thus no inheritance shall change

hands from *one* tribe to another, but every tribe of the children of Israel shall keep its own inheritance."

10 Just as the LORD commanded Moses, so did the daughters of Ze·loph'-e·had;

11 for Mah'lah, Tir'zah, Hog'lah, Mil'cah, and Noah, the daughters of Ze·loph'e·had, were married to the sons of their father's brothers.

12 They were married into the families of the children of Ma·nas'seh the son of Joseph, and their inheritance remained in the tribe of their father's family.

13 These *are* the commandments and the judgments which the LORD commanded the children of Israel by the hand of Moses in the plains of Mō'ab by the Jordan, *across from* Jericho.

DEUTERONOMY

THE PREVIOUS COMMAND TO ENTER CANAAN

THESE *are* the words which Moses spoke to all Israel on this side of the Jordan in the wilderness, in the plain*a* opposite Sūph,*b* between Par'an, Tō'phel, Lā'ban, Ha·zē'roth, and Diz'a·hab.

2 *It is* eleven days' *journey* from Hō'reb by way of Mount Sē'ir to Kā'desh Bar·nē'a.

3 Now it came to pass in the fortieth year, in the eleventh month, on the first *day* of the month, *that* Moses spoke to the children of Israel according to all that the LORD had given him as commandments to them,

4 after he had killed Sī'hon king of the Am'o·rītes, who dwelt in Hesh'bon, and Og king of Bā'shan, who dwelt at Ash'ta·roth in*a* Ed'-rē·ī.

5 On this side of the Jordan in the land of Mō'ab, Moses began to explain this law, saying,

6 "The LORD our God spoke to us in Hō'reb, saying: 'You have dwelt long enough at this mountain.

7 'Turn and take your journey, and go to the mountains of the Am'o·rītes, to all the neighboring *places* in the plain,*a* in the mountains and in the lowland, in the South and on the seacoast, to the land of the Cā'naan·ītes and to Lebanon, as far as the great river, the River Eū·phrā'tēs.

8 'See, I have set the land before you; go in and possess the land which the LORD swore to your fathers—to Abraham, Isaac, and Jacob—to give to them and their descendants after them.'

TRIBAL LEADERS APPOINTED

9 "And I spoke to you at that time, saying: 'I alone am not able to bear you.

10 'The LORD your God has multiplied you, and here you *are* today, as the stars of heaven in multitude.

11 'May the LORD God of your fathers make you a thousand times more numerous than you are, and bless you as He has promised you!

12 'How can I alone bear your problems and your burdens and your complaints?

13 'Choose wise, understanding, and knowledgeable men from among your tribes, and I will make them heads over you.'

14 "And you answered me and said, 'The thing which you have told *us* to do *is* good.'

15 "So I took the heads of your tribes, wise and knowledgeable men, and made them heads over you, leaders of thousands, leaders of hundreds, leaders of fifties, leaders of tens, and officers for your tribes.

16 "Then I commanded your judges at that time, saying, 'Hear *the cases* between your brethren, and judge righteously between a man and his brother or the stranger who is with him.

17 'You shall not show partiality in judgment; you shall hear the small as well as the great; you shall not be afraid in any man's presence, for the judgment *is* God's. The case that is too hard for you, bring to me, and I will hear it.'

1:1 *a*Hebrew *arabah* *b*One manuscript of the Septuagint, also Targum and Vulgate, read *Red Sea.*
1:4 *a*Septuagint, Syriac, and Vulgate read *and* (compare Joshua 12:4). 1:7 *a*Hebrew *arabah*

18 "And I commanded you at that time all the things which you should do.

ISRAEL'S REFUSAL TO ENTER THE LAND

19 "So we departed from Hō′reb, and went through all that great and terrible wilderness which you saw on the way to the mountains of the Am′-o·rītes, as the LORD our God had commanded us. Then we came to Kā′desh Bar·nē′a.

20 "And I said to you, 'You have come to the mountains of the Am′o·rītes, which the LORD our God is giving us.

21 'Look, the LORD your God has set the land before you; go up and possess it, as the LORD God of your fathers has spoken to you; do not fear or be discouraged.'

22 "And every one of you came near to me and said, 'Let us send men before us, and let them search out the land for us, and bring back word to us of the way by which we should go up, and of the cities into which we shall come.'

23 "The plan pleased me well; so I took twelve of your men, one man from each tribe.

24 "And they departed and went up into the mountains, and came to the Valley of Esh′col, and spied it out.

25 "They also took some of the fruit of the land in their hands and brought it down to us; and they brought back word to us, saying, 'It is a good land which the LORD our God is giving us.'

26 "Nevertheless you would not go up, but rebelled against the command of the LORD your God;

27 "and you complained in your tents, and said, 'Because the LORD hates us, He has brought us out of the land of Egypt to deliver us into the hand of the Am′o·rītes, to destroy us.

28 'Where can we go up? Our brethren have discouraged our hearts, saying, "The people are greater and taller than we; the cities are great and fortified up to heaven; moreover we have seen the sons of the An′a-kim there." '

29 "Then I said to you, 'Do not be terrified, or afraid of them.

30 'The LORD your God, who goes before you, He will fight for you, according to all He did for you in Egypt before your eyes,

31 'and in the wilderness where you saw how the LORD your God carried you, as a man carries his son, in all the way that you went until you came to this place.'

32 "Yet, for all that, you did not believe the LORD your God,

33 "who went in the way before you to search out a place for you to pitch your tents, to show you the way you should go, in the fire by night and in the cloud by day.

THE PENALTY FOR ISRAEL'S REBELLION

34 "And the LORD heard the sound of your words, and was angry, and took an oath, saying,

35 'Surely not one of these men of this evil generation shall see that good land of which I swore to give to your fathers,

36 'except Caleb the son of Je·phūn′neh; he shall see it, and to him and his children I am giving the land on which he walked, because he wholly followed the LORD.'

37 "The LORD was also angry with me for your sakes, saying, 'Even you shall not go in there.

38 'Joshua the son of Nun, who stands before you, he shall go in

there. Encourage him, for he shall cause Israel to inherit it.

39 'Moreover your little ones and your children, who you say will be victims, who today have no knowledge of good and evil, they shall go in there; to them I will give it, and they shall possess it.

40 'But *as for* you, turn and take your journey into the wilderness by the Way of the Red Sea.'

41 "Then you answered and said to me, 'We have sinned against the LORD; we will go up and fight, just as the LORD our God commanded us.' And when everyone of you had girded on his weapons of war, you were ready to go up into the mountain.

42 "And the LORD said to me, 'Tell them, "Do not go up nor fight, for I *am* not among you; lest you be defeated before your enemies."'

43 "So I spoke to you; yet you would not listen, but rebelled against the command of the LORD, and presumptuously went up into the mountain.

44 "And the Am'o·rītes who dwelt in that mountain came out against you and chased you as bees do, and drove you back from Sē'ir to Hor'mah.

45 "Then you returned and wept before the LORD, but the LORD would not listen to your voice nor give ear to you.

46 "So you remained in Kā'desh many days, according to the days that you spent *there*.

THE DESERT YEARS

2 "Then we turned and journeyed into the wilderness of the Way of the Red Sea, as the LORD spoke to me, and we skirted Mount Sē'ir for many days.

2 "And the LORD spoke to me, saying:

3 'You have skirted this mountain long enough; turn northward.

4 'And command the people, saying, "You *are about to* pass through the territory of your brethren, the descendants of Esau, who live in Sē'ir; and they will be afraid of you. Therefore watch yourselves carefully.

5 "Do not meddle with them, for I will not give you *any* of their land, no, not so much as one footstep, because I have given Mount Sē'ir to Esau *as* a possession.

6 "You shall buy food from them with money, that you may eat; and you shall also buy water from them with money, that you may drink.

7 "For the LORD your God has blessed you in all the work of your hand. He knows your trudging through this great wilderness. These forty years the LORD your God *has been* with you; you have lacked nothing."'

8 "And when we passed beyond our brethren, the descendants of Esau who dwell in Sē'ir, away from the road of the plain, away from Ē'lath and Ē'zi·on Gē'ber, we turned and passed by way of the Wilderness of Mō'ab.

9 "Then the LORD said to me, 'Do not harass Mō'ab, nor contend with them in battle, for I will not give you *any* of their land *as* a possession, because I have given Ar to the descendants of Lot *as* a possession.' "

10 (The Ē'mim had dwelt there in times past, a people as great and numerous and tall as the An'a·kim.

11 They were also regarded as giants,*a* like the An'a·kim, but the Mō'ab·ītes call them Ē'mim.

12 The Hor'ītes formerly dwelt in Sē'ir, but the descendants of Esau dispossessed them and destroyed them from before them, and dwelt in their place, just as Israel did to the

2:11 *a*Hebrew *rephaim*

land of their possession which the LORD gave them.)

13 " 'Now rise and cross over the Valley of the Zē′red.' So we crossed over the Valley of the Zē′red.

14 "And the time we took to come from Kā′desh Bar·nē′a until we crossed over the Valley of the Zē′red *was* thirty-eight years, until all the generation of the men of war was consumed from the midst of the camp, just as the LORD had sworn to them.

15 "For indeed the hand of the LORD was against them, to destroy them from the midst of the camp until they were consumed.

16 "So it was, when all the men of war had finally perished from among the people,

17 "that the LORD spoke to me, saying:

18 'This day you are to cross over at Ar, the boundary of Mō′ab.

19 'And *when* you come near the people of Am′mon, do not harass them or meddle with them, for I will not give you *any* of the land of the people of Am′mon *as* a possession, because I have given it to the descendants of Lot *as* a possession.' "

20 (That was also regarded as a land of giants;*a* giants formerly dwelt there. But the Am′mon·ītes call them Zam·zum′mim,

21 a people as great and numerous and tall as the An′a·kim. But the LORD destroyed them before them, and they dispossessed them and dwelt in their place,

22 just as He had done for the descendants of Esau, who dwelt in Sē′ir, when He destroyed the Hor′ītes from before them. They dispossessed them and dwelt in their place, even to this day.

23 And the Av′im, who dwelt in villages as far as Gā′za—the Caph′to·rim, who came from Caph′tor, destroyed them and dwelt in their place.)

24 " 'Rise, take your journey, and cross over the River Ar′non. Look, I have given into your hand Sī′hon the Am′o·rīte, king of Hesh′bon, and his land. Begin to possess *it,* and engage him in battle.

25 'This day I will begin to put the dread and fear of you upon the nations under the whole heaven, who shall hear the report of you, and shall tremble and be in anguish because of you.'

KING SIHON DEFEATED

26 "And I sent messengers from the Wilderness of Ked′e·moth to Sī′hon king of Hesh′bon, with words of peace, saying,

27 'Let me pass through your land; I will keep strictly to the road, and I will turn neither to the right nor to the left.

28 'You shall sell me food for money, that I may eat, and give me water for money, that I may drink; only let me pass through on foot,

29 'just as the descendants of Esau who dwell in Sē′ir and the Mō′ab·ītes who dwell in Ar did for me, until I cross the Jordan to the land which the LORD our God is giving us.'

30 "But Sī′hon king of Hesh′bon would not let us pass through, for the LORD your God hardened his spirit and made his heart obstinate, that He might deliver him into your hand, as *it is* this day.

31 "And the LORD said to me, 'See, I have begun to give Sī′hon and his land over to you. Begin to possess *it,* that you may inherit his land.'

32 "Then Sī′hon and all his people came out against us to fight at Jā′haz.

2:20 *a*Hebrew *rephaim*

33 "And the LORD our God delivered him over to us; so we defeated him, his sons, and all his people.

34 "We took all his cities at that time, and we utterly destroyed the men, women, and little ones of every city; we left none remaining.

35 "We took only the livestock as plunder for ourselves, with the spoil of the cities which we took.

36 "From A·rō′er, which *is* on the bank of the River Ar′non, and *from* the city that *is* in the ravine, as far as Gil′ē·ad, there was not one city too strong for us; the LORD our God delivered all to us.

37 "Only you did not go near the land of the people of Am′mon—anywhere along the River Jab′bok, or to the cities of the mountains, or wherever the LORD our God had forbidden us.

KING OG DEFEATED

3 "Then we turned and went up the road to Bā′shan; and Og king of Bā′shan came out against us, he and all his people, to battle at Ed′rē·ī.

2 "And the LORD said to me, 'Do not fear him, for I have delivered him and all his people and his land into your hand; you shall do to him as you did to Sī′hon king of the Am′o·rītes, who dwelt at Hesh′bon.'

3 "So the LORD our God also delivered into our hands Og king of Bā′shan, with all his people, and we attacked him until he had no survivors remaining.

4 "And we took all his cities at that time; there was not a city which we did not take from them: sixty cities, all the region of Ar′gob, the kingdom of Og in Bā′shan.

5 "All these cities *were* fortified with high walls, gates, and bars, besides a great many rural towns.

6 "And we utterly destroyed them, as we did to Sī′hon king of Hesh′bon, utterly destroying the men, women, and children of every city.

7 "But all the livestock and the spoil of the cities we took as booty for ourselves.

8 "And at that time we took the land from the hand of the two kings of the Am′o·rītes who *were* on this side of the Jordan, from the River Ar′non to Mount Her′mon

9 "(the Sī·dō′ni·ans call Her′mon Sir′i·on, and the Am′o·rītes call it Sē′nir),

10 "all the cities of the plain, all Gil′ē·ad, and all Bā′shan, as far as Sal′cah and Ed′rē·ī, cities of the kingdom of Og in Bā′shan.

11 "For only Og king of Bā′shan remained of the remnant of the giants.*a* Indeed his bedstead *was* an iron bedstead. (*Is* it not in Rab′bah of the people of Am′mon?) Nine cubits *is* its length and four cubits its width, according to the standard cubit.

THE LAND EAST OF THE JORDAN DIVIDED

12 "And this land, *which* we possessed at that time, from A·rō′er, which *is* by the River Ar′non, and half the mountains of Gil′ē·ad and its cities, I gave to the Reū′ben·ītes and the Gad′ītes.

13 "The rest of Gil′ē·ad, and all Bā′shan, the kingdom of Og, I gave to half the tribe of Ma·nas′seh. (All the region of Ar′gob, with all Bā′shan, was called the land of the giants.*a*

14 "Jā′ir the son of Ma·nas′seh took all the region of Ar′gob, as far as the border of the Gesh′ū·rītes and the Mā′a·cha·thītes, and called Bā′shan after his own name, Hā′voth Jā′ir,*a* to this day.)

3:11 *a*Hebrew *rephaim*   3:13 *a*Hebrew *rephaim*
3:14 *a*Literally *Towns of Jair*

15 "Also I gave Gil'e·ad to Mā'-chir.

16 "And to the Reū'ben·ites and the Gad'ites I gave from Gil'ē·ad as far as the River Ar'non, the middle of the river as *the* border, as far as the River Jab'bok, the border of the people of Am'mon;

17 "the plain also, with the Jordan as *the* border, from Chin'ne·reth as far as the east side of the Sea of the Ar'a·bah (the Salt Sea), below the slopes of Pis'gah.

18 "Then I commanded you at that time, saying: 'The LORD your God has given you this land to possess. All you men of valor shall cross over armed before your brethren, the children of Israel.

19 'But your wives, your little ones, and your livestock (I know that you have much livestock) shall stay in your cities which I have given you,

20 'until the LORD has given rest to your brethren as to you, and they also possess the land which the LORD your God is giving them beyond the Jordan. Then each of you may return to his possession which I have given you.'

21 "And I commanded Joshua at that time, saying, 'Your eyes have seen all that the LORD your God has done to these two kings; so will the LORD do to all the kingdoms through which you pass.

22 'You must not fear them, for the LORD your God Himself fights for you.'

MOSES FORBIDDEN TO ENTER THE LAND

23 "Then I pleaded with the LORD at that time, saying:

24 'O Lord GOD, You have begun to show Your servant Your greatness and Your mighty hand, for what god

Prayers

Deuteronomy 3:23–27

For forty years Moses had led the people of Israel toward the Promised Land. He had gone through many, many tough times. At last he and his people were at the borders of the Promised Land. "Let me go in," Moses begged God. But God said no. Sometimes God says no to something we want very much. You have never wanted anything more than Moses wanted to go into the Promised Land. But God would not let Moses have what he wanted most. Trust God. He knows what is best for you. Accept it!

is there in heaven or on earth who can do *anything* like Your works and Your mighty *deeds?*

25 'I pray, let me cross over and see the good land beyond the Jordan, those pleasant mountains, and Lebanon.'

26 "But the LORD was angry with me on your account, and would not listen to me. So the LORD said to me: 'Enough of that! Speak no more to Me of this matter.

27 'Go up to the top of Pis'gah, and lift your eyes toward the west, the north, the south, and the east; behold *it* with your eyes, for you shall not cross over this Jordan.

28 'But command Joshua, and encourage him and strengthen him; for he shall go over before this people, and he shall cause them to inherit the land which you will see.'

29 "So we stayed in the valley opposite Beth Pē'or.

*T*hank You, God, for giving us water.

———

Genesis 1:6–10

We can know what God wants by reading His Word.

———

Exodus 33:13

You cannot hide your sin by sweeping it under the rug.

———————

Numbers 32:23

*M*other and father will teach me the Word of God, the Bible.

Deuteronomy 4:10

MOSES COMMANDS OBEDIENCE

4 "Now, O Israel, listen to the statutes and the judgments which I teach you to observe, that you may live, and go in and possess the land which the LORD God of your fathers is giving you.

2 "You shall not add to the word which I command you, nor take from it, that you may keep the commandments of the LORD your God which I command you.

3 "Your eyes have seen what the LORD did at Bā'al Pē'or; for the LORD your God has destroyed from among you all the men who followed Bā'al of Pē'or.

4 "But you who held fast to the LORD your God *are* alive today, every one of you.

5 "Surely I have taught you statutes and judgments, just as the LORD my God commanded me, that you should act according *to them* in the land which you go to possess.

6 "Therefore be careful to observe *them;* for this *is* your wisdom and your understanding in the sight of the peoples who will hear all these statutes, and say, 'Surely this great nation *is* a wise and understanding people.'

7 "For what great nation *is there* that has God *so* near to it, as the LORD our God *is* to us, for whatever *reason* we may call upon Him?

8 "And what great nation *is there* that has *such* statutes and righteous judgments as are in all this law which I set before you this day?

9 "Only take heed to yourself, and diligently keep yourself, lest you forget the things your eyes have seen, and lest they depart from your heart all the days of your life. And teach them to your children and your grandchildren,

10 "*especially concerning* the day you stood before the LORD your God in Hō'reb, when the LORD said to me, 'Gather the people to Me, and I will let them hear My words, that they may learn to fear Me all the days they live on the earth, and *that* they may teach their children.'

11 "Then you came near and stood at the foot of the mountain, and the mountain burned with fire to the midst of heaven, with darkness, cloud, and thick darkness.

12 "And the LORD spoke to you out of the midst of the fire. You heard the sound of the words, but saw no form; *you* only *heard* a voice.

13 "So He declared to you His covenant which He commanded you to perform, the Ten Commandments; and He wrote them on two tablets of stone.

14 "And the LORD commanded me at that time to teach you statutes and judgments, that you might observe them in the land which you cross over to possess.

BEWARE OF IDOLATRY

15 "Take careful heed to yourselves, for you saw no form when the LORD spoke to you at Hō'reb out of the midst of the fire,

16 "lest you act corruptly and make for yourselves a carved image in the form of any figure: the likeness of male or female,

17 "the likeness of any animal that *is* on the earth or the likeness of any winged bird that flies in the air,

18 "the likeness of anything that creeps on the ground or the likeness of any fish that *is* in the water beneath the earth.

19 "And *take heed,* lest you lift your eyes to heaven, and *when* you see the sun, the moon, and the stars, all the host of heaven, you feel driven to worship them and serve them, which

THE MOST WONDERFUL GIFTS OF ALL Deuteronomy 4:7

What kind of gifts do you like to get for Christmas or birthdays? Most boys and girls like things that mother or father can buy at the store. Those are OK gifts. But they are not the most wonderful gifts of all. This mother is giving her little girl one of the most wonderful gifts of all. She is reading to her. She is giving herself to her little girl. Isn't that special?

1. Would you rather have a new toy or have your parents do things with you?
2. Read Deuteronomy 4:7. Would you rather have God or the things He has made?
3. Do you think your parents and God would rather have your love than anything you could buy for them? The most wonderful gifts of all are *not* things. They are gifts of yourself, your time, and your helpfulness.

For more on *Building Family Memories* turn to page 285
For more on *Giving* turn to page 292

WHAT SHOULD I LEARN MOST? Deuteronomy 4:10

What do you learn at school? It's important that we learn many things, isn't it? But of all the things we learn, what is the most important?

1. The last half of Deuteronomy 4:10 tells us what is the most important to learn. What is it? Why is this so important? Deuteronomy 5:1 is a follow-up verse. "Statutes and judgments" refers to God's Word.
2. Don't stop learning the things you must learn at school. But don't stop learning about God and His Word either. That is the most important learning of all.
3. How can you learn more about God and His Word? Will you be sure to learn something from His Word today?

For more on *What Should I Do?* turn to page 273
For more on *Bible* turn to page 497

the LORD your God has given to all the peoples under the whole heaven as a heritage.

20 "But the LORD has taken you and brought you out of the iron furnace, out of Egypt, to be His people, an inheritance, as you are this day.

21 "Furthermore the LORD was angry with me for your sakes, and swore that I would not cross over the Jordan, and that I would not enter the good land which the LORD your God is giving you as an inheritance.

22 "But I must die in this land, I must not cross over the Jordan; but you shall cross over and possess that good land.

23 "Take heed to yourselves, lest you forget the covenant of the LORD your God which He made with you, and make for yourselves a carved image in the form of anything which the LORD your God has forbidden you.

24 "For the LORD your God *is* a consuming fire, a jealous God.

25 "When you beget children and grandchildren and have grown old in the land, and act corruptly and make a carved image in the form of anything, and do evil in the sight of the LORD your God to provoke Him to anger,

26 "I call heaven and earth to witness against you this day, that you will soon utterly perish from the land which you cross over the Jordan to possess; you will not prolong *your* days in it, but will be utterly destroyed.

27 "And the LORD will scatter you among the peoples, and you will be left few in number among the nations where the LORD will drive you.

28 "And there you will serve gods, the work of men's hands, wood and stone, which neither see nor hear nor eat nor smell.

29 "But from there you will seek the LORD your God, and you will find *Him* if you seek Him with all your heart and with all your soul.

30 "When you are in distress, and all

these things come upon you in the latter days, when you turn to the LORD your God and obey His voice

31 "(for the LORD your God *is* a merciful God), He will not forsake you nor destroy you, nor forget the covenant of your fathers which He swore to them.

32 "For ask now concerning the days that are past, which were before you, since the day that God created man on the earth, and *ask* from one end of heaven to the other, whether *any* great *thing* like this has happened, or *anything* like it has been heard.

33 "Did *any* people *ever* hear the voice of God speaking out of the midst of the fire, as you have heard, and live?

34 "Or did God *ever* try to go *and* take for Himself a nation from the midst of *another* nation, by trials, by signs, by wonders, by war, by a mighty hand and an outstretched arm, and by great terrors, according to all that the LORD your God did for you in Egypt before your eyes?

35 "To you it was shown, that you might know that the LORD Himself *is* God; *there is* none other besides Him.

36 "Out of heaven He let you hear His voice, that He might instruct you; on earth He showed you His great fire, and you heard His words out of the midst of the fire.

37 "And because He loved your fathers, therefore He chose their descendants after them; and He brought you out of Egypt with His Presence, with His mighty power,

38 "driving out from before you nations greater and mightier than you, to bring you in, to give you their land *as* an inheritance, as *it is* this day.

39 "Therefore know this day, and consider *it* in your heart, that the LORD Himself *is* God in heaven above and on the earth beneath; *there is* no other.

40 "You shall therefore keep His statutes and His commandments which I command you today, that it may go well with you and with your children after you, and that you may prolong *your* days in the land which the LORD your God is giving you for all time."

CITIES OF REFUGE EAST OF THE JORDAN

41 Then Moses set apart three cities on this side of the Jordan, toward the rising of the sun,

42 that the manslayer might flee there, who kills his neighbor unintentionally, without having hated him in time past, and that by fleeing to one of these cities he might live:

43 Bē′zer in the wilderness on the plateau for the Reū′ben·ītes, Rā′moth in Gil′ē·ad for the Gad′ītes, and Gō′lan in Bā′shan for the Ma·nas′sītes.

INTRODUCTION TO GOD'S LAW

44 Now this *is* the law which Moses set before the children of Israel.

45 These *are* the testimonies, the statutes, and the judgments which Moses spoke to the children of Israel after they came out of Egypt,

46 on this side of the Jordan, in the valley opposite Beth Pē′or, in the land of Sī′hon king of the Am′o·rītes, who dwelt at Hesh′bon, whom Moses and the children of Israel defeated after they came out of Egypt.

47 And they took possession of his land and the land of Og king of Bā′shan, two kings of the Am′o·rītes, who *were* on this side of the Jordan, toward the rising of the sun,

48 from A·rō′er, which *is* on the bank of the River Ar′non, even to Mount Sī′on*a* (that is, Her′mon),

4:48 *a*Syriac reads *Sirion* (compare 3:9).

What Should I Do?

YOU SHOULDN'T DO THAT! Deuteronomy 5:11

"There's a stump down there," said Teri. "Let's slide down the hill over here." But Tim wouldn't listen to Teri. He thought he knew more than she. Now look what happened. What should Tim say to Teri?

1. Sometimes mother or father says, "You shouldn't do that." But you don't want to listen. Then you get into trouble. Should you listen to them?
2. Sometimes brother or sister says, "You shouldn't do that." But you don't want to listen. Then you get into trouble. Should you listen to him or her?
3. Deuteronomy 5:11 is one of several commands that says, "You shall not." God tells you in His Word, "You shouldn't do that." Now do you want to listen to Him? What should you do?

For more on *What Should I Do?* turn to page 275
For more on *Obeying* turn to page 289

49 and all the plain on the east side of the Jordan as far as the Sea of the Ar'a·bah, below the slopes of Pis'gah.

THE TEN COMMANDMENTS REVIEWED

5 And Moses called all Israel, and said to them: "Hear, O Israel, the statutes and judgments which I speak in your hearing today, that you may learn them and be careful to observe them.

2 "The LORD our God made a covenant with us in Hō'reb.

3 "The LORD did not make this covenant with our fathers, but with us, those who *are* here today, all of us who *are* alive.

4 "The LORD talked with you face to face on the mountain from the midst of the fire.

5 "I stood between the LORD and you at that time, to declare to you the word of the LORD; for you were afraid because of the fire, and you did not go up the mountain. *He* said:

6 'I *am* the LORD your God who brought you out of the land of Egypt, out of the house of bondage.

7 'You shall have no other gods before Me.

8 'You shall not make for yourself a carved image—any likeness *of anything* that *is* in heaven above, or that *is* in the earth beneath, or that *is* in the water under the earth;

9 you shall not bow down to them nor serve them. For I, the LORD your God, *am* a jealous God, visiting the iniquity of the fathers upon the children to the third and fourth *generations* of those who hate Me,

10 but showing mercy to thousands, to those who love Me and keep My commandments.

11 'You shall not take the name of the LORD your God in vain, for the LORD will not hold *him* guiltless who takes His name in vain.

12 'Observe the Sabbath day, to keep it holy, as the LORD your God commanded you.

13 Six days you shall labor and do all your work,

14 but the seventh day *is* the Sabbath of the LORD your God. *In it* you shall do no work: you, nor your son, nor your daughter, nor your male servant, nor your female servant, nor your ox, nor your donkey, nor any of your cattle, nor your stranger who *is* within your gates, that your male servant and your female servant may rest as well as you.

15 And remember that you were a slave in the land of Egypt, and the LORD your God brought you out from there by a mighty hand and by an outstretched arm; therefore the LORD your God commanded you to keep the Sabbath day.

16 'Honor your father and your mother, as the LORD your God has commanded you, that your days may be long, and that it may be well with you in the land which the LORD your God is giving you.

17 'You shall not murder.

18 'You shall not commit adultery.

19 'You shall not steal.

20 'You shall not bear false witness against your neighbor.

21 'You shall not covet your neighbor's wife; and you shall not desire your neighbor's house, his field, his male servant, his female servant, his ox, his donkey, or anything that *is* your neighbor's.'

What Should I Do?

LUCY'S NEW FRIEND   Deuteronomy 5:16

Lucy has found a new friend. "What should I do?" she asks her new friend. Lucy sassed her mother this morning. That made her mother sad. It made Lucy sad, too. Lucy went outside to find a friend to help her. Perhaps a friend could tell her what she should do now.

1. Is it wrong to sass your mother or father? Why?
2. You wouldn't sass your parents, would you? But what if you forget some time and do it? What should you do? What should you say to your parents then? How about "I'm sorry, please forgive me?" Do you think that would help?
3. Ask your mother or father what they would like for you to say. Will you remember to say that if you forget and sass one of them?
4. Look up Deuteronomy 5:16. What does it say about sassing your father or mother? Who commanded you to show honor to your parents?

For more on *What Should I Do?* turn to page 289
For more on *Forgiveness* turn to page 502

22 "These words the LORD spoke to all your assembly, in the mountain from the midst of the fire, the cloud, and the thick darkness, with a loud voice; and He added no more. And He wrote them on two tablets of stone and gave them to me.

THE PEOPLE AFRAID OF GOD'S PRESENCE

23 "So it was, when you heard the voice from the midst of the darkness, while the mountain was burning with fire, that you came near to me, all the heads of your tribes and your elders.
24 "And you said: 'Surely the LORD our God has shown us His glory and His greatness, and we have heard His voice from the midst of the fire. We have seen this day that God speaks with man; yet he *still* lives.
25 'Now therefore, why should we die? For this great fire will consume us; if we hear the voice of the LORD our God anymore, then we shall die.
26 'For who *is there* of all flesh who has heard the voice of the living God speaking from the midst of the fire, as we *have,* and lived?
27 'You go near and hear all that the LORD our God may say, and tell us all that the LORD our God says to you, and we will hear and do *it.*'
28 "Then the LORD heard the voice of your words when you spoke to me, and the LORD said to me: 'I have heard the voice of the words of this people which they have spoken to you. They are right *in* all that they have spoken.
29 'Oh, that they had such a heart in them that they would fear Me and always keep all My commandments, that it might be well with them and with their children forever!
30 'Go and say to them, "Return to your tents."

31 'But as for you, stand here by Me, and I will speak to you all the commandments, the statutes, and the judgments which you shall teach them, that they may observe *them* in the land which I am giving them to possess.'
32 "Therefore you shall be careful to do as the LORD your God has commanded you; you shall not turn aside to the right hand or to the left.
33 "You shall walk in all the ways which the LORD your God has commanded you, that you may live and *that it may be* well with you, and *that* you may prolong *your* days in the land which you shall possess.

THE GREATEST COMMANDMENT

6 "Now this *is* the commandment, *and these are* the statutes and judgments which the LORD your God has commanded to teach you, that you may observe *them* in the land which you are crossing over to possess,
2 "that you may fear the LORD your God, to keep all His statutes and His commandments which I command you, you and your son and your grandson, all the days of your life, and that your days may be prolonged.
3 "Therefore hear, O Israel, and be careful to observe *it,* that it may be well with you, and that you may multiply greatly as the LORD God of your fathers has promised you—'a land flowing with milk and honey.'a
4 "Hear, O Israel: The LORD our God, the LORD *is* one!a
5 "You shall love the LORD your God with all your heart, with all your soul, and with all your strength.
6 "And these words which I command you today shall be in your heart.

6:3 aExodus 3:8   6:4 aOr *The LORD is our God, the LORD alone* (that is, the only one)

Favorite Bible Words

TEACHING Deuteronomy 6:4–7

Who Will Teach Me about God?

Sometimes parents wish an angel could come and help them with their children. Sometimes it seems as if even an angel could not help. Being a parent isn't easy. Ask your parents! But parents do want to teach their children about God and His Word. They want to teach their children what the Bible says. Are you listening?

1. Do you want to learn from your parents? What do you want to learn?
2. Parents, what do you want to teach your children? Do you?
3. If parents don't teach children about God and His Word, who will? Parents, teach! Children, listen and learn!
4. Look up Deuteronomy 6:4–7. What does it say? What does it mean to you?

For more on *Favorite Bible Words* turn to page 498
For more on *Family* turn to page 285

7 "You shall teach them diligently to your children, and shall talk of them when you sit in your house, when you walk by the way, when you lie down, and when you rise up.

8 "You shall bind them as a sign on your hand, and they shall be as frontlets between your eyes.

9 "You shall write them on the doorposts of your house and on your gates.

CAUTION AGAINST DISOBEDIENCE

10 "So it shall be, when the LORD your God brings you into the land of which He swore to your fathers, to Abraham, Isaac, and Jacob, to give you large and beautiful cities which you did not build,

11 "houses full of all good things, which you did not fill, hewn-out wells which you did not dig, vineyards and olive trees which you did not plant— when you have eaten and are full—

12 "*then* beware, lest you forget the LORD who brought you out of the land of Egypt, from the house of bondage.

13 "You shall fear the LORD your God and serve Him, and shall take oaths in His name.

14 "You shall not go after other gods, the gods of the peoples who *are* all around you

15 "(for the LORD your God *is* a jealous God among you), lest the anger of the LORD your God be aroused against you and destroy you from the face of the earth.

16 "You shall not tempt the LORD your God as you tempted *Him* in Mas'sah.

17 "You shall diligently keep the commandments of the LORD your God, His testimonies, and His statutes which He has commanded you.

18 "And you shall do *what is* right and good in the sight of the LORD, that it may be well with you, and that you may go in and possess the good land of which the LORD swore to your fathers,

19 "to cast out all your enemies from before you, as the LORD has spoken.

20 "When your son asks you in time to come, saying, 'What *is the meaning of* the testimonies, the statutes, and the judgments which the LORD our God has commanded you?'

21 "then you shall say to your son: 'We were slaves of Pharaoh in Egypt, and the LORD brought us out of Egypt with a mighty hand;

22 'and the LORD showed signs and wonders before our eyes, great and severe, against Egypt, Pharaoh, and all his household.

23 'Then He brought us out from there, that He might bring us in, to give us the land of which He swore to our fathers.

24 'And the LORD commanded us to observe all these statutes, to fear the LORD our God, for our good always, that He might preserve us alive, as *it is* this day.

25 'Then it will be righteousness for us, if we are careful to observe all these commandments before the LORD our God, as He has commanded us.'

A CHOSEN PEOPLE

7 "When the LORD your God brings you into the land which you go to possess, and has cast out many nations before you, the Hit′tītes and the Gir′ga·shītes and the Am′o·rītes and the Cā′naan·ītes and the Per′iz·zītes and the Hī′vītes and the Jeb′ū·sītes, seven nations greater and mightier than you,

2 "and when the LORD your God delivers them over to you, you shall conquer them *and* utterly destroy them. You shall make no covenant with them nor show mercy to them.

3 "Nor shall you make marriages with them. You shall not give your daughter to their son, nor take their daughter for your son.

4 "For they will turn your sons away from following Me, to serve other gods; so the anger of the LORD will be aroused against you and destroy you suddenly.

5 "But thus you shall deal with them: you shall destroy their altars, and break down their *sacred* pillars, and cut down their wooden images,*a* and burn their carved images with fire.

6 "For you *are* a holy people to the LORD your God; the LORD your God has chosen you to be a people for Himself, a special treasure above all the peoples on the face of the earth.

7 "The LORD did not set His love on you nor choose you because you were more in number than any other people, for you were the least of all peoples;

8 "but because the LORD loves you, and because He would keep the oath which He swore to your fathers, the LORD has brought you out with a mighty hand, and redeemed you from the house of bondage, from the hand of Pharaoh king of Egypt.

9 "Therefore know that the LORD your God, He *is* God, the faithful God who keeps covenant and mercy for a thousand generations with those who love Him and keep His commandments;

10 "and He repays those who hate Him to their face, to destroy them. He will not be slack with him who hates Him; He will repay him to his face.

11 "Therefore you shall keep the commandment, the statutes, and the judgments which I command you today, to observe them.

7:5 *a*Hebrew *Asherim,* Canaanite deities

BLESSINGS OF OBEDIENCE

12 "Then it shall come to pass, because you listen to these judgments, and keep and do them, that the LORD your God will keep with you the covenant and the mercy which He swore to your fathers.

13 "And He will love you and bless you and multiply you; He will also bless the fruit of your womb and the fruit of your land, your grain and your new wine and your oil, the increase of your cattle and the offspring of your flock, in the land of which He swore to your fathers to give you.

14 "You shall be blessed above all peoples; there shall not be a male or female barren among you or among your livestock.

15 "And the LORD will take away from you all sickness, and will afflict you with none of the terrible diseases of Egypt which you have known, but will lay *them* on all those who hate you.

16 "Also you shall destroy all the peoples whom the LORD your God delivers over to you; your eye shall have no pity on them; nor shall you serve their gods, for that *will be* a snare to you.

17 "If you should say in your heart, 'These nations are greater than I; how can I dispossess them?'—

18 "you shall not be afraid of them, *but* you shall remember well what the LORD your God did to Pharaoh and to all Egypt:

19 "the great trials which your eyes saw, the signs and the wonders, the mighty hand and the outstretched arm, by which the LORD your God brought you out. So shall the LORD your God do to all the peoples of whom you are afraid.

20 "Moreover the LORD your God will send the hornet among them until those who are left, who hide themselves from you, are destroyed.

21 "You shall not be terrified of them; for the LORD your God, the great and awesome God, *is* among you.

22 "And the LORD your God will drive out those nations before you little by little; you will be unable to destroy them at once, lest the beasts of the field become *too* numerous for you.

23 "But the LORD your God will deliver them over to you, and will inflict defeat upon them until they are destroyed.

24 "And He will deliver their kings into your hand, and you will destroy their name from under heaven; no one shall be able to stand against you until you have destroyed them.

25 "You shall burn the carved images of their gods with fire; you shall not covet the silver or gold *that is* on them, nor take *it* for yourselves, lest you be snared by it; for it *is* an abomination to the LORD your God.

26 "Nor shall you bring an abomination into your house, lest you be doomed to destruction like it. You shall utterly detest it and utterly abhor it, for it *is* an accursed thing.

REMEMBER THE LORD YOUR GOD

8 "Every commandment which I command you today you must be careful to observe, that you may live and multiply, and go in and possess the land of which the LORD swore to your fathers.

2 "And you shall remember that the LORD your God led you all the way these forty years in the wilderness, to humble you *and* test you, to know what *was* in your heart, whether you would keep His commandments or not.

3 "So He humbled you, allowed you to hunger, and fed you with manna which you did not know nor did your fathers know, that He might make you know that man shall not live by bread alone; but man lives by every *word* that proceeds from the mouth of the LORD.

4 "Your garments did not wear out on you, nor did your foot swell these forty years.

5 "You should know in your heart that as a man chastens his son, *so* the LORD your God chastens you.

6 "Therefore you shall keep the commandments of the LORD your God, to walk in His ways and to fear Him.

7 "For the LORD your God is bringing you into a good land, a land of brooks of water, of fountains and springs, that flow out of valleys and hills;

8 "a land of wheat and barley, of vines and fig trees and pomegranates, a land of olive oil and honey;

9 "a land in which you will eat bread without scarcity, in which you will lack nothing; a land whose stones *are* iron and out of whose hills you can dig copper.

10 "When you have eaten and are full, then you shall bless the LORD your God for the good land which He has given you.

11 "Beware that you do not forget the LORD your God by not keeping His commandments, His judgments, and His statutes which I command you today,

12 "lest—*when* you have eaten and are full, and have built beautiful houses and dwell *in them;*

13 "and *when* your herds and your flocks multiply, and your silver and your gold are multiplied, and all that you have is multiplied;

14 "when your heart is lifted up, and you forget the LORD your God who brought you out of the land of Egypt, from the house of bondage;

15 "who led you through that great and terrible wilderness, *in which were* fiery serpents and scorpions and thirsty land where there was no water; who brought water for you out of the flinty rock;

16 "who fed you in the wilderness with manna, which your fathers did not know, that He might humble you and that He might test you, to do you good in the end—

17 "then you say in your heart, 'My power and the might of my hand have gained me this wealth.'

18 "And you shall remember the LORD your God, for *it is* He who gives you power to get wealth, that He may establish His covenant which He swore to your fathers, as *it is* this day.

19 "Then it shall be, if you by any means forget the LORD your God, and follow other gods, and serve them and worship them, I testify against you this day that you shall surely perish.

20 "As the nations which the LORD destroys before you, so you shall perish, because you would not be obedient to the voice of the LORD your God.

ISRAEL'S REBELLIONS REVIEWED

9 "Hear, O Israel: You *are* to cross over the Jordan today, and go in to dispossess nations greater and mightier than yourself, cities great and fortified up to heaven,

2 "a people great and tall, the descendants of the An'a·kim, whom you know, and *of whom* you heard *it said,* 'Who can stand before the descendants of Ā'nak?'

3 "Therefore understand today that the LORD your God *is* He who goes over before you *as* a consuming fire.

He will destroy them and bring them down before you; so you shall drive them out and destroy them quickly, as the LORD has said to you.

4 "Do not think in your heart, after the LORD your God has cast them out before you, saying, 'Because of my righteousness the LORD has brought me in to possess this land'; but *it is* because of the wickedness of these nations *that* the LORD is driving them out from before you.

5 "*It is* not because of your righteousness or the uprightness of your heart *that* you go in to possess their land, but because of the wickedness of these nations *that* the LORD your God drives them out from before you, and that He may fulfill the word which the LORD swore to your fathers, to Abraham, Isaac, and Jacob.

6 "Therefore understand that the LORD your God is not giving you this good land to possess because of your righteousness, for you *are* a stiff-necked people.

7 "Remember! Do not forget how you provoked the LORD your God to wrath in the wilderness. From the day that you departed from the land of Egypt until you came to this place, you have been rebellious against the LORD.

8 "Also in Hō'reb you provoked the LORD to wrath, so that the LORD was angry *enough* with you to have destroyed you.

9 "When I went up into the mountain to receive the tablets of stone, the tablets of the covenant which the LORD made with you, then I stayed on the mountain forty days and forty nights. I neither ate bread nor drank water.

10 "Then the LORD delivered to me two tablets of stone written with the finger of God, and on them *were* all the words which the LORD had spoken to you on the mountain from the midst of the fire in the day of the assembly.

11 "And it came to pass, at the end of forty days and forty nights, *that* the LORD gave me the two tablets of stone, the tablets of the covenant.

12 "Then the LORD said to me, 'Arise, go down quickly from here, for your people whom you brought out of Egypt have acted corruptly; they have quickly turned aside from the way which I commanded them; they have made themselves a molded image.'

13 "Furthermore the LORD spoke to me, saying, 'I have seen this people, and indeed they are a stiff-necked people.

14 'Let Me alone, that I may destroy them and blot out their name from under heaven; and I will make of you a nation mightier and greater than they.'

15 "So I turned and came down from the mountain, and the mountain burned with fire; and the two tablets of the covenant *were* in my two hands.

16 "And I looked, and behold, you had sinned against the LORD your God—had made for yourselves a molded calf! You had turned aside quickly from the way which the LORD had commanded you.

17 "Then I took the two tablets and threw them out of my two hands and broke them before your eyes.

18 "And I fell down before the LORD, as at the first, forty days and forty nights; I neither ate bread nor drank water, because of all your sin which you committed in doing wickedly in the sight of the LORD, to provoke Him to anger.

19 "For I was afraid of the anger and hot displeasure with which the LORD was angry with you, to destroy you. But the LORD listened to me at that time also.

20 "And the LORD was very angry with Aaron *and* would have destroyed him; so I prayed for Aaron also at the same time.

21 "Then I took your sin, the calf which you had made, and burned it with fire and crushed it *and* ground *it* very small, until it was as fine as dust; and I threw its dust into the brook that descended from the mountain.

22 "Also at Tab′e·rah and Mas′sah and Kib′roth Hat·tā′a·vah you provoked the LORD to wrath.

23 "Likewise, when the LORD sent you from Kā′desh Bar·nē′a, saying, 'Go up and possess the land which I have given you,' then you rebelled against the commandment of the LORD your God, and you did not believe Him nor obey His voice.

24 "You have been rebellious against the LORD from the day that I knew you.

25 "Thus I prostrated myself before the LORD; forty days and forty nights I kept prostrating myself, because the LORD had said He would destroy you.

26 "Therefore I prayed to the LORD, and said: 'O Lord GOD, do not destroy Your people and Your inheritance whom You have redeemed through Your greatness, whom You have brought out of Egypt with a mighty hand.

27 'Remember Your servants, Abraham, Isaac, and Jacob; do not look on the stubbornness of this people, or on their wickedness or their sin,

28 'lest the land from which You brought us should say, "Because the LORD was not able to bring them to the land which He promised them, and because He hated them, He has brought them out to kill them in the wilderness."

29 'Yet they *are* Your people and Your inheritance, whom You brought

out by Your mighty power and by Your outstretched arm.'

THE SECOND PAIR OF TABLETS

10 "At that time the LORD said to me, 'Hew for yourself two tablets of stone like the first, and come up to Me on the mountain and make yourself an ark of wood.

2 'And I will write on the tablets the words that were on the first tablets, which you broke; and you shall put them in the ark.'

3 "So I made an ark of acacia wood, hewed two tablets of stone like the first, and went up the mountain, having the two tablets in my hand.

4 "And He wrote on the tablets according to the first writing, the Ten Commandments, which the LORD had spoken to you in the mountain from the midst of the fire in the day of the assembly; and the LORD gave them to me.

5 "Then I turned and came down from the mountain, and put the tablets in the ark which I had made; and there they are, just as the LORD commanded me."

6 (Now the children of Israel journeyed from the wells of Ben′ē Jā′akan to Mō·sē′rah, where Aaron died, and where he was buried; and El·ē·ā′zar his son ministered as priest in his stead.

7 From there they journeyed to Gud′gō·dah, and from Gud′gō·dah to Jot′ba·thah, a land of rivers of water.

8 At that time the LORD separated the tribe of Levi to bear the ark of the covenant of the LORD, to stand before the LORD to minister to Him and to bless in His name, to this day.

9 Therefore Levi has no portion nor inheritance with his brethren; the LORD *is* his inheritance, just as the LORD your God promised him.)

10 "As at the first time, I stayed in the mountain forty days and forty nights; the LORD also heard me at that time, *and* the LORD chose not to destroy you.

11 "Then the LORD said to me, 'Arise, begin *your* journey before the people, that they may go in and possess the land which I swore to their fathers to give them.'

THE ESSENCE OF THE LAW

12 "And now, Israel, what does the LORD your God require of you, but to fear the LORD your God, to walk in all His ways and to love Him, to serve the LORD your God with all your heart and with all your soul,

13 "*and* to keep the commandments of the LORD and His statutes which I command you today for your good?

14 "Indeed heaven and the highest heavens belong to the LORD your God, *also* the earth with all that *is* in it.

15 "The LORD delighted only in your fathers, to love them; and He chose their descendants after them, you above all peoples, as *it is* this day.

16 "Therefore circumcise the foreskin of your heart, and be stiffnecked no longer.

17 "For the LORD your God *is* God of gods and Lord of lords, the great God, mighty and awesome, who shows no partiality nor takes a bribe.

18 "He administers justice for the fatherless and the widow, and loves the stranger, giving him food and clothing.

19 "Therefore love the stranger, for you were strangers in the land of Egypt.

20 "You shall fear the LORD your God; you shall serve Him, and to Him you shall hold fast, and take oaths in His name.

21 "He *is* your praise, and He *is* your God, who has done for you these

---

> ### *Praises*
> Deuteronomy 10:21
>
> God is our praise. Why? He has done so many wonderful things for us. Could you write all of God's wonderful gifts on a sheet of paper? Or would you need two or three or more sheets of paper? Try it sometime. Make a list of all that God has given you. Praise Him for each one.

---

great and awesome things which your eyes have seen.

22 "Your fathers went down to Egypt with seventy persons, and now the LORD your God has made you as the stars of heaven in multitude.

LOVE AND OBEDIENCE REWARDED

11 "Therefore you shall love the LORD your God, and keep His charge, His statutes, His judgments, and His commandments always.

2 "Know today that I do not *speak* with your children, who have not known and who have not seen the chastening of the LORD your God, His greatness and His mighty hand and His outstretched arm—

3 "His signs and His acts which He did in the midst of Egypt, to Pharaoh king of Egypt, and to all his land;

4 "what He did to the army of Egypt, to their horses and their chariots: how He made the waters of the Red Sea overflow them as they pursued you, and *how* the LORD has destroyed them to this day;

5 "what He did for you in the wilderness until you came to this place;

6 "and what He did to Dā′than and A·bī′ram the sons of E·lī′ab, the son

of Reuben: how the earth opened its mouth and swallowed them up, their households, their tents, and all the substance that *was* in their possession, in the midst of all Israel—

7 "but your eyes have seen every great act of the LORD which He did.

8 "Therefore you shall keep every commandment which I command you today, that you may be strong, and go in and possess the land which you cross over to possess,

9 "and that you may prolong *your* days in the land which the LORD swore to give your fathers, to them and their descendants, 'a land flowing with milk and honey.'a

10 "For the land which you go to possess *is* not like the land of Egypt from which you have come, where you sowed your seed and watered *it* by foot, as a vegetable garden;

11 "but the land which you cross over to possess *is* a land of hills and valleys, which drinks water from the rain of heaven,

12 "a land for which the LORD your God cares; the eyes of the LORD your God *are* always on it, from the beginning of the year to the very end of the year.

13 'And it shall be that if you earnestly obey My commandments which I command you today, to love the LORD your God and serve Him with all your heart and with all your soul,

14 'then Ia will give *you* the rain for your land in its season, the early rain and the latter rain, that you may gather in your grain, your new wine, and your oil.

15 'And I will send grass in your fields for your livestock, that you may eat and be filled.'

16 "Take heed to yourselves, lest your heart be deceived, and you turn aside and serve other gods and worship them,

17 "lest the LORD's anger be aroused against you, and He shut up the heavens so that there be no rain, and the land yield no produce, and you perish quickly from the good land which the LORD is giving you.

18 "Therefore you shall lay up these words of mine in your heart and in your soul, and bind them as a sign on your hand, and they shall be as frontlets between your eyes.

19 "You shall teach them to your children, speaking of them when you sit in your house, when you walk by the way, when you lie down, and when you rise up.

20 "And you shall write them on the doorposts of your house and on your gates,

21 "that your days and the days of your children may be multiplied in the land of which the LORD swore to your fathers to give them, like the days of the heavens above the earth.

22 "For if you carefully keep all these commandments which I command you to do—to love the LORD your God, to walk in all His ways, and to hold fast to Him—

23 "then the LORD will drive out all these nations from before you, and you will dispossess greater and mightier nations than yourselves.

24 "Every place on which the sole of your foot treads shall be yours: from the wilderness and Lebanon, from the river, the River Eū·phrā'tēs, even to the Western Sea,a shall be your territory.

25 "No man shall be able to stand against you; the LORD your God will put the dread of you and the fear of you upon all the land where you tread, just as He has said to you.

11:9 aExodus 3:8   11:14 aFollowing Masoretic Text and Targum; Samaritan Pentateuch, Septuagint, and Vulgate read *He*.   11:24 aThat is, the Mediterranean

MY DOLL, YOUR DOLL Deuteronomy 11:18–21

I remember the day my mother gave me the doll. I was a little girl. Today I am giving it to you. Take good care of it and give it to your little girl. I remember the day my father gave me the watch. I was just a boy. Today I am giving it to you. Take good care of it and give it to your little boy. I remember . . . and I rejoice.

1. Do you have a family keepsake? What is it? Who gave it to you? Will you give it to someone?
2. Family keepsakes can be family treasures, not because they are valuable, but because they help us remember someone wonderful from yesterday.
3. God's Word helps us remember the Lord. Would you like to read it daily and share it with your family?

For more on *Family Memories* turn to page 406
For more on *Family* turn to page 406

26 "Behold, I set before you today a blessing and a curse:

27 "the blessing, if you obey the commandments of the LORD your God which I command you today;

28 "and the curse, if you do not obey the commandments of the LORD your God, but turn aside from the way which I command you today, to go after other gods which you have not known.

29 "Now it shall be, when the LORD your God has brought you into the land which you go to possess, that you shall put the blessing on Mount Ger′i·zim and the curse on Mount Ē′bal.

30 "*Are* they not on the other side of the Jordan, toward the setting sun, in the land of the Cā′naan·ītes who dwell in the plain opposite Gil′gal, beside the terebinth trees of Mō′reh?

31 "For you will cross over the Jordan and go in to possess the land which the LORD your God is giving you, and you will possess it and dwell in it.

32 "And you shall be careful to observe all the statutes and judgments which I set before you today.

A PRESCRIBED PLACE OF WORSHIP

12 "These *are* the statutes and judgments which you shall be careful to observe in the land which the LORD God of your fathers is giving you to possess, all the days that you live on the earth.

2 "You shall utterly destroy all the places where the nations which you shall dispossess served their gods, on the high mountains and on the hills and under every green tree.

3 "And you shall destroy their altars, break their *sacred* pillars, and burn their wooden images with fire; you shall cut down the carved images of their gods and destroy their names from that place.

4 "You shall not worship the LORD your God *with* such *things.*

5 "But you shall seek the place where the LORD your God chooses, out of all your tribes, to put His name for His dwelling place; and there you shall go.

6 "There you shall take your burnt offerings, your sacrifices, your tithes, the heave offerings of your hand, your vowed offerings, your freewill offerings, and the firstborn of your herds and flocks.

7 "And there you shall eat before the LORD your God, and you shall rejoice in all to which you have put your hand, you and your households, in which the LORD your God has blessed you.

8 "You shall not at all do as we are doing here today—every man doing whatever *is* right in his own eyes—

9 "for as yet you have not come to the rest and the inheritance which the LORD your God is giving you.

10 "But *when* you cross over the Jordan and dwell in the land which the LORD your God is giving you to inherit, and He gives you rest from all your enemies round about, so that you dwell in safety,

11 "then there will be the place where the LORD your God chooses to make His name abide. There you shall bring all that I command you: your burnt offerings, your sacrifices, your tithes, the heave offerings of your hand, and all your choice offerings which you vow to the LORD.

12 "And you shall rejoice before the LORD your God, you and your sons and your daughters, your male and female servants, and the Lē′vīte who *is* within your gates, since he has no portion nor inheritance with you.

13 "Take heed to yourself that you do

not offer your burnt offerings in every place that you see;

14 "but in the place which the LORD chooses, in one of your tribes, there you shall offer your burnt offerings, and there you shall do all that I command you.

15 "However, you may slaughter and eat meat within all your gates, whatever your heart desires, according to the blessing of the LORD your God which He has given you; the unclean and the clean may eat of it, of the gazelle and the deer alike.

16 "Only you shall not eat the blood; you shall pour it on the earth like water.

17 "You may not eat within your gates the tithe of your grain or your new wine or your oil, of the firstborn of your herd or your flock, of any of your offerings which you vow, of your freewill offerings, or of the heave offering of your hand.

18 "But you must eat them before the LORD your God in the place which the LORD your God chooses, you and your son and your daughter, your male servant and your female servant, and the Lē'vīte who is within your gates; and you shall rejoice before the LORD your God in all to which you put your hands.

19 "Take heed to yourself that you do not forsake the Lē'vīte as long as you live in your land.

20 "When the LORD your God enlarges your border as He has promised you, and you say, 'Let me eat meat,' because you long to eat meat, you may eat as much meat as your heart desires.

21 "If the place where the LORD your God chooses to put His name is too far from you, then you may slaughter from your herd and from your flock which the LORD has given you, just as I have commanded you, and you may eat within your gates as much as your heart desires.

22 "Just as the gazelle and the deer are eaten, so you may eat them; the unclean and the clean alike may eat them.

23 "Only be sure that you do not eat the blood, for the blood is the life; you may not eat the life with the meat.

24 "You shall not eat it; you shall pour it on the earth like water.

25 "You shall not eat it, that it may go well with you and your children after you, when you do what is right in the sight of the LORD.

26 "Only the holy things which you have, and your vowed offerings, you shall take and go to the place which the LORD chooses.

27 "And you shall offer your burnt offerings, the meat and the blood, on the altar of the LORD your God; and the blood of your sacrifices shall be poured out on the altar of the LORD your God, and you shall eat the meat.

28 "Observe and obey all these words which I command you, that it may go well with you and your children after you forever, when you do what is good and right in the sight of the LORD your God.

BEWARE OF FALSE GODS

29 "When the LORD your God cuts off from before you the nations which you go to dispossess, and you displace them and dwell in their land,

30 "take heed to yourself that you are not ensnared to follow them, after they are destroyed from before you, and that you do not inquire after their gods, saying, 'How did these nations serve their gods? I also will do likewise.'

31 "You shall not worship the LORD your God in that way; for every abomination to the LORD which He hates they have done to their gods;

for they burn even their sons and daughters in the fire to their gods.

32 "Whatever I command you, be careful to observe it; you shall not add to it nor take away from it.

PUNISHMENT OF APOSTATES

13 "If there arises among you a prophet or a dreamer of dreams, and he gives you a sign or a wonder,

2 "and the sign or the wonder comes to pass, of which he spoke to you, saying, 'Let us go after other gods'—which you have not known—'and let us serve them,'

3 "you shall not listen to the words of that prophet or that dreamer of dreams, for the LORD your God is testing you to know whether you love the LORD your God with all your heart and with all your soul.

4 "You shall walk after the LORD your God and fear Him, and keep His commandments and obey His voice; you shall serve Him and hold fast to Him.

5 "But that prophet or that dreamer of dreams shall be put to death, because he has spoken in order to turn *you* away from the LORD your God, who brought you out of the land of Egypt and redeemed you from the house of bondage, to entice you from the way in which the LORD your God commanded you to walk. So you shall put away the evil from your midst.

6 "If your brother, the son of your mother, your son or your daughter, the wife of your bosom, or your friend who is as your own soul, secretly entices you, saying, 'Let us go and serve other gods,' which you have not known, neither you nor your fathers,

7 "of the gods of the people which *are* all around you, near to you or far off from you, from *one* end of the earth to the *other* end of the earth,

8 "you shall not consent to him or listen to him, nor shall your eye pity him, nor shall you spare him or conceal him;

9 "but you shall surely kill him; your hand shall be first against him to put him to death, and afterward the hand of all the people.

10 "And you shall stone him with stones until he dies, because he sought to entice you away from the LORD your God, who brought you out of the land of Egypt, from the house of bondage.

11 "So all Israel shall hear and fear, and not again do such wickedness as this among you.

12 "If you hear someone in one of your cities, which the LORD your God gives you to dwell in, saying,

13 'Corrupt men have gone out from among you and enticed the inhabitants of their city, saying, "Let us go and serve other gods" '—which you have not known—

14 "then you shall inquire, search out, and ask diligently. And *if it is* indeed true *and* certain *that* such an abomination was committed among you,

15 "you shall surely strike the inhabitants of that city with the edge of the sword, utterly destroying it, all that is in it and its livestock—with the edge of the sword.

16 "And you shall gather all its plunder into the middle of the street, and completely burn with fire the city and all its plunder, for the LORD your God. It shall be a heap forever; it shall not be built again.

17 "So none of the accursed things shall remain in your hand, that the LORD may turn from the fierceness of His anger and show you mercy, have compassion on you and multiply you, just as He swore to your fathers,

FOLLOW ME Deuteronomy 13:6–8

"Follow me," a friend says. But you know he wants you to do something you shouldn't do. "Follow me," another friend says. But God would not be pleased if you did. "Follow me," another friend says. But your parents would not be pleased if you did. "Follow Me," Jesus says. Should you?

1. Why should you not follow the wrong friends?
2. Should you follow your parents and what they say? Why?
3. Should you follow God and what He says? Why?

For more on *What Should I Do?* turn to page 301
For more on *Obeying* turn to page 428

18 "because you have listened to the voice of the LORD your God, to keep all His commandments which I command you today, to do *what is* right in the eyes of the LORD your God.

IMPROPER MOURNING

14 "You *are* the children of the LORD your God; you shall not cut yourselves nor shave the front of your head for the dead.
2 "For you *are* a holy people to the LORD your God, and the LORD has chosen you to be a people for Himself, a special treasure above all the peoples who *are* on the face of the earth.

CLEAN AND UNCLEAN MEAT

3 "You shall not eat any detestable thing.
4 "These *are* the animals which you may eat: the ox, the sheep, the goat,
5 "the deer, the gazelle, the roe deer, the wild goat, the mountain goat,*a* the antelope, and the mountain sheep.
6 "And you may eat every animal with cloven hooves, having the hoof split into two parts, *and that* chews the cud, among the animals.
7 "Nevertheless, of those that chew the cud or have cloven hooves, you shall not eat, *such as* these: the camel, the hare, and the rock hyrax; for they chew the cud but do not have cloven hooves; they *are* unclean for you.
8 "Also the swine is unclean for you, because it has cloven hooves, yet *does* not *chew* the cud; you shall not eat their flesh or touch their dead carcasses.
9 "These you may eat of all that *are* in the waters: you may eat all that have fins and scales.
10 "And whatever does not have fins

and scales you shall not eat; it *is* unclean for you.
11 "All clean birds you may eat.
12 "But these you shall not eat: the eagle, the vulture, the buzzard,
13 "the red kite, the falcon, and the kite after their kinds;
14 "every raven after its kind;
15 "the ostrich, the short-eared owl, the sea gull, and the hawk after their kinds;
16 "the little owl, the screech owl, the white owl,
17 "the jackdaw, the carrion vulture, the fisher owl,
18 "the stork, the heron after its kind, and the hoopoe and the bat.
19 "Also every creeping thing that flies is unclean for you; they shall not be eaten.
20 "You may eat all clean birds.
21 "You shall not eat anything that dies *of itself;* you may give it to the alien who *is* within your gates, that he may eat it, or you may sell it to a foreigner; for you *are* a holy people to the LORD your God. You shall not boil a young goat in its mother's milk.

TITHING PRINCIPLES

22 "You shall truly tithe all the increase of your grain that the field produces year by year.
23 "And you shall eat before the LORD your God, in the place where He chooses to make His name abide, the tithe of your grain and your new wine and your oil, of the firstborn of your herds and your flocks, that you may learn to fear the LORD your God always.
24 "But if the journey is too long for you, so that you are not able to carry *the tithe, or* if the place where the LORD your God chooses to put His

14:5 *a*Or *addax*

name is too far from you, when the LORD your God has blessed you,

25 "then you shall exchange *it* for money, take the money in your hand, and go to the place which the LORD your God chooses.

26 "And you shall spend that money for whatever your heart desires: for oxen or sheep, for wine or similar drink, for whatever your heart desires; you shall eat there before the LORD your God, and you shall rejoice, you and your household.

27 "You shall not forsake the Lē′vīte who *is* within your gates, for he has no part nor inheritance with you.

28 "At the end of *every* third year you shall bring out the tithe of your produce of that year and store *it* up within your gates.

29 "And the Lē′vīte, because he has no portion nor inheritance with you, and the stranger and the fatherless and the widow who *are* within your gates, may come and eat and be satisfied, that the LORD your God may bless you in all the work of your hand which you do.

DEBTS CANCELED EVERY SEVEN YEARS

15 "At the end of *every* seven years you shall grant a release *of debts*.

2 "And this *is* the form of the release: Every creditor who has lent *anything* to his neighbor shall release *it;* he shall not require *it* of his neighbor or his brother, because it is called the LORD's release.

3 "Of a foreigner you may require *it;* but you shall give up your claim to what is owed by your brother,

4 "except when there may be no poor among you; for the LORD will greatly bless you in the land which the LORD your God is giving you to possess *as* an inheritance—

5 "only if you carefully obey the voice of the LORD your God, to observe with care all these commandments which I command you today.

6 "For the LORD your God will bless you just as He promised you; you shall lend to many nations, but you shall not borrow; you shall reign over many nations, but they shall not reign over you.

GENEROSITY TO THE POOR

7 "If there is among you a poor man of your brethren, within any of the gates in your land which the LORD your God is giving you, you shall not harden your heart nor shut your hand from your poor brother,

8 "but you shall open your hand wide to him and willingly lend him sufficient for his need, whatever he needs.

9 "Beware lest there be a wicked thought in your heart, saying, 'The seventh year, the year of release, is at hand,' and your eye be evil against your poor brother and you give him nothing, and he cry out to the LORD against you, and it become sin among you.

10 "You shall surely give to him, and your heart should not be grieved when you give to him, because for this thing the LORD your God will bless you in all your works and in all to which you put your hand.

11 "For the poor will never cease from the land; therefore I command you, saying, 'You shall open your hand wide to your brother, to your poor and your needy, in your land.'

THE LAW CONCERNING BONDSERVANTS

12 "If your brother, a Hebrew man, or a Hebrew woman, is sold to you and serves you six years, then in the

Values

GIVING Deuteronomy 15:7, 8

What Shall I Give?

A poor child has no toys. Which of your toys would you give him? Would you give him one that is broken or one that isn't? Would you give him an old toy or a newer one? Would you give him one you don't like or one that you do like? Would you give him one that you think he would like or one that he probably would not like? What kind of giving is your giving?

1. What is this boy giving another poor boy? How do you know that boy is poor? Why do you think the first boy is not poor?
2. Do you think this is a special gift? Or is it something the little boy really doesn't want?
3. Why do you think this boy is giving something special to the poor boy? Why not give something junky?

For more on *Values* turn to page 321
For more on *Giving* turn to page 498

seventh year you shall let him go free from you.

13 "And when you send him away free from you, you shall not let him go away empty-handed;

14 "you shall supply him liberally from your flock, from your threshing floor, and from your winepress. *From what* the LORD has blessed you with, you shall give to him.

15 "You shall remember that you were a slave in the land of Egypt, and the LORD your God redeemed you; therefore I command you this thing today.

16 "And if it happens that he says to you, 'I will not go away from you,' because he loves you and your house, since he prospers with you,

17 "then you shall take an awl and thrust *it* through his ear to the door, and he shall be your servant forever. Also to your female servant you shall do likewise.

18 "It shall not seem hard to you when you send him away free from you; for he has been worth a double hired servant in serving you six years. Then the LORD your God will bless you in all that you do.

THE LAW CONCERNING FIRSTBORN ANIMALS

19 "All the firstborn males that come from your herd and your flock you shall sanctify to the LORD your God; you shall do no work with the firstborn of your herd, nor shear the firstborn of your flock.

20 "You and your household shall eat *it* before the LORD your God year by year in the place which the LORD chooses.

21 "But if there is a defect in it, *if it is* lame or blind *or has* any serious defect, you shall not sacrifice it to the LORD your God.

22 "You may eat it within your gates;

the unclean and the clean *person* alike *may eat it,* as *if it were* a gazelle or a deer.

23 "Only you shall not eat its blood; you shall pour it on the ground like water.

THE PASSOVER REVIEWED

16 "Observe the month of Ā'bib, and keep the Passover to the LORD your God, for in the month of Ā'bib the LORD your God brought you out of Egypt by night.

2 "Therefore you shall sacrifice the Passover to the LORD your God, from the flock and the herd, in the place where the LORD chooses to put His name.

3 "You shall eat no leavened bread with it; seven days you shall eat unleavened bread with it, *that is,* the bread of affliction (for you came out of the land of Egypt in haste), that you may remember the day in which you came out of the land of Egypt all the days of your life.

4 "And no leaven shall be seen among you in all your territory for seven days, nor shall *any* of the meat which you sacrifice the first day at twilight remain overnight until morning.

5 "You may not sacrifice the Passover within any of your gates which the LORD your God gives you;

6 "but at the place where the LORD your God chooses to make His name abide, there you shall sacrifice the Passover at twilight, at the going down of the sun, at the time you came out of Egypt.

7 "And you shall roast and eat *it* in the place which the LORD your God chooses, and in the morning you shall turn and go to your tents.

8 "Six days you shall eat unleavened bread, and on the seventh day

there *shall be* a sacred assembly to the LORD your God. You shall do no work *on it*.

THE FEAST OF WEEKS REVIEWED

9 "You shall count seven weeks for yourself; begin to count the seven weeks from *the time* you begin *to put* the sickle to the grain.

10 "Then you shall keep the Feast of Weeks to the LORD your God with the tribute of a freewill offering from your hand, which you shall give as the LORD your God blesses you.

11 "You shall rejoice before the LORD your God, you and your son and your daughter, your male servant and your female servant, the Lē'vīte who *is* within your gates, the stranger and the fatherless and the widow who *are* among you, at the place where the LORD your God chooses to make His name abide.

12 "And you shall remember that you were a slave in Egypt, and you shall be careful to observe these statutes.

THE FEAST OF TABERNACLES REVIEWED

13 "You shall observe the Feast of Tabernacles seven days, when you have gathered from your threshing floor and from your winepress.

14 "And you shall rejoice in your feast, you and your son and your daughter, your male servant and your female servant and the Lē'vīte, the stranger and the fatherless and the widow, who *are* within your gates.

15 "Seven days you shall keep a sacred feast to the LORD your God in the place which the LORD chooses, because the LORD your God will bless you in all your produce and in all the work of your hands, so that you surely rejoice.

16 "Three times a year all your males shall appear before the LORD your God in the place which He chooses: at the Feast of Unleavened Bread, at the Feast of Weeks, and at the Feast of Tabernacles; and they shall not appear before the LORD empty-handed.

17 "Every man *shall give* as he is able, according to the blessing of the LORD your God which He has given you.

JUSTICE MUST BE ADMINISTERED

18 "You shall appoint judges and officers in all your gates, which the LORD your God gives you, according to your tribes, and they shall judge the people with just judgment.

19 "You shall not pervert justice; you shall not show partiality, nor take a bribe, for a bribe blinds the eyes of the wise and twists the words of the righteous.

20 "You shall follow what is altogether just, that you may live and inherit the land which the LORD your God is giving you.

21 "You shall not plant for yourself any tree, as a wooden image, near the altar which you build for yourself to the LORD your God.

22 "You shall not set up a sacred pillar, which the LORD your God hates.

17 "You shall not sacrifice to the LORD your God a bull or sheep which has any blemish *or* defect, for that *is* an abomination to the LORD your God.

2 "If there is found among you, within any of your gates which the LORD your God gives you, a man or a woman who has been wicked in the sight of the LORD your God, in transgressing His covenant,

3 "who has gone and served other gods and worshiped them, either the sun or moon or any of the host of heaven, which I have not commanded,

4 "and it is told you, and you hear *of it,* then you shall inquire diligently. And if *it is* indeed true *and* certain that such an abomination has been committed in Israel,

5 "then you shall bring out to your gates that man or woman who has committed that wicked thing, and shall stone to death that man or woman with stones.

6 "Whoever is deserving of death shall be put to death on the testimony of two or three witnesses; he shall not be put to death on the testimony of one witness.

7 "The hands of the witnesses shall be the first against him to put him to death, and afterward the hands of all the people. So you shall put away the evil from among you.

8 "If a matter arises which is too hard for you to judge, between degrees of guilt for bloodshed, between one judgment or another, or between one punishment or another, matters of controversy within your gates, then you shall arise and go up to the place which the LORD your God chooses.

9 "And you shall come to the priests, the Lē'vītes, and to the judge *there* in those days, and inquire *of them;* they shall pronounce upon you the sentence of judgment.

10 "You shall do according to the sentence which they pronounce upon you in that place which the LORD chooses. And you shall be careful to do according to all that they order you.

11 "According to the sentence of the law in which they instruct you, according to the judgment which they tell you, you shall do; you shall not turn aside *to* the right hand or *to* the left from the sentence which they pronounce upon you.

12 "Now the man who acts presumptuously and will not heed the priest who stands to minister there before the LORD your God, or the judge, that man shall die. So you shall put away the evil from Israel.

13 "And all the people shall hear and fear, and no longer act presumptuously.

PRINCIPLES GOVERNING KINGS

14 "When you come to the land which the LORD your God is giving you, and possess it and dwell in it, and say, 'I will set a king over me like all the nations that *are* around me,'

15 "you shall surely set a king over you whom the LORD your God chooses; *one* from among your brethren you shall set as king over you; you may not set a foreigner over you, who *is* not your brother.

16 "But he shall not multiply horses for himself, nor cause the people to return to Egypt to multiply horses, for the LORD has said to you, 'You shall not return that way again.'

17 "Neither shall he multiply wives for himself, lest his heart turn away; nor shall he greatly multiply silver and gold for himself.

18 "Also it shall be, when he sits on the throne of his kingdom, that he shall write for himself a copy of this law in a book, from *the one* before the priests, the Lē'vītes.

19 "And it shall be with him, and he shall read it all the days of his life, that he may learn to fear the LORD his God and be careful to observe all the words of this law and these statutes,

20 "that his heart may not be lifted above his brethren, that he may not turn aside from the commandment *to* the right hand or *to* the left, and that

he may prolong *his* days in his kingdom, he and his children in the midst of Israel.

THE PORTION OF THE PRIESTS AND LEVITES

18 "The priests, the Lē'vītes—all the tribe of Levi—shall have no part nor inheritance with Israel; they shall eat the offerings of the LORD made by fire, and His portion.

2 "Therefore they shall have no inheritance among their brethren; the LORD is their inheritance, as He said to them.

3 "And this shall be the priest's due from the people, from those who offer a sacrifice, whether *it is* bull or sheep: they shall give to the priest the shoulder, the cheeks, and the stomach.

4 "The firstfruits of your grain and your new wine and your oil, and the first of the fleece of your sheep, you shall give him.

5 "For the LORD your God has chosen him out of all your tribes to stand to minister in the name of the LORD, him and his sons forever.

6 "So if a Lē'vīte comes from any of your gates, from where he dwells among all Israel, and comes with all the desire of his mind to the place which the LORD chooses,

7 "then he may serve in the name of the LORD his God as all his brethren the Lē'vītes *do,* who stand there before the LORD.

8 "They shall have equal portions to eat, besides what comes from the sale of his inheritance.

AVOID WICKED CUSTOMS

9 "When you come into the land which the LORD your God is giving you, you shall not learn to follow the abominations of those nations.

10 "There shall not be found among you *anyone* who makes his son or his daughter pass through the fire, *or one* who practices witchcraft, *or* a soothsayer, or one who interprets omens, or a sorcerer,

11 "or one who conjures spells, or a medium, or a spiritist, or one who calls up the dead.

12 "For all who do these things *are* an abomination to the LORD, and because of these abominations the LORD your God drives them out from before you.

13 "You shall be blameless before the LORD your God.

14 "For these nations which you will dispossess listened to soothsayers and diviners; but as for you, the LORD your God has not appointed such for you.

A NEW PROPHET LIKE MOSES

15 "The LORD your God will raise up for you a Prophet like me from your midst, from your brethren. Him you shall hear,

16 "according to all you desired of the LORD your God in Hō'reb in the day of the assembly, saying, 'Let me not hear again the voice of the LORD my God, nor let me see this great fire anymore, lest I die.'

17 "And the LORD said to me: 'What they have spoken is good.

18 'I will raise up for them a Prophet like you from among their brethren, and will put My words in His mouth, and He shall speak to them all that I command Him.

19 'And it shall be *that* whoever will not hear My words, which He speaks in My name, I will require *it* of him.

20 'But the prophet who presumes to speak a word in My name, which I have not commanded him to speak, or who speaks in the name of other gods, that prophet shall die.'

21 "And if you say in your heart, 'How shall we know the word which the LORD has not spoken?'—
22 "when a prophet speaks in the name of the LORD, if the thing does not happen or come to pass, that *is* the thing which the LORD has not spoken; the prophet has spoken it presumptuously; you shall not be afraid of him.

THREE CITIES OF REFUGE

19 "When the LORD your God has cut off the nations whose land the LORD your God is giving you, and you dispossess them and dwell in their cities and in their houses,
2 "you shall separate three cities for yourself in the midst of your land which the LORD your God is giving you to possess.
3 "You shall prepare roads for yourself, and divide into three parts the territory of your land which the LORD your God is giving you to inherit, that any manslayer may flee there.
4 "And this *is* the case of the manslayer who flees there, that he may live: Whoever kills his neighbor unintentionally, not having hated him in time past—
5 "as when *a man* goes to the woods with his neighbor to cut timber, and his hand swings a stroke with the ax to cut down the tree, and the head slips from the handle and strikes his neighbor so that he dies—he shall flee to one of these cities and live;
6 "lest the avenger of blood, while his anger is hot, pursue the manslayer and overtake him, because the way is long, and kill him, though he *was* not deserving of death, since he had not hated the victim in time past.
7 "Therefore I command you, say-ing, 'You shall separate three cities for yourself.'
8 "Now if the LORD your God enlarges your territory, as He swore to your fathers, and gives you the land which He promised to give to your fathers,
9 "and if you keep all these commandments and do them, which I command you today, to love the LORD your God and to walk always in His ways, then you shall add three more cities for yourself besides these three,
10 "lest innocent blood be shed in the midst of your land which the LORD your God is giving you *as* an inheritance, and *thus* guilt of bloodshed be upon you.
11 "But if anyone hates his neighbor, lies in wait for him, rises against him and strikes him mortally, so that he dies, and he flees to one of these cities,
12 "then the elders of his city shall send and bring him from there, and deliver him over to the hand of the avenger of blood, that he may die.
13 "Your eye shall not pity him, but you shall put away *the guilt of* innocent blood from Israel, that it may go well with you.

PROPERTY BOUNDARIES

14 "You shall not remove your neighbor's landmark, which the men of old have set, in your inheritance which you will inherit in the land that the LORD your God is giving you to possess.

THE LAW CONCERNING WITNESSES

15 "One witness shall not rise against a man concerning any iniquity or any sin that he commits; by the mouth of two or three witnesses the matter shall be established.
16 "If a false witness rises against

any man to testify against him of wrongdoing,

17 "then both men in the controversy shall stand before the LORD, before the priests and the judges who serve in those days.

18 "And the judges shall make careful inquiry, and indeed, *if* the witness *is* a false witness, who has testified falsely against his brother,

19 "then you shall do to him as he thought to have done to his brother; so you shall put away the evil from among you.

20 "And those who remain shall hear and fear, and hereafter they shall not again commit such evil among you.

21 "Your eye shall not pity: life *shall be* for life, eye for eye, tooth for tooth, hand for hand, foot for foot.

PRINCIPLES GOVERNING WARFARE

20 "When you go out to battle against your enemies, and see horses and chariots *and* people more numerous than you, do not be afraid of them; for the LORD your God *is* with you, who brought you up from the land of Egypt.

2 "So it shall be, when you are on the verge of battle, that the priest shall approach and speak to the people.

3 "And he shall say to them, 'Hear, O Israel: Today you are on the verge of battle with your enemies. Do not let your heart faint, do not be afraid, and do not tremble or be terrified because of them;

4 'for the LORD your God *is* He who goes with you, to fight for you against your enemies, to save you.'

5 "Then the officers shall speak to the people, saying: 'What man *is there* who has built a new house and has not dedicated it? Let him go and return to his house, lest he die in the battle and another man dedicate it.

6 'Also what man *is there* who has planted a vineyard and has not eaten of it? Let him go and return to his house, lest he die in the battle and another man eat of it.

7 'And what man *is there* who is betrothed to a woman and has not married her? Let him go and return to his house, lest he die in the battle and another man marry her.'

8 "The officers shall speak further to the people, and say, 'What man *is there who is* fearful and fainthearted? Let him go and return to his house, lest the heart of his brethren faint[a] like his heart.'

9 "And so it shall be, when the officers have finished speaking to the people, that they shall make captains of the armies to lead the people.

10 "When you go near a city to fight against it, then proclaim an offer of peace to it.

11 "And it shall be that if they accept your offer of peace, and open to you, then all the people *who are* found in it shall be placed under tribute to you, and serve you.

12 "Now if *the city* will not make peace with you, but makes war against you, then you shall besiege it.

13 "And when the LORD your God delivers it into your hands, you shall strike every male in it with the edge of the sword.

14 "But the women, the little ones, the livestock, and all that is in the city, all its spoil, you shall plunder for yourself; and you shall eat the enemies' plunder which the LORD your God gives you.

15 "Thus you shall do to all the cities *which are* very far from you, which *are* not of the cities of these nations.

16 "But of the cities of these peoples which the LORD your God gives you

---

20:8 [a]Following Masoretic Text and Targum; Samaritan Pentateuch, Septuagint, Syriac, and Vulgate read *lest he make his brother's heart faint.*

as an inheritance, you shall let nothing that breathes remain alive,

17 "but you shall utterly destroy them: the Hit'tīte and the Am'o·rīte and the Cā'naan·īte and the Per'-iz·zīte and the Hī'vīte and the Jeb'-ū·sīte, just as the LORD your God has commanded you,

18 "lest they teach you to do according to all their abominations which they have done for their gods, and you sin against the LORD your God.

19 "When you besiege a city for a long time, while making war against it to take it, you shall not destroy its trees by wielding an ax against them; if you can eat of them, do not cut them down to use in the siege, for the tree of the field *is* man's *food*.

20 "Only the trees which you know *are* not trees for food you may destroy and cut down, to build siegeworks against the city that makes war with you, until it is subdued.

THE LAW CONCERNING UNSOLVED MURDER

21 "If *anyone* is found slain, lying in the field in the land which the LORD your God is giving you to possess, *and* it is not known who killed him,

2 "then your elders and your judges shall go out and measure *the distance* from the slain man to the surrounding cities.

3 "And it shall be *that* the elders of the city nearest to the slain man will take a heifer which has not been worked *and* which has not pulled with a yoke.

4 "The elders of that city shall bring the heifer down to a valley with flowing water, which is neither plowed nor sown, and they shall break the heifer's neck there in the valley.

5 "Then the priests, the sons of Levi, shall come near, for the LORD your God has chosen them to minister to Him and to bless in the name of the LORD; by their word every controversy and every assault shall be *settled*.

6 "And all the elders of that city nearest to the slain *man* shall wash their hands over the heifer whose neck was broken in the valley.

7 "Then they shall answer and say, 'Our hands have not shed this blood, nor have our eyes seen *it*.

8 'Provide atonement, O LORD, for Your people Israel, whom You have redeemed, and do not lay innocent blood to the charge of Your people Israel.' And atonement shall be provided on their behalf for the blood.

9 "So you shall put away the *guilt of* innocent blood from among you when you do *what is* right in the sight of the LORD.

FEMALE CAPTIVES

10 "When you go out to war against your enemies, and the LORD your God delivers them into your hand, and you take them captive,

11 "and you see among the captives a beautiful woman, and desire her and would take her for your wife,

12 "then you shall bring her home to your house, and she shall shave her head and trim her nails.

13 "She shall put off the clothes of her captivity, remain in your house, and mourn her father and her mother a full month; after that you may go in to her and be her husband, and she shall be your wife.

14 "And it shall be, if you have no delight in her, then you shall set her free, but you certainly shall not sell her for money; you shall not treat her brutally, because you have humbled her.

FIRSTBORN INHERITANCE RIGHTS

15 "If a man has two wives, one loved and the other unloved, and they have borne him children, *both* the loved and the unloved, and *if* the firstborn son is of her who is unloved,
16 "then it shall be, on the day he bequeaths his possessions to his sons, *that* he must not bestow firstborn status on the son of the loved wife in preference to the son of the unloved, the *true* firstborn.
17 "But he shall acknowledge the son of the unloved wife *as* the firstborn by giving him a double portion of all that he has, for he *is* the beginning of his strength; the right of the firstborn *is* his.

THE REBELLIOUS SON

18 "If a man has a stubborn and rebellious son who will not obey the voice of his father or the voice of his mother, and *who,* when they have chastened him, will not heed them,
19 "then his father and his mother shall take hold of him and bring him out to the elders of his city, to the gate of his city.
20 "And they shall say to the elders of his city, 'This son of ours is stubborn and rebellious; he will not obey our voice; he is a glutton and a drunkard.'
21 "Then all the men of his city shall stone him to death with stones; so you shall put away the evil from among you, and all Israel shall hear and fear.

MISCELLANEOUS LAWS

22 "If a man has committed a sin deserving of death, and he is put to death, and you hang him on a tree,
23 "his body shall not remain overnight on the tree, but you shall surely bury him that day, so that you do not defile the land which the LORD your God is giving you *as* an inheritance; for he who is hanged *is* accursed of God.

22 "You shall not see your brother's ox or his sheep going astray, and hide yourself from them; you shall certainly bring them back to your brother.
2 "And if your brother *is* not near you, or if you do not know him, then you shall bring it to your own house, and it shall remain with you until your brother seeks it; then you shall restore it to him.
3 "You shall do the same with his donkey, and so shall you do with his garment; with any lost thing of your brother's, which he has lost and you have found, you shall do likewise; you must not hide yourself.
4 "You shall not see your brother's donkey or his ox fall down along the road, and hide yourself from them; you shall surely help him lift *them* up again.
5 "A woman shall not wear anything that pertains to a man, nor shall a man put on a woman's garment, for all who do so *are* an abomination to the LORD your God.
6 "If a bird's nest happens to be before you along the way, in any tree or on the ground, with young ones or eggs, with the mother sitting on the young or on the eggs, you shall not take the mother with the young;
7 "you shall surely let the mother go, and take the young for yourself, that it may be well with you and *that* you may prolong *your* days.
8 "When you build a new house, then you shall make a parapet for your roof, that you may not bring guilt of bloodshed on your household if anyone falls from it.
9 "You shall not sow your vineyard

What Should I Do?

SHOULD I GAIN FROM YOUR LOSS? Deuteronomy 22:1–3

Someone has a car accident. Her purse is lying on the road. Should you take it? Someone has dropped some money. You know who dropped it. Should you keep it? Someone has lost some school notes. You know where they are. But you're trying to make a better grade. If you tell your schoolmate where they are, this person will make a better grade. But should you gain from this person's loss? What should you do?

1. Would you really want to gain from someone's loss? Why not?
2. Would you rather lose to help someone else gain? Why?
3. Would you rather have less if mother or father could have more? Or would you rather have more if mother or father had to have less?

For more on *What Should I Do?* turn to page 317
For more on *Honesty* turn to page 1005

with different kinds of seed, lest the yield of the seed which you have sown and the fruit of your vineyard be defiled.

10 "You shall not plow with an ox and a donkey together.

11 "You shall not wear a garment of different sorts, *such as* wool and linen mixed together.

12 "You shall make tassels on the four corners of the clothing with which you cover *yourself.*

LAWS OF SEXUAL MORALITY

13 "If any man takes a wife, and goes in to her, and detests her,

14 "and charges her with shameful conduct, and brings a bad name on her, and says, 'I took this woman, and when I came to her I found she *was* not a virgin,'

15 "then the father and mother of the young woman shall take and bring out *the evidence of* the young woman's virginity to the elders of the city at the gate.

16 "And the young woman's father shall say to the elders, 'I gave my daughter to this man as wife, and he detests her.

17 'Now he has charged her with shameful conduct, saying, "I found your daughter *was* not a virgin," and yet these *are the evidences of* my daughter's virginity.' And they shall spread the cloth before the elders of the city.

18 "Then the elders of that city shall take that man and punish him;

19 "and they shall fine him one hundred *shekels* of silver and give *them* to the father of the young woman, because he has brought a bad name on a virgin of Israel. And she shall be his wife; he cannot divorce her all his days.

20 "But if the thing is true, *and evi-* dences *of* virginity are not found for the young woman,

21 "then they shall bring out the young woman to the door of her father's house, and the men of her city shall stone her to death with stones, because she has done a disgraceful thing in Israel, to play the harlot in her father's house. So you shall put away the evil from among you.

22 "If a man is found lying with a woman married to a husband, then both of them shall die—the man that lay with the woman, and the woman; so you shall put away the evil from Israel.

23 "If a young woman *who is* a virgin is betrothed to a husband, and a man finds her in the city and lies with her,

24 "then you shall bring them both out to the gate of that city, and you shall stone them to death with stones, the young woman because she did not cry out in the city, and the man because he humbled his neighbor's wife; so you shall put away the evil from among you.

25 "But if a man finds a betrothed young woman in the countryside, and the man forces her and lies with her, then only the man who lay with her shall die.

26 "But you shall do nothing to the young woman; *there is* in the young woman no sin *deserving* of death, for just as when a man rises against his neighbor and kills him, even so *is* this matter.

27 "For he found her in the countryside, *and* the betrothed young woman cried out, but *there was* no one to save her.

28 "If a man finds a young woman *who is* a virgin, who is not betrothed, and he seizes her and lies with her, and they are found out,

29 "then the man who lay with her shall give to the young woman's father fifty *shekels* of silver, and she

shall be his wife because he has humbled her; he shall not be permitted to divorce her all his days.

30 "A man shall not take his father's wife, nor uncover his father's bed.

THOSE EXCLUDED FROM THE CONGREGATION

23 "He who is emasculated by crushing or mutilation shall not enter the assembly of the LORD.

2 "One of illegitimate birth shall not enter the assembly of the LORD; even to the tenth generation none of his *descendants* shall enter the assembly of the LORD.

3 "An Am′mon·īte or Mō′ab·īte shall not enter the assembly of the LORD; even to the tenth generation none of his *descendants* shall enter the assembly of the LORD forever,

4 "because they did not meet you with bread and water on the road when you came out of Egypt, and because they hired against you Bā′laam the son of Bē′or from Pē′thor of Mes·o·po·tā′mi·a,ᵃ to curse you.

5 "Nevertheless the LORD your God would not listen to Bā′laam, but the LORD your God turned the curse into a blessing for you, because the LORD your God loves you.

6 "You shall not seek their peace nor their prosperity all your days forever.

7 "You shall not abhor an Ē′dom·īte, for he *is* your brother. You shall not abhor an Egyptian, because you were an alien in his land.

8 "The children of the third generation born to them may enter the assembly of the LORD.

CLEANLINESS OF THE CAMP SITE

9 "When the army goes out against your enemies, then keep yourself from every wicked thing.

10 "If there is any man among you who becomes unclean by some occurrence in the night, then he shall go outside the camp; he shall not come inside the camp.

11 "But it shall be, when evening comes, that he shall wash with water; and when the sun sets, he may come into the camp.

12 "Also you shall have a place outside the camp, where you may go out;

13 "and you shall have an implement among your equipment, and when you sit down outside, you shall dig with it and turn and cover your refuse.

14 "For the LORD your God walks in the midst of your camp, to deliver you and give your enemies over to you; therefore your camp shall be holy, that He may see no unclean thing among you, and turn away from you.

MISCELLANEOUS LAWS

15 "You shall not give back to his master the slave who has escaped from his master to you.

16 "He may dwell with you in your midst, in the place which he chooses within one of your gates, where it seems best to him; you shall not oppress him.

17 "There shall be no *ritual* harlotᵃ of the daughters of Israel, or a pervertedᵇ one of the sons of Israel.

18 "You shall not bring the wages of a harlot or the price of a dog to the house of the LORD your God for any vowed offering, for both of these *are* an abomination to the LORD your God.

19 "You shall not charge interest to your brother—interest on money *or*

23:4 ᵃHebrew *Aram Naharaim*   23:17 ᵃHebrew *qedeshah*, feminine of *qadesh* (see note b)   ᵇHebrew *qadesh*, that is, one practicing sodomy and prostitution in religious rituals

food *or* anything that is lent out at interest.

20 "To a foreigner you may charge interest, but to your brother you shall not charge interest, that the LORD your God may bless you in all to which you set your hand in the land which you are entering to possess.

21 "When you make a vow to the LORD your God, you shall not delay to pay it; for the LORD your God will surely require it of you, and it would be sin to you.

22 "But if you abstain from vowing, it shall not be sin to you.

23 "That which has gone from your lips you shall keep and perform, for you voluntarily vowed to the LORD your God what you have promised with your mouth.

24 "When you come into your neighbor's vineyard, you may eat your fill of grapes at your pleasure, but you shall not put *any* in your container.

25 "When you come into your neighbor's standing grain, you may pluck the heads with your hand, but you shall not use a sickle on your neighbor's standing grain.

LAW CONCERNING DIVORCE

24 "When a man takes a wife and marries her, and it happens that she finds no favor in his eyes because he has found some uncleanness in her, and he writes her a certificate of divorce, puts *it* in her hand, and sends her out of his house,

2 "when she has departed from his house, and goes and becomes another man's *wife,*

3 "*if* the latter husband detests her and writes her a certificate of divorce, puts *it* in her hand, and sends her out of his house, or if the latter husband dies who took her as his wife,

4 "*then* her former husband who divorced her must not take her back to be his wife after she has been defiled; for that *is* an abomination before the LORD, and you shall not bring sin on the land which the LORD your God is giving you *as* an inheritance.

MISCELLANEOUS LAWS

5 "When a man has taken a new wife, he shall not go out to war or be charged with any business; he shall be free at home one year, and bring happiness to his wife whom he has taken.

6 "No man shall take the lower or the upper millstone in pledge, for he takes *one's* living in pledge.

7 "If a man is found kidnapping any of his brethren of the children of Israel, and mistreats him or sells him, then that kidnapper shall die; and you shall put away the evil from among you.

8 "Take heed in an outbreak of leprosy, that you carefully observe and do according to all that the priests, the Lē′vītes, shall teach you; just as I commanded them, *so* you shall be careful to do.

9 "Remember what the LORD your God did to Miriam on the way when you came out of Egypt!

10 "When you lend your brother anything, you shall not go into his house to get his pledge.

11 "You shall stand outside, and the man to whom you lend shall bring the pledge out to you.

12 "And if the man *is* poor, you shall not keep his pledge overnight.

13 "You shall in any case return the pledge to him again when the sun goes down, that he may sleep in his own garment and bless you; and it shall be righteousness to you before the LORD your God.

14 "You shall not oppress a hired servant *who is* poor and needy, *whether*

one of your brethren or one of the aliens who *is* in your land within your gates.

15 "Each day you shall give *him* his wages, and not let the sun go down on it, for he *is* poor and has set his heart on it; lest he cry out against you to the LORD, and it be sin to you.

16 "Fathers shall not be put to death for *their* children, nor shall children be put to death for *their* fathers; a person shall be put to death for his own sin.

17 "You shall not pervert justice due the stranger or the fatherless, nor take a widow's garment as a pledge.

18 "But you shall remember that you were a slave in Egypt, and the LORD your God redeemed you from there; therefore I command you to do this thing.

19 "When you reap your harvest in your field, and forget a sheaf in the field, you shall not go back to get it; it shall be for the stranger, the fatherless, and the widow, that the LORD your God may bless you in all the work of your hands.

20 "When you beat your olive trees, you shall not go over the boughs again; it shall be for the stranger, the fatherless, and the widow.

21 "When you gather the grapes of your vineyard, you shall not glean *it* afterward; it shall be for the stranger, the fatherless, and the widow.

22 "And you shall remember that you were a slave in the land of Egypt; therefore I command you to do this thing.

25 "If there is a dispute between men, and they come to court, that *the judges* may judge them, and they justify the righteous and condemn the wicked,

2 "then it shall be, if the wicked man deserves to be beaten, that the judge will cause him to lie down and be beaten in his presence, according to his guilt, with a certain number of blows.

3 "Forty blows he may give him *and* no more, lest he should exceed this and beat him with many blows above these, and your brother be humiliated in your sight.

4 "You shall not muzzle an ox while it treads out *the grain.*

MARRIAGE DUTY OF THE SURVIVING BROTHER

5 "If brothers dwell together, and one of them dies and has no son, the widow of the dead man shall not be *married* to a stranger outside *the family;* her husband's brother shall go in to her, take her as his wife, and perform the duty of a husband's brother to her.

6 "And it shall be *that* the firstborn son which she bears will succeed to the name of his dead brother, that his name may not be blotted out of Israel.

7 "But if the man does not want to take his brother's wife, then let his brother's wife go up to the gate to the elders, and say, 'My husband's brother refuses to raise up a name to his brother in Israel; he will not perform the duty of my husband's brother.'

8 "Then the elders of his city shall call him and speak to him. But *if* he stands firm and says, 'I do not want to take her,'

9 "then his brother's wife shall come to him in the presence of the elders, remove his sandal from his foot, spit in his face, and answer and say, 'So shall it be done to the man who will not build up his brother's house.'

10 "And his name shall be called in Israel, 'The house of him who had his sandal removed.'

MISCELLANEOUS LAWS

11 "If *two* men fight together, and the wife of one draws near to rescue her husband from the hand of the one attacking him, and puts out her hand and seizes him by the genitals,

12 "then you shall cut off her hand; your eye shall not pity *her*.

13 "You shall not have in your bag differing weights, a heavy and a light.

14 "You shall not have in your house differing measures, a large and a small.

15 "You shall have a perfect and just weight, a perfect and just measure, that your days may be lengthened in the land which the LORD your God is giving you.

16 "For all who do such things, all who behave unrighteously, *are* an abomination to the LORD your God.

DESTROY THE AMALEKITES

17 "Remember what Am′a·lek did to you on the way as you were coming out of Egypt,

18 "how he met you on the way and attacked your rear ranks, all the stragglers at your rear, when you *were* tired and weary; and he did not fear God.

19 "Therefore it shall be, when the LORD your God has given you rest from your enemies all around, in the land which the LORD your God is giving you to possess *as* an inheritance, *that* you will blot out the remembrance of Am′a·lek from under heaven. You shall not forget.

OFFERINGS OF FIRSTFRUITS AND TITHES

26 "And it shall be, when you come into the land which the LORD your God is giving you *as* an inheritance, and you possess it and dwell in it,

2 "that you shall take some of the first of all the produce of the ground, which you shall bring from your land that the LORD your God is giving you, and put *it* in a basket and go to the place where the LORD your God chooses to make His name abide.

3 "And you shall go to the one who is priest in those days, and say to him, 'I declare today to the LORD your[a] God that I have come to the country which the LORD swore to our fathers to give us.'

4 "Then the priest shall take the basket out of your hand and set it down before the altar of the LORD your God.

5 "And you shall answer and say before the LORD your God: 'My father *was* a Syrian,[a] about to perish, and he went down to Egypt and dwelt there, few in number; and there he became a nation, great, mighty, and populous.

6 'But the Egyptians mistreated us, afflicted us, and laid hard bondage on us.

7 'Then we cried out to the LORD God of our fathers, and the LORD heard our voice and looked on our affliction and our labor and our oppression.

8 'So the LORD brought us out of Egypt with a mighty hand and with an outstretched arm, with great terror and with signs and wonders.

9 'He has brought us to this place and has given us this land, "a land flowing with milk and honey";[a]

10 'and now, behold, I have brought the firstfruits of the land which you, O LORD, have given me.' Then you shall set it before the LORD your God, and worship before the LORD your God.

26:3 [a]Septuagint reads *my*   26:5 [a]Or *Aramean*
26:9 [a]Exodus 3:8

11 "So you shall rejoice in every good *thing* which the LORD your God has given to you and your house, you and the Lē′vīte and the stranger who *is* among you.

12 "When you have finished laying aside all the tithe of your increase in the third year—the year of tithing—and have given *it* to the Lē′vīte, the stranger, the fatherless, and the widow, so that they may eat within your gates and be filled,

13 "then you shall say before the LORD your God: 'I have removed the holy *tithe* from *my* house, and also have given them to the Lē′vīte, the stranger, the fatherless, and the widow, according to all Your commandments which You have commanded me; I have not transgressed Your commandments, nor have I forgotten *them*.

14 'I have not eaten any of it when in mourning, nor have I removed *any* of it for an unclean *use,* nor given *any* of it for the dead. I have obeyed the voice of the LORD my God, and have done according to all that You have commanded me.

15 'Look down from Your holy habitation, from heaven, and bless Your people Israel and the land which You have given us, just as You swore to our fathers, "a land flowing with milk and honey." '*a*

A SPECIAL PEOPLE OF GOD

16 "This day the LORD your God commands you to observe these statutes and judgments; therefore you shall be careful to observe them with all your heart and with all your soul.

17 "Today you have proclaimed the LORD to be your God, and that you will walk in His ways and keep His statutes, His commandments, and His judgments, and that you will obey His voice.

18 "Also today the LORD has proclaimed you to be His special people, just as He promised you, that *you* should keep all His commandments,

19 "and that He will set you high above all nations which He has made, in praise, in name, and in honor, and that you may be a holy people to the LORD your God, just as He has spoken."

THE LAW INSCRIBED ON STONES

27 Now Moses, with the elders of Israel, commanded the people, saying: "Keep all the commandments which I command you today.

2 "And it shall be, on the day when you cross over the Jordan to the land which the LORD your God is giving you, that you shall set up for yourselves large stones, and whitewash them with lime.

3 "You shall write on them all the words of this law, when you have crossed over, that you may enter the land which the LORD your God is giving you, 'a land flowing with milk and honey,'*a* just as the LORD God of your fathers promised you.

4 "Therefore it shall be, when you have crossed over the Jordan, *that* on Mount Ē′bal you shall set up these stones, which I command you today, and you shall whitewash them with lime.

5 "And there you shall build an altar to the LORD your God, an altar of stones; you shall not use an iron *tool* on them.

6 "You shall build with whole stones the altar of the LORD your God, and offer burnt offerings on it to the LORD your God.

7 "You shall offer peace offerings, and shall eat there, and rejoice before the LORD your God.

26:15 *a*Exodus 3:8   27:3 *a*Exodus 3:8

8 "And you shall write very plainly on the stones all the words of this law."

9 Then Moses and the priests, the Lē′vītes, spoke to all Israel, saying, "Take heed and listen, O Israel: This day you have become the people of the LORD your God.

10 "Therefore you shall obey the voice of the LORD your God, and observe His commandments and His statutes which I command you today."

CURSES PRONOUNCED FROM MOUNT EBAL

11 And Moses commanded the people on the same day, saying,

12 "These shall stand on Mount Ger′i·zim to bless the people, when you have crossed over the Jordan: Sim′e·on, Levi, Judah, Is′sa·char, Joseph, and Benjamin;

13 "and these shall stand on Mount Ē′bal to curse: Reuben, Gad, Ash′er, Zeb′u·lun, Dan, and Naph′ta·lī.

14 "And the Lē′vītes shall speak with a loud voice and say to all the men of Israel:

15 'Cursed is the one who makes a carved or molded image, an abomination to the LORD, the work of the hands of the craftsman, and sets it up in secret.'

"And all the people shall answer and say, 'Amen!'

16 'Cursed is the one who treats his father or his mother with contempt.'

"And all the people shall say, 'Amen!'

17 'Cursed is the one who moves his neighbor's landmark.'

"And all the people shall say, 'Amen!'

18 'Cursed is the one who makes the blind to wander off the road.'

"And all the people shall say, 'Amen!'

19 'Cursed is the one who perverts the justice due the stranger, the fatherless, and widow.'

"And all the people shall say, 'Amen!'

20 'Cursed is the one who lies with his father's wife, because he has uncovered his father's bed.'

"And all the people shall say, 'Amen!'

21 'Cursed is the one who lies with any kind of animal.'

"And all the people shall say, 'Amen!'

22 'Cursed is the one who lies with his sister, the daughter of his father or the daughter of his mother.'

"And all the people shall say, 'Amen!'

23 'Cursed is the one who lies with his mother-in-law.'

"And all the people shall say, 'Amen!'

24 'Cursed is the one who attacks his neighbor secretly.'

"And all the people shall say, 'Amen!'

25 'Cursed is the one who takes a bribe to slay an innocent person.'

"And all the people shall say, 'Amen!'

26 'Cursed is the one who does not confirm all the words of this law.'

"And all the people shall say, 'Amen!'

BLESSINGS ON OBEDIENCE

28 "Now it shall come to pass, if you diligently obey the voice of the LORD your God, to observe carefully all His commandments which I command you today, that the LORD your God will set you high above all nations of the earth.

2 "And all these blessings shall come upon you and overtake you, because you obey the voice of the LORD your God:

3 "Blessed *shall* you *be* in the city, and blessed *shall* you *be* in the country.

4 "Blessed *shall be* the fruit of your body, the produce of your ground and the increase of your herds, the increase of your cattle and the offspring of your flocks.

5 "Blessed *shall be* your basket and your kneading bowl.

6 "Blessed *shall* you *be* when you come in, and blessed *shall* you *be* when you go out.

7 "The LORD will cause your enemies who rise against you to be defeated before your face; they shall come out against you one way and flee before you seven ways.

8 "The LORD will command the blessing on you in your storehouses and in all to which you set your hand, and He will bless you in the land which the LORD your God is giving you.

9 "The LORD will establish you as a holy people to Himself, just as He has sworn to you, if you keep the commandments of the LORD your God and walk in His ways.

10 "Then all peoples of the earth shall see that you are called by the name of the LORD, and they shall be afraid of you.

11 "And the LORD will grant you plenty of goods, in the fruit of your body, in the increase of your livestock, and in the produce of your ground, in the land of which the LORD swore to your fathers to give you.

12 "The LORD will open to you His good treasure, the heavens, to give the rain to your land in its season, and to bless all the work of your hand. You shall lend to many nations, but you shall not borrow.

13 "And the LORD will make you the head and not the tail; you shall be above only, and not be beneath, if you heed the commandments of the LORD your God, which I command you today, and are careful to observe *them*.

14 "So you shall not turn aside from any of the words which I command you this day, *to* the right or the left, to go after other gods to serve them.

CURSES ON DISOBEDIENCE

15 "But it shall come to pass, if you do not obey the voice of the LORD your God, to observe carefully all His commandments and His statutes which I command you today, that all these curses will come upon you and overtake you:

16 "Cursed *shall* you *be* in the city, and cursed *shall* you *be* in the country.

17 "Cursed *shall be* your basket and your kneading bowl.

18 "Cursed *shall be* the fruit of your body and the produce of your land, the increase of your cattle and the offspring of your flocks.

19 "Cursed *shall* you *be* when you come in, and cursed *shall* you *be* when you go out.

20 "The LORD will send on you cursing, confusion, and rebuke in all that you set your hand to do, until you are destroyed and until you perish quickly, because of the wickedness of your doings in which you have forsaken Me.

21 "The LORD will make the plague cling to you until He has consumed you from the land which you are going to possess.

22 "The LORD will strike you with consumption, with fever, with inflammation, with severe burning fever, with the sword, with scorching, and with mildew; they shall pursue you until you perish.

23 "And your heavens which *are* over your head shall be bronze, and the earth which is under you *shall be* iron.

24 "The LORD will change the rain of your land to powder and dust; from the heaven it shall come down on you until you are destroyed.

25 "The LORD will cause you to be defeated before your enemies; you shall go out one way against them and flee seven ways before them; and you shall become troublesome to all the kingdoms of the earth.

26 "Your carcasses shall be food for all the birds of the air and the beasts of the earth, and no one shall frighten *them* away.

27 "The LORD will strike you with the boils of Egypt, with tumors, with the scab, and with the itch, from which you cannot be healed.

28 "The LORD will strike you with madness and blindness and confusion of heart.

29 "And you shall grope at noonday, as a blind man gropes in darkness; you shall not prosper in your ways; you shall be only oppressed and plundered continually, and no one shall save *you.*

30 "You shall betroth a wife, but another man shall lie with her; you shall build a house, but you shall not dwell in it; you shall plant a vineyard, but shall not gather its grapes.

31 "Your ox *shall be* slaughtered before your eyes, but you shall not eat of it; your donkey *shall be* violently taken away from before you, and shall not be restored to you; your sheep *shall be* given to your enemies, and you shall have no one to rescue *them.*

32 "Your sons and your daughters *shall be* given to another people, and your eyes shall look and fail *with longing* for them all day long; and *there shall be* no strength in your hand.

33 "A nation whom you have not known shall eat the fruit of your land and the produce of your labor, and you shall be only oppressed and crushed continually.

34 "So you shall be driven mad because of the sight which your eyes see.

35 "The LORD will strike you in the knees and on the legs with severe boils which cannot be healed, and from the sole of your foot to the top of your head.

36 "The LORD will bring you and the king whom you set over you to a nation which neither you nor your fathers have known, and there you shall serve other gods—wood and stone.

37 "And you shall become an astonishment, a proverb, and a byword among all nations where the LORD will drive you.

38 "You shall carry much seed out to the field but gather little in, for the locust shall consume it.

39 "You shall plant vineyards and tend *them,* but you shall neither drink *of* the wine nor gather the *grapes;* for the worms shall eat them.

40 "You shall have olive trees throughout all your territory, but you shall not anoint *yourself* with the oil; for your olives shall drop off.

41 "You shall beget sons and daughters, but they shall not be yours; for they shall go into captivity.

42 "Locusts shall consume all your trees and the produce of your land.

43 "The alien who *is* among you shall rise higher and higher above you, and you shall come down lower and lower.

44 "He shall lend to you, but you shall not lend to him; he shall be the head, and you shall be the tail.

45 "Moreover all these curses shall come upon you and pursue and overtake you, until you are destroyed, because you did not obey the voice of the LORD your God, to keep His com-

mandments and His statutes which He commanded you.

46 "And they shall be upon you for a sign and a wonder, and on your descendants forever.

47 "Because you did not serve the LORD your God with joy and gladness of heart, for the abundance of everything,

48 "therefore you shall serve your enemies, whom the LORD will send against you, in hunger, in thirst, in nakedness, and in need of everything; and He will put a yoke of iron on your neck until He has destroyed you.

49 "The LORD will bring a nation against you from afar, from the end of the earth, *as swift* as the eagle flies, a nation whose language you will not understand,

50 "a nation of fierce countenance, which does not respect the elderly nor show favor to the young.

51 "And they shall eat the increase of your livestock and the produce of your land, until you are destroyed; they shall not leave you grain or new wine or oil, *or* the increase of your cattle or the offspring of your flocks, until they have destroyed you.

52 "They shall besiege you at all your gates until your high and fortified walls, in which you trust, come down throughout all your land; and they shall besiege you at all your gates throughout all your land which the LORD your God has given you.

53 "You shall eat the fruit of your own body, the flesh of your sons and your daughters whom the LORD your God has given you, in the siege and desperate straits in which your enemy shall distress you.

54 "The sensitive and very refined man among you will be hostile toward his brother, toward the wife of his bosom, and toward the rest of his children whom he leaves behind,

55 "so that he will not give any of them the flesh of his children whom he will eat, because he has nothing left in the siege and desperate straits in which your enemy shall distress you at all your gates.

56 "The tender and delicate woman among you, who would not venture to set the sole of her foot on the ground because of her delicateness and sensitivity, will refuse[a] to the husband of her bosom, and to her son and her daughter,

57 "her placenta which comes out from between her feet and her children whom she bears; for she will eat them secretly for lack of everything in the siege and desperate straits in which your enemy shall distress you at all your gates.

58 "If you do not carefully observe all the words of this law that are written in this book, that you may fear this glorious and awesome name, THE LORD YOUR GOD,

59 "then the LORD will bring upon you and your descendants extraordinary plagues—great and prolonged plagues—and serious and prolonged sicknesses.

60 "Moreover He will bring back on you all the diseases of Egypt, of which you were afraid, and they shall cling to you.

61 "Also every sickness and every plague, which *is* not written in this Book of the Law, will the LORD bring upon you until you are destroyed.

62 "You shall be left few in number, whereas you were as the stars of heaven in multitude, because you would not obey the voice of the LORD your God.

63 "And it shall be, *that* just as the LORD rejoiced over you to do you good and multiply you, so the LORD will rejoice over you to destroy you and

28:56 [a]Literally *her eye shall be evil toward*

bring you to nothing; and you shall be plucked from off the land which you go to possess.

64 "Then the LORD will scatter you among all peoples, from one end of the earth to the other, and there you shall serve other gods, which neither you nor your fathers have known—wood and stone.

65 "And among those nations you shall find no rest, nor shall the sole of your foot have a resting place; but there the LORD will give you a trembling heart, failing eyes, and anguish of soul.

66 "Your life shall hang in doubt before you; you shall fear day and night, and have no assurance of life.

67 "In the morning you shall say, 'Oh, that it were evening!' And at evening you shall say, 'Oh, that it were morning!' because of the fear which terrifies your heart, and because of the sight which your eyes see.

68 "And the LORD will take you back to Egypt in ships, by the way of which I said to you, 'You shall never see it again.' And there you shall be offered for sale to your enemies as male and female slaves, but no one will buy you."

THE COVENANT RENEWED IN MOAB

29 These *are* the words of the covenant which the LORD commanded Moses to make with the children of Israel in the land of Mō'ab, besides the covenant which He made with them in Hō'reb.

2 Now Moses called all Israel and said to them: "You have seen all that the LORD did before your eyes in the land of Egypt, to Pharaoh and to all his servants and to all his land—

3 "the great trials which your eyes have seen, the signs, and those great wonders.

4 "Yet the LORD has not given you a heart to perceive and eyes to see and ears to hear, to this *very* day.

5 "And I have led you forty years in the wilderness. Your clothes have not worn out on you, and your sandals have not worn out on your feet.

6 "You have not eaten bread, nor have you drunk wine or *similar* drink, that you may know that I *am* the LORD your God.

7 "And when you came to this place, Sī'hon king of Hesh'bon and Og king of Bā'shan came out against us to battle, and we conquered them.

8 "We took their land and gave it as an inheritance to the Reū'ben-ītes, to the Gad'ītes, and to half the tribe of Ma-nas'seh.

9 "Therefore keep the words of this covenant, and do them, that you may prosper in all that you do.

10 "All of you stand today before the LORD your God: your leaders and your tribes and your elders and your officers, all the men of Israel,

11 "your little ones and your wives—also the stranger who *is* in your camp, from the one who cuts your wood to the one who draws your water—

12 "that you may enter into covenant with the LORD your God, and into His oath, which the LORD your God makes with you today,

13 "that He may establish you today as a people for Himself, and *that* He may be God to you, just as He has spoken to you, and just as He has sworn to your fathers, to Abraham, Isaac, and Jacob.

14 "I make this covenant and this oath, not with you alone,

15 "but with *him* who stands here with us today before the LORD our God, as well as with *him* who *is* not here with us today

16 (for you know that we dwelt in the land of Egypt and that we came through the nations which you passed by,

17 and you saw their abominations and their idols which *were* among them—wood and stone and silver and gold);

18 "so that there may not be among you man or woman or family or tribe, whose heart turns away today from the LORD our God, to go *and* serve the gods of these nations, and that there may not be among you a root bearing bitterness or wormwood;

19 "and so it may not happen, when he hears the words of this curse, that he blesses himself in his heart, saying, 'I shall have peace, even though I follow the dictates*a* of my heart'—as though the drunkard could be included with the sober.

20 "The LORD would not spare him; for then the anger of the LORD and His jealousy would burn against that man, and every curse that is written in this book would settle on him, and the LORD would blot out his name from under heaven.

21 "And the LORD would separate him from all the tribes of Israel for adversity, according to all the curses of the covenant that are written in this Book of the Law,

22 "so that the coming generation of your children who rise up after you, and the foreigner who comes from a far land, would say, when they see the plagues of that land and the sicknesses which the LORD has laid on it:

23 'The whole land *is* brimstone, salt, and burning; it is not sown, nor does it bear, nor does any grass grow there, like the overthrow of Sod'om and Go·mor'rah, Ad'mah, and Ze-boi'im, which the LORD overthrew in His anger and His wrath.'

24 "All nations would say, 'Why has the LORD done so to this land? What does the heat of this great anger mean?'

25 "Then *people* would say: 'Because they have forsaken the covenant of the LORD God of their fathers, which He made with them when He brought them out of the land of Egypt;

26 'for they went and served other gods and worshiped them, gods that they did not know and that He had not given to them.

27 'Then the anger of the LORD was aroused against this land, to bring on it every curse that is written in this book.

28 'And the LORD uprooted them from their land in anger, in wrath, and in great indignation, and cast them into another land, as *it is* this day.'

29 "The secret *things belong* to the LORD our God, but those *things which are* revealed *belong* to us and to our children forever, that *we* may do all the words of this law.

THE BLESSING OF RETURNING TO GOD

30 "Now it shall come to pass, when all these things come upon you, the blessing and the curse which I have set before you, and you call *them* to mind among all the nations where the LORD your God drives you,

2 "and you return to the LORD your God and obey His voice, according to all that I command you today, you and your children, with all your heart and with all your soul,

3 "that the LORD your God will bring you back from captivity, and have compassion on you, and gather you again from all the nations where the LORD your God has scattered you.

29:19 *a*Or *stubbornness*

4   "If *any* of you are driven out to the farthest *parts* under heaven, from there the LORD your God will gather you, and from there He will bring you.

5   "Then the LORD your God will bring you to the land which your fathers possessed, and you shall possess it. He will prosper you and multiply you more than your fathers.

6   "And the LORD your God will circumcise your heart and the heart of your descendants, to love the LORD your God with all your heart and with all your soul, that you may live.

7   "Also the LORD your God will put all these curses on your enemies and on those who hate you, who persecuted you.

8   "And you will again obey the voice of the LORD and do all His commandments which I command you today.

9   "The LORD your God will make you abound in all the work of your hand, in the fruit of your body, in the increase of your livestock, and in the produce of your land for good. For the LORD will again rejoice over you for good as He rejoiced over your fathers,

10   "if you obey the voice of the LORD your God, to keep His commandments and His statutes which are written in this Book of the Law, *and* if you turn to the LORD your God with all your heart and with all your soul.

THE CHOICE OF LIFE OR DEATH

11   "For this commandment which I command you today *is* not *too* mysterious for you, nor *is* it far off.

12   "It *is* not in heaven, that you should say, 'Who will ascend into heaven for us and bring it to us, that we may hear it and do it?'

13   "Nor *is* it beyond the sea, that you should say, 'Who will go over the sea for us and bring it to us, that we may hear it and do it?'

14   "But the word *is* very near you, in your mouth and in your heart, that you may do it.

15   "See, I have set before you today life and good, death and evil,

16   "in that I command you today to love the LORD your God, to walk in His ways, and to keep His commandments, His statutes, and His judgments, that you may live and multiply; and the LORD your God will bless you in the land which you go to possess.

17   "But if your heart turns away so that you do not hear, and are drawn away, and worship other gods and serve them,

18   "I announce to you today that you shall surely perish; you shall not prolong *your* days in the land which you cross over the Jordan to go in and possess.

19   "I call heaven and earth as witnesses today against you, *that* I have set before you life and death, blessing and cursing; therefore choose life, that both you and your descendants may live;

20   "that you may love the LORD your God, that you may obey His voice, and that you may cling to Him, for He *is* your life and the length of your days; and that you may dwell in the land which the LORD swore to your fathers, to Abraham, Isaac, and Jacob, to give them."

JOSHUA THE NEW LEADER OF ISRAEL

31 Then Moses went and spoke these words to all Israel.

2   And he said to them: "I *am* one hundred and twenty years old today. I can no longer go out and come in. Also the LORD has said to me, 'You shall not cross over this Jordan.'

3 "The LORD your God Himself crosses over before you; He will destroy these nations from before you, and you shall dispossess them. Joshua himself crosses over before you, just as the LORD has said.

4 "And the LORD will do to them as He did to Sī'hon and Og, the kings of the Am'o·rītes and their land, when He destroyed them.

5 "The LORD will give them over to you, that you may do to them according to every commandment which I have commanded you.

6 "Be strong and of good courage, do not fear nor be afraid of them; for the LORD your God, He is the One who goes with you. He will not leave you nor forsake you."

7 Then Moses called Joshua and said to him in the sight of all Israel, "Be strong and of good courage, for you must go with this people to the land which the LORD has sworn to their fathers to give them, and you shall cause them to inherit it.

8 "And the LORD, He is the One who goes before you. He will be with you, He will not leave you nor forsake you; do not fear nor be dismayed."

THE LAW TO BE READ EVERY SEVEN YEARS

9 So Moses wrote this law and delivered it to the priests, the sons of Levi, who bore the ark of the covenant of the LORD, and to all the elders of Israel.

10 And Moses commanded them, saying: "At the end of every seven years, at the appointed time in the year of release, at the Feast of Tabernacles,

11 "when all Israel comes to appear before the LORD your God in the place which He chooses, you shall read this law before all Israel in their hearing.

12 "Gather the people together, men and women and little ones, and the stranger who is within your gates, that they may hear and that they may learn to fear the LORD your God and carefully observe all the words of this law,

13 "and that their children, who have not known it, may hear and learn to fear the LORD your God as long as you live in the land which you cross the Jordan to possess."

PREDICTION OF ISRAEL'S REBELLION

14 Then the LORD said to Moses, "Behold, the days approach when you must die; call Joshua, and present yourselves in the tabernacle of meeting, that I may inaugurate him." So Moses and Joshua went and presented themselves in the tabernacle of meeting.

15 Now the LORD appeared at the tabernacle in a pillar of cloud, and the pillar of cloud stood above the door of the tabernacle.

16 And the LORD said to Moses: "Behold, you will rest with your fathers; and this people will rise and play the harlot with the gods of the foreigners of the land, where they go to be among them, and they will forsake Me and break My covenant which I have made with them.

17 "Then My anger shall be aroused against them in that day, and I will forsake them, and I will hide My face from them, and they shall be devoured. And many evils and troubles shall befall them, so that they will say in that day, 'Have not these evils come upon us because our God is not among us?'

18 "And I will surely hide My face in that day because of all the evil which they have done, in that they have turned to other gods.

19 "Now therefore, write down this

song for yourselves, and teach it to the children of Israel; put it in their mouths, that this song may be a witness for Me against the children of Israel.

20 "When I have brought them to the land flowing with milk and honey, of which I swore to their fathers, and they have eaten and filled themselves and grown fat, then they will turn to other gods and serve them; and they will provoke Me and break My covenant.

21 "Then it shall be, when many evils and troubles have come upon them, that this song will testify against them as a witness; for it will not be forgotten in the mouths of their descendants, for I know the inclination of their behavior today, even before I have brought them to the land of which I swore *to give them*."

22 Therefore Moses wrote this song the same day, and taught it to the children of Israel.

23 Then He inaugurated Joshua the son of Nun, and said, "Be strong and of good courage; for you shall bring the children of Israel into the land of which I swore to them, and I will be with you."

24 So it was, when Moses had completed writing the words of this law in a book, when they were finished,

25 that Moses commanded the Lē'-vītes, who bore the ark of the covenant of the LORD, saying:

26 "Take this Book of the Law, and put it beside the ark of the covenant of the LORD your God, that it may be there as a witness against you;

27 "for I know your rebellion and your stiff neck. *If* today, while I am yet alive with you, you have been rebellious against the LORD, then how much more after my death?

28 "Gather to me all the elders of your tribes, and your officers, that I may speak these words in their hearing and call heaven and earth to witness against them.

29 "For I know that after my death you will become utterly corrupt, and turn aside from the way which I have commanded you. And evil will befall you in the latter days, because you will do evil in the sight of the LORD, to provoke Him to anger through the work of your hands."

THE SONG OF MOSES

30 Then Moses spoke in the hearing of all the assembly of Israel the words of this song until they were ended:

32 "Give ear, O heavens, and I
            will speak;
      And hear, O earth, the words of
            my mouth.
2   Let my teaching drop as the rain,
      My speech distill as the dew,
      As raindrops on the tender herb,
      And as showers on the grass.
3   For I proclaim the name of the
            LORD:
      Ascribe greatness to our God.
4   *He is* the Rock, His work *is*
            perfect;
      For all His ways *are* justice,
      A God of truth and without
            injustice;
      Righteous and upright *is* He.

5   "They have corrupted themselves;
      They are not His children,
      Because of their blemish:
      A perverse and crooked
            generation.
6   Do you thus deal with the LORD,
      O foolish and unwise people?
      Is He not your Father, *who*
            bought you?
      Has He not made you and
            established you?

WHEN LOVE LEAVES A DIRTY SHIRT   Deuteronomy 32:3, 4

A little friend wants to tell you he loves you. But he forgot to clean his muddy paws. Now you have a shirt with muddy paw prints. Should you get angry at him? What should you do? Your little brother or sister wants to hug mother. But he or she forgot to wash off the peanut butter and jam from their hands. Love leaves a blouse with peanut butter and jam fingerprints. Should mother get angry at your little brother or sister? What should she do?

1. Is love always perfect? Do expressions of love sometimes leave paw prints or peanut butter and jam marks? Can you think of other problems that have come from true expressions of love?
2. If genuine love is expressed, should you be angry at paw prints or jam marks? Or do these just come along at times? What should you do about them?
3. One Person is perfect. Who is He? All He does is perfect. Read Deuteronomy 32:3, 4. But since we are not God, our ways are not perfect. Even our expressions of love may leave peanut butter and jam marks.

For more on *What Should I Do?* turn to page 356
For more on *Love* turn to page 321

7 "Remember the days of old,
Consider the years of many
generations.
Ask your father, and he will show
you;
Your elders, and they will tell
you:

8 When the Most High divided
their inheritance to the nations,
When He separated the sons of
Adam,
He set the boundaries of the
peoples
According to the number of the
children of Israel.

9 For the LORD's portion is His
people;
Jacob is the place of His
inheritance.

10 "He found him in a desert land
And in the wasteland, a howling
wilderness;
He encircled him, He instructed
him,
He kept him as the apple of His
eye.

11 As an eagle stirs up its nest,
Hovers over its young,
Spreading out its wings, taking
them up,
Carrying them on its wings,

12 So the LORD alone led him,
And there was no foreign god with
him.

13 "He made him ride in the heights
of the earth,
That he might eat the produce of
the fields;
He made him draw honey from
the rock,
And oil from the flinty rock;

14 Curds from the cattle, and milk of
the flock,
With fat of lambs;
And rams of the breed of Bā'shan,
and goats,
With the choicest wheat;

And you drank wine, the blood of
the grapes.

15 "But Jesh'ū·run grew fat and
kicked;
You grew fat, you grew thick,
You are obese!
Then he forsook God who made
him,
And scornfully esteemed the Rock
of his salvation.

16 They provoked Him to jealousy
with foreign gods;
With abominations they provoked
Him to anger.

17 They sacrificed to demons, not to
God,
To gods they did not know,
To new gods, new arrivals
That your fathers did not fear.

18 Of the Rock who begot you, you
are unmindful,
And have forgotten the God who
fathered you.

19 "And when the LORD saw it, He
spurned them,
Because of the provocation of His
sons and His daughters.

20 And He said: 'I will hide My face
from them,
I will see what their end will be,
For they are a perverse
generation,
Children in whom is no faith.

21 They have provoked Me to
jealousy by what is not God;
They have moved Me to anger by
their foolish idols.
But I will provoke them to
jealousy by those who are not a
nation;
I will move them to anger by a
foolish nation.

22 For a fire is kindled in My anger,
And shall burn to the lowest hell;
It shall consume the earth with
her increase,

And set on fire the foundations of
the mountains.

23 'I will heap disasters on them;
I will spend My arrows on them.
24 *They shall be* wasted with hunger,
Devoured by pestilence and bitter
destruction;
I will also send against them the
teeth of beasts,
With the poison of serpents of the
dust.
25 The sword shall destroy outside;
There shall be terror within
For the young man and virgin,
The nursing child with the man of
gray hairs.
26 I would have said, "I will dash
them in pieces,
I will make the memory of them
to cease from among men,"
27 Had I not feared the wrath of the
enemy,
Lest their adversaries should
misunderstand,
Lest they should say, "Our hand
is high;
And it is not the LORD who has
done all this." '

28 "For they *are* a nation void of
counsel,
Nor *is there any* understanding in
them.
29 Oh, that they were wise, *that* they
understood this,
That they would consider their
latter end!
30 How could one chase a thousand,
And two put ten thousand to
flight,
Unless their Rock had sold them,
And the LORD had surrendered
them?
31 For their rock *is* not like our
Rock,
Even our enemies themselves
being judges.

32 For their vine *is* of the vine of
Sod'om
And of the fields of Go·mor'rah;
Their grapes *are* grapes of gall,
Their clusters *are* bitter.
33 Their wine *is* the poison of
serpents,
And the cruel venom of cobras.

34 'Is this not laid up in store with
Me,
Sealed up among My treasures?
35 Vengeance is Mine, and
recompense;
Their foot shall slip in *due* time;
For the day of their calamity *is* at
hand,
And the things to come hasten
upon them.'

36 "For the LORD will judge His
people
And have compassion on His
servants,
When He sees that *their* power is
gone,
And *there is* no one *remaining,*
bond or free.
37 He will say: 'Where *are* their
gods,
The rock in which they sought
refuge?
38 Who ate the fat of their sacrifices,
And drank the wine of their drink
offering?
Let them rise and help you,
And be your refuge.

39 'Now see that I, *even* I, *am* He,
And *there is* no God besides Me;
I kill and I make alive;
I wound and I heal;
Nor *is there any* who can deliver
from My hand.
40 For I raise My hand to heaven,
And say, "*As* I live forever,
41 If I whet My glittering sword,
And My hand takes hold on
judgment,

I will render vengeance to My
    enemies,
And repay those who hate Me.
42 I will make My arrows drunk
    with blood,
And My sword shall devour flesh,
With the blood of the slain and
    the captives,
From the heads of the leaders of
    the enemy." '

43 "Rejoice, O Gentiles, *with* His
    people;*a*
For He will avenge the blood of
    His servants,
And render vengeance to His
    adversaries;
He will provide atonement for His
    land *and* His people."

44 So Moses came with Joshua*a* the
son of Nun and spoke all the words of
this song in the hearing of the people.
45 Moses finished speaking all these
words to all Israel,
46 and he said to them: "Set your
hearts on all the words which I testify among you today, which you shall
command your children to be careful to observe—all the words of this
law.
47 "For it *is* not a futile thing for
you, because it *is* your life, and by
this word you shall prolong *your* days
in the land which you cross over the
Jordan to possess."

MOSES TO DIE ON MOUNT NEBO

48 Then the LORD spoke to Moses
that very same day, saying:
49 "Go up this mountain of the
Ab'a·rim, Mount Nē'bō, which *is* in
the land of Mō'ab, across from Jericho; view the land of Cā'naan, which
I give to the children of Israel as a
possession;
50 "and die on the mountain which

you ascend, and be gathered to your
people, just as Aaron your brother
died on Mount Hor and was gathered
to his people;
51 "because you trespassed against
Me among the children of Israel at
the waters of Mer'i·bah Kā'desh, in
the Wilderness of Zin, because you
did not hallow Me in the midst of the
children of Israel.
52 "Yet you shall see the land before
you, though you shall not go there,
into the land which I am giving to the
children of Israel."

MOSES' FINAL BLESSING ON ISRAEL

33 Now this *is* the blessing with
which Moses the man of God blessed
the children of Israel before his
death.
2   And he said:

"The LORD came from Sinai,
And dawned on them from Sē'ir;
He shone forth from Mount
    Par'an,
And He came with ten thousands
    of saints;
From His right hand
Came a fiery law for them.
3   Yes, He loves the people;
All His saints *are* in Your hand;
They sit down at Your feet;
Everyone receives Your words.
4   Moses commanded a law for us,
A heritage of the congregation of
    Jacob.
5   And He was King in Jesh'ū·run,
When the leaders of the people
    were gathered,
All the tribes of Israel together.

6 "Let Reuben live, and not die,
Nor let his men be few."

32:43 *a*A Dead Sea Scroll fragment adds *And let all
the* gods *(angels) worship Him* (compare Septuagint
and Hebrews 1:6).   32:44 *a*Hebrew *Hoshea*
(compare Numbers 13:8, 16)

HUMILITY Deuteronomy 33:3

Who Thinks You're Number 1?

Who thinks you're number 1? Does God? Read Deuteronomy 33:3. God loves all of His people. You *are* number 1 with Him. Who thinks you're number 1? Does your puppy? That's love. Aren't you glad your puppy or kitty thinks you're number 1? Aren't you glad they love you that much? Who thinks you're number 1? Perhaps mother or father thinks you're a number 1 girl or boy. Aren't you glad they love you that much?

1. Have you ever thanked your mother or father for their love for you? Why not now?
2. Have you ever shown your puppy or kitty love because they love you? Why not now?
3. Have you ever shown God how much you love Him the way He loves you? Why not now?

For more on *Values* turn to page 401
For more on *Love* turn to page 948

7 And this he said of Judah:

"Hear, LORD, the voice of Judah,
And bring him to his people;
Let his hands be sufficient for
  him,
And may You be a help against
  his enemies."

8 And of Levi he said:

"*Let* Your Thum'mim and Your
  Ū'rim *be* with Your holy one,
Whom You tested at Mas'sah,
And with whom You contended at
  the waters of Mer'i·bah,
9 Who says of his father and
  mother,
'I have not seen them';
Nor did he acknowledge his
  brothers,
Or know his own children;
For they have observed Your word
And kept Your covenant.
10 They shall teach Jacob Your
  judgments,
And Israel Your law.
They shall put incense before You,
And a whole burnt sacrifice on
  Your altar.
11 Bless his substance, LORD,
And accept the work of his hands;
Strike the loins of those who rise
  against him,
And of those who hate him, that
  they rise not again."

12 Of Benjamin he said:

"The beloved of the LORD shall
  dwell in safety by Him,
Who shelters him all the day long;
And he shall dwell between His
  shoulders."

13 And of Joseph he said:

"Blessed of the LORD *is* his land,
With the precious things of
  heaven, with the dew,
And the deep lying beneath,

┌─────────────────────────────┐
│ ■ *Promises* ■   │
│   │
│ Deuteronomy 33:12   │
│   │
│ God promised to be our shelter. │
│ He promised to protect us. If a │
│ big rainstorm comes, we want a │
│ shelter, don't we? If the sun │
│ beats down on us on a hot sum- │
│ mer day, what do we want? We │
│ want a shelter, don't we? When │
│ troubles come, we want God as │
│ our shelter. He has promised │
│ that He will be our shelter. │
│ Thank You, God!   │
└─────────────────────────────┘

14 With the precious fruits of the
  sun,
With the precious produce of the
  months,
15 With the best things of the
  ancient mountains,
With the precious things of the
  everlasting hills,
16 With the precious things of the
  earth and its fullness,
And the favor of Him who dwelt
  in the bush.
Let *the blessing* come 'on the head
  of Joseph,
And on the crown of the head of
  him *who was* separate from his
  brothers.'a
17 His glory *is like* a firstborn bull,
And his horns *like* the horns of
  the wild ox;
Together with them
He shall push the peoples
To the ends of the earth;
They *are* the ten thousands of
  Ē'phra·im,
And they *are* the thousands of
  Ma·nas'seh."

18 And of Zeb'ū·lun he said:

33:16 aGenesis 49:26

"Rejoice, Zeb′u·lun, in your going
out,
And Is′sa·char in your tents!
19 They shall call the peoples *to* the
mountain;
There they shall offer sacrifices of
righteousness;
For they shall partake *of* the
abundance of the seas
And *of* treasures hidden in the
sand."

20 And of Gad he said:

"Blessed *is* he who enlarges Gad;
He dwells as a lion,
And tears the arm and the crown
of his head.
21 He provided the first *part* for
himself,
Because a lawgiver's portion was
reserved there.
He came *with* the heads of the
people;
He administered the justice of the
LORD,
And His judgments with Israel."

22 And of Dan he said:

"Dan *is* a lion's whelp;
He shall leap from Bā′shan."

23 And of Naph′ta·lī he said:

"O Naph′ta·lī, satisfied with favor,
And full of the blessing of the
LORD,
Possess the west and the south."

24 And of Ash′er he said:

"Ash′er *is* most blessed of sons;
Let him be favored by his
brothers,
And let him dip his foot in oil.
25 Your sandals *shall be* iron and
bronze;
As your days, *so shall* your
strength *be*.

26 "*There is* no one like the God of
Jesh′u·run,
Who rides the heavens to help
you,
And in His excellency on the
clouds.
27 The eternal God *is your* refuge,
And underneath *are* the
everlasting arms;
He will thrust out the enemy
from before you,
And will say, 'Destroy!'
28 Then Israel shall dwell in safety,
The fountain of Jacob alone,
In a land of grain and new wine;
His heavens shall also drop dew.
29 Happy *are* you, O Israel!
Who *is* like you, a people saved by
the LORD,
The shield of your help
And the sword of your majesty!
Your enemies shall submit to you,
And you shall tread down their
high places."

MOSES DIES ON MOUNT NEBO

34 Then Moses went up from the
plains of Mō′ab to Mount Nē′bō, to
the top of Pis′gah, which is across
from Jericho. And the LORD showed
him all the land of Gil′e·ad as far as
Dan,
2 all Naph′ta·lī and the land of
Ē′phra·im and Ma·nas′seh, all the
land of Judah as far as the Western
Sea,*a*
3 the South, and the plain of the
Valley of Jericho, the city of palm
trees, as far as Zō′ar.
4 Then the LORD said to him, "This
is the land of which I swore to give
Abraham, Isaac, and Jacob, saying, 'I
will give it to your descendants.' I
have caused you to see *it* with your
eyes, but you shall not cross over
there."

34:2 *a*That is, the Mediterranean

5 So Moses the servant of the LORD died there in the land of Mō′ab, according to the word of the LORD.

6 And He buried him in a valley in the land of Mō′ab, opposite Beth Pē′or; but no one knows his grave to this day.

7 Moses *was* one hundred and twenty years old when he died. His eyes were not dim nor his natural vigor diminished.

8 And the children of Israel wept for Moses in the plains of Mō′ab thirty days. So the days of weeping *and* mourning for Moses ended.

9 Now Joshua the son of Nun was full of the spirit of wisdom, for Moses had laid his hands on him; so the children of Israel heeded him, and did as the LORD had commanded Moses.

10 But since then there has not arisen in Israel a prophet like Moses, whom the LORD knew face to face,

11 in all the signs and wonders which the LORD sent him to do in the land of Egypt, before Pharaoh, before all his servants, and in all his land,

12 and by all that mighty power and all the great terror which Moses performed in the sight of all Israel.

JOSHUA

GOD'S COMMISSION TO JOSHUA

AFTER the death of Moses the servant of the LORD, it came to pass that the LORD spoke to Joshua the son of Nun, Moses' assistant, saying:

2 "Moses My servant is dead. Now therefore, arise, go over this Jordan, you and all this people, to the land which I am giving to them—the children of Israel.

3 "Every place that the sole of your foot will tread upon I have given you, as I said to Moses.

4 "From the wilderness and this Lebanon as far as the great river, the River Eū·phrā′tēs, all the land of the Hit′tītes, and to the Great Sea toward the going down of the sun, shall be your territory.

5 "No man shall *be able to* stand before you all the days of your life; as I was with Moses, *so* I will be with you. I will not leave you nor forsake you.

6 "Be strong and of good courage, for to this people you shall divide as an inheritance the land which I swore to their fathers to give them.

7 "Only be strong and very courageous, that you may observe to do according to all the law which Moses My servant commanded you; do not turn from it to the right hand or to the left, that you may prosper wherever you go.

8 "This Book of the Law shall not depart from your mouth, but you shall meditate in it day and night, that you may observe to do according to all that is written in it. For then you will make your way prosperous, and then you will have good success.

9 "Have I not commanded you? Be strong and of good courage; do not be afraid, nor be dismayed, for the LORD your God *is* with you wherever you go."

THE ORDER TO CROSS THE JORDAN

10 Then Joshua commanded the officers of the people, saying,

11 "Pass through the camp and command the people, saying, 'Prepare provisions for yourselves, for within three days you will cross over this Jordan, to go in to possess the land which the LORD your God is giving you to possess.'"

12 And to the Reū′ben·ītes, the Gad′ītes, and half the tribe of Manas′seh Joshua spoke, saying,

13 "Remember the word which Moses the servant of the LORD commanded you, saying, 'The LORD your God is giving you rest and is giving you this land.'

14 "Your wives, your little ones, and your livestock shall remain in the land which Moses gave you on this side of the Jordan. But you shall pass before your brethren armed, all your mighty men of valor, and help them,

15 "until the LORD has given your brethren rest, as He *gave* you, and they also have taken possession of the land which the LORD your God is giving them. Then you shall return to the land of your possession and enjoy it, which Moses the LORD's servant gave you on this side of the Jordan toward the sunrise."

16 So they answered Joshua, saying, "All that you command us we will do, and wherever you send us we will go.

17 "Just as we heeded Moses in all things, so we will heed you. Only the LORD your God be with you, as He was with Moses.

18 "Whoever rebels against your command and does not heed your

words, in all that you command him, shall be put to death. Only be strong and of good courage."

RAHAB HIDES THE SPIES

2 Now Joshua the son of Nun sent out two men from Acacia Grove*a* to spy secretly, saying, "Go, view the land, especially Jericho." So they went, and came to the house of a harlot named Rā′hab, and lodged there. 2 And it was told the king of Jericho, saying, "Behold, men have come here tonight from the children of Israel to search out the country." 3 So the king of Jericho sent to Rā′hab, saying, "Bring out the men who have come to you, who have entered your house, for they have come to search out all the country." 4 Then the woman took the two men and hid them. So she said, "Yes, the men came to me, but I did not know where they *were* from. 5 "And it happened as the gate was being shut, when it was dark, that the men went out. Where the men went I do not know; pursue them quickly, for you may overtake them." 6 (But she had brought them up to the roof and hidden them with the stalks of flax, which she had laid in order on the roof.) 7 Then the men pursued them by the road to the Jordan, to the fords. And as soon as those who pursued them had gone out, they shut the gate. 8 Now before they lay down, she came up to them on the roof, 9 and said to the men: "I know that the LORD has given you the land, that the terror of you has fallen on us, and that all the inhabitants of the land are fainthearted because of you. 10 "For we have heard how the LORD dried up the water of the Red Sea for you when you came out of Egypt, and

what you did to the two kings of the Am′o·rītes who *were* on the other side of the Jordan, Sī′hon and Og, whom you utterly destroyed. 11 "And as soon as we heard *these things,* our hearts melted; neither did there remain any more courage in anyone because of you, for the LORD your God, He *is* God in heaven above and on earth beneath. 12 "Now therefore, I beg you, swear to me by the LORD, since I have shown you kindness, that you also will show kindness to my father's house, and give me a true token, 13 "and spare my father, my mother, my brothers, my sisters, and all that they have, and deliver our lives from death." 14 So the men answered her, "Our lives for yours, if none of you tell this business of ours. And it shall be, when the LORD has given us the land, that we will deal kindly and truly with you." 15 Then she let them down by a rope through the window, for her house *was* on the city wall; she dwelt on the wall. 16 And she said to them, "Get to the mountain, lest the pursuers meet you. Hide there three days, until the pursuers have returned. Afterward you may go your way." 17 So the men said to her: "We *will be* blameless of this oath of yours which you have made us swear, 18 "unless, *when* we come into the land, you bind this line of scarlet cord in the window through which you let us down, and unless you bring your father, your mother, your brothers, and all your father's household to your own home. 19 "So it shall be *that* whoever goes outside the doors of your house into the street, his blood *shall be* on his

2:1 *a*Hebrew *Shittim*

own head, and we *will be* guiltless. And whoever is with you in the house, his blood *shall be* on our head if a hand is laid on him.

20 "And if you tell this business of ours, then we will be free from your oath which you made us swear."

21 Then she said, "According to your words, so *be* it." And she sent them away, and they departed. And she bound the scarlet cord in the window.

22 They departed and went to the mountain, and stayed there three days until the pursuers returned. The pursuers sought *them* all along the way, but did not find *them*.

23 So the two men returned, descended from the mountain, and crossed over; and they came to Joshua the son of Nun, and told him all that had befallen them.

24 And they said to Joshua, "Truly the LORD has delivered all the land into our hands, for indeed all the inhabitants of the country are faint-hearted because of us."

ISRAEL CROSSES THE JORDAN

3 Then Joshua rose early in the morning; and they set out from Acacia Grove*a* and came to the Jordan, he and all the children of Israel, and lodged there before they crossed over.

2 So it was, after three days, that the officers went through the camp;

3 and they commanded the people, saying, "When you see the ark of the covenant of the LORD your God, and the priests, the Lē'vītes, bearing it, then you shall set out from your place and go after it.

4 "Yet there shall be a space between you and it, about two thousand cubits by measure. Do not come near it, that you may know the way by which you must go, for you have not passed *this* way before."

5 And Joshua said to the people,

"Sanctify yourselves, for tomorrow the LORD will do wonders among you."

6 Then Joshua spoke to the priests, saying, "Take up the ark of the covenant and cross over before the people." So they took up the ark of the covenant and went before the people.

7 And the LORD said to Joshua, "This day I will begin to exalt you in the sight of all Israel, that they may know that, as I was with Moses, *so* I will be with you.

8 "You shall command the priests who bear the ark of the covenant, saying, 'When you have come to the edge of the water of the Jordan, you shall stand in the Jordan.' "

9 So Joshua said to the children of Israel, "Come here, and hear the words of the LORD your God."

10 And Joshua said, "By this you shall know that the living God *is* among you, and *that* He will without fail drive out from before you the Cā'naan·ītes and the Hit'tītes and the Hī'vītes and the Per'iz·zītes and the Gir'ga·shītes and the Am'o·rītes and the Jeb'ū·sītes:

11 "Behold, the ark of the covenant of the Lord of all the earth is crossing over before you into the Jordan.

12 "Now therefore, take for yourselves twelve men from the tribes of Israel, one man from every tribe.

13 "And it shall come to pass, as soon as the soles of the feet of the priests who bear the ark of the LORD, the Lord of all the earth, shall rest in the waters of the Jordan, *that* the waters of the Jordan shall be cut off, the waters that come down from upstream, and they shall stand as a heap."

14 So it was, when the people set out from their camp to cross over the

3:1 *a*Hebrew *Shittim*

Jordan, with the priests bearing the ark of the covenant before the people, 15 and as those who bore the ark came to the Jordan, and the feet of the priests who bore the ark dipped in the edge of the water (for the Jordan overflows all its banks during the whole time of harvest), 16 that the waters which came down from upstream stood *still, and* rose in a heap very far away at Adam, the city that *is* beside Zar'e·tan. So the waters that went down into the Sea of the Ar'a·bah, the Salt Sea, failed, *and* were cut off; and the people crossed over opposite Jericho. 17 Then the priests who bore the ark of the covenant of the LORD stood firm on dry ground in the midst of the Jordan; and all Israel crossed over on dry ground, until all the people had crossed completely over the Jordan.

THE MEMORIAL STONES

4 And it came to pass, when all the people had completely crossed over the Jordan, that the LORD spoke to Joshua, saying: 2 "Take for yourselves twelve men from the people, one man from every tribe, 3 "and command them, saying, 'Take for yourselves twelve stones from here, out of the midst of the Jordan, from the place where the priests' feet stood firm. You shall carry them over with you and leave them in the lodging place where you lodge tonight.' " 4 Then Joshua called the twelve men whom he had appointed from the children of Israel, one man from every tribe; 5 and Joshua said to them: "Cross over before the ark of the LORD your God into the midst of the Jordan, and each one of you take up a stone on his shoulder, according to the number of the tribes of the children of Israel, 6 "that this may be a sign among you when your children ask in time to come, saying, 'What do these stones *mean* to you?' 7 "Then you shall answer them that the waters of the Jordan were cut off before the ark of the covenant of the LORD; when it crossed over the Jordan, the waters of the Jordan were cut off. And these stones shall be for a memorial to the children of Israel forever." 8 And the children of Israel did so, just as Joshua commanded, and took up twelve stones from the midst of the Jordan, as the LORD had spoken to Joshua, according to the number of the tribes of the children of Israel, and carried them over with them to the place where they lodged, and laid them down there. 9 Then Joshua set up twelve stones in the midst of the Jordan, in the place where the feet of the priests who bore the ark of the covenant stood; and they are there to this day. 10 So the priests who bore the ark stood in the midst of the Jordan until everything was finished that the LORD had commanded Joshua to speak to the people, according to all that Moses had commanded Joshua; and the people hurried and crossed over. 11 Then it came to pass, when all the people had completely crossed over, that the ark of the LORD and the priests crossed over in the presence of the people. 12 And the men of Reuben, the men of Gad, and half the tribe of Ma·nas'seh crossed over armed before the children of Israel, as Moses had spoken to them. 13 About forty thousand prepared for war crossed over before the LORD for battle, to the plains of Jericho. 14 On that day the LORD exalted

Joshua in the sight of all Israel; and they feared him, as they had feared Moses, all the days of his life.

15 Then the LORD spoke to Joshua, saying,

16 "Command the priests who bear the ark of the Testimony to come up from the Jordan."

17 Joshua therefore commanded the priests, saying, "Come up from the Jordan."

18 And it came to pass, when the priests who bore the ark of the covenant of the LORD had come from the midst of the Jordan, *and* the soles of the priests' feet touched the dry land, that the waters of the Jordan returned to their place and overflowed all its banks as before.

19 Now the people came up from the Jordan on the tenth *day* of the first month, and they camped in Gil'gal on the east border of Jericho.

20 And those twelve stones which they took out of the Jordan, Joshua set up in Gil'gal.

21 Then he spoke to the children of Israel, saying: "When your children ask their fathers in time to come, saying, 'What *are* these stones?'

22 "then you shall let your children know, saying, 'Israel crossed over this Jordan on dry land';

23 "for the LORD your God dried up the waters of the Jordan before you until you had crossed over, as the LORD your God did to the Red Sea, which He dried up before us until we had crossed over,

24 "that all the peoples of the earth may know the hand of the LORD, that it *is* mighty, that you may fear the LORD your God forever."

THE SECOND GENERATION CIRCUMCISED

5 So it was, when all the kings of the Am'o·rītes who *were* on the west side of the Jordan, and all the kings of the Cā'naan·ītes who *were* by the sea, heard that the LORD had dried up the waters of the Jordan from before the children of Israel until we[a] had crossed over, that their heart melted; and there was no spirit in them any longer because of the children of Israel.

2 At that time the LORD said to Joshua, "Make flint knives for yourself, and circumcise the sons of Israel again the second time."

3 So Joshua made flint knives for himself, and circumcised the sons of Israel at the hill of the foreskins.[a]

4 And this *is* the reason why Joshua circumcised them: All the people who came out of Egypt *who were* males, all the men of war, had died in the wilderness on the way, after they had come out of Egypt.

5 For all the people who came out had been circumcised, but all the people born in the wilderness, on the way as they came out of Egypt, had not been circumcised.

6 For the children of Israel walked forty years in the wilderness, till all the people *who were* men of war, who came out of Egypt, were consumed, because they did not obey the voice of the LORD—to whom the LORD swore that He would not show them the land which the LORD had sworn to their fathers that He would give us, "a land flowing with milk and honey."[a]

7 Then Joshua circumcised their sons *whom* He raised up in their place; for they were uncircumcised, because they had not been circumcised on the way.

5:1 [a]Following Kethib; Qere, some Hebrew manuscripts and editions, Septuagint, Syriac, Targum, and Vulgate read *they*.   5:3 [a]Hebrew *Gibeath Haaraloth*   5:6 [a]Exodus 3:8

8   So it was, when they had finished circumcising all the people, that they stayed in their places in the camp till they were healed.

9   Then the LORD said to Joshua, "This day I have rolled away the reproach of Egypt from you." Therefore the name of the place is called Gil'gal[a] to this day.

10   Now the children of Israel camped in Gil'gal, and kept the Passover on the fourteenth day of the month at twilight on the plains of Jericho.

11   And they ate of the produce of the land on the day after the Passover, unleavened bread and parched grain, on the very same day.

12   Then the manna ceased on the day after they had eaten the produce of the land; and the children of Israel no longer had manna, but they ate the food of the land of Cā'naan that year.

THE COMMANDER OF THE ARMY OF THE LORD

13   And it came to pass, when Joshua was by Jericho, that he lifted his eyes and looked, and behold, a Man stood opposite him with His sword drawn in His hand. And Joshua went to Him and said to Him, "*Are* You for us or for our adversaries?"

14   So He said, "No, but *as* Commander of the army of the LORD I have now come." And Joshua fell on his face to the earth and worshiped, and said to Him, "What does my Lord say to His servant?"

15   Then the Commander of the LORD's army said to Joshua, "Take your sandal off your foot, for the place where you stand *is* holy." And Joshua did so.

THE DESTRUCTION OF JERICHO

It had been forty years since the people of Israel left Egypt. Now they were finally entering the Promised Land. But there was still much work to do. Many enemies had to be conquered. Here is the first enemy the people faced. After this strange battle, there was no doubt that God was leading Israel's army!

6   Now Jericho was securely shut up because of the children of Israel; none went out, and none came in.

2   And the LORD said to Joshua: "See! I have given Jericho into your hand, its king, *and* the mighty men of valor.

3   "You shall march around the city, all *you* men of war; you shall go all around the city once. This you shall do six days.

4   "And seven priests shall bear seven trumpets of rams' horns before the ark. But the seventh day you shall march around the city seven times, and the priests shall blow the trumpets.

5   "It shall come to pass, when they make a long *blast* with the ram's horn, *and* when you hear the sound of the trumpet, that all the people shall shout with a great shout; then the wall of the city will fall down flat. And the people shall go up every man straight before him."

6   Then Joshua the son of Nun called the priests and said to them, "Take up the ark of the covenant, and let seven priests bear seven trumpets of rams' horns before the ark of the LORD."

7   And he said to the people, "Proceed, and march around the city, and

5:9 [a]Literally *Rolling*

let him who is armed advance before the ark of the LORD."

8 So it was, when Joshua had spoken to the people, that the seven priests bearing the seven trumpets of rams' horns before the LORD advanced and blew the trumpets, and the ark of the covenant of the LORD followed them.

9 The armed men went before the priests who blew the trumpets, and the rear guard came after the ark, while *the priests* continued blowing the trumpets.

10 Now Joshua had commanded the people, saying, "You shall not shout or make any noise with your voice, nor shall a word proceed out of your mouth, until the day I say to you, 'Shout!' Then you shall shout."

11 So he had the ark of the LORD circle the city, going around *it* once. Then they came into the camp and lodged in the camp.

12 And Joshua rose early in the morning, and the priests took up the ark of the LORD.

13 Then seven priests bearing seven trumpets of rams' horns before the ark of the LORD went on continually and blew with the trumpets. And the armed men went before them. But the rear guard came after the ark of the LORD, while *the priests* continued blowing the trumpets.

14 And the second day they marched around the city once and returned to the camp. So they did six days.

15 But it came to pass on the seventh day that they rose early, about the dawning of the day, and marched around the city seven times in the same manner. On that day only they marched around the city seven times.

16 And the seventh time it happened, when the priests blew the trumpets, that Joshua said to the people: "Shout, for the LORD has given you the city!

17 "Now the city shall be doomed by the LORD to destruction, it and all who *are* in it. Only Rā′hab the harlot shall live, she and all who *are* with her in the house, because she hid the messengers that we sent.

18 "And you, by all means abstain from the accursed things, lest you become accursed when you take of the accursed things, and make the camp of Israel a curse, and trouble it.

19 "But all the silver and gold, and vessels of bronze and iron, *are* consecrated to the LORD; they shall come into the treasury of the LORD."

20 So the people shouted when *the priests* blew the trumpets. And it happened when the people heard the sound of the trumpet, and the people shouted with a great shout, that the wall fell down flat. Then the people went up into the city, every man straight before him, and they took the city.

21 And they utterly destroyed all that *was* in the city, both man and woman, young and old, ox and sheep and donkey, with the edge of the sword.

22 But Joshua had said to the two men who had spied out the country, "Go into the harlot's house, and from there bring out the woman and all that she has, as you swore to her."

23 And the young men who had been spies went in and brought out Rā′hab, her father, her mother, her brothers, and all that she had. So they brought out all her relatives and left them outside the camp of Israel.

24 But they burned the city and all that *was* in it with fire. Only the silver and gold, and the vessels of bronze and iron, they put into the treasury of the house of the LORD.

25 And Joshua spared Rā′hab the harlot, her father's household, and all that she had. So she dwells in Israel to this day, because she hid the

messengers whom Joshua sent to spy out Jericho.

26 Then Joshua charged *them* at that time, saying, "Cursed *be* the man before the LORD who rises up and builds this city Jericho; he shall lay its foundation with his firstborn, and with his youngest he shall set up its gates."

27 So the LORD was with Joshua, and his fame spread throughout all the country.

Bible Quiz

Joshua 6   **Jericho's Walls Fall Down**

1. Once a day, for six days, the army of Israel had to do this. What was it?
2. What did they do on the seventh day to get into the city?
3. Who was saved from the battle? Do you know why Rahab was saved?
4. If you were a soldier in Israel's army, how would you feel about having God on your side? Do you know that if you believe in Jesus, God *is* on your side? He will help you fight against the evil forces that try to keep you from doing what is good and right.

DEFEAT AT AI

7 But the children of Israel committed a trespass regarding the accursed things, for Ā'chan the son of Car'mī, the son of Zab'dī,[a] the son of Zē'rah, of the tribe of Judah, took of

the accursed things; so the anger of the LORD burned against the children of Israel.

2 Now Joshua sent men from Jericho to Aī, which *is* beside Beth Ā'ven, on the east side of Beth'el, and spoke to them, saying, "Go up and spy out the country." So the men went up and spied out Aī.

3 And they returned to Joshua and said to him, "Do not let all the people go up, but let about two or three thousand men go up and attack Aī. Do not weary all the people there, for *the people of Aī are few.*"

4 So about three thousand men went up there from the people, but they fled before the men of Aī.

5 And the men of Aī struck down about thirty-six men, for they chased them *from* before the gate as far as Sheb'a·rim, and struck them down on the descent; therefore the hearts of the people melted and became like water.

6 Then Joshua tore his clothes, and fell to the earth on his face before the ark of the LORD until evening, he and the elders of Israel; and they put dust on their heads.

7 And Joshua said, "Alas, Lord GOD, why have You brought this people over the Jordan at all—to deliver us into the hand of the Am'o·rītes, to destroy us? Oh, that we had been content, and dwelt on the other side of the Jordan!

8 "O Lord, what shall I say when Israel turns its back before its enemies?

9 "For the Cā'naan·ītes and all the inhabitants of the land will hear *it,* and surround us, and cut off our name from the earth. Then what will You do for Your great name?"

7:1 [a]Called *Zimri* in 1 Chronicles 2:6

THE SIN OF ACHAN

10 So the LORD said to Joshua: "Get up! Why do you lie thus on your face?
11 "Israel has sinned, and they have also transgressed My covenant which I commanded them. For they have even taken some of the accursed things, and have both stolen and deceived; and they have also put *it* among their own stuff.
12 "Therefore the children of Israel could not stand before their enemies, *but* turned *their* backs before their enemies, because they have become doomed to destruction. Neither will I be with you anymore, unless you destroy the accursed from among you.
13 "Get up, sanctify the people, and say, 'Sanctify yourselves for tomorrow, because thus says the LORD God of Israel: "*There is* an accursed thing in your midst, O Israel; you cannot stand before your enemies until you take away the accursed thing from among you."
14 'In the morning therefore you shall be brought according to your tribes. And it shall be *that* the tribe which the LORD takes shall come according to families; and the family which the LORD takes shall come by households; and the household which the LORD takes shall come man by man.
15 'Then it shall be *that* he who is taken with the accursed thing shall be burned with fire, he and all that he has, because he has transgressed the covenant of the LORD, and because he has done a disgraceful thing in Israel.' "
16 So Joshua rose early in the morning and brought Israel by their tribes, and the tribe of Judah was taken.
17 He brought the clan of Judah, and he took the family of the Zar'-hites; and he brought the family of the Zar'hites man by man, and Zab'dī was taken.
18 Then he brought his household man by man, and Ā'chan the son of Car'mī, the son of Zab'dī, the son of Zē'rah, of the tribe of Judah, was taken.
19 Now Joshua said to Ā'chan, "My son, I beg you, give glory to the LORD God of Israel, and make confession to Him, and tell me now what you have done; do not hide *it* from me."
20 And Ā'chan answered Joshua and said, "Indeed I have sinned against the LORD God of Israel, and this is what I have done:
21 "When I saw among the spoils a beautiful Babylonian garment, two hundred shekels of silver, and a wedge of gold weighing fifty shekels, I coveted them and took them. And there they are, hidden in the earth in the midst of my tent, with the silver under it."
22 So Joshua sent messengers, and they ran to the tent; and there it was, hidden in his tent, with the silver under it.
23 And they took them from the midst of the tent, brought them to Joshua and to all the children of Israel, and laid them out before the LORD.
24 Then Joshua, and all Israel with him, took Ā'chan the son of Zē'rah, the silver, the garment, the wedge of gold, his sons, his daughters, his oxen, his donkeys, his sheep, his tent, and all that he had, and they brought them to the Valley of Ā'chor.
25 And Joshua said, "Why have you troubled us? The LORD will trouble you this day." So all Israel stoned him with stones; and they burned them with fire after they had stoned them with stones.
26 Then they raised over him a great heap of stones, still there to this day. So the LORD turned from the fierce-

ness of His anger. Therefore the name of that place has been called the Valley of Ā'chor[a] to this day.

THE FALL OF AI

8 Now the LORD said to Joshua: "Do not be afraid, nor be dismayed; take all the people of war with you, and arise, go up to Aī. See, I have given into your hand the king of Aī, his people, his city, and his land. 2 "And you shall do to Aī and its king as you did to Jericho and its king. Only its spoil and its cattle you shall take as booty for yourselves. Lay an ambush for the city behind it."

3 So Joshua arose, and all the people of war, to go up against Aī; and Joshua chose thirty thousand mighty men of valor and sent them away by night. 4 And he commanded them, saying: "Behold, you shall lie in ambush against the city, behind the city. Do not go very far from the city, but all of you be ready. 5 "Then I and all the people who *are* with me will approach the city; and it will come about, when they come out against us as at the first, that we shall flee before them. 6 "For they will come out after us till we have drawn them from the city, for they will say, 'They are fleeing before us as at the first.' Therefore we will flee before them. 7 "Then you shall rise from the ambush and seize the city, for the LORD your God will deliver it into your hand. 8 "And it will be, when you have taken the city, *that* you shall set the city on fire. According to the commandment of the LORD you shall do. See, I have commanded you." 9 Joshua therefore sent them out;

and they went to lie in ambush, and stayed between Beth'el and Aī, on the west side of Aī; but Joshua lodged that night among the people.

10 Then Joshua rose up early in the morning and mustered the people, and went up, he and the elders of Israel, before the people to Aī. 11 And all the people of war who *were* with him went up and drew near; and they came before the city and camped on the north side of Aī. Now a valley *lay* between them and Aī. 12 So he took about five thousand men and set them in ambush between Beth'el and Aī, on the west side of the city. 13 And when they had set the people, all the army that *was* on the north of the city, and its rear guard on the west of the city, Joshua went that night into the midst of the valley.

14 Now it happened, when the king of Aī saw *it,* that the men of the city hurried and rose early and went out against Israel to battle, he and all his people, at an appointed place before the plain. But he did not know that *there was* an ambush against him behind the city. 15 And Joshua and all Israel made as if they were beaten before them, and fled by the way of the wilderness. 16 So all the people who *were* in Aī were called together to pursue them. And they pursued Joshua and were drawn away from the city. 17 There was not a man left in Aī or Beth'el who did not go out after Israel. So they left the city open and pursued Israel.

18 Then the LORD said to Joshua, "Stretch out the spear that *is* in your hand toward Aī, for I will give it into your hand." And Joshua stretched

7:26 [a]Literally *Trouble*

out the spear that *was* in his hand toward the city.

19 So *those in* ambush arose quickly out of their place; they ran as soon as he had stretched out his hand, and they entered the city and took it, and hurried to set the city on fire.

20 And when the men of Aī looked behind them, they saw, and behold, the smoke of the city ascended to heaven. So they had no power to flee this way or that way, and the people who had fled to the wilderness turned back on the pursuers.

21 Now when Joshua and all Israel saw that the ambush had taken the city and that the smoke of the city ascended, they turned back and struck down the men of Aī.

22 Then the others came out of the city against them; so they were *caught* in the midst of Israel, some on this side and some on that side. And they struck them down, so that they let none of them remain or escape.

23 But the king of Aī they took alive, and brought him to Joshua.

24 And it came to pass when Israel had made an end of slaying all the inhabitants of Aī in the field, in the wilderness where they pursued them, and when they all had fallen by the edge of the sword until they were consumed, that all the Israelites returned to Aī and struck it with the edge of the sword.

25 So it was *that* all who fell that day, both men and women, *were* twelve thousand—all the people of Aī.

26 For Joshua did not draw back his hand, with which he stretched out the spear, until he had utterly destroyed all the inhabitants of Aī.

27 Only the livestock and the spoil of that city Israel took as booty for themselves, according to the word of the LORD which He had commanded Joshua.

28 So Joshua burned Aī and made it a heap forever, a desolation to this day.

29 And the king of Aī he hanged on a tree until evening. And as soon as the sun was down, Joshua commanded that they should take his corpse down from the tree, cast it at the entrance of the gate of the city, and raise over it a great heap of stones *that remains* to this day.

JOSHUA RENEWS THE COVENANT

30 Now Joshua built an altar to the LORD God of Israel in Mount Ē′bal,

31 as Moses the servant of the LORD had commanded the children of Israel, as it is written in the Book of the Law of Moses: "an altar of whole stones over which no man has wielded an iron *tool.*"[a] And they offered on it burnt offerings to the LORD, and sacrificed peace offerings.

32 And there, in the presence of the children of Israel, he wrote on the stones a copy of the law of Moses, which he had written.

33 Then all Israel, with their elders and officers and judges, stood on either side of the ark before the priests, the Lē′vītes, who bore the ark of the covenant of the LORD, the stranger as well as he who was born among them. Half of them *were* in front of Mount Ger′i·zim and half of them in front of Mount Ē′bal, as Moses the servant of the LORD had commanded before, that they should bless the people of Israel.

34 And afterward he read all the words of the law, the blessings and the cursings, according to all that is written in the Book of the Law.

35 There was not a word of all that Moses had commanded which Joshua did not read before all the assembly

8:31 [a]Deuteronomy 27:5, 6

of Israel, with the women, the little ones, and the strangers who were living among them.

THE TREATY WITH THE GIBEONITES

9 And it came to pass when all the kings who *were* on this side of the Jordan, in the hills and in the lowland and in all the coasts of the Great Sea toward Lebanon—the Hit'tīte, the Am'o·rīte, the Cā'naan·īte, the Per'iz·zīte, the Hī'vīte, and the Jeb'ū·sīte—heard *about it,*

2 that they gathered together to fight with Joshua and Israel with one accord.

3 But when the inhabitants of Gib'ē·on heard what Joshua had done to Jericho and Aī,

4 they worked craftily, and went and pretended to be ambassadors. And they took old sacks on their donkeys, old wineskins torn and mended,

5 old and patched sandals on their feet, and old garments on themselves; and all the bread of their provision was dry *and* moldy.

6 And they went to Joshua, to the camp at Gil'gal, and said to him and to the men of Israel, "We have come from a far country; now therefore, make a covenant with us."

7 Then the men of Israel said to the Hī'vītes, "Perhaps you dwell among us; so how can we make a covenant with you?"

8 But they said to Joshua, "We *are* your servants." And Joshua said to them, "Who *are* you, and where do you come from?"

9 So they said to him: "From a very far country your servants have come, because of the name of the LORD your God; for we have heard of His fame, and all that He did in Egypt,

10 "and all that He did to the two kings of the Am'o·rītes who *were* beyond the Jordan—to Sī'hon king of Hesh'bon, and Og king of Bā'shan, who was at Ash'ta·roth.

11 "Therefore our elders and all the inhabitants of our country spoke to us, saying, 'Take provisions with you for the journey, and go to meet them, and say to them, "We *are* your servants; now therefore, make a covenant with us." '

12 "This bread of ours we took hot *for* our provision from our houses on the day we departed to come to you. But now look, it is dry and moldy.

13 "And these wineskins which we filled *were* new, and see, they are torn; and these our garments and our sandals have become old because of the very long journey."

14 Then the men of Israel took some of their provisions; but they did not ask counsel of the LORD.

15 So Joshua made peace with them, and made a covenant with them to let them live; and the rulers of the congregation swore to them.

16 And it happened at the end of three days, after they had made a covenant with them, that they heard that they *were* their neighbors who dwelt near them.

17 Then the children of Israel journeyed and came to their cities on the third day. Now their cities *were* Gib'ē·on, Chē·phī'rah, Be·er'oth, and Kir'jath Jē'a·rim.

18 But the children of Israel did not attack them, because the rulers of the congregation had sworn to them by the LORD God of Israel. And all the congregation complained against the rulers.

19 Then all the rulers said to all the congregation, "We have sworn to them by the LORD God of Israel; now therefore, we may not touch them.

20 "This we will do to them: We will let them live, lest wrath be upon us

because of the oath which we swore to them."

21 And the rulers said to them, "Let them live, but let them be wood-cutters and water carriers for all the congregation, as the rulers had promised them."

22 Then Joshua called for them, and he spoke to them, saying, "Why have you deceived us, saying, 'We *are* very far from you,' when you dwell near us?

23 "Now therefore, you *are* cursed, and none of you shall be freed from being slaves—woodcutters and water carriers for the house of my God."

24 So they answered Joshua and said, "Because your servants were clearly told that the LORD your God commanded His servant Moses to give you all the land, and to destroy all the inhabitants of the land from before you; therefore we were very much afraid for our lives because of you, and have done this thing.

25 "And now, here we are, in your hands; do with us as it seems good and right to do to us."

26 So he did to them, and delivered them out of the hand of the children of Israel, so that they did not kill them.

27 And that day Joshua made them woodcutters and water carriers for the congregation and for the altar of the LORD, in the place which He would choose, even to this day.

THE SUN STANDS STILL

10 Now it came to pass when A·dō′ni-Zē′dek king of Jerusalem heard how Joshua had taken Aī and had utterly destroyed it—as he had done to Jericho and its king, so he had done to Aī and its king—and how the inhabitants of Gib′ē·on had made peace with Israel and were among them,

2 that they feared greatly, because Gib′ē·on *was* a great city, like one of the royal cities, and because it *was* greater than Aī, and all its men *were* mighty.

3 Therefore A·dō′ni-Zē′dek king of Jerusalem sent to Hō′ham king of Hē′bron, Pī′ram king of Jar′muth, Ja·phī′a king of Lā′chish, and Dē′bir king of Eg′lon, saying,

4 "Come up to me and help me, that we may attack Gib′ē·on, for it has made peace with Joshua and with the children of Israel."

5 Therefore the five kings of the Am′o·rītes, the king of Jerusalem, the king of Hē′bron, the king of Jar′muth, the king of Lā′chish, *and* the king of Eg′lon, gathered together and went up, they and all their armies, and camped before Gib′ē·on and made war against it.

6 And the men of Gib′ē·on sent to Joshua at the camp at Gil′gal, saying, "Do not forsake your servants; come up to us quickly, save us and help us, for all the kings of the Am′o·rītes who dwell in the mountains have gathered together against us."

7 So Joshua ascended from Gil′gal, he and all the people of war with him, and all the mighty men of valor.

8 And the LORD said to Joshua, "Do not fear them, for I have delivered them into your hand; not a man of them shall stand before you."

9 Joshua therefore came upon them suddenly, having marched all night from Gil′gal.

10 So the LORD routed them before Israel, killed them with a great slaughter at Gib′ē·on, chased them along the road that goes to Beth Hor′on, and struck them down as far as A·zē′kah and Mak·kē′dah.

11 And it happened, as they fled before Israel *and* were on the descent of Beth Hor′on, that the LORD cast

down large hailstones from heaven on them as far as A·zē′kah, and they died. *There were* more who died from the hailstones than the children of Israel killed with the sword.

12 Then Joshua spoke to the LORD in the day when the LORD delivered up the Am′o·rītes before the children of Israel, and he said in the sight of Israel:

"Sun, stand still over Gib′ē·on;
    And Moon, in the Valley of
      Aī′ja·lon."
13 So the sun stood still,
    And the moon stopped,
    Till the people had revenge
    Upon their enemies.

Is this not written in the Book of Jā′sher? So the sun stood still in the midst of heaven, and did not hasten to go *down* for about a whole day.
14 And there has been no day like that, before it or after it, that the LORD heeded the voice of a man; for the LORD fought for Israel.
15 Then Joshua returned, and all Israel with him, to the camp at Gil′gal.

THE AMORITE KINGS EXECUTED

16 But these five kings had fled and hidden themselves in a cave at Mak·kē′dah.
17 And it was told Joshua, saying, "The five kings have been found hidden in the cave at Mak·kē′dah."
18 So Joshua said, "Roll large stones against the mouth of the cave, and set men by it to guard them.
19 "And do not stay *there* yourselves, *but* pursue your enemies, and attack their rear *guard*. Do not allow them to enter their cities, for the LORD your God has delivered them into your hand."
20 Then it happened, while Joshua and the children of Israel made an

end of slaying them with a very great slaughter, till they had finished, that those who escaped entered fortified cities.
21 And all the people returned to the camp, to Joshua at Mak·kē′dah, in peace. No one moved his tongue against any of the children of Israel.
22 Then Joshua said, "Open the mouth of the cave, and bring out those five kings to me from the cave."
23 And they did so, and brought out those five kings to him from the cave: the king of Jerusalem, the king of Hē′bron, the king of Jar′muth, the king of Lā′chish, *and* the king of Eg′lon.
24 So it was, when they brought out those kings to Joshua, that Joshua called for all the men of Israel, and said to the captains of the men of war who went with him, "Come near, put your feet on the necks of these kings." And they drew near and put their feet on their necks.
25 Then Joshua said to them, "Do not be afraid, nor be dismayed; be strong and of good courage, for thus the LORD will do to all your enemies against whom you fight."
26 And afterward Joshua struck them and killed them, and hanged them on five trees; and they were hanging on the trees until evening.
27 So it was at the time of the going down of the sun *that* Joshua commanded, and they took them down from the trees, cast them into the cave where they had been hidden, and laid large stones against the cave's mouth, *which remain* until this very day.

CONQUEST OF THE SOUTHLAND

28 On that day Joshua took Mak·kē′dah, and struck it and its king with the edge of the sword. He ut-

terly destroyed them[a]—all the people who *were* in it. He let none remain. He also did to the king of Mak·kē′dah as he had done to the king of Jericho.

29 Then Joshua passed from Mak·kē′dah, and all Israel with him, to Lib′nah; and they fought against Lib′-nah.

30 And the LORD also delivered it and its king into the hand of Israel; he struck it and all the people who *were* in it with the edge of the sword. He let none remain in it, but did to its king as he had done to the king of Jericho.

31 Then Joshua passed from Lib′-nah, and all Israel with him, to Lā′-chish; and they encamped against it and fought against it.

32 And the LORD delivered Lā′chish into the hand of Israel, who took it on the second day, and struck it and all the people who *were* in it with the edge of the sword, according to all that he had done to Lib′nah.

33 Then Hō′ram king of Gē′zer came up to help Lā′chish; and Joshua struck him and his people, until he left him none remaining.

34 From Lā′chish Joshua passed to Eg′lon, and all Israel with him; and they encamped against it and fought against it.

35 They took it on that day and struck it with the edge of the sword; all the people who *were* in it he utterly destroyed that day, according to all that he had done to Lā′chish.

36 So Joshua went up from Eg′lon, and all Israel with him, to Hē′bron; and they fought against it.

37 And they took it and struck it with the edge of the sword—its king, all its cities, and all the people who *were* in it; he left none remaining, according to all that he had done to Eg′lon, but utterly destroyed it and all the people who *were* in it.

38 Then Joshua returned, and all Israel with him, to Dē′bir; and they fought against it.

39 And he took it and its king and all its cities; they struck them with the edge of the sword and utterly destroyed all the people who *were* in it. He left none remaining; as he had done to Hē′bron, so he did to Dē′bir and its king, as he had done also to Lib′nah and its king.

40 So Joshua conquered all the land: the mountain country and the South[a] and the lowland and the wilderness slopes, and all their kings; he left none remaining, but utterly destroyed all that breathed, as the LORD God of Israel had commanded.

41 And Joshua conquered them from Kā′desh Bar·nē′a as far as Gā′za, and all the country of Gō′shen, even as far as Gib′e·on.

42 All these kings and their land Joshua took at one time, because the LORD God of Israel fought for Israel.

43 Then Joshua returned, and all Israel with him, to the camp at Gil′gal.

THE NORTHERN CONQUEST

11 And it came to pass, when Jā′bin king of Hā′zor heard *these things,* that he sent to Jō′bab king of Mā′don, to the king of Shim′ron, to the king of Ach′shaph,

2 and to the kings who *were* from the north, in the mountains, in the plain south of Chin′ne·roth, in the lowland, and in the heights of Dor on the west,

3 to the Cā′naan·ites in the east and in the west, the Am′o·rīte, the Hit′tīte, the Per′iz·zīte, the Jeb′u·sīte in the mountains, and the Hī′vīte below Her′mon in the land of Miz′pah.

10:28 [a]Following Masoretic Text and most authorities; many Hebrew manuscripts, some manuscripts of the Septuagint, and some manuscripts of the Targum read *it.*　　10:40 [a]Hebrew *Negev,* and so throughout this book

4 So they went out, they and all their armies with them, *as* many people *as* the sand that *is* on the seashore in multitude, with very many horses and chariots.

5 And when all these kings had met together, they came and camped together at the waters of Mē′rom to fight against Israel.

6 But the LORD said to Joshua, "Do not be afraid because of them, for tomorrow about this time I will deliver all of them slain before Israel. You shall hamstring their horses and burn their chariots with fire."

7 So Joshua and all the people of war with him came against them suddenly by the waters of Mē′rom, and they attacked them.

8 And the LORD delivered them into the hand of Israel, who defeated them and chased them to Greater Sī′don, to the Brook Mis′re·photh,*a* and to the Valley of Miz′pah eastward; they attacked them until they left none of them remaining.

9 So Joshua did to them as the LORD had told him: he hamstrung their horses and burned their chariots with fire.

10 Joshua turned back at that time and took Hā′zor, and struck its king with the sword; for Hā′zor was formerly the head of all those kingdoms.

11 And they struck all the people who *were* in it with the edge of the sword, utterly destroying *them*. There was none left breathing. Then he burned Hā′zor with fire.

12 So all the cities of those kings, and all their kings, Joshua took and struck with the edge of the sword. He utterly destroyed them, as Moses the servant of the LORD had commanded.

13 But *as for* the cities that stood on their mounds,*a* Israel burned none of them, except Hā′zor only, *which* Joshua burned.

14 And all the spoil of these cities and the livestock, the children of Israel took as booty for themselves; but they struck every man with the edge of the sword until they had destroyed them, and they left none breathing.

15 As the LORD had commanded Moses his servant, so Moses commanded Joshua, and so Joshua did. He left nothing undone of all that the LORD had commanded Moses.

SUMMARY OF JOSHUA'S CONQUESTS

16 Thus Joshua took all this land: the mountain country, all the South, all the land of Gō′shen, the lowland, and the Jordan plain*a*—the mountains of Israel and its lowlands,

17 from Mount Hā′lak and the ascent to Sē′ir, even as far as Bā′al Gad in the Valley of Lebanon below Mount Her′mon. He captured all their kings, and struck them down and killed them.

18 Joshua made war a long time with all those kings.

19 There was not a city that made peace with the children of Israel, except the Hī′vites, the inhabitants of Gib′ē·on. All *the others* they took in battle.

20 For it was of the LORD to harden their hearts, that they should come against Israel in battle, that He might utterly destroy them, *and* that they might receive no mercy, but that He might destroy them, as the LORD had commanded Moses.

21 And at that time Joshua came and cut off the An′a·kim from the mountains: from Hē′bron, from Dē′bir, from Ā′nab, from all the mountains of Judah, and from all the mountains of Israel; Joshua utterly destroyed them with their cities.

11:8 *a*Hebrew *Misrephoth Maim*   11:13 *a*Hebrew *tel,* a heap of successive city ruins
11:16 *a*Hebrew *arabah*

22 None of the An'a·kim were left in the land of the children of Israel; they remained only in Gā'za, in Gath, and in Ash'dod.

23 So Joshua took the whole land, according to all that the LORD had said to Moses; and Joshua gave it as an inheritance to Israel according to their divisions by their tribes. Then the land rested from war.

THE KINGS CONQUERED BY MOSES

12 These *are* the kings of the land whom the children of Israel defeated, and whose land they possessed on the other side of the Jordan toward the rising of the sun, from the River Ar'non to Mount Her'mon, and all the eastern Jordan plain:

2 *One king was* Sī'hon king of the Am'o·rītes, who dwelt in Hesh'bon *and* ruled half of Gil'ē·ad, from A·rō'er, which is on the bank of the River Ar'non, from the middle of that river, even as far as the River Jab'bok, *which is* the border of the Am'mon·ītes,

3 and the eastern Jordan plain from the Sea of Chin'ne·roth as far as the Sea of the Ar'a·bah (the Salt Sea), the road to Beth Jesh'i·moth, and southward below the slopes of Pis'gah.

4 *The other king was* Og king of Bā'shan and his territory, *who was* of the remnant of the giants, who dwelt at Ash'ta·roth and at Ed'rē·ī,

5 and reigned over Mount Her'mon, over Sal'cah, over all Bā'shan, as far as the border of the Gesh'ū·rītes and the Mā'a·cha·thītes, and over half of Gil'ē·ad *to* the border of Sī'hon king of Hesh'bon.

6 These Moses the servant of the LORD and the children of Israel had conquered; and Moses the servant of the LORD had given it *as* a possession to the Reū'ben·ītes, the Gad'ītes, and half the tribe of Ma·nas'seh.

THE KINGS CONQUERED BY JOSHUA

7 And these *are* the kings of the country which Joshua and the children of Israel conquered on this side of the Jordan, on the west, from Bā'al Gad in the Valley of Lebanon as far as Mount Hā'lak and the ascent to Sē'ir, which Joshua gave to the tribes of Israel *as* a possession according to their divisions,

8 in the mountain country, in the lowlands, in the *Jordan* plain, in the slopes, in the wilderness, and in the South—the Hit'tītes, the Am'o·rītes, the Cā'naan·ītes, the Per'iz·zītes, the Hī'vītes, and the Jeb'ū·sītes:

9 the king of Jericho, one; the king of Ai, which *is* beside Beth'el, one;

10 the king of Jerusalem, one; the king of Hē'bron, one;

11 the king of Jar'muth, one; the king of Lā'chish, one;

12 the king of Eg'lon, one; the king of Gē'zer, one;

13 the king of Dē'bir, one; the king of Gē'der, one;

14 the king of Hor'mah, one; the king of Ar'ad, one;

15 the king of Lib'nah, one; the king of A·dul'lam, one;

16 the king of Mak·kē'dah, one; the king of Beth'el, one;

17 the king of Tap'pū·ah, one; the king of Hē'pher, one;

18 the king of Ā'phek, one; the king of La·shar'on, one;

19 the king of Mā'don, one; the king of Hā'zor, one;

20 the king of Shim'ron Mē'ron, one; the king of Ach'shaph, one;

21 the king of Tā'a·nach, one; the king of Me·gid'dō, one;

22 the king of Kē'desh, one; the king of Jok'nē·am in Car'mel, one;

23 the king of Dor in the heights of

Dor, one; the king of the people of Gil'gal, one;

24 the king of Tir'zah, one—all the kings, thirty-one.

REMAINING LAND TO BE CONQUERED

13 Now Joshua was old, advanced in years. And the LORD said to him: "You are old, advanced in years, and there remains very much land yet to be possessed.

2 "This is the land that yet remains: all the territory of the Philis'tines and all *that of* the Gesh'ū-rītes,

3 "from Sī'hor, which *is* east of Egypt, as far as the border of Ek'ron northward (*which* is counted as Cā'naan·ite); the five lords of the Phi·lis'tines—the Gā'zītes, the Ash'-dod·ītes, the Ash'ke·lon·ītes, the Git'-tītes, and the Ek'ron·ītes; also the Av'ītes;

4 "from the south, all the land of the Cā'naan·ītes, and Me·ar'ah that belongs to the Sī·dō'ni·ans as far as Ā'phek, to the border of the Am'-o·rītes;

5 "the land of the Gē'bal·ites,*a* and all Lebanon, toward the sunrise, from Bā'al Gad below Mount Her'mon as far as the entrance to Hā'math;

6 "all the inhabitants of the mountains from Lebanon as far as the Brook Mis're·photh,*a and* all the Sī·dō'ni·ans—them I will drive out from before the children of Israel; only divide it by lot to Israel as an inheritance, as I have commanded you.

7 "Now therefore, divide this land as an inheritance to the nine tribes and half the tribe of Ma·nas'seh."

THE LAND DIVIDED EAST OF THE JORDAN

8 With the other half-tribe the Reū'ben·ites and the Gad'ites re-ceived their inheritance, which Moses had given them, beyond the Jordan eastward, as Moses the servant of the LORD had given them:

9 from A·rō'er which *is* on the bank of the River Ar'non, and the town that *is* in the midst of the ravine, and all the plain of Med'e·ba as far as Dī'bon;

10 all the cities of Sī'hon king of the Am'o·rītes, who reigned in Hesh'bon, as far as the border of the children of Am'mon;

11 Gil'ē·ad, and the border of the Gesh'ū·rītes and Mā'a·cha·thītes, all Mount Her'mon, and all Bā'shan as far as Sal'cah;

12 all the kingdom of Og in Bā'shan, who reigned in Ash'ta·roth and Ed'-rē·ī, who remained of the remnant of the giants; for Moses had defeated and cast out these.

13 Nevertheless the children of Israel did not drive out the Gesh'ū·rītes or the Mā'a·cha·thītes, but the Gesh'ū·rītes and the Mā'a·cha·thītes dwell among the Israelites until this day.

14 Only to the tribe of Levi he had given no inheritance; the sacrifices of the LORD God of Israel made by fire *are* their inheritance, as He said to them.

THE LAND OF REUBEN

15 And Moses had given to the tribe of the children of Reuben *an inheritance* according to their families.

16 Their territory was from A·rō'er, which *is* on the bank of the River Ar'non, and the city that *is* in the midst of the ravine, and all the plain by Med'e·ba;

17 Hesh'bon and all its cities that *are* in the plain: Dī'bon, Bā'moth Bā'al, Beth Bā'al Mē'on,

---

13:5 *a*Or *Giblites*   13:6 *a*Hebrew *Misrephoth Maim*

18 Ja·ha'za, Ked'e·moth, Meph'a-ath,

19 Kir·jath'a·im, Sib'mah, Zē'reth Shā'har on the mountain of the valley,

20 Beth Pē'or, the slopes of Pis'gah, and Beth Jesh'i·moth—

21 all the cities of the plain and all the kingdom of Sī'hon king of the Am'o·rītes, who reigned in Hesh'bon, whom Moses had struck with the princes of Mid'i·an: Ē'vī, Rē'kem, Zūr, Hur, and Rē'ba, who *were* princes of Sī'hon dwelling in the country.

22 The children of Israel also killed with the sword Bā'laam the son of Bē'or, the soothsayer, among those who were killed by them.

23 And the border of the children of Reuben was the bank of the Jordan. This *was* the inheritance of the children of Reuben according to their families, the cities and their villages.

THE LAND OF GAD

24 Moses also had given *an inheritance* to the tribe of Gad, to the children of Gad according to their families.

25 Their territory was Jā'zer, and all the cities of Gil'e·ad, and half the land of the Am'mon·ītes as far as A·rō'er, which *is* before Rab'bah,

26 and from Hesh'bon to Rā'math Miz'pah and Bet'ō·nim, and from Mā·ha·na'im to the border of Dē'bir,

27 and in the valley Beth Hā'ram, Beth Nim'rah, Suc'coth, and Zā'-phon, the rest of the kingdom of Sī'-hon king of Hesh'bon, with the Jordan as *its* border, as far as the edge of the Sea of Chin'ne·reth, on the other side of the Jordan eastward.

28 This *is* the inheritance of the children of Gad according to their families, the cities and their villages.

HALF THE TRIBE OF MANASSEH (EAST)

29 Moses also had given *an inheritance* to half the tribe of Ma·nas'seh; it was for half the tribe of the children of Ma·nas'seh according to their families:

30 Their territory was from Mā-ha·na'im, all Bā'shan, all the kingdom of Og king of Bā'shan, and all the towns of Jā'ir which are in Bā'shan, sixty cities;

31 half of Gil'e·ad, and Ash'ta·roth and Ed'rē·ī, cities of the kingdom of Og in Bā'shan, *were* for the children of Mā'chir the son of Ma·nas'seh, for half of the children of Mā'chir according to their families.

32 These *are the areas* which Moses had distributed as an inheritance in the plains of Mō'ab on the other side of the Jordan, by Jericho eastward.

33 But to the tribe of Levi Moses had given no inheritance; the LORD God of Israel *was* their inheritance, as He had said to them.

THE LAND DIVIDED WEST OF THE JORDAN

14 These *are the areas* which the children of Israel inherited in the land of Cā'naan, which El·ē·ā'zar the priest, Joshua the son of Nun, and the heads of the fathers of the tribes of the children of Israel distributed as an inheritance to them.

2 Their inheritance *was* by lot, as the LORD had commanded by the hand of Moses, for the nine tribes and the half-tribe.

3 For Moses had given the inheritance of the two tribes and the half-tribe on the other side of the Jordan; but to the Lē'vītes he had given no inheritance among them.

4 For the children of Joseph were two tribes: Ma·nas'seh and

Ē'phra·im. And they gave no part to the Lē'vītes in the land, except cities to dwell in, with their common-lands for their livestock and their property.

5 As the LORD had commanded Moses, so the children of Israel did; and they divided the land.

CALEB INHERITS HEBRON

6 Then the children of Judah came to Joshua in Gil'gal. And Caleb the son of Je·phūn'neh the Kē'niz·zīte said to him: "You know the word which the LORD said to Moses the man of God concerning you and me in Kā'desh Bar·nē'a.

7 "I was forty years old when Moses the servant of the LORD sent me from Kā'desh Bar·nē'a to spy out the land, and I brought back word to him as it was in my heart.

8 "Nevertheless my brethren who went up with me made the heart of the people melt, but I wholly followed the LORD my God.

9 "So Moses swore on that day, saying, 'Surely the land where your foot has trodden shall be your inheritance and your children's forever, because you have wholly followed the LORD my God.'

10 "And now, behold, the LORD has kept me alive, as He said, these forty-five years, ever since the LORD spoke this word to Moses while Israel wandered in the wilderness; and now, here I am this day, eighty-five years old.

11 "As yet I am as strong this day as on the day that Moses sent me; just as my strength was then, so now is my strength for war, both for going out and for coming in.

12 "Now therefore, give me this mountain of which the LORD spoke in that day; for you heard in that day how the An'a·kim were there, and that the cities were great and forti-

fied. It may be that the LORD will be with me, and I shall be able to drive them out as the LORD said."

13 And Joshua blessed him, and gave Hē'bron to Caleb the son of Je·phūn'neh as an inheritance.

14 Hē'bron therefore became the inheritance of Caleb the son of Je·phūn'neh the Kē'niz·zīte to this day, because he wholly followed the LORD God of Israel.

15 And the name of Hē'bron formerly was Kir'jath Ar'ba (Ar'ba was the greatest man among the An'a·kim). Then the land had rest from war.

THE LAND OF JUDAH

15 So this was the lot of the tribe of the children of Judah according to their families: The border of Ē'dom at the Wilderness of Zin southward was the extreme southern boundary.

2 And their southern border began at the shore of the Salt Sea, from the bay that faces southward.

3 Then it went out to the southern side of the Ascent of Ak·rab'bim, passed along to Zin, ascended on the south side of Kā'desh Bar·nē'a, passed along to Hez'ron, went up to Ā'dar, and went around to Kar'ka·a.

4 From there it passed toward Az'mon and went out to the Brook of Egypt; and the border ended at the sea. This shall be your southern border.

5 The east border was the Salt Sea as far as the mouth of the Jordan. And the border on the northern quarter began at the bay of the sea at the mouth of the Jordan.

6 The border went up to Beth Hog'lah and passed north of Beth Ar'a·bah; and the border went up to the stone of Bō'han the son of Reuben.

7 Then the border went up toward Dē′bir from the Valley of Ā′chor, and it turned northward toward Gil′gal, which *is* before the Ascent of A·dum′mim, which *is* on the south side of the valley. The border continued toward the waters of En Shem′esh and ended at En Rō′gel.

8 And the border went up by the Valley of the Son of Hin′nom to the southern slope of the Jeb′ū·sīte *city* (which *is* Jerusalem). The border went up to the top of the mountain that *lies* before the Valley of Hin′nom westward, which *is* at the end of the Valley of Reph′a·im*ᵃ* northward.

9 Then the border went around from the top of the hill to the fountain of the water of Neph·tō′ah, and extended to the cities of Mount Ē′phron. And the border went around to Bā′a·lah (which *is* Kir′jath Jē′a·rim).

10 Then the border turned westward from Bā′a·lah to Mount Sē′ir, passed along to the side of Mount Jē′a·rim on the north (which *is* Ches′a·lon), went down to Beth Shem′esh, and passed on to Tim′nah.

11 And the border went out to the side of Ek′ron northward. Then the border went around to Shic′ron, passed along to Mount Bā′a·lah, and extended to Jab′nē·el; and the border ended at the sea.

12 The west border *was* the coastline of the Great Sea. This *is* the boundary of the children of Judah all around according to their families.

CALEB OCCUPIES HEBRON AND DEBIR

13 Now to Caleb the son of Je·phŭn′neh he gave a share among the children of Judah, according to the commandment of the LORD to Joshua, *namely,* Kir′jath Ar′ba, which *is* Hē′bron (*Ar′ba was* the father of Ā′nak).

14 Caleb drove out the three sons of Ā′nak from there: Shē′shai, A·hī′man, and Tal′maī, the children of Ā′nak.

15 Then he went up from there to the inhabitants of Dē′bir (formerly the name of Dē′bir *was* Kir′jath Sē′pher).

16 And Caleb said, "He who attacks Kir′jath Sē′pher and takes it, to him I will give Ach′sah my daughter as wife."

17 So Oth′ni·el the son of Kē′naz, the brother of Caleb, took it; and he gave him Ach′sah his daughter as wife.

18 Now it was so, when she came *to him,* that she persuaded him to ask her father for a field. So she dismounted from *her* donkey, and Caleb said to her, "What do you wish?"

19 She answered, "Give me a blessing; since you have given me land in the South, give me also springs of water." So he gave her the upper springs and the lower springs.

THE CITIES OF JUDAH

20 This *was* the inheritance of the tribe of the children of Judah according to their families:

21 The cities at the limits of the tribe of the children of Judah, toward the border of Ē′dom in the South, were Kab′zē·el, Ē′der, Jā′gur,

22 Kinah, Di·mō′nah, A·dā′dah,

23 Kē′desh, Hā′zor, Ith′nan,

24 Ziph, Tē′lem, Be·ā′loth,

25 Hā′zor, Ha·dat′tah, Ker′i·oth, Hez′ron (which *is* Hā′zor),

26 Ā′mam, Shē′ma, Mō′la·dah,

27 Hā′zar Gad′dah, Hesh′mon, Beth Pē′let,

28 Hā′zar Shū′al, Bē·er·shē′ba, Biz·joth′jah,

15:8 *ᵃ*Literally *Giants*

29 Bā′a·lah, Ī′jim, Ē′zem,
30 El·tō′lad, Chē′sil, Hor′mah,
31 Zik′lag, Mad·man′nah, San-san′nah,
32 Le·bā′oth, Shil′him, Ā′in, and Rim′mon: all the cities *are* twenty-nine, with their villages.
33 In the lowland: Esh′tā·ol, Zō′rah, Ash′nah,
34 Za·nō′ah, En Gan′nim, Tap′pū·ah, Ē′nam,
35 Jar′muth, A·dul′lam, Sō′cōh, A·zē′kah,
36 Sha·rā′im, Ad·i·thā′im, Ge·dē′rah, and Ged·e·rō·thā′im: fourteen cities with their villages;
37 Zē′nan, Ha·dash′ah, Migdal Gad,
38 Dil′e·an, Miz′pah, Jok′the·el,
39 Lā′chish, Boz′kath, Eg′lon,
40 Cab′bon, Lah′mas,[a] Kith′lish,
41 Ge·dē′roth, Beth Dā′gon, Nā′a·mah, and Mak·kē′dah: sixteen cities with their villages;
42 Lib′nah, Ē′ther, Ā′shan,
43 Jiph′tah, Ash′nah, Nē′zib,
44 Kē·ī′lah, Ach′zib, and Ma·rē′shah: nine cities with their villages;
45 Ek′ron, with its towns and villages;
46 from Ek′ron to the sea, all that *lay* near Ash′dod, with their villages;
47 Ash′dod with its towns and villages, Gā′za with its towns and villages—as far as the Brook of Egypt and the Great Sea with *its* coastline.
48 And in the mountain country: Shā′mir, Jat′tir, Sō′chōh,
49 Dan′nah, Kir′jath San′nah (which *is* Dē′bir),
50 Ā′nab, Esh′te·mōh, Ā′nim,
51 Gō′shen, Hō′lon, and Gī′lōh: eleven cities with their villages;
52 Arab, Dū′mah, Esh′e·an,
53 Jā′num, Beth Tap′pū·ah, A·phē′kah,
54 Hum′tah, Kir′jath Ar′ba (which *is* Hē′bron), and Zī′or: nine cities with their villages;
55 Mā′on, Car′mel, Ziph, Jut′tah,

56 Jez′re·el, Jok′de·am, Za·nō′ah,
57 Kāin, Gib′e·ah, and Tim′nah: ten cities with their villages;
58 Hal′hul, Beth Zūr, Gē′dor,
59 Mā′a·rath, Beth Ā′noth, and El′tē·kon: six cities with their villages;
60 Kir′jath Bā′al (which *is* Kir′jath Jē′a·rim) and Rab′bah: two cities with their villages.
61 In the wilderness: Beth Ar′a·bah, Mid′din, Se·cā′cah,
62 Nib′shan, the City of Salt, and En Ge′di: six cities with their villages.
63 As for the Jeb′ū·sītes, the inhabitants of Jerusalem, the children of Judah could not drive them out; but the Jeb′ū·sītes dwell with the children of Judah at Jerusalem to this day.

EPHRAIM AND WEST MANASSEH

16 The lot fell to the children of Joseph from the Jordan, by Jericho, to the waters of Jericho on the east, to the wilderness that goes up from Jericho through the mountains to Beth′el,
2 then went out from Beth′el to Luz,[a] passed along to the border of the Ar′chītes at At′a·roth,
3 and went down westward to the boundary of the Japh′let·ītes, as far as the boundary of Lower Beth Hor′on to Gē′zer; and it ended at the sea.
4 So the children of Joseph, Ma·nas′seh and Ē′phra·im, took their inheritance.

THE LAND OF EPHRAIM

5 The border of the children of Ē′phra·im, according to their families, was *thus:* The border of their in-

15:40 [a]Or *Lahmam*   16:2 [a]Septuagint reads *Bethel* (that is, Luz).

heritance on the east side was At'-a·roth Ad'dar as far as Upper Beth Hor'on.

6 And the border went out toward the sea on the north side of Mich·me'thath; then the border went around eastward to Tā'a·nath Shī'-lōh, and passed by it on the east of Ja·nō'hah.

7 Then it went down from Ja-nō'hah to At'a·roth and Nā'a·rah,a reached to Jericho, and came out at the Jordan.

8 The border went out from Tap'pū·ah westward to the Brook Kā'nah, and it ended at the sea. This *was* the inheritance of the tribe of the children of Ē'phra·im according to their families.

9 The separate cities for the children of Ē'phra·im *were* among the inheritance of the children of Ma-nas'seh, all the cities with their villages.

10 And they did not drive out the Cā'naan·ītes who dwelt in Gē'zer; but the Cā'naan·ītes dwell among the Ē'phra·im·ītes to this day and have become forced laborers.

THE OTHER HALF-TRIBE OF MANASSEH (WEST)

17 There was also a lot for the tribe of Ma·nas'seh, for he *was* the firstborn of Joseph: *namely* for Mā'chir the firstborn of Ma·nas'seh, the father of Gil'ē·ad, because he was a man of war; therefore he was given Gil'ē·ad and Bā'shan.

2 And there was *a lot* for the rest of the children of Ma·nas'seh according to their families: for the children of Ā·bi·ē'zer,a the children of Hē'lek, the children of As'ri·el, the children of Shē'chem, the children of Hē'pher, and the children of She·mī'da; these *were* the male children of Ma·nas'seh

the son of Joseph according to their families.

3 But Ze·loph'e·had the son of Hē'pher, the son of Gil'ē·ad, the son of Mā'chir, the son of Ma·nas'seh, had no sons, but only daughters. And these *are* the names of his daughters: Mah'lah, Noah, Hog'lah, Mil'cah, and Tir'zah.

4 And they came near before El·ē·ā'zar the priest, before Joshua the son of Nun, and before the rulers, saying, "The LORD commanded Moses to give us an inheritance among our brothers." Therefore, according to the commandment of the LORD, he gave them an inheritance among their father's brothers.

5 Ten shares fell to Ma·nas'seh, besides the land of Gil'ē·ad and Bā'-shan, which *were* on the other side of the Jordan,

6 because the daughters of Ma-nas'seh received an inheritance among his sons; and the rest of Ma-nas'seh's sons had the land of Gil'-ē·ad.

7 And the territory of Ma·nas'seh was from Ash'er to Mich·me'thath, that *lies* east of Shē'chem; and the border went along south to the inhabitants of En Tap'pū·ah.

8 Ma·nas'seh had the land of Tap'-pū·ah, but Tap'pū·ah on the border of Ma·nas'seh *belonged* to the children of Ē'phra·im.

9 And the border descended to the Brook Kā'nah, southward to the brook. These cities of Ē'phra·im *are* among the cities of Ma·nas'seh. The border of Ma·nas'seh *was* on the north side of the brook; and it ended at the sea.

10 Southward *it was* Ē'phra·im's, northward *it was* Ma·nas'seh's, and the sea was its border. Ma·nas'seh's

16:7 aOr *Naaran* (compare 1 Chronicles 7:28)
17:2 aCalled *Jeezer* in Numbers 26:30

territory was adjoining Ash'er on the north and Is'sa·char on the east.

11 And in Is'sa·char and in Ash'er, Ma·nas'seh had Beth Shē'an and its towns, Ib'lē·am and its towns, the inhabitants of Dor and its towns, the inhabitants of En Dor and its towns, the inhabitants of Tā'a·nach and its towns, and the inhabitants of Me·gid'dō and its towns—three hilly regions.

12 Yet the children of Ma·nas'seh could not drive out *the inhabitants of* those cities, but the Cā'naan·ites were determined to dwell in that land.

13 And it happened, when the children of Israel grew strong, that they put the Cā'naan·ites to forced labor, but did not utterly drive them out.

MORE LAND FOR EPHRAIM AND MANASSEH

14 Then the children of Joseph spoke to Joshua, saying, "Why have you given us *only* one lot and one share to inherit, since we *are* a great people, inasmuch as the LORD has blessed us until now?"

15 So Joshua answered them, "If you *are* a great people, *then* go up to the forest *country* and clear a place for yourself there in the land of the Per'iz·zites and the giants, since the mountains of Ē'phra·im are too confined for you."

16 But the children of Joseph said, "The mountain country is not enough for us; and all the Cā'naan·ites who dwell in the land of the valley have chariots of iron, *both those* who *are* of Beth Shē'an and its towns and *those* who *are* of the Valley of Jez're·el."

17 And Joshua spoke to the house of Joseph—to Ē'phra·im and Ma·nas'-seh—saying, "You *are* a great people and have great power; you shall not have *only* one lot,

18 "but the mountain country shall be yours. Although it *is* wooded, you shall cut it down, and its farthest extent shall be yours; for you shall drive out the Cā'naan·ites, though they have iron chariots *and* are strong."

THE REMAINDER OF THE LAND DIVIDED

18 Now the whole congregation of the children of Israel assembled together at Shī'lōh, and set up the tabernacle of meeting there. And the land was subdued before them.

2 But there remained among the children of Israel seven tribes which had not yet received their inheritance.

3 Then Joshua said to the children of Israel: "How long will you neglect to go and possess the land which the LORD God of your fathers has given you?

4 "Pick out from among you three men for *each* tribe, and I will send them; they shall rise and go through the land, survey it according to their inheritance, and come *back* to me.

5 "And they shall divide it into seven parts. Judah shall remain in their territory on the south, and the house of Joseph shall remain in their territory on the north.

6 "You shall therefore survey the land in seven parts and bring *the survey* here to me, that I may cast lots for you here before the LORD our God.

7 "But the Lē'vites have no part among you, for the priesthood of the LORD *is* their inheritance. And Gad, Reuben, and half the tribe of Ma·nas'seh have received their inheritance beyond the Jordan on the east, which Moses the servant of the LORD gave them."

8 Then the men arose to go away;

and Joshua charged those who went to survey the land, saying, "Go, walk through the land, survey it, and come back to me, that I may cast lots for you here before the LORD in Shī'lōh."

9 So the men went, passed through the land, and wrote the survey in a book in seven parts by cities; and they came to Joshua at the camp in Shī'lōh.

10 Then Joshua cast lots for them in Shī'lōh before the LORD, and there Joshua divided the land to the children of Israel according to their divisions.

THE LAND OF BENJAMIN

11 Now the lot of the tribe of the children of Benjamin came up according to their families, and the territory of their lot came out between the children of Judah and the children of Joseph.

12 Their border on the north side began at the Jordan, and the border went up to the side of Jericho on the north, and went up through the mountains westward; it ended at the Wilderness of Beth Ā'ven.

13 The border went over from there toward Luz, to the side of Luz (which is Beth'el) southward; and the border descended to At'a·roth Ad'dar, near the hill that lies on the south side of Lower Beth Hor'on.

14 Then the border extended around the west side to the south, from the hill that lies before Beth Hor'on southward; and it ended at Kir'jath Bā'al (which is Kir'jath Jē'a·rim), a city of the children of Judah. This was the west side.

15 The south side began at the end of Kir'jath Jē'a·rim, and the border extended on the west and went out to the spring of the waters of Neph·tō'ah.

16 Then the border came down to the end of the mountain that lies before the Valley of the Son of Hin'nom, which is in the Valley of the Reph'-a·im[a] on the north, descended to the Valley of Hin'nom, to the side of the Jeb'ū·sīte city on the south, and descended to En Rō'gel.

17 And it went around from the north, went out to En Shem'esh, and extended toward Ge·lī'loth, which is before the Ascent of A·dum'mim, and descended to the stone of Bō'han the son of Reuben.

18 Then it passed along toward the north side of Ar'a·bah,[a] and went down to Ar'a·bah.

19 And the border passed along to the north side of Beth Hog'lah; then the border ended at the north bay at the Salt Sea, at the south end of the Jordan. This was the southern boundary.

20 The Jordan was its border on the east side. This was the inheritance of the children of Benjamin, according to its boundaries all around, according to their families.

21 Now the cities of the tribe of the children of Benjamin, according to their families, were Jericho, Beth Hog'lah, Ē'mek Kē'ziz,

22 Beth Ar'a·bah, Zem·a·rā'im, Beth'el,

23 Av'im, Par'ah, Oph'rah,

24 Chē'phar Ha·am'mo·nī, Oph'nī, and Gā'ba: twelve cities with their villages;

25 Gib'e·on, Rā'mah, Be·er'oth,

26 Miz'pah, Chē·phī'rah, Mō'zah,

27 Rē'kem, Ir'pē·el, Tar'a·lah,

28 Zē'lah, Ē'leph, Jē'bus (which is Jerusalem), Gib'ē·ath, and Kir'jath: fourteen cities with their villages. This was the inheritance of the children of Benjamin according to their families.

18:16 [a]Literally Giants 18:18 [a]Or Beth Arabah (compare 15:6 and 18:22)

SIMEON'S INHERITANCE WITH JUDAH

19 The second lot came out for Sim'ē·on, for the tribe of the children of Sim'ē·on according to their families. And their inheritance was within the inheritance of the children of Judah.

2 They had in their inheritance Bē·er·shē'ba (Shē'ba), Mō'la·dah,

3 Hā'zar Shū'al, Bā'lah, Ē'zem,

4 El·tō'lad, Bē'thul, Hor'mah,

5 Zik'lag, Beth Mar'ca·both, Hā'zar Sū'sah,

6 Beth Le·bā'oth, and Sha·rū'hen: thirteen cities and their villages;

7 Ā'in, Rim'mon, Ē'ther, and Ā'shan: four cities and their villages;

8 and all the villages that *were* all around these cities as far as Bā'a·lath Bē'er, Rā'mah of the South. This *was* the inheritance of the tribe of the children of Sim'ē·on according to their families.

9 The inheritance of the children of Sim'ē·on *was included* in the share of the children of Judah, for the share of the children of Judah was too much for them. Therefore the children of Sim'ē·on had *their* inheritance within the inheritance of that people.

THE LAND OF ZEBULUN

10 The third lot came out for the children of Zeb'ū·lun according to their families, and the border of their inheritance was as far as Sā'rid.

11 Their border went toward the west and to Mar'a·lah, went to Dab'ba·sheth, and extended along the brook that is east of Jok'nē·am.

12 Then from Sā'rid it went eastward toward the sunrise along the border of Chis'loth Tā'bor, and went out toward Dab'e·rath, bypassing Ja·phī'a.

13 And from there it passed along on the east of Gath Hē'pher, toward Eth Kā'zin, and extended to Rim'mon, which borders on Nē'ah.

14 Then the border went around it on the north side of Han·na'thon, and it ended in the Valley of Jiph'thah El.

15 Included were Kat'tath, Na·hal'lal, Shim'ron, I'da·lah, and Bethlehem: twelve cities with their villages.

16 This *was* the inheritance of the children of Zeb'ū·lun according to their families, these cities with their villages.

THE LAND OF ISSACHAR

17 The fourth lot came out to Is'sa·char, for the children of Is'sa·char according to their families.

18 And their territory went to Jez'rē·el, and *included* Che·sul'loth, Shū'nem,

19 Haph·rā'im, Shī'on, A·nā'ha·rath,

20 Rab'bith, Kish'i·on, Ā'bez,

21 Rē'meth, En Gan'nim, En Had'dah, and Beth Paz'zez.

22 And the border reached to Tā'bor, Shā·ha·zi'mah, and Beth Shem'esh; their border ended at the Jordan: sixteen cities with their villages.

23 This *was* the inheritance of the tribe of the children of Is'sa·char according to their families, the cities and their villages.

THE LAND OF ASHER

24 The fifth lot came out for the tribe of the children of Ash'er according to their families.

25 And their territory included Hel'kath, Hā'li, Bē'ten, Ach'shaph,

26 A·lam'me·lech, Ā'mad, and Mī'shal; it reached to Mount Car'mel westward, along *the Brook* Shī'hor Lib'nath.

27 It turned toward the sunrise to Beth Dā'gon; and it reached to

Zeb′u·lun and to the Valley of Jiph′thah El, then northward beyond Beth Ē′mek and Nē·ī′el, bypassing Cā′bul *which was* on the left,

28 including Ē′bron,*a* Rē′hob, Ham′-mon, and Kā′nah, as far as Greater Sī′don.

29 And the border turned to Rā′mah and to the fortified city of Tȳre; then the border turned to Hō′sah, and ended at the sea by the region of Ach′zib.

30 Also Um′mah, Ā′phek, and Rē′-hob *were included:* twenty-two cities with their villages.

31 This *was* the inheritance of the tribe of the children of Ash′er according to their families, these cities with their villages.

THE LAND OF NAPHTALI

32 The sixth lot came out to the children of Naph′ta·lī, for the children of Naph′ta·lī according to their families.

33 And their border began at Hē′-leph, enclosing the territory from the terebinth tree in Zā·a·nan′nim, Ad′-a·mī Nē′keb, and Jab′nē·el, as far as Lak′kum; it ended at the Jordan.

34 From Hē′leph the border extended westward to Az′noth Tā′bor, and went out from there toward Huk′kok; it adjoined Zeb′u·lun on the south side and Ash′er on the west side, and ended at Judah by the Jordan toward the sunrise.

35 And the fortified cities *are* Zid′-dim, Zer, Ham′math, Rak′kath, Chin′ne·reth,

36 Ad′a·mah, Rā′mah, Hā′zor,

37 Kē′desh, Ed′rē·ī, En Hā′zor,

38 Ī′ron, Migdal El, Hō′rem, Beth Ā′nath, and Beth Shem′esh: nineteen cities with their villages.

39 This *was* the inheritance of the tribe of the children of Naph′ta·lī according to their families, the cities and their villages.

THE LAND OF DAN

40 The seventh lot came out for the tribe of the children of Dan according to their families.

41 And the territory of their inheritance was Zō′rah, Esh′tā·ol, Ir Shem′esh,

42 Shā·a·lab′bin, Aī′ja·lon, Jeth′lah,

43 Ē′lon, Tim′nah, Ek′ron,

44 El′tē·keh, Gib′be·thon, Bā′a·lath,

45 Jē′hud, Ben′ē Be′rak, Gath Rim′mon,

46 Me Jar′kon, and Rak′kon, with the region near Jop′pa.

47 And the border of the children of Dan went beyond these, because the children of Dan went up to fight against Lē′shem and took it; and they struck it with the edge of the sword, took possession of it, and dwelt in it. They called Lē′shem, Dan, after the name of Dan their father.

48 This *is* the inheritance of the tribe of the children of Dan according to their families, these cities with their villages.

JOSHUA'S INHERITANCE

49 When they had made an end of dividing the land as an inheritance according to their borders, the children of Israel gave an inheritance among them to Joshua the son of Nun.

50 According to the word of the LORD they gave him the city which he asked for, Tim′nath Sē′rah in the mountains of Ē′phra·im; and he built the city and dwelt in it.

51 These *were* the inheritances which El·ē·ā′zar the priest, Joshua the son of Nun, and the heads of the fathers of the tribes of the children of

19:28 *a*Following Masoretic Text, Targum, and Vulgate; a few Hebrew manuscripts read *Abdon* (compare 21:30 and 1 Chronicles 6:74).

Israel divided as an inheritance by lot in Shī′lōh before the LORD, at the door of the tabernacle of meeting. So they made an end of dividing the country.

THE CITIES OF REFUGE

20 The LORD also spoke to Joshua, saying,

2 "Speak to the children of Israel, saying: 'Appoint for yourselves cities of refuge, of which I spoke to you through Moses,

3 'that the slayer who kills a person accidentally *or* unintentionally may flee there; and they shall be your refuge from the avenger of blood.

4 'And when he flees to one of those cities, and stands at the entrance of the gate of the city, and declares his case in the hearing of the elders of that city, they shall take him into the city as one of them, and give him a place, that he may dwell among them.

5 'Then if the avenger of blood pursues him, they shall not deliver the slayer into his hand, because he struck his neighbor unintentionally, but did not hate him beforehand.

6 'And he shall dwell in that city until he stands before the congregation for judgment, *and* until the death of the one who is high priest in those days. Then the slayer may return and come to his own city and his own house, to the city from which he fled.' "

7 So they appointed Ke′desh in Galilee, in the mountains of Naph′ta·lī, Shē′chem in the mountains of Ē′phra·im, and Kir′jath Ar′ba (which *is* Hē′bron) in the mountains of Judah.

8 And on the other side of the Jordan, by Jericho eastward, they assigned Bē′zer in the wilderness on the plain, from the tribe of Reuben, Rā′moth in Gil′e·ad, from the tribe of Gad, and Gō′lan in Bā′shan, from the tribe of Ma·nas′seh.

9 These were the cities appointed for all the children of Israel and for the stranger who dwelt among them, that whoever killed a person accidentally might flee there, and not die by the hand of the avenger of blood until he stood before the congregation.

CITIES OF THE LEVITES

21 Then the heads of the fathers' *houses* of the Lē′vītes came near to El·e·ā′zar the priest, to Joshua the son of Nun, and to the heads of the fathers' *houses* of the tribes of the children of Israel.

2 And they spoke to them at Shī′lōh in the land of Cā′naan, saying, "The LORD commanded through Moses to give us cities to dwell in, with their common-lands for our livestock."

3 So the children of Israel gave to the Lē′vītes from their inheritance, at the commandment of the LORD, these cities and their common-lands:

4 Now the lot came out for the families of the Kō′hath·ītes. And the children of Aaron the priest, *who were* of the Lē′vītes, had thirteen cities by lot from the tribe of Judah, from the tribe of Sim′e·on, and from the tribe of Benjamin.

5 The rest of the children of Kō′hath had ten cities by lot from the families of the tribe of Ē′phra·im, from the tribe of Dan, and from the half-tribe of Ma·nas′seh.

6 And the children of Ger′shon had thirteen cities by lot from the families of the tribe of Is′sa·char, from the tribe of Ash′er, from the tribe of Naph′ta·lī, and from the half-tribe of Ma·nas′seh in Bā′shan.

7 The children of Me·rar′ī according

to their families had twelve cities from the tribe of Reuben, from the tribe of Gad, and from the tribe of Zeb′ū·lun.

8 And the children of Israel gave these cities with their common-lands by lot to the Lē′vītes, as the LORD had commanded by the hand of Moses.

9 So they gave from the tribe of the children of Judah and from the tribe of the children of Sim′e·on these cities which are designated by name,

10 which were for the children of Aaron, one of the families of the Kō′hath·ītes, *who were* of the children of Levi; for the lot was theirs first.

11 And they gave them Kir′jath Ar′ba (*Ar′ba was* the father of Ā′nak), which *is* Hē′bron, in the mountains of Judah, with the common-land surrounding it.

12 But the fields of the city and its villages they gave to Caleb the son of Je·phūn′neh as his possession.

13 Thus to the children of Aaron the priest they gave Hē′bron with its common-land (a city of refuge for the slayer), Lib′nah with its common-land,

14 Jat′tir with its common-land, Esh·te·mō′a with its common-land,

15 Hō′lon with its common-land, Dē′bir with its common-land,

16 Ā′in with its common-land, Jut′tah with its common-land, and Beth Shem′esh with its common-land: nine cities from those two tribes;

17 and from the tribe of Benjamin, Gib′e·on with its common-land, Gē′ba with its common-land,

18 An′a·thoth with its common-land, and Al′mon with its common-land: four cities.

19 All the cities of the children of Aaron, the priests, *were* thirteen cities with their common-lands.

20 And the families of the children of Kō′hath, the Lē′vītes, the rest of the children of Kō′hath, even they had the cities of their lot from the tribe of Ē′phra·im.

21 For they gave them Shē′chem with its common-land in the mountains of Ē′phra·im (a city of refuge for the slayer), Gē′zer with its common-land,

22 Kib′zā·im with its common-land, and Beth Hor′on with its common-land: four cities;

23 and from the tribe of Dan, El′te·keh with its common-land, Gib′be·thon with its common-land,

24 Aī′ja·lon with its common-land, *and* Gath Rim′mon with its common-land: four cities;

25 and from the half-tribe of Manas′seh, Tā′nach with its common-land and Gath Rim′mon with its common-land: two cities.

26 All the ten cities with their common-lands were for the rest of the families of the children of Kō′hath.

27 Also to the children of Ger′shon, of the families of the Lē′vītes, from the *other* half-tribe of Ma·nas′seh, *they gave* Gō′lan in Bā′shan with its common-land (a city of refuge for the slayer), and Be Esh′te·rah with its common-land: two cities;

28 and from the tribe of Is′sa·char, Kish′i·on with its common-land, Dab′e·rath with its common-land,

29 Jar′muth with its common-land, *and* En Gan′nim with its common-land: four cities;

30 and from the tribe of Ash′er, Mī′shal with its common-land, Ab′don with its common-land,

31 Hel′kath with its common-land, and Rē′hob with its common-land: four cities;

32 and from the tribe of Naph′ta·lī, Kē′desh in Galilee with its common-land (a city of refuge for the slayer),

ABOUT GOD'S PROMISES Joshua 21:45

Does God Keep His Promises? Do You?

Have you been to a wedding lately? Do you remember the bride and groom giving each other a ring to wear? This ring reminds them of their wedding vows, or promises. When two people get married they promise many things—to love each other, to help each other, to take care of each other, to forgive each other, and to stay with each other "until God separates them through death." We should keep our promises, shouldn't we? But does God keep His?

1. Read Joshua 21:45 and the last sentence of Joshua 23:14. Did God keep His promises to the people of Israel when they were in the wilderness? What do these verses say?
2. Read 2 Corinthians 1:20. What is this saying? Is this not another way of saying "God keeps His promises?"
3. Read 2 Thessalonians 3:3. Is God faithful? Faithful people keep their promises. Should you and I keep our promises? Why?

For more on *What the Bible Says* turn to page 462
For more on *God's Promises* turn to page 958

Ham'moth Dor with its common-land, and Kar'tan with its common-land: three cities.

33 All the cities of the Ger'shon·ites according to their families *were* thirteen cities with their common-lands.

34 And to the families of the children of Me·rar'ī, the rest of the Lē'vītes, from the tribe of Zeb'ū·lun, Jok'-nē·am with its common-land, Kar'tah with its common-land,

35 Dim'nah with its common-land, *and* Na·hal'al with its common-land: four cities;

36 and from the tribe of Reuben, Bē'zer with its common-land, Jā'haz with its common-land,

37 Ked'e·moth with its common-land, and Meph'a·ath with its common-land: four cities;*a*

38 and from the tribe of Gad, Rā'moth in Gil'ē·ad with its common-land (a city of refuge for the slayer), Mā·ha·na'im with its common-land,

39 Hesh'bon with its common-land, *and* Jā'zer with its common-land: four cities in all.

40 So all the cities for the children of Me·rar'ī according to their families, the rest of the families of the Lē'-vītes, were *by* their lot twelve cities.

41 All the cities of the Lē'vītes within the possession of the children of Israel *were* forty-eight cities with their common-lands.

42 Every one of these cities had its common-land surrounding it; thus *were* all these cities.

THE PROMISE FULFILLED

43 So the LORD gave to Israel all the land of which He had sworn to give to their fathers, and they took possession of it and dwelt in it.

44 The LORD gave them rest all around, according to all that He had sworn to their fathers. And not a man of all their enemies stood against them; the LORD delivered all their enemies into their hand.

45 Not a word failed of any good thing which the LORD had spoken to the house of Israel. All came to pass.

EASTERN TRIBES RETURN TO THEIR LANDS

22 Then Joshua called the Reū'ben·ītes, the Gad'ītes, and half the tribe of Ma·nas'seh,

2 and said to them: "You have kept all that Moses the servant of the LORD commanded you, and have obeyed my voice in all that I commanded you.

3 "You have not left your brethren these many days, up to this day, but have kept the charge of the commandment of the LORD your God.

4 "And now the LORD your God has given rest to your brethren, as He promised them; now therefore, return and go to your tents *and* to the land of your possession, which Moses the servant of the LORD gave you on the other side of the Jordan.

5 "But take careful heed to do the commandment and the law which Moses the servant of the LORD commanded you, to love the LORD your God, to walk in all His ways, to keep His commandments, to hold fast to Him, and to serve Him with all your heart and with all your soul."

6 So Joshua blessed them and sent them away, and they went to their tents.

7 Now to half the tribe of Ma·nas'-seh Moses had given a possession in Bā'shan, but to the *other* half of it Joshua gave *a possession* among their brethren on this side of the Jordan, westward. And indeed, when

---

21:37 *a*Following Septuagint and Vulgate (compare 1 Chronicles 6:78, 79); Masoretic Text, Bomberg, and Targum omit verses 36 and 37.

What Should I Do?

CAUGHT BETWEEN TWO FRIENDS Joshua 22:10–13, 32, 33

Wesley is caught between two friends. Kitty and Puppy are playing. That's OK if they don't hurt anyone or anything. But Wesley happened to be there. So when Puppy ran round and round, guess what happened to Wesley? That's why Wesley is caught between two friends. Sometimes you will be caught between two friends. You may not be tied up in ropes, but you may be asked to take sides in a quarrel or to favor one friend above another. What should you do?

1. How did Wesley get tied up with Puppy's rope?
2. Have you ever been caught between two friends? What happened? What should you have done? What did you do?
3. What should you do when one friend wants you to take sides or favor one friend above another? What would Jesus want you to do?

For more on *What Should I Do?* turn to page 372
For more on *Peacemaking* turn to page 1020

Joshua sent them away to their tents, he blessed them,

8 and spoke to them, saying, "Return with much riches to your tents, with very much livestock, with silver, with gold, with bronze, with iron, and with very much clothing. Divide the spoil of your enemies with your brethren."

9 So the children of Reuben, the children of Gad, and half the tribe of Ma·nas′seh returned, and departed from the children of Israel at Shī′lōh, which *is* in the land of Cā′naan, to go to the country of Gil′ē·ad, to the land of their possession, which they had obtained according to the word of the LORD by the hand of Moses.

AN ALTAR BY THE JORDAN

10 And when they came to the region of the Jordan which *is* in the land of Cā′naan, the children of Reuben, the children of Gad, and half the tribe of Ma·nas′seh built an altar there by the Jordan—a great, impressive altar.

11 Now the children of Israel heard *someone* say, "Behold, the children of Reuben, the children of Gad, and half the tribe of Ma·nas′seh have built an altar on the frontier of the land of Cā′naan, in the region of the Jordan—on the children of Israel's side."

12 And when the children of Israel heard *of it,* the whole congregation of the children of Israel gathered together at Shī′lōh to go to war against them.

13 Then the children of Israel sent Phin′e·has the son of El·ē·ā′zar the priest to the children of Reuben, to the children of Gad, and to half the tribe of Ma·nas′seh, into the land of Gil′ē·ad,

14 and with him ten rulers, one ruler each from the chief house of every tribe of Israel; and each one *was* the head of the house of his father among the divisions[a] of Israel.

15 Then they came to the children of Reuben, to the children of Gad, and to half the tribe of Ma·nas′seh, to the land of Gil′ē·ad, and they spoke with them, saying,

16 "Thus says the whole congregation of the LORD: 'What treachery *is* this that you have committed against the God of Israel, to turn away this day from following the LORD, in that you have built for yourselves an altar, that you might rebel this day against the LORD?

17 '*Is* the iniquity of Pē′or not enough for us, from which we are not cleansed till this day, although there was a plague in the congregation of the LORD,

18 'but that you must turn away this day from following the LORD? And it shall be, if you rebel today against the LORD, that tomorrow He will be angry with the whole congregation of Israel.

19 'Nevertheless, if the land of your possession *is* unclean, *then* cross over to the land of the possession of the LORD, where the LORD's tabernacle stands, and take possession among us; but do not rebel against the LORD, nor rebel against us, by building yourselves an altar besides the altar of the LORD our God.

20 'Did not Ā′chan the son of Zē′rah commit a trespass in the accursed thing, and wrath fell on all the congregation of Israel? And that man did not perish alone in his iniquity.' "

21 Then the children of Reuben, the children of Gad, and half the tribe of Ma·nas′seh answered and said to the heads of the divisions[a] of Israel:

22 "The LORD God of gods, the LORD God of gods, He knows, and let Israel

22:14 [a]Literally *thousands*   22:21 [a]Literally *thousands*

itself know—if *it is* in rebellion, or if in treachery against the LORD, do not save us this day.

23 "If we have built ourselves an altar to turn from following the LORD, or if to offer on it burnt offerings or grain offerings, or if to offer peace offerings on it, let the LORD Himself require *an account*.

24 "But in fact we have done it for fear, for a reason, saying, 'In time to come your descendants may speak to our descendants, saying, "What have you to do with the LORD God of Israel?

25 "For the LORD has made the Jordan a border between you and us, *you* children of Reuben and children of Gad. You have no part in the LORD." So your descendants would make our descendants cease fearing the LORD.'

26 "Therefore we said, 'Let us now prepare to build ourselves an altar, not for burnt offering nor for sacrifice,

27 'but *that* it *may be* a witness between you and us and our generations after us, that we may perform the service of the LORD before Him with our burnt offerings, with our sacrifices, and with our peace offerings; that your descendants may not say to our descendants in time to come, "You have no part in the LORD." '

28 "Therefore we said that it will be, when they say *this* to us or to our generations in time to come, that we may say, 'Here is the replica of the altar of the LORD which our fathers made, though not for burnt offerings nor for sacrifices; but it *is* a witness between you and us.'

29 "Far be it from us that we should rebel against the LORD, and turn *from following* the LORD *this* day, to build an altar for burnt offerings, for grain offerings, or for sacrifices, besides the altar of the LORD our God which *is* before His tabernacle."

30 Now when Phin'e·has the priest and the rulers of the congregation, the heads of the divisions[a] of Israel who *were* with him, heard the words that the children of Reuben, the children of Gad, and the children of Ma·nas'seh spoke, it pleased them.

31 Then Phin'e·has the son of El·ē·ā'zar the priest said to the children of Reuben, the children of Gad, and the children of Ma·nas'seh, "This day we perceive that the LORD *is* among us, because you have not committed this treachery against the LORD. Now you have delivered the children of Israel out of the hand of the LORD."

32 And Phin'e·has the son of El·ē·ā'zar the priest, and the rulers, returned from the children of Reuben and the children of Gad, from the land of Gil'ē·ad to the land of Cā'naan, to the children of Israel, and brought back word to them.

33 So the thing pleased the children of Israel, and the children of Israel blessed God; they spoke no more of going against them in battle, to destroy the land where the children of Reuben and Gad dwelt.

34 The children of Reuben and the children of Gad[a] called the altar, *Witness,* "For *it is* a witness between us that the LORD *is* God."

JOSHUA'S FAREWELL ADDRESS

23 Now it came to pass, a long time after the LORD had given rest to Israel from all their enemies round about, that Joshua was old, advanced in age.

2 And Joshua called for all Israel, for their elders, for their heads, for their judges, and for their officers, and said to them: "I am old, advanced in age.

22:30 [a]Literally *thousands*   22:34 [a]Septuagint adds *and half the tribe of Manasseh*

3 "You have seen all that the LORD your God has done to all these nations because of you, for the LORD your God *is* He who has fought for you.

4 "See, I have divided to you by lot these nations that remain, to be an inheritance for your tribes, from the Jordan, with all the nations that I have cut off, as far as the Great Sea westward.

5 "And the LORD your God will expel them from before you and drive them out of your sight. So you shall possess their land, as the LORD your God promised you.

6 "Therefore be very courageous to keep and to do all that is written in the Book of the Law of Moses, lest you turn aside from it to the right hand or to the left,

7 "*and* lest you go among these nations, these who remain among you. You shall not make mention of the name of their gods, nor cause *anyone* to swear *by them;* you shall not serve them nor bow down to them,

8 "but you shall hold fast to the LORD your God, as you have done to this day.

9 "For the LORD has driven out from before you great and strong nations; but *as for* you, no one has been able to stand against you to this day.

10 "One man of you shall chase a thousand, for the LORD your God *is* He who fights for you, as He promised you.

11 "Therefore take careful heed to yourselves, that you love the LORD your God.

12 "Or else, if indeed you do go back, and cling to the remnant of these nations—these that remain among you—and make marriages with them, and go in to them and they to you,

13 "know for certain that the LORD your God will no longer drive out

these nations from before you. But they shall be snares and traps to you, and scourges on your sides and thorns in your eyes, until you perish from this good land which the LORD your God has given you.

14 "Behold, this day I *am* going the way of all the earth. And you know in all your hearts and in all your souls that not one thing has failed of all the good things which the LORD your God spoke concerning you. All have come to pass for you; not one word of them has failed.

15 "Therefore it shall come to pass, that as all the good things have come upon you which the LORD your God promised you, so the LORD will bring upon you all harmful things, until He has destroyed you from this good land which the LORD your God has given you.

16 "When you have transgressed the covenant of the LORD your God, which He commanded you, and have gone and served other gods, and bowed down to them, then the anger of the LORD will burn against you, and you shall perish quickly from the good land which He has given you."

THE COVENANT AT SHECHEM

24 Then Joshua gathered all the tribes of Israel to Shē′chem and called for the elders of Israel, for their heads, for their judges, and for their officers; and they presented themselves before God.

2 And Joshua said to all the people, "Thus says the LORD God of Israel: 'Your fathers, *including* Tē′rah, the father of Abraham and the father of Nā′hor, dwelt on the other side of the River[a] in old times; and they served other gods.

24:2 [a]Hebrew *Nahar,* the Euphrates, and so in verses 3, 14, and 15

3 'Then I took your father Abraham from the other side of the River, led him throughout all the land of Cā′naan, and multiplied his descendants and gave him Isaac.

4 'To Isaac I gave Jacob and Esau. To Esau I gave the mountains of Sē′ir to possess, but Jacob and his children went down to Egypt.

5 'Also I sent Moses and Aaron, and I plagued Egypt, according to what I did among them. Afterward I brought you out.

6 'Then I brought your fathers out of Egypt, and you came to the sea; and the Egyptians pursued your fathers with chariots and horsemen to the Red Sea.

7 'So they cried out to the LORD; and He put darkness between you and the Egyptians, brought the sea upon them, and covered them. And your eyes saw what I did in Egypt. Then you dwelt in the wilderness a long time.

8 'And I brought you into the land of the Am′o·rītes, who dwelt on the other side of the Jordan, and they fought with you. But I gave them into your hand, that you might possess their land, and I destroyed them from before you.

9 'Then Bā′lak the son of Zip′por, king of Mō′ab, arose to make war against Israel, and sent and called Bā′laam the son of Bē′or to curse you.

10 'But I would not listen to Bā′laam; therefore he continued to bless you. So I delivered you out of his hand.

11 'Then you went over the Jordan and came to Jericho. And the men of Jericho fought against you—also the Am′o·rītes, the Per′iz·zītes, the Cā′naan·ītes, the Hit′tītes, the Gir′ga·shītes, the Hī′vītes, and the Jeb′ū·sītes. But I delivered them into your hand.

12 'I sent the hornet before you which drove them out from before you, also the two kings of the Am′o·rītes, but not with your sword or with your bow.

13 'I have given you a land for which you did not labor, and cities which you did not build, and you dwell in them; you eat of the vineyards and olive groves which you did not plant.'

14 "Now therefore, fear the LORD, serve Him in sincerity and in truth, and put away the gods which your fathers served on the other side of the River and in Egypt. Serve the LORD!

15 "And if it seems evil to you to serve the LORD, choose for yourselves this day whom you will serve, whether the gods which your fathers served that *were* on the other side of the River, or the gods of the Am′o·rītes, in whose land you dwell. But as for me and my house, we will serve the LORD."

16 So the people answered and said: "Far be it from us that we should forsake the LORD to serve other gods;

17 "for the LORD our God *is* He who brought us and our fathers up out of the land of Egypt, from the house of bondage, who did those great signs in our sight, and preserved us in all the way that we went and among all the people through whom we passed.

18 "And the LORD drove out from before us all the people, including the Am′o·rītes who dwelt in the land. We also will serve the LORD, for He *is* our God."

19 But Joshua said to the people, "You cannot serve the LORD, for He *is* a holy God. He *is* a jealous God; He will not forgive your transgressions nor your sins.

20 "If you forsake the LORD and serve foreign gods, then He will turn and do you harm and consume you, after He has done you good."

21 And the people said to Joshua, "No, but we will serve the LORD!"

22 So Joshua said to the people, "You *are* witnesses against yourselves that you have chosen the LORD for yourselves, to serve Him." And they said, "*We are* witnesses!"

23 "Now therefore," *he said,* "put away the foreign gods which *are* among you, and incline your heart to the LORD God of Israel."

24 And the people said to Joshua, "The LORD our God we will serve, and His voice we will obey!"

25 So Joshua made a covenant with the people that day, and made for them a statute and an ordinance in Shē'chem.

26 Then Joshua wrote these words in the Book of the Law of God. And he took a large stone, and set it up there under the oak that *was* by the sanctuary of the LORD.

27 And Joshua said to all the people, "Behold, this stone shall be a witness to us, for it has heard all the words of the LORD which He spoke to us. It shall therefore be a witness to you, lest you deny your God."

28 So Joshua let the people depart, each to his own inheritance.

DEATH OF JOSHUA AND ELEAZAR

29 Now it came to pass after these things that Joshua the son of Nun, the servant of the LORD, died, *being* one hundred and ten years old.

30 And they buried him within the border of his inheritance at Tim'nath Sē'rah, which *is* in the mountains of Ē'phra·im, on the north side of Mount Gā'ash.

31 Israel served the LORD all the days of Joshua, and all the days of the elders who outlived Joshua, who had known all the works of the LORD which He had done for Israel.

32 The bones of Joseph, which the children of Israel had brought up out of Egypt, they buried at Shē'chem, in the plot of ground which Jacob had bought from the sons of Hā'mor the father of Shē'chem for one hundred pieces of silver, and which had become an inheritance of the children of Joseph.

33 And El·ē·ā'zar the son of Aaron died. They buried him in a hill *belonging to* Phin'e·has his son, which was given to him in the mountains of Ē'phra·im.

The Book of
JUDGES

THE CONTINUING CONQUEST OF CANAAN

NOW after the death of Joshua it came to pass that the children of Israel asked the LORD, saying, "Who shall be first to go up for us against the Cā'naan·ītes to fight against them?"

2   And the LORD said, "Judah shall go up. Indeed I have delivered the land into his hand."

3   So Judah said to Sim'ē·on his brother, "Come up with me to my allotted territory, that we may fight against the Cā'naan·ītes; and I will likewise go with you to your allotted territory." And Sim'ē·on went with him.

4   Then Judah went up, and the LORD delivered the Cā'naan·ītes and the Per'iz·zītes into their hand; and they killed ten thousand men at Bē'zek.

5   And they found A·dō'ni-Bē'zek in Bē'zek, and fought against him; and they defeated the Cā'naan·ītes and the Per'iz·zītes.

6   Then A·dō'ni-Bē'zek fled, and they pursued him and caught him and cut off his thumbs and big toes.

7   And A·dō'ni-Bē'zek said, "Seventy kings with their thumbs and big toes cut off used to gather scraps under my table; as I have done, so God has repaid me." Then they brought him to Jerusalem, and there he died.

8   Now the children of Judah fought against Jerusalem and took it; they struck it with the edge of the sword and set the city on fire.

9   And afterward the children of Judah went down to fight against the Cā'naan·ītes who dwelt in the mountains, in the South,a and in the lowland.

10   Then Judah went against the Cā'naan·ītes who dwelt in Hē'bron. (Now the name of Hē'bron was formerly Kir'jath Ar'ba.) And they killed Shē'shai, A·hī'man, and Tal'maī.

11   From there they went against the inhabitants of Dē'bir. (The name of Dē'bir was formerly Kir'jath Sē'pher.)

12   Then Caleb said, "Whoever attacks Kir'jath Sē'pher and takes it, to him I will give my daughter Ach'sah as wife."

13   And Oth'ni·el the son of Kē'naz, Caleb's younger brother, took it; so he gave him his daughter Ach'sah as wife.

14   Now it happened, when she came to him, that she urged hima to ask her father for a field. And she dismounted from her donkey, and Caleb said to her, "What do you wish?"

15   So she said to him, "Give me a blessing; since you have given me land in the South, give me also springs of water." And Caleb gave her the upper springs and the lower springs.

16   Now the children of the Ken'īte, Moses' father-in-law, went up from the City of Palms with the children of Judah into the Wilderness of Judah, which lies in the South near Ar'ad; and they went and dwelt among the people.

17   And Judah went with his brother Sim'ē·on, and they attacked the Cā'naan·ītes who inhabited Zē'phath, and utterly destroyed it. So the name of the city was called Hor'mah.

18   Also Judah took Gā'za with its

1:9 aHebrew Negev, and so throughout this book
1:14 aSeptuagint and Vulgate read he urged her.

territory, Ash′ke·lon with its territory, and Ek′ron with its territory.

19 So the LORD was with Judah. And they drove out the mountaineers, but they could not drive out the inhabitants of the lowland, because they had chariots of iron.

20 And they gave Hē′bron to Caleb, as Moses had said. Then he expelled from there the three sons of Ā′nak.

21 But the children of Benjamin did not drive out the Jeb′ū·sītes who inhabited Jerusalem; so the Jeb′ū·sītes dwell with the children of Benjamin in Jerusalem to this day.

22 And the house of Joseph also went up against Beth′el, and the LORD *was* with them.

23 So the house of Joseph sent men to spy out Beth′el. (The name of the city *was* formerly Luz.)

24 And when the spies saw a man coming out of the city, they said to him, "Please show us the entrance to the city, and we will show you mercy."

25 So he showed them the entrance to the city, and they struck the city with the edge of the sword; but they let the man and all his family go.

26 And the man went to the land of the Hit′tītes, built a city, and called its name Luz, which *is* its name to this day.

INCOMPLETE CONQUEST OF THE LAND

27 However, Ma·nas′seh did not drive out *the inhabitants of* Beth Shē′an and its villages, or Tā′a·nach and its villages, or the inhabitants of Dor and its villages, or the inhabitants of Ib′lē·am and its villages, or the inhabitants of Me·gid′dō and its villages; for the Cā′naan·ītes were determined to dwell in that land.

28 And it came to pass, when Israel was strong, that they put the Cā′-naan·ītes under tribute, but did not completely drive them out.

29 Nor did Ē′phra·im drive out the Cā′naan·ītes who dwelt in Gē′zer; so the Cā′naan·ītes dwelt in Gē′zer among them.

30 Nor did Zeb′ū·lun drive out the inhabitants of Kit′ron or the inhabitants of Na·hal′ol; so the Cā′naan·ītes dwelt among them, and were put under tribute.

31 Nor did Ash′er drive out the inhabitants of Ac′cō or the inhabitants of Sī′don, or of Ah′lab, Ach′zib, Hel′bah, Ā′phik, or Rē′hob.

32 So the Ash′er·ītes dwelt among the Cā′naan·ītes, the inhabitants of the land; for they did not drive them out.

33 Nor did Naph′ta·lī drive out the inhabitants of Beth Shem′esh or the inhabitants of Beth Ā′nath; but they dwelt among the Cā′naan·ītes, the inhabitants of the land. Nevertheless the inhabitants of Beth Shem′esh and Beth Ā′nath were put under tribute to them.

34 And the Am′o·rītes forced the children of Dan into the mountains, for they would not allow them to come down to the valley;

35 and the Am′o·rītes were determined to dwell in Mount Hē′res, in Aī′ja·lon, and in Shā·al′bim;[a] yet when the strength of the house of Joseph became greater, they were put under tribute.

36 Now the boundary of the Am′o·rītes *was* from the Ascent of Ak·rab′-bim, from Sē′la, and upward.

ISRAEL'S DISOBEDIENCE

2 Then the Angel of the LORD came up from Gil′gal to Bō′chim, and said: "I led you up from Egypt and brought you to the land of which I swore to

1:35 ᵃSpelled *Shaalabbin* in Joshua 19:42

your fathers; and I said, 'I will never break My covenant with you.

2 'And you shall make no covenant with the inhabitants of this land; you shall tear down their altars.' But you have not obeyed My voice. Why have you done this?

3 "Therefore I also said, 'I will not drive them out before you; but they shall be *thorns* in your side,*a* and their gods shall be a snare to you.' "

4 So it was, when the Angel of the LORD spoke these words to all the children of Israel, that the people lifted up their voices and wept.

5 Then they called the name of that place Bō'chim;*a* and they sacrificed there to the LORD.

6 And when Joshua had dismissed the people, the children of Israel went each to his own inheritance to possess the land.

DEATH OF JOSHUA

7 So the people served the LORD all the days of Joshua, and all the days of the elders who outlived Joshua, who had seen all the great works of the LORD which He had done for Israel.

8 Now Joshua the son of Nun, the servant of the LORD, died *when he was* one hundred and ten years old.

9 And they buried him within the border of his inheritance at Tim'nath Hē'res, in the mountains of Ē'phra·im, on the north side of Mount Gā'ash.

10 When all that generation had been gathered to their fathers, another generation arose after them who did not know the LORD nor the work which He had done for Israel.

ISRAEL'S UNFAITHFULNESS

11 Then the children of Israel did evil in the sight of the LORD, and served the Bā'als;

12 and they forsook the LORD God of their fathers, who had brought them out of the land of Egypt; and they followed other gods from *among* the gods of the people who *were* all around them, and they bowed down to them; and they provoked the LORD to anger.

13 They forsook the LORD and served Bā'al and the Ash'to·reths.*a*

14 And the anger of the LORD was hot against Israel. So He delivered them into the hands of plunderers who despoiled them; and He sold them into the hands of their enemies all around, so that they could no longer stand before their enemies.

15 Wherever they went out, the hand of the LORD was against them for calamity, as the LORD had said, and as the LORD had sworn to them. And they were greatly distressed.

16 Nevertheless, the LORD raised up judges who delivered them out of the hand of those who plundered them.

17 Yet they would not listen to their judges, but they played the harlot with other gods, and bowed down to them. They turned quickly from the way in which their fathers walked, in obeying the commandments of the LORD; they did not do so.

18 And when the LORD raised up judges for them, the LORD was with the judge and delivered them out of the hand of their enemies all the days of the judge; for the LORD was moved to pity by their groaning because of those who oppressed them and harassed them.

19 And it came to pass, when the judge was dead, that they reverted and behaved more corruptly than their fathers, by following other gods, to serve them and bow down to them. They did not cease from their own doings nor from their stubborn way.

2:3 *a*Septuagint, Targum, and Vulgate read *enemies to you*.   2:5 *a*Literally *Weeping*
2:13 *a*Canaanite goddesses

20 Then the anger of the LORD was hot against Israel; and He said, "Because this nation has transgressed My covenant which I commanded their fathers, and has not heeded My voice,

21 "I also will no longer drive out before them any of the nations which Joshua left when he died,

22 "so that through them I may test Israel, whether they will keep the ways of the LORD, to walk in them as their fathers kept *them,* or not."

23 Therefore the LORD left those nations, without driving them out immediately; nor did He deliver them into the hand of Joshua.

THE NATIONS REMAINING IN THE LAND

3 Now these *are* the nations which the LORD left, that He might test Israel by them, *that is,* all who had not known any of the wars in Cā′naan

2 (*this was* only so that the generations of the children of Israel might be taught to know war, at least those who had not formerly known it),

3 *namely,* five lords of the Phi·lis′tines, all the Cā′naan·ites, the Sī·dō′ni·ans, and the Hī′vites who dwelt in Mount Lebanon, from Mount Bā′al Her′mon to the entrance of Hā′math.

4 And they were *left, that He might* test Israel by them, to know whether they would obey the commandments of the LORD, which He had commanded their fathers by the hand of Moses.

5 Thus the children of Israel dwelt among the Cā′naan·ites, the Hit′tites, the Am′o·rites, the Per′iz·zites, the Hī′vites, and the Jeb′u·sites.

6 And they took their daughters to be their wives, and gave their daughters to their sons; and they served their gods.

OTHNIEL

7 So the children of Israel did evil in the sight of the LORD. They forgot the LORD their God, and served the Bā′als and A·shē′rahs.*a*

8 Therefore the anger of the LORD was hot against Israel, and He sold them into the hand of Cū′shan-Rish·a·thā′im king of Mes·o·po·tā′mi·a; and the children of Israel served Cū′shan-Rish·a·thā′im eight years.

9 When the children of Israel cried out to the LORD, the LORD raised up a deliverer for the children of Israel, who delivered them: Oth′ni·el the son of Kē′naz, Caleb's younger brother.

10 The Spirit of the LORD came upon him, and he judged Israel. He went out to war, and the LORD delivered Cū′shan-Rish·a·thā′im king of Mes·o·po·tā′mi·a into his hand; and his hand prevailed over Cū′shan-Rish·a·thā′im.

11 So the land had rest for forty years. Then Oth′ni·el the son of Kē′naz died.

EHUD

12 And the children of Israel again did evil in the sight of the LORD. So the LORD strengthened Eg′lon king of Mō′ab against Israel, because they had done evil in the sight of the LORD.

13 Then he gathered to himself the people of Am′mon and Am′a·lek, went and defeated Israel, and took possession of the City of Palms.

14 So the children of Israel served Eg′lon king of Mō′ab eighteen years.

15 But when the children of Israel cried out to the LORD, the LORD raised up a deliverer for them: Ē′hud the son of Gē′ra, the Ben′ja·mite, a left-handed man. By him the children

3:7 *a*Name or symbol for Canaanite goddesses

of Israel sent tribute to Eg′lon king of Mō′ab.

16 Now Ē′hud made himself a dagger (it was double-edged and a cubit in length) and fastened it under his clothes on his right thigh.

17 So he brought the tribute to Eg′lon king of Mō′ab. (Now Eg′lon *was* a very fat man.)

18 And when he had finished presenting the tribute, he sent away the people who had carried the tribute.

19 But he himself turned back from the stone images that *were* at Gil′gal, and said, "I have a secret message for you, O king." He said, "Keep silence!" And all who attended him went out from him.

20 So Ē′hud came to him (now he was sitting upstairs in his cool private chamber). Then Ē′hud said, "I have a message from God for you." So he arose from *his* seat.

21 Then Ē′hud reached with his left hand, took the dagger from his right thigh, and thrust it into his belly.

22 Even the hilt went in after the blade, and the fat closed over the blade, for he did not draw the dagger out of his belly; and his entrails came out.

23 Then Ē′hud went out through the porch and shut the doors of the upper room behind him and locked them.

24 When he had gone out, Eg′lon′sᵃ servants came to look, and *to their* surprise, the doors of the upper room were locked. So they said, "He is probably attending to his needs in the cool chamber."

25 So they waited till they were embarrassed, and still he had not opened the doors of the upper room. Therefore they took the key and opened *them*. And there was their master, fallen dead on the floor.

26 But Ē′hud had escaped while they delayed, and passed beyond the stone images and escaped to Sē·ī′rah.

27 And it happened, when he ar-rived, that he blew the trumpet in the mountains of Ē′phra·im, and the children of Israel went down with him from the mountains; and he led them.

28 Then he said to them, "Follow *me,* for the LORD has delivered your enemies the Mō′ab·ītes into your hand." So they went down after him, seized the fords of the Jordan leading to Mō′ab, and did not allow anyone to cross over.

29 And at that time they killed about ten thousand men of Mō′ab, all stout men of valor; not a man escaped.

30 So Mō′ab was subdued that day under the hand of Israel. And the land had rest for eighty years.

SHAMGAR

31 After him was Sham′gar the son of Ā′nath, who killed six hundred men of the Phi·lis′tines with an ox goad; and he also delivered Israel.

DEBORAH

The people of Israel had lived in the Promised Land for many years now. They forgot about God. They no longer obeyed Him and worshipped Him. So God let evil nations invade the land. When the people of Israel called to God for help, He rescued them. He gave them leaders, called judges, who taught the people how to obey God again. This is a story about how one of those leaders, a woman named Deborah, helped Israel defeat a mighty enemy army.

4 When Ē′hud was dead, the children of Israel again did evil in the sight of the LORD.

3:24 ᵃLiterally *his*

2   So the LORD sold them into the hand of Jā′bin king of Cā′naan, who reigned in Hā′zor. The commander of his army *was* Sis′e·ra, who dwelt in Ha·rō′sheth Ha·goy′im.

3   And the children of Israel cried out to the LORD; for Jā′bin had nine hundred chariots of iron, and for twenty years he had harshly oppressed the children of Israel.

4   Now Deb′or·ah, a prophetess, the wife of Lap′i·doth, was judging Israel at that time.

5   And she would sit under the palm tree of Deb′or·ah between Rā′mah and Beth′el in the mountains of Ē′phra·im. And the children of Israel came up to her for judgment.

6   Then she sent and called for Bar′ak the son of A·bin′ō·am from Kē′desh in Naph′ta·lī, and said to him, "Has not the LORD God of Israel commanded, 'Go and deploy *troops* at Mount Tā′bor; take with you ten thousand men of the sons of Naph′ta·lī and of the sons of Zeb′ū·lun;

7   'and against you I will deploy Sis′e·ra, the commander of Jā′bin's army, with his chariots and his multitude at the River Kī′shon; and I will deliver him into your hand'?"

8   And Bar′ak said to her, "If you will go with me, then I will go; but if you will not go with me, I will not go!"

9   So she said, "I will surely go with you; nevertheless there will be no glory for you in the journey you are taking, for the LORD will sell Sis′e·ra into the hand of a woman." Then Deb′or·ah arose and went with Bar′-ak to Kē′desh.

10   And Bar′ak called Zeb′ū·lun and Naph′ta·lī to Kē′desh; he went up with ten thousand men under his command,*a* and Deb′or·ah went up with him.

11   Now Hē′ber the Ken′īte, of the children of Hō′bab the father-in-law

of Moses, had separated himself from the Ken′ītes and pitched his tent near the terebinth tree at Zā·a·nā′im, which *is* beside Kē′desh.

12   And they reported to Sis′e·ra that Bar′ak the son of A·bin′ō·am had gone up to Mount Tā′bor.

13   So Sis′e·ra gathered together all his chariots, nine hundred chariots of iron, and all the people who *were* with him, from Ha·rō′sheth Ha-goy′im to the River Kī′shon.

14   Then Deb′or·ah said to Bar′ak, "Up! For this *is* the day in which the LORD has delivered Sis′e·ra into your hand. Has not the LORD gone out before you?" So Bar′ak went down from Mount Tā′bor with ten thousand men following him.

15   And the LORD routed Sis′e·ra and all *his* chariots and all *his* army with the edge of the sword before Bar′ak; and Sis′e·ra alighted from *his* chariot and fled away on foot.

16   But Bar′ak pursued the chariots and the army as far as Ha·rō′sheth Ha·goy′im, and all the army of Sis′e·ra fell by the edge of the sword; not a man was left.

17   However, Sis′e·ra had fled away on foot to the tent of Jā′el, the wife of Hē′ber the Ken′īte; for *there was* peace between Jā′bin king of Hā′zor and the house of Hē′ber the Ken′īte.

18   And Jā′el went out to meet Sis′e·ra, and said to him, "Turn aside, my lord, turn aside to me; do not fear." And when he had turned aside with her into the tent, she covered him with a blanket.

19   Then he said to her, "Please give me a little water to drink, for I am thirsty." So she opened a jug of milk, gave him a drink, and covered him.

20   And he said to her, "Stand at the door of the tent, and if any man comes and inquires of you, and says,

---

4:10 *a*Literally *at his feet*

'Is there any man here?' you shall say, 'No.' "

21 Then Jā'el, Hē'ber's wife, took a tent peg and took a hammer in her hand, and went softly to him and drove the peg into his temple, and it went down into the ground; for he was fast asleep and weary. So he died.

22 And then, as Bar'ak pursued Sis'era, Jā'el came out to meet him, and said to him, "Come, I will show you the man whom you seek." And when he went into her *tent,* there lay Sis'era, dead with the peg in his temple.

23 So on that day God subdued Jā'bin king of Cā'naan in the presence of the children of Israel.

Bible Quiz

Judges 4 **The Story of Deborah**

1. Who was the judge (leader) of Israel?
2. What did she tell Barak, her army commander, to do? Why do you think Barak wanted Deborah to go along to the battle?
3. Who was Sisera? How many chariots did he have? What were they made of?
4. Was Sisera killed by a mighty warrior with a powerful weapon? How was he killed?
5. God likes to surprise us. He often uses people we would never think of to carry out His plans. Do you feel that God could never ask you to do something great for Him? Then you may be just the kind of person He is looking for.

---

24 And the hand of the children of Israel grew stronger and stronger against Jā'bin king of Cā'naan, until they had destroyed Jā'bin king of Cā'naan.

THE SONG OF DEBORAH

5 Then Deb'or·ah and Bar'ak the son of A·bin'ō·am sang on that day, saying:

2 "When leaders lead in Israel,
　　When the people willingly offer
　　　themselves,
　　Bless the LORD!

3 "Hear, O kings! Give ear,
　　　O princes!
　　I, *even* I, will sing to the LORD;
　　I will sing praise to the LORD God
　　　of Israel.

4 "LORD, when You went out from
　　　Sē'ir,
　　When You marched from the field
　　　of Ē'dom,
　　The earth trembled and the
　　　heavens poured,
　　The clouds also poured water;
5 The mountains gushed before the
　　　LORD,
　　This Sinai, before the LORD God
　　　of Israel.

6 "In the days of Sham'gar, son of
　　　Ā'nath,
　　In the days of Jā'el,
　　The highways were deserted,
　　And the travelers walked along
　　　the byways.
7 Village life ceased, it ceased in
　　　Israel,
　　Until I, Deb'or·ah, arose,
　　Arose a mother in Israel.
8 They chose new gods;
　　Then *there was* war in the gates;
　　Not a shield or spear was seen
　　　among forty thousand in Israel.

9 My heart *is* with the rulers of
   Israel
   Who offered themselves willingly
   with the people.
   Bless the LORD!

10 "Speak, you who ride on white
   donkeys,
   Who sit in judges' attire,
   And who walk along the road.

11 Far from the noise of the archers,
   among the watering places,
   There they shall recount the
   righteous acts of the LORD,
   The righteous acts *for* His
   villagers in Israel;
   Then the people of the LORD shall
   go down to the gates.

12 "Awake, awake, Deb′or·ah!
   Awake, awake, sing a song!
   Arise, Bar′ak, and lead your
   captives away,
   O son of A·bin′ō·am!

13 "Then the survivors came down,
   the people against the nobles;
   The LORD came down for me
   against the mighty.

14 From Ē′phra·im *were* those whose
   roots were in Am′a·lek.
   After you, Benjamin, with your
   peoples,
   From Mā′chir rulers came down,
   And from Zeb′ū·lun those who
   bear the recruiter's staff.

15 And the princes of Is′sa·char*a*
   were with Deb′or·ah;
   As Is′sa·char, so *was* Bar′ak
   Sent into the valley under his
   command;*b*
   Among the divisions of Reuben
   There were great resolves of
   heart.

16 Why did you sit among the
   sheepfolds,
   To hear the pipings for the flocks?
   The divisions of Reuben have
   great searchings of heart.

17 Gil′ē·ad stayed beyond the
   Jordan,
   And why did Dan remain on
   ships?*a*
   Ash′er continued at the seashore,
   And stayed by his inlets.

18 Zeb′ū·lun *is* a people *who*
   jeopardized their lives to the
   point of death,
   Naph′ta·lī also, on the heights of
   the battlefield.

19 "The kings came *and* fought,
   Then the kings of Cā′naan fought
   In Tā′a·nach, by the waters of
   Me·gid′dō;
   They took no spoils of silver.

20 They fought from the heavens;
   The stars from their courses
   fought against Sis′e·ra.

21 The torrent of Kī′shon swept
   them away,
   That ancient torrent, the torrent
   of Kī′shon.
   O my soul, march on in strength!

22 Then the horses' hooves pounded,
   The galloping, galloping of his
   steeds.

23 'Curse Mē′roz,' said the angel*a* of
   the LORD,
   'Curse its inhabitants bitterly,
   Because they did not come to the
   help of the LORD,
   To the help of the LORD against
   the mighty.'

24 "Most blessed among women is
   Jā′el,
   The wife of Hē′ber the Ken′īte;
   Blessed is she among women in
   tents.

25 He asked for water, she gave
   milk;
   She brought out cream in a lordly
   bowl.

5:15 *a*Following Septuagint, Syriac, Targum, and
Vulgate; Masoretic Text reads *And my princes in Is-
sachar.*   *b*Literally *at his feet*   5:17 *a*Or *at ease*
5:23 *a*Or *Angel*

26 She stretched her hand to the
    tent peg,
  Her right hand to the workmen's
    hammer;
  She pounded Sis′e·ra, she pierced
    his head,
  She split and struck through his
    temple.
27 At her feet he sank, he fell, he lay
    still;
  At her feet he sank, he fell;
  Where he sank, there he fell dead.

28 "The mother of Sis′e·ra looked
    through the window,
  And cried out through the lattice,
  'Why is his chariot so long in
    coming?
  Why tarries the clatter of his
    chariots?'
29 Her wisest ladies answered her,
  Yes, she answered herself,
30 'Are they not finding and dividing
    the spoil:
  To every man a girl or two;
  For Sis′e·ra, plunder of dyed
    garments,
  Plunder of garments embroidered
    and dyed,
  Two pieces of dyed embroidery for
    the neck of the looter?'

31 "Thus let all Your enemies perish,
    O LORD!
  But let those who love Him be like
    the sun
  When it comes out in full
    strength."

So the land had rest for forty years.

MIDIANITES OPPRESS ISRAEL

6 Then the children of Israel did evil in the sight of the LORD. So the LORD delivered them into the hand of Mid′i·an for seven years,
2 and the hand of Mid′i·an prevailed against Israel. Because of the Mid′i·an·ītes, the children of Israel made for themselves the dens, the caves, and the strongholds which are in the mountains.
3 So it was, whenever Israel had sown, Mid′i·an·ītes would come up; also A·mal′e·kītes and the people of the East would come up against them.
4 Then they would encamp against them and destroy the produce of the earth as far as Gā′za, and leave no sustenance for Israel, neither sheep nor ox nor donkey.
5 For they would come up with their livestock and their tents, coming in as numerous as locusts; both they and their camels were without number; and they would enter the land to destroy it.
6 So Israel was greatly impoverished because of the Mid′i·an·ītes, and the children of Israel cried out to the LORD.
7 And it came to pass, when the children of Israel cried out to the LORD because of the Mid′i·an·ītes,
8 that the LORD sent a prophet to the children of Israel, who said to them, "Thus says the LORD God of Israel: 'I brought you up from Egypt and brought you out of the house of bondage;
9 'and I delivered you out of the hand of the Egyptians and out of the hand of all who oppressed you, and drove them out before you and gave you their land.
10 'Also I said to you, "I am the LORD your God; do not fear the gods of the Am′o·rītes, in whose land you dwell." But you have not obeyed My voice.' "

GIDEON

11 Now the Angel of the LORD came and sat under the terebinth tree which was in Oph′rah, which belonged to Jō′ash the A·bi·ez′rīte,

while his son Gideon threshed wheat in the winepress, in order to hide *it* from the Mid′i·an·ites.

12 And the Angel of the LORD appeared to him, and said to him, "The LORD *is* with you, you mighty man of valor!"

13 Gideon said to Him, "O my lord,*a* if the LORD is with us, why then has all this happened to us? And where *are* all His miracles which our fathers told us about, saying, 'Did not the LORD bring us up from Egypt?' But now the LORD has forsaken us and delivered us into the hands of the Mid′i·an·ites."

14 Then the LORD turned to him and said, "Go in this might of yours, and you shall save Israel from the hand of the Mid′i·an·ites. Have I not sent you?"

15 So he said to Him, "O my Lord,*a* how can I save Israel? Indeed my clan *is* the weakest in Ma·nas′seh, and I *am* the least in my father's house."

16 And the LORD said to him, "Surely I will be with you, and you shall defeat the Mid′i·an·ites as one man."

17 Then he said to Him, "If now I have found favor in Your sight, then show me a sign that it is You who talk with me.

18 "Do not depart from here, I pray, until I come to You and bring out my offering and set *it* before You." And He said, "I will wait until you come back."

19 So Gideon went in and prepared a young goat, and unleavened bread from an ephah of flour. The meat he put in a basket, and he put the broth in a pot; and he brought *them* out to Him under the terebinth tree and presented *them*.

20 The Angel of God said to him, "Take the meat and the unleavened bread and lay *them* on this rock, and pour out the broth." And he did so.

21 Then the Angel of the LORD put out the end of the staff that *was* in His hand, and touched the meat and the unleavened bread; and fire rose out of the rock and consumed the meat and the unleavened bread. And the Angel of the LORD departed out of his sight.

22 Now Gideon perceived that He *was* the Angel of the LORD. So Gideon said, "Alas, O Lord GOD! For I have seen the Angel of the LORD face to face."

23 Then the LORD said to him, "Peace *be* with you; do not fear, you shall not die."

24 So Gideon built an altar there to the LORD, and called it The-LORD-*Is*-Peace.*a* To this day it *is* still in Oph′rah of the Ā·bi·ez′rites.

25 Now it came to pass the same night that the LORD said to him, "Take your father's young bull, the second bull of seven years old, and tear down the altar of Bā′al that your father has, and cut down the wooden image*a* that *is* beside it;

26 "and build an altar to the LORD your God on top of this rock in the proper arrangement, and take the second bull and offer a burnt sacrifice with the wood of the image which you shall cut down."

27 So Gideon took ten men from among his servants and did as the LORD had said to him. But because he feared his father's household and the men of the city too much to do *it* by day, he did *it* by night.

GIDEON DESTROYS THE ALTAR OF BAAL

28 And when the men of the city arose early in the morning, there was

6:13 *a*Hebrew *adoni*, used of man   6:15 *a*Hebrew *Adonai*, used of God   6:24 *a*Hebrew *YHWH Shalom*   6:25 *a*Hebrew *Asherah*, a Canaanite goddess

What Should I Do?

THE BEST BECAME WORST Judges 6:13–16

"I'll have the best dinner in town for you tonight," she said. Now look at it. Even a doggie wouldn't eat that dinner.

1. Do you ever promise something special? But it all goes wrong? What should you do? What should you say?
2. Do you ever expect something wonderful to happen, but something terrible comes instead? What should you do? What should you say? Should you blame God? Read Judges 6:13–16.
3. Don't always expect the very best and the worst may not seem so bad. Don't always promise the moon and something a little closer to home may not seem so bad. Unrealistic expectations will usually disappoint us.

For more on *What Should I Do?* turn to page 455
For more on *Facing Trials* turn to page 455

the altar of Bā′al, torn down; and the wooden image that *was* beside it was cut down, and the second bull was being offered on the altar *which had been* built.

29 So they said to one another, "Who has done this thing?" And when they had inquired and asked, they said, "Gideon the son of Jō′ash has done this thing."

30 Then the men of the city said to Jō′ash, "Bring out your son, that he may die, because he has torn down the altar of Bā′al, and because he has cut down the wooden image that *was* beside it."

31 But Jō′ash said to all who stood against him, "Would you plead for Bā′al? Would you save him? Let the one who would plead for him be put to death by morning! If he *is* a god, let him plead for himself, because his altar has been torn down!"

32 Therefore on that day he called him Jer·ub·bā′al,ᵃ saying, "Let Bā′al plead against him, because he has torn down his altar."

33 Then all the Mid′i·an·ītes and A·mal′e·kītes, the people of the East, gathered together; and they crossed over and encamped in the Valley of Jez′re·el.

34 But the Spirit of the LORD came upon Gideon; then he blew the trumpet, and the Ā·bi·ez′rītes gathered behind him.

35 And he sent messengers throughout all Ma·nas′seh, who also gathered behind him. He also sent messengers to Ash′er, Zeb′ū·lun, and Naph′ta·lī; and they came up to meet them.

THE SIGN OF THE FLEECE

36 So Gideon said to God, "If You will save Israel by my hand as You have said—

37 "look, I shall put a fleece of wool on the threshing floor; if there is dew

Prayers

Judges 6:36, 37

God promised to help Gideon defeat his enemies. But Gideon wanted to know for sure. "If you will truly do this, send dew on this sheepskin," Gideon asked. It was a prayer for a sign that God would keep His promise. For some reason, God honored this prayer. Should we ask God for signs that He will keep His promises to us? We don't need these signs as Gideon did. We have the Bible, with many, many stories to show that God does keep His promises. Gideon did not have that. For us to ask for a sign today would be doubting what we know about God in His Word. Do you ever wonder if God will keep His promises? Don't pray for a sign. Go to God's Word and see what He has done. Then pray a prayer of thanksgiving for keeping His promises to you.

on the fleece only, and *it is* dry on all the ground, then I shall know that You will save Israel by my hand, as You have said."

38 And it was so. When he rose early the next morning and squeezed the fleece together, he wrung the dew out of the fleece, a bowlful of water.

39 Then Gideon said to God, "Do not be angry with me, but let me speak just once more: Let me test, I pray, just once more with the fleece; let it now be dry only on the fleece, but on all the ground let there be dew."

40 And God did so that night. It was dry on the fleece only, but there was dew on all the ground.

6:32 ᵃLiterally *Let Baal Plead*

GIDEON'S VALIANT THREE HUNDRED

*How could an army of 300 win
a war against thousands?
Watch them!*

7 Then Jer·ub·bā'al (that *is,* Gid-eon) and all the people who *were* with him rose early and encamped beside the well of Har'od, so that the camp of the Mid'i·an·ītes was on the north side of them by the hill of Mō'reh in the valley.

2 And the LORD said to Gideon, "The people who *are* with you *are* too many for Me to give the Mid'i·an·ītes into their hands, lest Israel claim glory for itself against Me, saying, 'My own hand has saved me.'

3 "Now therefore, proclaim in the hearing of the people, saying, 'Who-ever *is* fearful and afraid, let him turn and depart at once from Mount Gil'ē·ad.' " And twenty-two thousand of the people returned, and ten thou-sand remained.

4 But the LORD said to Gideon, "The people *are* still *too* many; bring them down to the water, and I will test them for you there. Then it will be, *that* of whom I say to you, 'This one shall go with you,' the same shall go with you; and of whomever I say to you, 'This one shall not go with you,' the same shall not go."

5 So he brought the people down to the water. And the LORD said to Gid-eon, "Everyone who laps from the wa-ter with his tongue, as a dog laps, you shall set apart by himself; like-wise everyone who gets down on his knees to drink."

6 And the number of those who lapped, *putting* their hand to their mouth, was three hundred men; but all the rest of the people got down on their knees to drink water.

7 Then the LORD said to Gideon, "By the three hundred men who lapped I will save you, and deliver the Mid'i·an·ītes into your hand. Let all the *other* people go, every man to his place."

8 So the people took provisions and their trumpets in their hands. And he sent away all *the rest of* Israel, every man to his tent, and retained those three hundred men. Now the camp of Mid'i·an was below him in the valley.

9 It happened on the same night that the LORD said to him, "Arise, go down against the camp, for I have de-livered it into your hand.

10 "But if you are afraid to go down, go down to the camp with Pū'rah your servant,

11 "and you shall hear what they say; and afterward your hands shall be strengthened to go down against the camp." Then he went down with Pū'rah his servant to the outpost of the armed men who *were* in the camp.

12 Now the Mid'i·an·ītes and A·mal'-e·kītes, all the people of the East, were lying in the valley as numerous as locusts; and their camels *were* without number, as the sand by the seashore in multitude.

13 And when Gideon had come, there was a man telling a dream to his companion. He said, "I have had a dream: *To my* surprise, a loaf of bar-ley bread tumbled into the camp of Mid'i·an; it came to a tent and struck it so that it fell and overturned, and the tent collapsed."

14 Then his companion answered and said, "This *is* nothing else but the sword of Gideon the son of Jō'ash, a man of Israel! Into his hand God has delivered Mid'i·an and the whole camp."

15 And so it was, when Gideon heard the telling of the dream and its inter-pretation, that he worshiped. He re-turned to the camp of Israel, and

said, "Arise, for the LORD has delivered the camp of Mid′i·an into your hand."

16 Then he divided the three hundred men *into* three companies, and he put a trumpet into every man's hand, with empty pitchers, and torches inside the pitchers.

17 And he said to them, "Look at me and do likewise; watch, and when I come to the edge of the camp you shall do as I do:

18 "When I blow the trumpet, I and all who *are* with me, then you also blow the trumpets on every side of the whole camp, and say, '*The sword of* the LORD and of Gideon!' "

19 So Gideon and the hundred men who *were* with him came to the outpost of the camp at the beginning of the middle watch, just as they had posted the watch; and they blew the trumpets and broke the pitchers that *were* in their hands.

20 Then the three companies blew the trumpets and broke the pitchers—they held the torches in their left hands and the trumpets in their right hands for blowing—and they cried, "The sword of the LORD and of Gideon!"

21 And every man stood in his place all around the camp; and the whole army ran and cried out and fled.

22 When the three hundred blew the trumpets, the LORD set every man's sword against his companion throughout the whole camp; and the army fled to Beth Acacia,*a* toward Zer′e·rah, as far as the border of Abel Me·hō′lah, by Tab′bath.

23 And the men of Israel gathered together from Naph′ta·lī, Ash′er, and all Ma·nas′seh, and pursued the Mid′i·an·ītes.

24 Then Gideon sent messengers throughout all the mountains of Ē′phra·im, saying, "Come down against the Mid′i·an·ītes, and seize

from them the watering places as far as Beth Ba′rah and the Jordan." Then all the men of Ē′phra·im gathered together and seized the watering places as far as Beth Ba′rah and the Jordan.

25 And they captured two princes of the Mid′i·an·ītes, Or′eb and Zē′eb. They killed Or′eb at the rock of Or′eb, and Zē′eb they killed at the winepress of Zē′eb. They pursued Mid′i·an and brought the heads of Or′eb and Zē′eb to Gideon on the other side of the Jordan.

☑ *Bible Quiz*

Judges 7 **Gideon's Army of 300**

1. How big was Gideon's army? How did God cut the number of Gideon's soldiers?

2. Why do you think God made Gideon's army smaller?

3. How did God help this little army beat the bigger army?

GIDEON SUBDUES THE MIDIANITES

8 Now the men of Ē′phra·im said to him, "Why have you done this to us by not calling us when you went to fight with the Mid′i·an·ītes?" And they reprimanded him sharply.

2 So he said to them, "What have I done now in comparison with you? *Is* not the gleaning *of the grapes* of Ē′phra·im better than the vintage of Ā·bi·ē′zer?

3 "God has delivered into your hands the princes of Mid′i·an, Or′eb and Zē′eb. And what was I able to do in comparison with you?" Then their

7:22 *a*Hebrew *Beth Shittah*

anger toward him subsided when he said that.

4 When Gideon came to the Jordan, he and the three hundred men who *were* with him crossed over, exhausted but still in pursuit.

5 Then he said to the men of Suc'coth, "Please give loaves of bread to the people who follow me, for they are exhausted, and I am pursuing Zē'bah and Zal·mun'na, kings of Mid'i·an."

6 And the leaders of Suc'coth said, "*Are* the hands of Zē'bah and Zal·mun'na now in your hand, that we should give bread to your army?"

7 So Gideon said, "For this cause, when the LORD has delivered Zē'bah and Zal·mun'na into my hand, then I will tear your flesh with the thorns of the wilderness and with briers!"

8 Then he went up from there to Pe·nū'el and spoke to them in the same way. And the men of Pe·nū'el answered him as the men of Suc'coth had answered.

9 So he also spoke to the men of Pe·nū'el, saying, "When I come back in peace, I will tear down this tower!"

10 Now Zē'bah and Zal·mun'na *were* at Kar'kor, and their armies with them, about fifteen thousand, all who were left of all the army of the people of the East; for one hundred and twenty thousand men who drew the sword had fallen.

11 Then Gideon went up by the road of those who dwell in tents on the east of Nō'bah and Jog'be·hah; and he attacked the army while the camp felt secure.

12 When Zē'bah and Zal·mun'na fled, he pursued them; and he took the two kings of Mid'i·an, Zē'bah and Zal·mun'na, and routed the whole army.

13 Then Gideon the son of Jō'ash returned from battle, from the Ascent of Hē'res.

14 And he caught a young man of the men of Suc'coth and interrogated him; and he wrote down for him the leaders of Suc'coth and its elders, seventy-seven men.

15 Then he came to the men of Suc'coth and said, "Here are Zē'bah and Zal·mun'na, about whom you ridiculed me, saying, '*Are* the hands of Zē'bah and Zal·mun'na now in your hand, that we should give bread to your weary men?' "

16 And he took the elders of the city, and thorns of the wilderness and briers, and with them he taught the men of Suc'coth.

17 Then he tore down the tower of Pe·nū'el and killed the men of the city.

18 And he said to Zē'bah and Zal·mun'na, "What kind of men *were they* whom you killed at Tā'bor?" So they answered, "As you *are,* so *were* they; each one resembled the son of a king."

19 Then he said, "They *were* my brothers, the sons of my mother. *As* the LORD lives, if you had let them live, I would not kill you."

20 And he said to Jē'ther his firstborn, "Rise, kill them!" But the youth would not draw his sword; for he was afraid, because he *was* still a youth.

21 So Zē'bah and Zal·mun'na said, "Rise yourself, and kill us; for as a man *is, so is* his strength." So Gideon arose and killed Zē'bah and Zal·mun'na, and took the crescent ornaments that *were* on their camels' necks.

GIDEON'S EPHOD

22 Then the men of Israel said to Gideon, "Rule over us, both you and your son, and your grandson also; for you have delivered us from the hand of Mid'i·an."

23 But Gideon said to them, "I will

not rule over you, nor shall my son rule over you; the LORD shall rule over you."

24 Then Gideon said to them, "I would like to make a request of you, that each of you would give me the earrings from his plunder." For they had golden earrings, because they *were* Ish'ma·el·ītes.

25 So they answered, "We will gladly give *them*." And they spread out a garment, and each man threw into it the earrings from his plunder.

26 Now the weight of the gold earrings that he requested was one thousand seven hundred *shekels* of gold, besides the crescent ornaments, pendants, and purple robes which *were* on the kings of Mid'i·an, and besides the chains that *were* around their camels' necks.

27 Then Gideon made it into an ephod and set it up in his city, Oph'rah. And all Israel played the harlot with it there. It became a snare to Gideon and to his house.

28 Thus Mid'i·an was subdued before the children of Israel, so that they lifted their heads no more. And the country was quiet for forty years in the days of Gideon.

DEATH OF GIDEON

29 Then Jer·ub·bā'al the son of Jō'ash went and dwelt in his own house.

30 Gideon had seventy sons who were his own offspring, for he had many wives.

31 And his concubine who *was* in Shē'chem also bore him a son, whose name he called A·bim'e·lech.

32 Now Gideon the son of Jō'ash died at a good old age, and was buried in the tomb of Jō'ash his father, in Oph'rah of the Ā·bi·ez'rītes.

33 So it was, as soon as Gideon was dead, that the children of Israel again played the harlot with the Bā'als, and made Bā'al-Be'rith their god.

34 Thus the children of Israel did not remember the LORD their God, who had delivered them from the hands of all their enemies on every side;

35 nor did they show kindness to the house of Jer·ub·bā'al (Gideon) in accordance with the good he had done for Israel.

ABIMELECH'S CONSPIRACY

9 Then A·bim'e·lech the son of Jer·ub·bā'al went to Shē'chem, to his mother's brothers, and spoke with them and with all the family of the house of his mother's father, saying,

2 "Please speak in the hearing of all the men of Shē'chem: 'Which is better for you, that all seventy of the sons of Jer·ub·bā'al reign over you, or that one reign over you?' Remember that I *am* your own flesh and bone."

3 And his mother's brothers spoke all these words concerning him in the hearing of all the men of Shē'chem; and their heart was inclined to follow A·bim'e·lech, for they said, "He is our brother."

4 So they gave him seventy *shekels* of silver from the temple of Bā'al-Be'rith, with which A·bim'e·lech hired worthless and reckless men; and they followed him.

5 Then he went to his father's house at Oph'rah and killed his brothers, the seventy sons of Jer·ub·bā'al, on one stone. But Jō'tham the youngest son of Jer·ub·bā'al was left, because he hid himself.

6 And all the men of Shē'chem gathered together, all of Beth Mil'lō, and they went and made A·bim'e·lech king beside the terebinth tree at the pillar that *was* in Shē'chem.

The Parable of the Trees

7 Now when they told Jō′tham, he went and stood on top of Mount Ger′i·zim, and lifted his voice and cried out. And he said to them:

"Listen to me, you men of
  Shē′chem,
That God may listen to you!

8 "The trees once went forth to
    anoint a king over them.
  And they said to the olive tree,
  'Reign over us!'
9 But the olive tree said to them,
  'Should I cease giving my oil,
  With which they honor God and
    men,
  And go to sway over trees?'

10 "Then the trees said to the fig tree,
  'You come *and* reign over us!'
11 But the fig tree said to them,
  'Should I cease my sweetness and
    my good fruit,
  And go to sway over trees?'

12 "Then the trees said to the vine,
  'You come *and* reign over us!'
13 But the vine said to them,
  'Should I cease my new wine,
  Which cheers *both* God and men,
  And go to sway over trees?'

14 "Then all the trees said to the
    bramble,
  'You come *and* reign over us!'
15 And the bramble said to the trees,
  'If in truth you anoint me as king
    over you,
  Then come *and* take shelter in my
    shade;
  But if not, let fire come out of the
    bramble
  And devour the cedars of
    Lebanon!'

16 "Now therefore, if you have acted in truth and sincerity in making A·bim′e·lech king, and if you have dealt well with Jer·ub·bā′al and his house, and have done to him as he deserves—
17 "for my father fought for you, risked his life, and delivered you out of the hand of Mid′i·an;
18 "but you have risen up against my father's house this day, and killed his seventy sons on one stone, and made A·bim′e·lech, the son of his female servant, king over the men of Shē′chem, because he is your brother—
19 "if then you have acted in truth and sincerity with Jer·ub·bā′al and with his house this day, *then* rejoice in A·bim′e·lech, and let him also rejoice in you.
20 "But if not, let fire come from A·bim′e·lech and devour the men of Shē′chem and Beth Mil′lō; and let fire come from the men of Shē′chem and from Beth Mil′lō and devour A·bim′e·lech!"
21 And Jō′tham ran away and fled; and he went to Bē′er and dwelt there, for fear of A·bim′e·lech his brother.

Downfall of Abimelech

22 After A·bim′e·lech had reigned over Israel three years,
23 God sent a spirit of ill will between A·bim′e·lech and the men of Shē′chem; and the men of Shē′chem dealt treacherously with A·bim′e·lech,
24 that the crime *done* to the seventy sons of Jer·ub·bā′al might be settled and their blood be laid on A·bim′-e·lech their brother, who killed them, and on the men of Shē′chem, who aided him in the killing of his brothers.
25 And the men of Shē′chem set men in ambush against him on the tops of the mountains, and they robbed all

who passed by them along that way; and it was told A·bim′e·lech.

26 Now Gā′al the son of Ē′bed came with his brothers and went over to Shē′chem; and the men of Shē′chem put their confidence in him.

27 So they went out into the fields, and gathered *grapes* from their vineyards and trod *them,* and made merry. And they went into the house of their god, and ate and drank, and cursed A·bim′e·lech.

28 Then Gā′al the son of Ē′bed said, "Who *is* A·bim′e·lech, and who *is* Shē′chem, that we should serve him? *Is he* not the son of Jer·ub·bā′al, and *is not* Zē′bul his officer? Serve the men of Hā′mor the father of Shē′chem; but why should we serve him? 29 "If only this people were under my authority!*a* Then I would remove A·bim′e·lech." So he*b* said to A·bim′e·lech, "Increase your army and come out!"

30 When Zē′bul, the ruler of the city, heard the words of Gā′al the son of Ē′bed, his anger was aroused.

31 And he sent messengers to A·bim′e·lech secretly, saying, "Take note! Gā′al the son of Ē′bed and his brothers have come to Shē′chem; and here they are, fortifying the city against you.

32 "Now therefore, get up by night, you and the people who *are* with you, and lie in wait in the field.

33 "And it shall be, as soon as the sun is up in the morning, *that* you shall rise early and rush upon the city; and *when* he and the people who are with him come out against you, you may then do to them as you find opportunity."

34 So A·bim′e·lech and all the people who *were* with him rose by night, and lay in wait against Shē′chem in four companies.

35 When Gā′al the son of Ē′bed went out and stood in the entrance to the city gate, A·bim′e·lech and the people who *were* with him rose from lying in wait.

36 And when Gā′al saw the people, he said to Zē′bul, "Look, people are coming down from the tops of the mountains!" But Zē′bul said to him, "You see the shadows of the mountains as *if they were* men."

37 So Gā′al spoke again and said, "See, people are coming down from the center of the land, and another company is coming from the Diviners'*a* Terebinth Tree."

38 Then Zē′bul said to him, "Where indeed *is* your mouth now, with which you said, 'Who is A·bim′e·lech, that we should serve him?' *Are* not these the people whom you despised? Go out, if you will, and fight with them now."

39 So Gā′al went out, leading the men of Shē′chem, and fought with A·bim′e·lech.

40 And A·bim′e·lech chased him, and he fled from him; and many fell wounded, to the *very* entrance of the gate.

41 Then A·bim′e·lech dwelt at A·rū′mah, and Zē′bul drove out Gā′al and his brothers, so that they would not dwell in Shē′chem.

42 And it came about on the next day that the people went out into the field, and they told A·bim′e·lech.

43 So he took his people, divided them into three companies, and lay in wait in the field. And he looked, and there were the people, coming out of the city; and he rose against them and attacked them.

44 Then A·bim′e·lech and the company that *was* with him rushed forward and stood at the entrance of the gate of the city; and the *other* two

9:29 *a*Literally *hand*　*b*Following Masoretic Text and Targum; Dead Sea Scrolls read *they;* Septuagint reads *I.*　9:37 *a*Hebrew *Meonenim*

companies rushed upon all who *were* in the fields and killed them.

45 So A·bim′e·lech fought against the city all that day; he took the city and killed the people who *were* in it; and he demolished the city and sowed it with salt.

46 Now when all the men of the tower of Shē′chem had heard *that,* they entered the stronghold of the temple of the god Be′rith.

47 And it was told A·bim′e·lech that all the men of the tower of Shē′chem were gathered together.

48 Then A·bim′e·lech went up to Mount Zal′mon, he and all the people who *were* with him. And A·bim′e·lech took an ax in his hand and cut down a bough from the trees, and took it and laid *it* on his shoulder; then he said to the people who were with him, "What you have seen me do, make haste *and* do as I *have done.*"

49 So each of the people likewise cut down his own bough and followed A·bim′e·lech, put *them* against the stronghold, and set the stronghold on fire above them, so that all the people of the tower of Shē′chem died, about a thousand men and women.

50 Then A·bim′e·lech went to Thē′-bez, and he encamped against Thē′bez and took it.

51 But there was a strong tower in the city, and all the men and women—all the people of the city—fled there and shut themselves in; then they went up to the top of the tower.

52 So A·bim′e·lech came as far as the tower and fought against it; and he drew near the door of the tower to burn it with fire.

53 But a certain woman dropped an upper millstone on A·bim′e·lech's head and crushed his skull.

54 Then he called quickly to the young man, his armorbearer, and said to him, "Draw your sword and kill me, lest men say of me, 'A woman killed him.'" So his young man thrust him through, and he died.

55 And when the men of Israel saw that A·bim′e·lech was dead, they departed, every man to his place.

56 Thus God repaid the wickedness of A·bim′e·lech, which he had done to his father by killing his seventy brothers.

57 And all the evil of the men of Shē′chem God returned on their own heads, and on them came the curse of Jō′tham the son of Jer·ub·bā′al.

TOLA

10 After A·bim′e·lech there arose to save Israel Tō′la the son of Pū′ah, the son of Dodo, a man of Is′sa·char; and he dwelt in Shā′mir in the mountains of Ē′phra·im.

2 He judged Israel twenty-three years; and he died and was buried in Shā′mir.

JAIR

3 After him arose Jā′ir, a Gil′e·ad-īte; and he judged Israel twenty-two years.

4 Now he had thirty sons who rode on thirty donkeys; they also had thirty towns, which are called "Hā′-voth Jā′ir"[a] to this day, which *are* in the land of Gil′e·ad.

5 And Jā′ir died and was buried in Cā′mon.

ISRAEL OPPRESSED AGAIN

6 Then the children of Israel again did evil in the sight of the LORD, and served the Bā′als and the Ash′to-reths, the gods of Syria, the gods of Sī′don, the gods of Mō′ab, the gods of the people of Am′mon, and the gods

---

10:4 [a]Literally *Towns of Jair* (compare Numbers 32:41 and Deuteronomy 3:14)

of the Phi·lis'tines; and they forsook the LORD and did not serve Him.

7   So the anger of the LORD was hot against Israel; and He sold them into the hands of the Phi·lis'tines and into the hands of the people of Am'mon.

8   From that year they harassed and oppressed the children of Israel for eighteen years—all the children of Israel who *were* on the other side of the Jordan in the land of the Am'o·rītes, in Gil'ē·ad.

9   Moreover the people of Am'mon crossed over the Jordan to fight against Judah also, against Benjamin, and against the house of Ē'phra·im, so that Israel was severely distressed.

10   And the children of Israel cried out to the LORD, saying, "We have sinned against You, because we have both forsaken our God and served the Bā'als!"

11   So the LORD said to the children of Israel, "*Did I* not *deliver you* from the Egyptians and from the Am'o·rītes and from the people of Am'mon and from the Phi·lis'tines?

12   "Also the Sī·dō'ni·ans and A·mal'e·kītes and Mā'on·ītes*a* oppressed you; and you cried out to Me, and I delivered you from their hand.

13   "Yet you have forsaken Me and served other gods. Therefore I will deliver you no more.

14   "Go and cry out to the gods which you have chosen; let them deliver you in your time of distress."

15   And the children of Israel said to the LORD, "We have sinned! Do to us whatever seems best to You; only deliver us this day, we pray."

16   So they put away the foreign gods from among them and served the LORD. And His soul could no longer endure the misery of Israel.

17   Then the people of Am'mon gathered together and encamped in Gil'ē·ad. And the children of Israel assembled together and encamped in Miz'pah.

18   And the people, the leaders of Gil'ē·ad, said to one another, "Who *is* the man who will begin the fight against the people of Am'mon? He shall be head over all the inhabitants of Gil'ē·ad."

JEPHTHAH

11 Now Jeph'thah the Gil'ē·ad·īte was a mighty man of valor, but he *was* the son of a harlot; and Gil'ē·ad begot Jeph'thah.

2   Gil'ē·ad's wife bore sons; and when his wife's sons grew up, they drove Jeph'thah out, and said to him, "You shall have no inheritance in our father's house, for you *are* the son of another woman."

3   Then Jeph'thah fled from his brothers and dwelt in the land of Tob; and worthless men banded together with Jeph'thah and went out *raiding* with him.

4   It came to pass after a time that the people of Am'mon made war against Israel.

5   And so it was, when the people of Am'mon made war against Israel, that the elders of Gil'ē·ad went to get Jeph'thah from the land of Tob.

6   Then they said to Jeph'thah, "Come and be our commander, that we may fight against the people of Am'mon."

7   So Jeph'thah said to the elders of Gil'ē·ad, "Did you not hate me, and expel me from my father's house? Why have you come to me now when you are in distress?"

8   And the elders of Gil'ē·ad said to Jeph'thah, "That is why we have turned again to you now, that you may go with us and fight against the

10:12 *a*Some Septuagint manuscripts read *Midianites.*

people of Am'mon, and be our head over all the inhabitants of Gil'ē·ad."

9 So Jeph'thah said to the elders of Gil'ē·ad, "If you take me back home to fight against the people of Am'mon, and the LORD delivers them to me, shall I be your head?"

10 And the elders of Gil'ē·ad said to Jeph'thah, "The LORD will be a witness between us, if we do not do according to your words."

11 Then Jeph'thah went with the elders of Gil'ē·ad, and the people made him head and commander over them; and Jeph'thah spoke all his words before the LORD in Miz'pah.

12 Now Jeph'thah sent messengers to the king of the people of Am'mon, saying, "What do you have against me, that you have come to fight against me in my land?"

13 And the king of the people of Am'mon answered the messengers of Jeph'thah, "Because Israel took away my land when they came up out of Egypt, from the Ar'non as far as the Jab'bok, and to the Jordan. Now therefore, restore those *lands* peaceably."

14 So Jeph'thah again sent messengers to the king of the people of Am'mon,

15 and said to him, "Thus says Jeph'thah: 'Israel did not take away the land of Mō'ab, nor the land of the people of Am'mon;

16 'for when Israel came up from Egypt, they walked through the wilderness as far as the Red Sea and came to Kā'desh.

17 'Then Israel sent messengers to the king of Ē'dom, saying, "Please let me pass through your land." But the king of Ē'dom would not heed. And in like manner they sent to the king of Mō'ab, but he would not *consent*. So Israel remained in Kā'desh.

18 'And they went along through the wilderness and bypassed the land of Ē'dom and the land of Mō'ab, came to the east side of the land of Mō'ab, and encamped on the other side of the Ar'non. But they did not enter the border of Mō'ab, for the Ar'non *was* the border of Mō'ab.

19 'Then Israel sent messengers to Sī'hon king of the Am'o·rītes, king of Hesh'bon; and Israel said to him, "Please let us pass through your land into our place."

20 'But Sī'hon did not trust Israel to pass through his territory. So Sī'hon gathered all his people together, encamped in Jā'haz, and fought against Israel.

21 'And the LORD God of Israel delivered Sī'hon and all his people into the hand of Israel, and they defeated them. Thus Israel gained possession of all the land of the Am'o·rītes, who inhabited that country.

22 'They took possession of all the territory of the Am'o·rītes, from the Ar'non to the Jab'bok and from the wilderness to the Jordan.

23 'And now the LORD God of Israel has dispossessed the Am'o·rītes from before His people Israel; should you then possess it?

24 'Will you not possess whatever Chē'mosh your god gives you to possess? So whatever the LORD our God takes possession of before us, we will possess.

25 'And now, *are* you any better than Bā'lak the son of Zip'por, king of Mō'ab? Did he ever strive against Israel? Did he ever fight against them?

26 'While Israel dwelt in Hesh'bon and its villages, in A·rō'er and its villages, and in all the cities along the banks of the Ar'non, for three hundred years, why did you not recover *them* within that time?

27 'Therefore I have not sinned against you, but you wronged me by fighting against me. May the LORD, the Judge, render judgment this day

between the children of Israel and the people of Am'mon.' "

28 However, the king of the people of Am'mon did not heed the words which Jeph'thah sent him.

JEPHTHAH'S VOW AND VICTORY

29 Then the Spirit of the LORD came upon Jeph'thah, and he passed through Gil'ē·ad and Ma·nas'seh, and passed through Miz'pah of Gil'ē·ad; and from Miz'pah of Gil'ē·ad he advanced *toward* the people of Am'-mon.

30 And Jeph'thah made a vow to the LORD, and said, "If You will indeed deliver the people of Am'mon into my hands,

31 "then it will be that whatever comes out of the doors of my house to meet me, when I return in peace from the people of Am'mon, shall surely be the LORD's, and I will offer it up as a burnt offering."

32 So Jeph'thah advanced toward the people of Am'mon to fight against them, and the LORD delivered them into his hands.

33 And he defeated them from A·rō'er as far as Min'nith—twenty cities—and to Abel Ker'a·mim,*a* with a very great slaughter. Thus the people of Am'mon were subdued before the children of Israel.

JEPHTHAH'S DAUGHTER

34 When Jeph'thah came to his house at Miz'pah, there was his daughter, coming out to meet him with timbrels and dancing; and she *was his* only child. Besides her he had neither son nor daughter.

35 And it came to pass, when he saw her, that he tore his clothes, and said, "Alas, my daughter! You have brought me very low! You are among those who trouble me! For I have given my word to the LORD, and I cannot go back on it."

36 So she said to him, "My father, *if* you have given your word to the LORD, do to me according to what has gone out of your mouth, because the LORD has avenged you of your enemies, the people of Am'mon."

37 Then she said to her father, "Let this thing be done for me: let me alone for two months, that I may go and wander on the mountains and bewail my virginity, my friends and I."

38 So he said, "Go." And he sent her away *for* two months; and she went with her friends, and bewailed her virginity on the mountains.

39 And it was so at the end of two months that she returned to her father, and he carried out his vow with her which he had vowed. She knew no man. And it became a custom in Israel

40 *that* the daughters of Israel went four days each year to lament the daughter of Jeph'thah the Gil'ē·ad-īte.

JEPHTHAH'S CONFLICT WITH EPHRAIM

12 Then the men of Ē'phra·im gathered together, crossed over toward Zā'phon, and said to Jeph'thah, "Why did you cross over to fight against the people of Am'mon, and did not call us to go with you? We will burn your house down on you with fire!"

2 And Jeph'thah said to them, "My people and I were in a great struggle with the people of Am'mon; and when I called you, you did not deliver me out of their hands.

3 "So when I saw that you would not deliver *me,* I took my life in my

11:33 *a*Literally *Plain of Vineyards* ·

hands and crossed over against the people of Am'mon; and the LORD delivered them into my hand. Why then have you come up to me this day to fight against me?"

4 Now Jeph'thah gathered together all the men of Gil'e·ad and fought against Ē'phra·im. And the men of Gil'e·ad defeated Ē'phra·im, because they said, "You Gil'e·ad-ites *are* fugitives of Ē'phra·im among the Ē'phra·im·ītes *and* among the Ma·nas'sītes."

5 The Gil'e·ad-ites seized the fords of the Jordan before the Ē'phraim-ītes *arrived.* And when *any* Ē'phra·im·īte who escaped said, "Let me cross over," the men of Gil'e·ad would say to him, "*Are* you an Ē'phraim-īte?" If he said, "No,"

6 then they would say to him, "Then say, 'Shib'bo·leth'!" And he would say, "Sib'bo·leth," for he could not pronounce *it* right. Then they would take him and kill him at the fords of the Jordan. There fell at that time forty-two thousand Ē'phraim-ītes.

7 And Jeph'thah judged Israel six years. Then Jeph'thah the Gil'e·ad-īte died and was buried in among the cities of Gil'e·ad.

IBZAN, ELON, AND ABDON

8 After him, Ib'zan of Bethlehem judged Israel.

9 He had thirty sons. And he gave away thirty daughters in marriage, and brought in thirty daughters from elsewhere for his sons. He judged Israel seven years.

10 Then Ib'zan died and was buried at Bethlehem.

11 After him, Ē'lon the Zeb'ū·lun·īte judged Israel. He judged Israel ten years.

12 And Ē'lon the Zeb'ū·lun·īte died and was buried at Aī'ja·lon in the country of Zeb'ū·lun.

13 After him, Ab'don the son of Hil'lel the Pir'a·thon·īte judged Israel.

14 He had forty sons and thirty grandsons, who rode on seventy young donkeys. He judged Israel eight years.

15 Then Ab'don the son of Hil'lel the Pir'a·thon·īte died and was buried in Pir'a·thon in the land of Ē'phra·im, in the mountains of the A·mal'e·kītes.

THE BIRTH OF SAMSON

13 Again the children of Israel did evil in the sight of the LORD, and the LORD delivered them into the hand of the Phi·lis'tines for forty years.

2 Now there was a certain man from Zō'rah, of the family of the Dan'ītes, whose name *was* Ma·nō'ah; and his wife *was* barren and had no children.

3 And the Angel of the LORD appeared to the woman and said to her, "Indeed now, you are barren and have borne no children, but you shall conceive and bear a son.

4 "Now therefore, please be careful not to drink wine or *similar* drink, and not to eat anything unclean.

5 "For behold, you shall conceive and bear a son. And no razor shall come upon his head, for the child shall be a Naz'ir·īte to God from the womb; and he shall begin to deliver Israel out of the hand of the Phi·lis'tines."

6 So the woman came and told her husband, saying, "A Man of God came to me, and His countenance *was* like the countenance of the Angel of God, very awesome; but I did not ask Him where He *was* from, and He did not tell me His name.

7 "And He said to me, 'Behold, you shall conceive and bear a son. Now drink no wine or *similar* drink, nor

eat anything unclean, for the child shall be a Naz′ir·īte to God from the womb to the day of his death.'"

8 Then Ma·nō′ah prayed to the LORD, and said, "O my Lord, please let the Man of God whom You sent come to us again and teach us what we shall do for the child who will be born."

9 And God listened to the voice of Ma·nō′ah, and the Angel of God came to the woman again as she was sitting in the field; but Ma·nō′ah her husband *was* not with her.

10 Then the woman ran in haste and told her husband, and said to him, "Look, the Man who came to me the *other* day has just now appeared to me!"

11 So Ma·nō′ah arose and followed his wife. When he came to the Man, he said to Him, "Are You the Man who spoke to this woman?" And He said, "I *am*."

12 Ma·nō′ah said, "Now let Your words come *to pass!* What will be the boy's rule of life, and his work?"

13 So the Angel of the LORD said to Ma·nō′ah, "Of all that I said to the woman let her be careful.

14 "She may not eat anything that comes from the vine, nor may she drink wine or *similar* drink, nor eat anything unclean. All that I commanded her let her observe."

15 Then Ma·nō′ah said to the Angel of the LORD, "Please let us detain You, and we will prepare a young goat for You."

16 And the Angel of the LORD said to Ma·nō′ah, "Though you detain Me, I will not eat your food. But if you offer a burnt offering, you must offer it to the LORD." (For Ma·nō′ah did not know He *was* the Angel of the LORD.)

17 Then Ma·nō′ah said to the Angel of the LORD, "What *is* Your name, that when Your words come *to pass* we may honor You?"

18 And the Angel of the LORD said to him, "Why do you ask My name, seeing it *is* wonderful?"

19 So Ma·nō′ah took the young goat with the grain offering, and offered it upon the rock to the LORD. And He did a wondrous thing while Ma·nō′ah and his wife looked on—

20 it happened as the flame went up toward heaven from the altar—the Angel of the LORD ascended in the flame of the altar! When Ma·nō′ah and his wife saw *this,* they fell on their faces to the ground.

21 When the Angel of the LORD appeared no more to Ma·nō′ah and his wife, then Ma·nō′ah knew that He *was* the Angel of the LORD.

22 And Ma·nō′ah said to his wife, "We shall surely die, because we have seen God!"

23 But his wife said to him, "If the LORD had desired to kill us, He would not have accepted a burnt offering and a grain offering from our hands, nor would He have shown us all these *things,* nor would He have told us *such things* as these at this time."

24 So the woman bore a son and called his name Samson; and the child grew, and the LORD blessed him.

25 And the Spirit of the LORD began to move upon him at Mā′ha·neh Dan*a* between Zō′rah and Esh′tā·ol.

SAMSON'S PHILISTINE WIFE

14 Now Samson went down to Tim′nah, and saw a woman in Tim′nah of the daughters of the Phi·lis′tines.

2 So he went up and told his father and mother, saying, "I have seen a woman in Tim′nah of the daughters of the Phi·lis′tines; now therefore, get her for me as a wife."

3 Then his father and mother said

13:25 *a*Literally *Camp of Dan* (compare 18:12)

to him, "*Is there* no woman among the daughters of your brethren, or among all my people, that you must go and get a wife from the uncircumcised Phi·lis'tines?" And Samson said to his father, "Get her for me, for she pleases me well."

4　But his father and mother did not know that it was of the LORD—that He was seeking an occasion to move against the Phi·lis'tines. For at that time the Phi·lis'tines had dominion over Israel.

5　So Samson went down to Tim'nah with his father and mother, and came to the vineyards of Tim'nah.

Now *to his* surprise, a young lion *came* roaring against him.

6　And the Spirit of the LORD came mightily upon him, and he tore the lion apart as one would have torn apart a young goat, though *he had* nothing in his hand. But he did not tell his father or his mother what he had done.

7　Then he went down and talked with the woman; and she pleased Samson well.

8　After some time, when he returned to get her, he turned aside to see the carcass of the lion. And behold, a swarm of bees and honey *were* in the carcass of the lion.

9　He took some of it in his hands and went along, eating. When he came to his father and mother, he gave *some* to them, and they also ate. But he did not tell them that he had taken the honey out of the carcass of the lion.

10　So his father went down to the woman. And Samson gave a feast there, for young men used to do so.

11　And it happened, when they saw him, that they brought thirty companions to be with him.

12　Then Samson said to them, "Let me pose a riddle to you. If you can correctly solve and explain it to me within the seven days of the feast, then I will give you thirty linen garments and thirty changes of clothing.

13　"But if you cannot explain *it* to me, then you shall give me thirty linen garments and thirty changes of clothing." And they said to him, "Pose your riddle, that we may hear it."

14　So he said to them:

"Out of the eater came something
　　to eat,
　And out of the strong came
　　something sweet."

Now for three days they could not explain the riddle.

15　But it came to pass on the seventh[a] day that they said to Samson's wife, "Entice your husband, that he may explain the riddle to us, or else we will burn you and your father's house with fire. Have you invited us in order to take what is ours? *Is that* not *so?*"

16　Then Samson's wife wept on him, and said, "You only hate me! You do not love me! You have posed a riddle to the sons of my people, but you have not explained *it* to me." And he said to her, "Look, I have not explained *it* to my father or my mother; so should I explain *it* to you?"

17　Now she had wept on him the seven days while their feast lasted. And it happened on the seventh day that he told her, because she pressed him so much. Then she explained the riddle to the sons of her people.

18　So the men of the city said to him on the seventh day before the sun went down:

"What *is* sweeter than honey?
　And what *is* stronger than a
　　lion?"

14:15 [a]Following Masoretic Text, Targum, and Vulgate; Septuagint and Syriac read *fourth.*

And he said to them:

"If you had not plowed with my
  heifer,
You would not have solved my
  riddle!"

19 Then the Spirit of the LORD came
upon him mightily, and he went down
to Ash'ke·lon and killed thirty of
their men, took their apparel, and
gave the changes *of clothing* to those
who had explained the riddle. So his
anger was aroused, and he went back
up to his father's house.
20 And Samson's wife was *given* to
his companion, who had been his best
man.

SAMSON DEFEATS THE PHILISTINES

15 After a while, in the time of
wheat harvest, it happened that
Samson visited his wife with a young
goat. And he said, "Let me go in to
my wife, into *her* room." But her father would not permit him to go in.
2 Her father said, "I really thought
that you thoroughly hated her; therefore I gave her to your companion. *Is*
not her younger sister better than
she? Please, take her instead."
3 And Samson said to them, "This
time I shall be blameless regarding
the Phi·lis'tines if I harm them!"
4 Then Samson went and caught
three hundred foxes; and he took
torches, turned *the foxes* tail to tail,
and put a torch between each pair of
tails.
5 When he had set the torches on
fire, he let *the foxes* go into the standing grain of the Phi·lis'tines, and
burned up both the shocks and the
standing grain, as well as the vineyards *and* olive groves.
6 Then the Phi·lis'tines said, "Who
has done this?" And they answered,
"Samson, the son-in-law of the Tim'-

nīte, because he has taken his wife
and given her to his companion." So
the Phi·lis'tines came up and burned
her and her father with fire.
7 Samson said to them, "Since you
would do a thing like this, I will
surely take revenge on you, and after
that I will cease."
8 So he attacked them hip and
thigh with a great slaughter; then he
went down and dwelt in the cleft of
the rock of Ē'tam.
9 Now the Phi·lis'tines went up, encamped in Judah, and deployed
themselves against Lē'hi.
10 And the men of Judah said, "Why
have you come up against us?" So
they answered, "We have come up to
arrest Samson, to do to him as he has
done to us."
11 Then three thousand men of Judah went down to the cleft of the rock
of Ē'tam, and said to Samson, "Do
you not know that the Phi·lis'tines
rule over us? What *is* this you have
done to us?" And he said to them, "As
they did to me, so I have done to
them."
12 But they said to him, "We have
come down to arrest you, that we
may deliver you into the hand of the
Phi·lis'tines." Then Samson said to
them, "Swear to me that you will not
kill me yourselves."
13 So they spoke to him, saying, "No,
but we will tie you securely and deliver you into their hand; but we will
surely not kill you." And they bound
him with two new ropes and brought
him up from the rock.
14 When he came to Lē'hi, the Philis'tines came shouting against him.
Then the Spirit of the LORD came
mightily upon him; and the ropes
that *were* on his arms became like
flax that is burned with fire, and his
bonds broke loose from his hands.
15 He found a fresh jawbone of a
donkey, reached out his hand and

took it, and killed a thousand men with it.

16 Then Samson said:

"With the jawbone of a donkey,
Heaps upon heaps,
With the jawbone of a donkey
I have slain a thousand men!"

17 And so it was, when he had finished speaking, that he threw the jawbone from his hand, and called that place Rā'math Lē'hi.*a*

18 Then he became very thirsty; so he cried out to the LORD and said, "You have given this great deliverance by the hand of Your servant; and now shall I die of thirst and fall into the hand of the uncircumcised?"

19 So God split the hollow place that *is* in Lē'hi,*a* and water came out, and he drank; and his spirit returned, and he revived. Therefore he called its name En Hak'ko·rē,*b* which is in Lē'hi to this day.

20 And he judged Israel twenty years in the days of the Phi·lis'tines.

SAMSON AND DELILAH

Samson was the strongest man in the world—on the outside. But on the inside he was very weak. This story tells you why.

16 Now Samson went to Gā'za and saw a harlot there, and went in to her.

2 *When* the Gā'zītes *were told,* "Samson has come here!" they surrounded *the place* and lay in wait for him all night at the gate of the city. They were quiet all night, saying, "In the morning, when it is daylight, we will kill him."

3 And Samson lay *low* till midnight; then he arose at midnight, took hold of the doors of the gate of the city and the two gateposts, pulled them up, bar and all, put *them* on his shoulders, and carried them to the top of the hill that faces Hē'bron.

4 Afterward it happened that he loved a woman in the Valley of Sō'rek, whose name *was* Dē·lī'lah.

5 And the lords of the Phi·lis'tines came up to her and said to her, "Entice him, and find out where his great strength *lies,* and by what *means* we may overpower him, that we may bind him to afflict him; and every one of us will give you eleven hundred *pieces* of silver."

6 So Dē·lī'lah said to Samson, "Please tell me where your great strength *lies,* and with what you may be bound to afflict you."

7 And Samson said to her, "If they bind me with seven fresh bowstrings, not yet dried, then I shall become weak, and be like any *other* man."

8 So the lords of the Phi·lis'tines brought up to her seven fresh bowstrings, not yet dried, and she bound him with them.

9 Now *men were* lying in wait, staying with her in the room. And she said to him, "The Phi·lis'tines *are* upon you, Samson!" But he broke the bowstrings as a strand of yarn breaks when it touches fire. So the secret of his strength was not known.

10 Then Dē·lī'lah said to Samson, "Look, you have mocked me and told me lies. Now, please tell me what you may be bound with."

11 So he said to her, "If they bind me securely with new ropes that have never been used, then I shall become weak, and be like any *other* man."

12 Therefore Dē·lī'lah took new ropes and bound him with them, and said to him, "The Phi·lis'tines *are* upon you, Samson!" And *men were* ly-

15:17 *a*Literally *Jawbone Height*   15:19 *a*Literally *Jawbone* (compare verse 14) *b*Literally *Spring of the Caller*

ing in wait, staying in the room. But he broke them off his arms like a thread.
13 Dē·lī'lah said to Samson, "Until now you have mocked me and told me lies. Tell me what you may be bound with." And he said to her, "If you weave the seven locks of my head into the web of the loom"—
14 So she wove *it* tightly with the batten of the loom, and said to him, "The Phi·lis'tines *are* upon you, Samson!" But he awoke from his sleep, and pulled out the batten and the web from the loom.
15 Then she said to him, "How can you say, 'I love you,' when your heart *is* not with me? You have mocked me these three times, and have not told me where your great strength *lies*."
16 And it came to pass, when she pestered him daily with her words and pressed him, *so* that his soul was vexed to death,
17 that he told her all his heart, and said to her, "No razor has ever come upon my head, for I *have been* a Naz'-ir·īte to God from my mother's womb. If I am shaven, then my strength will leave me, and I shall become weak, and be like any *other* man."
18 When Dē·lī'lah saw that he had told her all his heart, she sent and called for the lords of the Phi·lis'-tines, saying, "Come up once more, for he has told me all his heart." So the lords of the Phi·lis'-tines came up to her and brought the money in their hand.
19 Then she lulled him to sleep on her knees, and called for a man and had him shave off the seven locks of his head. Then she began to torment him,[a] and his strength left him.
20 And she said, "The Phi·lis'tines *are* upon you, Samson!" So he awoke from his sleep, and said, "I will go out as before, at other times, and shake myself free!" But he did not know

that the LORD had departed from him.
21 Then the Phi·lis'tines took him and put out his eyes, and brought him down to Gā'za. They bound him with bronze fetters, and he became a grinder in the prison.
22 However, the hair of his head began to grow again after it had been shaven.

SAMSON DIES WITH THE PHILISTINES

23 Now the lords of the Phi·lis'tines gathered together to offer a great sacrifice to Dā'gon their god, and to rejoice. And they said:

"Our god has delivered into our
      hands
   Samson our enemy!"

24 When the people saw him, they praised their god; for they said:

"Our god has delivered into our
      hands our enemy,
   The destroyer of our land,
   And the one who multiplied our
      dead."

25 So it happened, when their hearts were merry, that they said, "Call for Samson, that he may perform for us." So they called for Samson from the prison, and he performed for them. And they stationed him between the pillars.
26 Then Samson said to the lad who held him by the hand, "Let me feel the pillars which support the temple, so that I can lean on them."
27 Now the temple was full of men and women. All the lords of the Phi·lis'tines *were* there—about three thousand men and women on the roof watching while Samson performed.
28 Then Samson called to the LORD,

16:19 *a*Following Masoretic Text, Targum, and Vulgate; Septuagint reads *he began to be weak.*

saying, "O Lord GOD, remember me, I pray! Strengthen me, I pray, just this once, O God, that I may with one *blow* take vengeance on the Phi·lis′-tines for my two eyes!"

29 And Samson took hold of the two middle pillars which supported the temple, and he braced himself against them, one on his right and the other on his left.

30 Then Samson said, "Let me die with the Phi·lis′tines!" And he pushed with *all his* might, and the temple fell on the lords and all the people who *were* in it. So the dead that he killed at his death were more than he had killed in his life.

31 And his brothers and all his father's household came down and took him, and brought *him* up and buried him between Zō′rah and Esh′tā·ol in the tomb of his father Ma·nō′ah. He had judged Israel twenty years.

☑ Bible Quiz

Judges 16 **Samson: The Strong Weak Man**

1. How do you know Samson was a strong man?
2. How do you know he was weak on the inside? What does it mean to be weak on the inside?
3. Do you think things might have been different if Samson had weak muscles but was strong on the inside?
4. Do you spend more time exercising your physical muscles or your spiritual muscles?
5. How can you develop your character and become stronger on the inside?

MICAH'S IDOLATRY

17 Now there was a man from the mountains of Ē′phra·im, whose name *was* Mī′cah.

2 And he said to his mother, "The eleven hundred *shekels* of silver that were taken from you, and on which you put a curse, even saying it in my ears—here *is* the silver with me; I took it." And his mother said, "*May you be* blessed by the LORD, my son!"

3 So when he had returned the eleven hundred *shekels* of silver to his mother, his mother said, "I had wholly dedicated the silver from my hand to the LORD for my son, to make a carved image and a molded image; now therefore, I will return it to you."

4 Thus he returned the silver to his mother. Then his mother took two hundred *shekels* of silver and gave them to the silversmith, and he made it into a carved image and a molded image; and they were in the house of Mī′cah.

5 The man Mī′cah had a shrine, and made an ephod and household idols;*a* and he consecrated one of his sons, who became his priest.

6 In those days *there was* no king in Israel; everyone did *what was* right in his own eyes.

7 Now there was a young man from Bethlehem in Judah, of the family of Judah; he *was* a Lē′vīte, and was staying there.

8 The man departed from the city of Bethlehem in Judah to stay wherever he could find *a place*. Then he came to the mountains of Ē′phra·im, to the house of Mī′cah, as he journeyed.

9 And Mī′cah said to him, "Where do you come from?" So he said to him, "I *am* a Lē′vīte from Bethlehem in Judah, and I am on my way to find *a place* to stay."

17:5 *a*Hebrew *teraphim*

10 Mī′cah said to him, "Dwell with me, and be a father and a priest to me, and I will give you ten *shekels* of silver per year, a suit of clothes, and your sustenance." So the Lē′vīte went in.

11 Then the Lē′vīte was content to dwell with the man; and the young man became like one of his sons to him.

12 So Mī′cah consecrated the Lē′vīte, and the young man became his priest, and lived in the house of Mī′cah.

13 Then Mī′cah said, "Now I know that the LORD will be good to me, since I have a Lē′vīte as priest!"

THE DANITES ADOPT MICAH'S IDOLATRY

18 In those days *there was* no king in Israel. And in those days the tribe of the Dan′ītes was seeking an inheritance for itself to dwell in; for until that day *their* inheritance among the tribes of Israel had not fallen to them.

2 So the children of Dan sent five men of their family from their territory, men of valor from Zō′rah and Esh′tā·ol, to spy out the land and search it. They said to them, "Go, search the land." So they went to the mountains of Ē′phra·im, to the house of Mī′cah, and lodged there.

3 While they *were* at the house of Mī′cah, they recognized the voice of the young Lē′vīte. They turned aside and said to him, "Who brought you here? What are you doing in this *place?* What do you have here?"

4 He said to them, "Thus and so Mī′cah did for me. He has hired me, and I have become his priest."

5 So they said to him, "Please inquire of God, that we may know whether the journey on which we go will be prosperous."

6 And the priest said to them, "Go in peace. The presence of the LORD *be* with you on your way."

7 So the five men departed and went to Lā′ish. They saw the people who *were* there, how they dwelt safely, in the manner of the Sī·dō′ni·ans, quiet and secure. *There were* no rulers in the land who might put *them* to shame for anything. They *were* far from the Sī·dō′ni·ans, and they had no ties with anyone.*a*

8 Then *the spies* came back to their brethren at Zō′rah and Esh′tā·ol, and their brethren said to them, "What *is* your *report?*"

9 So they said, "Arise, let us go up against them. For we have seen the land, and indeed it *is* very good. *Would* you *do* nothing? Do not hesitate to go, *and* enter to possess the land.

10 "When you go, you will come to a secure people and a large land. For God has given it into your hands, a place where *there is* no lack of anything that *is* on the earth."

11 And six hundred men of the family of the Dan′ītes went from there, from Zō′rah and Esh′tā·ol, armed with weapons of war.

12 Then they went up and encamped in Kir′jath Jē′a·rim in Judah. (Therefore they call that place Mā′ha·neh Dan*a* to this day. There *it is*, west of Kir′jath Jē′a·rim.)

13 And they passed from there to the mountains of Ē′phra·im, and came to the house of Mī′cah.

14 Then the five men who had gone to spy out the country of Lā′ish answered and said to their brethren, "Do you know that there are in these houses an ephod, household idols, a

---

18:7 *a*Following Masoretic Text, Targum, and Vulgate; Septuagint reads *with Syria*.　　18:12 *a*Literally *Camp of Dan*

carved image, and a molded image? Now therefore, consider what you should do."

15 So they turned aside there, and came to the house of the young Lē'-vīte man—to the house of Mī'cah—and greeted him.

16 The six hundred men armed with their weapons of war, who *were* of the children of Dan, stood by the entrance of the gate.

17 Then the five men who had gone to spy out the land went up. Entering there, they took the carved image, the ephod, the household idols, and the molded image. The priest stood at the entrance of the gate with the six hundred men *who were* armed with weapons of war.

18 When these went into Mī'cah's house and took the carved image, the ephod, the household idols, and the molded image, the priest said to them, "What are you doing?"

19 And they said to him, "Be quiet, put your hand over your mouth, and come with us; be a father and a priest to us. *Is it* better for you to be a priest to the household of one man, or that you be a priest to a tribe and a family in Israel?"

20 So the priest's heart was glad; and he took the ephod, the household idols, and the carved image, and took his place among the people.

21 Then they turned and departed, and put the little ones, the livestock, and the goods in front of them.

22 When they were a good way from the house of Mī'cah, the men who *were* in the houses near Mī'cah's house gathered together and overtook the children of Dan.

23 And they called out to the children of Dan. So they turned around and said to Mī'cah, "What ails you, that you have gathered such a company?"

24 So he said, "You have taken away my gods which I made, and the priest, and you have gone away. Now what more do I have? How can you say to me, 'What ails you?' "

25 And the children of Dan said to him, "Do not let your voice be heard among us, lest angry men fall upon you, and you lose your life, with the lives of your household!"

26 Then the children of Dan went their way. And when Mī'cah saw that they *were* too strong for him, he turned and went back to his house.

DANITES SETTLE IN LAISH

27 So they took *the things* Mī'cah had made, and the priest who had belonged to him, and went to Lā'ish, to a people quiet and secure; and they struck them with the edge of the sword and burned the city with fire.

28 *There was* no deliverer, because it *was* far from Sī'don, and they had no ties with anyone. It was in the valley that belongs to Beth Rē'hob. So they rebuilt the city and dwelt there.

29 And they called the name of the city Dan, after the name of Dan their father, who was born to Israel. However, the name of the city formerly *was* Lā'ish.

30 Then the children of Dan set up for themselves the carved image; and Jonathan the son of Ger'shom, the son of Ma·nas'seh,[a] and his sons were priests to the tribe of Dan until the day of the captivity of the land.

31 So they set up for themselves Mī'cah's carved image which he made, all the time that the house of God was in Shī'lōh.

THE LEVITE'S CONCUBINE

19 And it came to pass in those days, when *there was* no king in Is-

18:30 [a]Septuagint and Vulgate read *Moses.*

rael, that there was a certain Lē′vīte staying in the remote mountains of Ē′phra·im. He took for himself a concubine from Bethlehem in Judah.

2 But his concubine played the harlot against him, and went away from him to her father's house at Bethlehem in Judah, and was there four whole months.

3 Then her husband arose and went after her, to speak kindly to her *and* bring her back, having his servant and a couple of donkeys with him. So she brought him into her father's house; and when the father of the young woman saw him, he was glad to meet him.

4 Now his father-in-law, the young woman's father, detained him; and he stayed with him three days. So they ate and drank and lodged there.

5 Then it came to pass on the fourth day that they arose early in the morning, and he stood to depart; but the young woman's father said to his son-in-law, "Refresh your heart with a morsel of bread, and afterward go your way."

6 So they sat down, and the two of them ate and drank together. Then the young woman's father said to the man, "Please be content to stay all night, and let your heart be merry."

7 And when the man stood to depart, his father-in-law urged him; so he lodged there again.

8 Then he arose early in the morning on the fifth day to depart, but the young woman's father said, "Please refresh your heart." So they delayed until afternoon; and both of them ate.

9 And when the man stood to depart—he and his concubine and his servant—his father-in-law, the young woman's father, said to him, "Look, the day is now drawing toward evening; please spend the night. See, the day is coming to an end; lodge here, that your heart may be merry. Tomorrow go your way early, so that you may get home."

10 However, the man was not willing to spend that night; so he rose and departed, and came to opposite Jē′bus (that *is,* Jerusalem). With him were the two saddled donkeys; his concubine *was* also with him.

11 They *were* near Jē′bus, and the day was far spent; and the servant said to his master, "Come, please, and let us turn aside into this city of the Jeb′u·sītes and lodge in it."

12 But his master said to him, "We will not turn aside here into a city of foreigners, who *are* not of the children of Israel; we will go on to Gib′-ē·ah."

13 So he said to his servant, "Come, let us draw near to one of these places, and spend the night in Gib′-ē·ah or in Rā′mah."

14 And they passed by and went their way; and the sun went down on them near Gib′ē·ah, which belongs to Benjamin.

15 They turned aside there to go in to lodge in Gib′ē·ah. And when he went in, he sat down in the open square of the city, for no one would take them into *his* house to spend the night.

16 Just then an old man came in from his work in the field at evening, who also *was* from the mountains of Ē′phra·im; he was staying in Gib′ē·ah, whereas the men of the place *were* Ben′ja·mītes.

17 And when he raised his eyes, he saw the traveler in the open square of the city; and the old man said, "Where are you going, and where do you come from?"

18 So he said to him, "We *are* passing from Bethlehem in Judah toward the remote mountains of Ē′phra·im; I *am* from there. I went to Bethlehem in Judah; *now* I am going to the

house of the LORD. But there *is* no one who will take me into his house,
19 "although we have both straw and fodder for our donkeys, and bread and wine for myself, for your female servant, and for the young man *who is* with your servant; *there is* no lack of anything."
20 And the old man said, "Peace *be* with you! However, *let* all your needs *be* my responsibility; only do not spend the night in the open square."
21 So he brought him into his house, and gave fodder to the donkeys. And they washed their feet, and ate and drank.

GIBEAH'S CRIME

22 As they were enjoying themselves, suddenly certain men of the city, perverted men,ᵃ surrounded the house *and* beat on the door. They spoke to the master of the house, the old man, saying, "Bring out the man who came to your house, that we may know him *carnally!*"
23 But the man, the master of the house, went out to them and said to them, "No, my brethren! I beg you, do not act *so* wickedly! Seeing this man has come into my house, do not commit this outrage.
24 "Look, *here is* my virgin daughter and *the man's*ᵃ concubine; let me bring them out now. Humble them, and do with them as you please; but to this man do not do such a vile thing!"
25 But the men would not heed him. So the man took his concubine and brought *her* out to them. And they knew her and abused her all night until morning; and when the day began to break, they let her go.
26 Then the woman came as the day was dawning, and fell down at the door of the man's house where her master *was*, till it was light.

27 When her master arose in the morning, and opened the doors of the house and went out to go his way, there was his concubine, fallen *at* the door of the house with her hands on the threshold.
28 And he said to her, "Get up and let us be going." But there was no answer. So the man lifted her onto the donkey; and the man got up and went to his place.
29 When he entered his house he took a knife, laid hold of his concubine, and divided her into twelve pieces, limb by limb,ᵃ and sent her throughout all the territory of Israel.
30 And so it was that all who saw it said, "No such deed has been done or seen from the day that the children of Israel came up from the land of Egypt until this day. Consider it, confer, and speak up!"

ISRAEL'S WAR WITH THE BENJAMITES

20 So all the children of Israel came out, from Dan to Bē·er·shē'ba, as well as from the land of Gil'ē·ad, and the congregation gathered together as one man before the LORD at Miz'pah.
2 And the leaders of all the people, all the tribes of Israel, presented themselves in the assembly of the people of God, four hundred thousand foot soldiers who drew the sword.
3 (Now the children of Benjamin heard that the children of Israel had gone up to Miz'pah.) Then the children of Israel said, "Tell *us,* how did this wicked deed happen?"
4 So the Lē'vīte, the husband of the woman who was murdered, answered and said, "My concubine and I went into Gib'ē·ah, which belongs to Benjamin, to spend the night.

19:22 ᵃLiterally *sons of Belial*   19:24 ᵃLiterally *his*   19:29 ᵃLiterally *with her bones*

5 "And the men of Gib′ē·ah rose against me, and surrounded the house at night because of me. They intended to kill me, but instead they ravished my concubine so that she died.

6 "So I took hold of my concubine, cut her in pieces, and sent her throughout all the territory of the inheritance of Israel, because they committed lewdness and outrage in Israel.

7 "Look! All of you *are* children of Israel; give your advice and counsel here and now!"

8 So all the people arose as one man, saying, "None *of us* will go to his tent, nor will any turn back to his house;

9 "but now this *is* the thing which we will do to Gib′ē·ah: *We will go up* against it by lot.

10 "We will take ten men out of *every* hundred throughout all the tribes of Israel, a hundred out of *every* thousand, and a thousand out of *every* ten thousand, to make provisions for the people, that when they come to Gib′ē·ah in Benjamin, they may repay all the vileness that they have done in Israel."

11 So all the men of Israel were gathered against the city, united together as one man.

12 Then the tribes of Israel sent men through all the tribe of Benjamin, saying, "What *is* this wickedness that has occurred among you?

13 "Now therefore, deliver up the men, the perverted men*a* who *are* in Gib′ē·ah, that we may put them to death and remove the evil from Israel!" But the children of Benjamin would not listen to the voice of their brethren, the children of Israel.

14 Instead, the children of Benjamin gathered together from their cities to Gib′ē·ah, to go to battle against the children of Israel.

15 And from their cities at that time the children of Benjamin numbered twenty-six thousand men who drew the sword, besides the inhabitants of Gib′ē·ah, who numbered seven hundred select men.

16 Among all this people *were* seven hundred select men *who were* left-handed; every one could sling a stone at a hair's *breadth* and not miss.

17 Now besides Benjamin, the men of Israel numbered four hundred thousand men who drew the sword; all of these *were* men of war.

18 Then the children of Israel arose and went up to the house of God*a* to inquire of God. They said, "Which of us shall go up first to battle against the children of Benjamin?" The LORD said, "Judah first!"

19 So the children of Israel rose in the morning and encamped against Gib′ē·ah.

20 And the men of Israel went out to battle against Benjamin, and the men of Israel put themselves in battle array to fight against them at Gib′ē·ah.

21 Then the children of Benjamin came out of Gib′ē·ah, and on that day cut down to the ground twenty-two thousand men of the Israelites.

22 And the people, that is, the men of Israel, encouraged themselves and again formed the battle line at the place where they had put themselves in array on the first day.

23 Then the children of Israel went up and wept before the LORD until evening, and asked counsel of the LORD, saying, "Shall I again draw near for battle against the children of my brother Benjamin?" And the LORD said, "Go up against him."

24 So the children of Israel approached the children of Benjamin on the second day.

20:13 *a*Literally *sons of Belial*   20:18 *a*Or *Bethel*

25 And Benjamin went out against them from Gib′ē·ah on the second day, and cut down to the ground eighteen thousand more of the children of Israel; all these drew the sword.

26 Then all the children of Israel, that is, all the people, went up and came to the house of God*a* and wept. They sat there before the LORD and fasted that day until evening; and they offered burnt offerings and peace offerings before the LORD.

27 So the children of Israel inquired of the LORD (the ark of the covenant of God *was* there in those days,

28 and Phin′e·has the son of El·e·ā′zar, the son of Aaron, stood before it in those days), saying, "Shall I yet again go out to battle against the children of my brother Benjamin, or shall I cease?" And the LORD said, "Go up, for tomorrow I will deliver them into your hand."

29 Then Israel set men in ambush all around Gib′ē·ah.

30 And the children of Israel went up against the children of Benjamin on the third day, and put themselves in battle array against Gib′ē·ah as at the other times.

31 So the children of Benjamin went out against the people, *and* were drawn away from the city. They began to strike down *and* kill some of the people, as at the other times, in the highways (one of which goes up to Beth′el and the other to Gib′ē·ah) and in the field, about thirty men of Israel.

32 And the children of Benjamin said, "They *are* defeated before us, as at first." But the children of Israel said, "Let us flee and draw them away from the city to the highways."

33 So all the men of Israel rose from their place and put themselves in battle array at Bā′al Tā′mar. Then Israel's men in ambush burst forth from their position in the plain of Gē′ba.

34 And ten thousand select men from all Israel came against Gib′ē·ah, and the battle was fierce. But *the Ben′ja·mites*a* did not know that disaster *was* upon them.

35 The LORD defeated Benjamin before Israel. And the children of Israel destroyed that day twenty-five thousand one hundred Ben′ja·mites; all these drew the sword.

36 So the children of Benjamin saw that they were defeated. The men of Israel had given ground to the Ben′ja·mites, because they relied on the men in ambush whom they had set against Gib′ē·ah.

37 And the men in ambush quickly rushed upon Gib′ē·ah; the men in ambush spread out and struck the whole city with the edge of the sword.

38 Now the appointed signal between the men of Israel and the men in ambush was that they would make a great cloud of smoke rise up from the city,

39 whereupon the men of Israel would turn in battle. Now Benjamin had begun to strike *and* kill about thirty of the men of Israel. For they said, "Surely they are defeated before us, as *in* the first battle."

40 But when the cloud began to rise from the city in a column of smoke, the Ben′ja·mites looked behind them, and there was the whole city going up *in smoke* to heaven.

41 And when the men of Israel turned back, the men of Benjamin panicked, for they saw that disaster had come upon them.

42 Therefore they turned *their backs* before the men of Israel in the direction of the wilderness; but the battle overtook them, and whoever *came*

20:26 *a*Or *Bethel*   20:34 *a*Literally *they*

out of the cities they destroyed in their midst.

43 They surrounded the Ben′ja-mītes, chased them, *and* easily trampled them down as far as the front of Gib′ē·ah toward the east.

44 And eighteen thousand men of Benjamin fell; all these *were* men of valor.

45 Then they*ª* turned and fled toward the wilderness to the rock of Rim′mon; and they cut down five thousand of them on the highways. Then they pursued them relentlessly up to Gī′dom, and killed two thousand of them.

46 So all who fell of Benjamin that day were twenty-five thousand men who drew the sword; all these *were* men of valor.

47 But six hundred men turned and fled toward the wilderness to the rock of Rim′mon, and they stayed at the rock of Rim′mon for four months.

48 And the men of Israel turned back against the children of Benjamin, and struck them down with the edge of the sword—from *every* city, men and beasts, all who were found. They also set fire to all the cities they came to.

WIVES PROVIDED FOR THE BENJAMITES

21 Now the men of Israel had sworn an oath at Miz′pah, saying, "None of us shall give his daughter to Benjamin as a wife."

2 Then the people came to the house of God,*ª* and remained there before God till evening. They lifted up their voices and wept bitterly,

3 and said, "O LORD God of Israel, why has this come to pass in Israel, that today there should be one tribe *missing* in Israel?"

4 So it was, on the next morning, that the people rose early and built an altar there, and offered burnt offerings and peace offerings.

5 The children of Israel said, "Who *is there* among all the tribes of Israel who did not come up with the assembly to the LORD?" For they had made a great oath concerning anyone who had not come up to the LORD at Miz′-pah, saying, "He shall surely be put to death."

6 And the children of Israel grieved for Benjamin their brother, and said, "One tribe is cut off from Israel today.

7 "What shall we do for wives for those who remain, seeing we have sworn by the LORD that we will not give them our daughters as wives?"

8 And they said, "What one *is there* from the tribes of Israel who did not come up to Miz′pah to the LORD?" And, in fact, no one had come to the camp from Jā′besh Gil′e·ad to the assembly.

9 For when the people were counted, indeed, not one of the inhabitants of Jā′besh Gil′e·ad *was* there.

10 So the congregation sent out there twelve thousand of their most valiant men, and commanded them, saying, "Go and strike the inhabitants of Jā′besh Gil′e·ad with the edge of the sword, including the women and children.

11 "And this *is* the thing that you shall do: You shall utterly destroy every male, and every woman who has known a man intimately."

12 So they found among the inhabitants of Jā′besh Gil′e·ad four hundred young virgins who had not known a man intimately; and they brought them to the camp at Shī′lōh, which is in the land of Cā′naan.

13 Then the whole congregation sent *word* to the children of Benjamin who *were* at the rock of Rim′mon, and announced peace to them.

20:45 *ª*Septuagint reads *the rest.*   21:2 *ª*Or *Bethel*

14 So Benjamin came back at that time, and they gave them the women whom they had saved alive of the women of Jā′besh Gil′e·ad; and yet they had not found enough for them.

15 And the people grieved for Benjamin, because the LORD had made a void in the tribes of Israel.

16 Then the elders of the congregation said, "What shall we do for wives for those who remain, since the women of Benjamin have been destroyed?"

17 And they said, "*There must be* an inheritance for the survivors of Benjamin, that a tribe may not be destroyed from Israel.

18 "However, we cannot give them wives from our daughters, for the children of Israel have sworn an oath, saying, 'Cursed *be* the one who gives a wife to Benjamin.' "

19 Then they said, "In fact, *there is* a yearly feast of the LORD in Shī′lōh, which *is* north of Beth′el, on the east side of the highway that goes up from Beth′el to Shē′chem, and south of Le-bō′nah."

20 Therefore they instructed the children of Benjamin, saying, "Go, lie in wait in the vineyards,

21 "and watch; and just when the daughters of Shī′lōh come out to perform their dances, then come out from the vineyards, and every man catch a wife for himself from the daughters of Shī′lōh; then go to the land of Benjamin.

22 "Then it shall be, when their fathers or their brothers come to us to complain, that we will say to them, 'Be kind to them for our sakes, because we did not take a wife for any of them in the war; for *it is* not as *though* you have given the *women* to them at this time, making yourselves guilty of your oath.' "

23 And the children of Benjamin did so; they took enough wives for their number from those who danced, whom they caught. Then they went and returned to their inheritance, and they rebuilt the cities and dwelt in them.

24 So the children of Israel departed from there at that time, every man to his tribe and family; they went out from there, every man to his inheritance.

25 In those days *there was* no king in Israel; everyone did *what was* right in his own eyes.

The Book of
RUTH

ELIMELECH'S FAMILY GOES TO MOAB

NOW it came to pass, in the days when the judges ruled, that there was a famine in the land. And a certain man of Bethlehem, Judah, went to dwell in the country of Mō′ab, he and his wife and his two sons.
2 The name of the man *was* Ē·lim′-e·lech, the name of his wife *was* Nā′o·mī, and the names of his two sons *were* Mah′lon and Chil′i·on— Eph′ra·thītes of Bethlehem, Judah. And they went to the country of Mō′ab and remained there.
3 Then Ē·lim′e·lech, Nā′o·mī′s husband, died; and she was left, and her two sons.
4 Now they took wives of the women of Mō′ab: the name of the one *was* Or′pah, and the name of the other Ruth. And they dwelt there about ten years.
5 Then both Mah′lon and Chil′i·on also died; so the woman survived her two sons and her husband.

NAOMI RETURNS WITH RUTH

6 Then she arose with her daughters-in-law that she might return from the country of Mō′ab, for she had heard in the country of Mō′ab that the LORD had visited His people by giving them bread.
7 Therefore she went out from the place where she was, and her two daughters-in-law with her; and they went on the way to return to the land of Judah.
8 And Nā′o·mī said to her two daughters-in-law, "Go, return each to her mother's house. The LORD deal kindly with you, as you have dealt with the dead and with me.
9 "The LORD grant that you may find rest, each in the house of her husband." So she kissed them, and they lifted up their voices and wept.
10 And they said to her, "Surely we will return with you to your people."
11 But Nā′o·mī said, "Turn back, my daughters; why will you go with me? *Are* there still sons in my womb, that they may be your husbands?
12 "Turn back, my daughters, go— for I am too old to have a husband. If I should say I have hope, *if* I should have a husband tonight and should also bear sons,
13 "would you wait for them till they were grown? Would you restrain yourselves from having husbands? No, my daughters; for it grieves me very much for your sakes that the hand of the LORD has gone out against me!"
14 Then they lifted up their voices and wept again; and Or′pah kissed her mother-in-law, but Ruth clung to her.
15 And she said, "Look, your sister-in-law has gone back to her people and to her gods; return after your sister-in-law."
16 But Ruth said:

"Entreat me not to leave you,
Or to turn back from following
after you;
For wherever you go, I will go;
And wherever you lodge, I will
lodge;
Your people *shall be* my people,
And your God, my God.
17 Where you die, I will die,
And there will I be buried.
The LORD do so to me, and more
also,
If *anything but* death parts you
and me."

18 When she saw that she was determined to go with her, she stopped speaking to her.

19 Now the two of them went until they came to Bethlehem. And it happened, when they had come to Bethlehem, that all the city was excited because of them; and the women said, "Is this Nā′o·mī?"

20 But she said to them, "Do not call me Nā′o·mī;a call me Mar′a,b for the Almighty has dealt very bitterly with me.

21 "I went out full, and the LORD has brought me home again empty. Why do you call me Nā′o·mī, since the LORD has testified against me, and the Almighty has afflicted me?"

22 So Nā′o·mī returned, and Ruth the Mō′ab·ī·tess her daughter-in-law with her, who returned from the country of Mō′ab. Now they came to Bethlehem at the beginning of barley harvest.

RUTH MEETS BOAZ

2 There was a relative of Nā′o·mī's husband, a man of great wealth, of the family of Ē·lim′e·lech. His name *was* Bō′az.

2 So Ruth the Mō′ab·ī·tess said to Nā′o·mī, "Please let me go to the field, and glean heads of grain after *him* in whose sight I may find favor." And she said to her, "Go, my daughter."

3 Then she left, and went and gleaned in the field after the reapers. And she happened to come to the part of the field *belonging* to Bō′az, who *was* of the family of Ē·lim′e·lech.

4 Now behold, Bō′az came from Bethlehem, and said to the reapers, "The LORD *be* with you!" And they answered him, "The LORD bless you!"

5 Then Bō′az said to his servant who was in charge of the reapers, "Whose young woman *is* this?"

6 So the servant who was in charge of the reapers answered and said, "It *is* the young Mō′ab·īte woman who came back with Nā′o·mī from the country of Mō′ab.

7 "And she said, 'Please let me glean and gather after the reapers among the sheaves.' So she came and has continued from morning until now, though she rested a little in the house."

8 Then Bō′az said to Ruth, "You will listen, my daughter, will you not? Do not go to glean in another field, nor go from here, but stay close by my young women.

9 "*Let* your eyes *be* on the field which they reap, and go after them. Have I not commanded the young men not to touch you? And when you are thirsty, go to the vessels and drink from what the young men have drawn."

10 So she fell on her face, bowed down to the ground, and said to him, "Why have I found favor in your eyes, that you should take notice of me, since I *am* a foreigner?"

11 And Bō′az answered and said to her, "It has been fully reported to me, all that you have done for your mother-in-law since the death of your husband, and *how* you have left your father and your mother and the land of your birth, and have come to a people whom you did not know before.

12 "The LORD repay your work, and a full reward be given you by the LORD God of Israel, under whose wings you have come for refuge."

13 Then she said, "Let me find favor in your sight, my lord; for you have comforted me, and have spoken kindly to your maidservant, though I am not like one of your maidservants."

14 Now Bō′az said to her at meal-

1:20 aLiterally *Pleasant*   bLiterally *Bitter*

HELPFULNESS Ruth 2:11, 12

Let Me Help You

Have you ever cut your finger? Who put a bandage on your cut for you? Have you ever needed some medicine? Who helped you get it? Have you ever needed other things? Who helped you? Is Jesus pleased when we are good helpers?

1. Do your parents help you do things? What?
2. Does God help you do things? What?
3. Ruth helped her mother-in-law (Ruth 2:11, 12). Do you help your parents or God do things? What?
4. Think of some ways you can be a helper for others. Will you do one today?

For more on *Values* turn to page 428
For more on *Helpfulness* turn to page 723

time, "Come here, and eat of the bread, and dip your piece of bread in the vinegar." So she sat beside the reapers, and he passed parched *grain* to her; and she ate and was satisfied, and kept some back.

15 And when she rose up to glean, Bō'az commanded his young men, saying, "Let her glean even among the sheaves, and do not reproach her.

16 "Also let *grain* from the bundles fall purposely for her; leave *it* that she may glean, and do not rebuke her."

17 So she gleaned in the field until evening, and beat out what she had gleaned, and it was about an ephah of barley.

18 Then she took *it* up and went into the city, and her mother-in-law saw what she had gleaned. So she brought out and gave to her what she had kept back after she had been satisfied.

19 And her mother-in-law said to her, "Where have you gleaned today? And where did you work? Blessed be the one who took notice of you." So she told her mother-in-law with whom she had worked, and said, "The man's name with whom I worked today *is* Bō'az."

20 Then Nā'o·mī said to her daughter-in-law, "Blessed *be* he of the LORD, who has not forsaken His kindness to the living and the dead!" And Nā'-o·mī said to her, "This man *is* a relation of ours, one of our close relatives."

21 Ruth the Mō'ab·ī·tess said, "He also said to me, 'You shall stay close by my young men until they have finished all my harvest.'"

22 And Nā'o·mī said to Ruth her daughter-in-law, "*It is* good, my daughter, that you go out with his young women, and that people do not meet you in any other field."

23 So she stayed close by the young women of Bō'az, to glean until the end of barley harvest and wheat harvest; and she dwelt with her mother-in-law.

RUTH'S REDEMPTION ASSURED

3 Then Nā'o·mī her mother-in-law said to her, "My daughter, shall I not seek security for you, that it may be well with you?

2 "Now Bō'az, whose young women you were with, *is he* not our relative? In fact, he is winnowing barley tonight at the threshing floor.

3 "Therefore wash yourself and anoint yourself, put on your *best* garment and go down to the threshing floor; *but* do not make yourself known to the man until he has finished eating and drinking.

4 "Then it shall be, when he lies down, that you shall notice the place where he lies; and you shall go in, uncover his feet, and lie down; and he will tell you what you should do."

5 And she said to her, "All that you say to me I will do."

6 So she went down to the threshing floor and did according to all that her mother-in-law instructed her.

7 And after Bō'az had eaten and drunk, and his heart was cheerful, he went to lie down at the end of the heap of grain; and she came softly, uncovered his feet, and lay down.

8 Now it happened at midnight that the man was startled, and turned himself; and there, a woman was lying at his feet.

9 And he said, "Who *are* you?" So she answered, "I *am* Ruth, your maidservant. Take your maidservant under your wing,*a* for you are a close relative."

10 Then he said, "Blessed *are* you of

3:9 *a*Or *Spread the corner of your garment over your maidservant*

the LORD, my daughter! For you have shown more kindness at the end than at the beginning, in that you did not go after young men, whether poor or rich.

11 "And now, my daughter, do not fear. I will do for you all that you request, for all the people of my town know that you *are* a virtuous woman.

12 "Now it is true that I *am* a close relative; however, there is a relative closer than I.

13 "Stay this night, and in the morning it shall be *that* if he will perform the duty of a close relative for you—good; let him do it. But if he does not want to perform the duty for you, then I will perform the duty for you, *as* the LORD lives! Lie down until morning."

14 So she lay at his feet until morning, and she arose before one could recognize another. Then he said, "Do not let it be known that the woman came to the threshing floor."

15 Also he said, "Bring the shawl that *is* on you and hold it." And when she held it, he measured six *ephahs* of barley, and laid *it* on her. Then she*a* went into the city.

16 When she came to her mother-in-law, she said, "*Is* that you, my daughter?" Then she told her all that the man had done for her.

17 And she said, "These six *ephahs* of barley he gave me; for he said to me, 'Do not go empty-handed to your mother-in-law.' "

18 Then she said, "Sit still, my daughter, until you know how the matter will turn out; for the man will not rest until he has concluded the matter this day."

BOAZ REDEEMS RUTH

4 Now Bō'az went up to the gate and sat down there; and behold, the close relative of whom Bō'az had spoken came by. So Bō'az said, "Come aside, friend,*a* sit down here." So he came aside and sat down.

2   And he took ten men of the elders of the city, and said, "Sit down here." So they sat down.

3   Then he said to the close relative, "Nā'o·mī, who has come back from the country of Mō'ab, sold the piece of land which *belonged* to our brother Ē·lim'e·lech.

4   "And I thought to inform you, saying, 'Buy *it* back in the presence of the inhabitants and the elders of my people. If you will redeem *it*, redeem *it;* but if you*a* will not redeem *it, then* tell me, that I may know; for *there is* no one but you to redeem *it,* and I *am* next after you.' " And he said, "I will redeem *it.*"

5   Then Bō'az said, "On the day you buy the field from the hand of Nā'-o·mī, you must also buy *it* from Ruth the Mō'ab·ī·tess, the wife of the dead, to perpetuate*a* the name of the dead through his inheritance."

6   And the close relative said, "I cannot redeem *it* for myself, lest I ruin my own inheritance. You redeem my right of redemption for yourself, for I cannot redeem *it.*"

7   Now this *was the custom* in former times in Israel concerning redeeming and exchanging, to confirm anything: one man took off his sandal and gave *it* to the other, and this *was* a confirmation in Israel.

8   Therefore the close relative said to Bō'az, "Buy *it* for yourself." So he took off his sandal.

9   And Bō'az said to the elders and all the people, "You *are* witnesses this

3:15 *a*Many Hebrew manuscripts, Syriac, and Vulgate read *she;* Masoretic Text, Septuagint, and Targum read *he.*   4:1 *a*Hebrew *peloni almoni;* literally *so and so*   4:4 *a*Following many Hebrew manuscripts, Septuagint, Syriac, Targum, and Vulgate; Masoretic Text reads *he.*   4:5 *a*Literally *raise up*

day that I have bought all that was Ē·lim′e·lech's, and all that *was* Chil′-i·on's and Mah′lon's, from the hand of Nā′o·mī.

10 "Moreover, Ruth the Mō′ab·ī·tess, the widow of Mah′lon, I have acquired as my wife, to perpetuate the name of the dead through his inheritance, that the name of the dead may not be cut off from among his brethren and from his position at the gate.*a* You *are* witnesses this day."

11 And all the people who *were* at the gate, and the elders, said, "*We are* witnesses. The LORD make the woman who is coming to your house like Rachel and Leah, the two who built the house of Israel; and may you prosper in Eph′ra·thah and be famous in Bethlehem.

12 "May your house be like the house of Per′ez, whom Tā′mar bore to Judah, because of the offspring which the LORD will give you from this young woman."

DESCENDANTS OF BOAZ AND RUTH

13 So Bō′az took Ruth and she became his wife; and when he went in to her, the LORD gave her conception, and she bore a son.

14 Then the women said to Nā′o·mī, "Blessed *be* the LORD, who has not left you this day without a close relative; and may his name be famous in Israel!

15 "And may he be to you a restorer of life and a nourisher of your old age; for your daughter-in-law, who loves you, who is better to you than seven sons, has borne him."

16 Then Nā′o·mī took the child and laid him on her bosom, and became a nurse to him.

17 Also the neighbor women gave him a name, saying, "There is a son born to Nā′o·mī." And they called his name Ō′bed. He *is* the father of Jesse, the father of David.

18 Now this *is* the genealogy of Per′ez: Per′ez begot Hez′ron;

19 Hez′ron begot Ram, and Ram begot Am·min′a·dab;

20 Am·min′a·dab begot Nah′shon, and Nah′shon begot Sal′mon;*a*

21 Sal′mon begot Bō′az, and Bō′az begot Ō′bed;

22 Ō′bed begot Jesse, and Jesse begot David.

4:10 *a*Probably his civic office   4:20 *a*Hebrew *Salmah*

The First Book of
SAMUEL

THE FAMILY OF ELKANAH

NOW there was a certain man of Rā·ma·thā′im Zō′phim, of the mountains of Ē′phra·im, and his name *was* El·kā′nah the son of Je·rō′ham, the son of E·lī′hū,*a* the son of Tō′hū,*b* the son of Zuph, an Ē′phra·im·īte.

2 And he had two wives: the name of one *was* Hannah, and the name of the other Pe·nin′nah. Pe·nin′nah had children, but Hannah had no children.

3 This man went up from his city yearly to worship and sacrifice to the LORD of hosts in Shī′lōh. Also the two sons of Ē′lī, Hoph′nī and Phin′-e·has, the priests of the LORD, *were* there.

4 And whenever the time came for El·kā′nah to make an offering, he would give portions to Pe·nin′nah his wife and to all her sons and daughters.

5 But to Hannah he would give a double portion, for he loved Hannah, although the LORD had closed her womb.

6 And her rival also provoked her severely, to make her miserable, because the LORD had closed her womb.

7 So it was, year by year, when she went up to the house of the LORD, that she provoked her; therefore she wept and did not eat.

HANNAH'S VOW

8 Then El·kā′nah her husband said to her, "Hannah, why do you weep? Why do you not eat? And why is your heart grieved? *Am* I not better to you than ten sons?"

9 So Hannah arose after they had finished eating and drinking in Shī′-lōh. Now Ē′lī the priest was sitting on the seat by the doorpost of the tabernacle*a* of the LORD.

10 And she *was* in bitterness of soul, and prayed to the LORD and wept in anguish.

Prayers

1 Samuel 1:11

Have you ever wanted something very much? Hannah did. She wanted a son more than you have ever wanted anything. When you want something very much, what do you do? Do you ever ask God to help you? Hannah did. She also made a promise to God. If God would give her a son, she would give her son back to God. He would become God's helper. Hannah kept her promise. Be careful when you promise God something. Be sure to do it. If you say to God, "If You will give me something I want, I will do something for You," be sure to do it.

---

11 Then she made a vow and said, "O LORD of hosts, if You will indeed look on the affliction of Your maidservant and remember me, and not forget Your maidservant, but will give Your maidservant a male child, then I will give him to the LORD all the days of his life, and no razor shall come upon his head."

12 And it happened, as she continued praying before the LORD, that Ē′lī watched her mouth.

1:1 *a*Spelled *Eliel* in 1 Chronicles 6:34   *b*Spelled *Toah* in 1 Chronicles 6:34   1:9 *a*Hebrew *heykal*, palace or temple

SOMEONE SPECIAL IN OUR FAMILY 1 Samuel 1:19, 20

A new person has joined our family. She's only a tiny baby. But she's suddenly the star of the show. Everyone with a heart loves a baby. "Isn't she cute?" grandma says. "May I hold her?" sister asks. "May I feed her?" says brother. "I love you," grandpa tells her. Even uncles and aunts and cousins and friends and neighbors say special things about the new baby. She is truly a VIP, a very important person. Think of all the wonderful family memories this little baby is helping you build. Thank You, God!

1. Thank You, God, for a new family member. Help me make her a special part of our family.
2. Thank You, God, for a new friend. Help me show this new baby what a true friend a family member should be.
3. Thank You, God, for a new person who can do great things for You. Help me to help her learn how to please You and serve You.
4. Thank You, God, for the wonderful memories we are building with this new family member, new friend, and new special VIP.

For more on *Family Memories* turn to page 723
For more on *Family* turn to page 492

13 Now Hannah spoke in her heart; only her lips moved, but her voice was not heard. Therefore Ē′lī thought she was drunk.

14 So Ē′lī said to her, "How long will you be drunk? Put your wine away from you!"

15 But Hannah answered and said, "No, my lord, I *am* a woman of sorrowful spirit. I have drunk neither wine nor intoxicating drink, but have poured out my soul before the Lord.

16 "Do not consider your maidservant a wicked woman,*a* for out of the abundance of my complaint and grief I have spoken until now."

17 Then Ē′lī answered and said, "Go in peace, and the God of Israel grant your petition which you have asked of Him."

18 And she said, "Let your maidservant find favor in your sight." So the woman went her way and ate, and her face was no longer *sad*.

Samuel Is Born and Dedicated

19 Then they rose early in the morning and worshiped before the Lord, and returned and came to their house at Rā′mah. And El·kā′nah knew Hannah his wife, and the Lord remembered her.

20 So it came to pass in the process of time that Hannah conceived and bore a son, and called his name Samuel,*a* *saying,* "Because I have asked for him from the Lord."

21 Now the man El·kā′nah and all his house went up to offer to the Lord the yearly sacrifice and his vow.

22 But Hannah did not go up, for she said to her husband, "*Not* until the child is weaned; then I will take him, that he may appear before the Lord and remain there forever."

23 So El·kā′nah her husband said to her, "Do what seems best to you; wait until you have weaned him. Only let

the Lord establish His*a* word." Then the woman stayed and nursed her son until she had weaned him.

24 Now when she had weaned him, she took him up with her, with three bulls,*a* one ephah of flour, and a skin of wine, and brought him to the house of the Lord in Shī′lōh. And the child *was* young.

25 Then they slaughtered a bull, and brought the child to Ē′lī.

26 And she said, "O my lord! As your soul lives, my lord, I *am* the woman who stood by you here, praying to the Lord.

27 "For this child I prayed, and the Lord has granted me my petition which I asked of Him.

28 "Therefore I also have lent him to the Lord; as long as he lives he shall be lent to the Lord." So they worshiped the Lord there.

Hannah's Prayer

2 And Hannah prayed and said:

"My heart rejoices in the Lord;
My horn*a* is exalted in the Lord.
I smile at my enemies,
Because I rejoice in Your
　　salvation.

2 "No one is holy like the Lord,
For *there is* none besides You,
Nor *is there* any rock like our
　　God.

3 "Talk no more so very proudly;
Let no arrogance come from your
　　mouth,
For the Lord *is* the God of
　　knowledge;
And by Him actions are weighed.

1:16 *a*Literally *daughter of Belial* 　　1:20 *a*Literally *Heard by God* 　　1:23 *a*Following Masoretic Text, Targum, and Vulgate; Dead Sea Scrolls, Septuagint, and Syriac read *your.* 　　1:24 *a*Dead Sea Scrolls, Septuagint, and Syriac read *a three-year-old bull.* 　　2:1 *a*That is, strength

4 "The bows of the mighty men *are*
  broken,
  And those who stumbled are
  girded with strength.
5 *Those who were* full have hired
  themselves out for bread,
  And the hungry have ceased *to
  hunger.*
  Even the barren has borne seven,
  And she who has many children
  has become feeble.

6 "The LORD kills and makes alive;
  He brings down to the grave and
  brings up.
7 The LORD makes poor and makes
  rich;
  He brings low and lifts up.
8 He raises the poor from the dust
  And lifts the beggar from the ash
  heap,
  To set *them* among princes
  And make them inherit the
  throne of glory.

  "For the pillars of the earth *are*
  the LORD's,
  And He has set the world upon
  them.

"For by strength no man shall
  prevail.
10 The adversaries of the LORD shall
  be broken in pieces;
  From heaven He will thunder
  against them.
  The LORD will judge the ends of
  the earth.

  "He will give strength to His king,
  And exalt the horn of His
  anointed."

11 Then El·kā′nah went to his house
at Rā′mah. But the child ministered
to the LORD before Ē′lī the priest.

THE WICKED SONS OF ELI

12 Now the sons of Ē′lī *were* corrupt;a they did not know the LORD.
13 And the priests' custom with the
people *was that* when any man offered a sacrifice, the priest's servant
would come with a three-pronged
fleshhook in his hand while the meat
was boiling.
14 Then he would thrust *it* into the
pan, or kettle, or caldron, or pot; and
the priest would take for himself all
that the fleshhook brought up. So
they did in Shī′lōh to all the Israelites who came there.
15 Also, before they burned the fat,
the priest's servant would come and
say to the man who sacrificed, "Give
meat for roasting to the priest, for he
will not take boiled meat from you,
but raw."
16 And *if* the man said to him, "They
should really burn the fat first; *then*
you may take *as much* as your heart
desires," he would then answer him,
"*No,* but you must give *it* now; and if
not, I will take *it* by force."
17 Therefore the sin of the young
men was very great before the LORD,

┌─────────────────────────────┐
│ ◼ *Promises* ◼ │
│ │
│ 1 Samuel 2:9 │
│ │
│ Do you remember the song that │
│ says, "Be careful little feet │
│ where you go"? Our feet need a │
│ guard, someone to guard where │
│ they go. God has promised to be │
│ that guard. He will guard the │
│ feet of His people. But those peo- │
│ ple who don't know God don't │
│ have a guard. No wonder their │
│ feet take them to terrible places. │
└─────────────────────────────┘

9 He will guard the feet of His
  saints,
  But the wicked shall be silent in
  darkness.

2:12 aLiterally *sons of Belial*

for men abhorred the offering of the LORD.

SAMUEL'S CHILDHOOD MINISTRY

18 But Samuel ministered before the LORD, *even as* a child, wearing a linen ephod.
19 Moreover his mother used to make him a little robe, and bring *it* to him year by year when she came up with her husband to offer the yearly sacrifice.
20 And Ē'lī would bless El·kā'nah and his wife, and say, "The LORD give you descendants from this woman for the loan that was given to the LORD." Then they would go to their own home.
21 And the LORD visited Hannah, so that she conceived and bore three sons and two daughters. Meanwhile the child Samuel grew before the LORD.

PROPHECY AGAINST ELI'S HOUSEHOLD

22 Now Ē'lī was very old; and he heard everything his sons did to all Israel,*a* and how they lay with the women who assembled at the door of the tabernacle of meeting.
23 So he said to them, "Why do you do such things? For I hear of your evil dealings from all the people.
24 "No, my sons! For *it is* not a good report that I hear. You make the LORD's people transgress.
25 "If one man sins against another, God will judge him. But if a man sins against the LORD, who will intercede for him?" Nevertheless they did not heed the voice of their father, because the LORD desired to kill them.
26 And the child Samuel grew in stature, and in favor both with the LORD and men.
27 Then a man of God came to Ē'lī and said to him, "Thus says the LORD: 'Did I not clearly reveal Myself to the house of your father when they were in Egypt in Pharaoh's house?
28 'Did I not choose him out of all the tribes of Israel *to be* My priest, to offer upon My altar, to burn incense, and to wear an ephod before Me? And did I not give to the house of your father all the offerings of the children of Israel made by fire?
29 'Why do you kick at My sacrifice and My offering which I have commanded *in My* dwelling place, and honor your sons more than Me, to make yourselves fat with the best of all the offerings of Israel My people?'
30 "Therefore the LORD God of Israel says: 'I said indeed *that* your house and the house of your father would walk before Me forever.' But now the LORD says: 'Far be it from Me; for those who honor Me I will honor, and those who despise Me shall be lightly esteemed.
31 'Behold, the days are coming that I will cut off your arm and the arm of your father's house, so that there will not be an old man in your house.
32 'And you will see an enemy *in My* dwelling place, *despite* all the good which God does for Israel. And there shall not be an old man in your house forever.
33 'But any of your men *whom* I do not cut off from My altar shall consume your eyes and grieve your heart. And all the descendants of your house shall die in the flower of their age.
34 'Now this *shall be* a sign to you that will come upon your two sons, on Hoph'nī and Phin'e·has: in one day they shall die, both of them.
35 'Then I will raise up for Myself a faithful priest *who* shall do according to what *is* in My heart and in My

2:22 *a*Following Masoretic Text, Targum, and Vulgate; Dead Sea Scrolls and Septuagint omit the rest of this verse.

mind. I will build him a sure house, and he shall walk before My anointed forever.

36 'And it shall come to pass that everyone who is left in your house will come *and* bow down to him for a piece of silver and a morsel of bread, and say, "Please, put me in one of the priestly positions, that I may eat a piece of bread." ' "

SAMUEL'S FIRST PROPHECY

A boy had just gone to bed one night when God came to speak to him. This is what God told him.

3 Now the boy Samuel ministered to the LORD before Ē′lī. And the word of the LORD was rare in those days; *there was* no widespread revelation.

2   And it came to pass at that time, while Ē′lī *was* lying down in his place, and when his eyes had begun to grow so dim that he could not see,

3   and before the lamp of God went out in the tabernacle*a* of the LORD where the ark of God *was,* and while Samuel was lying down,

4   that the LORD called Samuel. And he answered, "Here I am!"

5   So he ran to Ē′lī and said, "Here I am, for you called me." And he said, "I did not call; lie down again." And he went and lay down.

6   Then the LORD called yet again, "Samuel!" So Samuel arose and went to Ē′lī, and said, "Here I am, for you called me." He answered, "I did not call, my son; lie down again."

7   (Now Samuel did not yet know the LORD, nor was the word of the LORD yet revealed to him.)

8   And the LORD called Samuel again the third time. So he arose and went to Ē′lī, and said, "Here I am, for you did call me." Then Ē′lī perceived that the LORD had called the boy.

9   Therefore Ē′lī said to Samuel, "Go, lie down; and it shall be, if He calls you, that you must say, 'Speak, LORD, for Your servant hears.' " So Samuel went and lay down in his place.

10   Now the LORD came and stood and called as at other times, "Samuel! Samuel!" And Samuel answered, "Speak, for Your servant hears."

11   Then the LORD said to Samuel: "Behold, I will do something in Israel at which both ears of everyone who hears it will tingle.

12   "In that day I will perform against Ē′lī all that I have spoken concerning his house, from beginning to end.

13   "For I have told him that I will judge his house forever for the iniquity which he knows, because his sons made themselves vile, and he did not restrain them.

14   "And therefore I have sworn to the house of Ē′lī that the iniquity of Ē′lī's house shall not be atoned for by sacrifice or offering forever."

15   So Samuel lay down until morning,*a* and opened the doors of the house of the LORD. And Samuel was afraid to tell Ē′lī the vision.

16   Then Ē′lī called Samuel and said, "Samuel, my son!" He answered, "Here I am."

17   And he said, "What *is* the word that *the LORD* spoke to you? Please do not hide *it* from me. God do so to you, and more also, if you hide anything from me of all the things that He said to you."

18   Then Samuel told him everything, and hid nothing from him. And he said, "It *is* the LORD. Let Him do what seems good to Him."

19   So Samuel grew, and the LORD

3:3 *a*Hebrew *heykal,* palace or temple
3:15 *a*Following Masoretic Text, Targum, and Vulgate; Septuagint adds *and he arose in the morning.*

☑ *Bible Quiz*

1 Samuel 3 **God Speaks to Samuel**

1. What was the boy's name?
2. Where did he live? Who took care of him?
3. Who called Samuel during the night? Who did Samuel think called him?
4. What did Eli tell Samuel to say the next time he heard the voice call him?
5. Can you talk with God? How can you listen to God?

---

was with him and let none of his words fall to the ground.

20 And all Israel from Dan to Bē·er·shē′ba knew that Samuel *had been* established as a prophet of the LORD. 21 Then the LORD appeared again in Shī′lōh. For the LORD revealed Himself to Samuel in Shī′lōh by the word of the LORD.

4 And the word of Samuel came to all Israel.*a*

THE ARK OF GOD CAPTURED

The ark of the covenant was a beautiful golden chest. Inside the golden chest were the Ten Commandments written on tablets of stone. These were the very same stone tablets God had given to Moses hundreds of years before. They had God's own handwriting on them. How precious the ark of the covenant was to the people of Israel. But then they lost it. This is how it happened.

Now Israel went out to battle against the Phi·lis′tines, and en-camped beside Eb·e·nē′zer; and the Phi·lis′tines encamped in Ā′phek. 2 Then the Phi·lis′tines put themselves in battle array against Israel. And when they joined battle, Israel was defeated by the Phi·lis′tines, who killed about four thousand men of the army in the field. 3 And when the people had come into the camp, the elders of Israel said, "Why has the LORD defeated us today before the Phi·lis′tines? Let us bring the ark of the covenant of the LORD from Shī′lōh to us, that when it comes among us it may save us from the hand of our enemies." 4 So the people sent to Shī′lōh, that they might bring from there the ark of the covenant of the LORD of hosts, who dwells *between* the cherubim. And the two sons of Ē′lī, Hoph′nī and Phin′e·has, *were* there with the ark of the covenant of God.

5 And when the ark of the covenant of the LORD came into the camp, all Israel shouted so loudly that the earth shook. 6 Now when the Phi·lis′tines heard the noise of the shout, they said, "What *does* the sound of this great shout in the camp of the Hebrews *mean?*" Then they understood that the ark of the LORD had come into the camp. 7 So the Phi·lis′tines were afraid, for they said, "God has come into the camp!" And they said, "Woe to us! For such a thing has never happened before. 8 "Woe to us! Who will deliver us from the hand of these mighty gods? These *are* the gods who struck the Egyptians with all the plagues in the wilderness.

4:1 *a*Following Masoretic Text and Targum; Septuagint and Vulgate add *And it came to pass in those days that the Philistines gathered themselves together to fight;* Septuagint adds further *against Israel.*

9 "Be strong and conduct your-selves like men, you Phi·lis′tines, that you do not become servants of the Hebrews, as they have been to you. Conduct yourselves like men, and fight!"

10 So the Phi·lis′tines fought, and Is-rael was defeated, and every man fled to his tent. There was a very great slaughter, and there fell of Is-rael thirty thousand foot soldiers.

11 Also the ark of God was captured; and the two sons of Ē′lī, Hoph′nī and Phin′e·has, died.

DEATH OF ELI

12 Then a man of Benjamin ran from the battle line the same day, and came to Shī′lōh with his clothes torn and dirt on his head.

13 Now when he came, there was Ē′lī, sitting on a seat by the wayside watching,*a* for his heart trembled for the ark of God. And when the man came into the city and told *it,* all the city cried out.

14 When Ē′lī heard the noise of the outcry, he said, "What *does* the sound of this tumult *mean?*" And the man came quickly and told Ē′lī.

15 Ē′lī was ninety-eight years old, and his eyes were so dim that he could not see.

16 Then the man said to Ē′lī, "I *am* he who came from the battle. And I fled today from the battle line." And he said, "What happened, my son?"

17 So the messenger answered and said, "Israel has fled before the Phi-lis′tines, and there has been a great slaughter among the people. Also your two sons, Hoph′nī and Phin′-e·has, are dead; and the ark of God has been captured."

18 Then it happened, when he made mention of the ark of God, that Ē′lī fell off the seat backward by the side of the gate; and his neck was broken

and he died, for the man was old and heavy. And he had judged Israel forty years.

ICHABOD

19 Now his daughter-in-law, Phin′-e·has' wife, was with child, *due* to be delivered; and when she heard the news that the ark of God was cap-tured, and that her father-in-law and her husband were dead, she bowed herself and gave birth, for her labor pains came upon her.

20 And about the time of her death the women who stood by her said to her, "Do not fear, for you have borne a son." But she did not answer, nor did she regard *it.*

4:13 *a*Following Masoretic Text and Vulgate; Sep-tuagint reads *beside the gate watching the road.*

✓ *Bible Quiz*

1 Samuel 4 **The Ark of the Covenant Is Captured**

1. Who was the enemy that came to fight Israel? Who won the first battle?

2. What did the soldiers of Israel bring to the next battle? Why do you think they did this?

3. Who won the next battle? Why didn't the ark help Israel win? Do you think the soldiers put more faith in the ark than in the God who gave it to them?

4. Are there any things God has given you that are more important to you than God Himself? How can we make God most important in our lives?

21 Then she named the child Ich′a-bod,[a] saying, "The glory has departed from Israel!" because the ark of God had been captured and because of her father-in-law and her husband.
22 And she said, "The glory has departed from Israel, for the ark of God has been captured."

THE PHILISTINES AND THE ARK

The Philistines took the ark of the covenant from Israel. But they didn't keep it for long! God wanted His people—the people of Israel—to have the ark, not the Philistines. Here are the terrible things that began happening to the Philistines as long as they had the ark.

5 Then the Phi·lis′tines took the ark of God and brought it from Eb·e-nē′zer to Ash′dod.
2 When the Phi·lis′tines took the ark of God, they brought it into the house of Dā′gon[a] and set it by Dā′-gon.
3 And when the people of Ash′dod arose early in the morning, there was Dā′gon, fallen on its face to the earth before the ark of the LORD. So they took Dā′gon and set it in its place again.
4 And when they arose early the next morning, there was Dā′gon, fallen on its face to the ground before the ark of the LORD. The head of Dā′gon and both the palms of its hands *were* broken off on the threshold; only Dā′gon's torso[a] was left of it.
5 Therefore neither the priests of Dā′gon nor any who come into Dā′-gon's house tread on the threshold of Dā′gon in Ash′dod to this day.

6 But the hand of the LORD was heavy on the people of Ash′dod, and He ravaged them and struck them with tumors,[a] *both* Ash′dod and its territory.
7 And when the men of Ash′dod saw how *it was,* they said, "The ark of the God of Israel must not remain with us, for His hand is harsh toward us and Dā′gon our god."
8 Therefore they sent and gathered to themselves all the lords of the Phi-lis′tines, and said, "What shall we do with the ark of the God of Israel?" And they answered, "Let the ark of the God of Israel be carried away to Gath." So they carried the ark of the God of Israel away.
9 So it was, after they had carried it away, that the hand of the LORD was against the city with a very great destruction; and He struck the men of the city, both small and great, and tumors broke out on them.
10 Therefore they sent the ark of God to Ek′ron. So it was, as the ark of God came to Ek′ron, that the Ek′ron·ītes cried out, saying, "They have brought the ark of the God of Israel to us, to kill us and our people!"
11 So they sent and gathered together all the lords of the Phi·lis′-tines, and said, "Send away the ark of the God of Israel, and let it go back to its own place, so that it does not kill us and our people." For there was a deadly destruction throughout all the city; the hand of God was very heavy there.
12 And the men who did not die were stricken with the tumors, and the cry of the city went up to heaven.

4:21 [a]Literally *Inglorious*   5:2 [a]A Philistine idol   5:4 [a]Following Septuagint, Syriac, Targum, and Vulgate; Masoretic Text reads *Dagon.*
5:6 [a]Probably bubonic plague. Septuagint and Vulgate add here *And in the midst of their land rats sprang up, and there was a great death panic in the city.*

The Ark Returned to Israel

6 Now the ark of the LORD was in the country of the Phi·lis′tines seven months.

2 And the Phi·lis′tines called for the priests and the diviners, saying, "What shall we do with the ark of the LORD? Tell us how we should send it to its place."

3 So they said, "If you send away the ark of the God of Israel, do not send it empty; but by all means return *it* to Him *with* a trespass offering. Then you will be healed, and it will be known to you why His hand is not removed from you."

4 Then they said, "What *is* the trespass offering which we shall return to Him?" They answered, "Five golden tumors and five golden rats, *according to* the number of the lords of the Phi·lis′tines. For the same plague *was* on all of you and on your lords.

5 "Therefore you shall make images of your tumors and images of your rats that ravage the land, and you shall give glory to the God of Israel; perhaps He will lighten His hand from you, from your gods, and from your land.

6 "Why then do you harden your hearts as the Egyptians and Pharaoh hardened their hearts? When He did mighty things among them, did they not let the people go, that they might depart?

7 "Now therefore, make a new cart, take two milk cows which have never been yoked, and hitch the cows to the cart; and take their calves home, away from them.

8 "Then take the ark of the LORD and set it on the cart; and put the articles of gold which you are returning to Him *as* a trespass offering in a chest by its side. Then send it away, and let it go.

9 "And watch: if it goes up the road to its own territory, to Beth Shem′esh, *then* He has done us this great evil. But if not, then we shall know that *it is* not His hand *that* struck us—it happened to us by chance."

10 Then the men did so; they took two milk cows and hitched them to the cart, and shut up their calves at home.

11 And they set the ark of the LORD on the cart, and the chest with the gold rats and the images of their tumors.

12 Then the cows headed straight for the road to Beth Shem′esh, *and* went along the highway, lowing as they went, and did not turn aside to the right hand or the left. And the lords of the Phi·lis′tines went after them to the border of Beth Shem′esh.

13 Now *the people of* Beth Shem′esh *were* reaping their wheat harvest in the valley; and they lifted their eyes and saw the ark, and rejoiced to see *it*.

14 Then the cart came into the field of Joshua of Beth Shem′esh, and stood there; a large stone *was* there. So they split the wood of the cart and offered the cows as a burnt offering to the LORD.

15 The Lē′vītes took down the ark of the LORD and the chest that *was* with it, in which *were* the articles of gold, and put *them* on the large stone. Then the men of Beth Shem′esh offered burnt offerings and made sacrifices the same day to the LORD.

16 So when the five lords of the Phi·lis′tines had seen *it,* they returned to Ek′ron the same day.

17 These *are* the golden tumors which the Phi·lis′tines returned *as* a trespass offering to the LORD: one for Ash′dod, one for Gā′za, one for Ash′ke·lon, one for Gath, one for Ek′ron;

18 and the golden rats, *according to* the number of all the cities of the Phi·lis′tines *belonging* to the five

lords, *both* fortified cities and country villages, even as far as the large *stone of* Abel on which they set the ark of the LORD, *which stone remains* to this day in the field of Joshua of Beth Shem′esh.

19 Then He struck the men of Beth Shem′esh, because they had looked into the ark of the LORD. He struck fifty thousand and seventy men*a* of the people, and the people lamented because the LORD had struck the people with a great slaughter.

THE ARK AT KIRJATH JEARIM

20 And the men of Beth Shem′esh said, "Who is able to stand before this holy LORD God? And to whom shall it go up from us?"

21 So they sent messengers to the inhabitants of Kir′jath Jē′a·rim, saying, "The Phi·lis′tines have brought back the ark of the LORD; come down *and* take it up with you."

7 Then the men of Kir′jath Jē′a·rim came and took the ark of the LORD, and brought it into the house of A·bin′a·dab on the hill, and consecrated El·ē·ā′zar his son to keep the ark of the LORD.

SAMUEL JUDGES ISRAEL

2 So it was that the ark remained in Kir′jath Jē′a·rim a long time; it was there twenty years. And all the house of Israel lamented after the LORD.

3 Then Samuel spoke to all the house of Israel, saying, "If you return to the LORD with all your hearts, *then* put away the foreign gods and the Ash′to·reths*a* from among you, and prepare your hearts for the LORD, and serve Him only; and He will deliver you from the hand of the Phi·lis′tines."

4 So the children of Israel put away the Bā′als and the Ash′to·reths,*a* and served the LORD only.

5 And Samuel said, "Gather all Israel to Miz′pah, and I will pray to the LORD for you."

6 So they gathered together at Miz′pah, drew water, and poured *it* out before the LORD. And they fasted that day, and said there, "We have sinned against the LORD." And Samuel judged the children of Israel at Miz′pah.

7 Now when the Phi·lis′tines heard that the children of Israel had gathered together at Miz′pah, the lords of the Phi·lis′tines went up against Israel. And when the children of Israel heard *of it,* they were afraid of the Phi·lis′tines.

8 So the children of Israel said to Samuel, "Do not cease to cry out to the LORD our God for us, that He may save us from the hand of the Phi·lis′tines."

☑ *Bible Quiz*

1 Samuel 5:1—7:2 **The Philistines Return the Ark of the Covenant**

1. When the Philistines put the ark in front of their idols what happened?

2. What other things happened to the Philistines when they had the ark?

3. What did the Philistines learn about the power of God?

4. Can you think of anything or anyone more powerful than God?

6:19 *a*Or *He struck seventy men of the people and fifty oxen of a man*   7:3 *a*Canaanite goddesses
7:4 *a*Canaanite goddesses

9 And Samuel took a suckling lamb and offered *it as* a whole burnt offering to the LORD. Then Samuel cried out to the LORD for Israel, and the LORD answered him.

10 Now as Samuel was offering up the burnt offering, the Phi·lis′tines drew near to battle against Israel. But the LORD thundered with a loud thunder upon the Phi·lis′tines that day, and so confused them that they were overcome before Israel.

11 And the men of Israel went out of Miz′pah and pursued the Phi·lis′tines, and drove them back as far as below Beth Car.

12 Then Samuel took a stone and set *it* up between Miz′pah and Shen, and called its name Eb·e·ne′zer,^a saying, "Thus far the LORD has helped us."

13 So the Phi·lis′tines were subdued, and they did not come anymore into the territory of Israel. And the hand of the LORD was against the Phi·lis′tines all the days of Samuel.

14 Then the cities which the Phi·lis′tines had taken from Israel were restored to Israel, from Ek′ron to Gath; and Israel recovered its territory from the hands of the Phi·lis′tines. Also there was peace between Israel and the Am′o·rites.

15 And Samuel judged Israel all the days of his life.

16 He went from year to year on a circuit to Beth′el, Gil′gal, and Miz′pah, and judged Israel in all those places.

17 But he always returned to Rā′mah, for his home *was* there. There he judged Israel, and there he built an altar to the LORD.

ISRAEL DEMANDS A KING

8 Now it came to pass when Samuel was old that he made his sons judges over Israel.

2 The name of his firstborn was Jō′el, and the name of his second, A·bī′jah; *they were* judges in Bē·er·she′ba.

3 But his sons did not walk in his ways; they turned aside after dishonest gain, took bribes, and perverted justice.

4 Then all the elders of Israel gathered together and came to Samuel at Rā′mah,

5 and said to him, "Look, you are old, and your sons do not walk in your ways. Now make us a king to judge us like all the nations."

6 But the thing displeased Samuel when they said, "Give us a king to judge us." So Samuel prayed to the LORD.

7 And the LORD said to Samuel, "Heed the voice of the people in all that they say to you; for they have not rejected you, but they have rejected Me, that I should not reign over them.

8 "According to all the works which they have done since the day that I brought them up out of Egypt, even to this day—with which they have forsaken Me and served other gods—so they are doing to you also.

9 "Now therefore, heed their voice. However, you shall solemnly forewarn them, and show them the behavior of the king who will reign over them."

10 So Samuel told all the words of the LORD to the people who asked him for a king.

11 And he said, "This will be the behavior of the king who will reign over you: He will take your sons and appoint *them* for his own chariots and *to be* his horsemen, and *some* will run before his chariots.

12 "He will appoint captains over his thousands and captains over his

7:12 ^aLiterally *Stone of Help*

fifties, *will set some* to plow his ground and reap his harvest, and *some* to make his weapons of war and equipment for his chariots.

13 "He will take your daughters *to be* perfumers, cooks, and bakers.

14 "And he will take the best of your fields, your vineyards, and your olive groves, and give *them* to his servants.

15 "He will take a tenth of your grain and your vintage, and give it to his officers and servants.

16 "And he will take your male servants, your female servants, your finest young men,*a* and your donkeys, and put *them* to his work.

17 "He will take a tenth of your sheep. And you will be his servants.

18 "And you will cry out in that day because of your king whom you have chosen for yourselves, and the LORD will not hear you in that day."

19 Nevertheless the people refused to obey the voice of Samuel; and they said, "No, but we will have a king over us,

20 "that we also may be like all the nations, and that our king may judge us and go out before us and fight our battles."

21 And Samuel heard all the words of the people, and he repeated them in the hearing of the LORD.

22 So the LORD said to Samuel, "Heed their voice, and make them a king." And Samuel said to the men of Israel, "Every man go to his city."

SAUL CHOSEN TO BE KING

9 There was a man of Benjamin whose name *was* Kish the son of A·bī′el, the son of Zē′ror, the son of Be·chō′rath, the son of A·phī′ah, a Ben′ja·mīte, a mighty man of power.

2   And he had a choice and handsome son whose name *was* Saul.

There was not a more handsome person than he among the children of Israel. From his shoulders upward *he was* taller than any of the people.

3   Now the donkeys of Kish, Saul's father, were lost. And Kish said to his son Saul, "Please take one of the servants with you, and arise, go and look for the donkeys."

4   So he passed through the mountains of Ē′phra·im and through the land of Shal′i·sha, but they did not find *them*. Then they passed through the land of Shā′a·lim, and *they were* not *there*. Then he passed through the land of the Ben′ja·mītes, but they did not find *them*.

5   When they had come to the land of Zuph, Saul said to his servant who *was* with him, "Come, let us return, lest my father cease *caring* about the donkeys and become worried about us."

6   And he said to him, "Look now, *there is* in this city a man of God, and *he is* an honorable man; all that he says surely comes to pass. So let us go there; perhaps he can show us the way that we should go."

7   Then Saul said to his servant, "But look, *if* we go, what shall we bring the man? For the bread in our vessels is all gone, and *there is* no present to bring to the man of God. What do we have?"

8   And the servant answered Saul again and said, "Look, I have here at hand one-fourth of a shekel of silver. I will give *that* to the man of God, to tell us our way."

9   (Formerly in Israel, when a man went to inquire of God, he spoke thus: "Come, let us go to the seer"; for *he who is* now *called* a prophet was formerly called a seer.)

10 Then Saul said to his servant, "Well said; come, let us go." So they

---

8:16 *a*Septuagint reads *cattle*.

went to the city where the man of God *was*.

11 As they went up the hill to the city, they met some young women going out to draw water, and said to them, "Is the seer here?"

12 And they answered them and said, "Yes, there he is, just ahead of you. Hurry now; for today he came to this city, because there is a sacrifice of the people today on the high place.

13 "As soon as you come into the city, you will surely find him before he goes up to the high place to eat. For the people will not eat until he comes, because he must bless the sacrifice; afterward those who are invited will eat. Now therefore, go up, for about this time you will find him."

14 So they went up to the city. As they were coming into the city, there was Samuel, coming out toward them on his way up to the high place.

15 Now the LORD had told Samuel in his ear the day before Saul came, saying,

16 "Tomorrow about this time I will send you a man from the land of Benjamin, and you shall anoint him commander over My people Israel, that he may save My people from the hand of the Phi·lis'tines; for I have looked upon My people, because their cry has come to Me."

17 So when Samuel saw Saul, the LORD said to him, "There he is, the man of whom I spoke to you. This one shall reign over My people."

18 Then Saul drew near to Samuel in the gate, and said, "Please tell me, where *is* the seer's house?"

19 Samuel answered Saul and said, "I *am* the seer. Go up before me to the high place, for you shall eat with me today; and tomorrow I will let you go and will tell you all that *is* in your heart.

20 "But as for your donkeys that were lost three days ago, do not be anxious about them, for they have been found. And on whom *is* all the desire of Israel? *Is it* not on you and on all your father's house?"

21 And Saul answered and said, "*Am I not a Ben'ja·mīte, of the smallest of the tribes of Israel, and my family the least of all the families of the tribe*[a] *of Benjamin? Why then do you speak like this to me?*"

22 Now Samuel took Saul and his servant and brought them into the hall, and had them sit in the place of honor among those who were invited; there *were* about thirty persons.

23 And Samuel said to the cook, "Bring the portion which I gave you, of which I said to you, 'Set it apart.' "

24 So the cook took up the thigh with its upper part and set *it* before Saul. And *Samuel* said, "Here it is, what was kept back. *It* was set apart for you. Eat; for until this time it has been kept for you, since I said I invited the people." So Saul ate with Samuel that day.

25 When they had come down from the high place into the city, *Samuel* spoke with Saul on the top of the house.[a]

26 They arose early; and it was about the dawning of the day that Samuel called to Saul on the top of the house, saying, "Get up, that I may send you on your way." And Saul arose, and both of them went outside, he and Samuel.

SAUL ANOINTED KING

27 As they were going down to the outskirts of the city, Samuel said to Saul, "Tell the servant to go on ahead of us." And he went on. "But you

---

9:21 [a]Literally *tribes*   9:25 [a]Following Masoretic Text and Targum; Septuagint omits *He spoke with Saul on the top of the house;* Septuagint and Vulgate add *And he prepared a bed for Saul on the top of the house, and he slept.*

stand here awhile, that I may announce to you the word of God."

10 Then Samuel took a flask of oil and poured *it* on his head, and kissed him and said: "*Is it* not because the LORD has anointed you commander over His inheritance?*a*

2 "When you have departed from me today, you will find two men by Rachel's tomb in the territory of Benjamin at Zel′zah; and they will say to you, 'The donkeys which you went to look for have been found. And now your father has ceased caring about the donkeys and is worrying about you, saying, "What shall I do about my son?" '

3 "Then you shall go on forward from there and come to the terebinth tree of Tā′bor. There three men going up to God at Beth′el will meet you, one carrying three young goats, another carrying three loaves of bread, and another carrying a skin of wine.

4 "And they will greet you and give you two *loaves* of bread, which you shall receive from their hands.

5 "After that you shall come to the hill of God where the Phi·lis′tine garrison *is*. And it will happen, when you have come there to the city, that you will meet a group of prophets coming down from the high place with a stringed instrument, a tambourine, a flute, and a harp before them; and they will be prophesying.

6 "Then the Spirit of the LORD will come upon you, and you will prophesy with them and be turned into another man.

7 "And let it be, when these signs come to you, *that* you do as the occasion demands; for God *is* with you.

8 "You shall go down before me to Gil′gal; and surely I will come down to you to offer burnt offerings *and* make sacrifices of peace offerings. Seven days you shall wait, till I come

to you and show you what you should do."

9 So it was, when he had turned his back to go from Samuel, that God gave him another heart; and all those signs came to pass that day.

10 When they came there to the hill, there was a group of prophets to meet him; then the Spirit of God came upon him, and he prophesied among them.

11 And it happened, when all who knew him formerly saw that he indeed prophesied among the prophets, that the people said to one another, "What *is* this *that* has come upon the son of Kish? *Is* Saul also among the prophets?"

12 Then a man from there answered and said, "But who *is* their father?" Therefore it became a proverb: "*Is* Saul also among the prophets?"

13 And when he had finished prophesying, he went to the high place.

14 Then Saul's uncle said to him and his servant, "Where did you go?" So he said, "To look for the donkeys. When we saw that *they were* nowhere *to be found,* we went to Samuel."

15 And Saul's uncle said, "Tell me, please, what Samuel said to you."

16 So Saul said to his uncle, "He told us plainly that the donkeys had been found." But about the matter of the kingdom, he did not tell him what Samuel had said.

SAUL PROCLAIMED KING

17 Then Samuel called the people together to the LORD at Miz′pah,

18 and said to the children of Israel, "Thus says the LORD God of Israel: 'I

10:1 *a*Following Masoretic Text, Targum, and Vulgate; Septuagint reads *His people Israel; and you shall rule the people of the Lord;* Septuagint and Vulgate add *And you shall deliver His people from the hands of their enemies all around them. And this shall be a sign to you, that God has anointed you to be a prince.*

brought up Israel out of Egypt, and delivered you from the hand of the Egyptians *and* from the hand of all kingdoms and from those who oppressed you.'

19 "But you have today rejected your God, who Himself saved you from all your adversities and your tribulations; and you have said to Him, 'No, set a king over us!' Now therefore, present yourselves before the LORD by your tribes and by your clans."*a*

20 And when Samuel had caused all the tribes of Israel to come near, the tribe of Benjamin was chosen.

21 When he had caused the tribe of Benjamin to come near by their families, the family of Mā'trī was chosen. And Saul the son of Kish was chosen. But when they sought him, he could not be found.

22 Therefore they inquired of the LORD further, "Has the man come here yet?" And the LORD answered, "There he is, hidden among the equipment."

23 So they ran and brought him from there; and when he stood among the people, he was taller than any of the people from his shoulders upward.

24 And Samuel said to all the people, "Do you see him whom the LORD has chosen, that *there is* no one like him among all the people?" So all the people shouted and said, "Long live the king!"

25 Then Samuel explained to the people the behavior of royalty, and wrote *it* in a book and laid *it* up before the LORD. And Samuel sent all the people away, every man to his house.

26 And Saul also went home to Gib'ē·ah; and valiant *men* went with him, whose hearts God had touched.

27 But some rebels said, "How can this man save us?" So they despised him, and brought him no presents. But he held his peace.

SAUL SAVES JABESH GILEAD

11 Then Nā'hash the Am'mon·īte came up and encamped against Jā'besh Gil'ē·ad; and all the men of Jā'besh said to Nā'hash, "Make a covenant with us, and we will serve you."

2 And Nā'hash the Am'mon·īte answered them, "On this *condition* I will make *a covenant* with you, that I may put out all your right eyes, and bring reproach on all Israel."

3 Then the elders of Jā'besh said to him, "Hold off for seven days, that we may send messengers to all the territory of Israel. And then, if *there is* no one to save us, we will come out to you."

4 So the messengers came to Gib'ē·ah of Saul and told the news in the hearing of the people. And all the people lifted up their voices and wept.

5 Now there was Saul, coming behind the herd from the field; and Saul said, "What *troubles* the people, that they weep?" And they told him the words of the men of Jā'besh.

6 Then the Spirit of God came upon Saul when he heard this news, and his anger was greatly aroused.

7 So he took a yoke of oxen and cut them in pieces, and sent *them* throughout all the territory of Israel by the hands of messengers, saying, "Whoever does not go out with Saul and Samuel to battle, so it shall be done to his oxen." And the fear of the LORD fell on the people, and they came out with one consent.

8 When he numbered them in Bē'zek, the children of Israel were three hundred thousand, and the men of Judah thirty thousand.

9 And they said to the messengers who came, "Thus you shall say to the

10:19 *a*Literally *thousands*

men of Jā′besh Gil′ē·ad: 'Tomorrow, by *the time* the sun is hot, you shall have help.' " Then the messengers came and reported *it* to the men of Jā′besh, and they were glad.

10 Therefore the men of Jā′besh said, "Tomorrow we will come out to you, and you may do with us whatever seems good to you."

11 So it was, on the next day, that Saul put the people in three companies; and they came into the midst of the camp in the morning watch, and killed Am′mon·ītes until the heat of the day. And it happened that those who survived were scattered, so that no two of them were left together.

12 Then the people said to Samuel, "Who *is* he who said, 'Shall Saul reign over us?' Bring the men, that we may put them to death."

13 But Saul said, "Not a man shall be put to death this day, for today the LORD has accomplished salvation in Israel."

14 Then Samuel said to the people, "Come, let us go to Gil′gal and renew the kingdom there."

15 So all the people went to Gil′gal, and there they made Saul king before the LORD in Gil′gal. There they made sacrifices of peace offerings before the LORD, and there Saul and all the men of Israel rejoiced greatly.

SAMUEL'S ADDRESS AT SAUL'S CORONATION

12 Now Samuel said to all Israel: "Indeed I have heeded your voice in all that you said to me, and have made a king over you.

2 "And now here is the king, walking before you; and I am old and grayheaded, and look, my sons *are* with you. I have walked before you from my childhood to this day.

3 "Here I am. Witness against me before the LORD and before His anointed: Whose ox have I taken, or whose donkey have I taken, or whom have I cheated? Whom have I oppressed, or from whose hand have I received *any* bribe with which to blind my eyes? I will restore *it* to you."

4 And they said, "You have not cheated us or oppressed us, nor have you taken anything from any man's hand."

5 Then he said to them, "The LORD *is* witness against you, and His anointed *is* witness this day, that you have not found anything in my hand." And they answered, "*He is* witness."

6 Then Samuel said to the people, "*It is* the LORD who raised up Moses and Aaron, and who brought your fathers up from the land of Egypt.

7 "Now therefore, stand still, that I may reason with you before the LORD concerning all the righteous acts of the LORD which He did to you and your fathers:

8 "When Jacob had gone into Egypt,*a* and your fathers cried out to the LORD, then the LORD sent Moses and Aaron, who brought your fathers out of Egypt and made them dwell in this place.

9 "And when they forgot the LORD their God, He sold them into the hand of Sis′e·ra, commander of the army of Hā′zor, into the hand of the Phi·lis′tines, and into the hand of the king of Mō′ab; and they fought against them.

10 "Then they cried out to the LORD, and said, 'We have sinned, because we have forsaken the LORD and served the Bā′als and Ash′to·reths;*a* but now deliver us from the hand of our enemies, and we will serve You.'

12:8 *a*Following Masoretic Text, Targum, and Vulgate; Septuagint adds *and the Egyptians afflicted them.* 12:10 *a*Canaanite goddesses

11 "And the LORD sent Jer·ub·bā′al,*a* Bē′dan,*b* Jeph′thah, and Samuel,*c* and delivered you out of the hand of your enemies on every side; and you dwelt in safety.

12 "And when you saw that Nā′hash king of the Am′mon·ites came against you, you said to me, 'No, but a king shall reign over us,' when the LORD your God *was* your king.

13 "Now therefore, here is the king whom you have chosen *and* whom you have desired. And take note, the LORD has set a king over you.

14 "If you fear the LORD and serve Him and obey His voice, and do not rebel against the commandment of the LORD, then both you and the king who reigns over you will continue following the LORD your God.

15 "However, if you do not obey the voice of the LORD, but rebel against the commandment of the LORD, then the hand of the LORD will be against you, as *it was* against your fathers.

16 "Now therefore, stand and see this great thing which the LORD will do before your eyes:

17 "*Is* today not the wheat harvest? I will call to the LORD, and He will send thunder and rain, that you may perceive and see that your wickedness *is* great, which you have done in the sight of the LORD, in asking a king for yourselves."

18 So Samuel called to the LORD, and the LORD sent thunder and rain that day; and all the people greatly feared the LORD and Samuel.

19 And all the people said to Samuel, "Pray for your servants to the LORD your God, that we may not die; for we have added to all our sins the evil of asking a king for ourselves."

20 Then Samuel said to the people, "Do not fear. You have done all this wickedness; yet do not turn aside from following the LORD, but serve the LORD with all your heart.

21 "And do not turn aside; for *then you would go* after empty things which cannot profit or deliver, for they *are* nothing.

22 "For the LORD will not forsake His people, for His great name's sake, because it has pleased the LORD to make you His people.

23 "Moreover, as for me, far be it from me that I should sin against the LORD in ceasing to pray for you; but I will teach you the good and the right way.

24 "Only fear the LORD, and serve Him in truth with all your heart; for consider what great things He has done for you.

25 "But if you still do wickedly, you shall be swept away, both you and your king."

SAUL'S UNLAWFUL SACRIFICE

King Saul was about to do something foolish. The people of Israel had wanted a king for many years. God finally let them make Saul their first king. Now Saul was about to lose his kingdom because he disobeyed God.

13 Saul reigned one year; and when he had reigned two years over Israel,*a*

2 Saul chose for himself three thousand *men* of Israel. Two thousand were with Saul in Mich′mash and in the mountains of Beth′el, and a thousand were with Jonathan in Gib′ē·ah of Benjamin. The rest of the people he sent away, every man to his tent.

3 And Jonathan attacked the garrison of the Phi·lis′tines that *was* in

12:11 *a*Syriac reads *Deborah;* Targum reads *Gideon.* *b*Septuagint and Syriac read *Barak;* Targum reads *Simson.* *c*Syriac reads *Simson.*
13:1 *a*The Hebrew is difficult (compare 2 Samuel 5:4; 2 Kings 14:2; see also 2 Samuel 2:10; Acts 13:21).

Gē′ba, and the Phi·lis′tines heard *of it*. Then Saul blew the trumpet throughout all the land, saying, "Let the Hebrews hear!"

4   Now all Israel heard it said *that* Saul had attacked a garrison of the Phi·lis′tines, and *that* Israel had also become an abomination to the Phi·lis′tines. And the people were called together to Saul at Gil′gal.

5   Then the Phi·lis′tines gathered together to fight with Israel, thirty*a* thousand chariots and six thousand horsemen, and people as the sand which *is* on the seashore in multitude. And they came up and encamped in Mich′mash, to the east of Beth Ā′ven.

6   When the men of Israel saw that they were in danger (for the people were distressed), then the people hid in caves, in thickets, in rocks, in holes, and in pits.

7   And *some of* the Hebrews crossed over the Jordan to the land of Gad and Gil′ē·ad. As for Saul, he *was* still in Gil′gal, and all the people followed him trembling.

8   Then he waited seven days, according to the time set by Samuel. But Samuel did not come to Gil′gal; and the people were scattered from him.

9   So Saul said, "Bring a burnt offering and peace offerings here to me." And he offered the burnt offering.

10   Now it happened, as soon as he had finished presenting the burnt offering, that Samuel came; and Saul went out to meet him, that he might greet him.

11   And Samuel said, "What have you done?" Saul said, "When I saw that the people were scattered from me, and *that* you did not come within the days appointed, and *that* the Phi·lis′- tines gathered together at Mich′- mash,

12   "then I said, 'The Phi·lis′tines will now come down on me at Gil′gal, and I have not made supplication to the LORD.' Therefore I felt compelled, and offered a burnt offering."

13   And Samuel said to Saul, "You have done foolishly. You have not kept the commandment of the LORD your God, which He commanded you. For now the LORD would have established your kingdom over Israel forever.

14   "But now your kingdom shall not continue. The LORD has sought for Himself a man after His own heart, and the LORD has commanded him *to be* commander over His people, because you have not kept what the LORD commanded you."

15   Then Samuel arose and went up

13:5 *a*Following Masoretic Text, Septuagint, Targum, and Vulgate; Syriac and some manuscripts of the Septuagint read *three*.

☑   *Bible Quiz*

1 Samuel 13:1–15   **Saul Disobeys God**

1.   What enemy army came out to fight Israel?
2.   What did Saul's soldiers do?
3.   Could Saul have helped them be less afraid? How? What did Saul do instead?
4.   Only a priest like Samuel could make a sacrifice to God. But Saul, seeing his soldiers running away, forgot to trust in God to help him. When you see trouble coming your way, don't give up on God. Be patient and wait for Him to help you. In what ways can you patiently wait for Him?

from Gil′gal to Gib′e·ah of Benja-
min.ᵃ And Saul numbered the people
present with him, about six hundred
men.

NO WEAPONS FOR THE ARMY

16 Saul, Jonathan his son, and the
people present with them remained
in Gib′e·ah of Benjamin. But the Phi-
lis′tines encamped in Mich′mash.
17 Then raiders came out of the
camp of the Phi·lis′tines in three
companies. One company turned onto
the road to Oph′rah, to the land of
Shū′al,
18 another company turned to the
road to Beth Hor′on, and another
company turned to the road of the
border that overlooks the Valley of
Ze·bō′im toward the wilderness.
19 Now there was no blacksmith to
be found throughout all the land of
Israel, for the Phi·lis′tines said, "Lest
the Hebrews make swords or spears."
20 But all the Israelites would go
down to the Phi·lis′tines to sharpen
each man's plowshare, his mattock,
his ax, and his sickle;
21 and the charge for a sharpening
was a pimᵃ for the plowshares, the
mattocks, the forks, and the axes,
and to set the points of the goads.
22 So it came about, on the day of
battle, that there was neither sword
nor spear found in the hand of any of
the people who were with Saul and
Jonathan. But they were found with
Saul and Jonathan his son.
23 And the garrison of the Phi·lis′-
tines went out to the pass of Mich′-
mash.

JONATHAN DEFEATS THE
PHILISTINES

14 Now it happened one day that
Jonathan the son of Saul said to the
young man who bore his armor,
"Come, let us go over to the Phi·lis′-
tines' garrison that is on the other
side." But he did not tell his father.
2 And Saul was sitting in the outskirts of Gib′e·ah under a pomegranate tree which is in Mig′ron. The people who were with him were about six
hundred men.
3 A·hī′jah the son of A·hī′tub, Ich′-
a·bod's brother, the son of Phin′e·has,
the son of Ē′lī, the LORD's priest in
Shī′lōh, was wearing an ephod. But
the people did not know that Jonathan had gone.
4 Between the passes, by which
Jonathan sought to go over to the
Phi·lis′tines' garrison, there was a
sharp rock on one side and a sharp
rock on the other side. And the name
of one was Bō′zez, and the name of
the other Sē′neh.
5 The front of one faced northward
opposite Mich′mash, and the other
southward opposite Gib′e·ah.
6 Then Jonathan said to the young
man who bore his armor, "Come, let
us go over to the garrison of these
uncircumcised; it may be that the
LORD will work for us. For nothing restrains the LORD from saving by
many or by few."
7 So his armorbearer said to him,
"Do all that is in your heart. Go then;
here I am with you, according to your
heart."
8 Then Jonathan said, "Very well,
let us cross over to these men, and we
will show ourselves to them.
9 "If they say thus to us, 'Wait until
we come to you,' then we will stand
still in our place and not go up to
them.
10 "But if they say thus, 'Come up to

13:15 ᵃFollowing Masoretic Text and Targum; Septuagint and Vulgate add And the rest of the people
went up after Saul to meet the people who fought
against them, going from Gilgal to Gibeah in the
hill of Benjamin.
13:21 ᵃAbout two-thirds shekel weight

us,' then we will go up. For the LORD has delivered them into our hand, and this *will be* a sign to us."

11 So both of them showed themselves to the garrison of the Phi·lis'-tines. And the Phi·lis'tines said, "Look, the Hebrews are coming out of the holes where they have hidden."

12 Then the men of the garrison called to Jonathan and his armorbearer, and said, "Come up to us, and we will show you something." Jonathan said to his armorbearer, "Come up after me, for the LORD has delivered them into the hand of Israel."

13 And Jonathan climbed up on his hands and knees with his armorbearer after him; and they fell before Jonathan. And as he came after him, his armorbearer killed them.

14 That first slaughter which Jonathan and his armorbearer made was about twenty men within about half an acre of land.*a*

15 And there was trembling in the camp, in the field, and among all the people. The garrison and the raiders also trembled; and the earth quaked, so that it was a very great trembling.

16 Now the watchmen of Saul in Gib'ē·ah of Benjamin looked, and *there* was the multitude, melting away; and they went here and there.

17 Then Saul said to the people who *were* with him, "Now call the roll and see who has gone from us." And when they had called the roll, surprisingly, Jonathan and his armorbearer *were* not *there*.

18 And Saul said to A·hī'jah, "Bring the ark*a* of God here" (for at that time the ark*b* of God was with the children of Israel).

19 Now it happened, while Saul talked to the priest, that the noise which *was* in the camp of the Phi·lis'tines continued to increase; so Saul said to the priest, "Withdraw your hand."

20 Then Saul and all the people who *were* with him assembled, and they went to the battle; and indeed every man's sword was against his neighbor, *and there was* very great confusion.

21 Moreover the Hebrews *who* were with the Phi·lis'tines before that time, who went up with them into the camp *from the* surrounding *country,* they also joined the Israelites who *were* with Saul and Jonathan.

22 Likewise all the men of Israel who had hidden in the mountains of Ē'phra·im, *when* they heard that the Phi·lis'tines fled, they also followed hard after them in the battle.

23 So the LORD saved Israel that day, and the battle shifted to Beth Ā'ven.

SAUL'S RASH OATH

24 And the men of Israel were distressed that day, for Saul had placed the people under oath, saying, "Cursed *is* the man who eats *any* food until evening, before I have taken vengeance on my enemies." So none of the people tasted food.

25 Now all *the people* of the land came to a forest; and there was honey on the ground.

26 And when the people had come into the woods, there was the honey, dripping; but no one put his hand to his mouth, for the people feared the oath.

27 But Jonathan had not heard his father charge the people with the oath; therefore he stretched out the end of the rod that *was* in his hand and dipped it in a honeycomb, and put his hand to his mouth; and his countenance brightened.

14:14 *a*Literally *half the area plowed by a yoke* (of oxen in a day)　14:18 *a*Following Masoretic Text, Targum, and Vulgate; Septuagint reads *ephod.* *b*Following Masoretic Text, Targum, and Vulgate; Septuagint reads *ephod.*

28 Then one of the people said, "Your father strictly charged the people with an oath, saying, 'Cursed *is* the man who eats food this day.' " And the people were faint.

29 But Jonathan said, "My father has troubled the land. Look now, how my countenance has brightened because I tasted a little of this honey.

30 "How much better if the people had eaten freely today of the spoil of their enemies which they found! For now would there not have been a much greater slaughter among the Phi·lis′tines?"

31 Now they had driven back the Phi·lis′tines that day from Mich′- mash to Aī′ja·lon. So the people were very faint.

32 And the people rushed on the spoil, and took sheep, oxen, and calves, and slaughtered *them* on the ground; and the people ate *them* with the blood.

33 Then they told Saul, saying, "Look, the people are sinning against the LORD by eating with the blood!" So he said, "You have dealt treacherously; roll a large stone to me this day."

34 Then Saul said, "Disperse yourselves among the people, and say to them, 'Bring me here every man's ox and every man's sheep, slaughter *them* here, and eat; and do not sin against the LORD by eating with the blood.' " So every one of the people brought his ox with him that night, and slaughtered *it* there.

35 Then Saul built an altar to the LORD. This was the first altar that he built to the LORD.

36 Now Saul said, "Let us go down after the Phi·lis′tines by night, and plunder them until the morning light; and let us not leave a man of them." And they said, "Do whatever seems good to you." Then the priest said, "Let us draw near to God here."

37 So Saul asked counsel of God, "Shall I go down after the Phi·lis′- tines? Will You deliver them into the hand of Israel?" But He did not answer him that day.

38 And Saul said, "Come over here, all you chiefs of the people, and know and see what this sin was today.

39 "For *as* the LORD lives, who saves Israel, though it be in Jonathan my son, he shall surely die." But not a man among all the people answered him.

40 Then he said to all Israel, "You be on one side, and my son Jonathan and I will be on the other side." And the people said to Saul, "Do what seems good to you."

41 Therefore Saul said to the LORD God of Israel, "Give a perfect *lot.*"a So Saul and Jonathan were taken, but the people escaped.

42 And Saul said, "Cast *lots* between my son Jonathan and me." So Jonathan was taken.

43 Then Saul said to Jonathan, "Tell me what you have done." And Jonathan told him, and said, "I only tasted a little honey with the end of the rod that *was* in my hand. So now I must die!"

44 Saul answered, "God do so and more also; for you shall surely die, Jonathan."

45 But the people said to Saul, "Shall Jonathan die, who has accomplished this great deliverance in Israel? Certainly not! *As* the LORD lives, not one hair of his head shall fall to the ground, for he has worked with God this day." So the people rescued Jonathan, and he did not die.

46 Then Saul returned from pursu-

14:41 aFollowing Masoretic Text and Targum; Septuagint and Vulgate read *Why do You not answer Your servant today? If the injustice is with me or Jonathan my son, O LORD God of Israel, give proof; and if You say it is with Your people Israel, give holiness.*

ing the Phi·lis'tines, and the Phi·lis'tines went to their own place.

SAUL'S CONTINUING WARS

47 So Saul established his sovereignty over Israel, and fought against all his enemies on every side, against Mō'ab, against the people of Am'mon, against Ē'dom, against the kings of Zō'bah, and against the Phi·lis'tines. Wherever he turned, he harassed *them.ᵃ*

48 And he gathered an army and attacked the A·mal'e·kītes, and delivered Israel from the hands of those who plundered them.

49 The sons of Saul were Jonathan, Jish'ū·ī,ᵃ and Mal·chī·shū'a. And the names of his two daughters *were these:* the name of the firstborn Mē'rab, and the name of the younger Mī'chal.

50 The name of Saul's wife *was* A·hin'ō·am the daughter of A·him'a·az. And the name of the commander of his army *was* Abner the son of Ner, Saul's uncle.

51 Kish *was* the father of Saul, and Ner the father of Abner *was* the son of A·bī'el.

52 Now there was fierce war with the Phi·lis'tines all the days of Saul. And when Saul saw any strong man or any valiant man, he took him for himself.

SAUL SPARES KING AGAG

15 Samuel also said to Saul, "The LORD sent me to anoint you king over His people, over Israel. Now therefore, heed the voice of the words of the LORD.

2 "Thus says the LORD of hosts: 'I will punish Am'a·lek *for* what he did to Israel, how he ambushed him on the way when he came up from Egypt.

3 'Now go and attack Am'a·lek, and utterly destroy all that they have, and do not spare them. But kill both man and woman, infant and nursing child, ox and sheep, camel and donkey.'"

4 So Saul gathered the people together and numbered them in Te·lā'im, two hundred thousand foot soldiers and ten thousand men of Judah.

5 And Saul came to a city of Am'a·lek, and lay in wait in the valley.

6 Then Saul said to the Ken'ītes, "Go, depart, get down from among the A·mal'e·kītes, lest I destroy you with them. For you showed kindness to all the children of Israel when they came up out of Egypt." So the Ken'ītes departed from among the A·mal'e·kītes.

7 And Saul attacked the A·mal'e·kītes, from Hav'i·lah all the way to Shūr, which is east of Egypt.

8 He also took Ā'gag king of the A·mal'e·kītes alive, and utterly destroyed all the people with the edge of the sword.

9 But Saul and the people spared Ā'gag and the best of the sheep, the oxen, the fatlings, the lambs, and all *that was* good, and were unwilling to utterly destroy them. But everything despised and worthless, that they utterly destroyed.

SAUL REJECTED AS KING

10 Now the word of the LORD came to Samuel, saying,

11 "I greatly regret that I have set up Saul *as* king, for he has turned back from following Me, and has not performed My commandments." And it grieved Samuel, and he cried out to the LORD all night.

14:47 ᵃSeptuagint and Vulgate read *prospered.*
14:49 ᵃCalled *Abinadab* in 1 Chronicles 8:33 and 9:39

OBEDIENCE 1 Samuel 15:22, 23

Stop Means Stop

Keith saw the stop sign. He knew that it meant *stop*. But he wanted to keep going. Now look what happened. Keith didn't keep on going. He stopped, but not the way the stop sign said. What would you like to say to Keith?

1. What does the sign say? Did Keith obey it? Why not?
2. What happened when Keith did not obey? What would have happened if he had obeyed?
3. What do you think could happen if you do not obey God? What do you think could happen if you do not obey your parents? Would you rather obey? Why?

For more on *Values* turn to page 440
For more on *Obeying* turn to page 840

12 So when Samuel rose early in the morning to meet Saul, it was told Samuel, saying, "Saul went to Car'mel, and indeed, he set up a monument for himself; and he has gone on around, passed by, and gone down to Gil'gal."

13 Then Samuel went to Saul, and Saul said to him, "Blessed *are* you of the LORD! I have performed the commandment of the LORD."

14 But Samuel said, "What then *is* this bleating of the sheep in my ears, and the lowing of the oxen which I hear?"

15 And Saul said, "They have brought them from the A·mal'e·kītes; for the people spared the best of the sheep and the oxen, to sacrifice to the LORD your God; and the rest we have utterly destroyed."

16 Then Samuel said to Saul, "Be quiet! And I will tell you what the LORD said to me last night." And he said to him, "Speak on."

17 So Samuel said, "When you *were* little in your own eyes, *were* you not head of the tribes of Israel? And did not the LORD anoint you king over Israel?

18 "Now the LORD sent you on a mission, and said, 'Go, and utterly destroy the sinners, the A·mal'e·kītes, and fight against them until they are consumed.'

19 "Why then did you not obey the voice of the LORD? Why did you swoop down on the spoil, and do evil in the sight of the LORD?"

20 And Saul said to Samuel, "But I have obeyed the voice of the LORD, and gone on the mission on which the LORD sent me, and brought back Ā'gag king of Am'a·lek; I have utterly destroyed the A·mal'e·kītes.

21 "But the people took of the plunder, sheep and oxen, the best of the things which should have been ut-terly destroyed, to sacrifice to the LORD your God in Gil'gal."

22 So Samuel said:

"Has the LORD *as great* delight in
    burnt offerings and sacrifices,
  As in obeying the voice of the
    LORD?
  Behold, to obey is better than
    sacrifice,
  And to heed than the fat of rams.
23 For rebellion *is as* the sin of
    witchcraft,
  And stubbornness *is as* iniquity
    and idolatry.
  Because you have rejected the
    word of the LORD,
  He also has rejected you from
    being king."

24 Then Saul said to Samuel, "I have sinned, for I have transgressed the commandment of the LORD and your words, because I feared the people and obeyed their voice.

25 "Now therefore, please pardon my sin, and return with me, that I may worship the LORD."

26 But Samuel said to Saul, "I will not return with you, for you have rejected the word of the LORD, and the LORD has rejected you from being king over Israel."

27 And as Samuel turned around to go away, *Saul* seized the edge of his robe, and it tore.

28 So Samuel said to him, "The LORD has torn the kingdom of Israel from you today, and has given it to a neighbor of yours, *who is* better than you.

29 "And also the Strength of Israel will not lie nor relent. For He *is* not a man, that He should relent."

30 Then he said, "I have sinned; *yet* honor me now, please, before the elders of my people and before Israel, and return with me, that I may worship the LORD your God."

31 So Samuel turned back after Saul, and Saul worshiped the LORD.

32 Then Samuel said, "Bring Ā'gag king of the A·mal'e·kītes here to me." So Ā'gag came to him cautiously. And Ā'gag said, "Surely the bitterness of death is past."

33 But Samuel said, "As your sword has made women childless, so shall your mother be childless among women." And Samuel hacked Ā'gag in pieces before the LORD in Gil'gal.

34 Then Samuel went to Rā'mah, and Saul went up to his house at Gib'ē·ah of Saul.

35 And Samuel went no more to see Saul until the day of his death. Nevertheless Samuel mourned for Saul, and the LORD regretted that He had made Saul king over Israel.

DAVID ANOINTED KING

King Saul had disobeyed God again and again. So God was going to choose a new king who would obey. This is who God chose.

16 Now the LORD said to Samuel, "How long will you mourn for Saul, seeing I have rejected him from reigning over Israel? Fill your horn with oil, and go; I am sending you to Jesse the Beth'le·hem-īte. For I have provided Myself a king among his sons."

2 And Samuel said, "How can I go? If Saul hears *it*, he will kill me." But the LORD said, "Take a heifer with you, and say, 'I have come to sacrifice to the LORD.'

3 "Then invite Jesse to the sacrifice, and I will show you what you shall do; you shall anoint for Me the one I name to you."

4 So Samuel did what the LORD said, and went to Bethlehem. And the elders of the town trembled at his coming, and said, "Do you come peaceably?"

5 And he said, "Peaceably; I have come to sacrifice to the LORD. Sanctify yourselves, and come with me to the sacrifice." Then he consecrated Jesse and his sons, and invited them to the sacrifice.

6 So it was, when they came, that he looked at E·lī'ab and said, "Surely the LORD's anointed *is* before Him!"

7 But the LORD said to Samuel, "Do not look at his appearance or at his physical stature, because I have refused him. For *the LORD does* not *see* as man sees;*a* for man looks at the outward appearance, but the LORD looks at the heart."

8 So Jesse called A·bin'a·dab, and made him pass before Samuel. And he said, "Neither has the LORD chosen this one."

9 Then Jesse made Sham'mah pass by. And he said, "Neither has the LORD chosen this one."

10 Thus Jesse made seven of his sons pass before Samuel. And Samuel said to Jesse, "The LORD has not chosen these."

11 And Samuel said to Jesse, "Are all the young men here?" Then he said, "There remains yet the youngest, and there he is, keeping the sheep." And Samuel said to Jesse, "Send and bring him. For we will not sit down*a* till he comes here."

12 So he sent and brought him in. Now he *was* ruddy, with bright eyes, and good-looking. And the LORD said, "Arise, anoint him; for this *is* the one!"

13 Then Samuel took the horn of oil and anointed him in the midst of his brothers; and the Spirit of the LORD

16:7 *a*Septuagint reads *For God does not see as man sees;* Targum reads *It is not by the appearance of a man;* Vulgate reads *Nor do I judge according to the looks of a man.*   16:11 *a*Following Septuagint and Vulgate; Masoretic Text reads *turn around;* Targum and Syriac read *turn away.*

Bible Quiz

1 Samuel 16:1–13 **The Boy Who Would Become King**

1. Where did Samuel go to find the new king? What was his name?
2. Why did Samuel think Eliab was the man God wanted as king?
3. Why didn't anyone think of David as God's choice?
4. You don't have to be strong, pretty, handsome, popular, or important to be chosen by God to do special things. You just need to be willing to obey Him.

came upon David from that day forward. So Samuel arose and went to Rā′mah.

A DISTRESSING SPIRIT TROUBLES SAUL

14 But the Spirit of the LORD departed from Saul, and a distressing spirit from the LORD troubled him.
15 And Saul's servants said to him, "Surely, a distressing spirit from God is troubling you.
16 "Let our master now command your servants, *who are* before you, to seek out a man *who is* a skillful player on the harp. And it shall be that he will play it with his hand when the distressing spirit from God is upon you, and you shall be well."
17 So Saul said to his servants, "Provide me now a man who can play well, and bring *him* to me."
18 Then one of the servants answered and said, "Look, I have seen a son of Jesse the Beth′le·hem·īte, *who is* skillful in playing, a mighty man of valor, a man of war, prudent in speech, and a handsome person; and the LORD *is* with him."
19 Therefore Saul sent messengers to Jesse, and said, "Send me your son David, who *is* with the sheep."
20 And Jesse took a donkey *loaded with* bread, a skin of wine, and a young goat, and sent *them* by his son David to Saul.
21 So David came to Saul and stood before him. And he loved him greatly, and he became his armorbearer.
22 Then Saul sent to Jesse, saying, "Please let David stand before me, for he has found favor in my sight."
23 And so it was, whenever the spirit from God was upon Saul, that David would take a harp and play *it* with his hand. Then Saul would become refreshed and well, and the distressing spirit would depart from him.

DAVID AND GOLIATH

What would you do if a nine-foot giant came running toward you with a sword? Here's what young David did.

17 Now the Phi·lis′tines gathered their armies together to battle, and were gathered at Sō′chōh, which *belongs* to Judah; they encamped between Sō′chōh and A·zē′kah, in Ē′phes Dam′mim.
2 And Saul and the men of Israel were gathered together, and they encamped in the Valley of Ē′lah, and drew up in battle array against the Phi·lis′tines.
3 The Phi·lis′tines stood on a mountain on one side, and Israel stood on a mountain on the other side, with a valley between them.
4 And a champion went out from the camp of the Phi·lis′tines, named Goliath, from Gath, whose height *was* six cubits and a span.

5 *He had* a bronze helmet on his head, and he *was* armed with a coat of mail, and the weight of the coat *was* five thousand shekels of bronze.

6 And *he had* bronze armor on his legs and a bronze javelin between his shoulders.

7 Now the staff of his spear *was* like a weaver's beam, and his iron spearhead *weighed* six hundred shekels; and a shield-bearer went before him.

8 Then he stood and cried out to the armies of Israel, and said to them, "Why have you come out to line up for battle? *Am* I not a Phi·lis'tine, and you the servants of Saul? Choose a man for yourselves, and let him come down to me.

9 "If he is able to fight with me and kill me, then we will be your servants. But if I prevail against him and kill him, then you shall be our servants and serve us."

10 And the Phi·lis'tine said, "I defy the armies of Israel this day; give me a man, that we may fight together."

11 When Saul and all Israel heard these words of the Phi·lis'tine, they were dismayed and greatly afraid.

12 Now David *was* the son of that Eph'ra·thīte of Bethlehem Judah, whose name *was* Jesse, and who had eight sons. And the man was old, advanced *in years,* in the days of Saul.

13 The three oldest sons of Jesse had gone to follow Saul to the battle. The names of his three sons who went to the battle *were* E·lī'ab the firstborn, next to him A·bin'a·dab, and the third Sham'mah.

14 David *was* the youngest. And the three oldest followed Saul.

15 But David occasionally went and returned from Saul to feed his father's sheep at Bethlehem.

16 And the Phi·lis'tine drew near and presented himself forty days, morning and evening.

17 Then Jesse said to his son David, "Take now for your brothers an ephah of this dried *grain* and these ten loaves, and run to your brothers at the camp.

18 "And carry these ten cheeses to the captain of *their* thousand, and see how your brothers fare, and bring back news of them."

19 Now Saul and they and all the men of Israel *were* in the Valley of Ē'lah, fighting with the Phi·lis'tines.

20 So David rose early in the morning, left the sheep with a keeper, and took *the things* and went as Jesse had commanded him. And he came to the camp as the army was going out to the fight and shouting for the battle.

21 For Israel and the Phi·lis'tines had drawn up in battle array, army against army.

22 And David left his supplies in the hand of the supply keeper, ran to the army, and came and greeted his brothers.

23 Then as he talked with them, there was the champion, the Phi·lis'tine of Gath, Goliath by name, coming up from the armies of the Phi·lis'tines; and he spoke according to the same words. So David heard *them.*

24 And all the men of Israel, when they saw the man, fled from him and were dreadfully afraid.

25 So the men of Israel said, "Have you seen this man who has come up? Surely he has come up to defy Israel; and it shall be *that* the man who kills him the king will enrich with great riches, will give him his daughter, and give his father's house exemption *from taxes* in Israel."

26 Then David spoke to the men who stood by him, saying, "What shall be done for the man who kills this Phi·lis'tine and takes away the reproach from Israel? For who *is* this uncircumcised Phi·lis'tine, that he should defy the armies of the living God?"

27 And the people answered him in this manner, saying, "So shall it be done for the man who kills him."

28 Now E·lī′ab his oldest brother heard when he spoke to the men; and E·lī′ab's anger was aroused against David, and he said, "Why did you come down here? And with whom have you left those few sheep in the wilderness? I know your pride and the insolence of your heart, for you have come down to see the battle."

29 And David said, "What have I done now? *Is there* not a cause?"

30 Then he turned from him toward another and said the same thing; and these people answered him as the first ones *did.*

31 Now when the words which David spoke were heard, they reported *them* to Saul; and he sent for him.

32 Then David said to Saul, "Let no man's heart fail because of him; your servant will go and fight with this Phi·lis′tine."

33 And Saul said to David, "You are not able to go against this Phi·lis′tine to fight with him; for you *are* a youth, and he a man of war from his youth."

34 But David said to Saul, "Your servant used to keep his father's sheep, and when a lion or a bear came and took a lamb out of the flock,

35 "I went out after it and struck it, and delivered *the lamb* from its mouth; and when it arose against me, I caught *it* by its beard, and struck and killed it.

36 "Your servant has killed both lion and bear; and this uncircumcised Phi·lis′tine will be like one of them, seeing he has defied the armies of the living God."

37 Moreover David said, "The LORD, who delivered me from the paw of the lion and from the paw of the bear, He will deliver me from the hand of this Phi·lis′tine." And Saul said to David, "Go, and the LORD be with you!"

38 So Saul clothed David with his armor, and he put a bronze helmet on his head; he also clothed him with a coat of mail.

39 David fastened his sword to his armor and tried to walk, for he had not tested *them.* And David said to Saul, "I cannot walk with these, for I have not tested *them.*" So David took them off.

40 Then he took his staff in his hand; and he chose for himself five smooth stones from the brook, and put them in a shepherd's bag, in a pouch which he had, and his sling was in his hand. And he drew near to the Phi·lis′tine.

41 So the Phi·lis′tine came, and began drawing near to David, and the man who bore the shield *went* before him.

42 And when the Phi·lis′tine looked about and saw David, he disdained him; for he was *only* a youth, ruddy and good-looking.

43 So the Phi·lis′tine said to David, "*Am* I a dog, that you come to me with sticks?" And the Phi·lis′tine cursed David by his gods.

44 And the Phi·lis′tine said to David, "Come to me, and I will give your flesh to the birds of the air and the beasts of the field!"

45 Then David said to the Phi·lis′-tine, "You come to me with a sword, with a spear, and with a javelin. But I come to you in the name of the LORD of hosts, the God of the armies of Israel, whom you have defied.

46 "This day the LORD will deliver you into my hand, and I will strike you and take your head from you. And this day I will give the carcasses of the camp of the Phi·lis′tines to the birds of the air and the wild beasts of the earth, that all the earth may know that there is a God in Israel.

47 "Then all this assembly shall know that the LORD does not save

with sword and spear; for the battle *is* the LORD's, and He will give you into our hands."

48 So it was, when the Phi·lis'tine arose and came and drew near to meet David, that David hurried and ran toward the army to meet the Phi·lis'tine.

49 Then David put his hand in his bag and took out a stone; and he slung *it* and struck the Phi·lis'tine in his forehead, so that the stone sank into his forehead, and he fell on his face to the earth.

50 So David prevailed over the Phi·lis'tine with a sling and a stone, and struck the Phi·lis'tine and killed him. But *there was* no sword in the hand of David.

51 Therefore David ran and stood over the Phi·lis'tine, took his sword and drew it out of its sheath and killed him, and cut off his head with it. And when the Phi·lis'tines saw that their champion was dead, they fled.

52 Now the men of Israel and Judah arose and shouted, and pursued the Phi·lis'tines as far as the entrance of the valley[a] and to the gates of Ek'ron. And the wounded of the Phi·lis'tines fell along the road to Shā·a·rā'im, even as far as Gath and Ek'ron.

53 Then the children of Israel returned from chasing the Phi·lis'tines, and they plundered their tents.

54 And David took the head of the Phi·lis'tine and brought it to Jerusalem, but he put his armor in his tent.

55 When Saul saw David going out against the Phi·lis'tine, he said to Abner, the commander of the army, "Abner, whose son *is* this youth?" And Abner said, "As your soul lives, O king, I do not know."

56 So the king said, "Inquire whose son this young man *is*."

57 Then, as David returned from the

☑ Bible Quiz

1 Samuel 17 David Fights the Giant Goliath

1. Was Goliath a Philistine or an Israelite? How tall was he?
2. What was the dare Goliath made to the Israelite soldiers?
3. Who was the only one not afraid of Goliath? Why was he not afraid?
4. How did David kill Goliath?
5. Do you have any problems that seem too big to beat? Is any problem too big for God? How can you trust Him to help?

---

slaughter of the Phi·lis'tine, Abner took him and brought him before Saul with the head of the Phi·lis'tine in his hand.

58 And Saul said to him, "Whose son *are* you, young man?" So David answered, "*I am* the son of your servant Jesse the Beth'le·hem·ite."

SAUL RESENTS DAVID

Everyone was talking about David the giant–killer. King Saul was getting jealous. He was planning to hurt David. He was about to become David's enemy. Meanwhile David and Jonathan, Saul's son, were becoming the best of friends.

18 Now when he had finished speaking to Saul, the soul of Jona-

17:52 [a]Following Masoretic Text, Syriac, Targum, and Vulgate; Septuagint reads *Gath*.

Do You Need Friends? 1 Samuel 18:1–4

"I don't need friends," a girl said. "I do," said another girl. Which girl was right?

1. Do you need friends? Why?
2. Read the story of David and Jonathan (1 Samuel 18:1–4). Did they need friends?
3. What can you do for friends?
4. Why should you ask Jesus to be your very best friend?

For more on *Family Friends* turn to page 758
For more on *Friendship* turn to page 440

than was knit to the soul of David, and Jonathan loved him as his own soul.

2 Saul took him that day, and would not let him go home to his father's house anymore.

3 Then Jonathan and David made a covenant, because he loved him as his own soul.

4 And Jonathan took off the robe that *was* on him and gave it to David, with his armor, even to his sword and his bow and his belt.

5 So David went out wherever Saul sent him, *and* behaved wisely. And Saul set him over the men of war, and he was accepted in the sight of all the people and also in the sight of Saul's servants.

6 Now it had happened as they were coming *home,* when David was returning from the slaughter of the Phi·lis′tine, that the women had come out of all the cities of Israel, singing and dancing, to meet King Saul, with tambourines, with joy, and with musical instruments.

7 So the women sang as they danced, and said:

"Saul has slain his thousands,
And David his ten thousands."

8 Then Saul was very angry, and the saying displeased him; and he said, "They have ascribed to David ten thousands, and to me they have ascribed *only* thousands. Now *what* more can he have but the kingdom?"

9 So Saul eyed David from that day forward.

10 And it happened on the next day that the distressing spirit from God came upon Saul, and he prophesied inside the house. So David played *music* with his hand, as at other times; but *there was* a spear in Saul's hand.

11 And Saul cast the spear, for he said, "I will pin David to the wall!" But David escaped his presence twice.

12 Now Saul was afraid of David, because the LORD was with him, but had departed from Saul.

13 Therefore Saul removed him from his presence, and made him his captain over a thousand; and he went out and came in before the people.

14 And David behaved wisely in all his ways, and the LORD *was* with him.

15 Therefore, when Saul saw that he behaved very wisely, he was afraid of him.

16 But all Israel and Judah loved David, because he went out and came in before them.

Bible Quiz

1 Samuel 18:1–16 **Two Friends and One Enemy**

1. Were David and Jonathan good friends or great friends? How do you know?
2. What did Jonathan give David to show his friendship? Do you think true friends can ever stop being friends? Why not?
3. Why did a song make Saul angry and jealous?
4. How did Saul try to hurt David?
5. When we are jealous of someone we may become angry at her. When we are angry at someone we may want to hurt him. How can we keep from becoming jealous in the first place? What could Saul have done?

DAVID MARRIES MICHAL

17 Then Saul said to David, "Here is my older daughter Mē′rab; I will give her to you as a wife. Only be valiant for me, and fight the LORD'S battles." For Saul thought, "Let my hand not be against him, but let the hand of the Phi·lis′tines be against him."

18 So David said to Saul, "Who *am* I, and what *is* my life *or* my father's family in Israel, that I should be son-in-law to the king?"

19 But it happened at the time when Mē′rab, Saul's daughter, should have been given to David, that she was given to Ā′dri·el the Me·hō′la·thīte as a wife.

20 Now Mī′chal, Saul's daughter, loved David. And they told Saul, and the thing pleased him.

21 So Saul said, "I will give her to him, that she may be a snare to him, and that the hand of the Phi·lis′tines may be against him." Therefore Saul said to David a second time, "You shall be my son-in-law today."

22 And Saul commanded his servants, "Communicate with David secretly, and say, 'Look, the king has delight in you, and all his servants love you. Now therefore, become the king's son-in-law.' "

23 So Saul's servants spoke those words in the hearing of David. And David said, "Does it seem to you *a* light *thing* to be a king's son-in-law, seeing I *am* a poor and lightly esteemed man?"

24 And the servants of Saul told him, saying, "In this manner David spoke."

25 Then Saul said, "Thus you shall say to David: 'The king does not desire any dowry but one hundred foreskins of the Phi·lis′tines, to take vengeance on the king's enemies.' " But Saul thought to make David fall by the hand of the Phi·lis′tines.

26 So when his servants told David these words, it pleased David well to become the king's son-in-law. Now the days had not expired;

27 therefore David arose and went, he and his men, and killed two hundred men of the Phi·lis′tines. And David brought their foreskins, and they gave them in full count to the king, that he might become the king's son-in-law. Then Saul gave him Mī′chal his daughter as a wife.

28 Thus Saul saw and knew that the LORD *was* with David, and *that* Mī′chal, Saul's daughter, loved him;

29 and Saul was still more afraid of David. So Saul became David's enemy continually.

30 Then the princes of the Phi·lis′tines went out *to war.* And so it was, whenever they went out, *that* David behaved more wisely than all the servants of Saul, so that his name became highly esteemed.

SAUL PERSECUTES DAVID

19 Now Saul spoke to Jonathan his son and to all his servants, that they should kill David; but Jonathan, Saul's son, delighted greatly in David.

2 So Jonathan told David, saying, "My father Saul seeks to kill you. Therefore please be on your guard until morning, and stay in a secret *place* and hide.

3 "And I will go out and stand beside my father in the field where you *are,* and I will speak with my father about you. Then what I observe, I will tell you."

4 Thus Jonathan spoke well of David to Saul his father, and said to him, "Let not the king sin against his servant, against David, because he has not sinned against you, and

because his works *have been* very good toward you.
5 "For he took his life in his hands and killed the Phi·lis'tine, and the LORD brought about a great deliverance for all Israel. You saw *it* and rejoiced. Why then will you sin against innocent blood, to kill David without a cause?"
6 So Saul heeded the voice of Jonathan, and Saul swore, "*As* the LORD lives, he shall not be killed."
7 Then Jonathan called David, and Jonathan told him all these things. So Jonathan brought David to Saul, and he was in his presence as in times past.
8 And there was war again; and David went out and fought with the Phi·lis'tines, and struck them with a mighty blow, and they fled from him.
9 Now the distressing spirit from the LORD came upon Saul as he sat in his house with his spear in his hand. And David was playing *music* with *his* hand.
10 Then Saul sought to pin David to the wall with the spear, but he slipped away from Saul's presence; and he drove the spear into the wall. So David fled and escaped that night.
11 Saul also sent messengers to David's house to watch him and to kill him in the morning. And Mī'chal, David's wife, told him, saying, "If you do not save your life tonight, tomorrow you will be killed."
12 So Mī'chal let David down through a window. And he went and fled and escaped.
13 And Mī'chal took an image and laid *it* in the bed, put a cover of goats' *hair* for his head, and covered *it* with clothes.
14 So when Saul sent messengers to take David, she said, "He *is* sick."
15 Then Saul sent the messengers

back to see David, saying, "Bring him up to me in the bed, that I may kill him."
16 And when the messengers had come in, there was the image in the bed, with a cover of goats' *hair* for his head.
17 Then Saul said to Mī'chal, "Why have you deceived me like this, and sent my enemy away, so that he has escaped?" And Mī'chal answered Saul, "He said to me, 'Let me go! Why should I kill you?' "
18 So David fled and escaped, and went to Samuel at Rā'mah, and told him all that Saul had done to him. And he and Samuel went and stayed in Naī'oth.
19 Now it was told Saul, saying, "Take note, David *is* at Naī'oth in Rā'mah!"
20 Then Saul sent messengers to take David. And when they saw the group of prophets prophesying, and Samuel standing *as* leader over them, the Spirit of God came upon the messengers of Saul, and they also prophesied.
21 And when Saul was told, he sent other messengers, and they prophesied likewise. Then Saul sent messengers again the third time, and they prophesied also.
22 Then he also went to Rā'mah, and came to the great well that *is* at Sē'chu. So he asked, and said, "Where *are* Samuel and David?" And *someone* said, "Indeed *they are* at Naī'oth in Rā'mah."
23 So he went there to Naī'oth in Rā'mah. Then the Spirit of God was upon him also, and he went on and prophesied until he came to Naī'oth in Rā'mah.
24 And he also stripped off his clothes and prophesied before Samuel in like manner, and lay down naked all that day and all that night.

Therefore they say, "*Is* Saul also among the prophets?"*a*

JONATHAN'S LOYALTY TO DAVID

20 Then David fled from Naī'oth in Rā'mah, and went and said to Jonathan, "What have I done? What *is* my iniquity, and what *is* my sin before your father, that he seeks my life?"

2 So Jonathan said to him, "By no means! You shall not die! Indeed, my father will do nothing either great or small without first telling me. And why should my father hide this thing from me? It *is* not *so!*"

3 Then David took an oath again, and said, "Your father certainly knows that I have found favor in your eyes, and he has said, 'Do not let Jonathan know this, lest he be grieved.' But truly, *as* the LORD lives and *as* your soul lives, *there is* but a step between me and death."

4 So Jonathan said to David, "Whatever you yourself desire, I will do *it* for you."

5 And David said to Jonathan, "Indeed tomorrow *is* the New Moon, and I should not fail to sit with the king to eat. But let me go, that I may hide in the field until the third *day* at evening.

6 "If your father misses me at all, then say, 'David earnestly asked *permission* of me that he might run over to Bethlehem, his city, for *there is* a yearly sacrifice there for all the family.'

7 "If he says thus: '*It is* well,' your servant will be safe. But if he is very angry, be sure that evil is determined by him.

8 "Therefore you shall deal kindly with your servant, for you have brought your servant into a covenant of the LORD with you. Nevertheless, if there is iniquity in me, kill me yourself, for why should you bring me to your father?"

9 But Jonathan said, "Far be it from you! For if I knew certainly that evil was determined by my father to come upon you, then would I not tell you?"

10 Then David said to Jonathan, "Who will tell me, or what *if* your father answers you roughly?"

11 And Jonathan said to David, "Come, let us go out into the field." So both of them went out into the field.

12 Then Jonathan said to David: "The LORD God of Israel *is witness!* When I have sounded out my father sometime tomorrow, *or* the third *day,* and indeed *there is* good toward David, and I do not send to you and tell you,

13 "may the LORD do so and much more to Jonathan. But if it pleases my father *to do* you evil, then I will report it to you and send you away, that you may go in safety. And the LORD be with you as He has been with my father.

14 "And you shall not only show me the kindness of the LORD while I still live, that I may not die;

15 "but you shall not cut off your kindness from my house forever, no, not when the LORD has cut off every one of the enemies of David from the face of the earth."

16 So Jonathan made *a covenant* with the house of David, *saying,* "Let the LORD require *it* at the hand of David's enemies."

17 Now Jonathan again caused David to vow, because he loved him; for he loved him as he loved his own soul.

18 Then Jonathan said to David, "Tomorrow *is* the New Moon; and you

19:24 *a*Compare 1 Samuel 10:12

Values

FRIENDLINESS 1 Samuel 20:17

Different Kinds of Friends

These two friends are different, aren't they? What makes them different? They really *are* different, aren't they? But you can see that they are friends, can't you?

1. Must friends be exactly alike? Can friends be different?
2. Are all your friends exactly like you? How are some different?
3. Are you friendly to people who are different from you? Should you be?

For more on *Values* turn to page 467
For more on *Friendship* turn to page 487

will be missed, because your seat will
be empty.

19 "And *when* you have stayed three
days, go down quickly and come to
the place where you hid on the day of
the deed; and remain by the stone
Ē′zel.

20 "Then I will shoot three arrows to
the side, as though I shot at a target;

21 "and there I will send a lad, *saying,* 'Go, find the arrows.' If I expressly say to the lad, 'Look, the arrows *are* on this side of you; get them
and come'—then, as the LORD lives,
there is safety for you and no harm.

22 "But if I say thus to the young
man, 'Look, the arrows *are* beyond
you'—go your way, for the LORD has
sent you away.

23 "And as for the matter which you
and I have spoken of, indeed the
LORD *be* between you and me forever."

24 Then David hid in the field. And
when the New Moon had come, the
king sat down to eat the feast.

25 Now the king sat on his seat, as
at other times, on a seat by the wall.
And Jonathan arose,*a* and Abner sat
by Saul's side, but David's place was
empty.

26 Nevertheless Saul did not say
anything that day, for he thought,
"Something has happened to him; he
is unclean, surely he *is* unclean."

27 And it happened the next day, the
second *day* of the month, that David's
place was empty. And Saul said to
Jonathan his son, "Why has the son
of Jesse not come to eat, either yesterday or today?"

28 So Jonathan answered Saul, "David earnestly asked *permission* of me
to go to Bethlehem.

29 "And he said, 'Please let me go,
for our family has a sacrifice in the
city, and my brother has commanded
me *to be there.* And now, if I have
found favor in your eyes, please let

me get away and see my brothers.'
Therefore he has not come to the
king's table."

30 Then Saul's anger was aroused
against Jonathan, and he said to
him, "You son of a perverse, rebellious *woman!* Do I not know that you
have chosen the son of Jesse to your
own shame and to the shame of your
mother's nakedness?

31 "For as long as the son of Jesse
lives on the earth, you shall not be
established, nor your kingdom. Now
therefore, send and bring him to me,
for he shall surely die."

32 And Jonathan answered Saul his
father, and said to him, "Why should
he be killed? What has he done?"

33 Then Saul cast a spear at him to
kill him, by which Jonathan knew
that it was determined by his father
to kill David.

34 So Jonathan arose from the table
in fierce anger, and ate no food the
second day of the month, for he was
grieved for David, because his father
had treated him shamefully.

35 And so it was, in the morning,
that Jonathan went out into the field
at the time appointed with David,
and a little lad *was* with him.

36 Then he said to his lad, "Now run,
find the arrows which I shoot." As the
lad ran, he shot an arrow beyond
him.

37 When the lad had come to the
place where the arrow was which
Jonathan had shot, Jonathan cried
out after the lad and said, "*Is* not the
arrow beyond you?"

38 And Jonathan cried out after the
lad, "Make haste, hurry, do not delay!" So Jonathan's lad gathered up
the arrows and came back to his master.

39 But the lad did not know any-

20:25 *a*Following Masoretic Text, Syriac, Targum,
and Vulgate; Septuagint reads *he sat across from
Jonathan.*

thing. Only Jonathan and David knew of the matter.

40 Then Jonathan gave his weapons to his lad, and said to him, "Go, carry *them* to the city."

41 As soon as the lad had gone, David arose from *a place* toward the south, fell on his face to the ground, and bowed down three times. And they kissed one another; and they wept together, but David more so.

42 Then Jonathan said to David, "Go in peace, since we have both sworn in the name of the LORD, saying, 'May the LORD be between you and me, and between your descendants and my descendants, forever.' " So he arose and departed, and Jonathan went into the city.

DAVID AND THE HOLY BREAD

21 Now David came to Nob, to A·him′e·lech the priest. And A·him′e·lech was afraid when he met David, and said to him, "Why *are* you alone, and no one is with you?"

2 So David said to A·him′e·lech the priest, "The king has ordered me on some business, and said to me, 'Do not let anyone know anything about the business on which I send you, or what I have commanded you.' And I have directed *my* young men to such and such a place.

3 "Now therefore, what have you on hand? Give *me* five *loaves of* bread in my hand, or whatever can be found."

4 And the priest answered David and said, "*There is* no common bread on hand; but there is holy bread, if the young men have at least kept themselves from women."

5 Then David answered the priest, and said to him, "Truly, women *have been* kept from us about three days since I came out. And the vessels of the young men are holy, and *the*

bread is in effect common, even though it was consecrated in the vessel this day."

6 So the priest gave him holy *bread;* for there was no bread there but the showbread which had been taken from before the LORD, in order to put hot bread *in its place* on the day when it was taken away.

7 Now a certain man of the servants of Saul *was* there that day, detained before the LORD. And his name *was* Dō′eg, an Ē′dom·īte, the chief of the herdsmen who *belonged* to Saul.

8 And David said to A·him′e·lech, "Is there not here on hand a spear or a sword? For I have brought neither my sword nor my weapons with me, because the king's business required haste."

9 So the priest said, "The sword of Goliath the Phi·lis′tine, whom you killed in the Valley of Ē′lah, there it is, wrapped in a cloth behind the ephod. If you will take that, take *it.* For *there is* no other except that one here." And David said, "*There is* none like it; give it to me."

DAVID FLEES TO GATH

10 Then David arose and fled that day from before Saul, and went to Ā′chish the king of Gath.

11 And the servants of Ā′chish said to him, "*Is* this not David the king of the land? Did they not sing of him to one another in dances, saying:

'Saul has slain his thousands,
  And David his ten thousands'?"[a]

12 Now David took these words to heart, and was very much afraid of Ā′chish the king of Gath.

13 So he changed his behavior before them, pretended madness in their

21:11 [a]Compare 1 Samuel 18:7

hands, scratched on the doors of the gate, and let his saliva fall down on his beard.

14 Then Ā′chish said to his servants, "Look, you see the man is insane. Why have you brought him to me?

15 "Have I need of madmen, that you have brought this *fellow* to play the madman in my presence? Shall this *fellow* come into my house?"

DAVID'S FOUR HUNDRED MEN

22 David therefore departed from there and escaped to the cave of A·dul′lam. So when his brothers and all his father's house heard *it*, they went down there to him.

2 And everyone *who was* in distress, everyone who *was* in debt, and everyone *who was* discontented gathered to him. So he became captain over them. And there were about four hundred men with him.

3 Then David went from there to Miz′pah of Mō′ab; and he said to the king of Mō′ab, "Please let my father and mother come here with you, till I know what God will do for me."

4 So he brought them before the king of Mō′ab, and they dwelt with him all the time that David was in the stronghold.

5 Now the prophet Gad said to David, "Do not stay in the stronghold; depart, and go to the land of Judah." So David departed and went into the forest of Hē′reth.

SAUL MURDERS THE PRIESTS

6 When Saul heard that David and the men who *were* with him had been discovered—now Saul was staying in Gib′ē·ah under a tamarisk tree in Rā′mah, with his spear in his hand, and all his servants standing about him—

7 then Saul said to his servants who stood about him, "Hear now, you Ben′ja·mītes! Will the son of Jesse give every one of you fields and vineyards, *and* make you all captains of thousands and captains of hundreds?

8 "All of you have conspired against me, and *there is* no one who reveals to me that my son has made a covenant with the son of Jesse; and *there is* not one of you who is sorry for me or reveals to me that my son has stirred up my servant against me, to lie in wait, as *it is* this day."

9 Then answered Dō′eg the Ē′dom-īte, who was set over the servants of Saul, and said, "I saw the son of Jesse going to Nob, to A·him′e·lech the son of A·hī′tub.

10 "And he inquired of the LORD for him, gave him provisions, and gave him the sword of Goliath the Phi·lis′-tine."

11 So the king sent to call A·him′-e·lech the priest, the son of A·hī′tub, and all his father's house, the priests who *were* in Nob. And they all came to the king.

12 And Saul said, "Hear now, son of A·hī′tub!" He answered, "Here I am, my lord."

13 Then Saul said to him, "Why have you conspired against me, you and the son of Jesse, in that you have given him bread and a sword, and have inquired of God for him, that he should rise against me, to lie in wait, as it is this day?"

14 So A·him′e·lech answered the king and said, "And who among all your servants *is as* faithful as David, who is the king's son-in-law, who goes at your bidding, and is honorable in your house?

15 "Did I then begin to inquire of God for him? Far be it from me! Let not the king impute anything to his servant, *or* to any in the house of my father. For your servant knew nothing of all this, little or much."

16 And the king said, "You shall surely die, A·him'e·lech, you and all your father's house!"

17 Then the king said to the guards who stood about him, "Turn and kill the priests of the LORD, because their hand also *is* with David, and because they knew when he fled and did not tell it to me." But the servants of the king would not lift their hands to strike the priests of the LORD.

18 And the king said to Dō'eg, "You turn and kill the priests!" So Dō'eg the Ē'dom·īte turned and struck the priests, and killed on that day eighty-five men who wore a linen ephod.

19 Also Nob, the city of the priests, he struck with the edge of the sword, both men and women, children and nursing infants, oxen and donkeys and sheep—with the edge of the sword.

20 Now one of the sons of A·him'e·lech the son of A·hī'tub, named A·bī'a·thar, escaped and fled after David.

21 And A·bī'a·thar told David that Saul had killed the LORD's priests.

22 So David said to A·bī'a·thar, "I knew that day, when Dō'eg the Ē'dom·īte *was* there, that he would surely tell Saul. I have caused *the death* of all the persons of your father's house.

23 "Stay with me; do not fear. For he who seeks my life seeks your life, but with me you *shall be* safe."

David Saves the City of Keilah

23 Then they told David, saying, "Look, the Phi·lis'tines are fighting against Kē·ī'lah, and they are robbing the threshing floors."

2 Therefore David inquired of the LORD, saying, "Shall I go and attack these Phi·lis'tines?" And the LORD said to David, "Go and attack the Phi·lis'tines, and save Kē·ī'lah."

3 But David's men said to him, "Look, we are afraid here in Judah. How much more then if we go to Kē·ī'lah against the armies of the Phi·lis'tines?"

4 Then David inquired of the LORD once again. And the LORD answered him and said, "Arise, go down to Kē·ī'lah. For I will deliver the Phi·lis'tines into your hand."

5 And David and his men went to Kē·ī'lah and fought with the Phi·lis'tines, struck them with a mighty blow, and took away their livestock. So David saved the inhabitants of Kē·ī'lah.

6 Now it happened, when A·bī'a·thar the son of A·him'e·lech fled to David at Kē·ī'lah, *that* he went down *with* an ephod in his hand.

7 And Saul was told that David had gone to Kē·ī'lah. So Saul said, "God has delivered him into my hand, for he has shut himself in by entering a town that has gates and bars."

8 Then Saul called all the people together for war, to go down to Kē·ī'lah to besiege David and his men.

9 When David knew that Saul plotted evil against him, he said to A·bī'a·thar the priest, "Bring the ephod here."

10 Then David said, "O LORD God of Israel, Your servant has certainly heard that Saul seeks to come to Kē·ī'lah to destroy the city for my sake.

11 "Will the men of Kē·ī'lah deliver me into his hand? Will Saul come down, as Your servant has heard? O LORD God of Israel, I pray, tell Your servant." And the LORD said, "He will come down."

12 Then David said, "Will the men of Kē·ī'lah deliver me and my men into the hand of Saul?" And the LORD said, "They will deliver *you*."

13 So David and his men, about six hundred, arose and departed from Kē·ī'lah and went wherever they

could go. Then it was told Saul that David had escaped from Kĕ·ī'lah; so he halted the expedition.

DAVID IN WILDERNESS STRONGHOLDS

14 And David stayed in strongholds in the wilderness, and remained in the mountains in the Wilderness of Ziph. Saul sought him every day, but God did not deliver him into his hand.

15 So David saw that Saul had come out to seek his life. And David *was* in the Wilderness of Ziph in a forest.ᵃ

16 Then Jonathan, Saul's son, arose and went to David in the woods and strengthened his hand in God.

17 And he said to him, "Do not fear, for the hand of Saul my father shall not find you. You shall be king over Israel, and I shall be next to you. Even my father Saul knows that."

18 So the two of them made a covenant before the LORD. And David stayed in the woods, and Jonathan went to his own house.

19 Then the Ziph'ites came up to Saul at Gib'ē·ah, saying, "Is David not hiding with us in strongholds in the woods, in the hill of Ha·chī'lah, which *is* on the south of Jĕ·shī'mon?

20 "Now therefore, O king, come down according to all the desire of your soul to come down; and our part *shall be* to deliver him into the king's hand."

21 And Saul said, "Blessed *are* you of the LORD, for you have compassion on me.

22 "Please go and find out for sure, and see the place where his hideout is, *and* who has seen him there. For I am told he is very crafty.

23 "See therefore, and take knowledge of all the lurking places where he hides; and come back to me with certainty, and I will go with you. And

it shall be, if he is in the land, that I will search for him throughout all the clansᵃ of Judah."

24 So they arose and went to Ziph before Saul. But David and his men *were* in the Wilderness of Mā'on, in the plain on the south of Jĕ·shī'mon.

25 When Saul and his men went to seek *him,* they told David. Therefore he went down to the rock, and stayed in the Wilderness of Mā'on. And when Saul heard *that,* he pursued David in the Wilderness of Mā'on.

26 Then Saul went on one side of the mountain, and David and his men on the other side of the mountain. So David made haste to get away from Saul, for Saul and his men were encircling David and his men to take them.

27 But a messenger came to Saul, saying, "Hurry and come, for the Phi·lis'tines have invaded the land!"

28 Therefore Saul returned from pursuing David, and went against the Phi·lis'tines; so they called that place the Rock of Escape.ᵃ

29 Then David went up from there and dwelt in strongholds at En Ge'di.

DAVID SPARES SAUL

24 Now it happened, when Saul had returned from following the Phi·lis'tines, that it was told him, saying, "Take note! David *is* in the Wilderness of En Ge'di."

2 Then Saul took three thousand chosen men from all Israel, and went to seek David and his men on the Rocks of the Wild Goats.

3 So he came to the sheepfolds by the road, where there *was* a cave; and Saul went in to attend to his needs. (David and his men were staying in the recesses of the cave.)

23:15 ᵃOr *in Horesh*   23:23 ᵃLiterally *thousands*   23:28 ᵃHebrew *Sela Hammahlekoth*

4 Then the men of David said to him, "This is the day of which the LORD said to you, 'Behold, I will deliver your enemy into your hand, that you may do to him as it seems good to you.'" And David arose and secretly cut off a corner of Saul's robe.

5 Now it happened afterward that David's heart troubled him because he had cut Saul's *robe.*

6 And he said to his men, "The LORD forbid that I should do this thing to my master, the LORD's anointed, to stretch out my hand against him, seeing he *is* the anointed of the LORD."

7 So David restrained his servants with *these* words, and did not allow them to rise against Saul. And Saul got up from the cave and went on *his* way.

8 David also arose afterward, went out of the cave, and called out to Saul, saying, "My lord the king!" And when Saul looked behind him, David stooped with his face to the earth, and bowed down.

9 And David said to Saul: "Why do you listen to the words of men who say, 'Indeed David seeks your harm'?

10 "Look, this day your eyes have seen that the LORD delivered you today into my hand in the cave, and *someone* urged *me* to kill you. But *my eye* spared you, and I said, 'I will not stretch out my hand against my lord, for he *is* the LORD's anointed.'

11 "Moreover, my father, see! Yes, see the corner of your robe in my hand! For in that I cut off the corner of your robe, and did not kill you, know and see that *there is* neither evil nor rebellion in my hand, and I have not sinned against you. Yet you hunt my life to take it.

12 "Let the LORD judge between you and me, and let the LORD avenge me on you. But my hand shall not be against you.

13 "As the proverb of the ancients says, 'Wickedness proceeds from the wicked.' But my hand shall not be against you.

14 "After whom has the king of Israel come out? Whom do you pursue? A dead dog? A flea?

15 "Therefore let the LORD be judge, and judge between you and me, and see and plead my case, and deliver me out of your hand."

16 So it was, when David had finished speaking these words to Saul, that Saul said, "*Is* this your voice, my son David?" And Saul lifted up his voice and wept.

17 Then he said to David: "You *are* more righteous than I; for you have rewarded me with good, whereas I have rewarded you with evil.

18 "And you have shown this day how you have dealt well with me; for when the LORD delivered me into your hand, you did not kill me.

19 "For if a man finds his enemy, will he let him get away safely? Therefore may the LORD reward you with good for what you have done to me this day.

20 "And now I know indeed that you shall surely be king, and that the kingdom of Israel shall be established in your hand.

21 "Therefore swear now to me by the LORD that you will not cut off my descendants after me, and that you will not destroy my name from my father's house."

22 So David swore to Saul. And Saul went home, but David and his men went up to the stronghold.

DEATH OF SAMUEL

25 Then Samuel died; and the Israelites gathered together and lamented for him, and buried him at his home in Rā'mah. And David

arose and went down to the Wilderness of Par'an.[a]

DAVID AND THE WIFE OF NABAL

2 Now *there was* a man in Mā'on whose business *was* in Car'mel, and the man *was* very rich. He had three thousand sheep and a thousand goats. And he was shearing his sheep in Car'mel.

3 The name of the man *was* Nā'bal, and the name of his wife Ab'i·gāil. And *she was* a woman of good understanding and beautiful appearance; but the man *was* harsh and evil in *his* doings. He *was of the house of* Caleb.

4 When David heard in the wilderness that Nā'bal was shearing his sheep,

5 David sent ten young men; and David said to the young men, "Go up to Car'mel, go to Nā'bal, and greet him in my name.

6 "And thus you shall say to him who lives *in prosperity:* 'Peace *be* to you, peace to your house, and peace to all that you have!

7 'Now I have heard that you have shearers. Your shepherds were with us, and we did not hurt them, nor was there anything missing from them all the while they were in Car'mel.

8 'Ask your young men, and they will tell you. Therefore let *my* young men find favor in your eyes, for we come on a feast day. Please give whatever comes to your hand to your servants and to your son David.' "

9 So when David's young men came, they spoke to Nā'bal according to all these words in the name of David, and waited.

10 Then Nā'bal answered David's servants, and said, "Who *is* David, and who *is* the son of Jesse? There are many servants nowadays who break away each one from his master.

11 "Shall I then take my bread and my water and my meat that I have killed for my shearers, and give *it* to men when I do not know where they *are* from?"

12 So David's young men turned on their heels and went back; and they came and told him all these words.

13 Then David said to his men, "Every man gird on his sword." So every man girded on his sword, and David also girded on his sword. And about four hundred men went with David, and two hundred stayed with the supplies.

14 Now one of the young men told Ab'i·gāil, Nā'bal's wife, saying, "Look, David sent messengers from the wilderness to greet our master; and he reviled them.

15 "But the men *were* very good to us, and we were not hurt, nor did we miss anything as long as we accompanied them, when we were in the fields.

16 "They were a wall to us both by night and day, all the time we were with them keeping the sheep.

17 "Now therefore, know and consider what you will do, for harm is determined against our master and against all his household. For he *is such* a scoundrel[a] that *one* cannot speak to him."

18 Then Ab'i·gāil made haste and took two hundred *loaves* of bread, two skins of wine, five sheep already dressed, five seahs of roasted *grain,* one hundred clusters of raisins, and two hundred cakes of figs, and loaded *them* on donkeys.

19 And she said to her servants, "Go on before me; see, I am coming after you." But she did not tell her husband Nā'bal.

20 So it was, *as* she rode on the don-

25:1 [a]Following Masoretic Text, Syriac, Targum, and Vulgate; Septuagint reads *Maon.*
25:17 [a]Literally *son of Belial*

key, that she went down under cover of the hill; and there were David and his men, coming down toward her, and she met them.

21 Now David had said, "Surely in vain I have protected all that this *fellow* has in the wilderness, so that nothing was missed of all that *belongs* to him. And he has repaid me evil for good.

22 "May God do so, and more also, to the enemies of David, if I leave one male of all who *belong* to him by morning light."

23 Now when Ab′i·gāil saw David, she dismounted quickly from the donkey, fell on her face before David, and bowed down to the ground.

24 So she fell at his feet and said: "On me, my lord, *on* me *let* this iniquity *be!* And please let your maidservant speak in your ears, and hear the words of your maidservant.

25 "Please, let not my lord regard this scoundrel Nā′bal. For as his name *is,* so *is* he: Nā′bal*a is* his name, and folly *is* with him! But I, your maidservant, did not see the young men of my lord whom you sent.

26 "Now therefore, my lord, *as* the LORD lives and *as* your soul lives, since the LORD has held you back from coming to bloodshed and from avenging yourself with your own hand, now then, let your enemies and those who seek harm for my lord be as Nā′bal.

27 "And now this present which your maidservant has brought to my lord, let it be given to the young men who follow my lord.

28 "Please forgive the trespass of your maidservant. For the LORD will certainly make for my lord an enduring house, because my lord fights the battles of the LORD, and evil is not found in you throughout your days.

29 "Yet a man has risen to pursue you and seek your life, but the life of my lord shall be bound in the bundle of the living with the LORD your God; and the lives of your enemies He shall sling out, *as from* the pocket of a sling.

30 "And it shall come to pass, when the LORD has done for my lord according to all the good that He has spoken concerning you, and has appointed you ruler over Israel,

31 "that this will be no grief to you, nor offense of heart to my lord, either that you have shed blood without cause, or that my lord has avenged himself. But when the LORD has dealt well with my lord, then remember your maidservant."

32 Then David said to Ab′i·gāil: "Blessed *is* the LORD God of Israel, who sent you this day to meet me!

33 "And blessed *is* your advice and blessed *are* you, because you have kept me this day from coming to bloodshed and from avenging myself with my own hand.

34 "For indeed, *as* the LORD God of Israel lives, who has kept me back from hurting you, unless you had hurried and come to meet me, surely by morning light no males would have been left to Nā′bal!"

35 So David received from her hand what she had brought him, and said to her, "Go up in peace to your house. See, I have heeded your voice and respected your person."

36 Now Ab′i·gāil went to Nā′bal, and there he was, holding a feast in his house, like the feast of a king. And Nā′bal's heart *was* merry within him, for he *was* very drunk; therefore she told him nothing, little or much, until morning light.

37 So it was, in the morning, when the wine had gone from Nā′bal, and his wife had told him these things,

25:25 *a*Literally *Fool*

that his heart died within him, and he became *like* a stone.

38 Then it happened, *after* about ten days, that the LORD struck Nā′bal, and he died.

39 So when David heard that Nā′bal was dead, he said, "Blessed *be* the LORD, who has pleaded the cause of my reproach from the hand of Nā′bal, and has kept His servant from evil! For the LORD has returned the wickedness of Nā′bal on his own head." And David sent and proposed to Ab′i·gāil, to take her as his wife.

40 When the servants of David had come to Ab′i·gāil at Car′mel, they spoke to her saying, "David sent us to you, to ask you to become his wife."

41 Then she arose, bowed her face to the earth, and said, "Here is your maidservant, a servant to wash the feet of the servants of my lord."

42 So Ab′i·gāil rose in haste and rode on a donkey, attended by five of her maidens; and she followed the messengers of David, and became his wife.

43 David also took A·hin′ō·am of Jez′re·el, and so both of them were his wives.

44 But Saul had given Mī′chal his daughter, David's wife, to Pal′tī*a* the son of Lā′ish, who *was* from Gal′lim.

DAVID SPARES SAUL A SECOND TIME

Saul was so jealous of David that he decided to kill him. So David had to run away from the palace and go far out into the wilderness. But Saul went after him with his army. One night David crept down into Saul's camp. He could kill Saul and become king. Would he do it?

26 Now the Ziph′ītes came to Saul at Gib′ē·ah, saying, "Is David not hiding in the hill of Ha·chī′lah, opposite Jē·shī′mon?"

2 Then Saul arose and went down to the Wilderness of Ziph, having three thousand chosen men of Israel with him, to seek David in the Wilderness of Ziph.

3 And Saul encamped in the hill of Ha·chī′lah, which *is* opposite Jē·shī′mon, by the road. But David stayed in the wilderness, and he saw that Saul came after him into the wilderness.

4 David therefore sent out spies, and understood that Saul had indeed come.

5 So David arose and came to the place where Saul had encamped. And David saw the place where Saul lay, and Abner the son of Ner, the commander of his army. Now Saul lay within the camp, with the people encamped all around him.

6 Then David answered, and said to A·him′e·lech the Hit′tīte and to A·bi′shaī the son of Ze·rū′i·ah, brother of Jō′ab, saying, "Who will go down with me to Saul in the camp?" And A·bi′shaī said, "I will go down with you."

7 So David and A·bi′shaī came to the people by night; and there Saul lay sleeping within the camp, with his spear stuck in the ground by his head. And Abner and the people lay all around him.

8 Then A·bi′shaī said to David, "God has delivered your enemy into your hand this day. Now therefore, please, let me strike him at once with the spear, right to the earth; and I will not *have to strike* him a second time!"

9 But David said to A·bi′shaī, "Do not destroy him; for who can stretch out his hand against the LORD's anointed, and be guiltless?"

25:44 *a* Spelled *Paltiel* in 2 Samuel 3:15

10 David said furthermore, "*As the* LORD lives, the LORD shall strike him, or his day shall come to die, or he shall go out to battle and perish.

11 "The LORD forbid that I should stretch out my hand against the LORD's anointed. But please, take now the spear and the jug of water that *are* by his head, and let us go."

12 So David took the spear and the jug of water *by* Saul's head, and they got away; and no man saw or knew *it* or awoke. For they *were* all asleep, because a deep sleep from the LORD had fallen on them.

13 Now David went over to the other side, and stood on the top of a hill afar off, a great distance *being* between them.

14 And David called out to the people and to Abner the son of Ner, saying, "Do you not answer, Abner?" Then Abner answered and said, "Who *are* you, calling out to the king?"

15 So David said to Abner, "*Are* you not a man? And who *is* like you in Israel? Why then have you not guarded your lord the king? For one of the people came in to destroy your lord the king.

16 "This thing that you have done *is* not good. *As* the LORD lives, you deserve to die, because you have not guarded your master, the LORD's anointed. And now see where the king's spear *is,* and the jug of water that *was* by his head."

17 Then Saul knew David's voice, and said, "*Is* that your voice, my son David?" David said, "*It is* my voice, my lord, O king."

18 And he said, "Why does my lord thus pursue his servant? For what have I done, or what evil *is* in my hand?

19 "Now therefore, please, let my lord the king hear the words of his servant: If the LORD has stirred you up against me, let Him accept an of-

fering. But if *it is* the children of men, *may* they *be* cursed before the LORD, for they have driven me out this day from sharing in the inheritance of the LORD, saying, 'Go, serve other gods.'

20 "So now, do not let my blood fall to the earth before the face of the LORD. For the king of Israel has come out to seek a flea, as when one hunts a partridge in the mountains."

21 Then Saul said, "I have sinned. Return, my son David. For I will

---

☑ **Bible Quiz**

1 Samuel 26   **David Sneaks into Saul's Camp**

1. How many soldiers did Saul take with him to hunt for David?

2. Why do you think Saul was so afraid of David? Do you think he was more afraid of God than David? What could Saul have done to stop being afraid of God? Could he have asked God to forgive him? Could he have spent more time trying to help his people rather than chasing David?

3. What did David do when he crept into Saul's camp?

4. What did Abishai want to do to Saul? Why did David stop him?

5. Do you remember when God had decided that David would be the next king (1 Samuel 16)? Why was Saul wasting his time chasing David? Can God's plans ever be stopped?

harm you no more, because my life was precious in your eyes this day. Indeed I have played the fool and erred exceedingly."

22 And David answered and said, "Here is the king's spear. Let one of the young men come over and get it.

23 "May the LORD repay every man *for* his righteousness and his faithfulness; for the LORD delivered you into *my* hand today, but I would not stretch out my hand against the LORD's anointed.

24 "And indeed, as your life was valued much this day in my eyes, so let my life be valued much in the eyes of the LORD, and let Him deliver me out of all tribulation."

25 Then Saul said to David, "*May* you *be* blessed, my son David! You shall both do great things and also still prevail." So David went on his way, and Saul returned to his place.

DAVID ALLIED WITH THE PHILISTINES

27 And David said in his heart, "Now I shall perish someday by the hand of Saul. *There is* nothing better for me than that I should speedily escape to the land of the Phi·lis'tines; and Saul will despair of me, to seek me anymore in any part of Israel. So I shall escape out of his hand."

2 Then David arose and went over with the six hundred men who *were* with him to Ā'chish the son of Mā'-och, king of Gath.

3 So David dwelt with Ā'chish at Gath, he and his men, each man with his household, *and* David with his two wives, A·hin'ō·am the Jez'rē·el·ī·tess, and Ab'i·gāil the Car'mel·ī·tess, Nā'bal's widow.

4 And it was told Saul that David had fled to Gath; so he sought him no more.

5 Then David said to Ā'chish, "If I have now found favor in your eyes, let them give me a place in some town in the country, that I may dwell there. For why should your servant dwell in the royal city with you?"

6 So Ā'chish gave him Zik'lag that day. Therefore Zik'lag has belonged to the kings of Judah to this day.

7 Now the time that David dwelt in the country of the Phi·lis'tines was one full year and four months.

8 And David and his men went up and raided the Gesh'ū·rītes, the Gir'zītes,*a* and the A·mal'e·kītes. For those nations were the inhabitants of the land from of old, as you go to Shūr, even as far as the land of Egypt.

9 Whenever David attacked the land, he left neither man nor woman alive, but took away the sheep, the oxen, the donkeys, the camels, and the apparel, and returned and came to Ā'chish.

10 Then Ā'chish would say, "Where have you made a raid today?" And David would say, "Against the southern *area* of Judah, or against the southern *area* of the Je·rah'mē·el·ītes, or against the southern *area* of the Ken'ītes."

11 David would save neither man nor woman alive, to bring *news* to Gath, saying, "Lest they should inform on us, saying, 'Thus David did.'" And thus *was* his behavior all the time he dwelt in the country of the Phi·lis'tines.

12 So Ā'chish believed David, saying, "He has made his people Israel utterly abhor him; therefore he will be my servant forever."

28 Now it happened in those days that the Phi·lis'tines gathered their armies together for war, to fight with

27:8 *a*Or *Gezrites*

Israel. And Ā′chish said to David, "You assuredly know that you will go out with me to battle, you and your men."

2 So David said to Ā′chish, "Surely you know what your servant can do." And Ā′chish said to David, "Therefore I will make you one of my chief guardians forever."

SAUL CONSULTS A MEDIUM

3 Now Samuel had died, and all Israel had lamented for him and buried him in Rā′mah, in his own city. And Saul had put the mediums and the spiritists out of the land.

4 Then the Phi·lis′tines gathered together, and came and encamped at Shū′nem. So Saul gathered all Israel together, and they encamped at Gil·bō′a.

5 When Saul saw the army of the Phi·lis′tines, he was afraid, and his heart trembled greatly.

6 And when Saul inquired of the LORD, the LORD did not answer him, either by dreams or by Ū′rim or by the prophets.

7 Then Saul said to his servants, "Find me a woman who is a medium, that I may go to her and inquire of her." And his servants said to him, "In fact, there is a woman who is a medium at En Dor."

8 So Saul disguised himself and put on other clothes, and he went, and two men with him; and they came to the woman by night. And he said, "Please conduct a séance for me, and bring up for me the one I shall name to you."

9 Then the woman said to him, "Look, you know what Saul has done, how he has cut off the mediums and the spiritists from the land. Why then do you lay a snare for my life, to cause me to die?"

10 And Saul swore to her by the LORD, saying, "As the LORD lives, no punishment shall come upon you for this thing."

11 Then the woman said, "Whom shall I bring up for you?" And he said, "Bring up Samuel for me."

12 When the woman saw Samuel, she cried out with a loud voice. And the woman spoke to Saul, saying, "Why have you deceived me? For you are Saul!"

13 And the king said to her, "Do not be afraid. What did you see?" And the woman said to Saul, "I saw a spirit[a] ascending out of the earth."

14 So he said to her, "What is his form?" And she said, "An old man is coming up, and he is covered with a mantle." And Saul perceived that it was Samuel, and he stooped with his face to the ground and bowed down.

15 Now Samuel said to Saul, "Why have you disturbed me by bringing me up?" And Saul answered, "I am deeply distressed; for the Phi·lis′tines make war against me, and God has departed from me and does not answer me anymore, neither by prophets nor by dreams. Therefore I have called you, that you may reveal to me what I should do."

16 Then Samuel said: "So why do you ask me, seeing the LORD has departed from you and has become your enemy?

17 "And the LORD has done for Himself[a] as He spoke by me. For the LORD has torn the kingdom out of your hand and given it to your neighbor, David.

18 "Because you did not obey the voice of the LORD nor execute His fierce wrath upon Am′a·lek, therefore the LORD has done this thing to you this day.

19 "Moreover the LORD will also deliver Israel with you into the hand of

28:13 [a]Hebrew elohim   28:17 [a]Or him, that is, David

the Phi·lis′tines. And tomorrow you and your sons *will be* with me. The LORD will also deliver the army of Israel into the hand of the Phi·lis′tines.”

20 Immediately Saul fell full length on the ground, and was dreadfully afraid because of the words of Samuel. And there was no strength in him, for he had eaten no food all day or all night.

21 And the woman came to Saul and saw that he was severely troubled, and said to him, “Look, your maidservant has obeyed your voice, and I have put my life in my hands and heeded the words which you spoke to me.

22 “Now therefore, please, heed also the voice of your maidservant, and let me set a piece of bread before you; and eat, that you may have strength when you go on *your* way.”

23 But he refused and said, “I will not eat.” So his servants, together with the woman, urged him; and he heeded their voice. Then he arose from the ground and sat on the bed.

24 Now the woman had a fatted calf in the house, and she hastened to kill it. And she took flour and kneaded *it,* and baked unleavened bread from it.

25 So she brought *it* before Saul and his servants, and they ate. Then they rose and went away that night.

THE PHILISTINES REJECT DAVID

29 Then the Phi·lis′tines gathered together all their armies at Ā′phek, and the Israelites encamped by a fountain which *is* in Jez′rē·el.

2 And the lords of the Phi·lis′tines passed in review by hundreds and by thousands, but David and his men passed in review at the rear with Ā′chish.

3 Then the princes of the Phi·lis′-tines said, “What *are* these Hebrews *doing here?*” And Ā′chish said to the princes of the Phi·lis′tines, “*Is* this not David, the servant of Saul king of Israel, who has been with me these days, or these years? And to this day I have found no fault in him since he defected *to me.*”

4 But the princes of the Phi·lis′tines were angry with him; so the princes of the Phi·lis′tines said to him, “Make this fellow return, that he may go back to the place which you have appointed for him, and do not let him go down with us to battle, lest in the battle he become our adversary. For with what could he reconcile himself to his master, if not with the heads of these men?

5 “*Is* this not David, of whom they sang to one another in dances, saying:

‘Saul has slain his thousands,
And David his ten thousands’?”[a]

6 Then Ā′chish called David and said to him, “Surely, *as* the LORD lives, you have been upright, and your going out and your coming in with me in the army *is* good in my sight. For to this day I have not found evil in you since the day of your coming to me. Nevertheless the lords do not favor you.

7 “Therefore return now, and go in peace, that you may not displease the lords of the Phi·lis′tines.”

8 So David said to Ā′chish, “But what have I done? And to this day what have you found in your servant as long as I have been with you, that I may not go and fight against the enemies of my lord the king?”

9 Then Ā′chish answered and said to David, “I know that you *are* as good in my sight as an angel of God;

29:5 [a]Compare 1 Samuel 18:7

nevertheless the princes of the Phi·lis'tines have said, 'He shall not go up with us to the battle.'

10 "Now therefore, rise early in the morning with your master's servants who have come with you.*a* And as soon as you are up early in the morning and have light, depart."

11 So David and his men rose early to depart in the morning, to return to the land of the Phi·lis'tines. And the Phi·lis'tines went up to Jez're·el.

DAVID'S CONFLICT WITH THE AMALEKITES

30 Now it happened, when David and his men came to Zik'lag, on the third day, that the A·mal'e·kites had invaded the South and Zik'lag, attacked Zik'lag and burned it with fire,

2 and had taken captive the women and those who *were* there, from small to great; they did not kill anyone, but carried *them* away and went their way.

3 So David and his men came to the city, and there it was, burned with fire; and their wives, their sons, and their daughters had been taken captive.

4 Then David and the people who *were* with him lifted up their voices and wept, until they had no more power to weep.

5 And David's two wives, A·hin'-o·am the Jez're·el·i·tess, and Ab'i·gail the widow of Nā'bal the Car'mel·īte, had been taken captive.

6 Now David was greatly distressed, for the people spoke of stoning him, because the soul of all the people was grieved, every man for his sons and his daughters. But David strengthened himself in the LORD his God.

7 Then David said to A·bī'a·thar the priest, A·him'e·lech's son, "Please bring the ephod here to me." And A·bī'a·thar brought the ephod to David.

8 So David inquired of the LORD, saying, "Shall I pursue this troop? Shall I overtake them?" And He answered him, "Pursue, for you shall surely overtake *them* and without fail recover *all*."

9 So David went, he and the six hundred men who *were* with him, and came to the Brook Bē'sor, where those stayed who were left behind.

10 But David pursued, he and four hundred men; for two hundred stayed *behind,* who were so weary that they could not cross the Brook Bē'sor.

11 Then they found an Egyptian in the field, and brought him to David; and they gave him bread and he ate, and they let him drink water.

12 And they gave him a piece of a cake of figs and two clusters of raisins. So when he had eaten, his strength came back to him; for he had eaten no bread nor drunk water for three days and three nights.

13 Then David said to him, "To whom do you *belong,* and where *are* you from?" And he said, "I *am* a young man from Egypt, servant of an A·mal'e·kīte; and my master left me behind, because three days ago I fell sick.

14 "We made an invasion of the southern *area* of the Cher'e·thītes, in the *territory* which *belongs* to Judah, and of the southern *area* of Caleb; and we burned Zik'lag with fire."

15 And David said to him, "Can you take me down to this troop?" So he said, "Swear to me by God that

29:10 *a*Following Masoretic Text, Targum, and Vulgate; Septuagint adds *and go to the place which I have selected for you there; and set no bothersome word in your heart, for you are good before me. And rise on your way.*

What Should I Do?

You went fishing with a dozen or more lures. You spent lots of money to get to the best fishing place you could find. This time you would catch a really *big* one. But things didn't turn out quite that way. Now what? You plan something big, but it happens little. You look for something special, but all you can find is something ordinary. What should you do?

1. When things don't turn out right, do you grumble or complain?
2. When things don't turn out right, do you blame someone else?
3. When things don't turn out right, do you pray and ask God to help you? David did. Read 1 Samuel 30:6.
4. When things don't turn out right, do you thank God they weren't worse?

For more on *What Should I Do?* turn to page 487
For more on *Facing Trials* turn to page 766

you will neither kill me nor deliver me into the hands of my master, and I will take you down to this troop."

16 And when he had brought him down, there they were, spread out over all the land, eating and drinking and dancing, because of all the great spoil which they had taken from the land of the Phi·lis'tines and from the land of Judah.

17 Then David attacked them from twilight until the evening of the next day. Not a man of them escaped, except four hundred young men who rode on camels and fled.

18 So David recovered all that the A·mal'e·kītes had carried away, and David rescued his two wives.

19 And nothing of theirs was lacking, either small or great, sons or daughters, spoil or anything which they had taken from them; David recovered all.

20 Then David took all the flocks and herds they had driven before those *other* livestock, and said, "This *is* David's spoil."

21 Now David came to the two hundred men who had been so weary that they could not follow David, whom they also had made to stay at the Brook Bē'sor. So they went out to meet David and to meet the people who *were* with him. And when David came near the people, he greeted them.

22 Then all the wicked and worthless men*a* of those who went with David answered and said, "Because they did not go with us, we will not give them *any* of the spoil that we have recovered, except for every man's wife and children, that they may lead *them* away and depart."

23 But David said, "My brethren, you shall not do so with what the LORD has given us, who has pre-

served us and delivered into our hand the troop that came against us.

24 "For who will heed you in this matter? But as his part *is* who goes down to the battle, so *shall* his part *be* who stays by the supplies; they shall share alike."

25 So it was, from that day forward; he made it a statute and an ordinance for Israel to this day.

26 Now when David came to Zik'lag, he sent *some* of the spoil to the elders of Judah, to his friends, saying, "Here is a present for you from the spoil of the enemies of the LORD"—

27 to *those* who *were* in Beth'el, *those* who *were* in Rā'moth of the South, *those* who *were* in Jat'tir,

28 *those* who *were* in A·rō'er, *those* who *were* in Siph'moth, *those* who *were* in Esh·te·mō'a,

29 *those* who *were* in Rā'chal, *those* who *were* in the cities of the Je·rah'mē·el·ītes, *those* who *were* in the cities of the Ken'ītes,

30 *those* who *were* in Hor'mah, *those* who *were* in Chor·ash'an,*a* *those* who *were* in Ā'thach,

31 *those* who *were* in Hē'bron, and to all the places where David himself and his men were accustomed to rove.

The Tragic End of Saul and His Sons

31 Now the Phi·lis'tines fought against Israel; and the men of Israel fled from before the Phi·lis'tines, and fell slain on Mount Gil·bō'a.

2 Then the Phi·lis'tines followed hard after Saul and his sons. And the Phi·lis'tines killed Jonathan, A·bin'a·dab, and Mal·chī·shū'a, Saul's sons.

3 The battle became fierce against Saul. The archers hit him, and he

30:22 *a*Literally *men of Belial*   30:30 *a*Or *Bor-ashan*

was severely wounded by the archers.

4 Then Saul said to his armorbearer, "Draw your sword, and thrust me through with it, lest these uncircumcised men come and thrust me through and abuse me." But his armorbearer would not, for he was greatly afraid. Therefore Saul took a sword and fell on it.

5 And when his armorbearer saw that Saul was dead, he also fell on his sword, and died with him.

6 So Saul, his three sons, his armorbearer, and all his men died together that same day.

7 And when the men of Israel who *were* on the other side of the valley, and *those* who *were* on the other side of the Jordan, saw that the men of Israel had fled and that Saul and his sons were dead, they forsook the cities and fled; and the Phi·lis′tines came and dwelt in them.

8 So it happened the next day, when the Phi·lis′tines came to strip the slain, that they found Saul and his three sons fallen on Mount Gil·bo′a.

9 And they cut off his head and stripped off his armor, and sent *word* throughout the land of the Phi·lis′tines, to proclaim *it in* the temple of their idols and among the people.

10 Then they put his armor in the temple of the Ash′to·reths, and they fastened his body to the wall of Beth Shan.*a*

11 Now when the inhabitants of Ja′besh Gil′e·ad heard what the Phi·lis′tines had done to Saul,

12 all the valiant men arose and traveled all night, and took the body of Saul and the bodies of his sons from the wall of Beth Shan; and they came to Ja′besh and burned them there.

13 Then they took their bones and buried *them* under the tamarisk tree at Ja′besh, and fasted seven days.

31:10 *a*Spelled *Beth Shean* in Joshua 17:11 and elsewhere

The Second Book of
SAMUEL

THE REPORT OF SAUL'S DEATH

NOW it came to pass after the death of Saul, when David had returned from the slaughter of the A·mal′e·kītes, and David had stayed two days in Zik′lag,

2 on the third day, behold, it happened that a man came from Saul's camp with his clothes torn and dust on his head. So it was, when he came to David, that he fell to the ground and prostrated himself.

3 And David said to him, "Where have you come from?" So he said to him, "I have escaped from the camp of Israel."

4 Then David said to him, "How did the matter go? Please tell me." And he answered, "The people have fled from the battle, many of the people are fallen and dead, and Saul and Jonathan his son are dead also."

5 So David said to the young man who told him, "How do you know that Saul and Jonathan his son are dead?"

6 Then the young man who told him said, "As I happened by chance *to be* on Mount Gil·bō′a, there was Saul, leaning on his spear; and indeed the chariots and horsemen followed hard after him.

7 "Now when he looked behind him, he saw me and called to me. And I answered, 'Here I am.'

8 "And he said to me, 'Who *are* you?' So I answered him, 'I *am* an A·mal′e·kīte.'

9 "He said to me again, 'Please stand over me and kill me, for anguish has come upon me, but my life still *remains* in me.'

10 "So I stood over him and killed him, because I was sure that he could not live after he had fallen. And I took the crown that *was* on his head and the bracelet that *was* on his arm, and have brought them here to my lord."

11 Therefore David took hold of his own clothes and tore them, and *so did* all the men who *were* with him.

12 And they mourned and wept and fasted until evening for Saul and for Jonathan his son, for the people of the LORD and for the house of Israel, because they had fallen by the sword.

13 Then David said to the young man who told him, "Where *are* you from?" And he answered, "I *am* the son of an alien, an A·mal′e·kīte."

14 So David said to him, "How was it you were not afraid to put forth your hand to destroy the LORD's anointed?"

15 Then David called one of the young men and said, "Go near, *and* execute him!" And he struck him so that he died.

16 So David said to him, "Your blood *is* on your own head, for your own mouth has testified against you, saying, 'I have killed the LORD's anointed.' "

THE SONG OF THE BOW

17 Then David lamented with this lamentation over Saul and over Jonathan his son,

18 and he told *them* to teach the children of Judah *the Song of* the Bow; indeed *it is* written in the Book of Jā′sher:

19 "The beauty of Israel is slain on
    your high places!
    How the mighty have fallen!
20 Tell *it* not in Gath,
    Proclaim *it* not in the streets of
      Ash′ke·lon—

Lest the daughters of the
　Phi·lis′tines rejoice,
Lest the daughters of the
　uncircumcised triumph.

21 "O mountains of Gil·bō′a,
　Let there be no dew nor rain upon
　　you,
　Nor fields of offerings.
　For the shield of the mighty is
　　cast away there!
　The shield of Saul, not anointed
　　with oil.
22 From the blood of the slain,
　From the fat of the mighty,
　The bow of Jonathan did not turn
　　back,
　And the sword of Saul did not
　　return empty.

23 "Saul and Jonathan *were* beloved
　　and pleasant in their lives,
　And in their death they were not
　　divided;
　They were swifter than eagles,
　They were stronger than lions.

24 "O daughters of Israel, weep over
　　Saul,
　Who clothed you in scarlet, with
　　luxury;
　Who put ornaments of gold on
　　your apparel.

25 "How the mighty have fallen in the
　　midst of the battle!
　Jonathan *was* slain in your high
　　places.
26 I am distressed for you, my
　　brother Jonathan;
　You have been very pleasant to
　　me;
　Your love to me was wonderful,
　Surpassing the love of women.

27 "How the mighty have fallen,
　And the weapons of war
　　perished!"

DAVID ANOINTED KING OF JUDAH

2 It happened after this that David
inquired of the LORD, saying, "Shall I
go up to any of the cities of Judah?"
And the LORD said to him, "Go up."
David said, "Where shall I go up?"
And He said, "To Hē′bron."
2 So David went up there, and his
two wives also, A·hin′ō·am the Jez′-
rē·el·ī·tess, and Ab′i·gāil the widow
of Nā′bal the Car′mel·īte.
3 And David brought up the men
who *were* with him, every man with
his household. So they dwelt in the
cities of Hē′bron.
4 Then the men of Judah came, and
there they anointed David king over
the house of Judah. And they told
David, saying, "The men of Jā′besh
Gil′ē·ad *were the ones* who buried
Saul."
5 So David sent messengers to the
men of Jā′besh Gil′ē·ad, and said to
them, "You *are* blessed of the LORD,
for you have shown this kindness to
your lord, to Saul, and have buried
him.
6 "And now may the LORD show
kindness and truth to you. I also will
repay you this kindness, because you
have done this thing.
7 "Now therefore, let your hands be
strengthened, and be valiant; for
your master Saul is dead, and also
the house of Judah has anointed me
king over them."

ISHBOSHETH MADE KING OF ISRAEL

8 But Abner the son of Ner, commander of Saul's army, took Ish·bō′-
sheth[a] the son of Saul and brought
him over to Mā·ha·na′im;
9 and he made him king over Gil′-
ē·ad, over the Ash′ur·ītes, over Jez′-

2:8 [a]Called *Esh-Baal* in 1 Chronicles 8:33 and 9:39

rē·el, over Ē′phra·im, over Benjamin, and over all Israel.

10 Ish·bō′sheth, Saul's son, *was* forty years old when he began to reign over Israel, and he reigned two years. Only the house of Judah followed David.

11 And the time that David was king in Hē′bron over the house of Judah was seven years and six months.

ISRAEL AND JUDAH AT WAR

12 Now Abner the son of Ner, and the servants of Ish·bō′sheth the son of Saul, went out from Mā·ha·na′im to Gib′ē·on.

13 And Jō′ab the son of Ze·rū′i·ah, and the servants of David, went out and met them by the pool of Gib′ē·on. So they sat down, one on one side of the pool and the other on the other side of the pool.

14 Then Abner said to Jō′ab, "Let the young men now arise and compete before us." And Jō′ab said, "Let them arise."

15 So they arose and went over by number, twelve from Benjamin, *followers* of Ish·bō′sheth the son of Saul, and twelve from the servants of David.

16 And each one grasped his opponent by the head and *thrust* his sword in his opponent's side; so they fell down together. Therefore that place was called the Field of Sharp Swords,*a* which *is* in Gib′ē·on.

17 So there was a very fierce battle that day, and Abner and the men of Israel were beaten before the servants of David.

18 Now the three sons of Ze·rū′i·ah were there: Jō′ab and A·bi′shaī and As′a·hel. And As′a·hel *was* as fleet of foot as a wild gazelle.

19 So As′a·hel pursued Abner, and in going he did not turn to the right hand or to the left from following Abner.

20 Then Abner looked behind him and said, "*Are* you As′a·hel?" He answered, "I *am.*"

21 And Abner said to him, "Turn aside to your right hand or to your left, and lay hold on one of the young men and take his armor for yourself." But As′a·hel would not turn aside from following him.

22 So Abner said again to As′a·hel, "Turn aside from following me. Why should I strike you to the ground? How then could I face your brother Jō′ab?"

23 However, he refused to turn aside. Therefore Abner struck him in the stomach with the blunt end of the spear, so that the spear came out of his back; and he fell down there and died on the spot. So it was *that* as many as came to the place where As′a·hel fell down and died, stood still.

24 Jō′ab and A·bi′shaī also pursued Abner. And the sun was going down when they came to the hill of Am′mah, which *is* before Gī′ah by the road to the Wilderness of Gib′ē·on.

25 Now the children of Benjamin gathered together behind Abner and became a unit, and took their stand on top of a hill.

26 Then Abner called to Jō′ab and said, "Shall the sword devour forever? Do you not know that it will be bitter in the latter end? How long will it be then until you tell the people to return from pursuing their brethren?"

27 And Jō′ab said, "*As* God lives, unless you had spoken, surely then by morning all the people would have given up pursuing their brethren."

28 So Jō′ab blew a trumpet; and all the people stood still and did not pur-

2:16 *a*Hebrew *Helkath Hazzurim*

sue Israel anymore, nor did they fight anymore.

29 Then Abner and his men went on all that night through the plain, crossed over the Jordan, and went through all Bith′ron; and they came to Mā·ha·na′im.

30 So Jō′ab returned from pursuing Abner. And when he had gathered all the people together, there were missing of David's servants nineteen men and As′a·hel.

31 But the servants of David had struck down, of Benjamin and Abner's men, three hundred and sixty men who died.

32 Then they took up As′a·hel and buried him in his father's tomb, which was in Bethlehem. And Jō′ab and his men went all night, and they came to Hē′bron at daybreak.

3 Now there was a long war between the house of Saul and the house of David. But David grew stronger and stronger, and the house of Saul grew weaker and weaker.

SONS OF DAVID

2 Sons were born to David in Hē′bron: His firstborn was Am′non by A·hin′ō·am the Jez′re·el·ī·tess;

3 his second, Chil′e·ab, by Ab′i·gāil the widow of Nā′bal the Car′mel·īte; the third, Ab′sa·lom the son of Mā′-a·cah, the daughter of Tal′maī, king of Gē′shur;

4 the fourth, Ad·o·nī′jah the son of Hag′gith; the fifth, Sheph·a·tī′ah the son of A·bī′tal;

5 and the sixth, Ith′re·am, by David's wife Eg′lah. These were born to David in Hē′bron.

ABNER JOINS FORCES WITH DAVID

6 Now it was so, while there was war between the house of Saul and the house of David, that Abner was strengthening *his hold* on the house of Saul.

7 And Saul had a concubine, whose name *was* Riz′pah, the daughter of Ā′i·ah. So *Ish·bō′sheth* said to Abner, "Why have you gone in to my father's concubine?"

8 Then Abner became very angry at the words of Ish·bō′sheth, and said, "*Am* I a dog's head that belongs to Judah? Today I show loyalty to the house of Saul your father, to his brothers, and to his friends, and have not delivered you into the hand of David; and you charge me today with a fault concerning this woman?

9 "May God do so to Abner, and more also, if I do not do for David as the LORD has sworn to him—

10 "to transfer the kingdom from the house of Saul, and set up the throne of David over Israel and over Judah, from Dan to Bē·er·shē′ba."

11 And he could not answer Abner another word, because he feared him.

12 Then Abner sent messengers on his behalf to David, saying, "Whose *is* the land?" saying *also,* "Make your covenant with me, and indeed my hand *shall be* with you to bring all Israel to you."

13 And *David* said, "Good, I will make a covenant with you. But one thing I require of you: you shall not see my face unless you first bring Mī′chal, Saul's daughter, when you come to see my face."

14 So David sent messengers to Ish·bō′sheth, Saul's son, saying, "Give *me* my wife Mī′chal, whom I betrothed to myself for a hundred foreskins of the Phi·lis′tines."

15 And Ish·bō′sheth sent and took her from *her* husband, from Pal′ti·el*a* the son of Lā′ish.

16 Then her husband went along with her to Ba·hū′rim, weeping be-

3:15 *a*Spelled *Palti* in 1 Samuel 25:44

ABOUT GOD'S PROTECTION 2 Samuel 3:18

My Friendly Umbrella Protects Me

It's raining. It's pouring. Susan could get wet. But she won't. She remembered to bring her friendly umbrella. It will protect her from the rain. She also remembered to pray this morning. Do you think God will protect her from bad things?

1. How does an umbrella protect Susan from the rain?
2. Who can protect you from bad things? What kind of bad things?
3. Will you ask God to protect you today? Will you ask Him now?

For more on *What the Bible Says* turn to page 497
For more on *God's Care* turn to page 538

hind her. So Abner said to him, "Go, return!" And he returned.

17 Now Abner had communicated with the elders of Israel, saying, "In time past you were seeking for David *to be* king over you.

18 "Now then, do *it!* For the LORD has spoken of David, saying, 'By the hand of My servant David, I*a* will save My people Israel from the hand of the Phi·lis′tines and the hand of all their enemies.'"

19 And Abner also spoke in the hearing of Benjamin. Then Abner also went to speak in the hearing of David in Hē′bron all that seemed good to Israel and the whole house of Benjamin.

20 So Abner and twenty men with him came to David at Hē′bron. And David made a feast for Abner and the men who *were* with him.

21 Then Abner said to David, "I will arise and go, and gather all Israel to my lord the king, that they may make a covenant with you, and that you may reign over all that your heart desires." So David sent Abner away, and he went in peace.

JOAB MURDERS ABNER

22 At that moment the servants of David and Jō′ab came from a raid and brought much spoil with them. But Abner *was* not with David in Hē′bron, for he had sent him away, and he had gone in peace.

23 When Jō′ab and all the troops that *were* with him had come, they told Jō′ab, saying, "Abner the son of Ner came to the king, and he sent him away, and he has gone in peace."

24 Then Jō′ab came to the king and said, "What have you done? Look, Abner came to you; why *is* it *that* you sent him away, and he has already gone?

25 "Surely you realize that Abner the son of Ner came to deceive you, to know your going out and your coming in, and to know all that you are doing."

26 And when Jō′ab had gone from David's presence, he sent messengers after Abner, who brought him back from the well of Sī′rah. But David did not know *it.*

27 Now when Abner had returned to Hē′bron, Jō′ab took him aside in the gate to speak with him privately, and there stabbed him in the stomach, so that he died for the blood of As′a·hel his brother.

28 Afterward, when David heard *it,* he said, "My kingdom and I *are* guiltless before the LORD forever of the blood of Abner the son of Ner.

29 "Let it rest on the head of Jō′ab and on all his father's house; and let there never fail to be in the house of Jō′ab one who has a discharge or is a leper, who leans on a staff or falls by the sword, or who lacks bread."

30 So Jō′ab and A·bi′shaī his brother killed Abner, because he had killed their brother As′a·hel at Gib′ē·on in the battle.

DAVID'S MOURNING FOR ABNER

31 Then David said to Jō′ab and to all the people who were with him, "Tear your clothes, gird yourselves with sackcloth, and mourn for Abner." And King David followed the coffin.

32 So they buried Abner in Hē′bron; and the king lifted up his voice and wept at the grave of Abner, and all the people wept.

33 And the king sang *a lament* over Abner and said:

"Should Abner die as a fool dies?
34 Your hands were not bound

3:18 *a*Following many Hebrew manuscripts, Septuagint, Syriac, and Targum; Masoretic Text reads *he.*

Nor your feet put into fetters;
As a man falls before wicked men,
   so you fell."

Then all the people wept over him again.

35 And when all the people came to persuade David to eat food while it was still day, David took an oath, saying, "God do so to me, and more also, if I taste bread or anything else till the sun goes down!"

36 Now all the people took note *of it,* and it pleased them, since whatever the king did pleased all the people.

37 For all the people and all Israel understood that day that it had not been the king's *intent* to kill Abner the son of Ner.

38 Then the king said to his servants, "Do you not know that a prince and a great man has fallen this day in Israel?

39 "And I *am* weak today, though anointed king; and these men, the sons of Ze·rū'i·ah, *are* too harsh for me. The LORD shall repay the evildoer according to his wickedness."

ISHBOSHETH IS MURDERED

4 When Saul's son[a] heard that Abner had died in Hē'bron, he lost heart, and all Israel was troubled.

2 Now Saul's son *had* two men *who were* captains of troops. The name of one *was* Bā'a·nah and the name of the other Rē'chab, the sons of Rim'mon the Be·er'oth·īte, of the children of Benjamin. (For Be·er'oth also was *part* of Benjamin,

3 because the Be·er'oth·ītes fled to Git'ta·im and have been sojourners there until this day.)

4 Jonathan, Saul's son, had a son *who was* lame in *his* feet. He was five years old when the news about Saul and Jonathan came from Jez're·el; and his nurse took him up and fled.

And it happened, as she made haste to flee, that he fell and became lame. His name *was* Me·phib'o·sheth.[a]

5 Then the sons of Rim'mon the Be·er'oth·īte, Rē'chab and Bā'a·nah, set out and came at about the heat of the day to the house of Ish·bō'sheth, who was lying on his bed at noon.

6 And they came there, all the way into the house, *as though* to get wheat, and they stabbed him in the stomach. Then Rē'chab and Bā'a·nah his brother escaped.

7 For when they came into the house, he was lying on his bed in his bedroom; then they struck him and killed him, beheaded him and took his head, and were all night escaping through the plain.

8 And they brought the head of Ish·bō'sheth to David at Hē'bron, and said to the king, "Here is the head of Ish·bō'sheth, the son of Saul your enemy, who sought your life; and the LORD has avenged my lord the king this day of Saul and his descendants."

9 But David answered Rē'chab and Bā'a·nah his brother, the sons of Rim'mon the Be·er'oth·īte, and said to them, "*As* the LORD lives, who has redeemed my life from all adversity,

10 "when someone told me, saying, 'Look, Saul is dead,' thinking to have brought good news, I arrested him and had him executed in Zik'lag—the one who *thought* I would give him a reward for *his* news.

11 "How much more, when wicked men have killed a righteous person in his own house on his bed? Therefore, shall I not now require his blood at your hand and remove you from the earth?"

12 So David commanded his young men, and they executed them, cut off their hands and feet, and hanged

4:1 [a]That is, Ishbosheth   4:4 [a]Called *Merib-Baal* in 1 Chronicles 8:34 and 9:40

them by the pool in Hē′bron. But they took the head of Ish·bō′sheth and buried *it* in the tomb of Abner in Hē′bron.

DAVID REIGNS OVER ALL ISRAEL

5 Then all the tribes of Israel came to David at Hē′bron and spoke, saying, "Indeed we *are* your bone and your flesh.

2 "Also, in time past, when Saul was king over us, you were the one who led Israel out and brought them in; and the LORD said to you, 'You shall shepherd My people Israel, and be ruler over Israel.'"

3 Therefore all the elders of Israel came to the king at Hē′bron, and King David made a covenant with them at Hē′bron before the LORD. And they anointed David king over Israel.

4 David *was* thirty years old when he began to reign, *and* he reigned forty years.

5 In Hē′bron he reigned over Judah seven years and six months, and in Jerusalem he reigned thirty-three years over all Israel and Judah.

THE CONQUEST OF JERUSALEM

6 And the king and his men went to Jerusalem against the Jeb′ū·sītes, the inhabitants of the land, who spoke to David, saying, "You shall not come in here; but the blind and the lame will repel you," thinking, "David cannot come in here."

7 Nevertheless David took the stronghold of Zion (that *is,* the City of David).

8 Now David said on that day, "Whoever climbs up by way of the water shaft and defeats the Jeb′ū·sītes (the lame and the blind, *who are* hated by David's soul), *he shall be chief and captain.*"a Therefore they

say, "The blind and the lame shall not come into the house."

9 Then David dwelt in the stronghold, and called it the City of David. And David built all around from the Mil′lōa and inward.

10 So David went on and became great, and the LORD God of hosts *was* with him.

11 Then Hī′ram king of Tȳre sent messengers to David, and cedar trees, and carpenters and masons. And they built David a house.

12 So David knew that the LORD had established him as king over Israel, and that He had exalted His kingdom for the sake of His people Israel.

13 And David took more concubines and wives from Jerusalem, after he had come from Hē′bron. Also more sons and daughters were born to David.

14 Now these *are* the names of those who were born to him in Jerusalem: Sham′mū·a,a Shō′bab, Nathan, Solomon,

15 Ib′har, E·lish′ū·a,a Nē′pheg, Japhī′a,

16 E·lish′a·ma, E·lī′a·da, and E·liph′-e·let.

THE PHILISTINES DEFEATED

17 Now when the Phi·lis′tines heard that they had anointed David king over Israel, all the Phi·lis′tines went up to search for David. And David heard *of it* and went down to the stronghold.

18 The Phi·lis′tines also went and deployed themselves in the Valley of Reph′a·im.

19 So David inquired of the LORD, saying, "Shall I go up against the Phi·lis′tines? Will You deliver them

---

5:8 aCompare 1 Chronicles 11:6   5:9 aLiterally *The Landfill*   5:14 aSpelled *Shimea* in 1 Chronicles 3:5   5:15 aSpelled *Elishama* in 1 Chronicles 3:6

into my hand?" And the LORD said to David, "Go up, for I will doubtless deliver the Phi·lis'tines into your hand."

20 So David went to Bā'al Pe·rā'zim, and David defeated them there; and he said, "The LORD has broken through my enemies before me, like a breakthrough of water." Therefore he called the name of that place Bā'al Pe·rā'zim.*a*

21 And they left their images there, and David and his men carried them away.

22 Then the Phi·lis'tines went up once again and deployed themselves in the Valley of Reph'a·im.

23 Therefore David inquired of the LORD, and He said, "You shall not go up; circle around behind them, and come upon them in front of the mulberry trees.

24 "And it shall be, when you hear the sound of marching in the tops of the mulberry trees, then you shall advance quickly. For then the LORD will go out before you to strike the camp of the Phi·lis'tines."

25 And David did so, as the LORD commanded him; and he drove back the Phi·lis'tines from Gē'ba*a* as far as Gē'zer.

THE ARK BROUGHT TO JERUSALEM

6 Again David gathered all *the* choice *men* of Israel, thirty thousand.

2 And David arose and went with all the people who *were* with him from Bā'a·lē Judah to bring up from there the ark of God, whose name is called by the Name,*a* the LORD of Hosts, who dwells *between* the cherubim.

3 So they set the ark of God on a new cart, and brought it out of the house of A·bin'a·dab, which *was* on the hill; and Uz'zah and A·hī'ō, the sons of A·bin'a·dab, drove the new cart.*a*

4 And they brought it out of the house of A·bin'a·dab, which *was* on the hill, accompanying the ark of God; and A·hī'ō went before the ark.

5 Then David and all the house of Israel played *music* before the LORD on all kinds of *instruments of* fir wood, on harps, on stringed instruments, on tambourines, on sistrums, and on cymbals.

6 And when they came to Nā'chon's threshing floor, Uz'zah put out *his* hand to the ark of God and took hold of it, for the oxen stumbled.

7 Then the anger of the LORD was aroused against Uz'zah, and God struck him there for *his* error; and he died there by the ark of God.

8 And David became angry because of the LORD's outbreak against Uz'zah; and he called the name of the place Per'ez Uz'zah*a* to this day.

9 David was afraid of the LORD that day; and he said, "How can the ark of the LORD come to me?"

10 So David would not move the ark of the LORD with him into the City of David; but David took it aside into the house of Ō'bed-Ē'dom the Git'tīte.

11 The ark of the LORD remained in the house of Ō'bed-Ē'dom the Git'tīte three months. And the LORD blessed Ō'bed-Ē'dom and all his household.

12 Now it was told King David, saying, "The LORD has blessed the house of Ō'bed-Ē'dom and all that *belongs* to him, because of the ark of God." So David went and brought up the ark of God from the house of Ō'bed-

5:20 *a*Literally *Master of Breakthroughs*
5:25 *a*Following Masoretic Text, Targum, and Vulgate; Septuagint reads *Gibeon*.　　6:2 *a*Septuagint, Targum, and Vulgate omit *by the Name;* many Hebrew manuscripts and Syriac read *there.*
6:3 *a*Septuagint adds *with the ark.*　　6:8 *a*Literally *Outburst Against Uzzah*

SERVING 2 Samuel 6:5

Serve the Lord. But How?

Do you have a good voice? Serve the Lord with your voice. Do you play a musical instrument? Serve the Lord with that instrument. Do you have a special talent? Serve the Lord with your talent. Are you alive and breathing? Serve the Lord with life itself. Serve Him because of everything He is and everything He does for you.

1. What instrument do you play? Are you serving God with it? Will you?
2. Do you sing well? How can you serve God with your singing?
3. What other talent do you have? How can you serve God with that talent?

For more on *Values* turn to page 620
For more on *Serving* turn to page 620

Ē′dom to the City of David with gladness.

13 And so it was, when those bearing the ark of the LORD had gone six paces, that he sacrificed oxen and fatted sheep.

14 Then David danced before the LORD with all *his* might; and David *was* wearing a linen ephod.

15 So David and all the house of Israel brought up the ark of the LORD with shouting and with the sound of the trumpet.

16 Now as the ark of the LORD came into the City of David, Mī′chal, Saul's daughter, looked through a window and saw King David leaping and whirling before the LORD; and she despised him in her heart.

17 So they brought the ark of the LORD, and set it in its place in the midst of the tabernacle that David had erected for it. Then David offered burnt offerings and peace offerings before the LORD.

18 And when David had finished offering burnt offerings and peace offerings, he blessed the people in the name of the LORD of hosts.

19 Then he distributed among all the people, among the whole multitude of Israel, both the women and the men, to everyone a loaf of bread, a piece *of meat,* and a cake of raisins. So all the people departed, everyone to his house.

20 Then David returned to bless his household. And Mī′chal the daughter of Saul came out to meet David, and said, "How glorious was the king of Israel today, uncovering himself today in the eyes of the maids of his servants, as one of the base fellows shamelessly uncovers himself!"

21 So David said to Mī′chal, "*It was* before the LORD, who chose me instead of your father and all his house, to appoint me ruler over the people of the LORD, over Israel.

Therefore I will play *music* before the LORD.

22 "And I will be even more undignified than this, and will be humble in my own sight. But as for the maidservants of whom you have spoken, by them I will be held in honor."

23 Therefore Mī′chal the daughter of Saul had no children to the day of her death.

GOD'S COVENANT WITH DAVID

7 Now it came to pass when the king was dwelling in his house, and the LORD had given him rest from all his enemies all around,

2 that the king said to Nathan the prophet, "See now, I dwell in a house of cedar, but the ark of God dwells inside tent curtains."

3 Then Nathan said to the king, "Go, do all that *is* in your heart, for the LORD *is* with you."

4 But it happened that night that the word of the LORD came to Nathan, saying,

5 "Go and tell My servant David, 'Thus says the LORD: "Would you build a house for Me to dwell in?

6 "For I have not dwelt in a house since the time that I brought the children of Israel up from Egypt, even to this day, but have moved about in a tent and in a tabernacle.

7 "Wherever I have moved about with all the children of Israel, have I ever spoken a word to anyone from the tribes of Israel, whom I commanded to shepherd My people Israel, saying, 'Why have you not built Me a house of cedar?' " '

8 "Now therefore, thus shall you say to My servant David, 'Thus says the LORD of hosts: "I took you from the sheepfold, from following the sheep, to be ruler over My people, over Israel.

9 "And I have been with you wher-

ever you have gone, and have cut off all your enemies from before you, and have made you a great name, like the name of the great men who *are* on the earth.

10 "Moreover I will appoint a place for My people Israel, and will plant them, that they may dwell in a place of their own and move no more; nor shall the sons of wickedness oppress them anymore, as previously,

11 "since the time that I commanded judges *to be* over My people Israel, and have caused you to rest from all your enemies. Also the LORD tells you that He will make you a house.*a*

12 "When your days are fulfilled and you rest with your fathers, I will set up your seed after you, who will come from your body, and I will establish his kingdom.

13 "He shall build a house for My name, and I will establish the throne of his kingdom forever.

14 "I will be his Father, and he shall be My son. If he commits iniquity, I will chasten him with the rod of men and with the blows of the sons of men.

15 "But My mercy shall not depart from him, as I took *it* from Saul, whom I removed from before you.

16 "And your house and your kingdom shall be established forever before you.*a* Your throne shall be established forever." ' "

17 According to all these words and according to all this vision, so Nathan spoke to David.

DAVID'S THANKSGIVING TO GOD

18 Then King David went in and sat before the LORD; and he said: "Who *am* I, O Lord GOD? And what is my house, that You have brought me this far?

19 "And yet this was a small thing in Your sight, O Lord GOD; and You have also spoken of Your servant's house for a great while to come. *Is* this the manner of man, O Lord GOD?

20 "Now what more can David say to You? For You, Lord GOD, know Your servant.

21 "For Your word's sake, and according to Your own heart, You have done all these great things, to make Your servant know *them*.

22 "Therefore You are great, O Lord GOD.*a* For *there is* none like You, nor *is there any* God besides You, according to all that we have heard with our ears.

23 "And who *is* like Your people, like Israel, the one nation on the earth whom God went to redeem for Himself as a people, to make for Himself a name—and to do for Yourself great and awesome deeds for Your land—before Your people whom You redeemed for Yourself from Egypt, the nations, and their gods?

24 "For You have made Your people Israel Your very own people forever; and You, LORD, have become their God.

25 "Now, O LORD God, the word which You have spoken concerning Your servant and concerning his house, establish *it* forever and do as You have said.

26 "So let Your name be magnified forever, saying, 'The LORD of hosts *is* the God over Israel.' And let the house of Your servant David be established before You.

27 "For You, O LORD of hosts, God of Israel, have revealed *this* to Your servant, saying, 'I will build you a house.' Therefore Your servant has found it in his heart to pray this prayer to You.

28 "And now, O Lord GOD, You are God, and Your words are true, and

---

7:11 *a*That is, a royal dynasty   7:16 *a*Septuagint reads *Me*.   7:22 *a*Targum and Syriac read *O LORD God*.

▆ *Prayers* ▆

2 Samuel 7:18–29

Has God ever said no when you asked for something? You wanted something very much. You prayed for it. But it never came. How did you feel? David wanted to build God's house, the temple. God said no. He would let David's son Solomon build the temple. What would you say in your next prayer? David thanked God for letting his son do it. He did not complain to God. He did not question God. He merely said "thanks." Remember that the next time God says no.

You have promised this goodness to Your servant.
29 "Now therefore, let it please You to bless the house of Your servant, that it may continue before You forever; for You, O Lord GOD, have spoken *it,* and with Your blessing let the house of Your servant be blessed forever."

DAVID'S FURTHER CONQUESTS

8 After this it came to pass that David attacked the Phi·lis'tines and subdued them. And David took Meth'eg Am'mah from the hand of the Phi·lis'tines.
2 Then he defeated Mō'ab. Forcing them down to the ground, he measured them off with a line. With two lines he measured off those to be put to death, and with one full line those to be kept alive. So the Mō'ab·ites became David's servants, *and* brought tribute.
3 David also defeated Had·a·dē'zer the son of Rē'hob, king of Zō'bah, as

he went to recover his territory at the River Eū·phrā'tēs.
4 David took from him one thousand *chariots,* seven hundred[a] horsemen, and twenty thousand foot soldiers. Also David hamstrung all the chariot horses, except that he spared *enough* of them for one hundred chariots.
5 When the Syrians of Damascus came to help Had·a·dē'zer king of Zō'bah, David killed twenty-two thousand of the Syrians.
6 Then David put garrisons in Syria of Damascus; and the Syrians became David's servants, *and* brought tribute. So the LORD preserved David wherever he went.
7 And David took the shields of gold that had belonged to the servants of Had·a·dē'zer, and brought them to Jerusalem.
8 Also from Bē'tah[a] and from Berothai, cities of Had·a·dē'zer, King David took a large amount of bronze.
9 When Tō'ī[a] king of Hā'math heard that David had defeated all the army of Had·a·dē'zer,
10 then Tō'ī sent Jō'ram[a] his son to King David, to greet him and bless him, because he had fought against Had·a·dē'zer and defeated him (for Had·a·dē'zer had been at war with Tō'ī); and *Jō'ram* brought with him articles of silver, articles of gold, and articles of bronze.
11 King David also dedicated these to the LORD, along with the silver and gold that he had dedicated from all the nations which he had subdued—
12 from Syria,[a] from Mō'ab, from the people of Am'mon, from the Phi·lis'tines, from Am'a·lek, and from the

---

8:4 [a]Or *seven thousand* (compare 1 Chronicles 18:4)   8:8 [a]Spelled *Tibhath* in 1 Chronicles 18:8
8:9 [a]Spelled *Tou* in 1 Chronicles 18:9
8:10 [a]Spelled *Hadoram* in 1 Chronicles 18:10
8:12 [a]Septuagint, Syriac, and some Hebrew manuscripts read *Edom.*

spoil of Had·a·dē′zer the son of Rē′hob, king of Zō′bah.

13 And David made *himself* a name when he returned from killing eighteen thousand Syrians*a* in the Valley of Salt.

14 He also put garrisons in Ē′dom; throughout all Ē′dom he put garrisons, and all the Ē′dom·ītes became David's servants. And the LORD preserved David wherever he went.

DAVID'S ADMINISTRATION

15 So David reigned over all Israel; and David administered judgment and justice to all his people.

16 Jō′ab the son of Ze·rū′i·ah *was* over the army; Je·hosh′a·phat the son of A·hī′lud *was* recorder;

17 Zā′dok the son of A·hī′tub and A·him′e·lech the son of A·bī′a·thar *were* the priests; Se·rāi′ah*a* *was* the scribe;

18 Be·nā′i·ah the son of Je·hoi′a·da *was over* both the Cher′e·thītes and the Pel′eth·ītes; and David's sons were chief ministers.

DAVID'S KINDNESS TO MEPHIBOSHETH

David stayed out in the wilderness for many years, hiding from Saul. One day he got the news that Saul had been killed in battle. So David returned home. He became king, as God promised. If you had been David, would you have been afraid of Saul's family? Would you have worried that they would try to hurt you? What would you have done to them? Here's what David did.

9 Now David said, "Is there still anyone who is left of the house of Saul, that I may show him kindness for Jonathan's sake?"

2 And *there was* a servant of the house of Saul whose name *was* Zī′ba. So when they had called him to David, the king said to him, "*Are* you Zī′ba?" He said, "At your service!"

3 Then the king said, "*Is* there not still someone of the house of Saul, to whom I may show the kindness of God?" And Zī′ba said to the king, "There is still a son of Jonathan *who is* lame in *his* feet."

4 So the king said to him, "Where *is* he?" And Zī′ba said to the king, "Indeed he *is* in the house of Mā′chir the son of Am′mi·el, in Lo Dē′bar."

5 Then King David sent and brought him out of the house of Mā′chir the son of Am′mi·el, from Lo Dē′bar.

6 Now when Me·phib′o·sheth the son of Jonathan, the son of Saul, had come to David, he fell on his face and prostrated himself. Then David said, "Me·phib′o·sheth?" And he answered, "Here is your servant!"

7 So David said to him, "Do not fear, for I will surely show you kindness for Jonathan your father's sake, and will restore to you all the land of Saul your grandfather; and you shall eat bread at my table continually."

8 Then he bowed himself, and said, "What *is* your servant, that you should look upon such a dead dog as I?"

9 And the king called to Zī′ba, Saul's servant, and said to him, "I have given to your master's son all that belonged to Saul and to all his house.

10 "You therefore, and your sons and your servants, shall work the land for

8:13 *a*Septuagint, Syriac, and some Hebrew manuscripts read *Edomites* (compare 1 Chronicles 18:12).
8:17 *a*Spelled *Shavsha* in 1 Chronicles 18:16

him, and you shall bring in *the harvest,* that your master's son may have food to eat. But Me·phib′o·sheth your master's son shall eat bread at my table always." Now Zī′ba had fifteen sons and twenty servants.

11 Then Zī′ba said to the king, "According to all that my lord the king has commanded his servant, so will your servant do." "As for Me·phib′o·sheth," *said the king,* "he shall eat at my table*a* like one of the king's sons."

12 Me·phib′o·sheth had a young son whose name *was* Mī′cha. And all who dwelt in the house of Zī′ba *were* servants of Me·phib′o·sheth.

13 So Me·phib′o·sheth dwelt in Jerusalem, for he ate continually at the king's table. And he was lame in both his feet.

✓	*Bible Quiz*

2 Samuel 9 **David Is Kind to Mephibosheth**

1. David had many reasons to be unkind to Saul's family. Why do you think he chose to be kind to Mephibosheth?
2. How did David show kindness to Mephibosheth?
3. Do you think David might have acted differently if God's love wasn't in him?
4. How do you feel after you've been kind to someone? How do you feel after you've been mean to someone?
5. Does anything good ever come from being mean to someone? What good can come from being kind to someone?

THE AMMONITES AND SYRIANS DEFEATED

10 It happened after this that the king of the people of Am′mon died, and Hā′nun his son reigned in his place.

2 Then David said, "I will show kindness to Hā′nun the son of Nā′hash, as his father showed kindness to me." So David sent by the hand of his servants to comfort him concerning his father. And David's servants came into the land of the people of Am′mon.

3 And the princes of the people of Am′mon said to Hā′nun their lord, "Do you think that David really honors your father because he has sent comforters to you? Has David not *rather* sent his servants to you to search the city, to spy it out, and to overthrow it?"

4 Therefore Hā′nun took David's servants, shaved off half of their beards, cut off their garments in the middle, at their buttocks, and sent them away.

5 When they told David, he sent to meet them, because the men were greatly ashamed. And the king said, "Wait at Jericho until your beards have grown, and *then* return."

6 When the people of Am′mon saw that they had made themselves repulsive to David, the people of Am′mon sent and hired the Syrians of Beth Rē′hob and the Syrians of Zō′ba, twenty thousand foot soldiers; and from the king of Mā′a·cah one thousand men, and from Ish-Tob twelve thousand men.

7 Now when David heard *of it,* he sent Jō′ab and all the army of the mighty men.

8 Then the people of Am′mon came out and put themselves in battle ar-

9:11 *a*Septuagint reads *David's table.*

ray at the entrance of the gate. And the Syrians of Zō′ba, Beth Rē′hob, Ish-Tob, and Mā′a·cah *were* by themselves in the field.

9 When Jō′ab saw that the battle line was against him before and behind, he chose some of Israel's best and put *them* in battle array against the Syrians.

10 And the rest of the people he put under the command of A·bi′shaī his brother, that he might set *them* in battle array against the people of Am′mon.

11 Then he said, "If the Syrians are too strong for me, then you shall help me; but if the people of Am′mon are too strong for you, then I will come and help you.

12 "Be of good courage, and let us be strong for our people and for the cities of our God. And may the LORD do *what is* good in His sight."

13 So Jō′ab and the people who *were* with him drew near for the battle against the Syrians, and they fled before him.

14 When the people of Am′mon saw that the Syrians were fleeing, they also fled before A·bi′shaī, and entered the city. So Jō′ab returned from the people of Am′mon and went to Jerusalem.

15 When the Syrians saw that they had been defeated by Israel, they gathered together.

16 Then Had·a·dē′zer*a* sent and brought out the Syrians who *were* beyond the River,*b* and they came to Hē′lam. And Shō′bach the commander of Had·a·dē′zer's army *went* before them.

17 When it was told David, he gathered all Israel, crossed over the Jordan, and came to Hē′lam. And the Syrians set themselves in battle array against David and fought with him.

18 Then the Syrians fled before Is-

rael; and David killed seven hundred charioteers and forty thousand horsemen of the Syrians, and struck Shō′bach the commander of their army, who died there.

19 And when all the kings *who were* servants to Had·a·dē′zer*a* saw that they were defeated by Israel, they made peace with Israel and served them. So the Syrians were afraid to help the people of Am′mon anymore.

DAVID, BATHSHEBA, AND URIAH

11 It happened in the spring of the year, at the time when kings go out *to battle,* that David sent Jō′ab and his servants with him, and all Israel; and they destroyed the people of Am′mon and besieged Rab′bah. But David remained at Jerusalem.

2 Then it happened one evening that David arose from his bed and walked on the roof of the king's house. And from the roof he saw a woman bathing, and the woman *was* very beautiful to behold.

3 So David sent and inquired about the woman. And *someone* said, "*Is* this not Bath·shē′ba, the daughter of E·lī′am, the wife of Ū·rī′ah the Hit′tīte?"

4 Then David sent messengers, and took her; and she came to him, and he lay with her, for she was cleansed from her impurity; and she returned to her house.

5 And the woman conceived; so she sent and told David, and said, "I *am* with child."

6 Then David sent to Jō′ab, *saying,* "Send me Ū·rī′ah the Hit′tīte." And Jō′ab sent Ū·rī′ah to David.

7 When Ū·rī′ah had come to him, David asked how Jō′ab was doing,

---

10:16 *a*Hebrew *Hadarezer*   *b*That is, the Euphrates   10:19 *a*Hebrew *Hadarezer*

and how the people were doing, and how the war prospered.

8 And David said to Ū·rī′ah, "Go down to your house and wash your feet." So Ū·rī′ah departed from the king's house, and a gift *of food* from the king followed him.

9 But Ū·rī′ah slept at the door of the king's house with all the servants of his lord, and did not go down to his house.

10 So when they told David, saying, "Ū·rī′ah did not go down to his house," David said to Ū·rī′ah, "Did you not come from a journey? Why did you not go down to your house?"

11 And Ū·rī′ah said to David, "The ark and Israel and Judah are dwelling in tents, and my lord Jō′ab and the servants of my lord are encamped in the open fields. Shall I then go to my house to eat and drink, and to lie with my wife? *As* you live, and *as* your soul lives, I will not do this thing."

12 Then David said to Ū·rī′ah, "Wait here today also, and tomorrow I will let you depart." So Ū·rī′ah remained in Jerusalem that day and the next.

13 Now when David called him, he ate and drank before him; and he made him drunk. And at evening he went out to lie on his bed with the servants of his lord, but he did not go down to his house.

14 In the morning it happened that David wrote a letter to Jō′ab and sent *it* by the hand of Ū·rī′ah.

15 And he wrote in the letter, saying, "Set Ū·rī′ah in the forefront of the hottest battle, and retreat from him, that he may be struck down and die."

16 So it was, while Jō′ab besieged the city, that he assigned Ū·rī′ah to a place where he knew there *were* valiant men.

17 Then the men of the city came out and fought with Jō′ab. And *some* of the people of the servants of David fell; and Ū·rī′ah the Hit′tīte died also.

18 Then Jō′ab sent and told David all the things concerning the war,

19 and charged the messenger, saying, "When you have finished telling the matters of the war to the king,

20 "if it happens that the king's wrath rises, and he says to you: 'Why did you approach so near to the city when you fought? Did you not know that they would shoot from the wall?

21 'Who struck A·bim′e·lech the son of Je·rub′be·sheth?*a* Was it not a woman who cast a piece of a millstone on him from the wall, so that he died in Thē′bez? Why did you go near the wall?'—then you shall say, 'Your servant Ū·rī′ah the Hit′tīte is dead also.' "

22 So the messenger went, and came and told David all that Jō′ab had sent by him.

23 And the messenger said to David, "Surely the men prevailed against us and came out to us in the field; then we drove them back as far as the entrance of the gate.

24 "The archers shot from the wall at your servants; and *some* of the king's servants are dead, and your servant Ū·rī′ah the Hit′tīte is dead also."

25 Then David said to the messenger, "Thus you shall say to Jō′ab: 'Do not let this thing displease you, for the sword devours one as well as another. Strengthen your attack against the city, and overthrow it.' So encourage him."

26 When the wife of Ū·rī′ah heard that Ū·rī′ah her husband was dead, she mourned for her husband.

27 And when her mourning was over, David sent and brought her to his house, and she became his wife and bore him a son. But the thing

11:21 *a*Same as *Jerubbaal* (Gideon), Judges 6:32ff

that David had done displeased the
LORD.

NATHAN'S PARABLE AND DAVID'S CONFESSION

12 Then the LORD sent Nathan to
David. And he came to him, and said
to him: "There were two men in one
city, one rich and the other poor.
2 "The rich *man* had exceedingly
many flocks and herds.
3 "But the poor *man* had nothing,
except one little ewe lamb which he
had bought and nourished; and it
grew up together with him and with
his children. It ate of his own food
and drank from his own cup and lay
in his bosom; and it was like a
daughter to him.
4 "And a traveler came to the rich
man, who refused to take from his
own flock and from his own herd to
prepare one for the wayfaring man
who had come to him; but he took the
poor man's lamb and prepared it for
the man who had come to him."
5 So David's anger was greatly
aroused against the man, and he said
to Nathan, "*As* the LORD lives, the
man who has done this shall surely
die!
6 "And he shall restore fourfold for
the lamb, because he did this thing
and because he had no pity."
7 Then Nathan said to David, "You
are the man! Thus says the LORD God
of Israel: 'I anointed you king over Israel, and I delivered you from the
hand of Saul.
8 'I gave you your master's house
and your master's wives into your
keeping, and gave you the house of
Israel and Judah. And if *that had
been* too little, I also would have
given you much more!
9 'Why have you despised the commandment of the LORD, to do evil in
His sight? You have killed Ū·rī′ah the

Hit′tīte with the sword; you have
taken his wife *to be* your wife, and
have killed him with the sword of the
people of Am′mon.
10 'Now therefore, the sword shall
never depart from your house, because you have despised Me, and
have taken the wife of Ū·rī′ah the
Hit′tīte to be your wife.'
11 "Thus says the LORD: 'Behold, I
will raise up adversity against you
from your own house; and I will take
your wives before your eyes and give
them to your neighbor, and he shall
lie with your wives in the sight of
this sun.
12 'For you did *it* secretly, but I will
do this thing before all Israel, before
the sun.'"
13 So David said to Nathan, "I have
sinned against the LORD." And Nathan said to David, "The LORD also
has put away your sin; you shall not
die.
14 "However, because by this deed
you have given great occasion to the
enemies of the LORD to blaspheme,
the child also *who is* born to you shall
surely die."
15 Then Nathan departed to his
house.

THE DEATH OF DAVID'S SON

And the LORD struck the child
that Ū·rī′ah's wife bore to David, and
it became ill.
16 David therefore pleaded with God
for the child, and David fasted and
went in and lay all night on the
ground.
17 So the elders of his house arose
and went to him, to raise him up
from the ground. But he would not,
nor did he eat food with them.
18 Then on the seventh day it came
to pass that the child died. And the
servants of David were afraid to tell
him that the child was dead. For they

said, "Indeed, while the child was alive, we spoke to him, and he would not heed our voice. How can we tell him that the child is dead? He may do some harm!"

19 When David saw that his servants were whispering, David perceived that the child was dead. Therefore David said to his servants, "Is the child dead?" And they said, "He is dead."

20 So David arose from the ground, washed and anointed himself, and changed his clothes; and he went into the house of the LORD and worshiped. Then he went to his own house; and when he requested, they set food before him, and he ate.

21 Then his servants said to him, "What *is* this that you have done? You fasted and wept for the child *while he was* alive, but when the child died, you arose and ate food."

22 And he said, "While the child was alive, I fasted and wept; for I said, 'Who can tell *whether* the LORD*a* will be gracious to me, that the child may live?'

23 "But now he is dead; why should I fast? Can I bring him back again? I shall go to him, but he shall not return to me."

SOLOMON IS BORN

24 Then David comforted Bathshē′ba his wife, and went in to her and lay with her. So she bore a son, and he*a* called his name Solomon. Now the LORD loved him,

25 and He sent *word* by the hand of Nathan the prophet: So he*a* called his name Jed·i·dī′ah,*b* because of the LORD.

RABBAH IS CAPTURED

26 Now Jō′ab fought against Rab′bah of the people of Am′mon, and took the royal city.

27 And Jō′ab sent messengers to David, and said, "I have fought against Rab′bah, and I have taken the city's water *supply*.

28 "Now therefore, gather the rest of the people together and encamp against the city and take it, lest I take the city and it be called after my name."

29 So David gathered all the people together and went to Rab′bah, fought against it, and took it.

30 Then he took their king's crown from his head. Its weight *was* a talent of gold, with precious stones. And it was *set* on David's head. Also he brought out the spoil of the city in great abundance.

31 And he brought out the people who *were* in it, and put *them to work* with saws and iron picks and iron axes, and made them cross over to the brick works. So he did to all the cities of the people of Am′mon. Then David and all the people returned to Jerusalem.

AMNON AND TAMAR

13 After this Ab′sa·lom the son of David had a lovely sister, whose name *was* Tā′mar; and Am′non the son of David loved her.

2 Am′non was so distressed over his sister Tā′mar that he became sick; for she *was* a virgin. And it was improper for Am′non to do anything to her.

3 But Am′non had a friend whose name *was* Jon′a·dab the son of Shim′e·ah, David's brother. Now Jon′a·dab *was* a very crafty man.

4 And he said to him, "Why *are* you, the king's son, becoming thinner day

---

12:22 *a*A few Hebrew manuscripts and Syriac read *God.*   12:24 *a*Following Kethib, Septuagint, and Vulgate; Qere, a few Hebrew manuscripts, Syriac, and Targum read *she.*   12:25 *a*Qere, some Hebrew manuscripts, Syriac, and Targum read *she.*
*b*Literally *Beloved of the LORD*

after day? Will you not tell me?" Am′non said to him, "I love Tā′mar, my brother Ab′sa·lom's sister."

5 So Jon′a·dab said to him, "Lie down on your bed and pretend to be ill. And when your father comes to see you, say to him, 'Please let my sister Tā′mar come and give me food, and prepare the food in my sight, that I may see *it* and eat it from her hand.'"

6 Then Am′non lay down and pretended to be ill; and when the king came to see him, Am′non said to the king, "Please let Tā′mar my sister come and make a couple of cakes for me in my sight, that I may eat from her hand."

7 And David sent home to Tā′mar, saying, "Now go to your brother Am′non's house, and prepare food for him."

8 So Tā′mar went to her brother Am′non's house; and he was lying down. Then she took flour and kneaded *it,* made cakes in his sight, and baked the cakes.

9 And she took the pan and placed *them* out before him, but he refused to eat. Then Am′non said, "Have everyone go out from me." And they all went out from him.

10 Then Am′non said to Tā′mar, "Bring the food into the bedroom, that I may eat from your hand." And Tā′mar took the cakes which she had made, and brought *them* to Am′non her brother in the bedroom.

11 Now when she had brought *them* to him to eat, he took hold of her and said to her, "Come, lie with me, my sister."

12 But she answered him, "No, my brother, do not force me, for no such thing should be done in Israel. Do not do this disgraceful thing!

13 "And I, where could I take my shame? And as for you, you would be like one of the fools in Israel. Now therefore, please speak to the king; for he will not withhold me from you."

14 However, he would not heed her voice; and being stronger than she, he forced her and lay with her.

15 Then Am′non hated her exceedingly, so that the hatred with which he hated her *was* greater than the love with which he had loved her. And Am′non said to her, "Arise, be gone!"

16 So she said to him, "No, indeed! This evil of sending me away *is* worse than the other that you did to me." But he would not listen to her.

17 Then he called his servant who attended him, and said, "Here! Put this *woman* out, away from me, and bolt the door behind her."

18 Now she had on a robe of many colors, for the king's virgin daughters wore such apparel. And his servant put her out and bolted the door behind her.

19 Then Tā′mar put ashes on her head, and tore her robe of many colors that *was* on her, and laid her hand on her head and went away crying bitterly.

20 And Ab′sa·lom her brother said to her, "Has Am′non your brother been with you? But now hold your peace, my sister. He *is* your brother; do not take this thing to heart." So Tā′mar remained desolate in her brother Ab′sa·lom's house.

21 But when King David heard of all these things, he was very angry.

22 And Ab′sa·lom spoke to his brother Am′non neither good nor bad. For Ab′sa·lom hated Am′non, because he had forced his sister Tā′mar.

ABSALOM MURDERS AMNON

23 And it came to pass, after two full years, that Ab′sa·lom had sheep-

shearers in Bā'al Hā'zor, which *is* near Ē'phra·im; so Ab'sa·lom invited all the king's sons.

24 Then Ab'sa·lom came to the king and said, "Kindly note, your servant has sheepshearers; please, let the king and his servants go with your servant."

25 But the king said to Ab'sa·lom, "No, my son, let us not all go now, lest we be a burden to you." Then he urged him, but he would not go; and he blessed him.

26 Then Ab'sa·lom said, "If not, please let my brother Am'non go with us." And the king said to him, "Why should he go with you?"

27 But Ab'sa·lom urged him; so he let Am'non and all the king's sons go with him.

28 Now Ab'sa·lom had commanded his servants, saying, "Watch now, when Am'non's heart is merry with wine, and when I say to you, 'Strike Am'non!' then kill him. Do not be afraid. Have I not commanded you? Be courageous and valiant."

29 So the servants of Ab'sa·lom did to Am'non as Ab'sa·lom had commanded. Then all the king's sons arose, and each one got on his mule and fled.

30 And it came to pass, while they were on the way, that news came to David, saying, "Ab'sa·lom has killed all the king's sons, and not one of them is left!"

31 So the king arose and tore his garments and lay on the ground, and all his servants stood by with their clothes torn.

32 Then Jon'a·dab the son of Shim'-ē·ah, David's brother, answered and said, "Let not my lord suppose they have killed all the young men, the king's sons, for only Am'non is dead. For by the command of Ab'sa·lom this has been determined from the day that he forced his sister Tā'mar.

33 "Now therefore, let not my lord the king take the thing to his heart, to think that all the king's sons are dead. For only Am'non is dead."

ABSALOM FLEES TO GESHUR

34 Then Ab'sa·lom fled. And the young man who was keeping watch lifted his eyes and looked, and there, many people were coming from the road on the hillside behind him.*a*

35 And Jon'a·dab said to the king, "Look, the king's sons are coming; as your servant said, so it is."

36 So it was, as soon as he had finished speaking, that the king's sons indeed came, and they lifted up their voice and wept. Also the king and all his servants wept very bitterly.

37 But Ab'sa·lom fled and went to Tal'maī the son of Am·mī'hud, king of Gē'shur. And *David* mourned for his son every day.

38 So Ab'sa·lom fled and went to Gē'shur, and was there three years.

39 And King David*a* longed to go to*b* Ab'sa·lom. For he had been comforted concerning Am'non, because he was dead.

ABSALOM RETURNS TO JERUSALEM

14 So Jō'ab the son of Ze·rū'i·ah perceived that the king's heart *was* concerned about Ab'sa·lom.

2 And Jō'ab sent to Te·kō'a and brought from there a wise woman, and said to her, "Please pretend to be a mourner, and put on mourning apparel; do not anoint yourself with

13:34 *a*Septuagint adds *And the watchman went and told the king, and said, "I see men from the way of Horonaim, from the regions of the mountains."*
13:39 *a*Following Masoretic Text, Syriac, and Vulgate; Septuagint reads *the spirit of the king;* Targum reads *the soul of King David.*   *b*Following Masoretic Text and Targum; Septuagint and Vulgate read *ceased to pursue after.*

oil, but act like a woman who has been mourning a long time for the dead.

3 "Go to the king and speak to him in this manner." So Jō′ab put the words in her mouth.

4 And when the woman of Te·kō′a spoke*a* to the king, she fell on her face to the ground and prostrated herself, and said, "Help, O king!"

5 Then the king said to her, "What troubles you?" And she answered, "Indeed I *am* a widow, my husband is dead.

6 "Now your maidservant had two sons; and the two fought with each other in the field, and *there was* no one to part them, but the one struck the other and killed him.

7 "And now the whole family has risen up against your maidservant, and they said, 'Deliver him who struck his brother, that we may execute him for the life of his brother whom he killed; and we will destroy the heir also.' So they would extinguish my ember that is left, and leave to my husband *neither* name nor remnant on the earth."

8 Then the king said to the woman, "Go to your house, and I will give orders concerning you."

9 And the woman of Te·kō′a said to the king, "My lord, O king, *let* the iniquity *be* on me and on my father's house, and the king and his throne *be* guiltless."

10 So the king said, "Whoever says *anything* to you, bring him to me, and he shall not touch you anymore."

11 Then she said, "Please let the king remember the LORD your God, and do not permit the avenger of blood to destroy anymore, lest they destroy my son." And he said, "*As* the LORD lives, not one hair of your son shall fall to the ground."

12 Therefore the woman said,

"Please, let your maidservant speak *another* word to my lord the king." And he said, "Say on."

13 So the woman said: "Why then have you schemed such a thing against the people of God? For the king speaks this thing as one who is guilty, *in that* the king does not bring his banished one home again.

14 "For we will surely die and *become* like water spilled on the ground, which cannot be gathered up again. Yet God does not take away a life; but He devises means, so that His banished ones are not expelled from Him.

15 "Now therefore, I have come to speak of this thing to my lord the king because the people have made me afraid. And your maidservant said, 'I will now speak to the king; it may be that the king will perform the request of his maidservant.

16 'For the king will hear and deliver his maidservant from the hand of the man *who would* destroy me and my son together from the inheritance of God.'

17 "Your maidservant said, 'The word of my lord the king will now be comforting; for as the angel of God, so *is* my lord the king in discerning good and evil. And may the LORD your God be with you.' "

18 Then the king answered and said to the woman, "Please do not hide from me anything that I ask you." And the woman said, "Please, let my lord the king speak."

19 So the king said, "*Is* the hand of Jō′ab with you in all this?" And the woman answered and said, "*As* you live, my lord the king, no one can turn to the right hand or to the left from anything that my lord the king has spoken. For your servant Jō′ab commanded me, and he put all these

14:4 *a*Many Hebrew manuscripts, Septuagint, Syriac, and Vulgate read *came.*

words in the mouth of your maid-servant.

20 "To bring about this change of affairs your servant Jō'ab has done this thing; but my lord *is* wise, according to the wisdom of the angel of God, to know everything that *is* in the earth."

21 And the king said to Jō'ab, "All right, I have granted this thing. Go therefore, bring back the young man Ab'sa·lom."

22 Then Jō'ab fell to the ground on his face and bowed himself, and thanked the king. And Jō'ab said, "Today your servant knows that I have found favor in your sight, my lord, O king, in that the king has fulfilled the request of his servant."

23 So Jō'ab arose and went to Gē'shur, and brought Ab'sa·lom to Jerusalem.

24 And the king said, "Let him return to his own house, but do not let him see my face." So Ab'sa·lom returned to his own house, but did not see the king's face.

DAVID FORGIVES ABSALOM

25 Now in all Israel there was no one who was praised as much as Ab'sa·lom for his good looks. From the sole of his foot to the crown of his head there was no blemish in him.

26 And when he cut the hair of his head—at the end of every year he cut *it* because it was heavy on him— when he cut it, he weighed the hair of his head at two hundred shekels according to the king's standard.

27 To Ab'sa·lom were born three sons, and one daughter whose name *was* Tā'mar. She was a woman of beautiful appearance.

28 And Ab'sa·lom dwelt two full years in Jerusalem, but did not see the king's face.

29 Therefore Ab'sa·lom sent for Jō'ab, to send him to the king, but he would not come to him. And when he sent again the second time, he would not come.

30 So he said to his servants, "See, Jō'ab's field is near mine, and he has barley there; go and set it on fire." And Ab'sa·lom's servants set the field on fire.

31 Then Jō'ab arose and came to Ab'sa·lom's house, and said to him, "Why have your servants set my field on fire?"

32 And Ab'sa·lom answered Jō'ab, "Look, I sent to you, saying, 'Come here, so that I may send you to the king, to say, "Why have I come from Gē'shur? *It would be* better for me *to be* there still." ' Now therefore, let me see the king's face; but if there is iniquity in me, let him execute me."

33 So Jō'ab went to the king and told him. And when he had called for Ab'sa·lom, he came to the king and bowed himself on his face to the ground before the king. Then the king kissed Ab'sa·lom.

ABSALOM'S TREASON

15 After this it happened that Ab'sa·lom provided himself with chariots and horses, and fifty men to run before him.

2 Now Ab'sa·lom would rise early and stand beside the way to the gate. *So* it was, whenever anyone who had a lawsuit came to the king for a decision, that Ab'sa·lom would call to him and say, "What city *are* you from?" And he would say, "Your servant *is* from such and such a tribe of Israel."

3 Then Ab'sa·lom would say to him, "Look, your case *is* good and right; but *there is* no deputy of the king to hear you."

4 Moreover Ab'sa·lom would say, "Oh, that I were made judge in the

land, and everyone who has any suit or cause would come to me; then I would give him justice."

5 And *so* it was, whenever anyone came near to bow down to him, that he would put out his hand and take him and kiss him.

6 In this manner Ab′sa·lom acted toward all Israel who came to the king for judgment. So Ab′sa·lom stole the hearts of the men of Israel.

7 Now it came to pass after forty[a] years that Ab′sa·lom said to the king, "Please, let me go to Hē′bron and pay the vow which I made to the LORD.

8 "For your servant took a vow while I dwelt at Gē′shur in Syria, saying, 'If the LORD indeed brings me back to Jerusalem, then I will serve the LORD.' "

9 And the king said to him, "Go in peace." So he arose and went to Hē′bron.

10 Then Ab′sa·lom sent spies throughout all the tribes of Israel, saying, "As soon as you hear the sound of the trumpet, then you shall say, 'Ab′sa·lom reigns in Hē′bron!' "

11 And with Ab′sa·lom went two hundred men invited from Jerusalem, and they went along innocently and did not know anything.

12 Then Ab′sa·lom sent for A·hith′o·phel the Gī′lo·nīte, David's counselor, from his city—from Gī′lōh—while he offered sacrifices. And the conspiracy grew strong, for the people with Ab′sa·lom continually increased in number.

DAVID ESCAPES FROM JERUSALEM

13 Now a messenger came to David, saying, "The hearts of the men of Israel are with Ab′sa·lom."

14 So David said to all his servants who *were* with him at Jerusalem, "Arise, and let us flee, or we shall not escape from Ab′sa·lom. Make haste to depart, lest he overtake us suddenly and bring disaster upon us, and strike the city with the edge of the sword."

15 And the king's servants said to the king, "We *are* your servants, *ready to do* whatever my lord the king commands."

16 Then the king went out with all his household after him. But the king left ten women, concubines, to keep the house.

17 And the king went out with all the people after him, and stopped at the outskirts.

18 Then all his servants passed before him; and all the Cher′e·thītes, all the Pel′eth·ītes, and all the Git′tītes, six hundred men who had followed him from Gath, passed before the king.

19 Then the king said to It′tai the Git′tīte, "Why are you also going with us? Return and remain with the king. For you *are* a foreigner and also an exile from your own place.

20 "In fact, you came *only* yesterday. Should I make you wander up and down with us today, since I go I know not where? Return, and take your brethren back. Mercy and truth *be* with you."

21 But It′tai answered the king and said, "*As* the LORD lives, and *as* my lord the king lives, surely in whatever place my lord the king shall be, whether in death or life, even there also your servant will be."

22 So David said to It′tai, "Go, and cross over." Then It′tai the Git′tīte and all his men and all the little ones who *were* with him crossed over.

23 And all the country wept with a loud voice, and all the people crossed over. The king himself also crossed over the Brook Kid′ron, and all the

15:7 [a]Septuagint manuscripts, Syriac, and Josephus read *four.*

people crossed over toward the way of the wilderness.

24 There was Zā′dok also, and all the Lē′vītes with him, bearing the ark of the covenant of God. And they set down the ark of God, and A·bī′a·thar went up until all the people had finished crossing over from the city.

25 Then the king said to Zā′dok, "Carry the ark of God back into the city. If I find favor in the eyes of the LORD, He will bring me back and show me *both* it and His dwelling place.

26 "But if He says thus: 'I have no delight in you,' here I am, let Him do to me as seems good to Him."

27 The king also said to Zā′dok the priest, "*Are* you *not* a seer? Return to the city in peace, and your two sons with you, A·him′a·az your son, and Jonathan the son of A·bī′a·thar.

28 "See, I will wait in the plains of the wilderness until word comes from you to inform me."

29 Therefore Zā′dok and A·bī′a·thar carried the ark of God back to Jerusalem. And they remained there.

30 So David went up by the Ascent of the *Mount of* Olives, and wept as he went up; and he had his head covered and went barefoot. And all the people who *were* with him covered their heads and went up, weeping as they went up.

31 Then *someone* told David, saying, "A·hith′o·phel *is* among the conspirators with Ab′sa·lom." And David said, "O LORD, I pray, turn the counsel of A·hith′o·phel into foolishness!"

32 Now it happened when David had come to the top *of the mountain,* where he worshiped God—there was Hū′shai the Ar′chīte coming to meet him with his robe torn and dust on his head.

33 David said to him, "If you go on

with me, then you will become a burden to me.

34 "But if you return to the city, and say to Ab′sa·lom, 'I will be your servant, O king; *as I was* your father's servant previously, so I *will* now also *be* your servant,' then you may defeat the counsel of A·hith′o·phel for me.

35 "And *do* you not *have* Zā′dok and A·bī′a·thar the priests with you there? Therefore it will be *that* whatever you hear from the king's house, you shall tell to Zā′dok and A·bī′a·thar the priests.

36 "Indeed *they have* there with them their two sons, A·him′a·az, Zā′dok's *son,* and Jonathan, A·bī′a·thar's *son;* and by them you shall send me everything you hear."

37 So Hū′shai, David's friend, went into the city. And Ab′sa·lom came into Jerusalem.

MEPHIBOSHETH'S SERVANT

16 When David was a little past the top *of the mountain,* there was Zī′ba the servant of Me·phib′o·sheth, who met him with a couple of saddled donkeys, and on them two hundred *loaves* of bread, one hundred clusters of raisins, one hundred summer fruits, and a skin of wine.

2 And the king said to Zī′ba, "What do you mean to do with these?" So Zī′ba said, "The donkeys *are* for the king's household to ride on, the bread and summer fruit for the young men to eat, and the wine for those who are faint in the wilderness to drink."

3 Then the king said, "And where *is* your master's son?" And Zī′ba said to the king, "Indeed he is staying in Jerusalem, for he said, 'Today the house of Israel will restore the kingdom of my father to me.' "

4 So the king said to Zī′ba, "Here, all that *belongs* to Me·phib′o·sheth *is*

yours." And Zī'ba said, "I humbly bow before you, *that* I may find favor in your sight, my lord, O king!"

SHIMEI CURSES DAVID

5 Now when King David came to Ba·hū'rim, there was a man from the family of the house of Saul, whose name *was* Shim'ē·ī the son of Gē'ra, coming from there. He came out, cursing continuously as he came.

6 And he threw stones at David and at all the servants of King David. And all the people and all the mighty men *were* on his right hand and on his left.

7 Also Shim'ē·ī said thus when he cursed: "Come out! Come out! You bloodthirsty man, you rogue!

8 "The LORD has brought upon you all the blood of the house of Saul, in whose place you have reigned; and the LORD has delivered the kingdom into the hand of Ab'sa·lom your son. So now you *are caught* in your own evil, because you are a bloodthirsty man!"

9 Then A·bi'shaī the son of Ze·rū'i·ah said to the king, "Why should this dead dog curse my lord the king? Please, let me go over and take off his head!"

10 But the king said, "What have I to do with you, you sons of Ze·rū'i·ah? So let him curse, because the LORD has said to him, 'Curse David.' Who then shall say, 'Why have you done so?' "

11 And David said to A·bi'shaī and all his servants, "See how my son who came from my own body seeks my life. How much more now *may this* Ben'ja·mīte? Let him alone, and let him curse; for so the LORD has ordered him.

12 "It may be that the LORD will look on my affliction,*a* and that the LORD will repay me with good for his cursing this day."

13 And as David and his men went along the road, Shim'ē·ī went along the hillside opposite him and cursed as he went, threw stones at him and kicked up dust.

14 Now the king and all the people who *were* with him became weary; so they refreshed themselves there.

THE ADVICE OF AHITHOPHEL

15 Meanwhile Ab'sa·lom and all the people, the men of Israel, came to Jerusalem; and A·hith'o·phel *was* with him.

16 And so it was, when Hū'shai the Ar'chīte, David's friend, came to Ab'sa·lom, that Hū'shai said to Ab'sa·lom, "*Long* live the king! *Long* live the king!"

17 So Ab'sa·lom said to Hū'shai, "*Is* this your loyalty to your friend? Why did you not go with your friend?"

18 And Hū'shai said to Ab'sa·lom, "No, but whom the LORD and this people and all the men of Israel choose, his I will be, and with him I will remain.

19 "Furthermore, whom should I serve? *Should I* not *serve* in the presence of his son? As I have served in your father's presence, so will I be in your presence."

20 Then Ab'sa·lom said to A·hith'o·phel, "Give advice as to what we should do."

21 And A·hith'o·phel said to Ab'sa·lom, "Go in to your father's concubines, whom he has left to keep the house; and all Israel will hear that you are abhorred by your father. Then the hands of all who are with you will be strong."

16:12 *a*Following Kethib, Septuagint, Syriac, and Vulgate; Qere reads *my eyes;* Targum reads *tears of my eyes.*

22 So they pitched a tent for Ab'sa-lom on the top of the house, and Ab'sa-lom went in to his father's concubines in the sight of all Israel.

23 Now the advice of A·hith'o·phel, which he gave in those days, *was* as if one had inquired at the oracle of God. So *was* all the advice of A·hith'-o·phel both with David and with Ab'-sa·lom.

17

Moreover A·hith'o·phel said to Ab'sa·lom, "Now let me choose twelve thousand men, and I will arise and pursue David tonight.

2 "I will come upon him while he *is* weary and weak, and make him afraid. And all the people who *are* with him will flee, and I will strike only the king.

3 "Then I will bring back all the people to you. When all return except the man whom you seek, all the people will be at peace."

4 And the saying pleased Ab'sa·lom and all the elders of Israel.

THE ADVICE OF HUSHAI

5 Then Ab'sa·lom said, "Now call Hū'shai the Ar'chīte also, and let us hear what he says too."

6 And when Hū'shai came to Ab'sa·lom, Ab'sa·lom spoke to him, saying, "A·hith'o·phel has spoken in this manner. Shall we do as he says? If not, speak up."

7 So Hū'shai said to Ab'sa·lom: "The advice that A·hith'o·phel has given *is* not good at this time.

8 "For," said Hū'shai, "you know your father and his men, that they *are* mighty men, and they *are* enraged in their minds, like a bear robbed of her cubs in the field; and your father *is* a man of war, and will not camp with the people.

9 "Surely by now he is hidden in some pit, or in some *other* place. And it will be, when some of them are overthrown at the first, that whoever hears *it* will say, 'There is a slaughter among the people who follow Ab'sa·lom.'

10 "And even he *who is* valiant, whose heart *is* like the heart of a lion, will melt completely. For all Israel knows that your father *is* a mighty man, and *those* who *are* with him *are* valiant men.

11 "Therefore I advise that all Israel be fully gathered to you, from Dan to Bē·er·shē'ba, like the sand that *is* by the sea for multitude, and that you go to battle in person.

12 "So we will come upon him in some place where he may be found, and we will fall on him as the dew falls on the ground. And of him and all the men who *are* with him there shall not be left so much as one.

13 "Moreover, if he has withdrawn into a city, then all Israel shall bring ropes to that city; and we will pull it into the river, until there is not one small stone found there."

14 So Ab'sa·lom and all the men of Israel said, "The advice of Hū'shai the Ar'chīte *is* better than the advice of A·hith'o·phel." For the LORD had purposed to defeat the good advice of A·hith'o·phel, to the intent that the LORD might bring disaster on Ab'sa·lom.

HUSHAI WARNS DAVID TO ESCAPE

15 Then Hū'shai said to Zā'dok and A·bī'a·thar the priests, "Thus and so A·hith'o·phel advised Ab'sa·lom and the elders of Israel, and thus and so I have advised.

16 "Now therefore, send quickly and tell David, saying, 'Do not spend this night in the plains of the wilderness, but speedily cross over, lest the king and all the people who *are* with him be swallowed up.'"

17 Now Jonathan and A·him′a·az stayed at En Rō′gel, for they dared not be seen coming into the city; so a female servant would come and tell them, and they would go and tell King David.
18 Nevertheless a lad saw them, and told Ab′sa·lom. But both of them went away quickly and came to a man's house in Ba·hū′rim, who had a well in his court; and they went down into it.
19 Then the woman took and spread a covering over the well's mouth, and spread ground grain on it; and the thing was not known.
20 And when Ab′sa·lom's servants came to the woman at the house, they said, "Where *are* A·him′a·az and Jonathan?" So the woman said to them, "They have gone over the water brook." And when they had searched and could not find *them,* they returned to Jerusalem.
21 Now it came to pass, after they had departed, that they came up out of the well and went and told King David, and said to David, "Arise and cross over the water quickly. For thus has A·hith′o·phel advised against you."
22 So David and all the people who *were* with him arose and crossed over the Jordan. By morning light not one of them was left who had not gone over the Jordan.
23 Now when A·hith′o·phel saw that his advice was not followed, he saddled a donkey, and arose and went home to his house, to his city. Then he put his household in order, and hanged himself, and died; and he was buried in his father's tomb.
24 Then David went to Mā·ha·na′im. And Ab′sa·lom crossed over the Jordan, he and all the men of Israel with him.
25 And Ab′sa·lom made A·mā′sa captain of the army instead of Jō′ab.

This A·mā′sa *was* the son of a man whose name *was* Jith′ra,*a* an Israelite,*b* who had gone in to Ab′i·gail the daughter of Nā′hash, sister of Ze·rū′i·ah, Jō′ab's mother.
26 So Israel and Ab′sa·lom encamped in the land of Gil′ē·ad.
27 Now it happened, when David had come to Mā·ha·na′im, that Shō′bī the son of Nā′hash from Rab′bah of the people of Am′mon, Mā′chir the son of Am′mi·el from Lo Dē′bar, and Bar·zil′lai the Gil′ē·ad·īte from Rō′ge·lim,
28 brought beds and basins, earthen vessels and wheat, barley and flour, parched *grain* and beans, lentils and parched *seeds,*
29 honey and curds, sheep and cheese of the herd, for David and the people who *were* with him to eat. For they said, "The people are hungry and weary and thirsty in the wilderness."

ABSALOM'S DEFEAT AND DEATH

18 And David numbered the people who *were* with him, and set captains of thousands and captains of hundreds over them.
2 Then David sent out one third of the people under the hand of Jō′ab, one third under the hand of A·bi′shaī the son of Ze·rū′i·ah, Jō′ab's brother, and one third under the hand of It′taī the Git′tīte. And the king said to the people, "I also will surely go out with you myself."
3 But the people answered, "You shall not go out! For if we flee away, they will not care about us; nor if half of us die, will they care about us. But *you are* worth ten thousand of us

17:25 *a*Spelled *Jether* in 1 Chronicles 2:17 and elsewhere *b*Following Masoretic Text, some manuscripts of the Septuagint, and Targum; some manuscripts of the Septuagint read *Ishmaelite* (compare 1 Chronicles 2:17); Vulgate reads *of Jezrael.*

now. For you are now more help to us in the city."

4 Then the king said to them, "Whatever seems best to you I will do." So the king stood beside the gate, and all the people went out by hundreds and by thousands.

5 Now the king had commanded Jōʹab, Aʹbiʹshaī, and Itʹtaī, saying, "*Deal* gently for my sake with the young man Abʹsa·lom." And all the people heard when the king gave all the captains orders concerning Abʹsa·lom.

6 So the people went out into the field of battle against Israel. And the battle was in the woods of Ēʹphra·im.

7 The people of Israel were overthrown there before the servants of David, and a great slaughter of twenty thousand took place there that day.

8 For the battle there was scattered over the face of the whole countryside, and the woods devoured more people that day than the sword devoured.

9 Then Abʹsa·lom met the servants of David. Abʹsa·lom rode on a mule. The mule went under the thick boughs of a great terebinth tree, and his head caught in the terebinth; so he was left hanging between heaven and earth. And the mule which *was* under him went on.

10 Now a certain man saw *it* and told Jōʹab, and said, "I just saw Abʹsa·lom hanging in a terebinth tree!"

11 So Jōʹab said to the man who told him, "You just saw *him!* And why did you not strike him there to the ground? I would have given you ten *shekels* of silver and a belt."

12 But the man said to Jōʹab, "Though I were to receive a thousand *shekels* of silver in my hand, I would not raise my hand against the king's son. For in our hearing the king com-

manded you and A·biʹshaī and Itʹtaī, saying, 'Beware lest anyone *touch* the young man Abʹsa·lom!'*a*

13 "Otherwise I would have dealt falsely against my own life. For there is nothing hidden from the king, and you yourself would have set yourself against *me*."

14 Then Jōʹab said, "I cannot linger with you." And he took three spears in his hand and thrust them through Abʹsa·lom's heart, while he was *still* alive in the midst of the terebinth tree.

15 And ten young men who bore Jōʹab's armor surrounded Abʹsa·lom, and struck and killed him.

16 So Jōʹab blew the trumpet, and the people returned from pursuing Israel. For Jōʹab held back the people.

17 And they took Abʹsa·lom and cast him into a large pit in the woods, and laid a very large heap of stones over him. Then all Israel fled, everyone to his tent.

18 Now Abʹsa·lom in his lifetime had taken and set up a pillar for himself, which *is* in the King's Valley. For he said, "I have no son to keep my name in remembrance." He called the pillar after his own name. And to this day it is called Abʹsa·lom's Monument.

DAVID HEARS OF ABSALOM'S DEATH

19 Then A·himʹa·az the son of Zāʹdok said, "Let me run now and take the news to the king, how the LORD has avenged him of his enemies."

20 And Jōʹab said to him, "You shall not take the news this day, for you shall take the news another day. But today you shall take no news, because the king's son is dead."

21 Then Jōʹab said to the Cūʹshīte,

18:12 *a*The ancient versions read *'Protect the young man Absalom for me!'*

BAD NEWS FROM A GOOD FRIEND 2 Samuel 18:19–32

"Hello, Jon," Christopher says. "I have some news for you." Do you think Christopher's news is good news or bad news? How do you know? Do you think Christopher is a good friend or a bad friend? How do you know?

1. Should good friends share only good news? Should they also share bad news? Why?
2. If a friend can be helped by sharing bad news, will you share it? Why? If a friend can be hurt by sharing any news, will you share it? Why not?
3. Jesus is a good friend when He warns you about sin, isn't He? He is also a good friend when He shares the Good News about His love for you. Be sure to say thank you to Jesus for being your friend—even when He must bring bad news about sin.

For more on *What Should I Do?* turn to page 489
For more on *Friendship* turn to page 489

"Go, tell the king what you have seen." So the Cū′shīte bowed himself to Jō′ab and ran.

22 And A·him′a·az the son of Zā′dok said again to Jō′ab, "But whatever happens, please let me also run after the Cū′shīte." So Jō′ab said, "Why will you run, my son, since you have no news ready?"

23 "But whatever happens," *he said,* "let me run." So he said to him, "Run." Then A·him′a·az ran by way of the plain, and outran the Cū′shīte.

24 Now David was sitting between the two gates. And the watchman went up to the roof over the gate, to the wall, lifted his eyes and looked, and there was a man, running alone.

25 Then the watchman cried out and told the king. And the king said, "If he *is* alone, *there is* news in his mouth." And he came rapidly and drew near.

26 Then the watchman saw *another* man running, and the watchman called to the gatekeeper and said, "There is *another* man, running alone!" And the king said, "He also brings news."

27 So the watchman said, "I think the running of the first is like the running of A·him′a·az the son of Zā′dok." And the king said, "He *is* a good man, and comes with good news."

28 So A·him′a·az called out and said to the king, "All is well!" Then he bowed down with his face to the earth before the king, and said, "Blessed *be* the LORD your God, who has delivered up the men who raised their hand against my lord the king!"

29 The king said, "Is the young man Ab′sa·lom safe?" A·him′a·az answered, "When Jō′ab sent the king's servant and *me* your servant, I saw a great tumult, but I did not know what *it was about.*"

30 And the king said, "Turn aside *and* stand here." So he turned aside and stood still.

31 Just then the Cū′shīte came, and the Cū′shīte said, "There is good news, my lord the king! For the LORD has avenged you this day of all those who rose against you."

32 And the king said to the Cū′shīte, "Is the young man Ab′sa·lom safe?" So the Cū′shīte answered, "May the enemies of my lord the king, and all who rise against you to do harm, be like *that* young man!"

DAVID'S MOURNING FOR ABSALOM

33 Then the king was deeply moved, and went up to the chamber over the gate, and wept. And as he went, he said thus: "O my son Ab′sa·lom—my son, my son Ab′sa·lom—if only I had died in your place! O Ab′sa·lom my son, my son!"

19 And Jō′ab was told, "Behold, the king is weeping and mourning for Ab′sa·lom."

2 So the victory that day was *turned* into mourning for all the people. For the people heard it said that day, "The king is grieved for his son."

3 And the people stole back into the city that day, as people who are ashamed steal away when they flee in battle.

4 But the king covered his face, and the king cried out with a loud voice, "O my son Ab′sa·lom! O Ab′sa·lom, my son, my son!"

5 Then Jō′ab came into the house to the king, and said, "Today you have disgraced all your servants who today have saved your life, the lives of your sons and daughters, the lives of your wives and the lives of your concubines,

6 "in that you love your enemies and hate your friends. For you have declared today that you regard

What Should I Do?

DON'T HURT ME 2 Samuel 19:5–7

What should this nurse do? The patient is crying, isn't he? He is begging the nurse not to hurt him. But she must hurt him if she gives him a shot. And he needs the shot to keep from getting sick. What should she do? What would you do?

1. Sometimes we must hurt a friend a little to help him or her a lot. Can you think of some ways we do that? In 2 Samuel 19:5–7 Joab had to hurt his friend King David in order to help him.
2. What would you like to say to the nurse? What would you like to say to this patient?

For more on *What Should I Do?* turn to page 492
For more on *Friendship* turn to page 758

neither princes nor servants; for to-day I perceive that if Ab′sa·lom had lived and all of us had died today, then it would have pleased you well. 7 "Now therefore, arise, go out and speak comfort to your servants. For I swear by the LORD, if you do not go out, not one will stay with you this night. And that will be worse for you than all the evil that has befallen you from your youth until now."

8 Then the king arose and sat in the gate. And they told all the people, saying, "There is the king, sitting in the gate." So all the people came before the king. For everyone of Israel had fled to his tent.

DAVID RETURNS TO JERUSALEM

9 Now all the people were in a dispute throughout all the tribes of Israel, saying, "The king saved us from the hand of our enemies, he delivered us from the hand of the Phi·lis′tines, and now he has fled from the land because of Ab′sa·lom.
10 "But Ab′sa·lom, whom we anointed over us, has died in battle. Now therefore, why do you say nothing about bringing back the king?"
11 So King David sent to Zā′dok and A·bī′a·thar the priests, saying, "Speak to the elders of Judah, saying, 'Why are you the last to bring the king back to his house, since the words of all Israel have come to the king, to his *very* house?
12 'You *are* my brethren, you *are* my bone and my flesh. Why then are you the last to bring back the king?'
13 "And say to A·mā′sa, 'Are you not my bone and my flesh? God do so to me, and more also, if you are not commander of the army before me continually in place of Jō′ab.' "
14 So he swayed the hearts of all the men of Judah, just as *the heart of* one man, so that they sent *this word* to

the king: "Return, you and all your servants!"
15 Then the king returned and came to the Jordan. And Judah came to Gil′gal, to go to meet the king, to escort the king across the Jordan.
16 And Shim′e·ī the son of Gē′ra, a Ben′ja·mīte, who *was* from Ba·hū′-rim, hurried and came down with the men of Judah to meet King David.
17 *There were* a thousand men of Benjamin with him, and Zī′ba the servant of the house of Saul, and his fifteen sons and his twenty servants with him; and they went over the Jordan before the king.
18 Then a ferryboat went across to carry over the king's household, and to do what he thought good.

DAVID'S MERCY TO SHIMEI

Now Shim′e·ī the son of Gē′ra fell down before the king when he had crossed the Jordan.
19 Then he said to the king, "Do not let my lord impute iniquity to me, or remember what wrong your servant did on the day that my lord the king left Jerusalem, that the king should take *it* to heart.
20 "For I, your servant, know that I have sinned. Therefore here I am, the first to come today of all the house of Joseph to go down to meet my lord the king."
21 But A·bi′shaī the son of Ze·rū′i·ah answered and said, "Shall not Shim′e·ī be put to death for this, because he cursed the LORD's anointed?"
22 And David said, "What have I to do with you, you sons of Ze·rū′i·ah, that you should be adversaries to me today? Shall any man be put to death today in Israel? For do I not know that today I *am* king over Israel?"
23 Therefore the king said to

Shim'ē·ī, "You shall not die." And the king swore to him.

DAVID AND MEPHIBOSHETH MEET

24 Now Me·phib'o·sheth the son of Saul came down to meet the king. And he had not cared for his feet, nor trimmed his mustache, nor washed his clothes, from the day the king departed until the day he returned in peace.
25 So it was, when he had come to Jerusalem to meet the king, that the king said to him, "Why did you not go with me, Me·phib'o·sheth?"
26 And he answered, "My lord, O king, my servant deceived me. For your servant said, 'I will saddle a donkey for myself, that I may ride on it and go to the king,' because your servant is lame.
27 "And he has slandered your servant to my lord the king, but my lord the king is like the angel of God. Therefore do what is good in your eyes.
28 "For all my father's house were but dead men before my lord the king. Yet you set your servant among those who eat at your own table. Therefore what right have I still to cry out anymore to the king?"
29 So the king said to him, "Why do you speak anymore of your matters? I have said, 'You and Zī'ba divide the land.' "
30 Then Me·phib'o·sheth said to the king, "Rather, let him take it all, inasmuch as my lord the king has come back in peace to his own house."

DAVID'S KINDNESS TO BARZILLAI

31 And Bar·zil'laī the Gil'ē·ad·īte came down from Rō'ge·lim and went across the Jordan with the king, to escort him across the Jordan.
32 Now Bar·zil'laī was a very aged

man, eighty years old. And he had provided the king with supplies while he stayed at Mā·ha·na'im, for he was a very rich man.
33 And the king said to Bar·zil'laī, "Come across with me, and I will provide for you while you are with me in Jerusalem."
34 But Bar·zil'laī said to the king, "How long have I to live, that I should go up with the king to Jerusalem?
35 "I am today eighty years old. Can I discern between the good and bad? Can your servant taste what I eat or what I drink? Can I hear any longer the voice of singing men and singing women? Why then should your servant be a further burden to my lord the king?
36 "Your servant will go a little way across the Jordan with the king. And why should the king repay me with such a reward?
37 "Please let your servant turn back again, that I may die in my own city, near the grave of my father and mother. But here is your servant Chim'ham; let him cross over with my lord the king, and do for him what seems good to you."
38 And the king answered, "Chim'ham shall cross over with me, and I will do for him what seems good to you. Now whatever you request of me, I will do for you."
39 Then all the people went over the Jordan. And when the king had crossed over, the king kissed Bar·zil'laī and blessed him, and he returned to his own place.

THE QUARREL ABOUT THE KING

40 Now the king went on to Gil'gal, and Chim'ham[a] went on with him. And all the people of Judah escorted

19:40 [a]Masoretic Text reads Chimhan.

What Should I Do?

GOING BOTH WAYS AT THE SAME TIME? 2 Samuel 19:40–43

"Let's go this way," mother says. "No, I want to go that way," says father. "Let's go this way," says brother. "No, I want to go that way," says sister. What do you think will happen?

1. Can you go in opposite directions at the same time? Why not?
2. If two family members want to go in opposite directions, what will happen? Will either go the right way?
3. Why should family members work together and pull together? What happens when they don't?

For more on *What Should I Do?* turn to page 502
For more on *Family* turn to page 891

the king, and also half the people of Israel.

41 Just then all the men of Israel came to the king, and said to the king, "Why have our brethren, the men of Judah, stolen you away and brought the king, his household, and all David's men with him across the Jordan?"

42 So all the men of Judah answered the men of Israel, "Because the king *is* a close relative of ours. Why then are you angry over this matter? Have we ever eaten at the king's *expense?* Or has he given us any gift?"

43 And the men of Israel answered the men of Judah, and said, "We have ten shares in the king; therefore we also have more *right* to David than you. Why then do you despise us— were we not the first to advise bringing back our king?" Yet the words of the men of Judah were fiercer than the words of the men of Israel.

THE REBELLION OF SHEBA

20 And there happened to be there a rebel,*a* whose name *was* Shē′ba the son of Bich′rī, a Ben′jamīte. And he blew a trumpet, and said:

"We have no share in David,
　Nor do we have inheritance in the
　　son of Jesse;
Every man to his tents, O Israel!"

2 So every man of Israel deserted David, *and* followed Shē′ba the son of Bich′rī. But the men of Judah, from the Jordan as far as Jerusalem, remained loyal to their king.

3 Now David came to his house at Jerusalem. And the king took the ten women, his concubines whom he had left to keep the house, and put them in seclusion and supported them, but

did not go in to them. So they were shut up to the day of their death, living in widowhood.

4 And the king said to A·mā′sa, "Assemble the men of Judah for me within three days, and be present here yourself."

5 So A·mā′sa went to assemble *the men of* Judah. But he delayed longer than the set time which David had appointed him.

6 And David said to A·bi′shaī, "Now Shē′ba the son of Bich′rī will do us more harm than Ab′sa·lom. Take your lord's servants and pursue him, lest he find for himself fortified cities, and escape us."

7 So Jō′ab's men, with the Cher′e·thītes, the Pel′eth·ītes, and all the mighty men, went out after him. And they went out of Jerusalem to pursue Shē′ba the son of Bich′rī.

8 When they *were* at the large stone which *is* in Gib′e·on, A·mā′sa came before them. Now Jō′ab was dressed in battle armor; on it was a belt *with* a sword fastened in its sheath at his hips; and as he was going forward, it fell out.

9 Then Jō′ab said to A·mā′sa, "*Are* you in health, my brother?" And Jō′ab took A·mā′sa by the beard with his right hand to kiss him.

10 But A·mā′sa did not notice the sword that *was* in Jō′ab's hand. And he struck him with it in the stomach, and his entrails poured out on the ground; and he did not *strike* him again. Thus he died. Then Jō′ab and A·bi′shaī his brother pursued Shē′ba the son of Bich′rī.

11 Meanwhile one of Jō′ab's men stood near A·mā′sa, and said, "Whoever favors Jō′ab and whoever *is* for David—follow Jō′ab!"

12 But A·mā′sa wallowed in *his* blood in the middle of the highway.

20:1 *a*Literally *man of Belial*

And when the man saw that all the people stood still, he moved A·mā′sa from the highway to the field and threw a garment over him, when he saw that everyone who came upon him halted.

13 When he was removed from the highway, all the people went on after Jō′ab to pursue Shē′ba the son of Bich′rī.

14 And he went through all the tribes of Israel to Abel and Beth Mā′a·chah and all the Be′rītes. So they were gathered together and also went after Shē′ba.ᵃ

15 Then they came and besieged him in Abel of Beth Mā′a·chah; and they cast up a siege mound against the city, and it stood by the rampart. And all the people who *were* with Jō′ab battered the wall to throw it down.

16 Then a wise woman cried out from the city, "Hear, hear! Please say to Jō′ab, 'Come nearby, that I may speak with you.' "

17 When he had come near to her, the woman said, "*Are* you Jō′ab?" He answered, "I *am*." Then she said to him, "Hear the words of your maidservant." And he answered, "I am listening."

18 So she spoke, saying, "They used to talk in former times, saying, 'They shall surely seek *guidance* at Abel,' and so they would end *disputes*.

19 "I *am among the* peaceable *and* faithful in Israel. You seek to destroy a city and a mother in Israel. Why would you swallow up the inheritance of the LORD?"

20 And Jō′ab answered and said, "Far be it, far be it from me, that I should swallow up or destroy!

21 "That *is* not so. But a man from the mountains of Ē′phra·im, Shē′ba the son of Bich′rī by name, has raised his hand against the king, against David. Deliver him only, and I will depart from the city." So the woman

said to Jō′ab, "Watch, his head will be thrown to you over the wall."

22 Then the woman in her wisdom went to all the people. And they cut off the head of Shē′ba the son of Bich′rī, and threw *it* out to Jō′ab. Then he blew a trumpet, and they withdrew from the city, every man to his tent. So Jō′ab returned to the king at Jerusalem.

DAVID'S GOVERNMENT OFFICERS

23 And Jō′ab *was* over all the army of Israel; Be·nā′i·ah the son of Je·hoi′a·da *was* over the Cher′e·thītes and the Pel′eth·ītes;

24 A·dor′am *was* in charge of revenue; Je·hosh′a·phat the son of A·hī′lud *was* recorder;

25 Shē′va *was* scribe; Zā′dok and A·bī′a·thar *were* the priests;

26 and Ī′ra the Jā′i·rīte was a chief minister under David.

DAVID AVENGES THE GIBEONITES

21 Now there was a famine in the days of David for three years, year after year; and David inquired of the LORD. And the LORD answered, "*It is* because of Saul and *his* bloodthirsty house, because he killed the Gib′e·on·ītes."

2 So the king called the Gib′e·on·ītes and spoke to them. Now the Gib′e·on·ītes *were* not of the children of Israel, but of the remnant of the Am′o·rītes; the children of Israel had sworn protection to them, but Saul had sought to kill them in his zeal for the children of Israel and Judah.

3 Therefore David said to the Gib′e·on·ītes, "What shall I do for you? And with what shall I make atonement, that you may bless the inheritance of the LORD?"

20:14 ᵃLiterally *him*

4   And the Gib′ē·on·ītes said to him,
"We will have no silver or gold from
Saul or from his house, nor shall you
kill any man in Israel for us." So he
said, "Whatever you say, I will do for
you."
5   Then they answered the king, "As
for the man who consumed us and
plotted against us, *that* we should be
destroyed from remaining in any of
the territories of Israel,
6   "let seven men of his descendants
be delivered to us, and we will hang
them before the LORD in Gib′ē·ah of
Saul, *whom* the LORD chose." And the
king said, "I will give *them*."
7   But the king spared Me·phib′-
o·sheth the son of Jonathan, the son
of Saul, because of the LORD's oath
that *was* between them, between David and Jonathan the son of Saul.
8   So the king took Ar·mō′nī and
Me·phib′o·sheth, the two sons of
Riz′pah the daughter of Ā′i·ah, whom
she bore to Saul, and the five sons of
Mī′chal*a* the daughter of Saul, whom
she brought up for Ā′dri·el the son of
Bar·zil′lai the Me·hō′la·thīte;
9   and he delivered them into the
hands of the Gib′ē·on·ītes, and they
hanged them on the hill before the
LORD. So they fell, *all* seven together,
and were put to death in the days of
harvest, in the first *days,* in the beginning of barley harvest.
10   Now Riz′pah the daughter of
Ā′i·ah took sackcloth and spread it
for herself on the rock, from the beginning of harvest until the late rains
poured on them from heaven. And
she did not allow the birds of the air
to rest on them by day nor the beasts
of the field by night.
11   And David was told what Riz′pah
the daughter of Ā′i·ah, the concubine
of Saul, had done.
12   Then David went and took the
bones of Saul, and the bones of Jonathan his son, from the men of Jā′besh

Gil′ē·ad who had stolen them from
the street of Beth Shan,*a* where the
Phi·lis′tines had hung them up, after
the Phi·lis′tines had struck down
Saul in Gil·bō′a.
13   So he brought up the bones of
Saul and the bones of Jonathan his
son from there; and they gathered
the bones of those who had been
hanged.
14   They buried the bones of Saul and
Jonathan his son in the country of
Benjamin in Zē′lah, in the tomb of
Kish his father. So they performed all
that the king commanded. And after
that God heeded the prayer for the
land.

PHILISTINE GIANTS DESTROYED

15   When the Phi·lis′tines were at
war again with Israel, David and his
servants with him went down and
fought against the Phi·lis′tines; and
David grew faint.
16   Then Ish′bi-Bē′nob, who *was* one
of the sons of the giant, the weight of
whose bronze spear *was* three hundred *shekels,* who was bearing a new
sword, thought he could kill David.
17   But A·bi′shaī the son of Ze·rū′i·ah
came to his aid, and struck the
Phi·lis′tine and killed him. Then the
men of David swore to him, saying,
"You shall go out no more with us to
battle, lest you quench the lamp of Israel."
18   Now it happened afterward that
there was again a battle with the Phi-
lis′tines at Gob. Then Sib′be·chaī the
Hū′sha·thīte killed Saph,*a* who *was*
one of the sons of the giant.
19   Again there was war at Gob with
the Phi·lis′tines, where El·hā′nan the

21:8 *a*Or *Merab* (compare 1 Samuel 18:19 and
25:44; 2 Samuel 3:14 and 6:23)   21:12 *a*Spelled
Beth Shean in Joshua 17:11 and elsewhere
21:18 *a*Spelled *Sippai* in 1 Chronicles 20:4

son of Jā′a·rē-Or′e·gim*a* the Beth′le-hem·īte killed *the brother of* Goliath the Git′tīte, the shaft of whose spear *was* like a weaver's beam. 20 Yet again there was war at Gath, where there was a man of *great* stature, who had six fingers on each hand and six toes on each foot, twenty-four in number; and he also was born to the giant. 21 So when he defied Israel, Jonathan the son of Shim′e·a,*a* David's brother, killed him. 22 These four were born to the giant in Gath, and fell by the hand of David and by the hand of his servants.

PRAISE FOR GOD'S DELIVERANCE

22 Then David spoke to the LORD the words of this song, on the day when the LORD had delivered him from the hand of all his enemies, and from the hand of Saul. 2 And he said:*a*

"The LORD *is* my rock and my fortress and my deliverer;
3 The God of my strength, in whom I will trust;
My shield and the horn of my salvation,
My stronghold and my refuge;
My Savior, You save me from violence.
4 I will call upon the LORD, *who is worthy* to be praised;
So shall I be saved from my enemies.

5 "When the waves of death surrounded me,
The floods of ungodliness made me afraid.
6 The sorrows of Shē′ōl surrounded me;
The snares of death confronted me.

7 In my distress I called upon the LORD,
And cried out to my God;
He heard my voice from His temple,
And my cry *entered* His ears.

8 "Then the earth shook and trembled;
The foundations of heaven*a* quaked and were shaken,
Because He was angry.
9 Smoke went up from His nostrils,
And devouring fire from His mouth;
Coals were kindled by it.
10 He bowed the heavens also, and came down
With darkness under His feet.
11 He rode upon a cherub, and flew;
And He was seen*a* upon the wings of the wind.
12 He made darkness canopies around Him,
Dark waters *and* thick clouds of the skies.
13 From the brightness before Him
Coals of fire were kindled.

14 "The LORD thundered from heaven,
And the Most High uttered His voice.
15 He sent out arrows and scattered them;
Lightning bolts, and He vanquished them.
16 Then the channels of the sea were seen,
The foundations of the world were uncovered,
At the rebuke of the LORD,

21:19 *a*Spelled *Jair* in 1 Chronicles 20:5
21:21 *a*Spelled *Shammah* in 1 Samuel 16:9 and elsewhere   22:2 *a*Compare Psalm 18
22:8 *a*Following Masoretic Text, Septuagint, and Targum; Syriac and Vulgate read *hills* (compare Psalm 18:7).   22:11 *a*Following Masoretic Text and Septuagint; many Hebrew manuscripts, Syriac, and Vulgate read *He flew* (compare Psalm 18:10); Targum reads *He spoke with power.*

At the blast of the breath of His
  nostrils.

17 "He sent from above, He took me,
  He drew me out of many waters.
18 He delivered me from my strong
  enemy,
  From those who hated me;
  For they were too strong for me.
19 They confronted me in the day of
  my calamity,
  But the LORD was my support.
20 He also brought me out into a
  broad place;
  He delivered me because He
  delighted in me.

21 "The LORD rewarded me according
  to my righteousness;
  According to the cleanness of my
  hands
  He has recompensed me.
22 For I have kept the ways of the
  LORD,
  And have not wickedly departed
  from my God.
23 For all His judgments *were* before
  me;
  And *as for* His statutes, I did not
  depart from them.
24 I was also blameless before Him,
  And I kept myself from my
  iniquity.

25 Therefore the LORD has
  recompensed me according
  to my righteousness,
  According to my cleanness in His
  eyes.*a*

26 "With the merciful You will show
  Yourself merciful;
  With a blameless man You will
  show Yourself blameless;
27 With the pure You will show
  Yourself pure;
  And with the devious You will
  show Yourself shrewd.
28 You will save the humble people;
  But Your eyes *are* on the haughty,
  that You may bring *them* down.

29 "For You *are* my lamp, O LORD;
  The LORD shall enlighten my
  darkness.
30 For by You I can run against a
  troop;
  By my God I can leap over a wall.
31 *As for* God, His way *is* perfect;
  The word of the LORD *is* proven;
  He *is* a shield to all who trust in
  Him.

32 "For who *is* God, except the LORD?

22:25 *a*Septuagint, Syriac, and Vulgate read *the cleanness of my hands in His sight* (compare Psalm 18:24); Targum reads *my cleanness before His word.*

THANKSGIVING 2 Samuel 22:50

A Gift Worth More than Jewels

What is the most precious gift you can give to God? Is it the largest diamond in the world? Is it the biggest emerald or ruby or other precious stone? Is it gold or silver? What is it?

1. Read 2 Samuel 22:50. We should give some of our money, or jewels and gold, to God's helpers for God's work. That's how God's helpers can keep on doing His work. But God Himself doesn't need these things. What does this verse say we should give Him? What gift would He appreciate most?

2. Why are praise and thanksgiving to God such wonderful gifts? Why are these more wonderful than jewels and gold? Will you give God the precious gift of praise today? Will you do it now?

For more on *Favorite Bible Words* turn to page 624
For more on *Giving* turn to page 572

And who *is* a rock, except our
    God?
33 God *is* my strength *and* power,*a*
And He makes my*b* way perfect.
34 He makes my*a* feet like the *feet* of
    deer,
And sets me on my high places.
35 He teaches my hands to make
    war,
So that my arms can bend a bow
    of bronze.

36 "You have also given me the shield
    of Your salvation;
Your gentleness has made me
    great.
37 You enlarged my path under me;
So my feet did not slip.

38 "I have pursued my enemies and
    destroyed them;
Neither did I turn back again till
    they were destroyed.
39 And I have destroyed them and
    wounded them,
So that they could not rise;
They have fallen under my feet.

40 For You have armed me with
    strength for the battle;
You have subdued under me those
    who rose against me.
41 You have also given me the necks
    of my enemies,
So that I destroyed those who
    hated me.
42 They looked, but *there was* none
    to save;
Even to the LORD, but He did not
    answer them.
43 Then I beat them as fine as the
    dust of the earth;
I trod them like dirt in the
    streets,
And I spread them out.

44 "You have also delivered me from
    the strivings of my people;

22:33 *a*Dead Sea Scrolls, Septuagint, Syriac, and Vulgate read *It is God who arms me with strength* (compare Psalm 18:32); Targum reads *It is God who sustains me with strength.* *b*Following Qere, Septuagint, Syriac, Targum, and Vulgate (compare Psalm 18:32); Kethib reads *His.* 22:34 *a*Following Qere, Septuagint, Syriac, Targum, and Vulgate (compare Psalm 18:33); Kethib reads *His.*

You have kept me as the head of
the nations.
A people I have not known shall
serve me.
45 The foreigners submit to me;
As soon as they hear, they obey
me.
46 The foreigners fade away,
And come frightened*a* from their
hideouts.

47 "The LORD lives!
Blessed *be* my Rock!
Let God be exalted,
The Rock of my salvation!
48 *It is* God who avenges me,
And subdues the peoples under
me;
49 He delivers me from my enemies.
You also lift me up above those
who rise against me;
You have delivered me from the
violent man.
50 Therefore I will give thanks to
You, O LORD, among the
Gentiles,
And sing praises to Your name.

51 "*He is* the tower of salvation to His
king,
And shows mercy to His anointed,
To David and his descendants
forevermore."

DAVID'S LAST WORDS

23 Now these *are* the last words
of David.

Thus says David the son of Jesse;
Thus says the man raised up on
high,
The anointed of the God of Jacob,
And the sweet psalmist of Israel:

2 "The Spirit of the LORD spoke by
me,
And His word *was* on my tongue.

3 The God of Israel said,
The Rock of Israel spoke to me:
'He who rules over men *must be*
just,
Ruling in the fear of God.
4 And *he shall be* like the light of
the morning *when* the sun
rises,
A morning without clouds,
Like the tender grass *springing*
out of the earth,
By clear shining after rain.'

5 "Although my house *is* not so with
God,
Yet He has made with me an
everlasting covenant,
Ordered in all *things* and secure.
For *this is* all my salvation and
all *my* desire;
Will He not make *it* increase?
6 But *the sons* of rebellion *shall* all
be as thorns thrust away,
Because they cannot be taken
with hands.
7 But the man *who* touches them
Must be armed with iron and the
shaft of a spear,
And they shall be utterly burned
with fire in *their* place."

DAVID'S MIGHTY MEN

8 These *are* the names of the
mighty men whom David had: Jō'-
sheb-Bas·shē'beth*a* the Tach'mo·nīte,
chief among the captains.*b* He was
called Ad'i·nō the Ez'nīte, because he
had killed eight hundred men at one
time.
9 And after him *was* El·ē·ā'zar the
son of Dodo,*a* the A·hō'hīte, *one of the
three mighty men with David when

22:46 *a*Following Septuagint, Targum, and Vulgate
(compare Psalm 18:45); Masoretic Text reads *gird
themselves.*   23:8 *a*Literally *One Who Sits in the
Seat* (compare 1 Chronicles 11:11) *b*Following Masoretic Text and Targum; Septuagint and Vulgate
read *the three.*   23:9 *a*Spelled *Dodai* in 1 Chronicles 27:4

they defied the Phi·lis'tines *who* were gathered there for battle, and the men of Israel had retreated.

10 He arose and attacked the Phi·lis'tines until his hand was weary, and his hand stuck to the sword. The LORD brought about a great victory that day; and the people returned after him only to plunder.

11 And after him *was* Sham'mah the son of Ā'gee the Har'a·rīte. The Phi·lis'tines had gathered together into a troop where there was a piece of ground full of lentils. So the people fled from the Phi·lis'tines.

12 But he stationed himself in the middle of the field, defended it, and killed the Phi·lis'tines. So the LORD brought about a great victory.

13 Then three of the thirty chief men went down at harvest time and came to David at the cave of A·dul'lam. And the troop of Phi·lis'tines encamped in the Valley of Reph'a·im.

14 David *was* then in the stronghold, and the garrison of the Phi·lis'tines *was* then *in* Bethlehem.

15 And David said with longing, "Oh, that someone would give me a drink of the water from the well of Bethlehem, which *is* by the gate!"

16 So the three mighty men broke through the camp of the Phi·lis'tines, drew water from the well of Bethlehem that *was* by the gate, and took it and brought *it* to David. Nevertheless he would not drink it, but poured it out to the LORD.

17 And he said, "Far be it from me, O LORD, that I should do this! Is *this* not the blood of the men who went in *jeopardy of* their lives?" Therefore he would not drink it. These things were done by the three mighty men.

18 Now A·bi'shaī the brother of Jō'ab, the son of Ze·rū'i·ah, was chief of *another* three.ᵃ He lifted his spear against three hundred *men,* killed them, and won a name among *these* three.

19 Was he not the most honored of three? Therefore he became their captain. However, he did not attain to the *first* three.

20 Be·nā'i·ah *was* the son of Je·hoi'a·da, the son of a valiant man from Kab'zē·el, who had done many deeds. He had killed two lion-like heroes of Mō'ab. He also had gone down and killed a lion in the midst of a pit on a snowy day.

21 And he killed an Egyptian, a spectacular man. The Egyptian *had* a spear in his hand; so he went down to him with a staff, wrested the spear out of the Egyptian's hand, and killed him with his own spear.

22 These *things* Be·nā'i·ah the son of Je·hoi'a·da did, and won a name among three mighty men.

23 He was more honored than the thirty, but he did not attain to the *first* three. And David appointed him over his guard.

24 As'a·hel the brother of Jō'ab *was* one of the thirty; El·hā'nan the son of Dodo of Bethlehem,

25 Sham'mah the Har'od·īte, E·lī'ka the Har'od·īte,

26 Hē'lez the Pal'tīte, Ī'ra the son of Ik'kesh the Te·kō'īte,

27 Ā·bi·ē'zer the An'a·thoth·īte, Me·bun'nai the Hū'sha·thīte,

28 Zal'mon the A·hō'hīte, Mā'ha·raī the Ne·toph'a·thīte,

29 Hē'leb the son of Bā'a·nah (the Ne·toph'a·thīte), It'tai the son of Rī'bai from Gib'ē·ah of the children of Benjamin,

30 Be·nā'i·ah a Pir'a·thon·īte, Hid'daī from the brooks of Gā'ash,

31 Ā'bi-Al'bon the Ar'ba·thīte, Az'ma·veth the Bar·hū'mīte,

23:18 ᵃFollowing Masoretic Text, Septuagint, and Vulgate; some Hebrew manuscripts and Syriac read *thirty;* Targum reads *the mighty men.*

32 Ē·lī'ah·ba the Shā·al'bon·īte (of the sons of Jā'shen), Jonathan,

33 Sham'mah the Har'a·rīte, A·hī'am the son of Shar'ar the Har'a·rīte,

34 E·liph'e·let the son of A·has'baī, the son of the Mā'a·cha·thīte, E·lī'am the son of A·hith'o·phel the Gī'lo·nīte,

35 Hez'raīa the Car'mel·īte, Pā'a·raī the Ar'bīte,

36 Ī'gal the son of Nathan of Zō'bah, Bā'nī the Gad'īte,

37 Zē'lek the Am'mon·īte, Nā'ha·raī the Be·er'oth·īte (armorbearer of Jō'ab the son of Ze·rū'i·ah),

38 Ī'ra the Ith'rīte, Gā'reb the Ith'rīte,

39 and Ū·rī'ah the Hit'tīte: thirty-seven in all.

DAVID'S CENSUS OF ISRAEL AND JUDAH

24 Again the anger of the LORD was aroused against Israel, and He moved David against them to say, "Go, number Israel and Judah."

2 So the king said to Jō'ab the commander of the army who *was* with him, "Now go throughout all the tribes of Israel, from Dan to Bē·er·shē'ba, and count the people, that I may know the number of the people."

3 And Jō'ab said to the king, "Now may the LORD your God add to the people a hundred times more than there are, and may the eyes of my lord the king see *it*. But why does my lord the king desire this thing?"

4 Nevertheless the king's word prevailed against Jō'ab and against the captains of the army. Therefore Jō'ab and the captains of the army went out from the presence of the king to count the people of Israel.

5 And they crossed over the Jordan and camped in A·rō'er, on the right side of the town which *is* in the midst of the ravine of Gad, and toward Jā'zer.

6 Then they came to Gil'ē·ad and to the land of Tah'tim Hod'shī; they came to Dan Jā'an and around to Sī'don;

7 and they came to the stronghold of Tyre and to all the cities of the Hī'vītes and the Cā'naan·ītes. Then they went out to South Judah *as far as* Bē·er·shē'ba.

8 So when they had gone through all the land, they came to Jerusalem at the end of nine months and twenty days.

9 Then Jō'ab gave the sum of the number of the people to the king. And there were in Israel eight hundred thousand valiant men who drew the sword, and the men of Judah were five hundred thousand men.

THE JUDGMENT ON DAVID'S SIN

10 And David's heart condemned him after he had numbered the people. So David said to the LORD, "I have sinned greatly in what I have done; but now, I pray, O LORD, take away the iniquity of Your servant, for I have done very foolishly."

11 Now when David arose in the morning, the word of the LORD came to the prophet Gad, David's seer, saying,

12 "Go and tell David, 'Thus says the LORD: "I offer you three *things;* choose one of them for yourself, that I may do *it* to you." ' "

13 So Gad came to David and told him; and he said to him, "Shall sevena years of famine come to you in your land? Or shall you flee three months before your enemies, while they pursue you? Or shall there be three days' plague in your land? Now

23:35 aSpelled *Hezro* in 1 Chronicles 11:37
24:13 aFollowing Masoretic Text, Syriac, Targum, and Vulgate; Septuagint reads *three* (compare 1 Chronicles 21:12).

WHAT DO I DO WITH MISTAKES? 2 Samuel 24:10

Which boy has made a mistake? "I'm sorry," he says. Now he will turn his board up the right way. Everyone will be happy now.

1. Do you ever make mistakes? What are some mistakes that you have made?
2. What should you say when you make a mistake? What should you do then? Will that make you happy?
3. When you do something wrong, what should you say to God? What should you do to make things right? Will that make you happy?

For more on *What Should I Do?* turn to page 510
For more on *Forgiveness* turn to page 778

consider and see what answer I should take back to Him who sent me."

14 And David said to Gad, "I am in great distress. Please let us fall into the hand of the LORD, for His mercies *are* great; but do not let me fall into the hand of man."

15 So the LORD sent a plague upon Israel from the morning till the appointed time. From Dan to Bē·er-shē'ba seventy thousand men of the people died.

16 And when the angel[a] stretched out His hand over Jerusalem to destroy it, the LORD relented from the destruction, and said to the angel who was destroying the people, "It is enough; now restrain your hand." And the angel of the LORD was by the threshing floor of A·rau'nah[b] the Jeb'ū·sīte.

17 Then David spoke to the LORD when he saw the angel who was striking the people, and said, "Surely I have sinned, and I have done wickedly; but these sheep, what have they done? Let Your hand, I pray, be against me and against my father's house."

THE ALTAR ON THE THRESHING FLOOR

18 And Gad came that day to David and said to him, "Go up, erect an altar to the LORD on the threshing floor of A·rau'nah the Jeb'ū·sīte."

19 So David, according to the word of Gad, went up as the LORD commanded.

20 Now A·rau'nah looked, and saw the king and his servants coming toward him. So A·rau'nah went out and bowed before the king with his face to the ground.

21 Then A·rau'nah said, "Why has my lord the king come to his servant?" And David said, "To buy the threshing floor from you, to build an altar to the LORD, that the plague may be withdrawn from the people."

22 Now A·rau'nah said to David, "Let my lord the king take and offer up whatever *seems* good to him. Look, *here are* oxen for burnt sacrifice, and threshing implements and the yokes of the oxen for wood.

23 "All these, O king, A·rau'nah has given to the king." And A·rau'nah said to the king, "May the LORD your God accept you."

24 Then the king said to A·rau'nah, "No, but I will surely buy *it* from you for a price; nor will I offer burnt offerings to the LORD my God with that which costs me nothing." So David bought the threshing floor and the oxen for fifty shekels of silver.

25 And David built there an altar to the LORD, and offered burnt offerings and peace offerings. So the LORD heeded the prayers for the land, and the plague was withdrawn from Israel.

24:16 [a]Or *Angel*   [b]Spelled *Ornan* in 1 Chronicles 21:15

The First Book of the
KINGS

NOW King David was old, advanced in years; and they put covers on him, but he could not get warm.
2 Therefore his servants said to him, "Let a young woman, a virgin, be sought for our lord the king, and let her stand before the king, and let her care for him; and let her lie in your bosom, that our lord the king may be warm."
3 So they sought for a lovely young woman throughout all the territory of Israel, and found Ab′i·shag the Shū′nam·mīte, and brought her to the king.
4 The young woman *was* very lovely; and she cared for the king, and served him; but the king did not know her.
5 Then Ad·o·nī′jah the son of Hag′-gith exalted himself, saying, "I will be king"; and he prepared for himself chariots and horsemen, and fifty men to run before him.
6 (And his father had not rebuked him at any time by saying, "Why have you done so?" He *was* also very good-looking. *His mother* had borne him after Ab′sa·lom.)
7 Then he conferred with Jō′ab the son of Ze·rū′i·ah and with A·bī′a·thar the priest, and they followed and helped Ad·o·nī′jah.
8 But Zā′dok the priest, Be·nā′i·ah the son of Je·hoi′a·da, Nathan the prophet, Shim′e·ī, Rē′ī, and the mighty men who *belonged* to David were not with Ad·o·nī′jah.
9 And Ad·o·nī′jah sacrificed sheep and oxen and fattened cattle by the stone of Zō′he·leth, which *is* by En Rō′gel; he also invited all his brothers, the king's sons, and all the men of Judah, the king's servants.
10 But he did not invite Nathan the prophet, Be·nā′i·ah, the mighty men, or Solomon his brother.
11 So Nathan spoke to Bath·shē′ba the mother of Solomon, saying, "Have you not heard that Ad·o·nī′jah the son of Hag′gith has become king, and David our lord does not know *it?*
12 "Come, please, let me now give you advice, that you may save your own life and the life of your son Solomon.
13 "Go immediately to King David and say to him, 'Did you not, my lord, O king, swear to your maidservant, saying, "Assuredly your son Solomon shall reign after me, and he shall sit on my throne"? Why then has Ad·o·nī′jah become king?'
14 "Then, while you are still talking there with the king, I also will come in after you and confirm your words."
15 So Bath·shē′ba went into the chamber to the king. (Now the king was very old, and Ab′i·shag the Shū′nam·mīte was serving the king.)
16 And Bath·shē′ba bowed and did homage to the king. Then the king said, "What is your wish?"
17 Then she said to him, "My lord, you swore by the LORD your God to your maidservant, *saying,* 'Assuredly Solomon your son shall reign after me, and he shall sit on my throne.'
18 "So now, look! Ad·o·nī′jah has become king; and now, my lord the king, you do not know about *it.*
19 "He has sacrificed oxen and fattened cattle and sheep in abundance, and has invited all the sons of the king, A·bī′a·thar the priest, and Jō′ab the commander of the army; but Solomon your servant he has not invited.
20 "And as for you, my lord, O king, the eyes of all Israel *are* on you, that you should tell them who will sit on the throne of my lord the king after him.

21 "Otherwise it will happen, when my lord the king rests with his fathers, that I and my son Solomon will be counted as offenders."

22 And just then, while she was still talking with the king, Nathan the prophet also came in.

23 So they told the king, saying, "Here is Nathan the prophet." And when he came in before the king, he bowed down before the king with his face to the ground.

24 And Nathan said, "My lord, O king, have you said, 'Ad·o·ni′jah shall reign after me, and he shall sit on my throne'?

25 "For he has gone down today, and has sacrificed oxen and fattened cattle and sheep in abundance, and has invited all the king's sons, and the commanders of the army, and A·bi′-a·thar the priest; and look! They are eating and drinking before him; and they say, 'Long live King Ad·o·ni′jah!'

26 "But he has not invited me—me your servant—nor Za′dok the priest, nor Be·na′i·ah the son of Je·hoi′a·da, nor your servant Solomon.

27 "Has this thing been done by my lord the king, and you have not told your servant who should sit on the throne of my lord the king after him?"

David Proclaims Solomon King

28 Then King David answered and said, "Call Bath·she′ba to me." So she came into the king's presence and stood before the king.

29 And the king took an oath and said, "As the LORD lives, who has redeemed my life from every distress,

30 "just as I swore to you by the LORD God of Israel, saying, 'Assuredly Solomon your son shall be king after me, and he shall sit on my throne in my place,' so I certainly will do this day."

31 Then Bath·she′ba bowed with *her* face to the earth, and paid homage to the king, and said, "Let my lord King David live forever!"

32 And King David said, "Call to me Za′dok the priest, Nathan the prophet, and Be·na′i·ah the son of Je·hoi′a·da." So they came before the king.

33 The king also said to them, "Take with you the servants of your lord, and have Solomon my son ride on my own mule, and take him down to Gi′hon.

34 "There let Za′dok the priest and Nathan the prophet anoint him king over Israel; and blow the horn, and say, '*Long* live King Solomon!'

35 "Then you shall come up after him, and he shall come and sit on my throne, and he shall be king in my place. For I have appointed him to be ruler over Israel and Judah."

36 Be·na′i·ah the son of Je·hoi′a·da answered the king and said, "Amen! May the LORD God of my lord the king say so *too*.

37 "As the LORD has been with my lord the king, even so may He be with Solomon, and make his throne greater than the throne of my lord King David."

38 So Za′dok the priest, Nathan the prophet, Be·na′i·ah the son of Je·hoi′a·da, the Cher′e·thites, and the Pel′eth·ites went down and had Solomon ride on King David's mule, and took him to Gi′hon.

39 Then Za′dok the priest took a horn of oil from the tabernacle and anointed Solomon. And they blew the horn, and all the people said, "*Long* live King Solomon!"

40 And all the people went up after him; and the people played the flutes and rejoiced with great joy, so that the earth *seemed to* split with their sound.

41 Now Ad·o·ni′jah and all the

guests who *were* with him heard *it* as they finished eating. And when Jō'ab heard the sound of the horn, he said, "Why *is* the city in such a noisy uproar?"

42 While he was still speaking, there came Jonathan, the son of A·bī'a·thar the priest. And Ad·o·nī'jah said to him, "Come in, for you *are* a prominent man, and bring good news."

43 Then Jonathan answered and said to Ad·o·nī'jah, "No! Our lord King David has made Solomon king.

44 "The king has sent with him Zā'-dok the priest, Nathan the prophet, Be·nā'i·ah the son of Je·hoi'a·da, the Cher'e·thītes, and the Pel'eth·ītes; and they have made him ride on the king's mule.

45 "So Zā'dok the priest and Nathan the prophet have anointed him king at Gī'hon; and they have gone up from there rejoicing, so that the city is in an uproar. This *is* the noise that you have heard.

46 "Also Solomon sits on the throne of the kingdom.

47 "And moreover the king's servants have gone to bless our lord King David, saying, 'May God make the name of Solomon better than your name, and may He make his throne greater than your throne.' Then the king bowed himself on the bed.

48 "Also the king said thus, 'Blessed *be* the LORD God of Israel, who has given *one* to sit on my throne this day, while my eyes see *it!*' "

49 So all the guests who were with Ad·o·nī'jah were afraid, and arose, and each one went his way.

50 Now Ad·o·nī'jah was afraid of Solomon; so he arose, and went and took hold of the horns of the altar.

51 And it was told Solomon, saying, "Indeed Ad·o·nī'jah is afraid of King Solomon; for look, he has taken hold of the horns of the altar, saying, 'Let King Solomon swear to me today that he will not put his servant to death with the sword.' "

52 Then Solomon said, "If he proves himself a worthy man, not one hair of him shall fall to the earth; but if wickedness is found in him, he shall die."

53 So King Solomon sent them to bring him down from the altar. And he came and fell down before King Solomon; and Solomon said to him, "Go to your house."

DAVID'S INSTRUCTIONS TO SOLOMON

2 Now the days of David drew near that he should die, and he charged Solomon his son, saying:

2 "I go the way of all the earth; be strong, therefore, and prove yourself a man.

3 "And keep the charge of the LORD your God: to walk in His ways, to keep His statutes, His commandments, His judgments, and His testimonies, as it is written in the Law of Moses, that you may prosper in all that you do and wherever you turn;

4 "that the LORD may fulfill His word which He spoke concerning me, saying, 'If your sons take heed to their way, to walk before Me in truth with all their heart and with all their soul,' He said, 'you shall not lack a man on the throne of Israel.'

5 "Moreover you know also what Jō'ab the son of Ze·rū'i·ah did to me, *and* what he did to the two commanders of the armies of Israel, to Abner the son of Ner and A·mā'sa the son of Jē'ther, whom he killed. And he shed the blood of war in peacetime, and put the blood of war on his belt that *was* around his waist, and on his sandals that *were* on his feet.

6 "Therefore do according to your wisdom, and do not let his gray hair go down to the grave in peace.

7 "But show kindness to the sons of Bar·zil'lai the Gil'e·ad·ite, and let them be among those who eat at your table, for so they came to me when I fled from Ab'sa·lom your brother.

8 "And see, *you have* with you Shim'e·i the son of Gē'ra, a Ben'ja·mīte from Ba·hū'rim, who cursed me with a malicious curse in the day when I went to Mā·ha·na'im. But he came down to meet me at the Jordan, and I swore to him by the LORD, saying, 'I will not put you to death with the sword.'

9 "Now therefore, do not hold him guiltless, for you *are* a wise man and know what you ought to do to him; but bring his gray hair down to the grave with blood."

DEATH OF DAVID

10 So David rested with his fathers, and was buried in the City of David.

11 The period that David reigned over Israel *was* forty years; seven years he reigned in Hē'bron, and in Jerusalem he reigned thirty-three years.

12 Then Solomon sat on the throne of his father David; and his kingdom was firmly established.

SOLOMON EXECUTES ADONIJAH

13 Now Ad·o·nī'jah the son of Hag'gith came to Bath·shē'ba the mother of Solomon. So she said, "Do you come peaceably?" And he said, "Peaceably."

14 Moreover he said, "I have something *to say* to you." And she said, "Say it."

15 Then he said, "You know that the kingdom was mine, and all Israel had set their expectations on me, that I should reign. However, the kingdom has been turned over, and has be-come my brother's; for it was his from the LORD.

16 "Now I ask one petition of you; do not deny me." And she said to him, "Say it."

17 Then he said, "Please speak to King Solomon, for he will not refuse you, that he may give me Ab'i·shag the Shū'nam·mīte as wife."

18 So Bath·shē'ba said, "Very well, I will speak for you to the king."

19 Bath·shē'ba therefore went to King Solomon, to speak to him for Ad·o·nī'jah. And the king rose up to meet her and bowed down to her, and sat down on his throne and had a throne set for the king's mother; so she sat at his right hand.

20 Then she said, "I desire one small petition of you; do not refuse me." And the king said to her, "Ask it, my mother, for I will not refuse you."

21 So she said, "Let Ab'i·shag the Shū'nam·mīte be given to Ad·o·nī'jah your brother as wife."

22 And King Solomon answered and said to his mother, "Now why do you ask Ab'i·shag the Shū'nam·mīte for Ad·o·nī'jah? Ask for him the kingdom also—for he *is* my older brother—for him, and for A·bī'a·thar the priest, and for Jō'ab the son of Ze·rū'i·ah."

23 Then King Solomon swore by the LORD, saying, "May God do so to me, and more also, if Ad·o·nī'jah has not spoken this word against his own life!

24 "Now therefore, *as* the LORD lives, who has confirmed me and set me on the throne of David my father, and who has established a house[a] for me, as He promised, Ad·o·nī'jah shall be put to death today!"

25 So King Solomon sent by the hand of Be·nā'iah the son of Je·hoi'a·da; and he struck him down, and he died.

2:24 [a]That is, a royal dynasty

ABIATHAR EXILED, JOAB EXECUTED

26 And to A·bī'a·thar the priest the king said, "Go to An'a·thoth, to your own fields, for you *are* deserving of death; but I will not put you to death at this time, because you carried the ark of the Lord GOD before my father David, and because you were afflicted every time my father was afflicted."

27 So Solomon removed A·bī'a·thar from being priest to the LORD, that he might fulfill the word of the LORD which He spoke concerning the house of Ē'lī at Shī'lōh.

28 Then news came to Jō'ab, for Jō'ab had defected to Ad·o·nī'jah, though he had not defected to Ab'sa·lom. So Jō'ab fled to the tabernacle of the LORD, and took hold of the horns of the altar.

29 And King Solomon was told, "Jō'ab has fled to the tabernacle of the LORD; there *he is,* by the altar." Then Solomon sent Be·nā'i·ah the son of Je·hoi'a·da, saying, "Go, strike him down."

30 So Be·nā'i·ah went to the tabernacle of the LORD, and said to him, "Thus says the king, 'Come out!' " And he said, "No, but I will die here." And Be·nā'i·ah brought back word to the king, saying, "Thus said Jō'ab, and thus he answered me."

31 Then the king said to him, "Do as he has said, and strike him down and bury him, that you may take away from me and from the house of my father the innocent blood which Jō'ab shed.

32 "So the LORD will return his blood on his head, because he struck down two men more righteous and better than he, and killed them with the sword—Abner the son of Ner, the commander of the army of Israel, and A·mā'sa the son of Jē'ther, the com-mander of the army of Judah—though my father David did not know *it.*

33 "Their blood shall therefore return upon the head of Jō'ab and upon the head of his descendants forever. But upon David and his descendants, upon his house and his throne, there shall be peace forever from the LORD."

34 So Be·nā'i·ah the son of Je·hoi'-a·da went up and struck and killed him; and he was buried in his own house in the wilderness.

35 The king put Be·nā'i·ah the son of Je·hoi'a·da in his place over the army, and the king put Zā'dok the priest in the place of A·bī'a·thar.

SHIMEI EXECUTED

36 Then the king sent and called for Shim'ē·ī, and said to him, "Build yourself a house in Jerusalem and dwell there, and do not go out from there anywhere.

37 "For it shall be, on the day you go out and cross the Brook Kid'ron, know for certain you shall surely die; your blood shall be on your own head."

38 And Shim'ē·ī said to the king, "The saying *is* good. As my lord the king has said, so your servant will do." So Shim'ē·ī dwelt in Jerusalem many days.

39 Now it happened at the end of three years, that two slaves of Shim'ē·ī ran away to Ā'chish the son of Mā'a·chah, king of Gath. And they told Shim'ē·ī, saying, "Look, your slaves *are* in Gath!"

40 So Shim'ē·ī arose, saddled his donkey, and went to Ā'chish at Gath to seek his slaves. And Shim'ē·ī went and brought his slaves from Gath.

41 And Solomon was told that

Shim′ē·ī had gone from Jerusalem to Gath and had come back.

42 Then the king sent and called for Shim′ē·ī, and said to him, "Did I not make you swear by the LORD, and warn you, saying, 'Know for certain that on the day you go out and travel anywhere, you shall surely die'? And you said to me, 'The word I have heard *is* good.'

43 "Why then have you not kept the oath of the LORD and the commandment that I gave you?"

44 The king said moreover to Shim′ē·ī, "You know, as your heart acknowledges, all the wickedness that you did to my father David; therefore the LORD will return your wickedness on your own head.

45 "But King Solomon *shall be* blessed, and the throne of David shall be established before the LORD forever."

46 So the king commanded Be·nā′-i·ah the son of Je·hoi′a·da; and he went out and struck him down, and he died. Thus the kingdom was established in the hand of Solomon.

SOLOMON REQUESTS WISDOM

3 Now Solomon made a treaty with Pharaoh king of Egypt, and married Pharaoh's daughter; then he brought her to the City of David until he had finished building his own house, and the house of the LORD, and the wall all around Jerusalem.

2 Meanwhile the people sacrificed at the high places, because there was no house built for the name of the LORD until those days.

3 And Solomon loved the LORD, walking in the statutes of his father David, except that he sacrificed and burned incense at the high places.

David was king for 40 years. Then he died and his son Solomon became king. One night God visited Solomon. God told Solomon he could have anything he wanted. He just had to ask. What would you have asked?

4 Now the king went to Gib′ē·on to sacrifice there, for that *was* the great high place: Solomon offered a thousand burnt offerings on that altar.

5 At Gib′ē·on the LORD appeared to Solomon in a dream by night; and God said, "Ask! What shall I give you?"

6 And Solomon said: "You have shown great mercy to Your servant David my father, because he walked before You in truth, in righteousness, and in uprightness of heart with You; You have continued this great kindness for him, and You have given him a son to sit on his throne, as *it is* this day.

7 "Now, O LORD my God, You have made Your servant king instead of my father David, but I *am* a little child; I do not know *how* to go out or come in.

8 "And Your servant *is* in the midst of Your people whom You have chosen, a great people, too numerous to be numbered or counted.

9 "Therefore give to Your servant an understanding heart to judge Your people, that I may discern between good and evil. For who is able to judge this great people of Yours?"

10 The speech pleased the LORD, that Solomon had asked this thing.

11 Then God said to him: "Because you have asked this thing, and have not asked long life for yourself, nor have asked riches for yourself, nor have asked the life of your enemies, but have asked for yourself understanding to discern justice,

12 "behold, I have done according to

THE BIG-LITTLE CHAMP 1 Kings 3:5–10

That's a big, big ball, and such a little guy. He wants to play in the NFL, but he's not really big enough yet for the sandlot team. Now what? What should he do?

1. Will a professional NFL football team sign up a preschool kid for the team? Why not? What should the preschool kid do if he wants to play football?

2. Can a toddler drive the school bus? Why not? Can a little boy fly an airplane or a little girl drive a tank? Why not? Should they? Why not?

3. What happens when we dream bigger than we can do? It's good to dream, isn't it? But it's also good to dream dreams that we can accomplish. When our dreams are bigger than we are, we may face some *big* disappointments when they don't happen.

4. When you dream dreams, hitch them to your prayers. Ask God to help you get what He wants you to have. Like King Solomon, ask for something that will please God (1 Kings 3:5–10).

For more on *What Should I Do?* turn to page 543
For more on *Prayer* turn to page 586

your words; see, I have given you a wise and understanding heart, so that there has not been anyone like you before you, nor shall any like you arise after you.

13 "And I have also given you what you have not asked: both riches and honor, so that there shall not be anyone like you among the kings all your days.

14 "So if you walk in My ways, to keep My statutes and My commandments, as your father David walked, then I will lengthen your days."

15 Then Solomon awoke; and indeed it had been a dream. And he came to Jerusalem and stood before the ark of the covenant of the LORD, offered up burnt offerings, offered peace offerings, and made a feast for all his servants.

SOLOMON'S WISE JUDGMENT

16 Now two women *who were* harlots came to the king, and stood before him.

17 And one woman said, "O my lord, this woman and I dwell in the same house; and I gave birth while she *was* in the house.

18 "Then it happened, the third day after I had given birth, that this woman also gave birth. And we *were* together; no one *was* with us in the house, except the two of us in the house.

19 "And this woman's son died in the night, because she lay on him.

20 "So she arose in the middle of the night and took my son from my side, while your maidservant slept, and laid him in her bosom, and laid her dead child in my bosom.

21 "And when I rose in the morning to nurse my son, there he was, dead. But when I had examined him in the morning, indeed, he was not my son whom I had borne."

22 Then the other woman said, "No! But the living one *is* my son, and the dead one *is* your son." And the first woman said, "No! But the dead one *is* your son, and the living one *is* my son." Thus they spoke before the king.

23 And the king said, "The one says, 'This *is* my son, who lives, and your son *is* the dead one'; and the other says, 'No! But your son *is* the dead one, and my son *is* the living one.' "

24 Then the king said, "Bring me a sword." So they brought a sword before the king.

25 And the king said, "Divide the living child in two, and give half to one, and half to the other."

26 Then the woman whose son *was* living spoke to the king, for she yearned with compassion for her son; and she said, "O my lord, give her the living child, and by no means kill him!" But the other said, "Let him be neither mine nor yours, *but* divide *him*."

27 So the king answered and said, "Give the first woman the living child, and by no means kill him; she *is* his mother."

✓   *Bible Quiz*

1 Kings 3:4–28   **Solomon Asks God for Wisdom**

1. How did Solomon feel about God?
2. What did God offer to give Solomon? What did Solomon choose?
3. Why did Solomon choose wisdom?
4. Did God give Solomon what he asked for?
5. Do you know what wisdom is? Why is it so important to be wise?

28 And all Israel heard of the judgment which the king had rendered; and they feared the king, for they saw that the wisdom of God *was* in him to administer justice.

SOLOMON'S ADMINISTRATION

4 So King Solomon was king over all Israel.

2 And these *were* his officials: Az·a·rī′ah the son of Zā′dok, the priest;

3 El·i·hor′eph and A·hī′jah, the sons of Shī′sha, scribes; Je·hosh′a·phat the son of A·hī′lud, the recorder;

4 Be·nā′i·ah the son of Je·hoi′a·da, over the army; Zā′dok and A·bī′a·thar, the priests;

5 Az·a·rī′ah the son of Nathan, over the officers; Zā′bud the son of Nathan, a priest *and* the king's friend;

6 A·hī′shar, over the household; and Ad·o·nī′ram the son of Ab′da, over the labor force.

7 And Solomon had twelve governors over all Israel, who provided food for the king and his household; each one made provision for one month of the year.

8 These *are* their names: Ben-Hur,*a* in the mountains of Ē′phra·im;

9 Ben-Dē′ker,*a* in Mā′kaz, Shā·al′bim, Beth Shem′esh, and Ē′lon Beth Hā′nan;

10 Ben-Hē′sed,*a* in A·rūb′both; to him *belonged* Sō′chōh and all the land of Hē′pher;

11 Ben-A·bin′a·dab,*a in* all the regions of Dor; he had Tā′phath the daughter of Solomon as wife;

12 Bā′a·na the son of A·hī′lud, *in* Tā′a·nach, Me·gid′dō, and all Beth Shē′an, which *is* beside Zar′e·tan below Jez′re·el, from Beth Shē′an to Abel Me·hō′lah, as far as the other side of Jok′ne·am;

13 Ben-Gē′ber,*a* in Rā′moth Gil′e·ad; to him *belonged* the towns of Jā′ir

the son of Ma·nas′seh, in Gil′e·ad; to him *also belonged* the region of Ar′gob in Bā′shan—sixty large cities with walls and bronze gate-bars;

14 A·hin′a·dab the son of Id′dō, *in* Mā·ha·na′im;

15 A·him′a·az, in Naph′ta·lī; he also took Bas′e·math the daughter of Solomon as wife;

16 Bā′a·nah the son of Hū′shai, in Ash′er and Ā′loth;

17 Je·hosh′a·phat the son of Pa·rū′ah, in Is′sa·char;

18 Shim′e·ī the son of Ē′lah, in Benjamin;

19 Gē′ber the son of Ū′rī, in the land of Gil′e·ad, *in* the country of Sī′hon king of the Am′o·rītes, and of Og king of Bā′shan. *He was* the only governor who *was* in the land.

PROSPERITY AND WISDOM OF SOLOMON'S REIGN

20 Judah and Israel *were* as numerous as the sand by the sea in multitude, eating and drinking and rejoicing.

21 So Solomon reigned over all kingdoms from the River*a to* the land of the Phi·lis′tines, as far as the border of Egypt. *They* brought tribute and served Solomon all the days of his life.

22 Now Solomon's provision for one day was thirty kors of fine flour, sixty kors of meal,

23 ten fatted oxen, twenty oxen from the pastures, and one hundred sheep, besides deer, gazelles, roebucks, and fatted fowl.

24 For he had dominion over all *the region* on this side of the River*a* from Tiph′sah even to Gā′za, namely over

4:8 *a*Literally *Son of Hur*   4:9 *a*Literally *Son of Deker*   4:10 *a*Literally *Son of Hesed*
4:11 *a*Literally *Son of Abinadab*   4:13 *a*Literally *Son of Geber*   4:21 *a*That is, the Euphrates
4:24 *a*That is, the Euphrates

all the kings on this side of the River; and he had peace on every side all around him.

25 And Judah and Israel dwelt safely, each man under his vine and his fig tree, from Dan as far as Bē·er·shē'ba, all the days of Solomon.

26 Solomon had forty*ᵃ* thousand stalls of horses for his chariots, and twelve thousand horsemen.

27 And these governors, each man in his month, provided food for King Solomon and for all who came to King Solomon's table. There was no lack in their supply.

28 They also brought barley and straw to the proper place, for the horses and steeds, each man according to his charge.

29 And God gave Solomon wisdom and exceedingly great understanding, and largeness of heart like the sand on the seashore.

30 Thus Solomon's wisdom excelled the wisdom of all the men of the East and all the wisdom of Egypt.

31 For he was wiser than all men— than Ē'than the Ez'ra·hīte, and Hē'man, Chal'col, and Dar'da, the sons of Mā'hol; and his fame was in all the surrounding nations.

32 He spoke three thousand proverbs, and his songs were one thousand and five.

33 Also he spoke of trees, from the cedar tree of Lebanon even to the hyssop that springs out of the wall; he spoke also of animals, of birds, of creeping things, and of fish.

34 And men of all nations, from all the kings of the earth who had heard of his wisdom, came to hear the wisdom of Solomon.

SOLOMON PREPARES TO BUILD THE TEMPLE

5 Now Hī'ram king of Tȳre sent his servants to Solomon, because he heard that they had anointed him king in place of his father, for Hī'ram had always loved David.

2 Then Solomon sent to Hī'ram, saying:

3 You know how my father David could not build a house for the name of the LORD his God because of the wars which were fought against him on every side, until the LORD put *his foesᵃ* under the soles of his feet.

4 But now the LORD my God has given me rest on every side; *there is* neither adversary nor evil occurrence.

5 And behold, I propose to build a house for the name of the LORD my God, as the LORD spoke to my father David, saying, "Your son, whom I will set on your throne in your place, he shall build the house for My name."

6 Now therefore, command that they cut down cedars for me from Lebanon; and my servants will be with your servants, and I will pay you wages for your servants according to whatever you say. For you know *there is* none among us who has skill to cut timber like the Sī·dō'ni·ans.

7 So it was, when Hī'ram heard the words of Solomon, that he rejoiced greatly and said,

Blessed *be* the LORD this day, for He has given David a wise son over this great people!

8 Then Hī'ram sent to Solomon, saying:

4:26 ᵃFollowing Masoretic Text and most other authorities; some manuscripts of the Septuagint read *four* (compare 2 Chronicles 9:25).   5:3 ᵃLiterally *them*

I have considered *the message* which you sent me, *and* I will do all you desire concerning the cedar and cypress logs.

9 My servants shall bring *them* down from Lebanon to the sea; I will float them in rafts by sea to the place you indicate to me, and will have them broken apart there; then you can take *them* away. And you shall fulfill my desire by giving food for my household.

10 Then Hī′ram gave Solomon cedar and cypress logs *according to* all his desire.

11 And Solomon gave Hī′ram twenty thousand kors of wheat *as* food for his household, and twenty*a* kors of pressed oil. Thus Solomon gave to Hī′ram year by year.

12 So the LORD gave Solomon wisdom, as He had promised him; and there was peace between Hī′ram and Solomon, and the two of them made a treaty together.

13 Then King Solomon raised up a labor force out of all Israel; and the labor force was thirty thousand men.

14 And he sent them to Lebanon, ten thousand a month in shifts: they were one month in Lebanon *and* two months at home; Ad·o·nī′ram *was* in charge of the labor force.

15 Solomon had seventy thousand who carried burdens, and eighty thousand who quarried *stone* in the mountains,

16 besides three thousand three hundred*a* from the chiefs of Solomon's deputies, who supervised the people who labored in the work.

17 And the king commanded them to quarry large stones, costly stones, *and* hewn stones, to lay the foundation of the temple.*a*

18 So Solomon's builders, Hī′ram's builders, and the Gē′bal·ites quarried *them;* and they prepared timber and stones to build the temple.

SOLOMON BUILDS THE TEMPLE

6 And it came to pass in the four hundred and eightieth*a* year after the children of Israel had come out of the land of Egypt, in the fourth year of Solomon's reign over Israel, in the month of Ziv, which *is* the second month, that he began to build the house of the LORD.

2 Now the house which King Solomon built for the LORD, its length *was* sixty cubits, its width twenty, and its height thirty cubits.

3 The vestibule in front of the sanctuary*a* of the house *was* twenty cubits long across the width of the house, *and* the width of *the vestibule*b *extended* ten cubits from the front of the house.

4 And he made for the house windows with beveled frames.

5 Against the wall of the temple he built chambers all around, *against* the walls of the temple, all around the sanctuary and the inner sanctuary.*a* Thus he made side chambers all around it.

6 The lowest chamber *was* five cubits wide, the middle *was* six cubits wide, and the third *was* seven cubits wide; for he made narrow ledges around the outside of the temple, so that *the support beams* would not be fastened into the walls of the temple.

5:11 *a*Following Masoretic Text, Targum, and Vulgate; Septuagint and Syriac read *twenty thousand.*
5:16 *a*Following Masoretic Text, Targum, and Vulgate; Septuagint reads *three thousand six hundred.*
5:17 *a*Literally *house,* and so frequently throughout this book   6:1 *a*Following Masoretic Text, Targum, and Vulgate; Septuagint reads *fortieth.*
6:3 *a*Hebrew *heykal;* here the main room of the temple, elsewhere called the holy place (compare Exodus 26:33 and Ezekiel 41:1)   *b*Literally *it*
6:5 *a*Hebrew *debir;* here the inner room of the temple, elsewhere called the Most Holy Place (compare verse 16)

7 And the temple, when it was being built, was built with stone finished at the quarry, so that no hammer or chisel *or* any iron tool was heard in the temple while it was being built.

8 The doorway for the middle story*a was* on the right side of the temple. They went up by stairs to the middle *story,* and from the middle to the third.

9 So he built the temple and finished it, and he paneled the temple with beams and boards of cedar.

10 And he built side chambers against the entire temple, each five cubits high; they were attached to the temple with cedar beams.

11 Then the word of the LORD came to Solomon, saying:

12 "*Concerning* this temple which you are building, if you walk in My statutes, execute My judgments, keep all My commandments, and walk in them, then I will perform My word with you, which I spoke to your father David.

13 "And I will dwell among the children of Israel, and will not forsake My people Israel."

14 So Solomon built the temple and finished it.

15 And he built the inside walls of the temple with cedar boards; from the floor of the temple to the ceiling he paneled the inside with wood; and he covered the floor of the temple with planks of cypress.

16 Then he built the twenty-cubit room at the rear of the temple, from floor to ceiling, with cedar boards; he built *it* inside as the inner sanctuary, as the Most Holy *Place.*

17 And in front of it the temple sanctuary was forty cubits *long.*

18 The inside of the temple was cedar, carved with ornamental buds and open flowers. All *was* cedar; there was no stone *to be* seen.

19 And he prepared the inner sanctuary inside the temple, to set the ark of the covenant of the LORD there.

20 The inner sanctuary *was* twenty cubits long, twenty cubits wide, and twenty cubits high. He overlaid it with pure gold, and overlaid the altar of cedar.

21 So Solomon overlaid the inside of the temple with pure gold. He stretched gold chains across the front of the inner sanctuary, and overlaid it with gold.

22 The whole temple he overlaid with gold, until he had finished all the temple; also he overlaid with gold the entire altar that *was* by the inner sanctuary.

23 Inside the inner sanctuary he made two cherubim *of* olive wood, *each* ten cubits high.

24 One wing of the cherub *was* five cubits, and the other wing of the cherub five cubits: ten cubits from the tip of one wing to the tip of the other.

25 And the other cherub *was* ten cubits; both cherubim *were* of the same size and shape.

26 The height of one cherub *was* ten cubits, and so *was* the other cherub.

27 Then he set the cherubim inside the inner room;*a* and they stretched out the wings of the cherubim so that the wing of the one touched *one* wall, and the wing of the other cherub touched the other wall. And their wings touched each other in the middle of the room.

28 Also he overlaid the cherubim with gold.

29 Then he carved all the walls of the temple all around, both the inner and outer *sanctuaries,* with carved figures of cherubim, palm trees, and open flowers.

6:8 *a*Following Masoretic Text and Vulgate; Septuagint reads *upper story;* Targum reads *ground story.*   6:27 *a*Literally *house*

30 And the floor of the temple he overlaid with gold, both the inner and outer *sanctuaries.*

31 For the entrance of the inner sanctuary he made doors *of* olive wood; the lintel *and* doorposts *were* one-fifth *of the wall.*

32 The two doors *were of* olive wood; and he carved on them figures of cherubim, palm trees, and open flowers, and overlaid *them* with gold; and he spread gold on the cherubim and on the palm trees.

33 So for the door of the sanctuary he also made doorposts *of* olive wood, one-fourth *of the wall.*

34 And the two doors *were of* cypress wood; two panels *comprised* one folding door, and two panels *comprised* the other folding door.

35 Then he carved cherubim, palm trees, and open flowers *on them,* and overlaid *them* with gold applied evenly on the carved work.

36 And he built the inner court with three rows of hewn stone and a row of cedar beams.

37 In the fourth year the foundation of the house of the LORD was laid, in the month of Ziv.

38 And in the eleventh year, in the month of Bul, which is the eighth month, the house was finished in all its details and according to all its plans. So he was seven years in building it.

SOLOMON'S OTHER BUILDINGS

7 But Solomon took thirteen years to build his own house; so he finished all his house.

2 He also built the House of the Forest of Lebanon; its length *was* one hundred cubits, its width fifty cubits, and its height thirty cubits, with four rows of cedar pillars, and cedar beams on the pillars.

3 And *it was* paneled with cedar above the beams that *were* on forty-five pillars, fifteen *to* a row.

4 *There were* windows *with beveled frames in* three rows, and window *was* opposite window *in* three tiers.

5 And all the doorways and doorposts *had* rectangular frames; and window *was* opposite window *in* three tiers.

6 He also made the Hall of Pillars: its length *was* fifty cubits, and its width thirty cubits; and in front of them *was* a portico with pillars, and a canopy *was* in front of them.

7 Then he made a hall for the throne, the Hall of Judgment, where he might judge; and *it was* paneled with cedar from floor to ceiling.ᵃ

8 And the house where he dwelt *had* another court inside the hall, of like workmanship. Solomon also made a house like this hall for Pharaoh's daughter, whom he had taken *as wife.*

9 All these *were of* costly stones cut to size, trimmed with saws, inside and out, from the foundation to the eaves, and also on the outside to the great court.

10 The foundation *was of* costly stones, large stones, some ten cubits and some eight cubits.

11 And above *were* costly stones, hewn to size, and cedar wood.

12 The great court *was* enclosed with three rows of hewn stones and a row of cedar beams. So were the inner court of the house of the LORD and the vestibule of the temple.

HIRAM THE CRAFTSMAN

13 Now King Solomon sent and brought Hū′ramᵃ from Tȳre.

7:7 ᵃLiterally *floor,* that is, of the upper level
7:13 ᵃHebrew *Hiram* (compare 2 Chronicles 2:13, 14)

14 He *was* the son of a widow from the tribe of Naph'ta·lī, and his father *was* a man of Tȳre, a bronze worker; he was filled with wisdom and understanding and skill in working with all kinds of bronze work. So he came to King Solomon and did all his work.

THE BRONZE PILLARS FOR THE TEMPLE

15 And he cast two pillars of bronze, each one eighteen cubits high, and a line of twelve cubits measured the circumference of each.

16 Then he made two capitals *of* cast bronze, to set on the tops of the pillars. The height of one capital *was* five cubits, and the height of the other capital *was* five cubits.

17 *He made* a lattice network, with wreaths of chainwork, for the capitals which *were* on top of the pillars: seven chains for one capital and seven for the other capital.

18 So he made the pillars, and two rows of pomegranates above the network all around to cover the capitals that *were* on top; and thus he did for the other capital.

19 The capitals which *were* on top of the pillars in the hall *were* in the shape of lilies, four cubits.

20 The capitals on the two pillars also *had pomegranates* above, by the convex surface which *was* next to the network; and there *were* two hundred such pomegranates in rows on each of the capitals all around.

21 Then he set up the pillars by the vestibule of the temple; he set up the pillar on the right and called its name Jā'chin, and he set up the pillar on the left and called its name Bō'az.

22 The tops of the pillars were in the shape of lilies. So the work of the pillars was finished.

THE SEA AND THE OXEN

23 And he made the Sea of cast bronze, ten cubits from one brim to the other; *it was* completely round. Its height *was* five cubits, and a line of thirty cubits measured its circumference.

24 Below its brim *were* ornamental buds encircling it all around, ten to a cubit, all the way around the Sea. The ornamental buds *were* cast in two rows when it was cast.

25 It stood on twelve oxen: three looking toward the north, three looking toward the west, three looking toward the south, and three looking toward the east; the Sea *was set* upon them, and all their back parts *pointed* inward.

26 It *was* a handbreadth thick; and its brim was shaped like the brim of a cup, *like* a lily blossom. It contained two thousand*a* baths.

THE CARTS AND THE LAVERS

27 He also made ten carts of bronze; four cubits *was* the length of each cart, four cubits its width, and three cubits its height.

28 And this *was* the design of the carts: They had panels, and the panels *were* between frames;

29 on the panels that *were* between the frames *were* lions, oxen, and cherubim. And on the frames *was* a pedestal on top. Below the lions and oxen *were* wreaths of plaited work.

30 Every cart had four bronze wheels and axles of bronze, and its four feet had supports. Under the laver *were* supports of cast *bronze* beside each wreath.

31 Its opening inside the crown at the top *was* one cubit in diameter; and the opening *was* round, shaped

7:26 *a*Or *three thousand* (compare 2 Chronicles 4:5)

like a pedestal, one and a half cubits in outside diameter; and also on the opening *were* engravings, but the panels were square, not round.

32 Under the panels *were* the four wheels, and the axles of the wheels *were joined* to the cart. The height of a wheel *was* one and a half cubits.

33 The workmanship of the wheels *was* like the workmanship of a chariot wheel; their axle pins, their rims, their spokes, and their hubs *were* all of cast *bronze.*

34 And *there were* four supports at the four corners of each cart; its supports *were* part of the cart itself.

35 On the top of the cart, at the height of half a cubit, *it was* perfectly round. And on the top of the cart, its flanges and its panels *were* of the same casting.

36 On the plates of its flanges and on its panels he engraved cherubim, lions, and palm trees, wherever there was a clear space on each, with wreaths all around.

37 Thus he made the ten carts. All of them were of the same mold, one measure, *and* one shape.

38 Then he made ten lavers of bronze; each laver contained forty baths, *and* each laver *was* four cubits. On each of the ten carts *was* a laver.

39 And he put five carts on the right side of the house, and five on the left side of the house. He set the Sea on the right side of the house, toward the southeast.

FURNISHINGS OF THE TEMPLE

40 Hū′ram*ᵃ* made the lavers and the shovels and the bowls. So Hū′ram finished doing all the work that he was to do for King Solomon *for* the house of the LORD:

41 the two pillars, the *two* bowl-shaped capitals that *were* on top of the two pillars; the two networks covering the two bowl-shaped capitals which *were* on top of the pillars;

42 four hundred pomegranates for the two networks (two rows of pomegranates for each network, to cover the two bowl-shaped capitals that *were* on top of the pillars);

43 the ten carts, and ten lavers on the carts;

44 one Sea, and twelve oxen under the Sea;

45 the pots, the shovels, and the bowls. All these articles which Hū′ram*ᵃ* made for King Solomon *for* the house of the LORD *were of* burnished bronze.

46 In the plain of Jordan the king had them cast in clay molds, between Suc′coth and Zar′e·tan.

47 And Solomon did not weigh all the articles, because *there were* so many; the weight of the bronze was not determined.

48 Thus Solomon had all the furnishings made for the house of the LORD: the altar of gold, and the table of gold on which *was* the showbread;

49 the lampstands of pure gold, five on the right *side* and five on the left in front of the inner sanctuary, with the flowers and the lamps and the wick-trimmers of gold;

50 the basins, the trimmers, the bowls, the ladles, and the censers of pure gold; and the hinges of gold, *both* for the doors of the inner room (the Most Holy *Place*) *and* for the doors of the main hall of the temple.

51 So all the work that King Solomon had done for the house of the LORD was finished; and Solomon brought in the things which his father David had dedicated: the silver and the gold and the furnishings. He

7:40 *ᵃ*Hebrew *Hiram* (compare 2 Chronicles 2:13, 14)   7:45 *ᵃ*Hebrew *Hiram* (compare 2 Chronicles 2:13, 14)

put them in the treasuries of the house of the LORD.

THE ARK BROUGHT INTO THE TEMPLE

8 Now Solomon assembled the elders of Israel and all the heads of the tribes, the chief fathers of the children of Israel, to King Solomon in Jerusalem, that they might bring up the ark of the covenant of the LORD from the City of David, which *is* Zion.
2   Therefore all the men of Israel assembled with King Solomon at the feast in the month of Eth′a·nim, which *is* the seventh month.
3   So all the elders of Israel came, and the priests took up the ark.
4   Then they brought up the ark of the LORD, the tabernacle of meeting, and all the holy furnishings that *were* in the tabernacle. The priests and the Lē′vītes brought them up.
5   Also King Solomon, and all the congregation of Israel who were assembled with him, *were* with him before the ark, sacrificing sheep and oxen that could not be counted or numbered for multitude.
6   Then the priests brought in the ark of the covenant of the LORD to its place, into the inner sanctuary of the temple, to the Most Holy *Place,* under the wings of the cherubim.
7   For the cherubim spread *their* two wings over the place of the ark, and the cherubim overshadowed the ark and its poles.
8   The poles extended so that the ends of the poles could be seen from the holy *place,* in front of the inner sanctuary; but they could not be seen from outside. And they are there to this day.
9   Nothing *was* in the ark except the two tablets of stone which Moses put there at Hō′reb, when the LORD made

a covenant with the children of Israel, when they came out of the land of Egypt.
10   And it came to pass, when the priests came out of the holy *place,* that the cloud filled the house of the LORD,
11   so that the priests could not continue ministering because of the cloud; for the glory of the LORD filled the house of the LORD.
12   Then Solomon spoke:

"The LORD said He would dwell in the dark cloud.
13   I have surely built You an exalted house,
And a place for You to dwell in forever."

SOLOMON'S SPEECH AT COMPLETION OF THE WORK

14   Then the king turned around and blessed the whole assembly of Israel, while all the assembly of Israel was standing.
15   And he said: "Blessed *be* the LORD God of Israel, who spoke with His mouth to my father David, and with His hand has fulfilled *it,* saying,
16   'Since the day that I brought My people Israel out of Egypt, I have chosen no city from any tribe of Israel *in which* to build a house, that My name might be there; but I chose David to be over My people Israel.'
17   "Now it was in the heart of my father David to build a temple[a] for the name of the LORD God of Israel.
18   "But the LORD said to my father David, 'Whereas it was in your heart to build a temple for My name, you did well that it was in your heart.
19   'Nevertheless you shall not build the temple, but your son who will

8:17 [a]Literally *house,* and so in verses 18–20

come from your body, he shall build the temple for My name.'

20 "So the LORD has fulfilled His word which He spoke; and I have filled the position of my father David, and sit on the throne of Israel, as the LORD promised; and I have built a temple for the name of the LORD God of Israel.

21 "And there I have made a place for the ark, in which *is* the covenant of the LORD which He made with our fathers, when He brought them out of the land of Egypt."

SOLOMON'S PRAYER OF DEDICATION

22 Then Solomon stood before the altar of the LORD in the presence of all the assembly of Israel, and spread out his hands toward heaven;

23 and he said: "LORD God of Israel, *there is* no God in heaven above or on earth below like You, who keep *Your* covenant and mercy with Your servants who walk before You with all their hearts.

24 "You have kept what You promised Your servant David my father; You have both spoken with Your mouth and fulfilled *it* with Your hand, as *it is* this day.

25 "Therefore, LORD God of Israel, now keep what You promised Your servant David my father, saying, 'You shall not fail to have a man sit before Me on the throne of Israel, only if your sons take heed to their way, that they walk before Me as you have walked before Me.'

26 "And now I pray, O God of Israel, let Your word come true, which You have spoken to Your servant David my father.

27 "But will God indeed dwell on the earth? Behold, heaven and the heaven of heavens cannot contain You. How much less this temple which I have built!

28 "Yet regard the prayer of Your servant and his supplication, O LORD my God, and listen to the cry and the prayer which Your servant is praying before You today:

29 "that Your eyes may be open toward this temple night and day, toward the place of which You said, 'My name shall be there,' that You may hear the prayer which Your servant makes toward this place.

30 "And may You hear the supplication of Your servant and of Your people Israel, when they pray toward this place. Hear in heaven Your dwelling place; and when You hear, forgive.

31 "When anyone sins against his neighbor, and is forced to take an oath, and comes *and* takes an oath before Your altar in this temple,

32 "then hear in heaven, and act, and judge Your servants, condemning the wicked, bringing his way on his head, and justifying the righteous by giving him according to his righteousness.

33 "When Your people Israel are defeated before an enemy because they have sinned against You, and when they turn back to You and confess Your name, and pray and make supplication to You in this temple,

34 "then hear in heaven, and forgive the sin of Your people Israel, and bring them back to the land which You gave to their fathers.

35 "When the heavens are shut up and there is no rain because they have sinned against You, when they pray toward this place and confess Your name, and turn from their sin because You afflict them,

36 "then hear in heaven, and forgive the sin of Your servants, Your people Israel, that You may teach them the good way in which they should walk; and send rain on Your land which

You have given to Your people as an inheritance.

37 "When there is famine in the land, pestilence or blight or mildew, locusts or grasshoppers; when their enemy besieges them in the land of their cities; whatever plague or whatever sickness there is;

38 "whatever prayer, whatever supplication is made by anyone, or by all Your people Israel, when each one knows the plague of his own heart, and spreads out his hands toward this temple:

39 "then hear in heaven Your dwelling place, and forgive, and act, and give to everyone according to all his ways, whose heart You know (for You alone know the hearts of all the sons of men),

40 "that they may fear You all the days that they live in the land which You gave to our fathers.

41 "Moreover, concerning a foreigner, who is not of Your people Israel, but has come from a far country for Your name's sake

42 "(for they will hear of Your great name and Your strong hand and Your outstretched arm), when he comes and prays toward this temple,

43 "hear in heaven Your dwelling place, and do according to all for which the foreigner calls to You, that all peoples of the earth may know Your name and fear You, as do Your people Israel, and that they may know that this temple which I have built is called by Your name.

44 "When Your people go out to battle against their enemy, wherever You send them, and when they pray to the LORD toward the city which You have chosen and the temple which I have built for Your name,

45 "then hear in heaven their prayer and their supplication, and maintain their cause.

46 "When they sin against You (for there is no one who does not sin), and You become angry with them and deliver them to the enemy, and they take them captive to the land of the enemy, far or near;

47 "yet when they come to themselves in the land where they were carried captive, and repent, and make supplication to You in the land of those who took them captive, saying, 'We have sinned and done wrong, we have committed wickedness';

48 "and when they return to You with all their heart and with all their soul in the land of their enemies who led them away captive, and pray to You toward their land which You gave to their fathers, the city which You have chosen and the temple which I have built for Your name:

49 "then hear in heaven Your dwelling place their prayer and their supplication, and maintain their cause,

50 "and forgive Your people who have sinned against You, and all their transgressions which they have transgressed against You; and grant them compassion before those who took them captive, that they may have compassion on them

51 "(for they are Your people and Your inheritance, whom You brought out of Egypt, out of the iron furnace),

52 "that Your eyes may be open to the supplication of Your servant and the supplication of Your people Israel, to listen to them whenever they call to You.

53 "For You separated them from among all the peoples of the earth to be Your inheritance, as You spoke by Your servant Moses, when You brought our fathers out of Egypt, O Lord GOD."

SOLOMON BLESSES THE ASSEMBLY

54 And so it was, when Solomon had finished praying all this prayer and

supplication to the LORD, that he arose from before the altar of the LORD, from kneeling on his knees with his hands spread up to heaven.

55 Then he stood and blessed all the assembly of Israel with a loud voice, saying:

56 "Blessed be the LORD, who has given rest to His people Israel, according to all that He promised. There has not failed one word of all His good promise, which He promised through His servant Moses.

57 "May the LORD our God be with us, as He was with our fathers. May He not leave us nor forsake us,

58 "that He may incline our hearts to Himself, to walk in all His ways, and to keep His commandments and His statutes and His judgments, which He commanded our fathers.

59 "And may these words of mine, with which I have made supplication before the LORD, be near the LORD our God day and night, that He may maintain the cause of His servant and the cause of His people Israel, as each day may require,

60 "that all the peoples of the earth may know that the LORD is God; there is no other.

61 "Let your heart therefore be loyal to the LORD our God, to walk in His statutes and keep His commandments, as at this day."

SOLOMON DEDICATES THE TEMPLE

62 Then the king and all Israel with him offered sacrifices before the LORD.

63 And Solomon offered a sacrifice of peace offerings, which he offered to the LORD, twenty-two thousand bulls and one hundred and twenty thousand sheep. So the king and all the children of Israel dedicated the house of the LORD.

64 On the same day the king conse-crated the middle of the court that was in front of the house of the LORD; for there he offered burnt offerings, grain offerings, and the fat of the peace offerings, because the bronze altar that was before the LORD was too small to receive the burnt offerings, the grain offerings, and the fat of the peace offerings.

65 At that time Solomon held a feast, and all Israel with him, a great assembly from the entrance of Hā'math to the Brook of Egypt, before the LORD our God, seven days and seven more days—fourteen days.

66 On the eighth day he sent the people away; and they blessed the king, and went to their tents joyful and glad of heart for all the good that the LORD had done for His servant David, and for Israel His people.

GOD'S SECOND APPEARANCE TO SOLOMON

9 And it came to pass, when Solomon had finished building the house of the LORD and the king's house, and all Solomon's desire which he wanted to do,

2 that the LORD appeared to Solomon the second time, as He had appeared to him at Gib'ē·on.

3 And the LORD said to him: "I have heard your prayer and your supplication that you have made before Me; I have consecrated this house which you have built to put My name there forever, and My eyes and My heart will be there perpetually.

4 "Now if you walk before Me as your father David walked, in integrity of heart and in uprightness, to do according to all that I have commanded you, and if you keep My statutes and My judgments,

5 "then I will establish the throne of your kingdom over Israel forever, as I promised David your father, say-

ing, 'You shall not fail to have a man on the throne of Israel.'

6   "*But* if you or your sons at all turn from following Me, and do not keep My commandments *and* My statutes which I have set before you, but go and serve other gods and worship them,

7   "then I will cut off Israel from the land which I have given them; and this house which I have consecrated for My name I will cast out of My sight. Israel will be a proverb and a byword among all peoples.

8   "And *as for* this house, *which* is exalted, everyone who passes by it will be astonished and will hiss, and say, 'Why has the LORD done thus to this land and to this house?'

9   "Then they will answer, 'Because they forsook the LORD their God, who brought their fathers out of the land of Egypt, and have embraced other gods, and worshiped them and served them; therefore the LORD has brought all this calamity on them.' "

SOLOMON AND HIRAM EXCHANGE GIFTS

10 Now it happened at the end of twenty years, when Solomon had built the two houses, the house of the LORD and the king's house

11 (Hī′ram the king of Tȳre had supplied Solomon with cedar and cypress and gold, as much as he desired), *that* King Solomon then gave Hī′ram twenty cities in the land of Galilee.

12 Then Hī′ram went from Tȳre to see the cities which Solomon had given him, but they did not please him.

13 So he said, "What *kind of* cities *are* these which you have given me, my brother?" And he called them the land of Cā′bul,*a* as they are to this day.

14 Then Hī′ram sent the king one hundred and twenty talents of gold.

SOLOMON'S ADDITIONAL ACHIEVEMENTS

15 And this *is* the reason for the labor force which King Solomon raised: to build the house of the LORD, his own house, the Mil′lō,*a* the wall of Jerusalem, Hā′zor, Me·gid′dō, and Gē′zer.

16 (Pharaoh king of Egypt had gone up and taken Gē′zer and burned it with fire, had killed the Cā′naan·ītes who dwelt in the city, and had given it *as* a dowry to his daughter, Solomon's wife.)

17 And Solomon built Gē′zer, Lower Beth Hor′on,

18 Bā′a·lath, and Tad′mor in the wilderness, in the land *of Judah,*

19 all the storage cities that Solomon had, cities for his chariots and cities for his cavalry, and whatever Solomon desired to build in Jerusalem, in Lebanon, and in all the land of his dominion.

20 All the people *who were* left of the Am′o·rītes, Hit′tītes, Per′iz·zītes, Hī′vītes, and Jeb′ū·sītes, who *were* not of the children of Israel—

21 that is, their descendants who were left in the land after them, whom the children of Israel had not been able to destroy completely— from these Solomon raised forced labor, as it is to this day.

22 But of the children of Israel Solomon made no forced laborers, because they *were* men of war and his servants: his officers, his captains, commanders of his chariots, and his cavalry.

23 Others *were* chiefs of the officials who *were* over Solomon's work: five

9:13 *a*Literally *Good for Nothing*   9:15 *a*Literally *The Landfill*

hundred and fifty, who ruled over the people who did the work.

24 But Pharaoh's daughter came up from the City of David to her house which *Solomon*a had built for her. Then he built the Mil′lo.

25 Now three times a year Solomon offered burnt offerings and peace offerings on the altar which he had built for the LORD, and he burned incense with them *on the altar* that *was* before the LORD. So he finished the temple.

26 King Solomon also built a fleet of ships at E′zi·on Ge′ber, which *is* near E′latha on the shore of the Red Sea, in the land of E′dom.

27 Then Hi′ram sent his servants with the fleet, seamen who knew the sea, to work with the servants of Solomon.

28 And they went to O′phir, and acquired four hundred and twenty talents of gold from there, and brought *it* to King Solomon.

THE QUEEN OF SHEBA'S PRAISE OF SOLOMON

10 Now when the queen of She′ba heard of the fame of Solomon concerning the name of the LORD, she came to test him with hard questions.

2 She came to Jerusalem with a very great retinue, with camels that bore spices, very much gold, and precious stones; and when she came to Solomon, she spoke with him about all that was in her heart.

3 So Solomon answered all her questions; there was nothing so difficult for the king that he could not explain *it* to her.

4 And when the queen of She′ba had seen all the wisdom of Solomon, the house that he had built,

5 the food on his table, the seating

of his servants, the service of his waiters and their apparel, his cupbearers, and his entryway by which he went up to the house of the LORD, there was no more spirit in her.

6 Then she said to the king: "It was a true report which I heard in my own land about your words and your wisdom.

7 "However I did not believe the words until I came and saw with my own eyes; and indeed the half was not told me. Your wisdom and prosperity exceed the fame of which I heard.

8 "Happy *are* your men and happy *are* these your servants, who stand continually before you *and* hear your wisdom!

9 "Blessed be the LORD your God, who delighted in you, setting you on the throne of Israel! Because the LORD has loved Israel forever, therefore He made you king, to do justice and righteousness."

10 Then she gave the king one hundred and twenty talents of gold, spices in great quantity, and precious stones. There never again came such abundance of spices as the queen of She′ba gave to King Solomon.

11 Also, the ships of Hi′ram, which brought gold from O′phir, brought great *quantities* of almuga wood and precious stones from O′phir.

12 And the king made steps of the almug wood for the house of the LORD and for the king's house, also harps and stringed instruments for singers. There never again came such almug wood, nor has the like been seen to this day.

13 Now King Solomon gave the queen of She′ba all she desired, whatever she asked, besides what

9:24 aLiterally *he* (compare 2 Chronicles 8:11)
9:26 aHebrew *Eloth* (compare 2 Kings 14:22)
10:11 aOr *algum* (compare 2 Chronicles 9:10, 11)

Solomon had given her according to the royal generosity. So she turned and went to her own country, she and her servants.

SOLOMON'S GREAT WEALTH

14 The weight of gold that came to Solomon yearly was six hundred and sixty-six talents of gold,
15 besides *that* from the traveling merchants, from the income of traders, from all the kings of Arabia, and from the governors of the country.
16 And King Solomon made two hundred large shields *of* hammered gold; six hundred *shekels* of gold went into each shield.
17 He also *made* three hundred shields *of* hammered gold; three minas of gold went into each shield. The king put them in the House of the Forest of Lebanon.
18 Moreover the king made a great throne of ivory, and overlaid it with pure gold.
19 The throne had six steps, and the top of the throne *was* round at the back; *there were* armrests on either side of the place of the seat, and two lions stood beside the armrests.
20 Twelve lions stood there, one on each side of the six steps; nothing like *this* had been made for any *other* kingdom.
21 All King Solomon's drinking vessels *were* gold, and all the vessels of the House of the Forest of Lebanon *were* pure gold. Not *one was* silver, for this was accounted as nothing in the days of Solomon.
22 For the king had merchant ships*a* at sea with the fleet of Hī′ram. Once every three years the merchant ships came bringing gold, silver, ivory, apes, and monkeys.*b*
23 So King Solomon surpassed all the kings of the earth in riches and wisdom.
24 Now all the earth sought the presence of Solomon to hear his wisdom, which God had put in his heart.
25 Each man brought his present: articles of silver and gold, garments, armor, spices, horses, and mules, at a set rate year by year.
26 And Solomon gathered chariots and horsemen; he had one thousand four hundred chariots and twelve thousand horsemen, whom he stationed*a* in the chariot cities and with the king at Jerusalem.
27 The king made silver *as common* in Jerusalem as stones, and he made cedar trees as abundant as the sycamores which *are* in the lowland.
28 Also Solomon had horses imported from Egypt and Ke·veh′; the king's merchants bought them in Ke·veh′ at the *current* price.
29 Now a chariot that was imported from Egypt cost six hundred *shekels* of silver, and a horse one hundred and fifty; and thus, through their agents,*a* they exported *them* to all the kings of the Hit′tītes and the kings of Syria.

SOLOMON'S HEART TURNS FROM THE LORD

11 But King Solomon loved many foreign women, as well as the daughter of Pharaoh: women of the Mō′ab·ītes, Am′mon·ītes, Ē′dom·ītes, Sī·dō′ni·ans, *and* Hit′tītes—
2 from the nations of whom the LORD had said to the children of Israel, "You shall not intermarry with them, nor they with you. Surely they

10:22 *a*Literally *ships of Tarshish*, deep-sea vessels *b*Or *peacocks*   10:26 *a*Following Septuagint, Syriac, Targum, and Vulgate (compare 2 Chronicles 9:25); Masoretic Text reads *led*.   10:29 *a*Literally *by their hands*

will turn away your hearts after their gods." Solomon clung to these in love.

3 And he had seven hundred wives, princesses, and three hundred concubines; and his wives turned away his heart.

4 For it was so, when Solomon was old, that his wives turned his heart after other gods; and his heart was not loyal to the LORD his God, as *was* the heart of his father David.

5 For Solomon went after Ash'toreth the goddess of the Si·dō'ni·ans, and after Mil'com the abomination of the Am'mon·ites.

6 Solomon did evil in the sight of the LORD, and did not fully follow the LORD, as *did* his father David.

7 Then Solomon built a high place for Chē'mosh the abomination of Mō'ab, on the hill that *is* east of Jerusalem, and for Mō'lech the abomination of the people of Am'mon.

8 And he did likewise for all his foreign wives, who burned incense and sacrificed to their gods.

9 So the LORD became angry with Solomon, because his heart had turned from the LORD God of Israel, who had appeared to him twice,

10 and had commanded him concerning this thing, that he should not go after other gods; but he did not keep what the LORD had commanded.

11 Therefore the LORD said to Solomon, "Because you have done this, and have not kept My covenant and My statutes, which I have commanded you, I will surely tear the kingdom away from you and give it to your servant.

12 "Nevertheless I will not do it in your days, for the sake of your father David; I will tear it out of the hand of your son.

13 "However I will not tear away the whole kingdom; I will give one tribe to your son for the sake of my servant

David, and for the sake of Jerusalem which I have chosen."

ADVERSARIES OF SOLOMON

14 Now the LORD raised up an adversary against Solomon, Hā'dad the Ē'dom·īte; he *was* a descendant of the king in Ē'dom.

15 For it happened, when David was in Ē'dom, and Jō'ab the commander of the army had gone up to bury the slain, after he had killed every male in Ē'dom

16 (because for six months Jō'ab remained there with all Israel, until he had cut down every male in Ē'dom),

17 that Hā'dad fled to go to Egypt, he and certain Ē'dom·ītes of his father's servants with him. Hā'dad *was* still a little child.

18 Then they arose from Mid'i·an and came to Par'an; and they took men with them from Par'an and came to Egypt, to Pharaoh king of Egypt, who gave him a house, apportioned food for him, and gave him land.

19 And Hā'dad found great favor in the sight of Pharaoh, so that he gave him as wife the sister of his own wife, that is, the sister of Queen Tah'pe·nēs.

20 Then the sister of Tah'pe·nēs bore him Ge·nū'bath his son, whom Tah'pe·nēs weaned in Pharaoh's house. And Ge·nū'bath was in Pharaoh's household among the sons of Pharaoh.

21 So when Hā'dad heard in Egypt that David rested with his fathers, and that Jō'ab the commander of the army was dead, Hā'dad said to Pharaoh, "Let me depart, that I may go to my own country."

22 Then Pharaoh said to him, "But what have you lacked with me, that suddenly you seek to go to your own

country?" So he answered, "Nothing, but do let me go anyway."

23 And God raised up *another* adversary against him, Rē'zon the son of E·lī'a·dah, who had fled from his lord, Had·a·dē'zer king of Zō'bah.

24 So he gathered men to him and became captain over a band *of raiders,* when David killed those *of Zō' bah.* And they went to Damascus and dwelt there, and reigned in Damascus.

25 He was an adversary of Israel all the days of Solomon (besides the trouble that Hā'dad *caused*); and he abhorred Israel, and reigned over Syria.

JEROBOAM'S REBELLION

26 Then Solomon's servant, Jer·o·bō'am the son of Nē'bat, an Ē'phra·im·īte from Zer'e·da, whose mother's name *was* Ze·rū'ah, a widow, also rebelled against the king.

27 And this *is* what caused him to rebel against the king: Solomon had built the Mil'lō *and* repaired the damages to the City of David his father.

28 The man Jer·o·bō'am *was* a mighty man of valor; and Solomon, seeing that the young man was industrious, made him the officer over all the labor force of the house of Joseph.

29 Now it happened at that time, when Jer·o·bō'am went out of Jerusalem, that the prophet A·hī'jah the Shī'lo·nīte met him on the way; and he had clothed himself with a new garment, and the two *were* alone in the field.

30 Then A·hī'jah took hold of the new garment that *was* on him, and tore it *into* twelve pieces.

31 And he said to Jer·o·bō'am, "Take for yourself ten pieces, for thus says the LORD, the God of Israel: 'Behold, I will tear the kingdom out of the hand of Solomon and will give ten tribes to you

32 '(but he shall have one tribe for the sake of My servant David, and for the sake of Jerusalem, the city which I have chosen out of all the tribes of Israel),

33 'because they have[a] forsaken Me, and worshiped Ash'to·reth the goddess of the Sī·dō'ni·ans, Chē'mosh the god of the Mō'ab·ītes, and Mil'com the god of the people of Am'mon, and have not walked in My ways to do *what is* right in My eyes and *keep* My statutes and My judgments, as *did* his father David.

34 'However I will not take the whole kingdom out of his hand, because I have made him ruler all the days of his life for the sake of My servant David, whom I chose because he kept My commandments and My statutes.

35 'But I will take the kingdom out of his son's hand and give it to you— ten tribes.

36 'And to his son I will give one tribe, that My servant David may always have a lamp before Me in Jerusalem, the city which I have chosen for Myself, to put My name there.

37 'So I will take you, and you shall reign over all your heart desires, and you shall be king over Israel.

38 'Then it shall be, if you heed all that I command you, walk in My ways, and do *what is* right in My sight, to keep My statutes and My commandments, as My servant David did, then I will be with you and build for you an enduring house, as I built for David, and will give Israel to you.

39 'And I will afflict the descendants of David because of this, but not forever.' "

11:33 [a]Following Masoretic Text and Targum; Septuagint, Syriac, and Vulgate read *he has.*

40 Solomon therefore sought to kill Jer·o·bo'am. But Jer·o·bo'am arose and fled to Egypt, to Shi'shak king of Egypt, and was in Egypt until the death of Solomon.

DEATH OF SOLOMON

41 Now the rest of the acts of Solomon, all that he did, and his wisdom, *are* they not written in the book of the acts of Solomon?
42 And the period that Solomon reigned in Jerusalem over all Israel *was* forty years.
43 Then Solomon rested with his fathers, and was buried in the City of David his father. And Re·ho·bo'am his son reigned in his place.

THE REVOLT AGAINST REHOBOAM

12 And Re·ho·bo'am went to She'chem, for all Israel had gone to She'chem to make him king.
2 So it happened, when Jer·o·bo'am the son of Ne'bat heard *it* (he was still in Egypt, for he had fled from the presence of King Solomon and had been dwelling in Egypt),
3 that they sent and called him. Then Jer·o·bo'am and the whole assembly of Israel came and spoke to Re·ho·bo'am, saying,
4 "Your father made our yoke heavy; now therefore, lighten the burdensome service of your father, and his heavy yoke which he put on us, and we will serve you."
5 So he said to them, "Depart *for* three days, then come back to me." And the people departed.
6 Then King Re·ho·bo'am consulted the elders who stood before his father Solomon while he still lived, and he said, "How do you advise *me* to answer these people?"

7 And they spoke to him, saying, "If you will be a servant to these people today, and serve them, and answer them, and speak good words to them, then they will be your servants forever."
8 But he rejected the advice which the elders had given him, and consulted the young men who had grown up with him, who stood before him.
9 And he said to them, "What advice do you give? How should we answer this people who have spoken to me, saying, 'Lighten the yoke which your father put on us'?"
10 Then the young men who had grown up with him spoke to him, saying, "Thus you should speak to this people who have spoken to you, saying, 'Your father made our yoke heavy, but you make *it* lighter on us'—thus you shall say to them: 'My little *finger* shall be thicker than my father's waist!
11 'And now, whereas my father put a heavy yoke on you, I will add to your yoke; my father chastised you with whips, but I will chastise you with scourges!' "*a*
12 So Jer·o·bo'am and all the people came to Re·ho·bo'am the third day, as the king had directed, saying, "Come back to me the third day."
13 Then the king answered the people roughly, and rejected the advice which the elders had given him;
14 and he spoke to them according to the advice of the young men, saying, "My father made your yoke heavy, but I will add to your yoke; my father chastised you with whips, but I will chastise you with scourges!"*a*
15 So the king did not listen to the people; for the turn *of events* was from the LORD, that He might fulfill His word, which the LORD had spo-

12:11 *a*Literally *scorpions*   12:14 *a*Literally *scorpions*

ken by A·hī'jah the Shī'lo·nīte to
Jer·o·bō'am the son of Nē'bat.
16 Now when all Israel saw that the
king did not listen to them, the people answered the king, saying:

"What share have we in David?
  We have no inheritance in the son
    of Jesse.
  To your tents, O Israel!
  Now, see to your own house,
    O David!"

So Israel departed to their tents.
17 But Rē·ho·bō'am reigned over the
children of Israel who dwelt in the
cities of Judah.
18 Then King Rē·ho·bō'am sent
A·dor'am, who *was* in charge of the
revenue; but all Israel stoned him
with stones, and he died. Therefore
King Rē·ho·bō'am mounted his chariot in haste to flee to Jerusalem.
19 So Israel has been in rebellion
against the house of David to this
day.
20 Now it came to pass when all Israel heard that Jer·o·bō'am had come
back, they sent for him and called
him to the congregation, and made
him king over all Israel. There
was none who followed the house
of David, but the tribe of Judah
only.
21 And when Rē·ho·bō'am came to
Jerusalem, he assembled all the
house of Judah with the tribe of Benjamin, one hundred and eighty thousand chosen *men* who were warriors,
to fight against the house of Israel,
that he might restore the kingdom to
Rē·ho·bō'am the son of Solomon.
22 But the word of God came to
She·māi'ah the man of God, saying,
23 "Speak to Rē·ho·bō'am the son of
Solomon, king of Judah, to all the
house of Judah and Benjamin, and to
the rest of the people, saying,
24 'Thus says the LORD: "You shall

not go up nor fight against your
brethren the children of Israel. Let
every man return to his house, for
this thing is from Me." ' " Therefore
they obeyed the word of the LORD,
and turned back, according to the
word of the LORD.

JEROBOAM'S GOLD CALVES

25 Then Jer·o·bō'am built Shē'chem
in the mountains of Ē'phra·im, and
dwelt there. Also he went out from
there and built Pe·nū'el.
26 And Jer·o·bō'am said in his heart,
"Now the kingdom may return to the
house of David:
27 "If these people go up to offer sacrifices in the house of the LORD at Jerusalem, then the heart of this people
will turn back to their lord, Rē·ho·
bō'am king of Judah, and they will
kill me and go back to Rē·ho·bō'am
king of Judah."
28 Therefore the king asked advice,
made two calves of gold, and said to
the people, "It is too much for you to
go up to Jerusalem. Here are your
gods, O Israel, which brought you up
from the land of Egypt!"
29 And he set up one in Beth'el, and
the other he put in Dan.
30 Now this thing became a sin, for
the people went *to worship* before the
one as far as Dan.
31 He made shrines[a] on the high
places, and made priests from every
class of people, who were not of the
sons of Levi.
32 Jer·o·bō'am ordained a feast on
the fifteenth day of the eighth month,
like the feast that *was* in Judah, and
offered sacrifices on the altar. So he
did at Beth'el, sacrificing to the
calves that he had made. And at
Beth'el he installed the priests of the
high places which he had made.

12:31 [a]Literally *a house*

33 So he made offerings on the altar which he had made at Beth'el on the fifteenth day of the eighth month, in the month which he had devised in his own heart. And he ordained a feast for the children of Israel, and offered sacrifices on the altar and burned incense.

THE MESSAGE OF THE MAN OF GOD

13 And behold, a man of God went from Judah to Beth'el by the word of the LORD, and Jer·o·bō'am stood by the altar to burn incense. 2 Then he cried out against the altar by the word of the LORD, and said, "O altar, altar! Thus says the LORD: 'Behold, a child, Jō·sī'ah by name, shall be born to the house of David; and on you he shall sacrifice the priests of the high places who burn incense on you, and men's bones shall be burned on you.'" 3 And he gave a sign the same day, saying, "This *is* the sign which the LORD has spoken: Surely the altar shall split apart, and the ashes on it shall be poured out." 4 So it came to pass when King Jer·o·bō'am heard the saying of the man of God, who cried out against the altar in Beth'el, that he stretched out his hand from the altar, saying, "Arrest him!" Then his hand, which he stretched out toward him, withered, so that he could not pull it back to himself. 5 The altar also was split apart, and the ashes poured out from the altar, according to the sign which the man of God had given by the word of the LORD. 6 Then the king answered and said to the man of God, "Please entreat the favor of the LORD your God, and pray for me, that my hand may be restored to me." So the man of God en-treated the LORD, and the king's hand was restored to him, and became as before. 7 Then the king said to the man of God, "Come home with me and refresh yourself, and I will give you a reward." 8 But the man of God said to the king, "If you were to give me half your house, I would not go in with you; nor would I eat bread nor drink water in this place. 9 "For so it was commanded me by the word of the LORD, saying, 'You shall not eat bread, nor drink water, nor return by the same way you came.'" 10 So he went another way and did not return by the way he came to Beth'el.

DEATH OF THE MAN OF GOD

11 Now an old prophet dwelt in Beth'el, and his sons came and told him all the works that the man of God had done that day in Beth'el; they also told their father the words which he had spoken to the king. 12 And their father said to them, "Which way did he go?" For his sons had seen[a] which way the man of God went who came from Judah. 13 Then he said to his sons, "Saddle the donkey for me." So they saddled the donkey for him; and he rode on it, 14 and went after the man of God, and found him sitting under an oak. Then he said to him, "*Are* you the man of God who came from Judah?" And he said, "I *am.*" 15 Then he said to him, "Come home with me and eat bread." 16 And he said, "I cannot return with you nor go in with you; neither

13:12 [a]Septuagint, Syriac, Targum, and Vulgate read *showed him.*

can I eat bread nor drink water with you in this place.

17 "For I have been told by the word of the LORD, 'You shall not eat bread nor drink water there, nor return by going the way you came.' "

18 He said to him, "I too *am* a prophet as you *are,* and an angel spoke to me by the word of the LORD, saying, 'Bring him back with you to your house, that he may eat bread and drink water.' " (He was lying to him.)

19 So he went back with him, and ate bread in his house, and drank water.

20 Now it happened, as they sat at the table, that the word of the LORD came to the prophet who had brought him back;

21 and he cried out to the man of God who came from Judah, saying, "Thus says the LORD: 'Because you have disobeyed the word of the LORD, and have not kept the commandment which the LORD your God commanded you,

22 'but you came back, ate bread, and drank water in the place of which *the LORD* said to you, "Eat no bread and drink no water," your corpse shall not come to the tomb of your fathers.' "

23 So it was, after he had eaten bread and after he had drunk, that he saddled the donkey for him, the prophet whom he had brought back.

24 When he was gone, a lion met him on the road and killed him. And his corpse was thrown on the road, and the donkey stood by it. The lion also stood by the corpse.

25 And there, men passed by and saw the corpse thrown on the road, and the lion standing by the corpse. Then they went and told *it* in the city where the old prophet dwelt.

26 Now when the prophet who had brought him back from the way heard *it,* he said, "It *is* the man of God who was disobedient to the word of the LORD. Therefore the LORD has delivered him to the lion, which has torn him and killed him, according to the word of the LORD which He spoke to him."

27 And he spoke to his sons, saying, "Saddle the donkey for me." So they saddled *it.*

28 Then he went and found his corpse thrown on the road, and the donkey and the lion standing by the corpse. The lion had not eaten the corpse nor torn the donkey.

29 And the prophet took up the corpse of the man of God, laid it on the donkey, and brought it back. So the old prophet came to the city to mourn, and to bury him.

30 Then he laid the corpse in his own tomb; and they mourned over him, *saying,* "Alas, my brother!"

31 So it was, after he had buried him, that he spoke to his sons, saying, "When I am dead, then bury me in the tomb where the man of God *is* buried; lay my bones beside his bones.

32 "For the saying which he cried out by the word of the LORD against the altar in Beth'el, and against all the shrines*a* on the high places which *are* in the cities of Samaria, will surely come to pass."

33 After this event Jer·o·bō'am did not turn from his evil way, but again he made priests from every class of people for the high places; whoever wished, he consecrated him, and he became *one* of the priests of the high places.

34 And this thing was the sin of the house of Jer·o·bō'am, so as to exterminate and destroy *it* from the face of the earth.

13:32 *a*Literally *houses*

JUDGMENT ON THE HOUSE OF JEROBOAM

14 At that time A·bī′jah the son of Jer·o·bō′am became sick.
2 And Jer·o·bō′am said to his wife, "Please arise, and disguise yourself, that they may not recognize you as the wife of Jer·o·bō′am, and go to Shī′loh. Indeed, A·hī′jah the prophet *is* there, who told me that *I would be* king over this people.
3 "Also take with you ten loaves, *some* cakes, and a jar of honey, and go to him; he will tell you what will become of the child."
4 And Jer·o·bō′am's wife did so; she arose and went to Shī′loh, and came to the house of A·hī′jah. But A·hī′jah could not see, for his eyes were glazed by reason of his age.
5 Now the LORD had said to A·hī′-jah, "Here is the wife of Jer·o·bō′am, coming to ask you something about her son, for he *is* sick. Thus and thus you shall say to her; for it will be, when she comes in, that she will pretend *to be* another *woman*."
6 And so it was, when A·hī′jah heard the sound of her footsteps as she came through the door, he said, "Come in, wife of Jer·o·bō′am. Why do you pretend *to be* another *person?* For I *have been* sent to you *with* bad news.
7 "Go, tell Jer·o·bō′am, 'Thus says the LORD God of Israel: "Because I exalted you from among the people, and made you ruler over My people Israel,
8 "and tore the kingdom away from the house of David, and gave it to you; and *yet* you have not been as My servant David, who kept My commandments and who followed Me with all his heart, to do only *what was* right in My eyes;
9 "but you have done more evil than all who were before you, for you have gone and made for yourself other gods and molded images to provoke Me to anger, and have cast Me behind your back—
10 "therefore behold! I will bring disaster on the house of Jer·o·bō′am, and will cut off from Jer·o·bō′am every male in Israel, bond and free; I will take away the remnant of the house of Jer·o·bō′am, as one takes away refuse until it is all gone.
11 "The dogs shall eat whoever belongs to Jer·o·bō′am and dies in the city, and the birds of the air shall eat whoever dies in the field; for the LORD has spoken!" '
12 "Arise therefore, go to your own house. When your feet enter the city, the child shall die.
13 "And all Israel shall mourn for him and bury him, for he is the only one of Jer·o·bō′am who shall come to the grave, because in him there is found something good toward the LORD God of Israel in the house of Jer·o·bō′am.
14 "Moreover the LORD will raise up for Himself a king over Israel who shall cut off the house of Jer·o·bō′am; this is the day. What? Even now!
15 "For the LORD will strike Israel, as a reed is shaken in the water. He will uproot Israel from this good land which He gave to their fathers, and will scatter them beyond the River,[a] because they have made their wooden images,[b] provoking the LORD to anger.
16 "And He will give Israel up because of the sins of Jer·o·bō′am, who sinned and who made Israel sin."
17 Then Jer·o·bō′am's wife arose and departed, and came to Tir′zah. When she came to the threshold of the house, the child died.

14:15 [a]That is, the Euphrates   [b]Hebrew *Asherim*, Canaanite deities

18 And they buried him; and all Israel mourned for him, according to the word of the LORD which He spoke through His servant A·hī′jah the prophet.

DEATH OF JEROBOAM

19 Now the rest of the acts of Jer-o·bō′am, how he made war and how he reigned, indeed they *are* written in the book of the chronicles of the kings of Israel.
20 The period that Jer·o·bō′am reigned *was* twenty-two years. So he rested with his fathers. Then Nā′dab his son reigned in his place.

REHOBOAM REIGNS IN JUDAH

21 And Rē·ho·bō′am the son of Solomon reigned in Judah. Rē·ho·bō′am *was* forty-one years old when he became king. He reigned seventeen years in Jerusalem, the city which the LORD had chosen out of all the tribes of Israel, to put His name there. His mother's name *was* Nā′a·mah, an Am′mon·ī·tess.
22 Now Judah did evil in the sight of the LORD, and they provoked Him to jealousy with their sins which they committed, more than all that their fathers had done.
23 For they also built for themselves high places, *sacred* pillars, and wooden images on every high hill and under every green tree.
24 And there were also perverted persons[a] in the land. They did according to all the abominations of the nations which the LORD had cast out before the children of Israel.
25 It happened in the fifth year of King Rē·ho·bō′am *that* Shī′shak king of Egypt came up against Jerusalem.
26 And he took away the treasures of the house of the LORD and the treasures of the king's house; he took away everything. He also took away all the gold shields which Solomon had made.
27 Then King Rē·ho·bō′am made bronze shields in their place, and committed *them* to the hands of the captains of the guard, who guarded the doorway of the king's house.
28 And whenever the king entered the house of the LORD, the guards carried them, then brought them back into the guardroom.
29 Now the rest of the acts of Rē·ho·bō′am, and all that he did, *are* they not written in the book of the chronicles of the kings of Judah?
30 And there was war between Rē·ho·bō′am and Jer·o·bō′am all *their* days.
31 So Rē·ho·bō′am rested with his fathers, and was buried with his fathers in the City of David. His mother's name *was* Nā′a·mah, an Am′mon·ī·tess. Then A·bī′jam[a] his son reigned in his place.

ABIJAM REIGNS IN JUDAH

15 In the eighteenth year of King Jer·o·bō′am the son of Nē′bat, A·bī′-jam became king over Judah.
2 He reigned three years in Jerusalem. His mother's name *was* Mā′a-chah the granddaughter of A·bish′-a·lom.
3 And he walked in all the sins of his father, which he had done before him; his heart was not loyal to the LORD his God, as was the heart of his father David.
4 Nevertheless for David's sake the LORD his God gave him a lamp in

14:24 [a]Hebrew *qadesh*, that is, one practicing sodomy and prostitution in religious rituals
14:31 [a]Spelled *Abijah* in 2 Chronicles 12:16ff

Jerusalem, by setting up his son after him and by establishing Jerusalem;

5 because David did *what was* right in the eyes of the LORD, and had not turned aside from anything that He commanded him all the days of his life, except in the matter of Ū·rī'ah the Hit'tīte.

6 And there was war between Rē·ho·bō'am*a* and Jer·o·bō'am all the days of his life.

7 Now the rest of the acts of A·bī'jam, and all that he did, *are* they not written in the book of the chronicles of the kings of Judah? And there was war between A·bī'jam and Jer·o·bō'am.

8 So A·bī'jam rested with his fathers, and they buried him in the City of David. Then Ā'sa his son reigned in his place.

ASA REIGNS IN JUDAH

9 In the twentieth year of Jer·o·bō'am king of Israel, Ā'sa became king over Judah.

10 And he reigned forty-one years in Jerusalem. His grandmother's name *was* Mā'a·chah the granddaughter of A·bish'a·lom.

11 Ā'sa did *what was* right in the eyes of the LORD, as *did* his father David.

12 And he banished the perverted persons*a* from the land, and removed all the idols that his fathers had made.

13 Also he removed Mā'a·chah his grandmother from *being* queen mother, because she had made an obscene image of A·shē'rah.*a* And Ā'sa cut down her obscene image and burned *it* by the Brook Kid'ron.

14 But the high places were not removed. Nevertheless Ā'sa's heart was loyal to the LORD all his days.

15 He also brought into the house of

the LORD the things which his father had dedicated, and the things which he himself had dedicated: silver and gold and utensils.

16 Now there was war between Ā'sa and Bā'a·sha king of Israel all their days.

17 And Bā'a·sha king of Israel came up against Judah, and built Rā'mah, that he might let none go out or come in to Ā'sa king of Judah.

18 Then Ā'sa took all the silver and gold *that was* left in the treasuries of the house of the LORD and the treasuries of the king's house, and delivered them into the hand of his servants. And King Ā'sa sent them to Ben-Hā'dad the son of Tab·rim'mon, the son of Hē'zi·on, king of Syria, who dwelt in Damascus, saying,

19 "*Let there be* a treaty between you and me, as there was between my father and your father. See, I have sent you a present of silver and gold. Come and break your treaty with Bā'a·sha king of Israel, so that he will withdraw from me."

20 So Ben-Hā'dad heeded King Ā'sa, and sent the captains of his armies against the cities of Israel. He attacked Ī'jon, Dan, Abel Beth Mā'a·chah, and all Chin'ne·roth, with all the land of Naph'ta·lī.

21 Now it happened, when Bā'a·sha heard *it,* that he stopped building Rā'mah, and remained in Tir'zah.

22 Then King Ā'sa made a proclamation throughout all Judah; none *was* exempted. And they took away the stones and timber of Rā'mah, which Bā'a·sha had used for building; and with them King Ā'sa built Gē'ba of Benjamin, and Miz'pah.

15:6 *a*Following Masoretic Text, Septuagint, Targum, and Vulgate; some Hebrew manuscripts and Syriac read *Abijam.*   15:12 *a*Hebrew *qedeshim,* that is, those practicing sodomy and prostitution in religious rituals   15:13 *a*A Canaanite goddess

23 The rest of all the acts of Ā′sa, all his might, all that he did, and the cities which he built, *are* they not written in the book of the chronicles of the kings of Judah? But in the time of his old age he was diseased in his feet.

24 So Ā′sa rested with his fathers, and was buried with his fathers in the City of David his father. Then Je·hosh′a·phat his son reigned in his place.

NADAB REIGNS IN ISRAEL

25 Now Nā′dab the son of Jer·o·bō′am became king over Israel in the second year of Ā′sa king of Judah, and he reigned over Israel two years.

26 And he did evil in the sight of the LORD, and walked in the way of his father, and in his sin by which he had made Israel sin.

27 Then Bā′a·sha the son of A·hī′jah, of the house of Is′sa·char, conspired against him. And Bā′a·sha killed him at Gib′be·thon, which *belonged* to the Phi·lis′tines, while Nā′dab and all Israel laid siege to Gib′be·thon.

28 Bā′a·sha killed him in the third year of Ā′sa king of Judah, and reigned in his place.

29 And it was so, when he became king, *that* he killed all the house of Jer·o·bō′am. He did not leave to Jer·o·bō′am anyone that breathed, until he had destroyed him, according to the word of the LORD which He had spoken by His servant A·hī′jah the Shī′lo·nīte,

30 because of the sins of Jer·o·bō′am, which he had sinned and by which he had made Israel sin, because of his provocation with which he had provoked the LORD God of Israel to anger.

31 Now the rest of the acts of Nā′dab, and all that he did, *are* they

not written in the book of the chronicles of the kings of Israel?

32 And there was war between Ā′sa and Bā′a·sha king of Israel all their days.

BAASHA REIGNS IN ISRAEL

33 In the third year of Ā′sa king of Judah, Bā′a·sha the son of A·hī′jah became king over all Israel in Tir′zah, and *reigned* twenty-four years.

34 He did evil in the sight of the LORD, and walked in the way of Jer·o·bō′am, and in his sin by which he had made Israel sin.

16 Then the word of the LORD came to Jē′hū the son of Ha·nā′nī, against Bā′a·sha, saying:

2 "Inasmuch as I lifted you out of the dust and made you ruler over My people Israel, and you have walked in the way of Jer·o·bō′am, and have made My people Israel sin, to provoke Me to anger with their sins,

3 "surely I will take away the posterity of Bā′a·sha and the posterity of his house, and I will make your house like the house of Jer·o·bō′am the son of Nē′bat.

4 "The dogs shall eat whoever belongs to Bā′a·sha and dies in the city, and the birds of the air shall eat whoever dies in the fields."

5 Now the rest of the acts of Bā′a·sha, what he did, and his might, *are* they not written in the book of the chronicles of the kings of Israel?

6 So Bā′a·sha rested with his fathers and was buried in Tir′zah. Then Ē′lah his son reigned in his place.

7 And also the word of the LORD came by the prophet Jē′hū the son of Ha·nā′nī against Bā′a·sha and his house, because of all the evil that he did in the sight of the LORD in pro-

voking Him to anger with the work of his hands, in being like the house of Jer·o·bō′am, and because he killed them.

ELAH REIGNS IN ISRAEL

8 In the twenty-sixth year of Ā′sa king of Judah, Ē′lah the son of Bā′-a·sha became king over Israel, *and reigned* two years in Tir′zah.
9 Now his servant Zim′rī, commander of half *his* chariots, conspired against him as he was in Tir′zah drinking himself drunk in the house of Ar′za, steward of *his* house in Tir′zah.
10 And Zim′rī went in and struck him and killed him in the twenty-seventh year of Ā′sa king of Judah, and reigned in his place.
11 Then it came to pass, when he began to reign, as soon as he was seated on his throne, *that* he killed all the household of Bā′a·sha; he did not leave him one male, neither of his relatives nor of his friends.
12 Thus Zim′rī destroyed all the household of Bā′a·sha, according to the word of the LORD, which He spoke against Bā′a·sha by Jē′hū the prophet,
13 for all the sins of Bā′a·sha and the sins of Ē′lah his son, by which they had sinned and by which they had made Israel sin, in provoking the LORD God of Israel to anger with their idols.
14 Now the rest of the acts of Ē′lah, and all that he did, *are* they not written in the book of the chronicles of the kings of Israel?

ZIMRI REIGNS IN ISRAEL

15 In the twenty-seventh year of Ā′sa king of Judah, Zim′rī had reigned in Tir′zah seven days. And the people *were* encamped against Gib′be·thon, which *belonged* to the Phi·lis′tines.
16 Now the people *who were* encamped heard it said, "Zim′rī has conspired and also has killed the king." So all Israel made Om′rī, the commander of the army, king over Israel that day in the camp.
17 Then Om′rī and all Israel with him went up from Gib′be·thon, and they besieged Tir′zah.
18 And it happened, when Zim′rī saw that the city was taken, that he went into the citadel of the king's house and burned the king's house down upon himself with fire, and died,
19 because of the sins which he had committed in doing evil in the sight of the LORD, in walking in the way of Jer·o·bō′am, and in his sin which he had committed to make Israel sin.
20 Now the rest of the acts of Zim′rī, and the treason he committed, *are* they not written in the book of the chronicles of the kings of Israel?

OMRI REIGNS IN ISRAEL

21 Then the people of Israel were divided into two parts: half of the people followed Tib′nī the son of Gī′nath, to make him king, and half followed Om′rī.
22 But the people who followed Om′rī prevailed over the people who followed Tib′nī the son of Gī′nath. So Tib′nī died and Om′rī reigned.
23 In the thirty-first year of Ā′sa king of Judah, Om′rī became king over Israel, *and reigned* twelve years. Six years he reigned in Tir′zah.
24 And he bought the hill of Samaria from Shē′mer for two talents of silver; then he built on the hill, and called the name of the city which he built, Samaria, after the name of Shē′mer, owner of the hill.

25 Om′rī did evil in the eyes of the LORD, and did worse than all who *were* before him.

26 For he walked in all the ways of Jer·o·bō′am the son of Nē′bat, and in his sin by which he had made Israel sin, provoking the LORD God of Israel to anger with their idols.

27 Now the rest of the acts of Om′rī which he did, and the might that he showed, *are* they not written in the book of the chronicles of the kings of Israel?

28 So Om′rī rested with his fathers and was buried in Samaria. Then Ā′hab his son reigned in his place.

AHAB REIGNS IN ISRAEL

29 In the thirty-eighth year of Ā′sa king of Judah, Ā′hab the son of Om′rī became king over Israel; and Ā′hab the son of Om′rī reigned over Israel in Samaria twenty-two years.

30 Now Ā′hab the son of Om′rī did evil in the sight of the LORD, more than all who *were* before him.

31 And it came to pass, as though it had been a trivial thing for him to walk in the sins of Jer·o·bō′am the son of Nē′bat, that he took as wife Jez′e·bel the daughter of Eth·bā′al, king of the Sī·dō′ni·ans; and he went and served Bā′al and worshiped him.

32 Then he set up an altar for Bā′al in the temple of Bā′al, which he had built in Samaria.

33 And Ā′hab made a wooden image.ᵃ Ā′hab did more to provoke the LORD God of Israel to anger than all the kings of Israel who were before him.

34 In his days Hī′el of Beth′el built Jericho. He laid its foundation with A·bī′ram his firstborn, and with his youngest *son* Sē′gub he set up its gates, according to the word of the LORD, which He had spoken through Joshua the son of Nun.ᵃ

ELIJAH PROCLAIMS A DROUGHT

Like his father David, Solomon was king for 40 years. Israel was at peace. But after Solomon died, many evil kings came to the throne. They told the people to stop obeying God. The worst of these kings was Ahab. He thought no one was mightier than he. But God was about to show him who was really in charge.

17 And E·lī′jah the Tish′bīte, of the inhabitants of Gil′ē·ad, said to Ā′hab, "As the LORD God of Israel lives, before whom I stand, there shall not be dew nor rain these years, except at my word."

2 Then the word of the LORD came to him, saying,

3 "Get away from here and turn eastward, and hide by the Brook Chē′rith, which flows into the Jordan.

4 "And it will be *that* you shall drink from the brook, and I have commanded the ravens to feed you there."

5 So he went and did according to the word of the LORD, for he went and stayed by the Brook Chē′rith, which flows into the Jordan.

6 The ravens brought him bread and meat in the morning, and bread and meat in the evening; and he drank from the brook.

7 And it happened after a while that the brook dried up, because there had been no rain in the land.

ELIJAH AND THE WIDOW

8 Then the word of the LORD came to him, saying,

16:33 ᵃHebrew *Asherah,* a Canaanite goddess
16:34 ᵃCompare Joshua 6:26

ABOUT GOD'S PROVISION 1 Kings 17:1–6

Will You Take Care of Me?

The girl is taking care of her kitty. You can see that she loves her kitty. She feeds her kitty and provides a nice basket where Kitty can sleep. She provides a blanket to cover Kitty. She even talks to Kitty when she tucks Kitty into bed at night. Parents provide loving care for you, too. And of course God provides everything you have. Thank You, God.

1. What is the girl providing for Kitty? How do you know she loves Kitty?
2. What do your parents provide for you? How do you know they love you?
3. What does God provide for you? How do you know that He loves you?

For more on *What the Bible Says* turn to page 712

For more on *God's Care* turn to page 543

9 "Arise, go to Zar′e·phath, which *belongs* to Si′don, and dwell there. See, I have commanded a widow there to provide for you."

10 So he arose and went to Zar′e·phath. And when he came to the gate of the city, indeed a widow *was* there gathering sticks. And he called to her and said, "Please bring me a little water in a cup, that I may drink."

11 And as she was going to get *it,* he called to her and said, "Please bring me a morsel of bread in your hand."

12 So she said, "As the LORD your God lives, I do not have bread, only a handful of flour in a bin, and a little oil in a jar; and see, I *am* gathering a couple of sticks that I may go in and prepare it for myself and my son, that we may eat it, and die."

13 And E·li′jah said to her, "Do not fear; go *and* do as you have said, but make me a small cake from it first, and bring *it* to me; and afterward make *some* for yourself and your son.

14 "For thus says the LORD God of Israel: 'The bin of flour shall not be used up, nor shall the jar of oil run dry, until the day the LORD sends rain on the earth.'"

15 So she went away and did according to the word of E·li′jah; and she and he and her household ate for *many* days.

16 The bin of flour was not used up, nor did the jar of oil run dry, according to the word of the LORD which He spoke by E·li′jah.

ELIJAH REVIVES THE WIDOW'S SON

17 Now it happened after these things *that* the son of the woman who owned the house became sick. And his sickness was so serious that there was no breath left in him.

18 So she said to E·li′jah, "What have I to do with you, O man of God? Have you come to me to bring my sin to remembrance, and to kill my son?"

19 And he said to her, "Give me your son." So he took him out of her arms and carried him to the upper room where he was staying, and laid him on his own bed.

20 Then he cried out to the LORD and said, "O LORD my God, have You also brought tragedy on the widow with whom I lodge, by killing her son?"

21 And he stretched himself out on the child three times, and cried out to the LORD and said, "O LORD my God, I pray, let this child's soul come back to him."

22 Then the LORD heard the voice of E·li′jah; and the soul of the child came back to him, and he revived.

23 And E·li′jah took the child and brought him down from the upper room into the house, and gave him to his mother. And E·li′jah said, "See, your son lives!"

24 Then the woman said to E·li′jah, "Now by this I know that you *are* a man of God, *and* that the word of the LORD in your mouth *is* the truth."

☑   *Bible Quiz*

1 Kings 17 **Ahab and Elijah**

1. Who came to talk to Ahab? What did Elijah tell Ahab?
2. This made Ahab angry. What did Elijah have to do then?
3. How did Elijah get his food when he lived by the brook?
4. When the brook dried up, where did Elijah go?
5. How did the widow help Elijah? How did Elijah help the widow?

ELIJAH'S MESSAGE TO AHAB

There are two kinds of prophets: prophets of God and false prophets. Elijah was a prophet of God. He urged people to worship only God and obey Him. Ahab had false prophets. They told the king whatever he wanted to hear. They didn't believe God was the one true God—until they met Elijah on a mountain!

18 And it came to pass *after* many days that the word of the LORD came to E·lī′jah, in the third year, saying, "Go, present yourself to Ā′hab, and I will send rain on the earth."

2 So E·lī′jah went to present himself to Ā′hab; and *there was* a severe famine in Samaria.

3 And Ā′hab had called Ō·ba·dī′ah, who *was* in charge of *his* house. (Now Ō·ba·dī′ah feared the LORD greatly.

4 For so it was, while Jez′e·bel massacred the prophets of the LORD, that Ō·ba·dī′ah had taken one hundred prophets and hidden them, fifty to a cave, and had fed them with bread and water.)

5 And Ā′hab had said to Ō·ba·dī′ah, "Go into the land to all the springs of water and to all the brooks; perhaps we may find grass to keep the horses and mules alive, so that we will not have to kill any livestock."

6 So they divided the land between them to explore it; Ā′hab went one way by himself, and Ō·ba·dī′ah went another way by himself.

7 Now as Ō·ba·dī′ah was on his way, suddenly E·lī′jah met him; and he recognized him, and fell on his face, and said, "*Is* that you, my lord E·lī′jah?"

8 And he answered him, "*It is* I. Go, tell your master, 'E·lī′jah *is here.*'"

9 So he said, "How have I sinned, that you are delivering your servant into the hand of Ā′hab, to kill me?

10 "*As* the LORD your God lives, there is no nation or kingdom where my master has not sent someone to hunt for you; and when they said, '*He is* not *here*,' he took an oath from the kingdom or nation that they could not find you.

11 "And now you say, 'Go, tell your master, "E·lī′jah *is here*" '!

12 "And it shall come to pass, *as soon as* I am gone from you, that the Spirit of the LORD will carry you to a place I do not know; so when I go and tell Ā′hab, and he cannot find you, he will kill me. But I your servant have feared the LORD from my youth.

13 "Was it not reported to my lord what I did when Jez′e·bel killed the prophets of the LORD, how I hid one hundred men of the LORD's prophets, fifty to a cave, and fed them with bread and water?

14 "And now you say, 'Go, tell your master, "E·lī′jah *is here.*" ' He will kill me!"

15 Then E·lī′jah said, "*As* the LORD of hosts lives, before whom I stand, I will surely present myself to him today."

16 So Ō·ba·dī′ah went to meet Ā′hab, and told him; and Ā′hab went to meet E·lī′jah.

17 Then it happened, when Ā′hab saw E·lī′jah, that Ā′hab said to him, "*Is that* you, O troubler of Israel?"

18 And he answered, "I have not troubled Israel, but you and your father's house *have,* in that you have forsaken the commandments of the LORD and have followed the Bā′als.

19 "Now therefore, send *and* gather all Israel to me on Mount Car′mel, the four hundred and fifty prophets of Bā′al, and the four hundred

prophets of A·shē′rah,*a* who eat at Jez′e·bel's table."

ELIJAH'S MOUNT CARMEL VICTORY

20 So Ā′hab sent for all the children of Israel, and gathered the prophets together on Mount Car′mel.

21 And E·lī′jah came to all the people, and said, "How long will you falter between two opinions? If the LORD *is* God, follow Him; but if Bā′al, follow him." But the people answered him not a word.

22 Then E·lī′jah said to the people, "I alone am left a prophet of the LORD; but Bā′al's prophets *are* four hundred and fifty men.

23 "Therefore let them give us two bulls; and let them choose one bull for themselves, cut it in pieces, and lay *it* on the wood, but put no fire *under it;* and I will prepare the other bull, and lay *it* on the wood, but put no fire *under it.*

24 "Then you call on the name of your gods, and I will call on the name of the LORD; and the God who answers by fire, He is God." So all the people answered and said, "It is well spoken."

25 Now E·lī′jah said to the prophets of Bā′al, "Choose one bull for yourselves and prepare *it* first, for you *are* many; and call on the name of your god, but put no fire *under it.*"

26 So they took the bull which was given them, and they prepared *it,* and called on the name of Bā′al from morning even till noon, saying, "O Bā′al, hear us!" But *there was* no voice; no one answered. Then they leaped about the altar which they had made.

27 And so it was, at noon, that E·lī′jah mocked them and said, "Cry aloud, for he *is* a god; either he is meditating, or he is busy, or he is on a journey, *or* perhaps he is sleeping and must be awakened."

28 So they cried aloud, and cut themselves, as was their custom, with knives and lances, until the blood gushed out on them.

29 And when midday was past, they prophesied until the *time* of the offering of the *evening* sacrifice. But *there was* no voice; no one answered, no one paid attention.

30 Then E·lī′jah said to all the people, "Come near to me." So all the people came near to him. And he repaired the altar of the LORD *that was* broken down.

31 And E·lī′jah took twelve stones, according to the number of the tribes of the sons of Jacob, to whom the word of the LORD had come, saying, "Israel shall be your name."*a*

32 Then with the stones he built an altar in the name of the LORD; and he made a trench around the altar large enough to hold two seahs of seed.

33 And he put the wood in order, cut the bull in pieces, and laid *it* on the wood, and said, "Fill four waterpots with water, and pour *it* on the burnt sacrifice and on the wood."

34 Then he said, "Do *it* a second time," and they did *it* a second time; and he said, "Do *it* a third time," and they did *it* a third time.

35 So the water ran all around the altar; and he also filled the trench with water.

36 And it came to pass, at *the time of* the offering of the *evening* sacrifice, that E·lī′jah the prophet came near and said, "LORD God of Abraham, Isaac, and Israel, let it be known this day that You *are* God in Israel and I *am* Your servant, and *that* I have done all these things at Your word.

37 "Hear me, O LORD, hear me, that

---

this people may know that You *are* the LORD God, and *that* You have turned their hearts back *to You* again."

38 Then the fire of the LORD fell and consumed the burnt sacrifice, and the wood and the stones and the dust, and it licked up the water that *was* in the trench.

39 Now when all the people saw *it,* they fell on their faces; and they said, "The LORD, He *is* God! The LORD, He *is* God!"

40 And E·lī′jah said to them, "Seize the prophets of Bā′al! Do not let one of them escape!" So they seized them; and E·lī′jah brought them down to the Brook Kī′shon and executed them there.

THE DROUGHT ENDS

41 Then E·lī′jah said to Ā′hab, "Go up, eat and drink; for *there is* the sound of abundance of rain."

42 So Ā′hab went up to eat and drink. And E·lī′jah went up to the top of Car′mel; then he bowed down on the ground, and put his face between his knees,

43 and said to his servant, "Go up now, look toward the sea." So he went up and looked, and said, "*There is* nothing." And seven times he said, "Go again."

44 Then it came to pass the seventh *time,* that he said, "There is a cloud, as small as a man's hand, rising out of the sea!" So he said, "Go up, say to Ā′hab, 'Prepare *your chariot,* and go down before the rain stops you.'"

45 Now it happened in the meantime that the sky became black with clouds and wind, and there was a heavy rain. So Ā′hab rode away and went to Jez′rē·el.

46 Then the hand of the LORD came upon E·lī′jah; and he girded up his loins and ran ahead of Ā′hab to the entrance of Jez′rē·el.

☑ ***Bible Quiz***

1 Kings 18 **Elijah and the False Prophets**

1. How long had it been since rain fell on Israel?
2. Whom did Ahab blame for the drought? Who was really to blame? Why?
3. What was the name of the god Ahab and his prophets worshiped?
4. What did Elijah suggest to show who was the one true God?
5. What strange things did the prophets of Baal do to get their fire started? Did anything happen? What did Elijah do? What happened? Who do you believe is the one true God?

ELIJAH ESCAPES FROM JEZEBEL

19 And Ā′hab told Jez′e·bel all that E·lī′jah had done, also how he had executed all the prophets with the sword.

2 Then Jez′e·bel sent a messenger to E·lī′jah, saying, "So let the gods do *to me,* and more also, if I do not make your life as the life of one of them by tomorrow about this time."

3 And when he saw *that,* he arose and ran for his life, and went to Bē·er·shē′ba, which *belongs* to Judah, and left his servant there.

4 But he himself went a day's journey into the wilderness, and came and sat down under a broom tree.

WHEN I'M LONELY OR AFRAID 1 Kings 19:4–8

Denny is lonely. Or is he afraid. Or perhaps he is sad or feeling hurt. Denny needs a big hug. Or does he need to give someone a big hug?

1. Why do you think Denny needs a hug?
2. When do you feel the need for a hug? Why?
3. Has one of your parents hugged you today? Have you hugged them? Why not do that now and say "thank you" for something.
4. Jesus is always with us. He said so. Is that like a hug? How?

For more on *What Should I Do?* turn to page 572
For more on *God's Care* turn to page 645

And he prayed that he might die, and said, "It is enough! Now, LORD, take my life, for I *am* no better than my fathers!"

5 Then as he lay and slept under a broom tree, suddenly an angel[a] touched him, and said to him, "Arise *and* eat."

6 Then he looked, and there by his head *was* a cake baked on coals, and a jar of water. So he ate and drank, and lay down again.

7 And the angel[a] of the LORD came back the second time, and touched him, and said, "Arise *and* eat, because the journey *is* too great for you."

8 So he arose, and ate and drank; and he went in the strength of that food forty days and forty nights as far as Hō′reb, the mountain of God.

9 And there he went into a cave, and spent the night in that place; and behold, the word of the LORD *came* to him, and He said to him, "What are you doing here, E·lī′jah?"

10 So he said, "I have been very zealous for the LORD God of hosts; for the children of Israel have forsaken Your covenant, torn down Your altars, and killed Your prophets with the sword. I alone am left; and they seek to take my life."

GOD'S REVELATION TO ELIJAH

11 Then He said, "Go out, and stand on the mountain before the LORD." And behold, the LORD passed by, and a great and strong wind tore into the mountains and broke the rocks in pieces before the LORD, *but* the LORD *was* not in the wind; and after the wind an earthquake, *but* the LORD *was* not in the earthquake;

12 and after the earthquake a fire, *but* the LORD *was* not in the fire; and after the fire a still small voice.

13 So it was, when E·lī′jah heard *it*,

that he wrapped his face in his mantle and went out and stood in the entrance of the cave. Suddenly a voice *came* to him, and said, "What are you doing here, E·lī′jah?"

14 And he said, "I have been very zealous for the LORD God of hosts; because the children of Israel have forsaken Your covenant, torn down Your altars, and killed Your prophets with the sword. I alone am left; and they seek to take my life."

15 Then the LORD said to him: "Go, return on your way to the Wilderness of Damascus; and when you arrive, anoint Haz′a·el *as* king over Syria.

16 "Also you shall anoint Jē′hū the son of Nim′shī *as* king over Israel. And E·lī′sha the son of Shā′phat of Abel Me·hō′lah you shall anoint *as* prophet in your place.

17 "It shall be *that* whoever escapes the sword of Haz′a·el, Jē′hū will kill; and whoever escapes the sword of Jē′hū, E·lī′sha will kill.

18 "Yet I have reserved seven thousand in Israel, all whose knees have not bowed to Bā′al, and every mouth that has not kissed him."

ELISHA FOLLOWS ELIJAH

19 So he departed from there, and found E·lī′sha the son of Shā′phat, who *was* plowing *with* twelve yoke *of* oxen before him, and he was with the twelfth. Then E·lī′jah passed by him and threw his mantle on him.

20 And he left the oxen and ran after E·lī′jah, and said, "Please let me kiss my father and my mother, and *then* I will follow you." And he said to him, "Go back again, for what have I done to you?"

21 So *E·li′sha* turned back from him, and took a yoke of oxen and slaughtered them and boiled their flesh, us-

19:5 *a*Or Angel   19:7 *a*Or Angel

ing the oxen's equipment, and gave it to the people, and they ate. Then he arose and followed E·li'jah, and became his servant.

Ahab Defeats the Syrians

20 Now Ben-Hā'dad the king of Syria gathered all his forces together; thirty-two kings *were* with him, with horses and chariots. And he went up and besieged Samaria, and made war against it.

2 Then he sent messengers into the city to Ā'hab king of Israel, and said to him, "Thus says Ben-Hā'dad:

3 'Your silver and your gold *are* mine; your loveliest wives and children are mine.' "

4 And the king of Israel answered and said, "My lord, O king, just as you say, I and all that I have *are* yours."

5 Then the messengers came back and said, "Thus speaks Ben-Hā'dad, saying, 'Indeed I have sent to you, saying, "You shall deliver to me your silver and your gold, your wives and your children";

6 'but I will send my servants to you tomorrow about this time, and they shall search your house and the houses of your servants. And it shall be, *that* whatever is pleasant in your eyes, they will put in their hands and take *it*.' "

7 So the king of Israel called all the elders of the land, and said, "Notice, please, and see how this *man* seeks trouble, for he sent to me for my wives, my children, my silver, and my gold; and I did not deny him."

8 And all the elders and all the people said to him, "Do not listen or consent."

9 Therefore he said to the messengers of Ben-Hā'dad, "Tell my lord the king, 'All that you sent for to your servant the first time I will do, but this thing I cannot do.' " And the messengers departed and brought back word to him.

10 Then Ben-Hā'dad sent to him and said, "The gods do so to me, and more also, if enough dust is left of Samaria for a handful for each of the people who follow me."

11 So the king of Israel answered and said, "Tell *him,* 'Let not the one who puts on *his armor* boast like the one who takes *it off*.' "

12 And it happened when *Ben-Hā'dad* heard this message, as he and the kings *were* drinking at the command post, that he said to his servants, "Get ready." And they got ready to attack the city.

13 Suddenly a prophet approached Ā'hab king of Israel, saying, "Thus says the LORD: 'Have you seen all this great multitude? Behold, I will deliver it into your hand today, and you shall know that I *am* the LORD.' "

14 So Ā'hab said, "By whom?" And he said, "Thus says the LORD: 'By the young leaders of the provinces.' " Then he said, "Who will set the battle in order?" And he answered, "You."

15 Then he mustered the young leaders of the provinces, and there were two hundred and thirty-two; and after them he mustered all the people, all the children of Israel— seven thousand.

16 So they went out at noon. Meanwhile Ben-Hā'dad and the thirty-two kings helping him were getting drunk at the command post.

17 The young leaders of the provinces went out first. And Ben-Hā'dad sent out *a patrol,* and they told him, saying, "Men are coming out of Samaria!"

18 So he said, "If they have come out for peace, take them alive; and if they have come out for war, take them alive."

19 Then these young leaders of the provinces went out of the city with the army which followed them.

20 And each one killed his man; so the Syrians fled, and Israel pursued them; and Ben-Hā′dad the king of Syria escaped on a horse with the cavalry.

21 Then the king of Israel went out and attacked the horses and chariots, and killed the Syrians with a great slaughter.

22 And the prophet came to the king of Israel and said to him, "Go, strengthen yourself; take note, and see what you should do, for in the spring of the year the king of Syria will come up against you."

The Syrians Again Defeated

23 Then the servants of the king of Syria said to him, "Their gods are gods of the hills. Therefore they were stronger than we; but if we fight against them in the plain, surely we will be stronger than they.

24 "So do this thing: Dismiss the kings, each from his position, and put captains in their places;

25 "and you shall muster an army like the army that you have lost, horse for horse and chariot for chariot. Then we will fight against them in the plain; surely we will be stronger than they." And he listened to their voice and did so.

26 So it was, in the spring of the year, that Ben-Hā′dad mustered the Syrians and went up to Ā′phek to fight against Israel.

27 And the children of Israel were mustered and given provisions, and they went against them. Now the children of Israel encamped before them like two little flocks of goats, while the Syrians filled the countryside.

28 Then a man of God came and spoke to the king of Israel, and said, "Thus says the LORD: 'Because the Syrians have said, "The LORD is God of the hills, but He is not God of the valleys," therefore I will deliver all this great multitude into your hand, and you shall know that I am the LORD.' "

29 And they encamped opposite each other for seven days. So it was that on the seventh day the battle was joined; and the children of Israel killed one hundred thousand foot soldiers of the Syrians in one day.

30 But the rest fled to Ā′phek, into the city; then a wall fell on twenty-seven thousand of the men who were left. And Ben-Hā′dad fled and went into the city, into an inner chamber.

Ahab's Treaty with Ben-Hadad

31 Then his servants said to him, "Look now, we have heard that the kings of the house of Israel are merciful kings. Please, let us put sackcloth around our waists and ropes around our heads, and go out to the king of Israel; perhaps he will spare your life."

32 So they wore sackcloth around their waists and put ropes around their heads, and came to the king of Israel and said, "Your servant Ben-Hā′dad says, 'Please let me live.' " And he said, "Is he still alive? He is my brother."

33 Now the men were watching closely to see whether any sign of mercy would come from him; and they quickly grasped at this word and said, "Your brother Ben-Hā′dad." So he said, "Go, bring him." Then Ben-Hā′dad came out to him; and he had him come up into the chariot.

34 So Ben-Hā′dad said to him, "The cities which my father took from your father I will restore; and you may set

up marketplaces for yourself in Damascus, as my father did in Samaria." Then Ā'hab said, "I will send you away with this treaty." So he made a treaty with him and sent him away.

AHAB CONDEMNED

35 Now a certain man of the sons of the prophets said to his neighbor by the word of the LORD, "Strike me, please." And the man refused to strike him.

36 Then he said to him, "Because you have not obeyed the voice of the LORD, surely, as soon as you depart from me, a lion shall kill you." And as soon as he left him, a lion found him and killed him.

37 And he found another man, and said, "Strike me, please." So the man struck him, inflicting a wound.

38 Then the prophet departed and waited for the king by the road, and disguised himself with a bandage over his eyes.

39 Now as the king passed by, he cried out to the king and said, "Your servant went out into the midst of the battle; and there, a man came over and brought a man to me, and said, 'Guard this man; if by any means he is missing, your life shall be for his life, or else you shall pay a talent of silver.'

40 "While your servant was busy here and there, he was gone." Then the king of Israel said to him, "So shall your judgment be; you yourself have decided it."

41 And he hastened to take the bandage away from his eyes; and the king of Israel recognized him as one of the prophets.

42 Then he said to him, "Thus says the LORD: 'Because you have let slip out of your hand a man whom I appointed to utter destruction, there-

fore your life shall go for his life, and your people for his people.' "

43 So the king of Israel went to his house sullen and displeased, and came to Samaria.

NABOTH IS MURDERED FOR HIS VINEYARD

21 And it came to pass after these things that Nā'both the Jez'rē·el·īte had a vineyard which was in Jez'rē·el, next to the palace of Ā'hab king of Samaria.

2 So Ā'hab spoke to Nā'both, saying, "Give me your vineyard, that I may have it for a vegetable garden, because it is near, next to my house; and for it I will give you a vineyard better than it. Or, if it seems good to you, I will give you its worth in money."

3 But Nā'both said to Ā'hab, "The LORD forbid that I should give the inheritance of my fathers to you!"

4 So Ā'hab went into his house sullen and displeased because of the word which Nā'both the Jez'rē·el·īte had spoken to him; for he had said, "I will not give you the inheritance of my fathers." And he lay down on his bed, and turned away his face, and would eat no food.

5 But Jez'e·bel his wife came to him, and said to him, "Why is your spirit so sullen that you eat no food?"

6 He said to her, "Because I spoke to Nā'both the Jez'rē·el·īte, and said to him, 'Give me your vineyard for money; or else, if it pleases you, I will give you another vineyard for it.' And he answered, 'I will not give you my vineyard.' "

7 Then Jez'e·bel his wife said to him, "You now exercise authority over Israel! Arise, eat food, and let your heart be cheerful; I will give you the vineyard of Nā'both the Jez'rē·el·īte."

8 And she wrote letters in Ā'hab's name, sealed *them* with his seal, and sent the letters to the elders and the nobles who *were* dwelling in the city with Nā'both.
9 She wrote in the letters, saying,

Proclaim a fast, and seat Nā'both with high honor among the people;
10 and seat two men, scoundrels, before him to bear witness against him, saying, "You have blasphemed God and the king." *Then* take him out, and stone him, that he may die.

11 So the men of his city, the elders and nobles who were inhabitants of his city, did as Jez'e·bel had sent to them, as it *was* written in the letters which she had sent to them.
12 They proclaimed a fast, and seated Nā'both with high honor among the people.
13 And two men, scoundrels, came in and sat before him; and the scoundrels witnessed against him, against Nā'both, in the presence of the people, saying, "Nā'both has blasphemed God and the king!" Then they took him outside the city and stoned him with stones, so that he died.
14 Then they sent to Jez'e·bel, saying, "Nā'both has been stoned and is dead."
15 And it came to pass, when Jez'e·bel heard that Nā'both had been stoned and was dead, that Jez'e·bel said to Ā'hab, "Arise, take possession of the vineyard of Nā'both the Jez're·el·ite, which he refused to give you for money; for Nā'both is not alive, but dead."
16 So it was, when Ā'hab heard that Nā'both was dead, that Ā'hab got up and went down to take possession of the vineyard of Nā'both the Jez're·el·ite.

THE LORD CONDEMNS AHAB

17 Then the word of the LORD came to E·lī'jah the Tish'bīte, saying,
18 "Arise, go down to meet Ā'hab king of Israel, who *lives* in Samaria. There *he is,* in the vineyard of Nā'both, where he has gone down to take possession of it.
19 "You shall speak to him, saying, 'Thus says the LORD: "Have you murdered and also taken possession?" ' And you shall speak to him, saying, 'Thus says the LORD: "In the place where dogs licked the blood of Nā'-both, dogs shall lick your blood, even yours." ' "
20 So Ā'hab said to E·lī'jah, "Have you found me, O my enemy?" And he answered, "I have found *you,* because you have sold yourself to do evil in the sight of the LORD:
21 'Behold, I will bring calamity on you. I will take away your posterity, and will cut off from Ā'hab every male in Israel, both bond and free.
22 'I will make your house like the house of Jer·o·bō'am the son of Nē'-bat, and like the house of Bā'a·sha the son of A·hī'jah, because of the provocation with which you have provoked *Me* to anger, and made Israel sin.'
23 "And concerning Jez'e·bel the LORD also spoke, saying, 'The dogs shall eat Jez'e·bel by the wall[a] of Jez're·el.'
24 "The dogs shall eat whoever belongs to Ā'hab and dies in the city, and the birds of the air shall eat whoever dies in the field."
25 But there was no one like Ā'hab who sold himself to do wickedness in the sight of the LORD, because Jez'e·bel his wife stirred him up.
26 And he behaved very abominably

21:23 [a]Following Masoretic Text and Septuagint; some Hebrew manuscripts, Syriac, Targum, and Vulgate read *plot of ground* (compare 2 Kings 9:36).

in following idols, according to all *that* the Am′o·rītes had done, whom the LORD had cast out before the children of Israel.

27 So it was, when Ā′hab heard those words, that he tore his clothes and put sackcloth on his body, and fasted and lay in sackcloth, and went about mourning.

28 And the word of the LORD came to E·lī′jah the Tish′bīte, saying,

29 "See how Ā′hab has humbled himself before Me? Because he has humbled himself before Me, I will not bring the calamity in his days. In the days of his son I will bring the calamity on his house."

MICAIAH WARNS AHAB

22 Now three years passed without war between Syria and Israel.

2 Then it came to pass, in the third year, that Je·hosh′a·phat the king of Judah went down to *visit* the king of Israel.

3 And the king of Israel said to his servants, "Do you know that Rā′moth in Gil′ē·ad *is* ours, but we hesitate to take it out of the hand of the king of Syria?"

4 So he said to Je·hosh′a·phat, "Will you go with me to fight at Rā′moth Gil′ē·ad?" Je·hosh′a·phat said to the king of Israel, "I *am* as you *are,* my people as your people, my horses as your horses."

5 Also Je·hosh′a·phat said to the king of Israel, "Please inquire for the word of the LORD today."

6 Then the king of Israel gathered the prophets together, about four hundred men, and said to them, "Shall I go against Rā′moth Gil′ē·ad to fight, or shall I refrain?" So they said, "Go up, for the Lord will deliver *it* into the hand of the king."

7 And Je·hosh′a·phat said, "*Is there* not still a prophet of the LORD here, that we may inquire of Him?"*a*

8 So the king of Israel said to Je·hosh′a·phat, "*There is* still one man, Mī·cāi′ah the son of Im′lah, by whom we may inquire of the LORD; but I hate him, because he does not prophesy good concerning me, but evil." And Je·hosh′a·phat said, "Let not the king say such things!"

9 Then the king of Israel called an officer and said, "Bring Mī·cāi′ah the son of Im′lah quickly!"

10 The king of Israel and Je·hosh′a·phat the king of Judah, having put on *their* robes, sat each on his throne, at a threshing floor at the entrance of the gate of Samaria; and all the prophets prophesied before them.

11 Now Zed·e·kī′ah the son of Che·nā′a·nah had made horns of iron for himself; and he said, "Thus says the LORD: 'With these you shall gore the Syrians until they are destroyed.'"

12 And all the prophets prophesied so, saying, "Go up to Rā′moth Gil′ē·ad and prosper, for the LORD will deliver *it* into the king's hand."

13 Then the messenger who had gone to call Mī·cāi′ah spoke to him, saying, "Now listen, the words of the prophets with one accord encourage the king. Please, let your word be like the word of one of them, and speak encouragement."

14 And Mī·cāi′ah said, "*As* the LORD lives, whatever the LORD says to me, that I will speak."

15 Then he came to the king; and the king said to him, "Mī·cāi′ah, shall we go to war against Rā′moth Gil′ē·ad, or shall we refrain?" And he answered him, "Go and prosper, for the LORD will deliver *it* into the hand of the king!"

16 So the king said to him, "How many times shall I make you swear

22:7 *a* Or *him*

that you tell me nothing but the truth in the name of the LORD?"

17 Then he said, "I saw all Israel scattered on the mountains, as sheep that have no shepherd. And the LORD said, 'These have no master. Let each return to his house in peace.' "

18 And the king of Israel said to Je·hosh'a·phat, "Did I not tell you he would not prophesy good concerning me, but evil?"

19 Then *Mī·cāi'ah* said, "Therefore hear the word of the LORD: I saw the LORD sitting on His throne, and all the host of heaven standing by, on His right hand and on His left.

20 "And the LORD said, 'Who will persuade Ā'hab to go up, that he may fall at Rā'moth Gil'ē·ad?' So one spoke in this manner, and another spoke in that manner.

21 "Then a spirit came forward and stood before the LORD, and said, 'I will persuade him.'

22 "The LORD said to him, 'In what way?' So he said, 'I will go out and be a lying spirit in the mouth of all his prophets.' And the LORD said, 'You shall persuade *him,* and also prevail. Go out and do so.'

23 "Therefore look! The LORD has put a lying spirit in the mouth of all these prophets of yours, and the LORD has declared disaster against you."

24 Now Zed·e·kī'ah the son of Che·nā'a·nah went near and struck Mī·cāi'ah on the cheek, and said, "Which way did the spirit from the LORD go from me to speak to you?"

25 And Mī·cāi'ah said, "Indeed, you shall see on that day when you go into an inner chamber to hide!"

26 So the king of Israel said, "Take Mī·cāi'ah, and return him to Ā'mon the governor of the city and to Jō'ash the king's son;

27 "and say, 'Thus says the king: "Put this *fellow* in prison, and feed him with bread of affliction and water of affliction, until I come in peace." ' "

28 But Mī·cāi'ah said, "If you ever return in peace, the LORD has not spoken by me." And he said, "Take heed, all you people!"

AHAB DIES IN BATTLE

29 So the king of Israel and Je·hosh'a·phat the king of Judah went up to Rā'moth Gil'ē·ad.

30 And the king of Israel said to Je·hosh'a·phat, "I will disguise myself and go into battle; but you put on your robes." So the king of Israel disguised himself and went into battle.

31 Now the king of Syria had commanded the thirty-two captains of his chariots, saying, "Fight with no one small or great, but only with the king of Israel."

32 So it was, when the captains of the chariots saw Je·hosh'a·phat, that they said, "Surely it *is* the king of Israel!" Therefore they turned aside to fight against him, and Je·hosh'a·phat cried out.

33 And it happened, when the captains of the chariots saw that it *was* not the king of Israel, that they turned back from pursuing him.

34 Now a *certain* man drew a bow at random, and struck the king of Israel between the joints of his armor. So he said to the driver of his chariot, "Turn around and take me out of the battle, for I am wounded."

35 The battle increased that day; and the king was propped up in his chariot, facing the Syrians, and died at evening. The blood ran out from the wound onto the floor of the chariot.

36 Then, as the sun was going down, a shout went throughout the army, saying, "Every man to his city, and every man to his own country!"

37 So the king died, and was brought to Samaria. And they buried the king in Samaria.

38 Then *someone* washed the chariot at a pool in Samaria, and the dogs licked up his blood while the harlots bathed,[a] according to the word of the LORD which He had spoken.

39 Now the rest of the acts of Ā′hab, and all that he did, the ivory house which he built and all the cities that he built, *are* they not written in the book of the chronicles of the kings of Israel?

40 So Ā′hab rested with his fathers. Then Ā·ha·zī′ah his son reigned in his place.

JEHOSHAPHAT REIGNS IN JUDAH

41 Je·hosh′a·phat the son of Ā′sa had become king over Judah in the fourth year of Ā′hab king of Israel.

42 Je·hosh′a·phat *was* thirty-five years old when he became king, and he reigned twenty-five years in Jerusalem. His mother's name *was* A·zū′bah the daughter of Shil′hī.

43 And he walked in all the ways of his father Ā′sa. He did not turn aside from them, doing *what was* right in the eyes of the LORD. Nevertheless the high places were not taken away, *for* the people offered sacrifices and burned incense on the high places.

44 Also Je·hosh′a·phat made peace with the king of Israel.

45 Now the rest of the acts of Je·hosh′a·phat, the might that he showed, and how he made war, *are* they not written in the book of the chronicles of the kings of Judah?

46 And the rest of the perverted persons,[a] who remained in the days of his father Ā′sa, he banished from the land.

47 *There was* then no king in Ē′dom, only a deputy of the king.

48 Je·hosh′a·phat made merchant ships[a] to go to Ō′phir for gold; but they never sailed, for the ships were wrecked at Ē′zi·on Gē′ber.

49 Then Ā·ha·zī′ah the son of Ā′hab said to Je·hosh′a·phat, "Let my servants go with your servants in the ships." But Je·hosh′a·phat would not.

50 And Je·hosh′a·phat rested with his fathers, and was buried with his fathers in the City of David his father. Then Je·hō′ram his son reigned in his place.

AZHAZZIAH REIGNS IN ISRAEL

51 Ā·ha·zī′ah the son of Ā′hab became king over Israel in Samaria in the seventeenth year of Je·hosh′a·phat king of Judah, and reigned two years over Israel.

52 He did evil in the sight of the LORD, and walked in the way of his father and in the way of his mother and in the way of Jer·o·bō′am the son of Nē′bat, who had made Israel sin;

53 for he served Bā′al and worshiped him, and provoked the LORD God of Israel to anger, according to all that his father had done.

22:38 [a]Syriac and Targum read *they washed his armor.*   22:46 [a]Hebrew *qadesh,* that is, one practicing sodomy and prostitution in religious rituals   22:48 [a]Or *ships of Tarshish*

GOD JUDGES AHAZIAH

MOAB rebelled against Israel after the death of Ā′hab.

2 Now Ā·ha·zī′ah fell through the lattice of his upper room in Samaria, and was injured; so he sent messengers and said to them, "Go, inquire of Bā′ al-Zē′bub, the god of Ek′ron, whether I shall recover from this injury."

3 But the angel*a* of the LORD said to E·lī′jah the Tish′bīte, "Arise, go up to meet the messengers of the king of Samaria, and say to them, '*Is it* because *there is* no God in Israel *that* you are going to inquire of Bā′ al-Zē′bub, the god of Ek′ron?'

4 "Now therefore, thus says the LORD: 'You shall not come down from the bed to which you have gone up, but you shall surely die.' " So E·lī′jah departed.

5 And when the messengers returned to him, he said to them, "Why have you come back?"

6 So they said to him, "A man came up to meet us, and said to us, 'Go, return to the king who sent you, and say to him, "Thus says the LORD: '*Is it* because *there is* no God in Israel *that* you are sending to inquire of Bā′al-Zē′bub, the god of Ek′ron? Therefore you shall not come down from the bed to which you have gone up, but you shall surely die.' " ' "

7 Then he said to them, "What kind of man *was it* who came up to meet you and told you these words?"

8 So they answered him, "A hairy man wearing a leather belt around his waist." And he said, "It *is* E·lī′jah the Tish′bīte."

9 Then the king sent to him a captain of fifty with his fifty men. So he went up to him; and there he was, sitting on the top of a hill. And he spoke to him: "Man of God, the king has said, 'Come down!' "

10 So E·lī′jah answered and said to the captain of fifty, "If I *am* a man of God, then let fire come down from heaven and consume you and your fifty men." And fire came down from heaven and consumed him and his fifty.

11 Then he sent to him another captain of fifty with his fifty men. And he answered and said to him: "Man of God, thus has the king said, 'Come down quickly!' "

12 So E·lī′jah answered and said to them, "If I *am* a man of God, let fire come down from heaven and consume you and your fifty men." And the fire of God came down from heaven and consumed him and his fifty.

13 Again, he sent a third captain of fifty with his fifty men. And the third captain of fifty went up, and came and fell on his knees before E·lī′jah, and pleaded with him, and said to him: "Man of God, please let my life and the life of these fifty servants of yours be precious in your sight.

14 "Look, fire has come down from heaven and burned up the first two captains of fifties with their fifties. But let my life now be precious in your sight."

15 And the angel*a* of the LORD said to E·lī′jah, "Go down with him; do not be afraid of him." So he arose and went down with him to the king.

16 Then he said to him, "Thus says the LORD: 'Because you have sent messengers to inquire of Bā′ al-Zē′bub, the god of Ek′ron, *is it* be-

1:3 *a*Or Angel   1:15 *a*Or Angel

cause *there is* no God in Israel to inquire of His word? Therefore you shall not come down from the bed to which you have gone up, but you shall surely die.' "

17 So Ā·ha·zī′ah died according to the word of the LORD which E·lī′jah had spoken. Because he had no son, Je·hō′ram*a* became king in his place, in the second year of Je·hō′ram the son of Je·hosh′a·phat, king of Judah.

18 Now the rest of the acts of Ā·ha·zī′ah which he did, *are* they not written in the book of the chronicles of the kings of Israel?

ELIJAH ASCENDS TO HEAVEN

There are only two men who never died. Elijah was one of them. This is how he went straight to heaven without dying.

2 And it came to pass, when the LORD was about to take up E·lī′jah into heaven by a whirlwind, that E·lī′jah went with E·lī′sha from Gil′gal.

2 Then E·lī′jah said to E·lī′sha, "Stay here, please, for the LORD has sent me on to Beth′el." But E·lī′sha said, "*As* the LORD lives, and *as* your soul lives, I will not leave you!" So they went down to Beth′el.

3 Now the sons of the prophets who *were* at Beth′el came out to E·lī′sha, and said to him, "Do you know that the LORD will take away your master from over you today?" And he said, "Yes, I know; keep silent!"

4 Then E·lī′jah said to him, "E·lī′-sha, stay here, please, for the LORD has sent me on to Jericho." But he said, "*As* the LORD lives, and *as* your soul lives, I will not leave you!" So they came to Jericho.

5 Now the sons of the prophets who *were* at Jericho came to E·lī′sha and said to him, "Do you know that the LORD will take away your master from over you today?" So he answered, "Yes, I know; keep silent!"

6 Then E·lī′jah said to him, "Stay here, please, for the LORD has sent me on to the Jordan." But he said, "*As* the LORD lives, and *as* your soul lives, I will not leave you!" So the two of them went on.

7 And fifty men of the sons of the prophets went and stood facing *them* at a distance, while the two of them stood by the Jordan.

8 Now E·lī′jah took his mantle, rolled *it* up, and struck the water; and it was divided this way and that, so that the two of them crossed over on dry ground.

9 And so it was, when they had crossed over, that E·lī′jah said to E·lī′sha, "Ask! What may I do for you, before I am taken away from you?" E·lī′sha said, "Please let a double portion of your spirit be upon me."

10 So he said, "You have asked a hard thing. *Nevertheless,* if you see me *when I am* taken from you, it shall be so for you; but if not, it shall not be *so.*"

11 Then it happened, as they continued on and talked, that suddenly a chariot of fire *appeared* with horses of fire, and separated the two of them; and E·lī′jah went up by a whirlwind into heaven.

12 And E·lī′sha saw *it,* and he cried out, "My father, my father, the chariot of Israel and its horsemen!" So he saw him no more. And he took hold of his own clothes and tore them into two pieces.

13 He also took up the mantle of E·lī′jah that had fallen from him, and went back and stood by the bank of the Jordan.

1:17 *a*The son of Ahab king of Israel (compare 3:1)

14 Then he took the mantle of E·lī′jah that had fallen from him, and struck the water, and said, "Where *is* the LORD God of E·lī′jah?" And when he also had struck the water, it was divided this way and that; and E·lī′sha crossed over.

☑ *Bible Quiz*

2 Kings 2:1–14 **Elijah Goes to Heaven in a Chariot of Fire**

1. What carried Elijah up to heaven?

2. Who saw Elijah go? Why was it important for Elisha to see Elijah go up to heaven?

3. How do you know that Elijah was a great man of God?

---

15 Now when the sons of the prophets who *were* from Jericho saw him, they said, "The spirit of E·lī′jah rests on E·lī′sha." And they came to meet him, and bowed to the ground before him.
16 Then they said to him, "Look now, there are fifty strong men with your servants. Please let them go and search for your master, lest perhaps the Spirit of the LORD has taken him up and cast him upon some mountain or into some valley." And he said, "You shall not send anyone."
17 But when they urged him till he was ashamed, he said, "Send *them!*" Therefore they sent fifty men, and they searched for three days but did not find him.
18 And when they came back to him, for he had stayed in Jericho, he said to them, "Did I not say to you, 'Do not go'?"

ELISHA PERFORMS MIRACLES

19 Then the men of the city said to E·lī′sha, "Please notice, the situation of this city *is* pleasant, as my lord sees; but the water *is* bad, and the ground barren."
20 And he said, "Bring me a new bowl, and put salt in it." So they brought *it* to him.
21 Then he went out to the source of the water, and cast in the salt there, and said, "Thus says the LORD: 'I have healed this water; from it there shall be no more death or barrenness.'"
22 So the water remains healed to this day, according to the word of E·lī′sha which he spoke.
23 Then he went up from there to Beth′el; and as he was going up the road, some youths came from the city and mocked him, and said to him, "Go up, you baldhead! Go up, you baldhead!"
24 So he turned around and looked at them, and pronounced a curse on them in the name of the LORD. And two female bears came out of the woods and mauled forty-two of the youths.
25 Then he went from there to Mount Car′mel, and from there he returned to Samaria.

MOAB REBELS AGAINST ISRAEL

3 Now Je·hō′ram the son of Ā′hab became king over Israel at Samaria in the eighteenth year of Je·hosh′a·phat king of Judah, and reigned twelve years.
2 And he did evil in the sight of the LORD, but not like his father and mother; for he put away the *sacred* pillar of Bā′al that his father had made.
3 Nevertheless he persisted in the sins of Jer·o·bō′am the son of Nē′bat,

who had made Israel sin; he did not depart from them.

4 Now Mē′sha king of Mō′ab was a sheepbreeder, and he regularly paid the king of Israel one hundred thousand lambs and the wool of one hundred thousand rams.

5 But it happened, when Ā′hab died, that the king of Mō′ab rebelled against the king of Israel.

6 So King Je·hō′ram went out of Samaria at that time and mustered all Israel.

7 Then he went and sent to Je·hosh′a·phat king of Judah, saying, "The king of Mō′ab has rebelled against me. Will you go with me to fight against Mō′ab?" And he said, "I will go up; I am as you are, my people as your people, my horses as your horses."

8 Then he said, "Which way shall we go up?" And he answered, "By way of the Wilderness of Ē′dom."

9 So the king of Israel went with the king of Judah and the king of Ē′dom, and they marched on that roundabout route seven days; and there was no water for the army, nor for the animals that followed them.

10 And the king of Israel said, "Alas! For the LORD has called these three kings together to deliver them into the hand of Mō′ab."

11 But Je·hosh′a·phat said, "Is there no prophet of the LORD here, that we may inquire of the LORD by him?" So one of the servants of the king of Israel answered and said, "E·lī′sha the son of Shā′phat is here, who poured water on the hands of E·lī′jah."

12 And Je·hosh′a·phat said, "The word of the LORD is with him." So the king of Israel and Je·hosh′a·phat and the king of Ē′dom went down to him.

13 Then E·lī′sha said to the king of Israel, "What have I to do with you? Go to the prophets of your father and the prophets of your mother." But the king of Israel said to him, "No, for the LORD has called these three kings together to deliver them into the hand of Mō′ab."

14 And E·lī′sha said, "As the LORD of hosts lives, before whom I stand, surely were it not that I regard the presence of Je·hosh′a·phat king of Judah, I would not look at you, nor see you.

15 "But now bring me a musician." Then it happened, when the musician played, that the hand of the LORD came upon him.

16 And he said, "Thus says the LORD: 'Make this valley full of ditches.'

17 "For thus says the LORD: 'You shall not see wind, nor shall you see rain; yet that valley shall be filled with water, so that you, your cattle, and your animals may drink.'

18 "And this is a simple matter in the sight of the LORD; He will also deliver the Mō′ab·ītes into your hand.

19 "Also you shall attack every fortified city and every choice city, and shall cut down every good tree, and stop up every spring of water, and ruin every good piece of land with stones."

20 Now it happened in the morning, when the grain offering was offered, that suddenly water came by way of Ē′dom, and the land was filled with water.

21 And when all the Mō′ab·ītes heard that the kings had come up to fight against them, all who were able to bear arms and older were gathered; and they stood at the border.

22 Then they rose up early in the morning, and the sun was shining on the water; and the Mō′ab·ītes saw the water on the other side as red as blood.

23 And they said, "This is blood; the kings have surely struck swords and have killed one another; now therefore, Mō′ab, to the spoil!"

24 So when they came to the camp of Israel, Israel rose up and attacked the Mō′ab·ītes, so that they fled before them; and they entered *their* land, killing the Mō′ab·ītes.

25 Then they destroyed the cities, and each man threw a stone on every good piece of land and filled it; and they stopped up all the springs of water and cut down all the good trees. But they left the stones of Kir Har′a·seth *intact.* However the slingers surrounded and attacked it.

26 And when the king of Mō′ab saw that the battle was too fierce for him, he took with him seven hundred men who drew swords, to break through to the king of Ē′dom, but they could not.

27 Then he took his eldest son who would have reigned in his place, and offered him *as* a burnt offering upon the wall; and there was great indignation against Israel. So they departed from him and returned to *their own* land.

ELISHA AND THE WIDOW'S OIL

Elijah had gone to heaven. Now Elisha was God's prophet. God helped Elisha do many miracles. Here are some of them.

4 A certain woman of the wives of the sons of the prophets cried out to E·lī′sha, saying, "Your servant my husband is dead, and you know that your servant feared the LORD. And the creditor is coming to take my two sons to be his slaves."

2 So E·lī′sha said to her, "What shall I do for you? Tell me, what do you have in the house?" And she said, "Your maidservant has nothing in the house but a jar of oil."

3 Then he said, "Go, borrow vessels from everywhere, from all your neighbors—empty vessels; do not gather just a few.

4 "And when you have come in, you shall shut the door behind you and your sons; then pour it into all those vessels, and set aside the full ones."

5 So she went from him and shut the door behind her and her sons, who brought *the vessels* to her; and she poured *it* out.

6 Now it came to pass, when the vessels were full, that she said to her son, "Bring me another vessel." And he said to her, "*There is* not another vessel." So the oil ceased.

7 Then she came and told the man of God. And he said, "Go, sell the oil and pay your debt; and you *and* your sons live on the rest."

ELISHA RAISES THE SHUNAMMITE'S SON

8 Now it happened one day that E·lī′sha went to Shū′nem, where there *was* a notable woman, and she persuaded him to eat some food. So it was, as often as he passed by, he would turn in there to eat some food.

9 And she said to her husband, "Look now, I know that this *is* a holy man of God, who passes by us regularly.

10 "Please, let us make a small upper room on the wall; and let us put a bed for him there, and a table and a chair and a lampstand; so it will be, whenever he comes to us, he can turn in there."

11 And it happened one day that he came there, and he turned in to the upper room and lay down there.

12 Then he said to Ge·hā′zī his servant, "Call this Shū′nam·mīte woman." When he had called her, she stood before him.

13 And he said to him, "Say now to her, 'Look, you have been concerned

*W*hen the wrong friends say, "Follow me," I will stay.
When Jesus says, "Follow Me," I will go.

Deuteronomy 13:6–8

My umbrella protects me from rain;
My God protects me from bad things.

———

2 Samuel 3:18

"Please" and *"Thank you"* are special words,
even when talking with God.

1 Chronicles 29:13

*W*hen we pray, we talk to God.

———

Nehemiah 1:5, 6

for us with all this care. What *can I* do for you? Do you want me to speak on your behalf to the king or to the commander of the army?' " She answered, "I dwell among my own people."

14 So he said, "What then *is* to be done for her?" And Ge·hā′zī answered, "Actually, she has no son, and her husband is old."

15 So he said, "Call her." When he had called her, she stood in the doorway.

16 Then he said, "About this time next year you shall embrace a son." And she said, "No, my lord. Man of God, do not lie to your maidservant!"

17 But the woman conceived, and bore a son when the appointed time had come, of which E·lī′sha had told her.

18 And the child grew. Now it happened one day that he went out to his father, to the reapers.

19 And he said to his father, "My head, my head!" So he said to a servant, "Carry him to his mother."

20 When he had taken him and brought him to his mother, he sat on her knees till noon, and *then* died.

21 And she went up and laid him on the bed of the man of God, shut *the door* upon him, and went out.

22 Then she called to her husband, and said, "Please send me one of the young men and one of the donkeys, that I may run to the man of God and come back."

23 So he said, "Why are you going to him today? *It is* neither the New Moon nor the Sabbath." And she said, "*It is* well."

24 Then she saddled a donkey, and said to her servant, "Drive, and go forward; do not slacken the pace for me unless I tell you."

25 And so she departed, and went to the man of God at Mount Car′mel.

So it was, when the man of God saw her afar off, that he said to his servant Ge·hā′zī, "Look, the Shū′nam·mīte woman!

26 "Please run now to meet her, and say to her, '*Is it* well with you? *Is it* well with your husband? *Is it* well with the child?' " And she answered, "*It is* well."

27 Now when she came to the man of God at the hill, she caught him by the feet, but Ge·hā′zī came near to push her away. But the man of God said, "Let her alone; for her soul *is* in deep distress, and the LORD has hidden *it* from me, and has not told me."

28 So she said, "Did I ask a son of my lord? Did I not say, 'Do not deceive me'?"

29 Then he said to Ge·hā′zī, "Get yourself ready, and take my staff in your hand, and be on your way. If you meet anyone, do not greet him; and if anyone greets you, do not answer him; but lay my staff on the face of the child."

30 And the mother of the child said, "*As* the LORD lives, and *as* your soul lives, I will not leave you." So he arose and followed her.

31 Now Ge·hā′zī went on ahead of them, and laid the staff on the face of the child; but *there was* neither voice nor hearing. Therefore he went back to meet him, and told him, saying, "The child has not awakened."

32 When E·lī′sha came into the house, there was the child, lying dead on his bed.

33 He went in therefore, shut the door behind the two of them, and prayed to the LORD.

34 And he went up and lay on the child, and put his mouth on his mouth, his eyes on his eyes, and his hands on his hands; and he stretched himself out on the child, and the flesh of the child became warm.

35 He returned and walked back and forth in the house, and again went up

and stretched himself out on him;
then the child sneezed seven times,
and the child opened his eyes.

36 And he called Ge·hā′zī and said,
"Call this Shū′nam·mīte woman." So
he called her. And when she came in
to him, he said, "Pick up your son."
37 So she went in, fell at his feet,
and bowed to the ground; then she
picked up her son and went out.

☑ Bible Quiz

2 Kings 4:1–37 **Elisha Raises a Boy to Life**

1. Why was the widow so sad? How did Elisha help?
2. Elisha met a woman from Shunem. What did she want so much? How did Elisha help?
3. What happened to the woman's son? How did Elisha help again?
4. Who really performed these miracles? Do you think God can still do miracles? What miracles do we see around us every day?

ELISHA PURIFIES THE POT OF STEW

38 And E·lī′sha returned to Gil′gal,
and *there was* a famine in the land.
Now the sons of the prophets *were*
sitting before him; and he said to his
servant, "Put on the large pot, and
boil stew for the sons of the
prophets."
39 So one went out into the field to
gather herbs, and found a wild vine,
and gathered from it a lapful of wild
gourds, and came and sliced *them*
into the pot of stew, though they did
not know *what they were*.

40 Then they served it to the men to
eat. Now it happened, as they were
eating the stew, that they cried out
and said, "Man of God, *there is* death
in the pot!" And they could not eat *it*.
41 So he said, "Then bring some
flour." And he put *it* into the pot, and
said, "Serve *it* to the people, that they
may eat." And there was nothing
harmful in the pot.

ELISHA FEEDS ONE HUNDRED MEN

42 Then a man came from Bā′al
Shal′i·sha, and brought the man of
God bread of the firstfruits, twenty
loaves of barley bread, and newly
ripened grain in his knapsack. And
he said, "Give *it* to the people, that
they may eat."
43 But his servant said, "What?
Shall I set this before one hundred
men?" He said again, "Give it to the
people, that they may eat; for thus
says the LORD: 'They shall eat and
have *some* left over.' "
44 So he set *it* before them; and they
ate and had *some* left over, according
to the word of the LORD.

NAAMAN'S LEPROSY HEALED

*This is a story about a man
who took a bath in dirty water,
and became clean!*

5 Now Nā′a·man, commander of
the army of the king of Syria, was a
great and honorable man in the eyes
of his master, because by him the
LORD had given victory to Syria. He
was also a mighty man of valor, *but* a
leper.
2 And the Syrians had gone out on
raids, and had brought back captive a
young girl from the land of Israel.
She waited on Nā′a·man's wife.
3 Then she said to her mistress, "If
only my master *were* with the

prophet who *is* in Samaria! For he would heal him of his leprosy."

4 And *Nā′a·man* went in and told his master, saying, "Thus and thus said the girl who *is* from the land of Israel."

5 Then the king of Syria said, "Go now, and I will send a letter to the king of Israel." So he departed and took with him ten talents of silver, six thousand *shekels* of gold, and ten changes of clothing.

6 Then he brought the letter to the king of Israel, which said,

Now be advised, when this letter comes to you, that I have sent Nā′a·man my servant to you, that you may heal him of his leprosy.

7 And it happened, when the king of Israel read the letter, that he tore his clothes and said, "*Am* I God, to kill and make alive, that this man sends a man to me to heal him of his leprosy? Therefore please consider, and see how he seeks a quarrel with me."

8 So it was, when E·lī′sha the man of God heard that the king of Israel had torn his clothes, that he sent to the king, saying, "Why have you torn your clothes? Please let him come to me, and he shall know that there is a prophet in Israel."

9 Then Nā′a·man went with his horses and chariot, and he stood at the door of E·lī′sha's house.

10 And E·lī′sha sent a messenger to him, saying, "Go and wash in the Jordan seven times, and your flesh shall be restored to you, and *you shall* be clean."

11 But Nā′a·man became furious, and went away and said, "Indeed, I said to myself, 'He will surely come out *to me,* and stand and call on the name of the LORD his God, and wave his hand over the place, and heal the leprosy.'

12 "*Are* not the A·bā′nah*a* and the Phar′par, the rivers of Damascus, better than all the waters of Israel? Could I not wash in them and be clean?" So he turned and went away in a rage.

13 And his servants came near and spoke to him, and said, "My father, *if* the prophet had told you *to do* something great, would you not have done *it?* How much more then, when he says to you, 'Wash, and be clean'?"

14 So he went down and dipped seven times in the Jordan, according to the saying of the man of God; and his flesh was restored like the flesh of a little child, and he was clean.

5:12 *a*Following Kethib, Septuagint, and Vulgate; Qere, Syriac, and Targum read *Amanah.*

☑ *Bible Quiz*

2 Kings 5:1–14 **Naaman Is Healed of Leprosy**

1. What country was Naaman from? What was his job?
2. What terrible disease did Naaman have?
3. Who told him about Elisha?
4. What did Elisha tell Naaman to do to get healed? What did Naaman do first?
5. What happened when Naaman washed in the river?
6. Some things God asks us to do are hard, or they may embarrass us before our friends (like reading the Bible or praying). But God knows what is best for us. Will you faithfully obey all that He asks you to do?

15 And he returned to the man of God, he and all his aides, and came and stood before him; and he said, "Indeed, now I know that *there is* no God in all the earth, except in Israel; now therefore, please take a gift from your servant."
16 But he said, "*As* the LORD lives, before whom I stand, I will receive nothing." And he urged him to take *it,* but he refused.
17 So Nā′a·man said, "Then, if not, please let your servant be given two mule-loads of earth; for your servant will no longer offer either burnt offering or sacrifice to other gods, but to the LORD.
18 "Yet in this thing may the LORD pardon your servant: when my master goes into the temple of Rim′mon to worship there, and he leans on my hand, and I bow down in the temple of Rim′mon—when I bow down in the temple of Rim′mon, may the LORD please pardon your servant in this thing."
19 Then he said to him, "Go in peace." So he departed from him a short distance.

GEHAZI'S GREED

20 But Ge·hā′zī, the servant of E·lī′sha the man of God, said, "Look, my master has spared Nā′a·man this Syrian, while not receiving from his hands what he brought; but *as* the LORD lives, I will run after him and take something from him."
21 So Ge·hā′zī pursued Nā′a·man. When Nā′a·man saw *him* running after him, he got down from the chariot to meet him, and said, "*Is* all well?"
22 And he said, "All *is* well. My master has sent me, saying, 'Indeed, just now two young men of the sons of the prophets have come to me from the mountains of Ē′phra·im. Please give

them a talent of silver and two changes of garments.' "
23 So Nā′a·man said, "Please, take two talents." And he urged him, and bound two talents of silver in two bags, with two changes of garments, and handed *them* to two of his servants; and they carried *them* on ahead of him.
24 When he came to the citadel, he took *them* from their hand, and stored *them* away in the house; then he let the men go, and they departed.
25 Now he went in and stood before his master. E·lī′sha said to him, "Where *did you go,* Ge·hā′zī?" And he said, "Your servant did not go anywhere."
26 Then he said to him, "Did not my heart go *with you* when the man turned back from his chariot to meet you? *Is it* time to receive money and to receive clothing, olive groves and vineyards, sheep and oxen, male and female servants?
27 "Therefore the leprosy of Nā′a·man shall cling to you and your descendants forever." And he went out from his presence leprous, *as white* as snow.

THE FLOATING AX HEAD

6 And the sons of the prophets said to E·lī′sha, "See now, the place where we dwell with you is too small for us.
2 "Please, let us go to the Jordan, and let every man take a beam from there, and let us make there a place where we may dwell." So he answered, "Go."
3 Then one said, "Please consent to go with your servants." And he answered, "I will go."
4 So he went with them. And when they came to the Jordan, they cut down trees.
5 But as one was cutting down a

tree, the iron *ax head* fell into the water; and he cried out and said, "Alas, master! For it was borrowed."

6 So the man of God said, "Where did it fall?" And he showed him the place. So he cut off a stick, and threw *it* in there; and he made the iron float.

7 Therefore he said, "Pick *it* up for yourself." So he reached out his hand and took it.

THE BLINDED SYRIANS CAPTURED

Elisha and his servant were in trouble. The king of Syria had sent a large army to capture them. Elisha and his servant were surrounded. But things sometimes look worse than they really are. Elisha asked God to help his servant see the invisible army that would fight for them.

8 Now the king of Syria was making war against Israel; and he consulted with his servants, saying, "My camp *will be* in such and such a place."

9 And the man of God sent to the king of Israel, saying, "Beware that you do not pass this place, for the Syrians are coming down there."

10 Then the king of Israel sent *someone* to the place of which the man of God had told him. Thus he warned him, and he was watchful there, not just once or twice.

11 Therefore the heart of the king of Syria was greatly troubled by this thing; and he called his servants and said to them, "Will you not show me which of us *is* for the king of Israel?"

12 And one of his servants said, "None, my lord, O king; but E·li′sha, the prophet who *is* in Israel, tells the king of Israel the words that you speak in your bedroom."

13 So he said, "Go and see where he *is*, that I may send and get him." And it was told him, saying, "Surely *he is* in Dō′than."

14 Therefore he sent horses and chariots and a great army there, and they came by night and surrounded the city.

15 And when the servant of the man of God arose early and went out, there was an army, surrounding the city with horses and chariots. And his servant said to him, "Alas, my master! What shall we do?"

16 So he answered, "Do not fear, for those who *are* with us *are* more than those who *are* with them."

17 And E·li′sha prayed, and said, "LORD, I pray, open his eyes that he may see." Then the LORD opened the eyes of the young man, and he saw. And behold, the mountain *was* full of horses and chariots of fire all around E·li′sha.

18 So when *the Syrians* came down to him, E·li′sha prayed to the LORD, and said, "Strike this people, I pray, with blindness." And He struck them with blindness according to the word of E·li′sha.

19 Now E·li′sha said to them, "This *is* not the way, nor *is* this the city. Follow me, and I will bring you to the man whom you seek." But he led them to Samaria.

20 So it was, when they had come to Samaria, that E·li′sha said, "LORD, open the eyes of these *men*, that they may see." And the LORD opened their eyes, and they saw; and there *they were*, inside Samaria!

21 Now when the king of Israel saw them, he said to E·li′sha, "My father, shall I kill *them*? Shall I kill *them*?"

22 But he answered, "You shall not kill *them*. Would you kill those whom you have taken captive with your sword and your bow? Set food and

water before them, that they may eat and drink and go to their master."
23 Then he prepared a great feast for them; and after they ate and drank, he sent them away and they went to their master. So the bands of Syrian *raiders* came no more into the land of Israel.

☑   *Bible Quiz*

2 Kings 6:8–23 **Elisha and the Angel Army**

1. Why was the king of Syria so angry at Elisha?
2. What did the king of Syria do?
3. What couldn't Elisha's servant see? No wonder Elisha wasn't afraid!
4. Do you think God is more powerful than your enemies? The next time you see no way out of your trouble, remember God has armies of angels watching over you.

SYRIA BESIEGES SAMARIA IN FAMINE

24 And it happened after this that Ben-Hā′dad king of Syria gathered all his army, and went up and besieged Samaria.
25 And there was a great famine in Samaria; and indeed they besieged it until a donkey's head was *sold* for eighty *shekels* of silver, and one-fourth of a kab of dove droppings for five *shekels* of silver.
26 Then, as the king of Israel was passing by on the wall, a woman cried out to him, saying, "Help, my lord, O king!"

27 And he said, "If the LORD does not help you, where can I find help for you? From the threshing floor or from the winepress?"
28 Then the king said to her, "What is troubling you?" And she answered, "This woman said to me, 'Give your son, that we may eat him today, and we will eat my son tomorrow.'
29 "So we boiled my son, and ate him. And I said to her on the next day, 'Give your son, that we may eat him'; but she has hidden her son."
30 Now it happened, when the king heard the words of the woman, that he tore his clothes; and as he passed by on the wall, the people looked, and there underneath *he had* sackcloth on his body.
31 Then he said, "God do so to me and more also, if the head of E·lī′sha the son of Shā′phat remains on him today!"
32 But E·lī′sha was sitting in his house, and the elders were sitting with him. And *the king* sent a man ahead of him, but before the messenger came to him, he said to the elders, "Do you see how this son of a murderer has sent someone to take away my head? Look, when the messenger comes, shut the door, and hold him fast at the door. *Is* not the sound of his master's feet behind him?"
33 And while he was still talking with them, there was the messenger, coming down to him; and then *the king* said, "Surely this calamity *is* from the LORD; why should I wait for the LORD any longer?"

7 Then E·lī′sha said, "Hear the word of the LORD. Thus says the LORD: 'Tomorrow about this time a seah of fine flour *shall be sold* for a shekel, and two seahs of barley for a shekel, at the gate of Samaria.'"
2 So an officer on whose hand the king leaned answered the man of God

and said, "Look, *if* the LORD would make windows in heaven, could this thing be?" And he said, "In fact, you shall see *it* with your eyes, but you shall not eat of it."

THE SYRIANS FLEE

3 Now there were four leprous men at the entrance of the gate; and they said to one another, "Why are we sitting here until we die?

4 "If we say, 'We will enter the city,' the famine *is* in the city, and we shall die there. And if we sit here, we die also. Now therefore, come, let us surrender to the army of the Syrians. If they keep us alive, we shall live; and if they kill us, we shall only die."

5 And they rose at twilight to go to the camp of the Syrians; and when they had come to the outskirts of the Syrian camp, to their surprise no one *was* there.

6 For the LORD had caused the army of the Syrians to hear the noise of chariots and the noise of horses—the noise of a great army; so they said to one another, "Look, the king of Israel has hired against us the kings of the Hit′tītes and the kings of the Egyptians to attack us!"

7 Therefore they arose and fled at twilight, and left the camp intact—their tents, their horses, and their donkeys—and they fled for their lives.

8 And when these lepers came to the outskirts of the camp, they went into one tent and ate and drank, and carried from it silver and gold and clothing, and went and hid *them;* then they came back and entered another tent, and carried *some* from there *also,* and went and hid *it.*

9 Then they said to one another, "We are not doing right. This day *is* a day of good news, and we remain silent. If we wait until morning light, some punishment will come upon us. Now therefore, come, let us go and tell the king's household."

10 So they went and called to the gatekeepers of the city, and told them, saying, "We went to the Syrian camp, and surprisingly no one *was* there, not a human sound—only horses and donkeys tied, and the tents intact."

11 And the gatekeepers called out, and they told *it* to the king's household inside.

12 So the king arose in the night and said to his servants, "Let me now tell you what the Syrians have done to us. They know that we *are* hungry; therefore they have gone out of the camp to hide themselves in the field, saying, 'When they come out of the city, we shall catch them alive, and get into the city.' "

13 And one of his servants answered and said, "Please, let several *men* take five of the remaining horses which are left in the city. Look, they *may either become* like all the multitude of Israel that are left in it; or indeed, *I say,* they *may become* like all the multitude of Israel left from those who are consumed; so let us send them and see."

14 Therefore they took two chariots with horses; and the king sent them in the direction of the Syrian army, saying, "Go and see."

15 And they went after them to the Jordan; and indeed all the road *was* full of garments and weapons which the Syrians had thrown away in their haste. So the messengers returned and told the king.

16 Then the people went out and plundered the tents of the Syrians. So a seah of fine flour was *sold* for a shekel, and two seahs of barley for a shekel, according to the word of the LORD.

17 Now the king had appointed the

officer on whose hand he leaned to have charge of the gate. But the people trampled him in the gate, and he died, just as the man of God had said, who spoke when the king came down to him.

18 So it happened just as the man of God had spoken to the king, saying, "Two seahs of barley for a shekel, and a seah of fine flour for a shekel, shall be *sold* tomorrow about this time in the gate of Samaria."

19 Then that officer had answered the man of God, and said, "Now look, *if* the LORD would make windows in heaven, could such a thing be?" And he had said, "In fact, you shall see *it* with your eyes, but you shall not eat of it."

20 And so it happened to him, for the people trampled him in the gate, and he died.

THE KING RESTORES THE SHUNAMMITE'S LAND

8 Then E·lī′sha spoke to the woman whose son he had restored to life, saying, "Arise and go, you and your household, and stay wherever you can; for the LORD has called for a famine, and furthermore, it will come upon the land for seven years."

2 So the woman arose and did according to the saying of the man of God, and she went with her household and dwelt in the land of the Phi·lis′tines seven years.

3 It came to pass, at the end of seven years, that the woman returned from the land of the Phi·lis′tines; and she went to make an appeal to the king for her house and for her land.

4 Then the king talked with Ge·hā′zī, the servant of the man of God, saying, "Tell me, please, all the great things E·lī′sha has done."

5 Now it happened, as he was telling the king how he had restored the dead to life, that there was the woman whose son he had restored to life, appealing to the king for her house and for her land. And Ge·hā′zī said, "My lord, O king, this *is* the woman, and this *is* her son whom E·lī′sha restored to life."

6 And when the king asked the woman, she told him. So the king appointed a certain officer for her, saying, "Restore all that *was* hers, and all the proceeds of the field from the day that she left the land until now."

DEATH OF BEN-HADAD

7 Then E·lī′sha went to Damascus, and Ben-Hā′dad king of Syria was sick; and it was told him, saying, "The man of God has come here."

8 And the king said to Haz′a·el, "Take a present in your hand, and go to meet the man of God, and inquire of the LORD by him, saying, 'Shall I recover from this disease?' "

9 So Haz′a·el went to meet him and took a present with him, of every good thing of Damascus, forty camel-loads; and he came and stood before him, and said, "Your son Ben-Hā′dad king of Syria has sent me to you, saying, 'Shall I recover from this disease?' "

10 And E·lī′sha said to him, "Go, say to him, 'You shall certainly recover.' However the LORD has shown me that he will really die."

11 Then he set his countenance in a stare until he was ashamed; and the man of God wept.

12 And Haz′a·el said, "Why is my lord weeping?" He answered, "Because I know the evil that you will do to the children of Israel: Their strongholds you will set on fire, and their young men you will kill with the sword; and you will dash their

children, and rip open their women with child."

13 So Haz′a·el said, "But what *is* your servant—a dog, that he should do this gross thing?" And E·li′sha answered, "The LORD has shown me that you *will become* king over Syria."

14 Then he departed from E·li′sha, and came to his master, who said to him, "What did E·li′sha say to you?" And he answered, "He told me you would surely recover."

15 But it happened on the next day that he took a thick cloth and dipped *it* in water, and spread *it* over his face so that he died; and Haz′a·el reigned in his place.

JEHORAM REIGNS IN JUDAH

16 Now in the fifth year of Jo′ram the son of A′hab, king of Israel, Je·hosh′a·phat *having been* king of Judah, Je·ho′ram the son of Je-hosh′a·phat began to reign as king of Judah.

17 He was thirty-two years old when he became king, and he reigned eight years in Jerusalem.

18 And he walked in the way of the kings of Israel, just as the house of A′hab had done, for the daughter of A′hab was his wife; and he did evil in the sight of the LORD.

19 Yet the LORD would not destroy Judah, for the sake of his servant David, as He promised him to give a lamp to him *and* his sons forever.

20 In his days E′dom revolted against Judah's authority, and made a king over themselves.

21 So Jo′ram^a went to Za′ir, and all his chariots with him. Then he rose by night and attacked the E′dom·ites who had surrounded him and the captains of the chariots; and the troops fled to their tents.

22 Thus E′dom has been in revolt against Judah's authority to this day. And Lib′nah revolted at that time.

23 Now the rest of the acts of Jo′-ram, and all that he did, *are* they not written in the book of the chronicles of the kings of Judah?

24 So Jo′ram rested with his fathers, and was buried with his fathers in the City of David. Then A·ha·zi′ah his son reigned in his place.

AHAZIAH REIGNS IN JUDAH

25 In the twelfth year of Jo′ram the son of A′hab, king of Israel, A·ha-zi′ah the son of Je·ho′ram, king of Judah, began to reign.

26 A·ha·zi′ah *was* twenty-two years old when he became king, and he reigned one year in Jerusalem. His mother's name *was* Ath·a·li′ah the granddaughter of Om′ri, king of Israel.

27 And he walked in the way of the house of A′hab, and did evil in the sight of the LORD, like the house of A′hab, for he *was* the son-in-law of the house of A′hab.

28 Now he went with Jo′ram the son of A′hab to war against Haz′a·el king of Syria at Ra′moth Gil′e·ad; and the Syrians wounded Jo′ram.

29 Then King Jo′ram went back to Jez′re·el to recover from the wounds which the Syrians had inflicted on him at Ra′mah, when he fought against Haz′a·el king of Syria. And A·ha·zi′ah the son of Je·ho′ram, king of Judah, went down to see Jo′ram the son of A′hab in Jez′re·el, because he was sick.

JEHU ANOINTED KING OF ISRAEL

9 And E·li′sha the prophet called one of the sons of the prophets, and

8:21 ^aSpelled *Jehoram* in verse 16

said to him, "Get yourself ready, take this flask of oil in your hand, and go to Rā′moth Gil′ē·ad.

2 "Now when you arrive at that place, look there for Jē′hū the son of Je·hosh′a·phat, the son of Nim′shī, and go in and make him rise up from among his associates, and take him to an inner room.

3 "Then take the flask of oil, and pour *it* on his head, and say, 'Thus says the LORD: "I have anointed you king over Israel." ' Then open the door and flee, and do not delay."

4 So the young man, the servant of the prophet, went to Rā′moth Gil′ē·ad.

5 And when he arrived, there *were* the captains of the army sitting; and he said, "I have a message for you, Commander." Jē′hū said, "For which *one* of us?" And he said, "For you, Commander."

6 Then he arose and went into the house. And he poured the oil on his head, and said to him, "Thus says the LORD God of Israel: 'I have anointed you king over the people of the LORD, over Israel.

7 'You shall strike down the house of Ā′hab your master, that I may avenge the blood of My servants the prophets, and the blood of all the servants of the LORD, at the hand of Jez′e·bel.

8 'For the whole house of Ā′hab shall perish; and I will cut off from Ā′hab all the males in Israel, both bond and free.

9 'So I will make the house of Ā′hab like the house of Jer·o·bō′am the son of Nē′bat, and like the house of Bā′a·sha the son of A·hī′jah.

10 'The dogs shall eat Jez′e·bel on the plot *of ground* at Jez′rē·el, and *there shall be* none to bury *her.* ' " And he opened the door and fled.

11 Then Jē′hū came out to the ser-

vants of his master, and *one* said to him, "*Is* all well? Why did this madman come to you?" And he said to them, "You know the man and his babble."

12 And they said, "A lie! Tell us now." So he said, "Thus and thus he spoke to me, saying, 'Thus says the LORD: "I have anointed you king over Israel." ' "

13 Then each man hastened to take his garment and put *it* under him on the top of the steps; and they blew trumpets, saying, "Jē′hū is king!"

JORAM OF ISRAEL KILLED

14 So Jē′hū the son of Je·hosh′a·phat, the son of Nim′shī, conspired against Jō′ram. (Now Jō′ram had been defending Rā′moth Gil′ē·ad, he and all Israel, against Haz′a·el king of Syria.

15 But King Jō′ram had returned to Jez′rē·el to recover from the wounds which the Syrians had inflicted on him when he fought with Haz′a·el king of Syria.) And Jē′hū said, "If you are so minded, let no one leave *or* escape from the city to go and tell *it* in Jez′rē·el."

16 So Jē′hū rode in a chariot and went to Jez′rē·el, for Jō′ram was laid up there; and Ā·ha·zī′ah king of Judah had come down to see Jō′ram.

17 Now a watchman stood on the tower in Jez′rē·el, and he saw the company of Jē′hū as he came, and said, "I see a company of men." And Jō′ram said, "Get a horseman and send him to meet them, and let him say, '*Is it* peace?' "

18 So the horseman went to meet him, and said, "Thus says the king: '*Is it* peace?' " And Jē′hū said, "What have you to do with peace? Turn around and follow me." So the watchman reported, saying, "The messen-

ger went to them, but is not coming back."

19 Then he sent out a second horseman who came to them, and said, "Thus says the king: '*Is it* peace?' " And Jē'hū answered, "What have you to do with peace? Turn around and follow me."

20 So the watchman reported, saying, "He went up to them and is not coming back; and the driving *is* like the driving of Jē'hū the son of Nim'shī, for he drives furiously!"

21 Then Jō'ram said, "Make ready." And his chariot was made ready. Then Jō'ram king of Israel and Ā·ha·zī'ah king of Judah went out, each in his chariot; and they went out to meet Jē'hū, and met him on the property of Nā'both the Jez'rē-el·īte.

22 Now it happened, when Jō'ram saw Jē'hū, that he said, "*Is it* peace, Jē'hū?" So he answered, "What peace, as long as the harlotries of your mother Jez'e·bel and her witchcraft *are so* many?"

23 Then Jō'ram turned around and fled, and said to Ā·ha·zī'ah, "Treachery, Ā·ha·zī'ah!"

24 Now Jē'hū drew his bow with full strength and shot Je·hō'ram between his arms; and the arrow came out at his heart, and he sank down in his chariot.

25 Then *Jē'hū* said to Bid'kar his captain, "Pick *him* up, *and* throw him into the tract of the field of Nā'both the Jez'rē-el·īte; for remember, when you and I were riding together behind Ā'hab his father, that the LORD laid this burden upon him:

26 'Surely I saw yesterday the blood of Nā'both and the blood of his sons,' says the LORD, 'and I will repay you in this plot,' says the LORD. Now therefore, take *and* throw him on the plot *of ground,* according to the word of the LORD."

AHAZIAH OF JUDAH KILLED

27 But when Ā·ha·zī'ah king of Judah saw *this,* he fled by the road to Beth Hag'gan.*a* So Jē'hū pursued him, and said, "Shoot him also in the chariot." *And they shot him* at the Ascent of Gur, which is by Ib'lē·am. Then he fled to Me·gid'dō, and died there.

28 And his servants carried him in the chariot to Jerusalem, and buried him in his tomb with his fathers in the City of David.

29 In the eleventh year of Jō'ram the son of Ā'hab, Ā·ha·zī'ah had become king over Judah.

JEZEBEL'S VIOLENT DEATH

30 Now when Jē'hū had come to Jez'rē·el, Jez'e·bel heard *of it;* and she put paint on her eyes and adorned her head, and looked through a window.

31 Then, as Jē'hū entered at the gate, she said, "*Is it* peace, Zim'rī, murderer of your master?"

32 And he looked up at the window, and said, "Who *is* on my side? Who?" So two *or* three eunuchs looked out at him.

33 Then he said, "Throw her down." So they threw her down, and *some* of her blood spattered on the wall and on the horses; and he trampled her underfoot.

34 And when he had gone in, he ate and drank. Then he said, "Go now, see to this accursed *woman,* and bury her, for she was a king's daughter."

35 So they went to bury her, but they found no more of her than the skull and the feet and the palms of *her* hands.

36 Therefore they came back and told him. And he said, "This *is* the

9:27 *a*Literally *The Garden House*

word of the LORD, which He spoke by His servant E·lī′jah the Tish′bīte, saying, 'On the plot *of ground* at Jez′rē·el dogs shall eat the flesh of Jez′e·bel;a

37 'and the corpse of Jez′e·bel shall be as refuse on the surface of the field, in the plot at Jez′rē·el, so that they shall not say, "Here *lies* Jez′e-bel." ' "

AHAB'S SEVENTY SONS KILLED

10 Now Ā′hab had seventy sons in Samaria. And Jē′hū wrote and sent letters to Samaria, to the rulers of Jez′rē·el,a to the elders, and to those who reared Ā′hab's *sons,* saying:

2 Now as soon as this letter comes to you, since your master's sons *are* with you, and you have chariots and horses, a fortified city also, and weapons,

3 choose the best qualified of your master's sons, set *him* on his father's throne, and fight for your master's house.

4 But they were exceedingly afraid, and said, "Look, two kings could not stand up to him; how then can we stand?"

5 And he who *was* in charge of the house, and he who *was* in charge of the city, the elders also, and those who reared *the sons,* sent to Jē′hū, saying, "We *are* your servants, we will do all you tell us; but we will not make anyone king. Do *what is* good in your sight."

6 Then he wrote a second letter to them, saying:

If you *are* for me and will obey my voice, take the heads of the men, your master's sons, and come to me at Jez′rē·el by this time tomorrow.

Now the king's sons, seventy persons, *were* with the great men of the city, *who* were rearing them.

7 So it was, when the letter came to them, that they took the king's sons and slaughtered seventy persons, put their heads in baskets and sent *them* to him at Jez′rē·el.

8 Then a messenger came and told him, saying, "They have brought the heads of the king's sons." And he said, "Lay them in two heaps at the entrance of the gate until morning."

9 So it was, in the morning, that he went out and stood, and said to all the people, "You *are* righteous. Indeed I conspired against my master and killed him; but who killed all these?

10 "Know now that nothing shall fall to the earth of the word of the LORD which the LORD spoke concerning the house of Ā′hab; for the LORD has done what He spoke by His servant E·lī′jah."

11 So Jē′hū killed all who remained of the house of Ā′hab in Jez′rē·el, and all his great men and his close acquaintances and his priests, until he left him none remaining.

AHAZIAH'S FORTY-TWO BROTHERS KILLED

12 And he arose and departed and went to Samaria. On the way, at Beth Ē′keda of the Shepherds,

13 Jē′hū met with the brothers of Ā·ha·zī′ah king of Judah, and said, "Who *are* you?" So they answered, "We *are* the brothers of Ā·ha·zī′ah; we have come down to greet the sons of the king and the sons of the queen mother."

14 And he said, "Take them alive!" So they took them alive, and killed

9:36 *a*1 Kings 21:23   10:1 *a*Following Masoretic Text, Syriac, and Targum; Septuagint reads *Samaria;* Vulgate reads *city.*   10:12 *a*Or *The Shearing House*

them at the well of Beth Ē′ked, forty-two men; and he left none of them.

THE REST OF AHAB'S FAMILY KILLED

15 Now when he departed from there, he met Je·hon′a·dab the son of Rē′chab, *coming* to meet him; and he greeted him and said to him, "Is your heart right, as my heart *is* toward your heart?" And Je·hon′a·dab answered, "It is." *Jē′hū* said, "If it is, give *me* your hand." So he gave *him* his hand, and he took him up to him into the chariot.
16 Then he said, "Come with me, and see my zeal for the LORD." So they had him ride in his chariot.
17 And when he came to Samaria, he killed all who remained to Ā′hab in Samaria, till he had destroyed them, according to the word of the LORD which He spoke to E·lī′jah.

WORSHIPERS OF BAAL KILLED

18 Then Jē′hū gathered all the people together, and said to them, "Ā′hab served Bā′al a little, Jē′hū will serve him much.
19 "Now therefore, call to me all the prophets of Bā′al, all his servants, and all his priests. Let no one be missing, for I have a great sacrifice for Bā′al. Whoever is missing shall not live." But Jē′hū acted deceptively, with the intent of destroying the worshipers of Bā′al.
20 And Jē′hū said, "Proclaim a solemn assembly for Bā′al." So they proclaimed *it.*
21 Then Jē′hū sent throughout all Israel; and all the worshipers of Bā′al came, so that there was not a man left who did not come. So they came into the temple*a* of Bā′al, and the temple of Bā′al was full from one end to the other.
22 And he said to the one in charge of the wardrobe, "Bring out vestments for all the worshipers of Bā′al." So he brought out vestments for them.
23 Then Jē′hū and Je·hon′a·dab the son of Rē′chab went into the temple of Bā′al, and said to the worshipers of Bā′al, "Search and see that no servants of the LORD are here with you, but only the worshipers of Bā′al."
24 So they went in to offer sacrifices and burnt offerings. Now Jē′hū had appointed for himself eighty men on the outside, and had said, "*If* any of the men whom I have brought into your hands escapes, *whoever lets him escape, it shall be* his life for the life of the other."
25 Now it happened, as soon as he had made an end of offering the burnt offering, that Jē′hū said to the guard and to the captains, "Go in *and* kill them; let no one come out!" And they killed them with the edge of the sword; then the guards and the officers threw *them* out, and went into the inner room of the temple of Bā′al.
26 And they brought the *sacred* pillars out of the temple of Bā′al and burned them.
27 Then they broke down the *sacred* pillar of Bā′al, and tore down the temple of Bā′al and made it a refuse dump to this day.
28 Thus Jē′hū destroyed Bā′al from Israel.
29 However Jē′hū did not turn away from the sins of Jer·o·bō′am the son of Nē′bat, who had made Israel sin, *that is,* from the golden calves that *were* at Beth′el and Dan.
30 And the LORD said to Jē′hū, "Because you have done well in doing *what is* right in My sight, *and* have done to the house of Ā′hab all that *was* in My heart, your sons shall sit

10:21 *a*Literally *house,* and so elsewhere in this chapter

on the throne of Israel to the fourth *generation*."

31 But Jē'hū took no heed to walk in the law of the LORD God of Israel with all his heart; for he did not depart from the sins of Jer·o·bō'am, who had made Israel sin.

DEATH OF JEHU

32 In those days the LORD began to cut off *parts* of Israel; and Haz'a·el conquered them in all the territory of Israel

33 from the Jordan eastward: all the land of Gil'ē·ad—Gad, Reuben, and Ma·nas'seh—from A·rō'er, which *is* by the River Ar'non, including Gil'ē·ad and Bā'shan.

34 Now the rest of the acts of Jē'hū, all that he did, and all his might, *are* they not written in the book of the chronicles of the kings of Israel?

35 So Jē'hū rested with his fathers, and they buried him in Samaria. Then Je·hō'a·haz his son reigned in his place.

36 And the period that Jē'hū reigned over Israel in Samaria *was* twenty-eight years.

ATHALIAH REIGNS IN JUDAH

11 When Ath·a·lī'ah the mother of Ā·ha·zī'ah saw that her son was dead, she arose and destroyed all the royal heirs.

2 But Je·hosh'e·ba, the daughter of King Jō'ram, sister of Ā·ha·zī'ah, took Jō'ash the son of Ā·ha·zī'ah, and stole him away from among the king's sons *who were* being murdered; and they hid him and his nurse in the bedroom, from Ath·a·lī'ah, so that he was not killed.

3 So he was hidden with her in the house of the LORD for six years, while Ath·a·lī'ah reigned over the land.

JOASH CROWNED KING OF JUDAH

4 In the seventh year Je·hoi'a·da sent and brought the captains of hundreds—of the bodyguards and the escorts—and brought them into the house of the LORD to him. And he made a covenant with them and took an oath from them in the house of the LORD, and showed them the king's son.

5 Then he commanded them, saying, "This *is* what you shall do: One-third of you who come on duty on the Sabbath shall be keeping watch over the king's house,

6 "one-third *shall be* at the gate of Sūr, and one-third at the gate behind the escorts. You shall keep the watch of the house, lest it be broken down.

7 "The two contingents of you who go off duty on the Sabbath shall keep the watch of the house of the LORD for the king.

8 "But you shall surround the king on all sides, every man with his weapons in his hand; and whoever comes within range, let him be put to death. You are to be with the king as he goes out and as he comes in."

9 So the captains of the hundreds did according to all that Je·hoi'a·da the priest commanded. Each of them took his men who were to be on duty on the Sabbath, with those who were going off duty on the Sabbath, and came to Je·hoi'a·da the priest.

10 And the priest gave the captains of hundreds the spears and shields which *had belonged* to King David, that were in the temple of the LORD.

11 Then the escorts stood, every man with his weapons in his hand, all around the king, from the right side of the temple to the left side of the temple, by the altar and the house.

12 And he brought out the king's son, put the crown on him, and *gave*

him the Testimony;*a* they made him king and anointed him, and they clapped their hands and said, "Long live the king!"

DEATH OF ATHALIAH

13 Now when Ath·a·lī'ah heard the noise of the escorts *and* the people, she came to the people *in* the temple of the LORD.
14 When she looked, there was the king standing by a pillar according to custom; and the leaders and the trumpeters were by the king. All the people of the land were rejoicing and blowing trumpets. So Ath·a·lī'ah tore her clothes and cried out, "Treason! Treason!"
15 And Je·hoi'a·da the priest commanded the captains of the hundreds, the officers of the army, and said to them, "Take her outside under guard, and slay with the sword whoever follows her." For the priest had said, "Do not let her be killed in the house of the LORD."
16 So they seized her; and she went by way of the horses' entrance *into* the king's house, and there she was killed.
17 Then Je·hoi'a·da made a covenant between the LORD, the king, and the people, that they should be the LORD's people, and *also* between the king and the people.
18 And all the people of the land went to the temple of Bā'al, and tore it down. They thoroughly broke in pieces its altars and images, and killed Mat'tan the priest of Bā'al before the altars. And the priest appointed officers over the house of the LORD.
19 Then he took the captains of hundreds, the bodyguards, the escorts, and all the people of the land; and they brought the king down from the house of the LORD, and went by way

of the gate of the escorts to the king's house. Then he sat on the throne of the kings.
20 So all the people of the land rejoiced; and the city was quiet, for they had slain Ath·a·lī'ah with the sword *in* the king's house.
21 Je·hō'ash *was* seven years old when he became king.

JEHOASH REPAIRS THE TEMPLE

12 In the seventh year of Jē'hū, Je·hō'ash*a* became king, and he reigned forty years in Jerusalem. His mother's name *was* Zib'i·ah of Bē·er·shē'ba.
2 Je·hō'ash did *what was* right in the sight of the LORD all the days in which Je·hoi'a·da the priest instructed him.
3 But the high places were not taken away; the people still sacrificed and burned incense on the high places.
4 And Je·hō'ash said to the priests, "All the money of the dedicated gifts that are brought into the house of the LORD—each man's census money, each man's assessment money*a*—and all the money that a man purposes in his heart to bring into the house of the LORD,
5 "let the priests take *it* themselves, each from his constituency; and let them repair the damages of the temple, wherever any dilapidation is found."
6 Now it was so, by the twenty-third year of King Je·hō'ash, *that* the priests had not repaired the damages of the temple.
7 So King Je·hō'ash called Je·hoi'a·da the priest and the *other* priests, and said to them, "Why have you not

11:12 *a*That is, the Law (compare Exodus 25:16, 21 and Deuteronomy 31:9)   12:1 *a*Spelled *Joash* in 11:2ff   12:4 *a*Compare Leviticus 27:2ff

SHOULD I HURT A LITTLE TO HELP A LOT? 2 Kings 12:4, 5

Wendy has saved money for a long time. She wants to give it to Jesus for something special. But her money is in her piggy bank. Now what should she do? To get her money she must break her piggy bank. If she doesn't break it, she can't give her money to Jesus. What should she do?

1. Why is Wendy sad? What must she do to give her money to Jesus?
2. Which is more important, giving money to Jesus or keeping her piggy bank?
3. What would you like to say to Wendy? What would you like to say to you?

For more on *What Should I Do?* turn to page 586
For more on *Giving* turn to page 632

repaired the damages of the temple? Now therefore, do not take *more* money from your constituency, but deliver it for repairing the damages of the temple."

8 And the priests agreed that they would neither receive *more* money from the people, nor repair the damages of the temple.

9 Then Je·hoi'a·da the priest took a chest, bored a hole in its lid, and set it beside the altar, on the right side as one comes into the house of the LORD; and the priests who kept the door put there all the money brought into the house of the LORD.

10 So it was, whenever they saw that *there was* much money in the chest, that the king's scribe and the high priest came up and put it in bags, and counted the money that was found in the house of the LORD.

11 Then they gave the money, which had been apportioned, into the hands of those who did the work, who had the oversight of the house of the LORD; and they paid it out to the carpenters and builders who worked on the house of the LORD,

12 and to masons and stonecutters, and for buying timber and hewn stone, to repair the damage of the house of the LORD, and for all that was paid out to repair the temple.

13 However there were not made for the house of the LORD basins of silver, trimmers, sprinkling-bowls, trumpets, any articles of gold or articles of silver, from the money brought into the house of the LORD.

14 But they gave that to the workmen, and they repaired the house of the LORD with it.

15 Moreover they did not require an account from the men into whose hand they delivered the money to be paid to workmen, for they dealt faithfully.

16 The money from the trespass offerings and the money from the sin offerings was not brought into the house of the LORD. It belonged to the priests.

HAZAEL THREATENS JERUSALEM

17 Haz'a·el king of Syria went up and fought against Gath, and took it; then Haz'a·el set his face to go up to Jerusalem.

18 And Je·ho'ash king of Judah took all the sacred things that his fathers, Je·hosh'a·phat and Je·ho'ram and A·ha·zī'ah, kings of Judah, had dedicated, and his own sacred things, and all the gold found in the treasuries of the house of the LORD and in the king's house, and sent *them* to Haz'a·el king of Syria. Then he went away from Jerusalem.

DEATH OF JOASH

19 Now the rest of the acts of Jō'-ash,*a* and all that he did, *are* they not written in the book of the chronicles of the kings of Judah?

20 And his servants arose and formed a conspiracy, and killed Jō'-ash in the house of the Mil'lō,*a* which goes down to Sil'la.

21 For Joz'a·char*a* the son of Shim'-ē·ath and Je·hō'za·bad the son of Shō'mer,*b* his servants, struck him. So he died, and they buried him with his fathers in the City of David. Then Am·a·zī'ah his son reigned in his place.

JEHOAHAZ REIGNS IN ISRAEL

13 In the twenty-third year of Jō'ash*a* the son of A·ha·zī'ah, king of

---

12:19 *a*Spelled *Jehoash* in 12:1ff   12:20 *a*Literally *The Landfill*   12:21 *a*Called *Zabad* in 2 Chronicles 24:26   *b*Called *Shimrith* in 2 Chronicles 24:26   13:1 *a*Spelled *Jehoash* in 12:1ff

Judah, Je·hō'a·haz the son of Jē'hū became king over Israel in Samaria, *and reigned* seventeen years.

2 And he did evil in the sight of the LORD, and followed the sins of Jer·o·bō'am the son of Nē'bat, who had made Israel sin. He did not depart from them.

3 Then the anger of the LORD was aroused against Israel, and He delivered them into the hand of Haz'a·el king of Syria, and into the hand of Ben-Hā'dad the son of Haz'a·el, all *their* days.

4 So Je·hō'a·haz pleaded with the LORD, and the LORD listened to him; for He saw the oppression of Israel, because the king of Syria oppressed them.

5 Then the LORD gave Israel a deliverer, so that they escaped from under the hand of the Syrians; and the children of Israel dwelt in their tents as before.

6 Nevertheless they did not depart from the sins of the house of Jer·o·bō'am, who had made Israel sin, *but* walked in them; and the wooden image*a* also remained in Samaria.

7 For He left of the army of Je·hō'a·haz only fifty horsemen, ten chariots, and ten thousand foot soldiers; for the king of Syria had destroyed them and made them like the dust at threshing.

8 Now the rest of the acts of Je·hō'a·haz, all that he did, and his might, *are* they not written in the book of the chronicles of the kings of Israel?

9 So Je·hō'a·haz rested with his fathers, and they buried him in Samaria. Then Jō'ash his son reigned in his place.

JEHOASH REIGNS IN ISRAEL

10 In the thirty-seventh year of Jō'ash king of Judah, Je·hō'ash*a* the son of Je·hō'a·haz became king over Israel in Samaria, *and reigned* sixteen years.

11 And he did evil in the sight of the LORD. He did not depart from all the sins of Jer·o·bō'am the son of Nē'bat, who made Israel sin, *but* walked in them.

12 Now the rest of the acts of Jō'ash, all that he did, and his might with which he fought against Am·a·zī'ah king of Judah, *are* they not written in the book of the chronicles of the kings of Israel?

13 So Jō'ash rested with his fathers. Then Jer·o·bō'am sat on his throne. And Jō'ash was buried in Samaria with the kings of Israel.

DEATH OF ELISHA

14 E·lī'sha had become sick with the illness of which he would die. Then Jō'ash the king of Israel came down to him, and wept over his face, and said, "O my father, my father, the chariots of Israel and their horsemen!"

15 And E·lī'sha said to him, "Take a bow and some arrows." So he took himself a bow and some arrows.

16 Then he said to the king of Israel, "Put your hand on the bow." So he put his hand *on it,* and E·lī'sha put his hands on the king's hands.

17 And he said, "Open the east window"; and he opened *it.* Then E·lī'sha said, "Shoot"; and he shot. And he said, "The arrow of the LORD's deliverance and the arrow of deliverance from Syria; for you must strike the Syrians at Ā'phek till you have destroyed *them.*"

18 Then he said, "Take the arrows"; so he took *them.* And he said to the

13:6 *a*Hebrew *Asherah,* a Canaanite goddess
13:10 *a*Spelled *Joash* in verse 9

king of Israel, "Strike the ground"; so he struck three times, and stopped.

19 And the man of God was angry with him, and said, "You should have struck five or six times; then you would have struck Syria till you had destroyed *it!* But now you will strike Syria *only* three times."

20 Then E·lī′sha died, and they buried him. And the *raiding* bands from Mō′ab invaded the land in the spring of the year.

21 So it was, as they were burying a man, that suddenly they spied a band *of raiders;* and they put the man in the tomb of E·lī′sha; and when the man was let down and touched the bones of E·lī′sha, he revived and stood on his feet.

Israel Recaptures Cities from Syria

22 And Haz′a·el king of Syria oppressed Israel all the days of Je·hō′-a·haz.

23 But the LORD was gracious to them, had compassion on them, and regarded them, because of His covenant with Abraham, Isaac, and Jacob, and would not yet destroy them or cast them from His presence.

24 Now Haz′a·el king of Syria died. Then Ben-Hā′dad his son reigned in his place.

25 And Je·hō′ash*a* the son of Je·hō′-a·haz recaptured from the hand of Ben-Hā′dad, the son of Haz′a·el, the cities which he had taken out of the hand of Je·hō′a·haz his father by war. Three times Jō′ash defeated him and recaptured the cities of Israel.

Amaziah Reigns in Judah

14 In the second year of Jō′ash the son of Je·hō′a·haz, king of Israel,

Am·a·zī′ah the son of Jō′ash, king of Judah, became king.

2 He was twenty-five years old when he became king, and he reigned twenty-nine years in Jerusalem. His mother's name was Je·hō·ad′dan of Jerusalem.

3 And he did *what was* right in the sight of the LORD, yet not like his father David; he did everything as his father Jō′ash had done.

4 However the high places were not taken away, and the people still sacrificed and burned incense on the high places.

5 Now it happened, as soon as the kingdom was established in his hand, that he executed his servants who had murdered his father the king.

6 But the children of the murderers he did not execute, according to what is written in the Book of the Law of Moses, in which the LORD commanded, saying, "Fathers shall not be put to death for their children, nor shall children be put to death for their fathers; but a person shall be put to death for his own sin."*a*

7 He killed ten thousand Ē′dom·ītes in the Valley of Salt, and took Sē′la by war, and called its name Jok′the·el to this day.

8 Then Am·a·zī′ah sent messengers to Je·hō′ash*a* the son of Je·hō′a·haz, the son of Jē′hū, king of Israel, saying, "Come, let us face one another *in battle.*"

9 And Je·hō′ash king of Israel sent to Am·a·zī′ah king of Judah, saying, "The thistle that *was* in Lebanon sent to the cedar that *was* in Lebanon, saying, 'Give your daughter to my son as wife'; and a wild beast that *was* in Lebanon passed by and trampled the thistle.

13:25 *a*Spelled *Joash* in verses 12–14, 25
14:6 *a*Deuteronomy 24:16   14:8 *a*Spelled *Joash* in 13:12ff and 2 Chronicles 25:17ff

10 "You have indeed defeated Ē'dom, and your heart has lifted you up. Glory *in that,* and stay at home; for why should you meddle with trouble so that you fall—you and Judah with you?"

11 But Am·a·zī'ah would not heed. Therefore Je·hō'ash king of Israel went out; so he and Am·a·zī'ah king of Judah faced one another at Beth Shem'esh, which *belongs* to Judah.

12 And Judah was defeated by Israel, and every man fled to his tent.

13 Then Je·hō'ash king of Israel captured Am·a·zī'ah king of Judah, the son of Je·hō'ash, the son of Ā·ha·zī'ah, at Beth Shem'esh; and he went to Jerusalem, and broke down the wall of Jerusalem from the Gate of Ē'phra·im to the Corner Gate—four hundred cubits.

14 And he took all the gold and silver, all the articles that were found in the house of the LORD and in the treasuries of the king's house, and hostages, and returned to Samaria.

15 Now the rest of the acts of Je·hō'ash which he did—his might, and how he fought with Am·a·zī'ah king of Judah—*are* they not written in the book of the chronicles of the kings of Israel?

16 So Je·hō'ash rested with his fathers, and was buried in Samaria with the kings of Israel. Then Jer·o·bō'am his son reigned in his place.

17 Am·a·zī'ah the son of Jō'ash, king of Judah, lived fifteen years after the death of Je·hō'ash the son of Je·hō'a·haz, king of Israel.

18 Now the rest of the acts of Am·a·zī'ah, *are* they not written in the book of the chronicles of the kings of Judah?

19 And they formed a conspiracy against him in Jerusalem, and he fled to Lā'chish; but they sent after him to Lā'chish and killed him there.

20 Then they brought him on horses, and he was buried at Jerusalem with his fathers in the City of David.

21 And all the people of Judah took Az·a·rī'ah,*a* who *was* sixteen years old, and made him king instead of his father Am·a·zī'ah.

22 He built Ē'lath and restored it to Judah, after the king rested with his fathers.

JEROBOAM II REIGNS IN ISRAEL

23 In the fifteenth year of Am·a·zī'ah the son of Jō'ash, king of Judah, Jer·o·bō'am the son of Jō'ash, king of Israel, became king in Samaria, *and reigned* forty-one years.

24 And he did evil in the sight of the LORD; he did not depart from all the sins of Jer·o·bō'am the son of Nē'bat, who had made Israel sin.

25 He restored the territory of Israel from the entrance of Hā'math to the Sea of the Ar'a·bah, according to the word of the LORD God of Israel, which He had spoken through His servant Jonah the son of A·mit'taī, the prophet who *was* from Gath Hē'pher.

26 For the LORD saw *that* the affliction of Israel *was* very bitter; and whether bond or free, there was no helper for Israel.

27 And the LORD did not say that He would blot out the name of Israel from under heaven; but He saved them by the hand of Jer·o·bō'am the son of Jō'ash.

28 Now the rest of the acts of Jer·o·bō'am, and all that he did—his might, how he made war, and how he recaptured for Israel, from Damascus and Hā'math, *what had belonged* to Judah—*are* they not written in the book of the chronicles of the kings of Israel?

29 So Jer·o·bō'am rested with his fa-

14:21 *a*Called *Uzziah* in 2 Chronicles 26:1ff, Isaiah 6:1, and elsewhere

thers, the kings of Israel. Then Zech·a·rī'ah his son reigned in his place.

AZARIAH REIGNS IN JUDAH

15 In the twenty-seventh year of Jer·o·bō'am king of Israel, Az·a·rī'ah the son of Am·a·zī'ah, king of Judah, became king.
2 He was sixteen years old when he became king, and he reigned fifty-two years in Jerusalem. His mother's name *was* Jech·o·lī'ah of Jerusalem.
3 And he did *what was* right in the sight of the LORD, according to all that his father Am·a·zī'ah had done,
4 except that the high places were not removed; the people still sacrificed and burned incense on the high places.
5 Then the LORD struck the king, so that he was a leper until the day of his death; so he dwelt in an isolated house. And Jō'tham the king's son *was* over the *royal* house, judging the people of the land.
6 Now the rest of the acts of Az·a·rī'ah, and all that he did, *are* they not written in the book of the chronicles of the kings of Judah?
7 So Az·a·rī'ah rested with his fathers, and they buried him with his fathers in the City of David. Then Jō'tham his son reigned in his place.

ZECHARIAH REIGNS IN ISRAEL

8 In the thirty-eighth year of Az·a·rī'ah king of Judah, Zech·a·rī'ah the son of Jer·o·bō'am reigned over Israel in Samaria six months.
9 And he did evil in the sight of the LORD, as his fathers had done; he did not depart from the sins of Jer·o·bō'am the son of Nē'bat, who had made Israel sin.
10 Then Shal'lum the son of Jā'besh conspired against him, and struck and killed him in front of the people; and he reigned in his place.
11 Now the rest of the acts of Zech·a·rī'ah, indeed they *are* written in the book of the chronicles of the kings of Israel.
12 This *was* the word of the LORD which He spoke to Jē'hū, saying, "Your sons shall sit on the throne of Israel to the fourth *generation.*"ᵃ And so it was.

SHALLUM REIGNS IN ISRAEL

13 Shal'lum the son of Jā'besh became king in the thirty-ninth year of Uz·zī'ahᵃ king of Judah; and he reigned a full month in Samaria.
14 For Men'a·hem the son of Gā'dī went up from Tir'zah, came to Samaria, and struck Shal'lum the son of Jā'besh in Samaria and killed him; and he reigned in his place.
15 Now the rest of the acts of Shal'lum, and the conspiracy which he led, indeed they *are* written in the book of the chronicles of the kings of Israel.
16 Then from Tir'zah, Men'a·hem attacked Tiph'sah, all who *were* there, and its territory. Because they did not surrender, therefore he attacked *it*. All the women there who were with child he ripped open.

MENAHEM REIGNS IN ISRAEL

17 In the thirty-ninth year of Az·a·rī'ah king of Judah, Men'a·hem the son of Gā'dī became king over Israel, *and reigned* ten years in Samaria.
18 And he did evil in the sight of the LORD; he did not depart all his days from the sins of Jer·o·bō'am the son of Nē'bat, who had made Israel sin.
19 Pūlᵃ king of Assyria came against

15:12 ᵃ2 Kings 10:30   15:13 ᵃCalled *Azariah* in 14:21ff and 15:1ff   15:19 ᵃThat is, Tiglath-Pileser III (compare verse 29)

the land; and Men'a·hem gave Pūl a thousand talents of silver, that his hand might be with him to strengthen the kingdom under his control.

20 And Men'a·hem exacted the money from Israel, from all the very wealthy, from each man fifty shekels of silver, to give to the king of Assyria. So the king of Assyria turned back, and did not stay there in the land.

21 Now the rest of the acts of Men'a·hem, and all that he did, *are* they not written in the book of the chronicles of the kings of Israel?

22 So Men'a·hem rested with his fathers. Then Pek·a·hī'ah his son reigned in his place.

PEKAHIAH REIGNS IN ISRAEL

23 In the fiftieth year of Az·a·rī'ah king of Judah, Pek·a·hī'ah the son of Men'a·hem became king over Israel in Samaria, *and reigned* two years.

24 And he did evil in the sight of the LORD; he did not depart from the sins of Jer·o·bō'am the son of Nē'bat, who had made Israel sin.

25 Then Pē'kah the son of Rem·a·lī'ah, an officer of his, conspired against him and killed him in Samaria, in the citadel of the king's house, along with Ar'gob and A·ri'eh; and with him were fifty men of Gil'ē·ad. He killed him and reigned in his place.

26 Now the rest of the acts of Pek·a·hī'ah, and all that he did, indeed they *are* written in the book of the chronicles of the kings of Israel.

PEKAH REIGNS IN ISRAEL

27 In the fifty-second year of Az·a·rī'ah king of Judah, Pē'kah the son of Rem·a·lī'ah became king over Israel in Samaria, *and reigned* twenty years.

28 And he did evil in the sight of the LORD; he did not depart from the sins of Jer·o·bō'am the son of Nē'bat, who had made Israel sin.

29 In the days of Pē'kah king of Israel, Tig'lath-Pī·lē'ser king of Assyria came and took Ī'jon, Abel Beth Mā'a·chah, Ja·nō'ah, Kē'desh, Hā'zor, Gil'ē·ad, and Galilee, all the land of Naph'ta·lī; and he carried them captive to Assyria.

30 Then Hō·shē'a the son of Ē'lah led a conspiracy against Pē'kah the son of Rem·a·lī'ah, and struck and killed him; so he reigned in his place in the twentieth year of Jō'tham the son of Uz·zī'ah.

31 Now the rest of the acts of Pē'kah, and all that he did, indeed they *are* written in the book of the chronicles of the kings of Israel.

JOTHAM REIGNS IN JUDAH

32 In the second year of Pē'kah the son of Rem·a·lī'ah, king of Israel, Jō'tham the son of Uz·zī'ah, king of Judah, began to reign.

33 He was twenty-five years old when he became king, and he reigned sixteen years in Jerusalem. His mother's name *was* Je·rū'sha[a] the daughter of Zā'dok.

34 And he did *what was* right in the sight of the LORD; he did according to all that his father Uz·zī'ah had done.

35 However the high places were not removed; the people still sacrificed and burned incense on the high places. He built the Upper Gate of the house of the LORD.

36 Now the rest of the acts of Jō'tham, and all that he did, *are* they not written in the book of the chronicles of the kings of Judah?

15:33 [a]Spelled *Jerushah* in 2 Chronicles 27:1

37 In those days the LORD began to send Rē′zin king of Syria and Pē′kah the son of Rem·a·lī′ah against Judah.

38 So Jō′tham rested with his fathers, and was buried with his fathers in the City of David his father. Then Ā′haz his son reigned in his place.

AHAZ REIGNS IN JUDAH

16 In the seventeenth year of Pē′kah the son of Rem·a·lī′ah, Ā′haz the son of Jō′tham, king of Judah, began to reign.

2 Ā′haz *was* twenty years old when he became king, and he reigned sixteen years in Jerusalem; and he did not do *what was* right in the sight of the LORD his God, as his father David *had done.*

3 But he walked in the way of the kings of Israel; indeed he made his son pass through the fire, according to the abominations of the nations whom the LORD had cast out from before the children of Israel.

4 And he sacrificed and burned incense on the high places, on the hills, and under every green tree.

5 Then Rē′zin king of Syria and Pē′kah the son of Rem·a·lī′ah, king of Israel, came up to Jerusalem to *make* war; and they besieged Ā′haz but could not overcome *him.*

6 At that time Rē′zin king of Syria captured Ē′lath for Syria, and drove the men of Judah from Ē′lath. Then the Ē′dom·ites*ᵃ* went to Ē′lath, and dwell there to this day.

7 So Ā′haz sent messengers to Tig′lath-Pī·lē′ser king of Assyria, saying, "I *am* your servant and your son. Come up and save me from the hand of the king of Syria and from the hand of the king of Israel, who rise up against me."

8 And Ā′haz took the silver and gold that was found in the house of the LORD, and in the treasuries of the king's house, and sent *it as* a present to the king of Assyria.

9 So the king of Assyria heeded him; for the king of Assyria went up against Damascus and took it, carried *its people* captive to Kir, and killed Rē′zin.

10 Now King Ā′haz went to Damascus to meet Tig′lath-Pī·lē′ser king of Assyria, and saw an altar that *was* at Damascus; and King Ā′haz sent to Ū·rī′jah the priest the design of the altar and its pattern, according to all its workmanship.

11 Then Ū·rī′jah the priest built an altar according to all that King Ā′haz had sent from Damascus. So Ū·rī′jah the priest made *it* before King Ā′haz came back from Damascus.

12 And when the king came back from Damascus, the king saw the altar; and the king approached the altar and made offerings on it.

13 So he burned his burnt offering and his grain offering; and he poured his drink offering and sprinkled the blood of his peace offerings on the altar.

14 He also brought the bronze altar which *was* before the LORD, from the front of the temple—from between the *new* altar and the house of the LORD—and put it on the north side of the *new* altar.

15 Then King Ā′haz commanded Ū·rī′jah the priest, saying, "On the great *new* altar burn the morning burnt offering, the evening grain offering, the king's burnt sacrifice, and his grain offering, with the burnt offering of all the people of the land, their grain offering, and their drink offerings; and sprinkle on it all the blood of the burnt offering and all the

16:6 *ᵃ*Some ancient authorities read *Syrians.*

blood of the sacrifice. And the bronze altar shall be for me to inquire *by.*"

16 Thus did Ū·rī'jah the priest, according to all that King Ā'haz commanded.

17 And King Ā'haz cut off the panels of the carts, and removed the lavers from them; and he took down the Sea from the bronze oxen that *were* under it, and put it on a pavement of stones.

18 Also he removed the Sabbath pavilion which they had built in the temple, and he removed the king's outer entrance from the house of the LORD, on account of the king of Assyria.

19 Now the rest of the acts of Ā'haz which he did, *are* they not written in the book of the chronicles of the kings of Judah?

20 So Ā'haz rested with his fathers, and was buried with his fathers in the City of David. Then Hez·e·kī'ah his son reigned in his place.

HOSHEA REIGNS IN ISRAEL

17 In the twelfth year of Ā'haz king of Judah, Hō·shē'a the son of Ē'lah became king of Israel in Samaria, *and he reigned* nine years.

2 And he did evil in the sight of the LORD, but not as the kings of Israel who were before him.

3 Shal·man·ē'ser king of Assyria came up against him; and Hō·shē'a became his vassal, and paid him tribute money.

4 And the king of Assyria uncovered a conspiracy by Hō·shē'a; for he had sent messengers to So, king of Egypt, and brought no tribute to the king of Assyria, as *he had done* year by year. Therefore the king of Assyria shut him up, and bound him in prison.

ISRAEL CARRIED CAPTIVE TO ASSYRIA

5 Now the king of Assyria went throughout all the land, and went up to Samaria and besieged it for three years.

6 In the ninth year of Hō·shē'a, the king of Assyria took Samaria and carried Israel away to Assyria, and placed them in Hā'lah and by the Hā'bor, the River of Gō'zan, and in the cities of the Mēdes.

7 For so it was that the children of Israel had sinned against the LORD their God, who had brought them up out of the land of Egypt, from under the hand of Pharaoh king of Egypt; and they had feared other gods,

8 and had walked in the statutes of the nations whom the LORD had cast out from before the children of Israel, and of the kings of Israel, which they had made.

9 Also the children of Israel secretly did against the LORD their God things that *were* not right, and they built for themselves high places in all their cities, from watchtower to fortified city.

10 They set up for themselves *sacred* pillars and wooden images*a* on every high hill and under every green tree.

11 There they burned incense on all the high places, like the nations whom the LORD had carried away before them; and they did wicked things to provoke the LORD to anger,

12 for they served idols, of which the LORD had said to them, "You shall not do this thing."

13 Yet the LORD testified against Israel and against Judah, by all of His prophets, every seer, saying, "Turn from your evil ways, and keep My commandments *and* My statutes, according to all the law which I com-

17:10 *a*Hebrew *Asherim,* Canaanite deities

manded your fathers, and which I sent to you by My servants the prophets."

14 Nevertheless they would not hear, but stiffened their necks, like the necks of their fathers, who did not believe in the LORD their God.

15 And they rejected His statutes and His covenant that He had made with their fathers, and His testimonies which He had testified against them; they followed idols, became idolaters, and *went* after the nations who *were* all around them, *concerning* whom the LORD had charged them that they should not do like them.

16 So they left all the commandments of the LORD their God, made for themselves a molded image *and* two calves, made a wooden image and worshiped all the host of heaven, and served Bā′al.

17 And they caused their sons and daughters to pass through the fire, practiced witchcraft and soothsaying, and sold themselves to do evil in the sight of the LORD, to provoke Him to anger.

18 Therefore the LORD was very angry with Israel, and removed them from His sight; there was none left but the tribe of Judah alone.

19 Also Judah did not keep the commandments of the LORD their God, but walked in the statutes of Israel which they made.

20 And the LORD rejected all the descendants of Israel, afflicted them, and delivered them into the hand of plunderers, until He had cast them from His sight.

21 For He tore Israel from the house of David, and they made Jer·o·bō′am the son of Nē′bat king. Then Jer·o·bō′am drove Israel from following the LORD, and made them commit a great sin.

22 For the children of Israel walked in all the sins of Jer·o·bō′am which he did; they did not depart from them,

23 until the LORD removed Israel out of His sight, as He had said by all His servants the prophets. So Israel was carried away from their own land to Assyria, *as it is* to this day.

ASSYRIA RESETTLES SAMARIA

24 Then the king of Assyria brought *people* from Babylon, Cū′thah, Ā′va, Hā′math, and from Seph·ar·vā′im, and placed *them* in the cities of Samaria instead of the children of Israel; and they took possession of Samaria and dwelt in its cities.

25 And it was so, at the beginning of their dwelling there, *that* they did not fear the LORD; therefore the LORD sent lions among them, which killed *some* of them.

26 So they spoke to the king of Assyria, saying, "The nations whom you have removed and placed in the cities of Samaria do not know the rituals of the God of the land; therefore He has sent lions among them, and indeed, they are killing them because they do not know the rituals of the God of the land."

27 Then the king of Assyria commanded, saying, "Send there one of the priests whom you brought from there; let him go and dwell there, and let him teach them the rituals of the God of the land."

28 Then one of the priests whom they had carried away from Samaria came and dwelt in Beth′el, and taught them how they should fear the LORD.

29 However every nation continued to make gods of its own, and put *them* in the shrines on the high places which the Samaritans had made, *every* nation in the cities where they dwelt.

30 The men of Babylon made

Suc'coth Be·noth', the men of Cūth made Ner'gal, the men of Hā'math made A·shī'ma,

31 and the Av'ītes made Nib'haz and Tar'tak; and the Se·phar'vītes burned their children in fire to A·dram'me·lech and A·nam'me·lech, the gods of Seph·ar·vā'im.

32 So they feared the LORD, and from every class they appointed for themselves priests of the high places, who sacrificed for them in the shrines of the high places.

33 They feared the LORD, yet served their own gods—according to the rituals of the nations from among whom they were carried away.

34 To this day they continue practicing the former rituals; they do not fear the LORD, nor do they follow their statutes or their ordinances, or the law and commandment which the LORD had commanded the children of Jacob, whom He named Israel,

35 with whom the LORD had made a covenant and charged them, saying: "You shall not fear other gods, nor bow down to them nor serve them nor sacrifice to them;

36 "but the LORD, who brought you up from the land of Egypt with great power and an outstretched arm, Him you shall fear, Him you shall worship, and to Him you shall offer sacrifice.

37 "And the statutes, the ordinances, the law, and the commandment which He wrote for you, you shall be careful to observe forever; you shall not fear other gods.

38 "And the covenant that I have made with you, you shall not forget, nor shall you fear other gods.

39 "But the LORD your God you shall fear; and He will deliver you from the hand of all your enemies."

40 However they did not obey, but they followed their former rituals.

41 So these nations feared the LORD, yet served their carved images; also their children and their children's children have continued doing as their fathers did, even to this day.

HEZEKIAH REIGNS IN JUDAH

18 Now it came to pass in the third year of Hō·shē'a the son of Ē'lah, king of Israel, *that* Hez·e·kī'ah the son of Ā'haz, king of Judah, began to reign.

2 He was twenty-five years old when he became king, and he reigned twenty-nine years in Jerusalem. His mother's name *was* Ā'bī*a* the daughter of Zech·a·rī'ah.

3 And he did *what was* right in the sight of the LORD, according to all that his father David had done.

4 He removed the high places and broke the *sacred* pillars, cut down the wooden image*a* and broke in pieces the bronze serpent that Moses had made; for until those days the children of Israel burned incense to it, and called it Ne·hush'tan.*b*

5 He trusted in the LORD God of Israel, so that after him was none like him among all the kings of Judah, nor who were before him.

6 For he held fast to the LORD; he did not depart from following Him, but kept His commandments, which the LORD had commanded Moses.

7 The LORD was with him; he prospered wherever he went. And he rebelled against the king of Assyria and did not serve him.

8 He subdued the Phi·lis'tines, as far as Gā'za and its territory, from watchtower to fortified city.

9 Now it came to pass in the fourth year of King Hez·e·kī'ah, which *was* the seventh year of Hō·shē'a the son

18:2 *a*Called *Abijah* in 2 Chronicles 29:1ff
18:4 *a*Hebrew *Asherah*, a Canaanite goddess
*b*Literally *Bronze Thing*

of Ē′lah, king of Israel, *that* Shal-man·ē′ser king of Assyria came up against Samaria and besieged it.

10 And at the end of three years they took it. In the sixth year of Hez·e·kī′ah, that *is,* the ninth year of Hō-shē′a king of Israel, Samaria was taken.

11 Then the king of Assyria carried Israel away captive to Assyria, and put them in Hā′lah and by the Hā′bor, the River of Gō′zan, and in the cities of the Mēdes,

12 because they did not obey the voice of the LORD their God, but transgressed His covenant *and* all that Moses the servant of the LORD had commanded; and they would nei-ther hear nor do *them.*

13 And in the fourteenth year of King Hez·e·kī′ah, Sen·nach′e·rib king of Assyria came up against all the fortified cities of Judah and took them.

14 Then Hez·e·kī′ah king of Judah sent to the king of Assyria at Lā′-chish, saying, "I have done wrong; turn away from me; whatever you impose on me I will pay." And the king of Assyria assessed Hez·e·kī′ah king of Judah three hundred talents of silver and thirty talents of gold.

15 So Hez·e·kī′ah gave *him* all the silver that was found in the house of the LORD and in the treasuries of the king's house.

16 At that time Hez·e·kī′ah stripped *the gold from* the doors of the temple of the LORD, and *from* the pillars which Hez·e·kī′ah king of Judah had overlaid, and gave it to the king of Assyria.

SENNACHERIB BOASTS AGAINST THE LORD

17 Then the king of Assyria sent *the* Tartan,*a the* Rab·sar′is,*b and the* Rab′sha·keh*c* from Lā′chish, with a great army against Jerusalem, to King Hez·e·kī′ah. And they went up and came to Jerusalem. When they had come up, they went and stood by the aqueduct from the upper pool, which *was* on the highway to the Fuller's Field.

18 And when they had called to the king, E·lī′a·kim the son of Hil·kī′ah, who *was* over the household, Sheb′na the scribe, and Jō′ah the son of Ā′saph, the recorder, came out to them.

19 Then *the* Rab′sha·keh said to them, "Say now to Hez·e·kī′ah, 'Thus says the great king, the king of As-syria: "What confidence *is* this in which you trust?

20 "You speak of *having* plans and power for war; but *they are* mere words. And in whom do you trust, that you rebel against me?

21 "Now look! You are trusting in the staff of this broken reed, Egypt, on which if a man leans, it will go into his hand and pierce it. So *is* Pharaoh king of Egypt to all who trust in him.

22 "But if you say to me, 'We trust in the LORD our God,' *is* it not He whose high places and whose altars Hez-e·kī′ah has taken away, and said to Judah and Jerusalem, 'You shall wor-ship before this altar in Jerusa-lem'?" '

23 "Now therefore, I urge you, give a pledge to my master the king of As-syria, and I will give you two thou-sand horses—if you are able on your part to put riders on them!

24 "How then will you repel one cap-tain of the least of my master's ser-vants, and put your trust in Egypt for chariots and horsemen?

25 "Have I now come up without the LORD against this place to destroy it?

18:17 *a*A title, probably *Commander in Chief*   *b*A title, probably *Chief Officer*   *c*A title, probably *Chief of Staff* or *Governor*

The LORD said to me, 'Go up against this land, and destroy it.' "

26 Then E·li'a·kim the son of Hil·ki'ah, Sheb'na, and Jo'ah said to *the* Rab'sha·keh, "Please speak to your servants in Ar·a·ma'ic, for we understand *it;* and do not speak to us in Hebrew[a] in the hearing of the people who *are* on the wall."

27 But *the* Rab'sha·keh said to them, "Has my master sent me to your master and to you to speak these words, and not to the men who sit on the wall, who will eat and drink their own waste with you?"

28 Then *the* Rab'sha·keh stood and called out with a loud voice in Hebrew, and spoke, saying, "Hear the word of the great king, the king of Assyria!

29 "Thus says the king: 'Do not let Hez·e·ki'ah deceive you, for he shall not be able to deliver you from his hand;

30 'nor let Hez·e·ki'ah make you trust in the LORD, saying, "The LORD will surely deliver us; this city shall not be given into the hand of the king of Assyria." '

31 "Do not listen to Hez·e·ki'ah; for thus says the king of Assyria: 'Make *peace* with me by a present and come out to me; and every one of you eat from his own vine and every one from his own fig tree, and every one of you drink the waters of his own cistern;

32 'until I come and take you away to a land like your own land, a land of grain and new wine, a land of bread and vineyards, a land of olive groves and honey, that you may live and not die. But do not listen to Hez·e·ki'ah, lest he persuade you, saying, "The LORD will deliver us."

33 'Has any of the gods of the nations at all delivered its land from the hand of the king of Assyria?

34 'Where *are* the gods of Ha'math and Ar'pad? Where *are* the gods of

Seph·ar·va'im and He'na and I'vah? Indeed, have they delivered Samaria from my hand?

35 'Who among all the gods of the lands have delivered their countries from my hand, that the LORD should deliver Jerusalem from my hand?' "

36 But the people held their peace and answered him not a word; for the king's commandment was, "Do not answer him."

37 Then E·li'a·kim the son of Hil·ki'ah, who *was* over the household, Sheb'na the scribe, and Jo'ah the son of A'saph, the recorder, came to Hez·e·ki'ah with *their* clothes torn, and told him the words of *the* Rab'-sha·keh.

ISAIAH ASSURES DELIVERANCE

19 And so it was, when King Hez·e·ki'ah heard *it,* that he tore his clothes, covered himself with sackcloth, and went into the house of the LORD.

2 Then he sent E·li'a·kim, who *was* over the household, Sheb'na the scribe, and the elders of the priests, covered with sackcloth, to I·sai'ah the prophet, the son of A'moz.

3 And they said to him, "Thus says Hez·e·ki'ah: 'This day *is* a day of trouble, and rebuke, and blasphemy; for the children have come to birth, but *there is* no strength to bring them forth.

4 'It may be that the LORD your God will hear all the words of *the* Rab'-sha·keh, whom his master the king of Assyria has sent to reproach the living God, and will rebuke the words which the LORD your God has heard. Therefore lift up *your* prayer for the remnant that is left.' "

5 So the servants of King Hez·e·ki'ah came to I·sai'ah.

18:26 [a]Literally *Judean*

6 And Ī·sāi′ah said to them, "Thus you shall say to your master, 'Thus says the LORD: "Do not be afraid of the words which you have heard, with which the servants of the king of Assyria have blasphemed Me.
7 "Surely I will send a spirit upon him, and he shall hear a rumor and return to his own land; and I will cause him to fall by the sword in his own land." ' "

SENNACHERIB'S THREAT AND HEZEKIAH'S PRAYER

8 Then *the* Rab′sha·keh returned and found the king of Assyria warring against Lib′nah, for he heard that he had departed from Lā′chish.
9 And the king heard concerning Tir·hā′kah king of Ethiopia, "Look, he has come out to make war with you." So he again sent messengers to Hez·e·kī′ah, saying,
10 "Thus you shall speak to Hez·e·kī′ah king of Judah, saying: 'Do not let your God in whom you trust deceive you, saying, "Jerusalem shall not be given into the hand of the king of Assyria."
11 'Look! You have heard what the kings of Assyria have done to all lands by utterly destroying them; and shall you be delivered?
12 'Have the gods of the nations delivered those whom my fathers have destroyed, Gō′zan and Har′an and Rē′zeph, and the people of Eden who *were* in Te·las′sar?
13 'Where *is* the king of Hā′math, the king of Ar′pad, and the king of the city of Seph·ar·vā′im, Hē′na, and Ī′vah?' "
14 And Hez·e·kī′ah received the letter from the hand of the messengers, and read it; and Hez·e·kī′ah went up to the house of the LORD, and spread it before the LORD.

15 Then Hez·e·kī′ah prayed before the LORD, and said: "O LORD God of Israel, *the One* who dwells *between* the cherubim, You are God, You alone, of all the kingdoms of the earth. You have made heaven and earth.
16 "Incline Your ear, O LORD, and hear; open Your eyes, O LORD, and see; and hear the words of Sen-nach′e·rib, which he has sent to reproach the living God.
17 "Truly, LORD, the kings of Assyria have laid waste the nations and their lands,
18 "and have cast their gods into the fire; for they *were* not gods, but the work of men's hands—wood and stone. Therefore they destroyed them.
19 "Now therefore, O LORD our God, I pray, save us from his hand, that all the kingdoms of the earth may know that You *are* the LORD God, You alone."

Prayers

2 Kings 19:14–20

What do you do when something seems impossible? Do you give up? Do you cry and moan? What do you do when you're scared? What do you do when you don't know what to do? The king of Assyria sent a great army to capture Jerusalem. Hezekiah knew he did not have an army big enough to win. The Assyrians were cruel. They would capture and torture him and his people. What would you do if you were Hezekiah? Hezekiah prayed. He begged God for help. Then God answered and helped. When you really need help, ask God.

WHEN THINGS SEEM UPSIDE DOWN 2 Kings 19:14–20

Sometimes it seems that the world is upside down. You thought things were OK, but they suddenly seem out of order. Is it you, or is it the rest of the world?

1. Do you ever feel that things are upside down, out of sync? What do you do then?
2. When that happens, do you blame everything else, or do you ask what you should do? How about praying? How about asking the Lord to help you cope? How about asking the Lord to help you see things the way you should?

For more on *What Should I Do?* turn to page 593

For more on *Prayer* turn to page 645

THE WORD OF THE LORD CONCERNING SENNACHERIB

20 Then Ī·sāi′ah the son of Ā′moz sent to Hez·e·kī′ah, saying, "Thus says the LORD God of Israel: 'Because you have prayed to Me against Sennach′e·rib king of Assyria, I have heard.'

21 "This *is* the word which the LORD has spoken concerning him:

'The virgin, the daughter of Zion,
Has despised you, laughed you to
    scorn;
The daughter of Jerusalem
Has shaken *her* head behind your
    back!

22 'Whom have you reproached and
    blasphemed?
Against whom have you raised
    your voice,
And lifted up your eyes on high?
Against the Holy *One* of Israel.

23 By your messengers you have
    reproached the Lord,
And said: "By the multitude of my
    chariots
I have come up to the height of
    the mountains,
To the limits of Lebanon;
I will cut down its tall cedars
And its choice cypress trees;
I will enter the extremity of its
    borders,
To its fruitful forest.

24 I have dug and drunk strange
    water,
And with the soles of my feet I
    have dried up
All the brooks of defense."

25 'Did you not hear long ago
How I made it,
From ancient times that I formed
    it?
Now I have brought it to pass,
That you should be

For crushing fortified cities *into*
    heaps of ruins.

26 Therefore their inhabitants had
    little power;
They were dismayed and
    confounded;
They were *as* the grass of the field
And the green herb,
As the grass on the housetops
And *grain* blighted before it is
    grown.

27 'But I know your dwelling place,
Your going out and your coming
    in,
And your rage against Me.

28 Because your rage against Me
    and your tumult
Have come up to My ears,
Therefore I will put My hook in
    your nose
And My bridle in your lips,
And I will turn you back
By the way which you came.

29 'This *shall be* a sign to you:

You shall eat this year such as
    grows of itself,
And in the second year what
    springs from the same;
Also in the third year sow and
    reap,
Plant vineyards and eat the fruit
    of them.

30 And the remnant who have
    escaped of the house of Judah
Shall again take root downward,
And bear fruit upward.

31 For out of Jerusalem shall go a
    remnant,
And those who escape from
    Mount Zion.
The zeal of the LORD of hosts[a] will
    do this.'

19:31 [a]Following many Hebrew manuscripts and ancient versions (compare Isaiah 37:32); Masoretic Text omits *of hosts*.

32 "Therefore thus says the LORD concerning the king of Assyria:

'He shall not come into this city,
Nor shoot an arrow there,
Nor come before it with shield,
Nor build a siege mound against it.
33 By the way that he came,
By the same shall he return;
And he shall not come into this city,'
Says the LORD.
34 'For I will defend this city, to save it
For My own sake and for My servant David's sake.' "

SENNACHERIB'S DEFEAT AND DEATH

35 And it came to pass on a certain night that the angel[a] of the LORD went out, and killed in the camp of the Assyrians one hundred and eighty-five thousand; and when *people* arose early in the morning, there were the corpses—all dead.
36 So Sen·nach'e·rib king of Assyria departed and went away, returned *home,* and remained at Nin'e·veh.
37 Now it came to pass, as he was worshiping in the temple of Nis'roch his god, that his sons A·dram'me·lech and Sha·rē'zer struck him down with the sword; and they escaped into the land of Ar'a·rat. Then Ē·sar·had'don his son reigned in his place.

HEZEKIAH'S LIFE EXTENDED

20 In those days Hez·e·kī'ah was sick and near death. And Ī·sāi'ah the prophet, the son of Ā'moz, went to him and said to him, "Thus says the LORD: 'Set your house in order, for you shall die, and not live.' "

2 Then he turned his face toward the wall, and prayed to the LORD, saying,
3 "Remember now, O LORD, I pray, how I have walked before You in truth and with a loyal heart, and have done *what was* good in Your sight." And Hez·e·kī'ah wept bitterly.
4 And it happened, before Ī·sāi'ah had gone out into the middle court, that the word of the LORD came to him, saying,
5 "Return and tell Hez·e·kī'ah the leader of My people, 'Thus says the LORD, the God of David your father: "I have heard your prayer, I have seen your tears; surely I will heal you. On the third day you shall go up to the house of the LORD.
6 "And I will add to your days fifteen years. I will deliver you and this city from the hand of the king of Assyria; and I will defend this city for My own sake, and for the sake of My servant David." ' "
7 Then Ī·sāi'ah said, "Take a lump of figs." So they took and laid *it* on the boil, and he recovered.
8 And Hez·e·kī'ah said to Ī·sāi'ah, "What *is* the sign that the LORD will heal me, and that I shall go up to the house of the LORD the third day?"
9 Then Ī·sāi'ah said, "This is the sign to you from the LORD, that the LORD will do the thing which He has spoken: *shall* the shadow go forward ten degrees or go backward ten degrees?"
10 And Hez·e·kī'ah answered, "It is an easy thing for the shadow to go down ten degrees; no, but let the shadow go backward ten degrees."
11 So Ī·sāi'ah the prophet cried out to the LORD, and He brought the shadow ten degrees backward, by

19:35 *a*Or *Angel*

which it had gone down on the sundial of Ā'haz.

THE BABYLONIAN ENVOYS

12 At that time Be·rō'dach-Bal'a·dan[a] the son of Bal'a·dan, king of Babylon, sent letters and a present to Hez·e·kī'ah, for he heard that Hez·e·kī'ah had been sick. **13** And Hez·e·kī'ah was attentive to them, and showed them all the house of his treasures—the silver and gold, the spices and precious ointment, and all[a] his armory—all that was found among his treasures. There was nothing in his house or in all his dominion that Hez·e·kī'ah did not show them. **14** Then Ī·sāi'ah the prophet went to King Hez·e·kī'ah, and said to him, "What did these men say, and from where did they come to you?" So Hez·e·kī'ah said, "They came from a far country, from Babylon." **15** And he said, "What have they seen in your house?" So Hez·e·kī'ah answered, "They have seen all that is in my house; there is nothing among my treasures that I have not shown them." **16** Then Ī·sāi'ah said to Hez·e·kī'ah, "Hear the word of the LORD: **17** 'Behold, the days are coming when all that is in your house, and what your fathers have accumulated until this day, shall be carried to Babylon; nothing shall be left,' says the LORD. **18** 'And they shall take away some of your sons who will descend from you, whom you will beget; and they shall be eunuchs in the palace of the king of Babylon.' " **19** So Hez·e·kī'ah said to Ī·sāi'ah, "The word of the LORD which you have spoken is good!" For he said, "Will there not be peace and truth at least in my days?"

DEATH OF HEZEKIAH

20 Now the rest of the acts of Hez·e·kī'ah—all his might, and how he made a pool and a tunnel and brought water into the city—are they not written in the book of the chronicles of the kings of Judah? **21** So Hez·e·kī'ah rested with his fathers. Then Ma·nas'seh his son reigned in his place.

MANASSEH REIGNS IN JUDAH

21 Ma·nas'seh was twelve years old when he became king, and he reigned fifty-five years in Jerusalem. His mother's name was Heph'zi·bah. **2** And he did evil in the sight of the LORD, according to the abominations of the nations whom the LORD had cast out before the children of Israel. **3** For he rebuilt the high places which Hez·e·kī'ah his father had destroyed; he raised up altars for Bā'al, and made a wooden image,[a] as Ā'hab king of Israel had done; and he worshiped all the host of heaven[b] and served them. **4** He also built altars in the house of the LORD, of which the LORD had said, "In Jerusalem I will put My name." **5** And he built altars for all the host of heaven in the two courts of the house of the LORD. **6** Also he made his son pass through the fire, practiced soothsaying, used witchcraft, and consulted spiritists and mediums. He did much evil in the sight of the LORD, to provoke Him to anger. **7** He even set a carved image of

20:12 [a]Spelled *Merodach-Baladan* in Isaiah 39:1
20:13 [a]Following many Hebrew manuscripts, Syriac, and Targum; Masoretic Text omits *all*.
21:3 [a]Hebrew *Asherah,* a Canaanite goddess
[b]The gods of the Assyrians

A·she′rah[a] that he had made, in the house of which the LORD had said to David and to Solomon his son, "In this house and in Jerusalem, which I have chosen out of all the tribes of Israel, I will put My name forever;

8 "and I will not make the feet of Israel wander anymore from the land which I gave their fathers—only if they are careful to do according to all that I have commanded them, and according to all the law that My servant Moses commanded them."

9 But they paid no attention, and Ma·nas′seh seduced them to do more evil than the nations whom the LORD had destroyed before the children of Israel.

10 And the LORD spoke by His servants the prophets, saying,

11 "Because Ma·nas′seh king of Judah has done these abominations (he has acted more wickedly than all the Am′o·rītes who were before him, and has also made Judah sin with his idols),

12 "therefore thus says the LORD God of Israel: 'Behold, I am bringing such calamity upon Jerusalem and Judah, that whoever hears of it, both his ears will tingle.

13 'And I will stretch over Jerusalem the measuring line of Samaria and the plummet of the house of Ā′hab; I will wipe Jerusalem as one wipes a dish, wiping it and turning it upside down.

14 'So I will forsake the remnant of My inheritance and deliver them into the hand of their enemies; and they shall become victims of plunder to all their enemies,

15 'because they have done evil in My sight, and have provoked Me to anger since the day their fathers came out of Egypt, even to this day.' "

16 Moreover Ma·nas′seh shed very much innocent blood, till he had filled Jerusalem from one end to another, besides his sin by which he made Judah sin, in doing evil in the sight of the LORD.

17 Now the rest of the acts of Ma·nas′seh—all that he did, and the sin that he committed—are they not written in the book of the chronicles of the kings of Judah?

18 So Ma·nas′seh rested with his fathers, and was buried in the garden of his own house, in the garden of Uz′za. Then his son Ā′mon reigned in his place.

AMON'S REIGN AND DEATH

19 Ā′mon was twenty-two years old when he became king, and he reigned two years in Jerusalem. His mother's name was Me·shul′le·meth the daughter of Ha′ruz of Jot′bah.

20 And he did evil in the sight of the LORD, as his father Ma·nas′seh had done.

21 So he walked in all the ways that his father had walked; and he served the idols that his father had served, and worshiped them.

22 He forsook the LORD God of his fathers, and did not walk in the way of the LORD.

23 Then the servants of Ā′mon conspired against him, and killed the king in his own house.

24 But the people of the land executed all those who had conspired against King Ā′mon. Then the people of the land made his son Jō·sī′ah king in his place.

25 Now the rest of the acts of Ā′mon which he did, are they not written in the book of the chronicles of the kings of Judah?

26 And he was buried in his tomb in the garden of Uz′za. Then Jō·sī′ah his son reigned in his place.

21:7 [a]A Canaanite goddess

JOSIAH REIGNS IN JUDAH

22 Jō·sī′ah *was* eight years old when he became king, and he reigned thirty-one years in Jerusalem. His mother's name *was* Je·dī′dah the daughter of A·dāi′ah of Boz′kath.

2 And he did *what was* right in the sight of the LORD, and walked in all the ways of his father David; he did not turn aside to the right hand or to the left.

HILKIAH FINDS THE BOOK OF THE LAW

3 Now it came to pass, in the eighteenth year of King Jō·sī′ah, *that* the king sent Shā′phan the scribe, the son of Az·a·lī′ah, the son of Me-shul′lam, to the house of the LORD, saying:

4 "Go up to Hil·kī′ah the high priest, that he may count the money which has been brought into the house of the LORD, which the door-keepers have gathered from the people.

5 "And let them deliver it into the hand of those doing the work, who are the overseers in the house of the LORD; let them give it to those who *are* in the house of the LORD doing the work, to repair the damages of the house—

6 "to carpenters and builders and masons—and to buy timber and hewn stone to repair the house.

7 "However there need be no accounting made with them of the money delivered into their hand, because they deal faithfully."

8 Then Hil·kī′ah the high priest said to Shā′phan the scribe, "I have found the Book of the Law in the house of the LORD." And Hil·kī′ah gave the book to Shā′phan, and he read it.

9 So Shā′phan the scribe went to the king, bringing the king word, saying, "Your servants have gathered the money that was found in the house, and have delivered it into the hand of those who do the work, who oversee the house of the LORD."

10 Then Shā′phan the scribe showed the king, saying, "Hil·kī′ah the priest has given me a book." And Shā′phan read it before the king.

11 Now it happened, when the king heard the words of the Book of the Law, that he tore his clothes.

12 Then the king commanded Hil-kī′ah the priest, A·hī′kam the son of Shā′phan, Ach′bor*a* the son of Mī-chaī′ah, Shā′phan the scribe, and A·saī′ah a servant of the king, saying,

13 "Go, inquire of the LORD for me, for the people and for all Judah, concerning the words of this book that has been found; for great *is* the wrath of the LORD that is aroused against us, because our fathers have not obeyed the words of this book, to do according to all that is written concerning us."

14 So Hil·kī′ah the priest, A·hī′kam, Ach′bor, Shā′phan, and A·saī′ah went to Hul′dah the prophetess, the wife of Shal′lum the son of Tik′vah, the son of Har′has, keeper of the wardrobe. (She dwelt in Jerusalem in the Second Quarter.) And they spoke with her.

15 Then she said to them, "Thus says the LORD God of Israel, 'Tell the man who sent you to Me,

16 "Thus says the LORD: 'Behold, I will bring calamity on this place and on its inhabitants—all the words of the book which the king of Judah has read—

17 'because they have forsaken Me and burned incense to other gods,

22:12 *aAbdon the son of Micah* in 2 Chronicles 34:20

that they might provoke Me to anger with all the works of their hands. Therefore My wrath shall be aroused against this place and shall not be quenched.' "'

18 "But as for the king of Judah, who sent you to inquire of the LORD, in this manner you shall speak to him, 'Thus says the LORD God of Israel: "*Concerning* the words which you have heard—

19 "because your heart was tender, and you humbled yourself before the LORD when you heard what I spoke against this place and against its inhabitants, that they would become a desolation and a curse, and you tore your clothes and wept before Me, I also have heard *you*," says the LORD.

20 "Surely, therefore, I will gather you to your fathers, and you shall be gathered to your grave in peace; and your eyes shall not see all the calamity which I will bring on this place." ' " So they brought back word to the king.

JOSIAH RESTORES TRUE WORSHIP

23 Now the king sent them to gather all the elders of Judah and Jerusalem to him.

2 The king went up to the house of the LORD with all the men of Judah, and with him all the inhabitants of Jerusalem—the priests and the prophets and all the people, both small and great. And he read in their hearing all the words of the Book of the Covenant which had been found in the house of the LORD.

3 Then the king stood by a pillar and made a covenant before the LORD, to follow the LORD and to keep His commandments and His testimonies and His statutes, with all *his* heart and all *his* soul, to perform the words of this covenant that were written in this book. And all the people took a stand for the covenant.

4 And the king commanded Hilkī'ah the high priest, the priests of the second order, and the doorkeepers, to bring out of the temple of the LORD all the articles that were made for Bā'al, for A·shē'rah,*a* and for all the host of heaven;*b* and he burned them outside Jerusalem in the fields of Kid'ron, and carried their ashes to Beth'el.

5 Then he removed the idolatrous priests whom the kings of Judah had ordained to burn incense on the high places in the cities of Judah and in the places all around Jerusalem, and those who burned incense to Bā'al, to the sun, to the moon, to the constellations, and to all the host of heaven.

6 And he brought out the wooden image*a* from the house of the LORD, to the Brook Kid'ron outside Jerusalem, burned it at the Brook Kid'ron and ground *it* to ashes, and threw its ashes on the graves of the common people.

7 Then he tore down the *ritual* booths of the perverted persons*a* that *were* in the house of the LORD, where the women wove hangings for the wooden image.

8 And he brought all the priests from the cities of Judah, and defiled the high places where the priests had burned incense, from Gē'ba to Bē·er·shē'ba; also he broke down the high places at the gates which *were* at the entrance of the Gate of Joshua the governor of the city, which *were* to the left of the city gate.

9 Nevertheless the priests of the high places did not come up to the altar of the LORD in Jerusalem, but

23:4 *a*A Canaanite goddess   *b*The gods of the Assyrians   23:6 *a*Hebrew *Asherah*, a Canaanite goddess   23:7 *a*Hebrew *qedeshim,* that is, those practicing sodomy and prostitution in religious rituals

What Should I Do?

GOOD EATING AND GOOD READING GO TOGETHER 2 Kings 23:1–3

When do you have Bible time in your house? Why not have it after breakfast, lunch, or dinner? Good reading and good eating go together. Feeding the body, feeding the mind, and feeding the soul are fun to do together.

1. Why should good eating and good reading fit together well? How are they alike?
2. Do you like mealtime with the family? Try to make that a happy time. You can make it even happier to add Bible time to mealtime.

For more on *What Should I Do?* turn to page 631
For more on *Bible* turn to page 731

they ate unleavened bread among their brethren.

10 And he defiled Tō'pheth, which *is* in the Valley of the Son*a* of Hin'nom, that no man might make his son or his daughter pass through the fire to Mō'lech.

11 Then he removed the horses that the kings of Judah had dedicated to the sun, at the entrance to the house of the LORD, by the chamber of Nā'than-Mē'lech, the officer who *was* in the court; and he burned the chariots of the sun with fire.

12 The altars that *were* on the roof, the upper chamber of Ā'haz, which the kings of Judah had made, and the altars which Ma·nas'seh had made in the two courts of the house of the LORD, the king broke down and pulverized there, and threw their dust into the Brook Kid'ron.

13 Then the king defiled the high places that *were* east of Jerusalem, which *were* on the south of the Mount of Corruption, which Solomon king of Israel had built for Ash'to·reth the abomination of the Sī·dō'ni·ans, for Chē'mosh the abomination of the Mō'ab·ītes, and for Mil'com the abomination of the people of Am'mon.

14 And he broke in pieces the *sacred* pillars and cut down the wooden images, and filled their places with the bones of men.

15 Moreover the altar that *was* at Beth'el, *and* the high place which Jer·o·bō'am the son of Nē'bat, who made Israel sin, had made, both that altar and the high place he broke down; and he burned the high place *and* crushed *it* to powder, and burned the wooden image.

16 As Jō·sī'ah turned, he saw the tombs that *were* there on the mountain. And he sent and took the bones out of the tombs and burned *them* on the altar, and defiled it according to the word of the LORD which the man of God proclaimed, who proclaimed these words.

17 Then he said, "What gravestone *is* this that I see?" So the men of the city told him, "*It is* the tomb of the man of God who came from Judah and proclaimed these things which you have done against the altar of Beth'el."

18 And he said, "Let him alone; let no one move his bones." So they let his bones alone, with the bones of the prophet who came from Samaria.

19 Now Jō·sī'ah also took away all the shrines of the high places that *were* in the cities of Samaria, which the kings of Israel had made to provoke the LORD*a* to anger; and he did to them according to all the deeds he had done in Beth'el.

20 He executed all the priests of the high places who *were* there, on the altars, and burned men's bones on them; and he returned to Jerusalem.

21 Then the king commanded all the people, saying, "Keep the Passover to the LORD your God, as *it is* written in this Book of the Covenant."

22 Such a Passover surely had never been held since the days of the judges who judged Israel, nor in all the days of the kings of Israel and the kings of Judah.

23 But in the eighteenth year of King Jō·sī'ah this Passover was held before the LORD in Jerusalem.

24 Moreover Jō·sī'ah put away those who consulted mediums and spiritists, the household gods and idols, all the abominations that were seen in the land of Judah and in Jerusalem, that he might perform the words of the law which were written in the book that Hil·kī'ah the priest found in the house of the LORD.

23:10 *a*Kethib reads *Sons.*   23:19 *a*Following Septuagint, Syriac, and Vulgate; Masoretic Text and Targum omit *the LORD.*

25 Now before him there was no king like him, who turned to the LORD with all his heart, with all his soul, and with all his might, according to all the Law of Moses; nor after him did *any* arise like him.

IMPENDING JUDGMENT ON JUDAH

26 Nevertheless the LORD did not turn from the fierceness of His great wrath, with which His anger was aroused against Judah, because of all the provocations with which Manas′seh had provoked Him.
27 And the LORD said, "I will also remove Judah from My sight, as I have removed Israel, and will cast off this city Jerusalem which I have chosen, and the house of which I said, 'My name shall be there.' "*a*

JOSIAH DIES IN BATTLE

28 Now the rest of the acts of Jō-sī′ah, and all that he did, *are* they not written in the book of the chronicles of the kings of Judah?
29 In his days Pharaoh Nē′cho king of Egypt went to the aid of the king of Assyria, to the River Eū·phrā′tēs; and King Jō·sī′ah went against him. And *Pharaoh Nē′cho* killed him at Me·gid′dō when he confronted him.
30 Then his servants moved his body in a chariot from Me·gid′dō, brought him to Jerusalem, and buried him in his own tomb. And the people of the land took Je·hō′a·haz the son of Jō·sī′ah, anointed him, and made him king in his father's place.

THE REIGN AND CAPTIVITY OF JEHOAHAZ

31 Je·hō′a·haz *was* twenty-three years old when he became king, and he reigned three months in Jerusa-lem. His mother's name *was* Ha-mū′tal the daughter of Jer·e·mī′ah of Lib′nah.
32 And he did evil in the sight of the LORD, according to all that his fathers had done.
33 Now Pharaoh Nē′cho put him in prison at Rib′lah in the land of Hā′math, that he might not reign in Jerusalem; and he imposed on the land a tribute of one hundred talents of silver and a talent of gold.
34 Then Pharaoh Nē′cho made E·lī′-a·kim the son of Jō·sī′ah king in place of his father Jō·sī′ah, and changed his name to Je·hoi′a·kim. And *Pharaoh* took Je·hō′a·haz and went to Egypt, and he*a* died there.

JEHOIAKIM REIGNS IN JUDAH

35 So Je·hoi′a·kim gave the silver and gold to Pharaoh; but he taxed the land to give money according to the command of Pharaoh; he exacted the silver and gold from the people of the land, from every one according to his assessment, to give *it* to Pharaoh Nē′cho.
36 Je·hoi′a·kim *was* twenty-five years old when he became king, and he reigned eleven years in Jerusa-lem. His mother's name *was* Ze·bū′-dah the daughter of Pe·dāi′ah of Rū′mah.
37 And he did evil in the sight of the LORD, according to all that his fathers had done.

JUDAH OVERRUN BY ENEMIES

24 In his days Ne·bū·chad·nez′zar king of Babylon came up, and Je-hoi′a·kim became his vassal *for* three years. Then he turned and rebelled against him.

23:27 *a*1 Kings 8:29   23:34 *a*That is, Jehoahaz

2　And the LORD sent against him *raiding* bands of Chal·dē'ans, bands of Syrians, bands of Mō'ab·ītes, and bands of the people of Am'mon; He sent them against Judah to destroy it, according to the word of the LORD which He had spoken by His servants the prophets.

3　Surely at the commandment of the LORD *this* came upon Judah, to remove *them* from His sight because of the sins of Ma·nas'seh, according to all that he had done,

4　and also because of the innocent blood that he had shed; for he had filled Jerusalem with innocent blood, which the LORD would not pardon.

5　Now the rest of the acts of Je·hoi'a·kim, and all that he did, *are* they not written in the book of the chronicles of the kings of Judah?

6　So Je·hoi'a·kim rested with his fathers. Then Je·hoi'a·chin his son reigned in his place.

7　And the king of Egypt did not come out of his land anymore, for the king of Babylon had taken all that belonged to the king of Egypt from the Brook of Egypt to the River Eū·phrā'tēs.

THE REIGN AND CAPTIVITY OF JEHOIACHIN

8　Je·hoi'a·chin *was* eighteen years old when he became king, and he reigned in Jerusalem three months. His mother's name *was* Ne·hush'ta the daughter of El·nā'than of Jerusalem.

9　And he did evil in the sight of the LORD, according to all that his father had done.

10　At that time the servants of Ne·bū·chad·nez'zar king of Babylon came up against Jerusalem, and the city was besieged.

11　And Ne·bū·chad·nez'zar king of Babylon came against the city, as his servants were besieging it.

12　Then Je·hoi'a·chin king of Judah, his mother, his servants, his princes, and his officers went out to the king of Babylon; and the king of Babylon, in the eighth year of his reign, took him prisoner.

THE CAPTIVITY OF JERUSALEM

13　And he carried out from there all the treasures of the house of the LORD and the treasures of the king's house, and he cut in pieces all the articles of gold which Solomon king of Israel had made in the temple of the LORD, as the LORD had said.

14　Also he carried into captivity all Jerusalem: all the captains and all the mighty men of valor, ten thousand captives, and all the craftsmen and smiths. None remained except the poorest people of the land.

15　And he carried Je·hoi'a·chin captive to Babylon. The king's mother, the king's wives, his officers, and the mighty of the land he carried into captivity from Jerusalem to Babylon.

16　All the valiant men, seven thousand, and craftsmen and smiths, one thousand, all *who were* strong *and* fit for war, these the king of Babylon brought captive to Babylon.

ZEDEKIAH REIGNS IN JUDAH

17　Then the king of Babylon made Mat·ta·nī'ah, *Je·hoi'a·chin's*[a] uncle, king in his place, and changed his name to Zed·e·kī'ah.

18　Zed·e·kī'ah *was* twenty-one years old when he became king, and he reigned eleven years in Jerusalem. His mother's name *was* Ha·mū'tal the daughter of Jer·e·mī'ah of Lib'nah.

24:17 [a]Literally *his*

19 He also did evil in the sight of the LORD, according to all that Je·hoi′-a·kim had done.
20 For because of the anger of the LORD *this* happened in Jerusalem and Judah, that He finally cast them out from His presence. Then Zed-e·kī′ah rebelled against the king of Babylon.

THE FALL AND CAPTIVITY OF JUDAH

25 Now it came to pass in the ninth year of his reign, in the tenth month, on the tenth *day* of the month, *that* Ne·bū·chad·nez′zar king of Babylon and all his army came against Jerusalem and encamped against it; and they built a siege wall against it all around.
2 So the city was besieged until the eleventh year of King Zed·e·kī′ah.
3 By the ninth *day* of the *fourth* month the famine had become so severe in the city that there was no food for the people of the land.
4 Then the city wall was broken through, and all the men of war *fled* at night by way of the gate between two walls, which was by the king's garden, even though the Chal·dē′ans *were* still encamped all around against the city. And the king^a went by way of the plain.^b
5 But the army of the Chal·dē′ans pursued the king, and they overtook him in the plains of Jericho. All his army was scattered from him.
6 So they took the king and brought him up to the king of Babylon at Rib′lah, and they pronounced judgment on him.
7 Then they killed the sons of Zed·e·kī′ah before his eyes, put out the eyes of Zed·e·kī′ah, bound him with bronze fetters, and took him to Babylon.
8 And in the fifth month, on the seventh *day* of the month (which *was* the nineteenth year of King Ne·bū·chad·nez′zar king of Babylon), Ne·bū·za·rad′an the captain of the guard, a servant of the king of Babylon, came to Jerusalem.
9 He burned the house of the LORD and the king's house; all the houses of Jerusalem, that is, all the houses of the great, he burned with fire.
10 And all the army of the Chal-dē′ans who *were with* the captain of the guard broke down the walls of Jerusalem all around.
11 Then Ne·bū·za·rad′an the captain of the guard carried away captive the rest of the people *who* remained in the city and the defectors who had deserted to the king of Babylon, with the rest of the multitude.
12 But the captain of the guard left *some* of the poor of the land as vine-dressers and farmers.
13 The bronze pillars that *were* in the house of the LORD, and the carts and the bronze Sea that *were* in the house of the LORD, the Chal·dē′ans broke in pieces, and carried their bronze to Babylon.
14 They also took away the pots, the shovels, the trimmers, the spoons, and all the bronze utensils with which the priests ministered.
15 The firepans and the basins, the things of solid gold and solid silver, the captain of the guard took away.
16 The two pillars, one Sea, and the carts, which Solomon had made for the house of the LORD, the bronze of all these articles was beyond measure.
17 The height of one pillar *was* eighteen cubits, and the capital on it *was* of bronze. The height of the capital was three cubits, and the network and pomegranates all around the

25:4 ^aLiterally *he*   ^bOr *Arabah,* that is, the Jordan Valley

capital were all of bronze. The second pillar was the same, with a network.

18 And the captain of the guard took Se·rāi′ah the chief priest, Zeph·a·nī′ah the second priest, and the three doorkeepers.

19 He also took out of the city an officer who had charge of the men of war, five men of the king's close associates who were found in the city, the chief recruiting officer of the army, who mustered the people of the land, and sixty men of the people of the land *who were* found in the city.

20 So Ne·bū·za·rad′an, captain of the guard, took these and brought them to the king of Babylon at Rib′lah.

21 Then the king of Babylon struck them and put them to death at Rib′lah in the land of Hā′math. Thus Judah was carried away captive from its own land.

GEDALIAH MADE GOVERNOR OF JUDAH

22 Then he made Ged·a·lī′ah the son of A·hī′kam, the son of Shā′phan, governor over the people who remained in the land of Judah, whom Ne·bū·chad·nez′zar king of Babylon had left.

23 Now when all the captains of the armies, they and *their* men, heard that the king of Babylon had made Ged·a·lī′ah governor, they came to Ged·a·lī′ah at Miz′pah—Ish′ma·el the son of Neth·a·nī′ah, Jō·hā′nan the son of Ca·rē′ah, Se·rāi′ah the son of Tan′hu·meth the Ne·toph′a·thīte, and Jā·az·a·nī′ah*ª* the son of a Mā′a·cha·thīte, they and their men.

24 And Ged·a·lī′ah took an oath before them and their men, and said to

them, "Do not be afraid of the servants of the Chal·dē′ans. Dwell in the land and serve the king of Babylon, and it shall be well with you."

25 But it happened in the seventh month that Ish′ma·el the son of Neth·a·nī′ah, the son of E·lish′a·ma, of the royal family, came with ten men and struck and killed Ged·a·lī′ah, the Jews, as well as the Chal·dē′ans who were with him at Miz′pah.

26 And all the people, small and great, and the captains of the armies, arose and went to Egypt; for they were afraid of the Chal·dē′ans.

JEHOIACHIN RELEASED FROM PRISON

27 Now it came to pass in the thirty-seventh year of the captivity of Je·hoi′a·chin king of Judah, in the twelfth month, on the twenty-seventh *day* of the month, *that* E′vil-Me·rō′dach*ª* king of Babylon, in the year that he began to reign, released Je·hoi′a·chin king of Judah from prison.

28 He spoke kindly to him, and gave him a more prominent seat than those of the kings who *were* with him in Babylon.

29 So Je·hoi′a·chin changed from his prison garments, and he ate bread regularly before the king all the days of his life.

30 And as for his provisions, *there was* a regular ration given him by the king, a portion for each day, all the days of his life.

25:23 *ª*Spelled *Jezaniah* in Jeremiah 40:8
25:27 *ª*Literally *Man of Marduk*

The First Book of the
CHRONICLES

THE FAMILY OF ADAM—SETH TO ABRAHAM

ADAM, Seth, Ē'nosh,
2 Cā·ī'nan,*a* Ma·hal'a·lel, Jar'ed,
3 Ē'noch, Me·thū'se·lah, Lā'mech,
4 Noah,*a* Shem, Ham, and Jā'-pheth.
5 The sons of Jā'pheth *were* Gō'-mer, Mā'gog, Mā'daī, Jā'van, Tū'bal, Mē'shech, and Tī'ras.
6 The sons of Gō'mer *were* Ash'ke·naz, Dī'phath,*a* and Tō·gar'-mah.
7 The sons of Jā'van *were* E·li'shah, Tar·shish'ah,*a* Kit'tim, and Rod'-a·nim.*b*
8 The sons of Ham *were* Cush, Miz'ra·im, Put, and Cā'naan.
9 The sons of Cush *were* Sē'ba, Hav'i·lah, Sab'ta,*a* Rā'a·ma,*b* and Sab'te·cha. The sons of Rā'a·ma *were* Shē'ba and Dē'dan.
10 Cush begot Nim'rod; he began to be a mighty one on the earth.
11 Miz'ra·im begot Lū'dim, An'a-mim, Le·hā'bim, Naph'tū·him,
12 Path·rū'sim, Cas·lū'him (from whom came the Phi·lis'tines and the Caph'to·rim).
13 Cā'naan begot Sī'don, his first-born, and Heth;
14 the Jeb'ū·sīte, the Am'o·rīte, and the Gir'ga·shīte;
15 the Hī'vīte, the Ar'kīte, and the Sī'nīte;
16 the Ar'vad·īte, the Zem'a·rīte, and the Hā'math·īte.
17 The sons of Shem *were* Ē'lam, As'shur, Ar·phā'xad, Lud, Ar'am, Uz, Hul, Gē'ther, and Mē'shech.*a*
18 Ar·phā'xad begot Shē'lah, and Shē'lah begot Ē'ber.
19 To Ē'ber were born two sons: the name of one *was* Pē'leg,*a* for in his

days the earth was divided; and his brother's name *was* Jok'tan.
20 Jok'tan begot Al·mō'dad, Shē'-leph, Hā·zar·mā'veth, Jē'rah,
21 Ha·dor'am, Ū'zal, Dik'lah,
22 Ē'bal,*a* A·bim'a·el, Shē'ba,
23 Ō'phir, Hav'i·lah, and Jō'bab. All these *were* the sons of Jok'tan.
24 Shem, Ar·phā'xad, Shē'lah,
25 Ē'ber, Pē'leg, Rē'ū,
26 Sē'rug, Nā'hor, Tē'rah,
27 and Abram, who *is* Abraham.
28 The sons of Abraham *were* Isaac and Ish'ma·el.

THE FAMILY OF ISHMAEL

29 These *are* their genealogies: The firstborn of Ish'ma·el *was* Ne·bā'joth; then Kē'dar, Ad'bē·el, Mib'sam,
30 Mish'ma, Dū'mah, Mas'sa, Hā'-dad,*a* Tē'ma,
31 Jē'tur, Nā'phish, and Ked'e·mah. These *were* the sons of Ish'ma·el.

THE FAMILY OF KETURAH

32 Now the sons born to Ke·tū'rah, Abraham's concubine, *were* Zim'ran, Jok'shan, Mē'dan, Mid'i·an, Ish'bak, and Shū'ah. The sons of Jok'shan *were* Shē'ba and Dē'dan.
33 The sons of Mid'i·an *were* Ē'phah, Ē'pher, Hā'noch, A·bī'da, and El-dā'ah. All these were the children of Ke·tū'rah.

1:2 *a*Hebrew *Qenan* 1:4 *a*Following Masoretic Text and Vulgate; Septuagint adds *the sons of Noah*. 1:6 *a*Spelled *Riphath* in Genesis 10:3
1:7 *a*Spelled *Tarshish* in Genesis 10:4 *b*Spelled *Dodanim* in Genesis 10:4 1:9 *a*Spelled *Sabtah* in Genesis 10:7 *b*Spelled *Raamah* in Genesis 10:7
1:17 *a*Spelled *Mash* in Genesis 10:23 1:19 *a*Literally *Division* 1:22 *a*Spelled *Obal* in Genesis 10:28 1:30 *a*Spelled *Hadar* in Genesis 25:15

THE FAMILY OF ISAAC

34 And Abraham begot Isaac. The sons of Isaac *were* Esau and Israel.
35 The sons of Esau *were* E·lī′phaz, Reū′el, Jē′ush, Jā′a·lam, and Kō′rah.
36 And the sons of E·li′phaz *were* Tē′man, Ō′mar, Zē′phī,*a* Gā′tam, *and* Kē′naz; and *by* Tim′na,*b* Am′a·lek.
37 The sons of Reū′el *were* Nā′hath, Zē′rah, Sham′mah, and Miz′zah.

THE FAMILY OF SEIR

38 The sons of Sē′ir *were* Lō′tan, Shō′bal, Zib′e·on, An′ah, Dī′shon, Ē′zer, and Dī′shan.
39 And the sons of Lō′tan *were* Hō′rī and Hō′mam; Lō′tan's sister *was* Tim′na.
40 The sons of Shō′bal *were* Al′i·an,*a* Man′a·hath, Ē′bal, Shē′phī,*b* and Ō′nam. The sons of Zib′e·on *were* Ā′jah and An′ah.
41 The son of An′ah *was* Dī′shon. The sons of Dī′shon *were* Ham′ran,*a* Esh′ban, Ith′ran, and Chē′ran.
42 The sons of Ē′zer *were* Bil′han, Zā′a·van, *and* Jā′a·kan.*a* The sons of Dī′shan *were* Uz and Ar′an.

THE KINGS OF EDOM

43 Now these *were* the kings who reigned in the land of Ē′dom before a king reigned over the children of Israel: Bē′la the son of Bē′or, and the name of his city was Din′ha·bah.
44 And when Bē′la died, Jō′bab the son of Zē′rah of Boz′rah reigned in his place.
45 When Jō′bab died, Hū′sham of the land of the Tē′man·ites reigned in his place.
46 And when Hū′sham died, Hā′dad the son of Bē′dad, who attacked Mid′i·an in the field of Mō′ab, reigned in his place. The name of his city *was* Ā′vith.

47 When Hā′dad died, Sam′lah of Mas·rē′kah reigned in his place.
48 And when Sam′lah died, Saul of Re·hō′both-by-the-River reigned in his place.
49 When Saul died, Bā′al-Hā′nan the son of Ach′bor reigned in his place.
50 And when Bā′al-Hā′nan died, Hā′dad*a* reigned in his place; and the name of his city was Pā′ī.*b* His wife's name was Me·het′a·bel the daughter of Mā′tred, the daughter of Mez′a·hab.
51 Hā′dad died also. And the chiefs of Ē′dom were Chief Tim′nah, Chief Al′i·ah,*a* Chief Jē′theth,
52 Chief A·hol·i·bā′mah, Chief Ē′lah, Chief Pī′non,
53 Chief Kē′naz, Chief Tē′man, Chief Mib′zar,
54 Chief Mag′di·el, and Chief Ī′ram. These *were* the chiefs of Ē′dom.

THE FAMILY OF ISRAEL

2 These *were* the sons of Israel: Reuben, Sim′e·on, Levi, Judah, Is′sa·char, Zeb′u·lun,
2 Dan, Joseph, Benjamin, Naph′ta·lī, Gad, and Ash′er.

FROM JUDAH TO DAVID

3 The sons of Judah *were* Er, Ō′nan, and Shē′lah. *These* three were born to him by the daughter of Shū′a, the Cā′naan·ī·tess. Er, the firstborn of Judah, was wicked in the sight of the LORD; so He killed him.
4 And Tā′mar, his daughter-in-law,

1:36 *a*Spelled *Zepho* in Genesis 36:11   *b*Compare Genesis 36:12   1:40 *a*Spelled *Alvan* in Genesis 36:23   *b*Spelled *Shepho* in Genesis 36:23
1:41 *a*Spelled *Hemdan* in Genesis 36:26
1:42 *a*Spelled *Akan* in Genesis 36:27
1:50 *a*Spelled *Hadar* in Genesis 36:39   *b*Spelled *Pau* in Genesis 36:39   1:51 *a*Spelled *Alvah* in Genesis 36:40

bore him Per′ez and Zē′rah. All the sons of Judah *were* five.

5   The sons of Per′ez *were* Hez′ron and Hā′mul.

6   The sons of Zē′rah *were* Zim′rī, Ē′than, Hē′man, Cal′col, and Dar′a—five of them in all.

7   The son of Car′mī *was* Ā′char,*a* the troubler of Israel, who transgressed in the accursed thing.

8   The son of Ē′than *was* Az·a·rī′ah.

9   Also the sons of Hez′ron who were born to him *were* Je·rah′mē·el, Ram, and Che·lū′bai.*a*

10   Ram begot Am·min′a·dab, and Am·min′a·dab begot Nah′shon, leader of the children of Judah;

11   Nah′shon begot Sal′ma,*a* and Sal′ma begot Bō′az;

12   Bō′az begot Ō′bed, and Ō′bed begot Jesse;

13   Jesse begot E·lī′ab his firstborn, A·bin′a·dab the second, Shim′ē·a*a* the third,

14   Ne·than′el the fourth, Rad′daī the fifth,

15   Ō′zem the sixth, *and* David the seventh.

16   Now their sisters *were* Ze·rū′i·ah and Ab′i·gāil. And the sons of Ze·rū′i·ah *were* A·bi′shaī, Jō′ab, and As′a·hel—three.

17   Ab′i·gāil bore A·mā′sa; and the father of A·mā′sa *was* Jē′ther the Ish′ma·el·īte.*a*

THE FAMILY OF HEZRON

18   Caleb the son of Hez′ron had children by A·zū′bah, *his* wife, and by Jer′i·oth. Now these were her sons: Jē′sher, Shō′bab, and Ar′don.

19   When A·zū′bah died, Caleb took Eph′rath*a* as his wife, who bore him Hur.

20   And Hur begot Ū′rī, and Ū′rī begot Bez′a·lel.

21   Now afterward Hez′ron went in to the daughter of Mā′chir the father of Gil′ē·ad, whom he married when he *was* sixty years old; and she bore him Sē′gub.

22   Sē′gub begot Jā′ir, who had twenty-three cities in the land of Gil′ē·ad.

23   (Gē′shur and Syria took from them the towns of Jā′ir, with Kē′nath and its towns—sixty towns.) All these *belonged to* the sons of Mā′chir the father of Gil′ē·ad.

24   After Hez′ron died in Caleb Eph′ra·thah, Hez′ron′s wife A·bī′jah bore him Ash′hur the father of Te·kō′a.

THE FAMILY OF JERAHMEEL

25   The sons of Je·rah′mē·el, the firstborn of Hez′ron, *were* Ram, the firstborn, and Bū′nah, Ō′ren, Ō′zem, *and* A·hī′jah.

26   Je·rah′mē·el had another wife, whose name was At′a·rah; she was the mother of Ō′nam.

27   The sons of Ram, the firstborn of Je·rah′mē·el, were Mā′az, Jā′min, and Ē′ker.

28   The sons of Ō′nam were Sham′maī and Jā′da. The sons of Sham′maī *were* Nā′dab and A·bī′shur.

29   And the name of the wife of A·bī′shur *was* Ab·i·hā′il, and she bore him Ah′ban and Mō′lid.

30   The sons of Nā′dab *were* Sē′led and Ap′pa·im; Sē′led died without children.

31   The son of Ap′pa·im *was* Ish′ī, the son of Ish′ī *was* Shē′shan, and Shē′shan′s son *was* Ah′laī.

32   The sons of Jā′da, the brother of Sham′maī, *were* Jē′ther and Jonathan; Jē′ther died without children.

2:7 *a*Spelled *Achan* in Joshua 7:1 and elsewhere
2:9 *a*Spelled *Caleb* in 2:18, 42   2:11 *a*Spelled *Salmon* in Ruth 4:21 and Luke 3:32
2:13 *a*Spelled *Shammah* in 1 Samuel 16:9 and elsewhere   2:17 *a*Compare 2 Samuel 17:25
2:19 *a*Spelled *Ephrathah* elsewhere

33 The sons of Jonathan *were* Pē′-leth and Zā′za. These were the sons of Je·rah′mē·el.

34 Now Shē′shan had no sons, only daughters. And Shē′shan had an Egyptian servant whose name *was* Jar′ha.

35 Shē′shan gave his daughter to Jar′ha his servant as wife, and she bore him At′taī.

36 At′taī begot Nathan, and Nathan begot Zā′bad;

37 Zā′bad begot Eph′lal, and Eph′lal begot Ō′bed;

38 Ō′bed begot Jē′hū, and Jē′hū begot Az·a·rī′ah;

39 Az·a·rī′ah begot Hē′lez, and Hē′lez begot El·e·ā′sah;

40 El·e·ā′sah begot Sis′maī, and Sis′maī begot Shal′lum;

41 Shal′lum begot Jek·a·mī′ah, and Jek·a·mī′ah begot E·lish′a·ma.

THE FAMILY OF CALEB

42 The descendants of Caleb the brother of Je·rah′mē·el *were* Mē′sha, his firstborn, who was the father of Ziph, and the sons of Ma·rē′shah the father of Hē′bron.

43 The sons of Hē′bron *were* Kō′rah, Tap′pū·ah, Rē′kem, and Shē′ma.

44 Shē′ma begot Rā′ham the father of Jor·kō′am, and Rē′kem begot Sham′maī.

45 And the son of Sham′maī *was* Mā′on, and Mā′on *was* the father of Beth Zūr.

46 Ē′phah, Caleb's concubine, bore Har′an, Mō′za, and Gā′zez; and Har′an begot Gā′zez.

47 And the sons of Jah′daī *were* Rē′gem, Jō′tham, Gē′shan, Pē′let, Ē′phah, and Shā′aph.

48 Mā′a·chah, Caleb's concubine, bore Shē′ber and Tir′hā·nah.

49 She also bore Shā′aph the father of Mad·man′nah, Shē′va the father of Mach·bē′nah and the father of Gib′ē·a. And the daughter of Caleb *was* Ach′sah.

50 These were the descendants of Caleb: The sons of Hur, the firstborn of Eph′ra·thah, *were* Shō′bal the father of Kir′jath Jē′a·rim,

51 Sal′ma the father of Bethlehem, *and* Har′eph the father of Beth Gā′der.

52 And Shō′bal the father of Kir′jath Jē′a·rim had descendants: Ha·rō′eh, *and* half of the *families of* Ma·nū′-hoth.*a*

53 The families of Kir′jath Jē′a·rim *were* the Ith′rītes, the Pū′thītes, the Shū′ma·thītes, and the Mish′ra·ītes. From these came the Zō′ra·thītes and the Esh′ta·o·lītes.

54 The sons of Sal′ma *were* Bethlehem, the Ne·toph′a·thītes, At′roth Beth Jō′ab, half of the Ma·nā′heth-ītes, and the Zō′rītes.

55 And the families of the scribes who dwelt at Jā′bez *were* the Tī′-ra·thītes, the Shim′ē·a·thītes, *and* the Sū′cha·thītes. These *were* the Ken′ītes who came from Ham′math, the father of the house of Rē′chab.

THE FAMILY OF DAVID

3 Now these were the sons of David who were born to him in Hē′bron: The firstborn *was* Am′non, by A·hin′ō·am the Jez′rē·el·ī·tess; the second, Daniel,*a* by Ab′i·gāil the Car′mel·ī·tess;

2 the third, Ab′sa·lom the son of Mā′a·cah, the daughter of Tal′maī, king of Gē′shur; the fourth, Ad·o·nī′jah the son of Hag′gith;

3 the fifth, Sheph·a·tī′ah, by A·bī′-tal; the sixth, Ith′rē·am, by his wife Eg′lah;

4 *These* six were born to him in

2:52 *a*Same as *the Manahethites,* verse 54
3:1 *a*Called *Chileab* in 2 Samuel 3:3

Hē'bron. There he reigned seven years and six months, and in Jerusalem he reigned thirty-three years.

5 And these were born to him in Jerusalem: Shim'ē·a,[a] Shō'bab, Nathan, and Solomon—four by Bath-shū'a[b] the daughter of Am'mi·el.[c]

6 Also *there* were Ib'har, E·lish'a·ma,[a] E·liph'e·let,[b]

7 Nō'gah, Nē'pheg, Ja·phī'a,

8 E·lish'a·ma, E·lī'a·da,[a] and E·liph'e·let—nine *in all*.

9 *These were* all the sons of David, besides the sons of the concubines, and Tā'mar their sister.

The Family of Solomon

10 Solomon's son *was* Rē·ho·bō'am; A·bī'jah[a] *was* his son, Ā'sa his son, Je·hosh'a·phat his son,

11 Jō'ram[a] his son, Ā·ha·zī'ah his son, Jō'ash[b] his son,

12 Am·a·zī'ah his son, Az·a·rī'ah[a] his son, Jō'tham his son,

13 Ā'haz his son, Hez·e·kī'ah his son, Ma·nas'seh his son,

14 Ā'mon his son, *and* Jō·sī'ah his son.

15 The sons of Jō·sī'ah *were* Jō·hā'-nan the firstborn, the second Je·hoi'a·kim, the third Zed·e·kī'ah, and the fourth Shal'lum.[a]

16 The sons of Je·hoi'a·kim *were* Jec·o·nī'ah his son *and* Zed·e·kī'ah[a] his son.

The Family of Jeconiah

17 And the sons of Jec·o·nī'ah[a] *were* As'sir,[b] She·al'ti·el his son,

18 *and* Mal·chi'ram, Pe·dāi'ah, Shen·az'zar, Jec·a·mī'ah, Hosh'a·ma, and Ned·a·bī'ah.

19 The sons of Pe·dāi'ah *were* Ze·rub'ba·bel and Shim'ē·ī. The sons of Ze·rub'ba·bel *were* Me·shul'lam, Han·a·nī'ah, She·lō'mith their sister,

20 and Ha·shū'bah, Ō'hel, Ber·e·chī'ah, Has·a·dī'ah, and Jū'shab-Hē'sed—five *in all*.

21 The sons of Han·a·nī'ah *were* Pel·a·tī'ah and Je·shā'i·ah, the sons of Reph·āi'ah, the sons of Ar'nan, the sons of Ō·ba·dī'ah, and the sons of Shech·a·nī'ah.

22 The son of Shech·a·nī'ah was She·māi'ah. The sons of She·māi'ah *were* Hat'tush, Ī'gal, Ba·rī'ah, Nē·a·rī'ah, and Shā'phat—six *in all*.

23 The sons of Nē·a·rī'ah *were* Eli·ō·ē'naī, Hez·e·kī'ah, and Az·rī'kam—three *in all*.

24 The sons of El·i·ō·ē'naī *were* Hod·a·vī'ah, E·lī'a·shib, Pe·lāi'ah, Ak'kub, Jō·hā'nan, De·lāi'ah, and A·nā'ni—seven *in all*.

The Family of Judah

4 The sons of Judah *were* Per'ez, Hez'ron, Car'mī, Hur, and Shō'bal.

2 And Rē·āi'ah the son of Shō'bal begot Jā'hath, and Jā'hath begot A·hū'mai and Lā'had. These *were* the families of the Zō'ra·thites.

3 These *were* the sons *of the father* of Ē'tam: Jez'rē·el, Ish'ma, and Id'bash; and the name of their sister *was* Haz·e·lel·pō'ni;

4 and Pe·nū'el *was* the father of Gē'dor, and Ē'zer *was the* father of Hū'shah. These *were* the sons of Hur, the firstborn of Eph'ra·thah the father of Bethlehem.

5 And Ash'hur the father of Te·kō'a had two wives, Hē'lah and Nā'a·rah.

3:5 [a]Spelled *Shammua* in 14:4 and 2 Samuel 5:14 [b]Spelled *Bathsheba* in 2 Samuel 11:3 [c]Called *Eliam* in 2 Samuel 11:3 3:6 [a]Spelled *Elishua* in 14:5 and 2 Samuel 5:15 [b]Spelled *Elpelet* in 14:5 3:8 [a]Spelled *Beeliada* in 14:7 3:10 [a]Spelled *Abijam* in 1 Kings 15:1 3:11 [a]Spelled *Jehoram* in 2 Kings 1:17 and 8:16 [b]Spelled *Jehoash* in 2 Kings 12:1 3:12 [a]Called *Uzziah* in Isaiah 6:1 3:15 [a]Called *Jehoahaz* in 2 Kings 23:31 3:16 [a]Compare 2 Kings 24:17 3:17 [a]Also called *Coniah* in Jeremiah 22:24 and *Jehoiachin* in 2 Kings 24:8 [b]Or *Jeconiah the captive were*

6 Nā′a·rah bore him A·huz′zam, Hē′pher, Tē′me·nī, and Hā·a·hash′-ta·rī. These *were* the sons of Nā′a-rah.
7 The sons of Hē′lah *were* Zē′reth, Zō′har, and Eth′nan;
8 and Koz begot A′nub, Zō·bē′bah, and the families of A·har′hel the son of Har′um.
9 Now Jā′bez was more honorable than his brothers, and his mother called his name Jā′bez,*a* saying, "Because I bore *him* in pain."
10 And Jā′bez called on the God of Israel saying, "Oh, that You would bless me indeed, and enlarge my territory, that Your hand would be with me, and that You would keep *me* from evil, that I may not cause pain!" So God granted him what he requested.

■ *Prayers* ■

1 Chronicles 4:10

You may want to pray the prayer of Jabez often, "That You would keep me from evil, that I may not cause pain." When we do bad things we hurt others, such as parents or friends, and we hurt God. We cause them pain. We also hurt ourselves and cause ourselves pain. There is so much evil around us, so much temptation. Pray often for God to keep you from yielding to it. If you do, you will cause yourself, others and God great pain.

---

11 Chē′lub the brother of Shū′hah begot Mē′hir, who *was* the father of Esh′ton.
12 And Esh′ton begot Beth-Rā′pha, Pa·sē′ah, and Te·hin′nah the father of Ir-Nā′hash. These *were* the men of Rē′chah.
13 The sons of Kē′naz *were* Oth′ni·el and Se·rāi′ah. The sons of Oth′ni·el *were* Hā′thath,*a*
14 and Me·on′o·thai *who* begot Oph′rah. Se·rāi′ah begot Jō′ab the father of Ge Ha·ra′shim,*a* for they were craftsmen.
15 The sons of Caleb the son of Je·phūn′neh *were* Ī′rū, Ē′lah, and Nā′am. The son of Ē′lah *was* Kē′naz.
16 The sons of Je·hal′le·lel *were* Ziph, Zī′phah, Tir′i·a, and As′a·rel.
17 The sons of Ez′rah *were* Jē′ther, Mē′red, Ē′pher, and Jā′lon. And Mē′red's wife*a* bore Miriam, Sham′-mai, and Ish′bah the father of Esh-te·mō′a.
18 (His wife Jē·hu·dī′jah*a* bore Jē′red the father of Gē′dor, Hē′ber the father of Sō′chōh, and Je·kū′thi·el the father of Za·nō′ah.) And these were the sons of Bith′i·ah the daughter of Pharaoh, whom Mē′red took.
19 The sons of Hō·dī′ah's wife, the sister of Nā′ham, *were* the fathers of Kē·ī′lah the Gar′mite and of Esh-te·mō′a the Mā′a·cha·thite.
20 And the sons of Shī′mon *were* Am′non, Rin′nah, Ben-Hā′nan, and Tī′lon. And the sons of Ish′ī *were* Zō′heth and Ben-Zō′heth.
21 The sons of Shē′lah the son of Judah *were* Er the father of Lē′cah, Lā′a·dah the father of Ma·rē′shah, and the families of the house of the linen workers of the house of Ash′-bē·a;
22 also Jō′kim, the men of Cho·zē′ba, and Jō′ash; Sar′aph, who ruled in Mō′ab, and Ja·shū′bī-Lē′hem. Now the records are ancient.
23 These *were* the potters and those who dwell at Ne·tā′im*a* and Ge·dē′-rah;*b* there they dwelt with the king for his work.

4:9 *a*Literally *He Will Cause Pain*   4:13 *a*Septuagint and Vulgate add *and Meonothai*.
4:14 *a*Literally *Valley of Craftsmen*   4:17 *a*Literally *she*   4:18 *a*Or *His Judean wife*   4:23 *a*Literally *Plants*   *b*Literally *Hedges*

The Family of Simeon

24 The sons of Sim'e·on *were* Nem'-ū·el, Jā'min, Jā'rib,*a* Zē'rah,*b and* Shā'ūl,
25 Shal'lum his son, Mib'sam his son, and Mish'ma his son.
26 And the sons of Mish'ma *were* Ham'ū·el his son, Zac'chur his son, and Shim'ē·ī his son.
27 Shim'ē·ī had sixteen sons and six daughters; but his brothers did not have many children, nor did any of their families multiply as much as the children of Judah.
28 They dwelt at Bē·er·shē'ba, Mō'la·dah, Hā'zar Shū'al,
29 Bil'hah, Ē'zem, Tō'lad,
30 Be·thū'el, Hor'mah, Zik'lag,
31 Beth Mar'ca·both, Hā'zar Sū'sim, Beth Bi'ri, and at Shā·a·rā'im. These *were* their cities until the reign of David.
32 And their villages *were* Ē'tam, Ā'in, Rim'mon, Tō'chen, and Ā'shan—five cities—
33 and all the villages that *were* around these cities as far as Bā'al.*a* These *were* their dwelling places, and they maintained their genealogy:
34 Me·shō'bab, Jam'lech, and Jō'-shah the son of Am·a·zī'ah;
35 Jō'el, and Jē'hū the son of Josh·i·bī'ah, the son of Se·rāi'ah, the son of As'i·el;
36 El·i·ō·ē'naī, Jā·a·kō'bah, Jesh-ō·hāi'ah, A·sāi'ah, Ad'i·el, Je·sim'i·el, and Be·nā'i·ah;
37 Zī'za the son of Shī'phī, the son of Al'lon, the son of Je·daī'ah, the son of Shim'rī, the son of She·māi'ah—
38 these mentioned by name *were* leaders in their families, and their father's house increased greatly.
39 So they went to the entrance of Gē'dor, as far as the east side of the valley, to seek pasture for their flocks.
40 And they found rich, good pas-ture, and the land *was* broad, quiet, and peaceful; for some Ham'ītes formerly lived there.
41 These recorded by name came in the days of Hez·e·kī'ah king of Judah; and they attacked their tents and the Me·ū'nītes who were found there, and utterly destroyed them, as it is to this day. So they dwelt in their place, because *there was* pasture for their flocks there.
42 Now *some* of them, five hundred men of the sons of Sim'e·on, went to Mount Sē'ir, having as their captains Pel·a·tī'ah, Nē·a·rī'ah, Reph·āi'ah, and Uz'zi·el, the sons of Ish'ī.
43 And they defeated the rest of the A·mal'e·kītes who had escaped. They have dwelt there to this day.

The Family of Reuben

5 Now the sons of Reuben the firstborn of Israel—he *was* indeed the firstborn, but because he defiled his father's bed, his birthright was given to the sons of Joseph, the son of Israel, so that the genealogy is not listed according to the birthright;
2 yet Judah prevailed over his brothers, and from him *came* a ruler, although the birthright was Joseph's—
3 the sons of Reuben the firstborn of Israel were Hā'noch, Pal'lū, Hez'ron, and Car'mī.
4 The sons of Jō'el *were* She·māi'ah his son, Gog his son, Shim'ē·ī his son,
5 Mī'cah his son, Rē·āi'ah his son, Bā'al his son,
6 and Be·er'ah his son, whom Tig'lath-Pī·lē'ser*a* king of Assyria carried into captivity. He *was* leader of the Reū'ben·ītes.

4:24 *a*Called *Jachin* in Genesis 46:10   *b*Called *Zohar* in Genesis 46:10   4:33 *a*Or *Baalath Beer* (compare Joshua 19:8)   5:6 *a*Hebrew *Tilgath-Pilneser*

7 And his brethren by their families, when the genealogy of their generations was registered: the chief, Je·ī′el, and Zech·a·rī′ah,

8 and Bē′la the son of Ā′zaz, the son of Shē′ma, the son of Jō′el, who dwelt in A·rō′er, as far as Nē′bo and Bā′al Mē′on.

9 Eastward they settled as far as the entrance of the wilderness this side of the River Eū·phrā′tēs, because their cattle had multiplied in the land of Gil′ē·ad.

10 Now in the days of Saul they made war with the Hag′rītes, who fell by their hand; and they dwelt in their tents throughout the entire *area* east of Gil′ē·ad.

THE FAMILY OF GAD

11 And the children of Gad dwelt next to them in the land of Bā′shan as far as Sal′cah:

12 Jō′el *was* the chief, Shā′pham the next, then Jā′a·naī and Shā′phat in Bā′shan,

13 and their brethren of their father's house: Michael, Me·shul′lam, Shē′ba, Jō′raī, Jā′chan, Zī′a, and Ē′ber—seven *in all.*

14 These *were* the children of Ab·i·hā′il the son of Hū′rī, the son of Ja·rō′ah, the son of Gil′ē·ad, the son of Michael, the son of Je·shish′aī, the son of Jah′dō, the son of Buz;

15 Ā′hī the son of Ab′di·el, the son of Gū′nī, *was* chief of their father's house.

16 And *the Gad′ītes* dwelt in Gil′ē·ad, in Bā′shan and in its villages, and in all the common-lands of Sharon within their borders.

17 All these were registered by genealogies in the days of Jō′tham king of Judah, and in the days of Jer·o·bō′am king of Israel.

18 The sons of Reuben, the Gad′ītes, and half the tribe of Ma·nas′seh *had*

forty-four thousand seven hundred and sixty valiant men, men able to bear shield and sword, to shoot with the bow, and skillful in war, who went to war.

19 They made war with the Hag′rītes, Jē′tur, Nā′phish, and Nō′dab.

20 And they were helped against them, and the Hag′rītes were delivered into their hand, and all who *were* with them, for they cried out to God in the battle. He heeded their prayer, because they put their trust in Him.

21 Then they took away their livestock—fifty thousand of their camels, two hundred and fifty thousand of their sheep, and two thousand of their donkeys—also one hundred thousand of their men;

22 for many fell dead, because the war *was* God's. And they dwelt in their place until the captivity.

THE FAMILY OF MANASSEH (EAST)

23 So the children of the half-tribe of Ma·nas′seh dwelt in the land. Their *numbers* increased from Bā′shan to Bā′al Her′mon, that is, to Sē′nir, or Mount Her′mon.

24 These *were* the heads of their fathers' houses: Ē′pher, Ish′ī, E·lī′el, Az′ri·el, Jer·e·mī′ah, Hod·a·vī′ah, and Jah′di·el. They were mighty men of valor, famous men, *and* heads of their fathers' houses.

25 And they were unfaithful to the God of their fathers, and played the harlot after the gods of the peoples of the land, whom God had destroyed before them.

26 So the God of Israel stirred up the spirit of Pūl king of Assyria, that is, Tig′lath-Pī·lē′ser[a] king of Assyria. He carried the Reū′ben·ītes, the Gad′ītes, and the half-tribe of Ma·nas′seh

5:26 [a]Hebrew *Tilgath-Pilneser*

into captivity. He took them to Hā′lah, Hā′bor, Hā′ra, and the river of Gō′zan to this day.

THE FAMILY OF LEVI

6 The sons of Levi *were* Ger′shon, Kō′hath, and Me·rar′ī.

2 The sons of Kō′hath *were* Am′-ram, Iz′har, Hē′bron, and Uz′zi·el.

3 The children of Am′ram *were* Aaron, Moses, and Miriam. And the sons of Aaron *were* Nā′dab, A·bī′hū, El·ē·ā′zar, and Ith′a·mar.

4 El·ē·ā′zar begot Phin′e·has, *and* Phin′e·has begot Ab·i·shū′a;

5 Ab·i·shū′a begot Buk′kī, and Buk′kī begot Uz′zī;

6 Uz′zī begot Zer·a·hī′ah, and Zer·a·hī′ah begot Me·rā′i·oth;

7 Me·rā′i·oth begot Am·a·rī′ah, and Am·a·rī′ah begot A·hī′tub;

8 A·hī′tub begot Zā′dok, and Zā′dok begot A·him′a·az;

9 A·him′a·az begot Az·a·rī′ah, and Az·a·rī′ah begot Jō·hā′nan;

10 Jō·hā′nan begot Az·a·rī′ah (it was he who ministered as priest in the temple that Solomon built in Jerusalem);

11 Az·a·rī′ah begot Am·a·rī′ah, and Am·a·rī′ah begot A·hī′tub;

12 A·hī′tub begot Zā′dok, and Zā′dok begot Shal′lum;

13 Shal′lum begot Hil·kī′ah, and Hil·kī′ah begot Az·a·rī′ah;

14 Az·a·rī′ah begot Se·rāi′ah, and Se·rāi′ah begot Je·hoz′a·dak.

15 Je·hoz′a·dak went *into captivity* when the LORD carried Judah and Jerusalem into captivity by the hand of Ne·bū·chad·nez′zar.

16 The sons of Levi *were* Ger′shon,*a* Kō′hath, and Me·rar′ī.

17 These are the names of the sons of Ger′shon: Lib′nī and Shim′ē·ī.

18 The sons of Kō′hath *were* Am′-ram, Iz′har, Hē′bron, and Uz′-zi·el.

19 The sons of Me·rar′ī *were* Mah′lī and Mū′shī. Now these *are* the families of the Lē′vītes according to their fathers:

20 Of Ger′shon *were* Lib′nī his son, Jā′hath his son, Zim′mah his son,

21 Jō′ah his son, Id′dō his son, Zē′-rah his son, *and* Jē·ath′e·raī his son.

22 The sons of Kō′hath *were* Am-min′a·dab his son, Kō′rah his son, As′sir his son,

23 El·kā′nah his son, E·bī′a·saph his son, As′sir his son,

24 Tā′hath his son, Ū·rī′el his son, Uz·zī′ah his son, and Shā′ul his son.

25 The sons of El·kā′nah *were* A·mā′saī and A·hī′moth.

26 *As for* El·kā′nah,*a* the sons of El·kā′nah *were* Zō′phaī*b* his son, Nā′hath*c* his son,

27 E·lī′ab*a* his son, Je·rō′ham his son, *and* El·kā′nah his son.

28 The sons of Samuel *were* Jō′el*a* the firstborn, and A·bī′jah the second.*b*

29 The sons of Me·rar′ī *were* Mah′lī, Lib′nī his son, Shim′ē·ī his son, Uz′zah his son,

30 Shim′ē·a his son, Hag·gī′ah his son, *and* A·sāi′ah his son.

MUSICIANS IN THE HOUSE OF THE LORD

31 Now these are the men whom David appointed over the service of song in the house of the LORD, after the ark came to rest.

32 They were ministering with music before the dwelling place of the tabernacle of meeting, until Solomon had built the house of the LORD in

6:16 *a*Hebrew *Gershom* (alternate spelling of *Gershon*, as in verses 1, 17, 20, 43, 62, and 71)
6:26 *a*Compare verse 35   *b*Spelled *Zuph* in verse 35 and 1 Samuel 1:1   *c*Compare verse 34
6:27 *a*Compare verse 34   6:28 *a*Following Septuagint, Syriac, and Arabic (compare verse 33 and 1 Samuel 8:2)   *b*Hebrew *Vasheni*

Jerusalem, and they served in their office according to their order.

33 And these *are* the ones who ministered with their sons: Of the sons of the Kō'hath·ites *were* Hē'man the singer, the son of Jō'el, the son of Samuel,

34 the son of El·kā'nah, the son of Je·rō'ham, the son of E·lī'el,*a* the son of Tō'ah,*b*

35 the son of Zuph, the son of El·kā'nah, the son of Mā'hath, the son of A·mā'saī,

36 the son of El·kā'nah, the son of Jō'el, the son of Az·a·rī'ah, the son of Zeph·a·nī'ah,

37 the son of Tā'hath, the son of As'sir, the son of E·bī'a·saph, the son of Kō'rah,

38 the son of Iz'har, the son of Kō'hath, the son of Levi, the son of Israel.

39 And his brother Ā'saph, who stood at his right hand, *was* Ā'saph the son of Ber·a·chī'ah, the son of Shim'ē·a,

40 the son of Michael, the son of Bā·a·sē'i·ah, the son of Mal·chī'jah,

41 the son of Eth'nī, the son of Zē'rah, the son of A·dāi'ah,

42 the son of Ē'than, the son of Zim'mah, the son of Shim'ē·ī,

43 the son of Jā'hath, the son of Ger'shon, the son of Levi.

44 Their brethren, the sons of Me·rar'ī, on the left hand, *were* Ē'than the son of Kish'ī, the son of Ab'dī, the son of Mal'luch,

45 the son of Hash·a·bī'ah, the son of Am·a·zī'ah, the son of Hil·kī'ah,

46 the son of Am'zī, the son of Bā'nī, the son of Shā'mer,

47 the son of Mah'lī, the son of Mū'shī, the son of Me·rar'ī, the son of Levi.

48 And their brethren, the Lē'vītes, *were* appointed to every kind of service of the tabernacle of the house of God.

The Family of Aaron

49 But Aaron and his sons offered sacrifices on the altar of burnt offering and on the altar of incense, for all the work of the Most Holy *Place,* and to make atonement for Israel, according to all that Moses the servant of God had commanded.

50 Now these *are* the sons of Aaron: El·ē·ā'zar his son, Phin'e·has his son, Ab·i·shū'a his son,

51 Buk'kī his son, Uz'zī his son, Zer·a·hī'ah his son,

52 Me·rā'i·oth his son, Am·a·rī'ah his son, A·hī'tub his son,

53 Zā'dok his son, *and* A·him'a·az his son.

Dwelling Places of the Levites

54 Now these *are* their dwelling places throughout their settlements in their territory, for they were *given* by lot to the sons of Aaron, of the family of the Kō'hath·ites:

55 They gave them Hē'bron in the land of Judah, with its surrounding common-lands.

56 But the fields of the city and its villages they gave to Caleb the son of Je·phūn'neh.

57 And to the sons of Aaron they gave *one of* the cities of refuge, Hē'bron; also Lib'nah with its common-lands, Jat'tir, Esh·te·mō'a with its common-lands,

58 Hī'len*a* with its common-lands, Dē'bir with its common-lands,

59 Ā'shan*a* with its common-lands, and Beth Shem'esh with its common-lands.

60 And from the tribe of Benjamin: Gē'ba with its common-lands, Al'e·meth*a* with its common-lands, and

6:34 *a*Spelled *Elihu* in 1 Samuel 1:1   *b*Spelled *Tohu* in 1 Samuel 1:1   6:58 *a*Spelled *Holon* in Joshua 21:15   6:59 *a*Spelled *Ain* in Joshua 21:16   6:60 *a*Spelled *Almon* in Joshua 21:18

An'a·thoth with its common-lands. All their cities among their families *were* thirteen.

61 To the rest of the family of the tribe of the Kō'hath·ites *they gave* by lot ten cities from half the tribe of Ma·nas'seh.

62 And to the sons of Ger'shon, throughout their families, *they gave* thirteen cities from the tribe of Is'sa·char, from the tribe of Ash'er, from the tribe of Naph'ta·lī, and from the tribe of Ma·nas'seh in Bā'shan.

63 To the sons of Me·rar'ī, throughout their families, *they gave* twelve cities from the tribe of Reuben, from the tribe of Gad, and from the tribe of Zeb'ū·lun.

64 So the children of Israel gave *these* cities with their common-lands to the Lē'vītes.

65 And they gave by lot from the tribe of the children of Judah, from the tribe of the children of Sim'ē·on, and from the tribe of the children of Benjamin these cities which are called by *their* names.

66 Now some of the families of the sons of Kō'hath *were given* cities as their territory from the tribe of Ē'phra·im.

67 And they gave them *one of* the cities of refuge, Shē'chem with its common-lands, in the mountains of Ē'phra·im, also Gē'zer with its common-lands,

68 Jok'mē·am with its common-lands, Beth Hor'on with its common-lands,

69 Aī'ja·lon with its common-lands, and Gath Rim'mon with its common-lands.

70 And from the half-tribe of Ma·nas'seh: Ā'ner with its common-lands and Bil'ē·am with its common-lands, for the rest of the family of the sons of Kō'hath.

71 From the family of the half-tribe of Ma·nas'seh the sons of Ger'shon *were given* Gō'lan in Bā'shan with its common-lands and Ash'ta·roth with its common-lands.

72 And from the tribe of Is'sa·char: Kē'desh with its common-lands, Dab'e·rath with its common-lands,

73 Rā'moth with its common-lands, and Ā'nem with its common-lands.

74 And from the tribe of Ash'er: Mā'shal with its common-lands, Ab'don with its common-lands,

75 Hū'kok with its common-lands, and Rē'hob with its common-lands.

76 And from the tribe of Naph'ta·lī: Kē'desh in Galilee with its common-lands, Ham'mon with its common-lands, and Kir·jath'a·im with its common-lands.

77 From the tribe of Zeb'ū·lun the rest of the children of Me·rar'ī *were given* Rim'mon[a] with its common-lands and Tā'bor with its common-lands.

78 And on the other side of the Jordan, across from Jericho, on the east side of the Jordan, *they were given* from the tribe of Reuben: Bē'zer in the wilderness with its common-lands, Jah'zah with its common-lands,

79 Ked'e·moth with its common-lands, and Meph'a·ath with its common-lands.

80 And from the tribe of Gad: Rā'moth in Gil'ē·ad with its common-lands, Mā·ha·na'im with its common-lands,

81 Hesh'bon with its common-lands, and Jā'zer with its common-lands.

THE FAMILY OF ISSACHAR

7 The sons of Is'sa·char *were* Tō'la, Pū'ah,[a] Jash'ub, and Shim'ron—four *in all.*

6:77 [a]Hebrew *Rimmono,* alternate spelling of *Rimmon;* see 4:32   7:1 [a]Spelled *Puvah* in Genesis 46:13

2 The sons of Tō'la *were* Uz'zī, Reph·āi'ah, Jē'ri·el, Jah'maī, Jib'sam, and She·mū'el, heads of their father's house. *The sons* of Tō'la *were* mighty men of valor in their generations; their number in the days of David *was* twenty-two thousand six hundred.

3 The son of Uz'zī *was* Iz·ra·hī'ah, and the sons of Iz·ra·hī'ah *were* Michael, Ō·ba·dī'ah, Jō'el, and Ish·ī'ah. All five of them *were* chief men.

4 And with them, by their generations, according to their fathers' houses, *were* thirty-six thousand troops ready for war; for they had many wives and sons.

5 Now their brethren among all the families of Is'sa·char *were* mighty men of valor, listed by their genealogies, eighty-seven thousand in all.

THE FAMILY OF BENJAMIN

6 *The sons* of Benjamin *were* Bē'la, Bē'cher, and Je·dī'a·el—three *in all*.

7 The sons of Bē'la were Ez'bon, Uz'zī, Uz'zi·el, Jer'i·moth, and Iri—five *in all*. They *were* heads of *their* fathers' houses, and they were listed by their genealogies, twenty-two thousand and thirty-four mighty men of valor.

8 The sons of Bē'cher *were* Ze·mī'rah, Jō'ash, El·i·ē'zer, El·i·ō·ē'naī, Om'rī, Jer'i·moth, A·bī'jah, An'a·thoth, and Al'e·meth. All these *are* the sons of Bē'cher.

9 And they were recorded by genealogy according to their generations, heads of their fathers' houses, twenty thousand two hundred mighty men of valor.

10 The son of Je·dī'a·el *was* Bil'han, and the sons of Bil'han *were* Jē'ush, Benjamin, Ē'hud, Che·nā'a·nah, Zē'than, Thar'shish, and A·hish'a·har.

11 All these sons of Je·dī'a·el *were* heads of their fathers' houses; *there were* seventeen thousand two hundred mighty men of valor fit to go out for war *and* battle.

12 Shup'pim and Hup'pim[a] *were* the sons of Ir, *and* Hū'shim *was* the son of Ā'her.

THE FAMILY OF NAPHTALI

13 The sons of Naph'ta·lī *were* Jah'zi·el,[a] Gū'nī, Jē'zer, and Shal'lum,[b] the sons of Bil'hah.

THE FAMILY OF MANASSEH (WEST)

14 The descendants of Ma·nas'seh: his Syrian concubine bore him Mā'chir the father of Gil'ē·ad, the father of As'ri·el.[a]

15 Mā'chir took as his wife *the sister* of Hup'pim and Shup'pim,[a] whose name *was* Mā'a·chah. The name of *Gil'ē·ad's* grandson[b] *was* Ze·loph'e·had,[c] but Ze·loph'e·had begot only daughters.

16 (Mā'a·chah the wife of Mā'chir bore a son, and she called his name Pē'resh. The name of his brother *was* Shē'resh, and his sons *were* Ū'lam and Rā'kem.

17 The son of Ū'lam *was* Bē'dan.) These *were* the descendants of Gil'ē·ad the son of Mā'chir, the son of Ma·nas'seh.

18 His sister Ham·mo'le·keth bore Ish'hod, Ā·bi·ē'zer, and Mah'lah.

19 And the sons of She·mī'da were A·hī'an, Shē'chem, Lik'hī, and A·nī'am.

THE FAMILY OF EPHRAIM

20 The sons of Ē'phra·im *were* Shū'the·lah, Bē'red his son, Tā'hath

---

7:12 [a]Called *Hupham* in Numbers 26:39
7:13 [a]Spelled *Jahzeel* in Genesis 46:24   [b]Spelled *Shillem* in Genesis 46:24   7:14 [a]The son of Gilead (compare Numbers 26:30, 31)
7:15 [a]Compare verse 12   [b]Literally *the second* [c]Compare Numbers 26:30–33

his son, El′a·dah his son, Tā′hath his son,

21 Zā′bad his son, Shū′the·lah his son, and Ē′zer and Ē′lē·ad. The men of Gath who were born in *that* land killed *them* because they came down to take away their cattle.

22 Then Ē′phra·im their father mourned many days, and his brethren came to comfort him.

23 And when he went in to his wife, she conceived and bore a son; and he called his name Bē·rī′ah,*a* because tragedy had come upon his house.

24 Now his daughter *was* Shē′e·rah, who built Lower and Upper Beth Hor′on and Uz′zen Shē′e·rah;

25 and Rē′phah *was* his son, *as well as* Rē′sheph, and Tē′lah his son, Tā′han his son,

26 Lā′a·dan his son, Am·mī′hud his son, E·lish′a·ma his son,

27 Nun*a* his son, and Joshua his son.

28 Now their possessions and dwelling places *were* Beth′el and its towns: to the east Nā′a·ran, to the west Gē′zer and its towns, and Shē′chem and its towns, as far as Āy′yah*a* and its towns;

29 and by the borders of the children of Ma·nas′seh *were* Beth Shē′an and its towns, Tā′a·nach and its towns, Me·gid′dō and its towns, Dor and its towns. In these dwelt the children of Joseph, the son of Israel.

The Family of Asher

30 The sons of Ash′er *were* Im′nah, Ish′vah, Ish′vī, Bē·rī′ah, and their sister Sē′rah.

31 The sons of Bē·rī′ah *were* Hē′ber and Mal′chi·el, who was the father of Bir′za·ith.*a*

32 And Hē′ber begot Japh′let, Shō′mer,*a* Hō′tham,*b* and their sister Shū′a.

33 The sons of Japh′let *were* Pā′- sach, Bim′hal, and Ash′vath. These *were* the children of Japh′let.

34 The sons of Shē′mer *were* Ā′hi, Rōh′gah, Je·hub′bah, and Ar′am.

35 And the sons of his brother Hē′lem *were* Zō′phah, Im′na, Shē′lesh, and Ā′mal.

36 The sons of Zō′phah *were* Sū′ah, Har′ne·pher, Shū′al, Bē′rī, Im′rah,

37 Bē′zer, Hod, Sham′ma, Shil′shah, Jith′ran,*a* and Be·ē′ra.

38 The sons of Jē′ther *were* Je·phūn′neh, Pis′pah, and Ar′a.

39 The sons of Ul′la *were* Ā′rah, Han′i·el, and Rī·zī′a.

40 All these *were* the children of Ash′er, heads of *their* fathers′ houses, choice men, mighty men of valor, chief leaders. And they were recorded by genealogies among the army fit for battle; their number *was* twenty-six thousand.

The Family Tree of King Saul of Benjamin

8 Now Benjamin begot Bē′la his firstborn, Ash′bel the second, A′har·ah*a* the third,

2 Nō′hah the fourth, and Rā′pha the fifth.

3 The sons of Bē′la *were* Ad′dar,*a* Gē′ra, A·bī′hud,

4 Ab·i·shū′a, Nā′a·man, A·hō′ah,

5 Gē′ra, She·phū′phan, and Hū′ram.

6 These *are* the sons of Ē′hud, who were the heads of the fathers′ *houses* of the inhabitants of Gē′ba, and who forced them to move to Man′a·hath:

7 Nā′a·man, A·hī′jah, and Gē′ra

7:23 *a*Literally *In Tragedy*   7:27 *a*Hebrew *Non*
7:28 *a*Many Hebrew manuscripts, Bomberg, Septuagint, Targum, and Vulgate read *Gazza.*
7:31 *a*Or *Birzavith* or *Birzoth*   7:32 *a*Spelled *Shemer* in verse 34   *b*Spelled *Helem* in verse 35
7:37 *a*Spelled *Jether* in verse 38   8:1 *a*Spelled *Ahiram* in Numbers 26:38   8:3 *a*Called *Ard* in Numbers 26:40

who forced them to move. He begot Uz′za and A·hī′hud.

8 Also Shā·ha·rā′im had children in the country of Mō′ab, after he had sent away Hū′shim and Bā′a·ra his wives.

9 By Hō′desh his wife he begot Jō′bab, Zib′i·a, Mē′sha, Mal′cam,

10 Jē′uz, Sa·chī′ah, and Mir′mah. These *were* his sons, heads of their fathers′ *houses*.

11 And by Hū′shim he begot A·bī′tub and El·pā′al.

12 The sons of El·pā′al *were* Ē′ber, Mī′sham, and Shē′med, who built Ō′nō and Lod with its towns;

13 and Bē·rī′ah and Shē′ma, who *were* heads of their fathers′ *houses* of the inhabitants of Aī′ja·lon, who drove out the inhabitants of Gath.

14 A·hī′ō, Shā′shak, Jer′e·moth,

15 Zeb·a·dī′ah, Ar′ad, Ē′der,

16 Michael, Is′pah, and Jō′ha *were* the sons of Bē·rī′ah.

17 Zeb·a·dī′ah, Me·shul′lam, Hiz′kī, Hē′ber,

18 Ish′me·raī, Jiz·lī′ah, and Jō′bab *were* the sons of El·pā′al.

19 Jā′kim, Zich′rī, Zab′dī,

20 E·li·ē′naī, Zil′le·thaī, E·lī′el,

21 A·dāi′ah, Be·rā′i·ah, and Shim′rath *were* the sons of Shim′ē·ī.

22 Ish′pan, Ē′ber, E·lī′el,

23 Ab′don, Zich′rī, Hā′nan,

24 Han·a·nī′ah, Ē′lam, An·to·thī′jah,

25 Iph·dē′i·ah, and Pe·nū′el *were* the sons of Shā′shak.

26 Sham′she·raī, Shē·ha·rī′ah, Ath·a·lī′ah,

27 Jā·ar·e·shī′ah, E·lī′jah, and Zich′rī *were* the sons of Je·rō′ham.

28 These *were* heads of the fathers′ *houses* by their generations, chief men. These dwelt in Jerusalem.

29 Now the father of Gib′ē·on, whose wife′s name *was* Mā′a·cah, dwelt at Gib′ē·on.

30 And his firstborn son *was* Ab′don, then Zūr, Kish, Bā′al, Nā′dab,

31 Gē′dor, A·hī′ō, Zē′cher,

32 and Mik′loth, *who* begot Shim′ē·ah.[a] They also dwelt alongside their relatives in Jerusalem, with their brethren.

33 Ner[a] begot Kish, Kish begot Saul, and Saul begot Jonathan, Mal·chī·shū′a, A·bin′a·dab,[b] and Esh-Bā′al.[c]

34 The son of Jonathan *was* Mer′ib-Bā′al,[a] and Mer′ib-Bā′al begot Mī′cah.

35 The sons of Mī′cah *were* Pī′thon, Mē′lech, Ta·rē′a, and Ā′haz.

36 And Ā′haz begot Je·hō′ad·dah;[a] Je·hō′ad·dah begot Al′e·meth, Az′ma·veth, and Zim′rī; and Zim′rī begot Mō′za.

37 Mō′za begot Bin′ē·a, Rā′phah[a] his son, El·e·ā′sah his son, *and* Ā′zel his son.

38 Ā′zel had six sons whose names *were* these: Az·rī′kam, Bō′che·rū, Ish′ma·el, Shē·a·rī′ah, Ō·ba·dī′ah, and Hā′nan. All these *were* the sons of Ā′zel.

39 And the sons of Ē′shek his brother *were* Ū′lam his firstborn, Jē′ush the second, and E·liph′e·let the third.

40 The sons of Ū′lam were mighty men of valor—archers. *They* had many sons and grandsons, one hundred and fifty *in all*. These *were* all sons of Benjamin.

9 So all Israel was recorded by genealogies, and indeed, they *were* inscribed in the book of the kings of Israel. But Judah was carried away captive to Babylon because of their unfaithfulness.

2 And the first inhabitants who

8:32 *a*Spelled *Shimeam* in 9:38   8:33 *a*Also the son of Gibeon (compare 9:36, 39)   *b*Called *Jishui* in 1 Samuel 14:49   *c*Called *Ishbosheth* in 2 Samuel 2:8 and elsewhere   8:34 *a*Called *Mephibosheth* in 2 Samuel 4:4   8:36 *a*Spelled *Jarah* in 9:42   8:37 *a*Spelled *Rephaiah* in 9:43

dwelt in their possessions in their cities *were* Israelites, priests, Lē'-vītes, and the Neth'i·nim.

DWELLERS IN JERUSALEM

3 Now in Jerusalem the children of Judah dwelt, and some of the children of Benjamin, and of the children of Ē'phra·im and Ma·nas'seh:
4 Ū'thaī the son of Am·mī'hud, the son of Om'rī, the son of Im'rī, the son of Bā'nī, of the descendants of Per'ez, the son of Judah.
5 Of the Shī'lo·nītes: A·sāi'ah the firstborn and his sons.
6 Of the sons of Zē'rah: Je·ū'el, and their brethren—six hundred and ninety.
7 Of the sons of Benjamin: Sal'lū the son of Me·shul'lam, the son of Hod·a·vī'ah, the son of Has·se·nū'ah;
8 Ib·nē'i·ah the son of Je·rō'ham; Ē'lah the son of Uz'zī, the son of Mich'rī; Me·shul'lam the son of Sheph·a·tī'ah, the son of Reū'el, the son of Ib·nī'jah;
9 and their brethren, according to their generations—nine hundred and fifty-six. All these men *were* heads of a father's *house* in their fathers' houses.

THE PRIESTS AT JERUSALEM

10 Of the priests: Je·daī'ah, Je-hoi'a·rib, and Jā'chin;
11 Az·a·rī'ah the son of Hil·kī'ah, the son of Me·shul'lam, the son of Zā'dok, the son of Me·rā'i·oth, the son of A·hī'tub, the officer over the house of God;
12 A·dāi'ah the son of Je·rō'ham, the son of Pash'ur, the son of Mal·chī'jah; Mā'a·saī the son of Ad'i·el, the son of Jah'ze·rah, the son of Me·shul'lam, the son of Me·shil'le·mith, the son of Im'mer;

13 and their brethren, heads of their fathers' *houses*—one thousand seven hundred and sixty. *They were* very able men for the work of the service of the house of God.

THE LEVITES AT JERUSALEM

14 Of the Lē'vītes: She·māi'ah the son of Has'shub, the son of Az·rī'-kam, the son of Hash·a·bī'ah, of the sons of Me·rar'ī;
15 Bak·bak'kar, Hē'resh, Gā'lal, and Mat·ta·nī'ah the son of Mī'cah, the son of Zich'rī, the son of Ā'saph;
16 Ō·ba·dī'ah the son of She·māi'ah, the son of Gā'lal, the son of Je-dū'thun; and Ber·e·chī'ah the son of Ā'sa, the son of El·kā'nah, who lived in the villages of the Ne·toph'a·thītes.

THE LEVITE GATEKEEPERS

17 And the gatekeepers *were* Shal'-lum, Ak'kub, Tal'mon, A·hī'man, and their brethren. Shal'lum *was* the chief.
18 Until then *they had been* gate-keepers for the camps of the children of Levi at the King's Gate on the east.
19 Shal'lum the son of Kō're, the son of E·bī'a·saph, the son of Kō'rah, and his brethren, from his father's house, the Kō'ra·hītes, *were* in charge of the work of the service, gatekeepers of the tabernacle. Their fathers had been keepers of the entrance to the camp of the LORD.
20 And Phin'e·has the son of El·ē-ā'zar had been the officer over them in time past; the LORD *was* with him.
21 Zech·a·rī'ah the son of Me·shel-e·mī'ah *was* keeper of the door of the tabernacle of meeting.
22 All those chosen as gatekeepers *were* two hundred and twelve. They were recorded by their genealogy, in their villages. David and Samuel the

seer had appointed them to their trusted office.

23 So they and their children *were* in charge of the gates of the house of the LORD, the house of the tabernacle, by assignment.

24 The gatekeepers were assigned to the four directions: the east, west, north, and south.

25 And their brethren in their villages *had* to come with them from time to time for seven days.

26 For in this trusted office *were* four chief gatekeepers; they were Lē′vītes. And they had charge over the chambers and treasuries of the house of God.

27 And they lodged *all* around the house of God because they *had* the responsibility, and they *were* in charge of opening *it* every morning.

OTHER LEVITE RESPONSIBILITIES

28 Now *some* of them were in charge of the serving vessels, for they brought them in and took them out by count.

29 *Some* of them *were* appointed over the furnishings and over all the implements of the sanctuary, and over the fine flour and the wine and the oil and the incense and the spices.

30 And *some* of the sons of the priests made the ointment of the spices.

31 Mat·ti·thī′ah of the Lē′vītes, the firstborn of Shal′lum the Kō′ra·hīte, had the trusted office over the things that were baked in the pans.

32 And some of their brethren of the sons of the Kō′hath·ītes *were* in charge of preparing the showbread for every Sabbath.

33 These are the singers, heads of the fathers′ *houses* of the Lē′vītes, *who lodged* in the chambers, *and* were free *from other duties;* for they

were employed in *that* work day and night.

34 These heads of the fathers′ *houses* of the Lē′vītes *were* heads throughout their generations. They dwelt at Jerusalem.

THE FAMILY OF KING SAUL

35 Je·ī′el the father of Gib′ē·on, whose wife′s name *was* Mā′a·cah, dwelt at Gib′ē·on.

36 His firstborn son *was* Ab′don, then Zūr, Kish, Bā′al, Ner, Nā′dab,

37 Gē′dor, A·hī′ō, Zech·a·rī′ah,*a* and Mik′loth.

38 And Mik′loth begot Shim′ē·am.*a* They also dwelt alongside their relatives in Jerusalem, with their brethren.

39 Ner begot Kish, Kish begot Saul, and Saul begot Jonathan, Mal·chī·shū′a, A·bin′a·dab, and Esh-Bā′al.

40 The son of Jonathan *was* Mer′ib-Bā′al, and Mer′ib-Bā′al begot Mī′-cah.

41 The sons of Mī′cah *were* Pī′thon, Mē′lech, Tah′rē·a,*a and* Ā′haz.*b*

42 And Ā′haz begot Jar′ah;*a* Jar′ah begot Al′e·meth, Az′ma·veth, and Zim′rī; and Zim′rī begot Mō′za;

43 Mō′za begot Bin′ē·a, Reph·āi′ah*a* his son, El·e·ā′sah his son, and Ā′zel his son.

44 And Ā′zel had six sons whose names *were* these: Az·rī′kam, Bō′-che·rū, Ish′ma·el, Shē·a·rī′ah, Ō·ba-dī′ah, and Hā′nan; these *were* the sons of Ā′zel.

TRAGIC END OF SAUL AND HIS SONS

10 Now the Phi·lis′tines fought against Israel; and the men of Israel

fled from before the Phi·lis′tines, and fell slain on Mount Gil·bo′a.

2　Then the Phi·lis′tines followed hard after Saul and his sons. And the Phi·lis′tines killed Jonathan, A·bin′a·dab, and Mal·chi·shu′a, Saul's sons.

3　The battle became fierce against Saul. The archers hit him, and he was wounded by the archers.

4　Then Saul said to his armorbearer, "Draw your sword, and thrust me through with it, lest these uncircumcised men come and abuse me." But his armorbearer would not, for he was greatly afraid. Therefore Saul took a sword and fell on it.

5　And when his armorbearer saw that Saul was dead, he also fell on his sword and died.

6　So Saul and his three sons died, and all his house died together.

7　And when all the men of Israel who *were* in the valley saw that they had fled and that Saul and his sons were dead, they forsook their cities and fled; then the Phi·lis′tines came and dwelt in them.

8　So it happened the next day, when the Phi·lis′tines came to strip the slain, that they found Saul and his sons fallen on Mount Gil·bo′a.

9　And they stripped him and took his head and his armor, and sent word *throughout* the land of the Philis′tines to proclaim the news *in the temple* of their idols and among the people.

10　Then they put his armor in the temple of their gods, and fastened his head in the temple of Da′gon.

11　And when all Ja′besh Gil′e·ad heard all that the Phi·lis′tines had done to Saul,

12　all the valiant men arose and took the body of Saul and the bodies of his sons; and they brought them to Ja′besh, and buried their bones under the tamarisk tree at Ja′besh, and fasted seven days.

13　So Saul died for his unfaithfulness which he had committed against the LORD, because he did not keep the word of the LORD, and also because he consulted a medium for guidance.

14　But *he* did not inquire of the LORD; therefore He killed him, and turned the kingdom over to David the son of Jesse.

DAVID MADE KING OVER ALL ISRAEL

11 Then all Israel came together to David at He′bron, saying, "Indeed we *are* your bone and your flesh.

2　"Also, in time past, even when Saul was king, you *were* the one who led Israel out and brought them in; and the LORD your God said to you, 'You shall shepherd My people Israel, and be ruler over My people Israel.' "

3　Therefore all the elders of Israel came to the king at He′bron, and David made a covenant with them at He′bron before the LORD. And they anointed David king over Israel, according to the word of the LORD by Samuel.

THE CITY OF DAVID

4　And David and all Israel went to Jerusalem, which is Je′bus, where the Jeb′u·sites *were*, the inhabitants of the land.

5　But the inhabitants of Je′bus said to David, "You shall not come in here!" Nevertheless David took the stronghold of Zion (that is, the City of David).

6　Now David said, "Whoever attacks the Jeb′u·sites first shall be chief and captain." And Jo′ab the son of Ze·ru′i·ah went up first, and became chief.

7　Then David dwelt in the strong-

hold; therefore they called it the City of David.

8 And he built the city around it, from the Mil′lō*a* to the surrounding area. Jō′ab repaired the rest of the city.

9 So David went on and became great, and the LORD of hosts *was* with him.

THE MIGHTY MEN OF DAVID

10 Now these *were* the heads of the mighty men whom David had, who strengthened themselves with him in his kingdom, with all Israel, to make him king, according to the word of the LORD concerning Israel.

11 And this *is* the number of the mighty men whom David had: Ja-shō′bē-am the son of a Hach′mo-nite, chief of the captains;*a* he had lifted up his spear against three hundred, killed *by him* at one time.

12 After him *was* El·ē·ā′zar the son of Dodo, the A·hō′hīte, who *was one* of the three mighty men.

13 He was with David at Pas·dam′-mim. Now there the Phi·lis′tines were gathered for battle, and there was a piece of ground full of barley. So the people fled from the Phi·lis′tines.

14 But they stationed themselves in the middle of *that* field, defended it, and killed the Phi·lis′tines. So the LORD brought about a great victory.

15 Now three of the thirty chief men went down to the rock to David, into the cave of A·dul′lam; and the army of the Phi·lis′tines encamped in the Valley of Reph′a·im.

16 David *was* then in the stronghold, and the garrison of the Phi·lis′tines *was* then in Bethlehem.

17 And David said with longing, "Oh, that someone would give me a drink of water from the well of Bethlehem, which is by the gate!"

18 So the three broke through the camp of the Phi·lis′tines, drew water from the well of Bethlehem that *was* by the gate, and took *it* and brought *it* to David. Nevertheless David would not drink it, but poured it out to the LORD.

19 And he said, "Far be it from me, O my God, that I should do this! Shall I drink the blood of these men *who have put* their lives *in jeopardy?* For at the risk of their lives they brought it." Therefore he would not drink it. These things were done by the three mighty men.

20 A·bi′shaī the brother of Jō′ab was chief of *another* three.*a* He had lifted up his spear against three hundred *men,* killed *them,* and won a name among *these* three.

21 Of the three he was more honored than the other two men. Therefore he became their captain. However he did not attain to the *first* three.

22 Be·nā′i·ah was the son of Je-hoi′a·da, the son of a valiant man from Kab′zē·el, who had done many deeds. He had killed two lion-like he-roes of Mō′ab. He also had gone down and killed a lion in the midst of a pit on a snowy day.

23 And he killed an Egyptian, a man of *great* height, five cubits tall. In the Egyptian's hand *there was* a spear like a weaver's beam; and he went down to him with a staff, wrested the spear out of the Egyptian's hand, and killed him with his own spear.

24 These *things* Be·nā′i·ah the son of Je·hoi′a·da did, and won a name among three mighty men.

25 Indeed he was more honored than the thirty, but he did not attain to the *first* three. And David appointed him over his guard.

11:8 *a*Literally *The Landfill*   11:11 *a*Following Qere; Kethib, Septuagint, and Vulgate read *the thirty* (compare 2 Samuel 23:8).   11:20 *a*Following Masoretic Text, Septuagint, and Vulgate; Syriac reads *thirty.*

26 Also the mighty warriors *were* As'a·hel the brother of Jō'ab, El·hā'nan the son of Dodo of Bethlehem,

27 Sham'moth the Ha'rō·rīte,*a* Hē'lez the Pel'o·nīte,*b*

28 Ī'ra the son of Ik'kesh the Te·kō'īte, Ā·bi·ē'zer the An'a·thoth·īte,

29 Sib'be·chaī the Hū'sha·thīte, Ī'laī the A·hō'hīte,

30 Mā'ha·raī the Ne·toph'a·thīte, Hē'led*a* the son of Bā'a·nah the Ne·toph'a·thīte,

31 Ith'aī*a* the son of Rī'baī of Gib'ē·ah, of the sons of Benjamin, Be·nā'i·ah the Pir'a·thon·īte,

32 Hū'raī*a* of the brooks of Gā'ash, A·bī'el*b* the Ar'ba·thīte,

33 Az'ma·veth the Ba·har'um·īte,*a* Ē·lī'ah·ba the Shā·al'bon·īte,

34 the sons of Hā'shem the Gī'zō·nīte, Jonathan the son of Shā'geh the Har'a·rīte,

35 A·hī'am the son of Sā'car the Har'a·rīte, E·lī'phal the son of Ūr,

36 Hē'pher the Me·chē'ra·thīte, A·hī'jah the Pel'o·nīte,

37 Hez'rō the Car'mel·īte, Nā'a·raī the son of Ez'baī,

38 Jō'el the brother of Nathan, Mib'har the son of Hag'rī,

39 Zē'lek the Am'mon·īte, Nā'ha·raī the Be·rō'thīte*a* (the armorbearer of Jō'ab the son of Ze·rū'i·ah),

40 Ī'ra the Ith'rīte, Gā'reb the Ith'rīte,

41 Ū·rī'ah the Hit'tīte, Zā'bad the son of Ah'laī,

42 Ad'i·na the son of Shī'za the Reū'ben·īte (a chief of the Reū'ben·ītes) and thirty with him,

43 Hā'nan the son of Mā'a·chah, Josh'a·phat the Mith'nīte,

44 Uz·zī'a the Ash'te·ra·thīte, Shā'ma and Je·ī'el the sons of Hō'tham the A·rō'er·īte,

45 Je·dī'a·el the son of Shim'rī, and Jō'ha his brother, the Tī'zīte,

46 E·lī'el the Mā'ha·vīte, Jer'i·baī

and Josh·a·vī'ah the sons of El'nā·am, Ith'mah the Mō'ab·īte,

47 E·lī'el, Ō'bed, and Jā·a·sī'el the Me·zō'ba·īte.

THE GROWTH OF DAVID'S ARMY

12 Now these *were* the men who came to David at Zik'lag while he was still a fugitive from Saul the son of Kish; and they *were* among the mighty men, helpers in the war,

2 armed with bows, using both the right hand and the left in *hurling* stones and *shooting* arrows with the bow. *They were* of Benjamin, Saul's brethren.

3 The chief *was* Ā·hi·ē'zer, then Jō'ash, the sons of She·mā'ah the Gib'ē·a·thīte; Jē'zi·el and Pē'let the sons of Az'ma·veth; Ber'a·chah, and Jē'hū the An'a·thoth·īte;

4 Ish·mā'i·ah the Gib'ē·on·īte, a mighty man among the thirty, and over the thirty; Jer·e·mī'ah, Ja·hā'zi·el, Jō·hā'nan, and Joz'a·bad the Ge·dē'ra·thīte;

5 E·lū'zaī, Jer'i·moth, Bē·a·lī'ah, Shem·a·rī'ah, and Sheph·a·tī'ah the Ha·rū'phite;

6 El·kā'nah, Jis·shī'ah, Az'a·rel, Jō·ē'zer, and Ja·shō'bē·am, the Kō'ra·hītes;

7 and Jō·ē'lah and Zeb·a·dī'ah the sons of Je·rō'ham of Gē'dor.

8 *Some* Gad'ītes joined David at the stronghold in the wilderness, mighty men of valor, men trained for battle, who could handle shield and spear, whose faces *were* *like* the faces of lions, and *were* as swift as gazelles on the mountains:

11:27 *a*Spelled *Harodite* in 2 Samuel 23:25
*b*Called *Paltite* in 2 Samuel 23:26
11:30 *a*Spelled *Heleb* in 2 Samuel 23:29 and *Heldai* in 1 Chronicles 27:15   11:31 *a*Spelled *Ittai* in 2 Samuel 23:29   11:32 *a*Spelled *Hiddai* in 2 Samuel 23:30   *b*Spelled *Abi-Albon* in 2 Samuel 23:31   11:33 *a*Spelled *Barhumite* in 2 Samuel 23:31   11:39 *a*Spelled *Beerothite* in 2 Samuel 23:37

9 Ē'zer the first, Ō·ba·dī'ah the second, E·lī'ab the third,

10 Mish·man'nah the fourth, Jer·e·mī'ah the fifth,

11 At'taī the sixth, E·lī'el the seventh,

12 Jō·hā'nan the eighth, El·zā'bad the ninth,

13 Jer·e·mī'ah the tenth, and Mach'ba·naī the eleventh.

14 These *were* from the sons of Gad, captains of the army; the least was over a hundred, and the greatest was over a thousand.

15 These *are* the ones who crossed the Jordan in the first month, when it had overflowed all its banks; and they put to flight all *those* in the valleys, to the east and to the west.

16 Then some of the sons of Benjamin and Judah came to David at the stronghold.

17 And David went out to meet them, and answered and said to them, "If you have come peaceably to me to help me, my heart will be united with you; but if to betray me to my enemies, since *there is* no wrong in my hands, may the God of our fathers look and bring judgment."

18 Then the Spirit came upon A·mā'saī, chief of the captains, *and* he said:

"*We are* yours, O David;
We *are* on your side, O son of
   Jesse!
Peace, peace to you,
And peace to your helpers!
For your God helps you."

So David received them, and made them captains of the troop.

19 And *some* from Ma·nas'seh defected to David when he was going with the Phi·lis'tines to battle against Saul; but they did not help them, for the lords of the Phi·lis'tines sent him away by agreement, saying, "He may defect to his master Saul *and endanger* our heads."

20 When he went to Zik'lag, those of Ma·nas'seh who defected to him were Ad'nah, Joz'a·bad, Je·dī'a·el, Michael, Joz'a·bad, E·lī'hū, and Zil'le·thaī, captains of the thousands who *were* from Ma·nas'seh.

21 And they helped David against the bands *of raiders,* for they *were* all mighty men of valor, and they were captains in the army.

22 For at *that* time they came to David day by day to help him, until *it was* a great army, like the army of God.

DAVID'S ARMY AT HEBRON

23 Now these *were* the numbers of the divisions *that were* equipped for war, *and* came to David at Hē'bron to turn *over* the kingdom of Saul to him, according to the word of the LORD:

24 of the sons of Judah bearing shield and spear, six thousand eight hundred armed for war;

25 of the sons of Sim'e·on, mighty men of valor fit for war, seven thousand one hundred;

26 of the sons of Levi four thousand six hundred;

27 Je·hoi'a·da, the leader of the Aaronites, and with him three thousand seven hundred;

28 Zā'dok, a young man, a valiant warrior, and from his father's house twenty-two captains;

29 of the sons of Benjamin, relatives of Saul, three thousand (until then the greatest part of them had remained loyal to the house of Saul);

30 of the sons of Ē'phra·im twenty thousand eight hundred, mighty men

of valor, famous men throughout their father's house;

31 of the half-tribe of Ma·nas'seh eighteen thousand, who were designated by name to come and make David king;

32 of the sons of Is'sa·char who had understanding of the times, to know what Israel ought to do, their chiefs were two hundred; and all their brethren were at their command;

33 of Zeb'u·lun there were fifty thousand who went out to battle, expert in war with all weapons of war, stouthearted men who could keep ranks;

34 of Naph'ta·li one thousand captains, and with them thirty-seven thousand with shield and spear;

35 of the Dan'ites who could keep battle formation, twenty-eight thousand six hundred;

36 of Ash'er, those who could go out to war, able to keep battle formation, forty thousand;

37 of the Reu'ben·ites and the Gad'ites and the half-tribe of Ma·nas'seh, from the other side of the Jordan, one hundred and twenty thousand armed for battle with every *kind* of weapon of war.

38 All these men of war, who could keep ranks, came to He'bron with a loyal heart, to make David king over all Israel; and all the rest of Israel *were* of one mind to make David king.

39 And they were there with David three days, eating and drinking, for their brethren had prepared for them.

40 Moreover those who were near to them, from as far away as Is'sa·char and Zeb'u·lun and Naph'ta·li, were bringing food on donkeys and camels, on mules and oxen—provisions of flour and cakes of figs and cakes of raisins, wine and oil and oxen and sheep abundantly, for *there was* joy in Israel.

THE ARK BROUGHT FROM KIRJATH JEARIM

13 Then David consulted with the captains of thousands and hundreds, *and* with every leader.

2 And David said to all the assembly of Israel, "If *it seems* good to you, and if it is of the LORD our God, let us send out to our brethren everywhere *who are* left in all the land of Israel, and with them to the priests and Le'vites *who are* in their cities *and* their common-lands, that they may gather together to us;

3 "and let us bring the ark of our God back to us, for we have not inquired at it since the days of Saul."

4 Then all the assembly said that they would do so, for the thing was right in the eyes of all the people.

5 So David gathered all Israel together, from Shi'hor in Egypt to as far as the entrance of Ha'math, to bring the ark of God from Kir'jath Je'a·rim.

6 And David and all Israel went up to Ba'a·lah,[a] to Kir'jath Je'a·rim, which belonged to Judah, to bring up from there the ark of God the LORD, who dwells *between* the cherubim, where *His* name is proclaimed.

7 So they carried the ark of God on a new cart from the house of A·bin'a·dab, and Uz'za and A·hi'o drove the cart.

8 Then David and all Israel played *music* before God with all *their* might, with singing, on harps, on stringed instruments, on tambourines, on cymbals, and with trumpets.

9 And when they came to Chi'don's[a] threshing floor, Uz'za put out his hand to hold the ark, for the oxen stumbled.

13:6 [a]Called *Baale Judah* in 2 Samuel 6:2
13:9 [a]Called *Nachon* in 2 Samuel 6:6

Values

GIVING 1 Chronicles 13:8

What Shall I Give to Jesus?

Do you remember the story of the Little Drummer Boy? He had no gift to give to the Baby Jesus, or so he thought. But he learned to give the best gift he had, some music with his drum. What do you think about that?

1. Look up Romans 12:6, especially the first half. Did the Little Drummer Boy use his gift "according to the grace given him?"
2. What are your best gifts? Read 1 Chronicles 13:8. Do you sing well? Sing for Jesus. Do you play an instrument well? Do it for Jesus. Do you help others well? Do that for Jesus. What else do you do well? What should you do with that good gift?

For more on *Values* turn to page 632
For more on *Serving* turn to page 908

10 Then the anger of the LORD was aroused against Uz′za, and He struck him because he put his hand to the ark; and he died there before God.

11 And David became angry because of the LORD's outbreak against Uz′za; therefore that place is called Per′ez Uz′za*a* to this day.

12 David was afraid of God that day, saying, "How can I bring the ark of God to me?"

13 So David would not move the ark with him into the City of David, but took it aside into the house of Ō′bed-Ē′dom the Git′tīte.

14 The ark of God remained with the family of Ō′bed-Ē′dom in his house three months. And the LORD blessed the house of Ō′bed-Ē′dom and all that he had.

DAVID ESTABLISHED AT JERUSALEM

14 Now Hī′ram king of Tȳre sent messengers to David, and cedar trees, with masons and carpenters, to build him a house.

2 So David knew that the LORD had established him as king over Israel, for his kingdom was highly exalted for the sake of His people Israel.

3 Then David took more wives in Jerusalem, and David begot more sons and daughters.

4 And these are the names of his children whom he had in Jerusalem: Sham′mū·a,*a* Shō′bab, Nathan, Solomon,

5 Ib′har, E·lish′ū·a,*a* El′pe·let,*b*

6 Nō′gah, Nē′pheg, Ja·phī′a,

7 E·lish′a·ma, Bē·e·lī′a·da,*a* and E·liph′e·let.

THE PHILISTINES DEFEATED

8 Now when the Phi·lis′tines heard that David had been anointed king over all Israel, all the Phi·lis′tines went up to search for David. And David heard *of it* and went out against them.

9 Then the Phi·lis′tines went and made a raid on the Valley of Reph′a·im.

10 And David inquired of God, saying, "Shall I go up against the Phi·lis′tines? Will You deliver them into my hand?" The LORD said to him, "Go up, for I will deliver them into your hand."

11 So they went up to Bā′al Pe·rā′zim, and David defeated them there. Then David said, "God has broken through my enemies by my hand like a breakthrough of water." Therefore they called the name of that place Bā′al Pe·rā′zim.*a*

12 And when they left their gods there, David gave a commandment, and they were burned with fire.

13 Then the Phi·lis′tines once again made a raid on the valley.

14 Therefore David inquired again of God, and God said to him, "You shall not go up after them; circle around them, and come upon them in front of the mulberry trees.

15 "And it shall be, when you hear a sound of marching in the tops of the mulberry trees, then you shall go out to battle, for God has gone out before you to strike the camp of the Phi·lis′tines."

16 So David did as God commanded him, and they drove back the army of the Phi·lis′tines from Gib′e·on as far as Gē′zer.

17 Then the fame of David went out into all lands, and the LORD brought the fear of him upon all nations.

13:11 *a*Literally *Outburst Against Uzza*
14:4 *a*Spelled *Shimea* in 3:5　　14:5 *a*Spelled *Elishama* in 3:6　　*b*Spelled *Eliphelet* in 3:6
14:7 *a*Spelled *Eliada* in 3:8　　14:11 *a*Literally *Master of Breakthroughs*

THE ARK BROUGHT TO JERUSALEM

15 *David* built houses for himself in the City of David; and he prepared a place for the ark of God, and pitched a tent for it.

2 Then David said, "No one may carry the ark of God but the Lē′vītes, for the LORD has chosen them to carry the ark of God and to minister before Him forever."

3 And David gathered all Israel together at Jerusalem, to bring up the ark of the LORD to its place, which he had prepared for it.

4 Then David assembled the children of Aaron and the Lē′vītes:

5 of the sons of Kō′hath, Ū·rī′el the chief, and one hundred and twenty of his brethren;

6 of the sons of Me·rar′ī, A·sāi′ah the chief, and two hundred and twenty of his brethren;

7 of the sons of Ger′shom, Jō′el the chief, and one hundred and thirty of his brethren;

8 of the sons of E·li·zā′phan, She·māi′ah the chief, and two hundred of his brethren;

9 of the sons of Hē′bron, E·lī′el the chief, and eighty of his brethren;

10 of the sons of Uz′zi·el, Am·min′a·dab the chief, and one hundred and twelve of his brethren.

11 And David called for Zā′dok and A·bī′a·thar the priests, and for the Lē′vītes: for Ū·rī′el, A·sāi′ah, Jō′el, She·māi′ah, E·lī′el, and Am·min′a·dab.

12 He said to them, "You *are* the heads of the fathers' *houses* of the Lē′vītes; sanctify yourselves, you and your brethren, that you may bring up the ark of the LORD God of Israel to *the place* I have prepared for it.

13 "For because you *did* not *do it* the first *time,* the LORD our God broke out against us, because we did not consult Him about the proper order."

14 So the priests and the Lē′vītes sanctified themselves to bring up the ark of the LORD God of Israel.

15 And the children of the Lē′vītes bore the ark of God on their shoulders, by its poles, as Moses had commanded according to the word of the LORD.

16 Then David spoke to the leaders of the Lē′vītes to appoint their brethren *to be* the singers accompanied by instruments of music, stringed instruments, harps, and cymbals, by raising the voice with resounding joy.

17 So the Lē′vītes appointed Hē′man the son of Jō′el; and of his brethren, Ā′saph the son of Ber·e·chī′ah; and of their brethren, the sons of Me·rar′ī, Ē′than the son of Kū·shā′i·ah;

18 and with them their brethren of the second *rank:* Zech·a·rī′ah, Ben,*a* Ja·ā′zi·el, She·mir′a·moth, Je·hī′el, Un′nī, E·lī′ab, Be·nā′i·ah, Mā·a·sēi′ah, Mat·ti·thī′ah, E·liph′e·leh, Mik·nē′i·ah, Ō′bed-Ē′dom, and Je·ī′el, the gatekeepers;

19 the singers, Hē′man, Ā′saph, and Ē′than, *were* to sound the cymbals of bronze;

20 Zech·a·rī′ah, Ā′zi·el, She·mir′a·moth, Je·hī′el, Un′nī, E·lī′ab, Mā·a·sēi′ah, and Be·nā′i·ah, with strings according to Al′a·moth;

21 Mat·ti·thī′ah, E·liph′e·leh, Mik·nē′i·ah, Ō′bed-Ē′dom, Je·ī′el, and Az·a·zī′ah, to direct with harps on the Shem′i·nith;

22 Chen·a·nī′ah, leader of the Lē′vītes, was instructor *in charge of* the music, because he *was* skillful;

23 Ber·e·chī′ah and El·kā′nah *were* doorkeepers for the ark;

24 Sheb·a·nī′ah, Josh′a·phat, Ne-

15:18 *a*Following Masoretic Text and Vulgate; Septuagint omits *Ben.*

than'el, A·mā'saī, Zech·a·rī'ah, Be·nā'i·ah, and El·i·ē'zer, the priests, were to blow the trumpets before the ark of God; and Ō'bed-Ē'dom and Je·hī'ah, doorkeepers for the ark.

25 So David, the elders of Israel, and the captains over thousands went to bring up the ark of the covenant of the LORD from the house of Ō'bed-Ē'dom with joy.

26 And so it was, when God helped the Lē'vītes who bore the ark of the covenant of the LORD, that they offered seven bulls and seven rams.

27 David was clothed with a robe of fine linen, as were all the Lē'vītes who bore the ark, the singers, and Chen·a·nī'ah the music master *with* the singers. David also wore a linen ephod.

28 Thus all Israel brought up the ark of the covenant of the LORD with shouting and with the sound of the horn, with trumpets and with cymbals, making music with stringed instruments and harps.

29 And it happened, *as* the ark of the covenant of the LORD came to the City of David, that Mī'chal, Saul's daughter, looked through a window and saw King David whirling and playing music; and she despised him in her heart.

THE ARK PLACED
IN THE TABERNACLE

16 So they brought the ark of God, and set it in the midst of the tabernacle that David had erected for it. Then they offered burnt offerings and peace offerings before God.

2 And when David had finished offering the burnt offerings and the peace offerings, he blessed the people in the name of the LORD.

3 Then he distributed to everyone of Israel, both man and woman, to everyone a loaf of bread, a piece *of meat,* and a cake of raisins.

4 And he appointed some of the Lē'vītes to minister before the ark of the LORD, to commemorate, to thank, and to praise the LORD God of Israel:

5 Ā'saph the chief, and next to him Zech·a·rī'ah, *then* Je·ī'el, She·mir'a-moth, Je·hī'el, Mat·ti·thī'ah, E·lī'ab, Be·nā'i·ah, and Ō'bed-Ē'dom: Je·ī'el with stringed instruments and harps, but Ā'saph made music with cymbals;

6 Be·nā'i·ah and Ja·hā'zi·el the priests regularly *blew* the trumpets before the ark of the covenant of God.

DAVID'S SONG OF THANKSGIVING

7 On that day David first delivered *this psalm* into the hand of Ā'saph and his brethren, to thank the LORD:

8 Oh, give thanks to the LORD!
  Call upon His name;
  Make known His deeds among
    the peoples!
9 Sing to Him, sing psalms to Him;
  Talk of all His wondrous works!
10 Glory in His holy name;
  Let the hearts of those rejoice
    who seek the LORD!
11 Seek the LORD and His strength;
  Seek His face evermore!
12 Remember His marvelous works
    which He has done,
  His wonders, and the judgments
    of His mouth,
13 O seed of Israel His servant,
  You children of Jacob, His chosen
    ones!

14 He *is* the LORD our God;
  His judgments *are* in all the
    earth.
15 Remember His covenant forever,
  The word which He commanded,
    for a thousand generations,

REMEMBER 1 Chronicles 16:11, 12

Remember Good Things. Remember God's Things.

Weddings are happy times. There's always a person taking pictures so people can remember those happy times. Christmas is a happy time. Someone often takes pictures at Christmas so they can remember the happy times. Picture taking is common at other happy events, too. That's so we can remember the good things, the happy times. We do like to remember good things, don't we? But do we also like to remember God's things, the good times we have with Him?

1. Read 1 Chronicles 16:11, 12. This is part of a psalm to the Lord. What does it say we should remember?
2. What special things has the Lord done for you? How do you plan to remember them?
3. Read 1 Corinthians 11:24, 25. What do we remember each time we take communion? How is that like taking a picture at a very special time?

For more on *Favorite Bible Words* turn to page 714
For more on *Thankfulness* turn to page 807

16 *The covenant which* He made
    with Abraham,
    And His oath to Isaac,
17 And confirmed it to Jacob for a
    statute,
    To Israel *for* an everlasting
    covenant,
18 Saying, "To you I will give the
    land of Cā′naan
    As the allotment of your
    inheritance,"
19 When you were few in number,
    Indeed very few, and strangers in
    it.
20 When they went from one nation
    to another,
    And from *one* kingdom to another
    people,
21 He permitted no man to do them
    wrong;
    Yes, He rebuked kings for their
    sakes,
22 *Saying,* "Do not touch My
    anointed ones,
    And do My prophets no harm."*a*

23 Sing to the LORD, all the earth;
    Proclaim the good news of His
    salvation from day to day.
24 Declare His glory among the
    nations,
    His wonders among all peoples.

25 For the LORD *is* great and greatly
    to be praised;
    He *is* also to be feared above all
    gods.
26 For all the gods of the peoples *are*
    idols,
    But the LORD made the heavens.
27 Honor and majesty *are* before
    Him;
    Strength and gladness are in His
    place.

28 Give to the LORD, O families of
    the peoples,
    Give to the LORD glory and
    strength.
29 Give to the LORD the glory *due*
    His name;
    Bring an offering, and come
    before Him.
    Oh, worship the LORD in the
    beauty of holiness!
30 Tremble before Him, all the earth.
    The world also is firmly
    established,
    It shall not be moved.

31 Let the heavens rejoice, and let
    the earth be glad;
    And let them say among the
    nations, "The LORD reigns."
32 Let the sea roar, and all its
    fullness;
    Let the field rejoice, and all that
    is in it.
33 Then the trees of the woods shall
    rejoice before the LORD,
    For He is coming to judge the
    earth.*a*

34 Oh, give thanks to the LORD, for
    He is good!
    For His mercy *endures* forever.*a*
35 And say, "Save us, O God of our
    salvation;
    Gather us together, and deliver us
    from the Gentiles,
    To give thanks to Your holy name,
    To triumph in Your praise."

36 Blessed *be* the LORD God of Israel
    From everlasting to everlasting!*a*

And all the people said, "Amen!" and
praised the LORD.

REGULAR WORSHIP MAINTAINED

37 So he left Ā′saph and his brothers
there before the ark of the covenant

16:22 *a*Compare verses 8–22 with Psalm 105:1–15
16:33 *a*Compare verses 23–33 with Psalm 96:1–13
16:34 *a*Compare verse 34 with Psalm 106:1
16:36 *a*Compare verses 35, 36 with Psalm 106:47,
48

of the LORD to minister before the ark regularly, as every day's work required;

38 and Ō'bed-Ē'dom with his sixty-eight brethren, including Ō'bed-Ē'dom the son of Je·dū'thun, and Hō'sah, *to be* gatekeepers;

39 and Zā'dok the priest and his brethren the priests, before the tabernacle of the LORD at the high place that *was* at Gib'ē·on,

40 to offer burnt offerings to the LORD on the altar of burnt offering regularly morning and evening, and *to do* according to all that is written in the Law of the LORD which He commanded Israel;

41 and with them Hē'man and Je·dū'thun and the rest who were chosen, who were designated by name, to give thanks to the LORD, because His mercy *endures* forever;

42 and with them Hē'man and Je·dū'thun, to sound aloud with trumpets and cymbals and the musical instruments of God. Now the sons of Je·dū'thun *were* gatekeepers.

43 Then all the people departed, every man to his house; and David returned to bless his house.

GOD'S COVENANT WITH DAVID

17 Now it came to pass, when David was dwelling in his house, that David said to Nathan the prophet, "See now, I dwell in a house of cedar, but the ark of the covenant of the LORD *is* under tent curtains."

2 Then Nathan said to David, "Do all that *is* in your heart, for God *is* with you."

3 But it happened that night that the word of God came to Nathan, saying,

4 "Go and tell My servant David, 'Thus says the LORD: "You shall not build Me a house to dwell in.

5 "For I have not dwelt in a house since the time that I brought up Israel, even to this day, but have gone from tent to tent, and from *one* tabernacle *to another*.

6 "Wherever I have moved about with all Israel, have I ever spoken a word to any of the judges of Israel, whom I commanded to shepherd My people, saying, 'Why have you not built Me a house of cedar?' " '

7 "Now therefore, thus shall you say to My servant David, 'Thus says the LORD of hosts: "I took you from the sheepfold, from following the sheep, to be ruler over My people Israel.

8 "And I have been with you wherever you have gone, and have cut off all your enemies from before you, and have made you a name like the name of the great men who *are* on the earth.

9 "Moreover I will appoint a place for My people Israel, and will plant them, that they may dwell in a place of their own and move no more; nor shall the sons of wickedness oppress them anymore, as previously,

10 "since the time that I commanded judges *to be* over My people Israel. Also I will subdue all your enemies. Furthermore I tell you that the LORD will build you a house.*a*

11 "And it shall be, when your days are fulfilled, when you must go *to be* with your fathers, that I will set up your seed after you, who will be of your sons; and I will establish his kingdom.

12 "He shall build Me a house, and I will establish his throne forever.

13 "I will be his Father, and he shall be My son; and I will not take My mercy away from him, as I took *it* from *him* who was before you.

14 "And I will establish him in My

17:10 *a*That is, a royal dynasty

house and in My kingdom forever; and his throne shall be established forever.' "

15 According to all these words and according to all this vision, so Nathan spoke to David.

16 Then King David went in and sat before the LORD; and he said: "Who *am* I, O LORD God? And what is my house, that You have brought me this far?

17 "And *yet* this was a small thing in Your sight, O God; and You have *also* spoken of Your servant's house for a great while to come, and have regarded me according to the rank of a man of high degree, O LORD God.

18 "What more can David *say* to You for the honor of Your servant? For You know Your servant.

19 "O LORD, for Your servant's sake, and according to Your own heart, You have done all this greatness, in making known all these great things.

20 "O LORD, *there is* none like You, nor *is there any* God besides You, according to all that we have heard with our ears.

21 "And who *is* like Your people Israel, the one nation on the earth whom God went to redeem for Himself *as* a people—to make for Yourself a name by great and awesome deeds, by driving out nations from before Your people whom You redeemed from Egypt?

22 "For You have made Your people Israel Your very own people forever; and You, LORD, have become their God.

23 "And now, O LORD, the word which You have spoken concerning Your servant and concerning his house, *let it* be established forever, and do as You have said.

24 "So let it be established, that Your name may be magnified forever, saying, 'The LORD of hosts, the God of Israel, *is* Israel's God.' And let the house of Your servant David be established before You.

25 "For You, O my God, have revealed to Your servant that You will build him a house. Therefore Your servant has found it *in his heart* to pray before You.

26 "And now, LORD, You are God, and have promised this goodness to Your servant.

27 "Now You have been pleased to bless the house of Your servant, that it may continue before You forever; for You have blessed it, O LORD, and *it shall be* blessed forever."

DAVID'S FURTHER CONQUESTS

18 After this it came to pass that David attacked the Phi·lis'tines, subdued them, and took Gath and its towns from the hand of the Phi·lis'tines.

2 Then he defeated Mō'ab, and the Mō'ab·ites became David's servants, *and* brought tribute.

3 And David defeated Had·a·dē'zer[a] king of Zō'bah *as far as* Hā'math, as he went to establish his power by the River Eū·phrā'tēs.

4 David took from him one thousand chariots, seven thousand[a] horsemen, and twenty thousand foot soldiers. Also David hamstrung all the chariot *horses,* except that he spared enough of them for one hundred chariots.

5 When the Syrians of Damascus came to help Had·a·dē'zer king of Zō'bah, David killed twenty-two thousand of the Syrians.

6 Then David put *garrisons* in Syria of Damascus; and the Syrians became David's servants, *and*

18:3 [a]Hebrew *Hadarezer,* and so throughout chapters 18 and 19 18:4 [a]Or *seven hundred* (compare 2 Samuel 8:4)

brought tribute. So the LORD preserved David wherever he went.

7   And David took the shields of gold that were on the servants of Had-a-dē′zer, and brought them to Jerusalem.

8   Also from Tib′hath*a* and from Chun, cities of Had-a-dē′zer, David brought a large amount of bronze, with which Solomon made the bronze Sea, the pillars, and the articles of bronze.

9   Now when Tō′ū*a* king of Hā′math heard that David had defeated all the army of Had-a-dē′zer king of Zō′bah,

10   he sent Ha-dor′am*a* his son to King David, to greet him and bless him, because he had fought against Had-a-dē′zer and defeated him (for Had-a-dē′zer had been at war with Tō′ū); and *Ha-dor′am brought with him* all kinds of articles of gold, silver, and bronze.

11   King David also dedicated these to the LORD, along with the silver and gold that he had brought from all *these* nations—from Ē′dom, from Mō′ab, from the people of Am′mon, from the Phi-lis′tines, and from Am′a-lek.

12   Moreover A-bi′shai the son of Ze-rū′i-ah killed eighteen thousand Ē′dom-ītes*a* in the Valley of Salt.

13   He also put garrisons in Ē′dom, and all the Ē′dom-ītes became David′s servants. And the LORD preserved David wherever he went.

DAVID′S ADMINISTRATION

14   So David reigned over all Israel, and administered judgment and justice to all his people.

15   Jō′ab the son of Ze-rū′i-ah *was* over the army; Je-hosh′a-phat the son of A-hī′lud *was* recorder;

16   Zā′dok the son of A-hī′tub and A-bim′e-lech the son of A-bī′a-thar *were* the priests; Shav′sha*a was* the scribe;

17   Be-nā′i-ah the son of Je-hoi′a-da *was* over the Cher′e-thītes and the Pel′eth-ītes; and David′s sons *were* chief ministers at the king′s side.

THE AMMONITES AND SYRIANS DEFEATED

19 It happened after this that Nā′hash the king of the people of Am′mon died, and his son reigned in his place.

2   Then David said, "I will show kindness to Hā′nun the son of Nā′hash, because his father showed kindness to me." So David sent messengers to comfort him concerning his father. And David′s servants came to Hā′nun in the land of the people of Am′mon to comfort him.

3   And the princes of the people of Am′mon said to Hā′nun, "Do you think that David really honors your father because he has sent comforters to you? Did his servants not come to you to search and to overthrow and to spy out the land?"

4   Therefore Hā′nun took David′s servants, shaved them, and cut off their garments in the middle, at their buttocks, and sent them away.

5   Then *some* went and told David about the men; and he sent to meet them, because the men were greatly ashamed. And the king said, "Wait at Jericho until your beards have grown, and *then* return."

6   When the people of Am′mon saw that they had made themselves repulsive to David, Hā′nun and the people of Am′mon sent a thousand talents of silver to hire for them-

18:8 *a*Spelled *Betah* in 2 Samuel 8:8
18:9 *a*Spelled *Toi* in 2 Samuel 8:9, 10
18:10 *a*Spelled *Joram* in 2 Samuel 8:10
18:12 *a*Or *Syrians* (compare 2 Samuel 8:13)
18:16 *a*Spelled *Seraiah* in 2 Samuel 8:17

selves chariots and horsemen from Mes·o·po·tā'mi·a,*a* from Syrian Mā'-a·cah, and from Zō'bah.*b*

7 So they hired for themselves thirty-two thousand chariots, with the king of Mā'a·cah and his people, who came and encamped before Med'e·ba. Also the people of Am'mon gathered together from their cities, and came to battle.

8 Now when David heard *of it,* he sent Jō'ab and all the army of the mighty men.

9 Then the people of Am'mon came out and put themselves in battle array before the gate of the city, and the kings who had come *were* by themselves in the field.

10 When Jō'ab saw that the battle line was against him before and behind, he chose some of Israel's best and put *them* in battle array against the Syrians.

11 And the rest of the people he put under the command of A·bi'shaī his brother, and they set *themselves* in battle array against the people of Am'mon.

12 Then he said, "If the Syrians are too strong for me, then you shall help me; but if the people of Am'mon are too strong for you, then I will help you.

13 "Be of good courage, and let us be strong for our people and for the cities of our God. And may the LORD do *what is* good in His sight."

14 So Jō'ab and the people who *were* with him drew near for the battle against the Syrians, and they fled before him.

15 When the people of Am'mon saw that the Syrians were fleeing, they also fled before A·bi'shaī his brother, and entered the city. So Jō'ab went to Jerusalem.

16 Now when the Syrians saw that they had been defeated by Israel, they sent messengers and brought the Syrians who were beyond the River,*a* and Shō'phach*b* the commander of Had·a·dē'zer's army *went* before them.

17 When it was told David, he gathered all Israel, crossed over the Jordan and came upon them, and set up in battle array against them. So when David had set up in *battle* array against the Syrians, they fought with him.

18 Then the Syrians fled before Israel; and David killed seven thousand*a* charioteers and forty thousand foot soldiers*b* of the Syrians, and killed Shō'phach the commander of the army.

19 And when the servants of Had·a·dē'zer saw that they were defeated by Israel, they made peace with David and became his servants. So the Syrians were not willing to help the people of Am'mon anymore.

RABBAH IS CONQUERED

20 It happened in the spring of the year, at the time kings go out *to battle,* that Jō'ab led out the armed forces and ravaged the country of the people of Am'mon, and came and besieged Rab'bah. But David stayed at Jerusalem. And Jō'ab defeated Rab'bah and overthrew it.

2 Then David took their king's crown from his head, and found it to weigh a talent of gold, and *there were* precious stones in it. And it was set on David's head. Also he brought out the spoil of the city in great abundance.

3 And he brought out the people who *were* in it, and put *them* to work*a*

19:6 *a*Hebrew *Aram Naharaim*   *b*Spelled *Zoba* in 2 Samuel 10:6   19:16 *a*That is, the Euphrates *b*Spelled *Shobach* in 2 Samuel 10:16
19:18 *a*Or *seven hundred* (compare 2 Samuel 10:18) *b*Or *horsemen* (compare 2 Samuel 10:18)
20:3 *a*Septuagint reads *cut them.*

with saws, with iron picks, and with axes. So David did to all the cities of the people of Am′mon. Then David and all the people returned *to* Jerusalem.

PHILISTINE GIANTS DESTROYED

4 Now it happened afterward that war broke out at Gē′zer with the Phi·lis′tines, at which time Sib′-be·chaī the Hū′sha·thīte killed Sip′paī,*a who was one* of the sons of the giant. And they were subdued.

5 Again there was war with the Phi·lis′tines, and El·hā′nan the son of Jā′ir*a* killed Lah′mī the brother of Goliath the Git′tīte, the shaft of whose spear *was* like a weaver's beam.

6 Yet again there was war at Gath, where there was a man of *great* stature, with twenty-four fingers and toes, six *on each hand* and six *on each foot;* and he also was born to the giant.

7 So when he defied Israel, Jonathan the son of Shim′ē·a,*a* David's brother, killed him.

8 These were born to the giant in Gath, and they fell by the hand of David and by the hand of his servants.

THE CENSUS OF ISRAEL AND JUDAH

21 Now Satan stood up against Israel, and moved David to number Israel.

2 So David said to Jō′ab and to the leaders of the people, "Go, number Israel from Bē·er·shē′ba to Dan, and bring the number of them to me that I may know *it.*"

3 And Jō′ab answered, "May the LORD make His people a hundred times more than they are. But, my lord the king, *are* they not all my lord's servants? Why then does my lord require this thing? Why should he be a cause of guilt in Israel?"

4 Nevertheless the king's word prevailed against Jō′ab. Therefore Jō′ab departed and went throughout all Israel and came to Jerusalem.

5 Then Jō′ab gave the sum of the number of the people to David. All Israel *had* one million one hundred thousand men who drew the sword, and Judah *had* four hundred and seventy thousand men who drew the sword.

6 But he did not count Levi and Benjamin among them, for the king's word was abominable to Jō′ab.

7 And God was displeased with this thing; therefore He struck Israel.

8 So David said to God, "I have sinned greatly, because I have done this thing; but now, I pray, take away the iniquity of Your servant, for I have done very foolishly."

9 Then the LORD spoke to Gad, David's seer, saying,

10 "Go and tell David, saying, 'Thus says the LORD: "I offer you three *things;* choose one of them for yourself, that I may do *it* to you." ' "

11 So Gad came to David and said to him, "Thus says the LORD: 'Choose for yourself,

12 'either three*a* years of famine, or three months to be defeated by your foes with the sword of your enemies overtaking *you,* or else for three days the sword of the LORD—the plague in the land, with the angel*b* of the LORD destroying throughout all the territory of Israel.' Now consider what answer I should take back to Him who sent me."

20:4 *aSpelled Saph in 2 Samuel 21:18
20:5 *aSpelled Jaare-Oregim in 2 Samuel 21:19
20:7 *aSpelled Shimeah in 2 Samuel 21:21 and *Shammah* in 1 Samuel 16:9   21:12 *aOr seven* (compare 2 Samuel 24:13)   *bOr Angel,* and so elsewhere in this chapter

SHOULD I DO IT? 1 Chronicles 21:1–4

This little boy can't decide what to do. He wants to do something. But he knows it is wrong. He knows it will not please God. He knows it will not please his parents. But he really *wants* to do it. What should he do?

1. What would you like to say to this boy? Why?
2. Should the boy do what he *wants* to do, but knows is wrong? Why not?

For more on *What Should I Do?* turn to page 654
For more on *Temptation* turn to page 810

GIVING   1 Chronicles 21:21–26

Giving Cheerfully

It's your birthday. Do I give you a gift because I should, or because I want to do it? It's Christmas. Does your mother give you a gift because she should, or because she wants to? Do I give wedding gifts or anniversary gifts or shower gifts or any other gifts because I should, or because I want to do it?

1. When do you give gifts? Why? Do you feel that you "ought to," or do you really want to?
2. When you give to Jesus, do you give because you should, or do you really want to give to Him? Which is better? Read 1 Chronicles 21:21–26. Did Ornan give because he wanted to?

For more on *Values* turn to page 645
For more on *Giving* turn to page 690

13 And David said to Gad, "I am in great distress. Please let me fall into the hand of the LORD, for His mercies *are* very great; but do not let me fall into the hand of man."

14 So the LORD sent a plague upon Israel, and seventy thousand men of Israel fell.

15 And God sent an angel to Jerusalem to destroy it. As he*a* was destroying, the LORD looked and relented of the disaster, and said to the angel who was destroying, "It is enough; now restrain your*b* hand." And the angel of the LORD stood by the threshing floor of Or'nan*c* the Jeb'-ū·sīte.

16 Then David lifted his eyes and saw the angel of the LORD standing between earth and heaven, having in his hand a drawn sword stretched out over Jerusalem. So David and the elders, clothed in sackcloth, fell on their faces.

17 And David said to God, "Was it not I who commanded the people to be numbered? I am the one who has sinned and done evil indeed; but these sheep, what have they done? Let Your hand, I pray, O LORD my God, be against me and my father's house, but not against Your people that they should be plagued."

18 Therefore, the angel of the LORD commanded Gad to say to David that David should go and erect an altar to the LORD on the threshing floor of Or'nan the Jeb'ū·sīte.

19 So David went up at the word of Gad, which he had spoken in the name of the LORD.

20 Now Or'nan turned and saw the angel; and his four sons *who were* with him hid themselves, but Or'nan continued threshing wheat.

21 So David came to Or'nan, and Or'nan looked and saw David. And he went out from the threshing floor, and bowed before David with *his* face to the ground.

22 Then David said to Or'nan, "Grant me the place of *this* threshing floor, that I may build an altar on it to the LORD. You shall grant it to me at the full price, that the plague may be withdrawn from the people."

23 But Or'nan said to David, "Take *it* to yourself, and let my lord the king do *what is* good in his eyes. Look, I *also* give *you* the oxen for burnt offerings, the threshing implements for wood, and the wheat for the grain offering; I give *it* all."

24 Then King David said to Or'nan, "No, but I will surely buy *it* for the full price, for I will not take what is yours for the LORD, nor offer burnt offerings with *that which* costs *me* nothing."

25 So David gave Or'nan six hundred shekels of gold by weight for the place.

26 And David built there an altar to the LORD, and offered burnt offerings and peace offerings, and called on the LORD; and He answered him from heaven by fire on the altar of burnt offering.

27 So the LORD commanded the angel, and he returned his sword to its sheath.

28 At that time, when David saw that the LORD had answered him on the threshing floor of Or'nan the Jeb'ū·sīte, he sacrificed there.

29 For the tabernacle of the LORD and the altar of the burnt offering, which Moses had made in the wilderness, *were* at that time at the high place in Gib'ē·on.

30 But David could not go before it to inquire of God, for he was afraid of the sword of the angel of the LORD.

21:15 *a*Or *He*   *b*Or *Your*   *c*Spelled *Araunah* in 2 Samuel 24:16

David Prepares to Build the Temple

22 Then David said, "This *is* the house of the LORD God, and this *is* the altar of burnt offering for Israel."

2 So David commanded to gather the aliens who *were* in the land of Israel; and he appointed masons to cut hewn stones to build the house of God.

3 And David prepared iron in abundance for the nails of the doors of the gates and for the joints, and bronze in abundance beyond measure,

4 and cedar trees in abundance; for the Sī·dō'ni·ans and those from Tȳre brought much cedar wood to David.

5 Now David said, "Solomon my son *is* young and inexperienced, and the house to be built for the LORD *must be* exceedingly magnificent, famous and glorious throughout all countries. I will now make preparation for it." So David made abundant preparations before his death.

6 Then he called for his son Solomon, and charged him to build a house for the LORD God of Israel.

7 And David said to Solomon: "My son, as for me, it was in my mind to build a house to the name of the LORD my God;

8 "but the word of the LORD came to me, saying, 'You have shed much blood and have made great wars; you shall not build a house for My name, because you have shed much blood on the earth in My sight.

9 'Behold, a son shall be born to you, who shall be a man of rest; and I will give him rest from all his enemies all around. His name shall be Solomon,*a* for I will give peace and quietness to Israel in his days.

10 'He shall build a house for My name, and he shall be My son, and I *will be* his Father; and I will estab-lish the throne of his kingdom over Israel forever.'

11 "Now, my son, may the LORD be with you; and may you prosper, and build the house of the LORD your God, as He has said to you.

12 "Only may the LORD give you wisdom and understanding, and give you charge concerning Israel, that you may keep the law of the LORD your God.

13 "Then you will prosper, if you take care to fulfill the statutes and judgments with which the LORD charged Moses concerning Israel. Be strong and of good courage; do not fear nor be dismayed.

14 "Indeed I have taken much trouble to prepare for the house of the LORD one hundred thousand talents of gold and one million talents of silver, and bronze and iron beyond measure, for it is so abundant. I have prepared timber and stone also, and you may add to them.

15 "Moreover *there are* workmen with you in abundance: woodsmen and stonecutters, and all types of skillful men for every kind of work.

16 "Of gold and silver and bronze and iron *there is* no limit. Arise and begin working, and the LORD be with you."

17 David also commanded all the leaders of Israel to help Solomon his son, *saying,*

18 "*Is* not the LORD your God with you? And has He *not* given you rest on every side? For He has given the inhabitants of the land into my hand, and the land is subdued before the LORD and before His people.

19 "Now set your heart and your soul to seek the LORD your God. Therefore arise and build the sanctuary of the LORD God, to bring the ark of the covenant of the LORD and the holy ar-

22:9 *a*Literally *Peaceful*

ticles of God into the house that is to
be built for the name of the LORD."

THE DIVISIONS OF THE LEVITES

23 So when David was old and
full of days, he made his son Solomon
king over Israel.
2 And he gathered together all the
leaders of Israel, with the priests and
the Lē'vītes.
3 Now the Lē'vītes were numbered
from the age of thirty years and
above; and the number of individual
males was thirty-eight thousand.
4 Of these, twenty-four thousand
were to look after the work of the
house of the LORD, six thousand *were*
officers and judges,
5 four thousand *were* gatekeepers,
and four thousand praised the LORD
with *musical* instruments, "which I
made," *said David,* "for giving
praise."

Praises

1 Chronicles 23:5

David said he made musical instruments for four thousand musicians. These musicians praised God with their musical instruments that David made. Were these special instruments? David said he made these instruments especially to praise God. Do you think they gave better music because they were instruments to praise God? What about you and me? Were we made especially to praise God? Then our praise should be special.

6 Also David separated them into
divisions among the sons of Levi:
Ger'shon, Kō'hath, and Me·rar'ī.
7 Of the Ger'shon·ītes: Lā'a·dan[a]
and Shim'ē·ī.
8 The sons of Lā'a·dan: the first
Je·hī'el, then Zē'tham and Jō'el—
three *in all.*
9 The sons of Shim'ē·ī: She·lō'mith,
Hā'zi·el, and Har'an—three *in all.*
These were the heads of the fathers'
houses of Lā'a·dan.
10 And the sons of Shim'ē·ī: Jā'hath,
Zī'na,[a] Jē'ush, and Bē·rī'ah. These
were the four sons of Shim'ē·ī.
11 Jā'hath was the first and Zī'zah
the second. But Jē'ush and Bē·rī'ah
did not have many sons; therefore
they were assigned as one father's
house.
12 The sons of Kō'hath: Am'ram,
Iz'har, Hē'bron, and Uz'zi·el—four *in*
all.
13 The sons of Am'ram: Aaron and
Moses; and Aaron was set apart, he
and his sons forever, that he should
sanctify the most holy things, to burn
incense before the LORD, to minister
to Him, and to give the blessing in
His name forever.
14 Now the sons of Moses the man of
God were reckoned to the tribe of
Levi.
15 The sons of Moses *were* Ger'shon[a]
and El·i·ē'zer.
16 Of the sons of Ger'shon, She-
bū'el[a] *was* the first.
17 Of the descendants of El·i·ē'zer,
Rē·ha·bī'ah was the first. And El-
i·ē'zer had no other sons, but the sons
of Rē·ha·bī'ah were very many.
18 Of the sons of Iz'har, She·lō'mith
was the first.
19 Of the sons of Hē'bron, Je·rī'ah
was the first, Am·a·rī'ah the second,
Ja·hā'zi·el the third, and Jek·a·mē'am
the fourth.
20 Of the sons of Uz'zi·el, Mī'chah

23:7 [a]Spelled *Libni* in Exodus 6:17 23:10 [a]Septuagint and Vulgate read *Zizah* (compare verse 11).
23:15 [a]Hebrew *Gershom* (compare 6:16)
23:16 [a]Spelled *Shubael* in 24:20

was the first and Jes·shi′ah the second.

21 The sons of Me·rar′i *were* Mah′li and Mū′shi. The sons of Mah′li *were* El·ē·ā′zar and Kish.

22 And El·ē·ā′zar died, and had no sons, but only daughters; and their brethren, the sons of Kish, took them *as wives.*

23 The sons of Mū′shi *were* Mah′li, Ē′der, and Jer′e·moth—three *in all.*

24 These *were* the sons of Levi by their fathers′ houses—the heads of the fathers′ *houses* as they were counted individually by the number of their names, who did the work for the service of the house of the LORD, from the age of twenty years and above.

25 For David said, "The LORD God of Israel has given rest to His people, that they may dwell in Jerusalem forever";

26 and also to the Lē′vites, "They shall no longer carry the tabernacle, or any of the articles for its service."

27 For by the last words of David the Lē′vites *were* numbered from twenty years old and above;

28 because their duty *was* to help the sons of Aaron in the service of the house of the LORD, in the courts and in the chambers, in the purifying of all holy things and the work of the service of the house of God,

29 both with the showbread and the fine flour for the grain offering, with the unleavened cakes and *what is baked in* the pan, with what is mixed and with all kinds of measures and sizes;

30 to stand every morning to thank and praise the LORD, and likewise at evening;

31 and at every presentation of a burnt offering to the LORD on the Sabbaths and on the New Moons and on the set feasts, by number according to the ordinance governing them, regularly before the LORD;

32 and that they should attend to the needs of the tabernacle of meeting, the needs of the holy *place,* and the needs of the sons of Aaron their brethren in the work of the house of the LORD.

THE DIVISIONS OF THE PRIESTS

24 Now *these are* the divisions of the sons of Aaron. The sons of Aaron *were* Nā′dab, A·bī′hū, El·ē·ā′zar, and Ith′a·mar.

2 And Nā′dab and A·bī′hū died before their father, and had no children; therefore El·ē·ā′zar and Ith′a·mar ministered as priests.

3 Then David with Zā′dok of the sons of El·ē·ā′zar, and A·him′e·lech of the sons of Ith′a·mar, divided them according to the schedule of their service.

4 There were more leaders found of the sons of El·ē·ā′zar than of the sons of Ith′a·mar, and *thus* they were divided. Among the sons of El·ē·ā′zar *were* sixteen heads of *their* fathers′ houses, and eight heads of their fathers′ houses among the sons of Ith′a·mar.

5 Thus they were divided by lot, one group as another, for there were officials of the sanctuary and officials *of the house* of God, from the sons of El·ē·ā′zar and from the sons of Ith′a·mar.

6 And the scribe, She·māi′ah the son of Ne·than′el, *one of* the Lē′vites, wrote them down before the king, the leaders, Zā′dok the priest, A·him′-e·lech the son of A·bī′a·thar, and the heads of the fathers′ *houses* of the priests and Lē′vites, one father′s house taken for El·ē·ā′zar and *one* for Ith′a·mar.

7 Now the first lot fell to Je·hoi′a·rib, the second to Je·daī′ah,

8 the third to Hā′rim, the fourth to Se·ō′rim,

9 the fifth to Mal·chī′jah, the sixth to Mij′a·min,

10 the seventh to Hak′koz, the eighth to A·bī′jah,

11 the ninth to Jesh′ū·a, the tenth to Shec·a·nī′ah,

12 the eleventh to E·lī′a·shib, the twelfth to Jā′kim,

13 the thirteenth to Hup′pah, the fourteenth to Je·sheb′e·ab,

14 the fifteenth to Bil′gah, the sixteenth to Im′mer,

15 the seventeenth to Hē′zir, the eighteenth to Hap′piz·zez,a

16 the nineteenth to Peth·a·hī′ah, the twentieth to Je·hez′e·kel,a

17 the twenty-first to Jā′chin, the twenty-second to Gā′mul,

18 the twenty-third to De·laī′ah, the twenty-fourth to Mā·a·zī′ah.

19 This *was* the schedule of their service for coming into the house of the Lord according to their ordinance by the hand of Aaron their father, as the Lord God of Israel had commanded him.

Other Levites

20 And the rest of the sons of Levi: of the sons of Am′ram, Shū′ba·el;a of the sons of Shū′ba·el, Jeh·dē′i·ah.

21 Concerning Rē·ha·bī′ah, of the sons of Rē·ha·bī′ah, the first *was* Is·shī′ah.

22 Of the Iz′har·ites, She·lō′moth;a of the sons of She·lō′moth, Jā′hath.

23 Of the sons *of Hē′bron,a* Je·rī′ah *was the first,b* Am·a·rī′ah the second, Ja·hā′zi·el the third, *and* Jek·a·mē′am the fourth.

24 *Of* the sons of Uz′zi·el, Mī′chah; of the sons of Mī′chah, Shā′mir.

25 The brother of Mī′chah, Is·shī′ah; of the sons of Is·shī′ah, Zech·a·rī′ah.

26 The sons of Me·rar′ī *were* Mah′lī and Mū′shī; the son of Jā·a·zī′ah, Bē′no.

27 The sons of Me·rar′ī by Jā·a·zī′ah *were* Bē′no, Shō′ham, Zac′cur, and Ib′rī.

28 Of Mah′lī: El·ē·ā′zar, who had no sons.

29 Of Kish: the son of Kish, Je·rah′mē·el.

30 Also the sons of Mū′shī *were* Mah′lī, Ē′der, and Jer′i·moth. These *were* the sons of the Lē′vītes according to their fathers′ houses.

31 These also cast lots just as their brothers the sons of Aaron did, in the presence of King David, Zā′dok, A·him′e·lech, and the heads of the fathers′ *houses* of the priests and Lē′vītes. The chief fathers *did* just as their younger brethren.

The Musicians

25 Moreover David and the captains of the army separated for the service *some* of the sons of Ā′saph, of Hē′man, and of Je·dū′thun, who *should* prophesy with harps, stringed instruments, and cymbals. And the number of the skilled men performing their service was:

2 Of the sons of Ā′saph: Zac′cur, Joseph, Neth·a·nī′ah, and Ash·a·rē′lah;a the sons of Ā′saph *were* under the direction of Ā′saph, who prophesied according to the order of the king.

3 Of Je·dū′thun, the sons of Je-

24:15 aSeptuagint and Vulgate read *Aphses.*
24:16 aMasoretic Text reads *Jehezkel.*
24:20 aSpelled *Shebuel* in 23:16   24:22 aSpelled *Shelomith* in 23:18   24:23 aSupplied from 23:19 (following some Hebrew manuscripts and Septuagint manuscripts)   bSupplied from 23:19 (following some Hebrew manuscripts and Septuagint manuscripts)   25:2 aSpelled *Jesharelah* in verse 14

dū'thun: Ged·a·lī'ah, Zē'rī,[a] Je·shā'-i·ah, Shim'ē·ī, Hash·a·bī'ah, and Mat·ti·thī'ah, six,[b] under the direction of their father Je·dū'thun, who prophesied with a harp to give thanks and to praise the LORD.

4 Of Hē'man, the sons of Hē'man: Buk·kī'ah, Mat·ta·nī'ah, Uz'zi·el,[a] She·bū'el,[b] Jer'i·moth,[c] Han·a·nī'ah, Ha·nā'nī, E·lī'a·thah, Gid·dal'tī, Rō·mam'ti-Ē'zer, Josh·be·kash'ah, Mal·lō'thī, Hō'thir, and Ma·hā'zi·oth.

5 All these were the sons of Hē'man the king's seer in the words of God, to exalt his horn.[a] For God gave Hē'man fourteen sons and three daughters.

6 All these were under the direction of their father for the music in the house of the LORD, with cymbals, stringed instruments, and harps, for the service of the house of God. Ā'saph, Je·dū'thun, and Hē'man were under the authority of the king.

7 So the number of them, with their brethren who were instructed in the songs of the LORD, all who were skillful, was two hundred and eighty-eight.

8 And they cast lots for their duty, the small as well as the great, the teacher with the student.

9 Now the first lot for Ā'saph came out for Joseph; the second for Ged·a·lī'ah, him with his brethren and sons, twelve;

10 the third for Zac'cur, his sons and his brethren, twelve;

11 the fourth for Jiz'rī,[a] his sons and his brethren, twelve;

12 the fifth for Neth·a·nī'ah, his sons and his brethren, twelve;

13 the sixth for Buk·kī'ah, his sons and his brethren, twelve;

14 the seventh for Jesh·a·rē'lah,[a] his sons and his brethren, twelve;

15 the eighth for Je·shā'i·ah, his sons and his brethren, twelve;

16 the ninth for Mat·ta·nī'ah, his sons and his brethren, twelve;

17 the tenth for Shim'ē·ī, his sons and his brethren, twelve;

18 the eleventh for Az'a·rel,[a] his sons and his brethren, twelve;

19 the twelfth for Hash·a·bī'ah, his sons and his brethren, twelve;

20 the thirteenth for Shū'ba·el,[a] his sons and his brethren, twelve;

21 the fourteenth for Mat·ti·thī'ah, his sons and his brethren, twelve;

22 the fifteenth for Jer'e·moth,[a] his sons and his brethren, twelve;

23 the sixteenth for Han·a·nī'ah, his sons and his brethren, twelve;

24 the seventeenth for Josh·be·kash'ah, his sons and his brethren, twelve;

25 the eighteenth for Ha·nā'nī, his sons and his brethren, twelve;

26 the nineteenth for Mal·lō'thī, his sons and his brethren, twelve;

27 the twentieth for E·lī'a·thah, his sons and his brethren, twelve;

28 the twenty-first for Hō'thir, his sons and his brethren, twelve;

29 the twenty-second for Gid·dal'tī, his sons and his brethren, twelve;

30 the twenty-third for Ma·hā'zi·oth, his sons and his brethren, twelve;

31 the twenty-fourth for Rō·mam'ti-Ē'zer, his sons and his brethren, twelve.

THE GATEKEEPERS

26 Concerning the divisions of the gatekeepers: of the Kō'ra·hites,

---

25:3 [a]Spelled Jizri in verse 11 [b]Shimei, appearing in one Hebrew and several Septuagint manuscripts, completes the total of six sons (compare verse 17). 25:4 [a]Spelled Azarel in verse 18 [b]Spelled Shubael in verse 20 [c]Spelled Jeremoth in verse 22 25:5 [a]That is, to increase his power or influence 25:11 [a]Spelled Zeri in verse 3 25:14 [a]Spelled Asharelah in verse 2 25:18 [a]Spelled Uzziel in verse 4 25:20 [a]Spelled Shebuel in verse 4 25:22 [a]Spelled Jerimoth in verse 4

Me·shel·e·mī′ah the son of Kō′re, of the sons of Ā′saph.

2 And the sons of Me·shel·e·mī′ah *were* Zech·a·rī′ah the firstborn, Je·dī′a·el the second, Zeb·a·dī′ah the third, Jath′ni·el the fourth,

3 Ē′lam the fifth, Jē·hō·hā′nan the sixth, El·i·ē·hō·ē′naī the seventh.

4 Moreover the sons of Ō′bed-Ē′dom *were* She·māi′ah the firstborn, Je·hō′za·bad the second, Jō′ah the third, Sā′car the fourth, Ne·than′el the fifth,

5 Am′mi·el the sixth, Is′sa·char the seventh, Pē·ul′thaī the eighth; for God blessed him.

6 Also to She·māi′ah his son were sons born who governed their fathers' houses, because they *were* men of great ability.

7 The sons of She·māi′ah *were* Oth′nī, Reph′a·el, Ō′bed, and El·zā′·bad, whose brothers E·lī′hū and Sem·a·chī′ah *were* able men.

8 All these *were* of the sons of Ō′bed-Ē′dom, they and their sons and their brethren, able men with strength for the work: sixty-two of Ō′bed-Ē′dom.

9 And Me·shel·e·mī′ah had sons and brethren, eighteen able men.

10 Also Hō′sah, of the children of Me·rar′ī, had sons: Shim′rī the first (for *though* he was not the firstborn, his father made him the first),

11 Hil·kī′ah the second, Teb·a·lī′ah the third, Zech·a·rī′ah the fourth; all the sons and brethren of Hō′sah *were* thirteen.

12 Among these *were* the divisions of the gatekeepers, among the chief men, *having* duties just like their brethren, to serve in the house of the LORD.

13 And they cast lots for each gate, the small as well as the great, according to their father's house.

14 The lot for the East *Gate* fell to Shel·e·mī′ah. Then they cast lots *for* his son Zech·a·rī′ah, a wise counselor, and his lot came out for the North Gate;

15 to Ō′bed-Ē′dom the South Gate, and to his sons the storehouse.*a*

16 To Shup′pim and Hō′sah *the lot came out* for the West Gate, with the Shal′le·cheth Gate on the ascending highway—watchman opposite watchman.

17 On the east were *six* Lē′vites, on the north four each day, on the south four each day, and for the storehouse*a* two by two.

18 As for the Par′bar*a* on the west, *there were* four on the highway *and* two at the Par′bar.

19 These were the divisions of the gatekeepers among the sons of Kō′·rah and among the sons of Me·rar′ī.

THE TREASURIES AND OTHER DUTIES

20 Of the Lē′vites, A·hī′jah *was* over the treasuries of the house of God and over the treasuries of the dedicated things.

21 The sons of Lā′a·dan, the descendants of the Ger′shon·ītes of Lā′a·dan, heads of their fathers' *houses,* of Lā′a·dan the Ger′shon·īte: Je·hī′e·lī.

22 The sons of Je·hī′e·lī, Zē′tham and Jō′el his brother, *were* over the treasuries of the house of the LORD.

23 Of the Am′ram·ītes, the Iz′har·ītes, the Hē′bron·ītes, and the Uz′·zi·el·ītes:

24 She·bū′el the son of Ger′shom, the son of Moses, *was* overseer of the treasuries.

25 And his brethren by El·i·ē′zer *were* Rē·ha·bī′ah his son, Je·shā′i·ah his son, Jō′ram his son, Zich′rī his son, and She·lō′mith his son.

26:15 *a*Hebrew *asuppim*   26:17 *a*Hebrew *asuppim*   26:18 *a*Probably a court or colonnade extending west of the temple

26 This She·lō′mith and his brethren *were* over all the treasuries of the dedicated things which King David and the heads of fathers' *houses,* the captains over thousands and hundreds, and the captains of the army, had dedicated.

27 Some of the spoils won in battles they dedicated to maintain the house of the LORD.

28 And all that Samuel the seer, Saul the son of Kish, Abner the son of Ner, and Jō′ab the son of Ze·rū′i·ah had dedicated, every dedicated *thing,* was under the hand of She·lō′mith and his brethren.

29 Of the Iz′har·ites, Chen·a·nī′ah and his sons *performed* duties as officials and judges over Israel outside Jerusalem.

30 Of the Hē′bron·ites, Hash·a·bī′ah and his brethren, one thousand seven hundred able men, had the oversight of Israel on the west side of the Jordan for all the business of the LORD, and in the service of the king.

31 Among the Hē′bron·ites, Je·rī′jah *was* head of the Hē′bron·ites according to his genealogy of the fathers. In the fortieth year of the reign of David they were sought, and there were found among them capable men at Jā′zer of Gil′ē·ad.

32 And his brethren *were* two thousand seven hundred able men, heads of fathers' *houses,* whom King David made officials over the Reū′ben·ites, the Gad′ites, and the half-tribe of Ma·nas′seh, for every matter pertaining to God and the affairs of the king.

THE MILITARY DIVISIONS

27 And the children of Israel, according to their number, the heads of fathers' *houses,* the captains of thousands and hundreds and their officers, served the king in every matter of the *military* divisions. *These divisions* came in and went out month by month throughout all the months of the year, each division *having* twenty-four thousand.

2 Over the first division for the first month *was* Ja·shō′bē·am the son of Zab′di·el, and in his division *were* twenty-four thousand;

3 *he was* of the children of Per′ez, and the chief of all the captains of the army for the first month.

4 Over the division of the second month *was* Dō′dai*a* an A·hō′hite, and of his division Mik′loth also *was* the leader; in his division *were* twenty-four thousand.

5 The third captain of the army for the third month *was* Be·nā′i·ah, the son of Je·hoi′a·da the priest, who was chief; in his division *were* twenty-four thousand.

6 This was the Be·nā′i·ah *who was* mighty *among* the thirty, and was over the thirty; in his division *was* Am·miz′a·bad his son.

7 The fourth *captain* for the fourth month *was* As′a·hel the brother of Jō′ab, and Zeb·a·dī′ah his son after him; in his division *were* twenty-four thousand.

8 The fifth *captain* for the fifth month *was* Sham′huth*a* the Iz′ra·hite; in his division were twenty-four thousand.

9 The sixth *captain* for the sixth month *was* Ī′ra the son of Ik′kesh the Te·kō′ite; in his division *were* twenty-four thousand.

10 The seventh *captain* for the seventh month *was* Hē′lez the Pel′o·nite, of the children of Ē′phra·im; in his division *were* twenty-four thousand.

11 The eighth *captain* for the eighth month *was* Sib′be·chai the Hū′sha-

---

27:4 *a*Hebrew *Dodai,* usually spelled *Dodo* (compare 2 Samuel 23:9)   27:8 *a*Spelled *Shammoth* in 11:27 and *Shammah* in 2 Samuel 23:11

thīte, of the Zar'hītes; in his division *were* twenty-four thousand.

12 The ninth *captain* for the ninth month *was* Ā·bi·ē'zer the An'a·thoth·īte, of the Ben'ja·mītes; in his division *were* twenty-four thousand.

13 The tenth *captain* for the tenth month *was* Mā'ha·raī the Ne·toph'-a·thīte, of the Zar'hītes; in his division *were* twenty-four thousand.

14 The eleventh *captain* for the eleventh month *was* Be·nā'i·ah the Pir'a·thon·īte, of the children of Ē'phra·im; in his division *were* twenty-four thousand.

15 The twelfth *captain* for the twelfth month *was* Hel'daī[a] the Ne·toph'a·thīte, of Oth'ni·el; in his division *were* twenty-four thousand.

LEADERS OF TRIBES

16 Furthermore, over the tribes of Israel: the officer over the Reū'ben·ītes *was* El·i·ē'zer the son of Zich'rī; over the Sim'ē·on·ītes, Sheph·a·tī'ah the son of Mā'a·chah;

17 *over* the Lē'vītes, Hash·a·bī'ah the son of Ke·mū'el; over the Aa-ronites, Zā'dok;

18 *over* Judah, E·lī'hū, *one* of David's brothers; *over* Is'sa·char, Om'rī the son of Michael;

19 *over* Zeb'ū·lun, Ish·mā'i·ah the son of Ō·ba·dī'ah; *over* Naph'ta·lī, Jer'i·moth the son of Az'ri·el;

20 *over* the children of Ē'phra·im, Hō·shē'a the son of Az·a·zī'ah; *over* the half-tribe of Ma·nas'seh, Jō'el the son of Pe·dāi'ah;

21 *over* the half-*tribe* of Ma·nas'seh in Gil'ē·ad, Id'dō the son of Zech-a·rī'ah; *over* Benjamin, Jā·a·sī'el the son of Abner;

22 *over* Dan, Az'a·rel the son of Je·rō'ham. These *were* the leaders of the tribes of Israel.

23 But David did not take the number of those twenty years old and un-

der, because the LORD had said He would multiply Israel like the stars of the heavens.

24 Jō'ab the son of Ze·rū'i·ah began a census, but he did not finish, for wrath came upon Israel because of this census; nor was the number recorded in the account of the chronicles of King David.

OTHER STATE OFFICIALS

25 And Az'ma·veth the son of Ad'i·el *was* over the king's treasuries; and Je·hon'a·than the son of Uz·zī'ah was over the storehouses in the field, in the cities, in the villages, and in the fortresses.

26 Ez'rī the son of Chē'lub was over those who did the work of the field for tilling the ground.

27 And Shim'ē·ī the Rā'ma·thīte *was* over the vineyards, and Zab'dī the Shiph'mīte was over the produce of the vineyards for the supply of wine.

28 Bā'al-Hā'nan the Ge·dē'rīte was over the olive trees and the sycamore trees that *were* in the lowlands, and Jō'ash *was* over the store of oil.

29 And Shit'raī the Shar'on·īte *was* over the herds that fed in Sharon, and Shā'phat the son of Ad'lā·ī was over the herds *that were* in the valleys.

30 Ō'bil the Ish'ma·el·īte *was* over the camels, Jeh·dē'i·ah the Me·ron'-o·thīte *was* over the donkeys,

31 and Jā'ziz the Hag'rīte *was* over the flocks. All these *were* the officials over King David's property.

32 Also Je·hon'a·than, David's uncle, *was* a counselor, a wise man, and a scribe; and Je·hī'el the son of Hach'mo·nī *was* with the king's sons.

33 A·hith'o·phel *was* the king's coun-

27:15 [a]Spelled *Heled* in 11:30 and *Heleb* in 2 Samuel 23:29

selor, and Hū′shai the Ar′chīte *was* the king's companion.

34 After A·hith′o·phel *was* Je·hoi′a·da the son of Be·nā′i·ah, then A·bī′a·thar. And the general of the king's army *was* Jō′ab.

SOLOMON INSTRUCTED TO BUILD THE TEMPLE

28 Now David assembled at Jerusalem all the leaders of Israel: the officers of the tribes and the captains of the divisions who served the king, the captains over thousands and captains over hundreds, and the stewards over all the substance and possessions of the king and of his sons, with the officials, the valiant men, and all the mighty men of valor.

2 Then King David rose to his feet and said, "Hear me, my brethren and my people: I *had* it in my heart to build a house of rest for the ark of the covenant of the LORD, and for the footstool of our God, and had made preparations to build it.

3 "But God said to me, 'You shall not build a house for My name, because you *have been* a man of war and have shed blood.'

4 "However the LORD God of Israel chose me above all the house of my father to be king over Israel forever, for He has chosen Judah *to be* the ruler. And of the house of Judah, the house of my father, and among the sons of my father, He was pleased with me to make *me* king over all Israel.

5 "And of all my sons (for the LORD has given me many sons) He has chosen my son Solomon to sit on the throne of the kingdom of the LORD over Israel.

6 "Now He said to me, 'It is your son Solomon *who* shall build My house and My courts; for I have cho-

sen him *to be* My son, and I will be his Father.

7 'Moreover I will establish his kingdom forever, if he is steadfast to observe My commandments and My judgments, as it is this day.'

8 "Now therefore, in the sight of all Israel, the assembly of the LORD, and in the hearing of our God, be careful to seek out all the commandments of the LORD your God, that you may possess this good land, and leave *it* as an inheritance for your children after you forever.

Promises

1 Chronicles 28:9

David is talking with his son Solomon. He tells his son about a promise. Seek God and you will find Him. Turn against God and He will turn against you. Do you seek God each day? Do you remember to pray each day? Do you remember to read God's Word each day? Do you ask God to be with you each day? Seek Him and you will find Him.

9 "As for you, my son Solomon, know the God of your father, and serve Him with a loyal heart and with a willing mind; for the LORD searches all hearts and understands all the intent of the thoughts. If you seek Him, He will be found by you; but if you forsake Him, He will cast you off forever.

10 "Consider now, for the LORD has chosen you to build a house for the sanctuary; be strong, and do it."

11 Then David gave his son Solomon the plans for the vestibule, its houses, its treasuries, its upper chambers, its inner chambers, and the place of the mercy seat;

12 and the plans for all that he had by the Spirit, of the courts of the house of the LORD, of all the chambers all around, of the treasuries of the house of God, and of the treasuries for the dedicated things;

13 also for the division of the priests and the Lē´vītes, for all the work of the service of the house of the LORD, and for all the articles of service in the house of the LORD.

14 *He gave* gold by weight for *things* of gold, for all articles used in every kind of service; also *silver* for all articles of silver by weight, for all articles used in every kind of service;

15 the weight for the lampstands of gold, and their lamps of gold, by weight for each lampstand and its lamps; for the lampstands of silver by weight, for the lampstand and its lamps, according to the use of each lampstand.

16 And by weight *he gave* gold for the tables of the showbread, for each table, and silver for the tables of silver;

17 also pure gold for the forks, the basins, the pitchers of pure gold, and the golden bowls—*he gave gold* by weight for every bowl; and for the silver bowls, *silver* by weight for every bowl;

18 and refined gold by weight for the altar of incense, and for the construction of the chariot, that is, the gold cherubim that spread *their wings* and overshadowed the ark of the covenant of the LORD.

19 "All *this*," said David, "the LORD made me understand in writing, by *His* hand upon me, all the works of these plans."

20 And David said to his son Solomon, "Be strong and of good courage, and do *it;* do not fear nor be dismayed, for the LORD God—my God—*will be* with you. He will not leave you nor forsake you, until you

have finished all the work for the service of the house of the LORD.

21 "*Here are* the divisions of the priests and the Lē´vītes for all the service of the house of God; and every willing craftsman *will be* with you for all manner of workmanship, for every kind of service; also the leaders and all the people *will be* completely at your command."

OFFERINGS FOR BUILDING THE TEMPLE

29 Furthermore King David said to all the assembly: "My son Solomon, whom alone God has chosen, *is* young and inexperienced; and the work *is* great, because the temple[a] *is* not for man but for the LORD God.

2 "Now for the house of my God I have prepared with all my might: gold for *things to be made of* gold, silver for *things of* silver, bronze for *things of* bronze, iron for *things of* iron, wood for *things of* wood, onyx stones, *stones* to be set, glistening stones of various colors, all kinds of precious stones, and marble slabs in abundance.

3 "Moreover, because I have set my affection on the house of my God, I have given to the house of my God, over and above all that I have prepared for the holy house, my own special treasure of gold and silver:

4 "three thousand talents of gold, of the gold of Ō´phir, and seven thousand talents of refined silver, to overlay the walls of the houses;

5 "the gold for *things of* gold and the silver for *things of* silver, and for all kinds of work *to be done* by the hands of craftsmen. Who *then* is will-

29:1 *ª*Literally *palace*

ing to consecrate himself this day to the LORD?"

6 Then the leaders of the fathers' *houses,* leaders of the tribes of Israel, the captains of thousands and of hundreds, with the officers over the king's work, offered willingly.

7 They gave for the work of the house of God five thousand talents and ten thousand darics of gold, ten thousand talents of silver, eighteen thousand talents of bronze, and one hundred thousand talents of iron.

8 And whoever had *precious* stones gave *them* to the treasury of the house of the LORD, into the hand of Je·hī′el*ª* the Ger′shon·īte.

9 Then the people rejoiced, for they had offered willingly, because with a loyal heart they had offered willingly to the LORD; and King David also rejoiced greatly.

DAVID'S PRAISE TO GOD

10 Therefore David blessed the LORD before all the assembly; and David said:

"Blessed are You, LORD God of
    Israel, our Father, forever and
    ever.
11 Yours, O LORD, *is* the greatness,
The power and the glory,
The victory and the majesty;
For all *that is* in heaven and in
    earth *is Yours;*
Yours *is* the kingdom, O LORD,
And You are exalted as head over
    all.
12 Both riches and honor *come* from
    You,
And You reign over all.
In Your hand *is* power and might;
In Your hand *it is* to make great
And to give strength to all.

13 "Now therefore, our God,
We thank You
And praise Your glorious name.

14 But who *am* I, and who *are* my
    people,
That we should be able to offer so
    willingly as this?
For all things *come* from You,
And of Your own we have given
    You.
15 For we *are* aliens and pilgrims
    before You,
As *were* all our fathers;
Our days on earth *are* as a
    shadow,
And without hope.

16 "O LORD our God, all this abundance that we have prepared to build You a house for Your holy name is from Your hand, and *is* all Your own.

17 "I know also, my God, that You test the heart and have pleasure in uprightness. As for me, in the uprightness of my heart I have willingly offered all these *things;* and now with joy I have seen Your people, who are present here to offer willingly to You.

18 "O LORD God of Abraham, Isaac, and Israel, our fathers, keep this forever in the intent of the thoughts of the heart of Your people, and fix their heart toward You.

19 "And give my son Solomon a loyal heart to keep Your commandments and Your testimonies and Your statutes, to do all *these things,* and to build the temple*ª* for which I have made provision."

20 Then David said to all the assembly, "Now bless the LORD your God." So all the assembly blessed the LORD God of their fathers, and bowed their heads and prostrated themselves before the LORD and the king.

SOLOMON ANOINTED KING

21 And they made sacrifices to the LORD and offered burnt offerings to the LORD on the next day: a thousand

---

29:8 *ª*Possibly the same as *Jehieli* (compare 26:21, 22)   29:19 *ª*Literally *palace*

Values

THANKFULNESS   1 Chronicles 29:13

Please and Thank You

"Please" and "thank you" are two special words. "Please" is a "help me" word. It opens doors to good things and sometimes brings good gifts. "Thank you" says "You're special. You did something special for me."

1. Allan is praying. Do you think he is saying "please" to the Lord? Or is he saying "thank You"?

2. Will you say "please" to the Lord today? What will you ask Him to do?

3. Will you say "thank You" to the Lord today? What has He done for you?

For more on *Values* turn to page 690
For more on *Prayer* turn to page 714

bulls, a thousand rams, a thousand lambs, with their drink offerings, and sacrifices in abundance for all Israel.

22 So they ate and drank before the LORD with great gladness on that day. And they made Solomon the son of David king the second time, and anointed *him* before the LORD *to be* the leader, and Zā′dok *to be* priest.

23 Then Solomon sat on the throne of the LORD as king instead of David his father, and prospered; and all Israel obeyed him.

24 All the leaders and the mighty men, and also all the sons of King David, submitted themselves to King Solomon.

25 So the LORD exalted Solomon exceedingly in the sight of all Israel, and bestowed on him *such* royal majesty as had not been on any king before him in Israel.

THE CLOSE OF DAVID'S REIGN

26 Thus David the son of Jesse reigned over all Israel.

27 And the period that he reigned over Israel *was* forty years; seven years he reigned in Hē′bron, and thirty-three *years* he reigned in Jerusalem.

28 So he died in a good old age, full of days and riches and honor; and Solomon his son reigned in his place.

29 Now the acts of King David, first and last, indeed they *are* written in the book of Samuel the seer, in the book of Nathan the prophet, and in the book of Gad the seer,

30 with all his reign and his might, and the events that happened to him, to Israel, and to all the kingdoms of the lands.

SOLOMON REQUESTS WISDOM

NOW Solomon the son of David was strengthened in his kingdom, and the LORD his God *was* with him and exalted him exceedingly.

2 And Solomon spoke to all Israel, to the captains of thousands and of hundreds, to the judges, and to every leader in all Israel, the heads of the fathers' *houses.*

3 Then Solomon, and all the assembly with him, went to the high place that *was* at Gib′e·on; for the tabernacle of meeting with God was there, which Moses the servant of the LORD had made in the wilderness.

4 But David had brought up the ark of God from Kir′jath Je′a·rim to *the place* David had prepared for it, for he had pitched a tent for it at Jerusalem.

5 Now the bronze altar that Bez′-a·lel the son of Ū′rī, the son of Hur, had made, he put*a* before the tabernacle of the LORD; Solomon and the assembly sought Him *there.*

6 And Solomon went up there to the bronze altar before the LORD, which *was* at the tabernacle of meeting, and offered a thousand burnt offerings on it.

7 On that night God appeared to Solomon, and said to him, "Ask! What shall I give you?"

8 And Solomon said to God: "You have shown great mercy to David my father, and have made me king in his place.

9 "Now, O LORD God, let Your promise to David my father be established, for You have made me king over a people like the dust of the earth in multitude.

10 "Now give me wisdom and knowl-edge, that I may go out and come in before this people; for who can judge this great people of Yours?"

11 Then God said to Solomon: "Because this was in your heart, and you have not asked riches or wealth or honor or the life of your enemies, nor have you asked long life—but have asked wisdom and knowledge for yourself, that you may judge My people over whom I have made you king—

12 "wisdom and knowledge *are* granted to you; and I will give you riches and wealth and honor, such as none of the kings have had who *were* before you, nor shall any after you have the like."

SOLOMON'S MILITARY AND ECONOMIC POWER

13 So Solomon came to Jerusalem from the high place that *was* at Gib′e·on, from before the tabernacle of meeting, and reigned over Israel.

14 And Solomon gathered chariots and horsemen; he had one thousand four hundred chariots and twelve thousand horsemen, whom he stationed in the chariot cities and with the king in Jerusalem.

15 Also the king made silver and gold as common in Jerusalem as stones, and he made cedars as abundant as the sycamores which *are* in the lowland.

16 And Solomon had horses imported from Egypt and Ke·veh′; the king's merchants bought them in Ke·veh′ at the *current* price.

17 They also acquired and imported from Egypt a chariot for six hundred

1:5 *a*Some authorities read *it was there.*

shekels of silver, and a horse for one hundred and fifty; thus, through their agents,[a] they exported them to all the kings of the Hit'tītes and the kings of Syria.

SOLOMON PREPARES TO BUILD THE TEMPLE

2 Then Solomon determined to build a temple for the name of the LORD, and a royal house for himself.
2 Solomon selected seventy thousand men to bear burdens, eighty thousand to quarry *stone* in the mountains, and three thousand six hundred to oversee them.
3 Then Solomon sent to Hī'ram[a] king of Tȳre, saying:

As you have dealt with David my father, and sent him cedars to build himself a house to dwell in, *so deal with me.*
4 Behold, I am building a temple for the name of the LORD my God, to dedicate *it* to Him, to burn before Him sweet incense, for the continual showbread, for the burnt offerings morning and evening, on the Sabbaths, on the New Moons, and on the set feasts of the LORD our God. This *is an ordinance* forever to Israel.
5 And the temple which I build *will be* great, for our God is greater than all gods.
6 But who is able to build Him a temple, since heaven and the heaven of heavens cannot contain Him? Who *am* I then, that I should build Him a temple, except to burn sacrifice before Him?
7 Therefore send me at once a man skillful to work in gold and silver, in bronze and iron, in purple and crimson and blue, who has skill to engrave with the skillful men who

are with me in Judah and Jerusalem, whom David my father provided.
8 Also send me cedar and cypress and algum logs from Lebanon, for I know that your servants have skill to cut timber in Lebanon; and indeed my servants *will be* with your servants,
9 to prepare timber for me in abundance, for the temple which I am about to build *shall be* great and wonderful.
10 And indeed I will give to your servants, the woodsmen who cut timber, twenty thousand kors of ground wheat, twenty thousand kors of barley, twenty thousand baths of wine, and twenty thousand baths of oil.

11 Then Hī'ram king of Tȳre answered in writing, which he sent to Solomon:

Because the LORD loves His people, He has made you king over them.

12 Hī'ram[a] also said:

Blessed *be* the LORD God of Israel, who made heaven and earth, for He has given King David a wise son, endowed with prudence and understanding, who will build a temple for the LORD and a royal house for himself!
13 And now I have sent a skillful man, endowed with understanding, Hū'ram[a] my master[b] *craftsman*
14 (the son of a woman of the daughters of Dan, and his father

---

1:17 [a]Literally *by their hands*   2:3 [a]Hebrew *Huram* (compare 1 Kings 5:1)   2:12 [a]Hebrew *Huram* (compare 1 Kings 5:1)   2:13 [a]Spelled *Hiram* in 1 Kings 7:13   [b]Literally *father* (compare 1 Kings 7:13, 14)

was a man of Tȳre), skilled to work in gold and silver, bronze and iron, stone and wood, purple and blue, fine linen and crimson, and to make any engraving and to accomplish any plan which may be given to him, with your skillful men and with the skillful men of my lord David your father.

15 Now therefore, the wheat, the barley, the oil, and the wine which my lord has spoken of, let him send to his servants.

16 And we will cut wood from Lebanon, as much as you need; we will bring it to you in rafts by sea to Jop′pa, and you will carry it up to Jerusalem.

17 Then Solomon numbered all the aliens who *were* in the land of Israel, after the census in which David his father had numbered them; and there were found to be one hundred and fifty-three thousand six hundred.

18 And he made seventy thousand of them bearers of burdens, eighty thousand stonecutters in the mountain, and three thousand six hundred overseers to make the people work.

Solomon Builds the Temple

3 Now Solomon began to build the house of the LORD at Jerusalem on Mount Mō·rī′ah, where *the LORD*a had appeared to his father David, at the place that David had prepared on the threshing floor of Or′nan*b* the Jeb′ū·sīte.

2 And he began to build on the second *day* of the second month in the fourth year of his reign.

3 This is the foundation which Solomon laid for building the house of God: The length *was* sixty cubits (by cubits according to the former measure) and the width twenty cubits.

4 And the vestibule that *was* in front *of the sanctuary*a was twenty cubits long across the width of the house, and the height *was* one hundred and*b* twenty. He overlaid the inside with pure gold.

5 The larger room*a* he paneled with cypress which he overlaid with fine gold, and he carved palm trees and chainwork on it.

6 And he decorated the house with precious stones for beauty, and the gold *was* gold from Par·vā′im.

7 He also overlaid the house—the beams and doorposts, its walls and doors—with gold; and he carved cherubim on the walls.

8 And he made the Most Holy Place. Its length was according to the width of the house, twenty cubits, and its width twenty cubits. He overlaid it with six hundred talents of fine gold.

9 The weight of the nails *was* fifty shekels of gold; and he overlaid the upper area with gold.

10 In the Most Holy Place he made two cherubim, fashioned by carving, and overlaid them with gold.

11 The wings of the cherubim *were* twenty cubits in *overall* length: one wing *of the one cherub was* five cubits, touching the wall of the room, and the other wing *was* five cubits, touching the wing of the other cherub;

12 *one* wing of the other cherub *was* five cubits, touching the wall of the room, and the other wing *also was*

3:1 aLiterally *He,* following Masoretic Text and Vulgate; Septuagint reads *the* LORD; Targum reads *the Angel of the* LORD. bSpelled *Araunah* in 2 Samuel 24:16ff   3:4 aThe main room of the temple; elsewhere called the holy place (compare 1 Kings 6:3)   bFollowing Masoretic Text, Septuagint, and Vulgate; Arabic, some manuscripts of the Septuagint, and Syriac omit *one hundred and.* 3:5 aLiterally *house*

five cubits, touching the wing of the other cherub.

13 The wings of these cherubim spanned twenty cubits overall. They stood on their feet, and they faced inward.

14 And he made the veil of blue, purple, crimson, and fine linen, and wove cherubim into it.

15 Also he made in front of the temple[a] two pillars thirty-five[b] cubits high, and the capital that *was* on the top of each of *them* was five cubits.

16 He made wreaths of chainwork, as in the inner sanctuary, and put *them* on top of the pillars; and he made one hundred pomegranates, and put *them* on the wreaths of chainwork.

17 Then he set up the pillars before the temple, one on the right hand and the other on the left; he called the name of the one on the right hand Jā′chin, and the name of the one on the left Bō′az.

FURNISHINGS OF THE TEMPLE

4 Moreover he made a bronze altar: twenty cubits was its length, twenty cubits its width, and ten cubits its height.

2 Then he made the Sea of cast *bronze,* ten cubits from one brim to the other; *it was* completely round. Its height *was* five cubits, and a line of thirty cubits measured its circumference.

3 And under it *was* the likeness of oxen encircling it all around, ten to a cubit, all the way around the Sea. The oxen *were* cast in two rows, when it was cast.

4 It stood on twelve oxen: three looking toward the north, three looking toward the west, three looking toward the south, and three looking toward the east; the Sea *was set* upon them, and all their back parts *pointed* inward.

5 It *was* a handbreadth thick; and its brim was shaped like the brim of a cup, *like* a lily blossom. It contained three thousand[a] baths.

6 He also made ten lavers, and put five on the right side and five on the left, to wash in them; such things as they offered for the burnt offering they would wash in them, but the Sea *was* for the priests to wash in.

7 And he made ten lampstands of gold according to their design, and set *them* in the temple, five on the right side and five on the left.

8 He also made ten tables, and placed *them* in the temple, five on the right side and five on the left. And he made one hundred bowls of gold.

9 Furthermore he made the court of the priests, and the great court and doors for the court; and he overlaid these doors with bronze.

10 He set the Sea on the right side, toward the southeast.

11 Then Hū′ram made the pots and the shovels and the bowls. So Hū′ram finished doing the work that he was to do for King Solomon for the house of God:

12 the two pillars and the bowl-shaped capitals *that were* on top of the two pillars; the two networks covering the two bowl-shaped capitals which *were* on top of the pillars;

13 four hundred pomegranates for the two networks (two rows of pomegranates for each network, to cover the two bowl-shaped capitals that *were* on the pillars);

14 he also made carts and the lavers on the carts;

15 one Sea and twelve oxen under it;

3:15 [a]Literally *house* [b]Or *eighteen* (compare 1 Kings 7:15; 2 Kings 25:17; and Jeremiah 52:21)
4:5 [a]Or *two thousand* (compare 1 Kings 7:26)

16 also the pots, the shovels, the forks—and all their articles Hū′ram his master*a craftsman* made of burnished bronze for King Solomon for the house of the LORD.

17 In the plain of Jordan the king had them cast in clay molds, between Suc′coth and Zer′e·dah.*a*

18 And Solomon had all these articles made in such great abundance that the weight of the bronze was not determined.

19 Thus Solomon had all the furnishings made for the house of God: the altar of gold and the tables on which *was* the showbread;

20 the lampstands with their lamps of pure gold, to burn in the prescribed manner in front of the inner sanctuary,

21 with the flowers and the lamps and the wick-trimmers of gold, of purest gold;

22 the trimmers, the bowls, the ladles, and the censers of pure gold. As for the entry of the sanctuary, its inner doors to the Most Holy *Place,* and the doors of the main hall of the temple, *were* gold.

5 So all the work that Solomon had done for the house of the LORD was finished; and Solomon brought in the things which his father David had dedicated: the silver and the gold and all the furnishings. And he put *them* in the treasuries of the house of God.

THE ARK BROUGHT
INTO THE TEMPLE

2 Now Solomon assembled the elders of Israel and all the heads of the tribes, the chief fathers of the children of Israel, in Jerusalem, that they might bring the ark of the covenant of the LORD up from the City of David, which *is* Zion.

3 Therefore all the men of Israel assembled with the king at the feast, which *was* in the seventh month.

4 So all the elders of Israel came, and the Lē′vītes took up the ark.

5 Then they brought up the ark, the tabernacle of meeting, and all the holy furnishings that *were* in the tabernacle. The priests and the Lē′vītes brought them up.

6 Also King Solomon, and all the congregation of Israel who were assembled with him before the ark, were sacrificing sheep and oxen that could not be counted or numbered for multitude.

7 Then the priests brought in the ark of the covenant of the LORD to its place, into the inner sanctuary of the temple,*a* to the Most Holy *Place,* under the wings of the cherubim.

8 For the cherubim spread *their* wings over the place of the ark, and the cherubim overshadowed the ark and its poles.

9 The poles extended so that the ends of the poles of the ark could be seen from *the holy place,* in front of the inner sanctuary; but they could not be seen from outside. And they are there to this day.

10 Nothing was in the ark except the two tablets which Moses put *there* at Hō′reb, when the LORD made *a covenant* with the children of Israel, when they had come out of Egypt.

11 And it came to pass when the priests came out of the *Most* Holy *Place* (for all the priests who *were* present had sanctified themselves, without keeping to their divisions),

12 and the Lē′vītes *who were* the singers, all those of Ā′saph and Hē′man and Je·dū′thun, with their

---

4:16 *a*Literally *father*   4:17 *a*Spelled *Zaretan* in 1 Kings 7:46   5:7 *a*Literally *house*

sons and their brethren, stood at the east end of the altar, clothed in white linen, having cymbals, stringed instruments and harps, and with them one hundred and twenty priests sounding with trumpets—

13 indeed it came to pass, when the trumpeters and singers *were* as one, to make one sound to be heard in praising and thanking the LORD, and when they lifted up their voice with the trumpets and cymbals and instruments of music, and praised the LORD, *saying:*

"*For He is* good,
    For His mercy *endures* forever,"a

that the house, the house of the LORD, was filled with a cloud,

---

Praises

2 Chronicles 5:13

A great choir and orchestra were like one voice in the temple, God's house. What were they doing? Praising and thanking God. Suddenly it was clear that God was there to receive His praise. When you praise God with all your heart, He is there to hear you. That's exciting, isn't it?

---

14 so that the priests could not continue ministering because of the cloud; for the glory of the LORD filled the house of God.

6

Then Solomon spoke:

"The LORD said He would dwell in
    the dark cloud.
2   I have surely built You an exalted
    house,
    And a place for You to dwell in
    forever."

SOLOMON'S SPEECH UPON COMPLETION OF THE WORK

3   Then the king turned around and blessed the whole assembly of Israel, while all the assembly of Israel was standing.
4   And he said: "Blessed *be* the LORD God of Israel, who has fulfilled with His hands *what* He spoke with His mouth to my father David, saying,
5   'Since the day that I brought My people out of the land of Egypt, I have chosen no city from any tribe of Israel *in which* to build a house, that My name might be there, nor did I choose any man to be a ruler over My people Israel.
6   'Yet I have chosen Jerusalem, that My name may be there, and I have chosen David to be over My people Israel.'
7   "Now it was in the heart of my father David to build a templea for the name of the LORD God of Israel.
8   "But the LORD said to my father David, 'Whereas it was in your heart to build a temple for My name, you did well in that it was in your heart.
9   'Nevertheless you shall not build the temple, but your son who will come from your body, he shall build the temple for My name.'
10   "So the LORD has fulfilled His word which He spoke, and I have filled the position of my father David, and sit on the throne of Israel, as the LORD promised; and I have built the temple for the name of the LORD God of Israel.
11   "And there I have put the ark, in which *is* the covenant of the LORD which He made with the children of Israel."

5:13 aCompare Psalm 106:1   6:7 aLiterally *house,* and so in verses 8–10

SOLOMON'S PRAYER OF DEDICATION

12 Then *Solomon*a stood before the altar of the LORD in the presence of all the assembly of Israel, and spread out his hands

13 (for Solomon had made a bronze platform five cubits long, five cubits wide, and three cubits high, and had set it in the midst of the court; and he stood on it, knelt down on his knees before all the assembly of Israel, and spread out his hands toward heaven);

14 and he said: "LORD God of Israel, *there is* no God in heaven or on earth like You, who keep *Your* covenant and mercy with Your servants who walk before You with all their hearts.

15 "You have kept what You promised Your servant David my father; You have both spoken with Your mouth and fulfilled *it* with Your hand, as *it is* this day.

16 "Therefore, LORD God of Israel, now keep what You promised Your servant David my father, saying, 'You shall not fail to have a man sit before Me on the throne of Israel, only if your sons take heed to their way, that they walk in My law as you have walked before Me.'

17 "And now, O LORD God of Israel, let Your word come true, which You have spoken to Your servant David.

18 "But will God indeed dwell with men on the earth? Behold, heaven and the heaven of heavens cannot contain You. How much less this templea which I have built!

19 "Yet regard the prayer of Your servant and his supplication, O LORD my God, and listen to the cry and the prayer which Your servant is praying before You:

20 "that Your eyes may be open toward this temple day and night, toward the place where *You* said *You would* put Your name, that You may hear the prayer which Your servant makes toward this place.

21 "And may You hear the supplications of Your servant and of Your people Israel, when they pray toward this place. Hear from heaven Your dwelling place, and when You hear, forgive.

22 "If anyone sins against his neighbor, and is forced to take an oath, and comes *and* takes an oath before Your altar in this temple,

23 "then hear from heaven, and act, and judge Your servants, bringing retribution on the wicked by bringing his way on his own head, and justifying the righteous by giving him according to his righteousness.

24 "Or if Your people Israel are defeated before an enemy because they have sinned against You, and return and confess Your name, and pray and make supplication before You in this temple,

25 "then hear from heaven and forgive the sin of Your people Israel, and bring them back to the land which You gave to them and their fathers.

26 "When the heavens are shut up and there is no rain because they have sinned against You, when they pray toward this place and confess Your name, and turn from their sin because You afflict them,

27 "then hear *in* heaven, and forgive the sin of Your servants, Your people Israel, that You may teach them the good way in which they should walk; and send rain on Your land which You have given to Your people as an inheritance.

28 "When there is famine in the land, pestilence or blight or mildew, locusts or grasshoppers; when their enemies besiege them in the land of

6:12 aLiterally *he* (compare 1 Kings 8:22)
6:18 aLiterally *house*

What Should I Do?

ARE YOU WITH ME? 2 Chronicles 6:19–21

When you're in a strange place, would you like a friend with you? When a storm is coming, would you like your parents with you? When you're feeling sad and lonely, would you like Jesus with you? Emily thought she was alone. But now she knows that she isn't.

1. Do you ever feel alone? Would you like someone with you?
2. When would you like a friend with you?
3. When would you like parents with you?
4. When would you like Jesus with you? He said He will be with you anywhere, at any time. Thank You, Jesus.

For more on *What Should I Do?* turn to page 731
For more on *God's Care* turn to page 712

their cities; whatever plague or whatever sickness *there is;*

29 "whatever prayer, whatever supplication is *made* by anyone, or by all Your people Israel, when each one knows his own burden and his own grief, and spreads out his hands to this temple:

30 "then hear from heaven Your dwelling place, and forgive, and give to everyone according to all his ways, whose heart You know (for You alone know the hearts of the sons of men),

31 "that they may fear You, to walk in Your ways as long as they live in the land which You gave to our fathers.

32 "Moreover, concerning a foreigner, who is not of Your people Israel, but has come from a far country for the sake of Your great name and Your mighty hand and Your outstretched arm, when they come and pray in this temple;

33 "then hear from heaven Your dwelling place, and do according to all for which the foreigner calls to You, that all peoples of the earth may know Your name and fear You, as *do* Your people Israel, and that they may know that this temple which I have built is called by Your name.

34 "When Your people go out to battle against their enemies, wherever You send them, and when they pray to You toward this city which You have chosen and the temple which I have built for Your name,

35 "then hear from heaven their prayer and their supplication, and maintain their cause.

36 "When they sin against You (for *there is* no one who does not sin), and You become angry with them and deliver them to the enemy, and they take them captive to a land far or near;

37 "*yet* when they come to themselves in the land where they were carried captive, and repent, and make supplication to You in the land of their captivity, saying, 'We have sinned, we have done wrong, and have committed wickedness';

38 "and *when* they return to You with all their heart and with all their soul in the land of their captivity, where they have been carried captive, and pray toward their land which You gave to their fathers, the city which You have chosen, and toward the temple which I have built for Your name:

39 "then hear from heaven Your dwelling place their prayer and their supplications, and maintain their cause, and forgive Your people who have sinned against You.

40 "Now, my God, I pray, let Your eyes be open and *let* Your ears *be* attentive to the prayer *made* in this place.

41 "Now therefore,
Arise, O Lord God, to Your
　resting place,
You and the ark of Your strength.
Let Your priests, O Lord God, be
　clothed with salvation,
And let Your saints rejoice in
　goodness.

42 "O Lord God, do not turn away the
　face of Your Anointed;
Remember the mercies of Your
　servant David."*a*

SOLOMON DEDICATES THE TEMPLE

7 When Solomon had finished praying, fire came down from heaven and consumed the burnt offering and the sacrifices; and the glory of the Lord filled the temple.*a*

2 And the priests could not enter the house of the Lord, because the

6:42 *a*Compare Psalm 132:8–10　7:1 *a*Literally *house*

glory of the LORD had filled the LORD's house.

3 When all the children of Israel saw how the fire came down, and the glory of the LORD on the temple, they bowed their faces to the ground on the pavement, and worshiped and praised the LORD, *saying:*

"For *He is* good,
For His mercy *endures* forever."[a]

4 Then the king and all the people offered sacrifices before the LORD.

5 King Solomon offered a sacrifice of twenty-two thousand bulls and one hundred and twenty thousand sheep. So the king and all the people dedicated the house of God.

6 And the priests attended to their services; the Lē′vītes also with instruments of the music of the LORD, which King David had made to praise the LORD, saying, "For His mercy *endures* forever,"[a] whenever David offered praise by their ministry. The priests sounded trumpets opposite them, while all Israel stood.

7 Furthermore Solomon consecrated the middle of the court that *was* in front of the house of the LORD; for there he offered burnt offerings and the fat of the peace offerings, because the bronze altar which Solomon had made was not able to receive the burnt offerings, the grain offerings, and the fat.

8 At that time Solomon kept the feast seven days, and all Israel with him, a very great assembly from the entrance of Hā′math to the Brook of Egypt.[a]

9 And on the eighth day they held a sacred assembly, for they observed the dedication of the altar seven days, and the feast seven days.

10 On the twenty-third day of the seventh month he sent the people away to their tents, joyful and glad of heart for the good that the LORD had done for David, for Solomon, and for His people Israel.

11 Thus Solomon finished the house of the LORD and the king's house; and Solomon successfully accomplished all that came into his heart to make in the house of the LORD and in his own house.

GOD'S SECOND APPEARANCE TO SOLOMON

12 Then the LORD appeared to Solomon by night, and said to him: "I have heard your prayer, and have chosen this place for Myself as a house of sacrifice.

13 "When I shut up heaven and there is no rain, or command the locusts to devour the land, or send pestilence among My people,

14 "if My people who are called by My name will humble themselves, and pray and seek My face, and turn from their wicked ways, then I will hear from heaven, and will forgive their sin and heal their land.

◾ *Promises* ◾

2 Chronicles 7:14

Do you ever wish someone could wipe away all the bad things in your life? God can. He can and will forgive you. Here He promises that He will forgive and heal. But He also tells us what we must do. We must humble ourselves. We must pray. We must seek God. We must turn from our bad ways. *Then* He will forgive. He will do His part. Will you do yours?

7:3 [a]Compare Psalm 106:1   7:6 [a]Compare Psalm 106:1   7:8 [a]That is, the Shihor (compare 1 Chronicles 13:5)

15 "Now My eyes will be open and My ears attentive to prayer *made* in this place.

16 "For now I have chosen and sanctified this house, that My name may be there forever; and My eyes and My heart will be there perpetually.

17 "As for you, if you walk before Me as your father David walked, and do according to all that I have commanded you, and if you keep My statutes and My judgments,

18 "then I will establish the throne of your kingdom, as I covenanted with David your father, saying, 'You shall not fail *to have* a man as ruler in Israel.'

19 "But if you turn away and forsake My statutes and My commandments which I have set before you, and go and serve other gods, and worship them,

20 "then I will uproot them from My land which I have given them; and this house which I have sanctified for My name I will cast out of My sight, and will make it a proverb and a byword among all peoples.

21 "And *as for* this house, which is exalted, everyone who passes by it will be astonished and say, 'Why has the LORD done thus to this land and this house?'

22 "Then they will answer, 'Because they forsook the LORD God of their fathers, who brought them out of the land of Egypt, and embraced other gods, and worshiped them and served them; therefore He has brought all this calamity on them.'"

SOLOMON'S ADDITIONAL ACHIEVEMENTS

8 It came to pass at the end of twenty years, when Solomon had built the house of the LORD and his own house,

2   that the cities which Hī'ram*a* had given to Solomon, Solomon built them; and he settled the children of Israel there.

3   And Solomon went to Hā'math Zō'bah and seized it.

4   He also built Tad'mor in the wilderness, and all the storage cities which he built in Hā'math.

5   He built Upper Beth Hor'on and Lower Beth Hor'on, fortified cities *with* walls, gates, and bars,

6   also Bā'a·lath and all the storage cities that Solomon had, and all the chariot cities and the cities of the cavalry, and all that Solomon desired to build in Jerusalem, in Lebanon, and in all the land of his dominion.

7   All the people *who were* left of the Hit'tītes, Am'o·rītes, Per'iz·zītes, Hī'-vītes, and Jeb'ū·sītes, who *were* not of Israel—

8   that is, their descendants who were left in the land after them, whom the children of Israel did not destroy—from these Solomon raised forced labor, as it is to this day.

9   But Solomon did not make the children of Israel servants for his work. Some *were* men of war, captains of his officers, captains of his chariots, and his cavalry.

10 And others *were* chiefs of the officials of King Solomon: two hundred and fifty, who ruled over the people.

11 Now Solomon brought the daughter of Pharaoh up from the City of David to the house he had built for her, for he said, "My wife shall not dwell in the house of David king of Israel, because *the places* to which the ark of the LORD has come are holy."

12 Then Solomon offered burnt offerings to the LORD on the altar of the LORD which he had built before the vestibule,

8:2 *a*Hebrew *Huram* (compare 2 Chronicles 2:3)

13 according to the daily rate, offering according to the commandment of Moses, for the Sabbaths, the New Moons, and the three appointed yearly feasts—the Feast of Unleavened Bread, the Feast of Weeks, and the Feast of Tabernacles.

14 And, according to the order of David his father, he appointed the divisions of the priests for their service, the Lē'vītes for their duties (to praise and serve before the priests) as the duty of each day required, and the gatekeepers by their divisions at each gate; for so David the man of God had commanded.

15 They did not depart from the command of the king to the priests and Lē'vītes concerning any matter or concerning the treasuries.

16 Now all the work of Solomon was well-ordered from*a* the day of the foundation of the house of the LORD until it was finished. So the house of the LORD was completed.

17 Then Solomon went to Ē'zi·on Gē'ber and Ē'lath*a* on the seacoast, in the land of Ē'dom.

18 And Hī'ram sent him ships by the hand of his servants, and servants who knew the sea. They went with the servants of Solomon to Ō'phir, and acquired four hundred and fifty talents of gold from there, and brought it to King Solomon.

THE QUEEN OF SHEBA'S PRAISE OF SOLOMON

9 Now when the queen of Shē'ba heard of the fame of Solomon, she came to Jerusalem to test Solomon with hard questions, *having* a very great retinue, camels that bore spices, gold in abundance, and precious stones; and when she came to Solomon, she spoke with him about all that was in her heart.

2 So Solomon answered all her questions; there was nothing so difficult for Solomon that he could not explain it to her.

3 And when the queen of Shē'ba had seen the wisdom of Solomon, the house that he had built,

4 the food on his table, the seating of his servants, the service of his waiters and their apparel, his cupbearers and their apparel, and his entryway by which he went up to the house of the LORD, there was no more spirit in her.

5 Then she said to the king: "*It was* a true report which I heard in my own land about your words and your wisdom.

6 "However I did not believe their words until I came and saw with my own eyes; and indeed the half of the greatness of your wisdom was not told me. You exceed the fame of which I heard.

7 "Happy *are* your men and happy *are* these your servants, who stand continually before you and hear your wisdom!

8 "Blessed be the LORD your God, who delighted in you, setting you on His throne *to be* king for the LORD your God! Because your God has loved Israel, to establish them forever, therefore He made you king over them, to do justice and righteousness."

9 And she gave the king one hundred and twenty talents of gold, spices in great abundance, and precious stones; there never were any spices such as those the queen of Shē'ba gave to King Solomon.

10 Also, the servants of Hī'ram and the servants of Solomon, who brought gold from Ō'phir, brought algum*a* wood and precious stones.

8:16 *a*Following Septuagint, Syriac, and Vulgate; Masoretic Text reads *as far as.*   8:17 *a*Hebrew *Eloth* (compare 2 Kings 14:22)   9:10 *a*Or *almug* (compare 1 Kings 10:11, 12)

11 And the king made walkways *of* the alguma wood for the house of the LORD and for the king's house, also harps and stringed instruments for singers; and there were none such *as these* seen before in the land of Judah.

12 Now King Solomon gave to the queen of Shē′ba all she desired, whatever she asked, *much more* than she had brought to the king. So she turned and went to her own country, she and her servants.

SOLOMON'S GREAT WEALTH

13 The weight of gold that came to Solomon yearly was six hundred and sixty-six talents of gold,

14 besides *what* the traveling merchants and traders brought. And all the kings of Arabia and governors of the country brought gold and silver to Solomon.

15 And King Solomon made two hundred large shields of hammered gold; six hundred *shekels* of hammered gold went into each shield.

16 *He* also *made* three hundred shields of hammered gold; three hundred *shekelsa* of gold went into each shield. The king put them in the House of the Forest of Lebanon.

17 Moreover the king made a great throne of ivory, and overlaid it with pure gold.

18 The throne *had* six steps, with a footstool of gold, *which were* fastened to the throne; there were armrests on either side of the place of the seat, and two lions stood beside the armrests.

19 Twelve lions stood there, one on each side of the six steps; nothing like *this* had been made for any *other* kingdom.

20 All King Solomon's drinking vessels *were* gold, and all the vessels of the House of the Forest of Lebanon were pure gold. Not *one was* silver, for this was accounted as nothing in the days of Solomon.

21 For the king's ships went to Tar′-shish with the servants of Hī′ram.a Once every three years the merchant shipsb came, bringing gold, silver, ivory, apes, and monkeys.c

22 So King Solomon surpassed all the kings of the earth in riches and wisdom.

23 And all the kings of the earth sought the presence of Solomon to hear his wisdom, which God had put in his heart.

24 Each man brought his present: articles of silver and gold, garments, armor, spices, horses, and mules, at a set rate year by year.

25 Solomon had four thousand stalls for horses and chariots, and twelve thousand horsemen whom he stationed in the chariot cities and with the king at Jerusalem.

26 So he reigned over all the kings from the Rivera to the land of the Phi·lis′tines, as far as the border of Egypt.

27 The king made silver *as common* in Jerusalem as stones, and he made cedar trees as abundant as the sycamores which *are* in the lowland.

28 And they brought horses to Solomon from Egypt and from all lands.

DEATH OF SOLOMON

29 Now the rest of the acts of Solomon, first and last, *are* they not written in the book of Nathan the prophet, in the prophecy of A·hī′jah the Shī′lo·nīte, and in the visions of Id′do the seer concerning Jer·o·bō′am the son of Nē′bat?

9:11 aOr *almug* (compare 1 Kings 10:11, 12)
9:16 aOr *three minas* (compare 1 Kings 10:17)
9:21 aHebrew *Huram* (compare 1 Kings 10:22)
bLiterally *ships of Tarshish*, deep-sea vessels   cOr
peacocks   9:26 aThat is, the Euphrates

30 Solomon reigned in Jerusalem over all Israel forty years.

31 Then Solomon rested with his fathers, and was buried in the City of David his father. And Rē·ho·bō′am his son reigned in his place.

THE REVOLT AGAINST REHOBOAM

10 And Rē·ho·bō′am went to Shē′chem, for all Israel had gone to Shē′chem to make him king.

2 So it happened, when Jer·o·bō′am the son of Nē′bat heard *it* (he was in Egypt, where he had fled from the presence of King Solomon), that Jer·o·bō′am returned from Egypt.

3 Then they sent for him and called him. And Jer·o·bō′am and all Israel came and spoke to Rē·ho·bō′am, saying,

4 "Your father made our yoke heavy; now therefore, lighten the burdensome service of your father and his heavy yoke which he put on us, and we will serve you."

5 So he said to them, "Come back to me after three days." And the people departed.

6 Then King Rē·ho·bō′am consulted the elders who stood before his father Solomon while he still lived, saying, "How do you advise *me* to answer these people?"

7 And they spoke to him, saying, "If you are kind to these people, and please them, and speak good words to them, they will be your servants forever."

8 But he rejected the advice which the elders had given him, and consulted the young men who had grown up with him, who stood before him.

9 And he said to them, "What advice do you give? How should we answer this people who have spoken to me, saying, 'Lighten the yoke which your father put on us'?"

10 Then the young men who had grown up with him spoke to him, saying, "Thus you should speak to the people who have spoken to you, saying, 'Your father made our yoke heavy, but you make *it* lighter on us'—thus you shall say to them: 'My little *finger* shall be thicker than my father's waist!

11 'And now, whereas my father put a heavy yoke on you, I will add to your yoke; my father chastised you with whips, but I *will chastise you* with scourges!' "a

12 So Jer·o·bō′am and all the people came to Rē·ho·bō′am on the third day, as the king had directed, saying, "Come back to me the third day."

13 Then the king answered them roughly. King Rē·ho·bō′am rejected the advice of the elders,

14 and he spoke to them according to the advice of the young men, saying, "My fathera made your yoke heavy, but I will add to it; my father chastised you with whips, but I *will chastise you* with scourges!"b

15 So the king did not listen to the people; for the turn *of events* was from God, that the LORD might fulfill His word, which He had spoken by the hand of A·hī′jah the Shī′lo·nīte to Jer·o·bō′am the son of Nē′bat.

16 Now when all Israel *saw* that the king did not listen to them, the people answered the king, saying:

"What share have we in David?
    We have no inheritance in the son
        of Jesse.
    Every man to your tents,
        O Israel!
    Now see to your own house,
        O David!"

10:11 aLiterally *scorpions*   10:14 aFollowing many Hebrew manuscripts, Septuagint, Syriac, and Vulgate (compare verse 10 and 1 Kings 12:14); Masoretic Text reads *I*.   bLiterally *scorpions*

So all Israel departed to their tents.
17 But Rē·ho·bō′am reigned over the children of Israel who dwelt in the cities of Judah.
18 Then King Rē·ho·bō′am sent Ha·dor′am, who *was* in charge of revenue; but the children of Israel stoned him with stones, and he died. Therefore King Rē·ho·bō′am mounted *his* chariot in haste to flee to Jerusalem.
19 So Israel has been in rebellion against the house of David to this day.

11 Now when Rē·ho·bō′am came to Jerusalem, he assembled from the house of Judah and Benjamin one hundred and eighty thousand chosen *men* who were warriors, to fight against Israel, that he might restore the kingdom to Rē·ho·bō′am.
2 But the word of the LORD came to She·māi′ah the man of God, saying,
3 "Speak to Rē·ho·bō′am the son of Solomon, king of Judah, and to all Israel in Judah and Benjamin, saying,
4 'Thus says the LORD: "You shall not go up or fight against your brethren! Let every man return to his house, for this thing is from Me." ' " Therefore they obeyed the words of the LORD, and turned back from attacking Jer·o·bō′am.

REHOBOAM FORTIFIES THE CITIES

5 So Rē·ho·bō′am dwelt in Jerusalem, and built cities for defense in Judah.
6 And he built Bethlehem, Ē′tam, Te·kō′a,
7 Beth Zūr, Sō′chōh, A·dul′lam,
8 Gath, Ma·rē′shah, Ziph,
9 Ad·o·rā′im, Lā′chish, A·zē′kah,
10 Zō′rah, Aī′ja·lon, and Hē′bron, which are in Judah and Benjamin, fortified cities.
11 And he fortified the strongholds, and put captains in them, and stores of food, oil, and wine.
12 Also in every city *he put* shields and spears, and made them very strong, having Judah and Benjamin on his side.

PRIESTS AND LEVITES MOVE TO JUDAH

13 And from all their territories the priests and the Lē′vītes who *were* in all Israel took their stand with him.
14 For the Lē′vītes left their common-lands and their possessions and came to Judah and Jerusalem, for Jer·o·bō′am and his sons had rejected them from serving as priests to the LORD.
15 Then he appointed for himself priests for the high places, for the demons, and the calf idols which he had made.
16 And after *the Lē′vites left,ᵃ* those from all the tribes of Israel, such as set their heart to seek the LORD God of Israel, came to Jerusalem to sacrifice to the LORD God of their fathers.
17 So they strengthened the kingdom of Judah, and made Rē·ho·bō′am the son of Solomon strong for three years, because they walked in the way of David and Solomon for three years.

THE FAMILY OF REHOBOAM

18 Then Rē·ho·bō′am took for himself as wife Mā′ha·lath the daughter of Jer′i·moth the son of David, *and of* Ab·i·hā′il the daughter of E·lī′ah the son of Jesse.
19 And she bore him children: Jē′ush, Sham·a·rī′ah, and Zā′ham.
20 After her he took Mā′a·chah the

11:16 ᵃLiterally *after them*

granddaughter[a] of Ab'sa·lom; and she bore him A·bi'jah, At'taī, Zī'za, and She·lō'mith.

21 Now Rē·ho·bō'am loved Mā'a·chah the granddaughter of Ab'sa·lom more than all his wives and his concubines; for he took eighteen wives and sixty concubines, and begot twenty-eight sons and sixty daughters.

22 And Rē·ho·bō'am appointed A·bi'jah the son of Mā'a·chah as chief, *to be* leader among his brothers; for he *intended* to make him king.

23 He dealt wisely, and dispersed some of his sons throughout all the territories of Judah and Benjamin, to every fortified city; and he gave them provisions in abundance. He also sought many wives *for them.*

EGYPT ATTACKS JUDAH

12 Now it came to pass, when Rē·ho·bō'am had established the kingdom and had strengthened himself, that he forsook the law of the LORD, and all Israel along with him.

2 And it happened in the fifth year of King Rē·ho·bō'am *that* Shī'shak king of Egypt came up against Jerusalem, because they had transgressed against the LORD,

3 with twelve hundred chariots, sixty thousand horsemen, and people without number who came with him out of Egypt—the Lū'bim and the Suk'ki·im and the Ethiopians.

4 And he took the fortified cities of Judah and came to Jerusalem.

5 Then She·mai'ah the prophet came to Rē·ho·bō'am and the leaders of Judah, who were gathered together in Jerusalem because of Shī'shak, and said to them, "Thus says the LORD: 'You have forsaken Me, and therefore I also have left you in the hand of Shī'shak.'"

6 So the leaders of Israel and the king humbled themselves; and they said, "The LORD *is* righteous."

7 Now when the LORD saw that they humbled themselves, the word of the LORD came to She·mai'ah, saying, "They have humbled themselves; *therefore* I will not destroy them, but I will grant them some deliverance. My wrath shall not be poured out on Jerusalem by the hand of Shī'shak.

8 "Nevertheless they will be his servants, that they may distinguish My service from the service of the kingdoms of the nations."

9 So Shī'shak king of Egypt came up against Jerusalem, and took away the treasures of the house of the LORD and the treasures of the king's house; he took everything. He also carried away the gold shields which Solomon had made.

10 Then King Rē·ho·bō'am made bronze shields in their place, and committed *them* to the hands of the captains of the guard, who guarded the doorway of the king's house.

11 And whenever the king entered the house of the LORD, the guard would go and bring them out; then they would take them back into the guardroom.

12 When he humbled himself, the wrath of the LORD turned from him, so as not to destroy *him* completely; and things also went well in Judah.

THE END OF REHOBOAM'S REIGN

13 Thus King Rē·ho·bō'am strengthened himself in Jerusalem and reigned. Now Rē·ho·bō'am *was* forty-one years old when he became king; and he reigned seventeen years in Jerusalem, the city which the LORD had chosen out of all the tribes of Israel,

---

11:20 [a]Literally *daughter,* but in the broader sense of granddaughter (compare 2 Chronicles 13:2)

to put His name there. His mother's name *was* Nā'a·mah, an Am'mon·ī·tess.

14 And he did evil, because he did not prepare his heart to seek the LORD.

15 The acts of Rē·ho·bō'am, first and last, *are* they not written in the book of She·māi'ah the prophet, and of Id'dō the seer concerning genealogies? And *there were* wars between Rē·ho·bō'am and Jer·o·bō'am all their days.

16 So Rē·ho·bō'am rested with his fathers, and was buried in the City of David. Then A·bī'jah[a] his son reigned in his place.

ABIJAH REIGNS IN JUDAH

13 In the eighteenth year of King Jer·o·bō'am, A·bī'jah became king over Judah.

2 He reigned three years in Jerusalem. His mother's name *was* Mī·chaī'ah[a] the daughter of Ū·rī'el of Gib'ē·ah. And there was war between A·bī'jah and Jer·o·bō'am.

3 A·bī'jah set the battle in order with an army of valiant warriors, four hundred thousand choice men. Jer·o·bō'am also drew up in battle formation against him with eight hundred thousand choice men, mighty men of valor.

4 Then A·bī'jah stood on Mount Zem·a·rā'im, which *is* in the mountains of Ē'phra·im, and said, "Hear me, Jer·o·bō'am and all Israel:

5 "Should you not know that the LORD God of Israel gave the dominion over Israel to David forever, to him and his sons, by a covenant of salt?

6 "Yet Jer·o·bō'am the son of Nē'bat, the servant of Solomon the son of David, rose up and rebelled against his lord.

7 "Then worthless rogues gathered to him, and strengthened themselves against Rē·ho·bō'am the son of Solomon, when Rē·ho·bō'am was young and inexperienced and could not withstand them.

8 "And now you think to withstand the kingdom of the LORD, which is in the hand of the sons of David; and you *are* a great multitude, and with you are the gold calves which Jer·o·bō'am made for you as gods.

9 "Have you not cast out the priests of the LORD, the sons of Aaron, and the Lē'vītes, and made for yourselves priests, like the peoples of *other* lands, so that whoever comes to consecrate himself with a young bull and seven rams may be a priest of *things that are* not gods?

10 "But as for us, the LORD *is* our God, and we have not forsaken Him; and the priests who minister to the LORD *are* the sons of Aaron, and the Lē'vītes *attend* to *their* duties.

11 "And they burn to the LORD every morning and every evening burnt sacrifices and sweet incense; *they* also *set* the showbread *in order on* the pure *gold* table, and the lampstand of gold with its lamps to burn every evening; for we keep the command of the LORD our God, but you have forsaken Him.

12 "Now look, God Himself is with us as *our* head, and His priests with sounding trumpets to sound the alarm against you. O children of Israel, do not fight against the LORD God of your fathers, for you shall not prosper!"

13 But Jer·o·bō'am caused an ambush to go around behind them; so they were in front of Judah, and the ambush *was* behind them.

14 And when Judah looked around,

12:16 [a]Spelled *Abijam* in 1 Kings 14:31
13:2 [a]Spelled *Maachah* in 11:20, 21 and 1 Kings 15:2

to their surprise the battle line *was* at both front and rear; and they cried out to the LORD, and the priests sounded the trumpets.

15 Then the men of Judah gave a shout; and as the men of Judah shouted, it happened that God struck Jer·o·bō′am and all Israel before A·bī′jah and Judah.

16 And the children of Israel fled before Judah, and God delivered them into their hand.

17 Then A·bī′jah and his people struck them with a great slaughter; so five hundred thousand choice men of Israel fell slain.

18 Thus the children of Israel were subdued at that time; and the children of Judah prevailed, because they relied on the LORD God of their fathers.

19 And A·bī′jah pursued Jer·o·bō′am and took cities from him: Beth′el with its villages, Je·shā′nah with its villages, and Ē′phra·in*a* with its villages.

20 So Jer·o·bō′am did not recover strength again in the days of A·bī′jah; and the LORD struck him, and he died.

21 But A·bī′jah grew mighty, married fourteen wives, and begot twenty-two sons and sixteen daughters.

22 Now the rest of the acts of A·bī′jah, his ways, and his sayings *are* written in the annals of the prophet Id′dō.

14 So A·bī′jah rested with his fathers, and they buried him in the City of David. Then Ā′sa his son reigned in his place. In his days the land was quiet for ten years.

ASA REIGNS IN JUDAH

2 Ā′sa did *what was* good and right in the eyes of the LORD his God,

3 for he removed the altars of the foreign *gods* and the high places, and broke down the *sacred* pillars and cut down the wooden images.

4 He commanded Judah to seek the LORD God of their fathers, and to observe the law and the commandment.

5 He also removed the high places and the incense altars from all the cities of Judah, and the kingdom was quiet under him.

6 And he built fortified cities in Judah, for the land had rest; he had no war in those years, because the LORD had given him rest.

7 Therefore he said to Judah, "Let us build these cities and make walls around *them,* and towers, gates, and bars, *while* the land *is* yet before us, because we have sought the LORD our God; we have sought *Him,* and He has given us rest on every side." So they built and prospered.

8 And Ā′sa had an army of three hundred thousand from Judah who carried shields and spears, and from Benjamin two hundred and eighty thousand men who carried shields and drew bows; all these *were* mighty men of valor.

9 Then Zē′rah the Ethiopian came out against them with an army of a million men and three hundred chariots, and he came to Ma·rē′shah.

10 So Ā′sa went out against him, and they set the troops in battle array in the Valley of Zeph′a·thah at Ma·rē′shah.

11 And Ā′sa cried out to the LORD his God, and said, "LORD, *it is* nothing for You to help, whether with many or with those who have no power; help us, O LORD our God, for we rest on You, and in Your name we go against this multitude. O LORD, You *are* our God; do not let man prevail against You!"

13:19 *a*Or *Ephron*

12 So the LORD struck the Ethiopians before Ā′sa and Judah, and the Ethiopians fled.

Prayers

2 Chronicles 14:11, 12

How would you like to fight an army with a million soldiers? You know you can't win. There are too many. Some people would feel like running away. Not Asa. He prayed. "Help!" he cried out. Then God helped him. Remember that the next time you face something too big for you. Pray "Help!" Do you think He will?

---

13 And Ā′sa and the people who *were* with him pursued them to Gē′rar. So the Ethiopians were overthrown, and they could not recover, for they were broken before the LORD and His army. And they carried away very much spoil.
14 Then they defeated all the cities around Gē′rar, for the fear of the LORD came upon them; and they plundered all the cities, for there was exceedingly much spoil in them.
15 They also attacked the livestock enclosures, and carried off sheep and camels in abundance, and returned to Jerusalem.

THE REFORMS OF ASA

15 Now the Spirit of God came upon Az·a·rī′ah the son of Ō′ded.
2 And he went out to meet Ā′sa, and said to him: "Hear me, Ā′sa, and all Judah and Benjamin. The LORD *is* with you while you are with Him. If you seek Him, He will be found by you; but if you forsake Him, He will forsake you.

Promises

2 Chronicles 15:2

Do you want God with you? Seek Him. Do you want to find God? Seek Him. Do you want God to turn against you? Of course not! But He will if you turn against God. But who wants that? You want God with you, don't you?

---

3 "For a long time Israel *has been* without the true God, without a teaching priest, and without law;
4 "but when in their trouble they turned to the LORD God of Israel, and sought Him, He was found by them.
5 "And in those times *there was* no peace to the one who went out, nor to the one who came in, but great turmoil *was* on all the inhabitants of the lands.
6 "So nation was destroyed by nation, and city by city, for God troubled them with every adversity.
7 "But you, be strong and do not let your hands be weak, for your work shall be rewarded!"
8 And when Ā′sa heard these words and the prophecy of Ō′ded*ᵃ* the prophet, he took courage, and removed the abominable idols from all the land of Judah and Benjamin and from the cities which he had taken in the mountains of Ē′phra·im; and he restored the altar of the LORD that *was* before the vestibule of the LORD.
9 Then he gathered all Judah and Benjamin, and those who dwelt with them from Ē′phra·im, Ma·nas′seh, and Sim′ē·on, for they came over to him in great numbers from Israel when they saw that the LORD his God was with him.

15:8 ᵃFollowing Masoretic Text and Septuagint; Syriac and Vulgate read *Azariah the son of Oded* (compare verse 1).

10 So they gathered together at Jerusalem in the third month, in the fifteenth year of the reign of Ā'sa.

11 And they offered to the LORD at that time seven hundred bulls and seven thousand sheep from the spoil they had brought.

12 Then they entered into a covenant to seek the LORD God of their fathers with all their heart and with all their soul;

13 and whoever would not seek the LORD God of Israel was to be put to death, whether small or great, whether man or woman.

14 Then they took an oath before the LORD with a loud voice, with shouting and trumpets and rams' horns.

15 And all Judah rejoiced at the oath, for they had sworn with all their heart and sought Him with all their soul; and He was found by them, and the LORD gave them rest all around.

16 Also he removed Mā'a·chah, the mother of Ā'sa the king, from *being* queen mother, because she had made an obscene image of A·shē'rah;*a* and Ā'sa cut down her obscene image, then crushed and burned *it* by the Brook Kid'ron.

17 But the high places were not removed from Israel. Nevertheless the heart of Ā'sa was loyal all his days.

18 He also brought into the house of God the things that his father had dedicated and that he himself had dedicated: silver and gold and utensils.

19 And there was no war until the thirty-fifth year of the reign of Ā'sa.

ASA'S TREATY WITH SYRIA

16 In the thirty-sixth year of the reign of Ā'sa, Bā'a·sha king of Israel came up against Judah and built Rā'mah, that he might let none go out or come in to Ā'sa king of Judah.

2 Then Ā'sa brought silver and gold from the treasuries of the house of the LORD and of the king's house, and sent to Ben-Hā'dad king of Syria, who dwelt in Damascus, saying,

3 "*Let there be* a treaty between you and me, as there was between my father and your father. See, I have sent you silver and gold; come, break your treaty with Bā'a·sha king of Israel, so that he will withdraw from me."

4 So Ben-Hā'dad heeded King Ā'sa, and sent the captains of his armies against the cities of Israel. They attacked Ī'jon, Dan, Abel Mā'im, and all the storage cities of Naph'ta·lī.

5 Now it happened, when Bā'a·sha heard *it,* that he stopped building Rā'mah and ceased his work.

6 Then King Ā'sa took all Judah, and they carried away the stones and timber of Rā'mah, which Bā'a·sha had used for building; and with them he built Gē'ba and Miz'pah.

HANANI'S MESSAGE TO ASA

7 And at that time Ha·nā'nī the seer came to Ā'sa king of Judah, and said to him: "Because you have relied on the king of Syria, and have not relied on the LORD your God, therefore the army of the king of Syria has escaped from your hand.

8 "Were the Ethiopians and the Lū'bim not a huge army with very many chariots and horsemen? Yet, because you relied on the LORD, He delivered them into your hand.

9 "For the eyes of the LORD run to and fro throughout the whole earth, to show Himself strong on behalf of *those* whose heart *is* loyal to Him. In this you have done foolishly; there-

15:16 *a*A Canaanite deity

fore from now on you shall have wars."

10 Then Ā′sa was angry with the seer, and put him in prison, for *he was* enraged at him because of this. And Ā′sa oppressed *some* of the people at that time.

ILLNESS AND DEATH OF ASA

11 Note that the acts of Ā′sa, first and last, are indeed written in the book of the kings of Judah and Israel. 12 And in the thirty-ninth year of his reign, Ā′sa became diseased in his feet, and his malady was severe; yet in his disease he did not seek the LORD, but the physicians.
13 So Ā′sa rested with his fathers; he died in the forty-first year of his reign.
14 They buried him in his own tomb, which he had made for himself in the City of David; and they laid him in the bed which was filled with spices and various ingredients prepared in a mixture of ointments. They made a very great burning for him.

JEHOSHAPHAT REIGNS IN JUDAH

17 Then Je·hosh′a·phat his son reigned in his place, and strengthened himself against Israel.
2 And he placed troops in all the fortified cities of Judah, and set garrisons in the land of Judah and in the cities of Ē′phra·im which Ā′sa his father had taken.
3 Now the LORD was with Je·hosh′-a·phat, because he walked in the former ways of his father David; he did not seek the Bā′als,
4 but sought the God[a] of his father, and walked in His commandments and not according to the acts of Israel.
5 Therefore the LORD established

the kingdom in his hand; and all Judah gave presents to Je·hosh′a·phat, and he had riches and honor in abundance.
6 And his heart took delight in the ways of the LORD; moreover he removed the high places and wooden images from Judah.
7 Also in the third year of his reign he sent his leaders, Ben-Hā′il, Ō·ba·dī′ah, Zech·a·rī′ah, Ne·than′el, and Mī·chaī′ah, to teach in the cities of Judah.
8 And with them *he sent* Lē′vītes: She·māi′ah, Neth·a·nī′ah, Zeb·a·dī′ah, As′a·hel, She·mir′a·moth, Je·hon′-a·than, Ad·o·nī′jah, Tō·bī′jah, and Tob·ad·o·nī′jah—the Lē′vītes; and with them E·lish′a·ma and Je·hō′ram, the priests.
9 So they taught in Judah, and *had* the Book of the Law of the LORD with them; they went throughout all the cities of Judah and taught the people.
10 And the fear of the LORD fell on all the kingdoms of the lands that *were* around Judah, so that they did not make war against Je·hosh′a·phat.
11 Also *some* of the Phi·lis′tines brought Je·hosh′a·phat presents and silver as tribute; and the Arabians brought him flocks, seven thousand seven hundred rams and seven thousand seven hundred male goats.
12 So Je·hosh′a·phat became increasingly powerful, and he built fortresses and storage cities in Judah.
13 He had much property in the cities of Judah; and the men of war, mighty men of valor, *were* in Jerusalem.
14 These *are* their numbers, according to their fathers' houses. Of Judah, the captains of thousands: Ad′nah the captain, and with him three hundred thousand mighty men of valor;

17:4 [a]Septuagint reads LORD God.

15 and next to him *was* Jĕ·hō·hā′nan the captain, and with him two hundred and eighty thousand;

16 and next to him *was* Am·a·sī′ah the son of Zich′rī, who willingly offered himself to the LORD, and with him two hundred thousand mighty men of valor.

17 Of Benjamin: E·lī′a·da a mighty man of valor, and with him two hundred thousand men armed with bow and shield;

18 and next to him *was* Je·hō′za·bad, and with him one hundred and eighty thousand prepared for war.

19 These served the king, besides those the king put in the fortified cities throughout all Judah.

MICAIAH WARNS AHAB

18 Je·hosh′a·phat had riches and honor in abundance; and by marriage he allied himself with Ā′hab.

2 After some years he went down to *visit* Ā′hab in Samaria; and Ā′hab killed sheep and oxen in abundance for him and the people who were with him, and persuaded him to go up *with him* to Rā′moth Gil′ē·ad.

3 So Ā′hab king of Israel said to Je·hosh′a·phat king of Judah, "Will you go with me *against* Rā′moth Gil′ē·ad?" And he answered him, "I *am* as you *are,* and my people as your people; *we will be* with you in the war."

4 Also Je·hosh′a·phat said to the king of Israel, "Please inquire for the word of the LORD today."

5 Then the king of Israel gathered the prophets together, four hundred men, and said to them, "Shall we go to war against Rā′moth Gil′ē·ad, or shall I refrain?" So they said, "Go up, for God will deliver it into the king's hand."

6 But Je·hosh′a·phat said, *"Is there* not still a prophet of the LORD here, that we may inquire of Him?"*a*

7 So the king of Israel said to Je·hosh′a·phat, *"There is* still one man by whom we may inquire of the LORD; but I hate him, because he never prophesies good concerning me, but always evil. He *is* Mī·cāi′ah the son of Im′la." And Je·hosh′a·phat said, "Let not the king say such things!"

8 Then the king of Israel called one *of his* officers and said, "Bring Mī·cāi′ah the son of Im′la quickly!"

9 The king of Israel and Je·hosh′a·phat king of Judah, clothed in *their* robes, sat each on his throne; and they sat at a threshing floor at the entrance of the gate of Samaria; and all the prophets prophesied before them.

10 Now Zed·e·kī′ah the son of Che·nā′a·nah had made horns of iron for himself; and he said, "Thus says the LORD: 'With these you shall gore the Syrians until they are destroyed.' "

11 And all the prophets prophesied so, saying, "Go up to Rā′moth Gil′ē·ad and prosper, for the LORD will deliver *it* into the king's hand."

12 Then the messenger who had gone to call Mī·cāi′ah spoke to him, saying, "Now listen, the words of the prophets with one accord encourage the king. Therefore please let your word be like *the word of* one of them, and speak encouragement."

13 And Mī·cāi′ah said, *"As* the LORD lives, whatever my God says, that I will speak."

14 Then he came to the king; and the king said to him, "Mī·cāi′ah, shall we go to war against Rā′moth Gil′ē·ad, or shall I refrain?" And he said, "Go and prosper, and they shall be delivered into your hand!"

15 So the king said to him, "How many times shall I make you swear

18:6 *a*Or *him*

that you tell me nothing but the truth in the name of the LORD?"

16 Then he said, "I saw all Israel scattered on the mountains, as sheep that have no shepherd. And the LORD said, 'These have no master. Let each return to his house in peace.' "

17 And the king of Israel said to Je·hosh'a·phat, "Did I not tell you he would not prophesy good concerning me, but evil?"

18 Then Mī·cāi'ah said, "Therefore hear the word of the LORD: I saw the LORD sitting on His throne, and all the host of heaven standing on His right hand and His left.

19 "And the LORD said, 'Who will persuade Ā'hab king of Israel to go up, that he may fall at Rā'moth Gil'ē·ad?' So one spoke in this manner, and another spoke in that manner.

20 "Then a spirit came forward and stood before the LORD, and said, 'I will persuade him.' The LORD said to him, 'In what way?'

21 "So he said, 'I will go out and be a lying spirit in the mouth of all his prophets.' And the LORD said, 'You shall persuade him and also prevail; go out and do so.'

22 "Therefore look! The LORD has put a lying spirit in the mouth of these prophets of yours, and the LORD has declared disaster against you."

23 Then Zed·e·kī'ah the son of Che·nā'a·nah went near and struck Mī·cāi'ah on the cheek, and said, "Which way did the spirit from the LORD go from me to speak to you?"

24 And Mī·cāi'ah said, "Indeed you shall see on that day when you go into an inner chamber to hide!"

25 Then the king of Israel said, "Take Mī·cāi'ah, and return him to Ā'mon the governor of the city and to Jō'ash the king's son;

26 "and say, 'Thus says the king: "Put this *fellow* in prison, and feed him with bread of affliction and water of affliction, until I return in peace." ' "

27 But Mī·cāi'ah said, "If you ever return in peace, the LORD has not spoken by me." And he said, "Take heed, all you people!"

AHAB DIES IN BATTLE

28 So the king of Israel and Je·hosh'a·phat the king of Judah went up to Rā'moth Gil'ē·ad.

29 And the king of Israel said to Je·hosh'a·phat, "I will disguise myself and go into battle; but you put on your robes." So the king of Israel disguised himself, and they went into battle.

30 Now the king of Syria had commanded the captains of the chariots who *were* with him, saying, "Fight with no one small or great, but only with the king of Israel."

31 So it was, when the captains of the chariots saw Je·hosh'a·phat, that they said, "It *is* the king of Israel!" Therefore they surrounded him to attack; but Je·hosh'a·phat cried out, and the LORD helped him, and God diverted them from him.

32 For so it was, when the captains of the chariots saw that it was not the king of Israel, that they turned back from pursuing him.

33 Now a certain man drew a bow at random, and struck the king of Israel between the joints of his armor. So he said to the driver of his chariot, "Turn around and take me out of the battle, for I am wounded."

34 The battle increased that day, and the king of Israel propped *himself* up in *his* chariot facing the Syrians until evening; and about the time of sunset he died.

19 Then Je·hosh'a·phat the king of Judah returned safely to his house in Jerusalem.

2 And Jē'hū the son of Ha·nā'nī the seer went out to meet him, and said to King Je·hosh'a·phat, "Should you help the wicked and love those who hate the LORD? Therefore the wrath of the LORD *is* upon you.

3 "Nevertheless good things are found in you, in that you have removed the wooden images from the land, and have prepared your heart to seek God."

THE REFORMS OF JEHOSHAPHAT

4 So Je·hosh'a·phat dwelt at Jerusalem; and he went out again among the people from Bē·er·shē'ba to the mountains of Ē'phra·im, and brought them back to the LORD God of their fathers.

5 Then he set judges in the land throughout all the fortified cities of Judah, city by city,

6 and said to the judges, "Take heed to what you are doing, for you do not judge for man but for the LORD, who *is* with you in the judgment.

7 "Now therefore, let the fear of the LORD be upon you; take care and do *it,* for *there is* no iniquity with the LORD our God, no partiality, nor taking of bribes."

8 Moreover in Jerusalem, for the judgment of the LORD and for controversies, Je·hosh'a·phat appointed some of the Lē'vītes and priests, and some of the chief fathers of Israel, when they returned to Jerusalem.*a*

9 And he commanded them, saying, "Thus you shall act in the fear of the LORD, faithfully and with a loyal heart:

10 "Whatever case comes to you from your brethren who dwell in their cities, whether of bloodshed or offenses against law or commandment, against statutes or ordinances, you shall warn them, lest they trespass against the LORD and wrath come upon you and your brethren. Do this, and you will not be guilty.

11 "And take notice: Am·a·rī'ah the chief priest *is* over you in all matters of the LORD; and Zeb·a·dī'ah the son of Ish'ma·el, the ruler of the house of Judah, for all the king's matters; also the Lē'vītes *will be* officials before you. Behave courageously, and the LORD will be with the good."

AMMON, MOAB, AND MOUNT SEIR DEFEATED

20 It happened after this *that* the people of Mō'ab with the people of Am'mon, and *others* with them besides the Am'mon·ītes,*a* came to battle against Je·hosh'a·phat.

2 Then some came and told Je·hosh'a·phat, saying, "A great multitude is coming against you from beyond the sea, from Syria;*a* and they are in Haz'a·zon Tā'mar" (which *is* En Ge'di).

3 And Je·hosh'a·phat feared, and set himself to seek the LORD, and proclaimed a fast throughout all Judah.

4 So Judah gathered together to ask *help* from the LORD; and from all the cities of Judah they came to seek the LORD.

5 Then Je·hosh'a·phat stood in the assembly of Judah and Jerusalem, in the house of the LORD, before the new court,

6 and said: "O LORD God of our fathers, *are* You not God in heaven, and do You *not* rule over all the kingdoms of the nations, and in Your hand *is*

19:8 *a*Septuagint and Vulgate read *for the inhabitants of Jerusalem.* 20:1 *a*Following Masoretic Text and Vulgate; Septuagint reads *Meunites* (compare 26:7). 20:2 *a*Following Masoretic Text, Septuagint, and Vulgate; some Hebrew manuscripts and Old Latin read *Edom.*

there not power and might, so that no one is able to withstand You?

7 "*Are* You not our God, *who* drove out the inhabitants of this land before Your people Israel, and gave it to the descendants of Abraham Your friend forever?

8 "And they dwell in it, and have built You a sanctuary in it for Your name, saying,

9 'If disaster comes upon us—sword, judgment, pestilence, or famine—we will stand before this temple and in Your presence (for Your name *is* in this temple), and cry out to You in our affliction, and You will hear and save.'

10 "And now, here are the people of Am′mon, Mō′ab, and Mount Sē′ir—whom You would not let Israel invade when they came out of the land of Egypt, but they turned from them and did not destroy them—

11 "here they are, rewarding us by coming to throw us out of Your possession which You have given us to inherit.

12 "O our God, will You not judge them? For we have no power against this great multitude that is coming against us; nor do we know what to do, but our eyes *are* upon You."

13 Now all Judah, with their little ones, their wives, and their children, stood before the LORD.

14 Then the Spirit of the LORD came upon Ja·hā′zi·el the son of Zech·a·rī′ah, the son of Be·nā′i·ah, the son of Je·ī′el, the son of Mat·ta·nī′ah, a Lē′vite of the sons of Ā′saph, in the midst of the assembly.

15 And he said, "Listen, all you of Judah and you inhabitants of Jerusalem, and you, King Je·hosh′a·phat! Thus says the LORD to you: 'Do not be afraid nor dismayed because of this great multitude, for the battle *is* not yours, but God's.

16 'Tomorrow go down against them. They will surely come up by the Ascent of Ziz, and you will find them at the end of the brook before the Wilderness of Je·rū′el.

17 'You will not *need* to fight in this *battle*. Position yourselves, stand still and see the salvation of the LORD, who is with you, O Judah and Jerusalem!' Do not fear or be dismayed; tomorrow go out against them, for the LORD *is* with you."

18 And Je·hosh′a·phat bowed his head with *his* face to the ground, and all Judah and the inhabitants of Jerusalem bowed before the LORD, worshiping the LORD.

19 Then the Lē′vites of the children of the Kō′hath·ites and of the children of the Kō′ra·hītes stood up to praise the LORD God of Israel with voices loud and high.

20 So they rose early in the morning and went out into the Wilderness of Te·kō′a; and as they went out, Je·hosh′a·phat stood and said, "Hear me, O Judah and you inhabitants of Jerusalem: Believe in the LORD your God, and you shall be established; believe His prophets, and you shall prosper."

Praises

2 Chronicles 20:21

Who ever heard of praise as a weapon in war? Jehoshaphat did! Faced with the ugliness of war and death, he appointed people to praise God. They were even to praise the beauty of God's holiness. God used their praise as a weapon of war, to help them win. Are you fighting some battles? Are you struggling with something? Try praising God! Praise the beauty of God's holiness.

21 And when he had consulted with the people, he appointed those who should sing to the LORD, and who should praise the beauty of holiness, as they went out before the army and were saying:

"Praise the LORD,
For His mercy *endures* forever."*a*

22 Now when they began to sing and to praise, the LORD set ambushes against the people of Am′mon, Mō′ab, and Mount Sē′ir, who had come against Judah; and they were defeated.
23 For the people of Am′mon and Mō′ab stood up against the inhabitants of Mount Sē′ir to utterly kill and destroy *them*. And when they had made an end of the inhabitants of Sē′ir, they helped to destroy one another.
24 So when Judah came to a place overlooking the wilderness, they looked toward the multitude; and there *were* their dead bodies, fallen on the earth. No one had escaped.
25 When Je·hosh′a·phat and his people came to take away their spoil, they found among them an abundance of valuables on the dead bodies,*a* and precious jewelry, which they stripped off for themselves, more than they could carry away; and they were three days gathering the spoil because there was so much.
26 And on the fourth day they assembled in the Valley of Ber′a·chah, for there they blessed the LORD; therefore the name of that place was called The Valley of Ber′a·chah*a* until this day.
27 Then they returned, every man of Judah and Jerusalem, with Je·hosh′a·phat in front of them, to go back to Jerusalem with joy, for the LORD had made them rejoice over their enemies.

28 So they came to Jerusalem, with stringed instruments and harps and trumpets, to the house of the LORD.
29 And the fear of God was on all the kingdoms of *those* countries when they heard that the LORD had fought against the enemies of Israel.
30 Then the realm of Je·hosh′a·phat was quiet, for his God gave him rest all around.

THE END OF JEHOSHAPHAT'S REIGN

31 So Je·hosh′a·phat was king over Judah. *He was* thirty-five years old when he became king, and he reigned twenty-five years in Jerusalem. His mother's name *was* A·zū′bah the daughter of Shil′hī.
32 And he walked in the way of his father Ā′sa, and did not turn aside from it, doing *what was* right in the sight of the LORD.
33 Nevertheless the high places were not taken away, for as yet the people had not directed their hearts to the God of their fathers.
34 Now the rest of the acts of Je·hosh′a·phat, first and last, indeed they *are* written in the book of Jē′hū the son of Ha·nā′nī, which *is* mentioned in the book of the kings of Israel.
35 After this Je·hosh′a·phat king of Judah allied himself with Ā·ha·zī′ah king of Israel, who acted very wickedly.
36 And he allied himself with him to make ships to go to Tar′shish, and they made the ships in Ē′zi·on Gē′-ber.
37 But El·i·ē′zer the son of Dō′da·vah of Ma·rē′shah prophesied against Je·hosh′a·phat, saying, "Because you

20:21 *a*Compare Psalm 106:1   20:25 *a*A few Hebrew manuscripts, Old Latin, and Vulgate read *garments*; Septuagint reads *armor*.   20:26 *a*Literally *Blessing*

have allied yourself with Ā·ha·zī'ah, the LORD has destroyed your works." Then the ships were wrecked, so that they were not able to go to Tar'shish.

JEHORAM REIGNS IN JUDAH

21 And Je·hosh'a·phat rested with his fathers, and was buried with his fathers in the City of David. Then Je·hō'ram his son reigned in his place.
2 He had brothers, the sons of Je·hosh'a·phat: Az·a·rī'ah, Je·hī'el, Zech·a·rī'ah, Az'ar·ya·hu, Michael, and Sheph·a·tī'ah; all these *were* the sons of Je·hosh'a·phat king of Israel.
3 Their father gave them great gifts of silver and gold and precious things, with fortified cities in Judah; but he gave the kingdom to Je·hō'ram, because he *was* the firstborn.
4 Now when Je·hō'ram was established over the kingdom of his father, he strengthened himself and killed all his brothers with the sword, and also *others* of the princes of Israel.
5 Je·hō'ram *was* thirty-two years old when he became king, and he reigned eight years in Jerusalem.
6 And he walked in the way of the kings of Israel, just as the house of Ā'hab had done, for he had the daughter of Ā'hab as a wife; and he did evil in the sight of the LORD.
7 Yet the LORD would not destroy the house of David, because of the covenant that He had made with David, and since He had promised to give a lamp to him and to his sons forever.
8 In his days Ē'dom revolted against Judah's authority, and made a king over themselves.
9 So Je·hō'ram went out with his officers, and all his chariots with him. And he rose by night and at-tacked the Ē'dom·ites who had sur-rounded him and the captains of the chariots.
10 Thus Ē'dom has been in revolt against Judah's authority to this day. At that time Lib'nah revolted against his rule, because he had forsaken the LORD God of his fathers.
11 Moreover he made high places in the mountains of Judah, and caused the inhabitants of Jerusalem to commit harlotry, and led Judah astray.
12 And a letter came to him from E·lī'jah the prophet, saying,

Thus says the LORD God of your father David:
Because you have not walked in the ways of Je·hosh'a·phat your father, or in the ways of Ā'sa king of Judah,
13 but have walked in the way of the kings of Israel, and have made Judah and the inhabitants of Jerusalem to play the harlot like the harlotry of the house of Ā'hab, and also have killed your brothers, those of your father's household, *who were* better than yourself,
14 behold, the LORD will strike your people with a serious affliction— your children, your wives, and all your possessions;
15 and you *will become* very sick with a disease of your intestines, until your intestines come out by reason of the sickness, day by day.

16 Moreover the LORD stirred up against Je·hō'ram the spirit of the Phi·lis'tines and the Arabians who *were* near the Ethiopians.
17 And they came up into Judah and invaded it, and carried away all the possessions that were found in the king's house, and also his sons and his wives, so that there was not a son

left to him except Je·hō′a·haz,a the youngest of his sons.

18 After all this the LORD struck him in his intestines with an incurable disease.

19 Then it happened in the course of time, after the end of two years, that his intestines came out because of his sickness; so he died in severe pain. And his people made no burning for him, like the burning for his fathers.

20 He was thirty-two years old when he became king. He reigned in Jerusalem eight years and, to no one's sorrow, departed. However they buried him in the City of David, but not in the tombs of the kings.

AHAZIAH REIGNS IN JUDAH

22 Then the inhabitants of Jerusalem made Ā·ha·zī′ah his youngest son king in his place, for the raiders who came with the Arabians into the camp had killed all the older *sons.* So Ā·ha·zī′ah the son of Je·hō′ram, king of Judah, reigned.

2 Ā·ha·zī′ah *was* forty-twoa years old when he became king, and he reigned one year in Jerusalem. His mother's name *was* Ath·a·lī′ah the granddaughter of Om′rī.

3 He also walked in the ways of the house of Ā′hab, for his mother advised him to do wickedly.

4 Therefore he did evil in the sight of the LORD, like the house of Ā′hab; for they were his counselors after the death of his father, to his destruction.

5 He also followed their advice, and went with Je·hō′rama the son of Ā′hab king of Israel to war against Haz′a·el king of Syria at Rā′moth Gil′ē·ad; and the Syrians wounded Jō′ram.

6 Then he returned to Jez′rē·el to recover from the wounds which he had received at Rā′mah, when he

fought against Haz′a·el king of Syria. And Az·a·rī′aha the son of Je·hō′ram, king of Judah, went down to see Je·hō′ram the son of Ā′hab in Jez′rē·el, because he was sick.

7 His going to Jō′ram was God's occasion for Ā·ha·zī′ah's downfall; for when he arrived, he went out with Je·hō′ram against Jē′hu the son of Nim′shī, whom the LORD had anointed to cut off the house of Ā′hab.

8 And it happened, when Jē′hu was executing judgment on the house of Ā′hab, and found the princes of Judah and the sons of Ā·ha·zī′ah's brothers who served Ā·ha·zī′ah, that he killed them.

9 Then he searched for Ā·ha·zī′ah; and they caught him (he was hiding in Samaria), and brought him to Jē′hu. When they had killed him, they buried him, "because," they said, "he is the son of Je·hosh′a·phat, who sought the LORD with all his heart." So the house of Ā·ha·zī′ah had no one to assume power over the kingdom.

ATHALIAH REIGNS IN JUDAH

10 Now when Ath·a·lī′ah the mother of Ā·ha·zī′ah saw that her son was dead, she arose and destroyed all the royal heirs of the house of Judah.

11 But Jē·hō·shab′e·ath,a the daughter of the king, took Jō′ash the son of Ā·ha·zī′ah, and stole him away from among the king's sons who were being murdered, and put him and his nurse in a bedroom. So Jē·hō·shab′e·ath, the daughter of King Je·hō′ram, the wife of Je·hoi′a·da the priest

21:17 aElsewhere called *Ahaziah* (compare 2 Chronicles 22:1)   22:2 aOr *twenty-two* (compare 2 Kings 8:26)   22:5 aAlso spelled *Joram* (compare verses 5 and 7; 2 Kings 8:28; and elsewhere)   22:6 aSome Hebrew manuscripts, Septuagint, Syriac, Vulgate, and 2 Kings 8:29 read *Ahaziah.*   22:11 aSpelled *Jehosheba* in 2 Kings 11:2

(for she was the sister of Ā·ha·zī′ah), hid him from Ath·a·lī′ah so that she did not kill him.

12 And he was hidden with them in the house of God for six years, while Ath·a·lī′ah reigned over the land.

JOASH CROWNED KING OF JUDAH

23 In the seventh year Je·hoi′a·da strengthened himself, *and made a* covenant with the captains of hundreds: Az·a·rī′ah the son of Je·rō′-ham, Ish′ma·el the son of Jē·hō·hā′-nan, Az·a·rī′ah the son of Ō′bed, Mā·a·sēi′ah the son of A·dāi′ah, and El·i·shā′phat the son of Zich′rī.

2 And they went throughout Judah and gathered the Lē′vītes from all the cities of Judah, and the chief fathers of Israel, and they came to Jerusalem.

3 Then all the assembly made a covenant with the king in the house of God. And he said to them, "Behold, the king's son shall reign, as the LORD has said of the sons of David.

4 "This *is* what you shall do: One-third of you entering on the Sabbath, of the priests and the Lē′vītes, *shall be* keeping watch over the doors;

5 "one-third *shall be* at the king's house; and one-third at the Gate of the Foundation. All the people *shall be* in the courts of the house of the LORD.

6 "But let no one come into the house of the LORD except the priests and those of the Lē′vītes who serve. They may go in, for they *are* holy; but all the people shall keep the watch of the LORD.

7 "And the Lē′vītes shall surround the king on all sides, every man with his weapons in his hand; and whoever comes into the house, let him be put to death. You are to be with the king when he comes in and when he goes out."

8 So the Lē′vītes and all Judah did according to all that Je·hoi′a·da the priest commanded. And each man took his men who were to be on duty on the Sabbath, with those who were going *off duty* on the Sabbath; for Je·hoi′a·da the priest had not dismissed the divisions.

9 And Je·hoi′a·da the priest gave to the captains of hundreds the spears and the large and small shields which *had belonged* to King David, that *were* in the temple of God.

10 Then he set all the people, every man with his weapon in his hand, from the right side of the temple to the left side of the temple, along by the altar and by the temple, all around the king.

11 And they brought out the king's son, put the crown on him, *gave him* the Testimony,*a* and made him king. Then Je·hoi′a·da and his sons anointed him, and said, "*Long* live the king!"

DEATH OF ATHALIAH

12 Now when Ath·a·lī′ah heard the noise of the people running and praising the king, she came to the people *in* the temple of the LORD.

13 When she looked, there was the king standing by his pillar at the entrance; and the leaders and the trumpeters *were* by the king. All the people of the land were rejoicing and blowing trumpets, also the singers with musical instruments, and those who led in praise. So Ath·a·lī′ah tore her clothes and said, "Treason! Treason!"

14 And Je·hoi′a·da the priest brought out the captains of hundreds who were set over the army, and said to them, "Take her outside under guard,

23:11 *a*That is, the Law (compare Exodus 25:16, 21; 31:18)

and slay with the sword whoever follows her." For the priest had said, "Do not kill her in the house of the LORD."

15 So they seized her; and she went by way of the entrance of the Horse Gate *into* the king's house, and they killed her there.

16 Then Je·hoi′a·da made a covenant between himself, the people, and the king, that they should be the LORD's people.

17 And all the people went to the temple*a* of Bā′al, and tore it down. They broke in pieces its altars and images, and killed Mat′tan the priest of Bā′al before the altars.

18 Also Je·hoi′a·da appointed the oversight of the house of the LORD to the hand of the priests, the Lē′vites, whom David had assigned in the house of the LORD, to offer the burnt offerings of the LORD, as *it is* written in the Law of Moses, with rejoicing and with singing, *as it was established* by David.

19 And he set the gatekeepers at the gates of the house of the LORD, so that no one *who was* in any way unclean should enter.

20 Then he took the captains of hundreds, the nobles, the governors of the people, and all the people of the land, and brought the king down from the house of the LORD; and they went through the Upper Gate to the king's house, and set the king on the throne of the kingdom.

21 So all the people of the land rejoiced; and the city was quiet, for they had slain Ath·a·lī′ah with the sword.

JOASH REPAIRS THE TEMPLE

24 Jō′ash *was* seven years old when he became king, and he reigned forty years in Jerusalem. His mother's name *was* Zib′i·ah of Bē·er·shē′ba.

2 Jō′ash did *what was* right in the sight of the LORD all the days of Je·hoi′a·da the priest.

3 And Je·hoi′a·da took two wives for him, and he had sons and daughters.

4 Now it happened after this *that* Jō′ash set his heart on repairing the house of the LORD.

5 Then he gathered the priests and the Lē′vites, and said to them, "Go out to the cities of Judah, and gather from all Israel money to repair the house of your God from year to year, and see that you do it quickly." However the Lē′vites did not do it quickly.

6 So the king called Je·hoi′a·da the chief *priest,* and said to him, "Why have you not required the Lē′vites to bring in from Judah and from Jerusalem the collection, *according to the commandment* of Moses the servant of the LORD and of the assembly of Israel, for the tabernacle of witness?"

7 For the sons of Ath·a·lī′ah, that wicked woman, had broken into the house of God, and had also presented all the dedicated things of the house of the LORD to the Bā′als.

8 Then at the king's command they made a chest, and set it outside at the gate of the house of the LORD.

9 And they made a proclamation throughout Judah and Jerusalem to bring to the LORD the collection *that* Moses the servant of God *had imposed* on Israel in the wilderness.

10 Then all the leaders and all the people rejoiced, brought their contributions, and put *them* into the chest until all had given.

11 So it was, at that time, when the chest was brought to the king's official by the hand of the Lē′vites, and when they saw that *there was* much

23:17 *a*Literally *house*

money, that the king's scribe and the high priest's officer came and emptied the chest, and took it and returned it to its place. Thus they did day by day, and gathered money in abundance.

12 The king and Je·hoi′a·da gave it to those who did the work of the service of the house of the LORD; and they hired masons and carpenters to repair the house of the LORD, and also those who worked in iron and bronze to restore the house of the LORD.

13 So the workmen labored, and the work was completed by them; they restored the house of God to its original condition and reinforced it.

14 When they had finished, they brought the rest of the money before the king and Je·hoi′a·da; they made from it articles for the house of the LORD, articles for serving and offering, spoons and vessels of gold and silver. And they offered burnt offerings in the house of the LORD continually all the days of Je·hoi′a·da.

APOSTASY OF JOASH

15 But Je·hoi′a·da grew old and was full of days, and he died; *he was* one hundred and thirty years old when he died.

16 And they buried him in the City of David among the kings, because he had done good in Israel, both toward God and His house.

17 Now after the death of Je·hoi′a·da the leaders of Judah came and bowed down to the king. And the king listened to them.

18 Therefore they left the house of the LORD God of their fathers, and served wooden images and idols; and wrath came upon Judah and Jerusalem because of their trespass.

19 Yet He sent prophets to them, to bring them back to the LORD; and they testified against them, but they would not listen.

20 Then the Spirit of God came upon Zech·a·rī′ah the son of Je·hoi′a·da the priest, who stood above the people, and said to them, "Thus says God: 'Why do you transgress the commandments of the LORD, so that you cannot prosper? Because you have forsaken the LORD, He also has forsaken you.' "

21 So they conspired against him, and at the command of the king they stoned him with stones in the court of the house of the LORD.

22 Thus Jō′ash the king did not remember the kindness which Je·hoi′a·da his father had done to him, but killed his son; and as he died, he said, "The LORD look on *it,* and repay!"

DEATH OF JOASH

23 So it happened in the spring of the year *that* the army of Syria came up against him; and they came to Judah and Jerusalem, and destroyed all the leaders of the people from among the people, and sent all their spoil to the king of Damascus.

24 For the army of the Syrians came with a small company of men; but the LORD delivered a very great army into their hand, because they had forsaken the LORD God of their fathers. So they executed judgment against Jō′ash.

25 And when they had withdrawn from him (for they left him severely wounded), his own servants conspired against him because of the blood of the sons[a] of Je·hoi′a·da the priest, and killed him on his bed. So he died. And they buried him in the City of David, but they did not bury him in the tombs of the kings.

24:25 [a]Septuagint and Vulgate read *son* (compare verses 20–22).

26 These are the ones who conspired against him: Zā′bad*a* the son of Shim′ē·ath the Am′mon·ī·tess, and Je·hō′za·bad the son of Shim′rith*b* the Mō′ab·ī·tess.

27 Now *concerning* his sons, and the many oracles about him, and the repairing of the house of God, indeed they *are* written in the annals of the book of the kings. Then Am·a·zī′ah his son reigned in his place.

AMAZIAH REIGNS IN JUDAH

25 Am·a·zī′ah *was* twenty-five years old *when* he became king, and he reigned twenty-nine years in Jerusalem. His mother's name *was* Jē·hō·ad′dan of Jerusalem.
2 And he did *what was* right in the sight of the LORD, but not with a loyal heart.
3 Now it happened, as soon as the kingdom was established for him, that he executed his servants who had murdered his father the king.
4 However he did not execute their children, but *did* as *it is* written in the Law in the Book of Moses, where the LORD commanded, saying, "The fathers shall not be put to death for their children, nor shall the children be put to death for their fathers; but a person shall die for his own sin."*a*

THE WAR AGAINST EDOM

5 Moreover Am·a·zī′ah gathered Judah together and set over them captains of thousands and captains of hundreds, according to *their* fathers' houses, throughout all Judah and Benjamin; and he numbered them from twenty years old and above, and found them to be three hundred thousand choice *men, able* to go to war, who could handle spear and shield.
6 He also hired one hundred thousand mighty men of valor from Israel for one hundred talents of silver.
7 But a man of God came to him, saying, "O king, do not let the army of Israel go with you, for the LORD *is* not with Israel—*not with* any of the children of Ē′phra·im.
8 "But if you go, be gone! Be strong in battle! *Even so,* God shall make you fall before the enemy; for God has power to help and to overthrow."
9 Then Am·a·zī′ah said to the man of God, "But what *shall we* do about the hundred talents which I have given to the troops of Israel?" And the man of God answered, "The LORD is able to give you much more than this."
10 So Am·a·zī′ah discharged the troops that had come to him from Ē′phra·im, to go back home. Therefore their anger was greatly aroused against Judah, and they returned home in great anger.
11 Then Am·a·zī′ah strengthened himself, and leading his people, he went to the Valley of Salt and killed ten thousand of the people of Sē′ir.
12 Also the children of Judah took captive ten thousand alive, brought them to the top of the rock, and cast them down from the top of the rock, so that they all were dashed in pieces.
13 But as for the soldiers of the army which Am·a·zī′ah had discharged, so that they would not go with him to battle, they raided the cities of Judah from Samaria to Beth Hor′on, killed three thousand in them, and took much spoil.
14 Now it was so, after Am·a·zī′ah came from the slaughter of the Ē′dom·ītes, that he brought the gods of the people of Sē′ir, set them up *to*

24:26 *a*Or *Jozachar* (compare 2 Kings 12:21)   *b*Or *Shomer* (compare 2 Kings 12:21)
25:4 *a*Deuteronomy 24:16

be his gods, and bowed down before them and burned incense to them.

15 Therefore the anger of the LORD was aroused against Am·a·zī'ah, and He sent him a prophet who said to him, "Why have you sought the gods of the people, which could not rescue their own people from your hand?"

16 So it was, as he talked with him, that *the king* said to him, "Have we made you the king's counselor? Cease! Why should you be killed?" Then the prophet ceased, and said, "I know that God has determined to destroy you, because you have done this and have not heeded my advice."

ISRAEL DEFEATS JUDAH

17 Now Am·a·zī'ah king of Judah asked advice and sent to Jō'ash[a] the son of Je·hō'a·haz, the son of Jē'hū, king of Israel, saying, "Come, let us face one another *in battle*."

18 And Jō'ash king of Israel sent to Am·a·zī'ah king of Judah, saying, "The thistle that *was* in Lebanon sent to the cedar that was in Lebanon, saying, 'Give your daughter to my son as wife'; and a wild beast that *was* in Lebanon passed by and trampled the thistle.

19 "Indeed you say that you have defeated the Ē'dom·ītes, and your heart is lifted up to boast. Stay at home now; why should you meddle with trouble, that you should fall—you and Judah with you?"

20 But Am·a·zī'ah would not heed, for it *came* from God, that He might give them into the hand *of their enemies,* because they sought the gods of Ē'dom.

21 So Jō'ash king of Israel went out; and he and Am·a·zī'ah king of Judah faced one another at Beth Shem'esh, which *belongs* to Judah.

22 And Judah was defeated by Israel, and every man fled to his tent.

23 Then Jō'ash the king of Israel captured Am·a·zī'ah king of Judah, the son of Jō'ash, the son of Je·hō'a·haz, at Beth Shem'esh; and he brought him to Jerusalem, and broke down the wall of Jerusalem from the Gate of Ē'phra·im to the Corner Gate—four hundred cubits.

24 And *he took* all the gold and silver, all the articles that were found in the house of God with Ō'bed-Ē'dom, the treasures of the king's house, and hostages, and returned to Samaria.

DEATH OF AMAZIAH

25 Am·a·zī'ah the son of Jō'ash, king of Judah, lived fifteen years after the death of Jō'ash the son of Je·hō'a·haz, king of Israel.

26 Now the rest of the acts of Am·a·zī'ah, from first to last, indeed *are* they not written in the book of the kings of Judah and Israel?

27 After the time that Am·a·zī'ah turned away from following the LORD, they made a conspiracy against him in Jerusalem, and he fled to Lā'chish; but they sent after him to Lā'chish and killed him there.

28 Then they brought him on horses and buried him with his fathers in the City of Judah.

UZZIAH REIGNS IN JUDAH

26 Now all the people of Judah took Uz·zī'ah,[a] who *was* sixteen years old, and made him king instead of his father Am·a·zī'ah.

2 He built Ē'lath[a] and restored it to Judah, after the king rested with his fathers.

3 Uz·zī'ah *was* sixteen years old

25:17 [a]Spelled *Jehoash* in 2 Kings 14:8ff
26:1 [a]Called *Azariah* in 2 Kings 14:21ff
26:2 [a]Hebrew *Eloth*

when he became king, and he reigned fifty-two years in Jerusalem. His mother's name was Jech·o·lī'ah of Jerusalem.

4 And he did *what was* right in the sight of the LORD, according to all that his father Am·a·zī'ah had done.

5 He sought God in the days of Zech·a·rī'ah, who had understanding in the visions[a] of God; and as long as he sought the LORD, God made him prosper.

6 Now he went out and made war against the Phi·lis'tines, and broke down the wall of Gath, the wall of Jab'neh, and the wall of Ash'dod; and he built cities *around* Ash'dod and among the Phi·lis'tines.

7 God helped him against the Phi·lis'tines, against the Arabians who lived in Gur Bā'al, and against the Me·ū'nītes.

8 Also the Am'mon·ītes brought tribute to Uz·zī'ah. His fame spread as far as the entrance of Egypt, for he became exceedingly strong.

9 And Uz·zī'ah built towers in Jerusalem at the Corner Gate, at the Valley Gate, and at the corner buttress of the wall; then he fortified them.

10 Also he built towers in the desert. He dug many wells, for he had much livestock, both in the lowlands and in the plains; *he also had* farmers and vinedressers in the mountains and in Car'mel, for he loved the soil.

11 Moreover Uz·zī'ah had an army of fighting men who went out to war by companies, according to the number on their roll as prepared by Je·ī'el the scribe and Mā·a·sēi'ah the officer, under the hand of Han·a·nī'ah, *one of* the king's captains.

12 The total number of chief officers[a] of the mighty men of valor *was* two thousand six hundred.

13 And under their authority *was* an army of three hundred and seven thousand five hundred, that made

war with mighty power, to help the king against the enemy.

14 Then Uz·zī'ah prepared for them, for the entire army, shields, spears, helmets, body armor, bows, and slings *to cast* stones.

15 And he made devices in Jerusalem, invented by skillful men, to be on the towers and the corners, to shoot arrows and large stones. So his fame spread far and wide, for he was marvelously helped till he became strong.

THE PENALTY FOR UZZIAH'S PRIDE

16 But when he was strong his heart was lifted up, to *his* destruction, for he transgressed against the LORD his God by entering the temple of the LORD to burn incense on the altar of incense.

17 So Az·a·rī'ah the priest went in after him, and with him were eighty priests of the LORD—valiant men.

18 And they withstood King Uz·zī'ah, and said to him, "*It is* not for you, Uz·zī'ah, to burn incense to the LORD, but for the priests, the sons of Aaron, who are consecrated to burn incense. Get out of the sanctuary, for you have trespassed! You *shall have* no honor from the LORD God."

19 Then Uz·zī'ah became furious; and he *had* a censer in his hand to burn incense. And while he was angry with the priests, leprosy broke out on his forehead, before the priests in the house of the LORD, beside the incense altar.

20 And Az·a·rī'ah the chief priest and all the priests looked at him, and there, on his forehead, he *was* leprous; so they thrust him out of that place. Indeed he also hurried to get

26:5 [a]Several Hebrew manuscripts, Septuagint, Syriac, Targum, and Arabic read *fear*.
26:12 [a]Literally *chief fathers*

out, because the LORD had struck him.

21 King Uz·zī'ah was a leper until the day of his death. He dwelt in an isolated house, because he was a leper; for he was cut off from the house of the LORD. Then Jō'tham his son *was* over the king's house, judging the people of the land.

22 Now the rest of the acts of Uz·zī'ah, from first to last, the prophet Ī·sāi'ah the son of Ā'moz wrote.

23 So Uz·zī'ah rested with his fathers, and they buried him with his fathers in the field of burial which *belonged* to the kings, for they said, "He is a leper." Then Jō'tham his son reigned in his place.

JOTHAM REIGNS IN JUDAH

27 Jō'tham *was* twenty-five years old when he became king, and he reigned sixteen years in Jerusalem. His mother's name *was* Je·rū'shah[a] the daughter of Zā'dok.

2 And he did *what was* right in the sight of the LORD, according to all that his father Uz·zī'ah had done (although he did not enter the temple of the LORD). But still the people acted corruptly.

3 He built the Upper Gate of the house of the LORD, and he built extensively on the wall of Ō'phel.

4 Moreover he built cities in the mountains of Judah, and in the forests he built fortresses and towers.

5 He also fought with the king of the Am'mon·ītes and defeated them. And the people of Am'mon gave him in that year one hundred talents of silver, ten thousand kors of wheat, and ten thousand of barley. The people of Am'mon paid this to him in the second and third years also.

6 So Jō'tham became mighty, be-

cause he prepared his ways before the LORD his God.

7 Now the rest of the acts of Jō'tham, and all his wars and his ways, indeed they *are* written in the book of the kings of Israel and Judah.

8 He was twenty-five years old when he became king, and he reigned sixteen years in Jerusalem.

9 So Jō'tham rested with his fathers, and they buried him in the City of David. Then Ā'haz his son reigned in his place.

AHAZ REIGNS IN JUDAH

28 Ā'haz *was* twenty years old when he became king, and he reigned sixteen years in Jerusalem; and he did not do *what was* right in the sight of the LORD, as his father David *had done.*

2 For he walked in the ways of the kings of Israel, and made molded images for the Bā'als.

3 He burned incense in the Valley of the Son of Hin'nom, and burned his children in the fire, according to the abominations of the nations whom the LORD had cast out before the children of Israel.

4 And he sacrificed and burned incense on the high places, on the hills, and under every green tree.

SYRIA AND ISRAEL DEFEAT JUDAH

5 Therefore the LORD his God delivered him into the hand of the king of Syria. They defeated him, and carried away a great multitude of them as captives, and brought *them* to Damascus. Then he was also delivered into the hand of the king of Israel, who defeated him with a great slaughter.

27:1 [a]Spelled *Jerusha* in 2 Kings 15:33

6 For Pē'kah the son of Rem·a·lī'ah killed one hundred and twenty thousand in Judah in one day, all valiant men, because they had forsaken the LORD God of their fathers.

7 Zich'rī, a mighty man of Ē'phra·im, killed Mā·a·sēi'ah the king's son, Az·rī'kam the officer over the house, and El·kā'nah *who was* second to the king.

8 And the children of Israel carried away captive of their brethren two hundred thousand women, sons, and daughters; and they also took away much spoil from them, and brought the spoil to Samaria.

ISRAEL RETURNS THE CAPTIVES

9 But a prophet of the LORD was there, whose name *was* Ō'ded; and he went out before the army that came to Samaria, and said to them: "Look, because the LORD God of your fathers was angry with Judah, He has delivered them into your hand; but you have killed them in a rage *that* reaches up to heaven.

10 "And now you propose to force the children of Judah and Jerusalem to be your male and female slaves; *but are* you not also guilty before the LORD your God?

11 "Now hear me, therefore, and return the captives, whom you have taken captive from your brethren, for the fierce wrath of the LORD *is* upon you."

12 Then some of the heads of the children of Ē'phra·im, Az·a·rī'ah the son of Jō·hā'nan, Ber·e·chī'ah the son of Me·shil'le·moth, Jē·hiz·kī'ah the son of Shal'lum, and A·mā'sa the son of Had'laī, stood up against those who came from the war,

13 and said to them, "You shall not bring the captives here, for we *already* have offended the LORD. You intend to add to our sins and to our

guilt; for our guilt is great, and *there is* fierce wrath against Israel."

14 So the armed men left the captives and the spoil before the leaders and all the assembly.

15 Then the men who were designated by name rose up and took the captives, and from the spoil they clothed all who were naked among them, dressed them and gave them sandals, gave them food and drink, and anointed them; and they let all the feeble ones ride on donkeys. So they brought them to their brethren at Jericho, the city of palm trees. Then they returned to Samaria.

ASSYRIA REFUSES TO HELP JUDAH

16 At the same time King Ā'haz sent to the kings[a] of Assyria to help him.

17 For again the Ē'dom·ītes had come, attacked Judah, and carried away captives.

18 The Phi·lis'tines also had invaded the cities of the lowland and of the South of Judah, and had taken Beth Shem'esh, Aī'ja·lon, Ge·dē'roth, Sō'chōh with its villages, Tim'nah with its villages, and Gim'zō with its villages; and they dwelt there.

19 For the LORD brought Judah low because of Ā'haz king of Israel, for he had encouraged moral decline in Judah and had been continually unfaithful to the LORD.

20 Also Tig'lath-Pī·lē'ser[a] king of Assyria came to him and distressed him, and did not assist him.

21 For Ā'haz took part *of the treasures* from the house of the LORD, from the house of the king, and from the leaders, and he gave *it* to the king of Assyria; but he did not help him.

28:16 [a]Septuagint, Syriac, and Vulgate read *king* (compare verse 20).   28:20 [a]Hebrew *Tilgath-Pilneser*

APOSTASY AND DEATH OF AHAZ

22 Now in the time of his distress King Ā′haz became increasingly unfaithful to the LORD. This *is that* King Ā′haz.
23 For he sacrificed to the gods of Damascus which had defeated him, saying, "Because the gods of the kings of Syria help them, I will sacrifice to them that they may help me." But they were the ruin of him and of all Israel.
24 So Ā′haz gathered the articles of the house of God, cut in pieces the articles of the house of God, shut up the doors of the house of the LORD, and made for himself altars in every corner of Jerusalem.
25 And in every single city of Judah he made high places to burn incense to other gods, and provoked to anger the LORD God of his fathers.
26 Now the rest of his acts and all his ways, from first to last, indeed they *are* written in the book of the kings of Judah and Israel.
27 So Ā′haz rested with his fathers, and they buried him in the city, in Jerusalem; but they did not bring him into the tombs of the kings of Israel. Then Hez·e·kī′ah his son reigned in his place.

HEZEKIAH REIGNS IN JUDAH

29 Hez·e·kī′ah became king *when he was* twenty-five years old, and he reigned twenty-nine years in Jerusalem. His mother's name *was* A·bī′jah*ᵃ* the daughter of Zech·a·rī′ah.
2 And he did *what was* right in the sight of the LORD, according to all that his father David had done.

HEZEKIAH CLEANSES THE TEMPLE

3 In the first year of his reign, in the first month, he opened the doors of the house of the LORD and repaired them.
4 Then he brought in the priests and the Lē′vītes, and gathered them in the East Square,
5 and said to them: "Hear me, Lē′vītes! Now sanctify yourselves, sanctify the house of the LORD God of your fathers, and carry out the rubbish from the holy *place*.
6 "For our fathers have trespassed and done evil in the eyes of the LORD our God; they have forsaken Him, have turned their faces away from the dwelling place of the LORD, and turned *their* backs *on Him*.
7 "They have also shut up the doors of the vestibule, put out the lamps, and have not burned incense or offered burnt offerings in the holy *place* to the God of Israel.
8 "Therefore the wrath of the LORD fell upon Judah and Jerusalem, and He has given them up to trouble, to desolation, and to jeering, as you see with your eyes.
9 "For indeed, because of this our fathers have fallen by the sword; and our sons, our daughters, and our wives *are* in captivity.
10 "Now *it is* in my heart to make a covenant with the LORD God of Israel, that His fierce wrath may turn away from us.
11 "My sons, do not be negligent now, for the LORD has chosen you to stand before Him, to serve Him, and that you should minister to Him and burn incense."
12 Then these Lē′vītes arose: Mā′hath the son of A·mā′saī and Jō′el the son of Az·a·rī′ah, of the sons of the Kō′hath·ītes; of the sons of Me·rar′ī, Kish the son of Ab′dī and Az·a·rī′ah the son of Je·hal′le·lel; of the Ger′shon·ītes, Jō′ah the son of Zim′mah and Eden the son of Jō′ah;

29:1 *ᵃ*Spelled *Abi* in 2 Kings 18:2

13 of the sons of E·li·zā′phan, Shim′rī and Je·ī′el; of the sons of Ā′saph, Zech·a·rī′ah and Mat·ta·nī′ah;

14 of the sons of Hē′man, Je·hī′el and Shim′ē·ī; and of the sons of Je·dū′thun, She·māi′ah and Uz′zi·el.

15 And they gathered their brethren, sanctified themselves, and went according to the commandment of the king, at the words of the LORD, to cleanse the house of the LORD.

16 Then the priests went into the inner part of the house of the LORD to cleanse it, and brought out all the debris that they found in the temple of the LORD to the court of the house of the LORD. And the Lē′vītes took it out and carried it to the Brook Kid′ron.

17 Now they began to sanctify on the first day of the first month, and on the eighth day of the month they came to the vestibule of the LORD. So they sanctified the house of the LORD in eight days, and on the sixteenth day of the first month they finished.

18 Then they went in to King Hez·e·kī′ah and said, "We have cleansed all the house of the LORD, the altar of burnt offerings with all its articles, and the table of the showbread with all its articles.

19 "Moreover all the articles which King Ā′haz in his reign had cast aside in his transgression we have prepared and sanctified; and there they are, before the altar of the LORD."

HEZEKIAH RESTORES TEMPLE WORSHIP

20 Then King Hez·e·kī′ah rose early, gathered the rulers of the city, and went up to the house of the LORD.

21 And they brought seven bulls, seven rams, seven lambs, and seven male goats for a sin offering for the kingdom, for the sanctuary, and for Judah. Then he commanded the priests, the sons of Aaron, to offer them on the altar of the LORD.

22 So they killed the bulls, and the priests received the blood and sprinkled it on the altar. Likewise they killed the rams and sprinkled the blood on the altar. They also killed the lambs and sprinkled the blood on the altar.

23 Then they brought out the male goats for the sin offering before the king and the assembly, and they laid their hands on them.

24 And the priests killed them; and they presented their blood on the altar as a sin offering to make an atonement for all Israel, for the king commanded that the burnt offering and the sin offering be made for all Israel.

25 And he stationed the Lē′vītes in the house of the LORD with cymbals, with stringed instruments, and with harps, according to the commandment of David, of Gad the king's seer, and of Nathan the prophet; for thus was the commandment of the LORD by his prophets.

26 The Lē′vītes stood with the instruments of David, and the priests with the trumpets.

27 Then Hez·e·kī′ah commanded them to offer the burnt offering on the altar. And when the burnt offering began, the song of the LORD also began, with the trumpets and with the instruments of David king of Israel.

28 So all the assembly worshiped, the singers sang, and the trumpeters sounded; all this continued until the burnt offering was finished.

29 And when they had finished offering, the king and all who were present with him bowed and worshiped.

30 Moreover King Hez·e·kī′ah and the leaders commanded the Lē′vītes to sing praise to the LORD with the

words of David and of Ā′saph the seer. So they sang praises with gladness, and they bowed their heads and worshiped.

■ **Praises** ■

2 Chronicles 29:30

These people sang their praises with gladness. How do you sing at church and Sunday School? Do you sing to God with gladness? Or do you sing because you have to sing? Do you sing with joy? Or do you just get through the song? Sing praises to God with gladness. That's what praise is all about, isn't it?

---

31 Then Hez·e·kī′ah answered and said, "Now *that* you have consecrated yourselves to the LORD, come near, and bring sacrifices and thank offerings into the house of the LORD." So the assembly brought in sacrifices and thank offerings, and as many as were of a willing heart *brought* burnt offerings.
32 And the number of the burnt offerings which the assembly brought was seventy bulls, one hundred rams, *and* two hundred lambs; all these *were* for a burnt offering to the LORD.
33 The consecrated things *were* six hundred bulls and three thousand sheep.
34 But the priests were too few, so that they could not skin all the burnt offerings; therefore their brethren the Lē′vītes helped them until the work was ended and until the *other* priests had sanctified themselves, for the Lē′vītes were more diligent in sanctifying themselves than the priests.
35 Also the burnt offerings *were* in abundance, with the fat of the peace offerings and *with* the drink offerings

for *every* burnt offering. So the service of the house of the LORD was set in order.
36 Then Hez·e·kī′ah and all the people rejoiced that God had prepared the people, since the events took place so suddenly.

HEZEKIAH KEEPS THE PASSOVER

30 And Hez·e·kī′ah sent to all Israel and Judah, and also wrote letters to Ē′phra·im and Ma·nas′seh, that they should come to the house of the LORD at Jerusalem, to keep the Passover to the LORD God of Israel.
2 For the king and his leaders and all the assembly in Jerusalem had agreed to keep the Passover in the second month.
3 For they could not keep it at the regular time,a because a sufficient number of priests had not consecrated themselves, nor had the people gathered together at Jerusalem.
4 And the matter pleased the king and all the assembly.
5 So they resolved to make a proclamation throughout all Israel, from Bē·er·shē′ba to Dan, that they should come to keep the Passover to the LORD God of Israel at Jerusalem, since they had not done *it* for a long *time* in the *prescribed* manner.
6 Then the runners went throughout all Israel and Judah with the letters from the king and his leaders, and spoke according to the command of the king: "Children of Israel, return to the LORD God of Abraham, Isaac, and Israel; then He will return to the remnant of you who have escaped from the hand of the kings of Assyria.
7 "And do not be like your fathers and your brethren, who trespassed

---

30:3 aThat is, the first month (compare Leviticus 23:5); literally *at that time*

against the LORD God of their fathers, so that He gave them up to desolation, as you see.

8 "Now do not be stiff-necked, as your fathers *were, but* yield yourselves to the LORD; and enter His sanctuary, which He has sanctified forever, and serve the LORD your God, that the fierceness of His wrath may turn away from you.

9 "For if you return to the LORD, your brethren and your children *will be treated* with compassion by those who lead them captive, so that they may come back to this land; for the LORD your God *is* gracious and merciful, and will not turn *His* face from you if you return to Him."

10 So the runners passed from city to city through the country of Ē'phra·im and Ma·nas'seh, as far as Zeb'ū·lun; but they laughed at them and mocked them.

11 Nevertheless some from Ash'er, Ma·nas'seh, and Zeb'ū·lun humbled themselves and came to Jerusalem.

12 Also the hand of God was on Judah to give them singleness of heart to obey the command of the king and the leaders, at the word of the LORD.

13 Now many people, a very great assembly, gathered at Jerusalem to keep the Feast of Unleavened Bread in the second month.

14 They arose and took away the altars that *were* in Jerusalem, and they took away all the incense altars and cast *them* into the Brook Kid'ron.

15 Then they slaughtered the Passover *lambs* on the fourteenth *day* of the second month. The priests and the Lē'vītes were ashamed, and sanctified themselves, and brought the burnt offerings to the house of the LORD.

16 They stood in their place according to their custom, according to the Law of Moses the man of God; the priests sprinkled the blood *received* from the hand of the Lē'vītes.

17 For *there were* many in the assembly who had not sanctified themselves; therefore the Lē'vītes had charge of the slaughter of the Passover *lambs* for everyone *who was* not clean, to sanctify *them* to the LORD.

18 For a multitude of the people, many from Ē'phra·im, Ma·nas'seh, Is'sa·char, and Zeb'ū·lun, had not cleansed themselves, yet they ate the Passover contrary to what was written. But Hez·e·kī'ah prayed for them, saying, "May the good LORD provide atonement for everyone

19 "*who* prepares his heart to seek God, the LORD God of his fathers, though *he is* not *cleansed* according to the purification of the sanctuary."

20 And the LORD listened to Hez·e·kī'ah and healed the people.

21 So the children of Israel who were present at Jerusalem kept the Feast of Unleavened Bread seven days with great gladness; and the Lē'vītes and the priests praised the LORD day by day, *singing* to the LORD, accompanied by loud instruments.

22 And Hez·e·kī'ah gave encouragement to all the Lē'vītes who taught the good knowledge of the LORD; and they ate throughout the feast seven days, offering peace offerings and making confession to the LORD God of their fathers.

23 Then the whole assembly agreed to keep *the feast* another seven days, and they kept it *another* seven days with gladness.

24 For Hez·e·kī'ah king of Judah gave to the assembly a thousand bulls and seven thousand sheep, and the leaders gave to the assembly a thousand bulls and ten thousand sheep; and a great number of priests sanctified themselves.

25 The whole assembly of Judah rejoiced, also the priests and Lē'vītes,

all the assembly that came from Israel, the sojourners who came from the land of Israel, and those who dwelt in Judah.

26 So there was great joy in Jerusalem, for since the time of Solomon the son of David, king of Israel, *there had* been nothing like this in Jerusalem.

27 Then the priests, the Lē'vītes, arose and blessed the people, and their voice was heard; and their prayer came *up* to His holy dwelling place, to heaven.

THE REFORMS OF HEZEKIAH

31 Now when all this was finished, all Israel who were present went out to the cities of Judah and broke the sacred pillars in pieces, cut down the wooden images, and threw down the high places and the altars—from all Judah, Benjamin, Ē'phra·im, and Ma·nas'seh—until they had utterly destroyed them all. Then all the children of Israel returned to their own cities, every man to his possession.

2 And Hez·e·kī'ah appointed the divisions of the priests and the Lē'vītes according to their divisions, each man according to his service, the priests and Lē'vītes for burnt offerings and peace offerings, to serve, to give thanks, and to praise in the gates of the camp*a* of the LORD.

3 The king also *appointed* a portion of his possessions for the burnt offerings: for the morning and evening burnt offerings, the burnt offerings for the Sabbaths and the New Moons and the set feasts, as *it is* written in the Law of the LORD.

4 Moreover he commanded the people who dwelt in Jerusalem to contribute support for the priests and the Lē'vītes, that they might devote themselves to the Law of the LORD.

5 As soon as the commandment was circulated, the children of Israel brought in abundance the firstfruits of grain and wine, oil and honey, and of all the produce of the field; and they brought in abundantly the tithe of everything.

6 And the children of Israel and Judah, who dwelt in the cities of Judah, brought the tithe of oxen and sheep; also the tithe of holy things which were consecrated to the LORD their God they laid in heaps.

7 In the third month they began laying them in heaps, and they finished in the seventh month.

8 And when Hez·e·kī'ah and the leaders came and saw the heaps, they blessed the LORD and His people Israel.

9 Then Hez·e·kī'ah questioned the priests and the Lē'vītes concerning the heaps.

10 And Az·a·rī'ah the chief priest, from the house of Zā'dok, answered him and said, "Since *the people* began to bring the offerings into the house of the LORD, we have had enough to eat and have plenty left, for the LORD has blessed His people; and what is left *is* this great abundance."

11 Now Hez·e·kī'ah commanded *them* to prepare rooms in the house of the LORD, and they prepared them.

12 Then they faithfully brought in the offerings, the tithes, and the dedicated things; Con·o·nī'ah the Lē'vīte had charge of them, and Shim'e·ī his brother *was* the next.

13 Je·hī'el, Az·a·zī'ah, Nā'hath, As'a·hel, Jer'i·moth, Joz'a·bad, E·lī'el, Is·ma·chī'ah, Mā'hath, and Be·nā'i·ah *were* overseers under the hand of Con·o·nī'ah and Shim'e·ī his brother, at the commandment of Hez·e·kī'ah the king and Az·a·rī'ah the ruler of the house of God.

31:2 *a*That is, the temple

14 Kō're the son of Im'nah the Lē'-vīte, the keeper of the East Gate, *was* over the freewill offerings to God, to distribute the offerings of the LORD and the most holy things.

15 And under him *were* Eden, Min'-ia·min, Jesh'ū·a, She·māi'ah, Am·a·rī'ah, and Shec·a·nī'ah, *his* faithful assistants in the cities of the priests, to distribute allotments to their brethren by divisions, to the great as well as the small.

16 Besides those males from three years old and up who were written in the genealogy, they distributed to everyone who entered the house of the LORD his daily portion for the work of his service, by his division,

17 and to the priests who were written in the genealogy according to their father's house, and to the Lē'vītes from twenty years old and up according to their work, by their divisions,

18 and to all who were written in the genealogy—their little ones and their wives, their sons and daughters, the whole company of them—for in their faithfulness they sanctified themselves in holiness.

19 Also for the sons of Aaron the priests, *who were* in the fields of the common-lands of their cities, in every single city, *there were* men who were designated by name to distribute portions to all the males among the priests and to all who were listed by genealogies among the Lē'vītes.

20 Thus Hez·e·kī'ah did throughout all Judah, and he did what *was* good and right and true before the LORD his God.

21 And in every work that he began in the service of the house of God, in the law and in the commandment, to seek his God, he did *it* with all his heart. So he prospered.

SENNACHERIB BOASTS AGAINST THE LORD

32 After these deeds of faithfulness, Sen·nach'e·rib king of Assyria came and entered Judah; he encamped against the fortified cities, thinking to win them over to himself.

2 And when Hez·e·kī'ah saw that Sen·nach'e·rib had come, and that his purpose was to make war against Jerusalem,

3 he consulted with his leaders and commanders[a] to stop the water from the springs which *were* outside the city; and they helped him.

4 Thus many people gathered together who stopped all the springs and the brook that ran through the land, saying, "Why should the kings[a] of Assyria come and find much water?"

5 And he strengthened himself, built up all the wall that was broken, raised *it* up to the towers, and *built* another wall outside; also he repaired the Mil'lō[a] *in* the City of David, and made weapons and shields in abundance.

6 Then he set military captains over the people, gathered them together to him in the open square of the city gate, and gave them encouragement, saying,

7 "Be strong and courageous; do not be afraid nor dismayed before the king of Assyria, nor before all the multitude that *is* with him; for *there are* more with us than with him.

8 "With him *is* an arm of flesh; but with us *is* the LORD our God, to help us and to fight our battles." And the people were strengthened by the words of Hez·e·kī'ah king of Judah.

9 After this Sen·nach'e·rib king of

32:3 [a]Literally *mighty men*   32:4 [a]Following Masoretic Text and Vulgate; Arabic, Septuagint, and Syriac read *king.*   32:5 [a]Literally *The Landfill*

Assyria sent his servants to Jerusalem (but he and all the forces with him *laid siege* against Lā′chish), to Hez·e·kī′ah king of Judah, and to all Judah who *were* in Jerusalem, saying,

10 "Thus says Sen·nach′e·rib king of Assyria: 'In what do you trust, that you remain under siege in Jerusalem?

11 'Does not Hez·e·kī′ah persuade you to give yourselves over to die by famine and by thirst, saying, "The LORD our God will deliver us from the hand of the king of Assyria"?

12 'Has not the same Hez·e·kī′ah taken away His high places and His altars, and commanded Judah and Jerusalem, saying, "You shall worship before one altar and burn incense on it"?

13 'Do you not know what I and my fathers have done to all the peoples of *other* lands? Were the gods of the nations of those lands in any way able to deliver their lands out of my hand?

14 'Who *was there* among all the gods of those nations that my fathers utterly destroyed that could deliver his people from my hand, that your God should be able to deliver you from my hand?

15 'Now therefore, do not let Hez·e·kī′ah deceive you or persuade you like this, and do not believe him; for no god of any nation or kingdom was able to deliver his people from my hand or the hand of my fathers. How much less will your God deliver you from my hand?' "

16 Furthermore, his servants spoke against the LORD God and against His servant Hez·e·kī′ah.

17 He also wrote letters to revile the LORD God of Israel, and to speak against Him, saying, "As the gods of the nations of *other* lands have not delivered their people from my hand, so the God of Hez·e·kī′ah will not deliver His people from my hand."

18 Then they called out with a loud voice in Hebrew[a] to the people of Jerusalem who *were* on the wall, to frighten them and trouble them, that they might take the city.

19 And they spoke against the God of Jerusalem, as against the gods of the people of the earth—the work of men's hands.

SENNACHERIB'S DEFEAT AND DEATH

20 Now because of this King Hez·e·kī′ah and the prophet Ī·sāi′ah, the son of Ā′moz, prayed and cried out to heaven.

21 Then the LORD sent an angel who cut down every mighty man of valor, leader, and captain in the camp of the king of Assyria. So he returned shamefaced to his own land. And when he had gone into the temple of his god, some of his own offspring struck him down with the sword there.

22 Thus the LORD saved Hez·e·kī′ah and the inhabitants of Jerusalem from the hand of Sen·nach′e·rib the king of Assyria, and from the hand of all *others,* and guided them[a] on every side.

23 And many brought gifts to the LORD at Jerusalem, and presents to Hez·e·kī′ah king of Judah, so that he was exalted in the sight of all nations thereafter.

HEZEKIAH HUMBLES HIMSELF

24 In those days Hez·e·kī′ah was sick and near death, and he prayed to the LORD; and He spoke to him and gave him a sign.

32:18 *a*Literally *Judean*   32:22 *a*Septuagint reads *gave them rest;* Vulgate reads *gave them treasures.*

GIVING 2 Chronicles 32:23

What Should We Give?

Sometimes we think that the only thing we can give is money. That's not true, is it? Look at this little plant. It needs water so it can grow. Carol will give it a drink of water. That's a gift of life for this little plant. Can you think of some other gifts you can give that are more important than money?

1. Would this little plant rather have money or water? Why?
2. Would a little bird rather have a chest of treasure or some bird food? Why?
3. A person is dying of thirst in a desert. Would that person rather have a cup of water or a cup of gold?
4. A person is dying of starvation. Would that person rather have a plate of food or a plate of money?
5. A person doesn't know Jesus. Is it more important to share Jesus with that person or write a check to that person?

For more on *Values* turn to page 701
For more on *Giving* turn to page 701

25 But Hez·e·kī′ah did not repay according to the favor *shown* him, for his heart was lifted up; therefore wrath was looming over him and over Judah and Jerusalem.
26 Then Hez·e·kī′ah humbled himself for the pride of his heart, he and the inhabitants of Jerusalem, so that the wrath of the LORD did not come upon them in the days of Hez·e·kī′ah.

HEZEKIAH'S WEALTH AND HONOR

27 Hez·e·kī′ah had very great riches and honor. And he made himself treasuries for silver, for gold, for precious stones, for spices, for shields, and for all kinds of desirable items;
28 storehouses for the harvest of grain, wine, and oil; and stalls for all kinds of livestock, and folds for flocks.*a*
29 Moreover he provided cities for himself, and possessions of flocks and herds in abundance; for God had given him very much property.
30 This same Hez·e·kī′ah also stopped the water outlet of Upper Gī′hon, and brought the water by tunnel*a* to the west side of the City of David. Hez·e·kī′ah prospered in all his works.
31 However, *regarding* the ambassadors of the princes of Babylon, whom they sent to him to inquire about the wonder that was *done* in the land, God withdrew from him, in order to test him, that He might know all *that was* in his heart.

DEATH OF HEZEKIAH

32 Now the rest of the acts of Hez·e·kī′ah, and his goodness, indeed they *are* written in the vision of Ī·sāi′ah the prophet, the son of Ā′moz, *and* in the book of the kings of Judah and Israel.
33 So Hez·e·kī′ah rested with his fa-

thers, and they buried him in the upper tombs of the sons of David; and all Judah and the inhabitants of Jerusalem honored him at his death. Then Ma·nas′seh his son reigned in his place.

MANASSEH REIGNS IN JUDAH

33 Ma·nas′seh *was* twelve years old when he became king, and he reigned fifty-five years in Jerusalem.
2 But he did evil in the sight of the LORD, according to the abominations of the nations whom the LORD had cast out before the children of Israel.
3 For he rebuilt the high places which Hez·e·kī′ah his father had broken down; he raised up altars for the Bā′als, and made wooden images; and he worshiped all the host of heaven*a* and served them.
4 He also built altars in the house of the LORD, of which the LORD had said, "In Jerusalem shall My name be forever."
5 And he built altars for all the host of heaven in the two courts of the house of the LORD.
6 Also he caused his sons to pass through the fire in the Valley of the Son of Hin′nom; he practiced soothsaying, used witchcraft and sorcery, and consulted mediums and spiritists. He did much evil in the sight of the LORD, to provoke Him to anger.
7 He even set a carved image, the idol which he had made, in the house of God, of which God had said to David and to Solomon his son, "In this house and in Jerusalem, which I

32:28 *a*Following Septuagint and Vulgate; Arabic and Syriac omit *folds for flocks;* Masoretic Text reads *flocks for sheepfolds.*   32:30 *a*Literally *brought it straight* (compare 2 Kings 20:20)
33:3 *a*The gods of the Assyrians

have chosen out of all the tribes of Israel, I will put My name forever;

8 "and I will not again remove the foot of Israel from the land which I have appointed for your fathers— only if they are careful to do all that I have commanded them, according to the whole law and the statutes and the ordinances by the hand of Moses."

9 So Ma·nas'seh seduced Judah and the inhabitants of Jerusalem to do more evil than the nations whom the LORD had destroyed before the children of Israel.

MANASSEH RESTORED AFTER REPENTANCE

10 And the LORD spoke to Ma·nas'-seh and his people, but they would not listen.

11 Therefore the LORD brought upon them the captains of the army of the king of Assyria, who took Ma·nas'seh with hooks,*a* bound him with bronze *fetters,* and carried him off to Babylon.

12 Now when he was in affliction, he implored the LORD his God, and humbled himself greatly before the God of his fathers,

13 and prayed to Him; and He received his entreaty, heard his supplication, and brought him back to Jerusalem into his kingdom. Then Ma·nas'seh knew that the LORD *was* God.

14 After this he built a wall outside the City of David on the west side of Gi'hon, in the valley, as far as the entrance of the Fish Gate; and *it* enclosed O'phel, and he raised it to a very great height. Then he put military captains in all the fortified cities of Judah.

15 He took away the foreign gods and the idol from the house of the LORD, and all the altars that he had built in the mount of the house of the LORD and in Jerusalem; and he cast *them* out of the city.

16 He also repaired the altar of the LORD, sacrificed peace offerings and thank offerings on it, and commanded Judah to serve the LORD God of Israel.

17 Nevertheless the people still sacrificed on the high places, *but* only to the LORD their God.

DEATH OF MANASSEH

18 Now the rest of the acts of Ma-nas'seh, his prayer to his God, and the words of the seers who spoke to him in the name of the LORD God of Israel, indeed they *are written* in the book*a* of the kings of Israel.

19 Also his prayer and *how God* received his entreaty, and all his sin and trespass, and the sites where he built high places and set up wooden images and carved images, before he was humbled, indeed they *are* written among the sayings of Hō'zā·ī.*a*

20 So Ma·nas'seh rested with his fathers, and they buried him in his own house. Then his son Ā'mon reigned in his place.

AMON'S REIGN AND DEATH

21 Ā'mon *was* twenty-two years old when he became king, and he reigned two years in Jerusalem.

22 But he did evil in the sight of the LORD, as his father Ma·nas'seh had done; for Ā'mon sacrificed to all the carved images which his father Ma-nas'seh had made, and served them.

23 And he did not humble himself before the LORD, as his father Ma-

---

33:11 *a*That is, nose hooks (compare 2 Kings 19:28)
33:18 *a*Literally *words*   33:19 *a*Septuagint reads *the seers.*

nas'seh had humbled himself; but Ā'mon trespassed more and more.

24 Then his servants conspired against him, and killed him in his own house.

25 But the people of the land executed all those who had conspired against King Ā'mon. Then the people of the land made his son Jō·sī'ah king in his place.

JOSIAH REIGNS IN JUDAH

This is a story about a boy king who helped an entire nation follow God.

34 Jō·sī'ah *was* eight years old when he became king, and he reigned thirty-one years in Jerusalem.

2 And he did *what was* right in the sight of the LORD, and walked in the ways of his father David; *he* did *not* turn aside to the right hand or to the left.

3 For in the eighth year of his reign, while he was still young, he began to seek the God of his father David; and in the twelfth year he began to purge Judah and Jerusalem of the high places, the wooden images, the carved images, and the molded images.

4 They broke down the altars of the Bā'als in his presence, and the incense altars which *were* above them he cut down; and the wooden images, the carved images, and the molded images he broke in pieces, and made dust of them and scattered *it* on the graves of those who had sacrificed to them.

5 He also burned the bones of the priests on their altars, and cleansed Judah and Jerusalem.

6 And *so he did* in the cities of Ma·nas'seh, Ē'phra·im, and Sim'ē·on, as far as Naph'ta·lī and all around, with axes.*a*

7 When he had broken down the altars and the wooden images, had beaten the carved images into powder, and cut down all the incense altars throughout all the land of Israel, he returned to Jerusalem.

HILKIAH FINDS THE BOOK OF THE LAW

8 In the eighteenth year of his reign, when he had purged the land and the temple,*a* he sent Shā'phan the son of Az·a·lī'ah, Mā·a·sēi'ah the governor of the city, and Jō'ah the son of Jō'a·haz the recorder, to repair the house of the LORD his God.

9 When they came to Hil·kī'ah the high priest, they delivered the money that was brought into the house of God, which the Lē'vītes who kept the doors had gathered from the hand of Ma·nas'seh and Ē'phra·im, from all the remnant of Israel, from all Judah and Benjamin, and *which* they had brought back to Jerusalem.

10 Then they put *it* in the hand of the foremen who had the oversight of the house of the LORD; and they gave it to the workmen who worked in the house of the LORD, to repair and restore the house.

11 They gave *it* to the craftsmen and builders to buy hewn stone and timber for beams, and to floor the houses which the kings of Judah had destroyed.

12 And the men did the work faithfully. Their overseers *were* Jā'hath and Ō·ba·dī'ah the Lē'vītes, of the sons of Me·rar'ī, and Zech·a·rī'ah and Me·shul'lam, of the sons of the Kō'hath·ītes, to supervise. *Others of* the Lē'vītes, all of whom were skillful with instruments of music,

13 *were* over the burden bearers and *were* overseers of all who did work in

34:6 *a*Literally *swords*   34:8 *a*Literally *house*

any kind of service. And *some* of the Lē′vītes *were* scribes, officers, and gatekeepers.

14 Now when they brought out the money that was brought into the house of the LORD, Hil·kī′ah the priest found the Book of the Law of the LORD *given* by Moses.

15 Then Hil·kī′ah answered and said to Shā′phan the scribe, "I have found the Book of the Law in the house of the LORD." And Hil·kī′ah gave the book to Shā′phan.

16 So Shā′phan carried the book to the king, bringing the king word, saying, "All that was committed to your servants they are doing.

17 "And they have gathered the money that was found in the house of the LORD, and have delivered it into the hand of the overseers and the workmen."

18 Then Shā′phan the scribe told the king, saying, "Hil·kī′ah the priest has given me a book." And Shā′phan read it before the king.

19 Thus it happened, when the king heard the words of the Law, that he tore his clothes.

20 Then the king commanded Hil·kī′ah, A·hī′kam the son of Shā′phan, Ab′don[a] the son of Mī′cah, Shā′phan the scribe, and A·sāi′ah a servant of the king, saying,

21 "Go, inquire of the LORD for me, and for those who are left in Israel and Judah, concerning the words of the book that is found; for great *is* the wrath of the LORD that is poured out on us, because our fathers have not kept the word of the LORD, to do according to all that is written in this book."

22 So Hil·kī′ah and those the king *had appointed* went to Hul′dah the prophetess, the wife of Shal′lum the son of Tok′hath,[a] the son of Has′rah,[b] keeper of the wardrobe. (She dwelt in Jerusalem in the Second Quarter.) And they spoke to her to that *effect*.

23 Then she answered them, "Thus says the LORD God of Israel, 'Tell the man who sent you to Me,

24 "Thus says the LORD: 'Behold, I will bring calamity on this place and on its inhabitants, all the curses that are written in the book which they have read before the king of Judah,

25 'because they have forsaken Me and burned incense to other gods, that they might provoke Me to anger with all the works of their hands. Therefore My wrath will be poured out on this place, and not be quenched.' " '

26 "But as for the king of Judah, who sent you to inquire of the LORD, in this manner you shall speak to him, 'Thus says the LORD God of Israel: "*Concerning* the words which you have heard—

27 "because your heart was tender, and you humbled yourself before God when you heard His words against this place and against its inhabitants, and you humbled yourself before Me, and you tore your clothes and wept before Me, I also have heard *you,*" says the LORD.

28 "Surely I will gather you to your fathers, and you shall be gathered to your grave in peace; and your eyes shall not see all the calamity which I will bring on this place and its inhabitants." ' " So they brought back word to the king.

JOSIAH RESTORES TRUE WORSHIP

29 Then the king sent and gathered all the elders of Judah and Jerusalem.

30 The king went up to the house of

34:20 [a]*Achbor the son of Michaiah* in 2 Kings 22:12
34:22 [a]Spelled *Tikvah* in 2 Kings 22:14   [b]Spelled *Harhas* in 2 Kings 22:14

the LORD, with all the men of Judah and the inhabitants of Jerusalem—the priests and the Lē'vītes, and all the people, great and small. And he read in their hearing all the words of the Book of the Covenant which had been found in the house of the LORD. 31 Then the king stood in his place and made a covenant before the LORD, to follow the LORD, and to keep His commandments and His testimonies and His statutes with all his heart and all his soul, to perform the words of the covenant that were written in this book.
32 And he made all who were present in Jerusalem and Benjamin take a stand. So the inhabitants of Jerusalem did according to the covenant of God, the God of their fathers.
33 Thus Jō·sī'ah removed all the abominations from all the country that *belonged* to the children of Israel, and made all who were present in Israel diligently serve the LORD their God. All his days they did not

depart from following the LORD God of their fathers.

JOSIAH KEEPS THE PASSOVER

35 Now Jō·sī'ah kept a Passover to the LORD in Jerusalem, and they slaughtered the Passover *lambs* on the fourteenth *day* of the first month.
2   And he set the priests in their duties and encouraged them for the service of the house of the LORD.
3   Then he said to the Lē'vītes who taught all Israel, who were holy to the LORD: "Put the holy ark in the house which Solomon the son of David, king of Israel, built. *It shall* no longer *be* a burden on *your* shoulders. Now serve the LORD your God and His people Israel.
4   "Prepare *yourselves* according to your fathers' houses, according to your divisions, following the written instruction of David king of Israel and the written instruction of Solomon his son.
5   "And stand in the holy *place* according to the divisions of the fathers' houses of your brethren the *lay* people, and *according to* the division of the father's house of the Lē'vītes.
6   "So slaughter the Passover *offerings*, consecrate yourselves, and prepare *them* for your brethren, that *they* may do according to the word of the LORD by the hand of Moses."
7   Then Jō·sī'ah gave the *lay* people lambs and young goats from the flock, all for Passover *offerings* for all who were present, to the number of thirty thousand, as well as three thousand cattle; these *were* from the king's possessions.
8   And his leaders gave willingly to the people, to the priests, and to the Lē'vītes. Hil·kī'ah, Zech·a·rī'ah, and Je·hī'el, rulers of the house of God, gave to the priests for the Passover

---

☑	*Bible Quiz*

2 Chronicles 34 **Josiah, the Boy King**

1. What was the name of this boy king? How old was he when he became king?
2. How do you know he tried to follow God?
3. As Hilkiah the priest was cleaning the temple, what did he find? Do you know what this special book was?
4. Why was it so important for Josiah to do what the book said? Why is it important for you to do what the Bible says?

offerings two thousand six hundred *from the flock,* and three hundred cattle.

9 Also Con·a·nī′ah, his brothers She·māi′ah and Ne·than′el, and Hash·a·bī′ah and Je·ī′el and Joz′a·bad, chief of the Lē′vītes, gave to the Lē′vītes for Passover *offerings* five thousand *from the flock* and five hundred cattle.

10 So the service was prepared, and the priests stood in their places, and the Lē′vītes in their divisions, according to the king's command.

11 And they slaughtered the Passover *offerings;* and the priests sprinkled *the blood* with their hands, while the Lē′vītes skinned *the animals.*

12 Then they removed the burnt offerings that *they* might give them to the divisions of the fathers' houses of the *lay* people, to offer to the LORD, as *it is* written in the Book of Moses. And so *they did* with the cattle.

13 Also they roasted the Passover *offerings* with fire according to the ordinance; but the *other* holy *offerings* they boiled in pots, in caldrons, and in pans, and divided *them* quickly among all the *lay* people.

14 Then afterward they prepared portions for themselves and for the priests, because the priests, the sons of Aaron, *were busy* in offering burnt offerings and fat until night; therefore the Lē′vītes prepared portions for themselves and for the priests, the sons of Aaron.

15 And the singers, the sons of Ā′saph, *were* in their places, according to the command of David, Ā′saph, Hē′man, and Je·dū′thun the king's seer. Also the gatekeepers *were* at each gate; they did not have to leave their position, because their brethren the Lē′vītes prepared portions for them.

16 So all the service of the LORD was prepared the same day, to keep the Passover and to offer burnt offerings on the altar of the LORD, according to the command of King Jō·sī′ah.

17 And the children of Israel who were present kept the Passover at that time, and the Feast of Unleavened Bread for seven days.

18 There had been no Passover kept in Israel like that since the days of Samuel the prophet; and none of the kings of Israel had kept such a Passover as Jō·sī′ah kept, with the priests and the Lē′vītes, all Judah and Israel who were present, and the inhabitants of Jerusalem.

19 In the eighteenth year of the reign of Jō·sī′ah this Passover was kept.

JOSIAH DIES IN BATTLE

20 After all this, when Jō·sī′ah had prepared the temple, Nē′cho king of Egypt came up to fight against Car′chem·ish by the Eū·phrā′tēs; and Jō·sī′ah went out against him.

21 But he sent messengers to him, saying, "What have I to do with you, king of Judah? *I have* not *come* against you this day, but against the house with which I have war; for God commanded me to make haste. Refrain *from meddling with* God, who *is* with me, lest He destroy you."

22 Nevertheless Jō·sī′ah would not turn his face from him, but disguised himself so that he might fight with him, and did not heed the words of Nē′cho from the mouth of God. So he came to fight in the Valley of Me·gid′dō.

23 And the archers shot King Jō·sī′ah; and the king said to his servants, "Take me away, for I am severely wounded."

24 His servants therefore took him out of that chariot and put him in the second chariot that he had, and they

brought him to Jerusalem. So he died, and was buried in *one of* the tombs of his fathers. And all Judah and Jerusalem mourned for Jō·sī'ah.

25 Jer·e·mī'ah also lamented for Jō·sī'ah. And to this day all the singing men and the singing women speak of Jō·sī'ah in their lamentations. They made it a custom in Israel; and indeed they *are* written in the Laments.

26 Now the rest of the acts of Jōsī'ah and his goodness, according to *what was* written in the Law of the LORD,

27 and his deeds from first to last, indeed they *are* written in the book of the kings of Israel and Judah.

THE REIGN AND CAPTIVITY OF JEHOAHAZ

36 Then the people of the land took Je·hō'a·haz the son of Jō·sī'ah, and made him king in his father's place in Jerusalem.

2 Je·hō'a·haz*a was* twenty-three years old when he became king, and he reigned three months in Jerusalem.

3 Now the king of Egypt deposed him at Jerusalem; and he imposed on the land a tribute of one hundred talents of silver and a talent of gold.

4 Then the king of Egypt made Je·hō'a·haz's*a* brother E·lī'a·kim king over Judah and Jerusalem, and changed his name to Je·hoi'a·kim. And Nē'cho took Je·hō'a·haz*b* his brother and carried him off to Egypt.

THE REIGN AND CAPTIVITY OF JEHOIAKIM

5 Je·hoi'a·kim *was* twenty-five years old when he became king, and he reigned eleven years in Jerusa-

lem. And he did evil in the sight of the LORD his God.

6 Ne·bū·chad·nez'zar king of Babylon came up against him, and bound him in bronze *fetters* to carry him off to Babylon.

7 Ne·bū·chad·nez'zar also carried off *some* of the articles from the house of the LORD to Babylon, and put them in his temple at Babylon.

8 Now the rest of the acts of Je·hoi'a·kim, the abominations which he did, and what was found against him, indeed they *are* written in the book of the kings of Israel and Judah. Then Je·hoi'a·chin his son reigned in his place.

THE REIGN AND CAPTIVITY OF JEHOIACHIN

9 Je·hoi'a·chin *was* eight*a* years old when he became king, and he reigned in Jerusalem three months and ten days. And he did evil in the sight of the LORD.

10 At the turn of the year King Ne·bū·chad·nez'zar summoned *him* and took him to Babylon, with the costly articles from the house of the LORD, and made Zed·e·kī'ah, *Je·hoi'a·kim's*a brother, king over Judah and Jerusalem.

ZEDEKIAH REIGNS IN JUDAH

11 Zed·e·kī'ah *was* twenty-one years old when he became king, and he reigned eleven years in Jerusalem.

12 He did evil in the sight of the LORD his God, *and* did not humble himself before Jer·e·mī'ah the prophet, *who spoke* from the mouth of the LORD.

36:2 *a*Masoretic Text reads *Joahaz*.   36:4 *a*Literally *his*   *b*Masoretic Text reads *Joahaz*.
36:9 *a*Some Hebrew manuscripts, Septuagint, Syriac, and 2 Kings 24:8 read *eighteen*.   36:10 *a*Literally *his* (compare 2 Kings 24:17)

13 And he also rebelled against King Ne·bu·chad·nez'zar, who had made him swear *an oath* by God; but he stiffened his neck and hardened his heart against turning to the LORD God of Israel.

14 Moreover all the leaders of the priests and the people transgressed more and more, *according* to all the abominations of the nations, and defiled the house of the LORD which He had consecrated in Jerusalem.

THE FALL OF JERUSALEM

15 And the LORD God of their fathers sent *warnings* to them by His messengers, rising up early and sending *them,* because He had compassion on His people and on His dwelling place. 16 But they mocked the messengers of God, despised His words, and scoffed at His prophets, until the wrath of the LORD arose against His people, till *there was* no remedy. 17 Therefore He brought against them the king of the Chal·de'ans, who killed their young men with the sword in the house of their sanctuary, and had no compassion on young man or virgin, on the aged or the weak; He gave *them* all into his hand. 18 And all the articles from the house of God, great and small, the treasures of the house of the LORD, and the treasures of the king and of his leaders, all *these* he took to Babylon.

19 Then they burned the house of God, broke down the wall of Jerusalem, burned all its palaces with fire, and destroyed all its precious possessions. 20 And those who escaped from the sword he carried away to Babylon, where they became servants to him and his sons until the rule of the kingdom of Persia, 21 to fulfill the word of the LORD by the mouth of Jer·e·mi'ah, until the land had enjoyed her Sabbaths. As long as she lay desolate she kept Sabbath, to fulfill seventy years.

THE PROCLAMATION OF CYRUS

22 Now in the first year of Cyrus king of Persia, that the word of the LORD by the mouth of Jer·e·mi'ah might be fulfilled, the LORD stirred up the spirit of Cyrus king of Persia, so that he made a proclamation throughout all his kingdom, and also *put it* in writing, saying,

23 Thus says Cyrus king of Persia:
All the kingdoms of the earth the
LORD God of heaven has given
me. And He has commanded
me to build Him a house
at Jerusalem which is in
Judah. Who *is* among you of all
His people? May the LORD his
God *be* with him, and let him
go up!

The Book of
EZRA

END OF THE BABYLONIAN CAPTIVITY

N OW in the first year of Cyrus king of Persia, that the word of the LORD by the mouth of Jer·e·mī′ah might be fulfilled, the LORD stirred up the spirit of Cyrus king of Persia, so that he made a proclamation throughout all his kingdom, and also *put it* in writing, saying,

2 Thus says Cyrus king of Persia: All the kingdoms of the earth the LORD God of heaven has given me. And He has commanded me to build Him a house at Jerusalem which *is* in Judah.
3 Who *is* among you of all His people? May his God be with him, and let him go up to Jerusalem which *is* in Judah, and build the house of the LORD God of Israel (He *is* God), which *is* in Jerusalem.
4 And whoever is left in any place where he dwells, let the men of his place help him with silver and gold, with goods and livestock, besides the freewill offerings for the house of God which *is* in Jerusalem.

5 Then the heads of the fathers' *houses* of Judah and Benjamin, and the priests and the Lē′vītes, with all whose spirits God had moved, arose to go up and build the house of the LORD which *is* in Jerusalem.
6 And all those who *were* around them encouraged them with articles of silver and gold, with goods and livestock, and with precious things, besides all *that* was willingly offered.
7 King Cyrus also brought out the articles of the house of the LORD, which Ne·bū·chad·nez′zar had taken from Jerusalem and put in the temple of his gods;
8 and Cyrus king of Persia brought them out by the hand of Mith′re·dath the treasurer, and counted them out to Shesh·baz′zar the prince of Judah.
9 This *is* the number of them: thirty gold platters, one thousand silver platters, twenty-nine knives,
10 thirty gold basins, four hundred and ten silver basins of a similar *kind, and* one thousand other articles.
11 All the articles of gold and silver *were* five thousand four hundred. All *these* Shesh·baz′zar took with the captives who were brought from Babylon to Jerusalem.

THE CAPTIVES WHO RETURNED TO JERUSALEM

2 Now[a] these *are* the people of the province who came back from the captivity, of those who had been carried away, whom Ne·bū·chad·nez′zar the king of Babylon had carried away to Babylon, and who returned to Jerusalem and Judah, everyone to his *own* city.
2 *Those* who came with Ze·rub′ba·bel *were* Jesh′ū·a, Nē·he·mī′ah, Se·rāi′ah, Rē·el·āi′ah, Mor′de·caī, Bil′shan, Mis′par,[a] Big′vaī, Rē′hum,[b] *and* Bā′a·nah. The number of the men of the people of Israel:
3 the people of Pā′rosh, two thousand one hundred and seventy-two;
4 the people of Sheph·a·tī′ah, three hundred and seventy-two;

2:1 [a]Compare this chapter with Nehemiah 7:6–73.
2:2 [a]Spelled *Mispereth* in Nehemiah 7:7   [b]Spelled *Nehum* in Nehemiah 7:7

5 the people of Ā′rah, seven hundred and seventy-five;

6 the people of Pā′hath-Mō′ab, of the people of Jesh′ū·a *and* Jō′ab, two thousand eight hundred and twelve;

7 the people of Ē′lam, one thousand two hundred and fifty-four;

8 the people of Zat′tū, nine hundred and forty-five;

9 the people of Zac′caī, seven hundred and sixty;

10 the people of Bā′nī,*a* six hundred and forty-two;

11 the people of Bē′baī, six hundred and twenty-three;

12 the people of Az′gad, one thousand two hundred and twenty-two;

13 the people of Ad·o·nī′kam, six hundred and sixty-six;

14 the people of Big′vaī, two thousand and fifty-six;

15 the people of Ā′din, four hundred and fifty-four;

16 the people of Ā′ter of Hez·e·kī′ah, ninety-eight;

17 the people of Bē′zaī, three hundred and twenty-three;

18 the people of Jō′rah,*a* one hundred and twelve;

19 the people of Hā′shum, two hundred and twenty-three;

20 the people of Gib′bar,*a* ninety-five;

21 the people of Bethlehem, one hundred and twenty-three;

22 the men of Ne·toph′ah, fifty-six;

23 the men of An′a·thoth, one hundred and twenty-eight;

24 the people of Az′ma·veth,*a* forty-two;

25 the people of Kir′jath Ar′im,*a* Chē·phī′rah, and Be·er′oth, seven hundred and forty-three;

26 the people of Rā′mah and Gē′ba, six hundred and twenty-one;

27 the men of Mich′mas, one hundred and twenty-two;

28 the men of Beth′el and Aī, two hundred and twenty-three;

29 the people of Nē′bō, fifty-two;

30 the people of Mag′bish, one hundred and fifty-six;

31 the people of the other Ē′lam, one thousand two hundred and fifty-four;

32 the people of Hā′rim, three hundred and twenty;

33 the people of Lod, Hā′did, and Ō′nō, seven hundred and twenty-five;

34 the people of Jericho, three hundred and forty-five;

35 the people of Se·nā′ah, three thousand six hundred and thirty.

36 The priests: the sons of Je·daī′ah, of the house of Jesh′ū·a, nine hundred and seventy-three;

37 the sons of Im′mer, one thousand and fifty-two;

38 the sons of Pash′hur, one thousand two hundred and forty-seven;

39 the sons of Hā′rim, one thousand and seventeen.

40 The Lē′vītes: the sons of Jesh′ū·a and Kad′mi·el, of the sons of Hod·a·vī′ah,*a* seventy-four.

41 The singers: the sons of Ā′saph, one hundred and twenty-eight.

42 The sons of the gatekeepers: the sons of Shal′lum, the sons of Ā′ter, the sons of Tal′mon, the sons of Ak′kub, the sons of Ha·tī′ta, and the sons of Shō′baī, one hundred and thirty-nine *in* all.

43 The Neth′i·nim: the sons of Zī′ha, the sons of Ha·sū′pha, the sons of Tab·bā′oth,

44 the sons of Kē′ros, the sons of Sī′a·ha,*a* the sons of Pā′don,

45 the sons of Le·bā′nah, the sons of Hag′a·bah, the sons of Ak′kub,

46 the sons of Hā′gab, the sons of Shal′maī, the sons of Hā′nan,

---

2:10 *a*Spelled *Binnui* in Nehemiah 7:15
2:18 *a*Called *Hariph* in Nehemiah 7:24
2:20 *a*Called *Gibeon* in Nehemiah 7:25
2:24 *a*Called *Beth Azmaveth* in Nehemiah 7:28
2:25 *a*Called *Kirjath Jearim* in Nehemiah 7:29
2:40 *a*Spelled *Hodevah* in Nehemiah 7:43
2:44 *a*Spelled *Sia* in Nehemiah 7:47

GIVING Ezra 2:68, 69

A Gift for Me

A mother and father had a wedding anniversary. He bought her a gift and she bought him a gift. What if he had bought her a football? Do you think she would like that best? What if she had bought him a book on sewing or knitting? Do you think he would like that better than a football? Most men would rather have the football, though some very fine men may like to sew or knit. Probably fewer moms like to play football, but some may. This couple didn't give those gifts. Instead, he gave her the book and she gave him the football. They like these gifts very much.

1. Do you like to give gifts that please the other person?
2. Do you like to give gifts that please your parents?
3. Do you like to give gifts that please God? What kind of gifts can you give to please Him?

For more on *Values* turn to page 754
For more on *Giving* turn to page 754

47 the sons of Gid'del, the sons of Gā'har, the sons of Rē·āi'ah,

48 the sons of Rē'zin, the sons of Ne·kō'da, the sons of Gaz'zam,

49 the sons of Uz'za, the sons of Pa·sē'ah, the sons of Bē'sai,

50 the sons of As'nah, the sons of Me·ū'nim, the sons of Ne·phū'sim,*a*

51 the sons of Bak'buk, the sons of Ha·kū'pha, the sons of Har'hur,

52 the sons of Baz'luth,*a* the sons of Me·hī'da, the sons of Har'sha,

53 the sons of Bar'kos, the sons of Sis'e·ra, the sons of Tam'ah,

54 the sons of Ne·zī'ah, and the sons of Ha·tī'pha.

55 The sons of Solomon's servants: the sons of Sō'tai, the sons of Sō'-phe·reth, the sons of Pe·rū'da,*a*

56 the sons of Jā'a·la, the sons of Dar'kon, the sons of Gid'del,

57 the sons of Sheph·a·tī'ah, the sons of Hat'til, the sons of Poch'e·reth of Ze·bā'im, and the sons of Ā'mī.*a*

58 All the Neth'i·nim and the children of Solomon's servants were three hundred and ninety-two.

59 And these *were* the ones who came up from Tel Mē'lah, Tel Har'-sha, Chē'rub, Ad'dan,*a* and Im'mer; but they could not identify their father's house or their genealogy,*b* whether they *were* of Israel:

60 the sons of De·lai'ah, the sons of Tō·bī'ah, and the sons of Ne·kō'da, six hundred and fifty-two;

61 and of the sons of the priests: the sons of Ha·bai'ah, the sons of Koz,*a* and the sons of Bar·zil'lai, who took a wife of the daughters of Bar·zil'lai the Gil'e·ad·ite, and was called by their name.

62 These sought their listing *among* those who were registered by genealogy, but they were not found; therefore they *were excluded* from the priesthood as defiled.

63 And the governor*a* said to them that they should not eat of the most holy things till a priest could consult with the U'rim and Thum'mim.

64 The whole assembly together *was* forty-two thousand three hundred *and* sixty,

65 besides their male and female servants, of whom *there were* seven thousand three hundred and thirty-seven; and they had two hundred men and women singers.

66 Their horses *were* seven hundred and thirty-six, their mules two hundred and forty-five,

67 their camels four hundred and thirty-five, and *their* donkeys six thousand seven hundred and twenty.

68 *Some* of the heads of the fathers' *houses,* when they came to the house of the LORD which *is* in Jerusalem, offered freely for the house of God, to erect it in its place:

69 According to their ability, they gave to the treasury for the work sixty-one thousand gold drachmas, five thousand minas of silver, and one hundred priestly garments.

70 So the priests and the Lē'vites, *some* of the people, the singers, the gatekeepers, and the Neth'i·nim, dwelt in their cities, and all Israel in their cities.

WORSHIP RESTORED AT JERUSALEM

3 And when the seventh month had come, and the children of Israel *were* in the cities, the people gathered together as one man to Jerusalem.

2 Then Jesh'ū·a the son of Jō'za-dak*a* and his brethren the priests,

---

2:50 *a*Spelled *Nephishesim* in Nehemiah 7:52
2:52 *a*Spelled *Bazlith* in Nehemiah 7:54
2:55 *a*Spelled *Perida* in Nehemiah 7:57
2:57 *a*Spelled *Amon* in Nehemiah 7:59
2:59 *a*Spelled *Addon* in Nehemiah 7:61   *b*Literally *seed*   2:61 *a*Or *Hakkoz*   2:63 *a*Hebrew *Tir-shatha*   3:2 *a*Spelled *Jehozadak* in 1 Chronicles 6:14

and Ze·rub′ba·bel the son of She-al′ti·el and his brethren, arose and built the altar of the God of Israel, to offer burnt offerings on it, as *it is* written in the Law of Moses the man of God. 3 Though fear *had come* upon them because of the people of those countries, they set the altar on its bases; and they offered burnt offerings on it to the LORD, *both* the morning and evening burnt offerings. 4 They also kept the Feast of Tabernacles, as *it is* written, and *offered* the daily burnt offerings in the number required by ordinance for each day. 5 Afterwards *they offered* the regular burnt offering, and *those* for New Moons and for all the appointed feasts of the LORD that were consecrated, and *those* of everyone who willingly offered a freewill offering to the LORD. 6 From the first day of the seventh month they began to offer burnt offerings to the LORD, although the foundation of the temple of the LORD had not been laid. 7 They also gave money to the masons and the carpenters, and food, drink, and oil to the people of Sī′don and Tȳre to bring cedar logs from Lebanon to the sea, to Jop′pa, according to the permission which they had from Cyrus king of Persia.

RESTORATION OF THE TEMPLE BEGINS

8 Now in the second month of the second year of their coming to the house of God at Jerusalem, Ze·rub′ba·bel the son of She·al′ti·el, Jesh′ū·a the son of Jō′za·dak,*a* and the rest of their brethren the priests and the Lē′vītes, and all those who had come out of the captivity to Jerusalem, began *work* and appointed the Lē′vītes

from twenty years old and above to oversee the work of the house of the LORD. 9 Then Jesh′ū·a *with* his sons and brothers, Kad′mi·el *with* his sons, and the sons of Judah,*a* arose as one to oversee those working on the house of God: the sons of Hen′a·dad *with* their sons and their brethren the Lē′vītes. 10 When the builders laid the foundation of the temple of the LORD, the priests stood*a* in their apparel with trumpets, and the Lē′vītes, the sons of Ā′saph, with cymbals, to praise the LORD, according to the ordinance of David king of Israel.

Praises

Ezra 3:11

What would cause you to praise God? Would you praise Him if He gave you a new bike? What if He gave you some other special gift? These people praised God for His house. Do you ever praise God for His house where you go? Would you like to do that today?

---

11 And they sang responsively, praising and giving thanks to the LORD:

"For *He is* good,
For His mercy *endures* forever toward Israel."*a*

Then all the people shouted with a great shout, when they praised the

---

3:8 *a*Spelled *Jehozadak* in 1 Chronicles 6:14
3:9 *a*Or *Hodaviah* (compare 2:40)   3:10 *a*Following Septuagint, Syriac, and Vulgate; Masoretic Text reads *they stationed the priests.*   3:11 *a*Compare Psalm 136:1

LORD, because the foundation of the house of the LORD was laid.

12 But many of the priests and Lē'vītes and heads of the fathers' *houses,* old men who had seen the first temple, wept with a loud voice when the foundation of this temple was laid before their eyes. Yet many shouted aloud for joy,

13 so that the people could not discern the noise of the shout of joy from the noise of the weeping of the people, for the people shouted with a loud shout, and the sound was heard afar off.

RESISTANCE TO REBUILDING THE TEMPLE

4 Now when the adversaries of Judah and Benjamin heard that the descendants of the captivity were building the temple of the LORD God of Israel,

2 they came to Ze·rub'ba·bel and the heads of the fathers' *houses,* and said to them, "Let us build with you, for we seek your God as you *do;* and we have sacrificed to Him since the days of Ē·sar·had'don king of Assyria, who brought us here."

3 But Ze·rub'ba·bel and Jesh'ū·a and the rest of the heads of the fathers' *houses* of Israel said to them, "You may do nothing with us to build a house for our God; but we alone will build to the LORD God of Israel, as King Cyrus the king of Persia has commanded us."

4 Then the people of the land tried to discourage the people of Judah. They troubled them in building,

5 and hired counselors against them to frustrate their purpose all the days of Cyrus king of Persia, even until the reign of Da·rī'us king of Persia.

REBUILDING OF JERUSALEM OPPOSED

6 In the reign of A·has·ū·ē'rus, in the beginning of his reign, they wrote an accusation against the inhabitants of Judah and Jerusalem.

7 In the days of Ar·ta·xerx'ēs also, Bish'lam, Mith're·dath, Tā'bel, and the rest of their companions wrote to Ar·ta·xerx'ēs king of Persia; and the letter *was* written in Ar·a·mā'ic script, and translated into the Ar·a·mā'ic language.

8 Rē'hum[a] the commander and Shim'shaī the scribe wrote a letter against Jerusalem to King Ar·ta·xerx'ēs in this fashion:

9 From[a] Rē'hum the commander, Shim'shaī the scribe, and the rest of their companions— *representatives* of the Dī'na·ītes, the A·phar'sath·chītes, the Tar'pel·ītes, the people of Persia and Ē'rech and Babylon and Shū'shan,[b] the De·hā'vītes, the Ē'lam·ītes,

10 and the rest of the nations whom the great and noble Os·nap'per took captive and settled in the cities of Samaria and the remainder beyond the River[a]— and so forth.[b]

11 (This *is* a copy of the letter that they sent him)

To King Ar·ta·xerx'ēs from your servants, the men *of the region* beyond the River, and so forth:[a]

12 Let it be known to the king that the Jews who came up from you have come to us at Jerusalem,

---

4:8 [a]The original language of Ezra 4:8 through 6:18 is Aramaic.   4:9 [a]Literally *Then*   [b]Or *Susa*
4:10 [a]That is, the Euphrates   [b]Literally *and now*
4:11 [a]Literally *and now*

and are building the rebellious and evil city, and are finishing *its* walls and repairing the foundations.

13 Let it now be known to the king that, if this city is built and the walls completed, they will not pay tax, tribute, or custom, and the king's treasury will be diminished.

14 Now because we receive support from the palace, it was not proper for us to see the king's dishonor; therefore we have sent and informed the king,

15 that search may be made in the book of the records of your fathers. And you will find in the book of the records and know that this city *is* a rebellious city, harmful to kings and provinces, and that they have incited sedition within the city in former times, for which cause this city was destroyed.

16 We inform the king that if this city is rebuilt and its walls are completed, the result will be that you will have no dominion beyond the River.

17 The king sent an answer:

To Rē′hum the commander, *to* Shim′shaī the scribe, *to* the rest of their companions who dwell in Samaria, and *to* the remainder beyond the River:

Peace, and so forth.*a*

18 The letter which you sent to us has been clearly read before me.

19 And I gave the command, and a search has been made, and it was found that this city in former times has revolted against kings, and rebellion and sedition have been fostered in it.

20 There have also been mighty kings over Jerusalem, who have ruled over all *the region* beyond the River; and tax, tribute, and custom were paid to them.

21 Now give the command to make these men cease, that this city may not be built until the command is given by me.

22 Take heed now that you do not fail to do this. Why should damage increase to the hurt of the kings?

23 Now when the copy of King Ar·ta·xerx′ēs' letter *was* read before Rē′hum, Shim′shaī the scribe, and their companions, they went up in haste to Jerusalem against the Jews, and by force of arms made them cease.

24 Thus the work of the house of God which *is* at Jerusalem ceased, and it was discontinued until the second year of the reign of Da·rī′us king of Persia.

RESTORATION OF THE TEMPLE RESUMED

5 Then the prophet Hag′gai and Zech·a·rī′ah the son of Id′do, prophets, prophesied to the Jews who *were* in Judah and Jerusalem, in the name of the God of Israel, *who was* over them.

2 So Ze·rub′ba·bel the son of She·al′ti·el and Jesh′ū·a the son of Jō′za·dak*a* rose up and began to build the house of God which *is* in Jerusalem; and the prophets of God *were* with them, helping them.

3 At the same time Tat′te·nai the governor of *the region* beyond the River*a* and Shē′thar-Boz′nai and their companions came to them and

4:17 *a*Literally *and now*   5:2 *a*Spelled *Je-hozadak* in 1 Chronicles 6:14   5:3 *a*That is, the Euphrates

spoke thus to them: "Who has commanded you to build this temple and finish this wall?"

4 Then, accordingly, we told them the names of the men who were constructing this building.

5 But the eye of their God was upon the elders of the Jews, so that they could not make them cease till a report could go to Da·rī′us. Then a written answer was returned concerning this *matter.*

6 This is a copy of the letter that Tat′te·naī sent:

The governor of *the region* beyond the River, and Shē′thar-Boz′nai, and his companions, the Persians who *were in the region* beyond the River, to Da·rī′us the king.

7 (They sent a letter to him, in which was written thus)

To Da·rī′us the king:

All peace.

8 Let it be known to the king that we went into the province of Judea, to the temple of the great God, which is being built with heavy stones, and timber is being laid in the walls; and this work goes on diligently and prospers in their hands.

9 Then we asked those elders, *and* spoke thus to them: "Who commanded you to build this temple and to finish these walls?"

10 We also asked them their names to inform you, that we might write the names of the men who *were* chief among them.

11 And thus they returned us an answer, saying: "We are the servants of the God of heaven and earth, and we are rebuilding the temple that was built many years ago, which a great king of Israel built and completed.

12 "But because our fathers provoked the God of heaven to wrath, He gave them into the hand of Ne·bu·chad·nez′zar king of Babylon, the Chal·dē′an, *who* destroyed this temple and carried the people away to Babylon.

13 "However, in the first year of Cyrus king of Babylon, King Cyrus issued a decree to build this house of God.

14 "Also, the gold and silver articles of the house of God, which Ne·bu·chad·nez′zar had taken from the temple that *was* in Jerusalem and carried into the temple of Babylon—those King Cyrus took from the temple of Babylon, and they were given to one named Shesh·baz′zar, whom he had made governor.

15 "And he said to him, 'Take these articles; go, carry them to the temple *site* that *is* in Jerusalem, and let the house of God be rebuilt on its former site.'

16 "Then the same Shesh·baz′zar came *and* laid the foundation of the house of God which *is* in Jerusalem; but from that time even until now it has been under construction, and it is not finished."

17 Now therefore, if *it seems* good to the king, let a search be made in the king's treasure house, which *is* there in Babylon, whether it is *so* that a decree was issued by King Cyrus to build this house of God at Jerusalem, and let the king send us his pleasure concerning this *matter.*

THE DECREE OF DARIUS

6 Then King Da·rī′us issued a decree, and a search was made in the

archives,[a] where the treasures were stored in Babylon.

2　And at Ach′me·tha,[a] in the palace that *is* in the province of Media, a scroll was found, and in it a record *was* written thus:

3　In the first year of King Cyrus, King Cyrus issued a decree *concerning* the house of God at Jerusalem: "Let the house be rebuilt, the place where they offered sacrifices; and let the foundations of it be firmly laid, its height sixty cubits *and* its width sixty cubits,

4　*with* three rows of heavy stones and one row of new timber. Let the expenses be paid from the king's treasury.

5　Also let the gold and silver articles of the house of God, which Ne·bū·chad·nez′zar took from the temple which *is* in Jerusalem and brought to Babylon, be restored and taken back to the temple which *is* in Jerusalem, *each* to its place; and deposit *them* in the house of God"—

6　Now *therefore,* Tat′te·nai, governor of *the region* beyond the River, and Shē′thar-Boz′nai, and your companions the Persians who *are* beyond the River, keep yourselves far from there.

7　Let the work of this house of God alone; let the governor of the Jews and the elders of the Jews build this house of God on its site.

8　Moreover I issue a decree *as to* what you shall do for the elders of these Jews, for the building of this house of God: Let the cost be paid at the king's expense from taxes *on the region* beyond the River; this is to be given immediately to these men, so that they are not hindered.

9　And whatever they need— young bulls, rams, and lambs for the burnt offerings of the God of heaven, wheat, salt, wine, and oil, according to the request of the priests who *are* in Jerusalem—let it be given them day by day without fail,

10　that they may offer sacrifices of sweet aroma to the God of heaven, and pray for the life of the king and his sons.

11　Also I issue a decree that whoever alters this edict, let a timber be pulled from his house and erected, and let him be hanged on it; and let his house be made a refuse heap because of this.

12　And may the God who causes His name to dwell there destroy any king or people who put their hand to alter it, or to destroy this house of God which is in Jerusalem. I Da·rī′us issue a decree; let it be done diligently.

The Temple Completed and Dedicated

13　Then Tat′te·nai, governor of *the region* beyond the River, Shē′thar-Boz′nai, and their companions diligently did according to what King Da·rī′us had sent.

14　So the elders of the Jews built, and they prospered through the prophesying of Hag′gai the prophet and Zech·a·rī′ah the son of Id′dō. And they built and finished *it,* according to the commandment of the God of Israel, and according to the command of Cyrus, Da·rī′us, and Ar·ta·xerx′ēs king of Persia.

6:1 [a]Literally *house of the scrolls*　6:2 [a]Probably *Ecbatana,* the ancient capital of Media

15 Now the temple was finished on the third day of the month of Ā′dar, which was in the sixth year of the reign of King Da·rī′us.

16 Then the children of Israel, the priests and the Lē′vītes and the rest of the descendants of the captivity, celebrated the dedication of this house of God with joy.

17 And they offered sacrifices at the dedication of this house of God, one hundred bulls, two hundred rams, four hundred lambs, and as a sin offering for all Israel twelve male goats, according to the number of the tribes of Israel.

18 They assigned the priests to their divisions and the Lē′vītes to their divisions, over the service of God in Jerusalem, as it is written in the Book of Moses.

The Passover Celebrated

19 And the descendants of the captivity kept the Passover on the fourteenth *day* of the first month.

20 For the priests and the Lē′vītes had purified themselves; all of them *were ritually* clean. And they slaughtered the Passover *lambs* for all the descendants of the captivity, for their brethren the priests, and for themselves.

21 Then the children of Israel who had returned from the captivity ate together with all who had separated themselves from the filth of the nations of the land in order to seek the LORD God of Israel.

22 And they kept the Feast of Unleavened Bread seven days with joy; for the LORD made them joyful, and turned the heart of the king of Assyria toward them, to strengthen their hands in the work of the house of God, the God of Israel.

The Arrival of Ezra

7 Now after these things, in the reign of Ar·ta·xerx′ēs king of Persia, Ezra the son of Se·rāi′ah, the son of Az·a·rī′ah, the son of Hil·kī′ah,

2 the son of Shal′lum, the son of Zā′dok, the son of A·hī′tub,

3 the son of Am·a·rī′ah, the son of Az·a·rī′ah, the son of Me·rā′i·oth,

4 the son of Zer·a·hī′ah, the son of Uz′zī, the son of Buk′kī,

5 the son of Ab·i·shū′a, the son of Phin′e·has, the son of El·ē·ā′zar, the son of Aaron the chief priest—

6 this Ezra came up from Babylon; and he *was* a skilled scribe in the Law of Moses, which the LORD God of Israel had given. The king granted him all his request, according to the hand of the LORD his God upon him.

7 *Some* of the children of Israel, the priests, the Lē′vītes, the singers, the gatekeepers, and the Neth′i·nim came up to Jerusalem in the seventh year of King Ar·ta·xerx′ēs.

8 And Ezra came to Jerusalem in the fifth month, which *was* in the seventh year of the king.

9 On the first *day* of the first month he began *his* journey from Babylon, and on the first *day* of the fifth month he came to Jerusalem, according to the good hand of his God upon him.

10 For Ezra had prepared his heart to seek the Law of the LORD, and to do *it,* and to teach statutes and ordinances in Israel.

The Letter of Artaxerxes to Ezra

11 This *is* a copy of the letter that King Ar·ta·xerx′ēs gave Ezra the priest, the scribe, expert in the words of the commandments of the LORD, and of His statutes to Israel:

12 Ar·ta·xerx'ēs,*a* king of kings,

To Ezra the priest, a scribe of the Law of the God of heaven:

Perfect *peace,* and so forth.*b*

13 I issue a decree that all those of the people of Israel and the priests and Lē'vītes in my realm, who volunteer to go up to Jerusalem, may go with you.

14 And whereas you are being sent by the king and his seven counselors to inquire concerning Judah and Jerusalem, with regard to the Law of your God which *is* in your hand;

15 and *whereas you are* to carry the silver and gold which the king and his counselors have freely offered to the God of Israel, whose dwelling *is* in Jerusalem;

16 and *whereas* all the silver and gold that you may find in all the province of Babylon, along with the freewill offering of the people and the priests, *are to be* freely offered for the house of their God in Jerusalem—

17 now therefore, be careful to buy with this money bulls, rams, and lambs, with their grain offerings and their drink offerings, and offer them on the altar of the house of your God in Jerusalem.

18 And whatever seems good to you and your brethren to do with the rest of the silver and the gold, do it according to the will of your God.

19 Also the articles that are given to you for the service of the house of your God, deliver in full before the God of Jerusalem.

20 And whatever more may be needed for the house of your God, which you may have occasion to provide, pay *for it* from the king's treasury.

21 And I, *even* I, Ar·ta·xerx'ēs the king, issue a decree to all the treasurers who *are in the region* beyond the River, that whatever Ezra the priest, the scribe of the Law of the God of heaven, may require of you, let it be done diligently,

22 up to one hundred talents of silver, one hundred kors of wheat, one hundred baths of wine, one hundred baths of oil, and salt without prescribed limit.

23 Whatever is commanded by the God of heaven, let it diligently be done for the house of the God of heaven. For why should there be wrath against the realm of the king and his sons?

24 Also we inform you that it shall not be lawful to impose tax, tribute, or custom *on* any of the priests, Lē'vītes, singers, gatekeepers, Neth'i·nim, or servants of this house of God.

25 And you, Ezra, according to your God-given wisdom, set magistrates and judges who may judge all the people who *are in the region* beyond the River, all such as know the laws of your God; and teach those who do not know *them.*

26 Whoever will not observe the law of your God and the law of the king, let judgment be executed speedily on him, whether *it be* death, or banishment, or confiscation of goods, or imprisonment.

27 Blessed *be* the LORD God of our fathers, who has put *such a thing as* this in the king's heart, to beautify

---

7:12 *a*The original language of Ezra 7:12–26 is Aramaic.　*b*Literally *and now*

the house of the LORD which *is* in Jerusalem,

28 and has extended mercy to me before the king and his counselors, and before all the king's mighty princes.

So I was encouraged, as the hand of the LORD my God *was* upon me; and I gathered leading men of Israel to go up with me.

HEADS OF FAMILIES WHO RETURNED WITH EZRA

8 These *are* the heads of their fathers' *houses,* and *this is* the genealogy of those who went up with me from Babylon, in the reign of King Ar·ta·xerx′ēs:

2 of the sons of Phin′e·has, Ger′shom; of the sons of Ith′a·mar, Daniel; of the sons of David, Hat′tush;

3 of the sons of Shec·a·nī′ah, of the sons of Pā′rosh, Zech·a·rī′ah; and registered with him *were* one hundred and fifty males;

4 of the sons of Pā′hath-Mō′ab, El·i·ē·hō·ē′naī the son of Zer·a·hī′ah, and with him two hundred males;

5 of the sons of Shech·a·nī′ah,*a* Ben-Ja·hā′zi·el, and with him three hundred males;

6 of the sons of Ā′din, Ē′bed the son of Jonathan, and with him fifty males;

7 of the sons of Ē′lam, Je·shā′i·ah the son of Ath·a·lī′ah, and with him seventy males;

8 of the sons of Sheph·a·tī′ah, Zeb·a·dī′ah the son of Michael, and with him eighty males;

9 of the sons of Jō′ab, Ō·ba·dī′ah the son of Je·hī′el, and with him two hundred and eighteen males;

10 of the sons of She·lō′mith,*a* Ben-Jō·si·phī′ah, and with him one hundred and sixty males;

11 of the sons of Bē′baī, Zech·a·rī′ah

the son of Bē′baī, and with him twenty-eight males;

12 of the sons of Az′gad, Jō·hā′nan the son of Hak′ka·tan, and with him one hundred and ten males;

13 of the last sons of Ad·o·nī′kam, whose names *are* these—E·liph′e·let, Je·ī′el, and She·māi′ah—and with them sixty males;

14 also of the sons of Big′vaī, Ū′thaī and Zab′bud, and with them seventy males.

SERVANTS FOR THE TEMPLE

15 Now I gathered them by the river that flows to A·hā′va, and we camped there three days. And I looked among the people and the priests, and found none of the sons of Levi there.

16 Then I sent for El·i·ē′zer, Ar′i·el, She·māi′ah, El·nā′than, Jā′rib, E·nā′than, Nathan, Zech·a·rī′ah, and Me·shul′lam, leaders; also for Joi′a·rib and El·nā′than, men of understanding.

17 And I gave them a command for Id′dō the chief man at the place Cas·i·phī′a, and I told them what they should say to Id′dō *and* his brethren*a* the Neth′i·nim at the place Cas·i·phī′a—that they should bring us servants for the house of our God.

18 Then, by the good hand of our God upon us, they brought us a man of understanding, of the sons of Mah′li the son of Levi, the son of Israel, namely Sher·e·bī′ah, with his sons and brothers, eighteen men;

19 and Hash·a·bī′ah, and with him Je·shā′i·ah of the sons of Me·rar′i, his brothers and their sons, twenty men;

8:5 *a*Following Masoretic Text and Vulgate; Septuagint reads *the sons of Zatho, Shechaniah.*
8:10 *a*Following Masoretic Text and Vulgate; Septuagint reads *the sons of Banni, Shelomith.*
8:17 *a*Following Vulgate; Masoretic Text reads *to Iddo his brother;* Septuagint reads *to their brethren.*

20 also of the Neth′i·nim, whom David and the leaders had appointed for the service of the Lē′vites, two hundred and twenty Neth′i·nim. All of them were designated by name.

FASTING AND PRAYER FOR PROTECTION

21 Then I proclaimed a fast there at the river of A·hā′va, that we might humble ourselves before our God, to seek from Him the right way for us and our little ones and all our possessions.
22 For I was ashamed to request of the king an escort of soldiers and horsemen to help us against the enemy on the road, because we had spoken to the king, saying, "The hand of our God *is* upon all those for good who seek Him, but His power and His wrath *are* against all those who forsake Him."
23 So we fasted and entreated our God for this, and He answered our prayer.

Prayers

Ezra 8:21–23

Ezra needed special protection for a trip. He couldn't ask the king for the protection. He had already told the king that God would take care of him and his people. Now what should Ezra do? What would you do? Ezra did the right thing. He asked God to protect him and his people. Then God answered his prayer. Do you need protection from something? Ask God.

GIFTS FOR THE TEMPLE

24 And I separated twelve of the leaders of the priests—Sher·e·bī′ah, Hash·a·bī′ah, and ten of their brethren with them—
25 and weighed out to them the silver, the gold, and the articles, the offering for the house of our God which the king and his counselors and his princes, and all Israel *who were* present, had offered.
26 I weighed into their hand six hundred and fifty talents of silver, silver articles *weighing* one hundred talents, one hundred talents of gold,
27 twenty gold basins *worth* a thousand drachmas, and two vessels of fine polished bronze, precious as gold.
28 And I said to them, "You *are* holy to the LORD; the articles *are* holy also; and the silver and the gold *are* a freewill offering to the LORD God of your fathers.
29 "Watch and keep *them* until you weigh *them* before the leaders of the priests and the Lē′vites and heads of the fathers' *houses* of Israel in Jerusalem, *in* the chambers of the house of the LORD."
30 So the priests and the Lē′vites received the silver and the gold and the articles by weight, to bring *them* to Jerusalem to the house of our God.

THE RETURN TO JERUSALEM

31 Then we departed from the river of A·hā′va on the twelfth *day* of the first month, to go to Jerusalem. And the hand of our God was upon us, and He delivered us from the hand of the enemy and from ambush along the road.
32 So we came to Jerusalem, and stayed there three days.
33 Now on the fourth day the silver

ABOUT GOD'S PROTECTION Ezra 8:31

Wake Up!

This soldier is sleeping. But he shouldn't sleep. The enemy is coming. "Wake up!" an angel says. "Go there." Do you think the soldier will do what the angel says?

1. The angel is *protecting* the soldier from harm. Do you think the soldier will say "thank you"?
2. When God *protects* you from harm, will you remember to say "thank You"?
3. Do you remember to say "thank you" when your parents protect you from harm? Will you do that now?

For more on *What the Bible Says* turn to page 799
For more on *God's Care* turn to page 761

and the gold and the articles were weighed in the house of our God by the hand of Mer'e·moth the son of Ū·rī'ah the priest, and with him *was* El·ē·ā'zar the son of Phin'e·has; with them *were* the Lē'vītes, Joz'a·bad the son of Jesh'ū·a and Nō·a·dī'ah the son of Bin'nū·ī,

34 with the number *and* weight of everything. All the weight was written down at that time.

35 The children of those who had been carried away captive, who had come from the captivity, offered burnt offerings to the God of Israel: twelve bulls for all Israel, ninety-six rams, seventy-seven lambs, and twelve male goats *as* a sin offering. All *this was* a burnt offering to the LORD.

36 And they delivered the king's orders to the king's satraps and the governors *in the region* beyond the River. So they gave support to the people and the house of God.

INTERMARRIAGE WITH PAGANS

9 When these things were done, the leaders came to me, saying, "The people of Israel and the priests and the Lē'vītes have not separated themselves from the peoples of the lands, with respect to the abominations of the Cā'naan·ītes, the Hit'-tītes, the Per'iz·zītes, the Jeb'ū·sītes, the Am'mon·ītes, the Mō'ab·ītes, the Egyptians, and the Am'o·rītes.

2 "For they have taken some of their daughters *as wives* for themselves and their sons, so that the holy seed is mixed with the peoples of *those* lands. Indeed, the hand of the leaders and rulers has been foremost in this trespass."

3 So when I heard this thing, I tore my garment and my robe, and plucked out some of the hair of my head and beard, and sat down astonished.

4 Then everyone who trembled at the words of the God of Israel assembled to me, because of the transgression of those who had been carried away captive, and I sat astonished until the evening sacrifice.

5 At the evening sacrifice I arose from my fasting; and having torn my garment and my robe, I fell on my knees and spread out my hands to the LORD my God.

6 And I said: "O my God, I am too ashamed and humiliated to lift up my face to You, my God; for our iniquities have risen higher than *our* heads, and our guilt has grown up to the heavens.

7 "Since the days of our fathers to this day we *have been* very guilty, and for our iniquities we, our kings, *and* our priests have been delivered into the hand of the kings of the lands, to the sword, to captivity, to plunder, and to humiliation, as *it is* this day.

8 "And now for a little while grace has been *shown* from the LORD our God, to leave us a remnant to escape,

---

■ *Prayers* ■

Ezra 9:5–15

Ezra's people had married pagans. It was wrong. God was angry. So Ezra tore his clothes, pulled out some of his hair and trembled. Then he prayed a long prayer to God. He confessed the sin of the people. He begged God to forgive. When you know that you have done something very wrong, confess your sin to God. Beg Him to forgive you. He will.

PRAYER Ezra 9:5–15

Prayer Mail

This girl has two mailboxes. One is for Regular Mail. The other is for Air Mail. Do you think she could have a third for Prayer Mail?

1. Do you pray for others? Do you pray for parents? Do you pray, thanking God and praising Him? Perhaps you could call that Prayer Mail.
2. Why would you like others to pray for you? What would you like them to ask God to do for you?
3. Do you pray often for your parents? Do you pray often for others? Do you pray often to thank and praise God? Should you?

For more on *Favorite Bible Words* turn to page 719
For more on *Prayer* turn to page 719

and to give us a peg in His holy place, that our God may enlighten our eyes and give us a measure of revival in our bondage.

9 "For we *were* slaves. Yet our God did not forsake us in our bondage; but He extended mercy to us in the sight of the kings of Persia, to revive us, to repair the house of our God, to rebuild its ruins, and to give us a wall in Judah and Jerusalem.

10 "And now, O our God, what shall we say after this? For we have forsaken Your commandments,

11 "which You commanded by Your servants the prophets, saying, 'The land which you are entering to possess is an unclean land, with the uncleanness of the peoples of the lands, with their abominations which have filled it from one end to another with their impurity.

12 'Now therefore, do not give your daughters as wives for their sons, nor take their daughters to your sons; and never seek their peace or prosperity, that you may be strong and eat the good of the land, and leave *it* as an inheritance to your children forever.'

13 "And after all that has come upon us for our evil deeds and for our great guilt, since You our God have punished us less than our iniquities *deserve,* and have given us *such* deliverance as this,

14 "should we again break Your commandments, and join in marriage with the people *committing* these abominations? Would You not be angry with us until You had consumed *us,* so that *there would be* no remnant or survivor?

15 "O LORD God of Israel, You *are* righteous, for we are left as a remnant, as *it is* this day. Here we *are* before You, in our guilt, though no one can stand before You because of this!"

CONFESSION OF IMPROPER MARRIAGES

10 Now while Ezra was praying, and while he was confessing, weeping, and bowing down before the house of God, a very large assembly of men, women, and children gathered to him from Israel; for the people wept very bitterly.

2 And Shech·a·nī'ah the son of Je·hī'el, *one* of the sons of Ē'lam, spoke up and said to Ezra, "We have trespassed against our God, and have taken pagan wives from the peoples of the land; yet now there is hope in Israel in spite of this.

3 "Now therefore, let us make a covenant with our God to put away all these wives and those who have been born to them, according to the advice of my master and of those who tremble at the commandment of our God; and let it be done according to the law.

4 "Arise, for *this* matter *is* your *responsibility.* We also *are* with you. Be of good courage, and do *it.*"

5 Then Ezra arose, and made the leaders of the priests, the Lē'vītes, and all Israel swear an oath that they would do according to this word. So they swore an oath.

6 Then Ezra rose up from before the house of God, and went into the chamber of Jē·hō·hā'nan the son of E·lī'a·shib; and *when* he came there, he ate no bread and drank no water, for he mourned because of the guilt of those from the captivity.

7 And they issued a proclamation throughout Judah and Jerusalem to all the descendants of the captivity, that they must gather at Jerusalem,

8 and that whoever would not come within three days, according to the instructions of the leaders and elders, all his property would be confiscated,

and he himself would be separated from the assembly of those from the captivity.

9 So all the men of Judah and Benjamin gathered at Jerusalem within three days. It *was* the ninth month, on the twentieth of the month; and all the people sat in the open square of the house of God, trembling because of *this* matter and because of heavy rain.

10 Then Ezra the priest stood up and said to them, "You have transgressed and have taken pagan wives, adding to the guilt of Israel.

11 "Now therefore, make confession to the LORD God of your fathers, and do His will; separate yourselves from the peoples of the land, and from the pagan wives."

12 Then all the assembly answered and said with a loud voice, "Yes! As you have said, so we must do.

13 "But *there are* many people; *it is* the season for heavy rain, and we are not able to stand outside. Nor *is this* the work of one or two days, for *there are* many of us who have transgressed in this matter.

14 "Please, let the leaders of our entire assembly stand; and let all those in our cities who have taken pagan wives come at appointed times, together with the elders and judges of their cities, until the fierce wrath of our God is turned away from us in this matter."

15 Only Jonathan the son of As'a·hel and Jā·ha·zī'ah the son of Tik'vah opposed this, and Me·shul'lam and Shab'be·thaī the Lē'vīte gave them support.

16 Then the descendants of the captivity did so. And Ezra the priest, *with* certain heads of the fathers' *households,* were set apart by the fathers' *households,* each of them by name; and they sat down on the first day of the tenth month to examine the matter.

17 By the first day of the first month they finished *questioning* all the men who had taken pagan wives.

PAGAN WIVES PUT AWAY

18 And among the sons of the priests who had taken pagan wives *the following* were found of the sons of Jesh'ū·a the son of Jō'za·dak,*a* and his brothers: Mā·a·sēi'ah, El·i·ē'zer, Jā'rib, and Ged·a·lī'ah.

19 And they gave their promise that they would put away their wives; and *being* guilty, *they presented* a ram of the flock as their trespass offering.

20 Also of the sons of Im'mer: Ha·nā'nī and Zeb·a·dī'ah;

21 of the sons of Hā'rim: Mā·a·sēi'ah, E·lī'jah, She·māi'ah, Je·hī'el, and Uz·zī'ah;

22 of the sons of Pash'hur: El·i·ō·ē'naī, Mā·a·sēi'ah, Ish'ma·el, Ne·than'el, Joz'a·bad, and El·ā'sah.

23 Also of the Lē'vītes: Joz'a·bad, Shim'ē·ī, Ke·lāi'ah (the same *is* Ke·lī'ta), Peth·a·hī'ah, Judah, and El·i·ē'zer.

24 Also of the singers: E·lī'a·shib; and of the gatekeepers: Shal'lum, Tē'lem, and Ū'rī.

25 And others of Israel: of the sons of Pā'rosh: Ra·mī'ah, Je·zī'ah, Malchī'ah, Mij'a·min, El·ē·ā'zar, Malchī'jah, and Be·nā'i·ah;

26 of the sons of Ē'lam: Mat·ta·nī'ah, Zech·a·rī'ah, Je·hī'el, Ab'dī, Jer'e·moth, and E·lī'ah;

27 of the sons of Zat'tū: El·i·ō·ē'naī, E·lī'a·shib, Mat·ta·nī'ah, Jer'e·moth, Zā'bad, and A·zī'za;

28 of the sons of Bē'baī: Jē·hō·hā'nan, Han·a·nī'ah, Zab'baī, *and* Ath'laī;

29 of the sons of Bā'nī: Me·shul'lam,

10:18 *a*Spelled *Jehozadak* in 1 Chronicles 6:14

Mal'luch, A·dāi'ah, Jash'ub, Shē'al, *and* Rā'moth;a

30 of the sons of Pā'hath-Mō'ab: Ad'na, Chē'lal, Be·nā'i·ah, Mā·a·sēi'ah, Mat·ta·nī'ah, Bez'a·lel, Bin'nū·ī, and Ma·nas'seh;

31 *of* the sons of Hā'rim: El·i·ē'zer, Ish·ī'jah, Mal·chī'jah, She·māi'ah, Shim'ē·on,

32 Benjamin, Mal'luch, *and* Shem·a·rī'ah;

33 of the sons of Hā'shum: Mat·tē'nai, Mat·tat'tah, Zā'bad, E·liph'e·let, Jer'e·mai, Ma·nas'seh, *and* Shim'ē·ī;

34 of the sons of Bā'nī: Mā·a·dā'ī, Am'ram, Ū'el,

35 Be·nā'i·ah, Bē·dēi'ah, Chel'ūh,a

36 Va·nī'ah, Mer'e·moth, E·lī'a·shib,

37 Mat·ta·nī'ah, Mat·tē'nai, Jā'a·sai,a

38 Bā'nī, Bin'nū·ī, Shim'ē·ī,

39 Shel·e·mī'ah, Nathan, A·dāi'ah,

40 Mach·nad'e·bai, Shā'shai, Shā'rai,

41 Az'a·rel, Shel·e·mī'ah, Shem·a·rī'ah,

42 Shal'lum, Am·a·rī'ah, *and* Joseph;

43 of the sons of Nē'bō: Je·ī'el, Mat·ti·thī'ah, Zā'bad, Ze·bī'na, Jad'dai,a Jō'el, *and* Be·nā'i·ah.

44 All these had taken pagan wives, and *some* of them had wives *by whom* they had children.

10:29 aOr *Jeremoth*   10:35 aOr *Cheluhi,* or *Cheluhu*   10:37 aOr *Jaasu*   10:43 aOr *Jaddu*

The Book of
NEHEMIAH

NEHEMIAH PRAYS FOR HIS PEOPLE

THE words of Nē·he·mī′ah the son of Ha·cha·lī′ah.

It came to pass in the month of Chis′lev, *in* the twentieth year, as I was in Shū′shan*a* the citadel,

2 that Ha·nā′nī one of my brethren came with men from Judah; and I asked them concerning the Jews who had escaped, who had survived the captivity, and concerning Jerusalem.

3 And they said to me, "The survivors who are left from the captivity in the province *are* there in great distress and reproach. The wall of Jerusalem *is* also broken down, and its gates *are* burned with fire."

4 So it was, when I heard these words, that I sat down and wept, and mourned *for many* days; I was fasting and praying before the God of heaven.

5 And I said: "I pray, LORD God of heaven, O great and awesome God, *You* who keep *Your* covenant and mercy with those who love You*a* and observe Your*b* commandments,

6 "please let Your ear be attentive and Your eyes open, that You may hear the prayer of Your servant which I pray before You now, day and night, for the children of Israel Your servants, and confess the sins of the children of Israel which we have sinned against You. Both my father's house and I have sinned.

7 "We have acted very corruptly against You, and have not kept the commandments, the statutes, nor the ordinances which You commanded Your servant Moses.

8 "Remember, I pray, the word that You commanded Your servant Moses, saying, '*If* you are unfaithful, I will scatter you among the nations;*a*

9 'but *if* you return to Me, and keep My commandments and do them, though some of you were cast out to the farthest part of the heavens, *yet* I will gather them from there, and bring them to the place which I have chosen as a dwelling for My name.'*a*

10 "Now these *are* Your servants and Your people, whom You have redeemed by Your great power, and by Your strong hand.

11 "O Lord, I pray, please let Your ear be attentive to the prayer of Your servant, and to the prayer of Your servants who desire to fear Your name; and let Your servant prosper this day, I pray, and grant him mercy in the sight of this man." For I was the king's cupbearer.

◼ *Prayers* ◼

Nehemiah 1:4–11

The beautiful city of Jerusalem was destroyed. Its walls were torn down. Its gates were burned. When Nehemiah heard the news he cried. Then he fasted and prayed. He begged God to forgive his people. There is a time to confess to God that you are wrong. There is a time to beg God for forgiveness. Prayer is not always asking God for things. Sometimes it is telling God how wrong you are and asking Him to forgive.

1:1 *a*Or *Susa*   1:5 *a*Literally *Him*   *b*Literally *His*   1:8 *a*Leviticus 26:33   1:9 *a*Deuteronomy 30:2–5

PRAYER Nehemiah 1:5, 6

What Is Prayer?

What is this girl doing? Do you think she is praying? Yes, she is. She is talking to God. "Please help me, God," she is praying. Or she could be praying, "Thank You, God." Perhaps she is telling God that she loves Him. Or she could be telling God how wonderful He is. Would you like to talk with God now? What will you say?

1. Whom are we talking to when we pray? Why should we pray?
2. Do you like to talk to God? What do you like to say to Him?
3. Would you like to talk to God now?

For more on *Favorite Bible Words* turn to page 769
For more on *Prayer* turn to page 1114

NEHEMIAH SENT TO JUDAH

2 And it came to pass in the month of Nī′san, in the twentieth year of King Ar·ta·xerx′ēs, *when* wine *was* before him, that I took the wine and gave it to the king. Now I had never been sad in his presence before.
2 Therefore the king said to me, "Why *is* your face sad, since you *are* not sick? This *is* nothing but sorrow of heart." So I became dreadfully afraid,
3 and said to the king, "May the king live forever! Why should my face not be sad, when the city, the place of my fathers' tombs, *lies* waste, and its gates are burned with fire?"
4 Then the king said to me, "What do you request?" So I prayed to the God of heaven.
5 And I said to the king, "If it pleases the king, and if your servant has found favor in your sight, I ask that you send me to Judah, to the city of my fathers' tombs, that I may rebuild it."
6 Then the king said to me (the queen also sitting beside him), "How long will your journey be? And when will you return?" So it pleased the king to send me; and I set him a time.
7 Furthermore I said to the king, "If it pleases the king, let letters be given to me for the governors *of the region* beyond the River,*a* that they must permit me to pass through till I come to Judah,
8 "and a letter to Ā′saph the keeper of the king's forest, that he must give me timber to make beams for the gates of the citadel which *pertains* to the temple,*a* for the city wall, and for the house that I will occupy." And the king granted *them* to me according to the good hand of my God upon me.
9 Then I went to the governors *in* the region beyond the River, and gave them the king's letters. Now the king had sent captains of the army and horsemen with me.
10 When San·bal′lat the Hor′o·nīte and Tō·bī′ah the Am′mon·īte official*a* heard *of it,* they were deeply disturbed that a man had come to seek the well-being of the children of Israel.

NEHEMIAH VIEWS THE WALL OF JERUSALEM

11 So I came to Jerusalem and was there three days.
12 Then I arose in the night, I and a few men with me; I told no one what my God had put in my heart to do at Jerusalem; nor was there any animal with me, except the one on which I rode.
13 And I went out by night through the Valley Gate to the Serpent Well and the Refuse Gate, and viewed the walls of Jerusalem which were broken down and its gates which were burned with fire.
14 Then I went on to the Fountain Gate and to the King's Pool, but *there was* no room for the animal under me to pass.
15 So I went up in the night by the valley, and viewed the wall; then I turned back and entered by the Valley Gate, and so returned.
16 And the officials did not know where I had gone or what I had done; I had not yet told the Jews, the priests, the nobles, the officials, or the others who did the work.
17 Then I said to them, "You see the distress that we *are* in, how Jerusalem *lies* waste, and its gates are burned with fire. Come and let us

2:7 *a*That is, the Euphrates, and so elsewhere in this book   2:8 *a*Literally *house*   2:10 *a*Literally *servant,* and so elsewhere in this book

build the wall of Jerusalem, that we may no longer be a reproach."

18 And I told them of the hand of my God which had been good upon me, and also of the king's words that he had spoken to me. So they said, "Let us rise up and build." Then they set their hands to *this* good *work.*

19 But when San·bal′lat the Hor′o·nīte, Tō·bī′ah the Am′mon·īte official, and Gē′shem the Arab heard *of it,* they laughed at us and despised us, and said, "What *is* this thing that you are doing? Will you rebel against the king?"

20 So I answered them, and said to them, "The God of heaven Himself will prosper us; therefore we His servants will arise and build, but you have no heritage or right or memorial in Jerusalem."

REBUILDING THE WALL

3 Then E·lī′a·shib the high priest rose up with his brethren the priests and built the Sheep Gate; they consecrated it and hung its doors. They built as far as the Tower of the Hundred,*a and* consecrated it, then as far as the Tower of Ha·nan′el.

2 Next to *E·lī′a·shiba* the men of Jericho built. And next to them Zac′cur the son of Im′rī built.

3 Also the sons of Has·se·nā′ah built the Fish Gate; they laid its beams and hung its doors with its bolts and bars.

4 And next to them Mer′e·moth the son of Ū·rī′jah, the son of Koz,*a* made repairs. Next to them Me·shul′lam the son of Ber·e·chī′ah, the son of Me·shez′a·bel, made repairs. Next to them Zā′dok the son of Bā′a·na made repairs.

5 Next to them the Te·kō′ītes made repairs; but their nobles did not put

their shoulders*a* to the work of their Lord.

6 Moreover Je·hoi′a·da the son of Pa·sē′ah and Me·shul′lam the son of Bes·o·dēi′ah repaired the Old Gate; they laid its beams and hung its doors, with its bolts and bars.

7 And next to them Me·la·tī′ah the Gib′ē·on·īte, Jā′don the Me·ron′o·thīte, the men of Gib′ē·on and Miz′pah, repaired the residence*a* of the governor *of the region* beyond the River.

8 Next to him Uz′zi·el the son of Har·haī′ah, one of the goldsmiths, made repairs. Also next to him Han·a·nī′ah, one*a* of the perfumers, made repairs; and they fortified Jerusalem as far as the Broad Wall.

9 And next to them Reph·āi′ah the son of Hur, leader of half the district of Jerusalem, made repairs.

10 Next to them Je·daī′ah the son of Har·ū′maph made repairs in front of his house. And next to him Hat′tush the son of Ha·shab·nī′ah made repairs.

11 Mal·chī′jah the son of Hā′rim and Hash′ub the son of Pā′hath-Mō′ab repaired another section, as well as the Tower of the Ovens.

12 And next to him was Shal′lum the son of Hal·lō′hesh, leader of half the district of Jerusalem; he and his daughters made repairs.

13 Hā′nun and the inhabitants of Za·nō′ah repaired the Valley Gate. They built it, hung its doors with its bolts and bars, and *repaired* a thousand cubits of the wall as far as the Refuse Gate.

14 Mal·chī′jah the son of Rē′chab, leader of the district of Beth Hac′ce·rem, repaired the Refuse Gate; he

3:1 *a*Hebrew *Hammeah,* also at 12:39
3:2 *a*Literally *On his hand*   3:4 *a*Or *Hakkoz*
3:5 *a*Literally *necks*   3:7 *a*Literally *throne*
3:8 *a*Literally *the son*

built it and hung its doors with its bolts and bars.

15 Shal'lun the son of Col-Hō'zeh, leader of the district of Miz'pah, repaired the Fountain Gate; he built it, covered it, hung its doors with its bolts and bars, and repaired the wall of the Pool of Shē'lah by the King's Garden, as far as the stairs that go down from the City of David.

16 After him Nē·he·mī'ah the son of Az'buk, leader of half the district of Beth Zūr, made repairs as far as *the place* in front of the tombs[a] of David, to the man-made pool, and as far as the House of the Mighty.

17 After him the Lē'vites, *under* Rē'hum the son of Bā'nī, made repairs. Next to him Hash·a·bī'ah, leader of half the district of Kē·ī'lah, made repairs for his district.

18 After him their brethren, *under* Bav'a·ī[a] the son of Hen'a·dad, leader of the *other* half of the district of Kē·ī'lah, made repairs.

19 And next to him Ē'zer the son of Jesh'ū·a, the leader of Miz'pah, repaired another section in front of the Ascent to the Armory at the buttress.

20 After him Bar'uch the son of Zab'bai[a] carefully repaired the other section, from the buttress to the door of the house of E·lī'a·shib the high priest.

21 After him Mer'e·moth the son of Ū·rī'jah, the son of Koz,[a] repaired another section, from the door of the house of E·lī'a·shib to the end of the house of E·lī'a·shib.

22 And after him the priests, the men of the plain, made repairs.

23 After him Benjamin and Has'shub made repairs opposite their house. After them Az·a·rī'ah the son of Mā·a·sēi'ah, the son of An·a·nī'ah, made repairs by his house.

24 After him Bin'nū·ī the son of Hen'a·dad repaired another section, from the house of Az·a·rī'ah to the buttress, even as far as the corner.

25 Pā'lal the son of Ū'zaī *made repairs* opposite the buttress, and on the tower which projects from the king's upper house that *was* by the court of the prison. After him Pe·dāi'ah the son of Pā'rosh *made repairs*.

26 Moreover the Neth'i·nim who dwelt in Ō'phel *made repairs* as far as *the place* in front of the Water Gate toward the east, and on the projecting tower.

27 After them the Te·kō'ites repaired another section, next to the great projecting tower, and as far as the wall of Ō'phel.

28 Beyond the Horse Gate the priests made repairs, each in front of his *own* house.

29 After them Zā'dok the son of Im'mer made repairs in front of his *own* house. After him She·māi'ah the son of Shech·a·nī'ah, the keeper of the East Gate, made repairs.

30 After him Han·a·nī'ah the son of Shel·e·mī'ah, and Hā'nun, the sixth son of Zā'laph, repaired another section. After him Me·shul'lam the son of Ber·e·chī'ah made repairs in front of his dwelling.

31 After him Mal·chī'jah, one of the goldsmiths, made repairs as far as the house of the Neth'i·nim and of the merchants, in front of the Miph'kad[a] Gate, and as far as the upper room at the corner.

32 And between the upper room at the corner, as far as the Sheep Gate, the goldsmiths and the merchants made repairs.

3:16 [a]Septuagint, Syriac, and Vulgate read *tomb*.
3:18 [a]Following Masoretic Text and Vulgate; some Hebrew manuscripts, Septuagint, and Syriac read *Binnui* (compare verse 24).   3:20 [a]A few Hebrew manuscripts, Syriac, and Vulgate read *Zaccai*.
3:21 [a]Or *Hakkoz*   3:31 [a]Literally *Inspection* or *Recruiting*

FIX-UP TIME Nehemiah 3:32

This stick horse has a problem. The poor horse can't fix his problem, either. How can a stick horse glue his stick together? He has no hands. The only hands he has are Eric's hands. So guess what Eric is doing? He is fixing up his stick horse. Sometimes mother or father needs our hands to help fix up or clean up or tidy up or straighten up. They could do it. But they're so busy with other things. Your hands are truly helping hands. Do you help to fix up or tidy up when you can? Fix-up time is a time when you can share your hands with mother or father. So is clean-up time. And tidy-up time and straighten-up time. Will you do it?

1. Have you and your parents had a fix-up or tidy-up time at your house? What did you do?
2. Are you glad to use your hands to help mother or father fix up or tidy up or clean up?
3. What will you do today to help fix up or clean up or tidy up? Will you?

For more on *Family Memories* turn to page 891
For more on *Helpfulness* turn to page 789

The Wall Defended Against Enemies

4 But it so happened, when San-bal'lat heard that we were rebuilding the wall, that he was furious and very indignant, and mocked the Jews.

2 And he spoke before his brethren and the army of Samaria, and said, "What are these feeble Jews doing? Will they fortify themselves? Will they offer sacrifices? Will they complete it in a day? Will they revive the stones from the heaps of rubbish— *stones* that are burned?"

3 Now Tō·bī'ah the Am'mon·ite *was* beside him, and he said, "Whatever they build, if even a fox goes up *on it,* he will break down their stone wall."

4 Hear, O our God, for we are despised; turn their reproach on their own heads, and give them as plunder to a land of captivity!

5 Do not cover their iniquity, and do not let their sin be blotted out from before You; for they have provoked *You* to anger before the builders.

6 So we built the wall, and the entire wall was joined together up to half its *height,* for the people had a mind to work.

7 Now it happened, when San·bal'-lat, Tō·bī'ah, the Arabs, the Am'-mon·ites, and the Ash'dod·ites heard that the walls of Jerusalem were being restored and the gaps were beginning to be closed, that they became very angry,

8 and all of them conspired together to come *and* attack Jerusalem and create confusion.

9 Nevertheless we made our prayer to our God, and because of them we set a watch against them day and night.

10 Then Judah said, "The strength of the laborers is failing, and *there is* so much rubbish that we are not able to build the wall."

11 And our adversaries said, "They will neither know nor see anything, till we come into their midst and kill them and cause the work to cease."

12 So it was, when the Jews who dwelt near them came, that they told us ten times, "From whatever place you turn, *they will be* upon us."

13 Therefore I positioned *men* behind the lower parts of the wall, at the openings; and I set the people according to their families, with their swords, their spears, and their bows.

14 And I looked, and arose and said to the nobles, to the leaders, and to the rest of the people, "Do not be afraid of them. Remember the Lord, great and awesome, and fight for your brethren, your sons, your daughters, your wives, and your houses."

15 And it happened, when our enemies heard that it was known to us, and *that* God had brought their plot to nothing, that all of us returned to the wall, everyone to his work.

16 So it was, from that time on, *that* half of my servants worked at construction, while the other half held the spears, the shields, the bows, and *wore* armor; and the leaders *were* behind all the house of Judah.

17 Those who built on the wall, and those who carried burdens, loaded themselves so that with one hand they worked at construction, and with the other held a weapon.

18 Every one of the builders had his sword girded at his side as he built. And the one who sounded the trumpet *was* beside me.

19 Then I said to the nobles, the rulers, and the rest of the people, "The work *is* great and extensive, and we are separated far from one another on the wall.

20 "Wherever you hear the sound of

the trumpet, rally to us there. Our God will fight for us."

21 So we labored in the work, and half of *the men*[a] held the spears from daybreak until the stars appeared.

22 At the same time I also said to the people, "Let each man and his servant stay at night in Jerusalem, that they may be our guard by night and a working party by day."

23 So neither I, my brethren, my servants, nor the men of the guard who followed me took off our clothes, *except* that everyone took them off for washing.

Nehemiah Deals with Oppression

5 And there was a great outcry of the people and their wives against their Jewish brethren.

2 For there were those who said, "We, our sons, and our daughters *are* many; therefore let us get grain, that we may eat and live."

3 There were also *some* who said, "We have mortgaged our lands and vineyards and houses, that we might buy grain because of the famine."

4 There were also those who said, "We have borrowed money for the king's tax *on* our lands and vineyards.

5 "Yet now our flesh *is* as the flesh of our brethren, our children as their children; and indeed we are forcing our sons and our daughters to be slaves, and *some* of our daughters have been brought into slavery. *It is* not in our power *to redeem them,* for other men have our lands and vineyards."

6 And I became very angry when I heard their outcry and these words.

7 After serious thought, I rebuked the nobles and rulers, and said to them, "Each of you is exacting usury from his brother." So I called a great assembly against them.

8 And I said to them, "According to our ability we have redeemed our Jewish brethren who were sold to the nations. Now indeed, will you even sell your brethren? Or should they be sold to us?" Then they were silenced and found nothing *to say.*

9 Then I said, "What you are doing *is* not good. Should you not walk in the fear of our God because of the reproach of the nations, our enemies?

10 "I also, *with* my brethren and my servants, am lending them money and grain. Please, let us stop this usury!

11 "Restore now to them, even this day, their lands, their vineyards, their olive groves, and their houses, also a hundredth of the money and the grain, the new wine and the oil, that you have charged them."

12 So they said, "We will restore *it,* and will require nothing from them; we will do as you say." Then I called the priests, and required an oath from them that they would do according to this promise.

13 Then I shook out the fold of my garment[a] and said, "So may God shake out each man from his house, and from his property, who does not perform this promise. Even thus may he be shaken out and emptied." And all the assembly said, "Amen!" and praised the LORD. Then the people did according to this promise.

The Generosity of Nehemiah

14 Moreover, from the time that I was appointed to be their governor in the land of Judah, from the twentieth year until the thirty-second year of King Ar·ta·xerx′ēs, twelve years,

4:21 [a]Literally *them*   5:13 [a]Literally *my lap*

neither I nor my brothers ate the governor's provisions.

15 But the former governors who *were* before me laid burdens on the people, and took from them bread and wine, besides forty shekels of silver. Yes, even their servants bore rule over the people, but I did not do so, because of the fear of God.

16 Indeed, I also continued the work on this wall, and we[a] did not buy any land. All my servants *were* gathered there for the work.

17 And at my table *were* one hundred and fifty Jews and rulers, besides those who came to us from the nations around us.

18 Now *that* which was prepared daily *was* one ox *and* six choice sheep. Also fowl were prepared for me, and once every ten days an abundance of all kinds of wine. Yet in spite of this I did not demand the governor's provisions, because the bondage was heavy on this people.

19 Remember me, my God, for good, *according to* all that I have done for this people.

Conspiracy Against Nehemiah

6 Now it happened when San·bal'-lat, Tō·bī'ah, Gē'shem the Arab, and the rest of our enemies heard that I had rebuilt the wall, and *that* there were no breaks left in it (though at that time I had not hung the doors in the gates),

2 that San·bal'lat and Gē'shem sent to me, saying, "Come, let us meet together among the villages in the plain of Ō'nō." But they thought to do me harm.

3 So I sent messengers to them, saying, "I *am* doing a great work, so that I cannot come down. Why should the work cease while I leave it and go down to you?"

4 But they sent me this message four times, and I answered them in the same manner.

5 Then San·bal'lat sent his servant to me as before, the fifth time, with an open letter in his hand.

6 In it *was* written:

It is reported among the nations, and Gē'shem[a] says, *that* you and the Jews plan to rebel; therefore, according to these rumors, you are rebuilding the wall, that you may be their king.

7 And you have also appointed prophets to proclaim concerning you at Jerusalem, saying, "*There is* a king in Judah!" Now these matters will be reported to the king. So come, therefore, and let us consult together.

8 Then I sent to him, saying, "No such things as you say are being done, but you invent them in your own heart."

9 For they all *were trying to* make us afraid, saying, "Their hands will be weakened in the work, and it will not be done."

Now therefore, *O God,* strengthen my hands.

10 Afterward I came to the house of She·māi'ah the son of De·laī'ah, the son of Me·het'a·bel, who *was* a secret informer; and he said, "Let us meet together in the house of God, within the temple, and let us close the doors of the temple, for they are coming to kill you; indeed, at night they will come to kill you."

11 And I said, "Should such a man as I flee? And who *is there* such as I who would go into the temple to save his life? I will not go in!"

12 Then I perceived that God had

5:16 [a]Following Masoretic Text; Septuagint, Syriac, and Vulgate read *I.*   6:6 [a]Hebrew *Gashmu*

not sent him at all, but that he pronounced *this* prophecy against me because Tō·bī′ah and San·bal′lat had hired him.

13 For this reason he *was* hired, that I should be afraid and act that way and sin, so *that* they might have *cause* for an evil report, that they might reproach me.

14 My God, remember Tō·bī′ah and San·bal′lat, according to these their works, and the prophetess Nō·a·dī′ah and the rest of the prophets who would have made me afraid.

THE WALL COMPLETED

15 So the wall was finished on the twenty-fifth *day* of Ē′lul, in fifty-two days.

16 And it happened, when all our enemies heard *of it,* and all the nations around us saw *these things,* that they were very disheartened in their own eyes; for they perceived that this work was done by our God.

17 Also in those days the nobles of Judah sent many letters to Tō·bī′ah, and *the letters of* Tō·bī′ah came to them.

18 For many in Judah were pledged to him, because he was the son-in-law of Shech·a·nī′ah the son of Ā′rah, and his son Jē·hō·hā′nan had married the daughter of Me·shul′lam the son of Ber·e·chī′ah.

19 Also they reported his good deeds before me, and reported my words to him. Tō·bī′ah sent letters to frighten me.

7 Then it was, when the wall was built and I had hung the doors, when the gatekeepers, the singers, and the Lē′vītes had been appointed,

2 that I gave the charge of Jerusalem to my brother Ha·nā′nī, and Han·a·nī′ah the leader of the citadel,

for he *was* a faithful man and feared God more than many.

3 And I said to them, "Do not let the gates of Jerusalem be opened until the sun is hot; and while they stand *guard,* let them shut and bar the doors; and appoint guards from among the inhabitants of Jerusalem, one at his watch station and another in front of his own house."

THE CAPTIVES WHO RETURNED TO JERUSALEM

4 Now the city *was* large and spacious, but the people in it *were* few, and the houses *were* not rebuilt.

5 Then my God put it into my heart to gather the nobles, the rulers, and the people, that they might be registered by genealogy. And I found a register of the genealogy of those who had come up in the first *return,* and found written in it:

6 These[a] are the people of the province who came back from the captivity, of those who had been carried away, whom Ne·bū·chad·nez′zar the king of Babylon had carried away, and who returned to Jerusalem and Judah, everyone to his city.

7 Those who came with Ze·rub′ba·bel *were* Jesh′ū·a, Nē·he·mī′ah, Az·a·rī′ah, Rā·a·mī′ah, Nā·ham′a·nī, Mor′de·caī, Bil′shan, Mis′pe·reth,[a] Big′vaī, Nē′hum, and Bā′a·nah.

The number of the men of the people of Israel:

8 the sons of Pā′rosh, two thousand one hundred and seventy-two;

9 the sons of Sheph·a·tī′ah, three hundred and seventy-two;

7:6 [a]Compare verses 6–72 with Ezra 2:1–70
7:7 [a]Spelled *Mispar* in Ezra 2:2

10 the sons of Ā′rah, six hundred and fifty-two;

11 the sons of Pā′hath-Mō′ab, of the sons of Jesh′u·a and Jō′ab, two thousand eight hundred and eighteen;

12 the sons of Ē′lam, one thousand two hundred and fifty-four;

13 the sons of Zat′tū, eight hundred and forty-five;

14 the sons of Zac′cāi, seven hundred and sixty;

15 the sons of Bin′nū·ī,*a* six hundred and forty-eight;

16 the sons of Bē′bāi, six hundred and twenty-eight;

17 the sons of Az′gad, two thousand three hundred and twenty-two;

18 the sons of Ad·o·nī′kam, six hundred and sixty-seven;

19 the sons of Big′vāi, two thousand and sixty-seven;

20 the sons of Ā′din, six hundred and fifty-five;

21 the sons of Ā′ter of Hez·e·kī′ah, ninety-eight;

22 the sons of Hā′shum, three hundred and twenty-eight;

23 the sons of Bē′zāi, three hundred and twenty-four;

24 the sons of Hā′riph,*a* one hundred and twelve;

25 the sons of Gib′e·on,*a* ninety-five;

26 the men of Bethlehem and Ne·toph′ah, one hundred and eighty-eight;

27 the men of An′a·thoth, one hundred and twenty-eight;

28 the men of Beth Az′ma·veth,*a* forty-two;

29 the men of Kir′jath Jē′a·rim, Chē·phī′rah, and Be·er′oth, seven hundred and forty-three;

30 the men of Rā′mah and Gē′ba, six hundred and twenty-one;

31 the men of Mich′mas, one hundred and twenty-two;

32 the men of Beth′el and Aī, one hundred and twenty-three;

33 the men of the other Nē′bō, fifty-two;

34 the sons of the other Ē′lam, one thousand two hundred and fifty-four;

35 the sons of Hā′rim, three hundred and twenty;

36 the sons of Jericho, three hundred and forty-five;

37 the sons of Lod, Hā′did, and Ō′nō, seven hundred and twenty-one;

38 the sons of Se·nā′ah, three thousand nine hundred and thirty.

39 The priests: the sons of Je·dāi′ah, of the house of Jesh′u·a, nine hundred and seventy-three;

40 the sons of Im′mer, one thousand and fifty-two;

41 the sons of Pash′hur, one thousand two hundred and forty-seven;

42 the sons of Hā′rim, one thousand and seventeen;

43 The Lē′vītes: the sons of Jesh′u·a, of Kad′mi·el, *and* of the sons of Hō′de·vah,*a* seventy-four.

44 The singers: the sons of Ā′saph, one hundred and forty-eight.

45 The gatekeepers: the sons of Shal′lum, the sons of Ā′ter, the sons of Tal′mon, the sons of Ak′kub, the sons of Ha·tī′ta, the sons of Shō′bāi, one hundred and thirty-eight.

46 The Neth′i·nim: the sons of Zī′ha, the sons of Ha·sū′pha, the sons of Tab·bā′oth,

47 the sons of Kē′ros, the sons of Sī′a,*a* the sons of Pā′don,

48 the sons of Le·bā′na,*a* the sons of Hag′a·ba,*b* the sons of Sal′māi,*c*

7:15 *a*Spelled *Bani* in Ezra 2:10   7:24 *a*Called *Jorah* in Ezra 2:18   7:25 *a*Called *Gibbar* in Ezra 2:20   7:28 *a*Called *Azmaveth* in Ezra 2:24
7:43 *a*Spelled *Hodaviah* in Ezra 2:40
7:47 *a*Spelled *Siaha* in Ezra 2:44
7:48 *a*Masoretic Text reads *Lebanah.* *b*Masoretic Text reads *Hogabah.* *c*Or *Shalmai,* or *Shamlai*

49 the sons of Hāʹnan, the sons of Gidʹdel, the sons of Gāʹhar,

50 the sons of Rē·āiʹah, the sons of Rēʹzin, the sons of Ne·kōʹda,

51 the sons of Gazʹzam, the sons of Uzʹza, the sons of Pa·sēʹah,

52 the sons of Bēʹsai, the sons of Me·ūʹnim, the sons of Ne·phishʹe·sim,ᵃ

53 the sons of Bakʹbuk, the sons of Ha·kūʹpha, the sons of Harʹhur,

54 the sons of Bazʹlith,ᵃ the sons of Me·hīʹda, the sons of Harʹsha,

55 the sons of Barʹkos, the sons of Sisʹe·ra, the sons of Tamʹah,

56 the sons of Ne·zīʹah, and the sons of Ha·tīʹpha.

57 The sons of Solomon's servants: the sons of Sōʹtai, the sons of Sōʹphe·reth, the sons of Pe·rīʹda,ᵃ

58 the sons of Jāʹa·la, the sons of Darʹkon, the sons of Gidʹdel,

59 the sons of Sheph·a·tīʹah, the sons of Hatʹtil, the sons of Pochʹe·reth of Ze·bāʹim, and the sons of Āʹmon.ᵃ

60 All the Nethʹi·nim, and the sons of Solomon's servants, *were* three hundred and ninety-two.

61 And these *were* the ones who came up from Tel Mēʹlah, Tel Harʹsha, Chēʹrub, Adʹdon,ᵃ and Imʹmer, but they could not identify their father's house nor their lineage, whether they *were* of Israel:

62 the sons of De·laiʹah, the sons of Tō·bīʹah, the sons of Ne·kōʹda, six hundred and forty-two;

63 and of the priests: the sons of Ha·baiʹah, the sons of Koz,ᵃ the sons of Bar·zilʹlai, who took a wife of the daughters of Bar·zilʹlai the Gilʹe·ad·īte, and was called by their name.

64 These sought their listing *among* those who were registered by genealogy, but it was not found;

therefore they were excluded from the priesthood as defiled.

65 And the governorᵃ said to them that they should not eat of the most holy things till a priest could consult with the Ūʹrim and Thumʹmim.

66 Altogether the whole assembly *was* forty-two thousand three hundred and sixty,

67 besides their male and female servants, of whom *there were* seven thousand three hundred and thirty-seven; and they had two hundred and forty-five men and women singers.

68 Their horses were seven hundred and thirty-six, their mules two hundred and forty-five,

69 *their* camels four hundred and thirty-five, *and* donkeys six thousand seven hundred and twenty.

70 And some of the heads of the fathers' houses gave to the work. The governorᵃ gave to the treasury one thousand gold drachmas, fifty basins, and five hundred and thirty priestly garments.

71 Some of the heads of the fathers' *houses* gave to the treasury of the work twenty thousand gold drachmas, and two thousand two hundred silver minas.

72 And that which the rest of the people gave *was* twenty thousand gold drachmas, two thousand silver minas, and sixty-seven priestly garments.

73 So the priests, the Lēʹvites, the gatekeepers, the singers, *some* of the

7:52 ᵃSpelled *Nephusim* in Ezra 2:50
7:54 ᵃSpelled *Bazluth* in Ezra 2:52
7:57 ᵃSpelled *Peruda* in Ezra 2:55
7:59 ᵃSpelled *Ami* in Ezra 2:57   7:61 ᵃSpelled *Addan* in Ezra 2:59   7:63 ᵃOr *Hakkoz*
7:65 ᵃHebrew *Tirshatha*   7:70 ᵃHebrew *Tirshatha*

people, the Neth′i·nim, and all Israel dwelt in their cities.

EZRA READS THE LAW

When the seventh month came, the children of Israel *were* in their cities.

8 Now all the people gathered together as one man in the open square that *was* in front of the Water Gate; and they told Ezra the scribe to bring the Book of the Law of Moses, which the LORD had commanded Israel.
2 So Ezra the priest brought the Law before the assembly of men and women and all who *could* hear with understanding on the first day of the seventh month.
3 Then he read from it in the open square that *was* in front of the Water Gate from morning until midday, before the men and women and those who could understand; and the ears of all the people *were attentive* to the Book of the Law.
4 So Ezra the scribe stood on a platform of wood which they had made for the purpose; and beside him, at his right hand, stood Mat·ti·thī′ah, Shē′ma, A·naī′ah, Ū·rī′jah, Hil·kī′ah, and Mā·a·sēi′ah; and at his left hand Pe·dāi′ah, Mish′a·el, Mal·chī′jah, Hā′shum, Hash·ba·da′na, Zech·a·rī′ah, *and* Me·shul′lam.
5 And Ezra opened the book in the sight of all the people, for he was *standing* above all the people; and when he opened it, all the people stood up.
6 And Ezra blessed the LORD, the great God. Then all the people answered, "Amen, Amen!" while lifting up their hands. And they bowed their heads and worshiped the LORD with *their* faces to the ground.
7 Also Jesh′ū·a, Bā′nī, Sher·e·bī′ah, Jā′min, Ak′kub, Shab′be·thaī, Hō·dī′-

jah, Mā·a·sēi′ah, Ke·lī′ta, Az·a·rī′ah, Joz′a·bad, Hā′nan, Pe·lāi′ah, and the Lē′vītes, helped the people to understand the Law; and the people *stood* in their place.
8 So they read distinctly from the book, in the Law of God; and they gave the sense, and helped *them* to understand the reading.
9 And Nē·he·mī′ah, who *was* the governor,*a* Ezra the priest *and* scribe, and the Lē′vītes who taught the people said to all the people, "This day *is* holy to the LORD your God; do not mourn nor weep." For all the people wept, when they heard the words of the Law.
10 Then he said to them, "Go your way, eat the fat, drink the sweet, and send portions to those for whom nothing is prepared; for *this* day *is* holy to our Lord. Do not sorrow, for the joy of the LORD is your strength."
11 So the Lē′vītes quieted all the

8:9 *a*Hebrew *Tirshatha*

◼ *Promises* ◼

Nehemiah 8:10

Here's a special promise. The joy of the Lord is our strength. Do you ever feel weak? You need to build the joy of the Lord. Do you ever feel sad or downcast? Build the joy of the Lord. Do you ever feel lonely or sad? You need to build the joy of the Lord. How? The same way that we build the joy of our parents. Spend time with the Lord. Talk with Him. Listen to Him speak to you in His Word. Think about Him. Tell Him how much you love Him. The more time you spend with the Lord, the more your joy of the Lord will grow. Try it.

What Should I Do?

OUR BABY AND OUR BIBLE—WE LOVE THEM BOTH Nehemiah 8:1–3

This mother and father love their new baby. They want their baby to have the best in life. They want their baby to grow up to be a good person. And they want their baby to learn to love God and His Word. This mother and father also love the Word of God, the Bible. So they want the baby they love and the Word of God they love to get together. How do you think they will do that?

1. When your parents want to have Bible reading or devotions, remember, they love you and they love the Bible. They want you to love the Book they love so much. What do you think about that?
2. Do you want to love God? You will when you love to listen to His Word and do it. When parents want to share God's Word with you, thank them. Remember to thank God for His Word, too.

For more on *What Should I Do?* turn to page 778
For more on *Bible* turn to page 926

people, saying, "Be still, for the day *is* holy; do not be grieved."

12 And all the people went their way to eat and drink, to send portions and rejoice greatly, because they understood the words that were declared to them.

THE FEAST OF TABERNACLES

13 Now on the second day the heads of the fathers' *houses* of all the people, with the priests and Lē′vītes, were gathered to Ezra the scribe, in order to understand the words of the Law.

14 And they found written in the Law, which the LORD had commanded by Moses, that the children of Israel should dwell in booths during the feast of the seventh month,

15 and that they should announce and proclaim in all their cities and in Jerusalem, saying, "Go out to the mountain, and bring olive branches, branches of oil trees, myrtle branches, palm branches, and branches of leafy trees, to make booths, as *it is* written."

16 Then the people went out and brought *them* and made themselves booths, each one on the roof of his house, or in their courtyards or the courts of the house of God, and in the open square of the Water Gate and in the open square of the Gate of Ē′phra·im.

17 So the whole assembly of those who had returned from the captivity made booths and sat under the booths; for since the days of Joshua the son of Nun until that day the children of Israel had not done so. And there was very great gladness.

18 Also day by day, from the first day until the last day, he read from the Book of the Law of God. And they kept the feast seven days; and on the eighth day *there was* a sacred assembly, according to the *prescribed* manner.

THE PEOPLE CONFESS THEIR SINS

9 Now on the twenty-fourth day of this month the children of Israel were assembled with fasting, in sackcloth, and with dust on their heads.*a*

2 Then those of Israelite lineage separated themselves from all foreigners; and they stood and confessed their sins and the iniquities of their fathers.

3 And they stood up in their place and read from the Book of the Law of the LORD their God *for one*-fourth of the day; and *for another* fourth they confessed and worshiped the LORD their God.

4 Then Jesh′ū·a, Bā′nī, Kad′mi·el, Sheb·a·nī′ah, Bun′nī, Sher·e·bī′ah, Bā′nī, *and* Che·nā′nī stood on the stairs of the Lē′vītes and cried out with a loud voice to the LORD their God.

5 And the Lē′vītes, Jesh′ū·a, Kad′-mi·el, Bā′nī, Ha·shab·nī′ah, Sher·e-bī′ah, Hō·dī′jah, Sheb·a·nī′ah, *and* Peth·a·hī′ah, said:

"Stand up *and* bless the LORD your
    God
Forever and ever!

"Blessed be Your glorious name,
    Which is exalted above all
        blessing and praise!
6 You alone *are* the LORD;
    You have made heaven,
    The heaven of heavens, with all
        their host,
    The earth and everything on it,
    The seas and all that is in them,
    And You preserve them all.
    The host of heaven worships You.

9:1 *a*Literally *earth on them*

7 "You *are* the LORD God,
   Who chose Abram,
   And brought him out of Ūr of the
      Chal·dē′ans,
   And gave him the name
      Abraham;
8 You found his heart faithful
      before You,
   And made a covenant with him
   To give the land of the
      Cā′naan·ītes,
   The Hit′tītes, the Am′o·rītes,
   The Per′iz·zītes, the Jeb′ū·sītes,
   And the Gir′ga·shītes—
   To give *it* to his descendants.
   You have performed Your words,
   For You *are* righteous.

9 "You saw the affliction of our
      fathers in Egypt,
   And heard their cry by the Red
      Sea.
10 You showed signs and wonders
      against Pharaoh,
   Against all his servants,
   And against all the people of his
      land.
   For You knew that they acted
      proudly against them.
   So You made a name for Yourself,
      as *it is* this day.
11 And You divided the sea before
      them,
   So that they went through the
      midst of the sea on the dry
      land;
   And their persecutors You threw
      into the deep,
   As a stone into the mighty
      waters.

12 Moreover You led them by day
      with a cloudy pillar,
   And by night with a pillar of fire,
   To give them light on the road
   Which they should travel.

13 "You came down also on Mount
      Sinai,

And spoke with them from
   heaven,
And gave them just ordinances
   and true laws,
Good statutes and
   commandments.
14 You made known to them Your
   holy Sabbath,
And commanded them precepts,
   statutes and laws,
By the hand of Moses Your
   servant.
15 You gave them bread from heaven
   for their hunger,
And brought them water out of
   the rock for their thirst,
And told them to go in to possess
   the land
Which You had sworn to give
   them.

16 "But they and our fathers acted
   proudly,
Hardened their necks,
And did not heed Your
   commandments.
17 They refused to obey,
And they were not mindful of
   Your wonders

◼ *Promises* ◼

Nehemiah 9:17

Do you ever think God has fun
punishing you? He doesn't. He
really wants to forgive you. Here
is a special promise. God is always ready to forgive you. He is
a gracious person. He wants to
show you mercy. He doesn't get
angry easily. He has *much* kindness. He is always there to help
you. God has "fun" or delight in
forgiving and helping you, not
punishing you. But sometimes,
like a loving parent, He must
punish you to set you straight.

That You did among them.
But they hardened their necks,
And in their rebellion*a*
They appointed a leader
To return to their bondage.
But You *are* God,
Ready to pardon,
Gracious and merciful,
Slow to anger,
Abundant in kindness,
And did not forsake them.

18 "Even when they made a molded
    calf for themselves,
And said, 'This *is* your god
That brought you up out of
    Egypt,'
And worked great provocations,
19 Yet in Your manifold mercies
You did not forsake them in the
    wilderness.
The pillar of the cloud did not
    depart from them by day,
To lead them on the road;
Nor the pillar of fire by night,
To show them light,
And the way they should go.
20 You also gave Your good Spirit to
    instruct them,
And did not withhold Your manna
    from their mouth,
And gave them water for their
    thirst.
21 Forty years You sustained them
    in the wilderness;
They lacked nothing;
Their clothes did not wear out*a*
And their feet did not swell.

22 "Moreover You gave them
    kingdoms and nations,
And divided them into districts.*a*
So they took possession of the
    land of Sī′hon,
The land of*b* the king of
    Hesh′bon,
And the land of Og king of
    Bā′shan.

23 You also multiplied their children
    as the stars of heaven,
And brought them into the land
Which You had told their fathers
To go in and possess.
24 So the people went in
And possessed the land;
You subdued before them the
    inhabitants of the land,
The Cā′naan-ītes,
And gave them into their hands,
With their kings
And the people of the land,
That they might do with them as
    they wished.
25 And they took strong cities and a
    rich land,
And possessed houses full of all
    goods,
Cisterns *already* dug, vineyards,
    olive groves,
And fruit trees in abundance.
So they ate and were filled and
    grew fat,
And delighted themselves in Your
    great goodness.

26 "Nevertheless they were
    disobedient
And rebelled against You,
Cast Your law behind their backs
And killed Your prophets, who
    testified against them
To turn them to Yourself;
And they worked great
    provocations.
27 Therefore You delivered them into
    the hand of their enemies,
Who oppressed them;
And in the time of their trouble,
When they cried to You,
You heard from heaven;
And according to Your abundant
    mercies

9:17 *a*Following Masoretic Text and Vulgate; Septuagint reads *in Egypt.*   9:21 *a*Compare
Deuteronomy 29:5   9:22 *a*Literally *corners*
*b*Following Masoretic Text and Vulgate; Septuagint
omits *The land of.*

You gave them deliverers who
   saved them
From the hand of their enemies.

28 "But after they had rest,
   They again did evil before You.
   Therefore You left them in the
      hand of their enemies,
   So that they had dominion over
      them;
   Yet when they returned and cried
      out to You,
   You heard from heaven;
   And many times You delivered
      them according to Your mercies,
29 And testified against them,
   That You might bring them back
      to Your law.
   Yet they acted proudly,
   And did not heed Your
      commandments,
   But sinned against Your
      judgments,
   'Which if a man does, he shall live
      by them.'*a*
   And they shrugged their
      shoulders,
   Stiffened their necks,
   And would not hear.
30 Yet for many years You had
      patience with them,
   And testified against them by
      Your Spirit in Your prophets.
   Yet they would not listen;
   Therefore You gave them into the
      hand of the peoples of the
      lands.
31 Nevertheless in Your great mercy
   You did not utterly consume them
      nor forsake them;
   For You *are* God, gracious and
      merciful.

32 "Now therefore, our God,
   The great, the mighty, and
      awesome God,
   Who keeps covenant and mercy:
   Do not let all the trouble seem
      small before You

That has come upon us,
Our kings and our princes,
Our priests and our prophets,
Our fathers and on all Your
   people,
From the days of the kings of
   Assyria until this day.
33 However You *are* just in all that
   has befallen us;
   For You have dealt faithfully,
   But we have done wickedly.
34 Neither our kings nor our princes,
   Our priests nor our fathers,
   Have kept Your law,
   Nor heeded Your commandments
      and Your testimonies,
   With which You testified against
      them.
35 For they have not served You in
      their kingdom,
   Or in the many good *things* that
      You gave them,
   Or in the large and rich land
      which You set before them;
   Nor did they turn from their
      wicked works.

36 "Here we *are,* servants today!
   And the land that You gave to our
      fathers,
   To eat its fruit and its bounty,
   Here we *are,* servants in it!
37 And it yields much increase to the
      kings
   You have set over us,
   Because of our sins;
   Also they have dominion over our
      bodies and our cattle
   At their pleasure;
   And we *are* in great distress.

38 "And because of all this,
   We make a sure *covenant* and
      write *it;*
   Our leaders, our Lē′vītes, *and* our
      priests seal *it.*"

9:29 *a*Leviticus 18:5

THE PEOPLE WHO SEALED THE COVENANT

10 Now those who placed *their* seal on *the document were:*

Nē·he·mī'ah the governor, the son of Hac·a·lī'ah, and Zed·e·kī'ah,

2 Se·rāi'ah, Az·a·rī'ah, Jer·e·mī'ah,

3 Pash'hur, Am·a·rī'ah, Mal·chī'jah,

4 Hat'tush, Sheb·a·nī'ah, Mal'luch,

5 Hā'rim, Mer'e·moth, Ō·ba·dī'ah,

6 Daniel, Gin'e·thon, Bar'uch,

7 Me·shul'lam, A·bī'jah, Mij'a·min,

8 Mā·a·zī'ah, Bil'gai, *and* She·māi'ah. These *were* the priests.

9 The Lē'vites: Jesh'ū·a the son of Az·a·nī'ah, Bin'nū·ī of the sons of Hen'a·dad, *and* Kad'mi·el.

10 Their brethren: Sheb·a·nī'ah, Hō·dī'jah, Ke·lī'ta, Pe·lāi'ah, Hā'nan,

11 Mī'cha, Rē'hob, Hash·a·bī'ah,

12 Zac'cur, Sher·e·bī'ah, Sheb·a·nī'ah,

13 Hō·dī'jah, Bā'ni, *and* Be·nī'nū.

14 The leaders of the people: Pā'rosh, Pā'hath-Mō'ab, Ē'lam, Zat'-tū, Bā'ni,

15 Bun'ni, Az'gad, Bē'bai,

16 Ad·o·nī'jah, Big'vai, Ā'din,

17 Ā'ter, Hez·e·kī'ah, Az'zur,

18 Hō·dī'jah, Hā'shum, Bē'zai,

19 Hā'riph, An'a·thoth, Nē'bai,

20 Mag'pi·ash, Me·shul'lam, Hē'zir,

21 Me·shez'a·bel, Zā'dok, Jad'dū·a,

22 Pel·a·tī'ah, Hā'nan, A·nai'ah,

23 Hō·shē'a, Han·a·nī'ah, Has'shub,

24 Hal·lō'hesh, Pil'ha, Shō'bek,

25 Rē'hum, Ha·shab'nah, Mā·a·sēi'ah,

26 A·hī'jah, Hā'nan, Ā'nan,

27 Mal'luch, Hā'rim, *and* Bā'a·nah.

THE COVENANT THAT WAS SEALED

28 Now the rest of the people—the priests, the Lē'vites, the gatekeepers, the singers, the Neth'i·nim, and all those who had separated themselves from the peoples of the lands to the Law of God, their wives, their sons, and their daughters, everyone who had knowledge and understanding—

29 these joined with their brethren, their nobles, and entered into a curse and an oath to walk in God's Law, which was given by Moses the servant of God, and to observe and do all the commandments of the LORD our Lord, and His ordinances and His statutes:

30 We would not give our daughters as wives to the peoples of the land, nor take their daughters for our sons;

31 *if* the peoples of the land brought wares or any grain to sell on the Sabbath day, we would not buy it from them on the Sabbath, or on a holy day; and we would forego the seventh year's *produce* and the exacting of every debt.

32 Also we made ordinances for ourselves, to exact from ourselves yearly one-third of a shekel for the service of the house of our God:

33 for the showbread, for the regular grain offering, for the regular burnt offering of the Sabbaths, the New Moons, and the set feasts; for the holy things, for the sin offerings to make atonement for Israel, and all the work of the house of our God.

34 We cast lots among the priests, the Lē'vites, and the people, for *bringing* the wood offering into the house of our God, according to our fathers' houses, at the appointed times year by year, to burn on the altar of the LORD our God as *it is* written in the Law.

35 And *we made ordinances* to bring the firstfruits of our ground and the firstfruits of all fruit of all trees, year by year, to the house of the LORD;

36 to bring the firstborn of our sons and our cattle, as *it is* written in the Law, and the firstborn of our herds

and our flocks, to the house of our God, to the priests who minister in the house of our God;

37 to bring the firstfruits of our dough, our offerings, the fruit from all kinds of trees, *the* new wine and oil, to the priests, to the storerooms of the house of our God; and to bring the tithes of our land to the Lē'vītes, for the Lē'vītes should receive the tithes in all our farming communities.

38 And the priest, the descendant of Aaron, shall be with the Lē'vītes when the Lē'vītes receive tithes; and the Lē'vītes shall bring up a tenth of the tithes to the house of our God, to the rooms of the storehouse.

39 For the children of Israel and the children of Levi shall bring the offering of the grain, of the new wine and the oil, to the storerooms where the articles of the sanctuary *are, where* the priests who minister and the gatekeepers and the singers *are;* and we will not neglect the house of our God.

THE PEOPLE DWELLING IN JERUSALEM

11 Now the leaders of the people dwelt at Jerusalem; the rest of the people cast lots to bring one out of ten to dwell in Jerusalem, the holy city, and nine-tenths *were to dwell* in *other* cities.

2 And the people blessed all the men who willingly offered themselves to dwell at Jerusalem.

3 These *are* the heads of the province who dwelt in Jerusalem. (But in the cities of Judah everyone dwelt in his own possession in their cities—Israelites, priests, Lē'vītes, Neth'i·nim, and descendants of Solomon's servants.)

4 Also in Jerusalem dwelt *some* of the children of Judah and of the children of Benjamin.

The children of Judah: A·thaī'ah the son of Uz·zī'ah, the son of Zech·a·rī'ah, the son of Am·a·rī'ah, the son of Sheph·a·tī'ah, the son of Ma·hal'·a·lel, of the children of Per'ez;

5 and Mā·a·sēi'ah the son of Bar'uch, the son of Col-Hō'zeh, the son of Ha·zaī'ah, the son of A·dāi'ah, the son of Joi'a·rib, the son of Zech·a·rī'ah, the son of Shi·lō'nī.

6 All the sons of Per'ez who dwelt at Jerusalem *were* four hundred and sixty-eight valiant men.

7 And these are the sons of Benjamin: Sal'lū the son of Me·shul'lam, the son of Jō'ed, the son of Pe·dāi'ah, the son of Kō·laī'ah, the son of Mā·a·sēi'ah, the son of Ith'i·el, the son of Je·shā'i·ah;

8 and after him Gab·bā'ī *and* Sal'·laī, nine hundred and twenty-eight.

9 Jō'el the son of Zich'rī *was* their overseer, and Judah the son of Se·nū'ah*a was* second over the city.

10 Of the priests: Je·dāi'ah the son of Joi'a·rib, and Jā'chin;

11 Se·rāi'ah the son of Hil·kī'ah, the son of Me·shul'lam, the son of Zā'·dok, the son of Me·rā'i·oth, the son of A·hī'tub, *was* the leader of the house of God.

12 Their brethren who did the work of the house *were* eight hundred and twenty-two; and A·dāi'ah the son of Je·rō'ham, the son of Pel·a·lī'ah, the son of Am'zī, the son of Zech·a·rī'ah, the son of Pash'hur, the son of Mal·chī'jah,

13 and his brethren, heads of the fathers' *houses, were* two hundred and forty-two; and A·mash'aī the son of Az'a·rel, the son of Ah'zaī, the son of Me·shil'le·moth, the son of Im'mer,

14 and their brethren, mighty men

11:9 *aOr Hassenuah*

of valor, *were* one hundred and twenty-eight. Their overseer *was* Zab′di·el the son of *one of* the great men.*a*

15 Also of the Lē′vītes: She·māi′ah the son of Has′shub, the son of Az·rī′kam, the son of Hash·a·bī′ah, the son of Bun′nī;

16 Shab′be·thaī and Joz′a·bad, of the heads of the Lē′vītes, *had* the oversight of the business outside of the house of God;

17 Mat·ta·nī′ah the son of Mī′cha,*a* the son of Zab′dī, the son of Ā′saph, the leader *who* began the thanksgiving with prayer; Bak·bū·kī′ah, the second among his brethren; and Ab′da the son of Sham′mū·a, the son of Gā′lal, the son of Je·dū′thun.

18 All the Lē′vītes in the holy city *were* two hundred and eighty-four.

19 Moreover the gatekeepers, Ak′kub, Tal′mon, and their brethren who kept the gates, *were* one hundred and seventy-two.

20 And the rest of Israel, of the priests *and* Lē′vītes, *were* in all the cities of Judah, everyone in his inheritance.

21 But the Neth′i·nim dwelt in Ō′phel. And Zī′ha and Gish′pa *were* over the Neth′i·nim.

22 Also the overseer of the Lē′vītes at Jerusalem *was* Uz′zī the son of Bā′nī, the son of Hash·a·bī′ah, the son of Mat·ta·nī′ah, the son of Mī′cha, of the sons of Ā′saph, the singers in charge of the service of the house of God.

23 For *it was* the king's command concerning them that a certain portion should be for the singers, a quota day by day.

24 Peth·a·hī′ah the son of Me·shez′a·bel, of the children of Zē′rah the son of Judah, *was* the king's deputy*a* in all matters concerning the people.

The People Dwelling Outside Jerusalem

25 And as for the villages with their fields, *some* of the children of Judah dwelt in Kir′jath Ar′ba and its villages, Dī′bon and its villages, Je·kab′zē·el and its villages;

26 in Jesh′ū·a, Mō′la·dah, Beth Pē′let,

27 Hā′zar Shū′al, and Bē·er·shē′ba and its villages;

28 in Zik′lag and Mē·cō′nah and its villages;

29 in En Rim′mon, Zō′rah, Jar′muth,

30 Za·nō′ah, A·dul′lam, and their villages; in Lā′chish and its fields; in A·zē′kah and its villages. They dwelt from Bē·er·shē′ba to the Valley of Hin′nom.

31 Also the children of Benjamin from Gē′ba *dwelt* in Mich′mash, Āi′ja, and Beth′el, and their villages;

32 in An′a·thoth, Nob, An·a·nī′ah;

33 in Hā′zor, Rā′mah, Git′ta·im;

34 in Hā′did, Ze·bō′im, Ne·bal′lat;

35 in Lod, Ō′nō, *and* the Valley of Craftsmen.

36 Some of the Judean divisions of Lē′vītes *were* in Benjamin.

The Priests and Levites

12 Now these *are* the priests and the Lē′vītes who came up with Ze·rub′ba·bel the son of She·al′ti·el, and Jesh′ū·a: Se·rāi′ah, Jer·e·mī′ah, Ezra,

2 Am·a·rī′ah, Mal′luch, Hat′tush,

3 Shech·a·nī′ah, Rē′hum, Mer′e·moth,

4 Id′dō, Gin′ne·thoi,*a* A·bī′jah,

5 Mij′a·min, Mā·a·dī′ah, Bil′gah,

6 She·māi′ah, Joi′a·rib, Je·daī′ah,

7 Sal′lū, Ā′mok, Hil·kī′ah, *and* Je·daī′ah.

11:14 *a*Or *the son of Haggedolim*   11:17 *a*Or *Michah*   11:24 *a*Literally *at the king's hand* 12:4 *a*Or *Ginnethon* (compare verse 16)

These *were* the heads of the priests and their brethren in the days of Jesh′ū·a.

8 Moreover the Lē′vītes *were* Jesh′ū·a, Bin′nū·ī, Kad′mi·el, Sher·e·bī′ah, Judah, *and* Mat·ta·nī′ah *who led* the thanksgiving *psalms,* he and his brethren.

9 Also Bak·bū·kī′ah and Un′nī, their brethren, *stood* across from them in *their* duties.

10 Jesh′ū·a begot Joi′a·kim, Joi′a·kim begot E·lī′a·shib, E·lī′a·shib begot Joi′a·da,

11 Joi′a·da begot Jonathan, and Jonathan begot Jad′dū·a.

12 Now in the days of Joi′a·kim, the priests, the heads of the fathers′ *houses were:* of Se·rāi′ah, Me·rāi′ah; of Jer·e·mī′ah, Han·a·nī′ah;

13 of Ezra, Me·shul′lam; of Am·a·rī′ah, Jē·hō·hā′nan;

14 of Mel′i·chū,*a* Jonathan; of Sheb·a·nī′ah,*b* Joseph;

15 of Hā′rim,*a* Ad′na; of Me·rā′i·oth,*b* Hel′kaī;

16 of Id′dō, Zech·a·rī′ah; of Gin′e·thon, Me·shul′lam;

17 of A·bī′jah, Zich′rī; *the son of* Min′ja·min;*a* of Mō·a·dī′ah,*b* Pil′taī;

18 of Bil′gah, Sham′mū·a; of She·māi′ah, Je·hon′a·than;

19 of Joi′ā·rib, Mat·tē′naī; of Je·daī′ah, Uz′zī;

20 of Sal′laī,*a* Kal′laī; of Ā′mok, Ē′ber;

21 of Hil·kī′ah, Hash·a·bī′ah; *and* of Je·daī′ah, Ne·than′el.

22 During the reign of Da·rī′us the Persian, a record *was also kept* of the Lē′vītes and priests *who had been* heads of their fathers′ *houses* in the days of E·lī′a·shib, Joi′a·da, Jō·hā′nan, and Jad′dū·a.

23 The sons of Levi, the heads of the fathers′ *houses* until the days of Jō·hā′nan the son of E·lī′a·shib, *were* written in the book of the chronicles.

24 And the heads of the Lē′vītes *were* Hash·a·bī′ah, Sher·e·bī′ah, and Jesh′ū·a the son of Kad′mi·el, with their brothers across from them, to praise *and* give thanks, group alternating with group, according to the command of David the man of God.

25 Mat·ta·nī′ah, Bak·bū·kī′ah, Ō·ba·dī′ah, Me·shul′lam, Tal′mon, and Ak′kub *were* gatekeepers keeping the watch at the storerooms of the gates.

26 These *lived* in the days of Joi′a·kim the son of Jesh′ū·a¯, the son of Jō′za·dak,*a* and in the days of Nē·he·mī′ah the governor, and of Ezra the priest, the scribe.

NEHEMIAH DEDICATES THE WALL

27 Now at the dedication of the wall of Jerusalem they sought out the Lē′vītes in all their places, to bring them to Jerusalem to celebrate the dedication with gladness, both with thanksgivings and singing, *with* cymbals and stringed instruments and harps.

28 And the sons of the singers gathered together from the countryside around Jerusalem, from the villages of the Ne·toph′a·thītes,

29 from the house of Gil′gal, and from the fields of Gē′ba and Az′ma·veth; for the singers had built themselves villages all around Jerusalem.

30 Then the priests and Lē′vītes purified themselves, and purified the people, the gates, and the wall.

31 So I brought the leaders of Judah up on the wall, and appointed two large thanksgiving choirs. *One* went

12:14 *a*Or *Malluch* (compare verse 2)   *b*Or *Shechaniah* (compare verse 3)   12:15 *a*Or *Rehum* (compare verse 3)   *b*Or *Meremoth* (compare verse 3)   12:17 *a*Or *Mijamin* (compare verse 5)   *b*Or *Maadiah* (compare verse 5)   12:20 *a*Or *Sallu* (compare verse 7)   12:26 *a*Spelled *Jehozadak* in 1 Chronicles 6:14

to the right hand on the wall toward the Refuse Gate.

32 After them went Hō·shaī′ah and half of the leaders of Judah,

33 and Az·a·rī′ah, Ezra, Me·shul′-lam,

34 Judah, Benjamin, She·māi′ah, Jer·e·mī′ah,

35 and some of the priests' sons with trumpets—Zech·a·rī′ah the son of Jonathan, the son of She·māi′ah, the son of Mat·ta·nī′ah, the son of Mī-chaī′ah, the son of Zac′cur, the son of Ā′saph,

36 and his brethren, She·māi′ah, Az′a·rel, Mil′a·lai, Gil′a·lai, Mā′aī, Ne·than′el, Judah, *and* Ha·nā′nī, with the musical instruments of David the man of God. Ezra the scribe *went* before them.

37 By the Fountain Gate, in front of them, they went up the stairs of the City of David, on the stairway of the wall, beyond the house of David, as far as the Water Gate eastward.

38 The other thanksgiving choir went the opposite *way,* and I *was* behind them with half of the people on the wall, going past the Tower of the Ovens as far as the Broad Wall,

39 and above the Gate of Ē′phra·im, above the Old Gate, above the Fish Gate, the Tower of Ha·nan′el, the Tower of the Hundred, as far as the Sheep Gate; and they stopped by the Gate of the Prison.

40 So the two thanksgiving choirs stood in the house of God, likewise I and the half of the rulers with me;

41 and the priests, E·lī′a·kim, Mā-a·sēi′ah, Min′ja·min,[a] Mī·chaī′ah, El-i·ō·ē′naī, Zech·a·rī′ah, *and* Han·a·nī′ah, with trumpets;

42 also Mā·a·sēi′ah, She·māi′ah, El·e·ā′zar, Uz′zī, Jē·hō·hā′nan, Mal-chī′jah, Ē′lam, and Ē′zer. The singers sang loudly with Jez·ra·hī′ah the director.

43 Also that day they offered great

sacrifices, and rejoiced, for God had made them rejoice with great joy; the women and the children also rejoiced, so that the joy of Jerusalem was heard afar off.

TEMPLE RESPONSIBILITIES

44 And at the same time some were appointed over the rooms of the storehouse for the offerings, the first-fruits, and the tithes, to gather into them from the fields of the cities the portions specified by the Law for the priests and Lē′vītes; for Judah rejoiced over the priests and Lē′vītes who ministered.

45 Both the singers and the gate-keepers kept the charge of their God and the charge of the purification, according to the command of David *and* Solomon his son.

46 For in the days of David and Ā′saph of old *there were* chiefs of the singers, and songs of praise and thanksgiving to God.

47 In the days of Ze·rub′ba·bel and in the days of Nē·he·mī′ah all Israel gave the portions for the singers and

12:41 ᵃOr *Mijamin* (compare verse 5)

Praises

Nehemiah 12:46

Someone was looking back at "the good old days." In those days there were chiefs of the singers, and songs of praise and thanksgiving. Do you ever think of someone who praised God? Was it a parent or grandparent? Will someone remember you some day as a person who praised God often? Would you like to be remembered that way?

the gatekeepers, a portion for each day. They also consecrated *holy things* for the Lē′vītes, and the Lē′vītes consecrated *them* for the children of Aaron.

PRINCIPLES OF SEPARATION

13 On that day they read from the Book of Moses in the hearing of the people, and in it was found written that no Am′mon-īte or Mō′ab-īte should ever come into the assembly of God, 2 because they had not met the children of Israel with bread and water, but hired Bā′laam against them to curse them. However, our God turned the curse into a blessing. 3 So it was, when they had heard the Law, that they separated all the mixed multitude from Israel.

THE REFORMS OF NEHEMIAH

4 Now before this, E·lī′a·shib the priest, having authority over the storerooms of the house of our God, *was* allied with Tō·bī′ah. 5 And he had prepared for him a large room, where previously they had stored the grain offerings, the frankincense, the articles, the tithes of grain, the new wine and oil, which were commanded *to be given* to the Lē′vītes and singers and gatekeepers, and the offerings for the priests. 6 But during all this I was not in Jerusalem, for in the thirty-second year of Ar·ta·xerx′ēs king of Babylon I had returned to the king. Then after certain days I obtained leave from the king, 7 and I came to Jerusalem and discovered the evil that E·lī′a·shib had done for Tō·bī′ah, in preparing a room for him in the courts of the house of God.

8 And it grieved me bitterly; therefore I threw all the household goods of Tō·bī′ah out of the room. 9 Then I commanded them to cleanse the rooms; and I brought back into them the articles of the house of God, with the grain offering and the frankincense.

10 I also realized that the portions for the Lē′vītes had not been given *them;* for each of the Lē′vītes and the singers who did the work had gone back to his field. 11 So I contended with the rulers, and said, "Why is the house of God forsaken?" And I gathered them together and set them in their place. 12 Then all Judah brought the tithe of the grain and the new wine and the oil to the storehouse. 13 And I appointed as treasurers over the storehouse Shel·e·mī′ah the priest and Zā′dok the scribe, and of the Lē′vītes, Pe·dāi′ah; and next to them *was* Hā′nan the son of Zac′cur, the son of Mat·ta·nī′ah; for they were considered faithful, and their task *was* to distribute to their brethren. 14 Remember me, O my God, concerning this, and do not wipe out my good deeds that I have done for the house of my God, and for its services!

15 In those days I saw *people* in Judah treading wine presses on the Sabbath, and bringing in sheaves, and loading donkeys with wine, grapes, figs, and all *kinds of* burdens, which they brought into Jerusalem on the Sabbath day. And I warned *them* about the day on which they were selling provisions. 16 Men of Tȳre dwelt there also, who brought in fish and all kinds of goods, and sold *them* on the Sabbath to the children of Judah, and in Jerusalem. 17 Then I contended with the nobles of Judah, and said to them, "What

evil thing *is* this that you do, by which you profane the Sabbath day?

18 "Did not your fathers do thus, and did not our God bring all this disaster on us and on this city? Yet you bring added wrath on Israel by profaning the Sabbath."

19 So it was, at the gates of Jerusalem, as it began to be dark before the Sabbath, that I commanded the gates to be shut, and charged that they must not be opened till after the Sabbath. Then I posted *some* of my servants at the gates, *so that* no burdens would be brought in on the Sabbath day.

20 Now the merchants and sellers of all kinds of wares lodged outside Jerusalem once or twice.

21 Then I warned them, and said to them, "Why do you spend the night around the wall? If you do *so* again, I will lay hands on you!" From that time on they came no *more* on the Sabbath.

22 And I commanded the Lē'vītes that they should cleanse themselves, and that they should go and guard the gates, to sanctify the Sabbath day.

Remember me, O my God, *concerning* this also, and spare me according to the greatness of Your mercy!

23 In those days I also saw Jews *who* had married women of Ash'dod, Am'mon, *and* Mō'ab.

24 And half of their children spoke the language of Ash'dod, and could not speak the language of Judah, but spoke according to the language of one or the other people.

25 So I contended with them and cursed them, struck some of them and pulled out their hair, and made them swear by God, *saying,* "You shall not give your daughters as wives to their sons, nor take their daughters for your sons or yourselves.

26 "Did not Solomon king of Israel sin by these things? Yet among many nations there was no king like him, who was beloved of his God; and God made him king over all Israel. Nevertheless pagan women caused even him to sin.

27 "Should we then hear of your doing all this great evil, transgressing against our God by marrying pagan women?"

28 And *one* of the sons of Joi'a·da, the son of E·lī'a·shib the high priest, *was* a son-in-law of San·bal'lat the Hor'o·nīte; therefore I drove him from me.

29 Remember them, O my God, because they have defiled the priesthood and the covenant of the priesthood and the Lē'vītes.

30 Thus I cleansed them of everything pagan. I also assigned duties to the priests and the Lē'vītes, each to his service,

31 and *to bringing* the wood offering and the firstfruits at appointed times.

Remember me, O my God, for good!

The Book of
ESTHER

THE KING DETHRONES QUEEN VASHTI

A young woman named Esther was a captive in a foreign land. This is the story of how she became queen and saved her people from a madman who wanted to destroy them.

NOW it came to pass in the days of A·has·u·ē′rus[a] (this *was* the A·has·u·ē′rus who reigned over one hundred and twenty-seven provinces, from India to Ethiopia),

2 in those days when King A·has·u·ē′rus sat on the throne of his kingdom, which *was* in Shū′shan[a] the citadel,

3 *that* in the third year of his reign he made a feast for all his officials and servants—the powers of Persia and Media, the nobles, and the princes of the provinces *being* before him—

4 when he showed the riches of his glorious kingdom and the splendor of his excellent majesty for many days, one hundred and eighty days *in all.*

5 And when these days were completed, the king made a feast lasting seven days for all the people who were present in Shū′shan the citadel, from great to small, in the court of the garden of the king's palace.

6 *There were* white and blue linen *curtains* fastened with cords of fine linen and purple on silver rods and marble pillars; *and the* couches *were* of gold and silver on a *mosaic* pavement of alabaster, turquoise, and white and black marble.

7 And they served drinks in golden vessels, each vessel being different from the other, with royal wine in abundance, according to the generosity of the king.

8 In accordance with the law, the drinking was not compulsory; for so the king had ordered all the officers of his household, that they should do according to each man's pleasure.

9 Queen Vash′tī also made a feast for the women *in* the royal palace which *belonged* to King A·has·u·ē′rus.

10 On the seventh day, when the heart of the king was merry with wine, he commanded Me·hū′man, Biz′tha, Har·bō′na, Big′tha, A·bag′-tha, Zē′thar, and Car′cas, seven eunuchs who served in the presence of King A·has·u·ē′rus,

11 to bring Queen Vash′tī before the king, *wearing* her royal crown, in order to show her beauty to the people and the officials, for she *was* beautiful to behold.

12 But Queen Vash′tī refused to come at the king's command *brought* by *his* eunuchs; therefore the king was furious, and his anger burned within him.

13 Then the king said to the wise men who understood the times (for this *was* the king's manner toward all who knew law and justice,

14 those closest to him *being* Car·shē′na, Shē′thar, Ad·mā′tha, Tar′shish, Mē′rēs, Mar·sē′na, and Mē·mū′can, the seven princes of Persia and Media, who had access to the king's presence, *and* who ranked highest in the kingdom):

15 "What *shall we* do to Queen Vash′tī, according to law, because she did not obey the command of King A·has·u·ē′rus *brought to her* by the eunuchs?"

1:1 [a]Generally identified with Xerxes I (485–464 B.C.)   1:2 [a]Or *Susa,* and so throughout this book

16 And Mē·mū'can answered before the king and the princes: "Queen Vash'tī has not only wronged the king, but also all the princes, and all the people who *are* in all the provinces of King A·has·ū·ē'rus.

17 "For the queen's behavior will become known to all women, so that they will despise their husbands in their eyes, when they report, 'King A·has·ū·ē'rus commanded Queen Vash'tī to be brought in before him, but she did not come.'

18 "This very day the *noble* ladies of Persia and Media will say to all the king's officials that they have heard of the behavior of the queen. Thus *there will be* excessive contempt and wrath.

19 "If it pleases the king, let a royal decree go out from him, and let it be recorded in the laws of the Persians and the Mēdes, so that it will not be altered, that Vash'tī shall come no more before King A·has·ū·ē'rus; and let the king give her royal position to another who is better than she.

20 "When the king's decree which he will make is proclaimed throughout all his empire (for it is great), all wives will honor their husbands, both great and small."

21 And the reply pleased the king and the princes, and the king did according to the word of Mē·mū'can.

22 Then he sent letters to all the king's provinces, to each province in its own script, and to every people in their own language, that each man should be master in his own house, and speak in the language of his own people.

ESTHER BECOMES QUEEN

2 After these things, when the wrath of King A·has·ū·ē'rus subsided, he remembered Vash'tī, what she had done, and what had been decreed against her.

2 Then the king's servants who attended him said: "Let beautiful young virgins be sought for the king;

3 "and let the king appoint officers in all the provinces of his kingdom, that they may gather all the beautiful young virgins to Shū'shan the citadel, into the women's quarters, under the custody of Heg'aī[a] the king's eunuch, custodian of the women. And let beauty preparations be given *them.*

4 "Then let the young woman who pleases the king be queen instead of Vash'tī." This thing pleased the king, and he did so.

5 In Shū'shan the citadel there was a certain Jew whose name *was* Mor'de·caī the son of Jā'ir, the son of Shim'ē·ī, the son of Kish, a Ben'ja-mīte.

6 *Kish*[a] had been carried away from Jerusalem with the captives who had been captured with Jec·o·nī'ah[b] king of Judah, whom Ne·bū·chad·nez'zar the king of Babylon had carried away.

7 And *Mor'de·caī* had brought up Ha·das'sah, that *is,* Esther, his uncle's daughter, for she had neither father nor mother. The young woman *was* lovely and beautiful. When her father and mother died, Mor'de·caī took her as his own daughter.

8 So it was, when the king's command and decree were heard, and when many young women were gathered at Shū'shan the citadel, *under* the custody of Heg'aī, that Esther also was taken to the king's palace, into the care of Heg'aī the custodian of the women.

9 Now the young woman pleased him, and she obtained his favor; so

2:3 [a]Hebrew *Hege* 2:6 [a]Literally *Who* [b]Same as *Jehoiachin,* 2 Kings 24:6 and elsewhere

he readily gave beauty preparations to her, besides her allowance. Then seven choice maidservants were provided for her from the king's palace, and he moved her and her maidservants to the best *place* in the house of the women.

10 Esther had not revealed her people or family, for Mor′de·caī had charged her not to reveal *it*.

11 And every day Mor′de·caī paced in front of the court of the women's quarters, to learn of Esther's welfare and what was happening to her.

12 Each young woman's turn came to go in to King A·has·u·ē′rus after she had completed twelve months' preparation, according to the regulations for the women, for thus were the days of their preparation apportioned: six months with oil of myrrh, and six months with perfumes and preparations for beautifying women.

13 Thus *prepared, each* young woman went to the king, and she was given whatever she desired to take with her from the women's quarters to the king's palace.

14 In the evening she went, and in the morning she returned to the second house of the women, to the custody of Sha·ash′gaz, the king's eunuch who kept the concubines. She would not go in to the king again unless the king delighted in her and called for her by name.

15 Now when the turn came for Esther the daughter of Ab·i·hā′il the uncle of Mor′de·caī, who had taken her as his daughter, to go in to the king, she requested nothing but what Heg′aī the king's eunuch, the custodian of the women, advised. And Esther obtained favor in the sight of all who saw her.

16 So Esther was taken to King A·has·ū·ē′rus, into his royal palace, in the tenth month, which *is* the month of Tē′beth, in the seventh year of his reign.

17 The king loved Esther more than all the *other* women, and she obtained grace and favor in his sight more than all the virgins; so he set the royal crown upon her head and made her queen instead of Vash′tī.

18 Then the king made a great feast, the Feast of Esther, for all his officials and servants; and he proclaimed a holiday in the provinces and gave gifts according to the generosity of a king.

☑ *Bible Quiz*

Esther 1:1—2:18 **Esther Becomes Queen**

1. What did King Ahasuerus want Queen Vashti to do at the party? What did Vashti do? What happened to Queen Vashti?

2. Who became queen after Vashti?

3. Who took care of Esther when she was a girl?

4. Ahasuerus didn't realize it, but it was really God who put Esther on the throne. If you read the rest of the book of Esther you'll find out why.

5. What special plans might God have for you?

MORDECAI DISCOVERS A PLOT

19 When virgins were gathered together a second time, Mor′de·caī sat within the king's gate.

20 *Now* Esther had not revealed her family and her people, just as Mor′de·caī had charged her, for Esther

obeyed the command of Mor′de·caī as when she was brought up by him.

21 In those days, while Mor′de·caī sat within the king's gate, two of the king's eunuchs, Big′than and Tē′resh, doorkeepers, became furious and sought to lay hands on King A·has·ū·ē′rus.

22 So the matter became known to Mor′de·caī, who told Queen Esther, and Esther informed the king in Mor′de·caī's name.

23 And when an inquiry was made into the matter, it was confirmed, and both were hanged on a gallows; and it was written in the book of the chronicles in the presence of the king.

HAMAN'S CONSPIRACY AGAINST THE JEWS

The king had a wicked prime minister named Haman. Haman was about to deceive the king into doing something so terrible that even Queen Esther's life would be in danger.

3 After these things King A·has·ū·ē′rus promoted Hā′man, the son of Ham·me·dā′tha the Ag′ag·īte, and advanced him and set his seat above all the princes who *were* with him.

2 And all the king's servants who *were* within the king's gate bowed and paid homage to Hā′man, for so the king had commanded concerning him. But Mor′de·caī would not bow or pay homage.

3 Then the king's servants who *were* within the king's gate said to Mor′de·caī, "Why do you transgress the king's command?"

4 Now it happened, when they spoke to him daily and he would not listen to them, that they told *it* to Hā′man, to see whether Mor′de·caī's

words would stand; for *Mor′de·caī* had told them that he *was* a Jew.

5 When Hā′man saw that Mor′de·caī did not bow or pay him homage, Hā′man was filled with wrath.

6 But he disdained to lay hands on Mor′de·caī alone, for they had told him of the people of Mor′de·caī. Instead, Hā′man sought to destroy all the Jews who *were* throughout the whole kingdom of A·has·ū·ē′rus—the people of Mor′de·caī.

7 In the first month, which is the month of Nī′san, in the twelfth year of King A·has·ū·ē′rus, they cast Pūr (that *is*, the lot), before Hā′man to determine the day and the month,*a* until *it fell on the* twelfth *month,b* which *is* the month of Ā′dar.

8 Then Hā′man said to King A·has·ū·ē′rus, "There is a certain people scattered and dispersed among the people in all the provinces of your kingdom; their laws *are* different from all *other* people's, and they do not keep the king's laws. Therefore it *is* not fitting for the king to let them remain.

9 "If it pleases the king, let *a decree* be written that they be destroyed, and I will pay ten thousand talents of silver into the hands of those who do the work, to bring *it* into the king's treasuries."

10 So the king took his signet ring from his hand and gave it to Hā′man, the son of Ham·me·dā′tha the Ag′ag·īte, the enemy of the Jews.

11 And the king said to Hā′man, "The money and the people *are* given to you, to do with them as seems good to you."

12 Then the king's scribes were called on the thirteenth day of the

3:7 *a*Septuagint adds *to destroy the people of Mordecai in one day;* Vulgate adds *the nation of the Jews should be destroyed.* *b*Following Masoretic Text and Vulgate; Septuagint reads *and the lot fell on the fourteenth of the month.*

first month, and *a decree* was written according to all that Hā′man commanded—to the king's satraps, to the governors who *were* over each province, to the officials of all people, to every province according to its script, and to every people in their language. In the name of King A·has·ū·ē′rus it was written, and sealed with the king's signet ring.

13 And the letters were sent by couriers into all the king's provinces, to destroy, to kill, and to annihilate all the Jews, both young and old, little children and women, in one day, on the thirteenth *day* of the twelfth *month,* which *is* the month of Ā′dar, and to plunder their possessions.*a*

14 A copy of the document was to be issued as law in every province, being published for all people, that they should be ready for that day.

15 The couriers went out, hastened by the king's command; and the decree was proclaimed in Shū′shan the citadel. So the king and Hā′man sat down to drink, but the city of Shū′shan was perplexed.

ESTHER AGREES TO HELP THE JEWS

4 When Mor′de·caī learned all that had happened, he tore his clothes and put on sackcloth and ashes, and went out into the midst of the city. He cried out with a loud and bitter cry.

2 He went as far as the front of the king's gate, for no one *might* enter the king's gate clothed with sackcloth.

3 And in every province where the king's command and decree arrived, *there was* great mourning among the Jews, with fasting, weeping, and wailing; and many lay in sackcloth and ashes.

4 So Esther's maids and eunuchs came and told her, and the queen was deeply distressed. Then she sent garments to clothe Mor′de·caī and take his sackcloth away from him, but he would not accept *them.*

5 Then Esther called Hā′thach, *one* of the king's eunuchs whom he had appointed to attend her, and she gave him a command concerning Mor′de·caī, to learn what and why this *was.*

6 So Hā′thach went out to Mor′de·caī in the city square that *was* in front of the king's gate.

7 And Mor′de·caī told him all that had happened to him, and the sum of money that Hā′man had promised to pay into the king's treasuries to destroy the Jews.

8 He also gave him a copy of the written decree for their destruction, which was given at Shū′shan, that he might show it to Esther and explain it to her, and that he might command her to go in to the king to make supplication to him and plead before him for her people.

9 So Hā′thach returned and told Esther the words of Mor′de·caī.

10 Then Esther spoke to Hā′thach, and gave him a command for Mor′de·caī:

11 "All the king's servants and the people of the king's provinces know that any man or woman who goes into the inner court to the king, who has not been called, *he has* but one law: put *all* to death, except the one to whom the king holds out the golden scepter, that he may live. Yet I myself have not been called to go in to the king these thirty days."

12 So they told Mor′de·caī Esther's words.

13 And Mor′de·caī told *them* to answer Esther: "Do not think in your heart that you will escape in the

---

3:13 *a*Septuagint adds the text of the letter here.

king's palace any more than all the other Jews.

14 "For if you remain completely silent at this time, relief and deliverance will arise for the Jews from another place, but you and your father's house will perish. Yet who knows whether you have come to the kingdom for *such* a time as this?"

15 Then Esther told *them* to reply to Mor′de·caī:

16 "Go, gather all the Jews who are present in Shū′shan, and fast for me; neither eat nor drink for three days, night or day. My maids and I will fast likewise. And so I will go to the king, which *is* against the law; and if I perish, I perish!"

---

17 So Mor′de·caī went his way and did according to all that Esther commanded him.[a]

ESTHER'S BANQUET

Haman deceived the king. His plan to destroy the Jews was now a law. It seemed that nothing could stop this terrible thing from happening. But there was something Haman didn't understand. God controls all things. And God was not on Haman's side!

---

5 Now it happened on the third day that Esther put on *her* royal *robes* and stood in the inner court of the king's palace, across from the king's house, while the king sat on his royal throne in the royal house, facing the entrance of the house.[a]

2 So it was, when the king saw Queen Esther standing in the court, *that* she found favor in his sight, and the king held out to Esther the golden scepter that *was* in his hand. Then Esther went near and touched the top of the scepter.

3 And the king said to her, "What do you wish, Queen Esther? What *is* your request? It shall be given to you—up to half the kingdom!"

4 So Esther answered, "If it pleases the king, let the king and Hā′man come today to the banquet that I have prepared for him."

5 Then the king said, "Bring Hā′man quickly, that he may do as Esther has said." So the king and Hā′man went to the banquet that Esther had prepared.

6 At the banquet of wine the king said to Esther, "What *is* your peti-

---

4:17 [a]Septuagint adds a prayer of Mordecai here.
5:1 [a]Septuagint adds many extra details in verses 1 and 2.

tion? It shall be granted you. What *is* your request, up to half the kingdom? It shall be done!"

7 Then Esther answered and said, "My petition and request *is this:*

8 "If I have found favor in the sight of the king, and if it pleases the king to grant my petition and fulfill my request, then let the king and Hā′man come to the banquet which I will prepare for them, and tomorrow I will do as the king has said."

HAMAN'S PLOT AGAINST MORDECAI

9 So Hā′man went out that day joyful and with a glad heart; but when Hā′man saw Mor′de·caī in the king's gate, and that he did not stand or tremble before him, he was filled with indignation against Mor′de·caī.

10 Nevertheless Hā′man restrained himself and went home, and he sent and called for his friends and his wife Zē′resh.

11 Then Hā′man told them of his great riches, the multitude of his children, everything in which the king had promoted him, and how he had advanced him above the officials and servants of the king.

12 Moreover Hā′man said, "Besides, Queen Esther invited no one but me to come in with the king to the banquet that she prepared; and tomorrow I am again invited by her, along with the king.

13 "Yet all this avails me nothing, so long as I see Mor′de·caī the Jew sitting at the king's gate."

14 Then his wife Zē′resh and all his friends said to him, "Let a gallows be made, fifty cubits high, and in the morning suggest to the king that Mor′de·caī be hanged on it; then go merrily with the king to the banquet." And the thing pleased Hā-man; so he had the gallows made.

THE KING HONORS MORDECAI

6 That night the king could not sleep. So one was commanded to bring the book of the records of the chronicles; and they were read before the king.

2 And it was found written that Mor′de·caī had told of Big·thā′na and Tē′resh, two of the king's eunuchs, the doorkeepers who had sought to lay hands on King A·has·ū·ē′rus.

3 Then the king said, "What honor or dignity has been bestowed on Mor′de·caī for this?" And the king's servants who attended him said, "Nothing has been done for him."

4 So the king said, "Who *is* in the court?" Now Hā′man had *just* entered the outer court of the king's palace to suggest that the king hang Mor′de·caī on the gallows that he had prepared for him.

5 The king's servants said to him, "Hā′man is there, standing in the court." And the king said, "Let him come in."

6 So Hā′man came in, and the king asked him, "What shall be done for the man whom the king delights to honor?" Now Hā′man thought in his heart, "Whom would the king delight to honor more than me?"

7 And Hā′man answered the king, "*For* the man whom the king delights to honor,

8 "let a royal robe be brought which the king has worn, and a horse on which the king has ridden, which has a royal crest placed on its head.

9 "Then let this robe and horse be delivered to the hand of one of the king's most noble princes, that he may array the man whom the king delights to honor. Then parade him on horseback through the city square, and proclaim before him: 'Thus shall it be done to the man whom the king delights to honor!' "

10 Then the king said to Hā′man, "Hurry, take the robe and the horse, as you have suggested, and do so for Mor′de·caī the Jew who sits within the king's gate! Leave nothing undone of all that you have spoken."

11 So Hā′man took the robe and the horse, arrayed Mor′de·caī and led him on horseback through the city square, and proclaimed before him, "Thus shall it be done to the man whom the king delights to honor!"

12 Afterward Mor′de·caī went back to the king's gate. But Hā′man hurried to his house, mourning and with his head covered.

13 When Hā′man told his wife Zē′resh and all his friends everything that had happened to him, his wise men and his wife Zē′resh said to him, "If Mor′de·caī, before whom you have begun to fall, is of Jewish descent, you will not prevail against him but will surely fall before him."

14 While they *were* still talking with him, the king's eunuchs came, and hastened to bring Hā′man to the banquet which Esther had prepared.

HAMAN HANGED INSTEAD OF MORDECAI

7 So the king and Hā′man went to dine with Queen Esther.

2 And on the second day, at the banquet of wine, the king again said to Esther, "What *is* your petition, Queen Esther? It shall be granted you. And what *is* your request, up to half the kingdom? It shall be done!"

3 Then Queen Esther answered and said, "If I have found favor in your sight, O king, and if it pleases the king, let my life be given me at my petition, and my people at my request.

4 "For we have been sold, my people and I, to be destroyed, to be killed, and to be annihilated. Had we been sold as male and female slaves, I would have held my tongue, although the enemy could never compensate for the king's loss."

5 So King A·has·u·ē′rus answered and said to Queen Esther, "Who is he, and where is he, who would dare presume in his heart to do such a thing?"

6 And Esther said, "The adversary and enemy *is* this wicked Hā′man!" So Hā′man was terrified before the king and queen.

7 Then the king arose in his wrath from the banquet of wine *and went* into the palace garden; but Hā′man stood before Queen Esther, pleading for his life, for he saw that evil was determined against him by the king.

✓ Bible Quiz

Esther 5—7 **Haman Is Defeated**

1. Esther did something very courageous. What was it? What did the king hold out to her that spared her life?

2. How did Haman feel when he was invited to a banquet with Esther and the king? Now who was deceiving whom?

3. What did the king do one night when he couldn't sleep? What did he find?

4. What did the king ask Haman to do to Mordecai? How did this make Haman feel? Do you think Haman deserved it for the way he treated Mordecai?

5. How was Haman punished by the king?

8 When the king returned from the palace garden to the place of the banquet of wine, Hā′man had fallen across the couch where Esther *was.* Then the king said, "Will he also assault the queen while I *am* in the house?" As the word left the king's mouth, they covered Hā′man's face.

9 Now Har·bō′nah, one of the eunuchs, said to the king, "Look! The gallows, fifty cubits high, which Hā′-man made for Mor′de·caī, who spoke good on the king's behalf, is standing at the house of Hā′man." Then the king said, "Hang him on it!"

10 So they hanged Hā′man on the gallows that he had prepared for Mor′de·caī. Then the king's wrath subsided.

ESTHER SAVES THE JEWS

8 On that day King A·has·ū·ē′rus gave Queen Esther the house of Hā′man, the enemy of the Jews. And Mor′de·caī came before the king, for Esther had told how he *was related* to her.

2 So the king took off his signet ring, which he had taken from Hā′-man, and gave it to Mor′de·caī; and Esther appointed Mor′de·caī over the house of Hā′man.

3 Now Esther spoke again to the king, fell down at his feet, and implored him with tears to counteract the evil of Hā′man the Ag′ag·īte, and the scheme which he had devised against the Jews.

4 And the king held out the golden scepter toward Esther. So Esther arose and stood before the king,

5 and said, "If it pleases the king, and if I have found favor in his sight and the thing *seems* right to the king and I am pleasing in his eyes, let it

be written to revoke the letters devised by Hā′man, the son of Ham·me·dā′tha the Ag′ag·īte, which he wrote to annihilate the Jews who *are* in all the king's provinces.

6 "For how can I endure to see the evil that will come to my people? Or how can I endure to see the destruction of my countrymen?"

7 Then King A·has·ū·ē′rus said to Queen Esther and Mor′de·caī the Jew, "Indeed, I have given Esther the house of Hā′man, and they have hanged him on the gallows because he *tried to* lay his hand on the Jews.

8 "You yourselves write *a decree* concerning the Jews, as you please, in the king's name, and seal *it* with the king's signet ring; for whatever is written in the king's name and sealed with the king's signet ring no one can revoke."

9 So the king's scribes were called at that time, in the third month, which *is* the month of Sī′van, on the twenty-third *day;* and it was written, according to all that Mor′de·caī commanded, to the Jews, the satraps, the governors, and the princes of the provinces from India to Ethiopia, one hundred and twenty-seven provinces *in all,* to every province in its own script, to every people in their own language, and to the Jews in their own script and language.

10 And he wrote in the name of King A·has·ū·ē′rus, sealed *it* with the king's signet ring, and sent letters by couriers on horseback, riding on royal horses bred from swift steeds.*a*

11 By these letters the king permitted the Jews who *were* in every city to gather together and protect their lives—to destroy, kill, and annihilate all the forces of any people or province that would assault them,

8:10 *a*Literally *sons of the swift horses*

both little children and women, and to plunder their possessions,

12 on one day in all the provinces of King A·has·ū·ē'rus, on the thirteenth *day* of the twelfth month, which *is* the month of Ā'dar.*a*

13 A copy of the document was to be issued as a decree in every province and published for all people, so that the Jews would be ready on that day to avenge themselves on their enemies.

14 The couriers who rode on royal horses went out, hastened and pressed on by the king's command. And the decree was issued in Shū'shan the citadel.

15 So Mor'de·caī went out from the presence of the king in royal apparel of blue and white, with a great crown of gold and a garment of fine linen and purple; and the city of Shū'shan rejoiced and was glad.

16 The Jews had light and gladness, joy and honor.

17 And in every province and city, wherever the king's command and decree came, the Jews had joy and gladness, a feast and a holiday. Then many of the people of the land became Jews, because fear of the Jews fell upon them.

THE JEWS DESTROY THEIR TORMENTORS

9 Now in the twelfth month, that *is,* the month of Ā'dar, on the thirteenth day, *the time* came for the king's command and his decree to be executed. On the day that the enemies of the Jews had hoped to overpower them, the opposite occurred, in that the Jews themselves overpowered those who hated them.

2 The Jews gathered together in their cities throughout all the provinces of King A·has·ū·ē'rus to lay hands on those who sought their harm. And no one could withstand them, because fear of them fell upon all people.

3 And all the officials of the provinces, the satraps, the governors, and all those doing the king's work, helped the Jews, because the fear of Mor'de·caī fell upon them.

4 For Mor'de·caī *was* great in the king's palace, and his fame spread throughout all the provinces; for this man Mor'de·caī became increasingly prominent.

5 Thus the Jews defeated all their enemies with the stroke of the sword, with slaughter and destruction, and did what they pleased with those who hated them.

6 And in Shū'shan the citadel the Jews killed and destroyed five hundred men.

7 Also Par·shan·dā'tha, Dal'phon, As·pā'tha,

8 Pō·rā'tha, A·dā'li·a, Ar·i·dā'tha,

9 Par·mash'ta, Ar'i·saī, Ar'i·daī, and Va·jez'a·tha—

10 the ten sons of Hā'man the son of Ham·me·dā'tha, the enemy of the Jews—they killed; but they did not lay a hand on the plunder.

11 On that day the number of those who were killed in Shū'shan the citadel was brought to the king.

12 And the king said to Queen Esther, "The Jews have killed and destroyed five hundred men in Shū'shan the citadel, and the ten sons of Hā'man. What have they done in the rest of the king's provinces? Now what *is* your petition? It shall be granted to you. Or what *is* your further request? It shall be done."

13 Then Esther said, "If it pleases the king, let it be granted to the Jews

8:12 *a*Septuagint adds the text of the letter here.

who *are* in Shū′shan to do again tomorrow according to today's decree, and let Hā′man's ten sons be hanged on the gallows."

14 So the king commanded this to be done; the decree was issued in Shū′shan, and they hanged Hā′man's ten sons.

15 And the Jews who *were* in Shū′shan gathered together again on the fourteenth day of the month of Ā′dar and killed three hundred men at Shū′shan; but they did not lay a hand on the plunder.

16 The remainder of the Jews in the king's provinces gathered together and protected their lives, had rest from their enemies, and killed seventy-five thousand of their enemies; but they did not lay a hand on the plunder.

17 *This was* on the thirteenth day of the month of Ā′dar. And on the fourteenth of *the month*[a] they rested and made it a day of feasting and gladness.

THE FEAST OF PURIM

18 But the Jews who *were* at Shū′shan assembled together on the thirteenth *day,* as well as on the fourteenth; and on the fifteenth of *the month*[a] they rested, and made it a day of feasting and gladness.

19 Therefore the Jews of the villages who dwelt in the unwalled towns celebrated the fourteenth day of the month of Ā′dar *with* gladness and feasting, as a holiday, and for sending presents to one another.

20 And Mor′de·caī wrote these things and sent letters to all the Jews, near and far, who *were* in all the provinces of King A·has·ū·ē′rus,

21 to establish among them that they should celebrate yearly the four-

teenth and fifteenth days of the month of Ā′dar,

22 as the days on which the Jews had rest from their enemies, as the month which was turned from sorrow to joy for them, and from mourning to a holiday; that they should make them days of feasting and joy, of sending presents to one another and gifts to the poor.

23 So the Jews accepted the custom which they had begun, as Mor′de·caī had written to them,

24 because Hā′man, the son of Hamme·dā′tha the Ag′ag·īte, the enemy of all the Jews, had plotted against the Jews to annihilate them, and had cast Pūr (that *is,* the lot), to consume them and destroy them;

25 but when *Esther*[a] came before the king, he commanded by letter that this[b] wicked plot which *Hā′man* had devised against the Jews should return on his own head, and that he and his sons should be hanged on the gallows.

26 So they called these days Pūr′im, after the name Pūr. Therefore, because of all the words of this letter, what they had seen concerning this matter, and what had happened to them,

27 the Jews established and imposed it upon themselves and their descendants and all who would join them, that without fail they should celebrate these two days every year, according to the written *instructions* and according to the *prescribed* time,

28 *that* these days *should be* remembered and kept throughout every generation, every family, every province, and every city, that these days of Pūr′im should not fail *to be observed* among the Jews, and *that*

9:17 [a]Literally *it*   9:18 [a]Literally *it*
9:25 [a]Literally *she* or *it*   [b]Literally *his*

Values

GIVING Esther 9:19

Happy Birthday to You!

It's your birthday. Happy birthday to you! Today we will celebrate the day you were born. Perhaps someone will give you a birthday gift. Or someone may give you a birthday cake. Giving good things is a wonderful way to say, "Happy birthday to you."

1. What special things do you get on your birthday? Would you *get* these things if someone did not *give* them to you?
2. Why is *giving* a wonderful way to say "happy birthday?" Why not *keeping* something from you, or *taking* something from you? What does God think of giving?

For more on *Values* turn to page 763
For more on *Giving* turn to page 1309

the memory of them should not perish among their descendants.

29 Then Queen Esther, the daughter of Ab·i·hā′il, with Mor′de·caī the Jew, wrote with full authority to confirm this second letter about Pūr′im.

30 And *Mor′de·caī* sent letters to all the Jews, to the one hundred and twenty-seven provinces of the kingdom of A·has·ū·ē′rus, *with* words of peace and truth,

31 to confirm these days of Pūr′im at their *appointed* time, as Mor′de·caī the Jew and Queen Esther had prescribed for them, and as they had decreed for themselves and their descendants concerning matters of their fasting and lamenting.

32 So the decree of Esther confirmed these matters of Pūr′im, and it was written in the book.

MORDECAI'S ADVANCEMENT

10 And King A·has·ū·ē′rus imposed tribute on the land and *on* the islands of the sea.

2 Now all the acts of his power and his might, and the account of the greatness of Mor′de·caī, to which the king advanced him, *are* they not written in the book of the chronicles of the kings of Media and Persia?

3 For Mor′de·caī the Jew *was* second to King A·has·ū·ē′rus, and was great among the Jews and well received by the multitude of his brethren, seeking the good of his people and speaking peace to all his countrymen.ᵃ

10:3 ᵃLiterally *seed*. Septuagint and Vulgate add a dream of Mordecai here; Vulgate adds six more chapters.

The Book of
JOB

Job and His Family in Uz

THERE was a man in the land of Uz, whose name *was* Job; and that man was blameless and upright, and one who feared God and shunned evil.

2 And seven sons and three daughters were born to him.

3 Also, his possessions were seven thousand sheep, three thousand camels, five hundred yoke of oxen, five hundred female donkeys, and a very large household, so that this man was the greatest of all the people of the East.

4 And his sons would go and feast *in their* houses, each on his *appointed* day, and would send and invite their three sisters to eat and drink with them.

5 So it was, when the days of feasting had run their course, that Job would send and sanctify them, and he would rise early in the morning and offer burnt offerings *according to* the number of them all. For Job said, "It may be that my sons have sinned and cursed[a] God in their hearts." Thus Job did regularly.

Satan Attacks Job's Character

6 Now there was a day when the sons of God came to present themselves before the LORD, and Satan[a] also came among them.

7 And the LORD said to Satan, "From where do you come?" So Satan answered the LORD and said, "From going to and fro on the earth, and from walking back and forth on it."

8 Then the LORD said to Satan, "Have you considered My servant Job, that *there is* none like him on the earth, a blameless and upright man, one who fears God and shuns evil?"

9 So Satan answered the LORD and said, "Does Job fear God for nothing?

10 "Have You not made a hedge around him, around his household, and around all that he has on every side? You have blessed the work of his hands, and his possessions have increased in the land.

11 "But now, stretch out Your hand and touch all that he has, and he will surely curse You to Your face!"

12 And the LORD said to Satan, "Behold, all that he has *is* in your power; only do not lay a hand on his *person.*" So Satan went out from the presence of the LORD.

Job Loses His Property and Children

13 Now there was a day when his sons and daughters *were* eating and drinking wine in their oldest brother's house;

14 and a messenger came to Job and said, "The oxen were plowing and the donkeys feeding beside them,

15 "when the Sa·bē′ans[a] raided *them* and took them away—indeed they have killed the servants with the edge of the sword; and I alone have escaped to tell you!"

16 While he *was* still speaking, another also came and said, "The fire of God fell from heaven and burned up the sheep and the servants, and consumed them; and I alone have escaped to tell you!"

17 While he *was* still speaking, an-

1:5 [a]Literally *blessed,* but used here in the evil sense, and so in verse 11 and 2:5, 9   1:6 [a]Literally *the Adversary,* and so throughout this book   1:15 [a]Literally *Sheba* (compare 6:19)

other also came and said, "The Chal-dē'ans formed three bands, raided the camels and took them away, yes, and killed the servants with the edge of the sword; and I alone have escaped to tell you!"

18 While he *was* still speaking, another also came and said, "Your sons and daughters *were* eating and drinking wine in their oldest brother's house,

19 "and suddenly a great wind came from across*a* the wilderness and struck the four corners of the house, and it fell on the young people, and they are dead; and I alone have escaped to tell you!"

20 Then Job arose, tore his robe, and shaved his head; and he fell to the ground and worshiped.

21 And he said:

"Naked I came from my mother's
    womb,
And naked shall I return there.
The LORD gave, and the LORD has
    taken away;
Blessed be the name of the LORD."

22 In all this Job did not sin nor charge God with wrong.

SATAN ATTACKS JOB'S HEALTH

2 Again there was a day when the sons of God came to present themselves before the LORD, and Satan came also among them to present himself before the LORD.

2 And the LORD said to Satan, "From where do you come?" So Satan answered the LORD and said, "From going to and fro on the earth, and from walking back and forth on it."

3 Then the LORD said to Satan, "Have you considered My servant Job, that *there is* none like him on the earth, a blameless and upright man, one who fears God and shuns evil? And still he holds fast to his integrity, although you incited Me against him, to destroy him without cause."

4 So Satan answered the LORD and said, "Skin for skin! Yes, all that a man has he will give for his life.

5 "But stretch out Your hand now, and touch his bone and his flesh, and he will surely curse You to Your face!"

6 And the LORD said to Satan, "Behold, he *is* in your hand, but spare his life."

7 So Satan went out from the presence of the LORD, and struck Job with painful boils from the sole of his foot to the crown of his head.

8 And he took for himself a potsherd with which to scrape himself while he sat in the midst of the ashes.

9 Then his wife said to him, "Do you still hold fast to your integrity? Curse God and die!"

10 But he said to her, "You speak as one of the foolish women speaks. Shall we indeed accept good from God, and shall we not accept adversity?" In all this Job did not sin with his lips.

JOB'S THREE FRIENDS

11 Now when Job's three friends heard of all this adversity that had come upon him, each one came from his own place—E·lī'phaz the Tē'-man·īte, Bil'dad the Shū'hīte, and Zō'phar the Nā'a·ma·thīte. For they had made an appointment together to come and mourn with him, and to comfort him.

12 And when they raised their eyes from afar, and did not recognize him, they lifted their voices and wept; and each one tore his robe and sprinkled dust on his head toward heaven.

1:19 *a*Septuagint omits *across*.

Family Friends

THE NEWEST FRIEND OF ALL Job 2:11

This boy has just met the newest friend of all. The little bird has just hatched, and the boy is the first to welcome it into the world. "Welcome, little bird," he said. "I'm your newest friend."

1. Who is your newest friend? Have you done something kind or special for that newest friend?
2. Do you know someone who has accepted Jesus as newest Friend? How can you help that person with the newest Friend? Think of some ways, then try to do one each day.

For more on *Family Friends* turn to page 987
For more on *Friendship* turn to page 763

13 So they sat down with him on the ground seven days and seven nights, and no one spoke a word to him, for they saw that *his* grief was very great.

JOB DEPLORES HIS BIRTH

3 After this Job opened his mouth and cursed the day of his *birth.*

2 And Job spoke, and said:

3 "May the day perish on which I was born,
And the night *in which* it was said,
'A male child is conceived.'

4 May that day be darkness;
May God above not seek it,
Nor the light shine upon it.

5 May darkness and the shadow of death claim it;
May a cloud settle on it;
May the blackness of the day terrify it.

6 *As for* that night, may darkness seize it;
May it not rejoice*a* among the days of the year,
May it not come into the number of the months.

7 Oh, may that night be barren!
May no joyful shout come into it!

8 May those curse it who curse the day,
Those who are ready to arouse Le·vī′a·than.

9 May the stars of its morning be dark;
May it look for light, but *have* none,
And not see the dawning of the day;

10 Because it did not shut up the doors of my *mother's* womb,
Nor hide sorrow from my eyes.

11 "Why did I not die at birth?
Why did I *not* perish when I came from the womb?

12 Why did the knees receive me?
Or why the breasts, that I should nurse?

13 For now I would have lain still and been quiet,
I would have been asleep;
Then I would have been at rest

14 With kings and counselors of the earth,
Who built ruins for themselves,

15 Or with princes who had gold,
Who filled their houses *with* silver;

16 Or *why* was I not hidden like a stillborn child,
Like infants who never saw light?

17 There the wicked cease *from* troubling,
And there the weary are at rest.

18 *There* the prisoners rest together;
They do not hear the voice of the oppressor.

19 The small and great are there,
And the servant *is* free from his master.

20 "Why is light given to him who is in misery,
And life to the bitter of soul,

21 Who long for death, but it does not *come,*
And search for it more than hidden treasures;

22 Who rejoice exceedingly,
And are glad when they can find the grave?

23 *Why is light given* to a man whose way is hidden,
And whom God has hedged in?

24 For my sighing comes before I eat,*a*
And my groanings pour out like water.

25 For the thing I greatly feared has come upon me,
And what I dreaded has happened to me.

3:6 *a*Septuagint, Syriac, Targum, and Vulgate read *be joined.*   3:24 *a*Literally *my bread*

26 I am not at ease, nor am I quiet;
   I have no rest, for trouble comes."

ELIPHAZ: JOB HAS SINNED

4 Then E·li′phaz the Tē′man·īte answered and said:

2 "*If* one attempts a word with you,
      will you become weary?
   But who can withhold himself
      from speaking?
3 Surely you have instructed many,
   And you have strengthened weak
      hands.
4 Your words have upheld him who
      was stumbling,
   And you have strengthened the
      feeble knees;
5 But now it comes upon you, and
      you are weary;
   It touches you, and you are
      troubled.
6 *Is* not your reverence your
      confidence?
   And the integrity of your ways
      your hope?

7 "Remember now, who *ever*
      perished being innocent?
   Or where were the upright *ever*
      cut off?
8 Even as I have seen,
   Those who plow iniquity
   And sow trouble reap the same.
9 By the blast of God they perish,
   And by the breath of His anger
      they are consumed.
10 The roaring of the lion,
   The voice of the fierce lion,
   And the teeth of the young lions
      are broken.
11 The old lion perishes for lack of
      prey,
   And the cubs of the lioness are
      scattered.

12 "Now a word was secretly brought
      to me,

   And my ear received a whisper of
      it.
13 In disquieting thoughts from the
      visions of the night,
   When deep sleep falls on men,
14 Fear came upon me, and
      trembling,
   Which made all my bones shake.
15 Then a spirit passed before my
      face;
   The hair on my body stood up.
16 It stood still,
   But I could not discern its
      appearance.
   A form *was* before my eyes;
   There was silence;
   Then I heard a voice *saying:*
17 'Can a mortal be more righteous
      than God?
   Can a man be more pure than his
      Maker?
18 If He puts no trust in His
      servants,
   If He charges His angels with
      error,
19 How much more those who dwell
      in houses of clay,
   Whose foundation is in the dust,
   Who are crushed before a moth?
20 They are broken in pieces from
      morning till evening;
   They perish forever, with no one
      regarding.
21 Does not their own excellence go
      away?
   They die, even without wisdom.'

ELIPHAZ: JOB IS CHASTENED BY GOD

5 "Call out now;
   Is there anyone who will answer
      you?
   And to which of the holy ones will
      you turn?
2 For wrath kills a foolish man,
   And envy slays a simple one.
3 I have seen the foolish taking
      root,

HE GIVES RAIN ON THE EARTH, / AND SENDS WATERS ON THE FIELDS.
Job 5:10

Who Sends the Rain?

The sky gets dark. Lightning flashes. Thunder rumbles. Rain falls and waters the garden and flowers and fields. Without the rain we would have no crops or flowers or gardens or lawns. But who sends the rain?

1. Can you make it rain? Can your friends make it rain?
2. Who makes the rain? Why does He send it?
3. Have you thanked our loving God for rain and sunshine? Why not do it now?

For more on *Favorite Family Verses* turn to page 766
For more on *God's Care* turn to page 829

But suddenly I cursed his
    dwelling place.
4 His sons are far from safety,
They are crushed in the gate,
And *there is* no deliverer.
5 Because the hungry eat up his
    harvest,
Taking it even from the thorns,*a*
And a snare snatches their
    substance.*b*
6 For affliction does not come from
    the dust,
Nor does trouble spring from the
    ground;
7 Yet man is born to trouble,
As the sparks fly upward.

8 "But as for me, I would seek God,
And to God I would commit my
    cause—
9 Who does great things, and
    unsearchable,
Marvelous things without
    number.
10 He gives rain on the earth,
And sends waters on the fields.
11 He sets on high those who are
    lowly,
And those who mourn are lifted to
    safety.

12 He frustrates the devices of the
    crafty,
So that their hands cannot carry
    out their plans.
13 He catches the wise in their own
    craftiness,
And the counsel of the cunning
    comes quickly upon them.
14 They meet with darkness in the
    daytime,
And grope at noontime as in the
    night.
15 But He saves the needy from the
    sword,
From the mouth of the mighty,
And from their hand.
16 So the poor have hope,
And injustice shuts her mouth.

17 "Behold, happy *is* the man whom
    God corrects;
Therefore do not despise the
    chastening of the Almighty.
18 For He bruises, but He binds up;

5:5 *a*Septuagint reads *They shall not be taken from
evil men;* Vulgate reads *And the armed man shall
take him by violence.* *b*Septuagint reads *The
might shall draw them off;* Vulgate reads *And the
thirsty shall drink up their riches.*

He wounds, but His hands make
whole.

19 He shall deliver you in six
troubles,
Yes, in seven no evil shall touch
you.

20 In famine He shall redeem you
from death,
And in war from the power of the
sword.

21 You shall be hidden from the
scourge of the tongue,
And you shall not be afraid of
destruction when it comes.

22 You shall laugh at destruction
and famine,
And you shall not be afraid of the
beasts of the earth.

23 For you shall have a covenant
with the stones of the field,
And the beasts of the field shall
be at peace with you.

24 You shall know that your tent *is*
in peace;
You shall visit your dwelling and
find nothing amiss.

25 You shall also know that your
descendants *shall be* many,
And your offspring like the grass
of the earth.

26 You shall come to the grave at a
full age,
As a sheaf of grain ripens in its
season.

27 Behold, this we have searched
out;
It *is* true.
Hear it, and know for yourself."

JOB: MY COMPLAINT IS JUST

6 Then Job answered and said:

2 "Oh, that my grief were fully
weighed,
And my calamity laid with it on
the scales!

3 For then it would be heavier than
the sand of the sea—

Therefore my words have been
rash.

4 For the arrows of the Almighty
are within me;
My spirit drinks in their poison;
The terrors of God are arrayed
against me.

5 Does the wild donkey bray when
it has grass,
Or does the ox low over its
fodder?

6 Can flavorless food be eaten
without salt?
Or is there *any* taste in the white
of an egg?

7 My soul refuses to touch them;
They *are* as loathsome food to me.

8 "Oh, that I might have my request,
That God would grant *me* the
thing that I long for!

9 That it would please God to crush
me,
That He would loose His hand
and cut me off!

10 Then I would still have comfort;
Though in anguish I would exult,
He will not spare;
For I have not concealed the
words of the Holy One.

11 "What strength do I have, that I
should hope?
And what *is* my end, that I should
prolong my life?

12 *Is* my strength the strength of
stones?
Or is my flesh bronze?

13 *Is* my help not within me?
And is success driven from me?

14 "To him who is afflicted, kindness
should be shown by his friend,
Even though he forsakes the fear
of the Almighty.

15 My brothers have dealt
deceitfully like a brook,
Like the streams of the brooks
that pass away,

Values

KINDNESS Job 6:14

A Time for Kindness

When was the last time you were sick? How did you feel? Did you want others to be mean to you at that time? Was this a time for kindness? Did you want your family and friends to be even more kind than usual when you were sick? Mark isn't feeling well. You know how much he appreciates it when his sister Maria reads to him. That's very kind of her, isn't it? How do you think Mark will treat Maria when she is sick next time?

1. Think of the kindest person you know. Who is it? What does this person do that you think is so kind?
2. How can you be kind to your family or friends? Think of several ways. Which can you do today?

For more on *Values* turn to page 789
For more on *Friendship* turn to page 820

16 Which are dark because of the ice,
And into which the snow
vanishes.
17 When it is warm, they cease to
flow;
When it is hot, they vanish from
their place.
18 The paths of their way turn aside,
They go nowhere and perish.
19 The caravans of Tē′ma look,
The travelers of Shē′ba hope for
them.
20 They are disappointed because
they were confident;
They come there and are
confused.
21 For now you are nothing,
You see terror and are afraid.
22 Did I ever say, 'Bring *something*
to me'?
Or, 'Offer a bribe for me from your
wealth'?
23 Or, 'Deliver me from the enemy's
hand'?
Or, 'Redeem me from the hand of
oppressors'?

24 "Teach me, and I will hold my
tongue;
Cause me to understand wherein
I have erred.
25 How forceful are right words!
But what does your arguing
prove?
26 Do you intend to rebuke *my*
words,
And the speeches of a desperate
one, *which are* as wind?
27 Yes, you overwhelm the
fatherless,
And you undermine your friend.
28 Now therefore, be pleased to look
at me;
For I would never lie to your face.
29 Yield now, let there be no
injustice!
Yes, concede, my righteousness
still stands!
30 Is there injustice on my tongue?

Cannot my taste discern the
unsavory?

JOB: MY SUFFERING IS COMFORTLESS

7 "*Is there* not a time of hard
service for man on earth?
Are not his days also like the days
of a hired man?
2 Like a servant who earnestly
desires the shade,
And like a hired man who eagerly
looks for his wages,
3 So I have been allotted months of
futility,
And wearisome nights have been
appointed to me.
4 When I lie down, I say, 'When
shall I arise,
And the night be ended?'
For I have had my fill of tossing
till dawn.
5 My flesh is caked with worms and
dust,
My skin is cracked and breaks out
afresh.

6 "My days are swifter than a
weaver's shuttle,
And are spent without hope.
7 Oh, remember that my life *is* a
breath!
My eye will never again see good.
8 The eye of him who sees me will
see me no *more;*
While your *eyes* are upon me, I
shall no longer *be.*
9 *As* the cloud disappears and
vanishes away,
So he who goes down to the grave
does not come up.
10 He shall never return to his
house,
Nor shall his place know him
anymore.

11 "Therefore I will not restrain my
mouth;

I will speak in the anguish of my
   spirit;
I will complain in the bitterness
   of my soul.
12 *Am* I a sea, or a sea serpent,
   That You set a guard over me?
13 When I say, 'My bed will comfort
   me,
   My couch will ease my complaint,'
14 Then You scare me with dreams
   And terrify me with visions,
15 So that my soul chooses
   strangling
   And death rather than my body.*a*
16 I loathe *my life;*
   I would not live forever.
   Let me alone,
   For my days *are but* a breath.

17 "What *is* man, that You should
   exalt him,
   That You should set Your heart on
   him,
18 That You should visit him every
   morning,
   And test him every moment?
19 How long?
   Will You not look away from me,
   And let me alone till I swallow my
   saliva?
20 Have I sinned?
   What have I done to You,
   O watcher of men?
   Why have You set me as Your
   target,
   So that I am a burden to myself?*a*
21 Why then do You not pardon my
   transgression,
   And take away my iniquity?
   For now I will lie down in the
   dust,
   And You will seek me diligently,
   But I *will* no longer *be.*"

BILDAD: JOB SHOULD REPENT

8 Then Bil′dad the Shū′hīte answered and said:

2 "How long will you speak these
   things,
   And the words of your mouth *be*
   like a strong wind?
3 Does God subvert judgment?
   Or does the Almighty pervert
   justice?
4 If your sons have sinned against
   Him,
   He has cast them away for their
   transgression.
5 If you would earnestly seek God
   And make your supplication to
   the Almighty,
6 If you *were* pure and upright,
   Surely now He would awake for
   you,
   And prosper your rightful
   dwelling place.
7 Though your beginning was
   small,
   Yet your latter end would
   increase abundantly.

8 "For inquire, please, of the former
   age,
   And consider the things
   discovered by their fathers;
9 For we *were born* yesterday, and
   know nothing,
   Because our days on earth *are* a
   shadow.
10 Will they not teach you and tell
   you,
   And utter words from their heart?

11 "Can the papyrus grow up without
   a marsh?
   Can the reeds flourish without
   water?
12 While it *is* yet green *and* not cut
   down,
   It withers before any *other* plant.
13 So *are* the paths of all who forget
   God;

7:15 *a*Literally *my bones*   7:20 *a*Following
Masoretic Text, Targum, and Vulgate; Septuagint
and Jewish tradition read *to You.*

Favorite Family Verses

HE WILL FILL YOUR MOUTH WITH LAUGHING, / AND YOUR LIPS WITH REJOICING. Job 8:21

A Time to Laugh and Sing

The sun is shining. Flowers are blooming. The sky is blue. Everything is going the right way for Grace. It's easy to laugh and whistle and sing when the world is smiling at you. But we also need to laugh and whistle and sing when the sun isn't shining and things are not all OK.

1. Is it easy to be joyful when things are all OK? Why?
2. Is it hard to be joyful when things are not all OK? Why?
3. Jesus can help you be joyful, even when things are not OK. Ask Him. Parents also may help you be joyful in tough times. Do you help them also when things are tough for them?

For more on *Favorite Family Verses* turn to page 825
For more on *Facing Trials* turn to page 870

And the hope of the hypocrite
    shall perish,
14 Whose confidence shall be cut off,
    And whose trust *is* a spider's web.
15 He leans on his house, but it does
    not stand.
    He holds it fast, but it does not
    endure.
16 He grows green in the sun,
    And his branches spread out in
    his garden.
17 His roots wrap around the rock
    heap,
    And look for a place in the stones.
18 If he is destroyed from his place,
    Then *it* will deny him, *saying,* 'I
    have not seen you.'

19 "Behold, this is the joy of His way,
    And out of the earth others will
    grow.
20 Behold, God will not cast away
    the blameless,
    Nor will He uphold the evildoers.
21 He will yet fill your mouth with
    laughing,
    And your lips with rejoicing.
22 Those who hate you will be
    clothed with shame,
    And the dwelling place of the
    wicked will come to nothing."*a*

JOB: THERE IS NO MEDIATOR

9 Then Job answered and said:

2 "Truly I know *it is* so,
    But how can a man be righteous
    before God?
3 If one wished to contend with
    Him,
    He could not answer Him one
    time out of a thousand.
4 *God is* wise in heart and mighty
    in strength.
    Who has hardened *himself*
    against Him and prospered?
5 He removes the mountains, and
    they do not know

When He overturns them in His
    anger;
6 He shakes the earth out of its
    place,
    And its pillars tremble;
7 He commands the sun, and it
    does not rise;
    He seals off the stars;
8 He alone spreads out the
    heavens,
    And treads on the waves of the
    sea;
9 He made the Bear, Ō·rī′on, and
    the Plēi′a·dēs,
    And the chambers of the south;
10 He does great things past finding
    out,
    Yes, wonders without number.
11 If He goes by me, I do not see
    Him;
    If He moves past, I do not
    perceive Him;
12 If He takes away, who can hinder
    Him?
    Who can say to Him, 'What are
    You doing?'
13 God will not withdraw His
    anger,
    The allies of the proud*a* lie
    prostrate beneath Him.

14 "How then can I answer Him,
    And choose my words *to reason*
    with Him?
15 For though I were righteous, I
    could not answer Him;
    I would beg mercy of my Judge.
16 If I called and He answered me,
    I would not believe that He was
    listening to my voice.
17 For He crushes me with a
    tempest,
    And multiplies my wounds
    without cause.
18 He will not allow me to catch my
    breath,
    But fills me with bitterness.

8:22 *a*Literally *will not be*   9:13 *a*Hebrew *rahab*

19 If *it is a matter* of strength,
   indeed *He is* strong;
   And if of justice, who will appoint
   my day *in court?*
20 Though I were righteous, my own
   mouth would condemn me;
   Though I *were* blameless, it would
   prove me perverse.

21 "I am blameless, yet I do not know
   myself;
   I despise my life.
22 It *is* all one *thing;*
   Therefore I say, 'He destroys the
   blameless and the wicked.'
23 If the scourge slays suddenly,
   He laughs at the plight of the
   innocent.
24 The earth is given into the hand
   of the wicked.
   He covers the faces of its judges.
   If it is not *He,* who else could it
   be?

25 "Now my days are swifter than a
   runner;
   They flee away, they see no good.
26 They pass by like swift ships,
   Like an eagle swooping on its
   prey.
27 If I say, 'I will forget my
   complaint,
   I will put off my sad face and
   wear a smile,'
28 I am afraid of all my sufferings;
   I know that You will not hold me
   innocent.
29 *If* I am condemned,
   Why then do I labor in vain?
30 If I wash myself with snow water,
   And cleanse my hands with soap,
31 Yet You will plunge me into the
   pit,
   And my own clothes will abhor
   me.

32 "For *He is* not a man, as I *am,*
   That I may answer Him,

And that we should go to court
   together.
33 Nor is there any mediator
   between us,
   Who may lay his hand on us both.
34 Let Him take His rod away from
   me,
   And do not let dread of Him
   terrify me.
35 *Then* I would speak and not fear
   Him,
   But it is not so with me.

JOB: I WOULD PLEAD WITH GOD

10 "My soul loathes my life;
   I will give free course to my
   complaint,
   I will speak in the bitterness of
   my soul.
2 I will say to God, 'Do not condemn
   me;
   Show me why You contend with
   me.
3 *Does it* seem good to You that You
   should oppress,
   That You should despise the work
   of Your hands,
   And smile on the counsel of the
   wicked?
4 Do You have eyes of flesh?
   Or do You see as man sees?
5 *Are* Your days like the days of a
   mortal man?
   Are Your years like the days of a
   mighty man,
6 That You should seek for my
   iniquity
   And search out my sin,
7 Although You know that I am not
   wicked,
   And *there is* no one who can
   deliver from Your hand?

8 'Your hands have made me and
   fashioned me,
   An intricate unity;
   Yet You would destroy me.

9 Remember, I pray, that You have
made me like clay.
And will You turn me into dust
again?
10 Did You not pour me out like
milk,
And curdle me like cheese,
11 Clothe me with skin and flesh,
And knit me together with bones
and sinews?
12 You have granted me life and
favor,
And Your care has preserved my
spirit.

13 'And these *things* You have hidden
in Your heart;
I know that this *was* with You:
14 If I sin, then You mark me,
And will not acquit me of my
iniquity.
15 If I am wicked, woe to me;
Even *if* I am righteous, I cannot
lift up my head.
I am full of disgrace;
See my misery!
16 If *my head* is exalted,
You hunt me like a fierce
lion,

And again You show Yourself
awesome against me.
17 You renew Your witnesses against
me,
And increase Your indignation
toward me;
Changes and war are *ever* with
me.

18 'Why then have You brought me
out of the womb?
Oh, that I had perished and no
eye had seen me!
19 I would have been as though I
had not been.
I would have been carried from
the womb to the grave.
20 Are not my days few?
Cease! Leave me alone, that I
may take a little comfort,
21 Before I go *to the place from
which* I shall not return,
To the land of darkness and the
shadow of death,
22 A land as dark as darkness *itself,*
As the shadow of death, without
any order,
Where even the light *is* like
darkness.' "

ZOPHAR URGES JOB TO REPENT

11 Then Zō′phar the Nā′a·ma-
thīte answered and said:

2 "Should not the multitude of words
  be answered?
 And should a man full of talk be
  vindicated?
3 Should your empty talk make
  men hold their peace?
 And when you mock, should no
  one rebuke you?
4 For you have said,
 'My doctrine *is* pure,
 And I am clean in your eyes.'
5 But oh, that God would speak,
 And open His lips against you,
6 That He would show you the
  secrets of wisdom!
 For *they would* double *your*
  prudence.
 Know therefore that God exacts
  from you
 Less than your iniquity *deserves*.

7 "Can you search out the deep
  things of God?
 Can you find out the limits of the
  Almighty?
8 *They are* higher than heaven—
  what can you do?
 Deeper than Shē′ōl—what can
  you know?
9 Their measure *is* longer than the
  earth
 And broader than the sea.

10 "If He passes by, imprisons, and
  gathers *to judgment,*
 Then who can hinder Him?
11 For He knows deceitful men;
 He sees wickedness also.
 Will He not then consider *it?*
12 For an empty-headed man will be
  wise,
 When a wild donkey's colt is born
  a man.

13 "If you would prepare your heart,
 And stretch out your hands
  toward Him;
14 If iniquity *were* in your hand, *and
 you* put it far away,
 And would not let wickedness
  dwell in your tents;
15 Then surely you could lift up your
  face without spot;
 Yes, you could be steadfast, and
  not fear;
16 Because you would forget *your*
  misery,
 And remember *it* as waters *that
 have* passed away,
17 And *your* life would be brighter
  than noonday.
 Though you were dark, you would
  be like the morning.
18 And you would be secure, because
  there is hope;
 Yes, you would dig *around you,
 and* take your rest in safety.
19 You would also lie down, and no
  one would make *you* afraid;
 Yes, many would court your favor.
20 But the eyes of the wicked will
  fail,
 And they shall not escape,
 And their hope—loss of life!"

JOB ANSWERS HIS CRITICS

12 Then Job answered and said:

2 "No doubt you *are* the people,
 And wisdom will die with you!
3 But I have understanding as well
  as you;
 I *am* not inferior to you.
 Indeed, who does not *know* such
  things as these?

4 "I am one mocked by his friends,
 Who called on God, and He
  answered him,
 The just and blameless *who is*
  ridiculed.

5 A lamp[a] is despised in the
  thought of one who is at ease;
  It is made ready for those whose
  feet slip.
6 The tents of robbers prosper,
  And those who provoke God are
  secure—
  In what God provides by His
  hand.

7 "But now ask the beasts, and they
  will teach you;
  And the birds of the air, and they
  will tell you;
8 Or speak to the earth, and it will
  teach you;
  And the fish of the sea will
  explain to you.
9 Who among all these does not
  know
  That the hand of the LORD has
  done this,
10 In whose hand *is* the life of every
  living thing,
  And the breath of all mankind?
11 Does not the ear test words
  And the mouth taste its food?
12 Wisdom *is* with aged men,
  And with length of days,
  understanding.

13 "With Him *are* wisdom and
  strength,
  He has counsel and
  understanding.
14 If He breaks *a thing* down, it
  cannot be rebuilt;
  If He imprisons a man, there can
  be no release.
15 If He withholds the waters, they
  dry up;
  If He sends them out, they
  overwhelm the earth.
16 With Him *are* strength and
  prudence.
  The deceived and the deceiver *are*
  His.
17 He leads counselors away
  plundered,

  And makes fools of the judges.
18 He loosens the bonds of kings,
  And binds their waist with a belt.
19 He leads princes[a] away
  plundered,
  And overthrows the mighty.
20 He deprives the trusted ones of
  speech,
  And takes away the discernment
  of the elders.
21 He pours contempt on princes,
  And disarms the mighty.
22 He uncovers deep things out of
  darkness,
  And brings the shadow of death
  to light.
23 He makes nations great, and
  destroys them;
  He enlarges nations, and guides
  them.
24 He takes away the
  understanding[a] of the chiefs
  of the people of the earth,
  And makes them wander in a
  pathless wilderness.
25 They grope in the dark without
  light,
  And He makes them stagger like
  a drunken *man.*

13

"Behold, my eye has seen all
  this,
  My ear has heard and understood
  it.
2 What you know, I also know;
  I *am* not inferior to you.
3 But I would speak to the
  Almighty,
  And I desire to reason with God.
4 But you forgers of lies,
  You *are* all worthless physicians.
5 Oh, that you would be silent,
  And it would be your wisdom!
6 Now hear my reasoning,
  And heed the pleadings of my
  lips.

12:5 [a]Or *disaster*   12:19 [a]Literally *priests,* but
not in a technical sense   12:24 [a]Literally *heart*

7 Will you speak wickedly for God,
   And talk deceitfully for Him?
8 Will you show partiality for Him?
   Will you contend for God?
9 Will it be well when He searches
   you out?
   Or can you mock Him as one
   mocks a man?
10 He will surely rebuke you
   If you secretly show partiality.
11 Will not His excellence make you
   afraid,
   And the dread of Him fall upon
   you?
12 Your platitudes *are* proverbs of
   ashes,
   Your defenses are defenses of clay.

13 "Hold your peace with me, and let
   me speak,
   Then let come on me what *may!*
14 Why do I take my flesh in my
   teeth,
   And put my life in my hands?
15 Though He slay me, yet will I
   trust Him.
   Even so, I will defend my own
   ways before Him.
16 He also *shall* be my salvation,
   For a hypocrite could not come
   before Him.
17 Listen carefully to my speech,
   And to my declaration with your
   ears.
18 See now, I have prepared *my* case,
   I know that I shall be vindicated.
19 Who *is* he *who* will contend with
   me?
   If now I hold my tongue, I perish.

JOB'S DESPONDENT PRAYER

20 "Only two *things* do not do to me,
   Then I will not hide myself from
   You:
21 Withdraw Your hand far from me,
   And let not the dread of You make
   me afraid.
22 Then call, and I will answer;

   Or let me speak, then You
   respond to me.
23 How many *are* my iniquities and
   sins?
   Make me know my transgression
   and my sin.
24 Why do You hide Your face,
   And regard me as Your enemy?

Prayers

Job 13:24

"Why do you hide Your face from me?" Job prayed. Do you ever feel that God is hiding? Do you ever wish He could stand there with you? Do you ever feel that God is far, far away? The Bible tells us that God is with us always. He is not far away. We can't see His face because God is too wonderful for us to see. Our human eyes could not look at Him. But He is there, beside you. He is not hiding. When you pray, you are talking with someone very close, someone who is always with you. Does that help you pray more often?

---

25 Will You frighten a leaf driven to
   and fro?
   And will You pursue dry stubble?
26 For You write bitter things
   against me,
   And make me inherit the
   iniquities of my youth.
27 You put my feet in the stocks,
   And watch closely all my paths.
   You set a limit[a] for the soles of
   my feet.

28 "Man[a] decays like a rotten thing,
   Like a garment that is moth-
   eaten.

13:27 [a]Literally *inscribe a print*   13:28 [a]Literally *He*

14
"Man *who is* born of woman
Is of few days and full of trouble.

2 He comes forth like a flower and
fades away;
He flees like a shadow and does
not continue.

3 And do You open Your eyes on
such a one,
And bring me[a] to judgment with
Yourself?

4 Who can bring a clean *thing* out
of an unclean?
No one!

5 Since his days *are* determined,
The number of his months *is* with
You;
You have appointed his limits, so
that he cannot pass.

6 Look away from him that he may
rest,
Till like a hired man he finishes
his day.

7 "For there is hope for a tree,
If it is cut down, that it will
sprout again,
And that its tender shoots will
not cease.

8 Though its root may grow old in
the earth,
And its stump may die in the
ground,

9 *Yet* at the scent of water it will
bud
And bring forth branches like a
plant.

10 But man dies and is laid away;
Indeed he breathes his last
And where *is* he?

11 *As* water disappears from the
sea,
And a river becomes parched and
dries up,

12 So man lies down and does not
rise.
Till the heavens *are* no more,
They will not awake
Nor be roused from their sleep.

13 "Oh, that You would hide me in
the grave,
That You would conceal me until
Your wrath is past,
That You would appoint me a set
time, and remember me!

14 If a man dies, shall he live *again?*
All the days of my hard service I
will wait,
Till my change comes.

15 You shall call, and I will answer
You;
You shall desire the work of Your
hands.

16 For now You number my steps,
But do not watch over my sin.

17 My transgression *is* sealed up in a
bag,
And You cover[a] my iniquity.

18 "But *as* a mountain falls *and*
crumbles away,
And *as* a rock is moved from its
place;

19 *As* water wears away stones,
And as torrents wash away the
soil of the earth;
So You destroy the hope of man.

20 You prevail forever against him,
and he passes on;
You change his countenance and
send him away.

21 His sons come to honor, and he
does not know *it;*
They are brought low, and he does
not perceive *it.*

22 But his flesh will be in pain over
it,
And his soul will mourn over it."

ELIPHAZ ACCUSES JOB OF FOLLY

15
Then E·lī′phaz the Tē′man·īte
answered and said:

2 "Should a wise man answer with
empty knowledge,

14:3 [a]Septuagint, Syriac, and Vulgate read *him.*
14:17 [a]Literally *plaster over*

And fill himself with the east wind?

3 Should he reason with unprofitable talk,
Or by speeches with which he can do no good?

4 Yes, you cast off fear,
And restrain prayer before God.

5 For your iniquity teaches your mouth,
And you choose the tongue of the crafty.

6 Your own mouth condemns you, and not I;
Yes, your own lips testify against you.

7 "Are you the first man who was born?
Or were you made before the hills?

8 Have you heard the counsel of God?
Do you limit wisdom to yourself?

9 What do you know that we do not know?
What do you understand that is not in us?

10 Both the gray-haired and the aged are among us,
Much older than your father.

11 Are the consolations of God too small for you,
And the word spoken gently^a with you?

12 Why does your heart carry you away,
And what do your eyes wink at,

13 That you turn your spirit against God,
And let such words go out of your mouth?

14 "What is man, that he could be pure?
And he who is born of a woman, that he could be righteous?

15 If God puts no trust in His saints,

And the heavens are not pure in His sight,

16 How much less man, who is abominable and filthy,
Who drinks iniquity like water!

17 "I will tell you, hear me;
What I have seen I will declare,

18 What wise men have told,
Not hiding anything received from their fathers,

19 To whom alone the land was given,
And no alien passed among them:

20 The wicked man writhes with pain all his days,
And the number of years is hidden from the oppressor.

21 Dreadful sounds are in his ears;
In prosperity the destroyer comes upon him.

22 He does not believe that he will return from darkness,
For a sword is waiting for him.

23 He wanders about for bread, saying, 'Where is it?'
He knows that a day of darkness is ready at his hand.

24 Trouble and anguish make him afraid;
They overpower him, like a king ready for battle.

25 For he stretches out his hand against God,
And acts defiantly against the Almighty,

26 Running stubbornly against Him
With his strong, embossed shield.

27 "Though he has covered his face with his fatness,
And made his waist heavy with fat,

28 He dwells in desolate cities,
In houses which no one inhabits,
Which are destined to become ruins.

15:11 ^aSeptuagint reads a secret thing.

29 He will not be rich,
Nor will his wealth continue,
Nor will his possessions
overspread the earth.
30 He will not depart from darkness;
The flame will dry out his
branches,
And by the breath of His mouth
he will go away.
31 Let him not trust in futile *things,*
deceiving himself,
For futility will be his reward.
32 It will be accomplished before his
time,
And his branch will not be green.
33 He will shake off his unripe grape
like a vine,
And cast off his blossom like an
olive tree.
34 For the company of hypocrites
will be barren,
And fire will consume the tents of
bribery.
35 They conceive trouble and bring
forth futility;
Their womb prepares deceit."

JOB REPROACHES HIS PITILESS FRIENDS

16 Then Job answered and said:

2 "I have heard many such things;
Miserable comforters *are* you all!
3 Shall words of wind have an
end?
Or what provokes you that you
answer?
4 I also could speak as you *do,*
If your soul were in my soul's
place.
I could heap up words against
you,
And shake my head at you;
5 *But* I would strengthen you with
my mouth,
And the comfort of my lips would
relieve *your* grief.

6 "Though I speak, my grief is not
relieved;
And *if* I remain silent, how am I
eased?
7 But now He has worn me out;
You have made desolate all my
company.
8 You have shriveled me up,
And it is a witness *against me;*
My leanness rises up against me
And bears witness to my face.
9 He tears *me* in His wrath, and
hates me;
He gnashes at me with His teeth;
My adversary sharpens His gaze
on me.
10 They gape at me with their
mouth,
They strike me reproachfully on
the cheek,
They gather together against me.
11 God has delivered me to the
ungodly,
And turned me over to the hands
of the wicked.
12 I was at ease, but He has
shattered me;
He also has taken *me* by my neck,
and shaken me to pieces;
He has set me up for His
target,
13 His archers surround me.
He pierces my heart[a] and does
not pity;
He pours out my gall on the
ground.
14 He breaks me with wound upon
wound;
He runs at me like a warrior.[a]

15 "I have sewn sackcloth over my
skin,
And laid my head[a] in the dust.
16 My face is flushed from weeping,
And on my eyelids *is* the shadow
of death;

16:13 [a]Literally *kidneys*   16:14 [a]Vulgate reads
giant.   16:15 [a]Literally *horn*

17 Although no violence *is* in my
hands,
And my prayer *is* pure.
18 "O earth, do not cover my blood,
And let my cry have no *resting*
place!
19 Surely even now my witness *is* in
heaven,
And my evidence *is* on high.
20 My friends scorn me;
My eyes pour out *tears* to God.
21 Oh, that one might plead for a
man with God,
As a man *pleads* for his neighbor!
22 For when a few years are
finished,
I shall go the way of no return.

JOB PRAYS FOR RELIEF

17 "My spirit is broken,
My days are extinguished,
The grave *is ready* for me.
2 *Are* not mockers with me?
And does not my eye dwell on
their provocation?

3 "Now put down a pledge for me
with Yourself.
Who *is* he *who* will shake hands
with me?
4 For You have hidden their heart
from understanding;
Therefore You will not exalt *them.*
5 He who speaks flattery to *his*
friends,
Even the eyes of his children will
fail.

6 "But He has made me a byword of
the people,
And I have become one in whose
face men spit.
7 My eye has also grown dim
because of sorrow,
And all my members *are* like
shadows.
8 Upright *men* are astonished at
this,

And the innocent stirs himself up
against the hypocrite.
9 Yet the righteous will hold to his
way,
And he who has clean hands will
be stronger and stronger.

10 "But please, come back again, all
of you,*a*
For I shall not find *one* wise *man*
among you.
11 My days are past,
My purposes are broken off,
Even the thoughts of my heart.
12 They change the night into day;
'The light *is* near,' *they say,* in the
face of darkness.
13 If I wait *for* the grave *as* my
house,
If I make my bed in the darkness,
14 If I say to corruption, 'You *are* my
father,'
And to the worm, 'You *are* my
mother and my sister,'
15 Where then *is* my hope?
As for my hope, who can see it?
16 *Will* they go down to the gates of
Shē′ōl?
Shall *we have* rest together in the
dust?"

BILDAD: THE WICKED
ARE PUNISHED

18 Then Bil′dad the Shū′hīte answered and said:

2 "How long *till* you put an end to
words?
Gain understanding, and
afterward we will speak.
3 Why are we counted as beasts,
And regarded as stupid in your
sight?

17:10 *a*Following some Hebrew manuscripts, Septuagint, Syriac, and Vulgate; Masoretic Text and
Targum read *all of them.*

4 You who tear yourself in anger,
  Shall the earth be forsaken for
    you?
  Or shall the rock be removed from
    its place?

5 "The light of the wicked indeed
    goes out,
  And the flame of his fire does not
    shine.
6 The light is dark in his tent,
  And his lamp beside him is put
    out.
7 The steps of his strength are
    shortened,
  And his own counsel casts him
    down.
8 For he is cast into a net by his
    own feet,
  And he walks into a snare.
9 The net takes *him* by the
    heel,
  And a snare lays hold of him.
10 A noose *is* hidden for him on the
    ground,
  And a trap for him in the road.
11 Terrors frighten him on every
    side,
  And drive him to his feet.
12 His strength is starved,
  And destruction *is* ready at his
    side.
13 It devours patches of his skin;
  The firstborn of death devours his
    limbs.
14 He is uprooted from the shelter of
    his tent,
  And they parade him before the
    king of terrors.
15 They dwell in his tent *who are*
    none of his;
  Brimstone is scattered on his
    dwelling.
16 His roots are dried out below,
  And his branch withers above.
17 The memory of him perishes from
    the earth,
  And he has no name among the
    renowned.*a*

18 He is driven from light into
    darkness,
  And chased out of the world.
19 He has neither son nor posterity
    among his people,
  Nor any remaining in his
    dwellings.
20 Those in the west are astonished
    at his day,
  As those in the east are
    frightened.
21 Surely such *are* the dwellings of
    the wicked,
  And this *is* the place *of him who*
    does not know God."

JOB TRUSTS IN HIS REDEEMER

19 Then Job answered and said:

2 "How long will you torment my
    soul,
  And break me in pieces with
    words?
3 These ten times you have
    reproached me;
  You are not ashamed *that* you
    have wronged me.*a*
4 And if indeed I have erred,
  My error remains with me.
5 If indeed you exalt *yourselves*
    against me,
  And plead my disgrace against
    me,
6 Know then that God has wronged
    me,
  And has surrounded me with His
    net.

7 "If I cry out concerning wrong, I
    am not heard.
  If I cry aloud, *there is* no justice.
8 He has fenced up my way, so that
    I cannot pass;

18:17 *a*Literally *before the outside,* meaning distinguished, famous   19:3 *a*A Jewish tradition
reads *make yourselves strange to me.*

THERE'S A SPIDER IN MY SKY Job 19:6–12

Have you ever found a fly in your soup, or a spider in your room? Have you ever found a piece of cardboard in your ice cream or a cherry pit in your cherry pie? What should you do?

1. When something isn't quite right, do you fuss or argue or blame someone? Or do you keep on going without making a big fuss? What should you do?
2. When your brother or sister or friend accidentally does something bad to you, do you argue or fuss or blame him or her? Or do you forgive and go on joyfully? What should you do?
3. Read Job's complaint against God in Job 19:6–12. When you think God has let something bad happen to you, do you blame God and make a big deal about it? Or do you thank God that it wasn't worse and go on joyfully? What should you do?

For more on *What Should I Do?* turn to page 807
For more on *Forgiveness* turn to page 857

And He has set darkness in my
paths.
9 He has stripped me of my glory,
And taken the crown *from* my
head.
10 He breaks me down on every side,
And I am gone;
My hope He has uprooted like a
tree.
11 He has also kindled His wrath
against me,
And He counts me as *one of* His
enemies.
12 His troops come together
And build up their road against
me;
They encamp all around my tent.

13 "He has removed my brothers far
from me,
And my acquaintances are
completely estranged from me.
14 My relatives have failed,
And my close friends have
forgotten me.
15 Those who dwell in my house,
and my maidservants,
Count me as a stranger;
I am an alien in their sight.
16 I call my servant, but he gives no
answer;
I beg him with my mouth.
17 My breath is offensive to my
wife,
And I am repulsive to the
children of my own body.
18 Even young children despise me;
I arise, and they speak against
me.
19 All my close friends abhor me,
And those whom I love have
turned against me.
20 My bone clings to my skin and to
my flesh,
And I have escaped by the skin of
my teeth.

21 "Have pity on me, have pity on me,
O you my friends,

For the hand of God has struck
me!
22 Why do you persecute me as God
does,
And are not satisfied with my
flesh?

23 "Oh, that my words were written!
Oh, that they were inscribed in a
book!
24 That they were engraved on a
rock
With an iron pen and lead,
forever!
25 For I know *that* my Redeemer
lives,
And He shall stand at last on the
earth;
26 And after my skin is destroyed,
this *I know,*
That in my flesh I shall see God,
27 Whom I shall see for myself,
And my eyes shall behold, and
not another.
How my heart yearns within
me!
28 If you should say, 'How shall we
persecute him?'—
Since the root of the matter is
found in me,
29 Be afraid of the sword for
yourselves;
For wrath *brings* the punishment
of the sword,
That you may know *there is* a
judgment."

ZOPHAR'S SERMON ON THE
WICKED MAN

20 Then Zō′phar the Nā′a·ma-
thīte answered and said:

2 "Therefore my anxious thoughts
make me answer,
Because of the turmoil within me.
3 I have heard the rebuke that
reproaches me,

And the spirit of my understanding causes me to answer.

4 "Do you *not* know this of old,
Since man was placed on earth,
5 That the triumphing of the wicked is short,
And the joy of the hypocrite is *but* for a moment?
6 Though his haughtiness mounts up to the heavens,
And his head reaches to the clouds,
7 *Yet* he will perish forever like his own refuse;
Those who have seen him will say, 'Where is he?'
8 He will fly away like a dream, and not be found;
Yes, he will be chased away like a vision of the night.
9 The eye *that* saw him will *see him* no more,
Nor will his place behold him anymore.
10 His children will seek the favor of the poor,
And his hands will restore his wealth.
11 His bones are full of his youthful vigor,
But it will lie down with him in the dust.

12 "Though evil is sweet in his mouth,
And he hides it under his tongue,
13 *Though* he spares it and does not forsake it,
But still keeps it in his mouth,
14 *Yet* his food in his stomach turns sour;
It becomes cobra venom within him.
15 He swallows down riches
And vomits them up again;
God casts them out of his belly.

16 He will suck the poison of cobras;
The viper's tongue will slay him.
17 He will not see the streams,
The rivers flowing with honey and cream.
18 He will restore that for which he labored,
And will not swallow *it* down;
From the proceeds of business He will get no enjoyment.
19 For he has oppressed *and* forsaken the poor,
He has violently seized a house which he did not build.

20 "Because he knows no quietness in his heart,a
He will not save anything he desires.
21 Nothing is left for him to eat;
Therefore his well-being will not last.
22 In his self-sufficiency he will be in distress;
Every hand of misery will come against him.
23 *When* he is about to fill his stomach,
God will cast on him the fury of His wrath,
And will rain *it* on him while he is eating.
24 He will flee from the iron weapon;
A bronze bow will pierce him through.
25 It is drawn, and comes out of the body;
Yes, the glittering *point comes* out of his gall.
Terrors *come* upon him;
26 Total darkness *is* reserved for his treasures.
An unfanned fire will consume him;
It shall go ill with him who is left in his tent.

20:20 ^aLiterally *belly*

27 The heavens will reveal his
      iniquity,
   And the earth will rise up against
      him.
28 The increase of his house will
      depart,
   And his goods will flow away in
      the day of His wrath.
29 This *is* the portion from God for a
      wicked man,
   The heritage appointed to him by
      God."

JOB'S DISCOURSE ON THE WICKED

21 Then Job answered and said:

2 "Listen carefully to my speech,
   And let this be your consolation.
3 Bear with me that I may speak,
   And after I have spoken, keep
      mocking.

4 "As for me, *is* my complaint
      against man?
   And if *it were,* why should I not be
      impatient?
5 Look at me and be astonished;
   Put *your* hand over *your* mouth.
6 Even when I remember I am
      terrified,
   And trembling takes hold of my
      flesh.
7 Why do the wicked live *and*
      become old,
   Yes, become mighty in power?
8 Their descendants are established
      with them in their sight,
   And their offspring before their
      eyes.
9 Their houses *are* safe from fear,
   Neither *is* the rod of God upon
      them.
10 Their bull breeds without failure;
   Their cow calves without
      miscarriage.
11 They send forth their little ones
      like a flock,
   And their children dance.

12 They sing to the tambourine and
      harp,
   And rejoice to the sound of the
      flute.
13 They spend their days in wealth,
   And in a moment go down to the
      grave.*a*
14 Yet they say to God, 'Depart from
      us,
   For we do not desire the
      knowledge of Your ways.
15 Who *is* the Almighty, that we
      should serve Him?
   And what profit do we have if we
      pray to Him?'
16 Indeed their prosperity *is* not in
      their hand;
   The counsel of the wicked is far
      from me.

17 "How often is the lamp of the
      wicked put out?
   How often does their destruction
      come upon them,
   The sorrows *God* distributes in
      His anger?
18 They are like straw before the
      wind,
   And like chaff that a storm
      carries away.
19 *They say,* 'God lays up one's*a*
      iniquity for his children';
   Let Him recompense him, that he
      may know *it.*
20 Let his eyes see his destruction,
   And let him drink of the wrath of
      the Almighty.
21 For what does he care about his
      household after him,
   When the number of his months
      is cut in half?

22 "Can *anyone* teach God knowledge,
   Since He judges those on high?
23 One dies in his full strength,
   Being wholly at ease and
      secure;

21:13 *a*Or *Sheol*   21:19 *a*Literally *his*

24 His pails[a] are full of milk,
And the marrow of his bones is
   moist.
25 Another man dies in the
   bitterness of his soul,
Never having eaten with
   pleasure.
26 They lie down alike in the dust,
And worms cover them.

27 "Look, I know your thoughts,
And the schemes *with which* you
   would wrong me.
28 For you say,
 'Where *is* the house of the prince?
 And where *is* the tent,[a]
 The dwelling place of the wicked?'
29 Have you not asked those who
   travel the road?
And do you not know their signs?
30 For the wicked are reserved for
   the day of doom;
They shall be brought out on the
   day of wrath.
31 Who condemns his way to his
   face?
And who repays him *for what* he
   has done?
32 Yet he shall be brought to the
   grave,
And a vigil kept over the tomb.
33 The clods of the valley shall be
   sweet to him;
Everyone shall follow him,
As countless *have gone* before
   him.
34 How then can you comfort me
   with empty words,
Since falsehood remains in your
   answers?"

ELIPHAZ ACCUSES JOB
OF WICKEDNESS

22 Then E·lĭ′phaz the Tē′man·ite
answered and said:

2 "Can a man be profitable to God,
Though he who is wise may be
   profitable to himself?

3 *Is it* any pleasure to the Almighty
   that you are righteous?
Or *is it* gain *to Him* that you
   make your ways blameless?

4 "Is it because of your fear of Him
   that He corrects you,
And enters into judgment with
   you?
5 *Is* not your wickedness great,
And your iniquity without end?
6 For you have taken pledges from
   your brother for no reason,
And stripped the naked of their
   clothing.
7 You have not given the weary
   water to drink,
And you have withheld bread
   from the hungry.
8 But the mighty man possessed
   the land,
And the honorable man dwelt in
   it.
9 You have sent widows away
   empty,
And the strength of the fatherless
   was crushed.
10 Therefore snares *are* all around
   you,
And sudden fear troubles you,
11 Or darkness *so that* you cannot
   see;
And an abundance of water
   covers you.

12 "Is not God in the height of
   heaven?
And see the highest stars, how
   lofty they are!
13 And you say, 'What does God
   know?
Can He judge through the deep
   darkness?
14 Thick clouds cover Him, so that
   He cannot see,

21:24 [a]Septuagint and Vulgate read *bowels;* Syriac
reads *sides;* Targum reads *breasts.*   21:28 [a]Vul-
gate omits *the tent.*

And He walks above the circle of
    heaven.'
15 Will you keep to the old way
    Which wicked men have trod,
16 Who were cut down before their
    time,
    Whose foundations were swept
    away by a flood?
17 They said to God, 'Depart from
    us!
    What can the Almighty do to
    them?'a
18 Yet He filled their houses with
    good *things;*
    But the counsel of the wicked is
    far from me.

19 "The righteous see *it* and are
    glad,
    And the innocent laugh at
    them:
20 'Surely our adversariesa are cut
    down,
    And the fire consumes their
    remnant.'

21 "Now acquaint yourself with Him,
    and be at peace;
    Thereby good will come to you.
22 Receive, please, instruction from
    His mouth,
    And lay up His words in your
    heart.
23 If you return to the Almighty, you
    will be built up;
    You will remove iniquity far from
    your tents.
24 Then you will lay your gold in the
    dust,
    And the *gold* of Ō'phir among the
    stones of the brooks.
25 Yes, the Almighty will be your
    golda
    And your precious silver;
26 For then you will have your
    delight in the Almighty,
    And lift up your face to God.
27 You will make your prayer to
    Him,

He will hear you,
    And you will pay your vows.
28 You will also declare a thing,
    And it will be established for
    you;
    So light will shine on your ways.
29 When they cast *you* down, and
    you say, 'Exaltation *will come!*'
    Then He will save the humble
    person.
30 He will *even* deliver one who is
    not innocent;
    Yes, he will be delivered by the
    purity of your hands."

JOB PROCLAIMS GOD'S RIGHTEOUS JUDGMENTS

23 Then Job answered and said:

2 "Even today my complaint is
    bitter;
    Mya hand is listless because of
    my groaning.
3 Oh, that I knew where I might
    find Him,
    That I might come to His seat!
4 I would present *my* case before
    Him,
    And fill my mouth with
    arguments.
5 I would know the words *which* He
    would answer me,
    And understand what He would
    say to me.
6 Would He contend with me in His
    great power?
    No! But He would take *note* of
    me.
7 There the upright could reason
    with Him,
    And I would be delivered forever
    from my Judge.

22:17 aSeptuagint and Syriac read *us.*
22:20 aSeptuagint reads *substance.*   22:25 aThe
ancient versions suggest *defense;* Hebrew reads
gold as in verse 24.   23:2 aFollowing Masoretic
Text, Targum, and Vulgate; Septuagint and Syriac
read *His.*

8 "Look, I go forward, but He is not
  there,
  And backward, but I cannot
  perceive Him;
9 When He works on the left hand,
  I cannot behold *Him;*
  When He turns to the right hand,
  I cannot see *Him.*
10 But He knows the way that I
  take;
  When He has tested me, I shall
  come forth as gold.
11 My foot has held fast to His
  steps;
  I have kept His way and not
  turned aside.
12 I have not departed from the
  commandment of His lips;
  I have treasured the words of His
  mouth
  More than my necessary *food.*

13 "But He *is* unique, and who can
  make Him change?
  And *whatever* His soul desires,
  that He does.
14 For He performs *what is*
  appointed for me,
  And many such *things are* with
  Him.
15 Therefore I am terrified at His
  presence;
  When I consider *this,* I am afraid
  of Him.
16 For God made my heart weak,
  And the Almighty terrifies me;
17 Because I was not cut off from the
  presence of darkness,
  And He did *not* hide deep
  darkness from my face.

JOB COMPLAINS OF VIOLENCE ON THE EARTH

24 "*Since* times are not hidden
  from the Almighty,
  Why do those who know Him see
  not His days?

2 "*Some* remove landmarks;
  They seize flocks violently and
  feed *on them;*
3 They drive away the donkey of
  the fatherless;
  They take the widow's ox as a
  pledge.
4 They push the needy off the road;
  All the poor of the land are forced
  to hide.
5 Indeed, *like* wild donkeys in the
  desert,
  They go out to their work,
  searching for food.
  The wilderness *yields* food for
  them *and* for *their* children.
6 They gather their fodder in the
  field
  And glean in the vineyard of the
  wicked.
7 They spend the night naked,
  without clothing,
  And have no covering in the cold.
8 They are wet with the showers of
  the mountains,
  And huddle around the rock for
  want of shelter.

9 "*Some* snatch the fatherless from
  the breast,
  And take a pledge from the poor.
10 They cause *the poor* to go naked,
  without clothing;
  And they take away the sheaves
  from the hungry.
11 They press out oil within their
  walls,
  And tread winepresses, yet suffer
  thirst.
12 The dying groan in the city,
  And the souls of the wounded cry
  out;
  Yet God does not charge *them*
  with wrong.

13 "There are those who rebel against
  the light;
  They do not know its ways
  Nor abide in its paths.

14 The murderer rises with the light;
He kills the poor and needy;
And in the night he is like a thief.
15 The eye of the adulterer waits for
the twilight,
Saying, 'No eye will see me';
And he disguises *his* face.
16 In the dark they break into
houses
Which they marked for
themselves in the daytime;
They do not know the light.
17 For the morning is the same to
them as the shadow of death;
If *someone* recognizes *them,*
They are in the terrors of the
shadow of death.

18 "They *should be* swift on the face
of the waters,
Their portion *should be* cursed in
the earth,
So that no *one would* turn into
the way of their vineyards.
19 As drought and heat consume the
snow waters,
So the grave[a] consumes those who
have sinned.
20 The womb *should* forget him,
The worm *should* feed sweetly on
him;
He *should* be remembered no
more,
And wickedness *should* be broken
like a tree.
21 For he preys on the barren *who*
do not bear,
And does no good for the widow.

22 "But *God* draws the mighty away
with His power;
He rises up, but no *man* is sure of
life.
23 He gives them security, and they
rely *on it;*
Yet His eyes *are* on their ways.
24 They are exalted for a little while,
Then they are gone.
They are brought low;

They are taken out of the way
like all *others;*
They dry out like the heads of
grain.

25 "Now if *it is* not *so,* who will prove
me a liar,
And make my speech worth
nothing?"

BILDAD: HOW CAN MAN BE RIGHTEOUS?

25
Then Bil′dad the Shū′hīte answered and said:

2 "Dominion and fear *belong* to Him;
He makes peace in His high
places.
3 Is there any number to His
armies?
Upon whom does His light not
rise?
4 How then can man be righteous
before God?
Or how can he be pure *who is*
born of a woman?
5 If even the moon does not shine,
And the stars are not pure in His
sight,
6 How much less man, *who is* a
maggot,
And a son of man, *who is* a
worm?"

JOB: MAN'S FRAILTY AND GOD'S MAJESTY

26
But Job answered and said:

2 "How have you helped *him who is*
without power?
How have you saved the arm *that
has* no strength?
3 How have you counseled *one who
has* no wisdom?

24:19 [a]Or *Sheol*

And *how* have you declared sound
advice to many?

4 To whom have you uttered
words?
And whose spirit came from you?

5 "The dead tremble,
Those under the waters and those
inhabiting them.

6 She′ōl *is* naked before Him,
And Destruction has no covering.

7 He stretches out the north over
empty space;
He hangs the earth on nothing.

8 He binds up the water in His
thick clouds,
Yet the clouds are not broken
under it.

9 He covers the face of *His* throne,
And spreads His cloud over it.

10 He drew a circular horizon on the
face of the waters,
At the boundary of light and
darkness.

11 The pillars of heaven tremble,
And are astonished at His rebuke.

12 He stirs up the sea with His
power,
And by His understanding He
breaks up the storm.

13 By His Spirit He adorned the
heavens;
His hand pierced the fleeing
serpent.

14 Indeed these *are* the mere edges
of His ways,
And how small a whisper we hear
of Him!
But the thunder of His power who
can understand?"

JOB MAINTAINS HIS INTEGRITY

27 Moreover Job continued his
discourse, and said:

2 "*As* God lives, *who* has taken away
my justice,

And the Almighty, *who* has made
my soul bitter,

3 As long as my breath *is* in me,
And the breath of God in my
nostrils,

4 My lips will not speak
wickedness,
Nor my tongue utter deceit.

5 Far be it from me
That I should say you are right;
Till I die I will not put away my
integrity from me.

6 My righteousness I hold fast, and
will not let it go;
My heart shall not reproach *me*
as long as I live.

7 "May my enemy be like the
wicked,
And he who rises up against me
like the unrighteous.

8 For what is the hope of the
hypocrite,
Though he may gain *much,*
If God takes away his life?

9 Will God hear his cry
When trouble comes upon him?

10 Will he delight himself in the
Almighty?
Will he always call on God?

11 "I will teach you about the hand of
God;
What *is* with the Almighty I will
not conceal.

12 Surely all of you have seen *it;*
Why then do you behave with
complete nonsense?

13 "This is the portion of a wicked
man with God,
And the heritage of oppressors,
received from the Almighty:

14 If his children are multiplied, *it is*
for the sword;
And his offspring shall not be
satisfied with bread.

15 Those who survive him shall be
buried in death,

And their*a* widows shall not
weep,

16 Though he heaps up silver like
dust,
And piles up clothing like clay—

17 He may pile *it* up, but the just
will wear *it,*
And the innocent will divide the
silver.

18 He builds his house like a moth,*a*
Like a booth *which* a watchman
makes.

19 The rich man will lie down,
But not be gathered *up;a*
He opens his eyes,
And he *is* no more.

20 Terrors overtake him like a
flood;
A tempest steals him away in the
night.

21 The east wind carries him away,
and he is gone;
It sweeps him out of his place.

22 It hurls against him and does not
spare;
He flees desperately from its
power.

23 *Men* shall clap their hands at
him,
And shall hiss him out of his
place.

JOB'S DISCOURSE ON WISDOM

28

"Surely there is a mine for
silver,
And a place *where* gold is refined.

2 Iron is taken from the earth,
And copper *is* smelted *from* ore.

3 *Man* puts an end to darkness,
And searches every recess
For ore in the darkness and the
shadow of death.

4 He breaks open a shaft away from
people;
In places forgotten by feet
They hang far away from men;
They swing to and fro.

5 *As for* the earth, from it comes
bread,
But underneath it is turned up as
by fire;

6 Its stones *are* the source of
sapphires,
And it contains gold dust.

7 *That* path no bird knows,
Nor has the falcon's eye seen it.

8 The proud lions*a* have not
trodden it,
Nor has the fierce lion passed
over it.

9 He puts his hand on the flint;
He overturns the mountains at
the roots.

10 He cuts out channels in the
rocks,
And his eye sees every precious
thing.

11 He dams up the streams from
trickling;
What is hidden he brings forth to
light.

12 "But where can wisdom be found?
And where *is* the place of
understanding?

13 Man does not know its value,
Nor is it found in the land of the
living.

14 The deep says, '*It is* not in me';
And the sea says, '*It is* not with
me.'

15 It cannot be purchased for gold,
Nor can silver be weighed *for* its
price.

16 It cannot be valued in the gold of
Ō′phir,
In precious onyx or sapphire.

17 Neither gold nor crystal can equal
it,

27:15 *a*Literally *his*   27:18 *a*Following Masoretic Text and Vulgate; Septuagint and Syriac read
spider (compare 8:14); Targum reads *decay.*
27:19 *a*Following Masoretic Text and Targum; Septuagint and Syriac read *But shall not add* (that is,
do it again); Vulgate reads *But take away nothing.*
28:8 *a*Literally *sons of pride,* figurative of the great
lions

Nor can it be exchanged for
jewelry of fine gold.
18 No mention shall be made of coral
or quartz,
For the price of wisdom *is* above
rubies.
19 The topaz of Ethiopia cannot
equal it,
Nor can it be valued in pure gold.

20 "From where then does wisdom
come?
And where *is* the place of
understanding?
21 It is hidden from the eyes of all
living,
And concealed from the birds of
the air.
22 Destruction and Death say,
'We have heard a report about it
with our ears.'
23 God understands its way,
And He knows its place.
24 For He looks to the ends of the
earth,
And sees under the whole
heavens,
25 To establish a weight for the
wind,
And apportion the waters by
measure.
26 When He made a law for the rain,
And a path for the thunderbolt,
27 Then He saw wisdom*a* and
declared it;
He prepared it, indeed, He
searched it out.
28 And to man He said,
'Behold, the fear of the Lord, that
is wisdom,
And to depart from evil *is*
understanding.' "

JOB'S SUMMARY DEFENSE

29 Job further continued his discourse, and said:

2 "Oh, that I were as *in* months
past,

As *in* the days *when* God watched
over me;
3 When His lamp shone upon my
head,
And when by His light I walked
through darkness;
4 Just as I was in the days of my
prime,
When the friendly counsel of God
was over my tent;
5 When the Almighty *was* yet with
me,
When my children *were* around
me;
6 When my steps were bathed with
cream,*a*
And the rock poured out rivers of
oil for me!

7 "When I went out to the gate by
the city,
When I took my seat in the open
square,
8 The young men saw me and hid,
And the aged arose *and* stood;
9 The princes refrained from
talking,
And put *their* hand on their
mouth;
10 The voice of nobles was hushed,
And their tongue stuck to the roof
of their mouth.
11 When the ear heard, then it
blessed me,
And when the eye saw, then it
approved me;
12 Because I delivered the poor who
cried out,
The fatherless and *the one who*
had no helper.
13 The blessing of a perishing *man*
came upon me,
And I caused the widow's heart to
sing for joy.
14 I put on righteousness, and it
clothed me;

28:27 *a*Literally *it*   29:6 *a*Masoretic Text reads
wrath; ancient versions and some Hebrew manuscripts read *cream* (compare 20:17).

HELPFULNESS Job 29:12

Let Me Help You

Someone is hurting. This little lamb needs a helper. But look! She does have a helper. Do you see what the helper is doing?

1. Do you know someone who is sad or hurting? Do you know someone who needs a helper?
2. Should you laugh at this person? Should you make fun of this person? Should you ignore this person? Should you help this person?
3. Which will make this person happier? Which will please your parents the most? Which will please Jesus the most? Which will please you the most?

For more on *Values* turn to page 824
For more on *Helpfulness* turn to page 1015

My justice *was* like a robe and a turban.

15 I *was* eyes to the blind,
And I *was* feet to the lame.

16 I *was* a father to the poor,
And I searched out the case *that* I did not know.

17 I broke the fangs of the wicked,
And plucked the victim from his teeth.

18 "Then I said, 'I shall die in my nest,
And multiply *my* days as the sand.

19 My root *is* spread out to the waters,
And the dew lies all night on my branch.

20 My glory *is* fresh within me,
And my bow is renewed in my hand.'

21 "*Men* listened to me and waited,
And kept silence for my counsel.

22 After my words they did not speak again,
And my speech settled on them *as* dew.

23 They waited for me *as* for the rain,
And they opened their mouth wide *as* for the spring rain.

24 *If* I mocked at them, they did not believe *it,*
And the light of my countenance they did not cast down.

25 I chose the way for them, and sat as chief;
So I dwelt as a king in the army,
As one *who* comforts mourners.

30
"But now they mock at me,
men younger than I,
Whose fathers I disdained to put with the dogs of my flock.

2 Indeed, what *profit* is the strength of their hands to me?
Their vigor has perished.

3 *They are* gaunt from want and famine,
Fleeing late to the wilderness, desolate and waste,

4 Who pluck mallow by the bushes,
And broom tree roots *for* their food.

5 They were driven out from among *men,*
They shouted at them as *at* a thief.

6 *They had* to live in the clefts of the valleys,
In caves of the earth and the rocks.

7 Among the bushes they brayed,
Under the nettles they nestled.

8 *They were* sons of fools,
Yes, sons of vile men;
They were scourged from the land.

9 "And now I am their taunting song;
Yes, I am their byword.

10 They abhor me, they keep far from me;
They do not hesitate to spit in my face.

11 Because He has loosed my[a] bowstring and afflicted me,
They have cast off restraint before me.

12 At *my* right *hand* the rabble arises;
They push away my feet,
And they raise against me their ways of destruction.

13 They break up my path,
They promote my calamity;
They have no helper.

14 They come as broad breakers;
Under the ruinous storm they roll along.

15 Terrors are turned upon me;
They pursue my honor as the wind,

30:11 [a]Following Masoretic Text, Syriac, and Targum; Septuagint and Vulgate read *His.*

And my prosperity has passed
   like a cloud.

16 "And now my soul is poured out
   because of my *plight;*
The days of affliction take hold of
   me.
17 My bones are pierced in me at
   night,
And my gnawing pains take no
   rest.
18 By great force my garment is
   disfigured;
It binds me about as the collar of
   my coat.
19 He has cast me into the mire,
And I have become like dust and
   ashes.

20 "I cry out to You, but You do not
   answer me;
I stand up, and You regard me.
21 *But* You have become cruel to me;
With the strength of Your hand
   You oppose me.
22 You lift me up to the wind and
   cause me to ride *on it;*
You spoil my success.
23 For I know *that* You will bring me
   to death,
And *to* the house appointed for all
   living.

24 "Surely He would not stretch out
   His hand against a heap of
   ruins,
If they cry out when He destroys
   it.
25 Have I not wept for him who was
   in trouble?
Has *not* my soul grieved for the
   poor?
26 But when I looked for good, evil
   came *to me;*
And when I waited for light, then
   came darkness.
27 My heart is in turmoil and cannot
   rest;
Days of affliction confront me.

28 I go about mourning, but not in
   the sun;
I stand up in the assembly *and*
   cry out for help.
29 I am a brother of jackals,
And a companion of ostriches.
30 My skin grows black and falls
   from me;
My bones burn with fever.
31 My harp is *turned* to mourning,
And my flute to the voice of those
   who weep.

31

  "I have made a covenant with
   my eyes;
Why then should I look upon a
   young woman?
2 For what *is* the allotment of God
   from above,
And the inheritance of the
   Almighty from on high?
3 *Is* it not destruction for the
   wicked,
And disaster for the workers of
   iniquity?
4 Does He not see my ways,
And count all my steps?

5 "If I have walked with falsehood,
Or if my foot has hastened to
   deceit,
6 Let me be weighed on honest
   scales,
That God may know my integrity.
7 If my step has turned from the
   way,
Or my heart walked after my
   eyes,
Or if any spot adheres to my
   hands,
8 *Then* let me sow, and another
   eat;
Yes, let my harvest be rooted
   out.

9 "If my heart has been enticed by a
   woman,
Or *if* I have lurked at my
   neighbor's door,

10 *Then* let my wife grind for
 another,
 And let others bow down over her.
11 For that *would be* wickedness;
 Yes, it *would be* iniquity *deserving
 of* judgment.
12 For that *would be* a fire *that*
 consumes to destruction,
 And would root out all my
 increase.

13 "If I have despised the cause of my
 male or female servant
 When they complained against
 me,
14 What then shall I do when God
 rises up?
 When He punishes, how shall I
 answer Him?
15 Did not He who made me in the
 womb make them?
 Did not the same One fashion us
 in the womb?

16 "If I have kept the poor from *their*
 desire,
 Or caused the eyes of the widow
 to fail,
17 Or eaten my morsel by myself,
 So that the fatherless could not
 eat of it
18 (But from my youth I reared him
 as a father,
 And from my mother's womb I
 guided *the widow*ᵃ);
19 If I have seen anyone perish for
 lack of clothing,
 Or any poor *man* without
 covering;
20 If his heartᵃ has not blessed
 me,
 And *if* he was *not* warmed with
 the fleece of my sheep;
21 If I have raised my hand against
 the fatherless,
 When I saw I had help in the
 gate;
22 *Then* let my arm fall from my
 shoulder,

 Let my arm be torn from the
 socket.
23 For destruction *from* God *is* a
 terror to me,
 And because of His magnificence I
 cannot endure.

24 "If I have made gold my hope,
 Or said to fine gold, '*You are* my
 confidence';
25 If I have rejoiced because my
 wealth *was* great,
 And because my hand had gained
 much;
26 If I have observed the sunᵃ when
 it shines,
 Or the moon moving *in*
 brightness,
27 So that my heart has been
 secretly enticed,
 And my mouth has kissed my
 hand;
28 This also *would be* an iniquity
 deserving of judgment,
 For I would have denied God *who
 is* above.

29 "If I have rejoiced at the
 destruction of him who hated
 me,
 Or lifted myself up when evil
 found him
30 (Indeed I have not allowed my
 mouth to sin
 By asking for a curse on his soul);
31 If the men of my tent have not
 said,
 'Who is there that has not been
 satisfied with his meat?'
32 (*But* no sojourner had to lodge in
 the street,
 For I have opened my doors to the
 travelerᵃ);
33 If I have covered my
 transgressions as Adam,

31:18 ᵃLiterally *her* (compare verse 16)
31:20 ᵃLiterally *loins*   31:26 ᵃLiterally *light*
31:32 ᵃFollowing Septuagint, Syriac, Targum, and
Vulgate; Masoretic Text reads *road*.

By hiding my iniquity in my
    bosom,
34 Because I feared the great
    multitude,
And dreaded the contempt of
    families,
So that I kept silence
And did not go out of the door—
35 Oh, that I had one to hear me!
Here is my mark.
Oh, that the Almighty would
    answer me,
That my Prosecutor had written a
    book!
36 Surely I would carry it on my
    shoulder,
And bind it on me *like* a crown;
37 I would declare to Him the
    number of my steps;
Like a prince I would approach
    Him.

38 "If my land cries out against me,
And its furrows weep together;
39 If I have eaten its fruit*a* without
    money,
Or caused its owners to lose their
    lives;
40 *Then* let thistles grow instead of
    wheat,
And weeds instead of barley."

The words of Job are ended.

ELIHU CONTRADICTS JOB'S FRIENDS

32 So these three men ceased answering Job, because he *was* righteous in his own eyes.
2 Then the wrath of E·liʹhū, the son
of Barʹa·chel the Būzʹīte, of the family of Ram, was aroused against Job;
his wrath was aroused because he
justified himself rather than God.
3 Also against his three friends his
wrath was aroused, because they had
found no answer, and *yet* had condemned Job.
4 Now because they *were* years

older than he, E·liʹhū had waited to
speak to Job.*a*
5 When E·liʹhū saw that *there was*
no answer in the mouth of these
three men, his wrath was aroused.
6 So E·liʹhū, the son of Barʹa·chel
the Būzʹīte, answered and said:

"I *am* young in years, and you *are*
    very old;
Therefore I was afraid,
And dared not declare my opinion
    to you.
7 I said, 'Age*a* should speak,
And multitude of years should
    teach wisdom.'
8 But *there is* a spirit in man,
And the breath of the Almighty
    gives him understanding.
9 Great men*a* are not *always* wise,
Nor do the aged *always*
    understand justice.

10 "Therefore I say, 'Listen to me,
I also will declare my opinion.'
11 Indeed I waited for your words,
I listened to your reasonings,
    while you searched out what to
    say.
12 I paid close attention to you;
And surely not one of you
    convinced Job,
Or answered his words—
13 Lest you say,
'We have found wisdom';
God will vanquish him, not man.
14 Now he has not directed *his*
    words against me;
So I will not answer him with
    your words.

15 "They are dismayed and answer no
    more;
Words escape them.
16 And I have waited, because they
    did not speak,

31:39 *a*Literally *its strength*   32:4 *a*Vulgate
reads *till Job had spoken.*   32:7 *a*Literally *Days,*
that is, years   32:9 *a*Or *Men of many years*

Because they stood still *and*
    answered no more.

17 I also will answer my part,
    I too will declare my opinion.

18 For I am full of words;
    The spirit within me compels me.

19 Indeed my belly *is* like wine *that*
    has no vent;
    It is ready to burst like new
    wineskins.

20 I will speak, that I may find
    relief;
    I must open my lips and answer.

21 Let me not, I pray, show partiality
    to anyone;
    Nor let me flatter any man.

22 For I do not know how to flatter,
    Else my Maker would soon take
    me away.

ELIHU CONTRADICTS JOB

33 "But please, Job, hear my
    speech,
    And listen to all my words.

2 Now, I open my mouth;
    My tongue speaks in my mouth.

3 My words *come* from my upright
    heart;
    My lips utter pure knowledge.

4 The Spirit of God has made me,
    And the breath of the Almighty
    gives me life.

5 If you can answer me,
    Set *your words* in order before
    me;
    Take your stand.

6 Truly I *am* as your spokesman[a]
    before God;
    I also have been formed out of
    clay.

7 Surely no fear of me will terrify
    you,
    Nor will my hand be heavy on
    you.

8 "Surely you have spoken in my
    hearing,
    And I have heard the sound of
    your words, *saying,*

9 'I *am* pure, without transgression;
    I *am* innocent, and *there is* no
    iniquity in me.

10 Yet He finds occasions against
    me,
    He counts me as His enemy;

11 He puts my feet in the stocks,
    He watches all my paths.'

12 "Look, *in* this you are not
    righteous.
    I will answer you,
    For God is greater than man.

13 Why do you contend with Him?
    For He does not give an
    accounting of any of His words.

14 For God may speak in one way, or
    in another,
    Yet man does not perceive it.

15 In a dream, in a vision of the
    night,
    When deep sleep falls upon men,
    While slumbering on their beds,

16 Then He opens the ears of men,
    And seals their instruction.

17 In order to turn man *from his*
    deed,
    And conceal pride from man,

18 He keeps back his soul from the
    Pit,
    And his life from perishing by the
    sword.

19 "*Man* is also chastened with pain
    on his bed,
    And with strong *pain* in many of
    his bones,

20 So that his life abhors bread,
    And his soul succulent food.

21 His flesh wastes away from
    sight,
    And his bones stick out *which
    once* were not seen.

22 Yes, his soul draws near the Pit,
    And his life to the executioners.

33:6 [a]Literally *as your mouth*

23 "If there is a messenger for him,
   A mediator, one among a
      thousand,
   To show man His uprightness,
24 Then He is gracious to him, and
      says,
   'Deliver him from going down to
      the Pit;
   I have found a ransom';
25 His flesh shall be young like a
      child's,
   He shall return to the days of his
      youth.
26 He shall pray to God, and He will
      delight in him,
   He shall see His face with joy,
   For He restores to man His
      righteousness.
27 Then he looks at men and says,
   'I have sinned, and perverted
      what was right,
   And it did not profit me.'
28 He will redeem his*a* soul from
      going down to the Pit,
   And his*b* life shall see the light.

29 "Behold, God works all these
      things,
   Twice, in fact, three times with a
      man,
30 To bring back his soul from the
      Pit,
   That he may be enlightened with
      the light of life.

31 "Give ear, Job, listen to me;
   Hold your peace, and I will
      speak.
32 If you have anything to say,
      answer me;
   Speak, for I desire to justify you.
33 If not, listen to me;
   Hold your peace, and I will teach
      you wisdom."

ELIHU PROCLAIMS GOD'S JUSTICE

34 E·li′hū further answered and
said:

2 "Hear my words, you wise *men*;
   Give ear to me, you who have
      knowledge.
3 For the ear tests words
   As the palate tastes food.
4 Let us choose justice for
      ourselves;
   Let us know among ourselves
      what *is* good.

5 "For Job has said, 'I am righteous,
   But God has taken away my
      justice;
6 Should I lie concerning my
      right?
   My wound *is* incurable, *though I
      am* without transgression.'
7 What man *is* like Job,
   Who drinks scorn like water,
8 Who goes in company with the
      workers of iniquity,
   And walks with wicked men?
9 For he has said, 'It profits a man
      nothing
   That he should delight in God.'

10 "Therefore listen to me, you men of
      understanding:
   Far be it from God *to do*
      wickedness,
   And *from* the Almighty to *commit*
      iniquity.
11 For He repays man *according to*
      his work,
   And makes man to find a reward
      according to *his* way.
12 Surely God will never do
      wickedly,
   Nor will the Almighty pervert
      justice.
13 Who gave Him charge over the
      earth?
   Or who appointed *Him over* the
      whole world?
14 If He should set His heart on it,
   If He should gather to Himself
      His Spirit and His breath,

33:28 *a*Or *my* (Kethib)   *b*Or *my* (Kethib)

15 All flesh would perish together,
   And man would return to dust.

16 "If *you have* understanding, hear
      this;
   Listen to the sound of my words:
17 Should one who hates justice
      govern?
   Will you condemn *Him who is*
      most just?
18 *Is it fitting* to say to a king, 'You
      are worthless,'
   And to nobles, 'You *are* wicked'?
19 Yet He is not partial to princes,
   Nor does He regard the rich more
      than the poor;
   For they *are* all the work of His
      hands.
20 In a moment they die, in the
      middle of the night;
   The people are shaken and pass
      away;
   The mighty are taken away
      without a hand.

21 "For His eyes *are* on the ways of
      man,
   And He sees all his steps.
22 There is no darkness nor shadow
      of death
   Where the workers of iniquity
      may hide themselves.
23 For He need not further consider
      a man,
   That he should go before God in
      judgment.
24 He breaks in pieces mighty men
      without inquiry,
   And sets others in their place.
25 Therefore He knows their works;
   He overthrows *them* in the
      night,
   And they are crushed.
26 He strikes them as wicked *men*
   In the open sight of others,
27 Because they turned back from
      Him,
   And would not consider any of
      His ways,

28 So that they caused the cry of the
      poor to come to Him;
   For He hears the cry of the
      afflicted.
29 When He gives quietness, who
      then can make trouble?
   And when He hides *His* face, who
      then can see Him,
   Whether *it is* against a nation or
      a man alone?—
30 That the hypocrite should not
      reign,
   Lest the people be ensnared.

31 "For has *anyone* said to God,
   'I have borne *chastening;*
   I will offend no more;
32 Teach me *what* I do not see;
   If I have done iniquity, I will do
      no more'?
33 Should He repay *it* according to
      your *terms,*
   Just because you disavow it?
   You must choose, and not I;
   Therefore speak what you know.

34 "Men of understanding say to me,
   Wise men who listen to me:
35 'Job speaks without knowledge,
   His words *are* without wisdom.'
36 Oh, that Job were tried to the
      utmost,
   Because *his* answers *are like*
      those of wicked men!
37 For he adds rebellion to his sin;
   He claps *his hands* among us,
   And multiplies his words against
      God."

ELIHU CONDEMNS
SELF-RIGHTEOUSNESS

35 Moreover E·li′hu answered
and said:

2 "Do you think this is right?
   Do you say,
   'My righteousness is more than
      God's'?

3 For you say,
   'What advantage will it be to
        You?
   What profit shall I have, more
        than *if* I had sinned?'

4 "I will answer you,
   And your companions with you.
5 Look to the heavens and see;
   And behold the clouds—
   They are higher than you.
6 If you sin, what do you
        accomplish against Him?
   Or, *if* your transgressions are
        multiplied, what do you do to
        Him?
7 If you are righteous, what do you
        give Him?
   Or what does He receive from
        your hand?
8 Your wickedness affects a man
        such as you,
   And your righteousness a son of
        man.

9 "Because of the multitude of
        oppressions they cry out;
   They cry out for help because of
        the arm of the mighty.
10 But no one says, 'Where *is* God
        my Maker,
   Who gives songs in the night,
11 Who teaches us more than the
        beasts of the earth,
   And makes us wiser than the
        birds of heaven?'
12 There they cry out, but He does
        not answer,
   Because of the pride of evil men.
13 Surely God will not listen to
        empty *talk*,
   Nor will the Almighty regard it.
14 Although you say you do not see
        Him,
   Yet justice *is* before Him, and you
        must wait for Him.
15 And now, because He has not
        punished in His anger,
   Nor taken much notice of folly,

16 Therefore Job opens his mouth in
        vain;
   He multiplies words without
        knowledge."

ELIHU PROCLAIMS GOD'S GOODNESS

36 E·lī′hū also proceeded and
said:

2 "Bear with me a little, and I will
        show you
   That *there are* yet words to speak
        on God's behalf.
3 I will fetch my knowledge from
        afar;
   I will ascribe righteousness to my
        Maker.
4 For truly my words *are* not false;
   One who is perfect in knowledge
        is with you.

5 "Behold, God *is* mighty, but
        despises *no one;*
   He is mighty in strength of
        understanding.
6 He does not preserve the life of
        the wicked,
   But gives justice to the oppressed.
7 He does not withdraw His eyes
        from the righteous;
   But *they are* on the throne with
        kings,
   For He has seated them forever,
   And they are exalted.
8 And if *they are* bound in fetters,
   Held in the cords of affliction,
9 Then He tells them their work
        and their transgressions—
   That they have acted defiantly.
10 He also opens their ear to
        instruction,
   And commands that they turn
        from iniquity.
11 If they obey and serve *Him,*
   They shall spend their days in
        prosperity,
   And their years in pleasures.

12 But if they do not obey,
They shall perish by the sword,
And they shall die without
   knowledge.*a*

13 "But the hypocrites in heart store
   up wrath;
They do not cry for help when He
   binds them.
14 They die in youth,
And their life *ends* among the
   perverted persons.*a*
15 He delivers the poor in their
   affliction,
And opens their ears in
   oppression.

16 "Indeed He would have brought
   you out of dire distress,
Into a broad place where *there is*
   no restraint;
And what is set on your table
   would be full of richness.
17 But you are filled with the
   judgment due the wicked;
Judgment and justice take hold *of*
   you.
18 Because *there is* wrath, *beware*
   lest He take you away with *one*
   blow;
For a large ransom would not
   help you avoid *it.*
19 Will your riches,
Or all the mighty forces,
Keep you from distress?
20 Do not desire the night,
When people are cut off in their
   place.
21 Take heed, do not turn to iniquity,
For you have chosen this rather
   than affliction.

22 "Behold, God is exalted by His
   power;
Who teaches like Him?
23 Who has assigned Him His way,
Or who has said, 'You have done
   wrong'?

Elihu Proclaims God's Majesty

24 "Remember to magnify His work,
Of which men have sung.
25 Everyone has seen it;
Man looks on *it* from afar.

26 "Behold, God *is* great, and we do
   not know *Him;*
Nor can the number of His years
   be discovered.
27 For He draws up drops of water,
Which distill as rain from the
   mist,
28 Which the clouds drop down
And pour abundantly on man.
29 Indeed, can *anyone* understand
   the spreading of clouds,
The thunder from His canopy?
30 Look, He scatters His light upon
   it,
And covers the depths of the
   sea.
31 For by these He judges the
   peoples;
He gives food in abundance.
32 He covers *His* hands with
   lightning,
And commands it to strike.
33 His thunder declares it,
The cattle also, concerning the
   rising *storm.*

37 "At this also my heart
   trembles,
And leaps from its place.
2 Hear attentively the thunder of
   His voice,
And the rumbling *that* comes
   from His mouth.
3 He sends it forth under the whole
   heaven,
His lightning to the ends of the
   earth.
4 After it a voice roars;

36:12 *a*Masoretic Text reads *as one without knowledge.*   36:14 *a*Hebrew *qedeshim,* that is, those
practicing sodomy and prostitution in religious rituals

ABOUT GOD'S WONDERS Job 37:14–16

God Gives Us Little Surprise Boxes

You open a shell. Surprise! There is a beautiful pearl. You plant some seeds. Surprise! They grow into colorful flowers. You put brown tulip bulbs into the ground. Next spring, surprise! There is a rainbow of colors bursting forth. You crack a nut. Surprise! There is a walnut or hickory nut or some other tasty nut for you to eat. God gives us hundreds of little surprise boxes for us to open. When we do, we are surprised with color or taste or smell. Thank You, God, for little surprise boxes.

1. Can you think of different kinds of surprise boxes that God gives us?
2. Are you grateful that God gives us surprise boxes?
3. Will you thank Him, now?

For more on *What the Bible Says* turn to page 802
For more on *God's Creation* turn to page 802

He thunders with His majestic
voice,
And He does not restrain them
when His voice is heard.
5 God thunders marvelously with
His voice;
He does great things which we
cannot comprehend.
6 For He says to the snow, 'Fall *on*
the earth';
Likewise to the gentle rain and
the heavy rain of His strength.
7 He seals the hand of every man,
That all men may know His work.
8 The beasts go into dens,
And remain in their lairs.
9 From the chamber *of the south*
comes the whirlwind,
And cold from the scattering
winds *of the north*.
10 By the breath of God ice is given,
And the broad waters are frozen.
11 Also with moisture He saturates
the thick clouds;
He scatters His bright clouds.
12 And they swirl about, being
turned by His guidance,
That they may do whatever He
commands them
On the face of the whole earth.*a*
13 He causes it to come,
Whether for correction,
Or for His land,
Or for mercy.

14 "Listen to this, O Job;
Stand still and consider the
wondrous works of God.
15 Do you know when God
dispatches them,
And causes the light of His cloud
to shine?
16 Do you know how the clouds are
balanced,
Those wondrous works of Him
who is perfect in knowledge?
17 Why *are* your garments hot,
When He quiets the earth by the
south *wind?*

18 With Him, have you spread out
the skies,
Strong as a cast metal mirror?

19 "Teach us what we should say to
Him,
For we can prepare nothing
because of the darkness.
20 Should He be told that I *wish to*
speak?
If a man were to speak, surely he
would be swallowed up.
21 Even now *men* cannot look at the
light *when it is* bright in the
skies,
When the wind has passed and
cleared them.
22 He comes from the north *as*
golden *splendor;*
With God *is* awesome majesty.
23 *As for* the Almighty, we cannot
find Him;
He is excellent in power,
In judgment and abundant
justice;
He does not oppress.
24 Therefore men fear Him;
He shows no partiality to any *who*
are wise of heart."

The Lord Reveals His Omnipotence to Job

38 Then the Lord answered Job
out of the whirlwind, and said:

2 "Who *is* this who darkens counsel
By words without knowledge?
3 Now prepare yourself like a man;
I will question you, and you shall
answer Me.

4 "Where were you when I laid the
foundations of the earth?
Tell *Me,* if you have
understanding.

37:12 *a*Literally *the world of the earth*

5 Who determined its
   measurements?
   Surely you know!
   Or who stretched the line upon it?
6 To what were its foundations
   fastened?
   Or who laid its cornerstone,
7 When the morning stars sang
   together,
   And all the sons of God shouted
   for joy?

8 "Or *who* shut in the sea with
   doors,
   When it burst forth *and* issued
   from the womb;
9 When I made the clouds its
   garment,
   And thick darkness its swaddling
   band;
10 When I fixed My limit for it,
   And set bars and doors;
11 When I said,
   'This far you may come, but no
   farther,
   And here your proud waves must
   stop!'

12 "Have you commanded the
   morning since your days *began,*
   And caused the dawn to know its
   place,
13 That it might take hold of the
   ends of the earth,
   And the wicked be shaken out of
   it?
14 It takes on form like clay *under* a
   seal,
   And stands out like a garment.
15 From the wicked their light is
   withheld,
   And the upraised arm is broken.

16 "Have you entered the springs of
   the sea?
   Or have you walked in search of
   the depths?
17 Have the gates of death been
   revealed to you?

Or have you seen the doors of the
   shadow of death?
18 Have you comprehended the
   breadth of the earth?
   Tell *Me,* if you know all this.

19 "Where *is* the way *to* the dwelling
   of light?
   And darkness, where *is* its place,
20 That you may take it to its
   territory,
   That you may know the paths *to*
   its home?
21 Do you know *it,* because you were
   born then,
   Or *because* the number of your
   days *is* great?

22 "Have you entered the treasury of
   snow,
   Or have you seen the treasury of
   hail,
23 Which I have reserved for the
   time of trouble,
   For the day of battle and war?
24 By what way is light diffused,
   Or the east wind scattered over
   the earth?

25 "Who has divided a channel for the
   overflowing *water,*
   Or a path for the thunderbolt,
26 To cause it to rain on a land
   where there is no one,
   A wilderness in which *there is* no
   man;
27 To satisfy the desolate waste,
   And cause to spring forth the
   growth of tender grass?
28 Has the rain a father?
   Or who has begotten the drops of
   dew?
29 From whose womb comes the ice?
   And the frost of heaven, who
   gives it birth?
30 The waters harden like stone,
   And the surface of the deep is
   frozen.

31 "Can you bind the cluster of the
    Plēi'a·dēs,
  Or loose the belt of Ō·rī'on?
32 Can you bring out Maz'za·roth[a]
    in its season?
  Or can you guide the Great Bear
    with its cubs?
33 Do you know the ordinances of
    the heavens?
  Can you set their dominion over
    the earth?

34 "Can you lift up your voice to the
    clouds,
  That an abundance of water may
    cover you?
35 Can you send out lightnings, that
    they may go,
  And say to you, 'Here we *are!*'?
36 Who has put wisdom in the
    mind?[a]
  Or who has given understanding
    to the heart?
37 Who can number the clouds by
    wisdom?
  Or who can pour out the bottles of
    heaven,

38 When the dust hardens in
    clumps,
  And the clods cling together?

39 "Can you hunt the prey for the
    lion,
  Or satisfy the appetite of the
    young lions,
40 When they crouch in *their* dens,
  Or lurk in their lairs to lie in
    wait?
41 Who provides food for the raven,
  When its young ones cry to God,
  And wander about for lack of
    food?

39

"Do you know the time when
    the wild mountain goats
    bear young?
  Or can you mark when the deer
    gives birth?
2 Can you number the months *that*
    they fulfill?

38:32 [a]Literally *Constellations*   38:36 [a]Literally *inward parts*

Or do you know the time when
   they bear young?
3 They bow down,
   They bring forth their young,
   They deliver their offspring.*a*
4 Their young ones are healthy,
   They grow strong with grain;
   They depart and do not return to
   them.

5 "Who set the wild donkey free?
   Who loosed the bonds of the
   onager,
6 Whose home I have made the
   wilderness,
   And the barren land his dwelling?
7 He scorns the tumult of the city;
   He does not heed the shouts of
   the driver.
8 The range of the mountains *is* his
   pasture,
   And he searches after every green
   thing.

9 "Will the wild ox be willing to
   serve you?
   Will he bed by your manger?
10 Can you bind the wild ox in the
   furrow with ropes?
   Or will he plow the valleys behind
   you?
11 Will you trust him because his
   strength *is* great?
   Or will you leave your labor to
   him?
12 Will you trust him to bring home
   your grain,
   And gather it to your threshing
   floor?

13 "The wings of the ostrich wave
   proudly,
   But are her wings and pinions
   like the kindly stork's?
14 For she leaves her eggs on the
   ground,
   And warms them in the dust;
15 She forgets that a foot may crush
   them,

Or that a wild beast may break
   them.
16 She treats her young harshly, as
   though *they were* not hers;
   Her labor is in vain, without
   concern,
17 Because God deprived her of
   wisdom,
   And did not endow her with
   understanding.
18 When she lifts herself on high,
   She scorns the horse and its rider.

19 "Have you given the horse
   strength?
   Have you clothed his neck with
   thunder?*a*
20 Can you frighten him like a
   locust?
   His majestic snorting strikes
   terror.
21 He paws in the valley, and
   rejoices in *his* strength;
   He gallops into the clash of
   arms.
22 He mocks at fear, and is not
   frightened;
   Nor does he turn back from the
   sword.
23 The quiver rattles against him,
   The glittering spear and javelin.
24 He devours the distance with
   fierceness and rage;
   Nor does he come to a halt
   because the trumpet *has*
   sounded.
25 At *the blast of* the trumpet he
   says, 'Aha!'
   He smells the battle from afar,
   The thunder of captains and
   shouting.

26 "Does the hawk fly by your
   wisdom,
   And spread its wings toward the
   south?

39:3 *a*Literally *pangs,* figurative of offspring
39:19 *a*Or *a mane*

27 Does the eagle mount up at your
command,
And make its nest on high?
28 On the rock it dwells and resides,
On the crag of the rock and the
stronghold.
29 From there it spies out the prey;
Its eyes observe from afar.
30 Its young ones suck up blood;
And where the slain *are,* there it
is."

40 Moreover the LORD answered Job, and said:

2 "Shall the one who contends with
the Almighty correct *Him?*
He who rebukes God, let him
answer it."

JOB'S RESPONSE TO GOD

3 Then Job answered the LORD and
said:

4 "Behold, I am vile;
What shall I answer You?
I lay my hand over my mouth.
5 Once I have spoken, but I will not
answer;
Yes, twice, but I will proceed no
further."

GOD'S CHALLENGE TO JOB

6 Then the LORD answered Job out
of the whirlwind, and said:

7 "Now prepare yourself like a man;
I will question you, and you shall
answer Me:

8 "Would you indeed annul My
judgment?
Would you condemn Me that you
may be justified?
9 Have you an arm like God?
Or can you thunder with a voice
like His?

10 Then adorn yourself *with* majesty
and splendor,
And array yourself with glory and
beauty.
11 Disperse the rage of your wrath;
Look on everyone *who is* proud,
and humble him.
12 Look on everyone *who is* proud,
and bring him low;
Tread down the wicked in their
place.
13 Hide them in the dust together,
Bind their faces in hidden
darkness.
14 Then I will also confess to you
That your own right hand can
save you.

15 "Look now at the behemoth,*a*
which I made *along* with you;
He eats grass like an ox.
16 See now, his strength *is* in his
hips,
And his power *is* in his stomach
muscles.
17 He moves his tail like a cedar;
The sinews of his thighs are
tightly knit.
18 His bones *are like* beams of
bronze,
His ribs like bars of iron.
19 He *is* the first of the ways of
God;
Only He who made him can bring
near His sword.
20 Surely the mountains yield food
for him,
And all the beasts of the field play
there.
21 He lies under the lotus trees,
In a covert of reeds and marsh.
22 The lotus trees cover him *with*
their shade;
The willows by the brook
surround him.
23 Indeed the river may rage,
Yet he is not disturbed;

40:15 *a*A large animal, exact identity unknown

He is confident, though the
    Jordan gushes into his mouth,
24 *Though* he takes it in his eyes,
    Or one pierces *his* nose with a
    snare.

41 "Can you draw out
    Le·vī′a·than*ª* with a hook,
    Or *snare* his tongue with a line
    which you lower?
2 Can you put a reed through his
    nose,
    Or pierce his jaw with a hook?
3 Will he make many supplications
    to you?
    Will he speak softly to you?
4 Will he make a covenant with
    you?
    Will you take him as a servant
    forever?
5 Will you play with him as *with* a
    bird,
    Or will you leash him for your
    maidens?
6 Will *your* companions make a
    banquet*ª* of him?
    Will they apportion him among
    the merchants?
7 Can you fill his skin with
    harpoons,
    Or his head with fishing spears?
8 Lay your hand on him;
    Remember the battle—
    Never do it again!
9 Indeed, *any* hope of *overcoming*
    him is false;
    Shall *one not* be overwhelmed at
    the sight of him?
10 No one *is so* fierce that he would
    dare stir him up.
    Who then is able to stand against
    Me?
11 Who has preceded Me, that I
    should pay *him?*
    Everything under heaven is Mine.

12 "I will not conceal*ª* his limbs,
    His mighty power, or his graceful
    proportions.
13 Who can remove his outer coat?
    Who can approach *him* with a
    double bridle?
14 Who can open the doors of his
    face,
    With his terrible teeth all around?
15 *His* rows of scales are *his* pride,
    Shut up tightly *as with* a seal;
16 One is so near another
    That no air can come between
    them;
17 They are joined one to another,
    They stick together and cannot be
    parted.
18 His sneezings flash forth light,
    And his eyes *are* like the eyelids
    of the morning.
19 Out of his mouth go burning
    lights;
    Sparks of fire shoot out.
20 Smoke goes out of his nostrils,
    As *from* a boiling pot and burning
    rushes.
21 His breath kindles coals,
    And a flame goes out of his
    mouth.
22 Strength dwells in his neck,
    And sorrow dances before him.
23 The folds of his flesh are joined
    together;
    They are firm on him and cannot
    be moved.
24 His heart is as hard as stone,
    Even as hard as the lower
    millstone.
25 When he raises himself up, the
    mighty are afraid;
    Because of his crashings they are
    beside*ª* themselves.
26 *Though* the sword reaches him, it
    cannot avail;
    Nor does spear, dart, or javelin.
27 He regards iron as straw,
    And bronze as rotten wood.
28 The arrow cannot make him flee;

41:1 *ª*A large sea creature, exact identity unknown
41:6 *ª*Or *bargain over him*   41:12 *ª*Literally
keep silent about   41:25 *ª*Or *purify themselves*

Slingstones become like stubble
to him.

29 Darts are regarded as straw;
He laughs at the threat of
javelins.

30 His undersides *are* like sharp
potsherds;
He spreads pointed *marks* in the
mire.

31 He makes the deep boil like a pot;
He makes the sea like a pot of
ointment.

32 He leaves a shining wake behind
him;
One would think the deep had
white hair.

33 On earth there is nothing like
him,
Which is made without fear.

34 He beholds every high *thing;*
He *is* king over all the children of
pride."

JOB'S REPENTANCE AND RESTORATION

42 Then Job answered the LORD
and said:

2 "I know that You can do
everything,
And that no purpose *of Yours* can
be withheld from You.

3 *You asked,* 'Who *is* this who hides
counsel without knowledge?'
Therefore I have uttered what I
did not understand,
Things too wonderful for me,
which I did not know.

4 Listen, please, and let me speak;
You said, 'I will question you, and
you shall answer Me.'

5 "I have heard of You by the
hearing of the ear,
But now my eye sees You.

6 Therefore I abhor *myself,*
And repent in dust and ashes."

Prayers

Job 42:2, 3

The Lord had shown Job wonderful things. Job, of course, did not have our Bible, so he missed many wonderful things that we know about God. But God gave a special message to Job and helped him see great wonders. What would you say if God showed you the deep secrets of His Creation? What would you say if God told you things that no one else had ever heard. Job prayed, "I know You can do everything . . . things too wonderful for me, which I did not know." Have you ever prayed for wisdom? Have you ever prayed for God to help you see life more clearly? Have you ever prayed for God to help you understand His Word better? Why not do that now?

---

7 And so it was, after the LORD had
spoken these words to Job, that the
LORD said to E·lī′phaz the Tē′man·ite,
"My wrath is aroused against you
and your two friends, for you have
not spoken of Me *what is* right, as My
servant Job *has.*

8 "Now therefore, take for yourselves seven bulls and seven rams, go
to My servant Job, and offer up for
yourselves a burnt offering; and My
servant Job shall pray for you. For I
will accept him, lest I deal with you
according to your folly; because you
have not spoken of Me *what is* right,
as My servant Job *has.*"

9 So E·lī′phaz the Tē′man·ite and
Bil′dad the Shū′hite *and* Zō′phar the
Nā′a·ma·thite went and did as the
LORD commanded them; for the LORD
had accepted Job.

What Should I Do?

WHEN YOU PLAY WITH YOUR TOYS? Job 42:10–12

Do you have some nice toys? When do you play with them? Have you ever thought about praying each time you play with your toys? Why should you do that?

1. Who gave you most of your toys? But who helped mother or father earn the money to buy your toys?
2. Would you like to thank your parents for the toys they gave you? Would you like to thank the Lord for helping them earn the money for your toys?

For more on *What Should I Do?* turn to page 831
For more on *Thankfulness* turn to page 902

10 And the LORD restored Job's losses*a* when he prayed for his friends. Indeed the LORD gave Job twice as much as he had before.

11 Then all his brothers, all his sisters, and all those who had been his acquaintances before, came to him and ate food with him in his house; and they consoled him and comforted him for all the adversity that the LORD had brought upon him. Each one gave him a piece of silver and each a ring of gold.

12 Now the LORD blessed the latter *days* of Job more than his beginning; for he had fourteen thousand sheep, six thousand camels, one thousand yoke of oxen, and one thousand female donkeys.

13 He also had seven sons and three daughters.

14 And he called the name of the first Je·mī'mah, the name of the second Ke·zī'ah, and the name of the third Ker'en-Hap'puch.

15 In all the land were found no women *so* beautiful as the daughters of Job; and their father gave them an inheritance among their brothers.

16 After this Job lived one hundred and forty years, and saw his children and grandchildren *for* four generations.

17 So Job died, old and full of days.

42:10 *a*Literally *Job's captivity,* that is, what was captured from Job

The Book of
PSALMS

BOOK ONE
Psalms 1—41

PSALM 1

THE WAY OF THE RIGHTEOUS AND THE END OF THE UNGODLY

BLESSED *is* the man
　Who walks not in the counsel of
　　the ungodly,
　　Nor stands in the path of
　　　sinners,
　　Nor sits in the seat of the
　　　scornful;
2 But his delight *is* in the law of the
　　LORD,
　　And in His law he meditates
　　　day and night.
3 He shall be like a tree
　　Planted by the rivers of water,
　　That brings forth its fruit in its
　　　season,
　　Whose leaf also shall not
　　　wither;
　And whatever he does shall
　　prosper.

4 The ungodly *are* not so,
　But *are* like the chaff which the
　　wind drives away.
5 Therefore the ungodly shall not
　　stand in the judgment,
　　Nor sinners in the congregation of
　　the righteous.

6 For the LORD knows the way of
　　the righteous,
　But the way of the ungodly shall
　　perish.

PSALM 2

THE MESSIAH'S TRIUMPH AND KINGDOM

WHY do the nations rage,
　And the people plot a vain thing?

2 The kings of the earth set
　　themselves,
　　And the rulers take counsel
　　　together,
　Against the LORD and against His
　　Anointed, *saying,*
3 "Let us break Their bonds in
　　pieces
　And cast away Their cords from
　　us."

4 He who sits in the heavens shall
　　laugh;
　The LORD shall hold them in
　　derision.
5 Then He shall speak to them in
　　His wrath,
　And distress them in His deep
　　displeasure:
6 "Yet I have set My King
　On My holy hill of Zion."

7 "I will declare the decree:
　The LORD has said to Me,
　'You *are* My Son,
　Today I have begotten You.
8 Ask of Me, and I will give *You*
　The nations *for* Your inheritance,
　And the ends of the earth *for* Your
　　possession.
9 You shall break*a* them with a rod
　　of iron;
　You shall dash them to pieces like
　　a potter's vessel.' "

10 Now therefore, be wise, O kings;
　Be instructed, you judges of the
　　earth.
11 Serve the LORD with fear,
　And rejoice with trembling.
12 Kiss the Son,*a* lest He*b* be angry,

2:9 *a*Following Masoretic Text and Targum; Septuagint, Syriac, and Vulgate read *rule* (compare Revelation 2:27). 2:12 *a*Septuagint and Vulgate read *Embrace discipline;* Targum reads *Receive instruction.* *b*Septuagint reads *the LORD.*

ABOUT GOD'S GUIDANCE Psalm 1:6

Which Way Are You Going?

Are you going this way, or are you going that way? Are you going the right way, or are you going the wrong way? Or do you know which way you are going?

1. This boy is going somewhere, but where is he going? What do you think?
2. Where do you learn the wrong way to go? Do some friends try to show you? Do things you read, or things you watch on TV, show you the wrong way? What else can show you the wrong way to go?
3. Where do you learn the right way to go? Read Psalm 1:6. Do you read the Bible each day? Does someone read it to you each day? Have you read your Bible today? Will you?

For more on *What the Bible Says* turn to page 819

For more on *Temptation* turn to page 831

And you perish *in* the way,
When His wrath is kindled but a
     little.
Blessed *are* all those who put
     their trust in Him.

PSALM 3

THE LORD HELPS HIS TROUBLED PEOPLE

A Psalm of David when he fled from
Ab′sa·lom his son.

LORD, how they have increased
     who trouble me!
Many *are* they who rise up
     against me.
2 Many *are* they who say of me,
     "There is no help for him in God."
                           Sē′lah

3 But You, O LORD, *are* a shield for
     me,
My glory and the One who lifts up
     my head.
4 I cried to the LORD with my
     voice,
And He heard me from His holy
     hill.   Sē′lah

5 I lay down and slept;
I awoke, for the LORD sustained
     me.
6 I will not be afraid of ten
     thousands of people
Who have set *themselves* against
     me all around.

7 Arise, O LORD;
Save me, O my God!
For You have struck all my
     enemies on the cheekbone;
You have broken the teeth of the
     ungodly.
8 Salvation *belongs* to the LORD.
Your blessing *is* upon Your people.
                           Sē′lah

PSALM 4

THE SAFETY OF THE FAITHFUL

To the Chief Musician. With stringed instruments.
A Psalm of David.

HEAR me when I call, O God of my
     righteousness!
You have relieved me in *my*
     distress;
Have mercy on me, and hear my
     prayer.

2 How long, O you sons of men,
Will you turn my glory to
     shame?
How long will you love
     worthlessness
And seek falsehood?   Sē′lah
3 But know that the LORD has set
     apart[a] for Himself him who is
     godly;
The LORD will hear when I call to
     Him.

4 Be angry, and do not sin.
Meditate within your heart on
     your bed, and be still.   Sē′lah
5 Offer the sacrifices of
     righteousness,
And put your trust in the LORD.

6 *There are* many who say,
     "Who will show us *any* good?"
LORD, lift up the light of Your
     countenance upon us.
7 You have put gladness in my
     heart,
More than in the season that
     their grain and wine increased.
8 I will both lie down in peace, and
     sleep;
For You alone, O LORD, make me
     dwell in safety.

4:3 [a]Many Hebrew manuscripts, Septuagint, Targum, and Vulgate read *made wonderful.*

PSALM 5

A PRAYER FOR GUIDANCE

*To the Chief Musician. With flutes.ᵃ
A Psalm of David.*

GIVE ear to my words, O LORD,
Consider my meditation.
2 Give heed to the voice of my cry,
My King and my God,
For to You I will pray.

■ *Prayers* ■

Psalm 5:3

There is something wonderful about starting the day with the Lord. The Psalmist reminds us of this. Listen to his prayer, "My voice You shall hear in the morning, O Lord." Do you remember to pray each morning? Can you think of a better way to begin each day?

---

3 My voice You shall hear in the
morning, O LORD;
In the morning I will direct *it* to
You,
And I will look up.

4 For You *are* not a God who takes
pleasure in wickedness,
Nor shall evil dwell with You.
5 The boastful shall not stand in
Your sight;
You hate all workers of iniquity.
6 You shall destroy those who speak
falsehood;
The LORD abhors the bloodthirsty
and deceitful man.

7 But as for me, I will come into
Your house in the multitude of
Your mercy;
In fear of You I will worship
toward Your holy temple.

8 Lead me, O LORD, in Your
righteousness because of my
enemies;
Make Your way straight before
my face.

9 For *there is* no faithfulness in
their mouth;
Their inward part *is* destruction;
Their throat *is* an open tomb;
They flatter with their tongue.
10 Pronounce them guilty, O God!
Let them fall by their own
counsels;
Cast them out in the multitude of
their transgressions,
For they have rebelled against
You.

11 But let all those rejoice who put
their trust in You;
Let them ever shout for joy,
because You defend them;
Let those also who love Your
name
Be joyful in You.
12 For You, O LORD, will bless the
righteous;
With favor You will surround him
as *with* a shield.

PSALM 6

A PRAYER OF FAITH IN TIME OF DISTRESS

*To the Chief Musician. With stringed instruments.
On an eight-stringed harp.ᵃ A Psalm of David.*

O LORD, do not rebuke me in Your
anger,
Nor chasten me in Your hot
displeasure.
2 Have mercy on me, O LORD, for I
am weak;
O LORD, heal me, for my bones
are troubled.

5:title ᵃHebrew *nehiloth*   6:title ᵃHebrew *shem-inith*

3 My soul also is greatly troubled;
  But You, O LORD—how long?

4 Return, O LORD, deliver me!
  Oh, save me for Your mercies'
  sake!

5 For in death *there is* no
  remembrance of You;
  In the grave who will give You
  thanks?

6 I am weary with my groaning;
  All night I make my bed swim;
  I drench my couch with my tears.

7 My eye wastes away because of
  grief;
  It grows old because of all my
  enemies.

8 Depart from me, all you workers
  of iniquity;
  For the LORD has heard the voice
  of my weeping.

9 The LORD has heard my
  supplication;
  The LORD will receive my prayer.

10 Let all my enemies be ashamed
  and greatly troubled;
  Let them turn back *and* be
  ashamed suddenly.

PSALM 7

PRAYER AND PRAISE FOR DELIVERANCE
FROM ENEMIES

A Meditation*a* of David, which he sang to the LORD
concerning the words of Cush, a Ben′ja·mīte.

O LORD my God, in You I put my
  trust;
  Save me from all those who
  persecute me;
  And deliver me,

2 Lest they tear me like a lion,
  Rending *me* in pieces, while *there
  is* none to deliver.

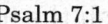

Prayers

Psalm 7:1

Where do you put your trust today? Honestly, are you trusting
in other people more than the
Lord? Are you trusting in yourself more than the Lord? Whom
do you trust most? Listen to the
Psalm writer pray, "O Lord my
God, in You I put my trust." Is
that a good idea? Can you think
of anyone more trustworthy
than the Lord?

3 O LORD my God, if I have done
  this:
  If there is iniquity in my hands,

4 If I have repaid evil to him who
  was at peace with me,
  Or have plundered my enemy
  without cause,

5 Let the enemy pursue me and
  overtake *me;*
  Yes, let him trample my life to the
  earth,
  And lay my honor in the dust.
                              Sē′lah

6 Arise, O LORD, in Your anger;
  Lift Yourself up because of the
  rage of my enemies;
  Rise up for me*a to* the judgment
  You have commanded!

7 So the congregation of the peoples
  shall surround You;
  For their sakes, therefore, return
  on high.

8 The LORD shall judge the peoples;
  Judge me, O LORD, according to
  my righteousness,
  And according to my integrity
  within me.

7:title *a*Hebrew *Shiggaion*   7:6 *a*Following
Masoretic Text, Targum, and Vulgate; Septuagint
reads *O LORD my God.*

9 Oh, let the wickedness of the
   wicked come to an end,
   But establish the just;
   For the righteous God tests the
   hearts and minds.
10 My defense *is* of God,
   Who saves the upright in heart.

11 God *is* a just judge,
   And God is angry *with the wicked*
   every day.
12 If he does not turn back,
   He will sharpen His sword;
   He bends His bow and makes it
   ready.
13 He also prepares for Himself
   instruments of death;
   He makes His arrows into fiery
   shafts.

14 Behold, *the wicked* brings forth
   iniquity;
   Yes, he conceives trouble and
   brings forth falsehood.
15 He made a pit and dug it out,
   And has fallen into the ditch
   which he made.
16 His trouble shall return upon his
   own head,
   And his violent dealing shall
   come down on his own crown.

17 I will praise the LORD according
   to His righteousness,
   And will sing praise to the name
   of the LORD Most High.

PSALM 8

THE GLORY OF THE LORD IN CREATION

To the Chief Musician. On the instrument of Gath.*a*
A Psalm of David.

O LORD, our Lord,
   How excellent *is* Your name in all
   the earth,
   Who have set Your glory above
   the heavens!

2 Out of the mouth of babes and
   nursing infants
   You have ordained strength,
   Because of Your enemies,
   That You may silence the enemy
   and the avenger.

3 When I consider Your heavens,
   the work of Your fingers,
   The moon and the stars, which
   You have ordained,
4 What is man that You are
   mindful of him,
   And the son of man that You visit
   him?
5 For You have made him a little
   lower than the angels,*a*
   And You have crowned him with
   glory and honor.

6 You have made him to have
   dominion over the works of
   Your hands;
   You have put all *things* under his
   feet,
7 All sheep and oxen—
   Even the beasts of the field,
8 The birds of the air,
   And the fish of the sea
   That pass through the paths of
   the seas.

9 O LORD, our Lord,
   How excellent *is* Your name in all
   the earth!

PSALM 9

PRAYER AND THANKSGIVING FOR THE LORD'S RIGHTEOUS JUDGMENTS

To the Chief Musician. To *the tune of* "Death of the
Son."*a* A Psalm of David.

I WILL praise *You,* O LORD, with my
   whole heart;

8:title *a*Hebrew *Al Gittith*   8:5 *a*Hebrew *Elohim, God;* Septuagint, Syriac, Targum, and Jewish
tradition translate as *angels.*   9:title *a*Hebrew
Muth Labben

Praises

Psalm 9:1

I will praise You, O Lord, with my whole heart. Not a small part of it. I will praise You with my *whole* heart. Not for a little time only. I will praise You with my whole heart *all* of the time. Not only when You give me something. I will praise You when You tell me maybe. I will even praise You when You say no. I will praise You with all I am and have. Praise the Lord.

I will tell of all Your marvelous works.

2 I will be glad and rejoice in You;
I will sing praise to Your name,
 O Most High.

3 When my enemies turn back,
They shall fall and perish at Your presence.
4 For You have maintained my right and my cause;
You sat on the throne judging in righteousness.
5 You have rebuked the nations,
You have destroyed the wicked;
You have blotted out their name forever and ever.

6 O enemy, destructions are finished forever!
And you have destroyed cities;
Even their memory has perished.
7 But the LORD shall endure forever;
He has prepared His throne for judgment.
8 He shall judge the world in righteousness,
And He shall administer judgment for the peoples in uprightness.

9 The LORD also will be a refuge for the oppressed,
A refuge in times of trouble.
10 And those who know Your name will put their trust in You;
For You, LORD, have not forsaken those who seek You.

11 Sing praises to the LORD, who dwells in Zion!
Declare His deeds among the people.
12 When He avenges blood, He remembers them;
He does not forget the cry of the humble.

13 Have mercy on me, O LORD!
Consider my trouble from those who hate me,
You who lift me up from the gates of death,
14 That I may tell of all Your praise
In the gates of the daughter of Zion.
I will rejoice in Your salvation.

15 The nations have sunk down in the pit *which* they made;
In the net which they hid, their own foot is caught.
16 The LORD is known *by* the judgment He executes;
The wicked is snared in the work of his own hands.
  Meditation.*a*   Sē'lah

17 The wicked shall be turned into hell,
And all the nations that forget God.
18 For the needy shall not always be forgotten;
The expectation of the poor shall *not* perish forever.

19 Arise, O LORD,
Do not let man prevail;

9:16 *a*Hebrew *Higgaion*

Let the nations be judged in Your
   sight.
20 Put them in fear, O LORD,
   That the nations may know
      themselves *to be but* men.
                              Sē′lah

PSALM 10

A SONG OF CONFIDENCE IN GOD'S
      TRIUMPH OVER EVIL

WHY do You stand afar off,
      O LORD?
Why do You hide in times of
      trouble?
2 The wicked in *his* pride
      persecutes the poor;
   Let them be caught in the plots
      which they have devised.

3 For the wicked boasts of his
      heart's desire;
   He blesses the greedy *and*
      renounces the LORD.
4 The wicked in his proud
      countenance does not seek
      God;
   God *is* in none of his thoughts.

5 His ways are always prospering;
   Your judgments *are* far above, out
      of his sight;
   As for all his enemies, he sneers
      at them.
6 He has said in his heart, "I shall
      not be moved;
   I shall never be in adversity."
7 His mouth is full of cursing and
      deceit and oppression;
   Under his tongue *is* trouble and
      iniquity.

8 He sits in the lurking places of
      the villages;
   In the secret places he murders
      the innocent;

His eyes are secretly fixed on the
      helpless.
9 He lies in wait secretly, as a lion
      in his den;
   He lies in wait to catch the
      poor;
   He catches the poor when he
      draws him into his net.
10 So he crouches, he lies low,
   That the helpless may fall by his
      strength.
11 He has said in his heart,
   "God has forgotten;
   He hides His face;
   He will never see."

12 Arise, O LORD!
   O God, lift up Your hand!
   Do not forget the humble.
13 Why do the wicked renounce
      God?
   He has said in his heart,
   "You will not require *an account.*"

14 But You have seen, for You
      observe trouble and grief,
   To repay *it* by Your hand.
   The helpless commits himself to
      You;
   You are the helper of the
      fatherless.
15 Break the arm of the wicked and
      the evil *man;*
   Seek out his wickedness *until* You
      find none.

16 The LORD *is* King forever and
      ever;
   The nations have perished out of
      His land.
17 LORD, You have heard the desire
      of the humble;
   You will prepare their heart;
   You will cause Your ear to hear,
18 To do justice to the fatherless and
      the oppressed,
   That the man of the earth may
      oppress no more.

PSALM 11

FAITH IN THE LORD'S RIGHTEOUSNESS

To the Chief Musician. A Psalm of David.

IN the LORD I put my trust;
  How can you say to my soul,
  "Flee *as* a bird to your mountain"?
2 For look! The wicked bend *their*
    bow,
  They make ready their arrow on
    the string,
  That they may shoot secretly at
    the upright in heart.
3 If the foundations are destroyed,
  What can the righteous do?

4 The LORD *is* in His holy temple,
  The LORD's throne *is* in heaven;
  His eyes behold,
  His eyelids test the sons of men.
5 The LORD tests the righteous,
  But the wicked and the one who
    loves violence His soul hates.
6 Upon the wicked He will rain
    coals;
  Fire and brimstone and a burning
    wind
  Shall be the portion of their
    cup.

7 For the LORD *is* righteous,
  He loves righteousness;
  His countenance beholds the
    upright.*a*

PSALM 12

MAN'S TREACHERY AND GOD'S CONSTANCY

To the Chief Musician. On an eight-stringed harp.*a*
A Psalm of David.

HELP, LORD, for the godly man
  ceases!

Prayers

Psalm 12:1

Here's a simple prayer. "Help,
Lord." Tuck that into your memory. You'll need that prayer a
dozen times each day, or more.
"Help, Lord. Something is too
big for me. Help Lord. I don't
feel I can do this. Help Lord. I
don't know which way to go.
Help, Lord. I need You."

For the faithful disappear from
    among the sons of men.
2 They speak idly everyone with his
    neighbor;
  With flattering lips *and* a double
    heart they speak.

3 May the LORD cut off all flattering
    lips,
  And the tongue that speaks proud
    things,
4 Who have said,
  "With our tongue we will prevail;
  Our lips *are* our own;
  Who *is* lord over us?"

5 "For the oppression of the poor, for
    the sighing of the needy,
  Now I will arise," says the LORD;
  "I will set *him* in the safety for
    which he yearns."

6 The words of the LORD *are* pure
    words,
  Like silver tried in a furnace of
    earth,
  Purified seven times.
7 You shall keep them, O LORD,
  You shall preserve them from this
    generation forever.

11:7 *a*Or *The upright beholds His countenance*
12:title *a*Hebrew *sheminith*

8 The wicked prowl on every side,
When vileness is exalted among
the sons of men.

PSALM 13

TRUST IN THE SALVATION OF THE LORD

To the Chief Musician. A Psalm of David.

HOW long, O LORD? Will You
forget me forever?
How long will You hide Your face
from me?
2 How long shall I take counsel in
my soul,
Having sorrow in my heart daily?
How long will my enemy be
exalted over me?

3 Consider *and* hear me, O LORD
my God;
Enlighten my eyes,
Lest I sleep the *sleep of* death;
4 Lest my enemy say,
"I have prevailed against him";
Lest those who trouble me rejoice
when I am moved.

5 But I have trusted in Your mercy;
My heart shall rejoice in Your
salvation.
6 I will sing to the LORD,
Because He has dealt bountifully
with me.

PSALM 14

FOLLY OF THE GODLESS, AND GOD'S FINAL TRIUMPH

To the Chief Musician. A Psalm of David.

THE fool has said in his heart,
"*There is* no God."
They are corrupt,
They have done abominable
works,
There is none who does good.

2 The LORD looks down from
heaven upon the children of
men,
To see if there are any who
understand, who seek God.
3 They have all turned aside,
They have together become
corrupt;
There is none who does good,
No, not one.

4 Have all the workers of iniquity
no knowledge,
Who eat up my people *as* they eat
bread,
And do not call on the LORD?
5 There they are in great fear,
For God *is* with the generation of
the righteous.
6 You shame the counsel of the
poor,
But the LORD *is* his refuge.

7 Oh, that the salvation of Israel
would come out of Zion!
When the LORD brings back the
captivity of His people,
Let Jacob rejoice *and* Israel be
glad.

PSALM 15

THE CHARACTER OF THOSE WHO MAY DWELL WITH THE LORD

A Psalm of David.

LORD, who may abide in Your
tabernacle?
Who may dwell in Your holy hill?

2 He who walks uprightly,
And works righteousness,
And speaks the truth in his
heart;
3 He *who* does not backbite with his
tongue,
Nor does evil to his neighbor,
Nor does he take up a reproach
against his friend;

What the Bible Says

ABOUT GOD'S GUIDANCE Psalm 16:7, 8

Who Will Show Me the Right Way?

Do you have special plans for tomorrow? Do you dream about something, plan for something special? Who will help you make your plans happen?

1. What special plans do you have? What do you hope you can do that you are not doing now?
2. Who will help you do what you want? Will your enemies? Will your friends? Will your parents? Will God?
3. Read Psalm 16:7, 8. What does this tell you about the Person who will help you carry out your plans? What should you ask Him to do?

For more on *What the Bible Says* turn to page 820
For more on *God's Guidance* turn to page 975

4 In whose eyes a vile person is
    despised,
    But he honors those who fear
      the LORD;
    He *who* swears to his own hurt
      and does not change;
5 He *who* does not put out his
    money at usury,
    Nor does he take a bribe
      against the innocent.

He who does these *things* shall
    never be moved.

PSALM 16

THE HOPE OF THE FAITHFUL, AND THE MESSIAH'S VICTORY

A Mich'tam of David.

PRESERVE me, O God, for in You I
    put my trust.

2 *O my soul,* you have said to the
    LORD,
  "You *are* my Lord,
    My goodness is nothing apart
      from You."

3 As for the saints who *are* on the
    earth,
  "They are the excellent ones, in
      whom is all my delight."

4 Their sorrows shall be multiplied
    who hasten *after* another *god;*
    Their drink offerings of blood I
      will not offer,
    Nor take up their names on my
      lips.

5 O LORD, *You are* the portion of my
    inheritance and my cup;
    You maintain my lot.
6 The lines have fallen to me in
    pleasant *places;*
    Yes, I have a good inheritance.

7 I will bless the LORD who has
    given me counsel;
    My heart also instructs me in the
      night seasons.
8 I have set the LORD always before
    me;
    Because *He is* at my right hand I
      shall not be moved.

9 Therefore my heart is glad, and
    my glory rejoices;
    My flesh also will rest in hope.

What the Bible Says

ABOUT GOD'S PRESENCE Psalm 16:11

Are You With Me?

Do you see that little kitty with her friend? Kitty isn't exactly a VIP, but she's there. When you need someone with you, you're glad to have a friend. Sometimes even a kitty will do. But think how much more wonderful it is to know that your parents are with you. They are much more important than Kitty. And think how extra special wonderful it is when God is with you. He is a million times more important to have with you than Kitty, isn't He?

1. Are you with me, Kitty? Thank you. I'm glad.
2. Are you with me, mother and father? Thank you. I'm very glad.
3. Are you with me, God? Thank You, thank You, thank You. Read Psalm 16:11. How much joy do you think "fullness of joy" is? Do you suppose you're so happy that you are just filled to the brim with joy?

For more on *What the Bible Says* turn to page 833
For more on *Friendship* turn to page 851

10 For You will not leave my soul in
   Shē′ōl,
   Nor will You allow Your Holy One
      to see corruption.
11 You will show me the path of life;
   In Your presence *is* fullness of joy;
   At Your right hand *are* pleasures
      forevermore.

PSALM 17

PRAYER WITH CONFIDENCE IN FINAL SALVATION

A Prayer of David.

HEAR a just cause, O LORD,
   Attend to my cry;
   Give ear to my prayer *which is*
      not from deceitful lips.
2 Let my vindication come from
      Your presence;
   Let Your eyes look on the things
      that are upright.
3 You have tested my heart;
   You have visited *me* in the night;
   You have tried me and have found
      nothing;
   I have purposed that my mouth
      shall not transgress.
4 Concerning the works of men,
   By the word of Your lips,
   I have kept away from the paths
      of the destroyer.
5 Uphold my steps in Your paths,
   That my footsteps may not slip.

6 I have called upon You, for You
      will hear me, O God;
   Incline Your ear to me, *and* hear
      my speech.
7 Show Your marvelous loving
      kindness by Your right hand,
   O You who save those who trust
      in You
   From those who rise up *against*
      them.
8 Keep me as the apple of Your eye;
   Hide me under the shadow of
      Your wings,

9 From the wicked who oppress me,
   From my deadly enemies who
      surround me.

10 They have closed up their fat
      hearts;
   With their mouths they speak
      proudly.
11 They have now surrounded us in
      our steps;
   They have set their eyes,
      crouching down to the earth,
12 As a lion is eager to tear his prey,
   And like a young lion lurking in
      secret places.

13 Arise, O LORD,
   Confront him, cast him down;
   Deliver my life from the wicked
      with Your sword,
14 With Your hand from men,
      O LORD,
   From men of the world *who have*
      their portion in *this* life,
   And whose belly You fill with
      Your hidden treasure.
   They are satisfied with children,
   And leave the rest of their
      possession for their babes.

15 As for me, I will see Your face in
      righteousness;
   I shall be satisfied when I awake
      in Your likeness.

PSALM 18

GOD THE SOVEREIGN SAVIOR

To the Chief Musician. A Psalm of
David the servant of the LORD, who
spoke to the LORD the words of this
song on the day that the LORD
delivered him from the hand of all his
enemies and from the hand of Saul.
And he said:

I WILL love You, O LORD, my
   strength.

2   The LORD is my rock and my
     fortress and my deliverer;
     My God, my strength, in whom I
     will trust;
     My shield and the horn of my
     salvation, my stronghold.
3   I will call upon the LORD, *who is
     worthy* to be praised;
     So shall I be saved from my
     enemies.

4   The pangs of death surrounded
     me,
     And the floods of ungodliness
     made me afraid.
5   The sorrows of Shē′ōl surrounded
     me;
     The snares of death confronted
     me.
6   In my distress I called upon the
     LORD,
     And cried out to my God;
     He heard my voice from His
     temple,
     And my cry came before Him,
     even to His ears.

7   Then the earth shook and
     trembled;
     The foundations of the hills also
     quaked and were shaken,
     Because He was angry.
8   Smoke went up from His
     nostrils,
     And devouring fire from His
     mouth;
     Coals were kindled by it.
9   He bowed the heavens also, and
     came down
     With darkness under His feet.
10   And He rode upon a cherub, and
     flew;
     He flew upon the wings of the
     wind.
11   He made darkness His secret
     place;
     His canopy around Him *was* dark
     waters
     And thick clouds of the skies.

12   From the brightness before Him,
     His thick clouds passed with
     hailstones and coals of fire.

13   The LORD thundered from
     heaven,
     And the Most High uttered His
     voice,
     Hailstones and coals of fire.[a]
14   He sent out His arrows and
     scattered the foe,
     Lightnings in abundance, and He
     vanquished them.
15   Then the channels of the sea were
     seen,
     The foundations of the world were
     uncovered
     At Your rebuke, O LORD,
     At the blast of the breath of Your
     nostrils.

16   He sent from above, He took
     me;
     He drew me out of many waters.
17   He delivered me from my strong
     enemy,
     From those who hated me,
     For they were too strong for me.
18   They confronted me in the day of
     my calamity,
     But the LORD was my support.
19   He also brought me out into a
     broad place;
     He delivered me because He
     delighted in me.

20   The LORD rewarded me according
     to my righteousness;
     According to the cleanness of my
     hands
     He has recompensed me.
21   For I have kept the ways of the
     LORD,
     And have not wickedly departed
     from my God.

18:13 [a]Following Masoretic Text, Targum, and Vulgate; a few Hebrew manuscripts and Septuagint omit *Hailstones and coals of fire.*

22 For all His judgments *were* before
   me,
   And I did not put away His
   statutes from me.
23 I was also blameless before Him,
   And I kept myself from my
   iniquity.
24 Therefore the LORD has
   recompensed me according to
   my righteousness,
   According to the cleanness of my
   hands in His sight.

25 With the merciful You will show
   Yourself merciful;
   With a blameless man You will
   show Yourself blameless;
26 With the pure You will show
   Yourself pure;
   And with the devious You will
   show Yourself shrewd.
27 For You will save the humble
   people,
   But will bring down haughty
   looks.

28 For You will light my lamp;
   The LORD my God will enlighten
   my darkness.
29 For by You I can run against a
   troop,
   By my God I can leap over a
   wall.
30 *As for* God, His way *is* perfect;
   The word of the LORD is proven;
   He *is* a shield to all who trust in
   Him.

31 For who *is* God, except the
   LORD?
   And who *is* a rock, except our
   God?
32 *It is* God who arms me with
   strength,
   And makes my way perfect.
33 He makes my feet like the *feet of*
   deer,
   And sets me on my high places.

34 He teaches my hands to make
   war,
   So that my arms can bend a bow
   of bronze.
35 You have also given me the shield
   of Your salvation;
   Your right hand has held me up,
   Your gentleness has made me
   great.
36 You enlarged my path under me,
   So my feet did not slip.

37 I have pursued my enemies and
   overtaken them;
   Neither did I turn back again till
   they were destroyed.
38 I have wounded them,
   So that they could not rise;
   They have fallen under my feet.
39 For You have armed me with
   strength for the battle;
   You have subdued under me those
   who rose up against me.
40 You have also given me the necks
   of my enemies,
   So that I destroyed those who
   hated me.
41 They cried out, but *there was*
   none to save;
   Even to the LORD, but He did not
   answer them.
42 Then I beat them as fine as the
   dust before the wind;
   I cast them out like dirt in the
   streets.

43 You have delivered me from the
   strivings of the people;
   You have made me the head of
   the nations;
   A people I have not known shall
   serve me.
44 As soon as they hear of me they
   obey me;
   The foreigners submit to me.
45 The foreigners fade away,
   And come frightened from their
   hideouts.

HUMILITY Psalm 18:27

Good Pride and Bad Pride—Which Is Which?

Do you see that special cap this boy is wearing? He is graduating from a school. Perhaps he is older than he looks and is graduating from college. Or he could be graduating from high school or some other school. Graduation is a special time. It's a time when we remember how hard we worked to get through school. It could be a time to be boastful and proud. "Look what I have done!" the graduate could say. "Look how important I am!" or "I'm smarter than you." But this boy is kneeling. He is praying to God. He isn't that kind of proud. He is humble. He's thanking God for helping him through school.

1. "I'm proud of you," mother says. Is this pride wrong? No, because mother is honoring you. "I'm smarter than you," or "I'm better than you," or "I don't need God." Is this pride wrong? Yes, because you are honoring yourself rather than God and others.
2. Do you think you're better or smarter or better looking than someone else? What's wrong with that? Do you think you know more than God or that you don't need God? What's wrong with that?
3. What does humility mean? It means honoring someone, especially God, more than yourself. It means not thinking more of yourself than you should. Why should you want to be humble?

For more on *Values* turn to page 857
For more on *Humility* turn to page 965

46 The LORD lives!
Blessed *be* my Rock!
Let the God of my salvation be
exalted.
47 *It is* God who avenges me,
And subdues the peoples under
me;
48 He delivers me from my enemies.
You also lift me up above those
who rise against me;
You have delivered me from the
violent man.
49 Therefore I will give thanks to
You, O LORD, among the
Gentiles,
And sing praises to Your name.

50 Great deliverance He gives to His
king,
And shows mercy to His anointed,
To David and his descendants
forevermore.

PSALM 19

THE PERFECT REVELATION OF THE LORD

To the Chief Musician. A Psalm of David.

THE heavens declare the glory of
God;
And the firmament shows His
handiwork.
2 Day unto day utters speech,
And night unto night reveals
knowledge.
3 *There is* no speech nor language
Where their voice is not heard.
4 Their line[a] has gone out through
all the earth,

19:4 [a]Septuagint, Syriac, and Vulgate read *sound;* Targum reads *business.*

And their words to the end of the world.

In them He has set a tabernacle for the sun,
5 Which *is* like a bridegroom coming out of his chamber,
And rejoices like a strong man to run its race.
6 Its rising *is* from one end of heaven,
And its circuit to the other end;
And there is nothing hidden from its heat.

7 The law of the LORD *is* perfect, converting the soul;
The testimony of the LORD *is* sure, making wise the simple;
8 The statutes of the LORD *are* right, rejoicing the heart;
The commandment of the LORD *is* pure, enlightening the eyes;
9 The fear of the LORD *is* clean, enduring forever;
The judgments of the LORD *are* true *and* righteous altogether.
10 More to be desired *are they* than gold,
Yea, than much fine gold;
Sweeter also than honey and the honeycomb.
11 Moreover by them Your servant is warned,
And in keeping them *there is* great reward.

12 Who can understand *his* errors? Cleanse me from secret *faults.*
13 Keep back Your servant also from presumptuous *sins;*
Let them not have dominion over me.
Then I shall be blameless,
And I shall be innocent of great transgression.

14 Let the words of my mouth and the meditation of my heart

Be acceptable in Your sight,
O LORD, my strength and my Redeemer.

PSALM 20

THE ASSURANCE OF GOD'S SAVING WORK

To the Chief Musician. A Psalm of David.

MAY the LORD answer you in the day of trouble;
May the name of the God of Jacob defend you;
2 May He send you help from the sanctuary,
And strengthen you out of Zion;
3 May He remember all your offerings,
And accept your burnt sacrifice.
Sē′lah

4 May He grant you according to your heart's *desire,*
And fulfill all your purpose.
5 We will rejoice in your salvation,
And in the name of our God we will set up *our* banners!
May the LORD fulfill all your petitions.

6 Now I know that the LORD saves His anointed;
He will answer him from His holy heaven
With the saving strength of His right hand.

7 Some *trust* in chariots, and some in horses;
But we will remember the name of the LORD our God.
8 They have bowed down and fallen;
But we have risen and stand upright.

9　Save, LORD!
　　May the King answer us when we
　　　call.

PSALM 21

JOY IN THE SALVATION OF THE LORD

To the Chief Musician. A Psalm of David.

THE king shall have joy in Your
　　strength, O LORD;
　　And in Your salvation how greatly
　　　shall he rejoice!
2　You have given him his heart's
　　　desire,
　　And have not withheld the
　　　request of his lips.　　　　Sē′lah

3　For You meet him with the
　　　blessings of goodness;
　　You set a crown of pure gold upon
　　　his head.
4　He asked life from You, *and* You
　　　gave *it* to him—
　　Length of days forever and ever.
5　His glory *is* great in Your
　　　salvation;
　　Honor and majesty You have
　　　placed upon him.
6　For You have made him most
　　　blessed forever;
　　You have made him exceedingly
　　　glad with Your presence.
7　For the king trusts in the LORD,
　　And through the mercy of the
　　　Most High he shall not be
　　　moved.

8　Your hand will find all Your
　　　enemies;
　　Your right hand will find those
　　　who hate You.
9　You shall make them as a fiery
　　　oven in the time of Your anger;
　　The LORD shall swallow them up
　　　in His wrath,
　　And the fire shall devour them.

10　Their offspring You shall destroy
　　　from the earth,
　　And their descendants from
　　　among the sons of men.
11　For they intended evil against
　　　You;
　　They devised a plot *which* they
　　　are not able *to perform.*
12　Therefore You will make them
　　　turn their back;
　　You will make ready *Your arrows*
　　　on Your string toward their
　　　faces.

13　Be exalted, O LORD, in Your own
　　　strength!
　　We will sing and praise Your
　　　power.

PSALM 22

THE SUFFERING, PRAISE, AND POSTERITY OF THE MESSIAH

To the Chief Musician. Set to "The Deer of the
Dawn."*a* A Psalm of David.

MY God, My God, why have You
　　forsaken Me?
　　Why are You so far from helping
　　　Me,
　　And from the words of My
　　　groaning?
2　O My God, I cry in the daytime,
　　but You do not hear;
　　And in the night season, and am
　　　not silent.

3　But You *are* holy,
　　Enthroned in the praises of
　　　Israel.
4　Our fathers trusted in You;
　　They trusted, and You delivered
　　　them.

22:title *a*Hebrew *Aijeleth Hashahar*

5 They cried to You, and were
    delivered;
    They trusted in You, and were not
    ashamed.

6 But I *am* a worm, and no man;
    A reproach of men, and despised
    by the people.
7 All those who see Me ridicule Me;
    They shoot out the lip, they shake
    the head, *saying*,
8 "He trusted[a] in the LORD, let Him
    rescue Him;
    Let Him deliver Him, since He
    delights in Him!"

9 But You *are* He who took Me out
    of the womb;
    You made Me trust *while* on My
    mother's breasts.
10 I was cast upon You from birth.
    From My mother's womb
    You *have been* My God.
11 Be not far from Me,
    For trouble *is* near;
    For *there is* none to help.

12 Many bulls have surrounded Me;
    Strong *bulls* of Bā′shan have
    encircled Me.
13 They gape at Me *with* their
    mouths,
    Like a raging and roaring lion.

14 I am poured out like water,
    And all My bones are out of joint;
    My heart is like wax;
    It has melted within Me.
15 My strength is dried up like a
    potsherd,
    And My tongue clings to My jaws;
    You have brought Me to the dust
    of death.

16 For dogs have surrounded Me;
    The congregation of the wicked
    has enclosed Me.
    They pierced[a] My hands and My
    feet;

17 I can count all My bones.
    They look *and* stare at Me.
18 They divide My garments among
    them,
    And for My clothing they cast
    lots.

19 But You, O LORD, do not be far
    from Me;
    O My Strength, hasten to help
    Me!
20 Deliver Me from the sword,
    My precious *life* from the power of
    the dog.
21 Save Me from the lion's mouth
    And from the horns of the wild
    oxen!

    You have answered Me.

22 I will declare Your name to My
    brethren;
    In the midst of the assembly I
    will praise You.
23 You who fear the LORD, praise
    Him!
    All you descendants of Jacob,
    glorify Him,
    And fear Him, all you offspring of
    Israel!
24 For He has not despised nor
    abhorred the affliction of the
    afflicted;
    Nor has He hidden His face from
    Him;
    But when He cried to Him, He
    heard.

25 My praise *shall be* of You in the
    great assembly;
    I will pay My vows before those
    who fear Him.
26 The poor shall eat and be
    satisfied;

22:8 [a]Septuagint, Syriac, and Vulgate read *hoped;*
Targum reads *praised.*   22:16 [a]Following some
Hebrew manuscripts, Septuagint, Syriac, Vulgate;
Masoretic Text reads *Like a lion.*

THE LORD IS MY SHEPHERD; I SHALL NOT WANT. Psalm 23:1

The Lord Is My Shepherd

The Lord is my shepherd. He is like the shepherds in Bible times. They took care of their sheep. They fed their sheep. They led their sheep. They protected their sheep. The Lord does all of these things for me, and more! What a good shepherd He is.

1. Read all of Psalm 23. How is the Lord like a Bible-time shepherd?
2. Are you happy that the Lord is like a shepherd to you? Why? What does the Lord do for you?
3. Have you thanked the Lord today for food, clothing, protection, and the other "shepherd gifts" that He has given you? Why not thank Him now for each one?

For more on *Favorite Family Verses* turn to page 858
For more on *God's Care* turn to page 833

Those who seek Him will praise
   the LORD.
Let your heart live forever!

27 All the ends of the world
Shall remember and turn to the
   LORD,
And all the families of the nations
Shall worship before You.*a*
28 For the kingdom *is* the LORD's,
And He rules over the nations.

29 All the prosperous of the earth
Shall eat and worship;
All those who go down to the dust
Shall bow before Him,
Even he who cannot keep himself
   alive.

30 A posterity shall serve Him.
It will be recounted of the Lord to
   the *next* generation,
31 They will come and declare His
   righteousness to a people who
   will be born,
That He has done *this*.

PSALM 23

THE LORD THE SHEPHERD OF HIS PEOPLE

A Psalm of David.

THE LORD *is* my shepherd;
   I shall not want.
2 He makes me to lie down in green
      pastures;
   He leads me beside the still
      waters.
3 He restores my soul;
   He leads me in the paths of
      righteousness
   For His name's sake.

4 Yea, though I walk through the
      valley of the shadow of death,
   I will fear no evil;
   For You *are* with me;
   Your rod and Your staff, they
      comfort me.

22:27 *a*Following Masoretic Text, Septuagint, and
Targum; Arabic, Syriac, and Vulgate read *Him*.

5 You prepare a table before me in
  the presence of my enemies;
You anoint my head with oil;
My cup runs over.

6 Surely goodness and mercy shall
  follow me
All the days of my life;
And I will dwell*a* in the house of
  the LORD
Forever.

PSALM 24

THE KING OF GLORY AND HIS KINGDOM

A Psalm of David.

THE earth *is* the LORD's, and all its
  fullness,
The world and those who dwell
  therein.

2 For He has founded it upon the
  seas,
And established it upon the
  waters.

3 Who may ascend into the hill of
  the LORD?
Or who may stand in His holy
  place?

4 He who has clean hands and a
  pure heart,
Who has not lifted up his soul to
  an idol,
Nor sworn deceitfully.

5 He shall receive blessing from the
  LORD,
And righteousness from the God
  of his salvation.

6 This *is* Jacob, the generation of
  those who seek Him,
Who seek Your face.   Sē'lah

7 Lift up your heads, O you gates!
And be lifted up, you everlasting
  doors!
And the King of glory shall come
  in.

8 Who *is* this King of glory?

The LORD strong and mighty,
The LORD mighty in battle.

9 Lift up your heads, O you gates!
Lift up, you everlasting doors!
And the King of glory shall come
  in.

10 Who is this King of glory?
The LORD of hosts,
He *is* the King of glory.   Sē'lah

PSALM 25

A PLEA FOR DELIVERANCE AND FORGIVENESS

A Psalm of David.

TO You, O LORD, I lift up my soul.

2 O my God, I trust in You;
Let me not be ashamed;
Let not my enemies triumph over
  me.

3 Indeed, let no one who waits on
  You be ashamed;
Let those be ashamed who deal
  treacherously without cause.

4 Show me Your ways, O LORD;
Teach me Your paths.

5 Lead me in Your truth and teach
  me,
For You *are* the God of my
  salvation;
On You I wait all the day.

23:6 *a*Following Septuagint, Syriac, Targum, and
Vulgate; Masoretic Text reads *return*.

◼ *Prayers* ◼

Psalm 25:4, 5

Show me Your ways, O Lord.
Have you prayed that prayer
lately? Would you rather do
what *you* want to do? Or would
you rather have the Lord show
you what He wants? Show me
Your ways, O Lord!

WHAT ARE YOU WATCHING? Psalm 25:15

Psalm 25:15 says, "My eyes are ever toward the Lord." Are your eyes on the Lord more than the TV screen? Are they on the Lord more than magazines that you shouldn't see? Are they on the Lord more than on bad things people want you to do? What are you watching?

1. Read Psalm 25:15 again. What does this say to you?
2. Why should you be careful what you watch on TV? Why should you be careful not to look at dirty pictures? Why should you be careful not to keep your eyes on bad things that bad friends want you to see? Where should your eyes look? What would please Jesus?

For more on *What Should I Do?* turn to page 840
For more on *Temptation* turn to page 1000

6 Remember, O LORD, Your tender
   mercies and Your loving
   kindnesses,
   For they *are* from of old.
7 Do not remember the sins of my
   youth, nor my transgressions;
   According to Your mercy
   remember me,
   For Your goodness' sake, O LORD.

8 Good and upright *is* the LORD;
   Therefore He teaches sinners in
   the way.
9 The humble He guides in justice,
   And the humble He teaches His
   way.
10 All the paths of the LORD *are*
    mercy and truth,
    To such as keep His covenant and
    His testimonies.
11 For Your name's sake, O LORD,
    Pardon my iniquity, for it *is* great.

12 Who *is* the man that fears the
    LORD?
    Him shall He*a* teach in the way
    He*b* chooses.
13 He himself shall dwell in
    prosperity,
    And his descendants shall inherit
    the earth.
14 The secret of the LORD *is* with
    those who fear Him,
    And He will show them His
    covenant.
15 My eyes *are* ever toward the
    LORD,
    For He shall pluck my feet out of
    the net.

16 Turn Yourself to me, and have
    mercy on me,
    For I *am* desolate and afflicted.
17 The troubles of my heart have
    enlarged;
    Bring me out of my distresses!
18 Look on my affliction and my
    pain,
    And forgive all my sins.

19 Consider my enemies, for they are
    many;
    And they hate me with cruel
    hatred.
20 Keep my soul, and deliver me;
    Let me not be ashamed, for I put
    my trust in You.
21 Let integrity and uprightness
    preserve me,
    For I wait for You.

22 Redeem Israel, O God,
    Out of all their troubles!

PSALM 26

A PRAYER FOR DIVINE SCRUTINY AND REDEMPTION

A Psalm of David.

VINDICATE me, O LORD,
   For I have walked in my integrity.
   I have also trusted in the LORD;
   I shall not slip.
2 Examine me, O LORD, and prove
   me;
   Try my mind and my heart.
3 For Your lovingkindness *is* before
   my eyes,
   And I have walked in Your truth.
4 I have not sat with idolatrous
   mortals,
   Nor will I go in with hypocrites.
5 I have hated the assembly of
   evildoers,
   And will not sit with the wicked.

6 I will wash my hands in
   innocence;
   So I will go about Your altar,
   O LORD,
7 That I may proclaim with the
   voice of thanksgiving,
   And tell of all Your wondrous
   works.

25:12 *a*Or he   *b*Or he

ABOUT GOD'S PROTECTION Psalm 27:4, 5

When Trouble Comes . . . What Then?

Who protects you when trouble comes? An umbrella or old newspaper can protect us from some drops of rain. But what about bigger trouble? Does mother or father protect you? Would your puppy protect you? Now what about *really big* trouble? Who can protect you from that?

1. Read Psalm 27:4, 5. Who will protect us in times of trouble? Can you think of some wonderful ways that God protects His own?
2. Read Psalm 46:1–3. Can God protect us in times of *big* trouble? What will you remember to do the next time you have *big* trouble?

For more on *What the Bible Says* turn to page 843
For more on *God's Care* turn to page 867

8 Lord, I have loved the habitation
   of Your house,
   And the place where Your glory
      dwells.

9 Do not gather my soul with
      sinners,
   Nor my life with bloodthirsty
      men,
10 In whose hands *is* a sinister
      scheme,
   And whose right hand is full of
      bribes.

11 But as for me, I will walk in my
      integrity;
   Redeem me and be merciful to
      me.
12 My foot stands in an even place;
   In the congregations I will bless
      the Lord.

PSALM 27

AN EXUBERANT DECLARATION OF FAITH

A Psalm of David.

THE Lord *is* my light and my
      salvation;
   Whom shall I fear?
   The Lord *is* the strength of my
      life;
   Of whom shall I be afraid?
2 When the wicked came against
      me
   To eat up my flesh,
   My enemies and foes,
   They stumbled and fell.
3 Though an army may encamp
      against me,
   My heart shall not fear;
   Though war may rise against
      me,
   In this I *will be* confident.

4 One *thing* I have desired of the
      Lord,
   That will I seek:
   That I may dwell in the house of
      the Lord
   All the days of my life,
   To behold the beauty of the
      Lord,
   And to inquire in His temple.
5 For in the time of trouble
   He shall hide me in His pavilion;
   In the secret place of His
      tabernacle
   He shall hide me;

He shall set me high upon a
    rock.

6 And now my head shall be lifted
    up above my enemies all
    around me;
Therefore I will offer sacrifices of
    joy in His tabernacle;
I will sing, yes, I will sing praises
    to the LORD.

7 Hear, O LORD, *when* I cry with my
    voice!
Have mercy also upon me, and
    answer me.
8 *When You said,* "Seek My face,"
My heart said to You, "Your face,
    LORD, I will seek."
9 Do not hide Your face from me;
Do not turn Your servant away in
    anger;
You have been my help;
Do not leave me nor forsake me,
O God of my salvation.
10 When my father and my mother
    forsake me,
Then the LORD will take care of
    me.

11 Teach me Your way, O LORD,
And lead me in a smooth path,
    because of my enemies.
12 Do not deliver me to the will of
    my adversaries;
For false witnesses have risen
    against me,
And such as breathe out violence.
13 *I would have lost heart,* unless I
    had believed
That I would see the goodness of
    the LORD
In the land of the living.

14 Wait on the LORD;
Be of good courage,
And He shall strengthen your
    heart;
Wait, I say, on the LORD!

PSALM 28

REJOICING IN ANSWERED PRAYER

A Psalm of David.

TO You I will cry, O LORD my
    Rock:
Do not be silent to me,
Lest, if You *are* silent to me,
I become like those who go down
    to the pit.
2 Hear the voice of my
    supplications
When I cry to You,
When I lift up my hands toward
    Your holy sanctuary.

3 Do not take me away with the
    wicked
And with the workers of iniquity,
Who speak peace to their
    neighbors,
But evil *is* in their hearts.
4 Give them according to their
    deeds,
And according to the wickedness
    of their endeavors;
Give them according to the work
    of their hands;
Render to them what they
    deserve.
5 Because they do not regard the
    works of the LORD,
Nor the operation of His hands,
He shall destroy them
And not build them up.

6 Blessed *be* the LORD,
Because He has heard the voice of
    my supplications!
7 The LORD *is* my strength and my
    shield;
My heart trusted in Him, and I
    am helped;
Therefore my heart greatly
    rejoices,
And with my song I will praise
    Him.

8 The LORD *is* their strength,*a*
And He *is* the saving refuge of
His anointed.
9 Save Your people,
And bless Your inheritance;
Shepherd them also,
And bear them up forever.

PSALM 29

PRAISE TO GOD IN HIS HOLINESS AND MAJESTY

A Psalm of David.

GIVE unto the LORD, O you mighty
ones,
Give unto the LORD glory and
strength.
2 Give unto the LORD the glory due
to His name;
Worship the LORD in the beauty of
holiness.

3 The voice of the LORD *is* over the
waters;
The God of glory thunders;
The LORD *is* over many waters.
4 The voice of the LORD *is*
powerful;
The voice of the LORD *is* full of
majesty.

5 The voice of the LORD breaks the
cedars,
Yes, the LORD splinters the cedars
of Lebanon.
6 He makes them also skip like a
calf,
Lebanon and Sir′i·on like a young
wild ox.
7 The voice of the LORD divides the
flames of fire.

8 The voice of the LORD shakes the
wilderness;
The LORD shakes the Wilderness
of Kā′desh.

9 The voice of the LORD makes the
deer give birth,
And strips the forests bare;
And in His temple everyone says,
"Glory!"

10 The LORD sat *enthroned* at the
Flood,
And the LORD sits as King
forever.
11 The LORD will give strength to
His people;
The LORD will bless His people
with peace.

PSALM 30

THE BLESSEDNESS OF ANSWERED PRAYER

A Psalm. A Song at the dedication of the house of David.

I WILL extol You, O LORD, for
You have lifted me up,
And have not let my foes rejoice
over me.
2 O LORD my God, I cried out to
You,
And You healed me.
3 O LORD, You brought my soul up
from the grave;
You have kept me alive, that I
should not go down to the pit.*a*

4 Sing praise to the LORD, you
saints of His,
And give thanks at the
remembrance of His holy
name.*a*
5 For His anger *is but for* a
moment,
His favor *is for* life;

28:8 *a*Following Masoretic Text and Targum; Septuagint, Syriac, and Vulgate read *the strength of
His people.*   30:3 *a*Following Qere and Targum;
Kethib, Septuagint, Syriac, and Vulgate read *from
those who descend to the pit.*   30:4 *a*Or *His holiness*

Weeping may endure for a night,
But joy *comes* in the morning.

6　Now in my prosperity I said,
"I shall never be moved."
7　LORD, by Your favor You have
made my mountain stand
strong;
You hid Your face, *and* I was
troubled.

8　I cried out to You, O LORD;
And to the LORD I made
supplication:
9　"What profit *is there* in my blood,
When I go down to the pit?
Will the dust praise You?
Will it declare Your truth?
10　Hear, O LORD, and have mercy on
me;
LORD, be my helper!"

11　You have turned for me my
mourning into dancing;
You have put off my sackcloth and
clothed me with gladness,
12　To the end that *my* glory may sing
praise to You and not be silent.
O LORD my God, I will give
thanks to You forever.

PSALM 31

THE LORD A FORTRESS IN ADVERSITY

To the Chief Musician. A Psalm of David.

IN You, O LORD, I put my trust;
Let me never be ashamed;
Deliver me in Your righteousness.
2　Bow down Your ear to me,
Deliver me speedily;
Be my rock of refuge,
A fortress of defense to save me.

3　For You *are* my rock and my
fortress;

Therefore, for Your name's sake,
Lead me and guide me.
4　Pull me out of the net which they
have secretly laid for me,
For You *are* my strength.
5　Into Your hand I commit my
spirit;
You have redeemed me, O LORD
God of truth.

6　I have hated those who regard
useless idols;
But I trust in the LORD.
7　I will be glad and rejoice in Your
mercy,
For You have considered my
trouble;
You have known my soul in
adversities,
8　And have not shut me up into the
hand of the enemy;
You have set my feet in a wide
place.

9　Have mercy on me, O LORD, for I
am in trouble;
My eye wastes away with grief,
Yes, my soul and my body!
10　For my life is spent with grief,
And my years with sighing;
My strength fails because of my
iniquity,
And my bones waste away.
11　I am a reproach among all my
enemies,
But especially among my
neighbors,
And *am* repulsive to my
acquaintances;
Those who see me outside flee
from me.
12　I am forgotten like a dead man,
out of mind;
I am like a broken vessel.
13　For I hear the slander of many;
Fear *is* on every side;
While they take counsel together
against me,

They scheme to take away my life.

14 But as for me, I trust in You, O LORD;
I say, "You *are* my God."
15 My times *are* in Your hand;
Deliver me from the hand of my enemies,
And from those who persecute me.
16 Make Your face shine upon Your servant;
Save me for Your mercies' sake.
17 Do not let me be ashamed, O LORD, for I have called upon You;
Let the wicked be ashamed;
Let them be silent in the grave.
18 Let the lying lips be put to silence,
Which speak insolent things proudly and contemptuously against the righteous.

19 Oh, how great *is* Your goodness,
Which You have laid up for those who fear You,
Which You have prepared for those who trust in You
In the presence of the sons of men!
20 You shall hide them in the secret place of Your presence
From the plots of man;
You shall keep them secretly in a pavilion
From the strife of tongues.

21 Blessed *be* the LORD,
For He has shown me His marvelous kindness in a strong city!
22 For I said in my haste,
"I am cut off from before Your eyes";
Nevertheless You heard the voice of my supplications
When I cried out to You.

23 Oh, love the LORD, all you His saints!
For the LORD preserves the faithful,
And fully repays the proud person.
24 Be of good courage,
And He shall strengthen your heart,
All you who hope in the LORD.

PSALM 32

THE JOY OF FORGIVENESS

A Psalm of David. A Contemplation.[a]

BLESSED *is he whose* transgression *is* forgiven,
Whose sin *is* covered.
2 Blessed *is* the man to whom the LORD does not impute iniquity,
And in whose spirit *there is* no deceit.

3 When I kept silent, my bones grew old
Through my groaning all the day long.
4 For day and night Your hand was heavy upon me;
My vitality was turned into the drought of summer.   Sē′lah
5 I acknowledged my sin to You,
And my iniquity I have not hidden.
I said, "I will confess my transgressions to the LORD,"
And You forgave the iniquity of my sin.   Sē′lah

6 For this cause everyone who is godly shall pray to You
In a time when You may be found;
Surely in a flood of great waters
They shall not come near him.

32:title [a]Hebrew *Maschil*

7 You *are* my hiding place;
You shall preserve me from
trouble;
You shall surround me with songs
of deliverance. Sē′lah

8 I will instruct you and teach you
in the way you should go;
I will guide you with My eye.

9 Do not be like the horse *or* like
the mule,
Which have no understanding,
Which must be harnessed with
bit and bridle,
Else they will not come near you.

10 Many sorrows *shall be* to the
wicked;
But he who trusts in the LORD,
mercy shall surround him.

11 Be glad in the LORD and rejoice,
you righteous;
And shout for joy, all *you* upright
in heart!

PSALM 33

THE SOVEREIGNTY OF THE LORD IN CREATION AND HISTORY

REJOICE in the LORD, O you
righteous!
For praise from the upright is
beautiful.

2 Praise the LORD with the harp;
Make melody to Him with an
instrument of ten strings.

3 Sing to Him a new song;
Play skillfully with a shout of
joy.

4 For the word of the LORD *is* right,
And all His work *is done* in
truth.

5 He loves righteousness and
justice;
The earth is full of the goodness
of the LORD.

6 By the word of the LORD the
heavens were made,
And all the host of them by the
breath of His mouth.

7 He gathers the waters of the sea
together as a heap;*a*
He lays up the deep in
storehouses.

8 Let all the earth fear the LORD;
Let all the inhabitants of the
world stand in awe of Him.

9 For He spoke, and it was *done;*
He commanded, and it stood fast.

10 The LORD brings the counsel of
the nations to nothing;
He makes the plans of the peoples
of no effect.

11 The counsel of the LORD stands
forever,
The plans of His heart to all
generations.

12 Blessed *is* the nation whose God
is the LORD,
The people He has chosen as His
own inheritance.

13 The LORD looks from heaven;
He sees all the sons of men.

14 From the place of His dwelling He
looks
On all the inhabitants of the
earth;

15 He fashions their hearts
individually;
He considers all their works.

16 No king *is* saved by the multitude
of an army;
A mighty man is not delivered by
great strength.

17 A horse *is* a vain hope for safety;
Neither shall it deliver *any* by its
great strength.

18 Behold, the eye of the LORD *is* on
those who fear Him,

33:7 *a*Septuagint, Targum, and Vulgate read *in a vessel.*

On those who hope in His mercy,
19 To deliver their soul from death,
And to keep them alive in
famine.

20 Our soul waits for the LORD;
He *is* our help and our shield.
21 For our heart shall rejoice in
Him,
Because we have trusted in His
holy name.
22 Let Your mercy, O LORD, be upon
us,
Just as we hope in You.

PSALM 34

THE HAPPINESS OF THOSE WHO TRUST
IN GOD

A Psalm of David when he pretended madness
before A·bim′e·lech, who drove him away, and he
departed.

I WILL bless the LORD at all times;
His praise *shall* continually *be* in
my mouth.
2 My soul shall make its boast in
the LORD;
The humble shall hear *of it* and
be glad.
3 Oh, magnify the LORD with me,
And let us exalt His name
together.

4 I sought the LORD, and He heard
me,
And delivered me from all my
fears.
5 They looked to Him and were
radiant,
And their faces were not
ashamed.
6 This poor man cried out, and the
LORD heard *him*,
And saved him out of all his
troubles.

7 The angel*a* of the LORD encamps
all around those who fear Him,
And delivers them.

8 Oh, taste and see that the LORD *is*
good;
Blessed *is* the man *who* trusts in
Him!
9 Oh, fear the LORD, you His saints!
There is no want to those who
fear Him.
10 The young lions lack and suffer
hunger;
But those who seek the LORD
shall not lack any good *thing*.

11 Come, you children, listen to me;
I will teach you the fear of the
LORD.
12 Who *is* the man *who* desires life,
And loves *many* days, that he
may see good?
13 Keep your tongue from evil,
And your lips from speaking
deceit.
14 Depart from evil and do good;
Seek peace and pursue it.

15 The eyes of the LORD *are* on the
righteous,
And His ears *are open* to their cry.
16 The face of the LORD *is* against
those who do evil,
To cut off the remembrance of
them from the earth.

17 *The righteous* cry out, and the
LORD hears,
And delivers them out of all their
troubles.
18 The LORD *is* near to those who
have a broken heart,
And saves such as have a contrite
spirit.

19 Many *are* the afflictions of the
righteous,

34:7 *a*Or *Angel*

But the LORD delivers him out of
  them all.
20 He guards all his bones;
   Not one of them is broken.
21 Evil shall slay the wicked,
   And those who hate the righteous
     shall be condemned.
22 The LORD redeems the soul of His
     servants,
   And none of those who trust in
     Him shall be condemned.

PSALM 35

THE LORD THE AVENGER OF HIS PEOPLE

A Psalm of David.

PLEAD *my cause*, O LORD, with
   those who strive with me;
   Fight against those who fight
     against me.
2 Take hold of shield and buckler,
   And stand up for my help.
3 Also draw out the spear,
   And stop those who pursue me.

Say to my soul,
   "I *am* your salvation."

4 Let those be put to shame and
     brought to dishonor
   Who seek after my life;
   Let those be turned back and
     brought to confusion
   Who plot my hurt.
5 Let them be like chaff before the
     wind,
   And let the angel*a* of the LORD
     chase *them*.
6 Let their way be dark and
     slippery,
   And let the angel of the LORD
     pursue them.
7 For without cause they have
     hidden their net for me *in* a pit,
   Which they have dug without
     cause for my life.
8 Let destruction come upon him
     unexpectedly,
   And let his net that he has hidden
     catch himself;

35:5 *a*Or Angel

Into that very destruction let him
    fall.

9 And my soul shall be joyful in the
    LORD;
  It shall rejoice in His salvation.
10 All my bones shall say,
  "LORD, who is like You,
  Delivering the poor from him who
    is too strong for him,
  Yes, the poor and the needy from
    him who plunders him?"

11 Fierce witnesses rise up;
  They ask me things that I do not
    know.
12 They reward me evil for good,
  To the sorrow of my soul.
13 But as for me, when they were
    sick,
  My clothing was sackcloth;
  I humbled myself with fasting;
  And my prayer would return to
    my own heart.
14 I paced about as though he were
    my friend or brother;
  I bowed down heavily, as one who
    mourns for his mother.

15 But in my adversity they rejoiced
  And gathered together;
  Attackers gathered against me,
  And I did not know it;
  They tore at me and did not cease;
16 With ungodly mockers at feasts
  They gnashed at me with their
    teeth.

17 Lord, how long will You look on?
  Rescue me from their
    destructions,
  My precious life from the lions.
18 I will give You thanks in the great
    assembly;
  I will praise You among many
    people.

19 Let them not rejoice over me who
  are wrongfully my enemies;

Nor let them wink with the eye
  who hate me without a cause.
20 For they do not speak peace,
  But they devise deceitful
    matters
  Against the quiet ones in the
    land.
21 They also opened their mouth
    wide against me,
  And said, "Aha, aha!
  Our eyes have seen it."

22 This You have seen, O LORD;
  Do not keep silence.
  O Lord, do not be far from me.
23 Stir up Yourself, and awake to my
    vindication,
  To my cause, my God and my
    Lord.
24 Vindicate me, O LORD my God,
    according to Your
    righteousness;
  And let them not rejoice over
    me.
25 Let them not say in their hearts,
  "Ah, so we would have it!"
  Let them not say, "We have
    swallowed him up."

26 Let them be ashamed and
    brought to mutual confusion
  Who rejoice at my hurt;
  Let them be clothed with shame
    and dishonor
  Who exalt themselves against
    me.

27 Let them shout for joy and be
    glad,
  Who favor my righteous cause;
  And let them say continually,
  "Let the LORD be magnified,
  Who has pleasure in the
    prosperity of His servant."
28 And my tongue shall speak of
    Your righteousness
  And of Your praise all the day
    long.

PSALM 36

MAN'S WICKEDNESS AND GOD'S PERFECTIONS

To the Chief Musician. A Psalm of David the
servant of the LORD.

AN oracle within my heart
    concerning the transgression of
    the wicked:
There is no fear of God before his
    eyes.
2   For he flatters himself in his own
        eyes,
    When he finds out his iniquity
        and when he hates.
3   The words of his mouth *are*
        wickedness and deceit;
    He has ceased to be wise *and* to
        do good.
4   He devises wickedness on his
        bed;
    He sets himself in a way *that is*
        not good;
    He does not abhor evil.

5   Your mercy, O LORD, *is* in the
        heavens;
    Your faithfulness *reaches* to the
        clouds.
6   Your righteousness *is* like the
        great mountains;
    Your judgments *are* a great deep;
    O LORD, You preserve man and
        beast.

7   How precious *is* Your
        lovingkindness, O God!
    Therefore the children of men put
        their trust under the shadow of
        Your wings.
8   They are abundantly satisfied
        with the fullness of Your house,
    And You give them drink from the
        river of Your pleasures.
9   For with You *is* the fountain of
        life;
    In Your light we see light.

10   Oh, continue Your lovingkindness
        to those who know You,
    And Your righteousness to the
        upright in heart.
11   Let not the foot of pride come
        against me,
    And let not the hand of the
        wicked drive me away.
12   There the workers of iniquity
        have fallen;
    They have been cast down and
        are not able to rise.

PSALM 37

THE HERITAGE OF THE RIGHTEOUS AND THE CALAMITY OF THE WICKED

A Psalm of David.

DO not fret because of evildoers,
    Nor be envious of the workers of
        iniquity.
2   For they shall soon be cut down
        like the grass,
    And wither as the green herb.

3   Trust in the LORD, and do good;
    Dwell in the land, and feed on His
        faithfulness.
4   Delight yourself also in the LORD,
    And He shall give you the desires
        of your heart.

5   Commit your way to the LORD,
    Trust also in Him,
    And He shall bring *it* to pass.
6   He shall bring forth your
        righteousness as the light,
    And your justice as the noonday.

7   Rest in the LORD, and wait
        patiently for Him;
    Do not fret because of him who
        prospers in his way,
    Because of the man who brings
        wicked schemes to pass.
8   Cease from anger, and forsake
        wrath;
    Do not fret—*it* only *causes* harm.

ABOUT GOD'S TREASURE Psalm 37:4

What's the Most Valuable Thing on Earth?

Suppose you had to give up every thing except one. What would you keep? Would it be your TV? Would it be your mother or father? Or would it be your piggy bank? What would it be?

1. Is money worth more to you than your parents? Is it worth more than your Bible?
2. Is TV worth more than God? Do you spend more time each day with the TV or with God?

For more on *What the Bible Says* turn to page 893

For more on *Choices* turn to page 932

9 For evildoers shall be cut off;
But those who wait on the LORD,
They shall inherit the earth.

10 For yet a little while and the
wicked *shall be* no *more;*
Indeed, you will look carefully for
his place,
But it *shall be* no *more.*

11 But the meek shall inherit the
earth,
And shall delight themselves in
the abundance of peace.

12 The wicked plots against the just,
And gnashes at him with his
teeth.

13 The Lord laughs at him,
For He sees that his day is
coming.

14 The wicked have drawn the sword
And have bent their bow,
To cast down the poor and needy,
To slay those who are of upright
conduct.

15 Their sword shall enter their own
heart,
And their bows shall be broken.

16 A little that a righteous man has
Is better than the riches of many
wicked.

17 For the arms of the wicked shall
be broken,
But the LORD upholds the
righteous.

18 The LORD knows the days of the
upright,
And their inheritance shall be
forever.

19 They shall not be ashamed in the
evil time,
And in the days of famine they
shall be satisfied.

20 But the wicked shall perish;
And the enemies of the LORD,
Like the splendor of the meadows,
shall vanish.
Into smoke they shall vanish
away.

21 The wicked borrows and does not
repay,
But the righteous shows mercy
and gives.

22 For *those* blessed by Him shall
inherit the earth,
But *those* cursed by Him shall be
cut off.

23 The steps of a *good* man are
ordered by the LORD,
And He delights in his way.

24 Though he fall, he shall not be
utterly cast down;
For the LORD upholds *him with*
His hand.

25 I have been young, and *now* am
old;
Yet I have not seen the righteous
forsaken,
Nor his descendants begging
bread.

26 *He is* ever merciful, and lends;
And his descendants *are* blessed.

27 Depart from evil, and do good;
And dwell forevermore.

28 For the LORD loves justice,
And does not forsake His saints;
They are preserved forever,
But the descendants of the
wicked shall be cut off.

29 The righteous shall inherit the
land,
And dwell in it forever.

30 The mouth of the righteous
speaks wisdom,
And his tongue talks of justice.

31 The law of his God *is* in his
heart;
None of his steps shall slide.

32 The wicked watches the
righteous,
And seeks to slay him.

33 The LORD will not leave him in
his hand,

I will keep my eyes always on the Lord.

———

Psalm 25:15

God tells His angels to watch over us.

Psalm 91:11, 12

*J*esus is our Shepherd; we are His sheep.

———

Psalm 100:3

*F*lowers may last only a short time, but the word of God lasts forever.

—————

Isaiah 40:8

Nor condemn him when he is
judged.

34 Wait on the LORD,
And keep His way,
And He shall exalt you to inherit
the land;
When the wicked are cut off, you
shall see *it.*
35 I have seen the wicked in great
power,
And spreading himself like a
native green tree.
36 Yet he passed away,*a* and behold,
he *was* no *more;*
Indeed I sought him, but he could
not be found.
37 Mark the blameless *man,* and
observe the upright;
For the future of *that* man *is*
peace.
38 But the transgressors shall be
destroyed together;
The future of the wicked shall be
cut off.

39 But the salvation of the righteous
is from the LORD;
He is their strength in the time of
trouble.
40 And the LORD shall help them
and deliver them;
He shall deliver them from the
wicked,
And save them,
Because they trust in Him.

PSALM 38

PRAYER IN TIME OF CHASTENING

A Psalm of David. To bring to remembrance.

O LORD, do not rebuke me in Your
wrath,
Nor chasten me in Your hot
displeasure!

2 For Your arrows pierce me deeply,
And Your hand presses me down.

3 *There is* no soundness in my flesh
Because of Your anger,
Nor *any* health in my bones
Because of my sin.
4 For my iniquities have gone over
my head;
Like a heavy burden they are too
heavy for me.
5 My wounds are foul *and* festering
Because of my foolishness.

6 I am troubled, I am bowed down
greatly;
I go mourning all the day long.
7 For my loins are full of
inflammation,
And *there is* no soundness in my
flesh.
8 I am feeble and severely broken;
I groan because of the turmoil of
my heart.

9 Lord, all my desire *is* before You;
And my sighing is not hidden
from You.
10 My heart pants, my strength fails
me;
As for the light of my eyes, it also
has gone from me.

11 My loved ones and my friends
stand aloof from my plague,
And my relatives stand afar off.
12 Those also who seek my life lay
snares *for me;*
Those who seek my hurt speak of
destruction,
And plan deception all the day
long.

13 But I, like a deaf *man,* do not
hear;

37:36 *a*Following Masoretic Text, Septuagint, and
Targum; Syriac and Vulgate read *I passed by.*

And *I am* like a mute *who* does
not open his mouth.
14 Thus I am like a man who does
not hear,
And in whose mouth *is* no
response.

15 For in You, O LORD, I hope;
You will hear, O Lord my God.
16 For I said, "*Hear me,* lest they
rejoice over me,
Lest, when my foot slips, they
exalt *themselves* against me."

17 For I *am* ready to fall,
And my sorrow *is* continually
before me.
18 For I will declare my iniquity;
I will be in anguish over my sin.
19 But my enemies *are* vigorous, *and*
they are strong;
And those who hate me
wrongfully have multiplied.
20 Those also who render evil for
good,
They are my adversaries, because
I follow *what is* good.

21 Do not forsake me, O LORD;
O my God, be not far from me!
22 Make haste to help me,
O Lord, my salvation!

PSALM 39

PRAYER FOR WISDOM AND FORGIVENESS

To the Chief Musician. To Je·dū'thun.
A Psalm of David.

I SAID, "I will guard my ways,
Lest I sin with my tongue;
I will restrain my mouth with a
muzzle,
While the wicked are before me."
2 I was mute with silence,
I held my peace *even* from good;
And my sorrow was stirred up.

3 My heart was hot within me;
While I was musing, the fire
burned.
Then I spoke with my tongue:

4 "LORD, make me to know my end,
And what *is* the measure of my
days,
That I may know how frail I *am.*
5 Indeed, You have made my days
as handbreadths,
And my age *is* as nothing before
You;
Certainly every man at his best
state *is* but vapor.   Sē'lah
6 Surely every man walks about
like a shadow;
Surely they busy themselves in
vain;
He heaps up *riches,*
And does not know who will
gather them.

7 "And now, Lord, what do I wait
for?
My hope *is* in You.
8 Deliver me from all my
transgressions;
Do not make me the reproach of
the foolish.
9 I was mute, I did not open my
mouth,
Because it was You who did *it.*
10 Remove Your plague from me;
I am consumed by the blow of
Your hand.
11 When with rebukes You correct
man for iniquity,
You make his beauty melt away
like a moth;
Surely every man *is* vapor.
     Sē'lah

12 "Hear my prayer, O LORD,
And give ear to my cry;
Do not be silent at my tears;
For I *am* a stranger with You,
A sojourner, as all my fathers
were.

13 Remove Your gaze from me, that I
    may regain strength,
    Before I go away and am no
    more."

PSALM 40

FAITH PERSEVERING IN TRIAL

To the Chief Musician. A Psalm of David.

I WAITED patiently for the LORD;
    And He inclined to me,
    And heard my cry.
2 He also brought me up out of a
    horrible pit,
    Out of the miry clay,
    And set my feet upon a rock,
    And established my steps.

Praises

Psalm 40:3

When God takes us from terrible
things, He puts a new song in
our mouth. We feel like singing
praises to God. Has God taken
something bad out of your life?
Did you praise Him? Will you
praise Him?

---

3 He has put a new song in my
    mouth—
    Praise to our God;
    Many will see *it* and fear,
    And will trust in the LORD.

4 Blessed *is* that man who makes
    the LORD his trust,
    And does not respect the proud,
    nor such as turn aside to lies.
5 Many, O LORD my God, *are* Your
    wonderful works
    Which You have done;
    And Your thoughts toward us
    Cannot be recounted to You in
    order;

If I would declare and speak *of*
    them,
    They are more than can be
    numbered.

6 Sacrifice and offering You did not
    desire;
    My ears You have opened.
    Burnt offering and sin offering
    You did not require.
7 Then I said, "Behold, I come;
    In the scroll of the book *it is*
    written of me.
8 I delight to do Your will, O my
    God,
    And Your law *is* within my heart."

9 I have proclaimed the good news
    of righteousness
    In the great assembly;
    Indeed, I do not restrain my lips,
    O LORD, You Yourself know.
10 I have not hidden Your
    righteousness within my heart;
    I have declared Your faithfulness
    and Your salvation;
    I have not concealed Your
    lovingkindness and Your truth
    From the great assembly.

11 Do not withhold Your tender
    mercies from me, O LORD;
    Let Your lovingkindness and Your
    truth continually preserve me.
12 For innumerable evils have
    surrounded me;
    My iniquities have overtaken me,
    so that I am not able to look
    up;
    They are more than the hairs of
    my head;
    Therefore my heart fails me.
13 Be pleased, O LORD, to deliver
    me;
    O LORD, make haste to help me!
14 Let them be ashamed and
    brought to mutual confusion
    Who seek to destroy my life;

Let them be driven backward and
brought to dishonor
Who wish me evil.
15 Let them be confounded because
of their shame,
Who say to me, "Aha, aha!"

16 Let all those who seek You rejoice
and be glad in You;
Let such as love Your salvation
say continually,
"The LORD be magnified!"
17 But I *am* poor and needy;
Yet the LORD thinks upon me.
You *are* my help and my
deliverer;
Do not delay, O my God.

PSALM 41

THE BLESSING AND SUFFERING OF THE GODLY

To the Chief Musician. A Psalm of David.

BLESSED *is* he who considers the
poor;
The LORD will deliver him in time
of trouble.
2 The LORD will preserve him and
keep him alive,
And he will be blessed on the
earth;
You will not deliver him to the
will of his enemies.
3 The LORD will strengthen him on
his bed of illness;
You will sustain him on his
sickbed.

4 I said, "LORD, be merciful to me;
Heal my soul, for I have sinned
against You."
5 My enemies speak evil of me:
"When will he die, and his name
perish?"
6 And if he comes to see *me,* he
speaks lies;

His heart gathers iniquity to
itself;
When he goes out, he tells *it.*

7 All who hate me whisper together
against me;
Against me they devise my hurt.
8 "An evil disease," *they say,* "clings
to him.
And *now* that he lies down, he
will rise up no more."
9 Even my own familiar friend in
whom I trusted,
Who ate my bread,
Has lifted up *his* heel against me.

10 But You, O LORD, be merciful to
me, and raise me up,
That I may repay them.
11 By this I know that You are well
pleased with me,
Because my enemy does not
triumph over me.
12 As for me, You uphold me in my
integrity,
And set me before Your face
forever.

13 Blessed *be* the LORD God of Israel
From everlasting to everlasting!
Amen and Amen.

BOOK TWO

Psalms 42—72

PSALM 42

YEARNING FOR GOD IN THE MIDST OF DISTRESSES

To the Chief Musician.
A Contemplation[a] of the sons of Kō′rah.

AS the deer pants for the water
brooks,

42:title [a]Hebrew *Maschil*

So pants my soul for You, O God.

2　My soul thirsts for God, for the
　　living God.
　When shall I come and appear
　　before God?[a]

3　My tears have been my food day
　　and night,
　While they continually say to me,
　"Where *is* your God?"

4　When I remember these *things,*
　I pour out my soul within me.
　For I used to go with the
　　multitude;
　I went with them to the house of
　　God,
　With the voice of joy and praise,
　With a multitude that kept a
　　pilgrim feast.

5　Why are you cast down, O my
　　soul?
　And *why* are you disquieted
　　within me?
　Hope in God, for I shall yet praise
　　Him
　For the help of His countenance.[a]

6　O my God,[a] my soul is cast down
　　within me;
　Therefore I will remember You
　　from the land of the Jordan,
　And from the heights of Her′mon,
　From the Hill Mī′zar.

7　Deep calls unto deep at the noise
　　of Your waterfalls;
　All Your waves and billows have
　　gone over me.

8　The LORD will command His
　　lovingkindness in the daytime,
　And in the night His song *shall be*
　　with me—
　A prayer to the God of my life.

9　I will say to God my Rock,
　"Why have You forgotten me?
　Why do I go mourning because of
　　the oppression of the enemy?"

10　*As* with a breaking of my bones,
　　My enemies reproach me,
　While they say to me all day long,
　"Where *is* your God?"

11　Why are you cast down, O my
　　soul?
　And why are you disquieted
　　within me?
　Hope in God;
　For I shall yet praise Him,
　The help of my countenance and
　　my God.

PSALM 43

PRAYER TO GOD IN TIME OF TROUBLE

VINDICATE me, O God,
　And plead my cause against an
　　ungodly nation;
　Oh, deliver me from the deceitful
　　and unjust man!

2　For You *are* the God of my
　　strength;
　Why do You cast me off?
　Why do I go mourning because of
　　the oppression of the enemy?

3　Oh, send out Your light and Your
　　truth!
　Let them lead me;
　Let them bring me to Your holy
　　hill
　And to Your tabernacle.

4　Then I will go to the altar of God,
　To God my exceeding joy;
　And on the harp I will praise You,
　O God, my God.

42:2 [a]Following Masoretic Text and Vulgate; some
Hebrew manuscripts, Septuagint, Syriac, and Targum read *I see the face of God.*　42:5 [a]Following
Masoretic Text and Targum; a few Hebrew manuscripts, Septuagint, Syriac, and Vulgate read *The
help of my countenance, my God.*　42:6 [a]Follow-
ing Masoretic Text and Targum; a few Hebrew
manuscripts, Septuagint, Syriac, and Vulgate put
my God at the end of verse 5.

5 Why are you cast down, O my
　　soul?
And why are you disquieted
　　within me?
Hope in God;
For I shall yet praise Him,
The help of my countenance and
　　my God.

PSALM 44

REDEMPTION REMEMBERED IN PRESENT DISHONOR

To the Chief Musician.
A Contemplation*a* of the sons of Kō'rah.

WE have heard with our ears,
　　O God,
Our fathers have told us,
The deeds You did in their days,
In days of old:
2 You drove out the nations with
　　Your hand,
But them You planted;
You afflicted the peoples, and cast
　　them out.
3 For they did not gain possession
　　of the land by their own sword,
Nor did their own arm save
　　them;
But it was Your right hand, Your
　　arm, and the light of Your
　　countenance,
Because You favored them.

4 You are my King, O God;*a*
Command*b* victories for Jacob.
5 Through You we will push down
　　our enemies;
Through Your name we will
　　trample those who rise up
　　against us.
6 For I will not trust in my bow,
Nor shall my sword save me.
7 But You have saved us from our
　　enemies,

And have put to shame those who
　　hated us.
8 In God we boast all day long,
And praise Your name forever.
　　　　　　　　　　Sē'lah

9 But You have cast *us* off and put
　　us to shame,
And You do not go out with our
　　armies.
10 You make us turn back from the
　　enemy,
And those who hate us have
　　taken spoil for themselves.
11 You have given us up like sheep
　　intended for food,
And have scattered us among the
　　nations.
12 You sell Your people for *next to*
　　nothing,
And are not enriched by selling
　　them.

13 You make us a reproach to our
　　neighbors,
A scorn and a derision to those all
　　around us.
14 You make us a byword among the
　　nations,
A shaking of the head among the
　　peoples.
15 My dishonor *is* continually before
　　me,
And the shame of my face has
　　covered me,
16 Because of the voice of him who
　　reproaches and reviles,
Because of the enemy and the
　　avenger.

17 All this has come upon us;
But we have not forgotten You,
Nor have we dealt falsely with
　　Your covenant.
18 Our heart has not turned back,

44:title *a*Hebrew *Maschil*　　44:4 *a*Following
Masoretic Text and Targum; Septuagint and Vulgate read *and my God.*　*b*Following Masoretic Text
and Targum; Septuagint, Syriac, and Vulgate read
Who commands.

Nor have our steps departed from
  Your way;

19 But You have severely broken us
  in the place of jackals,
  And covered us with the shadow
  of death.

20 If we had forgotten the name of
  our God,
  Or stretched out our hands to a
  foreign god,

21 Would not God search this out?
  For He knows the secrets of the
  heart.

22 Yet for Your sake we are killed all
  day long;
  We are accounted as sheep for the
  slaughter.

23 Awake! Why do You sleep,
  O Lord?
  Arise! Do not cast *us* off forever.

24 Why do You hide Your face,
  And forget our affliction and our
  oppression?

25 For our soul is bowed down to the
  dust;
  Our body clings to the ground.

26 Arise for our help,
  And redeem us for Your mercies'
  sake.

PSALM 45

THE GLORIES OF THE MESSIAH AND HIS BRIDE

To the Chief Musician. Set to "The Lilies."*a*
A Contemplation*b* of the sons of Kō′rah.
A Song of Love.

MY heart is overflowing with a
  good theme;
  I recite my composition
  concerning the King;
  My tongue *is* the pen of a ready
  writer.

2 You are fairer than the sons of
  men;
  Grace is poured upon Your lips;
  Therefore God has blessed You
  forever.

45:title *a*Hebrew *Shoshannim*   *b*Hebrew *Maschil*

3　Gird Your sword upon *Your* thigh,
　　O Mighty One,
　With Your glory and Your majesty.
4　And in Your majesty ride
　　prosperously because of truth,
　　humility, *and* righteousness;
　And Your right hand shall teach
　　You awesome things.
5　Your arrows *are* sharp in the
　　heart of the King's enemies;
　The peoples fall under You.

6　Your throne, O God, *is* forever
　　and ever;
　A scepter of righteousness *is* the
　　scepter of Your kingdom.
7　You love righteousness and hate
　　wickedness;
　Therefore God, Your God, has
　　anointed You
　With the oil of gladness more
　　than Your companions.
8　All Your garments are scented
　　with myrrh and aloes *and*
　　cassia,
　Out of the ivory palaces, by which
　　they have made You glad.
9　Kings' daughters *are* among Your
　　honorable women;
　At Your right hand stands the
　　queen in gold from Ō′phir.

10　Listen, O daughter,
　　Consider and incline your ear;
　Forget your own people also, and
　　your father's house;
11　So the King will greatly desire
　　your beauty;
　Because He *is* your Lord, worship
　　Him.
12　And the daughter of Tȳre *will*
　　come with a gift;
　The rich among the people will
　　seek your favor.

13　The royal daughter *is* all glorious
　　within *the palace;*
　Her clothing *is* woven with gold.

14　She shall be brought to the King
　　in robes of many colors;
　The virgins, her companions who
　　follow her, shall be brought to
　　You.
15　With gladness and rejoicing they
　　shall be brought;
　They shall enter the King's
　　palace.

16　Instead of Your fathers shall be
　　Your sons,
　Whom You shall make princes in
　　all the earth.
17　I will make Your name to be
　　remembered in all generations;
　Therefore the people shall praise
　　You forever and ever.

PSALM 46

GOD THE REFUGE OF HIS PEOPLE AND CONQUEROR OF THE NATIONS

To the Chief Musician. A Psalm of the sons of
Kō′rah. A Song for Al′a·moth.

GOD *is* our refuge and strength,
　A very present help in trouble.
2　Therefore we will not fear,
　　Even though the earth be
　　removed,
　And though the mountains be
　　carried into the midst of the
　　sea;
3　*Though* its waters roar *and* be
　　troubled,
　Though the mountains shake
　　with its swelling.　　Sē′lah

4　*There is* a river whose streams
　　shall make glad the city of
　　God,
　The holy *place* of the tabernacle of
　　the Most High.
5　God *is* in the midst of her, she
　　shall not be moved;

God shall help her, just at the
 break of dawn.
6 The nations raged, the kingdoms
 were moved;
He uttered His voice, the earth
 melted.

7 The LORD of hosts *is* with us;
The God of Jacob *is* our refuge.
                                Sē′lah

8 Come, behold the works of the
 LORD,
Who has made desolations in the
 earth.
9 He makes wars cease to the end
 of the earth;
He breaks the bow and cuts the
 spear in two;
He burns the chariot in the fire.

10 Be still, and know that I *am* God;
I will be exalted among the
 nations,
I will be exalted in the earth!

11 The LORD of hosts *is* with us;
The God of Jacob *is* our refuge.
                                Sē′lah

PSALM 47

PRAISE TO GOD, THE RULER OF THE EARTH

To the Chief Musician. A Psalm of the sons of
 Kō′rah.

OH, clap your hands, all you
 peoples!
Shout to God with the voice of
 triumph!
2 For the LORD Most High *is*
 awesome;
He is a great King over all the
 earth.
3 He will subdue the peoples under
 us,
And the nations under our feet.

4 He will choose our inheritance for
 us,
The excellence of Jacob whom He
 loves.   Sē′lah

5 God has gone up with a shout,
The LORD with the sound of a
 trumpet.
6 Sing praises to God, sing praises!
Sing praises to our King, sing
 praises!
7 For God *is* the King of all the
 earth;
Sing praises with understanding.

8 God reigns over the nations;
God sits on His holy throne.
9 The princes of the people have
 gathered together,
The people of the God of
 Abraham.
For the shields of the earth
 belong to God;
He is greatly exalted.

PSALM 48

THE GLORY OF GOD IN ZION

A Song. A Psalm of the sons of Kō′rah.

GREAT *is* the LORD, and greatly to
 be praised
In the city of our God,
In His holy mountain.
2 Beautiful in elevation,
The joy of the whole earth,
Is Mount Zion *on* the sides of the
 north,
The city of the great King.
3 God *is* in her palaces;
He is known as her refuge.

4 For behold, the kings assembled,
They passed by together.
5 They saw *it, and* so they
 marveled;

They were troubled, they
hastened away.

6 Fear took hold of them there,
And pain, as of a woman in birth
pangs,

7 *As when* You break the ships of
Tar'shish
With an east wind.

8 As we have heard,
So we have seen
In the city of the LORD of hosts,
In the city of our God:
God will establish it forever.

Sē'lah

9 We have thought, O God, on Your
lovingkindness,
In the midst of Your temple.

Praises

Psalm 48:10

Praise to God goes out to the
ends of the earth. In every nation someone is praising God.
Think of all these Christians
throughout the world. Think of
them praising God like a great
choir. Would you like to join
them. Praise God now!

---

10 According to Your name, O God,
So *is* Your praise to the ends of
the earth;
Your right hand is full of
righteousness.

11 Let Mount Zion rejoice,
Let the daughters of Judah be
glad,
Because of Your judgments.

12 Walk about Zion,
And go all around her.
Count her towers;

13 Mark well her bulwarks;
Consider her palaces;

That you may tell *it* to the
generation following.

14 For this *is* God,
Our God forever and ever;
He will be our guide
Even to death.*a*

The Lord of hosts is with us;
The God of Jacob is our refuge.

PSALM 49

THE CONFIDENCE OF THE FOOLISH

To the Chief Musician. A Psalm of the sons of
Kō'rah.

HEAR this, all peoples;
Give ear, all inhabitants of the
world,

2 Both low and high,
Rich and poor together.

3 My mouth shall speak wisdom,
And the meditation of my heart
shall give understanding.

4 I will incline my ear to a
proverb;
I will disclose my dark saying on
the harp.

5 Why should I fear in the days of
evil,
When the iniquity at my heels
surrounds me?

6 Those who trust in their wealth
And boast in the multitude of
their riches,

7 None *of them* can by any means
redeem *his* brother,
Nor give to God a ransom for
him—

8 For the redemption of their souls
is costly,
And it shall cease forever—

9 That he should continue to live
eternally,
And not see the Pit.

48:14 *a*Following Masoretic Text and Syriac; Septuagint and Vulgate read *Forever.*

10 For he sees wise men die;
   Likewise the fool and the
      senseless person perish,
   And leave their wealth to
      others.
11 Their inner thought *is that* their
      houses *will last* forever,*a*
   Their dwelling places to all
      generations;
   They call *their* lands after their
      own names.
12 Nevertheless man, *though* in
      honor, does not remain;*a*
   He is like the beasts *that* perish.

13 This is the way of those who *are*
      foolish,
   And of their posterity who
      approve their sayings.   Sē′lah
14 Like sheep they are laid in the
      grave;
   Death shall feed on them;
   The upright shall have dominion
      over them in the morning;
   And their beauty shall be
      consumed in the grave, far from
      their dwelling.
15 But God will redeem my soul
      from the power of the grave,
   For He shall receive me.   Sē′lah

16 Do not be afraid when one
      becomes rich,
   When the glory of his house is
      increased;
17 For when he dies he shall carry
      nothing away;
   His glory shall not descend after
      him.
18 Though while he lives he blesses
      himself
   (For *men* will praise you when
      you do well for yourself),
19 He shall go to the generation of
      his fathers;
   They shall never see light.
20 A man *who is* in honor, yet does
      not understand,
   Is like the beasts *that* perish.

PSALM 50

GOD THE RIGHTEOUS JUDGE

A Psalm of Ā′saph.

THE Mighty One, God the LORD,
   Has spoken and called the earth
   From the rising of the sun to its
      going down.
2   Out of Zion, the perfection of
      beauty,
   God will shine forth.
3   Our God shall come, and shall not
      keep silent;
   A fire shall devour before Him,
   And it shall be very tempestuous
      all around Him.
4   He shall call to the heavens from
      above,
   And to the earth, that He may
      judge His people:
5   "Gather My saints together to Me,
   Those who have made a covenant
      with Me by sacrifice."
6   Let the heavens declare His
      righteousness,
   For God Himself *is* Judge.
                              Sē′lah

7   "Hear, O My people, and I will
      speak,
   O Israel, and I will testify against
      you;
   I *am* God, your God!
8   I will not rebuke you for your
      sacrifices
   Or your burnt offerings,
   Which are continually before Me.
9   I will not take a bull from your
      house,
   Nor goats out of your folds.

49:11 *a*Septuagint, Syriac, Targum, and Vulgate
read *Their graves shall be their houses forever*.
49:12 *a*Following Masoretic Text and Targum; Septuagint, Syriac, and Vulgate read *understand* (compare verse 20).

10 For every beast of the forest *is*
   Mine,
   And the cattle on a thousand
   hills.
11 I know all the birds of the
   mountains,
   And the wild beasts of the field
   are Mine.

12 "If I were hungry, I would not tell
   you;
   For the world *is* Mine, and all its
   fullness.
13 Will I eat the flesh of bulls,
   Or drink the blood of goats?
14 Offer to God thanksgiving,
   And pay your vows to the Most
   High.
15 Call upon Me in the day of
   trouble;
   I will deliver you, and you shall
   glorify Me."

16 But to the wicked God says:
   "What *right* have you to declare
   My statutes,
   Or take My covenant in your
   mouth,
17 Seeing you hate instruction
   And cast My words behind you?
18 When you saw a thief, you
   consented[a] with him,
   And have been a partaker with
   adulterers.
19 You give your mouth to evil,
   And your tongue frames deceit.
20 You sit *and* speak against your
   brother;
   You slander your own mother's
   son.
21 These *things* you have done, and I
   kept silent;
   You thought that I was altogether
   like you;
   But I will rebuke you,
   And set *them* in order before your
   eyes.

22 "Now consider this, you who forget
   God,

Lest I tear *you* in pieces,
And *there be* none to deliver:
23 Whoever offers praise glorifies
   Me;
   And to him who orders *his*
   conduct *aright*
   I will show the salvation of God."

PSALM 51

A PRAYER OF REPENTANCE

To the Chief Musician. A Psalm of David when
Nathan the prophet went to him, after he had gone
in to Bath·shē'ba.

HAVE mercy upon me, O God,
   According to Your lovingkindness;
   According to the multitude of
   Your tender mercies,
   Blot out my transgressions.
2 Wash me thoroughly from my
   iniquity,
   And cleanse me from my sin.

3 For I acknowledge my
   transgressions,
   And my sin *is* always before me.
4 Against You, You only, have I
   sinned,
   And done *this* evil in Your sight—
   That You may be found just when
   You speak,[a]
   And blameless when You judge.

5 Behold, I was brought forth in
   iniquity,
   And in sin my mother conceived
   me.
6 Behold, You desire truth in the
   inward parts,
   And in the hidden *part* You will
   make me to know wisdom.

50:18 [a]Septuagint, Syriac, Targum, and Vulgate
read *ran*.   51:4 [a]Septuagint, Targum, and Vulgate read *in Your words*.

CLEANLINESS   Psalm 51:2, 7, 10

Is Cleanliness Next to Godliness?

Have you heard the old saying, "Cleanliness is next to godliness?" Psalm 51 tells us about the way God washes and cleans our hearts when we ask Him. He "cleanses me from my sin" (v. 2). He makes us clean, as fresh and spotless as new-fallen snow (v. 7). He creates a clean heart in me (v. 10). That's clean, isn't it? So if we want to keep our outward appearance as fresh and clean as our inner person, we should really scrub, shouldn't we?

1. How clean does God make our hearts, minds, and souls when we ask Him to forgive us and make us His people?
2. How clean should we try to be on the outside to match God's cleansing on the inside?

For more on *Values* turn to page 908

For more on *Forgiveness* turn to page 858

CREATE IN ME A CLEAN HEART, O GOD. Psalm 51:10

Can I Make a Clean Heart?

Kelly has a wonderful idea. "I will make a new heart," she says. "I will make a new heart that is clean." Kelly thinks her heart is a little dirty. She has been thinking some bad thoughts. She has been saying some bad words. Kelly wants a new heart. Can she make a new heart? Can she make a new heart that is clean?

1. Can you make a new heart? Can you cut a new heart from some paper?
2. How can you get a clean heart? Read Psalm 51:10. What does it say? Who can give you a clean heart?
3. Jesus died to take away our sin. That's the way we get a clean heart. We ask Jesus to take away our sin. We ask Him to make our heart clean. He will. Ask Him.

For more on *Favorite Family Verses* turn to page 902
For more on *Forgiveness* turn to page 945

7 Purge me with hyssop, and I shall
   be clean;
   Wash me, and I shall be whiter
   than snow.
8 Make me hear joy and gladness,
   That the bones You have broken
   may rejoice.
9 Hide Your face from my sins,
   And blot out all my iniquities.

10 Create in me a clean heart,
   O God,
   And renew a steadfast spirit
   within me.
11 Do not cast me away from Your
   presence,
   And do not take Your Holy Spirit
   from me.
12 Restore to me the joy of Your
   salvation,
   And uphold me *by Your* generous
   Spirit.
13 *Then* I will teach transgressors
   Your ways,
   And sinners shall be converted to
   You.

14 Deliver me from the guilt of
   bloodshed, O God,
   The God of my salvation,
   And my tongue shall sing aloud of
   Your righteousness.
15 O Lord, open my lips,
   And my mouth shall show forth
   Your praise.
16 For You do not desire sacrifice, or
   else I would give *it;*
   You do not delight in burnt
   offering.
17 The sacrifices of God *are* a broken
   spirit,
   A broken and a contrite heart—
   These, O God, You will not
   despise.

18 Do good in Your good pleasure to
   Zion;
   Build the walls of Jerusalem.

19 Then You shall be pleased with
   the sacrifices of righteousness,
   With burnt offering and whole
   burnt offering;
   Then they shall offer bulls on
   Your altar.

PSALM 52

THE END OF THE WICKED AND THE PEACE OF THE GODLY

To the Chief Musician. A Contemplation[a] of David when Dō′eg the Ē′dom·īte went and told Saul, and said to him, "David has gone to the house of A·him′e·lech."

WHY do you boast in evil,
   O mighty man?
   The goodness of God *endures*
   continually.
2 Your tongue devises destruction,
   Like a sharp razor, working
   deceitfully.
3 You love evil more than good,
   Lying rather than speaking
   righteousness.   Sē′lah
4 You love all devouring words,
   You deceitful tongue.

5 God shall likewise destroy you
   forever;
   He shall take you away, and pluck
   you out of *your* dwelling place,
   And uproot you from the land of
   the living.   Sē′lah
6 The righteous also shall see and
   fear,
   And shall laugh at him, *saying,*
7 "Here is the man *who* did not
   make God his strength,
   But trusted in the abundance of
   his riches,
   And strengthened himself in his
   wickedness."

52:title *a*Hebrew *Maschil*

8 But I *am* like a green olive tree in
   the house of God;
  I trust in the mercy of God
   forever and ever.
9 I will praise You forever,
  Because You have done *it;*
  And in the presence of Your saints
   I will wait on Your name, for *it is*
   good.

PSALM 53

FOLLY OF THE GODLESS, AND THE RESTORATION OF ISRAEL

To the Chief Musician. Set to "Mā′ha·lath."
A Contemplation*a* of David.

THE fool has said in his heart,
  "There is no God."
  They are corrupt, and have done
   abominable iniquity;
  There is none who does good.

2 God looks down from heaven
   upon the children of men,
  To see if there are *any* who
   understand, who seek God.
3 Every one of them has turned
   aside;
  They have together become
   corrupt;
  There is none who does good,
  No, not one.

4 Have the workers of iniquity no
   knowledge,
  Who eat up my people *as* they eat
   bread,
  And do not call upon God?
5 There they are in great fear
  Where no fear was,
  For God has scattered the bones
   of him who encamps against
   you;
  You have put *them* to shame,
  Because God has despised them.

6 Oh, that the salvation of Israel
   would come out of Zion!
  When God brings back the
   captivity of His people,
  Let Jacob rejoice *and* Israel be
   glad.

PSALM 54

ANSWERED PRAYER FOR DELIVERANCE FROM ADVERSARIES

To the Chief Musician. With stringed instruments.*a*
A Contemplation*b* of David when the Ziph′ītes
went and said to Saul, "Is David not hiding
with us?"

SAVE me, O God, by Your name,
  And vindicate me by Your
   strength.
2 Hear my prayer, O God;
  Give ear to the words of my
   mouth.
3 For strangers have risen up
   against me,
  And oppressors have sought after
   my life;
  They have not set God before
   them.   Sē′lah

4 Behold, God *is* my helper;
  The Lord *is* with those who
   uphold my life.
5 He will repay my enemies for
   their evil.
  Cut them off in Your truth.

6 I will freely sacrifice to You;
  I will praise Your name, O LORD,
   for *it is* good.
7 For He has delivered me out of all
   trouble;
  And my eye has seen *its desire*
   upon my enemies.

53:title *a*Hebrew *Maschil*   54:title *a*Hebrew
neginoth *b*Hebrew *Maschil*

PSALM 55

TRUST IN GOD CONCERNING THE
TREACHERY OF FRIENDS

To the Chief Musician. With stringed instruments.*a*
A Contemplation*b* of David.

G IVE ear to my prayer, O God,
And do not hide Yourself from my
supplication.
2 Attend to me, and hear me;
I am restless in my complaint,
and moan noisily,
3 Because of the voice of the
enemy,
Because of the oppression of the
wicked;
For they bring down trouble upon
me,
And in wrath they hate me.

4 My heart is severely pained
within me,
And the terrors of death have
fallen upon me.
5 Fearfulness and trembling have
come upon me,
And horror has overwhelmed
me.
6 So I said, "Oh, that I had wings
like a dove!
I would fly away and be at rest.
7 Indeed, I would wander far off,
And remain in the wilderness.
Sē′lah
8 I would hasten my escape
From the windy storm *and*
tempest."

9 Destroy, O Lord, *and* divide their
tongues,
For I have seen violence and
strife in the city.
10 Day and night they go around it
on its walls;
Iniquity and trouble *are* also in
the midst of it.
11 Destruction *is* in its midst;

Oppression and deceit do not
depart from its streets.

12 For *it is* not an enemy *who*
reproaches me;
Then I could bear *it.*
Nor *is it* one *who* hates me who
has exalted *himself* against me;
Then I could hide from him.
13 But *it was* you, a man my equal,
My companion and my
acquaintance.
14 We took sweet counsel together,
And walked to the house of God
in the throng.

15 Let death seize them;
Let them go down alive into hell,
For wickedness *is* in their
dwellings *and* among them.

16 As for me, I will call upon God,
And the LORD shall save me.
17 Evening and morning and at noon
I will pray, and cry aloud,
And He shall hear my voice.
18 He has redeemed my soul in
peace from the battle *that was*
against me,
For there were many against me.
19 God will hear, and afflict them,
Even He who abides from of old.
Sē′lah
Because they do not change,
Therefore they do not fear God.

20 He has put forth his hands
against those who were at
peace with him;
He has broken his covenant.
21 *The words* of his mouth were
smoother than butter,
But war *was* in his heart;
His words were softer than oil,
Yet they *were* drawn swords.

22 Cast your burden on the LORD,
And He shall sustain you;

55:title *a*Hebrew *neginoth*   *b*Hebrew *Maschil*

He shall never permit the
  righteous to be moved.

23 But You, O God, shall bring them
    down to the pit of destruction;
  Bloodthirsty and deceitful men
    shall not live out half their
    days;
  But I will trust in You.

PSALM 56

PRAYER FOR RELIEF FROM TORMENTORS

To the Chief Musician. Set to "The Silent Dove in
Distant Lands."a A Mich'tam of David when the
Phi·lis'tines captured him in Gath.

BE merciful to me, O God, for man
    would swallow me up;
  Fighting all day he oppresses
    me.
2 My enemies would hound *me* all
    day,
  For *there are* many who fight
    against me, O Most High.

3 Whenever I am afraid,
  I will trust in You.
4 In God (I will praise His word),
  In God I have put my trust;
  I will not fear.
  What can flesh do to me?

5 All day they twist my words;
  All their thoughts *are* against me
    for evil.
6 They gather together,
  They hide, they mark my steps,
  When they lie in wait for my life.
7 Shall they escape by iniquity?
  In anger cast down the peoples,
    O God!

8 You number my wanderings;
  Put my tears into Your bottle;
  Are they not in Your book?
9 When I cry out *to You,*
  Then my enemies will turn back;

This I know, because God *is* for
  me.
10 In God (I will praise *His* word),
  In the LORD (I will praise *His*
    word),
11 In God I have put my trust;
  I will not be afraid.
  What can man do to me?

Praises

Psalm 56:12, 13

I will praise God for delivering
me from death, for letting me
live with Him forever in heaven.
Do you praise God for saving
you? Do you praise Him for forgiving your sins? Do you praise
Him for letting you live with
Him forever?

---

12 Vows *made* to You *are binding*
    upon me, O God;
  I will render praises to You,
13 For You have delivered my soul
    from death.
  Have You not *kept* my feet from
    falling,
  That I may walk before God
  In the light of the living?

PSALM 57

PRAYER FOR SAFETY FROM ENEMIES

To the Chief Musician. Set to "Do Not Destroy."a
A Mich'tam of David when he fled from Saul into
the cave.

BE merciful to me, O God, be
    merciful to me!
  For my soul trusts in You;
  And in the shadow of Your wings
    I will make my refuge,
  Until *these* calamities have
    passed by.

56:title aHebrew *Jonath Elem Rechokim*
57:title aHebrew *Al Tashcheth*

2 I will cry out to God Most High,
   To God who performs *all things*
     for me.
3 He shall send from heaven and
     save me;
   He reproaches the one who would
     swallow me up.   Sē'lah
   God shall send forth His mercy
     and His truth.

4 My soul *is* among lions;
   I lie *among* the sons of men
   Who are set on fire,
   Whose teeth *are* spears and
     arrows,
   And their tongue a sharp sword.
5 Be exalted, O God, above the
     heavens;
   Let Your glory *be* above all the
     earth.

6 They have prepared a net for my
     steps;
   My soul is bowed down;
   They have dug a pit before me;
   Into the midst of it they
     themselves have fallen.   Sē'lah

7 My heart is steadfast, O God, my
     heart is steadfast;
   I will sing and give praise.
8 Awake, my glory!
   Awake, lute and harp!
   I will awaken the dawn.

9 I will praise You, O Lord, among
     the peoples;
   I will sing to You among the
     nations.
10 For Your mercy reaches unto the
     heavens,
   And Your truth unto the clouds.

11 Be exalted, O God, above the
     heavens;
   Let Your glory *be* above all the
     earth.

PSALM 58

THE JUST JUDGMENT OF THE WICKED

To the Chief Musician. Set to "Do Not Destroy."*a*
A Mich'tam of David.

DO you indeed speak
     righteousness, you silent ones?
   Do you judge uprightly, you sons
     of men?
2 No, in heart you work
     wickedness;
   You weigh out the violence of your
     hands in the earth.

3 The wicked are estranged from
     the womb;
   They go astray as soon as they
     are born, speaking lies.
4 Their poison *is* like the poison of a
     serpent;
   They are like the deaf cobra *that*
     stops its ear,
5 Which will not heed the voice of
     charmers,
   Charming ever so skillfully.

6 Break their teeth in their mouth,
     O God!
   Break out the fangs of the young
     lions, O LORD!
7 Let them flow away as waters
     which run continually;
   When he bends *his bow,*
   Let his arrows be as if cut in
     pieces.
8 *Let them be* like a snail which
     melts away as it goes,
   Like a stillborn child of a woman,
     that they may not see the sun.

9 Before your pots can feel *the
     burning* thorns,
   He shall take them away as with
     a whirlwind,
   As in His living and burning
     wrath.

58:title *a*Hebrew *Al Tashcheth*

10 The righteous shall rejoice when
he sees the vengeance;
He shall wash his feet in the
blood of the wicked,

11 So that men will say,
"Surely *there is* a reward for the
righteous;
Surely He is God who judges in
the earth."

PSALM 59

THE ASSURED JUDGMENT OF THE
WICKED

To the Chief Musician. Set to "Do Not Destroy."*a*
A Mich'tam of David when Saul sent men, and they
watched the house in order to kill him.

DELIVER me from my enemies, O
my God;
Defend me from those who rise up
against me.

2 Deliver me from the workers of
iniquity,
And save me from bloodthirsty
men.

3 For look, they lie in wait for my
life;
The mighty gather against me,
Not *for* my transgression nor *for*
my sin, O LORD.

4 They run and prepare themselves
through no fault *of mine.*

Awake to help me, and behold!

5 You therefore, O LORD God of
hosts, the God of Israel,
Awake to punish all the nations;
Do not be merciful to any wicked
transgressors.   Sē'lah

6 At evening they return,
They growl like a dog,
And go all around the city.

7 Indeed, they belch with their
mouth;

Swords *are* in their lips;
For *they say,* "Who hears?"

8 But You, O LORD, shall laugh at
them;
You shall have all the nations in
derision.

9 I will wait for You, O You his
Strength;*a*
For God *is* my defense.

10 My God of mercy*a* shall come to
meet me;
God shall let me see *my desire* on
my enemies.

11 Do not slay them, lest my people
forget;
Scatter them by Your power,
And bring them down,
O Lord our shield.

12 *For* the sin of their mouth *and*
the words of their lips,
Let them even be taken in their
pride,
And for the cursing and lying
which they speak.

13 Consume *them* in wrath, consume
them,
That they *may* not *be;*
And let them know that God rules
in Jacob
To the ends of the earth.   Sē'lah

14 And at evening they return,
They growl like a dog,
And go all around the city.

15 They wander up and down for
food,
And howl*a* if they are not
satisfied.

59:title *a*Hebrew *Al Tashcheth*   59:9 *a*Following
Masoretic Text and Syriac; some Hebrew manuscripts, Septuagint, Targum, and Vulgate read *my*
Strength.   59:10 *a*Following Qere; some Hebrew
manuscripts, Septuagint, and Vulgate read *My*
God, His mercy; Kethib, some Hebrew manuscripts
and Targum read *O God, my mercy;* Syriac reads
O God, Your mercy.   59:15 *a*Following Septuagint and Vulgate; Masoretic Text, Syriac, and Targum read *spend the night.*

16 But I will sing of Your power;
   Yes, I will sing aloud of Your
      mercy in the morning;
   For You have been my defense
   And refuge in the day of my
      trouble.
17 To You, O my Strength, I will sing
      praises;
   For God is my defense,
   My God of mercy.

PSALM 60

URGENT PRAYER FOR THE RESTORED FAVOR OF GOD

To the Chief Musician. Set to "Lily of the
Testimony."ᵃ A Mich'tam of David.
For teaching. When he fought against
Mes·o·po·tā'mi·a and Syria of Zō'bah,
and Jō'ab returned and killed twelve thousand
Ē'dom-ites in the Valley of Salt.

O GOD, You have cast us off;
   You have broken us down;
   You have been displeased;
   Oh, restore us again!
2 You have made the earth
      tremble;
   You have broken it;
   Heal its breaches, for it is
      shaking.
3 You have shown Your people hard
      things;
   You have made us drink the wine
      of confusion.

4 You have given a banner to those
      who fear You,
   That it may be displayed because
      of the truth.   Sē'lah
5 That Your beloved may be
      delivered,
   Save with Your right hand, and
      hear me.

6 God has spoken in His holiness:
   "I will rejoice;
   I will divide Shē'chem

And measure out the Valley of
   Suc'coth.
7 Gil'ē·ad is Mine, and Ma·nas'seh
      is Mine;
   Ē'phra·im also is the helmet for
      My head;
   Judah is My lawgiver.
8 Mō'ab is My washpot;
   Over Ē'dom I will cast My shoe;
   Phi·lis'ti·a, shout in triumph
      because of Me."

9 Who will bring me to the strong
      city?
   Who will lead me to Ē'dom?
10 Is it not You, O God, who cast us
      off?
   And You, O God, who did not go
      out with our armies?
11 Give us help from trouble,
   For the help of man is useless.
12 Through God we will do valiantly,
   For it is He who shall tread down
      our enemies.ᵃ

PSALM 61

ASSURANCE OF GOD'S ETERNAL PROTECTION

To the Chief Musician. On a stringed instrument.ᵃ
A Psalm of David.

HEAR my cry, O God;
   Attend to my prayer.
2 From the end of the earth I will
      cry to You,
   When my heart is overwhelmed;
   Lead me to the rock that is higher
      than I.

3 For You have been a shelter for
      me,
   A strong tower from the enemy.
4 I will abide in Your tabernacle
      forever;

60:title ᵃHebrew Shushan Eduth
60:12 ᵃCompare verses 5–12 with 108:6–13
61:title ᵃHebrew neginah

I will trust in the shelter of Your
   wings.   Sē'lah

5 For You, O God, have heard my
   vows;
   You have given *me* the heritage of
     those who fear Your name.
6 You will prolong the king's life,
   His years as many generations.
7 He shall abide before God forever.
   Oh, prepare mercy and truth,
   which may preserve him!

8 So I will sing praise to Your name
   forever,
   That I may daily perform my
     vows.

PSALM 62

A CALM RESOLVE TO WAIT FOR THE
SALVATION OF GOD

To the Chief Musician. To Je·dū'thun.
A Psalm of David.

TRULY my soul silently *waits* for
   God;
   From Him *comes* my salvation.
2 He only *is* my rock and my
     salvation;
   He is my defense;
   I shall not be greatly moved.

3 How long will you attack a man?
   You shall be slain, all of you,
   Like a leaning wall and a
     tottering fence.
4 They only consult to cast *him*
     down from his high position;
   They delight in lies;
   They bless with their mouth,
   But they curse inwardly.   Sē'lah

5 My soul, wait silently for God
     alone,
   For my expectation *is* from Him.
6 He only *is* my rock and my
     salvation;
   He is my defense;

I shall not be moved.
7 In God *is* my salvation and my
     glory;
   The rock of my strength,
   And my refuge, *is* in God.

8 Trust in Him at all times, you
     people;
   Pour out your heart before Him;
   God *is* a refuge for us.   Sē'lah

9 Surely men of low degree *are* a
     vapor,
   Men of high degree *are* a lie;
   If they are weighed on the scales,
   They *are* altogether *lighter* than
     vapor.
10 Do not trust in oppression,
   Nor vainly hope in robbery;
   If riches increase,
   Do not set *your* heart *on them.*

11 God has spoken once,
   Twice I have heard this:
   That power *belongs* to God.
12 Also to You, O Lord, *belongs*
     mercy;
   For You render to each one
     according to his work.

PSALM 63

JOY IN THE FELLOWSHIP OF GOD

A Psalm of David when he was in the wilderness of
Judah.

O GOD, You *are* my God;
   Early will I seek You;
   My soul thirsts for You;
   My flesh longs for You
   In a dry and thirsty land
   Where there is no water.
2 So I have looked for You in the
     sanctuary,
   To see Your power and Your glory.

3 Because Your lovingkindness *is*
     better than life,
   My lips shall praise You.

THE BEST OF PLANS SOMETIMES CRASH Psalm 62:8

You planned a special picnic for weeks. Your plans always pictured a sunny day. But the rain poured on the day of the picnic. You planned a party. Every detail was just right. But something kept all your friends from coming. The best of plans sometimes crash. So what should I do when that happens?

1. Have some of your plans gone wrong? What happened? What did you do then?
2. When bad things happen, what do you say? What should you say?
3. Read Psalm 62:8. When should we trust in the Lord? Should we trust in Him during good times only? How much should we trust Him in bad times?

For more on *What Should I Do?* turn to page 870
For more on *God's Care* turn to page 899

4 Thus I will bless You while I live;
I will lift up my hands in Your
name.
5 My soul shall be satisfied as with
marrow and fatness,
And my mouth shall praise You
with joyful lips.

6 When I remember You on my bed,
I meditate on You in the *night*
watches.
7 Because You have been my help,
Therefore in the shadow of Your
wings I will rejoice.
8 My soul follows close behind
You;
Your right hand upholds me.

9 But those *who* seek my life, to
destroy *it,*
Shall go into the lower parts of
the earth.
10 They shall fall by the sword;
They shall be a portion for
jackals.

11 But the king shall rejoice in
God;
Everyone who swears by Him
shall glory;
But the mouth of those who speak
lies shall be stopped.

PSALM 64

OPPRESSED BY THE WICKED BUT
REJOICING IN THE LORD

To the Chief Musician. A Psalm of David.

HEAR my voice, O God, in my
meditation;
Preserve my life from fear of the
enemy.
2 Hide me from the secret plots of
the wicked,
From the rebellion of the workers
of iniquity,

3 Who sharpen their tongue like a
sword,
And bend *their bows to shoot* their
arrows—bitter words,
4 That they may shoot in secret at
the blameless;
Suddenly they shoot at him and
do not fear.

5 They encourage themselves *in* an
evil matter;
They talk of laying snares
secretly;
They say, "Who will see them?"
6 They devise iniquities:
"We have perfected a shrewd
scheme."
Both the inward thought and the
heart of man are deep.

7 But God shall shoot at them *with*
an arrow;
Suddenly they shall be wounded.
8 So He will make them stumble
over their own tongue;
All who see them shall flee
away.
9 All men shall fear,
And shall declare the work of
God;
For they shall wisely consider His
doing.

10 The righteous shall be glad in the
LORD, and trust in Him.
And all the upright in heart shall
glory.

PSALM 65

PRAISE TO GOD FOR HIS SALVATION AND
PROVIDENCE

To the Chief Musician. A Psalm of David. A Song.

PRAISE is awaiting You, O God, in
Zion;

And to You the vow shall be performed.

2 O You who hear prayer,
To You all flesh will come.

3 Iniquities prevail against me;
As for our transgressions,
You will provide atonement for them.

4 Blessed *is the man* You choose,
And cause to approach *You,*
That he may dwell in Your courts.
We shall be satisfied with the goodness of Your house,
Of Your holy temple.

5 *By* awesome deeds in righteousness You will answer us,
O God of our salvation,
You who are the confidence of all the ends of the earth,
And of the far-off seas;

6 Who established the mountains by His strength,
Being clothed with power;

7 You who still the noise of the seas,
The noise of their waves,
And the tumult of the peoples.

8 They also who dwell in the farthest parts are afraid of Your signs;
You make the outgoings of the morning and evening rejoice.

9 You visit the earth and water it,
You greatly enrich it;
The river of God is full of water;
You provide their grain,
For so You have prepared it.

10 You water its ridges abundantly,
You settle its furrows;
You make it soft with showers,
You bless its growth.

11 You crown the year with Your goodness,

And Your paths drip *with* abundance.

12 They drop *on* the pastures of the wilderness,
And the little hills rejoice on every side.

13 The pastures are clothed with flocks;
The valleys also are covered with grain;
They shout for joy, they also sing.

PSALM 66

PRAISE TO GOD FOR HIS AWESOME WORKS

To the Chief Musician. A Song. A Psalm.

MAKE a joyful shout to God, all the earth!

2 Sing out the honor of His name;
Make His praise glorious.

3 Say to God,
"How awesome are Your works!
Through the greatness of Your power
Your enemies shall submit themselves to You.

4 All the earth shall worship You
And sing praises to You;
They shall sing praises *to* Your name."   Sē′lah

5 Come and see the works of God;
He is awesome *in His* doing toward the sons of men.

6 He turned the sea into dry *land;*
They went through the river on foot.
There we will rejoice in Him.

7 He rules by His power forever;
His eyes observe the nations;
Do not let the rebellious exalt themselves.   Sē′lah

SOMETHING GOOD FROM MY TROUBLE Psalm 66:10–12

Oh, no! Tim dropped his ice cream. "What can I do?" Tim asks. "I can't pick it up and eat it. But I wish someone could have it."

1. How did Tim's wish come true? Who can eat Tim's ice cream now?
2. What was bad about Tim's trouble? But what good came from Tim's trouble?
3. Will you remember this the next time you have trouble? Ask God to help something good come from it. Do you think He will?

For more on *What Should I Do?* turn to page 883
For more on *Facing Trials* turn to page 917

8 Oh, bless our God, you peoples!
  And make the voice of His praise
    to be heard,
9 Who keeps our soul among the
    living,
  And does not allow our feet to be
    moved.
10 For You, O God, have tested us;
  You have refined us as silver is
    refined.
11 You brought us into the net;
  You laid affliction on our backs.
12 You have caused men to ride over
    our heads;
  We went through fire and through
    water;
  But You brought us out to rich
    fulfillment.

13 I will go into Your house with
    burnt offerings;
  I will pay You my vows,
14 Which my lips have uttered
  And my mouth has spoken when I
    was in trouble.
15 I will offer You burnt sacrifices of
    fat animals,
  With the sweet aroma of rams;
  I will offer bulls with goats.
                                    Sē′lah

16 Come *and* hear, all you who fear
    God,
  And I will declare what He has
    done for my soul.
17 I cried to Him with my mouth,
  And He was extolled with my
    tongue.
18 If I regard iniquity in my heart,
  The Lord will not hear.
19 *But* certainly God has heard
    me;
  He has attended to the voice of
    my prayer.

20 Blessed *be* God,
  Who has not turned away my
    prayer,
  Nor His mercy from me!

PSALM 67

AN INVOCATION AND A DOXOLOGY

To the Chief Musician. On stringed instruments.*a*
A Psalm. A Song.

GOD be merciful to us and bless
    us,
  And cause His face to shine upon
    us,   Sē′lah
2 That Your way may be known on
    earth,
  Your salvation among all nations.

3 Let the peoples praise You,
    O God;
  Let all the peoples praise You.
4 Oh, let the nations be glad and
    sing for joy!
  For You shall judge the people
    righteously,
  And govern the nations on earth.
                                    Sē′lah

5 Let the peoples praise You,
    O God;
  Let all the peoples praise You.
6 *Then* the earth shall yield her
    increase;
  God, our own God, shall bless
    us.
7 God shall bless us,
  And all the ends of the earth shall
    fear Him.

PSALM 68

THE GLORY OF GOD IN HIS GOODNESS
TO ISRAEL

To the Chief Musician. A Psalm of David. A Song.

LET God arise,
    Let His enemies be scattered;
    Let those also who hate Him flee
      before Him.

67:title *a*Hebrew *neginoth*

2 As smoke is driven away,
So drive *them* away;
As wax melts before the fire,
So let the wicked perish at the
presence of God.
3 But let the righteous be glad;
Let them rejoice before God;
Yes, let them rejoice exceedingly.

4 Sing to God, sing praises to His
name;
Extol Him who rides on the
clouds,*a*
By His name YAH,
And rejoice before Him.

5 A father of the fatherless, a
defender of widows,
Is God in His holy habitation.
6 God sets the solitary in families;
He brings out those who are
bound into prosperity;
But the rebellious dwell in a dry
land.

7 O God, when You went out before
Your people,
When You marched through the
wilderness,   Sē′lah
8 The earth shook;
The heavens also dropped *rain* at
the presence of God;
Sinai itself *was moved* at the
presence of God, the God of
Israel.
9 You, O God, sent a plentiful rain,
Whereby You confirmed Your
inheritance,
When it was weary.
10 Your congregation dwelt in it;
You, O God, provided from Your
goodness for the poor.

11 The Lord gave the word;
Great *was* the company of those
who proclaimed *it:*
12 "Kings of armies flee, they flee,
And she who remains at home
divides the spoil.

13 Though you lie down among the
sheepfolds,
You will be like the wings of a
dove covered with silver,
And her feathers with yellow
gold."
14 When the Almighty scattered
kings in it,
It was *white* as snow in Zal′mon.

15 A mountain of God *is* the
mountain of Bā′shan;
A mountain *of many* peaks *is* the
mountain of Bā′shan.
16 Why do you fume with envy, you
mountains of *many* peaks?
This is the mountain *which* God
desires to dwell in;
Yes, the LORD will dwell *in it*
forever.

17 The chariots of God *are* twenty
thousand,
Even thousands of thousands;
The Lord is among them *as in*
Sinai, in the Holy *Place.*
18 You have ascended on high,
You have led captivity captive;
You have received gifts among
men,
Even *from* the rebellious,
That the LORD God might dwell
there.

19 Blessed *be* the Lord,
Who daily loads us *with benefits,*
The God of our salvation!
Sē′lah
20 Our God *is* the God of salvation;
And to GOD the Lord *belong*
escapes from death.

21 But God will wound the head of
His enemies,
The hairy scalp of the one who
still goes on in his trespasses.

68:4 *a*Masoretic Text reads *deserts;* Targum reads
heavens (compare verse 34 and Isaiah 19:1).

22 The Lord said, "I will bring back
from Bā′shan,
I will bring *them* back from the
depths of the sea,
23 That your foot may crush *them*[a]
in blood,
And the tongues of your dogs *may
have* their portion from *your*
enemies."

24 They have seen Your procession,
O God,
The procession of my God, my
King, into the sanctuary.
25 The singers went before, the
players on instruments
followed after;
Among *them were* the maidens
playing timbrels.
26 Bless God in the congregations,
The Lord, from the fountain of
Israel.
27 There *is* little Benjamin, their
leader,
The princes of Judah *and* their
company,
The princes of Zeb′ū·lun *and* the
princes of Naph′ta·lī.

28 Your God has commanded[a] your
strength;
Strengthen, O God, what You
have done for us.
29 Because of Your temple at
Jerusalem,
Kings will bring presents to You.
30 Rebuke the beasts of the reeds,
The herd of bulls with the calves
of the peoples,
Till everyone submits himself
with pieces of silver.
Scatter the peoples *who* delight in
war.
31 Envoys will come out of Egypt;
Ethiopia will quickly stretch out
her hands to God.

32 Sing to God, you kingdoms of the
earth;

Oh, sing praises to the Lord,
                              Sē′lah
33 To Him who rides on the heaven
of heavens, *which were* of old!
Indeed, He sends out His voice, a
mighty voice.
34 Ascribe strength to God;
His excellence *is* over Israel,
And His strength *is* in the
clouds.
35 O God, *You are* more awesome
than Your holy places.
The God of Israel *is* He who gives
strength and power to *His*
people.

Blessed *be* God!

PSALM 69

An Urgent Plea for Help in Trouble

To the Chief Musician. Set to "The Lilies."[a]
A Psalm of David.

Save me, O God!
For the waters have come up to
my neck.
2 I sink in deep mire,
Where *there is* no standing;
I have come into deep waters,
Where the floods overflow me.
3 I am weary with my crying;
My throat is dry;
My eyes fail while I wait for my
God.

4 Those who hate me without a
cause
Are more than the hairs of my
head;
They are mighty who would
destroy me,
Being my enemies wrongfully;

68:23 [a]Septuagint, Syriac, Targum, and Vulgate
read *you may dip your foot.*   68:28 [a]Septuagint,
Syriac, Targum, and Vulgate read *Command, O
God.*   69:title [a]Hebrew *Shoshannim*

Though I have stolen nothing,
I *still* must restore *it*.

5 O God, You know my foolishness;
And my sins are not hidden from
You.
6 Let not those who wait for You,
O Lord GOD of hosts, be
ashamed because of me;
Let not those who seek You be
confounded because of me,
O God of Israel.
7 Because for Your sake I have
borne reproach;
Shame has covered my face.
8 I have become a stranger to my
brothers,
And an alien to my mother's
children;
9 Because zeal for Your house has
eaten me up,
And the reproaches of those who
reproach You have fallen on me.
10 When I wept *and chastened* my
soul with fasting,
That became my reproach.
11 I also made sackcloth my
garment;
I became a byword to them.
12 Those who sit in the gate speak
against me,
And I *am* the song of the
drunkards.

13 But as for me, my prayer *is* to
You,
O LORD, *in* the acceptable time;
O God, in the multitude of Your
mercy,
Hear me in the truth of Your
salvation.
14 Deliver me out of the mire,
And let me not sink;
Let me be delivered from those
who hate me,
And out of the deep waters.
15 Let not the floodwater overflow
me,
Nor let the deep swallow me up;

And let not the pit shut its mouth
on me.

16 Hear me, O LORD, for Your
lovingkindness *is* good;
Turn to me according to the
multitude of Your tender
mercies.
17 And do not hide Your face from
Your servant,
For I am in trouble;
Hear me speedily.
18 Draw near to my soul, *and*
redeem it;
Deliver me because of my
enemies.

19 You know my reproach, my
shame, and my dishonor;
My adversaries *are* all before You.
20 Reproach has broken my heart,
And I am full of heaviness;
I looked *for someone* to take pity,
but *there was* none;
And for comforters, but I found
none.
21 They also gave me gall for my
food,
And for my thirst they gave me
vinegar to drink.

22 Let their table become a snare
before them,
And their well-being a trap.
23 Let their eyes be darkened, so
that they do not see;
And make their loins shake
continually.
24 Pour out Your indignation upon
them,
And let Your wrathful anger take
hold of them.
25 Let their dwelling place be
desolate;
Let no one live in their tents.
26 For they persecute the *ones* You
have struck,
And talk of the grief of those You
have wounded.
27 Add iniquity to their iniquity,

And let them not come into Your
 righteousness.

28 Let them be blotted out of the
 book of the living,
 And not be written with the
 righteous.

29 But I *am* poor and sorrowful;
 Let Your salvation, O God, set me
 up on high.

30 I will praise the name of God with
 a song,
 And will magnify Him with
 thanksgiving.

31 *This* also shall please the LORD
 better than an ox *or* bull,
 Which has horns and hooves.

32 The humble shall see *this and* be
 glad;
 And you who seek God, your
 hearts shall live.

33 For the LORD hears the poor,
 And does not despise His
 prisoners.

34 Let heaven and earth praise Him,
 The seas and everything that
 moves in them.

35 For God will save Zion
 And build the cities of Judah,
 That they may dwell there and
 possess it.

36 Also, the descendants of His
 servants shall inherit it,
 And those who love His name
 shall dwell in it.

PSALM 70

PRAYER FOR RELIEF FROM ADVERSARIES

*To the Chief Musician. A Psalm of David. To bring
to remembrance.*

MAKE *haste,* O God, to deliver me!
 Make haste to help me, O LORD!

2 Let them be ashamed and
 confounded
Who seek my life;
 Let them be turned back[a] and
 confused
Who desire my hurt.

3 Let them be turned back because
 of their shame,
 Who say, "Aha, aha!"

4 Let all those who seek You rejoice
 and be glad in You;
 And let those who love Your
 salvation say continually,
"Let God be magnified!"

5 But I *am* poor and needy;
 Make haste to me, O God!
 You *are* my help and my
 deliverer;
 O LORD, do not delay.

PSALM 71

GOD THE ROCK OF SALVATION

IN You, O LORD, I put my trust;
 Let me never be put to shame.

2 Deliver me in Your righteousness,
 and cause me to escape;
 Incline Your ear to me, and save
 me.

3 Be my strong refuge,
 To which I may resort
 continually;
 You have given the
 commandment to save me,
 For You *are* my rock and my
 fortress.

4 Deliver me, O my God, out of the
 hand of the wicked,
 Out of the hand of the
 unrighteous and cruel man.

5 For You are my hope, O Lord
 GOD;
 You are my trust from my youth.

70:2 [a]Following Masoretic Text, Septuagint, Targum, and Vulgate; some Hebrew manuscripts and Syriac read *be appalled* (compare 40:15).

6 By You I have been upheld from
   birth;
   You are He who took me out of my
     mother's womb.
   My praise *shall be* continually of
     You.

7 I have become as a wonder to
     many,
   But You *are* my strong refuge.

▪ *Praises* ▪

Psalm 71:8

Is your mouth filled with praise
for God? Or do you find some
place for dirty words? Is your
mouth filled with praise for
God? Or do you let yourself say
mean things to a friend? Is your
mouth filled with praise for
God? Or do you say something to
hurt your parents? Fill your
mouth with words of praise.

---

8 Let my mouth be filled *with* Your
     praise
   And with Your glory all the day.

9 Do not cast me off in the time of
     old age;
   Do not forsake me when my
     strength fails.
10 For my enemies speak against
     me;
   And those who lie in wait for my
     life take counsel together,
11 Saying, "God has forsaken him;
   Pursue and take him, for *there is*
     none to deliver *him.*"

12 O God, do not be far from me;
   O my God, make haste to help
     me!
13 Let them be confounded *and*
     consumed

Who are adversaries of my life;
   Let them be covered *with*
     reproach and dishonor
   Who seek my hurt.

▪ *Praises* ▪

Psalm 71:14

I will praise You more and more.
Do you praise God more today
than ever before? Or are you
praising Him less than before?
The Psalmist said he praised
God more and more. Each day
he praised God more than the
day before. Why? Each day we
praise Him, we realize even
more how much He has done for
us.

---

14 But I will hope continually,
   And will praise You yet more and
     more.
15 My mouth shall tell of Your
     righteousness
   And Your salvation all the day,
   For I do not know *their* limits.
16 I will go in the strength of the
     Lord GOD;
   I will make mention of Your
     righteousness, of Yours only.

17 O God, You have taught me from
     my youth;
   And to this *day* I declare Your
     wondrous works.
18 Now also when *I am* old and
     grayheaded,
   O God, do not forsake me,
   Until I declare Your strength to
     this generation,
   Your power to everyone *who* is to
     come.

19 Also Your righteousness, O God,
     is very high,
   You who have done great things;
   O God, who *is* like You?

20 *You,* who have shown me great
   and severe troubles,
   Shall revive me again,
   And bring me up again from the
   depths of the earth.
21 You shall increase my greatness,
   And comfort me on every side.

22 Also with the lute I will praise
   You—
   And Your faithfulness, O my
   God!
   To You I will sing with the harp,
   O Holy One of Israel.
23 My lips shall greatly rejoice when
   I sing to You,
   And my soul, which You have
   redeemed.
24 My tongue also shall talk of Your
   righteousness all the day long;
   For they are confounded,
   For they are brought to shame
   Who seek my hurt.

PSALM 72

GLORY AND UNIVERSALITY OF THE
MESSIAH'S REIGN

A Psalm of Solomon.

GIVE the king Your judgments,
   O God,
   And Your righteousness to the
   king's Son.
2 He will judge Your people with
   righteousness,
   And Your poor with justice.
3 The mountains will bring peace to
   the people,
   And the little hills, by
   righteousness.
4 He will bring justice to the poor of
   the people;
   He will save the children of the
   needy,
   And will break in pieces the
   oppressor.

5 They shall fear You*a*
   As long as the sun and moon
   endure,
   Throughout all generations.
6 He shall come down like rain
   upon the grass before mowing,
   Like showers *that* water the
   earth.
7 In His days the righteous shall
   flourish,
   And abundance of peace,
   Until the moon is no more.

8 He shall have dominion also from
   sea to sea,
   And from the River to the ends of
   the earth.
9 Those who dwell in the
   wilderness will bow before
   Him,
   And His enemies will lick the
   dust.
10 The kings of Tar′shish and of the
   isles
   Will bring presents;
   The kings of Shē′ba and Sē′ba
   Will offer gifts.
11 Yes, all kings shall fall down
   before Him;
   All nations shall serve Him.

12 For He will deliver the needy
   when he cries,
   The poor also, and *him* who has
   no helper.
13 He will spare the poor and needy,
   And will save the souls of the
   needy.
14 He will redeem their life from
   oppression and violence;
   And precious shall be their blood
   in His sight.

15 And He shall live;
   And the gold of Shē′ba will be
   given to Him;

72:5 *a*Following Masoretic Text and Targum; Septuagint and Vulgate read *They shall continue.*

Prayer also will be made for Him
continually,
And daily He shall be praised.

16 There will be an abundance of
grain in the earth,
On the top of the mountains;
Its fruit shall wave like Lebanon;
And *those* of the city shall flourish
like grass of the earth.

17 His name shall endure forever;
His name shall continue as long
as the sun.
And *men* shall be blessed in Him;
All nations shall call Him blessed.

18 Blessed *be* the LORD God, the God
of Israel,
Who only does wondrous things!
19 And blessed *be* His glorious name
forever!
And let the whole earth be filled
with His glory.
Amen and Amen.

20 The prayers of David the son of
Jesse are ended.

BOOK THREE

Psalms 73—89

PSALM 73

THE TRAGEDY OF THE WICKED, AND THE
BLESSEDNESS OF TRUST IN GOD

A Psalm of Ā'saph.

TRULY God *is* good to Israel,
To such as are pure in heart.
2 But as for me, my feet had almost
stumbled;
My steps had nearly slipped.
3 For I *was* envious of the boastful,
When I saw the prosperity of the
wicked.

4 For *there are* no pangs in their
death,
But their strength *is* firm.
5 They *are* not in trouble *as other*
men,
Nor are they plagued like *other*
men.
6 Therefore pride serves as their
necklace;
Violence covers them *like* a
garment.
7 Their eyes bulge*a* with
abundance;
They have more than heart could
wish.
8 They scoff and speak wickedly
concerning oppression;
They speak loftily.
9 They set their mouth against the
heavens,
And their tongue walks through
the earth.

10 Therefore his people return
here,
And waters of a full *cup* are
drained by them.
11 And they say, "How does God
know?
And is there knowledge in the
Most High?"
12 Behold, these *are* the ungodly,
Who are always at ease;
They increase *in* riches.
13 Surely I have cleansed my heart
in vain,
And washed my hands in
innocence.
14 For all day long I have been
plagued,
And chastened every morning.

15 If I had said, "I will speak
thus,"
Behold, I would have been untrue
to the generation of Your
children.

73:7 *a*Targum reads *face bulges;* Septuagint, Syriac, and Vulgate read *iniquity bulges.*

16 When I thought *how* to
   understand this,
   It *was* too painful for me—
17 Until I went into the sanctuary of
   God;
   Then I understood their end.

18 Surely You set them in slippery
   places;
   You cast them down to
   destruction.
19 Oh, how they are *brought* to
   desolation, as in a moment!
   They are utterly consumed with
   terrors.
20 As a dream when *one* awakes,
   So, Lord, when You awake,
   You shall despise their image.

21 Thus my heart was grieved,
   And I was vexed in my mind.
22 I *was* so foolish and ignorant;
   I was *like* a beast before You.
23 Nevertheless I *am* continually
   with You;
   You hold *me* by my right hand.
24 You will guide me with Your
   counsel,
   And afterward receive me *to*
   glory.

25 Whom have I in heaven *but*
   You?
   And *there is* none upon earth *that*
   I desire besides You.
26 My flesh and my heart fail;
   But God *is* the strength of my
   heart and my portion forever.

27 For indeed, those who are far
   from You shall perish;
   You have destroyed all those who
   desert You for harlotry.
28 But *it is* good for me to draw near
   to God;
   I have put my trust in the Lord
   GOD,
   That I may declare all Your
   works.

PSALM 74

A PLEA FOR RELIEF FROM OPPRESSORS

A Contemplation[a] of Ā′saph.

O GOD, why have You cast *us* off
   forever?
   Why does Your anger smoke
   against the sheep of Your
   pasture?
2 Remember Your congregation,
   which You have purchased of
   old,
   The tribe of Your inheritance,
   which You have redeemed—
   This Mount Zion where You have
   dwelt.
3 Lift up Your feet to the perpetual
   desolations.
   The enemy has damaged
   everything in the sanctuary.
4 Your enemies roar in the midst of
   Your meeting place;
   They set up their banners *for*
   signs.
5 They seem like men who lift up
   Axes among the thick trees.
6 And now they break down its
   carved work, all at once,
   With axes and hammers.
7 They have set fire to Your
   sanctuary;
   They have defiled the dwelling
   place of Your name to the
   ground.
8 They said in their hearts,
   "Let us destroy them altogether."
   They have burned up all the
   meeting places of God in the
   land.
9 We do not see our signs;
   There is no longer any
   prophet;
   Nor *is there* any among us who
   knows how long.

74:title [a]Hebrew *Maschil*

10 O God, how long will the
    adversary reproach?
  Will the enemy blaspheme Your
    name forever?
11 Why do You withdraw Your hand,
    even Your right hand?
  Take it out of Your bosom and
    destroy *them*.
12 For God *is* my King from of old,
  Working salvation in the midst of
    the earth.
13 You divided the sea by Your
    strength;
  You broke the heads of the sea
    serpents in the waters.
14 You broke the heads of
    Le·vī′a·than in pieces,
  And gave him *as* food to the
    people inhabiting the
    wilderness.
15 You broke open the fountain and
    the flood;
  You dried up mighty rivers.
16 The day *is* Yours, the night also *is*
    Yours;
  You have prepared the light and
    the sun.
17 You have set all the borders of the
    earth;
  You have made summer and
    winter.

18 Remember this, *that* the enemy
    has reproached, O Lord,
  And *that* a foolish people has
    blasphemed Your name.
19 Oh, do not deliver the life of
    Your turtledove to the wild
    beast!
  Do not forget the life of Your poor
    forever.
20 Have respect to the covenant;
  For the dark places of the earth
    are full of the haunts of
    cruelty.
21 Oh, do not let the oppressed
    return ashamed!
  Let the poor and needy praise
    Your name.

22 Arise, O God, plead Your own
    cause;
  Remember how the foolish man
    reproaches You daily.
23 Do not forget the voice of Your
    enemies;
  The tumult of those who rise up
    against You increases
    continually.

PSALM 75

Thanksgiving for God's Righteous Judgment

To the Chief Musician. Set to "Do Not Destroy."[a]
A Psalm of Ā′saph. A Song.

WE give thanks to You, O God, we
    give thanks!
  For Your wondrous works declare
    that Your name is near.

2 "When I choose the proper time,
    I will judge uprightly.
3 The earth and all its inhabitants
    are dissolved;
  I set up its pillars firmly.   Sē′lah

4 "I said to the boastful, 'Do not deal
    boastfully,'
  And to the wicked, 'Do not lift up
    the horn.
5 Do not lift up your horn on
    high;
  Do *not* speak with a stiff neck.' "

6 For exaltation *comes* neither from
    the east
  Nor from the west nor from the
    south.
7 But God *is* the Judge:
  He puts down one,
  And exalts another.
8 For in the hand of the Lord *there*
    is a cup,
  And the wine is red;

75:title *a*Hebrew *Al Tashcheth*

It is fully mixed, and He pours it
out;
Surely its dregs shall all the
wicked of the earth
Drain *and* drink down.

9 But I will declare forever,
I will sing praises to the God of
Jacob.

10 "All the horns of the wicked I will
also cut off,
But the horns of the righteous
shall be exalted."

PSALM 76

THE MAJESTY OF GOD IN JUDGMENT

To the Chief Musician. On stringed instruments.*a*
A Psalm of Ā′saph. A Song.

IN Judah God *is* known;
His name *is* great in Israel.
2 In Sā′lem*a* also is His tabernacle,
And His dwelling place in Zion.
3 There He broke the arrows of the
bow,
The shield and sword of battle.
Sē′lah

4 You *are* more glorious and
excellent
Than the mountains of prey.
5 The stouthearted were
plundered;
They have sunk into their sleep;
And none of the mighty men
have found the use of their
hands.
6 At Your rebuke, O God of Jacob,
Both the chariot and horse were
cast into a dead sleep.

7 You, Yourself, *are* to be feared;
And who may stand in Your
presence
When once You are angry?

8 You caused judgment to be heard
from heaven;
The earth feared and was still,
9 When God arose to judgment,
To deliver all the oppressed of the
earth. Sē′lah

10 Surely the wrath of man shall
praise You;
With the remainder of wrath You
shall gird Yourself.

11 Make vows to the LORD your God,
and pay *them;*
Let all who are around Him bring
presents to Him who ought to
be feared.
12 He shall cut off the spirit of
princes;
He is awesome to the kings of the
earth.

PSALM 77

THE CONSOLING MEMORY OF GOD'S REDEMPTIVE WORKS

To the Chief Musician. To Je·dū′thun.
A Psalm of Ā′saph.

I CRIED out to God with my voice—
To God with my voice;
And He gave ear to me.
2 In the day of my trouble I sought
the Lord;
My hand was stretched out in the
night without ceasing;
My soul refused to be comforted.
3 I remembered God, and was
troubled;
I complained, and my spirit was
overwhelmed. Sē′lah

4 You hold my eyelids *open;*
I am so troubled that I cannot
speak.

76:title *a*Hebrew *neginoth*   76:2 *a*That is, Jerusalem

5 I have considered the days of old,
  The years of ancient times.
6 I call to remembrance my song in
    the night;
  I meditate within my heart,
  And my spirit makes diligent
    search.

7 Will the Lord cast off forever?
  And will He be favorable no
    more?
8 Has His mercy ceased forever?
  Has *His* promise failed
    forevermore?
9 Has God forgotten to be gracious?
  Has He in anger shut up His
    tender mercies?   Sē′lah

10 And I said, "This *is* my anguish;
   But I will remember the years of
     the right hand of the Most
     High."
11 I will remember the works of the
     LORD;
   Surely I will remember Your
     wonders of old.
12 I will also meditate on all Your
     work,
   And talk of Your deeds.
13 Your way, O God, *is* in the
     sanctuary;
   Who *is* so great a God as *our*
     God?
14 You *are* the God who does
     wonders;
   You have declared Your strength
     among the peoples.
15 You have with *Your* arm
     redeemed Your people,
   The sons of Jacob and Joseph.
                                Sē′lah

16 The waters saw You, O God;
   The waters saw You, they were
     afraid;
   The depths also trembled.
17 The clouds poured out water;
   The skies sent out a sound;
   Your arrows also flashed about.

18 The voice of Your thunder *was* in
     the whirlwind;
   The lightnings lit up the world;
   The earth trembled and shook.
19 Your way *was* in the sea,
   Your path in the great waters,
   And Your footsteps were not
     known.
20 You led Your people like a flock
   By the hand of Moses and Aaron.

PSALM 78

GOD'S KINDNESS TO REBELLIOUS ISRAEL

A Contemplation[a] of Ā′saph.

GIVE ear, O my people, *to* my law;
  Incline your ears to the words of
    my mouth.
2 I will open my mouth in a
    parable;
  I will utter dark sayings of old,
3 Which we have heard and known,
  And our fathers have told us.
4 We will not hide *them* from their
    children,
  Telling to the generation to come
    the praises of the LORD,
  And His strength and His
    wonderful works that He has
    done.

5 For He established a testimony in
    Jacob,
  And appointed a law in Israel,
  Which He commanded our
    fathers,
  That they should make them
    known to their children;
6 That the generation to come
    might know *them,*
  The children *who* would be born,
  That they may arise and declare
    them to their children,
7 That they may set their hope in
    God,

78:title *a*Hebrew *Maschil*

TELLING A FRIEND ABOUT A FRIEND Psalm 78:4

Bob is pretending. You like to do that, don't you? He is pretending to sail far away. He will tell a new friend there about an old Friend here. He will tell faraway people about his Friend, Jesus.

1. Is Jesus your friend?
2. Do you want others to be His friends, too? Will you tell them about your Friend, Jesus?
3. Someday you may want to tell friends far away. But why not start with friends and neighbors nearby now?

For more on *What Should I Do?* turn to page 917
For more on *Sharing* turn to page 951

And not forget the works of God,
But keep His commandments;
8 And may not be like their fathers,
A stubborn and rebellious
generation,
A generation *that* did not set its
heart aright,
And whose spirit was not faithful
to God.

9 The children of Ē'phra·im, *being*
armed *and* carrying bows,
Turned back in the day of battle.
10 They did not keep the covenant of
God;
They refused to walk in His law,
11 And forgot His works
And His wonders that He had
shown them.

12 Marvelous things He did in the
sight of their fathers,
In the land of Egypt, *in* the field
of Zō'an.
13 He divided the sea and caused
them to pass through;
And He made the waters stand
up like a heap.
14 In the daytime also He led them
with the cloud,
And all the night with a light of
fire.
15 He split the rocks in the
wilderness,
And gave *them* drink in
abundance like the depths.
16 He also brought streams out of
the rock,
And caused waters to run down
like rivers.

17 But they sinned even more
against Him
By rebelling against the Most
High in the wilderness.
18 And they tested God in their
heart
By asking for the food of their
fancy.

19 Yes, they spoke against God:
They said, "Can God prepare a
table in the wilderness?
20 Behold, He struck the rock,
So that the waters gushed out,
And the streams overflowed.
Can He give bread also?
Can He provide meat for His
people?"

21 Therefore the LORD heard *this*
and was furious;
So a fire was kindled against
Jacob,
And anger also came up against
Israel,
22 Because they did not believe in
God,
And did not trust in His
salvation.
23 Yet He had commanded the
clouds above,
And opened the doors of heaven,
24 Had rained down manna on them
to eat,
And given them of the bread of
heaven.
25 Men ate angels' food;
He sent them food to the full.

26 He caused an east wind to blow in
the heavens;
And by His power He brought in
the south wind.
27 He also rained meat on them like
the dust,
Feathered fowl like the sand of
the seas;
28 And He let *them* fall in the midst
of their camp,
All around their dwellings.
29 So they ate and were well filled,
For He gave them their own
desire.
30 They were not deprived of their
craving;
But while their food *was* still in
their mouths,

31 The wrath of God came against
   them,
   And slew the stoutest of them,
   And struck down the choice *men*
   of Israel.

32 In spite of this they still sinned,
   And did not believe in His
   wondrous works.

33 Therefore their days He
   consumed in futility,
   And their years in fear.

34 When He slew them, then they
   sought Him;
   And they returned and sought
   earnestly for God.

35 Then they remembered that God
   was their rock,
   And the Most High God their
   Redeemer.

36 Nevertheless they flattered Him
   with their mouth,
   And they lied to Him with their
   tongue;

37 For their heart was not steadfast
   with Him,
   Nor were they faithful in His
   covenant.

38 But He, *being* full of compassion,
   forgave *their* iniquity,
   And did not destroy *them*.
   Yes, many a time He turned His
   anger away,
   And did not stir up all His wrath;

39 For He remembered that they
   were but flesh,
   A breath that passes away and
   does not come again.

40 How often they provoked Him in
   the wilderness,
   And grieved Him in the desert!

41 Yes, again and again they
   tempted God,
   And limited the Holy One of
   Israel.

42 They did not remember His
   power:

The day when He redeemed them
   from the enemy,

43 When He worked His signs in
   Egypt,
   And His wonders in the field of
   Zō'an;

44 Turned their rivers into blood,
   And their streams, that they
   could not drink.

45 He sent swarms of flies among
   them, which devoured them,
   And frogs, which destroyed
   them.

46 He also gave their crops to the
   caterpillar,
   And their labor to the locust.

47 He destroyed their vines with
   hail,
   And their sycamore trees with
   frost.

48 He also gave up their cattle to the
   hail,
   And their flocks to fiery lightning.

49 He cast on them the fierceness of
   His anger,
   Wrath, indignation, and trouble,
   By sending angels of destruction
   among them.

50 He made a path for His anger;
   He did not spare their soul from
   death,
   But gave their life over to the
   plague,

51 And destroyed all the firstborn in
   Egypt,
   The first of *their* strength in the
   tents of Ham.

52 But He made His own people go
   forth like sheep,
   And guided them in the
   wilderness like a flock;

53 And He led them on safely, so
   that they did not fear;
   But the sea overwhelmed their
   enemies.

54 And He brought them to His holy
   border,
   This mountain *which* His right
   hand had acquired.

55 He also drove out the nations
before them,
Allotted them an inheritance by
survey,
And made the tribes of Israel
dwell in their tents.

56 Yet they tested and provoked the
Most High God,
And did not keep His testimonies,
57 But turned back and acted
unfaithfully like their fathers;
They were turned aside like a
deceitful bow.
58 For they provoked Him to anger
with their high places,
And moved Him to jealousy with
their carved images.
59 When God heard *this,* He was
furious,
And greatly abhorred Israel,
60 So that He forsook the tabernacle
of Shī'lōh,
The tent He had placed among
men,
61 And delivered His strength into
captivity,
And His glory into the enemy's
hand.
62 He also gave His people over to
the sword,
And was furious with His
inheritance.
63 The fire consumed their young
men,
And their maidens were not given
in marriage.
64 Their priests fell by the sword,
And their widows made no
lamentation.

65 Then the Lord awoke as *from*
sleep,
Like a mighty man who shouts
because of wine.
66 And He beat back His enemies;
He put them to a perpetual
reproach.

67 Moreover He rejected the tent of
Joseph,
And did not choose the tribe of
Ē'phra·im,
68 But chose the tribe of Judah,
Mount Zion which He loved.
69 And He built His sanctuary like
the heights,
Like the earth which He has
established forever.
70 He also chose David His servant,
And took him from the
sheepfolds;
71 From following the ewes that had
young He brought him,
To shepherd Jacob His people,
And Israel His inheritance.
72 So he shepherded them according
to the integrity of his heart,
And guided them by the
skillfulness of his hands.

PSALM 79

A Dirge and a Prayer for Israel, Destroyed by Enemies

A Psalm of Ā'saph.

O GOD, the nations have come into
Your inheritance;
Your holy temple they have
defiled;
They have laid Jerusalem in
heaps.
2 The dead bodies of Your servants
They have given *as* food for the
birds of the heavens,
The flesh of Your saints to the
beasts of the earth.
3 Their blood they have shed like
water all around Jerusalem,
And *there was* no one to bury
them.
4 We have become a reproach to our
neighbors,
A scorn and derision to those who
are around us.

5 How long, LORD?
Will You be angry forever?
Will Your jealousy burn like fire?
6 Pour out Your wrath on the
nations that do not know You,
And on the kingdoms that do not
call on Your name.
7 For they have devoured Jacob,
And laid waste his dwelling place.

8 Oh, do not remember former
iniquities against us!
Let Your tender mercies come
speedily to meet us,
For we have been brought very
low.
9 Help us, O God of our salvation,
For the glory of Your name;
And deliver us, and provide
atonement for our sins,
For Your name's sake!
10 Why should the nations say,
"Where *is* their God?"
Let there be known among the
nations in our sight
The avenging of the blood of Your
servants *which has been* shed.

11 Let the groaning of the prisoner
come before You;

Praises

Psalm 79:13

Has a grandparent given you
something special? Has a parent
given you something special?
The most special gift of all to
give another generation is
praise for God. Praise God. Your
parents will rejoice. Praise God.
Some day your children will be
glad. Praise God. Is your brother
or sister happy to hear it? Praise
God. What will your uncles and
aunts and cousins think? Praise
God. What a gift to all generations.

According to the greatness of Your
power
Preserve those who are appointed
to die;
12 And return to our neighbors
sevenfold into their bosom
Their reproach with which they
have reproached You, O Lord.

13 So we, Your people and sheep of
Your pasture,
Will give You thanks forever;
We will show forth Your praise to
all generations.

PSALM 80

PRAYER FOR ISRAEL'S RESTORATION

To the Chief Musician. Set to "The Lilies."[a]
A Testimony[b] of Ā'saph. A Psalm.

GIVE ear, O Shepherd of Israel,
You who lead Joseph like a
flock;
You who dwell *between* the
cherubim, shine forth!
2 Before Ē'phra·im, Benjamin, and
Ma·nas'seh,
Stir up Your strength,
And come *and* save us!

3 Restore us, O God;
Cause Your face to shine,
And we shall be saved!

4 O LORD God of hosts,
How long will You be angry
Against the prayer of Your
people?
5 You have fed them with the bread
of tears,
And given them tears to drink in
great measure.
6 You have made us a strife to our
neighbors,

80:title [a]Hebrew *Shoshannim* [b]Hebrew *Eduth*

And our enemies laugh among
themselves.

7 Restore us, O God of hosts;
Cause Your face to shine,
And we shall be saved!

8 You have brought a vine out of
Egypt;
You have cast out the nations,
and planted it.

9 You prepared *room* for it,
And caused it to take deep root,
And it filled the land.

10 The hills were covered with its
shadow,
And the mighty cedars with its
boughs.

11 She sent out her boughs to the
Sea,*a*
And her branches to the River.*b*

12 Why have You broken down her
hedges,
So that all who pass by the way
pluck her *fruit?*

13 The boar out of the woods uproots
it,
And the wild beast of the field
devours it.

14 Return, we beseech You, O God of
hosts;
Look down from heaven and see,
And visit this vine

15 And the vineyard which Your
right hand has planted,
And the branch *that* You made
strong for Yourself.

16 *It is* burned with fire, *it is* cut
down;
They perish at the rebuke of Your
countenance.

17 Let Your hand be upon the man of
Your right hand,
Upon the son of man *whom* You
made strong for Yourself.

18 Then we will not turn back from
You;

Revive us, and we will call upon
Your name.

19 Restore us, O LORD God of
hosts;
Cause Your face to shine,
And we shall be saved!

PSALM 81

AN APPEAL FOR ISRAEL'S REPENTANCE

To the Chief Musician. On an instrument of Gath.*a*
A Psalm of Ā'saph.

Sing aloud to God our strength;
Make a joyful shout to the God of
Jacob.

2 Raise a song and strike the
timbrel,
The pleasant harp with the lute.

3 Blow the trumpet at the time of
the New Moon,
At the full moon, on our solemn
feast day.

4 For this *is* a statute for Israel,
A law of the God of Jacob.

5 This He established in Joseph *as*
a testimony,
When He went throughout the
land of Egypt,
Where I heard a language I did
not understand.

6 "I removed his shoulder from the
burden;
His hands were freed from the
baskets.

7 You called in trouble, and I
delivered you;
I answered you in the secret place
of thunder;
I tested you at the waters of
Mer'i·bah.   Sē'lah

80:11 *a*That is, the Mediterranean   *b*That is, the
Euphrates   81:title *a*Hebrew *Al Gittith*

8 "Hear, O My people, and I will
    admonish you!
  O Israel, if you will listen to Me!
9 There shall be no foreign god
    among you;
  Nor shall you worship any foreign
    god.
10 I *am* the LORD your God,
  Who brought you out of the land
    of Egypt;
  Open your mouth wide, and I will
    fill it.

11 "But My people would not heed My
    voice,
  And Israel would *have* none of
    Me.
12 So I gave them over to their own
    stubborn heart,
  To walk in their own counsels.

13 "Oh, that My people would listen
    to Me,
  That Israel would walk in My
    ways!
14 I would soon subdue their
    enemies,
  And turn My hand against their
    adversaries.
15 The haters of the LORD would
    pretend submission to Him,
  But their fate would endure
    forever.
16 He would have fed them also with
    the finest of wheat;
  And with honey from the rock I
    would have satisfied you."

PSALM 82

A PLEA FOR JUSTICE

A Psalm of Ā'saph.

GOD stands in the congregation of
  the mighty;
  He judges among the gods.*a*
2 How long will you judge unjustly,

And show partiality to the
    wicked?   Sē'lah
3 Defend the poor and fatherless;
  Do justice to the afflicted and
    needy.
4 Deliver the poor and needy;
  Free *them* from the hand of the
    wicked.

5 They do not know, nor do they
    understand;
  They walk about in darkness;
  All the foundations of the earth
    are unstable.

6 I said, "You *are* gods,*a*
  And all of you *are* children of the
    Most High.
7 But you shall die like men,
  And fall like one of the princes."

8 Arise, O God, judge the earth;
  For You shall inherit all nations.

PSALM 83

PRAYER TO FRUSTRATE CONSPIRACY
AGAINST ISRAEL

A Song. A Psalm of Ā'saph.

DO not keep silent, O God!
  Do not hold Your peace,
  And do not be still, O God!
2 For behold, Your enemies make a
    tumult;
  And those who hate You have
    lifted up their head.
3 They have taken crafty counsel
    against Your people,
  And consulted together against
    Your sheltered ones.
4 They have said, "Come, and let us
    cut them off from *being* a
    nation,

82:1 *a*Hebrew *elohim*, mighty *ones; that is, the
judges   82:6 *a*Hebrew *elohim*, mighty *ones; that
is, the judges

That the name of Israel may be
remembered no more."

5 For they have consulted together
with one consent;
They form a confederacy against
You:

6 The tents of Ē′dom and the
Ish′ma·el·ītes;
Mō′ab and the Hag′rītes;

7 Gē′bal, Am′mon, and Am′a·lek;
Phi·lis′ti·a with the inhabitants of
Tȳre;

8 Assyria also has joined with
them;
They have helped the children of
Lot.   Sē′lah

9 Deal with them as *with* Mid′i·an,
As *with* Sis′e·ra,
As *with* Jā′bin at the Brook
Kī′shon,

10 Who perished at En Dor,
Who became *as* refuse on the
earth.

11 Make their nobles like Or′eb and
like Zē′eb,
Yes, all their princes like Zē′bah
and Zal·mun′na,

12 Who said, "Let us take for
ourselves
The pastures of God for a
possession."

13 O my God, make them like the
whirling dust,
Like the chaff before the wind!

14 As the fire burns the woods,
And as the flame sets the
mountains on fire,

15 So pursue them with Your
tempest,
And frighten them with Your
storm.

16 Fill their faces with shame,
That they may seek Your name,
O Lord.

17 Let them be confounded and
dismayed forever;

Yes, let them be put to shame and
perish,

18 That they may know that You,
whose name alone *is* the Lord,
Are the Most High over all the
earth.

PSALM 84

THE BLESSEDNESS OF DWELLING IN THE HOUSE OF GOD

To the Chief Musician. On an instrument of Gath.*a*
A Psalm of the sons of Kō′rah.

HOW lovely *is* Your tabernacle,
O Lord of hosts!

2 My soul longs, yes, even faints
For the courts of the Lord;
My heart and my flesh cry out for
the living God.

3 Even the sparrow has found a
home,
And the swallow a nest for
herself,
Where she may lay her young—
Even Your altars, O Lord of hosts,
My King and my God.

4 Blessed *are* those who dwell in
Your house;
They will still be praising You.
      Sē′lah

5 Blessed *is* the man whose
strength *is* in You,
Whose heart *is* set on pilgrimage.

6 *As they* pass through the Valley of
Bā′ca,
They make it a spring;
The rain also covers it with
pools.

7 They go from strength to
strength;
Each one appears before God in
Zion.*a*

84:title *a*Hebrew *Al Gittith*   84:7 *a*Septuagint,
Syriac, and Vulgate read *The God of gods shall be
seen.*

WHERE DID YOU SLEEP LAST NIGHT? Psalm 84:3

Have you ever gone camping as a family? If you have, what do you remember? Do you sometimes laugh about sleeping in a tent and the problems you had? Sleeping in a tent or in a motel room or at an uncle's house or some other strange place can build family memories. How many memories do you have concerning places you and your family have slept?

1. What fun memories do you have of camping or sleeping at some other place? Talk about them together now.
2. Sleeping away from home is trying to make a "home away from home." What "home" stuff do you take with you to your "home away from home?" Do you take your pillow? Why? Do you take some favorite stuffed animals, books, or games? Why? Do you take certain ways of doing things? What? Why? Do you brush your teeth and do certain things away from home that you do at home? What? Why?
3. When you're away from home, how can you help each other as a family do "home" things? Why should you?
4. Read Psalm 84:3. What "home" did the sparrow find in God's house? How can God's house be something of a "home away from home" to your family? What kinds of "home" things can you do there?

For more on *Family Memories* turn to page 936
For more on *Family* turn to page 968

8 O LORD God of hosts, hear my
    prayer;
  Give ear, O God of Jacob!   Sē′lah
9 O God, behold our shield,
  And look upon the face of Your
    anointed.

10 For a day in Your courts *is* better
    than a thousand.
  I would rather be a doorkeeper in
    the house of my God
  Than dwell in the tents of
    wickedness.
11 For the LORD God *is* a sun and
    shield;
  The LORD will give grace and
    glory;
  No good *thing* will He withhold
  From those who walk uprightly.

12 O LORD of hosts,
  Blessed *is* the man who trusts in
    You!

PSALM 85

PRAYER THAT THE LORD WILL RESTORE FAVOR TO THE LAND

To the Chief Musician. A Psalm of the sons of
Kō′rah.

LORD, You have been favorable to
    Your land;
  You have brought back the
    captivity of Jacob.
2 You have forgiven the iniquity of
    Your people;
  You have covered all their sin.
                                Sē′lah
3 You have taken away all Your
    wrath;
  You have turned from the
    fierceness of Your anger.

4 Restore us, O God of our
    salvation,

And cause Your anger toward us
  to cease.
5 Will You be angry with us
  forever?
  Will You prolong Your anger to all
  generations?
6 Will You not revive us again,
  That Your people may rejoice in
  You?
7 Show us Your mercy, LORD,
  And grant us Your salvation.

8 I will hear what God the LORD
  will speak,
  For He will speak peace
  To His people and to His saints;
  But let them not turn back to
  folly.
9 Surely His salvation is near to
  those who fear Him,
  That glory may dwell in our land.

10 Mercy and truth have met
  together;
  Righteousness and peace have
  kissed.
11 Truth shall spring out of the
  earth,
  And righteousness shall look
  down from heaven.
12 Yes, the LORD will give what is
  good;
  And our land will yield its
  increase.
13 Righteousness will go before Him,
  And shall make His footsteps our
  pathway.

PSALM 86

PRAYER FOR MERCY, WITH MEDITATION ON THE EXCELLENCIES OF THE LORD

A Prayer of David.

BOW down Your ear, O LORD, hear
me;
For I am poor and needy.

2 Preserve my life, for I am holy;
  You are my God;
  Save Your servant who trusts in
  You!
3 Be merciful to me, O Lord,
  For I cry to You all day long.
4 Rejoice the soul of Your servant,
  For to You, O Lord, I lift up my
  soul.
5 For You, Lord, are good, and
  ready to forgive,
  And abundant in mercy to all
  those who call upon You.

6 Give ear, O LORD, to my prayer;
  And attend to the voice of my
  supplications.
7 In the day of my trouble I will call
  upon You,
  For You will answer me.

8 Among the gods there is none like
  You, O Lord;
  Nor are there any works like Your
  works.
9 All nations whom You have made
  Shall come and worship before
  You, O Lord,
  And shall glorify Your name.
10 For You are great, and do
  wondrous things;
  You alone are God.

11 Teach me Your way, O LORD;
  I will walk in Your truth;
  Unite my heart to fear Your
  name.
12 I will praise You, O Lord my God,
  with all my heart,
  And I will glorify Your name
  forevermore.
13 For great is Your mercy toward
  me,
  And You have delivered my soul
  from the depths of Shĕ′ōl.

14 O God, the proud have risen
  against me,

ABOUT GOD'S LOVE Psalm 86:9

Is God the God of Our Nation Only?

Did God make the people of our nation only? Or did He make all people of all the earth? Does God provide for the people of our nation only? Or does He provide for the people of all the earth? Does God love the people of our nation only? Or does He love all people of all the earth? Should only the people of our nation praise God? Or should all people of all the earth praise Him? Read Psalm 86:9. What does it say?

1. Which people did God make? Do you think He wants all people to love Him?
2. Does God take care of us only? Which people receive daily blessings from Him?
3. If all people receive His love and blessings, then which people *should* praise Him?
4. Will you praise Him today for all He has done for you?

For more on *What the Bible Says* turn to page 899
For more on *Praise* turn to page 1348

And a mob of violent *men* have
  sought my life,
And have not set You before
  them.
15 But You, O Lord, *are* a God full of
  compassion, and gracious,
Longsuffering and abundant in
  mercy and truth.

16 Oh, turn to me, and have mercy
  on me!
Give Your strength to Your
  servant,
And save the son of Your
  maidservant.
17 Show me a sign for good,
That those who hate me may see
  it and be ashamed,
Because You, LORD, have helped
  me and comforted me.

PSALM 87

THE GLORIES OF THE CITY OF GOD

A Psalm of the sons of Kō′rah. A Song.

HIS foundation *is* in the holy
  mountains.
2 The LORD loves the gates of
  Zion
More than all the dwellings of
  Jacob.
3 Glorious things are spoken of
  you,
O city of God!   Sē′lah

4 "I will make mention of Rā′hab
  and Babylon to those who know
  Me;
Behold, O Phi·lis′ti·a and Tyre,
  with Ethiopia:
'This *one* was born there.' "

5 And of Zion it will be said,
"This *one* and that *one* were born
  in her;

And the Most High Himself shall
  establish her."
6 The LORD will record,
When He registers the peoples:
"This *one* was born there."   Sē′lah

7 Both the singers and the players
  on instruments *say,*
"All my springs *are* in you."

PSALM 88

A PRAYER FOR HELP IN DESPONDENCY

A Song. A Psalm of the sons of Kō′rah.
To the Chief Musician.
Set to "Mā′ha·lath Le·an′noth."
A Contemplation[a] of Hē′man the Ez′ra·hīte.

O LORD, God of my salvation,
  I have cried out day and night
  before You.
2 Let my prayer come before
  You;
Incline Your ear to my cry.

3 For my soul is full of troubles,
And my life draws near to the
  grave.
4 I am counted with those who go
  down to the pit;
I am like a man *who has* no
  strength,
5 Adrift among the dead,
Like the slain who lie in the
  grave,
Whom You remember no more,
And who are cut off from Your
  hand.

6 You have laid me in the lowest
  pit,
In darkness, in the depths.
7 Your wrath lies heavy upon
  me,
And You have afflicted *me* with all
  Your waves.   Sē′lah

88:title [a]Hebrew *Maschil*

8 You have put away my
  acquaintances far from me;
  You have made me an
    abomination to them;
  I am shut up, and I cannot get
    out;
9 My eye wastes away because of
    affliction.

  Lord, I have called daily upon
    You;
  I have stretched out my hands to
    You.
10 Will You work wonders for the
    dead?
  Shall the dead arise *and* praise
    You?   Sē'lah
11 Shall Your lovingkindness be
    declared in the grave?
  Or Your faithfulness in the place
    of destruction?
12 Shall Your wonders be known in
    the dark?
  And Your righteousness in the
    land of forgetfulness?

13 But to You I have cried out,
    O Lord,
  And in the morning my prayer
    comes before You.
14 Lord, why do You cast off my
    soul?
  Why do You hide Your face from
    me?
15 I *have been* afflicted and ready to
    die from *my* youth;
  I suffer Your terrors;
  I am distraught.
16 Your fierce wrath has gone over
    me;
  Your terrors have cut me off.
17 They came around me all day
    long like water;
  They engulfed me altogether.
18 Loved one and friend You have
    put far from me,
  And my acquaintances into
    darkness.

PSALM 89

Remembering the Covenant with David, and Sorrow for Lost Blessings

A Contemplation[a] *of* Ē'than the Ez'ra·hīte.

I WILL sing of the mercies of the
    Lord forever;
  With my mouth will I make
    known Your faithfulness to all
    generations.
2 For I have said, "Mercy shall be
    built up forever;
  Your faithfulness You shall
    establish in the very heavens."

3 "I have made a covenant with My
    chosen,
  I have sworn to My servant
    David:
4 'Your seed I will establish
    forever,
  And build up your throne to all
    generations.' "   Sē'lah

5 And the heavens will praise Your
    wonders, O Lord;
  Your faithfulness also in the
    assembly of the saints.
6 For who in the heavens can be
    compared to the Lord?
  Who among the sons of the
    mighty can be likened to the
    Lord?
7 God is greatly to be feared in the
    assembly of the saints,
  And to be held in reverence by all
    those around Him.
8 O Lord God of hosts,
  Who *is* mighty like You, O Lord?
  Your faithfulness also surrounds
    You.
9 You rule the raging of the sea;
  When its waves rise, You still
    them.

89:title [a]Hebrew *Maschil*

10 You have broken Rā′hab in
pieces, as one who is slain;
You have scattered Your enemies
with Your mighty arm.

11 The heavens *are* Yours, the earth
also *is* Yours;
The world and all its fullness, You
have founded them.

12 The north and the south, You
have created them;
Tā′bor and Her′mon rejoice in
Your name.

13 You have a mighty arm;
Strong is Your hand, *and* high is
Your right hand.

14 Righteousness and justice *are* the
foundation of Your throne;
Mercy and truth go before Your
face.

15 Blessed *are* the people who know
the joyful sound!
They walk, O LORD, in the light of
Your countenance.

16 In Your name they rejoice all day
long,
And in Your righteousness they
are exalted.

17 For You *are* the glory of their
strength,
And in Your favor our horn is
exalted.

18 For our shield *belongs* to the
LORD,
And our king to the Holy One of
Israel.

19 Then You spoke in a vision to
Your holy one,*a*
And said: "I have given help to
one who is mighty;
I have exalted one chosen from
the people.

20 I have found My servant
David;
With My holy oil I have anointed
him,

21 With whom My hand shall be
established;

Also My arm shall strengthen
him.

22 The enemy shall not outwit him,
Nor the son of wickedness afflict
him.

23 I will beat down his foes before
his face,
And plague those who hate him.

24 "But My faithfulness and My
mercy *shall be* with him,
And in My name his horn shall be
exalted.

25 Also I will set his hand over the
sea,
And his right hand over the
rivers.

26 He shall cry to Me, 'You *are* my
Father,
My God, and the rock of my
salvation.'

27 Also I will make him *My*
firstborn,
The highest of the kings of the
earth.

28 My mercy I will keep for him
forever,
And My covenant shall stand firm
with him.

29 His seed also I will make *to
endure* forever,
And his throne as the days of
heaven.

30 "If his sons forsake My law
And do not walk in My
judgments,

31 If they break My statutes
And do not keep My
commandments,

32 Then I will punish their
transgression with the rod,
And their iniquity with stripes.

33 Nevertheless My lovingkindness I
will not utterly take from him,
Nor allow My faithfulness to fail.

89:19 *a*Following many Hebrew manuscripts;
Masoretic Text, Septuagint, Targum, and Vulgate
read *holy ones.*

34 My covenant I will not break,
   Nor alter the word that has gone
      out of My lips.
35 Once I have sworn by My
      holiness;
   I will not lie to David:
36 His seed shall endure forever,
   And his throne as the sun before
      Me;
37 It shall be established forever like
      the moon,
   Even *like* the faithful witness in
      the sky."   Sē′lah

38 But You have cast off and
      abhorred,
   You have been furious with Your
      anointed.
39 You have renounced the covenant
      of Your servant;
   You have profaned his crown *by*
      casting it to the ground.
40 You have broken down all his
      hedges;
   You have brought his strongholds
      to ruin.
41 All who pass by the way plunder
      him;
   He is a reproach to his
      neighbors.
42 You have exalted the right hand
      of his adversaries;
   You have made all his enemies
      rejoice.
43 You have also turned back the
      edge of his sword,
   And have not sustained him in
      the battle.
44 You have made his glory cease,
   And cast his throne down to the
      ground.
45 The days of his youth You have
      shortened;
   You have covered him with
      shame.   Sē′lah

46 How long, LORD?
   Will You hide Yourself forever?
   Will Your wrath burn like fire?

47 Remember how short my time is;
   For what futility have You
      created all the children of
      men?
48 What man can live and not see
      death?
   Can he deliver his life from the
      power of the grave?   Sē′lah

49 Lord, where *are* Your former
      lovingkindnesses,
   Which You swore to David in Your
      truth?
50 Remember, Lord, the reproach of
      Your servants—
   How I bear in my bosom *the*
      reproach of all the many
      peoples,
51 With which Your enemies have
      reproached, O LORD,
   With which they have reproached
      the footsteps of Your anointed.

52 Blessed *be* the LORD forevermore!
   Amen and Amen.

BOOK FOUR
Psalms 90—106

PSALM 90

THE ETERNITY OF GOD, AND MAN'S FRAILTY

A Prayer of Moses the man of God.

L ORD, You have been our dwelling
      place[a] in all generations.
2 Before the mountains were
      brought forth,
   Or ever You had formed the earth
      and the world,
   Even from everlasting to
      everlasting, You *are* God.

90:1 [a]Septuagint, Targum, and Vulgate read
refuge.

3 You turn man to destruction,
And say, "Return, O children of
men."
4 For a thousand years in Your
sight
Are like yesterday when it is past,
And *like* a watch in the night.
5 You carry them away *like* a flood;
They are like a sleep.
In the morning they are like grass
which grows up:
6 In the morning it flourishes and
grows up;
In the evening it is cut down and
withers.

7 For we have been consumed by
Your anger,
And by Your wrath we are
terrified.
8 You have set our iniquities before
You,
Our secret *sins* in the light of
Your countenance.
9 For all our days have passed
away in Your wrath;
We finish our years like a sigh.
10 The days of our lives *are* seventy
years;
And if by reason of strength *they
are* eighty years,
Yet their boast *is* only labor and
sorrow;
For it is soon cut off, and we fly
away.
11 Who knows the power of Your
anger?
For as the fear of You, *so is* Your
wrath.
12 So teach *us* to number our days,
That we may gain a heart of
wisdom.

13 Return, O LORD!
How long?
And have compassion on Your
servants.
14 Oh, satisfy us early with Your
mercy,

That we may rejoice and be glad
all our days!
15 Make us glad according to the
days *in which* You have
afflicted us,
The years *in which* we have seen
evil.
16 Let Your work appear to Your
servants,
And Your glory to their children.
17 And let the beauty of the LORD
our God be upon us,
And establish the work of our
hands for us;
Yes, establish the work of our
hands.

PSALM 91

SAFETY OF ABIDING IN THE PRESENCE
OF GOD

HE who dwells in the secret place
of the Most High
Shall abide under the shadow of
the Almighty.
2 I will say of the LORD, "He is my
refuge and my fortress;
My God, in Him I will trust."

3 Surely He shall deliver you from
the snare of the fowler[a]
And from the perilous pestilence.
4 He shall cover you with His
feathers,
And under His wings you shall
take refuge;
His truth *shall be your* shield and
buckler.
5 You shall not be afraid of the
terror by night,
Nor of the arrow *that* flies by day,
6 *Nor* of the pestilence *that* walks
in darkness,
Nor of the destruction *that* lays
waste at noonday.

91:3 [a]That is, one who catches birds in a trap or
snare

ABOUT ANGELS Psalm 91:11, 12

Are Angels Helping You?

Someone is watching you. Someone is taking care of you. Do parents do these things? Yes. Does God do these things? Yes. But someone else watches over you to help you do what you should. The Bible tells us that God gives His angels to watch over us and keep us in the right ways (read Psalm 91:11). We are not sure how they look. But they do watch over us. Thank You, God, for angels to watch over us and keep us in the right way.

1. Are you ever tempted to do something wrong? But do you often feel that you shouldn't do what you're tempted to do?
2. What keeps us from doing wrong? Do you want to do wrong when you know it will not please your parents? Do you want to do it when you know it will not please God? Perhaps an angel or two is tugging at us, too, trying to keep us from doing it. Read Psalm 91:11 again. Read it two or three times. What does it say?
3. Would you like to thank God now for sending angels to guard you?

For more on *What the Bible Says* turn to page 948
For more on *God's Care* turn to page 906

7 A thousand may fall at your side,
And ten thousand at your right
hand;
But it shall not come near you.
8 Only with your eyes shall you
look,
And see the reward of the wicked.

9 Because you have made the LORD,
who is my refuge,
Even the Most High, your
dwelling place,
10 No evil shall befall you,
Nor shall any plague come near
your dwelling;
11 For He shall give His angels
charge over you,
To keep you in all your ways.
12 In *their* hands they shall bear you
up,
Lest you dash your foot against a
stone.
13 You shall tread upon the lion and
the cobra,
The young lion and the serpent
you shall trample underfoot.

14 "Because he has set his love upon
Me, therefore I will deliver
him;
I will set him on high, because he
has known My name.
15 He shall call upon Me, and I will
answer him;
I *will be* with him in trouble;
I will deliver him and honor him.
16 With long life I will satisfy him,
And show him My salvation."

PSALM 92

PRAISE TO THE LORD FOR HIS LOVE AND FAITHFULNESS

A Psalm. A Song for the Sabbath day.

*I*T is good to give thanks to the
LORD,
And to sing praises to Your name,
O Most High;
2 To declare Your lovingkindness in
the morning,
And Your faithfulness every
night,
3 On an instrument of ten strings,
On the lute,
And on the harp,
With harmonious sound.
4 For You, LORD, have made me
glad through Your work;
I will triumph in the works of
Your hands.

5 O LORD, how great are Your
works!
Your thoughts are very deep.
6 A senseless man does not know,
Nor does a fool understand this.
7 When the wicked spring up like
grass,
And when all the workers of
iniquity flourish,
It is that they may be destroyed
forever.

8 But You, LORD, *are* on high
forevermore.
9 For behold, Your enemies,
O LORD,
For behold, Your enemies shall
perish;
All the workers of iniquity shall
be scattered.

10 But my horn You have exalted
like a wild ox;
I have been anointed with fresh
oil.
11 My eye also has seen *my desire* on
my enemies;
My ears hear *my desire* on the
wicked
Who rise up against me.

12 The righteous shall flourish like a
palm tree,
He shall grow like a cedar in
Lebanon.

13 Those who are planted in the
   house of the LORD
   Shall flourish in the courts of our
   God.
14 They shall still bear fruit in old
   age;
   They shall be fresh and
   flourishing,
15 To declare that the LORD is
   upright;
   He is my rock, and *there is* no
   unrighteousness in Him.

PSALM 93

THE ETERNAL REIGN OF THE LORD

THE LORD reigns, He is clothed
   with majesty;
   The LORD is clothed,
   He has girded Himself with
   strength.
   Surely the world is established, so
   that it cannot be moved.
2 Your throne *is* established from of
   old;
   You *are* from everlasting.

3 The floods have lifted up, O LORD,
   The floods have lifted up their
   voice;
   The floods lift up their waves.
4 The LORD on high *is* mightier
   Than the noise of many waters,
   Than the mighty waves of the
   sea.

5 Your testimonies are very sure;
   Holiness adorns Your house,
   O LORD, forever.

PSALM 94

GOD THE REFUGE OF THE RIGHTEOUS

O LORD God, to whom vengeance
   belongs—

O God, to whom vengeance
   belongs, shine forth!
2 Rise up, O Judge of the earth;
   Render punishment to the proud.
3 LORD, how long will the wicked,
   How long will the wicked
   triumph?

4 They utter speech, *and* speak
   insolent things;
   All the workers of iniquity boast
   in themselves.
5 They break in pieces Your people,
   O LORD,
   And afflict Your heritage.
6 They slay the widow and the
   stranger,
   And murder the fatherless.
7 Yet they say, "The LORD does not
   see,
   Nor does the God of Jacob
   understand."

8 Understand, you senseless among
   the people;
   And *you* fools, when will you be
   wise?
9 He who planted the ear, shall He
   not hear?
   He who formed the eye, shall He
   not see?
10 He who instructs the nations,
   shall He not correct,
   He who teaches man knowledge?
11 The LORD knows the thoughts of
   man,
   That they *are* futile.

12 Blessed *is* the man whom You
   instruct, O LORD,
   And teach out of Your law,
13 That You may give him rest from
   the days of adversity,
   Until the pit is dug for the
   wicked.
14 For the LORD will not cast off His
   people,
   Nor will He forsake His
   inheritance.

LET US COME BEFORE HIS PRESENCE WITH THANKSGIVING; / LET US SHOUT JOYFULLY TO HIM WITH PSALMS. Psalm 95:2

Whom Should We Thank on Thanksgiving?

Thanksgiving is a time to say thanks, isn't it? Otherwise why would it be called Thanksgiving? But whom should we thank on Thanksgiving?

1. Would you like to thank mother and father on Thanksgiving for all they do for you and all they give you? That's a good idea, isn't it?
2. But Psalm 95:2 tells us about another Person we should thank. Who is He? Why should we thank the Lord? What has He done for you?

For more on *Favorite Family Verses* turn to page 906
For more on *Thankfulness* turn to page 953

15 But judgment will return to
    righteousness,
    And all the upright in heart will
    follow it.

16 Who will rise up for me against
    the evildoers?
    Who will stand up for me against
    the workers of iniquity?

17 Unless the LORD *had been* my
    help,
    My soul would soon have settled
    in silence.

18 If I say, "My foot slips,"
    Your mercy, O LORD, will hold me
    up.

19 In the multitude of my anxieties
    within me,
    Your comforts delight my soul.

20 Shall the throne of iniquity, which
    devises evil by law,
    Have fellowship with You?

21 They gather together against the
    life of the righteous,
    And condemn innocent blood.

22 But the LORD has been my
    defense,
    And my God the rock of my
    refuge.

23 He has brought on them their
    own iniquity,
    And shall cut them off in their
    own wickedness;
    The LORD our God shall cut them
    off.

PSALM 95

A CALL TO WORSHIP AND OBEDIENCE

O H come, let us sing to the LORD!
    Let us shout joyfully to the Rock
    of our salvation.

2 Let us come before His presence
    with thanksgiving;
    Let us shout joyfully to Him with
    psalms.

3 For the LORD *is* the great God,
    And the great King above all
    gods.

4 In His hand *are* the deep places of
    the earth;
    The heights of the hills *are* His
    also.

5 The sea *is* His, for He made it;
    And His hands formed the dry
    land.

6 Oh come, let us worship and bow
    down;

Let us kneel before the LORD our
   Maker.
7 For He *is* our God,
And we *are* the people of His
   pasture,
And the sheep of His hand.

Today, if you will hear His voice:
8 "Do not harden your hearts, as in
   the rebellion,*a*
As *in* the day of trial*b* in the
   wilderness,
9 When your fathers tested Me;
They tried Me, though they saw
   My work.
10 For forty years I was grieved with
   that generation,
And said, 'It *is* a people who go
   astray in their hearts,
And they do not know My ways.'
11 So I swore in My wrath,
'They shall not enter My rest.' "

PSALM 96

A SONG OF PRAISE TO GOD COMING IN JUDGMENT

O H, sing to the LORD a new song!
Sing to the LORD, all the earth.
2 Sing to the LORD, bless His name;
Proclaim the good news of His
   salvation from day to day.
3 Declare His glory among the
   nations,
His wonders among all peoples.

4 For the LORD *is* great and greatly
   to be praised;
He *is* to be feared above all gods.
5 For all the gods of the peoples *are*
   idols,
But the LORD made the heavens.
6 Honor and majesty *are* before
   Him;
Strength and beauty *are* in His
   sanctuary.

7 Give to the LORD, O families of
   the peoples,

Give to the LORD glory and
   strength.
8 Give to the LORD the glory *due*
   His name;
Bring an offering, and come into
   His courts.
9 Oh, worship the LORD in the
   beauty of holiness!
Tremble before Him, all the earth.

10 Say among the nations, "The
   LORD reigns;
The world also is firmly
   established,
It shall not be moved;
He shall judge the peoples
   righteously."

11 Let the heavens rejoice, and let
   the earth be glad;
Let the sea roar, and all its
   fullness;
12 Let the field be joyful, and all that
   is in it.
Then all the trees of the woods
   will rejoice before the LORD.
13 For He is coming, for He is
   coming to judge the earth.
He shall judge the world with
   righteousness,
And the peoples with His truth.

PSALM 97

A SONG OF PRAISE TO THE SOVEREIGN LORD

T HE LORD reigns;
Let the earth rejoice;
Let the multitude of isles be glad!

2 Clouds and darkness surround
   Him;
Righteousness and justice *are* the
   foundation of His throne.
3 A fire goes before Him,

95:8 *a*Or *Meribah*   *b*Or *Massah*

And burns up His enemies round
about.

4 His lightnings light the world;
The earth sees and trembles.
5 The mountains melt like wax at
the presence of the LORD,
At the presence of the Lord of the
whole earth.
6 The heavens declare His
righteousness,
And all the peoples see His glory.

7 Let all be put to shame who serve
carved images,
Who boast of idols.
Worship Him, all *you* gods.
8 Zion hears and is glad,
And the daughters of Judah
rejoice
Because of Your judgments,
O LORD.
9 For You, LORD, *are* most high
above all the earth;
You are exalted far above all gods.

10 You who love the LORD, hate evil!
He preserves the souls of His
saints;
He delivers them out of the hand
of the wicked.
11 Light is sown for the righteous,
And gladness for the upright in
heart.
12 Rejoice in the LORD, you
righteous,
And give thanks at the
remembrance of His holy
name.*a*

PSALM 98

A SONG OF PRAISE TO THE LORD FOR HIS SALVATION AND JUDGMENT

A Psalm.

OH, sing to the LORD a new song!
For He has done marvelous
things;

His right hand and His holy arm
have gained Him the victory.
2 The LORD has made known His
salvation;
His righteousness He has
revealed in the sight of the
nations.
3 He has remembered His mercy
and His faithfulness to the
house of Israel;
All the ends of the earth have
seen the salvation of our God.

4 Shout joyfully to the LORD, all the
earth;
Break forth in song, rejoice, and
sing praises.
5 Sing to the LORD with the harp,
With the harp and the sound of a
psalm,
6 With trumpets and the sound of a
horn;
Shout joyfully before the LORD,
the King.

7 Let the sea roar, and all its
fullness,
The world and those who dwell in
it;
8 Let the rivers clap *their* hands;
Let the hills be joyful together
before the LORD,
9 For He is coming to judge the
earth.
With righteousness He shall
judge the world,
And the peoples with equity.

PSALM 99

PRAISE TO THE LORD FOR HIS HOLINESS

THE LORD reigns;
Let the peoples tremble!
He dwells *between* the cherubim;
Let the earth be moved!

97:12 *a*Or *His holiness*

2 The LORD *is* great in Zion,
And He *is* high above all the
peoples.
3 Let them praise Your great and
awesome name—
He *is* holy.

4 The King's strength also loves
justice;
You have established equity;
You have executed justice and
righteousness in Jacob.
5 Exalt the LORD our God,
And worship at His footstool—
He *is* holy.

6 Moses and Aaron were among His
priests,
And Samuel *was* among those
who called upon His name;
They called upon the LORD, and
He answered them.
7 He spoke to them in the cloudy
pillar;
They kept His testimonies and
the ordinance He gave them.

8 You answered them, O LORD our
God;
You were to them God-Who-
Forgives,
Though You took vengeance on
their deeds.
9 Exalt the LORD our God,
And worship at His holy hill;
For the LORD our God *is* holy.

PSALM 100

A SONG OF PRAISE FOR THE LORD'S
FAITHFULNESS TO HIS PEOPLE

A Psalm of Thanksgiving.

MAKE a joyful shout to the LORD,
all you lands!
2 Serve the LORD with gladness;
Come before His presence with
singing.

3 Know that the LORD, He *is* God;
It is He *who* has made us, and not
we ourselves;[a]
We are His people and the sheep
of His pasture.

4 Enter into His gates with
thanksgiving,
And into His courts with praise.
Be thankful to Him, *and* bless His
name.
5 For the LORD *is* good;
His mercy *is* everlasting,
And His truth *endures* to all
generations.

PSALM 101

PROMISED FAITHFULNESS TO THE LORD

A Psalm of David.

I WILL sing of mercy and justice;
To You, O LORD, I will sing
praises.

2 I will behave wisely in a perfect
way.
Oh, when will You come to me?
I will walk within my house with
a perfect heart.

3 I will set nothing wicked before
my eyes;
I hate the work of those who fall
away;
It shall not cling to me.
4 A perverse heart shall depart
from me;
I will not know wickedness.

5 Whoever secretly slanders his
neighbor,
Him I will destroy;

100:3 [a]Following Kethib, Septuagint, and Vulgate;
Qere, many Hebrew manuscripts, and Targum read
we are His.

WE ARE HIS PEOPLE AND THE SHEEP OF HIS PASTURE. Psalm 100:3

Are We Sheep?

Would you like to memorize the last part of Psalm 100:3? God says we are His people. He also says we are His sheep. Are we really like sheep? God says we are. That's because His people follow Him as sheep follow a shepherd. That's also because we let Him take care of us, as a shepherd takes care of his sheep. Are you glad Jesus is your shepherd? Are you glad He leads you? Are you glad He takes care of you?

1. Read John 10:11 and 10:14. What is Jesus saying?
2. How did Jesus give His life for us? How can we give our lives for Him?
3. Jesus died for us. But He wants us to live for Him. Will you?

For more on *Favorite Family Verses* turn to page 926
For more on *God's Care* turn to page 938

The one who has a haughty look
  and a proud heart,
Him I will not endure.

6 My eyes *shall be* on the faithful of
    the land,
  That they may dwell with me;
  He who walks in a perfect
    way,
  He shall serve me.
7 He who works deceit shall not
    dwell within my house;
  He who tells lies shall not
    continue in my presence.
8 Early I will destroy all the wicked
    of the land,
  That I may cut off all the
    evildoers from the city of the
    LORD.

PSALM 102

THE LORD'S ETERNAL LOVE

*A Prayer of the afflicted, when he is overwhelmed
and pours out his complaint before the LORD.*

HEAR my prayer, O LORD,
  And let my cry come to You.
2 Do not hide Your face from me in
    the day of my trouble;
  Incline Your ear to me;
  In the day that I call, answer me
    speedily.

3 For my days are consumed like
    smoke,
  And my bones are burned like a
    hearth.
4 My heart is stricken and withered
    like grass,
  So that I forget to eat my bread.
5 Because of the sound of my
    groaning
  My bones cling to my skin.
6 I am like a pelican of the
    wilderness;
  I am like an owl of the desert.

7 I lie awake,
  And am like a sparrow alone on
    the housetop.

8 My enemies reproach me all day
    long;
  Those who deride me swear an
    oath against me.
9 For I have eaten ashes like bread,
  And mingled my drink with
    weeping,
10 Because of Your indignation and
    Your wrath;
  For You have lifted me up and
    cast me away.
11 My days *are* like a shadow that
    lengthens,
  And I wither away like grass.

12 But You, O LORD, shall endure
    forever,
  And the remembrance of Your
    name to all generations.
13 You will arise *and* have mercy on
    Zion;
  For the time to favor her,
  Yes, the set time, has come.
14 For Your servants take pleasure
    in her stones,
  And show favor to her dust.
15 So the nations shall fear the
    name of the LORD,
  And all the kings of the earth
    Your glory.
16 For the LORD shall build up Zion;
  He shall appear in His glory.
17 He shall regard the prayer of the
    destitute,
  And shall not despise their
    prayer.

18 This will be written for the
    generation to come,
  That a people yet to be created
    may praise the LORD.
19 For He looked down from the
    height of His sanctuary;
  From heaven the LORD viewed the
    earth,

SERVING Psalm 102:22

Let Me Serve You

This lady is a waitress in a restaurant. Sometimes she is called a server, because her job is to serve people who eat there. She gives them menus. She brings them water. She pours coffee when they want it. She takes their order for food. Then she brings the food to them. Would you say that she is serving people? This lady makes others happy. And that should make her happy.

1. The Bible says we should serve others. We should also serve the Lord.
2. Read Galatians 5:13. What does it say about serving others?
3. Read Psalm 100:2. What does it say about serving the Lord?
4. Are you pleased when you can please your parents and the Lord?

For more on *Values* turn to page 951
For more on *Serving* turn to page 1024

20 To hear the groaning of the
    prisoner,
To release those appointed to
    death,
21 To declare the name of the LORD
    in Zion,
And His praise in Jerusalem,
22 When the peoples are gathered
    together,
And the kingdoms, to serve the
    LORD.

23 He weakened my strength in the
    way;
He shortened my days.
24 I said, "O my God,
Do not take me away in the midst
    of my days;
Your years *are* throughout all
    generations.
25 Of old You laid the foundation of
    the earth,
And the heavens *are* the work of
    Your hands.
26 They will perish, but You will
    endure;
Yes, they will all grow old like a
    garment;
Like a cloak You will change
    them,
And they will be changed.
27 But You *are* the same,
And Your years will have no end.
28 The children of Your servants will
    continue,
And their descendants will be
    established before You."

PSALM 103

PRAISE FOR THE LORD'S MERCIES

A Psalm of David.

BLESS the LORD, O my soul;
And all that is within me, *bless*
    His holy name!
2 Bless the LORD, O my soul,
And forget not all His benefits:

3 Who forgives all your iniquities,
Who heals all your diseases,
4 Who redeems your life from
    destruction,
Who crowns you with
    lovingkindness and tender
    mercies,
5 Who satisfies your mouth with
    good *things,*
So that your youth is renewed
    like the eagle's.

6 The LORD executes righteousness
And justice for all who are
    oppressed.
7 He made known His ways to
    Moses,
His acts to the children of Israel.
8 The LORD *is* merciful and
    gracious,
Slow to anger, and abounding in
    mercy.
9 He will not always strive *with us,*
Nor will He keep *His anger*
    forever.
10 He has not dealt with us
    according to our sins,
Nor punished us according to our
    iniquities.

11 For as the heavens are high above
    the earth,
So great is His mercy toward
    those who fear Him;
12 As far as the east is from the
    west,
So far has He removed our
    transgressions from us.
13 As a father pities *his* children,
So the LORD pities those who fear
    Him.
14 For He knows our frame;
He remembers that we *are* dust.

15 *As for* man, his days *are* like
    grass;
As a flower of the field, so he
    flourishes.
16 For the wind passes over it, and it
    is gone,

And its place remembers it no
more.*a*

17 But the mercy of the LORD *is* from
everlasting to everlasting
On those who fear Him,
And His righteousness to
children's children,
18 To such as keep His covenant,
And to those who remember His
commandments to do them.

19 The LORD has established His
throne in heaven,
And His kingdom rules over all.

20 Bless the LORD, you His angels,
Who excel in strength, who do His
word,
Heeding the voice of His word.
21 Bless the LORD, all *you* His hosts,
You ministers of His, who do His
pleasure.
22 Bless the LORD, all His works,
In all places of His dominion.

Bless the LORD, O my soul!

PSALM 104

PRAISE TO THE SOVEREIGN LORD FOR HIS CREATION AND PROVIDENCE

BLESS the LORD, O my soul!

O LORD my God, You are very
great:
You are clothed with honor and
majesty,
2 Who cover *Yourself* with light as
with a garment,
Who stretch out the heavens like
a curtain.

3 He lays the beams of His upper
chambers in the waters,
Who makes the clouds His
chariot,

Who walks on the wings of the
wind,
4 Who makes His angels spirits,
His ministers a flame of fire.

5 *You who* laid the foundations of
the earth,
So *that* it should not be moved
forever,
6 You covered it with the deep as
with a garment;
The waters stood above the
mountains.
7 At Your rebuke they fled;
At the voice of Your thunder they
hastened away.
8 They went up over the
mountains;
They went down into the valleys,
To the place which You founded
for them.
9 You have set a boundary that
they may not pass over,
That they may not return to cover
the earth.

10 He sends the springs into the
valleys;
They flow among the hills.
11 They give drink to every beast of
the field;
The wild donkeys quench their
thirst.
12 By them the birds of the heavens
have their home;
They sing among the branches.
13 He waters the hills from His
upper chambers;
The earth is satisfied with the
fruit of Your works.

14 He causes the grass to grow for
the cattle,
And vegetation for the service of
man,
That he may bring forth food from
the earth,

103:16 *a*Compare Job 7:10

15 And wine *that* makes glad the
  heart of man,
  Oil to make *his* face shine,
  And bread *which* strengthens
  man's heart.
16 The trees of the Lord are full *of
  sap,*
  The cedars of Lebanon which He
  planted,
17 Where the birds make their nests;
  The stork has her home in the fir
  trees.
18 The high hills *are* for the wild
  goats;
  The cliffs are a refuge for the rock
  badgers.*a*

19 He appointed the moon for
  seasons;
  The sun knows its going down.
20 You make darkness, and it is
  night,
  In which all the beasts of the
  forest creep about.
21 The young lions roar after their
  prey,
  And seek their food from God.
22 *When* the sun rises, they gather
  together
  And lie down in their dens.
23 Man goes out to his work
  And to his labor until the
  evening.

24 O Lord, how manifold are Your
  works!
  In wisdom You have made them
  all.
  The earth is full of Your
  possessions—
25 This great and wide sea,
  In which *are* innumerable
  teeming things,
  Living things both small and
  great.
26 There the ships sail about;
  There is that Le·vī′a·than
  Which You have made to play
  there.

27 These all wait for You,
  That You may give *them* their
  food in due season.
28 *What* You give them they gather
  in;
  You open Your hand, they are
  filled with good.
29 You hide Your face, they are
  troubled;
  You take away their breath, they
  die and return to their dust.
30 You send forth Your Spirit, they
  are created;
  And You renew the face of the
  earth.

31 May the glory of the Lord endure
  forever;
  May the Lord rejoice in His
  works.
32 He looks on the earth, and it
  trembles;
  He touches the hills, and they
  smoke.

Praises

Psalm 104:33

How long will you praise God? A minute? An hour? A day? Longer? What about all through your life? Of course you can't praise Him every minute. But find some time to praise God every day, several times each day. You will form a habit that will stay with you all through your life.

---

33 I will sing to the Lord as long as I
  live;
  I will sing praise to my God while
  I have my being.
34 May my meditation be sweet to
  Him;
  I will be glad in the Lord.

104:18 *a*Or *rock hyrax* (compare Leviticus 11:5)

35 May sinners be consumed from
      the earth,
   And the wicked be no more.

   Bless the LORD, O my soul!
   Praise the LORD!

PSALM 105

THE ETERNAL FAITHFULNESS OF THE
LORD

OH, give thanks to the LORD!
   Call upon His name;
   Make known His deeds among
      the peoples!
2 Sing to Him, sing psalms to Him;
   Talk of all His wondrous works!
3 Glory in His holy name;
   Let the hearts of those rejoice
      who seek the LORD!
4 Seek the LORD and His strength;
   Seek His face evermore!
5 Remember His marvelous works
      which He has done,
   His wonders, and the judgments
      of His mouth,
6 O seed of Abraham His servant,
   You children of Jacob, His chosen
      ones!

7 He *is* the LORD our God;
   His judgments *are* in all the earth.
8 He remembers His covenant
      forever,
   The word *which* He commanded,
      for a thousand generations,
9 *The covenant* which He made
      with Abraham,
   And His oath to Isaac,
10 And confirmed it to Jacob for a
      statute,
   To Israel *as* an everlasting
      covenant,
11 Saying, "To you I will give the
      land of Cā′naan
   As the allotment of your
      inheritance,"

12 When they were few in number,
   Indeed very few, and strangers in
      it.
13 When they went from one nation
      to another,
   From *one* kingdom to another
      people,
14 He permitted no one to do them
      wrong;
   Yes, He rebuked kings for their
      sakes,
15 *Saying,* "Do not touch My
      anointed ones,
   And do My prophets no harm."

16 Moreover He called for a famine
      in the land;
   He destroyed all the provision of
      bread.
17 He sent a man before them—
   Joseph—*who* was sold as a slave.
18 They hurt his feet with fetters,
   He was laid in irons.
19 Until the time that his word came
      to pass,
   The word of the LORD tested him.
20 The king sent and released him,
   The ruler of the people let him go
      free.
21 He made him lord of his house,
   And ruler of all his possessions,
22 To bind his princes at his
      pleasure,
   And teach his elders wisdom.

23 Israel also came into Egypt,
   And Jacob dwelt in the land of
      Ham.
24 He increased His people greatly,
   And made them stronger than
      their enemies.
25 He turned their heart to hate His
      people,
   To deal craftily with His servants.

26 He sent Moses His servant,
   And Aaron whom He had chosen.

27 They performed His signs among
them,
And wonders in the land of Ham.
28 He sent darkness, and made *it*
dark;
And they did not rebel against
His word.
29 He turned their waters into blood,
And killed their fish.
30 Their land abounded with frogs,
Even in the chambers of their
kings.
31 He spoke, and there came swarms
of flies,
And lice in all their territory.
32 He gave them hail for rain,
And flaming fire in their land.
33 He struck their vines also, and
their fig trees,
And splintered the trees of their
territory.
34 He spoke, and locusts came,
Young locusts without number,
35 And ate up all the vegetation in
their land,
And devoured the fruit of their
ground.
36 He also destroyed all the firstborn
in their land,
The first of all their strength.

37 He also brought them out with
silver and gold,
And *there was* none feeble among
His tribes.
38 Egypt was glad when they
departed,
For the fear of them had fallen
upon them.
39 He spread a cloud for a covering,
And fire to give light in the night.
40 *The people* asked, and He brought
quail,
And satisfied them with the bread
of heaven.
41 He opened the rock, and water
gushed out;
It ran in the dry places *like* a
river.

42 For He remembered His holy
promise,
And Abraham His servant.
43 He brought out His people with
joy,
His chosen ones with gladness.
44 He gave them the lands of the
Gentiles,
And they inherited the labor of
the nations,
45 That they might observe His
statutes
And keep His laws.

Praise the LORD!

PSALM 106

JOY IN FORGIVENESS OF ISRAEL'S SINS

PRAISE the LORD!

Oh, give thanks to the LORD, for
He is good!
For His mercy *endures* forever.
2 Who can utter the mighty acts of
the LORD?
Who can declare all His praise?
3 Blessed *are* those who keep
justice,
And he who does*a* righteousness
at all times!

4 Remember me, O LORD, with the
favor *You have toward* Your
people.
Oh, visit me with Your
salvation,
5 That I may see the benefit of Your
chosen ones,
That I may rejoice in the gladness
of Your nation,
That I may glory with Your
inheritance.

106:3 *a*Septuagint, Syriac, Targum, and Vulgate
read *those who do.*

6 We have sinned with our fathers,
  We have committed iniquity,
  We have done wickedly.
7 Our fathers in Egypt did not
    understand Your wonders;
  They did not remember the
    multitude of Your mercies,
  But rebelled by the sea—the
    Red Sea.

8 Nevertheless He saved them for
    His name's sake,
  That He might make His mighty
    power known.
9 He rebuked the Red Sea also, and
    it dried up;
  So He led them through the
    depths,
  As through the wilderness.
10 He saved them from the hand of
    him who hated *them,*
  And redeemed them from the
    hand of the enemy.
11 The waters covered their
    enemies;
  There was not one of them left.
12 Then they believed His words;
  They sang His praise.

13 They soon forgot His works;
  They did not wait for His counsel,
14 But lusted exceedingly in the
    wilderness,
  And tested God in the desert.
15 And He gave them their request,
  But sent leanness into their soul.

16 When they envied Moses in the
    camp,
  And Aaron the saint of the LORD,
17 The earth opened up and
    swallowed Dā′than,
  And covered the faction of
    A·bī′ram.
18 A fire was kindled in their
    company;
  The flame burned up the wicked.

19 They made a calf in Hō′reb,
  And worshiped the molded image.

20 Thus they changed their glory
  Into the image of an ox that eats
    grass.
21 They forgot God their Savior,
  Who had done great things in
    Egypt,
22 Wondrous works in the land of
    Ham,
  Awesome things by the Red Sea.
23 Therefore He said that He would
    destroy them,
  Had not Moses His chosen one
    stood before Him in the breach,
  To turn away His wrath, lest He
    destroy *them.*

24 Then they despised the pleasant
    land;
  They did not believe His word,
25 But complained in their tents,
  And did not heed the voice of the
    LORD.
26 Therefore He raised up His hand
    in an oath against them,
  To overthrow them in the
    wilderness,
27 To overthrow their descendants
    among the nations,
  And to scatter them in the lands.

28 They joined themselves also to
    Bā′al of Pē′or,
  And ate sacrifices made to the
    dead.
29 Thus they provoked *Him* to anger
    with their deeds,
  And the plague broke out among
    them.
30 Then Phin′e·has stood up and
    intervened,
  And the plague was stopped.
31 And that was accounted to him
    for righteousness
  To all generations forevermore.

32 They angered *Him* also at the
    waters of strife,[a]

106:32 [a]Or *Meribah*

So that it went ill with Moses on
   account of them;
33 Because they rebelled against His
   Spirit,
So that he spoke rashly with his
   lips.

34 They did not destroy the peoples,
Concerning whom the Lord had
   commanded them,
35 But they mingled with the
   Gentiles
And learned their works;
36 They served their idols,
Which became a snare to them.
37 They even sacrificed their sons
And their daughters to demons,
38 And shed innocent blood,
The blood of their sons and
   daughters,
Whom they sacrificed to the idols
   of Cā′naan;
And the land was polluted with
   blood.
39 Thus they were defiled by their
   own works,
And played the harlot by their
   own deeds.

40 Therefore the wrath of the Lord
   was kindled against His people,
So that He abhorred His own
   inheritance.
41 And He gave them into the hand
   of the Gentiles,
And those who hated them ruled
   over them.
42 Their enemies also oppressed
   them,
And they were brought into
   subjection under their hand.
43 Many times He delivered them;
But they rebelled in their counsel,
And were brought low for their
   iniquity.

44 Nevertheless He regarded their
   affliction,
When He heard their cry;

45 And for their sake He
   remembered His covenant,
And relented according to the
   multitude of His mercies.
46 He also made them to be pitied
By all those who carried them
   away captive.

47 Save us, O Lord our God,
And gather us from among the
   Gentiles,
To give thanks to Your holy name,
To triumph in Your praise.

48 Blessed *be* the Lord God of Israel
From everlasting to everlasting!
And let all the people say,
   "Amen!"

Praise the Lord!

BOOK FIVE

Psalms 107—150

PSALM 107

Thanksgiving to the Lord for His
Great Works of Deliverance

O H, give thanks to the Lord, for
   He is good!
For His mercy *endures* forever.
2 Let the redeemed of the Lord say
   so,
Whom He has redeemed from the
   hand of the enemy,
3 And gathered out of the lands,
From the east and from the west,
From the north and from the
   south.

4 They wandered in the wilderness
   in a desolate way;
They found no city to dwell in.
5 Hungry and thirsty,
Their soul fainted in them.
6 Then they cried out to the Lord
   in their trouble,

And He delivered them out of
their distresses.

7 And He led them forth by the
right way,
That they might go to a city for a
dwelling place.

8 Oh, that *men* would give thanks
to the LORD *for* His goodness,
And *for* His wonderful works to
the children of men!

9 For He satisfies the longing soul,
And fills the hungry soul with
goodness.

10 Those who sat in darkness and in
the shadow of death,
Bound in affliction and irons—

11 Because they rebelled against the
words of God,
And despised the counsel of the
Most High,

12 Therefore He brought down their
heart with labor;
They fell down, and *there was*
none to help.

13 Then they cried out to the LORD
in their trouble,
And He saved them out of their
distresses.

14 He brought them out of darkness
and the shadow of death,
And broke their chains in
pieces.

15 Oh, that *men* would give thanks
to the LORD *for* His goodness,
And *for* His wonderful works to
the children of men!

16 For He has broken the gates of
bronze,
And cut the bars of iron in two.

17 Fools, because of their
transgression,
And because of their iniquities,
were afflicted.

18 Their soul abhorred all manner of
food,
And they drew near to the gates
of death.

19 Then they cried out to the LORD
in their trouble,
And He saved them out of their
distresses.

20 He sent His word and healed
them,
And delivered *them* from their
destructions.

21 Oh, that *men* would give thanks
to the LORD *for* His goodness,
And *for* His wonderful works to
the children of men!

22 Let them sacrifice the sacrifices of
thanksgiving,
And declare His works with
rejoicing.

23 Those who go down to the sea in
ships,
Who do business on great
waters,

24 They see the works of the LORD,
And His wonders in the deep.

25 For He commands and raises the
stormy wind,
Which lifts up the waves of the
sea.

26 They mount up to the heavens,
They go down again to the
depths;
Their soul melts because of
trouble.

27 They reel to and fro, and stagger
like a drunken man,
And are at their wits' end.

28 Then they cry out to the LORD in
their trouble,
And He brings them out of their
distresses.

29 He calms the storm,
So that its waves are still.

30 Then they are glad because they
are quiet;
So He guides them to their
desired haven.

31 Oh, that *men* would give thanks
to the LORD *for* His goodness,
And *for* His wonderful works to
the children of men!

What Should I Do?

WHEN TROUBLE COMES Psalm 107:13

Trouble will come. It comes to all of us. Mother has had her share of trouble. Father has had his share of trouble. Perhaps you have, too. Everyone you meet has some trouble. We *will* have some trouble. Expect it. The question is, what will you do when trouble comes?

1. You could complain. It will make you feel miserable, but will it take your trouble away?
2. You can blame someone else, *anyone* else, even God. But will that take your trouble away?
3. Oh, yes! You can pray! Prayer may not take your trouble away, but God will help you conquer your trouble. Sometimes that's even better than taking your trouble away.
4. Read Psalm 107:13. What happens when you pray? What does God do?

For more on *What Should I Do?* turn to page 932
For more on *Facing Trials* turn to page 936

32 Let them exalt Him also in the
assembly of the people,
And praise Him in the company
of the elders.

33 He turns rivers into a
wilderness,
And the watersprings into dry
ground;

34 A fruitful land into barrenness,
For the wickedness of those who
dwell in it.

35 He turns a wilderness into pools
of water,
And dry land into watersprings.

36 There He makes the hungry
dwell,
That they may establish a city for
a dwelling place,

37 And sow fields and plant
vineyards,
That they may yield a fruitful
harvest.

38 He also blesses them, and they
multiply greatly;
And He does not let their cattle
decrease.

39 When they are diminished and
brought low
Through oppression, affliction
and sorrow,

40 He pours contempt on princes,
And causes them to wander in the
wilderness *where there is* no
way;

41 Yet He sets the poor on high, far
from affliction,
And makes *their* families like a
flock.

42 The righteous see *it* and rejoice,
And all iniquity stops its
mouth.

43 Whoever *is* wise will observe
these *things,*
And they will understand the
lovingkindness of the LORD.

PSALM 108

ASSURANCE OF GOD'S VICTORY OVER ENEMIES

A Song. A Psalm of David.

O GOD, my heart is steadfast;
I will sing and give praise, even
with my glory.

2 Awake, lute and harp!
I will awaken the dawn.

3 I will praise You, O LORD, among
the peoples,
And I will sing praises to You
among the nations.

4 For Your mercy *is* great above the
heavens,
And Your truth *reaches* to the
clouds.

5 Be exalted, O God, above the
heavens,
And Your glory above all the
earth;

6 That Your beloved may be
delivered,
Save *with* Your right hand, and
hear me.

7 God has spoken in His holiness:
"I will rejoice;
I will divide Shē'chem
And measure out the Valley of
Suc'coth.

8 Gil'ē·ad *is* Mine; Ma·nas'seh *is*
Mine;
Ē'phra·im also *is* the helmet for
My head;
Judah *is* My lawgiver.

9 Mō'ab *is* My washpot;
Over Ē'dom I will cast My shoe;
Over Phi·lis'ti·a I will triumph."

10 Who will bring me *into* the strong
city?
Who will lead me to Ē'dom?

11 *Is it* not *You,* O God, *who* cast us
off?

And *You,* O God, *who* did not go
out with our armies?

12 Give us help from trouble,
For the help of man is useless.

13 Through God we will do valiantly,
For *it is* He *who* shall tread down
our enemies.[a]

PSALM 109

PLEA FOR JUDGMENT OF FALSE ACCUSERS

To the Chief Musician. A Psalm of David.

D O not keep silent,
O God of my praise!

2 For the mouth of the wicked and
the mouth of the deceitful
Have opened against me;
They have spoken against me
with a lying tongue.

3 They have also surrounded me
with words of hatred,
And fought against me without a
cause.

4 In return for my love they are my
accusers,
But I *give myself to* prayer.

5 Thus they have rewarded me evil
for good,
And hatred for my love.

6 Set a wicked man over him,
And let an accuser[a] stand at his
right hand.

7 When he is judged, let him be
found guilty,
And let his prayer become sin.

8 Let his days be few,
And let another take his office.

9 Let his children be fatherless,
And his wife a widow.

10 Let his children continually be
vagabonds, and beg;
Let them seek *their bread*[a] also
from their desolate places.

11 Let the creditor seize all that he
has,

And let strangers plunder his
labor.

12 Let there be none to extend mercy
to him,
Nor let there be any to favor his
fatherless children.

13 Let his posterity be cut off,
And in the generation following
let their name be blotted out.

14 Let the iniquity of his fathers be
remembered before the LORD,
And let not the sin of his mother
be blotted out.

15 Let them be continually before
the LORD,
That He may cut off the memory
of them from the earth;

16 Because he did not remember to
show mercy,
But persecuted the poor and
needy man,
That he might even slay the
broken in heart.

17 As he loved cursing, so let it come
to him;
As he did not delight in blessing,
so let it be far from him.

18 As he clothed himself with
cursing as with his garment,
So let it enter his body like water,
And like oil into his bones.

19 Let it be to him like the garment
which covers him,
And for a belt with which he girds
himself continually.

20 *Let* this *be* the LORD's reward to
my accusers,
And to those who speak evil
against my person.

21 But You, O GOD the Lord,
Deal with me for Your name's
sake;
Because Your mercy *is* good,
deliver me.

108:13 [a]Compare verses 6–13 with 60:5–12
109:6 [a]Hebrew *satan*   109:10 [a]Following
Masoretic Text and Targum; Septuagint and Vulgate read *be cast out.*

22 For I *am* poor and needy,
And my heart is wounded within
me.
23 I am gone like a shadow when it
lengthens;
I am shaken off like a locust.
24 My knees are weak through
fasting,
And my flesh is feeble from lack
of fatness.
25 I also have become a reproach to
them;
When they look at me, they shake
their heads.

26 Help me, O LORD my God!
Oh, save me according to Your
mercy,
27 That they may know that this *is*
Your hand—
That You, LORD, have done it!
28 Let them curse, but You bless;
When they arise, let them be
ashamed,
But let Your servant rejoice.
29 Let my accusers be clothed with
shame,
And let them cover themselves
with their own disgrace as with
a mantle.

30 I will greatly praise the LORD
with my mouth;
Yes, I will praise Him among the
multitude.
31 For He shall stand at the right
hand of the poor,
To save *him* from those who
condemn him.

PSALM 110

ANNOUNCEMENT OF THE MESSIAH'S REIGN

A Psalm of David.

THE LORD said to my Lord,
"Sit at My right hand,
Till I make Your enemies Your
footstool."
2 The LORD shall send the rod of
Your strength out of Zion.
Rule in the midst of Your
enemies!

3 Your people *shall be* volunteers
In the day of Your power;
In the beauties of holiness, from
the womb of the morning,
You have the dew of Your youth.
4 The LORD has sworn
And will not relent,
"You *are* a priest forever
According to the order of
Mel·chiz′e·dek."

5 The Lord *is* at Your right hand;
He shall execute kings in the day
of His wrath.
6 He shall judge among the nations,
He shall fill *the places* with dead
bodies,
He shall execute the heads of
many countries.
7 He shall drink of the brook by the
wayside;
Therefore He shall lift up the
head.

PSALM 111

PRAISE TO GOD FOR HIS FAITHFULNESS AND JUSTICE

PRAISE the LORD!

I will praise the LORD with *my*
whole heart,
In the assembly of the upright
and *in* the congregation.
2 The works of the LORD *are* great,
Studied by all who have pleasure
in them.
3 His work *is* honorable and
glorious,
And His righteousness endures
forever.

4 He has made His wonderful
works to be remembered;
The LORD *is* gracious and full of
compassion.
5 He has given food to those who
fear Him;
He will ever be mindful of His
covenant.
6 He has declared to His people the
power of His works,
In giving them the heritage of the
nations.

7 The works of His hands *are* verity
and justice;
All His precepts *are* sure.
8 They stand fast forever and ever,
And are done in truth and
uprightness.
9 He has sent redemption to His
people;
He has commanded His covenant
forever:
Holy and awesome *is* His name.

10 The fear of the LORD *is* the
beginning of wisdom;
A good understanding have all
those who do *His*
commandments.
His praise endures forever.

PSALM 112

THE BLESSED STATE OF THE RIGHTEOUS

P RAISE the LORD!

Blessed *is* the man *who* fears the
LORD,
Who delights greatly in His
commandments.

2 His descendants will be mighty
on earth;
The generation of the upright will
be blessed.
3 Wealth and riches *will be* in his
house,

> *Praises*
>
> Psalm 112:1
>
> Praise the Lord! How often do
> you say these words? When?
> Why do you say them? Do you
> honor the Lord? Do you delight
> in His Words? The Lord says you
> will be blessed if you do. Praise
> God because you honor Him.
> Praise God because you delight
> in Him.

And his righteousness endures
forever.
4 Unto the upright there arises
light in the darkness;
He is gracious, and full of
compassion, and righteous.
5 A good man deals graciously and
lends;
He will guide his affairs with
discretion.
6 Surely he will never be shaken;
The righteous will be in
everlasting remembrance.
7 He will not be afraid of evil
tidings;
His heart is steadfast, trusting in
the LORD.
8 His heart *is* established;
He will not be afraid,
Until he sees *his desire* upon his
enemies.

9 He has dispersed abroad,
He has given to the poor;
His righteousness endures
forever;
His horn will be exalted with
honor.
10 The wicked will see *it* and be
grieved;
He will gnash his teeth and melt
away;
The desire of the wicked shall
perish.

PSALM 113

THE MAJESTY AND CONDESCENSION OF GOD

PRAISE the LORD!

Praise, O servants of the LORD,
Praise the name of the LORD!
2 Blessed be the name of the LORD
From this time forth and
forevermore!
3 From the rising of the sun to its
going down
The LORD's name *is* to be praised.

4 The LORD *is* high above all
nations,
His glory above the heavens.
5 Who *is* like the LORD our God,
Who dwells on high,
6 Who humbles Himself to behold
The things that are in the
heavens and in the earth?

7 He raises the poor out of the dust,
And lifts the needy out of the ash
heap,
8 That He may seat *him* with
princes—
With the princes of His people.
9 He grants the barren woman a
home,
Like a joyful mother of children.

Praise the LORD!

PSALM 114

THE POWER OF GOD IN HIS DELIVERANCE OF ISRAEL

WHEN Israel went out of Egypt,
The house of Jacob from a people
of strange language,
2 Judah became His sanctuary,
And Israel His dominion.

3 The sea saw *it* and fled;
Jordan turned back.
4 The mountains skipped like rams,
The little hills like lambs.
5 What ails you, O sea, that you
fled?
O Jordan, *that* you turned back?
6 O mountains, *that* you skipped
like rams?
O little hills, like lambs?

7 Tremble, O earth, at the presence
of the Lord,
At the presence of the God of
Jacob,
8 Who turned the rock *into* a pool of
water,
The flint into a fountain of
waters.

PSALM 115

THE FUTILITY OF IDOLS AND THE TRUSTWORTHINESS OF GOD

NOT unto us, O LORD, not unto us,
But to Your name give glory,
Because of Your mercy,
Because of Your truth.
2 Why should the Gentiles say,
"So where *is* their God?"

3 But our God *is* in heaven;
He does whatever He pleases.
4 Their idols *are* silver and gold,
The work of men's hands.
5 They have mouths, but they do
not speak;
Eyes they have, but they do not
see;
6 They have ears, but they do not
hear;
Noses they have, but they do not
smell;
7 They have hands, but they do not
handle;
Feet they have, but they do not
walk;

Nor do they mutter through their
    throat.
8 Those who make them are like
    them;
So is everyone who trusts in
    them.

9 O Israel, trust in the LORD;
He *is* their help and their shield.
10 O house of Aaron, trust in the
    LORD;
He *is* their help and their shield.
11 You who fear the LORD, trust in
    the LORD;
He *is* their help and their shield.

12 The LORD has been mindful of *us;*
He will bless us;
He will bless the house of Israel;
He will bless the house of Aaron.
13 He will bless those who fear the
    LORD,
Both small and great.

14 May the LORD give you increase
    more and more,
You and your children.
15 *May* you *be* blessed by the LORD,
Who made heaven and earth.

16 The heaven, *even* the heavens, *are*
    the LORD's;
But the earth He has given to the
    children of men.
17 The dead do not praise the LORD,
Nor any who go down into silence.
18 But we will bless the LORD
From this time forth and
    forevermore.

Praise the LORD!

PSALM 116

THANKSGIVING FOR DELIVERANCE FROM
DEATH

I LOVE the LORD, because He has
heard

My voice *and* my supplications.
2 Because He has inclined His ear
    to me,
Therefore I will call *upon Him* as
    long as I live.

3 The pains of death surrounded
    me,
And the pangs of Shē′ōl laid hold
    of me;
I found trouble and sorrow.
4 Then I called upon the name of
    the LORD:
"O LORD, I implore You, deliver my
    soul!"

5 Gracious *is* the LORD, and
    righteous;
Yes, our God *is* merciful.
6 The LORD preserves the simple;
I was brought low, and He saved
    me.
7 Return to your rest, O my soul,
For the LORD has dealt
    bountifully with you.

8 For You have delivered my soul
    from death,
My eyes from tears,
And my feet from falling.
9 I will walk before the LORD
In the land of the living.
10 I believed, therefore I spoke,
"I am greatly afflicted."
11 I said in my haste,
"All men *are* liars."

12 What shall I render to the
    LORD
For all His benefits toward me?
13 I will take up the cup of
    salvation,
And call upon the name of the
    LORD.
14 I will pay my vows to the LORD
Now in the presence of all His
    people.

15 Precious in the sight of the LORD
   Is the death of His saints.

16 O LORD, truly I *am* Your servant;
   I *am* Your servant, the son of Your
      maidservant;
   You have loosed my bonds.
17 I will offer to You the sacrifice of
      thanksgiving,
   And will call upon the name of
      the LORD.

18 I will pay my vows to the LORD
   Now in the presence of all His
      people,
19 In the courts of the LORD's
      house,
   In the midst of you, O Jerusalem.

   Praise the LORD!

PSALM 117

LET ALL PEOPLES PRAISE THE LORD

PRAISE the LORD, all you
      Gentiles!
   Laud Him, all you peoples!
2 For His merciful kindness is great
      toward us,
   And the truth of the LORD
      endures forever.

   Praise the LORD!

PSALM 118

PRAISE TO GOD FOR HIS EVERLASTING
MERCY

OH, give thanks to the LORD, for
   He is good!
   For His mercy *endures* forever.

2 Let Israel now say,
   "His mercy *endures* forever."
3 Let the house of Aaron now
      say,
   "His mercy *endures* forever."
4 Let those who fear the LORD now
      say,
   "His mercy *endures* forever."

5 I called on the LORD in distress;
   The LORD answered me *and set
      me* in a broad place.
6 The LORD *is* on my side;
   I will not fear.
   What can man do to me?
7 The LORD is for me among those
      who help me;
   Therefore I shall see *my desire* on
      those who hate me.
8 *It is* better to trust in the LORD
   Than to put confidence in man.
9 *It is* better to trust in the LORD
   Than to put confidence in
      princes.

10 All nations surrounded me,
   But in the name of the LORD I will
      destroy them.
11 They surrounded me,
   Yes, they surrounded me;
   But in the name of the LORD I will
      destroy them.
12 They surrounded me like bees;
   They were quenched like a fire of
      thorns;
   For in the name of the LORD I will
      destroy them.
13 You pushed me violently, that I
      might fall,
   But the LORD helped me.
14 The LORD *is* my strength and
      song,
   And He has become my
      salvation.ᵃ

15 The voice of rejoicing and
      salvation

118:14 ᵃCompare Exodus 15:2

Is in the tents of the righteous;
The right hand of the LORD does
valiantly.

16 The right hand of the LORD is
exalted;
The right hand of the LORD does
valiantly.

17 I shall not die, but live,
And declare the works of the
LORD.

18 The LORD has chastened me
severely,
But He has not given me over to
death.

19 Open to me the gates of
righteousness;
I will go through them,
And I will praise the LORD.

20 This is the gate of the LORD,
Through which the righteous
shall enter.

21 I will praise You,
For You have answered me,
And have become my salvation.

22 The stone *which* the builders
rejected
Has become the chief
cornerstone.

23 This was the LORD's doing;
It *is* marvelous in our eyes.

24 This *is* the day the LORD has
made;
We will rejoice and be glad in it.

25 Save now, I pray, O LORD;
O LORD, I pray, send now
prosperity.

26 Blessed *is* he who comes in the
name of the LORD!
We have blessed you from the
house of the LORD.

27 God *is* the LORD,
And He has given us light;
Bind the sacrifice with cords to
the horns of the altar.

28 You *are* my God, and I will praise
You;
You are my God, I will exalt You.

29 Oh, give thanks to the LORD, for
He is good!
For His mercy *endures* forever.

PSALM 119

MEDITATIONS ON THE EXCELLENCIES OF THE WORD OF GOD

א ALEPH

BLESSED *are* the undefiled in the
way,
Who walk in the law of the
LORD!

2 Blessed *are* those who keep His
testimonies,
Who seek Him with the whole
heart!

3 They also do no iniquity;
They walk in His ways.

4 You have commanded *us*
To keep Your precepts diligently.

5 Oh, that my ways were directed
To keep Your statutes!

6 Then I would not be ashamed,
When I look into all Your
commandments.

7 I will praise You with uprightness
of heart,
When I learn Your righteous
judgments.

8 I will keep Your statutes;
Oh, do not forsake me utterly!

ב BETH

9 How can a young man cleanse his
way?
By taking heed according to Your
word.

10 With my whole heart I have
sought You;
Oh, let me not wander from Your
commandments!

Favorite Family Verses

YOUR WORD I HAVE HIDDEN IN MY HEART, / THAT I MIGHT NOT SIN AGAINST YOU. Psalm 119:11

Can I Put a Book in My Heart?
How do you put a book like the Bible into your heart? Can you push the whole Bible down inside you? Or is there another way?

1. Read Psalm 119:11. Why should we hide God's Word in our heart?
2. How do you hide God's Word in your heart? Do you read your Bible each day? Will that help you hide it in your heart? Do you ever memorize God's Word? Will that help you hide it in your heart?

For more on *Favorite Family Verses* turn to page 930
For more on *Bible* turn to page 930

11 Your word I have hidden in my
    heart,
That I might not sin against
    You.
12 Blessed *are* You, O LORD!
Teach me Your statutes.
13 With my lips I have declared
All the judgments of Your
    mouth.
14 I have rejoiced in the way of Your
    testimonies,
As *much as* in all riches.
15 I will meditate on Your precepts,
And contemplate Your ways.
16 I will delight myself in Your
    statutes;
I will not forget Your word.

ג GIMEL
17 Deal bountifully with Your
    servant,
That I may live and keep Your
    word.
18 Open my eyes, that I may see
Wondrous things from Your law.
19 I *am* a stranger in the earth;
Do not hide Your commandments
    from me.
20 My soul breaks with longing
For Your judgments at all times.

21 You rebuke the proud—the
    cursed,
Who stray from Your
    commandments.
22 Remove from me reproach and
    contempt,
For I have kept Your
    testimonies.
23 Princes also sit *and* speak against
    me,
But Your servant meditates on
    Your statutes.
24 Your testimonies also *are* my
    delight
And my counselors.

ד DALETH
25 My soul clings to the dust;
Revive me according to Your
    word.
26 I have declared my ways, and You
    answered me;
Teach me Your statutes.
27 Make me understand the way of
    Your precepts;
So shall I meditate on Your
    wonderful works.
28 My soul melts from heaviness;
Strengthen me according to Your
    word.

29 Remove from me the way of
      lying,
   And grant me Your law
      graciously.
30 I have chosen the way of truth;
   Your judgments I have laid *before
      me.*
31 I cling to Your testimonies;
   O LORD, do not put me to shame!
32 I will run the course of Your
      commandments,
   For You shall enlarge my heart.

ה HE

33 Teach me, O LORD, the way of
      Your statutes,
   And I shall keep it *to* the end.
34 Give me understanding, and I
      shall keep Your law;
   Indeed, I shall observe it with *my*
      whole heart.
35 Make me walk in the path of Your
      commandments,
   For I delight in it.
36 Incline my heart to Your
      testimonies,
   And not to covetousness.
37 Turn away my eyes from looking
      at worthless things,
   And revive me in Your way.*a*
38 Establish Your word to Your
      servant,
   Who *is devoted* to fearing You.
39 Turn away my reproach which I
      dread,
   For Your judgments *are* good.
40 Behold, I long for Your precepts;
   Revive me in Your
      righteousness.

ו WAW

41 Let Your mercies come also to me,
      O LORD—
   Your salvation according to Your
      word.
42 So shall I have an answer for him
      who reproaches me,
   For I trust in Your word.

43 And take not the word of truth
      utterly out of my mouth,
   For I have hoped in Your
      ordinances.
44 So shall I keep Your law
      continually,
   Forever and ever.
45 And I will walk at liberty,
   For I seek Your precepts.
46 I will speak of Your testimonies
      also before kings,
   And will not be ashamed.
47 And I will delight myself in Your
      commandments,
   Which I love.
48 My hands also I will lift up to
      Your commandments,
   Which I love,
   And I will meditate on Your
      statutes.

ז ZAYIN

49 Remember the word to Your
      servant,
   Upon which You have caused me
      to hope.
50 This *is* my comfort in my
      affliction,
   For Your word has given me life.
51 The proud have me in great
      derision,
   Yet I do not turn aside from Your
      law.
52 I remembered Your judgments of
      old, O LORD,
   And have comforted myself.
53 Indignation has taken hold of
      me
   Because of the wicked, who
      forsake Your law.
54 Your statutes have been my
      songs
   In the house of my pilgrimage.
55 I remember Your name in the
      night, O LORD,
   And I keep Your law.

119:37 *a*Following Masoretic Text, Septuagint, and
Vulgate; Targum reads *Your words.*

56 This has become mine,
Because I kept Your precepts.

ה HETH

57 *You are* my portion, O LORD;
I have said that I would keep
Your words.
58 I entreated Your favor with *my*
whole heart;
Be merciful to me according to
Your word.
59 I thought about my ways,
And turned my feet to Your
testimonies.
60 I made haste, and did not
delay
To keep Your commandments.
61 The cords of the wicked have
bound me,
But I have not forgotten Your
law.
62 At midnight I will rise to give
thanks to You,
Because of Your righteous
judgments.
63 I *am* a companion of all who fear
You,
And of those who keep Your
precepts.
64 The earth, O LORD, is full of Your
mercy;
Teach me Your statutes.

ט TETH

65 You have dealt well with Your
servant,
O LORD, according to Your
word.
66 Teach me good judgment and
knowledge,
For I believe Your
commandments.
67 Before I was afflicted I went
astray,
But now I keep Your word.
68 You *are* good, and do good;
Teach me Your statutes.

69 The proud have forged a lie
against me,
But I will keep Your precepts with
my whole heart.
70 Their heart is as fat as grease,
But I delight in Your law.
71 *It is* good for me that I have been
afflicted,
That I may learn Your
statutes.
72 The law of Your mouth *is* better
to me
Than thousands of *coins of* gold
and silver.

י YOD

73 Your hands have made me and
fashioned me;
Give me understanding, that I
may learn Your
commandments.
74 Those who fear You will be glad
when they see me,
Because I have hoped in Your
word.
75 I know, O LORD, that Your
judgments *are* right,
And *that* in faithfulness You have
afflicted me.
76 Let, I pray, Your merciful
kindness be for my comfort,
According to Your word to Your
servant.
77 Let Your tender mercies come to
me, that I may live;
For Your law *is* my delight.
78 Let the proud be ashamed,
For they treated me wrongfully
with falsehood;
But I will meditate on Your
precepts.
79 Let those who fear You turn to
me,
Those who know Your
testimonies.
80 Let my heart be blameless
regarding Your statutes,
That I may not be ashamed.

כ **KAPH**

81 My soul faints for Your
     salvation,
     But I hope in Your word.

82 My eyes fail *from searching* Your
     word,
     Saying, "When will You comfort
     me?"

83 For I have become like a wineskin
     in smoke,
     Yet I do not forget Your statutes.

84 How many *are* the days of Your
     servant?
     When will You execute
     judgment on those who
     persecute me?

85 The proud have dug pits for
     me,
     Which *is* not according to Your
     law.

86 All Your commandments *are*
     faithful;
     They persecute me wrongfully;
     Help me!

87 They almost made an end of me
     on earth,
     But I did not forsake Your
     precepts.

88 Revive me according to Your
     lovingkindness,
     So that I may keep the testimony
     of Your mouth.

ל **LAMED**

89 Forever, O LORD,
     Your word is settled in heaven.

90 Your faithfulness *endures* to all
     generations;
     You established the earth, and it
     abides.

91 They continue this day according
     to Your ordinances,
     For all *are* Your servants.

92 Unless Your law *had been* my
     delight,
     I would then have perished in my
     affliction.

93 I will never forget Your precepts,

For by them You have given me
     life.

94 I *am* Yours, save me;
     For I have sought Your precepts.

95 The wicked wait for me to
     destroy me,
     But I will consider Your
     testimonies.

96 I have seen the consummation of
     all perfection,
     But Your commandment *is*
     exceedingly broad.

מ **MEM**

97 Oh, how I love Your law!
     It *is* my meditation all the day.

98 You, through Your
     commandments, make me
     wiser than my enemies;
     For they *are* ever with me.

99 I have more understanding than
     all my teachers,
     For Your testimonies *are* my
     meditation.

100 I understand more than the
     ancients,
     Because I keep Your precepts.

101 I have restrained my feet from
     every evil way,
     That I may keep Your word.

102 I have not departed from Your
     judgments,
     For You Yourself have taught
     me.

103 How sweet are Your words to my
     taste,
     Sweeter than honey to my
     mouth!

104 Through Your precepts I get
     understanding;
     Therefore I hate every false
     way.

נ **NUN**

105 Your word *is* a lamp to my feet
     And a light to my path.

106 I have sworn and confirmed

YOUR WORD IS A LAMP TO MY FEET / AND A LIGHT TO MY PATH.
Psalm 119:105

A Flashlight Book

Wouldn't you be surprised if you opened a book and light shone from it? That's what happens when you read your Bible. It isn't the kind of light that comes from a flashlight. It's a special kind of light that shows you where to go and what to do.

1. What does Psalm 119:105 say? What does it mean?
2. What kind of light comes from the Bible, God's Word?
3. What does the light from the Bible show you? What does it help you do?

For more on *Favorite Family Verses* turn to page 938
For more on *Bible* turn to page 948

That I will keep Your righteous judgments.
107 I am afflicted very much;
Revive me, O LORD, according to Your word.
108 Accept, I pray, the freewill offerings of my mouth,
O LORD,
And teach me Your judgments.
109 My life *is* continually in my hand,
Yet I do not forget Your law.
110 The wicked have laid a snare for me,
Yet I have not strayed from Your precepts.
111 Your testimonies I have taken as a heritage forever,
For they *are* the rejoicing of my heart.
112 I have inclined my heart to perform Your statutes
Forever, to the very end.

ס SAMEK

113 I hate the double-minded,
But I love Your law.

114 You *are* my hiding place and my shield;
I hope in Your word.
115 Depart from me, you evildoers,
For I will keep the commandments of my God!
116 Uphold me according to Your word, that I may live;
And do not let me be ashamed of my hope.
117 Hold me up, and I shall be safe,
And I shall observe Your statutes continually.
118 You reject all those who stray from Your statutes,
For their deceit *is* falsehood.
119 You put away all the wicked of the earth *like* dross;
Therefore I love Your testimonies.
120 My flesh trembles for fear of You,
And I am afraid of Your judgments.

ע AYIN

121 I have done justice and righteousness;

Do not leave me to my
oppressors.

122 Be surety for Your servant for
good;
Do not let the proud oppress
me.

123 My eyes fail *from seeking* Your
salvation
And Your righteous word.

124 Deal with Your servant
according to Your mercy,
And teach me Your statutes.

125 I *am* Your servant;
Give me understanding,
That I may know Your
testimonies.

126 *It is* time for *You* to act,
O LORD,
For they have regarded Your law
as void.

127 Therefore I love Your
commandments
More than gold, yes, than fine
gold!

128 Therefore all *Your* precepts
concerning all *things*
I consider *to be* right;
I hate every false way.

פ PE

129 Your testimonies are wonderful;
Therefore my soul keeps them.

130 The entrance of Your words gives
light;
It gives understanding to the
simple.

131 I opened my mouth and panted,
For I longed for Your
commandments.

132 Look upon me and be merciful to
me,
As Your custom *is* toward those
who love Your name.

133 Direct my steps by Your word,
And let no iniquity have
dominion over me.

134 Redeem me from the oppression
of man,
That I may keep Your precepts.

135 Make Your face shine upon Your
servant,
And teach me Your statutes.

136 Rivers of water run down from
my eyes,
Because *men* do not keep Your
law.

צ TSADDE

137 Righteous *are* You, O LORD,
And upright *are* Your judgments.

138 Your testimonies, *which* You
have commanded,
Are righteous and very faithful.

139 My zeal has consumed me,
Because my enemies have
forgotten Your words.

140 Your word *is* very pure;
Therefore Your servant loves it.

141 I *am* small and despised,
Yet I do not forget Your precepts.

142 Your righteousness *is* an
everlasting righteousness,
And Your law *is* truth.

143 Trouble and anguish have
overtaken me,
Yet Your commandments *are* my
delights.

144 The righteousness of Your
testimonies *is* everlasting;
Give me understanding, and I
shall live.

ק QOPH

145 I cry out with *my* whole heart;
Hear me, O LORD!
I will keep Your statutes.

146 I cry out to You;
Save me, and I will keep Your
testimonies.

147 I rise before the dawning of the
morning,
And cry for help;
I hope in Your word.

148 My eyes are awake through the
night watches,
That I may meditate on Your
word.

KEEPING LIFE IN BALANCE Psalm 119:130

Do you ever feel as if you are juggling too many things? You have school work and homework and chores and playing with your friend and a dozen or so other things. Ask your mother or father if they ever feel that way, too.

1. How many things are you trying to do? Do you feel there are too many? Talk with mother or father. Ask how they feel about the things they are trying to "juggle."
2. When life seems too complicated, ask God to help you. Read Psalm 119:130. How do the wise words from God's Word bring understanding and simplicity?

For more on *What Should I Do?* turn to page 971
For more on *Choices* turn to page 1267

149 Hear my voice according to Your
  lovingkindness;
    O LORD, revive me according to
    Your justice.
150 They draw near who follow after
  wickedness;
    They are far from Your law.
151 You *are* near, O LORD,
    And all Your commandments *are*
    truth.
152 Concerning Your testimonies,
    I have known of old that You
    have founded them forever.

ר RESH

153 Consider my affliction and
  deliver me,
    For I do not forget Your law.
154 Plead my cause and redeem me;
    Revive me according to Your
    word.
155 Salvation *is* far from the wicked,
    For they do not seek Your
    statutes.
156 Great *are* Your tender mercies,
    O LORD;
    Revive me according to Your
    judgments.
157 Many *are* my persecutors and
  my enemies,
    Yet I do not turn from Your
    testimonies.
158 I see the treacherous, and am
  disgusted,
    Because they do not keep Your
    word.
159 Consider how I love Your
  precepts;
    Revive me, O LORD, according to
    Your lovingkindness.
160 The entirety of Your word *is*
  truth,
    And every one of Your righteous
    judgments *endures* forever.

ש SHIN

161 Princes persecute me without a
  cause,

But my heart stands in awe of
  Your word.
162 I rejoice at Your word
    As one who finds great treasure.
163 I hate and abhor lying,
    But I love Your law.
164 Seven times a day I praise You,
    Because of Your righteous
    judgments.
165 Great peace have those who love
  Your law,
    And nothing causes them to
    stumble.
166 LORD, I hope for Your salvation,
    And I do Your commandments.
167 My soul keeps Your testimonies,
    And I love them exceedingly.
168 I keep Your precepts and Your
  testimonies,
    For all my ways *are* before You.

ת TAU

169 Let my cry come before You,
    O LORD;
    Give me understanding
    according to Your word.
170 Let my supplication come before
  You;
    Deliver me according to Your
    word.
171 My lips shall utter praise,
    For You teach me Your statutes.
172 My tongue shall speak of Your
  word,
    For all Your commandments *are*
    righteousness.
173 Let Your hand become my help,
    For I have chosen Your precepts.
174 I long for Your salvation,
    O LORD,
    And Your law *is* my delight.
175 Let my soul live, and it shall
  praise You;
    And let Your judgments help me.
176 I have gone astray like a lost
  sheep;
    Seek Your servant,
    For I do not forget Your
    commandments.

PSALM 120

PLEA FOR RELIEF FROM BITTER FOES

A Song of Ascents.

IN my distress I cried to the LORD,
And He heard me.
2 Deliver my soul, O LORD, from
lying lips
And from a deceitful tongue.

3 What shall be given to you,
Or what shall be done to you,
You false tongue?
4 Sharp arrows of the warrior,
With coals of the broom tree!

5 Woe is me, that I dwell in
Mē′shech,
That I dwell among the tents of
Kē′dar!
6 My soul has dwelt too long
With one who hates peace.
7 I *am for* peace;
But when I speak, they *are* for war.

PSALM 121

GOD THE HELP OF THOSE WHO SEEK HIM

A Song of Ascents.

I WILL lift up my eyes to the hills—
From whence comes my help?
2 My help *comes* from the LORD,
Who made heaven and earth.

3 He will not allow your foot to be
moved;
He who keeps you will not
slumber.
4 Behold, He who keeps Israel
Shall neither slumber nor sleep.

5 The LORD *is* your keeper;
The LORD *is* your shade at your
right hand.

6 The sun shall not strike you by
day,
Nor the moon by night.

7 The LORD shall preserve you from
all evil;
He shall preserve your soul.
8 The LORD shall preserve your
going out and your coming in
From this time forth, and even
forevermore.

PSALM 122

THE JOY OF GOING TO THE HOUSE OF THE LORD

A Song of Ascents. Of David.

I WAS glad when they said to me,
"Let us go into the house of the
LORD."
2 Our feet have been standing
Within your gates, O Jerusalem!

3 Jerusalem is built
As a city that is compact together,
4 Where the tribes go up,
The tribes of the LORD,
To the Testimony of Israel,
To give thanks to the name of the
LORD.
5 For thrones are set there for
judgment,
The thrones of the house of
David.

6 Pray for the peace of Jerusalem:
"May they prosper who love you.
7 Peace be within your walls,
Prosperity within your palaces."
8 For the sake of my brethren and
companions,
I will now say, "Peace *be* within
you."
9 Because of the house of the LORD
our God
I will seek your good.

PSALM 123

PRAYER FOR RELIEF FROM CONTEMPT

A Song of Ascents.

UNTO You I lift up my eyes,
O You who dwell in the heavens.
2 Behold, as the eyes of servants
look to the hand of their
masters,
As the eyes of a maid to the hand
of her mistress,
So our eyes *look* to the LORD our
God,
Until He has mercy on us.

3 Have mercy on us, O LORD, have
mercy on us!
For we are exceedingly filled with
contempt.
4 Our soul is exceedingly filled
With the scorn of those who are at
ease,
With the contempt of the proud.

PSALM 124

THE LORD THE DEFENSE OF HIS PEOPLE

A Song of Ascents. Of David.

"IF it had not been the LORD who
was on our side,"
Let Israel now say—
2 "If it had not been the LORD who
was on our side,
When men rose up against us,
3 Then they would have swallowed
us alive,
When their wrath was kindled
against us;
4 Then the waters would have
overwhelmed us,
The stream would have gone over
our soul;
5 Then the swollen waters
Would have gone over our soul."

6 Blessed *be* the LORD,
Who has not given us *as* prey to
their teeth.
7 Our soul has escaped as a bird
from the snare of the fowlers;*a*
The snare is broken, and we have
escaped.
8 Our help *is* in the name of the
LORD,
Who made heaven and earth.

PSALM 125

THE LORD THE STRENGTH OF HIS PEOPLE

A Song of Ascents.

THOSE who trust in the LORD
Are like Mount Zion,
Which cannot be moved, *but*
abides forever.
2 As the mountains surround
Jerusalem,
So the LORD surrounds His people
From this time forth and forever.

3 For the scepter of wickedness
shall not rest
On the land allotted to the
righteous,
Lest the righteous reach out their
hands to iniquity.

4 Do good, O LORD, to *those who are*
good,
And to *those who are* upright in
their hearts.

5 As for such as turn aside to their
crooked ways,
The LORD shall lead them away
With the workers of iniquity.

Peace *be* upon Israel!

124:7 *a*That is, persons who catch birds in a trap or
snare

DO YOU REMEMBER THAT EGG ON THE FLOOR? Psalm 126:2, 3

Do you remember when you flipped that pancake and it fell on you? Do you remember when you flipped an egg and it went on the floor? Do you remember when you spilled the glass of milk on your best dress? Sometimes we laugh together when we remember things like these. At the time they weren't funny. Now they are. Perhaps they should have caused us to laugh when they happened. Perhaps we should learn to laugh a little more, even when eggs fall on the floor. What do you think?

1. What "eggs on the floor" kind of things have happened in your family lately? Did you laugh together? Or did you yell at each other?
2. What will you do the next time something like this happens?
3. Does God want us to have fun together?

For more on *Family Memories* turn to page 968
For more on *Facing Trials* turn to page 1059

PSALM 126

A JOYFUL RETURN TO ZION

A Song of Ascents.

WHEN the LORD brought back the
captivity of Zion,
We were like those who dream.
2 Then our mouth was filled with
laughter,
And our tongue with singing.
Then they said among the
nations,
"The LORD has done great things
for them."
3 The LORD has done great things
for us,
And we are glad.

4 Bring back our captivity,
O LORD,
As the streams in the South.

5 Those who sow in tears
Shall reap in joy.
6 He who continually goes forth
weeping,
Bearing seed for sowing,
Shall doubtless come again with
rejoicing,
Bringing his sheaves *with him.*

PSALM 127

LABORING AND PROSPERING WITH THE
LORD

A Song of Ascents. Of Solomon.

UNLESS the LORD builds the
house,
They labor in vain who build it;
Unless the LORD guards the city,
The watchman stays awake in
vain.
2 *It is* vain for you to rise up early,
To sit up late,

To eat the bread of sorrows;
For so He gives His beloved
sleep.

3 Behold, children *are* a heritage
from the LORD,
The fruit of the womb *is* a reward.
4 Like arrows in the hand of a
warrior,
So *are* the children of one's youth.
5 Happy *is* the man who has his
quiver full of them;
They shall not be ashamed,
But shall speak with their
enemies in the gate.

PSALM 128

BLESSINGS OF THOSE WHO FEAR THE
LORD

A Song of Ascents.

BLESSED *is* every one who fears
the LORD,
Who walks in His ways.

2 When you eat the labor of your
hands,
You *shall be* happy, and *it shall be*
well with you.
3 Your wife *shall be* like a fruitful
vine
In the very heart of your house,
Your children like olive plants
All around your table.
4 Behold, thus shall the man be
blessed
Who fears the LORD.

5 The LORD bless you out of Zion,
And may you see the good of
Jerusalem
All the days of your life.
6 Yes, may you see your children's
children.

Peace *be* upon Israel!

Favorite Family Verses

HE GIVES HIS BELOVED SLEEP. Psalm 127:2

Is Sleep a Gift?

Has someone ever said to you, "I could not get to sleep last night. I'm *so* tired." Perhaps this person was worried about something. Or perhaps this person had too much coffee or chocolate that night. Sometimes older people can't sleep well. Anyone who hasn't slept well will tell you that sleep is more important than money. The wealthiest king in the world, who could not sleep, would give half his kingdom to sleep well again. So where does sleep come from? Where do we get it?

1. Read Psalm 127:2. Who gives His beloved sleep?
2. Read Ecclesiastes 5:12. Will money buy sleep? Is sleep really a gift from God then? That's what the Bible tells us in Psalm 127:2, isn't it?
3. Have you thanked God lately for the gift of sleep? Would you like to do that now?

For more on *Favorite Family Verses* turn to page 945
For more on *God's Care* turn to page 1018

PSALM 129

SONG OF VICTORY OVER ZION'S ENEMIES

A Song of Ascents.

"**M**ANY a time they have afflicted me from my youth,"
Let Israel now say—
2 "Many a time they have afflicted me from my youth;
Yet they have not prevailed against me.
3 The plowers plowed on my back;
They made their furrows long."
4 The LORD *is* righteous;
He has cut in pieces the cords of the wicked.

5 Let all those who hate Zion
Be put to shame and turned back.
6 Let them be as the grass *on* the housetops,
Which withers before it grows up,
7 With which the reaper does not fill his hand,
Nor he who binds sheaves, his arms.
8 Neither let those who pass by them say,
"The blessing of the LORD *be* upon you;
We bless you in the name of the LORD!"

PSALM 130

WAITING FOR THE REDEMPTION OF THE LORD

A Song of Ascents.

OUT of the depths I have cried to You, O LORD;
2 Lord, hear my voice!

Let Your ears be attentive
To the voice of my supplications.

3 If You, LORD, should mark iniquities,
O Lord, who could stand?
4 But *there is* forgiveness with You,
That You may be feared.

5 I wait for the LORD, my soul waits,
And in His word I do hope.
6 My soul *waits* for the Lord
More than those who watch for the morning—
Yes, more than those who watch for the morning.

7 O Israel, hope in the LORD;
For with the LORD *there is* mercy,
And with Him *is* abundant redemption.
8 And He shall redeem Israel
From all his iniquities.

PSALM 131

SIMPLE TRUST IN THE LORD

A Song of Ascents. Of David.

LORD, my heart is not haughty,
Nor my eyes lofty.
Neither do I concern myself with great matters,
Nor with things too profound for me.

2 Surely I have calmed and quieted my soul,
Like a weaned child with his mother;
Like a weaned child *is* my soul within me.

3 O Israel, hope in the LORD
From this time forth and forever.

PSALM 132

THE ETERNAL DWELLING OF GOD IN ZION

A Song of Ascents.

Lord, remember David
  And all his afflictions;
2 How he swore to the LORD,
  And vowed to the Mighty One of
    Jacob:
3 "Surely I will not go into the
    chamber of my house,
  Or go up to the comfort of my
    bed;
4 I will not give sleep to my eyes
  Or slumber to my eyelids,
5 Until I find a place for the LORD,
  A dwelling place for the Mighty
    One of Jacob."

6 Behold, we heard of it in
    Eph′ra·thah;
  We found it in the fields of the
    woods.*a*
7 Let us go into His tabernacle;
  Let us worship at His footstool.
8 Arise, O LORD, to Your resting
    place,
  You and the ark of Your strength.
9 Let Your priests be clothed with
    righteousness,
  And let Your saints shout for joy.

10 For Your servant David's sake,
  Do not turn away the face of Your
    Anointed.

11 The LORD has sworn *in* truth to
    David;
  He will not turn from it:
  "I will set upon your throne the
    fruit of your body.
12 If your sons will keep My
    covenant
  And My testimony which I shall
    teach them,
  Their sons also shall sit upon
    your throne forevermore."

13 For the LORD has chosen Zion;
  He has desired *it* for His dwelling
    place:
14 "This *is* My resting place forever;
  Here I will dwell, for I have
    desired it.
15 I will abundantly bless her
    provision;
  I will satisfy her poor with
    bread.
16 I will also clothe her priests with
    salvation,
  And her saints shall shout aloud
    for joy.
17 There I will make the horn of
    David grow;
  I will prepare a lamp for My
    Anointed.
18 His enemies I will clothe with
    shame,
  But upon Himself His crown shall
    flourish."

PSALM 133

BLESSED UNITY OF THE PEOPLE OF GOD

A Song of Ascents. Of David.

Behold, how good and how
    pleasant *it is*
  For brethren to dwell together in
    unity!

2 *It is* like the precious oil upon the
    head,
  Running down on the beard,
  The beard of Aaron,
  Running down on the edge of his
    garments.
3 *It is* like the dew of Her′mon,
  Descending upon the mountains
    of Zion;
  For there the LORD commanded
    the blessing—
  Life forevermore.

132:6 *a*Hebrew *Jaar*

PSALM 134

PRAISING THE LORD IN HIS HOUSE AT NIGHT

A Song of Ascents.

BEHOLD, bless the LORD,
All *you* servants of the LORD,
Who by night stand in the house
of the LORD!
2　Lift up your hands *in* the
sanctuary,
And bless the LORD.

3　The LORD who made heaven and
earth
Bless you from Zion!

PSALM 135

PRAISE TO GOD IN CREATION AND REDEMPTION

PRAISE the LORD!

Praise the name of the LORD;
Praise *Him,* O you servants of the
LORD!
2　You who stand in the house of the
LORD,
In the courts of the house of our
God,

Praises

Psalm 135:3

Why should we praise the Lord?
Because He is good. He not only
does good things. He *is* good.
Praise the Lord. Why should we
praise the Lord? Because we
honor His name. His name is
wonderful. He is the Lord God,
Creator of all things. Do you
think He deserves some praise?
Then praise Him.

3　Praise the LORD, for the LORD *is*
good;
Sing praises to His name, for *it is*
pleasant.
4　For the LORD has chosen Jacob for
Himself,
Israel for His special treasure.

5　For I know that the LORD *is* great,
And our Lord *is* above all gods.
6　Whatever the LORD pleases He
does,
In heaven and in earth,
In the seas and in all deep places.
7　He causes the vapors to ascend
from the ends of the earth;
He makes lightning for the rain;
He brings the wind out of His
treasuries.

8　He destroyed the firstborn of
Egypt,
Both of man and beast.
9　He sent signs and wonders into
the midst of you, O Egypt,
Upon Pharaoh and all his
servants.
10　He defeated many nations
And slew mighty kings—
11　Sī′hon king of the Am′o·rītes,
Og king of Bā′shan,
And all the kingdoms of
Cā′naan—
12　And gave their land *as* a
heritage,
A heritage to Israel His people.

13　Your name, O LORD, *endures*
forever,
Your fame, O LORD, throughout
all generations.
14　For the LORD will judge His
people,
And He will have compassion on
His servants.

15　The idols of the nations *are* silver
and gold,
The work of men's hands.

16 They have mouths, but they do
not speak;
Eyes they have, but they do not
see;
17 They have ears, but they do not
hear;
Nor is there *any* breath in their
mouths.
18 Those who make them are like
them;
So is everyone who trusts in
them.

19 Bless the LORD, O house of Israel!
Bless the LORD, O house of
Aaron!
20 Bless the LORD, O house of Levi!
You who fear the LORD, bless the
LORD!
21 Blessed be the LORD out of Zion,
Who dwells in Jerusalem!

Praise the LORD!

PSALM 136

THANKSGIVING TO GOD FOR HIS ENDURING MERCY

OH, give thanks to the LORD, for
He is good!
For His mercy *endures* forever.
2 Oh, give thanks to the God of
gods!
For His mercy *endures* forever.
3 Oh, give thanks to the Lord of
lords!
For His mercy *endures* forever:

4 To Him who alone does great
wonders,
For His mercy *endures* forever;
5 To Him who by wisdom made the
heavens,
For His mercy *endures* forever;
6 To Him who laid out the earth
above the waters,
For His mercy *endures* forever;

7 To Him who made great lights,
For His mercy *endures*
forever—
8 The sun to rule by day,
For His mercy *endures* forever;
9 The moon and stars to rule by
night,
For His mercy *endures* forever.

10 To Him who struck Egypt in their
firstborn,
For His mercy *endures* forever;
11 And brought out Israel from
among them,
For His mercy *endures* forever;
12 With a strong hand, and with an
outstretched arm,
For His mercy *endures* forever;
13 To Him who divided the Red Sea
in two,
For His mercy *endures* forever;
14 And made Israel pass through the
midst of it,
For His mercy *endures* forever;
15 But overthrew Pharaoh and his
army in the Red Sea,
For His mercy *endures* forever;
16 To Him who led His people
through the wilderness,
For His mercy *endures* forever;
17 To Him who struck down great
kings,
For His mercy *endures* forever;
18 And slew famous kings,
For His mercy *endures*
forever—
19 Sī'hon king of the Am'o·rītes,
For His mercy *endures* forever;
20 And Og king of Bā'shan,
For His mercy *endures*
forever—
21 And gave their land as a heritage,
For His mercy *endures* forever;
22 A heritage to Israel His servant,
For His mercy *endures* forever.

23 Who remembered us in our lowly
state,
For His mercy *endures* forever;

24 And rescued us from our enemies,
　　For His mercy *endures* forever;
25 Who gives food to all flesh,
　　For His mercy *endures* forever.

26 Oh, give thanks to the God of
　　heaven!
　　For His mercy *endures* forever.

PSALM 137

LONGING FOR ZION IN A FOREIGN LAND

BY the rivers of Babylon,
　　There we sat down, yea, we wept
　　When we remembered Zion.
2 We hung our harps
　　Upon the willows in the midst of
　　it.
3 For there those who carried us
　　away captive asked of us a
　　song,
　　And those who plundered us
　　requested mirth,
　　Saying, "Sing us *one* of the songs
　　of Zion!"

4 How shall we sing the LORD's
　　song
　　In a foreign land?
5 If I forget you, O Jerusalem,
　　Let my right hand forget *its skill!*
6 If I do not remember you,
　　Let my tongue cling to the roof of
　　my mouth—
　　If I do not exalt Jerusalem
　　Above my chief joy.

7 Remember, O LORD, against the
　　sons of Ē'dom
　　The day of Jerusalem,
　　Who said, "Raze *it,* raze *it,*
　　To its very foundation!"

8 O daughter of Babylon, who are
　　to be destroyed,
　　Happy the one who repays you as
　　you have served us!

9 Happy the one who takes and
　　dashes
　　Your little ones against the rock!

PSALM 138

THE LORD'S GOODNESS TO THE FAITHFUL

A Psalm of David.

I WILL praise You with my whole
　　heart;
　　Before the gods I will sing praises
　　to You.
2 I will worship toward Your holy
　　temple,
　　And praise Your name
　　For Your lovingkindness and Your
　　truth;
　　For You have magnified Your
　　word above all Your name.
3 In the day when I cried out, You
　　answered me,
　　And made me bold *with* strength
　　in my soul.

4 All the kings of the earth shall
　　praise You, O LORD,
　　When they hear the words of Your
　　mouth.
5 Yes, they shall sing of the ways of
　　the LORD,
　　For great *is* the glory of the LORD.
6 Though the LORD *is* on high,
　　Yet He regards the lowly;
　　But the proud He knows from
　　afar.

7 Though I walk in the midst of
　　trouble, You will revive me;
　　You will stretch out Your hand
　　Against the wrath of my enemies,
　　And Your right hand will save
　　me.
8 The LORD will perfect *that which*
　　concerns me;
　　Your mercy, O LORD, *endures*
　　forever;

Do not forsake the works of Your hands.

PSALM 139

GOD'S PERFECT KNOWLEDGE OF MAN

For the Chief Musician. A Psalm of David.

O LORD, You have searched me and known *me*.
2 You know my sitting down and my rising up;
You understand my thought afar off.
3 You comprehend my path and my lying down,
And are acquainted with all my ways.
4 For *there is* not a word on my tongue,
But behold, O LORD, You know it altogether.
5 You have hedged me behind and before,
And laid Your hand upon me.
6 *Such* knowledge *is* too wonderful for me;
It is high, I cannot *attain* it.

7 Where can I go from Your Spirit?
Or where can I flee from Your presence?
8 If I ascend into heaven, You *are* there;
If I make my bed in hell, behold, You *are there*.
9 *If* I take the wings of the morning,
And dwell in the uttermost parts of the sea,
10 Even there Your hand shall lead me,
And Your right hand shall hold me.
11 If I say, "Surely the darkness shall fall*a* on me,"

Even the night shall be light about me;
12 Indeed, the darkness shall not hide from You,
But the night shines as the day;
The darkness and the light *are* both alike *to You*.

13 For You formed my inward parts;
You covered me in my mother's womb.
14 I will praise You, for I am fearfully *and* wonderfully made;*a*
Marvelous are Your works,
And *that* my soul knows very well.
15 My frame was not hidden from You,
When I was made in secret,
And skillfully wrought in the lowest parts of the earth.
16 Your eyes saw my substance, being yet unformed.
And in Your book they all were written,
The days fashioned for me,
When *as yet there were* none of them.

17 How precious also are Your thoughts to me, O God!
How great is the sum of them!
18 *If* I should count them, they would be more in number than the sand;
When I awake, I am still with You.

19 Oh, that You would slay the wicked, O God!
Depart from me, therefore, you bloodthirsty men.

139:11 *a*Vulgate and Symmachus read *cover*.
139:14 *a*Following Masoretic Text and Targum; Septuagint, Syriac, and Vulgate read *You are fearfully wonderful*.

SEARCH ME, O GOD, AND KNOW MY HEART; / TRY ME, AND KNOW MY ANXIETIES; / AND SEE IF THERE IS ANY WICKED WAY IN ME, / AND LEAD ME IN THE WAY EVERLASTING. Psalm 139:23, 24

Can God See Your Heart?

The Psalmist prayed that God would search him and know his heart. But can God see your heart? Psalm 44:21 tells us that God knows the secrets of the heart. You cannot hide the least little thing from Him. Would you like to pray what the Psalmist prayed, that if God sees any wicked way in you, He will lead you in His ways.

1. What do you think God sees in your heart right now? Is there anything you would not want Him to see? If there is, ask Him to take it away.
2. Then pray the prayer of the Psalmist in Psalm 51:10, "Create in me a clean heart, O God." It is not enough to merely remove something bad. Ask Him to make you clean in His eyes. That happens when Jesus forgives our sin and becomes our Savior.

For more on *Favorite Family Verses* turn to page 958
For more on *Forgiveness* turn to page 978

20 For they speak against You
    wickedly;
    Your enemies take *Your name* in
    vain.*a*
21 Do I not hate them, O LORD, who
    hate You?
    And do I not loathe those who rise
    up against You?
22 I hate them with perfect hatred;
    I count them my enemies.

23 Search me, O God, and know my
    heart;
    Try me, and know my anxieties;
24 And see if *there is any* wicked way
    in me,
    And lead me in the way
    everlasting.

PSALM 140

PRAYER FOR DELIVERANCE FROM EVIL MEN

To the Chief Musician. A Psalm of David.

DELIVER me, O LORD, from evil
    men;
    Preserve me from violent men,
2 Who plan evil things in *their*
    hearts;
    They continually gather together
    for war.
3 They sharpen their tongues like a
    serpent;
    The poison of asps *is* under their
    lips.   Sē′lah

4 Keep me, O LORD, from the hands
    of the wicked;
    Preserve me from violent men,
    Who have purposed to make my
    steps stumble.
5 The proud have hidden a snare
    for me, and cords;
    They have spread a net by the
    wayside;
    They have set traps for me.
                    Sē′lah

6 I said to the LORD: "You *are* my
    God;
    Hear the voice of my
    supplications, O LORD.
7 O GOD the Lord, the strength of
    my salvation,
    You have covered my head in the
    day of battle.
8 Do not grant, O LORD, the desires
    of the wicked;
    Do not further his *wicked*
    scheme,
    Lest they be exalted.   Sē′lah

9 "*As for* the head of those who
    surround me,
    Let the evil of their lips cover
    them;
10 Let burning coals fall upon them;
    Let them be cast into the fire,
    Into deep pits, that they rise not
    up again.
11 Let not a slanderer be established
    in the earth;
    Let evil hunt the violent man to
    overthrow *him*."

12 I know that the LORD will
    maintain
    The cause of the afflicted,
    And justice for the poor.
13 Surely the righteous shall give
    thanks to Your name;
    The upright shall dwell in Your
    presence.

PSALM 141

PRAYER FOR SAFEKEEPING FROM WICKEDNESS

A Psalm of David.

LORD, I cry out to You;
    Make haste to me!

139:20 *a*Septuagint and Vulgate read *They take
your cities in vain.*

Give ear to my voice when I cry
out to You.

2 Let my prayer be set before You
as incense,
The lifting up of my hands *as* the
evening sacrifice.

3 Set a guard, O LORD, over my
mouth;
Keep watch over the door of my
lips.

4 Do not incline my heart to any
evil thing,
To practice wicked works
With men who work iniquity;
And do not let me eat of their
delicacies.

5 Let the righteous strike me;
It shall be a kindness.
And let him rebuke me;
It shall be as excellent oil;
Let my head not refuse it.

For still my prayer *is* against the
deeds of the wicked.
6 Their judges are overthrown by
the sides of the cliff,
And they hear my words, for they
are sweet.
7 Our bones are scattered at the
mouth of the grave,
As when one plows and breaks up
the earth.

8 But my eyes *are* upon You, O GOD
the Lord;
In You I take refuge;
Do not leave my soul destitute.
9 Keep me from the snares they
have laid for me,
And from the traps of the workers
of iniquity.
10 Let the wicked fall into their own
nets,
While I escape safely.

PSALM 142

A PLEA FOR RELIEF FROM PERSECUTORS

A Contemplation[a] of David. A Prayer when he was
in the cave.

I CRY out to the LORD with my
voice;
With my voice to the LORD I make
my supplication.
2 I pour out my complaint before
Him;
I declare before Him my trouble.

3 When my spirit was overwhelmed
within me,
Then You knew my path.
In the way in which I walk
They have secretly set a snare for
me.
4 Look on *my* right hand and see,
For *there is* no one who
acknowledges me;
Refuge has failed me;
No one cares for my soul.

5 I cried out to You, O LORD:
I said, "You *are* my refuge,
My portion in the land of the
living.
6 Attend to my cry,
For I am brought very low;
Deliver me from my persecutors,
For they are stronger than I.
7 Bring my soul out of prison,
That I may praise Your name;
The righteous shall surround me,
For You shall deal bountifully
with me."

PSALM 143

AN EARNEST APPEAL FOR GUIDANCE
AND DELIVERANCE

A Psalm of David.

H EAR my prayer, O LORD,
Give ear to my supplications!

142:title [a]Hebrew *Maschil*

What the Bible Says

ABOUT GOD'S LOVE Psalm 143:8

A Love Letter from God

Did you know that God wrote a love letter to you? "Dear (your name), I love you. Signed, God." This love letter is special. It's called the Bible.

1. In the Bible God tells you many times, "I love you." Read Psalm 51:1; 52:8; 63:3; 94:18; and 143:8. Do you think God loves you?
2. How much does God love you? Read John 3:16. How much do you love God? How much should you love God?

For more on *What the Bible Says* turn to page 1018
For more on *Bible* turn to page 981

In Your faithfulness answer me,
And in Your righteousness.

2 Do not enter into judgment with
Your servant,
For in Your sight no one living is
righteous.

3 For the enemy has persecuted my
soul;
He has crushed my life to the
ground;
He has made me dwell in
darkness,
Like those who have long been
dead.

4 Therefore my spirit is
overwhelmed within me;
My heart within me is distressed.

5 I remember the days of old;
I meditate on all Your works;
I muse on the work of Your hands.

6 I spread out my hands to You;
My soul *longs* for You like a
thirsty land.   Sē'lah

7 Answer me speedily, O LORD;
My spirit fails!
Do not hide Your face from me,
Lest I be like those who go down
into the pit.

8 Cause me to hear Your
lovingkindness in the morning,
For in You do I trust;
Cause me to know the way in
which I should walk,
For I lift up my soul to You.

9 Deliver me, O LORD, from my
enemies;
In You I take shelter.*a*

10 Teach me to do Your will,
For You *are* my God;
Your Spirit *is* good.
Lead me in the land of
uprightness.

11 Revive me, O LORD, for Your
name's sake!

For Your righteousness' sake
bring my soul out of trouble.

12 In Your mercy cut off my enemies,
And destroy all those who afflict
my soul;
For I *am* Your servant.

PSALM 144

A SONG TO THE LORD WHO PRESERVES AND PROSPERS HIS PEOPLE

A Psalm of David.

BLESSED *be* the LORD my Rock,
Who trains my hands for war,
And my fingers for battle—

2 My lovingkindness and my
fortress,
My high tower and my deliverer,
My shield and *the One* in whom I
take refuge,
Who subdues my people*a* under
me.

3 LORD, what *is* man, that You take
knowledge of him?
Or the son of man, that You are
mindful of him?

4 Man is like a breath;
His days *are* like a passing
shadow.

5 Bow down Your heavens, O LORD,
and come down;
Touch the mountains, and they
shall smoke.

6 Flash forth lightning and scatter
them;
Shoot out Your arrows and
destroy them.

7 Stretch out Your hand from
above;
Rescue me and deliver me out of
great waters,

143:9 *a*Septuagint and Vulgate read *To You I flee.*
144:2 *a*Following Masoretic Text, Septuagint, and
Vulgate; Syriac and Targum read *the peoples* (compare 18:47).

From the hand of foreigners,
8 Whose mouth speaks lying words,
And whose right hand *is* a right
hand of falsehood.

9 I will sing a new song to You,
O God;
On a harp of ten strings I will
sing praises to You,
10 *The One* who gives salvation to
kings,
Who delivers David His servant
From the deadly sword.

11 Rescue me and deliver me from
the hand of foreigners,
Whose mouth speaks lying words,
And whose right hand *is* a right
hand of falsehood—
12 That our sons *may be* as plants
grown up in their youth;
That our daughters *may be* as
pillars,
Sculptured in palace style;
13 *That* our barns *may be* full,
Supplying all kinds of produce;
That our sheep may bring forth
thousands
And ten thousands in our fields;
14 *That* our oxen *may be* well laden;
That there be no breaking in or
going out;
That there be no outcry in our
streets.
15 Happy *are* the people who are in
such a state;
Happy *are* the people whose God
is the LORD!

PSALM 145

A SONG OF GOD'S MAJESTY AND LOVE

A Praise of David.

I WILL extol You, my God, O King;
And I will bless Your name
forever and ever.

2 Every day I will bless You,
And I will praise Your name
forever and ever.
3 Great *is* the LORD, and greatly to
be praised;
And His greatness *is*
unsearchable.
4 One generation shall praise Your
works to another,
And shall declare Your mighty
acts.
5 I[a] will meditate on the glorious
splendor of Your majesty,
And on Your wondrous works.[b]
6 *Men* shall speak of the might of
Your awesome acts,
And I will declare Your greatness.
7 They shall utter the memory of
Your great goodness,
And shall sing of Your
righteousness.
8 The LORD *is* gracious and full of
compassion,
Slow to anger and great in mercy.
9 The LORD *is* good to all,
And His tender mercies *are* over
all His works.
10 All Your works shall praise You,
O LORD,
And Your saints shall bless You.
11 They shall speak of the glory of
Your kingdom,
And talk of Your power,
12 To make known to the sons of
men His mighty acts,
And the glorious majesty of His
kingdom.
13 Your kingdom *is* an everlasting
kingdom,
And Your dominion *endures*
throughout all generations.[a]

145:5 [a]Following Masoretic Text and Targum;
Dead Sea Scrolls, Septuagint, Syriac, and Vulgate
read *They.*   [b]Literally *on the words of Your wondrous works*   145:13 [a]Following Masoretic Text
and Targum; Dead Sea Scrolls, Septuagint, Syriac,
and Vulgate add *The LORD is faithful in all His
words, And holy in all His works.*

14 The LORD upholds all who fall,
And raises up all *who are* bowed down.

15 The eyes of all look expectantly to You,
And You give them their food in due season.

16 You open Your hand
And satisfy the desire of every living thing.

17 The LORD *is* righteous in all His ways,
Gracious in all His works.

18 The LORD *is* near to all who call upon Him,
To all who call upon Him in truth.

19 He will fulfill the desire of those who fear Him;
He also will hear their cry and save them.

20 The LORD preserves all who love Him,
But all the wicked He will destroy.

21 My mouth shall speak the praise of the LORD,
And all flesh shall bless His holy name
Forever and ever.

PSALM 146

THE HAPPINESS OF THOSE WHOSE HELP IS THE LORD

PRAISE the LORD!

Praise the LORD, O my soul!
2 While I live I will praise the LORD;
I will sing praises to my God while I have my being.

3 Do not put your trust in princes,
Nor in a son of man, in whom *there is* no help.

4 His spirit departs, he returns to his earth;
In that very day his plans perish.

5 Happy *is he* who *has* the God of Jacob for his help,
Whose hope *is* in the LORD his God,

6 Who made heaven and earth,
The sea, and all that *is* in them;
Who keeps truth forever,

7 Who executes justice for the oppressed,

Who gives food to the hungry.
The LORD gives freedom to the
prisoners.

8 The LORD opens *the eyes of* the
blind;
The LORD raises those who are
bowed down;
The LORD loves the righteous.
9 The LORD watches over the
strangers;
He relieves the fatherless and
widow;
But the way of the wicked He
turns upside down.

10 The LORD shall reign forever—
Your God, O Zion, to all
generations.

Praise the LORD!

PSALM 147

PRAISE TO GOD FOR HIS WORD AND
PROVIDENCE

PRAISE the LORD!
For *it is* good to sing praises to
our God;
For *it is* pleasant, *and* praise is
beautiful.

2 The LORD builds up Jerusalem;
He gathers together the outcasts
of Israel.

Praises

Psalm 147:1

Praise God! Why? Because it is
good. It is pleasant. It is beautiful. Those are three good reasons
to praise God. Can you think of
other good reasons? There are
many.

---

3 He heals the brokenhearted
And binds up their wounds.
4 He counts the number of the
stars;
He calls them all by name.
5 Great *is* our Lord, and mighty in
power;
His understanding *is* infinite.
6 The LORD lifts up the humble;
He casts the wicked down to the
ground.

7 Sing to the LORD with
thanksgiving;
Sing praises on the harp to our
God,
8 Who covers the heavens with
clouds,
Who prepares rain for the earth,
Who makes grass to grow on the
mountains.
9 He gives to the beast its food,
And to the young ravens that cry.

10 He does not delight in the
strength of the horse;
He takes no pleasure in the legs
of a man.
11 The LORD takes pleasure in those
who fear Him,
In those who hope in His mercy.

12 Praise the LORD, O Jerusalem!
Praise your God, O Zion!
13 For He has strengthened the bars
of your gates;
He has blessed your children
within you.
14 He makes peace *in* your borders,
And fills you with the finest
wheat.

15 He sends out His command *to the*
earth;
His word runs very swiftly.
16 He gives snow like wool;
He scatters the frost like ashes;
17 He casts out His hail like morsels;
Who can stand before His cold?

THANKFULNESS Psalm 147:7

Thank You!

Look at the special gift someone gave this girl. She has been praying for a kitty for a long time. So you know how much she has wanted one. Now someone has given it to her. Do you think it was her mother or father? What do you think this girl will say to them? Do you think she will say "Thank you?" She may even say, "Thank you, thank you, thank you."

1. Has someone given you something special? Who? What did they give? Did you say "thank you?"
2. What special gifts have your parents given to you? Have you said "thank you?" Would you like to thank them now for something?
3. What special gifts has God given you today? Would you like to say "thank You" to Him now?

For more on *Values* turn to page 965
For more on *Thankfulness* turn to page 1229

18 He sends out His word and melts
    them;
    He causes His wind to blow, *and*
    the waters flow.

19 He declares His word to Jacob,
    His statutes and His judgments
    to Israel.
20 He has not dealt thus with any
    nation;
    And *as for His* judgments, they
    have not known them.

Praise the LORD!

PSALM 148

PRAISE TO THE LORD FROM CREATION

PRAISE the LORD!

Praise the LORD from the
    heavens;
Praise Him in the heights!
2 Praise Him, all His angels;
    Praise Him, all His hosts!
3 Praise Him, sun and moon;
    Praise Him, all you stars of light!
4 Praise Him, you heavens of
    heavens,
    And you waters above the
    heavens!

5 Let them praise the name of the
    LORD,
    For He commanded and they
    were created.
6 He also established them forever
    and ever;
    He made a decree which shall not
    pass away.

7 Praise the LORD from the earth,
    You great sea creatures and all
    the depths;
8 Fire and hail, snow and clouds;
    Stormy wind, fulfilling His word;
9 Mountains and all hills;
    Fruitful trees and all cedars;

10 Beasts and all cattle;
    Creeping things and flying fowl;
11 Kings of the earth and all
    peoples;
    Princes and all judges of the
    earth;
12 Both young men and maidens;
    Old men and children.

13 Let them praise the name of the
    LORD,
    For His name alone is exalted;
    His glory *is* above the earth and
    heaven.
14 And He has exalted the horn of
    His people,
    The praise of all His saints—
    Of the children of Israel,
    A people near to Him.

Praise the LORD!

PSALM 149

PRAISE TO GOD FOR HIS SALVATION AND
JUDGMENT

PRAISE the LORD!

Sing to the LORD a new song,
And His praise in the assembly of
    saints.

2 Let Israel rejoice in their Maker;
    Let the children of Zion be joyful
    in their King.
3 Let them praise His name with
    the dance;
    Let them sing praises to Him
    with the timbrel and harp.
4 For the LORD takes pleasure in
    His people;
    He will beautify the humble with
    salvation.

5 Let the saints be joyful in glory;
    Let them sing aloud on their
    beds.
6 *Let* the high praises of God *be* in
    their mouth,

And a two-edged sword in their
  hand,
7 To execute vengeance on the
    nations,
  And punishments on the peoples;
8 To bind their kings with chains,
  And their nobles with fetters of
    iron;
9 To execute on them the written
    judgment—
  This honor have all His saints.

  Praise the LORD!

PSALM 150

LET ALL THINGS PRAISE THE LORD

PRAISE the LORD!

  Praise God in His sanctuary;
  Praise Him in His mighty
    firmament!

2 Praise Him for His mighty acts;
  Praise Him according to His
    excellent greatness!

3 Praise Him with the sound of the
    trumpet;

Praises

Psalm 150

Here is a chapter of praise to
God. Where should we praise
God? In His house. Anywhere
and everywhere in the world.
Why should we praise God? For
the wonderful things He has
done. For the wonderful Person
He is. With what things should
we praise God? With musical instruments of all kinds. With
every breath we breathe. Praise
the Lord.

  Praise Him with the lute and
    harp!
4 Praise Him with the timbrel and
    dance;
  Praise Him with stringed
    instruments and flutes!
5 Praise Him with loud cymbals;
  Praise Him with clashing
    cymbals!

6 Let everything that has breath
    praise the LORD.

  Praise the LORD!

The Book of
PROVERBS

THE BEGINNING OF KNOWLEDGE

THE proverbs of Solomon the son of David, king of Israel:

2 To know wisdom and instruction,
   To perceive the words of
      understanding,
3 To receive the instruction of
      wisdom,
   Justice, judgment, and equity;
4 To give prudence to the simple,
   To the young man knowledge and
      discretion—
5 A wise *man* will hear and
      increase learning,
   And a man of understanding will
      attain wise counsel,
6 To understand a proverb and an
      enigma,
   The words of the wise and their
      riddles.

7 The fear of the LORD *is* the
      beginning of knowledge,
   But fools despise wisdom and
      instruction.

SHUN EVIL COUNSEL

8 My son, hear the instruction of
      your father,
   And do not forsake the law of
      your mother;
9 For they *will be* a graceful
      ornament on your head,
   And chains about your neck.

10 My son, if sinners entice you,
   Do not consent.
11 If they say, "Come with us,
   Let us lie in wait to *shed* blood;
   Let us lurk secretly for the
      innocent without cause;
12 Let us swallow them alive like
   Shē′ōl,*a*

And whole, like those who go
      down to the Pit;
13 We shall find all *kinds* of precious
      possessions,
   We shall fill our houses with
      spoil;
14 Cast in your lot among us,
   Let us all have one purse"—
15 My son, do not walk in the way
      with them,
   Keep your foot from their path;
16 For their feet run to evil,
   And they make haste to shed
      blood.
17 Surely, in vain the net is spread
   In the sight of any bird;
18 But they lie in wait for their *own*
      blood,
   They lurk secretly for their *own*
      lives.
19 So *are* the ways of everyone who
      is greedy for gain;
   It takes away the life of its
      owners.

THE CALL OF WISDOM

20 Wisdom calls aloud outside;
   She raises her voice in the open
      squares.
21 She cries out in the chief
      concourses,*a*
   At the openings of the gates in
      the city
   She speaks her words:
22 "How long, you simple ones, will
      you love simplicity?
   For scorners delight in their
      scorning,
   And fools hate knowledge.
23 Turn at my rebuke;

1:12 *a*Or *the grave*   1:21 *a*Septuagint, Syriac,
and Targum read *top of the walls;* Vulgate reads *the
head of multitudes.*

Surely I will pour out my spirit on
  you;
I will make my words known to
  you.
24 Because I have called and you
  refused,
I have stretched out my hand and
  no one regarded,
25 Because you disdained all my
  counsel,
And would have none of my
  rebuke,
26 I also will laugh at your calamity;
I will mock when your terror
  comes,
27 When your terror comes like a
  storm,
And your destruction comes like a
  whirlwind,
When distress and anguish come
  upon you.

28 "Then they will call on me, but I
  will not answer;
They will seek me diligently, but
  they will not find me.
29 Because they hated knowledge
And did not choose the fear of the
  LORD,
30 They would have none of my
  counsel
And despised my every rebuke.
31 Therefore they shall eat the fruit
  of their own way,
And be filled to the full with their
  own fancies.
32 For the turning away of the
  simple will slay them,
And the complacency of fools will
  destroy them;
33 But whoever listens to me will
  dwell safely,
And will be secure, without fear
  of evil."

THE VALUE OF WISDOM

2 My son, if you receive my words,
And treasure my commands
  within you,

2 So that you incline your ear to
  wisdom,
And apply your heart to
  understanding;
3 Yes, if you cry out for
  discernment,
And lift up your voice for
  understanding,
4 If you seek her as silver,
And search for her as for hidden
  treasures;
5 Then you will understand the fear
  of the LORD,
And find the knowledge of God.
6 For the LORD gives wisdom;
From His mouth come knowledge
  and understanding;
7 He stores up sound wisdom for
  the upright;
He is a shield to those who walk
  uprightly;
8 He guards the paths of justice,
And preserves the way of His
  saints.
9 Then you will understand
  righteousness and justice,
Equity and every good path.
10 When wisdom enters your heart,
And knowledge is pleasant to
  your soul,
11 Discretion will preserve you;
Understanding will keep you,
12 To deliver you from the way of
  evil,
From the man who speaks
  perverse things,
13 From those who leave the paths
  of uprightness
To walk in the ways of
  darkness;
14 Who rejoice in doing evil,
And delight in the perversity of
  the wicked;
15 Whose ways are crooked,
And who are devious in their
  paths;
16 To deliver you from the immoral
  woman,

From the seductress *who* flatters with her words,

17 Who forsakes the companion of her youth,
And forgets the covenant of her God.

18 For her house leads down to death,
And her paths to the dead;

19 None who go to her return,
Nor do they regain the paths of life—

20 So you may walk in the way of goodness,
And keep *to* the paths of righteousness.

21 For the upright will dwell in the land,
And the blameless will remain in it;

22 But the wicked will be cut off from the earth,
And the unfaithful will be uprooted from it.

GUIDANCE FOR THE YOUNG

3 My son, do not forget my law,
But let your heart keep my commands;

2 For length of days and long life
And peace they will add to you.

3 Let not mercy and truth forsake you;
Bind them around your neck,
Write them on the tablet of your heart,

4 *And* so find favor and high esteem
In the sight of God and man.

5 Trust in the LORD with all your heart,
And lean not on your own understanding;

6 In all your ways acknowledge Him,
And He shall direct*a* your paths.

3:6 *a*Or *make smooth* or *straight*

7 Do not be wise in your own eyes;
Fear the LORD and depart from
evil.
8 It will be health to your flesh,*a*
And strength*b* to your bones.

9 Honor the LORD with your
possessions,
And with the firstfruits of all your
increase;
10 So your barns will be filled with
plenty,
And your vats will overflow with
new wine.

11 My son, do not despise the
chastening of the LORD,
Nor detest His correction;
12 For whom the LORD loves He
corrects,
Just as a father the son *in whom*
he delights.

13 Happy *is* the man *who* finds
wisdom,
And the man *who* gains
understanding;
14 For her proceeds *are* better than
the profits of silver,
And her gain than fine gold.
15 She *is* more precious than rubies,
And all the things you may desire
cannot compare with her.
16 Length of days *is* in her right
hand,
In her left hand riches and honor.
17 Her ways *are* ways of
pleasantness,
And all her paths *are* peace.
18 She *is* a tree of life to those who
take hold of her,
And happy *are all* who retain her.

19 The LORD by wisdom founded the
earth;
By understanding He established
the heavens;
20 By His knowledge the depths
were broken up,
And clouds drop down the dew.

21 My son, let them not depart from
your eyes—
Keep sound wisdom and
discretion;
22 So they will be life to your soul
And grace to your neck.
23 Then you will walk safely in your
way,
And your foot will not stumble.
24 When you lie down, you will not
be afraid;
Yes, you will lie down and your
sleep will be sweet.
25 Do not be afraid of sudden terror,
Nor of trouble from the wicked
when it comes;
26 For the LORD will be your
confidence,
And will keep your foot from
being caught.

27 Do not withhold good from those
to whom it is due,
When it is in the power of your
hand to do *so*.
28 Do not say to your neighbor,
"Go, and come back,
And tomorrow I will give *it*,"
When *you have* it with you.
29 Do not devise evil against your
neighbor,
For he dwells by you for safety's
sake.
30 Do not strive with a man without
cause,
If he has done you no harm.

31 Do not envy the oppressor,
And choose none of his ways;
32 For the perverse *person* is an
abomination to the LORD,
But His secret counsel *is* with the
upright.
33 The curse of the LORD *is* on the
house of the wicked,
But He blesses the home of the
just.

3:8 *a*Literally *navel,* figurative of the body   *b*Literally *drink* or *refreshment*

34 Surely He scorns the scornful,
   But gives grace to the humble.
35 The wise shall inherit glory,
   But shame shall be the legacy of
      fools.

SECURITY IN WISDOM

4 Hear, *my* children, the
      instruction of a father,
   And give attention to know
      understanding;
2 For I give you good doctrine:
   Do not forsake my law.
3 When I was my father's son,
   Tender and the only one in the
      sight of my mother,
4 He also taught me, and said to
      me:
   "Let your heart retain my words;
   Keep my commands, and live.
5 Get wisdom! Get understanding!
   Do not forget, nor turn away from
      the words of my mouth.
6 Do not forsake her, and she will
      preserve you;
   Love her, and she will keep you.
7 Wisdom *is* the principal thing;
   Therefore get wisdom.
   And in all your getting, get
      understanding.
8 Exalt her, and she will promote
      you;
   She will bring you honor, when
      you embrace her.
9 She will place on your head an
      ornament of grace;
   A crown of glory she will deliver
      to you."

10 Hear, my son, and receive my
      sayings,
   And the years of your life will be
      many.
11 I have taught you in the way of
      wisdom;
   I have led you in right paths.
12 When you walk, your steps will
      not be hindered,

And when you run, you will not
   stumble.
13 Take firm hold of instruction, do
      not let go;
   Keep her, for she *is* your life.

14 Do not enter the path of the
      wicked,
   And do not walk in the way of
      evil.
15 Avoid it, do not travel on it;
   Turn away from it and pass on.
16 For they do not sleep unless they
      have done evil;
   And their sleep is taken away
      unless they make *someone* fall.
17 For they eat the bread of
      wickedness,
   And drink the wine of violence.

18 But the path of the just *is* like the
      shining sun,*a*
   That shines ever brighter unto
      the perfect day.
19 The way of the wicked *is* like
      darkness;
   They do not know what makes
      them stumble.

20 My son, give attention to my
      words;
   Incline your ear to my sayings.
21 Do not let them depart from your
      eyes;
   Keep them in the midst of your
      heart;
22 For they *are* life to those who find
      them,
   And health to all their flesh.
23 Keep your heart with all
      diligence,
   For out of it *spring* the issues of
      life.
24 Put away from you a deceitful
      mouth,
   And put perverse lips far from
      you.

4:18 *a*Literally *light*

25 Let your eyes look straight ahead,
And your eyelids look right before
you.
26 Ponder the path of your feet,
And let all your ways be
established.
27 Do not turn to the right or the
left;
Remove your foot from evil.

THE PERIL OF ADULTERY

5 My son, pay attention to my
wisdom;
Lend your ear to my
understanding,
2 That you may preserve
discretion,
And your lips may keep
knowledge.
3 For the lips of an immoral woman
drip honey,
And her mouth *is* smoother than
oil;
4 But in the end she is bitter as
wormwood,
Sharp as a two-edged sword.
5 Her feet go down to death,
Her steps lay hold of hell.*a*
6 Lest you ponder *her* path of life—
Her ways are unstable;
You do not know *them*.

7 Therefore hear me now, *my*
children,
And do not depart from the words
of my mouth.
8 Remove your way far from her,
And do not go near the door of her
house,
9 Lest you give your honor to
others,
And your years to the cruel *one;*
10 Lest aliens be filled with your
wealth,
And your labors *go* to the house of
a foreigner;
11 And you mourn at last,

When your flesh and your body
are consumed,
12 And say:
"How I have hated instruction,
And my heart despised correction!
13 I have not obeyed the voice of my
teachers,
Nor inclined my ear to those who
instructed me!
14 I was on the verge of total ruin,
In the midst of the assembly and
congregation."

15 Drink water from your own
cistern,
And running water from your
own well.
16 Should your fountains be
dispersed abroad,
Streams of water in the streets?
17 Let them be only your own,
And not for strangers with you.
18 Let your fountain be blessed,
And rejoice with the wife of your
youth.
19 *As a* loving deer and a graceful
doe,
Let her breasts satisfy you at all
times;
And always be enraptured with
her love.
20 For why should you, my son, be
enraptured by an immoral
woman,
And be embraced in the arms of a
seductress?

21 For the ways of man *are* before
the eyes of the LORD,
And He ponders all his paths.
22 His own iniquities entrap the
wicked *man,*
And he is caught in the cords of
his sin.
23 He shall die for lack of
instruction,
And in the greatness of his folly
he shall go astray.

5:5 *a*Or *Sheol*

DANGEROUS PROMISES

6 My son, if you become surety for
    your friend,
  If you have shaken hands in
    pledge for a stranger,
2 You are snared by the words of
    your mouth;
  You are taken by the words of
    your mouth.
3 So do this, my son, and deliver
    yourself;
  For you have come into the hand
    of your friend:
  Go and humble yourself;
  Plead with your friend.
4 Give no sleep to your eyes,
  Nor slumber to your eyelids.
5 Deliver yourself like a gazelle
    from the hand *of the hunter,*
  And like a bird from the hand of
    the fowler.*a*

THE FOLLY OF INDOLENCE

6 Go to the ant, you sluggard!
  Consider her ways and be wise,
7 Which, having no captain,
  Overseer or ruler,
8 Provides her supplies in the
    summer,
  And gathers her food in the
    harvest.
9 How long will you slumber,
    O sluggard?
  When will you rise from your
    sleep?
10 A little sleep, a little slumber,
  A little folding of the hands to
    sleep—
11 So shall your poverty come on you
    like a prowler,
  And your need like an armed
    man.

THE WICKED MAN

12 A worthless person, a wicked
    man,
  Walks with a perverse mouth;

13 He winks with his eyes,
  He shuffles his feet,
  He points with his fingers;
14 Perversity *is* in his heart,
  He devises evil continually,
  He sows discord.
15 Therefore his calamity shall come
    suddenly;
  Suddenly he shall be broken
    without remedy.

16 These six *things* the LORD hates,
  Yes, seven *are* an abomination to
    Him:
17 A proud look,
  A lying tongue,
  Hands that shed innocent blood,
18 A heart that devises wicked
    plans,
  Feet that are swift in running to
    evil,
19 A false witness *who* speaks lies,
  And one who sows discord among
    brethren.

BEWARE OF ADULTERY

20 My son, keep your father's
    command,
  And do not forsake the law of
    your mother.
21 Bind them continually upon your
    heart;
  Tie them around your neck.
22 When you roam, they*a* will lead
    you;
  When you sleep, they will keep
    you;
  And *when* you awake, they will
    speak with you.
23 For the commandment *is* a lamp,
  And the law a light;
  Reproofs of instruction *are* the
    way of life,
24 To keep you from the evil woman,
  From the flattering tongue of a
    seductress.

6:5 *a*That is, one who catches birds in a trap or
snare   6:22 *a*Literally *it*

25 Do not lust after her beauty in
      your heart,
   Nor let her allure you with her
      eyelids.
26 For by means of a harlot
   A man is reduced to a crust of
      bread;
   And an adulteress*a* will prey
      upon his precious life.
27 Can a man take fire to his bosom,
   And his clothes not be burned?
28 Can one walk on hot coals,
   And his feet not be seared?
29 So *is* he who goes in to his
      neighbor's wife;
   Whoever touches her shall not be
      innocent.

30 *People* do not despise a thief
   If he steals to satisfy himself
      when he is starving.
31 Yet *when* he is found, he must
      restore sevenfold;
   He may have to give up all the
      substance of his house.
32 Whoever commits adultery with a
      woman lacks understanding;
   He *who* does so destroys his own
      soul.
33 Wounds and dishonor he will get,
   And his reproach will not be
      wiped away.
34 For jealousy *is* a husband's
      fury;
   Therefore he will not spare in the
      day of vengeance.
35 He will accept no recompense,
   Nor will he be appeased though
      you give many gifts.

7 My son, keep my words,
   And treasure my commands
      within you.
2 Keep my commands and live,
   And my law as the apple of your
      eye.
3 Bind them on your fingers;
   Write them on the tablet of your
      heart.

4 Say to wisdom, "You *are* my
      sister,"
   And call understanding *your*
      nearest kin,
5 That they may keep you from the
      immoral woman,
   From the seductress *who* flatters
      with her words.

THE CRAFTY HARLOT

6 For at the window of my house
   I looked through my lattice,
7 And saw among the simple,
   I perceived among the youths,
   A young man devoid of
      understanding,
8 Passing along the street near her
      corner;
   And he took the path to her house
9 In the twilight, in the evening,
   In the black and dark night.

10 And there a woman met him,
   With the attire of a harlot, and a
      crafty heart.
11 She *was* loud and rebellious,
   Her feet would not stay at home.
12 At times *she was* outside, at times
      in the open square,
   Lurking at every corner.
13 So she caught him and kissed
      him;
   With an impudent face she said to
      him:
14 "*I* have peace offerings with me;
   Today I have paid my vows.
15 So I came out to meet you,
   Diligently to seek your face,
   And I have found you.
16 I have spread my bed with
      tapestry,
   Colored coverings of Egyptian
      linen.
17 I have perfumed my bed
   With myrrh, aloes, and
      cinnamon.

6:26 *a*Literally *a man's wife,* that is, of another

18 Come, let us take our fill of love
  until morning;
  Let us delight ourselves with love.
19 For my husband *is* not at home;
  He has gone on a long journey;
20 He has taken a bag of money with
  him,
  And will come home on the
  appointed day."

21 With her enticing speech she
  caused him to yield,
  With her flattering lips she
  seduced him.
22 Immediately he went after her, as
  an ox goes to the slaughter,
  Or as a fool to the correction of
  the stocks,*a*
23 Till an arrow struck his liver.
  As a bird hastens to the snare,
  He did not know it *would cost* his
  life.

24 Now therefore, listen to me, my
  children;
  Pay attention to the words of my
  mouth:
25 Do not let your heart turn aside
  to her ways,
  Do not stray into her paths;
26 For she has cast down many
  wounded,
  And all who were slain by her
  were strong *men*.
27 Her house *is* the way to hell,*a*
  Descending to the chambers of
  death.

THE EXCELLENCE OF WISDOM

8 Does not wisdom cry out,
  And understanding lift up her
  voice?
2 She takes her stand on the top of
  the high hill,
  Beside the way, where the paths
  meet.
3 She cries out by the gates, at the
  entry of the city,

At the entrance of the doors:
4 "To you, O men, I call,
  And my voice *is* to the sons of
  men.
5 O you simple ones, understand
  prudence,
  And you fools, be of an
  understanding heart.
6 Listen, for I will speak of
  excellent things,
  And from the opening of my lips
  will come right things;
7 For my mouth will speak truth;
  Wickedness *is* an abomination to
  my lips.
8 All the words of my mouth *are*
  with righteousness;
  Nothing crooked or perverse *is* in
  them.
9 They *are* all plain to him who
  understands,
  And right to those who find
  knowledge.
10 Receive my instruction, and not
  silver,
  And knowledge rather than
  choice gold;
11 For wisdom *is* better than rubies,
  And all the things one may
  desire cannot be compared with
  her.

12 "I, wisdom, dwell with prudence,
  And find out knowledge *and*
  discretion.
13 The fear of the LORD *is* to hate
  evil;
  Pride and arrogance and the evil
  way
  And the perverse mouth I hate.
14 Counsel *is* mine, and sound
  wisdom;
  I *am* understanding, I have
  strength.
15 By me kings reign,
  And rulers decree justice.

7:22 *a*Septuagint, Syriac, and Targum read *as a
dog to bonds*; Vulgate reads *as a lamb . . . to
bonds.*   7:27 *a*Or *Sheol*

HUMILITY Proverbs 8:13

I'm First!

"I'm first!" Have you ever said that? "I get the biggest piece of pie. I get the bathroom before you. I was here first. I was playing with these toys first." What do all of these mean?

1. "I'm first" means I'm better or I'm smarter or I'm more important or I'm the one who should be ahead of you. Is this pride or humility?
2. Read Psalm 25:9. What does the Lord do for humble people? What does the Lord think of arrogant pride? Read Proverbs 8:13. What does it say?

For more on *Values* turn to page 1000
For more on *Humility* turn to page 1586

16 By me princes rule, and nobles,
   All the judges of the earth.*a*
17 I love those who love me,
   And those who seek me diligently
      will find me.
18 Riches and honor *are* with me,
   Enduring riches and
      righteousness.
19 My fruit *is* better than gold, yes,
      than fine gold,
   And my revenue than choice
      silver.
20 I traverse the way of
      righteousness,
   In the midst of the paths of
      justice,
21 That I may cause those who love
      me to inherit wealth,
   That I may fill their treasuries.

22 "The LORD possessed me at the
      beginning of His way,
   Before His works of old.
23 I have been established from
      everlasting,
   From the beginning, before there
      was ever an earth.
24 When *there were* no depths I was
      brought forth,
   When *there were* no fountains
      abounding with water.
25 Before the mountains were
      settled,
   Before the hills, I was brought
      forth;
26 While as yet He had not made the
      earth or the fields,
   Or the primal dust of the
      world.
27 When He prepared the heavens, I
      was there,
   When He drew a circle on the face
      of the deep,
28 When He established the clouds
      above,
   When He strengthened the
      fountains of the deep,
29 When He assigned to the sea its
      limit,

So that the waters would not
   transgress His command,
When He marked out the
   foundations of the earth,
30 Then I was beside Him as a
   master craftsman;*a*
And I was daily *His* delight,
Rejoicing always before Him,
31 Rejoicing in His inhabited world,
And my delight *was* with the sons
   of men.

32 "Now therefore, listen to me, my
   children,
For blessed *are those who* keep
   my ways.
33 Hear instruction and be wise,
And do not disdain *it*.
34 Blessed is the man who listens to
   me,
Watching daily at my gates,
Waiting at the posts of my doors.
35 For whoever finds me finds life,
And obtains favor from the
   LORD;
36 But he who sins against me
   wrongs his own soul;
All those who hate me love
   death."

THE WAY OF WISDOM

9 Wisdom has built her house,
She has hewn out her seven
   pillars;
2 She has slaughtered her meat,
She has mixed her wine,
She has also furnished her table.
3 She has sent out her maidens,
She cries out from the highest
   places of the city,
4 "Whoever *is* simple, let him turn
   in here!"
As for him who lacks
   understanding, she says to him,

8:16 *a*Masoretic Text, Syriac, Targum, and Vulgate
read *righteousness;* Septuagint, Bomberg, and some
manuscripts and editions read *earth.*   8:30 *a*A
Jewish tradition reads *one brought up.*

5 "Come, eat of my bread
   And drink of the wine I have
      mixed.
6 Forsake foolishness and live,
   And go in the way of
      understanding.

7 "He who corrects a scoffer gets
      shame for himself,
   And he who rebukes a wicked
      man only harms himself.
8 Do not correct a scoffer, lest he
      hate you;
   Rebuke a wise *man,* and he will
      love you.
9 Give *instruction* to a wise *man,*
      and he will be still wiser;
   Teach a just *man,* and he will
      increase in learning.

10 "The fear of the LORD *is* the
      beginning of wisdom,
   And the knowledge of the Holy
      One is understanding.
11 For by me your days will be
      multiplied,
   And years of life will be added to
      you.
12 If you are wise, you are wise for
      yourself,
   And *if* you scoff, you will bear *it*
      alone."

THE WAY OF FOLLY

13 A foolish woman is clamorous;
   She is simple, and knows nothing.
14 For she sits at the door of her
      house,
   On a seat *by* the highest places of
      the city,
15 To call to those who pass by,
   Who go straight on their way:
16 "Whoever *is* simple, let him turn
      in here";
   And *as for* him who lacks
      understanding, she says to
      him,

17 "Stolen water is sweet,
   And bread *eaten* in secret is
      pleasant."
18 But he does not know that the
      dead *are* there,
   That her guests *are* in the depths
      of hell.*a*

WISE SAYINGS OF SOLOMON

10 The proverbs of Solomon:

A wise son makes a glad father,
But a foolish son *is* the grief of his
   mother.

2 Treasures of wickedness profit
      nothing,
   But righteousness delivers from
      death.
3 The LORD will not allow the
      righteous soul to famish,
   But He casts away the desire of
      the wicked.

4 He who has a slack hand becomes
      poor,
   But the hand of the diligent
      makes rich.
5 He who gathers in summer is a
      wise son;
   He who sleeps in harvest is a son
      who causes shame.

6 Blessings *are* on the head of the
      righteous,
   But violence covers the mouth of
      the wicked.
7 The memory of the righteous *is*
      blessed,
   But the name of the wicked will
      rot.

8 The wise in heart will receive
      commands,
   But a prating fool will fall.

9:18 *a*Or *Sheol*

Family Memories

WONDERFUL MEMORIES Proverbs 10:7

Do you remember a special Christmas or birthday? Do you remember a special family vacation or trip you took together? Do you remember wonderful things? If so, you probably remember times when you honored God and your family more than the times when you did something bad. Remembering bad things often makes us sad. We wish those memories would rot, don't we? But we wish godly memories, good memories, would stay with us as long as we live.

1. What are some of your best family memories? What did you do? Why do you feel so good about those memories?
2. What are some of your worst memories? Do you think God is pleased with the things that caused those memories?
3. Read Proverbs 10:7. Try to say this verse in your own way of talking. What would you say?
4. Thank You, God, for good memories!

For more on *Family Memories* turn to page 1229
For more on *Family* turn to page 983

9 He who walks with integrity
   walks securely,
   But he who perverts his ways will
   become known.

10 He who winks with the eye causes
   trouble,
   But a prating fool will fall.

11 The mouth of the righteous *is* a
   well of life,
   But violence covers the mouth of
   the wicked.

12 Hatred stirs up strife,
   But love covers all sins.

13 Wisdom is found on the lips of
   him who has understanding,
   But a rod *is* for the back of him
   who is devoid of understanding.

14 Wise *people* store up knowledge,
   But the mouth of the foolish *is*
   near destruction.

15 The rich man's wealth is his
   strong city;
   The destruction of the poor is
   their poverty.

16 The labor of the righteous *leads* to
   life,
   The wages of the wicked to sin.

17 He who keeps instruction *is in*
   the way of life,
   But he who refuses correction
   goes astray.

18 Whoever hides hatred *has* lying
   lips,
   And whoever spreads slander *is* a
   fool.

19 In the multitude of words sin is
   not lacking,
   But he who restrains his lips *is*
   wise.

20 The tongue of the righteous *is*
   choice silver;

The heart of the wicked *is worth*
little.

21 The lips of the righteous feed
   many,
   But fools die for lack of wisdom.*a*

22 The blessing of the LORD makes
   one rich,
   And He adds no sorrow with it.

23 To do evil *is* like sport to a fool,
   But a man of understanding has
   wisdom.

24 The fear of the wicked will come
   upon him,
   And the desire of the righteous
   will be granted.

25 When the whirlwind passes by,
   the wicked *is* no *more,*
   But the righteous *has* an
   everlasting foundation.

26 As vinegar to the teeth and smoke
   to the eyes,
   So *is* the lazy *man* to those who
   send him.

27 The fear of the LORD prolongs
   days,
   But the years of the wicked will
   be shortened.

28 The hope of the righteous *will be*
   gladness,
   But the expectation of the wicked
   will perish.

29 The way of the LORD *is* strength
   for the upright,
   But destruction *will come* to the
   workers of iniquity.

30 The righteous will never be
   removed,
   But the wicked will not inhabit
   the earth.

31 The mouth of the righteous brings
   forth wisdom,

10:21 *a*Literally *heart*

But the perverse tongue will be
cut out.
32 The lips of the righteous know
what is acceptable,
But the mouth of the wicked *what
is* perverse.

11

Dishonest scales *are* an
abomination to the LORD,
But a just weight *is* His delight.

2 When pride comes, then comes
shame;
But with the humble *is* wisdom.

3 The integrity of the upright will
guide them,
But the perversity of the
unfaithful will destroy them.
4 Riches do not profit in the day of
wrath,
But righteousness delivers from
death.
5 The righteousness of the
blameless will direct[a] his way
aright,
But the wicked will fall by his
own wickedness.
6 The righteousness of the upright
will deliver them,
But the unfaithful will be caught
by *their* lust.

7 When a wicked man dies, his
expectation will perish,
And the hope of the unjust
perishes.
8 The righteous is delivered from
trouble,
And it comes to the wicked
instead.
9 The hypocrite with *his* mouth
destroys his neighbor,
But through knowledge the
righteous will be delivered.
10 When it goes well with the
righteous, the city rejoices;
And when the wicked perish,
there is jubilation.

11 By the blessing of the upright the
city is exalted,
But it is overthrown by the mouth
of the wicked.

12 He who is devoid of wisdom
despises his neighbor,
But a man of understanding holds
his peace.

13 A talebearer reveals secrets,
But he who is of a faithful spirit
conceals a matter.

14 Where *there is* no counsel, the
people fall;
But in the multitude of counselors
there is safety.

15 He who is surety for a stranger
will suffer,
But one who hates being surety is
secure.

16 A gracious woman retains honor,
But ruthless *men* retain riches.
17 The merciful man does good for
his own soul,
But *he who is* cruel troubles his
own flesh.
18 The wicked *man* does deceptive
work,
But he who sows righteousness
will have a sure reward.
19 As righteousness *leads* to life,
So he who pursues evil *pursues it*
to his own death.
20 Those who are of a perverse heart
are an abomination to the
LORD,
But *the* blameless in their ways
are His delight.
21 *Though they* join forces,[a] the
wicked will not go unpunished;
But the posterity of the righteous
will be delivered.

11:5 [a]Or *make smooth* or *straight*   11:21 [a]Liter-
ally *hand to hand*

What Should I Do?

WHEN I KNOW A SECRET Proverbs 11:13

"I know a secret. I'll tell you, but you must not tell anyone else." That's what Holly is saying to Hank. How long do you think it will be before Hank will say the same thing to another friend?

1. What is a secret? If a secret is *really* a secret, should we tell anyone else about it?
2. Look up Proverbs 11:13. The Bible tells us what we should do about secrets.
3. Do you know a secret about someone? Should you tell someone else about it? Why not?

For more on *What Should I Do?* turn to page 975
For more on *Friendship* turn to page 984

22 *As* a ring of gold in a swine's
snout,
So is a lovely woman who lacks
discretion.

23 The desire of the righteous *is* only
good,
But the expectation of the wicked
is wrath.

24 There is *one* who scatters, yet
increases more;
And there is *one* who withholds
more than is right,
But it *leads* to poverty.
25 The generous soul will be made
rich,
And he who waters will also be
watered himself.
26 The people will curse him who
withholds grain,
But blessing *will be* on the head
of him who sells *it.*

27 He who earnestly seeks good finds
favor,
But trouble will come to him who
seeks *evil.*

28 He who trusts in his riches will
fall,
But the righteous will flourish
like foliage.

29 He who troubles his own house
will inherit the wind,
And the fool *will be* servant to the
wise of heart.

30 The fruit of the righteous *is a* tree
of life,
And he who wins souls *is* wise.

31 If the righteous will be
recompensed on the earth,
How much more the ungodly and
the sinner.

12 Whoever loves instruction
loves knowledge,
But he who hates correction *is*
stupid.

2 A good *man* obtains favor from
the LORD,
But a man of wicked intentions
He will condemn.

3 A man is not established by
wickedness,
But the root of the righteous
cannot be moved.

4 An excellent^a wife *is* the crown of
her husband,
But she who causes shame *is* like
rottenness in his bones.

5 The thoughts of the righteous *are*
right,
But the counsels of the wicked *are*
deceitful.
6 The words of the wicked *are,* "Lie
in wait for blood,"
But the mouth of the upright will
deliver them.

7 The wicked are overthrown and
are no more,
But the house of the righteous
will stand.

8 A man will be commended
according to his wisdom,
But he who is of a perverse heart
will be despised.

9 Better *is the one* who is slighted
but has a servant,
Than he who honors himself but
lacks bread.

10 A righteous *man* regards the life
of his animal,

12:4 ^aLiterally *A wife of valor*

But the tender mercies of the
wicked *are* cruel.

11 He who tills his land will be
satisfied with bread,
But he who follows frivolity *is*
devoid of understanding.*a*

12 The wicked covet the catch of evil
men,
But the root of the righteous
yields *fruit.*

13 The wicked is ensnared by the
transgression of *his* lips,
But the righteous will come
through trouble.

14 A man will be satisfied with good
by the fruit of *his* mouth,
And the recompense of a man's
hands will be rendered to him.

15 The way of a fool *is* right in his
own eyes,
But he who heeds counsel *is* wise.

16 A fool's wrath is known at once,
But a prudent *man* covers shame.

17 He *who* speaks truth declares
righteousness,
But a false witness, deceit.

18 There is one who speaks like the
piercings of a sword,
But the tongue of the wise
promotes health.

19 The truthful lip shall be
established forever,
But a lying tongue *is* but for a
moment.

20 Deceit is in the heart of those who
devise evil,
But counselors of peace have joy.

21 No grave trouble will overtake
the righteous,
But the wicked shall be filled with
evil.

22 Lying lips *are* an abomination to
the LORD,
But those who deal truthfully *are*
His delight.

23 A prudent man conceals
knowledge,
But the heart of fools proclaims
foolishness.

24 The hand of the diligent will rule,
But the lazy *man* will be put to
forced labor.

25 Anxiety in the heart of man
causes depression,
But a good word makes it glad.

26 The righteous should choose his
friends carefully,
For the way of the wicked leads
them astray.

27 The lazy *man* does not roast what
he took in hunting,
But diligence *is* man's precious
possession.

28 In the way of righteousness *is* life,
And in *its* pathway *there is* no
death.

13 A wise son *heeds* his father's
instruction,
But a scoffer does not listen to
rebuke.

2 A man shall eat well by the fruit
of *his* mouth,
But the soul of the unfaithful
feeds on violence.

3 He who guards his mouth
preserves his life,
But he who opens wide his lips
shall have destruction.

4 The soul of a lazy *man* desires,
and *has* nothing;
But the soul of the diligent shall
be made rich.

5 A righteous *man* hates lying,
But a wicked *man* is loathsome
and comes to shame.

12:11 *a*Literally *heart*

6 Righteousness guards *him whose*
    way is blameless,
  But wickedness overthrows the
    sinner.

7 There is one who makes himself
    rich, yet *has* nothing;
  And one who makes himself poor,
    yet *has* great riches.

8 The ransom of a man's life *is* his
    riches,
  But the poor does not hear
    rebuke.

9 The light of the righteous rejoices,
  But the lamp of the wicked will be
    put out.

10 By pride comes nothing but strife,
   But with the well-advised *is*
     wisdom.

11 Wealth *gained by* dishonesty will
     be diminished,
   But he who gathers by labor will
     increase.

12 Hope deferred makes the heart
     sick,
   But *when* the desire comes, it is a
     tree of life.

13 He who despises the word will be
     destroyed,
   But he who fears the
     commandment will be
     rewarded.

14 The law of the wise *is* a fountain
     of life,
   To turn *one* away from the snares
     of death.

15 Good understanding gains favor,
   But the way of the unfaithful *is*
     hard.

16 Every prudent *man* acts with
     knowledge,
   But a fool lays open *his* folly.

17 A wicked messenger falls into
     trouble,
   But a faithful ambassador *brings*
     health.

18 Poverty and shame *will come* to
     him who disdains correction,
   But he who regards a rebuke will
     be honored.

19 A desire accomplished is sweet to
     the soul,
   But *it is* an abomination to fools
     to depart from evil.

20 He who walks with wise *men* will
     be wise,
   But the companion of fools will be
     destroyed.

21 Evil pursues sinners,
   But to the righteous, good shall
     be repaid.

22 A good *man* leaves an inheritance
     to his children's children,
   But the wealth of the sinner is
     stored up for the righteous.

23 Much food *is in* the fallow *ground*
     of the poor,
   And for lack of justice there is
     waste.*a*

24 He who spares his rod hates his
     son,
   But he who loves him disciplines
     him promptly.

25 The righteous eats to the
     satisfying of his soul,
   But the stomach of the wicked
     shall be in want.

14 The wise woman builds her
     house,
   But the foolish pulls it down with
     her hands.

13:23 *a*Literally *what is swept away*

What Should I Do?

HELP ME, BUT DON'T HURT ME Proverbs 13:24

This little boy had a terrible problem. He had a very bad tooth. So he went to the dentist. "Help me, but don't hurt me," the boy said. But the dentist had to pull the boy's tooth. What should a dentist do? Do you think he can help his patients without hurting them?

1. Sometimes parents must hurt us a little to help us. Can you think of a time they hurt you a little so they could help you?
2. Sometimes God must hurt us a little to help us. Can you think of a time He hurt you a little to help you?
3. Should we say thank you to parents or God even when they hurt us if they really are helping us?

For more on *What Should I Do?* turn to page 978
For more on *God's Guidance* turn to page 1508

2 He who walks in his uprightness
      fears the LORD,
   But *he who is* perverse in his
      ways despises Him.

3 In the mouth of a fool *is* a rod of
      pride,
   But the lips of the wise will
      preserve them.

4 Where no oxen *are,* the trough *is*
      clean;
   But much increase *comes* by the
      strength of an ox.

5 A faithful witness does not lie,
   But a false witness will utter lies.

6 A scoffer seeks wisdom and does
      not *find it,*
   But knowledge *is* easy to him who
      understands.

7 Go from the presence of a foolish
      man,
   When you do not perceive *in him*
      the lips of knowledge.

8 The wisdom of the prudent *is* to
      understand his way,
   But the folly of fools *is* deceit.

9 Fools mock at sin,
   But among the upright *there is*
      favor.

10 The heart knows its own
      bitterness,
   And a stranger does not share its
      joy.

11 The house of the wicked will be
      overthrown,
   But the tent of the upright will
      flourish.

12 There is a way *that seems* right to
      a man,
   But its end *is* the way of death.

13 Even in laughter the heart may
      sorrow,

And the end of mirth *may be*
      grief.

14 The backslider in heart will be
      filled with his own ways,
   But a good man *will be satisfied*
      from above.*a*

15 The simple believes every word,
   But the prudent considers well
      his steps.

16 A wise *man* fears and departs
      from evil,
   But a fool rages and is
      self-confident.

17 A quick-tempered *man* acts
      foolishly,
   And a man of wicked intentions is
      hated.

18 The simple inherit folly,
   But the prudent are crowned with
      knowledge.

19 The evil will bow before the good,
   And the wicked at the gates of the
      righteous.

20 The poor *man* is hated even by
      his own neighbor,
   But the rich *has* many friends.

21 He who despises his neighbor
      sins;
   But he who has mercy on the
      poor, happy *is* he.

22 Do they not go astray who devise
      evil?
   But mercy and truth *belong* to
      those who devise good.

23 In all labor there is profit,
   But idle chatter*a* *leads* only to
      poverty.

24 The crown of the wise is their
      riches,
   But the foolishness of fools *is* folly.

14:14 *a*Literally *from above himself*   14:23 *a*Literally *talk of the lips*

25 A true witness delivers souls,
But a deceitful *witness* speaks
lies.

26 In the fear of the LORD *there is*
strong confidence,
And His children will have a
place of refuge.

27 The fear of the LORD *is* a fountain
of life,
To turn *one* away from the snares
of death.

28 In a multitude of people *is* a
king's honor,
But in the lack of people *is* the
downfall of a prince.

29 *He who is* slow to wrath has great
understanding,
But *he who is* impulsive[a] exalts
folly.

30 A sound heart *is* life to the body,
But envy *is* rottenness to the
bones.

31 He who oppresses the poor
reproaches his Maker,
But he who honors Him has
mercy on the needy.

32 The wicked is banished in his
wickedness,
But the righteous has a refuge in
his death.

33 Wisdom rests in the heart of him
who has understanding,
But *what is* in the heart of fools is
made known.

34 Righteousness exalts a nation,
But sin *is* a reproach to *any*
people.

35 The king's favor *is* toward a wise
servant,

But his wrath *is against* him who
causes shame.

15 A soft answer turns away
wrath,
But a harsh word stirs up anger.

2 The tongue of the wise uses
knowledge rightly,
But the mouth of fools pours forth
foolishness.

3 The eyes of the LORD *are* in every
place,
Keeping watch on the evil and the
good.

4 A wholesome tongue *is* a tree of
life,
But perverseness in it breaks the
spirit.

5 A fool despises his father's
instruction,
But he who receives correction is
prudent.

6 *In* the house of the righteous
there is much treasure,
But in the revenue of the wicked
is trouble.

7 The lips of the wise disperse
knowledge,
But the heart of the fool *does* not
do so.

8 The sacrifice of the wicked *is* an
abomination to the LORD,
But the prayer of the upright *is*
His delight.

9 The way of the wicked *is* an
abomination to the LORD,
But He loves him who follows
righteousness.

10 Harsh discipline *is* for him who
forsakes the way,

14:29 [a]Literally *short of spirit*

I'M SORRY Proverbs 15:1

These two people had a quarrel. One said something bad. The other grew angry. Both of them had their feelings hurt. Then one said, "I'm sorry." The other said, "Me, too." Now look what is happening.

1. Have you ever had a quarrel or argument? How did it start? Did it help you to love Jesus more?
2. Have you ever stopped an argument or quarrel by saying, "I'm sorry"? Why is this a good idea?
3. Why is Jesus pleased when we stop a quarrel or argument by saying, "I'm sorry"? Why is He pleased when we tell Him, "I'm sorry for my sin"? Have you?

For more on *What Should I Do?* turn to page 1005
For more on *Forgiveness* turn to page 1453

And he who hates correction will die.

11 Hell[a] and Destruction[b] *are* before the LORD;
So how much more the hearts of the sons of men.

12 A scoffer does not love one who corrects him,
Nor will he go to the wise.

13 A merry heart makes a cheerful countenance,
But by sorrow of the heart the spirit is broken.

14 The heart of him who has understanding seeks knowledge,
But the mouth of fools feeds on foolishness.

15 All the days of the afflicted *are* evil,
But he who is of a merry heart *has* a continual feast.

16 Better *is* a little with the fear of the LORD,
Than great treasure with trouble.

17 Better *is* a dinner of herbs[a] where love is,
Than a fatted calf with hatred.

18 A wrathful man stirs up strife,
But *he who is* slow to anger allays contention.

19 The way of the lazy *man* is like a hedge of thorns,
But the way of the upright *is* a highway.

20 A wise son makes a father glad,
But a foolish man despises his mother.

21 Folly *is* joy *to him who is* destitute of discernment,

But a man of understanding walks uprightly.

22 Without counsel, plans go awry,
But in the multitude of counselors they are established.

23 A man has joy by the answer of his mouth,
And a word *spoken* in due season, how good *it is!*

24 The way of life *winds* upward for the wise,
That he may turn away from hell[a] below.

25 The LORD will destroy the house of the proud,
But He will establish the boundary of the widow.

26 The thoughts of the wicked *are* an abomination to the LORD,
But *the words* of the pure *are* pleasant.

27 He who is greedy for gain troubles his own house,
But he who hates bribes will live.

28 The heart of the righteous studies how to answer,
But the mouth of the wicked pours forth evil.

29 The LORD *is* far from the wicked,
But He hears the prayer of the righteous.

30 The light of the eyes rejoices the heart,
And a good report makes the bones healthy.[a]

15:11 [a]Or *Sheol* [b]Hebrew *Abaddon*   15:17 [a]Or *vegetables*   15:24 [a]Or *Sheol*   15:30 [a]Literally *fat*

31 The ear that hears the rebukes of
    life
    Will abide among the wise.
32 He who disdains instruction
    despises his own soul,
    But he who heeds rebuke gets
    understanding.
33 The fear of the LORD *is* the
    instruction of wisdom,
    And before honor *is* humility.

16
    The preparations of the heart
    belong to man,
    But the answer of the tongue *is*
    from the LORD.

2 All the ways of a man *are* pure in
    his own eyes,
    But the LORD weighs the spirits.

3 Commit your works to the LORD,
    And your thoughts will be
    established.

4 The LORD has made all for
    Himself,
    Yes, even the wicked for the day
    of doom.

5 Everyone proud in heart *is* an
    abomination to the LORD;
    Though they join forces,*a* none
    will go unpunished.

6 In mercy and truth
    Atonement is provided for
    iniquity;
    And by the fear of the LORD *one*
    departs from evil.

7 When a man's ways please the
    LORD,
    He makes even his enemies to be
    at peace with him.

8 Better *is* a little with
    righteousness,
    Than vast revenues without
    justice.

9 A man's heart plans his way,
    But the LORD directs his steps.

10 Divination *is* on the lips of the
    king;
    His mouth must not transgress in
    judgment.
11 Honest weights and scales *are* the
    LORD's;
    All the weights in the bag *are* His
    work.
12 *It is* an abomination for kings to
    commit wickedness,
    For a throne is established by
    righteousness.
13 Righteous lips *are* the delight of
    kings,
    And they love him who speaks
    what is right.
14 As messengers of death *is* the
    king's wrath,
    But a wise man will appease it.
15 In the light of the king's face *is*
    life,
    And his favor *is* like a cloud of the
    latter rain.

16 How much better to get wisdom
    than gold!
    And to get understanding is to be
    chosen rather than silver.

17 The highway of the upright *is* to
    depart from evil;
    He who keeps his way preserves
    his soul.

18 Pride *goes* before destruction,
    And a haughty spirit before a fall.
19 Better *to be* of a humble spirit
    with the lowly,
    Than to divide the spoil with the
    proud.

20 He who heeds the word wisely
    will find good,
    And whoever trusts in the LORD,
    happy *is* he.

16:5 *a*Literally *hand to hand*

WISDOM Proverbs 16:23

Wise Men with Good Gifts

Do you remember the story about three Wise Men, or Magi? They were wise because they gave their best gifts to Jesus. Read Proverbs 16:23. You can be a Wise Boy or a Wise Girl by letting your heart teach your lips what to say. If you have a wise heart, it will teach your lips to say wise things. Ask the Lord to give you a wise heart. Then you can say wise things.

1. Who can give you a wise heart? How can that help you say wise things?
2. You will have a wise heart as you read wise words from God's Word. God's Word will give you a great gift—a wise heart.

For more on *Favorite Bible Words* turn to page 983
For more on *Bible* turn to page 1092

21 The wise in heart will be called
    prudent,
And sweetness of the lips
    increases learning.

22 Understanding *is* a wellspring of
    life to him who has it.
But the correction of fools *is* folly.

23 The heart of the wise teaches his
    mouth,
And adds learning to his lips.

24 Pleasant words *are like* a
    honeycomb,
Sweetness to the soul and health
    to the bones.

25 There is a way *that seems* right to
    a man,
But its end *is* the way of death.

26 The person who labors, labors for
    himself,
For his *hungry* mouth drives him
    on.

27 An ungodly man digs up evil,
And *it is* on his lips like a burning
    fire.
28 A perverse man sows strife,
And a whisperer separates the
    best of friends.
29 A violent man entices his
    neighbor,
And leads him in a way *that is*
    not good.
30 He winks his eye to devise
    perverse things;
He purses his lips *and* brings
    about evil.

31 The silver-haired head *is* a crown
    of glory,
If it is found in the way of
    righteousness.

32 *He who is* slow to anger *is* better
    than the mighty,
And he who rules his spirit than
    he who takes a city.

33 The lot is cast into the lap,
But its every decision *is* from the
    LORD.

17 Better *is* a dry morsel with
    quietness,
Than a house full of feasting[a]
    with strife.

2 A wise servant will rule over a
    son who causes shame,
And will share an inheritance
    among the brothers.

3 The refining pot *is* for silver and
    the furnace for gold,
But the LORD tests the hearts.

4 An evildoer gives heed to false
    lips;
A liar listens eagerly to a spiteful
    tongue.

5 He who mocks the poor
    reproaches his Maker;
He who is glad at calamity will
    not go unpunished.

6 Children's children *are* the crown
    of old men,
And the glory of children *is* their
    father.

7 Excellent speech is not becoming
    to a fool,
Much less lying lips to a prince.

8 A present *is* a precious stone in
    the eyes of its possessor;
Wherever he turns, he prospers.

9 He who covers a transgression
    seeks love,
But he who repeats a matter
    separates friends.

17:1 [a]Or *sacrificial meals*

CROWN Proverbs 17:6

Grandpa's and Grandma's Crown

Did you know that grandpa and grandma have a crown? Do you know what it is? You'll be very surprised to learn what their crown is when you read Proverbs 17:6.

1. Did you read Proverbs 17:6? What is grandpa's and grandma's crown? Is it you?
2. Why are grandchildren a crown to grandparents? Why are they so special?
3. Would you like to talk with grandpa and grandma about this? Would you like to tell them how special they are to you? Perhaps they will tell you how special you are to them.

For more on *Favorite Bible Words* turn to page 1010
For more on *Family* turn to page 992

10 Rebuke is more effective for a
 wise *man*
 Than a hundred blows on a fool.

11 An evil *man* seeks only rebellion;
 Therefore a cruel messenger will
 be sent against him.

12 Let a man meet a bear robbed of
 her cubs,
 Rather than a fool in his folly.

13 Whoever rewards evil for good,
 Evil will not depart from his
 house.

14 The beginning of strife *is like*
 releasing water;
 Therefore stop contention before a
 quarrel starts.

15 He who justifies the wicked, and
 he who condemns the just,
 Both of them alike *are* an
 abomination to the LORD.

16 Why *is there* in the hand of a fool
 the purchase price of wisdom,
 Since *he has* no heart *for it?*

17 A friend loves at all times,
 And a brother is born for
 adversity.

18 A man devoid of understanding
 shakes hands in a pledge,
 And becomes surety for his
 friend.

19 He who loves transgression loves
 strife,
 And he who exalts his gate seeks
 destruction.

20 He who has a deceitful heart finds
 no good,
 And he who has a perverse
 tongue falls into evil.

21 He who begets a scoffer *does so* to
 his sorrow,
 And the father of a fool has no joy.

22 A merry heart does good, like
 medicine,*a*

17:22 *a*Or *makes medicine even better*

A FRIEND LOVES AT ALL TIMES. Proverbs 17:17

When You Need a Friend

Sometimes trouble comes fast. Everything looks great. Then suddenly, *snap!*— like the trap that caught this little mouse, you're caught. You need a friend. This mouse is certainly glad for a friend. What would he do without a friend to help him?

1. What happened to the mouse? Why is he so glad to have a friend? What is the friend doing for the mouse?
2. Has something bad happened to you lately? What? Did a friend help you? Who?
3. How did your friend help?
4. Has your mother or father been a good friend for you when you needed them?
5. Have you been a good friend when someone needed you? What did you do?

For more on *Favorite Family Verses* turn to page 992
For more on *Friendship* turn to page 987

But a broken spirit dries the bones.

23 A wicked *man* accepts a bribe behind the back[a]
To pervert the ways of justice.

24 Wisdom *is* in the sight of him who has understanding,
But the eyes of a fool *are* on the ends of the earth.

25 A foolish son *is* a grief to his father,
And bitterness to her who bore him.

26 Also, to punish the righteous *is* not good,
Nor to strike princes for *their* uprightness.

27 He who has knowledge spares his words,
And a man of understanding is of a calm spirit.

28 Even a fool is counted wise when he holds his peace;
When he shuts his lips, he is considered perceptive.

18 A man who isolates himself seeks his own desire;
He rages against all wise judgment.

2 A fool has no delight in understanding,
But in expressing his own heart.

3 When the wicked comes, contempt comes also;
And with dishonor *comes* reproach.

4 The words of a man's mouth *are* deep waters;
The wellspring of wisdom *is* a flowing brook.

5 *It is* not good to show partiality to the wicked,
Or to overthrow the righteous in judgment.

6 A fool's lips enter into contention,
And his mouth calls for blows.

7 A fool's mouth *is* his destruction,
And his lips *are* the snare of his soul.

8 The words of a talebearer *are* like tasty trifles,[a]
And they go down into the inmost body.

9 He who is slothful in his work
Is a brother to him who is a great destroyer.

10 The name of the LORD is a strong tower;
The righteous run to it and are safe.

11 The rich man's wealth is his strong city,
And like a high wall in his own esteem.

12 Before destruction the heart of a man is haughty,
And before honor *is* humility.

13 He who answers a matter before he hears *it,*
It *is* folly and shame to him.

14 The spirit of a man will sustain him in sickness,
But who can bear a broken spirit?

15 The heart of the prudent acquires knowledge,
And the ear of the wise seeks knowledge.

16 A man's gift makes room for him,
And brings him before great men.

17:23 [a]Literally *from the bosom*   18:8 [a]A Jewish tradition reads *wounds.*

17 The first *one* to plead his cause
    seems right,
    Until his neighbor comes and
    examines him.

18 Casting lots causes contentions to
    cease,
    And keeps the mighty apart.

19 A brother offended *is harder to*
    win than a strong city,
    And contentions *are* like the bars
    of a castle.

20 A man's stomach shall be
    satisfied from the fruit of his
    mouth;
    From the produce of his lips he
    shall be filled.

21 Death and life *are* in the power of
    the tongue,
    And those who love it will eat its
    fruit.

22 *He who* finds a wife finds a good
    thing,
    And obtains favor from the LORD.

23 The poor *man* uses entreaties,
    But the rich answers roughly.

24 A man *who has* friends must
    himself be friendly,*a*
    But there is a friend *who* sticks
    closer than a brother.

19 Better *is* the poor who walks
    in his integrity
    Than *one who is* perverse in his
    lips, and is a fool.

2 Also it is not good *for* a soul *to be*
    without knowledge,
    And he sins who hastens with *his*
    feet.

3 The foolishness of a man twists
    his way,

And his heart frets against the
    LORD.

4 Wealth makes many friends,
    But the poor is separated from his
    friend.

5 A false witness will not go
    unpunished,
    And *he who* speaks lies will not
    escape.

6 Many entreat the favor of the
    nobility,
    And every man *is* a friend to one
    who gives gifts.

7 All the brothers of the poor hate
    him;
    How much more do his friends go
    far from him!
    He may pursue *them with* words,
    yet they abandon *him.*

8 He who gets wisdom loves his
    own soul;
    He who keeps understanding will
    find good.

9 A false witness will not go
    unpunished,
    And *he who* speaks lies shall
    perish.

10 Luxury is not fitting for a fool,
    Much less for a servant to rule
    over princes.

11 The discretion of a man makes
    him slow to anger,
    And his glory *is* to overlook a
    transgression.

12 The king's wrath *is* like the
    roaring of a lion,
    But his favor *is* like dew on the
    grass.

18:24 *a*Following Greek manuscripts, Syriac, Targum, and Vulgate; Masoretic Text reads *may come to ruin.*

GOOD FRIENDS AND GOOD GIFTS GO TOGETHER Proverbs 19:6

Good friends like to give good gifts. Good friends and good gifts go together. You may have friends without giving gifts, of course, but if you have good friends you like to give them good things or do good things for them.

1. Think of three good friends. Have you done something special for them? Have they done something special for you?
2. Think of these three good friends again. Have you given good gifts to them? Have they given good gifts to you?
3. Now read Proverbs 19:6. What does this say? If we're friends because of good gifts, that's not very good friendship. But if we give gifts because we're friends, that is good friendship.

For more on *Family Friends* turn to page 1683
For more on *Friendship* turn to page 1002

13 A foolish son *is* the ruin of his
   father,
   And the contentions of a wife *are*
   a continual dripping.

14 Houses and riches *are* an
   inheritance from fathers,
   But a prudent wife *is* from the
   LORD.

15 Laziness casts *one* into a deep
   sleep,
   And an idle person will suffer
   hunger.

16 He who keeps the commandment
   keeps his soul,
   But he who is careless*a* of his
   ways will die.

17 He who has pity on the poor lends
   to the LORD,
   And He will pay back what he has
   given.

18 Chasten your son while there is
   hope,
   And do not set your heart on his
   destruction.*a*

19 *A man of* great wrath will suffer
   punishment;
   For if you rescue *him,* you will
   have to do it again.

20 Listen to counsel and receive
   instruction,
   That you may be wise in your
   latter days.

21 There are many plans in a man's
   heart,
   Nevertheless the LORD's counsel—
   that will stand.

22 What is desired in a man is
   kindness,
   And a poor man is better than a
   liar.

23 The fear of the LORD *leads* to life,
   And *he who has it* will abide in
   satisfaction;
   He will not be visited with evil.

24 A lazy *man* buries his hand in the
   bowl,*a*
   And will not so much as bring it
   to his mouth again.

25 Strike a scoffer, and the simple
   will become wary;
   Rebuke one who has
   understanding, *and* he will
   discern knowledge.

26 He who mistreats *his* father *and*
   chases away *his* mother
   Is a son who causes shame and
   brings reproach.

27 Cease listening to instruction, my
   son,
   And you will stray from the words
   of knowledge.

28 A disreputable witness scorns
   justice,
   And the mouth of the wicked
   devours iniquity.

29 Judgments are prepared for
   scoffers,
   And beatings for the backs of
   fools.

20 Wine *is* a mocker,
   Strong drink *is* a brawler,
   And whoever is led astray by it is
   not wise.

2 The wrath*a* of a king *is* like the
   roaring of a lion;
   Whoever provokes him to anger
   sins *against* his own life.

19:16 *a*Literally *despises,* figurative of recklessness
or carelessness   19:18 *a*Literally *to put him to
death;* a Jewish tradition reads *on his crying.*
19:24 *a*Septuagint and Syriac read *bosom;* Targum
and Vulgate read *armpit.*   20:2 *a*Literally *fear
or terror* which is produced by the king's wrath

3   *It is* honorable for a man to stop
striving,
Since any fool can start a quarrel.

4   The lazy *man* will not plow
because of winter;
He will beg during harvest and
have nothing.

5   Counsel in the heart of man *is*
like deep water,
But a man of understanding will
draw it out.

6   Most men will proclaim each his
own goodness,
But who can find a faithful man?

7   The righteous *man* walks in his
integrity;
His children *are* blessed after
him.

8   A king who sits on the throne of
judgment
Scatters all evil with his eyes.

9   Who can say, "I have made my
heart clean,
I am pure from my sin"?

10   Diverse weights *and* diverse
measures,
They *are* both alike, an
abomination to the LORD.

11   Even a child is known by his
deeds,
Whether what he does *is* pure
and right.

12   The hearing ear and the seeing
eye,
The LORD has made them both.

13   Do not love sleep, lest you come to
poverty;
Open your eyes, *and* you will be
satisfied with bread.

14   "*It is* good for nothing,"a cries the
buyer;
But when he has gone his way,
then he boasts.

15   There is gold and a multitude of
rubies,
But the lips of knowledge *are* a
precious jewel.

16   Take the garment of one who is
surety *for* a stranger,
And hold it as a pledge *when it* is
for a seductress.

17   Bread gained by deceit *is* sweet to
a man,
But afterward his mouth will be
filled with gravel.

18   Plans are established by counsel;
By wise counsel wage war.

19   He who goes about *as* a
talebearer reveals secrets;
Therefore do not associate with
one who flatters with his lips.

20   Whoever curses his father or his
mother,
His lamp will be put out in deep
darkness.

21   An inheritance gained hastily at
the beginning
Will not be blessed at the end.

22   Do not say, "I will recompense
evil";
Wait for the LORD, and He will
save you.

23   Diverse weights *are* an
abomination to the LORD,
And dishonest scales *are* not good.

24   A man's steps *are* of the LORD;
How then can a man understand
his own way?

20:14 aLiterally *evil, evil*

25 *It is* a snare for a man to devote
  rashly *something as* holy,
  And afterward to reconsider *his*
  vows.

26 A wise king sifts out the wicked,
  And brings the threshing wheel
  over them.

27 The spirit of a man *is* the lamp of
  the Lord,
  Searching all the inner depths of
  his heart.*a*

28 Mercy and truth preserve the
  king,
  And by lovingkindness he upholds
  his throne.

29 The glory of young men *is* their
  strength,
  And the splendor of old men *is*
  their gray head.

30 Blows that hurt cleanse away
  evil,
  As *do* stripes the inner depths of
  the heart.*a*

21 The king's heart *is* in the hand
  of the Lord,
  Like the rivers of water;
  He turns it wherever He wishes.

2 Every way of a man *is* right in his
  own eyes,
  But the Lord weighs the hearts.

3 To do righteousness and justice
  Is more acceptable to the Lord
  than sacrifice.

4 A haughty look, a proud heart,
  And the plowing*a* of the wicked
  are sin.

5 The plans of the diligent *lead*
  surely to plenty,

But *those of* everyone *who is*
  hasty, surely to poverty.

6 Getting treasures by a lying
  tongue
  Is the fleeting fantasy of those
  who seek death.*a*

7 The violence of the wicked will
  destroy them,*a*
  Because they refuse to do justice.

8 The way of a guilty man *is*
  perverse;*a*
  But *as for* the pure, his work *is*
  right.

9 Better to dwell in a corner of a
  housetop,
  Than in a house shared with a
  contentious woman.

10 The soul of the wicked desires
  evil;
  His neighbor finds no favor in his
  eyes.

11 When the scoffer is punished, the
  simple is made wise;
  But when the wise is instructed,
  he receives knowledge.

12 The righteous *God* wisely
  considers the house of the
  wicked,
  Overthrowing the wicked for *their*
  wickedness.

13 Whoever shuts his ears to the cry
  of the poor
  Will also cry himself and not be
  heard.

20:27 *a*Literally *the rooms of the belly*
20:30 *a*Literally *the rooms of the belly*   21:4 *a*Or
lamp   21:6 *a*Septuagint reads *Pursue vanity on
the snares of death;* Vulgate reads *Is vain and foolish, and shall stumble on the snares of death;* Targum reads *They shall be destroyed, and they shall
fall who seek death.*   21:7 *a*Literally *drag them
away*   21:8 *a*Or *The way of a man is perverse
and strange*

14 A gift in secret pacifies anger,
And a bribe behind the back,*a*
strong wrath.

15 *It is* a joy for the just to do justice,
But destruction *will come* to the
workers of iniquity.

16 A man who wanders from the way
of understanding
Will rest in the assembly of the
dead.

17 He who loves pleasure *will be* a
poor man;
He who loves wine and oil will not
be rich.

18 The wicked *shall be* a ransom for
the righteous,
And the unfaithful for the
upright.

19 Better to dwell in the wilderness,
Than with a contentious and
angry woman.

20 *There is* desirable treasure,
And oil in the dwelling of the
wise,
But a foolish man squanders it.

21 He who follows righteousness and
mercy
Finds life, righteousness and
honor.

22 A wise *man* scales the city of the
mighty,
And brings down the trusted
stronghold.

23 Whoever guards his mouth and
tongue
Keeps his soul from troubles.

24 A proud *and* haughty *man*—
"Scoffer" *is* his name;
He acts with arrogant pride.

25 The desire of the lazy *man* kills
him,
For his hands refuse to labor.

26 He covets greedily all day long,
But the righteous gives and does
not spare.

27 The sacrifice of the wicked *is* an
abomination;
How much more *when* he brings
it with wicked intent!

28 A false witness shall perish,
But the man who hears *him* will
speak endlessly.

29 A wicked man hardens his face,
But *as for* the upright, he
establishes*a* his way.

30 *There is* no wisdom or
understanding
Or counsel against the LORD.

31 The horse *is* prepared for the day
of battle,
But deliverance *is* of the LORD.

22 A *good* name is to be chosen
rather than great riches,
Loving favor rather than silver
and gold.

2 The rich and the poor have this in
common,
The LORD *is* the maker of them
all.

3 A prudent *man* foresees evil and
hides himself,
But the simple pass on and are
punished.

4 By humility *and* the fear of the
LORD
Are riches and honor and life.

21:14 *a*Literally *in the bosom*   21:29 *a*Qere and
Septuagint read *understands.*

Favorite Family Verses

TRAIN UP A CHILD IN THE WAY HE SHOULD GO, / AND WHEN HE IS OLD HE WILL NOT DEPART FROM IT. Proverbs 22:6

What Do You Want to Become?

"What do you want to be when you grow up, Brian?" someone asks. "A cowboy," says Brian. That's why Brian is riding his horse and wearing his cowboy hat now. "What do you *really* want to be when you grow up, Brian?" someone asks. "Just like dad," said Brian. Dad is a Christian. He reads his Bible. He loves Jesus. He does happy things with his family. He takes time to play with Brian. The first person was really asking, "What do you want to *do* when you grow up?" The second person was asking, "What do you want to *be* when you grow up?"

1. What's the difference between what you want to *do* and what you want to *be* when you grow up? What was the difference with Brian?
2. Why did Brian want to be just like dad? How was dad "training up his child in the way he should go?"
3. What can you and your family do now that will help you become what you should be later?

For more on *Favorite Family Verses* turn to page 995
For more on *Family* turn to page 1360

5 Thorns *and* snares *are* in the way
of the perverse;
He who guards his soul will be far
from them.

6 Train up a child in the way he
should go,
And when he is old he will not
depart from it.

7 The rich rules over the poor,
And the borrower *is* servant to
the lender.

8 He who sows iniquity will reap
sorrow,
And the rod of his anger will fail.

9 He who has a generous eye will
be blessed,
For he gives of his bread to the
poor.

10 Cast out the scoffer, and
contention will leave;
Yes, strife and reproach will
cease.

11 He who loves purity of heart
And has grace on his lips,
The king *will be* his friend.

12 The eyes of the LORD preserve
knowledge,
But He overthrows the words of
the faithless.

13 The lazy *man* says, "*There is* a
lion outside!
I shall be slain in the streets!"

14 The mouth of an immoral woman
is a deep pit;
He who is abhorred by the LORD
will fall there.

15 Foolishness *is* bound up in the
heart of a child;
The rod of correction will drive it
far from him.

16 He who oppresses the poor to
increase his *riches,*
And he who gives to the rich, will
surely *come* to poverty.

SAYINGS OF THE WISE

17 Incline your ear and hear the
words of the wise,
And apply your heart to my
knowledge;

18 For *it is* a pleasant thing if you
keep them within you;
Let them all be fixed upon your
lips,

19 So that your trust may be in the
LORD;
I have instructed you today, even
you.

20 Have I not written to you
excellent things
Of counsels and knowledge,

21 That I may make you know the
certainty of the words of truth,
That you may answer words of
truth
To those who send to you?

22 Do not rob the poor because he *is*
poor,
Nor oppress the afflicted at the
gate;

23 For the LORD will plead their
cause,
And plunder the soul of those who
plunder them.

24 Make no friendship with an angry
man,
And with a furious man do not go,

25 Lest you learn his ways
And set a snare for your soul.

26 Do not be one of those who shakes
hands in a pledge,
One of those who is surety for
debts;

27 If you have nothing *with which* to
pay,

Why should he take away your
bed from under you?

28 Do not remove the ancient
landmark
Which your fathers have set.

29 Do you see a man *who* excels in
his work?
He will stand before kings;
He will not stand before unknown
men.

23 When you sit down to eat with
a ruler,
Consider carefully what *is* before
you;
2 And put a knife to your throat
If you *are* a man given to
appetite.
3 Do not desire his delicacies,
For they *are* deceptive food.

4 Do not overwork to be rich;
Because of your own
understanding, cease!
5 Will you set your eyes on that
which is not?
For *riches* certainly make
themselves wings;
They fly away like an eagle
toward heaven.

6 Do not eat the bread of a miser,ᵃ
Nor desire his delicacies;
7 For as he thinks in his heart, so *is*
he.
"Eat and drink!" he says to you,
But his heart is not with you.
8 The morsel you have eaten, you
will vomit up,
And waste your pleasant words.

9 Do not speak in the hearing of a
fool,
For he will despise the wisdom of
your words.

10 Do not remove the ancient
landmark,

Nor enter the fields of the
fatherless;
11 For their Redeemer *is* mighty;
He will plead their cause against
you.

12 Apply your heart to instruction,
And your ears to words of
knowledge.

13 Do not withhold correction from a
child,
For *if* you beat him with a rod, he
will not die.
14 You shall beat him with a rod,
And deliver his soul from hell.ᵃ

15 My son, if your heart is wise,
My heart will rejoice—indeed, I
myself;
16 Yes, my inmost being will rejoice
When your lips speak right
things.

17 Do not let your heart envy
sinners,
But *be zealous* for the fear of the
LORD all the day;
18 For surely there is a hereafter,
And your hope will not be cut off.

19 Hear, my son, and be wise;
And guide your heart in the
way.
20 Do not mix with winebibbers,
Or with gluttonous eaters of
meat;
21 For the drunkard and the glutton
will come to poverty,
And drowsiness will clothe *a man*
with rags.

22 Listen to your father who begot
you,
And do not despise your mother
when she is old.

23:6 ᵃLiterally *one who has an evil eye*
23:14 ᵃOr *Sheol*

MY SON, GIVE ME YOUR HEART. Proverbs 23:26

My Best Gift for Jesus

What can I give Jesus to say "I love You"? Should I give Him money? Yes, I can give money for Jesus' work. Should I give Him my talents? Yes, I can sing or play or do other things to show Jesus I love Him. Should I give Him my time? Yes, I can do special things that Jesus wants me to do for others. But what does He want most? I think He wants me to give myself. Sometimes we say that is "giving our heart." That's another way of saying, "Jesus, I'm giving myself to You." That's the gift Jesus wants most.

1. Have you given your "heart" or life to Jesus? Have you ever told Him that you want Him to be your Savior?
2. Wouldn't this be a good time to say that to Jesus, if you haven't done it yet?

For more on *Favorite Family Verses* turn to page 1002
For more on *Dedication* turn to page 1474

23 Buy the truth, and do not sell *it,*
    Also wisdom and instruction and
    understanding.

24 The father of the righteous will
    greatly rejoice,
    And he who begets a wise *child*
    will delight in him.
25 Let your father and your mother
    be glad,
    And let her who bore you rejoice.

26 My son, give me your heart,
    And let your eyes observe my
    ways.
27 For a harlot *is* a deep pit,
    And a seductress *is* a narrow
    well.
28 She also lies in wait as *for* a
    victim,
    And increases the unfaithful
    among men.

29 Who has woe?
    Who has sorrow?
    Who has contentions?
    Who has complaints?
    Who has wounds without cause?
    Who has redness of eyes?
30 Those who linger long at the
    wine,
    Those who go in search of mixed
    wine.
31 Do not look on the wine when it is
    red,
    When it sparkles in the cup,
    When it swirls around smoothly;
32 At the last it bites like a serpent,
    And stings like a viper.
33 Your eyes will see strange things,
    And your heart will utter
    perverse things.
34 Yes, you will be like one who lies
    down in the midst of the sea,
    Or like one who lies at the top of
    the mast, *saying:*
35 "They have struck me, but I was
    not hurt;

They have beaten me, but I did
    not feel *it.*
When shall I awake, that I may
    seek another *drink?*"

24 Do not be envious of evil men,
    Nor desire to be with them;
2 For their heart devises violence,
    And their lips talk of
    troublemaking.

3 Through wisdom a house is built,
    And by understanding it is
    established;
4 By knowledge the rooms are filled
    With all precious and pleasant
    riches.

5 A wise man *is* strong,
    Yes, a man of knowledge
    increases strength;
6 For by wise counsel you will wage
    your own war,
    And in a multitude of counselors
    there is safety.

7 Wisdom *is* too lofty for a fool;
    He does not open his mouth in the
    gate.

8 He who plots to do evil
    Will be called a schemer.
9 The devising of foolishness *is* sin,
    And the scoffer *is* an abomination
    to men.

10 *If* you faint in the day of
    adversity,
    Your strength *is* small.

11 Deliver *those who* are drawn
    toward death,
    And hold back *those* stumbling to
    the slaughter.
12 If you say, "Surely we did not
    know this,"
    Does not He who weighs the
    hearts consider *it?*

He who keeps your soul, does He
not know *it?*
And will He *not* render to *each*
man according to his deeds?

13 My son, eat honey because *it is*
good,
And the honeycomb *which is*
sweet to your taste;
14 So *shall* the knowledge of wisdom
be to your soul;
If you have found *it,* there is a
prospect,
And your hope will not be cut off.

15 Do not lie in wait, O wicked *man,*
against the dwelling of the
righteous;
Do not plunder his resting place;
16 For a righteous *man* may fall
seven times
And rise again,
But the wicked shall fall by
calamity.

17 Do not rejoice when your enemy
falls,
And do not let your heart be glad
when he stumbles;
18 Lest the LORD see *it,* and it
displease Him,
And He turn away His wrath
from him.

19 Do not fret because of evildoers,
Nor be envious of the wicked;
20 For there will be no prospect for
the evil *man;*
The lamp of the wicked will be
put out.

21 My son, fear the LORD and the
king;
Do not associate with those given
to change;
22 For their calamity will rise
suddenly,
And who knows the ruin those
two can bring?

FURTHER SAYINGS OF THE WISE

23 These *things* also *belong* to the
wise:

It is not good to show partiality in
judgment.
24 He who says to the wicked, "You
are righteous,"
Him the people will curse;
Nations will abhor him.
25 But those who rebuke *the wicked*
will have delight,
And a good blessing will come
upon them.

26 He who gives a right answer
kisses the lips.

27 Prepare your outside work,
Make it fit for yourself in the
field;
And afterward build your house.

28 Do not be a witness against your
neighbor without cause,
For would you deceive*a* with your
lips?
29 Do not say, "I will do to him just
as he has done to me;
I will render to the man according
to his work."

30 I went by the field of the lazy
man,
And by the vineyard of the man
devoid of understanding;
31 And there it was, all overgrown
with thorns;
Its surface was covered with
nettles;
Its stone wall was broken down.
32 When I saw *it,* I considered *it*
well;
I looked on *it and* received
instruction:
33 A little sleep, a little slumber,

24:28 *a*Septuagint and Vulgate read *Do not deceive.*

A little folding of the hands to rest;

34 So shall your poverty come *like* a prowler,
And your need like an armed man.

FURTHER WISE SAYINGS OF SOLOMON

25 These also *are* proverbs of Solomon which the men of Hez·e·kī′ah king of Judah copied:

2 *It is* the glory of God to conceal a matter,
But the glory of kings *is* to search out a matter.

3 *As* the heavens for height and the earth for depth,
So the heart of kings *is* unsearchable.

4 Take away the dross from silver,
And it will go to the silversmith *for* jewelry.

5 Take away the wicked from before the king,
And his throne will be established in righteousness.

6 Do not exalt yourself in the presence of the king,
And do not stand in the place of the great;

7 For *it is* better that he say to you, "Come up here,"
Than that you should be put lower in the presence of the prince,
Whom your eyes have seen.

8 Do not go hastily to court;
For what will you do in the end,
When your neighbor has put you to shame?

9 Debate your case with your neighbor,
And do not disclose the secret to another;

10 Lest he who hears *it* expose your shame,
And your reputation be ruined.

11 A word fitly spoken *is like* apples of gold
In settings of silver.

12 *Like* an earring of gold and an ornament of fine gold
Is a wise rebuker to an obedient ear.

13 Like the cold of snow in time of harvest
Is a faithful messenger to those who send him,
For he refreshes the soul of his masters.

14 Whoever falsely boasts of giving
Is like clouds and wind without rain.

15 By long forbearance a ruler is persuaded,
And a gentle tongue breaks a bone.

16 Have you found honey?
Eat only as much as you need,
Lest you be filled with it and vomit.

17 Seldom set foot in your neighbor's house,
Lest he become weary of you and hate you.

18 A man who bears false witness against his neighbor
Is like a club, a sword, and a sharp arrow.

19 Confidence in an unfaithful *man* in time of trouble
Is like a bad tooth and a foot out of joint.

20 *Like* one who takes away a
garment in cold weather,
And like vinegar on soda,
Is one who sings songs to a heavy
heart.

21 If your enemy is hungry, give him
bread to eat;
And if he is thirsty, give him
water to drink;

22 For *so* you will heap coals of fire
on his head,
And the LORD will reward you.

23 The north wind brings forth rain,
And a backbiting tongue an angry
countenance.

24 *It is* better to dwell in a corner of
a housetop,
Than in a house shared with a
contentious woman.

25 *As* cold water to a weary soul,
So *is* good news from a far
country.

26 A righteous *man* who falters
before the wicked
Is like a murky spring and a
polluted well.

27 *It is* not good to eat much honey;
So to seek one's own glory *is not*
glory.

28 Whoever *has* no rule over his own
spirit
Is like a city broken down,
without walls.

26
As snow in summer and rain
in harvest,
So honor is not fitting for a fool.

2 Like a flitting sparrow, like a
flying swallow,
So a curse without cause shall not
alight.

3 A whip for the horse,
A bridle for the donkey,
And a rod for the fool's back.

4 Do not answer a fool according to
his folly,
Lest you also be like him.

5 Answer a fool according to his
folly,
Lest he be wise in his own eyes.

6 He who sends a message by the
hand of a fool
Cuts off *his own* feet *and* drinks
violence.

7 *Like* the legs of the lame that
hang limp
Is a proverb in the mouth of fools.

8 Like one who binds a stone in a
sling
Is he who gives honor to a fool.

9 *Like* a thorn *that* goes into the
hand of a drunkard
Is a proverb in the mouth of fools.

10 The great *God* who formed
everything
Gives the fool *his* hire and the
transgressor *his* wages.*a*

11 As a dog returns to his own
vomit,
So a fool repeats his folly.

12 Do you see a man wise in his own
eyes?
There is more hope for a fool than
for him.

13 The lazy *man* says, "*There is* a
lion in the road!
A fierce lion *is* in the streets!"

14 *As* a door turns on its hinges,
So *does* the lazy *man* on his bed.

15 The lazy *man* buries his hand in
the bowl;*a*
It wearies him to bring it back to
his mouth.

16 The lazy *man is* wiser in his own
eyes
Than seven men who can answer
sensibly.

26:10 *a*The Hebrew is difficult; ancient and modern
translators differ greatly. 26:15 *a*Compare 19:24

SELF-CONTROL Proverbs 25:28

Are You Like a City With Broken-Down Walls?

Proverbs 25:28 says, "Whoever has no rule over his own spirit is like a city broken down, without walls." Some translations use the word "self-control" instead of "no rule over his own spirit." In Bible times, city walls were important. They protected cities from the enemy. They kept the people inside safe. When the walls were broken down, the city could be defeated. Is that the way you are when you put aside your self-control? Are you like a walled city whose walls have just fallen down?

1. Think of some temptations that have come to you in the last few days. Did you resist them? Did you have self-control?
2. Are you ever tempted to eat too much, or be too lazy, or do something you shouldn't do? Don't be like a beautiful city whose walls have just fallen down. Use your self-control.
3. Next time you are tempted to eat too much or do what you shouldn't do, ask God to help you. He will help you use your self-control.

For more on *Values* turn to page 1015
For more on *Temptation* turn to page 1320

17 He who passes by *and* meddles in
   a quarrel not his own
   Is like one who takes a dog by the
   ears.

18 Like a madman who throws
   firebrands, arrows, and death,
19 *Is* the man *who* deceives his
   neighbor,
   And says, "I was only joking!"

20 Where *there is* no wood, the fire
   goes out;
   And where *there is* no talebearer,
   strife ceases.
21 *As* charcoal *is* to burning coals,
   and wood to fire,
   So *is* a contentious man to kindle
   strife.
22 The words of a talebearer *are* like
   tasty trifles,
   And they go down into the inmost
   body.

23 Fervent lips with a wicked heart
   Are like earthenware covered
   with silver dross.

24 He who hates, disguises *it* with
   his lips,
   And lays up deceit within himself;
25 When he speaks kindly, do not
   believe him,
   For *there are* seven abominations
   in his heart;
26 *Though his* hatred is covered by
   deceit,
   His wickedness will be revealed
   before the assembly.

27 Whoever digs a pit will fall into it,
   And he who rolls a stone will
   have it roll back on him.

28 A lying tongue hates *those who
   are* crushed by it,
   And a flattering mouth works
   ruin.

27 Do not boast about tomorrow,
   For you do not know what a day
   may bring forth.

2 Let another man praise you, and
   not your own mouth;
   A stranger, and not your own lips.

3 A stone *is* heavy and sand *is*
   weighty,
   But a fool's wrath *is* heavier than
   both of them.

4 Wrath *is* cruel and anger a
   torrent,
   But who *is* able to stand before
   jealousy?

5 Open rebuke *is* better
   Than love carefully concealed.

6 Faithful *are* the wounds of a
   friend,
   But the kisses of an enemy *are*
   deceitful.

7 A satisfied soul loathes the
   honeycomb,
   But to a hungry soul every bitter
   thing *is* sweet.

8 Like a bird that wanders from its
   nest
   Is a man who wanders from his
   place.

9 Ointment and perfume delight
   the heart,
   And the sweetness of a man's
   friend *gives delight* by hearty
   counsel.

10 Do not forsake your own friend or
   your father's friend,
   Nor go to your brother's house in
   the day of your calamity;
   Better *is* a neighbor nearby than
   a brother far away.

DO NOT FORSAKE YOUR OWN FRIEND OR YOUR FATHER'S FRIEND.
Proverbs 27:10

My Good Friend

"You are my good friend," this little boy tells his teddy bear. Do you know why? Teddy always loves this boy the same. When the boy is sad, Teddy loves him the same. When the boy is happy, Teddy loves him the same. When the boy is naughty, Teddy still loves him the same. And Teddy loves him the same when the boy is good. Read Proverbs 17:17. God tells us that a good friend loves a friend at all times. A good friend's love is always there. Is that why Jesus is our very best friend? Does He ever love us less than He did the day before?

1. Read John 3:16. How much does God love us? How much does Jesus love us?
2. How much should we love God? How much should we love Jesus?

For more on *Favorite Family Verses* turn to page 1056
For more on *Friendship* turn to page 1013

11 My son, be wise, and make my
heart glad,
That I may answer him who
reproaches me.

12 A prudent *man* foresees evil and
hides himself;
The simple pass on *and* are
punished.

13 Take the garment of him who is
surety for a stranger,
And hold it in pledge *when* he is
surety for a seductress.

14 He who blesses his friend with a
loud voice, rising early in the
morning,
It will be counted a curse to him.

15 A continual dripping on a very
rainy day
And a contentious woman are
alike;
16 Whoever restrains her restrains
the wind,
And grasps oil with his right
hand.

17 *As* iron sharpens iron,
So a man sharpens the
countenance of his friend.

18 Whoever keeps the fig tree will
eat its fruit;
So he who waits on his master
will be honored.

19 As in water face *reflects* face,
So a man's heart *reveals* the man.

20 Hell*a* and Destruction*b* are never
full;
So the eyes of man are never
satisfied.

21 The refining pot *is* for silver and
the furnace for gold,
And a man *is valued* by what
others say of him.

22 Though you grind a fool in a
mortar with a pestle along with
crushed grain,
Yet his foolishness will not depart
from him.

23 Be diligent to know the state of
your flocks,
And attend to your herds;
24 For riches *are* not forever,
Nor does a crown *endure* to all
generations.
25 *When* the hay is removed, and the
tender grass shows itself,
And the herbs of the mountains
are gathered in,
26 The lambs *will provide* your
clothing,
And the goats the price of a field;
27 *You shall have* enough goats' milk
for your food,
For the food of your household,
And the nourishment of your
maidservants.

28 The wicked flee when no one
pursues,
But the righteous are bold as a
lion.

2 Because of the transgression of a
land, many *are* its princes;
But by a man of understanding
and knowledge
Right will be prolonged.

3 A poor man who oppresses the
poor
Is like a driving rain which leaves
no food.

4 Those who forsake the law praise
the wicked,
But such as keep the law contend
with them.

5 Evil men do not understand
justice,

27:20 *a*Or *Sheol* *b*Hebrew *Abaddon*

But those who seek the LORD
understand all.

6 Better *is* the poor who walks in
his integrity
Than one perverse *in his* ways,
though he *be* rich.

7 Whoever keeps the law *is* a
discerning son,
But a companion of gluttons
shames his father.

8 One who increases his
possessions by usury and
extortion
Gathers it for him who will pity
the poor.

9 One who turns away his ear from
hearing the law,
Even his prayer *is* an
abomination.

10 Whoever causes the upright to go
astray in an evil way,
He himself will fall into his own
pit;
But the blameless will inherit
good.

11 The rich man *is* wise in his own
eyes,
But the poor who has
understanding searches him
out.

12 When the righteous rejoice, *there
is* great glory;
But when the wicked arise, men
hide themselves.

13 He who covers his sins will not
prosper,
But whoever confesses and
forsakes *them* will have mercy.

14 Happy *is* the man who is always
reverent,

But he who hardens his heart will
fall into calamity.

15 *Like* a roaring lion and a charging
bear
Is a wicked ruler over poor
people.

16 A ruler who lacks understanding
is a great oppressor,
But he who hates covetousness
will prolong *his* days.

17 A man burdened with bloodshed
will flee into a pit;
Let no one help him.

18 Whoever walks blamelessly will
be saved,
But *he who is* perverse *in his*
ways will suddenly fall.

19 He who tills his land will have
plenty of bread,
But he who follows frivolity will
have poverty enough!

20 A faithful man will abound with
blessings,
But he who hastens to be rich will
not go unpunished.

21 To show partiality *is* not good,
Because for a piece of bread a
man will transgress.

22 A man with an evil eye hastens
after riches,
And does not consider that
poverty will come upon him.

23 He who rebukes a man will find
more favor afterward
Than he who flatters with the
tongue.

24 Whoever robs his father or his
mother,
And says, "*It is* no transgression,"

What Should I Do?

SAYING THE RIGHT THING   Proverbs 28:23

Ned wants to sound good when he plays his horn. But he doesn't. That's because he has just started playing the horn. Ned also doesn't like to practice. Nell is listening to Ned. She knows he doesn't sound good. But she doesn't want to hurt his feelings. What should Nell say?

1.   Should we tell a person something is good when it isn't?
2.   Should we say what is true even when it hurts a friend's feelings?
3.   What are some ways to say what is true but not hurt a friend's feelings? What if Nell said, "I like it"? What if she said, "You're doing OK, keep practicing"? What if she said, "You're getting better every day"?

For more on *What Should I Do?* turn to page 1013
For more on *Honesty* turn to page 1383

The same *is* companion to a
destroyer.

25 He who is of a proud heart stirs
up strife,
But he who trusts in the LORD
will be prospered.

26 He who trusts in his own heart is
a fool,
But whoever walks wisely will be
delivered.

Promises

Proverbs 28:27

Do you like to give to those who
have less than you? God makes
a special promise here. If you do
this, you will never be poor. In
other places God says we will
lose what we have if we try to
hoard it. Do you want to lose
everything? Try to keep everything? Do you want to have
enough for tomorrow? Give to
God today. God takes care of
those who give cheerfully.

---

27 He who gives to the poor will not
lack,
But he who hides his eyes will
have many curses.

28 When the wicked arise, men hide
themselves;
But when they perish, the
righteous increase.

29 He who is often rebuked, *and*
hardens *his* neck,
Will suddenly be destroyed, and
that without remedy.

2 When the righteous are in
authority, the people rejoice;

But when a wicked *man* rules,
the people groan.

3 Whoever loves wisdom makes his
father rejoice,
But a companion of harlots
wastes *his* wealth.

4 The king establishes the land by
justice,
But he who receives bribes
overthrows it.

5 A man who flatters his neighbor
Spreads a net for his feet.

6 By transgression an evil man is
snared,
But the righteous sings and
rejoices.

7 The righteous considers the cause
of the poor,
But the wicked does not
understand *such* knowledge.

8 Scoffers set a city aflame,
But wise *men* turn away wrath.

9 *If* a wise man contends with a
foolish man,
Whether *the fool* rages or laughs,
there is no peace.

10 The bloodthirsty hate the
blameless,
But the upright seek his
well-being.[a]

11 A fool vents all his feelings,[a]
But a wise *man* holds them back.

12 If a ruler pays attention to lies,
All his servants *become* wicked.

13 The poor *man* and the oppressor
have this in common:

29:10 [a]Literally *soul*　　　29:11 [a]Literally *spirit*

The LORD gives light to the eyes
of both.

14 The king who judges the poor
with truth,
His throne will be established
forever.

15 The rod and rebuke give wisdom,
But a child left *to himself* brings
shame to his mother.

16 When the wicked are multiplied,
transgression increases;
But the righteous will see their
fall.

17 Correct your son, and he will give
you rest;
Yes, he will give delight to your
soul.

18 Where *there is* no revelation,*a* the
people cast off restraint;
But happy *is* he who keeps the
law.

19 A servant will not be corrected by
mere words;
For though he understands, he
will not respond.

20 Do you see a man hasty in his
words?
There is more hope for a fool than
for him.

21 He who pampers his servant from
childhood
Will have him as a son in the
end.

22 An angry man stirs up strife,
And a furious man abounds in
transgression.

23 A man's pride will bring him low,
But the humble in spirit will
retain honor.

24 Whoever is a partner with a thief
hates his own life;
He swears to tell the truth,*a* but
reveals nothing.

25 The fear of man brings a snare,
But whoever trusts in the LORD
shall be safe.

26 Many seek the ruler's favor,
But justice for man *comes* from
the LORD.

27 An unjust man *is* an abomination
to the righteous,
And *he who is* upright in the way
is an abomination to the
wicked.

THE WISDOM OF AGUR

30 The words of Āʹgur the son of
Jāʹkeh, *his* utterance. This man de-
clared to Ithʹi·el—to Ithʹi·el and
Ūʹcal:

2 Surely I *am* more stupid than *any*
man,
And do not have the
understanding of a man.
3 I neither learned wisdom
Nor have knowledge of the Holy
One.

4 Who has ascended into heaven, or
descended?
Who has gathered the wind in His
fists?
Who has bound the waters in a
garment?
Who has established all the ends
of the earth?
What *is* His name, and what *is*
His Son's name,
If you know?

29:18 *a*Or *prophetic vision*   29:24 *a*Literally
hears the adjuration

5 Every word of God *is* pure;
  He *is* a shield to those who put
    their trust in Him.
6 Do not add to His words,
  Lest He rebuke you, and you be
    found a liar.

7 Two *things* I request of You
  (Deprive me not before I die):
8 Remove falsehood and lies far
    from me;
  Give me neither poverty nor
    riches—
  Feed me with the food allotted to
    me;
9 Lest I be full and deny *You,*
  And say, "Who *is* the LORD?"
  Or lest I be poor and steal,
  And profane the name of my God.

10 Do not malign a servant to his
    master,
  Lest he curse you, and you be
    found guilty.

11 *There is* a generation *that* curses
    its father,
  And does not bless its mother.
12 *There is* a generation *that is* pure
    in its own eyes,
  Yet is not washed from its
    filthiness.
13 *There is* a generation—oh, how
    lofty are their eyes!
  And their eyelids are lifted up.
14 *There is* a generation whose teeth
    are like swords,
  And whose fangs *are like* knives,
  To devour the poor from off the
    earth,
  And the needy from *among* men.

15 The leech has two daughters—
  Give *and* Give!

  There are three *things that* are
    never satisfied,
  Four never say, "Enough!":
16 The grave,*a*

The barren womb,
  The earth *that* is not satisfied
    with water—
  And the fire never says,
    "Enough!"

17 The eye *that* mocks *his* father,
  And scorns obedience to *his*
    mother,
  The ravens of the valley will pick
    it out,
  And the young eagles will eat it.

18 There are three *things which* are
    too wonderful for me,
  Yes, four *which* I do not
    understand:
19 The way of an eagle in the air,
  The way of a serpent on a rock,
  The way of a ship in the midst of
    the sea,
  And the way of a man with a
    virgin.

20 This *is* the way of an adulterous
    woman:
  She eats and wipes her mouth,
  And says, "I have done no
    wickedness."

21 For three *things* the earth is
    perturbed,
  Yes, for four it cannot bear up:
22 For a servant when he reigns,
  A fool when he is filled with food,
23 A hateful *woman* when she is
    married,
  And a maidservant who succeeds
    her mistress.

24 There are four *things which* are
    little on the earth,
  But they *are* exceedingly wise:
25 The ants *are* a people not strong,
  Yet they prepare their food in the
    summer;
26 The rock badgers*a* are a feeble
    folk,

30:16 *a*Or Sheol   30:26 *a*Or hyraxes

Yet they make their homes in the crags;

27 The locusts have no king,
Yet they all advance in ranks;

28 The spider*a* skillfully grasps with its hands,
And it is in kings' palaces.

29 There are three *things which* are majestic in pace,
Yes, four *which* are stately in walk:

30 A lion, *which is* mighty among beasts
And does not turn away from any;

31 A greyhound,*a*
A male goat also,
And a king *whose* troops *are* with him.*b*

32 If you have been foolish in exalting yourself,
Or if you have devised evil, *put your* hand on *your* mouth.

33 For *as* the churning of milk produces butter,
And wringing the nose produces blood,
So the forcing of wrath produces strife.

THE WORDS OF KING LEMUEL'S MOTHER

31 The words of King Lem′ū·el, the utterance which his mother taught him:

2 What, my son?
And what, son of my womb?
And what, son of my vows?

3 Do not give your strength to women,
Nor your ways to that which destroys kings.

4 *It is* not for kings, O Lem′ū·el,
It is not for kings to drink wine,

Nor for princes intoxicating drink;

5 Lest they drink and forget the law,
And pervert the justice of all the afflicted.

6 Give strong drink to him who is perishing,
And wine to those who are bitter of heart.

7 Let him drink and forget his poverty,
And remember his misery no more.

8 Open your mouth for the speechless,
In the cause of all *who are* appointed to die.*a*

9 Open your mouth, judge righteously,
And plead the cause of the poor and needy.

THE VIRTUOUS WIFE

10 Who*a* can find a virtuous*b* wife?
For her worth *is* far above rubies.

11 The heart of her husband safely trusts her;
So he will have no lack of gain.

12 She does him good and not evil
All the days of her life.

13 She seeks wool and flax,
And willingly works with her hands.

14 She is like the merchant ships,
She brings her food from afar.

15 She also rises while it is yet night,
And provides food for her household,
And a portion for her maidservants.

30:28 *a*Or *lizard*   30:31 *a*Exact identity unknown   *b*A Jewish tradition reads *a king against whom there is no uprising.*   31:8 *a*Literally *sons of passing away*   31:10 *a*Verses 10 through 31 are an alphabetic acrostic in Hebrew (compare Psalm 119).   *b*Literally *a wife of valor,* in the sense of all forms of excellence

GODLY Proverbs 31:10–31

What Is a Godly Person?

Do you know a godly person? What is that person like? Do you know an ungodly person? What is that person like? Which kind of person would you rather become? Why?

1. Think of some qualities that make a godly person attractive? What are they? Which of these would you like to have?
2. Think of some qualities that make an ungodly person unattractive? What are they? Which of these would you *not* like to have?
3. How is a godly person like Jesus? How should you be like Jesus?

For more on *Favorite Bible Words* turn to page 1168
For more on *Godliness* turn to page 1792

16 She considers a field and buys
   it;
   From her profits she plants a
   vineyard.
17 She girds herself with strength,
   And strengthens her arms.
18 She perceives that her
   merchandise *is* good,
   And her lamp does not go out by
   night.
19 She stretches out her hands to
   the distaff,
   And her hand holds the spindle.
20 She extends her hand to the
   poor,
   Yes, she reaches out her hands to
   the needy.
21 She is not afraid of snow for her
   household,
   For all her household *is* clothed
   with scarlet.
22 She makes tapestry for herself;
   Her clothing *is* fine linen and
   purple.
23 Her husband is known in the
   gates,
   When he sits among the elders of
   the land.

24 She makes linen garments and
   sells *them,*
   And supplies sashes for the
   merchants.
25 Strength and honor *are* her
   clothing;
   She shall rejoice in time to come.
26 She opens her mouth with
   wisdom,
   And on her tongue *is* the law of
   kindness.
27 She watches over the ways of her
   household,
   And does not eat the bread of
   idleness.
28 Her children rise up and call her
   blessed;
   Her husband *also,* and he praises
   her:
29 "Many daughters have done well,
   But you excel them all."
30 Charm *is* deceitful and beauty *is*
   passing,
   But a woman *who* fears the LORD,
   she shall be praised.
31 Give her of the fruit of her hands,
   And let her own works praise her
   in the gates.

The Book of
ECCLESIASTES

THE VANITY OF LIFE

THE words of the Preacher, the son of David, king in Jerusalem.

2 "Vanity*a* of vanities," says the
 Preacher;
 "Vanity of vanities, all *is* vanity."

3 What profit has a man from all
  his labor
 In which he toils under the sun?
4 *One* generation passes away, and
  another generation comes;
 But the earth abides forever.
5 The sun also rises, and the sun
  goes down,
 And hastens to the place where it
  arose.
6 The wind goes toward the south,
 And turns around to the north;
 The wind whirls about
  continually,
 And comes again on its circuit.
7 All the rivers run into the sea,
 Yet the sea *is* not full;
 To the place from which the rivers
  come,
 There they return again.
8 All things *are* full of labor;
 Man cannot express *it*.
 The eye is not satisfied with
  seeing,
 Nor the ear filled with hearing.

9 That which has been *is* what will
  be,
 That which *is* done is what will be
  done,
 And *there is* nothing new under
  the sun.
10 Is there anything of which it may
  be said,
 "See, this *is* new"?
 It has already been in ancient
  times before us.

11 *There is* no remembrance of
  former *things,*
 Nor will there be any
  remembrance of *things* that are
  to come
 By *those* who will come after.

THE GRIEF OF WISDOM

12 I, the Preacher, was king over Israel in Jerusalem.
13 And I set my heart to seek and
search out by wisdom concerning all
that is done under heaven; this burdensome task God has given to the
sons of man, by which they may be
exercised.
14 I have seen all the works that are
done under the sun; and indeed, all *is*
vanity and grasping for the wind.

15 *What is* crooked cannot be made
  straight,
 And what is lacking cannot be
  numbered.

16 I communed with my heart, saying, "Look, I have attained greatness,
and have gained more wisdom than
all who were before me in Jerusalem.
My heart has understood great wisdom and knowledge."
17 And I set my heart to know wisdom and to know madness and folly. I
perceived that this also is grasping
for the wind.

18 For in much wisdom *is* much
  grief,
 And he who increases knowledge
  increases sorrow.

1:2 *a*Or *Absurdity, Frustration, Futility, Nonsense;*
and so throughout this book

THE VANITY OF PLEASURE

2 I said in my heart, "Come now, I will test you with mirth; therefore enjoy pleasure"; but surely, this also *was* vanity.
2 I said of laughter—"Madness!"; and of mirth, "What does it accomplish?"
3 I searched in my heart *how* to gratify my flesh with wine, while guiding my heart with wisdom, and how to lay hold on folly, till I might see what *was* good for the sons of men to do under heaven all the days of their lives.
4 I made my works great, I built myself houses, and planted myself vineyards.
5 I made myself gardens and orchards, and I planted all *kinds* of fruit trees in them.
6 I made myself water pools from which to water the growing trees of the grove.
7 I acquired male and female servants, and had servants born in my house. Yes, I had greater possessions of herds and flocks than all who were in Jerusalem before me.
8 I also gathered for myself silver and gold and the special treasures of kings and of the provinces. I acquired male and female singers, the delights of the sons of men, *and* musical instruments*a* of all kinds.
9 So I became great and excelled more than all who were before me in Jerusalem. Also my wisdom remained with me.

10 Whatever my eyes desired I did
    not keep from them.
I did not withhold my heart from
    any pleasure,
For my heart rejoiced in all my
    labor;
And this was my reward from all
    my labor.

11 Then I looked on all the works
    that my hands had done
And on the labor in which I had
    toiled;
And indeed all *was* vanity and
    grasping for the wind.
There was no profit under the
    sun.

THE END OF THE WISE AND THE FOOL

12 Then I turned myself to consider
    wisdom and madness and folly;
For what *can* the man *do* who
    succeeds the king?—
Only what he has already done.
13 Then I saw that wisdom excels
    folly
As light excels darkness.
14 The wise man's eyes *are* in his
    head,
But the fool walks in darkness.
Yet I myself perceived
That the same event happens to
    them all.

15 So I said in my heart,
"As it happens to the fool,
It also happens to me,
And why was I then more wise?"
Then I said in my heart,
"This also *is* vanity."
16 For *there is* no more
    remembrance of the wise than
    of the fool forever,
Since all that now *is* will be
    forgotten in the days to come.
And how does a wise *man* die?
As the fool!

17 Therefore I hated life because the work that was done under the sun *was* distressing to me, for all *is* vanity and grasping for the wind.
18 Then I hated all my labor in which I had toiled under the sun, because I must leave it to the man who will come after me.

2:8 *a*Exact meaning unknown

19 And who knows whether he will be wise or a fool? Yet he will rule over all my labor in which I toiled and in which I have shown myself wise under the sun. This also *is* vanity.
20 Therefore I turned my heart and despaired of all the labor in which I had toiled under the sun.
21 For there is a man whose labor *is* with wisdom, knowledge, and skill; yet he must leave his heritage to a man who has not labored for it. This also *is* vanity and a great evil.
22 For what has man for all his labor, and for the striving of his heart with which he has toiled under the sun?
23 For all his days *are* sorrowful, and his work burdensome; even in the night his heart takes no rest. This also is vanity.
24 Nothing *is* better for a man *than* that he should eat and drink, and *that* his soul should enjoy good in his labor. This also, I saw, was from the hand of God.
25 For who can eat, or who can have enjoyment, more than I?*a*
26 For *God* gives wisdom and knowl-

edge and joy to a man who *is* good in His sight; but to the sinner He gives the work of gathering and collecting, that he may give to *him who is* good before God. This also *is* vanity and grasping for the wind.

EVERYTHING HAS ITS TIME

3 To everything *there is* a season,
A time for every purpose under
  heaven:

2 A time to be born,
  And a time to die;
A time to plant,
  And a time to pluck *what is*
    planted;
3 A time to kill,
  And a time to heal;
A time to break down,
  And a time to build up;
4 A time to weep,
  And a time to laugh;
A time to mourn,
  And a time to dance;

2:25 *a*Following Masoretic Text, Targum, and Vulgate; some Hebrew manuscripts, Septuagint, and Syriac read *without Him.*

5 A time to cast away stones,
   And a time to gather stones;
   A time to embrace,
   And a time to refrain from
      embracing;
6 A time to gain,
   And a time to lose;
   A time to keep,
   And a time to throw away;
7 A time to tear,
   And a time to sew;
   A time to keep silence,
   And a time to speak;
8 A time to love,
   And a time to hate;
   A time of war,
   And a time of peace.

THE GOD-GIVEN TASK

9 What profit has the worker from that in which he labors?
10 I have seen the God-given task with which the sons of men are to be occupied.
11 He has made everything beautiful in its time. Also He has put eternity in their hearts, except that no one can find out the work that God does from beginning to end.
12 I know that nothing *is* better for them than to rejoice, and to do good in their lives,
13 and also that every man should eat and drink and enjoy the good of all his labor—it *is* the gift of God.

14 I know that whatever God does,
   It shall be forever.
   Nothing can be added to it,
   And nothing taken from it.
   God does *it,* that men should fear
      before Him.
15 That which is has already been,
   And what is to be has already
      been;
   And God requires an account of
      what is past.

INJUSTICE SEEMS TO PREVAIL

16 Moreover I saw under the sun:

   In the place of judgment,
   Wickedness *was* there;
   And *in* the place of righteousness,
   Iniquity *was* there.

17 I said in my heart,

   "God shall judge the righteous and
      the wicked,
   For *there is* a time there for every
      purpose and for every work."

18 I said in my heart, "Concerning the condition of the sons of men, God tests them, that they may see that they themselves are *like* animals."
19 For what happens to the sons of men also happens to animals; one thing befalls them: as one dies, so dies the other. Surely, they all have one breath; man has no advantage over animals, for all *is* vanity.
20 All go to one place: all are from the dust, and all return to dust.
21 Who knows the spirit of the sons of men, which goes upward, and the spirit of the animal, which goes down to the earth?[a]
22 So I perceived that nothing *is* better than that a man should rejoice in his own works, for that *is* his heritage. For who can bring him to see what will happen after him?

4 Then I returned and considered all the oppression that is done under the sun:

   And look! The tears of the
      oppressed,
   But they have no comforter—

3:21 [a]Septuagint, Syriac, Targum, and Vulgate read *Who knows whether the spirit . . . goes upward, and whether . . . goes downward to the earth?*

HELPFULNESS Ecclesiastes 4:9, 10

Let Me Give You a Push

Melanie wants to take some gifts to a friend. She has them wrapped. She is dressed up and ready to go on her sled. But something is wrong. She has no one to push it or pull it. Mike sees her. He wants to help. What should he do?

1. What is Mike doing for Melanie? Why do you think he is doing that?
2. How can you help a friend? How can you help your parents? How can you help God? Will you?

For more on *Values* turn to page 1035
For more on *Helpfulness* turn to page 1683

On the side of their oppressors
   there is power,
But they have no comforter.
2 Therefore I praised the dead who
   were already dead,
   More than the living who are still
   alive.
3 Yet, better than both *is he* who
   has never existed,
   Who has not seen the evil work
   that is done under the sun.

THE VANITY OF SELFISH TOIL

4 Again, I saw that for all toil and
every skillful work a man is envied
by his neighbor. This also *is* vanity
and grasping for the wind.

5 The fool folds his hands
   And consumes his own flesh.
6 Better a handful *with* quietness
   Than both hands full, *together
   with* toil and grasping for the
   wind.

7 Then I returned, and I saw vanity
under the sun:

8 There is one alone, without
   companion:
   He has neither son nor
   brother.
   Yet *there is* no end to all his
   labors,
   Nor is his eye satisfied with
   riches.
   But he never asks,
   "For whom do I toil and deprive
   myself of good?"
   This also *is* vanity and a grave
   misfortune.

THE VALUE OF A FRIEND

9 Two *are* better than one,
   Because they have a good reward
   for their labor.

10 For if they fall, one will lift up his
   companion.
   But woe to him *who is* alone when
   he falls,
   For *he has* no one to help him up.
11 Again, if two lie down together,
   they will keep warm;
   But how can one be warm *alone?*
12 Though one may be overpowered
   by another, two can withstand
   him.
   And a threefold cord is not
   quickly broken.

POPULARITY PASSES AWAY

13 Better a poor and wise youth
   Than an old and foolish king who
   will be admonished no more.
14 For he comes out of prison to be
   king,
   Although he was born poor in his
   kingdom.
15 I saw all the living who walk
   under the sun;
   They were with the second youth
   who stands in his place.
16 *There was* no end of all the people
   over whom he was made king;
   Yet those who come afterward
   will not rejoice in him.
   Surely this also *is* vanity and
   grasping for the wind.

FEAR GOD, KEEP YOUR VOWS

5 Walk prudently when you go to
the house of God; and draw near to
hear rather than to give the sacrifice
of fools, for they do not know that
they do evil.

2 Do not be rash with your mouth,
   And let not your heart utter
   anything hastily before God.
   For God *is* in heaven, and you on
   earth;

Therefore let your words be
few.
3 For a dream comes through much
activity,
And a fool's voice *is known* by *his*
many words.

4 When you make a vow to God, do
not delay to pay it;
For *He has* no pleasure in fools.
Pay what you have vowed—
5 Better not to vow than to vow and
not pay.

6 Do not let your mouth cause your
flesh to sin, nor say before the messenger *of God* that it *was* an error.
Why should God be angry at your excuse[a] and destroy the work of your
hands?
7 For in the multitude of dreams
and many words *there is* also vanity.
But fear God.

THE VANITY OF GAIN AND HONOR

8 If you see the oppression of the
poor, and the violent perversion of
justice and righteousness in a province, do not marvel at the matter; for
high official watches over high official, and higher officials are over
them.
9 Moreover the profit of the land is
for all; *even* the king is served from
the field.

10 He who loves silver will not be
satisfied with silver;
Nor he who loves abundance,
with increase.
This also *is* vanity.

11 When goods increase,
They increase who eat them;
So what profit have the owners
Except to see *them* with their
eyes?

12 The sleep of a laboring man *is*
sweet,
Whether he eats little or much;
But the abundance of the rich will
not permit him to sleep.

13 There is a severe evil *which* I
have seen under the sun:
Riches kept for their owner to his
hurt.
14 But those riches perish through
misfortune;
When he begets a son, *there is*
nothing in his hand.
15 As he came from his mother's
womb, naked shall he return,
To go as he came;
And he shall take nothing from
his labor
Which he may carry away in his
hand.

16 And this also *is* a severe evil—
Just exactly as he came, so shall
he go.
And what profit has he who has
labored for the wind?
17 All his days he also eats in
darkness,
And *he has* much sorrow and
sickness and anger.

18 Here is what I have seen: *It is*
good and fitting *for one* to eat and
drink, and to enjoy the good of all his
labor in which he toils under the sun
all the days of his life which God
gives him; for it *is* his heritage.
19 As for every man to whom God
has given riches and wealth, and
given him power to eat of it, to receive his heritage and rejoice in his
labor—this *is* the gift of God.
20 For he will not dwell unduly on
the days of his life, because God
keeps *him* busy with the joy of his
heart.

5:6 [a]Literally *voice*

What the Bible Says

ABOUT GOD'S GIVING Ecclesiastes 5:19

Heavenly Gifts

God's gifts come from God. Surprised? But think about that. God's gifts really do come from God. That's awesome! This morning God gave you sunshine and clouds, perhaps a little rain, a blue sky, green grass, and birds to sing. He gave you a thousand gifts—big and little. *But these gifts came from God,* not the person next door, not even from the most important king. They came from God the Creator. Awesome!

1. Read the first part of James 1:17. What does it say?
2. Did you think when you saw the sunrise, "God gave this to me?" Did you think that when you ate your breakfast? Did you think that when you saw beautiful clouds, or heard birds singing, or smelled flowers? You should!
3. What will you remember to think the next time you see a gift from God? Will you thank Him?

For more on *What the Bible Says* turn to page 1027
For more on *God's Care* turn to page 1056

6 There is an evil which I have seen under the sun, and it *is* common among men:

2 A man to whom God has given riches and wealth and honor, so that he lacks nothing for himself of all he desires; yet God does not give him power to eat of it, but a foreigner consumes it. This *is* vanity, and it *is* an evil affliction.

3 If a man begets a hundred *children* and lives many years, so that the days of his years are many, but his soul is not satisfied with goodness, or indeed he has no burial, I say *that* a stillborn child *is* better than he—

4 for it comes in vanity and departs in darkness, and its name is covered with darkness.

5 Though it has not seen the sun or known *anything,* this has more rest than that man,

6 even if he lives a thousand years twice—but has not seen goodness. Do not all go to one place?

7 All the labor of man *is* for his mouth,
And yet the soul is not satisfied.

8 For what more has the wise *man* than the fool?
What does the poor man have,
Who knows *how* to walk before the living?

9 Better *is* the sight of the eyes than the wandering of desire.
This also *is* vanity and grasping for the wind.

10 Whatever one is, he has been named already,
For it is known that he *is* man;
And he cannot contend with Him who is mightier than he.

11 Since there are many things that increase vanity,
How *is* man the better?

12 For who knows what *is* good for man in life, all the days of his vain life which he passes like a shadow? Who can tell a man what will happen after him under the sun?

The Value of Practical Wisdom

7 A good name *is* better than precious ointment,
And the day of death than the day of one's birth;

2 Better to go to the house of mourning
Than to go to the house of feasting,
For that *is* the end of all men;
And the living will take *it* to heart.

Sorrow *is* better than laughter,
For by a sad countenance the heart is made better.

4 The heart of the wise *is* in the house of mourning,
But the heart of fools *is* in the house of mirth.

5 *It is* better to hear the rebuke of the wise
Than for a man to hear the song of fools.

6 For like the crackling of thorns under a pot,
So *is* the laughter of the fool.
This also is vanity.

7 Surely oppression destroys a wise *man's* reason,
And a bribe debases the heart.

8 The end of a thing *is* better than its beginning;
The patient in spirit *is* better than the proud in spirit.

9 Do not hasten in your spirit to be angry,
For anger rests in the bosom of fools.

What Should I Do?

WHEN A FRIEND TRIES TO HURT A FRIEND Ecclesiastes 7:9

Look what Megan found. Kitty is a good friend. So is Megan's goldfish. Megan's good friend is trying to hurt another good friend. What should Megan do?

1. What is Kitty trying to do? Why is this wrong?
2. What should Megan do? Why?
3. What should you do when one friend tries to hurt another friend? Why? What would Jesus want you to do?

For more on *What Should I Do?* turn to page 1024
For more on *Peacemaking* turn to page 1452

10 Do not say,
　"Why were the former days better
　　than these?"
　For you do not inquire wisely
　　concerning this.

11 Wisdom *is* good with an
　　inheritance,
　And profitable to those who see
　　the sun.
12 For wisdom *is* a defense *as* money
　　is a defense,
　But the excellence of knowledge *is*
　　that wisdom gives life to those
　　who have it.

13 Consider the work of God;
　For who can make straight what
　　He has made crooked?
14 In the day of prosperity be joyful,
　But in the day of adversity
　　consider:
　Surely God has appointed the one
　　as well as the other,
　So that man can find out nothing
　　that will come after him.

15 I have seen everything in my days
of vanity:

　There is a just *man* who perishes
　　in his righteousness,
　And there is a wicked *man* who
　　prolongs *life* in his wickedness.

16 Do not be overly righteous,
　Nor be overly wise:
　Why should you destroy yourself?
17 Do not be overly wicked,
　Nor be foolish:
　Why should you die before your
　　time?
18 *It is* good that you grasp this,
　And also not remove your hand
　　from the other;
　For he who fears God will escape
　　them all.

19 Wisdom strengthens the wise
　More than ten rulers of the city.

20 For *there is* not a just man on
　　earth who does good
　And does not sin.

21 Also do not take to heart
　　everything people say,
　Lest you hear your servant
　　cursing you.
22 For many times, also, your own
　　heart has known
　That even you have cursed
　　others.

23 All this I have proved by wisdom.
　I said, "I will be wise";
　But it *was* far from me.
24 As for that which is far off and
　　exceedingly deep,
　Who can find it out?
25 I applied my heart to know,
　To search and seek out wisdom
　　and the reason *of things,*
　To know the wickedness of folly,
　Even of foolishness *and*
　　madness.
26 And I find more bitter than
　　death
　The woman whose heart *is* snares
　　and nets,
　Whose hands *are* fetters.
　He who pleases God shall escape
　　from her,
　But the sinner shall be trapped
　　by her.

27 "Here is what I have found," says
　　the Preacher,
　"*Adding* one thing to the other to
　　find out the reason,
28 Which my soul still seeks but I
　　cannot find:
　One man among a thousand I
　　have found,
　But a woman among all these I
　　have not found.
29 Truly, this only I have found:
　That God made man upright,
　But they have sought out many
　　schemes."

8 Who *is* like a wise *man?*
And who knows the
    interpretation of a thing?
A man's wisdom makes his face
    shine,
And the sternness of his face is
    changed.

OBEY AUTHORITIES FOR GOD'S SAKE

2 I *say,* "Keep the king's commandment for the sake of your oath to God.
3 "Do not be hasty to go from his presence. Do not take your stand for an evil thing, for he does whatever pleases him."

4 Where the word of a king *is, there*
    is power;
And who may say to him, "What
    are you doing?"
5 He who keeps his command
    will experience nothing
    harmful;
And a wise man's heart discerns
    both time and judgment,
6 Because for every matter there is
    a time and judgment,
Though the misery of man
    increases greatly.
7 For he does not know what will
    happen;
So who can tell him when it will
    occur?
8 No one has power over the spirit
    to retain the spirit,
And no one has power in the day
    of death.
There is no release from that war,
And wickedness will not deliver
    those who are given to it.

9 All this I have seen, and applied my heart to every work that is done under the sun: *There is* a time in which one man rules over another to his own hurt.

DEATH COMES TO ALL

10 Then I saw the wicked buried, who had come and gone from the place of holiness, and they were forgotten[a] in the city where they had so done. This also *is* vanity.
11 Because the sentence against an evil work is not executed speedily, therefore the heart of the sons of men is fully set in them to do evil.
12 Though a sinner does evil a hundred *times,* and his *days* are prolonged, yet I surely know that it will be well with those who fear God, who fear before Him.
13 But it will not be well with the wicked; nor will he prolong *his* days, *which are* as a shadow, because he does not fear before God.
14 There is a vanity which occurs on earth, that there are just *men* to whom it happens according to the work of the wicked; again, there are wicked *men* to whom it happens according to the work of the righteous. I said that this also *is* vanity.
15 So I commended enjoyment, because a man has nothing better under the sun than to eat, drink, and be merry; for this will remain with him in his labor *all* the days of his life which God gives him under the sun.
16 When I applied my heart to know wisdom and to see the business that is done on earth, even though one sees no sleep day or night,
17 then I saw all the work of God, that a man cannot find out the work that is done under the sun. For though a man labors to discover *it,* yet he will not find *it;* moreover, though a wise *man* attempts to know *it,* he will not be able to find *it.*

9 For I considered all this in my heart, so that I could declare it all:

8:10 [a]Some Hebrew manuscripts, Septuagint, and Vulgate read *praised.*

that the righteous and the wise and their works *are* in the hand of God. People know neither love nor hatred *by* anything *they see* before them.

2 All things *come* alike to all:

One event *happens* to the
    righteous and the wicked;
To the good,*a* the clean, and the
    unclean;
To him who sacrifices and him
    who does not sacrifice.
As is the good, so *is* the sinner;
He who takes an oath as *he* who
    fears an oath.

3 This *is* an evil in all that is done under the sun: that one thing *happens* to all. Truly the hearts of the sons of men are full of evil; madness *is* in their hearts while they live, and after that *they go* to the dead.
4 But for him who is joined to all the living there is hope, for a living dog is better than a dead lion.

5 For the living know that they will
    die;
But the dead know nothing,
And they have no more reward,
For the memory of them is
    forgotten.
6 Also their love, their hatred,
    and their envy have now
    perished;
Nevermore will they have a
    share
In anything done under the sun.

7 Go, eat your bread with joy,
And drink your wine with a
    merry heart;
For God has already accepted
    your works.
8 Let your garments always be
    white,
And let your head lack no oil.

9 Live joyfully with the wife whom you love all the days of your vain life which He has given you under the sun, all your days of vanity; for that *is* your portion in life, and in the labor which you perform under the sun.
10 Whatever your hand finds to do, do *it* with your might; for *there is* no work or device or knowledge or wisdom in the grave where you are going.
11 I returned and saw under the sun that—

The race *is* not to the swift,
Nor the battle to the strong,
Nor bread to the wise,
Nor riches to men of
    understanding,
Nor favor to men of skill;
But time and chance happen to
    them all.
12 For man also does not know his
    time:
Like fish taken in a cruel net,
Like birds caught in a snare,
So the sons of men *are* snared in
    an evil time,
When it falls suddenly upon
    them.

WISDOM SUPERIOR TO FOLLY

13 This wisdom I have also seen under the sun, and it *seemed* great to me:
14 *There was* a little city with few men in it; and a great king came against it, besieged it, and built great snares*a* around it.
15 Now there was found in it a poor wise man, and he by his wisdom delivered the city. Yet no one remembered that same poor man.

9:2 *a*Septuagint, Syriac, and Vulgate read *good and bad*.   9:14 *a*Septuagint, Syriac, and Vulgate read *bulwarks*.

16 Then I said:

"Wisdom *is* better than strength.
Nevertheless the poor man's
wisdom *is* despised,
And his words are not heard.
17 Words of the wise, *spoken* quietly,
should be heard
Rather than the shout of a ruler
of fools.
18 Wisdom *is* better than weapons of
war;
But one sinner destroys much
good."

10 Dead flies putrefy[a] the
perfumer's ointment,
And cause it to give off a foul
odor;
So does a little folly to one
respected for wisdom *and*
honor.
2 A wise man's heart *is* at his right
hand,
But a fool's heart at his left.

3 Even when a fool walks along the
way,
He lacks wisdom,
And he shows everyone *that* he *is*
a fool.
4 If the spirit of the ruler rises
against you,
Do not leave your post;
For conciliation pacifies great
offenses.

5 There is an evil I have seen under
the sun,
As an error proceeding from the
ruler:
6 Folly is set in great dignity,
While the rich sit in a lowly place.
7 I have seen servants on horses,
While princes walk on the ground
like servants.

8 He who digs a pit will fall into it,
And whoever breaks through a
wall will be bitten by a serpent.

10:1 [a]Targum and Vulgate omit *putrefy*.

9 He who quarries stones may be
    hurt by them,
And he who splits wood may be
    endangered by it.
10 If the ax is dull,
And one does not sharpen the
    edge,
Then he must use more strength;
But wisdom brings success.

11 A serpent may bite when *it is* not
    charmed;
The babbler is no different.
12 The words of a wise man's mouth
    are gracious,
But the lips of a fool shall
    swallow him up;
13 The words of his mouth begin
    with foolishness,
And the end of his talk *is* raving
    madness.
14 A fool also multiplies words.
No man knows what is to be;
Who can tell him what will be
    after him?
15 The labor of fools wearies them,
For they do not even know how to
    go to the city!

16 Woe to you, O land, when your
    king *is* a child,
And your princes feast in the
    morning!
17 Blessed *are* you, O land, when
    your king *is* the son of nobles,
And your princes feast at the
    proper time—
For strength and not for
    drunkenness!
18 Because of laziness the building
    decays,
And through idleness of hands
    the house leaks.
19 A feast is made for laughter,
And wine makes merry;
But money answers everything.

20 Do not curse the king, even in
    your thought;

Do not curse the rich, even in
    your bedroom;
For a bird of the air may carry
    your voice,
And a bird in flight may tell the
    matter.

THE VALUE OF DILIGENCE

11 Cast your bread upon the
    waters,
For you will find it after many
    days.
2 Give a serving to seven, and also
    to eight,
For you do not know what evil
    will be on the earth.

3 If the clouds are full of rain,
They empty *themselves* upon the
    earth;
And if a tree falls to the south or
    the north,
In the place where the tree falls,
    there it shall lie.
4 He who observes the wind will
    not sow,
And he who regards the clouds
    will not reap.

5 As you do not know what *is* the
    way of the wind,*a*
Or how the bones *grow* in the
    womb of her who is with
    child,
So you do not know the works of
    God who makes everything.
6 In the morning sow your
    seed,
And in the evening do not
    withhold your hand;
For you do not know which will
    prosper,
Either this or that,
Or whether both alike *will be*
    good.

11:5 *a*Or *spirit*

7   Truly the light is sweet,
And *it is* pleasant for the eyes to
   behold the sun;
8   But if a man lives many years
And rejoices in them all,
Yet let him remember the days of
   darkness,
For they will be many.
All that is coming *is* vanity.

SEEK GOD IN EARLY LIFE

9   Rejoice, O young man, in your
   youth,
And let your heart cheer you in
   the days of your youth;
Walk in the ways of your heart,
And in the sight of your eyes;
But know that for all these
God will bring you into
   judgment.
10   Therefore remove sorrow from
   your heart,
And put away evil from your
   flesh,
For childhood and youth *are*
   vanity.

12 Remember now your Creator
in the days of your youth,
Before the difficult days come,
And the years draw near when
   you say,
"I have no pleasure in them":
2   While the sun and the light,
The moon and the stars,
Are not darkened,
And the clouds do not return after
   the rain;
3   In the day when the keepers of
   the house tremble,
And the strong men bow down;
When the grinders cease because
   they are few,
And those that look through the
   windows grow dim;
4   When the doors are shut in the
   streets,

And the sound of grinding is
   low;
When one rises up at the sound of
   a bird,
And all the daughters of music
   are brought low.
5   Also they are afraid of height,
And of terrors in the way;
When the almond tree blossoms,
The grasshopper is a burden,
And desire fails.
For man goes to his eternal
   home,
And the mourners go about the
   streets.

6   *Remember your Creator* before
   the silver cord is loosed,[a]
Or the golden bowl is broken,
Or the pitcher shattered at the
   fountain,
Or the wheel broken at the well.
7   Then the dust will return to the
   earth as it was,
And the spirit will return to God
   who gave it.

8   "Vanity of vanities," says the
   Preacher,
"All *is* vanity."

THE WHOLE DUTY OF MAN

9   And moreover, because the
Preacher was wise, he still taught
the people knowledge; yes, he pondered and sought out *and* set in order
many proverbs.
10 The Preacher sought to find acceptable words; and *what was* written *was* upright—words of truth.
11 The words of the wise are like
goads, and the words of scholars[a] are
like well-driven nails, given by one
Shepherd.

12:6 [a]Following Qere and Targum; Kethib reads *removed;* Septuagint and Vulgate read *broken.*
12:11 [a]Literally *masters of the assemblies*

ABOUT GOD THE CREATOR Ecclesiastes 12:1

Who Is the Creator?

Look at the flowers! How beautiful. But who made them? Look at the clouds in the sky. How wonderful! But who made them? Who made the mountains and the oceans, the lakes and trees and birds and everything bright and beautiful? Who is the Creator?

1. Read Genesis, chapter 1. What did you learn about the Creator?
2. What should we think about the Creator? Read Ecclesiastes 12:1. When should we think about Him?
3. Read Colossians 1:15–18. What does this say about the Creator?
4. Have you thanked the Lord today for making you and the wonderful world where you live? Why not do that now? Then help Him take good care of it.

For more on *What the Bible Says* turn to page 1105
For more on *God's Creation* turn to page 1105

12 And further, my son, be admonished by these. Of making many books *there is* no end, and much study *is* wearisome to the flesh.

13 Let us hear the conclusion of the whole matter:

Fear God and keep His
   commandments,
For this is man's all.
14 For God will bring every work
   into judgment,
Including every secret thing,
Whether good or evil.

The
SONG OF SOLOMON

THE song of songs, which *is* Solomon's.

THE BANQUET

The Shulamite[a]

2 Let him kiss me with the kisses of
    his mouth—
    For your[b] love *is* better than
    wine.
3 Because of the fragrance of your
    good ointments,
    Your name *is* ointment poured
    forth;
    Therefore the virgins love you.
4 Draw me away!

The Daughters of Jerusalem

We will run after you.[a]

The Shulamite

The king has brought me into his
chambers.

The Daughters of Jerusalem

We will be glad and rejoice in
you.[b]

We will remember your[c] love
more than wine.

The Shulamite

Rightly do they love you.[d]

5 I *am* dark, but lovely,
    O daughters of Jerusalem,
    Like the tents of Kē'dar,
    Like the curtains of Solomon.
6 Do not look upon me, because I
    am dark,
    Because the sun has tanned me.
    My mother's sons were angry
    with me;
    They made me the keeper of the
    vineyards,

But my own vineyard I have not
kept.

(To Her Beloved)

7 Tell me, O you whom I love,
    Where you feed *your flock,*
    Where you make *it* rest at noon.
    For why should I be as one who
    veils herself[a]
    By the flocks of your companions?

The Beloved

8 If you do not know, O fairest
    among women,
    Follow in the footsteps of the
    flock,
    And feed your little goats
    Beside the shepherds' tents.
9 I have compared you, my love,
    To my filly among Pharaoh's
    chariots.
10 Your cheeks are lovely with
    ornaments,
    Your neck with chains *of gold.*

The Daughters of Jerusalem

11 We will make you[a] ornaments of
    gold
    With studs of silver.

The Shulamite

12 While the king *is* at his table,
    My spikenard sends forth its
    fragrance.
13 A bundle of myrrh *is* my beloved
    to me,

1:2 [a]A Palestinian young woman (compare 6:13).
The speaker and audience are identified according
to the number, gender, and person of the Hebrew
words. Occasionally the identity is not certain.
[b]Masculine singular, that is, the Beloved
1:4 [a]Masculine singular, that is, the Beloved
[b]Feminine singular, that is, the Shulamite [c]Mas-
culine singular, that is, the Beloved [d]Masculine
singular, that is, the Beloved   1:7 [a]Septuagint,
Syriac, and Vulgate read *wanders.*   1:11 [a]Femi-
nine singular, that is, the Shulamite

That lies all night between my breasts.

14 My beloved *is* to me a cluster of henna *blooms*
In the vineyards of En Ge'di.

The Beloved

15 Behold, you *are* fair, my love!
Behold, you *are* fair!
You *have* dove's eyes.

The Shulamite

16 Behold, you *are* handsome, my beloved!
Yes, pleasant!
Also our bed *is* green.

17 The beams of our houses *are* cedar,
And our rafters of fir.

2 I *am* the rose of Sharon,
And the lily of the valleys.

The Beloved

2 Like a lily among thorns,
So *is* my love among the daughters.

The Shulamite

3 Like an apple tree among the trees of the woods,
So *is* my beloved among the sons.
I sat down in his shade with great delight,
And his fruit *was* sweet to my taste.

The Shulamite to the Daughters of Jerusalem

4 He brought me to the banqueting house,
And his banner over me *was* love.

5 Sustain me with cakes of raisins,
Refresh me with apples,
For I *am* lovesick.

6 His left hand *is* under my head,
And his right hand embraces me.

7 I charge you, O daughters of Jerusalem,
By the gazelles or by the does of the field,
Do not stir up nor awaken love
Until it pleases.

THE BELOVED'S REQUEST

The Shulamite

8 The voice of my beloved!
Behold, he comes
Leaping upon the mountains,
Skipping upon the hills.

9 My beloved is like a gazelle or a young stag.
Behold, he stands behind our wall;
He is looking through the windows,
Gazing through the lattice.

10 My beloved spoke, and said to me:
"Rise up, my love, my fair one,
And come away.

11 For lo, the winter is past,
The rain is over *and* gone.

12 The flowers appear on the earth;
The time of singing has come,
And the voice of the turtledove
Is heard in our land.

13 The fig tree puts forth her green figs,
And the vines *with* the tender grapes
Give a good smell.
Rise up, my love, my fair one,
And come away!

14 "O my dove, in the clefts of the rock,
In the secret *places* of the cliff,
Let me see your face,
Let me hear your voice;
For your voice *is* sweet,
And your face *is* lovely."

Her Brothers

15 Catch us the foxes,
  The little foxes that spoil the
    vines,
  For our vines *have* tender grapes.

The Shulamite

16 My beloved *is* mine, and I *am* his.
  He feeds *his flock* among the
    lilies.

(To Her Beloved)

17 Until the day breaks
  And the shadows flee away,
  Turn, my beloved,
  And be like a gazelle
  Or a young stag
  Upon the mountains of Bē′ther.*a*

A Troubled Night

The Shulamite

3 By night on my bed I sought the
  one I love;
  I sought him, but I did not find
    him.
2 "I will rise now," *I said,*
  "And go about the city;
  In the streets and in the squares
  I will seek the one I love."
  I sought him, but I did not find
    him.
3 The watchmen who go about the
    city found me;
  I said,
  "Have you seen the one I love?"

4 Scarcely had I passed by them,
  When I found the one I love.
  I held him and would not let him
    go,
  Until I had brought him to the
    house of my mother,
  And into the chamber of her who
    conceived me.

5 I charge you, O daughters of
  Jerusalem,

By the gazelles or by the does of
  the field,
Do not stir up nor awaken love
Until it pleases.

The Coming of Solomon

The Shulamite

6 Who *is* this coming out of the
    wilderness
  Like pillars of smoke,
  Perfumed with myrrh and
    frankincense,
  With all the merchant's fragrant
    powders?
7 Behold, it *is* Solomon's couch,
  With sixty valiant men around it,
  Of the valiant of Israel.
8 They all hold swords,
  Being expert in war.
  Every man *has* his sword on his
    thigh
  Because of fear in the night.

9 Of the wood of Lebanon
  Solomon the King
  Made himself a palanquin:*a*
10 He made its pillars *of* silver,
  Its support *of* gold,
  Its seat *of* purple,
  Its interior paved *with* love
  By the daughters of Jerusalem.
11 Go forth, O daughters of Zion,
  And see King Solomon with the
    crown
  With which his mother crowned
    him
  On the day of his wedding,
  The day of the gladness of his
    heart.

The Beloved

4 Behold, you *are* fair, my love!
  Behold, you *are* fair!

2:17 *a*Literally *Separation*   3:9 *a*A portable enclosed chair

You *have* dove's eyes behind your
    veil.
Your hair *is* like a flock of goats,
Going down from Mount
    Gil′ē·ad.
2 Your teeth *are* like a flock of
    shorn *sheep*
Which have come up from the
    washing,
Every one of which bears twins,
And none *is* barren among
    them.
3 Your lips *are* like a strand of
    scarlet,
And your mouth is lovely.
Your temples behind your veil
Are like a piece of pomegranate.
4 Your neck *is* like the tower of
    David,
Built for an armory,
On which hang a thousand
    bucklers,
All shields of mighty men.
5 Your two breasts *are* like two
    fawns,
Twins of a gazelle,
Which feed among the lilies.

6 Until the day breaks
And the shadows flee away,
I will go my way to the mountain
    of myrrh
And to the hill of frankincense.

7 You *are* all fair, my love,
And *there is* no spot in you.
8 Come with me from Lebanon, *my*
    spouse,
With me from Lebanon.
Look from the top of A·ma′na,
From the top of Sē′nir and
    Her′mon,
From the lions' dens,
From the mountains of the
    leopards.

9 You have ravished my heart,
My sister, *my* spouse;
You have ravished my heart

With one *look* of your eyes,
With one link of your necklace.
10 How fair is your love,
My sister, *my* spouse!
How much better than wine is
    your love,
And the scent of your perfumes
Than all spices!
11 Your lips, O *my* spouse,
Drip as the honeycomb;
Honey and milk *are* under your
    tongue;
And the fragrance of your
    garments
Is like the fragrance of
    Lebanon.

12 A garden enclosed
Is my sister, *my* spouse,
A spring shut up,
A fountain sealed.
13 Your plants *are* an orchard of
    pomegranates
With pleasant fruits,
Fragrant henna with
    spikenard,
14 Spikenard and saffron,
Calamus and cinnamon,
With all trees of frankincense,
Myrrh and aloes,
With all the chief spices—
15 A fountain of gardens,
A well of living waters,
And streams from Lebanon.

The Shulamite

16 Awake, O north *wind,*
And come, O south!
Blow upon my garden,
That its spices may flow out.
Let my beloved come to his
    garden
And eat its pleasant fruits.

The Beloved

5 I have come to my garden, my
    sister, *my* spouse;

I have gathered my myrrh with
my spice;
I have eaten my honeycomb with
my honey;
I have drunk my wine with my
milk.

(To His Friends)
Eat, O friends!
Drink, yes, drink deeply,
O beloved ones!

THE SHULAMITE'S
TROUBLED EVENING

The Shulamite
2 I sleep, but my heart is awake;
It is the voice of my beloved!
He knocks, *saying,*
"Open for me, my sister, my love,
My dove, my perfect one;
For my head is covered with
dew,
My locks with the drops of the
night."

3 I have taken off my robe;
How can I put it on *again?*
I have washed my feet;
How can I defile them?
4 My beloved put his hand
By the latch *of the door,*
And my heart yearned for him.
5 I arose to open for my beloved,
And my hands dripped *with*
myrrh,
My fingers with liquid myrrh,
On the handles of the lock.

6 I opened for my beloved,
But my beloved had turned away
and was gone.
My heart leaped up when he
spoke.
I sought him, but I could not find
him;
I called him, but he gave me no
answer.

7 The watchmen who went about
the city found me.
They struck me, they wounded
me;
The keepers of the walls
Took my veil away from me.
8 I charge you, O daughters of
Jerusalem,
If you find my beloved,
That you tell him I *am*
lovesick!

The Daughters of Jerusalem
9 What *is* your beloved
More than *another* beloved,
O fairest among women?
What *is* your beloved
More than *another* beloved,
That you so charge us?

The Shulamite
10 My beloved *is* white and
ruddy,
Chief among ten thousand.
11 His head *is like* the finest gold;
His locks *are* wavy,
And black as a raven.
12 His eyes *are* like doves
By the rivers of waters,
Washed with milk,
And fitly set.
13 His cheeks *are* like a bed of
spices,
Banks of scented herbs.
His lips *are* lilies,
Dripping liquid myrrh.

14 His hands *are* rods of gold
Set with beryl.
His body *is* carved ivory
Inlaid *with* sapphires.
15 His legs *are* pillars of marble
Set on bases of fine gold.
His countenance *is* like
Lebanon,
Excellent as the cedars.
16 His mouth *is* most sweet,
Yes, he *is* altogether lovely.

This *is* my beloved,
And this *is* my friend,
O daughters of Jerusalem!

The Daughters of Jerusalem

6 Where has your beloved gone,
O fairest among women?
Where has your beloved turned
aside,
That we may seek him with you?

The Shulamite

2 My beloved has gone to his
garden,
To the beds of spices,
To feed *his flock* in the gardens,
And to gather lilies.
3 I *am* my beloved's,
And my beloved *is* mine.
He feeds *his flock* among the
lilies.

PRAISE OF THE
SHULAMITE'S BEAUTY

The Beloved

4 O my love, you *are as* beautiful as
Tir′zah,
Lovely as Jerusalem,
Awesome as *an army* with
banners!
5 Turn your eyes away from me,
For they have overcome me.
Your hair *is* like a flock of goats
Going down from Gil′ē·ad.
6 Your teeth *are* like a flock of
sheep
Which have come up from the
washing;
Every one bears twins,
And none *is* barren among them.
7 Like a piece of pomegranate
Are your temples behind your
veil.
8 There are sixty queens
And eighty concubines,
And virgins without number.

9 My dove, my perfect one,
Is the only one,
The only one of her mother,
The favorite of the one who bore
her.
The daughters saw her
And called her blessed,
The queens and the concubines,
And they praised her.

10 Who is she who looks forth as the
morning,
Fair as the moon,
Clear as the sun,
Awesome as *an army* with
banners?

The Shulamite

11 I went down to the garden of nuts
To see the verdure of the valley,
To see whether the vine had
budded
And the pomegranates had
bloomed.
12 Before I was even aware,
My soul had made me
As the chariots of my noble
people.ᵃ

The Beloved and His Friends

13 Return, return, O Shū′lam·īte;
Return, return, that we may look
upon you!

The Shulamite

What would you see in the
Shū′lam·īte—
As it were, the dance of the two
camps?ᵃ

EXPRESSIONS OF PRAISE

The Beloved

7 How beautiful are your feet in
sandals,

6:12 ᵃHebrew *Ammi Nadib*   6:13 ᵃHebrew *Mahanaim*

LOVE Song of Solomon 6:4

Do You Love Someone? Say So!

Do you love your brother or sister? Say so. Do you love your mother or father? Say so. Do you love Jesus? Say so.

1. How is this boy showing that he loves someone? Will that make someone happy?
2. Have you told your parents today that you love them? Why not now? Have you told Jesus today that you love Him? Why not now?

For more on *Values* turn to page 1036
For more on *Love* turn to page 1036

LOVE Song of Solomon 7:11, 12

Hitting a Bull's-Eye with Love Every Time

Does it really work that way? In archery or marksmanship, hitting the bull's-eye is like a home run in baseball or a touchdown in football. Do even the best baseball players hit a home run every time? Do even the best football players make a touchdown every time? They are content with little gains toward a big goal. Could that be the best way with love? Instead of a bull's-eye, or a touchdown, or a home run every time, how about small steps of progress?

1. Why don't baseball players make home runs every time? Why don't football players make touchdowns every time? Why don't archers or marksmen hit the bull's-eye every time?
2. Do even the best of people expect little problems in family living or community or church life? Why? What should you do about these little problems?

For more on *Values* turn to page 1111
For more on *Love* turn to page 1363

O prince's daughter!
The curves of your thighs *are* like
    jewels,
The work of the hands of a
    skillful workman.
2 Your navel *is* a rounded goblet;
It lacks no blended beverage.
Your waist *is* a heap of wheat
Set about with lilies.
3 Your two breasts *are* like two
    fawns,
Twins of a gazelle.
4 Your neck *is* like an ivory tower,
Your eyes *like* the pools in
    Hesh'bon
By the gate of Bath Rab'bim.
Your nose *is* like the tower of
    Lebanon
Which looks toward Damascus.
5 Your head *crowns* you like *Mount*
    Car'mel,
And the hair of your head *is* like
    purple;
A king *is* held captive by *your*
    tresses.

6 How fair and how pleasant you
    are,
O love, with your delights!
7 This stature of yours is like a
    palm tree,
And your breasts *like* its clusters.
8 I said, "I will go up to the palm
    tree,
I will take hold of its branches."
Let now your breasts be like
    clusters of the vine,
The fragrance of your breath like
    apples,
9 And the roof of your mouth like
    the best wine.

The Shulamite

  The wine goes *down* smoothly for
    my beloved,
Moving gently the lips of
    sleepers.*a*
10 I *am* my beloved's,
And his desire *is* toward me.

11 Come, my beloved,
Let us go forth to the field;
Let us lodge in the villages.
12 Let us get up early to the
    vineyards;
Let us see if the vine has budded,
Whether the grape blossoms are
    open,
And the pomegranates are in
    bloom.
There I will give you my love.
13 The mandrakes give off a
    fragrance,
And at our gates *are* pleasant
    fruits,
All manner, new and old,
Which I have laid up for you, my
    beloved.

8 Oh, that you were like my
    brother,
Who nursed at my mother's
    breasts!
If I should find you outside,
I would kiss you;
I would not be despised.
2 I would lead you *and* bring you
Into the house of my mother,
She *who* used to instruct me.
I would cause you to drink of
    spiced wine,
Of the juice of my pomegranate.

(To the Daughters of Jerusalem)

3 His left hand *is* under my head,
And his right hand embraces me.
4 I charge you, O daughters of
    Jerusalem,
Do not stir up nor awaken love
Until it pleases.

LOVE RENEWED IN LEBANON

A Relative

5 Who *is* this coming up from the
    wilderness,
Leaning upon her beloved?

7:9 *a*Septuagint, Syriac, and Vulgate read *lips and*
teeth.

I awakened you under the apple
tree.
There your mother brought you
forth;
There she *who* bore you brought
you forth.

The Shulamite to Her Beloved

6 Set me as a seal upon your heart,
As a seal upon your arm;
For love *is as* strong as death,
Jealousy *as* cruel as the grave;*a*
Its flames *are* flames of fire,
A most vehement*b* flame.

7 Many waters cannot quench love,
Nor can the floods drown it.
If a man would give for love
All the wealth of his house,
It would be utterly despised.

The Shulamite's Brothers

8 We have a little sister,
And she has no breasts.
What shall we do for our sister
In the day when she is spoken
for?
9 If she *is* a wall,
We will build upon her
A battlement of silver;
And if she *is* a door,
We will enclose her
With boards of cedar.

The Shulamite

10 I *am* a wall,
And my breasts like towers;
Then I became in his eyes
As one who found peace.
11 Solomon had a vineyard at Bā′al
Hā′mon;
He leased the vineyard to
keepers;
Everyone was to bring for its fruit
A thousand silver coins.

(To Solomon)

12 My own vineyard *is* before me.
You, O Solomon, *may have* a
thousand,
And those who tend its fruit two
hundred.

The Beloved

13 You who dwell in the gardens,
The companions listen for your
voice—
Let me hear it!

The Shulamite

14 Make haste, my beloved,
And be like a gazelle
Or a young stag
On the mountains of spices.

8:6 *a*Or *Sheol*   *b*Literally *A flame of* YAH (a poetic
form of *YHWH,* the LORD)

The Book of
ISAIAH

THE vision of Ī·saī′ah the son of Ā′moz, which he saw concerning Judah and Jerusalem in the days of Uz·zī′ah, Jō′tham, Ā′haz, *and* Hez·e·kī′ah, kings of Judah.

THE WICKEDNESS OF JUDAH

2 Hear, O heavens, and give ear,
    O earth!
 For the LORD has spoken:
 "I have nourished and brought up
    children,
 And they have rebelled against
    Me;
3 The ox knows its owner
 And the donkey its master's crib;
 But Israel does not know,
 My people do not consider."

4 Alas, sinful nation,
 A people laden with iniquity,
 A brood of evildoers,
 Children who are corrupters!
 They have forsaken the LORD,
 They have provoked to anger
 The Holy One of Israel,
 They have turned away
    backward.

5 Why should you be stricken
    again?
 You will revolt more and more.
 The whole head is sick,
 And the whole heart faints.
6 From the sole of the foot even to
    the head,
 There is no soundness in it,
 But wounds and bruises and
    putrefying sores;
 They have not been closed or
    bound up,
 Or soothed with ointment.

7 Your country *is* desolate,
 Your cities *are* burned with fire;

Strangers devour your land in
    your presence;
 And *it is* desolate, as overthrown
    by strangers.
8 So the daughter of Zion is left as
    a booth in a vineyard,
 As a hut in a garden of
    cucumbers,
 As a besieged city.
9 Unless the LORD of hosts
 Had left to us a very small
    remnant,
 We would have become like
    Sod′om,
 We would have been made like
    Go·mor′rah.

10 Hear the word of the LORD,
 You rulers of Sod′om;
 Give ear to the law of our God,
 You people of Go·mor′rah:
11 "To what purpose *is* the multitude
    of your sacrifices to Me?"
 Says the LORD.
 "I have had enough of burnt
    offerings of rams
 And the fat of fed cattle.
 I do not delight in the blood of
    bulls,
 Or of lambs or goats.

12 "When you come to appear before
    Me,
 Who has required this from your
    hand,
 To trample My courts?
13 Bring no more futile sacrifices;
 Incense is an abomination to
    Me.
 The New Moons, the Sabbaths,
    and the calling of assemblies—
 I cannot endure iniquity and the
    sacred meeting.
14 Your New Moons and your
    appointed feasts
 My soul hates;

They are a trouble to Me,
I am weary of bearing *them*.

15 When you spread out your hands,
   I will hide My eyes from you;
   Even though you make many
     prayers,
   I will not hear.
   Your hands are full of blood.

16 "Wash yourselves, make
    yourselves clean;
   Put away the evil of your doings
    from before My eyes.
   Cease to do evil,
17 Learn to do good;
   Seek justice,
   Rebuke the oppressor;[a]
   Defend the fatherless,
   Plead for the widow.

Promises

Isaiah 1:18

Do you ever feel sad because you have said bad things? Are you ever sorry because you have done bad things? Those bad things are sins. They are like big red blotches on your life. But God promises to make them as white as snow, as clean as snowflakes that fall. He will do this when we are truly sorry that we have sinned. He will do this when we ask Him to forgive us. Will you?

---

18 "Come now, and let us reason
    together,"
   Says the LORD,
  "Though your sins are like scarlet,
   They shall be as white as snow;
   Though they are red like crimson,
   They shall be as wool.
19 If you are willing and obedient,
   You shall eat the good of the land;
20 But if you refuse and rebel,

You shall be devoured by the
    sword";
For the mouth of the LORD has
   spoken.

THE DEGENERATE CITY

21 How the faithful city has become
    a harlot!
   It was full of justice;
   Righteousness lodged in it,
   But now murderers.
22 Your silver has become dross,
   Your wine mixed with water.
23 Your princes *are* rebellious,
   And companions of thieves;
   Everyone loves bribes,
   And follows after rewards.
   They do not defend the fatherless,
   Nor does the cause of the widow
    come before them.

24 Therefore the Lord says,
   The LORD of hosts, the Mighty
    One of Israel,
  "Ah, I will rid Myself of My
    adversaries,
   And take vengeance on My
    enemies.
25 I will turn My hand against you,
   And thoroughly purge away your
    dross,
   And take away all your alloy.
26 I will restore your judges as at
    the first,
   And your counselors as at the
    beginning.
   Afterward you shall be called the
    city of righteousness, the
    faithful city."

27 Zion shall be redeemed with
    justice,
   And her penitents with
    righteousness.
28 The destruction of transgressors
    and of sinners *shall be* together,

1:17 [a]Some ancient versions read *the oppressed.*

And those who forsake the LORD
    shall be consumed.
29 For they[a] shall be ashamed of the
    terebinth trees
    Which you have desired;
    And you shall be embarrassed
      because of the gardens
    Which you have chosen.
30 For you shall be as a terebinth
      whose leaf fades,
    And as a garden that has no
      water.
31 The strong shall be as tinder,
    And the work of it as a spark;
    Both will burn together,
    And no one shall quench *them.*

THE FUTURE HOUSE OF GOD

2 The word that Ī·sāi'ah the son of Ā'moz saw concerning Judah and Jerusalem.

2 Now it shall come to pass in the
      latter days
    That the mountain of the LORD's
      house
    Shall be established on the top of
      the mountains,
    And shall be exalted above the
      hills;
    And all nations shall flow to it.
3 Many people shall come and say,
    "Come, and let us go up to the
      mountain of the LORD,
    To the house of the God of Jacob;
    He will teach us His ways,
    And we shall walk in His paths."
    For out of Zion shall go forth the
      law,
    And the word of the LORD from
      Jerusalem.
4 He shall judge between the
      nations,
    And rebuke many people;
    They shall beat their swords into
      plowshares,
    And their spears into pruning
      hooks;

Nation shall not lift up sword
    against nation,
Neither shall they learn war
    anymore.

THE DAY OF THE LORD

5 O house of Jacob, come and let us
      walk
    In the light of the LORD.

6 For You have forsaken Your
      people, the house of Jacob,
    Because they are filled with
      eastern ways;
    They *are* soothsayers like the
      Phi·lis'tines,
    And they are pleased with the
      children of foreigners.
7 Their land is also full of silver
      and gold,
    And there is no end to their
      treasures;
    Their land is also full of horses,
    And there is no end to their
      chariots.
8 Their land is also full of idols;
    They worship the work of their
      own hands,
    That which their own fingers
      have made.
9 People bow down,
    And each man humbles himself;
    Therefore do not forgive them.

10 Enter into the rock, and hide in
      the dust,
    From the terror of the LORD
    And the glory of His majesty.
11 The lofty looks of man shall be
      humbled,
    The haughtiness of men shall be
      bowed down,
    And the LORD alone shall be
      exalted in that day.

1:29 [a]Following Masoretic Text, Septuagint, and Vulgate; some Hebrew manuscripts and Targum read *you.*

12 For the day of the LORD of hosts
  Shall come upon everything
    proud and lofty,
  Upon everything lifted up—
  And it shall be brought low—
13 Upon all the cedars of Lebanon
    that are high and lifted up,
  And upon all the oaks of Bā′shan;
14 Upon all the high mountains,
  And upon all the hills *that are*
    lifted up;
15 Upon every high tower,
  And upon every fortified wall;
16 Upon all the ships of Tar′shish,
  And upon all the beautiful
    sloops.
17 The loftiness of man shall be
    bowed down,
  And the haughtiness of men shall
    be brought low;
  The LORD alone will be exalted in
    that day,
18 But the idols He shall utterly
    abolish.

19 They shall go into the holes of the
    rocks,
  And into the caves of the earth,
  From the terror of the LORD
  And the glory of His majesty,
  When He arises to shake the
    earth mightily.

20 In that day a man will cast away
    his idols of silver
  And his idols of gold,
  Which they made, *each* for
    himself to worship,
  To the moles and bats,
21 To go into the clefts of the rocks,
  And into the crags of the rugged
    rocks,
  From the terror of the LORD
  And the glory of His majesty,
  When He arises to shake the
    earth mightily.

22 Sever yourselves from such a
    man,

Whose breath *is* in his nostrils;
  For of what account is he?

JUDGMENT ON JUDAH AND JERUSALEM

3 For behold, the Lord, the LORD of
    hosts,
  Takes away from Jerusalem and
    from Judah
  The stock and the store,
  The whole supply of bread and
    the whole supply of water;
2 The mighty man and the man of
    war,
  The judge and the prophet,
  And the diviner and the elder;
3 The captain of fifty and the
    honorable man,
  The counselor and the skillful
    artisan,
  And the expert enchanter.

4 "I will give children *to be* their
    princes,
  And babes shall rule over them.
5 The people will be oppressed,
  Every one by another and every
    one by his neighbor;
  The child will be insolent toward
    the elder,
  And the base toward the
    honorable."

6 When a man takes hold of his
    brother
  In the house of his father, *saying,*
  "You have clothing;
  You be our ruler,
  And *let* these ruins *be* under your
    power,"a
7 In that day he will protest,
    saying,
  "I cannot cure *your* ills,
  For in my house *is* neither food
    nor clothing;

3:6 aLiterally *hand*

Do not make me a ruler of the
   people."

8 For Jerusalem stumbled,
   And Judah is fallen,
   Because their tongue and their
     doings
   Are against the LORD,
   To provoke the eyes of His glory.
9 The look on their countenance
     witnesses against them,
   And they declare their sin as
     Sod'om;
   They do not hide *it*.
   Woe to their soul!
   For they have brought evil upon
     themselves.

10 "Say to the righteous that *it shall
     be* well *with them,*
   For they shall eat the fruit of
     their doings.
11 Woe to the wicked! *It shall be* ill
     with him,
   For the reward of his hands shall
     be given him.
12 *As for* My people, children *are*
     their oppressors,
   And women rule over them.
   O My people! Those who lead you
     cause *you* to err,
   And destroy the way of your
     paths."

OPPRESSION AND LUXURY CONDEMNED

13 The LORD stands up to plead,
   And stands to judge the people.
14 The LORD will enter into
     judgment
   With the elders of His people
   And His princes:
   "For you have eaten up the
     vineyard;
   The plunder of the poor *is* in your
     houses.
15 What do you mean by crushing
     My people

And grinding the faces of the
   poor?"
   Says the Lord GOD of hosts.

16 Moreover the LORD says:

   "Because the daughters of Zion are
     haughty,
   And walk with outstretched necks
   And wanton eyes,
   Walking and mincing *as* they go,
   Making a jingling with their feet,
17 Therefore the Lord will strike
     with a scab
   The crown of the head of the
     daughters of Zion,
   And the LORD will uncover their
     secret parts."

18 In that day the Lord will take
     away the finery:
   The jingling anklets, the scarves,
     and the crescents;
19 The pendants, the bracelets, and
     the veils;
20 The headdresses, the leg
     ornaments, and the headbands;
   The perfume boxes, the charms,
21   and the rings;
   The nose jewels,
22   the festal apparel, and the
     mantles;
   The outer garments, the purses,
23   and the mirrors;
   The fine linen, the turbans, and
     the robes.

24 And so it shall be:

   Instead of a sweet smell there
     will be a stench;
   Instead of a sash, a rope;
   Instead of well-set hair, baldness;
   Instead of a rich robe, a girding of
     sackcloth;
   And branding instead of beauty.
25 Your men shall fall by the sword,
   And your mighty in the war.

26 Her gates shall lament and
     mourn,
   And she *being* desolate shall sit
     on the ground.

4 And in that day seven women
     shall take hold of one man,
     saying,
   "We will eat our own food and
     wear our own apparel;
   Only let us be called by your
     name,
   To take away our reproach."

THE RENEWAL OF ZION

2 In that day the Branch of the
     LORD shall be beautiful and
     glorious;
   And the fruit of the earth *shall be*
     excellent and appealing
   For those of Israel who have
     escaped.

3 And it shall come to pass that *he
who is* left in Zion and remains in Jerusalem will be called holy—everyone who is recorded among the living
in Jerusalem.
4 When the Lord has washed away
the filth of the daughters of Zion, and
purged the blood of Jerusalem from
her midst, by the spirit of judgment
and by the spirit of burning,
5 then the LORD will create above
every dwelling place of Mount Zion,
and above her assemblies, a cloud
and smoke by day and the shining of
a flaming fire by night. For over all
the glory there *will be* a covering.
6 And there will be a tabernacle for
shade in the daytime from the heat,
for a place of refuge, and for a shelter
from storm and rain.

GOD'S DISAPPOINTING VINEYARD

5 Now let me sing to my
     Well-beloved

A song of my Beloved regarding
     His vineyard:

My Well-beloved has a vineyard
   On a very fruitful hill.
2 He dug it up and cleared out its
     stones,
   And planted it with the choicest
     vine.
   He built a tower in its midst,
   And also made a winepress in
     it;
   So He expected *it* to bring forth
     good grapes,
   But it brought forth wild grapes.

3 "And now, O inhabitants of
     Jerusalem and men of Judah,
   Judge, please, between Me and
     My vineyard.
4 What more could have been done
     to My vineyard
   That I have not done in it?
   Why then, when I expected *it* to
     bring forth *good* grapes,
   Did it bring forth wild grapes?
5 And now, please let Me tell you
     what I will do to My vineyard:
   I will take away its hedge, and it
     shall be burned;
   And break down its wall, and it
     shall be trampled down.
6 I will lay it waste;
   It shall not be pruned or dug,
   But there shall come up briers
     and thorns.
   I will also command the
     clouds
   That they rain no rain on it."

7 For the vineyard of the LORD of
     hosts *is* the house of Israel,
   And the men of Judah are His
     pleasant plant.
   He looked for justice, but behold,
     oppression;
   For righteousness, but behold, a
     cry *for help.*

IMPENDING JUDGMENT ON EXCESSES

8 Woe to those who join house to
   house;
   They add field to field,
   Till *there is* no place
   Where they may dwell alone in
   the midst of the land!
9 In my hearing the LORD of hosts
   said,
   "Truly, many houses shall be
   desolate,
   Great and beautiful ones, without
   inhabitant.
10 For ten acres of vineyard shall
   yield one bath,
   And a homer of seed shall yield
   one ephah."

11 Woe to those who rise early in the
   morning,
   That they may follow intoxicating
   drink;
   Who continue until night, *till*
   wine inflames them!
12 The harp and the strings,
   The tambourine and flute,
   And wine are in their feasts;
   But they do not regard the work
   of the LORD,
   Nor consider the operation of His
   hands.

13 Therefore my people have gone
   into captivity,
   Because *they have* no knowledge;
   Their honorable men *are*
   famished,
   And their multitude dried up
   with thirst.
14 Therefore Shē′ōl has enlarged
   itself
   And opened its mouth beyond
   measure;
   Their glory and their multitude
   and their pomp,
   And he who is jubilant, shall
   descend into it.
15 People shall be brought down,
   Each man shall be humbled,
   And the eyes of the lofty shall be
   humbled.
16 But the LORD of hosts shall be
   exalted in judgment,
   And God who is holy shall be
   hallowed in righteousness.
17 Then the lambs shall feed in their
   pasture,
   And in the waste places of the fat
   ones strangers shall eat.

18 Woe to those who draw iniquity
   with cords of vanity,
   And sin as if with a cart rope;
19 That say, "Let Him make speed
   and hasten His work,
   That we may see *it;*
   And let the counsel of the Holy
   One of Israel draw near and
   come,
   That we may know *it.*"

20 Woe to those who call evil good,
   and good evil;
   Who put darkness for light, and
   light for darkness;
   Who put bitter for sweet, and
   sweet for bitter!

21 Woe to *those who are* wise in their
   own eyes,
   And prudent in their own sight!

22 Woe to men mighty at drinking
   wine,
   Woe to men valiant for mixing
   intoxicating drink,
23 Who justify the wicked for a
   bribe,
   And take away justice from the
   righteous man!

24 Therefore, as the fire devours the
   stubble,
   And the flame consumes the
   chaff,
   So their root will be as
   rottenness,

And their blossom will ascend
like dust;
Because they have rejected the
law of the LORD of hosts,
And despised the word of the
Holy One of Israel.

25 Therefore the anger of the LORD is
aroused against His people;
He has stretched out His hand
against them
And stricken them,
And the hills trembled.
Their carcasses *were* as refuse in
the midst of the streets.

For all this His anger is not
turned away,
But His hand *is* stretched out
still.

26 He will lift up a banner to the
nations from afar,
And will whistle to them from the
end of the earth;
Surely they shall come with
speed, swiftly.

27 No one will be weary or stumble
among them,
No one will slumber or sleep;
Nor will the belt on their loins be
loosed,
Nor the strap of their sandals be
broken;

28 Whose arrows *are* sharp,
And all their bows bent;
Their horses' hooves will seem
like flint,
And their wheels like a
whirlwind.

29 Their roaring *will be* like a
lion,
They will roar like young
lions;
Yes, they will roar
And lay hold of the prey;
They will carry *it* away safely,
And no one will deliver.

30 In that day they will roar against
them

Like the roaring of the sea.
And if *one* looks to the land,
Behold, darkness *and* sorrow;
And the light is darkened by the
clouds.

ISAIAH CALLED TO BE A PROPHET

6 In the year that King Uz·zi′ah
died, I saw the Lord sitting on a
throne, high and lifted up, and the
train of His *robe* filled the temple.
2 Above it stood seraphim; each one
had six wings: with two he covered
his face, with two he covered his feet,
and with two he flew.
3 And one cried to another and
said:

"Holy, holy, holy *is* the LORD of
hosts;
The whole earth *is* full of His
glory!"

4 And the posts of the door were
shaken by the voice of him who cried
out, and the house was filled with
smoke.
5 So I said:

"Woe *is* me, for I am undone!
Because I *am* a man of unclean
lips,
And I dwell in the midst of a
people of unclean lips;
For my eyes have seen the King,
The LORD of hosts."

6 Then one of the seraphim flew to
me, having in his hand a live coal
which he had taken with the tongs
from the altar.
7 And he touched my mouth *with it,*
and said:

"Behold, this has touched your
lips;
Your iniquity is taken away,
And your sin purged."

8 Also I heard the voice of the Lord, saying:

> "Whom shall I send,
> And who will go for Us?"

Then I said, "Here *am* I! Send me."
9 And He said, "Go, and tell this people:

> 'Keep on hearing, but do not
>   understand;
> Keep on seeing, but do not
>   perceive.'

10 "Make the heart of this people
>   dull,
> And their ears heavy,
> And shut their eyes;
> Lest they see with their eyes,
> And hear with their ears,
> And understand with their heart,
> And return and be healed."

11 Then I said, "Lord, how long?"
And He answered:

> "Until the cities are laid waste and
>   without inhabitant,
> The houses are without a man,
> The land is utterly desolate,

12 The LORD has removed men far
>   away,
> And the forsaken places *are* many
>   in the midst of the land.
13 But yet a tenth *will be* in it,
> And will return and be for
>   consuming,
> As a terebinth tree or as an oak,
> Whose stump *remains* when it is
>   cut down.
> So the holy seed *shall be* its
>   stump."

ISAIAH SENT TO KING AHAZ

7 Now it came to pass in the days of Ā'haz the son of Jō'tham, the son of Uz·zī'ah, king of Judah, *that* Rē'zin king of Syria and Pē'kah the son of Rem·a·lī'ah, king of Israel, went up to Jerusalem to *make* war against it, but could not prevail against it.
2 And it was told to the house of David, saying, "Syria's forces are deployed in Ē'phra·im." So his heart and the heart of his people were moved as the trees of the woods are moved with the wind.
3 Then the LORD said to Ī·sāi'ah, "Go out now to meet Ā'haz, you and Shē'ar-Jā'shub[a] your son, at the end of the aqueduct from the upper pool, on the highway to the Fuller's Field,
4 "and say to him: 'Take heed, and be quiet; do not fear or be fainthearted for these two stubs of smoking firebrands, for the fierce anger of Rē'zin and Syria, and the son of Rem·a·lī'ah.
5 'Because Syria, Ē'phra·im, and the son of Rem·a·lī'ah have plotted evil against you, saying,
6 "Let us go up against Judah and trouble it, and let us make a gap in its wall for ourselves, and set a king over them, the son of Tā'bel"—

7:3 [a]Literally *A Remnant Shall Return*

7 'thus says the Lord GOD:

"It shall not stand,
　Nor shall it come to pass.
8 For the head of Syria *is*
　　Damascus,
　And the head of Damascus *is*
　　Rē′zin.
　Within sixty-five years Ē′phra·im
　　will be broken,
　So that it will not *be* a people.
9 The head of Ē′phra·im *is*
　　Samaria,
　And the head of Samaria *is*
　　Rem·a·lī′ah's son.
　If you will not believe,
　Surely you shall not be
　　established." ' "

THE IMMANUEL PROPHECY

10 Moreover the LORD spoke again to Ā′haz, saying,
11 "Ask a sign for yourself from the LORD your God; ask it either in the depth or in the height above."
12 But Ā′haz said, "I will not ask, nor will I test the LORD!"
13 Then he said, "Hear now, O house of David! *Is it* a small thing for you to weary men, but will you weary my God also?
14 "Therefore the Lord Himself will give you a sign: Behold, the virgin shall conceive and bear a Son, and shall call His name Im·man′ū·el.*a*
15 "Curds and honey He shall eat, that He may know to refuse the evil and choose the good.
16 "For before the Child shall know to refuse the evil and choose the good, the land that you dread will be forsaken by both her kings.
17 "The LORD will bring the king of Assyria upon you and your people and your father's house—days that have not come since the day that Ē′phra·im departed from Judah."

18 And it shall come to pass in that day
　That the LORD will whistle for the
　　fly
　That *is* in the farthest part of the
　　rivers of Egypt,
　And for the bee that *is* in the land
　　of Assyria.
19 They will come, and all of them
　　will rest
　In the desolate valleys and in the
　　clefts of the rocks,
　And on all thorns and in all
　　pastures.

20 In the same day the Lord will
　　shave with a hired razor,
　With those from beyond the
　　River,*a* with the king of
　　Assyria,
　The head and the hair of the legs,
　And will also remove the beard.

21 It shall be in that day
　That a man will keep alive a
　　young cow and two sheep;
22 So it shall be, from the abundance
　　of milk they give,
　That he will eat curds;
　For curds and honey everyone
　　will eat who is left in the land.

23 It shall happen in that day,
　That wherever there could be a
　　thousand vines
　Worth a thousand *shekels* of
　　silver,
　It will be for briers and thorns.
24 With arrows and bows men will
　　come there,
　Because all the land will become
　　briers and thorns.

25 And to any hill which could be
　　dug with the hoe,
　You will not go there for fear of
　　briers and thorns;

7:14 *a*Literally *God-With-Us*　　7:20 *a*That is, the Euphrates

But it will become a range for
  oxen
And a place for sheep to roam.

ASSYRIA WILL INVADE THE LAND

8 Moreover the LORD said to me,
"Take a large scroll, and write on it
with a man's pen concerning Mā′her-
Shal′al-Hash-Baz.*a*
2   "And I will take for Myself faithful witnesses to record, Ū·rī′ah the
priest and Zech·a·rī′ah the son of
Je·ber·e·chī′ah."
3   Then I went to the prophetess,
and she conceived and bore a son.
Then the LORD said to me, "Call his
name Mā′her-Shal′al-Hash-Baz;
4   "for before the child shall have
knowledge to cry 'My father' and 'My
mother,' the riches of Damascus and
the spoil of Samaria will be taken
away before the king of Assyria."
5   The LORD also spoke to me again,
saying:

6   "Inasmuch as these people
    refused
  The waters of Shī·lō′ah that flow
    softly,
  And rejoice in Rē′zin and in
    Rem·a·lī′ah's son;
7   Now therefore, behold, the Lord
    brings up over them
  The waters of the River,*a* strong
    and mighty—
  The king of Assyria and all his
    glory;
  He will go up over all his
    channels
  And go over all his banks.
8   He will pass through Judah,
  He will overflow and pass over,
  He will reach up to the neck;
  And the stretching out of his
    wings
  Will fill the breadth of Your land,
    O Im·man′u·el.*a*

9   "Be shattered, O you peoples, and
    be broken in pieces!
  Give ear, all you from far
    countries.
  Gird yourselves, but be broken in
    pieces;
  Gird yourselves, but be broken in
    pieces.
10   Take counsel together, but it will
    come to nothing;
  Speak the word, but it will not
    stand,
  For God *is* with us."*a*

FEAR GOD, HEED HIS WORD

11   For the LORD spoke thus to me
with a strong hand, and instructed
me that I should not walk in the way
of this people, saying:

12 "Do not say, 'A conspiracy,'
  Concerning all that this people
    call a conspiracy,
  Nor be afraid of their threats, nor
    be troubled.
13   The LORD of hosts, Him you shall
    hallow;
  Let Him *be* your fear,
  And *let* Him *be* your dread.
14   He will be as a sanctuary,
  But a stone of stumbling and a
    rock of offense
  To both the houses of Israel,
  As a trap and a snare to the
    inhabitants of Jerusalem.
15   And many among them shall
    stumble;
  They shall fall and be broken,
  Be snared and taken."

16   Bind up the testimony,
  Seal the law among my
    disciples.
17   And I will wait on the LORD,

8:1 *a*Literally *Speed the Spoil, Hasten the Booty*
8:7 *a*That is, the Euphrates   8:8 *a*Literally *God-*
With-Us   8:10 *a*Hebrew *Immanuel*

Who hides His face from the
  house of Jacob;
And I will hope in Him.
18 Here am I and the children whom
  the LORD has given me!
We are for signs and wonders in
  Israel
From the LORD of hosts,
Who dwells in Mount Zion.

19 And when they say to you, "Seek those who are mediums and wizards, who whisper and mutter," should not a people seek their God? *Should they seek* the dead on behalf of the living?
20 To the law and to the testimony! If they do not speak according to this word, *it is* because *there is* no light in them.
21 They will pass through it hard-pressed and hungry; and it shall happen, when they are hungry, that they will be enraged and curse their king and their God, and look upward.
22 Then they will look to the earth, and see trouble and darkness, gloom of anguish; and *they will be* driven into darkness.

THE GOVERNMENT OF THE PROMISED SON

9 Nevertheless the gloom *will* not
  be upon her who *is* distressed,
As when at first He lightly
  esteemed
The land of Zeb′ū·lun and the
  land of Naph′ta·lī,
And afterward more heavily
  oppressed *her,*
By the way of the sea, beyond the
  Jordan,
In Galilee of the Gentiles.
2 The people who walked in
  darkness
Have seen a great light;
Those who dwelt in the land of
  the shadow of death,
Upon them a light has shined.

3 You have multiplied the nation
And increased its joy;[a]
They rejoice before You
According to the joy of harvest,
As *men* rejoice when they divide
  the spoil.
4 For You have broken the yoke of
  his burden
And the staff of his shoulder,
The rod of his oppressor,
As in the day of Mid′i·an.
5 For every warrior's sandal from
  the noisy battle,
And garments rolled in blood,
Will be used for burning *and* fuel
  of fire.

6 For unto us a Child is born,
Unto us a Son is given;
And the government will be upon
  His shoulder.
And His name will be called
Wonderful, Counselor, Mighty
  God,
Everlasting Father, Prince of
  Peace.
7 Of the increase of *His* government
  and peace
There will be no end,
Upon the throne of David and
  over His kingdom,
To order it and establish it with
  judgment and justice
From that time forward, even
  forever.
The zeal of the LORD of hosts will
  perform this.

THE PUNISHMENT OF SAMARIA

8 The Lord sent a word against
  Jacob,
And it has fallen on Israel.
9 All the people will know—
Ē′phra·im and the inhabitant of
  Samaria—

9:3 [a]Following Qere and Targum; Kethib and Vulgate read *not increased joy;* Septuagint reads *Most of the people You brought down in Your joy.*

Who say in pride and arrogance of
heart:

10 "The bricks have fallen down,
But we will rebuild with hewn
stones;
The sycamores are cut down,
But we will replace *them* with
cedars."

11 Therefore the LORD shall set up
The adversaries of Rē′zin against
him,
And spur his enemies on,

12 The Syrians before and the
Phi·lis′tines behind;
And they shall devour Israel with
an open mouth.

For all this His anger is not
turned away,
But His hand *is* stretched out
still.

13 For the people do not turn to Him
who strikes them,
Nor do they seek the LORD of
hosts.

14 Therefore the LORD will cut off
head and tail from Israel,
Palm branch and bulrush in one
day.

15 The elder and honorable, he *is* the
head;
The prophet who teaches lies, he
is the tail.

16 For the leaders of this people
cause *them* to err,
And *those who are* led by them
are destroyed.

17 Therefore the Lord will have no
joy in their young men,
Nor have mercy on their
fatherless and widows;
For everyone *is* a hypocrite and
an evildoer,
And every mouth speaks folly.

For all this His anger is not
turned away,

But His hand *is* stretched out
still.

18 For wickedness burns as the fire;
It shall devour the briers and
thorns,
And kindle in the thickets of the
forest;
They shall mount up *like* rising
smoke.

19 Through the wrath of the LORD of
hosts
The land is burned up,
And the people shall be as fuel for
the fire;
No man shall spare his brother.

20 And he shall snatch on the right
hand
And be hungry;
He shall devour on the left hand
And not be satisfied;
Every man shall eat the flesh of
his own arm.

21 Ma·nas′seh *shall devour*
Ē′phra·im, and Ē′phra·im
Ma·nas′seh;
Together they *shall be* against
Judah.

For all this His anger is not
turned away,
But His hand *is* stretched out
still.

10 "Woe to those who decree
unrighteous decrees,
Who write misfortune,
Which they have prescribed

2 To rob the needy of justice,
And to take what is right from
the poor of My people,
That widows may be their prey,
And *that* they may rob the
fatherless.

3 What will you do in the day of
punishment,
And in the desolation *which* will
come from afar?
To whom will you flee for help?

And where will you leave your
glory?

4 Without Me they shall bow down
among the prisoners,
And they shall fall among the
slain."

For all this His anger is not
turned away,
But His hand is stretched out
still.

ARROGANT ASSYRIA ALSO JUDGED

5 "Woe to Assyria, the rod of My
anger
And the staff in whose hand is My
indignation.
6 I will send him against an
ungodly nation,
And against the people of My
wrath
I will give him charge,
To seize the spoil, to take the
prey,
And to tread them down like the
mire of the streets.
7 Yet he does not mean so,
Nor does his heart think so;
But it is in his heart to destroy,
And cut off not a few nations.
8 For he says,
'Are not my princes altogether
kings?
9 Is not Cal'nō like Car'chem·ish?
Is not Hā'math like Ar'pad?
Is not Samaria like Damascus?
10 As my hand has found the
kingdoms of the idols,
Whose carved images excelled
those of Jerusalem and
Samaria,
11 As I have done to Samaria and
her idols,
Shall I not do also to Jerusalem
and her idols?' "

12 Therefore it shall come to pass,
when the Lord has performed all His

work on Mount Zion and on Jerusalem, that He will say, "I will punish
the fruit of the arrogant heart of the
king of Assyria, and the glory of his
haughty looks."
13 For he says:

"By the strength of my hand I
have done it,
And by my wisdom, for I am
prudent;
Also I have removed the
boundaries of the people,
And have robbed their treasuries;
So I have put down the
inhabitants like a valiant man.
14 My hand has found like a nest the
riches of the people,
And as one gathers eggs that are
left,
I have gathered all the earth;
And there was no one who moved
his wing,
Nor opened his mouth with even
a peep."

15 Shall the ax boast itself against
him who chops with it?
Or shall the saw exalt itself
against him who saws with it?
As if a rod could wield itself
against those who lift it up,
Or as if a staff could lift up, as if
it were not wood!
16 Therefore the Lord, the Lorda of
hosts,
Will send leanness among his fat
ones;
And under his glory
He will kindle a burning
Like the burning of a fire.
17 So the Light of Israel will be for a
fire,
And his Holy One for a flame;
It will burn and devour
His thorns and his briers in one
day.

10:16 aFollowing Bomberg; Masoretic Text and
Dead Sea Scrolls read YHWH (the Lord).

18 And it will consume the glory of
    his forest and of his fruitful
    field,
    Both soul and body;
    And they will be as when a sick
    man wastes away.
19 Then the rest of the trees of his
    forest
    Will be so few in number
    That a child may write them.

The Returning Remnant of Israel

20 And it shall come to pass in that
    day
    That the remnant of Israel,
    And such as have escaped of the
    house of Jacob,
    Will never again depend on him
    who defeated them,
    But will depend on the LORD, the
    Holy One of Israel, in truth.
21 The remnant will return, the
    remnant of Jacob,
    To the Mighty God.
22 For though your people, O Israel,
    be as the sand of the sea,
    A remnant of them will return;
    The destruction decreed shall
    overflow with righteousness.
23 For the Lord GOD of hosts
    Will make a determined end
    In the midst of all the land.

24 Therefore thus says the Lord GOD
of hosts: "O My people, who dwell in
Zion, do not be afraid of the Assyrian.
He shall strike you with a rod and lift
up his staff against you, in the manner of Egypt.
25 "For yet a very little while and
the indignation will cease, as will My
anger in their destruction."
26 And the LORD of hosts will stir up
a scourge for him like the slaughter
of Mid′i·an at the rock of Or′eb; *as*
His rod was on the sea, so will He lift
it up in the manner of Egypt.

27 It shall come to pass in that day
    That his burden will be taken
    away from your shoulder,
    And his yoke from your neck,
    And the yoke will be destroyed
    because of the anointing oil.

28 He has come to Ai′ath,
    He has passed Mig′ron;
    At Mich′mash he has attended to
    his equipment.
29 They have gone along the ridge,
    They have taken up lodging at
    Gē′ba.
    Rā′mah is afraid,
    Gib′ē·ah of Saul has fled.
30 Lift up your voice,
    O daughter of Gal′lim!
    Cause it to be heard as far as
    Lā′ish—
    O poor An′a·thoth!*a*
31 Mad·mē′nah has fled,
    The inhabitants of Gē′bim seek
    refuge.
32 As yet he will remain at Nob that
    day;
    He will shake his fist at the
    mount of the daughter of Zion,
    The hill of Jerusalem.

33 Behold, the Lord,
    The LORD of hosts,
    Will lop off the bough with terror;
    Those of high stature *will be*
    hewn down,
    And the haughty will be humbled.
34 He will cut down the thickets of
    the forest with iron,
    And Lebanon will fall by the
    Mighty One.

The Reign of Jesse's Offspring

11 There shall come forth a Rod
    from the stem of Jesse,

10:30 *a*Following Masoretic Text, Targum, and Vulgate; Septuagint and Syriac read *Listen to her,*
O Anathoth.

And a Branch shall grow out of
his roots.
2 The Spirit of the LORD shall rest
upon Him,
The Spirit of wisdom and
understanding,
The Spirit of counsel and might,
The Spirit of knowledge and of
the fear of the LORD.

3 His delight *is* in the fear of the
LORD,
And He shall not judge by the
sight of His eyes,
Nor decide by the hearing of His
ears;
4 But with righteousness He shall
judge the poor,
And decide with equity for the
meek of the earth;
He shall strike the earth with the
rod of His mouth,
And with the breath of His lips
He shall slay the wicked.
5 Righteousness shall be the belt of
His loins,
And faithfulness the belt of His
waist.

6 "The wolf also shall dwell with the
lamb,
The leopard shall lie down with
the young goat,
The calf and the young lion and
the fatling together;
And a little child shall lead
them.
7 The cow and the bear shall
graze;
Their young ones shall lie down
together;
And the lion shall eat straw like
the ox.
8 The nursing child shall play by
the cobra's hole,
And the weaned child shall put
his hand in the viper's den.
9 They shall not hurt nor destroy in
all My holy mountain,

For the earth shall be full of the
knowledge of the LORD
As the waters cover the sea.

10 "And in that day there shall be a
Root of Jesse,
Who shall stand as a banner to
the people;
For the Gentiles shall seek Him,
And His resting place shall be
glorious."

11 It shall come to pass in that
day
That the Lord shall set His hand
again the second time
To recover the remnant of His
people who are left,
From Assyria and Egypt,
From Path'ros and Cush,
From Ē'lam and Shī'nar,
From Hā'math and the islands of
the sea.

12 He will set up a banner for the
nations,
And will assemble the outcasts of
Israel,
And gather together the
dispersed of Judah
From the four corners of the
earth.
13 Also the envy of Ē'phra·im shall
depart,
And the adversaries of Judah
shall be cut off;
Ē'phra·im shall not envy Judah,
And Judah shall not harass
Ē'phra·im.
14 But they shall fly down upon the
shoulder of the Phi·lis'tines
toward the west;
Together they shall plunder the
people of the East;
They shall lay their hand on
Ē'dom and Mō'ab;
And the people of Am'mon shall
obey them.

15 The LORD will utterly destroy*a*
    the tongue of the Sea of Egypt;
With His mighty wind He will
    shake His fist over the River,*b*
And strike it in the seven
    streams,
And make *men* cross over
    dry-shod.
16 There will be a highway for the
    remnant of His people
Who will be left from Assyria,
As it was for Israel
In the day that he came up from
    the land of Egypt.

A HYMN OF PRAISE

12 And in that day you will say:

"O LORD, I will praise You;
    Though You were angry with me,
Your anger is turned away, and
    You comfort me.
2 Behold, God *is* my salvation,
I will trust and not be afraid;
'For YAH, the LORD, *is* my strength
    and song;
He also has become my
    salvation.' "*a*

3 Therefore with joy you will draw
    water
From the wells of salvation.

4 And in that day you will say:

"Praise the LORD, call upon His
    name;
Declare His deeds among the
    peoples,
Make mention that His name is
    exalted.
5 Sing to the LORD,
For He has done excellent things;
This *is* known in all the earth.
6 Cry out and shout, O inhabitant
    of Zion,
For great *is* the Holy One of
    Israel in your midst!"

PROCLAMATION AGAINST BABYLON

13 The burden against Babylon
which Ī·sāi′ah the son of Ā′moz saw.

2 "Lift up a banner on the high
    mountain,
Raise your voice to them;
Wave your hand, that they may
    enter the gates of the nobles.
3 I have commanded My sanctified
    ones;
I have also called My mighty ones
    for My anger—
Those who rejoice in My
    exaltation."

4 The noise of a multitude in the
    mountains,
Like that of many people!
A tumultuous noise of the
    kingdoms of nations gathered
    together!
The LORD of hosts musters
The army for battle.
5 They come from a far country,
From the end of heaven—
The LORD and His weapons of
    indignation,
To destroy the whole land.

6 Wail, for the day of the LORD *is* at
    hand!
It will come as destruction from
    the Almighty.
7 Therefore all hands will be limp,
Every man's heart will melt,
8 And they will be afraid.
Pangs and sorrows will take hold
    of *them;*
They will be in pain as a woman
    in childbirth;
They will be amazed at one
    another;
Their faces *will be like* flames.

11:15 *a*Following Masoretic Text and Vulgate; Septuagint, Syriac, and Targum read *dry up.*   *b*That
is, the Euphrates   12:2 *a*Exodus 15:2

Favorite Family Verses

I WILL TRUST AND NOT BE AFRAID.   Isaiah 12:2

God is Here!

Lightning flashes. Thunder rolls. Jason is afraid. Should he be afraid?

1. Who makes the thunder and lightning?
2. Who made you?
3. Is God there with Jason? Is He with you when you are afraid of something?
4. Is God bigger and stronger than all the thunder and lightning? Can He protect you from them? Ask Him to take care of you. Ask Him to keep you from being afraid.

For more on *Favorite Family Verses* turn to page 1092
For more on *God's Care* turn to page 1094

9 Behold, the day of the Lord
comes,
  Cruel, with both wrath and fierce
anger,
  To lay the land desolate;
  And He will destroy its sinners
from it.
10 For the stars of heaven and their
constellations
  Will not give their light;
  The sun will be darkened in its
going forth,
  And the moon will not cause its
light to shine.

11 "I will punish the world for *its* evil,
  And the wicked for their iniquity;
  I will halt the arrogance of the
proud,
  And will lay low the haughtiness
of the terrible.
12 I will make a mortal more rare
than fine gold,
  A man more than the golden
wedge of Ō′phir.
13 Therefore I will shake the
heavens,
  And the earth will move out of
her place,
  In the wrath of the Lord of hosts
  And in the day of His fierce anger.
14 It shall be as the hunted gazelle,
  And as a sheep that no man takes
up;
  Every man will turn to his own
people,
  And everyone will flee to his own
land.
15 Everyone who is found will be
thrust through,
  And everyone who is captured
will fall by the sword.
16 Their children also will be dashed
to pieces before their eyes;
  Their houses will be plundered
  And their wives ravished.

17 "Behold, I will stir up the Mēdes
against them,

Who will not regard silver;
  And *as for* gold, they will not
delight in it.
18 Also *their* bows will dash the
young men to pieces,
  And they will have no pity on the
fruit of the womb;
  Their eye will not spare children.
19 And Babylon, the glory of
kingdoms,
  The beauty of the Chal·dē′ans′
pride,
  Will be as when God overthrew
Sod′om and Go·mor′rah.
20 It will never be inhabited,
  Nor will it be settled from
generation to generation;
  Nor will the Arabian pitch tents
there,
  Nor will the shepherds make
their sheepfolds there.
21 But wild beasts of the desert will
lie there,
  And their houses will be full of
owls;
  Ostriches will dwell there,
  And wild goats will caper there.
22 The hyenas will howl in their
citadels,
  And jackals in their pleasant
palaces.
  Her time *is* near to come,
  And her days will not be
prolonged."

Mercy on Jacob

14 For the Lord will have mercy
on Jacob, and will still choose Israel,
and settle them in their own land.
The strangers will be joined with
them, and they will cling to the house
of Jacob.
2   Then people will take them and
bring them to their place, and the
house of Israel will possess them for
servants and maids in the land of the
Lord; they will take them captive

whose captives they were, and rule over their oppressors.

FALL OF THE KING OF BABYLON

3 It shall come to pass in the day the LORD gives you rest from your sorrow, and from your fear and the hard bondage in which you were made to serve, 4 that you will take up this proverb against the king of Babylon, and say:

"How the oppressor has ceased,
The golden*a* city ceased!
5 The LORD has broken the staff of
the wicked,
The scepter of the rulers;
6 He who struck the people in
wrath with a continual stroke,
He who ruled the nations in
anger,
Is persecuted *and* no one
hinders.
7 The whole earth is at rest *and*
quiet;
They break forth into singing.
8 Indeed the cypress trees rejoice
over you,
And the cedars of Lebanon,
Saying, 'Since you were cut down,
No woodsman has come up
against us.'

9 "Hell from beneath is excited
about you,
To meet *you* at your coming;
It stirs up the dead for you,
All the chief ones of the earth;
It has raised up from their
thrones
All the kings of the nations.
10 They all shall speak and say to
you:
'Have you also become as weak as
we?
Have you become like us?
11 Your pomp is brought down to
Shē´ōl,

And the sound of your stringed
instruments;
The maggot is spread under you,
And worms cover you.'

THE FALL OF LUCIFER

12 "How you are fallen from heaven,
O Lū´ci·fer,*a* son of the morning!
How you are cut down to the
ground,
You who weakened the nations!
13 For you have said in your heart:
'I will ascend into heaven,
I will exalt my throne above the
stars of God;
I will also sit on the mount of the
congregation
On the farthest sides of the north;
14 I will ascend above the heights of
the clouds,
I will be like the Most High.'
15 Yet you shall be brought down to
Shē´ōl,
To the lowest depths of the Pit.

16 "Those who see you will gaze at
you,
And consider you, *saying*:
'*Is* this the man who made the
earth tremble,
Who shook kingdoms,
17 Who made the world as a
wilderness
And destroyed its cities,
Who did not open the house of his
prisoners?'

18 "All the kings of the nations,
All of them, sleep in glory,
Everyone in his own house;
19 But you are cast out of your grave
Like an abominable branch,
Like the garment of those who are
slain,
Thrust through with a sword,

14:4 *a*Or *insolent*   14:12 *a*Literally *Day Star*

Who go down to the stones of the
   pit,
Like a corpse trodden underfoot.
20 You will not be joined with them
      in burial,
   Because you have destroyed your
      land
   And slain your people.
   The brood of evildoers shall never
      be named.
21 Prepare slaughter for his children
   Because of the iniquity of their
      fathers,
   Lest they rise up and possess the
      land,
   And fill the face of the world with
      cities."

BABYLON DESTROYED

22 "For I will rise up against them,"
      says the LORD of hosts,
   "And cut off from Babylon the
      name and remnant,
   And offspring and posterity," says
      the LORD.

23 "I will also make it a possession
      for the porcupine,
   And marshes of muddy water;
   I will sweep it with the broom of
      destruction," says the LORD of
      hosts.

ASSYRIA DESTROYED

24 The LORD of hosts has sworn,
      saying,
   "Surely, as I have thought, so it
      shall come to pass,
   And as I have purposed, *so it*
      shall stand:
25 That I will break the Assyrian in
      My land,
   And on My mountains tread him
      underfoot.
   Then his yoke shall be removed
      from them,
   And his burden removed from
      their shoulders.
26 This *is* the purpose that is
      purposed against the whole
      earth,

And this *is* the hand that is
stretched out over all the
nations.

27 For the LORD of hosts has
purposed,
And who will annul *it?*
His hand *is* stretched out,
And who will turn it back?"

PHILISTIA DESTROYED

28 This is the burden which came in
the year that King Ā´haz died.

29 "Do not rejoice, all you of
Phi·lis´ti·a,
Because the rod that struck you is
broken;
For out of the serpent's roots will
come forth a viper,
And its offspring *will be* a fiery
flying serpent.

30 The firstborn of the poor will feed,
And the needy will lie down in
safety;
I will kill your roots with famine,
And it will slay your remnant.

31 Wail, O gate! Cry, O city!
All you of Phi·lis´ti·a *are*
dissolved;
For smoke will come from the
north,
And no one *will be* alone in his
appointed times."

32 What will they answer the
messengers of the nation?
That the LORD has founded Zion,
And the poor of His people shall
take refuge in it.

PROCLAMATION AGAINST MOAB

15 The burden against Mō´ab.

Because in the night Ar of Mō´ab
is laid waste
And destroyed,

Because in the night Kir of Mō´ab
is laid waste
And destroyed,

2 He has gone up to the temple*a*
and Di´bon,
To the high places to weep.
Mō´ab will wail over Nē´bō and
over Med´e·ba;
On all their heads *will be*
baldness,
And every beard cut off.

3 In their streets they will clothe
themselves with sackcloth;
On the tops of their houses
And in their streets
Everyone will wail, weeping
bitterly.

4 Hesh´bon and Ē·le·ā´leh will cry
out,
Their voice shall be heard as far
as Jā´haz;
Therefore the armed soldiers*a* of
Mō´ab will cry out;
His life will be burdensome to
him.

5 "My heart will cry out for Mō´ab;
His fugitives *shall flee* to Zō´ar,
Like a three-year-old heifer.*a*
For by the Ascent of Lū´hith
They will go up with weeping;
For in the way of Hor·ō·nā´im
They will raise up a cry of
destruction,

6 For the waters of Nim´rim will be
desolate,
For the green grass has withered
away;
The grass fails, there is nothing
green.

7 Therefore the abundance they
have gained,
And what they have laid up,
They will carry away to the Brook
of the Willows.

15:2 *a*Hebrew *bayith*, literally *house*
15:4 *a*Following Masoretic Text, Targum, and Vulgate; Septuagint and Syriac read *loins.*
15:5 *a*Or *The Third Eglath,* an unknown city (compare Jeremiah 48:34)

8 For the cry has gone all around
  　　the borders of Mō′ab,
  Its wailing to Eg·lā′im
  And its wailing to Bē′er Ē′lim.
9 For the waters of Dī′mon[a] will be
  　　full of blood;
  Because I will bring more upon
  　　Dī′mon,[b]
  Lions upon him who escapes from
  　　Mō′ab,
  And on the remnant of the
  　　land."

MOAB DESTROYED

16 Send the lamb to the ruler of
  　　the land,
  From Sē′la to the wilderness,
  To the mount of the daughter of
  　　Zion.
2 For it shall be as a wandering
  　　bird thrown out of the nest;
  So shall be the daughters of
  　　Mō′ab at the fords of the
  　　Ar′non.

3 "Take counsel, execute judgment;
  Make your shadow like the night
  　　in the middle of the day;
  Hide the outcasts,
  Do not betray him who escapes.
4 Let My outcasts dwell with you,
  　　O Mō′ab;
  Be a shelter to them from the face
  　　of the spoiler.
  For the extortioner is at an end,
  Devastation ceases,
  The oppressors are consumed out
  　　of the land.
5 In mercy the throne will be
  　　established;
  And One will sit on it in truth, in
  　　the tabernacle of David,
  Judging and seeking justice and
  　　hastening righteousness."

6 We have heard of the pride of
  　　Mō′ab—
  He is very proud—

Of his haughtiness and his pride
  　　and his wrath;
But his lies *shall* not *be* so.
7 Therefore Mō′ab shall wail for
  　　Mō′ab;
  Everyone shall wail.
  For the foundations of Kir
  　　Har′e·seth you shall mourn;
  Surely *they are* stricken.

8 For the fields of Hesh′bon
  　　languish,
  And the vine of Sib′mah;
  The lords of the nations have
  　　broken down its choice plants,
  Which have reached to Jā′zer
  And wandered through the
  　　wilderness.
  Her branches are stretched out,
  They are gone over the sea.
9 Therefore I will bewail the vine of
  　　Sib′mah,
  With the weeping of Jā′zer;
  I will drench you with my tears,
  O Hesh′bon and Ē·le·ā′leh;
  For battle cries have fallen
  Over your summer fruits and
  　　your harvest.

10 Gladness is taken away,
  And joy from the plentiful field;
  In the vineyards there will be no
  　　singing,
  Nor will there be shouting;
  No treaders will tread out wine in
  　　the presses;
  I have made their shouting cease.
11 Therefore my heart shall resound
  　　like a harp for Mō′ab,
  And my inner being for Kir
  　　Hē′res.

12 And it shall come to pass,
  When it is seen that Mō′ab is
  　　weary on the high place,

15:9 [a]Following Masoretic Text and Targum; Dead
Sea Scrolls and Vulgate read *Dibon;* Septuagint
reads *Rimon.* [b]Following Masoretic Text and Targum; Dead Sea Scrolls and Vulgate read *Dibon;*
Septuagint reads *Rimon.*

That he will come to his
    sanctuary to pray;
But he will not prevail.

13 This *is* the word which the LORD
has spoken concerning Mō′ab since
that time.
14 But now the LORD has spoken,
saying, "Within three years, as the
years of a hired man, the glory of
Mō′ab will be despised with all that
great multitude, and the remnant
will be very small *and* feeble."

PROCLAMATION AGAINST SYRIA
AND ISRAEL

17 The burden against Damascus.

"Behold, Damascus will cease from
    being a city,
And it will be a ruinous heap.
2   The cities of A·rō′er *are*
       forsaken;*a*
    They will be for flocks
    Which lie down, and no one will
       make *them* afraid.
3   The fortress also will cease from
       Ē′phra·im,
    The kingdom from Damascus,
    And the remnant of Syria;
    They will be as the glory of the
       children of Israel,"
    Says the LORD of hosts.

4   "In that day it shall come to pass
    That the glory of Jacob will wane,
    And the fatness of his flesh grow
       lean.
5   It shall be as when the harvester
       gathers the grain,
    And reaps the heads with his
       arm;
    It shall be as he who gathers
       heads of grain
    In the Valley of Reph′a·im.
6   Yet gleaning grapes will be left in
       it,
    Like the shaking of an olive tree,

Two *or* three olives at the top of
    the uppermost bough,
Four *or* five in its most fruitful
    branches,"
Says the LORD God of Israel.

7   In that day a man will look to his
       Maker,
    And his eyes will have respect for
       the Holy One of Israel.
8   He will not look to the altars,
    The work of his hands;
    He will not respect what his
       fingers have made,
    Nor the wooden images*a* nor the
       incense altars.

9   In that day his strong cities will
       be as a forsaken bough*a*
    And an uppermost branch,*b*
    Which they left because of the
       children of Israel;
    And there will be desolation.

10   Because you have forgotten the
       God of your salvation,
    And have not been mindful of the
       Rock of your stronghold,
    Therefore you will plant pleasant
       plants
    And set out foreign seedlings;
11   In the day you will make your
       plant to grow,
    And in the morning you will make
       your seed to flourish;
    But the harvest *will be* a heap of
       ruins
    In the day of grief and desperate
       sorrow.

12   Woe to the multitude of many
       people

17:2 *a*Following Masoretic Text and Vulgate; Septuagint reads *It shall be forsaken forever;* Targum
reads *Its cities shall be forsaken and desolate.*
17:8 *a*Hebrew *Asherim,* Canaanite deities
17:9 *a*Septuagint reads *Hivites;* Targum reads *laid
waste;* Vulgate reads *as the plows.* *b*Septuagint
reads *Amorites;* Targum reads *in ruins;* Vulgate
reads *corn.*

Who make a noise like the roar of
the seas,
And to the rushing of nations
That make a rushing like the
rushing of mighty waters!
13 The nations will rush like the
rushing of many waters;
But *God* will rebuke them and
they will flee far away,
And be chased like the chaff of
the mountains before the wind,
Like a rolling thing before the
whirlwind.
14 Then behold, at eventide, trouble!
And before the morning, he *is* no
more.
This *is* the portion of those who
plunder us,
And the lot of those who rob us.

PROCLAMATION AGAINST ETHIOPIA

18 Woe to the land shadowed
with buzzing wings,
Which *is* beyond the rivers of
Ethiopia,
2 Which sends ambassadors by sea,
Even in vessels of reed on the
waters, *saying,*
"Go, swift messengers, to a nation
tall and smooth *of* skin,
To a people terrible from their
beginning onward,
A nation powerful and treading
down,
Whose land the rivers divide."

3 All inhabitants of the world and
dwellers on the earth:
When he lifts up a banner on the
mountains, you see *it;*
And when he blows a trumpet,
you hear *it.*
4 For so the LORD said to me,
"I will take My rest,
And I will look from My dwelling
place
Like clear heat in sunshine,

Like a cloud of dew in the heat of
harvest."
5 For before the harvest, when the
bud is perfect
And the sour grape is ripening in
the flower,
He will both cut off the sprigs
with pruning hooks
And take away *and* cut down the
branches.
6 They will be left together for the
mountain birds of prey
And for the beasts of the earth;
The birds of prey will summer on
them,
And all the beasts of the earth
will winter on them.

7 In that time a present will be
brought to the LORD of hosts
From^a a people tall and smooth *of
skin,*
And from a people terrible from
their beginning onward,
A nation powerful and treading
down,
Whose land the rivers divide—
To the place of the name of the
LORD of hosts,
To Mount Zion.

PROCLAMATION AGAINST EGYPT

19 The burden against Egypt.

Behold, the LORD rides on a swift
cloud,
And will come into Egypt;
The idols of Egypt will totter at
His presence,
And the heart of Egypt will melt
in its midst.

2 "I will set Egyptians against
Egyptians;

18:7 ^aFollowing Dead Sea Scrolls, Septuagint, and
Vulgate; Masoretic Text omits *From;* Targum reads
To.

Everyone will fight against his
brother,
And everyone against his
neighbor,
City against city, kingdom against
kingdom.

3 The spirit of Egypt will fail in its
midst;
I will destroy their counsel,
And they will consult the idols
and the charmers,
The mediums and the sorcerers.

4 And the Egyptians I will give
Into the hand of a cruel master,
And a fierce king will rule over
them,"
Says the Lord, the LORD of hosts.

5 The waters will fail from the sea,
And the river will be wasted and
dried up.

6 The rivers will turn foul;
The brooks of defense will be
emptied and dried up;
The reeds and rushes will wither.

7 The papyrus reeds by the River,
by the mouth of the River,
And everything sown by the
River,a
Will wither, be driven away, and
be no more.

8 The fishermen also will mourn;
All those will lament who cast
hooks into the River,
And they will languish who
spread nets on the waters.

9 Moreover those who work in fine
flax
And those who weave fine fabric
will be ashamed;

10 And its foundations will be
broken.
All who make wages will be
troubled of soul.

11 Surely the princes of Zō′an are
fools;
Pharaoh's wise counselors give
foolish counsel.

How do you say to Pharaoh, "I am
the son of the wise,
The son of ancient kings?"

12 Where are they?
Where are your wise men?
Let them tell you now,
And let them know what the
LORD of hosts has purposed
against Egypt.

13 The princes of Zō′an have become
fools;
The princes of Nopha are
deceived;
They have also deluded Egypt,
Those who are the mainstay of its
tribes.

14 The LORD has mingled a perverse
spirit in her midst;
And they have caused Egypt to
err in all her work,
As a drunken man staggers in his
vomit.

15 Neither will there be any work for
Egypt,
Which the head or tail,
Palm branch or bulrush,
may do.a

16 In that day Egypt will be like
women, and will be afraid and fear
because of the waving of the hand of
the LORD of hosts, which He waves
over it.

17 And the land of Judah will be a
terror to Egypt; everyone who makes
mention of it will be afraid in himself, because of the counsel of the
LORD of hosts which He has determined against it.

EGYPT, ASSYRIA, AND ISRAEL BLESSED

18 In that day five cities in the land
of Egypt will speak the language of
Ca′naan and swear by the LORD of

19:7 aThat is, the Nile　　19:13 aThat is, ancient
Memphis　　19:15 aCompare Isaiah 9:14–16

hosts; one will be called the City of Destruction.a

19 In that day there will be an altar to the LORD in the midst of the land of Egypt, and a pillar to the LORD at its border.

20 And it will be for a sign and for a witness to the LORD of hosts in the land of Egypt; for they will cry to the LORD because of the oppressors, and He will send them a Savior and a Mighty One, and He will deliver them.

21 Then the LORD will be known to Egypt, and the Egyptians will know the LORD in that day, and will make sacrifice and offering; yes, they will make a vow to the LORD and perform *it.*

22 And the LORD will strike Egypt, He will strike and heal *it;* they will return to the LORD, and He will be entreated by them and heal them.

23 In that day there will be a highway from Egypt to Assyria, and the Assyrian will come into Egypt and the Egyptian into Assyria, and the Egyptians will serve with the Assyrians.

24 In that day Israel will be one of three with Egypt and Assyria—a blessing in the midst of the land,

25 whom the LORD of hosts shall bless, saying, "Blessed *is* Egypt My people, and Assyria the work of My hands, and Israel My inheritance."

THE SIGN AGAINST EGYPT AND ETHIOPIA

20 In the year that Tartan*a* came to Ash′dod, when Sar′gon the king of Assyria sent him, and he fought against Ash′dod and took it,

2 at the same time the LORD spoke by Ī·sāi′ah the son of Ā′moz, saying, "Go, and remove the sackcloth from your body, and take your sandals off

your feet." And he did so, walking naked and barefoot.

3 Then the LORD said, "Just as My servant Ī·sāi′ah has walked naked and barefoot three years *for* a sign and a wonder against Egypt and Ethiopia,

4 "so shall the king of Assyria lead away the Egyptians as prisoners and the Ethiopians as captives, young and old, naked and barefoot, with their buttocks uncovered, to the shame of Egypt.

5 "Then they shall be afraid and ashamed of Ethiopia their expectation and Egypt their glory.

6 "And the inhabitant of this territory will say in that day, 'Surely such *is* our expectation, wherever we flee for help to be delivered from the king of Assyria; and how shall we escape?' "

THE FALL OF BABYLON PROCLAIMED

21 The burden against the Wilderness of the Sea.

As whirlwinds in the South pass through,
So it comes from the desert, from a terrible land.
2 A distressing vision is declared to me;
The treacherous dealer deals treacherously,
And the plunderer plunders.
Go up, O Ē′lam!
Besiege, O Media!
All its sighing I have made to cease.

3 Therefore my loins are filled with pain;

19:18 *a*Some Hebrew manuscripts, Arabic, Dead Sea Scrolls, Targum, and Vulgate read *Sun;* Septuagint reads *Asedek* (literally *Righteousness*).
20:1 *a*Or *the Commander in Chief*

Pangs have taken hold of me, like
the pangs of a woman in labor.
I was distressed when *I* heard *it;*
I was dismayed when *I* saw *it.*

4 My heart wavered, fearfulness
frightened me;
The night for which I longed He
turned into fear for me.

5 Prepare the table,
Set a watchman in the tower,
Eat and drink.
Arise, you princes,
Anoint the shield!

6 For thus has the Lord said to me:
"Go, set a watchman,
Let him declare what he sees."

7 And he saw a chariot *with* a pair
of horsemen,
A chariot of donkeys, *and* a
chariot of camels,
And he listened earnestly with
great care.

8 Then he cried, "A lion,*a* my Lord!
I stand continually on the
watchtower in the daytime;
I have sat at my post every night.

9 And look, here comes a chariot of
men *with* a pair of horsemen!"
Then he answered and said,
"Babylon is fallen, is fallen!
And all the carved images of her
gods
He has broken to the ground."

10 Oh, my threshing and the grain of
my floor!
That which I have heard from the
LORD of hosts,
The God of Israel,
I have declared to you.

PROCLAMATION AGAINST EDOM

11 The burden against Dū′mah.

He calls to me out of Sē′ir,
"Watchman, what of the night?
Watchman, what of the night?"

12 The watchman said,
"The morning comes, and also the
night.
If you will inquire, inquire;
Return! Come back!"

PROCLAMATION AGAINST ARABIA

13 The burden against Arabia.

In the forest in Arabia you will
lodge,
O you traveling companies of
Ded′an·ites.

14 O inhabitants of the land of
Tē′ma,
Bring water to him who is thirsty;
With their bread they met him
who fled.

15 For they fled from the swords,
from the drawn sword,
From the bent bow, and from the
distress of war.

16 For thus the LORD has said to me:
"Within a year, according to the year
of a hired man, all the glory of Kē′dar
will fail;

17 "and the remainder of the number
of archers, the mighty men of the
people of Kē′dar, will be diminished;
for the LORD God of Israel has spoken
it."

PROCLAMATION AGAINST JERUSALEM

22 The burden against the Valley
of Vision.

What ails you now, that you have
all gone up to the housetops,
2 You who are full of noise,
A tumultuous city, a joyous city?
Your slain *men are* not slain with
the sword,
Nor dead in battle.

21:8 *a*Dead Sea Scrolls read *Then the observer
cried.*

3 All your rulers have fled together;
They are captured by the archers.
All who are found in you are
bound together;
They have fled from afar.
4 Therefore I said, "Look away from
me,
I will weep bitterly;
Do not labor to comfort me
Because of the plundering of the
daughter of my people."

5 For *it is* a day of trouble and
treading down and perplexity
By the Lord GOD of hosts
In the Valley of Vision—
Breaking down the walls
And of crying to the mountain.
6 Ē′lam bore the quiver
With chariots of men *and*
horsemen,
And Kir uncovered the shield.
7 It shall come to pass *that* your
choicest valleys
Shall be full of chariots,
And the horsemen shall set
themselves in array at the
gate.

8 He removed the protection of
Judah.
You looked in that day to the
armor of the House of the
Forest;
9 You also saw the damage to the
city of David,
That it was great;
And you gathered together the
waters of the lower pool.
10 You numbered the houses of
Jerusalem,
And the houses you broke down
To fortify the wall.
11 You also made a reservoir
between the two walls
For the water of the old pool.
But you did not look to its Maker,
Nor did you have respect for Him
who fashioned it long ago.

12 And in that day the Lord GOD of
hosts
Called for weeping and for
mourning,
For baldness and for girding with
sackcloth.
13 But instead, joy and gladness,
Slaying oxen and killing sheep,
Eating meat and drinking
wine:
"Let us eat and drink, for
tomorrow we die!"

14 Then it was revealed in my
hearing by the LORD of hosts,
"Surely for this iniquity there will
be no atonement for you,
Even to your death," says the
Lord GOD of hosts.

THE JUDGMENT ON SHEBNA

15 Thus says the Lord GOD of hosts:

"Go, proceed to this steward,
To Sheb′na, who *is* over the
house, *and say:*
16 'What have you here, and whom
have you here,
That you have hewn a sepulcher
here,
As he who hews himself a
sepulcher on high,
Who carves a tomb for himself in
a rock?
17 Indeed, the LORD will throw you
away violently,
O mighty man,
And will surely seize you.
18 He will surely turn violently and
toss you like a ball
Into a large country;
There you shall die, and there
your glorious chariots
Shall be the shame of your
master's house.
19 So I will drive you out of your
office,

And from your position he will pull you down.*a*

20 'Then it shall be in that day,
That I will call My servant
E·lī′a·kim the son of Hil·kī′ah;
21 I will clothe him with your robe
And strengthen him with your belt;
I will commit your responsibility into his hand.
He shall be a father to the inhabitants of Jerusalem
And to the house of Judah.
22 The key of the house of David
I will lay on his shoulder;
So he shall open, and no one shall shut;
And he shall shut, and no one shall open.
23 I will fasten him *as* a peg in a secure place,
And he will become a glorious throne to his father's house.

24 'They will hang on him all the glory of his father's house, the offspring and the posterity, all vessels of small quantity, from the cups to all the pitchers.
25 'In that day,' says the LORD of hosts, 'the peg that is fastened in the secure place will be removed and be cut down and fall, and the burden that *was* on it will be cut off; for the LORD has spoken.' "

PROCLAMATION AGAINST TYRE

23

The burden against Tyre.

Wail, you ships of Tar′shish!
For it is laid waste,
So that there is no house, no harbor;
From the land of Cyprus*a* it is revealed to them.

2 Be still, you inhabitants of the coastland,
You merchants of Sī′don,
Whom those who cross the sea have filled.*a*
3 And on great waters the grain of Shī′hor,
The harvest of the River,*a* *is* her revenue;
And she is a marketplace for the nations.

4 Be ashamed, O Sī′don;
For the sea has spoken,
The strength of the sea, saying,
"I do not labor, nor bring forth children;
Neither do I rear young men,
Nor bring up virgins."
5 When the report *reaches* Egypt,
They also will be in agony at the report of Tyre.

6 Cross over to Tar′shish;
Wail, you inhabitants of the coastland!
7 *Is* this your joyous *city,*
Whose antiquity *is* from ancient days,
Whose feet carried her far off to dwell?
8 Who has taken this counsel against Tyre, the crowning *city,*
Whose merchants *are* princes,
Whose traders *are* the honorable of the earth?
9 The LORD of hosts has purposed it,
To bring to dishonor the pride of all glory,
To bring into contempt all the honorable of the earth.

22:19 *a*Septuagint omits *he will pull you down;* Syriac, Targum, and Vulgate read *I will pull you down.*   23:1 *a*Hebrew *Kittim,* western lands, especially Cyprus   23:2 *a*Following Masoretic Text and Vulgate; Septuagint and Targum read *Passing over the water;* Dead Sea Scrolls read *Your messengers passing over the sea.*   23:3 *a*That is, the Nile

10 Overflow through your land like
      the River,*a*
   O daughter of Tar′shish;
   There is no more strength.
11 He stretched out His hand over
      the sea,
   He shook the kingdoms;
   The LORD has given a
      commandment against Cā′naan
   To destroy its strongholds.
12 And He said, "You will rejoice no
      more,
   O you oppressed virgin daughter
      of Sī′don.
   Arise, cross over to Cyprus;
   There also you will have no rest."

13 Behold, the land of the
      Chal·dē′ans,
   This people *which* was not;
   Assyria founded it for wild beasts
      of the desert.
   They set up its towers,
   They raised up its palaces,
   And brought it to ruin.

14 Wail, you ships of Tar′shish!
   For your strength is laid waste.

15 Now it shall come to pass in that
day that Tȳre will be forgotten seventy years, according to the days of
one king. At the end of seventy years
it will happen to Tȳre as *in* the song
of the harlot:

16 "Take a harp, go about the city,
   You forgotten harlot;
   Make sweet melody, sing many
      songs,
   That you may be remembered."

17 And it shall be, at the end of seventy years, that the LORD will deal
with Tȳre. She will return to her
hire, and commit fornication with all
the kingdoms of the world on the face
of the earth.
18 Her gain and her pay will be set

apart for the LORD; it will not be treasured nor laid up, for her gain will be
for those who dwell before the LORD,
to eat sufficiently, and for fine clothing.

IMPENDING JUDGMENT ON THE EARTH

24 Behold, the LORD makes the
      earth empty and makes it
      waste,
   Distorts its surface
   And scatters abroad its
      inhabitants.
2 And it shall be:
   As with the people, so with the
      priest;
   As with the servant, so with his
      master;
   As with the maid, so with her
      mistress;
   As with the buyer, so with the
      seller;
   As with the lender, so with the
      borrower;
   As with the creditor, so with the
      debtor.
3 The land shall be entirely
      emptied and utterly plundered,
   For the LORD has spoken this
      word.

4 The earth mourns *and* fades
      away,
   The world languishes *and* fades
      away;
   The haughty people of the earth
      languish.
5 The earth is also defiled under its
      inhabitants,
   Because they have transgressed
      the laws,
   Changed the ordinance,
   Broken the everlasting covenant.
6 Therefore the curse has devoured
      the earth,

23:10 *a*That is, the Nile

And those who dwell in it are
   desolate.
Therefore the inhabitants of the
   earth are burned,
And few men *are* left.

7 The new wine fails, the vine
   languishes,
All the merry-hearted sigh.
8 The mirth of the tambourine
   ceases,
The noise of the jubilant ends,
The joy of the harp ceases.
9 They shall not drink wine with a
   song;
Strong drink is bitter to those
   who drink it.
10 The city of confusion is broken
   down;
Every house is shut up, so that
   none may go in.
11 *There is* a cry for wine in the
   streets,
All joy is darkened,
The mirth of the land is gone.
12 In the city desolation is left,
And the gate is stricken with
   destruction.
13 When it shall be thus in the midst
   of the land among the people,
It shall be like the shaking of an
   olive tree,
Like the gleaning of grapes when
   the vintage is done.

14 They shall lift up their voice, they
   shall sing;
For the majesty of the LORD
They shall cry aloud from the sea.
15 Therefore glorify the LORD in the
   dawning light,
The name of the LORD God of
   Israel in the coastlands of the
   sea.
16 From the ends of the earth we
   have heard songs:
"Glory to the righteous!"
But I said, "I am ruined, ruined!
Woe to me!

The treacherous dealers have
   dealt treacherously,
Indeed, the treacherous dealers
   have dealt very treacherously."

17 Fear and the pit and the snare
Are upon you, O inhabitant of the
   earth.
18 And it shall be
That he who flees from the noise
   of the fear
Shall fall into the pit,
And he who comes up from the
   midst of the pit
Shall be caught in the snare;
For the windows from on high are
   open,
And the foundations of the earth
   are shaken.

19 The earth is violently broken,
The earth is split open,
The earth is shaken exceedingly.
20 The earth shall reel to and fro
   like a drunkard,
And shall totter like a hut;
Its transgression shall be heavy
   upon it,
And it will fall, and not rise
   again.

21 It shall come to pass in that day
That the LORD will punish on
   high the host of exalted ones,
And on the earth the kings of the
   earth.
22 They will be gathered together,
As prisoners are gathered in the
   pit,
And will be shut up in the
   prison;
After many days they will be
   punished.
23 Then the moon will be disgraced
And the sun ashamed;
For the LORD of hosts will reign
On Mount Zion and in Jerusalem
And before His elders,
   gloriously.

Praises

Isaiah 25:1

Why should we praise God? This Bible verse tells us. First, He is our God. We should praise Him for that. He has done wonderful things for us. We should praise Him for that. He has counseled us with wisdom and truth. That certainly should cause us to praise Him.

PRAISE TO GOD

25 O LORD, You *are* my God.
I will exalt You,
I will praise Your name,
For You have done wonderful
    things;
Your counsels of old *are*
    faithfulness *and* truth.

2 For You have made a city a ruin,
A fortified city a ruin,
A palace of foreigners to be a city
    no more;
It will never be rebuilt.

3 Therefore the strong people will
    glorify You;
The city of the terrible nations
    will fear You.

4 For You have been a strength to
    the poor,
A strength to the needy in his
    distress,
A refuge from the storm,
A shade from the heat;
For the blast of the terrible
    ones *is* as a storm *against* the
    wall.

5 You will reduce the noise of
    aliens,
As heat in a dry place;
As heat in the shadow of a
    cloud,
The song of the terrible ones will
    be diminished.

6 And in this mountain
The LORD of hosts will make for
    all people
A feast of choice pieces,
A feast of wines on the lees,
Of fat things full of marrow,
Of well-refined wines on the lees.

7 And He will destroy on this
    mountain
The surface of the covering cast
    over all people,
And the veil that is spread over
    all nations.

8 He will swallow up death forever,
And the Lord GOD will wipe away
    tears from all faces;
The rebuke of His people
He will take away from all the
    earth;
For the LORD has spoken.

9 And it will be said in that day:
"Behold, this *is* our God;
We have waited for Him, and He
    will save us.
This *is* the LORD;
We have waited for Him;
We will be glad and rejoice in His
    salvation."

10 For on this mountain the hand of
    the LORD will rest,
And Mō′ab shall be trampled
    down under Him,
As straw is trampled down for the
    refuse heap.

11 And He will spread out His hands
    in their midst
As a swimmer reaches out to
    swim,
And He will bring down their
    pride
Together with the trickery of their
    hands.

12 The fortress of the high fort of
    your walls
He will bring down, lay low,
And bring to the ground, down to
    the dust.

A Song of Salvation

26 In that day this song will be sung in the land of Judah:

"We have a strong city;
God will appoint salvation *for*
    walls and bulwarks.
2 Open the gates,
That the righteous nation which
    keeps the truth may enter in.

Promises

Isaiah 26:3

What do you think about most of the time? Do you think of things you want? Do you think of TV programs? Do you think of ways to please your friends? Do you spend any time thinking about God? Here's a promise from God. When you think about God, He will give you peace. Today, think about God often. Does He bring more peace to your mind? He will!

---

3 You will keep *him* in perfect
    peace,
Whose mind *is* stayed *on You,*
Because he trusts in You.
4 Trust in the LORD forever,
For in YAH, the LORD, *is*
    everlasting strength.*a*
5 For He brings down those who
    dwell on high,
The lofty city;
He lays it low,
He lays it low to the ground,
He brings it down to the dust.
6 The foot shall tread it down—
The feet of the poor
And the steps of the needy."

7 The way of the just *is*
    uprightness;

O Most Upright,
You weigh the path of the just.
8 Yes, in the way of Your
    judgments,
O LORD, we have waited for You;
The desire of *our* soul *is* for Your
    name
And for the remembrance of You.
9 With my soul I have desired You
    in the night,
Yes, by my spirit within me I will
    seek You early;
For when Your judgments *are* in
    the earth,
The inhabitants of the world will
    learn righteousness.

10 Let grace be shown to the wicked,
Yet he will not learn
    righteousness;
In the land of uprightness he will
    deal unjustly,
And will not behold the majesty of
    the LORD.
11 LORD, *when* Your hand is lifted
    up, they will not see.
But they will see and be ashamed
For *their* envy of people;
Yes, the fire of Your enemies shall
    devour them.

12 LORD, You will establish peace for
    us,
For You have also done all our
    works in us.
13 O LORD our God, masters besides
    You
Have had dominion over us;
But by You only we make mention
    of Your name.
14 *They are* dead, they will not live;
They are deceased, they will not
    rise.
Therefore You have punished and
    destroyed them,
And made all their memory to
    perish.

26:4 *a*Or *Rock of Ages*

15 You have increased the nation,
   O LORD,
   You have increased the nation;
   You are glorified;
   You have expanded all the
   borders of the land.

16 LORD, in trouble they have visited
   You,
   They poured out a prayer *when*
   Your chastening *was* upon
   them.
17 As a woman with child
   Is in pain and cries out in her
   pangs,
   When she draws near the time of
   her delivery,
   So have we been in Your sight,
   O LORD.
18 We have been with child, we have
   been in pain;
   We have, as it were, brought forth
   wind;
   We have not accomplished any
   deliverance in the earth,
   Nor have the inhabitants of the
   world fallen.

19 Your dead shall live;
   Together with my dead body*a* they
   shall arise.
   Awake and sing, you who dwell in
   dust;
   For your dew *is like* the dew of
   herbs,
   And the earth shall cast out the
   dead.

TAKE REFUGE FROM THE
COMING JUDGMENT

20 Come, my people, enter your
   chambers,
   And shut your doors behind you;
   Hide yourself, as it were, for a
   little moment,
   Until the indignation is past.
21 For behold, the LORD comes out of
   His place

To punish the inhabitants of the
earth for their iniquity;
The earth will also disclose her
blood,
And will no more cover her slain.

27 In that day the LORD with His
severe sword, great and
strong,
Will punish Le·vī′a·than the
fleeing serpent,
Le·vī′a·than that twisted serpent;
And He will slay the reptile that
is in the sea.

THE RESTORATION OF ISRAEL

2 In that day sing to her,
   "A vineyard of red wine!*a*
3 I, the LORD, keep it,
   I water it every moment;
   Lest any hurt it,
   I keep it night and day.
4 Fury *is* not in Me.
   Who would set briers *and* thorns
   Against Me in battle?
   I would go through them,
   I would burn them together.
5 Or let him take hold of My
   strength,
   That he may make peace with
   Me;
   And he shall make peace with
   Me."

6 Those who come He shall cause to
   take root in Jacob;
   Israel shall blossom and bud,
   And fill the face of the world with
   fruit.

7 Has He struck Israel as He struck
   those who struck him?

26:19 *a*Following Masoretic Text and Vulgate; Syriac and Targum read *their dead bodies;* Septuagint
reads *those in the tombs.*   27:2 *a*Following Masoretic Text (Kittel's *Biblia Hebraica*), Bomberg, and
Vulgate; Masoretic Text (*Biblia Hebraica Stutt-
gartensia*), some Hebrew manuscripts, and Septuagint read *delight;* Targum reads *choice vineyard.*

Or has He been slain according to
the slaughter of those who were
slain by Him?

8 In measure, by sending it away,
You contended with it.
He removes *it* by His rough wind
In the day of the east wind.

9 Therefore by this the iniquity of
Jacob will be covered;
And this *is* all the fruit of taking
away his sin:
When he makes all the stones of
the altar
Like chalkstones that are beaten
to dust,
Wooden images*a* and incense
altars shall not stand.

10 Yet the fortified city *will be*
desolate,
The habitation forsaken and left
like a wilderness;
There the calf will feed, and there
it will lie down
And consume its branches.

11 When its boughs are withered,
they will be broken off;
The women come *and* set them on
fire.
For it *is* a people of no
understanding;
Therefore He who made them will
not have mercy on them,
And He who formed them will
show them no favor.

12 And it shall come to pass in that
day
That the LORD will thresh,
From the channel of the River*a* to
the Brook of Egypt;
And you will be gathered one by
one,
O you children of Israel.

13 So it shall be in that day:
The great trumpet will be blown;
They will come, who are about to
perish in the land of Assyria,

And they who are outcasts in the
land of Egypt,
And shall worship the LORD in the
holy mount at Jerusalem.

WOE TO EPHRAIM AND JERUSALEM

28 Woe to the crown of pride, to
the drunkards of Ē′phra·im,
Whose glorious beauty *is* a fading
flower
Which *is* at the head of the
verdant valleys,
To those who are overcome with
wine!

2 Behold, the Lord has a mighty
and strong one,
Like a tempest of hail and a
destroying storm,
Like a flood of mighty waters
overflowing,
Who will bring *them* down to the
earth with *His* hand.

3 The crown of pride, the
drunkards of Ē′phra·im,
Will be trampled underfoot;

4 And the glorious beauty is a
fading flower
Which *is* at the head of the
verdant valley,
Like the first fruit before the
summer,
Which an observer sees;
He eats it up while it is still in his
hand.

5 In that day the LORD of hosts will
be
For a crown of glory and a diadem
of beauty
To the remnant of His people,

6 For a spirit of justice to him who
sits in judgment,
And for strength to those who
turn back the battle at the
gate.

27:9 *a*Hebrew *Asherim,* Canaanite deities
27:12 *a*That is, the Euphrates

7 But they also have erred through
wine,
And through intoxicating drink
are out of the way;
The priest and the prophet have
erred through intoxicating
drink,
They are swallowed up by wine,
They are out of the way through
intoxicating drink;
They err in vision, they stumble
in judgment.
8 For all tables are full of vomit
and filth;
No place *is* clean.

9 "Whom will he teach knowledge?
And whom will he make to
understand the message?
Those *just* weaned from milk?
Those *just* drawn from the
breasts?
10 For precept *must be* upon precept,
precept upon precept,
Line upon line, line upon line,
Here a little, there a little."

11 For with stammering lips and
another tongue
He will speak to this people,
12 To whom He said, "This *is* the
rest *with which*
You may cause the weary to rest,"
And, "This *is* the refreshing";
Yet they would not hear.
13 But the word of the LORD was to
them,
"Precept upon precept, precept
upon precept,
Line upon line, line upon line,
Here a little, there a little,"
That they might go and fall
backward, and be broken
And snared and caught.

14 Therefore hear the word of the
LORD, you scornful men,
Who rule this people who *are* in
Jerusalem,

15 Because you have said, "We have
made a covenant with death,
And with Shē′ōl we are in
agreement.
When the overflowing scourge
passes through,
It will not come to us,
For we have made lies our refuge,
And under falsehood we have
hidden ourselves."

A CORNERSTONE IN ZION

16 Therefore thus says the Lord
GOD:

"Behold, I lay in Zion a stone for a
foundation,
A tried stone, a precious
cornerstone, a sure foundation;
Whoever believes will not act
hastily.
17 Also I will make justice the
measuring line,
And righteousness the plummet;
The hail will sweep away the
refuge of lies,
And the waters will overflow the
hiding place.
18 Your covenant with death will be
annulled,
And your agreement with Shē′ōl
will not stand;
When the overflowing scourge
passes through,
Then you will be trampled down
by it.
19 As often as it goes out it will take
you;
For morning by morning it will
pass over,
And by day and by night;
It will be a terror just to
understand the report."

20 For the bed is too short to stretch
out *on,*
And the covering so narrow that
one cannot wrap himself *in it.*

21 For the LORD will rise up as *at*
   Mount Pe·rā′zim,
He will be angry as in the Valley
   of Gib′ē·on—
That He may do His work, His
   awesome work,
And bring to pass His act, His
   unusual act.
22 Now therefore, do not be mockers,
Lest your bonds be made strong;
For I have heard from the Lord
   GOD of hosts,
A destruction determined even
   upon the whole earth.

LISTEN TO THE TEACHING OF GOD

23 Give ear and hear my voice,
Listen and hear my speech.
24 Does the plowman keep plowing
   all day to sow?
Does he keep turning his soil and
   breaking the clods?
25 When he has leveled its surface,
Does he not sow the black
   cummin
And scatter the cummin,
Plant the wheat in rows,
The barley in the appointed place,
And the spelt in its place?
26 For He instructs him in right
   judgment,
His God teaches him.

27 For the black cummin is not
   threshed with a threshing
   sledge,
Nor is a cartwheel rolled over the
   cummin;
But the black cummin is beaten
   out with a stick,
And the cummin with a rod.
28 Bread *flour* must be ground;
Therefore he does not thresh it
   forever,
Break *it with* his cartwheel,
Or crush it *with* his horsemen.
29 This also comes from the LORD of
   hosts,

Who is wonderful in counsel *and*
   excellent in guidance.

WOE TO JERUSALEM

29 "Woe to Ar′i·el,[a] to Ar′i·el, the
   city *where* David dwelt!
Add year to year;
Let feasts come around.
2 Yet I will distress Ar′i·el;
There shall be heaviness and
   sorrow,
And it shall be to Me as Ar′i·el.
3 I will encamp against you all
   around,
I will lay siege against you with a
   mound,
And I will raise siegeworks
   against you.
4 You shall be brought down,
You shall speak out of the ground;
Your speech shall be low, out of
   the dust;
Your voice shall be like a
   medium's, out of the
   ground;
And your speech shall whisper
   out of the dust.

5 "Moreover the multitude of your
   foes
Shall be like fine dust,
And the multitude of the terrible
   ones
Like chaff that passes away;
Yes, it shall be in an instant,
   suddenly.
6 You will be punished by the LORD
   of hosts
With thunder and earthquake
   and great noise,
With storm and tempest
And the flame of devouring fire.
7 The multitude of all the nations
   who fight against Ar′i·el,
Even all who fight against her
   and her fortress,

29:1 *a*That is, Jerusalem

And distress her,
Shall be as a dream of a night
vision.
8 It shall even be as when a hungry
man dreams,
And look—he eats;
But he awakes, and his soul is
still empty;
Or as when a thirsty man
dreams,
And look—he drinks;
But he awakes, and indeed *he is*
faint,
And his soul still craves:
So the multitude of all the
nations shall be,
Who fight against Mount Zion."

THE BLINDNESS OF DISOBEDIENCE

9 Pause and wonder!
Blind yourselves and be blind!
They are drunk, but not with
wine;
They stagger, but not with
intoxicating drink.
10 For the LORD has poured out on
you
The spirit of deep sleep,
And has closed your eyes, namely,
the prophets;
And He has covered your heads,
namely, the seers.

11 The whole vision has become to
you like the words of a book that is
sealed, which *men* deliver to one who
is literate, saying, "Read this,
please." And he says, "I cannot, for it
is sealed."
12 Then the book is delivered to one
who is illiterate, saying, "Read this,
please." And he says, "I am not literate."
13 Therefore the Lord said:

"Inasmuch as these people draw
near with their mouths
And honor Me with their lips,

But have removed their hearts far
from Me,
And their fear toward Me is
taught by the commandment of
men,
14 Therefore, behold, I will again do
a marvelous work
Among this people,
A marvelous work and a wonder;
For the wisdom of their wise *men*
shall perish,
And the understanding of their
prudent *men* shall be hidden."

15 Woe to those who seek deep to
hide their counsel far from the
LORD,
And their works are in the
dark;
They say, "Who sees us?" and,
"Who knows us?"
16 Surely you have things turned
around!
Shall the potter be esteemed as
the clay;
For shall the thing made say of
him who made it,
"He did not make me"?
Or shall the thing formed say of
him who formed it,
"He has no understanding"?

FUTURE RECOVERY OF WISDOM

17 *Is* it not yet a very little while
Till Lebanon shall be turned into
a fruitful field,
And the fruitful field be esteemed
as a forest?
18 In that day the deaf shall hear
the words of the book,
And the eyes of the blind shall see
out of obscurity and out of
darkness.
19 The humble also shall increase
their joy in the LORD,
And the poor among men shall
rejoice
In the Holy One of Israel.

20 For the terrible one is brought to
nothing,
The scornful one is consumed,
And all who watch for iniquity
are cut off—
21 Who make a man an offender by a
word,
And lay a snare for him who
reproves in the gate,
And turn aside the just by empty
words.

22 Therefore thus says the LORD,
who redeemed Abraham, concerning
the house of Jacob:

"Jacob shall not now be ashamed,
Nor shall his face now grow pale;
23 But when he sees his children,
The work of My hands, in his
midst,
They will hallow My name,
And hallow the Holy One of
Jacob,
And fear the God of Israel.
24 These also who erred in spirit will
come to understanding,
And those who complained will
learn doctrine."

FUTILE CONFIDENCE IN EGYPT

30 "Woe to the rebellious
children," says the LORD,
"Who take counsel, but not of Me,
And who devise plans, but not of
My Spirit,
That they may add sin to sin;
2 Who walk to go down to Egypt,
And have not asked My advice,
To strengthen themselves in the
strength of Pharaoh,
And to trust in the shadow of
Egypt!
3 Therefore the strength of
Pharaoh
Shall be your shame,
And trust in the shadow of Egypt
Shall be *your* humiliation.

4 For his princes were at Zō′an,
And his ambassadors came to
Hā′nēs.
5 They were all ashamed of a
people *who* could not benefit
them,
Or be help or benefit,
But a shame and also a
reproach."

6 The burden against the beasts of
the South.

Through a land of trouble and
anguish,
From which *came* the lioness and
lion,
The viper and fiery flying serpent,
They will carry their riches on the
backs of young donkeys,
And their treasures on the humps
of camels,
To a people *who* shall not profit;
7 For the Egyptians shall help in
vain and to no purpose.
Therefore I have called her
Rā′hab-Hem-Shē′beth.*a*

A REBELLIOUS PEOPLE

8 Now go, write it before them on a
tablet,
And note it on a scroll,
That it may be for time to come,
Forever and ever:
9 That this *is* a rebellious people,
Lying children,
Children *who* will not hear the
law of the LORD;
10 Who say to the seers, "Do not
see,"
And to the prophets, "Do not
prophesy to us right things;
Speak to us smooth things,
prophesy deceits.
11 Get out of the way,
Turn aside from the path,

30:7 *a*Literally *Rahab Sits Idle*

Cause the Holy One of Israel
To cease from before us."

12 Therefore thus says the Holy One
of Israel:

"Because you despise this word,
And trust in oppression and
perversity,
And rely on them,
13 Therefore this iniquity shall be to
you
Like a breach ready to fall,
A bulge in a high wall,
Whose breaking comes suddenly,
in an instant.
14 And He shall break it like the
breaking of the potter's vessel,
Which is broken in pieces;
He shall not spare.
So there shall not be found among
its fragments
A shard to take fire from the
hearth,
Or to take water from the
cistern."

15 For thus says the Lord GOD, the
Holy One of Israel:

"In returning and rest you shall be
saved;
In quietness and confidence shall
be your strength."
But you would not,
16 And you said, "No, for we will flee
on horses"—
Therefore you shall flee!
And, "We will ride on swift
horses"—
Therefore those who pursue you
shall be swift!

17 One thousand *shall flee* at the
threat of one,
At the threat of five you shall flee,
Till you are left as a pole on top of
a mountain
And as a banner on a hill.

GOD WILL BE GRACIOUS

18 Therefore the LORD will wait, that
He may be gracious to you;
And therefore He will be exalted,
that He may have mercy on
you.
For the LORD *is* a God of justice;
Blessed *are* all those who wait for
Him.

19 For the people shall dwell in Zion
at Jerusalem;
You shall weep no more.
He will be very gracious to you at
the sound of your cry;
When He hears it, He will answer
you.
20 And *though* the Lord gives you
The bread of adversity and the
water of affliction,
Yet your teachers will not be
moved into a corner anymore,
But your eyes shall see your
teachers.
21 Your ears shall hear a word
behind you, saying,
"This *is* the way, walk in it,"
Whenever you turn to the right
hand
Or whenever you turn to the left.
22 You will also defile the covering of
your images of silver,
And the ornament of your molded
images of gold.
You will throw them away as an
unclean thing;
You will say to them, "Get away!"

23 Then He will give the rain for
your seed
With which you sow the ground,
And bread of the increase of the
earth;
It will be fat and plentiful.
In that day your cattle will feed
In large pastures.
24 Likewise the oxen and the young
donkeys that work the ground

Will eat cured fodder,
Which has been winnowed with
the shovel and fan.

25 There will be on every high
mountain
And on every high hill
Rivers *and* streams of waters,
In the day of the great slaughter,
When the towers fall.

26 Moreover the light of the moon
will be as the light of the sun,
And the light of the sun will be
sevenfold,
As the light of seven days,
In the day that the LORD binds up
the bruise of His people
And heals the stroke of their
wound.

JUDGMENT ON ASSYRIA

27 Behold, the name of the LORD
comes from afar,
Burning *with* His anger,
And *His* burden *is* heavy;
His lips are full of indignation,
And His tongue like a devouring
fire.

28 His breath is like an overflowing
stream,
Which reaches up to the neck,
To sift the nations with the sieve
of futility;
And *there shall be* a bridle in the
jaws of the people,
Causing *them* to err.

29 You shall have a song
As in the night *when* a holy
festival is kept,
And gladness of heart as when
one goes with a flute,
To come into the mountain of the
LORD,
To the Mighty One of Israel.

30 The LORD will cause His glorious
voice to be heard,
And show the descent of His arm,
With the indignation of *His* anger

And the flame of a devouring fire,
With scattering, tempest, and
hailstones.

31 For through the voice of the LORD
Assyria will be beaten down,
As He strikes with the rod.

32 And *in* every place where the
staff of punishment passes,
Which the LORD lays on him,
It will be with tambourines and
harps;
And in battles of brandishing He
will fight with it.

33 For Tō'phet *was* established of
old,
Yes, for the king it is prepared.
He has made *it* deep and large;
Its pyre *is* fire with much wood;
The breath of the LORD, like a
stream of brimstone,
Kindles it.

THE FOLLY OF NOT TRUSTING GOD

31 Woe to those who go down to
Egypt for help,
And rely on horses,
Who trust in chariots because
they are many,
And in horsemen because they
are very strong,
But who do not look to the Holy
One of Israel,
Nor seek the LORD!

2 Yet He also *is* wise and will bring
disaster,
And will not call back His words,
But will arise against the house
of evildoers,
And against the help of those who
work iniquity.

3 Now the Egyptians *are* men, and
not God;
And their horses are flesh, and
not spirit.
When the LORD stretches out His
hand,
Both he who helps will fall,

And he who is helped will fall
    down;
They all will perish together.

God Will Deliver Jerusalem

4   For thus the LORD has spoken to
me:

"As a lion roars,
    And a young lion over his prey
    (When a multitude of shepherds
       is summoned against him,
    He will not be afraid of their
      voice
    Nor be disturbed by their noise),
    So the LORD of hosts will come
      down
    To fight for Mount Zion and for its
      hill.
5   Like birds flying about,
    So will the LORD of hosts defend
      Jerusalem.
    Defending, He will also deliver *it;*
    Passing over, He will preserve *it.*"

6   Return *to Him* against whom the
children of Israel have deeply revolted.
7   For in that day every man shall
throw away his idols of silver and his
idols of gold—sin, which your own
hands have made for yourselves.

8   "Then Assyria shall fall by a sword
    not of man,
    And a sword not of mankind shall
      devour him.
    But he shall flee from the sword,
    And his young men shall become
      forced labor.
9   He shall cross over to his
      stronghold for fear,
    And his princes shall be afraid of
      the banner,"
    Says the LORD,
    Whose fire *is* in Zion
    And whose furnace *is* in
      Jerusalem.

A Reign of Righteousness

32   Behold, a king will reign in
      righteousness,
    And princes will rule with justice.
2   A man will be as a hiding place
      from the wind,
    And a cover from the tempest,
    As rivers of water in a dry place,
    As the shadow of a great rock in a
      weary land.
3   The eyes of those who see will not
      be dim,
    And the ears of those who hear
      will listen.
4   Also the heart of the rash will
      understand knowledge,
    And the tongue of the stammerers
      will be ready to speak plainly.
5   The foolish person will no longer
      be called generous,
    Nor the miser said *to be* bountiful;
6   For the foolish person will speak
      foolishness,
    And his heart will work iniquity:
    To practice ungodliness,
    To utter error against the LORD,
    To keep the hungry unsatisfied,
    And he will cause the drink of the
      thirsty to fail.
7   Also the schemes of the schemer
      are evil;
    He devises wicked plans
    To destroy the poor with lying
      words,
    Even when the needy speaks
      justice.
8   But a generous man devises
      generous things,
    And by generosity he shall stand.

Consequences of Complacency

9   Rise up, you women who are at
      ease,
    Hear my voice;
    You complacent daughters,
    Give ear to my speech.

10 In a year and *some* days
You will be troubled, you
    complacent women;
For the vintage will fail,
The gathering will not come.
11 Tremble, you *women* who are at
    ease;
Be troubled, you complacent ones;
Strip yourselves, make yourselves
    bare,
And gird *sackcloth* on *your*
    waists.

12 People shall mourn upon their
    breasts
For the pleasant fields, for the
    fruitful vine.
13 On the land of my people will
    come up thorns *and* briers,
Yes, on all the happy homes *in*
    the joyous city;
14 Because the palaces will be
    forsaken,
The bustling city will be
    deserted.
The forts and towers will become
    lairs forever,
A joy of wild donkeys, a pasture of
    flocks—
15 Until the Spirit is poured upon us
    from on high,
And the wilderness becomes a
    fruitful field,
And the fruitful field is counted
    as a forest.

THE PEACE OF GOD'S REIGN

16 Then justice will dwell in the
    wilderness,
And righteousness remain in the
    fruitful field.
17 The work of righteousness will be
    peace,
And the effect of righteousness,
    quietness and assurance
    forever.
18 My people will dwell in a peaceful
    habitation,

In secure dwellings, and in quiet
    resting places,
19 Though hail comes down on the
    forest,
And the city is brought low in
    humiliation.

20 Blessed *are* you who sow beside
    all waters,
Who send out freely the feet of
    the ox and the donkey.

A PRAYER IN DEEP DISTRESS

33 Woe to you who plunder,
    though you *have* not *been*
    plundered;
And you who deal treacherously,
    though they have not dealt
    treacherously with you!
When you cease plundering,
You will be plundered;
When you make an end of dealing
    treacherously,
They will deal treacherously with
    you.

2 O LORD, be gracious to us;
We have waited for You.
Be their[a] arm every morning,
Our salvation also in the time of
    trouble.
3 At the noise of the tumult the
    people shall flee;
When You lift Yourself up, the
    nations shall be scattered;
4 And Your plunder shall be
    gathered
Like the gathering of the
    caterpillar;
As the running to and fro of
    locusts,
He shall run upon them.

5 The LORD is exalted, for He dwells
    on high;

33:2 [a]Septuagint omits *their;* Syriac, Targum, and
Vulgate read *our.*

He has filled Zion with justice
and righteousness.

6 Wisdom and knowledge will be
the stability of your times,
And the strength of salvation;
The fear of the LORD *is* His
treasure.

7 Surely their valiant ones shall cry
outside,
The ambassadors of peace shall
weep bitterly.

8 The highways lie waste,
The traveling man ceases.
He has broken the covenant,
He has despised the cities,*a*
He regards no man.

9 The earth mourns *and*
languishes,
Lebanon is shamed *and* shriveled;
Sharon is like a wilderness,
And Bā′shan and Car′mel shake
off *their fruits.*

IMPENDING JUDGMENT ON ZION

10 "Now I will rise," says the LORD;
"Now I will be exalted,
Now I will lift Myself up.

11 You shall conceive chaff,
You shall bring forth stubble;
Your breath, *as* fire, shall devour
you.

12 And the people shall be *like* the
burnings of lime;
Like thorns cut up they shall be
burned in the fire.

13 Hear, you *who are* afar off, what I
have done;
And you *who are* near,
acknowledge My might."

14 The sinners in Zion are afraid;
Fearfulness has seized the
hypocrites:
"Who among us shall dwell with
the devouring fire?
Who among us shall dwell with
everlasting burnings?"

15 He who walks righteously and
speaks uprightly,
He who despises the gain of
oppressions,
Who gestures with his hands,
refusing bribes,
Who stops his ears from hearing
of bloodshed,
And shuts his eyes from seeing
evil:

16 He will dwell on high;
His place of defense *will be* the
fortress of rocks;
Bread will be given him,
His water *will be* sure.

THE LAND OF THE MAJESTIC KING

17 Your eyes will see the King in His
beauty;
They will see the land that is very
far off.

18 Your heart will meditate on
terror:
"Where *is* the scribe?
Where *is* he who weighs?
Where *is* he who counts the
towers?"

19 You will not see a fierce people,
A people of obscure speech,
beyond perception,
Of a stammering tongue *that you*
cannot understand.

20 Look upon Zion, the city of our
appointed feasts;
Your eyes will see Jerusalem, a
quiet home,
A tabernacle *that* will not be
taken down;
Not one of its stakes will ever be
removed,
Nor will any of its cords be
broken.

33:8 *a*Following Masoretic Text and Vulgate; Dead
Sea Scrolls read *witnesses;* Septuagint omits *cities;*
Targum reads *They have been removed from their
cities.*

21 But there the majestic LORD *will
      be* for us
   A place of broad rivers *and*
      streams,
   In which no galley with oars will
      sail,
   Nor majestic ships pass by
22 (For the LORD *is* our Judge,
   The LORD *is* our Lawgiver,
   The LORD *is* our King;
   He will save us);
23 Your tackle is loosed,
   They could not strengthen their
      mast,
   They could not spread the sail.

   Then the prey of great plunder is
      divided;
   The lame take the prey.
24 And the inhabitant will not say,
   "I am sick";
   The people who dwell in it *will be*
      forgiven *their* iniquity.

JUDGMENT ON THE NATIONS

34 Come near, you nations, to
         hear;
   And heed, you people!
   Let the earth hear, and all that is
      in it,
   The world and all things that
      come forth from it.
2 For the indignation of the LORD *is*
      against all nations,
   And *His* fury against all their
      armies;
   He has utterly destroyed them,
   He has given them over to the
      slaughter.
3 Also their slain shall be thrown
      out;
   Their stench shall rise from their
      corpses,
   And the mountains shall be
      melted with their blood.
4   All the host of heaven shall be
      dissolved,

And the heavens shall be rolled
   up like a scroll;
All their host shall fall down
As the leaf falls from the vine,
And as *fruit* falling from a fig
   tree.

5 "For My sword shall be bathed in
      heaven;
   Indeed it shall come down on
      Ē'dom,
   And on the people of My curse, for
      judgment.
6 The sword of the LORD is filled
      with blood,
   It is made overflowing with
      fatness,
   With the blood of lambs and
      goats,
   With the fat of the kidneys of
      rams.
   For the LORD has a sacrifice in
      Boz'rah,
   And a great slaughter in the land
      of Ē'dom.
7 The wild oxen shall come down
      with them,
   And the young bulls with the
      mighty bulls;
   Their land shall be soaked with
      blood,
   And their dust saturated with
      fatness."

8 For *it is* the day of the LORD's
      vengeance,
   The year of recompense for the
      cause of Zion.
9 Its streams shall be turned into
      pitch,
   And its dust into brimstone;
   Its land shall become burning
      pitch.
10 It shall not be quenched night or
      day;
   Its smoke shall ascend forever.
   From generation to generation it
      shall lie waste;

No one shall pass through it
　　forever and ever.
11 But the pelican and the porcupine
　　shall possess it,
　　Also the owl and the raven shall
　　　dwell in it.
　　And He shall stretch out over it
　　The line of confusion and the
　　　stones of emptiness.
12 They shall call its nobles to the
　　　kingdom,
　　But none *shall be* there, and all
　　　its princes shall be nothing.

13 And thorns shall come up in its
　　palaces,
　　Nettles and brambles in its
　　　fortresses;
　　It shall be a habitation of
　　　jackals,
　　A courtyard for ostriches.
14 The wild beasts of the desert shall
　　also meet with the jackals,
　　And the wild goat shall bleat to
　　　its companion;
　　Also the night creature shall rest
　　　there,
　　And find for herself a place of
　　　rest.
15 There the arrow snake shall
　　make her nest and lay *eggs*
　　And hatch, and gather *them*
　　　under her shadow;
　　There also shall the hawks be
　　　gathered,
　　Every one with her mate.

16 "Search from the book of the LORD,
　　and read:
　　Not one of these shall fail;
　　Not one shall lack her mate.
　　For My mouth has commanded it,
　　and His Spirit has gathered
　　them.
17 He has cast the lot for them,
　　And His hand has divided it
　　among them with a measuring
　　line.
　　They shall possess it forever;

From generation to generation
　　they shall dwell in it."

THE FUTURE GLORY OF ZION

35 The wilderness and the
　　wasteland shall be glad for
　　them,
　　And the desert shall rejoice and
　　　blossom as the rose;
2 It shall blossom abundantly and
　　rejoice,
　　Even with joy and singing.
　　The glory of Lebanon shall be
　　　given to it,
　　The excellence of Car'mel and
　　　Sharon.
　　They shall see the glory of the
　　　LORD,
　　The excellency of our God.

3 Strengthen the weak hands,
　　And make firm the feeble knees.
4 Say to those *who are*
　　fearful-hearted,
　　"Be strong, do not fear!
　　Behold, your God will come *with*
　　　vengeance,
　　With the recompense of God;
　　He will come and save you."
5 Then the eyes of the blind shall
　　be opened,
　　And the ears of the deaf shall be
　　unstopped.
6 Then the lame shall leap like a
　　deer,
　　And the tongue of the dumb sing.
　　For waters shall burst forth in
　　　the wilderness,
　　And streams in the desert.
7 The parched ground shall become
　　a pool,
　　And the thirsty land springs of
　　water;
　　In the habitation of jackals,
　　where each lay,
　　There shall be grass with reeds
　　and rushes.

8 A highway shall be there, and a
    road,
And it shall be called the
    Highway of Holiness.
The unclean shall not pass over
    it,
But it *shall be* for others.
Whoever walks the road,
    although a fool,
Shall not go astray.
9 No lion shall be there,
Nor shall *any* ravenous beast go
    up on it;
It shall not be found there.
But the redeemed shall walk
    there,
10 And the ransomed of the LORD
    shall return,
And come to Zion with singing,
With everlasting joy on their
    heads.
They shall obtain joy and
    gladness,
And sorrow and sighing shall flee
    away.

SENNACHERIB BOASTS AGAINST THE LORD

36 Now it came to pass in the
fourteenth year of King Hez·e·kī′ah
that Sen·nach′e·rib king of Assyria
came up against all the fortified cities
of Judah and took them.
2 Then the king of Assyria sent *the*
Rab′sha·keh[a] with a great army from
Lā′chish to King Hez·e·kī′ah at Jerusalem. And he stood by the aqueduct
from the upper pool, on the highway
to the Fuller's Field.
3 And E·lī′a·kim the son of Hil-
kī′ah, who was over the household,
Sheb′na the scribe, and Jō′ah the son
of Ā′saph, the recorder, came out to
him.
4 Then *the* Rab′sha·keh said to
them, "Say now to Hez·e·kī′ah, 'Thus
says the great king, the king of As-

syria: "What confidence is this in
which you trust?
5 "I say you speak of having plans
and power for war; but *they are* mere
words. Now in whom do you trust,
that you rebel against me?
6 "Look! You are trusting in the
staff of this broken reed, Egypt, on
which if a man leans, it will go into
his hand and pierce it. So *is* Pharaoh
king of Egypt to all who trust in him.
7 "But if you say to me, 'We trust in
the LORD our God,' *is it* not He whose
high places and whose altars Hez·e·
kī′ah has taken away, and said to Judah and Jerusalem, 'You shall worship before this altar'?" '
8 "Now therefore, I urge you, give a
pledge to my master the king of Assyria, and I will give you two thousand horses—if you are able on your
part to put riders on them!
9 "How then will you repel one captain of the least of my master's servants, and put your trust in Egypt for
chariots and horsemen?
10 "Have I now come up without the
LORD against this land to destroy it?
The LORD said to me, 'Go up against
this land, and destroy it.' "
11 Then E·lī′a·kim, Sheb′na, and
Jō′ah said to *the* Rab′sha·keh,
"Please speak to your servants in
Ar·a·mā′ic, for we understand *it;* and
do not speak to us in Hebrew[a] in the
hearing of the people who *are* on the
wall."
12 But *the* Rab′sha·keh said, "Has
my master sent me to your master
and to you to speak these words, and
not to the men who sit on the wall,
who will eat and drink their own
waste with you?"
13 Then *the* Rab′sha·keh stood and
called out with a loud voice in Hebrew, and said, "Hear the words of

36:2 [a]A title, probably *Chief of Staff* or *Governor*
36:11 [a]Literally *Judean*

the great king, the king of Assyria!
14 "Thus says the king: 'Do not let
Hez·e·kī′ah deceive you, for he will
not be able to deliver you;
15 'nor let Hez·e·kī′ah make you
trust in the LORD, saying, "The LORD
will surely deliver us; this city will
not be given into the hand of the king
of Assyria." '
16 "Do not listen to Hez·e·kī′ah; for
thus says the king of Assyria: 'Make
peace with me *by a* present and come
out to me; and every one of you eat
from his own vine and every one from
his own fig tree, and every one of you
drink the waters of his own cistern;
17 'until I come and take you away
to a land like your own land, a land
of grain and new wine, a land of
bread and vineyards.
18 '*Beware* lest Hez·e·kī′ah persuade
you, saying, "The LORD will deliver
us." Has any one of the gods of the
nations delivered its land from the
hand of the king of Assyria?
19 'Where *are* the gods of Hā′math
and Ar′pad? Where *are* the gods of
Seph·ar·vā′im? Indeed, have they delivered Samaria from my hand?
20 'Who among all the gods of these
lands have delivered their countries
from my hand, that the LORD should
deliver Jerusalem from my hand?' "
21 But they held their peace and answered him not a word; for the king's
commandment was, "Do not answer
him."
22 Then E·lī′a·kim the son of Hil-
kī′ah, who *was* over the household,
Sheb′na the scribe, and Jō′ah the son
of Ā′saph, the recorder, came to
Hez·e·kī′ah with *their* clothes torn,
and told him the words of *the* Rab′-
sha·keh.

ISAIAH ASSURES DELIVERANCE

37 And so it was, when King
Hez·e·kī′ah heard *it,* that he tore his
clothes, covered himself with sackcloth, and went into the house of the
LORD.
2 Then he sent E·lī′a·kim, who *was*
over the household, Sheb′na the
scribe, and the elders of the priests,
covered with sackcloth, to Ī·sāi′ah the
prophet, the son of Ā′moz.
3 And they said to him, "Thus says
Hez·e·kī′ah: 'This day *is* a day of trouble and rebuke and blasphemy; for
the children have come to birth, but
there is no strength to bring them
forth.
4 'It may be that the LORD your God
will hear the words of *the* Rab′sha-
keh, whom his master the king of Assyria has sent to reproach the living
God, and will rebuke the words
which the LORD your God has heard.
Therefore lift up *your* prayer for the
remnant that is left.' "
5 So the servants of King Hez·e·
kī′ah came to Ī·sāi′ah.
6 And Ī·sāi′ah said to them, "Thus
you shall say to your master, 'Thus
says the LORD: "Do not be afraid of
the words which you have heard,
with which the servants of the king
of Assyria have blasphemed Me.
7 "Surely I will send a spirit upon
him, and he shall hear a rumor and
return to his own land; and I will
cause him to fall by the sword in his
own land." ' "

SENNACHERIB'S THREAT AND HEZEKIAH'S PRAYER

8 Then *the* Rab′sha·keh returned,
and found the king of Assyria
warring against Lib′nah, for he
heard that he had departed from
Lā′chish.
9 And the king heard concerning
Tir·hā′kah king of Ethiopia, "He has
come out to make war with you." So
when he heard *it,* he sent messengers
to Hez·e·kī′ah, saying,

10 "Thus you shall speak to Hez·e·kī′ah king of Judah, saying: 'Do not let your God in whom you trust deceive you, saying, "Jerusalem shall not be given into the hand of the king of Assyria."

11 'Look! You have heard what the kings of Assyria have done to all lands by utterly destroying them; and shall you be delivered?

12 'Have the gods of the nations delivered those whom my fathers have destroyed, Gō′zan and Har′an and Rē′zeph, and the people of Eden who *were* in Te·las′sar?

13 'Where *is* the king of Hā′math, the king of Ar′pad, and the king of the city of Seph·ar·vā′im, Hē′na, and Ī′vah?' "

14 And Hez·e·kī′ah received the letter from the hand of the messengers, and read it; and Hez·e·kī′ah went up to the house of the LORD, and spread it before the LORD.

15 Then Hez·e·kī′ah prayed to the LORD, saying:

16 "O LORD of hosts, God of Israel, *the One* who dwells *between* the cherubim, You *are* God, You alone, of all the kingdoms of the earth. You have made heaven and earth.

17 "Incline Your ear, O LORD, and hear; open Your eyes, O LORD, and see; and hear all the words of Sennach′e·rib, which he has sent to reproach the living God.

18 "Truly, LORD, the kings of Assyria have laid waste all the nations and their lands,

19 "and have cast their gods into the fire; for they *were* not gods, but the work of men's hands—wood and stone. Therefore they destroyed them.

20 "Now therefore, O LORD our God, save us from his hand, that all the kingdoms of the earth may know that You *are* the LORD, You alone."

THE WORD OF THE LORD CONCERNING SENNACHERIB

21 Then Ī·sāi′ah the son of Ā′moz sent to Hez·e·kī′ah, saying, "Thus says the LORD God of Israel, 'Because you have prayed to Me against Sennach′e·rib king of Assyria,

22 'this *is* the word which the LORD has spoken concerning him:

"The virgin, the daughter of Zion,
  Has despised you, laughed you to
    scorn;
  The daughter of Jerusalem
  Has shaken *her* head behind your
    back!

23 "Whom have you reproached and
    blasphemed?
  Against whom have you raised
    your voice,
  And lifted up your eyes on high?
  Against the Holy One of Israel.
24 By your servants you have
    reproached the Lord,
  And said, 'By the multitude of my
    chariots
  I have come up to the height of
    the mountains,
  To the limits of Lebanon;
  I will cut down its tall cedars
  And its choice cypress trees;
  I will enter its farthest height,
  To its fruitful forest.
25 I have dug and drunk water,
  And with the soles of my feet I
    have dried up
  All the brooks of defense.'

26 "Did you not hear long ago
  How I made it,
  From ancient times that I formed
    it?
  Now I have brought it to pass,
  That you should be
  For crushing fortified cities *into*
    heaps of ruins.

27 Therefore their inhabitants *had*
      little power;
   They were dismayed and
      confounded;
   They were *as* the grass of the field
   And the green herb,
   As the grass on the housetops
   And *grain* blighted before it is
      grown.

28 "But I know your dwelling place,
   Your going out and your coming
      in,
   And your rage against Me.
29 Because your rage against Me
      and your tumult
   Have come up to My ears,
   Therefore I will put My hook in
      your nose
   And My bridle in your lips,
   And I will turn you back
   By the way which you came." '

30 "This *shall be* a sign to you:

   You shall eat this year such as
      grows of itself,
   And the second year what springs
      from the same;
   Also in the third year sow and
      reap,
   Plant vineyards and eat the fruit
      of them.
31 And the remnant who have
      escaped of the house of Judah
   Shall again take root downward,
   And bear fruit upward.
32 For out of Jerusalem shall go a
      remnant,
   And those who escape from
      Mount Zion.
   The zeal of the LORD of hosts will
      do this.

33 "Therefore thus says the LORD
concerning the king of Assyria:

   'He shall not come into this city,
   Nor shoot an arrow there,

   Nor come before it with shield,
   Nor build a siege mound against
      it.
34 By the way that he came,
   By the same shall he return;
   And he shall not come into this
      city,'
   Says the LORD.
35 'For I will defend this city, to save
      it
   For My own sake and for My
      servant David's sake.' "

SENNACHERIB'S DEFEAT AND DEATH

36 Then the angel[a] of the LORD went
out, and killed in the camp of the Assyrians one hundred and eighty-five
thousand; and when *people* arose
early in the morning, there were the
corpses—all dead.
37 So Sen·nach'e·rib king of Assyria
departed and went away, returned
home, and remained at Nin'e·veh.
38 Now it came to pass, as he was
worshiping in the house of Nis'roch
his god, that his sons A·dram'me·lech
and Sha·rē'zer struck him down with
the sword; and they escaped into the
land of Ar'a·rat. Then Ē·sar·had'don
his son reigned in his place.

HEZEKIAH'S LIFE EXTENDED

38 In those days Hez·e·kī'ah was
sick and near death. And Ī·sāi'ah the
prophet, the son of Ā'moz, went to
him and said to him, "Thus says the
LORD: 'Set your house in order, for
you shall die and not live.' "
2 Then Hez·e·kī'ah turned his face
toward the wall, and prayed to the
LORD,
3 and said, "Remember now, O
LORD, I pray, how I have walked before You in truth and with a loyal

37:36 *a* Or *Angel*

◼ *Prayers* ◼

Isaiah 38:2, 3

Hezekiah was going to die. God told him so. "Prepare to die," God told him. Hezekiah cried. He begged God to hear his prayers and let him live. That's a big prayer, isn't it? But God listened and gave him another 15 years. Do you ever think something is too big for God? It isn't. God can do anything. But He will do only what He knows is best for you.

---

heart, and have done *what is* good in Your sight." And Hez·e·kī′ah wept bitterly.

4 And the word of the LORD came to Ī·sāi′ah, saying,

5 "Go and tell Hez·e·kī′ah, 'Thus says the LORD, the God of David your father: "I have heard your prayer, I have seen your tears; surely I will add to your days fifteen years.

6 "I will deliver you and this city from the hand of the king of Assyria, and I will defend this city." '

7 "And this *is* the sign to you from the LORD, that the LORD will do this thing which He has spoken:

8 "Behold, I will bring the shadow on the sundial, which has gone down with the sun on the sundial of Ā′haz, ten degrees backward." So the sun returned ten degrees on the dial by which it had gone down.

9 This is the writing of Hez·e·kī′ah king of Judah, when he had been sick and had recovered from his sickness:

10 I said,
"In the prime of my life
I shall go to the gates of Shē′ol;
I am deprived of the remainder of my years."

11 I said,
"I shall not see YAH,
The LORD*a* in the land of the living;
I shall observe man no more among the inhabitants of the world.*b*

12 My life span is gone,
Taken from me like a shepherd's tent;
I have cut off my life like a weaver.
He cuts me off from the loom;
From day until night You make an end of me.

13 I have considered until morning—
Like a lion,
So He breaks all my bones;
From day until night You make an end of me.

14 Like a crane *or* a swallow, so I chattered;
I mourned like a dove;
My eyes fail *from looking* upward.
O LORD,*a* I am oppressed;
Undertake for me!

15 "What shall I say?
He has both spoken to me,*a*
And He Himself has done *it.*
I shall walk carefully all my years
In the bitterness of my soul.

16 O Lord, by these *things men* live;
And in all these *things is* the life of my spirit;
So You will restore me and make me live.

17 Indeed *it was* for *my own* peace
That I had great bitterness;
But You have lovingly *delivered* my soul from the pit of corruption,

38:11 *a*Hebrew YAH, YAH   *b*Following some Hebrew manuscripts; Masoretic Text and Vulgate read *rest;* Septuagint omits *among the inhabitants of the world;* Targum reads *land.*   38:14 *a*Following Bomberg; Masoretic Text and Dead Sea Scrolls read *Lord.*   38:15 *a*Following Masoretic Text and Vulgate; Dead Sea Scrolls and Targum read *And shall I say to Him;* Septuagint omits first half of this verse.

For You have cast all my sins
behind Your back.
18 For Shē′ōl cannot thank You,
Death cannot praise You;
Those who go down to the pit
cannot hope for Your truth.
19 The living, the living man, he
shall praise You,
As I *do* this day;
The father shall make known
Your truth to the children.

20 "The LORD *was ready* to save me;
Therefore we will sing my songs
with stringed instruments
All the days of our life, in the
house of the LORD."

21 Now Ī·sāi′ah had said, "Let them
take a lump of figs, and apply *it* as a
poultice on the boil, and he shall recover."
22 And Hez·e·kī′ah had said, "What
is the sign that I shall go up to the
house of the LORD?"

THE BABYLONIAN ENVOYS

39 At that time Mer′o·dach-Bal′-
a·dan[a] the son of Bal′a·dan, king of
Babylon, sent letters and a present to
Hez·e·kī′ah, for he heard that he had
been sick and had recovered.
2   And Hez·e·kī′ah was pleased with
them, and showed them the house of
his treasures—the silver and gold,
the spices and precious ointment,
and all his armory—all that was
found among his treasures. There
was nothing in his house or in all his
dominion that Hez·e·kī′ah did not
show them.
3   Then Ī·sāi′ah the prophet went to
King Hez·e·kī′ah, and said to him,
"What did these men say, and from
where did they come to you?" So Hez-
e·kī′ah said, "They came to me from a
far country, from Babylon."

4   And he said, "What have they
seen in your house?" So Hez·e·kī′ah
answered, "They have seen all that *is*
in my house; there is nothing among
my treasures that I have not shown
them."
5   Then Ī·sāi′ah said to Hez·e·kī′ah,
"Hear the word of the LORD of hosts:
6   'Behold, the days are coming
when all that *is* in your house, and
what your fathers have accumulated
until this day, shall be carried to
Babylon; nothing shall be left,' says
the LORD.
7   'And they shall take away *some* of
your sons who will descend from you,
whom you will beget; and they shall
be eunuchs in the palace of the king
of Babylon.' "
8   So Hez·e·kī′ah said to Ī·sāi′ah,
"The word of the LORD which you
have spoken *is* good!" For he said, "At
least there will be peace and truth in
my days."

GOD'S PEOPLE ARE COMFORTED

40 "Comfort, yes, comfort My
people!"
Says your God.
2 "Speak comfort to Jerusalem, and
cry out to her,
That her warfare is ended,
That her iniquity is pardoned;
For she has received from the
LORD's hand
Double for all her sins."

3   The voice of one crying in the
wilderness:
"Prepare the way of the LORD;
Make straight in the desert[a]
A highway for our God.
4   Every valley shall be exalted
And every mountain and hill
brought low;

39:1 [a]Spelled *Berodach-Baladan* in 2 Kings 20:12
40:3 [a]Following Masoretic Text, Targum, and Vulgate; Septuagint omits *in the desert*.

THE GRASS WITHERS, THE FLOWER FADES, / BUT THE WORD OF OUR GOD STANDS FOREVER. Isaiah 40:8

Can You Keep Flowers Forever?

Do you like flowers? They are beautiful, aren't they? But many flowers last only a short time before they wither. When you see flowers wither, wood rotting, iron rusting and people growing old, you may ask, "Does anything last forever?"

1. Can you keep flowers forever? Why not?
2. Is there something that does last forever? What does Isaiah 40:8 tell us? Why is this so important to us? Thank You, God, for Your everlasting Word.
3. Since God's Word is so important, what should you do about it? Should you read it? Should you memorize it? Should you study it and apply it to your life? How? When? Will you do these things this week?

For more on *Favorite Family Verses* turn to page 1094
For more on *Bible* turn to page 1659

The crooked places shall be made
straight
And the rough places smooth;
5 The glory of the LORD shall be
revealed,
And all flesh shall see *it*
together;
For the mouth of the LORD has
spoken."

6 The voice said, "Cry out!"
And he*a* said, "What shall I
cry?"

"All flesh *is* grass,
And all its loveliness *is* like the
flower of the field.
7 The grass withers, the flower
fades,
Because the breath of the LORD
blows upon it;
Surely the people *are* grass.
8 The grass withers, the flower
fades,
But the word of our God stands
forever."

9 O Zion,
You who bring good tidings,
Get up into the high mountain;
O Jerusalem,
You who bring good tidings,
Lift up your voice with strength,
Lift *it* up, be not afraid;
Say to the cities of Judah,
"Behold your God!"

10 Behold, the Lord GOD shall come
with a strong *hand,*
And His arm shall rule for Him;
Behold, His reward *is* with Him,
And His work before Him.
11 He will feed His flock like a
shepherd;
He will gather the lambs with His
arm,
And carry *them* in His bosom,
And gently lead those who are
with young.

12 Who has measured the waters*a* in
the hollow of His hand,
Measured heaven with a span
And calculated the dust of the
earth in a measure?
Weighed the mountains in scales
And the hills in a balance?
13 Who has directed the Spirit of the
LORD,
Or *as* His counselor has taught
Him?
14 With whom did He take counsel,
and *who* instructed Him,
And taught Him in the path of
justice?
Who taught Him knowledge,
And showed Him the way of
understanding?

15 Behold, the nations *are* as a drop
in a bucket,
And are counted as the small dust
on the scales;
Look, He lifts up the isles as a
very little thing.
16 And Lebanon *is* not sufficient to
burn,
Nor its beasts sufficient for a
burnt offering.
17 All nations before Him *are* as
nothing,
And they are counted by Him less
than nothing and worthless.

18 To whom then will you liken God?
Or what likeness will you
compare to Him?
19 The workman molds an image,
The goldsmith overspreads it
with gold,
And the silversmith casts silver
chains.
20 Whoever *is* too impoverished for
such a contribution

40:6 *a*Following Masoretic Text and Targum; Dead
Sea Scrolls, Septuagint, and Vulgate read *I.*
40:12 *a*Following Masoretic Text, Septuagint, and
Vulgate; Dead Sea Scrolls read *waters of the sea;*
Targum reads *waters of the world.*

HE WILL FEED HIS FLOCK LIKE A SHEPHERD; / HE WILL GATHER THE LAMBS WITH HIS ARM, / AND CARRY THEM IN HIS BOSOM. Isaiah 40:11

Jesus, My Shepherd

Although written many years before Jesus' birth, Isaiah 40:11 tells us about Him. What will Jesus be like? He will take care of His people like a shepherd takes care of his sheep. He will make sure we have food and clothing. He will lead us in the right ways. He will protect us and comfort us. He will be our companion wherever we go. And He will love us more than anyone else can love us. Thank You, God, for this wonderful promise. Thank You, Jesus, for being our Good Shepherd.

1. What does Jesus do for us?
2. What would you like to say to Jesus now? Will you?
3. Read John 10:1–11, especially verse 11. Would you like to say "thank You, Jesus?" Why not?

For more on *Favorite Family Verses* turn to page 1237
For more on *God's Care* turn to page 1111

Chooses a tree *that* will not rot;
He seeks for himself a skillful
　workman
To prepare a carved image *that*
　will not totter.

21 Have you not known?
Have you not heard?
Has it not been told you from the
　beginning?
Have you not understood from the
　foundations of the earth?
22 *It is* He who sits above the circle
　of the earth,
And its inhabitants *are* like
　grasshoppers,
Who stretches out the heavens
　like a curtain,
And spreads them out like a tent
　to dwell in.
23 He brings the princes to nothing;
He makes the judges of the earth
　useless.

24 Scarcely shall they be planted,
Scarcely shall they be sown,
Scarcely shall their stock take
　root in the earth,
When He will also blow on them,
And they will wither,
And the whirlwind will take them
　away like stubble.

25 "To whom then will you liken Me,
Or *to whom* shall I be equal?"
　says the Holy One.
26 Lift up your eyes on high,
And see who has created these
　things,
Who brings out their host by
　number;
He calls them all by name,
By the greatness of His might
And the strength of *His* power;
Not one is missing.

27 Why do you say, O Jacob,
And speak, O Israel:
"My way is hidden from the LORD,

And my just claim is passed over
　by my God"?
28 Have you not known?
Have you not heard?
The everlasting God, the LORD,
The Creator of the ends of the
　earth,
Neither faints nor is weary.
His understanding is
　unsearchable.
29 He gives power to the weak,
And to *those who have* no might
　He increases strength.
30 Even the youths shall faint and
　be weary,
And the young men shall utterly
　fall,
31 But those who wait on the LORD
Shall renew *their* strength;
They shall mount up with wings
　like eagles,
They shall run and not be weary,
They shall walk and not faint.

ISRAEL ASSURED OF GOD'S HELP

41 "Keep silence before Me,
　　　O coastlands,
And let the people renew *their*
　strength!
Let them come near, then let
　them speak;
Let us come near together for
　judgment.

2 "Who raised up one from the east?
Who in righteousness called him
　to His feet?
Who gave the nations before him,
And made *him* rule over kings?
Who gave *them* as the dust *to* his
　sword,
As driven stubble to his bow?
3 Who pursued them, *and* passed
　safely
By the way *that* he had not gone
　with his feet?
4 Who has performed and done *it,*

Calling the generations from the
beginning?
'I, the LORD, am the first;
And with the last I *am* He.' "

5 The coastlands saw *it* and feared,
The ends of the earth were afraid;
They drew near and came.
6 Everyone helped his neighbor,
And said to his brother,
"Be of good courage!"
7 So the craftsman encouraged the
goldsmith;
He who smooths *with* the
hammer *inspired* him who
strikes the anvil,
Saying, "It *is* ready for the
soldering";
Then he fastened it with pegs,
That it might not totter.

8 "But you, Israel, *are* My servant,
Jacob whom I have chosen,
The descendants of Abraham My
friend.
9 *You* whom I have taken from the
ends of the earth,
And called from its farthest
regions,
And said to you,
'You *are* My servant,
I have chosen you and have not
cast you away:
10 Fear not, for I *am* with you;
Be not dismayed, for I *am* your
God.
I will strengthen you,
Yes, I will help you,
I will uphold you with My
righteous right hand.'

11 "Behold, all those who were
incensed against you
Shall be ashamed and disgraced;
They shall be as nothing,
And those who strive with you
shall perish.
12 You shall seek them and not find
them—

Those who contended with you.
Those who war against you
Shall be as nothing,
As a nonexistent thing.
13 For I, the LORD your God, will
hold your right hand,
Saying to you, 'Fear not, I will
help you.'

14 "Fear not, you worm Jacob,
You men of Israel!
I will help you," says the LORD
And your Redeemer, the Holy One
of Israel.
15 "Behold, I will make you into a
new threshing sledge with
sharp teeth;
You shall thresh the mountains
and beat *them* small,
And make the hills like chaff.
16 You shall winnow them, the wind
shall carry them away,
And the whirlwind shall scatter
them;
You shall rejoice in the LORD,
And glory in the Holy One of
Israel.

17 "The poor and needy seek water,
but *there is* none,
Their tongues fail for thirst.
I, the LORD, will hear them;
I, the God of Israel, will not
forsake them.
18 I will open rivers in desolate
heights,
And fountains in the midst of the
valleys;
I will make the wilderness a pool
of water,
And the dry land springs of
water.
19 I will plant in the wilderness the
cedar and the acacia tree,
The myrtle and the oil tree;
I will set in the desert the cypress
tree *and* the pine
And the box tree together,
20 That they may see and know,

And consider and understand
together,
That the hand of the LORD has
done this,
And the Holy One of Israel has
created it.

THE FUTILITY OF IDOLS

21 "Present your case," says the
LORD.
"Bring forth your strong *reasons*,"
says the King of Jacob.
22 "Let them bring forth and show us
what will happen;
Let them show the former things,
what they *were,*
That we may consider them,
And know the latter end of them;
Or declare to us things to come.
23 Show the things that are to come
hereafter,
That we may know that you *are*
gods;
Yes, do good or do evil,
That we may be dismayed and see
it together.
24 Indeed you *are* nothing,
And your work *is* nothing;
He who chooses you *is* an
abomination.

25 "I have raised up one from the
north,
And he shall come;
From the rising of the sun he
shall call on My name;
And he shall come against princes
as *though* mortar,
As the potter treads clay.
26 Who has declared from the
beginning, that we may know?
And former times, that we may
say, '*He is* righteous'?
Surely *there is* no one who shows,
Surely *there is* no one who
declares,
Surely *there is* no one who hears
your words.

27 The first time *I said* to Zion,
'Look, there they are!'
And I will give to Jerusalem one
who brings good tidings.
28 For I looked, and *there was* no
man;
I looked among them, but *there
was* no counselor,
Who, when I asked of them, could
answer a word.
29 Indeed they *are* all worthless;*a*
Their works *are* nothing;
Their molded images *are* wind
and confusion.

THE SERVANT OF THE LORD

42 "Behold! My Servant whom I
uphold,
My Elect One *in whom* My soul
delights!
I have put My Spirit upon Him;
He will bring forth justice to the
Gentiles.
2 He will not cry out, nor raise *His
voice,*
Nor cause His voice to be heard in
the street.
3 A bruised reed He will not break,
And smoking flax He will not
quench;
He will bring forth justice for
truth.
4 He will not fail nor be
discouraged,
Till He has established justice in
the earth;
And the coastlands shall wait for
His law."

5 Thus says God the LORD,
Who created the heavens and
stretched them out,
Who spread forth the earth and
that which comes from it,

41:29 *a*Following Masoretic Text and Vulgate; Dead
Sea Scrolls, Syriac, and Targum read *nothing;* Septuagint omits the first line.

Who gives breath to the people on
it,
And spirit to those who walk on
it:

6 "I, the LORD, have called You in
righteousness,
And will hold Your hand;
I will keep You and give You as a
covenant to the people,
As a light to the Gentiles,

7 To open blind eyes,
To bring out prisoners from the
prison,
Those who sit in darkness from
the prison house.

8 I *am* the LORD, that *is* My name;
And My glory I will not give to
another,
Nor My praise to carved images.

9 Behold, the former things have
come to pass,
And new things I declare;
Before they spring forth I tell you
of them."

PRAISE TO THE LORD

10 Sing to the LORD a new song,
And His praise from the ends of
the earth,
You who go down to the sea, and
all that is in it,

■ *Praises* **■**

Isaiah 42:10

Sing to the Lord a new song.
From the ends of the earth let
praise come forth to God. People
all over the world are praising
God with singing. People in
Africa sing praise to God. People
in Asia sing praise to God. People in Europe sing praise to God.
People in North America sing
praise to God. Are you singing
with them?

You coastlands and you
inhabitants of them!

11 Let the wilderness and its cities
lift up *their voice,*
The villages *that* Kē'dar inhabits.
Let the inhabitants of Sē'la sing,
Let them shout from the top of
the mountains.

12 Let them give glory to the LORD,
And declare His praise in the
coastlands.

13 The LORD shall go forth like a
mighty man;
He shall stir up *His* zeal like a
man of war.
He shall cry out, yes, shout aloud;
He shall prevail against His
enemies.

PROMISE OF THE LORD'S HELP

14 "I have held My peace a long time,
I have been still and restrained
Myself.
Now I will cry like a woman in
labor,
I will pant and gasp at once.

15 I will lay waste the mountains
and hills,
And dry up all their vegetation;
I will make the rivers coastlands,
And I will dry up the pools.

16 I will bring the blind by a way
they did not know;
I will lead them in paths they
have not known.
I will make darkness light before
them,
And crooked places straight.
These things I will do for them,
And not forsake them.

17 They shall be turned back,
They shall be greatly ashamed,
Who trust in carved images,
Who say to the molded images,
'You *are* our gods.'

18 "Hear, you deaf;
And look, you blind, that you may
see.

19 Who *is* blind but My servant,
Or deaf as My messenger *whom* I
send?
Who *is* blind as *he who is*
perfect,
And blind as the LORD's
servant?

20 Seeing many things, but you do
not observe;
Opening the ears, but he does not
hear."

ISRAEL'S OBSTINATE DISOBEDIENCE

21 The LORD is well pleased for His
righteousness' sake;
He will exalt the law and make *it*
honorable.

22 But this *is* a people robbed and
plundered;
All of them are snared in holes,
And they are hidden in prison
houses;
They are for prey, and no one
delivers;
For plunder, and no one says,
"Restore!"

23 Who among you will give ear to
this?
Who will listen and hear for the
time to come?

24 Who gave Jacob for plunder, and
Israel to the robbers?
Was it not the LORD,
He against whom we have
sinned?
For they would not walk in His
ways,
Nor were they obedient to His
law.

25 Therefore He has poured on him
the fury of His anger
And the strength of battle;
It has set him on fire all around,
Yet he did not know;
And it burned him,
Yet he did not take *it* to heart.

THE REDEEMER OF ISRAEL

43 But now, thus says the LORD,
who created you, O Jacob,
And He who formed you, O Israel:
"Fear not, for I have redeemed
you;
I have called *you* by your name;
You *are* Mine.

2 When you pass through the
waters, I *will be* with you;
And through the rivers, they shall
not overflow you.
When you walk through the fire,
you shall not be burned,
Nor shall the flame scorch you.

3 For I *am* the LORD your God,
The Holy One of Israel, your
Savior;
I gave Egypt for your ransom,
Ethiopia and Sē′ba in your
place.

4 Since you were precious in My
sight,
You have been honored,
And I have loved you;
Therefore I will give men for you,
And people for your life.

5 Fear not, for I *am* with you;
I will bring your descendants
from the east,
And gather you from the west;

6 I will say to the north, 'Give them
up!'
And to the south, 'Do not keep
them back!'
Bring My sons from afar,
And My daughters from the ends
of the earth—

7 Everyone who is called by My
name,
Whom I have created for My
glory;
I have formed him, yes, I have
made him."

8 Bring out the blind people who
have eyes,
And the deaf who have ears.

9 Let all the nations be gathered
    together,
And let the people be assembled.
Who among them can declare
    this,
And show us former things?
Let them bring out their
    witnesses, that they may be
    justified;
Or let them hear and say, "*It is*
    truth."
10 "You *are* My witnesses," says the
    LORD,
  "And My servant whom I have
    chosen,
  That you may know and believe
    Me,
  And understand that I *am* He.
  Before Me there was no God
    formed,
  Nor shall there be after Me.
11 I, *even* I, *am* the LORD,
  And besides Me *there is* no savior.
12 I have declared and saved,
  I have proclaimed,
  And *there was* no foreign *god*
    among you;
  Therefore you *are* My witnesses,"
  Says the LORD, "that I *am* God.
13 Indeed before the day *was,* I *am*
    He;
  And *there is* no one who can
    deliver out of My hand;
  I work, and who will reverse it?"

14 Thus says the LORD, your
    Redeemer,
  The Holy One of Israel:
  "For your sake I will send to
    Babylon,
  And bring them all down as
    fugitives—
  The Chal·dē′ans, who rejoice in
    their ships.
15 I *am* the LORD, your Holy One,
  The Creator of Israel, your King."

16 Thus says the LORD, who makes a
    way in the sea

And a path through the mighty
    waters,
17 Who brings forth the chariot and
    horse,
  The army and the power
  (They shall lie down together,
    they shall not rise;
  They are extinguished, they are
    quenched like a wick):
18 "Do not remember the former
    things,
  Nor consider the things of old.
19 Behold, I will do a new thing,
  Now it shall spring forth;
  Shall you not know it?
  I will even make a road in the
    wilderness
  And rivers in the desert.
20 The beast of the field will honor
    Me,
  The jackals and the ostriches,
  Because I give waters in the
    wilderness
  And rivers in the desert,
  To give drink to My people, My
    chosen.
21 This people I have formed for
    Myself;
  They shall declare My praise.

PLEADING WITH UNFAITHFUL ISRAEL

22 "But you have not called upon Me,
    O Jacob;
  And you have been weary of Me,
    O Israel.
23 You have not brought Me the
    sheep for your burnt offerings,
  Nor have you honored Me with
    your sacrifices.
  I have not caused you to serve
    with grain offerings,
  Nor wearied you with incense.
24 You have bought Me no sweet
    cane with money,
  Nor have you satisfied Me with
    the fat of your sacrifices;
  But you have burdened Me with
    your sins,

You have wearied Me with your
    iniquities.

25 "I, *even* I, *am* He who blots out
    your transgressions for My own
    sake;
    And I will not remember your
    sins.
26 Put Me in remembrance;
    Let us contend together;
    State your *case,* that you may be
    acquitted.
27 Your first father sinned,
    And your mediators have
    transgressed against Me.
28 Therefore I will profane the
    princes of the sanctuary;
    I will give Jacob to the curse,
    And Israel to reproaches.

GOD'S BLESSING ON ISRAEL

44 "Yet hear now, O Jacob My
    servant,
    And Israel whom I have chosen.
2 Thus says the LORD who made
    you
    And formed you from the womb,
    who will help you:
    'Fear not, O Jacob My servant;
    And you, Jesh'ū·run, whom I
    have chosen.
3 For I will pour water on him who
    is thirsty,
    And floods on the dry ground;
    I will pour My Spirit on your
    descendants,
    And My blessing on your
    offspring;
4 They will spring up among the
    grass
    Like willows by the watercourses.'
5 One will say, 'I *am* the LORD's';
    Another will call *himself* by the
    name of Jacob;
    Another will write *with* his hand,
    'The LORD's,'
    And name *himself* by the name of
    Israel.

THERE IS NO OTHER GOD

6 "Thus says the LORD, the King of
    Israel,
    And his Redeemer, the LORD of
    hosts:
    'I *am* the First and I *am* the
    Last;
    Besides Me *there is* no God.
7 And who can proclaim as I do?
    Then let him declare it and set it
    in order for Me,
    Since I appointed the ancient
    people.
    And the things that are coming
    and shall come,
    Let them show these to them.
8 Do not fear, nor be afraid;
    Have I not told you from that
    time, and declared *it?*
    You *are* My witnesses.
    Is there a God besides Me?
    Indeed *there is* no other Rock;
    I know not *one.*' "

IDOLATRY IS FOOLISHNESS

9 Those who make an image, all of
    them *are* useless,
    And their precious things shall
    not profit;
    They *are* their own witnesses;
    They neither see nor know, that
    they may be ashamed.
10 Who would form a god or mold an
    image
    That profits him nothing?
11 Surely all his companions would
    be ashamed;
    And the workmen, they *are* mere
    men.
    Let them all be gathered together,
    Let them stand up;
    Yet they shall fear,
    They shall be ashamed together.

12 The blacksmith with the tongs
    works one in the coals,
    Fashions it with hammers,

And works it with the strength of
his arms.
Even so, he is hungry, and his
strength fails;
He drinks no water and is faint.

13 The craftsman stretches out *his*
rule,
He marks one out with chalk;
He fashions it with a plane,
He marks it out with the
compass,
And makes it like the figure of a
man,
According to the beauty of a man,
that it may remain in the
house.

14 He cuts down cedars for himself,
And takes the cypress and the
oak;
He secures *it* for himself among
the trees of the forest.
He plants a pine, and the rain
nourishes *it*.

15 Then it shall be for a man to
burn,
For he will take some of it and
warm himself;
Yes, he kindles *it* and bakes
bread;
Indeed he makes a god and
worships *it;*
He makes it a carved image, and
falls down to it.

16 He burns half of it in the fire;
With this half he eats meat;
He roasts a roast, and is satisfied.
He even warms *himself* and
says,
"Ah! I am warm,
I have seen the fire."

17 And the rest of it he makes into a
god,
His carved image.
He falls down before it and
worships *it,*
Prays to it and says,
"Deliver me, for you *are* my god!"

18 They do not know nor
understand;
For He has shut their eyes, so
that they cannot see,
And their hearts, so that they
cannot understand.

19 And no one considers in his heart,
Nor *is there* knowledge nor
understanding to say,
"I have burned half of it in the fire,
Yes, I have also baked bread on
its coals;
I have roasted meat and eaten *it;*
And shall I make the rest of it an
abomination?
Shall I fall down before a block of
wood?"

20 He feeds on ashes;
A deceived heart has turned him
aside;
And he cannot deliver his soul,
Nor say, "Is there not a lie in my
right hand?"

ISRAEL IS NOT FORGOTTEN

21 "Remember these, O Jacob,
And Israel, for you *are* My
servant;
I have formed you, you *are* My
servant;
O Israel, you will not be forgotten
by Me!

22 I have blotted out, like a thick
cloud, your transgressions,
And like a cloud, your sins.
Return to Me, for I have
redeemed you."

23 Sing, O heavens, for the LORD has
done *it!*
Shout, you lower parts of the
earth;
Break forth into singing, you
mountains,
O forest, and every tree in it!
For the LORD has redeemed
Jacob,
And glorified Himself in Israel.

JUDAH WILL BE RESTORED

24 Thus says the LORD, your
　　Redeemer,
　　And He who formed you from the
　　womb:
　　"I *am* the LORD, who makes all
　　things,
　　Who stretches out the heavens all
　　alone,
　　Who spreads abroad the earth by
　　Myself;
25 Who frustrates the signs of the
　　babblers,
　　And drives diviners mad;
　　Who turns wise men backward,
　　And makes their knowledge
　　foolishness;
26 Who confirms the word of His
　　servant,
　　And performs the counsel of His
　　messengers;
　　Who says to Jerusalem, 'You shall
　　be inhabited,'
　　To the cities of Judah, 'You shall
　　be built,'
　　And I will raise up her waste
　　places;
27 Who says to the deep, 'Be dry!
　　And I will dry up your rivers';
28 Who says of Cyrus, '*He is* My
　　shepherd,
　　And he shall perform all My
　　pleasure,
　　Saying to Jerusalem, "You shall
　　be built,"
　　And to the temple, "Your
　　foundation shall be laid." '

CYRUS, GOD'S INSTRUMENT

45 "Thus says the LORD to His
　　anointed,
　　To Cyrus, whose right hand I
　　have held—
　　To subdue nations before him
　　And loose the armor of kings,
　　To open before him the double
　　doors,

So that the gates will not be shut:
2 'I will go before you
　　And make the crooked places[a]
　　straight;
　　I will break in pieces the gates of
　　bronze
　　And cut the bars of iron.
3 I will give you the treasures of
　　darkness
　　And hidden riches of secret
　　places,
　　That you may know that I, the
　　LORD,
　　Who call *you* by your name,
　　Am the God of Israel.
4 For Jacob My servant's sake,
　　And Israel My elect,
　　I have even called you by your
　　name;
　　I have named you, though you
　　have not known Me.
5 I *am* the LORD, and *there is* no
　　other;
　　There is no God besides Me.
　　I will gird you, though you have
　　not known Me,
6 That they may know from the
　　rising of the sun to its setting
　　That *there is* none besides Me.
　　I *am* the LORD, and *there is* no
　　other;
7 I form the light and create
　　darkness,
　　I make peace and create calamity;
　　I, the LORD, do all these *things.*'

8 "Rain down, you heavens, from
　　above,
　　And let the skies pour down
　　righteousness;
　　Let the earth open, let them bring
　　forth salvation,
　　And let righteousness spring up
　　together.
　　I, the LORD, have created it.

45:2 [a]Dead Sea Scrolls and Septuagint read *mountains;* Targum reads *I will trample down the walls;*
Vulgate reads *I will humble the great ones of the
earth.*

9 "Woe to him who strives with his
Maker!
Let the potsherd *strive* with the
potsherds of the earth!
Shall the clay say to him who
forms it, 'What are you
making?'
Or shall your handiwork *say,* 'He
has no hands'?
10 Woe to him who says to *his*
father, 'What are you
begetting?'
Or to the woman, 'What have you
brought forth?' "

11 Thus says the LORD,
The Holy One of Israel, and his
Maker:
"Ask Me of things to come
concerning My sons;
And concerning the work of My
hands, you command Me.
12 I have made the earth,
And created man on it.
I—My hands—stretched out the
heavens,
And all their host I have
commanded.
13 I have raised him up in
righteousness,
And I will direct all his ways;
He shall build My city
And let My exiles go free,
Not for price nor reward,"
Says the LORD of hosts.

THE LORD, THE ONLY SAVIOR

14 Thus says the LORD:

"The labor of Egypt and
merchandise of Cush
And of the Sa·bē'ans, men of
stature,
Shall come over to you, and they
shall be yours;
They shall walk behind you,
They shall come over in chains;
And they shall bow down to you.

They will make supplication to
you, *saying,* 'Surely God *is* in
you,
And *there is* no other;
There is no other God.' "

15 Truly You *are* God, who hide
Yourself,
O God of Israel, the Savior!
16 They shall be ashamed
And also disgraced, all of them;
They shall go in confusion
together,
Who are makers of idols.
17 *But* Israel shall be saved by the
LORD
With an everlasting salvation;
You shall not be ashamed or
disgraced
Forever and ever.

18 For thus says the LORD,
Who created the heavens,
Who is God,
Who formed the earth and made
it,
Who has established it,
Who did not create it in vain,
Who formed it to be inhabited:
"I *am* the LORD, and *there is* no
other.
19 I have not spoken in secret,
In a dark place of the earth;
I did not say to the seed of Jacob,
'Seek Me in vain';
I, the LORD, speak righteousness,
I declare things that are right.

20 "Assemble yourselves and come;
Draw near together,
You *who have* escaped from the
nations.
They have no knowledge,
Who carry the wood of their
carved image,
And pray to a god *that* cannot
save.
21 Tell and bring forth *your case;*

What the Bible Says

ABOUT GOD THE CREATOR Isaiah 45:18

Who Made the Ends of the Earth?

Do you see a bird? Who made it? Do you see a magnificent sunset? Who made it? Do you see a pretty flower in the pot? Who made it? Do you see your mother's smile? Who made her? Who made everything you see? Who made everything beyond what you can see, to the ends of the earth?

1. Who is the Creator? Can you create a world? Can you make a person? Why not?
2. What has the Creator done for you? Can you do all these things? Why not?
3. Read Isaiah 40:28. What does it tell you about the Creator?

For more on *What the Bible Says* turn to page 1121
For more on *God's Creation* turn to page 1121

Yes, let them take counsel
    together.
Who has declared this from
    ancient time?
Who has told it from that time?
Have not I, the LORD?
And *there is* no other God besides
    Me,
A just God and a Savior;
There is none besides Me.

22 "Look to Me, and be saved,
    All you ends of the earth!
    For I *am* God, and *there is* no
        other.
23 I have sworn by Myself;
    The word has gone out of My
        mouth *in* righteousness,
    And shall not return,
    That to Me every knee shall bow,
    Every tongue shall take an oath.
24 He shall say,
    'Surely in the LORD I have
        righteousness and strength.
    To Him *men* shall come,
    And all shall be ashamed
    Who are incensed against Him.
25 In the LORD all the descendants of
        Israel
    Shall be justified, and shall glory.'"

DEAD IDOLS AND THE LIVING GOD

46
Bel bows down, Nē′bō stoops;
    Their idols were on the beasts
        and on the cattle.
    Your carriages *were* heavily
        loaded,
    A burden to the weary *beast*.
2 They stoop, they bow down
        together;
    They could not deliver the
        burden,
    But have themselves gone into
        captivity.

3 "Listen to Me, O house of Jacob,
    And all the remnant of the house
        of Israel,

Who have been upheld *by Me*
    from birth,
Who have been carried from the
    womb:
4 Even to *your* old age, I *am* He,
    And *even* to gray hairs I will carry
        you!
    I have made, and I will bear;
    Even I will carry, and will deliver
        you.

5 "To whom will you liken Me, and
        make *Me* equal
    And compare Me, that we should
        be alike?
6 They lavish gold out of the bag,
    And weigh silver on the scales;
    They hire a goldsmith, and he
        makes it a god;
    They prostrate themselves, yes,
        they worship.
7 They bear it on the shoulder, they
        carry it
    And set it in its place, and it
        stands;
    From its place it shall not move.
    Though *one* cries out to it, yet it
        cannot answer
    Nor save him out of his trouble.

8 "Remember this, and show
        yourselves men;
    Recall to mind, O you
        transgressors.
9 Remember the former things of
        old,
    For I *am* God, and *there is* no
        other;
    I am God, and *there is* none like
        Me,
10 Declaring the end from the
        beginning,
    And from ancient times *things*
        that are not *yet* done,
    Saying, 'My counsel shall stand,
    And I will do all My pleasure,'
11 Calling a bird of prey from the
        east,

The man who executes My
    counsel, from a far country.
Indeed I have spoken *it;*
I will also bring it to pass.
I have purposed *it;*
I will also do it.

12 "Listen to Me, you stubborn-
    hearted,
Who *are* far from righteousness:
13 I bring My righteousness near, it
    shall not be far off;
My salvation shall not linger.
And I will place salvation in Zion,
For Israel My glory.

THE HUMILIATION OF BABYLON

47 "Come down and sit in the
    dust,
O virgin daughter of Babylon;
Sit on the ground without a
    throne,
O daughter of the Chal·dē′ans!
For you shall no more be called
Tender and delicate.
2 Take the millstones and grind
    meal.
Remove your veil,
Take off the skirt,
Uncover the thigh,
Pass through the rivers.
3 Your nakedness shall be
    uncovered,
Yes, your shame will be seen;
I will take vengeance,
And I will not arbitrate with a
    man."

4 *As for* our Redeemer, the LORD of
    hosts *is* His name,
The Holy One of Israel.

5 "Sit in silence, and go into
    darkness,
O daughter of the Chal·dē′ans;
For you shall no longer be called
The Lady of Kingdoms.

6 I was angry with My people;
I have profaned My inheritance,
And given them into your hand.
You showed them no mercy;
On the elderly you laid your yoke
    very heavily.
7 And you said, 'I shall be a lady
    forever,'
So that you did not take these
    things to heart,
Nor remember the latter end of
    them.

8 "Therefore hear this now, *you who*
    are given to pleasures,
Who dwell securely,
Who say in your heart,
'I *am,* and *there is* no one else
    besides me;
I shall not sit *as* a widow,
Nor shall I know the loss of
    children';
9 But these two *things* shall come
    to you
In a moment, in one day:
The loss of children, and
    widowhood.
They shall come upon you in their
    fullness
Because of the multitude of your
    sorceries,
For the great abundance of your
    enchantments.

10 "For you have trusted in your
    wickedness;
You have said, 'No one sees me';
Your wisdom and your knowledge
    have warped you;
And you have said in your
    heart,
'I *am,* and *there is* no one else
    besides me.'
11 Therefore evil shall come upon
    you;
You shall not know from where it
    arises.
And trouble shall fall upon you;
You will not be able to put it off.

And desolation shall come upon
   you suddenly,
Which you shall not know.

12 "Stand now with your
      enchantments
   And the multitude of your
      sorceries,
   In which you have labored from
      your youth—
   Perhaps you will be able to profit,
   Perhaps you will prevail.
13 You are wearied in the multitude
      of your counsels;
   Let now the astrologers, the
      stargazers,
   And the monthly prognosticators
   Stand up and save you
   From what shall come upon you.
14 Behold, they shall be as stubble,
   The fire shall burn them;
   They shall not deliver themselves
   From the power of the flame;
   It shall not *be* a coal to be
      warmed by,
   Nor a fire to sit before!
15 Thus shall they be to you
   With whom you have labored,
   Your merchants from your youth;
   They shall wander each one to his
      quarter.
   No one shall save you.

ISRAEL REFINED FOR GOD'S GLORY

48 "Hear this, O house of Jacob,
   Who are called by the name of
      Israel,
   And have come forth from the
      wellsprings of Judah;
   Who swear by the name of the
      LORD,
   And make mention of the God of
      Israel,
   But not in truth or in
      righteousness;
2 For they call themselves after the
   holy city,

And lean on the God of Israel;
The LORD of hosts *is* His name:

3 "I have declared the former things
      from the beginning;
   They went forth from My mouth,
      and I caused them to hear it.
   Suddenly I did *them,* and they
      came to pass.
4 Because I knew that you *were*
      obstinate,
   And your neck *was* an iron
      sinew,
   And your brow bronze,
5 Even from the beginning I have
      declared *it* to you;
   Before it came to pass I
      proclaimed *it* to you,
   Lest you should say, 'My idol has
      done them,
   And my carved image and my
      molded image
   Have commanded them.'

6 "You have heard;
   See all this.
   And will you not declare *it?*
   I have made you hear new things
      from this time,
   Even hidden things, and you did
      not know them.
7 They are created now and not
      from the beginning;
   And before this day you have not
      heard them,
   Lest you should say, 'Of course I
      knew them.'
8 Surely you did not hear,
   Surely you did not know;
   Surely from long ago your ear was
      not opened.
   For I knew that you would deal
      very treacherously,
   And were called a transgressor
      from the womb.

9 "For My name's sake I will defer
      My anger,

And *for* My praise I will restrain
   it from you,
So that I do not cut you off.
10 Behold, I have refined you, but
   not as silver;
I have tested you in the furnace of
   affliction.
11 For My own sake, for My own
   sake, I will do *it;*
For how should *My name* be
   profaned?
And I will not give My glory to
   another.

GOD'S ANCIENT PLAN
TO REDEEM ISRAEL

12 "Listen to Me, O Jacob,
And Israel, My called:
I *am* He, I *am* the First,
I *am* also the Last.
13 Indeed My hand has laid the
   foundation of the earth,
And My right hand has stretched
   out the heavens;
When I call to them,
They stand up together.

14 "All of you, assemble yourselves,
   and hear!
Who among them has declared
   these *things?*
The LORD loves him;
He shall do His pleasure on
   Babylon,
And His arm *shall be against* the
   Chal·dē'ans.
15 I, *even* I, have spoken;
Yes, I have called him,
I have brought him, and his way
   will prosper.

16 "Come near to Me, hear this:
I have not spoken in secret from
   the beginning;
From the time that it was, I *was*
   there.
And now the Lord GOD and His
   Spirit
Have[a] sent Me."

17 Thus says the LORD, your
   Redeemer,
The Holy One of Israel:
"I *am* the LORD your God,
Who teaches you to profit,
Who leads you by the way you
   should go.
18 Oh, that you had heeded My
   commandments!
Then your peace would have been
   like a river,
And your righteousness like the
   waves of the sea.
19 Your descendants also would have
   been like the sand,
And the offspring of your body
   like the grains of sand;
His name would not have been
   cut off
Nor destroyed from before Me."

20 Go forth from Babylon!
Flee from the Chal·dē'ans!
With a voice of singing,
Declare, proclaim this,
Utter it to the end of the earth;
Say, "The LORD has redeemed
   His servant Jacob!"
21 And they did not thirst
When He led them through the
   deserts;
He caused the waters to flow from
   the rock for them;
He also split the rock, and the
   waters gushed out.

22 "*There is* no peace," says the LORD,
   "for the wicked."

THE SERVANT, THE LIGHT
TO THE GENTILES

49 "Listen, O coastlands, to Me,
And take heed, you peoples from
   afar!
The LORD has called Me from the
   womb;

48:16 [a]The Hebrew verb is singular.

From the matrix of My mother He
has made mention of My name.

2 And He has made My mouth like
a sharp sword;
In the shadow of His hand He has
hidden Me,
And made Me a polished shaft;
In His quiver He has hidden Me."

3 "And He said to me,
'You *are* My servant, O Israel,
In whom I will be glorified.'

4 Then I said, 'I have labored in
vain,
I have spent my strength for
nothing and in vain;
Yet surely my just reward *is* with
the LORD,
And my work with my God.'"

5 "And now the LORD says,
Who formed Me from the womb *to
be* His Servant,
To bring Jacob back to Him,
So that Israel is gathered to Him*a*
(For I shall be glorious in the eyes
of the LORD,
And My God shall be My
strength),

6 Indeed He says,
'It is too small a thing that You
should be My Servant
To raise up the tribes of Jacob,
And to restore the preserved ones
of Israel;
I will also give You as a light to
the Gentiles,
That You should be My salvation
to the ends of the earth.'"

7 Thus says the LORD,
The Redeemer of Israel, their
Holy One,
To Him whom man despises,
To Him whom the nation abhors,
To the Servant of rulers:
"Kings shall see and arise,
Princes also shall worship,
Because of the LORD who is
faithful,

The Holy One of Israel;
And He has chosen You."

8 Thus says the LORD:

"In an acceptable time I have
heard You,
And in the day of salvation I have
helped You;
I will preserve You and give You
As a covenant to the people,
To restore the earth,
To cause them to inherit the
desolate heritages;

9 That You may say to the
prisoners, 'Go forth,'
To those who *are* in darkness,
'Show yourselves.'

"They shall feed along the roads,
And their pastures *shall be* on all
desolate heights.

10 They shall neither hunger nor
thirst,
Neither heat nor sun shall strike
them;
For He who has mercy on them
will lead them,
Even by the springs of water He
will guide them.

11 I will make each of My mountains
a road,
And My highways shall be
elevated.

12 Surely these shall come from afar;
Look! Those from the north and
the west,
And these from the land of
Sin'im."

13 Sing, O heavens!
Be joyful, O earth!
And break out in singing,
O mountains!
For the LORD has comforted His
people,
And will have mercy on His
afflicted.

49:5 *a*Qere, Dead Sea Scrolls, and Septuagint read
is gathered to Him; Kethib reads *is not gathered.*

FAILURE Isaiah 49:13

Who Can Help Me When I Fail?

"I failed!" That's what Frank said. He did not do well in school. That's why you see the tear in his eye. Even Puppy has a tear in her eye too.

1. Have you ever failed at something? What? Were you sad?
2. Did you want someone to help you feel better? Who?
3. Read Isaiah 49:13. God wants to comfort His people when they are sad. Jesus will help you when you fail. He will comfort you. Then He will help you do better. Ask Him!

For more on *Values* turn to page 1114
For more on *God's Care* turn to page 1136

God Will Remember Zion

14 But Zion said, "The LORD has
  forsaken me,
  And my Lord has forgotten me."

15 "Can a woman forget her nursing
  child,
  And not have compassion on the
  son of her womb?
  Surely they may forget,
  Yet I will not forget you.
16 See, I have inscribed you on the
  palms *of My hands;*
  Your walls *are* continually before
  Me.
17 Your sons*a* shall make haste;
  Your destroyers and those who
  laid you waste
  Shall go away from you.
18 Lift up your eyes, look around
  and see;
  All these gather together *and*
  come to you.
  As I live," says the LORD,
  "You shall surely clothe yourselves
  with them all as an ornament,
  And bind them *on you* as a bride
  does.

19 "For your waste and desolate
  places,
  And the land of your destruction,
  Will even now be too small for the
  inhabitants;
  And those who swallowed you up
  will be far away.
20 The children you will have,
  After you have lost the others,
  Will say again in your ears,
  'The place *is* too small for me;
  Give me a place where I may
  dwell.'
21 Then you will say in your heart,
  'Who has begotten these for me,
  Since I have lost my children and
  am desolate,
  A captive, and wandering to and
  fro?

And who has brought these up?
There I was, left alone;
But these, where *were* they?' "

22 Thus says the Lord GOD:

"Behold, I will lift My hand in an
  oath to the nations,
  And set up My standard for the
  peoples;
  They shall bring your sons in
  their arms,
  And your daughters shall be
  carried on *their* shoulders;
23 Kings shall be your foster fathers,
  And their queens your nursing
  mothers;
  They shall bow down to you with
  their faces to the earth,
  And lick up the dust of your feet.
  Then you will know that I *am* the
  LORD,
  For they shall not be ashamed
  who wait for Me."

24 Shall the prey be taken from the
  mighty,
  Or the captives of the righteous*a*
  be delivered?

25 But thus says the LORD:

"Even the captives of the mighty
  shall be taken away,
  And the prey of the terrible be
  delivered;
  For I will contend with him who
  contends with you,
  And I will save your children.
26 I will feed those who oppress you
  with their own flesh,
  And they shall be drunk with
  their own blood as with sweet
  wine.

49:17 *a*Dead Sea Scrolls, Septuagint, Targum, and
Vulgate read *builders.*   49:24 *a*Following
Masoretic Text and Targum; Dead Sea Scrolls,
Syriac, and Vulgate read *the mighty;* Septuagint
reads *unjustly.*

All flesh shall know
That I, the LORD, *am* your Savior,
And your Redeemer, the Mighty
  One of Jacob.'"

THE SERVANT, ISRAEL'S HOPE

50 Thus says the LORD:

"Where *is* the certificate of your
  mother's divorce,
Whom I have put away?
Or which of My creditors *is it* to
  whom I have sold you?
For your iniquities you have sold
  yourselves,
And for your transgressions your
  mother has been put away.
2 Why, when I came, *was there* no
  man?
Why, when I called, *was there*
  none to answer?
Is My hand shortened at all that
  it cannot redeem?
Or have I no power to deliver?
Indeed with My rebuke I dry up
  the sea,
I make the rivers a wilderness;
Their fish stink because *there is*
  no water,
And die of thirst.
3 I clothe the heavens with
  blackness,
And I make sackcloth their
  covering."

4 "The Lord GOD has given Me
The tongue of the learned,
That I should know how to speak
A word in season to *him who is*
  weary.
He awakens Me morning by
  morning,
He awakens My ear
To hear as the learned.
5 The Lord GOD has opened My ear;
And I was not rebellious,
Nor did I turn away.

6 I gave My back to those who
  struck *Me,*
And My cheeks to those who
  plucked out the beard;
I did not hide My face from shame
  and spitting.

7 "For the Lord GOD will help Me;
Therefore I will not be disgraced;
Therefore I have set My face like
  a flint,
And I know that I will not be
  ashamed.
8 *He is* near who justifies Me;
Who will contend with Me?
Let us stand together.
Who *is* My adversary?
Let him come near Me.
9 Surely the Lord GOD will help
  Me;
Who *is* he *who* will condemn Me?
Indeed they will all grow old like
  a garment;
The moth will eat them up.

10 "Who among you fears the LORD?
Who obeys the voice of His
  Servant?
Who walks in darkness
And has no light?
Let him trust in the name of the
  LORD
And rely upon his God.
11 Look, all you who kindle a fire,
Who encircle *yourselves* with
  sparks:
Walk in the light of your fire and
  in the sparks you have
  kindled—
This you shall have from My
  hand:
You shall lie down in torment.

THE LORD COMFORTS ZION

51 "Listen to Me, you who follow
  after righteousness,
You who seek the LORD:

JOYFULNESS Isaiah 50:4

Good Morning! Time to Wake Up!

It's wake-up time! Good morning! Do you like to wake up in the morning? It's time to get dressed and brush your teeth. Do you like to do that? It's also time for breakfast. Do you like to eat breakfast? What other very important thing should you do in the morning?

1. Do you like to say "good morning" to mother and father?
2. Do you like to say "good morning" to Jesus? Morning is a good time to pray to Him, isn't it?

For more on *Values* turn to page 1190
For more on *Prayer* turn to page 1339

Look to the rock *from which* you
were hewn,
And to the hole of the pit *from
which* you were dug.
2 Look to Abraham your father,
And to Sarah *who* bore you;
For I called him alone,
And blessed him and increased
him."

3 For the LORD will comfort Zion,
He will comfort all her waste
places;
He will make her wilderness like
Eden,
And her desert like the garden of
the LORD;
Joy and gladness will be found in
it,
Thanksgiving and the voice of
melody.

4 "Listen to Me, My people;
And give ear to Me, O My nation:
For law will proceed from Me,
And I will make My justice rest
As a light of the peoples.
5 My righteousness *is* near,
My salvation has gone forth,
And My arms will judge the
peoples;
The coastlands will wait upon Me,
And on My arm they will trust.
6 Lift up your eyes to the heavens,
And look on the earth beneath.
For the heavens will vanish away
like smoke,
The earth will grow old like a
garment,
And those who dwell in it will die
in like manner;
But My salvation will be forever,
And My righteousness will not be
abolished.

7 "Listen to Me, you who know
righteousness,
You people in whose heart *is* My
law:

Do not fear the reproach of men,
Nor be afraid of their insults.
8 For the moth will eat them up
like a garment,
And the worm will eat them like
wool;
But My righteousness will be
forever,
And My salvation from
generation to generation."

9 Awake, awake, put on strength,
O arm of the LORD!
Awake as in the ancient days,
In the generations of old.
Are You not *the arm* that cut
Rā′hab apart,
And wounded the serpent?
10 *Are* You not *the One* who dried up
the sea,
The waters of the great deep;
That made the depths of the sea a
road
For the redeemed to cross over?
11 So the ransomed of the LORD shall
return,
And come to Zion with singing,
With everlasting joy on their
heads.
They shall obtain joy and
gladness;
Sorrow and sighing shall flee
away.

12 "I, *even* I, *am* He who comforts
you.
Who *are* you that you should be
afraid
Of a man *who* will die,
And of the son of a man *who* will
be made like grass?
13 And you forget the LORD your
Maker,
Who stretched out the heavens
And laid the foundations of the
earth;
You have feared continually every
day

Because of the fury of the
oppressor,
When *he has* prepared to destroy.
And where *is* the fury of the
oppressor?

14 The captive exile hastens, that he
may be loosed,
That he should not die in the pit,
And that his bread should not
fail.

15 But I *am* the LORD your God,
Who divided the sea whose waves
roared—
The LORD of hosts *is* His name.

16 And I have put My words in your
mouth;
I have covered you with the
shadow of My hand,
That I may plant the heavens,
Lay the foundations of the earth,
And say to Zion, 'You *are* My
people.' "

GOD'S FURY REMOVED

17 Awake, awake!
Stand up, O Jerusalem,
You who have drunk at the hand
of the LORD
The cup of His fury;
You have drunk the dregs of the
cup of trembling,
And drained *it* out.

18 *There is* no one to guide her
Among all the sons she has
brought forth;
Nor *is there any* who takes her by
the hand
Among all the sons she has
brought up.

19 These two *things* have come to
you;
Who will be sorry for you?—
Desolation and destruction,
famine and sword—
By whom will I comfort you?

20 Your sons have fainted,
They lie at the head of all the
streets,

Like an antelope in a net;
They are full of the fury of the
LORD,
The rebuke of your God.

21 Therefore please hear this, you
afflicted,
And drunk but not with wine.

22 Thus says your Lord,
The LORD and your God,
Who pleads the cause of His
people:
"See, I have taken out of your
hand
The cup of trembling,
The dregs of the cup of My fury;
You shall no longer drink it.

23 But I will put it into the hand of
those who afflict you,
Who have said to you,*a*
'Lie down, that we may walk over
you.'
And you have laid your body like
the ground,
And as the street, for those who
walk over."

GOD REDEEMS JERUSALEM

52 Awake, awake!
Put on your strength, O Zion;
Put on your beautiful garments,
O Jerusalem, the holy city!
For the uncircumcised and the
unclean
Shall no longer come to you.

2 Shake yourself from the dust,
arise;
Sit down, O Jerusalem!
Loose yourself from the bonds of
your neck,
O captive daughter of Zion!

3 For thus says the LORD:

"You have sold yourselves for
nothing,

51:23 *a*Literally *your soul*

And you shall be redeemed
  without money."

4 For thus says the Lord GOD:

"My people went down at first
  Into Egypt to dwell there;
Then the Assyrian oppressed
  them without cause.
5 Now therefore, what have I here,"
  says the LORD,
"That My people are taken away
  for nothing?
Those who rule over them
  Make them wail,"*a* says the
  LORD,
"And My name *is* blasphemed
  continually every day.
6 Therefore My people shall know
  My name;
Therefore *they shall know* in that
  day
That I *am* He who speaks:
'Behold, *it is* I.' "

7 How beautiful upon the
  mountains
Are the feet of him who brings
  good news,
Who proclaims peace,
Who brings glad tidings of good
  things,
Who proclaims salvation,
Who says to Zion,
"Your God reigns!"
8 Your watchmen shall lift up *their*
  voices,
With their voices they shall sing
  together;
For they shall see eye to eye
When the LORD brings back Zion.
9 Break forth into joy, sing together,
You waste places of Jerusalem!
For the LORD has comforted His
  people,
He has redeemed Jerusalem.
10 The LORD has made bare His holy
  arm
In the eyes of all the nations;

And all the ends of the earth shall
  see
The salvation of our God.

11 Depart! Depart! Go out from
  there,
Touch no unclean *thing;*
Go out from the midst of her,
Be clean,
You who bear the vessels of the
  LORD.
12 For you shall not go out with
  haste,
Nor go by flight;
For the LORD will go before you,
And the God of Israel *will* be your
  rear guard.

THE SIN-BEARING SERVANT

13 Behold, My Servant shall deal
  prudently;
He shall be exalted and extolled
  and be very high.
14 Just as many were astonished at
  you,
So His visage was marred more
  than any man,
And His form more than the sons
  of men;
15 So shall He sprinkle*a* many
  nations.
Kings shall shut their mouths at
  Him;
For what had not been told them
  they shall see,
And what they had not heard
  they shall consider.

53
  Who has believed our report?
And to whom has the arm of the
  LORD been revealed?
2 For He shall grow up before Him
  as a tender plant,

52:5 *a*Dead Sea Scrolls read *Mock;* Septuagint
reads *Marvel and wail;* Targum reads *Boast themselves;* Vulgate reads *Treat them unjustly.*
52:15 *a*Or *startle*

And as a root out of dry ground.
He has no form or comeliness;
And when we see Him,
There is no beauty that we should
    desire Him.
3 He is despised and rejected by
    men,
A Man of sorrows and acquainted
    with grief.
And we hid, as it were, *our* faces
    from Him;
He was despised, and we did not
    esteem Him.

4 Surely He has borne our griefs
And carried our sorrows;
Yet we esteemed Him stricken,
Smitten by God, and afflicted.
5 But He *was* wounded for our
    transgressions,
He was bruised for our iniquities;
The chastisement for our peace
    was upon Him,
And by His stripes we are healed.
6 All we like sheep have gone
    astray;
We have turned, every one, to his
    own way;
And the Lord has laid on Him the
    iniquity of us all.

7 He was oppressed and He was
    afflicted,
Yet He opened not His mouth;
He was led as a lamb to the
    slaughter,
And as a sheep before its shearers
    is silent,
So He opened not His mouth.
8 He was taken from prison and
    from judgment,
And who will declare His
    generation?
For He was cut off from the land
    of the living;
For the transgressions of My
    people He was stricken.
9 And they[a] made His grave with
    the wicked—

But with the rich at His death,
Because He had done no violence,
Nor *was any* deceit in His mouth.

10 Yet it pleased the Lord to bruise
    Him;
He has put *Him* to grief.
When You make His soul an
    offering for sin,
He shall see *His* seed, He shall
    prolong *His* days,
And the pleasure of the Lord
    shall prosper in His hand.
11 He shall see the labor of His
    soul,[a] *and* be satisfied.
By His knowledge My righteous
    Servant shall justify many,
For He shall bear their iniquities.
12 Therefore I will divide Him a
    portion with the great,
And He shall divide the spoil with
    the strong,
Because He poured out His soul
    unto death,
And He was numbered with the
    transgressors,
And He bore the sin of many,
And made intercession for the
    transgressors.

A Perpetual Covenant of Peace

54 "Sing, O barren,
You *who* have not borne!
Break forth into singing, and cry
    aloud,
You *who* have not labored with
    child!
For more *are* the children of the
    desolate
Than the children of the married
    woman," says the Lord.
2 "Enlarge the place of your tent,
And let them stretch out the
    curtains of your dwellings;

53:9 [a]Literally *he* or *He*   53:11 [a]Following
Masoretic Text, Targum, and Vulgate; Dead Sea
Scrolls and Septuagint read *From the labor of His
soul He shall see light.*

Do not spare;
Lengthen your cords,
And strengthen your stakes.
3 For you shall expand to the right
    and to the left,
And your descendants will inherit
    the nations,
And make the desolate cities
    inhabited.

4 "Do not fear, for you will not be
    ashamed;
Neither be disgraced, for you will
    not be put to shame;
For you will forget the shame of
    your youth,
And will not remember the
    reproach of your widowhood
    anymore.
5 For your Maker is your husband,
The LORD of hosts is His name;
And your Redeemer is the Holy
    One of Israel;
He is called the God of the whole
    earth.
6 For the LORD has called you
Like a woman forsaken and
    grieved in spirit,
Like a youthful wife when you
    were refused,"
Says your God.
7 "For a mere moment I have
    forsaken you,
But with great mercies I will
    gather you.
8 With a little wrath I hid My face
    from you for a moment;
But with everlasting kindness I
    will have mercy on you,"
Says the LORD, your Redeemer.

9 "For this is like the waters of Noah
    to Me;
For as I have sworn
That the waters of Noah would no
    longer cover the earth,
So have I sworn
That I would not be angry with
    you, nor rebuke you.

10 For the mountains shall depart
And the hills be removed,
But My kindness shall not depart
    from you,
Nor shall My covenant of peace be
    removed,"
Says the LORD, who has mercy on
    you.

11 "O you afflicted one,
Tossed with tempest, and not
    comforted,
Behold, I will lay your stones with
    colorful gems,
And lay your foundations with
    sapphires.
12 I will make your pinnacles of
    rubies,
Your gates of crystal,
And all your walls of precious
    stones.
13 All your children shall be taught
    by the LORD,
And great shall be the peace of
    your children.
14 In righteousness you shall be
    established;
You shall be far from oppression,
    for you shall not fear;
And from terror, for it shall not
    come near you.
15 Indeed they shall surely
    assemble, but not because of
    Me.
Whoever assembles against you
    shall fall for your sake.

16 "Behold, I have created the
    blacksmith
Who blows the coals in the fire,
Who brings forth an instrument
    for his work;
And I have created the spoiler to
    destroy.
17 No weapon formed against you
    shall prosper,
And every tongue which rises
    against you in judgment
You shall condemn.

This *is* the heritage of the
    servants of the LORD,
And their righteousness *is* from
    Me,"
Says the LORD.

AN INVITATION TO ABUNDANT LIFE

55 "Ho! Everyone who thirsts,
    Come to the waters;
And you who have no money,
    Come, buy and eat.
Yes, come, buy wine and milk
Without money and without price.
2 Why do you spend money for
    what is not bread,
And your wages for *what* does not
    satisfy?
Listen carefully to Me, and eat
    what is good,
And let your soul delight itself in
    abundance.
3 Incline your ear, and come to Me.
Hear, and your soul shall live;
And I will make an everlasting
    covenant with you—
The sure mercies of David.
4 Indeed I have given him *as* a
    witness to the people,
A leader and commander for the
    people.
5 Surely you shall call a nation you
    do not know,
And nations *who* do not know you
    shall run to you,
Because of the LORD your God,
And the Holy One of Israel;
For He has glorified you."

6 Seek the LORD while He may be
    found,
Call upon Him while He is near.
7 Let the wicked forsake his way,
And the unrighteous man his
    thoughts;
Let him return to the LORD,
And He will have mercy on him;
And to our God,
For He will abundantly pardon.

8 "For My thoughts *are* not your
    thoughts,
Nor *are* your ways My ways," says
    the LORD.
9 "For *as* the heavens are higher
    than the earth,
So are My ways higher than your
    ways,
And My thoughts than your
    thoughts.

10 "For as the rain comes down, and
    the snow from heaven,
And do not return there,
But water the earth,
And make it bring forth and bud,
That it may give seed to the
    sower
And bread to the eater,
11 So shall My word be that goes
    forth from My mouth;
It shall not return to Me void,
But it shall accomplish what I
    please,
And it shall prosper *in the thing*
    for which I sent it.

12 "For you shall go out with joy,
And be led out with peace;
The mountains and the hills
Shall break forth into singing
    before you,
And all the trees of the field shall
    clap *their* hands.
13 Instead of the thorn shall come
    up the cypress tree,
And instead of the brier shall
    come up the myrtle tree;
And it shall be to the LORD for a
    name,
For an everlasting sign *that* shall
    not be cut off."

SALVATION FOR THE GENTILES

56 Thus says the LORD:
"Keep justice, and do
    righteousness,

What the Bible Says

ABOUT GOD'S PROVISION Isaiah 55:12, 13

It's Nothing But a Tree

It's nothing but a tree. Have you ever said that as you look at a tree? There are trees all around us. What's so special about a tree?

1. What if every tree on earth disappeared tonight? What difference would it make from now on?
2. What if every tree on earth had disappeared a hundred years ago? What would you *not* have today that you have? Look through your house. Make a list of everything you have that is made of wood—your house, furniture, toys. Pretend all wood is gone. What's missing? Even an armload of firewood is gone, isn't it?
3. Have you ever thought about the joy and delight associated with trees? Look up these Bible verses and talk about the family joys and delights you have had associated with trees: Psalm 96:11–13 and Isaiah 55:12, 13. You may wish to read the entire chapter of Isaiah 55 to capture the full delight and joy associated with the coming Messiah. Remember this was about 900 years before Jesus came, but it told of His coming.

For more on *What the Bible Says* turn to page 1136
For more on *God's Creation* turn to page 1377

For My salvation *is* about to
come,
And My righteousness to be
revealed.
2 Blessed *is* the man *who* does this,
And the son of man *who* lays hold
on it;
Who keeps from defiling the
Sabbath,
And keeps his hand from doing
any evil."

3 Do not let the son of the foreigner
Who has joined himself to the
LORD
Speak, saying,
"The LORD has utterly separated
me from His people";
Nor let the eunuch say,
"Here I am, a dry tree."
4 For thus says the LORD:

"To the eunuchs who keep My
Sabbaths,
And choose what pleases Me,
And hold fast My covenant,
5 Even to them I will give in My
house
And within My walls a place and
a name
Better than that of sons and
daughters;
I will give them*a* an everlasting
name
That shall not be cut off.

6 "Also the sons of the foreigner
Who join themselves to the LORD,
to serve Him,
And to love the name of the LORD,
to be His servants—

56:5 *a*Literally *him*

Everyone who keeps from defiling
　the Sabbath,
And holds fast My covenant—
7 Even them I will bring to My holy
　mountain,
And make them joyful in My
　house of prayer.
Their burnt offerings and their
　sacrifices
Will be accepted on My altar;
For My house shall be called a
　house of prayer for all nations."
8 The Lord GOD, who gathers the
　outcasts of Israel, says,
　"Yet I will gather to him
　Others besides those who are
　gathered to him."

ISRAEL'S IRRESPONSIBLE LEADERS

9 All you beasts of the field, come to
　devour,
All you beasts in the forest.
10 His watchmen *are* blind,
They are all ignorant;
They *are* all dumb dogs,
They cannot bark;
Sleeping, lying down, loving to
　slumber.
11 Yes, *they are* greedy dogs
Which never have enough.
And they *are* shepherds
Who cannot understand;
They all look to their own way,
Every one for his own gain,
From his *own* territory.
12 "Come," *one says,* "I will bring
　wine,
And we will fill ourselves with
　intoxicating drink;
Tomorrow will be as today,
And much more abundant."

ISRAEL'S FUTILE IDOLATRY

57 The righteous perishes,
And no man takes *it* to heart;
Merciful men *are* taken away,
While no one considers

That the righteous is taken away
　from evil.
2 He shall enter into peace;
They shall rest in their beds,
Each one walking *in* his
　uprightness.

3 "But come here,
You sons of the sorceress,
You offspring of the adulterer and
　the harlot!
4 Whom do you ridicule?
Against whom do you make a
　wide mouth
And stick out the tongue?
Are you not children of
　transgression,
Offspring of falsehood,
5 Inflaming yourselves with gods
　under every green tree,
Slaying the children in the
　valleys,
Under the clefts of the rocks?
6 Among the smooth *stones* of the
　stream
Is your portion;
They, they, *are* your lot!
Even to them you have poured a
　drink offering,
You have offered a grain offering.
Should I receive comfort in these?

7 "On a lofty and high mountain
You have set your bed;
Even there you went up
To offer sacrifice.
8 Also behind the doors and their
　posts
You have set up your
　remembrance;
For you have uncovered yourself
　to those other than Me,
And have gone up to them;
You have enlarged your bed
And made *a* covenant with them;
You have loved their bed,
Where you saw *their* nudity.*a*

57:8 *a*Literally *hand,* a euphemism

9 You went to the king with
     ointment,
And increased your perfumes;
You sent your messengers far off,
And *even* descended to Shē′ōl.
10 You are wearied in the length of
     your way;
Yet you did not say, 'There is no
     hope.'
You have found the life of your
     hand;
Therefore you were not grieved.

11 "And of whom have you been
     afraid, or feared,
That you have lied
And not remembered Me,
Nor taken *it* to your heart?
Is it not because I have held My
     peace from of old
That you do not fear Me?
12 I will declare your righteousness
And your works,
For they will not profit you.
13 When you cry out,
Let your collection *of idols* deliver
     you.
But the wind will carry them all
     away,
A breath will take *them*.
But he who puts his trust in Me
     shall possess the land,
And shall inherit My holy
     mountain."

HEALING FOR THE BACKSLIDER

14 And one shall say,
"Heap it up! Heap it up!
Prepare the way,
Take the stumbling block out of
     the way of My people."

15 For thus says the High and Lofty
     One
Who inhabits eternity, whose
     name *is* Holy:
"I dwell in the high and holy *place,*

With him *who* has a contrite and
     humble spirit,
To revive the spirit of the humble,
And to revive the heart of the
     contrite ones.
16 For I will not contend forever,
Nor will I always be angry;
For the spirit would fail before
     Me,
And the souls *which* I have made.
17 For the iniquity of his
     covetousness
I was angry and struck him;
I hid and was angry,
And he went on backsliding in the
     way of his heart.
18 I have seen his ways, and will
     heal him;
I will also lead him,
And restore comforts to him
And to his mourners.

19 "I create the fruit of the lips:
Peace, peace to *him who is* far off
     and to *him who is* near,"
Says the LORD,
"And I will heal him."
20 But the wicked *are* like the
     troubled sea,
When it cannot rest,
Whose waters cast up mire and
     dirt.

21 "*There is* no peace,"
Says my God, "for the wicked."

FASTING THAT PLEASES GOD

58 "Cry aloud, spare not;
Lift up your voice like a trumpet;
Tell My people their
     transgression,
And the house of Jacob their
     sins.
2 Yet they seek Me daily,
And delight to know My ways,
As a nation that did
     righteousness,

RAINY DAY SHARING Isaiah 58:7

It's raining. Katy has an umbrella. Karen doesn't. So Karen is getting wet.

1. What should Katy do? Why?
2. What should Karen say then? Why?
3. Think of something you can share today.

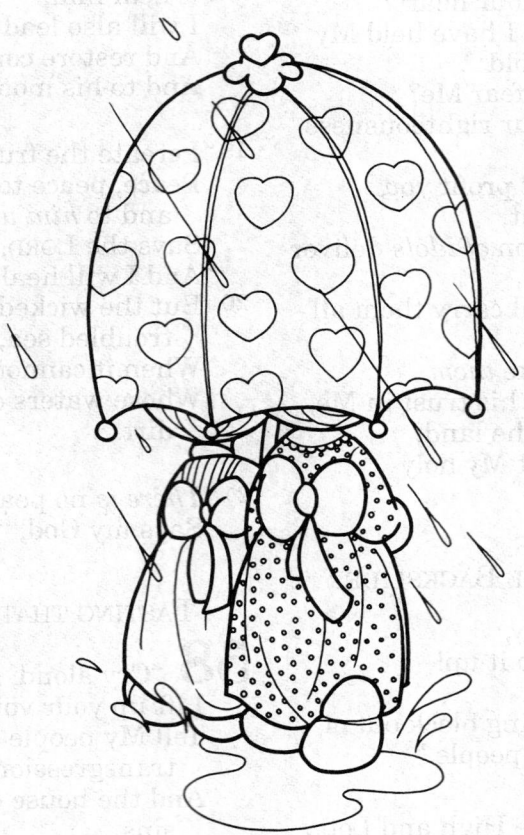

For more on *What Should I Do?* turn to page 1208
For more on *Sharing* turn to page 1464

And did not forsake the ordinance
    of their God.
They ask of Me the ordinances of
    justice;
They take delight in approaching
    God.
3 'Why have we fasted,' *they say,*
    'and You have not seen?
Why have we afflicted our souls,
    and You take no notice?'

    "In fact, in the day of your fast you
      find pleasure,
And exploit all your laborers.
4 Indeed you fast for strife and
    debate,
And to strike with the fist of
    wickedness.
You will not fast as *you do* this
    day,
To make your voice heard on high.
5 Is it a fast that I have chosen,
A day for a man to afflict his soul?
Is it to bow down his head like a
    bulrush,
And to spread out sackcloth and
    ashes?
Would you call this a fast,
And an acceptable day to the
    LORD?

6 "*Is* this not the fast that I have
    chosen:
To loose the bonds of wickedness,
To undo the heavy burdens,
To let the oppressed go free,
And that you break every yoke?
7 *Is it* not to share your bread with
    the hungry,
And that you bring to your house
    the poor who are cast out;
When you see the naked, that you
    cover him,
And not hide yourself from your
    own flesh?
8 Then your light shall break forth
    like the morning,
Your healing shall spring forth
    speedily,

And your righteousness shall go
    before you;
The glory of the LORD shall be
    your rear guard.

■ *Promises* ■

Isaiah 58:9

Has someone ever ignored you
when you tried to talk to him or
her? Do you ever feel that someone is not listening to you?
Here's a promise from God. Talk
to Him. He will *always* listen.
He will answer in the way He
knows is best. Pray! God listens.
Pray! God answers.

---

9 Then you shall call, and the LORD
    will answer;
You shall cry, and He will say,
    'Here I *am.*'

    "If you take away the yoke from
      your midst,
The pointing of the finger, and
    speaking wickedness,
10 *If* you extend your soul to the
    hungry
And satisfy the afflicted soul,
Then your light shall dawn in the
    darkness,
And your darkness shall *be* as the
    noonday.
11 The LORD will guide you
    continually,
And satisfy your soul in drought,
And strengthen your bones;
You shall be like a watered
    garden,
And like a spring of water, whose
    waters do not fail.
12 Those from among you
Shall build the old waste places;
You shall raise up the foundations
    of many generations;

And you shall be called the
  Repairer of the Breach,
The Restorer of Streets to Dwell
  In.

13 "If you turn away your foot from
    the Sabbath,
  From doing your pleasure on My
    holy day,
  And call the Sabbath a delight,
  The holy *day* of the LORD
    honorable,
  And shall honor Him, not doing
    your own ways,
  Nor finding your own pleasure,
  Nor speaking *your own* words,
14 Then you shall delight yourself in
    the LORD;
  And I will cause you to ride on the
    high hills of the earth,
  And feed you with the heritage of
    Jacob your father.
  The mouth of the LORD has
    spoken."

SEPARATED FROM GOD

59 Behold, the LORD's hand is not
    shortened,
  That it cannot save;
  Nor His ear heavy,
  That it cannot hear.
2 But your iniquities have
    separated you from your God;
  And your sins have hidden *His*
    face from you,
  So that He will not hear.
3 For your hands are defiled with
    blood,
  And your fingers with iniquity;
  Your lips have spoken lies,
  Your tongue has muttered
    perversity.

4 No one calls for justice,
  Nor does *any* plead for truth.
  They trust in empty words and
    speak lies;

They conceive evil and bring forth
  iniquity.
5 They hatch vipers' eggs and
    weave the spider's web;
  He who eats of their eggs dies,
  And *from* that which is crushed a
    viper breaks out.

6 Their webs will not become
    garments,
  Nor will they cover themselves
    with their works;
  Their works *are* works of iniquity,
  And the act of violence *is* in their
    hands.
7 Their feet run to evil,
  And they make haste to shed
    innocent blood;
  Their thoughts *are* thoughts of
    iniquity;
  Wasting and destruction *are* in
    their paths.
8 The way of peace they have not
    known,
  And *there is* no justice in their
    ways;
  They have made themselves
    crooked paths;
  Whoever takes that way shall not
    know peace.

SIN CONFESSED

9 Therefore justice is far from us,
  Nor does righteousness overtake
    us;
  We look for light, but there is
    darkness!
  For brightness, *but* we walk in
    blackness!
10 We grope for the wall like the
    blind,
  And we grope as if *we had* no
    eyes;
  We stumble at noonday as at
    twilight;
  We are as dead *men* in desolate
    places.
11 We all growl like bears,

And moan sadly like doves;
We look for justice, but *there is*
  none;
For salvation, *but* it is far from
  us.
12 For our transgressions are
  multiplied before You,
And our sins testify against us;
For our transgressions *are* with
  us,
And *as for* our iniquities, we
  know them:
13 In transgressing and lying
  against the LORD,
And departing from our God,
Speaking oppression and revolt,
Conceiving and uttering from the
  heart words of falsehood.
14 Justice is turned back,
And righteousness stands afar off;
For truth is fallen in the street,
And equity cannot enter.
15 So truth fails,
And he *who* departs from evil
  makes himself a prey.

THE REDEEMER OF ZION

Then the LORD saw *it,* and it
  displeased Him
That *there was* no justice.
16 He saw that *there was* no man,
And wondered that *there was* no
  intercessor;
Therefore His own arm brought
  salvation for Him;
And His own righteousness, it
  sustained Him.
17 For He put on righteousness as a
  breastplate,
And a helmet of salvation on His
  head;
He put on the garments of
  vengeance for clothing,
And was clad with zeal as a cloak.
18 According to *their* deeds,
  accordingly He will repay,
Fury to His adversaries,
Recompense to His enemies;

The coastlands He will fully
  repay.
19 So shall they fear
The name of the LORD from the
  west,
And His glory from the rising of
  the sun;
When the enemy comes in like a
  flood,
The Spirit of the LORD will lift up
  a standard against him.

20 "The Redeemer will come to Zion,
And to those who turn from
  transgression in Jacob,"
Says the LORD.

21 "As for Me," says the LORD, "this
is My covenant with them: My Spirit
who *is* upon you, and My words
which I have put in your mouth, shall
not depart from your mouth, nor
from the mouth of your descendants,
nor from the mouth of your descendants' descendants," says the LORD,
"from this time and forevermore."

THE GENTILES BLESS ZION

60 Arise, shine;
  For your light has come!
And the glory of the LORD is risen
  upon you.
2 For behold, the darkness shall
  cover the earth,
And deep darkness the people;
But the LORD will arise over you,
And His glory will be seen upon
  you.
3 The Gentiles shall come to your
  light,
And kings to the brightness of
  your rising.

4 "Lift up your eyes all around, and
  see:
They all gather together, they
  come to you;

Your sons shall come from afar,
And your daughters shall be
    nursed at *your* side.
5   Then you shall see and become
    radiant,
And your heart shall swell with
    joy;
Because the abundance of the sea
    shall be turned to you,
The wealth of the Gentiles shall
    come to you.
6   The multitude of camels shall
    cover your *land,*
The dromedaries of Mid′i·an and
    Ē′phah;
All those from Shē′ba shall come;
They shall bring gold and
    incense,
And they shall proclaim the
    praises of the LORD.
7   All the flocks of Kē′dar shall be
    gathered together to you,
The rams of Ne·bā′i·oth shall
    minister to you;
They shall ascend with
    acceptance on My altar,
And I will glorify the house of My
    glory.

8   "Who *are* these *who* fly like a
    cloud,
And like doves to their roosts?
9   Surely the coastlands shall wait
    for Me;
And the ships of Tar′shish *will
    come* first,
To bring your sons from afar,
Their silver and their gold with
    them,
To the name of the LORD your
    God,
And to the Holy One of Israel,
Because He has glorified you.

10 "The sons of foreigners shall build
    up your walls,
And their kings shall minister to
    you;
For in My wrath I struck you,

But in My favor I have had mercy
    on you.
11 Therefore your gates shall be
    open continually;
They shall not be shut day or
    night,
That *men* may bring to you the
    wealth of the Gentiles,
And their kings in procession.
12 For the nation and kingdom
    which will not serve you shall
    perish,
And *those* nations shall be utterly
    ruined.
13 "The glory of Lebanon shall come
    to you,
The cypress, the pine, and the box
    tree together,
To beautify the place of My
    sanctuary;
And I will make the place of My
    feet glorious.
14 Also the sons of those who
    afflicted you
Shall come bowing to you,
And all those who despised you
    shall fall prostrate at the soles
    of your feet;
And they shall call you The City
    of the LORD,
Zion of the Holy One of Israel.

15 "Whereas you have been forsaken
    and hated,
So that no one went through *you,*
I will make you an eternal
    excellence,
A joy of many generations.
16 You shall drink the milk of the
    Gentiles,
And milk the breast of kings;
You shall know that I, the LORD,
    am your Savior
And your Redeemer, the Mighty
    One of Jacob.

17 "Instead of bronze I will bring
    gold,

Instead of iron I will bring silver,
Instead of wood, bronze,
And instead of stones, iron.
I will also make your officers
   peace,
And your magistrates
   righteousness.
18 Violence shall no longer be heard
   in your land,
Neither wasting nor destruction
   within your borders;
But you shall call your walls
   Salvation,
And your gates Praise.

GOD THE GLORY OF HIS PEOPLE

19 "The sun shall no longer be your
   light by day,
Nor for brightness shall the moon
   give light to you;
But the LORD will be to you an
   everlasting light,
And your God your glory.
20 Your sun shall no longer go down,
Nor shall your moon withdraw
   itself;
For the LORD will be your
   everlasting light,
And the days of your mourning
   shall be ended.
21 Also your people *shall* all *be*
   righteous;
They shall inherit the land
   forever,
The branch of My planting,
The work of My hands,
That I may be glorified.
22 A little one shall become a
   thousand,
And a small one a strong nation.
I, the LORD, will hasten it in its
   time."

THE GOOD NEWS OF SALVATION

61 "The Spirit of the Lord GOD *is*
   upon Me,

Because the LORD has anointed
   Me
To preach good tidings to the
   poor;
He has sent Me to heal the
   brokenhearted,
To proclaim liberty to the
   captives,
And the opening of the prison to
   those who are bound;
2 To proclaim the acceptable year of
   the LORD,
And the day of vengeance of our
   God;
To comfort all who mourn,

Praises

Isaiah 61:3

Have you ever thought of praise as a piece of clothing? Isaiah speaks of it as a mantle, like a cloak. Have you ever seen bright happy clothing that seemed to praise the person who wears it? Could we wear our praise for God like a beautiful piece of clothing? Would others see it and say "praise the Lord"? Wear your praise for God like a beautiful coat.

3 To console those who mourn in
   Zion,
To give them beauty for ashes,
The oil of joy for mourning,
The garment of praise for the
   spirit of heaviness;
That they may be called trees of
   righteousness,
The planting of the LORD, that He
   may be glorified."

4 And they shall rebuild the old
   ruins,
They shall raise up the former
   desolations,

And they shall repair the ruined
cities,
The desolations of many
generations.

5 Strangers shall stand and feed
your flocks,
And the sons of the foreigner
Shall be your plowmen and your
vinedressers.

6 But you shall be named the
priests of the LORD,
They shall call you the servants of
our God.
You shall eat the riches of the
Gentiles,
And in their glory you shall
boast.

7 Instead of your shame *you shall
have* double *honor,*
And *instead of* confusion they
shall rejoice in their portion.
Therefore in their land they shall
possess double;
Everlasting joy shall be theirs.

8 "For I, the LORD, love justice;
I hate robbery for burnt offering;
I will direct their work in truth,
And will make with them an
everlasting covenant.

9 Their descendants shall be known
among the Gentiles,
And their offspring among the
people.
All who see them shall
acknowledge them,
That they *are* the posterity *whom*
the LORD has blessed."

10 I will greatly rejoice in the LORD,
My soul shall be joyful in my God;
For He has clothed me with the
garments of salvation,
He has covered me with the robe
of righteousness,
As a bridegroom decks *himself*
with ornaments,
And as a bride adorns *herself*
with her jewels.

11 For as the earth brings forth its
bud,
As the garden causes the things
that are sown in it to spring
forth,
So the Lord GOD will cause
righteousness and praise to
spring forth before all the
nations.

ASSURANCE OF ZION'S SALVATION

62 For Zion's sake I will not hold
My peace,
And for Jerusalem's sake I will
not rest,
Until her righteousness goes forth
as brightness,
And her salvation as a lamp *that*
burns.

2 The Gentiles shall see your
righteousness,
And all kings your glory.
You shall be called by a new
name,
Which the mouth of the LORD will
name.

3 You shall also be a crown of
glory
In the hand of the LORD,
And a royal diadem
In the hand of your God.

4 You shall no longer be termed
Forsaken,
Nor shall your land any more be
termed Desolate;
But you shall be called
Heph′zi·bah,*a* and your land
Beū′lah;*b*
For the LORD delights in you,
And your land shall be married.

5 For *as* a young man marries a
virgin,
So shall your sons marry you;
And *as* the bridegroom rejoices
over the bride,

62:4 *a*Literally *My Delight Is in Her*   *b*Literally
Married

So shall your God rejoice over
    you.

6 I have set watchmen on your
    walls, O Jerusalem;
  They shall never hold their peace
    day or night.
  You who make mention of the
    LORD, do not keep silent,
7 And give Him no rest till He
    establishes
  And till He makes Jerusalem a
    praise in the earth.

8 The LORD has sworn by His right
    hand
  And by the arm of His strength:
  "Surely I will no longer give your
    grain
  As food for your enemies;
  And the sons of the foreigner
    shall not drink your new wine,
  For which you have labored.
9 But those who have gathered it
    shall eat it,
  And praise the LORD;
  Those who have brought it
    together shall drink it in My
    holy courts."

10 Go through,
  Go through the gates!
  Prepare the way for the people;
  Build up,
  Build up the highway!
  Take out the stones,
  Lift up a banner for the peoples!

11 Indeed the LORD has proclaimed
  To the end of the world:
  "Say to the daughter of Zion,
  'Surely your salvation is coming;
  Behold, His reward *is* with
    Him,
  And His work before Him.' "
12 And they shall call them The
    Holy People,
  The Redeemed of the LORD;

And you shall be called Sought
    Out,
A City Not Forsaken.

THE LORD IN JUDGMENT AND SALVATION

63 Who *is* this who comes from
    Ē'dom,
  With dyed garments from
    Boz'rah,
  This *One who is* glorious in His
    apparel,
  Traveling in the greatness of His
    strength?—

  "I who speak in righteousness,
    mighty to save."

2 Why *is* Your apparel red,
  And Your garments like one who
    treads in the winepress?

3 "I have trodden the winepress
    alone,
  And from the peoples no one *was*
    with Me.
  For I have trodden them in My
    anger,
  And trampled them in My fury;
  Their blood is sprinkled upon My
    garments,
  And I have stained all My robes.
4 For the day of vengeance *is* in My
    heart,
  And the year of My redeemed has
    come.
5 I looked, but *there was* no one to
    help,
  And I wondered
  That *there was* no one to uphold;
  Therefore My own arm brought
    salvation for Me;
  And My own fury, it sustained
    Me.
6 I have trodden down the peoples
    in My anger,
  Made them drunk in My fury,

And brought down their strength
to the earth."

GOD'S MERCY REMEMBERED

7 I will mention the
lovingkindnesses of the LORD
And the praises of the LORD,
According to all that the LORD has
bestowed on us,
And the great goodness toward
the house of Israel,
Which He has bestowed on them
according to His mercies,
According to the multitude of His
lovingkindnesses.
8 For He said, "Surely they *are* My
people,
Children *who* will not lie."
So He became their Savior.
9 In all their affliction He was
afflicted,
And the Angel of His Presence
saved them;
In His love and in His pity He
redeemed them;
And He bore them and carried
them
All the days of old.
10 But they rebelled and grieved His
Holy Spirit;
So He turned Himself against
them as an enemy,
And He fought against them.

11 Then he remembered the days of
old,
Moses *and* his people, *saying:*
"Where *is* He who brought them
up out of the sea
With the shepherd of His flock?
Where *is* He who put His Holy
Spirit within them,
12 Who led *them* by the right hand of
Moses,
With His glorious arm,
Dividing the water before them
To make for Himself an
everlasting name,

13 Who led them through the deep,
As a horse in the wilderness,
That they might not stumble?"
14 As a beast goes down into the
valley,
And the Spirit of the LORD causes
him to rest,
So You lead Your people,
To make Yourself a glorious
name.

A PRAYER OF PENITENCE

15 Look down from heaven,
And see from Your habitation,
holy and glorious.
Where *are* Your zeal and Your
strength,
The yearning of Your heart and
Your mercies toward me?
Are they restrained?
16 Doubtless You *are* our Father,
Though Abraham was ignorant of
us,
And Israel does not acknowledge
us.
You, O LORD, *are* our Father;
Our Redeemer from Everlasting
is Your name.
17 O LORD, why have You made us
stray from Your ways,
And hardened our heart from
Your fear?
Return for Your servants' sake,
The tribes of Your inheritance.
18 Your holy people have possessed
it but a little while;
Our adversaries have trodden
down Your sanctuary.
19 We have become *like* those of old,
over whom You never ruled,
Those who were never called by
Your name.

64 Oh, that You would rend the
heavens!
That You would come down!

*J*esus, my Good Shepherd, will protect me and comfort me.

———

Isaiah 40:11

Good friends help to chase our tears away.

Jeremiah 31:13

*S*ing "Thank You" to the Lord when He does something wonderful.

———

Daniel 4:34

*P*rayer time is a "Thank-You-God" time.

———

Jonah 2:9

That the mountains might shake
  at Your presence—
2 As fire burns brushwood,
As fire causes water to boil—
To make Your name known to
  Your adversaries,
That the nations may tremble at
  Your presence!
3 When You did awesome things *for*
  which we did not look,
You came down,
The mountains shook at Your
  presence.
4 For since the beginning of the
  world
Men have not heard nor perceived
  by the ear,
Nor has the eye seen any God
  besides You,
Who acts for the one who waits
  for Him.
5 You meet him who rejoices and
  does righteousness,
Who remembers You in Your
  ways.
You are indeed angry, for we have
  sinned—
In these ways we continue;
And we need to be saved.

6 But we are all like an unclean
  thing,
And all our righteousnesses *are*
  like filthy rags;
We all fade as a leaf,
And our iniquities, like the wind,
Have taken us away.
7 And *there is* no one who calls on
  Your name,
Who stirs himself up to take hold
  of You;
For You have hidden Your face
  from us,
And have consumed us because of
  our iniquities.

8 But now, O LORD,
You *are* our Father;

We *are* the clay, and You our
  potter;
And all we *are* the work of Your
  hand.
9 Do not be furious, O LORD,
Nor remember iniquity forever;
Indeed, please look—we all *are*
  Your people!
10 Your holy cities are a wilderness,
Zion is a wilderness,
Jerusalem a desolation.
11 Our holy and beautiful temple,
Where our fathers praised You,
Is burned up with fire;
And all our pleasant things are
  laid waste.
12 Will You restrain Yourself because
  of these *things,* O LORD?
Will You hold Your peace, and
  afflict us very severely?

THE RIGHTEOUSNESS
OF GOD'S JUDGMENT

65 "I was sought by *those who* did
  not ask *for Me;*
I was found by *those who* did not
  seek Me.
I said, 'Here I am, here I am,'
To a nation *that* was not called by
  My name.
2 I have stretched out My hands all
  day long to a rebellious people,
Who walk in a way *that is* not
  good,
According to their own thoughts;
3 A people who provoke Me to
  anger continually to My face;
Who sacrifice in gardens,
And burn incense on altars of
  brick;
4 Who sit among the graves,
And spend the night in the tombs;
Who eat swine's flesh,
And the broth of abominable
  things is *in* their vessels;
5 Who say, 'Keep to yourself,
Do not come near me,
For I am holier than you!'

These *are* smoke in My nostrils,
A fire that burns all the day.

6 "Behold, *it is* written before Me:
    I will not keep silence, but will
      repay—
    Even repay into their bosom—
7 Your iniquities and the iniquities
      of your fathers together,"
    Says the LORD,
    "Who have burned incense on the
      mountains
    And blasphemed Me on the hills;
    Therefore I will measure their
      former work into their bosom."

8 Thus says the LORD:

    "As the new wine is found in the
      cluster,
    And *one* says, 'Do not destroy it,
    For a blessing *is* in it,'
    So will I do for My servants' sake,
    That I may not destroy them all.
9 I will bring forth descendants
      from Jacob,
    And from Judah an heir of My
      mountains;
    My elect shall inherit it,
    And My servants shall dwell
      there.
10 Sharon shall be a fold of flocks,
    And the Valley of Ā'chor a place
      for herds to lie down,
    For My people who have sought
      Me.

11 "But you *are* those who forsake the
      LORD,
    Who forget My holy mountain,
    Who prepare a table for Gad,*a*
    And who furnish a drink offering
      for Men'ī.*b*
12 Therefore I will number you for
      the sword,
    And you shall all bow down to the
      slaughter;
    Because, when I called, you did
      not answer;

When I spoke, you did not hear,
    But did evil before My eyes,
    And chose *that* in which I do not
      delight."

13 Therefore thus says the Lord
GOD:

    "Behold, My servants shall eat,
    But you shall be hungry;
    Behold, My servants shall drink,
    But you shall be thirsty;
    Behold, My servants shall rejoice,
    But you shall be ashamed;
14 Behold, My servants shall sing for
      joy of heart,
    But you shall cry for sorrow of
      heart,
    And wail for grief of spirit.
15 You shall leave your name as a
      curse to My chosen;
    For the Lord GOD will slay you,
    And call His servants by another
      name;
16 So that he who blesses himself in
      the earth
    Shall bless himself in the God of
      truth;
    And he who swears in the earth
    Shall swear by the God of truth;
    Because the former troubles are
      forgotten,
    And because they are hidden from
      My eyes.

THE GLORIOUS NEW CREATION

17 "For behold, I create new heavens
      and a new earth;
    And the former shall not be
      remembered or come to mind.
18 But be glad and rejoice forever in
      what I create;
    For behold, I create Jerusalem *as*
      a rejoicing,
    And her people a joy.

65:11 *a*Literally *Troop* or *Fortune,* a pagan deity
*b*Literally *Number* or *Destiny,* a pagan deity

19 I will rejoice in Jerusalem,
And joy in My people;
The voice of weeping shall no
longer be heard in her,
Nor the voice of crying.

20 "No more shall an infant from
there *live but a few* days,
Nor an old man who has not
fulfilled his days;
For the child shall die one
hundred years old,
But the sinner *being* one
hundred years old shall be
accursed.
21 They shall build houses and
inhabit *them;*
They shall plant vineyards and
eat their fruit.
22 They shall not build and another
inhabit;
They shall not plant and another
eat;
For as the days of a tree, *so shall
be* the days of My people,
And My elect shall long enjoy the
work of their hands.
23 They shall not labor in vain,
Nor bring forth children for
trouble;
For they *shall be* the descendants
of the blessed of the LORD,
And their offspring with them.

24 "It shall come to pass
That before they call, I will
answer;
And while they are still speaking,
I will hear.
25 The wolf and the lamb shall feed
together,
The lion shall eat straw like the
ox,
And dust *shall be* the serpent's
food.
They shall not hurt nor destroy in
all My holy mountain,"
Says the LORD.

TRUE WORSHIP AND FALSE

66 Thus says the LORD:

"Heaven *is* My throne,
And earth *is* My footstool.
Where *is* the house that you will
build Me?
And where *is* the place of My
rest?
2   For all those *things* My hand has
made,
And all those *things* exist,"
Says the LORD.
"But on this *one* will I look:
On *him who is* poor and of a
contrite spirit,
And who trembles at My word.

3 "He who kills a bull *is as if* he
slays a man;
He who sacrifices a lamb, *as if* he
breaks a dog's neck;
He who offers a grain offering, *as
if he offers* swine's blood;
He who burns incense, *as if* he
blesses an idol.
Just as they have chosen their
own ways,
And their soul delights in their
abominations,
4   So will I choose their delusions,
And bring their fears on them;
Because, when I called, no one
answered,
When I spoke they did not hear;
But they did evil before My
eyes,
And chose *that* in which I do not
delight."

THE LORD VINDICATES ZION

5   Hear the word of the LORD,
You who tremble at His word:
"Your brethren who hated you,
Who cast you out for My name's
sake, said,
'Let the LORD be glorified,

What the Bible Says

ABOUT GOD'S COMFORT   Isaiah 66:13

God Will Wipe Away Your Tears

Do you sometimes want to cry? Are you sometimes bruised or beat up or unhappy? You want someone to comfort you and wipe away your tears. Mother or father are often good tear wipers and comforters. So is God. He is always there to wipe away your tears and comfort you.

1. Read Isaiah 66:13. Who will comfort us like a mother comforts us? Why is that so important?
2. Do you comfort others who hurt? Can you think of some friends or family members who need comfort? Will you help to chase their tears away?

For more on *What the Bible Says* turn to page 1260
For more on *God's Care* turn to page 1237

That we may see your joy.'
But they shall be ashamed."

6   The sound of noise from the city!
A voice from the temple!
The voice of the LORD,
Who fully repays His enemies!

7   "Before she was in labor, she gave
birth;
Before her pain came,
She delivered a male child.
8   Who has heard such a thing?
Who has seen such things?
Shall the earth be made to give
birth in one day?
Or shall a nation be born at once?
For as soon as Zion was in labor,
She gave birth to her children.
9   Shall I bring to the time of birth,
and not cause delivery?" says
the LORD.
"Shall I who cause delivery shut
up *the womb?*" says your God.
10 "Rejoice with Jerusalem,
And be glad with her, all you who
love her;
Rejoice for joy with her, all you
who mourn for her;
11   That you may feed and be
satisfied
With the consolation of her
bosom,
That you may drink deeply and
be delighted
With the abundance of her glory."

12   For thus says the LORD:

"Behold, I will extend peace to her
like a river,
And the glory of the Gentiles like
a flowing stream.
Then you shall feed;
On *her* sides shall you be carried,
And be dandled on *her* knees.
13   As one whom his mother
comforts,
So I will comfort you;

And you shall be comforted in
Jerusalem."

THE REIGN AND INDIGNATION OF GOD

14   When you see *this,* your heart
shall rejoice,
And your bones shall flourish like
grass;
The hand of the LORD shall be
known to His servants,
And *His* indignation to His
enemies.
15   For behold, the LORD will come
with fire
And with His chariots, like a
whirlwind,
To render His anger with fury,
And His rebuke with flames of
fire.
16   For by fire and by His sword
The LORD will judge all flesh;
And the slain of the LORD shall be
many.

17 "Those who sanctify themselves
and purify themselves,
To go to the gardens
After an *idol* in the midst,
Eating swine's flesh and the
abomination and the mouse,
Shall be consumed together," says
the LORD.

18   "For I *know* their works and their
thoughts. It shall be that I will
gather all nations and tongues; and
they shall come and see My glory.
19   "I will set a sign among them; and
those among them who escape I will
send to the nations: *to* Tar′shish and
Pūl[a] and Lud, who draw the bow, and
Tū′bal and Jā′van, *to* the coastlands
afar off who have not heard My fame
nor seen My glory. And they shall declare My glory among the Gentiles.

66:19 [a]Following Masoretic Text and Targum; Septuagint reads *Put* (compare Jeremiah 46:9).

20 "Then they shall bring all your brethren for an offering to the LORD out of all nations, on horses and in chariots and in litters, on mules and on camels, to My holy mountain Jerusalem," says the LORD, "as the children of Israel bring an offering in a clean vessel into the house of the LORD.

21 "And I will also take some of them for priests *and* Lē′vītes," says the LORD.

22 "For as the new heavens and the
    new earth
  Which I will make shall remain
    before Me," says the LORD,

"So shall your descendants and
    your name remain.
23 And it shall come to pass
  That from one New Moon to
    another,
  And from one Sabbath to another,
  All flesh shall come to worship
    before Me," says the LORD.

24 "And they shall go forth and look
  Upon the corpses of the men
  Who have transgressed against
    Me.
  For their worm does not die,
  And their fire is not quenched.
  They shall be an abhorrence to all
    flesh."

The Book of

JEREMIAH

THE words of Jer·e·mī′ah the son of Hil·kī′ah, of the priests who *were* in An′a·thoth in the land of Benjamin,
2 to whom the word of the LORD came in the days of Jō·sī′ah the son of Ā′mon, king of Judah, in the thirteenth year of his reign.
3 It came also in the days of Je·hoi′a·kim the son of Jō·sī′ah, king of Judah, until the end of the eleventh year of Zed·e·kī′ah the son of Jō·sī′ah, king of Judah, until the carrying away of Jerusalem captive in the fifth month.

THE PROPHET IS CALLED

4 Then the word of the LORD came to me, saying:

5 "Before I formed you in the womb I knew you;
Before you were born I sanctified you;
I ordained you a prophet to the nations."

6 Then said I:

"Ah, Lord GOD!
Behold, I cannot speak, for I *am* a youth."

7 But the LORD said to me:

"Do not say, 'I *am* a youth,'
For you shall go to all to whom I send you,
And whatever I command you, you shall speak.
8 Do not be afraid of their faces,
For I *am* with you to deliver you," says the LORD.

9 Then the LORD put forth His hand and touched my mouth, and the LORD said to me:

"Behold, I have put My words in your mouth.
10 See, I have this day set you over the nations and over the kingdoms,
To root out and to pull down,
To destroy and to throw down,
To build and to plant."

11 Moreover the word of the LORD came to me, saying, "Jer·e·mī′ah, what do you see?" And I said, "I see a branch of an almond tree."
12 Then the LORD said to me, "You have seen well, for I am ready to perform My word."
13 And the word of the LORD came to me the second time, saying, "What do you see?" And I said, "I see a boiling pot, and it is facing away from the north."
14 Then the LORD said to me:

"Out of the north calamity shall break forth
On all the inhabitants of the land.
15 For behold, I am calling
All the families of the kingdoms of the north," says the LORD;

Promises

Jeremiah 1:8

Are you ever afraid of something? What do you do? Do you run? Do you try to handle this by yourself? God has a promise for you. He is with you. So you don't need to be afraid. God is bigger and stronger than anything in the world. When He is with you, stop being afraid. Pray and ask His help.

"They shall come and each one set
his throne
At the entrance of the gates of
Jerusalem,
Against all its walls all around,
And against all the cities of
Judah.
16 I will utter My judgments
Against them concerning all their
wickedness,
Because they have forsaken Me,
Burned incense to other gods,
And worshiped the works of their
own hands.

17 "Therefore prepare yourself and
arise,
And speak to them all that I
command you.
Do not be dismayed before their
faces,
Lest I dismay you before them.
18 For behold, I have made you this
day
A fortified city and an iron pillar,
And bronze walls against the
whole land—
Against the kings of Judah,
Against its princes,
Against its priests,
And against the people of the
land.
19 They will fight against you,
But they shall not prevail against
you.
For I am with you," says the
LORD, "to deliver you."

GOD'S CASE AGAINST ISRAEL

2 Moreover the word of the LORD
came to me, saying,
2 "Go and cry in the hearing of Jerusalem, saying, 'Thus says the
LORD:

"I remember you,
The kindness of your youth,
The love of your betrothal,

When you went after Me in the
wilderness,
In a land not sown.
3 Israel was holiness to the LORD,
The firstfruits of His increase.
All that devour him will offend;
Disaster will come upon them,"
says the LORD.' "

4 Hear the word of the LORD, O
house of Jacob and all the families of
the house of Israel.
5 Thus says the LORD:

"What injustice have your fathers
found in Me,
That they have gone far from Me,
Have followed idols,
And have become idolaters?
6 Neither did they say, 'Where is
the LORD,
Who brought us up out of the
land of Egypt,
Who led us through the
wilderness,
Through a land of deserts and
pits,
Through a land of drought and
the shadow of death,
Through a land that no one
crossed
And where no one dwelt?'
7 I brought you into a bountiful
country,
To eat its fruit and its goodness.
But when you entered, you defiled
My land
And made My heritage an
abomination.
8 The priests did not say, 'Where is
the LORD?'
And those who handle the law did
not know Me;
The rulers also transgressed
against Me;
The prophets prophesied by
Ba'al,
And walked after things that do
not profit.

9 "Therefore I will yet bring charges
  against you," says the LORD,
  "And against your children's
  children I will bring charges.
10 For pass beyond the coasts of
  Cyprus*a* and see,
  Send to Kē′dar*b* and consider
  diligently,
  And see if there has been such *a*
  thing.
11 Has a nation changed *its* gods,
  Which *are* not gods?
  But My people have changed
  their Glory
  For *what* does not profit.
12 Be astonished, O heavens, at this,
  And be horribly afraid;
  Be very desolate," says the LORD.
13 "For My people have committed
  two evils:
  They have forsaken Me, the
  fountain of living waters,
  And hewn themselves cisterns—
  broken cisterns that can hold
  no water.

14 "*Is* Israel a servant?
  Is he a homeborn *slave*?
  Why is he plundered?
15 The young lions roared at him,
  and growled;
  They made his land waste;
  His cities are burned, without
  inhabitant.
16 Also the people of Noph*a* and
  Tah′pan·hēs
  Have broken the crown of your
  head.
17 Have you not brought this on
  yourself,
  In that you have forsaken the
  LORD your God
  When He led you in the way?
18 And now why take the road to
  Egypt,
  To drink the waters of Sī′hor?
  Or why take the road to Assyria,
  To drink the waters of the
  River?*a*

19 Your own wickedness will correct
  you,
  And your backslidings will rebuke
  you.
  Know therefore and see that *it is*
  an evil and bitter *thing*
  That you have forsaken the LORD
  your God,
  And the fear of Me *is* not in you,"
  Says the Lord GOD of hosts.

20 "For of old I have broken your yoke
  and burst your bonds;
  And you said, 'I will not
  transgress,'
  When on every high hill and
  under every green tree
  You lay down, playing the harlot.
21 Yet I had planted you a noble
  vine, a seed of highest quality.
  How then have you turned before
  Me
  Into the degenerate plant of an
  alien vine?
22 For though you wash yourself
  with lye, and use much soap,
  Yet your iniquity is marked before
  Me," says the Lord GOD.

23 "How can you say, 'I am not
  polluted,
  I have not gone after the
  Bā′als'?
  See your way in the valley;
  Know what you have done:
  You are a swift dromedary
  breaking loose in her ways,
24 A wild donkey used to the
  wilderness,
  That sniffs at the wind in her
  desire;
  In her time of mating, who can
  turn her away?

2:10 *a*Hebrew *Kittim,* western lands, especially
Cyprus *b*In the northern Arabian desert, repre-
sentative of the eastern cultures 2:16 *a*That is,
Memphis in ancient Egypt 2:18 *a*That is, the
Euphrates

All those who seek her will not
   weary themselves;
In her month they will find her.
25 Withhold your foot from being
   unshod, and your throat from
   thirst.
But you said, 'There is no hope.
No! For I have loved aliens, and
   after them I will go.'

26 "As the thief is ashamed when he
   is found out,
So is the house of Israel ashamed;
They and their kings and their
   princes, and their priests and
   their prophets,
27 Saying to a tree, 'You *are* my
   father,'
And to a stone, 'You gave birth to
   me.'
For they have turned *their* back
   to Me, and not *their* face.
But in the time of their trouble
They will say, 'Arise and save us.'
28 But where *are* your gods that you
   have made for yourselves?
Let them arise,
If they can save you in the time of
   your trouble;
For *according to* the number of
   your cities
Are your gods, O Judah.

29 "Why will you plead with Me?
You all have transgressed against
   Me," says the LORD.
30 "In vain I have chastened your
   children;
They received no correction.
Your sword has devoured your
   prophets
Like a destroying lion.

31 "O generation, see the word of the
   LORD!
Have I been a wilderness to
   Israel,
Or a land of darkness?

Why do My people say, 'We are
   lords;
We will come no more to You'?
32 Can a virgin forget her
   ornaments,
Or a bride her attire?
Yet My people have forgotten Me
   days without number.

33 "Why do you beautify your way to
   seek love?
Therefore you have also taught
The wicked women your ways.
34 Also on your skirts is found
The blood of the lives of the poor
   innocents.
I have not found it by secret
   search,
But plainly on all these things.
35 Yet you say, 'Because I am
   innocent,
Surely His anger shall turn from
   me.'
Behold, I will plead My case
   against you,
Because you say, 'I have not
   sinned.'
36 Why do you gad about so much to
   change your way?
Also you shall be ashamed of
   Egypt as you were ashamed of
   Assyria.
37 Indeed you will go forth from
   him
With your hands on your head;
For the LORD has rejected your
   trusted allies,
And you will not prosper by them.

ISRAEL IS SHAMELESS

3 "They say, 'If a man divorces his
   wife,
And she goes from him
And becomes another man's,
May he return to her again?'
Would not that land be greatly
   polluted?

But you have played the harlot
   with many lovers;
Yet return to Me," says the LORD.

2 "Lift up your eyes to the desolate
   heights and see:
Where have you not lain *with
  men?*
By the road you have sat for them
Like an Arabian in the
  wilderness;
And you have polluted the land
With your harlotries and your
  wickedness.
3 Therefore the showers have been
   withheld,
And there has been no latter rain.
You have had a harlot's forehead;
You refuse to be ashamed.
4 Will you not from this time cry to
  Me,
'My Father, You *are* the guide of
  my youth?
5 Will He remain angry forever?
Will He keep it to the end?'
Behold, you have spoken and
  done evil things,
As you were able."

A CALL TO REPENTANCE

6 The LORD said also to me in the
days of Jō·sī′ah the king: "Have you
seen what backsliding Israel has
done? She has gone up on every high
mountain and under every green
tree, and there played the harlot.
7 "And I said, after she had done all
these *things,* 'Return to Me.' But she
did not return. And her treacherous
sister Judah saw it.
8 "Then I saw that for all the
causes for which backsliding Israel
had committed adultery, I had put
her away and given her a certificate
of divorce; yet her treacherous sister
Judah did not fear, but went and
played the harlot also.
9 "So it came to pass, through her

casual harlotry, that she defiled the
land and committed adultery with
stones and trees.
10 "And yet for all this her treacherous sister Judah has not turned to
Me with her whole heart, but in pretense," says the LORD.
11 Then the LORD said to me, "Backsliding Israel has shown herself more
righteous than treacherous Judah.
12 "Go and proclaim these words toward the north, and say:

'Return, backsliding Israel,' says
  the LORD;
'I will not cause My anger to fall
  on you.
For I *am* merciful,' says the LORD;
'I will not remain angry forever.
13 Only acknowledge your iniquity,
That you have transgressed
  against the LORD your God,
And have scattered your charms
To alien deities under every green
  tree,
And you have not obeyed My
  voice,' says the LORD.

14 "Return, O backsliding children,"
says the LORD; "for I am married to
you. I will take you, one from a city
and two from a family, and I will
bring you to Zion.
15 "And I will give you shepherds according to My heart, who will feed
you with knowledge and understanding.
16 "Then it shall come to pass, when
you are multiplied and increased in
the land in those days," says the
LORD, "that they will say no more,
'The ark of the covenant of the LORD.'
It shall not come to mind, nor shall
they remember it, nor shall they visit
it, nor shall it be made anymore.
17 "At that time Jerusalem shall be
called The Throne of the LORD, and
all the nations shall be gathered to it,
to the name of the LORD, to Jerusa-

lem. No more shall they follow the dictates of their evil hearts.

18 "In those days the house of Judah shall walk with the house of Israel, and they shall come together out of the land of the north to the land that I have given as an inheritance to your fathers.

19 "But I said:

'How can I put you among the children
And give you a pleasant land,
A beautiful heritage of the hosts of nations?'

"And I said:

'You shall call Me, "My Father,"
And not turn away from Me.'
20 Surely, *as* a wife treacherously departs from her husband,
So have you dealt treacherously with Me,
O house of Israel," says the LORD.

21 A voice was heard on the desolate heights,
Weeping *and* supplications of the children of Israel.
For they have perverted their way;
They have forgotten the LORD their God.

22 "Return, you backsliding children,
And I will heal your backslidings."

"Indeed we do come to You,
For You are the LORD our God.
23 Truly, in vain *is salvation hoped for* from the hills,
And from the multitude of mountains;
Truly, in the LORD our God
Is the salvation of Israel.
24 For shame has devoured

The labor of our fathers from our youth—
Their flocks and their herds,
Their sons and their daughters.
25 We lie down in our shame,
And our reproach covers us.
For we have sinned against the LORD our God,
We and our fathers,
From our youth even to this day,
And have not obeyed the voice of the LORD our God."

4 "If you will return, O Israel," says the LORD,
"Return to Me;
And if you will put away your abominations out of My sight,
Then you shall not be moved.
2 And you shall swear, 'The LORD lives,'
In truth, in judgment, and in righteousness;
The nations shall bless themselves in Him,
And in Him they shall glory."

3 For thus says the LORD to the men of Judah and Jerusalem:

"Break up your fallow ground,
And do not sow among thorns.
4 Circumcise yourselves to the LORD,
And take away the foreskins of your hearts,
You men of Judah and inhabitants of Jerusalem,
Lest My fury come forth like fire,
And burn so that no one can quench *it,*
Because of the evil of your doings."

AN IMMINENT INVASION

5 Declare in Judah and proclaim in Jerusalem, and say:

"Blow the trumpet in the land;
 Cry, 'Gather together,'
 And say, 'Assemble yourselves,
 And let us go into the fortified
    cities.'
6 Set up the standard toward Zion.
 Take refuge! Do not delay!
 For I will bring disaster from the
    north,
 And great destruction."

7 The lion has come up from his
    thicket,
 And the destroyer of nations is on
    his way.
 He has gone forth from his place
 To make your land desolate.
 Your cities will be laid waste,
 Without inhabitant.
8 For this, clothe yourself with
    sackcloth,
 Lament and wail.
 For the fierce anger of the LORD
 Has not turned back from us.

9 "And it shall come to pass in that
    day," says the LORD,
 "*That* the heart of the king shall
    perish,
 And the heart of the princes;
 The priests shall be astonished,
 And the prophets shall wonder."

10 Then I said, "Ah, Lord GOD!
 Surely You have greatly deceived
    this people and Jerusalem,
 Saying, 'You shall have peace,'
 Whereas the sword reaches to the
    heart."

11 At that time it will be said
 To this people and to Jerusalem,
 "A dry wind of the desolate heights
    blows in the wilderness
 Toward the daughter of My
    people—
 Not to fan or to cleanse—
12 A wind too strong for these will
    come for Me;

Now I will also speak judgment
    against them."

13 "Behold, he shall come up like
    clouds,
 And his chariots like a whirlwind.
 His horses are swifter than
    eagles.
 Woe to us, for we are plundered!"

14 O Jerusalem, wash your heart
    from wickedness,
 That you may be saved.
 How long shall your evil thoughts
    lodge within you?
15 For a voice declares from Dan
 And proclaims affliction from
    Mount Ē'phra·im:
16 "Make mention to the nations,
 Yes, proclaim against Jerusalem,
 That watchers come from a far
    country
 And raise their voice against the
    cities of Judah.
17 Like keepers of a field they are
    against her all around,
 Because she has been rebellious
    against Me," says the LORD.
18 "Your ways and your doings
 Have procured these *things* for
    you.
 This *is* your wickedness,
 Because it is bitter,
 Because it reaches to your heart."

SORROW FOR THE DOOMED NATION

19 O my soul, my soul!
 I am pained in my very heart!
 My heart makes a noise in me;
 I cannot hold my peace,
 Because you have heard, O my
    soul,
 The sound of the trumpet,
 The alarm of war.
20 Destruction upon destruction is
    cried,
 For the whole land is plundered.

Suddenly my tents are plundered,
And my curtains in a moment.
21 How long will I see the standard,
And hear the sound of the
trumpet?

22 "For My people *are* foolish,
They have not known Me.
They *are* silly children,
And they have no understanding.
They *are* wise to do evil,
But to do good they have no
knowledge."

23 I beheld the earth, and indeed *it
was* without form, and void;
And the heavens, they *had* no
light.
24 I beheld the mountains, and
indeed they trembled,
And all the hills moved back and
forth.
25 I beheld, and indeed *there was* no
man,
And all the birds of the heavens
had fled.
26 I beheld, and indeed the fruitful
land *was* a wilderness,
And all its cities were broken
down
At the presence of the LORD,
By His fierce anger.

27 For thus says the LORD:

"The whole land shall be desolate;
Yet I will not make a full end.
28 For this shall the earth mourn,
And the heavens above be black,
Because I have spoken.
I have purposed and will not
relent,
Nor will I turn back from it.
29 The whole city shall flee from the
noise of the horsemen and
bowmen.
They shall go into thickets and
climb up on the rocks.

Every city *shall be* forsaken,
And not a man shall dwell in it.

30 "And *when* you *are* plundered,
What will you do?
Though you clothe yourself with
crimson,
Though you adorn *yourself* with
ornaments of gold,
Though you enlarge your eyes
with paint,
In vain you will make yourself
fair;
Your lovers will despise you;
They will seek your life.

31 "For I have heard a voice as of a
woman in labor,
The anguish as of her who brings
forth her first child,
The voice of the daughter of Zion
bewailing herself;
She spreads her hands, *saying,*
'Woe *is* me now, for my soul is
weary
Because of murderers!'

THE JUSTICE OF GOD'S JUDGMENT

5 "Run to and fro through the
streets of Jerusalem;
See now and know;
And seek in her open places
If you can find a man,
If there is *anyone* who executes
judgment,
Who seeks the truth,
And I will pardon her.
2 Though they say, 'As the LORD
lives,'
Surely they swear falsely."

3 O LORD, *are* not Your eyes on the
truth?
You have stricken them,
But they have not grieved;
You have consumed them,
But they have refused to receive
correction.

They have made their faces
    harder than rock;
They have refused to return.

4 Therefore I said, "Surely these
    are poor.
They are foolish;
For they do not know the way of
    the LORD,
The judgment of their God.
5 I will go to the great men and
    speak to them,
For they have known the way of
    the LORD,
The judgment of their God."

But these have altogether broken
    the yoke
And burst the bonds.
6 Therefore a lion from the forest
    shall slay them,
A wolf of the deserts shall destroy
    them;
A leopard will watch over their
    cities.
Everyone who goes out from there
    shall be torn in pieces,
Because their transgressions are
    many;
Their backslidings have
    increased.

7 "How shall I pardon you for this?
Your children have forsaken Me
And sworn by *those that are* not
    gods.
When I had fed them to the full,
Then they committed adultery
And assembled themselves by
    troops in the harlots' houses.
8 They were *like* well-fed lusty
    stallions;
Every one neighed after his
    neighbor's wife.
9 Shall I not punish *them* for these
    things?" says the LORD.
"And shall I not avenge Myself on
    such a nation as this?

10 "Go up on her walls and destroy,
But do not make a complete end.
Take away her branches,
For they *are* not the LORD's.
11 For the house of Israel and the
    house of Judah
Have dealt very treacherously
    with Me," says the LORD.

12 They have lied about the LORD,
And said, "*It is* not He.
Neither will evil come upon us,
Nor shall we see sword or famine.
13 And the prophets become wind,
For the word *is* not in them.
Thus shall it be done to them."

14 Therefore thus says the LORD God
of hosts:

"Because you speak this word,
Behold, I will make My words in
    your mouth fire,
And this people wood,
And it shall devour them.
15 Behold, I will bring a nation
    against you from afar,
O house of Israel," says the LORD.
"It *is* a mighty nation,
It *is* an ancient nation,
A nation whose language you do
    not know,
Nor can you understand what
    they say.
16 Their quiver *is* like an open
    tomb;
They *are* all mighty men.
17 And they shall eat up your
    harvest and your bread,
Which your sons and daughters
    should eat.
They shall eat up your flocks and
    your herds;
They shall eat up your vines and
    your fig trees;
They shall destroy your fortified
    cities,
In which you trust, with the
    sword.

18 "Nevertheless in those days," says the LORD, "I will not make a complete end of you.

19 "And it will be when you say, 'Why does the LORD our God do all these *things* to us?' then you shall answer them, 'Just as you have forsaken Me and served foreign gods in your land, so you shall serve aliens in a land *that is* not yours.'

20 "Declare this in the house of Jacob
  And proclaim it in Judah, saying,
21 'Hear this now, O foolish people,
  Without understanding,
  Who have eyes and see not,
  And who have ears and hear not:
22 Do you not fear Me?' says the
    LORD.
  'Will you not tremble at My
    presence,
  Who have placed the sand as the
    bound of the sea,
  By a perpetual decree, that it
    cannot pass beyond it?
  And though its waves toss to and
    fro,
  Yet they cannot prevail;
  Though they roar, yet they cannot
    pass over it.
23 But this people has a defiant and
    rebellious heart;
  They have revolted and departed.
24 They do not say in their heart,
  "Let us now fear the LORD our
    God,
  Who gives rain, both the former
    and the latter, in its season.
  He reserves for us the appointed
    weeks of the harvest."
25 Your iniquities have turned these
    things away,
  And your sins have withheld good
    from you.

26 'For among My people are found
    wicked *men;*
  They lie in wait as one who sets
    snares;

They set a trap;
  They catch men.
27 As a cage is full of birds,
  So their houses *are* full of deceit.
  Therefore they have become great
    and grown rich.
28 They have grown fat, they are
    sleek;
  Yes, they surpass the deeds of the
    wicked;
  They do not plead the cause,
  The cause of the fatherless;
  Yet they prosper,
  And the right of the needy they do
    not defend.
29 Shall I not punish *them* for these
    things?' says the LORD.
  'Shall I not avenge Myself on such
    a nation as this?'

30 "An astonishing and horrible thing
  Has been committed in the land:
31 The prophets prophesy falsely,
  And the priests rule by their *own*
    power;
  And My people love *to have it* so.
  But what will you do in the end?

IMPENDING DESTRUCTION
FROM THE NORTH

6 "O you children of Benjamin,
Gather yourselves to flee from the
    midst of Jerusalem!
Blow the trumpet in Te·kō′a,
And set up a signal-fire in Beth
    Hac′ce·rem;
For disaster appears out of the
    north,
And great destruction.
2 I have likened the daughter of
    Zion
To a lovely and delicate woman.
3 The shepherds with their flocks
    shall come to her.
They shall pitch *their* tents
    against her all around.
Each one shall pasture in his own
    place."

4 "Prepare war against her;
    Arise, and let us go up at noon.
    Woe to us, for the day goes away,
    For the shadows of the evening
      are lengthening.
5   Arise, and let us go by night,
    And let us destroy her palaces."

6   For thus has the LORD of hosts
said:

    "Cut down trees,
    And build a mound against
      Jerusalem.
    This *is* the city to be punished.
    She *is* full of oppression in her
      midst.
7   As a fountain wells up with
      water,
    So she wells up with her
      wickedness.
    Violence and plundering are
      heard in her.
    Before Me continually *are* grief
      and wounds.
8   Be instructed, O Jerusalem,
    Lest My soul depart from you;
    Lest I make you desolate,
    A land not inhabited."

9   Thus says the LORD of hosts:

    "They shall thoroughly glean as a
      vine the remnant of Israel;
    As a grape-gatherer, put your
      hand back into the branches."

10   To whom shall I speak and give
      warning,
    That they may hear?
    Indeed their ear *is* uncircumcised,
    And they cannot give heed.
    Behold, the word of the LORD is a
      reproach to them;
    They have no delight in it.
11   Therefore I am full of the fury of
      the LORD.
    I am weary of holding *it* in.
    "I will pour it out on the children
      outside,

And on the assembly of young
    men together;
    For even the husband shall be
      taken with the wife,
    The aged with *him who is* full of
      days.
12   And their houses shall be turned
      over to others,
    Fields and wives together;
    For I will stretch out My hand
    Against the inhabitants of the
      land," says the LORD.
13 "Because from the least of them
      even to the greatest of them,
    Everyone *is* given to
      covetousness;
    And from the prophet even to the
      priest,
    Everyone deals falsely.
14   They have also healed the hurt of
      My people slightly,
    Saying, 'Peace, peace!'
    When *there is* no peace.
15   Were they ashamed when they
      had committed abomination?
    No! They were not at all
      ashamed;
    Nor did they know how to blush.
    Therefore they shall fall among
      those who fall;
    At the time I punish them,
    They shall be cast down," says the
      LORD.

16   Thus says the LORD:

    "Stand in the ways and see,
    And ask for the old paths, where
      the good way *is,*
    And walk in it;
    Then you will find rest for your
      souls.
    But they said, 'We will not walk
      in it.'
17   Also, I set watchmen over you,
      saying,
    'Listen to the sound of the
      trumpet!'
    But they said, 'We will not listen.'

18 Therefore hear, you nations,
And know, O congregation, what
is among them.
19 Hear, O earth!
Behold, I will certainly bring
calamity on this people—
The fruit of their thoughts,
Because they have not heeded My
words
Nor My law, but rejected it.
20 For what purpose to Me
Comes frankincense from She′ba,
And sweet cane from a far
country?
Your burnt offerings *are* not
acceptable,
Nor your sacrifices sweet to Me.″

21 Therefore thus says the LORD:

″Behold, I will lay stumbling
blocks before this people,
And the fathers and the sons
together shall fall on them.
The neighbor and his friend shall
perish.″

22 Thus says the LORD:

″Behold, a people comes from the
north country,
And a great nation will be raised
from the farthest parts of the
earth.
23 They will lay hold on bow and
spear;
They *are* cruel and have no
mercy;
Their voice roars like the sea;
And they ride on horses,
As men of war set in array
against you, O daughter of
Zion.″

24 We have heard the report of it;
Our hands grow feeble.
Anguish has taken hold of us,
Pain as of a woman in labor.
25 Do not go out into the field,
Nor walk by the way.

Because of the sword of the
enemy,
Fear *is* on every side.
26 O daughter of my people,
Dress in sackcloth
And roll about in ashes!
Make mourning *as for* an only
son, most bitter lamentation;
For the plunderer will suddenly
come upon us.

27 ″I have set you *as* an assayer *and*
a fortress among My people,
That you may know and test their
way.
28 They *are* all stubborn rebels,
walking as slanderers.
They are bronze and iron,
They *are* all corrupters;
29 The bellows blow fiercely,
The lead is consumed by the fire;
The smelter refines in vain,
For the wicked are not drawn off.
30 *People* will call them rejected
silver,
Because the LORD has rejected
them.″

TRUSTING IN LYING WORDS

7 The word that came to Jer·e-mī′ah from the LORD, saying,
2 ″Stand in the gate of the LORD's house, and proclaim there this word, and say, 'Hear the word of the LORD, all *you of* Judah who enter in at these gates to worship the LORD!' ″
3 Thus says the LORD of hosts, the God of Israel: ″Amend your ways and your doings, and I will cause you to dwell in this place.
4 ″Do not trust in these lying words, saying, 'The temple of the LORD, the temple of the LORD, the temple of the LORD *are* these.'
5 ″For if you thoroughly amend your ways and your doings, if you thoroughly execute judgment between a man and his neighbor,

6 "*if* you do not oppress the stranger, the fatherless, and the widow, and do not shed innocent blood in this place, or walk after other gods to your hurt,

7 "then I will cause you to dwell in this place, in the land that I gave to your fathers forever and ever.

8 "Behold, you trust in lying words that cannot profit.

9 "Will you steal, murder, commit adultery, swear falsely, burn incense to Bā′al, and walk after other gods whom you do not know,

10 "and *then* come and stand before Me in this house which is called by My name, and say, 'We are delivered to do all these abominations'?

11 "Has this house, which is called by My name, become a den of thieves in your eyes? Behold, I, even I, have seen *it*," says the LORD.

12 "But go now to My place which *was* in Shī′lōh, where I set My name at the first, and see what I did to it because of the wickedness of My people Israel.

13 "And now, because you have done all these works," says the LORD, "and I spoke to you, rising up early and speaking, but you did not hear, and I called you, but you did not answer,

14 "therefore I will do to the house which is called by My name, in which you trust, and to this place which I gave to you and your fathers, as I have done to Shī′lōh.

15 "And I will cast you out of My sight, as I have cast out all your brethren—the whole posterity of Ē′phra·im.

16 "Therefore do not pray for this people, nor lift up a cry or prayer for them, nor make intercession to Me; for I will not hear you.

17 "Do you not see what they do in the cities of Judah and in the streets of Jerusalem?

18 "The children gather wood, the fathers kindle the fire, and the women knead dough, to make cakes for the queen of heaven; and *they* pour out drink offerings to other gods, that they may provoke Me to anger.

19 "Do they provoke Me to anger?" says the LORD. "*Do they* not *provoke* themselves, to the shame of their own faces?"

20 Therefore thus says the Lord GOD: "Behold, My anger and My fury will be poured out on this place—on man and on beast, on the trees of the field and on the fruit of the ground. And it will burn and not be quenched."

21 Thus says the LORD of hosts, the God of Israel: "Add your burnt offerings to your sacrifices and eat meat.

22 "For I did not speak to your fathers, or command them in the day that I brought them out of the land of Egypt, concerning burnt offerings or sacrifices.

23 "But this is what I commanded

Promises

Jeremiah 7:23

Do you like to obey? Most people don't. Most people want to do what they want to do. Often this isn't the best for them. God's promise is simple. Obey Him, and He will be your God and you will be His people. Do what God says and it will be well with you. Ignore what God says and it may hurt you. Do you want what is best for you? Obey God. Do what He says. Do you want Him to be your God? Obey God. Do you want to be His person? Obey God. He promises to be your God and give you what is best if you obey Him.

them, saying, 'Obey My voice, and I will be your God, and you shall be My people. And walk in all the ways that I have commanded you, that it may be well with you.'

24 "Yet they did not obey or incline their ear, but followed the counsels *and* the dictates of their evil hearts, and went backward and not forward.

25 "Since the day that your fathers came out of the land of Egypt until this day, I have even sent to you all My servants the prophets, daily rising up early and sending *them*.

26 "Yet they did not obey Me or incline their ear, but stiffened their neck. They did worse than their fathers.

27 "Therefore you shall speak all these words to them, but they will not obey you. You shall also call to them, but they will not answer you.

JUDGMENT ON OBSCENE RELIGION

28 "So you shall say to them, 'This *is* a nation that does not obey the voice of the LORD their God nor receive correction. Truth has perished and has been cut off from their mouth.

29 'Cut off your hair and cast *it* away, and take up a lamentation on the desolate heights; for the LORD has rejected and forsaken the generation of His wrath.'

30 "For the children of Judah have done evil in My sight," says the LORD. "They have set their abominations in the house which is called by My name, to pollute it.

31 "And they have built the high places of Tō′phet, which *is* in the Valley of the Son of Hin′nom, to burn their sons and their daughters in the fire, which I did not command, nor did it come into My heart.

32 "Therefore behold, the days are coming," says the LORD, "when it will no more be called Tō′phet, or the Val-

ley of the Son of Hin′nom, but the Valley of Slaughter; for they will bury in Tō′phet until there is no room.

33 "The corpses of this people will be food for the birds of the heaven and for the beasts of the earth. And no one will frighten *them away*.

34 "Then I will cause to cease from the cities of Judah and from the streets of Jerusalem the voice of mirth and the voice of gladness, the voice of the bridegroom and the voice of the bride. For the land shall be desolate.

8 "At that time," says the LORD, "they shall bring out the bones of the kings of Judah, and the bones of its princes, and the bones of the priests, and the bones of the prophets, and the bones of the inhabitants of Jerusalem, out of their graves.

2 "They shall spread them before the sun and the moon and all the host of heaven, which they have loved and which they have served and after which they have walked, which they have sought and which they have worshiped. They shall not be gathered nor buried; they shall be like refuse on the face of the earth.

3 "Then death shall be chosen rather than life by all the residue of those who remain of this evil family, who remain in all the places where I have driven them," says the LORD of hosts.

THE PERIL OF FALSE TEACHING

4 "Moreover you shall say to them, 'Thus says the LORD:

"Will they fall and not rise?
Will one turn away and not
    return?
5 Why has this people slidden back,
    Jerusalem, in a perpetual
    backsliding?

They hold fast to deceit,
They refuse to return.

6 I listened and heard,
But they do not speak aright.
No man repented of his
wickedness,
Saying, 'What have I done?'
Everyone turned to his own
course,
As the horse rushes into the
battle.

7 "Even the stork in the heavens
Knows her appointed times;
And the turtledove, the swift, and
the swallow
Observe the time of their
coming.
But My people do not know the
judgment of the LORD.

8 "How can you say, 'We *are* wise,
And the law of the LORD *is* with
us'?
Look, the false pen of the scribe
certainly works falsehood.

9 The wise men are ashamed,
They are dismayed and taken.
Behold, they have rejected the
word of the LORD;
So what wisdom do they have?

10 Therefore I will give their wives
to others,
And their fields to those who will
inherit *them;*
Because from the least even to
the greatest
Everyone is given to
covetousness;
From the prophet even to the
priest
Everyone deals falsely.

11 For they have healed the hurt of
the daughter of My people
slightly,
Saying, 'Peace, peace!'
When *there is* no peace.

12 Were they ashamed when they
had committed abomination?
No! They were not at all
ashamed,
Nor did they know how to blush.
Therefore they shall fall among
those who fall;
In the time of their punishment
They shall be cast down," says the
LORD.

13 "I will surely consume them," says
the LORD.
"No grapes *shall be* on the vine,
Nor figs on the fig tree,
And the leaf shall fade;
And *the things* I have given them
shall pass away from them." ' "

14 "Why do we sit still?
Assemble yourselves,
And let us enter the fortified
cities,
And let us be silent there.
For the LORD our God has put us
to silence
And given us water of gall to
drink,
Because we have sinned against
the LORD.

15 "*We* looked for peace, but no good
came;
And for a time of health, and
there was trouble!

16 The snorting of His horses was
heard from Dan.
The whole land trembled at the
sound of the neighing of His
strong ones;
For they have come and devoured
the land and all that is in it,
The city and those who dwell in
it."

17 "For behold, I will send serpents
among you,
Vipers which cannot be charmed,
And they shall bite you," says the
LORD.

THE PROPHET MOURNS FOR THE PEOPLE

18 I would comfort myself in sorrow;
My heart *is* faint in me.
19 Listen! The voice,
The cry of the daughter of my
   people
From a far country:
"*Is* not the LORD in Zion?
Is not her King in her?"

"Why have they provoked Me to
   anger
With their carved images—
With foreign idols?"

20 "The harvest is past,
The summer is ended,
And we are not saved!"

21 For the hurt of the daughter of
   my people I am hurt.
I am mourning;
Astonishment has taken hold of
   me.
22 *Is there* no balm in Gil′ē·ad,
Is there no physician there?
Why then is there no recovery
For the health of the daughter of
   my people?

9 Oh, that my head were waters,
And my eyes a fountain of tears,
That I might weep day and night
For the slain of the daughter of
   my people!
2 Oh, that I had in the wilderness
A lodging place for travelers;
That I might leave my people,
And go from them!
For they *are* all adulterers,
An assembly of treacherous men.

3 "And *like* their bow they have bent
   their tongues *for* lies.
They are not valiant for the truth
   on the earth.

For they proceed from evil to evil,
And they do not know Me," says
   the LORD.
4 "Everyone take heed to his
   neighbor,
And do not trust any brother;
For every brother will utterly
   supplant,
And every neighbor will walk
   with slanderers.
5 Everyone will deceive his
   neighbor,
And will not speak the truth;
They have taught their tongue to
   speak lies;
They weary themselves to commit
   iniquity.
6 Your dwelling place *is* in the
   midst of deceit;
Through deceit they refuse to
   know Me," says the LORD.

7 Therefore thus says the LORD of
hosts:

"Behold, I will refine them and try
   them;
For how shall I deal with the
   daughter of My people?
8 Their tongue *is* an arrow shot out;
It speaks deceit;
One speaks peaceably to his
   neighbor with his mouth,
But in his heart he lies in wait.
9 Shall I not punish them for these
   things?" says the LORD.
"Shall I not avenge Myself on such
   a nation as this?"

10 I will take up a weeping and
   wailing for the mountains,
And for the dwelling places of the
   wilderness a lamentation,
Because they are burned up,
So that no one can pass through;
Nor can *men* hear the voice of the
   cattle.
Both the birds of the heavens and
   the beasts have fled;
They are gone.

11 "I will make Jerusalem a heap of ruins, a den of jackals.
I will make the cities of Judah desolate, without an inhabitant."

12 Who *is* the wise man who may understand this? And *who is he* to whom the mouth of the LORD has spoken, that he may declare it? Why does the land perish *and* burn up like a wilderness, so that no one can pass through?
13 And the LORD said, "Because they have forsaken My law which I set before them, and have not obeyed My voice, nor walked according to it,
14 "but they have walked according to the dictates of their own hearts and after the Bāʹals, which their fathers taught them,"
15 therefore thus says the LORD of hosts, the God of Israel: "Behold, I will feed them, this people, with wormwood, and give them water of gall to drink.
16 "I will scatter them also among the Gentiles, whom neither they nor their fathers have known. And I will send a sword after them until I have consumed them."

THE PEOPLE MOURN IN JUDGMENT

17 Thus says the LORD of hosts:

"Consider and call for the mourning women,
That they may come;
And send for skillful wailing women,
That they may come.
18 Let them make haste
And take up a wailing for us,
That our eyes may run with tears,
And our eyelids gush with water.
19 For a voice of wailing is heard from Zion:
'How we are plundered!

We are greatly ashamed,
Because we have forsaken the land,
Because we have been cast out of our dwellings.' "

20 Yet hear the word of the LORD, O women,
And let your ear receive the word of His mouth;
Teach your daughters wailing,
And everyone her neighbor a lamentation.
21 For death has come through our windows,
Has entered our palaces,
To kill off the children— *no longer to be* outside!
And the young men— *no longer* on the streets!

22 Speak, "Thus says the LORD:

'Even the carcasses of men shall fall as refuse on the open field,
Like cuttings after the harvester,
And no one shall gather *them*.' "

23 Thus says the LORD:

"Let not the wise *man* glory in his wisdom,
Let not the mighty *man* glory in his might,
Nor let the rich *man* glory in his riches;
24 But let him who glories glory in this,
That he understands and knows Me,
That I *am* the LORD, exercising lovingkindness, judgment, and righteousness in the earth.
For in these I delight," says the LORD.

25 "Behold, the days are coming," says the LORD, "that I will punish all

who are circumcised with the uncircumcised—

26 "Egypt, Judah, Ē′dom, the people of Am′mon, Mō′ab, and all *who are in* the farthest corners, who dwell in the wilderness. For all *these* nations *are* uncircumcised, and all the house of Israel *are* uncircumcised in the heart."

IDOLS AND THE TRUE GOD

10 Hear the word which the LORD speaks to you, O house of Israel.
2 Thus says the LORD:

"Do not learn the way of the
    Gentiles;
Do not be dismayed at the signs
    of heaven,
For the Gentiles are dismayed at
    them.
3 For the customs of the peoples *are*
    futile;
For *one* cuts a tree from the
    forest,
The work of the hands of the
    workman, with the ax.
4 They decorate it with silver and
    gold;
They fasten it with nails and
    hammers
So that it will not topple.
5 They *are* upright, like a palm
    tree,
And they cannot speak;
They must be carried,
Because they cannot go *by*
    themselves.
Do not be afraid of them,
For they cannot do evil,
Nor can they do any good."

6 Inasmuch as *there is* none like
    You, O LORD
    (You *are* great, and Your name *is*
    great in might),
7 Who would not fear You, O King
    of the nations?

For this is Your rightful due.
For among all the wise *men* of the
    nations,
And in all their kingdoms,
There is none like You.
8 But they are altogether
    dull-hearted and foolish;
A wooden idol *is* a worthless
    doctrine.
9 Silver is beaten into plates;
It is brought from Tar′shish,
And gold from Ū′phaz,
The work of the craftsman
And of the hands of the
    metalsmith;
Blue and purple *are* their
    clothing;
They *are* all the work of skillful
    men.
10 But the LORD *is* the true God;
He *is* the living God and the
    everlasting King.
At His wrath the earth will
    tremble,
And the nations will not be able
    to endure His indignation.

11 Thus you shall say to them: "The gods that have not made the heavens and the earth shall perish from the earth and from under these heavens."

12 He has made the earth by His
    power,
He has established the world by
    His wisdom,
And has stretched out the
    heavens at His discretion.
13 When He utters His voice,
There is a multitude of waters in
    the heavens:
"And He causes the vapors to
    ascend from the ends of the
    earth.
He makes lightning for the rain,
He brings the wind out of His
    treasuries."*a*

10:13 *a*Psalm 135:7

14 Everyone is dull-hearted, without
    knowledge;
  Every metalsmith is put to shame
    by an image;
  For his molded image *is*
    falsehood,
  And *there is* no breath in them.
15 They *are* futile, a work of errors;
  In the time of their punishment
    they shall perish.
16 The Portion of Jacob *is* not like
    them,
  For He *is* the Maker of all *things,*
  And Israel *is* the tribe of His
    inheritance;
  The LORD of hosts *is* His name.

THE COMING CAPTIVITY OF JUDAH

17 Gather up your wares from the
    land,
  O inhabitant of the fortress!

18 For thus says the LORD:

  "Behold, I will throw out at this
    time
  The inhabitants of the land,
  And will distress them,
  That they may find *it so.*"

19 Woe is me for my hurt!
  My wound is severe.
  But I say, "Truly this *is* an
    infirmity,
  And I must bear it."
20 My tent is plundered,
  And all my cords are broken;
  My children have gone from me,
  And they *are* no more.
  There is no one to pitch my tent
    anymore,
  Or set up my curtains.

21 For the shepherds have become
    dull-hearted,
  And have not sought the LORD;
  Therefore they shall not prosper,

  And all their flocks shall be
    scattered.
22 Behold, the noise of the report
    has come,
  And a great commotion out of the
    north country,
  To make the cities of Judah
    desolate, a den of jackals.

23 O LORD, I know the way of man *is*
    not in himself;
  It is not in man who walks to
    direct his own steps.
24 O LORD, correct me, but with
    justice;
  Not in Your anger, lest You bring
    me to nothing.
25 Pour out Your fury on the
    Gentiles, who do not know You,
  And on the families who do not
    call on Your name;
  For they have eaten up Jacob,
  Devoured him and consumed
    him,
  And made his dwelling place
    desolate.

THE BROKEN COVENANT

11 The word that came to Jer·e-
mī′ah from the LORD, saying,
2 "Hear the words of this covenant,
and speak to the men of Judah and to
the inhabitants of Jerusalem;
3 "and say to them, 'Thus says the
LORD God of Israel: "Cursed *is* the
man who does not obey the words of
this covenant
4 "which I commanded your fathers
in the day I brought them out of the
land of Egypt, from the iron furnace,
saying, 'Obey My voice, and do according to all that I command you; so
shall you be My people, and I will be
your God,'
5 "that I may establish the oath
which I have sworn to your fathers,
to give them 'a land flowing with

milk and honey,'ᵃ as *it is* this day.'"' And I answered and said, "So be it, LORD."

6 Then the LORD said to me, "Proclaim all these words in the cities of Judah and in the streets of Jerusalem, saying: 'Hear the words of this covenant and do them.

7 'For I earnestly exhorted your fathers in the day I brought them up out of the land of Egypt, until this day, rising early and exhorting, saying, "Obey My voice."

8 'Yet they did not obey or incline their ear, but everyone followed the dictates of his evil heart; therefore I will bring upon them all the words of this covenant, which I commanded *them* to do, but *which* they have not done.'"

9 And the LORD said to me, "A conspiracy has been found among the men of Judah and among the inhabitants of Jerusalem.

10 "They have turned back to the iniquities of their forefathers who refused to hear My words, and they have gone after other gods to serve them; the house of Israel and the house of Judah have broken My covenant which I made with their fathers."

11 Therefore thus says the LORD: "Behold, I will surely bring calamity on them which they will not be able to escape; and though they cry out to Me, I will not listen to them.

12 "Then the cities of Judah and the inhabitants of Jerusalem will go and cry out to the gods to whom they offer incense, but they will not save them at all in the time of their trouble.

13 "For *according to* the number of your cities were your gods, O Judah; and *according to* the number of the streets of Jerusalem you have set up altars to *that* shameful thing, altars to burn incense to Bāʹal.

14 "So do not pray for this people, or lift up a cry or prayer for them; for I will not hear *them* in the time that they cry out to Me because of their trouble.

15 "What has My beloved to do in My house,
Having done lewd deeds with many?
And the holy flesh has passed from you.
When you do evil, then you rejoice.

16 The LORD called your name,
Green Olive Tree, Lovely *and* of Good Fruit.
With the noise of a great tumult
He has kindled fire on it,
And its branches are broken.

17 "For the LORD of hosts, who planted you, has pronounced doom against you for the evil of the house of Israel and of the house of Judah, which they have done against themselves to provoke Me to anger in offering incense to Bāʹal."

JEREMIAH'S LIFE THREATENED

18 Now the LORD gave me knowledge *of it,* and I know *it;* for You showed me their doings.

19 But I *was* like a docile lamb brought to the slaughter; and I did not know that they had devised schemes against me, *saying,* "Let us destroy the tree with its fruit, and let us cut him off from the land of the living, that his name may be remembered no more."

20 But, O LORD of hosts,
You who judge righteously,
Testing the mind and the heart,
Let me see Your vengeance on them,

11:5 ᵃExodus 3:8

For to You I have revealed my
cause.

21 "Therefore thus says the LORD
concerning the men of An'a·thoth
who seek your life, saying, 'Do not
prophesy in the name of the LORD,
lest you die by our hand'—
22 "therefore thus says the LORD of
hosts: 'Behold, I will punish them.
The young men shall die by the
sword, their sons and their daughters
shall die by famine;
23 'and there shall be no remnant of
them, for I will bring catastrophe on
the men of An'a·thoth, *even* the year
of their punishment.'"

JEREMIAH'S QUESTION

12 Righteous *are* You, O LORD,
         when I plead with You;
    Yet let me talk with You about
       Your judgments.
    Why does the way of the wicked
       prosper?
    Why are those happy who deal so
       treacherously?
2   You have planted them, yes, they
       have taken root;
    They grow, yes, they bear fruit.
    You *are* near in their mouth
    But far from their mind.

3   But You, O LORD, know me;
    You have seen me,
    And You have tested my heart
       toward You.
    Pull them out like sheep for the
       slaughter,
    And prepare them for the day of
       slaughter.
4   How long will the land mourn,
    And the herbs of every field
       wither?
    The beasts and birds are
       consumed,
    For the wickedness of those who
       dwell there,

Because they said, "He will not
       see our final end."

THE LORD ANSWERS JEREMIAH

5   "If you have run with the footmen,
       and they have wearied you,
    Then how can you contend with
       horses?
    And *if* in the land of peace,
    In which you trusted, *they*
       wearied you,
    Then how will you do in the
       floodplain*a* of the Jordan?
6   For even your brothers, the house
       of your father,
    Even they have dealt
       treacherously with you;
    Yes, they have called a multitude
       after you.
    Do not believe them,
    Even though they speak smooth
       words to you.

7   "I have forsaken My house, I have
       left My heritage;
    I have given the dearly beloved of
       My soul into the hand of her
       enemies.
8   My heritage is to Me like a lion in
       the forest;
    It cries out against Me;
    Therefore I have hated it.
9   My heritage *is* to Me *like* a
       speckled vulture;
    The vultures all around *are*
       against her.
    Come, assemble all the beasts of
       the field,
    Bring them to devour!
10 "Many rulers*a* have destroyed My
       vineyard,
    They have trodden My portion
       underfoot;
    They have made My pleasant
       portion a desolate wilderness.

12:5 *a*Or *thicket*   12:10 *a*Literally *shepherds* or
pastors

11 They have made it desolate;
　　Desolate, it mourns to Me;
　　The whole land is made desolate,
　　Because no one takes *it* to heart.
12 The plunderers have come
　　On all the desolate heights in the
　　　wilderness,
　　For the sword of the LORD shall
　　　devour
　　From *one* end of the land to the
　　　other end of the land;
　　No flesh shall have peace.
13 They have sown wheat but reaped
　　　thorns;
　　They have put themselves to pain
　　　but do not profit.
　　But be ashamed of your harvest
　　Because of the fierce anger of the
　　LORD."

14 Thus says the LORD: "Against all
My evil neighbors who touch the inheritance which I have caused My
people Israel to inherit—behold, I
will pluck them out of their land and
pluck out the house of Judah from
among them.
15 "Then it shall be, after I have
plucked them out, that I will return
and have compassion on them and
bring them back, everyone to his heritage and everyone to his land.
16 "And it shall be, if they will learn
carefully the ways of My people, to
swear by My name, 'As the LORD
lives,' as they taught My people to
swear by Bā′al, then they shall be established in the midst of My people.
17 "But if they do not obey, I will utterly pluck up and destroy that nation," says the LORD.

SYMBOL OF THE LINEN SASH

13 Thus the LORD said to me: "Go
and get yourself a linen sash, and put
it around your waist, but do not put
it in water."

2　So I got a sash according to the
word of the LORD, and put *it* around
my waist.
3　And the word of the LORD came to
me the second time, saying,
4　"Take the sash that you acquired,
which *is* around your waist, and
arise, go to the Eū·phrā′tēs,*a* and
hide it there in a hole in the rock."
5　So I went and hid it by the Eū-
phrā′tēs, as the LORD commanded
me.
6　Now it came to pass after many
days that the LORD said to me,
"Arise, go to the Eū·phrā′tēs, and
take from there the sash which I
commanded you to hide there."
7　Then I went to the Eū·phrā′tēs
and dug, and I took the sash from the
place where I had hidden it; and
there was the sash, ruined. It was
profitable for nothing.
8　Then the word of the LORD came
to me, saying,
9　"Thus says the LORD: 'In this
manner I will ruin the pride of Judah
and the great pride of Jerusalem.
10　'This evil people, who refuse
to hear My words, who follow the
dictates of their hearts, and walk
after other gods to serve them and
worship them, shall be just like
this sash which is profitable for nothing.
11　'For as the sash clings to the
waist of a man, so I have caused
the whole house of Israel and the
whole house of Judah to cling to Me,'
says the LORD, 'that they may become
My people, for renown, for praise,
and for glory; but they would not
hear.'

SYMBOL OF THE WINE BOTTLES

12　"Therefore you shall speak to
them this word: 'Thus says the LORD

13:4 *a*Hebrew *Perath*

God of Israel: "Every bottle shall be filled with wine." ' And they will say to you, 'Do we not certainly know that every bottle will be filled with wine?'

13 "Then you shall say to them, 'Thus says the LORD: "Behold, I will fill all the inhabitants of this land— even the kings who sit on David's throne, the priests, the prophets, and all the inhabitants of Jerusalem— with drunkenness!

14 "And I will dash them one against another, even the fathers and the sons together," says the LORD. "I will not pity nor spare nor have mercy, but will destroy them." ' "

PRIDE PRECEDES CAPTIVITY

15 Hear and give ear:
Do not be proud,
For the LORD has spoken.
16 Give glory to the LORD your God
Before He causes darkness,
And before your feet stumble
On the dark mountains,
And while you are looking for
light,
He turns it into the shadow of
death
And makes it dense darkness.
17 But if you will not hear it,
My soul will weep in secret for
your pride;
My eyes will weep bitterly
And run down with tears,
Because the LORD's flock has been
taken captive.

18 Say to the king and to the queen
mother,
"Humble yourselves;
Sit down,
For your rule shall collapse, the
crown of your glory."
19 The cities of the South shall be
shut up,

And no one shall open them;
Judah shall be carried away
captive, all of it;
It shall be wholly carried away
captive.

20 Lift up your eyes and see
Those who come from the north.
Where is the flock that was given
to you,
Your beautiful sheep?
21 What will you say when He
punishes you?
For you have taught them
To be chieftains, to be head over
you.
Will not pangs seize you,
Like a woman in labor?
22 And if you say in your heart,
"Why have these things come upon
me?"
For the greatness of your
iniquity
Your skirts have been uncovered,
Your heels made bare.
23 Can the Ethiopian change his
skin or the leopard its spots?
Then may you also do good who
are accustomed to do evil.

24 "Therefore I will scatter them like
stubble
That passes away by the wind of
the wilderness.
25 This is your lot,
The portion of your measures
from Me," says the LORD,
"Because you have forgotten Me
And trusted in falsehood.
26 Therefore I will uncover your
skirts over your face,
That your shame may appear.
27 I have seen your adulteries
And your lustful neighings,
The lewdness of your harlotry,
Your abominations on the hills in
the fields.
Woe to you, O Jerusalem!
Will you still not be made clean?"

SWORD, FAMINE, AND PESTILENCE

14 The word of the LORD that came to Jer·e·mī'ah concerning the droughts.

2 "Judah mourns,
    And her gates languish;
    They mourn for the land,
    And the cry of Jerusalem has
        gone up.
3 Their nobles have sent their lads
        for water;
    They went to the cisterns *and*
        found no water.
    They returned with their vessels
        empty;
    They were ashamed and
        confounded
    And covered their heads.
4 Because the ground is parched,
    For there was no rain in the
        land,
    The plowmen were ashamed;
    They covered their heads.
5 Yes, the deer also gave birth in
        the field,
    But left because there was no
        grass.
6 And the wild donkeys stood in the
        desolate heights;
    They sniffed at the wind like
        jackals;
    Their eyes failed because *there
        was* no grass."

7 O LORD, though our iniquities
        testify against us,
    Do it for Your name's sake;
    For our backslidings are many,
    We have sinned against You.
8 O the Hope of Israel, his Savior in
        time of trouble,
    Why should You be like a
        stranger in the land,
    And like a traveler *who* turns
        aside to tarry for a night?
9 Why should You be like a man
        astonished,

Like a mighty one *who* cannot
        save?
    Yet You, O LORD, *are* in our midst,
    And we are called by Your name;
    Do not leave us!

10 Thus says the LORD to this people:

    "Thus they have loved to wander;
    They have not restrained their
        feet.
    Therefore the LORD does not
        accept them;
    He will remember their iniquity
        now,
    And punish their sins."

11 Then the LORD said to me, "Do not pray for this people, for *their* good.
12 "When they fast, I will not hear their cry; and when they offer burnt offering and grain offering, I will not accept them. But I will consume them by the sword, by the famine, and by the pestilence."
13 Then I said, "Ah, Lord GOD! Behold, the prophets say to them, 'You shall not see the sword, nor shall you have famine, but I will give you assured peace in this place.' "
14 And the LORD said to me, "The prophets prophesy lies in My name. I have not sent them, commanded them, nor spoken to them; they prophesy to you a false vision, divination, a worthless thing, and the deceit of their heart.
15 "Therefore thus says the LORD concerning the prophets who prophesy in My name, whom I did not send, and who say, 'Sword and famine shall not be in this land'—'By sword and famine those prophets shall be consumed!
16 'And the people to whom they prophesy shall be cast out in the streets of Jerusalem because of the

famine and the sword; they will have no one to bury them—them nor their wives, their sons nor their daughters—for I will pour their wickedness on them.'

17 "Therefore you shall say this word to them:

'Let my eyes flow with tears night
   and day,
And let them not cease;
For the virgin daughter of my
   people
Has been broken with a mighty
   stroke, with a very severe blow.
18 If I go out to the field,
Then behold, those slain with the
   sword!
And if I enter the city,
Then behold, those sick from
   famine!
Yes, both prophet and priest go
   about in a land they do not
   know.' "

THE PEOPLE PLEAD FOR MERCY

19 Have You utterly rejected Judah?
Has Your soul loathed Zion?
Why have You stricken us so that
   there is no healing for us?
We looked for peace, but *there
   was* no good;
And for the time of healing, and
   there was trouble.
20 We acknowledge, O LORD, our
   wickedness
And the iniquity of our fathers,
For we have sinned against You.
21 Do not abhor *us,* for Your name's
   sake;
Do not disgrace the throne of Your
   glory.
Remember, do not break Your
   covenant with us.
22 Are there any among the idols of
   the nations that can cause
   rain?
Or can the heavens give showers?

Are You not He, O LORD our God?
Therefore we will wait for You,
Since You have made all these.

THE LORD WILL NOT RELENT

15 Then the LORD said to me, "*Even* if Moses and Samuel stood before Me, My mind *would* not *be* favorable toward this people. Cast *them* out of My sight, and let them go forth.
2 "And it shall be, if they say to you, 'Where should we go?' then you shall tell them, 'Thus says the LORD:

"Such as *are* for death, to death;
And such as *are* for the sword, to
   the sword;
And such as *are* for the famine, to
   the famine;
And such as *are* for the captivity,
   to the captivity." '

3 "And I will appoint over them four forms *of destruction,*" says the LORD: "the sword to slay, the dogs to drag, the birds of the heavens and the beasts of the earth to devour and destroy.
4 "I will hand them over to trouble, to all kingdoms of the earth, because of Ma·nas′seh the son of Hez·e·kī′ah, king of Judah, for what he did in Jerusalem.

5 "For who will have pity on you,
   O Jerusalem?
Or who will bemoan you?
Or who will turn aside to ask how
   you are doing?
6 You have forsaken Me," says the
   LORD,
"You have gone backward.
Therefore I will stretch out My
   hand against you and destroy
   you;
I am weary of relenting!
7 And I will winnow them with a

winnowing fan in the gates of
the land;
I will bereave *them* of children;
I will destroy My people,
Since they do not return from
their ways.

8 Their widows will be increased to
Me more than the sand of the
seas;
I will bring against them,
Against the mother of the young
men,
A plunderer at noonday;
I will cause anguish and terror to
fall on them suddenly.

9 "She languishes who has borne
seven;
She has breathed her last;
Her sun has gone down
While *it was* yet day;
She has been ashamed and
confounded.
And the remnant of them I will
deliver to the sword
Before their enemies," says the
LORD.

JEREMIAH'S DEJECTION

10 Woe is me, my mother,
That you have borne me,
A man of strife and a man of
contention to the whole earth!
I have neither lent for interest,
Nor have men lent to me for
interest.
Every one of them curses me.

11 The LORD said:

"Surely it will be well with your
remnant;
Surely I will cause the enemy to
intercede with you
In the time of adversity and in
the time of affliction.

12 Can anyone break iron,
The northern iron and the
bronze?

13 Your wealth and your treasures
I will give as plunder without
price,
Because of all your sins,
Throughout your territories.

14 And I will make *you* cross over
with^a your enemies
Into a land *which* you do not
know;
For a fire is kindled in My anger,
Which shall burn upon you."

15 O LORD, You know;
Remember me and visit me,
And take vengeance for me on my
persecutors.
In Your enduring patience, do not
take me away.
Know that for Your sake I have
suffered rebuke.

16 Your words were found, and I ate
them,
And Your word was to me the joy
and rejoicing of my heart;
For I am called by Your name,
O LORD God of hosts.

17 I did not sit in the assembly of the
mockers,
Nor did I rejoice;
I sat alone because of Your hand,
For You have filled me with
indignation.

18 Why is my pain perpetual
And my wound incurable,
Which refuses to be healed?
Will You surely be to me like an
unreliable stream,
As waters *that* fail?

THE LORD REASSURES JEREMIAH

19 Therefore thus says the LORD:

"If you return,
Then I will bring you back;
You shall stand before Me;

15:14 ^a Following Masoretic Text and Vulgate; Septuagint, Syriac, and Targum read *cause you to serve*
(compare 17:4).

If you take out the precious from
  the vile,
You shall be as My mouth.
Let them return to you,
But you must not return to them.
20 And I will make you to this people
  a fortified bronze wall;
And they will fight against you,
But they shall not prevail against
  you;
For I *am* with you to save you
And deliver you," says the LORD.
21 "I will deliver you from the hand of
  the wicked,
And I will redeem you from the
  grip of the terrible."

JEREMIAH'S LIFE-STYLE AND MESSAGE

16 The word of the LORD also
came to me, saying,
2 "You shall not take a wife, nor
shall you have sons or daughters in
this place."
3 For thus says the LORD concerning the sons and daughters who are
born in this place, and concerning
their mothers who bore them and
their fathers who begot them in this
land:
4 "They shall die gruesome deaths;
they shall not be lamented nor shall
they be buried, *but* they shall be like
refuse on the face of the earth. They
shall be consumed by the sword and
by famine, and their corpses shall be
meat for the birds of heaven and for
the beasts of the earth."
5 For thus says the LORD: "Do not
enter the house of mourning, nor go
to lament or bemoan them; for I have
taken away My peace from this people," says the LORD, "lovingkindness
and mercies.
6 "Both the great and the small
shall die in this land. They shall not
be buried; neither shall men lament

for them, cut themselves, nor make
themselves bald for them.
7 "Nor shall *men* break *bread* in
mourning for them, to comfort them
for the dead; nor shall *men* give them
the cup of consolation to drink for
their father or their mother.
8 "Also you shall not go into the
house of feasting to sit with them, to
eat and drink."
9 For thus says the LORD of hosts,
the God of Israel: "Behold, I will
cause to cease from this place, before
your eyes and in your days, the voice
of mirth and the voice of gladness,
the voice of the bridegroom and the
voice of the bride.
10 "And it shall be, when you show
this people all these words, and they
say to you, 'Why has the LORD pronounced all this great disaster
against us? Or what *is* our iniquity?
Or what *is* our sin that we have committed against the LORD our God?'
11 "then you shall say to them, 'Because your fathers have forsaken
Me,' says the LORD; 'they have
walked after other gods and have
served them and worshiped them,
and have forsaken Me and not kept
My law.
12 'And you have done worse than
your fathers, for behold, each one follows the dictates of his own evil
heart, so that no one listens to Me.
13 'Therefore I will cast you out of
this land into a land that you do not
know, neither you nor your fathers;
and there you shall serve other gods
day and night, where I will not show
you favor.'

GOD WILL RESTORE ISRAEL

14 "Therefore behold, the days are
coming," says the LORD, "that it shall
no more be said, 'The LORD lives who
brought up the children of Israel
from the land of Egypt,'

15 "but, 'The LORD lives who brought up the children of Israel from the land of the north and from all the lands where He had driven them.' For I will bring them back into their land which I gave to their fathers.

16 "Behold, I will send for many fishermen," says the LORD, "and they shall fish them; and afterward I will send for many hunters, and they shall hunt them from every mountain and every hill, and out of the holes of the rocks.

17 "For My eyes *are* on all their ways; they are not hidden from My face, nor is their iniquity hidden from My eyes.

18 "And first I will repay double for their iniquity and their sin, because they have defiled My land; they have filled My inheritance with the carcasses of their detestable and abominable idols."

19 O LORD, my strength and my
⠀⠀⠀fortress,
⠀⠀My refuge in the day of affliction,
⠀⠀The Gentiles shall come to You
⠀⠀From the ends of the earth and
⠀⠀⠀say,
⠀⠀"Surely our fathers have inherited
⠀⠀⠀lies,
⠀⠀Worthlessness and unprofitable
⠀⠀⠀*things.*"
20 Will a man make gods for himself,
⠀⠀Which *are* not gods?

21 "Therefore behold, I will this once
⠀⠀⠀cause them to know,
⠀⠀I will cause them to know
⠀⠀My hand and My might;
⠀⠀And they shall know that My
⠀⠀⠀name *is* the LORD.

JUDAH'S SIN AND PUNISHMENT

17 "The sin of Judah *is* written
⠀⠀⠀with a pen of iron;

⠀⠀With the point of a diamond *it is*
⠀⠀⠀engraved
⠀⠀On the tablet of their heart,
⠀⠀And on the horns of your altars,
2 While their children remember
⠀⠀Their altars and their wooden
⠀⠀⠀imagesa
⠀⠀By the green trees on the high
⠀⠀⠀hills.
3 O My mountain in the field,
⠀⠀I will give as plunder your
⠀⠀⠀wealth, all your treasures,
⠀⠀*And* your high places of sin
⠀⠀⠀within all your borders.
4 And you, even yourself,
⠀⠀Shall let go of your heritage
⠀⠀⠀which I gave you;
⠀⠀And I will cause you to serve your
⠀⠀⠀enemies
⠀⠀In the land which you do not
⠀⠀⠀know;
⠀⠀For you have kindled a fire in My
⠀⠀⠀anger *which* shall burn
⠀⠀⠀forever."

5 Thus says the LORD:

"Cursed *is* the man who trusts in
⠀⠀⠀man
⠀⠀And makes flesh his strength,
⠀⠀Whose heart departs from the
⠀⠀⠀LORD.
6 For he shall be like a shrub in the
⠀⠀⠀desert,
⠀⠀And shall not see when good
⠀⠀⠀comes,
⠀⠀But shall inhabit the parched
⠀⠀⠀places in the wilderness,
⠀⠀*In* a salt land *which is* not
⠀⠀⠀inhabited.

7 "Blessed *is* the man who trusts in
⠀⠀⠀the LORD,
⠀⠀And whose hope is the LORD.
8 For he shall be like a tree planted
⠀⠀⠀by the waters,
⠀⠀Which spreads out its roots by the
⠀⠀⠀river,

17:2 ᵃHebrew *Asherim*, Canaanite deities

And will not fear*a* when heat
    comes;
But its leaf will be green,
And will not be anxious in the
    year of drought,
Nor will cease from yielding fruit.

9 "The heart *is* deceitful above all
    things,
    And desperately wicked;
    Who can know it?
10 I, the LORD, search the heart,
    I test the mind,
    Even to give every man according
      to his ways,
    According to the fruit of his
      doings.

11 "*As* a partridge that broods but
    does not hatch,
    So is he who gets riches, but not
      by right;
    It will leave him in the midst of
      his days,
    And at his end he will be a fool."

12 A glorious high throne from the
    beginning
    Is the place of our sanctuary.
13 O LORD, the hope of Israel,
    All who forsake You shall be
      ashamed.

    "Those who depart from Me
    Shall be written in the earth,
    Because they have forsaken the
      LORD,
    The fountain of living waters."

JEREMIAH PRAYS FOR DELIVERANCE

14 Heal me, O LORD, and I shall be
    healed;
    Save me, and I shall be saved,
    For You *are* my praise.
15 Indeed they say to me,
    "Where *is* the word of the LORD?
    Let it come now!"

Praises

Jeremiah 17:14

When you get well after being sick, do you praise God? He gave you healing, didn't He? When God rescues you from something bad, do you praise Him? He is the One who rescues you. Do you praise God for health? Do you praise Him for saving you from sin? When you do, God is *your* praise.

---

16 As for me, I have not hurried
    away from *being* a shepherd
    who follows You,
    Nor have I desired the woeful
      day;
    You know what came out of my
      lips;
    It was right there before You.
17 Do not be a terror to me;
    You *are* my hope in the day of
      doom.
18 Let them be ashamed who
    persecute me,
    But do not let me be put to
      shame;
    Let them be dismayed,
    But do not let me be dismayed.
    Bring on them the day of doom,
    And destroy them with double
      destruction!

HALLOW THE SABBATH DAY

19 Thus the LORD said to me: "Go and stand in the gate of the children of the people, by which the kings of Judah come in and by which they go out, and in all the gates of Jerusalem;
20 "and say to them, 'Hear the word of the LORD, you kings of Judah, and

17:8 *a*Qere and Targum read *see.*

SALVATION Jeremiah 17:14

Save Me!

Look at that one little angel. Something happened. He almost fell. But the other little angel saved him. He saved the little angel from falling. Do you think the angel who was falling cried out, "Save me!"?

1. When someone saves us, he or she keeps us from getting hurt. When God saves us, He keeps us from going to hell. He helps us go to heaven instead. Saving us is called salvation.
2. Have you ever asked God to save you? Do it now. He will.

For more on *Favorite Bible Words* turn to page 1309
For more on *Salvation* turn to page 1344

all Judah, and all the inhabitants of Jerusalem, who enter by these gates.

21 'Thus says the LORD: "Take heed to yourselves, and bear no burden on the Sabbath day, nor bring *it* in by the gates of Jerusalem;

22 "nor carry a burden out of your houses on the Sabbath day, nor do any work, but hallow the Sabbath day, as I commanded your fathers.

23 "But they did not obey nor incline their ear, but made their neck stiff, that they might not hear nor receive instruction.

24 "And it shall be, if you heed Me carefully," says the LORD, "to bring no burden through the gates of this city on the Sabbath day, but hallow the Sabbath day, to do no work in it,

25 "then shall enter the gates of this city kings and princes sitting on the throne of David, riding in chariots and on horses, they and their princes, accompanied by the men of Judah and the inhabitants of Jerusalem; and this city shall remain forever.

26 "And they shall come from the cities of Judah and from the places around Jerusalem, from the land of Benjamin and from the lowland, from the mountains and from the South, bringing burnt offerings and sacrifices, grain offerings and incense, bringing sacrifices of praise to the house of the LORD.

27 "But if you will not heed Me to hallow the Sabbath day, such as not carrying a burden when entering the gates of Jerusalem on the Sabbath day, then I will kindle a fire in its gates, and it shall devour the palaces of Jerusalem, and it shall not be quenched." ' "

THE POTTER AND THE CLAY

18 The word which came to Jeremī′ah from the LORD, saying:

2 "Arise and go down to the potter's house, and there I will cause you to hear My words."

3 Then I went down to the potter's house, and there he was, making something at the wheel.

4 And the vessel that he made of clay was marred in the hand of the potter; so he made it again into another vessel, as it seemed good to the potter to make.

5 Then the word of the LORD came to me, saying:

6 "O house of Israel, can I not do with you as this potter?" says the LORD. "Look, as the clay *is* in the potter's hand, so *are* you in My hand, O house of Israel!

7 "The instant I speak concerning a nation and concerning a kingdom, to pluck up, to pull down, and to destroy *it,*

8 "if that nation against whom I have spoken turns from its evil, I will relent of the disaster that I thought to bring upon it.

9 "And the instant I speak concerning a nation and concerning a kingdom, to build and to plant *it,*

10 "if it does evil in My sight so that it does not obey My voice, then I will relent concerning the good with which I said I would benefit it.

11 "Now therefore, speak to the men of Judah and to the inhabitants of Jerusalem, saying, 'Thus says the LORD: "Behold, I am fashioning a disaster and devising a plan against you. Return now every one from his evil way, and make your ways and your doings good." ' "

GOD'S WARNING REJECTED

12 And they said, "That is hopeless! So we will walk according to our own plans, and we will every one obey the dictates of his evil heart."

13 Therefore thus says the LORD:

"Ask now among the Gentiles,
  Who has heard such things?
The virgin of Israel has done a
  very horrible thing.
14 Will *a man* leave the snow water
  of Lebanon,
Which comes from the rock of the
  field?
Will the cold flowing waters be
  forsaken for strange waters?

15 "Because My people have forgotten
  Me,
They have burned incense to
  worthless idols.
And they have caused themselves
  to stumble in their ways,
From the ancient paths,
To walk in pathways and not on a
  highway,
16 To make their land desolate *and* a
  perpetual hissing;
Everyone who passes by it will be
  astonished
And shake his head.
17 I will scatter them as with an
  east wind before the enemy;
I will show them*a* the back and
  not the face
In the day of their calamity."

JEREMIAH PERSECUTED

18 Then they said, "Come and let us
devise plans against Jer·e·mī′ah; for
the law shall not perish from the
priest, nor counsel from the wise, nor
the word from the prophet. Come and
let us attack him with the tongue,
and let us not give heed to any of his
words."

19 Give heed to me, O LORD,
And listen to the voice of those
  who contend with me!
20 Shall evil be repaid for good?

For they have dug a pit for my
  life.
Remember that I stood before You
To speak good for them,
To turn away Your wrath from
  them.
21 Therefore deliver up their
  children to the famine,
And pour out their *blood*
By the force of the sword;
Let their wives *become* widows
And bereaved of their children.
Let their men be put to death,
Their young men *be* slain
By the sword in battle.
22 Let a cry be heard from their
  houses,
When You bring a troop suddenly
  upon them;
For they have dug a pit to take
  me,
And hidden snares for my feet.
23 Yet, LORD, You know all their
  counsel
Which is against me, to slay *me*.
Provide no atonement for their
  iniquity,
Nor blot out their sin from Your
  sight;
But let them be overthrown
  before You.
Deal *thus* with them
In the time of Your anger.

THE SIGN OF THE BROKEN FLASK

19 Thus says the LORD: "Go and
get a potter's earthen flask, and *take*
some of the elders of the people and
some of the elders of the priests.
2   "And go out to the Valley of the
Son of Hin′nom, which *is* by the entry of the Potsherd Gate; and proclaim there the words that I will tell
you,
3   "and say, 'Hear the word of the

18:17 *a*Following Septuagint, Syriac, Targum, and
Vulgate; Masoretic Text reads *look them in.*

LORD, O kings of Judah and inhabitants of Jerusalem. Thus says the LORD of hosts, the God of Israel: "Behold, I will bring such a catastrophe on this place, that whoever hears of it, his ears will tingle.

4 "Because they have forsaken Me and made this an alien place, because they have burned incense in it to other gods whom neither they, their fathers, nor the kings of Judah have known, and have filled this place with the blood of the innocents

5 "(they have also built the high places of Bāʹal, to burn their sons with fire *for* burnt offerings to Bāʹal, which I did not command or speak, nor did it come into My mind),

6 "therefore behold, the days are coming," says the LORD, "that this place shall no more be called Tōʹphet or the Valley of the Son of Hinʹnom, but the Valley of Slaughter.

7 "And I will make void the counsel of Judah and Jerusalem in this place, and I will cause them to fall by the sword before their enemies and by the hands of those who seek their lives; their corpses I will give as meat for the birds of the heaven and for the beasts of the earth.

8 "I will make this city desolate and a hissing; everyone who passes by it will be astonished and hiss because of all its plagues.

9 "And I will cause them to eat the flesh of their sons and the flesh of their daughters, and everyone shall eat the flesh of his friend in the siege and in the desperation with which their enemies and those who seek their lives shall drive them to despair."ʹ

10 "Then you shall break the flask in the sight of the men who go with you,

11 "and say to them, 'Thus says the LORD of hosts: "Even so I will break this people and this city, as *one* breaks a potter's vessel, which cannot be made whole again; and they shall bury *them* in Tōʹphet till *there is* no place to bury.

12 "Thus I will do to this place," says the LORD, "and to its inhabitants, and make this city like Tōʹphet.

13 "And the houses of Jerusalem and the houses of the kings of Judah shall be defiled like the place of Tōʹphet, because of all the houses on whose roofs they have burned incense to all the host of heaven, and poured out drink offerings to other gods." ' "

14 Then Jer·e·mīʹah came from Tōʹphet, where the LORD had sent him to prophesy; and he stood in the court of the Lord's house and said to all the people,

15 "Thus says the LORD of hosts, the God of Israel: 'Behold, I will bring on this city and on all her towns all the doom that I have pronounced against it, because they have stiffened their necks that they might not hear My words.' "

THE WORD OF GOD TO PASHHUR

20 Now Pashʹhur the son of Imʹmer, the priest who *was* also chief governor in the house of the LORD, heard that Jer·e·mīʹah prophesied these things.

2 Then Pashʹhur struck Jer·e·mīʹah the prophet, and put him in the stocks that *were* in the high gate of Benjamin, which *was* by the house of the LORD.

3 And it happened on the next day that Pashʹhur brought Jer·e·mīʹah out of the stocks. Then Jer·e·mīʹah said to him, "The LORD has not called your name Pashʹhur, but Māʹgor-Mis·sāʹbib.a

4 "For thus says the LORD: 'Behold, I will make you a terror to yourself and to all your friends; and they shall

20:3 aLiterally *Fear on Every Side*

fall by the sword of their enemies, and your eyes shall see *it*. I will give all Judah into the hand of the king of Babylon, and he shall carry them captive to Babylon and slay them with the sword.

5 'Moreover I will deliver all the wealth of this city, all its produce, and all its precious things; all the treasures of the kings of Judah I will give into the hand of their enemies, who will plunder them, seize them, and carry them to Babylon.

6 'And you, Pash'hur, and all who dwell in your house, shall go into captivity. You shall go to Babylon, and there you shall die, and be buried there, you and all your friends, to whom you have prophesied lies.' "

JEREMIAH'S UNPOPULAR MINISTRY

7 O LORD, You induced me, and I
    was persuaded;
  You are stronger than I, and have
    prevailed.
  I am in derision daily;
  Everyone mocks me.
8 For when I spoke, I cried out;
  I shouted, "Violence and plunder!"
  Because the word of the LORD was
    made to me
  A reproach and a derision daily.
9 Then I said, "I will not make
    mention of Him,
  Nor speak anymore in His name."
  But *His word* was in my heart
    like a burning fire
  Shut up in my bones;
  I was weary of holding *it* back,
  And I could not.
10 For I heard many mocking:
  "Fear on every side!"
  "Report," *they say,* "and we will
    report it!"
  All my acquaintances watched for
    my stumbling, *saying,*
  "Perhaps he can be induced;
  Then we will prevail against him,

And we will take our revenge on
    him."

11 But the LORD *is* with me as a
    mighty, awesome One.
  Therefore my persecutors will
    stumble, and will not prevail.
  They will be greatly ashamed, for
    they will not prosper.
  Their everlasting confusion will
    never be forgotten.
12 But, O LORD of hosts,
  You who test the righteous,
  And see the mind and heart,
  Let me see Your vengeance on
    them;
  For I have pleaded my cause
    before You.

Praises

Jeremiah 20:13

Here's something to stir our praise! When God helps a poor person, praise Him. When He helps a poor person survive evil, praise Him. Sing songs of praise. Pray prayers of praise. Praise God!

---

13 Sing to the LORD! Praise the
    LORD!
  For He has delivered the life of
    the poor
  From the hand of evildoers.

14 Cursed *be* the day in which I was
    born!
  Let the day not be blessed in
    which my mother bore me!
15 Let the man *be* cursed
  Who brought news to my father,
    saying,
  "A male child has been born to
    you!"
  Making him very glad.

16 And let that man be like the cities
   Which the LORD overthrew, and
      did not relent;
   Let him hear the cry in the
      morning
   And the shouting at noon,
17 Because he did not kill me from
      the womb,
   That my mother might have been
      my grave,
   And her womb always enlarged
      with me.
18 Why did I come forth from the
      womb to see labor and sorrow,
   That my days should be
      consumed with shame?

JERUSALEM'S DOOM IS SEALED

21 The word which came to Jer-e·mī′ah from the LORD when King Zed·e·kī′ah sent to him Pash′hur the son of Mel·chī′ah, and Zeph·a·nī′ah the son of Mā·a·sēi′ah, the priest, saying,
2 "Please inquire of the LORD for us, for Ne·bū·chad·nez′zar*a* king of Babylon makes war against us. Perhaps the LORD will deal with us according to all His wonderful works, that *the king* may go away from us."
3 Then Jer·e·mī′ah said to them, "Thus you shall say to Zed·e·kī′ah,
4 'Thus says the LORD God of Israel: "Behold, I will turn back the weapons of war that *are* in your hands, with which you fight against the king of Babylon and the Chal·dē′ans*a* who besiege you outside the walls; and I will assemble them in the midst of this city.
5 "I Myself will fight against you with an outstretched hand and with a strong arm, even in anger and fury and great wrath.
6 "I will strike the inhabitants of this city, both man and beast; they shall die of a great pestilence.
7 "And afterward," says the LORD,

"I will deliver Zed·e·kī′ah king of Judah, his servants and the people, and such as are left in this city from the pestilence and the sword and the famine, into the hand of Ne·bū·chad-nez′zar king of Babylon, into the hand of their enemies, and into the hand of those who seek their life; and he shall strike them with the edge of the sword. He shall not spare them, or have pity or mercy." '
8 "Now you shall say to this people, 'Thus says the LORD: "Behold, I set before you the way of life and the way of death.
9 "He who remains in this city shall die by the sword, by famine, and by pestilence; but he who goes out and defects to the Chal·dē′ans who besiege you, he shall live, and his life shall be as a prize to him.
10 "For I have set My face against this city for adversity and not for good," says the LORD. "It shall be given into the hand of the king of Babylon, and he shall burn it with fire." '

MESSAGE TO THE HOUSE OF DAVID

11 "And concerning the house of the king of Judah, *say,* 'Hear the word of the LORD,
12 'O house of David! Thus says the LORD:

"Execute judgment in the
      morning;
   And deliver *him who is* plundered
   Out of the hand of the oppressor,
   Lest My fury go forth like fire
   And burn so that no one can
      quench *it,*
   Because of the evil of your doings.

13 "Behold, I *am* against you,
   O inhabitant of the valley,

21:2 *a*Hebrew *Nebuchadrezzar,* and so elsewhere
21:4 *a*Or *Babylonians*

And rock of the plain," says the
LORD,
"Who say, 'Who shall come down
against us?
Or who shall enter our
dwellings?'
14 But I will punish you according to
the fruit of your doings," says
the LORD;
"I will kindle a fire in its forest,
And it shall devour all things
around it." ' "

22 Thus says the LORD: "Go down
to the house of the king of Judah, and
there speak this word,
2 "and say, 'Hear the word of the
LORD, O king of Judah, you who sit
on the throne of David, you and your
servants and your people who enter
these gates!
3 'Thus says the LORD: "Execute
judgment and righteousness, and deliver the plundered out of the hand of
the oppressor. Do no wrong and do no
violence to the stranger, the fatherless, or the widow, nor shed innocent
blood in this place.
4 "For if you indeed do this thing,
then shall enter the gates of this
house, riding on horses and in chariots, accompanied by servants and
people, kings who sit on the throne of
David.
5 "But if you will not hear these
words, I swear by Myself," says the
LORD, "that this house shall become a
desolation." ' "
6 For thus says the LORD to the
house of the king of Judah:

"You *are* Gil'ē·ad to Me,
The head of Lebanon;
Yet I surely will make you a
wilderness,
Cities *which* are not inhabited.
7 I will prepare destroyers against
you,
Everyone with his weapons;

They shall cut down your choice
cedars
And cast *them* into the fire.

8 "And many nations will pass by
this city; and everyone will say to his
neighbor, 'Why has the LORD done so
to this great city?'
9 "Then they will answer, 'Because
they have forsaken the covenant of
the LORD their God, and worshiped
other gods and served them.' "

10 Weep not for the dead, nor
bemoan him;
Weep bitterly for him who goes
away,
For he shall return no more,
Nor see his native country.

MESSAGE TO THE SONS OF JOSIAH

11 For thus says the LORD concerning Shal'lum[a] the son of Jō·sī'ah,
king of Judah, who reigned instead of
Jō·sī'ah his father, who went from
this place: "He shall not return here
anymore,
12 "but he shall die in the place
where they have led him captive, and
shall see this land no more.

13 "Woe to him who builds his house
by unrighteousness
And his chambers by injustice,
Who uses his neighbor's service
without wages
And gives him nothing for his
work,
14 Who says, 'I will build myself a
wide house with spacious
chambers,
And cut out windows for it,
Paneling *it* with cedar
And painting *it* with vermilion.'
15 "Shall you reign because you
enclose *yourself* in cedar?

22:11 [a]Also called *Jehoahaz*

Did not your father eat and drink,
And do justice and righteousness?
Then *it was* well with him.
16 He judged the cause of the poor
and needy;
Then *it was* well.
Was not this knowing Me?" says
the LORD.
17 "Yet your eyes and your heart *are*
for nothing but your
covetousness,
For shedding innocent blood,
And practicing oppression and
violence."

18 Therefore thus says the LORD concerning Je·hoi′a·kim the son of Jo-
si′ah, king of Judah:

"They shall not lament for him,
Saying, 'Alas, my brother!' or
'Alas, my sister!'
They shall not lament for him,
Saying, 'Alas, master!' or 'Alas,
his glory!'
19 He shall be buried with the burial
of a donkey,
Dragged and cast out beyond the
gates of Jerusalem.

20 "Go up to Lebanon, and cry out,
And lift up your voice in Ba′shan;
Cry from Ab′a·rim,
For all your lovers are destroyed.
21 I spoke to you in your prosperity,
But you said, 'I will not hear.'
This *has been* your manner from
your youth,
That you did not obey My voice.
22 The wind shall eat up all your
rulers,
And your lovers shall go into
captivity;
Surely then you will be ashamed
and humiliated
For all your wickedness.
23 O inhabitant of Lebanon,
Making your nest in the cedars,
How gracious will you be when
pangs come upon you,

Like the pain of a woman in
labor?

MESSAGE TO CONIAH

24 "*As* I live," says the LORD, "though
Co·ni′ah[a] the son of Je·hoi′a·kim,
king of Judah, were the signet on My
right hand, yet I would pluck you off;
25 "and I will give you into the hand
of those who seek your life, and into
the hand *of those* whose face you
fear—the hand of Ne·bu·chad·nez′zar
king of Babylon and the hand of the
Chal·de′ans.
26 "So I will cast you out, and your
mother who bore you, into another
country where you were not born;
and there you shall die.
27 "But to the land to which they desire to return, there they shall not return.

28 "Is this man Co·ni′ah a despised,
broken idol—
A vessel in which *is* no pleasure?
Why are they cast out, he and his
descendants,
And cast into a land which they
do not know?
29 O earth, earth, earth,
Hear the word of the LORD!
30 Thus says the LORD:
'Write this man down as childless,
A man *who* shall not prosper in
his days;
For none of his descendants shall
prosper,
Sitting on the throne of David,
And ruling anymore in Judah.' "

THE BRANCH OF RIGHTEOUSNESS

23
"Woe to the shepherds who destroy and scatter the sheep of My
pasture!" says the LORD.

22:24 ^aAlso called *Jeconiah* and *Jehoiachin*

2   Therefore thus says the LORD God of Israel against the shepherds who feed My people: "You have scattered My flock, driven them away, and not attended to them. Behold, I will attend to you for the evil of your doings," says the LORD.
3   "But I will gather the remnant of My flock out of all countries where I have driven them, and bring them back to their folds; and they shall be fruitful and increase.
4   "I will set up shepherds over them who will feed them; and they shall fear no more, nor be dismayed, nor shall they be lacking," says the LORD.

5   "Behold, *the* days are coming,"
        says the LORD,
    "That I will raise to David a
        Branch of righteousness;
    A King shall reign and prosper,
    And execute judgment and
        righteousness in the earth.
6   In His days Judah will be saved,
    And Israel will dwell safely;
    Now this *is* His name by which
    He will be called:

THE LORD OUR RIGHTEOUSNESS.*a*

7   "Therefore, behold, *the* days are coming," says the LORD, "that they shall no longer say, 'As the LORD lives who brought up the children of Israel from the land of Egypt,'
8   "but, 'As the LORD lives who brought up and led the descendants of the house of Israel from the north country and from all the countries where I had driven them.' And they shall dwell in their own land."

FALSE PROPHETS AND EMPTY ORACLES

9   My heart within me is broken
    Because of the prophets;
    All my bones shake.
    I am like a drunken man,
    And like a man whom wine has
        overcome,
    Because of the LORD,
    And because of His holy words.
10 For the land is full of adulterers;
    For because of a curse the land
        mourns.
    The pleasant places of the
        wilderness are dried up.
    Their course of life is evil,
    And their might *is* not right.

11 "For both prophet and priest are
        profane;
    Yes, in My house I have found
        their wickedness," says the
        LORD.
12 "Therefore their way shall be to
        them
    Like slippery *ways;*
    In the darkness they shall be
        driven on
    And fall in them;
    For I will bring disaster on them,
    The year of their punishment,"
        says the LORD.
13 "And I have seen folly in the
        prophets of Samaria:
    They prophesied by Bā'al
    And caused My people Israel to
        err.
14 Also I have seen a horrible thing
        in the prophets of Jerusalem:
    They commit adultery and walk
        in lies;
    They also strengthen the hands of
        evildoers,
    So that no one turns back from
        his wickedness.
    All of them are like Sod'om to Me,
    And her inhabitants like
        Go·mor'rah.

15 "Therefore thus says the LORD of hosts concerning the prophets:

23:6 *a*Hebrew *YHWH Tsidkenu*

'Behold, I will feed them with
    wormwood,
And make them drink the water
    of gall;
For from the prophets of
    Jerusalem
Profaneness has gone out into all
    the land.' "

16 Thus says the LORD of hosts:

"Do not listen to the words of the
    prophets who prophesy to you.
They make you worthless;
They speak a vision of their own
    heart,
Not from the mouth of the LORD.
17 They continually say to those who
    despise Me,
'The LORD has said, "You shall
    have peace" ';
And to everyone who walks
    according to the dictates of his
    own heart, they say,
'No evil shall come upon you.' "

18 For who has stood in the counsel
    of the LORD,
And has perceived and heard His
    word?
Who has marked His word and
    heard it?
19 Behold, a whirlwind of the LORD
    has gone forth in fury—
A violent whirlwind!
It will fall violently on the head of
    the wicked.
20 The anger of the LORD will not
    turn back
Until He has executed and
    performed the thoughts of His
    heart.
In the latter days you will
    understand it perfectly.

21 "I have not sent these prophets,
    yet they ran.
I have not spoken to them, yet
    they prophesied.

22 But if they had stood in My
    counsel,
And had caused My people to
    hear My words,
Then they would have turned
    them from their evil way
And from the evil of their doings.

23 "Am I a God near at hand," says
    the LORD,
"And not a God afar off?
24 Can anyone hide himself in secret
    places,
So I shall not see him?" says the
    LORD;
"Do I not fill heaven and earth?"
    says the LORD.

25 "I have heard what the prophets
have said who prophesy lies in My
name, saying, 'I have dreamed, I
have dreamed!'
26 "How long will this be in the
heart of the prophets who prophesy
lies? Indeed they are prophets of the
deceit of their own heart,
27 "who try to make My people forget My name by their dreams which
everyone tells his neighbor, as their
fathers forgot My name for Bā′al.

28 "The prophet who has a dream, let
    him tell a dream;
And he who has My word, let him
    speak My word faithfully.
What is the chaff to the wheat?"
    says the LORD.
29 "Is not My word like a fire?" says
    the LORD,
"And like a hammer that breaks
    the rock in pieces?

30 "Therefore behold, I am against
the prophets," says the LORD, "who
steal My words every one from his
neighbor.
31 "Behold, I am against the prophets," says the LORD, "who use their
tongues and say, 'He says.'

32 "Behold, I *am* against those who prophesy false dreams," says the LORD, "and tell them, and cause My people to err by their lies and by their recklessness. Yet I did not send them or command them; therefore they shall not profit this people at all," says the LORD.

33 "So when these people or the prophet or the priest ask you, saying, 'What is the oracle of the LORD?' you shall then say to them, 'What oracle?'ᵃ I will even forsake you," says the LORD.

34 "And *as for* the prophet and the priest and the people who say, 'The oracle of the LORD!' I will even punish that man and his house.

35 "Thus every one of you shall say to his neighbor, and every one to his brother, 'What has the LORD answered?' and, 'What has the LORD spoken?'

36 "And the oracle of the LORD you shall mention no more. For every man's word will be his oracle, for you have perverted the words of the living God, the LORD of hosts, our God.

37 "Thus you shall say to the prophet, 'What has the LORD answered you?' and, 'What has the LORD spoken?'

38 "But since you say, 'The oracle of the LORD!' therefore thus says the LORD: 'Because you say this word, "The oracle of the LORD!" and I have sent to you, saying, "Do not say, 'The oracle of the LORD!' "

39 'therefore behold, I, even I, will utterly forget you and forsake you, and the city that I gave you and your fathers, and *will cast you* out of My presence.

40 'And I will bring an everlasting reproach upon you, and a perpetual shame, which shall not be forgotten.' "

THE SIGN OF TWO BASKETS OF FIGS

24 The LORD showed me, and there were two baskets of figs set before the temple of the LORD, after Ne·bu·chad·nez′zar king of Babylon had carried away captive Jec·o·nī′ah the son of Je·hoi′a·kim, king of Judah, and the princes of Judah with the craftsmen and smiths, from Jerusalem, and had brought them to Babylon.

2 One basket *had* very good figs, like the figs *that are* first ripe; and the other basket *had* very bad figs which could not be eaten, they were so bad.

3 Then the LORD said to me, "What do you see, Jer·e·mī′ah?" And I said, "Figs, the good figs, very good; and the bad, very bad, which cannot be eaten, they are so bad."

4 Again the word of the LORD came to me, saying,

5 "Thus says the LORD, the God of Israel: 'Like these good figs, so will I acknowledge those who are carried away captive from Judah, whom I have sent out of this place for *their own* good, into the land of the Chaldē′ans.

6 'For I will set My eyes on them for good, and I will bring them back to this land; I will build them and not pull *them* down, and I will plant them and not pluck *them* up.

7 'Then I will give them a heart to know Me, that I *am* the LORD; and they shall be My people, and I will be their God, for they shall return to Me with their whole heart.

8 'And as the bad figs which cannot be eaten, they are so bad'—surely thus says the LORD—'so will I give up Zed·e·kī′ah the king of Judah, his princes, the residue of Jerusalem

23:33 ᵃSeptuagint, Targum, and Vulgate read 'You *are the burden.'*

who remain in this land, and those who dwell in the land of Egypt.

9 'I will deliver them to trouble into all the kingdoms of the earth, for *their* harm, *to be* a reproach and a byword, a taunt and a curse, in all places where I shall drive them.

10 'And I will send the sword, the famine, and the pestilence among them, till they are consumed from the land that I gave to them and their fathers.' "

SEVENTY YEARS OF DESOLATION

25 The word that came to Jer·e·mī'ah concerning all the people of Judah, in the fourth year of Je·hoi'a·kim the son of Jō·sī'ah, king of Judah (which *was* the first year of Ne·bū·chad·nez'zar king of Babylon),

2 which Jer·e·mī'ah the prophet spoke to all the people of Judah and to all the inhabitants of Jerusalem, saying:

3 "From the thirteenth year of Jō·sī'ah the son of Ā'mon, king of Judah, even to this day, this *is* the twenty-third year in which the word of the LORD has come to me; and I have spoken to you, rising early and speaking, but you have not listened.

4 "And the LORD has sent to you all His servants the prophets, rising early and sending *them,* but you have not listened nor inclined your ear to hear.

5 "They said, 'Repent now everyone of his evil way and his evil doings, and dwell in the land that the LORD has given to you and your fathers forever and ever.

6 'Do not go after other gods to serve them and worship them, and do not provoke Me to anger with the works of your hands; and I will not harm you.'

7 "Yet you have not listened to Me," says the LORD, "that you might provoke Me to anger with the works of your hands to your own hurt.

8 "Therefore thus says the LORD of hosts: 'Because you have not heard My words,

9 'behold, I will send and take all the families of the north,' says the LORD, 'and Ne·bū·chad·nez'zar the king of Babylon, My servant, and will bring them against this land, against its inhabitants, and against these nations all around, and will utterly destroy them, and make them an astonishment, a hissing, and perpetual desolations.

10 'Moreover I will take from them the voice of mirth and the voice of gladness, the voice of the bridegroom and the voice of the bride, the sound of the millstones and the light of the lamp.

11 'And this whole land shall be a desolation *and* an astonishment, and these nations shall serve the king of Babylon seventy years.

12 'Then it will come to pass, when seventy years are completed, *that* I will punish the king of Babylon and that nation, the land of the Chaldē'ans, for their iniquity,' says the LORD; 'and I will make it a perpetual desolation.

13 'So I will bring on that land all My words which I have pronounced against it, all that is written in this book, which Jer·e·mī'ah has prophesied concerning all the nations.

14 '(For many nations and great kings shall be served by them also; and I will repay them according to their deeds and according to the works of their own hands.)' "

JUDGMENT ON THE NATIONS

15 For thus says the LORD God of Israel to me: "Take this wine cup of fury from My hand, and cause all the

nations, to whom I send you, to drink it.

16 "And they will drink and stagger and go mad because of the sword that I will send among them."

17 Then I took the cup from the LORD's hand, and made all the nations drink, to whom the LORD had sent me:

18 Jerusalem and the cities of Judah, its kings and its princes, to make them a desolation, an astonishment, a hissing, and a curse, as *it is* this day;

19 Pharaoh king of Egypt, his servants, his princes, and all his people;

20 all the mixed multitude, all the kings of the land of Uz, all the kings of the land of the Phi·lis'tines (namely, Ash'ke·lon, Gā'za, Ek'ron, and the remnant of Ash'dod);

21 Ē'dom, Mō'ab, and the people of Am'mon;

22 all the kings of Tyre, all the kings of Sī'don, and the kings of the coastlands which *are* across the sea;

23 Dē'dan, Tē'ma, Buz, and all *who are* in the farthest corners;

24 all the kings of Arabia and all the kings of the mixed multitude who dwell in the desert;

25 all the kings of Zim'rī, all the kings of Ē'lam, and all the kings of the Mēdes;

26 all the kings of the north, far and near, one with another; and all the kingdoms of the world which *are* on the face of the earth. Also the king of Shē'shach*ᵃ* shall drink after them.

27 "Therefore you shall say to them, 'Thus says the LORD of hosts, the God of Israel: "Drink, be drunk, and vomit! Fall and rise no more, because of the sword which I will send among you." '

28 "And it shall be, if they refuse to take the cup from your hand to drink, then you shall say to them, 'Thus

says the LORD of hosts: "You shall certainly drink!

29 "For behold, I begin to bring calamity on the city which is called by My name, and should you be utterly unpunished? You shall not be unpunished, for I will call for a sword on all the inhabitants of the earth," says the LORD of hosts.'

30 "Therefore prophesy against them all these words, and say to them:

'The LORD will roar from on high,
And utter His voice from His holy
    habitation;
He will roar mightily against His
    fold.
He will give a shout, as those who
    tread *the grapes*,
Against all the inhabitants of the
    earth.
31 A noise will come to the ends of
    the earth—
For the LORD has a controversy
    with the nations;
He will plead His case with all
    flesh.
He will give those *who are* wicked
    to the sword,' says the LORD."

32 Thus says the LORD of hosts:

"Behold, disaster shall go forth
From nation to nation,
And a great whirlwind shall be
    raised up
From the farthest parts of the
    earth.

33 "And at that day the slain of the LORD shall be from *one* end of the earth even to the *other* end of the earth. They shall not be lamented, or gathered, or buried; they shall become refuse on the ground.

34 "Wail, shepherds, and cry!
    Roll about *in the ashes*,

25:26 ᵃA code word for Babylon (compare 51:41)

You leaders of the flock!
For the days of your slaughter
   and your dispersions are
   fulfilled;
You shall fall like a precious
   vessel.
35 And the shepherds will have no
   way to flee,
Nor the leaders of the flock to
   escape.
36 A voice of the cry of the
   shepherds,
And a wailing of the leaders to
   the flock *will be heard*.
For the LORD has plundered their
   pasture,
37 And the peaceful dwellings are
   cut down
Because of the fierce anger of the
   LORD.
38 He has left His lair like the lion;
For their land is desolate
Because of the fierceness of the
   Oppressor,
And because of His fierce anger.”

JEREMIAH SAVED FROM DEATH

26 In the beginning of the reign of Je·hoi′a·kim the son of Jō·sī′ah, king of Judah, this word came from the LORD, saying,
2 “Thus says the LORD: ‘Stand in the court of the LORD’s house, and speak to all the cities of Judah, which come to worship *in* the LORD’s house, all the words that I command you to speak to them. Do not diminish a word.
3 ‘Perhaps everyone will listen and turn from his evil way, that I may relent concerning the calamity which I purpose to bring on them because of the evil of their doings.’
4 “And you shall say to them, ‘Thus says the LORD: “If you will not listen to Me, to walk in My law which I have set before you,

5 “to heed the words of My servants the prophets whom I sent to you, both rising up early and sending *them* (but you have not heeded),
6 “then I will make this house like Shī′lōh, and will make this city a curse to all the nations of the earth.” ’ ”
7 So the priests and the prophets and all the people heard Jer·e·mī′ah speaking these words in the house of the LORD.
8 Now it happened, when Jer·e·mī′ah had made an end of speaking all that the LORD had commanded *him* to speak to all the people, that the priests and the prophets and all the people seized him, saying, “You will surely die!
9 “Why have you prophesied in the name of the LORD, saying, ‘This house shall be like Shī′lōh, and this city shall be desolate, without an inhabitant’?” And all the people were gathered against Jer·e·mī′ah in the house of the LORD.
10 When the princes of Judah heard these things, they came up from the king’s house to the house of the LORD and sat down in the entry of the New Gate of the LORD’s *house*.
11 And the priests and the prophets spoke to the princes and all the people, saying, “This man deserves to die! For he has prophesied against this city, as you have heard with your ears.”
12 Then Jer·e·mī′ah spoke to all the princes and all the people, saying: “The LORD sent me to prophesy against this house and against this city with all the words that you have heard.
13 “Now therefore, amend your ways and your doings, and obey the voice of the LORD your God; then the LORD will relent concerning the doom that He has pronounced against you.
14 “As for me, here I am, in your

hand; do with me as seems good and proper to you.

15 "But know for certain that if you put me to death, you will surely bring innocent blood on yourselves, on this city, and on its inhabitants; for truly the LORD has sent me to you to speak all these words in your hearing."

16 So the princes and all the people said to the priests and the prophets, "This man does not deserve to die. For he has spoken to us in the name of the LORD our God."

17 Then certain of the elders of the land rose up and spoke to all the assembly of the people, saying:

18 "Mī′cah of Mō′re·sheth prophesied in the days of Hez·e·kī′ah king of Judah, and spoke to all the people of Judah, saying, 'Thus says the LORD of hosts:

> "Zion shall be plowed *like* a field,
> Jerusalem shall become heaps of ruins,
> And the mountain of the temple*a*
> Like the bare hills of the forest." '*b*

19 "Did Hez·e·kī′ah king of Judah and all Judah ever put him to death? Did he not fear the LORD and seek the LORD's favor? And the LORD relented concerning the doom which He had pronounced against them. But we are doing great evil against ourselves."

20 Now there was also a man who prophesied in the name of the LORD, Ū·rī′jah the son of She·māi′ah of Kir′-jath Jē′a·rim, who prophesied against this city and against this land according to all the words of Jer·e·mī′ah.

21 And when Je·hoi′a·kim the king, with all his mighty men and all the princes, heard his words, the king sought to put him to death; but when Ū·rī′jah heard *it*, he was afraid and fled, and went to Egypt.

22 Then Je·hoi′a·kim the king sent men to Egypt: El·nā′than the son of Ach′bor, and *other* men *who went* with him to Egypt.

23 And they brought Ū·rī′jah from Egypt and brought him to Je·hoi′a·kim the king, who killed him with the sword and cast his dead body into the graves of the common people.

24 Nevertheless the hand of A·hī′-kam the son of Shā′phan was with Jer·e·mī′ah, so that they should not give him into the hand of the people to put him to death.

SYMBOL OF THE BONDS AND YOKES

27 In the beginning of the reign of Je·hoi′a·kim*a* the son of Jō·sī′ah, king of Judah, this word came to Jer·e·mī′ah from the LORD, saying,*b*

2 "Thus says the LORD to me: 'Make for yourselves bonds and yokes, and put them on your neck,

3 'and send them to the king of Ē′dom, the king of Mō′ab, the king of the Am′mon·ites, the king of Tȳre, and the king of Sī′don, by the hand of the messengers who come to Jerusalem to Zed·e·kī′ah king of Judah.

4 'And command them to say to their masters, "Thus says the LORD of hosts, the God of Israel—thus you shall say to your masters:

5 'I have made the earth, the man and the beast that *are* on the ground, by My great power and by My outstretched arm, and have given it to whom it seemed proper to Me.

6 'And now I have given all these lands into the hand of Ne·bū·chad-nez′zar the king of Babylon, My servant; and the beasts of the field I have also given him to serve him.

26:18 *a*Literally *house*   *b*Compare Micah 3:12
27:1 *a*Following Masoretic Text, Targum, and Vulgate; some Hebrew manuscripts, Arabic, and Syriac read *Zedekiah* (compare 27:3, 12; 28:1).   *b*Septuagint omits verse 1.

7 'So all nations shall serve him and his son and his son's son, until the time of his land comes; and then many nations and great kings shall make him serve them.

8 'And it shall be, *that* the nation and kingdom which will not serve Ne·bu·chad·nez′zar the king of Babylon, and which will not put its neck under the yoke of the king of Babylon, that nation I will punish,' says the LORD, 'with the sword, the famine, and the pestilence, until I have consumed them by his hand.

9 'Therefore do not listen to your prophets, your diviners, your dreamers, your soothsayers, or your sorcerers, who speak to you, saying, "You shall not serve the king of Babylon."

10 'For they prophesy a lie to you, to remove you far from your land; and I will drive you out, and you will perish.

11 'But the nations that bring their necks under the yoke of the king of Babylon and serve him, I will let them remain in their own land,' says the LORD, 'and they shall till it and dwell in it.' " ' "

12 I also spoke to Zed·e·kī′ah king of Judah according to all these words, saying, "Bring your necks under the yoke of the king of Babylon, and serve him and his people, and live!

13 "Why will you die, you and your people, by the sword, by the famine, and by the pestilence, as the LORD has spoken against the nation that will not serve the king of Babylon?

14 "Therefore do not listen to the words of the prophets who speak to you, saying, 'You shall not serve the king of Babylon,' for they prophesy a lie to you;

15 "for I have not sent them," says the LORD, "yet they prophesy a lie in My name, that I may drive you out, and that you may perish, you and the prophets who prophesy to you."

16 Also I spoke to the priests and to all this people, saying, "Thus says the LORD: 'Do not listen to the words of your prophets who prophesy to you, saying, "Behold, the vessels of the LORD's house will now shortly be brought back from Babylon"; for they prophesy a lie to you.

17 'Do not listen to them; serve the king of Babylon, and live! Why should this city be laid waste?

18 'But if they *are* prophets, and if the word of the LORD is with them, let them now make intercession to the LORD of hosts, that the vessels which are left in the house of the LORD, *in* the house of the king of Judah, and at Jerusalem, do not go to Babylon.'

19 "For thus says the LORD of hosts concerning the pillars, concerning the Sea, concerning the carts, and concerning the remainder of the vessels that remain in this city,

20 "which Ne·bu·chad·nez′zar king of Babylon did not take, when he carried away captive Jec·o·nī′ah the son of Je·hoi′a·kim, king of Judah, from Jerusalem to Babylon, and all the nobles of Judah and Jerusalem—

21 "yes, thus says the LORD of hosts, the God of Israel, concerning the vessels that remain in the house of the LORD, and in the house of the king of Judah and of Jerusalem:

22 'They shall be carried to Babylon, and there they shall be until the day that I visit them,' says the LORD. 'Then I will bring them up and restore them to this place.' "

HANANIAH'S FALSEHOOD AND DOOM

28 And it happened in the same year, at the beginning of the reign of Zed·e·kī′ah king of Judah, in the fourth year *and* in the fifth month, *that* Han·a·nī′ah the son of Ā′zur the prophet, who *was* from Gib′e·on,

spoke to me in the house of the LORD in the presence of the priests and of all the people, saying,

2 "Thus speaks the LORD of hosts, the God of Israel, saying: 'I have broken the yoke of the king of Babylon.

3 'Within two full years I will bring back to this place all the vessels of the LORD's house, that Ne·bū·chad·nez'zar king of Babylon took away from this place and carried to Babylon.

4 'And I will bring back to this place Jec·o·nī'ah the son of Je·hoi'a·kim, king of Judah, with all the captives of Judah who went to Babylon,' says the LORD, 'for I will break the yoke of the king of Babylon.'"

5 Then the prophet Jer·e·mī'ah spoke to the prophet Han·a·nī'ah in the presence of the priests and in the presence of all the people who stood in the house of the LORD,

6 and the prophet Jer·e·mī'ah said, "Amen! The LORD do so; the LORD perform your words which you have prophesied, to bring back the vessels of the LORD's house and all who were carried away captive, from Babylon to this place.

7 "Nevertheless hear now this word that I speak in your hearing and in the hearing of all the people:

8 "The prophets who have been before me and before you of old prophesied against many countries and great kingdoms—of war and disaster and pestilence.

9 "As for the prophet who prophesies of peace, when the word of the prophet comes to pass, the prophet will be known *as* one whom the LORD has truly sent."

10 Then Han·a·nī'ah the prophet took the yoke off the prophet Jer·e·mī'ah's neck and broke it.

11 And Han·a·nī'ah spoke in the presence of all the people, saying, "Thus says the LORD: 'Even so I will break the yoke of Ne·bū·chad·nez'zar king of Babylon from the neck of all nations within the space of two full years.'" And the prophet Jer·e·mī'ah went his way.

12 Now the word of the LORD came to Jer·e·mī'ah, after Han·a·nī'ah the prophet had broken the yoke from the neck of the prophet Jer·e·mī'ah, saying,

13 "Go and tell Han·a·nī'ah, saying, 'Thus says the LORD: "You have broken the yokes of wood, but you have made in their place yokes of iron."

14 'For thus says the LORD of hosts, the God of Israel: "I have put a yoke of iron on the neck of all these nations, that they may serve Ne·bū·chad·nez'zar king of Babylon; and they shall serve him. I have given him the beasts of the field also."'"

15 Then the prophet Jer·e·mī'ah said to Han·a·nī'ah the prophet, "Hear now, Han·a·nī'ah, the LORD has not sent you, but you make this people trust in a lie.

16 "Therefore thus says the LORD: 'Behold, I will cast you from the face of the earth. This year you shall die, because you have taught rebellion against the LORD.'"

17 So Han·a·nī'ah the prophet died the same year in the seventh month.

JEREMIAH'S LETTER
TO THE CAPTIVES

29 Now these *are* the words of the letter that Jer·e·mī'ah the prophet sent from Jerusalem to the remainder of the elders who were carried away captive—to the priests, the prophets, and all the people whom Ne·bū·chad·nez'zar had carried away captive from Jerusalem to Babylon.

2 (This happened after Jec·o·nī'ah the king, the queen mother, the eunuchs, the princes of Judah and Je-

rusalem, the craftsmen, and the smiths had departed from Jerusalem.)

3 *The letter was sent* by the hand of El·ā′sah the son of Shā′phan, and Gem·a·rī′ah the son of Hil·kī′ah, whom Zed·e·kī′ah king of Judah sent to Babylon, to Ne·bū·chad·nez′zar king of Babylon, saying,

4 Thus says the LORD of hosts, the God of Israel, to all who were carried away captive, whom I have caused to be carried away from Jerusalem to Babylon:

5 Build houses and dwell *in them;* plant gardens and eat their fruit.

6 Take wives and beget sons and daughters; and take wives for your sons and give your daughters to husbands, so that they may bear sons and daughters—that you may be increased there, and not diminished.

7 And seek the peace of the city where I have caused you to be carried away captive, and pray to the LORD for it; for in its peace you will have peace.

8 For thus says the LORD of hosts, the God of Israel: Do not let your prophets and your diviners who are in your midst deceive you, nor listen to your dreams which you cause to be dreamed.

9 For they prophesy falsely to you in My name; I have not sent them, says the LORD.

10 For thus says the LORD: After seventy years are completed at Babylon, I will visit you and perform My good word toward you, and cause you to return to this place.

11 For I know the thoughts that I think toward you, says the LORD, thoughts of peace and not of evil, to give you a future and a hope.

12 Then you will call upon Me and go and pray to Me, and I will listen to you.

■ Promises ■

Jeremiah 29:13

How can you find God? It's simple. Seek Him. He is not hiding. He wants you to find Him. Actually He is also searching for you. When you really and truly want to find God, He promises that you will find Him. That's a wonderful promise, isn't it?

---

13 And you will seek Me and find *Me,* when you search for Me with all your heart.

14 I will be found by you, says the LORD, and I will bring you back from your captivity; I will gather you from all the nations and from all the places where I have driven you, says the LORD, and I will bring you to the place from which I cause you to be carried away captive.

15 Because you have said, "The LORD has raised up prophets for us in Babylon"—

16 therefore thus says the LORD concerning the king who sits on the throne of David, concerning all the people who dwell in this city, and concerning your brethren who have not gone out with you into captivity—

17 thus says the LORD of hosts: Behold, I will send on them the sword, the famine, and the pestilence, and will make them like rotten figs that cannot be eaten, they are so bad.

18 And I will pursue them with the sword, with famine, and with pestilence; and I will deliver them

to trouble among all the kingdoms of the earth—to be a curse, an astonishment, a hissing, and a reproach among all the nations where I have driven them,

19 because they have not heeded My words, says the LORD, which I sent to them by My servants the prophets, rising up early and sending *them;* neither would you heed, says the LORD.

20 Therefore hear the word of the LORD, all you of the captivity, whom I have sent from Jerusalem to Babylon.

21 Thus says the LORD of hosts, the God of Israel, concerning Ā′hab the son of Kō·laī′ah, and Zed·e·kī′ah the son of Mā·a·sēi′ah, who prophesy a lie to you in My name: Behold, I will deliver them into the hand of Ne·bū·chad·nez′zar king of Babylon, and he shall slay them before your eyes.

22 And because of them a curse shall be taken up by all the captivity of Judah who *are* in Babylon, saying, "The LORD make you like Zed·e·kī′ah and Ā′hab, whom the king of Babylon roasted in the fire";

23 because they have done disgraceful things in Israel, have committed adultery with their neighbors' wives, and have spoken lying words in My name, which I have not commanded them. Indeed I know, and *am* a witness, says the LORD.

24 You shall also speak to She·māi′ah the Ne·hel′a·mīte, saying,

25 Thus speaks the LORD of hosts, the God of Israel, saying: You have sent letters in your name to all the people who *are* at Jerusalem, to Zeph·a·nī′ah the son of Mā·a·sēi′ah the priest, and to all the priests, saying,

26 "The LORD has made you priest instead of Je·hoi′a·da the priest, so that there should be officers *in* the house of the LORD over every man *who* is demented and considers himself a prophet, that you should put him in prison and in the stocks.

27 Now therefore, why have you not rebuked Jer·e·mī′ah of An′a·thoth who makes himself a prophet to you?

28 For he has sent to us *in* Babylon, saying, 'This *captivity is* long; build houses and dwell *in them,* and plant gardens and eat their fruit.' "

29 Now Zeph·a·nī′ah the priest read this letter in the hearing of Jer·e·mī′ah the prophet.

30 Then the word of the LORD came to Jer·e·mī′ah, saying:

31 Send to all those in captivity, saying, Thus says the LORD concerning She·māi′ah the Ne·hel′a·mīte: Because She·māi′ah has prophesied to you, and I have not sent him, and he has caused you to trust in a lie—

32 therefore thus says the LORD: Behold, I will punish She·māi′ah the Ne·hel′a·mīte and his family: he shall not have anyone to dwell among this people, nor shall he see the good that I will do for My people, says the LORD, because he has taught rebellion against the LORD.

RESTORATION OF ISRAEL AND JUDAH

30 The word that came to Jer·e·mī′ah from the LORD, saying,

2 "Thus speaks the LORD God of Is-

rael, saying: 'Write in a book for yourself all the words that I have spoken to you.

3 'For behold, the days are coming,' says the LORD, 'that I will bring back from captivity My people Israel and Judah,' says the LORD. 'And I will cause them to return to the land that I gave to their fathers, and they shall possess it.' "

4 Now these *are* the words that the LORD spoke concerning Israel and Judah.

5 "For thus says the LORD:

'We have heard a voice of
   trembling,
Of fear, and not of peace.
6 Ask now, and see,
Whether a man is ever in labor
   with child?
So why do I see every man *with*
   his hands on his loins
Like a woman in labor,
And all faces turned pale?
7 Alas! For that day *is* great,
So that none *is* like it;
And it *is* the time of Jacob's
   trouble,
But he shall be saved out of it.

8 'For it shall come to pass in that
   day,'
Says the LORD of hosts,
'That I will break his yoke from
   your neck,
And will burst your bonds;
Foreigners shall no more enslave
   them.
9 But they shall serve the LORD
   their God,
And David their king,
Whom I will raise up for them.

10 'Therefore do not fear, O My
   servant Jacob,' says the LORD,
'Nor be dismayed, O Israel;
For behold, I will save you from
   afar,

And your seed from the land of
   their captivity.
Jacob shall return, have rest and
   be quiet,
And no one shall make *him*
   afraid.
11 For I *am* with you,' says the
   LORD, 'to save you;
Though I make a full end of all
   nations where I have scattered
   you,
Yet I will not make a complete
   end of you.
But I will correct you in justice,
And will not let you go altogether
   unpunished.'

12 "For thus says the LORD:

'Your affliction *is* incurable,
Your wound *is* severe.
13 *There is* no one to plead your
   cause,
That you may be bound up;
You have no healing medicines.
14 All your lovers have forgotten
   you;
They do not seek you;
For I have wounded you with the
   wound of an enemy,
With the chastisement of a cruel
   one,
For the multitude of your
   iniquities,
Because your sins have increased.
15 Why do you cry about your
   affliction?
Your sorrow *is* incurable.
Because of the multitude of your
   iniquities,
Because your sins have
   increased,
I have done these things to you.
16 'Therefore all those who devour
   you shall be devoured;
And all your adversaries, every
   one of them, shall go into
   captivity;

Those who plunder you shall
become plunder,
And all who prey upon you I will
make a prey.
17 For I will restore health to you
And heal you of your wounds,'
says the LORD,
'Because they called you an
outcast *saying:*
"This *is* Zion;
No one seeks her." '

18 "Thus says the LORD:

'Behold, I will bring back the
captivity of Jacob's tents,
And have mercy on his dwelling
places;
The city shall be built upon its
own mound,
And the palace shall remain
according to its own plan.
19 Then out of them shall proceed
thanksgiving
And the voice of those who make
merry;
I will multiply them, and they
shall not diminish;
I will also glorify them, and they
shall not be small.
20 Their children also shall be as
before,
And their congregation shall be
established before Me;
And I will punish all who oppress
them.
21 Their nobles shall be from among
them,
And their governor shall come
from their midst;
Then I will cause him to draw
near,
And he shall approach Me;
For who *is* this who pledged his
heart to approach Me?' says the
LORD.
22 'You shall be My people,
And I will be your God.' "

23 Behold, the whirlwind of the
LORD
Goes forth with fury,
A continuing whirlwind;
It will fall violently on the head of
the wicked.
24 The fierce anger of the LORD will
not return until He has done it,
And until He has performed the
intents of His heart.

In the latter days you will
consider it.

THE REMNANT OF ISRAEL SAVED

31 "At the same time," says the
LORD, "I will be the God of all the
families of Israel, and they shall be
My people."
2   Thus says the LORD:

"The people who survived the
sword
Found grace in the wilderness—
Israel, when I went to give him
rest."

◼ *Promises* ◼

Jeremiah 31:3

God's most special promise of all
is the most simple. He promised
to love us. He not only promised
to love us, but to love us forever.
His love is an everlasting love.
Do you really want the most important Person of all to love you?
Do you want Him to love you forever? He promised that He
would. So what are you doing
about it?

---

3   The LORD has appeared of old to
me, *saying:*
"Yes, I have loved you with an
everlasting love;

Therefore with lovingkindness I
have drawn you.

4 Again I will build you, and you
shall be rebuilt,
O virgin of Israel!
You shall again be adorned with
your tambourines,
And shall go forth in the dances
of those who rejoice.

5 You shall yet plant vines on the
mountains of Samaria;
The planters shall plant and eat
them as ordinary food.

6 For there shall be a day
When the watchmen will cry on
Mount Ē′phra·im,
'Arise, and let us go up *to* Zion,
To the LORD our God.' ”

7 For thus says the LORD:

“Sing with gladness for Jacob,
And shout among the chief of the
nations;
Proclaim, give praise, and say,
'O LORD, save Your people,
The remnant of Israel!'

8 Behold, I will bring them from the
north country,
And gather them from the ends of
the earth,
Among them the blind and the
lame,
The woman with child
And the one who labors with
child, together;
A great throng shall return there.

9 They shall come with weeping,
And with supplications I will lead
them.
I will cause them to walk by the
rivers of waters,
In a straight way in which they
shall not stumble;
For I am a Father to Israel,
And Ē′phra·im *is* My firstborn.

10 “Hear the word of the LORD,
O nations,

And declare *it* in the isles afar off,
and say,
'He who scattered Israel will
gather him,
And keep him as a shepherd *does*
his flock.'

11 For the LORD has redeemed
Jacob,
And ransomed him from the hand
of one stronger than he.

12 Therefore they shall come and
sing in the height of Zion,
Streaming to the goodness of the
LORD—
For wheat and new wine and oil,
For the young of the flock and the
herd;
Their souls shall be like a
well-watered garden,
And they shall sorrow no more at
all.

13 “Then shall the virgin rejoice in
the dance,
And the young men and the old,
together;
For I will turn their mourning to
joy,
Will comfort them,
And make them rejoice rather
than sorrow.

14 I will satiate the soul of the
priests with abundance,
And My people shall be satisfied
with My goodness, says the
LORD.”

MERCY ON EPHRAIM

15 Thus says the LORD:

“A voice was heard in Rā′mah,
Lamentation *and* bitter weeping,
Rachel weeping for her children,
Refusing to be comforted for her
children,
Because they *are* no more.”

16 Thus says the LORD:

Values

FRIENDLINESS Jeremiah 31:13

Good Friends Are Tear Chasers

Good friends are tear chasers. When we're sad, or hurt, or lonely, we need a tear chaser. Who is a better tear chaser than a friend? Parents are good friends too when they help to chase our tears. And God is the best tear chaser of all, isn't He?

1. Dawn needs a tear chaser, doesn't she? What do you think made her cry?
2. How is David being Dawn's tear chaser? Do you think he will chase her tears away? How?
3. Who helps chase your tears away?
4. How can you be a tear chaser for a friend? Will you?

For more on *Values* turn to page 1320
For more on *Friendship* turn to page 1615

"Refrain your voice from weeping,
And your eyes from tears;
For your work shall be rewarded,
   says the LORD,
And they shall come back from
   the land of the enemy.
17 There is hope in your future, says
   the LORD,
That *your* children shall come
   back to their own border.

18 "I have surely heard Ē′phra·im
   bemoaning himself:
'You have chastised me, and I was
   chastised,
Like an untrained bull;
Restore me, and I will return,
For You *are* the LORD my God.
19 Surely, after my turning, I
   repented;
And after I was instructed, I
   struck myself on the thigh;
I was ashamed, yes, even
   humiliated,
Because I bore the reproach of my
   youth.'
20 *Is* Ē′phra·im My dear son?
Is he a pleasant child?
For though I spoke against him,
I earnestly remember him still;
Therefore My heart yearns for
   him;
I will surely have mercy on him,
   says the LORD.

21 "Set up signposts,
Make landmarks;
Set your heart toward the
   highway,
The way in *which* you went.
Turn back, O virgin of Israel,
Turn back to these your cities.
22 How long will you gad about,
O you backsliding daughter?
For the LORD has created a new
   thing in the earth—
A woman shall encompass a
   man."

FUTURE PROSPERITY OF JUDAH

23 Thus says the LORD of hosts, the God of Israel: "They shall again use this speech in the land of Judah and in its cities, when I bring back their captivity: 'The LORD bless you, O home of justice, *and* mountain of holiness!'
24 "And there shall dwell in Judah itself, and in all its cities together, farmers and those going out with flocks.
25 "For I have satiated the weary soul, and I have replenished every sorrowful soul."
26 After this I awoke and looked around, and my sleep was sweet to me.
27 "Behold, the days are coming, says the LORD, that I will sow the house of Israel and the house of Judah with the seed of man and the seed of beast.
28 "And it shall come to pass, *that* as I have watched over them to pluck up, to break down, to throw down, to destroy, and to afflict, so I will watch over them to build and to plant, says the LORD.
29 "In those days they shall say no more:

'The fathers have eaten sour
   grapes,
And the children's teeth are set
   on edge.'

30 "But every one shall die for his own iniquity; every man who eats the sour grapes, his teeth shall be set on edge.

A NEW COVENANT

31 "Behold, the days are coming, says the LORD, when I will make a new covenant with the house of Israel and with the house of Judah—

32 "not according to the covenant that I made with their fathers in the day *that* I took them by the hand to lead them out of the land of Egypt, My covenant which they broke, though I was a husband to them,*a* says the LORD.

33 "But this *is* the covenant that I will make with the house of Israel after those days, says the LORD: I will put My law in their minds, and write it on their hearts; and I will be their God, and they shall be My people.

34 "No more shall every man teach his neighbor, and every man his brother, saying, 'Know the LORD,' for they all shall know Me, from the least of them to the greatest of them, says the LORD. For I will forgive their iniquity, and their sin I will remember no more."

35 Thus says the LORD,
Who gives the sun for a light by
    day,
The ordinances of the moon and
    the stars for a light by night,
Who disturbs the sea,
And its waves roar
(The LORD of hosts *is* His name):

36 "If those ordinances depart
From before Me, says the LORD,
Then the seed of Israel shall also
    cease
From being a nation before Me
    forever."

37 Thus says the LORD:

"If heaven above can be
    measured,
And the foundations of the earth
    searched out beneath,
I will also cast off all the seed of
    Israel
For all that they have done, says
    the LORD.

38 "Behold, the days are coming, says the LORD, that the city shall be built for the LORD from the Tower of Ha·nan'el to the Corner Gate.

39 "The surveyor's line shall again extend straight forward over the hill Gā'reb; then it shall turn toward Gō'-ath.

40 "And the whole valley of the dead bodies and of the ashes, and all the fields as far as the Brook Kid'ron, to the corner of the Horse Gate toward the east, *shall be* holy to the LORD. It shall not be plucked up or thrown down anymore forever."

JEREMIAH BUYS A FIELD

32 The word that came to Jer·e-mī'ah from the LORD in the tenth year of Zed·e·kī'ah king of Judah, which was the eighteenth year of Ne·bū·chad·nez'zar.

2 For then the king of Babylon's army besieged Jerusalem, and Jer·e-mī'ah the prophet was shut up in the court of the prison, which *was in* the king of Judah's house.

3 For Zed·e·kī'ah king of Judah had shut him up, saying, "Why do you prophesy and say, 'Thus says the LORD: "Behold, I will give this city into the hand of the king of Babylon, and he shall take it;

4 "and Zed·e·kī'ah king of Judah shall not escape from the hand of the Chal·dē'ans, but shall surely be delivered into the hand of the king of Babylon, and shall speak with him face to face,*a* and see him eye to eye;

5 "then he shall lead Zed·e·kī'ah to Babylon, and there he shall be until I visit him," says the LORD; "though you fight with the Chal·dē'ans, you shall not succeed" '?"

31:32 *a*Following Masoretic Text, Targum, and Vulgate; Septuagint and Syriac read *and I turned away from them.*   32:4 *a*Literally *mouth to mouth*

6 And Jer·e·mī'ah said, "The word of the LORD came to me, saying,

7 'Behold, Han'a·mel the son of Shal'lum your uncle will come to you, saying, "Buy my field which *is* in An'a·thoth, for the right of redemption *is* yours to buy *it*."'

8 "Then Han'a·mel my uncle's son came to me in the court of the prison according to the word of the LORD, and said to me, 'Please buy my field that *is* in An'a·thoth, which *is* in the country of Benjamin; for the right of inheritance *is* yours, and the redemption yours; buy *it* for yourself.' Then I knew that this was the word of the LORD.

9 "So I bought the field from Han'a·mel, the son of my uncle who *was* in An'a·thoth, and weighed *out to* him the money—seventeen shekels of silver.

10 "And I signed the deed and sealed *it*, took witnesses, and weighed the money on the scales.

11 "So I took the purchase deed, *both* that which was sealed *according* to the law and custom, and that which was open;

12 "and I gave the purchase deed to Bar'uch the son of Ne·rī'ah, son of Mah'sēi·ah, in the presence of Han'a·mel my uncle's *son,* and in the presence of the witnesses who signed the purchase deed, before all the Jews who sat in the court of the prison.

13 "Then I charged Bar'uch before them, saying,

14 'Thus says the LORD of hosts, the God of Israel: "Take these deeds, both this purchase deed which is sealed and this deed which is open, and put them in an earthen vessel, that they may last many days."

15 'For thus says the LORD of hosts, the God of Israel: "Houses and fields and vineyards shall be possessed again in this land."'

JEREMIAH PRAYS FOR UNDERSTANDING

16 "Now when I had delivered the purchase deed to Bar'uch the son of Ne·rī'ah, I prayed to the LORD, saying:

17 'Ah, Lord GOD! Behold, You have made the heavens and the earth by Your great power and outstretched arm. There is nothing too hard for You.

18 '*You* show lovingkindness to thousands, and repay the iniquity of the fathers into the bosom of their children after them—the Great, the Mighty God, whose name *is* the LORD of hosts.

19 '*You are* great in counsel and mighty in work, for your eyes *are* open to all the ways of the sons of men, to give everyone according to his ways and according to the fruit of his doings.

Prayers

Jeremiah 32:16–25

It was a terrible time in Israel. The people had turned against God. Now He was letting the Babylonians capture Jerusalem. On the eve of the capture, God told Jeremiah to buy some land in Jerusalem. When a city is about to fall, it is *not* the time to buy land. But Jeremiah did what the Lord told him. Why? Jeremiah prayed and asked the Lord why. The Lord promised to bring His people back to Jerusalem. Someday He would give the city back to them. The Lord sees the future. We don't. We should keep praying to Him because He knows what is ahead and we don't.

20 'You have set signs and wonders in the land of Egypt, to this day, and in Israel and among *other* men; and You have made Yourself a name, as it is this day.

21 'You have brought Your people Israel out of the land of Egypt with signs and wonders, with a strong hand and an outstretched arm, and with great terror;

22 'You have given them this land, of which You swore to their fathers to give them—"a land flowing with milk and honey."*a*

23 'And they came in and took possession of it, but they have not obeyed Your voice or walked in Your law. They have done nothing of all that You commanded them to do; therefore You have caused all this calamity to come upon them.

24 'Look, the siege mounds! They have come to the city to take it; and the city has been given into the hand of the Chal·dē′ans who fight against it, because of the sword and famine and pestilence. What You have spoken has happened; there You see *it!*

25 'And You have said to me, O Lord GOD, "Buy the field for money, and take witnesses"!—yet the city has been given into the hand of the Chal·dē′ans.' "

GOD'S ASSURANCE
OF THE PEOPLE'S RETURN

26 Then the word of the LORD came to Jer·e·mī′ah, saying,

27 "Behold, I *am* the LORD, the God of all flesh. Is there anything too hard for Me?

28 "Therefore thus says the LORD: 'Behold, I will give this city into the hand of the Chal·dē′ans, into the hand of Ne·bū·chad·nez′zar king of Babylon, and he shall take it.

29 'And the Chal·dē′ans who fight against this city shall come and set fire to this city and burn it, with the houses on whose roofs they have offered incense to Bā′al and poured out drink offerings to other gods, to provoke Me to anger;

30 'because the children of Israel and the children of Judah have done only evil before Me from their youth. For the children of Israel have provoked Me only to anger with the work of their hands,' says the LORD.

31 'For this city has been to Me *a provocation of* My anger and My fury from the day that they built it, even to this day; so I will remove it from before My face

32 'because of all the evil of the children of Israel and the children of Judah, which they have done to provoke Me to anger—they, their kings, their princes, their priests, their prophets, the men of Judah, and the inhabitants of Jerusalem.

33 'And they have turned to Me the back, and not the face; though I taught them, rising up early and teaching *them,* yet they have not listened to receive instruction.

34 'But they set their abominations in the house which is called by My name, to defile it.

35 'And they built the high places of Bā′al which *are* in the Valley of the Son of Hin′nom, to cause their sons and their daughters to pass through *the fire* to Mō′lech, which I did not command them, nor did it come into My mind that they should do this abomination, to cause Judah to sin.'

36 "Now therefore, thus says the LORD, the God of Israel, concerning this city of which you say, 'It shall be delivered into the hand of the king of Babylon by the sword, by the famine, and by the pestilence':

37 'Behold, I will gather them out of all countries where I have driven

32:22 *a*Exodus 3:8

them in My anger, in My fury, and in great wrath; I will bring them back to this place, and I will cause them to dwell safely.

38 'They shall be My people, and I will be their God;

39 'then I will give them one heart and one way, that they may fear Me forever, for the good of them and their children after them.

40 'And I will make an everlasting covenant with them, that I will not turn away from doing them good; but I will put My fear in their hearts so that they will not depart from Me.

41 'Yes, I will rejoice over them to do them good, and I will assuredly plant them in this land, with all My heart and with all My soul.'

42 "For thus says the LORD: 'Just as I have brought all this great calamity on this people, so I will bring on them all the good that I have promised them.

43 'And fields will be bought in this land of which you say, "*It is* desolate, without man or beast; it has been given into the hand of the Chal·dē'-ans."

44 'Men will buy fields for money, sign deeds and seal *them,* and take witnesses, in the land of Benjamin, in the places around Jerusalem, in the cities of Judah, in the cities of the mountains, in the cities of the lowland, and in the cities of the South; for I will cause their captives to return,' says the LORD."

EXCELLENCE OF THE RESTORED NATION

33 Moreover the word of the LORD came to Jer·e·mī'ah a second time, while he was still shut up in the court of the prison, saying,

2 "Thus says the LORD who made it, the LORD who formed it to establish it (the LORD *is* His name):

┌─────────────────────────────┐
│ **Promises** │
│ Jeremiah 33:3 │
└─────────────────────────────┘

Can you ever say, "God is ignoring me"? Here is a special promise from God. Call and I will answer. He promised! But He promised even more. He will not only answer, He will do wonderful things for us when we ask. So what are you waiting for? Pray! Call on Him.

---

3 'Call to Me, and I will answer you, and show you great and mighty things, which you do not know.'

4 "For thus says the LORD, the God of Israel, concerning the houses of this city and the houses of the kings of Judah, which have been pulled down *to fortify*a against the siege mounds and the sword:

5 'They come to fight with the Chal·dē'ans, but *only* to fill their placesa with the dead bodies of men whom I will slay in My anger and My fury, all for whose wickedness I have hidden My face from this city.

6 'Behold, I will bring it health and healing; I will heal them and reveal to them the abundance of peace and truth.

7 'And I will cause the captives of Judah and the captives of Israel to return, and will rebuild those places as at the first.

8 'I will cleanse them from all their iniquity by which they have sinned against Me, and I will pardon all their iniquities by which they have sinned and by which they have transgressed against Me.

9 'Then it shall be to Me a name of joy, a praise, and an honor before all

33:4 aCompare Isaiah 22:10   33:5 aCompare 2 Kings 23:14

nations of the earth, who shall hear all the good that I do to them; they shall fear and tremble for all the goodness and all the prosperity that I provide for it.'

10 "Thus says the LORD: 'Again there shall be heard in this place—of which you say, "It *is* desolate, without man and without beast"—in the cities of Judah, in the streets of Jerusalem that are desolate, without man and without inhabitant and without beast,

11 'the voice of joy and the voice of gladness, the voice of the bridegroom and the voice of the bride, the voice of those who will say:

"Praise the LORD of hosts,
For the LORD *is* good,
For His mercy *endures* forever"—

and of those *who will* bring the sacrifice of praise into the house of the LORD. For I will cause the captives of the land to return as at the first,' says the LORD.

12 "Thus says the LORD of hosts: 'In this place which is desolate, without man and without beast, and in all its cities, there shall again be a dwelling place of shepherds causing *their* flocks to lie down.

13 'In the cities of the mountains, in the cities of the lowland, in the cities of the South, in the land of Benjamin, in the places around Jerusalem, and in the cities of Judah, the flocks shall again pass under the hands of him who counts *them,*' says the LORD.

14 'Behold, the days are coming,' says the LORD, 'that I will perform that good thing which I have promised to the house of Israel and to the house of Judah:

15 'In those days and at that time
I will cause to grow up to David
A Branch of righteousness;

He shall execute judgment and
righteousness in the earth.

16 In those days Judah will be saved,
And Jerusalem will dwell safely.
And this *is the name* by which she will be called:

**THE LORD OUR
RIGHTEOUSNESS.'***a***

17 "For thus says the LORD: 'David shall never lack a man to sit on the throne of the house of Israel;

18 'nor shall the priests, the Lē'vītes, lack a man to offer burnt offerings before Me, to kindle grain offerings, and to sacrifice continually.' "

THE PERMANENCE OF GOD'S COVENANT

19 And the word of the LORD came to Jer·e·mī'ah, saying,

20 "Thus says the LORD: 'If you can break My covenant with the day and My covenant with the night, so that there will not be day and night in their season,

21 'then My covenant may also be broken with David My servant, so that he shall not have a son to reign on his throne, and with the Lē'vītes, the priests, My ministers.

22 'As the host of heaven cannot be numbered, nor the sand of the sea measured, so will I multiply the descendants of David My servant and the Lē'vītes who minister to Me.' "

23 Moreover the word of the LORD came to Jer·e·mī'ah, saying,

24 "Have you not considered what these people have spoken, saying, 'The two families which the LORD has chosen, He has also cast them off'? Thus they have despised My people, as if they should no more be a nation before them.

33:16 *a*Compare 23:5, 6

25 "Thus says the LORD: 'If My covenant *is* not with day and night, *and if* I have not appointed the ordinances of heaven and earth,
26 'then I will cast away the descendants of Jacob and David My servant, *so* that I will not take *any* of his descendants *to be* rulers over the descendants of Abraham, Isaac, and Jacob. For I will cause their captives to return, and will have mercy on them.' "

ZEDEKIAH WARNED BY GOD

34 The word which came to Jer·e·mī′ah from the LORD, when Ne·bū·chad·nez′zar king of Babylon and all his army, all the kingdoms of the earth under his dominion, and all the people, fought against Jerusalem and all its cities, saying,
2 "Thus says the LORD, the God of Israel: 'Go and speak to Zed·e·kī′ah king of Judah and tell him, "Thus says the LORD: 'Behold, I will give this city into the hand of the king of Babylon, and he shall burn it with fire.
3 'And you shall not escape from his hand, but shall surely be taken and delivered into his hand; your eyes shall see the eyes of the king of Babylon, he shall speak with you face to face,ᵃ and you shall go to Babylon.' " '
4 "Yet hear the word of the LORD, O Zed·e·kī′ah king of Judah! Thus says the LORD concerning you: 'You shall not die by the sword.
5 'You shall die in peace; as in the ceremonies of your fathers, the former kings who were before you, so they shall burn incense for you and lament for you, *saying,* "Alas, lord!" For I have pronounced the word, says the LORD.' "
6 Then Jer·e·mī′ah the prophet spoke all these words to Zed·e·kī′ah king of Judah in Jerusalem,

7 when the king of Babylon's army fought against Jerusalem and all the cities of Judah that were left, against Lā′chish and A·zē′kah; for *only* these fortified cities remained of the cities of Judah.

TREACHEROUS TREATMENT OF SLAVES

8 *This is* the word that came to Jer·e·mī′ah from the LORD, after King Zed·e·kī′ah had made a covenant with all the people who *were* at Jerusalem to proclaim liberty to them:
9 that every man should set free his male and female slave—a Hebrew man or woman—that no one should keep a Jewish brother in bondage.
10 Now when all the princes and all the people, who had entered into the covenant, heard that everyone should set free his male and female slaves, that no one should keep them in bondage anymore, they obeyed and let *them* go.
11 But afterward they changed their minds and made the male and female slaves return, whom they had set free, and brought them into subjection as male and female slaves.
12 Therefore the word of the LORD came to Jer·e·mī′ah from the LORD, saying,
13 "Thus says the LORD, the God of Israel: 'I made a covenant with your fathers in the day that I brought them out of the land of Egypt, out of the house of bondage, saying,
14 "At the end of seven years let every man set free his Hebrew brother, who has been sold to him; and when he has served you six years, you shall let him go free from you." But your fathers did not obey Me nor incline their ear.
15 'Then you recently turned and did

34:3 ᵃLiterally *mouth to mouth*

what was right in My sight—every man proclaiming liberty to his neighbor; and you made a covenant before Me in the house which is called by My name.

16 'Then you turned around and profaned My name, and every one of you brought back his male and female slaves, whom he had set at liberty, at their pleasure, and brought them back into subjection, to be your male and female slaves.'

17 "Therefore thus says the LORD: 'You have not obeyed Me in proclaiming liberty, every one to his brother and every one to his neighbor. Behold, I proclaim liberty to you,' says the LORD—'to the sword, to pestilence, and to famine! And I will deliver you to trouble among all the kingdoms of the earth.

18 'And I will give the men who have transgressed My covenant, who have not performed the words of the covenant which they made before Me, when they cut the calf in two and passed between the parts of it—

19 'the princes of Judah, the princes of Jerusalem, the eunuchs, the priests, and all the people of the land who passed between the parts of the calf—

20 'I will give them into the hand of their enemies and into the hand of those who seek their life. Their dead bodies shall be for meat for the birds of the heaven and the beasts of the earth.

21 'And I will give Zed·e·kī'ah king of Judah and his princes into the hand of their enemies, into the hand of those who seek their life, and into the hand of the king of Babylon's army which has gone back from you.

22 'Behold, I will command,' says the LORD, 'and cause them to return to this city. They will fight against it and take it and burn it with fire; and

I will make the cities of Judah a desolation without inhabitant.'"

THE OBEDIENT RECHABITES

35 The word which came to Jer·e·mī'ah from the LORD in the days of Je·hoi'a·kim the son of Jō·sī'ah, king of Judah, saying,

2 "Go to the house of the Rē'chab-ites, speak to them, and bring them into the house of the LORD, into one of the chambers, and give them wine to drink."

3 Then I took Jā·az·a·nī'ah the son of Jer·e·mī'ah, the son of Ha·baz·zi·nī'ah, his brothers and all his sons, and the whole house of the Rē'chab-ites,

4 and I brought them into the house of the LORD, into the chamber of the sons of Hā'nan the son of Ig·da·lī'ah, a man of God, which *was* by the chamber of the princes, above the chamber of Mā·a·sēi'ah the son of Shal'lum, the keeper of the door.

5 Then I set before the sons of the house of the Rē'chab·ites bowls full of wine, and cups; and I said to them, "Drink wine."

6 But they said, "We will drink no wine, for Jon'a·dab the son of Rē'chab, our father, commanded us, saying, 'You shall drink no wine, you nor your sons, forever.

7 'You shall not build a house, sow seed, plant a vineyard, nor have *any of these;* but all your days you shall dwell in tents, that you may live many days in the land where you are sojourners.'

8 "Thus we have obeyed the voice of Jon'a·dab the son of Rē'chab, our father, in all that he charged us, to drink no wine all our days, we, our wives, our sons, or our daughters,

9 "nor to build ourselves houses to dwell in; nor do we have vineyard, field, or seed.

10 "But we have dwelt in tents, and have obeyed and done according to all that Jon′a·dab our father commanded us.

11 "But it came to pass, when Ne·bu-chad·nez′zar king of Babylon came up into the land, that we said, 'Come, let us go to Jerusalem for fear of the army of the Chal·de′ans and for fear of the army of the Syrians.' So we dwell at Jerusalem."

12 Then came the word of the LORD to Jer·e·mi′ah, saying,

13 "Thus says the LORD of hosts, the God of Israel: 'Go and tell the men of Judah and the inhabitants of Jerusalem, "Will you not receive instruction to obey My words?" says the LORD.

14 "The words of Jon′a·dab the son of Re′chab, which he commanded his sons, not to drink wine, are performed; for to this day they drink none, and obey their father's commandment. But although I have spoken to you, rising early and speaking, you did not obey Me.

15 "I have also sent to you all My servants the prophets, rising up early and sending them, saying, 'Turn now everyone from his evil way, amend your doings, and do not go after other gods to serve them; then you will dwell in the land which I have given you and your fathers.' But you have not inclined your ear, nor obeyed Me.

16 "Surely the sons of Jon′a·dab the son of Re′chab have performed the commandment of their father, which he commanded them, but this people has not obeyed Me." '

17 "Therefore thus says the LORD God of hosts, the God of Israel: 'Behold, I will bring on Judah and on all the inhabitants of Jerusalem all the doom that I have pronounced against them; because I have spoken to them but they have not heard, and I have called to them but they have not answered.' "

18 And Jer·e·mi′ah said to the house of the Re′chab·ites, "Thus says the LORD of hosts, the God of Israel: 'Because you have obeyed the commandment of Jon′a·dab your father, and kept all his precepts and done according to all that he commanded you,

19 'therefore thus says the LORD of hosts, the God of Israel: "Jon′a·dab the son of Re′chab shall not lack a man to stand before Me forever." ' "

THE SCROLL READ IN THE TEMPLE

36 Now it came to pass in the fourth year of Je·hoi′a·kim the son of Jo·si′ah, king of Judah, *that* this word came to Jer·e·mi′ah from the LORD, saying:

2 "Take a scroll of a book and write on it all the words that I have spoken to you against Israel, against Judah, and against all the nations, from the day I spoke to you, from the days of Jo·si′ah even to this day.

3 "It may be that the house of Judah will hear all the adversities which I purpose to bring upon them, that everyone may turn from his evil way, that I may forgive their iniquity and their sin."

4 Then Jer·e·mi′ah called Bar′uch the son of Ne·ri′ah; and Bar′uch wrote on a scroll of a book, at the instruction of Jer·e·mi′ah,ᵃ all the words of the LORD which He had spoken to him.

5 And Jer·e·mi′ah commanded Bar′uch, saying, "I *am* confined, I cannot go into the house of the LORD.

6 "You go, therefore, and read from the scroll which you have written at my instruction,ᵃ the words of the LORD, in the hearing of the people in the LORD's house on the day of fasting. And you shall also read them in

36:4 ᵃLiterally *from Jeremiah's mouth*
36:6 ᵃLiterally *from my mouth*

the hearing of all Judah who come from their cities.

7 "It may be that they will present their supplication before the LORD, and everyone will turn from his evil way. For great *is* the anger and the fury that the LORD has pronounced against this people."

8 And Bar'uch the son of Ne·rī'ah did according to all that Jer·e·mī'ah the prophet commanded him, reading from the book the words of the LORD in the LORD's house.

9 Now it came to pass in the fifth year of Je·hoi'a·kim the son of Jō·sī'ah, king of Judah, in the ninth month, *that* they proclaimed a fast before the LORD to all the people in Jerusalem, and to all the people who came from the cities of Judah to Jerusalem.

10 Then Bar'uch read from the book the words of Jer·e·mī'ah in the house of the LORD, in the chamber of Gem·a·rī'ah the son of Shā'phan the scribe, in the upper court at the entry of the New Gate of the LORD's house, in the hearing of all the people.

THE SCROLL READ IN THE PALACE

11 When Mī·chaī'ah the son of Gem·a·rī'ah, the son of Shā'phan, heard all the words of the LORD from the book,

12 he then went down to the king's house, into the scribe's chamber; and there all the princes were sitting— E·lish'a·ma the scribe, De·laī'ah the son of She·māi'ah, El·nā'than the son of Ach'bor, Gem·a·rī'ah the son of Shā'phan, Zed·e·kī'ah the son of Han·a·nī'ah, and all the princes.

13 Then Mī·chaī'ah declared to them all the words that he had heard when Bar'uch read the book in the hearing of the people.

14 Therefore all the princes sent Je·hū'dī the son of Neth·a·nī'ah, the son of Shel·e·mī'ah, the son of Cū'shī, to Bar'uch, saying, "Take in your hand the scroll from which you have read in the hearing of the people, and come." So Bar'uch the son of Ne·rī'ah took the scroll in his hand and came to them.

15 And they said to him, "Sit down now, and read it in our hearing." So Bar'uch read *it* in their hearing.

16 Now it happened, when they had heard all the words, that they looked in fear from one to another, and said to Bar'uch, "We will surely tell the king of all these words."

17 And they asked Bar'uch, saying, "Tell us now, how did you write all these words—at his instruction?"*a*

18 So Bar'uch answered them, "He proclaimed with his mouth all these words to me, and I wrote *them* with ink in the book."

19 Then the princes said to Bar'uch, "Go and hide, you and Jer·e·mī'ah; and let no one know where you are."

THE KING DESTROYS JEREMIAH'S SCROLL

20 And they went to the king, into the court; but they stored the scroll in the chamber of E·lish'a·ma the scribe, and told all the words in the hearing of the king.

21 So the king sent Je·hū'dī to bring the scroll, and he took it from E·lish'a·ma the scribe's chamber. And Je·hū'dī read it in the hearing of the king and in the hearing of all the princes who stood beside the king.

22 Now the king was sitting in the winter house in the ninth month, with *a fire* burning on the hearth before him.

23 And it happened, when Je·hū'dī had read three or four columns, *that the king* cut it with the scribe's knife

36:17 *a*Literally *with his mouth*

and cast *it* into the fire that *was* on the hearth, until all the scroll was consumed in the fire that *was* on the hearth.

24 Yet they were not afraid, nor did they tear their garments, the king nor any of his servants who heard all these words.

25 Nevertheless El·nā′than, De·laī′ah, and Gem·a·rī′ah implored the king not to burn the scroll; but he would not listen to them.

26 And the king commanded Je·rah′-mē·el the king's*a* son, Se·rāi′ah the son of Az′ri·el, and Shel·e·mī′ah the son of Ab·dē′el, to seize Bar′uch the scribe and Jer·e·mī′ah the prophet, but the LORD hid them.

JEREMIAH REWRITES THE SCROLL

27 Now after the king had burned the scroll with the words which Bar′uch had written at the instruction of Jer·e·mī′ah,*a* the word of the LORD came to Jer·e·mī′ah, saying:

28 "Take yet another scroll, and write on it all the former words that were in the first scroll which Je·hoi′a·kim the king of Judah has burned.

29 "And you shall say to Je·hoi′a·kim king of Judah, 'Thus says the LORD: "You have burned this scroll, saying, 'Why have you written in it that the king of Babylon will certainly come and destroy this land, and cause man and beast to cease from here?' "

30 'Therefore thus says the LORD concerning Je·hoi′a·kim king of Judah: "He shall have no one to sit on the throne of David, and his dead body shall be cast out to the heat of the day and the frost of the night.

31 "I will punish him, his family, and his servants for their iniquity; and I will bring on them, on the inhabitants of Jerusalem, and on the men of Judah all the doom that I have pronounced against them; but they did not heed." ' "

32 Then Jer·e·mī′ah took another scroll and gave it to Bar′uch the scribe, the son of Ne·rī′ah, who wrote on it at the instruction of Jer·e·mī′ah*a* all the words of the book which Je·hoi′a·kim king of Judah had burned in the fire. And besides, there were added to them many similar words.

ZEDEKIAH'S VAIN HOPE

37 Now King Zed·e·kī′ah the son of Jō·sī′ah reigned instead of Cō·nī′ah the son of Je·hoi′a·kim, whom Ne·bū·chad·nez′zar king of Babylon made king in the land of Judah.

2 But neither he nor his servants nor the people of the land gave heed to the words of the LORD which He spoke by the prophet Jer·e·mī′ah.

3 And Zed·e·kī′ah the king sent Je·hū′cal the son of Shel·e·mī′ah, and Zeph·a·nī′ah the son of Mā·a·sēi′ah, the priest, to the prophet Jer·e·mī′ah, saying, "Pray now to the LORD our God for us."

4 Now Jer·e·mī′ah was coming and going among the people, for they had not *yet* put him in prison.

5 Then Pharaoh's army came up from Egypt; and when the Chal·dē′ans who were besieging Jerusalem heard news of them, they departed from Jerusalem.

6 Then the word of the LORD came to the prophet Jer·e·mī′ah, saying,

7 "Thus says the LORD, the God of Israel, 'Thus you shall say to the king of Judah, who sent you to Me to inquire of Me: "Behold, Pharaoh's army which has come up to help you will return to Egypt, to their own land.

36:26 *a*Hebrew *Hammelech*   36:27 *a*Literally *from Jeremiah's mouth*   36:32 *a*Literally *from Jeremiah's mouth*

8 "And the Chal·dē'ans shall come back and fight against this city, and take it and burn it with fire." '

9 "Thus says the LORD: 'Do not deceive yourselves, saying, "The Chal·dē'ans will surely depart from us," for they will not depart.

10 'For though you had defeated the whole army of the Chal·dē'ans who fight against you, and there remained *only* wounded men among them, they would rise up, every man in his tent, and burn the city with fire.' "

JEREMIAH IMPRISONED

11 And it happened, when the army of the Chal·dē'ans left *the siege* of Jerusalem for fear of Pharaoh's army,

12 that Jer·e·mī'ah went out of Jerusalem to go into the land of Benjamin to claim his property there among the people.

13 And when he was in the Gate of Benjamin, a captain of the guard *was* there whose name *was* I·rī'jah the son of Shel·e·mī'ah, the son of Han·a·nī'ah; and he seized Jer·e·mī'ah the prophet, saying, "You are defecting to the Chal·dē'ans!"

14 Then Jer·e·mī'ah said, "False! I am not defecting to the Chal·dē'ans." But he did not listen to him. So I·rī'jah seized Jer·e·mī'ah and brought him to the princes.

15 Therefore the princes were angry with Jer·e·mī'ah, and they struck him and put him in prison in the house of Jonathan the scribe. For they had made that the prison.

16 When Jer·e·mī'ah entered the dungeon and the cells, and Jer·e·mī'ah had remained there many days,

17 then Zed·e·kī'ah the king sent and took him *out*. The king asked him secretly in his house, and said, "Is there *any* word from the LORD?" And Jer·e·mī'ah said, "There is." Then he said, "You shall be delivered into the hand of the king of Babylon!"

18 Moreover Jer·e·mī'ah said to King Zed·e·kī'ah, "What offense have I committed against you, against your servants, or against this people, that you have put me in prison?

19 "Where now *are* your prophets who prophesied to you, saying, 'The king of Babylon will not come against you or against this land'?

20 "Therefore please hear now, O my lord the king. Please, let my petition be accepted before you, and do not make me return to the house of Jonathan the scribe, lest I die there."

21 Then Zed·e·kī'ah the king commanded that they should commit Jer·e·mī'ah to the court of the prison, and that they should give him daily a piece of bread from the bakers' street, until all the bread in the city was gone. Thus Jer·e·mī'ah remained in the court of the prison.

JEREMIAH IN THE DUNGEON

38 Now Sheph·a·tī'ah the son of Mat'tan, Ged·a·lī'ah the son of Pash'hur, Jū'cal[a] the son of Shel·e·mī'ah, and Pash'hur the son of Mal·chī'ah heard the words that Jer·e·mī'ah had spoken to all the people, saying,

2 "Thus says the LORD: 'He who remains in this city shall die by the sword, by famine, and by pestilence; but he who goes over to the Chal·dē'ans shall live; his life shall be as a prize to him, and he shall live.'[a]

3 "Thus says the LORD: 'This city shall surely be given into the hand of the king of Babylon's army, which shall take it.' "

4 Therefore the princes said to the king, "Please, let this man be put to death, for thus he weakens the hands

38:1 [a]Same as *Jehucal* (compare 37:3)
38:2 [a]Compare 21:9

of the men of war who remain in this city, and the hands of all the people, by speaking such words to them. For this man does not seek the welfare of this people, but their harm."

5 Then Zed·e·kī′ah the king said, "Look, he *is* in your hand. For the king can *do* nothing against you."

6 So they took Jer·e·mī′ah and cast him into the dungeon of Mal·chī′ah the king's*a* son, which *was* in the court of the prison, and they let Jer·e·mī′ah down with ropes. And in the dungeon *there was* no water, but mire. So Jer·e·mī′ah sank in the mire.

7 Now Ē′bed-Mē′lech the Ethiopian, one of the eunuchs, who was in the king's house, heard that they had put Jer·e·mī′ah in the dungeon. When the king was sitting at the Gate of Benjamin,

8 Ē′bed-Mē′lech went out of the king's house and spoke to the king, saying:

9 "My lord the king, these men have done evil in all that they have done to Jer·e·mī′ah the prophet, whom they have cast into the dungeon, and he is likely to die from hunger in the place where he is. For *there is* no more bread in the city."

10 Then the king commanded Ē′bed-Mē′lech the Ethiopian, saying, "Take from here thirty men with you, and lift Jer·e·mī′ah the prophet out of the dungeon before he dies."

11 So Ē′bed-Mē′lech took the men with him and went into the house of the king under the treasury, and took from there old clothes and old rags, and let them down by ropes into the dungeon to Jer·e·mī′ah.

12 Then Ē′bed-Mē′lech the Ethiopian said to Jer·e·mī′ah, "Please put these old clothes and rags under your armpits, under the ropes." And Jer·e·mī′ah did so.

13 So they pulled Jer·e·mī′ah up with ropes and lifted him out of the dungeon. And Jer·e·mī′ah remained in the court of the prison.

ZEDEKIAH'S FEARS AND JEREMIAH'S ADVICE

14 Then Zed·e·kī′ah the king sent and had Jer·e·mī′ah the prophet brought to him at the third entrance of the house of the LORD. And the king said to Jer·e·mī′ah, "I will ask you something. Hide nothing from me."

15 Jer·e·mī′ah said to Zed·e·kī′ah, "If I declare *it* to you, will you not surely put me to death? And if I give you advice, you will not listen to me."

16 So Zed·e·kī′ah the king swore secretly to Jer·e·mī′ah, saying, "*As* the LORD lives, who made our very souls, I will not put you to death, nor will I give you into the hand of these men who seek your life."

17 Then Jer·e·mī′ah said to Zed·e·kī′ah, "Thus says the LORD, the God of hosts, the God of Israel: 'If you surely surrender to the king of Babylon's princes, then your soul shall live; this city shall not be burned with fire, and you and your house shall live.

18 'But if you do not surrender to the king of Babylon's princes, then this city shall be given into the hand of the Chal·dē′ans; they shall burn it with fire, and you shall not escape from their hand.'"

19 And Zed·e·kī′ah the king said to Jer·e·mī′ah, "I am afraid of the Jews who have defected to the Chal·dē′ans, lest they deliver me into their hand, and they abuse me."

20 But Jer·e·mī′ah said, "They shall not deliver *you*. Please, obey the voice of the LORD which I speak to you. So it shall be well with you, and your soul shall live.

38:6 *a*Hebrew *Hammelech*

21 "But if you refuse to surrender, this *is* the word that the LORD has shown me:

22 'Now behold, all the women who are left in the king of Judah's house *shall be* surrendered to the king of Babylon's princes, and those *women* shall say:

"Your close friends have set upon
  you
And prevailed against you;
Your feet have sunk in the mire,
And they have turned away
  again."

23 'So they shall surrender all your wives and children to the Chal-dē'ans. You shall not escape from their hand, but shall be taken by the hand of the king of Babylon. And you shall cause this city to be burned with fire.' "

24 Then Zed-e-kīah said to Jer-e-mī'ah, "Let no one know of these words, and you shall not die.

25 "But if the princes hear that I have talked with you, and they come to you and say to you, 'Declare to us now what you have said to the king, and also what the king said to you; do not hide *it* from us, and we will not put you to death,'

26 "then you shall say to them, 'I presented my request before the king, that he would not make me return to Jonathan's house to die there.' "

27 Then all the princes came to Jer-e-mī'ah and asked him. And he told them according to all these words that the king had commanded. So they stopped speaking with him, for the conversation had not been heard.

28 Now Jer-e-mī'ah remained in the court of the prison until the day that Jerusalem was taken. And he was *there* when Jerusalem was taken.

THE FALL OF JERUSALEM

39 In the ninth year of Zed-e-kī'ah king of Judah, in the tenth month, Ne-bū-chad-nez'zar king of Babylon and all his army came against Jerusalem, and besieged it.

2 In the eleventh year of Zed-e-kī'ah, in the fourth month, on the ninth *day* of the month, the city was penetrated.

3 Then all the princes of the king of Babylon came in and sat in the Middle Gate: Ner'gal-Sha-rē'zer, Sam'-gar-Nē'bō, Sar'se-chim, Rab-sar'is,a Ner'gal-Sa-rē'zer, Rab'mag,b with the rest of the princes of the king of Babylon.

4 So it was, when Zed-e-kī'ah the king of Judah and all the men of war saw them, that they fled and went out of the city by night, by way of the king's garden, by the gate between the two walls. And he went out by way of the plain.a

5 But the Chal-dē'an army pursued them and overtook Zed-e-kī'ah in the plains of Jericho. And when they had captured him, they brought him up to Ne-bū-chad-nez'zar king of Babylon, to Rib'lah in the land of Hā'math, where he pronounced judgment on him.

6 Then the king of Babylon killed the sons of Zed-e-kī'ah before his eyes in Rib'lah; the king of Babylon also killed all the nobles of Judah.

7 Moreover he put out Zed-e-kī'ah's eyes, and bound him with bronze fetters to carry him off to Babylon.

8 And the Chal-dē'ans burned the king's house and the houses of the people with fire, and broke down the walls of Jerusalem.

9 Then Ne-bū-za-rad'an the captain

39:3 aA title, probably *Chief Officer;* also verse 13
bA title, probably *Troop Commander;* also verse 13
39:4 aOr *the Arabah,* that is, the Jordan Valley

of the guard carried away captive to Babylon the remnant of the people who remained in the city and those who defected to him, with the rest of the people who remained.

10 But Ne·bu·za·rad'an the captain of the guard left in the land of Judah the poor people, who had nothing, and gave them vineyards and fields at the same time.

JEREMIAH GOES FREE

11 Now Ne·bu·chad·nez'zar king of Babylon gave charge concerning Jer·e·mi'ah to Ne·bu·za·rad'an the captain of the guard, saying,

12 "Take him and look after him, and do him no harm; but do to him just as he says to you."

13 So Ne·bu·za·rad'an the captain of the guard sent Ne·bu·shas'ban, Rab-sar'is, Ner'gal-Sha·re'zer, Rab'mag, and all the king of Babylon's chief officers;

14 then they sent *someone* to take Jer·e·mi'ah from the court of the prison, and committed him to Ged-a·li'ah the son of A·hi'kam, the son of Sha'phan, that he should take him home. So he dwelt among the people.

15 Meanwhile the word of the LORD had come to Jer·e·mi'ah while he was shut up in the court of the prison, saying,

16 "Go and speak to E'bed-Me'lech the Ethiopian, saying, 'Thus says the LORD of hosts, the God of Israel: "Behold, I will bring My words upon this city for adversity and not for good, and they shall be *performed* in that day before you.

17 "But I will deliver you in that day," says the LORD, "and you shall not be given into the hand of the men of whom you *are* afraid.

18 "For I will surely deliver you, and you shall not fall by the sword; but your life shall be as a prize to you, because you have put your trust in Me," says the LORD.' "

JEREMIAH WITH GEDALIAH THE GOVERNOR

40 The word that came to Jer·e·mi'ah from the LORD after Ne·bu·za·rad'an the captain of the guard had let him go from Ra'mah, when he had taken him bound in chains among all who were carried away captive from Jerusalem and Judah, who were carried away captive to Babylon.

2 And the captain of the guard took Jer·e·mi'ah and said to him: "The LORD your God has pronounced this doom on this place.

3 "Now the LORD has brought *it,* and has done just as He said. Because you *people* have sinned against the LORD, and not obeyed His voice, therefore this thing has come upon you.

4 "And now look, I free you this day from the chains that *were* on your hand. If it seems good to you to come with me to Babylon, come, and I will look after you. But if it seems wrong for you to come with me to Babylon, remain here. See, all the land *is* before you; wherever it seems good and convenient for you to go, go there."

5 Now while Jer·e·mi'ah had not yet gone back, *Ne·bu·za·rad'an* said, "Go back to Ged·a·li'ah the son of A·hi'-kam, the son of Sha'phan, whom the king of Babylon has made governor over the cities of Judah, and dwell with him among the people. Or go wherever it seems convenient for you to go." So the captain of the guard gave him rations and a gift and let him go.

6 Then Jer·e·mi'ah went to Ged·a·li'ah the son of A·hi'kam, to Miz'pah, and dwelt with him among the people who were left in the land.

7 And when all the captains of the armies who *were* in the fields, they and their men, heard that the king of Babylon had made Ged·a·lī′ah the son of A·hī′kam governor in the land, and had committed to him men, women, children, and the poorest of the land who had not been carried away captive to Babylon,

8 then they came to Ged·a·lī′ah at Miz′pah—Ish′ma·el the son of Neth·a·nī′ah, Jō·hā′nan and Jonathan the sons of Ka·rē′ah, Se·rāi′ah the son of Tan′hu·meth, the sons of Ē′phai the Ne·toph′a·thīte, and Jez·a·nī′ah*a* the son of a Mā′a·cha·thīte, they and their men.

9 And Ged·a·lī′ah the son of A·hī′- kam, the son of Shā′phan, took an oath before them and their men, saying, "Do not be afraid to serve the Chal·dē′ans. Dwell in the land and serve the king of Babylon, and it shall be well with you.

10 "As for me, I will indeed dwell at Miz′pah and serve the Chal·dē′ans who come to us. But you, gather wine and summer fruit and oil, put *them* in your vessels, and dwell in your cities that you have taken."

11 Likewise, when all the Jews who *were* in Mō′ab, among the Am′mon- ītes, in Ē′dom, and who *were* in all the countries, heard that the king of Babylon had left a remnant of Judah, and that he had set over them Ged- a·lī′ah the son of A·hī′kam, the son of Shā′phan,

12 then all the Jews returned out of all places where they had been driven, and came to the land of Ju- dah, to Ged·a·lī′ah at Miz′pah, and gathered wine and summer fruit in abundance.

13 Moreover Jō·hā′nan the son of Ka·rē′ah and all the captains of the forces that *were* in the fields came to Ged·a·lī′ah at Miz′pah,

14 and said to him, "Do you certainly know that Bā′a·lis the king of the Am′mon·ītes has sent Ish′ma·el the son of Neth·a·nī′ah to murder you?" But Ged·a·lī′ah the son of A·hī′kam did not believe them.

15 Then Jō·hā′nan the son of Ka·rē′ah spoke secretly to Ged·a·lī′ah in Miz′pah, saying, "Let me go, please, and I will kill Ish′ma·el the son of Neth·a·nī′ah, and no one will know *it*. Why should he murder you, so that all the Jews who are gathered to you would be scattered, and the remnant in Judah perish?"

16 But Ged·a·lī′ah the son of A·hī′- kam said to Jō·hā′nan the son of Ka- rē′ah, "You shall not do this thing, for you speak falsely concerning Ish′- ma·el."

INSURRECTION AGAINST GEDALIAH

41 Now it came to pass in the sev- enth month *that* Ish′ma·el the son of Neth·a·nī′ah, the son of E·lish′a·ma, of the royal family and of the officers of the king, came with ten men to Ged·a·lī′ah the son of A·hī′kam, at Miz′pah. And there they ate bread to- gether in Miz′pah.

2 Then Ish′ma·el the son of Neth- a·nī′ah, and the ten men who were with him, arose and struck Ged·a- lī′ah the son of A·hī′kam, the son of Shā′phan, with the sword, and killed him whom the king of Babylon had made governor over the land.

3 Ish′ma·el also struck down all the Jews who were with him, *that is,* with Ged·a·lī′ah at Miz′pah, and the Chal·dē′ans who were found there, the men of war.

4 And it happened, on the second day after he had killed Ged·a·lī′ah, when as yet no one knew *it*,

5 that certain men came from Shē′chem, from Shī′lōh, and from Sa-

40:8 *a*Spelled *Jaazaniah* in 2 Kings 25:23

maria, eighty men with their beards shaved and their clothes torn, having cut themselves, with offerings and incense in their hand, to bring *them* to the house of the LORD.

6 Now Ish'ma·el the son of Neth·a·nī'ah went out from Miz'pah to meet them, weeping as he went along; and it happened as he met them that he said to them, "Come to Ged·a·lī'ah the son of A·hī'kam!"

7 So it was, when they came into the midst of the city, that Ish'ma·el the son of Neth·a·nī'ah killed them *and cast them* into the midst of a pit, he and the men who were with him.

8 But ten men were found among them who said to Ish'ma·el, "Do not kill us, for we have treasures of wheat, barley, oil, and honey in the field." So he desisted and did not kill them among their brethren.

9 Now the pit into which Ish'ma·el had cast all the dead bodies of the men whom he had slain, because of Ged·a·lī'ah, *was* the same one Ā'sa the king had made for fear of Bā'a·sha king of Israel. Ish'ma·el the son of Neth·a·nī'ah filled it with *the* slain.

10 Then Ish'ma·el carried away captive all the rest of the people who *were* in Miz'pah, the king's daughters and all the people who remained in Miz'pah, whom Ne·bū·za·rad'an the captain of the guard had committed to Ged·a·lī'ah the son of A·hī'kam. And Ish'ma·el the son of Neth·a·nī'ah carried them away captive and departed to go over to the Am'mon·ītes.

11 But when Jō·hā'nan the son of Ka·rē'ah and all the captains of the forces that *were* with him heard of all the evil that Ish'ma·el the son of Neth·a·nī'ah had done,

12 they took all the men and went to fight with Ish'ma·el the son of Neth·a·nī'ah; and they found him by the great pool that *is* in Gib'e·on.

13 So it was, when all the people who *were* with Ish'ma·el saw Jō·hā'nan the son of Ka·rē'ah, and all the captains of the forces who *were* with him, that they were glad.

14 Then all the people whom Ish'ma·el had carried away captive from Miz'pah turned around and came back, and went to Jō·hā'nan the son of Ka·rē'ah.

15 But Ish'ma·el the son of Neth·a·nī'ah escaped from Jō·hā'nan with eight men and went to the Am'mon·ītes.

16 Then Jō·hā'nan the son of Ka·rē'ah, and all the captains of the forces that were with him, took from Miz'pah all the rest of the people whom he had recovered from Ish'ma·el the son of Neth·a·nī'ah after he had murdered Ged·a·lī'ah the son of A·hī'kam—the mighty men of war and the women and the children and the eunuchs, whom he had brought back from Gib'e·on.

17 And they departed and dwelt in the habitation of Chim'ham, which is near Bethlehem, as they went on their way to Egypt,

18 because of the Chal·dē'ans; for they were afraid of them, because Ish'ma·el the son of Neth·a·nī'ah had murdered Ged·a·lī'ah the son of A·hī'kam, whom the king of Babylon had made governor in the land.

THE FLIGHT TO EGYPT FORBIDDEN

42 Now all the captains of the forces, Jō·hā'nan the son of Ka·rē'ah, Jez·a·nī'ah the son of Hō·shaī'ah, and all the people, from the least to the greatest, came near

2 and said to Jer·e·mī'ah the prophet, "Please, let our petition be acceptable to you, and pray for us to the LORD your God, for all this remnant (since we are left *but* a few of many, as you can see),

HOW DOES LIFE LOOK FROM A MUD PUDDLE? Jeremiah 42:1–6

You want to break a pole vaulting record. You leap and soar, then land *splat* in a mud puddle. There are no new records, just an ugly puddle of mud. A puppy wants to please his master and jump through a hoop. How exciting when he leaps through the hoop the way he should. Then *splat* he lands in a mud puddle. A person does a beautiful parachute jump and soars through the air, only to land *splat* in a mud puddle. So how does life look from a mud puddle? What should you do then?

1. It's not fun to have great expectations, to want to soar like a bird, only to land in a mud puddle. It's not fun to have great dreams, only to have life drop you in the mud. But it does happen. Have you had something like that happen to you? What did you do?
2. The next time life drops you into a mud puddle, what *should* you do? Read Jeremiah 42:1–6. Times were tough for Jeremiah and his people. It was like sitting in a big mud puddle. What kind of help did they want? Whom did they ask to lead them? Should you ask the same Person? Will you?

For more on *What Should I Do?* turn to page 1238
For more on *Facing Trials* turn to page 1238

3 "that the LORD your God may show us the way in which we should walk and the thing we should do."

4 Then Jer·e·mi′ah the prophet said to them, "I have heard. Indeed, I will pray to the LORD your God according to your words, and it shall be, *that* whatever the LORD answers you, I will declare *it* to you. I will keep nothing back from you."

5 So they said to Jer·e·mi′ah, "Let the LORD be a true and faithful witness between us, if we do not do according to everything which the LORD your God sends us by you.

6 "Whether *it is* pleasing or displeasing, we will obey the voice of the LORD our God to whom we send you, that it may be well with us when we obey the voice of the LORD our God."

7 And it happened after ten days that the word of the LORD came to Jer·e·mi′ah.

8 Then he called Jō·hā′nan the son of Ka·rē′ah, all the captains of the forces which *were* with him, and all the people from the least even to the greatest,

9 and said to them, "Thus says the LORD, the God of Israel, to whom you sent me to present your petition before Him:

10 'If you will still remain in this land, then I will build you and not pull *you* down, and I will plant you and not pluck *you* up. For I relent concerning the disaster that I have brought upon you.

11 'Do not be afraid of the king of Babylon, of whom you are afraid; do not be afraid of him,' says the LORD, 'for I *am* with you, to save you and deliver you from his hand.

12 'And I will show you mercy, that he may have mercy on you and cause you to return to your own land.'

13 "But if you say, 'We will not dwell in this land,' disobeying the voice of the Lord your God,
14 "saying, 'No, but we will go to the land of Egypt where we shall see no war, nor hear the sound of the trumpet, nor be hungry for bread, and there we will dwell'—
15 "Then hear now the word of the Lord, O remnant of Judah! Thus says the Lord of hosts, the God of Israel: 'If you wholly set your faces to enter Egypt, and go to dwell there,
16 'then it shall be *that* the sword which you feared shall overtake you there in the land of Egypt; the famine of which you were afraid shall follow close after you there *in* Egypt; and there you shall die.
17 'So shall it be with all the men who set their faces to go to Egypt to dwell there. They shall die by the sword, by famine, and by pestilence. And none of them shall remain or escape from the disaster that I will bring upon them.'
18 "For thus says the Lord of hosts, the God of Israel: 'As My anger and My fury have been poured out on the inhabitants of Jerusalem, so will My fury be poured out on you when you enter Egypt. And you shall be an oath, an astonishment, a curse, and a reproach; and you shall see this place no more.'
19 "The Lord has said concerning you, O remnant of Judah, 'Do not go to Egypt!' Know certainly that I have admonished you this day.
20 "For you were hypocrites in your hearts when you sent me to the Lord your God, saying, 'Pray for us to the Lord our God, and according to all that the Lord your God says, so declare to us and we will do *it.*'
21 "And I have this day declared *it* to you, but you have not obeyed the voice of the Lord your God, or anything which He has sent you by me.

22 "Now therefore, know certainly that you shall die by the sword, by famine, and by pestilence in the place where you desire to go to dwell."

JEREMIAH TAKEN TO EGYPT

43 Now it happened, when Jer·e·mī'ah had stopped speaking to all the people all the words of the Lord their God, for which the Lord their God had sent him to them, all these words,
2 that Az·a·rī'ah the son of Hō·shaī'ah, Jō·hā'nan the son of Ka·rē'ah, and all the proud men spoke, saying to Jer·e·mī'ah, "You speak falsely! The Lord our God has not sent you to say, 'Do not go to Egypt to dwell there.'
3 "But Bar'uch the son of Ne·rī'ah has set you against us, to deliver us into the hand of the Chal·dē'ans, that they may put us to death or carry us away captive to Babylon."
4 So Jō·hā'nan the son of Ka·rē'ah, all the captains of the forces, and all the people would not obey the voice of the Lord, to remain in the land of Judah.
5 But Jō·hā'nan the son of Ka·rē'ah and all the captains of the forces took all the remnant of Judah who had returned to dwell in the land of Judah, from all nations where they had been driven—
6 men, women, children, the king's daughters, and every person whom Ne·bū·za·rad'an the captain of the guard had left with Ged·a·lī'ah the son of A·hī'kam, the son of Shā'phan, and Jer·e·mī'ah the prophet and Bar'uch the son of Ne·rī'ah.
7 So they went to the land of Egypt, for they did not obey the voice of the Lord. And they went as far as Tah'pan·hēs.
8 Then the word of the Lord came

to Jer·e·mī′ah in Tah′pan·hēs, saying,
9 "Take large stones in your hand,
and hide them in the sight of the men
of Judah, in the clay in the brick
courtyard which *is* at the entrance to
Pharaoh's house in Tah′pan·hēs;
10 "and say to them, 'Thus says the
LORD of hosts, the God of Israel: "Behold, I will send and bring Ne·bū-
chad·nez′zar the king of Babylon, My
servant, and will set his throne above
these stones that I have hidden. And
he will spread his royal pavilion over
them.
11 "When he comes, he shall strike
the land of Egypt *and deliver* to
death *those appointed* for death, and
to captivity *those appointed* for captivity, and to the sword *those appointed* for the sword.
12 "I*a* will kindle a fire in the houses
of the gods of Egypt, and he shall
burn them and carry them away captive. And he shall array himself with
the land of Egypt, as a shepherd puts
on his garment, and he shall go out
from there in peace.
13 "He shall also break the sacred
pillars of Beth Shem′esh*a* that *are* in
the land of Egypt; and the houses of
the gods of the Egyptians he shall
burn with fire." ' "

ISRAELITES WILL BE
PUNISHED IN EGYPT

44 The word that came to
Jer·e·mī′ah concerning all the Jews
who dwell in the land of Egypt, who
dwell at Mig′dōl, at Tah′pan·hēs, at
Noph,*a* and in the country of Path′-
ros, saying,
2 "Thus says the LORD of hosts, the
God of Israel: 'You have seen all the
calamity that I have brought on Jerusalem and on all the cities of Judah;
and behold, this day they *are* a desolation, and no one dwells in them,
3 'because of their wickedness

which they have committed to provoke Me to anger, in that they went
to burn incense *and* to serve other
gods whom they did not know, they
nor you nor your fathers.
4 'However I have sent to you all
My servants the prophets, rising
early and sending *them,* saying, "Oh,
do not do this abominable thing that
I hate!"
5 'But they did not listen or incline
their ear to turn from their wickedness, to burn no incense to other
gods.
6 'So My fury and My anger were
poured out and kindled in the cities
of Judah and in the streets of Jerusalem; and they are wasted *and* desolate, as it is this day.'
7 "Now therefore, thus says the
LORD, the God of hosts, the God of Israel: 'Why do you commit *this* great
evil against yourselves, to cut off
from you man and woman, child and
infant, out of Judah, leaving none to
remain,
8 'in that you provoke Me to wrath
with the works of your hands, burning incense to other gods in the land
of Egypt where you have gone to
dwell, that you may cut yourselves
off and be a curse and a reproach
among all the nations of the earth?
9 'Have you forgotten the wickedness of your fathers, the wickedness
of the kings of Judah, the wickedness
of their wives, your own wickedness,
and the wickedness of your wives,
which they committed in the land of
Judah and in the streets of Jerusalem?
10 'They have not been humbled, to
this day, nor have they feared; they
have not walked in My law or in My

43:12 *a*Following Masoretic Text and Targum; Septuagint, Syriac, and Vulgate read *He.*
43:13 *a*Literally *House of the Sun,* ancient On;
later called Heliopolis　　44:1 *a*That is, ancient
Memphis

statutes that I set before you and your fathers.'

11 "Therefore thus says the LORD of hosts, the God of Israel: 'Behold, I will set My face against you for catastrophe and for cutting off all Judah.

12 'And I will take the remnant of Judah who have set their faces to go into the land of Egypt to dwell there, and they shall all be consumed *and* fall in the land of Egypt. They shall be consumed by the sword *and* by famine. They shall die, from the least to the greatest, by the sword and by famine; and they shall be an oath, an astonishment, a curse and a reproach!

13 'For I will punish those who dwell in the land of Egypt, as I have punished Jerusalem, by the sword, by famine, and by pestilence,

14 'so that none of the remnant of Judah who have gone into the land of Egypt to dwell there shall escape or survive, lest they return to the land of Judah, to which they desire to return and dwell. For none shall return except those who escape.' "

15 Then all the men who knew that their wives had burned incense to other gods, with all the women who stood by, a great multitude, and all the people who dwelt in the land of Egypt, in Path′ros, answered Jer·e·mī′ah, saying:

16 "*As for* the word that you have spoken to us in the name of the LORD, we will not listen to you!

17 "But we will certainly do whatever has gone out of our own mouth, to burn incense to the queen of heaven and pour out drink offerings to her, as we have done, we and our fathers, our kings and our princes, in the cities of Judah and in the streets of Jerusalem. For *then* we had plenty of food, were well-off, and saw no trouble.

18 "But since we stopped burning incense to the queen of heaven and pouring out drink offerings to her, we have lacked everything and have been consumed by the sword and by famine."

19 *The women also said,* "And when we burned incense to the queen of heaven and poured out drink offerings to her, did we make cakes for her, to worship her, and pour out drink offerings to her without our husbands' *permission?*"

20 Then Jer·e·mī′ah spoke to all the people—the men, the women, and all the people who had given him *that* answer—saying:

21 "The incense that you burned in the cities of Judah and in the streets of Jerusalem, you and your fathers, your kings and your princes, and the people of the land, did not the LORD remember them, and did it *not* come into His mind?

22 "So the LORD could no longer bear *it,* because of the evil of your doings *and* because of the abominations which you committed. Therefore your land is a desolation, an astonishment, a curse, and without an inhabitant, as *it is* this day.

23 "Because you have burned incense and because you have sinned against the LORD, and have not obeyed the voice of the LORD or walked in His law, in His statutes or in His testimonies, therefore this calamity has happened to you, as *at* this day."

24 Moreover Jer·e·mī′ah said to all the people and to all the women, "Hear the word of the LORD, all Judah who *are* in the land of Egypt!

25 "Thus says the LORD of hosts, the God of Israel, saying: 'You and your wives have spoken with your mouths and fulfilled with your hands, saying, "We will surely keep our vows that we have made, to burn incense

to the queen of heaven and pour out drink offerings to her." You will surely keep your vows and perform your vows!'

26 "Therefore hear the word of the LORD, all Judah who dwell in the land of Egypt: 'Behold, I have sworn by My great name,' says the LORD, 'that My name shall no more be named in the mouth of any man of Judah in all the land of Egypt, saying, "The Lord GOD lives."

27 'Behold, I will watch over them for adversity and not for good. And all the men of Judah who *are* in the land of Egypt shall be consumed by the sword and by famine, until there is an end to them.

28 'Yet a small number who escape the sword shall return from the land of Egypt to the land of Judah; and all the remnant of Judah, who have gone to the land of Egypt to dwell there, shall know whose words will stand, Mine or theirs.

29 'And this *shall be* a sign to you,' says the LORD, 'that I will punish you in this place, that you may know that My words will surely stand against you for adversity.'

30 "Thus says the LORD: 'Behold, I will give Pharaoh Hoph'ra king of Egypt into the hand of his enemies and into the hand of those who seek his life, as I gave Zed·e·kī'ah king of Judah into the hand of Ne·bū·chad·nez'zar king of Babylon, his enemy who sought his life.'"

ASSURANCE TO BARUCH

45 The word that Jer·e·mī'ah the prophet spoke to Bar'uch the son of Ne·rī'ah, when he had written these words in a book at the instruction of Jer·e·mī'ah,[a] in the fourth year of Je·hoi'a·kim the son of Jō·sī'ah, king of Judah, saying,

2 "Thus says the LORD, the God of Israel, to you, O Bar'uch:

3 'You said, "Woe is me now! For the LORD has added grief to my sorrow. I fainted in my sighing, and I find no rest."'

4 "Thus you shall say to him, 'Thus says the LORD: "Behold, what I have built I will break down, and what I have planted I will pluck up, that is, this whole land.

5 "And do you seek great things for yourself? Do not seek *them;* for behold, I will bring adversity on all flesh," says the LORD. "But I will give your life to you as a prize in all places, wherever you go."'"

JUDGMENT ON EGYPT

46 The word of the LORD which came to Jer·e·mī'ah the prophet against the nations.

2 Against Egypt.

Concerning the army of Pharaoh Nē'cho, king of Egypt, which was by the River Eū·phrā'tēs in Car'chem-ish, and which Ne·bū·chad·nez'zar king of Babylon defeated in the fourth year of Je·hoi'a·kim the son of Jō·sī'ah, king of Judah:

3 "Order the buckler and shield,
And draw near to battle!
4 Harness the horses,
And mount up, you horsemen!
Stand forth with *your* helmets,
Polish the spears,
Put on the armor!
5 Why have I seen them dismayed
and turned back?
Their mighty ones are beaten down;
They have speedily fled,
And did not look back,
For fear was all around," says the LORD.

45:1 *a*Literally *from Jeremiah's mouth*

6 "Do not let the swift flee away,
　　Nor the mighty man escape;
　　They will stumble and fall
　　Toward the north, by the River
　　　Eū·phrā'tēs.

7 "Who *is* this coming up like a flood,
　　Whose waters move like the
　　　rivers?

8 Egypt rises up like a flood,
　　And *its* waters move like the
　　　rivers;
　　And he says, 'I will go up *and*
　　　cover the earth,
　　I will destroy the city and its
　　　inhabitants.'

9 Come up, O horses, and rage,
　　O chariots!
　　And let the mighty men come
　　　forth:
　　The Ethiopians and the Lib'yans
　　　who handle the shield,
　　And the Lyd'i·ans who handle
　　　and bend the bow.

10 For this *is* the day of the Lord
　　GOD of hosts,
　　A day of vengeance,
　　That He may avenge Himself on
　　　His adversaries.
　　The sword shall devour;
　　It shall be satiated and made
　　　drunk with their blood;
　　For the Lord GOD of hosts has a
　　　sacrifice
　　In the north country by the River
　　　Eū·phrā'tēs.

11 "Go up to Gil'ē·ad and take balm,
　　O virgin, the daughter of Egypt;
　　In vain you will use many
　　　medicines;
　　You shall not be cured.

12 The nations have heard of your
　　　shame,
　　And your cry has filled the land;
　　For the mighty man has stumbled
　　　against the mighty;
　　They both have fallen together."

BABYLONIA WILL STRIKE EGYPT

13 The word that the LORD spoke to
Jer·e·mī'ah the prophet, how Ne·bū-
chad·nez'zar king of Babylon would
come *and* strike the land of Egypt.

14 "Declare in Egypt, and proclaim in
　　　Mig'dōl;
　　Proclaim in Noph*a* and in
　　　Tah'pan·hēs;
　　Say, 'Stand fast and prepare
　　　yourselves,
　　For the sword devours all around
　　　you.'

15 Why are your valiant *men* swept
　　　away?
　　They did not stand
　　Because the LORD drove them
　　　away.

16 He made many fall;
　　Yes, one fell upon another.
　　And they said, 'Arise!
　　Let us go back to our own
　　　people
　　And to the land of our nativity
　　From the oppressing sword.'

17 They cried there,
　　'Pharaoh, king of Egypt, *is but* a
　　　noise.
　　He has passed by the appointed
　　　time!'

18 "*As* I live," says the King,
　　Whose name *is* the LORD of
　　　hosts,
　　"Surely as Tā'bor *is* among the
　　　mountains
　　And as Car'mel by the sea, *so* he
　　　shall come.

19 O you daughter dwelling in
　　　Egypt,
　　Prepare yourself to go into
　　　captivity!
　　For Noph*a* shall be waste and
　　　desolate, without inhabitant.

46:14 *a*That is, ancient Memphis　　46:19 *a*That
is, ancient Memphis

20 "Egypt *is* a very pretty heifer,
But destruction comes, it comes
from the north.
21 Also her mercenaries are in her
midst like fat bulls,
For they also are turned back,
They have fled away together.
They did not stand,
For the day of their calamity had
come upon them,
The time of their punishment.
22 Her noise shall go like a serpent,
For they shall march with an
army
And come against her with axes,
Like those who chop wood.

23 "They shall cut down her forest,"
says the LORD,
"Though it cannot be searched,
Because they *are* innumerable,
And more numerous than
grasshoppers.
24 The daughter of Egypt shall be
ashamed;
She shall be delivered into the
hand
Of the people of the north."

25 The LORD of hosts, the God of Israel, says: "Behold, I will bring punishment on Ā'mon*a* of No,*b* and
Pharaoh and Egypt, with their gods
and their kings—Pharaoh and those
who trust in him.
26 "And I will deliver them into the
hand of those who seek their lives,
into the hand of Ne·bū·chad·nez'zar
king of Babylon and the hand of his
servants. Afterward it shall be inhabited as in the days of old," says the
LORD.

GOD WILL PRESERVE ISRAEL

27 "But do not fear, O My servant
Jacob,
And do not be dismayed,
O Israel!

For behold, I will save you from
afar,
And your offspring from the land
of their captivity;
Jacob shall return, have rest and
be at ease;
No one shall make *him* afraid.
28 Do not fear, O Jacob My servant,"
says the LORD,
"For I *am* with you;
For I will make a complete end of
all the nations
To which I have driven you,
But I will not make a complete
end of you.
I will rightly correct you,
For I will not leave you wholly
unpunished."

JUDGMENT ON PHILISTIA

47 The word of the LORD that
came to Jer·e·mī'ah the prophet
against the Phi·lis'tines, before
Pharaoh attacked Gā'za.
2 Thus says the LORD:

"Behold, waters rise out of the
north,
And shall be an overflowing
flood;
They shall overflow the land and
all that is in it,
The city and those who dwell
within;
Then the men shall cry,
And all the inhabitants of the
land shall wail.
3 At the noise of the stamping
hooves of his strong horses,
At the rushing of his chariots,
At the rumbling of his wheels,
The fathers will not look back for
their children,
Lacking courage,
4 Because of the day that comes to
plunder all the Phi·lis'tines,

46:25 *a*A sun god   *b*That is, ancient Thebes

To cut off from Tȳre and Sī′don
　every helper who remains;
For the LORD shall plunder the
　Phi·lis′tines,
The remnant of the country of
　Caph′tor.
5 Baldness has come upon Gā′za,
　Ash′ke·lon is cut off
With the remnant of their
　valley.
How long will you cut yourself?

6 "O you sword of the LORD,
　How long until you are quiet?
Put yourself up into your
　scabbard,
Rest and be still!
7 How can it be quiet,
　Seeing the LORD has given it a
　charge
Against Ash′ke·lon and against
　the seashore?
There He has appointed it."

JUDGMENT ON MOAB

48 Against Mō′ab.
Thus says the LORD of hosts, the
God of Israel:

"Woe to Nē′bō!
　For it is plundered,
Kir·jath′a·im is shamed *and*
　taken;
The high stronghold*a* is shamed
　and dismayed—
2 No more praise of Mō′ab.
In Hesh′bon they have devised
　evil against her:
'Come, and let us cut her off as a
　nation.'
You also shall be cut down,
　O Madmen!*a*
The sword shall pursue you;
3 A voice of crying *shall be* from
　Hor·ō·nā′im:
'Plundering and great
　destruction!'

4 "Mō′ab is destroyed;
　Her little ones have caused a cry
　to be heard;*a*
5 For in the Ascent of Lū′hith they
　ascend with continual weeping;
For in the descent of Hor·ō·nā′im
　the enemies have heard a cry of
　destruction.

6 "Flee, save your lives!
　And be like the juniper*a* in the
　wilderness.
7 For because you have trusted in
　your works and your treasures,
You also shall be taken.
And Chē′mosh shall go forth into
　captivity,
His priests and his princes
　together.
8 And the plunderer shall come
　against every city;
No one shall escape.
The valley also shall perish,
And the plain shall be destroyed,
As the LORD has spoken.

9 "Give wings to Mō′ab,
　That she may flee and get away;
For her cities shall be desolate,
Without any to dwell in them.
10 Cursed *is* he who does the work of
　the LORD deceitfully,
And cursed *is* he who keeps back
　his sword from blood.

11 "Mō′ab has been at ease from his*a*
　youth;
He has settled on his dregs,
And has not been emptied from
　vessel to vessel,
Nor has he gone into captivity.
Therefore his taste remained in
　him,
And his scent has not changed.

48:1 *a*Hebrew *Misgab*　　48:2 *a*A city of Moab
48:4 *a*Following Masoretic Text, Targum, and Vulgate; Septuagint reads *Proclaim it in Zoar.*
48:6 *a*Or *Aroer,* a city of Moab　　48:11 *a*The Hebrew uses masculine and feminine pronouns inter-
changeably in this chapter.

12 "Therefore behold, the days are
         coming," says the LORD,
   "That I shall send him
         wine-workers
   Who will tip him over
   And empty his vessels
   And break the bottles.
13 Mō'ab shall be ashamed of
         Chē'mosh,
   As the house of Israel was
         ashamed of Beth'el, their
         confidence.

14 "How can you say, 'We *are* mighty
   And strong men for the war'?
15 Mō'ab is plundered and gone up
         from her cities;
   Her chosen young men have gone
         down to the slaughter," says the
         King,
   Whose name *is* the LORD of hosts.

16 "The calamity of Mō'ab *is* near at
         hand,
   And his affliction comes quickly.
17 Bemoan him, all you who are
         around him;
   And all you who know his name,
   Say, 'How the strong staff is
         broken,
   The beautiful rod!'

18 "O daughter inhabiting Dī'bon,
   Come down from *your* glory,
   And sit in thirst;
   For the plunderer of Mō'ab has
         come against you,
   He has destroyed your
         strongholds.
19 O inhabitant of A·rō'er,
   Stand by the way and watch;
   Ask him who flees
   And her who escapes;
   Say, 'What has happened?'
20 Mō'ab is shamed, for he is broken
         down.
   Wail and cry!
   Tell it in Ar'non, that Mō'ab is
         plundered.

21 "And judgment has come on the
         plain country:
   On Hō'lon and Jah'zah and
         Meph'a·ath,
22 On Dī'bon and Nē'bo and Beth
         Dib·la·thā'im,
23 On Kir·jath'a·im and Beth
         Gā'mūl and Beth Mē'on,
24 On Ker'i·oth and Boz'rah,
   On all the cities of the land of
         Mō'ab,
   Far or near.
25 The horn of Mō'ab is cut off,
   And his arm is broken," says the
         LORD.

26 "Make him drunk,
   Because he exalted *himself*
         against the LORD.
   Mō'ab shall wallow in his vomit,
   And he shall also be in derision.
27 For was not Israel a derision to
         you?
   Was he found among thieves?
   For whenever you speak of him,
   You shake *your head in scorn.*
28 You who dwell in Mō'ab,
   Leave the cities and dwell in the
         rock,
   And be like the dove *which* makes
         her nest
   In the sides of the cave's mouth.

29 "We have heard the pride of Mō'ab
   (He *is* exceedingly proud),
   Of his loftiness and arrogance
         and pride,
   And of the haughtiness of his
         heart."

30 "I know his wrath," says the LORD,
   "But it *is* not right;
   His lies have made nothing right.
31 Therefore I will wail for Mō'ab,
   And I will cry out for all Mō'ab;
   I^a will mourn for the men of Kir
         Hē'res.

48:31 ^aFollowing Dead Sea Scrolls, Septuagint,
and Vulgate; Masoretic Text reads *He.*

32 O vine of Sib'mah! I will weep for
    you with the weeping of Jā'zer.
Your plants have gone over the
    sea,
They reach to the sea of Jā'zer.
The plunderer has fallen on your
    summer fruit and your vintage.
33 Joy and gladness are taken
From the plentiful field
And from the land of Mō'ab;
I have caused wine to fail from
    the winepresses;
No one will tread with joyous
    shouting—
Not joyous shouting!

34 "From the cry of Hesh'bon to
    Ē·le·ā'leh and to Jā'haz
They have uttered their voice,
From Zō'ar to Hor·ō·nā'īm,
Like a three-year-old heifer;*a*
For the waters of Nim'rim also
    shall be desolate.

35 "Moreover," says the LORD,
"I will cause to cease in Mō'ab
The one who offers *sacrifices* in
    the high places
And burns incense to his gods.
36 Therefore My heart shall wail like
    flutes for Mō'ab,
And like flutes My heart shall
    wail
For the men of Kir Hē'res.
Therefore the riches they have
    acquired have perished.

37 "For every head *shall be* bald, and
    every beard clipped;
On all the hands *shall be* cuts,
    and on the loins sackcloth—
38 A general lamentation
On all the housetops of Mō'ab,
And in its streets;
For I have broken Mō'ab like a
    vessel in which *is* no pleasure,"
    says the LORD.
39 "They shall wail:
'How she is broken down!

How Mō'ab has turned her back
    with shame!'
So Mō'ab shall be a derision
And a dismay to all those about
    her."

40 For thus says the LORD:

"Behold, one shall fly like an eagle,
And spread his wings over Mō'ab.
41 Ker'i·oth is taken,
And the strongholds are
    surprised;
The mighty men's hearts in
    Mō'ab on that day shall be
Like the heart of a woman in
    birth pangs.
42 And Mō'ab shall be destroyed as
    a people,
Because he exalted *himself*
    against the LORD.
43 Fear and the pit and the snare
    shall be upon you,
O inhabitant of Mō'ab," says the
    LORD.
44 "He who flees from the fear shall
    fall into the pit,
And he who gets out of the pit
    shall be caught in the snare.
For upon Mō'ab, upon it I will
    bring
The year of their punishment,"
    says the LORD.

45 "Those who fled stood under the
    shadow of Hesh'bon
Because of exhaustion.
But a fire shall come out of
    Hesh'bon,
A flame from the midst of Sī'hon,
And shall devour the brow of
    Mō'ab,
The crown of the head of the sons
    of tumult.
46 Woe to you, O Mō'ab!
The people of Chē'mosh perish;

48:34 *a*Or *The Third Eglath,* an unknown city
(compare Isaiah 15:5)

For your sons have been taken
captive,
And your daughters captive.

47 "Yet I will bring back the captives
of Mō′ab
In the latter days," says the LORD.

Thus far *is* the judgment of
Mō′ab.

JUDGMENT ON AMMON

49 Against the Am′mon·ites.
Thus says the LORD:

"Has Israel no sons?
Has he no heir?
Why *then* does Mil′com*a* inherit
Gad,
And his people dwell in its cities?
2 Therefore behold, the days are
coming," says the LORD,
"That I will cause to be heard an
alarm of war
In Rab′bah of the Am′mon·ites;
It shall be a desolate mound,
And her villages shall be burned
with fire.
Then Israel shall take possession
of his inheritance," says the
LORD.

3 "Wail, O Hesh′bon, for Aī is
plundered!
Cry, you daughters of Rab′bah,
Gird yourselves with sackcloth!
Lament and run to and fro by the
walls;
For Mil′com shall go into
captivity
With his priests and his princes
together.
4 Why do you boast in the valleys,
Your flowing valley, O backsliding
daughter?
Who trusted in her treasures,
saying,
'Who will come against me?'

5 Behold, I will bring fear upon
you,"
Says the Lord GOD of hosts,
"From all those who are around
you;
You shall be driven out, everyone
headlong,
And no one will gather those who
wander off.
6 But afterward I will bring back
The captives of the people of
Am′mon," says the LORD.

JUDGMENT ON EDOM

7 Against Ē′dom.
Thus says the LORD of hosts:

"*Is* wisdom no more in Tē′man?
Has counsel perished from the
prudent?
Has their wisdom vanished?
8 Flee, turn back, dwell in the
depths, O inhabitants of
Dē′dan!
For I will bring the calamity of
Esau upon him,
The time *that* I will punish him.
9 If grape-gatherers came to you,
Would they not leave *some*
gleaning grapes?
If thieves by night,
Would they not destroy until they
have enough?
10 But I have made Esau bare;
I have uncovered his secret
places,*a*
And he shall not be able to hide
himself.
His descendants are plundered,
His brethren and his neighbors,
And he *is* no more.
11 Leave your fatherless children,
I will preserve *them* alive;
And let your widows trust in Me."

49:1 *a*Hebrew *Malcam,* literally *their king,* a god of
the Ammonites; also called *Molech* (compare verse
3)   49:10 *a*Compare Obadiah 5, 6

12 For thus says the LORD: "Behold, those whose judgment *was* not to drink of the cup have assuredly drunk. And *are* you the one who will altogether go unpunished? You shall not go unpunished, but you shall surely drink *of it*.
13 "For I have sworn by Myself," says the LORD, "that Boz′rah shall become a desolation, a reproach, a waste, and a curse. And all its cities shall be perpetual wastes."

14 I have heard a message from the
      LORD,
  And an ambassador has been sent
      to the nations:
  "Gather together, come against
      her,
  And rise up to battle!

15 "For indeed, I will make you small
      among nations,
  Despised among men.
16 Your fierceness has deceived you,
  The pride of your heart,
  O you who dwell in the clefts of
      the rock,
  Who hold the height of the hill!
  Though you make your nest as
      high as the eagle,
  I will bring you down from there,"
      says the LORD.*a*

17 "Ē′dom also shall be an
      astonishment;
  Everyone who goes by it will be
      astonished
  And will hiss at all its plagues.
18 As in the overthrow of Sod′om
      and Go·mor′rah
  And their neighbors," says the
      LORD,
  "No one shall remain there,
    Nor shall a son of man dwell in it.

19 "Behold, he shall come up like a
      lion from the floodplain*a* of the
      Jordan

  Against the dwelling place of the
      strong;
  But I will suddenly make him run
      away from her.
  And who *is* a chosen *man that* I
      may appoint over her?
  For who *is* like Me?
  Who will arraign Me?
  And who *is* that shepherd
  Who will withstand Me?"

20 Therefore hear the counsel of the
      LORD that He has taken against
      Ē′dom,
  And His purposes that He has
      proposed against the
      inhabitants of Tē′man:
  Surely the least of the flock shall
      draw them out;
  Surely He shall make their
      dwelling places desolate with
      them.
21 The earth shakes at the noise of
      their fall;
  At the cry its noise is heard at the
      Red Sea.
22 Behold, He shall come up and fly
      like the eagle,
  And spread His wings over
      Boz′rah;
  The heart of the mighty men of
      Ē′dom in that day shall be
  Like the heart of a woman in
      birth pangs.

JUDGMENT ON DAMASCUS

23 Against Damascus.

  "Hā′math and Ar′pad are shamed,
  For they have heard bad news.
  They are fainthearted;
  There is trouble on the sea;
  It cannot be quiet.
24 Damascus has grown feeble;
  She turns to flee,
  And fear has seized *her*.

49:16 *a*Compare Obadiah 3, 4   49:19 *a*Or
thicket

Anguish and sorrows have taken
her like a woman in labor.
25 Why is the city of praise not
deserted, the city of My joy?
26 Therefore her young men shall
fall in her streets,
And all the men of war shall be
cut off in that day," says the
LORD of hosts.
27 "I will kindle a fire in the wall of
Damascus,
And it shall consume the palaces
of Ben-Hā′dad."*a*

JUDGMENT ON KEDAR AND HAZOR

28 Against Kē′dar and against the
kingdoms of Hā′zor, which Ne·bū-
chad·nez′zar king of Babylon shall
strike.
Thus says the LORD:

"Arise, go up to Kē′dar,
And devastate the men of the
East!
29 Their tents and their flocks they
shall take away.
They shall take for themselves
their curtains,
All their vessels and their camels;
And they shall cry out to them,
'Fear *is* on every side!'

30 "Flee, get far away! Dwell in the
depths,
O inhabitants of Hā′zor!" says the
LORD.
"For Ne·bū·chad·nez′zar king of
Babylon has taken counsel
against you,
And has conceived a plan against
you.

31 "Arise, go up to the wealthy nation
that dwells securely," says the
LORD,
"Which has neither gates nor bars,
Dwelling alone.
32 Their camels shall be for booty,

And the multitude of their cattle
for plunder.
I will scatter to all winds those in
the farthest corners,
And I will bring their calamity
from all its sides," says the
LORD.
33 "Hā′zor shall be a dwelling for
jackals, a desolation forever;
No one shall reside there,
Nor son of man dwell in it."

JUDGMENT ON ELAM

34 The word of the LORD that came
to Jer·e·mī′ah the prophet against
Ē′lam, in the beginning of the reign
of Zed·e·kī′ah king of Judah, saying,
35 "Thus says the LORD of hosts:

'Behold, I will break the bow of
Ē′lam,
The foremost of their might.
36 Against Ē′lam I will bring the
four winds
From the four quarters of heaven,
And scatter them toward all those
winds;
There shall be no nations where
the outcasts of Ē′lam will not
go.
37 For I will cause Ē′lam to be
dismayed before their enemies
And before those who seek their
life.
I will bring disaster upon them,
My fierce anger,' says the LORD;
'And I will send the sword after
them
Until I have consumed them.
38 I will set My throne in Ē′lam,
And will destroy from there the
king and the princes,' says the
LORD.

39 'But it shall come to pass in the
latter days:

49:27 *a*Compare Amos 1:4

I will bring back the captives of
Ē′lam,' says the LORD."

JUDGMENT ON BABYLON
AND BABYLONIA

50 The word that the LORD spoke
against Babylon *and* against the land
of the Chal·dē′ans by Jer·e·mī′ah the
prophet.

2 "Declare among the nations,
Proclaim, and set up a standard;
Proclaim—do not conceal *it*—
Say, 'Babylon is taken, Bel is
shamed.
Mer′o·dach*a* is broken in pieces;
Her idols are humiliated,
Her images are broken in pieces.'
3 For out of the north a nation
comes up against her,
Which shall make her land
desolate,
And no one shall dwell therein.
They shall move, they shall
depart,
Both man and beast.

4 "In those days and in that time,"
says the LORD,
"The children of Israel shall come,
They and the children of Judah
together;
With continual weeping they
shall come,
And seek the LORD their God.
5 They shall ask the way to Zion,
With their faces toward it, *saying*,
'Come and let us join ourselves to
the LORD
In a perpetual covenant
That will not be forgotten.'

6 "My people have been lost sheep.
Their shepherds have led them
astray;
They have turned them away *on*
the mountains.

They have gone from mountain to
hill;
They have forgotten their resting
place.
7 All who found them have
devoured them;
And their adversaries said, 'We
have not offended,
Because they have sinned against
the LORD, the habitation of
justice,
The LORD, the hope of their
fathers.'

8 "Move from the midst of Babylon,
Go out of the land of the
Chal·dē′ans;
And be like the rams before the
flocks.
9 For behold, I will raise and cause
to come up against Babylon
An assembly of great nations
from the north country,
And they shall array themselves
against her;
From there she shall be captured.
Their arrows *shall be* like *those* of
an expert warrior;*a*
None shall return in vain.
10 And Chal·dē′a shall become
plunder;
All who plunder her shall be
satisfied," says the LORD.

11 "Because you were glad, because
you rejoiced,
You destroyers of My heritage,
Because you have grown fat like a
heifer threshing grain,
And you bellow like bulls,
12 Your mother shall be deeply
ashamed;
She who bore you shall be
ashamed.

50:2 *a*A Babylonian god; sometimes spelled *Marduk*   50:9 *a*Following some Hebrew manuscripts, Septuagint, and Syriac; Masoretic Text,
Targum, and Vulgate read *a warrior who makes
childless.*

Behold, the least of the nations
 shall be a wilderness,
A dry land and a desert.
13 Because of the wrath of the LORD
 She shall not be inhabited,
 But she shall be wholly desolate.
 Everyone who goes by Babylon
  shall be horrified
 And hiss at all her plagues.

14 "Put yourselves in array against
  Babylon all around,
 All you who bend the bow;
 Shoot at her, spare no arrows,
 For she has sinned against the
  LORD.
15 Shout against her all around;
 She has given her hand,
 Her foundations have fallen,
 Her walls are thrown down;
 For it *is* the vengeance of the
  LORD.
 Take vengeance on her.
 As she has done, so do to her.
16 Cut off the sower from Babylon,
 And him who handles the sickle
  at harvest time.
 For fear of the oppressing sword
 Everyone shall turn to his own
  people,
 And everyone shall flee to his own
  land.

17 "Israel *is* like scattered sheep;
 The lions have driven *him* away.
 First the king of Assyria devoured
  him;
 Now at last this
 Ne·bu·chad·nez'zar king of
  Babylon has broken his bones."

18 Therefore thus says the LORD of
hosts, the God of Israel:

 "Behold, I will punish the king of
  Babylon and his land,
 As I have punished the king of
  Assyria.

19 But I will bring back Israel to his
  home,
 And he shall feed on Car'mel and
  Ba'shan;
 His soul shall be satisfied on
  Mount E'phra·im and Gil'e·ad.
20 In those days and in that time,"
  says the LORD,
 "The iniquity of Israel shall be
  sought, but *there shall be* none;
 And the sins of Judah, but they
  shall not be found;
 For I will pardon those whom I
  preserve.

21 "Go up against the land of
  Mer·a·tha'im, against it,
 And against the inhabitants of
  Pe'kod.
 Waste and utterly destroy them,"
  says the LORD,
 "And do according to all that I
  have commanded you.
22 A sound of battle *is* in the land,
 And of great destruction.
23 How the hammer of the whole
  earth has been cut apart and
  broken!
 How Babylon has become a
  desolation among the nations!
 I have laid a snare for you;
24 You have indeed been trapped,
  O Babylon,
 And you were not aware;
 You have been found and also
  caught,
 Because you have contended
  against the LORD.
25 The LORD has opened His
  armory,
 And has brought out the weapons
  of His indignation;
 For this *is* the work of the Lord
  GOD of hosts
 In the land of the Chal·de'ans.
26 Come against her from the
  farthest border;
 Open her storehouses;
 Cast her up as heaps of ruins,

And destroy her utterly;
Let nothing of her be left.
27 Slay all her bulls,
Let them go down to the
   slaughter.
Woe to them!
For their day has come, the time
   of their punishment.
28 The voice of those who flee and
   escape from the land of Babylon
Declares in Zion the vengeance of
   the LORD our God,
The vengeance of His temple.

29 "Call together the archers against
   Babylon.
All you who bend the bow,
   encamp against it all around;
Let none of them escape.*a*
Repay her according to her work;
According to all she has done, do
   to her;
For she has been proud against
   the LORD,
Against the Holy One of Israel.
30 Therefore her young men shall
   fall in the streets,
And all her men of war shall be
   cut off in that day," says the
   LORD.
31 "Behold, I *am* against you,
O most haughty one!" says the
   Lord GOD of hosts;
"For your day has come,
The time *that* I will punish you.*a*
32 The most proud shall stumble
   and fall,
And no one will raise him up;
I will kindle a fire in his cities,
And it will devour all around
   him."

33 Thus says the LORD of hosts:

"The children of Israel *were*
   oppressed,
Along with the children of Judah;
All who took them captive have
   held them fast;

They have refused to let them go.
34 Their Redeemer *is* strong;
The LORD of hosts *is* His name.
He will thoroughly plead their
   case,
That He may give rest to the
   land,
And disquiet the inhabitants of
   Babylon.

35 "A sword *is* against the
   Chal·dē′ans," says the LORD,
"Against the inhabitants of
   Babylon,
And against her princes and her
   wise men.
36 A sword *is* against the
   soothsayers, and they will be
   fools.
A sword *is* against her mighty
   men, and they will be
   dismayed.
37 A sword *is* against their horses,
Against their chariots,
And against all the mixed peoples
   who *are* in her midst;
And they will become like women.
A sword *is* against her treasures,
   and they will be robbed.
38 A drought*a is* against her waters,
   and they will be dried up.
For it *is* the land of carved
   images,
And they are insane with *their*
   idols.

39 "Therefore the wild desert beasts
   shall dwell *there* with the
   jackals,
And the ostriches shall dwell in
   it.
It shall be inhabited no more
   forever,

50:29 *a*Qere, some Hebrew manuscripts, Septuagint, and Targum add *to her.*   50:31 *a*Following Masoretic Text and Targum; Septuagint and Vulgate read *The time of your punishment.*
50:38 *a*Following Masoretic Text, Targum, and Vulgate; Syriac reads *sword;* Septuagint omits *A drought is.*

Nor shall it be dwelt in from
  generation to generation.
40 As God overthrew Sod'om and
  Go·mor'rah
  And their neighbors," says the
  LORD,
  "So no one shall reside there,
  Nor son of man dwell in it.

41 "Behold, a people shall come from
  the north,
  And a great nation and many
  kings
  Shall be raised up from the ends
  of the earth.
42 They shall hold the bow and the
  lance;
  They are cruel and shall not show
  mercy.
  Their voice shall roar like the sea;
  They shall ride on horses,
  Set in array, like a man for the
  battle,
  Against you, O daughter of
  Babylon.

43 "The king of Babylon has heard
  the report about them,
  And his hands grow feeble;
  Anguish has taken hold of him,
  Pangs as of a woman in
  childbirth.

44 "Behold, he shall come up like a
  lion from the floodplain^a of the
  Jordan
  Against the dwelling place of the
  strong;
  But I will make them suddenly
  run away from her.
  And who is a chosen man that I
  may appoint over her?
  For who is like Me?
  Who will arraign Me?
  And who is that shepherd
  Who will withstand Me?"

45 Therefore hear the counsel of the
  LORD that He has taken against
  Babylon,

And His purposes that He has
  proposed against the land of
  the Chal·dē'ans:
  Surely the least of the flock shall
  draw them out;
  Surely He will make their
  dwelling place desolate with
  them.
46 At the noise of the taking of
  Babylon
  The earth trembles,
  And the cry is heard among the
  nations.

THE UTTER DESTRUCTION
OF BABYLON

51

Thus says the LORD:

"Behold, I will raise up against
  Babylon,
  Against those who dwell in Leb
  Kā'maī,^{a}
  A destroying wind.
2 And I will send winnowers to
  Babylon,
  Who shall winnow her and empty
  her land.
  For in the day of doom
  They shall be against her all
  around.
3 Against her let the archer bend
  his bow,
  And lift himself up against her in
  his armor.
  Do not spare her young men;
  Utterly destroy all her army.
4 Thus the slain shall fall in the
  land of the Chal·dē'ans,
  And those thrust through in her
  streets.
5 For Israel is not forsaken, nor
  Judah,
  By his God, the LORD of hosts,

50:44 ^{a}Or thicket   51:1 ^{a}A code word for
Chaldea (Babylonia); may be translated The Midst
of Those Who Rise Up Against Me

Though their land was filled with
sin against the Holy One of
Israel."

6 Flee from the midst of Babylon,
And every one save his life!
Do not be cut off in her iniquity,
For this *is* the time of the LORD's
vengeance;
He shall recompense her.
7 Babylon *was* a golden cup in the
LORD's hand,
That made all the earth drunk.
The nations drank her wine;
Therefore the nations are
deranged.
8 Babylon has suddenly fallen and
been destroyed.
Wail for her!
Take balm for her pain;
Perhaps she may be healed.

9 We would have healed Babylon,
But she is not healed.
Forsake her, and let us go
everyone to his own country;
For her judgment reaches to
heaven and is lifted up to the
skies.
10 The LORD has revealed our
righteousness.
Come and let us declare in Zion
the work of the LORD our God.

11 Make the arrows bright!
Gather the shields!
The LORD has raised up the spirit
of the kings of the Mēdes.
For His plan *is* against Babylon
to destroy it,
Because it *is* the vengeance of the
LORD,
The vengeance for His temple.
12 Set up the standard on the walls
of Babylon;
Make the guard strong,
Set up the watchmen,
Prepare the ambushes.

For the LORD has both devised
and done
What He spoke against the
inhabitants of Babylon.
13 O you who dwell by many waters,
Abundant in treasures,
Your end has come,
The measure of your
covetousness.
14 The LORD of hosts has sworn by
Himself:
"Surely I will fill you with men, as
with locusts,
And they shall lift up a shout
against you."

15 He has made the earth by His
power;
He has established the world by
His wisdom,
And stretched out the heaven by
His understanding.
16 When He utters *His* voice—
There is a multitude of waters in
the heavens:
"He causes the vapors to ascend
from the ends of the earth;
He makes lightnings for the rain;
He brings the wind out of His
treasuries."*a*

17 Everyone is dull-hearted, without
knowledge;
Every metalsmith is put to shame
by the carved image;
For his molded image *is*
falsehood,
And *there is* no breath in them.
18 They *are* futile, a work of errors;
In the time of their punishment
they shall perish.
19 The Portion of Jacob *is* not like
them,
For He *is* the Maker of all things;
And *Israel is* the tribe of His
inheritance.
The LORD of hosts *is* His name.

51:16 *a*Psalm 135:7

20 "You *are* My battle-ax *and*
       weapons of war:
   For with you I will break the
       nation in pieces;
   With you I will destroy kingdoms;
21 With you I will break in pieces
       the horse and its rider;
   With you I will break in pieces
       the chariot and its rider;
22 With you also I will break in
       pieces man and woman;
   With you I will break in pieces old
       and young;
   With you I will break in pieces
       the young man and the maiden;
23 With you also I will break in
       pieces the shepherd and his
       flock;
   With you I will break in pieces
       the farmer and his yoke of
       oxen;
   And with you I will break in
       pieces governors and rulers.

24 "And I will repay Babylon
   And all the inhabitants of
       Chal·dē′a
   For all the evil they have done
   In Zion in your sight," says the
       LORD.

25 "Behold, I *am* against you,
       O destroying mountain,
   Who destroys all the earth," says
       the LORD.
   "And I will stretch out My hand
       against you,
   Roll you down from the rocks,
   And make you a burnt mountain.
26 They shall not take from you a
       stone for a corner
   Nor a stone for a foundation,
   But you shall be desolate forever,"
       says the LORD.

27 Set up a banner in the land,
   Blow the trumpet among the
       nations!
   Prepare the nations against her,

   Call the kingdoms together
       against her:
   Ar′a·rat, Min′nī, and Ash′ke·naz.
   Appoint a general against her;
   Cause the horses to come up like
       the bristling locusts.
28 Prepare against her the nations,
   With the kings of the Mēdes,
   Its governors and all its rulers,
   All the land of his dominion.
29 And the land will tremble and
       sorrow;
   For every purpose of the LORD
       shall be performed against
       Babylon,
   To make the land of Babylon a
       desolation without inhabitant.
30 The mighty men of Babylon have
       ceased fighting,
   They have remained in their
       strongholds;
   Their might has failed,
   They became *like* women;
   They have burned her dwelling
       places,
   The bars of her *gate* are broken.
31 One runner will run to meet
       another,
   And one messenger to meet
       another,
   To show the king of Babylon that
       his city is taken on *all* sides;
32 The passages are blocked,
   The reeds they have burned with
       fire,
   And the men of war are terrified.

33 For thus says the LORD of hosts,
   the God of Israel:

   "The daughter of Babylon *is* like a
       threshing floor
   When it is time to thresh her;
   Yet a little while
   And the time of her harvest will
       come."

34 "Ne·bū·chad·nez′zar the king of
       Babylon

Has devoured me, he has crushed
   me;
He has made me an empty vessel,
He has swallowed me up like a
   monster;
He has filled his stomach with my
   delicacies,
He has spit me out.
35 Let the violence *done* to me and
   my flesh *be* upon Babylon,"
The inhabitant of Zion will say;
"And my blood *be* upon the
   inhabitants of Chal·dē′a!"
Jerusalem will say.

36 Therefore thus says the LORD:

"Behold, I will plead your case and
   take vengeance for you.
I will dry up her sea and make
   her springs dry.
37 Babylon shall become a heap,
A dwelling place for jackals,
An astonishment and a hissing,
Without an inhabitant.
38 They shall roar together like
   lions,
They shall growl like lions'
   whelps.
39 In their excitement I will prepare
   their feasts;
I will make them drunk,
That they may rejoice,
And sleep a perpetual sleep
And not awake," says the LORD.
40 "I will bring them down
Like lambs to the slaughter,
Like rams with male goats.

41 "Oh, how Shē′shach[a] is taken!
Oh, how the praise of the whole
   earth is seized!
How Babylon has become
   desolate among the nations!
42 The sea has come up over
   Babylon;
She is covered with the multitude
   of its waves.
43 Her cities are a desolation,

A dry land and a wilderness,
A land where no one dwells,
Through which no son of man
   passes.
44 I will punish Bel in Babylon,
And I will bring out of his mouth
   what he has swallowed;
And the nations shall not stream
   to him anymore.
Yes, the wall of Babylon shall fall.

45 "My people, go out of the midst of
   her!
And let everyone deliver himself
   from the fierce anger of the
   LORD.
46 And lest your heart faint,
And you fear for the rumor that
   will be heard in the land
(A rumor will come *one* year,
And after that, in *another* year
A rumor *will come,*
And violence in the land,
Ruler against ruler),
47 Therefore behold, the days are
   coming
That I will bring judgment on the
   carved images of Babylon;
Her whole land shall be ashamed,
And all her slain shall fall in her
   midst.
48 Then the heavens and the earth
   and all that *is* in them
Shall sing joyously over Babylon;
For the plunderers shall come to
   her from the north," says the
   LORD.

49 As Babylon *has caused* the slain
   of Israel to fall,
So at Babylon the slain of all the
   earth shall fall.
50 You who have escaped the sword,
Get away! Do not stand still!
Remember the LORD afar off,
And let Jerusalem come to your
   mind.

51:41 [a]A code word for Babylon (compare Jeremiah
25:26)

51 We are ashamed because we have
　　heard reproach.
　Shame has covered our faces,
　For strangers have come into the
　　sanctuaries of the LORD's house.

52 "Therefore behold, the days are
　　coming," says the LORD,
　"That I will bring judgment on her
　　carved images,
　And throughout all her land the
　　wounded shall groan.
53 Though Babylon were to mount
　　up to heaven,
　And though she were to fortify
　　the height of her strength,
　Yet from Me plunderers would
　　come to her," says the LORD.

54 The sound of a cry *comes* from
　　Babylon,
　And great destruction from the
　　land of the Chal·dē'ans,
55 Because the LORD is plundering
　　Babylon
　And silencing her loud voice,
　Though her waves roar like great
　　waters,
　And the noise of their voice is
　　uttered,
56 Because the plunderer comes
　　against her, against Babylon,
　And her mighty men are taken.
　Every one of their bows is broken;
　For the LORD *is* the God of
　　recompense,
　He will surely repay.

57 "And I will make drunk
　Her princes and wise men,
　Her governors, her deputies, and
　　her mighty men.
　And they shall sleep a perpetual
　　sleep
　And not awake," says the King,
　Whose name *is* the LORD of
　　hosts.

58 Thus says the LORD of hosts:

"The broad walls of Babylon shall
　　be utterly broken,
　And her high gates shall be
　　burned with fire;
　The people will labor in vain,
　And the nations, because of the
　　fire;
　And they shall be weary."

JEREMIAH'S COMMAND TO SERAIAH

59 The word which Jer·e·mī'ah the
prophet commanded Se·rāi'ah the
son of Ne·rī'ah, the son of Mah'sēi·ah,
when he went with Zed·e·kī'ah the
king of Judah to Babylon in the
fourth year of his reign. And Se-
rāi'ah *was* the quartermaster.
60 So Jer·e·mī'ah wrote in a book all
the evil that would come upon Babylon, all these words that are written
against Babylon.
61 And Jer·e·mī'ah said to Se·rāi'ah,
"When you arrive in Babylon and see
it, and read all these words,
62 "then you shall say, 'O LORD, You
have spoken against this place to cut
it off, so that none shall remain in it,
neither man nor beast, but it shall be
desolate forever.'
63 "Now it shall be, when you have
finished reading this book, *that* you
shall tie a stone to it and throw it out
into the Eū·phrā'tēs.
64 "Then you shall say, 'Thus Babylon shall sink and not rise from the
catastrophe that I will bring upon
her. And they shall be weary.'" Thus
far *are* the words of Jer·e·mī'ah.

THE FALL OF JERUSALEM REVIEWED

52 Zed·e·kī'ah *was* twenty-one
years old when he became king, and
he reigned eleven years in Jerusalem. His mother's name *was* Ha·mū'-
tal the daughter of Jer·e·mī'ah of
Lib'nah.

WHOM WOULD I CHOOSE FOR MY MOTHER?   Jeremiah 52:1

If I could choose my mother, whom would I choose? I would choose you, mother, because you do so many things for me. I would choose you, mother, because you smile at me. I would choose you, mother, because you love me. I would choose you, mother, because you love Jesus and are helping me love Him, too. I would choose you, mother, because there is no one else in the whole world as wonderful as you.

1. Have you said "thank you" to your mother today? Have you thanked her for all she does for you? Have you thanked her for taking care of you?
2. Have you helped your mother today? Have you helped her when she is too busy? Have you helped her to help you? Have you helped her to help Jesus? Ask her how you can be her helper.
3. Have you told your mother today that you love her? Is this a good time?

For more on *Family Memories* turn to page 1360
For more on *Thankfulness* turn to page 1329

2 He also did evil in the sight of the LORD, according to all that Je·hoi'a·kim had done.

3 For because of the anger of the LORD *this* happened in Jerusalem and Judah, till He finally cast them out from His presence. Then Zed·e·kī'ah rebelled against the king of Babylon.

4 Now it came to pass in the ninth year of his reign, in the tenth month, on the tenth *day* of the month, *that* Ne·bū·chad·nez'zar king of Babylon and all his army came against Jerusalem and encamped against it; and *they* built a siege wall against it all around.

5 So the city was besieged until the eleventh year of King Zed·e·kī'ah.

6 By the fourth month, on the ninth day of the month, the famine had become so severe in the city that there was no food for the people of the land.

7 Then the city wall was broken through, and all the men of war fled and went out of the city at night by way of the gate between the two walls, which *was* by the king's garden, even though the Chal·dē'ans *were* near the city all around. And they went by way of the plain.*a*

8 But the army of the Chal·dē'ans pursued the king, and they overtook Zed·e·kī'ah in the plains of Jericho. All his army was scattered from him.

9 So they took the king and brought him up to the king of Babylon at Rib'lah in the land of Hā'math, and he pronounced judgment on him.

10 Then the king of Babylon killed the sons of Zed·e·kī'ah before his eyes. And he killed all the princes of Judah in Rib'lah.

11 He also put out the eyes of Zed·e·kī'ah; and the king of Babylon bound him in bronze fetters, took him to Babylon, and put him in prison till the day of his death.

THE TEMPLE AND CITY PLUNDERED AND BURNED

12 Now in the fifth month, on the tenth *day* of the month (which *was* the nineteenth year of King Ne·bū·chad·nez'zar king of Babylon), Ne·bū·za·rad'an, the captain of the guard, *who* served the king of Babylon, came to Jerusalem.

13 He burned the house of the LORD and the king's house; all the houses of Jerusalem, that is, all the houses of the great, he burned with fire.

14 And all the army of the Chal·dē'ans who *were* with the captain of the guard broke down all the walls of Jerusalem all around.

15 Then Ne·bū·za·rad'an the captain of the guard carried away captive *some* of the poor people, the rest of the people who remained in the city, the defectors who had deserted to the king of Babylon, and the rest of the craftsmen.

16 But Ne·bū·za·rad'an the captain of the guard left *some* of the poor of the land as vinedressers and farmers.

17 The bronze pillars that *were* in the house of the LORD, and the carts and the bronze Sea that *were* in the house of the LORD, the Chal·dē'ans broke in pieces, and carried all their bronze to Babylon.

18 They also took away the pots, the shovels, the trimmers, the bowls, the spoons, and all the bronze utensils with which the priests ministered.

19 The basins, the firepans, the bowls, the pots, the lampstands, the spoons, and the cups, whatever *was* solid gold and whatever *was* solid silver, the captain of the guard took away.

20 The two pillars, one Sea, the twelve bronze bulls which *were* under

---

52:7 *a*Or *the Arabah,* that is, the Jordan Valley

it, and the carts, which King Solomon had made for the house of the LORD— the bronze of all these articles was beyond measure.

21 Now *concerning* the pillars: the height of one pillar *was* eighteen cubits, a measuring line of twelve cubits could measure its circumference, and its thickness *was* four fingers; *it was* hollow.

22 A capital of bronze *was* on it; and the height of one capital *was* five cubits, with a network and pomegranates all around the capital, all of bronze. The second pillar, with pomegranates was the same.

23 There were ninety-six pomegranates on the sides; all the pomegranates, all around on the network, *were* one hundred.

THE PEOPLE TAKEN CAPTIVE TO BABYLONIA

24 The captain of the guard took Se·rāi'ah the chief priest, Zeph·a·nī'ah the second priest, and the three doorkeepers.

25 He also took out of the city an officer who had charge of the men of war, seven men of the king's close associates who were found in the city, the principal scribe of the army who mustered the people of the land, and sixty men of the people of the land who were found in the midst of the city.

26 And Ne·bū·za·rad'an the captain of the guard took these and brought them to the king of Babylon at Rib'lah.

27 Then the king of Babylon struck them and put them to death at Rib'lah in the land of Hā'math. Thus Judah was carried away captive from its own land.

28 These *are* the people whom Ne·bū·chad·nez'zar carried away captive: in the seventh year, three thousand and twenty-three Jews;

29 in the eighteenth year of Ne·bū·chad·nez'zar he carried away captive from Jerusalem eight hundred and thirty-two persons;

30 in the twenty-third year of Ne·bū·chad·nez'zar, Ne·bū·za·rad'an the captain of the guard carried away captive of the Jews seven hundred and forty-five persons. All the persons *were* four thousand six hundred.

JEHOIACHIN RELEASED FROM PRISON

31 Now it came to pass in the thirty-seventh year of the captivity of Je·hoi'a·chin king of Judah, in the twelfth month, on the twenty-fifth *day* of the month, *that* Ē'vil-Me·rō'dach[a] king of Babylon, in the first *year* of his reign, lifted up the head of Je·hoi'a·chin king of Judah and brought him out of prison.

32 And he spoke kindly to him and gave him a more prominent seat than those of the kings who *were* with him in Babylon.

33 So Je·hoi'a·chin changed from his prison garments, and he ate bread regularly before the king all the days of his life.

34 And as for his provisions, there was a regular ration given him by the king of Babylon, a portion for each day until the day of his death, all the days of his life.

52:31 [a]Or *Awil-Marduk*

The Book of
LAMENTATIONS

JERUSALEM IN AFFLICTION

HOW lonely sits the city
That was full of people!
How like a widow is she,
Who *was* great among the
    nations!
The princess among the provinces
Has become a slave!

2 She weeps bitterly in the night,
Her tears *are* on her cheeks;
Among all her lovers
She has none to comfort *her*.
All her friends have dealt
    treacherously with her;
They have become her enemies.

3 Judah has gone into captivity,
Under affliction and hard
    servitude;
She dwells among the nations,
She finds no rest;
All her persecutors overtake her
    in dire straits.

4 The roads to Zion mourn
Because no one comes to the set
    feasts.
All her gates are desolate;
Her priests sigh,
Her virgins are afflicted,
And she *is* in bitterness.

5 Her adversaries have become the
    master,
Her enemies prosper;
For the LORD has afflicted her
Because of the multitude of her
    transgressions.
Her children have gone into
    captivity before the enemy.

6 And from the daughter of Zion
All her splendor has departed.

Her princes have become like
    deer
That find no pasture,
That flee without strength
Before the pursuer.

7 In the days of her affliction and
    roaming,
Jerusalem remembers all her
    pleasant things
That she had in the days of old.
When her people fell into the
    hand of the enemy,
With no one to help her,
The adversaries saw her
And mocked at her downfall.*a*

8 Jerusalem has sinned gravely,
Therefore she has become vile.*a*
All who honored her despise her
Because they have seen her
    nakedness;
Yes, she sighs and turns away.

9 Her uncleanness *is* in her skirts;
She did not consider her destiny;
Therefore her collapse was
    awesome;
She had no comforter.
"O LORD, behold my affliction,
For *the* enemy is exalted!"

10 The adversary has spread his
    hand
Over all her pleasant things;
For she has seen the nations
    enter her sanctuary,
Those whom You commanded
Not to enter Your assembly.

11 All her people sigh,
They seek bread;

1:7 *a*Vulgate reads *her Sabbaths.*   1:8 *a*Septuagint and Vulgate read *moved* or *removed.*

They have given their valuables
    for food to restore life.
"See, O LORD, and consider,
    For I am scorned."

12 "*Is it* nothing to you, all you who
    pass by?
Behold and see
If there is any sorrow like my
    sorrow,
Which has been brought on me,
Which the LORD has inflicted
In the day of His fierce anger.

13 "From above He has sent fire into
    my bones,
And it overpowered them;
He has spread a net for my feet
And turned me back;
He has made me desolate
And faint all the day.

14 "The yoke of my transgressions
    was bound;*a*
They were woven together by His
    hands,
And thrust upon my neck.
He made my strength fail;
The Lord delivered me into the
    hands of *those whom* I am not
    able to withstand.

15 "The Lord has trampled underfoot
    all my mighty *men* in my midst;
He has called an assembly
    against me
To crush my young men;
The Lord trampled *as* in a
    winepress
The virgin daughter of Judah.

16 "For these *things* I weep;
My eye, my eye overflows with
    water;
Because the comforter, who
    should restore my life,
Is far from me.
My children are desolate
Because the enemy prevailed."

17 Zion spreads out her hands,
But no one comforts her;
The LORD has commanded
    concerning Jacob
That those around him *become*
    his adversaries;
Jerusalem has become an unclean
    thing among them.

18 "The LORD is righteous,
For I rebelled against His
    commandment.
Hear now, all peoples,
And behold my sorrow;
My virgins and my young men
Have gone into captivity.

19 "I called for my lovers,
But they deceived me;
My priests and my elders
Breathed their last in the city,
While they sought food
To restore their life.

20 "See, O LORD, that I *am* in
    distress;
My soul is troubled;
My heart is overturned within
    me,
For I have been very rebellious.
Outside the sword bereaves,
At home *it is* like death.

21 "They have heard that I sigh,
But no one comforts me.
All my enemies have heard of my
    trouble;
They are glad that You have done
    it.
Bring on the day You have
    announced,
That they may become like me.

22 "Let all their wickedness come
    before You,

1:14 *a*Following Masoretic Text and Targum; Septuagint, Syriac, and Vulgate read *watched over*.

And do to them as You have done
to me
For all my transgressions;
For my sighs *are* many,
And my heart *is* faint."

GOD'S ANGER WITH JERUSALEM

2 How the Lord has covered the
daughter of Zion
With a cloud in His anger!
He cast down from heaven to the
earth
The beauty of Israel,
And did not remember His
footstool
In the day of His anger.

2 The Lord has swallowed up and
has not pitied
All the dwelling places of Jacob.
He has thrown down in His wrath
The strongholds of the daughter
of Judah;
He has brought *them* down to the
ground;
He has profaned the kingdom and
its princes.

3 He has cut off in fierce anger
Every horn of Israel;
He has drawn back His right
hand
From before the enemy.
He has blazed against Jacob like
a flaming fire
Devouring all around.

4 Standing like an enemy, He has
bent His bow;
With His right hand, like an
adversary,
He has slain all *who were*
pleasing to His eye;
On the tent of the daughter of
Zion,
He has poured out His fury like
fire.

5 The Lord was like an enemy.
He has swallowed up Israel,
He has swallowed up all her
palaces;
He has destroyed her
strongholds,
And has increased mourning and
lamentation
In the daughter of Judah.

6 He has done violence to His
tabernacle,
As if it were a garden;
He has destroyed His place of
assembly;
The LORD has caused
The appointed feasts and
Sabbaths to be forgotten in
Zion.
In His burning indignation He
has spurned the king and the
priest.

7 The Lord has spurned His altar,
He has abandoned His
sanctuary;
He has given up the walls of her
palaces
Into the hand of the enemy.
They have made a noise in the
house of the LORD
As on the day of a set feast.

8 The LORD has purposed to
destroy
The wall of the daughter of Zion.
He has stretched out a line;
He has not withdrawn His hand
from destroying;
Therefore He has caused the
rampart and wall to lament;
They languished together.

9 Her gates have sunk into the
ground;
He has destroyed and broken her
bars.
Her king and her princes *are*
among the nations;

The Law *is* no *more,*
And her prophets find no vision
from the LORD.

10 The elders of the daughter of Zion
Sit on the ground *and* keep
silence;
They throw dust on their heads
And gird themselves with
sackcloth.
The virgins of Jerusalem
Bow their heads to the ground.

11 My eyes fail with tears,
My heart is troubled;
My bile is poured on the ground
Because of the destruction of the
daughter of my people,
Because the children and the
infants
Faint in the streets of the city.

12 They say to their mothers,
"Where *is* grain and wine?"
As they swoon like the wounded
In the streets of the city,
As their life is poured out
In their mothers' bosom.

13 How shall I console you?
To what shall I liken you,
O daughter of Jerusalem?
What shall I compare with you,
that I may comfort you,
O virgin daughter of Zion?
For your ruin *is* spread wide as
the sea;
Who can heal you?

14 Your prophets have seen for you
False and deceptive visions;
They have not uncovered your
iniquity,
To bring back your captives,
But have envisioned for you false
prophecies and delusions.

15 All who pass by clap *their* hands
at you;

They hiss and shake their heads
At the daughter of Jerusalem:
"*Is* this the city that is called
'The perfection of beauty,
The joy of the whole earth'?"

16 All your enemies have opened
their mouth against you;
They hiss and gnash *their* teeth.
They say, "We have swallowed *her*
up!
Surely this *is* the day we have
waited for;
We have found *it,* we have seen
it!"

17 The LORD has done what He
purposed;
He has fulfilled His word
Which He commanded in days of
old.
He has thrown down and has not
pitied,
And He has caused an enemy to
rejoice over you;
He has exalted the horn of your
adversaries.

18 Their heart cried out to the
Lord,
"O wall of the daughter of Zion,
Let tears run down like a river
day and night;
Give yourself no relief;
Give your eyes no rest.

19 "Arise, cry out in the night,
At the beginning of the watches;
Pour out your heart like water
before the face of the Lord.
Lift your hands toward Him
For the life of your young
children,
Who faint from hunger at the
head of every street."

20 "See, O LORD, and consider!
To whom have You done this?

Should the women eat their
offspring,
The children they have cuddled?a
Should the priest and prophet be
slain
In the sanctuary of the Lord?

21 "Young and old lie
On the ground in the streets;
My virgins and my young men
Have fallen by the sword;
You have slain *them* in the day of
Your anger,
You have slaughtered *and* not
pitied.

22 "You have invited as to a feast day
The terrors that surround me.
In the day of the LORD's anger
There was no refugee or survivor.
Those whom I have borne and
brought up
My enemies have destroyed."

THE PROPHET'S ANGUISH
AND HOPE

3 I *am* the man *who* has seen
affliction by the rod of His
wrath.
2 He has led me and made *me* walk
In darkness and not *in* light.
3 Surely He has turned His hand
against me
Time and time again throughout
the day.

4 He has aged my flesh and my
skin,
And broken my bones.
5 He has besieged me
And surrounded *me* with
bitterness and woe.
6 He has set me in dark places
Like the dead of long ago.

7 He has hedged me in so that I
cannot get out;
He has made my chain heavy.

8 Even when I cry and shout,
He shuts out my prayer.
9 He has blocked my ways with
hewn stone;
He has made my paths crooked.

10 He *has been* to me a bear lying in
wait,
Like a lion in ambush.
11 He has turned aside my ways and
torn me in pieces;
He has made me desolate.
12 He has bent His bow
And set me up as a target for the
arrow.

13 He has caused the arrows of His
quiver
To pierce my loins.a
14 I have become the ridicule of all
my people—
Their taunting song all the day.
15 He has filled me with bitterness,
He has made me drink
wormwood.

16 He has also broken my teeth with
gravel,
And covered me with ashes.
17 You have moved my soul far from
peace;
I have forgotten prosperity.
18 And I said, "My strength and my
hope
Have perished from the LORD."

19 Remember my affliction and
roaming,
The wormwood and the gall.
20 My soul still remembers
And sinks within me.
21 This I recall to my mind,
Therefore I have hope.

22 *Through* the LORD's mercies we
are not consumed,
Because His compassions fail not.

2:20 aVulgate reads *a span long.*   3:13 aLiterally *kidneys*

HIS COMPASSIONS FAIL NOT, / THEY ARE NEW EVERY MORNING; / GREAT IS YOUR FAITHFULNESS. Lamentations 3:22, 23

Something New from God This Morning

What if you woke up each morning and found a new gift lying on your bed? Each one was different. There was never a boring gift, never the same gift, never a dull gift. A new fresh gift each morning! What a wonderful idea! That's what God has for us with each new day. He has a brand-new day waiting for us, and that day is a precious gift from Him, with many little gifts throughout the day.

1. The sunrise this morning brought a new day, and thus a new gift, from God. Thank You, God! But within that one new gift are many wonderful smaller gifts—things you see, smell, touch, taste, and experience. Can you name some of these wonderful gifts God gave you yesterday in His one great gift of a new day?
2. What will you do with each of these good gifts that God gives you today? What will you do with His special gift of the day?
3. Have you thanked God for His special gift of the day? Will you do that now?

For more on *Favorite Family Verses* turn to page 1344
For more on *God's Care* turn to page 1260

23 *They are* new every morning;
   Great *is* Your faithfulness.
24 "The LORD *is* my portion," says my soul,
   "Therefore I hope in Him!"

25 The LORD *is* good to those who wait for Him,
   To the soul *who* seeks Him.
26 *It is* good that *one* should hope and wait quietly
   For the salvation of the LORD.
27 *It is* good for a man to bear
   The yoke in his youth.

28 Let him sit alone and keep silent,
   Because *God* has laid *it* on him;
29 Let him put his mouth in the dust—
   There may yet be hope.

30 Let him give *his* cheek to the one who strikes him,
   And be full of reproach.

31 For the Lord will not cast off forever.
32 Though He causes grief,
   Yet He will show compassion
   According to the multitude of His mercies.
33 For He does not afflict willingly,
   Nor grieve the children of men.

34 To crush under one's feet
   All the prisoners of the earth,
35 To turn aside the justice *due* a man
   Before the face of the Most High,
36 Or subvert a man in his cause—
   The Lord does not approve.

What Should I Do?

WHEN MY BALLOON BURSTS Lamentations 3:31–33

Good things are often like a pretty balloon. They look so bright and beautiful. Then suddenly *poof!* The balloon bursts. Or are good things like a birthday cake with candles lit? Everything looks like a happy birthday. Then the cake drops on the floor. What should you do when your birthday cake plops on the floor or your balloon bursts?

1. Have you ever lost something very good or suddenly had it turn into something very bad? What did you do?
2. Have you ever had a fun time turn into a disaster? What did you do?
3. Have you ever had a happy day become a miserable day? What did you do?

For more on *What Should I Do?* turn to page 1267
For more on *Facing Trials* turn to page 1353

37 Who *is he who* speaks and it
   comes to pass,
   When the Lord has not
   commanded *it?*
38 *Is it* not from the mouth of the
   Most High
   That woe and well-being proceed?
39 Why should a living man
   complain,
   A man for the punishment of his
   sins?

40 Let us search out and examine
   our ways,
   And turn back to the LORD;
41 Let us lift our hearts and hands
   To God in heaven.
42 We have transgressed and
   rebelled;
   You have not pardoned.

43 You have covered *Yourself* with
   anger
   And pursued us;
   You have slain *and* not pitied.
44 You have covered Yourself with a
   cloud,
   That prayer should not pass
   through.
45 You have made us an offscouring
   and refuse
   In the midst of the peoples.

46 All our enemies
   Have opened their mouths
   against us.
47 Fear and a snare have come upon
   us,
   Desolation and destruction.
48 My eyes overflow with rivers of
   water
   For the destruction of the
   daughter of my people.

49 My eyes flow and do not cease,
   Without interruption,
50 Till the LORD from heaven
   Looks down and sees.
51 My eyes bring suffering to my
   soul

Because of all the daughters of
   my city.

52 My enemies without cause
   Hunted me down like a bird.
53 They silenced[a] my life in the pit
   And threw stones at me.
54 The waters flowed over my head;
   I said, "I am cut off!"

■ **Prayers** ■

Lamentations 3:55–57

Listen to Jeremiah's prayer. "I called on Your name, O Lord, From the lowest pit." Do you ever feel that you are praying from the bottom of the deepest, darkest pit? Now listen to the rest of Jeremiah's prayer. "You have heard my voice." Then the Lord said, "Do not fear!" The Lord hears our prayers, even from the deepest, darkest pit. Never think that the Lord is far away and is not listening. He is there, no matter where you are. He listens, no matter how bad things seem. He also reminds us, "Do not fear!"

---

55 I called on Your name, O LORD,
   From the lowest pit.
56 You have heard my voice:
   "Do not hide Your ear
   From my sighing, from my cry for
   help."
57 You drew near on the day I called
   on You,
   And said, "Do not fear!"

58 O Lord, You have pleaded the
   case for my soul;
   You have redeemed my life.

3:53 [a]Septuagint reads *put to death.*

59 O Lord, You have seen *how* I am
    wronged;
    Judge my case.
60 You have seen all their
    vengeance,
    All their schemes against me.

61 You have heard their reproach,
    O Lord,
    All their schemes against me,
62 The lips of my enemies
    And their whispering against me
    all the day.
63 Look at their sitting down and
    their rising up;
    I *am* their taunting song.

64 Repay them, O Lord,
    According to the work of their
    hands.
65 Give them a veiled[a] heart;
    Your curse *be* upon them!
66 In Your anger,
    Pursue and destroy them
    From under the heavens of the
    Lord.

The Degradation of Zion

4 How the gold has become dim!
    How changed the fine gold!
    The stones of the sanctuary are
    scattered
    At the head of every street.

2 The precious sons of Zion,
    Valuable as fine gold,
    How they are regarded as clay
    pots,
    The work of the hands of the
    potter!

3 Even the jackals present their
    breasts
    To nurse their young;
    But the daughter of my people *is*
    cruel,
    Like ostriches in the wilderness.

4 The tongue of the infant clings
    To the roof of its mouth for thirst;
    The young children ask for bread,
    But no one breaks *it* for them.

5 Those who ate delicacies
    Are desolate in the streets;
    Those who were brought up in
    scarlet
    Embrace ash heaps.

6 The punishment of the iniquity of
    the daughter of my people
    Is greater than the punishment of
    the sin of Sod′om,
    Which was overthrown in a
    moment,
    With no hand to help her!

7 Her Naz′ir-ites[a] were brighter
    than snow
    And whiter than milk;
    They were more ruddy in body
    than rubies,
    Like sapphire in their
    appearance.

8 *Now* their appearance is blacker
    than soot;
    They go unrecognized in the
    streets;
    Their skin clings to their bones,
    It has become as dry as wood.

9 *Those* slain by the sword are
    better off
    Than *those* who die of hunger;
    For these pine away,
    Stricken *for lack* of the fruits of
    the field.

10 The hands of the compassionate
    women
    Have cooked their own children;
    They became food for them
    In the destruction of the daughter
    of my people.

3:65 [a]A Jewish tradition reads *sorrow of.*
4:7 [a]Or *nobles*

11 The LORD has fulfilled His fury,
He has poured out His fierce
anger.
He kindled a fire in Zion,
And it has devoured its
foundations.

12 The kings of the earth,
And all inhabitants of the world,
Would not have believed
That the adversary and the
enemy
Could enter the gates of
Jerusalem—

13 Because of the sins of her
prophets
And the iniquities of her priests,
Who shed in her midst
The blood of the just.

14 They wandered blind in the
streets;
They have defiled themselves
with blood,
So that no one would touch their
garments.

15 They cried out to them,
"Go away, unclean!
Go away, go away,
Do not touch us!"
When they fled and wandered,
Those among the nations said,
"They shall no longer dwell *here*."

16 The face*a* of the LORD scattered
them;
He no longer regards them.
The people do not respect the
priests
Nor show favor to the elders.

17 Still our eyes failed us,
Watching vainly for our help;
In our watching we watched
For a nation *that* could not save
us.

18 They tracked our steps
So that we could not walk in our
streets.
Our end was near;
Our days were over,
For our end had come.

19 Our pursuers were swifter
Than the eagles of the heavens.
They pursued us on the
mountains
And lay in wait for us in the
wilderness.

20 The breath of our nostrils, the
anointed of the LORD,
Was caught in their pits,
Of whom we said, "Under his
shadow
We shall live among the nations."

21 Rejoice and be glad, O daughter
of Ē′dom,
You who dwell in the land of Uz!
The cup shall also pass over to
you
And you shall become drunk and
make yourself naked.

22 *The punishment of* your iniquity
is accomplished,
O daughter of Zion;
He will no longer send you into
captivity.
He will punish your iniquity,
O daughter of Ē′dom;
He will uncover your sins!

A PRAYER FOR RESTORATION

5 Remember, O LORD, what has
come upon us;
Look, and behold our reproach!

2 Our inheritance has been turned
over to aliens,
And our houses to foreigners.

4:16 *a*Targum reads *anger*.

3 We have become orphans and
waifs,
Our mothers *are* like widows.

4 We pay for the water we drink,
And our wood comes at a price.
5 *They* pursue at our heels;*a*
We labor *and* have no rest.
6 We have given our hand *to* the
Egyptians
And the Assyrians, to be satisfied
with bread.

7 Our fathers sinned *and are* no
more,
But we bear their iniquities.
8 Servants rule over us;
There is none to deliver *us* from
their hand.
9 We get our bread *at the risk* of our
lives,
Because of the sword in the
wilderness.

10 Our skin is hot as an oven,
Because of the fever of famine.
11 They ravished the women in Zion,
The maidens in the cities of
Judah.
12 Princes were hung up by their
hands,
And elders were not respected.
13 Young men ground at the
millstones;

Boys staggered under *loads of*
wood.
14 The elders have ceased *gathering*
at the gate,
And the young men from their
music.

15 The joy of our heart has ceased;
Our dance has turned into
mourning.
16 The crown has fallen *from* our
head.
Woe to us, for we have sinned!
17 Because of this our heart is faint;
Because of these *things* our eyes
grow dim;
18 Because of Mount Zion which is
desolate,
With foxes walking about on it.

19 You, O LORD, remain forever;
Your throne from generation to
generation.
20 Why do You forget us forever,
And forsake us for so long a
time?
21 Turn us back to You, O LORD, and
we will be restored;
Renew our days as of old,
22 Unless You have utterly rejected
us,
And are very angry with us!

5:5 *a*Literally *necks*

The Book of
EZEKIEL

Ezekiel's Vision of God

NOW it came to pass in the thirtieth year, in the fourth *month,* on the fifth *day* of the month, as I *was* among the captives by the River Chē'bar, *that* the heavens were opened and I saw visions[a] of God.

2 On the fifth *day* of the month, which *was* in the fifth year of King Je·hoi'a·chin's captivity,

3 the word of the LORD came expressly to E·zēk'i·el the priest, the son of Bū'zī, in the land of the Chaldē'ans[a] by the River Chē'bar; and the hand of the LORD was upon him there.

4 Then I looked, and behold, a whirlwind was coming out of the north, a great cloud with raging fire engulfing itself; and brightness *was* all around it and radiating out of its midst like the color of amber, out of the midst of the fire.

5 Also from within it *came* the likeness of four living creatures. And this *was* their appearance: they had the likeness of a man.

6 Each one had four faces, and each one had four wings.

7 Their legs *were* straight, and the soles of their feet *were* like the soles of calves' feet. They sparkled like the color of burnished bronze.

8 The hands of a man *were* under their wings on their four sides; and each of the four had faces and wings.

9 Their wings touched one another. *The creatures* did not turn when they went, but each one went straight forward.

10 As for the likeness of their faces, *each* had the face of a man; each of the four had the face of a lion on the right side, each of the four had the face of an ox on the left side, and each of the four had the face of an eagle.

11 Thus *were* their faces. Their wings stretched upward; two *wings* of each one touched one another, and two covered their bodies.

12 And each one went straight forward; they went wherever the spirit wanted to go, and they did not turn when they went.

13 As for the likeness of the living creatures, their appearance *was* like burning coals of fire, like the appearance of torches going back and forth among the living creatures. The fire was bright, and out of the fire went lightning.

14 And the living creatures ran back and forth, in appearance like a flash of lightning.

15 Now as I looked at the living creatures, behold, a wheel *was* on the earth beside each living creature with its four faces.

16 The appearance of the wheels and their workings *was* like the color of beryl, and all four had the same likeness. The appearance of their workings *was,* as it were, a wheel in the middle of a wheel.

17 When they moved, they went toward any one of four directions; they did not turn aside when they went.

18 As for their rims, they were so high they were awesome; and their rims *were* full of eyes, all around the four of them.

19 When the living creatures went, the wheels went beside them; and when the living creatures were lifted up from the earth, the wheels were lifted up.

1:1 [a]Following Masoretic Text, Septuagint, and Vulgate; Syriac and Targum read *a vision.*
1:3 [a]Or *Babylonians,* and so elsewhere in this book

20 Wherever the spirit wanted to go, they went, *because* there the spirit went; and the wheels were lifted together with them, for the spirit of the living creatures*a was* in the wheels.

21 When those went, *these* went; when those stood, *these* stood; and when those were lifted up from the earth, the wheels were lifted up together with them, for the spirit of the living creatures*a was* in the wheels.

22 The likeness of the firmament above the heads of the living creatures*a was* like the color of an awesome crystal, stretched out over their heads.

23 And under the firmament their wings *spread out* straight, one toward another. Each one had two which covered one side, and each one had two which covered the other side of the body.

24 When they went, I heard the noise of their wings, like the noise of many waters, like the voice of the Almighty, a tumult like the noise of an army; and when they stood still, they let down their wings.

25 A voice came from above the firmament that *was* over their heads; whenever they stood, they let down their wings.

26 And above the firmament over their heads *was* the likeness of a throne, in appearance like a sapphire stone; on the likeness of the throne *was* a likeness with the appearance of a man high above it.

27 Also from the appearance of His waist and upward I saw, as it were, the color of amber with the appearance of fire all around within it; and from the appearance of His waist and downward I saw, as it were, the appearance of fire with brightness all around.

28 Like the appearance of a rainbow in a cloud on a rainy day, so *was* the appearance of the brightness all around it. This *was* the appearance of the likeness of the glory of the Lord.

EZEKIEL SENT TO REBELLIOUS ISRAEL

So when I saw *it,* I fell on my face, and I heard a voice of One speaking.

2 And He said to me, "Son of man, stand on your feet, and I will speak to you."

2 Then the Spirit entered me when He spoke to me, and set me on my feet; and I heard Him who spoke to me.

3 And He said to me: "Son of man, I am sending you to the children of Israel, to a rebellious nation that has rebelled against Me; they and their fathers have transgressed against Me to this very day.

4 "For *they are* impudent and stubborn children. I am sending you to them, and you shall say to them, 'Thus says the Lord God.'

5 "As for them, whether they hear or whether they refuse—for they *are* a rebellious house—yet they will know that a prophet has been among them.

6 "And you, son of man, do not be afraid of them nor be afraid of their words, though briers and thorns *are* with you and you dwell among scorpions; do not be afraid of their words or dismayed by their looks, though they *are* a rebellious house.

7 "You shall speak My words to them, whether they hear or whether they refuse, for they *are* rebellious.

8 "But you, son of man, hear what I say to you. Do not be rebellious like

1:20 *a*Literally *living creature;* Septuagint and Vulgate read *spirit of life;* Targum reads *creatures.*
1:21 *a*Literally *living creature;* Septuagint and Vulgate read *spirit of life;* Targum reads *creatures.*
1:22 *a*Following Septuagint, Targum, and Vulgate; Masoretic Text reads *living creature.*

that rebellious house; open your mouth and eat what I give you."

9 Now when I looked, there was a hand stretched out to me; and behold, a scroll of a book *was* in it.

10 Then He spread it before me; and *there was* writing on the inside and on the outside, and written on it *were* lamentations and mourning and woe.

3 Moreover He said to me, "Son of man, eat what you find; eat this scroll, and go, speak to the house of Israel."

2 So I opened my mouth, and He caused me to eat that scroll.

3 And He said to me, "Son of man, feed your belly, and fill your stomach with this scroll that I give you." So I ate, and it was in my mouth like honey in sweetness.

4 Then He said to me: "Son of man, go to the house of Israel and speak with My words to them.

5 "For you *are* not sent to a people of unfamiliar speech and of hard language, *but* to the house of Israel,

6 "not to many people of unfamiliar speech and of hard language, whose words you cannot understand. Surely, had I sent you to them, they would have listened to you.

7 "But the house of Israel will not listen to you, because they will not listen to Me; for all the house of Israel *are* impudent and hard-hearted.

8 "Behold, I have made your face strong against their faces, and your forehead strong against their foreheads.

9 "Like adamant stone, harder than flint, I have made your forehead; do not be afraid of them, nor be dismayed at their looks, though they *are* a rebellious house."

10 Moreover He said to me: "Son of man, receive into your heart all My words that I speak to you, and hear with your ears.

11 "And go, get to the captives, to the children of your people, and speak to them and tell them, 'Thus says the Lord GOD,' whether they hear, or whether they refuse."

12 Then the Spirit lifted me up, and I heard behind me a great thunderous voice: "Blessed *is* the glory of the LORD from His place!"

13 *I* also *heard* the noise of the wings of the living creatures that touched one another, and the noise of the wheels beside them, and a great thunderous noise.

14 So the Spirit lifted me up and took me away, and I went in bitterness, in the heat of my spirit; but the hand of the LORD was strong upon me.

15 Then I came to the captives at Tel Ā'bib, who dwelt by the River Chē'-bar; and I sat where they sat, and remained there astonished among them seven days.

EZEKIEL IS A WATCHMAN

16 Now it came to pass at the end of seven days that the word of the LORD came to me, saying,

17 "Son of man, I have made you a watchman for the house of Israel; therefore hear a word from My mouth, and give them warning from Me:

18 "When I say to the wicked, 'You shall surely die,' and you give him no warning, nor speak to warn the wicked from his wicked way, to save his life, that same wicked *man* shall die in his iniquity; but his blood I will require at your hand.

19 "Yet, if you warn the wicked, and he does not turn from his wickedness, nor from his wicked way, he shall die in his iniquity; but you have delivered your soul.

20 "Again, when a righteous *man* turns from his righteousness and

commits iniquity, and I lay a stumbling block before him, he shall die; because you did not give him warning, he shall die in his sin, and his righteousness which he has done shall not be remembered; but his blood I will require at your hand.

21 "Nevertheless if you warn the righteous *man* that the righteous should not sin, and he does not sin, he shall surely live because he took warning; also you will have delivered your soul."

22 Then the hand of the LORD was upon me there, and He said to me, "Arise, go out into the plain, and there I shall talk with you."

23 So I arose and went out into the plain, and behold, the glory of the LORD stood there, like the glory which I saw by the River Chē′bar; and I fell on my face.

24 Then the Spirit entered me and set me on my feet, and spoke with me and said to me: "Go, shut yourself inside your house.

25 "And you, O son of man, surely they will put ropes on you and bind you with them, so that you cannot go out among them.

26 "I will make your tongue cling to the roof of your mouth, so that you shall be mute and not be one to rebuke them, for they *are* a rebellious house.

27 "But when I speak with you, I will open your mouth, and you shall say to them, 'Thus says the Lord GOD.' He who hears, let him hear; and he who refuses, let him refuse; for they *are* a rebellious house.

THE SIEGE OF JERUSALEM PORTRAYED

4 "You also, son of man, take a clay tablet and lay it before you, and portray on it a city, Jerusalem.

2 "Lay siege against it, build a siege wall against it, and heap up a mound against it; set camps against it also, and place battering rams against it all around.

3 "Moreover take for yourself an iron plate, and set it *as* an iron wall between you and the city. Set your face against it, and it shall be besieged, and you shall lay siege against it. This *will be* a sign to the house of Israel.

4 "Lie also on your left side, and lay the iniquity of the house of Israel upon it. *According* to the number of the days that you lie on it, you shall bear their iniquity.

5 "For I have laid on you the years of their iniquity, according to the number of the days, three hundred and ninety days; so you shall bear the iniquity of the house of Israel.

6 "And when you have completed them, lie again on your right side; then you shall bear the iniquity of the house of Judah forty days. I have laid on you a day for each year.

7 "Therefore you shall set your face toward the siege of Jerusalem; your arm *shall be* uncovered, and you shall prophesy against it.

8 "And surely I will restrain you so that you cannot turn from one side to another till you have ended the days of your siege.

9 "Also take for yourself wheat, barley, beans, lentils, millet, and spelt; put them into one vessel, and make bread of them for yourself. *During* the number of days that you lie on your side, three hundred and ninety days, you shall eat it.

10 "And your food which you eat *shall be* by weight, twenty shekels a day; from time to time you shall eat it.

11 "You shall also drink water by measure, one-sixth of a hin; from time to time you shall drink.

12 "And you shall eat it *as* barley cakes; and bake it using fuel of human waste in their sight."

13 Then the LORD said, "So shall the children of Israel eat their defiled bread among the Gentiles, where I will drive them."

14 So I said, "Ah, Lord GOD! Indeed I have never defiled myself from my youth till now; I have never eaten what died of itself or was torn by beasts, nor has abominable flesh ever come into my mouth."

15 Then He said to me, "See, I am giving you cow dung instead of human waste, and you shall prepare your bread over it."

16 Moreover He said to me, "Son of man, surely I will cut off the supply of bread in Jerusalem; they shall eat bread by weight and with anxiety, and shall drink water by measure and with dread,

17 "that they may lack bread and water, and be dismayed with one another, and waste away because of their iniquity.

A SWORD AGAINST JERUSALEM

5 "And you, son of man, take a sharp sword, take it as a barber's razor, and pass *it* over your head and your beard; then take scales to weigh and divide the hair.

2 "You shall burn with fire one-third in the midst of the city, when the days of the siege are finished; then you shall take one-third and strike around *it* with the sword, and one-third you shall scatter in the wind: I will draw out a sword after them.

3 "You shall also take a small number of them and bind them in the edge of your *garment.*

4 "Then take some of them again and throw them into the midst of the fire, and burn them in the fire. From there a fire will go out into all the house of Israel.

5 "Thus says the Lord GOD: 'This *is* Jerusalem; I have set her in the midst of the nations and the countries all around her.

6 'She has rebelled against My judgments by doing wickedness more than the nations, and against My statutes more than the countries that *are* all around her; for they have refused My judgments, and they have not walked in My statutes.'

7 "Therefore thus says the Lord GOD: 'Because you have multiplied *disobedience* more than the nations that *are* all around you, have not walked in My statutes nor kept My judgments, nor even done[a] according to the judgments of the nations that *are* all around you'—

8 "therefore thus says the Lord GOD: 'Indeed I, even I, *am* against you and will execute judgments in your midst in the sight of the nations.

9 'And I will do among you what I have never done, and the like of which I will never do again, because of all your abominations.

10 'Therefore fathers shall eat *their* sons in your midst, and sons shall eat their fathers; and I will execute judgments among you, and all of you who remain I will scatter to all the winds.

11 'Therefore, *as* I live,' says the Lord GOD, 'surely, because you have defiled My sanctuary with all your detestable things and with all your abominations, therefore I will also diminish *you;* My eye will not spare, nor will I have any pity.

12 'One-third of you shall die of the pestilence, and be consumed with

5:7 [a]Following Masoretic Text, Septuagint, Targum, and Vulgate; many Hebrew manuscripts and Syriac read *but have done* (compare 11:12).

famine in your midst; and one-third shall fall by the sword all around you; and I will scatter another third to all the winds, and I will draw out a sword after them.

13 'Thus shall My anger be spent, and I will cause My fury to rest upon them, and I will be avenged; and they shall know that I, the LORD, have spoken *it* in My zeal, when I have spent My fury upon them.

14 'Moreover I will make you a waste and a reproach among the nations that *are* all around you, in the sight of all who pass by.

15 'So it*a* shall be a reproach, a taunt, a lesson, and an astonishment to the nations that *are* all around you, when I execute judgments among you in anger and in fury and in furious rebukes. I, the LORD, have spoken.

16 'When I send against them the terrible arrows of famine which shall be for destruction, which I will send to destroy you, I will increase the famine upon you and cut off your supply of bread.

17 'So I will send against you famine and wild beasts, and they will bereave you. Pestilence and blood shall pass through you, and I will bring the sword against you. I, the LORD, have spoken.' "

JUDGMENT ON IDOLATROUS ISRAEL

6 Now the word of the LORD came to me, saying:

2 "Son of man, set your face toward the mountains of Israel, and prophesy against them,

3 "and say, 'O mountains of Israel, hear the word of the Lord GOD! Thus says the Lord GOD to the mountains, to the hills, to the ravines, and to the valleys: "Indeed I, *even* I, will bring a sword against you, and I will destroy your high places.

4 "Then your altars shall be desolate, your incense altars shall be broken, and I will cast down your slain *men* before your idols.

5 "And I will lay the corpses of the children of Israel before their idols, and I will scatter your bones all around your altars.

6 "In all your dwelling places the cities shall be laid waste, and the high places shall be desolate, so that your altars may be laid waste and made desolate, your idols may be broken and made to cease, your incense altars may be cut down, and your works may be abolished.

7 "The slain shall fall in your midst, and you shall know that I *am* the LORD.

8 "Yet I will leave a remnant, so that you may have *some* who escape the sword among the nations, when you are scattered through the countries.

9 "Then those of you who escape will remember Me among the nations where they are carried captive, because I was crushed by their adulterous heart which has departed from Me, and by their eyes which play the harlot after their idols; they will loathe themselves for the evils which they committed in all their abominations.

10 "And they shall know that I *am* the LORD; I have not said in vain that I would bring this calamity upon them."

11 'Thus says the Lord GOD: "Pound your fists and stamp your feet, and say, 'Alas, for all the evil abominations of the house of Israel! For they shall fall by the sword, by famine, and by pestilence.

12 'He who is far off shall die by the pestilence, he who is near shall fall

5:15 *a*Septuagint, Syriac, Targum, and Vulgate read *you*.

by the sword, and he who remains and is besieged shall die by the famine. Thus will I spend My fury upon them.

13 'Then you shall know that I *am* the LORD, when their slain are among their idols all around their altars, on every high hill, on all the mountaintops, under every green tree, and under every thick oak, wherever they offered sweet incense to all their idols.

14 'So I will stretch out My hand against them and make the land desolate, yes, more desolate than the wilderness toward Dib'lah, in all their dwelling places. Then they shall know that I *am* the LORD.' " ' "

JUDGMENT ON ISRAEL IS NEAR

7 Moreover the word of the LORD came to me, saying,

2 "And you, son of man, thus says the Lord GOD to the land of Israel:

'An end! The end has come upon the four corners of the land.

3 Now the end *has come* upon you, And I will send My anger against you; I will judge you according to your ways, And I will repay you for all your abominations.

4 My eye will not spare you, Nor will I have pity; But I will repay your ways, And your abominations will be in your midst; Then you shall know that I *am* the LORD!'

5 "Thus says the Lord GOD:

'A disaster, a singular disaster; Behold, it has come!

6 An end has come, The end has come;

It has dawned for you; Behold, it has come!

7 Doom has come to you, you who dwell in the land; The time has come, A day of trouble *is* near, And not of rejoicing in the mountains.

8 Now upon you I will soon pour out My fury, And spend My anger upon you; I will judge you according to your ways, And I will repay you for all your abominations.

9 'My eye will not spare, Nor will I have pity; I will repay you according to your ways, And your abominations will be in your midst. Then you shall know that I *am* the LORD who strikes.

10 'Behold, the day! Behold, it has come! Doom has gone out; The rod has blossomed, Pride has budded.

11 Violence has risen up into a rod of wickedness; None of them *shall remain,* None of their multitude, None of them; Nor *shall there be* wailing for them.

12 The time has come, The day draws near.

'Let not the buyer rejoice, Nor the seller mourn, For wrath *is* on their whole multitude.

13 For the seller shall not return to what has been sold, Though he may still be alive; For the vision concerns the whole multitude,

And it shall not turn back;
No one will strengthen himself
Who lives in iniquity.

14 'They have blown the trumpet and
   made everyone ready,
But no one goes to battle;
For My wrath *is* on all their
   multitude.
15 The sword *is* outside,
And the pestilence and famine
   within.
Whoever *is* in the field
Will die by the sword;
And whoever *is* in the city,
Famine and pestilence will
   devour him.

16 'Those who survive will escape
   and be on the mountains
Like doves of the valleys,
All of them mourning,
Each for his iniquity.
17 Every hand will be feeble,
And every knee will be *as* weak *as*
   water.
18 They will also be girded with
   sackcloth;
Horror will cover them;
Shame *will be* on every face,
Baldness on all their heads.

19 'They will throw their silver into
   the streets,
And their gold will be like refuse;
Their silver and their gold will
   not be able to deliver them
In the day of the wrath of the
   LORD;
They will not satisfy their souls,
Nor fill their stomachs,
Because it became their
   stumbling block of iniquity.

20 'As for the beauty of his
   ornaments,
He set it in majesty;
But they made from it

The images of their
   abominations—
Their detestable things;
Therefore I have made it
Like refuse to them.
21 I will give it as plunder
Into the hands of strangers,
And to the wicked of the earth as
   spoil;
And they shall defile it.
22 I will turn My face from them,
And they will defile My secret
   place;
For robbers shall enter it and
   defile it.

23 'Make a chain,
For the land is filled with crimes
   of blood,
And the city is full of violence.
24 Therefore I will bring the worst of
   the Gentiles,
And they will possess their
   houses;
I will cause the pomp of the
   strong to cease,
And their holy places shall be
   defiled.
25 Destruction comes;
They will seek peace, but *there
   shall be* none.
26 Disaster will come upon
   disaster,
And rumor will be upon rumor.
Then they will seek a vision from
   a prophet;
But the law will perish from the
   priest,
And counsel from the elders.

27 'The king will mourn,
The prince will be clothed with
   desolation,
And the hands of the common
   people will tremble.
I will do to them according to
   their way,
And according to what they
   deserve I will judge them;

Then they shall know that I *am* the LORD!' "

ABOMINATIONS IN THE TEMPLE

8 And it came to pass in the sixth year, in the sixth *month,* on the fifth *day* of the month, as I sat in my house with the elders of Judah sitting before me, that the hand of the Lord GOD fell upon me there.

2 Then I looked, and there was a likeness, like the appearance of fire— from the appearance of His waist and downward, fire; and from His waist and upward, like the appearance of brightness, like the color of amber.

3 He stretched out the form of a hand, and took me by a lock of my hair; and the Spirit lifted me up between earth and heaven, and brought me in visions of God to Jerusalem, to the door of the north gate of the inner *court,* where the seat of the image of jealousy *was,* which provokes to jealousy.

4 And behold, the glory of the God of Israel *was* there, like the vision that I saw in the plain.

5 Then He said to me, "Son of man, lift your eyes now toward the north." So I lifted my eyes toward the north, and there, north of the altar gate, was this image of jealousy in the entrance.

6 Furthermore He said to me, "Son of man, do you see what they are doing, the great abominations that the house of Israel commits here, to make Me go far away from My sanctuary? Now turn again, you will see greater abominations."

7 So He brought me to the door of the court; and when I looked, there was a hole in the wall.

8 Then He said to me, "Son of man, dig into the wall"; and when I dug into the wall, there was a door.

9 And He said to me, "Go in, and see the wicked abominations which they are doing there."

10 So I went in and saw, and there— every sort of creeping thing, abominable beasts, and all the idols of the house of Israel, portrayed all around on the walls.

11 And there stood before them seventy men of the elders of the house of Israel, and in their midst stood Jā·az·a·nī′ah the son of Shā′phan. Each man had a censer in his hand, and a thick cloud of incense went up.

12 Then He said to me, "Son of man, have you seen what the elders of the house of Israel do in the dark, every man in the room of his idols? For they say, 'The LORD does not see us, the LORD has forsaken the land.' "

13 And He said to me, "Turn again, *and* you will see greater abominations that they are doing."

14 So He brought me to the door of the north gate of the LORD's house; and to my dismay, women were sitting there weeping for Tam′mūz.

15 Then He said to me, "Have you seen *this,* O son of man? Turn again, you will see greater abominations than these."

16 So He brought me into the inner court of the LORD's house; and there, at the door of the temple of the LORD, between the porch and the altar, *were* about twenty-five men with their backs toward the temple of the LORD and their faces toward the east, and they were worshiping the sun toward the east.

17 And He said to me, "Have you seen *this,* O son of man? Is it a trivial thing to the house of Judah to commit the abominations which they commit here? For they have filled the land with violence; then they have returned to provoke Me to anger. Indeed they put the branch to their nose.

18 "Therefore I also will act in fury.

My eye will not spare nor will I have pity; and though they cry in My ears with a loud voice, I will not hear them."

THE WICKED ARE SLAIN

9 Then He called out in my hearing with a loud voice, saying, "Let those who have charge over the city draw near, each *with* a deadly weapon in his hand."

2   And suddenly six men came from the direction of the upper gate, which faces north, each with his battle-ax in his hand. One man among them *was* clothed with linen and had a writer's inkhorn at his side. They went in and stood beside the bronze altar.

3   Now the glory of the God of Israel had gone up from the cherub, where it had been, to the threshold of the temple.a And He called to the man clothed with linen, who *had* the writer's inkhorn at his side;

4   and the LORD said to him, "Go through the midst of the city, through the midst of Jerusalem, and put a mark on the foreheads of the men who sigh and cry over all the abominations that are done within it."

5   To the others He said in my hearing, "Go after him through the city and kill; do not let your eye spare, nor have any pity.

6   "Utterly slay old *and* young men, maidens and little children and women; but do not come near anyone on whom *is* the mark; and begin at My sanctuary." So they began with the elders who *were* before the temple.

7   Then He said to them, "Defile the temple, and fill the courts with the slain. Go out!" And they went out and killed in the city.

8   So it was, that while they were killing them, I was left *alone;* and I fell on my face and cried out, and said, "Ah, Lord GOD! Will You destroy all the remnant of Israel in pouring out Your fury on Jerusalem?"

9   Then He said to me, "The iniquity of the house of Israel and Judah *is* exceedingly great, and the land is full of bloodshed, and the city full of perversity; for they say, 'The LORD has forsaken the land, and the LORD does not see!'

10 "And as for Me also, My eye will neither spare, nor will I have pity, *but* I will recompense their deeds on their own head."

11 Just then, the man clothed with linen, who *had* the inkhorn at his side, reported back and said, "I have done as You commanded me."

THE GLORY DEPARTS
FROM THE TEMPLE

10 And I looked, and there in the firmament that was above the head of the cherubim, there appeared something like a sapphire stone, having the appearance of the likeness of a throne.

2   Then He spoke to the man clothed with linen, and said, "Go in among the wheels, under the cherub, fill your hands with coals of fire from among the cherubim, and scatter *them* over the city." And he went in as I watched.

3   Now the cherubim were standing on the south side of the templea when the man went in, and the cloud filled the inner court.

4   Then the glory of the LORD went up from the cherub, *and paused* over the threshold of the temple; and the house was filled with the cloud, and the court was full of the brightness of the LORD's glory.

5   And the sound of the wings of the

9:3 aLiterally *house*   10:3 aLiterally *house,* also in verses 4 and 18

cherubim was heard *even* in the outer court, like the voice of Almighty God when He speaks.

6 Then it happened, when He commanded the man clothed in linen, saying, "Take fire from among the wheels, from among the cherubim," that he went in and stood beside the wheels.

7 And the cherub stretched out his hand from among the cherubim to the fire that *was* among the cherubim, and took *some of it* and put *it* into the hands of the *man* clothed with linen, who took *it* and went out.

8 The cherubim appeared to have the form of a man's hand under their wings.

9 And when I looked, there were four wheels by the cherubim, one wheel by one cherub and another wheel by each other cherub; the wheels appeared *to have* the color of a beryl stone.

10 *As for* their appearance, all four looked alike—as it were, a wheel in the middle of a wheel.

11 When they went, they went toward *any of* their four directions; they did not turn aside when they went, but followed in the direction the head was facing. They did not turn aside when they went.

12 And their whole body, with their back, their hands, their wings, and the wheels that the four had, *were* full of eyes all around.

13 As for the wheels, they were called in my hearing, "Wheel."

14 Each one had four faces: the first face *was* the face of a cherub, the second face the face of a man, the third the face of a lion, and the fourth the face of an eagle.

15 And the cherubim were lifted up. This *was* the living creature I saw by the River Chē′bar.

16 When the cherubim went, the wheels went beside them; and when the cherubim lifted their wings to mount up from the earth, the same wheels also did not turn from beside them.

17 When *the cherubim*ᵃ stood still, *the wheels* stood still, and when *one*ᵇ was lifted up, *the other*ᶜ lifted itself up, for the spirit of the living creature *was* in them.

18 Then the glory of the LORD departed from the threshold of the temple and stood over the cherubim.

19 And the cherubim lifted their wings and mounted up from the earth in my sight. When they went out, the wheels *were* beside them; and they stood at the door of the east gate of the LORD's house, and the glory of the God of Israel *was* above them.

20 This *is* the living creature I saw under the God of Israel by the River Chē′bar, and I knew they *were* cherubim.

21 Each one had four faces and each one four wings, and the likeness of the hands of a man *was* under their wings.

22 And the likeness of their faces *was* the same *as* the faces which I had seen by the River Chē′bar, their appearance and their persons. They each went straight forward.

JUDGMENT ON WICKED COUNSELORS

11 Then the Spirit lifted me up and brought me to the East Gate of the LORD's house, which faces eastward; and there at the door of the gate were twenty-five men, among whom I saw Jā·az·a·nī′ah the son of Az′zur, and Pel·a·tī′ah the son of Be-nā′i·ah, princes of the people.

2 And He said to me: "Son of man,

10:17 ᵃLiterally *they* ᵇLiterally *they* ᶜLiterally *they*

these *are* the men who devise iniquity and give wicked counsel in this city,

3 "who say, '*The time is* not near to build houses; this *city is* the caldron, and we *are* the meat.'

4 "Therefore prophesy against them, prophesy, O son of man!"

5 Then the Spirit of the LORD fell upon me, and said to me, "Speak! 'Thus says the LORD: "Thus you have said, O house of Israel; for I know the things that come into your mind.

6 "You have multiplied your slain in this city, and you have filled its streets with the slain."

7 'Therefore thus says the Lord GOD: "Your slain whom you have laid in its midst, they *are* the meat, and this *city is* the caldron; but I shall bring you out of the midst of it.

8 "You have feared the sword; and I will bring a sword upon you," says the Lord GOD.

9 "And I will bring you out of its midst, and deliver you into the hands of strangers, and execute judgments on you.

10 "You shall fall by the sword. I will judge you at the border of Israel. Then you shall know that I *am* the LORD.

11 "This *city* shall not be your caldron, nor shall you be the meat in its midst. I will judge you at the border of Israel.

12 "And you shall know that I *am* the LORD; for you have not walked in My statutes nor executed My judgments, but have done according to the customs of the Gentiles which *are* all around you." ' "

13 Now it happened, while I was prophesying, that Pel·a·tī′ah the son of Be·nā′i·ah died. Then I fell on my face and cried with a loud voice, and said, "Ah, Lord GOD! Will You make a complete end of the remnant of Israel?"

GOD WILL RESTORE ISRAEL

14 Again the word of the LORD came to me, saying,

15 "Son of man, your brethren, your relatives, your countrymen, and all the house of Israel in its entirety, *are* those about whom the inhabitants of Jerusalem have said, 'Get far away from the LORD; this land has been given to us as a possession.'

16 "Therefore say, 'Thus says the Lord GOD: "Although I have cast them far off among the Gentiles, and although I have scattered them among the countries, yet I shall be a little sanctuary for them in the countries where they have gone." '

17 "Therefore say, 'Thus says the Lord GOD: "I will gather you from the peoples, assemble you from the countries where you have been scattered, and I will give you the land of Israel." '

18 "And they will go there, and they will take away all its detestable things and all its abominations from there.

19 "Then I will give them one heart, and I will put a new spirit within them,a and take the stony heart out of their flesh, and give them a heart of flesh,

20 "that they may walk in My statutes and keep My judgments and do them; and they shall be My people, and I will be their God.

21 "But *as for those* whose hearts follow the desire for their detestable things and their abominations, I will recompense their deeds on their own heads," says the Lord GOD.

22 So the cherubim lifted up their wings, with the wheels beside them, and the glory of the God of Israel *was* high above them.

23 And the glory of the LORD went

11:19 *a*Literally *you*

up from the midst of the city and stood on the mountain, which *is* on the east side of the city.

24 Then the Spirit took me up and brought me in a vision by the Spirit of God into Chal·dē´a,*a* to those in captivity. And the vision that I had seen went up from me.

25 So I spoke to those in captivity of all the things the LORD had shown me.

JUDAH'S CAPTIVITY PORTRAYED

12 Now the word of the LORD came to me, saying:

2 "Son of man, you dwell in the midst of a rebellious house, which has eyes to see but does not see, and ears to hear but does not hear; for they *are* a rebellious house.

3 "Therefore, son of man, prepare your belongings for captivity, and go into captivity by day in their sight. You shall go from your place into captivity to another place in their sight. It may be that they will consider, though they *are* a rebellious house.

4 "By day you shall bring out your belongings in their sight, as though going into captivity; and at evening you shall go in their sight, like those who go into captivity.

5 "Dig through the wall in their sight, and carry your belongings out through it.

6 "In their sight you shall bear *them* on *your* shoulders *and* carry *them* out at twilight; you shall cover your face, so that you cannot see the ground, for I have made you a sign to the house of Israel."

7 So I did as I was commanded. I brought out my belongings by day, as though going into captivity, and at evening I dug through the wall with my hand. I brought *them* out at twi-

light, *and* I bore *them* on *my* shoulder in their sight.

8 And in the morning the word of the LORD came to me, saying,

9 "Son of man, has not the house of Israel, the rebellious house, said to you, 'What are you doing?'

10 "Say to them, 'Thus says the Lord GOD: "This burden *concerns* the prince in Jerusalem and all the house of Israel who are among them." '

11 "Say, 'I *am* a sign to you. As I have done, so shall it be done to them; they shall be carried away into captivity.'

12 "And the prince who *is* among them shall bear *his belongings* on *his* shoulder at twilight and go out. They shall dig through the wall to carry *them* out through it. He shall cover his face, so that he cannot see the ground with *his* eyes.

13 "I will also spread My net over him, and he shall be caught in My snare. I will bring him to Babylon, *to* the land of the Chal·dē´ans; yet he shall not see it, though he shall die there.

14 "I will scatter to every wind all who *are* around him to help him, and all his troops; and I will draw out the sword after them.

15 "Then they shall know that I *am* the LORD, when I scatter them among the nations and disperse them throughout the countries.

16 "But I will spare a few of their men from the sword, from famine, and from pestilence, that they may declare all their abominations among the Gentiles wherever they go. Then they shall know that I *am* the LORD."

JUDGMENT NOT POSTPONED

17 Moreover the word of the LORD came to me, saying,

11:24 *a*Or *Babylon,* and so elsewhere in this book

18 "Son of man, eat your bread with quaking, and drink your water with trembling and anxiety.

19 "And say to the people of the land, 'Thus says the Lord GOD to the inhabitants of Jerusalem *and* to the land of Israel: "They shall eat their bread with anxiety, and drink their water with dread, so that her land may be emptied of all who are in it, because of the violence of all those who dwell in it.

20 "Then the cities that are inhabited shall be laid waste, and the land shall become desolate; and you shall know that I *am* the LORD."' "

21 And the word of the LORD came to me, saying,

22 "Son of man, what *is* this proverb *that* you *people* have about the land of Israel, which says, 'The days are prolonged, and every vision fails'?

23 "Tell them therefore, 'Thus says the Lord GOD: "I will lay this proverb to rest, and they shall no more use it as a proverb in Israel." But say to them, "The days are at hand, and the fulfillment of every vision.

24 "For no more shall there be any false vision or flattering divination within the house of Israel.

25 "For I *am* the LORD. I speak, and the word which I speak will come to pass; it will no more be postponed; for in your days, O rebellious house, I will say the word and perform it," says the Lord GOD.' "

26 Again the word of the LORD came to me, saying,

27 "Son of man, look, the house of Israel is saying, 'The vision that he sees *is* for many days *from now,* and he prophesies of times far off.'

28 "Therefore say to them, 'Thus says the Lord GOD: "None of My words will be postponed any more, but the word which I speak will be done," says the Lord GOD.' "

WOE TO FOOLISH PROPHETS

13 And the word of the LORD came to me, saying,

2 "Son of man, prophesy against the prophets of Israel who prophesy, and say to those who prophesy out of their own heart, 'Hear the word of the LORD!' "

3 Thus says the Lord GOD: "Woe to the foolish prophets, who follow their own spirit and have seen nothing!

4 "O Israel, your prophets are like foxes in the deserts.

5 "You have not gone up into the gaps to build a wall for the house of Israel to stand in battle on the day of the LORD.

6 "They have envisioned futility and false divination, saying, 'Thus says the LORD!' But the LORD has not sent them; yet they hope that the word may be confirmed.

7 "Have you not seen a futile vision, and have you not spoken false divination? You say, 'The LORD says,' but I have not spoken."

8 Therefore thus says the Lord GOD: "Because you have spoken nonsense and envisioned lies, therefore I *am* indeed against you," says the Lord GOD.

9 "My hand will be against the prophets who envision futility and who divine lies; they shall not be in the assembly of My people, nor be written in the record of the house of Israel, nor shall they enter into the land of Israel. Then you shall know that I *am* the Lord GOD.

10 "Because, indeed, because they have seduced My people, saying, 'Peace!' when *there is* no peace—and one builds a wall, and they plaster it with untempered *mortar*—

11 "say to those who plaster *it* with untempered *mortar,* that it will fall. There will be flooding rain, and you,

O great hailstones, shall fall; and a stormy wind shall tear *it* down.

12 "Surely, when the wall has fallen, will it not be said to you, 'Where *is* the mortar with which you plastered *it?'*"

13 Therefore thus says the Lord GOD: "I will cause a stormy wind to break forth in My fury; and there shall be a flooding rain in My anger, and great hailstones in fury to consume *it.*

14 "So I will break down the wall you have plastered with untempered *mortar,* and bring it down to the ground, so that its foundation will be uncovered; it will fall, and you shall be consumed in the midst of it. Then you shall know that I *am* the LORD.

15 "Thus will I accomplish My wrath on the wall and on those who have plastered it with untempered *mortar;* and I will say to you, 'The wall *is* no *more,* nor those who plastered it,

16 'that is, the prophets of Israel who prophesy concerning Jerusalem, and who see visions of peace for her when *there is* no peace,' " says the Lord GOD.

17 "Likewise, son of man, set your face against the daughters of your people, who prophesy out of their own heart; prophesy against them,

18 "and say, 'Thus says the Lord GOD: "Woe to the *women* who sew *magic* charms on their sleeves[a] and make veils for the heads of people of every height to hunt souls! Will you hunt the souls of My people, and keep yourselves alive?

19 "And will you profane Me among My people for handfuls of barley and for pieces of bread, killing people who should not die, and keeping people alive who should not live, by your lying to My people who listen to lies?"'

20 'Therefore thus says the Lord GOD: "Behold, I *am* against your *magic* charms by which you hunt souls there like birds. I will tear them from your arms, and let the souls go, the souls you hunt like birds.

21 "I will also tear off your veils and deliver My people out of your hand, and they shall no longer be as prey in your hand. Then you shall know that I *am* the LORD.

22 "Because with lies you have made the heart of the righteous sad, whom I have not made sad; and you have strengthened the hands of the wicked, so that he does not turn from his wicked way to save his life.

23 "Therefore you shall no longer envision futility nor practice divination; for I will deliver My people out of your hand, and you shall know that I *am* the LORD." ' "

IDOLATRY WILL BE PUNISHED

14 Now some of the elders of Israel came to me and sat before me.

2 And the word of the LORD came to me, saying,

3 "Son of man, these men have set up their idols in their hearts, and put before them that which causes them to stumble into iniquity. Should I let Myself be inquired of at all by them?

4 "Therefore speak to them, and say to them, 'Thus says the Lord GOD: "Everyone of the house of Israel who sets up his idols in his heart, and puts before him what causes him to stumble into iniquity, and then comes to the prophet, I the LORD will answer him who comes, according to the multitude of his idols,

5 "that I may seize the house of Israel by their heart, because they are all estranged from Me by their idols." '

13:18 [a]Literally *over all the joints of My hands;* Vulgate reads *under every elbow;* Septuagint and Targum read *on all elbows of the hands.*

6 "Therefore say to the house of Israel, 'Thus says the Lord GOD: "Repent, turn away from your idols, and turn your faces away from all your abominations.

7 "For anyone of the house of Israel, or of the strangers who dwell in Israel, who separates himself from Me and sets up his idols in his heart and puts before him what causes him to stumble into iniquity, then comes to a prophet to inquire of him concerning Me, I the LORD will answer him by Myself.

8 "I will set My face against that man and make him a sign and a proverb, and I will cut him off from the midst of My people. Then you shall know that I *am* the LORD.

9 "And if the prophet is induced to speak anything, I the LORD have induced that prophet, and I will stretch out My hand against him and destroy him from among My people Israel.

10 "And they shall bear their iniquity; the punishment of the prophet shall be the same as the punishment of the one who inquired,

11 "that the house of Israel may no longer stray from Me, nor be profaned anymore with all their transgressions, but that they may be My people and I may be their God," says the Lord GOD.' "

JUDGMENT ON PERSISTENT UNFAITHFULNESS

12 The word of the LORD came again to me, saying:

13 "Son of man, when a land sins against Me by persistent unfaithfulness, I will stretch out My hand against it; I will cut off its supply of bread, send famine on it, and cut off man and beast from it.

14 "Even *if* these three men, Noah, Daniel, and Job, were in it, they would deliver *only* themselves by their righteousness," says the Lord GOD.

15 "If I cause wild beasts to pass through the land, and they empty it, and make it so desolate that no man may pass through because of the beasts,

16 "*even though* these three men *were* in it, *as* I live," says the Lord GOD, "they would deliver neither sons nor daughters; only they would be delivered, and the land would be desolate.

17 "Or *if* I bring a sword on that land, and say, 'Sword, go through the land,' and I cut off man and beast from it,

18 "even *though* these three men *were* in it, *as* I live," says the Lord GOD, "they would deliver neither sons nor daughters, but only they themselves would be delivered.

19 "Or *if* I send a pestilence into that land and pour out My fury on it in blood, and cut off from it man and beast,

20 "even *though* Noah, Daniel, and Job *were* in it, *as* I live," says the Lord GOD, "they would deliver neither son nor daughter; they would deliver *only* themselves by their righteousness."

21 For thus says the Lord GOD: "How much more it shall be when I send My four severe judgments on Jerusalem—the sword and famine and wild beasts and pestilence—to cut off man and beast from it?

22 "Yet behold, there shall be left in it a remnant who will be brought out, *both* sons and daughters; surely they will come out to you, and you will see their ways and their doings. Then you will be comforted concerning the disaster that I have brought upon Jerusalem, all that I have brought upon it.

23 "And they will comfort you, when you see their ways and their doings;

and you shall know that I have done nothing without cause that I have done in it," says the Lord GOD.

THE OUTCAST VINE

15 Then the word of the LORD came to me, saying:

2 "Son of man, how is the wood of the vine *better* than any other wood, the vine branch which is among the trees of the forest?

3 "Is wood taken from it to make any object? Or can *men* make a peg from it to hang any vessel on?

4 "Instead, it is thrown into the fire for fuel; the fire devours both ends of it, and its middle is burned. Is it useful for *any* work?

5 "Indeed, when it was whole, no object could be made from it. How much less will it be useful for *any* work when the fire has devoured it, and it is burned?

6 "Therefore thus says the Lord GOD: 'Like the wood of the vine among the trees of the forest, which I have given to the fire for fuel, so I will give up the inhabitants of Jerusalem;

7 'and I will set My face against them. They will go out from *one* fire, but *another* fire shall devour them. Then you shall know that I *am* the LORD, when I set My face against them.

8 'Thus I will make the land desolate, because they have persisted in unfaithfulness,' says the Lord GOD."

GOD'S LOVE FOR JERUSALEM

16 Again the word of the LORD came to me, saying,

2 "Son of man, cause Jerusalem to know her abominations,

3 "and say, 'Thus says the Lord GOD to Jerusalem: "Your birth and your nativity *are* from the land of Cā'naan; your father *was* an Am'o·rīte and your mother a Hit'tīte.

4 "As for your nativity, on the day you were born your navel cord was not cut, nor were you washed in water to cleanse *you;* you were not rubbed with salt nor wrapped in swaddling cloths.

5 "No eye pitied you, to do any of these things for you, to have compassion on you; but you were thrown out into the open field, when you yourself were loathed on the day you were born.

6 "And when I passed by you and saw you struggling in your own blood, I said to you in your blood, 'Live!' Yes, I said to you in your blood, 'Live!'

7 "I made you thrive like a plant in the field; and you grew, matured, and became very beautiful. *Your* breasts were formed, your hair grew, but you *were* naked and bare.

8 "When I passed by you again and looked upon you, indeed your time *was* the time of love; so I spread My wing over you and covered your nakedness. Yes, I swore an oath to you and entered into a covenant with you, and you became Mine," says the Lord GOD.

9 "Then I washed you in water; yes, I thoroughly washed off your blood, and I anointed you with oil.

10 "I clothed you in embroidered cloth and gave you sandals of badger skin; I clothed you with fine linen and covered you with silk.

11 "I adorned you with ornaments, put bracelets on your wrists, and a chain on your neck.

12 "And I put a jewel in your nose, earrings in your ears, and a beautiful crown on your head.

13 "Thus you were adorned with gold and silver, and your clothing *was of*

ABOUT GOD'S PROVISION Ezekiel 16:19

Do You Have Enough to Eat?

Many people around the world do not have enough to eat. Some starve to death because they lack food. Did you have enough food to eat today? Did you have many wonderful foods? So what do you say to God about all the food you have?

1. What did you eat today? Did you have more than enough? Praise God for good food. Will you praise Him now?
2. Did you have the joy of eating with family or friends? Praise God for good food, friends and family. Will you praise Him now?

For more on *What the Bible Says* turn to page 1391
For more on *God's Care* turn to page 1391

fine linen, silk, and embroidered cloth. You ate *pastry of* fine flour, honey, and oil. You were exceedingly beautiful, and succeeded to royalty.

14 "Your fame went out among the nations because of your beauty, for it *was* perfect through My splendor which I had bestowed on you," says the Lord GOD.

JERUSALEM'S HARLOTRY

15 "But you trusted in your own beauty, played the harlot because of your fame, and poured out your harlotry on everyone passing by who *would have* it.

16 "You took some of your garments and adorned multicolored high places for yourself, and played the harlot on them. *Such* things should not happen, nor be.

17 "You have also taken your beautiful jewelry from My gold and My silver, which I had given you, and made for yourself male images and played the harlot with them.

18 "You took your embroidered garments and covered them, and you set My oil and My incense before them.

19 "Also My food which I gave you— the pastry of fine flour, oil, and honey *which* I fed you—you set it before them as sweet incense; and *so* it was," says the Lord GOD.

20 "Moreover you took your sons and your daughters, whom you bore to Me, and these you sacrificed to them to be devoured. *Were* your *acts* of harlotry a small matter,

21 "that you have slain My children and offered them up to them by causing them to pass through *the* fire?

22 "And in all your abominations and acts of harlotry you did not remember the days of your youth, when you were naked and bare, struggling in your blood.

23 "Then it was so, after all your wickedness—'Woe, woe to you!' says the Lord GOD—

24 "*that* you also built for yourself a shrine, and made a high place for yourself in every street.

25 "You built your high places at the head of every road, and made your beauty to be abhorred. You offered yourself to everyone who passed by, and multiplied your acts of harlotry.

26 "You also committed harlotry with the Egyptians, your very fleshly neighbors, and increased your acts of harlotry to provoke Me to anger.

27 "Behold, therefore, I stretched out My hand against you, diminished your allotment, and gave you up to the will of those who hate you, the daughters of the Phi·lis'tines, who were ashamed of your lewd behavior.

28 "You also played the harlot with the Assyrians, because you were insatiable; indeed you played the harlot with them and still were not satisfied.

29 "Moreover you multiplied your acts of harlotry as far as the land of the trader, Chal·dē'a; and even then you were not satisfied.

30 "How degenerate is your heart!" says the Lord GOD, "seeing you do all these *things,* the deeds of a brazen harlot.

JERUSALEM'S ADULTERY

31 "You erected your shrine at the head of every road, and built your high place in every street. Yet you were not like a harlot, because you scorned payment.

32 "*You are* an adulterous wife, *who* takes strangers instead of her husband.

33 "Men make payment to all harlots, but you made your payments to all your lovers, and hired them to come to you from all around for your harlotry.

34 "You are the opposite of *other* women in your harlotry, because no one solicited you to be a harlot. In that you gave payment but no payment was given you, therefore you are the opposite."

JERUSALEM'S LOVERS WILL ABUSE HER

35 'Now then, O harlot, hear the word of the LORD!
36 'Thus says the Lord GOD: "Because your filthiness was poured out and your nakedness uncovered in your harlotry with your lovers, and with all your abominable idols, and because of the blood of your children which you gave to them,
37 "surely, therefore, I will gather all your lovers with whom you took pleasure, all those you loved, *and* all those you hated; I will gather them from all around against you and will uncover your nakedness to them, that they may see all your nakedness.
38 "And I will judge you as women who break wedlock or shed blood are judged; I will bring blood upon you in fury and jealousy.
39 "I will also give you into their hand, and they shall throw down your shrines and break down your high places. They shall also strip you of your clothes, take your beautiful jewelry, and leave you naked and bare.
40 "They shall also bring up an assembly against you, and they shall stone you with stones and thrust you through with their swords.
41 "They shall burn your houses with fire, and execute judgments on you in the sight of many women; and I will make you cease playing the harlot, and you shall no longer hire lovers.

42 "So I will lay to rest My fury toward you, and My jealousy shall depart from you. I will be quiet, and be angry no more.
43 "Because you did not remember the days of your youth, but agitated Me[a] with all these *things,* surely I will also recompense your deeds on *your own* head," says the Lord GOD. "And you shall not commit lewdness in addition to all your abominations.

MORE WICKED THAN SAMARIA AND SODOM

44 "Indeed everyone who quotes proverbs will use *this* proverb against you: 'Like mother, like daughter!'
45 "You *are* your mother's daughter, loathing husband and children; and you *are* the sister of your sisters, who loathed their husbands and children; your mother *was* a Hit'tite and your father an Am'o·rīte.
46 "Your elder sister *is* Samaria, who dwells with her daughters to the north of you; and your younger sister, who dwells to the south of you, *is* Sod'om and her daughters.
47 "You did not walk in their ways nor act according to their abominations; but, as *if that were* too little, you became more corrupt than they in all your ways.
48 "*As* I live," says the Lord GOD, "neither your sister Sod'om nor her daughters have done as you and your daughters have done.
49 "Look, this was the iniquity of your sister Sod'om: She and her daughter had pride, fullness of food, and abundance of idleness; neither did she strengthen the hand of the poor and needy.

16:43 [a]Following Septuagint, Syriac, Targum, and Vulgate; Masoretic Text reads *were agitated with Me.*

50 "And they were haughty and committed abomination before Me; therefore I took them away as I saw fit.[a]

51 "Samaria did not commit half of your sins; but you have multiplied your abominations more than they, and have justified your sisters by all the abominations which you have done.

52 "You who judged your sisters, bear your own shame also, because the sins which you committed were more abominable than theirs; they are more righteous than you. Yes, be disgraced also, and bear your own shame, because you justified your sisters.

53 "When I bring back their captives, the captives of Sod'om and her daughters, and the captives of Samaria and her daughters, then *I will also bring back* the captives of your captivity among them,

54 "that you may bear your own shame and be disgraced by all that you did when you comforted them.

55 "When your sisters, Sod'om and her daughters, return to their former state, and Samaria and her daughters return to their former state, then you and your daughters will return to your former state.

56 "For your sister Sod'om was not a byword in your mouth in the days of your pride,

57 "before your wickedness was uncovered. It was like the time of the reproach of the daughters of Syria[a] and all *those* around her, and of the daughters of the Phi·lis'tines, who despise you everywhere.

58 "You have paid for your lewdness and your abominations," says the LORD.

59 'For thus says the Lord GOD: "I will deal with you as you have done, who despised the oath by breaking the covenant.

AN EVERLASTING COVENANT

60 "Nevertheless I will remember My covenant with you in the days of your youth, and I will establish an everlasting covenant with you.

61 "Then you will remember your ways and be ashamed, when you receive your older and your younger sisters; for I will give them to you for daughters, but not because of My covenant with you.

62 "And I will establish My covenant with you. Then you shall know that I *am* the LORD,

63 "that you may remember and be ashamed, and never open your mouth anymore because of your shame, when I provide you an atonement for all you have done," says the Lord GOD.' "

THE EAGLES AND THE VINE

17 And the word of the LORD came to me, saying,

2 "Son of man, pose a riddle, and speak a parable to the house of Israel,

3 "and say, 'Thus says the Lord GOD:

"A great eagle with large wings
        and long pinions,
    Full of feathers of various colors,
    Came to Lebanon
    And took from the cedar the
        highest branch.
4   He cropped off its topmost young
        twig
    And carried it to a land of trade;
    He set it in a city of merchants.
5   Then he took some of the seed of
        the land

16:50 [a]Vulgate reads *you saw*; Septuagint reads *he saw*; Targum reads *as was revealed to Me*.
16:57 [a]Following Masoretic Text, Septuagint, Targum, and Vulgate; many Hebrew manuscripts and Syriac read *Edom*.

And planted it in a fertile field;
He placed *it* by abundant waters
And set it like a willow tree.
6   And it grew and became a
    spreading vine of low stature;
Its branches turned toward him,
But its roots were under it.
So it became a vine,
Brought forth branches,
And put forth shoots.

7   "But there was another[a] great
    eagle with large wings and
    many feathers;
And behold, this vine bent its
    roots toward him,
And stretched its branches
    toward him,
From the garden terrace where it
    had been planted,
That he might water it.
8   It was planted in good soil by
    many waters,
To bring forth branches, bear
    fruit,
And become a majestic vine." '

9   "Say, 'Thus says the Lord GOD:

"Will it thrive?
Will he not pull up its roots,
Cut off its fruit,
And leave it to wither?
All of its spring leaves will wither,
And no great power or many
    people
Will be needed to pluck it up by
    its roots.
10 Behold, *it is* planted,
Will it thrive?
Will it not utterly wither when
    the east wind touches it?
It will wither in the garden
    terrace where it grew." ' "

11 Moreover the word of the LORD
came to me, saying,
12 "Say now to the rebellious house:
'Do you not know what these *things*
mean?' Tell *them*, 'Indeed the king of

Babylon went to Jerusalem and took
its king and princes, and led them
with him to Babylon.
13 'And he took the king's offspring,
made a covenant with him, and put
him under oath. He also took away
the mighty of the land,
14 'that the kingdom might be
brought low and not lift itself up, *but*
that by keeping his covenant it might
stand.
15 'But he rebelled against him by
sending his ambassadors to Egypt,
that they might give him horses and
many people. Will he prosper? Will he
who does such *things* escape? Can he
break a covenant and still be delivered?
16 'As I live,' says the Lord GOD,
'surely in the place *where* the king
dwells who made him king, whose
oath he despised and whose covenant
he broke—with him in the midst of
Babylon he shall die.
17 'Nor will Pharaoh with *his* mighty
army and great company do anything
in the war, when they heap up a
siege mound and build a wall to cut
off many persons.
18 'Since he despised the oath by
breaking the covenant, and in fact
gave his hand and still did all these
things, he shall not escape.' "
19 Therefore thus says the Lord
GOD: "*As* I live, surely My oath which
he despised, and My covenant which
he broke, I will recompense on his
own head.
20 "I will spread My net over him,
and he shall be taken in My snare. I
will bring him to Babylon and try
him there for the treason which he
committed against Me.
21 "All his fugitives[a] with all his

17:7 [a]Following Septuagint, Syriac, and Vulgate;
Masoretic Text and Targum read *one.*
17:21 [a]Following Masoretic Text and Vulgate;
many Hebrew manuscripts and Syriac read *choice
men;* Targum reads *mighty men;* Septuagint omits
All his fugitives.

troops shall fall by the sword, and those who remain shall be scattered to every wind; and you shall know that I, the LORD, have spoken."

ISRAEL EXALTED AT LAST

22 Thus says the Lord GOD: "I will take also *one* of the highest branches of the high cedar and set *it* out. I will crop off from the topmost of its young twigs a tender one, and will plant *it* on a high and prominent mountain.
23 "On the mountain height of Israel I will plant it; and it will bring forth boughs, and bear fruit, and be a majestic cedar. Under it will dwell birds of every sort; in the shadow of its branches they will dwell.
24 "And all the trees of the field shall know that I, the LORD, have brought down the high tree and exalted the low tree, dried up the green tree and made the dry tree flourish; I, the LORD, have spoken and have done *it*."

A FALSE PROVERB REFUTED

18 The word of the LORD came to me again, saying,
2 "What do you mean when you use this proverb concerning the land of Israel, saying:

'The fathers have eaten sour grapes,
And the children's teeth are set on edge'?

3 "*As* I live," says the Lord GOD, "you shall no longer use this proverb in Israel.

4 "Behold, all souls are Mine;
The soul of the father
As well as the soul of the son is Mine;
The soul who sins shall die.

5 But if a man is just
And does what is lawful and right;
6 If he has not eaten on the mountains,
Nor lifted up his eyes to the idols of the house of Israel,
Nor defiled his neighbor's wife,
Nor approached a woman during her impurity;
7 If he has not oppressed anyone,
But has restored to the debtor his pledge;
Has robbed no one by violence,
But has given his bread to the hungry
And covered the naked with clothing;
8 If he has not exacted usury
Nor taken any increase,
But has withdrawn his hand from iniquity
And executed true judgment between man and man;
9 *If* he has walked in My statutes
And kept My judgments faithfully—
He *is* just;
He shall surely live!"
Says the Lord GOD.

10 "If he begets a son *who is* a robber
Or a shedder of blood,
Who does any of these *things*
11 And does none of those *duties,*
But has eaten on the mountains
Or defiled his neighbor's wife;
12 If he has oppressed the poor and needy,
Robbed by violence,
Not restored the pledge,
Lifted his eyes to the idols,
Or committed abomination;
13 If he has exacted usury
Or taken increase—
Shall he then live?
He shall not live!
If he has done any of these abominations,

He shall surely die;
His blood shall be upon him.

14 "*If,* however, he begets a son
  Who sees all the sins which his
    father has done,
  And considers but does not do
    likewise;
15 *Who* has not eaten on the
    mountains,
  Nor lifted his eyes to the idols of
    the house of Israel,
  Nor defiled his neighbor's wife;
16 Has not oppressed anyone,
  Nor withheld a pledge,
  Nor robbed by violence,
  But has given his bread to the
    hungry
  And covered the naked with
    clothing;
17 *Who* has withdrawn his hand
    from the poor[a]
  And not received usury or
    increase,
  But has executed My judgments
  And walked in My statutes—
  He shall not die for the iniquity of
    his father;
  He shall surely live!

18 "*As for* his father,
  Because he cruelly oppressed,
  Robbed his brother by violence,
  And did what *is* not good among
    his people,
  Behold, he shall die for his
    iniquity.

TURN AND LIVE

19 "Yet you say, 'Why should the son
not bear the guilt of the father?' Because the son has done what is lawful
and right, and has kept all My
statutes and observed them, he shall
surely live.
20 "The soul who sins shall die. The
son shall not bear the guilt of the father, nor the father bear the guilt of
the son. The righteousness of the

righteous shall be upon himself, and
the wickedness of the wicked shall be
upon himself.

Promises

Ezekiel 18:21

How would you like to live forever in the most wonderful place
of all? That place is heaven. God
promises that you can live there
forever. How? If you turn from
your sins and live for God.
That's a promise, a promise from
God Himself. Will you do your
part?

---

21 "But if a wicked man turns from
all his sins which he has committed,
keeps all My statutes, and does what
is lawful and right, he shall surely
live; he shall not die.
22 "None of the transgressions which
he has committed shall be remembered against him; because of the
righteousness which he has done, he
shall live.
23 "Do I have any pleasure at all
that the wicked should die?" says the
Lord GOD, "*and* not that he should
turn from his ways and live?
24 "But when a righteous man turns
away from his righteousness and
commits iniquity, and does according
to all the abominations that the
wicked *man* does, shall he live? All
the righteousness which he has done
shall not be remembered; because of
the unfaithfulness of which he is
guilty and the sin which he has committed, because of them he shall die.
25 "Yet you say, 'The way of the Lord
is not fair.' Hear now, O house of Israel, is it not My way which is fair,
and your ways which are not fair?

18:17 [a]Following Masoretic Text, Targum, and Vulgate; Septuagint reads *iniquity* (compare verse 8).

26 "When a righteous *man* turns away from his righteousness, commits iniquity, and dies in it, it is because of the iniquity which he has done that he dies.
27 "Again, when a wicked *man* turns away from the wickedness which he committed, and does what is lawful and right, he preserves himself alive.
28 "Because he considers and turns away from all the transgressions which he committed, he shall surely live; he shall not die.
29 "Yet the house of Israel says, 'The way of the Lord is not fair.' O house of Israel, is it not My ways which are fair, and your ways which are not fair?
30 "Therefore I will judge you, O house of Israel, every one according to his ways," says the Lord GOD. "Repent, and turn from all your transgressions, so that iniquity will not be your ruin.
31 "Cast away from you all the transgressions which you have committed, and get yourselves a new heart and a new spirit. For why should you die, O house of Israel?
32 "For I have no pleasure in the death of one who dies," says the Lord GOD. "Therefore turn and live!"

ISRAEL DEGRADED

19 "Moreover take up a lamentation for the princes of Israel,
2 "and say:

'What *is* your mother? A lioness:
She lay down among the lions;
Among the young lions she
    nourished her cubs.
3 She brought up one of her cubs,
And he became a young lion;
He learned to catch prey,
And he devoured men.
4 The nations also heard of him;
He was trapped in their pit,
And they brought him with
    chains to the land of Egypt.

5 'When she saw that she waited,
    that her hope was lost,
  She took another of her cubs *and*
    made him a young lion.
6 He roved among the lions,
  And became a young lion;
  He learned to catch prey;
  He devoured men.
7 He knew their desolate places,*a*
  And laid waste their cities;
  The land with its fullness was
    desolated
  By the noise of his roaring.
8 Then the nations set against him
    from the provinces on every
    side,
  And spread their net over him;
  He was trapped in their pit.
9 They put him in a cage with
    chains,
  And brought him to the king of
    Babylon;
  They brought him in nets,
  That his voice should no longer be
    heard on the mountains of
    Israel.

10 'Your mother *was* like a vine in
    your bloodline,*a*
  Planted by the waters,
  Fruitful and full of branches
  Because of many waters.
11 She had strong branches for
    scepters of rulers.
  She towered in stature above the
    thick branches,
  And was seen in her height amid
    the dense foliage.
12 But she was plucked up in fury,
  She was cast down to the ground,
  And the east wind dried her fruit.
  Her strong branches were broken
    and withered;
  The fire consumed them.
13 And now she *is* planted in the
    wilderness,
  In a dry and thirsty land.
14 Fire has come out from a rod of
    her branches

  And devoured her fruit,
  So that she has no strong
    branch—a scepter for ruling.' "

This *is* a lamentation, and has become a lamentation.

THE REBELLIONS OF ISRAEL

20 It came to pass in the seventh
year, in the fifth *month,* on the tenth
day of the month, *that* certain of the
elders of Israel came to inquire of the
Lord, and sat before me.
2   Then the word of the Lord came
to me, saying,
3   "Son of man, speak to the elders
of Israel, and say to them, 'Thus says
the Lord God: "Have you come to inquire of Me? *As* I live," says the Lord
God, "I will not be inquired of by
you." '
4   "Will you judge them, son of man,
will you judge *them?* Then make
known to them the abominations of
their fathers.
5   "Say to them, 'Thus says the Lord
God: "On the day when I chose Israel
and raised My hand in an oath to the
descendants of the house of Jacob,
and made Myself known to them in
the land of Egypt, I raised My hand
in an oath to them, saying, 'I *am* the
Lord your God.'
6   "On that day I raised My hand in
an oath to them, to bring them out of
the land of Egypt into a land that I
had searched out for them, 'flowing
with milk and honey,'*a* the glory of all
lands.
7   "Then I said to them, 'Each of
you, throw away the abominations

19:7 *a*Septuagint reads *He stood in insolence;* Targum reads *He destroyed its palaces;* Vulgate reads
He learned to make widows.   19:10 *a*Literally
blood, following Masoretic Text, Syriac, and Vulgate; Septuagint reads *like a flower on a pomegranate tree;* Targum reads *in your likeness.*
20:6 *a*Exodus 3:8

which are before his eyes, and do not defile yourselves with the idols of Egypt. I *am* the LORD your God.'

8 "But they rebelled against Me and would not obey Me. They did not all cast away the abominations which were before their eyes, nor did they forsake the idols of Egypt. Then I said, 'I will pour out My fury on them and fulfill My anger against them in the midst of the land of Egypt.'

9 "But I acted for My name's sake, that it should not be profaned before the Gentiles among whom they *were,* in whose sight I had made Myself known to them, to bring them out of the land of Egypt.

10 "Therefore I made them go out of the land of Egypt and brought them into the wilderness.

11 "And I gave them My statutes and showed them My judgments, 'which, *if* a man does, he shall live by them.'*a*

12 "Moreover I also gave them My Sabbaths, to be a sign between them and Me, that they might know that I *am* the LORD who sanctifies them.

13 "Yet the house of Israel rebelled against Me in the wilderness; they did not walk in My statutes; they despised My judgments, 'which, *if* a man does, he shall live by them';*a* and they greatly defiled My Sabbaths. Then I said I would pour out My fury on them in the wilderness, to consume them.

14 "But I acted for My name's sake, that it should not be profaned before the Gentiles, in whose sight I had brought them out.

15 "So I also raised My hand in an oath to them in the wilderness, that I would not bring them into the land which I had given *them,* 'flowing with milk and honey,'*a* the glory of all lands,

16 "because they despised My judgments and did not walk in My

statutes, but profaned My Sabbaths; for their heart went after their idols.

17 "Nevertheless My eye spared them from destruction. I did not make an end of them in the wilderness.

18 "But I said to their children in the wilderness, 'Do not walk in the statutes of your fathers, nor observe their judgments, nor defile yourselves with their idols.

19 'I *am* the LORD your God: Walk in My statutes, keep My judgments, and do them;

20 'hallow My Sabbaths, and they will be a sign between Me and you, that you may know that I *am* the LORD your God.'

21 "Notwithstanding, the children rebelled against Me; they did not walk in My statutes, and were not careful to observe My judgments, 'which, *if* a man does, he shall live by them';*a* but they profaned My Sabbaths. Then I said I would pour out My fury on them and fulfill My anger against them in the wilderness.

22 "Nevertheless I withdrew My hand and acted for My name's sake, that it should not be profaned in the sight of the Gentiles, in whose sight I had brought them out.

23 "Also I raised My hand in an oath to those in the wilderness, that I would scatter them among the Gentiles and disperse them throughout the countries,

24 "because they had not executed My judgments, but had despised My statutes, profaned My Sabbaths, and their eyes were fixed on their fathers' idols.

25 "Therefore I also gave them up to statutes *that were* not good, and judgments by which they could not live;

26 "and I pronounced them unclean

20:11 *a*Leviticus 18:5   20:13 *a*Leviticus 18:5
20:15 *a*Exodus 3:8   20:21 *a*Leviticus 18:5

because of their ritual gifts, in that they caused all their firstborn to pass through *the fire,* that I might make them desolate and that they might know that I am the LORD." '

27 "Therefore, son of man, speak to the house of Israel, and say to them, 'Thus says the Lord GOD: "In this too your fathers have blasphemed Me, by being unfaithful to Me.

28 "When I brought them into the land *concerning* which I had raised My hand in an oath to give them, and they saw all the high hills and all the thick trees, there they offered their sacrifices and provoked Me with their offerings. There they also sent up their sweet aroma and poured out their drink offerings.

29 "Then I said to them, 'What *is* this high place to which you go?' So its name is called Bā′mahᵃ to this day." '

30 "Therefore say to the house of Israel, 'Thus says the Lord GOD: "Are you defiling yourselves in the manner of your fathers, and committing harlotry according to their abominations?

31 "For when you offer your gifts and make your sons pass through the fire, you defile yourselves with all your idols, even to this day. So shall I be inquired of by you, O house of Israel? *As* I live," says the Lord GOD, "I will not be inquired of by you.

32 "What you have in your mind shall never be, when you say, 'We will be like the Gentiles, like the families in other countries, serving wood and stone.'

GOD WILL RESTORE ISRAEL

33 "*As* I live," says the Lord GOD, "surely with a mighty hand, with an outstretched arm, and with fury poured out, I will rule over you.

34 "I will bring you out from the peoples and gather you out of the countries where you are scattered, with a mighty hand, with an outstretched arm, and with fury poured out.

35 "And I will bring you into the wilderness of the peoples, and there I will plead My case with you face to face.

36 "Just as I pleaded My case with your fathers in the wilderness of the land of Egypt, so I will plead My case with you," says the Lord GOD.

37 "I will make you pass under the rod, and I will bring you into the bond of the covenant;

38 "I will purge the rebels from among you, and those who transgress against Me; I will bring them out of the country where they dwell, but they shall not enter the land of Israel. Then you will know that I *am* the LORD.

39 "As for you, O house of Israel," thus says the Lord GOD: "Go, serve every one of you his idols—and hereafter—if you will not obey Me; but profane My holy name no more with your gifts and your idols.

40 "For on My holy mountain, on the mountain height of Israel," says the Lord GOD, "there all the house of Israel, all of them in the land, shall serve Me; there I will accept them, and there I will require your offerings and the firstfruits of your sacrifices, together with all your holy things.

41 "I will accept you as a sweet aroma when I bring you out from the peoples and gather you out of the countries where you have been scattered; and I will be hallowed in you before the Gentiles.

42 "Then you shall know that I *am* the LORD, when I bring you into the land of Israel, into the country for

20:29 ᵃLiterally *High Place*

which I raised My hand in an oath to give to your fathers.

43 "And there you shall remember your ways and all your doings with which you were defiled; and you shall loathe yourselves in your own sight because of all the evils that you have committed.

44 "Then you shall know that I *am* the LORD, when I have dealt with you for My name's sake, not according to your wicked ways nor according to your corrupt doings, O house of Israel," says the Lord GOD.' "

FIRE IN THE FOREST

45 Furthermore the word of the LORD came to me, saying,

46 "Son of man, set your face toward the south; preach against the south and prophesy against the forest land, the South,*a*

47 "and say to the forest of the South, 'Hear the word of the LORD! Thus says the Lord GOD: "Behold, I will kindle a fire in you, and it shall devour every green tree and every dry tree in you; the blazing flame shall not be quenched, and all faces from the south to the north shall be scorched by it.

48 "All flesh shall see that I, the LORD, have kindled it; it shall not be quenched." ' "

49 Then I said, "Ah, Lord GOD! They say of me, 'Does he not speak parables?' "

BABYLON, THE SWORD OF GOD

21 And the word of the LORD came to me, saying,

2 "Son of man, set your face toward Jerusalem, preach against the holy places, and prophesy against the land of Israel;

3 "and say to the land of Israel, 'Thus says the LORD: "Behold, I *am*

against you, and I will draw My sword out of its sheath and cut off both righteous and wicked from you.

4 "Because I will cut off both righteous and wicked from you, therefore My sword shall go out of its sheath against all flesh from south *to* north,

5 "that all flesh may know that I, the LORD, have drawn My sword out of its sheath; it shall not return anymore." '

6 "Sigh therefore, son of man, with a breaking heart, and sigh with bitterness before their eyes.

7 "And it shall be when they say to you, 'Why are you sighing?' that you shall answer, 'Because of the news; when it comes, every heart will melt, all hands will be feeble, every spirit will faint, and all knees will be weak *as* water. Behold, it is coming and shall be brought to pass,' says the Lord GOD."

8 Again the word of the LORD came to me, saying,

9 "Son of man, prophesy and say, 'Thus says the LORD!' Say:

'A sword, a sword is sharpened
And also polished!
10 Sharpened to make a dreadful
  slaughter,
Polished to flash like lightning!
Should we then make mirth?
It despises the scepter of My son,
As it does all wood.
11 And He has given it to be
  polished,
That it may be handled;
This sword is sharpened, and it is
  polished
To be given into the hand of the
  slayer.'

12 "Cry and wail, son of man;
For it will be against My people,
Against all the princes of Israel.

20:46 *a*Hebrew *Negev*

Terrors including the sword will
    be against My people;
Therefore strike *your* thigh.

13 "Because *it is* a testing,
    And what if *the sword* despises
      even the scepter?
    The scepter shall be no *more*,"

says the Lord GOD.

14 "You therefore, son of man,
    prophesy,
    And strike *your* hands together.
    The third time let the sword do
      double *damage*.
    It *is* the sword *that* slays,
    The sword that slays the great
      men,
    That enters their private
      chambers.
15 I have set the point of the sword
    against all their gates,
    That the heart may melt and
      many may stumble.
    Ah! *It is* made bright;
    It is grasped for slaughter:

16 "Swords at the ready!
    Thrust right!
    Set your blade!
    Thrust left—
    Wherever your edge is ordered!

17 "I also will beat My fists together,
    And I will cause My fury to rest;
    I, the LORD, have spoken."

18 The word of the LORD came to me
again, saying:
19 "And son of man, appoint for
yourself two ways for the sword of
the king of Babylon to go; both of
them shall go from the same land.
Make a sign; put *it* at the head of the
road to the city.
20 "Appoint a road for the sword to
go to Rab'bah of the Am'mon·ītes,

and to Judah, into fortified Jerusalem.
21 "For the king of Babylon stands
at the parting of the road, at the fork
of the two roads, to use divination: he
shakes the arrows, he consults the
images, he looks at the liver.
22 "In his right hand is the divination for Jerusalem: to set up battering rams, to call for a slaughter, to
lift the voice with shouting, to set
battering rams against the gates, to
heap up a *siege* mound, and to build a
wall.
23 "And it will be to them like a false
divination in the eyes of those who
have sworn oaths with them; but he
will bring their iniquity to remembrance, that they may be taken.
24 "Therefore thus says the Lord
GOD: 'Because you have made your
iniquity to be remembered, in that
your transgressions are uncovered, so
that in all your doings your sins appear—because you have come to remembrance, you shall be taken in
hand.
25 'Now to you, O profane, wicked
prince of Israel, whose day has come,
whose iniquity *shall* end,
26 'thus says the Lord GOD:

"Remove the turban, and take off
    the crown;
    Nothing *shall remain* the same.
    Exalt the humble, and humble
      the exalted.
27 Overthrown, overthrown,
    I will make it overthrown!
    It shall be no *longer*,
    Until He comes whose right it is,
    And I will give it *to Him*." '

A SWORD AGAINST THE AMMONITES

28 "And you, son of man, prophesy
and say, 'Thus says the Lord GOD
concerning the Am'mon·ītes and concerning their reproach,' and say:

'A sword, a sword *is* drawn,
Polished for slaughter,
For consuming, for flashing—
29 While they see false visions for
    you,
While they divine a lie to you,
To bring you on the necks of the
    wicked, the slain
Whose day has come,
Whose iniquity *shall* end.

30 'Return *it* to its sheath.
I will judge you
In the place where you were
    created,
In the land of your nativity.
31 I will pour out My indignation on
    you;
I will blow against you with the
    fire of My wrath,
And deliver you into the hands of
    brutal men *who are* skillful to
    destroy.
32 You shall be fuel for the fire;
Your blood shall be in the midst of
    the land.
You shall not be remembered,
For I the LORD have spoken.' "

SINS OF JERUSALEM

22 Moreover the word of the LORD
came to me, saying,
2 "Now, son of man, will you judge,
will you judge the bloody city? Yes,
show her all her abominations!
3 "Then say, 'Thus says the Lord
GOD: "The city sheds blood in her own
midst, that her time may come; and
she makes idols within herself to defile herself.
4 "You have become guilty by the
blood which you have shed, and have
defiled yourself with the idols which
you have made. You have caused
your days to draw near, and have
come to *the end of* your years; therefore I have made you a reproach to
the nations, and a mockery to all
countries.
5 "*Those* near and *those* far from
you will mock you as infamous *and*
full of tumult.
6 "Look, the princes of Israel: each
one has used his power to shed blood
in you.
7 "In you they have made light of
father and mother; in your midst
they have oppressed the stranger; in
you they have mistreated the fatherless and the widow.
8 "You have despised My holy
things and profaned My Sabbaths.
9 "In you are men who slander to
cause bloodshed; in you are those
who eat on the mountains; in your
midst they commit lewdness.
10 "In you men uncover their fathers' nakedness; in you they violate
women who are set apart during
their impurity.
11 "One commits abomination with
his neighbor's wife; another lewdly
defiles his daughter-in-law; and another in you violates his sister, his father's daughter.
12 "In you they take bribes to shed
blood; you take usury and increase;
you have made profit from your
neighbors by extortion, and have forgotten Me," says the Lord GOD.
13 "Behold, therefore, I beat My fists
at the dishonest profit which you
have made, and at the bloodshed
which has been in your midst.
14 "Can your heart endure, or can
your hands remain strong, in the
days when I shall deal with you?
I, the LORD, have spoken, and will
do *it*.
15 "I will scatter you among the nations, disperse you throughout the
countries, and remove your filthiness
completely from you.
16 "You shall defile yourself in the
sight of the nations; then you shall
know that I *am* the LORD." ' "

ISRAEL IN THE FURNACE

17 The word of the LORD came to me, saying,

18 "Son of man, the house of Israel has become dross to Me; they *are* all bronze, tin, iron, and lead, in the midst of a furnace; they have become dross from silver.

19 "Therefore thus says the Lord GOD: 'Because you have all become dross, therefore behold, I will gather you into the midst of Jerusalem.

20 '*As men* gather silver, bronze, iron, lead, and tin into the midst of a furnace, to blow fire on it, to melt *it;* so I will gather *you* in My anger and in My fury, and I will leave *you there* and melt you.

21 'Yes, I will gather you and blow on you with the fire of My wrath, and you shall be melted in its midst.

22 'As silver is melted in the midst of a furnace, so shall you be melted in its midst; then you shall know that I, the LORD, have poured out My fury on you.' "

ISRAEL'S WICKED LEADERS

23 And the word of the LORD came to me, saying,

24 "Son of man, say to her: 'You *are* a land that is not cleansed*a* or rained on in the day of indignation.'

25 "The conspiracy of her prophets*a* in her midst is like a roaring lion tearing the prey; they have devoured people; they have taken treasure and precious things; they have made many widows in her midst.

26 "Her priests have violated My law and profaned My holy things; they have not distinguished between the holy and unholy, nor have they made known *the difference* between the unclean and the clean; and they have hidden their eyes from My Sabbaths, so that I am profaned among them.

27 "Her princes in her midst *are* like wolves tearing the prey, to shed blood, to destroy people, and to get dishonest gain.

28 "Her prophets plastered them with untempered *mortar,* seeing false visions, and divining lies for them, saying, 'Thus says the Lord GOD,' when the LORD had not spoken.

29 "The people of the land have used oppressions, committed robbery, and mistreated the poor and needy; and they wrongfully oppress the stranger.

30 "So I sought for a man among them who would make a wall, and stand in the gap before Me on behalf of the land, that I should not destroy it; but I found no one.

31 "Therefore I have poured out My indignation on them; I have consumed them with the fire of My wrath; and I have recompensed their deeds on their own heads," says the Lord GOD.

TWO HARLOT SISTERS

23 The word of the LORD came again to me, saying:

2   "Son of man, there were two
      women,
    The daughters of one mother.
3   They committed harlotry in
      Egypt,
    They committed harlotry in their
      youth;
    Their breasts were there
      embraced,
    Their virgin bosom was there
      pressed.
4   Their names: Ō·hō'lah*a* the elder
    and Ō·hol'i·bah*b* her sister;

22:24 *a*Following Masoretic Text, Syriac, and Vulgate; Septuagint reads *showered upon.*
22:25 *a*Following Masoretic Text and Vulgate; Septuagint reads *princes;* Targum reads *scribes.*
23:4 *a*Literally *Her Own Tabernacle*   *b*Literally *My Tabernacle Is in Her*

They were Mine,
And they bore sons and
   daughters.
As for their names,
Samaria *is* Ō·hō′lah, and
   Jerusalem *is* Ō·hol′i·bah.

THE OLDER SISTER, SAMARIA

5 "Ō·hō′lah played the harlot even
   though she was Mine;
And she lusted for her lovers, the
   neighboring Assyrians,
6 *Who were* clothed in purple,
Captains and rulers,
All of them desirable young men,
Horsemen riding on horses.
7 Thus she committed her harlotry
   with them,
All of them choice men of Assyria;
And with all for whom she lusted,
With all their idols, she defiled
   herself.
8 She has never given up her
   harlotry *brought* from Egypt,
For in her youth they had lain
   with her,
Pressed her virgin bosom,
And poured out their immorality
   upon her.

9 "Therefore I have delivered her
Into the hand of her lovers,
Into the hand of the Assyrians,
For whom she lusted.
10 They uncovered her nakedness,
Took away her sons and
   daughters,
And slew her with the sword;
She became a byword among
   women,
For they had executed judgment
   on her.

THE YOUNGER SISTER, JERUSALEM

11 "Now although her sister Ō·hol′i-
bah saw *this,* she became more corrupt in her lust than she, and in her
harlotry more corrupt than her sister's harlotry.

12 "She lusted for the neighboring
   Assyrians,
Captains and rulers,
Clothed most gorgeously,
Horsemen riding on horses,
All of them desirable young men.
13 Then I saw that she was defiled;
Both *took* the same way.
14 But she increased her harlotry;
She looked at men portrayed on
   the wall,
Images of Chal·dē′ans portrayed
   in vermilion,
15 Girded with belts around their
   waists,
Flowing turbans on their heads,
All of them looking like captains,
In the manner of the Babylonians
   of Chal·dē′a,
The land of their nativity.
16 As soon as her eyes saw them,
She lusted for them
And sent messengers to them in
   Chal·dē′a.

17 "Then the Babylonians came to
   her, into the bed of love,
And they defiled her with their
   immorality;
So she was defiled by them, and
   alienated herself from them.
18 She revealed her harlotry and
   uncovered her nakedness.
Then I alienated Myself from
   her,
As I had alienated Myself from
   her sister.

19 "Yet she multiplied her harlotry
In calling to remembrance the
   days of her youth,
When she had played the harlot
   in the land of Egypt.
20 For she lusted for her paramours,
Whose flesh *is like* the flesh of
   donkeys,

And whose issue *is like* the issue of horses.
21 Thus you called to remembrance the lewdness of your youth,
When the Egyptians pressed your bosom
Because of your youthful breasts.

JUDGMENT ON JERUSALEM

22 "Therefore, Ō·hol′i·bah, thus says the Lord GOD:

'Behold, I will stir up your lovers against you,
From whom you have alienated yourself,
And I will bring them against you from every side:
23 The Babylonians,
All the Chal·dē′ans,
Pē′kod, Shō′a, Kō′a,
All the Assyrians with them,
All of them desirable young men,
Governors and rulers,
Captains and men of renown,
All of them riding on horses.
24 And they shall come against you
With chariots, wagons, and war-horses,
With a horde of people.
They shall array against you
Buckler, shield, and helmet all around.

'I will delegate judgment to them,
And they shall judge you according to their judgments.
25 I will set My jealousy against you,
And they shall deal furiously with you;
They shall remove your nose and your ears,
And your remnant shall fall by the sword;
They shall take your sons and your daughters,
And your remnant shall be devoured by fire.

26 They shall also strip you of your clothes
And take away your beautiful jewelry.

27 'Thus I will make you cease your lewdness and your harlotry
Brought from the land of Egypt,
So that you will not lift your eyes to them,
Nor remember Egypt anymore.'

28 "For thus says the Lord GOD: 'Surely I will deliver you into the hand of those you hate, into the hand *of those* from whom you alienated yourself.
29 'They will deal hatefully with you, take away all you have worked for, and leave you naked and bare. The nakedness of your harlotry shall be uncovered, both your lewdness and your harlotry.
30 'I will do these *things* to you because you have gone as a harlot after the Gentiles, because you have become defiled by their idols.
31 'You have walked in the way of your sister; therefore I will put her cup in your hand.'
32 "Thus says the Lord GOD:

'You shall drink of your sister's cup,
The deep and wide one;
You shall be laughed to scorn
And held in derision;
It contains much.
33 You will be filled with drunkenness and sorrow,
The cup of horror and desolation,
The cup of your sister Samaria.
34 You shall drink and drain it,
You shall break its shards,
And tear at your own breasts;
For I have spoken,'
Says the Lord GOD.

35 "Therefore thus says the Lord GOD:

'Because you have forgotten Me
and cast Me behind your back,
Therefore you shall bear the
penalty
Of your lewdness and your
harlotry.' "

BOTH SISTERS JUDGED

36 The LORD also said to me: "Son of man, will you judge Ō·hō′lah and Ō·hol′i·bah? Then declare to them their abominations.
37 "For they have committed adultery, and blood *is* on their hands. They have committed adultery with their idols, and even sacrificed their sons whom they bore to Me, passing them through *the fire,* to devour *them.*
38 "Moreover they have done this to Me: They have defiled My sanctuary on the same day and profaned My Sabbaths.
39 "For after they had slain their children for their idols, on the same day they came into My sanctuary to profane it; and indeed thus they have done in the midst of My house.
40 "Furthermore you sent for men to come from afar, to whom a messenger *was* sent; and there they came. And you washed yourself for them, painted your eyes, and adorned yourself with ornaments.
41 "You sat on a stately couch, with a table prepared before it, on which you had set My incense and My oil.
42 "The sound of a carefree multitude *was* with her, and Sa·bē′ans *were* brought from the wilderness with men of the common sort, who put bracelets on their wrists and beautiful crowns on their heads.
43 "Then I said concerning *her who had grown* old in adulteries, 'Will they commit harlotry with her now, and she *with them?*'
44 "Yet they went in to her, as men go in to a woman who plays the harlot; thus they went in to Ō·hō′lah and Ō·hol′i·bah, the lewd women.
45 "But righteous men will judge them after the manner of adulteresses, and after the manner of women who shed blood, because they *are* adulteresses, and blood *is* on their hands.
46 "For thus says the Lord GOD: 'Bring up an assembly against them, give them up to trouble and plunder.
47 'The assembly shall stone them with stones and execute them with their swords; they shall slay their sons and their daughters, and burn their houses with fire.
48 'Thus I will cause lewdness to cease from the land, that all women may be taught not to practice your lewdness.
49 'They shall repay you for your lewdness, and you shall pay for your idolatrous sins. Then you shall know that I *am* the Lord GOD.' "

SYMBOL OF THE COOKING POT

24 Again, in the ninth year, in the tenth month, on the tenth *day* of the month, the word of the LORD came to me, saying,
2 "Son of man, write down the name of the day, this very day—the king of Babylon started his siege against Jerusalem this very day.
3 "And utter a parable to the rebellious house, and say to them, 'Thus says the Lord GOD:

"Put on a pot, set *it* on,
And also pour water into it.
4 Gather pieces *of meat* in it,
Every good piece,
The thigh and the shoulder.
Fill *it* with choice cuts;
5 Take the choice of the flock.
Also pile *fuel* bones under it,

Make it boil well,
And let the cuts simmer in it."

6 'Therefore thus says the Lord GOD:

"Woe to the bloody city,
To the pot whose scum *is* in it,
And whose scum is not gone from
   it!
Bring it out piece by piece,
On which no lot has fallen.
7 For her blood is in her midst;
She set it on top of a rock;
She did not pour it on the ground,
To cover it with dust.
8 That it may raise up fury and
   take vengeance,
I have set her blood on top of a
   rock,
That it may not be covered."

9 'Therefore thus says the Lord GOD:

"Woe to the bloody city!
I too will make the pyre great.
10 Heap on the wood,
Kindle the fire;
Cook the meat well,
Mix in the spices,
And let the cuts be burned up.
11 "Then set the pot empty on the
   coals,
That it may become hot and its
   bronze may burn,
That its filthiness may be melted
   in it,
That its scum may be consumed.
12 She has grown weary with lies,
And her great scum has not gone
   from her.
Let her scum *be* in the fire!
13 In your filthiness *is* lewdness.
Because I have cleansed you, and
   you were not cleansed,
You will not be cleansed of your
   filthiness anymore,
Till I have caused My fury to rest
   upon you.

14 I, the LORD, have spoken *it;*
It shall come to pass, and I will do
   it;
I will not hold back,
Nor will I spare,
Nor will I relent;
According to your ways
And according to your deeds
They[a] will judge you,"
Says the Lord GOD.' "

THE PROPHET'S WIFE DIES

15 Also the word of the LORD came to me, saying,
16 "Son of man, behold, I take away from you the desire of your eyes with one stroke; yet you shall neither mourn nor weep, nor shall your tears run down.
17 "Sigh in silence, make no mourning for the dead; bind your turban on your head, and put your sandals on your feet; do not cover *your* lips, and do not eat man's bread *of sorrow.*"
18 So I spoke to the people in the morning, and at evening my wife died; and the next morning I did as I was commanded.
19 And the people said to me, "Will you not tell us what these *things signify* to us, that you behave so?"
20 Then I answered them, "The word of the LORD came to me, saying,
21 'Speak to the house of Israel, "Thus says the Lord GOD: 'Behold, I will profane My sanctuary, your arrogant boast, the desire of your eyes, the delight of your soul; and your sons and daughters whom you left behind shall fall by the sword.
22 'And you shall do as I have done; you shall not cover *your* lips nor eat man's bread *of sorrow.*
23 'Your turbans shall be on your heads and your sandals on your feet;

24:14 [a]Septuagint, Syriac, Targum, and Vulgate read *I.*

you shall neither mourn nor weep, but you shall pine away in your iniquities and mourn with one another.

24 'Thus E·zĕk′i·el is a sign to you; according to all that he has done you shall do; and when this comes, you shall know that I *am* the Lord GOD.' "

25 'And you, son of man—*will it* not *be* in the day when I take from them their stronghold, their joy and their glory, the desire of their eyes, and that on which they set their minds, their sons and their daughters:

26 'on that day one who escapes will come to you to let *you* hear *it* with *your* ears;

27 'on that day your mouth will be opened to him who has escaped; you shall speak and no longer be mute. Thus you will be a sign to them, and they shall know that I *am* the LORD.' "

PROCLAMATION AGAINST AMMON

25 The word of the LORD came to me, saying,

2 "Son of man, set your face against the Am′mon·ĭtes, and prophesy against them.

3 "Say to the Am′mon·ĭtes, 'Hear the word of the Lord GOD! Thus says the Lord GOD: "Because you said, 'Aha!' against My sanctuary when it was profaned, and against the land of Israel when it was desolate, and against the house of Judah when they went into captivity,

4 "indeed, therefore, I will deliver you as a possession to the men of the East, and they shall set their encampments among you and make their dwellings among you; they shall eat your fruit, and they shall drink your milk.

5 "And I will make Rab′bah a stable for camels and Am′mon a resting

place for flocks. Then you shall know that I *am* the LORD."

6 'For thus says the Lord GOD: "Because you clapped *your* hands, stamped your feet, and rejoiced in heart with all your disdain for the land of Israel,

7 "indeed, therefore, I will stretch out My hand against you, and give you as plunder to the nations; I will cut you off from the peoples, and I will cause you to perish from the countries; I will destroy you, and you shall know that I *am* the LORD."

PROCLAMATION AGAINST MOAB

8 'Thus says the Lord GOD: "Because Mō′ab and Sē′ir say, 'Look! The house of Judah *is* like all the nations,'

9 "therefore, behold, I will clear the territory of Mō′ab of cities, of the cities on its frontier, the glory of the country, Beth Jesh′i·moth, Bā′al Mē′on, and Kir·jath′a·im.

10 "To the men of the East I will give it as a possession, together with the Am′mon·ĭtes, that the Am′mon·ĭtes may not be remembered among the nations.

11 "And I will execute judgments upon Mō′ab, and they shall know that I *am* the LORD."

PROCLAMATION AGAINST EDOM

12 'Thus says the Lord GOD: "Because of what Ē′dom did against the house of Judah by taking vengeance, and has greatly offended by avenging itself on them,"

13 'therefore thus says the Lord GOD: "I will also stretch out My hand against Ē′dom, cut off man and beast from it, and make it desolate from Tē′man; Dē′dan shall fall by the sword.

14 "I will lay My vengeance on

Ē'dom by the hand of My people Israel, that they may do in Ē'dom according to My anger and according to
My fury; and they shall know My
vengeance," says the Lord GOD.

PROCLAMATION AGAINST PHILISTIA

15 'Thus says the Lord GOD: "Because the Phi·lis'tines dealt venge-
fully and took vengeance with a
spiteful heart, to destroy because of
the old hatred,"
16 'therefore thus says the Lord GOD:
"I will stretch out My hand against
the Phi·lis'tines, and I will cut off the
Cher'e·thītes and destroy the remnant of the seacoast.
17 "I will execute great vengeance on
them with furious rebukes; and they
shall know that I *am* the LORD, when
I lay My vengeance upon them." ' "

PROCLAMATION AGAINST TYRE

26 And it came to pass in the
eleventh year, on the first *day* of the
month, *that* the word of the LORD
came to me, saying,
2 "Son of man, because Tȳre has
said against Jerusalem, 'Aha! She is
broken who *was* the gateway of the
peoples; now she is turned over to
me; I shall be filled; she is laid
waste.'
3 "Therefore thus says the Lord
GOD: 'Behold, I *am* against you, O
Tȳre, and will cause many nations to
come up against you, as the sea
causes its waves to come up.
4 'And they shall destroy the walls
of Tȳre and break down her towers; I
will also scrape her dust from her,
and make her like the top of a rock.
5 'It shall be *a place for* spreading
nets in the midst of the sea, for I
have spoken,' says the Lord GOD; 'it
shall become plunder for the nations.
6 'Also her daughter *villages* which

are in the fields shall be slain by the
sword. Then they shall know that I
am the LORD.'
7 "For thus says the Lord GOD: 'Behold, I will bring against Tȳre from
the north Ne·bū·chad·nez'zar[a] king of
Babylon, king of kings, with horses,
with chariots, and with horsemen,
and an army with many people.
8 'He will slay with the sword your
daughter *villages* in the fields; he will
heap up a siege mound against you,
build a wall against you, and raise a
defense against you.
9 'He will direct his battering rams
against your walls, and with his axes
he will break down your towers.
10 'Because of the abundance of his
horses, their dust will cover you; your
walls will shake at the noise of the
horsemen, the wagons, and the chariots, when he enters your gates, as
men enter a city that has been
breached.
11 'With the hooves of his horses he
will trample all your streets; he will
slay your people by the sword, and
your strong pillars will fall to the
ground.
12 'They will plunder your riches
and pillage your merchandise; they
will break down your walls and destroy your pleasant houses; they will
lay your stones, your timber, and
your soil in the midst of the water.
13 'I will put an end to the sound of
your songs, and the sound of your
harps shall be heard no more.
14 'I will make you like the top of a
rock; you shall be *a place for* spreading nets, and you shall never be rebuilt, for I the LORD have spoken,'
says the Lord GOD.
15 "Thus says the Lord GOD to Tȳre:
'Will the coastlands not shake at the
sound of your fall, when the wounded

26:7 [a]Hebrew *Nebuchadrezzar,* and so elsewhere in
this book

cry, when slaughter is made in the midst of you?
16 'Then all the princes of the sea will come down from their thrones, lay aside their robes, and take off their embroidered garments; they will clothe themselves with trembling; they will sit on the ground, tremble *every* moment, and be astonished at you.
17 'And they will take up a lamentation for you, and say to you:

"How you have perished,
O one inhabited by seafaring men,
O renowned city,
Who was strong at sea,
She and her inhabitants,
Who caused their terror *to be* on all her inhabitants!
18 Now the coastlands tremble on the day of your fall;
Yes, the coastlands by the sea are troubled at your departure." '

19 "For thus says the Lord GOD: 'When I make you a desolate city, like cities that are not inhabited, when I bring the deep upon you, and great waters cover you,
20 'then I will bring you down with those who descend into the Pit, to the people of old, and I will make you dwell in the lowest part of the earth, in places desolate from antiquity, with those who go down to the Pit, so that you may never be inhabited; and I shall establish glory in the land of the living.
21 'I will make you a terror, and you *shall be* no *more;* though you are sought for, you will never be found again,' says the Lord GOD."

LAMENTATION FOR TYRE

27

The word of the LORD came again to me, saying,

2 "Now, son of man, take up a lamentation for Tyre,
3 "and say to Tyre, 'You who are situated at the entrance of the sea, merchant of the peoples on many coastlands, thus says the Lord GOD:

"O Tyre, you have said,
'I *am* perfect in beauty.'
4 Your borders *are* in the midst of the seas.
Your builders have perfected your beauty.
5 They made all *your* planks of fir trees from Sē'nir;
They took a cedar from Lebanon to make you a mast.
6 *Of* oaks from Bā'shan they made your oars;
The company of Ash'ur·ītes have inlaid your planks
With ivory from the coasts of Cyprus.a
7 Fine embroidered linen from Egypt was what you spread for your sail;
Blue and purple from the coasts of E·li'shah was what covered you.

8 "Inhabitants of Si'don and Ar'vad were your oarsmen;
Your wise men, O Tyre, were in you;
They became your pilots.
9 Elders of Gē'bal and its wise men Were in you to caulk your seams;
All the ships of the sea And their oarsmen were in you To market your merchandise.

10 "Those from Persia, Lyd'i·a,a and Lib'yab
Were in your army as men of war;
They hung shield and helmet in you;
They gave splendor to you.

27:6 aHebrew *Kittim,* western lands, especially Cyprus   27:10 aHebrew *Lud*   bHebrew *Put*

11 Men of Ar'vad with your army
　　 were on your walls *all* around,
　　 And the men of Gam'mad were in
　　　　 your towers;
　　 They hung their shields on your
　　　　 walls *all* around;
　　 They made your beauty perfect.

12 "Tar'shish *was* your merchant because of your many luxury goods.
They gave you silver, iron, tin, and
lead for your goods.
13 "Jā'van, Tū'bal, and Mē'shech
were your traders. They bartered human lives and vessels of bronze for
your merchandise.
14 "Those from the house of Tō·gar'-
mah traded for your wares with
horses, steeds, and mules.
15 "The men of Dē'dan *were* your
traders; many isles *were* the market
of your hand. They brought you ivory
tusks and ebony as payment.
16 "Syria *was* your merchant because of the abundance of goods you
made. They gave you for your wares
emeralds, purple, embroidery, fine
linen, corals, and rubies.
17 "Judah and the land of Israel
were your traders. They traded for
your merchandise wheat of Min'nith,
millet, honey, oil, and balm.
18 "Damascus *was* your merchant
because of the abundance of goods
you made, because of your many luxury items, with the wine of Hel'bon
and with white wool.
19 "Dan and Jā'van paid for your
wares, traversing back and forth.
Wrought iron, cassia, and cane were
among your merchandise.
20 "Dē'dan *was* your merchant in
saddlecloths for riding.
21 "Arabia and all the princes of Kē'-
dar *were* your regular merchants.
They traded with you in lambs, rams,
and goats.
22 "The merchants of Shē'ba and
Rā'a·mah *were* your merchants. They

traded for your wares the choicest
spices, all kinds of precious stones,
and gold.
23 "Har'an, Can'neh, Eden, the merchants of Shē'ba, Assyria, *and* Chil'-
mad *were* your merchants.
24 "These *were* your merchants in
choice items—in purple clothes, in
embroidered garments, in chests of
multicolored apparel, in sturdy woven cords, which were in your marketplace.

25 "The ships of Tar'shish were
　　　　 carriers of your merchandise.
　　 You were filled and very glorious
　　　　 in the midst of the seas.
26 Your oarsmen brought you into
　　　　 many waters,
　　 But the east wind broke you in
　　　　 the midst of the seas.

27 "Your riches, wares, and
　　　　 merchandise,
　　 Your mariners and pilots,
　　 Your caulkers and merchandisers,
　　 All your men of war who *are* in
　　　　 you,
　　 And the entire company which *is*
　　　　 in your midst,
　　 Will fall into the midst of the seas
　　　　 on the day of your ruin.
28 The common-land will shake at
　　　　 the sound of the cry of your
　　　　 pilots.

29 "All who handle the oar,
　　 The mariners,
　　 All the pilots of the sea
　　 Will come down from their ships
　　　　 and stand on the shore.
30 They will make their voice heard
　　　　 because of you;
　　 They will cry bitterly and cast
　　　　 dust on their heads;
　　 They will roll about in ashes;
31 They will shave themselves
　　　　 completely bald because of you,
　　 Gird themselves with sackcloth,

And weep for you
With bitterness of heart *and*
  bitter wailing.
32 In their wailing for you
They will take up a lamentation,
And lament for you:
'What *city is* like Tyre,
Destroyed in the midst of the sea?

33 'When your wares went out by
  sea,
You satisfied many people;
You enriched the kings of the
  earth
With your many luxury goods and
  your merchandise.
34 But you are broken by the seas in
  the depths of the waters;
Your merchandise and the entire
  company will fall in your midst.
35 All the inhabitants of the isles
  will be astonished at you;
Their kings will be greatly afraid,
And *their* countenance will be
  troubled.
36 The merchants among the peoples
  will hiss at you;
You will become a horror, and *be*
  no more forever.' " ' "

PROCLAMATION AGAINST THE KING OF TYRE

28 The word of the LORD came to me again, saying,
2 "Son of man, say to the prince of Tyre, 'Thus says the Lord GOD:

"Because your heart *is* lifted up,
And you say, 'I *am* a god,
I sit *in* the seat of gods,
In the midst of the seas,'
Yet you *are* a man, and not a god,
Though you set your heart as the
  heart of a god
3 (Behold, you *are* wiser than
  Daniel!
There is no secret that can be
  hidden from you!

4 With your wisdom and your
  understanding
You have gained riches for
  yourself,
And gathered gold and silver into
  your treasuries;
5 By your great wisdom in trade
  you have increased your riches,
And your heart is lifted up
  because of your riches),"

6 'Therefore thus says the Lord
GOD:

"Because you have set your heart
  as the heart of a god,
7 Behold, therefore, I will bring
  strangers against you,
The most terrible of the nations;
And they shall draw their swords
  against the beauty of your
  wisdom,
And defile your splendor.
8 They shall throw you down into
  the Pit,
And you shall die the death of the
  slain
In the midst of the seas.

9 "Will you still say before him who
  slays you,
'I *am* a god'?
But you *shall be* a man, and not a
  god,
In the hand of him who slays you.
10 You shall die the death of the
  uncircumcised
By the hand of aliens;
For I have spoken," says the Lord
  GOD.' "

LAMENTATION FOR THE KING OF TYRE

11 Moreover the word of the LORD came to me, saying,
12 "Son of man, take up a lamentation for the king of Tyre, and say to him, 'Thus says the Lord GOD:

"You *were* the seal of perfection,
Full of wisdom and perfect in
  beauty.
13 You were in Eden, the garden of
  God;
Every precious stone *was* your
  covering:
The sardius, topaz, and diamond,
Beryl, onyx, and jasper,
Sapphire, turquoise, and emerald
  with gold.
The workmanship of your
  timbrels and pipes
Was prepared for you on the day
  you were created.

14 "You *were* the anointed cherub who
  covers;
I established you;
You were on the holy mountain of
  God;
You walked back and forth in the
  midst of fiery stones.
15 You *were* perfect in your ways
  from the day you were created,
Till iniquity was found in you.

16 "By the abundance of your trading
You became filled with violence
  within,
And you sinned;
Therefore I cast you as a profane
  thing
Out of the mountain of God;
And I destroyed you, O covering
  cherub,
From the midst of the fiery
  stones.

17 "Your heart was lifted up because
  of your beauty;
You corrupted your wisdom for
  the sake of your splendor;
I cast you to the ground,
I laid you before kings,
That they might gaze at you.

18 "You defiled your sanctuaries
By the multitude of your
  iniquities,

By the iniquity of your trading;
Therefore I brought fire from your
  midst;
It devoured you,
And I turned you to ashes upon
  the earth
In the sight of all who saw you.
19 All who knew you among the
  peoples are astonished at you;
You have become a horror,
And *shall be* no more forever." ' "

PROCLAMATION AGAINST SIDON

20 Then the word of the LORD came
to me, saying,
21 "Son of man, set your face toward
Si'don, and prophesy against her,
22 "and say, 'Thus says the Lord
GOD:

"Behold, I *am* against you,
  O Si'don;
I will be glorified in your midst;
And they shall know that I *am*
  the LORD,
When I execute judgments in her
  and am hallowed in her.
23 For I will send pestilence upon
  her,
And blood in her streets;
The wounded shall be judged in
  her midst
By the sword against her on every
  side;
Then they shall know that I *am*
  the LORD.

24 "And there shall no longer be a
pricking brier or a painful thorn for
the house of Israel from among all
who are around them, who despise
them. Then they shall know that I
am the Lord GOD."

ISRAEL'S FUTURE BLESSING

25 'Thus says the Lord GOD: "When I
have gathered the house of Israel

from the peoples among whom they are scattered, and am hallowed in them in the sight of the Gentiles, then they will dwell in their own land which I gave to My servant Jacob. 26 "And they will dwell safely there, build houses, and plant vineyards; yes, they will dwell securely, when I execute judgments on all those around them who despise them. Then they shall know that I *am* the LORD their God." ' "

PROCLAMATION AGAINST EGYPT

29 In the tenth year, in the tenth *month,* on the twelfth *day* of the month, the word of the LORD came to me, saying, 2 "Son of man, set your face against Pharaoh king of Egypt, and prophesy against him, and against all Egypt. 3 "Speak, and say, 'Thus says the Lord GOD:

"Behold, I *am* against you,
  O Pharaoh king of Egypt,
  O great monster who lies in the
    midst of his rivers,
  Who has said, 'My River*a* *is* my
    own;
  I have made *it* for myself.'
4 But I will put hooks in your jaws,
  And cause the fish of your rivers
    to stick to your scales;
  I will bring you up out of the
    midst of your rivers,
  And all the fish in your rivers will
    stick to your scales.
5 I will leave you in the wilderness,
  You and all the fish of your
    rivers;
  You shall fall on the open field;
  You shall not be picked up or
    gathered.*a*
  I have given you as food
  To the beasts of the field
  And to the birds of the heavens.

6 "Then all the inhabitants of
    Egypt
  Shall know that I *am* the LORD,
  Because they have been a staff of
    reed to the house of Israel.
7 When they took hold of you with
    the hand,
  You broke and tore all their
    shoulders;*a*
  When they leaned on you,
  You broke and made all their
    backs quiver."

8 'Therefore thus says the Lord GOD: "Surely I will bring a sword upon you and cut off from you man and beast.
9 "And the land of Egypt shall become desolate and waste; then they will know that I *am* the LORD, because he said, 'The River *is* mine, and I have made *it.*'
10 "Indeed, therefore, I *am* against you and against your rivers, and I will make the land of Egypt utterly waste and desolate, from Mig'dōl*a* *to* Sȳē'nē, as far as the border of Ethiopia.
11 "Neither foot of man shall pass through it nor foot of beast pass through it, and it shall be uninhabited forty years.
12 "I will make the land of Egypt desolate in the midst of the countries *that are* desolate; and among the cities *that are* laid waste, her cities shall be desolate forty years; and I will scatter the Egyptians among the nations and disperse them throughout the countries."
13 'Yet, thus says the Lord GOD: "At the end of forty years I will gather the Egyptians from the peoples among whom they were scattered.

29:3 *a*That is, the Nile   29:5 *a*Following Masoretic Text, Septuagint, and Vulgate; some Hebrew manuscripts and Targum read *buried.*
29:7 *a*Following Masoretic Text and Vulgate; Septuagint and Syriac read *hand.*   29:10 *a*Or *tower*

14 "I will bring back the captives of Egypt and cause them to return to the land of Path'ros, to the land of their origin, and there they shall be a lowly kingdom.
15 "It shall be the lowliest of kingdoms; it shall never again exalt itself above the nations, for I will diminish them so that they will not rule over the nations anymore.
16 "No longer shall it be the confidence of the house of Israel, but will remind them of *their* iniquity when they turned to follow them. Then they shall know that I *am* the Lord GOD." ' "

BABYLONIA WILL PLUNDER EGYPT

17 And it came to pass in the twenty-seventh year, in the first *month,* on the first *day* of the month, *that* the word of the LORD came to me, saying,
18 "Son of man, Ne·bū·chad·nez'zar king of Babylon caused his army to labor strenuously against Tȳre; every head *was* made bald, and every shoulder rubbed raw; yet neither he nor his army received wages from Tȳre, for the labor which they expended on it.
19 "Therefore thus says the Lord GOD: 'Surely I will give the land of Egypt to Ne·bū·chad·nez'zar king of Babylon; he shall take away her wealth, carry off her spoil, and remove her pillage; and that will be the wages for his army.
20 'I have given him the land of Egypt *for* his labor, because they worked for Me,' says the Lord GOD.
21 'In that day I will cause the horn of the house of Israel to spring forth, and I will open your mouth to speak in their midst. Then they shall know that I *am* the LORD.' "

EGYPT AND HER ALLIES WILL FALL

30 The word of the LORD came to me again, saying,
2 "Son of man, prophesy and say, 'Thus says the Lord GOD:

"Wail, 'Woe to the day!'
3 For the day *is* near,
Even the day of the LORD *is* near;
It will be a day of clouds, the time of the Gentiles.
4 The sword shall come upon Egypt,
And great anguish shall be in Ethiopia,
When the slain fall in Egypt,
And they take away her wealth,
And her foundations are broken down.

5 "Ethiopia, Lib'ya,*a* Lyd'i·a,*b* all the mingled people, Chub, and the men of the lands who are allied, shall fall with them by the sword."
6 'Thus says the LORD:

"Those who uphold Egypt shall fall,
And the pride of her power shall come down.
From Mig'dōl *to* Sȳ·ē'nē
Those within her shall fall by the sword,"
Says the Lord GOD.

7 "They shall be desolate in the midst of the desolate countries,
And her cities shall be in the midst of the cities *that are* laid waste.
8 Then they will know that I *am* the LORD,
When I have set a fire in Egypt
And all her helpers are destroyed.
9 On that day messengers shall go forth from Me in ships

30:5 *a*Hebrew *Put*   *b*Hebrew *Lud*

To make the careless Ethiopians
    afraid,
And great anguish shall come
    upon them,
As on the day of Egypt;
For indeed it is coming!"

10 'Thus says the Lord GOD:

"I will also make a multitude of
    Egypt to cease
By the hand of Ne·bu·chad·nez'zar
    king of Babylon.
11 He and his people with him, the
    most terrible of the nations,
Shall be brought to destroy the
    land;
They shall draw their swords
    against Egypt,
And fill the land with the slain.
12 I will make the rivers dry,
And sell the land into the hand of
    the wicked;
I will make the land waste, and
    all that is in it,
By the hand of aliens.
I, the LORD, have spoken."

13 'Thus says the Lord GOD:

"I will also destroy the idols,
And cause the images to cease
    from Noph;a
There shall no longer be princes
    from the land of Egypt;
I will put fear in the land of
    Egypt.
14 I will make Path'ros desolate,
Set fire to Zo'an,
And execute judgments in No.a
15 I will pour My fury on Sin,a the
    strength of Egypt;
I will cut off the multitude of No,
16 And set a fire in Egypt;
Sin shall have great pain,
No shall be split open,
And Noph *shall be in* distress
    daily.
17 The young men of A'vena and Pi

Be'seth shall fall by the sword,
And these *cities* shall go into
    captivity.
18 At Te·haph'ne·hesa the day shall
    also be darkened,b
When I break the yokes of Egypt
    there.
And her arrogant strength shall
    cease in her;
As for her, a cloud shall cover her,
And her daughters shall go into
    captivity.
19 Thus I will execute judgments on
    Egypt,
Then they shall know that I *am*
    the LORD."'"

PROCLAMATION AGAINST PHARAOH

20 And it came to pass in the
eleventh year, in the first *month,* on
the seventh *day* of the month, *that*
the word of the LORD came to me,
saying,
21 "Son of man, I have broken the
arm of Pharaoh king of Egypt; and
see, it has not been bandaged for
healing, nor a splint put on to bind it,
to make it strong enough to hold a
sword.
22 "Therefore thus says the Lord
GOD: 'Surely I *am* against Pharaoh
king of Egypt, and will break his
arms, both the strong one and the
one that was broken; and I will make
the sword fall out of his hand.
23 'I will scatter the Egyptians
among the nations, and disperse
them throughout the countries.
24 'I will strengthen the arms of the
king of Babylon and put My sword in
his hand; but I will break Pharaoh's
arms, and he will groan before him

30:13 aThat is, ancient Memphis   30:14 aThat
is, ancient Thebes   30:15 aThat is, ancient
Pelusium   30:17 aThat is, ancient On (Heliopolis)   30:18 aSpelled *Tahpanhes* in Jeremiah 43:7
and elsewhere   bFollowing many Hebrew manuscripts, Bomberg, Septuagint, Syriac, Targum, and
Vulgate; Masoretic Text reads *refrained.*

with the groanings of a mortally wounded *man.*

25 'Thus I will strengthen the arms of the king of Babylon, but the arms of Pharaoh shall fall down; they shall know that I *am* the LORD, when I put My sword into the hand of the king of Babylon and he stretches it out against the land of Egypt.

26 'I will scatter the Egyptians among the nations and disperse them throughout the countries. Then they shall know that I *am* the LORD.' "

EGYPT CUT DOWN LIKE
A GREAT TREE

31 Now it came to pass in the eleventh year, in the third *month,* on the first *day* of the month, *that* the word of the LORD came to me, saying,

2 "Son of man, say to Pharaoh king of Egypt and to his multitude:

'Whom are you like in your
　greatness?
3 Indeed Assyria *was* a cedar in
　Lebanon,
With fine branches that shaded
　the forest,
And of high stature;
And its top was among the thick
　boughs.
4 The waters made it grow;
Underground waters gave it
　height,
With their rivers running around
　the place where it was planted,
And sent out rivulets to all the
　trees of the field.

5 'Therefore its height was exalted
　above all the trees of the field;
Its boughs were multiplied,
And its branches became long
　because of the abundance of
　water,
As it sent them out.

6 All the birds of the heavens made
　their nests in its boughs;
Under its branches all the beasts
　of the field brought forth their
　young;
And in its shadow all great
　nations made their home.

7 'Thus it was beautiful in greatness
　and in the length of its
　branches,
Because its roots reached to
　abundant waters.
8 The cedars in the garden of God
　could not hide it;
The fir trees were not like its
　boughs,
And the chestnut*a* trees were not
　like its branches;
No tree in the garden of God was
　like it in beauty.
9 I made it beautiful with a
　multitude of branches,
So that all the trees of Eden
　envied it,
That *were* in the garden of God.'

10 "Therefore thus says the Lord GOD: 'Because you have increased in height, and it set its top among the thick boughs, and its heart was lifted up in its height,

11 'therefore I will deliver it into the hand of the mighty one of the nations, and he shall surely deal with it; I have driven it out for its wickedness.

12 'And aliens, the most terrible of the nations, have cut it down and left it; its branches have fallen on the mountains and in all the valleys; its boughs lie broken by all the rivers of the land; and all the peoples of the earth have gone from under its shadow and left it.

13 'On its ruin will remain all the
　birds of the heavens,

31:8 *a*Hebrew *armon*

And all the beasts of the field will come to its branches—

14 'So that no trees by the waters may ever again exalt themselves for their height, nor set their tops among the thick boughs, that no tree which drinks water may ever be high enough to reach up to them.

'For they have all been delivered
  to death,
To the depths of the earth,
Among the children of men who
  go down to the Pit.'

15 "Thus says the Lord GOD: 'In the day when it went down to hell, I caused mourning. I covered the deep because of it. I restrained its rivers, and the great waters were held back. I caused Lebanon to mourn for it, and all the trees of the field wilted because of it.
16 'I made the nations shake at the sound of its fall, when I cast it down to hell together with those who descend into the Pit; and all the trees of Eden, the choice and best of Lebanon, all that drink water, were comforted in the depths of the earth.
17 'They also went down to hell with it, with those *slain* by the sword; and *those who were* its *strong* arm dwelt in its shadows among the nations.
18 'To which of the trees in Eden will you then be likened in glory and greatness? Yet you shall be brought down with the trees of Eden to the depths of the earth; you shall lie in the midst of the uncircumcised, with *those* slain by the sword. This *is* Pharaoh and all his multitude,' says the Lord GOD."

LAMENTATION FOR PHARAOH
AND EGYPT

32 And it came to pass in the twelfth year, in the twelfth *month,* on the first *day* of the month, *that* the word of the LORD came to me, saying,
2 "Son of man, take up a lamentation for Pharaoh king of Egypt, and say to him:

'You are like a young lion among
  the nations,
And you *are* like a monster in the
  seas,
Bursting forth in your rivers,
Troubling the waters with your
  feet,
And fouling their rivers.'

3 "Thus says the Lord GOD:

'I will therefore spread My net
  over you with a company of
  many people,
And they will draw you up in My
  net.
4 Then I will leave you on the land;
I will cast you out on the open
  fields,
And cause to settle on you all the
  birds of the heavens.
And with you I will fill the beasts
  of the whole earth.
5 I will lay your flesh on the
  mountains,
And fill the valleys with your
  carcass.

6 'I will also water the land with the
  flow of your blood,
Even to the mountains;
And the riverbeds will be full of
  you.
7 When *I* put out your light,
I will cover the heavens, and
  make its stars dark;
I will cover the sun with a cloud,
And the moon shall not give her
  light.
8 All the bright lights of the
  heavens I will make dark over
  you,

And bring darkness upon your
 land,'
Says the Lord GOD.

9 'I will also trouble the hearts of
many peoples, when I bring your destruction among the nations, into the
countries which you have not known.
10 'Yes, I will make many peoples astonished at you, and their kings shall
be horribly afraid of you when I bran-
dish My sword before them; and they
shall tremble *every* moment, every
man for his own life, in the day of
your fall.'
11 "For thus says the Lord GOD: 'The
sword of the king of Babylon shall
come upon you.
12 'By the swords of the mighty warriors, all of them the most terrible of
the nations, I will cause your multitude to fall.

 'They shall plunder the pomp of
  Egypt,
 And all its multitude shall be
  destroyed.
13 Also I will destroy all its animals
 From beside its great waters;
 The foot of man shall muddy
  them no more,
 Nor shall the hooves of animals
  muddy them.
14 Then I will make their waters
  clear,
 And make their rivers run like
  oil,'
Says the Lord GOD.

15 'When I make the land of Egypt
  desolate,
 And the country is destitute of all
  that once filled it,
 When I strike all who dwell in it,
 Then they shall know that I *am*
  the LORD.

16 'This *is* the lamentation
 With which they shall lament her;

The daughters of the nations
 shall lament her;
They shall lament for her, for
 Egypt,
And for all her multitude,'
Says the Lord GOD."

EGYPT AND OTHERS CONSIGNED
TO THE PIT

17 It came to pass also in the twelfth
year, on the fifteenth *day* of the
month, *that* the word of the LORD
came to me, saying:

18 "Son of man, wail over the
 multitude of Egypt,
 And cast them down to the depths
  of the earth,
 Her and the daughters of the
  famous nations,
 With those who go down to the
  Pit:
19 'Whom do you surpass in beauty?
 Go down, be placed with the
  uncircumcised.'
20 "They shall fall in the midst of
 those slain by the sword;
 She is delivered to the sword,
 Drawing her and all her
  multitudes.
21 The strong among the mighty
 Shall speak to him out of the
  midst of hell
 With those who help him:
 'They have gone down,
 They lie with the uncircumcised,
  slain by the sword.'

22 "Assyria *is* there, and all her
  company,
 With their graves all around her,
 All of them slain, fallen by the
  sword.
23 Her graves are set in the recesses
  of the Pit,
 And her company is all around
  her grave,

All of them slain, fallen by the
sword,
Who caused terror in the land of
the living.

24 "There *is* Ē'lam and all her
multitude,
All around her grave,
All of them slain, fallen by the
sword,
Who have gone down
uncircumcised to the lower
parts of the earth,
Who caused their terror in the
land of the living;
Now they bear their shame with
those who go down to the Pit.
25 They have set her bed in the
midst of the slain,
With all her multitude,
With her graves all around it,
All of them uncircumcised, slain
by the sword;
Though their terror was caused
In the land of the living,
Yet they bear their shame
With those who go down to the
Pit;
It was put in the midst of the
slain.

26 "There *are* Mē'shech and Tū'bal
and all their multitudes,
With all their graves around it,
All of them uncircumcised, slain
by the sword,
Though they caused their terror
in the land of the living.
27 They do not lie with the mighty
Who are fallen of the
uncircumcised,
Who have gone down to hell with
their weapons of war;
They have laid their swords
under their heads,
But their iniquities will be on
their bones,
Because of the terror of the
mighty in the land of the living.

28 Yes, you shall be broken in the
midst of the uncircumcised,
And lie with *those* slain by the
sword.

29 "There *is* Ē'dom,
Her kings and all her princes,
Who despite their might
Are laid beside *those* slain by the
sword;
They shall lie with the
uncircumcised,
And with those who go down to
the Pit.
30 There *are* the princes of the
north,
All of them, and all the
Sī·dō'ni·ans,
Who have gone down with the
slain
In shame at the terror which they
caused by their might;
They lie uncircumcised with *those*
slain by the sword,
And bear their shame with those
who go down to the Pit.

31 "Pharaoh will see them
And be comforted over all his
multitude,
Pharaoh and all his army,
Slain by the sword,"
Says the Lord GOD.

32 "For I have caused My terror in
the land of the living;
And he shall be placed in the
midst of the uncircumcised
With *those* slain by the sword,
Pharaoh and all his multitude,"
Says the Lord GOD.

THE WATCHMAN AND HIS MESSAGE

33 Again the word of the LORD
came to me, saying,
2 "Son of man, speak to the children of your people, and say to them:

'When I bring the sword upon a land, and the people of the land take a man from their territory and make him their watchman,

3 'when he sees the sword coming upon the land, if he blows the trumpet and warns the people,

4 'then whoever hears the sound of the trumpet and does not take warning, if the sword comes and takes him away, his blood shall be on his *own* head.

5 'He heard the sound of the trumpet, but did not take warning; his blood shall be upon himself. But he who takes warning will save his life.

6 'But if the watchman sees the sword coming and does not blow the trumpet, and the people are not warned, and the sword comes and takes *any* person from among them, he is taken away in his iniquity; but his blood I will require at the watchman's hand.'

7 "So you, son of man: I have made you a watchman for the house of Israel; therefore you shall hear a word from My mouth and warn them for Me.

8 "When I say to the wicked, 'O wicked *man,* you shall surely die!' and you do not speak to warn the wicked from his way, that wicked *man* shall die in his iniquity; but his blood I will require at your hand.

9 "Nevertheless if you warn the wicked to turn from his way, and he does not turn from his way, he shall die in his iniquity; but you have delivered your soul.

10 "Therefore you, O son of man, say to the house of Israel: 'Thus you say, "If our transgressions and our sins *lie* upon us, and we pine away in them, how can we then live?" '

11 "Say to them: '*As* I live,' says the Lord GOD, 'I have no pleasure in the death of the wicked, but that the wicked turn from his way and live. Turn, turn from your evil ways! For why should you die, O house of Israel?'

THE FAIRNESS OF GOD'S JUDGMENT

12 "Therefore you, O son of man, say to the children of your people: 'The righteousness of the righteous man shall not deliver him in the day of his transgression; as for the wickedness of the wicked, he shall not fall because of it in the day that he turns from his wickedness; nor shall the righteous be able to live because of *his righteousness* in the day that he sins.'

13 "When I say to the righteous *that* he shall surely live, but he trusts in his own righteousness and commits iniquity, none of his righteous works shall be remembered; but because of the iniquity that he has committed, he shall die.

14 "Again, when I say to the wicked, 'You shall surely die,' if he turns from his sin and does what is lawful and right,

15 "*if* the wicked restores the pledge, gives back what he has stolen, and walks in the statutes of life without committing iniquity, he shall surely live; he shall not die.

16 "None of his sins which he has committed shall be remembered against him; he has done what is lawful and right; he shall surely live.

17 "Yet the children of your people say, 'The way of the LORD is not fair.' But it is their way which is not fair!

18 "When the righteous turns from his righteousness and commits iniquity, he shall die because of it.

19 "But when the wicked turns from his wickedness and does what is lawful and right, he shall live because of it.

20 "Yet you say, 'The way of the LORD is not fair.' O house of Israel, I will

judge every one of you according to his own ways.”

THE FALL OF JERUSALEM

21 And it came to pass in the twelfth year of our captivity, in the tenth *month,* on the fifth *day* of the month, *that* one who had escaped from Jerusalem came to me and said, “The city has been captured!”
22 Now the hand of the LORD had been upon me the evening before the man came who had escaped. And He had opened my mouth; so when he came to me in the morning, my mouth was opened, and I was no longer mute.

THE CAUSE OF JUDAH'S RUIN

23 Then the word of the LORD came to me, saying:
24 “Son of man, they who inhabit those ruins in the land of Israel are saying, ‘Abraham was only one, and he inherited the land. But we *are* many; the land has been given to us as a possession.’
25 “Therefore say to them, ‘Thus says the Lord GOD: “You eat *meat* with blood, you lift up your eyes toward your idols, and shed blood. Should you then possess the land?
26 “You rely on your sword, you commit abominations, and you defile one another's wives. Should you then possess the land?”’
27 “Say thus to them, ‘Thus says the Lord GOD: “*As* I live, surely those who *are* in the ruins shall fall by the sword, and the one who *is* in the open field I will give to the beasts to be devoured, and those who *are* in the strongholds and caves shall die of the pestilence.
28 “For I will make the land most desolate, her arrogant strength shall cease, and the mountains of Israel

shall be so desolate that no one will pass through.
29 “Then they shall know that I *am* the LORD, when I have made the land most desolate because of all their abominations which they have committed.”’

HEARING AND NOT DOING

30 “As for you, son of man, the children of your people are talking about you beside the walls and in the doors of the houses; and they speak to one another, everyone saying to his brother, ‘Please come and hear what the word is that comes from the LORD.’
31 “So they come to you as people do, they sit before you *as* My people, and they hear your words, but they do not do them; for with their mouth they show much love, *but* their hearts pursue their *own* gain.
32 “Indeed you *are* to them as a very lovely song of one who has a pleasant voice and can play well on an instrument; for they hear your words, but they do not do them.
33 “And when this comes to pass—surely it will come—then they will know that a prophet has been among them.”

IRRESPONSIBLE SHEPHERDS

34 And the word of the LORD came to me, saying,
2 “Son of man, prophesy against the shepherds of Israel, prophesy and say to them, ‘Thus says the Lord GOD to the shepherds: “Woe to the shepherds of Israel who feed themselves! Should not the shepherds feed the flocks?
3 “You eat the fat and clothe yourselves with the wool; you slaughter the fatlings, *but* you do not feed the flock.

4 "The weak you have not strengthened, nor have you healed those who were sick, nor bound up the broken, nor brought back what was driven away, nor sought what was lost; but with force and cruelty you have ruled them.

5 "So they were scattered because *there was* no shepherd; and they became food for all the beasts of the field when they were scattered.

6 "My sheep wandered through all the mountains, and on every high hill; yes, My flock was scattered over the whole face of the earth, and no one was seeking or searching *for them.*"

7 'Therefore, you shepherds, hear the word of the LORD:

8 "*As* I live," says the Lord GOD, "surely because My flock became a prey, and My flock became food for every beast of the field, because *there was* no shepherd, nor did My shepherds search for My flock, but the shepherds fed themselves and did not feed My flock"—

9 'therefore, O shepherds, hear the word of the LORD!

10 'Thus says the Lord GOD: "Behold, I *am* against the shepherds, and I will require My flock at their hand; I will cause them to cease feeding the sheep, and the shepherds shall feed themselves no more; for I will deliver My flock from their mouths, that they may no longer be food for them."

GOD, THE TRUE SHEPHERD

11 'For thus says the Lord GOD: "Indeed I Myself will search for My sheep and seek them out.

12 "As a shepherd seeks out his flock on the day he is among his scattered sheep, so will I seek out My sheep and deliver them from all the places where they were scattered on a cloudy and dark day.

13 "And I will bring them out from the peoples and gather them from the countries, and will bring them to their own land; I will feed them on the mountains of Israel, in the valleys and in all the inhabited places of the country.

14 "I will feed them in good pasture, and their fold shall be on the high mountains of Israel. There they shall lie down in a good fold and feed in rich pasture on the mountains of Israel.

15 "I will feed My flock, and I will make them lie down," says the Lord GOD.

16 "I will seek what was lost and bring back what was driven away, bind up the broken and strengthen what was sick; but I will destroy the fat and the strong, and feed them in judgment."

17 'And *as for* you, O My flock, thus says the Lord GOD: "Behold, I shall judge between sheep and sheep, between rams and goats.

18 "*Is it* too little for you to have eaten up the good pasture, that you must tread down with your feet the residue of your pasture—and to have drunk of the clear waters, that you must foul the residue with your feet?

19 "And *as for* My flock, they eat what you have trampled with your feet, and they drink what you have fouled with your feet."

20 'Therefore thus says the Lord GOD to them: "Behold, I Myself will judge between the fat and the lean sheep.

21 "Because you have pushed with side and shoulder, butted all the weak ones with your horns, and scattered them abroad,

22 "therefore I will save My flock, and they shall no longer be a prey; and I will judge between sheep and sheep.

23 "I will establish one shepherd over them, and he shall feed them—

My servant David. He shall feed them and be their shepherd.

24 "And I, the LORD, will be their God, and My servant David a prince among them; I, the LORD, have spoken.

25 "I will make a covenant of peace with them, and cause wild beasts to cease from the land; and they will dwell safely in the wilderness and sleep in the woods.

26 "I will make them and the places all around My hill a blessing; and I will cause showers to come down in their season; there shall be showers of blessing.

27 "Then the trees of the field shall yield their fruit, and the earth shall yield her increase. They shall be safe in their land; and they shall know that I *am* the LORD, when I have broken the bands of their yoke and delivered them from the hand of those who enslaved them.

28 "And they shall no longer be a prey for the nations, nor shall beasts of the land devour them; but they shall dwell safely, and no one shall make *them* afraid.

29 "I will raise up for them a garden of renown, and they shall no longer be consumed with hunger in the land, nor bear the shame of the Gentiles anymore.

30 "Thus they shall know that I, the LORD their God, *am* with them, and they, the house of Israel, *are* My people," says the Lord GOD.' "

31 "You are My flock, the flock of My pasture; you *are* men, *and* I *am* your God," says the Lord GOD.

JUDGMENT ON MOUNT SEIR

35 Moreover the word of the LORD came to me, saying,

2 "Son of man, set your face against Mount Sē′ir and prophesy against it,

3 "and say to it, 'Thus says the Lord GOD:

"Behold, O Mount Sē′ir, I *am*
    against you;
I will stretch out My hand against
    you,
And make you most desolate;
4 I shall lay your cities waste,
And you shall be desolate.
Then you shall know that I *am*
    the LORD.

5 "Because you have had an ancient hatred, and have shed *the blood of* the children of Israel by the power of the sword at the time of their calamity, *when* their iniquity *came to an* end,

6 "therefore, *as* I live," says the Lord GOD, "I will prepare you for blood, and blood shall pursue you; since you have not hated blood, therefore blood shall pursue you.

7 "Thus I will make Mount Sē′ir most desolate, and cut off from it the one who leaves and the one who returns.

8 "And I will fill its mountains with the slain; on your hills and in your valleys and in all your ravines those who are slain by the sword shall fall.

9 "I will make you perpetually desolate, and your cities shall be uninhabited; then you shall know that I *am* the LORD.

10 "Because you have said, 'These two nations and these two countries shall be mine, and we will possess them,' although the LORD was there,

11 "therefore, *as* I live," says the Lord GOD, "I will do according to your anger and according to the envy which you showed in your hatred against them; and I will make Myself known among them when I judge you.

12 "Then you shall know that I *am* the LORD. I have heard all your

blasphemies which you have spoken against the mountains of Israel, saying, 'They are desolate; they are given to us to consume.'

13 "Thus with your mouth you have boasted against Me and multiplied your words against Me; I have heard *them*."

14 'Thus says the Lord GOD: "The whole earth will rejoice when I make you desolate.

15 "As you rejoiced because the inheritance of the house of Israel was desolate, so I will do to you; you shall be desolate, O Mount Sē'ir, as well as all of Ē'dom—all of it! Then they shall know that I *am* the LORD." '

BLESSING ON ISRAEL

36 "And you, son of man, prophesy to the mountains of Israel, and say, 'O mountains of Israel, hear the word of the LORD!

2 'Thus says the Lord GOD: "Because the enemy has said of you, 'Aha! The ancient heights have become our possession,' " '

3 "therefore prophesy, and say, 'Thus says the Lord GOD: "Because they made *you* desolate and swallowed you up on every side, so that you became the possession of the rest of the nations, and you are taken up by the lips of talkers and slandered by the people"—

4 'therefore, O mountains of Israel, hear the word of the Lord GOD! Thus says the Lord GOD to the mountains, the hills, the rivers, the valleys, the desolate wastes, and the cities that have been forsaken, which became plunder and mockery to the rest of the nations all around—

5 'therefore thus says the Lord GOD: "Surely I have spoken in My burning jealousy against the rest of the nations and against all Ē'dom, who

gave My land to themselves as a possession, with wholehearted joy *and* spiteful minds, in order to plunder its open country." '

6 "Therefore prophesy concerning the land of Israel, and say to the mountains, the hills, the rivers, and the valleys, 'Thus says the Lord GOD: "Behold, I have spoken in My jealousy and My fury, because you have borne the shame of the nations."

7 'Therefore thus says the Lord GOD: "I have raised My hand in an oath that surely the nations that *are* around you shall bear their own shame.

8 "But you, O mountains of Israel, you shall shoot forth your branches and yield your fruit to My people Israel, for they are about to come.

9 "For indeed I *am* for you, and I will turn to you, and you shall be tilled and sown.

10 "I will multiply men upon you, all the house of Israel, all of it; and the cities shall be inhabited and the ruins rebuilt.

11 "I will multiply upon you man and beast; and they shall increase and bear young; I will make you inhabited as in former times, and do better *for you* than at your beginnings. Then you shall know that I *am* the LORD.

12 "Yes, I will cause men to walk on you, My people Israel; they shall take possession of you, and you shall be their inheritance; no more shall you bereave them *of children*."

13 'Thus says the Lord GOD: "Because they say to you, 'You devour men and bereave your nation *of children*,'

14 "therefore you shall devour men no more, nor bereave your nation anymore," says the Lord GOD.

15 "Nor will I let you hear the taunts of the nations anymore, nor bear the reproach of the peoples anymore, nor

shall you cause your nation to stumble anymore," says the Lord GOD.' "

THE RENEWAL OF ISRAEL

16 Moreover the word of the LORD came to me, saying:

17 "Son of man, when the house of Israel dwelt in their own land, they defiled it by their own ways and deeds; to Me their way was like the uncleanness of a woman in her customary impurity.

18 "Therefore I poured out My fury on them for the blood they had shed on the land, and for their idols *with which* they had defiled it.

19 "So I scattered them among the nations, and they were dispersed throughout the countries; I judged them according to their ways and their deeds.

20 "When they came to the nations, wherever they went, they profaned My holy name—when they said of them, 'These *are* the people of the LORD, *and* yet they have gone out of His land.'

21 "But I had concern for My holy name, which the house of Israel had profaned among the nations wherever they went.

22 "Therefore say to the house of Israel, 'Thus says the Lord GOD: "I do not do *this* for your sake, O house of Israel, but for My holy name's sake, which you have profaned among the nations wherever you went.

23 "And I will sanctify My great name, which has been profaned among the nations, which you have profaned in their midst; and the nations shall know that I *am* the LORD," says the Lord GOD, "when I am hallowed in you before their eyes.

24 "For I will take you from among the nations, gather you out of all countries, and bring you into your own land.

25 "Then I will sprinkle clean water on you, and you shall be clean; I will cleanse you from all your filthiness and from all your idols.

■ *Promises* ■

Ezekiel 36:26, 27

The next time you face troubles, would you like God with you? Would it be even better if God is *in* you? Here's a special promise from God. He will let His Spirit live in us and help us live the way we should. He will give us a new heart—a heart in tune with God Himself. Ask Him to do this. Ask Him to be *your* God and live within you.

---

26 "I will give you a new heart and put a new spirit within you; I will take the heart of stone out of your flesh and give you a heart of flesh.

27 "I will put My Spirit within you and cause you to walk in My statutes, and you will keep My judgments and do *them*.

28 "Then you shall dwell in the land that I gave to your fathers; you shall be My people, and I will be your God.

29 "I will deliver you from all your uncleannesses. I will call for the grain and multiply it, and bring no famine upon you.

30 "And I will multiply the fruit of your trees and the increase of your fields, so that you need never again bear the reproach of famine among the nations.

31 "Then you will remember your evil ways and your deeds that *were* not good; and you will loathe yourselves in your own sight, for your iniquities and your abominations.

32 "Not for your sake do I do *this*,"

says the Lord GOD, "let it be known to you. Be ashamed and confounded for your own ways, O house of Israel!"

33 'Thus says the Lord GOD: "On the day that I cleanse you from all your iniquities, I will also enable *you* to dwell in the cities, and the ruins shall be rebuilt.

34 "The desolate land shall be tilled instead of lying desolate in the sight of all who pass by.

35 "So they will say, 'This land that was desolate has become like the garden of Eden; and the wasted, desolate, and ruined cities *are now* fortified *and* inhabited.'

36 "Then the nations which are left all around you shall know that I, the LORD, have rebuilt the ruined places *and* planted what was desolate. I, the LORD, have spoken *it,* and I will do *it.*"

37 'Thus says the Lord GOD: "I will also let the house of Israel inquire of Me to do this for them: I will increase their men like a flock.

38 "Like a flock *offered as* holy *sacrifices,* like the flock at Jerusalem on its feast days, so shall the ruined cities be filled with flocks of men. Then they shall know that I *am* the LORD."'"

THE DRY BONES LIVE

37 The hand of the LORD came upon me and brought me out in the Spirit of the LORD, and set me down in the midst of the valley; and it *was* full of bones.

2 Then He caused me to pass by them all around, and behold, *there were* very many in the open valley; and indeed *they were* very dry.

3 And He said to me, "Son of man, can these bones live?" So I answered, "O Lord GOD, You know."

4 Again He said to me, "Prophesy to these bones, and say to them, 'O dry bones, hear the word of the LORD!

5 'Thus says the Lord GOD to these bones: "Surely I will cause breath to enter into you, and you shall live.

6 "I will put sinews on you and bring flesh upon you, cover you with skin and put breath in you; and you shall live. Then you shall know that I *am* the LORD."'"

7 So I prophesied as I was commanded; and as I prophesied, there was a noise, and suddenly a rattling; and the bones came together, bone to bone.

8 Indeed, as I looked, the sinews and the flesh came upon them, and the skin covered them over; but *there was* no breath in them.

9 Also He said to me, "Prophesy to the breath, prophesy, son of man, and say to the breath, 'Thus says the Lord GOD: "Come from the four winds, O breath, and breathe on these slain, that they may live."'"

10 So I prophesied as He commanded me, and breath came into them, and they lived, and stood upon their feet, an exceedingly great army.

11 Then He said to me, "Son of man, these bones are the whole house of Israel. They indeed say, 'Our bones are dry, our hope is lost, and we ourselves are cut off!'

12 "Therefore prophesy and say to them, 'Thus says the Lord GOD: "Behold, O My people, I will open your graves and cause you to come up from your graves, and bring you into the land of Israel.

13 "Then you shall know that I *am* the LORD, when I have opened your graves, O My people, and brought you up from your graves.

14 "I will put My Spirit in you, and you shall live, and I will place you in your own land. Then you shall know

that I, the LORD, have spoken *it* and performed *it*," says the LORD.'"

ONE KINGDOM, ONE KING

15 Again the word of the LORD came to me, saying,

16 "As for you, son of man, take a stick for yourself and write on it: 'For Judah and for the children of Israel, his companions.' Then take another stick and write on it, 'For Joseph, the stick of Ē'phra·im, and *for* all the house of Israel, his companions.'

17 "Then join them one to another for yourself into one stick, and they will become one in your hand.

18 "And when the children of your people speak to you, saying, 'Will you not show us what you *mean* by these?'—

19 "say to them, 'Thus says the Lord GOD: "Surely I will take the stick of Joseph, which *is* in the hand of Ē'phra·im, and the tribes of Israel, his companions; and I will join them with it, with the stick of Judah, and make them one stick, and they will be one in My hand."'

20 "And the sticks on which you write will be in your hand before their eyes.

21 "Then say to them, 'Thus says the Lord GOD: "Surely I will take the children of Israel from among the nations, wherever they have gone, and will gather them from every side and bring them into their own land;

22 "and I will make them one nation in the land, on the mountains of Israel; and one king shall be king over them all; they shall no longer be two nations, nor shall they ever be divided into two kingdoms again.

23 "They shall not defile themselves anymore with their idols, nor with their detestable things, nor with any of their transgressions; but I will deliver them from all their dwelling

places in which they have sinned, and will cleanse them. Then they shall be My people, and I will be their God.

24 "David My servant *shall be* king over them, and they shall all have one shepherd; they shall also walk in My judgments and observe My statutes, and do them.

25 "Then they shall dwell in the land that I have given to Jacob My servant, where your fathers dwelt; and they shall dwell there, they, their children, and their children's children, forever; and My servant David *shall be* their prince forever.

26 "Moreover I will make a covenant of peace with them, and it shall be an everlasting covenant with them; I will establish them and multiply them, and I will set My sanctuary in their midst forevermore.

27 "My tabernacle also shall be with them; indeed I will be their God, and they shall be My people.

28 "The nations also will know that I, the LORD, sanctify Israel, when My sanctuary is in their midst forevermore."'"

GOG AND ALLIES ATTACK ISRAEL

38 Now the word of the LORD came to me, saying,

2 "Son of man, set your face against Gog, of the land of Mā'gog, the prince of Rosh,*a* Mē'shech, and Tū'bal, and prophesy against him,

3 "and say, 'Thus says the Lord GOD: "Behold, I *am* against you, O Gog, the prince of Rosh, Mē'shech, and Tū'bal.

4 "I will turn you around, put hooks into your jaws, and lead you out, with all your army, horses, and horsemen, all splendidly clothed, a great com-

---

38:2 *a*Targum, Vulgate, and Aquila read *chief prince of* (also verse 3).

pany *with* bucklers and shields, all of them handling swords.

5 "Persia, Ethiopia,*a* and Lib'ya*b* are with them, all of them *with* shield and helmet;

6 "Gō'mer and all its troops; the house of Tō·gar'mah *from* the far north and all its troops—many people *are* with you.

7 "Prepare yourself and be ready, you and all your companies that are gathered about you; and be a guard for them.

8 "After many days you will be visited. In the latter years you will come into the land of those brought back from the sword *and* gathered from many people on the mountains of Israel, which had long been desolate; they were brought out of the nations, and now all of them dwell safely.

9 "You will ascend, coming like a storm, covering the land like a cloud, you and all your troops and many peoples with you."

10 'Thus says the Lord GOD: "On that day it shall come to pass *that* thoughts will arise in your mind, and you will make an evil plan:

11 "You will say, 'I will go up against a land of unwalled villages; I will go to a peaceful people, who dwell safely, all of them dwelling without walls, and having neither bars nor gates'—

12 "to take plunder and to take booty, to stretch out your hand against the waste places *that are* again inhabited, and against a people gathered from the nations, who have acquired livestock and goods, who dwell in the midst of the land.

13 "Shē'ba, Dē'dan, the merchants of Tar'shish, and all their young lions will say to you, 'Have you come to take plunder? Have you gathered your army to take booty, to carry away silver and gold, to take away livestock and goods, to take great plunder?' "'

14 "Therefore, son of man, prophesy and say to Gog, 'Thus says the Lord GOD: "On that day when My people Israel dwell safely, will you not know *it?*

15 "Then you will come from your place out of the far north, you and many peoples with you, all of them riding on horses, a great company and a mighty army.

16 "You will come up against My people Israel like a cloud, to cover the land. It will be in the latter days that I will bring you against My land, so that the nations may know Me, when I am hallowed in you, O Gog, before their eyes."

17 'Thus says the Lord GOD: "Are *you* he of whom I have spoken in former days by My servants the prophets of Israel, who prophesied for years in those days that I would bring you against them?

JUDGMENT ON GOG

18 "And it will come to pass at the same time, when Gog comes against the land of Israel," says the Lord GOD, "*that* My fury will show in My face.

19 "For in My jealousy *and* in the fire of My wrath I have spoken: 'Surely in that day there shall be a great earthquake in the land of Israel,

20 'so that the fish of the sea, the birds of the heavens, the beasts of the field, all creeping things that creep on the earth, and all men who *are* on the face of the earth shall shake at My presence. The mountains shall be thrown down, the steep places shall fall, and every wall shall fall to the ground.'

21 "I will call for a sword against Gog throughout all My mountains,"

38:5 *a*Hebrew *Cush*   *b*Hebrew *Put*

says the Lord GOD. "Every man's sword will be against his brother.

22 "And I will bring him to judgment with pestilence and bloodshed; I will rain down on him, on his troops, and on the many peoples who *are* with him, flooding rain, great hailstones, fire, and brimstone.

23 "Thus I will magnify Myself and sanctify Myself, and I will be known in the eyes of many nations. Then they shall know that I *am* the LORD." '

GOG'S ARMIES DESTROYED

39 "And you, son of man, prophesy against Gog, and say, 'Thus says the Lord GOD: "Behold, I *am* against you, O Gog, the prince of Rosh,*a* Mē'-shech, and Tū'bal;

2 "and I will turn you around and lead you on, bringing you up from the far north, and bring you against the mountains of Israel.

3 "Then I will knock the bow out of your left hand, and cause the arrows to fall out of your right hand.

4 "You shall fall upon the mountains of Israel, you and all your troops and the peoples who *are* with you; I will give you to birds of prey of every sort and *to* the beasts of the field to be devoured.

5 "You shall fall on the open field; for I have spoken," says the Lord GOD.

6 "And I will send fire on Mā'gog and on those who live in security in the coastlands. Then they shall know that I *am* the LORD.

7 "So I will make My holy name known in the midst of My people Israel, and I will not *let them* profane My holy name anymore. Then the nations shall know that *I am* the LORD, the Holy One in Israel.

8 "Surely it is coming, and it shall

be done," says the Lord GOD. "This *is* the day of which I have spoken.

9 "Then those who dwell in the cities of Israel will go out and set on fire and burn the weapons, both the shields and bucklers, the bows and arrows, the javelins and spears; and they will make fires with them for seven years.

10 "They will not take wood from the field nor cut down *any* from the forests, because they will make fires with the weapons; and they will plunder those who plundered them, and pillage those who pillaged them," says the Lord GOD.

THE BURIAL OF GOG

11 "It will come to pass in that day *that* I will give Gog a burial place there in Israel, the valley of those who pass by east of the sea; and it will obstruct travelers, because there they will bury Gog and all his multitude. Therefore they will call *it* the Valley of Hā'mon Gog.*a*

12 "For seven months the house of Israel will be burying them, in order to cleanse the land.

13 "Indeed all the people of the land will be burying, and they will gain renown for it on the day that I am glorified," says the Lord GOD.

14 "They will set apart men regularly employed, with the help of a search party,*a* to pass through the land and bury those bodies remaining on the ground, in order to cleanse it. At the end of seven months they will make a search.

15 "The search party will pass through the land; and *when anyone* sees a man's bone, he shall set up a marker by it, till the buriers have

39:1 *a*Targum, Vulgate and Aquila read *chief prince of.*   39:11 *a*Literally *The Multitude of Gog*
39:14 *a*Literally *those who pass through*

buried it in the Valley of Hā′mon Gog.

16 *"The* name of *the* city *will* also *be* Ha·mō′nah. Thus they shall cleanse the land."'

A TRIUMPHANT FESTIVAL

17 "And as for you, son of man, thus says the Lord GOD, 'Speak to every sort of bird and to every beast of the field:

"Assemble yourselves and come;
  Gather together from all sides to
    My sacrificial meal
Which I am sacrificing for you,
A great sacrificial meal on the
    mountains of Israel,
That you may eat flesh and drink
    blood.
18 You shall eat the flesh of the
    mighty,
Drink the blood of the princes of
    the earth,
Of rams and lambs,
Of goats and bulls,
All of them fatlings of Bā′shan.
19 You shall eat fat till you are full,
And drink blood till you are
    drunk,
At My sacrificial meal
Which I am sacrificing for you.
20 You shall be filled at My table
With horses and riders,
With mighty men
And with all the men of war,"
  says the Lord GOD.

ISRAEL RESTORED TO THE LAND

21 "I will set My glory among the nations; all the nations shall see My judgment which I have executed, and My hand which I have laid on them.
22 "So the house of Israel shall know that I *am* the LORD their God from that day forward.

23 "The Gentiles shall know that the house of Israel went into captivity for their iniquity; because they were unfaithful to Me, therefore I hid My face from them. I gave them into the hand of their enemies, and they all fell by the sword.
24 "According to their uncleanness and according to their transgressions I have dealt with them, and hidden My face from them."'
25 "Therefore thus says the Lord GOD: 'Now I will bring back the captives of Jacob, and have mercy on the whole house of Israel; and I will be jealous for My holy name—
26 'after they have borne their shame, and all their unfaithfulness in which they were unfaithful to Me, when they dwelt safely in their *own* land and no one made *them* afraid.
27 'When I have brought them back from the peoples and gathered them out of their enemies' lands, and I am hallowed in them in the sight of many nations,
28 'then they shall know that I *am* the LORD their God, who sent them into captivity among the nations, but also brought them back to their land, and left none of them captive any longer.
29 'And I will not hide My face from them anymore; for I shall have poured out My Spirit on the house of Israel,' says the Lord GOD."

A NEW CITY, A NEW TEMPLE

40 In the twenty-fifth year of our captivity, at the beginning of the year, on the tenth *day* of the month, in the fourteenth year after the city was captured, on the very same day the hand of the LORD was upon me; and He took me there.
2 In the visions of God He took me into the land of Israel and set me on

a very high mountain; on it toward the south *was* something like the structure of a city.

3 He took me there, and behold, *there was* a man whose appearance *was* like the appearance of bronze. He had a line of flax and a measuring rod in his hand, and he stood in the gateway.

4 And the man said to me, "Son of man, look with your eyes and hear with your ears, and fix your mind on everything I show you; for you *were* brought here so that I might show *them* to you. Declare to the house of Israel everything you see."

5 Now there was a wall all around the outside of the temple.*a* In the man's hand was a measuring rod six cubits *long, each being a* cubit and a handbreadth; and he measured the width of the wall structure, one rod; and the height, one rod.

THE EASTERN GATEWAY
OF THE TEMPLE

6 Then he went to the gateway which faced east; and he went up its stairs and measured the threshold of the gateway, *which was* one rod wide, and the other threshold *was* one rod wide.

7 Each gate chamber *was* one rod long and one rod wide; between the gate chambers *was a space of* five cubits; and the threshold of the gateway by the vestibule of the inside gate *was* one rod.

8 He also measured the vestibule of the inside gate, one rod.

9 Then he measured the vestibule of the gateway, eight cubits; and the gateposts, two cubits. The vestibule of the gate *was* on the inside.

10 In the eastern gateway *were* three gate chambers on one side and three on the other; the three *were* all the same size; also the gateposts were of the same size on this side and that side.

11 He measured the width of the entrance to the gateway, ten cubits; *and* the length of the gate, thirteen cubits.

12 *There was* a space in front of the gate chambers, one cubit *on this side* and one cubit on that side; the gate chambers *were* six cubits on this side and six cubits on that side.

13 Then he measured the gateway from the roof of *one* gate chamber to the roof of the other; the width *was* twenty-five cubits, as door faces door.

14 He measured the gateposts, sixty cubits high, and the court all around the gateway *extended* to the gatepost.

15 *From* the front of the entrance gate to the front of the vestibule of the inner gate *was* fifty cubits.

16 *There were* beveled window *frames* in the gate chambers and in their intervening archways on the inside of the gateway all around, and likewise in the vestibules. *There were* windows all around on the inside. And on each gatepost *were* palm trees.

THE OUTER COURT

17 Then he brought me into the outer court; and *there were* chambers and a pavement made all around the court; thirty chambers faced the pavement.

18 The pavement was by the side of the gateways, corresponding to the length of the gateways; *this was* the lower pavement.

19 Then he measured the width from the front of the lower gateway to the front of the inner court exterior, one hundred cubits toward the east and the north.

40:5 *a*Literally *house,* and so elsewhere in this book

THE NORTHERN GATEWAY

20 On the outer court was also a gateway facing north, and he measured its length and its width.
21 Its gate chambers, three on this side and three on that side, its gateposts and its archways, had the same measurements as the first gate; its length *was* fifty cubits and its width twenty-five cubits.
22 Its windows and those of its archways, and also its palm trees, *had* the same measurements as the gateway facing east; it was ascended by seven steps, and its archway *was* in front of it.
23 A gate of the inner court was opposite the northern gateway, just as the eastern *gateway;* and he measured from gateway to gateway, one hundred cubits.

THE SOUTHERN GATEWAY

24 After that he brought me toward the south, and there a gateway was facing south; and he measured its gateposts and archways according to these same measurements.
25 *There were* windows in it and in its archways all around like those windows; its length *was* fifty cubits and its width twenty-five cubits.
26 Seven steps led up to it, and its archway *was* in front of them; and it had palm trees on its gateposts, one on this side and one on that side.
27 *There was* also a gateway on the inner court, facing south; and he measured from gateway to gateway toward the south, one hundred cubits.

GATEWAYS OF THE INNER COURT

28 Then he brought me to the inner court through the southern gateway; he measured the southern gateway according to these same measurements.
29 Also its gate chambers, its gateposts, and its archways *were* according to these same measurements; *there were* windows in it and in its archways all around; *it was* fifty cubits long and twenty-five cubits wide.
30 *There were* archways all around, twenty-five cubits long and five cubits wide.
31 Its archways faced the outer court, palm trees *were* on its gateposts, and going up to it *were* eight steps.
32 And he brought me into the inner court facing east; he measured the gateway according to these same measurements.
33 Also its gate chambers, its gateposts, and its archways *were* according to these same measurements; and *there were* windows in it and in its archways all around; *it was* fifty cubits long and twenty-five cubits wide.
34 Its archways faced the outer court, and palm trees *were* on its gateposts on this side and on that side; and going up to it *were* eight steps.
35 Then he brought me to the north gateway and measured *it* according to these same measurements—
36 also its gate chambers, its gateposts, and its archways. It had windows all around; its length *was* fifty cubits and its width twenty-five cubits.
37 Its gateposts faced the outer court, palm trees *were* on its gateposts on this side and on that side, and going up to it *were* eight steps.

WHERE SACRIFICES WERE PREPARED

38 *There was* a chamber and its entrance by the gateposts of the gateway, where they washed the burnt offering.

39 In the vestibule of the gateway *were* two tables on this side and two tables on that side, on which to slay the burnt offering, the sin offering, and the trespass offering.

40 At the outer side of the vestibule, as one goes up to the entrance of the northern gateway, *were* two tables; and on the other side of the vestibule of the gateway *were* two tables.

41 Four tables *were* on this side and four tables on that side, by the side of the gateway, eight tables on which they slaughtered *the sacrifices.*

42 *There were* also four tables of hewn stone for the burnt offering, one cubit and a half long, one cubit and a half wide, and one cubit high; on these they laid the instruments with which they slaughtered the burnt offering and the sacrifice.

43 Inside *were* hooks, a handbreadth wide, fastened all around; and the flesh of the sacrifices *was* on the tables.

CHAMBERS FOR SINGERS AND PRIESTS

44 Outside the inner gate *were* the chambers for the singers in the inner court, one facing south at the side of the northern gateway, and the other facing north at the side of the southern gateway.

45 Then he said to me, "This chamber which faces south *is* for the priests who have charge of the temple.

46 "The chamber which faces north *is* for the priests who have charge of the altar; these *are* the sons of Zā'-dok, from the sons of Levi, who come near the LORD to minister to Him."

DIMENSIONS OF THE INNER COURT AND VESTIBULE

47 And he measured the court, one hundred cubits long and one hundred cubits wide, foursquare. The altar *was* in front of the temple.

48 Then he brought me to the vestibule of the temple and measured the doorposts of the vestibule, five cubits on this side and five cubits on that side; and the width of the gateway was three cubits on this side and three cubits on that side.

49 The length of the vestibule *was* twenty cubits, and the width eleven cubits; and by the steps which led up to it *there were* pillars by the doorposts, one on this side and another on that side.

DIMENSIONS OF THE SANCTUARY

41 Then he brought me into the sanctuary*a* and measured the doorposts, six cubits wide on one side and six cubits wide on the other side—the width of the tabernacle.

2 The width of the entryway *was* ten cubits, and the side walls of the entrance *were* five cubits on this side and five cubits on the other side; and he measured its length, forty cubits, and its width, twenty cubits.

3 Also he went inside and measured the doorposts, two cubits; and the entrance, six cubits *high;* and the width of the entrance, seven cubits.

4 He measured the length, twenty cubits; and the width, twenty cubits, beyond the sanctuary; and he said to me, "This *is* the Most Holy *Place.*"

THE SIDE CHAMBERS ON THE WALL

5 Next, he measured the wall of the temple, six cubits. The width of each side chamber all around the temple *was* four cubits on every side.

6 The side chambers *were* in three

41:1 *a*Hebrew *heykal,* here the main room of the temple, sometimes called the *holy place* (compare Exodus 26:33)

stories, one above the other, thirty chambers in each story; they rested on ledges which *were* for the side chambers all around, that they might be supported, but not fastened to the wall of the temple.

7 As one went up from story to story, the side chambers became wider all around, because their supporting ledges in the wall of the temple ascended like steps; therefore the width of the structure increased as one went up *from* the lowest *story* to the highest by way of the middle one.

8 I also saw an elevation all around the temple; it was the foundation of the side chambers, a full rod, *that is,* six cubits *high.*

9 The thickness of the outer wall of the side chambers *was* five cubits, and so also the remaining terrace by the place of the side chambers of the temple.

10 And between *it and* the *wall* chambers was a width of twenty cubits all around the temple on every side.

11 The doors of the side chambers opened on the terrace, one door toward the north and another toward the south; and the width of the terrace *was* five cubits all around.

THE BUILDING AT THE WESTERN END

12 The building that faced the separating courtyard at its western end *was* seventy cubits wide; the wall of the building *was* five cubits thick all around, and its length ninety cubits.

DIMENSIONS AND DESIGN OF THE TEMPLE AREA

13 So he measured the temple, one hundred cubits long; and the separating courtyard with the building and its walls *was* one hundred cubits long;

14 also the width of the eastern face of the temple, including the separating courtyard, *was* one hundred cubits.

15 He measured the length of the building behind it, facing the separating courtyard, with its galleries on the one side and on the other side, one hundred cubits, as well as the inner temple and the porches of the court,

16 their doorposts and the beveled window frames. And the galleries all around their three stories opposite the threshold were paneled with wood from the ground to the windows—the windows were covered—

17 from the space above the door, even to the inner room,*a* as well as outside, and on every wall all around, inside and outside, by measure.

18 And *it was* made with cherubim and palm trees, a palm tree between cherub and cherub. *Each* cherub had two faces,

19 so that the face of a man *was* toward a palm tree on one side, and the face of a young lion toward a palm tree on the other side; thus *it was* made throughout the temple all around.

20 From the floor to the space above the door, and on the wall of the sanctuary, cherubim and palm trees *were* carved.

21 The doorposts of the temple *were* square, *as was* the front of the sanctuary; their appearance was similar.

22 The altar *was* of wood, three cubits high, and its length two cubits. Its corners, its length, and its sides *were* of wood; and he said to me, "This *is* the table that *is* before the LORD."

23 The temple and the sanctuary had two doors.

24 The doors had two panels *apiece,*

41:17 *a*Literally *house,* here *the Most Holy Place*

two folding panels: two *panels* for one door and two panels for the other *door.*

25 Cherubim and palm trees *were* carved on the doors of the temple just as they *were* carved on the walls. A wooden canopy *was* on the front of the vestibule outside.

26 *There were* beveled window *frames* and palm trees on one side and on the other, on the sides of the vestibule—also on the side chambers of the temple and on the canopies.

THE CHAMBERS FOR THE PRIESTS

42 Then he brought me out into the outer court, by the way toward the north; and he brought me into the chamber which *was* opposite the separating courtyard, and which *was* opposite the building toward the north.

2 Facing the length, *which was* one hundred cubits (the width was fifty cubits), was the north door.

3 Opposite the inner court of twenty *cubits,* and opposite the pavement of the outer court, *was* gallery against gallery in three *stories.*

4 In front of the chambers, toward the inside, *was* a walk ten cubits wide, at a distance of one cubit; and their doors faced north.

5 Now the upper chambers *were* shorter, because the galleries took away *space* from them more than from the lower and middle stories of the building.

6 For they *were* in three *stories* and did not have pillars like the pillars of the courts; therefore *the upper level* was shortened more than the lower and middle levels from the ground up.

7 And a wall which *was* outside ran parallel to the chambers, at the front of the chambers, toward the outer court; its length *was* fifty cubits.

8 The length of the chambers toward the outer court *was* fifty cubits, whereas that facing the temple *was* one hundred cubits.

9 At the lower chambers *was* the entrance on the east side, as one goes into them from the outer court.

10 Also *there were* chambers in the thickness of the wall of the court toward the east, opposite the separating courtyard and opposite the building.

11 *There was* a walk in front of them also, and their appearance *was* like the chambers which *were* toward the north; they *were* as long and as wide as the others, and all their exits and entrances *were* according to plan.

12 And corresponding to the doors of the chambers that *were* facing south, as one enters them, *there was* a door in front of the walk, the way directly in front of the wall toward the east.

13 Then he said to me, "The north chambers *and* the south chambers, which *are* opposite the separating courtyard, *are* the holy chambers where the priests who approach the LORD shall eat the most holy offerings. There they shall lay the most holy offerings—the grain offering, the sin offering, and the trespass offering—for the place *is* holy.

14 "When the priests enter them, they shall not go out of the holy *chamber* into the outer court; but there they shall leave their garments in which they minister, for they *are* holy. They shall put on other garments; then they may approach *that* which *is* for the people."

OUTER DIMENSIONS OF THE TEMPLE

15 Now when he had finished measuring the inner temple, he brought me out through the gateway that faces toward the east, and measured it all around.

16 He measured the east side with the measuring rod,*a* five hundred rods by the measuring rod all around.
17 He measured the north side, five hundred rods by the measuring rod all around.
18 He measured the south side, five hundred rods by the measuring rod.
19 He came around to the west side *and* measured five hundred rods by the measuring rod.
20 He measured it on the four sides; it had a wall all around, five hundred *cubits* long and five hundred wide, to separate the holy areas from the common.

THE TEMPLE, THE LORD'S DWELLING PLACE

43 Afterward he brought me to the gate, the gate that faces toward the east.
2 And behold, the glory of the God of Israel came from the way of the east. His voice *was* like the sound of many waters; and the earth shone with His glory.
3 *It was* like the appearance of the vision which I saw—like the vision which I saw when I*a* came to destroy the city. The visions *were* like the vision which I saw by the River Chē'-bar; and I fell on my face.
4 And the glory of the LORD came into the temple by way of the gate which faces toward the east.
5 The Spirit lifted me up and brought me into the inner court; and behold, the glory of the LORD filled the temple.
6 Then I heard *Him* speaking to me from the temple, while a man stood beside me.
7 And He said to me, "Son of man, *this is* the place of My throne and the place of the soles of My feet, where I will dwell in the midst of the children of Israel forever. No more shall the house of Israel defile My holy name, they nor their kings, by their harlotry or with the carcasses of their kings on their high places.
8 "When they set their threshold by My threshold, and their doorpost by My doorpost, with a wall between them and Me, they defiled My holy name by the abominations which they committed; therefore I have consumed them in My anger.
9 "Now let them put their harlotry and the carcasses of their kings far away from Me, and I will dwell in their midst forever.
10 "Son of man, describe the temple to the house of Israel, that they may be ashamed of their iniquities; and let them measure the pattern.
11 "And if they are ashamed of all that they have done, make known to them the design of the temple and its arrangement, its exits and its entrances, its entire design and all its ordinances, all its forms and all its laws. Write *it* down in their sight, so that they may keep its whole design and all its ordinances, and perform them.
12 "This *is* the law of the temple: The whole area surrounding the mountaintop *is* most holy. Behold, this *is* the law of the temple.

DIMENSIONS OF THE ALTAR

13 "These are the measurements of the altar in cubits (the *cubit is* one cubit and a handbreadth): the base one cubit high and one cubit wide, with a rim all around its edge of one span. This *is* the height of the altar:
14 "from the base on the ground to the lower ledge, two cubits; the width of the ledge, one cubit; from the smaller ledge to the larger ledge, four

---

42:16 *a*Compare 40:5   43:3 *a*Some Hebrew manuscripts and Vulgate read *He*.

OFFERING Ezekiel 43:24–27

What Will You Give in Your Offering?

What do you put in the offering at church or Sunday school? Most people put money. But in Bible times people often gave an animal for an offering. Sometimes they called it a sacrifice. This animal could not be just any old animal. It had to be perfect, the very best animal that they had. Do you think God still wants our best?

1. Do you give God the best time each day? Do you pray when you're feeling your best or when you're dead tired? Do you spend your best time watching TV?
2. Do you give God your best talents? If you do something very well, do you do it for God?
3. Do you give God only the money you don't need? Or do you give Him money you would really like to keep?

For more on *Favorite Bible Words* turn to page 1348
For more on *Giving* turn to page 1564

cubits; and the width of the ledge, *one* cubit.

15 "The altar hearth *is* four cubits high, with four horns extending upward from the hearth.

16 "The altar hearth *is* twelve cubits long, twelve wide, square at its four corners;

17 "the ledge, fourteen *cubits* long and fourteen wide on its four sides, with a rim of half a cubit around it; its base, one cubit all around; and its steps face toward the east."

CONSECRATING THE ALTAR

18 And He said to me, "Son of man, thus says the Lord GOD: 'These *are* the ordinances for the altar on the day when it is made, for sacrificing burnt offerings on it, and for sprinkling blood on it.

19 'You shall give a young bull for a sin offering to the priests, the Lē′vites, who are of the seed of Zā′dok,

who approach Me to minister to Me,' says the Lord GOD.

20 'You shall take some of its blood and put *it* on the four horns of the altar, on the four corners of the ledge, and on the rim around it; thus you shall cleanse it and make atonement for it.

21 'Then you shall also take the bull of the sin offering, and burn it in the appointed place of the temple, outside the sanctuary.

22 'On the second day you shall offer a kid of the goats without blemish for a sin offering; and they shall cleanse the altar, as they cleansed *it* with the bull.

23 'When you have finished cleansing *it,* you shall offer a young bull without blemish, and a ram from the flock without blemish.

24 'When you offer them before the LORD, the priests shall throw salt on them, and they will offer them up *as* a burnt offering to the LORD.

25 'Every day for seven days you shall prepare a goat *for* a sin offering; they shall also prepare a young bull and a ram from the flock, both without blemish.
26 'Seven days they shall make atonement for the altar and purify it, and so consecrate *it*.
27 'When these days are over it shall be, on the eighth day and thereafter, that the priests shall offer your burnt offerings and your peace offerings on the altar; and I will accept you,' says the Lord GOD."

THE EAST GATE AND THE PRINCE

44 Then He brought me back to the outer gate of the sanctuary which faces toward the east, but it *was* shut.
2 And the LORD said to me, "This gate shall be shut; it shall not be opened, and no man shall enter by it, because the LORD God of Israel has entered by it; therefore it shall be shut.
3 "*As for* the prince, *because* he *is* the prince, he may sit in it to eat bread before the LORD; he shall enter by way of the vestibule of the gateway, and go out the same way."

THOSE ADMITTED TO THE TEMPLE

4 Also He brought me by way of the north gate to the front of the temple; so I looked, and behold, the glory of the LORD filled the house of the LORD; and I fell on my face.
5 And the LORD said to me, "Son of man, mark well, see with your eyes and hear with your ears, all that I say to you concerning all the ordinances of the house of the LORD and all its laws. Mark well who may enter the house and all who go out from the sanctuary.

6 "Now say to the rebellious, to the house of Israel, 'Thus says the Lord GOD: "O house of Israel, let Us have no more of all your abominations.
7 "When you brought in foreigners, uncircumcised in heart and uncircumcised in flesh, to be in My sanctuary to defile it—My house—and when you offered My food, the fat and the blood, then they broke My covenant because of all your abominations.
8 "And you have not kept charge of My holy things, but you have set *others* to keep charge of My sanctuary for you."
9 'Thus says the Lord GOD: "No foreigner, uncircumcised in heart or uncircumcised in flesh, shall enter My sanctuary, including any foreigner who *is* among the children of Israel.

LAWS GOVERNING PRIESTS

10 "And the Lē′vītes who went far from Me, when Israel went astray, who strayed away from Me after their idols, they shall bear their iniquity.
11 "Yet they shall be ministers in My sanctuary, *as* gatekeepers of the house and ministers of the house; they shall slay the burnt offering and the sacrifice for the people, and they shall stand before them to minister to them.
12 "Because they ministered to them before their idols and caused the house of Israel to fall into iniquity, therefore I have raised My hand in an oath against them," says the Lord GOD, "that they shall bear their iniquity.
13 "And they shall not come near Me to minister to Me as priest, nor come near any of My holy things, nor into the Most Holy *Place;* but they shall bear their shame and their abominations which they have committed.

14 "Nevertheless I will make them keep charge of the temple, for all its work, and for all that has to be done in it.

15 "But the priests, the Lē′vītes, the sons of Zā′dok, who kept charge of My sanctuary when the children of Israel went astray from Me, they shall come near Me to minister to Me; and they shall stand before Me to offer to Me the fat and the blood," says the Lord GOD.

16 "They shall enter My sanctuary, and they shall come near My table to minister to Me, and they shall keep My charge.

17 "And it shall be, whenever they enter the gates of the inner court, that they shall put on linen garments; no wool shall come upon them while they minister within the gates of the inner court or within the house.

18 "They shall have linen turbans on their heads and linen trousers on their bodies; they shall not clothe themselves with *anything that causes* sweat.

19 "When they go out to the outer court, to the *outer* court to the people, they shall take off their garments in which they have ministered, leave them in the holy chambers, and put on other garments; and in their holy garments they shall not sanctify the people.

20 "They shall neither shave their heads nor let their hair grow long, but they shall keep their hair well trimmed.

21 "No priest shall drink wine when he enters the inner court.

22 "They shall not take as wife a widow or a divorced woman, but take virgins of the descendants of the house of Israel, or widows of priests.

23 "And they shall teach My people *the difference* between the holy and the unholy, and cause them to discern between the unclean and the clean.

24 "In controversy they shall stand as judges, *and* judge it according to My judgments. They shall keep My laws and My statutes in all My appointed meetings, and they shall hallow My Sabbaths.

25 "They shall not defile *themselves* by coming near a dead person. Only for father or mother, for son or daughter, for brother or unmarried sister may they defile themselves.

26 "After he is cleansed, they shall count seven days for him.

27 "And on the day that he goes to the sanctuary to minister in the sanctuary, he must offer his sin offering in the inner court," says the Lord GOD.

28 "It shall be, in regard to their inheritance, *that* I *am* their inheritance. You shall give them no possession in Israel, for I *am* their possession.

29 "They shall eat the grain offering, the sin offering, and the trespass offering; every dedicated thing in Israel shall be theirs.

30 "The best of all firstfruits of any kind, and every sacrifice of any kind from all your sacrifices, shall be the priest's; also you shall give to the priest the first of your ground meal, to cause a blessing to rest on your house.

31 "The priests shall not eat anything, bird or beast, that died naturally or was torn *by wild beasts*.

THE HOLY DISTRICT

45 "Moreover, when you divide the land by lot into inheritance, you shall set apart a district for the LORD, a holy section of the land; its length

shall be twenty-five thousand *cubits,* and the width ten thousand. It *shall be* holy throughout its territory all around.

2　"Of this there shall be a square plot for the sanctuary, five hundred by five hundred *rods,* with fifty cubits around it for an open space.

3　"So this is the district you shall measure: twenty-five thousand *cubits* long and ten thousand wide; in it shall be the sanctuary, the Most Holy *Place.*

4　"It shall be a holy *section* of the land, belonging to the priests, the ministers of the sanctuary, who come near to minister to the LORD; it shall be a place for their houses and a holy place for the sanctuary.

5　"*An area* twenty-five thousand *cubits* long and ten thousand wide shall belong to the Lē′vītes, the ministers of the temple; they shall have twenty chambers as a possession.*a*

PROPERTIES OF THE CITY AND THE PRINCE

6　"You shall appoint as the property of the city *an area* five thousand *cubits* wide and twenty-five thousand long, adjacent to the district of the holy *section;* it shall belong to the whole house of Israel.

7　"The prince shall have *a section* on one side and the other of the holy district and the city's property; and bordering on the holy district and the city's property, extending westward on the west side and eastward on the east side, the length *shall be* side by side with one of the *tribal* portions, from the west border to the east border.

8　"The land shall be his possession in Israel; and My princes shall no more oppress My people, but they shall give *the rest of* the land to the house of Israel, according to their tribes."

LAWS GOVERNING THE PRINCE

9　'Thus says the Lord GOD: "Enough, O princes of Israel! Remove violence and plundering, execute justice and righteousness, and stop dispossessing My people," says the Lord GOD.

10　"You shall have honest scales, an honest ephah, and an honest bath.

11　"The ephah and the bath shall be of the same measure, so that the bath contains one-tenth of a homer, and the ephah one-tenth of a homer; their measure shall be according to the homer.

12　"The shekel *shall be* twenty gerahs; twenty shekels, twenty-five shekels, *and* fifteen shekels shall be your mina.

13　"This *is* the offering which you shall offer: you shall give one-sixth of an ephah from a homer of wheat, and one-sixth of an ephah from a homer of barley.

14　"The ordinance concerning oil, the bath of oil, *is* one-tenth of a bath from a kor. A kor *is* a homer or ten baths, for ten baths *are* a homer.

15　"And one lamb shall be given from a flock of two hundred, from the rich pastures of Israel. These shall be for grain offerings, burnt offerings, and peace offerings, to make atonement for them," says the Lord GOD.

16　"All the people of the land shall give this offering for the prince in Israel.

17　"Then it shall be the prince's part *to give* burnt offerings, grain offerings, and drink offerings, at the

---

45:5 *a*Following Masoretic Text, Targum, and Vulgate; Septuagint reads *a possession, cities of dwelling.*

feasts, the New Moons, the Sabbaths, and at all the appointed seasons of the house of Israel. He shall prepare the sin offering, the grain offering, the burnt offering, and the peace offerings to make atonement for the house of Israel."

KEEPING THE FEASTS

18 'Thus says the Lord GOD: "In the first *month,* on the first *day* of the month, you shall take a young bull without blemish and cleanse the sanctuary.

19 "The priest shall take some of the blood of the sin offering and put *it* on the doorposts of the temple, on the four corners of the ledge of the altar, and on the gateposts of the gate of the inner court.

20 "And so you shall do on the seventh *day* of the month for everyone who has sinned unintentionally or in ignorance. Thus you shall make atonement for the temple.

21 "In the first *month,* on the fourteenth day of the month, you shall observe the Passover, a feast of seven days; unleavened bread shall be eaten.

22 "And on that day the prince shall prepare for himself and for all the people of the land a bull *for* a sin offering.

23 "On the seven days of the feast he shall prepare a burnt offering to the LORD, seven bulls and seven rams without blemish, daily for seven days, and a kid of the goats daily *for* a sin offering.

24 "And he shall prepare a grain offering of one ephah for each bull and one ephah for each ram, together with a hin of oil for each ephah.

25 "In the seventh *month,* on the fifteenth day of the month, at the feast, he shall do likewise for seven days, according to the sin offering, the burnt offering, the grain offering, and the oil."

THE MANNER OF WORSHIP

46 'Thus says the Lord GOD: "The gateway of the inner court that faces toward the east shall be shut the six working days; but on the Sabbath it shall be opened, and on the day of the New Moon it shall be opened.

2 "The prince shall enter by way of the vestibule of the gateway from the outside, and stand by the gatepost. The priests shall prepare his burnt offering and his peace offerings. He shall worship at the threshold of the gate. Then he shall go out, but the gate shall not be shut until evening.

3 "Likewise the people of the land shall worship at the entrance to this gateway before the LORD on the Sabbaths and the New Moons.

4 "The burnt offering that the prince offers to the LORD on the Sabbath day *shall be* six lambs without blemish, and a ram without blemish;

5 "and the grain offering *shall be* one ephah for a ram, and the grain offering for the lambs, as much as he wants to give, as well as a hin of oil with every ephah.

6 "On the day of the New Moon *it shall be* a young bull without blemish, six lambs, and a ram; they shall be without blemish.

7 "He shall prepare a grain offering of an ephah for a bull, an ephah for a ram, as much as he wants to give for the lambs, and a hin of oil with every ephah.

8 "When the prince enters, he shall go in by way of the vestibule of the gateway, and go out the same way.

9 "But when the people of the land come before the LORD on the appointed feast days, whoever enters by way of the north gate to worship

shall go out by way of the south gate; and whoever enters by way of the south gate shall go out by way of the north gate. He shall not return by way of the gate through which he came, but shall go out through the opposite gate.

10 "The prince shall then be in their midst. When they go in, he shall go in; and when they go out, he shall go out.

11 "At the festivals and the appointed feast days the grain offering shall be an ephah for a bull, an ephah for a ram, as much as he wants to give for the lambs, and a hin of oil with every ephah.

12 "Now when the prince makes a voluntary burnt offering or voluntary peace offering to the LORD, the gate that faces toward the east shall then be opened for him; and he shall prepare his burnt offering and his peace offerings as he did on the Sabbath day. Then he shall go out, and after he goes out the gate shall be shut.

13 "You shall daily make a burnt offering to the LORD of a lamb of the first year without blemish; you shall prepare it every morning.

14 "And you shall prepare a grain offering with it every morning, a sixth of an ephah, and a third of a hin of oil to moisten the fine flour. This grain offering is a perpetual ordinance, to be made regularly to the LORD.

15 "Thus they shall prepare the lamb, the grain offering, and the oil, as a regular burnt offering every morning."

THE PRINCE AND INHERITANCE LAWS

16 'Thus says the Lord GOD: "If the prince gives a gift of some of his inheritance to any of his sons, it shall belong to his sons; it is their possession by inheritance.

17 "But if he gives a gift of some of his inheritance to one of his servants, it shall be his until the year of liberty, after which it shall return to the prince. But his inheritance shall belong to his sons; it shall become theirs.

18 "Moreover the prince shall not take any of the people's inheritance by evicting them from their property; he shall provide an inheritance for his sons from his own property, so that none of My people may be scattered from his property." ' "

HOW THE OFFERINGS WERE PREPARED

19 Now he brought me through the entrance, which was at the side of the gate, into the holy chambers of the priests which face toward the north; and there a place was situated at their extreme western end.

20 And he said to me, "This is the place where the priests shall boil the trespass offering and the sin offering, and where they shall bake the grain offering, so that they do not bring them out into the outer court to sanctify the people."

21 Then he brought me out into the outer court and caused me to pass by the four corners of the court; and in fact, in every corner of the court there was another court.

22 In the four corners of the court were enclosed courts, forty cubits long and thirty wide; all four corners were the same size.

23 There was a row of building stones all around in them, all around the four of them; and cooking hearths were made under the rows of stones all around.

24 And he said to me, "These are the kitchens where the ministers of the temple shall boil the sacrifices of the people."

THE HEALING WATERS AND TREES

47 Then he brought me back to the door of the temple; and there was water, flowing from under the threshold of the temple toward the east, for the front of the temple faced east; the water was flowing from under the right side of the temple, south of the altar.

2 He brought me out by way of the north gate, and led me around on the outside to the outer gateway that faces east; and there was water, running out on the right side.

3 And when the man went out to the east with the line in his hand, he measured one thousand cubits, and he brought me through the waters; the water *came up to my* ankles.

4 Again he measured one thousand and brought me through the waters; the water *came up to my* knees. Again he measured one thousand and brought me through; the water *came up to my* waist.

5 Again he measured one thousand, *and it was* a river that I could not cross; for the water was too deep, water in which one must swim, a river that could not be crossed.

6 He said to me, "Son of man, have you seen *this?*" Then he brought me and returned me to the bank of the river.

7 When I returned, there, along the bank of the river, *were* very many trees on one side and the other.

8 Then he said to me: "This water flows toward the eastern region, goes down into the valley, and enters the sea. *When it* reaches the sea, *its* waters are healed.

9 "And it shall be *that* every living thing that moves, wherever the rivers go, will live. There will be a very great multitude of fish, because these waters go there; for they will be healed, and everything will live wherever the river goes.

10 "It shall be *that* fishermen will stand by it from En Ge′di to En Eg·la′im; they will be *places* for spreading their nets. Their fish will be of the same kinds as the fish of the Great Sea, exceedingly many.

11 "But its swamps and marshes will not be healed; they will be given over to salt.

12 "Along the bank of the river, on this side and that, will grow all *kinds of* trees used for food; their leaves will not wither, and their fruit will not fail. They will bear fruit every month, because their water flows from the sanctuary. Their fruit will be for food, and their leaves for medicine."

BORDERS OF THE LAND

13 Thus says the Lord GOD: "These *are* the borders by which you shall divide the land as an inheritance among the twelve tribes of Israel. Joseph *shall have two* portions.

14 "You shall inherit it equally with one another; for I raised My hand in an oath to give it to your fathers, and this land shall fall to you as your inheritance.

15 "This *shall be* the border of the land on the north: from the Great Sea, *by* the road to Heth′lon, as one goes to Zē′dad,

16 "Hā′math, Be·rō′thah, Sib′rā·im (which *is* between the border of Damascus and the border of Hā′math), to Hā′zar Hat′ti·con (which *is* on the border of Hau′ran).

17 "Thus the boundary shall be from the Sea to Hā′zar Ē′nan, the border of Damascus; and as for the north, northward, it is the border of Hā′-math. *This is* the north side.

18 "On the east side you shall mark out the border from between Hau′ran

and Damascus, and between Gil′e·ad and the land of Israel, along the Jordan, and along the eastern side of the sea. *This is* the east side.

19 "The south side, toward the South,ᵃ *shall be* from Tā′mar to the waters of Mer′i·bah by Kā′desh, along the brook to the Great Sea. *This is* the south side, toward the South.

20 "The west side *shall be* the Great Sea, from the *southern* boundary until one comes to a point opposite Hā′math. This *is* the west side.

21 "Thus you shall divide this land among yourselves according to the tribes of Israel.

22 "It shall be that you will divide it by lot as an inheritance for yourselves, and for the strangers who dwell among you and who bear children among you. They shall be to you as native-born among the children of Israel; they shall have an inheritance with you among the tribes of Israel.

23 "And it shall be *that* in whatever tribe the stranger dwells, there you shall give *him* his inheritance," says the Lord GOD.

DIVISION OF THE LAND

48 "Now these *are* the names of the tribes: From the northern border along the road to Heth′lon at the entrance of Hā′math, to Hā′zar Ē′nan, the border of Damascus northward, in the direction of Hā′math, *there shall be* one *section for* Dan from its east to its west side;

2 "by the border of Dan, from the east side to the west, one *section for* Ash′er;

3 "by the border of Ash′er, from the east side to the west, one *section for* Naph′ta·lī;

4 "by the border of Naph′ta·lī, from the east side to the west, one *section for* Ma·nas′seh;

5 "by the border of Ma·nas′seh, from the east side to the west, one *section for* Ē′phra·im;

6 "by the border of Ē′phra·im, from the east side to the west, one *section for* Reuben;

7 "by the border of Reuben, from the east side to the west, one *section for* Judah;

8 "by the border of Judah, from the east side to the west, shall be the district which you shall set apart, twenty-five thousand *cubits* in width, and *in* length the same as one of the *other* portions, from the east side to the west, with the sanctuary in the center.

9 "The district that you shall set apart for the LORD *shall be* twenty-five thousand *cubits* in length and ten thousand in width.

10 "To these—to the priests—the holy district shall belong: on the north twenty-five thousand *cubits in length,* on the west ten thousand in width, on the east ten thousand in width, and on the south twenty-five thousand in length. The sanctuary of the LORD shall be in the center.

11 "*It shall be* for the priests of the sons of Zā′dok, who are sanctified, who have kept My charge, who did not go astray when the children of Israel went astray, as the Lē′vites went astray.

12 "And *this* district of land that is set apart shall be to them a thing most holy by the border of the Lē′vites.

13 "Opposite the border of the priests, the Lē′vites *shall have an area* twenty-five thousand *cubits* in length and ten thousand in width; its entire length *shall be* twenty-five thousand and its width ten thousand.

14 "And they shall not sell or exchange any of it; they may not alien-

47:19 ᵃHebrew *Negev*

ate this best *part* of the land, for *it is* holy to the LORD.

15 "The five thousand *cubits* in width that remain, along the edge of the twenty-five thousand, shall be for general use by the city, for dwellings and common-land; and the city shall be in the center.

16 "These *shall be* its measurements: the north side four thousand five hundred *cubits,* the south side four thousand five hundred, the east side four thousand five hundred, and the west side four thousand five hundred.

17 "The common-land of the city shall be: to the north two hundred and fifty *cubits,* to the south two hundred and fifty, to the east two hundred and fifty, and to the west two hundred and fifty.

18 "The rest of the length, alongside the district of the holy *section, shall be* ten thousand *cubits* to the east and ten thousand to the west. It shall be adjacent to the district of the holy *section,* and its produce shall be food for the workers of the city.

19 "The workers of the city, from all the tribes of Israel, shall cultivate it.

20 "The entire district *shall be* twenty-five thousand *cubits* by twenty-five thousand *cubits,* four-square. You shall set apart the holy district with the property of the city.

21 "The rest *shall belong* to the prince, on one side and on the other of the holy district and of the city's property, next to the twenty-five thousand *cubits* of the *holy* district as far as the eastern border, and westward next to the twenty-five thousand as far as the western border, adjacent to the *tribal* portions; *it shall belong* to the prince. It shall be the holy district, and the sanctuary of the temple *shall be* in the center.

22 "Moreover, apart from the posses-sion of the Lē′vītes and the posses-sion of the city *which are* in the midst of what *belongs* to the prince, *the area* between the border of Judah and the border of Benjamin shall be-long to the prince.

23 "As for the rest of the tribes, from the east side to the west, Benjamin *shall have* one *section;*

24 "by the border of Benjamin, from the east side to the west, Sim′ē·on *shall have* one *section;*

25 "by the border of Sim′ē·on, from the east side to the west, Is′sa·char *shall have* one *section;*

26 "by the border of Is′sa·char, from the east side to the west, Zeb′ū·lun *shall have* one *section;*

27 "by the border of Zeb′ū·lun, from the east side to the west, Gad *shall have* one *section;*

28 "by the border of Gad, on the south side, toward the South,*a* the border shall be from Tā′mar *to* the waters of Mer′i·bah *by* Kā′desh, along the brook to the Great Sea.

29 "This *is* the land which you shall divide by lot as an inheritance among the tribes of Israel, and these *are* their portions," says the Lord GOD.

THE GATES OF THE CITY AND ITS NAME

30 "These *are* the exits of the city. On the north side, measuring four thou-sand five hundred *cubits*

31 "(the gates of the city *shall be* named after the tribes of Israel), the three gates northward: one gate for Reuben, one gate for Judah, and one gate for Levi;

32 "on the east side, four thousand five hundred *cubits,* three gates: one gate for Joseph, one gate for Benja-min, and one gate for Dan;

33 "on the south side, measuring

48:28 *a*Hebrew *Negev*

four thousand five hundred *cubits,* three gates: one gate for Sim'ē·on, one gate for Is'sa·char, and one gate for Zeb'ū·lun;

34 "on the west side, four thousand five hundred *cubits* with their three gates: one gate for Gad, one gate for

Ash'er, and one gate for Naph'ta·lī.

35 "All the way around *shall be* eighteen thousand *cubits;* and the name of the city from *that* day *shall be:* THE LORD *IS* THERE."a

48:35 aHebrew *YHWH Shammah*

The Book of
DANIEL

DANIEL AND HIS FRIENDS OBEY GOD

IN the third year of the reign of Je·hoi′a·kim king of Judah, Ne·bū·chad·nez′zar king of Babylon came to Jerusalem and besieged it.
2 And the Lord gave Je·hoi′a·kim king of Judah into his hand, with some of the articles of the house of God, which he carried into the land of Shī′nar to the house of his god; and he brought the articles into the treasure house of his god.
3 Then the king instructed Ash′-pe·naz, the master of his eunuchs, to bring some of the children of Israel and some of the king's descendants and some of the nobles,
4 young men in whom *there was* no blemish, but good-looking, gifted in all wisdom, possessing knowledge and quick to understand, who *had* ability to serve in the king's palace, and whom they might teach the language and literature of the Chal-dē′ans.
5 And the king appointed for them a daily provision of the king's delicacies and of the wine which he drank, and three years of training for them, so that at the end of *that time* they might serve before the king.
6 Now from among those of the sons of Judah were Daniel, Han·a·nī′ah, Mish′a·el, and Az·a·rī′ah.
7 To them the chief of the eunuchs gave names: he gave Daniel *the name* Bel·te·shaz′zar; to Han·a·nī′ah, Shad′-rach; to Mish′a·el, Mē′shach; and to Az·a·rī′ah, A·bed′-Ne·gō′.
8 But Daniel purposed in his heart that he would not defile himself with the portion of the king's delicacies, nor with the wine which he drank; therefore he requested of the chief of the eunuchs that he might not defile himself.
9 Now God had brought Daniel into the favor and goodwill of the chief of the eunuchs.
10 And the chief of the eunuchs said to Daniel, "I fear my lord the king, who has appointed your food and drink. For why should he see your faces looking worse than the young men who *are* your age? Then you would endanger my head before the king."
11 So Daniel said to the steward[a] whom the chief of the eunuchs had set over Daniel, Han·a·nī′ah, Mish′-a·el, and Az·a·rī′ah,
12 "Please test your servants for ten days, and let them give us vegetables to eat and water to drink.
13 "Then let our appearance be examined before you, and the appearance of the young men who eat the portion of the king's delicacies; and as you see fit, *so* deal with your servants."
14 So he consented with them in this matter, and tested them ten days.
15 And at the end of ten days their features appeared better and fatter in flesh than all the young men who ate the portion of the king's delicacies.
16 Thus the steward took away their portion of delicacies and the wine that they were to drink, and gave them vegetables.
17 As for these four young men, God gave them knowledge and skill in all literature and wisdom; and Daniel had understanding in all visions and dreams.
18 Now at the end of the days, when the king had said that they should be

1:11 *a*Hebrew *Melzar,* also in verse 16

TEMPTATION Daniel 1:8

No, Kitty, No!

Kitty, don't eat that little bird. You're my friend. The little bird is my friend, too. That's a no-no. Don't even think of it. Do you think parents ever say that to us? "No, no, don't even think of doing that!" They're trying to help you. They don't want you to hurt someone or do something wrong. Do you think God ever wants to say that to us? "No, no. Don't even think of doing that!" He's trying to help us. He doesn't want us to hurt someone or do something wrong. Thank you, parents. Thank You, God.

1. Have you been tempted to do something wrong? Did you feel that God or parents were saying, "Don't do that"?
2. When you are tempted to do wrong, what should you do? Should you ask God to help you not to do it? Should you talk about it with your parents?

For more on *Values* turn to page 1351
For more on *Temptation* turn to page 1805

brought in, the chief of the eunuchs brought them in before Ne·bu·chad·nez′zar.

19 Then the king interviewed them,*a* and among them all none was found like Daniel, Han·a·ni′ah, Mish′a·el, and Az·a·ri′ah; therefore they served before the king.

20 And in all matters of wisdom *and* understanding about which the king examined them, he found them ten times better than all the magicians *and* astrologers who *were* in all his realm.

21 Thus Daniel continued until the first year of King Cyrus.

NEBUCHADNEZZAR'S DREAM

2 Now in the second year of Ne·bu·chad·nez′zar's reign, Ne·bu·chad·nez′zar had dreams; and his spirit was *so* troubled that his sleep left him.

2 Then the king gave the command to call the magicians, the astrologers, the sorcerers, and the Chal·de′ans to tell the king his dreams. So they came and stood before the king.

3 And the king said to them, "I have had a dream, and my spirit is anxious to know the dream."

4 Then the Chal·de′ans spoke to the king in Ar·a·ma′ic,*a* "O king, live forever! Tell your servants the dream, and we will give the interpretation."

5 The king answered and said to the Chal·de′ans, "My decision is firm: if you do not make known the dream to me, and its interpretation, you shall be cut in pieces, and your houses shall be made an ash heap.

6 "However, if you tell the dream and its interpretation, you shall receive from me gifts, rewards, and great honor. Therefore tell me the dream and its interpretation."

7 They answered again and said, "Let the king tell his servants the dream, and we will give its interpretation."

8 The king answered and said, "I know for certain that you would gain time, because you see that my decision is firm:

9 "if you do not make known the dream to me, *there is only* one decree for you! For you have agreed to speak lying and corrupt words before me till the time has changed. Therefore tell me the dream, and I shall know that you can give me its interpretation."

10 The Chal·de′ans answered the king, and said, "There is not a man on earth who can tell the king's matter; therefore no king, lord, or ruler has *ever* asked such things of any magician, astrologer, or Chal·de′an.

11 "*It is* a difficult thing that the king requests, and there is no other who can tell it to the king except the gods, whose dwelling is not with flesh."

12 For this reason the king was angry and very furious, and gave the command to destroy all the wise *men* of Babylon.

13 So the decree went out, and they began killing the wise *men;* and they sought Daniel and his companions, to kill *them.*

GOD REVEALS NEBUCHADNEZZAR'S DREAM

14 Then with counsel and wisdom Daniel answered Ar′i·och, the captain of the king's guard, who had gone out to kill the wise *men* of Babylon;

15 he answered and said to Ar′i·och the king's captain, "Why is the decree from the king so urgent?" Then Ar′i·och made the decision known to Daniel.

16 So Daniel went in and asked the

1:19 *a*Literally *talked with them*   2:4 *a*The original language of Daniel 2:4b through 7:28 is Aramaic.

king to give him time, that he might tell the king the interpretation.

17 Then Daniel went to his house, and made the decision known to Han·a·nī′ah, Mish′a·el, and Az·a·rī′ah, his companions,

18 that they might seek mercies from the God of heaven concerning this secret, so that Daniel and his companions might not perish with the rest of the wise *men* of Babylon.

19 Then the secret was revealed to Daniel in a night vision. So Daniel blessed the God of heaven.

20 Daniel answered and said:

"Blessed be the name of God
    forever and ever,
For wisdom and might are His.
21 And He changes the times and
    the seasons;
He removes kings and raises up
    kings;
He gives wisdom to the wise
And knowledge to those who have
    understanding.
22 He reveals deep and secret
    things;
He knows what *is* in the
    darkness,
And light dwells with Him.

Praises

Daniel 2:23

Would you like to pray Daniel's prayer? He thanked God and praised Him for wisdom. Do you ever need help in making a decision? Ask God. Then praise Him. Do you ever need help to know what to do next? Ask God. Then praise Him. Praise God for wisdom. Praise God for showing you something you needed to see. Praise God!

---

23 "I thank You and praise You,
    O God of my fathers;
You have given me wisdom and
    might,
And have now made known to me
    what we asked of You,
For You have made known to us
    the king's demand."

DANIEL EXPLAINS THE DREAM

24 Therefore Daniel went to Ar′i·och, whom the king had appointed to destroy the wise *men* of Babylon. He went and said thus to him: "Do not destroy the wise *men* of Babylon; take me before the king, and I will tell the king the interpretation."

25 Then Ar′i·och quickly brought Daniel before the king, and said thus to him, "I have found a man of the captives[a] of Judah, who will make known to the king the interpretation."

26 The king answered and said to Daniel, whose name *was* Bel·te·shaz′zar, "Are you able to make known to me the dream which I have seen, and its interpretation?"

27 Daniel answered in the presence of the king, and said, "The secret which the king has demanded, the wise *men,* the astrologers, the magicians, and the soothsayers cannot declare to the king.

28 "But there is a God in heaven who reveals secrets, and He has made known to King Ne·bū·chad·nez′zar what will be in the latter days. Your dream, and the visions of your head upon your bed, were these:

29 "As for you, O king, thoughts came *to* your *mind while* on your bed, *about* what would come to pass after this; and He who reveals secrets has made known to you what will be.

30 "But as for me, this secret has not

2:25 [a]Literally *of the sons of the captivity*

been revealed to me because I have more wisdom than anyone living, but for *our* sakes who make known the interpretation to the king, and that you may know the thoughts of your heart.

31 "You, O king, were watching; and behold, a great image! This great image, whose splendor *was* excellent, stood before you; and its form *was* awesome.

32 "This image's head *was* of fine gold, its chest and arms of silver, its belly and thighs*a* of bronze,

33 "its legs of iron, its feet partly of iron and partly of clay.*a*

34 "You watched while a stone was cut out without hands, which struck the image on its feet of iron and clay, and broke them in pieces.

35 "Then the iron, the clay, the bronze, the silver, and the gold were crushed together, and became like chaff from the summer threshing floors; the wind carried them away so that no trace of them was found. And the stone that struck the image became a great mountain and filled the whole earth.

36 "This *is* the dream. Now we will tell the interpretation of it before the king.

37 "You, O king, *are* a king of kings. For the God of heaven has given you a kingdom, power, strength, and glory;

38 "and wherever the children of men dwell, or the beasts of the field and the birds of the heaven, He has given *them* into your hand, and has made you ruler over them all—you *are* this head of gold.

39 "But after you shall arise another kingdom inferior to yours; then another, a third kingdom of bronze, which shall rule over all the earth.

40 "And the fourth kingdom shall be as strong as iron, inasmuch as iron breaks in pieces and shatters every-

thing; and like iron that crushes, *that kingdom* will break in pieces and crush all the others.

41 "Whereas you saw the feet and toes, partly of potter's clay and partly of iron, the kingdom shall be divided; yet the strength of the iron shall be in it, just as you saw the iron mixed with ceramic clay.

42 "And *as* the toes of the feet *were* partly of iron and partly of clay, *so* the kingdom shall be partly strong and partly fragile.

43 "As you saw iron mixed with ceramic clay, they will mingle with the seed of men; but they will not adhere to one another, just as iron does not mix with clay.

44 "And in the days of these kings the God of heaven will set up a kingdom which shall never be destroyed; and the kingdom shall not be left to other people; it shall break in pieces and consume all these kingdoms, and it shall stand forever.

45 "Inasmuch as you saw that the stone was cut out of the mountain without hands, and that it broke in pieces the iron, the bronze, the clay, the silver, and the gold—the great God has made known to the king what will come to pass after this. The dream is certain, and its interpretation is sure."

DANIEL AND HIS FRIENDS PROMOTED

46 Then King Ne·bu·chad·nez'zar fell on his face, prostrate before Daniel, and commanded that they should present an offering and incense to him.

47 The king answered Daniel, and said, "Truly your God *is* the God of gods, the Lord of kings, and a

---

2:32 *a*Or *sides*　　2:33 *a*Or *baked clay,* and so in verses 34, 35, and 42

revealer of secrets, since you could reveal this secret."

48 Then the king promoted Daniel and gave him many great gifts; and he made him ruler over the whole province of Babylon, and chief administrator over all the wise *men* of Babylon.

49 Also Daniel petitioned the king, and he set Shad′rach, Mē′shach, and A·bed′-Ne·gō′ over the affairs of the province of Babylon; but Daniel *sat* in the gate[a] of the king.

THE IMAGE OF GOLD

Three men are thrown into a raging fire. But something amazing happens.

3 Ne·bu·chad·nez′zar the king made an image of gold, whose height *was* sixty cubits *and* its width six cubits. He set it up in the plain of Dū′ra, in the province of Babylon.

2 And King Ne·bu·chad·nez′zar sent *word* to gather together the satraps, the administrators, the governors, the counselors, the treasurers, the judges, the magistrates, and all the officials of the provinces, to come to the dedication of the image which King Ne·bu·chad·nez′zar had set up.

3 So the satraps, the administrators, the governors, the counselors, the treasurers, the judges, the magistrates, and all the officials of the provinces gathered together for the dedication of the image that King Ne·bu·chad·nez′zar had set up; and they stood before the image that Ne·bu·chad·nez′zar had set up.

4 Then a herald cried aloud: "To you it is commanded, O peoples, nations, and languages,

5 "*that* at the time you hear the sound of the horn, flute, harp, lyre, *and* psaltery, in symphony with all kinds of music, you shall fall down

and worship the gold image that King Ne·bu·chad·nez′zar has set up;

6 "and whoever does not fall down and worship shall be cast immediately into the midst of a burning fiery furnace."

7 So at that time, when all the people heard the sound of the horn, flute, harp, *and* lyre, in symphony with all kinds of music, all the people, nations, and languages fell down *and* worshiped the gold image which King Ne·bu·chad·nez′zar had set up.

DANIEL'S FRIENDS DISOBEY THE KING

8 Therefore at that time certain Chal·dē′ans came forward and accused the Jews.

9 They spoke and said to King Ne·bu·chad·nez′zar, "O king, live forever!

10 "You, O king, have made a decree that everyone who hears the sound of the horn, flute, harp, lyre, *and* psaltery, in symphony with all kinds of music, shall fall down and worship the gold image;

11 "and whoever does not fall down and worship shall be cast into the midst of a burning fiery furnace.

12 "There are certain Jews whom you have set over the affairs of the province of Babylon: Shad′rach, Mē′shach, and A·bed′-Ne·gō′; these men, O king, have not paid due regard to you. They do not serve your gods or worship the gold image which you have set up."

13 Then Ne·bu·chad·nez′zar, in rage and fury, gave the command to bring Shad′rach, Mē′shach, and A·bed′-Ne·gō′. So they brought these men before the king.

14 Ne·bu·chad·nez′zar spoke, saying to them, "*Is it* true, Shad′rach, Mē′shach, and A·bed′-Ne·gō′, *that* you do

2:49 [a]That is, the king's court

not serve my gods or worship the gold image which I have set up?

15 "Now if you are ready at the time you hear the sound of the horn, flute, harp, lyre, *and* psaltery, in symphony with all kinds of music, and you fall down and worship the image which I have made, *good!* But if you do not worship, you shall be cast immediately into the midst of a burning fiery furnace. And who *is* the god who will deliver you from my hands?"

16 Shad'rach, Mē'shach, and A·bed'-Ne·gō' answered and said to the king, "O Ne·bu·chad·nez'zar, we have no need to answer you in this matter.

17 "If that *is the case,* our God whom we serve is able to deliver us from the burning fiery furnace, and He will deliver *us* from your hand, O king.

18 "But if not, let it be known to you, O king, that we do not serve your gods, nor will we worship the gold image which you have set up."

Saved in Fiery Trial

19 Then Ne·bu·chad·nez'zar was full of fury, and the expression on his face changed toward Shad'rach, Mē'shach, and A·bed'-Ne·gō'. He spoke and commanded that they heat the furnace seven times more than it was usually heated.

20 And he commanded certain mighty men of valor who *were* in his army to bind Shad'rach, Mē'shach, and A·bed'-Ne·gō', *and* cast *them* into the burning fiery furnace.

21 Then these men were bound in their coats, their trousers, their turbans, and their *other* garments, and were cast into the midst of the burning fiery furnace.

22 Therefore, because the king's command was urgent, and the furnace exceedingly hot, the flame of the fire killed those men who took up Shad'rach, Mē'shach, and A·bed'-Ne·gō'.

23 And these three men, Shad'rach, Mē'shach, and A·bed'-Ne·gō', fell down bound into the midst of the burning fiery furnace.

24 Then King Ne·bu·chad·nez'zar was astonished; and he rose in haste *and* spoke, saying to his counselors, "Did we not cast three men bound into the midst of the fire?" They answered and said to the king, "True, O king."

25 "Look!" he answered, "I see four men loose, walking in the midst of the fire; and they are not hurt, and the form of the fourth is like the Son of God."*a*

Nebuchadnezzar Praises God

26 Then Ne·bu·chad·nez'zar went near the mouth of the burning fiery furnace *and* spoke, saying, "Shad'-rach, Mē'shach, and A·bed'-Ne·gō', servants of the Most High God, come out, and come *here.*" Then Shad'rach, Mē'shach, and A·bed'-Ne·gō' came from the midst of the fire.

27 And the satraps, administrators, governors, and the king's counselors gathered together, and they saw these men on whose bodies the fire had no power; the hair of their head was not singed nor were their garments affected, and the smell of fire was not on them.

28 Ne·bu·chad·nez'zar spoke, saying, "Blessed be the God of Shad'rach, Mē'shach, and A·bed'-Ne·gō', who sent His Angel*a* and delivered His servants who trusted in Him, and they have frustrated the king's word, and yielded their bodies, that they should not serve nor worship any god except their own God!

29 "Therefore I make a decree that

3:25 *a*Or *a son of the gods*   3:28 *a*Or *angel*

any people, nation, or language which speaks anything amiss against the God of Shad′rach, Mē′shach, and A·bed′-Ne·gō′ shall be cut in pieces, and their houses shall be made an ash heap; because there is no other God who can deliver like this."

30 Then the king promoted Shad′-rach, Mē′shach, and A·bed′-Ne·gō′ in the province of Babylon.

✓ ## Bible Quiz

Daniel 3 **Three Men in a Fiery Furnace**

1. Can you pronounce the name of the king in this story?
2. What did the king make on the plain of Dura?
3. What did he want everyone to do when they came to see the statue? Who wouldn't worship before it?
4. What did the king do to Shadrach, Meshach, and Abed–Nego? How do you know God was taking care of them?
5. What did the king say about God after this? Would the king have praised God if Shadrach, Meshach, and Abed–Nego had worshiped the statue? What can you do to show others how much you love God?

NEBUCHADNEZZAR'S SECOND DREAM

4 Ne·bū·chad·nez′zar the king,

To all peoples, nations, and languages that dwell in all the earth:

Peace be multiplied to you.

2 I thought it good to declare the signs and wonders that the Most High God has worked for me.

3 How great *are* His signs,
And how mighty His wonders!
His kingdom *is* an everlasting kingdom,
And His dominion *is* from generation to generation.

4 I, Ne·bū·chad·nez′zar, was at rest in my house, and flourishing in my palace.
5 I saw a dream which made me afraid, and the thoughts on my bed and the visions of my head troubled me.
6 Therefore I issued a decree to bring in all the wise *men* of Babylon before me, that they might make known to me the interpretation of the dream.
7 Then the magicians, the astrologers, the Chal·dē′ans, and the soothsayers came in, and I told them the dream; but they did not make known to me its interpretation.
8 But at last Daniel came before me (his name *is* Bel·te·shaz′zar, according to the name of my god; in him *is* the Spirit of the Holy God), and I told the dream before him, *saying:*
9 "Bel·te·shaz′zar, chief of the magicians, because I know that the Spirit of the Holy God *is* in you, and no secret troubles you, explain to me the visions of my dream that I have seen, and its interpretation.
10 "These *were* the visions of my head *while* on my bed:

I was looking, and behold,
A tree in the midst of the earth,
And its height was great.

11 The tree grew and became strong;
   Its height reached to the heavens,
   And it could be seen to the ends of
      all the earth.
12 Its leaves *were* lovely,
   Its fruit abundant,
   And in it *was* food for all.
   The beasts of the field found
      shade under it,
   The birds of the heavens dwelt in
      its branches,
   And all flesh was fed from it.

13 "I saw in the visions of my head
   while on my bed, and there was a
   watcher, a holy one, coming down
   from heaven.
14 He cried aloud and said thus:

   'Chop down the tree and cut off its
      branches,
   Strip off its leaves and scatter its
      fruit.
   Let the beasts get out from under
      it,
   And the birds from its branches.
15 Nevertheless leave the stump and
      roots in the earth,
   Bound with a band of iron and
      bronze,
   In the tender grass of the field.
   Let it be wet with the dew of
      heaven,
   And *let* him graze with the
      beasts
   On the grass of the earth.
16 Let his heart be changed from
      that of a man,
   Let him be given the heart of a
      beast,
   And let seven times*a* pass over
      him.

17 'This decision *is* by the decree of
      the watchers,
   And the sentence by the word of
      the holy ones,
   In order that the living may know

That the Most High rules in the
   kingdom of men,
   Gives it to whomever He will,
   And sets over it the lowest of
      men.'

18 "This dream I, King
   Ne·bu·chad·nez'zar, have seen.
   Now you, Bel·te·shaz'zar, declare
   its interpretation, since all the
   wise *men* of my kingdom are not
   able to make known to me the
   interpretation; but you *are* able,
   for the Spirit of the Holy God *is*
   in you."

DANIEL EXPLAINS THE SECOND DREAM

19 Then Daniel, whose name was
   Bel·te·shaz'zar, was astonished
   for a time, and his thoughts
   troubled him. *So* the king spoke,
   and said, "Bel·te·shaz'zar, do not
   let the dream or its interpretation
   trouble you." Bel·te·shaz'zar
   answered and said, "My lord, *may*
   the dream concern those who hate
   you, and its interpretation
   concern your enemies!
20 The tree that you saw, which
   grew and became strong, whose
   height reached to the heavens
   and which *could be seen* by all the
   earth,
21 whose leaves *were* lovely and its
   fruit abundant, in which *was* food
   for all, under which the beasts of
   the field dwelt, and in whose
   branches the birds of the heaven
   had their home—
22 it *is* you, O king, who have grown
   and become strong; for your
   greatness has grown and reaches
   to the heavens, and your
   dominion to the end of the earth.

4:16 *a*Possibly *seven years,* and so in verses 23, 25,
and 32

23 And inasmuch as the king saw a watcher, a holy one, coming down from heaven and saying, 'Chop down the tree and destroy it, but leave its stump and roots in the earth, *bound* with a band of iron and bronze in the tender grass of the field; let it be wet with the dew of heaven, and let him graze with the beasts of the field, till seven times pass over him';

24 this is the interpretation, O king, and this is the decree of the Most High, which has come upon my lord the king:

25 They shall drive you from men, your dwelling shall be with the beasts of the field, and they shall make you eat grass like oxen. They shall wet you with the dew of heaven, and seven times shall pass over you, till you know that the Most High rules in the kingdom of men, and gives it to whomever He chooses.

26 And inasmuch as they gave the command to leave the stump *and* roots of the tree, your kingdom shall be assured to you, after you come to know that Heaven rules.

27 Therefore, O king, let my advice be acceptable to you; break off your sins by *being* righteous, and your iniquities by showing mercy to *the* poor. Perhaps there may be a lengthening of your prosperity."

NEBUCHADNEZZAR'S HUMILIATION

28 All *this* came upon King Ne·bu·chad·nez'zar.

29 At the end of the twelve months he was walking about the royal palace of Babylon.

30 The king spoke, saying, "Is not this great Babylon, that I have built for a royal dwelling by my mighty power and for the honor of my majesty?"

31 While the word *was* still in the king's mouth, a voice fell from heaven: "King Ne·bu·chad·nez'zar, to you it is spoken: the kingdom has departed from you!

32 And they shall drive you from men, and your dwelling *shall be* with the beasts of the field. They shall make you eat grass like oxen; and seven times shall pass over you, until you know that the Most High rules in the kingdom of men, and gives it to whomever He chooses."

33 That very hour the word was fulfilled concerning Ne·bu·chad·nez'zar; he was driven from men and ate grass like oxen; his body was wet with the dew of heaven till his hair had grown like eagles' *feathers* and his nails like birds' *claws.*

NEBUCHADNEZZAR PRAISES GOD

34 And at the end of the time*a* I, Ne·bu·chad·nez'zar, lifted my eyes to heaven, and my understanding returned to me; and I blessed the Most High and praised and honored Him who lives forever:

For His dominion *is* an
    everlasting dominion,
And His kingdom *is* from
    generation to generation.

35 All the inhabitants of the earth
    are reputed as nothing;
He does according to His will in
    the army of heaven
And *among* the inhabitants of the
    earth.
No one can restrain His hand
Or say to Him, "What have You
    done?"

36 At the same time my reason returned to me, and for the glory

4:34 *a*Literally *days*

WHEN THE LORD DOES SOMETHING SPECIAL FOR ME   Daniel 4:34

Father or mother does something special for you. What do you do? What should you do? Brother or sister does something special for you. What do you do? What should you do? A friend does something special for you. What do you do? What should you do? The Lord does something special for you. What do you do? What should you do?

1. This girl is so happy. Something wonderful happened to her. The Lord did something special for her. How is she saying "Thank You" to the Lord?

2. Think of some other ways you can say "Thank You" to the Lord when He does something special for you. What are they? Will you do some today?

For more on *What Should I Do?* turn to page 1339
For more on *Thankfulness* turn to page 1370

of my kingdom, my honor and splendor returned to me. My counselors and nobles resorted to me, I was restored to my kingdom, and excellent majesty was added to me.

37 Now I, Ne·bu·chad·nez'zar, praise and extol and honor the King of heaven, all of whose works *are* truth, and His ways justice. And those who walk in pride He is able to put down.

BELSHAZZAR'S FEAST

5 Bel·shaz'zar the king made a great feast for a thousand of his lords, and drank wine in the presence of the thousand.

2 While he tasted the wine, Bel·shaz'zar gave the command to bring the gold and silver vessels which his father Ne·bu·chad·nez'zar had taken from the temple which *had been* in Jerusalem, that the king and his lords, his wives, and his concubines might drink from them.

3 Then they brought the gold vessels that had been taken from the temple of the house of God which *had been* in Jerusalem; and the king and his lords, his wives, and his concubines drank from them.

4 They drank wine, and praised the gods of gold and silver, bronze and iron, wood and stone.

5 In the same hour the fingers of a man's hand appeared and wrote opposite the lampstand on the plaster of the wall of the king's palace; and the king saw the part of the hand that wrote.

6 Then the king's countenance changed, and his thoughts troubled him, so that the joints of his hips were loosened and his knees knocked against each other.

7 The king cried aloud to bring in the astrologers, the Chal·dē'ans, and the soothsayers. The king spoke, saying to the wise *men* of Babylon, "Whoever reads this writing, and tells me its interpretation, shall be clothed with purple and *have* a chain of gold around his neck; and he shall be the third ruler in the kingdom."

8 Now all the king's wise *men* came, but they could not read the writing, or make known to the king its interpretation.

9 Then King Bel·shaz'zar was greatly troubled, his countenance was changed, and his lords were astonished.

10 The queen, because of the words of the king and his lords, came to the banquet hall. The queen spoke, saying, "O king, live forever! Do not let your thoughts trouble you, nor let your countenance change.

11 "There is a man in your kingdom in whom *is* the Spirit of the Holy God. And in the days of your father, light and understanding and wisdom, like the wisdom of the gods, were found in him; and King Ne·bu·chad·nez'zar your father—your father the king—made him chief of the magicians, astrologers, Chal·dē'ans, *and* soothsayers.

12 "Inasmuch as an excellent spirit, knowledge, understanding, interpreting dreams, solving riddles, and explaining enigmas[a] were found in this Daniel, whom the king named Bel·te·shaz'zar, now let Daniel be called, and he will give the interpretation."

THE WRITING ON THE WALL EXPLAINED

13 Then Daniel was brought in before the king. The king spoke, and said to Daniel, "*Are* you that Daniel who is one of the captives[a] from

5:12 [a]Literally *untying knots,* and so in verse 16
5:13 [a]Literally *of the sons of the captivity*

Judah, whom my father the king brought from Judah?

14 "I have heard of you, that the Spirit of God *is* in you, and *that* light and understanding and excellent wisdom are found in you.

15 "Now the wise *men,* the astrologers, have been brought in before me, that they should read this writing and make known to me its interpretation, but they could not give the interpretation of the thing.

16 "And I have heard of you, that you can give interpretations and explain enigmas. Now if you can read the writing and make known to me its interpretation, you shall be clothed with purple and *have* a chain of gold around your neck, and shall be the third ruler in the kingdom."

17 Then Daniel answered, and said before the king, "Let your gifts be for yourself, and give your rewards to another; yet I will read the writing to the king, and make known to him the interpretation.

18 "O king, the Most High God gave Ne·bu·chad·nez'zar your father a kingdom and majesty, glory and honor.

19 "And because of the majesty that He gave him, all peoples, nations, and languages trembled and feared before him. Whomever he wished, he executed; whomever he wished, he kept alive; whomever he wished, he set up; and whomever he wished, he put down.

20 "But when his heart was lifted up, and his spirit was hardened in pride, he was deposed from his kingly throne, and they took his glory from him.

21 "Then he was driven from the sons of men, his heart was made like the beasts, and his dwelling *was* with the wild donkeys. They fed him with grass like oxen, and his body was wet with the dew of heaven, till he knew that the Most High God rules in the kingdom of men, and appoints over it whomever He chooses.

22 "But you his son, Bel·shaz'zar, have not humbled your heart, although you knew all this.

23 "And you have lifted yourself up against the Lord of heaven. They have brought the vessels of His house before you, and you and your lords, your wives and your concubines, have drunk wine from them. And you have praised the gods of silver and gold, bronze and iron, wood and stone, which do not see or hear or know; and the God who *holds* your breath in His hand and owns all your ways, you have not glorified.

24 "Then the fingers*a* of the hand were sent from Him, and this writing was written.

25 "And this is the inscription that was written:

MENE,*a* MENE, TEKEL,*b* UPHARSIN.*c*

26 "This *is* the interpretation of *each* word. MENE: God has numbered your kingdom, and finished it;

27 "TEKEL: You have been weighed in the balances, and found wanting;

28 "PERES: Your kingdom has been divided, and given to the Medes and Persians."*a*

29 Then Bel·shaz'zar gave the command, and they clothed Daniel with purple and *put* a chain of gold around his neck, and made a proclamation concerning him that he should be the third ruler in the kingdom.

BELSHAZZAR'S FALL

30 That very night Bel·shaz'zar, king of the Chal·de'ans, was slain.

5:24 *a*Literally *palm*　　5:25 *a*Literally *a mina* (50 shekels) from the verb "to number"　*b*Literally *a shekel* from the verb "to weigh"　*c*Literally *and half-shekels* from the verb "to divide"
5:28 *a*Aramaic *Paras,* consonant with *Peres*

31 And Da·rī′us the Mēde received the kingdom, *being* about sixty-two years old.

THE PLOT AGAINST DANIEL

This is the story about a man who was thrown into a den of hungry lions because he prayed to God. If you knew this might happen to you, would you have the courage to keep praying?

6 It pleased Da·rī′us to set over the kingdom one hundred and twenty satraps, to be over the whole kingdom;

2 and over these, three governors, of whom Daniel *was* one, that the satraps might give account to them, so that the king would suffer no loss.

3 Then this Daniel distinguished himself above the governors and satraps, because an excellent spirit *was* in him; and the king gave thought to setting him over the whole realm.

4 So the governors and satraps sought to find *some* charge against Daniel concerning the kingdom; but they could find no charge or fault, because he *was* faithful; nor was there any error or fault found in him.

5 Then these men said, "We shall not find any charge against this Daniel unless we find *it* against him concerning the law of his God."

6 So these governors and satraps thronged before the king, and said thus to him: "King Da·rī′us, live forever!

7 "All the governors of the kingdom, the administrators and satraps, the counselors and advisors, have consulted together to establish a royal statute and to make a firm decree, that whoever petitions any god or man for thirty days, except you, O king, shall be cast into the den of lions.

8 "Now, O king, establish the decree and sign the writing, so that it cannot be changed, according to the law of the Mēdes and Persians, which does not alter."

9 Therefore King Da·rī′us signed the written decree.

DANIEL IN THE LIONS' DEN

10 Now when Daniel knew that the writing was signed, he went home. And in his upper room, with his windows open toward Jerusalem, he knelt down on his knees three times that day, and prayed and gave thanks before his God, as was his custom since early days.

11 Then these men assembled and found Daniel praying and making supplication before his God.

12 And they went before the king, and spoke concerning the king's decree: "Have you not signed a decree that every man who petitions any god or man within thirty days, except you, O king, shall be cast into the den of lions?" The king answered and said, "The thing *is* true, according to the law of the Mēdes and Persians, which does not alter."

13 So they answered and said before the king, "That Daniel, who is one of the captives[a] from Judah, does not show due regard for you, O king, or for the decree that you have signed, but makes his petition three times a day."

14 And the king, when he heard *these* words, was greatly displeased with himself, and set *his* heart on Daniel to deliver him; and he labored till the going down of the sun to deliver him.

6:13 [a]Literally *of the sons of the captivity*

15 Then these men approached the king, and said to the king, "Know, O king, that *it is* the law of the Mēdes and Persians that no decree or statute which the king establishes may be changed."

16 So the king gave the command, and they brought Daniel and cast *him* into the den of lions. *But* the king spoke, saying to Daniel, "Your God, whom you serve continually, He will deliver you."

17 Then a stone was brought and laid on the mouth of the den, and the king sealed it with his own signet ring and with the signets of his lords, that the purpose concerning Daniel might not be changed.

DANIEL SAVED FROM THE LIONS

18 Now the king went to his palace and spent the night fasting; and no musicians*a* were brought before him. Also his sleep went from him.

19 Then the king arose very early in the morning and went in haste to the den of lions.

20 And when he came to the den, he cried out with a lamenting voice to Daniel. The king spoke, saying to Daniel, "Daniel, servant of the living God, has your God, whom you serve continually, been able to deliver you from the lions?"

21 Then Daniel said to the king, "O king, live forever!

22 "My God sent His angel and shut the lions' mouths, so that they have not hurt me, because I was found innocent before Him; and also, O king, I have done no wrong before you."

23 Now the king was exceedingly glad for him, and commanded that they should take Daniel up out of the den. So Daniel was taken up out of the den, and no injury whatever was found on him, because he believed in his God.

DARIUS HONORS GOD

24 And the king gave the command, and they brought those men who had accused Daniel, and they cast *them* into the den of lions—them, their children, and their wives; and the

6:18 *a*Exact meaning unknown

☑ ***Bible Quiz***

Daniel 6 **Daniel in the Lions' Den**

1. What important position did Daniel have in the government?

2. Why did the other rulers become jealous of him? Why couldn't the other rulers get him in trouble?

3. What did they finally do to trap Daniel? Did this stop Daniel from praying to God? Should you let anyone stop you from worshiping God?

4. What did the king do when he found out Daniel had broken the new law? Did the king really want to hurt Daniel? How do you know?

5. What did the king find when he looked into the lions' den the next morning? Do you think the king would have believed in God if Daniel hadn't kept worshiping God and been thrown into the lions' den? Should anything stop you from talking to God and obeying Him? Can you think of any friends who need to know that you believe in God? How might this change their life?

lions overpowered them, and broke all their bones in pieces before they ever came to the bottom of the den.
25 Then King Da·rī′us wrote:

To all peoples, nations, and languages that dwell in all the earth:

Peace be multiplied to you.

26 I make a decree that in every dominion of my kingdom *men must* tremble and fear before the God of Daniel.

For He *is* the living God,
And steadfast forever;
His kingdom *is the one* which
    shall not be destroyed,
And His dominion *shall endure* to
    the end.
27 He delivers and rescues,
And He works signs and wonders
In heaven and on earth,
Who has delivered Daniel from
    the power of the lions.

28 So this Daniel prospered in the reign of Da·rī′us and in the reign of Cyrus the Persian.

VISION OF THE FOUR BEASTS

7 In the first year of Bel·shaz′zar king of Babylon, Daniel had a dream and visions of his head *while* on his bed. Then he wrote down the dream, telling the main facts.*a*
2 Daniel spoke, saying, "I saw in my vision by night, and behold, the four winds of heaven were stirring up the Great Sea.
3 "And four great beasts came up from the sea, each different from the other.
4 "The first *was* like a lion, and had eagle's wings. I watched till its wings were plucked off; and it was lifted up

from the earth and made to stand on two feet like a man, and a man's heart was given to it.
5 "And suddenly another beast, a second, like a bear. It was raised up on one side, and *had* three ribs in its mouth between its teeth. And they said thus to it: 'Arise, devour much flesh!'
6 "After this I looked, and there was another, like a leopard, which had on its back four wings of a bird. The beast also had four heads, and dominion was given to it.
7 "After this I saw in the night visions, and behold, a fourth beast, dreadful and terrible, exceedingly strong. It had huge iron teeth; it was devouring, breaking in pieces, and trampling the residue with its feet. It *was* different from all the beasts that *were* before it, and it had ten horns.
8 "I was considering the horns, and there was another horn, a little one, coming up among them, before whom three of the first horns were plucked out by the roots. And there, in this horn, *were* eyes like the eyes of a man, and a mouth speaking pompous words.

VISION OF THE ANCIENT OF DAYS

9 "I watched till thrones were put in
    place,
And the Ancient of Days was
    seated;
His garment *was* white as snow,
And the hair of His head *was* like
    pure wool.
His throne *was* a fiery flame,
Its wheels a burning fire;
10 A fiery stream issued
And came forth from before Him.
A thousand thousands ministered
    to Him;

7:1 *a*Literally *the head* (or *chief*) *of the words*

Ten thousand times ten thousand
  stood before Him.
The court*a* was seated,
And the books were opened.

11 "I watched then because of the sound of the pompous words which the horn was speaking; I watched till the beast was slain, and its body destroyed and given to the burning flame.

12 "As for the rest of the beasts, they had their dominion taken away, yet their lives were prolonged for a season and a time.

13 "I was watching in the night
  visions,
And behold, *One* like the Son of
  Man,
Coming with the clouds of
  heaven!
He came to the Ancient of Days,
And they brought Him near
  before Him.
14 Then to Him was given dominion
  and glory and a kingdom,
That all peoples, nations, and
  languages should serve Him.
His dominion *is* an everlasting
  dominion,
Which shall not pass away,
And His kingdom *the one*
Which shall not be destroyed.

DANIEL'S VISIONS INTERPRETED

15 "I, Daniel, was grieved in my spirit within *my* body, and the visions of my head troubled me.

16 "I came near to one of those who stood by, and asked him the truth of all this. So he told me and made known to me the interpretation of these things:

17 'Those great beasts, which are four, *are* four kings*a* which arise out of the earth.

18 'But the saints of the Most High shall receive the kingdom, and possess the kingdom forever, even forever and ever.'

19 "Then I wished to know the truth about the fourth beast, which was different from all the others, exceedingly dreadful, *with* its teeth of iron and its nails of bronze, *which* devoured, broke in pieces, and trampled the residue with its feet;

20 "and the ten horns that *were* on its head, and the other *horn* which came up, before which three fell, namely, that horn which had eyes and a mouth which spoke pompous words, whose appearance *was* greater than his fellows.

21 "I was watching; and the same horn was making war against the saints, and prevailing against them,

22 "until the Ancient of Days came, and a judgment was made *in favor* of the saints of the Most High, and the time came for the saints to possess the kingdom.

23 "Thus he said:

'The fourth beast shall be
A fourth kingdom on earth,
Which shall be different from all
  other kingdoms,
And shall devour the whole earth,
Trample it and break it in pieces.
24 The ten horns *are* ten kings
Who shall arise from this
  kingdom.
And another shall rise after them;
He shall be different from the
  first *ones,*
And shall subdue three kings.
25 He shall speak *pompous* words
  against the Most High,
Shall persecute*a* the saints of the
  Most High,
And shall intend to change times
  and law.

7:10 *a*Or *judgment*　　7:17 *a*Representing their kingdoms (compare verse 23)　　7:25 *a*Literally *wear out*

Then *the saints* shall be given
   into his hand
For a time and times and half a
   time.

26 'But the court shall be seated,
   And they shall take away his
     dominion,
   To consume and destroy *it* forever.

27 Then the kingdom and dominion,
   And the greatness of the
     kingdoms under the whole
     heaven,
   Shall be given to the people, the
     saints of the Most High.
   His kingdom *is* an everlasting
     kingdom,
   And all dominions shall serve and
     obey Him.'

28 "This *is* the end of the account.*a* As for me, Daniel, my thoughts greatly troubled me, and my countenance changed; but I kept the matter in my heart."

VISION OF A RAM AND A GOAT

8 In the third year of the reign of King Bel·shaz′zar a vision appeared *to* me—to me, Daniel—after the one that appeared to me the first time.
2 I saw in the vision, and it so happened while I was looking, that I *was* in Shū′shan, the citadel, which *is* in the province of Ē′lam; and I saw in the vision that I *was* by the River Ū′laī.
3 Then I lifted my eyes and saw, and there, standing beside the river, was a ram which had two horns, and the two horns *were* high; but one *was* higher than the other, and the higher *one* came up last.
4 I saw the ram pushing westward, northward, and southward, so that no animal could withstand him; nor *was there any* that could deliver from

his hand, but he did according to his will and became great.
5 And as I was considering, suddenly a male goat came from the west, across the surface of the whole earth, without touching the ground; and the goat *had* a notable horn between his eyes.
6 Then he came to the ram that had two horns, which I had seen standing beside the river, and ran at him with furious power.
7 And I saw him confronting the ram; he was moved with rage against him, attacked the ram, and broke his two horns. There was no power in the ram to withstand him, but he cast him down to the ground and trampled him; and there was no one that could deliver the ram from his hand.
8 Therefore the male goat grew very great; but when he became strong, the large horn was broken, and in place of it four notable ones came up toward the four winds of heaven.
9 And out of one of them came a little horn which grew exceedingly great toward the south, toward the east, and toward the Glorious *Land*.
10 And it grew up to the host of heaven; and it cast down *some* of the host and *some* of the stars to the ground, and trampled them.
11 He even exalted *himself* as high as the Prince of the host; and by him the daily *sacrifices* were taken away, and the place of His sanctuary was cast down.
12 Because of transgression, an army was given over *to the horn* to oppose the daily *sacrifices;* and he cast truth down to the ground. He did *all this* and prospered.
13 Then I heard a holy one speaking; and *another* holy one said to that certain *one* who was speaking, "How

7:28 *a*Literally *the word*

long *will* the vision *be, concerning* the daily *sacrifices* and the transgression of desolation, the giving of both the sanctuary and the host to be trampled underfoot?"

14 And he said to me, "For two thousand three hundred days;*a* then the sanctuary shall be cleansed."

GABRIEL INTERPRETS THE VISION

15 Then it happened, when I, Daniel, had seen the vision and was seeking the meaning, that suddenly there stood before me one having the appearance of a man.
16 And I heard a man's voice between *the banks of* the Ū′laī, who called, and said, "Gabriel, make this *man* understand the vision."
17 So he came near where I stood, and when he came I was afraid and fell on my face; but he said to me, "Understand, son of man, that the vision *refers* to the time of the end."
18 Now, as he was speaking with me, I was in a deep sleep with my face to the ground; but he touched me, and stood me upright.
19 And he said, "Look, I am making known to you what shall happen in the latter time of the indignation; for at the appointed time the end *shall be.*
20 "The ram which you saw, having the two horns—*they are* the kings of Media and Persia.
21 "And the male goat *is* the kingdom*a* of Greece. The large horn that *is* between its eyes *is* the first king.
22 "As for the broken *horn* and the four that stood up in its place, four kingdoms shall arise out of that nation, but not with its power.

23 "And in the latter time of their kingdom,
When the transgressors have reached their fullness,

A king shall arise,
Having fierce features,
Who understands sinister schemes.
24 His power shall be mighty, but not by his own power;
He shall destroy fearfully,
And shall prosper and thrive;
He shall destroy the mighty, and *also* the holy people.

25 "Through his cunning
He shall cause deceit to prosper under his rule;*a*
And he shall exalt *himself* in his heart.
He shall destroy many in *their* prosperity.
He shall even rise against the Prince of princes;
But he shall be broken without *human* means.*b*

26 "And the vision of the evenings and mornings
Which was told is true;
Therefore seal up the vision,
For *it refers* to many days *in the future.*"

27 And I, Daniel, fainted and was sick for days; afterward I arose and went about the king's business. I was astonished by the vision, but no one understood it.

DANIEL'S PRAYER FOR THE PEOPLE

9 In the first year of Da·rī′us the son of A·has·u·ē′rus, of the lineage of the Mēdes, who was made king over the realm of the Chal·dē′ans—
2 in the first year of his reign I, Daniel, understood by the books the number of the years *specified* by the

8:14 *a*Literally *evening-mornings*　8:21 *a*Literally *king,* representing his kingdom (compare 7:17, 23)　8:25 *a*Literally *hand*　*b*Literally *hand*

word of the LORD through Jer·e·mī′ah the prophet, that He would accomplish seventy years in the desolations of Jerusalem.

Prayers

Daniel 9:3–19

When Daniel prayed he stopped eating, put on rough sackcloth, and put ashes on himself. Most of us don't do that when we pray, do we? Then Daniel confessed the sin of his people. He reminded God that they had not obeyed Him. Then he begged God to forgive. When you know that you have done something terrible against God, confess what you have done. Beg Him to forgive you.

---

3 Then I set my face toward the Lord God to make request by prayer and supplications, with fasting, sackcloth, and ashes.

4 And I prayed to the LORD my God, and made confession, and said, "O Lord, great and awesome God, who keeps His covenant and mercy with those who love Him, and with those who keep His commandments,

5 "we have sinned and committed iniquity, we have done wickedly and rebelled, even by departing from Your precepts and Your judgments.

6 "Neither have we heeded Your servants the prophets, who spoke in Your name to our kings and our princes, to our fathers and all the people of the land.

7 "O Lord, righteousness belongs to You, but to us shame of face, as it is this day—to the men of Judah, to the inhabitants of Jerusalem and all Israel, those near and those far off in all the countries to which You have driven them, because of the unfaithfulness which they have committed against You.

8 "O Lord, to us belongs shame of face, to our kings, our princes, and our fathers, because we have sinned against You.

9 "To the Lord our God belong mercy and forgiveness, though we have rebelled against Him.

10 "We have not obeyed the voice of the LORD our God, to walk in His laws, which He set before us by His servants the prophets.

11 "Yes, all Israel has transgressed Your law, and has departed so as not to obey Your voice; therefore the curse and the oath written in the Law of Moses the servant of God have been poured out on us, because we have sinned against Him.

12 "And He has confirmed His words, which He spoke against us and against our judges who judged us, by bringing upon us a great disaster; for under the whole heaven such has never been done as what has been done to Jerusalem.

13 "As it is written in the Law of Moses, all this disaster has come upon us; yet we have not made our prayer before the LORD our God, that we might turn from our iniquities and understand Your truth.

14 "Therefore the LORD has kept the disaster in mind, and brought it upon us; for the LORD our God is righteous in all the works which He does, though we have not obeyed His voice.

15 "And now, O Lord our God, who brought Your people out of the land of Egypt with a mighty hand, and made Yourself a name, as it is this day—we have sinned, we have done wickedly!

16 "O Lord, according to all Your righteousness, I pray, let Your anger and Your fury be turned away from Your city Jerusalem, Your holy mountain; because for our sins, and for the

For more on *What Should I Do?* turn to page 1353
For more on *Prayer* turn to page 1871

iniquities of our fathers, Jerusalem and Your people *are* a reproach to all *those* around us.

17 "Now therefore, our God, hear the prayer of Your servant, and his supplications, and for the Lord's sake cause Your face to shine on Your sanctuary, which is desolate.

18 "O my God, incline Your ear and hear; open Your eyes and see our desolations, and the city which is called by Your name; for we do not present our supplications before You because of our righteous deeds, but because of Your great mercies.

19 "O Lord, hear! O Lord, forgive! O Lord, listen and act! Do not delay for Your own sake, my God, for Your city and Your people are called by Your name."

THE SEVENTY-WEEKS PROPHECY

20 Now while I *was* speaking, praying, and confessing my sin and the sin of my people Israel, and presenting my supplication before the LORD my God for the holy mountain of my God,

21 yes, while I *was* speaking in prayer, the man Gabriel, whom I had seen in the vision at the beginning, being caused to fly swiftly, reached me about the time of the evening offering.

22 And he informed *me,* and talked with me, and said, "O Daniel, I have now come forth to give you skill to understand.

23 "At the beginning of your supplications the command went out, and I have come to tell *you,* for you *are* greatly beloved; therefore consider the matter, and understand the vision:

24 "Seventy weeks*a* are determined
For your people and for your holy city,
To finish the transgression,
To make an end of*b* sins,

9:24 *a*Literally *sevens,* and so throughout the chapter *b*Following Qere, Septuagint, Syriac, and Vulgate; Kethib and Theodotion read *To seal up.*

To make reconciliation for
iniquity,
To bring in everlasting
righteousness,
To seal up vision and prophecy,
And to anoint the Most Holy.

25 "Know therefore and understand,
That from the going forth of the
command
To restore and build Jerusalem
Until Messiah the Prince,
There shall be seven weeks and
sixty-two weeks;
The street*a* shall be built again,
and the wall,*b*
Even in troublesome times.

26 "And after the sixty-two weeks
Messiah shall be cut off, but not
for Himself;
And the people of the prince who
is to come
Shall destroy the city and the
sanctuary.
The end of it *shall be* with a flood,
And till the end of the war
desolations are determined.
27 Then he shall confirm a covenant
with many for one week;
But in the middle of the week
He shall bring an end to sacrifice
and offering.
And on the wing of abominations
shall be one who makes
desolate,
Even until the consummation,
which is determined,
Is poured out on the desolate."

VISION OF THE GLORIOUS MAN

10 In the third year of Cyrus king
of Persia a message was revealed to
Daniel, whose name was called
Bel·te·shaz′zar. The message *was*
true, but the appointed time *was*
long;*a* and he understood the mes-

sage, and had understanding of the
vision.
2 In those days I, Daniel, was
mourning three full weeks.
3 I ate no pleasant food, no meat or
wine came into my mouth, nor did I
anoint myself at all, till three whole
weeks were fulfilled.
4 Now on the twenty-fourth day of
the first month, as I was by the side
of the great river, that *is*, the Tī′-
gris,*a*
5 I lifted my eyes and looked, and
behold, a certain man clothed in
linen, whose waist *was* girded with
gold of Ū′phaz!
6 His body *was* like beryl, his face
like the appearance of lightning, his
eyes like torches of fire, his arms and
feet like burnished bronze in color,
and the sound of his words like the
voice of a multitude.
7 And I, Daniel, alone saw the vision, for the men who were with me
did not see the vision; but a great terror fell upon them, so that they fled
to hide themselves.
8 Therefore I was left alone when
I saw this great vision, and no
strength remained in me; for my
vigor was turned to frailty in me, and
I retained no strength.
9 Yet I heard the sound of his
words; and while I heard the sound of
his words I was in a deep sleep on my
face, with my face to the ground.

PROPHECIES CONCERNING PERSIA AND GREECE

10 Suddenly, a hand touched me,
which made me tremble on my knees
and *on* the palms of my hands.
11 And he said to me, "O Daniel,
man greatly beloved, understand the
words that I speak to you, and stand

9:25 *a*Or *open square*   *b*Or *moat*   10:1 *a*Or *and
of great conflict*   10:4 *a*Hebrew *Hiddekel*

upright, for I have now been sent to you." While he was speaking this word to me, I stood trembling.

12 Then he said to me, "Do not fear, Daniel, for from the first day that you set your heart to understand, and to humble yourself before your God, your words were heard; and I have come because of your words.

13 "But the prince of the kingdom of Persia withstood me twenty-one days; and behold, Michael, one of the chief princes, came to help me, for I had been left alone there with the kings of Persia.

14 "Now I have come to make you understand what will happen to your people in the latter days, for the vision *refers* to *many* days yet *to come*."

15 When he had spoken such words to me, I turned my face toward the ground and became speechless.

16 And suddenly, *one* having the likeness of the sons*a* of men touched my lips; then I opened my mouth and spoke, saying to him who stood before me, "My lord, because of the vision my sorrows have overwhelmed me, and I have retained no strength.

17 "For how can this servant of my lord talk with you, my lord? As for me, no strength remains in me now, nor is any breath left in me."

18 Then again, *the one* having the likeness of a man touched me and strengthened me.

19 And he said, "O man greatly beloved, fear not! Peace *be* to you; be strong, yes, be strong!" So when he spoke to me I was strengthened, and said, "Let my lord speak, for you have strengthened me."

20 Then he said, "Do you know why I have come to you? And now I must return to fight with the prince of Persia; and when I have gone forth, indeed the prince of Greece will come.

21 "But I will tell you what is noted in the Scripture of Truth. (No one up-

holds me against these, except Michael your prince.

11 "Also in the first year of Da·rī′us the Mēde, I, *even* I, stood up to confirm and strengthen him.)

2 "And now I will tell you the truth: Behold, three more kings will arise in Persia, and the fourth shall be far richer than *them* all; by his strength, through his riches, he shall stir up all against the realm of Greece.

3 "Then a mighty king shall arise, who shall rule with great dominion, and do according to his will.

4 "And when he has arisen, his kingdom shall be broken up and divided toward the four winds of heaven, but not among his posterity nor according to his dominion with which he ruled; for his kingdom shall be uprooted, even for others besides these.

WARRING KINGS OF NORTH AND SOUTH

5 "Also the king of the South shall become strong, as well as *one* of his princes; and he shall gain power over him and have dominion. His dominion *shall be* a great dominion.

6 "And at the end of *some* years they shall join forces, for the daughter of the king of the South shall go to the king of the North to make an agreement; but she shall not retain the power of her authority,*a* and neither he nor his authority*b* shall stand; but she shall be given up, with those who brought her, and with him who begot her, and with him who strengthened her in *those* times.

7 "But from a branch of her roots *one* shall arise in his place, who shall come with an army, enter the fortress

---

10:16 *a*Theodotion and Vulgate read *the son;* Septuagint reads *a hand.*　　11:6 *a*Literally *arm*　*b*Literally *arm*

of the king of the North, and deal with them and prevail.

8 "And he shall also carry their gods captive to Egypt, with their princes*a and* their precious articles of silver and gold; and he shall continue *more* years than the king of the North.

9 "Also *the king of the North* shall come to the kingdom of the king of the South, but shall return to his own land.

10 "However his sons shall stir up strife, and assemble a multitude of great forces; and *one* shall certainly come and overwhelm and pass through; then he shall return to his fortress and stir up strife.

11 "And the king of the South shall be moved with rage, and go out and fight with him, with the king of the North, who shall muster a great multitude; but the multitude shall be given into the hand of his *enemy.*

12 "When he has taken away the multitude, his heart will be lifted up; and he will cast down tens of thousands, but he will not prevail.

13 "For the king of the North will return and muster a multitude greater than the former, and shall certainly come at the end of some years with a great army and much equipment.

14 "Now in those times many shall rise up against the king of the South. Also, violent men*a* of your people shall exalt themselves in fulfillment of the vision, but they shall fall.

15 "So the king of the North shall come and build a siege mound, and take a fortified city; and the forces*a* of the South shall not withstand *him.* Even his choice troops *shall have* no strength to resist.

16 "But he who comes against him shall do according to his own will, and no one shall stand against him. He shall stand in the Glorious Land with destruction in his power.*a*

17 "He shall also set his face to enter with the strength of his whole kingdom, and upright ones*a* with him; thus shall he do. And he shall give him the daughter of women to destroy it; but she shall not stand *with him,* or be for him.

18 "After this he shall turn his face to the coastlands, and shall take many. But a ruler shall bring the reproach against them to an end; and with the reproach removed, he shall turn back on him.

19 "Then he shall turn his face toward the fortress of his own land; but he shall stumble and fall, and not be found.

20 "There shall arise in his place one who imposes taxes *on* the glorious kingdom; but within a few days he shall be destroyed, but not in anger or in battle.

21 "And in his place shall arise a vile person, to whom they will not give the honor of royalty; but he shall come in peaceably, and seize the kingdom by intrigue.

22 "With the force*a* of a flood they shall be swept away from before him and be broken, and also the prince of the covenant.

23 "And after the league *is made* with him he shall act deceitfully, for he shall come up and become strong with a small *number of* people.

24 "He shall enter peaceably, even into the richest places of the province; and he shall do *what* his fathers have not done, nor his forefathers: he shall disperse among them the plunder, spoil, and riches; and he shall devise his plans against the strongholds, but *only* for a time.

25 "He shall stir up his power and his courage against the king of the

11:8 *a*Or *molded images* lit-erally *sons of breakage*　11:16 *a*Literally *hand*　11:14 *a*Or *robbers,* lit-erally *arms*　11:15 *a*Literally *arms*　11:17 *a*Or *bring equitable terms*　11:22 *a*Literally *arms*

South with a great army. And the king of the South shall be stirred up to battle with a very great and mighty army; but he shall not stand, for they shall devise plans against him.

26 "Yes, those who eat of the portion of his delicacies shall destroy him; his army shall be swept away, and many shall fall down slain.

27 "Both these kings' hearts *shall be* bent on evil, and they shall speak lies at the same table; but it shall not prosper, for the end *will* still *be* at the appointed time.

28 "While returning to his land with great riches, his heart shall be *moved* against the holy covenant; so he shall do *damage* and return to his own land.

THE NORTHERN KING'S BLASPHEMIES

29 "At the appointed time he shall return and go toward the south; but it shall not be like the former or the latter.

30 "For ships from Cyprus*a* shall come against him; therefore he shall be grieved, and return in rage against the holy covenant, and do *damage*. So he shall return and show regard for those who forsake the holy covenant.

31 "And forces*a* shall be mustered by him, and they shall defile the sanctuary fortress; then they shall take away the daily *sacrifices,* and place *there* the abomination of desolation.

32 "Those who do wickedly against the covenant he shall corrupt with flattery; but the people who know their God shall be strong, and carry out *great exploits*.

33 "And those of the people who understand shall instruct many; yet *for many* days they shall fall by sword and flame, by captivity and plundering.

34 "Now when they fall, they shall be aided with a little help; but many shall join with them by intrigue.

35 "And *some* of those of understanding shall fall, to refine them, purify *them,* and make *them* white, *until* the time of the end; because *it is* still for the appointed time.

36 "Then the king shall do according to his own will: he shall exalt and magnify himself above every god, shall speak blasphemies against the God of gods, and shall prosper till the wrath has been accomplished; for what has been determined shall be done.

37 "He shall regard neither the God*a* of his fathers nor the desire of women, nor regard any god; for he shall exalt himself above *them* all.

38 "But in their place he shall honor a god of fortresses; and a god which his fathers did not know he shall honor with gold and silver, with precious stones and pleasant things.

39 "Thus he shall act against the strongest fortresses with a foreign god, which he shall acknowledge, *and* advance *its* glory; and he shall cause them to rule over many, and divide the land for gain.

THE NORTHERN KING'S CONQUESTS

40 "At the time of the end the king of the South shall attack him; and the king of the North shall come against him like a whirlwind, with chariots, horsemen, and with many ships; and he shall enter the countries, overwhelm *them,* and pass through.

41 "He shall also enter the Glorious Land, and many *countries* shall be overthrown; but these shall escape from his hand: Ē'dom, Mō'ab, and the prominent people of Am'mon.

11:30 *a*Hebrew *Kittim,* western lands, especially Cyprus   11:31 *a*Literally *arms*   11:37 *a*Or *gods*

THOSE WHO ARE WISE SHALL SHINE / LIKE THE BRIGHTNESS OF THE FIRMAMENT, / AND THOSE WHO TURN MANY TO RIGHTEOUSNESS / LIKE THE STARS FOREVER AND EVER.   Daniel 12:3

Are You a Star?

We talk about movie stars and sports stars. That's because they "shine" a little brighter than some of the rest of us, at least in popularity and income. But that's *nothing!* Wait until you see the real stars—God's people who turn others to Him. Movie stars and sports stars may shine a little for a short time. But God's real stars will shine brightly forever and ever. Would you like to become a *real* star?

1. Have you ever dreamed of becoming a movie star or a sports star? Why?
2. Daniel 12:3 tells you how to become a much brighter star forever and ever. Read it again. How can you become one of God's stars? What do you need to do? Will you?

For more on *Favorite Family Verses* turn to page 1466
For more on *Salvation* turn to page 1480

42 "He shall stretch out his hand against the countries, and the land of Egypt shall not escape.

43 "He shall have power over the treasures of gold and silver, and over all the precious things of Egypt; also the Lib'yans and Ethiopians *shall follow* at his heels.

44 "But news from the east and the north shall trouble him; therefore he shall go out with great fury to destroy and annihilate many.

45 "And he shall plant the tents of his palace between the seas and the glorious holy mountain; yet he shall come to his end, and no one will help him.

PROPHECY OF THE END TIME

12 "At that time Michael shall stand up,
The great prince who stands *watch* over the sons of your people;
And there shall be a time of trouble,
Such as never was since there was a nation,
Even to that time.
And at that time your people shall be delivered,
Every one who is found written in the book.

2 And many of those who sleep in the dust of the earth shall awake,
Some to everlasting life,
Some to shame *and* everlasting contempt.

3 Those who are wise shall shine
Like the brightness of the firmament,
And those who turn many to righteousness
Like the stars forever and ever.

4 "But you, Daniel, shut up the words, and seal the book until the time of the end; many shall run to and fro, and knowledge shall increase."

5 Then I, Daniel, looked; and there stood two others, one on this riverbank and the other on that riverbank.

6 And *one* said to the man clothed in linen, who *was* above the waters of the river, "How long shall the fulfillment of these wonders *be?*"

7 Then I heard the man clothed in linen, who *was* above the waters of the river, when he held up his right hand and his left hand to heaven, and swore by Him who lives forever, that *it shall be* for a time, times, and half *a time;* and when the power of the holy people has been completely shattered, all these *things* shall be finished.

8 Although I heard, I did not understand. Then I said, "My lord, what *shall be* the end of these *things?*"

9 And he said, "Go *your way,* Daniel, for the words *are* closed up and sealed till the time of the end.

10 "Many shall be purified, made white, and refined, but the wicked shall do wickedly; and none of the wicked shall understand, but the wise shall understand.

11 "And from the time *that* the daily *sacrifice* is taken away, and the abomination of desolation is set up, *there shall be* one thousand two hundred and ninety days.

12 "Blessed *is* he who waits, and comes to the one thousand three hundred and thirty-five days.

13 "But you, go *your way* till the end; for you shall rest, and will arise to your inheritance at the end of the days."

The Book of
HOSEA

THE word of the LORD that came to Hō·sē′a the son of Be·ē′rī, in the days of Uz·zī′ah, Jō′tham, Ā′haz, *and* Hez-e·kī′ah, kings of Judah, and in the days of Jer·o·bō′am the son of Jō′ash, king of Israel.

THE FAMILY OF HOSEA

2 When the LORD began to speak by Hō·sē′a, the LORD said to Hō·sē′a:

"Go, take yourself a wife of
    harlotry
And children of harlotry,
For the land has committed great
    harlotry
By departing from the LORD."

3 So he went and took Gō′mer the daughter of Dib·lā′im, and she conceived and bore him a son.
4 Then the LORD said to him:

"Call his name Jez′re·el,
For in a little *while*
I will avenge the bloodshed of
    Jez′re·el on the house of Jē′hu,
And bring an end to the kingdom
    of the house of Israel.
5 It shall come to pass in that day
That I will break the bow of Israel
    in the Valley of Jez′re·el."

6 And she conceived again and bore a daughter. Then *God* said to him:

"Call her name Lō-Rū·ha′mah,a
For I will no longer have mercy
    on the house of Israel,
But I will utterly take them
    away.b
7 Yet I will have mercy on the
    house of Judah,

Will save them by the LORD their
    God,
And will not save them by bow,
Nor by sword or battle,
By horses or horsemen."

8 Now when she had weaned Lō-Rū·ha′mah, she conceived and bore a son.
9 Then *God* said:

"Call his name Lō-Am′mī,a
For you *are* not My people,
And I will not be your *God*.

THE RESTORATION OF ISRAEL

10 "Yet the number of the children of
    Israel
Shall be as the sand of the sea,
Which cannot be measured or
    numbered.
And it shall come to pass
In the place where it was said to
    them,
'You *are* not My people,'a
There it shall be said to them,
'*You* are sons of the living God.'
11 Then the children of Judah and
    the children of Israel
Shall be gathered together,
And appoint for themselves one
    head;
And they shall come up out of the
    land,
For great *will be* the day of
    Jez′re·el!

2
Say to your brethren, 'My people,'a
And to your sisters, 'Mercyb *is
    shown*.'

1:6 aLiterally *No-Mercy* bOr *That I may forgive them at all* 1:9 aLiterally *Not-My-People*
1:10 aHebrew *lo-ammi* (compare verse 9)
2:1 aHebrew *Ammi* (compare 1:9, 10) bHebrew *Ruhamah* (compare 1:6)

GOD'S UNFAITHFUL PEOPLE

2 "Bring charges against your
　　mother, bring charges;
　　For she *is* not My wife, nor *am* I
　　　her Husband!
　　Let her put away her harlotries
　　　from her sight,
　　And her adulteries from between
　　　her breasts;
3 Lest I strip her naked
　　And expose her, as in the day she
　　　was born,
　　And make her like a wilderness,
　　And set her like a dry land,
　　And slay her with thirst.

4 "I will not have mercy on her
　　children,
　　For they *are* the children of
　　　harlotry.
5 For their mother has played the
　　harlot;
　　She who conceived them has
　　　behaved shamefully.
　　For she said, 'I will go after my
　　　lovers,
　　Who give *me* my bread and my
　　　water,
　　My wool and my linen,
　　My oil and my drink.'

6 "Therefore, behold,
　　I will hedge up your way with
　　　thorns,
　　And wall her in,
　　So that she cannot find her
　　　paths.
7 She will chase her lovers,
　　But not overtake them;
　　Yes, she will seek them, but not
　　　find *them*.
　　Then she will say,
　　'I will go and return to my first
　　　husband,
　　For then *it was* better for me than
　　　now.'
8 For she did not know

That I gave her grain, new wine,
　　and oil,
　　And multiplied her silver and
　　　gold—
　　Which they prepared for Bāʹal.

9 "Therefore I will return and take
　　away
　　My grain in its time
　　And My new wine in its season,
　　And will take back My wool and
　　　My linen,
　　Given to cover her nakedness.
10 Now I will uncover her lewdness
　　in the sight of her lovers,
　　And no one shall deliver her from
　　　My hand.
11 I will also cause all her mirth to
　　cease,
　　Her feast days,
　　Her New Moons,
　　Her Sabbaths—
　　All her appointed feasts.

12 "And I will destroy her vines and
　　her fig trees,
　　Of which she has said,
　　'These *are* my wages that my
　　　lovers have given me.'
　　So I will make them a forest,
　　And the beasts of the field shall
　　　eat them.
13 I will punish her
　　For the days of the Bāʹals to
　　　which she burned incense.
　　She decked herself with her
　　　earrings and jewelry,
　　And went after her lovers;
　　But Me she forgot," says the
　　LORD.

GOD'S MERCY ON HIS PEOPLE

14 "Therefore, behold, I will allure
　　her,
　　Will bring her into the
　　　wilderness,
　　And speak comfort to her.

SINGING Hosea 2:15

What Kind of Song Shall We Sing?

We're ready to sing, but what shall we sing? How about a song of praise to the Lord? Has He done wonderful things for you? Praise Him with your singing. Are you glad you can know Him? Praise Him with your singing.

1. What has the Lord done for you? Praise Him!
2. Why do you think the Lord is so special? Praise Him!
3. What do you think the Lord will do for you today and tomorrow and the next day? Praise Him!

For more on *Favorite Bible Words* turn to page 1452
For more on *Praise* turn to page 1698

15 I will give her her vineyards from
  there,
  And the Valley of Ā′chor as a door
  of hope;
  She shall sing there,
  As in the days of her youth,
  As in the day when she came up
  from the land of Egypt.

16 "And it shall be, in that day,"
  Says the LORD,
  "*That* you will call Me 'My
  Husband,'*a*
  And no longer call Me 'My
  Master,'*b*
17 For I will take from her mouth
  the names of the Bā′als,
  And they shall be remembered by
  their name no more.
18 In that day I will make a
  covenant for them
  With the beasts of the field,
  With the birds of the air,
  And *with* the creeping things of
  the ground.
  Bow and sword of battle I will
  shatter from the earth,
  To make them lie down safely.

19 "I will betroth you to Me forever;
  Yes, I will betroth you to Me
  In righteousness and justice,
  In lovingkindness and mercy;
20 I will betroth you to Me in
  faithfulness,
  And you shall know the LORD.

21 "It shall come to pass in that day
  That I will answer," says the
  LORD;
  "I will answer the heavens,
  And they shall answer the earth.
22 The earth shall answer
  With grain,
  With new wine,
  And with oil;
  They shall answer Jez′re·el.*a*
23 Then I will sow her for Myself in
  the earth,

And I will have mercy on *her who
  had* not obtained mercy;*a*
Then I will say to *those who were*
  not My people,*b*
'You *are* My people!'
And they shall say, '*You are* my
  God!' "

ISRAEL WILL RETURN TO GOD

3 Then the LORD said to me, "Go
again, love a woman *who is* loved by
a lover*a* and is committing adultery,
just like the love of the LORD for the
children of Israel, who look to other
gods and love *the* raisin cakes *of the
pagans.*"
2 So I bought her for myself for fifteen *shekels* of silver, and one and
one-half homers of barley.
3 And I said to her, "You shall stay
with me many days; you shall not
play the harlot, nor shall you have a
man—so, too, *will* I *be* toward you."
4 For the children of Israel shall
abide many days without king or
prince, without sacrifice or sacred pillar, without ephod or teraphim.
5 Afterward the children of Israel
shall return and seek the LORD their
God and David their king. They shall
fear the LORD and His goodness in
the latter days.

GOD'S CHARGE AGAINST ISRAEL

4 Hear the word of the LORD,
  You children of Israel,
  For the LORD *brings* a charge
    against the inhabitants of the
    land:

"There is no truth or mercy
  Or knowledge of God in the land.
2 *By* swearing and lying,

2:16 *a*Hebrew *Ishi*   *b*Hebrew *Baali*
2:22 *a*Literally *God Will Sow*   2:23 *a*Hebrew *lo-
ruhamah*   *b*Hebrew *lo-ammi*   3:1 *a*Literally
friend or *husband*

Killing and stealing and
committing adultery,
They break all restraint,
With bloodshed upon bloodshed.
3 Therefore the land will mourn;
And everyone who dwells there
will waste away
With the beasts of the field
And the birds of the air;
Even the fish of the sea will be
taken away.

4 "Now let no man contend, or
rebuke another;
For your people *are* like those
who contend with the priest.
5 Therefore you shall stumble in
the day;
The prophet also shall stumble
with you in the night;
And I will destroy your mother.
6 My people are destroyed for lack
of knowledge.
Because you have rejected
knowledge,
I also will reject you from being
priest for Me;
Because you have forgotten the
law of your God,
I also will forget your children.

7 "The more they increased,
The more they sinned against Me;
I will change*a* their glory*b* into
shame.
8 They eat up the sin of My people;
They set their heart on their
iniquity.
9 And it shall be: like people, like
priest.
So I will punish them for their
ways,
And reward them for their deeds.
10 For they shall eat, but not have
enough;
They shall commit harlotry, but
not increase;
Because they have ceased obeying
the LORD.

THE IDOLATRY OF ISRAEL

11 "Harlotry, wine, and new wine
enslave the heart.
12 My people ask counsel from their
wooden *idols,*
And their staff informs them.
For the spirit of harlotry has
caused *them* to stray,
And they have played the harlot
against their God.
13 They offer sacrifices on the
mountaintops,
And burn incense on the hills,
Under oaks, poplars, and
terebinths,
Because their shade *is* good.
Therefore your daughters commit
harlotry,
And your brides commit adultery.

14 "I will not punish your daughters
when they commit harlotry,
Nor your brides when they
commit adultery;
For *the men* themselves go apart
with harlots,
And offer sacrifices with a ritual
harlot.*a*
Therefore people *who* do not
understand will be trampled.

15 "Though you, Israel, play the
harlot,
Let not Judah offend.
Do not come up to Gil'gal,
Nor go up to Beth Ā'ven,
Nor swear an oath, *saying,* 'As
the LORD lives'—

16 "For Israel is stubborn
Like a stubborn calf;
Now the LORD will let them
forage
Like a lamb in open country.

4:7 *a*Following Masoretic Text, Septuagint, and
Vulgate; scribal tradition, Syriac, and Targum read
They will change. *b*Following Masoretic Text, Septuagint, Syriac, Targum, and Vulgate; scribal tradition reads *My glory.*
4:14 *a*Compare Deuteronomy 23:18

Values

Are You Ever a Stubborn Donkey?

Did you ever see such a stubborn donkey? Caleb wants to lead him to his food and water. But that stubborn donkey doesn't want to go anywhere. That makes Caleb sad. His poor donkey will be hungry and thirsty, just because it is so stubborn. Caleb knows what is best for his donkey. But how can he give his donkey what is best when the donkey is so stubborn?

1. Why will this donkey not get what is best for it? Why will it miss its food and water?
2. Are you ever stubborn? You know that mother or father is trying to do what is best for you. But you just do *not* want to do it? Can they do what is best if you are stubborn?
3. Can God do what is best for you when you are stubborn? Stop it! Don't be like a stubborn donkey. Let parents and God do their best for you.

For more on *Values* turn to page 1363
For more on *Obeying* turn to page 1589

17 "Ē′phra·im *is* joined to idols,
Let him alone.
18 Their drink is rebellion,
They commit harlotry continually.
Her rulers dearly love dishonor.*a*
19 The wind has wrapped her up in
its wings,
And they shall be ashamed
because of their sacrifices.

IMPENDING JUDGMENT ON ISRAEL
AND JUDAH

5 "Hear this, O priests!
Take heed, O house of Israel!
Give ear, O house of the king!
For yours *is* the judgment,
Because you have been a snare to
Miz′pah
And a net spread on Tā′bor.
2 The revolters are deeply involved
in slaughter,
Though I rebuke them all.
3 I know Ē′phra·im,
And Israel is not hidden from
Me;
For now, O Ē′phra·im, you
commit harlotry;
Israel is defiled.

4 "They do not direct their deeds
Toward turning to their God,
For the spirit of harlotry is in
their midst,
And they do not know the LORD.
5 The pride of Israel testifies to his
face;
Therefore Israel and Ē′phra·im
stumble in their iniquity;
Judah also stumbles with them.

6 "With their flocks and herds
They shall go to seek the LORD,
But they will not find *Him;*
He has withdrawn Himself from
them.
7 They have dealt treacherously
with the LORD,

For they have begotten pagan
children.
Now a New Moon shall devour
them and their heritage.

8 "Blow the ram's horn in Gib′ē·ah,
The trumpet in Rā′mah!
Cry aloud *at* Beth Ā′ven,
'*Look* behind you, O Benjamin!'
9 Ē′phra·im shall be desolate in the
day of rebuke;
Among the tribes of Israel I make
known what is sure.

10 "The princes of Judah are like
those who remove a landmark;
I will pour out my wrath on them
like water.
11 Ē′phra·im is oppressed *and*
broken in judgment,
Because he willingly walked by
human precept.
12 Therefore I *will be* to Ē′phra·im
like a moth,
And to the house of Judah like
rottenness.

13 "When Ē′phra·im saw his sickness,
And Judah *saw* his wound,
Then Ē′phra·im went to Assyria
And sent to King Jā′reb;
Yet he cannot cure you,
Nor heal you of your wound.
14 For I *will be* like a lion to
Ē′phra·im,
And like a young lion to the house
of Judah.
I, *even* I, will tear *them* and go
away;
I will take *them* away, and no one
shall rescue.
15 I will return again to My place
Till they acknowledge their
offense.
Then they will seek My face;
In their affliction they will
earnestly seek Me."

4:18 *a*Hebrew is difficult; a Jewish tradition reads
Her rulers shamefully love, 'Give!'

WHEN TROUBLES GANG UP ON ME   Hosea 5:15

Do you ever feel like troubles gang up on you? Parents feel like that. Sometimes there are bills to pay and not enough money to pay them. Sometimes parents lose their jobs, or get hurt, or have a car accident, or have a dozen other troubles. Perhaps you feel like too many troubles are coming your way. What should you do when this happens?

1. Why do you think this lady is sad? Have troubles ganged up on her?
2. Have troubles ever ganged up on you? What happened? What did you do?
3. What should you do when troubles gang up on you? Which of the following should you do: (1) pray; (2) ask someone to help you; (3) ask someone to comfort you; (4) deal with one trouble at a time.

For more on *What Should I Do?* turn to page 1377
For more on *Facing Trials* turn to page 1758

A CALL TO REPENTANCE

6 Come, and let us return to the
LORD;
For He has torn, but He will heal
us;
He has stricken, but He will bind
us up.

■ *Promises* ■

Hosea 6:1

The people of Israel had to be
punished. They didn't like it.
God didn't like it. He said they
were "torn" and "stricken." But
after the punishment, God
wanted them back in a loving
relationship. Does that sound
like a loving parent? When you
do something bad, your parents
should punish you in some way,
shouldn't they? When you stop
doing something bad, it's time
for hugs and kisses. God promises to accept His people back
into a loving relationship after
punishment. That's good to know,
isn't it?

---

2   After two days He will revive us;
On the third day He will raise us
up,
That we may live in His sight.
3   Let us know,
Let us pursue the knowledge of
the LORD.
His going forth is established as
the morning;
He will come to us like the rain,
Like the latter *and* former rain to
the earth.

IMPENITENCE OF ISRAEL AND JUDAH

4   "O Ē'phra·im, what shall I do to
you?

O Judah, what shall I do to you?
For your faithfulness is like a
morning cloud,
And like the early dew it goes
away.
5   Therefore I have hewn *them* by
the prophets,
I have slain them by the words of
My mouth;
And your judgments *are like* light
that goes forth.
6   For I desire mercy and not
sacrifice,
And the knowledge of God more
than burnt offerings.

7   "But like men*a* they transgressed
the covenant;
There they dealt treacherously
with Me.
8   Gil'ē·ad *is* a city of evildoers
And defiled with blood.
9   As bands of robbers lie in wait for
a man,
So the company of priests murder
on the way to Shē'chem;
Surely they commit lewdness.
10 I have seen a horrible thing in the
house of Israel:
There *is* the harlotry of
Ē'phra·im;
Israel is defiled.
11 Also, O Judah, a harvest is
appointed for you,
When I return the captives of My
people.

7 "When I would have healed
Israel,
Then the iniquity of Ē'phra·im
was uncovered,
And the wickedness of Samaria.
For they have committed fraud;
A thief comes in;
A band of robbers takes spoil
outside.

6:7 *a*Or *like Adam*

2 They do not consider in their
      hearts
   That I remember all their
      wickedness;
   Now their own deeds have
      surrounded them;
   They are before My face.
3 They make a king glad with their
      wickedness,
   And princes with their lies.

4 "They *are* all adulterers.
   Like an oven heated by a
      baker—
   He ceases stirring *the fire* after
      kneading the dough,
   Until it is leavened.
5 In the day of our king
   Princes have made *him* sick,
      inflamed with wine;
   He stretched out his hand with
      scoffers.
6 They prepare their heart like an
      oven,
   While they lie in wait;
   Their baker*a* sleeps all night;
   In the morning it burns like a
      flaming fire.
7 They are all hot, like an oven,
   And have devoured their
      judges;
   All their kings have fallen.
   None among them calls upon
      Me.

8 "Ē′phra·im has mixed himself
      among the peoples;
   Ē′phra·im is a cake unturned.
9 Aliens have devoured his
      strength,
   But he does not know *it;*
   Yes, gray hairs are here and there
      on him,
   Yet he does not know *it.*
10 And the pride of Israel testifies to
      his face,
   But they do not return to the
      LORD their God,
   Nor seek Him for all this.

FUTILE RELIANCE ON THE NATIONS

11 "Ē′phra·im also is like a silly dove,
      without sense—
   They call to Egypt,
   They go to Assyria.
12 Wherever they go, I will spread
      My net on them;
   I will bring them down like birds
      of the air;
   I will chastise them
   According to what their
      congregation has heard.

13 "Woe to them, for they have fled
      from Me!
   Destruction to them,
   Because they have transgressed
      against Me!
   Though I redeemed them,
   Yet they have spoken lies against
      Me.
14 They did not cry out to Me with
      their heart
   When they wailed upon their
      beds.

   "They assemble together for*a*
      grain and new wine,
   They rebel against Me;*b*
15 Though I disciplined *and*
      strengthened their arms,
   Yet they devise evil against
      Me;
16 They return, *but* not to the Most
      High;*a*
   They are like a treacherous bow.
   Their princes shall fall by the
      sword
   For the cursings of their tongue.
   This *shall be* their derision in the
      land of Egypt.

7:6 *a*Following Masoretic Text and Vulgate; Syriac
and Targum read *Their anger;* Septuagint reads
Ephraim.   7:14 *a*Following Masoretic Text and
Targum; Vulgate reads *thought upon;* Septuagint
reads *slashed themselves for* (compare 1 Kings
18:28).   *b*Following Masoretic Text, Syriac, and
Targum; Septuagint omits *They rebel against Me;*
Vulgate reads *They departed from Me.*
7:16 *a*Or *upward*

THE APOSTASY OF ISRAEL

8 "Set the trumpet[a] to your mouth!
He shall come like an eagle
  against the house of the LORD,
Because they have transgressed
  My covenant
And rebelled against My law.
2 Israel will cry to Me,
  'My God, we know You!'
3 Israel has rejected the good;
  The enemy will pursue him.

4 "They set up kings, but not by Me;
  They made princes, but I did not
    acknowledge *them.*
  From their silver and gold
  They made idols for themselves—
  That they might be cut off.
5 Your calf is rejected, O Samaria!
  My anger is aroused against
    them—
  How long until they attain to
    innocence?
6 For from Israel *is* even this:
  A workman made it, and it *is* not
    God;
  But the calf of Samaria shall be
    broken to pieces.

7 "They sow the wind,
  And reap the whirlwind.
  The stalk has no bud;
  It shall never produce meal.
  If it should produce,
  Aliens would swallow it up.
8 Israel is swallowed up;
  Now they are among the Gentiles
  Like a vessel in which *is* no
    pleasure.
9 For they have gone up to Assyria,
  Like a wild donkey alone by itself;
  É'phra·im has hired lovers.
10 Yes, though they have hired
    among the nations,
  Now I will gather them;
  And they shall sorrow a little,[a]
  Because of the burden[b] of the
    king of princes.

11 "Because É'phra·im has made
    many altars for sin,
  They have become for him altars
    for sinning.
12 I have written for him the great
    things of My law,
  But they were considered a
    strange thing.
13 *For* the sacrifices of My offerings
    they sacrifice flesh and eat *it,*
  But the LORD does not accept
    them.
  Now He will remember their
    iniquity and punish their sins.
  They shall return to Egypt.

14 "For Israel has forgotten his
    Maker,
  And has built temples;[a]
  Judah also has multiplied
    fortified cities;
  But I will send fire upon his
    cities,
  And it shall devour his palaces."

JUDGMENT OF ISRAEL'S SIN

9 Do not rejoice, O Israel, with joy
  like *other* peoples,
  For you have played the harlot
    against your God.
  You have made love *for* hire on
    every threshing floor.
2 The threshing floor and the
    winepress
  Shall not feed them,
  And the new wine shall fail in
    her.

3 They shall not dwell in the LORD's
    land,
  But É'phra·im shall return to
    Egypt,
  And shall eat unclean *things* in
    Assyria.

8:1 [a]Hebrew *shophar,* ram's horn   8:10 [a]Or *begin to diminish*   [b]Or *oracle*   8:14 [a]Or *palaces*

4 They shall not offer wine *offerings*
to the LORD,
Nor shall their sacrifices be
pleasing to Him.
It shall be like bread of mourners
to them;
All who eat it shall be defiled.
For their bread *shall be* for their
own life;
It shall not come into the house of
the LORD.

5 What will you do in the appointed
day,
And in the day of the feast of the
LORD?

6 For indeed they are gone because
of destruction.
Egypt shall gather them up;
Memphis shall bury them.
Nettles shall possess their
valuables of silver;
Thorns *shall be* in their tents.

7 The days of punishment have
come;
The days of recompense have
come.
Israel knows!
The prophet *is* a fool,
The spiritual man *is* insane,
Because of the greatness of your
iniquity and great enmity.

8 The watchman of Ē′phra·im *is*
with my God;
But the prophet *is* a fowler's^a
snare in all his ways—
Enmity in the house of his God.

9 They are deeply corrupted,
As in the days of Gib′ē·ah.
He will remember their iniquity;
He will punish their sins.

10 "I found Israel
Like grapes in the wilderness;
I saw your fathers
As the firstfruits on the fig tree in
its first season.
But they went to Bā′al Pē′or,

And separated themselves *to that*
shame;
They became an abomination like
the thing they loved.

11 *As for* Ē′phra·im, their glory shall
fly away like a bird—
No birth, no pregnancy, and no
conception!

12 Though they bring up their
children,
Yet I will bereave them to the last
man.
Yes, woe to them when I depart
from them!

13 Just as I saw Ē′phra·im like Tȳre,
planted in a pleasant place,
So Ē′phra·im will bring out his
children to the murderer."

14 Give them, O LORD—
What will You give?
Give them a miscarrying womb
And dry breasts!

15 "All their wickedness *is* in Gil′gal,
For there I hated them.
Because of the evil of their deeds
I will drive them from My house;
I will love them no more.
All their princes *are* rebellious.

16 Ē′phra·im is stricken,
Their root is dried up;
They shall bear no fruit.
Yes, were they to bear children,
I would kill the darlings of their
womb."

17 My God will cast them away,
Because they did not obey Him;
And they shall be wanderers
among the nations.

ISRAEL'S SIN AND CAPTIVITY

10 Israel empties *his* vine;
He brings forth fruit for himself.

9:8 ^aThat is, one who catches birds in a trap or
snare

According to the multitude of his
fruit
He has increased the altars;
According to the bounty of his
land
They have embellished *his* sacred
pillars.
2 Their heart is divided;
Now they are held guilty.
He will break down their altars;
He will ruin their sacred pillars.

3 For now they say,
"We have no king,
Because we did not fear the
LORD.
And as for a king, what would he
do for us?"
4 They have spoken words,
Swearing falsely in making a
covenant.
Thus judgment springs up like
hemlock in the furrows of the
field.

5 The inhabitants of Samaria fear
Because of the calf*a* of Beth
Ā′ven.
For its people mourn for it,
And its priests shriek for it—
Because its glory has departed
from it.
6 *The idol* also shall be carried to
Assyria
As a present for King Jā′reb.
Ē′phra·im shall receive shame,
And Israel shall be ashamed of
his own counsel.

7 *As for* Samaria, her king is cut off
Like a twig on the water.
8 Also the high places of Ā′ven, the
sin of Israel,
Shall be destroyed.
The thorn and thistle shall grow
on their altars;
They shall say to the mountains,
"Cover us!"
And to the hills, "Fall on us!"

9 "O Israel, you have sinned from
the days of Gib′ē·ah;
There they stood.
The battle in Gib′ē·ah against the
children of iniquity*a*
Did not overtake them.
10 When *it is* My desire, I will
chasten them.
Peoples shall be gathered against
them
When I bind them for their two
transgressions.*a*
11 Ē′phra·im *is* a trained heifer
That loves to thresh *grain;*
But I harnessed her fair neck,
I will make Ē′phra·im pull *a plow.*
Judah shall plow;
Jacob shall break his clods."

12 Sow for yourselves righteousness;
Reap in mercy;
Break up your fallow ground,
For *it is* time to seek the LORD,
Till He comes and rains
righteousness on you.

13 You have plowed wickedness;
You have reaped iniquity.
You have eaten the fruit of lies,
Because you trusted in your own
way,
In the multitude of your mighty
men.
14 Therefore tumult shall arise
among your people,
And all your fortresses shall be
plundered
As Shal′man plundered Beth
Ar′bel in the day of battle—
A mother dashed in pieces upon
her children.
15 Thus it shall be done to you,
O Beth′el,
Because of your great
wickedness.

10:5 *a*Literally *calves*   10:9 *a*So read many
Hebrew manuscripts, Septuagint, and Vulgate;
Masoretic Text reads *unruliness.*   10:10 *a*Or *in
their two habitations*

At dawn the king of Israel
Shall be cut off utterly.

GOD'S CONTINUING LOVE FOR ISRAEL

11 "When Israel *was* a child, I
loved him,
And out of Egypt I called My son.
2   *As* they called them,*a*
So they went from them;*b*
They sacrificed to the Bā′als,
And burned incense to carved
images.

3   "I taught Ē′phra·im to walk,
Taking them by their arms;*a*
But they did not know that I
healed them.
4   I drew them with gentle cords,*a*
With bands of love,
And I was to them as those who
take the yoke from their neck.*b*
I stooped *and* fed them.

5   "He shall not return to the land of
Egypt;
But the Assyrian shall be his
king,
Because they refused to repent.
6   And the sword shall slash in his
cities,
Devour his districts,
And consume *them,*
Because of their own counsels.
7   My people are bent on backsliding
from Me.
Though they call to the Most
High,*a*
None at all exalt *Him.*

8   "How can I give you up,
Ē′phra·im?
How can I hand you over,
Israel?
How can I make you like
Ad′mah?
How can I set you like Ze·boi′im?

My heart churns within Me;
My sympathy is stirred.
9   I will not execute the fierceness of
My anger;
I will not again destroy
Ē′phra·im.
For I *am* God, and not man,
The Holy One in your midst;
And I will not come with terror.*a*

10 "They shall walk after the LORD.
He will roar like a lion.
When He roars,
Then *His* sons shall come
trembling from the west;
11 They shall come trembling like a
bird from Egypt,
Like a dove from the land of
Assyria.
And I will let them dwell in their
houses,"
Says the LORD.

GOD'S CHARGE AGAINST EPHRAIM

12 "Ē′phra·im has encircled Me with
lies,
And the house of Israel with
deceit;
But Judah still walks with God,
Even with the Holy One*a* *who is*
faithful.

12 "Ē′phra·im feeds on the wind,
And pursues the east wind;
He daily increases lies and
desolation.
Also they make a covenant with
the Assyrians,
And oil is carried to Egypt.

11:2 *a*Following Masoretic Text and Vulgate; Septuagint reads *Just as I called them;* Targum interprets as *I sent prophets to a thousand of them.*
*b*Following Masoretic Text, Targum, and Vulgate;
Septuagint reads *from My face.*   11:3 *a*Some
Hebrew manuscripts, Septuagint, Syriac, and Vulgate read *My arms.*   11:4 *a*Literally *cords of a
man* *b*Literally *jaws*   11:7 *a*Or *upward*
11:9 *a*Or *I will not enter a city*   11:12 *a*Or *holy
ones*

REMEMBER WHEN WE FLEW TO THE CLOUDS? Hosea 11:1–4

Do you remember when we flew kites? They seemed to touch the clouds. Do you remember when the string got a knot in it and we had to work together to get it out? Do you remember? I remember the kite and the clouds and the string. Those were fun. But most of all I remember that you were there, dad. That was more important than all the kites and clouds and string in the whole wide world. Do you remember? I'll never forget.

1. Family memories are often built of little things, like flying kites, more than of big things. When was the last time you built some family memories together?
2. What are some special memories you have of family togetherness? Would you like to make some memories today for tomorrow's memory bank?

For more on *Family Memories* turn to page 1807
For more on *Family* turn to page 1368

2   "The LORD also *brings* a charge
       against Judah,
       And will punish Jacob according
       to his ways;
       According to his deeds He will
       recompense him.
3   He took his brother by the heel in
       the womb,
       And in his strength he struggled
       with God.*a*
4   Yes, he struggled with the Angel
       and prevailed;
       He wept, and sought favor from
       Him.
       He found Him *in* Beth'el,
       And there He spoke to us—
5   That is, the LORD God of hosts.
       The LORD *is* His memorable
       name.
6   So you, by *the help of* your God,
       return;
       Observe mercy and justice,
       And wait on your God continually.

7   "A cunning Cā'naan·īte!
       Deceitful scales *are* in his hand;
       He loves to oppress.
8   And Ē'phra·im said,
       'Surely I have become rich,
       I have found wealth for myself;
       In all my labors
       They shall find in me no iniquity
         that *is* sin.'

9   "But I *am* the LORD your God,
       Ever since the land of Egypt;
       I will again make you dwell in
       tents,
       As in the days of the appointed
       feast.
10   I have also spoken by the
       prophets,
       And have multiplied visions;
       I have given symbols through the
       witness of the prophets."

11   Though Gil'e·ad *has* idols—
       Surely they are vanity—
       Though they sacrifice bulls in
       Gil'gal,
       Indeed their altars *shall be* heaps
       in the furrows of the field.
12   Jacob fled to the country of Syria;
       Israel served for a spouse,
       And for a wife he tended *sheep*.
13   By a prophet the LORD brought
       Israel out of Egypt,
       And by a prophet he was
       preserved.
14   Ē'phra·im provoked *Him* to anger
       most bitterly;
       Therefore his Lord will leave the
       guilt of his bloodshed upon him,
       And return his reproach upon
       him.

RELENTLESS JUDGMENT ON ISRAEL

13 When Ē'phra·im spoke,
         trembling,
       He exalted *himself* in Israel;
       But when he offended through
       Bā'al *worship*, he died.
2   Now they sin more and more,
       And have made for themselves
       molded images,
       Idols of their silver, according to
       their skill;
       All of it *is* the work of craftsmen.
       They say of them,
       "Let the men who sacrifice*a* kiss
       the calves!"
3   Therefore they shall be like the
       morning cloud
       And like the early dew that
       passes away,
       Like chaff blown off from a
       threshing floor
       And like smoke from a chimney.

4   "Yet I *am* the LORD your God
       Ever since the land of Egypt,

12:3 *a*Compare Genesis 32:28   13:2 *a*Or *those
who offer human sacrifice*

And you shall know no God but
    Me;
For *there is* no savior besides Me.

5 I knew you in the wilderness,
    In the land of great drought.
6 When they had pasture, they
    were filled;
    They were filled and their heart
    was exalted;
    Therefore they forgot Me.

7 "So I will be to them like a lion;
    Like a leopard by the road I will
    lurk;
8 I will meet them like a bear
    deprived *of her cubs;*
    I will tear open their rib cage,
    And there I will devour them like
    a lion.
    The wild beast shall tear them.

9 "O Israel, you are destroyed,*a*
    But your help*b is* from Me.
10 I will be your King;*a*
    Where *is any other,*
    That he may save you in all your
    cities?
    And your judges to whom you
    said,
    'Give me a king and princes'?
11 I gave you a king in My anger,
    And took *him* away in My wrath.

12 "The iniquity of Ē′phra·im *is*
    bound up;
    His sin *is* stored up.
13 The sorrows of a woman in
    childbirth shall come upon him.
    He *is* an unwise son,
    For he should not stay long where
    children are born.

14 "I will ransom them from the
    power of the grave;*a*
    I will redeem them from death.
    O Death, I will be your plagues!*b*
    O Grave,*c* I will be your
    destruction!*d*
    Pity is hidden from My eyes."

15 Though he is fruitful among *his*
    brethren,
    An east wind shall come;
    The wind of the LORD shall come
    up from the wilderness.
    Then his spring shall become dry,
    And his fountain shall be dried
    up.
    He shall plunder the treasury of
    every desirable prize.
16 Samaria is held guilty,*a*
    For she has rebelled against her
    God.
    They shall fall by the sword,
    Their infants shall be dashed in
    pieces,
    And their women with child
    ripped open.

ISRAEL RESTORED AT LAST

14 O Israel, return to the LORD
    your God,
    For you have stumbled because of
    your iniquity;
2 Take words with you,
    And return to the LORD.
    Say to Him,
    "Take away all iniquity;
    Receive *us* graciously,
    For we will offer the sacrifices*a* of
    our lips.
3 Assyria shall not save us,
    We will not ride on horses,
    Nor will we say anymore to the
    work of our hands,
    '*You are* our gods.'
    For in You the fatherless finds
    mercy."

4 "I will heal their backsliding,
    I will love them freely,

13:9 *a*Literally *it* or *he destroyed you* *b*Literally *in
your help*   13:10 *a*Septuagint, Syriac, Targum,
and Vulgate read *Where is your king?*
13:14 *a*Or *Sheol* *b*Septuagint reads *where is your
punishment?* *c*Or *Sheol* *d*Septuagint reads *where
is your sting?*   13:16 *a*Septuagint reads *shall be
disfigured*   14:2 *a*Literally *bull calves;* Septuagint reads *fruit.*

LOVE Hosea 14:4

I Love You

What are the most wonderful words in the world? Are they, "I hate you"? Are they "Gimme that"? Are they "That's mine"? What are they?

1. How would you feel if no one loved you? How would you feel if no one ever said, "I love you"?
2. How do you feel when mother or father says, "I love you"?
3. How do you feel when you read in your Bible that God loves you *very* much? Are you glad? Say, "Thank You, God."

For more on *Values* turn to page 1368
For more on *Love* turn to page 1415

Promises

Hosea 14:4

Do you know what backsliding is? When a Christian keeps on doing things that displease God, he or she is sliding back. They are not living for the Lord the way they once did. But God has a promise for backsliders. He will heal them. He will love them freely. He will turn His anger away from them. Are you not living for the Lord the way you once did? Ask Him to forgive you. Ask Him to heal you and love you freely. Ask Him to turn His anger from you. He will.

For My anger has turned away
from him.
5 I will be like the dew to Israel;
He shall grow like the lily,
And lengthen his roots like
Lebanon.
6 His branches shall spread;

His beauty shall be like an olive
tree,
And his fragrance like Lebanon.
7 Those who dwell under his
shadow shall return;
They shall be revived *like* grain,
And grow like a vine.
Their scent*a shall be* like the
wine of Lebanon.

8 "Ē'phra·im *shall say,*
'What have I to do anymore with
idols?'
I have heard and observed him.
I *am* like a green cypress tree;
Your fruit is found in Me."

9 Who *is* wise?
Let him understand these things.
Who is prudent?
Let him know them.
For the ways of the LORD *are*
right;
The righteous walk in them,
But transgressors stumble in
them.

14:7 *a*Literally *remembrance*

The Book of
JOEL

THE word of the LORD that came to Jō′el the son of Pe·thū′el.

THE LAND LAID WASTE

2 Hear this, you elders,
And give ear, all you inhabitants of the land!
Has *anything like* this happened in your days,
Or even in the days of your fathers?

3 Tell your children about it,
Let your children *tell* their children,
And their children another generation.

4 What the chewing locust[a] left, the swarming locust has eaten;
What the swarming locust left, the crawling locust has eaten;
And what the crawling locust left, the consuming locust has eaten.

5 Awake, you drunkards, and weep;
And wail, all you drinkers of wine,
Because of the new wine,
For it has been cut off from your mouth.

6 For a nation has come up against My land,
Strong, and without number;
His teeth *are* the teeth of a lion,
And he has the fangs of a fierce lion.

7 He has laid waste My vine,
And ruined My fig tree;
He has stripped it bare and thrown *it* away;
Its branches are made white.

8 Lament like a virgin girded with sackcloth
For the husband of her youth.

9 The grain offering and the drink offering
Have been cut off from the house of the LORD;
The priests mourn, who minister to the LORD.

10 The field is wasted,
The land mourns;
For the grain is ruined,
The new wine is dried up,
The oil fails.

11 Be ashamed, you farmers,
Wail, you vinedressers,
For the wheat and the barley;
Because the harvest of the field has perished.

12 The vine has dried up,
And the fig tree has withered;
The pomegranate tree,
The palm tree also,
And the apple tree—
All the trees of the field are withered;
Surely joy has withered away from the sons of men.

MOURNING FOR THE LAND

13 Gird yourselves and lament, you priests;
Wail, you who minister before the altar;
Come, lie all night in sackcloth,
You who minister to my God;
For the grain offering and the drink offering
Are withheld from the house of your God.

14 Consecrate a fast,
Call a sacred assembly;
Gather the elders
And all the inhabitants of the land

1:4 [a]Exact identity of these locusts is unknown.

Into the house of the LORD your
God,
And cry out to the LORD.

15 Alas for the day!
For the day of the LORD *is* at
hand;
It shall come as destruction from
the Almighty.
16 Is not the food cut off before our
eyes,
Joy and gladness from the house
of our God?
17 The seed shrivels under the clods,
Storehouses are in shambles;
Barns are broken down,
For the grain has withered.
18 How the animals groan!
The herds of cattle are restless,
Because they have no pasture;
Even the flocks of sheep suffer
punishment.*a*

19 O LORD, to You I cry out;
For fire has devoured the open
pastures,
And a flame has burned all the
trees of the field.
20 The beasts of the field also cry out
to You,
For the water brooks are dried
up,
And fire has devoured the open
pastures.

THE DAY OF THE LORD

2 Blow the trumpet in Zion,
And sound an alarm in My holy
mountain!
Let all the inhabitants of the land
tremble;
For the day of the LORD is coming,
For it is at hand:
2 A day of darkness and
gloominess,
A day of clouds and thick
darkness,

Like the morning *clouds* spread
over the mountains.
A people *come,* great and strong,
The like of whom has never been;
Nor will there ever be any *such*
after them,
Even for many successive
generations.

3 A fire devours before them,
And behind them a flame burns;
The land *is* like the Garden of
Eden before them,
And behind them a desolate
wilderness;
Surely nothing shall escape them.
4 Their appearance is like the
appearance of horses;
And like swift steeds, so they run.
5 With a noise like chariots
Over mountaintops they leap,
Like the noise of a flaming fire
that devours the stubble,
Like a strong people set in battle
array.

6 Before them the people writhe in
pain;
All faces are drained of color.*a*
7 They run like mighty men,
They climb the wall like men of
war;
Every one marches in formation,
And they do not break ranks.
8 They do not push one another;
Every one marches in his own
column.*a*
Though they lunge between the
weapons,
They are not cut down.*b*
9 They run to and fro in the city,
They run on the wall;
They climb into the houses,
They enter at the windows like a
thief.

1:18 *a*Septuagint and Vulgate read *are made desolate.*   2:6 *a*Septuagint, Targum, and Vulgate
read *gather blackness.*   2:8 *a*Literally *his own
highway*   *b*That is, they are not halted by losses

10 The earth quakes before them,
The heavens tremble;
The sun and moon grow dark,
And the stars diminish their
brightness.
11 The LORD gives voice before His
army,
For His camp is very great;
For strong *is the One* who
executes His word.
For the day of the LORD *is* great
and very terrible;
Who can endure it?

A CALL TO REPENTANCE

12 "Now, therefore," says the LORD,
"Turn to Me with all your heart,
With fasting, with weeping, and
with mourning."
13 So rend your heart, and not your
garments;
Return to the LORD your God,
For He *is* gracious and merciful,
Slow to anger, and of great
kindness;
And He relents from doing harm.
14 Who knows *if* He will turn and
relent,
And leave a blessing behind
Him—
A grain offering and a drink
offering
For the LORD your God?

15 Blow the trumpet in Zion,
Consecrate a fast,
Call a sacred assembly;
16 Gather the people,
Sanctify the congregation,
Assemble the elders,
Gather the children and nursing
babes;
Let the bridegroom go out from
his chamber,
And the bride from her dressing
room.
17 Let the priests, who minister to
the LORD,

Weep between the porch and the
altar;
Let them say, "Spare Your people,
O LORD,
And do not give Your heritage to
reproach,
That the nations should rule over
them.
Why should they say among the
peoples,
'Where *is* their God?' "

THE LAND REFRESHED

18 Then the LORD will be zealous for
His land,
And pity His people.
19 The LORD will answer and say to
His people,
"Behold, I will send you grain and
new wine and oil,
And you will be satisfied by them;
I will no longer make you a
reproach among the nations.

20 "But I will remove far from you the
northern *army,*
And will drive him away into a
barren and desolate land,
With his face toward the eastern
sea
And his back toward the western
sea;
His stench will come up,
And his foul odor will rise,
Because he has done monstrous
things."

21 Fear not, O land;
Be glad and rejoice,
For the LORD has done marvelous
things!
22 Do not be afraid, you beasts of the
field;
For the open pastures are
springing up,
And the tree bears its fruit;
The fig tree and the vine yield
their strength.

HONORING Joel 2:16

Honor the New First-Class Baby

The Bible tells us to honor our parents. We should certainly do that, shouldn't we? The Bible also tells us to honor God. We don't want to forget that, do we? And of course we should honor each other. But what about that brand-new baby. Should we honor him or her?

1. Should we honor parents? Why?
2. Should we honor God? Why?
3. Should we honor others? Why?
4. Should we honor a new baby? Why? Think of several good reasons to show honor to a newborn baby.

For more on *Values* turn to page 1370
For more on *Family* turn to page 1470

23 Be glad then, you children of
     Zion,
And rejoice in the LORD your God;
For He has given you the former
     rain faithfully,*a*
And He will cause the rain to
     come down for you—
The former rain,
And the latter rain in the first
     month.

24 The threshing floors shall be full
     of wheat,
And the vats shall overflow with
     new wine and oil.

25 "So I will restore to you the years
     that the swarming locust has
     eaten,
The crawling locust,
The consuming locust,
And the chewing locust,*a*
My great army which I sent
     among you.

Praises

Joel 2:26

Do you have enough to eat? Give praise to God. Do you have abundant food? Praise God. Do you have food with many good flavors? Thank You, God. Do you have breakfast, lunch, *and* dinner? Praise You, God. Do you enjoy picnics and snacks? Sing praise to God. Do you enjoy salads and a main meal and desserts? Praise God. Think of all the wonderful foods that God gives to you. Praise Him for them all.

---

26 You shall eat in plenty and be
     satisfied,
And praise the name of the LORD
     your God,

Who has dealt wondrously with
     you;
And My people shall never be put
     to shame.

27 Then you shall know that I *am* in
     the midst of Israel:
I *am* the LORD your God
And there is no other.
My people shall never be put to
     shame.

GOD'S SPIRIT POURED OUT

28 "And it shall come to pass
     afterward
That I will pour out My Spirit on
     all flesh;
Your sons and your daughters
     shall prophesy,
Your old men shall dream
     dreams,
Your young men shall see visions.

29 And also on *My* menservants and
     on *My* maidservants
I will pour out My Spirit in those
     days.

30 "And I will show wonders in the
     heavens and in the earth:
Blood and fire and pillars of
     smoke.

31 The sun shall be turned into
     darkness,
And the moon into blood,
Before the coming of the great
     and awesome day of the LORD.

32 And it shall come to pass
That whoever calls on the name
     of the LORD
Shall be saved.
For in Mount Zion and in
     Jerusalem there shall be
     deliverance,
As the LORD has said,
Among the remnant whom the
     LORD calls.

2:23 *a*Or *the teacher of righteousness*
2:25 *a*Compare 1:4

THANKFULNESS Joel 2:26

Thank God for Big Things and Little Things

What if you had the biggest Thanksgiving dinner in history? Would you thank God for it? What if you had nothing but a bowl of soup? Would you still thank God for it?

1. Should we thank God only for the very special things in life? What about the little things He gives us?
2. Think of the very best that God has given you. Did you thank Him for these things?
3. Now think of the very smallest, least significant things God has given you. Did you thank Him for those?

For more on *Values* turn to page 1383
For more on *Thankfulness* turn to page 1390

GOD JUDGES THE NATIONS

3 "For behold, in those days and at that time,
When I bring back the captives of Judah and Jerusalem,

2 I will also gather all nations,
And bring them down to the Valley of Je·hosh′a·phat;
And I will enter into judgment with them there
On account of My people, My heritage Israel,
Whom they have scattered among the nations;
They have also divided up My land.

3 They have cast lots for My people,
Have given a boy *as payment* for a harlot,
And sold a girl for wine, that they may drink.

4 "Indeed, what have you to do with Me,
O Tȳre and Sī′don, and all the coasts of Phi·lis′ti·a?
Will you retaliate against Me?
But if you retaliate against Me,
Swiftly and speedily I will return your retaliation upon your own head;

5 Because you have taken My silver and My gold,
And have carried into your temples My prized possessions.

6 Also the people of Judah and the people of Jerusalem
You have sold to the Greeks,
That you may remove them far from their borders.

7 "Behold, I will raise them Out of the place to which you have sold them,
And will return your retaliation upon your own head.

8 I will sell your sons and your daughters
Into the hand of the people of Judah,
And they will sell them to the Sa·bē′ans,a
To a people far off;
For the LORD has spoken."

9 Proclaim this among the nations:
"Prepare for war!
Wake up the mighty men,
Let all the men of war draw near,
Let them come up.

10 Beat your plowshares into swords
And your pruning hooks into spears;
Let the weak say, 'I *am* strong.'"

11 Assemble and come, all you nations,
And gather together all around.
Cause Your mighty ones to go down there, O LORD.

12 "Let the nations be wakened, and come up to the Valley of Je·hosh′a·phat;
For there I will sit to judge all the surrounding nations.

13 Put in the sickle, for the harvest is ripe.
Come, go down;
For the winepress is full,
The vats overflow—
For their wickedness *is* great."

14 Multitudes, multitudes in the valley of decision!
For the day of the LORD *is* near in the valley of decision.

15 The sun and moon will grow dark,
And the stars will diminish their brightness.

16 The LORD also will roar from Zion,
And utter His voice from Jerusalem;
The heavens and earth will shake;

3:8 aLiterally *Shebaites* (compare Isaiah 60:6 and Ezekiel 27:22)

■ *Promises* ■

Joel 3:16

You would not want the Lord to yell at you, would you? If He really yelled, this verse says the whole earth would shake! It's a good idea to love the Lord and stay close to Him. Instead of yelling at you, He will be your shelter. Do you ever want to be protected from something? You need a shelter. The Lord promises to be your shelter. Ask Him. Then walk in His ways.

But the LORD will be a shelter for
   His people,
And the strength of the children
   of Israel.

17 "So you shall know that I *am* the
   LORD your God,
Dwelling in Zion My holy
   mountain.
Then Jerusalem shall be holy,

And no aliens shall ever pass
   through her again."

GOD BLESSES HIS PEOPLE

18 And it will come to pass in that
   day
That the mountains shall drip
   with new wine,
The hills shall flow with milk,
And all the brooks of Judah shall
   be flooded with water;
A fountain shall flow from the
   house of the LORD
And water the Valley of Acacias.

19 "Egypt shall be a desolation,
And Ē'dom a desolate wilderness,
Because of violence *against* the
   people of Judah,
For they have shed innocent blood
   in their land.
20 But Judah shall abide forever,
And Jerusalem from generation
   to generation.
21 For I will acquit them of the guilt
   of bloodshed, whom I had not
   acquitted;
For the LORD dwells in Zion."

The Book of
AMOS

THE words of Ā′mos, who was among the sheepbreeders*a* of Te·kō′a, which he saw concerning Israel in the days of Uz·zī′ah king of Judah, and in the days of Jer·o·bō′am the son of Jō′ash, king of Israel, two years before the earthquake.

2 And he said:

"The LORD roars from Zion,
And utters His voice from
    Jerusalem;
The pastures of the shepherds
    mourn,
And the top of Car′mel withers."

JUDGMENT ON THE NATIONS

3 Thus says the LORD:

"For three transgressions of
    Damascus, and for four,
I will not turn away its
    punishment,
Because they have threshed
    Gil′e·ad with implements of
    iron.
4 But I will send a fire into the
    house of Haz′a·el,
Which shall devour the palaces of
    Ben-Hā′dad.
5 I will also break the *gate* bar of
    Damascus,
And cut off the inhabitant from
    the Valley of Ā′ven,
And the one who holds the
    scepter from Beth Eden.
The people of Syria shall go
    captive to Kir,"
Says the LORD.

6 Thus says the LORD:

"For three transgressions of Gā′za,
    and for four,

I will not turn away its
    punishment,
Because they took captive the
    whole captivity
To deliver *them* up to Ē′dom.
7 But I will send a fire upon the
    wall of Gā′za,
Which shall devour its palaces.
8 I will cut off the inhabitant from
    Ash′dod,
And the one who holds the
    scepter from Ash′ke·lon;
I will turn My hand against
    Ek′ron,
And the remnant of the
    Phi·lis′tines shall perish,"
Says the Lord GOD.

9 Thus says the LORD:

"For three transgressions of Tȳre,
    and for four,
I will not turn away its
    punishment,
Because they delivered up the
    whole captivity to Ē′dom,
And did not remember the
    covenant of brotherhood.
10 But I will send a fire upon the
    wall of Tȳre,
Which shall devour its palaces."

11 Thus says the LORD:

"For three transgressions of
    Ē′dom, and for four,
I will not turn away its
    punishment,
Because he pursued his brother
    with the sword,
And cast off all pity;
His anger tore perpetually,
And he kept his wrath forever.

1:1 *a*Compare 2 Kings 3:4

12 But I will send a fire upon
    Tē′man,
Which shall devour the palaces of
    Boz′rah.”

13 Thus says the LORD:

“For three transgressions of the
    people of Am′mon, and for four,
I will not turn away its
    punishment,
Because they ripped open the
    women with child in Gil′ē·ad,
That they might enlarge their
    territory.
14 But I will kindle a fire in the wall
    of Rab′bah,
And it shall devour its palaces,
Amid shouting in the day of
    battle,
And a tempest in the day of the
    whirlwind.
15 Their king shall go into captivity,
He and his princes together,”
Says the LORD.

2 Thus says the LORD:

“For three transgressions of
    Mō′ab, and for four,
I will not turn away its
    punishment,
Because he burned the bones of
    the king of Ē′dom to lime.
2 But I will send a fire upon Mō′ab,
And it shall devour the palaces of
    Ker′i·oth;
Mō′ab shall die with tumult,
With shouting *and* trumpet
    sound.
3 And I will cut off the judge from
    its midst,
And slay all its princes with him,”
Says the LORD.

JUDGMENT ON JUDAH

4 Thus says the LORD:

“For three transgressions of
    Judah, and for four,

I will not turn away its
    punishment,
Because they have despised the
    law of the LORD,
And have not kept His
    commandments.
Their lies lead them astray,
Lies which their fathers followed.
5 But I will send a fire upon Judah,
And it shall devour the palaces of
    Jerusalem.”

JUDGMENT ON ISRAEL

6 Thus says the LORD:

“For three transgressions of Israel,
    and for four,
I will not turn away its
    punishment,
Because they sell the righteous
    for silver,
And the poor for a pair of sandals.
7 They pant after[a] the dust of the
    earth *which is* on the head of
    the poor,
And pervert the way of the
    humble.
A man and his father go in to the
    same girl,
To defile My holy name.
8 They lie down by every altar on
    clothes taken in pledge,
And drink the wine of the
    condemned *in* the house of their
    god.

9 “Yet *it was* I *who* destroyed the
    Am′o·rīte before them,
Whose height *was* like the height
    of the cedars,
And he *was as* strong as the
    oaks;
Yet I destroyed his fruit above
And his roots beneath.
10 Also *it was* I *who* brought you up
    from the land of Egypt,

2:7 [a]Or *trample on*

And led you forty years through
the wilderness,
To possess the land of the
Am'o·rīte.
11 I raised up some of your sons as
prophets,
And some of your young men as
Naz'ir·ītes.
Is it not so, O you children of
Israel?"
Says the LORD.
12 "But you gave the Naz'ir·ītes wine
to drink,
And commanded the prophets
saying,
'Do not prophesy!'

13 "Behold, I am weighed down by
you,
As a cart full of sheaves is
weighed down.
14 Therefore flight shall perish from
the swift,
The strong shall not strengthen
his power,
Nor shall the mighty deliver
himself;
15 He shall not stand who handles
the bow,
The swift of foot shall not escape,
Nor shall he who rides a horse
deliver himself.
16 The most courageous men of
might
Shall flee naked in that day,"
Says the LORD.

AUTHORITY OF THE PROPHET'S MESSAGE

3 Hear this word that the LORD has
spoken against you, O children of Israel, against the whole family which
I brought up from the land of Egypt,
saying:

2 "You only have I known of all the
families of the earth;

Therefore I will punish you for all
your iniquities."

3 Can two walk together, unless
they are agreed?
4 Will a lion roar in the forest,
when he has no prey?
Will a young lion cry out of his
den, if he has caught nothing?
5 Will a bird fall into a snare on the
earth, where there is no trap
for it?
Will a snare spring up from the
earth, if it has caught nothing
at all?
6 If a trumpet is blown in a city,
will not the people be afraid?
If there is calamity in a city, will
not the LORD have done *it?*

7 Surely the Lord GOD does
nothing,
Unless He reveals His secret to
His servants the prophets.
8 A lion has roared!
Who will not fear?
The Lord GOD has spoken!
Who can but prophesy?

PUNISHMENT OF ISRAEL'S SINS

9 "Proclaim in the palaces at
Ash'dod,*a*
And in the palaces in the land of
Egypt, and say:
'Assemble on the mountains of
Samaria;
See great tumults in her midst,
And the oppressed within her.
10 For they do not know to do right,'
Says the LORD,
'Who store up violence and
robbery in their palaces.' "

11 Therefore thus says the Lord
GOD:

3:9 *a*Following Masoretic Text; Septuagint reads
Assyria.

"An adversary *shall be* all around the land;
He shall sap your strength from you,
And your palaces shall be plundered."

12 Thus says the LORD:

"As a shepherd takes from the mouth of a lion
Two legs or a piece of an ear,
So shall the children of Israel be taken out
Who dwell in Samaria—
In the corner of a bed and on the edge*a* of a couch!
13 Hear and testify against the house of Jacob,"
Says the Lord GOD, the God of hosts,
14 "That in the day I punish Israel for their transgressions,
I will also visit *destruction* on the altars of Beth'el;
And the horns of the altar shall be cut off
And fall to the ground.
15 I will destroy the winter house along with the summer house;
The houses of ivory shall perish,
And the great houses shall have an end,"
Says the LORD.

4 Hear this word, you cows of Bā'shan, who *are* on the mountain of Samaria,
Who oppress the poor,
Who crush the needy,
Who say to your husbands,*a*
"Bring *wine,* let us drink!"
2 The Lord GOD has sworn by His holiness:
"Behold, the days shall come upon you
When He will take you away with fishhooks,
And your posterity with fishhooks.

3 You will go out *through* broken *walls,*
Each one straight ahead of her,
And you will be cast into Har'mon,"
Says the LORD.

4 "Come to Beth'el and transgress,
At Gil'gal multiply transgression;
Bring your sacrifices every morning,
Your tithes every three days.*a*
5 Offer a sacrifice of thanksgiving with leaven,
Proclaim *and* announce the freewill offerings;
For this you love,
You children of Israel!"
Says the Lord GOD.

ISRAEL DID NOT
ACCEPT CORRECTION

6 "Also I gave you cleanness of teeth in all your cities.
And lack of bread in all your places;
Yet you have not returned to Me,"
Says the LORD.

7 "I also withheld rain from you,
When *there were* still three months to the harvest.
I made it rain on one city,
I withheld rain from another city.
One part was rained upon,
And where it did not rain the part withered.
8 So two *or* three cities wandered to another city to drink water,
But they were not satisfied;
Yet you have not returned to Me,"
Says the LORD.

9 "I blasted you with blight and mildew.

3:12 *a*The Hebrew is uncertain. 4:1 *a*Literally *their lords* or *their masters* 4:4 *a*Or *years* (compare Deuteronomy 14:28)

CAN YOU MAKE A BETTER FLOWER THAN GOD CAN MAKE? Amos 4:13

Have you ever said, "I wish I could stop the rain"? Or, "I wish I could make the sun shine today"? Or have you ever thought you could make a better tree or flower or bird or animal than God made? Barry tried to paint a beautiful flower. He tried many times. But none looked as good as the flower that God made. That's why Barry is framing God's flower, not his. The next time you don't like what God made, or did, ask if you could *really* do better?

1. Have you ever wished you could do something different from the way God did it? What?
2. Could you ever do better than God did? Why not?
3. Would you like to thank God now for all the beautiful and wonderful things He has done for you? Will you?

For more on *What Should I Do?* turn to page 1440
For more on *God's Creation* turn to page 1618

When your gardens increased,
Your vineyards,
Your fig trees,
And your olive trees,
The locust devoured *them;*
Yet you have not returned to Me,"
Says the LORD.

10 "I sent among you a plague after
    the manner of Egypt;
Your young men I killed with a
    sword,
Along with your captive horses;
I made the stench of your camps
    come up into your nostrils;
Yet you have not returned to Me,"
Says the LORD.

11 "I overthrew *some* of you,
As God overthrew Sod'om and
    Go·mor'rah,
And you were like a firebrand
    plucked from the burning;
Yet you have not returned to Me,"
Says the LORD.

12 "Therefore thus will I do to you,
    O Israel;
Because I will do this to you,
Prepare to meet your God,
    O Israel!"

13 For behold,
He who forms mountains,
And creates the wind,
Who declares to man what his*a*
    thought *is,*
And makes the morning
    darkness,
Who treads the high places of the
    earth—
The LORD God of hosts *is* His
    name.

A LAMENT FOR ISRAEL

5 Hear this word which I take up
against you, a lamentation, O house
of Israel:

2   The virgin of Israel has fallen;
She will rise no more.
She lies forsaken on her land;
There is no one to raise her up.

3   For thus says the Lord GOD:

"The city that goes out by a
    thousand
Shall have a hundred left,
And that which goes out by a
    hundred
Shall have ten left to the house of
    Israel."

A CALL TO REPENTANCE

4   For thus says the LORD to the
house of Israel:

"Seek Me and live;
5   But do not seek Beth'el,
Nor enter Gil'gal,
Nor pass over to Bē·er·shē'ba;
For Gil'gal shall surely go into
    captivity,
And Beth'el shall come to
    nothing.
6   Seek the LORD and live,
Lest He break out like fire *in* the
    house of Joseph,
And devour *it,*
With no one to quench *it* in
    Beth'el—
7   You who turn justice to
    wormwood,
And lay righteousness to rest in
    the earth!"

8   He made the Plēi'a·dēs and
    Ō·rī'on;
He turns the shadow of death into
    morning
And makes the day dark as night;
He calls for the waters of the sea
And pours them out on the face of
    the earth;
The LORD *is* His name.

4:13 *a* Or *His*

9   He rains ruin upon the strong,
    So that fury comes upon the
        fortress.

10 They hate the one who rebukes in
        the gate,
    And they abhor the one who
        speaks uprightly.
11 Therefore, because you tread
        down the poor
    And take grain taxes from him,
    Though you have built houses of
        hewn stone,
    Yet you shall not dwell in them;
    You have planted pleasant
        vineyards,
    But you shall not drink wine from
        them.
12 For I know your manifold
        transgressions
    And your mighty sins:
    Afflicting the just *and* taking
        bribes;
    Diverting the poor *from justice* at
        the gate.
13 Therefore the prudent keep silent
        at that time,
    For it *is* an evil time.

14 Seek good and not evil,
    That you may live;

So the LORD God of hosts will be
    with you,
As you have spoken.
15 Hate evil, love good;
    Establish justice in the gate.
    It may be that the LORD God of
        hosts
    Will be gracious to the remnant of
        Joseph.

THE DAY OF THE LORD

16 Therefore the LORD God of hosts,
the Lord, says this:

    "*There shall be* wailing in all
        streets,
    And they shall say in all the
        highways,
    'Alas! Alas!'
    They shall call the farmer to
        mourning,
    And skillful lamenters to wailing.
17 In all vineyards *there shall be*
        wailing,
    For I will pass through you,"
    Says the LORD.

18 Woe to you who desire the day of
        the LORD!
    For what good *is* the day of the
        LORD to you?
    It *will be* darkness, and not light.
19 It *will be* as though a man fled
        from a lion,
    And a bear met him!
    Or *as though* he went into the
        house,
    Leaned his hand on the wall,
    And a serpent bit him!
20 *Is* not the day of the LORD
        darkness, and not light?
    Is it not very dark, with no
        brightness in it?

21 "I hate, I despise your feast days,
    And I do not savor your sacred
        assemblies.

◼ *Promises* ◼

Amos 5:14

Honestly, would you rather be
bad or good? Would you rather
be evil or godly? This verse tells
you and me to seek good and not
evil. We should, shouldn't we?
Do you? Will you? If you do, God
has a special promise for you. He
will be *with* you as you have
asked Him to be. Having God
with us is special. You do want
that, don't you?

22 Though you offer Me burnt
offerings and your grain
offerings,
I will not accept *them,*
Nor will I regard your fattened
peace offerings.
23 Take away from Me the noise of
your songs,
For I will not hear the melody of
your stringed instruments.
24 But let justice run down like
water,
And righteousness like a mighty
stream.

25 "Did you offer Me sacrifices and
offerings
In the wilderness forty years,
O house of Israel?
26 You also carried Sik'kutha*a* your
king*b*
And Chī'un,*c* your idols,
The star of your gods,
Which you made for yourselves.
27 Therefore I will send you into
captivity beyond Damascus,"
Says the LORD, whose name *is* the
God of hosts.

WARNINGS TO ZION AND SAMARIA

6 Woe to you *who are* at ease in
Zion,
And trust in Mount Samaria,
Notable persons in the chief
nation,
To whom the house of Israel
comes!
2 Go over to Cal'neh and see;
And from there go to Hā'math the
great;
Then go down to Gath of the
Phi·lis'tines.
Are you better than these
kingdoms?
Or is their territory greater than
your territory?

3 *Woe to* you who put far off the day
of doom,
Who cause the seat of violence to
come near;
4 Who lie on beds of ivory,
Stretch out on your couches,
Eat lambs from the flock
And calves from the midst of the
stall;
5 Who sing idly to the sound of
stringed instruments,
And invent for yourselves musical
instruments like David;
6 Who drink wine from bowls,
And anoint yourselves with the
best ointments,
But are not grieved for the
affliction of Joseph.
7 Therefore they shall now go
captive as the first of the
captives,
And those who recline at
banquets shall be removed.

8 The Lord GOD has sworn by
Himself,
The LORD God of hosts says:
"I abhor the pride of Jacob,
And hate his palaces;
Therefore I will deliver up *the*
city
And all that is in it."

9 Then it shall come to pass, that if
ten men remain in one house, they
shall die. 10 And when a relative *of the dead,*
with one who will burn *the bodies,*
picks up the bodies*a* to take them out
of the house, he will say to one inside
the house, "*Are there* any more with
you?" Then someone will say, "None."
And he will say, "Hold your tongue!
For we dare not mention the name of
the LORD."

5:26 *a*A pagan deity *b*Septuagint and Vulgate
read *tabernacle of Moloch.* *c*A pagan deity
6:10 *a*Literally *bones*

11 For behold, the LORD gives a command:
He will break the great house into bits,
And the little house into pieces.

12 Do horses run on rocks?
Does *one* plow *there* with oxen?
Yet you have turned justice into gall,
And the fruit of righteousness into wormwood,

13 You who rejoice over Lo Dē′bar,*a*
Who say, "Have we not taken Kar·nā′im*b* for ourselves
By our own strength?"

14 "But, behold, I will raise up a nation against you,
O house of Israel,"
Says the LORD God of hosts;
"And they will afflict you from the entrance of Hā′math
To the Valley of the Ar′a·bah."

VISION OF THE LOCUSTS

7 Thus the Lord GOD showed me: Behold, He formed locust swarms at the beginning of the late crop; indeed *it was* the late crop after the king's mowings.
2 And so it was, when they had finished eating the grass of the land, that I said:

"O Lord GOD, forgive, I pray!
Oh, that Jacob may stand,
For he *is* small!"
3 *So* the LORD relented concerning this.
"It shall not be," said the LORD.

VISION OF THE FIRE

4 Thus the Lord GOD showed me: Behold, the Lord GOD called for conflict by fire, and it consumed the great deep and devoured the territory.
5 Then I said:

"O Lord GOD, cease, I pray!
Oh, that Jacob may stand,
For he *is* small!"
6 *So* the LORD relented concerning this.
"This also shall not be," said the Lord GOD.

VISION OF THE PLUMB LINE

7 Thus He showed me: Behold, the Lord stood on a wall *made* with a plumb line, with a plumb line in His hand.
8 And the LORD said to me, "Ā′mos, what do you see?" And I said, "A plumb line." Then the Lord said:

"Behold, I am setting a plumb line
In the midst of My people Israel;
I will not pass by them anymore.
9 The high places of Isaac shall be desolate,
And the sanctuaries of Israel shall be laid waste.
I will rise with the sword against the house of Jer·o·bō′am."

AMAZIAH'S COMPLAINT

10 Then Am·a·zī′ah the priest of Beth′el sent to Jer·o·bō′am king of Israel, saying, "Ā′mos has conspired against you in the midst of the house of Israel. The land is not able to bear all his words.
11 "For thus Ā′mos has said:

'Jer·o·bō′am shall die by the sword,
And Israel shall surely be led away captive
From their own land.' "

6:13 *a*Literally *Nothing* *b*Literally *Horns*, symbol of strength

12 Then Am·a·zī′ah said to Ā′mos:

"Go, you seer!
Flee to the land of Judah.
There eat bread,
And there prophesy.
13 But never again prophesy at
    Beth′el,
For it *is* the king's sanctuary,
And it *is* the royal residence."

14 Then Ā′mos answered, and said
to Am·a·zī′ah:

"I *was* no prophet,
Nor *was* I a son of a prophet,
But I *was* a sheepbreeder*a*
And a tender of sycamore fruit.
15 Then the LORD took me as I
    followed the flock,
And the LORD said to me,
'Go, prophesy to My people
    Israel.'
16 Now therefore, hear the word of
    the LORD:
You say, 'Do not prophesy against
    Israel,
And do not spout against the
    house of Isaac.'

17 "Therefore thus says the LORD:

'Your wife shall be a harlot in the
    city;
Your sons and daughters shall fall
    by the sword;
Your land shall be divided by
    survey line;
You shall die in a defiled land;
And Israel shall surely be led
    away captive
From his own land.' "

VISION OF THE SUMMER FRUIT

8 Thus the Lord GOD showed me:
Behold, a basket of summer fruit.
2 And He said, "Ā′mos, what do you

see?" So I said, "A basket of summer
fruit." Then the LORD said to me:

"The end has come upon My
    people Israel;
I will not pass by them anymore.
3 And the songs of the temple
Shall be wailing in that day,"
Says the Lord GOD—
"Many dead bodies everywhere,
They shall be thrown out in
    silence."

4 Hear this, you who swallow up*a*
    the needy,
And make the poor of the land
    fail,

5 Saying:

"When will the New Moon be past,
That we may sell grain?
And the Sabbath,
That we may trade wheat?
Making the ephah small and the
    shekel large,
Falsifying the scales by deceit,
6 That we may buy the poor for
    silver,
And the needy for a pair of
    sandals—
Even sell the bad wheat?"

7 The LORD has sworn by the pride
    of Jacob:
"Surely I will never forget any of
    their works.
8 Shall the land not tremble for
    this,
And everyone mourn who dwells
    in it?
All of it shall swell like the
    River,*a*

7:14 *a*Compare 2 Kings 3:4   8:4 *a*Or *trample on*
(compare 2:7)   8:8 *a*That is, the Nile; some
Hebrew manuscripts, Septuagint, Syriac, Targum,
and Vulgate read *River;* Masoretic Text reads *the
light.*

Values

HONESTY Amos 8:5

Should We Ever Cheat?
Have you ever seen someone cheating another person? Is that right? Is that something you should do? What do you think?

1. Why is it wrong to cheat? Is cheating the same as stealing?
2. Would you want others to cheat you? Why not?
3. Read the last phrase of Amos 8:5. "Falsifying the scales by deceit" is another way of saying cheating when you weigh something. People used balances as scales in Amos's time. Is there *ever* any time that we should cheat others?

For more on *Values* turn to page 1390
For more on *Honesty* turn to page 1670

Heave and subside
Like the River of Egypt.

9 "And it shall come to pass in that day," says the Lord GOD,
"That I will make the sun go down at noon,
And I will darken the earth in broad daylight;
10 I will turn your feasts into mourning,
And all your songs into lamentation;
I will bring sackcloth on every waist,
And baldness on every head;
I will make it like mourning for an only *son*,
And its end like a bitter day.

11 "Behold, the days are coming," says the Lord GOD,
"That I will send a famine on the land,
Not a famine of bread,
Nor a thirst for water,
But of hearing the words of the LORD.

12 They shall wander from sea to sea,
And from north to east;
They shall run to and fro, seeking the word of the LORD,
But shall not find *it*.

13 "In that day the fair virgins
And strong young men
Shall faint from thirst.
14 Those who swear by the sin[a] of Samaria,
Who say,
'As your god lives, O Dan!'
And, 'As the way of Bē·er·shē'ba lives!'
They shall fall and never rise again."

THE DESTRUCTION OF ISRAEL

9 I saw the Lord standing by the altar, and He said:

"Strike the doorposts, that the thresholds may shake,

8:14 [a]Or *Ashima,* a Syrian goddess

And break them on the heads of
them all.
I will slay the last of them with
the sword.
He who flees from them shall not
get away,
And he who escapes from them
shall not be delivered.

2 "Though they dig into hell,*a*
From there My hand shall take
them;
Though they climb up to heaven,
From there I will bring them
down;
3 And though they hide themselves
on top of Car′mel,
From there I will search and take
them;
Though they hide from My sight
at the bottom of the sea,
From there I will command the
serpent, and it shall bite
them;
4 Though they go into captivity
before their enemies,
From there I will command the
sword,
And it shall slay them.
I will set My eyes on them for
harm and not for good."

5 The Lord GOD of hosts,
He who touches the earth and it
melts,
And all who dwell there mourn;
All of it shall swell like the
River,*a*
And subside like the River of
Egypt.
6 He who builds His layers in the
sky,
And has founded His strata in the
earth;
Who calls for the waters of the
sea,
And pours them out on the face of
the earth—
The LORD *is* His name.

7 "*Are* you not like the people of
Ethiopia to Me,
O children of Israel?" says the
LORD.
"Did I not bring up Israel from the
land of Egypt,
The Phi·lis′tines from Caph′tor,
And the Syrians from Kir?

8 "Behold, the eyes of the Lord GOD
are on the sinful kingdom,
And I will destroy it from the face
of the earth;
Yet I will not utterly destroy the
house of Jacob,"
Says the LORD.

9 "For surely I will command,
And will sift the house of Israel
among all nations,
As *grain* is sifted in a sieve;
Yet not the smallest grain shall
fall to the ground.
10 All the sinners of My people shall
die by the sword,
Who say, 'The calamity shall not
overtake nor confront us.'

ISRAEL WILL BE RESTORED

11 "On that day I will raise up
The tabernacle*a* of David, which
has fallen down,
And repair its damages;
I will raise up its ruins,
And rebuild it as in the days of
old;
12 That they may possess the
remnant of E′dom,*a*
And all the Gentiles who are
called by My name,"
Says the LORD who does this
thing.

13 "Behold, the days are coming,"
says the LORD,

9:2 *a*Or *Sheol*   9:5 *a*That is, the Nile
9:11 *a*Literally *booth,* figure of a deposed dynasty
9:12 *a*Septuagint reads *mankind.*

"When the plowman shall overtake
the reaper,
And the treader of grapes him
who sows seed;
The mountains shall drip with
sweet wine,
And all the hills shall flow *with it.*
14 I will bring back the captives of
My people Israel;
They shall build the waste cities
and inhabit *them;*

They shall plant vineyards and
drink wine from them;
They shall also make gardens and
eat fruit from them.
15 I will plant them in their
land,
And no longer shall they be
pulled up
From the land I have given
them,"
Says the LORD your God.

The Book of
OBADIAH

The Coming Judgment on Edom

THE vision of Ō·ba·dī′ah.

Thus says the Lord GOD
 concerning Ē′dom
(We have heard a report from the
 LORD,
And a messenger has been sent
 among the nations, *saying,*
"Arise, and let us rise up against
 her for battle"):

2 "Behold, I will make you small
 among the nations;
You shall be greatly despised.
3 The pride of your heart has
 deceived you,
You who dwell in the clefts of the
 rock,
Whose habitation is high;
You who say in your heart,
'Who will bring me down to the
 ground?'
4 Though you ascend *as* high as the
 eagle,
And though you set your nest
 among the stars,
From there I will bring you
 down," says the LORD.

5 "If thieves had come to you,
If robbers by night—
Oh, how you will be cut off!—
Would they not have stolen till
 they had enough?
If grape-gatherers had come to
 you,
Would they not have left *some*
 gleanings?

6 "Oh, how Esau shall be searched
 out!
How his hidden treasures shall be
 sought after!
7 All the men in your confederacy
Shall force you to the border;
The men at peace with you
Shall deceive you *and* prevail
 against you.
Those who eat your bread shall
 lay a trap*a* for you.
No one is aware of it.

8 "Will I not in that day," says the
 LORD,
"Even destroy the wise *men* from
 Ē′dom,
And understanding from the
 mountains of Esau?
9 Then your mighty men,
 O Tē′man, shall be dismayed,
To the end that everyone from the
 mountains of Esau
May be cut off by slaughter.

Edom Mistreated His Brother

10 "For violence against your brother
 Jacob,
Shame shall cover you,
And you shall be cut off forever.
11 In the day that you stood on the
 other side—
In the day that strangers carried
 captive his forces,
When foreigners entered his gates
And cast lots for Jerusalem—
Even you *were* as one of them.

12 "But you should not have gazed on
 the day of your brother
In the day of his captivity;*a*
Nor should you have rejoiced over
 the children of Judah
In the day of their destruction;
Nor should you have spoken
 proudly
In the day of distress.

7 *a*Or *wound,* or *plot* 12 *a*Literally *on the day*
he became a foreigner

13 You should not have entered the
       gate of My people
In the day of their calamity.
Indeed, you should not have
       gazed on their affliction
In the day of their calamity,
Nor laid *hands* on their substance
In the day of their calamity.
14 You should not have stood at the
       crossroads
To cut off those among them who
       escaped;
Nor should you have delivered up
       those among them who
       remained
In the day of distress.

15 "For the day of the Lord upon all
       the nations *is* near;
As you have done, it shall be done
       to you;
Your reprisal shall return upon
       your own head.
16 For as you drank on My holy
       mountain,
So shall all the nations drink
       continually;
Yes, they shall drink, and
       swallow,
And they shall be as though they
       had never been.

ISRAEL'S FINAL TRIUMPH

17 "But on Mount Zion there shall be
       deliverance,
And there shall be holiness;

The house of Jacob shall possess
       their possessions.
18 The house of Jacob shall be a fire,
And the house of Joseph a flame;
But the house of Esau *shall be*
       stubble;
They shall kindle them and
       devour them,
And no survivor shall *remain* of
       the house of Esau,"
For the Lord has spoken.

19 The South*a* shall possess the
       mountains of Esau,
And the Lowland shall possess
       Phi·lis'ti·a.
They shall possess the fields of
       Ē'phra·im
And the fields of Samaria.
Benjamin *shall possess* Gil'ē·ad.
20 And the captives of this host of
       the children of Israel
Shall possess the land of the
       Cā'naan·ītes
As far as Zar'e·phath.
The captives of Jerusalem who
       are in Se·phar'ad
Shall possess the cities of the
       South.*a*
21 Then saviors*a* shall come to
       Mount Zion
To judge the mountains of Esau,
And the kingdom shall be the
       Lord's.

19 *a*Hebrew *Negev*   20 *a*Hebrew *Negev*
21 *a*Or *deliverers*

The Book of
JONAH

JONAH'S DISOBEDIENCE

Have you ever tried to run away? Jonah learned you cannot run away from God. But he had to be swallowed by a giant fish before he learned his lesson.

NOW the word of the LORD came to Jonah the son of A·mit′taī, saying, 2 "Arise, go to Nin′e·veh, that great city, and cry out against it; for their wickedness has come up before Me." 3 But Jonah arose to flee to Tar′shish from the presence of the LORD. He went down to Jop′pa, and found a ship going to Tar′shish; so he paid the fare, and went down into it, to go with them to Tar′shish from the presence of the LORD.

THE STORM AT SEA

4 But the LORD sent out a great wind on the sea, and there was a mighty tempest on the sea, so that the ship was about to be broken up. 5 Then the mariners were afraid; and every man cried out to his god, and threw the cargo that *was* in the ship into the sea, to lighten the load.ᵃ But Jonah had gone down into the lowest parts of the ship, had lain down, and was fast asleep. 6 So the captain came to him, and said to him, "What do you mean, sleeper? Arise, call on your God; perhaps your God will consider us, so that we may not perish." 7 And they said to one another, "Come, let us cast lots, that we may know for whose cause this trouble *has come* upon us." So they cast lots, and the lot fell on Jonah.

8 Then they said to him, "Please tell us! For whose cause *is* this trouble upon us? What is your occupation? And where do you come from? What is your country? And of what people are you?" 9 So he said to them, "I *am* a Hebrew; and I fear the LORD, the God of heaven, who made the sea and the dry *land.*"

JONAH THROWN INTO THE SEA

10 Then the men were exceedingly afraid, and said to him, "Why have you done this?" For the men knew that he fled from the presence of the LORD, because he had told them. 11 Then they said to him, "What shall we do to you that the sea may be calm for us?"—for the sea was growing more tempestuous. 12 And he said to them, "Pick me up and throw me into the sea; then the sea will become calm for you. For I know that this great tempest *is* because of me." 13 Nevertheless the men rowed hard to return to land, but they could not, for the sea continued to grow more tempestuous against them. 14 Therefore they cried out to the LORD and said, "We pray, O LORD, please do not let us perish for this man's life, and do not charge us with innocent blood; for You, O LORD, have done as it pleased You." 15 So they picked up Jonah and threw him into the sea, and the sea ceased from its raging. 16 Then the men feared the LORD exceedingly, and offered a sacrifice to the LORD and took vows.

1:5 ᵃLiterally *from upon them*

JONAH'S PRAYER AND DELIVERANCE

17 Now the LORD had prepared a great fish to swallow Jonah. And Jonah was in the belly of the fish three days and three nights.

---

2 Then Jonah prayed to the LORD his God from the fish's belly.
2 And he said:

"I cried out to the LORD because of my affliction,
And He answered me.

"Out of the belly of Shē′ōl I cried,
And You heard my voice.

3 For You cast me into the deep,
Into the heart of the seas,
And the floods surrounded me;
All Your billows and Your waves passed over me.
4 Then I said, 'I have been cast out of Your sight;
Yet I will look again toward Your holy temple.'
5 The waters surrounded me, *even* to my soul;
The deep closed around me;
Weeds were wrapped around my head.
6 I went down to the moorings of the mountains;
The earth with its bars *closed* behind me forever;
Yet You have brought up my life from the pit,
O LORD, my God.

7 "When my soul fainted within me,
I remembered the LORD;
And my prayer went *up* to You,
Into Your holy temple.

8 "Those who regard worthless idols
Forsake their own Mercy.
9 But I will sacrifice to You
With the voice of thanksgiving;
I will pay what I have vowed.
Salvation *is* of the LORD."

10 So the LORD spoke to the fish, and it vomited Jonah onto dry *land*.

JONAH PREACHES AT NINEVEH

3 Now the word of the LORD came to Jonah the second time, saying,
2 "Arise, go to Nin′e·veh, that great city, and preach to it the message that I tell you."
3 So Jonah arose and went to Nin′e·veh, according to the word of

Values

THANKFULNESS Jonah 2:9

Thank You, God

It's "Thank-You-God" time for Duane. It could be morning. It could be noon. It could be night. It could be time to eat or time for anything. Which time do you think it is?

1. What do you think Duane is saying to God?
2. Think of all the "Thank-You-God" times. What are they? Why?
3. Is it a "Thank-You-God" time now? Would you like to thank Him?

For more on *Values* turn to page 1415
For more on *Thankfulness* turn to page 109

the LORD. Now Nin'e·veh was an exceedingly great city, a three-day journey*a* *in extent.*

4 And Jonah began to enter the city on the first day's walk. Then he cried out and said, "Yet forty days, and Nin'e·veh shall be overthrown!"

THE PEOPLE OF NINEVEH BELIEVE

5 So the people of Nin'e·veh believed God, proclaimed a fast, and put on sackcloth, from the greatest to the least of them.

6 Then word came to the king of Nin'e·veh; and he arose from his throne and laid aside his robe, covered *himself* with sackcloth and sat in ashes.

7 And he caused *it* to be proclaimed and published throughout Nin'e·veh by the decree of the king and his nobles, saying,

Let neither man nor beast, herd nor flock, taste anything; do not let them eat, or drink water.

8 But let man and beast be covered with sackcloth, and cry mightily to God; yes, let every one turn from his evil way and from the violence that is in his hands.

9 Who can tell *if* God will turn and relent, and turn away from His fierce anger, so that we may not perish?

10 Then God saw their works, that they turned from their evil way; and God relented from the disaster that He had said He would bring upon them, and He did not do it.

JONAH'S ANGER AND GOD'S KINDNESS

4 But it displeased Jonah exceedingly, and he became angry.

2 So he prayed to the LORD, and said, "Ah, LORD, was not this what I said when I was still in my country? Therefore I fled previously to Tar'shish; for I know that You *are* a gracious and merciful God, slow to anger

3:3 *a*Exact meaning unknown

and abundant in lovingkindness, One who relents from doing harm.

3   "Therefore now, O LORD, please take my life from me, for *it is* better for me to die than to live!"

4   Then the LORD said, "*Is it* right for you to be angry?"

5   So Jonah went out of the city and sat on the east side of the city. There he made himself a shelter and sat under it in the shade, till he might see what would become of the city.

6   And the LORD God prepared a plant*a* and made it come up over Jonah, that it might be shade for his head to deliver him from his misery. So Jonah was very grateful for the plant.

7   But as morning dawned the next day God prepared a worm, and it *so* damaged the plant that it withered.

8   And it happened, when the sun arose, that God prepared a vehement east wind; and the sun beat on Jonah's head, so that he grew faint. Then he wished death for himself, and said, "*It is* better for me to die than to live."

9   Then God said to Jonah, "*Is it* right for you to be angry about the plant?" And he said, "*It is* right for me to be angry, even to death!"

10   But the LORD said, "You have had pity on the plant for which you have not labored, nor made it grow, which came up in a night and perished in a night.

11   "And should I not pity Nin′e·veh, that great city, in which are more than one hundred and twenty thousand persons who cannot discern between their right hand and their left—and much livestock?"

4:6 *a*Hebrew *kikayon,* exact identity unknown

The Book of
MICAH

THE word of the LORD that came to
Mī'cah of Mō're·sheth in the days of
Jō'tham, Ā'haz, *and* Hez·e·kī'ah,
kings of Judah, which he saw concerning Samaria and Jerusalem.

THE COMING JUDGMENT ON ISRAEL

2 Hear, all you peoples!
  Listen, O earth, and all that is in
    it!
  Let the Lord GOD be a witness
    against you,
  The Lord from His holy temple.

3 For behold, the LORD is coming
    out of His place;
  He will come down
  And tread on the high places of
    the earth.
4 The mountains will melt under
    Him,
  And the valleys will split
  Like wax before the fire,
  Like waters poured down a steep
    place.
5 All this is for the transgression of
    Jacob
  And for the sins of the house of
    Israel.
  What *is* the transgression of
    Jacob?
  Is it not Samaria?
  And what *are* the high places of
    Judah?
  Are they not Jerusalem?

6 "Therefore I will make Samaria a
    heap of ruins in the field,
  Places for planting a vineyard;
  I will pour down her stones into
    the valley,
  And I will uncover her
    foundations.
7 All her carved images shall be
    beaten to pieces,

And all her pay as a harlot shall
    be burned with the fire;
All her idols I will lay desolate,
For she gathered *it* from the pay
    of a harlot,
And they shall return to the pay
    of a harlot."

MOURNING FOR ISRAEL AND JUDAH

8 Therefore I will wail and howl,
  I will go stripped and naked;
  I will make a wailing like the
    jackals
  And a mourning like the
    ostriches
9 For her wounds *are* incurable.
  For it has come to Judah;
  It has come to the gate of My
    people—
  To Jerusalem.

10 Tell *it* not in Gath,
   Weep not at all;
   In Beth Aph'rah^a
   Roll yourself in the dust.
11 Pass by in naked shame, you
     inhabitant of Shā'phir;
   The inhabitant of Zā'a·nan^a does
     not go out.
   Beth E'zel mourns;
   Its place to stand is taken away
     from you.

12 For the inhabitant of Mā'roth
     pined^a for good,
   But disaster came down from the
     LORD
   To the gate of Jerusalem.
13 O inhabitant of Lā'chish,
   Harness the chariot to the swift
     steeds

(She *was* the beginning of sin to
the daughter of Zion),
For the transgressions of Israel
were found in you.

14 Therefore you shall give presents
to Mō′re·sheth Gath;*a*
The houses of Ach′zib*b* *shall be* a
lie to the kings of Israel.
15 I will yet bring an heir to you,
O inhabitant of Ma·rē′shah;*a*
The glory of Israel shall come to
A·dul′lam.
16 Make yourself bald and cut off
your hair,
Because of your precious children;
Enlarge your baldness like an
eagle,
For they shall go from you into
captivity.

WOE TO EVILDOERS

2 Woe to those who devise
iniquity,
And work out evil on their beds!
At morning light they practice it,
Because it is in the power of their
hand.
2 They covet fields and take *them*
by violence,
Also houses, and seize *them*.
So they oppress a man and his
house,
A man and his inheritance.

3 Therefore thus says the LORD:

"Behold, against this family I am
devising disaster,
From which you cannot remove
your necks;
Nor shall you walk haughtily,
For this *is* an evil time.
4 In that day *one* shall take up a
proverb against you,
And lament with a bitter
lamentation, saying:
'We are utterly destroyed!

He has changed the heritage of
my people;
How He has removed *it* from me!
To a turncoat He has divided our
fields.'"

5 Therefore you will have no one to
determine boundaries*a* by lot
In the assembly of the LORD.

LYING PROPHETS

6 "Do not prattle," *you say to those*
who prophesy.
So they shall not prophesy to
you;*a*
They shall not return insult for
insult.*b*
7 *You who are* named the house of
Jacob:
"Is the Spirit of the LORD
restricted?
Are these His doings?
Do not My words do good
To him who walks uprightly?

8 "Lately My people have risen up as
an enemy—
You pull off the robe with the
garment
From those who trust *you*, as they
pass by,
Like men returned from war.
9 The women of My people you cast
out
From their pleasant houses;
From their children
You have taken away My glory
forever.

10 "Arise and depart,
For this *is* not *your* rest;
Because it is defiled, it shall
destroy,

1:14 *a*Literally *Possession of Gath*   *b*Literally *Lie*
1:15 *a*Literally *Inheritance*   2:5 *a*Literally *one
casting a surveyor's line*   2:6 *a*Literally *to these*
*b*Vulgate reads *He shall not take shame.*

Yes, with utter destruction.
11 If a man should walk in a false
    spirit
    And speak a lie, *saying,*
    'I will prophesy to you of wine and
    drink,'
    Even he would be the prattler of
    this people.

ISRAEL RESTORED

12 "I will surely assemble all of you,
    O Jacob,
    I will surely gather the remnant
    of Israel;
    I will put them together like
    sheep of the fold,*a*
    Like a flock in the midst of their
    pasture;
    They shall make a loud noise
    because of *so many* people.
13 The one who breaks open will
    come up before them;
    They will break out,
    Pass through the gate,
    And go out by it;
    Their king will pass before them,
    With the LORD at their head."

WICKED RULERS AND PROPHETS

3 And I said:

    "Hear now, O heads of Jacob,
    And you rulers of the house of
    Israel:
    Is it not for you to know justice?
2   You who hate good and love evil;
    Who strip the skin from My
    people,*a*
    And the flesh from their bones;
3   Who also eat the flesh of My
    people,
    Flay their skin from them,
    Break their bones,
    And chop *them* in pieces
    Like *meat* for the pot,
    Like flesh in the caldron."

4   Then they will cry to the LORD,
    But He will not hear them;
    He will even hide His face from
    them at that time,
    Because they have been evil in
    their deeds.

5   Thus says the LORD concerning
    the prophets
    Who make my people stray;
    Who chant "Peace"
    While they chew with their teeth,
    But who prepare war against him
    Who puts nothing into their
    mouths:
6   "Therefore you shall have night
    without vision,
    And you shall have darkness
    without divination;
    The sun shall go down on the
    prophets,
    And the day shall be dark for
    them.
7   So the seers shall be ashamed,
    And the diviners abashed;
    Indeed they shall all cover their
    lips;
    For *there is* no answer from God."

8   But truly I am full of power by
    the Spirit of the LORD,
    And of justice and might,
    To declare to Jacob his
    transgression
    And to Israel his sin.
9   Now hear this,
    You heads of the house of Jacob
    And rulers of the house of Israel,
    Who abhor justice
    And pervert all equity,
10 Who build up Zion with
    bloodshed
    And Jerusalem with iniquity:
11 Her heads judge for a bribe,
    Her priests teach for pay,
    And her prophets divine for
    money.

2:12 *a*Hebrew *Bozrah*   3:2 *a*Literally *them*

Yet they lean on the LORD, and
   say,
"Is not the LORD among us?
No harm can come upon us."
12 Therefore because of you
Zion shall be plowed *like* a field,
Jerusalem shall become heaps of
   ruins,
And the mountain of the temple[a]
Like the bare hills of the forest.

THE LORD'S REIGN IN ZION

4 Now it shall come to pass in the
   latter days
That the mountain of the LORD's
   house
Shall be established on the top of
   the mountains,
And shall be exalted above the
   hills;
And peoples shall flow to it.
2 Many nations shall come and
   say,
"Come, and let us go up to the
   mountain of the LORD,
To the house of the God of Jacob;
He will teach us His ways,
And we shall walk in His paths."
For out of Zion the law shall go
   forth,
And the word of the LORD from
   Jerusalem.
3 He shall judge between many
   peoples,
And rebuke strong nations afar
   off;
They shall beat their swords into
   plowshares,
And their spears into pruning
   hooks;
Nation shall not lift up sword
   against nation,
Neither shall they learn war
   anymore.[a]

4 But everyone shall sit under his
   vine and under his fig tree,

And no one shall make *them*
   afraid;
For the mouth of the LORD of
   hosts has spoken.
5 For all people walk each in the
   name of his god,
But we will walk in the name of
   the LORD our God
Forever and ever.

ZION'S FUTURE TRIUMPH

6 "In that day," says the LORD,
"I will assemble the lame,
I will gather the outcast
And those whom I have afflicted;
7 I will make the lame a remnant,
And the outcast a strong nation;
So the LORD will reign over them
   in Mount Zion
From now on, even forever.
8 And you, O tower of the flock,
The stronghold of the daughter of
   Zion,
To you shall it come,
Even the former dominion shall
   come,
The kingdom of the daughter of
   Jerusalem."

9 Now why do you cry aloud?
Is there no king in your midst?
Has your counselor perished?
For pangs have seized you like a
   woman in labor.
10 Be in pain, and labor to bring
   forth,
O daughter of Zion,
Like a woman in birth pangs.
For now you shall go forth from
   the city,
You shall dwell in the field,
And to Babylon you shall go.
There you shall be delivered;
There the LORD will redeem you
From the hand of your enemies.

3:12 [a]Literally *house*   4:3 [a]Compare Isaiah
2:2–4

11 Now also many nations have
    gathered against you,
Who say, "Let her be defiled,
And let our eye look upon Zion."
12 But they do not know the
    thoughts of the LORD,
Nor do they understand His
    counsel;
For He will gather them like
    sheaves to the threshing floor.

13 "Arise and thresh, O daughter of
    Zion;
For I will make your horn iron,
And I will make your hooves
    bronze;
You shall beat in pieces many
    peoples;
I will consecrate their gain to the
    LORD,
And their substance to the Lord
    of the whole earth."

5 Now gather yourself in troops,
O daughter of troops;
He has laid siege against us;
They will strike the judge of
    Israel with a rod on the cheek.

THE COMING MESSIAH

2 "But you, Bethlehem Eph′ra·thah,
Though you are little among the
    thousands of Judah,
Yet out of you shall come forth to
    Me
The One to be Ruler in Israel,
Whose goings forth *are* from of
    old,
From everlasting."

3 Therefore He shall give them up,
Until the time *that* she who is in
    labor has given birth;
Then the remnant of His
    brethren
Shall return to the children of
    Israel.

■ *Promises* ■

Micah 5:2

God made a special promise to Bethlehem many, many years before the Baby Jesus came there. He promised that Jesus would be born. He promised that Jesus would be born in Bethlehem. God kept His promise. Jesus was born in Bethlehem. God remembers His promises for hundreds of years. That's special to know, isn't it? That reminds you that God will keep His promises to you for a long, long time.

---

4 And He shall stand and feed *His*
    flock
In the strength of the LORD,
In the majesty of the name of the
    LORD His God;
And they shall abide,
For now He shall be great
To the ends of the earth;
5 And this *One* shall be peace.

JUDGMENT ON ISRAEL'S ENEMIES

When the Assyrian comes into
    our land,
And when he treads in our
    palaces,
Then we will raise against him
Seven shepherds and eight
    princely men.
6 They shall waste with the sword
    the land of Assyria,
And the land of Nim′rod at its
    entrances;
Thus He shall deliver *us* from the
    Assyrian,
When he comes into our land
And when he treads within our
    borders.

7 Then the remnant of Jacob
Shall be in the midst of many
   peoples,
Like dew from the LORD,
Like showers on the grass,
That tarry for no man
Nor wait for the sons of men.
8 And the remnant of Jacob
Shall be among the Gentiles,
In the midst of many peoples,
Like a lion among the beasts of
   the forest,
Like a young lion among flocks of
   sheep,
Who, if he passes through,
Both treads down and tears in
   pieces,
And none can deliver.
9 Your hand shall be lifted against
   your adversaries,
And all your enemies shall be cut
   off.

10 "And it shall be in that day," says
   the LORD,
  "That I will cut off your horses
   from your midst
And destroy your chariots.
11 I will cut off the cities of your
   land
And throw down all your
   strongholds.
12 I will cut off sorceries from your
   hand,
And you shall have no
   soothsayers.
13 Your carved images I will also cut
   off,
And your sacred pillars from your
   midst;
You shall no more worship the
   work of your hands;
14 I will pluck your wooden images[a]
   from your midst;
Thus I will destroy your cities.
15 And I will execute vengeance in
   anger and fury
On the nations that have not
   heard."[a]

GOD PLEADS WITH ISRAEL

6 Hear now what the LORD says:

"Arise, plead your case before the
   mountains,
And let the hills hear your voice.
2 Hear, O you mountains, the
   LORD's complaint,
And you strong foundations of the
   earth;
For the LORD has a complaint
   against His people,
And He will contend with Israel.

3 "O My people, what have I done to
   you?
And how have I wearied you?
Testify against Me.
4 For I brought you up from the
   land of Egypt,
I redeemed you from the house of
   bondage;
And I sent before you Moses,
   Aaron, and Miriam.
5 O My people, remember now
What Bā'lak king of Mō'ab
   counseled,
And what Bā'laam the son of
   Bē'or answered him,
From Acacia Grove[a] to Gil'gal,
That you may know the
   righteousness of the LORD."

6 With what shall I come before the
   LORD,
And bow myself before the High
   God?
Shall I come before Him with
   burnt offerings,
With calves a year old?
7 Will the LORD be pleased with
   thousands of rams,
Ten thousand rivers of oil?
Shall I give my firstborn *for* my
   transgression,

5:14 [a]Hebrew *Asherim,* Canaanite deities
5:15 [a]Or *obeyed*   6:5 [a]Hebrew *Shittim* (compare Numbers 25:1; Joshua 2:1; 3:1)

The fruit of my body *for* the sin of
my soul?

8 He has shown you, O man, what
      is good;
   And what does the LORD require
      of you
   But to do justly,
   To love mercy,
   And to walk humbly with your
      God?

PUNISHMENT OF ISRAEL'S INJUSTICE

9 The LORD's voice cries to the
      city—
   Wisdom shall see Your name:

   "Hear the rod!
   Who has appointed it?
10 Are there yet the treasures of
      wickedness
   In the house of the wicked,
   And the short measure *that is* an
      abomination?
11 Shall I count pure *those* with the
      wicked scales,
   And with the bag of deceitful
      weights?
12 For her rich men are full of
      violence,
   Her inhabitants have spoken lies,
   And their tongue is deceitful in
      their mouth.

13 "Therefore I will also make *you*
      sick by striking you,
   By making *you* desolate because
      of your sins.
14 You shall eat, but not be satisfied;
   Hunger*a* *shall be* in your midst.
   You may carry *some* away,*b* but
      shall not save *them;*
   And what you do rescue I will
      give over to the sword.

15 "You shall sow, but not reap;
   You shall tread the olives, but not
      anoint yourselves with oil;

   And *make* sweet wine, but not
      drink wine.
16 For the statutes of Om′rī are
      kept;
   All the works of Ā′hab's house *are*
      done;
   And you walk in their counsels,
   That I may make you a
      desolation,
   And your inhabitants a hissing.
   Therefore you shall bear the
      reproach of My people."*a*

SORROW FOR ISRAEL'S SINS

7 Woe is me!
   For I am like those who gather
      summer fruits,
   Like those who glean vintage
      grapes;
   There is no cluster to eat
   Of the first-ripe fruit *which* my
      soul desires.
2 The faithful *man* has perished
      from the earth,
   And *there is* no one upright
      among men.
   They all lie in wait for blood;
   Every man hunts his brother with
      a net.

3 That they may successfully do
      evil with both hands—
   The prince asks *for gifts,*
   The judge *seeks* a bribe,
   And the great *man* utters his evil
      desire;
   So they scheme together.
4 The best of them *is* like a brier;
   The most upright *is sharper* than
      a thorn hedge;
   The day of your watchman and
      your punishment comes;
   Now shall be their perplexity.

6:14 *a*Or *Emptiness* or *Humiliation*   *b*Targum and
Vulgate read *You shall take hold.*   6:16 *a*Following Masoretic Text, Targum, and Vulgate; Septuagint reads *of nations.*

5 Do not trust in a friend;
Do not put your confidence in a
companion;
Guard the doors of your mouth
From her who lies in your bosom.
6 For son dishonors father,
Daughter rises against her
mother,
Daughter-in-law against her
mother-in-law;
A man's enemies *are* the men of
his own household.
7 Therefore I will look to the LORD;
I will wait for the God of my
salvation;
My God will hear me.

ISRAEL'S CONFESSION AND COMFORT

8 Do not rejoice over me, my
enemy;
When I fall, I will arise;
When I sit in darkness,
The LORD *will be* a light to me.
9 I will bear the indignation of the
LORD,
Because I have sinned against
Him,
Until He pleads my case
And executes justice for me.
He will bring me forth to the
light;
I will see His righteousness.
10 Then *she who is* my enemy will
see,
And shame will cover her who
said to me,
"Where is the LORD your God?"
My eyes will see her;
Now she will be trampled down
Like mud in the streets.

11 *In* the day when your walls are to
be built,
In that day the decree shall go far
and wide.*a*
12 *In* that day they*a* shall come to
you

From Assyria and the fortified
cities,*b*
From the fortress*c* to the River,*d*
From sea to sea,
And mountain *to* mountain.
13 Yet the land shall be desolate
Because of those who dwell in it,
And for the fruit of their deeds.

GOD WILL FORGIVE ISRAEL

14 Shepherd Your people with Your
staff,
The flock of Your heritage,
Who dwell solitarily *in* a
woodland,
In the midst of Car′mel;
Let them feed *in* Bā′shan and
Gil′ē·ad,
As in days of old.

15 "As in the days when you came out
of the land of Egypt,
I will show them*a* wonders."

16 The nations shall see and be
ashamed of all their might;
They shall put *their* hand over
their mouth;
Their ears shall be deaf.
17 They shall lick the dust like a
serpent;
They shall crawl from their holes
like snakes of the earth.
They shall be afraid of the LORD
our God,
And shall fear because of You.
18 Who *is* a God like You,
Pardoning iniquity
And passing over the
transgression of the remnant of
His heritage?

7:11 *a*Or *the boundary shall be extended*
7:12 *a*Literally *he,* collective of the captives   *b*Hebrew *arey mazor,* possibly *cities of Egypt*   *c*Hebrew
mazor, possibly *Egypt*   *d*That is, the Euphrates
7:15 *a*Literally *him,* collective for the captives

He does not retain His anger
    forever,
Because He delights *in* mercy.
19 He will again have compassion on
    us,
And will subdue our iniquities.

You will cast all our*ᵃ* sins
Into the depths of the sea.

20 You will give truth to
    Jacob
And mercy to Abraham,
Which You have sworn to our
    fathers
From days of old.

7:19 *ᵃLiterally their*

The Book of
NAHUM

T HE burden*a* against Nin′e·veh.
The book of the vision of Nā′hum the
El′kosh·ite.

GOD'S WRATH ON HIS ENEMIES

2 God *is* jealous, and the LORD
    avenges;
  The LORD avenges and *is* furious.
  The LORD will take vengeance on
    His adversaries,
  And He reserves *wrath* for His
    enemies;
3 The LORD *is* slow to anger and
    great in power,
  And will not at all acquit *the
    wicked.*

  The LORD has His way
  In the whirlwind and in the
    storm,
  And the clouds *are* the dust of His
    feet.
4 He rebukes the sea and makes it
    dry,

And dries up all the rivers.
Bā′shan and Car′mel wither,
And the flower of Lebanon wilts.
5 The mountains quake before Him,
  The hills melt,
  And the earth heaves*a* at His
    presence,
  Yes, the world and all who dwell
    in it.

6 Who can stand before His
    indignation?
  And who can endure the
    fierceness of His anger?
  His fury is poured out like fire,
  And the rocks are thrown down
    by Him.

7 The LORD *is* good,
  A stronghold in the day of
    trouble;
  And He knows those who trust in
    Him.
8 But with an overflowing flood
  He will make an utter end of its
    place,
  And darkness will pursue His
    enemies.

9 What do you conspire against the
    LORD?
  He will make an utter end *of it.*
  Affliction will not rise up a second
    time.
10 For while tangled *like* thorns,
   And while drunken *like*
     drunkards,
   They shall be devoured like
     stubble fully dried.
11 From you comes forth *one*
   Who plots evil against the LORD,
   A wicked counselor.

12 Thus says the LORD:

Promises

Nahum 1:7

Here's a great promise. The Lord
promises to be our stronghold.
That's like a castle or fortress.
When the day of trouble comes
we have a fortress that is more
powerful than any other in the
world. You don't have to build a
fortress when trouble comes. You
already have a fortress. It is the
Lord Himself. But you can't
stand outside the fortress and
let the enemy hurt you. You
must be *in* the fortress. You
must *let* the Lord be your
fortress.

1:1 *a*Or *oracle*   1:5 *a*Targum reads *burns.*

"Though *they are* safe, and
likewise many,
Yet in this manner they will be
cut down
When he passes through.
Though I have afflicted you,
I will afflict you no more;

13 For now I will break off his yoke
from you,
And burst your bonds apart."

14 The LORD has given a command
concerning you:
"Your name shall be perpetuated
no longer.
Out of the house of your gods
I will cut off the carved image and
the molded image.
I will dig your grave,
For you are vile."

15 Behold, on the mountains
The feet of him who brings good
tidings,
Who proclaims peace!
O Judah, keep your appointed
feasts,
Perform your vows.
For the wicked one shall no more
pass through you;
He is utterly cut off.

THE DESTRUCTION OF NINEVEH

2 He who scatters*a* has come up
before your face.
Man the fort!
Watch the road!
Strengthen *your* flanks!
Fortify *your* power mightily.

2 For the LORD will restore the
excellence of Jacob
Like the excellence of Israel,
For the emptiers have emptied
them out
And ruined their vine branches.

3 The shields of his mighty men *are*
made red,

The valiant men *are* in scarlet.
The chariots *come* with flaming
torches
In the day of his preparation,
And the spears are brandished.*a*

4 The chariots rage in the streets,
They jostle one another in the
broad roads;
They seem like torches,
They run like lightning.

5 He remembers his nobles;
They stumble in their walk;
They make haste to her walls,
And the defense is prepared.

6 The gates of the rivers are
opened,
And the palace is dissolved.

7 It is decreed:*a*
She shall be led away captive,
She shall be brought up;
And her maidservants shall lead
her as with the voice of doves,
Beating their breasts.

8 Though Nin'e·veh of old *was* like
a pool of water,
Now they flee away.
"Halt! Halt!" *they cry;*
But no one turns back.

9 Take spoil of silver!
Take spoil of gold!
There is no end of treasure,
Or wealth of every desirable
prize.

10 She is empty, desolate, and waste!
The heart melts, and the knees
shake;
Much pain *is* in every side,
And all their faces are drained of
color.*a*

11 Where *is* the dwelling of the lions,
And the feeding place of the
young lions,

2:1 *a*Vulgate reads *he who destroys.*   2:3 *a*Literally *the cypresses are shaken;* Septuagint and Syriac read *the horses rush about;* Vulgate reads *the
drivers are stupefied.*   2:7 *a*Hebrew *Huzzab*
2:10 *a*Compare Joel 2:6

Where the lion walked, the
    lioness *and* lion's cub,
And no one made *them* afraid?
12 The lion tore in pieces enough for
    his cubs,
    Killed for his lionesses,
    Filled his caves with prey,
    And his dens with flesh.

13 "Behold, I *am* against you," says
the LORD of hosts, "I will burn your*a*
chariots in smoke, and the sword
shall devour your young lions; I will
cut off your prey from the earth, and
the voice of your messengers shall be
heard no more."

THE WOE OF NINEVEH

3 Woe to the bloody city!
    It *is* all full of lies *and* robbery.
    Its victim never departs.
2 The noise of a whip
    And the noise of rattling wheels,
    Of galloping horses,
    Of clattering chariots!
3 Horsemen charge with bright
    sword and glittering spear.
    There is a multitude of slain,
    A great number of bodies,
    Countless corpses—
    They stumble over the corpses—
4 Because of the multitude of
    harlotries of the seductive
    harlot,
    The mistress of sorceries,
    Who sells nations through her
    harlotries,
    And families through her
    sorceries.

5 "Behold, I *am* against you," says
    the LORD of hosts;
"I will lift your skirts over your
    face,
    I will show the nations your
    nakedness,
    And the kingdoms your shame.

6 I will cast abominable filth upon
    you,
    Make you vile,
    And make you a spectacle.
7 It shall come to pass *that* all who
    look upon you
    Will flee from you, and say,
    'Nin'e·veh is laid waste!
    Who will bemoan her?'
    Where shall I seek comforters for
    you?"

8 Are you better than No Ā'mon*a*
    That was situated by the River,*b*
    That had the waters around her,
    Whose rampart *was* the sea,
    Whose wall *was* the sea?
9 Ethiopia and Egypt *were* her
    strength,
    And *it was* boundless;
    Put and Lū'bim were your*a*
    helpers.
10 Yet she *was* carried away,
    She went into captivity;
    Her young children also were
    dashed to pieces
    At the head of every street;
    They cast lots for her honorable
    men,
    And all her great men were bound
    in chains.
11 You also will be drunk;
    You will be hidden;
    You also will seek refuge from the
    enemy.

12 All your strongholds *are* fig trees
    with ripened figs:
    If they are shaken,
    They fall into the mouth of the
    eater.
13 Surely, your people in your midst
    are women!
    The gates of your land are wide
    open for your enemies;

2:13 *a*Literally *her*   3:8 *a*That is, ancient
Thebes; Targum and Vulgate read *populous Alexandria.* *b*Literally *rivers,* that is, the Nile and the
surrounding canals   3:9 *a*Septuagint reads *her.*

Fire shall devour the bars of your
   gates.

14 Draw your water for the siege!
   Fortify your strongholds!
   Go into the clay and tread the
      mortar!
   Make strong the brick kiln!
15 There the fire will devour you,
   The sword will cut you off;
   It will eat you up like a locust.

   Make yourself many—like the
      locust!
   Make yourself many— like the
      swarming locusts!
16 You have multiplied your
      merchants more than the
      stars of heaven.
   The locust plunders and flies
      away.
17 Your commanders *are* like
      swarming locusts,

And your generals like great
   grasshoppers,
Which camp in the hedges on a
   cold day;
When the sun rises they flee
   away,
And the place where they *are* is
   not known.

18 Your shepherds slumber, O king
      of Assyria;
   Your nobles rest *in the dust*.
   Your people are scattered on the
      mountains,
   And no one gathers them.
19 Your injury *has* no healing,
   Your wound is severe.
   All who hear news of you
   Will clap *their* hands over
      you,
   For upon whom has not your
      wickedness passed
      continually?

The Book of
HABAKKUK

THE burden[a] which the prophet Ha·bak′kuk saw.

THE PROPHET'S QUESTION

2 O LORD, how long shall I cry,
   And You will not hear?
   Even cry out to You, "Violence!"
   And You will not save.
3 Why do You show me iniquity,
   And cause *me* to see trouble?
   For plundering and violence *are*
      before me;
   There is strife, and contention
      arises.
4 Therefore the law is powerless,
   And justice never goes forth.
   For the wicked surround the
      righteous;
   Therefore perverse judgment
      proceeds.

THE LORD'S REPLY

5 "Look among the nations and
      watch—
   Be utterly astounded!
   For *I will* work a work in your
      days
   Which you would not believe,
      though it were told *you*.
6 For indeed I am raising up the
      Chal·dē′ans,
   A bitter and hasty nation
   Which marches through the
      breadth of the earth,
   To possess dwelling places *that
      are* not theirs.
7 They are terrible and dreadful;
   Their judgment and their dignity
      proceed from themselves.
8 Their horses also are swifter than
      leopards,
   And more fierce than evening
      wolves.
   Their chargers charge ahead;

Prayers

Habakkuk 1:2

Lord, You're not listening. That was Habakkuk's prayer. Lord, You're not helping me. That was also Habakkuk's prayer. Do you ever feel like praying those prayers? But you know that God is listening, don't you? You know that He answers, but He sometimes says no, or maybe, or wait. Remember, God *always* hears your prayers. He *always* listens. He *always* answers. His answer may not be the one you want. But it is the right answer. He knows what is best.

   Their cavalry comes from afar;
   They fly as the eagle *that* hastens
      to eat.
9 "They all come for violence;
   Their faces are set *like* the east
      wind.
   They gather captives like sand.
10 They scoff at kings,
   And princes are scorned by them.
   They deride every stronghold,
   For they heap up earthen *mounds*
      and seize it.
11 Then *his* mind[a] changes, and he
      transgresses;
   He commits offense,
   Ascribing this power to his god."

THE PROPHET'S SECOND QUESTION

12 Are You not from everlasting,
   O LORD my God, my Holy One?
   We shall not die.

1:1 [a]Or *oracle*   1:11 [a]Literally *spirit* or *wind*

O Lord, You have appointed them
    for judgment;
O Rock, You have marked them
    for correction.
13 *You are* of purer eyes than to
    behold evil,
And cannot look on wickedness.
Why do You look on those who
    deal treacherously,
And hold Your tongue when the
    wicked devours
A *person* more righteous than he?
14 *Why* do You make men like fish of
    the sea,
Like creeping things *that have* no
    ruler over them?
15 They take up all of them with a
    hook,
They catch them in their net,
And gather them in their dragnet.
Therefore they rejoice and are
    glad.
16 Therefore they sacrifice to their
    net,
And burn incense to their
    dragnet;
Because by them their share *is*
    sumptuous
And their food plentiful.
17 Shall they therefore empty their
    net,
And continue to slay nations
    without pity?

2 I will stand my watch
And set myself on the rampart,
And watch to see what He will
    say to me,
And what I will answer when I
    am corrected.

The Just Live by Faith

2 Then the Lord answered me and
said:

"Write the vision
And make *it* plain on tablets,
That he may run who reads it.

3 For the vision *is* yet for an
    appointed time;
But at the end it will speak, and
    it will not lie.
Though it tarries, wait for it;
Because it will surely come,
It will not tarry.

4 "Behold the proud,
His soul is not upright in him;
But the just shall live by his faith.

Woe to the Wicked

5 "Indeed, because he transgresses
    by wine,
He is a proud man,
And he does not stay at home.
Because he enlarges his desire as
    hell,*a*
And he *is* like death, and cannot
    be satisfied,
He gathers to himself all nations
And heaps up for himself all
    peoples.

6 "Will not all these take up a
    proverb against him,
And a taunting riddle against
    him, and say,
'Woe to him who increases
What is not his—how long?
And to him who loads himself
    with many pledges'?*a*
7 Will not your creditors*a* rise up
    suddenly?
Will they not awaken who oppress
    you?
And you will become their booty.
8 Because you have plundered
    many nations,
All the remnant of the people
    shall plunder you,
Because of men's blood
And the violence of the land *and*
    the city,
And of all who dwell in it.

2:5 *a*Or *Sheol*   2:6 *a*Syriac and Vulgate read
thick clay.   2:7 *a*Literally *those who bite you*

9 "Woe to him who covets evil gain
    for his house,
  That he may set his nest on high,
  That he may be delivered from
    the power of disaster!
10 You give shameful counsel to your
    house,
  Cutting off many peoples,
  And sin *against* your soul.
11 For the stone will cry out from
    the wall,
  And the beam from the timbers
    will answer it.

12 "Woe to him who builds a town
    with bloodshed,
  Who establishes a city by
    iniquity!
13 Behold, *is it* not of the LORD of
    hosts
  That the peoples labor to feed the
    fire,*a*

Promises

Habakkuk 2:14

Do you go to school? Do you ever think the world is full of information and knowledge? There is much to learn. But the Lord's knowledge would fill the world and spill over the sides. The Lord knows much, much more than all people together. He knows all that has happened. He knows all that *will* happen. He knows every person by name and what each one is thinking. The Lord knows every thought you think. He knows everything you have ever done. He knows everything you will ever do. What a lot to know! No library or computer program in the world has all that knowledge. It's good to seek His wisdom, isn't it?

  And nations weary themselves in
    vain?
14 For the earth will be filled
  With the knowledge of the glory
    of the LORD,
  As the waters cover the sea.

15 "Woe to him who gives drink to his
    neighbor,
  Pressing*a him to* your bottle,
  Even to make *him* drunk,
  That you may look on his
    nakedness!
16 You are filled with shame instead
    of glory.
  You also—drink!
  And be exposed as
    uncircumcised!*a*
  The cup of the LORD's right hand
    will be turned against you,
  And utter shame will be on your
    glory.
17 For the violence *done to* Lebanon
    will cover you,
  And the plunder of beasts *which*
    made them afraid,
  Because of men's blood
  And the violence of the land *and*
    the city,
  And of all who dwell in it.

18 "What profit is the image, that its
    maker should carve it,
  The molded image, a teacher of
    lies,
  That the maker of its mold should
    trust in it,
  To make mute idols?
19 Woe to him who says to wood,
    'Awake!'
  To silent stone, 'Arise! It shall
    teach!'
  Behold, it is overlaid with gold
    and silver,
  Yet in it there is no breath at all.

2:13 *a*Literally *for what satisfies fire,* that is, for what is of no lasting value   2:15 *a*Literally *Attaching* or *Joining*   2:16 *a*Dead Sea Scrolls and Septuagint read *And reel!;* Syriac and Vulgate read *And fall fast asleep!*

20 "But the LORD is in His holy
   temple.
      Let all the earth keep silence
         before Him."

THE PROPHET'S PRAYER

3 A prayer of Ha·bak'kuk the
prophet, on Shig·i·ōn'oth.a

2 O LORD, I have heard Your speech
      and was afraid;
   O LORD, revive Your work in the
      midst of the years!
   In the midst of the years make *it*
      known;
   In wrath remember mercy.

◼ *Praises* ◼

Habakkuk 3:3

"The earth was full of His
praise." Look at everything
around you on a beautiful day.
Look at the clouds and flowers
and trees and bushes. Are they
a praise to God? What about
the grass and birds and animals? Are they a praise to
God? Are flavors in foods a
praise to God? What about
wonderful smells in flowers?
What about the wonderful
things you hear? Does the
whole earth seem full of His
praise? It is!

---

3 God came from Tē'man,
   The Holy One from Mount
      Par'an.   Sē'lah

   His glory covered the heavens,
   And the earth was full of His
      praise.
4 *His* brightness was like the light;
   He had rays *flashing* from His
      hand,
   And there His power *was* hidden.

5 Before Him went pestilence,
   And fever followed at His feet.

6 He stood and measured the earth;
   He looked and startled the
      nations.
   And the everlasting mountains
      were scattered,
   The perpetual hills bowed.
   His ways *are* everlasting.
7 I saw the tents of Cūsh'an in
      affliction;
   The curtains of the land of
      Mid'i·an trembled.

8 O LORD, were *You* displeased with
      the rivers,
   Was Your anger against the
      rivers,
   Was Your wrath against the sea,
   That You rode on Your horses,
   Your chariots of salvation?
9 Your bow was made quite ready;
   Oaths were sworn over *Your*
      arrows.a   Sē'lah

   You divided the earth with rivers.
10 The mountains saw You *and*
      trembled;
   The overflowing of the water
      passed by.
   The deep uttered its voice,
   And lifted its hands on high.
11 The sun and moon stood still in
      their habitation;
   At the light of Your arrows they
      went,
   At the shining of Your glittering
      spear.

12 You marched through the land in
      indignation;
   You trampled the nations in
      anger.
13 You went forth for the salvation of
      Your people,

3:1 *a*Exact meaning unknown   3:9 *a*Literally
rods or *tribes* (compare verse 14)

For salvation with Your Anointed.
You struck the head from the
   house of the wicked,
By laying bare from foundation to
   neck.   Sē'lah

14 You thrust through with his own
   arrows
The head of his villages.
They came out like a whirlwind to
   scatter me;
Their rejoicing was like feasting
   on the poor in secret.

15 You walked through the sea with
   Your horses,
Through the heap of great waters.

16 When I heard, my body trembled;
My lips quivered at *the* voice;
Rottenness entered my bones;
And I trembled in myself,
That I might rest in the day of
   trouble.
When he comes up to the people,
He will invade them with his
   troops.

A HYMN OF FAITH

17 Though the fig tree may not
   blossom,
Nor fruit be on the vines;
Though the labor of the olive may
   fail,
And the fields yield no food;
Though the flock may be cut off
   from the fold,
And there be no herd in the
   stalls—

18 Yet I will rejoice in the LORD,
I will joy in the God of my
   salvation.

19 The LORD God*a* is my strength;
He will make my feet like deer's
   feet,
And He will make me walk on my
   high hills.

To the Chief Musician. With my
stringed instruments.

3:19 *a*Hebrew *YHWH Adonai*

The Book of
ZEPHANIAH

THE word of the LORD which came to Zeph·a·nī′ah the son of Cū′shī, the son of Ged·a·lī′ah, the son of Am·a·rī′ah, the son of Hez·e·kī′ah, in the days of Jō·sī′ah the son of Ā′mon, king of Judah.

THE GREAT DAY OF THE LORD

2 "I will utterly consume everything
  From the face of the land,"
  Says the LORD;
3 "I will consume man and beast;
  I will consume the birds of the
    heavens,
  The fish of the sea,
  And the stumbling blocksa along
    with the wicked.
  I will cut off man from the face of
    the land,"
  Says the LORD.

4 "I will stretch out My hand against
    Judah,
  And against all the inhabitants of
    Jerusalem.
  I will cut off every trace of Bā′al
    from this place,
  The names of the idolatrous
    priestsa with the *pagan*
    priests—
5 Those who worship the host of
    heaven on the housetops;
  Those who worship and swear
    oaths by the LORD,
  But who *also* swear by Mil′com;a
6 Those who have turned back from
    following the LORD,
  And have not sought the LORD,
    nor inquired of Him."

7 Be silent in the presence of the
    Lord GOD;
  For the day of the LORD *is* at
    hand,

For the LORD has prepared a
    sacrifice;
  He has inviteda His guests.

8 "And it shall be,
  In the day of the LORD's sacrifice,
  That I will punish the princes and
    the king's children,
  And all such as are clothed with
    foreign apparel.
9 In the same day I will punish
  All those who leap over the
    threshold,a
  Who fill their masters' houses
    with violence and deceit.

10 "And there shall be on that day,"
    says the LORD,
  "The sound of a mournful cry from
    the Fish Gate,
  A wailing from the Second
    Quarter,
  And a loud crashing from the
    hills.
11 Wail, you inhabitants of
    Mak′tesh!a
  For all the merchant people are
    cut down;
  All those who handle money are
    cut off.

12 "And it shall come to pass at that
    time
  That I will search Jerusalem with
    lamps,
  And punish the men
  Who are settled in complacency,a
  Who say in their heart,

1:3 aFigurative of idols   1:4 aHebrew *chemarim*
1:5 aOr *Malcam,* an Ammonite god, also called
Molech (compare Leviticus 18:21)   1:7 aLiterally *set apart, consecrated*   1:9 aCompare
1 Samuel 5:5   1:11 aLiterally *Mortar,* a market
district of Jerusalem   1:12 aLiterally *on their
lees,* that is, settled like the dregs of wine

'The LORD will not do good,
Nor will He do evil.'

13 Therefore their goods shall
    become booty,
And their houses a desolation;
They shall build houses, but not
    inhabit *them;*
They shall plant vineyards, but
    not drink their wine."

14 The great day of the LORD *is*
    near;
It is near and hastens quickly.
The noise of the day of the LORD
    is bitter;
There the mighty men shall cry
    out.
15 That day *is* a day of wrath,
A day of trouble and distress,
A day of devastation and
    desolation,
A day of darkness and
    gloominess,
A day of clouds and thick
    darkness,
16 A day of trumpet and alarm
Against the fortified cities
And against the high towers.

17 "I will bring distress upon men,
And they shall walk like blind
    men,
Because they have sinned against
    the LORD;
Their blood shall be poured out
    like dust,
And their flesh like refuse."

18 Neither their silver nor their
    gold
Shall be able to deliver them
In the day of the LORD's wrath;
But the whole land shall be
    devoured
By the fire of His jealousy,
For He will make speedy
    riddance
Of all those who dwell in the
    land.

A CALL TO REPENTANCE

2 Gather yourselves together, yes,
    gather together,
O undesirable[a] nation,
2 Before the decree is issued,
Or the day passes like chaff,
Before the LORD's fierce anger
    comes upon you,
Before the day of the LORD's anger
    comes upon you!
3 Seek the LORD, all you meek of
    the earth,
Who have upheld His justice.
Seek righteousness, seek
    humility.
It may be that you will be
    hidden
In the day of the LORD's anger.

JUDGMENT ON NATIONS

4 For Gā′za shall be forsaken,
And Ash′ke·lon desolate;
They shall drive out Ash′dod at
    noonday,
And Ek′ron shall be uprooted.
5 Woe to the inhabitants of the
    seacoast,
The nation of the Cher′e·thītes!
The word of the LORD *is* against
    you,
O Cā′naan, land of the
    Phi·lis′tines:
"I will destroy you;
So there shall be no inhabitant."

6 The seacoast shall be pastures,
With shelters[a] for shepherds and
    folds for flocks.
7 The coast shall be for the
    remnant of the house of Judah;
They shall feed *their* flocks
    there;
In the houses of Ash′ke·lon they
    shall lie down at evening.

2:1 [a]Or *shameless*   2:6 [a]Literally *excavations,*
either underground huts or cisterns

For the LORD their God will
   intervene for them,
And return their captives.

8 "I have heard the reproach of
   Mō′ab,
And the insults of the people of
   Am′mon,
With which they have reproached
   My people,
And made arrogant threats
   against their borders.
9 Therefore, as I live,"
Says the LORD of hosts, the God of
   Israel,
"Surely Mō′ab shall be like
   Sod′om,
And the people of Am′mon like
   Go·mor′rah—
Overrun with weeds and saltpits,
And a perpetual desolation.
The residue of My people shall
   plunder them,
And the remnant of My people
   shall possess them."

10 This they shall have for their
   pride,
Because they have reproached
   and made arrogant threats
Against the people of the LORD of
   hosts.
11 The LORD *will be* awesome to
   them,
For He will reduce to nothing all
   the gods of the earth;
People shall worship Him,
Each one from his place,
Indeed all the shores of the
   nations.

12 "You Ethiopians also,
You shall be slain by My sword."

13 And He will stretch out His hand
   against the north,
Destroy Assyria,
And make Nin′e·veh a desolation,
As dry as the wilderness.

14 The herds shall lie down in her
   midst,
Every beast of the nation.
Both the pelican and the bittern
Shall lodge on the capitals *of* her
   pillars;
Their voice shall sing in the
   windows;
Desolation *shall be* at the
   threshold;
For He will lay bare the cedar
   work.
15 This is the rejoicing city
That dwelt securely,
That said in her heart,
"I *am it,* and *there is* none besides
   me."
How has she become a desolation,
A place for beasts to lie down!
Everyone who passes by her
Shall hiss and shake his fist.

THE WICKEDNESS OF JERUSALEM

3 Woe to her who is rebellious and
   polluted,
To the oppressing city!
2 She has not obeyed *His* voice,
She has not received correction;
She has not trusted in the LORD,
She has not drawn near to her
   God.

3 Her princes in her midst *are*
   roaring lions;
Her judges *are* evening wolves
That leave not a bone till
   morning.
4 Her prophets are insolent,
   treacherous people;
Her priests have polluted the
   sanctuary,
They have done violence to the
   law.
5 The LORD *is* righteous in her
   midst,
He will do no unrighteousness.
Every morning He brings His
   justice to light;

He never fails,
But the unjust knows no shame.

6 "I have cut off nations,
Their fortresses are devastated;
I have made their streets
  desolate,
With none passing by.
Their cities are destroyed;
There is no one, no inhabitant.
7 I said, 'Surely you will fear Me,
You will receive instruction'—
So that her dwelling would not be
  cut off,
Despite everything for which I
  punished her.
But they rose early and corrupted
  all their deeds.

A FAITHFUL REMNANT

8 "Therefore wait for Me," says the
  LORD,
"Until the day I rise up for
  plunder;*a*
My determination *is* to gather the
  nations
To My assembly of kingdoms,
To pour on them My indignation,
All My fierce anger;
All the earth shall be devoured
With the fire of My jealousy.

9 "For then I will restore to the
  peoples a pure language,
That they all may call on the
  name of the LORD,
To serve Him with one accord.
10 From beyond the rivers of
  Ethiopia
My worshipers,
The daughter of My dispersed
  ones,
Shall bring My offering.
11 In that day you shall not be
  shamed for any of your deeds
In which you transgress against
  Me;
For then I will take away from
  your midst

Those who rejoice in your pride,
And you shall no longer be
  haughty
In My holy mountain.
12 I will leave in your midst
A meek and humble people,
And they shall trust in the name
  of the LORD.
13 The remnant of Israel shall do no
  unrighteousness
And speak no lies,
Nor shall a deceitful tongue be
  found in their mouth;
For they shall feed *their* flocks
  and lie down,
And no one shall make *them*
  afraid."

JOY IN GOD'S FAITHFULNESS

14 Sing, O daughter of Zion!
Shout, O Israel!
Be glad and rejoice with all *your*
  heart,
O daughter of Jerusalem!
15 The LORD has taken away your
  judgments,
He has cast out your enemy.
The King of Israel, the LORD, *is* in
  your midst;
You shall see*a* disaster no more.

16 In that day it shall be said to
  Jerusalem:
"Do not fear;
Zion, let not your hands be weak.
17 The LORD your God in your midst,
The Mighty One, will save;
He will rejoice over you with
  gladness,
He will quiet *you* with His love,
He will rejoice over you with
  singing."

3:8 *a*Septuagint and Syriac read *for witness;* Targum reads *for the day of My revelation for judgment;* Vulgate reads *for the day of My resurrection that is to come.*   3:15 *a*Some Hebrew manuscripts, Septuagint, and Bomberg read *see;* Masoretic Text and Vulgate read *fear.*

LOVE Zephaniah 3:17

If You Love Me, Say So

Do you love me? Please tell me. God loves you and me. He tells us many times in the Bible. Do you love God? Tell Him!

1. Sometimes Indians "talked" by sending smoke signals. What do you think this boy is saying?
2. Do you think this boy might send a smoke signal to God? What would he say?
3. What would you like to say to God? Will you?

For more on *Values* turn to page 1447

For more on *Love* turn to page 1454

18 "I will gather those who sorrow
     over the appointed assembly,
Who are among you,
To whom its reproach *is* a burden.

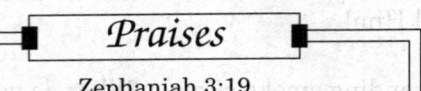

Praises

Zephaniah 3:19

"I will appoint them for praise,"
God said about some people. Do
you ever think that God appoints us to praise Him? God
puts us here on earth to bring
praise to Him. Are you doing
what God appointed you to do?

19   Behold, at that time
     I will deal with all who afflict you;
     I will save the lame,
     And gather those who were
        driven out;
     I will appoint them for praise and
        fame
     In every land where they were
        put to shame.
20   At that time I will bring you back,
     Even at the time I gather you;
     For I will give you fame and
        praise
     Among all the peoples of the
        earth,
     When I return your captives
        before your eyes,"
     Says the LORD.

The Book of
HAGGAI

THE COMMAND TO BUILD GOD'S HOUSE

IN the second year of King Da·rī'us, in the sixth month, on the first day of the month, the word of the LORD came by Hag'gaī the prophet to Ze·rub'ba·bel the son of She·al'ti·el, governor of Judah, and to Joshua the son of Je·hoz'a·dak, the high priest, saying,

2 "Thus speaks the LORD of hosts, saying: 'This people says, "The time has not come, the time that the LORD's house should be built." ' "

3 Then the word of the LORD came by Hag'gaī the prophet, saying,

4 "*Is it* time for you yourselves to dwell in your paneled houses, and this templea *to lie* in ruins?"

5 Now therefore, thus says the LORD of hosts: "Consider your ways!

6 "You have sown much, and bring
    in little;
  You eat, but do not have enough;
  You drink, but you are not filled
    with drink;
  You clothe yourselves, but no one
    is warm;
  And he who earns wages,
  Earns wages *to put* into a bag
    with holes."

7 Thus says the LORD of hosts: "Consider your ways!

8 "Go up to the mountains and bring wood and build the temple, that I may take pleasure in it and be glorified," says the LORD.

9 "*You* looked for much, but indeed *it came to* little; and when you brought it home, I blew it away. Why?" says the LORD of hosts. "Because of My house that *is in* ruins,

while every one of you runs to his own house.

10 "Therefore the heavens above you withhold the dew, and the earth withholds its fruit.

11 "For I called for a drought on the land and the mountains, on the grain and the new wine and the oil, on whatever the ground brings forth, on men and livestock, and on all the labor of *your* hands."

THE PEOPLE'S OBEDIENCE

12 Then Ze·rub'ba·bel the son of She·al'ti·el, and Joshua the son of Je·hoz'a·dak, the high priest, with all the remnant of the people, obeyed the voice of the LORD their God, and the words of Hag'gaī the prophet, as the LORD their God had sent him; and the people feared the presence of the LORD.

13 Then Hag'gaī, the LORD's messenger, spoke the LORD's message to the people, saying, "I *am* with you, says the LORD."

14 So the LORD stirred up the spirit of Ze·rub'ba·bel the son of She·al'ti·el, governor of Judah, and the spirit of Joshua the son of Je·hoz'a·dak, the high priest, and the spirit of all the remnant of the people; and they came and worked on the house of the LORD of hosts, their God,

15 on the twenty-fourth day of the sixth month, in the second year of King Da·rī'us.

THE COMING GLORY OF GOD'S HOUSE

2 In the seventh *month,* on the twenty-first of the month, the word of

1:4 aLiterally *house,* and so in verse 8

the LORD came by Hag'gaï the prophet, saying:

2 "Speak now to Ze·rub'ba·bel the son of She·al'ti·el, governor of Judah, and to Joshua the son of Je·hoz'a·dak, the high priest, and to the remnant of the people, saying:

3 'Who is left among you who saw this temple*a* in its former glory? And how do you see it now? In comparison with it, *is this* not in your eyes as nothing?

```
┌─────────────────────────────────┐
│  ◼▬▬▬   Promises   ▬▬▬◼         │
│                                 │
│         Haggai 2:4              │
│                                 │
│ The Lord had some work for      │
│ Haggai to do. He wanted Haggai  │
│ the prophet to relay some mes-  │
│ sages. "Be strong," God said    │
│ through Haggai. "Be strong be-  │
│ cause I am with you." Do you    │
│ ever feel weak? Do you ever wish│
│ you were stronger? But you don't│
│ know how to be strong. Here's   │
│ God's way. When you invite the  │
│ Lord to be with you, you *will* be │
│ strong. That's a promise. It's  │
│ God's promise.                  │
└─────────────────────────────────┘
```

4 'Yet now be strong, Ze·rub'ba·bel,' says the LORD; 'and be strong, Joshua, son of Je·hoz'a·dak, the high priest; and be strong, all you people of the land,' says the LORD, 'and work; for I *am* with you,' says the LORD of hosts.

5 'According to the word that I covenanted with you when you came out of Egypt, so My Spirit remains among you; do not fear!'

6 "For thus says the LORD of hosts: 'Once more (it *is* a little while) I will shake heaven and earth, the sea and dry land;

7 'and I will shake all nations, and they shall come to the Desire of All Nations,*a* and I will fill this temple with glory,' says the LORD of hosts.

8 'The silver *is* Mine, and the gold *is* Mine,' says the LORD of hosts.

9 'The glory of this latter temple shall be greater than the former,' says the LORD of hosts. 'And in this place I will give peace,' says the LORD of hosts."

THE PEOPLE ARE DEFILED

10 On the twenty-fourth *day* of the ninth *month,* in the second year of Da·rī'us, the word of the LORD came by Hag'gaï the prophet, saying,

11 "Thus says the LORD of hosts: 'Now, ask the priests *concerning the* law, saying,

12 "If one carries holy meat in the fold of his garment, and with the edge he touches bread or stew, wine or oil, or any food, will it become holy?" ' " Then the priests answered and said, "No."

13 And Hag'gaï said, "If *one who is* unclean *because* of a dead body touches any of these, will it be unclean?" So the priests answered and said, "It shall be unclean."

14 Then Hag'gaï answered and said, " 'So is this people, and so is this nation before Me,' says the LORD, 'and so is every work of their hands; and what they offer there is unclean.

PROMISED BLESSING

15 'And now, carefully consider from this day forward: from before stone was laid upon stone in the temple of the LORD—

16 'since those *days,* when *one* came to a heap of twenty ephahs, there were *but* ten; when *one* came to the

---

2:3 *a*Literally *house,* and so in verses 7 and 9
2:7 *a*Or *the desire of all nations*

wine vat to draw out fifty baths from the press, there were *but* twenty.

17 'I struck you with blight and mildew and hail in all the labors of your hands; yet you did not *turn* to Me,' says the LORD.

18 'Consider now from this day forward, from the twenty-fourth day of the ninth month, from the day that the foundation of the LORD's temple was laid—consider it:

19 'Is the seed still in the barn? As yet the vine, the fig tree, the pomegranate, and the olive tree have not yielded *fruit. But* from this day I will bless *you.*' "

ZERUBBABEL CHOSEN AS A SIGNET

20 And again the word of the LORD came to Hag'gaī on the twenty-fourth day of the month, saying,

21 "Speak to Ze·rub'ba·bel, governor of Judah, saying:

'I will shake heaven and earth.
22 I will overthrow the throne of
    kingdoms;
I will destroy the strength of the
    Gentile kingdoms.
I will overthrow the chariots
And those who ride in them;
The horses and their riders shall
    come down,
Every one by the sword of his
    brother.

23 'In that day,' says the LORD of hosts, 'I will take you, Ze·rub'ba·bel My servant, the son of She·al'ti·el,' says the LORD, 'and will make you like a signet *ring;* for I have chosen you,' says the LORD of hosts."

The Book of
ZECHARIAH

A CALL TO REPENTANCE

IN the eighth month of the second year of Da·rī′us, the word of the LORD came to Zech·a·rī′ah the son of Ber·e·chī′ah, the son of Id′dō the prophet, saying,

2 "The LORD has been very angry with your fathers.

3 "Therefore say to them, 'Thus says the LORD of hosts: "Return to Me," says the LORD of hosts, "and I will return to you," says the LORD of hosts.

4 "Do not be like your fathers, to whom the former prophets preached, saying, 'Thus says the LORD of hosts: "Turn now from your evil ways and your evil deeds." ' But they did not hear nor heed Me," says the LORD.

5 "Your fathers, where are they?
    And the prophets, do they live forever?
6 Yet surely My words and My statutes,
    Which I commanded My servants the prophets,
    Did they not overtake your fathers?

"So they returned and said:

'Just as the LORD of hosts determined to do to us,
    According to our ways and according to our deeds,
    So He has dealt with us.' " ' "

VISION OF THE HORSES

7 On the twenty-fourth day of the eleventh month, which is the month She·bat′, in the second year of Da·rī′us, the word of the LORD came to Zech·a·rī′ah the son of Ber·e·chī′ah, the son of Id′dō the prophet:

8 I saw by night, and behold, a man riding on a red horse, and it stood among the myrtle trees in the hollow; and behind him were horses: red, sorrel, and white.

9 Then I said, "My lord, what are these?" So the angel who talked with me said to me, "I will show you what they are."

10 And the man who stood among the myrtle trees answered and said, "These are the ones whom the LORD has sent to walk to and fro throughout the earth."

11 So they answered the Angel of the LORD, who stood among the myrtle trees, and said, "We have walked to and fro throughout the earth, and behold, all the earth is resting quietly."

THE LORD WILL COMFORT ZION

12 Then the Angel of the LORD answered and said, "O LORD of hosts, how long will You not have mercy on Jerusalem and on the cities of Judah, against which You were angry these seventy years?"

13 And the LORD answered the angel who talked to me, with good and comforting words.

14 So the angel who spoke with me said to me, "Proclaim, saying, 'Thus says the LORD of hosts:

"I am zealous for Jerusalem
    And for Zion with great zeal.
15 I am exceedingly angry with the nations at ease;
    For I was a little angry,
    And they helped—but with evil intent."

*J*esus said, "Let the little children come to Me."

———————

Matthew 19:14

*J*esus is the way to God. Follow Him.

———

John 14:6

When we share with others, Jesus is pleased.

———

Acts 2:44

*P*aint me a Christian. Tell everyone that I belong to Christ.

Acts 11:26

16 'Therefore thus says the LORD:

"I am returning to Jerusalem with
      mercy;
   My house shall be built in it,"
      says the LORD of hosts,
"And a *surveyor's* line shall be
      stretched out over Jerusalem." '

17 "Again proclaim, saying, 'Thus
says the LORD of hosts:

"My cities shall again spread out
      through prosperity;
   The LORD will again comfort
      Zion,
   And will again choose
      Jerusalem." ' "

VISION OF THE HORNS

18 Then I raised my eyes and looked,
and there *were* four horns.
19 And I said to the angel who
talked with me, "What *are* these?" So
he answered me, "These *are* the
horns that have scattered Judah, Israel, and Jerusalem."
20 Then the LORD showed me four
craftsmen.
21 And I said, "What are these coming to do?" So he said, "These *are* the
horns that scattered Judah, so that
no one could lift up his head; but the
craftsmen*a* are coming to terrify
them, to cast out the horns of the nations that lifted up *their* horn against
the land of Judah to scatter it."

VISION OF THE MEASURING LINE

2 Then I raised my eyes and looked,
and behold, a man with a measuring
line in his hand.
2 So I said, "Where are you going?"
And he said to me, "To measure Jerusalem, to see what *is* its width and
what *is* its length."

3 And there *was* the angel who
talked with me, going out; and another angel was coming out to meet
him,
4 who said to him, "Run, speak to
this young man, saying: 'Jerusalem
shall be inhabited *as* towns without
walls, because of the multitude of
men and livestock in it.
5 'For I,' says the LORD, 'will be a
wall of fire all around her, and I will
be the glory in her midst.' "

FUTURE JOY OF ZION AND
MANY NATIONS

6 "Up, up! Flee from the land of the
north," says the LORD; "for I have
spread you abroad like the four
winds of heaven," says the LORD.
7 "Up, Zion! Escape, you who dwell
with the daughter of Babylon."
8 For thus says the LORD of hosts:
"He sent Me after glory, to the nations which plunder you; for he who
touches you touches the apple of His
eye.
9 "For surely I will shake My hand
against them, and they shall become
spoil for their servants. Then you will
know that the LORD of hosts has sent
Me.
10 "Sing and rejoice, O daughter of
Zion! For behold, I am coming and I
will dwell in your midst," says the
LORD.
11 "Many nations shall be joined to
the LORD in that day, and they shall
become My people. And I will dwell
in your midst. Then you will know
that the LORD of hosts has sent Me to
you.
12 "And the LORD will take possession of Judah as His inheritance in
the Holy Land, and will again choose
Jerusalem.
13 "Be silent, all flesh, before the

1:21 *a*Literally *these*

Lord, for He is aroused from His holy habitation!"

Vision of the High Priest

3 Then he showed me Joshua the high priest standing before the Angel of the Lord, and Satan standing at his right hand to oppose him.
2 And the Lord said to Satan, "The Lord rebuke you, Satan! The Lord who has chosen Jerusalem rebuke you! *Is* this not a brand plucked from the fire?"
3 Now Joshua was clothed with filthy garments, and was standing before the Angel.
4 Then He answered and spoke to those who stood before Him, saying, "Take away the filthy garments from him." And to him He said, "See, I have removed your iniquity from you, and I will clothe you with rich robes."
5 And I said, "Let them put a clean turban on his head." So they put a clean turban on his head, and they put the clothes on him. And the Angel of the Lord stood by.

The Coming Branch

6 Then the Angel of the Lord admonished Joshua, saying,
7 "Thus says the Lord of hosts:

'If you will walk in My ways,
And if you will keep My
　command,
Then you shall also judge My
　house,
And likewise have charge of My
　courts;
I will give you places to walk
Among these who stand here.

8 'Hear, O Joshua, the high priest,
You and your companions who sit
　before you,

For they are a wondrous sign;
For behold, I am bringing forth
　My Servant the BRANCH.
9 For behold, the stone
That I have laid before Joshua:
Upon the stone *are* seven eyes.
Behold, I will engrave its
　inscription,'
Says the Lord of hosts,
'And I will remove the iniquity of
　that land in one day.
10 In that day,' says the Lord of
　hosts,
'Everyone will invite his neighbor
Under his vine and under his fig
　tree.' "

Vision of the Lampstand and Olive Trees

4 Now the angel who talked with me came back and wakened me, as a man who is wakened out of his sleep.
2 And he said to me, "What do you see?" So I said, "I am looking, and there *is* a lampstand of solid gold with a bowl on top of it, and on the *stand* seven lamps with seven pipes to the seven lamps.
3 "Two olive trees *are* by it, one at the right of the bowl and the other at its left."
4 So I answered and spoke to the angel who talked with me, saying, "What *are* these, my lord?"
5 Then the angel who talked with me answered and said to me, "Do you not know what these are?" And I said, "No, my lord."
6 So he answered and said to me:

"This *is* the word of the Lord to
　Ze·rub'ba·bel:
'Not by might nor by power, but by
　My Spirit,'
Says the Lord of hosts.
7 'Who *are* you, O great mountain?

ABOUT GOD'S POWER Zechariah 4:6

I'll Knock the Ball Over the Moon

Have you ever heard someone say, "I'll knock that ball over the moon"? That's quite far, isn't it? Have you ever thought you were almost as big as God, or could do something almost as well as God? Are you? Can you?

1. Whom do we need when we do God's work? Are you big enough to do God's work without God?
2. Read Zechariah 4:6. How do we do great things for God? Do we do them by our own strength or power? Or do we do them with God's help?

For more on *What the Bible Says* turn to page 1441
For more on *Serving* turn to page 1440

Before Ze·rub′ba·bel *you shall
    become* a plain!
And he shall bring forth the
    capstone
With shouts of "Grace, grace to
    it!" ' "

8 Moreover the word of the LORD
came to me, saying:

9 "The hands of Ze·rub′ba·bel
    Have laid the foundation of this
        temple;*a*
    His hands shall also finish *it.*
    Then you will know
    That the LORD of hosts has sent
        Me to you.
10 For who has despised the day of
        small things?
    For these seven rejoice to see
    The plumb line in the hand of
        Ze·rub′ba·bel.
    They are the eyes of the LORD,
    Which scan to and fro throughout
        the whole earth."

11 Then I answered and said to him,
"What *are* these two olive trees—at
the right of the lampstand and at its
left?"
12 And I further answered and said
to him, "What *are these* two olive
branches that *drip* into the recepta-
cles*a* of the two gold pipes from which
the golden *oil* drains?"
13 Then he answered me and said,
"Do you not know what these *are?*"
And I said, "No, my lord."
14 So he said, "These *are* the two
anointed ones, who stand beside the
Lord of the whole earth."

VISION OF THE FLYING SCROLL

5 Then I turned and raised my
eyes, and saw there a flying scroll.
2 And he said to me, "What do you
see?" So I answered, "I see a flying

scroll. Its length *is* twenty cubits and
its width ten cubits."
3 Then he said to me, "This *is* the
curse that goes out over the face of
the whole earth: 'Every thief shall be
expelled,' according *to* this side of
the scroll; and, 'Every perjurer shall
be expelled,' according *to* that side
of it."

4 "I will send out *the curse,*" says the
        LORD of hosts;
    "It shall enter the house of the
        thief
    And the house of the one who
        swears falsely by My name.
    It shall remain in the midst of his
        house
    And consume it, with its timber
        and stones."

VISION OF THE WOMAN IN A BASKET

5 Then the angel who talked with
me came out and said to me, "Lift
your eyes now, and see what this *is*
that goes forth."
6 So I asked, "What *is* it?" And he
said, "It *is* a basket*a* that is going
forth." He also said, "This *is* their re-
semblance throughout the earth:
7 "Here *is* a lead disc lifted up, and
this *is* a woman sitting inside the
basket";
8 then he said, "This *is* Wickedness!" And he thrust her down into
the basket, and threw the lead cover*a*
over its mouth.
9 Then I raised my eyes and looked,
and there *were* two women, coming
with the wind in their wings; for they
had wings like the wings of a stork,
and they lifted up the basket between
earth and heaven.
10 So I said to the angel who talked

4:9 *a*Literally *house*   4:12 *a*Literally *into the
hands of*   5:6 *a*Hebrew *ephah,* a measuring container, and so elsewhere   5:8 *a*Literally *stone*

with me, "Where are they carrying the basket?"

11 And he said to me, "To build a house for it in the land of Shī′nar;*a* when it is ready, *the basket* will be set there on its base."

VISION OF THE FOUR CHARIOTS

6 Then I turned and raised my eyes and looked, and behold, four chariots *were* coming from between two mountains, and the mountains *were* mountains of bronze.
2 With the first chariot *were* red horses, with the second chariot black horses,
3 with the third chariot white horses, and with the fourth chariot dappled horses—strong *steeds*.
4 Then I answered and said to the angel who talked with me, "What *are* these, my lord?"
5 And the angel answered and said to me, "These *are* four spirits of heaven, who go out from *their* station before the Lord of all the earth.
6 "The one with the black horses is going to the north country, the white are going after them, and the dappled are going toward the south country."
7 Then the strong *steeds* went out, eager to go, that they might walk to and fro throughout the earth. And He said, "Go, walk to and fro throughout the earth." So they walked to and fro throughout the earth.
8 And He called to me, and spoke to me, saying, "See, those who go toward the north country have given rest to My Spirit in the north country."

THE COMMAND TO CROWN JOSHUA

9 Then the word of the LORD came to me, saying:
10 "Receive *the gift* from the cap-

tives—from Hel′daī, Tō·bī′jah, and Je·daī′ah, who have come from Babylon—and go the same day and enter the house of Jō·sī′ah the son of Zeph-a·nī′ah.
11 "Take the silver and gold, make an elaborate crown, and set *it* on the head of Joshua the son of Je·hoz′a-dak, the high priest.
12 "Then speak to him, saying, 'Thus says the LORD of hosts, saying:

"Behold, the Man whose name *is*
 the BRANCH!
From His place He shall branch
 out,
And He shall build the temple of
 the LORD;
13 Yes, He shall build the temple of
 the LORD.
He shall bear the glory,
And shall sit and rule on His
 throne;
So He shall be a priest on His
 throne,
And the counsel of peace shall be
 between them both." '

14 "Now the elaborate crown shall be for a memorial in the temple of the LORD for Hē′lem,*a* Tō·bī′jah, Je-daī′ah, and Hen the son of Zeph·a·nī′ah.
15 "Even those from afar shall come and build the temple of the LORD. Then you shall know that the LORD of hosts has sent Me to you. And *this* shall come to pass if you diligently obey the voice of the LORD your God."

OBEDIENCE BETTER THAN FASTING

7 Now in the fourth year of King Da·rī′us it came to pass *that* the word

---

5:11 *a*That is, Babylon 6:14 *a*Following Masoretic Text, Targum, and Vulgate; Syriac reads *for Heldai* (compare verse 10); Septuagint reads *for the patient ones.*

of the LORD came to Zech·a·rī′ah, on the fourth day of the ninth month, Chis′lev,

2 when *the people*ᵃ sent She·rē′zer,ᵇ with Reg′em-Mel′ech and his men, *to* the house of God,ᶜ to pray before the LORD,

3 *and* to ask the priests who *were* in the house of the LORD of hosts, and the prophets, saying, "Should I weep in the fifth month and fast as I have done for so many years?"

4 Then the word of the LORD of hosts came to me, saying,

5 "Say to all the people of the land, and to the priests: 'When you fasted and mourned in the fifth and seventh *months* during those seventy years, did you really fast for Me—for Me?

6 'When you eat and when you drink, do you not eat and drink *for yourselves?*

7 'Should you* not *have obeyed* the words which the LORD proclaimed through the former prophets when Jerusalem and the cities around it were inhabited and prosperous, and the Southᵃ and the Lowland were inhabited?'"

DISOBEDIENCE RESULTED IN CAPTIVITY

8 Then the word of the LORD came to Zech·a·rī′ah, saying,

9 "Thus says the LORD of hosts:

'Execute true justice,
Show mercy and compassion
Everyone to his brother.

10 Do not oppress the widow or the fatherless,
The alien or the poor.
Let none of you plan evil in his heart
Against his brother.'

11 "But they refused to heed, shrugged their shoulders, and stopped their ears so that they could not hear.

12 "Yes, they made their hearts like flint, refusing to hear the law and the words which the LORD of hosts had sent by His Spirit through the former prophets. Thus great wrath came from the LORD of hosts.

13 "Therefore it happened, *that* just as He proclaimed and they would not hear, so they called out and I would not listen," says the LORD of hosts.

14 "But I scattered them with a whirlwind among all the nations which they had not known. Thus the land became desolate after them, so that no one passed through or returned; for they made the pleasant land desolate."

JERUSALEM, HOLY CITY OF THE FUTURE

8 Again the word of the LORD of hosts came, saying,

2 "Thus says the LORD of hosts:

'I am zealous for Zion with great zeal;
With great fervor I am zealous for her.'

3 "Thus says the LORD:

'I will return to Zion,
And dwell in the midst of Jerusalem.
Jerusalem shall be called the City of Truth,
The Mountain of the LORD of hosts,
The Holy Mountain.'

4 "Thus says the LORD of hosts:

7:2 ᵃLiterally *they* (compare verse 5) ᵇOr *Sar-Ezer* ᶜHebrew *Bethel* 7:7 ᵃHebrew *Negev*

'Old men and old women shall
   again sit
In the streets of Jerusalem,
Each one with his staff in his
   hand
Because of great age.
5 The streets of the city
Shall be full of boys and girls
Playing in its streets.'

6 "Thus says the LORD of hosts:

'If it is marvelous in the eyes of
   the remnant of this people in
   these days,
Will it also be marvelous in My
   eyes?'
Says the LORD of hosts.

7 "Thus says the LORD of hosts:

'Behold, I will save My people
   from the land of the east
And from the land of the west;
8 I will bring them *back,*
And they shall dwell in the midst
   of Jerusalem.
They shall be My people
And I will be their God,
In truth and righteousness.'

9 "Thus says the LORD of hosts:

'Let your hands be strong,
You who have been hearing in
   these days
These words by the mouth of the
   prophets,
Who *spoke* in the day the
   foundation was laid
For the house of the LORD of
   hosts,
That the temple might be built.
10 For before these days
There were no wages for man nor
   any hire for beast;
There was no peace from the

enemy for whoever went out or
   came in;
For I set all men, everyone,
   against his neighbor.

11 'But now I *will* not *treat* the remnant of this people as in the former
days,' says the LORD of hosts.

12 'For the seed *shall be* prosperous,
The vine shall give its fruit,
The ground shall give her
   increase,
And the heavens shall give their
   dew—
I will cause the remnant of this
   people
To possess all these.
13 And it shall come to pass
That just as you were a curse
   among the nations,
O house of Judah and house of
   Israel,
So I will save you, and you shall
   be a blessing.
Do not fear,
Let your hands be strong.'

14 "For thus says the LORD of hosts:

'Just as I determined to punish
   you
When your fathers provoked Me
   to wrath,'
Says the LORD of hosts,
'And I would not relent,
15 So again in these days
I am determined to do good
To Jerusalem and to the house of
   Judah.
Do not fear.
16 These *are* the things you shall
   do:
Speak each man the truth to his
   neighbor;
Give judgment in your gates for
   truth, justice, and peace;
17 Let none of you think evil in

your[a] heart against your
neighbor;
And do not love a false oath.
For all these *are things* that I
hate,'
Says the LORD."

18 Then the word of the LORD of
hosts came to me, saying,
19 "Thus says the LORD of hosts:

'The fast of the fourth *month,*
The fast of the fifth,
The fast of the seventh,
And the fast of the tenth,
Shall be joy and gladness and
cheerful feasts
For the house of Judah.
Therefore love truth and peace.'

20 "Thus says the LORD of hosts:

'Peoples shall yet come,
Inhabitants of many cities;
21 The inhabitants of one *city* shall
go to another, saying,
"Let us continue to go and pray
before the LORD,
And seek the LORD of hosts.
I myself will go also."
22 Yes, many peoples and strong
nations
Shall come to seek the LORD of
hosts in Jerusalem,
And to pray before the LORD.'

23 "Thus says the LORD of hosts: 'In
those days ten men from every language of the nations shall grasp the
sleeve of a Jewish man, saying, "Let
us go with you, for we have heard
that God *is* with you." ' "

ISRAEL DEFENDED
AGAINST ENEMIES

9 The burden[a] of the word of the
LORD

Against the land of Had'rach,
And Damascus its resting place
(For the eyes of men
And all the tribes of Israel
Are on the LORD);
2 Also *against* Hā'math, *which*
borders on it,
And *against* Tȳre and Sī'don,
though they are very wise.

3 For Tȳre built herself a tower,
Heaped up silver like the dust,
And gold like the mire of the
streets.
4 Behold, the LORD will cast her
out;
He will destroy her power in the
sea,
And she will be devoured by fire.

5 Ash'ke·lon shall see *it* and fear;
Gā'za also shall be very
sorrowful;
And Ek'ron, for He dried up her
expectation.
The king shall perish from Gā'za,
And Ash'ke·lon shall not be
inhabited.

6 "A mixed race shall settle in
Ash'dod,
And I will cut off the pride of the
Phi·lis'tines.
7 I will take away the blood from
his mouth,
And the abominations from
between his teeth.
But he who remains, even he
shall be for our God,
And shall be like a leader in
Judah,
And Ek'ron like a Jeb'ū·site.
8 I will camp around My house
Because of the army,
Because of him who passes by
and him who returns.

8:17 [a]Literally *his*   9:1 [a]Or *oracle*

No more shall an oppressor pass
through them,
For now I have seen with My
eyes.

THE COMING KING

9 "Rejoice greatly, O daughter of
Zion!
Shout, O daughter of Jerusalem!
Behold, your King is coming to
you;
He *is* just and having salvation,
Lowly and riding on a donkey,
A colt, the foal of a donkey.
10 I will cut off the chariot from
Ē′phra·im
And the horse from Jerusalem;
The battle bow shall be cut off.
He shall speak peace to the
nations;
His dominion *shall be* 'from sea to
sea,
And from the River to the ends of
the earth.'*a*

GOD WILL SAVE HIS PEOPLE

11 "As for you also,
Because of the blood of your
covenant,
I will set your prisoners free from
the waterless pit.
12 Return to the stronghold,
You prisoners of hope.
Even today I declare
That I will restore double to you.
13 For I have bent Judah, My *bow,*
Fitted the bow with Ē′phra·im,
And raised up your sons, O Zion,
Against your sons, O Greece,
And made you like the sword of a
mighty man."

14 Then the LORD will be seen over
them,
And His arrow will go forth like
lightning.

The Lord GOD will blow the
trumpet,
And go with whirlwinds from the
south.
15 The LORD of hosts will defend
them;
They shall devour and subdue
with slingstones.
They shall drink *and* roar as if
with wine;
They shall be filled *with blood*
like basins,
Like the corners of the altar.
16 The LORD their God will save
them in that day,
As the flock of His people.
For they *shall be like* the jewels of
a crown,
Lifted like a banner over His
land—
17 For how great is its*a* goodness
And how great its*b* beauty!
Grain shall make the young men
thrive,
And new wine the young women.

RESTORATION OF JUDAH AND ISRAEL

10 Ask the LORD for rain
In the time of the latter rain.*a*
The LORD will make flashing
clouds;
He will give them showers of
rain,
Grass in the field for everyone.

2 For the idols*a* speak delusion;
The diviners envision lies,
And tell false dreams;
They comfort in vain.
Therefore *the people* wend their
way like sheep;
They are in trouble because *there
is* no shepherd.

9:10 *a*Psalm 72:8   9:17 *a*Or *His* *b*Or *His*
10:1 *a*That is, spring rain   10:2 *a*Hebrew
teraphim

3 "My anger is kindled against the
  shepherds,
  And I will punish the goatherds.
  For the LORD of hosts will visit
  His flock,
  The house of Judah,
  And will make them as His royal
  horse in the battle.
4 From him comes the
  cornerstone,
  From him the tent peg,
  From him the battle bow,
  From him every ruler*a* together.
5 They shall be like mighty men,
  Who tread down *their enemies*
  In the mire of the streets in the
  battle.
  They shall fight because the LORD
  is with them,
  And the riders on horses shall be
  put to shame.

6 "I will strengthen the house of
  Judah,
  And I will save the house of
  Joseph.
  I will bring them back,
  Because I have mercy on them.
  They shall be as though I had not
  cast them aside;
  For I *am* the LORD their God,
  And I will hear them.
7 *Those of* Ē′phra·im shall be like a
  mighty man,
  And their heart shall rejoice as if
  with wine.
  Yes, their children shall see *it* and
  be glad;
  Their heart shall rejoice in the
  LORD.
8 I will whistle for them and gather
  them,
  For I will redeem them;
  And they shall increase as they
  once increased.

9 "I will sow them among the
  peoples,

And they shall remember Me in
  far countries;
They shall live, together with
  their children,
And they shall return.
10 I will also bring them back from
  the land of Egypt,
  And gather them from Assyria.
  I will bring them into the land of
  Gil′ē·ad and Lebanon,
  Until no *more room* is found for
  them.
11 He shall pass through the sea
  with affliction,
  And strike the waves of the
  sea:
  All the depths of the River*a* shall
  dry up.
  Then the pride of Assyria shall be
  brought down,
  And the scepter of Egypt shall
  depart.

12 "So I will strengthen them in the
  LORD,
  And they shall walk up and down
  in His name,"
  Says the LORD.

DESOLATION OF ISRAEL

11 Open your doors, O Lebanon,
  That fire may devour your
  cedars.
2 Wail, O cypress, for the cedar has
  fallen,
  Because the mighty *trees* are
  ruined.
  Wail, O oaks of Bā′shan,
  For the thick forest has come
  down.
3 *There is* the sound of wailing
  shepherds!
  For their glory is in ruins.
  There is the sound of roaring
  lions!

10:4 *a*Or *despot*   10:11 *a*That is, the Nile

For the pride*a* of the Jordan is in ruins.

PROPHECY OF THE SHEPHERDS

4 Thus says the LORD my God, "Feed the flock for slaughter,
5 "whose owners slaughter them and feel no guilt; those who sell them say, 'Blessed be the LORD, for I am rich'; and their shepherds do not pity them.
6 "For I will no longer pity the inhabitants of the land," says the LORD. "But indeed I will give everyone into his neighbor's hand and into the hand of his king. They shall attack the land, and I will not deliver *them* from their hand."
7 So I fed the flock for slaughter, in particular the poor of the flock.*a* I took for myself two staffs: the one I called Beauty,*b* and the other I called Bonds;*c* and I fed the flock.
8 I dismissed the three shepherds in one month. My soul loathed them, and their soul also abhorred me.
9 Then I said, "I will not feed you. Let what is dying die, and what is perishing perish. Let those that are left eat each other's flesh."
10 And I took my staff, Beauty, and cut it in two, that I might break the covenant which I had made with all the peoples.
11 So it was broken on that day. Thus the poor*a* of the flock, who were watching me, knew that it *was* the word of the LORD.
12 Then I said to them, "If it is agreeable to you, give *me* my wages; and if not, refrain." So they weighed out for my wages thirty *pieces* of silver.
13 And the LORD said to me, "Throw it to the potter"—that princely price they set on me. So I took the thirty *pieces* of silver and threw them into the house of the LORD for the potter.
14 Then I cut in two my other staff, Bonds, that I might break the brotherhood between Judah and Israel.
15 And the LORD said to me, "Next, take for yourself the implements of a foolish shepherd.
16 "For indeed I will raise up a shepherd in the land *who* will not care for those who are cut off, nor seek the young, nor heal those that are broken, nor feed those that still stand. But he will eat the flesh of the fat and tear their hooves in pieces.

17 "Woe to the worthless shepherd,
Who leaves the flock!
A sword *shall be* against his arm
And against his right eye;
His arm shall completely wither,
And his right eye shall be totally blinded."

THE COMING DELIVERANCE OF JUDAH

12 The burden*a* of the word of the LORD against Israel. Thus says the LORD, who stretches out the heavens, lays the foundation of the earth, and forms the spirit of man within him:
2 "Behold, I will make Jerusalem a cup of drunkenness to all the surrounding peoples, when they lay siege against Judah and Jerusalem.
3 "And it shall happen in that day that I will make Jerusalem a very heavy stone for all peoples; all who would heave it away will surely be cut in pieces, though all nations of the earth are gathered against it.
4 "In that day," says the LORD, "I

11:3 *a*Or *floodplain, thicket*   11:7 *a*Following Masoretic Text, Targum, and Vulgate; Septuagint reads *for the Canaanites.*   *b*Or *Grace,* and so in verse 10   *c*Or *Unity,* and so in verse 14   11:11 *a*Following Masoretic Text, Targum, and Vulgate; Septuagint reads *the Canaanites.*   12:1 *a*Or *oracle*

will strike every horse with confusion, and its rider with madness; I will open My eyes on the house of Judah, and will strike every horse of the peoples with blindness.

5 "And the governors of Judah shall say in their heart, 'The inhabitants of Jerusalem *are* my strength in the LORD of hosts, their God.'

6 "In that day I will make the governors of Judah like a firepan in the woodpile, and like a fiery torch in the sheaves; they shall devour all the surrounding peoples on the right hand and on the left, but Jerusalem shall be inhabited again in her own place—Jerusalem.

7 "The LORD will save the tents of Judah first, so that the glory of the house of David and the glory of the inhabitants of Jerusalem shall not become greater than that of Judah.

8 "In that day the LORD will defend the inhabitants of Jerusalem; the one who is feeble among them in that day shall be like David, and the house of David *shall be* like God, like the Angel of the LORD before them.

9 "It shall be in that day *that* I will seek to destroy all the nations that come against Jerusalem.

MOURNING FOR THE PIERCED ONE

10 "And I will pour on the house of David and on the inhabitants of Jerusalem the Spirit of grace and supplication; then they will look on Me whom they pierced. Yes, they will mourn for Him as one mourns for *his* only *son,* and grieve for Him as one grieves for a firstborn.

11 "In that day there shall be a great mourning in Jerusalem, like the mourning at Hā'dad Rim'mon in the plain of Me·gid'dō.*a*

12 "And the land shall mourn, every family by itself: the family of the house of David by itself, and their wives by themselves; the family of the house of Nathan by itself, and their wives by themselves;

13 "the family of the house of Levi by itself, and their wives by themselves; the family of Shim'ē·ī by itself, and their wives by themselves;

14 "all the families that remain, every family by itself, and their wives by themselves.

IDOLATRY CUT OFF

13 "In that day a fountain shall be opened for the house of David and for the inhabitants of Jerusalem, for sin and for uncleanness.

2 "It shall be in that day," says the LORD of hosts, "*that* I will cut off the names of the idols from the land, and they shall no longer be remembered. I will also cause the prophets and the unclean spirit to depart from the land.

3 "It shall come to pass *that* if anyone still prophesies, then his father and mother who begot him will say to him, 'You shall not live, because you have spoken lies in the name of the LORD.' And his father and mother who begot him shall thrust him through when he prophesies.

4 "And it shall be in that day *that* every prophet will be ashamed of his vision when he prophesies; they will not wear a robe of coarse hair to deceive.

5 "But he will say, 'I *am* no prophet, I *am* a farmer; for a man taught me to keep cattle from my youth.'

6 "And *one* will say to him, 'What are these wounds between your arms?'*a* Then he will answer, 'Those with which I was wounded in the house of my friends.'

12:11 *a*Hebrew *Megiddon*   13:6 *a*Or *hands*

THE SHEPHERD SAVIOR

7 "Awake, O sword, against My
   Shepherd,
   Against the Man who is My
   Companion,"
   Says the LORD of hosts.
   "Strike the Shepherd,
   And the sheep will be scattered;
   Then I will turn My hand against
   the little ones.
8 And it shall come to pass in all
   the land,"
   Says the LORD,
   "*That* two-thirds in it shall be cut
   off *and* die,
   But *one*-third shall be left in it:
9 I will bring the *one*-third through
   the fire,
   Will refine them as silver is
   refined,
   And test them as gold is tested.
   They will call on My name,
   And I will answer them.
   I will say, 'This *is* My people';
   And each one will say, 'The LORD
   is my God.' "

THE DAY OF THE LORD

14 Behold, the day of the LORD is
   coming,
   And your spoil will be divided in
   your midst.
2 For I will gather all the nations to
   battle against Jerusalem;
   The city shall be taken,
   The houses rifled,
   And the women ravished.
   Half of the city shall go into
   captivity,
   But the remnant of the people
   shall not be cut off from the
   city.

3 Then the LORD will go forth
   And fight against those nations,
   As He fights in the day of battle.

4 And in that day His feet will
   stand on the Mount of Olives,
   Which faces Jerusalem on the
   east.
   And the Mount of Olives shall be
   split in two,
   From east to west,
   Making a very large valley;
   Half of the mountain shall move
   toward the north
   And half of it toward the south.

5 Then you shall flee *through* My
   mountain valley,
   For the mountain valley shall
   reach to Ā´zal.
   Yes, you shall flee
   As you fled from the earthquake
   In the days of Uz·zī´ah king of
   Judah.

   Thus the LORD my God will
   come,
   And all the saints with You.*a*

6 It shall come to pass in that day
   That there will be no light;
   The lights will diminish.
7 It shall be one day
   Which is known to the LORD—
   Neither day nor night.
   But at evening time it shall
   happen
   That it will be light.

8 And in that day it shall be
   That living waters shall flow from
   Jerusalem,
   Half of them toward the eastern
   sea
   And half of them toward the
   western sea;
   In both summer and winter it
   shall occur.
9 And the LORD shall be King over
   all the earth.

14:5 *a*Or *you;* Septuagint, Targum, and Vulgate
read *Him.*

┌─────────────────────────────┐
│ ■ *Promises* ■ │
│   │
│   Zechariah 14:9   │
│   │
│ Here's a wonderful promise. │
│ Think of the most powerful peo- │
│ ple on earth today. The Lord is │
│ King over them. Think of the │
│ most powerful people of history. │
│ The Lord was King over them. │
│ Try to imagine the most power- │
│ ful kings or generals or world │
│ leaders to come. The Lord will be │
│ their King. The biggest and most │
│ powerful people will still have a │
│ King over them. He is the Lord. │
│ Aren't you happy He's on your │
│ side? He has promised that He │
│ will. │
└─────────────────────────────┘

In that day it shall be—
"The LORD *is* one,"*a*
And His name one.

10 All the land shall be turned into a plain from Gē´ba to Rim´mon south of Jerusalem. *Jerusalem*ª shall be raised up and inhabited in her place from Benjamin's Gate to the place of the First Gate and the Corner Gate, and *from* the Tower of Ha·nan´el to the king's winepresses.

11 *The people* shall dwell in it;
And no longer shall there be utter destruction,
But Jerusalem shall be safely inhabited.

12 And this shall be the plague with which the LORD will strike all the people who fought against Jerusalem:

Their flesh shall dissolve while they stand on their feet,
Their eyes shall dissolve in their sockets,

And their tongues shall dissolve in their mouths.

13 It shall come to pass in that day
That a great panic from the LORD will be among them.
Everyone will seize the hand of his neighbor,
And raise his hand against his neighbor's hand;

14 Judah also will fight at Jerusalem.
And the wealth of all the surrounding nations
Shall be gathered together:
Gold, silver, and apparel in great abundance.

15 Such also shall be the plague
On the horse *and* the mule,
On the camel and the donkey,
And on all the cattle that will be in those camps.
So *shall* this plague *be*.

THE NATIONS WORSHIP THE KING

16 And it shall come to pass *that* everyone who is left of all the nations which came against Jerusalem shall go up from year to year to worship the King, the LORD of hosts, and to keep the Feast of Tabernacles.
17 And it shall be *that* whichever of the families of the earth do not come up to Jerusalem to worship the King, the LORD of hosts, on them there will be no rain.
18 If the family of Egypt will not come up and enter in, they *shall have* no *rain;* they shall receive the plague with which the LORD strikes the nations who do not come up to keep the Feast of Tabernacles.
19 This shall be the punishment of

14:9 ªCompare Deuteronomy 6:4   14:10 ªLiterally *She*

Egypt and the punishment of all the nations that do not come up to keep the Feast of Tabernacles.

20 In that day "HOLINESS TO THE LORD" shall be *engraved* on the bells of the horses. The pots in the LORD's house shall be like the bowls before the altar.

21 Yes, every pot in Jerusalem and Judah shall be holiness to the LORD of hosts.*a* Everyone who sacrifices shall come and take them and cook in them. In that day there shall no longer be a Cā′naan-īte in the house of the LORD of hosts.

14:21 *a*Or *on every pot . . . shall be (engraved)* "HOLINESS TO THE LORD OF HOSTS"

The Book of
MALACHI

THE burden*a* of the word of the
LORD to Israel by Mal′a·chī.

ISRAEL BELOVED OF GOD

2 "I have loved you," says the LORD.
"Yet you say, 'In what way have
You loved us?'
Was not Esau Jacob's brother?"
Says the LORD.
"Yet Jacob I have loved;
3 But Esau I have hated,
And laid waste his mountains and
his heritage
For the jackals of the wilderness."

4 Even though Ē′dom has said,
"We have been impoverished,
But we will return and build the
desolate places,"

Thus says the LORD of hosts:

"They may build, but I will throw
down;
They shall be called the Territory
of Wickedness,
And the people against whom the
LORD will have indignation
forever.
5 Your eyes shall see,
And you shall say,
'The LORD is magnified beyond the
border of Israel.'

POLLUTED OFFERINGS

6 "A son honors *his* father,
And a servant *his* master.
If then I am the Father,
Where *is* My honor?
And if I *am* a Master,
Where *is* My reverence?
Says the LORD of hosts

To you priests who despise My
name.
Yet you say, 'In what way have we
despised Your name?'

7 "You offer defiled food on My altar,
But say,
'In what way have we defiled
You?'
By saying,
'The table of the LORD is
contemptible.'
8 And when you offer the blind as a
sacrifice,
Is it not evil?
And when you offer the lame and
sick,
Is it not evil?
Offer it then to your governor!
Would he be pleased with you?
Would he accept you favorably?"
Says the LORD of hosts.

9 "But now entreat God's favor,
That He may be gracious to us.
While this is being *done* by your
hands,
Will He accept you favorably?"
Says the LORD of hosts.
10 "Who *is there* even among you who
would shut the doors,
So that you would not kindle fire
on My altar in vain?
I have no pleasure in you,"
Says the LORD of hosts,
"Nor will I accept an offering from
your hands.
11 For from the rising of the sun,
even to its going down,
My name *shall be* great among
the Gentiles;
In every place incense *shall be*
offered to My name,
And a pure offering;

1:1 *a*Or *oracle*

For My name shall be great
 among the nations,"
Says the LORD of hosts.

12 "But you profane it,
 In that you say,
 'The table of the LORD[a] is defiled;
 And its fruit, its food, *is*
  contemptible.'
13 You also say,
 'Oh, what a weariness!'
 And you sneer at it,"
 Says the LORD of hosts.
 "And you bring the stolen, the
  lame, and the sick;
 Thus you bring an offering!
 Should I accept this from your
  hand?"
 Says the LORD.
14 "But cursed *be* the deceiver
 Who has in his flock a male,
 And takes a vow,
 But sacrifices to the Lord what is
  blemished—
 For I *am* a great King,"
 Says the LORD of hosts,
 "And My name *is to be* feared
  among the nations.

CORRUPT PRIESTS

2 "And now, O priests, this
 commandment is for you.
2 If you will not hear,
 And if you will not take *it* to
  heart,
 To give glory to My name,"
 Says the LORD of hosts,
 "I will send a curse upon you,
 And I will curse your blessings.
 Yes, I have cursed them already,
 Because you do not take *it* to
  heart.
3 "Behold, I will rebuke your
  descendants
 And spread refuse on your faces,
 The refuse of your solemn feasts;
 And *one* will take you away with
  it.

4 Then you shall know that I have
 sent this commandment to you,
 That My covenant with Levi may
  continue,"
 Says the LORD of hosts.
5 "My covenant was with him, *one* of
  life and peace,
 And I gave them to him *that he
  might* fear *Me*;
 So he feared Me
 And was reverent before My
  name.
6 The law of truth[a] was in his
  mouth,
 And injustice was not found on
  his lips.
 He walked with Me in peace and
  equity,
 And turned many away from
  iniquity.

7 "For the lips of a priest should
  keep knowledge,
 And *people* should seek the law
  from his mouth;
 For he is the messenger of the
  LORD of hosts.
8 But you have departed from the
  way;
 You have caused many to stumble
  at the law.
 You have corrupted the covenant
  of Levi,"
 Says the LORD of hosts.
9 "Therefore I also have made you
  contemptible and base
 Before all the people,
 Because you have not kept My
  ways
 But have shown partiality in the
  law."

TREACHERY OF INFIDELITY

10 Have we not all one Father?
 Has not one God created us?

1:12 [a]Following Bomberg; Masoretic Text reads
Lord.   2:6 [a]Or *true instruction*

Why do we deal treacherously
    with one another
By profaning the covenant of the
    fathers?
11 Judah has dealt treacherously,
And an abomination has been
    committed in Israel and in
    Jerusalem,
For Judah has profaned
The LORD's holy *institution* which
    He loves:
He has married the daughter of a
    foreign god.
12 May the LORD cut off from the
    tents of Jacob
The man who does this, being
    awake and aware,ᵃ
Yet who brings an offering to the
    LORD of hosts!

13 And this is the second thing you
    do:
You cover the altar of the LORD
    with tears,
With weeping and crying;
So He does not regard the offering
    anymore,
Nor receive *it* with goodwill from
    your hands.
14 Yet you say, "For what reason?"
Because the LORD has been
    witness
Between you and the wife of your
    youth,
With whom you have dealt
    treacherously;
Yet she is your companion
And your wife by covenant.
15 But did He not make *them* one,
Having a remnant of the Spirit?
And why one?
He seeks godly offspring.
Therefore take heed to your
    spirit,
And let none deal treacherously
    with the wife of his youth.

16 "For the LORD God of Israel says
That He hates divorce,

For it covers one's garment with
    violence,"
Says the LORD of hosts.
"Therefore take heed to your
    spirit,
That you do not deal
    treacherously."

17 You have wearied the LORD with
    your words;
Yet you say,
"In what way have we wearied
    Him?"
In that you say,
"Everyone who does evil
Is good in the sight of the LORD,
And He delights in them,"
Or, "Where *is* the God of justice?"

THE COMING MESSENGER

3 "Behold, I send My messenger,
And he will prepare the way
    before Me.
And the Lord, whom you seek,
Will suddenly come to His temple,
Even the Messenger of the
    covenant,
In whom you delight.
Behold, He is coming,"
Says the LORD of hosts.

2 "But who can endure the day of
    His coming?
And who can stand when He
    appears?
For He *is* like a refiner's fire
And like launderers' soap.
3 He will sit as a refiner and a
    purifier of silver;
He will purify the sons of Levi,
And purge them as gold and
    silver,
That they may offer to the LORD
An offering in righteousness.

2:12 ᵃTalmud and Vulgate read *teacher and student.*

4 "Then the offering of Judah and
     Jerusalem
     Will be pleasant to the LORD,
     As in the days of old,
     As in former years.
5 And I will come near you for
     judgment;
     I will be a swift witness
     Against sorcerers,
     Against adulterers,
     Against perjurers,
     Against those who exploit wage
     earners and widows and
     orphans,
     And against those who turn away
     an alien—
     Because they do not fear Me,"
     Says the LORD of hosts.

6 "For I *am* the LORD, I do not
     change;
     Therefore you are not consumed,
     O sons of Jacob.
7 Yet from the days of your fathers
     You have gone away from My
     ordinances
     And have not kept *them.*
     Return to Me, and I will return to
     you,"
     Says the LORD of hosts.
     "But you said,
     'In what way shall we return?'

DO NOT ROB GOD

8 "Will a man rob God?
     Yet you have robbed Me!
     But you say,
     'In what way have we robbed
     You?'
     In tithes and offerings.
9 You are cursed with a curse,
     For you have robbed Me,
     Even this whole nation.
10 Bring all the tithes into the
     storehouse,
     That there may be food in My
     house,
     And try Me now in this,"

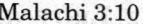

Promises

Malachi 3:10

Do you like to give to God? Do you like to give for God's work? God expects us to give cheerfully and generously. When we do, we have His special promise. He will give us more than we can dream. We must not give to get, for that is not giving. We must give to Him because we love Him. *Then* He will bless us. Try it, just for the joy of giving to the Lord.

     Says the LORD of hosts,
     "If I will not open for you the
     windows of heaven
     And pour out for you *such*
     blessing
     That *there will* not *be room*
     enough *to receive it.*

11 "And I will rebuke the devourer for
     your sakes,
     So that he will not destroy the
     fruit of your ground,
     Nor shall the vine fail to bear
     fruit for you in the field,"
     Says the LORD of hosts;
12 "And all nations will call you
     blessed,
     For you will be a delightful land,"
     Says the LORD of hosts.

THE PEOPLE COMPLAIN HARSHLY

13 "Your words have been harsh
     against Me,"
     Says the LORD,
     "Yet you say,
     'What have we spoken against
     You?'
14 You have said,
     'It is useless to serve God;

What Should I Do?

ONE SMALL LISTENER Malachi 3:14

This little boy is pretending that he is a great preacher. Thousands and thousands of people are listening to him. They have come for many miles to hear him. And hundreds will tell him what a great preacher he is. Then the little boy looks down. There aren't thousands. There is only one. Would he still do it? God asks you to do something for Him. Must you have a big reward? Or will you do it just for Him? Will you do it even if one person hears what you say, or what you sing, or what you play? What will you do to please God?

1. How many people did the boy pretend were listening to him? How many really were listening to him?
2. What did you learn from this? What would you do for Jesus, or for parents, or for a friend, if you got nothing for it? Why do we do special things for those we love?

For more on *What Should I Do?* turn to page 1459
For more on *Serving* turn to page 1447

ABOUT JESUS' HEALING Malachi 4:2

For Brokenhearted People

Do you know people who have felt brokenhearted? Perhaps a loved one died. Or something sad happened in their lives. Or they did something very wrong and felt sad for their sin. What did you wish you could do for them?

1. Read the first half of Malachi 4:2. This is a prophecy about the coming of Jesus Christ. He will have healing for sin and brokenheartedness.

2. What then can you do most for brokenhearted people? They will appreciate a sympathetic ear, of course. But ultimately they need what only Jesus can bring—His healing for brokenheartedness. Another prophet, Isaiah, told how He would do this. Read Isaiah 53:4, 5. Jesus was crucified, wounded, for our transgressions. He took our sins on the cross so we would not be punished for them. He is God's ultimate answer for the brokenhearted, especially those wounded by sin.

For more on *What the Bible Says* turn to page 1456
For more on *Healing* turn to page 1515

What profit *is it* that we have
 kept His ordinance,
And that we have walked as
 mourners
Before the LORD of hosts?

15 So now we call the proud blessed,
 For those who do wickedness are
 raised up;
 They even tempt God and go
 free.' "

A BOOK OF REMEMBRANCE

16 Then those who feared the LORD
 spoke to one another,
 And the LORD listened and heard
 them;
 So a book of remembrance was
 written before Him
 For those who fear the LORD
 And who meditate on His name.

17 "They shall be Mine," says the
 LORD of hosts,
 "On the day that I make them My
 jewels.*a*
 And I will spare them
 As a man spares his own son who
 serves him."
18 Then you shall again discern
 Between the righteous and the
 wicked,
 Between one who serves God
 And one who does not serve Him.

THE GREAT DAY OF GOD

4 "For behold, the day is coming,
 Burning like an oven,

And all the proud, yes, all who do
 wickedly will be stubble.
And the day which is coming
 shall burn them up,"
Says the LORD of hosts,
"That will leave them neither root
 nor branch.
2 But to you who fear My name
 The Sun of Righteousness shall
 arise
 With healing in His wings;
 And you shall go out
 And grow fat like stall-fed
 calves.
3 You shall trample the wicked,
 For they shall be ashes under the
 soles of your feet
 On the day that I do *this,*"
 Says the LORD of hosts.

4 "Remember the Law of Moses, My
 servant,
 Which I commanded him in
 Hō′reb for all Israel,
 With the statutes and
 judgments.
5 Behold, I will send you E·lī′jah
 the prophet
 Before the coming of the great
 and dreadful day of the LORD.
6 And he will turn
 The hearts of the fathers to the
 children,
 And the hearts of the children to
 their fathers,
 Lest I come and strike the earth
 with a curse."

3:17 *a*Literally *special treasure*

The
New Testament

The Gospel According to
MATTHEW

The Genealogy of Jesus Christ

THE book of the genealogy of Jesus Christ, the Son of David, the Son of Abraham:

2 Abraham begot Isaac, Isaac begot Jacob, and Jacob begot Judah and his brothers.

3 Judah begot Per′ez and Zē′rah by Tā′mar, Per′ez begot Hez′ron, and Hez′ron begot Ram.

4 Ram begot Am·min′a·dab, Am·min′a·dab begot Nah′shon, and Nah′shon begot Sal′mon.

5 Sal′mon begot Bō′az by Rā′hab, Bō′az begot Ō′bed by Ruth, Ō′bed begot Jesse,

6 and Jesse begot David the king.

David the king begot Solomon by her *who had been the wife*ᵃ of Ū·rī′ah.

7 Solomon begot Rē·ho·bō′am, Rē·ho·bō′am begot A·bī′jah, and A·bī′jah begot Ā′sa.ᵃ

8 Ā′sa begot Je·hosh′a·phat, Je·hosh′a·phat begot Jō′ram, and Jō′ram begot Uz·zī′ah.

9 Uz·zī′ah begot Jō′tham, Jō′tham begot Ā′haz, and Ā′haz begot Hez·e·kī′ah.

10 Hez·e·kī′ah begot Ma·nas′seh, Ma·nas′seh begot Ā′mon,ᵃ and Ā′mon begot Jō·sī′ah.

11 Jō·sī′ah begot Jec·o·nī′ah and his brothers about the time they were carried away to Babylon.

12 And after they were brought to Babylon, Jec·o·nī′ah begot She·al′ti·el, and She·al′ti·el begot Ze·rub′ba·bel.

13 Ze·rub′ba·bel begot A·bī′ud, A·bī′ud begot E·lī′a·kim, and E·lī′a·kim begot Ā′zor.

14 Ā′zor begot Zā′dok, Zā′dok begot Ā′chim, and Ā′chim begot E·lī′ud.

15 E·lī′ud begot El·e·ā′zar, El·e·ā′zar begot Mat′than, and Mat′than begot Jacob.

16 And Jacob begot Joseph the husband of Mary, of whom was born Jesus who is called Christ.

17 So all the generations from Abraham to David *are* fourteen generations, from David until the captivity in Babylon *are* fourteen generations, and from the captivity in Babylon until the Christ *are* fourteen generations.

Christ Born of Mary

18 Now the birth of Jesus Christ was as follows: After His mother Mary was betrothed to Joseph, before they came together, she was found with child of the Holy Spirit.

19 Then Joseph her husband, being a just *man*, and not wanting to make her a public example, was minded to put her away secretly.

20 But while he thought about these things, behold, an angel of the Lord appeared to him in a dream, saying, "Joseph, son of David, do not be afraid to take to you Mary your wife, for that which is conceived in her is of the Holy Spirit.

21 "And she will bring forth a Son, and you shall call His name JESUS, for He will save His people from their sins."

22 So all this was done that it might be fulfilled which was spoken by the Lord through the prophet, saying:

23 *"Behold, the virgin shall be with child, and bear a Son, and they shall call His name Im·man′ū·el,"*ᵃ which is translated, "God with us."

1:6 ᵃWords in italic type have been added for clarity. They are not found in the original Greek.
1:7 ᵃNU-Text reads *Asaph.* 1:10 ᵃNU-Text reads *Amos.* 1:23 ᵃIsaiah 7:14. Words in oblique type in the New Testament are quoted from the Old Testament.

24 Then Joseph, being aroused from sleep, did as the angel of the Lord commanded him and took to him his wife,

25 and did not know her till she had brought forth her firstborn Son.*a* And he called His name JESUS.

WISE MEN FROM THE EAST

When Jesus was born, a star shone over Bethlehem. Far, far away some important men saw the star and decided to follow it. They were happy they did.

2 Now after Jesus was born in Bethlehem of Judea in the days of Her′od the king, behold, wise men from the East came to Jerusalem,

2 saying, "Where is He who has been born King of the Jews? For we have seen His star in the East and have come to worship Him."

3 When Her′od the king heard *this,* he was troubled, and all Jerusalem with him.

4 And when he had gathered all the chief priests and scribes of the people together, he inquired of them where the Christ was to be born.

5 So they said to him, "In Bethlehem of Judea, for thus it is written by the prophet:

6 'But you, Bethlehem, *in the land of Judah,*
  Are not the least among the rulers of Judah;
  For out of you shall come a Ruler
  Who will shepherd My people Israel.' "*a*

7 Then Her′od, when he had secretly called the wise men, determined from them what time the star appeared.

8 And he sent them to Bethlehem and said, "Go and search carefully for the young Child, and when you have found *Him,* bring back word to me, that I may come and worship Him also."

9 When they heard the king, they departed; and behold, the star which they had seen in the East went before them, till it came and stood over where the young Child was.

10 When they saw the star, they rejoiced with exceedingly great joy.

11 And when they had come into the house, they saw the young Child with Mary His mother, and fell down and worshiped Him. And when they had opened their treasures, they presented gifts to Him: gold, frankincense, and myrrh.

12 Then, being divinely warned in a

1:25 *a*NU-Text reads *a Son.*   2:6 *a*Micah 5:2

☑ Bible Quiz

Matthew 2:1–12 **Wise Men Visit Jesus**

1. How do we know that the wise men believed Jesus was special?

2. Who was troubled when he heard the news of Jesus' birth?

3. What did the wise men give Jesus? Can you name each of the gifts?

4. Do you think King Herod wanted to worship Jesus? How did the wise men know to stay away from him on their way home?

5. What does it mean to give your best to Jesus? Do you think the wise men did this? How can you do this?

SERVING Matthew 2:11

How May I Serve the Newborn King?

Do you ever wish you could have done something special for Baby Jesus, the newborn King? But what? Here is one idea. Can you think of others?

1. What about serving Jesus now? Can you think of several ways you can serve Him?
2. Will you choose one way and do it today?

For more on *Values* turn to page 1453
For more on *Serving* turn to page 1546

dream that they should not return to Her′od, they departed for their own country another way.

THE FLIGHT INTO EGYPT

13 Now when they had departed, behold, an angel of the Lord appeared to Joseph in a dream, saying, "Arise, take the young Child and His mother, flee to Egypt, and stay there until I bring you word; for Her′od will seek the young Child to destroy Him."

14 When he arose, he took the young Child and His mother by night and departed for Egypt,

15 and was there until the death of Her′od, that it might be fulfilled which was spoken by the Lord through the prophet, saying, *"Out of Egypt I called My Son."ª*

MASSACRE OF THE INNOCENTS

16 Then Her′od, when he saw that he was deceived by the wise men, was exceedingly angry; and he sent forth and put to death all the male children who were in Bethlehem and in all its districts, from two years old and under, according to the time which he had determined from the wise men.

17 Then was fulfilled what was spoken by Jer·e·mī′ah the prophet, saying:

18 *"A voice was heard in Rā′mah,*
Lamentation, weeping, and great
    mourning,
Rachel weeping for her children,
Refusing to be comforted,
Because they are no more."ª

THE HOME IN NAZARETH

19 Now when Her′od was dead, behold, an angel of the Lord appeared in a dream to Joseph in Egypt,

20 saying, "Arise, take the young Child and His mother, and go to the land of Israel, for those who sought the young Child's life are dead."

21 Then he arose, took the young Child and His mother, and came into the land of Israel.

22 But when he heard that Ar·che·lā′us was reigning over Judea instead of his father Her′od, he was afraid to go there. And being warned by God in a dream, he turned aside into the region of Galilee.

23 And he came and dwelt in a city called Nazareth, that it might be fulfilled which was spoken by the prophets, "He shall be called a Naz′-a·rēne."

JOHN THE BAPTIST PREPARES THE WAY

Would you listen to a man who wore camel's hair and ate locusts? John may have dressed strangely, but God gave him one of the most special jobs in all the world—to prepare peoples' hearts for Jesus!

3 In those days John the Baptist came preaching in the wilderness of Judea,

2 and saying, "Repent, for the kingdom of heaven is at hand!"

3 For this is he who was spoken of by the prophet Ī·sāi′ah, saying:

"The voice of one crying in the
    wilderness:
'Prepare the way of the LORD;
Make His paths straight.' "ª

4 Now John himself was clothed in camel's hair, with a leather belt

2:15 ªHosea 11:1   2:18 ªJeremiah 31:15
3:3 ªIsaiah 40:3

around his waist; and his food was locusts and wild honey.

5 Then Jerusalem, all Judea, and all the region around the Jordan went out to him

6 and were baptized by him in the Jordan, confessing their sins.

7 But when he saw many of the Phar´i·sees and Sad´du·cees coming to his baptism, he said to them, "Brood of vipers! Who warned you to flee from the wrath to come?

8 "Therefore bear fruits worthy of repentance,

9 "and do not think to say to yourselves, 'We have Abraham as *our* father.' For I say to you that God is able to raise up children to Abraham from these stones.

10 "And even now the ax is laid to the root of the trees. Therefore every tree which does not bear good fruit is cut down and thrown into the fire.

11 "I indeed baptize you with water unto repentance, but He who is coming after me is mightier than I, whose sandals I am not worthy to carry. He will baptize you with the Holy Spirit and fire.*a*

12 "His winnowing fan *is* in His hand, and He will thoroughly clean out His threshing floor, and gather His wheat into the barn; but He will burn up the chaff with unquenchable fire."

JOHN BAPTIZES JESUS

13 Then Jesus came from Galilee to John at the Jordan to be baptized by him.

14 And John *tried to* prevent Him, saying, "I need to be baptized by You, and are You coming to me?"

15 But Jesus answered and said to him, "Permit *it to be so* now, for thus it is fitting for us to fulfill all righteousness." Then he allowed Him.

16 When He had been baptized, Jesus came up immediately from the water; and behold, the heavens were opened to Him, and He*a* saw the Spirit of God descending like a dove and alighting upon Him.

17 And suddenly a voice *came* from heaven, saying, "This is My beloved Son, in whom I am well pleased."

☑ *Bible Quiz*

Matthew 3:1–17 **John the Baptist**

1. Where did John do most of his preaching?
2. What did John tell the people to turn from? Whom did he tell them to turn to?
3. What did John wear? What did he eat?
4. What did Jesus ask John to do? Why didn't John want to do it?
5. What happened to Jesus after He was baptized?

SATAN TEMPTS JESUS

When the devil tempted Adam and Eve, they sinned. Could he get Jesus to sin, too?

4 Then Jesus was led up by the Spirit into the wilderness to be tempted by the devil.

2 And when He had fasted forty days and forty nights, afterward He was hungry.

3 Now when the tempter came to Him, he said, "If You are the Son of God, command that these stones become bread."

4 But He answered and said, "It is

3:11 *a*M-Text omits *and fire.*   3:16 *a*Or *he*

written, *'Man shall not live by bread alone, but by every word that proceeds from the mouth of God.'* "ᵃ

5 Then the devil took Him up into the holy city, set Him on the pinnacle of the temple,

6 and said to Him, "If You are the Son of God, throw Yourself down. For it is written:

'He shall give His angels charge over you,'

and,

'In their hands they shall bear you up,
Lest you dash your foot against a stone.' "ᵃ

7 Jesus said to him, "It is written again, *'You shall not tempt the LORD your God.'* "ᵃ

8 Again, the devil took Him up on an exceedingly high mountain, and showed Him all the kingdoms of the world and their glory.

9 And he said to Him, "All these things I will give You if You will fall down and worship me."

10 Then Jesus said to him, "Away with you,ᵃ Satan! For it is written, *'You shall worship the LORD your God, and Him only you shall serve.'* "ᵇ

11 Then the devil left Him, and behold, angels came and ministered to Him.

JESUS BEGINS HIS GALILEAN MINISTRY

12 Now when Jesus heard that John had been put in prison, He departed to Galilee.

13 And leaving Nazareth, He came and dwelt in Ca·per′na·um, which is by the sea, in the regions of Zeb′ū·lun and Naph′ta·lī,

14 that it might be fulfilled which was spoken by Ī·sāi′ah the prophet, saying:

15 *"The land of Zeb′ū·lun and the land of Naph′ta·lī,*
By the way of the sea, beyond the Jordan,
Galilee of the Gentiles:
16 *The people who sat in darkness have seen a great light,*
And upon those who sat in the region and shadow of death Light has dawned." ᵃ

17 From that time Jesus began to preach and to say, "Repent, for the kingdom of heaven is at hand."

FOUR FISHERMEN CALLED AS DISCIPLES

18 And Jesus, walking by the Sea of Galilee, saw two brothers, Simon

---

☑ *Bible Quiz*

Matthew 4:1–11 **Jesus Is Tempted**

1. How long was Jesus in the wilderness? What did He eat during this time?
2. Who came to tempt Jesus?
3. What three things did the devil try to get Jesus to do?
4. Did Jesus do what the devil wanted? Whenever He answered the devil, Jesus would say a Bible verse. How many Bible verses do you know? How can knowing Bible verses keep you from doing wrong?

4:4 ᵃDeuteronomy 8:3   4:6 ᵃPsalm 91:11, 12
4:7 ᵃDeuteronomy 6:16   4:10 ᵃM-Text reads *Get behind Me.* ᵇDeuteronomy 6:13
4:16 ᵃIsaiah 9:1, 2

called Peter, and Andrew his brother, casting a net into the sea; for they were fishermen.

19 Then He said to them, "Follow Me, and I will make you fishers of men."

20 They immediately left *their* nets and followed Him.

21 Going on from there, He saw two other brothers, James *the son* of Zeb'e·dee, and John his brother, in the boat with Zeb'e·dee their father, mending their nets. He called them,

22 and immediately they left the boat and their father, and followed Him.

■ *see Mark 1:16–20*

JESUS HEALS A GREAT MULTITUDE

23 And Jesus went about all Galilee, teaching in their synagogues, preaching the gospel of the kingdom, and healing all kinds of sickness and all kinds of disease among the people.

24 Then His fame went throughout all Syria; and they brought to Him all sick people who were afflicted with various diseases and torments, and those who were demon-possessed, epileptics, and paralytics; and He healed them.

25 Great multitudes followed Him— from Galilee, and *from* De·cap'o·lis, Jerusalem, Judea, and beyond the Jordan.

THE BEATITUDES

5 And seeing the multitudes, He went up on a mountain, and when He was seated His disciples came to Him.

2 Then He opened His mouth and taught them, saying:

3 "Blessed *are* the poor in spirit,
For theirs is the kingdom of
heaven.

4 Blessed *are* those who mourn,
For they shall be comforted.

5 Blessed *are* the meek,
For they shall inherit the
earth.

6 Blessed *are* those who hunger and
thirst for righteousness,
For they shall be filled.

7 Blessed *are* the merciful,
For they shall obtain mercy.

8 Blessed *are* the pure in heart,
For they shall see God.

9 Blessed *are* the peacemakers,
For they shall be called sons of
God.

10 Blessed are those who are
persecuted for righteousness'
sake,
For theirs is the kingdom of
heaven.

11 "Blessed are you when they revile and persecute you, and say all kinds of evil against you falsely for My sake.

12 "Rejoice and be exceedingly glad, for great *is* your reward in heaven, for so they persecuted the prophets who were before you.

BELIEVERS ARE SALT AND LIGHT

13 "You are the salt of the earth; but if the salt loses its flavor, how shall it be seasoned? It is then good for nothing but to be thrown out and trampled underfoot by men.

14 "You are the light of the world. A city that is set on a hill cannot be hidden.

15 "Nor do they light a lamp and put it under a basket, but on a lampstand, and it gives light to all *who are* in the house.

16 "Let your light so shine before men, that they may see your good works and glorify your Father in heaven.

PEACEMAKERS Matthew 5:9

Who Are the Peacemakers?

It isn't much fun to fight, is it? Someone always loses. Someone often gets hurt. You don't like to lose or get hurt, do you? Jesus said that people who stop fights are peacemakers. People who keep others from starting fights are peacemakers, too. They are blessed, or happy. Jesus said so.

1. Is it better to fight or to stop a fight? Why?
2. Is it better not to start a fight? Why?
3. What is a peacemaker?
4. Why is a peacemaker happy or blessed?
5. How can you be a peacemaker?

For more on *Favorite Bible Words* turn to page 1474
For more on *Peacemaking* turn to page 1830

Values

GIVING Matthew 5:23, 24

When Does God *Not* Want Our Gifts?

Did you know that God sometimes does *not* want our gifts? Does that seem possible? Would you ever not want gifts from someone you love? When could that be? When could God not want our gifts?

1. Read Matthew 5:23, 24. When does God not want our gift?
2. What must we do first before we give our gift to God?
3. Are you angry at someone? Do you hate someone? Is there something bad between you and someone? God wants you to make up with that person before you give to Him. Then He will want your gift.

For more on *Values* turn to page 1454
For more on *Forgiveness* turn to page 1459

CHRIST FULFILLS THE LAW

17 "Do not think that I came to destroy the Law or the Prophets. I did not come to destroy but to fulfill.

18 "For assuredly, I say to you, till heaven and earth pass away, one jot or one tittle will by no means pass from the law till all is fulfilled.

19 "Whoever therefore breaks one of the least of these commandments, and teaches men so, shall be called least in the kingdom of heaven; but whoever does and teaches *them,* he shall be called great in the kingdom of heaven.

20 "For I say to you, that unless your righteousness exceeds *the righteousness* of the scribes and Phar′i·sees, you will by no means enter the kingdom of heaven.

MURDER BEGINS IN THE HEART

21 "You have heard that it was said to those of old, '*You shall not murder,a* and whoever murders will be in danger of the judgment.'

22 "But I say to you that whoever is angry with his brother without a cause*a* shall be in danger of the judgment. And whoever says to his brother, 'Ra′ca!' shall be in danger of the council. But whoever says, 'You fool!' shall be in danger of hell fire.

23 "Therefore if you bring your gift to the altar, and there remember that your brother has something against you,

24 "leave your gift there before the altar, and go your way. First be reconciled to your brother, and then come and offer your gift.

25 "Agree with your adversary quickly, while you are on the way with him, lest your adversary deliver you to the judge, the judge hand you over to the officer, and you be thrown into prison.

26 "Assuredly, I say to you, you will by no means get out of there till you have paid the last penny.

5:21 *a*Exodus 20:13; Deuteronomy 5:17
5:22 *a*NU-Text omits *without a cause.*

Values

LOVING ENEMIES   Matthew 5:44

Can a Cat and a Mouse Be Friends?

Cats like to catch mice. Sometimes cats eat the mice they catch. You wouldn't think that a cat and a mouse could become friends, would you? But stranger things than that happen. When people love Jesus, enemies become friends. People who hated each other learn to love each other and work together for Jesus.

1. Read Matthew 5:44. What is Jesus asking us to do? Can you?
2. How could you ever love someone who hates you? What would happen to cause you to do that?
3. Would you do this for Jesus? Why?

For more on *Values* turn to page 1464
For more on *Love* turn to page 1486

ADULTERY IN THE HEART

27 "You have heard that it was said to those of old,*a* *'You shall not commit adultery.'b*

28 "But I say to you that whoever looks at a woman to lust for her has already committed adultery with her in his heart.

29 "If your right eye causes you to sin, pluck it out and cast *it* from you; for it is more profitable for you that one of your members perish, than for your whole body to be cast into hell.

30 "And if your right hand causes you to sin, cut it off and cast *it* from you; for it is more profitable for you that one of your members perish, than for your whole body to be cast into hell.

MARRIAGE IS SACRED AND BINDING

31 "Furthermore it has been said, 'Whoever divorces his wife, let him give her a certificate of divorce.'

32 "But I say to you that whoever divorces his wife for any reason except sexual immorality*a* causes her to commit adultery; and whoever marries a woman who is divorced commits adultery.

JESUS FORBIDS OATHS

33 "Again you have heard that it was said to those of old, 'You shall not swear falsely, but shall perform your oaths to the Lord.'

34 "But I say to you, do not swear at all: neither by heaven, for it is God's throne;

35 "nor by the earth, for it is His footstool; nor by Jerusalem, for it is the city of the great King.

36 "Nor shall you swear by your head, because you cannot make one hair white or black.

37 "But let your 'Yes' be 'Yes,' and your 'No,' 'No.' For whatever is more than these is from the evil one.

GO THE SECOND MILE

38 "You have heard that it was said, *'An eye for an eye and a tooth for a tooth.'a*

39 "But I tell you not to resist an evil person. But whoever slaps you on your right cheek, turn the other to him also.

40 "If anyone wants to sue you and take away your tunic, let him have *your* cloak also.

41 "And whoever compels you to go one mile, go with him two.

42 "Give to him who asks you, and from him who wants to borrow from you do not turn away.

LOVE YOUR ENEMIES

43 "You have heard that it was said, *'You shall love your neighbora* and hate your enemy.'

44 "But I say to you, love your enemies, bless those who curse you, do good to those who hate you, and pray for those who spitefully use you and persecute you,*a*

45 "that you may be sons of your Father in heaven; for He makes His sun rise on the evil and on the good, and sends rain on the just and on the unjust.

46 "For if you love those who love you, what reward have you? Do not even the tax collectors do the same?

47 "And if you greet your brethren*a* only, what do you do more *than others?* Do not even the tax collectors*b* do so?

5:27 *a*NU-Text and M-Text omit *to those of old.* *b*Exodus 20:14; Deuteronomy 5:18   5:32 *a*Or *fornication*   5:38 *a*Exodus 21:24; Leviticus 24:20; Deuteronomy 19:21   5:43 *a*Compare Leviticus 19:18   5:44 *a*NU-Text omits three clauses from this verse, leaving, *"But I say to you, love your enemies and pray for those who persecute you."* 5:47 *a*M-Text reads *friends.* *b*NU-Text reads *Gentiles.*

ABOUT GOD'S GIFTS Matthew 5:45

Does It Rain on Good People Only?

It's raining! The rain helps crops grow and gives us food. It helps flowers grow so we can enjoy them. But look! Is God sending rain only to people who are good? Will He keep it from raining for people who are bad?

1. Look up Matthew 5:45. Does God give rain to everyone or just to a few?
2. What if God gave rain only to rich people? What if He gave rain only to tall people or short people? What if He gave rain only to white people or black people or people in Asia? What if He gave rain only to good people? God sends His rain to everyone. Every person can have His gift of rain.
3. God also offers the gift of everlasting life to everyone. A person may be black or white, tall or short, fat or thin, old or young. God still offers His wonderful gift of everlasting life. *Anyone* may receive it. Thank You, God!

For more on *What the Bible Says* turn to page 1480
For more on *God's Care* turn to page 1466

48 "Therefore you shall be perfect, just as your Father in heaven is perfect.

DO GOOD TO PLEASE GOD

6 "Take heed that you do not do your charitable deeds before men, to be seen by them. Otherwise you have no reward from your Father in heaven.
2 "Therefore, when you do a charitable deed, do not sound a trumpet before you as the hypocrites do in the synagogues and in the streets, that they may have glory from men. Assuredly, I say to you, they have their reward.
3 "But when you do a charitable deed, do not let your left hand know what your right hand is doing,
4 "that your charitable deed may be in secret; and your Father who sees in secret will Himself reward you openly.*a*

THE MODEL PRAYER

5 "And when you pray, you shall not be like the hypocrites. For they love to pray standing in the synagogues and on the corners of the streets, that they may be seen by men. Assuredly, I say to you, they have their reward.
6 "But you, when you pray, go into your room, and when you have shut your door, pray to your Father who *is* in the secret *place;* and your Father who sees in secret will reward you openly.*a*
7 "And when you pray, do not use vain repetitions as the heathen *do.* For they think that they will be heard for their many words.

6:4 *a*NU-Text omits *openly.*   6:6 *a*NU-Text omits *openly.*

Prayers

Matthew 6:9–13

This is often called The Lord's Prayer. Jesus said this prayer should be our model. "In this manner, therefore, pray." Read the prayer several times. What do you see in it? Why do you think Jesus used this as our model prayer?

---

8 "Therefore do not be like them. For your Father knows the things you have need of before you ask Him.
9 "In this manner, therefore, pray:

Our Father in heaven,
Hallowed be Your name.
10 Your kingdom come.
Your will be done
On earth as *it is* in heaven.
11 Give us this day our daily bread.
12 And forgive us our debts,
As we forgive our debtors.
13 And do not lead us into temptation,
But deliver us from the evil one.
For Yours is the kingdom and the power and the glory forever.
Amen.*a*

14 "For if you forgive men their trespasses, your heavenly Father will also forgive you.
15 "But if you do not forgive men their trespasses, neither will your Father forgive your trespasses.

FASTING TO BE SEEN ONLY BY GOD

16 "Moreover, when you fast, do not be like the hypocrites, with a sad countenance. For they disfigure their faces that they may appear to men to be fasting. Assuredly, I say to you, they have their reward.
17 "But you, when you fast, anoint your head and wash your face,
18 "so that you do not appear to men to be fasting, but to your Father who *is* in the secret *place;* and your Father who sees in secret will reward you openly.*a*

LAY UP TREASURES IN HEAVEN

19 "Do not lay up for yourselves treasures on earth, where moth and rust destroy and where thieves break in and steal;
20 "but lay up for yourselves treasures in heaven, where neither moth nor rust destroys and where thieves do not break in and steal.
21 "For where your treasure is, there your heart will be also.

THE LAMP OF THE BODY

22 "The lamp of the body is the eye. If therefore your eye is good, your whole body will be full of light.
23 "But if your eye is bad, your whole body will be full of darkness. If therefore the light that is in you is darkness, how great *is* that darkness!

YOU CANNOT SERVE GOD AND RICHES

24 "No one can serve two masters; for either he will hate the one and love the other, or else he will be loyal to the one and despise the other. You cannot serve God and mammon.

DO NOT WORRY

25 "Therefore I say to you, do not worry about your life, what you will

---

6:13 *a*NU-Text omits *For Yours* through *Amen.*
6:18 *a*NU-Text and M-Text omit *openly.*

eat or what you will drink; nor about your body, what you will put on. Is not life more than food and the body more than clothing?

26 "Look at the birds of the air, for they neither sow nor reap nor gather into barns; yet your heavenly Father feeds them. Are you not of more value than they?

27 "Which of you by worrying can add one cubit to his stature?

28 "So why do you worry about clothing? Consider the lilies of the field, how they grow: they neither toil nor spin;

29 "and yet I say to you that even Solomon in all his glory was not arrayed like one of these.

30 "Now if God so clothes the grass of the field, which today is, and tomorrow is thrown into the oven, *will He* not much more *clothe* you, O you of little faith?

31 "Therefore do not worry, saying, 'What shall we eat?' or 'What shall we drink?' or 'What shall we wear?'

32 "For after all these things the Gentiles seek. For your heavenly Father knows that you need all these things.

33 "But seek first the kingdom of God and His righteousness, and all these things shall be added to you.

34 "Therefore do not worry about tomorrow, for tomorrow will worry about its own things. Sufficient for the day *is* its own trouble.

DO NOT JUDGE

7 "Judge not, that you be not judged.

2 "For with what judgment you judge, you will be judged; and with the measure you use, it will be measured back to you.

3 "And why do you look at the speck in your brother's eye, but do not consider the plank in your own eye?

4 "Or how can you say to your brother, 'Let me remove the speck from your eye'; and look, a plank *is* in your own eye?

5 "Hypocrite! First remove the plank from your own eye, and then you will see clearly to remove the speck from your brother's eye.

6 "Do not give what is holy to the dogs; nor cast your pearls before swine, lest they trample them under their feet, and turn and tear you in pieces.

KEEP ASKING, SEEKING, KNOCKING

7 "Ask, and it will be given to you; seek, and you will find; knock, and it will be opened to you.

8 "For everyone who asks receives, and he who seeks finds, and to him who knocks it will be opened.

9 "Or what man is there among you who, if his son asks for bread, will give him a stone?

10 "Or if he asks for a fish, will he give him a serpent?

11 "If you then, being evil, know how to give good gifts to your children, how much more will your Father who is in heaven give good things to those who ask Him!

12 "Therefore, whatever you want men to do to you, do also to them, for this is the Law and the Prophets.

THE NARROW WAY

13 "Enter by the narrow gate; for wide *is* the gate and broad *is* the way that leads to destruction, and there are many who go in by it.

14 "Because[a] narrow *is* the gate and difficult *is* the way which leads to life, and there are few who find it.

7:14 [a]NU-Text and M-Text read *How . . . !*

WHEN SOMEONE LAUGHS AT ME Matthew 7:12

You stumble and fall. Your friends laugh. Do you get angry? Something goes plop on your head. Your friends laugh. Do you get angry? You make a mistake. Your friends laugh. What do you do? What should you do?

1. What do you do when your friends laugh at you? What should you do?
2. Should you get angry or laugh with your friends? What do you want your friends to do when you laugh at their mistakes?
3. Read Matthew 7:12. This is the "Golden Rule." How do you think the Golden Rule applies here?

For more on *What Should I Do?* turn to page 1546
For more on *Forgiveness* turn to page 1563

You Will Know Them by Their Fruits

15 "Beware of false prophets, who come to you in sheep's clothing, but inwardly they are ravenous wolves.

16 "You will know them by their fruits. Do men gather grapes from thornbushes or figs from thistles?

17 "Even so, every good tree bears good fruit, but a bad tree bears bad fruit.

18 "A good tree cannot bear bad fruit, nor *can* a bad tree bear good fruit.

19 "Every tree that does not bear good fruit is cut down and thrown into the fire.

20 "Therefore by their fruits you will know them.

I Never Knew You

21 "Not everyone who says to Me, 'Lord, Lord,' shall enter the kingdom of heaven, but he who does the will of My Father in heaven.

22 "Many will say to Me in that day, 'Lord, Lord, have we not prophesied in Your name, cast out demons in Your name, and done many wonders in Your name?'

23 "And then I will declare to them, 'I never knew you; depart from Me, you who practice lawlessness!'

Build on the Rock

24 "Therefore whoever hears these sayings of Mine, and does them, I will liken him to a wise man who built his house on the rock:

25 "and the rain descended, the floods came, and the winds blew and beat on that house; and it did not fall, for it was founded on the rock.

26 "But everyone who hears these sayings of Mine, and does not do them, will be like a foolish man who built his house on the sand:

27 "and the rain descended, the floods came, and the winds blew and beat on that house; and it fell. And great was its fall."

28 And so it was, when Jesus had ended these sayings, that the people were astonished at His teaching,

29 for He taught them as one having authority, and not as the scribes.

Jesus Cleanses a Leper

8 When He had come down from the mountain, great multitudes followed Him.

2 And behold, a leper came and worshiped Him, saying, "Lord, if You are willing, You can make me clean."

3 Then Jesus put out *His* hand and touched him, saying, "I am willing; be cleansed." Immediately his leprosy was cleansed.

4 And Jesus said to him, "See that you tell no one; but go your way, show yourself to the priest, and offer the gift that Moses commanded, as a testimony to them."

Jesus Heals a Centurion's Servant

5 Now when Jesus had entered Ca·per'na·um, a centurion came to Him, pleading with Him,

6 saying, "Lord, my servant is lying at home paralyzed, dreadfully tormented."

7 And Jesus said to him, "I will come and heal him."

8 The centurion answered and said, "Lord, I am not worthy that You should come under my roof. But only speak a word, and my servant will be healed.

9 "For I also am a man under authority, having soldiers under me. And I say to this *one,* 'Go,' and he goes; and to another, 'Come,' and he

comes; and to my servant, 'Do this,' and he does *it*."

10 When Jesus heard *it*, He marveled, and said to those who followed, "Assuredly, I say to you, I have not found such great faith, not even in Israel!

11 "And I say to you that many will come from east and west, and sit down with Abraham, Isaac, and Jacob in the kingdom of heaven.

12 "But the sons of the kingdom will be cast out into outer darkness. There will be weeping and gnashing of teeth."

13 Then Jesus said to the centurion, "Go your way; and as you have believed, *so* let it be done for you." And his servant was healed that same hour.

PETER'S MOTHER-IN-LAW HEALED

14 Now when Jesus had come into Peter's house, He saw his wife's mother lying sick with a fever.

15 So He touched her hand, and the fever left her. And she arose and served them.*a*

MANY HEALED AFTER SABBATH SUNSET

16 When evening had come, they brought to Him many who were demon-possessed. And He cast out the spirits with a word, and healed all who were sick,

17 that it might be fulfilled which was spoken by Ī·sāi'ah the prophet, saying:

*"He Himself took our infirmities
And bore our sicknesses."a*

THE COST OF DISCIPLESHIP

18 And when Jesus saw great multitudes about Him, He gave a command to depart to the other side.

19 Then a certain scribe came and said to Him, "Teacher, I will follow You wherever You go."

20 And Jesus said to him, "Foxes have holes and birds of the air *have* nests, but the Son of Man has nowhere to lay *His* head."

21 Then another of His disciples said to Him, "Lord, let me first go and bury my father."

22 But Jesus said to him, "Follow Me, and let the dead bury their own dead."

WIND AND WAVE OBEY JESUS

23 Now when He got into a boat, His disciples followed Him.

24 And suddenly a great tempest arose on the sea, so that the boat was covered with the waves. But He was asleep.

25 Then His disciples came to *Him* and awoke Him, saying, "Lord, save us! We are perishing!"

26 But He said to them, "Why are you fearful, O you of little faith?" Then He arose and rebuked the winds and the sea, and there was a great calm.

27 So the men marveled, saying, "Who can this be, that even the winds and the sea obey Him?"

■ *see Mark 4:35–41*

TWO DEMON-POSSESSED MEN HEALED

28 When He had come to the other side, to the country of the Ger'ge-sēnes,*a* there met Him two demon-possessed *men*, coming out of the tombs, exceedingly fierce, so that no one could pass that way.

29 And suddenly they cried out, saying, "What have we to do with You,

8:15 *a*NU-Text and M-Text read *Him*.
8:17 *a*Isaiah 53:4   8:28 *a*NU-Text reads *Gadarenes*.

Jesus, You Son of God? Have You come here to torment us before the time?"

30 Now a good way off from them there was a herd of many swine feeding.

31 So the demons begged Him, saying, "If You cast us out, permit us to go away*a* into the herd of swine."

32 And He said to them, "Go." So when they had come out, they went into the herd of swine. And suddenly the whole herd of swine ran violently down the steep place into the sea, and perished in the water.

33 Then those who kept *them* fled; and they went away into the city and told everything, including what *had happened* to the demon-possessed *men.*

34 And behold, the whole city came out to meet Jesus. And when they saw Him, they begged *Him* to depart from their region.

JESUS FORGIVES AND HEALS A PARALYTIC

9 So He got into a boat, crossed over, and came to His own city.

2 Then behold, they brought to Him a paralytic lying on a bed. When Jesus saw their faith, He said to the paralytic, "Son, be of good cheer; your sins are forgiven you."

3 And at once some of the scribes said within themselves, "This Man blasphemes!"

4 But Jesus, knowing their thoughts, said, "Why do you think evil in your hearts?

5 "For which is easier, to say, 'Your sins are forgiven you,' or to say, 'Arise and walk'?

6 "But that you may know that the Son of Man has power on earth to forgive sins"—then He said to the paralytic, "Arise, take up your bed, and go to your house."

7 And he arose and departed to his house.

8 Now when the multitudes saw *it,* they marveled*a* and glorified God, who had given such power to men.

■ *see Mark 2:1–12*

MATTHEW THE TAX COLLECTOR

9 As Jesus passed on from there, He saw a man named Matthew sitting at the tax office. And He said to him, "Follow Me." So he arose and followed Him.

10 Now it happened, as Jesus sat at the table in the house, *that* behold, many tax collectors and sinners came and sat down with Him and His disciples.

11 And when the Phar'i·sees saw *it,* they said to His disciples, "Why does your Teacher eat with tax collectors and sinners?"

12 When Jesus heard *that,* He said to them, "Those who are well have no need of a physician, but those who are sick.

13 "But go and learn what *this* means: *'I desire mercy and not sacrifice.'a* For I did not come to call the righteous, but sinners, to repentance."*b*

JESUS IS QUESTIONED ABOUT FASTING

14 Then the disciples of John came to Him, saying, "Why do we and the Phar'i·sees fast often,*a* but Your disciples do not fast?"

15 And Jesus said to them, "Can the friends of the bridegroom mourn as long as the bridegroom is with them?

8:31 *a*NU-Text reads *send us.*   9:8 *a*NU-Text reads *were afraid.*   9:13 *a*Hosea 6:6   *b*NU-Text omits *to repentance.*   9:14 *a*NU-Text brackets *often* as disputed.

But the days will come when the bridegroom will be taken away from them, and then they will fast.

16 "No one puts a piece of unshrunk cloth on an old garment; for the patch pulls away from the garment, and the tear is made worse.

17 "Nor do they put new wine into old wineskins, or else the wineskins break, the wine is spilled, and the wineskins are ruined. But they put new wine into new wineskins, and both are preserved."

A GIRL RESTORED TO LIFE AND A WOMAN HEALED

18 While He spoke these things to them, behold, a ruler came and worshiped Him, saying, "My daughter has just died, but come and lay Your hand on her and she will live."

19 So Jesus arose and followed him, and so *did* His disciples.

20 And suddenly, a woman who had a flow of blood for twelve years came from behind and touched the hem of His garment.

21 For she said to herself, "If only I may touch His garment, I shall be made well."

22 But Jesus turned around, and when He saw her He said, "Be of good cheer, daughter; your faith has made you well." And the woman was made well from that hour.

23 When Jesus came into the ruler's house, and saw the flute players and the noisy crowd wailing,

24 He said to them, "Make room, for the girl is not dead, but sleeping." And they ridiculed Him.

25 But when the crowd was put outside, He went in and took her by the hand, and the girl arose.

26 And the report of this went out into all that land.

■ *see Luke 8:40–56*

TWO BLIND MEN HEALED

27 When Jesus departed from there, two blind men followed Him, crying out and saying, "Son of David, have mercy on us!"

28 And when He had come into the house, the blind men came to Him. And Jesus said to them, "Do you believe that I am able to do this?" They said to Him, "Yes, Lord."

29 Then He touched their eyes, saying, "According to your faith let it be to you."

30 And their eyes were opened. And Jesus sternly warned them, saying, "See *that* no one knows *it.*"

31 But when they had departed, they spread the news about Him in all that country.

A MUTE MAN SPEAKS

32 As they went out, behold, they brought to Him a man, mute and demon-possessed.

33 And when the demon was cast out, the mute spoke. And the multitudes marveled, saying, "It was never seen like this in Israel!"

34 But the Phar'i·sees said, "He casts out demons by the ruler of the demons."

THE COMPASSION OF JESUS

35 Then Jesus went about all the cities and villages, teaching in their synagogues, preaching the gospel of the kingdom, and healing every sickness and every disease among the people.a

36 But when He saw the multitudes, He was moved with compassion for them, because they were wearya and scattered, like sheep having no shepherd.

9:35 aNU-Text omits *among the people.*
9:36 aNU-Text and M-Text read *harassed.*

SHARING Matthew 10:8

Sharing What I Have

One little girl has a bowl of milk. But she has no kitty. Another little girl has a kitty. But she has no bowl of milk. "May I share my milk with your kitty?" one girl asks. "Would you like to play with my kitty and me?" the other girl asks. Do you think these two girls had fun together that day?

1. Which girl has something to share? How did each girl share with the other?
2. Why do you think these two girls had fun that day? Would they have had as much fun if they had not shared? Why not?
3. Look up Matthew 10:8. Read the second part of the verse. What does it say about sharing? What would you like to share today?

For more on *Values* turn to page 1524
For more on *Sharing* turn to page 1660

37 Then He said to His disciples, "The harvest truly *is* plentiful, but the laborers *are* few.
38 "Therefore pray the Lord of the harvest to send out laborers into His harvest."

THE TWELVE APOSTLES

10 And when He had called His twelve disciples to *Him,* He gave them power *over* unclean spirits, to cast them out, and to heal all kinds of sickness and all kinds of disease.
2 Now the names of the twelve apostles are these: first, Simon, who is called Peter, and Andrew his brother; James the *son* of Zeb′e·dee, and John his brother;
3 Philip and Bartholomew; Thomas and Matthew the tax collector; James the *son* of Al·phaē′us, and Leb·baē′us, whose surname was*a* Thad·daē′us;
4 Simon the Can′a·nīte,*a* and Judas Is·car′i·ot, who also betrayed Him.

SENDING OUT THE TWELVE

5 These twelve Jesus sent out and commanded them, saying: "Do not go into the way of the Gentiles, and do not enter a city of the Samaritans.
6 "But go rather to the lost sheep of the house of Israel.
7 "And as you go, preach, saying, 'The kingdom of heaven is at hand.'
8 "Heal the sick, cleanse the lepers, raise the dead,*a* cast out demons. Freely you have received, freely give.
9 "Provide neither gold nor silver nor copper in your money belts,
10 "nor bag for *your* journey, nor two tunics, nor sandals, nor staffs; for a worker is worthy of his food.
11 "Now whatever city or town you enter, inquire who in it is worthy, and stay there till you go out.
12 "And when you go into a household, greet it.

10:3 *a*NU-Text omits *Lebbaeus, whose surname was.*   10:4 *a*NU-Text reads *Cananaean.*
10:8 *a*NU-Text reads *raise the dead, cleanse the lepers;* M-Text omits *raise the dead.*

13 "If the household is worthy, let your peace come upon it. But if it is not worthy, let your peace return to you.

14 "And whoever will not receive you nor hear your words, when you depart from that house or city, shake off the dust from your feet.

15 "Assuredly, I say to you, it will be more tolerable for the land of Sod'om and Go·mor'rah in the day of judgment than for that city!

PERSECUTIONS ARE COMING

16 "Behold, I send you out as sheep in the midst of wolves. Therefore be wise as serpents and harmless as doves.

17 "But beware of men, for they will deliver you up to councils and scourge you in their synagogues.

18 "You will be brought before governors and kings for My sake, as a testimony to them and to the Gentiles.

19 "But when they deliver you up, do not worry about how or what you should speak. For it will be given to you in that hour what you should speak;

20 "for it is not you who speak, but the Spirit of your Father who speaks in you.

21 "Now brother will deliver up brother to death, and a father *his* child; and children will rise up against parents and cause them to be put to death.

22 "And you will be hated by all for My name's sake. But he who endures to the end will be saved.

23 "When they persecute you in this city, flee to another. For assuredly, I say to you, you will not have gone through the cities of Israel before the Son of Man comes.

24 "A disciple is not above *his* teacher, nor a servant above his master.

25 "It is enough for a disciple that he be like his teacher, and a servant like his master. If they have called the master of the house Bē·el'ze·bub,*a* how much more *will they call* those of his household!

26 "Therefore do not fear them. For there is nothing covered that will not be revealed, and hidden that will not be known.

JESUS TEACHES THE FEAR OF GOD

27 "Whatever I tell you in the dark, speak in the light; and what you hear in the ear, preach on the housetops.

28 "And do not fear those who kill the body but cannot kill the soul. But rather fear Him who is able to destroy both soul and body in hell.

29 "Are not two sparrows sold for a copper coin? And not one of them falls to the ground apart from your Father's will.

30 "But the very hairs of your head are all numbered.

31 "Do not fear therefore; you are of more value than many sparrows.

CONFESS CHRIST BEFORE MEN

32 "Therefore whoever confesses Me before men, him I will also confess before My Father who is in heaven.

33 "But whoever denies Me before men, him I will also deny before My Father who is in heaven.

CHRIST BRINGS DIVISION

34 "Do not think that I came to bring peace on earth. I did not come to bring peace but a sword.

35 "For I have come to *'set a man against his father, a daughter against her mother, and a daughter-in-law against her mother-in-law';*

10:25 *a*NU-Text and M-Text read *Beelzebul.*

ARE NOT TWO SPARROWS SOLD FOR A COPPER COIN? AND NOT ONE OF THEM FALLS TO THE GROUND APART FROM YOUR FATHER'S WILL.
Matthew 10:29

How Much Is a Bird Worth?

God knows every little bird in the world. Do you suppose He has given each one a name? He knows this little bird, too. He takes care of this little bird, and every other little bird in the world. So are you surprised that He takes care of you?

1. Who made each bird in the world? Who takes care of each one?
2. Who made you? Who takes care of you each day? How can you help Him?
3. What should you say to God for doing this?

For more on *Favorite Family Verses* turn to page 1470
For more on *God's Care* turn to page 1548

36 "and 'a man's enemies will be those of his own household.'ᵃ

37 "He who loves father or mother more than Me is not worthy of Me. And he who loves son or daughter more than Me is not worthy of Me.

38 "And he who does not take his cross and follow after Me is not worthy of Me.

39 "He who finds his life will lose it, and he who loses his life for My sake will find it.

A Cup of Cold Water

40 "He who receives you receives Me, and he who receives Me receives Him who sent Me.

41 "He who receives a prophet in the name of a prophet shall receive a prophet's reward. And he who receives a righteous man in the name of a righteous man shall receive a righteous man's reward.

42 "And whoever gives one of these little ones only a cup of cold water in the name of a disciple, assuredly, I say to you, he shall by no means lose his reward."

John the Baptist Sends Messengers to Jesus

11 Now it came to pass, when Jesus finished commanding His twelve disciples, that He departed from there to teach and to preach in their cities.

2 And when John had heard in prison about the works of Christ, he sent two ofᵃ his disciples

3 and said to Him, "Are You the Coming One, or do we look for another?"

4 Jesus answered and said to them, "Go and tell John the things which you hear and see:

5 "The blind see and the lame walk; the lepers are cleansed and the deaf hear; the dead are raised up and the poor have the gospel preached to them.

6 "And blessed is he who is not offended because of Me."

7 As they departed, Jesus began to say to the multitudes concerning John: "What did you go out into the wilderness to see? A reed shaken by the wind?

8 "But what did you go out to see? A man clothed in soft garments? Indeed, those who wear soft clothing are in kings' houses.

9 "But what did you go out to see? A prophet? Yes, I say to you, and more than a prophet.

10 "For this is he of whom it is written:

'Behold, I send My messenger
　　before Your face,
　Who will prepare Your way before
　　You.'ᵃ

11 "Assuredly, I say to you, among those born of women there has not risen one greater than John the Baptist; but he who is least in the kingdom of heaven is greater than he.

12 "And from the days of John the Baptist until now the kingdom of heaven suffers violence, and the violent take it by force.

13 "For all the prophets and the law prophesied until John.

14 "And if you are willing to receive it, he is E·li′jah who is to come.

15 "He who has ears to hear, let him hear!

16 "But to what shall I liken this generation? It is like children sitting in the marketplaces and calling to their companions,

17 "and saying:

10:36 ᵃMicah 7:6   11:2 ᵃNU-Text reads by for two of.   11:10 ᵃMalachi 3:1

'We played the flute for you,
　And you did not dance;
We mourned to you,
　And you did not lament.'

18 "For John came neither eating nor drinking, and they say, 'He has a demon.'

19 "The Son of Man came eating and drinking, and they say, 'Look, a glutton and a winebibber, a friend of tax collectors and sinners!' But wisdom is justified by her children."ᵃ

WOE TO THE IMPENITENT CITIES

20 Then He began to rebuke the cities in which most of His mighty works had been done, because they did not repent:

21 "Woe to you, Chō·rā′zin! Woe to you, Beth·sā′i·da! For if the mighty works which were done in you had been done in Tȳre and Sī′don, they would have repented long ago in sackcloth and ashes.

22 "But I say to you, it will be more tolerable for Tȳre and Sī′don in the day of judgment than for you.

23 "And you, Ca·per′na·um, who are exalted to heaven, will beᵃ brought down to Hā′dēs; for if the mighty works which were done in you had been done in Sod′om, it would have remained until this day.

24 "But I say to you that it shall be more tolerable for the land of Sod′om in the day of judgment than for you."

JESUS GIVES TRUE REST

25 At that time Jesus answered and said, "I thank You, Father, Lord of heaven and earth, that You have hidden these things from the wise and prudent and have revealed them to babes.

26 "Even so, Father, for so it seemed good in Your sight.

27 "All things have been delivered to Me by My Father, and no one knows the Son except the Father. Nor does anyone know the Father except the Son, and the one to whom the Son wills to reveal Him.

28 "Come to Me, all you who labor and are heavy laden, and I will give you rest.

29 "Take My yoke upon you and learn from Me, for I am gentle and lowly in heart, and you will find rest for your souls.

30 "For My yoke is easy and My burden is light."

JESUS IS LORD OF THE SABBATH

12 At that time Jesus went through the grainfields on the Sabbath. And His disciples were hungry, and began to pluck heads of grain and to eat.

2 And when the Phar′i·sees saw it, they said to Him, "Look, Your disciples are doing what is not lawful to do on the Sabbath!"

3 But He said to them, "Have you not read what David did when he was hungry, he and those who were with him:

4 "how he entered the house of God and ate the showbread which was not lawful for him to eat, nor for those who were with him, but only for the priests?

5 "Or have you not read in the law that on the Sabbath the priests in the temple profane the Sabbath, and are blameless?

6 "Yet I say to you that in this place there is One greater than the temple.

7 "But if you had known what this

11:19 ᵃNU-Text reads works.　11:23 ᵃNU-Text reads will you be exalted to heaven? No, you will be.

means, '*I desire mercy and not sacrifice,*'[a] you would not have condemned the guiltless.

8　"For the Son of Man is Lord even[a] of the Sabbath."

HEALING ON THE SABBATH

9　Now when He had departed from there, He went into their synagogue.

10　And behold, there was a man who had a withered hand. And they asked Him, saying, "Is it lawful to heal on the Sabbath?"—that they might accuse Him.

11　Then He said to them, "What man is there among you who has one sheep, and if it falls into a pit on the Sabbath, will not lay hold of it and lift *it* out?

12　"Of how much more value then is a man than a sheep? Therefore it is lawful to do good on the Sabbath."

13　Then He said to the man, "Stretch out your hand." And he stretched *it* out, and it was restored as whole as the other.

14　Then the Phar′i·sees went out and plotted against Him, how they might destroy Him.

BEHOLD, MY SERVANT

15　But when Jesus knew *it*, He withdrew from there. And great multitudes[a] followed Him, and He healed them all.

16　Yet He warned them not to make Him known,

17　that it might be fulfilled which was spoken by I·sai′ah the prophet, saying:

18　"*Behold! My Servant whom I have chosen,*
　　My Beloved in whom My soul is well pleased!
　　I will put My Spirit upon Him,

And He will declare justice to the Gentiles.

19　*He will not quarrel nor cry out,*
　　Nor will anyone hear His voice in the streets.

20　*A bruised reed He will not break,*
　　And smoking flax He will not quench,
　　Till He sends forth justice to victory;

21　*And in His name Gentiles will trust.*"[a]

A HOUSE DIVIDED CANNOT STAND

22　Then one was brought to Him who was demon-possessed, blind and mute; and He healed him, so that the blind and[a] mute man both spoke and saw.

23　And all the multitudes were amazed and said, "Could this be the Son of David?"

24　Now when the Phar′i·sees heard *it* they said, "This *fellow* does not cast out demons except by Be·el′ze·bub,[a] the ruler of the demons."

25　But Jesus knew their thoughts, and said to them: "Every kingdom divided against itself is brought to desolation, and every city or house divided against itself will not stand.

26　"If Satan casts out Satan, he is divided against himself. How then will his kingdom stand?

27　"And if I cast out demons by Be·el′ze·bub, by whom do your sons cast *them* out? Therefore they shall be your judges.

28　"But if I cast out demons by the Spirit of God, surely the kingdom of God has come upon you.

29　"Or how can one enter a strong man's house and plunder his goods,

---

12:7 [a]Hosea 6:6　　12:8 [a]NU-Text and M-Text omit *even*.　　12:15 [a]NU-Text brackets *multitudes* as disputed.　　12:21 [a]Isaiah 42:1–4　　12:22 [a]NU-Text omits *blind and*.　　12:24 [a]NU-Text and M-Text read *Beelzebul*.

unless he first binds the strong man? And then he will plunder his house.
30 "He who is not with Me is against Me, and he who does not gather with Me scatters abroad.

THE UNPARDONABLE SIN

31 "Therefore I say to you, every sin and blasphemy will be forgiven men, but the blasphemy *against* the Spirit will not be forgiven men.
32 "Anyone who speaks a word against the Son of Man, it will be forgiven him; but whoever speaks against the Holy Spirit, it will not be forgiven him, either in this age or in the *age* to come.

A TREE KNOWN BY ITS FRUIT

33 "Either make the tree good and its fruit good, or else make the tree bad and its fruit bad; for a tree is known by *its* fruit.

34 "Brood of vipers! How can you, being evil, speak good things? For out of the abundance of the heart the mouth speaks.
35 "A good man out of the good treasure of his heart[a] brings forth good things, and an evil man out of the evil treasure brings forth evil things.
36 "But I say to you that for every idle word men may speak, they will give account of it in the day of judgment.
37 "For by your words you will be justified, and by your words you will be condemned."

THE SCRIBES AND PHARISEES ASK FOR A SIGN

38 Then some of the scribes and Phar'i·sees answered, saying, "Teacher, we want to see a sign from You."
39 But He answered and said to

12:35 [a]NU-Text and M-Text omit *of his heart.*

them, "An evil and adulterous generation seeks after a sign, and no sign will be given to it except the sign of the prophet Jonah.

40 "For as Jonah was three days and three nights in the belly of the great fish, so will the Son of Man be three days and three nights in the heart of the earth.

41 "The men of Nin'e·veh will rise up in the judgment with this generation and condemn it, because they repented at the preaching of Jonah; and indeed a greater than Jonah *is* here.

42 "The queen of the South will rise up in the judgment with this generation and condemn it, for she came from the ends of the earth to hear the wisdom of Solomon; and indeed a greater than Solomon *is* here.

AN UNCLEAN SPIRIT RETURNS

43 "When an unclean spirit goes out of a man, he goes through dry places, seeking rest, and finds none.

44 "Then he says, 'I will return to my house from which I came.' And when he comes, he finds *it* empty, swept, and put in order.

45 "Then he goes and takes with him seven other spirits more wicked than himself, and they enter and dwell there; and the last *state* of that man is worse than the first. So shall it also be with this wicked generation."

JESUS' MOTHER AND BROTHERS SEND FOR HIM

46 While He was still talking to the multitudes, behold, His mother and brothers stood outside, seeking to speak with Him.

47 Then one said to Him, "Look, Your mother and Your brothers are standing outside, seeking to speak with You."

48 But He answered and said to the one who told Him, "Who is My mother and who are My brothers?"

49 And He stretched out His hand toward His disciples and said, "Here are My mother and My brothers!

50 "For whoever does the will of My Father in heaven is My brother and sister and mother."

THE PARABLE OF THE SOWER

Jesus loved to tell stories. Here is a story He told about a farmer. The stories Jesus told are often called parables. A parable is a story with a hidden meaning. Jesus explains the meaning of this parable, but usually He wants us to find the meaning.

13 On the same day Jesus went out of the house and sat by the sea.

2 And great multitudes were gathered together to Him, so that He got into a boat and sat; and the whole multitude stood on the shore.

3 Then He spoke many things to them in parables, saying: "Behold, a sower went out to sow.

4 "And as he sowed, some *seed* fell by the wayside; and the birds came and devoured them.

5 "Some fell on stony places, where they did not have much earth; and they immediately sprang up because they had no depth of earth.

6 "But when the sun was up they were scorched, and because they had no root they withered away.

7 "And some fell among thorns, and the thorns sprang up and choked them.

8 "But others fell on good ground and yielded a crop: some a hundredfold, some sixty, some thirty.

☑ *Bible Quiz*

Matthew 13:1–9, 18–23 **Parable of the Sower**

1. Jesus told this parable from an unusual place. Where was it?
2. Can you name the four different places the seeds fell when the sower threw them into the air?
3. Can you tell what happened to the seeds when they fell in each of those places?
4. Jesus was telling us that the four different places the seeds fell are like the four ways people respond to God's Word. What are those four ways?
5. Which way are you like? Have you accepted God's Word as the truth? Do you try to live by it?
6. Can you name some friends you know who are like the four different places the seeds fell? How can you help them be like the seeds that took root in the good soil?

---

9 "He who has ears to hear, let him hear!"

THE PURPOSE OF PARABLES

10 And the disciples came and said to Him, "Why do You speak to them in parables?"
11 He answered and said to them, "Because it has been given to you to know the mysteries of the kingdom of heaven, but to them it has not been given.

12 "For whoever has, to him more will be given, and he will have abundance; but whoever does not have, even what he has will be taken away from him.
13 "Therefore I speak to them in parables, because seeing they do not see, and hearing they do not hear, nor do they understand.
14 "And in them the prophecy of I-sāi′ah is fulfilled, which says:

'Hearing you will hear and shall
  not understand,
And seeing you will see and not
  perceive;
15 For the hearts of this people have
  grown dull.
Their ears are hard of hearing,
And their eyes they have closed,
Lest they should see with their
  eyes and hear with their ears,
Lest they should understand with
  their hearts and turn,
So that I should[a] heal them.'[b]

16 "But blessed are your eyes for they see, and your ears for they hear;
17 "for assuredly, I say to you that many prophets and righteous men desired to see what you see, and did not see it, and to hear what you hear, and did not hear it.

THE PARABLE OF THE SOWER EXPLAINED

18 "Therefore hear the parable of the sower:
19 "When anyone hears the word of the kingdom, and does not understand it, then the wicked one comes and snatches away what was sown in his heart. This is he who received seed by the wayside.
20 "But he who received the seed on

13:15 [a]NU-Text and M-Text read would. [b]Isaiah 6:9, 10

stony places, this is he who hears the word and immediately receives it with joy;

21 "yet he has no root in himself, but endures only for a while. For when tribulation or persecution arises because of the word, immediately he stumbles.

22 "Now he who received seed among the thorns is he who hears the word, and the cares of this world and the deceitfulness of riches choke the word, and he becomes unfruitful.

23 "But he who received seed on the good ground is he who hears the word and understands *it,* who indeed bears fruit and produces: some a hundredfold, some sixty, some thirty."

THE PARABLE OF THE WHEAT AND THE TARES

24 Another parable He put forth to them, saying: "The kingdom of heaven is like a man who sowed good seed in his field;

25 "but while men slept, his enemy came and sowed tares among the wheat and went his way.

26 "But when the grain had sprouted and produced a crop, then the tares also appeared.

27 "So the servants of the owner came and said to him, 'Sir, did you not sow good seed in your field? How then does it have tares?'

28 "He said to them, 'An enemy has done this.' The servants said to him, 'Do you want us then to go and gather them up?'

29 "But he said, 'No, lest while you gather up the tares you also uproot the wheat with them.

30 'Let both grow together until the harvest, and at the time of harvest I will say to the reapers, "First gather together the tares and bind them in bundles to burn them, but gather the wheat into my barn." ' "

THE PARABLE OF THE MUSTARD SEED

31 Another parable He put forth to them, saying: "The kingdom of heaven is like a mustard seed, which a man took and sowed in his field,

32 "which indeed is the least of all the seeds; but when it is grown it is greater than the herbs and becomes a tree, so that the birds of the air come and nest in its branches."

THE PARABLE OF THE LEAVEN

33 Another parable He spoke to them: "The kingdom of heaven is like leaven, which a woman took and hid in three measures[a] of meal till it was all leavened."

PROPHECY AND THE PARABLES

34 All these things Jesus spoke to the multitude in parables; and without a parable He did not speak to them,

35 that it might be fulfilled which was spoken by the prophet, saying:

"I will open My mouth in parables;
I will utter things kept secret
from the foundation of the
world."[a]

THE PARABLE OF THE TARES EXPLAINED

36 Then Jesus sent the multitude away and went into the house. And His disciples came to Him, saying, "Explain to us the parable of the tares of the field."

37 He answered and said to them: "He who sows the good seed is the Son of Man.

13:33 [a]Greek *sata,* approximately two pecks in all
13:35 [a]Psalm 78:2

TREASURE Matthew 13:44

What Is Worth the Most?

Do you have something worth more than a million pieces of gold? Do you have something worth more than 100 million pieces of gold? Would you sell your house for that? Would you sell some of your toys for that? Would you sell your mother or father for that? Would you take a million pieces of gold *not* to live in heaven? Jesus told a story about a pearl (read Matthew 13:45, 46). A man who bought and sold pearls found one that was more wonderful than all the pearls he had ever owned. He sold everything he owned and bought that pearl. Heaven is like that, Jesus said. When you hear about Jesus and heaven, you'll give up anything or everything to live with Him in heaven. Isn't living in heaven with Jesus worth more than anything else in the world?

1. How much is heaven worth? Would you give up heaven for a million pieces of gold?
2. Heaven is free. Jesus lets us go there without paying money for it. Thank You, Jesus.
3. Have you asked Jesus to be your Savior and let you live with Him in heaven someday? Would you like to do that now?

For more on *Favorite Bible Words* turn to page 1508

For more on *Dedication* turn to page 1779

38 "The field is the world, the good seeds are the sons of the kingdom, but the tares are the sons of the wicked *one*.

39 "The enemy who sowed them is the devil, the harvest is the end of the age, and the reapers are the angels.

40 "Therefore as the tares are gathered and burned in the fire, so it will be at the end of this age.

41 "The Son of Man will send out His angels, and they will gather out of His kingdom all things that offend, and those who practice lawlessness,

42 "and will cast them into the furnace of fire. There will be wailing and gnashing of teeth.

43 "Then the righteous will shine forth as the sun in the kingdom of their Father. He who has ears to hear, let him hear!

THE PARABLE OF
THE HIDDEN TREASURE

44 "Again, the kingdom of heaven is like treasure hidden in a field, which a man found and hid; and for joy over it he goes and sells all that he has and buys that field.

THE PARABLE OF
THE PEARL OF GREAT PRICE

45 "Again, the kingdom of heaven is like a merchant seeking beautiful pearls,

46 "who, when he had found one pearl of great price, went and sold all that he had and bought it.

THE PARABLE OF THE DRAGNET

47 "Again, the kingdom of heaven is like a dragnet that was cast into the sea and gathered some of every kind,

48 "which, when it was full, they drew to shore; and they sat down and gathered the good into vessels, but threw the bad away.

49 "So it will be at the end of the age. The angels will come forth, separate the wicked from among the just,

50 "and cast them into the furnace of fire. There will be wailing and gnashing of teeth."

51 Jesus said to them,*a* "Have you understood all these things?" They said to Him, "Yes, Lord."*b*

52 Then He said to them, "Therefore every scribe instructed concerning*a* the kingdom of heaven is like a householder who brings out of his treasure *things* new and old."

JESUS REJECTED AT NAZARETH

53 Now it came to pass, when Jesus had finished these parables, that He departed from there.

54 When He had come to His own country, He taught them in their synagogue, so that they were astonished and said, "Where did this *Man* get this wisdom and *these* mighty works?

55 "Is this not the carpenter's son? Is not His mother called Mary? And His brothers James, Jō'sēs,*a* Simon, and Judas?

56 "And His sisters, are they not all with us? Where then did this *Man* get all these things?"

57 So they were offended at Him. But Jesus said to them, "A prophet is not without honor except in his own country and in his own house."

58 Now He did not do many mighty works there because of their unbelief.

JOHN THE BAPTIST BEHEADED

14 At that time Her'od the tetrarch heard the report about Jesus

13:51 *a*NU-Text omits *Jesus said to them.* *b*NU-Text omits *Lord.* 13:52 *a*Or *for* 13:55 *a*NU-Text reads *Joseph.*

2 and said to his servants, "This is John the Baptist; he is risen from the dead, and therefore these powers are at work in him."

3 For Her'od had laid hold of John and bound him, and put *him* in prison for the sake of He·rō'di·as, his brother Philip's wife.

4 Because John had said to him, "It is not lawful for you to have her."

5 And although he wanted to put him to death, he feared the multitude, because they counted him as a prophet.

6 But when Her'od's birthday was celebrated, the daughter of He·rō'di·as danced before them and pleased Her'od.

7 Therefore he promised with an oath to give her whatever she might ask.

8 So she, having been prompted by her mother, said, "Give me John the Baptist's head here on a platter."

9 And the king was sorry; nevertheless, because of the oaths and because of those who sat with him, he commanded *it* to be given *to her*.

10 So he sent and had John beheaded in prison.

11 And his head was brought on a platter and given to the girl, and she brought *it* to her mother.

12 Then his disciples came and took away the body and buried it, and went and told Jesus.

FEEDING THE FIVE THOUSAND

13 When Jesus heard *it,* He departed from there by boat to a deserted place by Himself. But when the multitudes heard it, they followed Him on foot from the cities.

14 And when Jesus went out He saw a great multitude; and He was moved with compassion for them, and healed their sick.

15 When it was evening, His disciples came to Him, saying, "This is a deserted place, and the hour is already late. Send the multitudes away, that they may go into the villages and buy themselves food."

16 But Jesus said to them, "They do not need to go away. You give them something to eat."

17 And they said to Him, "We have here only five loaves and two fish."

18 He said, "Bring them here to Me."

19 Then He commanded the multitudes to sit down on the grass. And He took the five loaves and the two fish, and looking up to heaven, He blessed and broke and gave the loaves to the disciples; and the disciples gave to the multitudes.

20 So they all ate and were filled, and they took up twelve baskets full of the fragments that remained.

21 Now those who had eaten were about five thousand men, besides women and children.

■ *see John 6:1–15*

JESUS WALKS ON THE SEA

The disciples had never seen this before! They were fishermen, so they spent much time in their boats out on the sea. But what they saw frightened even these fishermen.

22 Immediately Jesus made His disciples get into the boat and go before Him to the other side, while He sent the multitudes away.

23 And when He had sent the multitudes away, He went up on the mountain by Himself to pray. Now when evening came, He was alone there.

24 But the boat was now in the middle of the sea,*a* tossed by the waves, for the wind was contrary.

14:24 *a*NU-Text reads *many furlongs away from the land.*

25 Now in the fourth watch of the night Jesus went to them, walking on the sea.

26 And when the disciples saw Him walking on the sea, they were troubled, saying, "It is a ghost!" And they cried out for fear.

27 But immediately Jesus spoke to them, saying, "Be of good cheer! It is I; do not be afraid."

28 And Peter answered Him and said, "Lord, if it is You, command me to come to You on the water."

29 So He said, "Come." And when Peter had come down out of the boat, he walked on the water to go to Jesus.

30 But when he saw that the wind *was* boisterous,*a* he was afraid; and beginning to sink he cried out, saying, "Lord, save me!"

31 And immediately Jesus stretched out *His* hand and caught him, and said to him, "O you of little faith, why did you doubt?"

32 And when they got into the boat, the wind ceased.

33 Then those who were in the boat came and*a* worshiped Him, saying, "Truly You are the Son of God."

☑ *Bible Quiz*

Matthew 14:22–33 **Jesus Walks on the Water**

1. Why did Jesus tell the disciples to go ahead without Him? What did He do with the people? What did He do up on the mountain?

2. In the meantime, what was happening out on the sea? How do you think the disciples were feeling without Jesus?

3. Do you think Jesus knew they were in trouble? Why?

4. Why were the disciples so afraid when they saw Jesus? Who did they think He was?

5. What did Peter do? Why couldn't he walk on the water?

6. What happened to the storm when Jesus stepped into the boat? How much do you trust Jesus? Do you believe He can rescue you from the troubles that come your way?

MANY TOUCH HIM AND ARE MADE WELL

34 When they had crossed over, they came to the land of*a* Gen·nes′a·ret.

35 And when the men of that place recognized Him, they sent out into all that surrounding region, brought to Him all who were sick,

36 and begged Him that they might only touch the hem of His garment. And as many as touched *it* were made perfectly well.

DEFILEMENT COMES FROM WITHIN

15 Then the scribes and Phar′i-sees who were from Jerusalem came to Jesus, saying,

2 "Why do Your disciples transgress the tradition of the elders? For they do not wash their hands when they eat bread."

3 He answered and said to them, "Why do you also transgress the commandment of God because of your tradition?

14:30 *a*NU-Text brackets *that* and *boisterous* as disputed.   14:33 *a*NU-Text omits *came and.*
14:34 *a*NU-Text reads *came to land at.*

4 "For God commanded, saying, *'Honor your father and your mother';a* and, *'He who curses father or mother, let him be put to death.'b*

5 "But you say, 'Whoever says to his father or mother, "Whatever profit you might have received from me *is a gift to God"*—

6 'then he need not honor his father or mother.'a Thus you have made the commandmentb of God of no effect by your tradition.

7 "Hypocrites! Well did Ī·sāi'ah prophesy about you, saying:

8 *'These people draw near to Me*
        with their mouth,
    Anda honor Me with their lips,
    But their heart is far from Me.
9 *And in vain they worship Me,*
    Teaching as doctrines the
        commandments of men.'"a

10 When He had called the multitude to *Himself*, He said to them, "Hear and understand:

11 "Not what goes into the mouth defiles a man; but what comes out of the mouth, this defiles a man."

12 Then His disciples came and said to Him, "Do You know that the Phar'i·sees were offended when they heard this saying?"

13 But He answered and said, "Every plant which My heavenly Father has not planted will be uprooted.

14 "Let them alone. They are blind leaders of the blind. And if the blind leads the blind, both will fall into a ditch."

15 Then Peter answered and said to Him, "Explain this parable to us."

16 So Jesus said, "Are you also still without understanding?

17 "Do you not yet understand that whatever enters the mouth goes into the stomach and is eliminated?

18 "But those things which proceed out of the mouth come from the heart, and they defile a man.

19 "For out of the heart proceed evil thoughts, murders, adulteries, fornications, thefts, false witness, blasphemies.

20 "These are *the things* which defile a man, but to eat with unwashed hands does not defile a man."

A GENTILE SHOWS HER FAITH

21 Then Jesus went out from there and departed to the region of Tȳre and Sī'don.

22 And behold, a woman of Cā'naan came from that region and cried out to Him, saying, "Have mercy on me, O Lord, Son of David! My daughter is severely demon-possessed."

23 But He answered her not a word. And His disciples came and urged Him, saying, "Send her away, for she cries out after us."

24 But He answered and said, "I was not sent except to the lost sheep of the house of Israel."

25 Then she came and worshiped Him, saying, "Lord, help me!"

26 But He answered and said, "It is not good to take the children's bread and throw *it* to the little dogs."

27 And she said, "Yes, Lord, yet even the little dogs eat the crumbs which fall from their masters' table."

28 Then Jesus answered and said to her, "O woman, great *is* your faith! Let it be to you as you desire." And her daughter was healed from that very hour.

JESUS HEALS GREAT MULTITUDES

29 Jesus departed from there, skirted the Sea of Galilee, and went

15:4 aExodus 20:12; Deuteronomy 5:16   bExodus 21:17   15:6 aNU-Text omits or mother.   bNU-Text reads word.   15:8 aNU-Text omits draw near to Me with their mouth, And.   15:9 aIsaiah 29:13

up on the mountain and sat down there.

30 Then great multitudes came to Him, having with them *the* lame, blind, mute, maimed, and many others; and they laid them down at Jesus' feet, and He healed them.

31 So the multitude marveled when they saw *the* mute speaking, *the* maimed made whole, *the* lame walking, and *the* blind seeing; and they glorified the God of Israel.

FEEDING THE FOUR THOUSAND

32 Now Jesus called His disciples to *Himself* and said, "I have compassion on the multitude, because they have now continued with Me three days and have nothing to eat. And I do not want to send them away hungry, lest they faint on the way."

33 Then His disciples said to Him, "Where could we get enough bread in the wilderness to fill such a great multitude?"

34 Jesus said to them, "How many loaves do you have?" And they said, "Seven, and a few little fish."

35 So He commanded the multitude to sit down on the ground.

36 And He took the seven loaves and the fish and gave thanks, broke *them* and gave *them* to His disciples; and the disciples *gave* to the multitude.

37 So they all ate and were filled, and they took up seven large baskets full of the fragments that were left.

38 Now those who ate were four thousand men, besides women and children.

39 And He sent away the multitude, got into the boat, and came to the region of Mag′da·la.*a*

THE PHARISEES AND SADDUCEES SEEK A SIGN

16 Then the Phar′i·sees and Sad′-du·cees came, and testing Him asked that He would show them a sign from heaven.

2 He answered and said to them, "When it is evening you say, '*It will be* fair weather, for the sky is red';

3 "and in the morning, '*It will be* foul weather today, for the sky is red and threatening.' Hypocrites!*a* You know how to discern the face of the sky, but you cannot *discern* the signs of the times.

4 "A wicked and adulterous generation seeks after a sign, and no sign shall be given to it except the sign of the prophet*a* Jonah." And He left them and departed.

THE LEAVEN OF THE PHARISEES AND SADDUCEES

5 Now when His disciples had come to the other side, they had forgotten to take bread.

6 Then Jesus said to them, "Take heed and beware of the leaven of the Phar′i·sees and the Sad′du·cees."

7 And they reasoned among themselves, saying, "*It is* because we have taken no bread."

8 But Jesus, being aware of *it,* said to them, "O you of little faith, why do you reason among yourselves because you have brought no bread?*a*

9 "Do you not yet understand, or remember the five loaves of the five thousand and how many baskets you took up?

10 "Nor the seven loaves of the four thousand and how many large baskets you took up?

11 "How is it you do not understand that I did not speak to you concerning bread?—*but* to beware of the leaven of the Phar′i·sees and Sad′du·cees."

15:39 *a*NU-Text reads *Magadan.*   16:3 *a*NU-Text omits *Hypocrites.*   16:4 *a*NU-Text omits *the prophet.*   16:8 *a*NU-Text reads *you have no bread.*

ABOUT GOD'S REWARDS Matthew 16:24–27

Does God Have Merit Badges for You?

Are you in a scouting program? If you are, you probably try to do special things to get merit badges. These are rewards for special things you have done. But what about God? Does He reward you for the good things you do? What does God ask you to do for your rewards?

1. Read Matthew 16:24–27. Can you get to heaven by doing good things? No, God will not reward you that way for the good things you do. To get to heaven you must give yourself to Jesus and follow Him.
2. What must we do for God's rewards? Matthew 16:24–27 tells us. When we become Christians, Jesus' followers, we must do Jesus' work. God will reward us for the good work we do for Him.

For more on *What the Bible Says* turn to page 1515
For more on *Salvation* turn to page 1483

12 Then they understood that He did not tell *them* to beware of the leaven of bread, but of the doctrine of the Phar′i·sees and Sad′du·cees.

PETER CONFESSES JESUS AS THE CHRIST

13 When Jesus came into the region of Caes·a·re′a Phi·lip′pi, He asked His disciples, saying, "Who do men say that I, the Son of Man, am?"
14 So they said, "Some *say* John the Baptist, some E·li′jah, and others Jer·e·mi′ah or one of the prophets."
15 He said to them, "But who do you say that I am?"
16 Simon Peter answered and said, "You are the Christ, the Son of the living God."
17 Jesus answered and said to him, "Blessed are you, Simon Bar-Jo′nah, for flesh and blood has not revealed *this* to you, but My Father who is in heaven.
18 "And I also say to you that you are Peter, and on this rock I will build My church, and the gates of Ha′des shall not prevail against it.
19 "And I will give you the keys of the kingdom of heaven, and whatever you bind on earth will be bound in heaven, and whatever you loose on earth will be loosed[a] in heaven."
20 Then He commanded His disciples that they should tell no one that He was Jesus the Christ.

JESUS PREDICTS HIS DEATH AND RESURRECTION

21 From that time Jesus began to show to His disciples that He must go to Jerusalem, and suffer many things from the elders and chief priests and scribes, and be killed, and be raised the third day.
22 Then Peter took Him aside and began to rebuke Him, saying, "Far be it from You, Lord; this shall not happen to You!"

16:19 [a]Or *will have been bound . . . will have been loosed*

23 But He turned and said to Peter, "Get behind Me, Satan! You are an offense to Me, for you are not mindful of the things of God, but the things of men."

TAKE UP THE CROSS AND FOLLOW HIM

24 Then Jesus said to His disciples, "If anyone desires to come after Me, let him deny himself, and take up his cross, and follow Me.
25 "For whoever desires to save his life will lose it, but whoever loses his life for My sake will find it.
26 "For what profit is it to a man if he gains the whole world, and loses his own soul? Or what will a man give in exchange for his soul?
27 "For the Son of Man will come in the glory of His Father with His angels, and then He will reward each according to his works.

JESUS TRANSFIGURED ON THE MOUNT

28 "Assuredly, I say to you, there are some standing here who shall not taste death till they see the Son of Man coming in His kingdom."

17 Now after six days Jesus took Peter, James, and John his brother, led them up on a high mountain by themselves;
2 and He was transfigured before them. His face shone like the sun, and His clothes became as white as the light.
3 And behold, Moses and E·li′jah appeared to them, talking with Him.
4 Then Peter answered and said to Jesus, "Lord, it is good for us to be here; if You wish, let us*a* make here three tabernacles: one for You, one for Moses, and one for E·li′jah."

5 While he was still speaking, behold, a bright cloud overshadowed them; and suddenly a voice came out of the cloud, saying, "This is My beloved Son, in whom I am well pleased. Hear Him!"
6 And when the disciples heard *it,* they fell on their faces and were greatly afraid.
7 But Jesus came and touched them and said, "Arise, and do not be afraid."
8 When they had lifted up their eyes, they saw no one but Jesus only.
9 Now as they came down from the mountain, Jesus commanded them, saying, "Tell the vision to no one until the Son of Man is risen from the dead."
10 And His disciples asked Him, saying, "Why then do the scribes say that E·li′jah must come first?"
11 Jesus answered and said to them, "Indeed, E·li′jah is coming first*a* and will restore all things.
12 "But I say to you that E·li′jah has come already, and they did not know him but did to him whatever they wished. Likewise the Son of Man is also about to suffer at their hands."
13 Then the disciples understood that He spoke to them of John the Baptist.

A BOY IS HEALED

14 And when they had come to the multitude, a man came to Him, kneeling down to Him and saying,
15 "Lord, have mercy on my son, for he is an epileptic*a* and suffers severely; for he often falls into the fire and often into the water.
16 "So I brought him to Your disciples, but they could not cure him."
17 Then Jesus answered and said,

17:4 *a*NU-Text reads *I will.*   17:11 *a*NU-Text omits *first.*   17:15 *a*Literally *moonstruck*

"O faithless and perverse generation, how long shall I be with you? How long shall I bear with you? Bring him here to Me."

18 And Jesus rebuked the demon, and it came out of him; and the child was cured from that very hour.

19 Then the disciples came to Jesus privately and said, "Why could we not cast it out?"

20 So Jesus said to them, "Because of your unbelief;a for assuredly, I say to you, if you have faith as a mustard seed, you will say to this mountain, 'Move from here to there,' and it will move; and nothing will be impossible for you.

21 "However, this kind does not go out except by prayer and fasting."a

JESUS AGAIN PREDICTS HIS DEATH AND RESURRECTION

22 Now while they were stayinga in Galilee, Jesus said to them, "The Son of Man is about to be betrayed into the hands of men,

23 "and they will kill Him, and the third day He will be raised up." And they were exceedingly sorrowful.

PETER AND HIS MASTER PAY THEIR TAXES

24 When they had come to Ca·per'-na·um,a those who received the *temple* tax came to Peter and said, "Does your Teacher not pay the *temple* tax?"

25 He said, "Yes." And when he had come into the house, Jesus anticipated him, saying, "What do you think, Simon? From whom do the kings of the earth take customs or taxes, from their sons or from strangers?"

26 Peter said to Him, "From strangers." Jesus said to him, "Then the sons are free.

27 "Nevertheless, lest we offend them, go to the sea, cast in a hook, and take the fish that comes up first. And when you have opened its mouth, you will find a piece of money;a take that and give it to them for Me and you."

WHO IS THE GREATEST?

18 At that time the disciples came to Jesus, saying, "Who then is greatest in the kingdom of heaven?"

2 Then Jesus called a little child to Him, set him in the midst of them,

3 and said, "Assuredly, I say to you, unless you are converted and become as little children, you will by no means enter the kingdom of heaven.

4 "Therefore whoever humbles himself as this little child is the greatest in the kingdom of heaven.

5 "Whoever receives one little child like this in My name receives Me.

JESUS WARNS OF OFFENSES

6 "But whoever causes one of these little ones who believe in Me to sin, it would be better for him if a millstone were hung around his neck, and he were drowned in the depth of the sea.

7 "Woe to the world because of offenses! For offenses must come, but woe to that man by whom the offense comes!

8 "If your hand or foot causes you to sin, cut it off and cast *it* from you. It is better for you to enter into life lame or maimed, rather than having two hands or two feet, to be cast into the everlasting fire.

17:20 aNU-Text reads *little faith.*   17:21 aNU-Text omits this verse.   17:22 aNU-Text reads *gathering together.*   17:24 aNU-Text reads *Capharnaum* (here and elsewhere).
17:27 aGreek *stater,* the exact amount to pay the temple tax (didrachma) for two

9 "And if your eye causes you to sin, pluck it out and cast *it* from you. It is better for you to enter into life with one eye, rather than having two eyes, to be cast into hell fire.

THE PARABLE OF THE LOST SHEEP

10 "Take heed that you do not despise one of these little ones, for I say to you that in heaven their angels always see the face of My Father who is in heaven.

11 "For the Son of Man has come to save that which was lost.a

12 "What do you think? If a man has a hundred sheep, and one of them goes astray, does he not leave the ninety-nine and go to the mountains to seek the one that is straying?

13 "And if he should find it, assuredly, I say to you, he rejoices more over that *sheep* than over the ninety-nine that did not go astray.

14 "Even so it is not the will of your Father who is in heaven that one of these little ones should perish.

DEALING WITH A SINNING BROTHER

15 "Moreover if your brother sins against you, go and tell him his fault between you and him alone. If he hears you, you have gained your brother.

16 "But if he will not hear, take with you one or two more, that *'by the mouth of two or three witnesses every word may be established.'a*

17 "And if he refuses to hear them, tell *it* to the church. But if he refuses even to hear the church, let him be to you like a heathen and a tax collector.

18 "Assuredly, I say to you, whatever you bind on earth will be bound in heaven, and whatever you loose on earth will be loosed in heaven.

19 "Again I saya to you that if two of you agree on earth concerning anything that they ask, it will be done for them by My Father in heaven.

18:11 aNU-Text omits this verse.
18:16 aDeuteronomy 19:15   18:19 aNU-Text and M-Text read *Again, assuredly, I say.*

20 "For where two or three are gathered together in My name, I am there in the midst of them."

THE PARABLE OF THE UNFORGIVING SERVANT

Could you forgive someone who was very mean to you? What if they were mean to you everyday—could you forgive them again and again? Here is a parable Jesus told about how we should forgive others.

21 Then Peter came to Him and said, "Lord, how often shall my brother sin against me, and I forgive him? Up to seven times?"

22 Jesus said to him, "I do not say to you, up to seven times, but up to seventy times seven.

23 "Therefore the kingdom of heaven is like a certain king who wanted to settle accounts with his servants.

24 "And when he had begun to settle accounts, one was brought to him who owed him ten thousand talents.

25 "But as he was not able to pay, his master commanded that he be sold, with his wife and children and all that he had, and that payment be made.

26 "The servant therefore fell down before him, saying, 'Master, have patience with me, and I will pay you all.'

27 "Then the master of that servant was moved with compassion, released him, and forgave him the debt.

28 "But that servant went out and found one of his fellow servants who owed him a hundred denarii; and he laid hands on him and took *him* by the throat, saying, 'Pay me what you owe!'

29 "So his fellow servant fell down at his feet*a* and begged him, saying, 'Have patience with me, and I will pay you all.'*b*

Bible Quiz

Matthew 18:21–35 **Parable of the Unforgiving Servant**

1. If someone keeps being mean to us, how many times did Jesus say we should forgive them? What do you think Jesus meant by saying "seventy times seven"?

2. In Jesus' parable, how many talents did the first servant owe the king? When the servant couldn't pay, what did the king want to do to get his money? Why do you think the king changed his mind and forgave the servant?

3. After he was forgiven, what did the servant do then? After he had just been forgiven by the king, how could he have been so mean as to not forgive someone else? What does this say about the kind of person he was?

4. What did the king do when he learned what his wicked servant had done? What will God do to those who will not forgive others?

5. Do you know someone whom you need to forgive? What did they do to hurt you? How can you forgive them?

18:29 *a*NU-Text omits *at his feet.* *b*NU-Text and M-Text omit *all.*

30 "And he would not, but went and threw him into prison till he should pay the debt.

31 "So when his fellow servants saw what had been done, they were very grieved, and came and told their master all that had been done.

32 "Then his master, after he had called him, said to him, 'You wicked servant! I forgave you all that debt because you begged me.

33 'Should you not also have had compassion on your fellow servant, just as I had pity on you?'

34 "And his master was angry, and delivered him to the torturers until he should pay all that was due to him.

35 "So My heavenly Father also will do to you if each of you, from his heart, does not forgive his brother his trespasses."*a*

MARRIAGE AND DIVORCE

19 Now it came to pass, when Jesus had finished these sayings, *that* He departed from Galilee and came to the region of Judea beyond the Jordan.

2 And great multitudes followed Him, and He healed them there.

3 The Phar'i·sees also came to Him, testing Him, and saying to Him, "Is it lawful for a man to divorce his wife for *just* any reason?"

4 And He answered and said to them, "Have you not read that He who made*a* them at the beginning 'made them male and female,'*b*

5 "and said, 'For this reason a man shall leave his father and mother and be joined to his wife, and the two shall become one flesh'?*a*

6 "So then, they are no longer two but one flesh. Therefore what God has joined together, let not man separate."

7 They said to Him, "Why then did Moses command to give a certificate of divorce, and to put her away?"

8 He said to them, "Moses, because of the hardness of your hearts, permitted you to divorce your wives, but from the beginning it was not so.

9 "And I say to you, whoever divorces his wife, except for sexual immorality,*a* and marries another, commits adultery; and whoever marries her who is divorced commits adultery."

10 His disciples said to Him, "If such is the case of the man with *his* wife, it is better not to marry."

JESUS TEACHES ON CELIBACY

11 But He said to them, "All cannot accept this saying, but only *those* to whom it has been given:

12 "For there are eunuchs who were born thus from *their* mother's womb, and there are eunuchs who were made eunuchs by men, and there are eunuchs who have made themselves eunuchs for the kingdom of heaven's sake. He who is able to accept *it,* let him accept *it.*"

JESUS BLESSES LITTLE CHILDREN

13 Then little children were brought to Him that He might put *His* hands on them and pray, but the disciples rebuked them.

14 But Jesus said, "Let the little children come to Me, and do not forbid them; for of such is the kingdom of heaven."

15 And He laid *His* hands on them and departed from there.

■ *see Mark 10:13–16*

18:35 *a*NU-Text omits *his trespasses.*
19:4 *a*NU-Text reads *created.*　*b*Genesis 1:27; 5:2
19:5 *a*Genesis 2:24　　19:9 *a*Or *fornication*

LET THE LITTLE CHILDREN COME TO ME. Matthew 19:14

Does Jesus Love Children?

Is Jesus just for big folks? Or does He really care for children? How do we know? Is there a way to be sure?

1. Read Matthew 19:14 again. Who said this? Read *all* of this verse. What else does it say about Jesus and the children?
2. Are you glad that Jesus loves children? Why? Have you thanked Him today that He loves you?

For more on *Favorite Family Verses* turn to page 1564
For more on *Love* turn to page 1524

Jesus Counsels the Rich Young Ruler

16 Now behold, one came and said to Him, "Good*a* Teacher, what good thing shall I do that I may have eternal life?"

17 So He said to him, "Why do you call Me good?*a* No one *is* good but One, *that is,* God.*b* But if you want to enter into life, keep the commandments."

18 He said to Him, "Which ones?" Jesus said, "*'You shall not murder,' 'You shall not commit adultery,' 'You shall not steal,' 'You shall not bear false witness,'*

19 *'Honor your father and your mother,'a* and, *'You shall love your neighbor as yourself.' "b*

20 The young man said to Him, "All these things I have kept from my youth.*a* What do I still lack?"

21 Jesus said to him, "If you want to be perfect, go, sell what you have and give to the poor, and you will have treasure in heaven; and come, follow Me."

22 But when the young man heard that saying, he went away sorrowful, for he had great possessions.

With God All Things Are Possible

23 Then Jesus said to His disciples, "Assuredly, I say to you that it is hard for a rich man to enter the kingdom of heaven.

24 "And again I say to you, it is easier for a camel to go through the eye of a needle than for a rich man to enter the kingdom of God."

25 When His disciples heard *it,* they were greatly astonished, saying, "Who then can be saved?"

26 But Jesus looked at *them* and said to them, "With men this is im-

possible, but with God all things are possible."

27 Then Peter answered and said to Him, "See, we have left all and followed You. Therefore what shall we have?"

28 So Jesus said to them, "Assuredly I say to you, that in the regeneration, when the Son of Man sits on the throne of His glory, you who have followed Me will also sit on twelve thrones, judging the twelve tribes of Israel.

29 "And everyone who has left houses or brothers or sisters or father or mother or wife*a* or children or lands, for My name's sake, shall receive a hundredfold, and inherit eternal life.

30 "But many *who are* first will be last, and the last first.

The Parable of the Workers in the Vineyard

Have you ever said, "That's not fair!"? Jesus told a story about some people who said that. What do you think He was trying to say by telling this story?

20 "For the kingdom of heaven is like a landowner who went out early in the morning to hire laborers for his vineyard.

2 "Now when he had agreed with the laborers for a denarius a day, he sent them into his vineyard.

3 "And he went out about the third hour and saw others standing idle in the marketplace,

4 "and said to them, 'You also go

19:16 *a*NU-Text omits *Good.*   19:17 *a*NU-Text reads *Why do you ask Me about what is good?* *b*NU-Text reads *There is One who is good.*
19:19 *a*Exodus 20:12–16; Deuteronomy 5:16–20 *b*Leviticus 19:18   19:20 *a*NU-Text omits *from my youth.*   19:29 *a*NU-Text omits *or wife.*

Bible Quiz

Matthew 20:1–16 **Parable of the Workers in the Vineyard**

1. Jesus told this story to help us understand what a certain kingdom is like. What is this special kingdom?

2. Early in the morning, the landowner hired some people to work in his vineyard. How much did he pay them?

3. Later in the day, the landowner hired some more people to work in his vineyard. How much did he pay them?

4. Near the end of the day, the landowner hired still more people to work in his vineyard. How much did he pay them? Did the workers hired early in the morning think this was fair? What do you think?

5. Jesus was saying that the most important thing is not how long someone has believed in Jesus, but that they do believe in Jesus.

6. Think about this. If you have older brothers or sisters, your parents don't love them more because they have been alive longer than you. They love you all the same. The love of Jesus is like that. He wants all of us to be happy when someone begins to believe in Him, no matter how old or young they may be.

into the vineyard, and whatever is right I will give you.' So they went.

5 "Again he went out about the sixth and the ninth hour, and did likewise.

6 "And about the eleventh hour he went out and found others standing idle,*a* and said to them, 'Why have you been standing here idle all day?'

7 "They said to him, 'Because no one hired us.' He said to them, 'You also go into the vineyard, and whatever is right you will receive.'*a*

8 "So when evening had come, the owner of the vineyard said to his steward, 'Call the laborers and give them *their* wages, beginning with the last to the first.'

9 "And when those came who *were hired* about the eleventh hour, they each received a denarius.

10 "But when the first came, they supposed that they would receive more; and they likewise received each a denarius.

11 "And when they had received *it,* they complained against the landowner,

12 "saying, 'These last *men* have worked *only* one hour, and you made them equal to us who have borne the burden and the heat of the day.'

13 "But he answered one of them and said, 'Friend, I am doing you no wrong. Did you not agree with me for a denarius?

14 'Take *what is* yours and go your way. I wish to give to this last man *the same* as to you.

15 'Is it not lawful for me to do what I wish with my own things? Or is your eye evil because I am good?'

16 "So the last will be first, and the first last. For many are called, but few chosen."*a*

20:6 *a*NU-Text omits *idle.*   20:7 *a*NU-Text omits the last clause of this verse.   20:16 *a*NU-Text omits the last sentence of this verse.

JESUS A THIRD TIME PREDICTS HIS DEATH AND RESURRECTION

17 Now Jesus, going up to Jerusalem, took the twelve disciples aside on the road and said to them,
18 "Behold, we are going up to Jerusalem, and the Son of Man will be betrayed to the chief priests and to the scribes; and they will condemn Him to death,
19 "and deliver Him to the Gentiles to mock and to scourge and to crucify. And the third day He will rise again."

GREATNESS IS SERVING

20 Then the mother of Zeb′e·dee's sons came to Him with her sons, kneeling down and asking something from Him.
21 And He said to her, "What do you wish?" She said to Him, "Grant that these two sons of mine may sit, one on Your right hand and the other on the left, in Your kingdom."
22 But Jesus answered and said, "You do not know what you ask. Are you able to drink the cup that I am about to drink, and be baptized with the baptism that I am baptized with?"*a* They said to Him, "We are able."
23 So He said to them, "You will indeed drink My cup, and be baptized with the baptism that I am baptized with;*a* but to sit on My right hand and on My left is not Mine to give, but *it is for those* for whom it is prepared by My Father."
24 And when the ten heard *it,* they were greatly displeased with the two brothers.
25 But Jesus called them to *Himself* and said, "You know that the rulers of the Gentiles lord it over them, and those who are great exercise authority over them.
26 "Yet it shall not be so among you;

but whoever desires to become great among you, let him be your servant.
27 "And whoever desires to be first among you, let him be your slave—
28 "just as the Son of Man did not come to be served, but to serve, and to give His life a ransom for many."

TWO BLIND MEN RECEIVE THEIR SIGHT

29 Now as they went out of Jericho, a great multitude followed Him.
30 And behold, two blind men sitting by the road, when they heard that Jesus was passing by, cried out, saying, "Have mercy on us, O Lord, Son of David!"
31 Then the multitude warned them that they should be quiet; but they cried out all the more, saying, "Have mercy on us, O Lord, Son of David!"
32 So Jesus stood still and called them, and said, "What do you want Me to do for you?"
33 They said to Him, "Lord, that our eyes may be opened."
34 So Jesus had compassion and touched their eyes. And immediately their eyes received sight, and they followed Him.
■ *see Mark 10:46–52*

THE TRIUMPHAL ENTRY

21 Now when they drew near Jerusalem, and came to Beth′pha·gē,*a* at the Mount of Olives, then Jesus sent two disciples,
2 saying to them, "Go into the village opposite you, and immediately you will find a donkey tied, and a colt with her. Loose *them* and bring *them* to Me.

20:22 *a*NU-Text omits *and be baptized with the baptism that I am baptized with.*   20:23 *a*NU-Text omits *and be baptized with the baptism that I am baptized with.*   21:1 *a*M-Text reads *Bethsphage.*

3 "And if anyone says anything to you, you shall say, 'The Lord has need of them,' and immediately he will send them."

4 All*a* this was done that it might be fulfilled which was spoken by the prophet, saying:

5 *"Tell the daughter of Zion,*
   'Behold, your King is coming to
      you,
   Lowly, and sitting on a donkey,
   A colt, the foal of a donkey.' "a

6 So the disciples went and did as Jesus commanded them.
7 They brought the donkey and the colt, laid their clothes on them, and set *Him*a on them.
8 And a very great multitude spread their clothes on the road; others cut down branches from the trees and spread *them* on the road.
9 Then the multitudes who went before and those who followed cried out, saying:

   "Hō·san'na to the Son of David!
   '*Blessed is He who comes in the*
      name of the LORD!'a
   Hō·san'na in the highest!"

10 And when He had come into Jerusalem, all the city was moved, saying, "Who is this?"
11 So the multitudes said, "This is Jesus, the prophet from Nazareth of Galilee."
■ *see Mark 11:1–11*

JESUS CLEANSES THE TEMPLE

Something terrible was
happening around God's
temple. Jesus was going to
stop it from happening any
longer.

12 Then Jesus went into the temple of God*a* and drove out all those who bought and sold in the temple, and overturned the tables of the money changers and the seats of those who sold doves.
13 And He said to them, "It is written, '*My house shall be called a house of prayer,*'a but you have made it a '*den of thieves.*' "b
14 Then *the* blind and *the* lame came to Him in the temple, and He healed them.
15 But when the chief priests and scribes saw the wonderful things that He did, and the children crying out in the temple and saying, "Hō·san'na to the Son of David!" they were indignant
16 and said to Him, "Do You hear what these are saying?" And Jesus said to them, "Yes. Have you never read,

   '*Out of the mouth of babes and*
      nursing infants
   You have perfected praise'?"a

17 Then He left them and went out of the city to Beth'a·ny, and He lodged there.

THE FIG TREE WITHERED

18 Now in the morning, as He returned to the city, He was hungry.
19 And seeing a fig tree by the road, He came to it and found nothing on it but leaves, and said to it, "Let no fruit grow on you ever again." Immediately the fig tree withered away.

THE LESSON OF THE WITHERED FIG TREE

20 And when the disciples saw *it,* they marveled, saying, "How did the fig tree wither away so soon?"
21 So Jesus answered and said to

21:4 *a*NU-Text omits *All.*   21:5 *a*Zechariah 9:9
21:7 *a*NU-Text reads *and He sat.*   21:9 *a*Psalm
118:26   21:12 *a*NU-Text omits *of God.*
21:13 *a*Isaiah 56:7   *b*Jeremiah 7:11
21:16 *a*Psalm 8:2

☑ *Bible Quiz*

Matthew 21:12–17 **Jesus Clears the Temple**

1. The merchants and money changers were turning the temple into a store. Why do you think this made Jesus angry?
2. What did Jesus do?
3. What did Jesus say that makes you think the merchants and money changers were not always being honest?
4. Make sure you are angry for the right reason. Jesus was angry because bad things were happening in God's house and innocent people were being cheated. Are there bad things you should be angry about? Are there other things you are angry at that you shouldn't be angry about?

them, "Assuredly, I say to you, if you have faith and do not doubt, you will not only do what was done to the fig tree, but also if you say to this mountain, 'Be removed and be cast into the sea,' it will be done.

22 "And whatever things you ask in prayer, believing, you will receive."

JESUS' AUTHORITY QUESTIONED

23 Now when He came into the temple, the chief priests and the elders of the people confronted Him as He was teaching, and said, "By what authority are You doing these things? And who gave You this authority?"

24 But Jesus answered and said to them, "I also will ask you one thing, which if you tell Me, I likewise will tell you by what authority I do these things:

25 "The baptism of John—where was it from? From heaven or from men?" And they reasoned among themselves, saying, "If we say, 'From heaven,' He will say to us, 'Why then did you not believe him?'

26 "But if we say, 'From men,' we fear the multitude, for all count John as a prophet."

27 So they answered Jesus and said, "We do not know." And He said to them, "Neither will I tell you by what authority I do these things.

THE PARABLE OF THE TWO SONS

28 "But what do you think? A man had two sons, and he came to the first and said, 'Son, go, work today in my vineyard.'

29 "He answered and said, 'I will not,' but afterward he regretted it and went.

30 "Then he came to the second and said likewise. And he answered and said, 'I *go,* sir,' but he did not go.

31 "Which of the two did the will of *his* father?" They said to Him, "The first." Jesus said to them, "Assuredly, I say to you that tax collectors and harlots enter the kingdom of God before you.

32 "For John came to you in the way of righteousness, and you did not believe him; but tax collectors and harlots believed him; and when you saw *it,* you did not afterward relent and believe him.

THE PARABLE OF
THE WICKED VINEDRESSERS

33 "Hear another parable: There was a certain landowner who planted a

vineyard and set a hedge around it, dug a winepress in it and built a tower. And he leased it to vinedressers and went into a far country.

34 "Now when vintage-time drew near, he sent his servants to the vinedressers, that they might receive its fruit.

35 "And the vinedressers took his servants, beat one, killed one, and stoned another.

36 "Again he sent other servants, more than the first, and they did likewise to them.

37 "Then last of all he sent his son to them, saying, 'They will respect my son.'

38 "But when the vinedressers saw the son, they said among themselves, 'This is the heir. Come, let us kill him and seize his inheritance.'

39 "So they took him and cast *him* out of the vineyard and killed *him.*

40 "Therefore, when the owner of the vineyard comes, what will he do to those vinedressers?"

41 They said to Him, "He will destroy those wicked men miserably, and lease *his* vineyard to other vinedressers who will render to him the fruits in their seasons."

42 Jesus said to them, "Have you never read in the Scriptures:

'The stone which the builders
　　rejected
Has become the chief cornerstone.
This was the LORD's doing,
And it is marvelous in our
　　eyes'?[a]

43 "Therefore I say to you, the kingdom of God will be taken from you and given to a nation bearing the fruits of it.

44 "And whoever falls on this stone will be broken; but on whomever it falls, it will grind him to powder."

45 Now when the chief priests and Phar'i·sees heard His parables, they perceived that He was speaking of them.

46 But when they sought to lay hands on Him, they feared the multitudes, because they took Him for a prophet.

THE PARABLE OF THE WEDDING FEAST

22 And Jesus answered and spoke to them again by parables and said:

2　"The kingdom of heaven is like a certain king who arranged a marriage for his son,

3　"and sent out his servants to call those who were invited to the wedding; and they were not willing to come.

4　"Again, he sent out other servants, saying, 'Tell those who are invited, "See, I have prepared my dinner; my oxen and fatted cattle *are* killed, and all things *are* ready. Come to the wedding."'

5　"But they made light of it and went their ways, one to his own farm, another to his business.

6　"And the rest seized his servants, treated *them* spitefully, and killed *them.*

7　"But when the king heard *about it,* he was furious. And he sent out his armies, destroyed those murderers, and burned up their city.

8　"Then he said to his servants, 'The wedding is ready, but those who were invited were not worthy.

9　'Therefore go into the highways, and as many as you find, invite to the wedding.'

10 "So those servants went out into the highways and gathered together

21:42 [a]Psalm 118:22, 23

all whom they found, both bad and good. And the wedding *hall* was filled with guests.

11 "But when the king came in to see the guests, he saw a man there who did not have on a wedding garment.

12 "So he said to him, 'Friend, how did you come in here without a wedding garment?' And he was speechless.

13 "Then the king said to the servants, 'Bind him hand and foot, take him away, and*a* cast *him* into outer darkness; there will be weeping and gnashing of teeth.'

14 "For many are called, but few *are* chosen."

THE PHARISEES: IS IT LAWFUL TO PAY TAXES TO CAESAR?

15 Then the Phar'i·sees went and plotted how they might entangle Him in *His* talk.

16 And they sent to Him their disciples with the He·rō'di·ans, saying, "Teacher, we know that You are true, and teach the way of God in truth; nor do You care about anyone, for You do not regard the person of men.

17 "Tell us, therefore, what do You think? Is it lawful to pay taxes to Caesar, or not?"

18 But Jesus perceived their wickedness, and said, "Why do you test Me, *you* hypocrites?

19 "Show Me the tax money." So they brought Him a denarius.

20 And He said to them, "Whose image and inscription *is* this?"

21 They said to Him, "Caesar's." And He said to them, "Render therefore to Caesar the things that are Caesar's, and to God the things that are God's."

22 When they had heard *these words,* they marveled, and left Him and went their way.

THE SADDUCEES: WHAT ABOUT THE RESURRECTION?

23 The same day the Sad'du·cees, who say there is no resurrection, came to Him and asked Him,

24 saying: "Teacher, Moses said that if a man dies, having no children, his brother shall marry his wife and raise up offspring for his brother.

25 "Now there were with us seven brothers. The first died after he had married, and having no offspring, left his wife to his brother.

26 "Likewise the second also, and the third, even to the seventh.

27 "Last of all the woman died also.

28 "Therefore, in the resurrection, whose wife of the seven will she be? For they all had her."

29 Jesus answered and said to them, "You are mistaken, not knowing the Scriptures nor the power of God.

30 "For in the resurrection they neither marry nor are given in marriage, but are like angels of God*a* in heaven.

31 "But concerning the resurrection of the dead, have you not read what was spoken to you by God, saying,

32 '*I am the God of Abraham, the God of Isaac, and the God of Jacob*'?*a* God is not the God of the dead, but of the living."

33 And when the multitudes heard *this,* they were astonished at His teaching.

THE SCRIBES: WHICH IS THE FIRST COMMANDMENT OF ALL?

34 But when the Phar'i·sees heard that He had silenced the Sad'du·cees, they gathered together.

35 Then one of them, a lawyer, asked

22:13 *a*NU-Text omits *take him away, and.*
22:30 *a*NU-Text omits *of God.*   22:32 *a*Exodus 3:6, 15

Him a question, testing Him, and saying,

36 "Teacher, which *is* the great commandment in the law?"

37 Jesus said to him, "*'You shall love the* LORD *your God with all your heart, with all your soul, and with all your mind.'ᵃ*

38 "This is *the* first and great commandment.

39 "And *the* second *is* like it: *'You shall love your neighbor as yourself.'ᵃ*

40 "On these two commandments hang all the Law and the Prophets."

JESUS: HOW CAN DAVID CALL HIS DESCENDANT LORD?

41 While the Phar'i·sees were gathered together, Jesus asked them,

42 saying, "What do you think about the Christ? Whose Son is He?" They said to Him, *"The Son* of David."

43 He said to them, "How then does David in the Spirit call Him *'Lord,'* saying:

44 *'The* LORD *said to my Lord,*
  "Sit at My right hand,
    Till I make Your enemies Your
      footstool"'?ᵃ

45 "If David then calls Him *'Lord,'* how is He his Son?"

46 And no one was able to answer Him a word, nor from that day on did anyone dare question Him anymore.

WOE TO THE SCRIBES AND PHARISEES

23 Then Jesus spoke to the multitudes and to His disciples,

2 saying: "The scribes and the Phar'i·sees sit in Moses' seat.

3 "Therefore whatever they tell you to observe,ᵃ *that* observe and do, but do not do according to their works; for they say, and do not do.

4 "For they bind heavy burdens, hard to bear, and lay *them* on men's shoulders; but they *themselves* will not move them with one of their fingers.

5 "But all their works they do to be seen by men. They make their phylacteries broad and enlarge the borders of their garments.

6 "They love the best places at feasts, the best seats in the synagogues,

7 "greetings in the marketplaces, and to be called by men, 'Rabbi, Rabbi.'

8 "But you, do not be called 'Rabbi'; for One is your Teacher, the Christ,ᵃ and you are all brethren.

9 "Do not call anyone on earth your father; for One is your Father, He who is in heaven.

10 "And do not be called teachers; for One is your Teacher, the Christ.

11 "But he who is greatest among you shall be your servant.

12 "And whoever exalts himself will be humbled, and he who humbles himself will be exalted.

13 "But woe to you, scribes and Phar'i·sees, hypocrites! For you shut up the kingdom of heaven against men; for you neither go in *yourselves,* nor do you allow those who are entering to go in.

14 "Woe to you, scribes and Phar'i·sees, hypocrites! For you devour widows' houses, and for a pretense make long prayers. Therefore you will receive greater condemnation.ᵃ

15 "Woe to you, scribes and Phar'i·sees, hypocrites! For you travel land and sea to win one proselyte, and

22:37 ᵃDeuteronomy 6:5   22:39 ᵃLeviticus 19:18   22:44 ᵃPsalm 110:1   23:3 ᵃNU-Text omits *to observe.*   23:8 ᵃNU-Text omits *the Christ.*   23:14 ᵃNU-Text omits this verse.

when he is won, you make him twice as much a son of hell as yourselves.

16 "Woe to you, blind guides, who say, 'Whoever swears by the temple, it is nothing; but whoever swears by the gold of the temple, he is obliged *to perform it.*'

17 "Fools and blind! For which is greater, the gold or the temple that sanctifies*a* the gold?

18 "And, 'Whoever swears by the altar, it is nothing; but whoever swears by the gift that is on it, he is obliged *to perform it.*'

19 "Fools and blind! For which is greater, the gift or the altar that sanctifies the gift?

20 "Therefore he who swears by the altar, swears by it and by all things on it.

21 "He who swears by the temple, swears by it and by Him who dwells*a* in it.

22 "And he who swears by heaven, swears by the throne of God and by Him who sits on it.

23 "Woe to you, scribes and Phar'i-sees, hypocrites! For you pay tithe of mint and anise and cummin, and have neglected the weightier *matters* of the law: justice and mercy and faith. These you ought to have done, without leaving the others undone.

24 "Blind guides, who strain out a gnat and swallow a camel!

25 "Woe to you, scribes and Phar'i-sees, hypocrites! For you cleanse the outside of the cup and dish, but inside they are full of extortion and self-indulgence.*a*

26 "Blind Phar'i·see, first cleanse the inside of the cup and dish, that the outside of them may be clean also.

27 "Woe to you, scribes and Phar'i-sees, hypocrites! For you are like whitewashed tombs which indeed appear beautiful outwardly, but inside are full of dead *men's* bones and all uncleanness.

28 "Even so you also outwardly appear righteous to men, but inside you are full of hypocrisy and lawlessness.

29 "Woe to you, scribes and Phar'i-sees, hypocrites! Because you build the tombs of the prophets and adorn the monuments of the righteous,

30 "and say, 'If we had lived in the days of our fathers, we would not have been partakers*a* with them in the blood of the prophets.'

31 "Therefore you are witnesses against yourselves that you are sons of those who murdered the prophets.

32 "Fill up, then, the measure of your fathers' *guilt.*

33 "Serpents, brood of vipers! How can you escape the condemnation of hell?

34 "Therefore, indeed, I send you prophets, wise men, and scribes: *some* of them you will kill and crucify, and *some* of them you will scourge in your synagogues and persecute from city to city,

35 "that on you may come all the righteous blood shed on the earth, from the blood of righteous Abel to the blood of Zech·a·rī'ah, son of Ber·e·chī'ah, whom you murdered between the temple and the altar.

36 "Assuredly, I say to you, all these things will come upon this generation.

JESUS LAMENTS OVER JERUSALEM

37 "O Jerusalem, Jerusalem, the one who kills the prophets and stones those who are sent to her! How often I wanted to gather your children together, as a hen gathers her chicks under *her* wings, but you were not willing!

38 "See! Your house is left to you desolate;

23:17 *a*NU-Text reads *sanctified.*
23:21 *a*M-Text reads *dwelt.* 23:25 *a*M-Text reads *unrighteousness.*

39 "for I say to you, you shall see Me no more till you say, *'Blessed is He who comes in the name of the* LORD!' "*a*

JESUS PREDICTS THE DESTRUCTION OF THE TEMPLE

24 Then Jesus went out and departed from the temple, and His disciples came up to show Him the buildings of the temple.
2   And Jesus said to them, "Do you not see all these things? Assuredly, I say to you, not *one* stone shall be left here upon another, that shall not be thrown down."

THE SIGNS OF THE TIMES AND THE END OF THE AGE

3   Now as He sat on the Mount of Olives, the disciples came to Him privately, saying, "Tell us, when will these things be? And what *will be* the sign of Your coming, and of the end of the age?"
4   And Jesus answered and said to them: "Take heed that no one deceives you.
5   "For many will come in My name, saying, 'I am the Christ,' and will deceive many.
6   "And you will hear of wars and rumors of wars. See that you are not troubled; for all*a these things* must come to pass, but the end is not yet.
7   "For nation will rise against nation, and kingdom against kingdom. And there will be famines, pestilences,*a* and earthquakes in various places.
8   "All these *are* the beginning of sorrows.
9   "Then they will deliver you up to tribulation and kill you, and you will be hated by all nations for My name's sake.

10   "And then many will be offended, will betray one another, and will hate one another.
11   "Then many false prophets will rise up and deceive many.
12   "And because lawlessness will abound, the love of many will grow cold.
13   "But he who endures to the end shall be saved.
14   "And this gospel of the kingdom will be preached in all the world as a witness to all the nations, and then the end will come.

THE GREAT TRIBULATION

15   "Therefore when you see the *'abomination of desolation,'a* spoken of by Daniel the prophet, standing in the holy place" (whoever reads, let him understand),
16   "then let those who are in Judea flee to the mountains.
17   "Let him who is on the housetop not go down to take anything out of his house.
18   "And let him who is in the field not go back to get his clothes.
19   "But woe to those who are pregnant and to those who are nursing babies in those days!
20   "And pray that your flight may not be in winter or on the Sabbath.
21   "For then there will be great tribulation, such as has not been since the beginning of the world until this time, no, nor ever shall be.
22   "And unless those days were shortened, no flesh would be saved; but for the elect's sake those days will be shortened.
23   "Then if anyone says to you, 'Look, here *is* the Christ!' or 'There!' do not believe *it*.
24   "For false christs and false

23:39 *a*Psalm 118:26   24:6 *a*NU-Text omits *all*. 24:7 *a*NU-Text omits *pestilences*.   24:15 *a*Daniel 11:31; 12:11

prophets will rise and show great signs and wonders to deceive, if possible, even the elect.

25 "See, I have told you beforehand.

26 "Therefore if they say to you, 'Look, He is in the desert!' do not go out; or 'Look, *He is* in the inner rooms!' do not believe *it*.

27 "For as the lightning comes from the east and flashes to the west, so also will the coming of the Son of Man be.

28 "For wherever the carcass is, there the eagles will be gathered together.

THE COMING OF THE SON OF MAN

29 "Immediately after the tribulation of those days the sun will be darkened, and the moon will not give its light; the stars will fall from heaven, and the powers of the heavens will be shaken.

30 "Then the sign of the Son of Man will appear in heaven, and then all the tribes of the earth will mourn, and they will see the Son of Man coming on the clouds of heaven with power and great glory.

31 "And He will send His angels with a great sound of a trumpet, and they will gather together His elect from the four winds, from one end of heaven to the other.

THE PARABLE OF THE FIG TREE

32 "Now learn this parable from the fig tree: When its branch has already become tender and puts forth leaves, you know that summer *is* near.

33 "So you also, when you see all these things, know that it*a* is near— at the doors!

34 "Assuredly, I say to you, this generation will by no means pass away till all these things take place.

35 "Heaven and earth will pass away, but My words will by no means pass away.

NO ONE KNOWS THE DAY OR HOUR

36 "But of that day and hour no one knows, not even the angels of heaven,*a* but My Father only.

37 "But as the days of Noah *were,* so also will the coming of the Son of Man be.

38 "For as in the days before the flood, they were eating and drinking, marrying and giving in marriage, until the day that Noah entered the ark,

39 "and did not know until the flood came and took them all away, so also will the coming of the Son of Man be.

40 "Then two *men* will be in the field: one will be taken and the other left.

41 "Two *women will be* grinding at the mill: one will be taken and the other left.

42 "Watch therefore, for you do not know what hour*a* your Lord is coming.

43 "But know this, that if the master of the house had known what hour the thief would come, he would have watched and not allowed his house to be broken into.

44 "Therefore you also be ready, for the Son of Man is coming at an hour you do not expect.

THE FAITHFUL SERVANT AND THE EVIL SERVANT

45 "Who then is a faithful and wise servant, whom his master made ruler over his household, to give them food in due season?

46 "Blessed *is* that servant whom his master, when he comes, will find so doing.

47 "Assuredly, I say to you that he

24:33 *a*Or *He* 　　24:36 *a*NU-Text adds *nor the Son.* 　　24:42 *a*NU-Text reads *day.*

will make him ruler over all his goods.

48 "But if that evil servant says in his heart, 'My master is delaying his coming,'ᵃ

49 "and begins to beat *his* fellow servants, and to eat and drink with the drunkards,

50 "the master of that servant will come on a day when he is not looking for *him* and at an hour that he is not aware of,

51 "and will cut him in two and appoint *him* his portion with the hypocrites. There shall be weeping and gnashing of teeth.

THE PARABLE OF THE WISE AND FOOLISH VIRGINS

25 "Then the kingdom of heaven shall be likened to ten virgins who took their lamps and went out to meet the bridegroom.

2   "Now five of them were wise, and five *were* foolish.

3   "Those who *were* foolish took their lamps and took no oil with them,

4   "but the wise took oil in their vessels with their lamps.

5   "But while the bridegroom was delayed, they all slumbered and slept.

6   "And at midnight a cry was *heard:* 'Behold, the bridegroom is coming;ᵃ go out to meet him!'

7   "Then all those virgins arose and trimmed their lamps.

8   "And the foolish said to the wise, 'Give us *some* of your oil, for our lamps are going out.'

9   "But the wise answered, saying, '*No,* lest there should not be enough for us and you; but go rather to those who sell, and buy for yourselves.'

10 "And while they went to buy, the bridegroom came, and those who were ready went in with him to the wedding; and the door was shut.

11 "Afterward the other virgins came also, saying, 'Lord, Lord, open to us!'

12 "But he answered and said, 'Assuredly, I say to you, I do not know you.'

13 "Watch therefore, for you know neither the day nor the hourᵃ in which the Son of Man is coming.

THE PARABLE OF THE TALENTS

A man was going on a trip. He would be away from home for a while. Who would do a good job of taking care of his things? Why is it important for us to know the answer to that question?

14 "For *the kingdom of heaven is* like a man traveling to a far country, *who* called his own servants and delivered his goods to them.

15 "And to one he gave five talents, to another two, and to another one, to each according to his own ability; and immediately he went on a journey.

16 "Then he who had received the five talents went and traded with them, and made another five talents.

17 "And likewise he who *had received* two gained two more also.

18 "But he who had received one went and dug in the ground, and hid his lord's money.

19 "After a long time the lord of those servants came and settled accounts with them.

20 "So he who had received five talents came and brought five other talents, saying, 'Lord, you delivered to me five talents; look, I have gained five more talents besides them.'

21 "His lord said to him, 'Well *done,* good and faithful servant; you were

---

24:48 ᵃNU-Text omits *his coming.*   25:6 ᵃNU-Text omits *is coming.*   25:13 ᵃNU-Text omits the rest of this verse.

faithful over a few things, I will make you ruler over many things. Enter into the joy of your lord.'

22 "He also who had received two talents came and said, 'Lord, you delivered to me two talents; look, I have gained two more talents besides them.'

23 "His lord said to him, 'Well *done*, good and faithful servant; you have been faithful over a few things, I will make you ruler over many things. Enter into the joy of your lord.'

24 "Then he who had received the one talent came and said, 'Lord, I knew you to be a hard man, reaping where you have not sown, and gathering where you have not scattered seed.

25 'And I was afraid, and went and hid your talent in the ground. Look, *there* you have *what is* yours.'

26 "But his lord answered and said to him, 'You wicked and lazy servant, you knew that I reap where I have not sown, and gather where I have not scattered seed.

27 'So you ought to have deposited my money with the bankers, and at my coming I would have received back my own with interest.

28 'Therefore take the talent from him, and give *it* to him who has ten talents.

29 'For to everyone who has, more will be given, and he will have abundance; but from him who does not have, even what he has will be taken away.

30 'And cast the unprofitable servant into the outer darkness. There will be weeping and gnashing of teeth.'

THE SON OF MAN WILL JUDGE THE NATIONS

31 "When the Son of Man comes in His glory, and all the holy[a] angels

---

☑ *Bible Quiz*

Matthew 25:14–30 **Parable of the Talents**

1. Jesus is trying to show us that the man traveling to a far country is like someone else. Who?
2. Jesus is trying to show us that the servants are like someone else. Who?
3. How many talents did Jesus give the first servant? How many did He give the second servant? The third?
4. What did each servant do with his talents?
5. Can you name some of the talents God has given you? Are you using them or wasting them? Those you waste you lose.
6. In what ways can you better use some of the talents God has given you?

---

with Him, then He will sit on the throne of His glory.

32 "All the nations will be gathered before Him, and He will separate them one from another, as a shepherd divides *his* sheep from the goats.

33 "And He will set the sheep on His right hand, but the goats on the left.

34 "Then the King will say to those on His right hand, 'Come, you blessed of My Father, inherit the kingdom prepared for you from the foundation of the world:

35 'for I was hungry and you gave Me food; I was thirsty and you gave

25:31 [a]NU-Text omits *holy*.

Me drink; I was a stranger and you took Me in;

36 'I *was* naked and you clothed Me; I was sick and you visited Me; I was in prison and you came to Me.'

37 "Then the righteous will answer Him, saying, 'Lord, when did we see You hungry and feed *You,* or thirsty and give *You* drink?

38 'When did we see You a stranger and take *You* in, or naked and clothe *You?*

39 'Or when did we see You sick, or in prison, and come to You?'

40 "And the King will answer and say to them, 'Assuredly, I say to you, inasmuch as you did *it* to one of the least of these My brethren, you did *it* to Me.'

41 "Then He will also say to those on the left hand, 'Depart from Me, you cursed, into the everlasting fire prepared for the devil and his angels:

42 'for I was hungry and you gave Me no food; I was thirsty and you gave Me no drink;

43 'I was a stranger and you did not take Me in, naked and you did not clothe Me, sick and in prison and you did not visit Me.'

44 "Then they also will answer Him,*a* saying, 'Lord, when did we see You hungry or thirsty or a stranger or naked or sick or in prison, and did not minister to You?'

45 "Then He will answer them, saying, 'Assuredly, I say to you, inasmuch as you did not do *it* to one of the least of these, you did not do *it* to Me.'

46 "And these will go away into everlasting punishment, but the righteous into eternal life."

THE PLOT TO KILL JESUS

26 Now it came to pass, when Jesus had finished all these sayings, *that* He said to His disciples,

2 "You know that after two days is the Passover, and the Son of Man will be delivered up to be crucified."

3 Then the chief priests, the scribes,*a* and the elders of the people assembled at the palace of the high priest, who was called Cā′i·a·phas,

4 and plotted to take Jesus by trickery and kill *Him.*

5 But they said, "Not during the feast, lest there be an uproar among the people."

THE ANOINTING AT BETHANY

6 And when Jesus was in Beth′a·ny at the house of Simon the leper,

7 a woman came to Him having an alabaster flask of very costly fragrant oil, and she poured *it* on His head as He sat *at the table.*

8 But when His disciples saw *it,* they were indignant, saying, "Why this waste?

9 "For this fragrant oil might have been sold for much and given to *the* poor."

10 But when Jesus was aware of *it,* He said to them, "Why do you trouble the woman? For she has done a good work for Me.

11 "For you have the poor with you always, but Me you do not have always.

12 "For in pouring this fragrant oil on My body, she did *it* for My burial.

13 "Assuredly, I say to you, wherever this gospel is preached in the whole world, what this woman has done will also be told as a memorial to her."

JUDAS AGREES TO BETRAY JESUS

14 Then one of the twelve, called Judas Is·car′i·ot, went to the chief priests

25:44 *a*NU-Text and M-Text omit *Him.*
26:3 *a*NU-Text omits *the scribes.*

15 and said, "What are you willing to give me if I deliver Him to you?" And they counted out to him thirty pieces of silver.

16 So from that time he sought opportunity to betray Him.

JESUS CELEBRATES PASSOVER WITH HIS DISCIPLES

Jesus is about to eat a meal with His disciples for the last time. But it wasn't food Jesus was interested in. He had some important things He needed to tell the disciples that would forever change their lives.

17 Now on the first *day of the* Feast of Unleavened Bread the disciples came to Jesus, saying to Him, "Where do You want us to prepare for You to eat the Passover?"

18 And He said, "Go into the city to a certain man, and say to him, 'The Teacher says, "My time is at hand; I will keep the Passover at your house with My disciples." ' "

19 So the disciples did as Jesus had directed them; and they prepared the Passover.

20 When evening had come, He sat down with the twelve.

21 Now as they were eating, He said, "Assuredly, I say to you, one of you will betray Me."

22 And they were exceedingly sorrowful, and each of them began to say to Him, "Lord, is it I?"

23 He answered and said, "He who dipped *his* hand with Me in the dish will betray Me.

24 "The Son of Man indeed goes just as it is written of Him, but woe to that man by whom the Son of Man is betrayed! It would have been good for that man if he had not been born."

25 Then Judas, who was betraying Him, answered and said, "Rabbi, is it I?" He said to him, "You have said it."

JESUS INSTITUTES THE LORD'S SUPPER

26 And as they were eating, Jesus took bread, blessed[a] and broke *it,* and gave *it* to the disciples and said, "Take, eat; this is My body."

27 Then He took the cup, and gave thanks, and gave *it* to them, saying, "Drink from it, all of you.

28 "For this is My blood of the new[a] covenant, which is shed for many for the remission of sins.

29 "But I say to you, I will not drink of this fruit of the vine from now on until that day when I drink it new with you in My Father's kingdom."

30 And when they had sung a hymn, they went out to the Mount of Olives.

JESUS PREDICTS PETER'S DENIAL

31 Then Jesus said to them, "All of you will be made to stumble because of Me this night, for it is written:

   '*I will strike the Shepherd,*
   And the sheep of the flock will be
     scattered.'[a]

32 "But after I have been raised, I will go before you to Galilee."

33 Peter answered and said to Him, "Even if all are made to stumble because of You, I will never be made to stumble."

34 Jesus said to him, "Assuredly, I say to you that this night, before the rooster crows, you will deny Me three times."

35 Peter said to Him, "Even if I have to die with You, I will not deny You!" And so said all the disciples.

26:26 [a]M-Text reads *gave thanks for.*
26:28 [a]NU-Text omits *new.*   26:31 [a]Zechariah 13:7

☑ *Bible Quiz*

Matthew 26:17–35 **The Last Supper**

1. What did Jesus say that someone would do to Him? Who was the one who would betray Jesus?
2. Why do you think each of the disciples asked if he was the one who would betray Jesus? Do you ever wonder if something could cause you to turn against Jesus? How can you stay close to Jesus so this won't happen?
3. When Jesus held the bread, what did He say it was? What did He say was in the cup?
4. What did Jesus and the disciples do just before they left for the Mount of Olives?
5. What did Jesus tell Peter he would do? Did Peter think he could ever deny he knew Jesus? If one of your friends, who is not a Christian, asked if you were a Christian, what would you say?

THE PRAYER IN THE GARDEN

36 Then Jesus came with them to a place called Geth·sem′a·nē, and said to the disciples, "Sit here while I go and pray over there."
37 And He took with Him Peter and the two sons of Zeb′e·dee, and He began to be sorrowful and deeply distressed.
38 Then He said to them, "My soul is exceedingly sorrowful, even to death. Stay here and watch with Me."

39 He went a little farther and fell on His face, and prayed, saying, "O My Father, if it is possible, let this cup pass from Me; nevertheless, not as I will, but as You *will*."
40 Then He came to the disciples and found them sleeping, and said to Peter, "What? Could you not watch with Me one hour?
41 "Watch and pray, lest you enter into temptation. The spirit indeed *is* willing, but the flesh *is* weak."
42 Again, a second time, He went away and prayed, saying, "O My Father, if this cup cannot pass away from Me unless*a* I drink it, Your will be done."
43 And He came and found them asleep again, for their eyes were heavy.
44 So He left them, went away again, and prayed the third time, saying the same words.
45 Then He came to His disciples and said to them, "Are *you* still sleeping and resting? Behold, the hour is at hand, and the Son of Man is being betrayed into the hands of sinners.
46 "Rise, let us be going. See, My betrayer is at hand."
■ *see Mark 14:32–42*

BETRAYAL AND ARREST IN GETHSEMANE

When Jesus finished praying in the garden He looked up and saw a large mob of people coming toward Him. He knew what they were going to do, but the disciples didn't. "What's going on?" they must have wondered.

47 And while He was still speaking, behold, Judas, one of the twelve, with

26:42 *a*NU-Text reads *if this may not pass away unless.*

a great multitude with swords and clubs, came from the chief priests and elders of the people.

48 Now His betrayer had given them a sign, saying, "Whomever I kiss, He is the One; seize Him."

49 Immediately he went up to Jesus and said, "Greetings, Rabbi!" and kissed Him.

50 But Jesus said to him, "Friend, why have you come?" Then they came and laid hands on Jesus and took Him.

51 And suddenly, one of those *who were* with Jesus stretched out *his* hand and drew his sword, struck the servant of the high priest, and cut off his ear.

52 But Jesus said to him, "Put your sword in its place, for all who take the sword will perish*a* by the sword.

53 "Or do you think that I cannot now pray to My Father, and He will provide Me with more than twelve legions of angels?

54 "How then could the Scriptures be fulfilled, that it must happen thus?"

55 In that hour Jesus said to the multitudes, "Have you come out, as against a robber, with swords and clubs to take Me? I sat daily with you, teaching in the temple, and you did not seize Me.

56 "But all this was done that the Scriptures of the prophets might be fulfilled." Then all the disciples forsook Him and fled.

JESUS FACES THE SANHEDRIN

57 And those who had laid hold of Jesus led *Him* away to Cā′i·a·phas the high priest, where the scribes and the elders were assembled.

58 But Peter followed Him at a distance to the high priest's courtyard. And he went in and sat with the servants to see the end.

59 Now the chief priests, the elders,*a* and all the council sought false testimony against Jesus to put Him to death,

60 but found none. Even though many false witnesses came forward, they found none.*a* But at last two false witnesses*b* came forward

61 and said, "This *fellow* said, 'I am able to destroy the temple of God and to build it in three days.' "

62 And the high priest arose and said to Him, "Do You answer nothing? What *is it* these men testify against You?"

63 But Jesus kept silent. And the high priest answered and said to Him, "I put You under oath by the living God: Tell us if You are the Christ, the Son of God!"

64 Jesus said to him, "*It is as you*

☑ *Bible Quiz*

Matthew 26:47–56 **Judas Betrays Jesus**

1. Was the mob large or small? Was it friendly or unfriendly? Why do you think Judas brought along such a large, well-armed mob of people?

2. How did Judas let the others know who Jesus was?

3. What did one of the disciples do to help? What did Jesus say to him? Why didn't Jesus need help?

4. What did the disciples do then? What would you have done?

26:52 *a*M-Text reads *die.*   26:59 *a*NU-Text omits *the elders.*   26:60 *a*NU-Text puts a comma after *but found none,* does not capitalize *Even,* and omits *they found none.*   *b*NU-Text omits *false witnesses.*

said. Nevertheless, I say to you, hereafter you will see the Son of Man sitting at the right hand of the Power, and coming on the clouds of heaven."

65 Then the high priest tore his clothes, saying, "He has spoken blasphemy! What further need do we have of witnesses? Look, now you have heard His blasphemy!

66 "What do you think?" They answered and said, "He is deserving of death."

67 Then they spat in His face and beat Him; and others struck *Him* with the palms of their hands,

68 saying, "Prophesy to us, Christ! Who is the one who struck You?"

PETER DENIES JESUS, AND WEEPS BITTERLY

69 Now Peter sat outside in the courtyard. And a servant girl came to him, saying, "You also were with Jesus of Galilee."

70 But he denied it before *them* all, saying, "I do not know what you are saying."

71 And when he had gone out to the gateway, another *girl* saw him and said to those *who were* there, "This *fellow* also was with Jesus of Nazareth."

72 But again he denied with an oath, "I do not know the Man!"

73 And a little later those who stood by came up and said to Peter, "Surely you also are *one* of them, for your speech betrays you."

74 Then he began to curse and swear, *saying,* "I do not know the Man!" Immediately a rooster crowed.

75 And Peter remembered the word of Jesus who had said to him, "Before the rooster crows, you will deny Me three times." So he went out and wept bitterly.

■ *see Luke 22:54–62*

JESUS HANDED OVER TO PONTIUS PILATE

27 When morning came, all the chief priests and elders of the people plotted against Jesus to put Him to death.

2 And when they had bound Him, they led Him away and delivered Him to Pon′ti·us[a] Pilate the governor.

JUDAS HANGS HIMSELF

3 Then Judas, His betrayer, seeing that He had been condemned, was remorseful and brought back the thirty pieces of silver to the chief priests and elders,

4 saying, "I have sinned by betraying innocent blood." And they said, "What *is that* to us? You see *to it!*"

5 Then he threw down the pieces of silver in the temple and departed, and went and hanged himself.

6 But the chief priests took the silver pieces and said, "It is not lawful to put them into the treasury, because they are the price of blood."

7 And they consulted together and bought with them the potter's field, to bury strangers in.

8 Therefore that field has been called the Field of Blood to this day.

9 Then was fulfilled what was spoken by Jer·e·mī′ah the prophet, saying, *"And they took the thirty pieces of silver, the value of Him who was priced,* whom they of the children of Israel priced,

10 *"and gave them for the potter's field, as the* LORD *directed me."*[a]

JESUS FACES PILATE

11 Now Jesus stood before the governor. And the governor asked Him, saying, "Are You the King of the

27:2 [a]NU-Text omits *Pontius.*   27:10 [a]Jeremiah 32:6–9

Jews?" Jesus said to him, "*It is as* you say."

12 And while He was being accused by the chief priests and elders, He answered nothing.

13 Then Pilate said to Him, "Do You not hear how many things they testify against You?"

14 But He answered him not one word, so that the governor marveled greatly.

TAKING THE PLACE OF BARABBAS

15 Now at the feast the governor was accustomed to releasing to the multitude one prisoner whom they wished.

16 And at that time they had a notorious prisoner called Ba·rab′bas.*a*

17 Therefore, when they had gathered together, Pilate said to them, "Whom do you want me to release to you? Ba·rab′bas, or Jesus who is called Christ?"

18 For he knew that they had handed Him over because of envy.

19 While he was sitting on the judgment seat, his wife sent to him, saying, "Have nothing to do with that just Man, for I have suffered many things today in a dream because of Him."

20 But the chief priests and elders persuaded the multitudes that they should ask for Ba·rab′bas and destroy Jesus.

21 The governor answered and said to them, "Which of the two do you want me to release to you?" They said, "Ba·rab′bas!"

22 Pilate said to them, "What then shall I do with Jesus who is called Christ?" *They* all said to him, "Let Him be crucified!"

23 Then the governor said, "Why, what evil has He done?" But they cried out all the more, saying, "Let Him be crucified!"

24 When Pilate saw that he could not prevail at all, but rather *that* a tumult was rising, he took water and washed *his* hands before the multitude, saying, "I am innocent of the blood of this just Person.*a* You see *to it.*"

25 And all the people answered and said, "His blood *be* on us and on our children."

26 Then he released Ba·rab′bas to them; and when he had scourged Jesus, he delivered *Him* to be crucified.

THE SOLDIERS MOCK JESUS

27 Then the soldiers of the governor took Jesus into the Prae·tō′ri·um and gathered the whole garrison around Him.

28 And they stripped Him and put a scarlet robe on Him.

29 When they had twisted a crown of thorns, they put *it* on His head, and a reed in His right hand. And they bowed the knee before Him and mocked Him, saying, "Hail, King of the Jews!"

30 Then they spat on Him, and took the reed and struck Him on the head.

31 And when they had mocked Him, they took the robe off Him, put His *own* clothes on Him, and led Him away to be crucified.

THE KING ON A CROSS

32 Now as they came out, they found a man of Cȳ·rē′nē, Simon by name. Him they compelled to bear His cross.

33 And when they had come to a place called Gol′go·tha, that is to say, Place of a Skull,

34 they gave Him sour*a* wine mingled with gall to drink. But when He had tasted *it*, He would not drink.

27:16 *a*NU-Text reads *Jesus Barabbas.*
27:24 *a*NU-Text omits *just.*   27:34 *a*NU-Text omits *sour.*

35 Then they crucified Him, and divided His garments, casting lots,*a* that it might be fulfilled which was spoken by the prophet:

"They divided My garments among them,
And for My clothing they cast lots."*b*

36 Sitting down, they kept watch over Him there.
37 And they put up over His head the accusation written against Him:

THIS IS JESUS THE KING OF THE JEWS.

38 Then two robbers were crucified with Him, one on the right and another on the left.
39 And those who passed by blasphemed Him, wagging their heads
40 and saying, "You who destroy the temple and build *it* in three days, save Yourself! If You are the Son of God, come down from the cross."
41 Likewise the chief priests also, mocking with the scribes and elders,*a* said,
42 "He saved others; Himself He cannot save. If He is the King of Israel,*a* let Him now come down from the cross, and we will believe Him.*b*
43 "He trusted in God; let Him deliver Him now if He will have Him; for He said, 'I am the Son of God.' "
44 Even the robbers who were crucified with Him reviled Him with the same thing.

Jesus Dies on the Cross

45 Now from the sixth hour until the ninth hour there was darkness over all the land.
46 And about the ninth hour Jesus cried out with a loud voice, saying, "Ē′li, Ē′li, la·ma′ sa·bach′tha·nī?" that is, *"My God, My God, why have You forsaken Me?"*a*

47 Some of those who stood there, when they heard *that,* said, "This Man is calling for E·li′jah!"
48 Immediately one of them ran and took a sponge, filled *it* with sour wine and put *it* on a reed, and offered it to Him to drink.
49 The rest said, "Let Him alone; let us see if E·li′jah will come to save Him."
50 And Jesus cried out again with a loud voice, and yielded up His spirit.
51 Then, behold, the veil of the temple was torn in two from top to bottom; and the earth quaked, and the rocks were split,
52 and the graves were opened; and many bodies of the saints who had fallen asleep were raised;
53 and coming out of the graves after His resurrection, they went into the holy city and appeared to many.
54 So when the centurion and those with him, who were guarding Jesus, saw the earthquake and the things that had happened, they feared greatly, saying, "Truly this was the Son of God!"
55 And many women who followed Jesus from Galilee, ministering to Him, were there looking on from afar,
56 among whom were Mary Mag′da·lēne, Mary the mother of James and Jō′ses,*a* and the mother of Zeb′e·dee's sons.

Jesus Buried in Joseph's Tomb

57 Now when evening had come, there came a rich man from Ar·i·ma·thē′a, named Joseph, who himself had also become a disciple of Jesus.
58 This man went to Pilate and

27:35 *a*NU-Text and M-Text omit the rest of this verse. *b*Psalm 22:18 27:41 *a*M-Text reads *with the scribes, the Pharisees, and the elders.* 27:42 *a*NU-Text reads *He is the King of Israel!* *b*NU-Text and M-Text read *we will believe in Him.* 27:46 *a*Psalm 22:1 27:56 *a*NU-Text reads *Joseph.*

asked for the body of Jesus. Then Pilate commanded the body to be given to him.

59 When Joseph had taken the body, he wrapped it in a clean linen cloth,

60 and laid it in his new tomb which he had hewn out of the rock; and he rolled a large stone against the door of the tomb, and departed.

61 And Mary Mag'da·lēne was there, and the other Mary, sitting opposite the tomb.

■ *see Mark 15*

PILATE SETS A GUARD

62 On the next day, which followed the Day of Preparation, the chief priests and Phar'i·sees gathered together to Pilate,

63 saying, "Sir, we remember, while He was still alive, how that deceiver said, 'After three days I will rise.'

64 "Therefore command that the tomb be made secure until the third day, lest His disciples come by night*a* and steal Him *away,* and say to the people, 'He has risen from the dead.' So the last deception will be worse than the first."

65 Pilate said to them, "You have a guard; go your way, make *it* as secure as you know how."

66 So they went and made the tomb secure, sealing the stone and setting the guard.

HE IS RISEN

Early in the morning, three days after Jesus died, some women came to Jesus' tomb to remember Him. What they saw would change the world forever.

28 Now after the Sabbath, as the first *day* of the week began to dawn, Mary Mag'da·lēne and the other Mary came to see the tomb.

2 And behold, there was a great earthquake; for an angel of the Lord descended from heaven, and came and rolled back the stone from the door,*a* and sat on it.

3 His countenance was like lightning, and his clothing as white as snow.

4 And the guards shook for fear of him, and became like dead *men.*

5 But the angel answered and said to the women, "Do not be afraid, for I know that you seek Jesus who was crucified.

6 "He is not here; for He is risen, as He said. Come, see the place where the Lord lay.

7 "And go quickly and tell His disciples that He is risen from the dead, and indeed He is going before you into Galilee; there you will see Him. Behold, I have told you."

8 So they went out quickly from the tomb with fear and great joy, and ran to bring His disciples word.

THE WOMEN WORSHIP THE RISEN LORD

9 And as they went to tell His disciples,*a* behold, Jesus met them, saying, "Rejoice!" So they came and held Him by the feet and worshiped Him.

10 Then Jesus said to them, "Do not be afraid. Go *and* tell My brethren to go to Galilee, and there they will see Me."

THE SOLDIERS ARE BRIBED

11 Now while they were going, behold, some of the guard came into the city and reported to the chief priests all the things that had happened.

12 When they had assembled with

27:64 *a*NU-Text omits *by night.* 28:2 *a*NU-Text omits *from the door.* 28:9 *a*NU-Text omits the first clause of this verse.

Favorite Bible Words

WITH Matthew 28:19, 20

Is Someone With You Right Now?

It's a dark night and you must walk home alone. "I will walk with you," says a friend. Does that make a difference? It's the middle of the night and a big storm comes with lightning and thunder. "I am with you," mother or father whispers as they slip into your room. Does that make a difference? You wonder how you will feel when you move to a new town, or start at a new school, or think about getting married someday. "I will be with you," the Lord says. Does that make a difference?

1. Who do you want with you when you are lonely or afraid? Your parents? Jesus?
2. Who do you want with you when you're going to a new place? Your parents? Jesus?
3. Who do you want with you today and tomorrow and the next day? Your parents? Jesus?
4. Read Matthew 28:20. Who is with you forever? Thank You, Jesus.

For more on *Favorite Bible Words* turn to page 1548
For more on *God's Guidance* turn to page 1749

Bible Quiz ✓

Matthew 28:1–20 **A Visit to Jesus' Tomb**

1. Can you name the two women who went to Jesus' tomb? What day was it?
2. Tell three things that happened as the women arrived at the tomb.
3. Describe what the angel looked like. What did he tell the women?
4. What two feelings did the women have as they ran to tell the disciples what had happened? Why do you think they felt both ways? Who met them along the road to help them with their fears?
5. What lies did the soldiers tell?
6. When Jesus met His disciples on a mountain, what did He tell them to do? The best news the world has ever known is that Jesus is risen from the dead! Why is this news so wonderful?

the elders and consulted together, they gave a large sum of money to the soldiers,

13 saying, "Tell them, 'His disciples came at night and stole Him *away* while we slept.'

14 "And if this comes to the governor's ears, we will appease him and make you secure."

15 So they took the money and did as they were instructed; and this saying is commonly reported among the Jews until this day.

THE GREAT COMMISSION

16 Then the eleven disciples went away into Galilee, to the mountain which Jesus had appointed for them.

17 When they saw Him, they worshiped Him; but some doubted.

18 And Jesus came and spoke to them, saying, "All authority has been given to Me in heaven and on earth.

19 "Go therefore*a* and make disciples of all the nations, baptizing them in the name of the Father and of the Son and of the Holy Spirit,

20 "teaching them to observe all things that I have commanded you; and lo, I am with you always, *even* to the end of the age." Amen.*a*

28:19 *a*M-Text omits *therefore*.   28:20 *a*NU-Text omits *Amen*.

The Gospel According to
MARK

John the Baptist Prepares the Way

THE beginning of the gospel of Jesus Christ, the Son of God.
2 As it is written in the Prophets:*a*

"Behold, I send My messenger
before Your face,
Who will prepare Your way before
You."*b*
3 "The voice of one crying in the
wilderness:
'Prepare the way of the LORD;
Make His paths straight.' "*a*

4 John came baptizing in the wilderness and preaching a baptism of repentance for the remission of sins.
5 Then all the land of Judea, and those from Jerusalem, went out to him and were all baptized by him in the Jordan River, confessing their sins.
6 Now John was clothed with camel's hair and with a leather belt around his waist, and he ate locusts and wild honey.
7 And he preached, saying, "There comes One after me who is mightier than I, whose sandal strap I am not worthy to stoop down and loose.
8 "I indeed baptized you with water, but He will baptize you with the Holy Spirit."

John Baptizes Jesus

9 It came to pass in those days *that* Jesus came from Nazareth of Galilee, and was baptized by John in the Jordan.
10 And immediately, coming up from*a* the water, He saw the heavens parting and the Spirit descending upon Him like a dove.
11 Then a voice came from heaven, "You are My beloved Son, in whom I am well pleased."
■ *see Matthew 3:1–17*

Satan Tempts Jesus

12 Immediately the Spirit drove Him into the wilderness.
13 And He was there in the wilderness forty days, tempted by Satan, and was with the wild beasts; and the angels ministered to Him.
■ *see Matthew 4:1–11*

Jesus Begins His Galilean Ministry

14 Now after John was put in prison, Jesus came to Galilee, preaching the gospel of the kingdom*a* of God,
15 and saying, "The time is fulfilled, and the kingdom of God is at hand. Repent, and believe in the gospel."

Four Fishermen Called as Disciples

*By the shore of the Sea of
Galilee, Jesus saw four men.
He called out to them to follow
Him and be His disciples.
Would they do it?*

16 And as He walked by the Sea of Galilee, He saw Simon and Andrew his brother casting a net into the sea; for they were fishermen.
17 Then Jesus said to them, "Follow

1:2 *a*NU-Text reads *Isaiah the prophet.* *b*Malachi 3:1   1:3 *a*Isaiah 40:3   1:10 *a*NU-Text reads *out of.*   1:14 *a*NU-Text omits *of the kingdom.*

Me, and I will make you become fishers of men."

18 They immediately left their nets and followed Him.

19 When He had gone a little farther from there, He saw James the *son* of Zeb′e·dee, and John his brother, who also *were* in the boat mending their nets.

20 And immediately He called them, and they left their father Zeb′e·dee in the boat with the hired servants, and went after Him.

☑️ *Bible Quiz*

Mark 1:16–20 **Four Men Follow Jesus**

1. Where was Jesus when He saw the four men?
2. What did the men do for a living? What kind of fishermen did Jesus want them to become?
3. What did the men do?
4. Have you decided to follow Jesus? If you had to give up everything to follow Him, would you do it?

JESUS CASTS OUT AN UNCLEAN SPIRIT

21 Then they went into Ca·per′-na·um, and immediately on the Sabbath He entered the synagogue and taught.

22 And they were astonished at His teaching, for He taught them as one having authority, and not as the scribes.

23 Now there was a man in their synagogue with an unclean spirit. And he cried out,

24 saying, "Let *us* alone! What have we to do with You, Jesus of Nazareth? Did You come to destroy us? I know who You are—the Holy One of God!"

25 But Jesus rebuked him, saying, "Be quiet, and come out of him!"

26 And when the unclean spirit had convulsed him and cried out with a loud voice, he came out of him.

27 Then they were all amazed, so that they questioned among themselves, saying, "What is this? What new doctrine *is* this? For with authority[a] He commands even the unclean spirits, and they obey Him."

28 And immediately His fame spread throughout all the region around Galilee.

PETER'S MOTHER-IN-LAW HEALED

29 Now as soon as they had come out of the synagogue, they entered the house of Simon and Andrew, with James and John.

30 But Simon's wife's mother lay sick with a fever, and they told Him about her at once.

31 So He came and took her by the hand and lifted her up, and immediately the fever left her. And she served them.

MANY HEALED AFTER SABBATH SUNSET

32 At evening, when the sun had set, they brought to Him all who were sick and those who were demon-possessed.

33 And the whole city was gathered together at the door.

34 Then He healed many who were sick with various diseases, and cast out many demons; and He did not

1:27 [a]NU-Text reads *What is this? A new doctrine with authority.*

allow the demons to speak, because they knew Him.

PREACHING IN GALILEE

35 Now in the morning, having risen a long while before daylight, He went out and departed to a solitary place; and there He prayed.
36 And Simon and those *who were* with Him searched for Him.
37 When they found Him, they said to Him, "Everyone is looking for You."
38 But He said to them, "Let us go into the next towns, that I may preach there also, because for this purpose I have come forth."
39 And He was preaching in their synagogues throughout all Galilee, and casting out demons.

JESUS CLEANSES A LEPER

40 Now a leper came to Him, imploring Him, kneeling down to Him and saying to Him, "If You are willing, You can make me clean."
41 Then Jesus, moved with compassion, stretched out *His* hand and touched him, and said to him, "I am willing; be cleansed."
42 As soon as He had spoken, immediately the leprosy left him, and he was cleansed.
43 And He strictly warned him and sent him away at once,
44 and said to him, "See that you say nothing to anyone; but go your way, show yourself to the priest, and offer for your cleansing those things which Moses commanded, as a testimony to them."
45 However, he went out and began to proclaim *it* freely, and to spread the matter, so that Jesus could no longer openly enter the city, but was outside in deserted places; and they came to Him from every direction.

JESUS FORGIVES AND HEALS A PARALYTIC

Four friends had to see Jesus. They knew that only He could help. But how could they get to Jesus? There were so many people around Him. Suddenly they got an idea that was sure to work!

2 And again He entered Ca·per'-na·um after *some* days, and it was heard that He was in the house.
2 Immediately[a] many gathered together, so that there was no longer room to receive *them,* not even near the door. And He preached the word to them.
3 Then they came to Him, bringing a paralytic who was carried by four *men.*
4 And when they could not come near Him because of the crowd, they uncovered the roof where He was. So when they had broken through, they let down the bed on which the paralytic was lying.
5 When Jesus saw their faith, He said to the paralytic, "Son, your sins are forgiven you."
6 And some of the scribes were sitting there and reasoning in their hearts,
7 "Why does this *Man* speak blasphemies like this? Who can forgive sins but God alone?"
8 But immediately, when Jesus perceived in His spirit that they reasoned thus within themselves, He said to them, "Why do you reason about these things in your hearts?
9 "Which is easier, to say to the paralytic, 'Your sins are forgiven you,' or to say, 'Arise, take up your bed and walk'?
10 "But that you may know that the

2:2 [a]NU-Text omits *Immediately.*

Son of Man has power on earth to forgive sins"—He said to the paralytic,

11 "I say to you, arise, take up your bed, and go to your house."

12 Immediately he arose, took up the bed, and went out in the presence of them all, so that all were amazed and glorified God, saying, "We never saw *anything* like this!"

✓ *Bible Quiz*

Mark 2:1–12 **Through the Roof to See Jesus**

1. What city was Jesus in? What happened when people found out He was there?
2. Why did the four men need to see Jesus?
3. How did they finally get their paralyzed friend to Jesus? How did Jesus help?
4. What do you think the paralyzed man said to his friends who helped him see Jesus? How much did these men care for their friend?
5. Do you have friends who need help? Do you have friends who need to find Jesus? How can you help them?

MATTHEW THE TAX COLLECTOR

13 Then He went out again by the sea; and all the multitude came to Him, and He taught them.

14 As He passed by, He saw Levi the *son* of Al·phaē′us sitting at the tax office. And He said to him, "Follow Me." So he arose and followed Him.

15 Now it happened, as He was dining in *Levi's* house, that many tax collectors and sinners also sat together with Jesus and His disciples; for there were many, and they followed Him.

16 And when the scribes and*a* Phar′i·sees saw Him eating with the tax collectors and sinners, they said to His disciples, "How *is it* that He eats and drinks with tax collectors and sinners?"

17 When Jesus heard *it,* He said to them, "Those who are well have no need of a physician, but those who are sick. I did not come to call *the* righteous, but sinners, to repentance."*a*

JESUS IS QUESTIONED ABOUT FASTING

18 The disciples of John and of the Phar′i·sees were fasting. Then they came and said to Him, "Why do the disciples of John and of the Phar′i·sees fast, but Your disciples do not fast?"

19 And Jesus said to them, "Can the friends of the bridegroom fast while the bridegroom is with them? As long as they have the bridegroom with them they cannot fast.

20 "But the days will come when the bridegroom will be taken away from them, and then they will fast in those days.

21 "No one sews a piece of unshrunk cloth on an old garment; or else the new piece pulls away from the old, and the tear is made worse.

22 "And no one puts new wine into old wineskins; or else the new wine bursts the wineskins, the wine is spilled, and the wineskins are ruined. But new wine must be put into new wineskins."

2:16 *a*NU-Text reads *of the.*   2:17 *a*NU-Text omits *to repentance.*

Jesus Is Lord of the Sabbath

23 Now it happened that He went through the grainfields on the Sabbath; and as they went His disciples began to pluck the heads of grain.
24 And the Phar′i·sees said to Him, "Look, why do they do what is not lawful on the Sabbath?"
25 But He said to them, "Have you never read what David did when he was in need and hungry, he and those with him:
26 "how he went into the house of God *in the days* of A·bī′a·thar the high priest, and ate the showbread, which is not lawful to eat except for the priests, and also gave some to those who were with him?"
27 And He said to them, "The Sabbath was made for man, and not man for the Sabbath.
28 "Therefore the Son of Man is also Lord of the Sabbath."

Healing on the Sabbath

3 And He entered the synagogue again, and a man was there who had a withered hand.
2 So they watched Him closely, whether He would heal him on the Sabbath, so that they might accuse Him.
3 And He said to the man who had the withered hand, "Step forward."
4 Then He said to them, "Is it lawful on the Sabbath to do good or to do evil, to save life or to kill?" But they kept silent.
5 And when He had looked around at them with anger, being grieved by the hardness of their hearts, He said to the man, "Stretch out your hand." And he stretched *it* out, and his hand was restored as whole as the other.*a*
6 Then the Phar′i·sees went out and immediately plotted with the He·rō′di·ans against Him, how they might destroy Him.

A Great Multitude Follows Jesus

7 But Jesus withdrew with His disciples to the sea. And a great multitude from Galilee followed Him, and from Judea
8 and Jerusalem and Id·ū·mē′a and beyond the Jordan; and those from Tyre and Sī′don, a great multitude, when they heard how many things He was doing, came to Him.
9 So He told His disciples that a small boat should be kept ready for Him because of the multitude, lest they should crush Him.
10 For He healed many, so that as many as had afflictions pressed about Him to touch Him.
11 And the unclean spirits, whenever they saw Him, fell down before Him and cried out, saying, "You are the Son of God."
12 But He sternly warned them that they should not make Him known.

The Twelve Apostles

Jesus needed people who would help Him do His work. He chose twelve special helpers who would follow Him. They were called disciples. Here are their names.

13 And He went up on the mountain and called to *Him* those He Himself wanted. And they came to Him.
14 Then He appointed twelve,*a* that they might be with Him and that He might send them out to preach,
15 and to have power to heal sicknesses and*a* to cast out demons:

3:5 *a*NU-Text omits *as whole as the other.*
3:14 *a*NU-Text adds *whom He also named apostles.*
3:15 *a*NU-Text omits *to heal sicknesses and.*

ABOUT GOD'S HEALING Mark 3:10

Who *Really* Heals You?

God has given you a wonderful body. When you cut it, He helps it heal. A doctor may help you know how to take care of your body. A doctor may give you some medicine to help you heal, but God is the Great Healer, the One who truly helps you get well. Thank You, God. I praise You for that.

1. When was the last time you were hurt? What happened? Did your body heal? Did you do it? Did God do it?
2. When was the last time you were sick? What happened? Some sick people don't get well, of course. We don't quite understand that, but we know that God knows what is best. But did you get well? If you got well, did you do it all by yourself? Did God do it?
3. Praise God for His gift of healing.

For more on *What the Bible Says* turn to page 1618
For more on *Healing* turn to page 1731

16 Simon,^{a} to whom He gave the name Peter;
17 James the *son* of Zeb′e·dee and John the brother of James, to whom He gave the name Bō·a·ner′gēs, that is, "Sons of Thunder";
18 Andrew, Philip, Bartholomew, Matthew, Thomas, James the *son* of Al·phaē′us, Thad·daē′us, Simon the Can′a·nīte;
19 and Judas Is·car′i·ot, who also betrayed Him. And they went into a house.

A HOUSE DIVIDED CANNOT STAND

20 Then the multitude came together again, so that they could not so much as eat bread.
21 But when His own people heard *about this,* they went out to lay hold of Him, for they said, "He is out of His mind."
22 And the scribes who came down from Jerusalem said, "He has Bē·el′-

Mark 3:13–19 **Jesus Chooses Twelve Disciples**

1. Can you name four of the disciples? Can you memorize all twelve names?
2. How would these disciples help Jesus?
3. What kinds of things can you do to help Jesus? Will you decide to follow Him all your life?
4. Which disciple would betray Jesus to His enemies? Would you like to be known for betraying Jesus?

3:16 ^{a}NU-Text reads *and He appointed the twelve: Simon . . . .*

ze·bub," and, "By the ruler of the demons He casts out demons."

23 So He called them to *Himself* and said to them in parables: "How can Satan cast out Satan?

24 "If a kingdom is divided against itself, that kingdom cannot stand.

25 "And if a house is divided against itself, that house cannot stand.

26 "And if Satan has risen up against himself, and is divided, he cannot stand, but has an end.

27 "No one can enter a strong man's house and plunder his goods, unless he first binds the strong man. And then he will plunder his house.

THE UNPARDONABLE SIN

28 "Assuredly, I say to you, all sins will be forgiven the sons of men, and whatever blasphemies they may utter;

29 "but he who blasphemes against the Holy Spirit never has forgiveness, but is subject to eternal condemnation"—

30 because they said, "He has an unclean spirit."

JESUS' MOTHER AND BROTHERS SEND FOR HIM

31 Then His brothers and His mother came, and standing outside they sent to Him, calling Him.

32 And a multitude was sitting around Him; and they said to Him, "Look, Your mother and Your brothers*a* are outside seeking You."

33 But He answered them, saying, "Who is My mother, or My brothers?"

34 And He looked around in a circle at those who sat about Him, and said, "Here are My mother and My brothers!

35 "For whoever does the will of God is My brother and My sister and mother."

THE PARABLE OF THE SOWER

4 And again He began to teach by the sea. And a great multitude was gathered to Him, so that He got into a boat and sat *in it* on the sea; and the whole multitude was on the land facing the sea.

2 Then He taught them many things by parables, and said to them in His teaching:

3 "Listen! Behold, a sower went out to sow.

4 "And it happened, as he sowed, *that* some *seed* fell by the wayside; and the birds of the air*a* came and devoured it.

5 "Some fell on stony ground, where it did not have much earth; and immediately it sprang up because it had no depth of earth.

6 "But when the sun was up it was scorched, and because it had no root it withered away.

7 "And some *seed* fell among thorns; and the thorns grew up and choked it, and it yielded no crop.

8 "But other *seed* fell on good ground and yielded a crop that sprang up, increased and produced: some thirtyfold, some sixty, and some a hundred."

9 And He said to them,*a* "He who has ears to hear, let him hear!"

THE PURPOSE OF PARABLES

10 But when He was alone, those around Him with the twelve asked Him about the parable.

11 And He said to them, "To you it has been given to know the mystery of the kingdom of God; but to those who are outside, all things come in parables,

3:32 *a*NU-Text and M-Text add *and Your sisters.*
4:4 *a*NU-Text and M-Text omit *of the air.*
4:9 *a*NU-Text and M-Text omit *to them.*

12 "so that

'Seeing they may see and not
   perceive,
And hearing they may hear and
   not understand;
Lest they should turn,
And their sins be forgiven
   them.' "a

THE PARABLE OF THE SOWER EXPLAINED

13 And He said to them, "Do you not understand this parable? How then will you understand all the parables?
14 "The sower sows the word.
15 "And these are the ones by the wayside where the word is sown. When they hear, Satan comes immediately and takes away the word that was sown in their hearts.
16 "These likewise are the ones sown on stony ground who, when they hear the word, immediately receive it with gladness;
17 "and they have no root in themselves, and so endure only for a time. Afterward, when tribulation or persecution arises for the word's sake, immediately they stumble.
18 "Now these are the ones sown among thorns; *they are* the ones who hear the word,
19 "and the cares of this world, the deceitfulness of riches, and the desires for other things entering in choke the word, and it becomes unfruitful.
20 "But these are the ones sown on good ground, those who hear the word, accept *it,* and bear fruit: some thirtyfold, some sixty, and some a hundred."
■ *see Matthew 13:1–9, 18–23*

LIGHT UNDER A BASKET

21 Also He said to them, "Is a lamp brought to be put under a basket or under a bed? Is it not to be set on a lampstand?
22 "For there is nothing hidden which will not be revealed, nor has anything been kept secret but that it should come to light.
23 "If anyone has ears to hear, let him hear."
24 Then He said to them, "Take heed what you hear. With the same measure you use, it will be measured to you; and to you who hear, more will be given.
25 "For whoever has, to him more will be given; but whoever does not have, even what he has will be taken away from him."

THE PARABLE OF THE GROWING SEED

26 And He said, "The kingdom of God is as if a man should scatter seed on the ground,
27 "and should sleep by night and rise by day, and the seed should sprout and grow, he himself does not know how.
28 "For the earth yields crops by itself: first the blade, then the head, after that the full grain in the head.
29 "But when the grain ripens, immediately he puts in the sickle, because the harvest has come."

THE PARABLE OF THE MUSTARD SEED

30 Then He said, "To what shall we liken the kingdom of God? Or with what parable shall we picture it?
31 "*It is* like a mustard seed which, when it is sown on the ground, is smaller than all the seeds on earth;
32 "but when it is sown, it grows up

4:12 aIsaiah 6:9, 10

and becomes greater than all herbs, and shoots out large branches, so that the birds of the air may nest under its shade."

JESUS' USE OF PARABLES

33 And with many such parables He spoke the word to them as they were able to hear *it.*
34 But without a parable He did not speak to them. And when they were alone, He explained all things to His disciples.

WIND AND WAVE OBEY JESUS

The disciples had never been more afraid. They thought they were going to die. But why should they be afraid? Jesus was with them!

---

35 On the same day, when evening had come, He said to them, "Let us cross over to the other side."
36 Now when they had left the multitude, they took Him along in the boat as He was. And other little boats were also with Him.
37 And a great windstorm arose, and the waves beat into the boat, so that it was already filling.
38 But He was in the stern, asleep on a pillow. And they awoke Him and said to Him, "Teacher, do You not care that we are perishing?"
39 Then He arose and rebuked the wind, and said to the sea, "Peace, be still!" And the wind ceased and there was a great calm.
40 But He said to them, "Why are you so fearful? How *is it* that you have no faith?"*a*
41 And they feared exceedingly, and said to one another, "Who can this be, that even the wind and the sea obey Him!"

Bible Quiz

Mark 4:35–41 **Jesus Stills a Storm**

1. What had Jesus been doing all day? See verses 33, 34. What time of day was it now?
2. Where did Jesus ask the disciples to take Him?
3. What happened when they were out on the sea? How do you know it was a bad storm? How did the disciples feel?
4. What was Jesus doing during the storm? Was He afraid?
5. How did the storm stop? When you think about it, is it surprising that the Creator of the world could stop a storm by speaking to it?
6. Do you think the disciples really understood yet who Jesus was? Do you know Jesus yet? Can you turn all your fears over to Him?

A DEMON-POSSESSED MAN HEALED

5 Then they came to the other side of the sea, to the country of the Gad′a·rēnes.*a*
2 And when He had come out of the boat, immediately there met Him out of the tombs a man with an unclean spirit,
3 who had *his* dwelling among the tombs; and no one could bind him,*a* not even with chains,

---

4:40 *a*NU-Text reads *Have you still no faith?*
5:1 *a*NU-Text reads *Gerasenes.*   5:3 *a*NU-Text adds *anymore.*

4 because he had often been bound with shackles and chains. And the chains had been pulled apart by him, and the shackles broken in pieces; neither could anyone tame him.

5 And always, night and day, he was in the mountains and in the tombs, crying out and cutting himself with stones.

6 When he saw Jesus from afar, he ran and worshiped Him.

7 And he cried out with a loud voice and said, "What have I to do with You, Jesus, Son of the Most High God? I implore You by God that You do not torment me."

8 For He said to him, "Come out of the man, unclean spirit!"

9 Then He asked him, "What *is* your name?" And he answered, saying, "My name *is* Legion; for we are many."

10 Also he begged Him earnestly that He would not send them out of the country.

11 Now a large herd of swine was feeding there near the mountains.

12 So all the demons begged Him, saying, "Send us to the swine, that we may enter them."

13 And at once Jesus*a* gave them permission. Then the unclean spirits went out and entered the swine (there were about two thousand); and the herd ran violently down the steep place into the sea, and drowned in the sea.

14 So those who fed the swine fled, and they told *it* in the city and in the country. And they went out to see what it was that had happened.

15 Then they came to Jesus, and saw the one *who had been* demon-possessed and had the legion, sitting and clothed and in his right mind. And they were afraid.

16 And those who saw it told them how it happened to him *who had* been demon-possessed, and about the swine.

17 Then they began to plead with Him to depart from their region.

18 And when He got into the boat, he who had been demon-possessed begged Him that he might be with Him.

19 However, Jesus did not permit him, but said to him, "Go home to your friends, and tell them what great things the Lord has done for you, and how He has had compassion on you."

20 And he departed and began to proclaim in De·cap'o·lis all that Jesus had done for him; and all marveled.

A GIRL RESTORED TO LIFE AND A WOMAN HEALED

21 Now when Jesus had crossed over again by boat to the other side, a great multitude gathered to Him; and He was by the sea.

22 And behold, one of the rulers of the synagogue came, Jā·ī'rus by name. And when he saw Him, he fell at His feet

23 and begged Him earnestly, saying, "My little daughter lies at the point of death. Come and lay Your hands on her, that she may be healed, and she will live."

24 So *Jesus* went with him, and a great multitude followed Him and thronged Him.

25 Now a certain woman had a flow of blood for twelve years,

26 and had suffered many things from many physicians. She had spent all that she had and was no better, but rather grew worse.

27 When she heard about Jesus, she came behind *Him* in the crowd and touched His garment.

28 For she said, "If only I may touch His clothes, I shall be made well."

5:13 *a*NU-Text reads *And He gave.*

29 Immediately the fountain of her blood was dried up, and she felt in *her* body that she was healed of the affliction.

30 And Jesus, immediately knowing in Himself that power had gone out of Him, turned around in the crowd and said, "Who touched My clothes?"

31 But His disciples said to Him, "You see the multitude thronging You, and You say, 'Who touched Me?'"

32 And He looked around to see her who had done this thing.

33 But the woman, fearing and trembling, knowing what had happened to her, came and fell down before Him and told Him the whole truth.

34 And He said to her, "Daughter, your faith has made you well. Go in peace, and be healed of your affliction."

35 While He was still speaking, *some* came from the ruler of the synagogue's *house* who said, "Your daughter is dead. Why trouble the Teacher any further?"

36 As soon as Jesus heard the word that was spoken, He said to the ruler of the synagogue, "Do not be afraid; only believe."

37 And He permitted no one to follow Him except Peter, James, and John the brother of James.

38 Then He came to the house of the ruler of the synagogue, and saw a tumult and those who wept and wailed loudly.

39 When He came in, He said to them, "Why make this commotion and weep? The child is not dead, but sleeping."

40 And they ridiculed Him. But when He had put them all outside, He took the father and the mother of the child, and those *who were* with Him, and entered where the child was lying.

41 Then He took the child by the hand, and said to her, "Tal′i·tha, cū′mi," which is translated, "Little girl, I say to you, arise."

42 Immediately the girl arose and walked, for she was twelve years *of age*. And they were overcome with great amazement.

43 But He commanded them strictly that no one should know it, and said that *something* should be given her to eat.

■ *see Luke 8:40–56*

JESUS REJECTED AT NAZARETH

6 Then He went out from there and came to His own country, and His disciples followed Him.

2 And when the Sabbath had come, He began to teach in the synagogue. And many hearing *Him* were astonished, saying, "Where *did* this Man *get* these things? And what wisdom *is* this which is given to Him, that such mighty works are performed by His hands!

3 "Is this not the carpenter, the Son of Mary, and brother of James, Jō′sēs, Judas, and Simon? And are not His sisters here with us?" So they were offended at Him.

4 But Jesus said to them, "A prophet is not without honor except in his own country, among his own relatives, and in his own house."

5 Now He could do no mighty work there, except that He laid His hands on a few sick people and healed *them*.

6 And He marveled because of their unbelief. Then He went about the villages in a circuit, teaching.

SENDING OUT THE TWELVE

7 And He called the twelve to *Himself,* and began to send them out two *by* two, and gave them power over unclean spirits.

8 He commanded them to take

nothing for the journey except a staff—no bag, no bread, no copper in *their* money belts—

9 but to wear sandals, and not to put on two tunics.

10 Also He said to them, "In whatever place you enter a house, stay there till you depart from that place.

11 "And whoever*a* will not receive you nor hear you, when you depart from there, shake off the dust under your feet as a testimony against them.*b* Assuredly, I say to you, it will be more tolerable for Sod'om and Go·mor'rah in the day of judgment than for that city!"

12 So they went out and preached that *people* should repent.

13 And they cast out many demons, and anointed with oil many who were sick, and healed *them.*

JOHN THE BAPTIST BEHEADED

14 Now King Her'od heard *of Him,* for His name had become well known. And he said, "John the Baptist is risen from the dead, and therefore these powers are at work in him."

15 Others said, "It is E·lī'jah." And others said, "It is the Prophet, or*a* like one of the prophets."

16 But when Her'od heard, he said, "This is John, whom I beheaded; he has been raised from the dead!"

17 For Her'od himself had sent and laid hold of John, and bound him in prison for the sake of He·rō'di·as, his brother Philip's wife; for he had married her.

18 Because John had said to Her'od, "It is not lawful for you to have your brother's wife."

19 Therefore He·rō'di·as held it against him and wanted to kill him, but she could not;

20 for Her'od feared John, knowing that he *was* a just and holy man, and he protected him. And when he heard him, he did many things, and heard him gladly.

21 Then an opportune day came when Her'od on his birthday gave a feast for his nobles, the high officers, and the chief *men* of Galilee.

22 And when He·rō'di·as' daughter herself came in and danced, and pleased Her'od and those who sat with him, the king said to the girl, "Ask me whatever you want, and I will give *it* to you."

23 He also swore to her, "Whatever you ask me, I will give you, up to half my kingdom."

24 So she went out and said to her mother, "What shall I ask?" And she said, "The head of John the Baptist!"

25 Immediately she came in with haste to the king and asked, saying, "I want you to give me at once the head of John the Baptist on a platter."

26 And the king was exceedingly sorry; *yet,* because of the oaths and because of those who sat with him, he did not want to refuse her.

27 Immediately the king sent an executioner and commanded his head to be brought. And he went and beheaded him in prison,

28 brought his head on a platter, and gave it to the girl; and the girl gave it to her mother.

29 When his disciples heard *of it,* they came and took away his corpse and laid it in a tomb.

FEEDING THE FIVE THOUSAND

30 Then the apostles gathered to Jesus and told Him all things, both what they had done and what they had taught.

31 And He said to them, "Come aside

6:11 *a*NU-Text reads *whatever place.* *b*NU-Text omits the rest of this verse. 6:15 *a*NU-Text and M-Text omit *or.*

by yourselves to a deserted place and rest a while." For there were many coming and going, and they did not even have time to eat.

32 So they departed to a deserted place in the boat by themselves.

33 But the multitudes*a* saw them departing, and many knew Him and ran there on foot from all the cities. They arrived before them and came together to Him.

34 And Jesus, when He came out, saw a great multitude and was moved with compassion for them, because they were like sheep not having a shepherd. So He began to teach them many things.

35 When the day was now far spent, His disciples came to Him and said, "This is a deserted place, and already the hour *is* late.

36 "Send them away, that they may go into the surrounding country and villages and buy themselves bread;*a* for they have nothing to eat."

37 But He answered and said to them, "You give them something to eat." And they said to Him, "Shall we go and buy two hundred denarii worth of bread and give them *something* to eat?"

38 But He said to them, "How many loaves do you have? Go and see." And when they found out they said, "Five, and two fish."

39 Then He commanded them to make them all sit down in groups on the green grass.

40 So they sat down in ranks, in hundreds and in fifties.

41 And when He had taken the five loaves and the two fish, He looked up to heaven, blessed and broke the loaves, and gave *them* to His disciples to set before them; and the two fish He divided among *them* all.

42 So they all ate and were filled.

43 And they took up twelve baskets full of fragments and of the fish.

44 Now those who had eaten the loaves were about*a* five thousand men.

■ *see John 6:1–15*

JESUS WALKS ON THE SEA

45 Immediately He made His disciples get into the boat and go before Him to the other side, to Beth·sā'i·da, while He sent the multitude away.

46 And when He had sent them away, He departed to the mountain to pray.

47 Now when evening came, the boat was in the middle of the sea; and He *was* alone on the land.

48 Then He saw them straining at rowing, for the wind was against them. Now about the fourth watch of the night He came to them, walking on the sea, and would have passed them by.

49 And when they saw Him walking on the sea, they supposed it was a ghost, and cried out;

50 for they all saw Him and were troubled. But immediately He talked with them and said to them, "Be of good cheer! It is I; do not be afraid."

51 Then He went up into the boat to them, and the wind ceased. And they were greatly amazed in themselves beyond measure, and marveled.

52 For they had not understood about the loaves, because their heart was hardened.

■ *see Matthew 14:22–33*

MANY TOUCH HIM AND ARE MADE WELL

53 When they had crossed over, they came to the land of Gen·nes'a·ret and anchored there.

6:33 *a*NU-Text and M-Text read *they.*
6:36 *a*NU-Text reads *something to eat* and omits the rest of this verse.   6:44 *a*NU-Text and M-Text omit *about.*

54 And when they came out of the boat, immediately the people recognized Him,

55 ran through that whole surrounding region, and began to carry about on beds those who were sick to wherever they heard He was.

56 Wherever He entered, into villages, cities, or the country, they laid the sick in the marketplaces, and begged Him that they might just touch the hem of His garment. And as many as touched Him were made well.

DEFILEMENT COMES FROM WITHIN

7 Then the Phar'i·sees and some of the scribes came together to Him, having come from Jerusalem.

2 Now when*a* they saw some of His disciples eat bread with defiled, that is, with unwashed hands, they found fault.

3 For the Phar'i·sees and all the Jews do not eat unless they wash *their* hands in a special way, holding the tradition of the elders.

4 *When they come* from the marketplace, they do not eat unless they wash. And there are many other things which they have received and hold, *like* the washing of cups, pitchers, copper vessels, and couches.

5 Then the Phar'i·sees and scribes asked Him, "Why do Your disciples not walk according to the tradition of the elders, but eat bread with unwashed hands?"

6 He answered and said to them, "Well did Ī·sāi'ah prophesy of you hypocrites, as it is written:

'This people honors Me with their
   lips,
But their heart is far from Me.

7 And in vain they worship Me,
Teaching *as* doctrines the
   commandments of men.'*a*

8 "For laying aside the commandment of God, you hold the tradition of men*a*—the washing of pitchers and cups, and many other such things you do."

9 He said to them, "*All too* well you reject the commandment of God, that you may keep your tradition.

10 "For Moses said, '*Honor your father and your mother*';*a* and, '*He who curses father or mother, let him be put to death.*'*b*

11 "But you say, 'If a man says to his father or mother, "Whatever profit you might have received from me *is* Cor'ban"—' (that is, a gift *to God*),

12 "then you no longer let him do anything for his father or his mother,

13 "making the word of God of no effect through your tradition which you have handed down. And many such things you do."

14 When He had called all the multitude to *Himself,* He said to them, "Hear Me, everyone, and understand:

15 "There is nothing that enters a man from outside which can defile him; but the things which come out of him, those are the things that defile a man.

16 "If anyone has ears to hear, let him hear!"*a*

17 When He had entered a house away from the crowd, His disciples asked Him concerning the parable.

18 So He said to them, "Are you thus without understanding also? Do you not perceive that whatever enters a man from outside cannot defile him,

19 "because it does not enter his heart but his stomach, and is eliminated, *thus* purifying all foods?"*a*

7:2 *a*NU-Text omits *when* and *they found fault.*
7:7 *a*Isaiah 29:13   7:8 *a*NU-Text omits the rest of this verse.   7:10 *a*Exodus 20:12; Deuteronomy 5:16   *b*Exodus 21:17   7:16 *a*NU-Text omits this verse.   7:19 *a*NU-Text ends quotation with *eliminated,* setting off the final clause as Mark's comment that Jesus has declared all foods clean.

LOVE Mark 7:10

Why Does Mother Do All She Does?

How many things does mother do for you each day? A dozen? Two dozen? Ask her to list some of the things she does. The list is much longer than you think. Sometimes it gets a little rough for mother, doing all the things she does for you. Why does she do it?

1. How many things did you count on mother's list of things she does for you? Did you know that she does that much for you?
2. Ask mother why she does all of these things. Now why would you like to do a few things for mother? Think of one that you can do for her today.

For more on *Values* turn to page 1631
For more on *Love* turn to page 1649

20 And He said, "What comes out of a man, that defiles a man.

21 "For from within, out of the heart of men, proceed evil thoughts, adulteries, fornications, murders,

22 "thefts, covetousness, wickedness, deceit, lewdness, an evil eye, blasphemy, pride, foolishness.

23 "All these evil things come from within and defile a man."

A Gentile Shows Her Faith

24 From there He arose and went to the region of Tȳre and Sī'don.ᵃ And He entered a house and wanted no one to know *it*, but He could not be hidden.

25 For a woman whose young daughter had an unclean spirit heard about Him, and she came and fell at His feet.

26 The woman was a Greek, a Sȳ'rō-Phoe·ni'cian by birth, and she kept asking Him to cast the demon out of her daughter.

27 But Jesus said to her, "Let the children be filled first, for it is not good to take the children's bread and throw *it* to the little dogs."

28 And she answered and said to Him, "Yes, Lord, yet even the little dogs under the table eat from the children's crumbs."

29 Then He said to her, "For this saying go your way; the demon has gone out of your daughter."

30 And when she had come to her house, she found the demon gone out, and her daughter lying on the bed.

Jesus Heals a Deaf-Mute

31 Again, departing from the region of Tȳre and Sī'don, He came through the midst of the region of De·cap'o·lis to the Sea of Galilee.

32 Then they brought to Him one who was deaf and had an impedi-ment in his speech, and they begged Him to put His hand on him.

33 And He took him aside from the multitude, and put His fingers in his ears, and He spat and touched his tongue.

34 Then, looking up to heaven, He sighed, and said to him, "Eph'pha-tha," that is, "Be opened."

35 Immediately his ears were opened, and the impediment of his tongue was loosed, and he spoke plainly.

36 Then He commanded them that they should tell no one; but the more He commanded them, the more widely they proclaimed *it*.

37 And they were astonished beyond measure, saying, "He has done all things well. He makes both the deaf to hear and the mute to speak."

Feeding the Four Thousand

8 In those days, the multitude being very great and having nothing to eat, Jesus called His disciples *to Him* and said to them,

2 "I have compassion on the multitude, because they have now continued with Me three days and have nothing to eat.

3 "And if I send them away hungry to their own houses, they will faint on the way; for some of them have come from afar."

4 Then His disciples answered Him, "How can one satisfy these people with bread here in the wilderness?"

5 He asked them, "How many loaves do you have?" And they said, "Seven."

6 So He commanded the multitude to sit down on the ground. And He took the seven loaves and gave thanks, broke *them* and gave *them* to

---

7:24 ᵃNU-Text omits *and Sidon.*

His disciples to set before *them;* and they set *them* before the multitude.

7 They also had a few small fish; and having blessed them, He said to set them also before *them.*

8 So they ate and were filled, and they took up seven large baskets of leftover fragments.

9 Now those who had eaten were about four thousand. And He sent them away,

10 immediately got into the boat with His disciples, and came to the region of Dal·ma·nu′tha.

THE PHARISEES SEEK A SIGN

11 Then the Phar′i·sees came out and began to dispute with Him, seeking from Him a sign from heaven, testing Him.

12 But He sighed deeply in His spirit, and said, "Why does this generation seek a sign? Assuredly, I say to you, no sign shall be given to this generation."

BEWARE OF THE LEAVEN OF THE PHARISEES AND HEROD

13 And He left them, and getting into the boat again, departed to the other side.

14 Now the disciples*a* had forgotten to take bread, and they did not have more than one loaf with them in the boat.

15 Then He charged them, saying, "Take heed, beware of the leaven of the Phar′i·sees and the leaven of Her′od."

16 And they reasoned among themselves, saying, *"It is* because we have no bread."

17 But Jesus, being aware of *it,* said to them, "Why do you reason because you have no bread? Do you not yet perceive nor understand? Is your heart still*a* hardened?

18 "Having eyes, do you not see? And having ears, do you not hear? And do you not remember?

19 "When I broke the five loaves for the five thousand, how many baskets full of fragments did you take up?" They said to Him, "Twelve."

20 "Also, when I broke the seven for the four thousand, how many large baskets full of fragments did you take up?" And they said, "Seven."

21 So He said to them, "How *is it* you do not understand?"

A BLIND MAN HEALED AT BETHSAIDA

22 Then He came to Beth·sā′i·da; and they brought a blind man to Him, and begged Him to touch him.

23 So He took the blind man by the hand and led him out of the town. And when He had spit on his eyes and put His hands on him, He asked him if he saw anything.

24 And he looked up and said, "I see men like trees, walking."

25 Then He put *His* hands on his eyes again and made him look up. And he was restored and saw everyone clearly.

26 Then He sent him away to his house, saying, "Neither go into the town, nor tell anyone in the town."*a*

PETER CONFESSES JESUS AS THE CHRIST

27 Now Jesus and His disciples went out to the towns of Caes·a·rē′a Phi·lip′pī; and on the road He asked His disciples, saying to them, "Who do men say that I am?"

28 So they answered, "John the Baptist; but some *say,* E·lī′jah; and others, one of the prophets."

8:14 *a*NU-Text and M-Text read *they.*
8:17 *a*NU-Text omits *still.*   8:26 *a*NU-Text reads "Do not even go into the town."

29 He said to them, "But who do you say that I am?" Peter answered and said to Him, "You are the Christ."
30 Then He strictly warned them that they should tell no one about Him.

Jesus Predicts His Death and Resurrection

31 And He began to teach them that the Son of Man must suffer many things, and be rejected by the elders and chief priests and scribes, and be killed, and after three days rise again.
32 He spoke this word openly. Then Peter took Him aside and began to rebuke Him.
33 But when He had turned around and looked at His disciples, He rebuked Peter, saying, "Get behind Me, Satan! For you are not mindful of the things of God, but the things of men."

Take Up the Cross and Follow Him

34 When He had called the people to *Himself,* with His disciples also, He said to them, "Whoever desires to come after Me, let him deny himself, and take up his cross, and follow Me.
35 "For whoever desires to save his life will lose it, but whoever loses his life for My sake and the gospel's will save it.
36 "For what will it profit a man if he gains the whole world, and loses his own soul?
37 "Or what will a man give in exchange for his soul?
38 "For whoever is ashamed of Me and My words in this adulterous and sinful generation, of him the Son of Man also will be ashamed when He comes in the glory of His Father with the holy angels."

Jesus Transfigured on the Mount

9 And He said to them, "Assuredly, I say to you that there are some standing here who will not taste death till they see the kingdom of God present with power."
2 Now after six days Jesus took Peter, James, and John, and led them up on a high mountain apart by themselves; and He was transfigured before them.
3 His clothes became shining, exceedingly white, like snow, such as no launderer on earth can whiten them.
4 And E·li′jah appeared to them with Moses, and they were talking with Jesus.
5 Then Peter answered and said to Jesus, "Rabbi, it is good for us to be here; and let us make three tabernacles: one for You, one for Moses, and one for E·li′jah"—
6 because he did not know what to say, for they were greatly afraid.
7 And a cloud came and overshadowed them; and a voice came out of the cloud, saying, "This is My beloved Son. Hear Him!"
8 Suddenly, when they had looked around, they saw no one anymore, but only Jesus with themselves.
9 Now as they came down from the mountain, He commanded them that they should tell no one the things they had seen, till the Son of Man had risen from the dead.
10 So they kept this word to themselves, questioning what the rising from the dead meant.
11 And they asked Him, saying, "Why do the scribes say that E·li′jah must come first?"
12 Then He answered and told them, "Indeed, E·li′jah is coming first and restores all things. And how is it written concerning the Son of Man,

that He must suffer many things and be treated with contempt?

13 "But I say to you that E·lī′jah has also come, and they did to him whatever they wished, as it is written of him."

A Boy Is Healed

14 And when He came to the disciples, He saw a great multitude around them, and scribes disputing with them.

15 Immediately, when they saw Him, all the people were greatly amazed, and running to *Him,* greeted Him.

16 And He asked the scribes, "What are you discussing with them?"

17 Then one of the crowd answered and said, "Teacher, I brought You my son, who has a mute spirit.

18 "And wherever it seizes him, it throws him down; he foams at the mouth, gnashes his teeth, and becomes rigid. So I spoke to Your disciples, that they should cast it out, but they could not."

19 He answered him and said, "O faithless generation, how long shall I be with you? How long shall I bear with you? Bring him to Me."

20 Then they brought him to Him. And when he saw Him, immediately the spirit convulsed him, and he fell on the ground and wallowed, foaming at the mouth.

21 So He asked his father, "How long has this been happening to him?" And he said, "From childhood.

22 "And often he has thrown him both into the fire and into the water to destroy him. But if You can do anything, have compassion on us and help us."

23 Jesus said to him, "If you can believe,*a* all things *are* possible to him who believes."

24 Immediately the father of the child cried out and said with tears, "Lord, I believe; help my unbelief!"

25 When Jesus saw that the people came running together, He rebuked the unclean spirit, saying to it: "Deaf and dumb spirit, I command you, come out of him and enter him no more!"

26 Then *the spirit* cried out, convulsed him greatly, and came out of him. And he became as one dead, so that many said, "He is dead."

27 But Jesus took him by the hand and lifted him up, and he arose.

28 And when He had come into the house, His disciples asked Him privately, "Why could we not cast it out?"

29 So He said to them, "This kind can come out by nothing but prayer and fasting."*a*

Jesus Again Predicts His Death and Resurrection

30 Then they departed from there and passed through Galilee, and He did not want anyone to know *it.*

31 For He taught His disciples and said to them, "The Son of Man is being betrayed into the hands of men, and they will kill Him. And after He is killed, He will rise the third day."

32 But they did not understand this saying, and were afraid to ask Him.

Who Is the Greatest?

33 Then He came to Ca·per′na·um. And when He was in the house He asked them, "What was it you disputed among yourselves on the road?"

34 But they kept silent, for on the road they had disputed among themselves who *would be the* greatest.

9:23 *a*NU-Text reads *" 'If You can!' All things. . . ."*
9:29 *a*NU-Text omits *and fasting.*

35 And He sat down, called the twelve, and said to them, "If anyone desires to be first, he shall be last of all and servant of all."
36 Then He took a little child and set him in the midst of them. And when He had taken him in His arms, He said to them,
37 "Whoever receives one of these little children in My name receives Me; and whoever receives Me, receives not Me but Him who sent Me."

JESUS FORBIDS SECTARIANISM

38 Now John answered Him, saying, "Teacher, we saw someone who does not follow us casting out demons in Your name, and we forbade him because he does not follow us."
39 But Jesus said, "Do not forbid him, for no one who works a miracle in My name can soon afterward speak evil of Me.
40 "For he who is not against us is on our*a* side.
41 "For whoever gives you a cup of water to drink in My name, because you belong to Christ, assuredly, I say to you, he will by no means lose his reward.

JESUS WARNS OF OFFENSES

42 "But whoever causes one of these little ones who believe in Me to stumble, it would be better for him if a millstone were hung around his neck, and he were thrown into the sea.
43 "If your hand causes you to sin, cut it off. It is better for you to enter into life maimed, rather than having two hands, to go to hell, into the fire that shall never be quenched—
44 "where

*'Their worm does not die,
And the fire is not quenched.'a*

45 "And if your foot causes you to sin, cut it off. It is better for you to enter life lame, rather than having two feet, to be cast into hell, into the fire that shall never be quenched—
46 "where

*'Their worm does not die,
And the fire is not quenched.'a*

47 "And if your eye causes you to sin, pluck it out. It is better for you to enter the kingdom of God with one eye, rather than having two eyes, to be cast into hell fire—
48 "where

*'Their worm does not die,
And the fire is not quenched.'a*

TASTELESS SALT IS WORTHLESS

49 "For everyone will be seasoned with fire,*a* and every sacrifice will be seasoned with salt.
50 "Salt *is* good, but if the salt loses its flavor, how will you season it? Have salt in yourselves, and have peace with one another."

MARRIAGE AND DIVORCE

10 Then He arose from there and came to the region of Judea by the other side of the Jordan. And multitudes gathered to Him again, and as He was accustomed, He taught them again.
2 The Phar′i·sees came and asked Him, "Is it lawful for a man to divorce *his* wife?" testing Him.
3 And He answered and said to them, "What did Moses command you?"
4 They said, "Moses permitted *a*

9:40 *a*M-Text reads *against you is on your side.*
9:44 *a*NU-Text omits this verse.   9:46 *a*NU-Text omits the last clause of verse 45 and all of verse 46.
9:48 *a*Isaiah 66:24   9:49 *a*NU-Text omits the rest of this verse.

man to write a certificate of divorce, and to dismiss *her*."

5 And Jesus answered and said to them, "Because of the hardness of your heart he wrote you this precept.

6 "But from the beginning of the creation, God *'made them male and female.'a*

7 *'For this reason a man shall leave his father and mother and be joined to his wife,*

8 *'and the two shall become one flesh';a* so then they are no longer two, but one flesh.

9 "Therefore what God has joined together, let not man separate."

10 In the house His disciples also asked Him again about the same *matter*.

11 So He said to them, "Whoever divorces his wife and marries another commits adultery against her.

12 "And if a woman divorces her husband and marries another, she commits adultery."

JESUS BLESSES LITTLE CHILDREN

Jesus loves children. And He knows that children can teach adults some important lessons about faith.

13 Then they brought little children to Him, that He might touch them; but the disciples rebuked those who brought *them.*

14 But when Jesus saw *it,* He was greatly displeased and said to them, "Let the little children come to Me, and do not forbid them; for of such is the kingdom of God.

15 "Assuredly, I say to you, whoever does not receive the kingdom of God as a little child will by no means enter it."

16 And He took them up in His arms, laid *His* hands on them, and blessed them.

☑ Bible Quiz

Mark 10:13–16 **Jesus Blesses the Children**

1. Why were some people bringing their children to Jesus?
2. What did the disciples try to do? Why do you think they did this?
3. What did Jesus say?
4. Why do you think Jesus said we need to receive the kingdom of God as a little child? Aren't children often more trusting than adults? Do you think Jesus was saying we need to trust Him with all our hearts in order to enter His kingdom?
5. What did Jesus do to the children then? Do you know that Jesus holds you in His arms each day?

JESUS COUNSELS THE RICH YOUNG RULER

17 Now as He was going out on the road, one came running, knelt before Him, and asked Him, "Good Teacher, what shall I do that I may inherit eternal life?"

18 So Jesus said to him, "Why do you call Me good? No one *is* good but One, *that is,* God.

19 "You know the commandments: *'Do not commit adultery,' 'Do not murder,' 'Do not steal,' 'Do not bear false witness,' 'Do not defraud,' 'Honor your father and your mother.'"a*

10:6 *a*Genesis 1:27; 5:2   10:8 *a*Genesis 2:24
10:19 *a*Exodus 20:12–16; Deuteronomy 5:16–20

20 And he answered and said to Him, "Teacher, all these things I have kept from my youth."

21 Then Jesus, looking at him, loved him, and said to him, "One thing you lack: Go your way, sell whatever you have and give to the poor, and you will have treasure in heaven; and come, take up the cross, and follow Me."

22 But he was sad at this word, and went away sorrowful, for he had great possessions.

WITH GOD ALL THINGS ARE POSSIBLE

23 Then Jesus looked around and said to His disciples, "How hard it is for those who have riches to enter the kingdom of God!"

24 And the disciples were astonished at His words. But Jesus answered again and said to them, "Children, how hard it is for those who trust in riches*a* to enter the kingdom of God!

25 "It is easier for a camel to go through the eye of a needle than for a rich man to enter the kingdom of God."

26 And they were greatly astonished, saying among themselves, "Who then can be saved?"

27 But Jesus looked at them and said, "With men *it is* impossible, but not with God; for with God all things are possible."

28 Then Peter began to say to Him, "See, we have left all and followed You."

29 So Jesus answered and said, "Assuredly, I say to you, there is no one who has left house or brothers or sisters or father or mother or wife*a* or children or lands, for My sake and the gospel's,

30 "who shall not receive a hundredfold now in this time—houses and brothers and sisters and mothers and children and lands, with persecutions—and in the age to come, eternal life.

31 "But many *who are* first will be last, and the last first."

JESUS A THIRD TIME PREDICTS HIS DEATH AND RESURRECTION

32 Now they were on the road, going up to Jerusalem, and Jesus was going before them; and they were amazed. And as they followed they were afraid. Then He took the twelve aside again and began to tell them the things that would happen to Him:

33 "Behold, we are going up to Jerusalem, and the Son of Man will be betrayed to the chief priests and to the scribes; and they will condemn Him to death and deliver Him to the Gentiles;

34 "and they will mock Him, and scourge Him, and spit on Him, and kill Him. And the third day He will rise again."

GREATNESS IS SERVING

35 Then James and John, the sons of Zeb′e·dee, came to Him, saying, "Teacher, we want You to do for us whatever we ask."

36 And He said to them, "What do you want Me to do for you?"

37 They said to Him, "Grant us that we may sit, one on Your right hand and the other on Your left, in Your glory."

38 But Jesus said to them, "You do not know what you ask. Are you able to drink the cup that I drink, and be baptized with the baptism that I am baptized with?"

39 They said to Him, "We are able."

10:24 *a*NU-Text omits *for those who trust in riches.*
10:29 *a*NU-Text omits *or wife.*

So Jesus said to them, "You will indeed drink the cup that I drink, and with the baptism I am baptized with you will be baptized;
40 "but to sit on My right hand and on My left is not Mine to give, but *it is for those* for whom it is prepared."
41 And when the ten heard *it,* they began to be greatly displeased with James and John.
42 But Jesus called them to *Himself* and said to them, "You know that those who are considered rulers over the Gentiles lord it over them, and their great ones exercise authority over them.
43 "Yet it shall not be so among you; but whoever desires to become great among you shall be your servant.
44 "And whoever of you desires to be first shall be slave of all.
45 "For even the Son of Man did not come to be served, but to serve, and to give His life a ransom for many."

JESUS HEALS BLIND BARTIMAEUS

Close your eyes. Try to keep them closed for five minutes. Can you do it? That may help you understand a little about what it's like to be blind. The man in this story was blind, and he wanted to see more than anything in the world. Then one day, he heard that Jesus was coming to his town.

46 Now they came to Jericho. As He went out of Jericho with His disciples and a great multitude, blind Bar·ti·mae′us, the son of Ti·mae′us, sat by the road begging.
47 And when he heard that it was Jesus of Nazareth, he began to cry out and say, "Jesus, Son of David, have mercy on me!"
48 Then many warned him to be quiet; but he cried out all the more, "Son of David, have mercy on me!"
49 So Jesus stood still and commanded him to be called. Then they called the blind man, saying to him, "Be of good cheer. Rise, He is calling you."
50 And throwing aside his garment, he rose and came to Jesus.
51 So Jesus answered and said to him, "What do you want Me to do for you?" The blind man said to Him, "Rab·bo′nī, that I may receive my sight."
52 Then Jesus said to him, "Go your way; your faith has made you well." And immediately he received his sight and followed Jesus on the road.

☑ Bible Quiz

Mark 10:46–52 **A Blind Man Sees**

1. What town was Jesus near when the blind man called to Him?
2. What was the blind man's name?
3. How did Bartimaeus try to get Jesus' attention? What did the people say to him? Can you think of any reason why these people would not want to help Bartimaeus?
4. Did Jesus want to help Bartimaeus? What did Jesus say Bartimaeus had that allowed him to see?
5. Bartimaeus truly believed that Jesus could help him. Do you believe that Jesus can help you when you need Him?

THE TRIUMPHAL ENTRY

*As Jesus rode into Jerusalem
on a colt, people from
everywhere came to greet Him.
What were they shouting about
Him?*

11 Now when they drew near Jerusalem, to Beth′pha·ge*ᵃ* and Beth′a·ny, at the Mount of Olives, He sent two of His disciples;
2 and He said to them, "Go into the village opposite you; and as soon as you have entered it you will find a colt tied, on which no one has sat. Loose it and bring *it.*
3 "And if anyone says to you, 'Why are you doing this?' say, 'The Lord has need of it,' and immediately he will send it here."
4 So they went their way, and found the*ᵃ* colt tied by the door outside on the street, and they loosed it.

☑ *Bible Quiz*

Mark 11:1–11   **A Triumphal Entry into Jerusalem**

1. What did Jesus send His disciples to find?
2. What did Jesus say might happen when the disciples found the colt? How do you think Jesus knew this?
3. Name two things the crowds spread on the road as Jesus rode into town.
4. The people of Israel had not had a king for over 500 years. They thought Jesus might be their king. But Jesus didn't want to be king of Israel. One day He will be King of all the earth!

---

5 But some of those who stood there said to them, "What are you doing, loosing the colt?"
6 And they spoke to them just as Jesus had commanded. So they let them go.
7 Then they brought the colt to Jesus and threw their clothes on it, and He sat on it.
8 And many spread their clothes on the road, and others cut down leafy branches from the trees and spread *them* on the road.
9 Then those who went before and those who followed cried out, saying:

"Hō·san′na!
'Blessed is He who comes in the
name of the LORD!'*ᵃ*
10 Blessed *is* the kingdom of our
father David
That comes in the name of the
Lord!*ᵃ*
Hō·san′na in the highest!"

11 And Jesus went into Jerusalem and into the temple. So when He had looked around at all things, as the hour was already late, He went out to Beth′a·ny with the twelve.

THE FIG TREE WITHERED

12 Now the next day, when they had come out from Beth′a·ny, He was hungry.
13 And seeing from afar a fig tree having leaves, He went to see if perhaps He would find something on it. When He came to it, He found nothing but leaves, for it was not the season for figs.
14 In response Jesus said to it, "Let

11:1 *ᵃ*M-Text reads *Bethsphage.*   11:4 *ᵃ*NU-Text and M-Text read *a.*   11:9 *ᵃ*Psalm 118:26
11:10 *ᵃ*NU-Text omits *in the name of the Lord.*

no one eat fruit from you ever again." And His disciples heard *it.*

JESUS CLEANSES THE TEMPLE

15 So they came to Jerusalem. Then Jesus went into the temple and began to drive out those who bought and sold in the temple, and overturned the tables of the money changers and the seats of those who sold doves.
16 And He would not allow anyone to carry wares through the temple.
17 Then He taught, saying to them, "Is it not written, *'My house shall be called a house of prayer for all nations'*?*a* But you have made it a *'den of thieves.'* "*b*
18 And the scribes and chief priests heard it and sought how they might destroy Him; for they feared Him, because all the people were astonished at His teaching.
19 When evening had come, He went out of the city.
■ *see Matthew 21:12–17*

THE LESSON OF THE WITHERED FIG TREE

20 Now in the morning, as they passed by, they saw the fig tree dried up from the roots.
21 And Peter, remembering, said to Him, "Rabbi, look! The fig tree which You cursed has withered away."
22 So Jesus answered and said to them, "Have faith in God.
23 "For assuredly, I say to you, whoever says to this mountain, 'Be removed and be cast into the sea,' and does not doubt in his heart, but believes that those things he says will be done, he will have whatever he says.
24 "Therefore I say to you, whatever things you ask when you pray, believe that you receive *them,* and you will have *them.*

FORGIVENESS AND PRAYER

25 "And whenever you stand praying, if you have anything against anyone, forgive him, that your Father in heaven may also forgive you your trespasses.
26 "But if you do not forgive, neither will your Father in heaven forgive your trespasses."*a*

JESUS' AUTHORITY QUESTIONED

27 Then they came again to Jerusalem. And as He was walking in the temple, the chief priests, the scribes, and the elders came to Him.
28 And they said to Him, "By what authority are You doing these things? And who gave You this authority to do these things?"
29 But Jesus answered and said to them, "I also will ask you one question; then answer Me, and I will tell you by what authority I do these things:
30 "The baptism of John—was it from heaven or from men? Answer Me."
31 And they reasoned among themselves, saying, "If we say, 'From heaven,' He will say, 'Why then did you not believe him?'
32 "But if we say, 'From men' "—they feared the people, for all counted John to have been a prophet indeed.
33 So they answered and said to Jesus, "We do not know." And Jesus answered and said to them, "Neither will I tell you by what authority I do these things."

11:17 *a*Isaiah 56:7 *b*Jeremiah 7:11
11:26 *a*NU-Text omits this verse.

The Parable of the Wicked Vinedressers

12 Then He began to speak to them in parables: "A man planted a vineyard and set a hedge around *it,* dug *a place for* the wine vat and built a tower. And he leased it to vinedressers and went into a far country.
2 "Now at vintage-time he sent a servant to the vinedressers, that he might receive some of the fruit of the vineyard from the vinedressers.
3 "And they took *him* and beat him and sent *him* away empty-handed.
4 "Again he sent them another servant, and at him they threw stones,*a* wounded *him* in the head, and sent *him* away shamefully treated.
5 "And again he sent another, and him they killed; and many others, beating some and killing some.
6 "Therefore still having one son, his beloved, he also sent him to them last, saying, 'They will respect my son.'
7 "But those vinedressers said among themselves, 'This is the heir. Come, let us kill him, and the inheritance will be ours.'
8 "So they took him and killed *him* and cast *him* out of the vineyard.
9 "Therefore what will the owner of the vineyard do? He will come and destroy the vinedressers, and give the vineyard to others.
10 "Have you not even read this Scripture:

'The stone which the builders
     rejected
Has become the chief cornerstone.
11 This was the LORD's doing,
And it is marvelous in our
     eyes'?"*a*

12 And they sought to lay hands on Him, but feared the multitude, for they knew He had spoken the parable against them. So they left Him and went away.

The Pharisees: Is It Lawful to Pay Taxes to Caesar?

13 Then they sent to Him some of the Phar'i·sees and the He·rō'di·ans, to catch Him in *His* words.
14 When they had come, they said to Him, "Teacher, we know that You are true, and care about no one; for You do not regard the person of men, but teach the way of God in truth. Is it lawful to pay taxes to Caesar, or not?
15 "Shall we pay, or shall we not pay?" But He, knowing their hypocrisy, said to them, "Why do you test Me? Bring Me a denarius that I may see *it.*"
16 So they brought *it.* And He said to them, "Whose image and inscription *is* this?" They said to Him, "Caesar's."
17 And Jesus answered and said to them, "Render to Caesar the things that are Caesar's, and to God the things that are God's." And they marveled at Him.

The Sadducees: What About the Resurrection?

18 Then *some* Sad'du·cees, who say there is no resurrection, came to Him; and they asked Him, saying:
19 "Teacher, Moses wrote to us that if a man's brother dies, and leaves *his* wife behind, and leaves no children, his brother should take his wife and raise up offspring for his brother.
20 "Now there were seven brothers. The first took a wife; and dying, he left no offspring.
21 "And the second took her, and he

12:4 *a*NU-Text omits *and at him they threw stones.*
12:11 *a*Psalm 118:22, 23

died; nor did he leave any offspring. And the third likewise.

22 "So the seven had her and left no offspring. Last of all the woman died also.

23 "Therefore, in the resurrection, when they rise, whose wife will she be? For all seven had her as wife."

24 Jesus answered and said to them, "Are you not therefore mistaken, because you do not know the Scriptures nor the power of God?

25 "For when they rise from the dead, they neither marry nor are given in marriage, but are like angels in heaven.

26 "But concerning the dead, that they rise, have you not read in the book of Moses, in the *burning* bush *passage,* how God spoke to him, saying, *'I am the God of Abraham, the God of Isaac, and the God of Jacob'?*a

27 "He is not the God of the dead, but the God of the living. You are therefore greatly mistaken."

THE SCRIBES: WHICH IS THE FIRST COMMANDMENT OF ALL?

28 Then one of the scribes came, and having heard them reasoning together, perceivinga that He had answered them well, asked Him, "Which is the first commandment of all?"

29 Jesus answered him, "The first of all the commandments *is:* 'Hear, O Israel, the Lord our God, the Lord is one.

30 'And you shall love the LORD your God with all your heart, with all your soul, with all your mind, and with all your strength.'a This *is* the first commandment.b

31 "And the second, like *it, is* this: 'You shall love your neighbor as yourself.'a There is no other commandment greater than these."

32 So the scribe said to Him, "Well

said, Teacher. You have spoken the truth, for there is one God, and there is no other but He.

33 "And to love Him with all the heart, with all the understanding, with all the soul,a and with all the strength, and to love one's neighbor as oneself, is more than all the whole burnt offerings and sacrifices."

34 Now when Jesus saw that he answered wisely, He said to him, "You are not far from the kingdom of God." But after that no one dared question Him.

JESUS: HOW CAN DAVID CALL HIS DESCENDANT LORD?

35 Then Jesus answered and said, while He taught in the temple, "How *is it* that the scribes say that the Christ is the Son of David?

36 "For David himself said by the Holy Spirit:

'The LORD said to my Lord,
"Sit at My right hand,
    Till I make Your enemies Your
        footstool." 'a

37 "Therefore David himself calls Him *'Lord';* how is He *then* his Son?" And the common people heard Him gladly.

BEWARE OF THE SCRIBES

38 Then He said to them in His teaching, "Beware of the scribes, who desire to go around in long robes, *love* greetings in the marketplaces,

39 "the best seats in the synagogues, and the best places at feasts,

40 "who devour widows' houses, and

12:26 aExodus 3:6, 15   12:28 aNU-Text reads *seeing.*   12:30 aDeuteronomy 6:4, 5   bNU-Text omits this sentence.   12:31 aLeviticus 19:18   12:33 aNU-Text omits *with all the soul.*   12:36 aPsalm 110:1

for a pretense make long prayers. These will receive greater condemnation."

THE WIDOW'S TWO MITES

Something was happening at the temple that would become an important lesson in giving for the disciples.

41 Now Jesus sat opposite the treasury and saw how the people put money into the treasury. And many *who were* rich put in much.
42 Then one poor widow came and threw in two mites,*a* which make a quadrans.
43 So He called His disciples to *Himself* and said to them, "Assuredly, I say to you that this poor widow has put in more than all those who have given to the treasury;

✓ Bible Quiz

Mark 12:41–44 **A Poor Widow Gives All She Has**

1. How much money did the widow throw into the treasury?
2. What would some of the rich people have thought about the amount she threw in? What did Jesus think about the amount she threw in?
3. The poor widow was willing to give all she had for God. God isn't asking us to give all our money to Jesus, but He is asking if we are willing to. If God asked you, how much would you be willing to give to Him?

---

44 "for they all put in out of their abundance, but she out of her poverty put in all that she had, her whole livelihood."

JESUS PREDICTS THE DESTRUCTION OF THE TEMPLE

13 Then as He went out of the temple, one of His disciples said to Him, "Teacher, see what manner of stones and what buildings *are here!*"
2 And Jesus answered and said to him, "Do you see these great buildings? Not *one* stone shall be left upon another, that shall not be thrown down."

THE SIGNS OF THE TIMES AND THE END OF THE AGE

3 Now as He sat on the Mount of Olives opposite the temple, Peter, James, John, and Andrew asked Him privately,
4 "Tell us, when will these things be? And what *will be* the sign when all these things will be fulfilled?"
5 And Jesus, answering them, began to say: "Take heed that no one deceives you.
6 "For many will come in My name, saying, 'I am *He,*' and will deceive many.
7 "But when you hear of wars and rumors of wars, do not be troubled; for *such things* must happen, but the end *is* not yet.
8 "For nation will rise against nation, and kingdom against kingdom. And there will be earthquakes in various places, and there will be famines and troubles.*a* These *are* the beginnings of sorrows.

12:42 *a*Greek *lepta,* very small copper coins worth a fraction of a penny   13:8 *a*NU-Text omits *and troubles.*

9 "But watch out for yourselves, for they will deliver you up to councils, and you will be beaten in the synagogues. You will be brought*a* before rulers and kings for My sake, for a testimony to them.
10 "And the gospel must first be preached to all the nations.
11 "But when they arrest *you* and deliver you up, do not worry beforehand, or premeditate*a* what you will speak. But whatever is given you in that hour, speak that; for it is not you who speak, but the Holy Spirit.
12 "Now brother will betray brother to death, and a father *his* child; and children will rise up against parents and cause them to be put to death.
13 "And you will be hated by all for My name's sake. But he who endures to the end shall be saved.

THE GREAT TRIBULATION

14 "So when you see the *'abomination of desolation,'a* spoken of by Daniel the prophet,*b* standing where it ought not" (let the reader understand), "then let those who are in Judea flee to the mountains.
15 "Let him who is on the housetop not go down into the house, nor enter to take anything out of his house.
16 "And let him who is in the field not go back to get his clothes.
17 "But woe to those who are pregnant and to those who are nursing babies in those days!
18 "And pray that your flight may not be in winter.
19 "For *in* those days there will be tribulation, such as has not been since the beginning of the creation which God created until this time, nor ever shall be.
20 "And unless the Lord had shortened those days, no flesh would be saved; but for the elect's sake, whom He chose, He shortened the days.
21 "Then if anyone says to you, 'Look, here *is* the Christ!' or, 'Look, *He is* there!' do not believe it.
22 "For false christs and false prophets will rise and show signs and wonders to deceive, if possible, even the elect.
23 "But take heed; see, I have told you all things beforehand.

THE COMING OF THE SON OF MAN

24 "But in those days, after that tribulation, the sun will be darkened, and the moon will not give its light;
25 "the stars of heaven will fall, and the powers in the heavens will be shaken.
26 "Then they will see the Son of Man coming in the clouds with great power and glory.
27 "And then He will send His angels, and gather together His elect from the four winds, from the farthest part of earth to the farthest part of heaven.

THE PARABLE OF THE FIG TREE

28 "Now learn this parable from the fig tree: When its branch has already become tender, and puts forth leaves, you know that summer is near.
29 "So you also, when you see these things happening, know that it*a* is near—at the doors!
30 "Assuredly, I say to you, this generation will by no means pass away till all these things take place.
31 "Heaven and earth will pass away, but My words will by no means pass away.

13:9 *a*NU-Text and M-Text read *will stand.*
13:11 *a*NU-Text omits *or premeditate.*
13:14 *a*Daniel 11:31; 12:11   *b*NU-Text omits *spoken of by Daniel the prophet.*   13:29 *a*Or *He*

No One Knows the Day or Hour

32 "But of that day and hour no one knows, not even the angels in heaven, nor the Son, but only the Father.

33 "Take heed, watch and pray; for you do not know when the time is.

34 *It is* like a man going to a far country, who left his house and gave authority to his servants, and to each his work, and commanded the door-keeper to watch.

35 "Watch therefore, for you do not know when the master of the house is coming—in the evening, at midnight, at the crowing of the rooster, or in the morning—

36 "lest, coming suddenly, he find you sleeping.

37 "And what I say to you, I say to all: Watch!"

The Plot to Kill Jesus

14 After two days it was the Passover and *the Feast* of Unleavened Bread. And the chief priests and the scribes sought how they might take Him by trickery and put *Him* to death.

2 But they said, "Not during the feast, lest there be an uproar of the people."

The Anointing at Bethany

3 And being in Beth′a·ny at the house of Simon the leper, as He sat at the table, a woman came having an alabaster flask of very costly oil of spikenard. Then she broke the flask and poured *it* on His head.

4 But there were some who were indignant among themselves, and said, "Why was this fragrant oil wasted?

5 "For it might have been sold for more than three hundred denarii and given to the poor." And they criticized her sharply.

6 But Jesus said, "Let her alone. Why do you trouble her? She has done a good work for Me.

7 "For you have the poor with you always, and whenever you wish you may do them good; but Me you do not have always.

8 "She has done what she could. She has come beforehand to anoint My body for burial.

9 "Assuredly, I say to you, wherever this gospel is preached in the whole world, what this woman has done will also be told as a memorial to her."

Judas Agrees to Betray Jesus

10 Then Judas Is·car′i·ot, one of the twelve, went to the chief priests to betray Him to them.

11 And when they heard *it,* they were glad, and promised to give him money. So he sought how he might conveniently betray Him.

Jesus Celebrates the Passover with His Disciples

12 Now on the first day of Unleavened Bread, when they killed the Passover *lamb,* His disciples said to Him, "Where do You want us to go and prepare, that You may eat the Passover?"

13 And He sent out two of His disciples and said to them, "Go into the city, and a man will meet you carrying a pitcher of water; follow him.

14 "Wherever he goes in, say to the master of the house, 'The Teacher says, "Where is the guest room in which I may eat the Passover with My disciples?" '

15 "Then he will show you a large upper room, furnished *and* prepared; there make ready for us."

16 So His disciples went out, and came into the city, and found it just as He had said to them; and they prepared the Passover.

17 In the evening He came with the twelve.

18 Now as they sat and ate, Jesus said, "Assuredly, I say to you, one of you who eats with Me will betray Me."

19 And they began to be sorrowful, and to say to Him one by one, "*Is it I?*" And another *said,* "*Is it I?*"*a*

20 He answered and said to them, "*It is* one of the twelve, who dips with Me in the dish.

21 "The Son of Man indeed goes just as it is written of Him, but woe to that man by whom the Son of Man is betrayed! It would have been good for that man if he had never been born."

JESUS INSTITUTES THE LORD'S SUPPER

22 And as they were eating, Jesus took bread, blessed and broke *it,* and gave *it* to them and said, "Take, eat;*a* this is My body."

23 Then He took the cup, and when He had given thanks He gave *it* to them, and they all drank from it.

24 And He said to them, "This is My blood of the new*a* covenant, which is shed for many.

25 "Assuredly, I say to you, I will no longer drink of the fruit of the vine until that day when I drink it new in the kingdom of God."

26 And when they had sung a hymn, they went out to the Mount of Olives.

JESUS PREDICTS PETER'S DENIAL

27 Then Jesus said to them, "All of you will be made to stumble because of Me this night,*a* for it is written:

'I will strike the Shepherd,
And the sheep will be scattered.'*b*

28 "But after I have been raised, I will go before you to Galilee."

29 Peter said to Him, "Even if all are made to stumble, yet I *will* not *be.*"

30 Jesus said to him, "Assuredly, I say to you that today, *even* this night, before the rooster crows twice, you will deny Me three times."

31 But he spoke more vehemently, "If I have to die with You, I will not deny You!" And they all said likewise.

■ see Matthew 26:17–35

THE PRAYER IN THE GARDEN

After their last supper together, Jesus and His disciples walked to the Garden of Gethsemane. It was night. Jesus knew that the next day He would be condemned to die. He needed to pray to God because He knew that He would soon be bearing the weight of all the sins of the world. This is what He prayed to God about.

32 Then they came to a place which was named Geth·sem′a·nē; and He said to His disciples, "Sit here while I pray."

33 And He took Peter, James, and John with Him, and He began to be troubled and deeply distressed.

34 Then He said to them, "My soul is exceedingly sorrowful, *even* to death. Stay here and watch."

35 He went a little farther, and fell

14:19 *a*NU-Text omits this sentence.
14:22 *a*NU-Text omits *eat.*   14:24 *a*NU-Text omits *new.*   14:27 *a*NU-Text omits *because of Me this night.* *b*Zechariah 13:7

on the ground, and prayed that if it were possible, the hour might pass from Him.

36 And He said, "Abba, Father, all things *are* possible for You. Take this cup away from Me; nevertheless, not what I will, but what You *will*."

37 Then He came and found them sleeping, and said to Peter, "Simon,

---

☑ *Bible Quiz*

Mark 14:32–42 **Jesus Prays in the Garden of Gethsemane**

1. What was the name of the place where Jesus stopped to pray?
2. Jesus took three disciples further into the garden with Him. Who were they?
3. What was Jesus feeling? Do you know why?
4. What did Jesus ask Peter, James, and John to do while He prayed? What did the three disciples do?
5. Jesus told Peter, James, and John that praying could help them stay away from something. What? How can praying help us avoid temptation?
6. What did Jesus talk to God about? What if God had not allowed Jesus to die for the sins of the world? What would our future be like? Can you thank Jesus that He was willing to suffer and die for us so that we might live with Him forever?

---

are you sleeping? Could you not watch one hour?

38 "Watch and pray, lest you enter into temptation. The spirit indeed *is* willing, but the flesh *is* weak."

39 Again He went away and prayed, and spoke the same words.

40 And when He returned, He found them asleep again, for their eyes were heavy; and they did not know what to answer Him.

41 Then He came the third time and said to them, "Are you still sleeping and resting? It is enough! The hour has come; behold, the Son of Man is being betrayed into the hands of sinners.

42 "Rise, let us be going. See, My betrayer is at hand."

BETRAYAL AND ARREST IN GETHSEMANE

43 And immediately, while He was still speaking, Judas, one of the twelve, with a great multitude with swords and clubs, came from the chief priests and the scribes and the elders.

44 Now His betrayer had given them a signal, saying, "Whomever I kiss, He is the One; seize Him and lead *Him* away safely."

45 As soon as he had come, immediately he went up to Him and said to Him, "Rabbi, Rabbi!" and kissed Him.

46 Then they laid their hands on Him and took Him.

47 And one of those who stood by drew his sword and struck the servant of the high priest, and cut off his ear.

48 Then Jesus answered and said to them, "Have you come out, as against a robber, with swords and clubs to take Me?

49 "I was daily with you in the temple teaching, and you did not seize

Me. But the Scriptures must be fulfilled."

50 Then they all forsook Him and fled.

A Young Man Flees Naked

51 Now a certain young man followed Him, having a linen cloth thrown around *his* naked *body*. And the young men laid hold of him,

52 and he left the linen cloth and fled from them naked.

■ *see Matthew 26:47–56*

Jesus Faces the Sanhedrin

53 And they led Jesus away to the high priest; and with him were assembled all the chief priests, the elders, and the scribes.

54 But Peter followed Him at a distance, right into the courtyard of the high priest. And he sat with the servants and warmed himself at the fire.

55 Now the chief priests and all the council sought testimony against Jesus to put Him to death, but found none.

56 For many bore false witness against Him, but their testimonies did not agree.

57 Then some rose up and bore false witness against Him, saying,

58 "We heard Him say, 'I will destroy this temple made with hands, and within three days I will build another made without hands.'"

59 But not even then did their testimony agree.

60 And the high priest stood up in the midst and asked Jesus, saying, "Do You answer nothing? What *is it* these men testify against You?"

61 But He kept silent and answered nothing. Again the high priest asked Him, saying to Him, "Are You the Christ, the Son of the Blessed?"

62 Jesus said, "I am. And you will see the Son of Man sitting at the right hand of the Power, and coming with the clouds of heaven."

63 Then the high priest tore his clothes and said, "What further need do we have of witnesses?

64 "You have heard the blasphemy! What do you think?" And they all condemned Him to be deserving of death.

65 Then some began to spit on Him, and to blindfold Him, and to beat Him, and to say to Him, "Prophesy!" And the officers struck Him with the palms of their hands.*a*

Peter Denies Jesus, and Weeps

66 Now as Peter was below in the courtyard, one of the servant girls of the high priest came.

67 And when she saw Peter warming himself, she looked at him and said, "You also were with Jesus of Nazareth."

68 But he denied it, saying, "I neither know nor understand what you are saying." And he went out on the porch, and a rooster crowed.

69 And the servant girl saw him again, and began to say to those who stood by, "This is one of them."

70 But he denied it again. And a little later those who stood by said to Peter again, "Surely you are *one* of them; for you are a Galilean, and your speech shows *it.*"*a*

71 Then he began to curse and swear, "I do not know this Man of whom you speak!"

72 A second time *the* rooster crowed. Then Peter called to mind the word that Jesus had said to him, "Before the rooster crows twice, you will deny Me three times." And when he thought about it, he wept.

■ *see Luke 22:54–62*

14:65 *a*NU-Text reads *received Him with slaps.*
14:70 *a*NU-Text omits *and your speech shows it.*

JESUS FACES PILATE

It was the darkest day in history. Jesus, God's Son was about to die on a cross. But God was in control. He planned it this way. Soon this darkest day would give way to the day of greatest hope for all the world!

15 Immediately, in the morning, the chief priests held a consultation with the elders and scribes and the whole council; and they bound Jesus, led *Him* away, and delivered *Him* to Pilate.

2 Then Pilate asked Him, "Are You the King of the Jews?" He answered and said to him, "*It is as* you say."

3 And the chief priests accused Him of many things, but He answered nothing.

4 Then Pilate asked Him again, saying, "Do You answer nothing? See how many things they testify against You!"a

5 But Jesus still answered nothing, so that Pilate marveled.

TAKING THE PLACE OF BARABBAS

6 Now at the feast he was accustomed to releasing one prisoner to them, whomever they requested.

7 And there was one named Barab'bas, *who was* chained with his fellow rebels; they had committed murder in the rebellion.

8 Then the multitude, crying aloud,a began to ask *him to do* just as he had always done for them.

9 But Pilate answered them, saying, "Do you want me to release to you the King of the Jews?"

10 For he knew that the chief priests had handed Him over because of envy.

11 But the chief priests stirred up the crowd, so that he should rather release Ba·rab'bas to them.

12 Pilate answered and said to them again, "What then do you want me to do *with Him* whom you call the King of the Jews?"

13 So they cried out again, "Crucify Him!"

14 Then Pilate said to them, "Why, what evil has He done?" But they cried out all the more, "Crucify Him!"

15 So Pilate, wanting to gratify the crowd, released Ba·rab'bas to them; and he delivered Jesus, after he had scourged *Him,* to be crucified.

THE SOLDIERS MOCK JESUS

16 Then the soldiers led Him away into the hall called Prae·tō'ri·um, and they called together the whole garrison.

17 And they clothed Him with purple; and they twisted a crown of thorns, put it on His *head,*

18 and began to salute Him, "Hail, King of the Jews!"

19 Then they struck Him on the head with a reed and spat on Him; and bowing the knee, they worshiped Him.

20 And when they had mocked Him, they took the purple off Him, put His own clothes on Him, and led Him out to crucify Him.

THE KING ON A CROSS

21 Then they compelled a certain man, Simon a Cȳ·rē'ni·an, the father of Alexander and Rū'fus, as he was coming out of the country and passing by, to bear His cross.

22 And they brought Him to the place Gol'go·tha, which is translated, Place of a Skull.

15:4 aNU-Text reads *of which they accuse You.*
15:8 aNU-Text reads *going up.*

23 Then they gave Him wine mingled with myrrh to drink, but He did not take *it*.
24 And when they crucified Him, they divided His garments, casting lots for them to determine what every man should take.
25 Now it was the third hour, and they crucified Him.
26 And the inscription of His accusation was written above:

THE KING OF THE JEWS.

27 With Him they also crucified two robbers, one on His right and the other on His left.
28 So the Scripture was fulfilled*a* which says, *"And He was numbered with the transgressors."b*
29 And those who passed by blasphemed Him, wagging their heads and saying, "Aha! *You* who destroy the temple and build *it* in three days,
30 "save Yourself, and come down from the cross!"
31 Likewise the chief priests also, mocking among themselves with the scribes, said, "He saved others; Himself He cannot save.
32 "Let the Christ, the King of Israel, descend now from the cross, that we may see and believe."*a* Even those who were crucified with Him reviled Him.

JESUS DIES ON THE CROSS

33 Now when the sixth hour had come, there was darkness over the whole land until the ninth hour.
34 And at the ninth hour Jesus cried out with a loud voice, saying, "Ē′lō·ī, Ē′lō·ī, la·ma′ sa·bach′tha·nī?" which is translated, *My God, My God, why have You forsaken Me?"a*
35 Some of those who stood by, when they heard *that,* said, "Look, He is calling for E·lī′jah!"
36 Then someone ran and filled a sponge full of sour wine, put *it* on a reed, and offered *it* to Him to drink, saying, "Let Him alone; let us see if E·lī′jah will come to take Him down."
37 And Jesus cried out with a loud voice, and breathed His last.
38 Then the veil of the temple was torn in two from top to bottom.
39 So when the centurion, who stood opposite Him, saw that He cried out like this and breathed His last,*a* he said, "Truly this Man was the Son of God!"
40 There were also women looking on from afar, among whom were Mary Mag′da·lēne, Mary the mother of James the Less and of Jō′sēs, and Sa·lō′mē,
41 who also followed Him and ministered to Him when He was in Galilee, and many other women who came up with Him to Jerusalem.

JESUS BURIED IN JOSEPH'S TOMB

42 Now when evening had come, because it was the Preparation Day, that is, the day before the Sabbath,
43 Joseph of Ar·i·ma·thē′a, a prominent council member, who was himself waiting for the kingdom of God, coming and taking courage, went in to Pilate and asked for the body of Jesus.
44 Pilate marveled that He was already dead; and summoning the centurion, he asked him if He had been dead for some time.
45 So when he found out from the centurion, he granted the body to Joseph.
46 Then he bought fine linen, took Him down, and wrapped Him in the linen. And he laid Him in a tomb which had been hewn out of the rock,

15:28 *a*Isaiah 53:12   *b*NU-Text omits this verse.
15:32 *a*M-Text reads *believe Him.*
15:34 *a*Psalm 22:1   15:39 *a*NU-Text reads *that He thus breathed His last.*

Mark 15 **Jesus Is Crucified**

1. Which man did the chief priests and scribes take Jesus to first?

2. Did Pilate find anything wrong with Jesus? How did he try to help Jesus?

3. Why didn't Pilate keep trying to help Jesus? Would you call Pilate a man of courage?

4. Who should have been crucified instead of Jesus?

5. What are some of the bad things the soldiers did to Jesus?

6. Name two things that happened when Jesus died.

7. What did the Roman soldier say about Jesus when He died?

8. Who offered to bury Jesus' body?

9. Jesus died for our sins so that we would not have to stay dead forever. Instead, we can now live with Him forever in heaven. Have you thanked Jesus lately for what He did for us?

and rolled a stone against the door of the tomb.

47 And Mary Mag′da·lēne and Mary *the mother* of Jō′sēs observed where He was laid.

He Is Risen

16 Now when the Sabbath was past, Mary Mag′da·lēne, Mary *the mother* of James, and Sa·lō′mē bought spices, that they might come and anoint Him.

2 Very early in the morning, on the first *day* of the week, they came to the tomb when the sun had risen.

3 And they said among themselves, "Who will roll away the stone from the door of the tomb for us?"

4 But when they looked up, they saw that the stone had been rolled away—for it was very large.

5 And entering the tomb, they saw a young man clothed in a long white robe sitting on the right side; and they were alarmed.

6 But he said to them, "Do not be alarmed. You seek Jesus of Nazareth, who was crucified. He is risen! He is not here. See the place where they laid Him.

7 "But go, tell His disciples—and Peter—that He is going before you into Galilee; there you will see Him, as He said to you."

8 So they went out quickly[a] and fled from the tomb, for they trembled and were amazed. And they said nothing to anyone, for they were afraid.

Mary Magdalene Sees the Risen Lord

9 Now when *He* rose early on the first *day* of the week, He appeared first to Mary Mag′da·lēne, out of whom He had cast seven demons.

10 She went and told those who had been with Him, as they mourned and wept.

11 And when they heard that He was alive and had been seen by her, they did not believe.

■ *see Matthew 28:1–20*

16:8 [a]NU-Text and M-Text omit *quickly*.

WHO WILL LISTEN TO ME? Mark 16:15, 16

Would you feed the birds at your bird feeder if only one little bird came to eat? Would you teach a Sunday School class if only one little child came to listen? Would you preach a sermon if only one poor person came to hear you? Would you talk about Jesus if you could talk to only one person?

1. Why do you tell others about Jesus? Must you have big crowds or big rewards?
2. Why do you share God's Word with others? Must you have important people listen or will one little child do?

For more on *What Should I Do?* turn to page 1563
For more on *Serving* turn to page 1790

JESUS APPEARS TO TWO DISCIPLES

12 After that, He appeared in another form to two of them as they walked and went into the country.
13 And they went and told *it* to the rest, *but* they did not believe them either.

THE GREAT COMMISSION

14 Later He appeared to the eleven as they sat at the table; and He rebuked their unbelief and hardness of heart, because they did not believe those who had seen Him after He had risen.
15 And He said to them, "Go into all the world and preach the gospel to every creature.
16 "He who believes and is baptized will be saved; but he who does not believe will be condemned.
17 "And these signs will follow those who believe: In My name they will cast out demons; they will speak with new tongues;
18 "they*a* will take up serpents; and if they drink anything deadly, it will by no means hurt them; they will lay hands on the sick, and they will recover."

CHRIST ASCENDS TO GOD'S RIGHT HAND

19 So then, after the Lord had spoken to them, He was received up into heaven, and sat down at the right hand of God.
20 And they went out and preached everywhere, the Lord working with *them* and confirming the word through the accompanying signs. Amen.*a*
■ *see Luke 24:13–53*

16:18 *a*NU-Text reads *and in their hands they will.*
16:20 *a*Verses 9–20 are bracketed in NU-Text as not original. They are lacking in Codex Sinaiticus and Codex Vaticanus, although nearly all other manuscripts of Mark contain them.

DEDICATION TO THEOPHILUS

INASMUCH as many have taken in hand to set in order a narrative of those things which have been fulfilled*a* among us,

2 just as those who from the beginning were eyewitnesses and ministers of the word delivered them to us,

3 it seemed good to me also, having had perfect understanding of all things from the very first, to write to you an orderly account, most excellent Thē·oph'i·lus,

4 that you may know the certainty of those things in which you were instructed.

JOHN'S BIRTH ANNOUNCED TO ZACHARIAS

5 There was in the days of Her'od, the king of Judea, a certain priest named Zach·a·rī'as, of the division of A·bī'jah. His wife *was* of the daughters of Aaron, and her name *was* Elizabeth.

6 And they were both righteous before God, walking in all the commandments and ordinances of the Lord blameless.

7 But they had no child, because Elizabeth was barren, and they were both well advanced in years.

8 So it was, that while he was serving as priest before God in the order of his division,

9 according to the custom of the priesthood, his lot fell to burn incense when he went into the temple of the Lord.

10 And the whole multitude of the people was praying outside at the hour of incense.

11 Then an angel of the Lord appeared to him, standing on the right side of the altar of incense.

12 And when Zach·a·rī'as saw *him,* he was troubled, and fear fell upon him.

13 But the angel said to him, "Do not be afraid, Zach·a·rī'as, for your prayer is heard; and your wife Elizabeth will bear you a son, and you shall call his name John.

14 "And you will have joy and gladness, and many will rejoice at his birth.

15 "For he will be great in the sight of the Lord, and shall drink neither wine nor strong drink. He will also be filled with the Holy Spirit, even from his mother's womb.

16 "And he will turn many of the children of Israel to the Lord their God.

17 "He will also go before Him in the spirit and power of E·lī'jah, *'to turn the hearts of the fathers to the children,'a* and the disobedient to the wisdom of the just, to make ready a people prepared for the Lord."

18 And Zach·a·rī'as said to the angel, "How shall I know this? For I am an old man, and my wife is well advanced in years."

19 And the angel answered and said to him, "I am Gabriel, who stands in the presence of God, and was sent to speak to you and bring you these glad tidings.

20 "But behold, you will be mute and not able to speak until the day these things take place, because you did not believe my words which will be fulfilled in their own time."

21 And the people waited for Zach·a·rī'as, and marveled that he lingered so long in the temple.

22 But when he came out, he could not speak to them; and they per-

1:1 *aOr are most surely believed*   1:17 *aMalachi 4:5, 6*

ANGELS Luke 1:11–20, 26–38

What Do Angels Do All Day?

Have you ever wondered about the angels in heaven? What do they do? Do they puff up the clouds and color the rainbows? The Bible doesn't say angels do those things, of course. But it does say something about angels.

1. Read Luke 1:11–20 and Luke 1:26–38. This angel brought special messages from God.
2. Read Psalm 91:11. God appoints angels to take care of us and watch over us.
3. Read Acts 8:26. Sometimes angels show us what to do or where to go.
4. Read Acts 12:7–11. God sometimes sends angels to get us out of trouble.

For more on *Favorite Bible Words* turn to page 1552
For more on *God's Care* turn to page 1578

ceived that he had seen a vision in the temple, for he beckoned to them and remained speechless.

23 So it was, as soon as the days of his service were completed, that he departed to his own house.

24 Now after those days his wife Elizabeth conceived; and she hid herself five months, saying,

25 "Thus the Lord has dealt with me, in the days when He looked on *me,* to take away my reproach among people."

CHRIST'S BIRTH ANNOUNCED TO MARY

What would you do if an angel suddenly appeared before you? What if the angel said he had wonderful news for you? This happened to a young woman named Mary. The news the angel gave her would change the world forever.

26 Now in the sixth month the angel Gabriel was sent by God to a city of Galilee named Nazareth,

27 to a virgin betrothed to a man whose name was Joseph, of the house of David. The virgin's name *was* Mary.

28 And having come in, the angel said to her, "Rejoice, highly favored *one,* the Lord *is* with you; blessed *are* you among women!"a

29 But when she saw *him,*a she was troubled at his saying, and considered what manner of greeting this was.

30 Then the angel said to her, "Do not be afraid, Mary, for you have found favor with God.

31 "And behold, you will conceive in your womb and bring forth a Son, and shall call His name JESUS.

32 "He will be great, and will be called the Son of the Highest; and the Lord God will give Him the throne of His father David.

33 "And He will reign over the house of Jacob forever, and of His kingdom there will be no end."

1:28 aNU-Text omits *blessed are you among women.* 1:29 aNU-Text omits *when she saw him.*

34 Then Mary said to the angel, "How can this be, since I do not know a man?"

35 And the angel answered and said to her, "*The* Holy Spirit will come upon you, and the power of the Highest will overshadow you; therefore, also, that Holy One who is to be born will be called the Son of God.

36 "Now indeed, Elizabeth your relative has also conceived a son in her old age; and this is now the sixth month for her who was called barren.

37 "For with God nothing will be impossible."

38 Then Mary said, "Behold the maidservant of the Lord! Let it be to me according to your word." And the angel departed from her.

☑ *Bible Quiz*

Luke 1:26–38 **An Angel Visits Mary**

1. What was the angel's name?
2. What did the angel say would happen to Mary?
3. What was Mary to name her Baby?
4. Why was this Baby so special?
5. Why do you believe that Jesus is God's Son?

MARY VISITS ELIZABETH

39 Now Mary arose in those days and went into the hill country with haste, to a city of Judah,

40 and entered the house of Zach·a·rī'as and greeted Elizabeth.

41 And it happened, when Elizabeth heard the greeting of Mary, that the babe leaped in her womb; and Elizabeth was filled with the Holy Spirit.

42 Then she spoke out with a loud voice and said, "Blessed *are* you among women, and blessed *is* the fruit of your womb!

43 "But why *is* this *granted* to me, that the mother of my Lord should come to me?

44 "For indeed, as soon as the voice of your greeting sounded in my ears, the babe leaped in my womb for joy.

45 "Blessed *is* she who believed, for there will be a fulfillment of those things which were told her from the Lord."

THE SONG OF MARY

46 And Mary said:

"My soul magnifies the Lord,
47 And my spirit has rejoiced in God my Savior.
48 For He has regarded the lowly state of His maidservant;
For behold, henceforth all generations will call me blessed.
49 For He who is mighty has done great things for me,
And holy *is* His name.
50 And His mercy *is* on those who fear Him
From generation to generation.
51 He has shown strength with His arm;
He has scattered *the* proud in the imagination of their hearts.
52 He has put down the mighty from *their* thrones,
And exalted *the* lowly.
53 He has filled *the* hungry with good things,
And *the* rich He has sent away empty.
54 He has helped His servant Israel,
In remembrance of *His* mercy,
55 As He spoke to our fathers,
To Abraham and to his seed forever."

56 And Mary remained with her about three months, and returned to her house.

BIRTH OF JOHN THE BAPTIST

57 Now Elizabeth's full time came for her to be delivered, and she brought forth a son.
58 When her neighbors and relatives heard how the Lord had shown great mercy to her, they rejoiced with her.

CIRCUMCISION OF JOHN THE BAPTIST

59 So it was, on the eighth day, that they came to circumcise the child; and they would have called him by the name of his father, Zach·a·rī'as.
60 His mother answered and said, "No; he shall be called John."
61 But they said to her, "There is no one among your relatives who is called by this name."
62 So they made signs to his father—what he would have him called.
63 And he asked for a writing tablet, and wrote, saying, "His name is John." So they all marveled.
64 Immediately his mouth was opened and his tongue *loosed,* and he spoke, praising God.
65 Then fear came on all who dwelt around them; and all these sayings were discussed throughout all the hill country of Judea.
66 And all those who heard *them* kept *them* in their hearts, saying, "What kind of child will this be?" And the hand of the Lord was with him.

ZACHARIAS' PROPHECY

67 Now his father Zach·a·rī'as was filled with the Holy Spirit, and prophesied, saying:

68 "Blessed *is* the Lord God of Israel,
For He has visited and redeemed His people,
69 And has raised up a horn of salvation for us
In the house of His servant David,
70 As He spoke by the mouth of His holy prophets,
Who *have been* since the world began,
71 That we should be saved from our enemies
And from the hand of all who hate us,
72 To perform the mercy *promised* to our fathers
And to remember His holy covenant,
73 The oath which He swore to our father Abraham:
74 To grant us that we,
Being delivered from the hand of our enemies,
Might serve Him without fear,
75 In holiness and righteousness before Him all the days of our life.

76 "And you, child, will be called the prophet of the Highest;
For you will go before the face of the Lord to prepare His ways,
77 To give knowledge of salvation to His people
By the remission of their sins,
78 Through the tender mercy of our God,
With which the Dayspring from on high has visited[a] us;
79 To give light to those who sit in darkness and the shadow of death,
To guide our feet into the way of peace."

1:78 [a]NU-Text reads *shall visit.*

80 So the child grew and became strong in spirit, and was in the deserts till the day of his manifestation to Israel.

CHRIST BORN OF MARY

Shepherds were watching their sheep on a quiet hillside outside Bethlehem. That night they would witness the most amazing event in history.

2 And it came to pass in those days *that* a decree went out from Caesar Au·gus′tus that all the world should be registered.
2 This census first took place while Qui·rin′i·us was governing Syria.
3 So all went to be registered, everyone to his own city.
4 Joseph also went up from Galilee, out of the city of Nazareth, into Judea, to the city of David, which is called Bethlehem, because he was of the house and lineage of David,
5 to be registered with Mary, his betrothed wife,*a* who was with child.
6 So it was, that while they were there, the days were completed for her to be delivered.
7 And she brought forth her firstborn Son, and wrapped Him in swaddling cloths, and laid Him in a manger, because there was no room for them in the inn.

GLORY IN THE HIGHEST

8 Now there were in the same country shepherds living out in the fields, keeping watch over their flock by night.
9 And behold,*a* an angel of the Lord stood before them, and the glory of the Lord shone around them, and they were greatly afraid.
10 Then the angel said to them, "Do not be afraid, for behold, I bring you good tidings of great joy which will be to all people.
11 "For there is born to you this day in the city of David a Savior, who is Christ the Lord.
12 "And this *will be* the sign to you: You will find a Babe wrapped in swaddling cloths, lying in a manger."
13 And suddenly there was with the angel a multitude of the heavenly host praising God and saying:

14 "Glory to God in the highest,
   And on earth peace, goodwill
      toward men!"*a*

15 So it was, when the angels had gone away from them into heaven, that the shepherds said to one another, "Let us now go to Bethlehem and see this thing that has come to pass, which the Lord has made known to us."
16 And they came with haste and

2:5 *a*NU-Text omits *wife*.   2:9 *a*NU-Text omits *behold*.   2:14 *a*NU-Text reads *toward men of goodwill*.

✓ Bible Quiz

Luke 2:1–20 **Jesus Is Born**

1. What was this amazing event in history? Why was it so important?
2. Why did Mary and Joseph have to go to Bethlehem?
3. Why couldn't Mary and Joseph stay at the inn?
4. What was Jesus' first crib?
5. How did the shepherds hear about Jesus? After they saw Jesus, were they excited to tell others about Him? How can you tell others about Him?

Favorite Bible Words

GOOD NEWS Luke 2:10, 11

Good News! Jesus Is Born!

It would really be bad news if Jesus had never been born. How would we ever find our way to heaven? How would we ever get our sins forgiven?

1. Why was the news of Jesus' birth such good news? What would we not have if Jesus had never come?
2. Are you excited about the good news of Jesus' birth? Are you thankful to Him that He came? Are you glad that He can be your Savior? Have you asked Him?

For more on *Favorite Bible Words* turn to page 1673
For more on *Salvation* turn to page 1636

found Mary and Joseph, and the Babe lying in a manger.

17 Now when they had seen *Him,* they made widely[a] known the saying which was told them concerning this Child.

18 And all those who heard *it* marveled at those things which were told them by the shepherds.

19 But Mary kept all these things and pondered *them* in her heart.

20 Then the shepherds returned, glorifying and praising God for all the things that they had heard and seen, as it was told them.

CIRCUMCISION OF JESUS

21 And when eight days were completed for the circumcision of the Child,[a] His name was called JESUS, the name given by the angel before He was conceived in the womb.

JESUS PRESENTED IN THE TEMPLE

22 Now when the days of her purification according to the law of Moses were completed, they brought Him to Jerusalem to present *Him* to the Lord

23 (as it is written in the law of the Lord, *"Every male who opens the womb shall be called holy to the LORD"*),[a]

24 and to offer a sacrifice according to what is said in the law of the Lord, *"A pair of turtledoves or two young pigeons."*[a]

SIMEON SEES GOD'S SALVATION

25 And behold, there was a man in Jerusalem whose name was Sim′e·on, and this man was just and devout, waiting for the Consolation of Israel, and the Holy Spirit was upon him.

26 And it had been revealed to him by the Holy Spirit that he would not see death before he had seen the Lord's Christ.

27 So he came by the Spirit into the temple. And when the parents brought in the Child Jesus, to do for Him according to the custom of the law,

28 he took Him up in his arms and blessed God and said:

29 "Lord, now You are letting Your
　　　servant depart in peace,
　　According to Your word;
30 For my eyes have seen Your
　　　salvation
31 Which You have prepared before
　　　the face of all peoples,
32 A light to *bring* revelation to the
　　　Gentiles,
　　And the glory of Your people
　　　Israel."

33 And Joseph and His mother[a] marveled at those things which were spoken of Him.

34 Then Sim′e·on blessed them, and said to Mary His mother, "Behold, this *Child* is destined for the fall and rising of many in Israel, and for a sign which will be spoken against

35 "(yes, a sword will pierce through your own soul also), that the thoughts of many hearts may be revealed."

ANNA BEARS WITNESS TO THE REDEEMER

36 Now there was one, Anna, a prophetess, the daughter of Phan′-ū·el, of the tribe of Ash′er. She was of a great age, and had lived with a husband seven years from her virginity;

37 and this woman *was* a widow of

2:17 [a]NU-Text omits *widely*.　　2:21 [a]NU-Text reads *for His circumcision.*　　2:23 [a]Exodus 13:2, 12, 15　　2:24 [a]Leviticus 12:8　　2:33 [a]NU-Text reads *And His father and mother.*

about eighty-four years,*a* who did not depart from the temple, but served *God* with fastings and prayers night and day.

38 And coming in that instant she gave thanks to the Lord,*a* and spoke of Him to all those who looked for redemption in Jerusalem.

THE FAMILY RETURNS TO NAZARETH

39 So when they had performed all things according to the law of the Lord, they returned to Galilee, to their *own* city, Nazareth.

40 And the Child grew and became strong in spirit,*a* filled with wisdom; and the grace of God was upon Him.

THE BOY JESUS AMAZES THE SCHOLARS

Jesus, a boy now, was talking to some teachers. But it was the teachers who were learning something!

41 His parents went to Jerusalem every year at the Feast of the Passover.

42 And when He was twelve years old, they went up to Jerusalem according to the custom of the feast.

43 When they had finished the days, as they returned, the Boy Jesus lingered behind in Jerusalem. And Joseph and His mother*a* did not know *it;*

44 but supposing Him to have been in the company, they went a day's journey, and sought Him among *their* relatives and acquaintances.

45 So when they did not find Him, they returned to Jerusalem, seeking Him.

46 Now so it was *that* after three days they found Him in the temple, sitting in the midst of the teachers, both listening to them and asking them questions.

47 And all who heard Him were astonished at His understanding and answers.

48 So when they saw Him, they were amazed; and His mother said to Him, "Son, why have You done this to us? Look, Your father and I have sought You anxiously."

49 And He said to them, "Why did you seek Me? Did you not know that I must be about My Father's business?"

50 But they did not understand the statement which He spoke to them.

JESUS ADVANCES IN WISDOM AND FAVOR

51 Then He went down with them and came to Nazareth, and was subject to them, but His mother kept all these things in her heart.

52 And Jesus increased in wisdom and stature, and in favor with God and men.

2:37 *a*NU-Text reads *a widow until she was eighty-four.*   2:38 *a*NU-Text reads *to God.*
2:40 *a*NU-Text omits *in spirit.*   2:43 *a*NU-Text reads *And His parents.*

☑   *Bible Quiz*

Luke 2:41–52 **Jesus Amazes the Teachers**

1. How old was Jesus?
2. Why were Jesus and His parents in Jerusalem?
3. Why didn't His parents miss Him when they left for home?
4. Where did His parents finally find Him? What was Jesus doing?
5. How can you tell from this story that Jesus is God's Son?

JOHN THE BAPTIST PREPARES THE WAY

3 Now in the fifteenth year of the reign of Tī·bē'ri·us Caesar, Pon'ti·us Pilate being governor of Judea, Her'od being tetrarch of Galilee, his brother Philip tetrarch of Ī·tu·rē'a and the region of Trach·o·nī'tis, and Lȳ·sā'ni·as tetrarch of Ab·i·lē'nē,

2 while An'nas and Cā'i·a·phas were high priests,*a* the word of God came to John the son of Zach·a·rī'as in the wilderness.

3 And he went into all the region around the Jordan, preaching a baptism of repentance for the remission of sins,

4 as it is written in the book of the words of Ī·sāi'ah the prophet, saying:

"The voice of one crying in the
        wilderness:
'Prepare the way of the LORD;
Make His paths straight.
5   Every valley shall be filled
And every mountain and hill
        brought low;
The crooked places shall be made
        straight
And the rough ways smooth;
6   And all flesh shall see the
        salvation of God.' "*a*

JOHN PREACHES TO THE PEOPLE

7 Then he said to the multitudes that came out to be baptized by him, "Brood of vipers! Who warned you to flee from the wrath to come?

8 "Therefore bear fruits worthy of repentance, and do not begin to say to yourselves, 'We have Abraham as *our* father.' For I say to you that God is able to raise up children to Abraham from these stones.

9 "And even now the ax is laid to the root of the trees. Therefore every tree which does not bear good fruit is cut down and thrown into the fire."

10 So the people asked him, saying, "What shall we do then?"

11 He answered and said to them, "He who has two tunics, let him give to him who has none; and he who has food, let him do likewise."

12 Then tax collectors also came to be baptized, and said to him, "Teacher, what shall we do?"

13 And he said to them, "Collect no more than what is appointed for you."

14 Likewise the soldiers asked him, saying, "And what shall we do?" So he said to them, "Do not intimidate anyone or accuse falsely, and be content with your wages."

15 Now as the people were in expectation, and all reasoned in their hearts about John, whether he was the Christ *or* not,

16 John answered, saying to all, "I indeed baptize you with water; but One mightier than I is coming, whose sandal strap I am not worthy to loose. He will baptize you with the Holy Spirit and fire.

17 "His winnowing fan *is* in His hand, and He will thoroughly clean out His threshing floor, and gather the wheat into His barn; but the chaff He will burn with unquenchable fire."

18 And with many other exhortations he preached to the people.

19 But Her'od the tetrarch, being rebuked by him concerning He·rō'di·as, his brother Philip's wife,*a* and for all the evils which Her'od had done,

20 also added this, above all, that he shut John up in prison.

3:2 *a*NU-Text and M-Text read *in the high priesthood of Annas and Caiaphas.*   3:6 *a*Isaiah 40:3–5   3:19 *a*NU-Text reads *his brother's wife.*

JOHN BAPTIZES JESUS

21 When all the people were baptized, it came to pass that Jesus also was baptized; and while He prayed, the heaven was opened.
22 And the Holy Spirit descended in bodily form like a dove upon Him, and a voice came from heaven which said, "You are My beloved Son; in You I am well pleased."

■ *see Matthew 3:1–17*

THE GENEALOGY OF JESUS CHRIST

23 Now Jesus Himself began *His* ministry *at* about thirty years of age, being (as was supposed) *the* son of Joseph, *the son* of Hē′li,
24 *the son* of Mat′that,*a the son* of Levi, *the son* of Mel′chī, *the son* of Jan′na, *the son* of Joseph,
25 *the son* of Mat·ta·thī′ah, *the son* of Ā′mos, *the son* of Nā′hum, *the son* of Es′lī, *the son* of Nag′ga·ī,
26 *the son* of Mā′ath, *the son* of Matta·thī′ah, *the son* of Sem′e·ī, *the son* of Joseph, *the son* of Judah,
27 *the son* of Jō·an′nas, *the son* of Rhē′sa, *the son* of Ze·rub′ba·bel, *the son* of She·al′ti·el, *the son* of Nē′rī,
28 *the son* of Mel′chī, *the son* of Ad′dī, *the son* of Cō′sam, *the son* of El·mō′dam, *the son* of Er,
29 *the son* of Jō′sē, *the son* of El·i·ē′zer, *the son* of Jō′rim, *the son* of Mat′that, *the son* of Levi,
30 *the son* of Sim′e·on, *the son* of Judah, *the son* of Joseph, *the son* of Jō′nan, *the son* of E·lī′a·kim,
31 *the son* of Mē′le·a, *the son* of Mē′nan, *the son* of Mat′ta·thah, *the son* of Nathan, *the son* of David,
32 *the son* of Jesse, *the son* of Ō′bed, *the son* of Bō′az, *the son* of Sal′mon, *the son* of Nah′shon,
33 *the son* of Am·min′a·dab, *the son* of Ram, *the son* of Hez′ron, *the son* of Per′ez, *the son* of Judah,
34 *the son* of Jacob, *the son* of Isaac, *the son* of Abraham, *the son* of Tē′rah, *the son* of Nā′hor,
35 *the son* of Sē′rug, *the son* of Rē′ū, *the son* of Pē′leg, *the son* of Ē′ber, *the son* of Shē′lah,
36 *the son* of Cā·ī′nan, *the son* of Ar·phā′xad, *the son* of Shem, *the son* of Noah, *the son* of Lā′mech,
37 *the son* of Me·thū′se·lah, *the son* of Ē′noch, *the son* of Jar′ed, *the son* of Ma·hal′a·lel, *the son* of Cā·ī′nan,
38 *the son* of Ē′nosh, *the son* of Seth, *the son* of Adam, *the son* of God.

SATAN TEMPTS JESUS

4 Then Jesus, being filled with the Holy Spirit, returned from the Jordan and was led by the Spirit into*a* the wilderness,
2 being tempted for forty days by the devil. And in those days He ate nothing, and afterward, when they had ended, He was hungry.
3 And the devil said to Him, "If You are the Son of God, command this stone to become bread."
4 But Jesus answered him, saying,*a* "It is written, *'Man shall not live by bread alone, but by every word of God.'"b*
5 Then the devil, taking Him up on a high mountain, showed Him*a* all the kingdoms of the world in a moment of time.
6 And the devil said to Him, "All this authority I will give You, and their glory; for *this* has been deliv-

---

3:24 *a*This and several other names in the genealogy are spelled somewhat differently in the NU-Text. Since the New King James Version uses the Old Testament spelling for persons mentioned in the New Testament, these variations, which come from the Greek, have not been footnoted.
4:1 *a*NU-Text reads *in.*   4:4 *a*Deuteronomy 8:3 *b*NU-Text omits *but by every word of God.*
4:5 *a*NU-Text reads *And taking Him up, he showed Him.*

ered to me, and I give it to whomever I wish.

7 "Therefore, if You will worship before me, all will be Yours."

8 And Jesus answered and said to him, "Get behind Me, Satan!^a For^b it is written, *'You shall worship the* LORD *your God, and Him only you shall serve.'*^c

9 Then he brought Him to Jerusalem, set Him on the pinnacle of the temple, and said to Him, "If You are the Son of God, throw Yourself down from here.

10 "For it is written:

'He shall give His angels charge over you,
To keep you,'

11 "and,

'In their hands they shall bear you up,
Lest you dash your foot against a stone.'"^a

12 And Jesus answered and said to him, "It has been said, *'You shall not tempt the* LORD *your God.'*"^a

13 Now when the devil had ended every temptation, he departed from Him until an opportune time.

■ *see Matthew 4:1–11*

JESUS BEGINS HIS GALILEAN MINISTRY

14 Then Jesus returned in the power of the Spirit to Galilee, and news of Him went out through all the surrounding region.

15 And He taught in their synagogues, being glorified by all.

JESUS REJECTED AT NAZARETH

16 So He came to Nazareth, where He had been brought up. And as His custom was, He went into the synagogue on the Sabbath day, and stood up to read.

17 And He was handed the book of the prophet I·sāi'ah. And when He had opened the book, He found the place where it was written:

18 *"The Spirit of the* LORD *is upon Me,*
    Because He has anointed Me
    To preach the gospel to the poor;
    He has sent Me to heal the brokenhearted,^a
    To proclaim liberty to the captives
    And recovery of sight to the blind,
    To set at liberty those who are oppressed;
19 *To proclaim the acceptable year of the* LORD."^a

20 Then He closed the book, and gave *it* back to the attendant and sat down. And the eyes of all who were in the synagogue were fixed on Him.

21 And He began to say to them, "Today this Scripture is fulfilled in your hearing."

22 So all bore witness to Him, and marveled at the gracious words which proceeded out of His mouth. And they said, "Is this not Joseph's son?"

23 He said to them, "You will surely say this proverb to Me, 'Physician, heal yourself! Whatever we have heard done in Ca·per'na·um,^a do also here in Your country.'"

24 Then He said, "Assuredly, I say to you, no prophet is accepted in his own country.

25 "But I tell you truly, many widows were in Israel in the days of E·lī'jah, when the heaven was shut up three

4:8 ^aNU-Text omits *Get behind Me, Satan.* ^bNU-Text and M-Text omit *For.* ^cDeuteronomy 6:13
4:11 ^aPsalm 91:11, 12   4:12 ^aDeuteronomy 6:16
4:18 ^aNU-Text omits *to heal the brokenhearted.*
4:19 ^aIsaiah 61:1, 2   4:23 ^aHere and elsewhere the NU-Text spelling is *Capharnaum.*

years and six months, and there was a great famine throughout all the land;

26 "but to none of them was E·lī′jah sent except to Zar′e·phath,*a in the region* of Sī′don, to a woman *who was* a widow.

27 "And many lepers were in Israel in the time of E·lī′sha the prophet, and none of them was cleansed except Nā′a·man the Syrian."

28 So all those in the synagogue, when they heard these things, were filled with wrath,

29 and rose up and thrust Him out of the city; and they led Him to the brow of the hill on which their city was built, that they might throw Him down over the cliff.

30 Then passing through the midst of them, He went His way.

JESUS CASTS OUT AN UNCLEAN SPIRIT

31 Then He went down to Ca·per′-na·um, a city of Galilee, and was teaching them on the Sabbaths.

32 And they were astonished at His teaching, for His word was with authority.

33 Now in the synagogue there was a man who had a spirit of an unclean demon. And he cried out with a loud voice,

34 saying, "Let *us* alone! What have we to do with You, Jesus of Nazareth? Did You come to destroy us? I know who You are—the Holy One of God!"

35 But Jesus rebuked him, saying, "Be quiet, and come out of him!" And when the demon had thrown him in *their* midst, it came out of him and did not hurt him.

36 Then they were all amazed and spoke among themselves, saying, "What a word this *is!* For with authority and power He commands the unclean spirits, and they come out."

37 And the report about Him went out into every place in the surrounding region.

PETER'S MOTHER-IN-LAW HEALED

38 Now He arose from the synagogue and entered Simon's house. But Simon's wife's mother was sick with a high fever, and they made request of Him concerning her.

39 So He stood over her and rebuked the fever, and it left her. And immediately she arose and served them.

MANY HEALED AFTER SABBATH SUNSET

40 When the sun was setting, all those who had any that were sick with various diseases brought them to Him; and He laid His hands on every one of them and healed them.

41 And demons also came out of many, crying out and saying, "You are the Christ,*a* the Son of God!" And He, rebuking *them,* did not allow them to speak, for they knew that He was the Christ.

JESUS PREACHES IN GALILEE

42 Now when it was day, He departed and went into a deserted place. And the crowd sought Him and came to Him, and tried to keep Him from leaving them;

43 but He said to them, "I must preach the kingdom of God to the other cities also, because for this purpose I have been sent."

44 And He was preaching in the synagogues of Galilee.*a*

4:26 *a*Greek *Sarepta*   4:41 *a*NU-Text omits *the Christ.*   4:44 *a*NU-Text reads *Judea.*

FOUR FISHERMEN CALLED AS DISCIPLES

Some men had been fishing all night, but they had not caught anything. They were discouraged. Jesus told them to try again. Would they do what He asked?

5 So it was, as the multitude pressed about Him to hear the word of God, that He stood by the Lake of Gen·nes′a·ret,
2 and saw two boats standing by the lake; but the fishermen had gone from them and were washing *their* nets.
3 Then He got into one of the boats, which was Simon's, and asked him to put out a little from the land. And He sat down and taught the multitudes from the boat.
4 When He had stopped speaking, He said to Simon, "Launch out into the deep and let down your nets for a catch."
5 But Simon answered and said to Him, "Master, we have toiled all night and caught nothing; nevertheless at Your word I will let down the net."
6 And when they had done this, they caught a great number of fish, and their net was breaking.
7 So they signaled to *their* partners in the other boat to come and help them. And they came and filled both the boats, so that they began to sink.
8 When Simon Peter saw *it,* he fell down at Jesus' knees, saying, "Depart from me, for I am a sinful man, O Lord!"
9 For he and all who were with him were astonished at the catch of fish which they had taken;
10 and so also *were* James and John, the sons of Zeb′e·dee, who were partners with Simon. And Jesus said to

Simon, "Do not be afraid. From now on you will catch men."
11 So when they had brought their boats to land, they forsook all and followed Him.

Bible Quiz

☑

Luke 5:1–11 A Great Catch of Fish

1. How many fish had the fishermen caught during the night?
2. Whom did Jesus tell to try again? How can you tell that Simon had great faith in Jesus?
3. What happened when the men went out and tried again?
4. What did Simon realize about Jesus after the great catch of fish?
5. What did Jesus say Simon would be fishing for now? How can you help Jesus fish for people?

JESUS CLEANSES A LEPER

12 And it happened when He was in a certain city, that behold, a man who was full of leprosy saw Jesus; and he fell on *his* face and implored Him, saying, "Lord, if You are willing, You can make me clean."
13 Then He put out *His* hand and touched him, saying, "I am willing; be cleansed." Immediately the leprosy left him.
14 And He charged him to tell no one, "But go and show yourself to the priest, and make an offering for your cleansing, as a testimony to them, just as Moses commanded."
15 However, the report went around

concerning Him all the more; and great multitudes came together to hear, and to be healed by Him of their infirmities.

16 So He Himself *often* withdrew into the wilderness and prayed.

JESUS FORGIVES AND HEALS A PARALYTIC

17 Now it happened on a certain day, as He was teaching, that there were Phar′i·sees and teachers of the law sitting by, who had come out of every town of Galilee, Judea, and Jerusalem. And the power of the Lord was *present* to heal them.*a*

18 Then behold, men brought on a bed a man who was paralyzed, whom they sought to bring in and lay before Him.

19 And when they could not find how they might bring him in, because of the crowd, they went up on the housetop and let him down with *his* bed through the tiling into the midst before Jesus.

20 When He saw their faith, He said to him, "Man, your sins are forgiven you."

21 And the scribes and the Phar′i·sees began to reason, saying, "Who is this who speaks blasphemies? Who can forgive sins but God alone?"

22 But when Jesus perceived their thoughts, He answered and said to them, "Why are you reasoning in your hearts?

23 "Which is easier, to say, 'Your sins are forgiven you,' or to say, 'Rise up and walk'?

24 "But that you may know that the Son of Man has power on earth to forgive sins"—He said to the man who was paralyzed, "I say to you, arise, take up your bed, and go to your house."

25 Immediately he rose up before them, took up what he had been lying on, and departed to his own house, glorifying God.

26 And they were all amazed, and they glorified God and were filled with fear, saying, "We have seen strange things today!"

■ *see Mark 2:1–12*

MATTHEW THE TAX COLLECTOR

27 After these things He went out and saw a tax collector named Levi, sitting at the tax office. And He said to him, "Follow Me."

28 So he left all, rose up, and followed Him.

29 Then Levi gave Him a great feast in his own house. And there were a great number of tax collectors and others who sat down with them.

30 And their scribes and the Phar′i·sees*a* complained against His disciples, saying, "Why do You eat and drink with tax collectors and sinners?"

31 Jesus answered and said to them, "Those who are well have no need of a physician, but those who are sick.

32 "I have not come to call *the* righteous, but sinners, to repentance."

JESUS IS QUESTIONED ABOUT FASTING

33 Then they said to Him, "Why do*a* the disciples of John fast often and make prayers, and likewise those of the Phar′i·sees, but Yours eat and drink?"

34 And He said to them, "Can you make the friends of the bridegroom fast while the bridegroom is with them?

35 "But the days will come when the bridegroom will be taken away from

5:17 *a*NU-Text reads *present with Him to heal.*
5:30 *a*NU-Text reads *But the Pharisees and their scribes.*　　5:33 *a*NU-Text omits *Why do,* making the verse a statement.

them; then they will fast in those days."

36 Then He spoke a parable to them: "No one puts a piece from a new garment on an old one;*a* otherwise the new makes a tear, and also the piece that was *taken* out of the new does not match the old.

37 "And no one puts new wine into old wineskins; or else the new wine will burst the wineskins and be spilled, and the wineskins will be ruined.

38 "But new wine must be put into new wineskins, and both are preserved.*a*

39 "And no one, having drunk old *wine,* immediately*a* desires new; for he says, 'The old is better.' "*b*

JESUS IS LORD OF THE SABBATH

6 Now it happened on the second Sabbath after the first*a* that He went through the grainfields. And His disciples plucked the heads of grain and ate *them,* rubbing *them* in *their* hands.

2 And some of the Phar'i·sees said to them, "Why are you doing what is not lawful to do on the Sabbath?"

3 But Jesus answering them said, "Have you not even read this, what David did when he was hungry, he and those who were with him:

4 "how he went into the house of God, took and ate the showbread, and also gave some to those with him, which is not lawful for any but the priests to eat?"

5 And He said to them, "The Son of Man is also Lord of the Sabbath."

HEALING ON THE SABBATH

6 Now it happened on another Sabbath, also, that He entered the synagogue and taught. And a man was there whose right hand was withered.

7 So the scribes and Phar'i·sees watched Him closely, whether He would heal on the Sabbath, that they might find an accusation against Him.

8 But He knew their thoughts, and said to the man who had the withered hand, "Arise and stand here." And he arose and stood.

9 Then Jesus said to them, "I will ask you one thing: Is it lawful on the Sabbath to do good or to do evil, to save life or to destroy?"*a*

10 And when He had looked around at them all, He said to the man,*a* "Stretch out your hand." And he did so, and his hand was restored as whole as the other.*b*

11 But they were filled with rage, and discussed with one another what they might do to Jesus.

THE TWELVE APOSTLES

12 Now it came to pass in those days that He went out to the mountain to pray, and continued all night in prayer to God.

13 And when it was day, He called His disciples to *Himself;* and from them He chose twelve whom He also named apostles:

14 Simon, whom He also named Peter, and Andrew his brother; James and John; Philip and Bartholomew;

15 Matthew and Thomas; James the *son* of Al·phae'us, and Simon called the Zealot;

16 Judas *the son* of James, and Judas Is·car'i·ot who also became a traitor.

■ *see Mark 3:13–19*

5:36 *a*NU-Text reads *No one tears a piece from a new garment and puts it on an old one.*
5:38 *a*NU-Text omits *and both are preserved.*
5:39 *a*NU-Text omits *immediately.* *b*NU-Text reads *good.* 6:1 *a*NU-Text reads *on a Sabbath.*
6:9 *a*M-Text reads *to kill.* 6:10 *a*NU-Text and M-Text read *to him.* *b*NU-Text omits *as whole as the other.*

JESUS HEALS A GREAT MULTITUDE

17 And He came down with them and stood on a level place with a crowd of His disciples and a great multitude of people from all Judea and Jerusalem, and from the seacoast of Tӯre and Sī′don, who came to hear Him and be healed of their diseases,
18 as well as those who were tormented with unclean spirits. And they were healed.
19 And the whole multitude sought to touch Him, for power went out from Him and healed *them* all.

THE BEATITUDES

20 Then He lifted up His eyes toward His disciples, and said:

"Blessed *are you* poor,
　　For yours is the kingdom of
　　God.
21 Blessed *are you* who hunger
　　now,
　　For you shall be filled.
　Blessed *are you* who weep now,
　　For you shall laugh.
22 Blessed are you when men hate
　　you,
　　And when they exclude you,
　　And revile *you,* and cast out
　　your name as evil,
　　For the Son of Man's sake.
23 Rejoice in that day and leap for
　　joy!
　　For indeed your reward *is* great
　　in heaven,
　　For in like manner their fathers
　　did to the prophets.

JESUS PRONOUNCES WOES

24 "But woe to you who are rich,
　　For you have received your
　　consolation.

25 Woe to you who are full,
　　For you shall hunger.
　Woe to you who laugh now,
　　For you shall mourn and
　　weep.
26 Woe to you*a* when all*b* men speak
　　well of you,
　　For so did their fathers to the
　　false prophets.

LOVE YOUR ENEMIES

27 "But I say to you who hear: Love your enemies, do good to those who hate you,
28 "bless those who curse you, and pray for those who spitefully use you.
29 "To him who strikes you on the *one* cheek, offer the other also. And from him who takes away your cloak, do not withhold *your* tunic either.
30 "Give to everyone who asks of you. And from him who takes away your goods do not ask *them* back.
31 "And just as you want men to do to you, you also do to them likewise.
32 "But if you love those who love you, what credit is that to you? For even sinners love those who love them.
33 "And if you do good to those who do good to you, what credit is that to you? For even sinners do the same.
34 "And if you lend *to those* from whom you hope to receive back, what credit is that to you? For even sinners lend to sinners to receive as much back.
35 "But love your enemies, do good, and lend, hoping for nothing in return; and your reward will be great, and you will be sons of the Most High. For He is kind to the unthankful and evil.

6:26 *a*NU-Text and M-Text omit *to you.* *b*M-Text omits *all.*

What Should I Do?

WHEN LIFE GETS ROUGH Luke 6:27, 28

What do you do when friends gang up on you? What do you do when friends make fun of you? What do you do when friends whisper about you to others? What do you do when friends don't act like friends? What *should* you do?

1. Do you remember the last time some of these things happened? What did you do?
2. What should you do when friends don't really act like friends? What would Jesus want you to do? Read Luke 6:27, 28. What is Jesus saying?

For more on *What Should I Do?* turn to page 1586
For more on *Forgiveness* turn to page 1592

GIVE, AND IT WILL BE GIVEN TO YOU . . . WITH THE SAME MEASURE THAT YOU USE, IT WILL BE MEASURED BACK TO YOU. Luke 6:38

Will You Give a Spoonful or a Bucketful?

How do you measure your giving—a spoonful or a bucketful? Are you a stingy giver or a generous giver? Will you give away only what you have, or will you even give yourself—your time, talent, and energy? What kind of a giver are you, anyway?

1. What does Luke 6:38 say to you about giving? If you give a spoonful of yourself away, how much should you expect in return, a bucketful? Why not?
2. How can you give yourself away? Think of several ways. Would you like to do one of them today?
3. When you were born, you were God's gift to your family. Are you still God's gift to your family each day? How?

For more on *Favorite Family Verses* turn to page 1578
For more on *Giving* turn to page 1641

36 "Therefore be merciful, just as your Father also is merciful.

DO NOT JUDGE

37 "Judge not, and you shall not be judged. Condemn not, and you shall not be condemned. Forgive, and you will be forgiven.

38 "Give, and it will be given to you: good measure, pressed down, shaken together, and running over will be put into your bosom. For with the same measure that you use, it will be measured back to you."

39 And He spoke a parable to them: "Can the blind lead the blind? Will they not both fall into the ditch?

40 "A disciple is not above his teacher, but everyone who is perfectly trained will be like his teacher.

41 "And why do you look at the speck in your brother's eye, but do not perceive the plank in your own eye?

42 "Or how can you say to your brother, 'Brother, let me remove the speck that *is* in your eye,' when you yourself do not see the plank that *is* in your own eye? Hypocrite! First remove the plank from your own eye, and then you will see clearly to remove the speck that is in your brother's eye.

A TREE IS KNOWN BY ITS FRUIT

43 "For a good tree does not bear bad fruit, nor does a bad tree bear good fruit.

44 "For every tree is known by its own fruit. For *men* do not gather figs from thorns, nor do they gather grapes from a bramble bush.

45 "A good man out of the good treasure of his heart brings forth good; and an evil man out of the evil treasure of his heart*a* brings forth evil. For out of the abundance of the heart his mouth speaks.

BUILD ON THE ROCK

46 "But why do you call Me 'Lord, Lord,' and not do the things which I say?

47 "Whoever comes to Me, and hears My sayings and does them, I will show you whom he is like:

48 "He is like a man building a house, who dug deep and laid the foundation on the rock. And when the flood arose, the stream beat vehemently against that house, and could not shake it, for it was founded on the rock.*a*

49 "But he who heard and did nothing is like a man who built a house on the earth without a foundation, against which the stream beat vehemently; and immediately it fell.*a* And the ruin of that house was great."

JESUS HEALS A CENTURION'S SERVANT

7 Now when He concluded all His sayings in the hearing of the people, He entered Ca·per′na·um.

2 And a certain centurion's servant, who was dear to him, was sick and ready to die.

3 So when he heard about Jesus, he sent elders of the Jews to Him, pleading with Him to come and heal his servant.

4 And when they came to Jesus, they begged Him earnestly, saying that the one for whom He should do this was deserving,

5 "for he loves our nation, and has built us a synagogue."

6 Then Jesus went with them. And when He was already not far from the house, the centurion sent friends to Him, saying to Him, "Lord, do not

6:45 *a*NU-Text omits *treasure of his heart.*
6:48 *a*NU-Text reads *for it was well built.*
6:49 *a*NU-Text reads *collapsed.*

trouble Yourself, for I am not worthy that You should enter under my roof.

7 "Therefore I did not even think myself worthy to come to You. But say the word, and my servant will be healed.

8 "For I also am a man placed under authority, having soldiers under me. And I say to one, 'Go,' and he goes; and to another, 'Come,' and he comes; and to my servant, 'Do this,' and he does *it*."

9 When Jesus heard these things, He marveled at him, and turned around and said to the crowd that followed Him, "I say to you, I have not found such great faith, not even in Israel!"

10 And those who were sent, returning to the house, found the servant well who had been sick.*a*

JESUS RAISES THE SON OF THE WIDOW OF NAIN

The town of Nain was not a happy place this day. A young man had died. His mother and friends were carrying his body to the graveyard. Jesus met them as He came into the town. He stopped by the coffin. Something wonderful was about to happen!

11 Now it happened, the day after, *that* He went into a city called Nā′in; and many of His disciples went with Him, and a large crowd.

12 And when He came near the gate of the city, behold, a dead man was being carried out, the only son of his mother; and she was a widow. And a large crowd from the city was with her.

13 When the Lord saw her, He had compassion on her and said to her, "Do not weep."

14 Then He came and touched the open coffin, and those who carried *him* stood still. And He said, "Young man, I say to you, arise."

15 So he who was dead sat up and began to speak. And He presented him to his mother.

16 Then fear came upon all, and they glorified God, saying, "A great prophet has risen up among us"; and, "God has visited His people."

17 And this report about Him went throughout all Judea and all the surrounding region.

☑ Bible Quiz

Luke 7:11–17 Why Jesus Stopped a Funeral

1. What did Jesus see as He came toward the city of Nain?
2. What did Jesus feel when He saw the mother?
3. How did Jesus help her?
4. What did the crowd do when they saw what happened?
5. What does this tell you about Jesus' power over death?

JOHN THE BAPTIST SENDS MESSENGERS TO JESUS

18 Then the disciples of John reported to him concerning all these things.

19 And John, calling two of his disciples to *him,* sent *them* to Jesus,*a* saying, "Are You the Coming One, or do we look for another?"

20 When the men had come to Him, they said, "John the Baptist has sent

---

7:10 *a*NU-Text omits *who had been sick.*
7:19 *a*NU-Text reads *the Lord.*

us to You, saying, 'Are You the Coming One, or do we look for another?' "

21 And that very hour He cured many of infirmities, afflictions, and evil spirits; and to many blind He gave sight.

22 Jesus answered and said to them, "Go and tell John the things you have seen and heard: that *the* blind see, *the* lame walk, *the* lepers are cleansed, *the* deaf hear, *the* dead are raised, *the* poor have the gospel preached to them.

23 "And blessed is *he* who is not offended because of Me."

24 When the messengers of John had departed, He began to speak to the multitudes concerning John: "What did you go out into the wilderness to see? A reed shaken by the wind?

25 "But what did you go out to see? A man clothed in soft garments? Indeed those who are gorgeously appareled and live in luxury are in kings' courts.

26 "But what did you go out to see? A prophet? Yes, I say to you, and more than a prophet.

27 "This is *he* of whom it is written:

'Behold, I send My messenger before Your face,
Who will prepare Your way before You.'a

28 "For I say to you, among those born of women there is not a greater prophet than John the Baptist;a but he who is least in the kingdom of God is greater than he."

29 And when all the people heard *Him,* even the tax collectors justified God, having been baptized with the baptism of John.

30 But the Phar'i·sees and lawyers rejected the will of God for themselves, not having been baptized by him.

31 And the Lord said,a "To what

then shall I liken the men of this generation, and what are they like?

32 "They are like children sitting in the marketplace and calling to one another, saying:

'We played the flute for you,
And you did not dance;
We mourned to you,
And you did not weep.'

33 "For John the Baptist came neither eating bread nor drinking wine, and you say, 'He has a demon.'

34 "The Son of Man has come eating and drinking, and you say, 'Look, a glutton and a winebibber, a friend of tax collectors and sinners!'

35 "But wisdom is justified by all her children."

A Sinful Woman Forgiven

36 Then one of the Phar'i·sees asked Him to eat with him. And He went to the Phar'i·see's house, and sat down to eat.

37 And behold, a woman in the city who was a sinner, when she knew that *Jesus* sat at the table in the Phar'i·see's house, brought an alabaster flask of fragrant oil,

38 and stood at His feet behind *Him* weeping; and she began to wash His feet with her tears, and wiped *them* with the hair of her head; and she kissed His feet and anointed *them* with the fragrant oil.

39 Now when the Phar'i·see who had invited Him saw *this,* he spoke to himself, saying, "This Man, if He were a prophet, would know who and what manner of woman *this is* who is touching Him, for she is a sinner."

40 And Jesus answered and said to him, "Simon, I have something to say to you." So he said, "Teacher, say it."

7:27 aMalachi 3:1   7:28 aNU-Text reads *there is none greater than John.*   7:31 aNU-Text and M-Text omit *And the Lord said.*

41 "There was a certain creditor who had two debtors. One owed five hundred denarii, and the other fifty.

42 "And when they had nothing with which to repay, he freely forgave them both. Tell Me, therefore, which of them will love him more?"

43 Simon answered and said, "I suppose the *one* whom he forgave more." And He said to him, "You have rightly judged."

44 Then He turned to the woman and said to Simon, "Do you see this woman? I entered your house; you gave Me no water for My feet, but she has washed My feet with her tears and wiped *them* with the hair of her head.

45 "You gave Me no kiss, but this woman has not ceased to kiss My feet since the time I came in.

46 "You did not anoint My head with oil, but this woman has anointed My feet with fragrant oil.

47 "Therefore I say to you, her sins, *which are* many, are forgiven, for she loved much. But to whom little is forgiven, *the same* loves little."

48 Then He said to her, "Your sins are forgiven."

49 And those who sat at the table with Him began to say to themselves, "Who is this who even forgives sins?"

50 Then He said to the woman, "Your faith has saved you. Go in peace."

Many Women Minister to Jesus

8 Now it came to pass, afterward, that He went through every city and village, preaching and bringing the glad tidings of the kingdom of God. And the twelve *were* with Him,

2 and certain women who had been healed of evil spirits and infirmities—Mary called Mag′da·lēne, out of whom had come seven demons,

3 and Jō·an′na the wife of Chū′za, Her′od's steward, and Susanna, and many others who provided for Him*a* from their substance.

The Parable of the Sower

4 And when a great multitude had gathered, and they had come to Him from every city, He spoke by a parable:

5 "A sower went out to sow his seed. And as he sowed, some fell by the wayside; and it was trampled down, and the birds of the air devoured it.

6 "Some fell on rock; and as soon as it sprang up, it withered away because it lacked moisture.

7 "And some fell among thorns, and the thorns sprang up with it and choked it.

8 "But others fell on good ground, sprang up, and yielded a crop a hundredfold." When He had said these things He cried, "He who has ears to hear, let him hear!"

The Purpose of Parables

9 Then His disciples asked Him, saying, "What does this parable mean?"

10 And He said, "To you it has been given to know the mysteries of the kingdom of God, but to the rest *it is given* in parables, that

'Seeing they may not see,
And hearing they may not
   understand.'*a*

The Parable of the Sower Explained

11 "Now the parable is this: The seed is the word of God.

8:3 *a*NU-Text and M-Text read *them.*
8:10 *a*Isaiah 6:9

12 "Those by the wayside are the ones who hear; then the devil comes and takes away the word out of their hearts, lest they should believe and be saved.

13 "But the ones on the rock *are those* who, when they hear, receive the word with joy; and these have no root, who believe for a while and in time of temptation fall away.

14 "Now the ones *that* fell among thorns are those who, when they have heard, go out and are choked with cares, riches, and pleasures of life, and bring no fruit to maturity.

15 "But the ones *that* fell on the good ground are those who, having heard the word with a noble and good heart, keep *it* and bear fruit with patience.

■ *see Matthew 13:1–9, 18–23*

THE PARABLE OF THE REVEALED LIGHT

16 "No one, when he has lit a lamp, covers it with a vessel or puts *it* under a bed, but sets *it* on a lampstand, that those who enter may see the light.

17 "For nothing is secret that will not be revealed, nor *anything* hidden that will not be known and come to light.

18 "Therefore take heed how you hear. For whoever has, to him *more* will be given; and whoever does not have, even what he seems to have will be taken from him."

JESUS' MOTHER AND BROTHERS COME TO HIM

19 Then His mother and brothers came to Him, and could not approach Him because of the crowd.

20 And it was told Him *by some,* who said, "Your mother and Your brothers are standing outside, desiring to see You."

21 But He answered and said to them, "My mother and My brothers are these who hear the word of God and do it."

WIND AND WAVE OBEY JESUS

22 Now it happened, on a certain day, that He got into a boat with His disciples. And He said to them, "Let us cross over to the other side of the lake." And they launched out.

23 But as they sailed He fell asleep. And a windstorm came down on the lake, and they were filling *with water,* and were in jeopardy.

24 And they came to Him and awoke Him, saying, "Master, Master, we are perishing!" Then He arose and rebuked the wind and the raging of the water. And they ceased, and there was a calm.

25 But He said to them, "Where is your faith?" And they were afraid, and marveled, saying to one another, "Who can this be? For He commands even the winds and water, and they obey Him!"

■ *see Mark 4:35–41*

A DEMON-POSSESSED MAN HEALED

26 Then they sailed to the country of the Gad'a·rēnes,[a] which is opposite Galilee.

27 And when He stepped out on the land, there met Him a certain man from the city who had demons for a long time. And he wore no clothes,[a] nor did he live in a house but in the tombs.

28 When he saw Jesus, he cried out, fell down before Him, and with a loud voice said, "What have I to do with

8:26 [a]NU-Text reads *Gerasenes.*   8:27 [a]NU-Text reads *who had demons and for a long time wore no clothes.*

You, Jesus, Son of the Most High God? I beg You, do not torment me!"

29 For He had commanded the unclean spirit to come out of the man. For it had often seized him, and he was kept under guard, bound with chains and shackles; and he broke the bonds and was driven by the demon into the wilderness.

30 Jesus asked him, saying, "What is your name?" And he said, "Legion," because many demons had entered him.

31 And they begged Him that He would not command them to go out into the abyss.

32 Now a herd of many swine was feeding there on the mountain. So they begged Him that He would permit them to enter them. And He permitted them.

33 Then the demons went out of the man and entered the swine, and the herd ran violently down the steep place into the lake and drowned.

34 When those who fed *them* saw what had happened, they fled and told *it* in the city and in the country.

35 Then they went out to see what had happened, and came to Jesus, and found the man from whom the demons had departed, sitting at the feet of Jesus, clothed and in his right mind. And they were afraid.

36 They also who had seen *it* told them by what means he who had been demon-possessed was healed.

37 Then the whole multitude of the surrounding region of the Gad′a-rēnes*a* asked Him to depart from them, for they were seized with great fear. And He got into the boat and returned.

38 Now the man from whom the demons had departed begged Him that he might be with Him. But Jesus sent him away, saying,

39 "Return to your own house, and tell what great things God has done for you." And he went his way and proclaimed throughout the whole city what great things Jesus had done for him.

A GIRL RESTORED TO LIFE AND A WOMAN HEALED

This would be a special day for a very sick woman and a very sick girl. They would meet Jesus. Will they also understand that Jesus can heal more than just their physical sickness?

40 So it was, when Jesus returned, that the multitude welcomed Him, for they were all waiting for Him.

41 And behold, there came a man named Jā-ī′rus, and he was a ruler of the synagogue. And he fell down at Jesus' feet and begged Him to come to his house,

42 for he had an only daughter about twelve years of age, and she was dying. But as He went, the multitudes thronged Him.

43 Now a woman, having a flow of blood for twelve years, who had spent all her livelihood on physicians and could not be healed by any,

44 came from behind and touched the border of His garment. And immediately her flow of blood stopped.

45 And Jesus said, "Who touched Me?" When all denied it, Peter and those with him*a* said, "Master, the multitudes throng and press You, and You say, 'Who touched Me?' "*b*

46 But Jesus said, "Somebody touched Me, for I perceived power going out from Me."

47 Now when the woman saw that she was not hidden, she came trem-

8:37 *a*NU-Text reads *Gerasenes.*   8:45 *a*NU-Text omits *and those with him.*   *b*NU-Text omits *and You say, 'Who touched Me?'*

bling; and falling down before Him, she declared to Him in the presence of all the people the reason she had touched Him and how she was healed immediately.

48 And He said to her, "Daughter, be of good cheer;a your faith has made you well. Go in peace."

49 While He was still speaking, someone came from the ruler of the synagogue's *house,* saying to him, "Your daughter is dead. Do not trouble the Teacher."a

50 But when Jesus heard *it,* He answered him, saying, "Do not be afraid; only believe, and she will be made well."

51 When He came into the house, He permitted no one to go ina except Peter, James, and John,b and the father and mother of the girl.

52 Now all wept and mourned for her; but He said, "Do not weep; she is not dead, but sleeping."

53 And they ridiculed Him, knowing that she was dead.

54 But He put them all outside,a took her by the hand and called, saying, "Little girl, arise."

55 Then her spirit returned, and she arose immediately. And He commanded that she be given *something* to eat.

56 And her parents were astonished, but He charged them to tell no one what had happened.

Bible Quiz

☑

Luke 8:40–56 **A Woman and a Girl Are Healed**

1. A man begged Jesus to help him. What was the man's name? What did he need Jesus for? How old was his daughter?

2. As Jesus went to help Jairus, what did a woman in the crowd do? How long had she been sick?

3. There were so many people pressing around Jesus. Why do you think this woman got well by touching Him? What did Jesus say she had that made her well?

4. What bad news did Jesus and Jairus get along the way? Did this discourage Jesus? What did He say to Jairus instead?

5. What happened to Jairus' daughter? Did Jairus believe Jesus?

SENDING OUT THE TWELVE

9 Then He called His twelve disciples together and gave them power and authority over all demons, and to cure diseases.

2 He sent them to preach the kingdom of God and to heal the sick.

3 And He said to them, "Take nothing for the journey, neither staffs nor bag nor bread nor money; and do not have two tunics apiece.

4 "Whatever house you enter, stay there, and from there depart.

5 "And whoever will not receive you, when you go out of that city, shake off the very dust from your feet as a testimony against them."

6 So they departed and went through the towns, preaching the gospel and healing everywhere.

8:48 aNU-Text omits *be of good cheer.*
8:49 aNU-Text adds *anymore.*   8:51 aNU-Text adds *with Him.*   bNU-Text and M-Text read *Peter, John, and James.*   8:54 aNU-Text omits *put them all outside.*

HEROD SEEKS TO SEE JESUS

7 Now Her′od the tetrarch heard of all that was done by Him; and he was perplexed, because it was said by some that John had risen from the dead,

8 and by some that E·lī′jah had appeared, and by others that one of the old prophets had risen again.

9 Her′od said, "John I have beheaded, but who is this of whom I hear such things?" So he sought to see Him.

FEEDING THE FIVE THOUSAND

10 And the apostles, when they had returned, told Him all that they had done. Then He took them and went aside privately into a deserted place belonging to the city called Beth-sā′i·da.

11 But when the multitudes knew it, they followed Him; and He received them and spoke to them about the kingdom of God, and healed those who had need of healing.

12 When the day began to wear away, the twelve came and said to Him, "Send the multitude away, that they may go into the surrounding towns and country, and lodge and get provisions; for we are in a deserted place here."

13 But He said to them, "You give them something to eat." And they said, "We have no more than five loaves and two fish, unless we go and buy food for all these people."

14 For there were about five thousand men. Then He said to His disciples, "Make them sit down in groups of fifty."

15 And they did so, and made them all sit down.

16 Then He took the five loaves and the two fish, and looking up to heaven, He blessed and broke them, and gave them to the disciples to set before the multitude.

17 So they all ate and were filled, and twelve baskets of the leftover fragments were taken up by them.
■ see John 6:1–15

PETER CONFESSES JESUS AS THE CHRIST

18 And it happened, as He was alone praying, that His disciples joined Him, and He asked them, saying, "Who do the crowds say that I am?"

19 So they answered and said, "John the Baptist, but some say E·lī′jah; and others say that one of the old prophets has risen again."

20 He said to them, "But who do you say that I am?" Peter answered and said, "The Christ of God."

JESUS PREDICTS HIS DEATH AND RESURRECTION

21 And He strictly warned and commanded them to tell this to no one,

22 saying, "The Son of Man must suffer many things, and be rejected by the elders and chief priests and scribes, and be killed, and be raised the third day."

TAKE UP THE CROSS AND FOLLOW HIM

23 Then He said to them all, "If anyone desires to come after Me, let him deny himself, and take up his cross daily,a and follow Me.

24 "For whoever desires to save his life will lose it, but whoever loses his life for My sake will save it.

25 "For what profit is it to a man if he gains the whole world, and is himself destroyed or lost?

9:23 aM-Text omits daily.

26 "For whoever is ashamed of Me and My words, of him the Son of Man will be ashamed when He comes in His *own* glory, and *in His* Father's, and of the holy angels.

JESUS TRANSFIGURED ON THE MOUNT

27 "But I tell you truly, there are some standing here who shall not taste death till they see the kingdom of God."

28 Now it came to pass, about eight days after these sayings, that He took Peter, John, and James and went up on the mountain to pray.

29 As He prayed, the appearance of His face was altered, and His robe *became* white *and* glistening.

30 And behold, two men talked with Him, who were Moses and E·li′jah,

31 who appeared in glory and spoke of His decease which He was about to accomplish at Jerusalem.

32 But Peter and those with him were heavy with sleep; and when they were fully awake, they saw His glory and the two men who stood with Him.

33 Then it happened, as they were parting from Him, *that* Peter said to Jesus, "Master, it is good for us to be here; and let us make three tabernacles: one for You, one for Moses, and one for E·li′jah"—not knowing what he said.

34 While he was saying this, a cloud came and overshadowed them; and they were fearful as they entered the cloud.

35 And a voice came out of the cloud, saying,*a* "This is My beloved Son.*a* Hear Him!"

36 When the voice had ceased, Jesus was found alone. But they kept quiet, and told no one in those days any of the things they had seen.

A BOY IS HEALED

37 Now it happened on the next day, when they had come down from the mountain, that a great multitude met Him.

38 Suddenly a man from the multitude cried out, saying, "Teacher, I implore You, look on my son, for he is my only child.

39 "And behold, a spirit seizes him, and he suddenly cries out; it convulses him so that he foams *at the mouth;* and it departs from him with great difficulty, bruising him.

40 "So I implored Your disciples to cast it out, but they could not."

41 Then Jesus answered and said, "O faithless and perverse generation, how long shall I be with you and bear with you? Bring your son here."

42 And as he was still coming, the demon threw him down and convulsed *him.* Then Jesus rebuked the unclean spirit, healed the child, and gave him back to his father.

JESUS AGAIN PREDICTS HIS DEATH

43 And they were all amazed at the majesty of God. But while everyone marveled at all the things which Jesus did, He said to His disciples,

44 "Let these words sink down into your ears, for the Son of Man is about to be betrayed into the hands of men."

45 But they did not understand this saying, and it was hidden from them so that they did not perceive it; and they were afraid to ask Him about this saying.

WHO IS THE GREATEST?

46 Then a dispute arose among them as to which of them would be greatest.

9:35 *a*NU-Text reads *This is My Son, the Chosen One.*

47 And Jesus, perceiving the thought of their heart, took a little child and set him by Him,
48 and said to them, "Whoever receives this little child in My name receives Me; and whoever receives Me receives Him who sent Me. For he who is least among you all will be great."

JESUS FORBIDS SECTARIANISM

49 Now John answered and said, "Master, we saw someone casting out demons in Your name, and we forbade him because he does not follow with us."
50 But Jesus said to him, "Do not forbid *him,* for he who is not against us*a* is on our*b* side."

A SAMARITAN VILLAGE REJECTS
THE SAVIOR

51 Now it came to pass, when the time had come for Him to be received up, that He steadfastly set His face to go to Jerusalem,
52 and sent messengers before His face. And as they went, they entered a village of the Samaritans, to prepare for Him.
53 But they did not receive Him, because His face was *set* for the journey to Jerusalem.
54 And when His disciples James and John saw *this,* they said, "Lord, do You want us to command fire to come down from heaven and consume them, just as E·li'jah did?"*a*
55 But He turned and rebuked them,*a* and said, "You do not know what manner of spirit you are of.
56 "For the Son of Man did not come to destroy men's lives but to save them."*a* And they went to another village.

THE COST OF DISCIPLESHIP

57 Now it happened as they journeyed on the road, *that* someone said to Him, "Lord, I will follow You wherever You go."
58 And Jesus said to him, "Foxes have holes and birds of the air *have* nests, but the Son of Man has nowhere to lay *His* head."
59 Then He said to another, "Follow Me." But he said, "Lord, let me first go and bury my father."
60 Jesus said to him, "Let the dead bury their own dead, but you go and preach the kingdom of God."
61 And another also said, "Lord, I will follow You, but let me first go *and* bid them farewell who are at my house."
62 But Jesus said to him, "No one, having put his hand to the plow, and looking back, is fit for the kingdom of God."

THE SEVENTY SENT OUT

10 After these things the Lord appointed seventy others also,*a* and sent them two by two before His face into every city and place where He Himself was about to go.
2   Then He said to them, "The harvest truly *is* great, but the laborers *are* few; therefore pray the Lord of the harvest to send out laborers into His harvest.
3   "Go your way; behold, I send you out as lambs among wolves.
4   "Carry neither money bag, knapsack, nor sandals; and greet no one along the road.
5   "But whatever house you enter, first say, 'Peace to this house.'
6   "And if a son of peace is there,

9:50 *a*NU-Text reads *you.* *b*NU-Text reads *your.*
9:54 *a*NU-Text omits *just as Elijah did.*
9:55 *a*NU-Text omits the rest of this verse.
9:56 *a*NU-Text omits the first sentence of this verse.   10:1 *a*NU-Text reads *seventy-two others.*

your peace will rest on it; if not, it will return to you.

7   "And remain in the same house, eating and drinking such things as they give, for the laborer is worthy of his wages. Do not go from house to house.

8   "Whatever city you enter, and they receive you, eat such things as are set before you.

9   "And heal the sick there, and say to them, 'The kingdom of God has come near to you.'

10   "But whatever city you enter, and they do not receive you, go out into its streets and say,

11   'The very dust of your city which clings to us*a* we wipe off against you. Nevertheless know this, that the kingdom of God has come near you.'

12   "But*a* I say to you that it will be more tolerable in that Day for Sod'om than for that city.

WOE TO THE IMPENITENT CITIES

13   "Woe to you, Chō·rā'zin! Woe to you, Beth·sā'i·da! For if the mighty works which were done in you had been done in Tȳre and Sī'don, they would have repented long ago, sitting in sackcloth and ashes.

14   "But it will be more tolerable for Tȳre and Sī'don at the judgment than for you.

15   "And you, Ca·per'na·um, who are exalted to heaven, will be brought down to Hā'dēs.*a*

16   "He who hears you hears Me, he who rejects you rejects Me, and he who rejects Me rejects Him who sent Me."

THE SEVENTY RETURN WITH JOY

17   Then the seventy*a* returned with joy, saying, "Lord, even the demons are subject to us in Your name."

18   And He said to them, "I saw Satan fall like lightning from heaven.

19   "Behold, I give you the authority to trample on serpents and scorpions, and over all the power of the enemy, and nothing shall by any means hurt you.

20   "Nevertheless do not rejoice in this, that the spirits are subject to you, but rather*a* rejoice because your names are written in heaven."

JESUS REJOICES IN THE SPIRIT

21   In that hour Jesus rejoiced in the Spirit and said, "I thank You, Father, Lord of heaven and earth, that You have hidden these things from *the* wise and prudent and revealed them to babes. Even so, Father, for so it seemed good in Your sight.

22   "All*a* things have been delivered to Me by My Father, and no one knows who the Son is except the Father, and who the Father is except the Son, and *the one* to whom the Son wills to reveal *Him.*"

23   Then He turned to *His* disciples and said privately, "Blessed *are* the eyes which see the things you see;

24   "for I tell you that many prophets and kings have desired to see what you see, and have not seen *it,* and to hear what you hear, and have not heard *it.*"

THE PARABLE OF THE GOOD SAMARITAN

Who is your neighbor? The person next door? Someone living on your street? Jesus gives us a surprising answer.

25   And behold, a certain lawyer stood up and tested Him, saying,

10:11 *a*NU-Text reads *our feet.*   10:12 *a*NU-Text and M-Text omit *But.*   10:15 *a*NU-Text reads *will you be exalted to heaven? You will be thrust down to Hades!*   10:17 *a*NU-Text reads *seventy-two.*   10:20 *a*NU-Text and M-Text omit *rather.*
10:22 *a*M-Text reads *And turning to the disciples He said,* "All . . . ."

"Teacher, what shall I do to inherit eternal life?"

26 He said to him, "What is written in the law? What is your reading *of it?*"

27 So he answered and said, "*'You shall love the* LORD *your God with all your heart, with all your soul, with all your strength, and with all your mind,'a and 'your neighbor as yourself.'*" *b*

28 And He said to him, "You have answered rightly; do this and you will live."

29 But he, wanting to justify himself, said to Jesus, "And who is my neighbor?"

30 Then Jesus answered and said: "A certain *man* went down from Jerusalem to Jericho, and fell among thieves, who stripped him of his clothing, wounded *him,* and departed, leaving *him* half dead.

31 "Now by chance a certain priest came down that road. And when he saw him, he passed by on the other side.

32 "Likewise a Lē'vīte, when he arrived at the place, came and looked, and passed by on the other side.

33 "But a certain Samaritan, as he journeyed, came where he was. And when he saw him, he had compassion.

34 "So he went to *him* and bandaged his wounds, pouring on oil and wine; and he set him on his own animal, brought him to an inn, and took care of him.

35 "On the next day, when he departed,*a* he took out two denarii, gave *them* to the innkeeper, and said to him, 'Take care of him; and whatever more you spend, when I come again, I will repay you.'

36 "So which of these three do you think was neighbor to him who fell among the thieves?"

37 And he said, "He who showed

mercy on him." Then Jesus said to him, "Go and do likewise."

MARY AND MARTHA WORSHIP AND SERVE

38 Now it happened as they went that He entered a certain village; and a certain woman named Martha welcomed Him into her house.

39 And she had a sister called Mary, who also sat at Jesus'*a* feet and heard His word.

40 But Martha was distracted with much serving, and she approached Him and said, "Lord, do You not care

10:27 *a*Deuteronomy 6:5   *b*Leviticus 19:18
10:35 *a*NU-Text omits *when he departed.*
10:39 *a*NU-Text reads *the Lord's.*

that my sister has left me to serve alone? Therefore tell her to help me." 41 And Jesus[a] answered and said to her, "Martha, Martha, you are worried and troubled about many things. 42 "But one thing is needed, and Mary has chosen that good part, which will not be taken away from her."

THE MODEL PRAYER

11 Now it came to pass, as He was praying in a certain place, when He ceased, *that* one of His disciples said to Him, "Lord, teach us to pray, as John also taught his disciples." 2 So He said to them, "When you pray, say:

Our Father in heaven,[a]
Hallowed be Your name.
Your kingdom come.[b]
Your will be done
On earth as *it is* in heaven.
3 Give us day by day our daily
bread.
4 And forgive us our sins,
For we also forgive everyone who
is indebted to us.
And do not lead us into
temptation,
But deliver us from the evil one."[a]

A FRIEND COMES AT MIDNIGHT

5 And He said to them, "Which of you shall have a friend, and go to him at midnight and say to him, 'Friend, lend me three loaves; 6 'for a friend of mine has come to me on his journey, and I have nothing to set before him'; 7 "and he will answer from within and say, 'Do not trouble me; the door is now shut, and my children are with me in bed; I cannot rise and give to you'?

8 "I say to you, though he will not rise and give to him because he is his friend, yet because of his persistence he will rise and give him as many as he needs.

KEEP ASKING, SEEKING, KNOCKING

9 "So I say to you, ask, and it will be given to you; seek, and you will find; knock, and it will be opened to you. 10 "For everyone who asks receives, and he who seeks finds, and to him who knocks it will be opened. 11 "If a son asks for bread[a] from any father among you, will he give him a stone? Or if *he asks* for a fish, will he give him a serpent instead of a fish? 12 "Or if he asks for an egg, will he offer him a scorpion? 13 "If you then, being evil, know how to give good gifts to your children, how much more will *your* heavenly Father give the Holy Spirit to those who ask Him!"

A HOUSE DIVIDED CANNOT STAND

14 And He was casting out a demon, and it was mute. So it was, when the demon had gone out, that the mute spoke; and the multitudes marveled. 15 But some of them said, "He casts out demons by Bē·el′ze·bub,[a] the ruler of the demons." 16 Others, testing *Him,* sought from Him a sign from heaven. 17 But He, knowing their thoughts, said to them: "Every kingdom divided against itself is brought to desolation, and a house *divided* against a house falls.

10:41 [a]NU-Text reads *the Lord.*   11:2 [a]NU-Text omits *Our* and *in heaven.*   [b]NU-Text omits the rest of this verse.   11:4 [a]NU-Text omits *But deliver us from the evil one.*   11:11 [a]NU-Text omits the words from *bread* through *for* in the next sentence.   11:15 [a]NU-Text and M-Text read *Beelzebul.*

GIVE US DAY BY DAY OUR DAILY BREAD. Luke 11:3

Where Does Food Come From?

It's dinner time, or lunch time, or breakfast time. You come to the table and it is always filled with good food. But where does it come from?

1. Who puts the food on your table? How does mother or father help put food on your table?
2. What other people help to put food on your table? Think about the grocery store people, the truck drivers who brought the food to the grocery stores, the companies that helped to produce and package it, and the farmers who raised it. Thank God for each person who helped you have good food today.
3. But who makes it possible for food to grow? Think of one food that you would have without God. Is there even one? No, not even one.
4. Would you like to thank God now for good food? Would you like to thank Him at each meal?

For more on *Favorite Family Verses* turn to page 1619
For more on *God's Care* turn to page 1647

18 "If Satan also is divided against himself, how will his kingdom stand? Because you say I cast out demons by Bē·el'ze·bub.

19 "And if I cast out demons by Bē·el'ze·bub, by whom do your sons cast *them* out? Therefore they will be your judges.

20 "But if I cast out demons with the finger of God, surely the kingdom of God has come upon you.

21 "When a strong man, fully armed, guards his own palace, his goods are in peace.

22 "But when a stronger than he comes upon him and overcomes him, he takes from him all his armor in which he trusted, and divides his spoils.

23 "He who is not with Me is against Me, and he who does not gather with Me scatters.

AN UNCLEAN SPIRIT RETURNS

24 "When an unclean spirit goes out of a man, he goes through dry places, seeking rest; and finding none, he says, 'I will return to my house from which I came.'

25 "And when he comes, he finds *it* swept and put in order.

26 "Then he goes and takes with *him* seven other spirits more wicked than himself, and they enter and dwell there; and the last *state* of that man is worse than the first."

KEEPING THE WORD

27 And it happened, as He spoke these things, that a certain woman from the crowd raised her voice and said to Him, "Blessed *is* the womb that bore You, and *the* breasts which nursed You!"

28 But He said, "More than that, blessed *are* those who hear the word of God and keep it!"

SEEKING A SIGN

29 And while the crowds were thickly gathered together, He began to say, "This is an evil generation. It seeks a sign, and no sign will be given to it except the sign of Jonah the prophet.*a*

30 "For as Jonah became a sign to the Nin'e·vītes, so also the Son of Man will be to this generation.

31 "The queen of the South will rise up in the judgment with the men of this generation and condemn them, for she came from the ends of the earth to hear the wisdom of Solomon; and indeed a greater than Solomon *is* here.

32 "The men of Nin'e·veh will rise up in the judgment with this generation and condemn it, for they repented at the preaching of Jonah; and indeed a greater than Jonah *is* here.

THE LAMP OF THE BODY

33 "No one, when he has lit a lamp, puts *it* in a secret place or under a basket, but on a lampstand, that those who come in may see the light.

34 "The lamp of the body is the eye. Therefore, when your eye is good, your whole body also is full of light. But when *your eye* is bad, your body also *is* full of darkness.

35 "Therefore take heed that the light which is in you is not darkness.

36 "If then your whole body *is* full of light, having no part dark, *the* whole *body* will be full of light, as when the bright shining of a lamp gives you light."

WOE TO THE PHARISEES AND LAWYERS

37 And as He spoke, a certain Phar'i·see asked Him to dine with

11:29 *a*NU-Text omits *the prophet.*

him. So He went in and sat down to eat.

38 When the Phar′i·see saw *it,* he marveled that He had not first washed before dinner.

39 Then the Lord said to him, "Now you Phar′i·sees make the outside of the cup and dish clean, but your inward part is full of greed and wickedness.

40 "Foolish ones! Did not He who made the outside make the inside also?

41 "But rather give alms of such things as you have; then indeed all things are clean to you.

42 "But woe to you Phar′i·sees! For you tithe mint and rue and all manner of herbs, and pass by justice and the love of God. These you ought to have done, without leaving the others undone.

43 "Woe to you Phar′i·sees! For you love the best seats in the synagogues and greetings in the marketplaces.

44 "Woe to you, scribes and Phar′i·sees, hypocrites!*a* For you are like graves which are not seen, and the men who walk over *them* are not aware *of them.*"

45 Then one of the lawyers answered and said to Him, "Teacher, by saying these things You reproach us also."

46 And He said, "Woe to you also, lawyers! For you load men with burdens hard to bear, and you yourselves do not touch the burdens with one of your fingers.

47 "Woe to you! For you build the tombs of the prophets, and your fathers killed them.

48 "In fact, you bear witness that you approve the deeds of your fathers; for they indeed killed them, and you build their tombs.

49 "Therefore the wisdom of God also said, 'I will send them prophets and apostles, and *some* of them they will kill and persecute,'

50 "that the blood of all the prophets which was shed from the foundation of the world may be required of this generation,

51 "from the blood of Abel to the blood of Zech·a·rī′ah who perished between the altar and the temple. Yes, I say to you, it shall be required of this generation.

52 "Woe to you lawyers! For you have taken away the key of knowledge. You did not enter in yourselves, and those who were entering in you hindered."

53 And as He said these things to them,*a* the scribes and the Phar′i·sees began to assail *Him* vehemently, and to cross-examine Him about many things,

54 lying in wait for Him, and seeking to catch Him in something He might say, that they might accuse Him.*a*

BEWARE OF HYPOCRISY

12 In the meantime, when an innumerable multitude of people had gathered together, so that they trampled one another, He began to say to His disciples first *of all,* "Beware of the leaven of the Phar′i·sees, which is hypocrisy.

2 "For there is nothing covered that will not be revealed, nor hidden that will not be known.

3 "Therefore whatever you have spoken in the dark will be heard in the light, and what you have spoken in the ear in inner rooms will be proclaimed on the housetops.

JESUS TEACHES THE FEAR OF GOD

4 "And I say to you, My friends, do not be afraid of those who kill the

11:44 *a*NU-Text omits *scribes and Pharisees, hypocrites.* 11:53 *a*NU-Text reads *And when He left there.* 11:54 *a*NU-Text omits *and seeking* and *that they might accuse Him.*

body, and after that have no more that they can do.

5 "But I will show you whom you should fear: Fear Him who, after He has killed, has power to cast into hell; yes, I say to you, fear Him!

6 "Are not five sparrows sold for two copper coins?a And not one of them is forgotten before God.

7 "But the very hairs of your head are all numbered. Do not fear therefore; you are of more value than many sparrows.

Confess Christ Before Men

8 "Also I say to you, whoever confesses Me before men, him the Son of Man also will confess before the angels of God.

9 "But he who denies Me before men will be denied before the angels of God.

10 "And anyone who speaks a word against the Son of Man, it will be forgiven him; but to him who blasphemes against the Holy Spirit, it will not be forgiven.

11 "Now when they bring you to the synagogues and magistrates and authorities, do not worry about how or what you should answer, or what you should say.

12 "For the Holy Spirit will teach you in that very hour what you ought to say."

The Parable of the Rich Fool

13 Then one from the crowd said to Him, "Teacher, tell my brother to divide the inheritance with me."

14 But He said to him, "Man, who made Me a judge or an arbitrator over you?"

15 And He said to them, "Take heed and beware of covetousness,a for one's life does not consist in the abundance of the things he possesses."

16 Then He spoke a parable to them, saying: "The ground of a certain rich man yielded plentifully.

17 "And he thought within himself, saying, 'What shall I do, since I have no room to store my crops?'

18 "So he said, 'I will do this: I will pull down my barns and build greater, and there I will store all my crops and my goods.

19 'And I will say to my soul, "Soul, you have many goods laid up for many years; take your ease; eat, drink, *and* be merry." '

20 "But God said to him, 'Fool! This night your soul will be required of you; then whose will those things be which you have provided?'

21 "So *is* he who lays up treasure for himself, and is not rich toward God."

Do Not Worry

22 Then He said to His disciples, "Therefore I say to you, do not worry about your life, what you will eat; nor about the body, what you will put on.

23 "Life is more than food, and the body *is more* than clothing.

24 "Consider the ravens, for they neither sow nor reap, which have neither storehouse nor barn; and God feeds them. Of how much more value are you than the birds?

25 "And which of you by worrying can add one cubit to his stature?

26 "If you then are not able to do *the* least, why are you anxious for the rest?

27 "Consider the lilies, how they grow: they neither toil nor spin; and yet I say to you, even Solomon in all his glory was not arrayed like one of these.

28 "If then God so clothes the grass,

12:6 aGreek *assarion,* a coin of very small value
12:15 aNU-Text reads *all covetousness.*

which today is in the field and tomorrow is thrown into the oven, how much more *will He clothe* you, O *you* of little faith?

29 "And do not seek what you should eat or what you should drink, nor have an anxious mind.

30 "For all these things the nations of the world seek after, and your Father knows that you need these things.

31 "But seek the kingdom of God, and all these things[a] shall be added to you.

32 "Do not fear, little flock, for it is your Father's good pleasure to give you the kingdom.

33 "Sell what you have and give alms; provide yourselves money bags which do not grow old, a treasure in the heavens that does not fail, where no thief approaches nor moth destroys.

34 "For where your treasure is, there your heart will be also.

THE FAITHFUL SERVANT AND THE EVIL SERVANT

35 "Let your waist be girded and *your* lamps burning;

36 "and you yourselves be like men who wait for their master, when he will return from the wedding, that when he comes and knocks they may open to him immediately.

37 "Blessed *are* those servants whom the master, when he comes, will find watching. Assuredly, I say to you that he will gird himself and have them sit down *to eat,* and will come and serve them.

38 "And if he should come in the second watch, or come in the third watch, and find *them* so, blessed are those servants.

39 "But know this, that if the master of the house had known what hour the thief would come, he would have watched and[a] not allowed his house to be broken into.

40 "Therefore you also be ready, for the Son of Man is coming at an hour you do not expect."

41 Then Peter said to Him, "Lord, do You speak this parable *only* to us, or to all *people?*"

42 And the Lord said, "Who then is that faithful and wise steward, whom *his* master will make ruler over his household, to give *them their* portion of food in due season?

43 "Blessed *is* that servant whom his master will find so doing when he comes.

44 "Truly, I say to you that he will make him ruler over all that he has.

45 "But if that servant says in his heart, 'My master is delaying his coming,' and begins to beat the male and female servants, and to eat and drink and be drunk,

46 "the master of that servant will come on a day when he is not looking for *him,* and at an hour when he is not aware, and will cut him in two and appoint *him* his portion with the unbelievers.

47 "And that servant who knew his master's will, and did not prepare *himself* or do according to his will, shall be beaten with many *stripes.*

48 "But he who did not know, yet committed things deserving of stripes, shall be beaten with few. For everyone to whom much is given, from him much will be required; and to whom much has been committed, of him they will ask the more.

CHRIST BRINGS DIVISION

49 "I came to send fire on the earth, and how I wish it were already kindled!

12:31 [a]NU-Text reads *His kingdom, and these things.*   12:39 [a]NU-Text reads *he would not have allowed.*

50 "But I have a baptism to be baptized with, and how distressed I am till it is accomplished!

51 "Do *you* suppose that I came to give peace on earth? I tell you, not at all, but rather division.

52 "For from now on five in one house will be divided: three against two, and two against three.

53 "Father will be divided against son and son against father, mother against daughter and daughter against mother, mother-in-law against her daughter-in-law and daughter-in-law against her mother-in-law."

DISCERN THE TIME

54 Then He also said to the multitudes, "Whenever you see a cloud rising out of the west, immediately you say, 'A shower is coming'; and so it is.

55 "And when you see the south wind blow, you say, 'There will be hot weather'; and there is.

56 "Hypocrites! You can discern the face of the sky and of the earth, but how *is it* you do not discern this time?

MAKE PEACE WITH YOUR ADVERSARY

57 "Yes, and why, even of yourselves, do you not judge what is right?

58 "When you go with your adversary to the magistrate, make every effort along the way to settle with him, lest he drag you to the judge, the judge deliver you to the officer, and the officer throw you into prison.

59 "I tell you, you shall not depart from there till you have paid the very last mite."

REPENT OR PERISH

13

There were present at that season some who told Him about the Galileans whose blood Pilate had mingled with their sacrifices.

2 And Jesus answered and said to them, "Do you suppose that these Galileans were worse sinners than all *other* Galileans, because they suffered such things?

3 "I tell you, no; but unless you repent you will all likewise perish.

4 "Or those eighteen on whom the tower in Sĭ-lō'am fell and killed them, do you think that they were worse sinners than all *other* men who dwelt in Jerusalem?

5 "I tell you, no; but unless you repent you will all likewise perish."

THE PARABLE OF THE BARREN FIG TREE

6 He also spoke this parable: "A certain *man* had a fig tree planted in his vineyard, and he came seeking fruit on it and found none.

7 "Then he said to the keeper of his vineyard, 'Look, for three years I have come seeking fruit on this fig tree and find none. Cut it down; why does it use up the ground?'

8 "But he answered and said to him, 'Sir, let it alone this year also, until I dig around it and fertilize *it*.

9 'And if it bears fruit, *well*. But if not, after that[a] you can cut it down.' "

A SPIRIT OF INFIRMITY

10 Now He was teaching in one of the synagogues on the Sabbath.

11 And behold, there was a woman who had a spirit of infirmity eighteen years, and was bent over and could in no way raise *herself* up.

12 But when Jesus saw her, He called *her* to *Him* and said to her,

13:9 [a]NU-Text reads *And if it bears fruit after that, well. But if not, you can cut it down.*

"Woman, you are loosed from your infirmity."

13 And He laid *His* hands on her, and immediately she was made straight, and glorified God.

14 But the ruler of the synagogue answered with indignation, because Jesus had healed on the Sabbath; and he said to the crowd, "There are six days on which men ought to work; therefore come and be healed on them, and not on the Sabbath day."

15 The Lord then answered him and said, "Hypocrite!a Does not each one of you on the Sabbath loose his ox or donkey from the stall, and lead *it* away to water it?

16 "So ought not this woman, being a daughter of Abraham, whom Satan has bound—think of it—for eighteen years, be loosed from this bond on the Sabbath?"

17 And when He said these things, all His adversaries were put to shame; and all the multitude rejoiced for all the glorious things that were done by Him.

THE PARABLE OF THE MUSTARD SEED

18 Then He said, "What is the kingdom of God like? And to what shall I compare it?

19 "It is like a mustard seed, which a man took and put in his garden; and it grew and became a largea tree, and the birds of the air nested in its branches."

THE PARABLE OF THE LEAVEN

20 And again He said, "To what shall I liken the kingdom of God?

21 "It is like leaven, which a woman took and hid in three measuresa of meal till it was all leavened."

THE NARROW WAY

22 And He went through the cities and villages, teaching, and journeying toward Jerusalem.

23 Then one said to Him, "Lord, are there few who are saved?" And He said to them,

24 "Strive to enter through the narrow gate, for many, I say to you, will seek to enter and will not be able.

25 "When once the Master of the house has risen up and shut the door, and you begin to stand outside and knock at the door, saying, 'Lord, Lord, open for us,' and He will answer and say to you, 'I do not know you, where you are from,'

26 "then you will begin to say, 'We ate and drank in Your presence, and You taught in our streets.'

27 "But He will say, 'I tell you I do not know you, where you are from. Depart from Me, all you workers of iniquity.'

28 "There will be weeping and gnashing of teeth, when you see Abraham and Isaac and Jacob and all the prophets in the kingdom of God, and yourselves thrust out.

29 "They will come from the east and the west, from the north and the south, and sit down in the kingdom of God.

30 "And indeed there are last who will be first, and there are first who will be last."

31 On that very daya some Phar'-i-sees came, saying to Him, "Get out and depart from here, for Her'od wants to kill You."

32 And He said to them, "Go, tell that fox, 'Behold, I cast out demons and perform cures today and tomor-

13:15 aNU-Text and M-Text read *Hypocrites.*
13:19 aNU-Text omits *large.*   13:21 aGreek *sata,* approximately two pecks in all
13:31 aNU-Text reads *In that very hour.*

row, and the third *day* I shall be perfected.'

33 "Nevertheless I must journey today, tomorrow, and the *day* following; for it cannot be that a prophet should perish outside of Jerusalem.

JESUS LAMENTS OVER JERUSALEM

34 "O Jerusalem, Jerusalem, the one who kills the prophets and stones those who are sent to her! How often I wanted to gather your children together, as a hen *gathers* her brood under *her* wings, but you were not willing!

35 "See! Your house is left to you desolate; and assuredly,a I say to you, you shall not see Me until *the time* comes when you say, 'Blessed is He who comes in the name of the LORD!'"b

A MAN WITH DROPSY HEALED ON THE SABBATH

14 Now it happened, as He went into the house of one of the rulers of the Phar'i·sees to eat bread on the Sabbath, that they watched Him closely.

2 And behold, there was a certain man before Him who had dropsy.

3 And Jesus, answering, spoke to the lawyers and Phar'i·sees, saying, "Is it lawful to heal on the Sabbath?"a

4 But they kept silent. And He took *him* and healed him, and let him go.

5 Then He answered them, saying, "Which of you, having a donkeya or an ox that has fallen into a pit, will not immediately pull him out on the Sabbath day?"

6 And they could not answer Him regarding these things.

TAKE THE LOWLY PLACE

7 So He told a parable to those who were invited, when He noted how they chose the best places, saying to them:

8 "When you are invited by anyone to a wedding feast, do not sit down in the best place, lest one more honorable than you be invited by him;

9 "and he who invited you and him come and say to you, 'Give place to this man,' and then you begin with shame to take the lowest place.

10 "But when you are invited, go and sit down in the lowest place, so that when he who invited you comes he may say to you, 'Friend, go up higher.' Then you will have glory in the presence of those who sit at the table with you.

11 "For whoever exalts himself will be humbled, and he who humbles himself will be exalted."

12 Then He also said to him who invited Him, "When you give a dinner or a supper, do not ask your friends, your brothers, your relatives, nor rich neighbors, lest they also invite you back, and you be repaid.

13 "But when you give a feast, invite *the* poor, *the* maimed, *the* lame, *the* blind.

14 "And you will be blessed, because they cannot repay you; for you shall be repaid at the resurrection of the just."

THE PARABLE OF THE GREAT SUPPER

15 Now when one of those who sat at the table with Him heard these things, he said to Him, "Blessed *is* he who shall eat breada in the kingdom of God!"

16 Then He said to him, "A certain

13:35 aNU-Text and M-Text omit *assuredly.*
bPsalm 118:26   14:3 aNU-Text adds *or not.*
14:5 aNU-Text and M-Text read *son.*
14:15 aM-Text reads *dinner.*

I FISHED FOR A WHALE AND CAUGHT A MINNOW Luke 14:27–33

Have you ever dreamed *big* dreams? You want to be rich or famous or muscular or beautiful or something. But things don't seem to work out quite that way. You went for a whale, but caught a minnow. You want *big* things, but always seem to get the little ones. What should you do then?

1. Should you blame God when things don't seem to work quite right? Is it really God's fault?
2. Should you blame others when things don't seem to work quite right? Is it always the fault of someone else?
3. Should you ask first "Was my dream too big?" Should you bring your million-dollar dreams down to ten-dollar ability to fulfill them? Read Luke 14:27–33. Ask two questions: "What am I able to do without God?" and "What is God able to do through me?" What's the difference?

For more on *What Should I Do?* turn to page 1589
For more on *Humility* turn to page 1737

man gave a great supper and invited many,

17 "and sent his servant at supper time to say to those who were invited, 'Come, for all things are now ready.'

18 "But they all with one *accord* began to make excuses. The first said to him, 'I have bought a piece of ground, and I must go and see it. I ask you to have me excused.'

19 "And another said, 'I have bought five yoke of oxen, and I am going to test them. I ask you to have me excused.'

20 "Still another said, 'I have married a wife, and therefore I cannot come.'

21 "So that servant came and reported these things to his master. Then the master of the house, being angry, said to his servant, 'Go out quickly into the streets and lanes of the city, and bring in here *the* poor and *the* maimed and *the* lame and *the* blind.'

22 "And the servant said, 'Master, it is done as you commanded, and still there is room.'

23 "Then the master said to the servant, 'Go out into the highways and hedges, and compel *them* to come in, that my house may be filled.

24 'For I say to you that none of those men who were invited shall taste my supper.' "

LEAVING ALL TO FOLLOW CHRIST

25 Now great multitudes went with Him. And He turned and said to them,

26 "If anyone comes to Me and does not hate his father and mother, wife and children, brothers and sisters, yes, and his own life also, he cannot be My disciple.

27 "And whoever does not bear his cross and come after Me cannot be My disciple.

28 "For which of you, intending to build a tower, does not sit down first

and count the cost, whether he has *enough* to finish *it*—

29 "lest, after he has laid the foundation, and is not able to finish, all who see *it* begin to mock him,

30 "saying, 'This man began to build and was not able to finish.'

31 "Or what king, going to make war against another king, does not sit down first and consider whether he is able with ten thousand to meet him who comes against him with twenty thousand?

32 "Or else, while the other is still a great way off, he sends a delegation and asks conditions of peace.

33 "So likewise, whoever of you does not forsake all that he has cannot be My disciple.

TASTELESS SALT IS WORTHLESS

34 "Salt *is* good; but if the salt has lost its flavor, how shall it be seasoned?

35 "It is neither fit for the land nor for the dunghill, *but* men throw it out. He who has ears to hear, let him hear!"

THE PARABLE OF THE LOST SHEEP

Some men were angry at Jesus because He was spending time with people who did not know God and were not obeying Him. Jesus had some stories for these angry men.

15 Then all the tax collectors and the sinners drew near to Him to hear Him.

2 And the Phar′i·sees and scribes complained, saying, "This Man receives sinners and eats with them."

3 So He spoke this parable to them, saying:

4 "What man of you, having a hundred sheep, if he loses one of them, does not leave the ninety-nine in the wilderness, and go after the one which is lost until he finds it?

5 "And when he has found *it,* he lays *it* on his shoulders, rejoicing.

6 "And when he comes home, he calls together *his* friends and neighbors, saying to them, 'Rejoice with me, for I have found my sheep which was lost!'

7 "I say to you that likewise there will be more joy in heaven over one sinner who repents than over ninety-nine just persons who need no repentance.

THE PARABLE OF THE LOST COIN

8 "Or what woman, having ten silver coins,[a] if she loses one coin, does

15:8 [a]Greek *drachma,* a valuable coin often worn in a ten-piece garland by married women

---

✓	*Bible Quiz*

Luke 15:1–10   **A Lost Sheep and a Lost Coin**

1. Why were the Pharisees and scribes angry at Jesus? What two stories did Jesus tell them?

2. Why do you think the shepherd went out to find his one lost sheep? What would have happened to the sheep if the shepherd had not gone out looking for it?

3. What would have happened to the coin if the woman had not looked for it?

4. How are sinners lost when they don't know Jesus? How will one of your friends come to know Jesus if you don't help that friend find Him?

not light a lamp, sweep the house, and search carefully until she finds *it?*

9 "And when she has found *it,* she calls *her* friends and neighbors together, saying, 'Rejoice with me, for I have found the piece which I lost!'

10 "Likewise, I say to you, there is joy in the presence of the angels of God over one sinner who repents."

The Parable of the Lost Son

Jesus tells a story about a son who went away from home, then decided to come back. What do you think Jesus was trying to tell us?

11 Then He said: "A certain man had two sons.

12 "And the younger of them said to *his* father, 'Father, give me the portion of goods that falls *to me.*' So he divided to them *his* livelihood.

13 "And not many days after, the younger son gathered all together, journeyed to a far country, and there wasted his possessions with prodigal living.

14 "But when he had spent all, there arose a severe famine in that land, and he began to be in want.

15 "Then he went and joined himself to a citizen of that country, and he sent him into his fields to feed swine.

16 "And he would gladly have filled his stomach with the pods that the swine ate, and no one gave him *anything.*

17 "But when he came to himself, he said, 'How many of my father's hired servants have bread enough and to spare, and I perish with hunger!

18 'I will arise and go to my father, and will say to him, "Father, I have sinned against heaven and before you,

19 "and I am no longer worthy to be called your son. Make me like one of your hired servants." '

20 "And he arose and came to his father. But when he was still a great way off, his father saw him and had compassion, and ran and fell on his neck and kissed him.

21 "And the son said to him, 'Father, I have sinned against heaven and in your sight, and am no longer worthy to be called your son.'

22 "But the father said to his servants, 'Bring*a* out the best robe and put *it* on him, and put a ring on his hand and sandals on *his* feet.

23 'And bring the fatted calf here and kill *it,* and let us eat and be merry;

24 'for this my son was dead and is alive again; he was lost and is found.' And they began to be merry.

25 "Now his older son was in the field. And as he came and drew near to the house, he heard music and dancing.

26 "So he called one of the servants and asked what these things meant.

27 "And he said to him, 'Your brother has come, and because he has received him safe and sound, your father has killed the fatted calf.'

28 "But he was angry and would not go in. Therefore his father came out and pleaded with him.

29 "So he answered and said to *his* father, 'Lo, these many years I have been serving you; I never transgressed your commandment at any time; and yet you never gave me a young goat, that I might make merry with my friends.

30 'But as soon as this son of yours came, who has devoured your livelihood with harlots, you killed the fatted calf for him.'

31 "And he said to him, 'Son, you are

15:22 *a*NU-Text reads *Quickly bring.*

SHOULD I EVER RUN AWAY? Luke 15:13

What if mother or father scolds me? Should I run away? What if mother or father won't let me do something I want to do? Should I run away? What if mother or father won't take me somewhere I want to go? Should I run away? Should I ever run away?

1. Is there ever a time to run away from home? Why not?
2. Think of three good reasons why it is very bad to run away from home.
3. Would running away please God? Why not?

For more on *What Should I Do?* turn to page 1592
For more on *Obeying* turn to page 1890

always with me, and all that I have is yours.

32 'It was right that we should make merry and be glad, for your brother was dead and is alive again, and was lost and is found.'"

☑	*Bible Quiz*

Luke 15:11–32 **The Lost Son**

1. What did the younger son ask of his father? What did the father do?
2. What did the younger son do with the money he got from his father?
3. What kind of work did the son do when he ran out of money? How did he feel then?
4. What did the son finally decide to do? Why do you think it was a hard decision for the son to go home?
5. What did the father do when he saw his son coming home? How did the older son feel about this? What did you learn about forgiveness?

THE PARABLE OF THE
UNJUST STEWARD

16 He also said to His disciples: "There was a certain rich man who had a steward, and an accusation was brought to him that this man was wasting his goods.

2 "So he called him and said to him, 'What is this I hear about you? Give an account of your stewardship, for you can no longer be steward.'

3 "Then the steward said within himself, 'What shall I do? For my master is taking the stewardship away from me. I cannot dig; I am ashamed to beg.

4 'I have resolved what to do, that when I am put out of the stewardship, they may receive me into their houses.'

5 "So he called every one of his master's debtors to *him,* and said to the first, 'How much do you owe my master?'

6 "And he said, 'A hundred measures*a* of oil.' So he said to him, 'Take your bill, and sit down quickly and write fifty.'

7 "Then he said to another, 'And how much do you owe?' So he said, 'A hundred measures*a* of wheat.' And he said to him, 'Take your bill, and write eighty.'

8 "So the master commended the unjust steward because he had dealt shrewdly. For the sons of this world are more shrewd in their generation than the sons of light.

9 "And I say to you, make friends for yourselves by unrighteous mammon, that when you fail,*a* they may receive you into an everlasting home.

10 "He who *is* faithful in *what is* least is faithful also in much; and he who is unjust in *what is* least is unjust also in much.

11 "Therefore if you have not been faithful in the unrighteous mammon, who will commit to your trust the true *riches?*

12 "And if you have not been faithful in what is another man's, who will give you what is your own?

13 "No servant can serve two masters; for either he will hate the one and love the other, or else he will be

16:6 *a*Greek *batos,* eight or nine gallons each (Old Testament *bath*)   16:7 *a*Greek *koros,* ten or twelve bushels each (Old Testament *kor*)
16:9 *a*NU-Text reads *it fails.*

loyal to the one and despise the other. You cannot serve God and mammon."

The Law, the Prophets, and the Kingdom

14 Now the Phar′i·sees, who were lovers of money, also heard all these things, and they derided Him.
15 And He said to them, "You are those who justify yourselves before men, but God knows your hearts. For what is highly esteemed among men is an abomination in the sight of God.
16 "The law and the prophets *were* until John. Since that time the kingdom of God has been preached, and everyone is pressing into it.
17 "And it is easier for heaven and earth to pass away than for one tittle of the law to fail.
18 "Whoever divorces his wife and marries another commits adultery; and whoever marries her who is divorced from *her* husband commits adultery.

The Rich Man and Lazarus

19 "There was a certain rich man who was clothed in purple and fine linen and fared sumptuously every day.
20 "But there was a certain beggar named Laz′a·rus, full of sores, who was laid at his gate,
21 "desiring to be fed with the crumbs which fell*a* from the rich man's table. Moreover the dogs came and licked his sores.
22 "So it was that the beggar died, and was carried by the angels to Abraham's bosom. The rich man also died and was buried.
23 "And being in torments in Hā′dēs, he lifted up his eyes and saw Abraham afar off, and Laz′a·rus in his bosom.
24 "Then he cried and said, 'Father Abraham, have mercy on me, and send Laz′a·rus that he may dip the tip of his finger in water and cool my tongue; for I am tormented in this flame.'
25 "But Abraham said, 'Son, remember that in your lifetime you received your good things, and likewise Laz′a·rus evil things; but now he is comforted and you are tormented.
26 'And besides all this, between us and you there is a great gulf fixed, so that those who want to pass from here to you cannot, nor can those from there pass to us.'
27 "Then he said, 'I beg you therefore, father, that you would send him to my father's house,
28 'for I have five brothers, that he may testify to them, lest they also come to this place of torment.'
29 "Abraham said to him, 'They have Moses and the prophets; let them hear them.'
30 "And he said, 'No, father Abraham; but if one goes to them from the dead, they will repent.'
31 "But he said to him, 'If they do not hear Moses and the prophets, neither will they be persuaded though one rise from the dead.'"

Jesus Warns of Offenses

17 Then He said to the disciples, "It is impossible that no offenses should come, but woe *to him* through whom they do come!
2 "It would be better for him if a millstone were hung around his neck, and he were thrown into the sea, than that he should offend one of these little ones.
3 "Take heed to yourselves. If your brother sins against you,*a* rebuke him; and if he repents, forgive him.

16:21 *a*NU-Text reads *with what fell.*
17:3 *a*NU-Text omits *against you.*

What Should I Do?

WHEN I HURT YOU Luke 17:3, 4

Do you ever say something that hurts a friend or family member? Do you ever do something that hurts a friend or family member? You know it when you hurt someone you love. Now what should you do?

1. When you hurt someone you love, should you say, "Why did you do that?" Should you say, "It's all your fault?" What should you say?
2. When you hurt someone you love, should you make fun of her because she is crying? Should you tell him, "You'll get over it" or "Why don't you toughen up?" What should you say?
3. When you hurt someone you love, should you say, "I'm sorry, forgive me"? What would you want others to do or say when they hurt you?

For more on *What Should I Do?* turn to page 1597
For more on *Forgiveness* turn to page 1597

4 "And if he sins against you seven times in a day, and seven times in a day returns to you,*a* saying, 'I repent,' you shall forgive him."

FAITH AND DUTY

5 And the apostles said to the Lord, "Increase our faith."
6 So the Lord said, "If you have faith as a mustard seed, you can say to this mulberry tree, 'Be pulled up by the roots and be planted in the sea,' and it would obey you.
7 "And which of you, having a servant plowing or tending sheep, will say to him when he has come in from the field, 'Come at once and sit down to eat'?
8 "But will he not rather say to him, 'Prepare something for my supper, and gird yourself and serve me till I have eaten and drunk, and afterward you will eat and drink'?
9 "Does he thank that servant because he did the things that were commanded him? I think not.*a*
10 "So likewise you, when you have done all those things which you are commanded, say, 'We are unprofitable servants. We have done what was our duty to do.' "

TEN LEPERS CLEANSED

Do you know what the word "contagious" means? If you touch a person with a contagious disease you get that disease, too. Ten men who had a contagious disease called leprosy came to Jesus for help. How would Jesus help them?

11 Now it happened as He went to Jerusalem that He passed through the midst of Samaria and Galilee.
12 Then as He entered a certain village, there met Him ten men who were lepers, who stood afar off.
13 And they lifted up *their* voices and said, "Jesus, Master, have mercy on us!"
14 So when He saw *them,* He said to them, "Go, show yourselves to the

17:4 *a*M-Text omits *to you.*   17:9 *a*NU-Text ends verse with *commanded;* M-Text omits *him.*

priests." And so it was that as they went, they were cleansed.

15 And one of them, when he saw that he was healed, returned, and with a loud voice glorified God,

16 and fell down on *his* face at His feet, giving Him thanks. And he was a Samaritan.

17 So Jesus answered and said, "Were there not ten cleansed? But where *are* the nine?

18 "Were there not any found who returned to give glory to God except this foreigner?"

19 And He said to him, "Arise, go your way. Your faith has made you well."

☑ *Bible Quiz*

Luke 17:11–19 **Jesus Heals Ten Lepers**

1. What was wrong with the ten men who came to see Jesus? A leper is a person who has leprosy. Look it up in the dictionary to see just how sick these men really were.

2. What can you find in this story that tells you these ten men had a very difficult life (see verses 12 and 13)?

3. What did Jesus do for them?

4. When the ten men were healed, how many came back to see Jesus? Why did this man come back?

5. Do you think it was important to Jesus that the man came back to thank Him? How do you think Jesus feels when you thank Him for all the good things He gives you?

THE COMING OF THE KINGDOM

20 Now when He was asked by the Phar'i-sees when the kingdom of God would come, He answered them and said, "The kingdom of God does not come with observation;

21 "nor will they say, 'See here!' or 'See there!'*a* For indeed, the kingdom of God is within you."

22 Then He said to the disciples, "The days will come when you will desire to see one of the days of the Son of Man, and you will not see *it*.

23 "And they will say to you, 'Look here!' or 'Look there!'*a* Do not go after *them* or follow *them*.

24 "For as the lightning that flashes out of one *part* under heaven shines to the other *part* under heaven, so also the Son of Man will be in His day.

25 "But first He must suffer many things and be rejected by this generation.

26 "And as it was in the days of Noah, so it will be also in the days of the Son of Man:

27 "They ate, they drank, they married wives, they were given in marriage, until the day that Noah entered the ark, and the flood came and destroyed them all.

28 "Likewise as it was also in the days of Lot: They ate, they drank, they bought, they sold, they planted, they built;

29 "but on the day that Lot went out of Sod'om it rained fire and brimstone from heaven and destroyed *them* all.

30 "Even so will it be in the day when the Son of Man is revealed.

31 "In that day, he who is on the housetop, and his goods *are* in the house, let him not come down to take

17:21 *a*NU-Text reverses *here* and *there*.
17:23 *a*NU-Text reverses *here* and *there*.

them away. And likewise the one who is in the field, let him not turn back.

32 "Remember Lot's wife.

33 "Whoever seeks to save his life will lose it, and whoever loses his life will preserve it.

34 "I tell you, in that night there will be two *men* in one bed: the one will be taken and the other will be left.

35 "Two *women* will be grinding together: the one will be taken and the other left.

36 "Two *men* will be in the field: the one will be taken and the other left."*a*

37 And they answered and said to Him, "Where, Lord?" So He said to them, "Wherever the body is, there the eagles will be gathered together."

THE PARABLE OF THE PERSISTENT WIDOW

18 Then He spoke a parable to them, that men always ought to pray and not lose heart,

2 saying: "There was in a certain city a judge who did not fear God nor regard man.

3 "Now there was a widow in that city; and she came to him, saying, 'Get justice for me from my adversary.'

4 "And he would not for a while; but afterward he said within himself, 'Though I do not fear God nor regard man,

5 'yet because this widow troubles me I will avenge her, lest by her continual coming she weary me.' "

6 Then the Lord said, "Hear what the unjust judge said.

7 "And shall God not avenge His own elect who cry out day and night to Him, though He bears long with them?

8 "I tell you that He will avenge them speedily. Nevertheless, when the Son of Man comes, will He really find faith on the earth?"

THE PARABLE OF THE PHARISEE AND THE TAX COLLECTOR

9 Also He spoke this parable to some who trusted in themselves that they were righteous, and despised others:

> ## Prayers
>
> Luke 18:9–14
>
> Here are two prayers. One was prayed by a religious leader, a proud man. The other was prayed by a man who knew he was a sinner. Which prayer would you rather pray? Why? Is prayer a time to tell God how good we are? Or is it rather a time to tell God how much we need Him?

---

10 "Two men went up to the temple to pray, one a Phar′i·see and the other a tax collector.

11 "The Phar′i·see stood and prayed thus with himself, 'God, I thank You that I am not like other men—extortioners, unjust, adulterers, or even as this tax collector.

12 'I fast twice a week; I give tithes of all that I possess.'

13 "And the tax collector, standing afar off, would not so much as raise *his* eyes to heaven, but beat his breast, saying, 'God, be merciful to me a sinner!'

14 "I tell you, this man went down to his house justified *rather* than the other; for everyone who exalts himself will be humbled, and he who humbles himself will be exalted."

17:36 *a*NU-Text and M-Text omit verse 36.

JESUS BLESSES LITTLE CHILDREN

15 Then they also brought infants to Him that He might touch them; but when the disciples saw *it,* they rebuked them.

16 But Jesus called them to *Him* and said, "Let the little children come to Me, and do not forbid them; for of such is the kingdom of God.

17 "Assuredly, I say to you, whoever does not receive the kingdom of God as a little child will by no means enter it."

■ *see Mark 10:13–16*

JESUS COUNSELS THE RICH YOUNG RULER

18 Now a certain ruler asked Him, saying, "Good Teacher, what shall I do to inherit eternal life?"

19 So Jesus said to him, "Why do you call Me good? No one *is* good but One, *that is,* God.

20 "You know the commandments: *'Do not commit adultery,' 'Do not murder,' 'Do not steal,' 'Do not bear false witness,' 'Honor your father and your mother.' "*[a]

21 And he said, "All these things I have kept from my youth."

22 So when Jesus heard these things, He said to him, "You still lack one thing. Sell all that you have and distribute to the poor, and you will have treasure in heaven; and come, follow Me."

23 But when he heard this, he became very sorrowful, for he was very rich.

WITH GOD ALL THINGS ARE POSSIBLE

24 And when Jesus saw that he became very sorrowful, He said, "How hard it is for those who have riches to enter the kingdom of God!

25 "For it is easier for a camel to go through the eye of a needle than for a rich man to enter the kingdom of God."

26 And those who heard it said, "Who then can be saved?"

27 But He said, "The things which are impossible with men are possible with God."

28 Then Peter said, "See, we have left all[a] and followed You."

29 So He said to them, "Assuredly, I say to you, there is no one who has left house or parents or brothers or wife or children, for the sake of the kingdom of God,

30 "who shall not receive many times more in this present time, and in the age to come eternal life."

JESUS A THIRD TIME PREDICTS HIS DEATH AND RESURRECTION

31 Then He took the twelve aside and said to them, "Behold, we are going up to Jerusalem, and all things that are written by the prophets concerning the Son of Man will be accomplished.

32 "For He will be delivered to the Gentiles and will be mocked and insulted and spit upon.

33 "They will scourge *Him* and kill Him. And the third day He will rise again."

34 But they understood none of these things; this saying was hidden from them, and they did not know the things which were spoken.

A BLIND MAN RECEIVES HIS SIGHT

35 Then it happened, as He was coming near Jericho, that a certain blind man sat by the road begging.

18:20 [a]Exodus 20:12–16; Deuteronomy 5:16–20
18:28 [a]NU-Text reads *our own.*

36 And hearing a multitude passing by, he asked what it meant.
37 So they told him that Jesus of Nazareth was passing by.
38 And he cried out, saying, "Jesus, Son of David, have mercy on me!"

Prayers

Luke 18:38–43

A blind man sat by the side of the road. Jesus came by. The man cried out an urgent prayer. "Jesus . . . have mercy on me." He wanted to see. He didn't care who heard him. He knew that Jesus could help him so he prayed desperately. "Have mercy on me." When you know that you have a need and that Jesus can help, will you be quiet? Or will you cry out urgently, "Have mercy on me"? Remember the blind man by the side of the road.

---

39 Then those who went before warned him that he should be quiet; but he cried out all the more, "Son of David, have mercy on me!"
40 So Jesus stood still and commanded him to be brought to Him. And when he had come near, He asked him,
41 saying, "What do you want Me to do for you?" He said, "Lord, that I may receive my sight."
42 Then Jesus said to him, "Receive your sight; your faith has made you well."
43 And immediately he received his sight, and followed Him, glorifying God. And all the people, when they saw it, gave praise to God.

■ see Mark 10:46–52

JESUS COMES TO ZACCHAEUS' HOUSE

Jesus was coming to town. So many people wanted to see Him that huge crowds lined the street. But one man knew he would not be able to see Jesus. He was too short. So this is what he did to see Jesus.

19 Then *Jesus* entered and passed through Jericho.
2 Now behold, *there was* a man named Zac·chae'us who was a chief tax collector, and he was rich.
3 And he sought to see who Jesus was, but could not because of the crowd, for he was of short stature.
4 So he ran ahead and climbed up into a sycamore tree to see Him, for He was going to pass that *way.*
5 And when Jesus came to the place, He looked up and saw him,a and said to him, "Zac·chae'us, make haste and come down, for today I must stay at your house."
6 So he made haste and came down, and received Him joyfully.
7 But when they saw *it,* they all complained, saying, "He has gone to be a guest with a man who is a sinner."
8 Then Zac·chae'us stood and said to the Lord, "Look, Lord, I give half of my goods to the poor; and if I have taken anything from anyone by false accusation, I restore fourfold."
9 And Jesus said to him, "Today salvation has come to this house, because he also is a son of Abraham;
10 "for the Son of Man has come to seek and to save that which was lost."

19:5 aNU-Text omits *and saw him.*

I'M SORRY! Luke 19:8

The boy with the fishing pole made a *big* mistake! What did he do? What do you think he will say to his little brother? "You're in the wrong place," or "Let go of my hook!"?

1. What do you say when you hurt someone? "Why were you standing there?" or "Why don't you get out of my way?"
2. What should you say when you hurt someone? "It's all your fault," or "I'm sorry"?

For more on *What Should I Do?* turn to page 1615
For more on *Forgiveness* turn to page 1631

THE PARABLE OF THE MINAS

11 Now as they heard these things, He spoke another parable, because He was near Jerusalem and because they thought the kingdom of God would appear immediately.

12 Therefore He said: "A certain nobleman went into a far country to receive for himself a kingdom and to return.

13 "So he called ten of his servants, delivered to them ten minas,*a* and said to them, 'Do business till I come.'

14 "But his citizens hated him, and sent a delegation after him, saying, 'We will not have this *man* to reign over us.'

15 "And so it was that when he returned, having received the kingdom, he then commanded these servants, to whom he had given the money, to be called to him, that he might know how much every man had gained by trading.

16 "Then came the first, saying, 'Master, your mina has earned ten minas.'

17 "And he said to him, 'Well *done*, good servant; because you were faithful in a very little, have authority over ten cities.'

18 "And the second came, saying, 'Master, your mina has earned five minas.'

19 "Likewise he said to him, 'You also be over five cities.'

20 "Then another came, saying, 'Master, here is your mina, which I have kept put away in a handkerchief.

21 'For I feared you, because you are an austere man. You collect what you did not deposit, and reap what you did not sow.'

22 "And he said to him, 'Out of your own mouth I will judge you, *you* wicked servant. You knew that I was an austere man, collecting what I did not deposit and reaping what I did not sow.

23 'Why then did you not put my money in the bank, that at my coming I might have collected it with interest?'

24 "And he said to those who stood by, 'Take the mina from him, and give *it* to him who has ten minas.'

25 ("But they said to him, 'Master, he has ten minas.')

19:13 *a*The *mina* (Greek *mna*, Hebrew *minah*) was worth about three months' salary.

26 'For I say to you, that to everyone who has will be given; and from him who does not have, even what he has will be taken away from him.
27 'But bring here those enemies of mine, who did not want me to reign over them, and slay *them* before me.' "

THE TRIUMPHAL ENTRY

28 When He had said this, He went on ahead, going up to Jerusalem.
29 And it came to pass, when He drew near to Beth′pha·gē*a* and Beth′a·ny, at the mountain called Ol′i·vet, *that* He sent two of His disciples,
30 saying, "Go into the village opposite *you,* where as you enter you will find a colt tied, on which no one has ever sat. Loose it and bring *it* here.
31 "And if anyone asks you, 'Why are you loosing *it?*' thus you shall say to him, 'Because the Lord has need of it.' "
32 So those who were sent went their way and found *it* just as He had said to them.
33 But as they were loosing the colt, the owners of it said to them, "Why are you loosing the colt?"
34 And they said, "The Lord has need of him."
35 Then they brought him to Jesus. And they threw their own clothes on the colt, and they set Jesus on him.
36 And as He went, *many* spread their clothes on the road.
37 Then, as He was now drawing near the descent of the Mount of Olives, the whole multitude of the disciples began to rejoice and praise God with a loud voice for all the mighty works they had seen,
38 saying:

" *Blessed is the King who comes in the name of the LORD!'a*
Peace in heaven and glory in the highest!"

39 And some of the Phar′i·sees called to Him from the crowd, "Teacher, rebuke Your disciples."
40 But He answered and said to them, "I tell you that if these should keep silent, the stones would immediately cry out."
■ *see Mark 11:1–11*

JESUS WEEPS OVER JERUSALEM

41 Now as He drew near, He saw the city and wept over it,
42 saying, "If you had known, even you, especially in this your day, the things *that make* for your peace! But now they are hidden from your eyes.
43 "For days will come upon you when your enemies will build an embankment around you, surround you and close you in on every side,
44 "and level you, and your children within you, to the ground; and they will not leave in you one stone upon another, because you did not know the time of your visitation."

JESUS CLEANSES THE TEMPLE

45 Then He went into the temple and began to drive out those who bought and sold in it,*a*
46 saying to them, "It is written, *'My house is*a *a house of prayer,'b* but you have made it a *'den of thieves.' "c*
47 And He was teaching daily in the temple. But the chief priests, the scribes, and the leaders of the people sought to destroy Him,
48 and were unable to do anything; for all the people were very attentive to hear Him.
■ *see Matthew 21:12–17*

19:29 *a*M-Text reads *Bethsphage.*
19:38 *a*Psalm 118:26   19:45 *a*NU-Text reads
those who were selling.   19:46 *a*NU-Text reads
shall be.   *b*Isaiah 56:7   *c*Jeremiah 7:11

JESUS' AUTHORITY QUESTIONED

20 Now it happened on one of those days, as He taught the people in the temple and preached the gospel, *that* the chief priests and the scribes, together with the elders, confronted *Him*

2 and spoke to Him, saying, "Tell us, by what authority are You doing these things? Or who is he who gave You this authority?"

3 But He answered and said to them, "I also will ask you one thing, and answer Me:

4 "The baptism of John—was it from heaven or from men?"

5 And they reasoned among themselves, saying, "If we say, 'From heaven,' He will say, 'Why then*a* did you not believe him?'

6 "But if we say, 'From men,' all the people will stone us, for they are persuaded that John was a prophet."

7 So they answered that they did not know where *it was* from.

8 And Jesus said to them, "Neither will I tell you by what authority I do these things."

THE PARABLE OF THE WICKED VINEDRESSERS

9 Then He began to tell the people this parable: "A certain man planted a vineyard, leased it to vinedressers, and went into a far country for a long time.

10 "Now at vintage-time he sent a servant to the vinedressers, that they might give him some of the fruit of the vineyard. But the vinedressers beat him and sent *him* away empty-handed.

11 "Again he sent another servant; and they beat him also, treated *him* shamefully, and sent *him* away empty-handed.

12 "And again he sent a third; and they wounded him also and cast *him* out.

13 "Then the owner of the vineyard said, 'What shall I do? I will send my beloved son. Probably they will respect *him* when they see him.'

14 "But when the vinedressers saw him, they reasoned among themselves, saying, 'This is the heir. Come, let us kill him, that the inheritance may be ours.'

15 "So they cast him out of the vineyard and killed *him.* Therefore what will the owner of the vineyard do to them?

16 "He will come and destroy those vinedressers and give the vineyard to others." And when they heard *it* they said, "Certainly not!"

17 Then He looked at them and said, "What then is this that is written:

'The stone which the builders
    rejected
Has become the chief
    cornerstone'?*a*

18 "Whoever falls on that stone will be broken; but on whomever it falls, it will grind him to powder."

19 And the chief priests and the scribes that very hour sought to lay hands on Him, but they feared the people*a*—for they knew He had spoken this parable against them.

THE PHARISEES: IS IT LAWFUL TO PAY TAXES TO CAESAR?

20 So they watched *Him,* and sent spies who pretended to be righteous, that they might seize on His words, in order to deliver Him to the power and the authority of the governor.

21 Then they asked Him, saying,

20:5 *a*NU-Text and M-Text omit *then.*
20:17 *a*Psalm 118:22   20:19 *a*M-Text reads *but they were afraid.*

"Teacher, we know that You say and teach rightly, and You do not show personal favoritism, but teach the way of God in truth:

22 "Is it lawful for us to pay taxes to Caesar or not?"

23 But He perceived their craftiness, and said to them, "Why do you test Me?*a*

24 "Show Me a denarius. Whose image and inscription does it have?" They answered and said, "Caesar's."

25 And He said to them, "Render therefore to Caesar the things that are Caesar's, and to God the things that are God's."

26 But they could not catch Him in His words in the presence of the people. And they marveled at His answer and kept silent.

THE SADDUCEES: WHAT ABOUT THE RESURRECTION?

27 Then some of the Sad′du·cees, who deny that there is a resurrection, came to *Him* and asked Him,

28 saying: "Teacher, Moses wrote to us *that* if a man's brother dies, having a wife, and he dies without children, his brother should take his wife and raise up offspring for his brother.

29 "Now there were seven brothers. And the first took a wife, and died without children.

30 "And the second*a* took her as wife, and he died childless.

31 "Then the third took her, and in like manner the seven also; and they left no children,*a* and died.

32 "Last of all the woman died also.

33 "Therefore, in the resurrection, whose wife does she become? For all seven had her as wife."

34 Jesus answered and said to them, "The sons of this age marry and are given in marriage.

35 "But those who are counted worthy to attain that age, and the resurrection from the dead, neither marry nor are given in marriage;

36 "nor can they die anymore, for they are equal to the angels and are sons of God, being sons of the resurrection.

37 "But even Moses showed in the *burning* bush *passage* that the dead are raised, when he called the Lord *'the God of Abraham, the God of Isaac, and the God of Jacob.'a*

38 "For He is not the God of the dead but of the living, for all live to Him."

39 Then some of the scribes answered and said, "Teacher, You have spoken well."

40 But after that they dared not question Him anymore.

JESUS: HOW CAN DAVID CALL HIS DESCENDANT LORD?

41 And He said to them, "How can they say that the Christ is the Son of David?

42 "Now David himself said in the Book of Psalms:

'The LORD said to my Lord,
"Sit at My right hand,
43 Till I make Your enemies Your footstool." 'a

44 "Therefore David calls Him *'Lord'*; how is He then his Son?"

BEWARE OF THE SCRIBES

45 Then, in the hearing of all the people, He said to His disciples,

46 "Beware of the scribes, who desire to go around in long robes, love greetings in the marketplaces, the best

20:23 *a*NU-Text omits *Why do you test Me?*
20:30 *a*NU-Text ends verse 30 here.
20:31 *a*NU-Text and M-Text read *the seven also left no children.*   20:37 *a*Exodus 3:6, 15
20:43 *a*Psalm 110:1

seats in the synagogues, and the best places at feasts,

47 "who devour widows' houses, and for a pretense make long prayers. These will receive greater condemnation."

THE WIDOW'S TWO MITES

21 And He looked up and saw the rich putting their gifts into the treasury,

2 and He saw also a certain poor widow putting in two mites.

3 So He said, "Truly I say to you that this poor widow has put in more than all;

4 "for all these out of their abundance have put in offerings for God,*a* but she out of her poverty put in all the livelihood that she had."

■ *see Mark 12:41–44*

JESUS PREDICTS THE DESTRUCTION OF THE TEMPLE

5 Then, as some spoke of the temple, how it was adorned with beautiful stones and donations, He said,

6 "These things which you see—the days will come in which not *one* stone shall be left upon another that shall not be thrown down."

THE SIGNS OF THE TIMES AND THE END OF THE AGE

7 So they asked Him, saying, "Teacher, but when will these things be? And what sign *will there be* when these things are about to take place?"

8 And He said: "Take heed that you not be deceived. For many will come in My name, saying, 'I am *He*,' and, 'The time has drawn near.' Therefore*a* do not go after them.

9 "But when you hear of wars and commotions, do not be terrified; for these things must come to pass first, but the end *will not come* immediately."

10 Then He said to them, "Nation will rise against nation, and kingdom against kingdom.

11 "And there will be great earthquakes in various places, and famines and pestilences; and there will be fearful sights and great signs from heaven.

12 "But before all these things, they will lay their hands on you and persecute *you,* delivering *you* up to the synagogues and prisons. You will be brought before kings and rulers for My name's sake.

13 "But it will turn out for you as an occasion for testimony.

14 "Therefore settle *it* in your hearts not to meditate beforehand on what you will answer;

15 "for I will give you a mouth and wisdom which all your adversaries will not be able to contradict or resist.

16 "You will be betrayed even by parents and brothers, relatives and friends; and they will put *some* of you to death.

17 "And you will be hated by all for My name's sake.

18 "But not a hair of your head shall be lost.

19 "By your patience possess your souls.

THE DESTRUCTION OF JERUSALEM

20 "But when you see Jerusalem surrounded by armies, then know that its desolation is near.

21 "Then let those who are in Judea flee to the mountains, let those who are in the midst of her depart, and let

21:4 *a*NU-Text omits *for God.*   21:8 *a*NU-Text omits *Therefore.*

not those who are in the country enter her.

22 "For these are the days of vengeance, that all things which are written may be fulfilled.

23 "But woe to those who are pregnant and to those who are nursing babies in those days! For there will be great distress in the land and wrath upon this people.

24 "And they will fall by the edge of the sword, and be led away captive into all nations. And Jerusalem will be trampled by Gentiles until the times of the Gentiles are fulfilled.

THE COMING OF THE SON OF MAN

25 "And there will be signs in the sun, in the moon, and in the stars; and on the earth distress of nations, with perplexity, the sea and the waves roaring;

26 "men's hearts failing them from fear and the expectation of those things which are coming on the earth, for the powers of the heavens will be shaken.

27 "Then they will see the Son of Man coming in a cloud with power and great glory.

28 "Now when these things begin to happen, look up and lift up your heads, because your redemption draws near."

THE PARABLE OF THE FIG TREE

29 Then He spoke to them a parable: "Look at the fig tree, and all the trees.

30 "When they are already budding, you see and know for yourselves that summer is now near.

31 "So you also, when you see these things happening, know that the kingdom of God is near.

32 "Assuredly, I say to you, this generation will by no means pass away till all things take place.

33 "Heaven and earth will pass away, but My words will by no means pass away.

THE IMPORTANCE OF WATCHING

34 "But take heed to yourselves, lest your hearts be weighed down with carousing, drunkenness, and cares of this life, and that Day come on you unexpectedly.

35 "For it will come as a snare on all those who dwell on the face of the whole earth.

36 "Watch therefore, and pray always that you may be counted worthy*a* to escape all these things that will come to pass, and to stand before the Son of Man."

37 And in the daytime He was teaching in the temple, but at night He went out and stayed on the mountain called Ol'i·vet.

38 Then early in the morning all the people came to Him in the temple to hear Him.

THE PLOT TO KILL JESUS

22 Now the Feast of Unleavened Bread drew near, which is called Passover.

2 And the chief priests and the scribes sought how they might kill Him, for they feared the people.

3 Then Satan entered Judas, surnamed Is·car'i·ot, who was numbered among the twelve.

4 So he went his way and conferred with the chief priests and captains, how he might betray Him to them.

5 And they were glad, and agreed to give him money.

21:36 *a*NU-Text reads *may have strength.*

6   So he promised and sought opportunity to betray Him to them in the absence of the multitude.

JESUS AND HIS DISCIPLES PREPARE THE PASSOVER

7   Then came the Day of Unleavened Bread, when the Passover must be killed.
8   And He sent Peter and John, saying, "Go and prepare the Passover for us, that we may eat."
9   So they said to Him, "Where do You want us to prepare?"
10   And He said to them, "Behold, when you have entered the city, a man will meet you carrying a pitcher of water; follow him into the house which he enters.
11   "Then you shall say to the master of the house, 'The Teacher says to you, "Where is the guest room where I may eat the Passover with My disciples?"'
12   "Then he will show you a large, furnished upper room; there make ready."
13   So they went and found it just as He had said to them, and they prepared the Passover.

JESUS INSTITUTES THE LORD'S SUPPER

14   When the hour had come, He sat down, and the twelve[a] apostles with Him.
15   Then He said to them, "With *fervent* desire I have desired to eat this Passover with you before I suffer;
16   "for I say to you, I will no longer eat of it until it is fulfilled in the kingdom of God."
17   Then He took the cup, and gave thanks, and said, "Take this and divide *it* among yourselves;
18   "for I say to you,[a] I will not drink of the fruit of the vine until the kingdom of God comes."
19   And He took bread, gave thanks and broke *it,* and gave *it* to them, saying, "This is My body which is given for you; do this in remembrance of Me."
20   Likewise He also *took* the cup after supper, saying, "This cup *is* the new covenant in My blood, which is shed for you.
21   "But behold, the hand of My betrayer *is* with Me on the table.
22   "And truly the Son of Man goes as it has been determined, but woe to that man by whom He is betrayed!"
23   Then they began to question among themselves, which of them it was who would do this thing.
■ *see Matthew 26:17–35*

THE DISCIPLES ARGUE ABOUT GREATNESS

24   Now there was also a dispute among them, as to which of them should be considered the greatest.
25   And He said to them, "The kings of the Gentiles exercise lordship over them, and those who exercise authority over them are called 'benefactors.'
26   "But not so *among* you; on the contrary, he who is greatest among you, let him be as the younger, and he who governs as he who serves.
27   "For who *is* greater, he who sits at the table, or he who serves? *Is* it not he who sits at the table? Yet I am among you as the One who serves.
28   "But you are those who have continued with Me in My trials.
29   "And I bestow upon you a kingdom, just as My Father bestowed *one* upon Me,
30   "that you may eat and drink at My table in My kingdom, and sit on

22:14 [a]NU-Text omits *twelve.*   22:18 [a]NU-Text adds *from now on.*

thrones judging the twelve tribes of Israel."

JESUS PREDICTS PETER'S DENIAL

31 And the Lord said,*a* "Simon, Simon! Indeed, Satan has asked for you, that he may sift *you* as wheat.

32 "But I have prayed for you, that your faith should not fail; and when you have returned to *Me,* strengthen your brethren."

33 But he said to Him, "Lord, I am ready to go with You, both to prison and to death."

34 Then He said, "I tell you, Peter, the rooster shall not crow this day before you will deny three times that you know Me."

SUPPLIES FOR THE ROAD

35 And He said to them, "When I sent you without money bag, knapsack, and sandals, did you lack anything?" So they said, "Nothing."

36 Then He said to them, "But now, he who has a money bag, let him take *it,* and likewise a knapsack; and he who has no sword, let him sell his garment and buy one.

37 "For I say to you that this which is written must still be accomplished in Me: *'And He was numbered with the transgressors.'a* For the things concerning Me have an end."

38 So they said, "Lord, look, here *are* two swords." And He said to them; "It is enough."

THE PRAYER IN THE GARDEN

39 Coming out, He went to the Mount of Olives, as He was accustomed, and His disciples also followed Him.

40 When He came to the place, He said to them, "Pray that you may not enter into temptation."

41 And He was withdrawn from them about a stone's throw, and He knelt down and prayed,

42 saying, "Father, if it is Your will, take this cup away from Me; nevertheless not My will, but Yours, be done."

43 Then an angel appeared to Him from heaven, strengthening Him.

44 And being in agony, He prayed more earnestly. Then His sweat became like great drops of blood falling down to the ground.*a*

45 When He rose up from prayer, and had come to His disciples, He found them sleeping from sorrow.

46 Then He said to them, "Why do you sleep? Rise and pray, lest you enter into temptation."

■ *see Mark 14:32–42*

BETRAYAL AND ARREST IN GETHSEMANE

47 And while He was still speaking, behold, a multitude; and he who was called Judas, one of the twelve, went before them and drew near to Jesus to kiss Him.

48 But Jesus said to him, "Judas, are you betraying the Son of Man with a kiss?"

49 When those around Him saw what was going to happen, they said to Him, "Lord, shall we strike with the sword?"

50 And one of them struck the servant of the high priest and cut off his right ear.

51 But Jesus answered and said, "Permit even this." And He touched his ear and healed him.

22:31 *a*NU-Text omits *And the Lord said.*
22:37 *a*Isaiah 53:12   22:44 *a*NU-Text brackets verses 43 and 44 as not in the original text.

52 Then Jesus said to the chief priests, captains of the temple, and the elders who had come to Him, "Have you come out, as against a robber, with swords and clubs?
53 "When I was with you daily in the temple, you did not try to seize Me. But this is your hour, and the power of darkness."

■ *see Matthew 26:47–56*

PETER DENIES JESUS, AND WEEPS BITTERLY

Peter waited in the courtyard to find out what would happen to Jesus. He knew the men inside wanted to hurt Jesus. He knew the men would want to hurt him too if they knew he was one of Jesus' disciples. Peter was afraid. Then someone looked at him and said, "That man was with Jesus!" What would Peter do? What would you do?

54 Having arrested Him, they led *Him* and brought Him into the high priest's house. But Peter followed at a distance.
55 Now when they had kindled a fire in the midst of the courtyard and sat down together, Peter sat among them.
56 And a certain servant girl, seeing him as he sat by the fire, looked intently at him and said, "This man was also with Him."
57 But he denied Him,*a* saying, "Woman, I do not know Him."
58 And after a little while another saw him and said, "You also are of them." But Peter said, "Man, I am not!"
59 Then after about an hour had passed, another confidently affirmed, saying, "Surely this *fellow* also was with Him, for he is a Galilean."

60 But Peter said, "Man, I do not know what you are saying!" Immediately, while he was still speaking, the rooster*a* crowed.
61 And the Lord turned and looked at Peter. Then Peter remembered the word of the Lord, how He had said to him, "Before the rooster crows,*a* you will deny Me three times."
62 So Peter went out and wept bitterly.

22:57 *a*NU-Text reads *denied it.*   22:60 *a*NU-Text and M-Text read *a rooster.*   22:61 *a*NU-Text adds *today.*

Bible Quiz

☑

Luke 22:54–62   **Peter Denies Jesus**

1. Where did the guards take Jesus after He was arrested? Did Peter want anyone to know he was following? How do you know that?
2. The first woman said she saw Peter with Jesus. What did Peter say?
3. How many times did Peter deny that he knew Jesus?
4. What happened after the third time? How did Peter feel then?
5. Have there been times when you have been afraid or embarrassed to tell others that you love Jesus? How do you think Jesus feels when we deny Him? If Jesus really is most important to us, then we must be ready to gladly and boldly tell others about Him.

JESUS MOCKED AND BEATEN

63 Now the men who held Jesus mocked Him and beat Him.
64 And having blindfolded Him, they struck Him on the face and asked Him,*a* saying, "Prophesy! Who is the one who struck You?"
65 And many other things they blasphemously spoke against Him.

JESUS FACES THE SANHEDRIN

66 As soon as it was day, the elders of the people, both chief priests and scribes, came together and led Him into their council, saying,
67 "If You are the Christ, tell us." But He said to them, "If I tell you, you will by no means believe.
68 "And if I also ask *you,* you will by no means answer Me or let *Me* go.*a*
69 "Hereafter the Son of Man will sit on the right hand of the power of God."
70 Then they all said, "Are You then the Son of God?" So He said to them, "You *rightly* say that I am."
71 And they said, "What further testimony do we need? For we have heard it ourselves from His own mouth."

JESUS HANDED OVER TO PONTIUS PILATE

23 Then the whole multitude of them arose and led Him to Pilate.
2 And they began to accuse Him, saying, "We found this *fellow* perverting the*a* nation, and forbidding to pay taxes to Caesar, saying that He Himself is Christ, a King."
3 Then Pilate asked Him, saying, "Are You the King of the Jews?" He answered him and said, "*It is as* you say."
4 So Pilate said to the chief priests and the crowd, "I find no fault in this Man."
5 But they were the more fierce, saying, "He stirs up the people, teaching throughout all Judea, beginning from Galilee to this place."

JESUS FACES HEROD

6 When Pilate heard of Galilee,*a* he asked if the Man were a Galilean.
7 And as soon as he knew that He belonged to Her′od's jurisdiction, he sent Him to Her′od, who was also in Jerusalem at that time.
8 Now when Her′od saw Jesus, he was exceedingly glad; for he had desired for a long *time* to see Him, because he had heard many things about Him, and he hoped to see some miracle done by Him.
9 Then he questioned Him with many words, but He answered him nothing.
10 And the chief priests and scribes stood and vehemently accused Him.
11 Then Her′od, with his men of war, treated Him with contempt and mocked *Him,* arrayed Him in a gorgeous robe, and sent Him back to Pilate.
12 That very day Pilate and Her′od became friends with each other, for previously they had been at enmity with each other.

TAKING THE PLACE OF BARABBAS

13 Then Pilate, when he had called together the chief priests, the rulers, and the people,
14 said to them, "You have brought this Man to me, as one who misleads the people. And indeed, having examined *Him* in your presence, I have

---

22:64 *a*NU-Text reads *And having blindfolded Him, they asked Him.*　22:68 *a*NU-Text omits *also* and *Me or let Me go.*　23:2 *a*NU-Text reads *our.*　23:6 *a*NU-Text omits *of Galilee.*

found no fault in this Man concerning those things of which you accuse Him;

15 "no, neither did Her′od, for I sent you back to him;*a* and indeed nothing deserving of death has been done by Him.

16 "I will therefore chastise Him and release *Him*"

17 (for it was necessary for him to release one to them at the feast).*a*

18 And they all cried out at once, saying, "Away with this *Man,* and release to us Ba·rab′bas"—

19 who had been thrown into prison for a certain rebellion made in the city, and for murder.

20 Pilate, therefore, wishing to release Jesus, again called out to them.

21 But they shouted, saying, "Crucify *Him,* crucify Him!"

22 Then he said to them the third time, "Why, what evil has He done? I have found no reason for death in Him. I will therefore chastise Him and let *Him* go."

23 But they were insistent, demanding with loud voices that He be crucified. And the voices of these men and of the chief priests prevailed.*a*

24 So Pilate gave sentence that it should be as they requested.

25 And he released to them*a* the one they requested, who for rebellion and murder had been thrown into prison; but he delivered Jesus to their will.

THE KING ON A CROSS

26 Now as they led Him away, they laid hold of a certain man, Simon a Cȳ·rē′ni·an, who was coming from the country, and on him they laid the cross that he might bear *it* after Jesus.

27 And a great multitude of the people followed Him, and women who also mourned and lamented Him.

28 But Jesus, turning to them, said, "Daughters of Jerusalem, do not weep for Me, but weep for yourselves and for your children.

29 "For indeed the days are coming in which they will say, 'Blessed *are* the barren, wombs that never bore, and breasts which never nursed!'

30 "Then they will begin '*to say to the mountains, "Fall on us!" and to the hills, "Cover us!"*a

31 "For if they do these things in the green wood, what will be done in the dry?"

32 There were also two others, criminals, led with Him to be put to death.

33 And when they had come to the place called Calvary, there they crucified Him, and the criminals, one on the right hand and the other on the left.

34 Then Jesus said, "Father, forgive them, for they do not know what they do."*a* And they divided His garments and cast lots.

23:15 *a*NU-Text reads *for he sent Him back to us.*
23:17 *a*NU-Text omits verse 17.   23:23 *a*NU-Text omits *and of the chief priests.*   23:25 *a*NU-Text and M-Text omit *to them.*   23:30 *a*Hosea 10:8   23:34 *a*NU-Text brackets the first sentence as a later addition.

◼ *Prayers* ◼

Luke 23:34

Jesus was nailed to the cross. He was dying in great pain. What would you expect Him to pray at that time? Would you expect Him to ask God to judge these wicked men? Would you expect Him to pray for His own suffering? This is what He prayed, "Father, forgive them, for they do not know what they do." When someone hurts you, do you pray for the Lord to forgive that person? Jesus did.

35 And the people stood looking on. But even the rulers with them sneered, saying, "He saved others; let Him save Himself if He is the Christ, the chosen of God."

36 The soldiers also mocked Him, coming and offering Him sour wine,

37 and saying, "If You are the King of the Jews, save Yourself."

38 And an inscription also was written over Him in letters of Greek, Latin, and Hebrew:a

THIS IS THE KING OF THE JEWS.

39 Then one of the criminals who were hanged blasphemed Him, saying, "If You are the Christ,a save Yourself and us."

40 But the other, answering, rebuked him, saying, "Do you not even fear God, seeing you are under the same condemnation?

41 "And we indeed justly, for we receive the due reward of our deeds; but this Man has done nothing wrong."

42 Then he said to Jesus, "Lord,a remember me when You come into Your kingdom."

43 And Jesus said to him, "Assuredly, I say to you, today you will be with Me in Paradise."

JESUS DIES ON THE CROSS

44 Now it wasa about the sixth hour, and there was darkness over all the earth until the ninth hour.

45 Then the sun was darkened,a and the veil of the temple was torn in two.

46 And when Jesus had cried out with a loud voice, He said, "Father, 'into Your hands I commit My spirit.' "a Having said this, He breathed His last.

47 So when the centurion saw what had happened, he glorified God, saying, "Certainly this was a righteous Man!"

48 And the whole crowd who came together to that sight, seeing what had been done, beat their breasts and returned.

49 But all His acquaintances, and the women who followed Him from Galilee, stood at a distance, watching these things.

JESUS BURIED IN JOSEPH'S TOMB

50 Now behold, *there was* a man named Joseph, a council member, a good and just man.

51 He had not consented to their decision and deed. *He was* from Ar·i·ma·thē′a, a city of the Jews, who himself was also waitinga for the kingdom of God.

52 This man went to Pilate and asked for the body of Jesus.

53 Then he took it down, wrapped it in linen, and laid it in a tomb *that was* hewn out of the rock, where no one had ever lain before.

54 That day was the Preparation, and the Sabbath drew near.

55 And the women who had come with Him from Galilee followed after, and they observed the tomb and how His body was laid.

56 Then they returned and prepared spices and fragrant oils. And they rested on the Sabbath according to the commandment.

■ *see Mark 15*

HE IS RISEN

24 Now on the first *day* of the week, very early in the morning,

---

23:38 aNU-Text omits *written* and *in letters of Greek, Latin, and Hebrew.*   23:39 aNU-Text reads *Are You not the Christ?*   23:42 aNU-Text reads *And he said, "Jesus, remember me.*   23:44 aNU-Text adds *already.*   23:45 aNU-Text reads *obscured.*   23:46 aPsalm 31:5   23:51 aNU-Text reads *who was waiting.*

they, and certain *other women* with them,a came to the tomb bringing the spices which they had prepared.

2   But they found the stone rolled away from the tomb.

3   Then they went in and did not find the body of the Lord Jesus.

4   And it happened, as they were greatlya perplexed about this, that behold, two men stood by them in shining garments.

5   Then, as they were afraid and bowed *their* faces to the earth, they said to them, "Why do you seek the living among the dead?

6   "He is not here, but is risen! Remember how He spoke to you when He was still in Galilee,

7   "saying, 'The Son of Man must be delivered into the hands of sinful men, and be crucified, and the third day rise again.'"

8   And they remembered His words.

9   Then they returned from the tomb and told all these things to the eleven and to all the rest.

10   It was Mary Mag′da·lene, Jō-an′na, Mary *the mother* of James, and the other *women* with them, who told these things to the apostles.

11   And their words seemed to them like idle tales, and they did not believe them.

12   But Peter arose and ran to the tomb; and stooping down, he saw the linen cloths lyinga by themselves; and he departed, marveling to himself at what had happened.

■ *see Matthew 28:1–20*

THE ROAD TO EMMAUS

Jesus had risen from the dead! But some of the disciples didn't know this yet. Jesus was about to surprise them!

13   Now behold, two of them were traveling that same day to a village called Em·mā′us, which was seven milesa from Jerusalem.

14   And they talked together of all these things which had happened.

15   So it was, while they conversed and reasoned, that Jesus Himself drew near and went with them.

16   But their eyes were restrained, so that they did not know Him.

17   And He said to them, "What kind of conversation *is* this that you have with one another as you walk and are sad?"a

18   Then the one whose name was Clē′o·pas answered and said to Him, "Are You the only stranger in Jerusalem, and have You not known the things which happened there in these days?"

19   And He said to them, "What things?" So they said to Him, "The things concerning Jesus of Nazareth, who was a Prophet mighty in deed and word before God and all the people,

20   "and how the chief priests and our rulers delivered Him to be condemned to death, and crucified Him.

21   "But we were hoping that it was He who was going to redeem Israel. Indeed, besides all this, today is the third day since these things happened.

22   "Yes, and certain women of our company, who arrived at the tomb early, astonished us.

23   "When they did not find His body, they came saying that they had also seen a vision of angels who said He was alive.

24   "And certain of those *who were* with us went to the tomb and found *it* just as the women had said; but Him they did not see."

24:1 aNU-Text omits *and certain other women with them.*   24:4 aNU-Text omits *greatly.*
24:12 aNU-Text omits *lying.*   24:13 aLiterally *sixty stadia*   24:17 aNU-Text reads *as you walk? And they stood still, looking sad.*

25 Then He said to them, "O foolish ones, and slow of heart to believe in all that the prophets have spoken!
26 "Ought not the Christ to have suffered these things and to enter into His glory?"
27 And beginning at Moses and all the Prophets, He expounded to them in all the Scriptures the things concerning Himself.

THE DISCIPLES' EYES OPENED

28 Then they drew near to the village where they were going, and He indicated that He would have gone farther.
29 But they constrained Him, saying, "Abide with us, for it is toward evening, and the day is far spent." And He went in to stay with them.
30 Now it came to pass, as He sat at the table with them, that He took bread, blessed and broke it, and gave it to them.
31 Then their eyes were opened and they knew Him; and He vanished from their sight.
32 And they said to one another, "Did not our heart burn within us while He talked with us on the road, and while He opened the Scriptures to us?"
33 So they rose up that very hour and returned to Jerusalem, and found the eleven and those who were with them gathered together,
34 saying, "The Lord is risen indeed, and has appeared to Simon!"
35 And they told about the things that had happened on the road, and how He was known to them in the breaking of bread.

JESUS APPEARS TO HIS DISCIPLES

36 Now as they said these things, Jesus Himself stood in the midst of them, and said to them, "Peace to you."
37 But they were terrified and frightened, and supposed they had seen a spirit.
38 And He said to them, "Why are you troubled? And why do doubts arise in your hearts?
39 "Behold My hands and My feet, that it is I Myself. Handle Me and see, for a spirit does not have flesh and bones as you see I have."
40 When He had said this, He showed them His hands and His feet.a
41 But while they still did not believe for joy, and marveled, He said to them, "Have you any food here?"
42 So they gave Him a piece of a broiled fish and some honeycomb.a
43 And He took it and ate in their presence.

THE SCRIPTURES OPENED

44 Then He said to them, "These are the words which I spoke to you while I was still with you, that all things must be fulfilled which were written in the Law of Moses and the Prophets and the Psalms concerning Me."
45 And He opened their understanding, that they might comprehend the Scriptures.
46 Then He said to them, "Thus it is written, and thus it was necessary for the Christ to suffer and to risea from the dead the third day,
47 "and that repentance and remission of sins should be preached in His name to all nations, beginning at Jerusalem.

24:40 aSome printed New Testaments omit this verse. It is found in nearly all Greek manuscripts.
24:42 aNU-Text omits and some honeycomb.
24:46 aNU-Text reads written, that the Christ should suffer and rise.

☑ *Bible Quiz*

Luke 24:13–53   **Jesus Goes Up to Heaven**

1. How many disciples were walking on the road to Emmaus?
2. Who joined them as they walked along? Did the disciples know who He was?
3. What did they talk about?
4. What happened as they sat at the table to eat?
5. How did Jesus show His other disciples that He really was alive?
6. After Jesus taught His disciples, where did He go? God has promised that one day Jesus will return to take all those who love Him to heaven. How can you make sure you go to heaven with Him?

---

48 "And you are witnesses of these things.
49 "Behold, I send the Promise of My Father upon you; but tarry in the city of Jerusalem*a* until you are endued with power from on high."

THE ASCENSION

50 And He led them out as far as Beth′a·ny, and He lifted up His hands and blessed them.
51 Now it came to pass, while He blessed them, that He was parted from them and carried up into heaven.
52 And they worshiped Him, and returned to Jerusalem with great joy,
53 and were continually in the temple praising and*a* blessing God. Amen.*b*

24:49 *a*NU-Text omits *of Jerusalem.*
24:53 *a*NU-Text omits *praising and.* *b*NU-Text omits *Amen.*

The Gospel According to
JOHN

The Eternal Word

IN the beginning was the Word, and the Word was with God, and the Word was God.

2 He was in the beginning with God.

3 All things were made through Him, and without Him nothing was made that was made.

4 In Him was life, and the life was the light of men.

5 And the light shines in the darkness, and the darkness did not comprehend*a* it.

John's Witness: The True Light

6 There was a man sent from God, whose name *was* John.

7 This man came for a witness, to bear witness of the Light, that all through him might believe.

8 He was not that Light, but *was sent* to bear witness of that Light.

9 That was the true Light which gives light to every man coming into the world.*a*

10 He was in the world, and the world was made through Him, and the world did not know Him.

11 He came to His own,*a* and His own*b* did not receive Him.

12 But as many as received Him, to them He gave the right to become children of God, to those who believe in His name:

13 who were born, not of blood, nor of the will of the flesh, nor of the will of man, but of God.

The Word Becomes Flesh

14 And the Word became flesh and dwelt among us, and we beheld His glory, the glory as of the only begotten of the Father, full of grace and truth.

15 John bore witness of Him and cried out, saying, "This was He of whom I said, 'He who comes after me is preferred before me, for He was before me.' "

16 And*a* of His fullness we have all received, and grace for grace.

17 For the law was given through Moses, *but* grace and truth came through Jesus Christ.

18 No one has seen God at any time. The only begotten Son,*a* who is in the bosom of the Father, He has declared *Him.*

A Voice in the Wilderness

19 Now this is the testimony of John, when the Jews sent priests and Lē′vītes from Jerusalem to ask him, "Who are you?"

20 He confessed, and did not deny, but confessed, "I am not the Christ."

21 And they asked him, "What then? Are you E·lī′jah?" He said, "I am not." "Are you the Prophet?" And he answered, "No."

22 Then they said to him, "Who are you, that we may give an answer to those who sent us? What do you say about yourself?"

23 He said: "I *am*

'The voice of one crying in the wilderness:
"Make straight the way of the LORD," '*a*

as the prophet I·sāi′ah said."

1:5 *a*Or *overcome*   1:9 *a*Or *That was the true Light which, coming into the world, gives light to every man.*   1:11 *a*That is, His own things or domain   *b*That is, His own people   1:16 *a*NU-Text reads *For.*   1:18 *a*NU-Text reads *only begotten God.*   1:23 *a*Isaiah 40:3

24 Now those who were sent were from the Phar′i·sees.

25 And they asked him, saying, "Why then do you baptize if you are not the Christ, nor E·lī′jah, nor the Prophet?"

26 John answered them, saying, "I baptize with water, but there stands One among you whom you do not know.

27 "It is He who, coming after me, is preferred before me, whose sandal strap I am not worthy to loose."

28 These things were done in Beth-ab′a·ra*a* beyond the Jordan, where John was baptizing.

THE LAMB OF GOD

29 The next day John saw Jesus coming toward him, and said, "Behold! The Lamb of God who takes away the sin of the world!

30 "This is He of whom I said, 'After me comes a Man who is preferred before me, for He was before me.'

31 "I did not know Him; but that He should be revealed to Israel, therefore I came baptizing with water."

32 And John bore witness, saying, "I saw the Spirit descending from heaven like a dove, and He remained upon Him.

33 "I did not know Him, but He who sent me to baptize with water said to me, 'Upon whom you see the Spirit descending, and remaining on Him, this is He who baptizes with the Holy Spirit.'

34 "And I have seen and testified that this is the Son of God."

THE FIRST DISCIPLES

35 Again, the next day, John stood with two of his disciples.

36 And looking at Jesus as He walked, he said, "Behold the Lamb of God!"

37 The two disciples heard him speak, and they followed Jesus.

38 Then Jesus turned, and seeing them following, said to them, "What do you seek?" They said to Him, "Rabbi" (which is to say, when translated, Teacher), "where are You staying?"

39 He said to them, "Come and see." They came and saw where He was staying, and remained with Him that day (now it was about the tenth hour).

40 One of the two who heard John *speak,* and followed Him, was Andrew, Simon Peter's brother.

41 He first found his own brother Simon, and said to him, "We have found the Messiah" (which is translated, the Christ).

42 And he brought him to Jesus. Now when Jesus looked at him, He said, "You are Simon the son of Jonah.*a* You shall be called Cē′phas" (which is translated, A Stone).

PHILIP AND NATHANAEL

43 The following day Jesus wanted to go to Galilee, and He found Philip and said to him, "Follow Me."

44 Now Philip was from Beth·sā′i·da, the city of Andrew and Peter.

45 Philip found Na·than′a·el and said to him, "We have found Him of whom Moses in the law, and also the prophets, wrote—Jesus of Nazareth, the son of Joseph."

46 And Na·than′a·el said to him, "Can anything good come out of Nazareth?" Philip said to him, "Come and see."

47 Jesus saw Na·than′a·el coming toward Him, and said of him, "Behold, an Israelite indeed, in whom is no deceit!

1:28 *a*NU-Text and M-Text read *Bethany.*
1:42 *a*NU-Text reads *John.*

GETTING GOOD FRIENDS TOGETHER John 1:43–49

Andrea's puppies want a good home. They want someone to love them and take care of them. Andrea wants this, too. And do you know what? Some of Andrea's friends want some puppies. They wish someone would come to their door with a puppy so they could take care of it. Do you think Andrea is having fun helping her friends and her puppies get together? Jesus wants your friends to be His friends. Your friends may want Jesus to be their friend. Would you have fun getting them together?

1. Why do you think Andrea is having fun?
2. Why is it fun getting good friends together?
3. Jesus wants your friends to be His friends. Do you think some of your friends want Jesus to be their friend?
4. Wouldn't it be fun to get your good friends together with your Friend Jesus? That's just what Philip did for Nathanael (read John 1:45).

For more on *What Should I Do?* turn to page 1641
For more on *Friendship* turn to page 1740

48 Na·than′a·el said to Him, "How do You know me?" Jesus answered and said to him, "Before Philip called you, when you were under the fig tree, I saw you."

49 Na·than′a·el answered and said to Him, "Rabbi, You are the Son of God! You are the King of Israel!"

50 Jesus answered and said to him, "Because I said to you, 'I saw you under the fig tree,' do you believe? You will see greater things than these."

51 And He said to him, "Most assuredly, I say to you, hereafter[a] you shall see heaven open, and the angels of God ascending and descending upon the Son of Man."

WATER TURNED TO WINE

2 On the third day there was a wedding in Cā′na of Galilee, and the mother of Jesus was there.

2 Now both Jesus and His disciples were invited to the wedding.

3 And when they ran out of wine, the mother of Jesus said to Him, "They have no wine."

4 Jesus said to her, "Woman, what does your concern have to do with Me? My hour has not yet come."

5 His mother said to the servants, "Whatever He says to you, do it."

6 Now there were set there six waterpots of stone, according to the manner of purification of the Jews, containing twenty or thirty gallons apiece.

7 Jesus said to them, "Fill the waterpots with water." And they filled them up to the brim.

8 And He said to them, "Draw some out now, and take it to the master of the feast." And they took it.

9 When the master of the feast had tasted the water that was made wine, and did not know where it came from

(but the servants who had drawn the water knew), the master of the feast called the bridegroom.

10 And he said to him, "Every man at the beginning sets out the good wine, and when the guests have well drunk, then the inferior. You have kept the good wine until now!"

11 This beginning of signs Jesus did in Cā′na of Galilee, and manifested His glory; and His disciples believed in Him.

12 After this He went down to Ca·per′na·um, He, His mother, His brothers, and His disciples; and they did not stay there many days.

JESUS CLEANSES THE TEMPLE

13 Now the Passover of the Jews was at hand, and Jesus went up to Jerusalem.

14 And He found in the temple those who sold oxen and sheep and doves, and the money changers doing business.

15 When He had made a whip of cords, He drove them all out of the temple, with the sheep and the oxen, and poured out the changers' money and overturned the tables.

16 And He said to those who sold doves, "Take these things away! Do not make My Father's house a house of merchandise!"

17 Then His disciples remembered that it was written, *"Zeal for Your house has eaten[a] Me up."*[b]

18 So the Jews answered and said to Him, "What sign do You show to us, since You do these things?"

19 Jesus answered and said to them, "Destroy this temple, and in three days I will raise it up."

20 Then the Jews said, "It has taken forty-six years to build this temple,

1:51 [a]NU-Text omits *hereafter.*   2:17 [a]NU-Text and M-Text read *will eat.*   [b]Psalm 69:9

and will You raise it up in three days?"

21 But He was speaking of the temple of His body.

22 Therefore, when He had risen from the dead, His disciples remembered that He had said this to them;a and they believed the Scripture and the word which Jesus had said.

THE DISCERNER OF HEARTS

23 Now when He was in Jerusalem at the Passover, during the feast, many believed in His name when they saw the signs which He did.

24 But Jesus did not commit Himself to them, because He knew all *men,*

25 and had no need that anyone should testify of man, for He knew what was in man.

THE NEW BIRTH

One night a man came to visit Jesus. This man wanted to keep his visit a secret. What did he want to talk about?

3 There was a man of the Phar'i-sees named Nic·o·dē'mus, a ruler of the Jews.

2 This man came to Jesus by night and said to Him, "Rabbi, we know that You are a teacher come from God; for no one can do these signs that You do unless God is with him."

3 Jesus answered and said to him, "Most assuredly, I say to you, unless one is born again, he cannot see the kingdom of God."

4 Nic·o·dē'mus said to Him, "How can a man be born when he is old? Can he enter a second time into his mother's womb and be born?"

5 Jesus answered, "Most assuredly, I say to you, unless one is born of water and the Spirit, he cannot enter the kingdom of God.

6 "That which is born of the flesh is flesh, and that which is born of the Spirit is spirit.

7 "Do not marvel that I said to you, 'You must be born again.'

8 "The wind blows where it wishes, and you hear the sound of it, but cannot tell where it comes from and where it goes. So is everyone who is born of the Spirit."

9 Nic·o·dē'mus answered and said to Him, "How can these things be?"

10 Jesus answered and said to him, "Are you the teacher of Israel, and do not know these things?

11 "Most assuredly, I say to you, We speak what We know and testify what We have seen, and you do not receive Our witness.

12 "If I have told you earthly things and you do not believe, how will you believe if I tell you heavenly things?

13 "No one has ascended to heaven but He who came down from heaven, *that is,* the Son of Man who is in heaven.a

14 "And as Moses lifted up the serpent in the wilderness, even so must the Son of Man be lifted up,

15 "that whoever believes in Him should not perish buta have eternal life.

16 "For God so loved the world that He gave His only begotten Son, that whoever believes in Him should not perish but have everlasting life.

17 "For God did not send His Son into the world to condemn the world, but that the world through Him might be saved.

18 "He who believes in Him is not condemned; but he who does not believe is condemned already, because he has not believed in the name of the only begotten Son of God.

2:22 aNU-Text and M-Text omit *to them.*
3:13 aNU-Text omits *who is in heaven.*
3:15 aNU-Text omits *not perish but.*

ABOUT GOD'S LOVE John 3:16

How Much Does God Love Me?

The world isn't merely a big globe, is it? The world is also all the people who live here. God loves the beautiful place He created. He takes good care of it and wants us to help Him. But even more, He loves us—all the people who live here.

1. How much does God love us? Read John 3:16. What does it say?
2. What did He do to say "I love you"?
3. What we should do to say "I love You" to God?

For more on *What the Bible Says* turn to page 1636
For more on *God's Creation* turn to page 1909

19 "And this is the condemnation, that the light has come into the world, and men loved darkness rather than light, because their deeds were evil.
20 "For everyone practicing evil hates the light and does not come to the light, lest his deeds should be exposed.
21 "But he who does the truth comes to the light, that his deeds may be clearly seen, that they have been done in God."

JOHN THE BAPTIST EXALTS CHRIST

22 After these things Jesus and His disciples came into the land of Judea, and there He remained with them and baptized.
23 Now John also was baptizing in Aē'non near Sā'lim, because there was much water there. And they came and were baptized.

24 For John had not yet been thrown into prison.

25 Then there arose a dispute between *some* of John's disciples and the Jews about purification.

26 And they came to John and said to him, "Rabbi, He who was with you beyond the Jordan, to whom you have testified—behold, He is baptizing, and all are coming to Him!"

27 John answered and said, "A man can receive nothing unless it has been given to him from heaven.

28 "You yourselves bear me witness, that I said, 'I am not the Christ,' but, 'I have been sent before Him.'

29 "He who has the bride is the bridegroom; but the friend of the bridegroom, who stands and hears him, rejoices greatly because of the bridegroom's voice. Therefore this joy of mine is fulfilled.

30 "He must increase, but I *must* decrease.

31 "He who comes from above is above all; he who is of the earth is earthly and speaks of the earth. He who comes from heaven is above all.

32 "And what He has seen and heard, that He testifies; and no one receives His testimony.

33 "He who has received His testimony has certified that God is true.

34 "For He whom God has sent speaks the words of God, for God does not give the Spirit by measure.

35 "The Father loves the Son, and has given all things into His hand.

36 "He who believes in the Son has everlasting life; and he who does not believe the Son shall not see life, but the wrath of God abides on him."

A Samaritan Woman Meets Her Messiah

4 Therefore, when the Lord knew that the Phar'i·sees had heard that Jesus made and baptized more disciples than John

2 (though Jesus Himself did not baptize, but His disciples),

3 He left Judea and departed again to Galilee.

4 But He needed to go through Samaria.

5 So He came to a city of Samaria which is called Sȳ'char, near the plot of ground that Jacob gave to his son Joseph.

6 Now Jacob's well was there. Jesus therefore, being wearied from *His* journey, sat thus by the well. It was about the sixth hour.

7 A woman of Samaria came to draw water. Jesus said to her, "Give Me a drink."

8 For His disciples had gone away into the city to buy food.

9 Then the woman of Samaria said to Him, "How is it that You, being a Jew, ask a drink from me, a Samaritan woman?" For Jews have no dealings with Samaritans.

10 Jesus answered and said to her, "If you knew the gift of God, and who it is who says to you, 'Give Me a drink,' you would have asked Him, and He would have given you living water."

11 The woman said to Him, "Sir, You have nothing to draw with, and the well is deep. Where then do You get that living water?

12 "Are You greater than our father Jacob, who gave us the well, and drank from it himself, as well as his sons and his livestock?"

13 Jesus answered and said to her, "Whoever drinks of this water will thirst again,

14 "but whoever drinks of the water that I shall give him will never thirst. But the water that I shall give him will become in him a fountain of water springing up into everlasting life."

15 The woman said to Him, "Sir, give me this water, that I may not thirst, nor come here to draw."

16 Jesus said to her, "Go, call your husband, and come here."

17 The woman answered and said, "I have no husband." Jesus said to her, "You have well said, 'I have no husband,'

18 "for you have had five husbands, and the one whom you now have is not your husband; in that you spoke truly."

19 The woman said to Him, "Sir, I perceive that You are a prophet.

20 "Our fathers worshiped on this mountain, and you *Jews* say that in Jerusalem is the place where one ought to worship."

21 Jesus said to her, "Woman, believe Me, the hour is coming when you will neither on this mountain, nor in Jerusalem, worship the Father.

22 "You worship what you do not know; we know what we worship, for salvation is of the Jews.

23 "But the hour is coming, and now is, when the true worshipers will worship the Father in spirit and truth; for the Father is seeking such to worship Him.

24 "God *is* Spirit, and those who worship Him must worship in spirit and truth."

25 The woman said to Him, "I know that Messiah is coming" (who is called Christ). "When He comes, He will tell us all things."

26 Jesus said to her, "I who speak to you am *He.*"

THE WHITENED HARVEST

27 And at this *point* His disciples came, and they marveled that He talked with a woman; yet no one said, "What do You seek?" or, "Why are You talking with her?"

28 The woman then left her waterpot, went her way into the city, and said to the men,

29 "Come, see a Man who told me all things that I ever did. Could this be the Christ?"

30 Then they went out of the city and came to Him.

31 In the meantime His disciples urged Him, saying, "Rabbi, eat."

32 But He said to them, "I have food to eat of which you do not know."

33 Therefore the disciples said to one another, "Has anyone brought Him *anything* to eat?"

34 Jesus said to them, "My food is to do the will of Him who sent Me, and to finish His work.

35 "Do you not say, 'There are still four months and *then* comes the harvest'? Behold, I say to you, lift up your eyes and look at the fields, for they are already white for harvest!

36 "And he who reaps receives wages, and gathers fruit for eternal life, that both he who sows and he who reaps may rejoice together.

37 "For in this the saying is true: 'One sows and another reaps.'

38 "I sent you to reap that for which you have not labored; others have labored, and you have entered into their labors."

THE SAVIOR OF THE WORLD

39 And many of the Samaritans of that city believed in Him because of the word of the woman who testified, "He told me all that I *ever* did."

40 So when the Samaritans had come to Him, they urged Him to stay with them; and He stayed there two days.

41 And many more believed because of His own word.

42 Then they said to the woman, "Now we believe, not because of what you said, for we ourselves have heard

Him and we know that this is indeed the Christ,*a* the Savior of the world."

WELCOME AT GALILEE

43 Now after the two days He departed from there and went to Galilee.

44 For Jesus Himself testified that a prophet has no honor in his own country.

45 So when He came to Galilee, the Galileans received Him, having seen all the things He did in Jerusalem at the feast; for they also had gone to the feast.

A NOBLEMAN'S SON HEALED

A man's son was very sick and about to die. The man wanted to take his son to see Jesus, who was in another town some distance away. But the boy was too sick to travel. So the man went to see Jesus anyway. How could Jesus heal the boy if he wasn't there?

46 So Jesus came again to Cā′na of Galilee where He had made the water wine. And there was a certain nobleman whose son was sick at Caper′na·um.

47 When he heard that Jesus had come out of Judea into Galilee, he went to Him and implored Him to come down and heal his son, for he was at the point of death.

48 Then Jesus said to him, "Unless you *people* see signs and wonders, you will by no means believe."

49 The nobleman said to Him, "Sir, come down before my child dies!"

50 Jesus said to him, "Go your way; your son lives." So the man believed the word that Jesus spoke to him, and he went his way.

51 And as he was now going down, his servants met him and told *him,* saying, "Your son lives!"

52 Then he inquired of them the hour when he got better. And they said to him, "Yesterday at the seventh hour the fever left him."

53 So the father knew that *it was* at the same hour in which Jesus said to him, "Your son lives." And he himself believed, and his whole household.

54 This again *is* the second sign Jesus did when He had come out of Judea into Galilee.

☑ *Bible Quiz*

John 4:46–54 **A Long Distance Healing**

1. Where was Jesus? Where did the nobleman and his son live?
2. What did the nobleman ask Jesus to do? How do you know that the nobleman loved his son?
3. Did Jesus go with the nobleman? What did He do instead?
4. The nobleman's son was healed, but something happened to the nobleman, too. What was it?
5. Why should Jesus' miracles help us believe that Jesus is God's Son?

A MAN HEALED AT THE POOL OF BETHESDA

5 After this there was a feast of the Jews, and Jesus went up to Jerusalem.

4:42 *a*NU-Text omits *the Christ.*

2 Now there is in Jerusalem by the Sheep *Gate* a pool, which is called in Hebrew, Be·thes′da,*a* having five porches.

3 In these lay a great multitude of sick people, blind, lame, paralyzed, waiting for the moving of the water.

4 For an angel went down at a certain time into the pool and stirred up the water; then whoever stepped in first, after the stirring of the water, was made well of whatever disease he had.*a*

5 Now a certain man was there who had an infirmity thirty-eight years.

6 When Jesus saw him lying there, and knew that he already had been *in that condition* a long time, He said to him, "Do you want to be made well?"

7 The sick man answered Him, "Sir, I have no man to put me into the pool when the water is stirred up; but while I am coming, another steps down before me."

8 Jesus said to him, "Rise, take up your bed and walk."

9 And immediately the man was made well, took up his bed, and walked. And that day was the Sabbath.

10 The Jews therefore said to him who was cured, "It is the Sabbath; it is not lawful for you to carry your bed."

11 He answered them, "He who made me well said to me, 'Take up your bed and walk.' "

12 Then they asked him, "Who is the Man who said to you, 'Take up your bed and walk'?"

13 But the one who was healed did not know who it was, for Jesus had withdrawn, a multitude being in *that* place.

14 Afterward Jesus found him in the temple, and said to him, "See, you have been made well. Sin no more, lest a worse thing come upon you."

15 The man departed and told the Jews that it was Jesus who had made him well.

HONOR THE FATHER AND THE SON

16 For this reason the Jews persecuted Jesus, and sought to kill Him,*a* because He had done these things on the Sabbath.

17 But Jesus answered them, "My Father has been working until now, and I have been working."

18 Therefore the Jews sought all the more to kill Him, because He not only broke the Sabbath, but also said that God was His Father, making Himself equal with God.

19 Then Jesus answered and said to them, "Most assuredly, I say to you, the Son can do nothing of Himself, but what He sees the Father do; for whatever He does, the Son also does in like manner.

20 "For the Father loves the Son, and shows Him all things that He Himself does; and He will show Him greater works than these, that you may marvel.

21 "For as the Father raises the dead and gives life to *them,* even so the Son gives life to whom He will.

22 "For the Father judges no one, but has committed all judgment to the Son,

23 "that all should honor the Son just as they honor the Father. He who does not honor the Son does not honor the Father who sent Him.

LIFE AND JUDGMENT ARE THROUGH THE SON

24 "Most assuredly, I say to you, he who hears My word and believes in

---

5:2 *a*NU-Text reads *Bethzatha.*   5:4 *a*NU-Text omits *waiting for the moving of the water* at the end of verse 3, and all of verse 4.   5:16 *a*NU-Text omits *and sought to kill Him.*

Him who sent Me has everlasting life, and shall not come into judgment, but has passed from death into life.

25 "Most assuredly, I say to you, the hour is coming, and now is, when the dead will hear the voice of the Son of God; and those who hear will live.

26 "For as the Father has life in Himself, so He has granted the Son to have life in Himself,

27 "and has given Him authority to execute judgment also, because He is the Son of Man.

28 "Do not marvel at this; for the hour is coming in which all who are in the graves will hear His voice

29 "and come forth—those who have done good, to the resurrection of life, and those who have done evil, to the resurrection of condemnation.

30 "I can of Myself do nothing. As I hear, I judge; and My judgment is righteous, because I do not seek My own will but the will of the Father who sent Me.

THE FOURFOLD WITNESS

31 "If I bear witness of Myself, My witness is not true.

32 "There is another who bears witness of Me, and I know that the witness which He witnesses of Me is true.

33 "You have sent to John, and he has borne witness to the truth.

34 "Yet I do not receive testimony from man, but I say these things that you may be saved.

35 "He was the burning and shining lamp, and you were willing for a time to rejoice in his light.

36 "But I have a greater witness than John's; for the works which the Father has given Me to finish—the very works that I do—bear witness of Me, that the Father has sent Me.

37 "And the Father Himself, who sent Me, has testified of Me. You have neither heard His voice at any time, nor seen His form.

38 "But you do not have His word abiding in you, because whom He sent, Him you do not believe.

39 "You search the Scriptures, for in them you think you have eternal life; and these are they which testify of Me.

40 "But you are not willing to come to Me that you may have life.

41 "I do not receive honor from men.

42 "But I know you, that you do not have the love of God in you.

43 "I have come in My Father's name, and you do not receive Me; if another comes in his own name, him you will receive.

44 "How can you believe, who receive honor from one another, and do not seek the honor that *comes* from the only God?

45 "Do not think that I shall accuse you to the Father; there is *one* who accuses you—Moses, in whom you trust.

46 "For if you believed Moses, you would believe Me; for he wrote about Me.

47 "But if you do not believe his writings, how will you believe My words?"

FEEDING THE FIVE THOUSAND

A boy packed a lunch and went to hear Jesus one day. And what a wonderful day it turned out to be! He would have quite a story to tell his friends for years to come.

6 After these things Jesus went over the Sea of Galilee, which is *the Sea* of Tī·bē′ri·as.

2 Then a great multitude followed

Him, because they saw His signs which He performed on those who were diseased.

3 And Jesus went up on the mountain, and there He sat with His disciples.

4 Now the Passover, a feast of the Jews, was near.

5 Then Jesus lifted up *His* eyes, and seeing a great multitude coming toward Him, He said to Philip, "Where shall we buy bread, that these may eat?"

6 But this He said to test him, for He Himself knew what He would do.

7 Philip answered Him, "Two hundred denarii worth of bread is not sufficient for them, that every one of them may have a little."

8 One of His disciples, Andrew, Simon Peter's brother, said to Him,

9 "There is a lad here who has five barley loaves and two small fish, but what are they among so many?"

10 Then Jesus said, "Make the people sit down." Now there was much grass in the place. So the men sat down, in number about five thousand.

11 And Jesus took the loaves, and when He had given thanks He distributed *them* to the disciples, and the disciples[a] to those sitting down; and likewise of the fish, as much as they wanted.

12 So when they were filled, He said to His disciples, "Gather up the fragments that remain, so that nothing is lost."

13 Therefore they gathered *them* up, and filled twelve baskets with the fragments of the five barley loaves which were left over by those who had eaten.

14 Then those men, when they had seen the sign that Jesus did, said, "This is truly the Prophet who is to come into the world."

JESUS WALKS ON THE SEA

15 Therefore when Jesus perceived that they were about to come and take Him by force to make Him king, He departed again to the mountain by Himself alone.

☑ Bible Quiz

John 6:1–15 **Jesus Feeds 5,000 with a Boy's Lunch**

1. Why did the crowds keep following Jesus? Where did Jesus go?
2. How did Jesus want to help all the people?
3. Did the disciples think it was possible to feed all these people? What did Jesus think?
4. How much food did the young boy bring with him? Did the disciples think this was enough? Did Jesus think this was enough?
5. How many people did Jesus feed with the boy's lunch? How much was left over?
6. What did the disciples say about Jesus after all the people had been fed? What would you have said about Jesus if you had been the young boy? Does this help you believe in Jesus as God's Son?

16 Now when evening came, His disciples went down to the sea,

17 got into the boat, and went over the sea toward Ca·per′na·um. And it

6:11 [a]NU-Text omits *to the disciples, and the disciples.*

was already dark, and Jesus had not come to them.

18 Then the sea arose because a great wind was blowing.

19 So when they had rowed about three or four miles,*a* they saw Jesus walking on the sea and drawing near the boat; and they were afraid.

20 But He said to them, "It is I; do not be afraid."

21 Then they willingly received Him into the boat, and immediately the boat was at the land where they were going.

■ *see Matthew 14:22–33*

THE BREAD FROM HEAVEN

22 On the following day, when the people who were standing on the other side of the sea saw that there was no other boat there, except that one which His disciples had entered,*a* and that Jesus had not entered the boat with His disciples, but His disciples had gone away alone—

23 however, other boats came from Tī·bē′ri·as, near the place where they ate bread after the Lord had given thanks—

24 when the people therefore saw that Jesus was not there, nor His disciples, they also got into boats and came to Ca·per′na·um, seeking Jesus.

25 And when they found Him on the other side of the sea, they said to Him, "Rabbi, when did You come here?"

26 Jesus answered them and said, "Most assuredly, I say to you, you seek Me, not because you saw the signs, but because you ate of the loaves and were filled.

27 "Do not labor for the food which perishes, but for the food which endures to everlasting life, which the Son of Man will give you, because God the Father has set His seal on Him."

28 Then they said to Him, "What shall we do, that we may work the works of God?"

29 Jesus answered and said to them, "This is the work of God, that you believe in Him whom He sent."

30 Therefore they said to Him, "What sign will You perform then, that we may see it and believe You? What work will You do?

31 "Our fathers ate the manna in the desert; as it is written, *'He gave them bread from heaven to eat.'* "*a*

32 Then Jesus said to them, "Most assuredly, I say to you, Moses did not give you the bread from heaven, but My Father gives you the true bread from heaven.

33 "For the bread of God is He who comes down from heaven and gives life to the world."

34 Then they said to Him, "Lord, give us this bread always."

35 And Jesus said to them, "I am the bread of life. He who comes to Me shall never hunger, and he who believes in Me shall never thirst.

36 "But I said to you that you have seen Me and yet do not believe.

37 "All that the Father gives Me will come to Me, and the one who comes to Me I will by no means cast out.

38 "For I have come down from heaven, not to do My own will, but the will of Him who sent Me.

39 "This is the will of the Father who sent Me, that of all He has given Me I should lose nothing, but should raise it up at the last day.

40 "And this is the will of Him who sent Me, that everyone who sees the Son and believes in Him may have everlasting life; and I will raise him up at the last day."

6:19 *a*Literally *twenty-five or thirty stadia*
6:22 *a*NU-Text omits *that* and *which His disciples had entered.*   6:31 *a*Exodus 16:4; Nehemiah 9:15; Psalm 78:24

REJECTED BY HIS OWN

41 The Jews then complained about Him, because He said, "I am the bread which came down from heaven."

42 And they said, "Is not this Jesus, the son of Joseph, whose father and mother we know? How is it then that He says, 'I have come down from heaven'?"

43 Jesus therefore answered and said to them, "Do not murmur among yourselves.

44 "No one can come to Me unless the Father who sent Me draws him; and I will raise him up at the last day.

45 "It is written in the prophets, *'And they shall all be taught by God.'a* Therefore everyone who has heard and learnedb from the Father comes to Me.

46 "Not that anyone has seen the Father, except He who is from God; He has seen the Father.

47 "Most assuredly, I say to you, he who believes in Mea has everlasting life.

48 "I am the bread of life.

49 "Your fathers ate the manna in the wilderness, and are dead.

50 "This is the bread which comes down from heaven, that one may eat of it and not die.

51 "I am the living bread which came down from heaven. If anyone eats of this bread, he will live forever; and the bread that I shall give is My flesh, which I shall give for the life of the world."

52 The Jews therefore quarreled among themselves, saying, "How can this Man give us *His* flesh to eat?"

53 Then Jesus said to them, "Most assuredly, I say to you, unless you eat the flesh of the Son of Man and drink His blood, you have no life in you.

54 "Whoever eats My flesh and drinks My blood has eternal life, and I will raise him up at the last day.

55 "For My flesh is food indeed,a and My blood is drink indeed.

56 "He who eats My flesh and drinks My blood abides in Me, and I in him.

57 "As the living Father sent Me, and I live because of the Father, so he who feeds on Me will live because of Me.

58 "This is the bread which came down from heaven—not as your fathers ate the manna, and are dead. He who eats this bread will live forever."

59 These things He said in the synagogue as He taught in Ca·per′na·um.

MANY DISCIPLES TURN AWAY

60 Therefore many of His disciples, when they heard *this,* said, "This is a hard saying; who can understand it?"

61 When Jesus knew in Himself that His disciples complained about this, He said to them, "Does this offend you?

62 *"What* then if you should see the Son of Man ascend where He was before?

63 "It is the Spirit who gives life; the flesh profits nothing. The words that I speak to you are spirit, and *they* are life.

64 "But there are some of you who do not believe." For Jesus knew from the beginning who they were who did not believe, and who would betray Him.

65 And He said, "Therefore I have said to you that no one can come to Me unless it has been granted to him by My Father."

66 From that *time* many of His disciples went back and walked with Him no more.

6:45 aIsaiah 54:13   bM-Text reads *hears and has learned.*   6:47 aNU-Text omits *in Me.*
6:55 aNU-Text reads *true food* and *true drink.*

67 Then Jesus said to the twelve, "Do you also want to go away?"

68 But Simon Peter answered Him, "Lord, to whom shall we go? You have the words of eternal life.

69 "Also we have come to believe and know that You are the Christ, the Son of the living God."a

70 Jesus answered them, "Did I not choose you, the twelve, and one of you is a devil?"

71 He spoke of Judas Is·car'i·ot, *the son* of Simon, for it was he who would betray Him, being one of the twelve.

JESUS' BROTHERS DISBELIEVE

7 After these things Jesus walked in Galilee; for He did not want to walk in Judea, because the Jewsa sought to kill Him.

2 Now the Jews' Feast of Tabernacles was at hand.

3 His brothers therefore said to Him, "Depart from here and go into Judea, that Your disciples also may see the works that You are doing.

4 "For no one does anything in secret while he himself seeks to be known openly. If You do these things, show Yourself to the world."

5 For even His brothers did not believe in Him.

6 Then Jesus said to them, "My time has not yet come, but your time is always ready.

7 "The world cannot hate you, but it hates Me because I testify of it that its works are evil.

8 "You go up to this feast. I am not yeta going up to this feast, for My time has not yet fully come."

9 When He had said these things to them, He remained in Galilee.

THE HEAVENLY SCHOLAR

10 But when His brothers had gone up, then He also went up to the feast, not openly, but as it were in secret.

11 Then the Jews sought Him at the feast, and said, "Where is He?"

12 And there was much complaining among the people concerning Him. Some said, "He is good"; others said, "No, on the contrary, He deceives the people."

13 However, no one spoke openly of Him for fear of the Jews.

14 Now about the middle of the feast Jesus went up into the temple and taught.

15 And the Jews marveled, saying, "How does this Man know letters, having never studied?"

16 Jesusa answered them and said, "My doctrine is not Mine, but His who sent Me.

17 "If anyone wills to do His will, he shall know concerning the doctrine, whether it is from God or *whether* I speak on My own *authority*.

18 "He who speaks from himself seeks his own glory; but He who seeks the glory of the One who sent Him is true, and no unrighteousness is in Him.

19 "Did not Moses give you the law, yet none of you keeps the law? Why do you seek to kill Me?"

20 The people answered and said, "You have a demon. Who is seeking to kill You?"

21 Jesus answered and said to them, "I did one work, and you all marvel.

22 "Moses therefore gave you circumcision (not that it is from Moses, but from the fathers), and you circumcise a man on the Sabbath.

23 "If a man receives circumcision on the Sabbath, so that the law of Moses should not be broken, are you angry with Me because I made a man completely well on the Sabbath?

6:69 aNU-Text reads *You are the Holy One of God.*
7:1 aThat is, the ruling authorities   7:8 aNU-Text omits *yet.*   7:16 aNU-Text and M-Text read *So Jesus.*

24 "Do not judge according to appearance, but judge with righteous judgment."

COULD THIS BE THE CHRIST?

25 Now some of them from Jerusalem said, "Is this not He whom they seek to kill?
26 "But look! He speaks boldly, and they say nothing to Him. Do the rulers know indeed that this is truly*a* the Christ?
27 "However, we know where this Man is from; but when the Christ comes, no one knows where He is from."
28 Then Jesus cried out, as He taught in the temple, saying, "You both know Me, and you know where I am from; and I have not come of Myself, but He who sent Me is true, whom you do not know.
29 "But*a* I know Him, for I am from Him, and He sent Me."
30 Therefore they sought to take Him; but no one laid a hand on Him, because His hour had not yet come.
31 And many of the people believed in Him, and said, "When the Christ comes, will He do more signs than these which this *Man* has done?"

JESUS AND THE RELIGIOUS LEADERS

32 The Phar′i·sees heard the crowd murmuring these things concerning Him, and the Phar′i·sees and the chief priests sent officers to take Him.
33 Then Jesus said to them,*a* "I shall be with you a little while longer, and *then* I go to Him who sent Me.
34 "You will seek Me and not find *Me,* and where I am you cannot come."
35 Then the Jews said among themselves, "Where does He intend to go that we shall not find Him? Does He

intend to go to the Dispersion among the Greeks and teach the Greeks?
36 "What is this thing that He said, 'You will seek Me and not find Me, and where I am you cannot come'?"

THE PROMISE OF THE HOLY SPIRIT

37 On the last day, that great *day* of the feast, Jesus stood and cried out, saying, "If anyone thirsts, let him come to Me and drink.
38 "He who believes in Me, as the Scripture has said, out of his heart will flow rivers of living water."
39 But this He spoke concerning the Spirit, whom those believing*a* in Him would receive; for the Holy*b* Spirit was not yet *given,* because Jesus was not yet glorified.

WHO IS HE?

40 Therefore many*a* from the crowd, when they heard this saying, said, "Truly this is the Prophet."
41 Others said, "This is the Christ." But some said, "Will the Christ come out of Galilee?
42 "Has not the Scripture said that the Christ comes from the seed of David and from the town of Bethlehem, where David was?"
43 So there was a division among the people because of Him.
44 Now some of them wanted to take Him, but no one laid hands on Him.

REJECTED BY THE AUTHORITIES

45 Then the officers came to the chief priests and Phar′i·sees, who said to them, "Why have you not brought Him?"

7:26 *a*NU-Text omits *truly.*   7:29 *a*NU-Text and M-Text omit *But.*   7:33 *a*NU-Text and M-Text omit *to them.*   7:39 *a*NU-Text reads *who believed.*   *b*NU-Text omits *Holy.*   7:40 *a*NU-Text reads *some.*

46 The officers answered, "No man ever spoke like this Man!"

47 Then the Phar′i·sees answered them, "Are you also deceived?

48 "Have any of the rulers or the Phar′i·sees believed in Him?

49 "But this crowd that does not know the law is accursed."

50 Nic·o·de′mus (he who came to Jesus by night,*a* being one of them) said to them,

51 "Does our law judge a man before it hears him and knows what he is doing?"

52 They answered and said to him, "Are you also from Galilee? Search and look, for no prophet has arisen*a* out of Galilee."

AN ADULTERESS FACES THE LIGHT OF THE WORLD

53 And everyone went to his *own* house.*a*

8 But Jesus went to the Mount of Olives.

2 Now early*a* in the morning He came again into the temple, and all the people came to Him; and He sat down and taught them.

3 Then the scribes and Phar′i·sees brought to Him a woman caught in adultery. And when they had set her in the midst,

4 they said to Him, "Teacher, this woman was caught*a* in adultery, in the very act.

5 "Now Moses, in the law, commanded*a* us that such should be stoned.*b* But what do You say?"*c*

6 This they said, testing Him, that they might have *something* of which to accuse Him. But Jesus stooped down and wrote on the ground with *His* finger, as though He did not hear.*a*

7 So when they continued asking Him, He raised Himself up*a* and said to them, "He who is without sin among you, let him throw a stone at her first."

8 And again He stooped down and wrote on the ground.

9 Then those who heard *it,* being convicted by *their* conscience,*a* went out one by one, beginning with the oldest *even* to the last. And Jesus was left alone, and the woman standing in the midst.

10 When Jesus had raised Himself up and saw no one but the woman, He said to her,*a* "Woman, where are those accusers of yours?*b* Has no one condemned you?"

11 She said, "No one, Lord." And Jesus said to her, "Neither do I condemn you; go and*a* sin no more."

12 Then Jesus spoke to them again, saying, "I am the light of the world. He who follows Me shall not walk in darkness, but have the light of life."

JESUS DEFENDS HIS SELF-WITNESS

13 The Phar′i·sees therefore said to Him, "You bear witness of Yourself; Your witness is not true."

14 Jesus answered and said to them, "Even if I bear witness of Myself, My witness is true, for I know where I came from and where I am going; but you do not know where I come from and where I am going.

7:50 *a*NU-Text reads *before.*   7:52 *a*NU-Text reads *is to rise.*   7:53 *a*The words *And everyone* through *sin no more* (8:11) are bracketed by NU-Text as not original. They are present in over 900 manuscripts.   8:2 *a*M-Text reads *very early.* 8:4 *a*M-Text reads *we found this woman.* 8:5 *a*M-Text reads *in our law Moses commanded.* *b*NU-Text and M-Text read *to stone such.* *c*M-Text adds *about her.*   8:6 *a*NU-Text and M-Text omit *as though He did not hear.*   8:7 *a*M-Text reads *He looked up.*   8:9 *a*NU-Text and M-Text omit *being convicted by their conscience.*   8:10 *a*NU-Text omits *and saw no one but the woman;* M-Text reads *He saw her and said.* *b*NU-Text and M-Text omit *of yours.*   8:11 *a*NU-Text and M-Text add *from now on.*

FORGIVING John 8:7

Am I Perfect?

Are you perfect? This boy isn't. He knows it. He knows that he has done wrong. So what should he do now?

1. When you do something wrong, should you lie about it? Should you try to cover it up? Should you tell the right person that you are sorry and ask forgiveness?
2. When a friend does something wrong to you, and asks you to forgive, what should you do? Should you try to hurt that person? Should you forgive that person? What would Jesus want you to do?
3. Look up John 8:7. A woman did wrong things. Men wanted to throw stones at her. "If you're perfect, if you've never done something wrong, throw the first stone," Jesus told them. No one threw a stone.
4. Are you perfect? Have you ever done something wrong? If you have, you may want to forgive others for wrong things when they ask you.

For more on *Values* turn to page 1649
For more on *Forgiveness* turn to page 1816

15 "You judge according to the flesh; I judge no one.

16 "And yet if I do judge, My judgment is true; for I am not alone, but I *am* with the Father who sent Me.

17 "It is also written in your law that the testimony of two men is true.

18 "I am One who bears witness of Myself, and the Father who sent Me bears witness of Me."

19 Then they said to Him, "Where is Your Father?" Jesus answered, "You know neither Me nor My Father. If you had known Me, you would have known My Father also."

20 These words Jesus spoke in the treasury, as He taught in the temple; and no one laid hands on Him, for His hour had not yet come.

JESUS PREDICTS HIS DEPARTURE

21 Then Jesus said to them again, "I am going away, and you will seek Me, and will die in your sin. Where I go you cannot come."

22 So the Jews said, "Will He kill Himself, because He says, 'Where I go you cannot come'?"

23 And He said to them, "You are from beneath; I am from above. You are of this world; I am not of this world.

24 "Therefore I said to you that you will die in your sins; for if you do not believe that I am *He,* you will die in your sins."

25 Then they said to Him, "Who are You?" And Jesus said to them, "Just what I have been saying to you from the beginning.

26 "I have many things to say and to judge concerning you, but He who sent Me is true; and I speak to the world those things which I heard from Him."

27 They did not understand that He spoke to them of the Father.

28 Then Jesus said to them, "When you lift up the Son of Man, then you will know that I am *He,* and *that* I do nothing of Myself; but as My Father taught Me, I speak these things.

29 "And He who sent Me is with Me. The Father has not left Me alone, for I always do those things that please Him."

30 As He spoke these words, many believed in Him.

THE TRUTH SHALL MAKE YOU FREE

31 Then Jesus said to those Jews who believed Him, "If you abide in My word, you are My disciples indeed.

32 "And you shall know the truth, and the truth shall make you free."

33 They answered Him, "We are Abraham's descendants, and have never been in bondage to anyone. How *can* You say, 'You will be made free'?"

34 Jesus answered them, "Most assuredly, I say to you, whoever commits sin is a slave of sin.

35 "And a slave does not abide in the house forever, *but* a son abides forever.

36 "Therefore if the Son makes you free, you shall be free indeed.

ABRAHAM'S SEED AND SATAN'S

37 "I know that you are Abraham's descendants, but you seek to kill Me, because My word has no place in you.

38 "I speak what I have seen with My Father, and you do what you have seen with[a] your father."

39 They answered and said to Him, "Abraham is our father." Jesus said to them, "If you were Abraham's children, you would do the works of Abraham.

40 "But now you seek to kill Me, a

8:38 [a]NU-Text reads *heard from.*

Man who has told you the truth which I heard from God. Abraham did not do this.

41 "You do the deeds of your father." Then they said to Him, "We were not born of fornication; we have one Father—God."

42 Jesus said to them, "If God were your Father, you would love Me, for I proceeded forth and came from God; nor have I come of Myself, but He sent Me.

43 "Why do you not understand My speech? Because you are not able to listen to My word.

44 "You are of *your* father the devil, and the desires of your father you want to do. He was a murderer from the beginning, and does not stand in the truth, because there is no truth in him. When he speaks a lie, he speaks from his own *resources,* for he is a liar and the father of it.

45 "But because I tell the truth, you do not believe Me.

46 "Which of you convicts Me of sin? And if I tell the truth, why do you not believe Me?

47 "He who is of God hears God's words; therefore you do not hear, because you are not of God."

BEFORE ABRAHAM WAS, I AM

48 Then the Jews answered and said to Him, "Do we not say rightly that You are a Samaritan and have a demon?"

49 Jesus answered, "I do not have a demon; but I honor My Father, and you dishonor Me.

50 "And I do not seek My *own* glory; there is One who seeks and judges.

51 "Most assuredly, I say to you, if anyone keeps My word he shall never see death."

52 Then the Jews said to Him, "Now we know that You have a demon! Abraham is dead, and the prophets;

and You say, 'If anyone keeps My word he shall never taste death.'

53 "Are You greater than our father Abraham, who is dead? And the prophets are dead. Who do You make Yourself out to be?"

54 Jesus answered, "If I honor Myself, My honor is nothing. It is My Father who honors Me, of whom you say that He is your[a] God.

55 "Yet you have not known Him, but I know Him. And if I say, 'I do not know Him,' I shall be a liar like you; but I do know Him and keep His word.

56 "Your father Abraham rejoiced to see My day, and he saw *it* and was glad."

57 Then the Jews said to Him, "You are not yet fifty years old, and have You seen Abraham?"

58 Jesus said to them, "Most assuredly, I say to you, before Abraham was, I AM."

59 Then they took up stones to throw at Him; but Jesus hid Himself and went out of the temple,[a] going through the midst of them, and so passed by.

A MAN BORN BLIND RECEIVES SIGHT

9 Now as *Jesus* passed by, He saw a man who was blind from birth.

2   And His disciples asked Him, saying, "Rabbi, who sinned, this man or his parents, that he was born blind?"

3   Jesus answered, "Neither this man nor his parents sinned, but that the works of God should be revealed in him.

4   "I[a] must work the works of Him who sent Me while it is day; *the* night is coming when no one can work.

8:54 [a]NU-Text and M-Text read *our.*
8:59 [a]NU-Text omits the rest of this verse.
9:4 [a]NU-Text reads *We.*

5 "As long as I am in the world, I am the light of the world."

6 When He had said these things, He spat on the ground and made clay with the saliva; and He anointed the eyes of the blind man with the clay.

7 And He said to him, "Go, wash in the pool of Sĭ·lō'am" (which is translated, Sent). So he went and washed, and came back seeing.

8 Therefore the neighbors and those who previously had seen that he was blind*a* said, "Is not this he who sat and begged?"

9 Some said, "This is he." Others said, "He is like him."*a* He said, "I am he."

10 Therefore they said to him, "How were your eyes opened?"

11 He answered and said, "A Man called Jesus made clay and anointed my eyes and said to me, 'Go to the pool of*a* Sĭ·lō'am and wash.' So I went and washed, and I received sight."

12 Then they said to him, "Where is He?" He said, "I do not know."

THE PHARISEES EXCOMMUNICATE THE HEALED MAN

13 They brought him who formerly was blind to the Phar'i·sees.

14 Now it was a Sabbath when Jesus made the clay and opened his eyes.

15 Then the Phar'i·sees also asked him again how he had received his sight. He said to them, "He put clay on my eyes, and I washed, and I see."

16 Therefore some of the Phar'i·sees said, "This Man is not from God, because He does not keep the Sabbath." Others said, "How can a man who is a sinner do such signs?" And there was a division among them.

17 They said to the blind man again, "What do you say about Him because He opened your eyes?" He said, "He is a prophet."

18 But the Jews did not believe concerning him, that he had been blind and received his sight, until they called the parents of him who had received his sight.

19 And they asked them, saying, "Is this your son, who you say was born blind? How then does he now see?"

20 His parents answered them and said, "We know that this is our son, and that he was born blind;

21 "but by what means he now sees we do not know, or who opened his eyes we do not know. He is of age; ask him. He will speak for himself."

22 His parents said these *things* because they feared the Jews, for the Jews had agreed already that if anyone confessed *that* He *was* Christ, he would be put out of the synagogue.

23 Therefore his parents said, "He is of age; ask him."

24 So they again called the man who was blind, and said to him, "Give God the glory! We know that this Man is a sinner."

25 He answered and said, "Whether He is a sinner *or not* I do not know. One thing I know: that though I was blind, now I see."

26 Then they said to him again, "What did He do to you? How did He open your eyes?"

27 He answered them, "I told you already, and you did not listen. Why do you want to hear *it* again? Do you also want to become His disciples?"

28 Then they reviled him and said, "You are His disciple, but we are Moses' disciples.

29 "We know that God spoke to Moses; *as for* this *fellow,* we do not know where He is from."

30 The man answered and said to them, "Why, this is a marvelous thing, that you do not know where

9:8 *a*NU-Text reads *a beggar.*   9:9 *a*NU-Text reads *"No, but he is like him."*   9:11 *a*NU-Text omits *the pool of.*

He is from; yet He has opened my eyes!

31 "Now we know that God does not hear sinners; but if anyone is a worshiper of God and does His will, He hears him.

32 "Since the world began it has been unheard of that anyone opened the eyes of one who was born blind.

33 "If this Man were not from God, He could do nothing."

34 They answered and said to him, "You were completely born in sins, and are you teaching us?" And they cast him out.

TRUE VISION AND TRUE BLINDNESS

35 Jesus heard that they had cast him out; and when He had found him, He said to him, "Do you believe in the Son of God?"*a*

36 He answered and said, "Who is He, Lord, that I may believe in Him?"

37 And Jesus said to him, "You have both seen Him and it is He who is talking with you."

38 Then he said, "Lord, I believe!" And he worshiped Him.

39 And Jesus said, "For judgment I have come into this world, that those who do not see may see, and that those who see may be made blind."

40 Then *some* of the Phar'i·sees who were with Him heard these words, and said to Him, "Are we blind also?"

41 Jesus said to them, "If you were blind, you would have no sin; but now you say, 'We see.' Therefore your sin remains.

JESUS THE TRUE SHEPHERD

10 "Most assuredly, I say to you, he who does not enter the sheepfold by the door, but climbs up some other way, the same is a thief and a robber.

2 "But he who enters by the door is the shepherd of the sheep.

3 "To him the doorkeeper opens, and the sheep hear his voice; and he calls his own sheep by name and leads them out.

4 "And when he brings out his own sheep, he goes before them; and the sheep follow him, for they know his voice.

5 "Yet they will by no means follow a stranger, but will flee from him, for they do not know the voice of strangers."

6 Jesus used this illustration, but they did not understand the things which He spoke to them.

JESUS THE GOOD SHEPHERD

7 Then Jesus said to them again, "Most assuredly, I say to you, I am the door of the sheep.

8 "All who *ever* came before Me*a* are thieves and robbers, but the sheep did not hear them.

9 "I am the door. If anyone enters by Me, he will be saved, and will go in and out and find pasture.

10 "The thief does not come except to steal, and to kill, and to destroy. I have come that they may have life, and that they may have *it* more abundantly.

11 "I am the good shepherd. The good shepherd gives His life for the sheep.

12 "But a hireling, *he who is* not the shepherd, one who does not own the sheep, sees the wolf coming and leaves the sheep and flees; and the wolf catches the sheep and scatters them.

13 "The hireling flees because he is a hireling and does not care about the sheep.

9:35 *a*NU-Text reads *Son of Man.*　　10:8 *a*M-Text omits *before Me.*

14 "I am the good shepherd; and I know My *sheep,* and am known by My own.

15 "As the Father knows Me, even so I know the Father; and I lay down My life for the sheep.

16 "And other sheep I have which are not of this fold; them also I must bring, and they will hear My voice; and there will be one flock *and* one shepherd.

17 "Therefore My Father loves Me, because I lay down My life that I may take it again.

18 "No one takes it from Me, but I lay it down of Myself. I have power to lay it down, and I have power to take it again. This command I have received from My Father."

19 Therefore there was a division again among the Jews because of these sayings.

20 And many of them said, "He has a demon and is mad. Why do you listen to Him?"

21 Others said, "These are not the words of one who has a demon. Can a demon open the eyes of the blind?"

THE SHEPHERD KNOWS HIS SHEEP

22 Now it was the Feast of Dedication in Jerusalem, and it was winter.

23 And Jesus walked in the temple, in Solomon's porch.

24 Then the Jews surrounded Him and said to Him, "How long do You keep us in doubt? If You are the Christ, tell us plainly."

25 Jesus answered them, "I told you, and you do not believe. The works that I do in My Father's name, they bear witness of Me.

26 "But you do not believe, because you are not of My sheep, as I said to you.a

27 "My sheep hear My voice, and I know them, and they follow Me.

28 "And I give them eternal life, and

10:26 aNU-Text omits *as I said to you.*

they shall never perish; neither shall anyone snatch them out of My hand.

29 "My Father, who has given *them* to Me, is greater than all; and no one is able to snatch *them* out of My Father's hand.

30 "I and *My* Father are one."

RENEWED EFFORTS TO STONE JESUS

31 Then the Jews took up stones again to stone Him.

32 Jesus answered them, "Many good works I have shown you from My Father. For which of those works do you stone Me?"

33 The Jews answered Him, saying, "For a good work we do not stone You, but for blasphemy, and because You, being a Man, make Yourself God."

34 Jesus answered them, "Is it not written in your law, *'I said, "You are gods"'?a*

35 "If He called them gods, to whom the word of God came (and the Scripture cannot be broken),

36 "do you say of Him whom the Father sanctified and sent into the world, 'You are blaspheming,' because I said, 'I am the Son of God'?

37 "If I do not do the works of My Father, do not believe Me;

38 "but if I do, though you do not believe Me, believe the works, that you may know and believe*a* that the Father *is* in Me, and I in Him."

39 Therefore they sought again to seize Him, but He escaped out of their hand.

THE BELIEVERS BEYOND JORDAN

40 And He went away again beyond the Jordan to the place where John was baptizing at first, and there He stayed.

41 Then many came to Him and said, "John performed no sign, but all the things that John spoke about this Man were true."

42 And many believed in Him there.

THE DEATH OF LAZARUS

When you are with Jesus, you never know when a miracle will happen. Jesus' friends learned this when He came to Bethany one day.

11 Now a certain *man* was sick, Laz'a·rus of Beth'a·ny, the town of Mary and her sister Martha.

2 It was *that* Mary who anointed the Lord with fragrant oil and wiped His feet with her hair, whose brother Laz'a·rus was sick.

3 Therefore the sisters sent to Him, saying, "Lord, behold, he whom You love is sick."

4 When Jesus heard *that,* He said, "This sickness is not unto death, but for the glory of God, that the Son of God may be glorified through it."

5 Now Jesus loved Martha and her sister and Laz'a·rus.

6 So, when He heard that he was sick, He stayed two more days in the place where He was.

7 Then after this He said to *the* disciples, "Let us go to Judea again."

8 *The* disciples said to Him, "Rabbi, lately the Jews sought to stone You, and are You going there again?"

9 Jesus answered, "Are there not twelve hours in the day? If anyone walks in the day, he does not stumble, because he sees the light of this world.

10 "But if one walks in the night, he stumbles, because the light is not in him."

11 These things He said, and after that He said to them, "Our friend

10:34 *a*Psalm 82:6   10:38 *a*NU-Text reads *understand.*

Laz′a·rus sleeps, but I go that I may wake him up.”

12 Then His disciples said, “Lord, if he sleeps he will get well.”

13 However, Jesus spoke of his death, but they thought that He was speaking about taking rest in sleep.

14 Then Jesus said to them plainly, “Laz′a·rus is dead.

15 “And I am glad for your sakes that I was not there, that you may believe. Nevertheless let us go to him.”

16 Then Thomas, who is called the Twin, said to his fellow disciples, “Let us also go, that we may die with Him.”

I Am the Resurrection and the Life

17 So when Jesus came, He found that he had already been in the tomb four days.

18 Now Beth′a·ny was near Jerusalem, about two miles[a] away.

19 And many of the Jews had joined the women around Martha and Mary, to comfort them concerning their brother.

20 Then Martha, as soon as she heard that Jesus was coming, went and met Him, but Mary was sitting in the house.

21 Now Martha said to Jesus, “Lord, if You had been here, my brother would not have died.

22 “But even now I know that whatever You ask of God, God will give You.”

23 Jesus said to her, “Your brother will rise again.”

24 Martha said to Him, “I know that he will rise again in the resurrection at the last day.”

25 Jesus said to her, “I am the resurrection and the life. He who believes in Me, though he may die, he shall live.

26 “And whoever lives and believes in Me shall never die. Do you believe this?”

27 She said to Him, “Yes, Lord, I believe that You are the Christ, the Son of God, who is to come into the world.”

Jesus and Death, the Last Enemy

28 And when she had said these things, she went her way and secretly called Mary her sister, saying, “The Teacher has come and is calling for you.”

29 As soon as she heard *that*, she arose quickly and came to Him.

30 Now Jesus had not yet come into the town, but was[a] in the place where Martha met Him.

31 Then the Jews who were with her in the house, and comforting her, when they saw that Mary rose up quickly and went out, followed her, saying, “She is going to the tomb to weep there.”[a]

32 Then, when Mary came where Jesus was, and saw Him, she fell down at His feet, saying to Him, “Lord, if You had been here, my brother would not have died.”

33 Therefore, when Jesus saw her weeping, and the Jews who came with her weeping, He groaned in the spirit and was troubled.

34 And He said, “Where have you laid him?” They said to Him, “Lord, come and see.”

35 Jesus wept.

36 Then the Jews said, “See how He loved him!”

37 And some of them said, “Could not this Man, who opened the eyes of the blind, also have kept this man from dying?”

11:18 *a*Literally *fifteen stadia*   11:30 *a*NU-Text adds *still*.   11:31 *a*NU-Text reads *supposing that she was going to the tomb to weep there.*

LAZARUS RAISED FROM THE DEAD

38 Then Jesus, again groaning in Himself, came to the tomb. It was a cave, and a stone lay against it.

39 Jesus said, "Take away the stone." Martha, the sister of him who was dead, said to Him, "Lord, by this time there is a stench, for he has been *dead* four days."

40 Jesus said to her, "Did I not say to you that if you would believe you would see the glory of God?"

41 Then they took away the stone *from the place* where the dead man was lying.*a* And Jesus lifted up *His* eyes and said, "Father, I thank You that You have heard Me.

42 "And I know that You always hear Me, but because of the people who are standing by I said *this,* that they may believe that You sent Me."

43 Now when He had said these things, He cried with a loud voice, "Laz′a·rus, come forth!"

44 And he who had died came out bound hand and foot with grave-clothes, and his face was wrapped with a cloth. Jesus said to them, "Loose him, and let him go."

THE PLOT TO KILL JESUS

45 Then many of the Jews who had come to Mary, and had seen the things Jesus did, believed in Him.

46 But some of them went away to the Phar′i·sees and told them the things Jesus did.

47 Then the chief priests and the Phar′i·sees gathered a council and said, "What shall we do? For this Man works many signs.

48 "If we let Him alone like this, everyone will believe in Him, and the Romans will come and take away both our place and nation."

49 And one of them, Cā′ia·phas, be-

☑ *Bible Quiz*

John 11:1–44 Jesus Raises Lazarus from the Dead

1. What was the name of the man who got sick and died? Can you give the names of his two sisters? What town did they live in?
2. Why didn't Jesus come right away when Mary and Martha sent a message that Lazarus was sick?
3. How can you tell that Jesus loved His friends?
4. How long had Lazarus been dead when Jesus arrived? What did He say to Lazarus? What happened then?
5. What did many people think about Jesus after they saw Lazarus alive again?

---

ing high priest that year, said to them, "You know nothing at all,

50 "nor do you consider that it is expedient for us*a* that one man should die for the people, and not that the whole nation should perish."

51 Now this he did not say on his own *authority;* but being high priest that year he prophesied that Jesus would die for the nation,

52 and not for that nation only, but also that He would gather together in one the children of God who were scattered abroad.

53 Then, from that day on, they plotted to put Him to death.

54 Therefore Jesus no longer walked openly among the Jews, but went

---

11:41 *a*NU-Text omits *from the place where the dead man was lying.*   11:50 *a*NU-Text reads *you.*

from there into the country near the wilderness, to a city called Ē′phra·im, and there remained with His disciples.

55 And the Passover of the Jews was near, and many went from the country up to Jerusalem before the Passover, to purify themselves.

56 Then they sought Jesus, and spoke among themselves as they stood in the temple, "What do you think—that He will not come to the feast?"

57 Now both the chief priests and the Phar′i·sees had given a command, that if anyone knew where He was, he should report *it,* that they might seize Him.

THE ANOINTING AT BETHANY

12 Then, six days before the Passover, Jesus came to Beth′a·ny, where Laz′a·rus was who had been dead,*a* whom He had raised from the dead.

2 There they made Him a supper; and Martha served, but Laz′a·rus was one of those who sat at the table with Him.

3 Then Mary took a pound of very costly oil of spikenard, anointed the feet of Jesus, and wiped His feet with her hair. And the house was filled with the fragrance of the oil.

4 But one of His disciples, Judas Is·car′i·ot, Simon's *son,* who would betray Him, said,

5 "Why was this fragrant oil not sold for three hundred denarii*a* and given to the poor?"

6 This he said, not that he cared for the poor, but because he was a thief, and had the money box; and he used to take what was put in it.

7 But Jesus said, "Let her alone; she has kept*a* this for the day of My burial.

8 "For the poor you have with you always, but Me you do not have always."

THE PLOT TO KILL LAZARUS

9 Now a great many of the Jews knew that He was there; and they came, not for Jesus' sake only, but that they might also see Laz′a·rus, whom He had raised from the dead.

10 But the chief priests plotted to put Laz′a·rus to death also,

11 because on account of him many of the Jews went away and believed in Jesus.

THE TRIUMPHAL ENTRY

12 The next day a great multitude that had come to the feast, when they heard that Jesus was coming to Jerusalem,

13 took branches of palm trees and went out to meet Him, and cried out:

"Hō·san′na!
'Blessed is He who comes in the
   name of the LORD!'*a*
The King of Israel!"

14 Then Jesus, when He had found a young donkey, sat on it; as it is written:

15 "Fear not, daughter of Zion;
Behold, your King is coming,
Sitting on a donkey's colt."*a*

16 His disciples did not understand these things at first; but when Jesus was glorified, then they remembered that these things were written about Him and *that* they had done these things to Him.

17 Therefore the people, who were

12:1 *a*NU-Text omits *who had been dead.*
12:5 *a*About one year's wages for a worker
12:7 *a*NU-Text reads *that she may keep.*
12:13 *a*Psalm 118:26   12:15 *a*Zechariah 9:9

What Should I Do?

WORMY GIFTS John 12:3–8

Glen has a gift for his teacher. He had two apples when he left home. He ate the good one. Now look what he is giving to his teacher. What would you like to say to Glen about his wormy gift?

1. Should you give your best or worst gift to someone you love? Why?
2. Should you say your best or worst words to your parents? Why?
3. Read John 12:3–8. Should you give your best or worst gifts to Jesus? Why?

For more on *What Should I Do?* turn to page 1659
For more on *Giving* turn to page 1706

with Him when He called Laz′a·rus out of his tomb and raised him from the dead, bore witness.

18 For this reason the people also met Him, because they heard that He had done this sign.

19 The Phar′i·sees therefore said among themselves, "You see that you are accomplishing nothing. Look, the world has gone after Him!"

■ *see Mark 11:1–11*

THE FRUITFUL GRAIN OF WHEAT

20 Now there were certain Greeks among those who came up to worship at the feast.

21 Then they came to Philip, who was from Beth·sā′i·da of Galilee, and asked him, saying, "Sir, we wish to see Jesus."

22 Philip came and told Andrew, and in turn Andrew and Philip told Jesus.

23 But Jesus answered them, saying, "The hour has come that the Son of Man should be glorified.

24 "Most assuredly, I say to you, unless a grain of wheat falls into the ground and dies, it remains alone; but if it dies, it produces much grain.

25 "He who loves his life will lose it, and he who hates his life in this world will keep it for eternal life.

26 "If anyone serves Me, let him follow Me; and where I am, there My servant will be also. If anyone serves Me, him *My* Father will honor.

JESUS PREDICTS HIS DEATH
ON THE CROSS

27 "Now My soul is troubled, and what shall I say? 'Father, save Me from this hour'? But for this purpose I came to this hour.

28 "Father, glorify Your name." Then a voice came from heaven, *saying,* "I have both glorified *it* and will glorify *it* again."

29 Therefore the people who stood by and heard *it* said that it had thundered. Others said, "An angel has spoken to Him."

30 Jesus answered and said, "This voice did not come because of Me, but for your sake.

31 "Now is the judgment of this world; now the ruler of this world will be cast out.

32 "And I, if I am lifted up from the earth, will draw all *peoples* to Myself."

33 This He said, signifying by what death He would die.

34 The people answered Him, "We have heard from the law that the Christ remains forever; and how *can* You say, 'The Son of Man must be lifted up'? Who is this Son of Man?"

35 Then Jesus said to them, "A little while longer the light is with you. Walk while you have the light, lest darkness overtake you; he who walks in darkness does not know where he is going.

36 "While you have the light, believe in the light, that you may become sons of light." These things Jesus spoke, and departed, and was hidden from them.

WHO HAS BELIEVED OUR REPORT?

37 But although He had done so many signs before them, they did not believe in Him,

38 that the word of Ī·sāi′ah the prophet might be fulfilled, which he spoke:

"Lord, who has believed our
   report?
And to whom has the arm of the
   LORD been revealed?"a

12:38 aIsaiah 53:1

39 Therefore they could not believe, because Ī·saī'ah said again:

40 *"He has blinded their eyes and hardened their hearts,*
Lest they should see with their eyes,
Lest they should understand with their hearts and turn,
So that I should heal them."a

41 These things Ī·saī'ah said when*a* he saw His glory and spoke of Him.

WALK IN THE LIGHT

42 Nevertheless even among the rulers many believed in Him, but because of the Phar'i·sees they did not confess *Him,* lest they should be put out of the synagogue;
43 for they loved the praise of men more than the praise of God.
44 Then Jesus cried out and said, "He who believes in Me, believes not in Me but in Him who sent Me.
45 "And he who sees Me sees Him who sent Me.
46 "I have come *as* a light into the world, that whoever believes in Me should not abide in darkness.
47 "And if anyone hears My words and does not believe,*a* I do not judge him; for I did not come to judge the world but to save the world.
48 "He who rejects Me, and does not receive My words, has that which judges him—the word that I have spoken will judge him in the last day.
49 "For I have not spoken on My own *authority;* but the Father who sent Me gave Me a command, what I should say and what I should speak.
50 "And I know that His command is everlasting life. Therefore, whatever I speak, just as the Father has told Me, so I speak."

JESUS WASHES THE DISCIPLES' FEET

13 Now before the Feast of the Passover, when Jesus knew that His hour had come that He should depart from this world to the Father, having loved His own who were in the world, He loved them to the end.
2 And supper being ended,*a* the devil having already put it into the heart of Judas Is·car'i·ot, Simon's *son,* to betray Him,
3 Jesus, knowing that the Father had given all things into His hands, and that He had come from God and was going to God,
4 rose from supper and laid aside His garments, took a towel and girded Himself.
5 After that, He poured water into a basin and began to wash the disciples' feet, and to wipe *them* with the towel with which He was girded.
6 Then He came to Simon Peter. And *Peter* said to Him, "Lord, are You washing my feet?"
7 Jesus answered and said to him, "What I am doing you do not understand now, but you will know after this."
8 Peter said to Him, "You shall never wash my feet!" Jesus answered him, "If I do not wash you, you have no part with Me."
9 Simon Peter said to Him, "Lord, not my feet only, but also *my* hands and *my* head!"
10 Jesus said to him, "He who is bathed needs only to wash *his* feet, but is completely clean; and you are clean, but not all of you."
11 For He knew who would betray Him; therefore He said, "You are not all clean."
12 So when He had washed their feet, taken His garments, and sat

12:40 *a*Isaiah 6:10   12:41 *a*NU-Text reads *because.*   12:47 *a*NU-Text reads *keep them.*
13:2 *a*NU-Text reads *And during supper.*

down again, He said to them, "Do you know what I have done to you?

13 "You call Me Teacher and Lord, and you say well, for *so* I am.

14 "If I then, *your* Lord and Teacher, have washed your feet, you also ought to wash one another's feet.

15 "For I have given you an example, that you should do as I have done to you.

16 "Most assuredly, I say to you, a servant is not greater than his master; nor is he who is sent greater than he who sent him.

17 "If you know these things, blessed are you if you do them.

JESUS IDENTIFIES HIS BETRAYER

18 "I do not speak concerning all of you. I know whom I have chosen; but that the Scripture may be fulfilled, *'He who eats bread with Me*a *has lifted up his heel against Me.'*b

19 "Now I tell you before it comes, that when it does come to pass, you may believe that I am *He.*

20 "Most assuredly, I say to you, he who receives whomever I send receives Me; and he who receives Me receives Him who sent Me."

21 When Jesus had said these things, He was troubled in spirit, and testified and said, "Most assuredly, I say to you, one of you will betray Me."

22 Then the disciples looked at one another, perplexed about whom He spoke.

23 Now there was leaning on Jesus' bosom one of His disciples, whom Jesus loved.

24 Simon Peter therefore motioned to him to ask who it was of whom He spoke.

25 Then, leaning back*a* on Jesus' breast, he said to Him, "Lord, who is it?"

26 Jesus answered, "It is he to whom

I shall give a piece of bread when I have dipped *it*." And having dipped the bread, He gave *it* to Judas Iscar′i·ot, *the son* of Simon.

27 Now after the piece of bread, Satan entered him. Then Jesus said to him, "What you do, do quickly."

28 But no one at the table knew for what reason He said this to him.

29 For some thought, because Judas had the money box, that Jesus had said to him, "Buy *those things* we need for the feast," or that he should give something to the poor.

30 Having received the piece of bread, he then went out immediately. And it was night.

■ *see Matthew 26:17–35*

THE NEW COMMANDMENT

31 So, when he had gone out, Jesus said, "Now the Son of Man is glorified, and God is glorified in Him.

32 "If God is glorified in Him, God will also glorify Him in Himself, and glorify Him immediately.

33 "Little children, I shall be with you a little while longer. You will seek Me; and as I said to the Jews, 'Where I am going, you cannot come,' so now I say to you.

34 "A new commandment I give to you, that you love one another; as I have loved you, that you also love one another.

35 "By this all will know that you are My disciples, if you have love for one another."

JESUS PREDICTS PETER'S DENIAL

36 Simon Peter said to Him, "Lord, where are You going?" Jesus answered him, "Where I am going you cannot follow Me now, but you shall follow Me afterward."

13:18 *a*NU-Text reads *My bread.*   *b*Psalm 41:9
13:25 *a*NU-Text and M-Text add *thus.*

37 Peter said to Him, "Lord, why can I not follow You now? I will lay down my life for Your sake."

38 Jesus answered him, "Will you lay down your life for My sake? Most assuredly, I say to you, the rooster shall not crow till you have denied Me three times.

THE WAY, THE TRUTH, AND THE LIFE

14 "Let not your heart be troubled; you believe in God, believe also in Me.

2 "In My Father's house are many mansions;a if *it were* not *so,* I would have told you. I go to prepare a place for you.b

3 "And if I go and prepare a place for you, I will come again and receive you to Myself; that where I am, *there* you may be also.

4 "And where I go you know, and the way you know."

5 Thomas said to Him, "Lord, we do not know where You are going, and how can we know the way?"

6 Jesus said to him, "I am the way, the truth, and the life. No one comes to the Father except through Me.

THE FATHER REVEALED

7 "If you had known Me, you would have known My Father also; and from now on you know Him and have seen Him."

8 Philip said to Him, "Lord, show us the Father, and it is sufficient for us."

9 Jesus said to him, "Have I been with you so long, and yet you have not known Me, Philip? He who has seen Me has seen the Father; so how can you say, 'Show us the Father'?

10 "Do you not believe that I am in the Father, and the Father in Me? The words that I speak to you I do not speak on My own *authority;* but the Father who dwells in Me does the works.

11 "Believe Me that I *am* in the Father and the Father in Me, or else believe Me for the sake of the works themselves.

THE ANSWERED PRAYER

12 "Most assuredly, I say to you, he who believes in Me, the works that I do he will do also; and greater *works* than these he will do, because I go to My Father.

13 "And whatever you ask in My name, that I will do, that the Father may be glorified in the Son.

14 "If you aska anything in My name, I will do *it.*

JESUS PROMISES ANOTHER HELPER

15 "If you love Me, keepa My commandments.

16 "And I will pray the Father, and He will give you another Helper, that He may abide with you forever—

17 "the Spirit of truth, whom the world cannot receive, because it neither sees Him nor knows Him; but you know Him, for He dwells with you and will be in you.

18 "I will not leave you orphans; I will come to you.

INDWELLING OF THE FATHER AND THE SON

19 "A little while longer and the world will see Me no more, but you will see Me. Because I live, you will live also.

14:2 aLiterally *dwellings* bNU-Text adds a word which would cause the text to read either *if it were not so, would I have told you that I go to prepare a place for you?* or *if it were not so I would have told you; for I go to prepare a place for you.*
14:14 aNU-Text adds *Me.*   14:15 aNU-Text reads *you will keep.*

JESUS SAID, . . . "I AM THE WAY." John 14:6

Which Way Is Right?

"Let's do this," a friend says. But you know that's wrong. God does not want you to do what your friend says. It's the wrong way. "Let's do that," another friend says. But what would your parents say? "Don't go that way," they would tell you. "Go this way," God says. Should you?

1. How do you know which way is right or wrong? What book tells you? Who wrote this book?
2. If someone tries to get you to go the wrong way, what should you do? What should you say? Why?
3. How do you know that you can trust Jesus? He is the way to God, you know. Will you follow Him?

For more on *Favorite Family Verses* turn to page 1728
For more on *Choices* turn to page 843

ABOUT GOD'S PRESENCE John 14:18

What Is an Orphan?

An orphan has lost both parents. But an orphan is not alone if she has new parents to love her and care for her. Jesus said, "I will not leave you orphans; I will come to you" (John 14:18). What do you think He meant?

1. How would you be like an orphan if God or Jesus left you all alone? How would you feel?
2. Why is God's presence important to you? Why are you glad to know that Jesus will never leave you? Thank You, God, for being with me. Thank You, Jesus, for never leaving me.

For more on *What the Bible Says* turn to page 1731
For more on *God's Care* turn to page 1776

20 "At that day you will know that I *am* in My Father, and you in Me, and I in you.

21 "He who has My commandments and keeps them, it is he who loves Me. And he who loves Me will be loved by My Father, and I will love him and manifest Myself to him."

22 Judas (not Is·car'i·ot) said to Him, "Lord, how is it that You will manifest Yourself to us, and not to the world?"

23 Jesus answered and said to him, "If anyone loves Me, he will keep My word; and My Father will love him, and We will come to him and make Our home with him.

24 "He who does not love Me does not keep My words; and the word which you hear is not Mine but the Father's who sent Me.

THE GIFT OF HIS PEACE

25 "These things I have spoken to you while being present with you.

26 "But the Helper, the Holy Spirit, whom the Father will send in My name, He will teach you all things, and bring to your remembrance all things that I said to you.

27 "Peace I leave with you, My peace I give to you; not as the world gives do I give to you. Let not your heart be troubled, neither let it be afraid.

28 "You have heard Me say to you, 'I am going away and coming *back* to you.' If you loved Me, you would rejoice because I said,*a* 'I am going to the Father,' for My Father is greater than I.

29 "And now I have told you before it comes, that when it does come to pass, you may believe.

30 "I will no longer talk much with you, for the ruler of this world is coming, and he has nothing in Me.

31 "But that the world may know that I love the Father, and as the Fa-ther gave Me commandment, so I do. Arise, let us go from here.

THE TRUE VINE

15 "I am the true vine, and My Father is the vinedresser.

2 "Every branch in Me that does not bear fruit He takes away;*a* and every *branch* that bears fruit He prunes, that it may bear more fruit.

3 "You are already clean because of the word which I have spoken to you.

4 "Abide in Me, and I in you. As the branch cannot bear fruit of itself, unless it abides in the vine, neither can you, unless you abide in Me.

5 "I am the vine, you *are* the branches. He who abides in Me, and I in him, bears much fruit; for without Me you can do nothing.

6 "If anyone does not abide in Me, he is cast out as a branch and is withered; and they gather them and throw *them* into the fire, and they are burned.

7 "If you abide in Me, and My words abide in you, you will*a* ask what you desire, and it shall be done for you.

8 "By this My Father is glorified, that you bear much fruit; so you will be My disciples.

LOVE AND JOY PERFECTED

9 "As the Father loved Me, I also have loved you; abide in My love.

10 "If you keep My commandments, you will abide in My love, just as I have kept My Father's commandments and abide in His love.

11 "These things I have spoken to you, that My joy may remain in you, and *that* your joy may be full.

12 "This is My commandment, that

14:28 *a*NU-Text omits *I said.*   15:2 *a*Or *lifts up*
15:7 *a*NU-Text omits *you will.*

LOVE John 15:12–14

Who Loves You Most?

Does your friend down the street love you most? Does your brother or sister love you most? Who does love you most? Who *really* loves you most?

1. Look up John 15:12–14. What is Jesus saying? Can anyone love us more than Jesus does? Why not?
2. Are you glad that Jesus loves you so much? Have you told Him so? Why not tell Him now?

JESUS LOVES ME

For more on *Values* turn to page 1666
For more on *Love* turn to page 1727

you love one another as I have loved you.

13 "Greater love has no one than this, than to lay down one's life for his friends.

14 "You are My friends if you do whatever I command you.

15 "No longer do I call you servants, for a servant does not know what his master is doing; but I have called you friends, for all things that I heard from My Father I have made known to you.

16 "You did not choose Me, but I chose you and appointed you that you should go and bear fruit, and *that* your fruit should remain, that whatever you ask the Father in My name He may give you.

17 "These things I command you, that you love one another.

THE WORLD'S HATRED

18 "If the world hates you, you know that it hated Me before *it hated* you.

19 "If you were of the world, the world would love its own. Yet because you are not of the world, but I chose you out of the world, therefore the world hates you.

20 "Remember the word that I said to you, 'A servant is not greater than his master.' If they persecuted Me, they will also persecute you. If they kept My word, they will keep yours also.

21 "But all these things they will do to you for My name's sake, because they do not know Him who sent Me.

22 "If I had not come and spoken to them, they would have no sin, but now they have no excuse for their sin.

23 "He who hates Me hates My Father also.

24 "If I had not done among them the works which no one else did, they would have no sin; but now they have

seen and also hated both Me and My Father.

25 "But *this happened* that the word might be fulfilled which is written in their law, *'They hated Me without a cause.'a*

THE COMING REJECTION

26 "But when the Helper comes, whom I shall send to you from the Father, the Spirit of truth who proceeds from the Father, He will testify of Me.

27 "And you also will bear witness, because you have been with Me from the beginning.

16 "These things I have spoken to you, that you should not be made to stumble.

2 "They will put you out of the synagogues; yes, the time is coming that whoever kills you will think that he offers God service.

3 "And these things they will do to you*a* because they have not known the Father nor Me.

4 "But these things I have told you, that when the*a* time comes, you may remember that I told you of them. And these things I did not say to you at the beginning, because I was with you.

THE WORK OF THE HOLY SPIRIT

5 "But now I go away to Him who sent Me, and none of you asks Me, 'Where are You going?'

6 "But because I have said these things to you, sorrow has filled your heart.

7 "Nevertheless I tell you the truth. It is to your advantage that I go away; for if I do not go away, the

15:25 *a*Psalm 69:4   16:3 *a*NU-Text and M-Text omit *to you.*   16:4 *a*NU-Text reads *their.*

Helper will not come to you; but if I depart, I will send Him to you.

8 "And when He has come, He will convict the world of sin, and of righteousness, and of judgment:

9 "of sin, because they do not believe in Me;

10 "of righteousness, because I go to My Father and you see Me no more;

11 "of judgment, because the ruler of this world is judged.

12 "I still have many things to say to you, but you cannot bear *them* now.

13 "However, when He, the Spirit of truth, has come, He will guide you into all truth; for He will not speak on His own *authority*, but whatever He hears He will speak; and He will tell you things to come.

14 "He will glorify Me, for He will take of what is Mine and declare *it* to you.

15 "All things that the Father has are Mine. Therefore I said that He will take of Mine and declare *it* to you.a

SORROW WILL TURN TO JOY

16 "A little while, and you will not see Me; and again a little while, and you will see Me, because I go to the Father."

17 Then *some* of His disciples said among themselves, "What is this that He says to us, 'A little while, and you will not see Me; and again a little while, and you will see Me'; and, 'because I go to the Father'?"

18 They said therefore, "What is this that He says, 'A little while'? We do not know what He is saying."

19 Now Jesus knew that they desired to ask Him, and He said to them, "Are you inquiring among yourselves about what I said, 'A little while, and you will not see Me; and again a little while, and you will see Me'?

20 "Most assuredly, I say to you that you will weep and lament, but the world will rejoice; and you will be sorrowful, but your sorrow will be turned into joy.

21 "A woman, when she is in labor, has sorrow because her hour has come; but as soon as she has given birth to the child, she no longer remembers the anguish, for joy that a human being has been born into the world.

22 "Therefore you now have sorrow; but I will see you again and your heart will rejoice, and your joy no one will take from you.

23 "And in that day you will ask Me nothing. Most assuredly, I say to you, whatever you ask the Father in My name He will give you.

24 "Until now you have asked nothing in My name. Ask, and you will receive, that your joy may be full.

JESUS CHRIST HAS OVERCOME THE WORLD

25 "These things I have spoken to you in figurative language; but the time is coming when I will no longer speak to you in figurative language, but I will tell you plainly about the Father.

26 "In that day you will ask in My name, and I do not say to you that I shall pray the Father for you;

27 "for the Father Himself loves you, because you have loved Me, and have believed that I came forth from God.

28 "I came forth from the Father and have come into the world. Again, I leave the world and go to the Father."

29 His disciples said to Him, "See, now You are speaking plainly, and using no figure of speech!

30 "Now we are sure that You know all things, and have no need that

16:15 aNU-Text and M-Text read *He takes of Mine and will declare it to you.*

anyone should question You. By this we believe that You came forth from God."

31 Jesus answered them, "Do you now believe?

32 "Indeed the hour is coming, yes, has now come, that you will be scattered, each to his own, and will leave Me alone. And yet I am not alone, because the Father is with Me.

33 "These things I have spoken to you, that in Me you may have peace. In the world you will^a have tribulation; but be of good cheer, I have overcome the world."

JESUS PRAYS FOR HIMSELF

17 Jesus spoke these words, lifted up His eyes to heaven, and said: "Father, the hour has come. Glorify Your Son, that Your Son also may glorify You,

2 "as You have given Him authority over all flesh, that He should^a give eternal life to as many as You have given Him.

3 "And this is eternal life, that they may know You, the only true God, and Jesus Christ whom You have sent.

4 "I have glorified You on the earth. I have finished the work which You have given Me to do.

5 "And now, O Father, glorify Me together with Yourself, with the glory which I had with You before the world was.

JESUS PRAYS FOR HIS DISCIPLES

6 "I have manifested Your name to the men whom You have given Me out of the world. They were Yours, You gave them to Me, and they have kept Your word.

7 "Now they have known that all things which You have given Me are from You.

Prayers

John 17

This is a long prayer from God the Son to God the Father. Jesus prayed to the Heavenly Father for Himself, for those close to Him, and for those who would yet believe in Him. When you pray, don't forget to pray for your own need. But remember also to pray for your family and friends. Pray for your church. Pray for all those close to you. But what about others across the world, people far away who believe in Jesus?

---

8 "For I have given to them the words which You have given Me; and they have received *them,* and have known surely that I came forth from You; and they have believed that You sent Me.

9 "I pray for them. I do not pray for the world but for those whom You have given Me, for they are Yours.

10 "And all Mine are Yours, and Yours are Mine, and I am glorified in them.

11 "Now I am no longer in the world, but these are in the world, and I come to You. Holy Father, keep through Your name those whom You have given Me,^{a} that they may be one as We *are.*

12 "While I was with them in the world,^{a} I kept them in Your name. Those whom You gave Me I have kept;^{b} and none of them is lost except

---

16:33 ^{a}NU-Text and M-Text omit *will.*
17:2 ^{a}M-Text reads *shall.*   17:11 ^{a}NU-Text and M-Text read *keep them through Your name which You have given Me.*   17:12 ^{a}NU-Text omits *in the world.* ^{b}NU-Text reads *in Your name which You gave Me. And I guarded them;* (or *it;*).

the son of perdition, that the Scripture might be fulfilled.

13 "But now I come to You, and these things I speak in the world, that they may have My joy fulfilled in themselves.

14 "I have given them Your word; and the world has hated them because they are not of the world, just as I am not of the world.

15 "I do not pray that You should take them out of the world, but that You should keep them from the evil one.

16 "They are not of the world, just as I am not of the world.

17 "Sanctify them by Your truth. Your word is truth.

18 "As You sent Me into the world, I also have sent them into the world.

19 "And for their sakes I sanctify Myself, that they also may be sanctified by the truth.

JESUS PRAYS FOR ALL BELIEVERS

20 "I do not pray for these alone, but also for those who will*a* believe in Me through their word;

21 "that they all may be one, as You, Father, *are* in Me, and I in You; that they also may be one in Us, that the world may believe that You sent Me.

22 "And the glory which You gave Me I have given them, that they may be one just as We are one:

23 "I in them, and You in Me; that they may be made perfect in one, and that the world may know that You have sent Me, and have loved them as You have loved Me.

24 "Father, I desire that they also whom You gave Me may be with Me where I am, that they may behold My glory which You have given Me; for You loved Me before the foundation of the world.

25 "O righteous Father! The world has not known You, but I have known

You; and these have known that You sent Me.

26 "And I have declared to them Your name, and will declare *it*, that the love with which You loved Me may be in them, and I in them."

BETRAYAL AND ARREST IN GETHSEMANE

18 When Jesus had spoken these words, He went out with His disciples over the Brook Kid'ron, where there was a garden, which He and His disciples entered.

2 And Judas, who betrayed Him, also knew the place; for Jesus often met there with His disciples.

3 Then Judas, having received a detachment *of troops,* and officers from the chief priests and Phar'i·sees, came there with lanterns, torches, and weapons.

4 Jesus therefore, knowing all things that would come upon Him, went forward and said to them, "Whom are you seeking?"

5 They answered Him, "Jesus of Nazareth." Jesus said to them, "I am *He.*" And Judas, who betrayed Him, also stood with them.

6 Now when He said to them, "I am *He,*" they drew back and fell to the ground.

7 Then He asked them again, "Whom are you seeking?" And they said, "Jesus of Nazareth."

8 Jesus answered, "I have told you that I am *He.* Therefore, if you seek Me, let these go their way,"

9 that the saying might be fulfilled which He spoke, "Of those whom You gave Me I have lost none."

10 Then Simon Peter, having a sword, drew it and struck the high priest's servant, and cut off his right

17:20 *a*NU-Text and M-Text omit *will.*

ear. The servant's name was Mal′-chus.

11 So Jesus said to Peter, "Put your sword into the sheath. Shall I not drink the cup which My Father has given Me?"

■ *see Matthew 26:47–56*

BEFORE THE HIGH PRIEST

12 Then the detachment *of troops* and the captain and the officers of the Jews arrested Jesus and bound Him.

13 And they led Him away to An′nas first, for he was the father-in-law of Cā′i·a·phas who was high priest that year.

14 Now it was Cā′i·a·phas who advised the Jews that it was expedient that one man should die for the people.

PETER DENIES JESUS

15 And Simon Peter followed Jesus, and so *did* another*a* disciple. Now that disciple was known to the high priest, and went with Jesus into the courtyard of the high priest.

16 But Peter stood at the door outside. Then the other disciple, who was known to the high priest, went out and spoke to her who kept the door, and brought Peter in.

17 Then the servant girl who kept the door said to Peter, "You are not also *one* of this Man's disciples, are you?" He said, "I am not."

18 Now the servants and officers who had made a fire of coals stood there, for it was cold, and they warmed themselves. And Peter stood with them and warmed himself.

JESUS QUESTIONED BY THE HIGH PRIEST

19 The high priest then asked Jesus about His disciples and His doctrine.

20 Jesus answered him, "I spoke openly to the world. I always taught in synagogues and in the temple, where the Jews always meet,*a* and in secret I have said nothing.

21 "Why do you ask Me? Ask those who have heard Me what I said to them. Indeed they know what I said."

22 And when He had said these things, one of the officers who stood by struck Jesus with the palm of his hand, saying, "Do You answer the high priest like that?"

23 Jesus answered him, "If I have spoken evil, bear witness of the evil; but if well, why do you strike Me?"

24 Then An′nas sent Him bound to Cā′i·a·phas the high priest.

PETER DENIES TWICE MORE

25 Now Simon Peter stood and warmed himself. Therefore they said to him, "You are not also *one* of His disciples, are you?" He denied *it* and said, "I am not!"

26 One of the servants of the high priest, a relative *of him* whose ear Peter cut off, said, "Did I not see you in the garden with Him?"

27 Peter then denied again; and immediately a rooster crowed.

■ *see Luke 22:54-62*

IN PILATE'S COURT

28 Then they led Jesus from Cā′i·a·phas to the Prae·tō′ri·um, and it was early morning. But they themselves did not go into the Prae·tō′ri·um, lest they should be defiled, but that they might eat the Passover.

29 Pilate then went out to them and said, "What accusation do you bring against this Man?"

30 They answered and said to him,

18:15 *a*M-Text reads *the other*.　18:20 *a*NU-Text reads *where all the Jews meet*.

"If He were not an evildoer, we would not have delivered Him up to you."

31 Then Pilate said to them, "You take Him and judge Him according to your law." Therefore the Jews said to him, "It is not lawful for us to put anyone to death,"

32 that the saying of Jesus might be fulfilled which He spoke, signifying by what death He would die.

33 Then Pilate entered the Prae·tō′-ri·um again, called Jesus, and said to Him, "Are You the King of the Jews?"

34 Jesus answered him, "Are you speaking for yourself about this, or did others tell you this concerning Me?"

35 Pilate answered, "Am I a Jew? Your own nation and the chief priests have delivered You to me. What have You done?"

36 Jesus answered, "My kingdom is not of this world. If My kingdom were of this world, My servants would fight, so that I should not be delivered to the Jews; but now My kingdom is not from here."

37 Pilate therefore said to Him, "Are You a king then?" Jesus answered, "You say *rightly* that I am a king. For this cause I was born, and for this cause I have come into the world, that I should bear witness to the truth. Everyone who is of the truth hears My voice."

38 Pilate said to Him, "What is truth?" And when he had said this, he went out again to the Jews, and said to them, "I find no fault in Him at all.

TAKING THE PLACE OF BARABBAS

39 "But you have a custom that I should release someone to you at the Passover. Do you therefore want me to release to you the King of the Jews?"

40 Then they all cried again, saying,

"Not this Man, but Ba·rab′bas!" Now Ba·rab′bas was a robber.

THE SOLDIERS MOCK JESUS

19 So then Pilate took Jesus and scourged *Him.*

2 And the soldiers twisted a crown of thorns and put *it* on His head, and they put on Him a purple robe.

3 Then they said,*a* "Hail, King of the Jews!" And they struck Him with their hands.

4 Pilate then went out again, and said to them, "Behold, I am bringing Him out to you, that you may know that I find no fault in Him."

PILATE'S DECISION

5 Then Jesus came out, wearing the crown of thorns and the purple robe. And *Pilate* said to them, "Behold the Man!"

6 Therefore, when the chief priests and officers saw Him, they cried out, saying, "Crucify *Him,* crucify *Him!*" Pilate said to them, "You take Him and crucify *Him,* for I find no fault in Him."

7 The Jews answered him, "We have a law, and according to our*a* law He ought to die, because He made Himself the Son of God."

8 Therefore, when Pilate heard that saying, he was the more afraid,

9 and went again into the Prae·tō′-ri·um, and said to Jesus, "Where are You from?" But Jesus gave him no answer.

10 Then Pilate said to Him, "Are You not speaking to me? Do You not know that I have power to crucify You, and power to release You?"

11 Jesus answered, "You could have no power at all against Me unless it

19:3 *a*NU-Text reads *And they came up to Him and said.* 19:7 *a*NU-Text reads *the law.*

had been given you from above. Therefore the one who delivered Me to you has the greater sin."

12 From then on Pilate sought to release Him, but the Jews cried out, saying, "If you let this Man go, you are not Caesar's friend. Whoever makes himself a king speaks against Caesar."

13 When Pilate therefore heard that saying, he brought Jesus out and sat down in the judgment seat in a place that is called *The* Pavement, but in Hebrew, Gab′ba·tha.

14 Now it was the Preparation Day of the Passover, and about the sixth hour. And he said to the Jews, "Behold your King!"

15 But they cried out, "Away with *Him,* away with *Him!* Crucify Him!" Pilate said to them, "Shall I crucify your King?" The chief priests answered, "We have no king but Caesar!"

16 Then he delivered Him to them to be crucified. So they took Jesus and led *Him* away.*a*

The King on a Cross

17 And He, bearing His cross, went out to a place called *the Place* of a Skull, which is called in Hebrew, Gol′go·tha,

18 where they crucified Him, and two others with Him, one on either side, and Jesus in the center.

19 Now Pilate wrote a title and put *it* on the cross. And the writing was:

JESUS OF NAZARETH,
THE KING OF THE JEWS.

20 Then many of the Jews read this title, for the place where Jesus was crucified was near the city; and it was written in Hebrew, Greek, *and* Latin.

21 Therefore the chief priests of the Jews said to Pilate, "Do not write, 'The King of the Jews,' but, 'He said, "I am the King of the Jews." ' "

22 Pilate answered, "What I have written, I have written."

23 Then the soldiers, when they had crucified Jesus, took His garments and made four parts, to each soldier a part, and also the tunic. Now the tunic was without seam, woven from the top in one piece.

24 They said therefore among themselves, "Let us not tear it, but cast lots for it, whose it shall be," that the Scripture might be fulfilled which says:

"They divided My garments among them,
And for My clothing they cast lots."*a*

Therefore the soldiers did these things.

Behold Your Mother

25 Now there stood by the cross of Jesus His mother, and His mother's sister, Mary the *wife* of Clō′pas, and Mary Mag′da·lēne.

26 When Jesus therefore saw His mother, and the disciple whom He loved standing by, He said to His mother, "Woman, behold your son!"

27 Then He said to the disciple, "Behold your mother!" And from that hour that disciple took her to his own *home.*

It Is Finished

28 After this, Jesus, knowing*a* that all things were now accomplished, that the Scripture might be fulfilled, said, "I thirst!"

29 Now a vessel full of sour wine was

19:16 *a*NU-Text omits *and led Him away.*
19:24 *a*Psalm 22:18   19:28 *a*M-Text reads *seeing.*

sitting there; and they filled a sponge with sour wine, put *it* on hyssop, and put *it* to His mouth.
30 So when Jesus had received the sour wine, He said, "It is finished!" And bowing His head, He gave up His spirit.

JESUS' SIDE IS PIERCED

31 Therefore, because it was the Preparation *Day,* that the bodies should not remain on the cross on the Sabbath (for that Sabbath was a high day), the Jews asked Pilate that their legs might be broken, and *that* they might be taken away.
32 Then the soldiers came and broke the legs of the first and of the other who was crucified with Him.
33 But when they came to Jesus and saw that He was already dead, they did not break His legs.
34 But one of the soldiers pierced His side with a spear, and immediately blood and water came out.
35 And he who has seen has testified, and his testimony is true; and he knows that he is telling the truth, so that you may believe.
36 For these things were done that the Scripture should be fulfilled, *"Not one of His bones shall be broken."a*
37 And again another Scripture says, *"They shall look on Him whom they pierced."a*

JESUS BURIED IN JOSEPH'S TOMB

38 After this, Joseph of Ar·i·ma-thē′a, being a disciple of Jesus, but secretly, for fear of the Jews, asked Pilate that he might take away the body of Jesus; and Pilate gave *him* permission. So he came and took the body of Jesus.
39 And Nic·o·dē′mus, who at first came to Jesus by night, also came,
bringing a mixture of myrrh and aloes, about a hundred pounds.
40 Then they took the body of Jesus, and bound it in strips of linen with the spices, as the custom of the Jews is to bury.
41 Now in the place where He was crucified there was a garden, and in the garden a new tomb in which no one had yet been laid.
42 So there they laid Jesus, because of the Jews' Preparation *Day,* for the tomb was nearby.
■ *see Mark 15*

THE EMPTY TOMB

20 Now on the first *day* of the week Mary Mag′da·lēne went to the tomb early, while it was still dark, and saw *that* the stone had been taken away from the tomb.
2 Then she ran and came to Simon Peter, and to the other disciple, whom Jesus loved, and said to them, "They have taken away the Lord out of the tomb, and we do not know where they have laid Him."
3 Peter therefore went out, and the other disciple, and were going to the tomb.
4 So they both ran together, and the other disciple outran Peter and came to the tomb first.
5 And he, stooping down and looking in, saw the linen cloths lying *there;* yet he did not go in.
6 Then Simon Peter came, following him, and went into the tomb; and he saw the linen cloths lying *there,*
7 and the handkerchief that had been around His head, not lying with the linen cloths, but folded together in a place by itself.
8 Then the other disciple, who came

19:36 *a*Exodus 12:46; Numbers 9:12; Psalm 34:20
19:37 *a*Zechariah 12:10

to the tomb first, went in also; and he saw and believed.

9 For as yet they did not know the Scripture, that He must rise again from the dead.

10 Then the disciples went away again to their own homes.

MARY MAGDALENE SEES THE RISEN LORD

11 But Mary stood outside by the tomb weeping, and as she wept she stooped down *and looked* into the tomb.

12 And she saw two angels in white sitting, one at the head and the other at the feet, where the body of Jesus had lain.

13 Then they said to her, "Woman, why are you weeping?" She said to them, "Because they have taken away my Lord, and I do not know where they have laid Him."

14 Now when she had said this, she turned around and saw Jesus standing *there,* and did not know that it was Jesus.

15 Jesus said to her, "Woman, why are you weeping? Whom are you seeking?" She, supposing Him to be the gardener, said to Him, "Sir, if You have carried Him away, tell me where You have laid Him, and I will take Him away."

16 Jesus said to her, "Mary!" She turned and said to Him,*a* "Rab·bo′nī!" (which is to say, Teacher).

17 Jesus said to her, "Do not cling to Me, for I have not yet ascended to My Father; but go to My brethren and say to them, 'I am ascending to My Father and your Father, and *to* My God and your God.' "

18 Mary Mag′da·lēne came and told the disciples that she had seen the Lord,*a* and *that* He had spoken these things to her.

■ *see Matthew 28:1–20*

THE APOSTLES COMMISSIONED

19 Then, the same day at evening, being the first *day* of the week, when the doors were shut where the disciples were assembled,*a* for fear of the Jews, Jesus came and stood in the midst, and said to them, "Peace *be* with you."

20 When He had said this, He showed them *His* hands and His side. Then the disciples were glad when they saw the Lord.

21 So Jesus said to them again, "Peace to you! As the Father has sent Me, I also send you."

22 And when He had said this, He breathed on *them,* and said to them, "Receive the Holy Spirit.

23 "If you forgive the sins of any, they are forgiven them; if you retain the *sins* of any, they are retained."

SEEING AND BELIEVING

24 Now Thomas, called the Twin, one of the twelve, was not with them when Jesus came.

25 The other disciples therefore said to him, "We have seen the Lord." So he said to them, "Unless I see in His hands the print of the nails, and put my finger into the print of the nails, and put my hand into His side, I will not believe."

26 And after eight days His disciples were again inside, and Thomas with them. Jesus came, the doors being shut, and stood in the midst, and said, "Peace to you!"

27 Then He said to Thomas, "Reach your finger here, and look at My hands; and reach your hand *here,* and put *it* into My side. Do not be unbelieving, but believing."

20:16 *a*NU-Text adds *in Hebrew.*   20:18 *a*NU-Text reads *disciples, "I have seen the Lord,"* . . .
20:19 *a*NU-Text omits *assembled.*

28 And Thomas answered and said to Him, "My Lord and my God!"
29 Jesus said to him, "Thomas,[a] because you have seen Me, you have believed. Blessed *are* those who have not seen and *yet* have believed."

THAT YOU MAY BELIEVE

30 And truly Jesus did many other signs in the presence of His disciples, which are not written in this book;
31 but these are written that you may believe that Jesus is the Christ, the Son of God, and that believing you may have life in His name.

BREAKFAST BY THE SEA

21 After these things Jesus showed Himself again to the disciples at the Sea of Tĭ·bē′ri·as, and in this way He showed *Himself*:
2 Simon Peter, Thomas called the Twin, Na·than′a·el of Cā′na in Galilee, the *sons* of Zeb′e·dee, and two others of His disciples were together.
3 Simon Peter said to them, "I am going fishing." They said to him, "We are going with you also." They went out and immediately[a] got into the boat, and that night they caught nothing.
4 But when the morning had now come, Jesus stood on the shore; yet the disciples did not know that it was Jesus.
5 Then Jesus said to them, "Children, have you any food?" They answered Him, "No."
6 And He said to them, "Cast the net on the right side of the boat, and you will find *some*." So they cast, and now they were not able to draw it in because of the multitude of fish.
7 Therefore that disciple whom Jesus loved said to Peter, "It is the Lord!" Now when Simon Peter heard

20:29 [a]NU-Text and M-Text omit *Thomas*.
21:3 [a]NU-Text omits *immediately*.

that it was the Lord, he put on *his* outer garment (for he had removed it), and plunged into the sea.

8 But the other disciples came in the little boat (for they were not far from land, but about two hundred cubits), dragging the net with fish.

9 Then, as soon as they had come to land, they saw a fire of coals there, and fish laid on it, and bread.

10 Jesus said to them, "Bring some of the fish which you have just caught."

11 Simon Peter went up and dragged the net to land, full of large fish, one hundred and fifty-three; and although there were so many, the net was not broken.

12 Jesus said to them, "Come *and* eat breakfast." Yet none of the disciples dared ask Him, "Who are You?"—knowing that it was the Lord.

13 Jesus then came and took the bread and gave it to them, and likewise the fish.

14 This *is* now the third time Jesus showed Himself to His disciples after He was raised from the dead.

JESUS RESTORES PETER

15 So when they had eaten breakfast, Jesus said to Simon Peter, "Simon, *son* of Jonah,[a] do you love Me more than these?" He said to Him, "Yes, Lord; You know that I love You." He said to him, "Feed My lambs."

16 He said to him again a second time, "Simon, *son* of Jonah,[a] do you love Me?" He said to Him, "Yes, Lord; You know that I love You." He said to him, "Tend My sheep."

17 He said to him the third time, "Simon, *son* of Jonah,[a] do you love Me?" Peter was grieved because He said to him the third time, "Do you love Me?" And he said to Him, "Lord, You know all things; You know that I love You." Jesus said to him, "Feed My sheep.

21:15 [a]NU-Text reads *John.*   21:16 [a]NU-Text reads *John.*   21:17 [a]NU-Text reads *John.*

18 "Most assuredly, I say to you, when you were younger, you girded yourself and walked where you wished; but when you are old, you will stretch out your hands, and another will gird you and carry *you* where you do not wish."

19 This He spoke, signifying by what death he would glorify God. And when He had spoken this, He said to him, "Follow Me."

THE BELOVED DISCIPLE AND HIS BOOK

20 Then Peter, turning around, saw the disciple whom Jesus loved following, who also had leaned on His breast at the supper, and said, "Lord, who is the one who betrays You?"

21 Peter, seeing him, said to Jesus, "But Lord, what *about* this man?"

22 Jesus said to him, "If I will that he remain till I come, what *is that* to you? You follow Me."

23 Then this saying went out among the brethren that this disciple would not die. Yet Jesus did not say to him that he would not die, but, "If I will that he remain till I come, what *is that* to you?"

24 This is the disciple who testifies of these things, and wrote these things; and we know that his testimony is true.

25 And there are also many other things that Jesus did, which if they were written one by one, I suppose that even the world itself could not contain the books that would be written. Amen.

THE ACTS
of the Apostles

PROLOGUE

THE former account I made, O Thē·oph'i·lus, of all that Jesus began both to do and teach,
2 until the day in which He was taken up, after He through the Holy Spirit had given commandments to the apostles whom He had chosen,
3 to whom He also presented Himself alive after His suffering by many infallible proofs, being seen by them during forty days and speaking of the things pertaining to the kingdom of God.

THE HOLY SPIRIT PROMISED

4 And being assembled together with *them,* He commanded them not to depart from Jerusalem, but to wait for the Promise of the Father, "which," *He said,* "you have heard from Me;
5 "for John truly baptized with water, but you shall be baptized with the Holy Spirit not many days from now."
6 Therefore, when they had come together, they asked Him, saying, "Lord, will You at this time restore the kingdom to Israel?"
7 And He said to them, "It is not for you to know times or seasons which the Father has put in His own authority.
8 "But you shall receive power when the Holy Spirit has come upon you; and you shall be witnesses to Me*a* in Jerusalem, and in all Judea and Samaria, and to the end of the earth."

JESUS ASCENDS TO HEAVEN

9 Now when He had spoken these things, while they watched, He was taken up, and a cloud received Him out of their sight.
10 And while they looked steadfastly toward heaven as He went up, behold, two men stood by them in white apparel,
11 who also said, "Men of Galilee, why do you stand gazing up into heaven? This *same* Jesus, who was taken up from you into heaven, will so come in like manner as you saw Him go into heaven."

THE UPPER ROOM PRAYER MEETING

12 Then they returned to Jerusalem from the mount called Ol'i·vet, which is near Jerusalem, a Sabbath day's journey.
13 And when they had entered, they went up into the upper room where they were staying: Peter, James, John, and Andrew; Philip and Thomas; Bartholomew and Matthew; James *the son* of Al·phaē'us and Simon the Zealot; and Judas *the son* of James.
14 These all continued with one accord in prayer and supplication,*a* with the women and Mary the mother of Jesus, and with His brothers.

MATTHIAS CHOSEN

15 And in those days Peter stood up in the midst of the disciples*a* (altogether the number of names was about a hundred and twenty), and said,
16 "Men *and* brethren, this Scripture had to be fulfilled, which the Holy

1:8 *a*NU-Text reads *My witnesses.* 1:14 *a*NU-Text omits *and supplication.* 1:15 *a*NU-Text reads *brethren.*

Spirit spoke before by the mouth of David concerning Judas, who became a guide to those who arrested Jesus;

17 "for he was numbered with us and obtained a part in this ministry."

18 (Now this man purchased a field with the wages of iniquity; and falling headlong, he burst open in the middle and all his entrails gushed out.

19 And it became known to all those dwelling in Jerusalem; so that field is called in their own language, Akel Da'ma, that is, Field of Blood.)

20 "For it is written in the Book of Psalms:

'Let his dwelling place be desolate,
And let no one live in it';a

and,

'Letb another take his office.'c

21 "Therefore, of these men who have accompanied us all the time that the Lord Jesus went in and out among us,

22 "beginning from the baptism of John to that day when He was taken up from us, one of these must become a witness with us of His resurrection."

23 And they proposed two: Joseph called Bar'sa·bas, who was surnamed Jus'tus, and Mat·thī'as.

24 And they prayed and said, "You, O Lord, who know the hearts of all, show which of these two You have chosen

25 "to take part in this ministry and apostleship from which Judas by transgression fell, that he might go to his own place."

26 And they cast their lots, and the lot fell on Mat·thī'as. And he was numbered with the eleven apostles.

COMING OF THE HOLY SPIRIT

Jesus had risen from the dead. The disciples saw Him rise up to heaven, and they knew He would return one day. But Jesus would not leave them alone. He was sending One who would comfort them and always be with them. This is how it happened.

2 When the Day of Pentecost had fully come, they were all with one accorda in one place.

2 And suddenly there came a sound from heaven, as of a rushing mighty wind, and it filled the whole house where they were sitting.

3 Then there appeared to them divided tongues, as of fire, and *one* sat upon each of them.

4 And they were all filled with the Holy Spirit and began to speak with other tongues, as the Spirit gave them utterance.

THE CROWD'S RESPONSE

5 And there were dwelling in Jerusalem Jews, devout men, from every nation under heaven.

6 And when this sound occurred, the multitude came together, and were confused, because everyone heard them speak in his own language.

7 Then they were all amazed and marveled, saying to one another, "Look, are not all these who speak Galileans?

8 "And how *is it that* we hear, each in our own language in which we were born?

9 "Par'thi·ans and Mēdes and

1:20 aPsalm 69:25 bPsalm 109:8 cGreek *episkopen*, position of overseer 2:1 aNU-Text reads *together*.

Ē'lam·ītes, those dwelling in Mes·o-po·tā'mi·a, Judea and Cap·pa·dō'ci·a, Pon'tus and Asia,

10 "Phryg'i·a and Pam·phyl'i·a, Egypt and the parts of Lib'ya adjoining Cȳ·rē'nē, visitors from Rome, both Jews and proselytes,

11 "Crē'tans and Arabs—we hear them speaking in our own tongues the wonderful works of God."

12 So they were all amazed and perplexed, saying to one another, "Whatever could this mean?"

13 Others mocking said, "They are full of new wine."

PETER'S SERMON

14 But Peter, standing up with the eleven, raised his voice and said to them, "Men of Judea and all who dwell in Jerusalem, let this be known to you, and heed my words.

15 "For these are not drunk, as you suppose, since it is *only* the third hour of the day.

16 "But this is what was spoken by the prophet Jō'el:

17 '*And it shall come to pass in the last days, says God,*
That I will pour out of My Spirit on all flesh;
Your sons and your daughters shall prophesy,
Your young men shall see visions,
Your old men shall dream dreams.

18 *And on My menservants and on My maidservants*
I will pour out My Spirit in those days;
And they shall prophesy.

19 *I will show wonders in heaven above*
And signs in the earth beneath:
Blood and fire and vapor of smoke.

20 *The sun shall be turned into darkness,*

And the moon into blood,
Before the coming of the great and awesome day of the LORD.

21 *And it shall come to pass*
That whoever calls on the name of the LORD
Shall be saved.'ᵃ

22 "Men of Israel, hear these words: Jesus of Nazareth, a Man attested by God to you by miracles, wonders, and signs which God did through Him in your midst, as you yourselves also know—

23 "Him, being delivered by the determined purpose and foreknowledge of God, you have takenᵃ by lawless hands, have crucified, and put to death;

24 "whom God raised up, having loosed the pains of death, because it

2:21 ᵃJoel 2:28–32　　2:23 ᵃNU-Text omits *have taken.*

Bible Quiz

Acts 2:1–24　**The Holy Spirit Comes**

1. What was the name of the day when God sent His Holy Spirit?
2. When the Holy Spirit came, what did it sound like at first?
3. What appeared on the disciples' heads?
4. Name one thing the Holy Spirit helped the disciples do.
5. Which disciple talked to the crowd about Jesus and the Holy Spirit?
6. Can you name some ways the Holy Spirit helps us today?

was not possible that He should be held by it.

25 "For David says concerning Him:

'I foresaw the Lord always before
    my face,
For He is at my right hand, that I
    may not be shaken.
26 Therefore my heart rejoiced, and
    my tongue was glad;
Moreover my flesh also will rest
    in hope.
27 For You will not leave my soul in
    Hā′dēs,
Nor will You allow Your Holy One
    to see corruption.
28 You have made known to me the
    ways of life;
You will make me full of joy in
    Your presence.'ᵃ

29 "Men *and* brethren, let *me* speak freely to you of the patriarch David, that he is both dead and buried, and his tomb is with us to this day.
30 "Therefore, being a prophet, and knowing that God had sworn with an oath to him that of the fruit of his body, according to the flesh, He would raise up the Christ to sit on his throne,ᵃ
31 "he, foreseeing this, spoke concerning the resurrection of the Christ, that His soul was not left in Hā′dēs, nor did His flesh see corruption.
32 "This Jesus God has raised up, of which we are all witnesses.
33 "Therefore being exalted to the right hand of God, and having received from the Father the promise of the Holy Spirit, He poured out this which you now see and hear.
34 "For David did not ascend into the heavens, but he says himself:

'The Lord said to my Lord,
"Sit at My right hand,
35 Till I make Your enemies Your
    footstool." 'ᵃ

36 "Therefore let all the house of Israel know assuredly that God has made this Jesus, whom you crucified, both Lord and Christ."
37 Now when they heard *this,* they were cut to the heart, and said to Peter and the rest of the apostles, "Men *and* brethren, what shall we do?"
38 Then Peter said to them, "Repent, and let every one of you be baptized in the name of Jesus Christ for the remission of sins; and you shall receive the gift of the Holy Spirit.
39 "For the promise is to you and to your children, and to all who are afar off, as many as the Lord our God will call."

A Vital Church Grows

40 And with many other words he testified and exhorted them, saying, "Be saved from this perverse generation."
41 Then those who gladlyᵃ received his word were baptized; and that day about three thousand souls were added *to them.*
42 And they continued steadfastly in the apostles' doctrine and fellowship, in the breaking of bread, and in prayers.
43 Then fear came upon every soul, and many wonders and signs were done through the apostles.
44 Now all who believed were together, and had all things in common,
45 and sold their possessions and goods, and divided them among all, as anyone had need.
46 So continuing daily with one accord in the temple, and breaking bread from house to house, they ate

2:28 ᵃPsalm 16:8–11   2:30 ᵃNU-Text omits *according to the flesh, He would raise up the Christ* and completes the verse with *He would seat one on his throne.*   2:35 ᵃPsalm 110:1   2:41 ᵃNU-Text omits *gladly.*

SHARING Acts 2:44

Share My Flower

Share my flower. Smell it with me. Share my food. Eat it with me. Share my toys. Play with me. Share my money. Buy something you really need.

1. What is this little girl sharing? Why do you think she is doing that?
2. What should we share with others? Why?
3. Why does sharing please Jesus?

For more on *Values* turn to page 1670
For more on *Sharing* turn to page 1869

their food with gladness and simplicity of heart,

47 praising God and having favor with all the people. And the Lord added to the church[a] daily those who were being saved.

A Lame Man Healed

3 Now Peter and John went up together to the temple at the hour of prayer, the ninth *hour*.

2 And a certain man lame from his mother's womb was carried, whom they laid daily at the gate of the temple which is called Beautiful, to ask alms from those who entered the temple;

3 who, seeing Peter and John about to go into the temple, asked for alms.

4 And fixing his eyes on him, with John, Peter said, "Look at us."

5 So he gave them his attention, expecting to receive something from them.

6 Then Peter said, "Silver and gold I do not have, but what I do have I give you: In the name of Jesus Christ of Nazareth, rise up and walk."

7 And he took him by the right hand and lifted *him* up, and immediately his feet and ankle bones received strength.

8 So he, leaping up, stood and walked and entered the temple with them—walking, leaping, and praising God.

9 And all the people saw him walking and praising God.

10 Then they knew that it was he who sat begging alms at the Beautiful Gate of the temple; and they were filled with wonder and amazement at what had happened to him.

Preaching in Solomon's Portico

11 Now as the lame man who was healed held on to Peter and John, all the people ran together to them in the porch which is called Solomon's, greatly amazed.

12 So when Peter saw *it,* he responded to the people: "Men of Israel, why do you marvel at this? Or why look so intently at us, as though by our own power or godliness we had made this man walk?

13 "The God of Abraham, Isaac, and Jacob, the God of our fathers, glorified His Servant Jesus, whom you delivered up and denied in the presence of Pilate, when he was determined to let *Him* go.

14 "But you denied the Holy One and the Just, and asked for a murderer to be granted to you,

15 "and killed the Prince of life, whom God raised from the dead, of which we are witnesses.

16 "And His name, through faith in His name, has made this man strong, whom you see and know. Yes, the faith which *comes* through Him has given him this perfect soundness in the presence of you all.

17 "Yet now, brethren, I know that you did *it* in ignorance, as *did* also your rulers.

18 "But those things which God foretold by the mouth of all His prophets, that the Christ would suffer, He has thus fulfilled.

19 "Repent therefore and be converted, that your sins may be blotted out, so that times of refreshing may come from the presence of the Lord,

20 "and that He may send Jesus Christ, who was preached to you before,[a]

21 "whom heaven must receive until the times of restoration of all things, which God has spoken by the mouth of all His holy prophets since the world began.

2:47 [a]NU-Text omits *to the church.*   3:20 [a]NU-Text and M-Text read *Christ Jesus, who was ordained for you before.*

22 "For Moses truly said to the fathers, *'The LORD your God will raise up for you a Prophet like me from your brethren. Him you shall hear in all things, whatever He says to you.*

23 *'And it shall be that every soul who will not hear that Prophet shall be utterly destroyed from among the people.'*ª

24 "Yes, and all the prophets, from Samuel and those who follow, as many as have spoken, have also foretoldª these days.

25 "You are sons of the prophets, and of the covenant which God made with our fathers, saying to Abraham, *'And in your seed all the families of the earth shall be blessed.'*ª

26 "To you first, God, having raised up His Servant Jesus, sent Him to bless you, in turning away every one *of you* from your iniquities."

PETER AND JOHN ARRESTED

4 Now as they spoke to the people, the priests, the captain of the temple, and the Sad'dū·cees came upon them,

2 being greatly disturbed that they taught the people and preached in Jesus the resurrection from the dead.

3 And they laid hands on them, and put *them* in custody until the next day, for it was already evening.

4 However, many of those who heard the word believed; and the number of the men came to be about five thousand.

ADDRESSING THE SANHEDRIN

5 And it came to pass, on the next day, that their rulers, elders, and scribes,

6 as well as An'nas the high priest, Cā'i·a·phas, John, and Alexander, and as many as were of the family of the high priest, were gathered together at Jerusalem.

7 And when they had set them in the midst, they asked, "By what power or by what name have you done this?"

8 Then Peter, filled with the Holy Spirit, said to them, "Rulers of the people and elders of Israel:

9 "If we this day are judged for a good deed *done* to a helpless man, by what means he has been made well,

10 "let it be known to you all, and to all the people of Israel, that by the name of Jesus Christ of Nazareth, whom you crucified, whom God raised from the dead, by Him this man stands here before you whole.

11 "This is the *'stone which was rejected by you builders, which has become the chief cornerstone.'*ª

12 "Nor is there salvation in any other, for there is no other name under heaven given among men by which we must be saved."

THE NAME OF JESUS FORBIDDEN

13 Now when they saw the boldness of Peter and John, and perceived that they were uneducated and untrained men, they marveled. And they realized that they had been with Jesus.

14 And seeing the man who had been healed standing with them, they could say nothing against it.

15 But when they had commanded them to go aside out of the council, they conferred among themselves,

16 saying, "What shall we do to these men? For, indeed, that a notable miracle has been done through them *is* evident to all who dwell in Jerusalem, and we cannot deny *it*.

17 "But so that it spreads no further among the people, let us severely threaten them, that from now on they speak to no man in this name."

3:23 ªDeuteronomy 18:15, 18, 19   3:24 ªNU-Text and M-Text read *proclaimed*.   3:25 ªGenesis 22:18; 26:4; 28:14   4:11 ªPsalm 118:22

18 So they called them and commanded them not to speak at all nor teach in the name of Jesus.

19 But Peter and John answered and said to them, "Whether it is right in the sight of God to listen to you more than to God, you judge.

20 "For we cannot but speak the things which we have seen and heard."

21 So when they had further threatened them, they let them go, finding no way of punishing them, because of the people, since they all glorified God for what had been done.

22 For the man was over forty years old on whom this miracle of healing had been performed.

PRAYER FOR BOLDNESS

23 And being let go, they went to their own *companions* and reported all that the chief priests and elders had said to them.

24 So when they heard that, they raised their voice to God with one accord and said: "Lord, You *are* God, who made heaven and earth and the sea, and all that is in them,

25 "who by the mouth of Your servant David*a* have said:

'Why did the nations rage,
And the people plot vain things?
26 The kings of the earth took their stand,
And the rulers were gathered together
Against the LORD and against His Christ.'*a*

27 "For truly against Your holy Servant Jesus, whom You anointed, both Her′od and Pon′ti·us Pilate, with the Gentiles and the people of Israel, were gathered together

28 "to do whatever Your hand and Your purpose determined before to be done.

29 "Now, Lord, look on their threats, and grant to Your servants that with all boldness they may speak Your word,

30 "by stretching out Your hand to heal, and that signs and wonders may be done through the name of Your holy Servant Jesus."

31 And when they had prayed, the place where they were assembled together was shaken; and they were all filled with the Holy Spirit, and they spoke the word of God with boldness.

SHARING IN ALL THINGS

32 Now the multitude of those who believed were of one heart and one soul; neither did anyone say that any of the things he possessed was his own, but they had all things in common.

33 And with great power the apostles gave witness to the resurrection of the Lord Jesus. And great grace was upon them all.

34 Nor was there anyone among them who lacked; for all who were possessors of lands or houses sold them, and brought the proceeds of the things that were sold,

35 and laid *them* at the apostles' feet; and they distributed to each as anyone had need.

36 And Jō′ses,*a* who was also named Bar′na·bas by the apostles (which is translated Son of Encouragement), a Lē′vīte of the country of Cyprus,

37 having land, sold *it,* and brought the money and laid *it* at the apostles' feet.

LYING TO THE HOLY SPIRIT

5 But a certain man named An·a·nī′as, with Sap·phī′ra his wife, sold a possession.

4:25 *a*NU-Text reads *who through the Holy Spirit, by the mouth of our father, Your servant David.*
4:26 *a*Psalm 2:1, 2　　4:36 *a*NU-Text reads *Joseph.*

Values

TRUTHFULNESS Acts 5:1–5

Telling the Truth

Do you see what Jeremy is giving his friend Jennifer? But listen! Do you hear what he is saying? "Jennifer, I have a *whole box* of candy for you. I'm giving it *all* to you."

1. Is Jeremy telling Jennifer the truth? How do you know?
2. Is a little lie OK? Why not? Is a little lie any better than a bigger lie? Why not? Read Acts 5:1–5. What does it say?
3. What do you think Jennifer should say to Jeremy? What would *you* say?

For more on *Values* turn to page 1679
For more on *Honesty* turn to page 117

2 And he kept back *part* of the proceeds, his wife also being aware *of it,* and brought a certain part and laid *it* at the apostles' feet.

3 But Peter said, "An·a·nī'as, why has Satan filled your heart to lie to the Holy Spirit and keep back *part* of the price of the land for yourself?

4 "While it remained, was it not your own? And after it was sold, was it not in your own control? Why have you conceived this thing in your heart? You have not lied to men but to God."

5 Then An·a·nī'as, hearing these words, fell down and breathed his last. So great fear came upon all those who heard these things.

6 And the young men arose and wrapped him up, carried *him* out, and buried *him.*

7 Now it was about three hours later when his wife came in, not knowing what had happened.

8 And Peter answered her, "Tell me whether you sold the land for so much?" She said, "Yes, for so much."

9 Then Peter said to her, "How is it that you have agreed together to test the Spirit of the Lord? Look, the feet of those who have buried your husband *are* at the door, and they will carry you out."

10 Then immediately she fell down at his feet and breathed her last. And the young men came in and found her dead, and carrying *her* out, buried *her* by her husband.

11 So great fear came upon all the church and upon all who heard these things.

CONTINUING POWER IN THE CHURCH

12 And through the hands of the apostles many signs and wonders were done among the people. And they were all with one accord in Solomon's Porch.

13 Yet none of the rest dared join them, but the people esteemed them highly.

14 And believers were increasingly added to the Lord, multitudes of both men and women,

15 so that they brought the sick out into the streets and laid *them* on beds and couches, that at least the shadow of Peter passing by might fall on some of them.

16 Also a multitude gathered from the surrounding cities to Jerusalem, bringing sick people and those who were tormented by unclean spirits, and they were all healed.

IMPRISONED APOSTLES FREED

17 Then the high priest rose up, and all those who *were* with him (which is the sect of the Sad'dū·cees), and they were filled with indignation,

18 and laid their hands on the apostles and put them in the common prison.

19 But at night an angel of the Lord opened the prison doors and brought them out, and said,

20 "Go, stand in the temple and speak to the people all the words of this life."

21 And when they heard *that,* they entered the temple early in the morning and taught. But the high priest and those with him came and called the council together, with all the elders of the children of Israel, and sent to the prison to have them brought.

APOSTLES ON TRIAL AGAIN

22 But when the officers came and did not find them in the prison, they returned and reported,

23 saying, "Indeed we found the prison shut securely, and the guards

standing outside[a] before the doors; but when we opened them, we found no one inside!"

24 Now when the high priest,[a] the captain of the temple, and the chief priests heard these things, they wondered what the outcome would be.

25 So one came and told them, saying,[a] "Look, the men whom you put in prison are standing in the temple and teaching the people!"

26 Then the captain went with the officers and brought them without violence, for they feared the people, lest they should be stoned.

27 And when they had brought them, they set *them* before the council. And the high priest asked them,

28 saying, "Did we not strictly command you not to teach in this name? And look, you have filled Jerusalem with your doctrine, and intend to bring this Man's blood on us!"

29 But Peter and the *other* apostles answered and said: "We ought to obey God rather than men.

30 "The God of our fathers raised up Jesus whom you murdered by hanging on a tree.

31 "Him God has exalted to His right hand *to be* Prince and Savior, to give repentance to Israel and forgiveness of sins.

32 "And we are His witnesses to these things, and *so* also *is* the Holy Spirit whom God has given to those who obey Him."

GAMALIEL'S ADVICE

33 When they heard *this*, they were furious and plotted to kill them.

34 Then one in the council stood up, a Phar'i·see named Ga·mā'li·el, a teacher of the law held in respect by all the people, and commanded them to put the apostles outside for a little while.

35 And he said to them: "Men of Is-rael, take heed to yourselves what you intend to do regarding these men.

36 "For some time ago Theū'das rose up, claiming to be somebody. A number of men, about four hundred, joined him. He was slain, and all who obeyed him were scattered and came to nothing.

37 "After this man, Judas of Galilee rose up in the days of the census, and drew away many people after him. He also perished, and all who obeyed him were dispersed.

38 "And now I say to you, keep away from these men and let them alone; for if this plan or this work is of men, it will come to nothing;

39 "but if it is of God, you cannot overthrow it—lest you even be found to fight against God."

40 And they agreed with him, and when they had called for the apostles and beaten *them,* they commanded that they should not speak in the name of Jesus, and let them go.

41 So they departed from the presence of the council, rejoicing that they were counted worthy to suffer shame for His[a] name.

42 And daily in the temple, and in every house, they did not cease teaching and preaching Jesus *as* the Christ.

SEVEN CHOSEN TO SERVE

6 Now in those days, when *the number of* the disciples was multiplying, there arose a complaint against the Hebrews by the Hel'len·ists,[a] because their widows were neglected in the daily distribution.

2 Then the twelve summoned the

5:23 [a]NU-Text and M-Text omit *outside.*
5:24 [a]NU-Text omits *the high priest.*
5:25 [a]NU-Text and M-Text omit *saying.*
5:41 [a]NU-Text reads *the name;* M-Text reads *the name of Jesus.* 6:1 [a]That is, Greek-speaking Jews

GOOD NEWS Acts 5:42

Bad News or Good News?

Do you ever read the newspaper? Do your parents read it? If you do, you read a lot of bad news. Newspapers tell us about the bad things that happen to people—wars, floods, fires, fights. Sometimes they tell us a little good news, but not much. But there is a special Book filled with Good News. Do you know what it is?

1. Ask mother or father to tell you about some of the bad news in today's newspaper. What is it?
2. Ask mother or father to tell you about the Good News in the Bible. What is the very best news of all? Read Acts 5:42 and Acts 17:18.

For more on *Favorite Bible Words* turn to page 1688
For more on *Bible* turn to page 1679

multitude of the disciples and said, "It is not desirable that we should leave the word of God and serve tables.

3 "Therefore, brethren, seek out from among you seven men of *good* reputation, full of the Holy Spirit and wisdom, whom we may appoint over this business;

4 "but we will give ourselves continually to prayer and to the ministry of the word."

5 And the saying pleased the whole multitude. And they chose Stephen, a man full of faith and the Holy Spirit, and Philip, Proch′o·rus, Nī·cā′nor, Tī′mon, Par′me·nas, and Nic′o·las, a proselyte from An′ti·och,

6 whom they set before the apostles; and when they had prayed, they laid hands on them.

7 Then the word of God spread, and the number of the disciples multiplied greatly in Jerusalem, and a great many of the priests were obedient to the faith.

STEPHEN ACCUSED OF BLASPHEMY

8 And Stephen, full of faith*a* and power, did great wonders and signs among the people.

9 Then there arose some from what is called the Synagogue of the Freedmen (Cȳ·rē′ni·ans, Alexandrians, and those from Ci·li′ci·a and Asia), disputing with Stephen.

10 And they were not able to resist the wisdom and the Spirit by which he spoke.

11 Then they secretly induced men to say, "We have heard him speak blasphemous words against Moses and God."

12 And they stirred up the people, the elders, and the scribes; and they came upon *him,* seized him, and brought *him* to the council.

13 They also set up false witnesses

who said, "This man does not cease to speak blasphemous*a* words against this holy place and the law;

14 "for we have heard him say that this Jesus of Nazareth will destroy this place and change the customs which Moses delivered to us."

15 And all who sat in the council, looking steadfastly at him, saw his face as the face of an angel.

STEPHEN'S ADDRESS: THE CALL OF ABRAHAM

7 Then the high priest said, "Are these things so?"

2 And he said, "Brethren and fathers, listen: The God of glory appeared to our father Abraham when he was in Mes·o·po·tā′mi·a, before he dwelt in Har′an,

3 "and said to him, *'Get out of your country and from your relatives, and come to a land that I will show you.'a*

4 "Then he came out of the land of the Chal·dē′ans and dwelt in Har′an. And from there, when his father was dead, He moved him to this land in which you now dwell.

5 "And *God* gave him no inheritance in it, not even *enough* to set his foot on. But even when *Abraham* had no child, He promised to give it to him for a possession, and to his descendants after him.

6 "But God spoke in this way: that his descendants would dwell in a foreign land, and that they would bring them into bondage and oppress *them* four hundred years.

7 *'And the nation to whom they will be in bondage I will judge,'a* said God, *'and after that they shall come out and serve Me in this place.'b*

8 "Then He gave him the covenant

6:8 *a*NU-Text reads *grace.* 6:13 *a*NU-Text omits *blasphemous.* 7:3 *a*Genesis 12:1
7:7 *a*Genesis 15:14 *b*Exodus 3:12

of circumcision; and so *Abraham* begot Isaac and circumcised him on the eighth day; and Isaac *begot* Jacob, and Jacob *begot* the twelve patriarchs.

THE PATRIARCHS IN EGYPT

9 "And the patriarchs, becoming envious, sold Joseph into Egypt. But God was with him

10 "and delivered him out of all his troubles, and gave him favor and wisdom in the presence of Pharaoh, king of Egypt; and he made him governor over Egypt and all his house.

11 "Now a famine and great trouble came over all the land of Egypt and Cā′naan, and our fathers found no sustenance.

12 "But when Jacob heard that there was grain in Egypt, he sent out our fathers first.

13 "And the second *time* Joseph was made known to his brothers, and Joseph's family became known to the Pharaoh.

14 "Then Joseph sent and called his father Jacob and all his relatives to *him,* seventy-five*a* people.

15 "So Jacob went down to Egypt; and he died, he and our fathers.

16 "And they were carried back to Shē′chem and laid in the tomb that Abraham bought for a sum of money from the sons of Hā′mor, *the father* of Shē′chem.

GOD DELIVERS ISRAEL BY MOSES

17 "But when the time of the promise drew near which God had sworn to Abraham, the people grew and multiplied in Egypt

18 "till another king arose who did not know Joseph.

19 "This man dealt treacherously with our people, and oppressed our forefathers, making them expose their babies, so that they might not live.

20 "At this time Moses was born, and was well pleasing to God; and he was brought up in his father's house for three months.

21 "But when he was set out, Pharaoh's daughter took him away and brought him up as her own son.

22 "And Moses was learned in all the wisdom of the Egyptians, and was mighty in words and deeds.

23 "Now when he was forty years old, it came into his heart to visit his brethren, the children of Israel.

24 "And seeing one of *them* suffer wrong, he defended and avenged him who was oppressed, and struck down the Egyptian.

25 "For he supposed that his brethren would have understood that God would deliver them by his hand, but they did not understand.

26 "And the next day he appeared to two of them as they were fighting, and *tried to* reconcile them, saying, 'Men, you are brethren; why do you wrong one another?'

27 "But he who did his neighbor wrong pushed him away, saying, *'Who made you a ruler and a judge over us?*

28 *'Do you want to kill me as you did the Egyptian yesterday?'a*

29 "Then, at this saying, Moses fled and became a dweller in the land of Mid′i·an, where he had two sons.

30 "And when forty years had passed, an Angel of the Lord*a* appeared to him in a flame of fire in a bush, in the wilderness of Mount Sinai.

31 "When Moses saw *it,* he marveled at the sight; and as he drew near to observe, the voice of the Lord came to him,

7:14 *a*Or *seventy* (compare Exodus 1:5)
7:28 *a*Exodus 2:14   7:30 *a*NU-Text omits *of the Lord.*

32 "saying, 'I am the God of your fathers—the God of Abraham, the God of Isaac, and the God of Jacob.'[a] And Moses trembled and dared not look.

33 'Then the LORD said to him, "Take your sandals off your feet, for the place where you stand is holy ground.

34 "I have surely seen the oppression of My people who are in Egypt; I have heard their groaning and have come down to deliver them. And now come, I will send you to Egypt." '[a]

35 "This Moses whom they rejected, saying, 'Who made you a ruler and a judge?'[a] is the one God sent to be a ruler and a deliverer by the hand of the Angel who appeared to him in the bush.

36 "He brought them out, after he had shown wonders and signs in the land of Egypt, and in the Red Sea, and in the wilderness forty years.

ISRAEL REBELS AGAINST GOD

37 "This is that Moses who said to the children of Israel,[a] 'The LORD your God will raise up for you a Prophet like me from your brethren. Him you shall hear.'[b]

38 "This is he who was in the congregation in the wilderness with the Angel who spoke to him on Mount Sinai, and with our fathers, the one who received the living oracles to give to us,

39 "whom our fathers would not obey, but rejected. And in their hearts they turned back to Egypt,

40 "saying to Aaron, 'Make us gods to go before us; as for this Moses who brought us out of the land of Egypt, we do not know what has become of him.'[a]

41 "And they made a calf in those days, offered sacrifices to the idol, and rejoiced in the works of their own hands.

42 "Then God turned and gave them up to worship the host of heaven, as it is written in the book of the Prophets:

'Did you offer Me slaughtered
  animals and sacrifices during
  forty years in the wilderness,
O house of Israel?

43 You also took up the tabernacle of
   Mō' loch,
And the star of your god
   Rem' phan,
Images which you made to
   worship;
And I will carry you away beyond
   Babylon.'[a]

GOD'S TRUE TABERNACLE

44 "Our fathers had the tabernacle of witness in the wilderness, as He appointed, instructing Moses to make it according to the pattern that he had seen,

45 "which our fathers, having received it in turn, also brought with Joshua into the land possessed by the Gentiles, whom God drove out before the face of our fathers until the days of David,

46 "who found favor before God and asked to find a dwelling for the God of Jacob,

47 "But Solomon built Him a house.

48 "However, the Most High does not dwell in temples made with hands, as the prophet says:

49 'Heaven is My throne,
  And earth is My footstool.
  What house will you build for Me?
    says the LORD,
  Or what is the place of My rest?

50 Has My hand not made all these
    things?'[a]

7:32 [a]Exodus 3:6, 15   7:34 [a]Exodus 3:5, 7, 8, 10
7:35 [a]Exodus 2:14   7:37 [a]Deuteronomy 18:15
[b]NU-Text and M-Text omit *Him you shall hear.*
7:40 [a]Exodus 32:1, 23   7:43 [a]Amos 5:25–27
7:50 [a]Isaiah 66:1, 2

Israel Resists the Holy Spirit

51 *"You* stiff-necked and uncircumcised in heart and ears! You always resist the Holy Spirit; as your fathers *did,* so *do* you.
52 "Which of the prophets did your fathers not persecute? And they killed those who foretold the coming of the Just One, of whom you now have become the betrayers and murderers,
53 "who have received the law by the direction of angels and have not kept *it."*

Stephen the Martyr

54 When they heard these things they were cut to the heart, and they gnashed at him with *their* teeth.
55 But he, being full of the Holy Spirit, gazed into heaven and saw the glory of God, and Jesus standing at the right hand of God,
56 and said, "Look! I see the heavens opened and the Son of Man standing at the right hand of God!"
57 Then they cried out with a loud voice, stopped their ears, and ran at him with one accord;
58 and they cast *him* out of the city and stoned *him.* And the witnesses laid down their clothes at the feet of a young man named Saul.
59 And they stoned Stephen as he was calling on *God* and saying, "Lord Jesus, receive my spirit."
60 Then he knelt down and cried out with a loud voice, "Lord, do not charge them with this sin." And when he had said this, he fell asleep.

Saul Persecutes the Church

8 Now Saul was consenting to his death. At that time a great persecution arose against the church which was at Jerusalem; and they were all scattered throughout the regions of Judea and Samaria, except the apostles.
2 And devout men carried Stephen *to his burial,* and made great lamentation over him.
3 As for Saul, he made havoc of the church, entering every house, and dragging off men and women, committing *them* to prison.

Christ Is Preached in Samaria

4 Therefore those who were scattered went everywhere preaching the word.
5 Then Philip went down to the[a] city of Samaria and preached Christ to them.
6 And the multitudes with one accord heeded the things spoken by Philip, hearing and seeing the miracles which he did.
7 For unclean spirits, crying with a loud voice, came out of many who were possessed; and many who were paralyzed and lame were healed.

Prayers

Acts 7:60

What would you pray if someone was throwing rocks at you? What would you say if someone hated you and tried to hurt you? Stephen prayed for the Lord to forgive these foolish people. Do you ever pray for those who hate you? Do you ever pray for the bully who wants to hurt you? Do you ever pray for those who make fun of you? Do you ever pray for those who won't play with you?

8:5 [a]Or *a*

8 And there was great joy in that city.

The Sorcerer's Profession of Faith

9 But there was a certain man called Simon, who previously practiced sorcery in the city and astonished the people of Samaria, claiming that he was someone great,
10 to whom they all gave heed, from the least to the greatest, saying, "This man is the great power of God."
11 And they heeded him because he had astonished them with his sorceries for a long time.
12 But when they believed Philip as he preached the things concerning the kingdom of God and the name of Jesus Christ, both men and women were baptized.
13 Then Simon himself also believed; and when he was baptized he continued with Philip, and was amazed, seeing the miracles and signs which were done.

The Sorcerer's Sin

14 Now when the apostles who were at Jerusalem heard that Samaria had received the word of God, they sent Peter and John to them,
15 who, when they had come down, prayed for them that they might receive the Holy Spirit.
16 For as yet He had fallen upon none of them. They had only been baptized in the name of the Lord Jesus.
17 Then they laid hands on them, and they received the Holy Spirit.
18 And when Simon saw that through the laying on of the apostles' hands the Holy Spirit was given, he offered them money,
19 saying, "Give me this power also, that anyone on whom I lay hands may receive the Holy Spirit."

20 But Peter said to him, "Your money perish with you, because you thought that the gift of God could be purchased with money!
21 "You have neither part nor portion in this matter, for your heart is not right in the sight of God.
22 "Repent therefore of this your wickedness, and pray God if perhaps the thought of your heart may be forgiven you.
23 "For I see that you are poisoned by bitterness and bound by iniquity."
24 Then Simon answered and said, "Pray to the Lord for me, that none of the things which you have spoken may come upon me."
25 So when they had testified and preached the word of the Lord, they returned to Jerusalem, preaching the gospel in many villages of the Samaritans.

Christ Is Preached to an Ethiopian

Philip was a person who loved to tell others about Jesus. He was helping many people become Christians. One day God sent Philip to tell a certain person about Jesus. Why was it so important that this person know about Jesus?

26 Now an angel of the Lord spoke to Philip, saying, "Arise and go toward the south along the road which goes down from Jerusalem to Gā'za." This is desert.
27 So he arose and went. And behold, a man of Ethiopia, a eunuch of great authority under Can·dā'cē the queen of the Ethiopians, who had charge of all her treasury, and had come to Jerusalem to worship,
28 was returning. And sitting in his chariot, he was reading Ī·sāi'ah the prophet.

Values

SHARING   Acts 8:30, 31

Praise God for Wonderful Things

Do you like to hear Bible stories? Do you like to share them with your little brother or sister? Bible stories tell us about the wonderful things God has done. There are many wonderful things. Thank You, God, for the wonderful things You have done. I will praise You for them.

1. Why do you like to hear Bible stories? When do you like to hear them?
2. Do you like to share Bible stories with others? With whom do you share them? Why?
3. What is this boy doing? Do you think sharing Bible stories makes him happy? He is praising God by sharing the wonderful things God has done in these Bible stories.

For more on *Values* turn to page 1706
For more on *Bible* turn to page 1743

29 Then the Spirit said to Philip, "Go near and overtake this chariot."
30 So Philip ran to him, and heard him reading the prophet Ī·sāi′ah, and said, "Do you understand what you are reading?"
31 And he said, "How can I, unless someone guides me?" And he asked Philip to come up and sit with him.
32 The place in the Scripture which he read was this:

> "He was led as a sheep to the
>   slaughter;
> And as a lamb before its shearer
>   is silent,
> So He opened not His mouth.
> 33 In His humiliation His justice
>   was taken away,
> And who will declare His
>   generation?
> For His life is taken from the
>   earth."ᵃ

34 So the eunuch answered Philip and said, "I ask you, of whom does the prophet say this, of himself or of some other man?"
35 Then Philip opened his mouth, and beginning at this Scripture, preached Jesus to him.
36 Now as they went down the road, they came to some water. And the eunuch said, "See, *here is* water. What hinders me from being baptized?"
37 Then Philip said, "If you believe with all your heart, you may." And he answered and said, "I believe that Jesus Christ is the Son of God."ᵃ
38 So he commanded the chariot to stand still. And both Philip and the eunuch went down into the water, and he baptized him.
39 Now when they came up out of the water, the Spirit of the Lord caught Philip away, so that the eunuch saw him no more; and he went on his way rejoicing.
40 But Philip was found at A·zō′tus. And passing through, he preached in

---

☑ Bible Quiz

Acts 8:26–40 **Philip and the Ethiopian**

1. Philip told many people about Jesus. Then an angel told him to go to the desert. Do you think Philip may have wondered why God would send him into the desert when he was helping so many people where he was?
2. Who did Philip find in the desert? Where was this person from?
3. What book of the Bible was the Ethiopian reading from? What did Philip ask him?
4. What did the Ethiopian have to believe in order to be baptized?
5. What happened to Philip after he baptized the Ethiopian? Do you think God had someone else in mind who needed to hear about Jesus?
6. The Ethiopian was from a far away country. The world was just learning about Jesus. Why do you think God wanted Philip to tell the Ethiopian about Jesus? When you tell others about Jesus, how might that help others come to know about Him?

8:33 ᵃIsaiah 53:7, 8   8:37 ᵃNU-Text and M-Text omit this verse. It is found in Western texts, including the Latin tradition.

all the cities till he came to Caes·a·rē′a.

THE DAMASCUS ROAD: SAUL CONVERTED

What dangerous but exciting days to be a Christian! God's Holy Spirit was helping the disciples do great miracles. Many people were becoming Christians. But there were some people who hated the Christians. One of those people was Saul. He was on his way to Damascus to hurt some of them. But Jesus met him on the way. Could Jesus change his mind?

9 Then Saul, still breathing threats and murder against the disciples of the Lord, went to the high priest
2 and asked letters from him to the synagogues of Damascus, so that if he found any who were of the Way, whether men or women, he might bring them bound to Jerusalem.
3 As he journeyed he came near Damascus, and suddenly a light shone around him from heaven.
4 Then he fell to the ground, and heard a voice saying to him, "Saul, Saul, why are you persecuting Me?"
5 And he said, "Who are You, Lord?" Then the Lord said, "I am Jesus, whom you are persecuting.*a* It *is* hard for you to kick against the goads."
6 So he, trembling and astonished, said, "Lord, what do You want me to do?" Then the Lord *said* to him, "Arise and go into the city, and you will be told what you must do."
7 And the men who journeyed with him stood speechless, hearing a voice but seeing no one.
8 Then Saul arose from the ground,

and when his eyes were opened he saw no one. But they led him by the hand and brought *him* into Damascus.
9 And he was three days without sight, and neither ate nor drank.

ANANIAS BAPTIZES SAUL

10 Now there was a certain disciple at Damascus named An·a·nī′as; and to him the Lord said in a vision, "An·a·nī′as." And he said, "Here I am, Lord."
11 So the Lord *said* to him, "Arise and go to the street called Straight, and inquire at the house of Judas for *one* called Saul of Tar′sus, for behold, he is praying.
12 "And in a vision he has seen a man named An·a·nī′as coming in and putting *his* hand on him, so that he might receive his sight."
13 Then An·a·nī′as answered, "Lord, I have heard from many about this man, how much harm he has done to Your saints in Jerusalem.
14 "And here he has authority from the chief priests to bind all who call on Your name."
15 But the Lord said to him, "Go, for he is a chosen vessel of Mine to bear My name before Gentiles, kings, and the children of Israel.
16 "For I will show him how many things he must suffer for My name's sake."
17 And An·a·nī′as went his way and entered the house; and laying his hands on him he said, "Brother Saul, the Lord Jesus,*a* who appeared to you on the road as you came, has sent me that you may receive your sight and be filled with the Holy Spirit."
18 Immediately there fell from his

9:5 *a*NU-Text and M-Text omit the last sentence of verse 5 and begin verse 6 with *But arise and go.*
9:17 *a*M-Text omits *Jesus.*

eyes *something* like scales, and he received his sight at once; and he arose and was baptized.

19 So when he had received food, he was strengthened. Then Saul spent some days with the disciples at Damascus.

SAUL PREACHES CHRIST

20 Immediately he preached the Christ[a] in the synagogues, that He is the Son of God.

21 Then all who heard were amazed, and said, "Is this not he who destroyed those who called on this name in Jerusalem, and has come here for that purpose, so that he might bring them bound to the chief priests?"

22 But Saul increased all the more in strength, and confounded the Jews who dwelt in Damascus, proving that this *Jesus* is the Christ.

SAUL ESCAPES DEATH

23 Now after many days were past, the Jews plotted to kill him.

24 But their plot became known to Saul. And they watched the gates day and night, to kill him.

25 Then the disciples took him by night and let *him* down through the wall in a large basket.

SAUL AT JERUSALEM

26 And when Saul had come to Jerusalem, he tried to join the disciples; but they were all afraid of him, and did not believe that he was a disciple.

27 But Bar'na·bas took him and brought *him* to the apostles. And he declared to them how he had seen the Lord on the road, and that He had spoken to him, and how he had preached boldly at Damascus in the name of Jesus.

28 So he was with them at Jerusalem, coming in and going out.

29 And he spoke boldly in the name of the Lord Jesus and disputed against the Hel'len·ists, but they attempted to kill him.

30 When the brethren found out, they brought him down to Caes·a·rē'a and sent him out to Tar'sus.

THE CHURCH PROSPERS

31 Then the churches[a] throughout all Judea, Galilee, and Samaria had peace and were edified. And walking

---

☑ *Bible Quiz*

Acts 9:1–22 **Jesus Meets Saul on the Damascus Road**

1. Where was Saul going? Why was he going there? Why wasn't it easy to be a Christian in those days?
2. What stopped Saul along the way? Who talked to him?
3. Where did Jesus tell Saul to go? Who came to tell Saul what to do?
4. When Jesus left, what was wrong with Saul? How long was Saul blind?
5. What great change happened in Saul? If Jesus can change an evil person like Saul, He can change anyone!
6. Who do you know who needs Jesus? Do you believe Jesus can change that person?

9:20 [a]NU-Text reads *Jesus.*   9:31 [a]NU-Text reads *church . . . was edified.*

AN EXTRA PUSH Acts 9:23–28

"I need an extra push," Allison said to Alan. So Alan gave her the extra push. Higher and higher went Allison. Without that extra push, Allison would have slowed down, then stopped.

1. Good friends give an extra push when needed. Saul needed an extra bit of help from a friend (Acts 9:23–28). But who would help? Saul's old friends were not his friends now. Then Barnabas came along. He gave Saul that "extra push" that Saul needed.
2. Does one of your friends need some kind of extra help? How can you help? Will you?
3. Are you glad when a friend gives you that extra push that you need? What should you say when a friend helps you?

For more on *Family Friends* turn to page 1830
For more on *Helpfulness* turn to page 62

in the fear of the Lord and in the comfort of the Holy Spirit, they were multiplied.

AENEAS HEALED

32 Now it came to pass, as Peter went through all *parts of the country,* that he also came down to the saints who dwelt in Lyd′da.

33 There he found a certain man named Aē·nē′as, who had been bedridden eight years and was paralyzed.

34 And Peter said to him, "Aē·nē′as, Jesus the Christ heals you. Arise and make your bed." Then he arose immediately.

35 So all who dwelt at Lyd′da and Sharon saw him and turned to the Lord.

DORCAS RESTORED TO LIFE

Many people were getting to know Jesus. When they did, things were different. And even if life got harder, they seemed to be happier. Dorcas was such a person. Then one day she got sick. But her sickness would help even more people know Jesus. Here's how.

36 At Jop′pa there was a certain disciple named Tab′i·tha, which is translated Dor′cas. This woman was full of good works and charitable deeds which she did.

37 But it happened in those days that she became sick and died. When they had washed her, they laid *her* in an upper room.

38 And since Lyd′da was near Jop′pa, and the disciples had heard that Peter was there, they sent two men to him, imploring *him* not to delay in coming to them.

39 Then Peter arose and went with them. When he had come, they brought *him* to the upper room. And all the widows stood by him weeping, showing the tunics and garments which Dor′cas had made while she was with them.

40 But Peter put them all out, and knelt down and prayed. And turning to the body he said, "Tab′i·tha, arise." And she opened her eyes, and when she saw Peter she sat up.

41 Then he gave her *his* hand and lifted her up; and when he had called the saints and widows, he presented her alive.

42 And it became known throughout all Jop′pa, and many believed on the Lord.

43 So it was that he stayed many days in Jop′pa with Simon, a tanner.

☑ *Bible Quiz*

Acts 9:36–43   **Peter Raises Dorcas to Life**

1. In what town did Dorcas live?
2. What kind of a person was she?
3. What happened to her?
4. What did Peter do when he arrived? Who helped Peter raise Dorcas from the dead?
5. What did many people do when they heard how Dorcas was raised to life?
6. What miracles do we see all around us that could help others believe in Jesus?

CORNELIUS SENDS A DELEGATION

10 There was a certain man in Caes·a·rē′a called Cornelius, a centurion of what was called the Italian Regiment,

2 a devout *man* and one who feared God with all his household, who gave alms generously to the people, and prayed to God always.
3 About the ninth hour of the day he saw clearly in a vision an angel of God coming in and saying to him, "Cornelius!"
4 And when he observed him, he was afraid, and said, "What is it, lord?" So he said to him, "Your prayers and your alms have come up for a memorial before God.
5 "Now send men to Jop′pa, and send for Simon whose surname is Peter.
6 "He is lodging with Simon, a tanner, whose house is by the sea.ᵃ He will tell you what you must do."
7 And when the angel who spoke to him had departed, Cornelius called two of his household servants and a devout soldier from among those who waited on him continually.
8 So when he had explained all *these* things to them, he sent them to Jop′pa.

PETER'S VISION

9 The next day, as they went on their journey and drew near the city, Peter went up on the housetop to pray, about the sixth hour.
10 Then he became very hungry and wanted to eat; but while they made ready, he fell into a trance
11 and saw heaven opened and an object like a great sheet bound at the four corners, descending to him and let down to the earth.
12 In it were all kinds of four-footed animals of the earth, wild beasts, creeping things, and birds of the air.
13 And a voice came to him, "Rise, Peter; kill and eat."
14 But Peter said, "Not so, Lord! For I have never eaten anything common or unclean."

15 And a voice *spoke* to him again the second time, "What God has cleansed you must not call common."
16 This was done three times. And the object was taken up into heaven again.

SUMMONED TO CAESAREA

17 Now while Peter wondered within himself what this vision which he had seen meant, behold, the men who had been sent from Cornelius had made inquiry for Simon's house, and stood before the gate.
18 And they called and asked whether Simon, whose surname was Peter, was lodging there.
19 While Peter thought about the vision, the Spirit said to him, "Behold, three men are seeking you.
20 "Arise therefore, go down and go with them, doubting nothing; for I have sent them."
21 Then Peter went down to the men who had been sent to him from Cornelius,ᵃ and said, "Yes, I am he whom you seek. For what reason have you come?"
22 And they said, "Cornelius *the* centurion, a just man, one who fears God and has a good reputation among all the nation of the Jews, was divinely instructed by a holy angel to summon you to his house, and to hear words from you."
23 Then he invited them in and lodged *them.* On the next day Peter went away with them, and some brethren from Jop′pa accompanied him.

PETER MEETS CORNELIUS

24 And the following day they entered Caes·a·re′a. Now Cornelius was

10:6 ᵃNU-Text and M-Text omit the last sentence of this verse.   10:21 ᵃNU-Text and M-Text omit *who had been sent to him from Cornelius.*

waiting for them, and had called together his relatives and close friends.

25 As Peter was coming in, Cornelius met him and fell down at his feet and worshiped *him.*

26 But Peter lifted him up, saying, "Stand up; I myself am also a man."

27 And as he talked with him, he went in and found many who had come together.

28 Then he said to them, "You know how unlawful it is for a Jewish man to keep company with or go to one of another nation. But God has shown me that I should not call any man common or unclean.

29 "Therefore I came without objection as soon as I was sent for. I ask, then, for what reason have you sent for me?"

30 So Cornelius said, "Four days ago I was fasting until this hour; and*a* at the ninth hour I prayed in my house, and behold, a man stood before me in bright clothing,

31 "and said, 'Cornelius, your prayer has been heard, and your alms are remembered in the sight of God.

32 'Send therefore to Jop'pa and call Simon here, whose surname is Peter. He is lodging in the house of Simon, a tanner, by the sea.*a* When he comes, he will speak to you.'

33 "So I sent to you immediately, and you have done well to come. Now therefore, we are all present before God, to hear all the things commanded you by God."

PREACHING TO CORNELIUS' HOUSEHOLD

34 Then Peter opened *his* mouth and said: "In truth I perceive that God shows no partiality.

35 "But in every nation whoever fears Him and works righteousness is accepted by Him.

36 "The word which *God* sent to the children of Israel, preaching peace through Jesus Christ—He is Lord of all—

37 "that word you know, which was proclaimed throughout all Judea, and began from Galilee after the baptism which John preached:

38 "how God anointed Jesus of Nazareth with the Holy Spirit and with power, who went about doing good and healing all who were oppressed by the devil, for God was with Him.

39 "And we are witnesses of all things which He did both in the land of the Jews and in Jerusalem, whom they*a* killed by hanging on a tree.

40 "Him God raised up on the third day, and showed Him openly,

41 "not to all the people, but to witnesses chosen before by God, *even* to us who ate and drank with Him after He arose from the dead.

42 "And He commanded us to preach to the people, and to testify that it is He who was ordained by God *to be* Judge of the living and the dead.

43 "To Him all the prophets witness that, through His name, whoever believes in Him will receive remission of sins."

THE HOLY SPIRIT FALLS ON THE GENTILES

44 While Peter was still speaking these words, the Holy Spirit fell upon all those who heard the word.

45 And those of the circumcision who believed were astonished, as many as came with Peter, because the gift of the Holy Spirit had been poured out on the Gentiles also.

46 For they heard them speak with tongues and magnify God. Then Peter answered,

10:30 *a*NU-Text reads *Four days ago to this hour, at the ninth hour.*   10:32 *a*NU-Text omits the last sentence of this verse.   10:39 *a*NU-Text and M-Text add *also.*

47 "Can anyone forbid water, that these should not be baptized who have received the Holy Spirit just as we *have?*"

48 And he commanded them to be baptized in the name of the Lord. Then they asked him to stay a few days.

PETER DEFENDS GOD'S GRACE

11 Now the apostles and brethren who were in Judea heard that the Gentiles had also received the word of God.

2 And when Peter came up to Jerusalem, those of the circumcision contended with him,

3 saying, "You went in to uncircumcised men and ate with them!"

4 But Peter explained *it* to them in order from the beginning, saying:

5 "I was in the city of Jop′pa praying; and in a trance I saw a vision, an object descending like a great sheet, let down from heaven by four corners; and it came to me.

6 "When I observed it intently and considered, I saw four-footed animals of the earth, wild beasts, creeping things, and birds of the air.

7 "And I heard a voice saying to me, 'Rise, Peter; kill and eat.'

8 "But I said, 'Not so, Lord! For nothing common or unclean has at any time entered my mouth.'

9 "But the voice answered me again from heaven, 'What God has cleansed you must not call common.'

10 "Now this was done three times, and all were drawn up again into heaven.

11 "At that very moment, three men stood before the house where I was, having been sent to me from Caesa·rē′a.

12 "Then the Spirit told me to go with them, doubting nothing. More-

over these six brethren accompanied me, and we entered the man's house.

13 "And he told us how he had seen an angel standing in his house, who said to him, 'Send men to Jop′pa, and call for Simon whose surname is Peter,

14 'who will tell you words by which you and all your household will be saved.'

15 "And as I began to speak, the Holy Spirit fell upon them, as upon us at the beginning.

16 "Then I remembered the word of the Lord, how He said, 'John indeed baptized with water, but you shall be baptized with the Holy Spirit.'

17 "If therefore God gave them the same gift as *He gave* us when we believed on the Lord Jesus Christ, who was I that I could withstand God?"

18 When they heard these things they became silent; and they glorified God, saying, "Then God has also granted to the Gentiles repentance to life."

BARNABAS AND SAUL AT ANTIOCH

19 Now those who were scattered after the persecution that arose over Stephen traveled as far as Phoe·ni′-ci·a, Cyprus, and An′ti·och, preaching the word to no one but the Jews only.

20 But some of them were men from Cyprus and Cȳ·rē′nē, who, when they had come to An′ti·och, spoke to the Hel′len·ists, preaching the Lord Jesus.

21 And the hand of the Lord was with them, and a great number believed and turned to the Lord.

22 Then news of these things came to the ears of the church in Jerusalem, and they sent out Bar′na·bas to go as far as An′ti·och.

23 When he came and had seen the grace of God, he was glad, and encouraged them all that with purpose

CHRISTIAN Acts 11:26

Branded for Jesus

Have you ever seen pictures of branded cattle or sheep? There is a little mark on the animal. It is a special shape or size or color. Wherever that animal goes, people know the animal's owner because they know the owner's mark or brand. "That sheep belongs to so-and-so," they say. When we become Christians, we wear the name Christian. Wherever we go, people say, "that person belongs to Christ." Sometimes Christians wear a pin or necklace shaped like a cross. That usually says to people, "I belong to Christ. I am a Christian."

1. Why do people brand their animals? What does it tell others?
2. How are we "branded" for Christ? What does that brand tell others?
3. Are you a Christian? Have you accepted Jesus as your Savior? If you have, do you want to tell others about Him? Why?

For more on *Favorite Bible Words* turn to page 1764
For more on *Salvation* turn to page 1728

of heart they should continue with the Lord.

24 For he was a good man, full of the Holy Spirit and of faith. And a great many people were added to the Lord.

25 Then Bar′na·bas departed for Tar′sus to seek Saul.

26 And when he had found him, he brought him to An′ti·och. So it was that for a whole year they assembled with the church and taught a great many people. And the disciples were first called Christians in An′ti·och.

RELIEF TO JUDEA

27 And in these days prophets came from Jerusalem to An′ti·och.

28 Then one of them, named Ag′a·bus, stood up and showed by the Spirit that there was going to be a great famine throughout all the world, which also happened in the days of Clau′di·us Caesar.

29 Then the disciples, each according to his ability, determined to send relief to the brethren dwelling in Judea.

30 This they also did, and sent it to the elders by the hands of Bar′na·bas and Saul.

HEROD'S VIOLENCE TO THE CHURCH

Herod the king didn't like Christians. He had already killed James the disciple. Now he arrested Peter and threw him into prison. What would happen to Peter?

12 Now about that time Her′od the king stretched out *his* hand to harass some from the church.

2 Then he killed James the brother of John with the sword.

3 And because he saw that it pleased the Jews, he proceeded further to seize Peter also. Now it was *during* the Days of Unleavened Bread.

4 So when he had arrested him, he put *him* in prison, and delivered *him* to four squads of soldiers to keep him, intending to bring him before the people after Passover.

PETER FREED FROM PRISON

5 Peter was therefore kept in prison, but constant[a] prayer was offered to God for him by the church.

6 And when Her′od was about to bring him out, that night Peter was sleeping, bound with two chains between two soldiers; and the guards before the door were keeping the prison.

7 Now behold, an angel of the Lord stood by *him,* and a light shone in the prison; and he struck Peter on the side and raised him up, saying, "Arise quickly!" And his chains fell off *his* hands.

8 Then the angel said to him, "Gird yourself and tie on your sandals"; and so he did. And he said to him, "Put on your garment and follow me."

9 So he went out and followed him, and did not know that what was done by the angel was real, but thought he was seeing a vision.

10 When they were past the first and the second guard posts, they came to the iron gate that leads to the city, which opened to them of its own accord; and they went out and went down one street, and immediately the angel departed from him.

11 And when Peter had come to himself, he said, "Now I know for certain that the Lord has sent His angel, and has delivered me from the hand of Her′od and *from* all the expectation of the Jewish people."

12 So, when he had considered *this,*

12:5 [a]NU-Text reads *constantly* (or *earnestly*).

he came to the house of Mary, the mother of John whose surname was Mark, where many were gathered together praying.

13 And as Peter knocked at the door of the gate, a girl named Rhō´da came to answer.

14 When she recognized Peter's voice, because of *her* gladness she did not open the gate, but ran in and announced that Peter stood before the gate.

15 But they said to her, "You are beside yourself!" Yet she kept insisting that it was so. So they said, "It is his angel."

16 Now Peter continued knocking; and when they opened *the door* and saw him, they were astonished.

17 But motioning to them with his hand to keep silent, he declared to them how the Lord had brought him out of the prison. And he said, "Go, tell these things to James and to the brethren." And he departed and went to another place.

18 Then, as soon as it was day, there was no small stir among the soldiers about what had become of Peter.

19 But when Her´od had searched for him and not found him, he examined the guards and commanded that *they* should be put to death. And he went down from Judea to Caes·a·rē´a, and stayed *there*.

HEROD'S VIOLENT DEATH

20 Now Her´od had been very angry with the people of Tȳre and Sī´don; but they came to him with one accord, and having made Blas´tus the king's personal aide their friend, they asked for peace, because their country was supplied with food by the king's *country*.

21 So on a set day Her´od, arrayed in royal apparel, sat on his throne and gave an oration to them.

☑ Bible Quiz

Acts 12:1–19 **An Angel Frees Peter from Prison**

1. Did Herod like the Christians? How do you know?
2. What did Herod do to Peter?
3. What were other Christians doing for Peter while he was in prison?
4. Who came to rescue Peter from prison? How did it happen?
5. Whose house did Peter go to?
6. Do you think the prayers of the Christians helped get Peter out of prison? Are there people you know who need help? Will you pray for them?

---

22 And the people kept shouting, "The voice of a god and not of a man!"

23 Then immediately an angel of the Lord struck him, because he did not give glory to God. And he was eaten by worms and died.

24 But the word of God grew and multiplied.

BARNABAS AND SAUL APPOINTED

25 And Bar´na·bas and Saul returned from[a] Jerusalem when they had fulfilled *their* ministry, and they also took with them John whose surname was Mark.

13 Now in the church that was at An´ti·och there were certain prophets and teachers: Bar´na·bas, Sim´e·on

12:25 [a]NU-Text and M-Text read *to*.

who was called Nī′ger, Lū′cius of Cȳ·rē′nē, Man′a·en who had been brought up with Her′od the tetrarch, and Saul.
2 As they ministered to the Lord and fasted, the Holy Spirit said, "Now separate to Me Bar′na·bas and Saul for the work to which I have called them."
3 Then, having fasted and prayed, and laid hands on them, they sent *them* away.

PREACHING IN CYPRUS

4 So, being sent out by the Holy Spirit, they went down to Se·leū′ci·a, and from there they sailed to Cyprus.
5 And when they arrived in Sal′a·mis, they preached the word of God in the synagogues of the Jews. They also had John as *their* assistant.
6 Now when they had gone through the island*a* to Pā′phos, they found a certain sorcerer, a false prophet, a Jew whose name *was* Bar-Jē′sus,
7 who was with the proconsul, Ser′gi·us Paul′us, an intelligent man. This man called for Bar′na·bas and Saul and sought to hear the word of God.
8 But El′y·mas the sorcerer (for so his name is translated) withstood them, seeking to turn the proconsul away from the faith.
9 Then Saul, who also *is called* Paul, filled with the Holy Spirit, looked intently at him
10 and said, "O full of all deceit and all fraud, *you* son of the devil, *you* enemy of all righteousness, will you not cease perverting the straight ways of the Lord?
11 "And now, indeed, the hand of the Lord *is* upon you, and you shall be blind, not seeing the sun for a time." And immediately a dark mist fell on him, and he went around seeking someone to lead him by the hand.

12 Then the proconsul believed, when he saw what had been done, being astonished at the teaching of the Lord.

AT ANTIOCH IN PISIDIA

13 Now when Paul and his party set sail from Pā′phos, they came to Per′ga in Pam·phyl′i·a; and John, departing from them, returned to Jerusalem.
14 But when they departed from Per′ga, they came to An′ti·och in Pisid′i·a, and went into the synagogue on the Sabbath day and sat down.
15 And after the reading of the Law and the Prophets, the rulers of the synagogue sent to them, saying, "Men *and* brethren, if you have any word of exhortation for the people, say on."
16 Then Paul stood up, and motioning with *his* hand said, "Men of Israel, and you who fear God, listen:
17 "The God of this people Israel*a* chose our fathers, and exalted the people when they dwelt as strangers in the land of Egypt, and with an uplifted arm He brought them out of it.
18 "Now for a time of about forty years He put up with their ways in the wilderness.
19 "And when He had destroyed seven nations in the land of Cā′naan, He distributed their land to them by allotment.
20 "After that He gave *them* judges for about four hundred and fifty years, until Samuel the prophet.
21 "And afterward they asked for a king; so God gave them Saul the son of Kish, a man of the tribe of Benjamin, for forty years.
22 "And when He had removed him, He raised up for them David as king,

13:6 *a*NU-Text reads *the whole island.*
13:17 *a*M-Text omits *Israel.*

to whom also He gave testimony and said, *'I have found David*ᵃ *the son* of Jesse, *a man after My own heart,* who will do all My will.'ᵇ

23 "From this man's seed, according to *the* promise, God raised up for Israel a Savior—Jesus—ᵃ

24 "after John had first preached, before His coming, the baptism of repentance to all the people of Israel.

25 "And as John was finishing his course, he said, 'Who do you think I am? I am not *He.* But behold, there comes One after me, the sandals of whose feet I am not worthy to loose.'

26 "Men *and* brethren, sons of the family of Abraham, and those among you who fear God, to you the word of this salvation has been sent.

27 "For those who dwell in Jerusalem, and their rulers, because they did not know Him, nor even the voices of the Prophets which are read every Sabbath, have fulfilled *them* in condemning *Him.*

28 "And though they found no cause for death *in Him,* they asked Pilate that He should be put to death.

29 "Now when they had fulfilled all that was written concerning Him, they took *Him* down from the tree and laid *Him* in a tomb.

30 "But God raised Him from the dead.

31 "He was seen for many days by those who came up with Him from Galilee to Jerusalem, who are His witnesses to the people.

32 "And we declare to you glad tidings—that promise which was made to the fathers.

33 "God has fulfilled this for us their children, in that He has raised up Jesus. As it is also written in the second Psalm:

'You are My Son,
Today I have begotten You.'ᵃ

34 "And that He raised Him from the dead, no more to return to corruption, He has spoken thus:

'I will give you the sure mercies of David.'ᵃ

35 "Therefore He also says in another *Psalm:*

'You will not allow Your Holy One to see corruption.'ᵃ

36 "For David, after he had served his own generation by the will of God, fell asleep, was buried with his fathers, and saw corruption;

37 "but He whom God raised up saw no corruption.

38 "Therefore let it be known to you, brethren, that through this Man is preached to you the forgiveness of sins;

39 "and by Him everyone who believes is justified from all things from which you could not be justified by the law of Moses.

40 "Beware therefore, lest what has been spoken in the prophets come upon you:

41 'Behold, you despisers,
Marvel and perish!
For I work a work in your days,
A work which you will by no
means believe,
Though one were to declare it
to you.' "ᵃ

BLESSING AND CONFLICT AT ANTIOCH

42 So when the Jews went out of the synagogue,ᵃ the Gentiles begged that

13:22 ᵃPsalm 89:20   ᵇ1 Samuel 13:14
13:23 ᵃM-Text reads *for Israel salvation.*
13:33 ᵃPsalm 2:7   13:34 ᵃIsaiah 55:3
13:35 ᵃPsalm 16:10   13:41 ᵃHabakkuk 1:5
13:42 ᵃOr *And when they went out of the synagogue of the Jews;* NU-Text reads *And when they went out of the synagogue, they begged.*

these words might be preached to them the next Sabbath.

43 Now when the congregation had broken up, many of the Jews and devout proselytes followed Paul and Bar′na·bas, who, speaking to them, persuaded them to continue in the grace of God.

44 On the next Sabbath almost the whole city came together to hear the word of God.

45 But when the Jews saw the multitudes, they were filled with envy; and contradicting and blaspheming, they opposed the things spoken by Paul.

46 Then Paul and Bar′na·bas grew bold and said, "It was necessary that the word of God should be spoken to you first; but since you reject it, and judge yourselves unworthy of everlasting life, behold, we turn to the Gentiles.

47 "For so the Lord has commanded us:

'I have set you as a light to the Gentiles,
That you should be for salvation to the ends of the earth.' "a

48 Now when the Gentiles heard this, they were glad and glorified the word of the Lord. And as many as had been appointed to eternal life believed.

49 And the word of the Lord was being spread throughout all the region.

50 But the Jews stirred up the devout and prominent women and the chief men of the city, raised up persecution against Paul and Bar′na·bas, and expelled them from their region.

51 But they shook off the dust from their feet against them, and came to Ĭ·cō′ni·um.

52 And the disciples were filled with joy and with the Holy Spirit.

AT ICONIUM

14 Now it happened in Ĭ·cō′ni·um that they went together to the synagogue of the Jews, and so spoke that a great multitude both of the Jews and of the Greeks believed.

2 But the unbelieving Jews stirred up the Gentiles and poisoned their minds against the brethren.

3 Therefore they stayed there a long time, speaking boldly in the Lord, who was bearing witness to the word of His grace, granting signs and wonders to be done by their hands.

4 But the multitude of the city was divided: part sided with the Jews, and part with the apostles.

5 And when a violent attempt was made by both the Gentiles and Jews, with their rulers, to abuse and stone them,

6 they became aware of it and fled to Lys′tra and Der′bē, cities of Lyc·a·ō′ni·a, and to the surrounding region.

7 And they were preaching the gospel there.

IDOLATRY AT LYSTRA

8 And in Lys′tra a certain man without strength in his feet was sitting, a cripple from his mother's womb, who had never walked.

9 *This* man heard Paul speaking. Paul, observing him intently and seeing that he had faith to be healed,

10 said with a loud voice, "Stand up straight on your feet!" And he leaped and walked.

11 Now when the people saw what Paul had done, they raised their voices, saying in the Lyc·a·ō′ni·an *language,* "The gods have come down to us in the likeness of men!"

12 And Bar′na·bas they called Zeūs,

13:47 *a*Isaiah 49:6

and Paul, Her'mēs, because he was the chief speaker.

13 Then the priest of Zeūs, whose temple was in front of their city, brought oxen and garlands to the gates, intending to sacrifice with the multitudes.

14 But when the apostles Bar'na·bas and Paul heard this, they tore their clothes and ran in among the multitude, crying out

15 and saying, "Men, why are you doing these things? We also are men with the same nature as you, and preach to you that you should turn from these useless things to the living God, who made the heaven, the earth, the sea, and all things that are in them,

16 "who in bygone generations allowed all nations to walk in their own ways.

17 "Nevertheless He did not leave Himself without witness, in that He did good, gave us rain from heaven and fruitful seasons, filling our hearts with food and gladness."

18 And with these sayings they could scarcely restrain the multitudes from sacrificing to them.

STONING, ESCAPE TO DERBE

19 Then Jews from An'ti·och and Ī·cō'ni·um came there; and having persuaded the multitudes, they stoned Paul and dragged him out of the city, supposing him to be dead.

20 However, when the disciples gathered around him, he rose up and went into the city. And the next day he departed with Bar'na·bas to Der'bē.

STRENGTHENING THE CONVERTS

21 And when they had preached the gospel to that city and made many

disciples, they returned to Lys'tra, Ī·cō'ni·um, and An'ti·och,

22 strengthening the souls of the disciples, exhorting them to continue in the faith, and saying, "We must through many tribulations enter the kingdom of God."

23 So when they had appointed elders in every church, and prayed with fasting, they commended them to the Lord in whom they had believed.

24 And after they had passed through Pi·sid'i·a, they came to Pamphyl'i·a.

25 Now when they had preached the word in Per'ga, they went down to At·ta·lī'a.

26 From there they sailed to An'ti·och, where they had been commended to the grace of God for the work which they had completed.

27 Now when they had come and gathered the church together, they reported all that God had done with them, and that He had opened the door of faith to the Gentiles.

28 So they stayed there a long time with the disciples.

CONFLICT OVER CIRCUMCISION

15 And certain men came down from Judea and taught the brethren, "Unless you are circumcised according to the custom of Moses, you cannot be saved."

2 Therefore, when Paul and Bar'na·bas had no small dissension and dispute with them, they determined that Paul and Bar'na·bas and certain others of them should go up to Jerusalem, to the apostles and elders, about this question.

3 So, being sent on their way by the church, they passed through Phoeni'ci·a and Samaria, describing the conversion of the Gentiles; and they caused great joy to all the brethren.

4 And when they had come to Jerusalem, they were received by the church and the apostles and the elders; and they reported all things that God had done with them.

5 But some of the sect of the Phar′i·sees who believed rose up, saying, "It is necessary to circumcise them, and to command *them* to keep the law of Moses."

THE JERUSALEM COUNCIL

6 Now the apostles and elders came together to consider this matter.

7 And when there had been much dispute, Peter rose up and said to them: "Men and brethren, you know that a good while ago God chose among us, that by my mouth the Gentiles should hear the word of the gospel and believe.

8 "So God, who knows the heart, acknowledged them by giving them the Holy Spirit, just as *He did* to us,

9 "and made no distinction between us and them, purifying their hearts by faith.

10 "Now therefore, why do you test God by putting a yoke on the neck of the disciples which neither our fathers nor we were able to bear?

11 "But we believe that through the grace of the Lord Jesus Christ*a* we shall be saved in the same manner as they."

12 Then all the multitude kept silent and listened to Bar′na·bas and Paul declaring how many miracles and wonders God had worked through them among the Gentiles.

13 And after they had become silent, James answered, saying, "Men *and* brethren, listen to me:

14 "Simon has declared how God at the first visited the Gentiles to take out of them a people for His name.

15 "And with this the words of the prophets agree, just as it is written:

16 'After this I will return
And will rebuild the tabernacle of
   David, which has fallen down;
I will rebuild its ruins,
And I will set it up;

17 So that the rest of mankind may
   seek the LORD,
Even all the Gentiles who are
   called by My name,
Says the LORD who does all these
   things.'*a*

18 "Known to God from eternity are all His works.*a*

19 "Therefore I judge that we should not trouble those from among the Gentiles who are turning to God,

20 "but that we write to them to abstain from things polluted by idols, *from* sexual immorality,*a from* things strangled, and *from* blood.

21 "For Moses has had throughout many generations those who preach him in every city, being read in the synagogues every Sabbath."

THE JERUSALEM DECREE

22 Then it pleased the apostles and elders, with the whole church, to send chosen men of their own company to An′ti·och with Paul and Bar′na·bas, *namely,* Judas who was also named Bar′sa·bas,*a* and Silas, leading men among the brethren.

23 They wrote this *letter* by them:

The apostles, the elders, and the brethren,

To the brethren who are of the Gentiles in An′ti·och, Syria, and Ci·li′ci·a:

Greetings.

15:11 *a*NU-Text and M-Text omit *Christ.*
15:17 *a*Amos 9:11, 12   15:18 *a*NU-Text (combining with verse 17) reads *Says the Lord, who makes these things known from eternity (of old).*
15:20 *a*Or *fornication*   15:22 *a*NU-Text and M-Text read *Barsabbas.*

24 Since we have heard that some who went out from us have troubled you with words, unsettling your souls, saying, *"You must* be circumcised and keep the law"*a*—to whom we gave no *such* commandment—

25 it seemed good to us, being assembled with one accord, to send chosen men to you with our beloved Bar'na·bas and Paul,

26 men who have risked their lives for the name of our Lord Jesus Christ.

27 We have therefore sent Judas and Silas, who will also report the same things by word of mouth.

28 For it seemed good to the Holy Spirit, and to us, to lay upon you no greater burden than these necessary things:

29 that you abstain from things offered to idols, from blood, from things strangled, and from sexual immorality.*a* If you keep yourselves from these, you will do well.

Farewell.

Continuing Ministry in Syria

30 So when they were sent off, they came to An'ti·och; and when they had gathered the multitude together, they delivered the letter.

31 When they had read it, they rejoiced over its encouragement.

32 Now Judas and Silas, themselves being prophets also, exhorted and strengthened the brethren with many words.

33 And after they had stayed *there* for a time, they were sent back with greetings from the brethren to the apostles.*a*

34 However, it seemed good to Silas to remain there.*a*

35 Paul and Bar'na·bas also re-

mained in An'ti·och, teaching and preaching the word of the Lord, with many others also.

Division over John Mark

36 Then after some days Paul said to Bar'na·bas, "Let us now go back and visit our brethren in every city where we have preached the word of the Lord, *and see* how they are doing."

37 Now Bar'na·bas was determined to take with them John called Mark.

38 But Paul insisted that they should not take with them the one who had departed from them in Pam·phyl'i·a, and had not gone with them to the work.

39 Then the contention became so sharp that they parted from one another. And so Bar'na·bas took Mark and sailed to Cyprus;

40 but Paul chose Silas and departed, being commended by the brethren to the grace of God.

41 And he went through Syria and Ci·li'ci·a, strengthening the churches.

Timothy Joins Paul and Silas

16 Then he came to Der'bē and Lys'tra. And behold, a certain disciple was there, named Timothy, *the* son of a certain Jewish woman who believed, but his father *was* Greek.

2 He was well spoken of by the brethren who were at Lys'tra and Ī·cō'ni·um.

3 Paul wanted to have him go on with him. And he took *him* and circumcised him because of the Jews who were in that region, for they all knew that his father was Greek.

4 And as they went through the

15:24 *a*NU-Text omits *saying, "You must be circumcised and keep the law."*   15:29 *a*Or *fornication*
15:33 *a*NU-Text reads *to those who had sent them.*
15:34 *a*NU-Text and M-Text omit this verse.

cities, they delivered to them the decrees to keep, which were determined by the apostles and elders at Jerusalem.

5 So the churches were strengthened in the faith, and increased in number daily.

THE MACEDONIAN CALL

6 Now when they had gone through Phryg'i·a and the region of Galatia, they were forbidden by the Holy Spirit to preach the word in Asia.
7 After they had come to Mys'i·a, they tried to go into Bi·thyn'i·a, but the Spirit[a] did not permit them.
8 So passing by Mys'i·a, they came down to Trō'as.
9 And a vision appeared to Paul in the night. A man of Mac·e·dō'ni·a stood and pleaded with him, saying, "Come over to Mac·e·dō'ni·a and help us."
10 Now after he had seen the vision, immediately we sought to go to Mac·e·dō'ni·a, concluding that the Lord had called us to preach the gospel to them.

LYDIA BAPTIZED AT PHILIPPI

11 Therefore, sailing from Trō'as, we ran a straight course to Sam'o·thrāce, and the next *day* came to Nē·ap'o·lis,
12 and from there to Phi·lip'pī, which is the foremost city of that part of Mac·e·dō'ni·a, a colony. And we were staying in that city for some days.
13 And on the Sabbath day we went out of the city to the riverside, where prayer was customarily made; and we sat down and spoke to the women who met *there.*
14 Now a certain woman named Lyd'i·a heard *us.* She was a seller of purple from the city of Thȳ·a·tī'ra,

who worshiped God. The Lord opened her heart to heed the things spoken by Paul.
15 And when she and her household were baptized, she begged *us,* saying, "If you have judged me to be faithful to the Lord, come to my house and stay." So she persuaded us.

PAUL AND SILAS IMPRISONED

Saul, the man who tried to hurt Christians, is now named Paul. After he met Jesus on the road to Damascus he became a missionary. He traveled all over that part of the world telling everyone about Jesus. Many became Christians. There were also some who tried to stop him. This is a story about how Paul was thrown into prison for helping someone.

16 Now it happened, as we went to prayer, that a certain slave girl possessed with a spirit of divination met us, who brought her masters much profit by fortune-telling.
17 This girl followed Paul and us, and cried out, saying, "These men are the servants of the Most High God, who proclaim to us the way of salvation."
18 And this she did for many days. But Paul, greatly annoyed, turned and said to the spirit, "I command you in the name of Jesus Christ to come out of her." And he came out that very hour.
19 But when her masters saw that their hope of profit was gone, they seized Paul and Silas and dragged *them* into the marketplace to the authorities.
20 And they brought them to the

16:7 [a]NU-Text adds *of Jesus.*

What Should I Do?

CAN YOU SING WHEN YOU DON'T FEEL LIKE SINGING? Acts 16:23–25

You're hurting. You're sad. You're lonely. Is it time to grumble? Or is it time to sing praises to God?

1. Read Acts 16:23–25. This is the story about Paul and Silas when they were beaten and thrown into a dungeon. Did they gripe or complain? Or did they do something else? What?
2. When you're sad or lonely or feel like griping or complaining, what should you do? Can you sing praises to God? Will you the next time you feel down?

For more on *What Should I Do?* turn to page 1743
For more on *Praise* turn to page 1811

magistrates, and said, "These men, being Jews, exceedingly trouble our city;
21 "and they teach customs which are not lawful for us, being Romans, to receive or observe."
22 Then the multitude rose up together against them; and the magistrates tore off their clothes and commanded *them* to be beaten with rods.
23 And when they had laid many stripes on them, they threw *them* into prison, commanding the jailer to keep them securely.
24 Having received such a charge, he put them into the inner prison and fastened their feet in the stocks.

THE PHILIPPIAN JAILER SAVED

25 But at midnight Paul and Silas were praying and singing hymns to God, and the prisoners were listening to them.
26 Suddenly there was a great earthquake, so that the foundations of the prison were shaken; and immediately all the doors were opened and everyone's chains were loosed.

27 And the keeper of the prison, awaking from sleep and seeing the prison doors open, supposing the prisoners had fled, drew his sword and was about to kill himself.
28 But Paul called with a loud voice, saying, "Do yourself no harm, for we are all here."
29 Then he called for a light, ran in, and fell down trembling before Paul and Silas.
30 And he brought them out and said, "Sirs, what must I do to be saved?"
31 So they said, "Believe on the Lord Jesus Christ, and you will be saved, you and your household."
32 Then they spoke the word of the Lord to him and to all who were in his house.
33 And he took them the same hour of the night and washed *their* stripes. And immediately he and all his family were baptized.
34 Now when he had brought them into his house, he set food before them; and he rejoiced, having believed in God with all his household.

☑ *Bible Quiz*

Acts 16:16–34 Paul and Silas in Prison

1. What was the slave girl's problem?
2. How did Paul help the slave girl? What happened then?
3. Who was Paul's helper? What did they do when they were thrown in prison? What would you have done?
4. What shook the prison? Why was the prison guard so afraid? What did he ask Paul?
5. How did Paul help him?
6. It wasn't good that Paul and Silas were thrown into prison, but God made something good come from it—the keeper of the prison became a Christian! Is there something happening in your life that is not good? Can you trust God to help something good come from it?

PAUL REFUSES TO DEPART SECRETLY

35 And when it was day, the magistrates sent the officers, saying, "Let those men go."

36 So the keeper of the prison reported these words to Paul, saying, "The magistrates have sent to let you go. Now therefore depart, and go in peace."

37 But Paul said to them, "They have beaten us openly, uncondemned Romans, *and* have thrown *us* into prison. And now do they put us out secretly? No indeed! Let them come themselves and get us out."

38 And the officers told these words to the magistrates, and they were afraid when they heard that they were Romans.

39 Then they came and pleaded with them and brought *them* out, and asked *them* to depart from the city.

40 So they went out of the prison and entered *the house of* Lyd′i·a; and when they had seen the brethren, they encouraged them and departed.

PREACHING CHRIST AT THESSALONICA

17 Now when they had passed through Am·phip′o·lis and A·pol·lo′ni·a, they came to Thes·sa·lo·ni′ca, where there was a synagogue of the Jews.

2 Then Paul, as his custom was, went in to them, and for three Sabbaths reasoned with them from the Scriptures,

3 explaining and demonstrating that the Christ had to suffer and rise again from the dead, and *saying,* "This Jesus whom I preach to you is the Christ."

4 And some of them were persuaded; and a great multitude of the devout Greeks, and not a few of the leading women, joined Paul and Silas.

ASSAULT ON JASON'S HOUSE

5 But the Jews who were not persuaded, becoming envious,*a* took some of the evil men from the marketplace, and gathering a mob, set all the city in an uproar and attacked the house of Jason, and sought to bring them out to the people.

6 But when they did not find them, they dragged Jason and some

17:5 *a*NU-Text omits *who were not persuaded;* M-Text omits *becoming envious.*

brethren to the rulers of the city, crying out, "These who have turned the world upside down have come here too.

7 "Jason has harbored them, and these are all acting contrary to the decrees of Caesar, saying there is another king—Jesus."

8 And they troubled the crowd and the rulers of the city when they heard these things.

9 So when they had taken security from Jason and the rest, they let them go.

MINISTERING AT BEREA

10 Then the brethren immediately sent Paul and Silas away by night to Be·rē′a. When they arrived, they went into the synagogue of the Jews.

11 These were more fair-minded than those in Thes·sa·lo·nī′ca, in that they received the word with all readiness, and searched the Scriptures daily *to find out* whether these things were so.

12 Therefore many of them believed, and also not a few of the Greeks, prominent women as well as men.

13 But when the Jews from Thes·sa·lo·nī′ca learned that the word of God was preached by Paul at Be·rē′a, they came there also and stirred up the crowds.

14 Then immediately the brethren sent Paul away, to go to the sea; but both Silas and Timothy remained there.

15 So those who conducted Paul brought him to Athens; and receiving a command for Silas and Timothy to come to him with all speed, they departed.

THE PHILOSOPHERS AT ATHENS

16 Now while Paul waited for them at Athens, his spirit was provoked within him when he saw that the city was given over to idols.

17 Therefore he reasoned in the synagogue with the Jews and with the *Gentile* worshipers, and in the marketplace daily with those who happened to be there.

18 Then[a] a certain Ep·i·cū·rē′an and Stoic philosophers encountered him. And some said, "What does this babbler want to say?" Others said, "He seems to be a proclaimer of foreign gods," because he preached to them Jesus and the resurrection.

19 And they took him and brought him to the Ar·e·op′a·gus, saying, "May we know what this new doctrine *is* of which you speak?

20 "For you are bringing some strange things to our ears. Therefore we want to know what these things mean."

21 For all the A·thē′ni·ans and the foreigners who were there spent their time in nothing else but either to tell or to hear some new thing.

ADDRESSING THE AREOPAGUS

22 Then Paul stood in the midst of the Ar·e·op′a·gus and said, "Men of Athens, I perceive that in all things you are very religious;

23 "for as I was passing through and considering the objects of your worship, I even found an altar with this inscription:

TO THE UNKNOWN GOD.

Therefore, the One whom you worship without knowing, Him I proclaim to you:

24 "God, who made the world and everything in it, since He is Lord of heaven and earth, does not dwell in temples made with hands.

25 "Nor is He worshiped with men's

17:18 [a]NU-Text and M-Text add *also*.

hands, as though He needed anything, since He gives to all life, breath, and all things.

26 "And He has made from one blood[a] every nation of men to dwell on all the face of the earth, and has determined their preappointed times and the boundaries of their dwellings,

27 "so that they should seek the Lord, in the hope that they might grope for Him and find Him, though He is not far from each one of us;

28 "for in Him we live and move and have our being, as also some of your own poets have said, 'For we are also His offspring.'

29 "Therefore, since we are the offspring of God, we ought not to think that the Divine Nature is like gold or silver or stone, something shaped by art and man's devising.

30 "Truly, these times of ignorance God overlooked, but now commands all men everywhere to repent,

31 "because He has appointed a day on which He will judge the world in righteousness by the Man whom He has ordained. He has given assurance of this to all by raising Him from the dead."

32 And when they heard of the resurrection of the dead, some mocked, while others said, "We will hear you again on this *matter*."

33 So Paul departed from among them.

34 However, some men joined him and believed, among them Dī·o·nys'i·us the Ar·e·op'a·gīte, a woman named Dam'a·ris, and others with them.

MINISTERING AT CORINTH

18 After these things Paul departed from Athens and went to Corinth.

2 And he found a certain Jew named A·qui'la, born in Pon'tus, who had recently come from Italy with his wife Pri·scil'la (because Clau'di·us had commanded all the Jews to depart from Rome); and he came to them.

3 So, because he was of the same trade, he stayed with them and worked; for by occupation they were tentmakers.

4 And he reasoned in the synagogue every Sabbath, and persuaded both Jews and Greeks.

5 When Silas and Timothy had come from Mac·e·dō'ni·a, Paul was compelled by the Spirit, and testified to the Jews *that* Jesus *is* the Christ.

6 But when they opposed him and blasphemed, he shook *his* garments and said to them, "Your blood *be* upon your *own* heads; I *am* clean. From now on I will go to the Gentiles."

7 And he departed from there and entered the house of a certain *man* named Jus'tus,[a] *one* who worshiped God, whose house was next door to the synagogue.

8 Then Cris'pus, the ruler of the synagogue, believed on the Lord with all his household. And many of the Corinthians, hearing, believed and were baptized.

9 Now the Lord spoke to Paul in the night by a vision, "Do not be afraid, but speak, and do not keep silent;

10 "for I am with you, and no one will attack you to hurt you; for I have many people in this city."

11 And he continued *there* a year and six months, teaching the word of God among them.

12 When Gal'li·ō was proconsul of A·chā'i·a, the Jews with one accord rose up against Paul and brought him to the judgment seat,

17:26 [a]NU-Text omits *blood*.   18:7 [a]NU-Text reads *Titius Justus*.

13 saying, "This *fellow* persuades men to worship God contrary to the law."

14 And when Paul was about to open *his* mouth, Gal'li·ō said to the Jews, "If it were a matter of wrongdoing or wicked crimes, O Jews, there would be reason why I should bear with you.

15 "But if it is a question of words and names and your own law, look *to it* yourselves; for I do not want to be a judge of such *matters.*"

16 And he drove them from the judgment seat.

17 Then all the Greeks*a* took Sos'the·nēs, the ruler of the synagogue, and beat *him* before the judgment seat. But Gal'li·ō took no notice of these things.

PAUL RETURNS TO ANTIOCH

18 So Paul still remained a good while. Then he took leave of the brethren and sailed for Syria, and Pri·scil'la and A·qui'la *were* with him. He had *his* hair cut off at Cen'chrē·a, for he had taken a vow.

19 And he came to Eph'e·sus, and left them there; but he himself entered the synagogue and reasoned with the Jews.

20 When they asked *him* to stay a longer time with them, he did not consent,

21 but took leave of them, saying, "I must by all means keep this coming feast in Jerusalem;*a* but I will return again to you, God willing." And he sailed from Eph'e·sus.

22 And when he had landed at Caes·a·rē'a, and gone up and greeted the church, he went down to An'ti·och.

23 After he had spent some time *there,* he departed and went over the region of Galatia and Phryg'i·a in order, strengthening all the disciples.

MINISTRY OF APOLLOS

24 Now a certain Jew named A·pol'los, born at Alexandria, an eloquent man *and* mighty in the Scriptures, came to Eph'e·sus.

25 This man had been instructed in the way of the Lord; and being fervent in spirit, he spoke and taught accurately the things of the Lord, though he knew only the baptism of John.

26 So he began to speak boldly in the synagogue. When A·qui'la and Pri·scil'la heard him, they took him aside and explained to him the way of God more accurately.

27 And when he desired to cross to A·chā'i·a, the brethren wrote, exhorting the disciples to receive him; and when he arrived, he greatly helped those who had believed through grace;

28 for he vigorously refuted the Jews publicly, showing from the Scriptures that Jesus is the Christ.

PAUL AT EPHESUS

19 And it happened, while A·pol'los was at Corinth, that Paul, having passed through the upper regions, came to Eph'e·sus. And finding some disciples

2 he said to them, "Did you receive the Holy Spirit when you believed?" So they said to him, "We have not so much as heard whether there is a Holy Spirit."

3 And he said to them, "Into what then were you baptized?" So they said, "Into John's baptism."

4 Then Paul said, "John indeed baptized with a baptism of repentance, saying to the people that they should believe on Him who would

18:17 *a*NU-Text reads *they all.*   18:21 *a*NU-Text omits *I must* through *Jerusalem.*

come after him, that is, on Christ Jesus."

5 When they heard *this,* they were baptized in the name of the Lord Jesus.

6 And when Paul had laid hands on them, the Holy Spirit came upon them, and they spoke with tongues and prophesied.

7 Now the men were about twelve in all.

8 And he went into the synagogue and spoke boldly for three months, reasoning and persuading concerning the things of the kingdom of God.

9 But when some were hardened and did not believe, but spoke evil of the Way before the multitude, he departed from them and withdrew the disciples, reasoning daily in the school of Tȳ·ran′nus.

10 And this continued for two years, so that all who dwelt in Asia heard the word of the Lord Jesus, both Jews and Greeks.

MIRACLES GLORIFY CHRIST

11 Now God worked unusual miracles by the hands of Paul,

12 so that even handkerchiefs or aprons were brought from his body to the sick, and the diseases left them and the evil spirits went out of them.

13 Then some of the itinerant Jewish exorcists took it upon themselves to call the name of the Lord Jesus over those who had evil spirits, saying, "Wea exorcise you by the Jesus whom Paul preaches."

14 Also there were seven sons of Scē′va, a Jewish chief priest, who did so.

15 And the evil spirit answered and said, "Jesus I know, and Paul I know; but who are you?"

16 Then the man in whom the evil spirit was leaped on them, overpowereda them, and prevailed against

them,b so that they fled out of that house naked and wounded.

17 This became known both to all Jews and Greeks dwelling in Eph′e·sus; and fear fell on them all, and the name of the Lord Jesus was magnified.

18 And many who had believed came confessing and telling their deeds.

19 Also, many of those who had practiced magic brought their books together and burned *them* in the sight of all. And they counted up the value of them, and *it* totaled fifty thousand *pieces* of silver.

20 So the word of the Lord grew mightily and prevailed.

THE RIOT AT EPHESUS

21 When these things were accomplished, Paul purposed in the Spirit, when he had passed through Mace·dō′ni·a and A·chā′i·a, to go to Jerusalem, saying, "After I have been there, I must also see Rome."

22 So he sent into Mac·e·dō′ni·a two of those who ministered to him, Timothy and Ē·ras′tus, but he himself stayed in Asia for a time.

23 And about that time there arose a great commotion about the Way.

24 For a certain man named De·mē′tri·us, a silversmith, who made silver shrines of Diana,a brought no small profit to the craftsmen.

25 He called them together with the workers of similar occupation, and said: "Men, you know that we have our prosperity by this trade.

26 "Moreover you see and hear that not only at Eph′e·sus, but throughout almost all Asia, this Paul has persuaded and turned away many people, saying that they are not gods which are made with hands.

19:13 aNU-Text reads *I.*   19:16 aM-Text reads *and they overpowered.* bNU-Text reads *both of them.*   19:24 aGreek *Artemis*

27 "So not only is this trade of ours in danger of falling into disrepute, but also the temple of the great goddess Diana may be despised and her magnificence destroyed,*a* whom all Asia and the world worship."

28 Now when they heard *this,* they were full of wrath and cried out, saying, "Great *is* Diana of the E·phē'-si·ans!"

29 So the whole city was filled with confusion, and rushed into the theater with one accord, having seized Gā'i·us and Ar·is·tar'chus, Mac·e-dō'ni·ans, Paul's travel companions.

30 And when Paul wanted to go in to the people, the disciples would not allow him.

31 Then some of the officials of Asia, who were his friends, sent to him pleading that he would not venture into the theater.

32 Some therefore cried one thing and some another, for the assembly was confused, and most of them did not know why they had come together.

33 And they drew Alexander out of the multitude, the Jews putting him forward. And Alexander motioned with his hand, and wanted to make his defense to the people.

34 But when they found out that he was a Jew, all with one voice cried out for about two hours, "Great *is* Diana of the E·phē'si·ans!"

35 And when the city clerk had quieted the crowd, he said: "Men of Eph'e·sus, what man is there who does not know that the city of the E·phē'si·ans is temple guardian of the great goddess Diana, and of the *image* which fell down from Zeūs?

36 "Therefore, since these things cannot be denied, you ought to be quiet and do nothing rashly.

37 "For you have brought these men here who are neither robbers of temples nor blasphemers of your*a* goddess.

38 "Therefore, if De·mē'tri·us and his fellow craftsmen have a case against anyone, the courts are open and there are proconsuls. Let them bring charges against one another.

39 "But if you have any other inquiry to make, it shall be determined in the lawful assembly.

40 "For we are in danger of being called in question for today's uproar, there being no reason which we may give to account for this disorderly gathering."

41 And when he had said these things, he dismissed the assembly.

JOURNEYS IN GREECE

20 After the uproar had ceased, Paul called the disciples to *himself,* embraced *them,* and departed to go to Mac·e·dō'ni·a.

2 Now when he had gone over that region and encouraged them with many words, he came to Greece

3 and stayed three months. And when the Jews plotted against him as he was about to sail to Syria, he decided to return through Mac·e-dō'ni·a.

4 And Sop'a·ter of Be·rē'a accompanied him to Asia—also Ar·is·tar'chus and Secundus of the Thes·sa·lō'-ni·ans, and Gā'i·us of Der'bē, and Timothy, and Tych'i·cus and Troph'-i·mus of Asia.

5 These men, going ahead, waited for us at Trō'as.

6 But we sailed away from Phi-lip'pī after the Days of Unleavened Bread, and in five days joined them at Trō'as, where we stayed seven days.

19:27 *a*NU-Text reads *she be deposed from her magnificence.*   19:37 *a*NU-Text reads *our.*

MINISTERING AT TROAS

7 Now on the first *day* of the week, when the disciples came together to break bread, Paul, ready to depart the next day, spoke to them and continued his message until midnight.
8 There were many lamps in the upper room where they*a* were gathered together.
9 And in a window sat a certain young man named Eū'ty·chus, who was sinking into a deep sleep. He was overcome by sleep; and as Paul continued speaking, he fell down from the third story and was taken up dead.
10 But Paul went down, fell on him, and embracing *him* said, "Do not trouble yourselves, for his life is in him."
11 Now when he had come up, had broken bread and eaten, and talked a long while, even till daybreak, he departed.
12 And they brought the young man in alive, and they were not a little comforted.

FROM TROAS TO MILETUS

13 Then we went ahead to the ship and sailed to As'sos, there intending to take Paul on board; for so he had given orders, intending himself to go on foot.
14 And when he met us at As'sos, we took him on board and came to Mit·y·lē'nē.
15 We sailed from there, and the next *day* came opposite Chī'os. The following *day* we arrived at Sā'mos and stayed at Trō·gyl'li·um. The next *day* we came to Mī·lē'tus.
16 For Paul had decided to sail past Eph'e·sus, so that he would not have to spend time in Asia; for he was hurrying to be at Jerusalem, if possible, on the Day of Pentecost.

THE EPHESIAN ELDERS EXHORTED

17 From Mī·lē'tus he sent to Eph'-e·sus and called for the elders of the church.
18 And when they had come to him, he said to them: "You know, from the first day that I came to Asia, in what manner I always lived among you,
19 "serving the Lord with all humility, with many tears and trials which happened to me by the plotting of the Jews;
20 "how I kept back nothing that was helpful, but proclaimed it to you, and taught you publicly and from house to house,
21 "testifying to Jews, and also to Greeks, repentance toward God and faith toward our Lord Jesus Christ.
22 "And see, now I go bound in the spirit to Jerusalem, not knowing the things that will happen to me there,
23 "except that the Holy Spirit testifies in every city, saying that chains and tribulations await me.
24 "But none of these things move me; nor do I count my life dear to myself,*a* so that I may finish my race with joy, and the ministry which I received from the Lord Jesus, to testify to the gospel of the grace of God.
25 "And indeed, now I know that you all, among whom I have gone preaching the kingdom of God, will see my face no more.
26 "Therefore I testify to you this day that I *am* innocent of the blood of all *men*.
27 "For I have not shunned to declare to you the whole counsel of God.
28 "Therefore take heed to yourselves and to all the flock, among which the Holy Spirit has made you overseers, to shepherd the church of

20:8 *a*NU-Text and M-Text read *we*.
20:24 *a*NU-Text reads *But I do not count my life of any value or dear to myself*.

God*a* which He purchased with His own blood.

29 "For I know this, that after my departure savage wolves will come in among you, not sparing the flock.

30 "Also from among yourselves men will rise up, speaking perverse things, to draw away the disciples after themselves.

31 "Therefore watch, and remember that for three years I did not cease to warn everyone night and day with tears.

32 "So now, brethren, I commend you to God and to the word of His grace, which is able to build you up and give you an inheritance among all those who are sanctified.

33 "I have coveted no one's silver or gold or apparel.

34 "Yes,*a* you yourselves know that these hands have provided for my necessities, and for those who were with me.

35 "I have shown you in every way, by laboring like this, that you must support the weak. And remember the words of the Lord Jesus, that He said, 'It is more blessed to give than to receive.' "

36 And when he had said these things, he knelt down and prayed with them all.

37 Then they all wept freely, and fell on Paul's neck and kissed him,

38 sorrowing most of all for the words which he spoke, that they would see his face no more. And they accompanied him to the ship.

WARNINGS ON THE JOURNEY TO JERUSALEM

21 Now it came to pass, that when we had departed from them and set sail, running a straight course we came to Cōs, the following *day* to Rhōdes, and from there to Pat′a·ra.

20:28 *a*M-Text reads *of the Lord and God.*
20:34 *a*NU-Text and M-Text omit *Yes.*

2 And finding a ship sailing over to Phoe·ni′ci·a, we went aboard and set sail.

3 When we had sighted Cyprus, we passed it on the left, sailed to Syria, and landed at Tȳre; for there the ship was to unload her cargo.

4 And finding disciples,*a* we stayed there seven days. They told Paul through the Spirit not to go up to Jerusalem.

5 When we had come to the end of those days, we departed and went on our way; and they all accompanied us, with wives and children, till *we were* out of the city. And we knelt down on the shore and prayed.

6 When we had taken our leave of one another, we boarded the ship, and they returned home.

7 And when we had finished *our* voyage from Tȳre, we came to Ptol·e·mā′is, greeted the brethren, and stayed with them one day.

8 On the next *day* we who were Paul's companions*a* departed and came to Caes·a·rē′a, and entered the house of Philip the evangelist, who was *one* of the seven, and stayed with him.

9 Now this man had four virgin daughters who prophesied.

10 And as we stayed many days, a certain prophet named Ag′a·bus came down from Judea.

11 When he had come to us, he took Paul's belt, bound his *own* hands and feet, and said, "Thus says the Holy Spirit, 'So shall the Jews at Jerusalem bind the man who owns this belt, and deliver *him* into the hands of the Gentiles.' "

12 Now when we heard these things, both we and those from that place pleaded with him not to go up to Jerusalem.

13 Then Paul answered, "What do you mean by weeping and breaking my heart? For I am ready not only to be bound, but also to die at Jerusalem for the name of the Lord Jesus."

14 So when he would not be persuaded, we ceased, saying, "The will of the Lord be done."

PAUL URGED TO MAKE PEACE

15 And after those days we packed and went up to Jerusalem.

16 Also some of the disciples from Caes·a·rē′a went with us and brought with them a certain Mnā′son of Cyprus, an early disciple, with whom we were to lodge.

17 And when we had come to Jerusalem, the brethren received us gladly.

18 On the following *day* Paul went in with us to James, and all the elders were present.

19 When he had greeted them, he told in detail those things which God had done among the Gentiles through his ministry.

20 And when they heard *it,* they glorified the Lord. And they said to him, "You see, brother, how many myriads of Jews there are who have believed, and they are all zealous for the law;

21 "but they have been informed about you that you teach all the Jews who are among the Gentiles to forsake Moses, saying that they ought not to circumcise *their* children nor to walk according to the customs.

22 "What then? The assembly must certainly meet, for they will hear that you have come.*a*

23 "Therefore do what we tell you: We have four men who have taken a vow.

24 "Take them and be purified with them, and pay their expenses so that they may shave *their* heads, and that

21:4 *a*NU-Text reads *the disciples.*   21:8 *a*NU-Text omits *who were Paul's companions.*
21:22 *a*NU-Text reads *What then is to be done? They will certainly.*

all may know that those things of which they were informed concerning you are nothing, but *that* you yourself also walk orderly and keep the law.

25 "But concerning the Gentiles who believe, we have written *and* decided that they should observe no such thing,a except that they should keep themselves from *things* offered to idols, from blood, from things strangled, and from sexual immorality."

ARRESTED IN THE TEMPLE

26 Then Paul took the men, and the next day, having been purified with them, entered the temple to announce the expiration of the days of purification, at which time an offering should be made for each one of them.

27 Now when the seven days were almost ended, the Jews from Asia, seeing him in the temple, stirred up the whole crowd and laid hands on him,

28 crying out, "Men of Israel, help! This is the man who teaches all *men* everywhere against the people, the law, and this place; and furthermore he also brought Greeks into the temple and has defiled this holy place."

29 (For they had previouslya seen Troph′i·mus the E·phe′si·an with him in the city, whom they supposed that Paul had brought into the temple.)

30 And all the city was disturbed; and the people ran together, seized Paul, and dragged him out of the temple; and immediately the doors were shut.

31 Now as they were seeking to kill him, news came to the commander of the garrison that all Jerusalem was in an uproar.

32 He immediately took soldiers and centurions, and ran down to them.

And when they saw the commander and the soldiers, they stopped beating Paul.

33 Then the commander came near and took him, and commanded *him* to be bound with two chains; and he asked who he was and what he had done.

34 And some among the multitude cried one thing and some another. So when he could not ascertain the truth because of the tumult, he commanded him to be taken into the barracks.

35 When he reached the stairs, he had to be carried by the soldiers because of the violence of the mob.

36 For the multitude of the people followed after, crying out, "Away with him!"

ADDRESSING THE JERUSALEM MOB

37 Then as Paul was about to be led into the barracks, he said to the commander, "May I speak to you?" He replied, "Can you speak Greek?

38 "Are you not the Egyptian who some time ago stirred up a rebellion and led the four thousand assassins out into the wilderness?"

39 But Paul said, "I am a Jew from Tar′sus, in Ci·li′ci·a, a citizen of no mean city; and I implore you, permit me to speak to the people."

40 So when he had given him permission, Paul stood on the stairs and motioned with his hand to the people. And when there was a great silence, he spoke to *them* in the Hebrew language, saying,

22 "Brethren and fathers, hear my defense before you now."

2 And when they heard that he spoke to them in the Hebrew lan-

21:25 aNU-Text omits *that they should observe no such thing, except.* 21:29 aM-Text omits *previously.*

*J*esus gives us a new life and makes us a new creation.

———

2 Corinthians 5:17

When we serve one another, we also serve the Lord.

Ephesians 6:7

*R*ejoice always in the Lord. Rejoice!

———

Philippians 4:4

*T*here will be no wheelchairs in heaven.

Revelation 21:4

guage, they kept all the more silent. Then he said:

3 "I am indeed a Jew, born in Tar'-sus of Ci·li'ci·a, but brought up in this city at the feet of Ga·ma'li·el, taught according to the strictness of our fathers' law, and was zealous toward God as you all are today.

4 "I persecuted this Way to the death, binding and delivering into prisons both men and women,

5 "as also the high priest bears me witness, and all the council of the elders, from whom I also received letters to the brethren, and went to Damascus to bring in chains even those who were there to Jerusalem to be punished.

6 "Now it happened, as I journeyed and came near Damascus at about noon, suddenly a great light from heaven shone around me.

7 "And I fell to the ground and heard a voice saying to me, 'Saul, Saul, why are you persecuting Me?'

8 "So I answered, 'Who are You, Lord?' And He said to me, 'I am Jesus of Nazareth, whom you are persecuting.'

9 "And those who were with me indeed saw the light and were afraid,a but they did not hear the voice of Him who spoke to me.

10 "So I said, 'What shall I do, Lord?' And the Lord said to me, 'Arise and go into Damascus, and there you will be told all things which are appointed for you to do.'

11 "And since I could not see for the glory of that light, being led by the hand of those who were with me, I came into Damascus.

12 "Then a certain An·a·ni'as, a devout man according to the law, having a good testimony with all the Jews who dwelt there,

13 "came to me; and he stood and said to me, 'Brother Saul, receive

your sight.' And at that same hour I looked up at him.

14 "Then he said, 'The God of our fathers has chosen you that you should know His will, and see the Just One, and hear the voice of His mouth.

15 'For you will be His witness to all men of what you have seen and heard.

16 'And now why are you waiting? Arise and be baptized, and wash away your sins, calling on the name of the Lord.'

17 "Now it happened, when I returned to Jerusalem and was praying in the temple, that I was in a trance

18 "and saw Him saying to me, 'Make haste and get out of Jerusalem quickly, for they will not receive your testimony concerning Me.'

19 "So I said, 'Lord, they know that in every synagogue I imprisoned and beat those who believe on You.

20 'And when the blood of Your martyr Stephen was shed, I also was standing by consenting to his death,a and guarding the clothes of those who were killing him.'

21 "Then He said to me, 'Depart, for I will send you far from here to the Gentiles.'"

PAUL'S ROMAN CITIZENSHIP

22 And they listened to him until this word, and *then* they raised their voices and said, "Away with such a *fellow* from the earth, for he is not fit to live!"

23 Then, as they cried out and tore off *their* clothes and threw dust into the air,

24 the commander ordered him to be brought into the barracks, and said that he should be examined under

22:9 aNU-Text omits *and were afraid.*
22:20 aNU-Text omits *to his death.*

scourging, so that he might know why they shouted so against him.

25 And as they bound him with thongs, Paul said to the centurion who stood by, "Is it lawful for you to scourge a man who is a Roman, and uncondemned?"

26 When the centurion heard *that,* he went and told the commander, saying, "Take care what you do, for this man is a Roman."

27 Then the commander came and said to him, "Tell me, are you a Roman?" He said, "Yes."

28 The commander answered, "With a large sum I obtained this citizenship." And Paul said, "But I was born *a citizen.*"

29 Then immediately those who were about to examine him withdrew from him; and the commander was also afraid after he found out that he was a Roman, and because he had bound him.

The Sanhedrin Divided

30 The next day, because he wanted to know for certain why he was accused by the Jews, he released him from *his* bonds, and commanded the chief priests and all their council to appear, and brought Paul down and set him before them.

23 Then Paul, looking earnestly at the council, said, "Men *and* brethren, I have lived in all good conscience before God until this day."

2 And the high priest An·a·nī′as commanded those who stood by him to strike him on the mouth.

3 Then Paul said to him, "God will strike you, *you* whitewashed wall! For you sit to judge me according to the law, and do you command me to be struck contrary to the law?"

4 And those who stood by said, "Do you revile God's high priest?"

5 Then Paul said, "I did not know, brethren, that he was the high priest; for it is written, *'You shall not speak evil of a ruler of your people.'* "a

6 But when Paul perceived that one part were Sad′du·cees and the other Phar′i·sees, he cried out in the council, "Men *and* brethren, I am a Phar′i·see, the son of a Phar′i·see; concerning the hope and resurrection of the dead I am being judged!"

7 And when he had said this, a dissension arose between the Phar′i·sees and the Sad′du·cees; and the assembly was divided.

8 For Sad′du·cees say that there is no resurrection—and no angel or spirit; but the Phar′i·sees confess both.

9 Then there arose a loud outcry. And the scribes of the Phar′i·sees' party arose and protested, saying, "We find no evil in this man; but if a spirit or an angel has spoken to him, let us not fight against God."a

10 Now when there arose a great dissension, the commander, fearing lest Paul might be pulled to pieces by them, commanded the soldiers to go down and take him by force from among them, and bring *him* into the barracks.

The Plot Against Paul

11 But the following night the Lord stood by him and said, "Be of good cheer, Paul; for as you have testified for Me in Jerusalem, so you must also bear witness at Rome."

12 And when it was day, some of the Jews banded together and bound themselves under an oath, saying

23:5 aExodus 22:28   23:9 aNU-Text omits last clause and reads *what if a spirit or an angel has spoken to him?*

that they would neither eat nor drink till they had killed Paul.

13 Now there were more than forty who had formed this conspiracy.

14 They came to the chief priests and elders, and said, "We have bound ourselves under a great oath that we will eat nothing until we have killed Paul.

15 "Now you, therefore, together with the council, suggest to the commander that he be brought down to you tomorrow,ᵃ as though you were going to make further inquiries concerning him; but we are ready to kill him before he comes near."

16 So when Paul's sister's son heard of their ambush, he went and entered the barracks and told Paul.

17 Then Paul called one of the centurions to *him* and said, "Take this young man to the commander, for he has something to tell him."

18 So he took him and brought *him* to the commander and said, "Paul the prisoner called me to *him* and asked *me* to bring this young man to you. He has something to say to you."

19 Then the commander took him by the hand, went aside, and asked privately, "What is it that you have to tell me?"

20 And he said, "The Jews have agreed to ask that you bring Paul down to the council tomorrow, as though they were going to inquire more fully about him.

21 "But do not yield to them, for more than forty of them lie in wait for him, men who have bound themselves by an oath that they will neither eat nor drink till they have killed him; and now they are ready, waiting for the promise from you."

22 So the commander let the young man depart, and commanded *him*, "Tell no one that you have revealed these things to me."

SENT TO FELIX

23 And he called for two centurions, saying, "Prepare two hundred soldiers, seventy horsemen, and two hundred spearmen to go to Caes·a·rē′a at the third hour of the night;

24 "and provide mounts to set Paul on, and bring *him* safely to Felix the governor."

25 He wrote a letter in the following manner:

26 Clau′di·us Lys′i·as,

To the most excellent governor Felix:

Greetings.

27 This man was seized by the Jews and was about to be killed by them. Coming with the troops I rescued him, having learned that he was a Roman.

28 And when I wanted to know the reason they accused him, I brought him before their council.

29 I found out that he was accused concerning questions of their law, but had nothing charged against him deserving of death or chains.

30 And when it was told me that the Jews lay in wait for the man,ᵃ I sent him immediately to you, and also commanded his accusers to state before you the charges against him.

Farewell.

31 Then the soldiers, as they were commanded, took Paul and brought *him* by night to An·tip′a·tris.

32 The next day they left the horsemen to go on with him, and returned to the barracks.

23:15 ᵃNU-Text omits *tomorrow.*   23:30 ᵃNU-Text reads *there would be a plot against the man.*

33 When they came to Caes·a·rē′a and had delivered the letter to the governor, they also presented Paul to him.

34 And when the governor had read *it*, he asked what province he was from. And when he understood that *he was* from Ci·li′ci·a,

35 he said, "I will hear you when your accusers also have come." And he commanded him to be kept in Her′od's Prae·tō′ri·um.

ACCUSED OF SEDITION

24 Now after five days An·a·nī′as the high priest came down with the elders and a certain orator *named* Ter·tul′lus. These gave evidence to the governor against Paul.

2 And when he was called upon, Ter·tul′lus began his accusation, saying: "Seeing that through you we enjoy great peace, and prosperity is being brought to this nation by your foresight,

3 "we accept *it* always and in all places, most noble Felix, with all thankfulness.

4 "Nevertheless, not to be tedious to you any further, I beg you to hear, by your courtesy, a few words from us.

5 "For we have found this man a plague, a creator of dissension among all the Jews throughout the world, and a ringleader of the sect of the Naz′a·rēnes.

6 "He even tried to profane the temple, and we seized him,*a* and wanted to judge him according to our law.

7 "But the commander Lys′i·as came by and with great violence took *him* out of our hands,

8 "commanding his accusers to come to you. By examining him yourself you may ascertain all these things of which we accuse him."

9 And the Jews also assented,*a*

maintaining that these things were so.

THE DEFENSE BEFORE FELIX

10 Then Paul, after the governor had nodded to him to speak, answered: "Inasmuch as I know that you have been for many years a judge of this nation, I do the more cheerfully answer for myself,

11 "because you may ascertain that it is no more than twelve days since I went up to Jerusalem to worship.

12 "And they neither found me in the temple disputing with anyone nor inciting the crowd, either in the synagogues or in the city.

13 "Nor can they prove the things of which they now accuse me.

14 "But this I confess to you, that according to the Way which they call a sect, so I worship the God of my fathers, believing all things which are written in the Law and in the Prophets.

15 "I have hope in God, which they themselves also accept, that there will be a resurrection of *the* dead,*a* both of *the* just and *the* unjust.

16 "This *being* so, I myself always strive to have a conscience without offense toward God and men.

17 "Now after many years I came to bring alms and offerings to my nation,

18 "in the midst of which some Jews from Asia found me purified in the temple, neither with a mob nor with tumult.

19 "They ought to have been here before you to object if they had anything against me.

24:6 *a*NU-Text ends the sentence here and omits the rest of verse 6, all of verse 7, and the first clause of verse 8.   24:9 *a*NU-Text and M-Text read *joined the attack.*   24:15 *a*NU-Text omits *of the dead.*

20 "Or else let those who are *here* themselves say if they found any wrongdoing*a* in me while I stood before the council,

21 "unless *it is* for this one statement which I cried out, standing among them, 'Concerning the resurrection of the dead I am being judged by you this day.' "

FELIX PROCRASTINATES

22 But when Felix heard these things, having more accurate knowledge of *the* Way, he adjourned the proceedings and said, "When Lys′i·as the commander comes down, I will make a decision on your case."

23 So he commanded the centurion to keep Paul and to let *him* have liberty, and told him not to forbid any of his friends to provide for or visit him.

24 And after some days, when Felix came with his wife Drū·sil′la, who was Jewish, he sent for Paul and heard him concerning the faith in Christ.

25 Now as he reasoned about righteousness, self-control, and the judgment to come, Felix was afraid and answered, "Go away for now; when I have a convenient time I will call for you."

26 Meanwhile he also hoped that money would be given him by Paul, that he might release him.*a* Therefore he sent for him more often and conversed with him.

27 But after two years Por′ci·us Fes′tus succeeded Felix; and Felix, wanting to do the Jews a favor, left Paul bound.

PAUL APPEALS TO CAESAR

25 Now when Fes′tus had come to the province, after three days he went up from Caes·a·rē′a to Jerusalem.

2   Then the high priest*a* and the chief men of the Jews informed him against Paul; and they petitioned him,

3   asking a favor against him, that he would summon him to Jerusalem—while *they* lay in ambush along the road to kill him.

4   But Fes′tus answered that Paul should be kept at Caes·a·rē′a, and that he himself was going *there* shortly.

5   "Therefore," he said, "let those who have authority among you go down with *me* and accuse this man, to see if there is any fault in him."

6   And when he had remained among them more than ten days, he went down to Caes·a·rē′a. And the next day, sitting on the judgment seat, he commanded Paul to be brought.

7   When he had come, the Jews who had come down from Jerusalem stood about and laid many serious complaints against Paul, which they could not prove,

8   while he answered for himself, "Neither against the law of the Jews, nor against the temple, nor against Caesar have I offended in anything at all."

9   But Fes′tus, wanting to do the Jews a favor, answered Paul and said, "Are you willing to go up to Jerusalem and there be judged before me concerning these things?"

10 So Paul said, "I stand at Caesar's judgment seat, where I ought to be judged. To the Jews I have done no wrong, as you very well know.

11 "For if I am an offender, or have

24:20 *a*NU-Text and M-Text read *say what wrongdoing they found.*   24:26 *a*NU-Text omits *that he might release him.*   25:2 *a*NU-Text reads *chief priests.*

committed anything deserving of death, I do not object to dying; but if there is nothing in these things of which these men accuse me, no one can deliver me to them. I appeal to Caesar."

12 Then Fes′tus, when he had conferred with the council, answered, "You have appealed to Caesar? To Caesar you shall go!"

PAUL BEFORE AGRIPPA

13 And after some days King A·grip′pa and Ber·nī′cē came to Caes·a·rē′a to greet Fes′tus.

14 When they had been there many days, Fes′tus laid Paul's case before the king, saying: "There is a certain man left a prisoner by Felix,

15 "about whom the chief priests and the elders of the Jews informed me, when I was in Jerusalem, asking for a judgment against him.

16 "To them I answered, 'It is not the custom of the Romans to deliver any man to destruction[a] before the accused meets the accusers face to face, and has opportunity to answer for himself concerning the charge against him.'

17 "Therefore when they had come together, without any delay, the next day I sat on the judgment seat and commanded the man to be brought in.

18 "When the accusers stood up, they brought no accusation against him of such things as I supposed,

19 "but had some questions against him about their own religion and about a certain Jesus, who had died, whom Paul affirmed to be alive.

20 "And because I was uncertain of such questions, I asked whether he was willing to go to Jerusalem and there be judged concerning these matters.

21 "But when Paul appealed to be reserved for the decision of Au·gus′tus, I commanded him to be kept till I could send him to Caesar."

22 Then A·grip′pa said to Fes′tus, "I also would like to hear the man myself." "Tomorrow," he said, "you shall hear him."

23 So the next day, when A·grip′pa and Ber·nī′cē had come with great pomp, and had entered the auditorium with the commanders and the prominent men of the city, at Fes′tus' command Paul was brought in.

24 And Fes′tus said: "King A·grip′pa and all the men who are here present with us, you see this man about whom the whole assembly of the Jews petitioned me, both at Jerusalem and here, crying out that he was not fit to live any longer.

25 "But when I found that he had committed nothing deserving of death, and that he himself had appealed to Au·gus′tus, I decided to send him.

26 "I have nothing certain to write to my lord concerning him. Therefore I have brought him out before you, and especially before you, King A·grip′pa, so that after the examination has taken place I may have something to write.

27 "For it seems to me unreasonable to send a prisoner and not to specify the charges against him."

PAUL'S EARLY LIFE

26 Then A·grip′pa said to Paul, "You are permitted to speak for yourself." So Paul stretched out his hand and answered for himself:

2 "I think myself happy, King A·grip′pa, because today I shall an-

25:16 [a]NU-Text omits to destruction, although it is implied.

swer for myself before you concerning all the things of which I am accused by the Jews,

3 "especially because you are expert in all customs and questions which have to do with the Jews. Therefore I beg you to hear me patiently.

4 "My manner of life from my youth, which was spent from the beginning among my own nation at Jerusalem, all the Jews know.

5 "They knew me from the first, if they were willing to testify, that according to the strictest sect of our religion I lived a Phar′i·see.

6 "And now I stand and am judged for the hope of the promise made by God to our fathers.

7 "To this *promise* our twelve tribes, earnestly serving *God* night and day, hope to attain. For this hope's sake, King A·grip′pa, I am accused by the Jews.

8 "Why should it be thought incredible by you that God raises the dead?

9 "Indeed, I myself thought I must do many things contrary to the name of Jesus of Nazareth.

10 "This I also did in Jerusalem, and many of the saints I shut up in prison, having received authority from the chief priests; and when they were put to death, I cast my vote against *them*.

11 "And I punished them often in every synagogue and compelled *them* to blaspheme; and being exceedingly enraged against them, I persecuted *them* even to foreign cities.

PAUL RECOUNTS HIS CONVERSION

12 "While thus occupied, as I journeyed to Damascus with authority and commission from the chief priests,

13 "at midday, O king, along the road I saw a light from heaven, brighter than the sun, shining around me and those who journeyed with me.

14 "And when we all had fallen to the ground, I heard a voice speaking to me and saying in the Hebrew language, 'Saul, Saul, why are you persecuting Me? *It is* hard for you to kick against the goads.'

15 "So I said, 'Who are You, Lord?' And He said, 'I am Jesus, whom you are persecuting.

16 'But rise and stand on your feet; for I have appeared to you for this purpose, to make you a minister and a witness both of the things which you have seen and of the things which I will yet reveal to you.

17 'I will deliver you from the *Jewish* people, as well as *from* the Gentiles, to whom I now*a* send you,

18 'to open their eyes, *in order* to turn *them* from darkness to light, and *from* the power of Satan to God, that they may receive forgiveness of sins and an inheritance among those who are sanctified by faith in Me.'

PAUL'S POST-CONVERSION LIFE

19 "Therefore, King A·grip′pa, I was not disobedient to the heavenly vision,

20 "but declared first to those in Damascus and in Jerusalem, and throughout all the region of Judea, and *then* to the Gentiles, that they should repent, turn to God, and do works befitting repentance.

21 "For these reasons the Jews seized me in the temple and tried to kill *me*.

22 "Therefore, having obtained help from God, to this day I stand, witnessing both to small and great,

26:17 *a*NU-Text and M-Text omit *now.*

saying no other things than those which the prophets and Moses said would come—

23 "that the Christ would suffer, that He would be the first to rise from the dead, and would proclaim light to the *Jewish* people and to the Gentiles."

AGRIPPA PARRIES PAUL'S CHALLENGE

24 Now as he thus made his defense, Fes'tus said with a loud voice, "Paul, you are beside yourself! Much learning is driving you mad!"
25 But he said, "I am not mad, most noble Fes'tus, but speak the words of truth and reason.
26 "For the king, before whom I also speak freely, knows these things; for I am convinced that none of these things escapes his attention, since this thing was not done in a corner.
27 "King A·grip'pa, do you believe the prophets? I know that you do believe."
28 Then A·grip'pa said to Paul, "You almost persuade me to become a Christian."
29 And Paul said, "I would to God that not only you, but also all who hear me today, might become both almost and altogether such as I am, except for these chains."
30 When he had said these things, the king stood up, as well as the governor and Ber·ni'cē and those who sat with them;
31 and when they had gone aside, they talked among themselves, saying, "This man is doing nothing deserving of death or chains."
32 Then A·grip'pa said to Fes'tus, "This man might have been set free if he had not appealed to Caesar."

THE VOYAGE TO ROME BEGINS

Once again Paul was a prisoner for telling people about Jesus. This time some soldiers would take him to Rome to stand trial. They had to travel by ship. But the ship ran into a terrible storm. Would they make it?

27 And when it was decided that we should sail to Italy, they delivered Paul and some other prisoners to *one* named Julius, a centurion of the Au·gus'tan Regiment.
2 So, entering a ship of Ad·ra·myt'ti·um, we put to sea, meaning to sail along the coasts of Asia. Ar·is·tar'chus, a Mac·e·dō'ni·an of Thes·sa·lo·ni'ca, was with us.
3 And the next *day* we landed at Si'don. And Julius treated Paul kindly and gave *him* liberty to go to his friends and receive care.
4 When we had put to sea from there, we sailed under *the shelter of* Cyprus, because the winds were contrary.
5 And when we had sailed over the sea which is off Ci·li'ci·a and Pam·phyl'i·a, we came to Mȳ'ra, *a city* of Ly'ci·a.
6 There the centurion found an Alexandrian ship sailing to Italy, and he put us on board.
7 When we had sailed slowly many days, and arrived with difficulty off Cni'dus, the wind not permitting us to proceed, we sailed under *the shelter of* Crēte off Sal·mō'nē.
8 Passing it with difficulty, we came to a place called Fair Havens, near the city *of* La·sē'a.

PAUL'S WARNING IGNORED

9 Now when much time had been spent, and sailing was now dan-

gerous because the Fast was already over, Paul advised them,

10 saying, "Men, I perceive that this voyage will end with disaster and much loss, not only of the cargo and ship, but also our lives."

11 Nevertheless the centurion was more persuaded by the helmsman and the owner of the ship than by the things spoken by Paul.

12 And because the harbor was not suitable to winter in, the majority advised to set sail from there also, if by any means they could reach Phoenix, a harbor of Crēte opening toward the southwest and northwest, *and* winter *there.*

IN THE TEMPEST

13 When the south wind blew softly, supposing that they had obtained *their* desire, putting out to sea, they sailed close by Crēte.

14 But not long after, a tempestuous head wind arose, called Eū·roc′ly-don.*a*

15 So when the ship was caught, and could not head into the wind, we let *her* drive.

16 And running under *the shelter of* an island called Clau′da,*a* we secured the skiff with difficulty.

17 When they had taken it on board, they used cables to undergird the ship; and fearing lest they should run aground on the Syr′tis*a Sands,* they struck sail and so were driven.

18 And because we were exceedingly tempest-tossed, the next *day* they lightened the ship.

19 On the third *day* we threw the ship's tackle overboard with our own hands.

20 Now when neither sun nor stars appeared for many days, and no small tempest beat on *us,* all hope that we would be saved was finally given up.

21 But after long abstinence from food, then Paul stood in the midst of them and said, "Men, you should have listened to me, and not have sailed from Crēte and incurred this disaster and loss.

22 "And now I urge you to take heart, for there will be no loss of life among you, but only of the ship.

23 "For there stood by me this night an angel of the God to whom I belong and whom I serve,

24 "saying, 'Do not be afraid, Paul; you must be brought before Caesar; and indeed God has granted you all those who sail with you.'

25 "Therefore take heart, men, for I believe God that it will be just as it was told me.

26 "However, we must run aground on a certain island."

27 Now when the fourteenth night had come, as we were driven up and down in the Ā·dri·at′ic *Sea,* about midnight the sailors sensed that they were drawing near some land.

28 And they took soundings and found *it* to be twenty fathoms; and when they had gone a little farther, they took soundings again and found *it* to be fifteen fathoms.

29 Then, fearing lest we should run aground on the rocks, they dropped four anchors from the stern, and prayed for day to come.

30 And as the sailors were seeking to escape from the ship, when they had let down the skiff into the sea, under pretense of putting out anchors from the prow,

31 Paul said to the centurion and the soldiers, "Unless these men stay in the ship, you cannot be saved."

32 Then the soldiers cut away the ropes of the skiff and let it fall off.

27:14 *a*NU-Text reads *Euraquilon.*
27:16 *a*NU-Text reads *Cauda.*   27:17 *a*M-Text reads *Syrtes.*

33 And as day was about to dawn, Paul implored *them* all to take food, saying, "Today is the fourteenth day you have waited and continued without food, and eaten nothing.
34 "Therefore I urge you to take nourishment, for this is for your survival, since not a hair will fall from the head of any of you."
35 And when he had said these things, he took bread and gave thanks to God in the presence of them all; and when he had broken *it* he began to eat.
36 Then they were all encouraged, and also took food themselves.
37 And in all we were two hundred and seventy-six persons on the ship.
38 So when they had eaten enough, they lightened the ship and threw out the wheat into the sea.

SHIPWRECKED ON MALTA

39 When it was day, they did not recognize the land; but they observed a bay with a beach, onto which they planned to run the ship if possible.
40 And they let go the anchors and left *them* in the sea, meanwhile loosing the rudder ropes; and they hoisted the mainsail to the wind and made for shore.
41 But striking a place where two seas met, they ran the ship aground; and the prow stuck fast and remained immovable, but the stern was being broken up by the violence of the waves.
42 And the soldiers' plan was to kill the prisoners, lest any of them should swim away and escape.
43 But the centurion, wanting to save Paul, kept them from *their* purpose, and commanded that those who could swim should jump *overboard* first and get to land,
44 and the rest, some on boards and some on *parts* of the ship. And so it was that they all escaped safely to land.

PAUL'S MINISTRY ON MALTA

28 Now when they had escaped, they then found out that the island was called Malta.
2 And the natives showed us unusual kindness; for they kindled a fire and made us all welcome, because of the rain that was falling and because of the cold.
3 But when Paul had gathered a bundle of sticks and laid *them* on the fire, a viper came out because of the heat, and fastened on his hand.
4 So when the natives saw the creature hanging from his hand, they said to one another, "No doubt this man is a murderer, whom, though he has escaped the sea, yet justice does not allow to live."
5 But he shook off the creature into the fire and suffered no harm.
6 However, they were expecting that he would swell up or suddenly fall down dead. But after they had looked for a long time and saw no harm come to him, they changed their minds and said that he was a god.
7 In that region there was an estate of the leading citizen of the island, whose name was Pub′li·us, who received us and entertained us courteously for three days.
8 And it happened that the father of Pub′li·us lay sick of a fever and dysentery. Paul went in to him and prayed, and he laid his hands on him and healed him.
9 So when this was done, the rest of those on the island who had diseases also came and were healed.
10 They also honored us in many ways; and when we departed, they provided such things as were necessary.

ARRIVAL AT ROME

11 After three months we sailed in an Alexandrian ship whose figurehead was the Twin Brothers, which had wintered at the island.
12 And landing at Syracuse, we stayed three days.
13 From there we circled round and reached Rhē′gi·um. And after one day the south wind blew; and the next day we came to Pū·tē′o·lī,
14 where we found brethren, and were invited to stay with them seven days. And so we went toward Rome.

15 And from there, when the brethren heard about us, they came to meet us as far as Ap′pi·ī Forum and Three Inns. When Paul saw them, he thanked God and took courage.
16 Now when we came to Rome, the centurion delivered the prisoners to the captain of the guard; but Paul was permitted to dwell by himself with the soldier who guarded him.

PAUL'S MINISTRY AT ROME

17 And it came to pass after three days that Paul called the leaders of the Jews together. So when they had come together, he said to them: "Men *and* brethren, though I have done nothing against our people or the customs of our fathers, yet I was delivered as a prisoner from Jerusalem into the hands of the Romans,
18 "who, when they had examined me, wanted to let *me* go, because there was no cause for putting me to death.
19 "But when the Jews*a* spoke against *it,* I was compelled to appeal to Caesar, not that I had anything of which to accuse my nation.
20 "For this reason therefore I have called for you, to see *you* and speak with *you,* because for the hope of Israel I am bound with this chain."
21 Then they said to him, "We neither received letters from Judea concerning you, nor have any of the brethren who came reported or spoken any evil of you.
22 "But we desire to hear from you what you think; for concerning this sect, we know that it is spoken against everywhere."
23 So when they had appointed him a day, many came to him at *his* lodging, to whom he explained and

28:19 *a*That is, the ruling authorities

solemnly testified of the kingdom of God, persuading them concerning Jesus from both the Law of Moses and the Prophets, from morning till evening.

24 And some were persuaded by the things which were spoken, and some disbelieved.

25 So when they did not agree among themselves, they departed after Paul had said one word: "The Holy Spirit spoke rightly through Ī·sāi'ah the prophet to our[a] fathers,

26 "saying,

'Go to this people and say:
"Hearing you will hear, and shall not understand;
And seeing you will see, and not perceive;
27 For the hearts of this people have grown dull.
Their ears are hard of hearing,
And their eyes they have closed,
Lest they should see with their eyes and hear with their ears,
Lest they should understand with their hearts and turn,
So that I should heal them." '[a]

28 "Therefore let it be known to you that the salvation of God has been sent to the Gentiles, and they will hear it!"

29 And when he had said these words, the Jews departed and had a great dispute among themselves.[a]

30 Then Paul dwelt two whole years in his own rented house, and received all who came to him,

31 preaching the kingdom of God and teaching the things which concern the Lord Jesus Christ with all confidence, no one forbidding him.

28:25 [a]NU-Text reads *your.*   28:27 [a]Isaiah 6:9, 10   28:29 [a]NU-Text omits this verse.

ROMANS

GREETING

PAUL, a bondservant of Jesus Christ, called *to be* an apostle, separated to the gospel of God
2 which He promised before through His prophets in the Holy Scriptures,
3 concerning His Son Jesus Christ our Lord, who was born of the seed of David according to the flesh,
4 *and* declared *to be* the Son of God with power according to the Spirit of holiness, by the resurrection from the dead.
5 Through Him we have received grace and apostleship for obedience to the faith among all nations for His name,
6 among whom you also are the called of Jesus Christ;

7 To all who are in Rome, beloved of God, called *to be* saints:

Grace to you and peace from God our Father and the Lord Jesus Christ.

DESIRE TO VISIT ROME

8 First, I thank my God through Jesus Christ for you all, that your faith is spoken of throughout the whole world.
9 For God is my witness, whom I serve with my spirit in the gospel of His Son, that without ceasing I make mention of you always in my prayers,
10 making request if, by some means, now at last I may find a way in the will of God to come to you.
11 For I long to see you, that I may impart to you some spiritual gift, so that you may be established—
12 that is, that I may be encouraged together with you by the mutual faith both of you and me.
13 Now I do not want you to be unaware, brethren, that I often planned to come to you (but was hindered until now), that I might have some fruit among you also, just as among the other Gentiles.
14 I am a debtor both to Greeks and to barbarians, both to wise and to unwise.
15 So, as much as is in me, *I am* ready to preach the gospel to you who are in Rome also.

THE JUST LIVE BY FAITH

16 For I am not ashamed of the gospel of Christ,*a* for it is the power of God to salvation for everyone who believes, for the Jew first and also for the Greek.
17 For in it the righteousness of God is revealed from faith to faith; as it is written, *"The just shall live by faith."a*

GOD'S WRATH
ON UNRIGHTEOUSNESS

18 For the wrath of God is revealed from heaven against all ungodliness and unrighteousness of men, who suppress the truth in unrighteousness,
19 because what may be known of God is manifest in them, for God has shown *it* to them.
20 For since the creation of the world His invisible *attributes* are clearly seen, being understood by the things that are made, *even* His eternal

1:16 *a*NU-Text omits *of Christ.*
1:17 *a*Habakkuk 2:4

power and Godhead, so that they are without excuse,

21 because, although they knew God, they did not glorify *Him* as God, nor were thankful, but became futile in their thoughts, and their foolish hearts were darkened.

22 Professing to be wise, they became fools,

23 and changed the glory of the incorruptible God into an image made like corruptible man—and birds and four-footed animals and creeping things.

24 Therefore God also gave them up to uncleanness, in the lusts of their hearts, to dishonor their bodies among themselves,

25 who exchanged the truth of God for the lie, and worshiped and served the creature rather than the Creator, who is blessed forever. Amen.

26 For this reason God gave them up to vile passions. For even their women exchanged the natural use for what is against nature.

27 Likewise also the men, leaving the natural use of the woman, burned in their lust for one another, men with men committing what is shameful, and receiving in themselves the penalty of their error which was due.

28 And even as they did not like to retain God in *their* knowledge, God gave them over to a debased mind, to do those things which are not fitting;

29 being filled with all unrighteousness, sexual immorality,*a* wickedness, covetousness, maliciousness; full of envy, murder, strife, deceit, evil-mindedness; *they are* whisperers,

30 backbiters, haters of God, violent, proud, boasters, inventors of evil things, disobedient to parents,

31 undiscerning, untrustworthy, unloving, unforgiving,*a* unmerciful;

32 who, knowing the righteous judgment of God, that those who practice

such things are deserving of death, not only do the same but also approve of those who practice them.

GOD'S RIGHTEOUS JUDGMENT

2 Therefore you are inexcusable, O man, whoever you are who judge, for in whatever you judge another you condemn yourself; for you who judge practice the same things.

2 But we know that the judgment of God is according to truth against those who practice such things.

3 And do you think this, O man, you who judge those practicing such things, and doing the same, that you will escape the judgment of God?

4 Or do you despise the riches of His goodness, forbearance, and long-suffering, not knowing that the goodness of God leads you to repentance?

5 But in accordance with your hardness and your impenitent heart you are treasuring up for yourself wrath in the day of wrath and revelation of the righteous judgment of God,

6 who *"will render to each one according to his deeds"*:*a*

7 eternal life to those who by patient continuance in doing good seek for glory, honor, and immortality;

8 but to those who are self-seeking and do not obey the truth, but obey unrighteousness—indignation and wrath,

9 tribulation and anguish, on every soul of man who does evil, of the Jew first and also of the Greek;

10 but glory, honor, and peace to everyone who works what is good, to the Jew first and also to the Greek.

11 For there is no partiality with God.

1:29 *a*NU-Text omits *sexual immorality.*
1:31 *a*NU-Text omits *unforgiving.*   2:6 *a*Psalm 62:12; Proverbs 24:12

12 For as many as have sinned without law will also perish without law, and as many as have sinned in the law will be judged by the law

13 (for not the hearers of the law *are* just in the sight of God, but the doers of the law will be justified;

14 for when Gentiles, who do not have the law, by nature do the things in the law, these, although not having the law, are a law to themselves,

15 who show the work of the law written in their hearts, their conscience also bearing witness, and between themselves *their* thoughts accusing or else excusing *them*)

16 in the day when God will judge the secrets of men by Jesus Christ, according to my gospel.

THE JEWS GUILTY AS THE GENTILES

17 Indeed*a* you are called a Jew, and rest on the law, and make your boast in God,

18 and know *His* will, and approve the things that are excellent, being instructed out of the law,

19 and are confident that you yourself are a guide to the blind, a light to those who are in darkness,

20 an instructor of the foolish, a teacher of babes, having the form of knowledge and truth in the law.

21 You, therefore, who teach another, do you not teach yourself? You who preach that a man should not steal, do you steal?

22 You who say, "Do not commit adultery," do you commit adultery? You who abhor idols, do you rob temples?

23 You who make your boast in the law, do you dishonor God through breaking the law?

24 For *"the name of God is blasphemed among the Gentiles because of you,"a* as it is written.

CIRCUMCISION OF NO AVAIL

25 For circumcision is indeed profitable if you keep the law; but if you are a breaker of the law, your circumcision has become uncircumcision.

26 Therefore, if an uncircumcised man keeps the righteous requirements of the law, will not his uncircumcision be counted as circumcision?

27 And will not the physically uncircumcised, if he fulfills the law, judge you who, *even* with *your* written *code* and circumcision, *are* a transgressor of the law?

28 For he is not a Jew who *is one* outwardly, nor *is* circumcision that which *is* outward in the flesh;

29 but *he is* a Jew who *is one* inwardly; and circumcision *is that* of the heart, in the Spirit, not in the letter; whose praise *is* not from men but from God.

GOD'S JUDGMENT DEFENDED

3 What advantage then has the Jew, or what *is* the profit of circumcision?

2 Much in every way! Chiefly because to them were committed the oracles of God.

3 For what if some did not believe? Will their unbelief make the faithfulness of God without effect?

4 Certainly not! Indeed, let God be true but every man a liar. As it is written:

> *"That You may be justified in Your words,*
> *And may overcome when You are judged."a*

5 But if our unrighteousness demonstrates the righteousness of

2:17 *a*NU-Text reads *But if.*　　2:24 *a*Isaiah 52:5; Ezekiel 36:22　　3:4 *a*Psalm 51:4

God, what shall we say? *Is* God unjust who inflicts wrath? (I speak as a man.)

6 Certainly not! For then how will God judge the world?

7 For if the truth of God has increased through my lie to His glory, why am I also still judged as a sinner?

8 And *why* not *say,* "Let us do evil that good may come"?—as we are slanderously reported and as some affirm that we say. Their condemnation is just.

ALL HAVE SINNED

9 What then? Are we better *than they?* Not at all. For we have previously charged both Jews and Greeks that they are all under sin.

10 As it is written:

"There is none righteous, no, not one;

11 There is none who understands; There is none who seeks after God.

12 They have all turned aside; They have together become unprofitable; There is none who does good, no, not one."*a*

13 "Their throat is an open tomb; With their tongues they have practiced deceit";*a* "The poison of asps is under their lips";*b*

14 "Whose mouth is full of cursing and bitterness."*a*

15 "Their feet are swift to shed blood;

16 Destruction and misery are in their ways;

17 And the way of peace they have not known."*a*

18 "There is no fear of God before their eyes."*a*

19 Now we know that whatever the law says, it says to those who are under the law, that every mouth may be stopped, and all the world may become guilty before God.

20 Therefore by the deeds of the law no flesh will be justified in His sight, for by the law *is* the knowledge of sin.

GOD'S RIGHTEOUSNESS THROUGH FAITH

21 But now the righteousness of God apart from the law is revealed, being witnessed by the Law and the Prophets,

22 even the righteousness of God, through faith in Jesus Christ, to all and on all*a* who believe. For there is no difference;

23 for all have sinned and fall short of the glory of God,

24 being justified freely by His grace through the redemption that is in Christ Jesus,

25 whom God set forth *as* a propitiation by His blood, through faith, to demonstrate His righteousness, because in His forbearance God had passed over the sins that were previously committed,

26 to demonstrate at the present time His righteousness, that He might be just and the justifier of the one who has faith in Jesus.

BOASTING EXCLUDED

27 Where *is* boasting then? It is excluded. By what law? Of works? No, but by the law of faith.

28 Therefore we conclude that a man is justified by faith apart from the deeds of the law.

29 Or *is He* the God of the Jews only? *Is He* not also the God of the Gentiles? Yes, of the Gentiles also,

---

3:12 *a*Psalms 14:1–3; 53:1–3; Ecclesiastes 7:20
3:13 *a*Psalm 5:9   *b*Psalm 140:3   3:14 *a*Psalm
10:7   3:17 *a*Isaiah 59:7, 8   3:18 *a*Psalm 36:1
3:22 *a*NU-Text omits *and on all.*

30 since *there is* one God who will justify the circumcised by faith and the uncircumcised through faith.

31 Do we then make void the law through faith? Certainly not! On the contrary, we establish the law.

ABRAHAM JUSTIFIED BY FAITH

4 What then shall we say that Abraham our father has found according to the flesh?*a*

2 For if Abraham was justified by works, he has *something* to boast about, but not before God.

3 For what does the Scripture say? *"Abraham believed God, and it was accounted to him for righteousness."a*

4 Now to him who works, the wages are not counted as grace but as debt.

DAVID CELEBRATES THE SAME TRUTH

5 But to him who does not work but believes on Him who justifies the ungodly, his faith is accounted for righteousness,

6 just as David also describes the blessedness of the man to whom God imputes righteousness apart from works:

7 *"Blessed are those whose lawless deeds are forgiven,*
And whose sins are covered;

8 *Blessed is the man to whom the* LORD *shall not impute sin."a*

ABRAHAM JUSTIFIED BEFORE CIRCUMCISION

9 *Does* this blessedness then *come* upon the circumcised *only,* or upon the uncircumcised also? For we say that faith was accounted to Abraham for righteousness.

10 How then was it accounted? While he was circumcised, or uncircumcised? Not while circumcised, but while uncircumcised.

11 And he received the sign of circumcision, a seal of the righteousness of the faith which *he had while still* uncircumcised, that he might be the father of all those who believe, though they are uncircumcised, that righteousness might be imputed to them also,

12 and the father of circumcision to those who not only *are* of the circumcision, but who also walk in the steps of the faith which our father Abraham *had while still* uncircumcised.

THE PROMISE GRANTED THROUGH FAITH

13 For the promise that he would be the heir of the world *was* not to Abraham or to his seed through the law, but through the righteousness of faith.

14 For if those who are of the law *are* heirs, faith is made void and the promise made of no effect,

15 because the law brings about wrath; for where there is no law *there is* no transgression.

16 Therefore *it is* of faith that *it might be* according to grace, so that the promise might be sure to all the seed, not only to those who are of the law, but also to those who are of the faith of Abraham, who is the father of us all

17 (as it is written, *"I have made you a father of many nations"a*) in the presence of Him whom he believed— God, who gives life to the dead and calls those things which do not exist as though they did;

4:1 *aOr Abraham our (fore)father according to the flesh has found?*   4:3 *aGenesis 15:6*
4:8 *aPsalm 32:1, 2*   4:17 *aGenesis 17:5*

18 who, contrary to hope, in hope believed, so that he became the father of many nations, according to what was spoken, *"So shall your descendants be."*a

19 And not being weak in faith, he did not consider his own body, already dead (since he was about a hundred years old), and the deadness of Sarah's womb.

20 He did not waver at the promise of God through unbelief, but was strengthened in faith, giving glory to God,

21 and being fully convinced that what He had promised He was also able to perform.

22 And therefore *"it was accounted to him for righteousness."*a

23 Now it was not written for his sake alone that it was imputed to him,

24 but also for us. It shall be imputed to us who believe in Him who raised up Jesus our Lord from the dead,

25 who was delivered up because of our offenses, and was raised because of our justification.

FAITH TRIUMPHS IN TROUBLE

5 Therefore, having been justified by faith, we havea peace with God through our Lord Jesus Christ,

2 through whom also we have access by faith into this grace in which we stand, and rejoice in hope of the glory of God.

3 And not only *that,* but we also glory in tribulations, knowing that tribulation produces perseverance;

4 and perseverance, character; and character, hope.

5 Now hope does not disappoint, because the love of God has been poured out in our hearts by the Holy Spirit who was given to us.

CHRIST IN OUR PLACE

6 For when we were still without strength, in due time Christ died for the ungodly.

7 For scarcely for a righteous man will one die; yet perhaps for a good man someone would even dare to die.

8 But God demonstrates His own love toward us, in that while we were still sinners, Christ died for us.

9 Much more then, having now been justified by His blood, we shall be saved from wrath through Him.

10 For if when we were enemies we were reconciled to God through the death of His Son, much more, having been reconciled, we shall be saved by His life.

11 And not only *that,* but we also rejoice in God through our Lord Jesus Christ, through whom we have now received the reconciliation.

DEATH IN ADAM, LIFE IN CHRIST

12 Therefore, just as through one man sin entered the world, and death through sin, and thus death spread to all men, because all sinned—

13 (For until the law sin was in the world, but sin is not imputed when there is no law.

14 Nevertheless death reigned from Adam to Moses, even over those who had not sinned according to the likeness of the transgression of Adam, who is a type of Him who was to come.

15 But the free gift *is* not like the offense. For if by the one man's offense many died, much more the grace of God and the gift by the grace of the one Man, Jesus Christ, abounded to many.

16 And the gift *is* not like *that which came* through the one who sinned.

4:18 aGenesis 15:5   4:22 aGenesis 15:6
5:1 aAnother ancient reading is, *let us have peace.*

LOVE Romans 5:8

What Is Love?

What would you say if someone asked you, "What is love?" Is it a warm, fuzzy feeling about someone? Or is it giving yourself away to someone? If a husband or wife gives self away to serve the other, is that showing love? When God gave His Son Jesus, was that love (read Romans 5:8)? Do you think God felt good when He gave us a new life through Jesus? His love was in giving. His delight was seeing us receive His gift.

1. Do you love mother and father? How much would you do for them? Do you show your love by giving? Do you feel warm and fuzzy because you gave to them? Why?
2. Do you love Jesus? How much would you do for Him? Do you show love when you give to Jesus? Does that help you feel warm and fuzzy when you give to Him? Why?

For more on *Values* turn to page 1737
For more on *Love* turn to page 1739

For the judgment *which came* from one *offense resulted* in condemnation, but the free gift *which came* from many offenses *resulted* in justification.

17 For if by the one man's offense death reigned through the one, much more those who receive abundance of grace and of the gift of righteousness will reign in life through the One, Jesus Christ.)

18 Therefore, as through one man's offense *judgment* came to all men, resulting in condemnation, even so through one Man's righteous act *the free gift came* to all men, resulting in justification of life.

19 For as by one man's disobedience many were made sinners, so also by one Man's obedience many will be made righteous.

20 Moreover the law entered that the offense might abound. But where sin abounded, grace abounded much more,

21 so that as sin reigned in death,

even so grace might reign through righteousness to eternal life through Jesus Christ our Lord.

DEAD TO SIN, ALIVE TO GOD

6 What shall we say then? Shall we continue in sin that grace may abound?

2 Certainly not! How shall we who died to sin live any longer in it?

3 Or do you not know that as many of us as were baptized into Christ Jesus were baptized into His death?

4 Therefore we were buried with Him through baptism into death, that just as Christ was raised from the dead by the glory of the Father, even so we also should walk in newness of life.

5 For if we have been united together in the likeness of His death, certainly we also shall be *in the likeness* of *His* resurrection,

6 knowing this, that our old man was crucified with *Him,* that the body

Favorite Family Verses

FOR THE WAGES OF SIN IS DEATH, BUT THE GIFT OF GOD IS ETERNAL LIFE IN CHRIST JESUS OUR LORD. Romans 6:23

The Best Gift of All

Have you ever earned some money? What work did you do to earn it? When we sin, we earn God's punishment. That's what He *should* pay us for our sin. But Jesus loves us. He died for us. He will give us a life that goes on forever and ever. It is a gift. We can't earn it. He just gives it to us when we ask. Thank You, Jesus.

1. Can you earn your way to heaven? Why not?
2. Can Jesus give you a life that goes on forever and ever? How do we get this wonderful eternal life?
3. Have you asked Jesus for this wonderful life in heaven? Ask Him! He wants to give it to you, *free!*

For more on *Favorite Family Verses* turn to page 1739
For more on *Salvation* turn to page 1764

of sin might be done away with, that we should no longer be slaves of sin.

7 For he who has died has been freed from sin.

8 Now if we died with Christ, we believe that we shall also live with Him,

9 knowing that Christ, having been raised from the dead, dies no more. Death no longer has dominion over Him.

10 For *the death* that He died, He died to sin once for all; but *the life* that He lives, He lives to God.

11 Likewise you also, reckon yourselves to be dead indeed to sin, but alive to God in Christ Jesus our Lord.

12 Therefore do not let sin reign in your mortal body, that you should obey it in its lusts.

13 And do not present your members *as* instruments of unrighteousness to sin, but present yourselves to God as being alive from the dead, and your members *as* instruments of righteousness to God.

14 For sin shall not have dominion over you, for you are not under law but under grace.

FROM SLAVES OF SIN TO SLAVES OF GOD

15 What then? Shall we sin because we are not under law but under grace? Certainly not!

16 Do you not know that to whom you present yourselves slaves to obey, you are that one's slaves whom you obey, whether of sin *leading* to death, or of obedience *leading* to righteousness?

17 But God be thanked that *though* you were slaves of sin, yet you obeyed from the heart that form of doctrine to which you were delivered.

18 And having been set free from sin, you became slaves of righteousness.

19 I speak in human *terms* because of the weakness of your flesh. For just as you presented your members

as slaves of uncleanness, and of lawlessness *leading* to *more* lawlessness, so now present your members *as* slaves *of* righteousness for holiness.

20 For when you were slaves of sin, you were free in regard to righteousness.

21 What fruit did you have then in the things of which you are now ashamed? For the end of those things *is* death.

22 But now having been set free from sin, and having become slaves of God, you have your fruit to holiness, and the end, everlasting life.

23 For the wages of sin *is* death, but the gift of God *is* eternal life in Christ Jesus our Lord.

FREED FROM THE LAW

7 Or do you not know, brethren (for I speak to those who know the law), that the law has dominion over a man as long as he lives?

2 For the woman who has a husband is bound by the law to *her* husband as long as he lives. But if the husband dies, she is released from the law of *her* husband.

3 So then if, while *her* husband lives, she marries another man, she will be called an adulteress; but if her husband dies, she is free from that law, so that she is no adulteress, though she has married another man.

4 Therefore, my brethren, you also have become dead to the law through the body of Christ, that you may be married to another—to Him who was raised from the dead, that we should bear fruit to God.

5 For when we were in the flesh, the sinful passions which were aroused by the law were at work in our members to bear fruit to death.

6 But now we have been delivered from the law, having died to what we were held by, so that we should serve in the newness of the Spirit and not *in* the oldness of the letter.

SIN'S ADVANTAGE IN THE LAW

7 What shall we say then? *Is* the law sin? Certainly not! On the contrary, I would not have known sin except through the law. For I would not have known covetousness unless the law had said, *"You shall not covet."*a

8 But sin, taking opportunity by the commandment, produced in me all *manner of evil* desire. For apart from the law sin *was* dead.

9 I was alive once without the law, but when the commandment came, sin revived and I died.

10 And the commandment, which *was* to *bring* life, I found to *bring* death.

11 For sin, taking occasion by the commandment, deceived me, and by it killed *me*.

12 Therefore the law *is* holy, and the commandment holy and just and good.

LAW CANNOT SAVE FROM SIN

13 Has then what is good become death to me? Certainly not! But sin, that it might appear sin, was producing death in me through what is good, so that sin through the commandment might become exceedingly sinful.

14 For we know that the law is spiritual, but I am carnal, sold under sin.

15 For what I am doing, I do not understand. For what I will to do, that I do not practice; but what I hate, that I do.

16 If, then, I do what I will not to do, I agree with the law that *it is* good.

17 But now, *it is* no longer I who do it, but sin that dwells in me.

7:7 *a*Exodus 20:17; Deuteronomy 5:21

18 For I know that in me (that is, in my flesh) nothing good dwells; for to will is present with me, but *how* to perform what is good I do not find.

19 For the good that I will *to do,* I do not do; but the evil I will not *to do,* that I practice.

20 Now if I do what I will not *to do,* it is no longer I who do it, but sin that dwells in me.

21 I find then a law, that evil is present with me, the one who wills to do good.

22 For I delight in the law of God according to the inward man.

23 But I see another law in my members, warring against the law of my mind, and bringing me into captivity to the law of sin which is in my members.

24 O wretched man that I am! Who will deliver me from this body of death?

25 I thank God—through Jesus Christ our Lord! So then, with the mind I myself serve the law of God, but with the flesh the law of sin.

FREE FROM INDWELLING SIN

8 *There* is therefore now no condemnation to those who are in Christ Jesus,*a* who do not walk according to the flesh, but according to the Spirit.

2 For the law of the Spirit of life in Christ Jesus has made me free from the law of sin and death.

3 For what the law could not do in that it was weak through the flesh, God *did* by sending His own Son in the likeness of sinful flesh, on account of sin: He condemned sin in the flesh,

4 that the righteous requirement of the law might be fulfilled in us who do not walk according to the flesh but according to the Spirit.

5 For those who live according to the flesh set their minds on the things of the flesh, but those *who live* according to the Spirit, the things of the Spirit.

6 For to be carnally minded *is* death, but to be spiritually minded *is* life and peace.

7 Because the carnal mind *is* enmity against God; for it is not subject to the law of God, nor indeed can be.

8 So then, those who are in the flesh cannot please God.

9 But you are not in the flesh but in the Spirit, if indeed the Spirit of God dwells in you. Now if anyone does not have the Spirit of Christ, he is not His.

10 And if Christ *is* in you, the body *is* dead because of sin, but the Spirit *is* life because of righteousness.

11 But if the Spirit of Him who raised Jesus from the dead dwells in you, He who raised Christ from the dead will also give life to your mortal bodies through His Spirit who dwells in you.

SONSHIP THROUGH THE SPIRIT

12 Therefore, brethren, we are debtors—not to the flesh, to live according to the flesh.

13 For if you live according to the flesh you will die; but if by the Spirit you put to death the deeds of the body, you will live.

14 For as many as are led by the Spirit of God, these are sons of God.

15 For you did not receive the spirit of bondage again to fear, but you received the Spirit of adoption by whom we cry out, "Abba, Father."

16 The Spirit Himself bears witness with our spirit that we are children of God,

17 and if children, then heirs—heirs of God and joint heirs with Christ, if

8:1 *a*NU-Text omits the rest of this verse.

ABOUT HEAVEN Romans 8:16–18

No Wheelchairs in Heaven

Do you know people who are sick or suffering? Do you know people who seem to have a lot of trouble? There is a lot of suffering and hurt here, but there is no suffering or pain or sorrow in heaven (read Revelation 21:4). Heaven is a perfect, glorious place. Sometimes people suffer here to help Jesus in His work. Is it worth it?

1. Read Romans 8:16–18. The glory of heaven is more wonderful than we can imagine. If we suffer a little for Jesus here, it's nothing compared to the glory of heaven.
2. Would you help Jesus do His work, even if you had to suffer a little now? What does Romans 8:16–18 say He will do for you?

For more on *What the Bible Says* turn to page 1776
For more on *Healing* turn to page 1441

indeed we suffer with *Him,* that we may also be glorified together.

From Suffering to Glory

18 For I consider that the sufferings of this present time are not worthy *to be compared* with the glory which shall be revealed in us.

19 For the earnest expectation of the creation eagerly waits for the revealing of the sons of God.

20 For the creation was subjected to futility, not willingly, but because of Him who subjected *it* in hope;

21 because the creation itself also will be delivered from the bondage of corruption into the glorious liberty of the children of God.

22 For we know that the whole creation groans and labors with birth pangs together until now.

23 Not only *that,* but we also who have the firstfruits of the Spirit, even we ourselves groan within ourselves, eagerly waiting for the adoption, the redemption of our body.

24 For we were saved in this hope, but hope that is seen is not hope; for why does one still hope for what he sees?

25 But if we hope for what we do not see, we eagerly wait for *it* with perseverance.

26 Likewise the Spirit also helps in our weaknesses. For we do not know what we should pray for as we ought, but the Spirit Himself makes intercession for us[a] with groanings which cannot be uttered.

27 Now He who searches the hearts knows what the mind of the Spirit *is,* because He makes intercession for the saints according to *the will of* God.

28 And we know that all things work together for good to those who love God, to those who are the called according to *His* purpose.

29 For whom He foreknew, He also predestined *to be* conformed to the image of His Son, that He might be the firstborn among many brethren.

30 Moreover whom He predestined, these He also called; whom He called, these He also justified; and whom He justified, these He also glorified.

God's Everlasting Love

31 What then shall we say to these things? If God *is* for us, who *can be* against us?

32 He who did not spare His own Son, but delivered Him up for us all, how shall He not with Him also freely give us all things?

33 Who shall bring a charge against God's elect? *It is* God who justifies.

34 Who *is* he who condemns? *It is* Christ who died, and furthermore is also risen, who is even at the right hand of God, who also makes intercession for us.

35 Who shall separate us from the love of Christ? *Shall* tribulation, or distress, or persecution, or famine, or nakedness, or peril, or sword?

36 As it is written:

> *"For Your sake we are killed all*
> *   day long;*
> *We are accounted as sheep for the*
> *   slaughter."[a]*

37 Yet in all these things we are more than conquerors through Him who loved us.

38 For I am persuaded that neither death nor life, nor angels nor principalities nor powers, nor things present nor things to come,

39 nor height nor depth, nor any other created thing, shall be able to separate us from the love of God which is in Christ Jesus our Lord.

8:26 [a]NU-Text omits *for us.*   8:36 [a]Psalm 44:22

ISRAEL'S REJECTION OF CHRIST

9 I tell the truth in Christ, I am not lying, my conscience also bearing me witness in the Holy Spirit,

2 that I have great sorrow and continual grief in my heart.

3 For I could wish that I myself were accursed from Christ for my brethren, my countrymen*a* according to the flesh,

4 who are Israelites, to whom *pertain* the adoption, the glory, the covenants, the giving of the law, the service *of God,* and the promises;

5 of whom *are* the fathers and from whom, according to the flesh, Christ *came,* who is over all, *the* eternally blessed God. Amen.

ISRAEL'S REJECTION AND GOD'S PURPOSE

6 But it is not that the word of God has taken no effect. For they *are* not all Israel who *are* of Israel,

7 nor *are they* all children because they are the seed of Abraham; but, *"In Isaac your seed shall be called."a*

8 That is, those who *are* the children of the flesh, these *are* not the children of God; but the children of the promise are counted as the seed.

9 For this *is* the word of promise: *"At this time I will come and Sarah shall have a son."a*

10 And not only *this,* but when Rebecca also had conceived by one man, *even* by our father Isaac

11 (for *the children* not yet being born, nor having done any good or evil, that the purpose of God according to election might stand, not of works but of Him who calls),

12 it was said to her, *"The older shall serve the younger."a*

13 As it is written, *"Jacob I have loved, but Esau I have hated."a*

ISRAEL'S REJECTION AND GOD'S JUSTICE

14 What shall we say then? *Is there* unrighteousness with God? Certainly not!

15 For He says to Moses, *"I will have mercy on whomever I will have mercy, and I will have compassion on whomever I will have compassion."a*

16 So then *it is* not of him who wills, nor of him who runs, but of God who shows mercy.

17 For the Scripture says to the Pharaoh, *"For this very purpose I have raised you up, that I may show My power in you, and that My name may be declared in all the earth."a*

18 Therefore He has mercy on whom He wills, and whom He wills He hardens.

19 You will say to me then, "Why does He still find fault? For who has resisted His will?"

20 But indeed, O man, who are you to reply against God? Will the thing formed say to him who formed *it,* "Why have you made me like this?"

21 Does not the potter have power over the clay, from the same lump to make one vessel for honor and another for dishonor?

22 *What* if God, wanting to show *His* wrath and to make His power known, endured with much longsuffering the vessels of wrath prepared for destruction,

23 and that He might make known the riches of His glory on the vessels of mercy, which He had prepared beforehand for glory,

24 *even* us whom He called, not of the Jews only, but also of the Gentiles?

9:3 *a*Or *relatives*　　9:7 *a*Genesis 21:12
9:9 *a*Genesis 18:10, 14　　9:12 *a*Genesis 25:23
9:13 *a*Malachi 1:2, 3　　9:15 *a*Exodus 33:19
9:17 *a*Exodus 9:16

25 As He says also in Hō·sē′a:

"I will call them My people, who
  were not My people,
And her beloved, who was not
  beloved."a
26 "And it shall come to pass in the
  place where it was said to
  them,
  'You are not My people,'
There they shall be called sons of
  the living God."a

27 Ī·sāi′ah also cries out concerning
Israel:a

"Though the number of the
  children of Israel be as the sand
  of the sea,
The remnant will be saved.
28 For He will finish the work and
  cut it short in righteousness,
Because the Lord will make a
  short work upon the earth."a

29 And as Ī·sāi′ah said before:

"Unless the Lord of Sab′a·ōtha
  had left us a seed,
We would have become like
  Sod′om,
And we would have been made
  like Go·mor′rah."b

PRESENT CONDITION OF ISRAEL

30 What shall we say then? That
Gentiles, who did not pursue righteousness, have attained to righteousness, even the righteousness of
faith;
31 but Israel, pursuing the law of
righteousness, has not attained to
the law of righteousness.a
32 Why? Because they did not seek it
by faith, but as it were, by the works
of the law.a For they stumbled at
that stumbling stone.

33 As it is written:

"Behold, I lay in Zion a stumbling
  stone and rock of offense,
And whoever believes on Him will
  not be put to shame."a

ISRAEL NEEDS THE GOSPEL

10 Brethren, my heart's desire
and prayer to God for Israela is that
they may be saved.
2 For I bear them witness that they
have a zeal for God, but not according
to knowledge.
3 For they being ignorant of God's
righteousness, and seeking to establish their own righteousness, have
not submitted to the righteousness of
God.
4 For Christ is the end of the law
for righteousness to everyone who believes.
5 For Moses writes about the righteousness which is of the law, "The
man who does those things shall live
by them."a
6 But the righteousness of faith
speaks in this way, "Do not say in
your heart, 'Who will ascend into
heaven?' "a (that is, to bring Christ
down from above)
7 or, " 'Who will descend into the
abyss?' "a (that is, to bring Christ up
from the dead).
8 But what does it say? "The word
is near you, in your mouth and in
your heart"a (that is, the word of
faith which we preach):
9 that if you confess with your

9:25 aHosea 2:23   9:26 aHosea 1:10
9:27 aIsaiah 10:22, 23   9:28 aNU-Text reads
*For the Lord will finish the work and cut it short
upon the earth.*   9:29 aLiterally, in Hebrew,
Hosts bIsaiah 1:9   9:31 aNU-Text omits *of
righteousness.*   9:32 aNU-Text reads *by works.*
9:33 aIsaiah 8:14; 28:16   10:1 aNU-Text reads
them.   10:5 aLeviticus 18:5   10:6 aDeuteronomy 30:12   10:7 aDeuteronomy 30:13
10:8 aDeuteronomy 30:14

mouth the Lord Jesus and believe in your heart that God has raised Him from the dead, you will be saved.

10 For with the heart one believes unto righteousness, and with the mouth confession is made unto salvation.

11 For the Scripture says, *"Whoever believes on Him will not be put to shame."ª*

12 For there is no distinction between Jew and Greek, for the same Lord over all is rich to all who call upon Him.

13 For *"whoever calls on the name of the LORD shall be saved."ª*

ISRAEL REJECTS THE GOSPEL

14 How then shall they call on Him in whom they have not believed? And how shall they believe in Him of whom they have not heard? And how shall they hear without a preacher?

15 And how shall they preach unless they are sent? As it is written:

"How beautiful are the feet of those who preach the gospel of peace,ª
Who bring glad tidings of good things!"b

16 But they have not all obeyed the gospel. For I·sāi′ah says, *"LORD, who has believed our report?"ª*

17 So then faith *comes* by hearing, and hearing by the word of God.

18 But I say, have they not heard? Yes indeed:

"Their sound has gone out to all the earth,
And their words to the ends of the world."ª

19 But I say, did Israel not know? First Moses says:

"I will provoke you to jealousy by those who are not a nation,
I will move you to anger by a foolish nation."ª

20 But I·sāi′ah is very bold and says:

"I was found by those who did not seek Me;
I was made manifest to those who did not ask for Me."ª

21 But to Israel he says:

"All day long I have stretched out My hands
To a disobedient and contrary people."ª

ISRAEL'S REJECTION NOT TOTAL

11 I say then, has God cast away His people? Certainly not! For I also am an Israelite, of the seed of Abraham, *of* the tribe of Benjamin.

2 God has not cast away His people whom He foreknew. Or do you not know what the Scripture says of E·lī′jah, how he pleads with God against Israel, saying,

3 *"LORD, they have killed Your prophets and torn down Your altars, and I alone am left, and they seek my life"?ª*

4 But what does the divine response say to him? *"I have reserved for Myself seven thousand men who have not bowed the knee to Bā′al."ª*

5 Even so then, at this present time there is a remnant according to the election of grace.

6 And if by grace, then *it is* no

10:11 ªIsaiah 28:16   10:13 ªJoel 2:32
10:15 ªNU-Text omits *preach the gospel of peace,*
Who. bIsaiah 52:7; Nahum 1:15   10:16 ªIsaiah
53:1   10:18 ªPsalm 19:4   10:19 ªDeuteronomy 32:21   10:20 ªIsaiah 65:1   10:21 ªIsaiah 65:2   11:3 ª1 Kings 19:10, 14
11:4 ª1 Kings 19:18

longer of works; otherwise grace is no longer grace.a But if *it is* of works, it is no longer grace; otherwise work is no longer work.

7 What then? Israel has not obtained what it seeks; but the elect have obtained it, and the rest were blinded.

8 Just as it is written:

> "God has given them a spirit of
>   stupor,
> Eyes that they should not see
> And ears that they should not
>   hear,
> To this very day."a

9 And David says:

> "Let their table become a snare
>   and a trap,
> A stumbling block and a
>   recompense to them.
> 10 Let their eyes be darkened, so
>   that they do not see,
> And bow down their back
>   always."a

ISRAEL'S REJECTION NOT FINAL

11 I say then, have they stumbled that they should fall? Certainly not! But through their fall, to provoke them to jealousy, salvation *has come* to the Gentiles.

12 Now if their fall *is* riches for the world, and their failure riches for the Gentiles, how much more their fullness!

13 For I speak to you Gentiles; inasmuch as I am an apostle to the Gentiles, I magnify my ministry,

14 if by any means I may provoke to jealousy *those who are* my flesh and save some of them.

15 For if their being cast away *is* the reconciling of the world, what *will* their acceptance *be* but life from the dead?

16 For if the firstfruit *is* holy, the lump *is* also *holy;* and if the root *is* holy, so *are* the branches.

17 And if some of the branches were broken off, and you, being a wild olive tree, were grafted in among them, and with them became a partaker of the root and fatness of the olive tree,

18 do not boast against the branches. But if you do boast, *remember that* you do not support the root, but the root supports you.

19 You will say then, "Branches were broken off that I might be grafted in."

20 Well *said.* Because of unbelief they were broken off, and you stand by faith. Do not be haughty, but fear.

21 For if God did not spare the natural branches, He may not spare you either.

22 Therefore consider the goodness and severity of God: on those who fell, severity; but toward you, goodness,a if you continue in *His* goodness. Otherwise you also will be cut off.

23 And they also, if they do not continue in unbelief, will be grafted in, for God is able to graft them in again.

24 For if you were cut out of the olive tree which is wild by nature, and were grafted contrary to nature into a cultivated olive tree, how much more will these, who *are* natural *branches,* be grafted into their own olive tree?

25 For I do not desire, brethren, that you should be ignorant of this mystery, lest you should be wise in your own opinion, that blindness in part has happened to Israel until the fullness of the Gentiles has come in.

26 And so all Israel will be saved,a as it is written:

11:6 aNU-Text omits the rest of this verse.
11:8 aDeuteronomy 29:4; Isaiah 29:10
11:10 aPsalm 69:22, 23   11:22 aNU-Text adds *of God.*   11:26 aOr *delivered*

HUMILITY Romans 12:3

What Does God Think of Pride?

Have you ever seen a proud person? What did you think of that person? What does God think of that person? Sometimes mother or father says, "I'm proud of you." That's great, isn't it? We want our parents to be proud of us, just as we are proud of them. But God doesn't want us to be too proud about ourselves or to think we are better than others. He doesn't want us to think more of ourselves than we ought to think. Let others praise you.

1. Read Romans 12:3. What is God saying? We are proud when we think we are bigger than we are, or more important than we are, or better than others, or smarter than others.

2. If mother says, "I'm proud of you," what does she mean? She means that she is pleased with the way you are living or things you are doing. She thinks highly of you. That's wonderful, isn't it? We want mother or father or others to be proud of the good things we do. We just should not be *a proud or arrogant person,* thinking we are big shots. God knows better.

3. What should you do when you catch yourself thinking those kinds of thoughts? Should you ask God to help you think the right things?

For more on *Values* turn to page 1753

For more on *Humility* turn to page 1880

"The Deliverer will come out of Zion,
And He will turn away ungodliness from Jacob;
27 *For this is My covenant with them,*
When I take away their sins."ᵃ

28 Concerning the gospel *they are* enemies for your sake, but concerning the election *they are* beloved for the sake of the fathers.
29 For the gifts and the calling of God *are* irrevocable.
30 For as you were once disobedient to God, yet have now obtained mercy through their disobedience,
31 even so these also have now been disobedient, that through the mercy shown you they also may obtain mercy.
32 For God has committed them all to disobedience, that He might have mercy on all.
33 Oh, the depth of the riches both of the wisdom and knowledge of God! How unsearchable *are* His judgments and His ways past finding out!

34 *"For who has known the mind of the LORD?*
Or who has become His counselor?"ᵃ
35 *"Or who has first given to Him*
And it shall be repaid to him?"ᵃ

36 For of Him and through Him and to Him *are* all things, to whom *be* glory forever. Amen.

LIVING SACRIFICES TO GOD

12 I beseech you therefore, brethren, by the mercies of God, that you present your bodies a living sacrifice, holy, acceptable to God, *which is* your reasonable service.
2 And do not be conformed to this world, but be transformed by the renewing of your mind, that you may prove what *is* that good and acceptable and perfect will of God.

SERVE GOD WITH SPIRITUAL GIFTS

3 For I say, through the grace given to me, to everyone who is among you, not to think *of himself* more highly than he ought to think, but to think soberly, as God has dealt to each one a measure of faith.
4 For as we have many members in one body, but all the members do not have the same function,
5 so we, *being* many, are one body in Christ, and individually members of one another.
6 Having then gifts differing according to the grace that is given to us, *let us use them:* if prophecy, *let us prophesy* in proportion to our faith;
7 or ministry, *let us use it* in *our* ministering; he who teaches, in teaching;
8 he who exhorts, in exhortation; he who gives, with liberality; he who leads, with diligence; he who shows mercy, with cheerfulness.

BEHAVE LIKE A CHRISTIAN

9 *Let* love *be* without hypocrisy. Abhor what is evil. Cling to what is good.
10 *Be* kindly affectionate to one another with brotherly love, in honor giving preference to one another;
11 not lagging in diligence, fervent in spirit, serving the Lord;
12 rejoicing in hope, patient in tribulation, continuing steadfastly in prayer;
13 distributing to the needs of the saints, given to hospitality.

11:27 ᵃIsaiah 59:20, 21   11:34 ᵃIsaiah 40:13; Jeremiah 23:18   11:35 ᵃJob 41:11

14 Bless those who persecute you; bless and do not curse.
15 Rejoice with those who rejoice, and weep with those who weep.
16 Be of the same mind toward one another. Do not set your mind on high things, but associate with the humble. Do not be wise in your own opinion.
17 Repay no one evil for evil. Have regard for good things in the sight of all men.
18 If it is possible, as much as depends on you, live peaceably with all men.
19 Beloved, do not avenge yourselves, but *rather* give place to wrath; for it is written, *"Vengeance is Mine, I will repay,"a* says the Lord.
20 Therefore

"If your enemy is hungry, feed him;
If he is thirsty, give him a drink;
For in so doing you will heap coals of fire on his head."a

21 Do not be overcome by evil, but overcome evil with good.

SUBMIT TO GOVERNMENT

13 Let every soul be subject to the governing authorities. For there is no authority except from God, and the authorities that exist are appointed by God.
2 Therefore whoever resists the authority resists the ordinance of God, and those who resist will bring judgment on themselves.
3 For rulers are not a terror to good works, but to evil. Do you want to be unafraid of the authority? Do what is good, and you will have praise from the same.
4 For he is God's minister to you for good. But if you do evil, be afraid; for he does not bear the sword in vain; for he is God's minister, an avenger to *execute* wrath on him who practices evil.
5 Therefore *you* must be subject, not only because of wrath but also for conscience' sake.
6 For because of this you also pay

12:19 aDeuteronomy 32:35   12:20 aProverbs 25:21, 22

REJOICE WITH THOSE WHO REJOICE, AND WEEP WITH THOSE WHO WEEP.
Romans 12:15

A Time for Hugs

This girl has just graduated. She has worked hard. She has done well. Now she has her diploma. She is about the happiest girl on earth. But some other people are happy, too. They are almost as happy as she. Her parents have their arms out to give her a big hug. And she wants that hug almost as much as she wants her diploma.

1. Why is this girl so happy? What has she done?
2. Why are her parents so happy? What are they doing?
3. Do you think this girl wants a big hug? Do you think her parents want to give her a big hug? There's a time for hugs. There's a time to be joyful because a friend or family member is joyful.
4. The next time a friend or family member rejoices because of something special, what will you do?

For more on *Favorite Family Verses* turn to page 1749
For more on *Friendship* turn to page 1825

taxes, for they are God's ministers attending continually to this very thing.

7 Render therefore to all their due: taxes to whom taxes *are due,* customs to whom customs, fear to whom fear, honor to whom honor.

LOVE YOUR NEIGHBOR

8 Owe no one anything except to love one another, for he who loves another has fulfilled the law.

9 For the commandments, *"You shall not commit adultery," "You shall not murder," "You shall not steal," "You shall not bear false witness,"a "You shall not covet,"b* and if *there is* any other commandment, are *all* summed up in this saying, namely, *"You shall love your neighbor as yourself."c*

10 Love does no harm to a neighbor; therefore love *is* the fulfillment of the law.

PUT ON CHRIST

11 And *do* this, knowing the time, that now *it is* high time to awake out of sleep; for now our salvation *is* nearer than when we *first* believed.

12 The night is far spent, the day is at hand. Therefore let us cast off the works of darkness, and let us put on the armor of light.

13 Let us walk properly, as in the day, not in revelry and drunkenness, not in lewdness and lust, not in strife and envy.

14 But put on the Lord Jesus Christ, and make no provision for the flesh, to *fulfill its* lusts.

THE LAW OF LIBERTY

14 Receive one who is weak in the faith, *but* not to disputes over doubtful things.

2 For one believes he may eat all things, but he who is weak eats *only* vegetables.

3 Let not him who eats despise him who does not eat, and let not him who does not eat judge him who eats; for God has received him.

4 Who are you to judge another's servant? To his own master he stands or falls. Indeed, he will be made to stand, for God is able to make him stand.

5 One person esteems *one* day above another; another esteems every day *alike.* Let each be fully convinced in his own mind.

6 He who observes the day, observes *it* to the Lord;a and he who does not observe the day, to the Lord he does not observe *it.* He who eats, eats to the Lord, for he gives God thanks; and he who does not eat, to the Lord he does not eat, and gives God thanks.

7 For none of us lives to himself, and no one dies to himself.

8 For if we live, we live to the Lord; and if we die, we die to the Lord. Therefore, whether we live or die, we are the Lord's.

9 For to this end Christ died and rosea and lived again, that He might be Lord of both the dead and the living.

10 But why do you judge your brother? Or why do you show contempt for your brother? For we shall all stand before the judgment seat of Christ.a

11 For it is written:

*"As I live, says the LORD,
Every knee shall bow to Me,*

13:9 aNU-Text omits *"You shall not bear false witness."* bExodus 20:13–15, 17; Deuteronomy 5:17–19, 21 cLeviticus 19:18   14:6 aNU-Text omits the rest of this sentence.   14:9 aNU-Text omits *and rose.*   14:10 aNU-Text reads *of God.*

And every tongue shall confess to God."a

12 So then each of us shall give account of himself to God.

13 Therefore let us not judge one another anymore, but rather resolve this, not to put a stumbling block or a cause to fall in *our* brother's way.

THE LAW OF LOVE

14 I know and am convinced by the Lord Jesus that *there is* nothing unclean of itself; but to him who considers anything to be unclean, to him *it is* unclean.

15 Yet if your brother is grieved because of *your* food, you are no longer walking in love. Do not destroy with your food the one for whom Christ died.

16 Therefore do not let your good be spoken of as evil;

17 for the kingdom of God is not eating and drinking, but righteousness and peace and joy in the Holy Spirit.

18 For he who serves Christ in these things*a is* acceptable to God and approved by men.

19 Therefore let us pursue the things *which make* for peace and the things by which one may edify another.

20 Do not destroy the work of God for the sake of food. All things indeed *are* pure, but *it is* evil for the man who eats with offense.

21 *It is* good neither to eat meat nor drink wine nor *do anything* by which your brother stumbles or is offended or is made weak.*a*

22 Do you have faith?*a* Have *it* to yourself before God. Happy *is* he who does not condemn himself in what he approves.

23 But he who doubts is condemned if he eats, because *he does* not *eat* from faith; for whatever *is* not from faith is sin.*a*

BEARING OTHERS' BURDENS

15 We then who are strong ought to bear with the scruples of the weak, and not to please ourselves.

2 Let each of us please *his* neighbor for *his* good, leading to edification.

3 For even Christ did not please Himself; but as it is written, *"The reproaches of those who reproached You fell on Me."a*

4 For whatever things were written before were written for our learning, that we through the patience and comfort of the Scriptures might have hope.

5 Now may the God of patience and comfort grant you to be like-minded toward one another, according to Christ Jesus,

6 that you may with one mind *and* one mouth glorify the God and Father of our Lord Jesus Christ.

GLORIFY GOD TOGETHER

7 Therefore receive one another, just as Christ also received us,*a* to the glory of God.

8 Now I say that Jesus Christ has become a servant to the circumcision for the truth of God, to confirm the promises *made* to the fathers,

9 and that the Gentiles might glorify God for *His* mercy, as it is written:

"For this reason I will confess to You among the Gentiles, And sing to Your name."a

10 And again he says:

14:11 *a*Isaiah 45:23   14:18 *a*NU-Text reads *this.* 14:21 *a*NU-Text omits *or is offended or is made weak.*   14:22 *a*NU-Text reads *The faith which you have—have.*   14:23 *a*M-Text puts Romans 16:25–27 here.   15:3 *a*Psalm 69:9 15:7 *a*NU-Text and M-Text read *you.* 15:9 *a*2 Samuel 22:50; Psalm 18:49

What Should I Do?

SHOULD I DO SOMETHING WITH MY BIBLE? Romans 15:4

Do you have a Bible? What should you do with it? Should you use it for a doorstop? Should you use it for a little table where you can set some plants? What should you do with your Bible?

1. Should you carry your Bible to church or Sunday school? Why? What should you do with it there?
2. Should you read from your Bible each day? Why? What should you do with what you learn?
3. Should you read your Bible to others? Why? What do you hope will happen?
4. Should you talk with others about the Bible and what it will do for you? Why?
5. What else should you do with your Bible?

For more on *What Should I Do?* turn to page 1758
For more on *Bible* turn to page 1872

"Rejoice, O Gentiles, with His
    people!"a

11 And again:

"Praise the LORD, all you Gentiles!
Laud Him, all you peoples!"a

12 And again, Ī·sāi′ah says:

"There shall be a root of Jesse;
And He who shall rise to reign
    over the Gentiles,
In Him the Gentiles shall hope."a

13 Now may the God of hope fill you with all joy and peace in believing, that you may abound in hope by the power of the Holy Spirit.

FROM JERUSALEM TO ILLYRICUM

14 Now I myself am confident concerning you, my brethren, that you also are full of goodness, filled with all knowledge, able also to admonish one another.a

15 Nevertheless, brethren, I have written more boldly to you on *some* points, as reminding you, because of the grace given to me by God,
16 that I might be a minister of Jesus Christ to the Gentiles, ministering the gospel of God, that the offering of the Gentiles might be acceptable, sanctified by the Holy Spirit.
17 Therefore I have reason to glory in Christ Jesus in the things *which pertain* to God.
18 For I will not dare to speak of any of those things which Christ has not accomplished through me, in word and deed, to make the Gentiles obedient—
19 in mighty signs and wonders, by the power of the Spirit of God, so that from Jerusalem and round about to Il·lyr′i·cum I have fully preached the gospel of Christ.
20 And so I have made it my aim to

15:10 aDeuteronomy 32:43   15:11 aPsalm 117:1
15:12 aIsaiah 11:10   15:14 aM-Text reads *others*.

preach the gospel, not where Christ was named, lest I should build on another man's foundation,

21 but as it is written:

"*To whom He was not announced,*
  they shall see;
And those who have not heard
  shall understand."*a*

PLAN TO VISIT ROME

22 For this reason I also have been much hindered from coming to you.

23 But now no longer having a place in these parts, and having a great desire these many years to come to you,

24 whenever I journey to Spain, I shall come to you.*a* For I hope to see you on my journey, and to be helped on my way there by you, if first I may enjoy your *company* for a while.

25 But now I am going to Jerusalem to minister to the saints.

26 For it pleased those from Mac·e·dō′ni·a and A·chā′i·a to make a certain contribution for the poor among the saints who are in Jerusalem.

27 It pleased them indeed, and they are their debtors. For if the Gentiles have been partakers of their spiritual things, their duty is also to minister to them in material things.

28 Therefore, when I have performed this and have sealed to them this fruit, I shall go by way of you to Spain.

29 But I know that when I come to you, I shall come in the fullness of the blessing of the gospel*a* of Christ.

30 Now I beg you, brethren, through the Lord Jesus Christ, and through the love of the Spirit, that you strive together with me in prayers to God for me,

31 that I may be delivered from those in Judea who do not believe, and that my service for Jerusalem may be acceptable to the saints,

32 that I may come to you with joy by the will of God, and may be refreshed together with you.

33 Now the God of peace *be* with you all. Amen.

SISTER PHOEBE COMMENDED

16 I commend to you Phoē′bē our sister, who is a servant of the church in Cen′chrē·a,

2 that you may receive her in the Lord in a manner worthy of the saints, and assist her in whatever business she has need of you; for indeed she has been a helper of many and of myself also.

GREETING ROMAN SAINTS

3 Greet Pri·scil′la and A·qui′la, my fellow workers in Christ Jesus,

4 who risked their own necks for my life, to whom not only I give thanks, but also all the churches of the Gentiles.

5 Likewise *greet* the church that is in their house. Greet my beloved E·paē′ne·tus, who is the firstfruits of A·chā′i·a*a* to Christ.

6 Greet Mary, who labored much for us.

7 Greet An·dron′i·cus and Jū′ni·a, my countrymen and my fellow prisoners, who are of note among the apostles, who also were in Christ before me.

8 Greet Am′pli·as, my beloved in the Lord.

9 Greet Ur·bā′nus, our fellow worker in Christ, and Stā′chys, my beloved.

10 Greet A·pel′lēs, approved in Christ. Greet those who are of the *household* of Ar·is·tob′ū·lus.

15:21 *a*Isaiah 52:15   15:24 *a*NU-Text omits *I shall come to you* (and joins *Spain* with the next sentence).   15:29 *a*NU-Text omits *of the gospel.* 16:5 *a*NU-Text reads *Asia.*

11 Greet He·rō′di·on, my country-man.*a* Greet those who are of the *household* of Nar·cis′sus who are in the Lord.

12 Greet Trȳ·phē′na and Trȳ·phō′sa, who have labored in the Lord. Greet the beloved Per′sis, who labored much in the Lord.

13 Greet Rū′fus, chosen in the Lord, and his mother and mine.

14 Greet A·syn′cri·tus, Phlē′gon, Her′mas, Pat′ro·bas, Her′mēs, and the brethren who are with them.

15 Greet Phi·lol′o·gus and Julia, Ne′re·us and his sister, and Ō·lym′pas, and all the saints who are with them.

16 Greet one another with a holy kiss. The*a* churches of Christ greet you.

AVOID DIVISIVE PERSONS

17 Now I urge you, brethren, note those who cause divisions and offenses, contrary to the doctrine which you learned, and avoid them.

18 For those who are such do not serve our Lord Jesus*a* Christ, but their own belly, and by smooth words and flattering speech deceive the hearts of the simple.

19 For your obedience has become known to all. Therefore I am glad on your behalf; but I want you to be wise in what is good, and simple concerning evil.

20 And the God of peace will crush Satan under your feet shortly. The grace of our Lord Jesus Christ *be* with you. Amen.

GREETINGS FROM PAUL'S FRIENDS

21 Timothy, my fellow worker, and Lū′cius, Jason, and Sō·sip′a·ter, my countrymen, greet you.

22 I, Ter′ti·us, who wrote *this* epistle, greet you in the Lord.

23 Gā′i·us, my host and *the host* of the whole church, greets you. Ē·ras′tus, the treasurer of the city, greets you, and Quar′tus, a brother.

24 The grace of our Lord Jesus Christ *be* with you all. Amen.*a*

BENEDICTION

25 Now to Him who is able to establish you according to my gospel and the preaching of Jesus Christ, according to the revelation of the mystery kept secret since the world began

26 but now made manifest, and by the prophetic Scriptures made known to all nations, according to the commandment of the everlasting God, for obedience to the faith—

27 to God, alone wise, *be* glory through Jesus Christ forever. Amen.*a*

16:11 *a*Or *relative*　　16:16 *a*NU-Text reads *All the churches.*　　16:18 *a*NU-Text and M-Text omit *Jesus.*　　16:24 *a*NU-Text omits this verse. 16:27 *a*M-Text puts Romans 16:25–27 after Romans 14:23.

The First Epistle of Paul the Apostle to the
CORINTHIANS

GREETING

PAUL, called *to be* an apostle of Jesus Christ through the will of God, and Sos'the·nēs *our* brother,

2 To the church of God which is at Corinth, to those who are sanctified in Christ Jesus, called *to be* saints, with all who in every place call on the name of Jesus Christ our Lord, both theirs and ours:

3 Grace to you and peace from God our Father and the Lord Jesus Christ.

SPIRITUAL GIFTS AT CORINTH

4 I thank my God always concerning you for the grace of God which was given to you by Christ Jesus,
5 that you were enriched in every thing by Him in all utterance and all knowledge,
6 even as the testimony of Christ was confirmed in you,
7 so that you come short in no gift, eagerly waiting for the revelation of our Lord Jesus Christ,
8 who will also confirm you to the end, *that you may be* blameless in the day of our Lord Jesus Christ.
9 God *is* faithful, by whom you were called into the fellowship of His Son, Jesus Christ our Lord.

SECTARIANISM IS SIN

10 Now I plead with you, brethren, by the name of our Lord Jesus Christ, that you all speak the same thing, and *that* there be no divisions among you, but *that* you be perfectly joined together in the same mind and in the same judgment.

11 For it has been declared to me concerning you, my brethren, by those of Chlō'ē's *household,* that there are contentions among you.
12 Now I say this, that each of you says, "I am of Paul," or "I am of A·pol'los," or "I am of Cē'phas," or "I am of Christ."
13 Is Christ divided? Was Paul crucified for you? Or were you baptized in the name of Paul?
14 I thank God that I baptized none of you except Cris'pus and Gā'i·us,
15 lest anyone should say that I had baptized in my own name.
16 Yes, I also baptized the household of Steph'a·nas. Besides, I do not know whether I baptized any other.
17 For Christ did not send me to baptize, but to preach the gospel, not with wisdom of words, lest the cross of Christ should be made of no effect.

CHRIST THE POWER AND WISDOM OF GOD

18 For the message of the cross is foolishness to those who are perishing, but to us who are being saved it is the power of God.
19 For it is written:

"*I will destroy the wisdom of the wise,
And bring to nothing the understanding of the prudent.*"[a]

20 Where *is* the wise? Where *is* the scribe? Where *is* the disputer of this age? Has not God made foolish the wisdom of this world?
21 For since, in the wisdom of God, the world through wisdom did not

1:19 [a]Isaiah 29:14

know God, it pleased God through the foolishness of the message preached to save those who believe.

22 For Jews request a sign, and Greeks seek after wisdom;

23 but we preach Christ crucified, to the Jews a stumbling block and to the Greeks*a* foolishness,

24 but to those who are called, both Jews and Greeks, Christ the power of God and the wisdom of God.

25 Because the foolishness of God is wiser than men, and the weakness of God is stronger than men.

GLORY ONLY IN THE LORD

26 For you see your calling, brethren, that not many wise according to the flesh, not many mighty, not many noble, *are called.*

27 But God has chosen the foolish things of the world to put to shame the wise, and God has chosen the weak things of the world to put to shame the things which are mighty;

28 and the base things of the world and the things which are despised God has chosen, and the things which are not, to bring to nothing the things that are,

29 that no flesh should glory in His presence.

30 But of Him you are in Christ Jesus, who became for us wisdom from God—and righteousness and sanctification and redemption—

31 that, as it is written, *"He who glories, let him glory in the LORD."a*

CHRIST CRUCIFIED

2 And I, brethren, when I came to you, did not come with excellence of speech or of wisdom declaring to you the testimony*a* of God.

2 For I determined not to know anything among you except Jesus Christ and Him crucified.

3 I was with you in weakness, in fear, and in much trembling.

4 And my speech and my preaching *were* not with persuasive words of human*a* wisdom, but in demonstration of the Spirit and of power,

5 that your faith should not be in the wisdom of men but in the power of God.

SPIRITUAL WISDOM

6 However, we speak wisdom among those who are mature, yet not the wisdom of this age, nor of the rulers of this age, who are coming to nothing.

7 But we speak the wisdom of God in a mystery, the hidden *wisdom* which God ordained before the ages for our glory,

8 which none of the rulers of this age knew; for had they known, they would not have crucified the Lord of glory.

9 But as it is written:

"Eye has not seen, nor ear heard,
Nor have entered into the heart of
man
The things which God has
prepared for those who love
Him."a

10 But God has revealed *them* to us through His Spirit. For the Spirit searches all things, yes, the deep things of God.

11 For what man knows the things of a man except the spirit of the man which is in him? Even so no one knows the things of God except the Spirit of God.

12 Now we have received, not the spirit of the world, but the Spirit who is from God, that we might know the

---

1:23 *a*NU-Text reads *Gentiles.*   1:31 *a*Jeremiah 9:24   2:1 *a*NU-Text reads *mystery.*
2:4 *a*NU-Text omits *human.*   2:9 *a*Isaiah 64:4

things that have been freely given to us by God.

13 These things we also speak, not in words which man's wisdom teaches but which the Holy[a] Spirit teaches, comparing spiritual things with spiritual.

14 But the natural man does not receive the things of the Spirit of God, for they are foolishness to him; nor can he know *them,* because they are spiritually discerned.

15 But he who is spiritual judges all things, yet he himself is *rightly* judged by no one.

16 For *"who has known the mind of the LORD that he may instruct Him?"*[a] But we have the mind of Christ.

SECTARIANISM IS CARNAL

3 And I, brethren, could not speak to you as to spiritual *people* but as to carnal, as to babes in Christ.

2 I fed you with milk and not with solid food; for until now you were not able *to receive it,* and even now you are still not able;

3 for you are still carnal. For where *there are* envy, strife, and divisions among you, are you not carnal and behaving like *mere* men?

4 For when one says, "I am of Paul," and another, "I *am* of A·pol'-los," are you not carnal?

WATERING, WORKING, WARNING

5 Who then is Paul, and who *is* A·pol'los, but ministers through whom you believed, as the Lord gave to each one?

6 I planted, A·pol'los watered, but God gave the increase.

7 So then neither he who plants is anything, nor he who waters, but God who gives the increase.

8 Now he who plants and he who

waters are one, and each one will receive his own reward according to his own labor.

9 For we are God's fellow workers; you are God's field, *you are* God's building.

10 According to the grace of God which was given to me, as a wise master builder I have laid the foundation, and another builds on it. But let each one take heed how he builds on it.

11 For no other foundation can anyone lay than that which is laid, which is Jesus Christ.

12 Now if anyone builds on this foundation *with* gold, silver, precious stones, wood, hay, straw,

13 each one's work will become clear; for the Day will declare it, because it will be revealed by fire; and the fire will test each one's work, of what sort it is.

14 If anyone's work which he has built on *it* endures, he will receive a reward.

15 If anyone's work is burned, he will suffer loss; but he himself will be saved, yet so as through fire.

16 Do you not know that you are the temple of God and *that* the Spirit of God dwells in you?

17 If anyone defiles the temple of God, God will destroy him. For the temple of God is holy, which *temple* you are.

AVOID WORLDLY WISDOM

18 Let no one deceive himself. If anyone among you seems to be wise in this age, let him become a fool that he may become wise.

19 For the wisdom of this world is foolishness with God. For it is written, *"He catches the wise in their own craftiness";*[a]

2:13 [a]NU-Text omits *Holy.*   2:16 [a]Isaiah 40:13
3:19 [a]Job 5:13

DO YOU NOT KNOW THAT YOU ARE THE TEMPLE OF GOD AND THAT THE SPIRIT OF GOD DWELLS IN YOU? 1 Corinthians 3:16

You Are a Temple!

Have you seen pictures of temples? They are *big* buildings where people worship God, or some other gods. They are something like a church. God says you are a temple, His temple, and that He lives in you. That happens, of course, when you become a Christian. So what difference does that make in our daily lives?

1. If God lives in you, what should you do about keeping your body, mind, and soul clean? Do you think God wants to live in a dirty mind, dirty soul, or dirty body?
2. If God lives in you, what should you do about reading His Word each day to help you know how to live? If you never read the Bible, God's Word, how would you know what to do with your temple of God?
3. If God lives in you, what should you do about praying each day? If God lives in you, what will He think if you never talk with Him?

For more on *Favorite Family Verses* turn to page 1773
For more on *God's Guidance* turn to page 819

20 and again, *"The LORD knows the thoughts of the wise, that they are futile."*a

21 Therefore let no one boast in men. For all things are yours:

22 whether Paul or A·pol′los or Cē′-phas, or the world or life or death, or things present or things to come—all are yours.

23 And you *are* Christ's, and Christ *is* God's.

STEWARDS OF THE MYSTERIES OF GOD

4 Let a man so consider us, as servants of Christ and stewards of the mysteries of God.

2 Moreover it is required in stewards that one be found faithful.

3 But with me it is a very small thing that I should be judged by you or by a human court.a In fact, I do not even judge myself.

4 For I know of nothing against myself, yet I am not justified by this; but He who judges me is the Lord.

5 Therefore judge nothing before the time, until the Lord comes, who will both bring to light the hidden things of darkness and reveal the counsels of the hearts. Then each one's praise will come from God.

FOOLS FOR CHRIST'S SAKE

6 Now these things, brethren, I have figuratively transferred to myself and A·pol′los for your sakes, that you may learn in us not to think beyond what is written, that none of you may be puffed up on behalf of one against the other.

7 For who makes you differ *from another?* And what do you have that you did not receive? Now if you did indeed receive *it,* why do you boast as if you had not received *it?*

8 You are already full! You are already rich! You have reigned as kings without us—and indeed I could wish you did reign, that we also might reign with you!

9 For I think that God has displayed us, the apostles, last, as men condemned to death; for we have been made a spectacle to the world, both to angels and to men.

10 We *are* fools for Christ's sake, but you *are* wise in Christ! We *are* weak, but you *are* strong! You *are* distinguished, but we *are* dishonored!

11 To the present hour we both hunger and thirst, and we are poorly clothed, and beaten, and homeless.

12 And we labor, working with our own hands. Being reviled, we bless; being persecuted, we endure;

13 being defamed, we entreat. We have been made as the filth of the world, the offscouring of all things until now.

PAUL'S PATERNAL CARE

14 I do not write these things to shame you, but as my beloved children I warn *you.*

15 For though you might have ten thousand instructors in Christ, yet *you do* not *have* many fathers; for in Christ Jesus I have begotten you through the gospel.

16 Therefore I urge you, imitate me.

17 For this reason I have sent Timothy to you, who is my beloved and faithful son in the Lord, who will remind you of my ways in Christ, as I teach everywhere in every church.

18 Now some are puffed up, as though I were not coming to you.

19 But I will come to you shortly, if the Lord wills, and I will know, not the word of those who are puffed up, but the power.

3:20 aPsalm 94:11   4:3 aLiterally *day*

20 For the kingdom of God *is* not in word but in power.
21 What do you want? Shall I come to you with a rod, or in love and a spirit of gentleness?

IMMORALITY DEFILES THE CHURCH

5 It is actually reported *that there is* sexual immorality among you, and such sexual immorality as is not even namedª among the Gentiles—that a man has his father's wife!
2 And you are puffed up, and have not rather mourned, that he who has done this deed might be taken away from among you.
3 For I indeed, as absent in body but present in spirit, have already judged (as though I were present) him who has so done this deed.
4 In the name of our Lord Jesus Christ, when you are gathered together, along with my spirit, with the power of our Lord Jesus Christ,
5 deliver such a one to Satan for the destruction of the flesh, that his spirit may be saved in the day of the Lord Jesus.ª
6 Your glorying *is* not good. Do you not know that a little leaven leavens the whole lump?
7 Therefore purge out the old leaven, that you may be a new lump, since you truly are unleavened. For indeed Christ, our Passover, was sacrificed for us.ª
8 Therefore let us keep the feast, not with old leaven, nor with the leaven of malice and wickedness, but with the unleavened *bread* of sincerity and truth.

IMMORALITY MUST BE JUDGED

9 I wrote to you in my epistle not to keep company with sexually immoral people.

10 Yet *I* certainly *did* not *mean* with the sexually immoral people of this world, or with the covetous, or extortioners, or idolaters, since then you would need to go out of the world.
11 But now I have written to you not to keep company with anyone named a brother, who is sexually immoral, or covetous, or an idolater, or a reviler, or a drunkard, or an extortioner—not even to eat with such a person.
12 For what *have* I *to do* with judging those also who are outside? Do you not judge those who are inside?
13 But those who are outside God judges. Therefore *"put away from yourselves the evil person."*ª

DO NOT SUE THE BRETHREN

6 Dare any of you, having a matter against another, go to law before the unrighteous, and not before the saints?
2 Do you not know that the saints will judge the world? And if the world will be judged by you, are you unworthy to judge the smallest matters?
3 Do you not know that we shall judge angels? How much more, things that pertain to this life?
4 If then you have judgments concerning things pertaining to this life, do you appoint those who are least esteemed by the church to judge?
5 I say this to your shame. Is it so, that there is not a wise man among you, not even one, who will be able to judge between his brethren?
6 But brother goes to law against brother, and that before unbelievers!
7 Now therefore, it is already an utter failure for you that you go to law against one another. Why do you not

5:1 ªNU-Text omits *named.*   5:5 ªNU-Text omits *Jesus.*   5:7 ªNU-Text omits *for us.*
5:13 ªDeuteronomy 17:7; 19:19; 22:21, 24; 24:7

rather accept wrong? Why do you not rather *let yourselves* be cheated?

8 No, you yourselves do wrong and cheat, and *you do* these things *to your* brethren!

9 Do you not know that the unrighteous will not inherit the kingdom of God? Do not be deceived. Neither fornicators, nor idolaters, nor adulterers, nor homosexuals,*a* nor sodomites,

10 nor thieves, nor covetous, nor drunkards, nor revilers, nor extortioners will inherit the kingdom of God.

11 And such were some of you. But you were washed, but you were sanctified, but you were justified in the name of the Lord Jesus and by the Spirit of our God.

GLORIFY GOD IN BODY AND SPIRIT

12 All things are lawful for me, but all things are not helpful. All things are lawful for me, but I will not be brought under the power of any.

13 Foods for the stomach and the stomach for foods, but God will destroy both it and them. Now the body *is* not for sexual immorality but for the Lord, and the Lord for the body.

14 And God both raised up the Lord and will also raise us up by His power.

15 Do you not know that your bodies are members of Christ? Shall I then take the members of Christ and make *them* members of a harlot? Certainly not!

16 Or do you not know that he who is joined to a harlot is one body *with her?* For *"the two,"* He says, *"shall become one flesh."a*

17 But he who is joined to the Lord is one spirit *with Him.*

18 Flee sexual immorality. Every sin that a man does is outside the body,

but he who commits sexual immorality sins against his own body.

19 Or do you not know that your body is the temple of the Holy Spirit *who is* in you, whom you have from God, and you are not your own?

20 For you were bought at a price; therefore glorify God in your body*a* and in your spirit, which are God's.

PRINCIPLES OF MARRIAGE

7 Now concerning the things of which you wrote to me: *It is* good for a man not to touch a woman.

2 Nevertheless, because of sexual immorality, let each man have his own wife, and let each woman have her own husband.

3 Let the husband render to his wife the affection due her, and likewise also the wife to her husband.

4 The wife does not have authority over her own body, but the husband *does.* And likewise the husband does not have authority over his own body, but the wife *does.*

5 Do not deprive one another except with consent for a time, that you may give yourselves to fasting and prayer; and come together again so that Satan does not tempt you because of your lack of self-control.

6 But I say this as a concession, not as a commandment.

7 For I wish that all men were even as I myself. But each one has his own gift from God, one in this manner and another in that.

8 But I say to the unmarried and to the widows: It is good for them if they remain even as I am;

9 but if they cannot exercise self-control, let them marry. For it is better to marry than to burn *with passion.*

6:9 *a*That is, catamites   6:16 *a*Genesis 2:24
6:20 *a*NU-Text ends the verse at *body.*

Values

CLEANLINESS 1 Corinthians 6:19, 20

Why Should I Take a Bath?

Are there times when you don't want to take a bath? Do you ever argue with your parents about doing this? But what if you stopped taking a bath? How long would your friends want to be around you?

1. Why should we keep our bodies clean? Read 1 Corinthians 6:19, 20. What does this say about taking good care of our bodies?
2. Would Jesus want you to stop taking a bath? Would it please God if you went around dirty and filthy all the time? Why not?
3. Who else would not be pleased if you stopped taking a bath or washing your hands? Would you be pleased?

For more on *Values* turn to page 1808
For more on *Responsibility* turn to page 1808

KEEP YOUR MARRIAGE VOWS

10 Now to the married I command, *yet* not I but the Lord: A wife is not to depart from *her* husband.

11 But even if she does depart, let her remain unmarried or be reconciled to *her* husband. And a husband is not to divorce *his* wife.

12 But to the rest I, not the Lord, say: If any brother has a wife who does not believe, and she is willing to live with him, let him not divorce her.

13 And a woman who has a husband who does not believe, if he is willing to live with her, let her not divorce him.

14 For the unbelieving husband is sanctified by the wife, and the unbelieving wife is sanctified by the husband; otherwise your children would be unclean, but now they are holy.

15 But if the unbeliever departs, let him depart; a brother or a sister is not under bondage in such *cases*. But God has called us to peace.

16 For how do you know, O wife, whether you will save *your* husband? Or how do you know, O husband, whether you will save *your* wife?

LIVE AS YOU ARE CALLED

17 But as God has distributed to each one, as the Lord has called each one, so let him walk. And so I ordain in all the churches.

18 Was anyone called while circumcised? Let him not become uncircumcised. Was anyone called while uncircumcised? Let him not be circumcised.

19 Circumcision is nothing and uncircumcision is nothing, but keeping the commandments of God *is what matters.*

20 Let each one remain in the same calling in which he was called.

21 Were you called *while* a slave? Do not be concerned about it; but if you can be made free, rather use *it*.

22 For he who is called in the Lord *while* a slave is the Lord's freedman. Likewise he who is called *while* free is Christ's slave.

23 You were bought at a price; do not become slaves of men.

24 Brethren, let each one remain with God in that *state* in which he was called.

TO THE UNMARRIED AND WIDOWS

25 Now concerning virgins: I have no commandment from the Lord; yet I give judgment as one whom the Lord in His mercy *has made* trustworthy.

26 I suppose therefore that this is good because of the present distress—that *it is* good for a man to remain as he is:

27 Are you bound to a wife? Do not seek to be loosed. Are you loosed from a wife? Do not seek a wife.

28 But even if you do marry, you have not sinned; and if a virgin marries, she has not sinned. Nevertheless such will have trouble in the flesh, but I would spare you.

29 But this I say, brethren, the time *is* short, so that from now on even those who have wives should be as though they had none,

30 those who weep as though they did not weep, those who rejoice as though they did not rejoice, those who buy as though they did not possess,

31 and those who use this world as not misusing *it*. For the form of this world is passing away.

32 But I want you to be without care. He who is unmarried cares for the things of the Lord—how he may please the Lord.

33 But he who is married cares about the things of the world—how he may please *his* wife.

34 There is*a* a difference between a wife and a virgin. The unmarried woman cares about the things of the Lord, that she may be holy both in body and in spirit. But she who is married cares about the things of the world—how she may please *her* husband.

35 And this I say for your own profit, not that I may put a leash on you, but for what is proper, and that you may serve the Lord without distraction.

36 But if any man thinks he is behaving improperly toward his virgin, if she is past the flower of youth, and thus it must be, let him do what he wishes. He does not sin; let them marry.

37 Nevertheless he who stands steadfast in his heart, having no necessity, but has power over his own will, and has so determined in his heart that he will keep his virgin,*a* does well.

38 So then he who gives *her*a in marriage does well, but he who does not give *her* in marriage does better.

39 A wife is bound by law as long as her husband lives; but if her husband dies, she is at liberty to be married to whom she wishes, only in the Lord.

40 But she is happier if she remains as she is, according to my judgment—and I think I also have the Spirit of God.

BE SENSITIVE TO CONSCIENCE

8 Now concerning things offered to idols: We know that we all have knowledge. Knowledge puffs up, but love edifies.

2 And if anyone thinks that he knows anything, he knows nothing yet as he ought to know.

3 But if anyone loves God, this one is known by Him.

4 Therefore concerning the eating of things offered to idols, we know that an idol *is* nothing in the world, and that *there is* no other God but one.

5 For even if there are so-called gods, whether in heaven or on earth (as there are many gods and many lords),

6 yet for us *there is* one God, the Father, of whom *are* all things, and we for Him; and one Lord Jesus Christ, through whom *are* all things, and through whom we *live*.

7 However, *there is* not in everyone that knowledge; for some, with consciousness of the idol, until now eat *it* as a thing offered to an idol; and their conscience, being weak, is defiled.

8 But food does not commend us to God; for neither if we eat are we the better, nor if we do not eat are we the worse.

9 But beware lest somehow this liberty of yours become a stumbling block to those who are weak.

10 For if anyone sees you who have knowledge eating in an idol's temple, will not the conscience of him who is weak be emboldened to eat those things offered to idols?

11 And because of your knowledge shall the weak brother perish, for whom Christ died?

12 But when you thus sin against the brethren, and wound their weak conscience, you sin against Christ.

13 Therefore, if food makes my brother stumble, I will never again eat meat, lest I make my brother stumble.

A PATTERN OF SELF-DENIAL

9 Am I not an apostle? Am I not free? Have I not seen Jesus Christ

---

7:34 *a*M-Text adds *also*.   7:37 *a*Or *virgin daughter*   7:38 *a*NU-Text reads *his own virgin.*

our Lord? Are you not my work in the Lord?

2 If I am not an apostle to others, yet doubtless I am to you. For you are the seal of my apostleship in the Lord.

3 My defense to those who examine me is this:

4 Do we have no right to eat and drink?

5 Do we have no right to take along a believing wife, as *do* also the other apostles, the brothers of the Lord, and Cē′phas?

6 Or *is it* only Bar′na·bas and I *who* have no right to refrain from working?

7 Who ever goes to war at his own expense? Who plants a vineyard and does not eat of its fruit? Or who tends a flock and does not drink of the milk of the flock?

8 Do I say these things as a *mere* man? Or does not the law say the same also?

9 For it is written in the law of Moses, *"You shall not muzzle an ox while it treads out the grain."[a]* Is it oxen God is concerned about?

10 Or does He say *it* altogether for our sakes? For our sakes, no doubt, *this* is written, that he who plows should plow in hope, and he who threshes in hope should be partaker of his hope.

11 If we have sown spiritual things for you, *is it* a great thing if we reap your material things?

12 If others are partakers of *this* right over you, *are* we not even more? Nevertheless we have not used this right, but endure all things lest we hinder the gospel of Christ.

13 Do you not know that those who minister the holy things eat *of the things* of the temple, and those who serve at the altar partake of *the offerings of* the altar?

14 Even so the Lord has commanded that those who preach the gospel should live from the gospel.

15 But I have used none of these things, nor have I written these things that it should be done so to me; for it *would be* better for me to die than that anyone should make my boasting void.

16 For if I preach the gospel, I have nothing to boast of, for necessity is laid upon me; yes, woe is me if I do not preach the gospel!

17 For if I do this willingly, I have a reward; but if against my will, I have been entrusted with a stewardship.

18 What is my reward then? That when I preach the gospel, I may present the gospel of Christ[a] without charge, that I may not abuse my authority in the gospel.

SERVING ALL MEN

19 For though I am free from all *men,* I have made myself a servant to all, that I might win the more;

20 and to the Jews I became as a Jew, that I might win Jews; to those *who are* under the law, as under the law,[a] that I might win those *who are* under the law;

21 to those *who are* without law, as without law (not being without law toward God,[a] but under law toward Christ[b]), that I might win those *who are* without law;

22 to the weak I became as[a] weak, that I might win the weak. I have become all things to all *men,* that I might by all means save some.

23 Now this I do for the gospel's sake, that I may be partaker of it with *you.*

9:9 [a]Deuteronomy 25:4   9:18 [a]NU-Text omits *of Christ.*   9:20 [a]NU-Text adds *though not being myself under the law.*   9:21 [a]NU-Text reads *God's law.* [b]NU-Text reads *Christ's law.*
9:22 [a]NU-Text omits *as.*

STRIVING FOR A CROWN

24 Do you not know that those who run in a race all run, but one receives the prize? Run in such a way that you may obtain *it*.

25 And everyone who competes *for the prize* is temperate in all things. Now they *do it* to obtain a perishable crown, but we *for* an imperishable *crown*.

26 Therefore I run thus: not with uncertainty. Thus I fight: not as *one who* beats the air.

27 But I discipline my body and bring *it* into subjection, lest, when I have preached to others, I myself should become disqualified.

OLD TESTAMENT EXAMPLES

10 Moreover, brethren, I do not want you to be unaware that all our fathers were under the cloud, all passed through the sea,

2 all were baptized into Moses in the cloud and in the sea,

3 all ate the same spiritual food,

4 and all drank the same spiritual drink. For they drank of that spiritual Rock that followed them, and that Rock was Christ.

5 But with most of them God was not well pleased, for *their bodies* were scattered in the wilderness.

6 Now these things became our examples, to the intent that we should not lust after evil things as they also lusted.

7 And do not become idolaters as *were* some of them. As it is written, *"The people sat down to eat and drink, and rose up to play."*[a]

8 Nor let us commit sexual immorality, as some of them did, and in one day twenty-three thousand fell;

9 nor let us tempt Christ, as some of them also tempted, and were destroyed by serpents;

10 nor complain, as some of them also complained, and were destroyed by the destroyer.

11 Now all[a] these things happened to them as examples, and they were written for our admonition, upon whom the ends of the ages have come.

12 Therefore let him who thinks he stands take heed lest he fall.

13 No temptation has overtaken you except such as is common to man; but God *is* faithful, who will not allow you to be tempted beyond what you are able, but with the temptation will also make the way of escape, that you may be able to bear *it*.

FLEE FROM IDOLATRY

14 Therefore, my beloved, flee from idolatry.

15 I speak as to wise men; judge for yourselves what I say.

16 The cup of blessing which we bless, is it not the communion of the blood of Christ? The bread which we break, is it not the communion of the body of Christ?

17 For we, *though* many, are one bread *and* one body; for we all partake of that one bread.

18 Observe Israel after the flesh: Are not those who eat of the sacrifices partakers of the altar?

19 What am I saying then? That an idol is anything, or what is offered to idols is anything?

20 Rather, that the things which the Gentiles sacrifice they sacrifice to demons and not to God, and I do not want you to have fellowship with demons.

21 You cannot drink the cup of the Lord and the cup of demons; you cannot partake of the Lord's table and of the table of demons.

10:7 [a]Exodus 32:6   10:11 [a]NU-Text omits *all*.

WHEN A ROCKING HORSE BECOMES A WILD STALLION

1 Corinthians 10:13

Did you ever think you were riding a little rocking horse, or stick horse, but it suddenly became a wild stallion? Did you ever plan a simple picnic, but it became so complicated that it turned into a disaster? Did you ever want to make something uncomplicated, but it became terribly confusing? Have you ever seen little things become big deals and you wished you had never started them? What should you do then?

1. What simple things have become almost too big for you to handle? What did you do about them? What should you do about them?
2. Does it ever seem that life sometimes gets too complicated, or has too many problems? What do you do? What should you do?
3. Read 1 Corinthians 10:13. Now read it using "problem" instead of "temptation." Everyone has big problems. You are not alone. But who can help you deal with them most? Thank You, God, for being my helper.
4. Whenever you face *big* problems, turn to God. He is much *bigger* than your *big* problems. He will help you.

For more on *What Should I Do?* turn to page 1766
For more on *Facing Trials* turn to page 1766

22 Or do we provoke the Lord to jealousy? Are we stronger than He?

ALL TO THE GLORY OF GOD

23 All things are lawful for me,*a* but not all things are helpful; all things are lawful for me,*b* but not all things edify.
24 Let no one seek his own, but each one the other's *well-being.*
25 Eat whatever is sold in the meat market, asking no questions for conscience' sake;
26 for *"the earth is the LORD's, and all its fullness."a*
27 If any of those who do not believe invites you *to dinner,* and you desire to go, eat whatever is set before you, asking no question for conscience' sake.
28 But if anyone says to you, "This was offered to idols," do not eat it for the sake of the one who told you, and for conscience' sake;*a* for *"the earth is the LORD's, and all its fullness."b*
29 "Conscience," I say, not your own, but that of the other. For why is my liberty judged by another *man's* conscience?
30 But if I partake with thanks, why am I evil spoken of for *the food* over which I give thanks?
31 Therefore, whether you eat or drink, or whatever you do, do all to the glory of God.
32 Give no offense, either to the Jews or to the Greeks or to the church of God,
33 just as I also please all *men* in all *things,* not seeking my own profit,

10:23 *a*NU-Text omits *for me.* *b*NU-Text omits *for me.* 10:26 *a*Psalm 24:1 10:28 *a*NU-Text omits the rest of this verse. *b*Psalm 24:1

but the *profit* of many, that they may be saved.

11 Imitate me, just as I also *imitate* Christ.

HEAD COVERINGS

2 Now I praise you, brethren, that you remember me in all things and keep the traditions just as I delivered *them* to you.
3 But I want you to know that the head of every man is Christ, the head of woman *is* man, and the head of Christ *is* God.
4 Every man praying or prophesying, having *his* head covered, dishonors his head.
5 But every woman who prays or prophesies with *her* head uncovered dishonors her head, for that is one and the same as if her head were shaved.
6 For if a woman is not covered, let her also be shorn. But if it is shameful for a woman to be shorn or shaved, let her be covered.
7 For a man indeed ought not to cover *his* head, since he is the image and glory of God; but woman is the glory of man.
8 For man is not from woman, but woman from man.
9 Nor was man created for the woman, but woman for the man.
10 For this reason the woman ought to have *a symbol of* authority on *her* head, because of the angels.
11 Nevertheless, neither *is* man independent of woman, nor woman independent of man, in the Lord.
12 For as woman *came* from man, even so man also *comes* through woman; but all things are from God.
13 Judge among yourselves. Is it proper for a woman to pray to God with her head uncovered?
14 Does not even nature itself teach you that if a man has long hair, it is a dishonor to him?
15 But if a woman has long hair, it is a glory to her; for *her* hair is given to her[a] for a covering.
16 But if anyone seems to be contentious, we have no such custom, nor *do* the churches of God.

CONDUCT AT THE LORD'S SUPPER

17 Now in giving these instructions I do not praise *you,* since you come together not for the better but for the worse.
18 For first of all, when you come together as a church, I hear that there are divisions among you, and in part I believe it.
19 For there must also be factions among you, that those who are approved may be recognized among you.
20 Therefore when you come together in one place, it is not to eat the Lord's Supper.
21 For in eating, each one takes his own supper ahead of *others;* and one is hungry and another is drunk.
22 What! Do you not have houses to eat and drink in? Or do you despise the church of God and shame those who have nothing? What shall I say to you? Shall I praise you in this? I do not praise *you.*

INSTITUTION OF THE LORD'S SUPPER

23 For I received from the Lord that which I also delivered to you: that the Lord Jesus on the *same* night in which He was betrayed took bread;
24 and when He had given thanks, He broke *it* and said, "Take, eat;[a] this is My body which is broken[b] for you; do this in remembrance of Me."

11:15 [a]M-Text omits *to her.*   11:24 [a]NU-Text omits *Take, eat.*   [b]NU-Text omits *broken.*

25 In the same manner *He* also *took* the cup after supper, saying, "This cup is the new covenant in My blood. This do, as often as you drink *it,* in remembrance of Me."

26 For as often as you eat this bread and drink this cup, you proclaim the Lord's death till He comes.

EXAMINE YOURSELF

27 Therefore whoever eats this bread or drinks *this* cup of the Lord in an unworthy manner will be guilty of the body and blood[a] of the Lord.

28 But let a man examine himself, and so let him eat of the bread and drink of the cup.

29 For he who eats and drinks in an unworthy manner[a] eats and drinks judgment to himself, not discerning the Lord's[b] body.

30 For this reason many *are* weak and sick among you, and many sleep.

31 For if we would judge ourselves, we would not be judged.

32 But when we are judged, we are chastened by the Lord, that we may not be condemned with the world.

33 Therefore, my brethren, when you come together to eat, wait for one another.

34 But if anyone is hungry, let him eat at home, lest you come together for judgment. And the rest I will set in order when I come.

SPIRITUAL GIFTS: UNITY IN DIVERSITY

12 Now concerning spiritual *gifts,* brethren, I do not want you to be ignorant:

2 You know that[a] you were Gentiles, carried away to these dumb idols, however you were led.

3 Therefore I make known to you that no one speaking by the Spirit of God calls Jesus accursed, and no one can say that Jesus is Lord except by the Holy Spirit.

4 There are diversities of gifts, but the same Spirit.

5 There are differences of ministries, but the same Lord.

6 And there are diversities of activities, but it is the same God who works all in all.

7 But the manifestation of the Spirit is given to each one for the profit *of all:*

8 for to one is given the word of wisdom through the Spirit, to another the word of knowledge through the same Spirit,

9 to another faith by the same Spirit, to another gifts of healings by the same[a] Spirit,

10 to another the working of miracles, to another prophecy, to another discerning of spirits, to another *different* kinds of tongues, to another the interpretation of tongues.

11 But one and the same Spirit works all these things, distributing to each one individually as He wills.

UNITY AND DIVERSITY IN ONE BODY

12 For as the body is one and has many members, but all the members of that one body, being many, are one body, so also *is* Christ.

13 For by one Spirit we were all baptized into one body—whether Jews or Greeks, whether slaves or free—and have all been made to drink into[a] one Spirit.

14 For in fact the body is not one member but many.

15 If the foot should say, "Because I am not a hand, I am not of the body," is it therefore not of the body?

11:27 [a]NU-Text and M-Text read *the blood.*
11:29 [a]NU-Text omits *in an unworthy manner.*
[b]NU-Text omits *Lord's.*   12:2 [a]NU-Text and M-Text add *when.*   12:9 [a]NU-Text reads *one.*
12:13 [a]NU-Text omits *into.*

16 And if the ear should say, "Because I am not an eye, I am not of the body," is it therefore not of the body?
17 If the whole body *were* an eye, where *would be* the hearing? If the whole *were* hearing, where *would be* the smelling?
18 But now God has set the members, each one of them, in the body just as He pleased.
19 And if they *were* all one member, where *would* the body *be?*
20 But now indeed *there are* many members, yet one body.
21 And the eye cannot say to the hand, "I have no need of you"; nor again the head to the feet, "I have no need of you."
22 No, much rather, those members of the body which seem to be weaker are necessary.
23 And those *members* of the body which we think to be less honorable, on these we bestow greater honor; and our unpresentable *parts* have greater modesty,
24 but our presentable *parts* have no need. But God composed the body, having given greater honor to that *part* which lacks it,
25 that there should be no schism in the body, but *that* the members should have the same care for one another.
26 And if one member suffers, all the members suffer with *it;* or if one member is honored, all the members rejoice with *it.*
27 Now you are the body of Christ, and members individually.
28 And God has appointed these in the church: first apostles, second prophets, third teachers, after that miracles, then gifts of healings, helps, administrations, varieties of tongues.
29 *Are* all apostles? *Are* all prophets? *Are* all teachers? *Are* all workers of miracles?

30 Do all have gifts of healings? Do all speak with tongues? Do all interpret?
31 But earnestly desire the best*a* gifts. And yet I show you a more excellent way.

The Greatest Gift

13 Though I speak with the tongues of men and of angels, but have not love, I have become sounding brass or a clanging cymbal.
2 And though I have *the gift of* prophecy, and understand all mysteries and all knowledge, and though I have all faith, so that I could remove mountains, but have not love, I am nothing.
3 And though I bestow all my goods to feed *the poor,* and though I give my body to be burned,*a* but have not love, it profits me nothing.
4 Love suffers long *and* is kind; love does not envy; love does not parade itself, is not puffed up;
5 does not behave rudely, does not seek its own, is not provoked, thinks no evil;
6 does not rejoice in iniquity, but rejoices in the truth;
7 bears all things, believes all things, hopes all things, endures all things.
8 Love never fails. But whether *there are* prophecies, they will fail; whether *there are* tongues, they will cease; whether *there is* knowledge, it will vanish away.
9 For we know in part and we prophesy in part.
10 But when that which is perfect has come, then that which is in part will be done away.
11 When I was a child, I spoke as a child, I understood as a child, I

12:31 *a*NU-Text reads *greater.*   13:3 *a*NU-Text reads *so I may boast.*

thought as a child; but when I became a man, I put away childish things.

12 For now we see in a mirror, dimly, but then face to face. Now I know in part, but then I shall know just as I also am known.

13 And now abide faith, hope, love, these three; but the greatest of these *is* love.

PROPHECY AND TONGUES

14 Pursue love, and desire spiritual *gifts,* but especially that you may prophesy.

2 For he who speaks in a tongue does not speak to men but to God, for no one understands *him;* however, in the spirit he speaks mysteries.

3 But he who prophesies speaks edification and exhortation and comfort to men.

4 He who speaks in a tongue edifies himself, but he who prophesies edifies the church.

5 I wish you all spoke with tongues, but even more that you prophesied; for[a] he who prophesies *is* greater than he who speaks with tongues, unless indeed he interprets, that the church may receive edification.

TONGUES MUST BE INTERPRETED

6 But now, brethren, if I come to you speaking with tongues, what shall I profit you unless I speak to you either by revelation, by knowledge, by prophesying, or by teaching?

7 Even things without life, whether flute or harp, when they make a sound, unless they make a distinction in the sounds, how will it be known what is piped or played?

8 For if the trumpet makes an uncertain sound, who will prepare for battle?

9 So likewise you, unless you utter by the tongue words easy to understand, how will it be known what is spoken? For you will be speaking into the air.

10 There are, it may be, so many kinds of languages in the world, and none of them *is* without significance.

11 Therefore, if I do not know the meaning of the language, I shall be a foreigner to him who speaks, and he who speaks *will be* a foreigner to me.

12 Even so you, since you are zealous for spiritual *gifts, let it be* for the edification of the church *that* you seek to excel.

13 Therefore let him who speaks in a tongue pray that he may interpret.

14 For if I pray in a tongue, my spirit prays, but my understanding is unfruitful.

15 What is *the conclusion* then? I will pray with the spirit, and I will also pray with the understanding. I will sing with the spirit, and I will also sing with the understanding.

16 Otherwise, if you bless with the spirit, how will he who occupies the place of the uninformed say "Amen" at your giving of thanks, since he does not understand what you say?

17 For you indeed give thanks well, but the other is not edified.

18 I thank my God I speak with tongues more than you all;

19 yet in the church I would rather speak five words with my understanding, that I may teach others also, than ten thousand words in a tongue.

TONGUES A SIGN TO UNBELIEVERS

20 Brethren, do not be children in understanding; however, in malice be babes, but in understanding be mature.

14:5 [a]NU-Text reads *and.*

21 In the law it is written:

"With men of other tongues and
  other lips
I will speak to this people;
And yet, for all that, they will not
  hear Me,"a

says the Lord.
22 Therefore tongues are for a sign, not to those who believe but to unbelievers; but prophesying is not for unbelievers but for those who believe.
23 Therefore if the whole church comes together in one place, and all speak with tongues, and there come in those who are uninformed or unbelievers, will they not say that you are out of your mind?
24 But if all prophesy, and an unbeliever or an uninformed person comes in, he is convinced by all, he is convicted by all.
25 And thusa the secrets of his heart are revealed; and so, falling down on his face, he will worship God and report that God is truly among you.

ORDER IN CHURCH MEETINGS

26 How is it then, brethren? Whenever you come together, each of you has a psalm, has a teaching, has a tongue, has a revelation, has an interpretation. Let all things be done for edification.
27 If anyone speaks in a tongue, let there be two or at the most three, each in turn, and let one interpret.
28 But if there is no interpreter, let him keep silent in church, and let him speak to himself and to God.
29 Let two or three prophets speak, and let the others judge.
30 But if anything is revealed to another who sits by, let the first keep silent.

31 For you can all prophesy one by one, that all may learn and all may be encouraged.
32 And the spirits of the prophets are subject to the prophets.
33 For God is not the author of confusion but of peace, as in all the churches of the saints.
34 Let youra women keep silent in the churches, for they are not permitted to speak; but they are to be submissive, as the law also says.
35 And if they want to learn something, let them ask their own husbands at home; for it is shameful for women to speak in church.
36 Or did the word of God come originally from you? Or was it you only that it reached?
37 If anyone thinks himself to be a prophet or spiritual, let him acknowledge that the things which I write to you are the commandments of the Lord.
38 But if anyone is ignorant, let him be ignorant.a
39 Therefore, brethren, desire earnestly to prophesy, and do not forbid to speak with tongues.
40 Let all things be done decently and in order.

THE RISEN CHRIST, FAITH'S REALITY

15 Moreover, brethren, I declare to you the gospel which I preached to you, which also you received and in which you stand,
2 by which also you are saved, if you hold fast that word which I preached to you—unless you believed in vain.
3 For I delivered to you first of all that which I also received: that

14:21 aIsaiah 28:11, 12　14:25 aNU-Text omits And thus.　14:34 aNU-Text omits your.
14:38 aNU-Text reads if anyone does not recognize this, he is not recognized.

RESURRECTION 1 Corinthians 15:12–20

New Life!

Have you ever planted a dry, brown tulip bulb in the fall? Next spring, what did you see? Was there a bright red tulip from it? The brown tulip bulb looked like it was dead. The green tulip plant with the red tulip looks very much alive! When you plant seeds, new life springs from them. Green plants grow, and flowers or vegetables come forth. That's a picture of resurrection. A person's body dies, just as Jesus' body died. But God raises it up to a new life.

1. Read 1 Corinthians 15:13, 14. Can we be raised from the dead without Jesus? Why not?
2. Are you glad Jesus arose from the dead? What does that tell you about resurrection? Is it real? The Bible teaches that Christians will rise from the dead some day. Just as Jesus arose from the dead, so we who believe in Him shall rise from the dead also.

For more on *Favorite Bible Words* turn to page 1786
For more on *Salvation* turn to page 1773

Christ died for our sins according to the Scriptures,

4 and that He was buried, and that He rose again the third day according to the Scriptures,

5 and that He was seen by Cē′phas, then by the twelve.

6 After that He was seen by over five hundred brethren at once, of whom the greater part remain to the present, but some have fallen asleep.

7 After that He was seen by James, then by all the apostles.

8 Then last of all He was seen by me also, as by one born out of due time.

9 For I am the least of the apostles, who am not worthy to be called an apostle, because I persecuted the church of God.

10 But by the grace of God I am what I am, and His grace toward me was not in vain; but I labored more abundantly than they all, yet not I, but the grace of God *which was* with me.

11 Therefore, whether *it was* I or they, so we preach and so you believed.

THE RISEN CHRIST, OUR HOPE

12 Now if Christ is preached that He has been raised from the dead, how do some among you say that there is no resurrection of the dead?

13 But if there is no resurrection of the dead, then Christ is not risen.

14 And if Christ is not risen, then our preaching *is* empty and your faith *is* also empty.

15 Yes, and we are found false witnesses of God, because we have testified of God that He raised up Christ, whom He did not raise up—if in fact the dead do not rise.

16 For if *the* dead do not rise, then Christ is not risen.

17 And if Christ is not risen, your

faith *is* futile; you are still in your sins!

18 Then also those who have fallen asleep in Christ have perished.

19 If in this life only we have hope in Christ, we are of all men the most pitiable.

THE LAST ENEMY DESTROYED

20 But now Christ is risen from the dead, *and* has become the firstfruits of those who have fallen asleep.

21 For since by man *came* death, by Man also *came* the resurrection of the dead.

22 For as in Adam all die, even so in Christ all shall be made alive.

23 But each one in his own order: Christ the firstfruits, afterward those *who are* Christ's at His coming.

24 Then *comes* the end, when He delivers the kingdom to God the Father, when He puts an end to all rule and all authority and power.

25 For He must reign till He has put all enemies under His feet.

26 The last enemy *that* will be destroyed *is* death.

27 For *"He has put all things under His feet."ᵃ* But when He says "all things are put under *Him,"* it is evident that He who put all things under Him is excepted.

28 Now when all things are made subject to Him, then the Son Himself will also be subject to Him who put all things under Him, that God may be all in all.

EFFECTS OF DENYING
THE RESURRECTION

29 Otherwise, what will they do who are baptized for the dead, if the dead do not rise at all? Why then are they baptized for the dead?

30 And why do we stand in jeopardy every hour?

31 I affirm, by the boasting in you which I have in Christ Jesus our Lord, I die daily.

32 If, in the manner of men, I have fought with beasts at Eph′e·sus, what advantage *is it* to me? If *the* dead do not rise, *"Let us eat and drink, for tomorrow we die!"ᵃ*

33 Do not be deceived: "Evil company corrupts good habits."

34 Awake to righteousness, and do not sin; for some do not have the knowledge of God. I speak *this* to your shame.

A GLORIOUS BODY

35 But someone will say, "How are the dead raised up? And with what body do they come?"

36 Foolish one, what you sow is not made alive unless it dies.

37 And what you sow, you do not sow that body that shall be, but mere grain—perhaps wheat or some other *grain.*

38 But God gives it a body as He pleases, and to each seed its own body.

39 All flesh *is* not the same flesh, but *there is* one *kind of* fleshᵃ of men, another flesh of animals, another of fish, *and* another of birds.

40 *There are* also celestial bodies and terrestrial bodies; but the glory of the celestial *is* one, and the *glory* of the terrestrial *is* another.

41 *There is* one glory of the sun, another glory of the moon, and another glory of the stars; for *one* star differs from *another* star in glory.

42 So also *is* the resurrection of the dead. *The body* is sown in corruption, it is raised in incorruption.

43 It is sown in dishonor, it is raised

15:27 ᵃPsalm 8:6   15:32 ᵃIsaiah 22:13
15:39 ᵃNU-Text and M-Text omit *of flesh.*

What Should I Do?

WHEN MY BALLOON BURSTS 1 Corinthians 15:57

Your balloon is so beautiful. You wish you could keep it forever, or at least for a day or two. But suddenly something comes along and your balloon bursts. Perhaps you have done something special. Is it a vacation you've planned for a long time. Now it's pouring rain. Or is it something special you have made? But an accident happens, and now it's a mess. Whatever it is, it's like a beautiful balloon that bursts. What should you do then?

1. What special thing have you had burst or go sour? What did you do? What should you do?
2. Perhaps your balloon that burst was really big, like the death of a loved one or family troubles or the time when mother or father lost their jobs. Can you have victory in the middle of bad defeat? Read 1 Corinthians 15:57. What does it say about victory in defeat? Who gives it? Remember to turn to Jesus next time your balloon, or your life, bursts on you.

For more on *What Should I Do?* turn to page 1800
For more on *Facing Trials* turn to page 1826

in glory. It is sown in weakness, it is raised in power.

44 It is sown a natural body, it is raised a spiritual body. There is a natural body, and there is a spiritual body.

45 And so it is written, *"The first man Adam became a living being."ª* The last Adam *became* a life-giving spirit.

46 However, the spiritual is not first, but the natural, and afterward the spiritual.

47 The first man *was* of the earth, *made* of dust; the second Man *is* the Lordª from heaven.

48 As *was* the *man* of dust, so also *are* those *who are* made of dust; and as *is* the heavenly *Man,* so also *are* those *who are* heavenly.

49 And as we have borne the image of the *man* of dust, we shall also bearª the image of the heavenly *Man.*

OUR FINAL VICTORY

50 Now this I say, brethren, that flesh and blood cannot inherit the kingdom of God; nor does corruption inherit incorruption.

51 Behold, I tell you a mystery: We shall not all sleep, but we shall all be changed—

52 in a moment, in the twinkling of an eye, at the last trumpet. For the trumpet will sound, and the dead will be raised incorruptible, and we shall be changed.

53 For this corruptible must put on incorruption, and this mortal *must* put on immortality.

54 So when this corruptible has put on incorruption, and this mortal has put on immortality, then shall be brought to pass the saying that is

15:45 ªGenesis 2:7   15:47 ªNU-Text omits *the Lord.*   15:49 ªM-Text reads *let us also bear.*

written: *"Death is swallowed up in victory."ᵃ*

55 *"O Death, where is your sting?ᵃ*
O Hā'dēs, where is your
victory?"ᵇ

56 The sting of death *is* sin, and the strength of sin *is* the law.
57 But thanks *be* to God, who gives us the victory through our Lord Jesus Christ.
58 Therefore, my beloved brethren, be steadfast, immovable, always abounding in the work of the Lord, knowing that your labor is not in vain in the Lord.

COLLECTION FOR THE SAINTS

16 Now concerning the collection for the saints, as I have given orders to the churches of Galatia, so you must do also:
2   On the first *day* of the week let each one of you lay something aside, storing up as he may prosper, that there be no collections when I come.
3   And when I come, whomever you approve by *your* letters I will send to bear your gift to Jerusalem.
4   But if it is fitting that I go also, they will go with me.

PERSONAL PLANS

5   Now I will come to you when I pass through Mac·e·dō'ni·a (for I am passing through Mac·e·dō'ni·a).
6   And it may be that I will remain, or even spend the winter with you, that you may send me on my journey, wherever I go.
7   For I do not wish to see you now on the way; but I hope to stay a while with you, if the Lord permits.
8   But I will tarry in Eph'e·sus until Pentecost.
9   For a great and effective door has

opened to me, and *there are* many adversaries.
10   And if Timothy comes, see that he may be with you without fear; for he does the work of the Lord, as I also *do.*
11   Therefore let no one despise him. But send him on his journey in peace, that he may come to me; for I am waiting for him with the brethren.
12   Now concerning *our* brother A·pol'los, I strongly urged him to come to you with the brethren, but he was quite unwilling to come at this time; however, he will come when he has a convenient time.

FINAL EXHORTATIONS

13   Watch, stand fast in the faith, be brave, be strong.
14   Let all *that* you *do* be done with love.
15   I urge you, brethren—you know the household of Steph'a·nas, that it is the firstfruits of A·chā'i·a, and *that* they have devoted themselves to the ministry of the saints—
16   that you also submit to such, and to everyone who works and labors with *us.*
17   I am glad about the coming of Steph'a·nas, For·tu·nā'tus, and A·chā'i·cus, for what was lacking on your part they supplied.
18   For they refreshed my spirit and yours. Therefore acknowledge such men.

GREETINGS AND A SOLEMN FAREWELL

19   The churches of Asia greet you. A·qui'la and Pri·scil'la greet you heartily in the Lord, with the church that is in their house.

15:54 ᵃIsaiah 25:8   15:55 ᵃHosea 13:14   ᵇNU-Text reads *O Death, where is your victory? O Death, where is your sting?*

20 All the brethren greet you. Greet one another with a holy kiss.

21 The salutation with my own hand—Paul's.

22 If anyone does not love the Lord Jesus Christ, let him be accursed.*a* O Lord, come!*b*

23 The grace of our Lord Jesus Christ *be* with you.

24 My love *be* with you all in Christ Jesus. Amen.

16:22 *a*Greek *anathema*   *b*Aramaic *Maranatha*

The Second Epistle of Paul the Apostle to the
CORINTHIANS

GREETING

PAUL, an apostle of Jesus Christ by the will of God, and Timothy *our* brother,

To the church of God which is at Corinth, with all the saints who are in all A·chā′i·a:

2 Grace to you and peace from God our Father and the Lord Jesus Christ.

COMFORT IN SUFFERING

3 Blessed *be* the God and Father of our Lord Jesus Christ, the Father of mercies and God of all comfort,
4 who comforts us in all our tribulation, that we may be able to comfort those who are in any trouble, with the comfort with which we ourselves are comforted by God.
5 For as the sufferings of Christ abound in us, so our consolation also abounds through Christ.
6 Now if we are afflicted, *it is* for your consolation and salvation, which is effective for enduring the same sufferings which we also suffer. Or if we are comforted, *it is* for your consolation and salvation.
7 And our hope for you *is* steadfast, because we know that as you are partakers of the sufferings, so also *you will partake* of the consolation.

DELIVERED FROM SUFFERING

8 For we do not want you to be ignorant, brethren, of our trouble which came to us in Asia: that we were burdened beyond measure, above strength, so that we despaired even of life.

9 Yes, we had the sentence of death in ourselves, that we should not trust in ourselves but in God who raises the dead,
10 who delivered us from so great a death, and does*a* deliver us; in whom we trust that He will still deliver *us,*
11 you also helping together in prayer for us, that thanks may be given by many persons on our*a* behalf for the gift *granted* to us through many.

PAUL'S SINCERITY

12 For our boasting is this: the testimony of our conscience that we conducted ourselves in the world in simplicity and godly sincerity, not with fleshly wisdom but by the grace of God, and more abundantly toward you.
13 For we are not writing any other things to you than what you read or understand. Now I trust you will understand, even to the end
14 (as also you have understood us in part), that we are your boast as you also *are* ours, in the day of the Lord Jesus.

SPARING THE CHURCH

15 And in this confidence I intended to come to you before, that you might have a second benefit—
16 to pass by way of you to Mac·e·dō′ni·a, to come again from Mac·e·dō′ni·a to you, and be helped by you on my way to Judea.
17 Therefore, when I was planning this, did I do it lightly? Or the things

1:10 *a*NU-Text reads *shall.*   1:11 *a*M-Text reads *your behalf.*

I plan, do I plan according to the flesh, that with me there should be Yes, Yes, and No, No?

18 But *as* God *is* faithful, our word to you was not Yes and No.

19 For the Son of God, Jesus Christ, who was preached among you by us—by me, Sil·vā′nus, and Timothy—was not Yes and No, but in Him was Yes.

20 For all the promises of God in Him *are* Yes, and in Him Amen, to the glory of God through us.

21 Now He who establishes us with you in Christ and has anointed us *is* God,

22 who also has sealed us and given us the Spirit in our hearts as a guarantee.

23 Moreover I call God as witness against my soul, that to spare you I came no more to Corinth.

24 Not that we have dominion over your faith, but are fellow workers for your joy; for by faith you stand.

2 But I determined this within myself, that I would not come again to you in sorrow.

2 For if I make you sorrowful, then who is he who makes me glad but the one who is made sorrowful by me?

FORGIVE THE OFFENDER

3 And I wrote this very thing to you, lest, when I came, I should have sorrow over those from whom I ought to have joy, having confidence in you all that my joy is *the joy* of you all.

4 For out of much affliction and anguish of heart I wrote to you, with many tears, not that you should be grieved, but that you might know the love which I have so abundantly for you.

5 But if anyone has caused grief, he has not grieved me, but all of you to some extent—not to be too severe.

6 This punishment which *was inflicted* by the majority *is* sufficient for such a man,

7 so that, on the contrary, you *ought* rather to forgive and comfort *him*, lest perhaps such a one be swallowed up with too much sorrow.

8 Therefore I urge you to reaffirm *your* love to him.

9 For to this end I also wrote, that I might put you to the test, whether you are obedient in all things.

10 Now whom you forgive anything, I also *forgive*. For if indeed I have forgiven anything, I have forgiven that one[a] for your sakes in the presence of Christ,

11 lest Satan should take advantage of us; for we are not ignorant of his devices.

TRIUMPH IN CHRIST

12 Furthermore, when I came to Trō′as to *preach* Christ's gospel, and a door was opened to me by the Lord,

13 I had no rest in my spirit, because I did not find Titus my brother; but taking my leave of them, I departed for Mac·e·dō′ni·a.

14 Now thanks *be* to God who always leads us in triumph in Christ, and through us diffuses the fragrance of His knowledge in every place.

15 For we are to God the fragrance of Christ among those who are being saved and among those who are perishing.

16 To the one *we are* the aroma of death *leading* to death, and to the other the aroma of life *leading* to life. And who *is* sufficient for these things?

17 For we are not, as so many,[a] peddling the word of God; but as of sin-

---

2:10 [a]NU-Text reads *For indeed, what I have forgiven, if I have forgiven anything, I did it.*
2:17 [a]M-Text reads *the rest.*

cerity, but as from God, we speak in the sight of God in Christ.

CHRIST'S EPISTLE

3 Do we begin again to commend ourselves? Or do we need, as some *others,* epistles of commendation to you or *letters* of commendation from you?
2 You are our epistle written in our hearts, known and read by all men;
3 clearly *you are* an epistle of Christ, ministered by us, written not with ink but by the Spirit of the living God, not on tablets of stone but on tablets of flesh, *that is,* of the heart.

THE SPIRIT, NOT THE LETTER

4 And we have such trust through Christ toward God.
5 Not that we are sufficient of ourselves to think of anything as *being* from ourselves, but our sufficiency *is* from God,
6 who also made us sufficient as ministers of the new covenant, not of the letter but of the Spirit;a for the letter kills, but the Spirit gives life.

GLORY OF THE NEW COVENANT

7 But if the ministry of death, written *and* engraved on stones, was glorious, so that the children of Israel could not look steadily at the face of Moses because of the glory of his countenance, which *glory* was passing away,
8 how will the ministry of the Spirit not be more glorious?
9 For if the ministry of condemnation *had* glory, the ministry of righteousness exceeds much more in glory.
10 For even what was made glorious had no glory in this respect, because of the glory that excels.

11 For if what is passing away *was* glorious, what remains *is* much more glorious.
12 Therefore, since we have such hope, we use great boldness of speech—
13 unlike Moses, *who* put a veil over his face so that the children of Israel could not look steadily at the end of what was passing away.
14 But their minds were blinded. For until this day the same veil remains unlifted in the reading of the Old Testament, because the *veil* is taken away in Christ.
15 But even to this day, when Moses is read, a veil lies on their heart.
16 Nevertheless when one turns to the Lord, the veil is taken away.
17 Now the Lord is the Spirit; and where the Spirit of the Lord *is,* there *is* liberty.
18 But we all, with unveiled face, beholding as in a mirror the glory of the Lord, are being transformed into the same image from glory to glory, just as by the Spirit of the Lord.

THE LIGHT OF CHRIST'S GOSPEL

4 Therefore, since we have this ministry, as we have received mercy, we do not lose heart.
2 But we have renounced the hidden things of shame, not walking in craftiness nor handling the word of God deceitfully, but by manifestation of the truth commending ourselves to every man's conscience in the sight of God.
3 But even if our gospel is veiled, it is veiled to those who are perishing,
4 whose minds the god of this age has blinded, who do not believe, lest the light of the gospel of the glory of Christ, who is the image of God, should shine on them.

3:6 aOr *spirit*

5 For we do not preach ourselves, but Christ Jesus the Lord, and ourselves your bondservants for Jesus' sake.

6 For it is the God who commanded light to shine out of darkness, who has shone in our hearts to *give* the light of the knowledge of the glory of God in the face of Jesus Christ.

CAST DOWN BUT UNCONQUERED

7 But we have this treasure in earthen vessels, that the excellence of the power may be of God and not of us.

8 *We are* hard-pressed on every side, yet not crushed; *we are* perplexed, but not in despair;

9 persecuted, but not forsaken; struck down, but not destroyed—

10 always carrying about in the body the dying of the Lord Jesus, that the life of Jesus also may be manifested in our body.

11 For we who live are always delivered to death for Jesus' sake, that the life of Jesus also may be manifested in our mortal flesh.

12 So then death is working in us, but life in you.

13 And since we have the same spirit of faith, according to what is written, *"I believed and therefore I spoke,"a* we also believe and therefore speak,

14 knowing that He who raised up the Lord Jesus will also raise us up with Jesus, and will present *us* with you.

15 For all things *are* for your sakes, that grace, having spread through the many, may cause thanksgiving to abound to the glory of God.

SEEING THE INVISIBLE

16 Therefore we do not lose heart. Even though our outward man is perishing, yet the inward *man* is being renewed day by day.

17 For our light affliction, which is but for a moment, is working for us a far more exceeding *and* eternal weight of glory,

18 while we do not look at the things which are seen, but at the things which are not seen. For the things which are seen *are* temporary, but the things which are not seen *are* eternal.

ASSURANCE OF THE RESURRECTION

5 For we know that if our earthly house, *this* tent, is destroyed, we have a building from God, a house not made with hands, eternal in the heavens.

2 For in this we groan, earnestly desiring to be clothed with our habitation which is from heaven,

3 if indeed, having been clothed, we shall not be found naked.

4 For we who are in *this* tent groan, being burdened, not because we want to be unclothed, but further clothed, that mortality may be swallowed up by life.

5 Now He who has prepared us for this very thing *is* God, who also has given us the Spirit as a guarantee.

6 So *we are* always confident, knowing that while we are at home in the body we are absent from the Lord.

7 For we walk by faith, not by sight.

8 We are confident, yes, well pleased rather to be absent from the body and to be present with the Lord.

THE JUDGMENT SEAT OF CHRIST

9 Therefore we make it our aim, whether present or absent, to be well pleasing to Him.

4:13 *a*Psalm 116:10

THEREFORE, IF ANYONE IS IN CHRIST, HE IS A NEW CREATION; OLD THINGS HAVE PASSED AWAY; BEHOLD, ALL THINGS HAVE BECOME NEW.

2 Corinthians 5:17

A New Life

When we accept Jesus as Savior, we become different. Jesus takes our sins away. He gives us a new life—which we call a Christian life. We love God now. We want to read His Word. We want to please Him. We want to tell others about Him. We're different, like this butterfly. A few minutes ago this little girl saw only an ugly, brown cocoon. Now she sees a beautiful butterfly.

1. Where did this butterfly come from? How is it different now from the way it was before?
2. How is a person who accepts Jesus different? Have you accepted Him? How should you be different? Are you?

For more on *Favorite Family Verses* turn to page 1779
For more on *Salvation* turn to page 1796

10 For we must all appear before the judgment seat of Christ, that each one may receive the things *done* in the body, according to what he has done, whether good or bad.

11 Knowing, therefore, the terror of the Lord, we persuade men; but we are well known to God, and I also trust are well known in your consciences.

BE RECONCILED TO GOD

12 For we do not commend ourselves again to you, but give you opportunity to boast on our behalf, that you may have *an answer* for those who boast in appearance and not in heart.

13 For if we are beside ourselves, *it is* for God; or if we are of sound mind, *it is* for you.

14 For the love of Christ compels us, because we judge thus: that if One died for all, then all died;

15 and He died for all, that those who live should live no longer for themselves, but for Him who died for them and rose again.

16 Therefore, from now on, we regard no one according to the flesh. Even though we have known Christ according to the flesh, yet now we know *Him thus* no longer.

17 Therefore, if anyone *is* in Christ, *he is* a new creation; old things have passed away; behold, all things have become new.

18 Now all things *are* of God, who has reconciled us to Himself through Jesus Christ, and has given us the ministry of reconciliation,

19 that is, that God was in Christ reconciling the world to Himself, not imputing their trespasses to them, and has committed to us the word of reconciliation.

20 Now then, we are ambassadors for Christ, as though God were pleading through us: we implore *you* on Christ's behalf, be reconciled to God.

21 For He made Him who knew no sin *to be* sin for us, that we might become the righteousness of God in Him.

MARKS OF THE MINISTRY

6 We then, *as* workers together *with Him* also plead with *you* not to receive the grace of God in vain.

2   For He says:

> "*In an acceptable time I have*
> *heard you,*
> *And in the day of salvation I have*
> *helped you.*"[a]

Behold, now *is* the accepted time; behold, now *is* the day of salvation.

3   We give no offense in anything, that our ministry may not be blamed.

4   But in all *things* we commend ourselves as ministers of God: in much patience, in tribulations, in needs, in distresses,

5   in stripes, in imprisonments, in tumults, in labors, in sleeplessness, in fastings;

6   by purity, by knowledge, by longsuffering, by kindness, by the Holy Spirit, by sincere love,

7   by the word of truth, by the power of God, by the armor of righteousness on the right hand and on the left,

8   by honor and dishonor, by evil report and good report; as deceivers, and *yet* true;

9   as unknown, and *yet* well known; as dying, and behold we live; as chastened, and *yet* not killed;

10 as sorrowful, yet always rejoicing; as poor, yet making many rich; as having nothing, and *yet* possessing all things.

6:2 [a]Isaiah 49:8

BE HOLY

11 O Corinthians! We have spoken openly to you, our heart is wide open. **12** You are not restricted by us, but you are restricted by your *own* affections. **13** Now in return for the same (I speak as to children), you also be open.

14 Do not be unequally yoked together with unbelievers. For what fellowship has righteousness with lawlessness? And what communion has light with darkness? **15** And what accord has Christ with Bē'li·al? Or what part has a believer with an unbeliever? **16** And what agreement has the temple of God with idols? For youᵃ are the temple of the living God. As God has said:

> *"I will dwell in them*
> *And walk among them.*
> *I will be their God,*
> *And they shall be My people."*ᵇ

17 Therefore

> *"Come out from among them*
> *And be separate, says the Lord.*
> *Do not touch what is unclean,*
> *And I will receive you."*ᵃ
> **18** *"I will be a Father to you,*
> *And you shall be My sons and*
>   *daughters,*
> *Says the LORD Almighty."*ᵃ

7 Therefore, having these promises, beloved, let us cleanse ourselves from all filthiness of the flesh and spirit, perfecting holiness in the fear of God.

THE CORINTHIANS' REPENTANCE

2 Open *your hearts* to us. We have wronged no one, we have corrupted no one, we have cheated no one.

3 I do not say *this* to condemn; for I have said before that you are in our hearts, to die together and to live together. **4** Great *is* my boldness of speech toward you, great *is* my boasting on your behalf. I am filled with comfort. I am exceedingly joyful in all our tribulation.

5 For indeed, when we came to Mac·e·dō'ni·a, our bodies had no rest, but we were troubled on every side. Outside *were* conflicts, inside *were* fears. **6** Nevertheless God, who comforts the downcast, comforted us by the coming of Titus, **7** and not only by his coming, but also by the consolation with which he was comforted in you, when he told us of your earnest desire, your mourning, your zeal for me, so that I rejoiced even more.

8 For even if I made you sorry with my letter, I do not regret it; though I did regret it. For I perceive that the same epistle made you sorry, though only for a while. **9** Now I rejoice, not that you were made sorry, but that your sorrow led to repentance. For you were made sorry in a godly manner, that you might suffer loss from us in nothing. **10** For godly sorrow produces repentance *leading* to salvation, not to be regretted; but the sorrow of the world produces death. **11** For observe this very thing, that you sorrowed in a godly manner: What diligence it produced in you, *what* clearing *of yourselves, what* indignation, *what* fear, *what* vehement desire, *what* zeal, *what* vindication! In all *things* you proved yourselves to be clear in this matter. **12** Therefore, although I wrote to

---

6:16 ᵃNU-Text reads *we.*   ᵇLeviticus 26:12; Jeremiah 32:38; Ezekiel 37:27   6:17 ᵃIsaiah 52:11; Ezekiel 20:34, 41   6:18 ᵃ2 Samuel 7:14

ABOUT GOD THE COMFORTER 2 Corinthians 7:6

Who Will Comfort Me?

Someone or something hurt Kitty. You can see the tear in her eye. Poor Kitty. She needs a comforter, someone to comfort her. But look. She has a comforter. Elsie sees how much Kitty hurts. So she stays there with Kitty to comfort her. It hurts Elsie to see how much Kitty hurts. That's why you see a tear in Elsie's eye also.

1. Do you know of someone who is hurting? Does this person need a comforter?
2. Could you be a comforter to that person? How? When? Why not now?
3. Look up Ecclesiastes 4:1. Why is it sad when hurting people have no one to comfort them?
4. Now look up 2 Corinthians 7:6. Who is our special Comforter? When can you ask Him to comfort you?

For more on *What the Bible Says* turn to page 1782
For more on *God's Care* turn to page 1837

you, *I did* not *do it* for the sake of him who had done the wrong, nor for the sake of him who suffered wrong, but that our care for you in the sight of God might appear to you.

THE JOY OF TITUS

13 Therefore we have been comforted in your comfort. And we rejoiced exceedingly more for the joy of Titus, because his spirit has been refreshed by you all.

14 For if in anything I have boasted to him about you, I am not ashamed. But as we spoke all things to you in truth, even so our boasting to Titus was found true.

15 And his affections are greater for you as he remembers the obedience of you all, how with fear and trembling you received him.

16 Therefore I rejoice that I have confidence in you in everything.

EXCEL IN GIVING

8 Moreover, brethren, we make known to you the grace of God bestowed on the churches of Mac·e·dō'-ni·a:

2 that in a great trial of affliction the abundance of their joy and their deep poverty abounded in the riches of their liberality.

3 For I bear witness that according to *their* ability, yes, and beyond *their* ability, *they were* freely willing,

4 imploring us with much urgency that we would receive*a* the gift and the fellowship of the ministering to the saints.

5 And not *only* as we had hoped, but they first gave themselves to the Lord, and *then* to us by the will of God.

6 So we urged Titus, that as he had begun, so he would also complete this grace in you as well.

7 But as you abound in everything—in faith, in speech, in knowledge, in all diligence, and in your love for us—*see* that you abound in this grace also.

CHRIST OUR PATTERN

8 I speak not by commandment, but I am testing the sincerity of your love by the diligence of others.

9 For you know the grace of our Lord Jesus Christ, that though He was rich, yet for your sakes He became poor, that you through His poverty might become rich.

10 And in this I give advice: It is to your advantage not only to be doing what you began and were desiring to do a year ago;

11 but now you also must complete the doing *of it;* that as *there was* a readiness to desire *it,* so *there* also *may be* a completion out of what *you* have.

12 For if there is first a willing mind, *it is* accepted according to what one has, *and* not according to what he does not have.

13 For *I do* not *mean* that others should be eased and you burdened;

14 but by an equality, *that* now at this time your abundance *may supply* their lack, that their abundance also may supply your lack—that there may be equality.

15 As it is written, *"He who gathered much had nothing left over, and he who gathered little had no lack."a*

COLLECTION FOR THE JUDEAN SAINTS

16 But thanks *be* to God who puts*a* the same earnest care for you into the heart of Titus.

8:4 *a*NU-Text and M-Text omit *that we would receive,* thus changing text to *urgency for the favor and fellowship . . . .*   8:15 *a*Exodus 16:18
8:16 *a*NU-Text reads *has put.*

17 For he not only accepted the exhortation, but being more diligent, he went to you of his own accord.

18 And we have sent with him the brother whose praise *is* in the gospel throughout all the churches,

19 and not only *that,* but who was also chosen by the churches to travel with us with this gift, which is administered by us to the glory of the Lord Himself and *to show* your ready mind,

20 avoiding this: that anyone should blame us in this lavish gift which is administered by us—

21 providing honorable things, not only in the sight of the Lord, but also in the sight of men.

22 And we have sent with them our brother whom we have often proved diligent in many things, but now much more diligent, because of the great confidence which *we have* in you.

23 If *anyone inquires* about Titus, *he is* my partner and fellow worker concerning you. Or if our brethren *are inquired about, they are* messengers of the churches, the glory of Christ.

24 Therefore show to them, and*a* before the churches the proof of your love and of our boasting on your behalf.

ADMINISTERING THE GIFT

9 Now concerning the ministering to the saints, it is superfluous for me to write to you;

2 for I know your willingness, about which I boast of you to the Mac·e·dō′ni·ans, that A·chā′i·a was ready a year ago; and your zeal has stirred up the majority.

3 Yet I have sent the brethren, lest our boasting of you should be in vain in this respect, that, as I said, you may be ready;

4 lest if *some* Mac·e·dō′ni·ans come with me and find you unprepared, we (not to mention you!) should be ashamed of this confident boasting.*a*

5 Therefore I thought it necessary to exhort the brethren to go to you ahead of time, and prepare your generous gift beforehand, which *you had* previously promised, that it may be ready as *a matter of* generosity and not as a grudging obligation.

THE CHEERFUL GIVER

6 But this *I say:* He who sows sparingly will also reap sparingly, and he who sows bountifully will also reap bountifully.

7 *So let* each one *give* as he purposes in his heart, not grudgingly or of necessity; for God loves a cheerful giver.

8 And God *is* able to make all grace abound toward you, that you, always having all sufficiency in all *things,* may have an abundance for every good work.

9 As it is written:

"He has dispersed abroad,
He has given to the poor;
His righteousness endures
    forever."a

10 Now may*a* He who supplies seed to the sower, and bread for food, supply and multiply the seed you have *sown* and increase the fruits of your righteousness,

11 while *you are* enriched in everything for all liberality, which causes thanksgiving through us to God.

12 For the administration of this service not only supplies the needs of the saints, but also is abounding through many thanksgivings to God,

8:24 *a*NU-Text and M-Text omit *and.*
9:4 *a*NU-Text reads *this confidence.*
9:9 *a*Psalm 112:9   9:10 *a*NU-Text reads *Now He who supplies . . . will supply . . . .*

13 while, through the proof of this ministry, they glorify God for the obedience of your confession to the gospel of Christ, and for *your* liberal sharing with them and all *men,*
14 and by their prayer for you, who long for you because of the exceeding grace of God in you.
15 Thanks *be* to God for His indescribable gift!

THE SPIRITUAL WAR

10 Now I, Paul, myself am pleading with you by the meekness and gentleness of Christ—who in presence *am* lowly among you, but being absent am bold toward you.
2 But I beg *you* that when I am present I may not be bold with that confidence by which I intend to be bold against some, who think of us as if we walked according to the flesh.
3 For though we walk in the flesh, we do not war according to the flesh.
4 For the weapons of our warfare *are* not carnal but mighty in God for pulling down strongholds,
5 casting down arguments and

every high thing that exalts itself against the knowledge of God, bringing every thought into captivity to the obedience of Christ,
6 and being ready to punish all disobedience when your obedience is fulfilled.

REALITY OF PAUL'S AUTHORITY

7 Do you look at things according to the outward appearance? If anyone is convinced in himself that he is Christ's, let him again consider this in himself, that just as he *is* Christ's, even so we *are* Christ's.a
8 For even if I should boast somewhat more about our authority, which the Lord gave usa for edification and not for your destruction, I shall not be ashamed—
9 lest I seem to terrify you by letters.
10 "For *his* letters," they say, "*are* weighty and powerful, but *his* bodily presence *is* weak, and *his* speech contemptible."

10:7 aNU-Text reads *even as we are.*
10:8 aNU-Text omits *us.*

11 Let such a person consider this, that what we are in word by letters when we are absent, such *we will* also *be* in deed when we are present.

LIMITS OF PAUL'S AUTHORITY

12 For we dare not class ourselves or compare ourselves with those who commend themselves. But they, measuring themselves by themselves, and comparing themselves among themselves, are not wise.
13 We, however, will not boast beyond measure, but within the limits of the sphere which God appointed us—a sphere which especially includes you.
14 For we are not overextending ourselves (as though *our authority* did not extend to you), for it was to you that we came with the gospel of Christ;
15 not boasting of things beyond measure, *that is,* in other men's labors, but having hope, *that* as your faith is increased, we shall be greatly enlarged by you in our sphere,
16 to preach the gospel in the *regions* beyond you, *and* not to boast in another man's sphere of accomplishment.
17 But *"he who glories, let him glory in the LORD."*a
18 For not he who commends himself is approved, but whom the Lord commends.

CONCERN FOR THEIR FAITHFULNESS

11 Oh, that you would bear with me in a little folly—and indeed you do bear with me.
2 For I am jealous for you with godly jealousy. For I have betrothed you to one husband, that I may present *you as* a chaste virgin to Christ.
3 But I fear, lest somehow, as the serpent deceived Eve by his crafti-

ness, so your minds may be corrupted from the simplicity*a* that is in Christ.
4 For if he who comes preaches another Jesus whom we have not preached, or *if* you receive a different spirit which you have not received, or a different gospel which you have not accepted—you may well put up with it!

PAUL AND FALSE APOSTLES

5 For I consider that I am not at all inferior to the most eminent apostles.
6 Even though *I am* untrained in speech, yet *I am* not in knowledge. But we have been thoroughly manifested*a* among you in all things.
7 Did I commit sin in humbling myself that you might be exalted, because I preached the gospel of God to you free of charge?
8 I robbed other churches, taking wages *from them* to minister to you.
9 And when I was present with you, and in need, I was a burden to no one, for what I lacked the brethren who came from Mac·e·dō′ni·a supplied. And in everything I kept myself from being burdensome to you, and so I will keep *myself.*
10 As the truth of Christ is in me, no one shall stop me from this boasting in the regions of A·chā′i·a.
11 Why? Because I do not love you? God knows!
12 But what I do, I will also continue to do, that I may cut off the opportunity from those who desire an opportunity to be regarded just as we are in the things of which they boast.
13 For such *are* false apostles, deceitful workers, transforming themselves into apostles of Christ.
14 And no wonder! For Satan himself transforms himself into an angel of light.

10:17 *a*Jeremiah 9:24   11:3 *a*NU-Text adds *and purity.*   11:6 *a*NU-Text omits *been.*

15 Therefore *it is* no great thing if his ministers also transform themselves into ministers of righteousness, whose end will be according to their works.

RELUCTANT BOASTING

16 I say again, let no one think me a fool. If otherwise, at least receive me as a fool, that I also may boast a little.

17 What I speak, I speak not according to the Lord, but as it were, foolishly, in this confidence of boasting.

18 Seeing that many boast according to the flesh, I also will boast.

19 For you put up with fools gladly, since you *yourselves* are wise!

20 For you put up with it if one brings you into bondage, if one devours *you,* if one takes *from you,* if one exalts himself, if one strikes you on the face.

21 To *our* shame I say that we were too weak for that! But in whatever anyone is bold—I speak foolishly—I am bold also.

SUFFERING FOR CHRIST

22 Are they Hebrews? So *am* I. Are they Israelites? So *am* I. Are they the seed of Abraham? So *am* I.

23 Are they ministers of Christ?—I speak as a fool—I *am* more: in labors more abundant, in stripes above measure, in prisons more frequently, in deaths often.

24 From the Jews five times I received forty *stripes* minus one.

25 Three times I was beaten with rods; once I was stoned; three times I was shipwrecked; a night and a day I have been in the deep;

26 *in* journeys often, *in* perils of waters, *in* perils of robbers, *in* perils of my own countrymen, *in* perils of the Gentiles, *in* perils in the city, *in* perils in the wilderness, *in* perils in the sea, *in* perils among false brethren;

27 in weariness and toil, in sleeplessness often, in hunger and thirst, in fastings often, in cold and nakedness—

28 besides the other things, what comes upon me daily: my deep concern for all the churches.

29 Who is weak, and I am not weak? Who is made to stumble, and I do not burn *with indignation?*

30 If I must boast, I will boast in the things which concern my infirmity.

31 The God and Father of our Lord Jesus Christ, who is blessed forever, knows that I am not lying.

32 In Damascus the governor, under Ar′e·tas the king, was guarding the city of the Dam′a·scēnes with a garrison, desiring to arrest me;

33 but I was let down in a basket through a window in the wall, and escaped from his hands.

THE VISION OF PARADISE

12 It is doubtless*a* not profitable for me to boast. I will come to visions and revelations of the Lord:

2 I know a man in Christ who fourteen years ago—whether in the body I do not know, or whether out of the body I do not know, God knows—such a one was caught up to the third heaven.

3 And I know such a man—whether in the body or out of the body I do not know, God knows—

4 how he was caught up into Paradise and heard inexpressible words, which it is not lawful for a man to utter.

5 Of such a one I will boast; yet of myself I will not boast, except in my infirmities.

12:1 *a*NU-Text reads *necessary, though not profitable, to boast.*

ABOUT GOD'S POWER 2 Corinthians 12:9, 10

Powerful Weakling

Do you ever feel like a weakling? Do you boys ever wish you were big and muscular, like a pro athlete? Do you girls ever wish you were like a beauty queen? Sometimes God makes the weakest people strong. Does that make sense? If not, read 2 Corinthians 12:9, 10.

1. You may have a weak or small body but be a powerfully strong Christian. God can help you do that.
2. You may not look at all like a beauty queen or movie star, but with God's help you can be the most beautiful Christian your friends have ever met.
3. Read 2 Corinthians 12:9, 10 again. There's the secret formula.

For more on *What the Bible Says* turn to page 1837
For more on *God's Promises* turn to page 1867

6 For though I might desire to boast, I will not be a fool; for I will speak the truth. But I refrain, lest anyone should think of me above what he sees me *to be* or hears from me.

THE THORN IN THE FLESH

7 And lest I should be exalted above measure by the abundance of the revelations, a thorn in the flesh was given to me, a messenger of Satan to buffet me, lest I be exalted above measure.
8 Concerning this thing I pleaded with the Lord three times that it might depart from me.
9 And He said to me, "My grace is sufficient for you, for My strength is made perfect in weakness." Therefore most gladly I will rather boast in my infirmities, that the power of Christ may rest upon me.
10 Therefore I take pleasure in infirmities, in reproaches, in needs, in persecutions, in distresses, for Christ's sake. For when I am weak, then I am strong.

SIGNS OF AN APOSTLE

11 I have become a fool in boasting;[a] you have compelled me. For I ought to have been commended by you; for in nothing was I behind the most eminent apostles, though I am nothing.
12 Truly the signs of an apostle were accomplished among you with all perseverance, in signs and wonders and mighty deeds.
13 For what is it in which you were inferior to other churches, except that I myself was not burdensome to you? Forgive me this wrong!

LOVE FOR THE CHURCH

14 Now *for* the third time I am ready to come to you. And I will not be burdensome to you; for I do not seek yours, but you. For the children ought not to lay up for the par-

12:11 [a]NU-Text omits *in boasting*.

ents, but the parents for the children.
15 And I will very gladly spend and be spent for your souls; though the more abundantly I love you, the less I am loved.
16 But be that *as it may,* I did not burden you. Nevertheless, being crafty, I caught you by cunning!
17 Did I take advantage of you by any of those whom I sent to you?
18 I urged Titus, and sent our brother with *him.* Did Titus take advantage of you? Did we not walk in the same spirit? Did *we* not *walk* in the same steps?
19 Again, do you think*a* that we excuse ourselves to you? We speak before God in Christ. But *we do* all things, beloved, for your edification.
20 For I fear lest, when I come, I shall not find you such as I wish, and *that* I shall be found by you such as you do not wish; lest *there be* contentions, jealousies, outbursts of wrath, selfish ambitions, backbitings, whisperings, conceits, tumults;
21 lest, when I come again, my God will humble me among you, and I shall mourn for many who have sinned before and have not repented of the uncleanness, fornication, and lewdness which they have practiced.

COMING WITH AUTHORITY

13 This *will be* the third *time* I am coming to you. *"By the mouth of two or three witnesses every word shall be established."a*
2 I have told you before, and foretell as if I were present the second time, and now being absent I write*a* to those who have sinned before, and to all the rest, that if I come again I will not spare—
3 since you seek a proof of Christ speaking in me, who is not weak toward you, but mighty in you.
4 For though He was crucified in weakness, yet He lives by the power of God. For we also are weak in Him, but we shall live with Him by the power of God toward you.
5 Examine yourselves *as to* whether you are in the faith. Test yourselves. Do you not know yourselves, that Jesus Christ is in you?—unless indeed you are disqualified.
6 But I trust that you will know that we are not disqualified.

PAUL PREFERS GENTLENESS

7 Now I*a* pray to God that you do no evil, not that we should appear approved, but that you should do what is honorable, though we may seem disqualified.
8 For we can do nothing against the truth, but for the truth.
9 For we are glad when we are weak and you are strong. And this also we pray, that you may be made complete.
10 Therefore I write these things being absent, lest being present I should use sharpness, according to the authority which the Lord has given me for edification and not for destruction.

GREETINGS AND BENEDICTION

11 Finally, brethren, farewell. Become complete. Be of good comfort, be of one mind, live in peace; and the God of love and peace will be with you.
12 Greet one another with a holy kiss.
13 All the saints greet you.
14 The grace of the Lord Jesus Christ, and the love of God, and the communion of the Holy Spirit *be* with you all. Amen.

12:19 *a*NU-Text reads *You have been thinking for a long time....*   13:1 *a*Deuteronomy 19:15
13:2 *a*NU-Text omits *I write.*   13:7 *a*NU-Text reads *we.*

GALATIANS

GREETING

PAUL, an apostle (not from men nor through man, but through Jesus Christ and God the Father who raised Him from the dead),

2 and all the brethren who are with me,

To the churches of Galatia:

3 Grace to you and peace from God the Father and our Lord Jesus Christ,

4 who gave Himself for our sins, that He might deliver us from this present evil age, according to the will of our God and Father,

5 to whom be glory forever and ever. Amen.

ONLY ONE GOSPEL

6 I marvel that you are turning away so soon from Him who called you in the grace of Christ, to a different gospel,

7 which is not another; but there are some who trouble you and want to pervert the gospel of Christ.

8 But even if we, or an angel from heaven, preach any other gospel to you than what we have preached to you, let him be accursed.

9 As we have said before, so now I say again, if anyone preaches any other gospel to you than what you have received, let him be accursed.

10 For do I now persuade men, or God? Or do I seek to please men? For if I still pleased men, I would not be a bondservant of Christ.

CALL TO APOSTLESHIP

11 But I make known to you, brethren, that the gospel which was preached by me is not according to man.

12 For I neither received it from man, nor was I taught it, but it came through the revelation of Jesus Christ.

13 For you have heard of my former conduct in Judaism, how I persecuted the church of God beyond measure and tried to destroy it.

14 And I advanced in Judaism beyond many of my contemporaries in my own nation, being more exceedingly zealous for the traditions of my fathers.

15 But when it pleased God, who separated me from my mother's womb and called me through His grace,

16 to reveal His Son in me, that I might preach Him among the Gentiles, I did not immediately confer with flesh and blood,

17 nor did I go up to Jerusalem to those who were apostles before me; but I went to Arabia, and returned again to Damascus.

CONTACTS AT JERUSALEM

18 Then after three years I went up to Jerusalem to see Peter,[a] and remained with him fifteen days.

19 But I saw none of the other apostles except James, the Lord's brother.

20 (Now concerning the things which I write to you, indeed, before God, I do not lie.)

21 Afterward I went into the regions of Syria and Ci·li′ci·a.

22 And I was unknown by face to the churches of Judea which were in Christ.

23 But they were hearing only, "He

1:18 ^aNU-Text reads Cephas.

who formerly persecuted us now preaches the faith which he once *tried to* destroy."

24 And they glorified God in me.

DEFENDING THE GOSPEL

2 Then after fourteen years I went up again to Jerusalem with Bar′na-bas, and also took Titus with *me*.

2 And I went up by revelation, and communicated to them that gospel which I preach among the Gentiles, but privately to those who were of reputation, lest by any means I might run, or had run, in vain.

3 Yet not even Titus who *was* with me, being a Greek, was compelled to be circumcised.

4 And *this occurred* because of false brethren secretly brought in (who came in by stealth to spy out our liberty which we have in Christ Jesus, that they might bring us into bondage),

5 to whom we did not yield submission even for an hour, that the truth of the gospel might continue with you.

6 But from those who seemed to be something—whatever they were, it makes no difference to me; God shows personal favoritism to no man—for those who seemed *to be something* added nothing to me.

7 But on the contrary, when they saw that the gospel for the uncircumcised had been committed to me, as *the gospel* for the circumcised *was* to Peter

8 (for He who worked effectively in Peter for the apostleship to the circumcised also worked effectively in me toward the Gentiles),

9 and when James, Cē′phas, and John, who seemed to be pillars, perceived the grace that had been given to me, they gave me and Bar′na·bas the right hand of fellowship, that we *should go* to the Gentiles and they to the circumcised.

10 *They desired* only that we should remember the poor, the very thing which I also was eager to do.

NO RETURN TO THE LAW

11 Now when Peter[a] had come to An′ti·och, I withstood him to his face, because he was to be blamed;

12 for before certain men came from James, he would eat with the Gentiles; but when they came, he withdrew and separated himself, fearing those who were of the circumcision.

13 And the rest of the Jews also played the hypocrite with him, so that even Bar′na·bas was carried away with their hypocrisy.

14 But when I saw that they were not straightforward about the truth of the gospel, I said to Peter before *them* all, "If you, being a Jew, live in the manner of Gentiles and not as the Jews, why do you[a] compel Gentiles to live as Jews?[b]

15 "We *who are* Jews by nature, and not sinners of the Gentiles,

16 "knowing that a man is not justified by the works of the law but by faith in Jesus Christ, even we have believed in Christ Jesus, that we might be justified by faith in Christ and not by the works of the law; for by the works of the law no flesh shall be justified.

17 "But if, while we seek to be justified by Christ, we ourselves also are found sinners, *is* Christ therefore a minister of sin? Certainly not!

18 "For if I build again those things which I destroyed, I make myself a transgressor.

19 "For I through the law died to the law that I might live to God.

2:11 [a]NU-Text reads *Cephas*.   2:14 [a]NU-Text reads *how can you*.   [b]Some interpreters stop the quotation here.

CRUCIFIED Galatians 2:20

For Me?

Roman soldiers nailed Jesus to a cross to die. They called that crucifixion. A person who died on a cross like that was crucified. Those people thought they were punishing Jesus. They didn't know that Jesus was dying for us. He had planned to do that. It was His way to help us get to heaven. When He died, He died for our sins, taking our sins upon Himself. In a way, we and our sins were there with Him. Do you think that is what Galatians 2:20 is saying?

1. Why did Jesus die on a cross? What was He doing for you and me?
2. How were we there with Him? What does Galatians 2:20 say?

For more on *Favorite Bible Words* turn to page 1796
For more on *Sin* turn to page 1793

20 "I have been crucified with Christ; it is no longer I who live, but Christ lives in me; and the *life* which I now live in the flesh I live by faith in the Son of God, who loved me and gave Himself for me.

21 "I do not set aside the grace of God; for if righteousness *comes* through the law, then Christ died in vain."

JUSTIFICATION BY FAITH

3 O foolish Galatians! Who has bewitched you that you should not obey the truth,*a* before whose eyes Jesus Christ was clearly portrayed among you*b* as crucified?

2 This only I want to learn from you: Did you receive the Spirit by the works of the law, or by the hearing of faith?

3 Are you so foolish? Having begun in the Spirit, are you now being made perfect by the flesh?

4 Have you suffered so many things in vain—if indeed *it was* in vain?

5 Therefore He who supplies the Spirit to you and works miracles among you, *does He do it* by the works of the law, or by the hearing of faith?—

6 just as Abraham *"believed God, and it was accounted to him for righteousness."a*

7 Therefore know that *only* those who are of faith are sons of Abraham.

8 And the Scripture, foreseeing that God would justify the Gentiles by faith, preached the gospel to Abraham beforehand, *saying, "In you all the nations shall be blessed."a*

9 So then those who *are* of faith are blessed with believing Abraham.

THE LAW BRINGS A CURSE

10 For as many as are of the works of the law are under the curse; for it is written, *"Cursed is everyone who does not continue in all things which are written in the book of the law, to do them."a*

11 But that no one is justified by the law in the sight of God *is* evident, for *"the just shall live by faith."a*

12 Yet the law is not of faith, but *"the man who does them shall live by them."a*

13 Christ has redeemed us from the curse of the law, having become a curse for us (for it is written, *"Cursed is everyone who hangs on a tree"a*),

14 that the blessing of Abraham might come upon the Gentiles in Christ Jesus, that we might receive the promise of the Spirit through faith.

THE CHANGELESS PROMISE

15 Brethren, I speak in the manner of men: Though *it is* only a man's covenant, yet *if it is* confirmed, no one annuls or adds to it.

16 Now to Abraham and his Seed were the promises made. He does not say, "And to seeds," as of many, but as of one, *"And to your Seed,"a* who is Christ.

17 And this I say, *that* the law, which was four hundred and thirty years later, cannot annul the covenant that was confirmed before by God in Christ,*a* that it should make the promise of no effect.

18 For if the inheritance *is* of the law, *it is* no longer of promise; but God gave *it* to Abraham by promise.

3:1 *a*NU-Text omits *that you should not obey the truth.*   *b*NU-Text omits *among you.*
3:6 *a*Genesis 15:6   3:8 *a*Genesis 12:3; 18:18; 22:18; 26:4; 28:14   3:10 *a*Deuteronomy 27:26
3:11 *a*Habakkuk 2:4   3:12 *a*Leviticus 18:5
3:13 *a*Deuteronomy 21:23   3:16 *a*Genesis 12:7; 13:15; 24:7   3:17 *a*NU-Text omits *in Christ.*

PURPOSE OF THE LAW

19 What purpose then *does* the law *serve?* It was added because of transgressions, till the Seed should come to whom the promise was made; *and it was* appointed through angels by the hand of a mediator.
20 Now a mediator does not *mediate* for one *only,* but God is one.
21 *Is* the law then against the promises of God? Certainly not! For if there had been a law given which could have given life, truly righteousness would have been by the law.
22 But the Scripture has confined all under sin, that the promise by faith in Jesus Christ might be given to those who believe.
23 But before faith came, we were kept under guard by the law, kept for the faith which would afterward be revealed.
24 Therefore the law was our tutor *to bring us* to Christ, that we might be justified by faith.
25 But after faith has come, we are no longer under a tutor.

SONS AND HEIRS

26 For you are all sons of God through faith in Christ Jesus.
27 For as many of you as were baptized into Christ have put on Christ.
28 There is neither Jew nor Greek, there is neither slave nor free, there is neither male nor female; for you are all one in Christ Jesus.
29 And if you *are* Christ's, then you are Abraham's seed, and heirs according to the promise.

4 Now I say *that* the heir, as long as he is a child, does not differ at all from a slave, though he is master of all,

2 but is under guardians and stewards until the time appointed by the father.
3 Even so we, when we were children, were in bondage under the elements of the world.
4 But when the fullness of the time had come, God sent forth His Son, born*a* of a woman, born under the law,
5 to redeem those who were under the law, that we might receive the adoption as sons.
6 And because you are sons, God has sent forth the Spirit of His Son into your hearts, crying out, "Abba, Father!"
7 Therefore you are no longer a slave but a son, and if a son, then an heir of*a* God through Christ.

FEARS FOR THE CHURCH

8 But then, indeed, when you did not know God, you served those which by nature are not gods.
9 But now after you have known God, or rather are known by God, how *is it that* you turn again to the weak and beggarly elements, to which you desire again to be in bondage?
10 You observe days and months and seasons and years.
11 I am afraid for you, lest I have labored for you in vain.
12 Brethren, I urge you to become like me, for I *became* like you. You have not injured me at all.
13 You know that because of physical infirmity I preached the gospel to you at the first.
14 And my trial which was in my flesh you did not despise or reject, but you received me as an angel of God, *even* as Christ Jesus.

4:4 *a*Or *made*   4:7 *a*NU-Text reads *through God* and omits *through Christ.*

15 What*a* then was the blessing you *enjoyed*? For I bear you witness that, if possible, you would have plucked out your own eyes and given them to me.

16 Have I therefore become your enemy because I tell you the truth?

17 They zealously court you, *but* for no good; yes, they want to exclude you, that you may be zealous for them.

18 But it is good to be zealous in a good thing always, and not only when I am present with you.

19 My little children, for whom I labor in birth again until Christ is formed in you,

20 I would like to be present with you now and to change my tone; for I have doubts about you.

TWO COVENANTS

21 Tell me, you who desire to be under the law, do you not hear the law?

22 For it is written that Abraham had two sons: the one by a bondwoman, the other by a freewoman.

23 But he *who was* of the bondwoman was born according to the flesh, and he of the freewoman through promise,

24 which things are symbolic. For these are the*a* two covenants: the one from Mount Sinai which gives birth to bondage, which is Hā′gar—

25 for this Hā′gar is Mount Sinai in Arabia, and corresponds to Jerusalem which now is, and is in bondage with her children—

26 but the Jerusalem above is free, which is the mother of us all.

27 For it is written:

"Rejoice, O barren,
 You who do not bear!
 Break forth and shout,

You who are not in labor!
 For the desolate has many more
 children
 Than she who has a husband."*a*

28 Now we, brethren, as Isaac *was*, are children of promise.

29 But, as he who was born according to the flesh then persecuted him *who was born* according to the Spirit, even so *it is* now.

30 Nevertheless what does the Scripture say? *"Cast out the bondwoman and her son, for the son of the bondwoman shall not be heir with the son of the freewoman.*"*a*

31 So then, brethren, we are not children of the bondwoman but of the free.

CHRISTIAN LIBERTY

5 Stand fast therefore in the liberty by which Christ has made us free,*a* and do not be entangled again with a yoke of bondage.

2 Indeed I, Paul, say to you that if you become circumcised, Christ will profit you nothing.

3 And I testify again to every man who becomes circumcised that he is a debtor to keep the whole law.

4 You have become estranged from Christ, you who *attempt to* be justified by law; you have fallen from grace.

5 For we through the Spirit eagerly wait for the hope of righteousness by faith.

6 For in Christ Jesus neither circumcision nor uncircumcision avails anything, but faith working through love.

4:15 *a*NU-Text reads *Where.*　　4:24 *a*NU-Text and M-Text omit *the.*　　4:27 *a*Isaiah 54:1
4:30 *a*Genesis 21:10　　5:1 *a*NU-Text reads *For freedom Christ has made us free; stand fast therefore.*

THROUGH LOVE SERVE ONE ANOTHER Galatians 5:13

How May I Serve You?

Does mother wash and iron your clothes? Is she serving you when she does that? What does father do to keep your family happy and well? Is he serving you when he does that? What do you do to help your family? Are you serving others when you do that?

1. How is this boy serving someone? Does that make the special someone happy?
2. Does serving someone make that person happy? Why? Does it make you happy when you serve someone? Why?
3. Read Galatians 5:13. What does the Lord want us to do? What is He saying?

For more on *Favorite Family Verses* turn to page 1792
For more on *Serving* turn to page 1803

LOVE FULFILLS THE LAW

7 You ran well. Who hindered you from obeying the truth?

8 This persuasion does not *come* from Him who calls you.

9 A little leaven leavens the whole lump.

10 I have confidence in you, in the Lord, that you will have no other mind; but he who troubles you shall bear his judgment, whoever he is.

11 And I, brethren, if I still preach circumcision, why do I still suffer persecution? Then the offense of the cross has ceased.

12 I could wish that those who trouble you would even cut themselves off!

13 For you, brethren, have been called to liberty; only do not *use* liberty as an opportunity for the flesh, but through love serve one another.

14 For all the law is fulfilled in one word, *even* in this: *"You shall love your neighbor as yourself."*a

15 But if you bite and devour one another, beware lest you be consumed by one another!

WALKING IN THE SPIRIT

16 I say then: Walk in the Spirit, and you shall not fulfill the lust of the flesh.

17 For the flesh lusts against the Spirit, and the Spirit against the flesh; and these are contrary to one another, so that you do not do the things that you wish.

18 But if you are led by the Spirit, you are not under the law.

19 Now the works of the flesh are evident, which are: adultery,a fornication, uncleanness, lewdness,

20 idolatry, sorcery, hatred, contentions, jealousies, outbursts of wrath, selfish ambitions, dissensions, heresies,

21 envy, murders,a drunkenness, revelries, and the like; of which I tell you beforehand, just as I also told *you* in time past, that those who practice such things will not inherit the kingdom of God.

22 But the fruit of the Spirit is love, joy, peace, longsuffering, kindness, goodness, faithfulness,

23 gentleness, self-control. Against such there is no law.

24 And those *who are* Christ's have crucified the flesh with its passions and desires.

25 If we live in the Spirit, let us also walk in the Spirit.

26 Let us not become conceited, provoking one another, envying one another.

BEAR AND SHARE THE BURDENS

6 Brethren, if a man is overtaken in any trespass, you who *are* spiritual restore such a one in a spirit of gentleness, considering yourself lest you also be tempted.

2 Bear one another's burdens, and so fulfill the law of Christ.

3 For if anyone thinks himself to be something, when he is nothing, he deceives himself.

4 But let each one examine his own work, and then he will have rejoicing in himself alone, and not in another.

5 For each one shall bear his own load.

BE GENEROUS AND DO GOOD

6 Let him who is taught the word share in all good things with him who teaches.

7 Do not be deceived, God is not mocked; for whatever a man sows, that he will also reap.

5:14 aLeviticus 19:18   5:19 aNU-Text omits *adultery.*   5:21 aNU-Text omits *murders.*

BUT THE FRUIT OF THE SPIRIT IS LOVE, JOY, PEACE, LONGSUFFERING, KINDNESS, GOODNESS, FAITHFULNESS, GENTLENESS, SELF-CONTROL.
Galatians 5:22, 23

Our Little Fruit Stand

Look at the little stand. Actually it is a fruit stand, even though it looks like a book stand. The fruit they are sharing is the fruit of the Spirit. When we let the Spirit of God live in us, He produces in us "fruit" such as love, joy, peace, and the others listed in Galatians 5:22, 23. In a way, we're like a little fruit stand. The fruit of God's Spirit looks attractive in our lives and others want it too. We don't sell this fruit. It's free. We share it with anyone who wants it. Thank You, Lord, for this wonderful fruit. And thank You that we can share it with others so that they will want it too.

1. How should you and I be like a little fruit stand?
2. What kind of fruit do we share there? How do we share it?
3. Do you think your friends see the love of God, the joy of God, and the peace of God in you? Do you want them to? Will you share?

For more on *Favorite Family Verses* turn to page 1793
For more on *Godliness* turn to page 1861

WHATEVER A MAN SOWS, THAT HE WILL ALSO REAP. Galatians 6:7

Do Apples Grow on Pear Trees?

You planted an apple tree. Will pears grow on it? You planted poppy seeds. Will you see tulips grow from them? Will peas grow from bean seeds or corn from pumpkin seeds? But what if you or I plant "sin"? Will godly things come from it?

1. What kind of plants and fruit grow from seeds? Read Genesis 1:11–13. What does it say about seeds and plants that grow from those seeds? Does God ever surprise you with plants that are different from the seeds you plant? Why not?

2. What kind of "fruit" do we reap from the "seeds" of sin? Read Galatians 6:7. What does it say?

3. If we want godliness in our lives, what kind of life should we live? What kind of "seeds" should we sow?

POPPY SEEDS

For more on *Favorite Family Verses* turn to page 1802
For more on *Sin* turn to page 6

8 For he who sows to his flesh will of the flesh reap corruption, but he who sows to the Spirit will of the Spirit reap everlasting life.

9 And let us not grow weary while doing good, for in due season we shall reap if we do not lose heart.

10 Therefore, as we have opportunity, let us do good to all, especially to those who are of the household of faith.

GLORY ONLY IN THE CROSS

11 See with what large letters I have written to you with my own hand!

12 As many as desire to make a good showing in the flesh, these *would* compel you to be circumcised, only that they may not suffer persecution for the cross of Christ.

13 For not even those who are circumcised keep the law, but they desire to have you circumcised that they may boast in your flesh.

14 But God forbid that I should boast except in the cross of our Lord Jesus Christ, by whom[a] the world has been crucified to me, and I to the world.

15 For in Christ Jesus neither circumcision nor uncircumcision avails anything, but a new creation.

BLESSING AND A PLEA

16 And as many as walk according to this rule, peace and mercy *be* upon them, and upon the Israel of God.

17 From now on let no one trouble me, for I bear in my body the marks of the Lord Jesus.

18 Brethren, the grace of our Lord Jesus Christ *be* with your spirit. Amen.

6:14 [a]Or *by which* (the cross)

EPHESIANS

GREETING

PAUL, an apostle of Jesus Christ by the will of God,

To the saints who are in Eph'e-sus, and faithful in Christ Jesus:

2 Grace to you and peace from God our Father and the Lord Jesus Christ.

REDEMPTION IN CHRIST

3 Blessed *be* the God and Father of our Lord Jesus Christ, who has blessed us with every spiritual bless-ing in the heavenly *places* in Christ,
4 just as He chose us in Him before the foundation of the world, that we should be holy and without blame be-fore Him in love,
5 having predestined us to adoption as sons by Jesus Christ to Himself, according to the good pleasure of His will,
6 to the praise of the glory of His grace, by which He made us accepted in the Beloved.
7 In Him we have redemption through His blood, the forgiveness of sins, according to the riches of His grace
8 which He made to abound toward us in all wisdom and prudence,
9 having made known to us the mystery of His will, according to His good pleasure which He purposed in Himself,
10 that in the dispensation of the fullness of the times He might gather together in one all things in Christ, both*a* which are in heaven and which are on earth—in Him.
11 In Him also we have obtained an inheritance, being predestined ac-cording to the purpose of Him who works all things according to the counsel of His will,
12 that we who first trusted in Christ should be to the praise of His glory.
13 In Him you also *trusted,* after you heard the word of truth, the gospel of your salvation; in whom also, having believed, you were sealed with the Holy Spirit of promise,
14 who*a* is the guarantee of our in-heritance until the redemption of the purchased possession, to the praise of His glory.

PRAYER FOR SPIRITUAL WISDOM

15 Therefore I also, after I heard of your faith in the Lord Jesus and your love for all the saints,
16 do not cease to give thanks for you, making mention of you in my prayers:
17 that the God of our Lord Jesus Christ, the Father of glory, may give to you the spirit of wisdom and reve-lation in the knowledge of Him,
18 the eyes of your understanding*a* being enlightened; that you may know what is the hope of His calling, what are the riches of the glory of His inheritance in the saints,
19 and what *is* the exceeding great-ness of His power toward us who be-lieve, according to the working of His mighty power
20 which He worked in Christ when He raised Him from the dead and seated *Him* at His right hand in the heavenly *places,*
21 far above all principality and

1:10 *a*NU-Text and M-Text omit *both.*
1:14 *a*NU-Text reads *which.*   1:18 *a*NU-Text and M-Text read *hearts.*

ADOPTION Ephesians 1:3–6

God's Adopted Children

We are God's twice-born children. First, He made us to be His children. He chose us, in Christ, from the beginning. But sin came between us and God. Sin spoiled our relationship to our Heavenly Father. Then, through Christ's death on the cross, God provided a new parent-child relationship. He adopted us. It is as if a child ran away and lost her "childness," only to have her parents choose her again by adopting her. It's a little hard to understand, but the important thing to remember is that God wants you as His child. He wants you so much that you are not only born to be His child, He has also adopted you as His child.

1. Do you know of someone who is adopted? This girl was not born to her adoptive parents, but they chose her. She is a "chosen child."
2. Read Ephesians 1:3–6. This tells us how we are "twice-born" children of God, born through the lineage of Creation to be His child, but when sin broke that relationship, born again through salvation in Christ—adopted this time by God to be His child.
3. Have you asked God, through Jesus, to make you His child by being born again? Would you like to do that?

For more on *Favorite Bible Words* turn to page 1836
For more on *Salvation* turn to page 1858

power and might and dominion, and every name that is named, not only in this age but also in that which is to come.

22 And He put all *things* under His feet, and gave Him *to be* head over all *things* to the church,

23 which is His body, the fullness of Him who fills all in all.

By Grace Through Faith

2 And you *He made alive,* who were dead in trespasses and sins,

2 in which you once walked according to the course of this world, according to the prince of the power of the air, the spirit who now works in the sons of disobedience,

3 among whom also we all once conducted ourselves in the lusts of our flesh, fulfilling the desires of the flesh and of the mind, and were by nature children of wrath, just as the others.

4 But God, who is rich in mercy, because of His great love with which He loved us,

5 even when we were dead in trespasses, made us alive together with Christ (by grace you have been saved),

6 and raised *us* up together, and made *us* sit together in the heavenly *places* in Christ Jesus,

7 that in the ages to come He might show the exceeding riches of His grace in *His* kindness toward us in Christ Jesus.

8 For by grace you have been saved through faith, and that not of yourselves; *it is* the gift of God,

9 not of works, lest anyone should boast.

10 For we are His workmanship, created in Christ Jesus for good works, which God prepared beforehand that we should walk in them.

Brought Near by His Blood

11 Therefore remember that you, once Gentiles in the flesh—who are called Uncircumcision by what is called the Circumcision made in the flesh by hands—

12 that at that time you were without Christ, being aliens from the commonwealth of Israel and strangers from the covenants of promise, having no hope and without God in the world.

13 But now in Christ Jesus you who once were far off have been brought near by the blood of Christ.

Christ Our Peace

14 For He Himself is our peace, who has made both one, and has broken down the middle wall of separation,

15 having abolished in His flesh the enmity, *that is,* the law of commandments *contained* in ordinances, so as to create in Himself one new man *from* the two, *thus* making peace,

16 and that He might reconcile them both to God in one body through the cross, thereby putting to death the enmity.

17 And He came and preached peace to you who were afar off and to those who were near.

18 For through Him we both have access by one Spirit to the Father.

Christ Our Cornerstone

19 Now, therefore, you are no longer strangers and foreigners, but fellow citizens with the saints and members of the household of God,

20 having been built on the foundation of the apostles and prophets, Jesus Christ Himself being the chief cornerstone,

21 in whom the whole building, being fitted together, grows into a holy temple in the Lord,

22 in whom you also are being built together for a dwelling place of God in the Spirit.

THE MYSTERY REVEALED

3 For this reason I, Paul, the prisoner of Christ Jesus for you Gentiles—

2 if indeed you have heard of the dispensation of the grace of God which was given to me for you,

3 how that by revelation He made known to me the mystery (as I have briefly written already,

4 by which, when you read, you may understand my knowledge in the mystery of Christ),

5 which in other ages was not made known to the sons of men, as it has now been revealed by the Spirit to His holy apostles and prophets:

6 that the Gentiles should be fellow heirs, of the same body, and partakers of His promise in Christ through the gospel,

7 of which I became a minister according to the gift of the grace of God given to me by the effective working of His power.

PURPOSE OF THE MYSTERY

8 To me, who am less than the least of all the saints, this grace was given, that I should preach among the Gentiles the unsearchable riches of Christ,

9 and to make all see what *is* the fellowship*a* of the mystery, which from the beginning of the ages has been hidden in God who created all things through Jesus Christ;*b*

10 to the intent that now the manifold wisdom of God might be made known by the church to the principalities and powers in the heavenly *places,*

11 according to the eternal purpose which He accomplished in Christ Jesus our Lord,

12 in whom we have boldness and access with confidence through faith in Him.

13 Therefore I ask that you do not lose heart at my tribulations for you, which is your glory.

APPRECIATION OF THE MYSTERY

14 For this reason I bow my knees to the Father of our Lord Jesus Christ,*a*

15 from whom the whole family in heaven and earth is named,

16 that He would grant you, according to the riches of His glory, to be strengthened with might through His Spirit in the inner man,

17 that Christ may dwell in your hearts through faith; that you, being rooted and grounded in love,

18 may be able to comprehend with all the saints what *is* the width and length and depth and height—

19 to know the love of Christ which passes knowledge; that you may be filled with all the fullness of God.

20 Now to Him who is able to do exceedingly abundantly above all that we ask or think, according to the power that works in us,

21 to Him *be* glory in the church by Christ Jesus to all generations, forever and ever. Amen.

WALK IN UNITY

4 I, therefore, the prisoner of the Lord, beseech you to walk worthy of

---

3:9 *a*NU-Text and M-Text read *stewardship* (dispensation). *b*NU-Text omits *through Jesus Christ.* 3:14 *a*NU-Text omits *of our Lord Jesus Christ.*

the calling with which you were called,

2 with all lowliness and gentleness, with longsuffering, bearing with one another in love,

3 endeavoring to keep the unity of the Spirit in the bond of peace.

4 *There is* one body and one Spirit, just as you were called in one hope of your calling;

5 one Lord, one faith, one baptism;

6 one God and Father of all, who *is* above all, and through all, and in you*a* all.

SPIRITUAL GIFTS

7 But to each one of us grace was given according to the measure of Christ's gift.

8 Therefore He says:

"When He ascended on high,
He led captivity captive,
And gave gifts to men."a

9 (Now this, *"He ascended"*—what does it mean but that He also first*a* descended into the lower parts of the earth?

10 He who descended is also the One who ascended far above all the heavens, that He might fill all things.)

11 And He Himself gave some *to be* apostles, some prophets, some evangelists, and some pastors and teachers,

12 for the equipping of the saints for the work of ministry, for the edifying of the body of Christ,

13 till we all come to the unity of the faith and of the knowledge of the Son of God, to a perfect man, to the measure of the stature of the fullness of Christ;

14 that we should no longer be chil-

dren, tossed to and fro and carried about with every wind of doctrine, by the trickery of men, in the cunning craftiness of deceitful plotting,

15 but, speaking the truth in love, may grow up in all things into Him who is the head—Christ—

16 from whom the whole body, joined and knit together by what every joint supplies, according to the effective working by which every part does its share, causes growth of the body for the edifying of itself in love.

THE NEW MAN

17 This I say, therefore, and testify in the Lord, that you should no longer walk as the rest of*a* the Gentiles walk, in the futility of their mind,

18 having their understanding darkened, being alienated from the life of God, because of the ignorance that is in them, because of the blindness of their heart;

19 who, being past feeling, have given themselves over to lewdness, to work all uncleanness with greediness.

20 But you have not so learned Christ,

21 if indeed you have heard Him and have been taught by Him, as the truth is in Jesus:

22 that you put off, concerning your former conduct, the old man which grows corrupt according to the deceitful lusts,

23 and be renewed in the spirit of your mind,

24 and that you put on the new man which was created according to God, in true righteousness and holiness.

4:6 *a*NU-Text omits *you;* M-Text reads *us.*
4:8 *a*Psalm 68:18   4:9 *a*NU-Text omits *first.*
4:17 *a*NU-Text omits *the rest of.*

WHAT DID THAT GIFT COST YOU? Ephesians 5:2

Every gift you give costs you something—money, time, talent, problems. If you make a gift, you may spend a lot of time, or you may have a lot of problems. If you sing your gift, you are giving talent. Perhaps you bought your gift. That cost money. How much did that last gift cost you—money, time, problems? Would you still give that gift if you had known then how much it would cost?

1. When God gave His Son to die on the cross, He gave the greatest gift ever given. It cost more than any other gift ever given. Do you think God was ever sorry that He had given such a costly gift?
2. Why do you think God gave this most costly gift? What did it have to do with loving you?
3. If you love someone very much, are you sorry that the special gift to that person cost a little more—money, time, problems? Why not?
4. What do love and gift-giving have to do with each other? Read Ephesians 5:2. What does it say about love and giving? Remember John 3:16? What does it say about love and giving?

For more on *What Should I Do?* turn to page 1818
For more on *Giving* turn to page 1884

DO NOT GRIEVE THE SPIRIT

25 Therefore, putting away lying, *"Let each one of you speak truth with his neighbor,"ᵃ* for we are members of one another.

26 *"Be angry, and do not sin":ᵃ* do not let the sun go down on your wrath,

27 nor give place to the devil.

28 Let him who stole steal no longer, but rather let him labor, working with *his* hands what is good, that he may have something to give him who has need.

29 Let no corrupt word proceed out of your mouth, but what is good for necessary edification, that it may impart grace to the hearers.

30 And do not grieve the Holy Spirit of God, by whom you were sealed for the day of redemption.

31 Let all bitterness, wrath, anger, clamor, and evil speaking be put away from you, with all malice.

32 And be kind to one another, tenderhearted, forgiving one another, even as God in Christ forgave you.

WALK IN LOVE

5 Therefore be imitators of God as dear children.

2 And walk in love, as Christ also has loved us and given Himself for us, an offering and a sacrifice to God for a sweet-smelling aroma.

3 But fornication and all uncleanness or covetousness, let it not even be named among you, as is fitting for saints;

4:25 ᵃZechariah 8:16   4:26 ᵃPsalm 4:4

4 neither filthiness, nor foolish talking, nor coarse jesting, which are not fitting, but rather giving of thanks.

5 For this you know,[a] that no fornicator, unclean person, nor covetous man, who is an idolater, has any inheritance in the kingdom of Christ and God.

6 Let no one deceive you with empty words, for because of these things the wrath of God comes upon the sons of disobedience.

7 Therefore do not be partakers with them.

WALK IN LIGHT

8 For you were once darkness, but now *you are* light in the Lord. Walk as children of light

9 (for the fruit of the Spirit[a] *is* in all goodness, righteousness, and truth),

10 finding out what is acceptable to the Lord.

11 And have no fellowship with the unfruitful works of darkness, but rather expose *them*.

12 For it is shameful even to speak of those things which are done by them in secret.

13 But all things that are exposed are made manifest by the light, for whatever makes manifest is light.

14 Therefore He says:

"Awake, you who sleep,
Arise from the dead,
And Christ will give you light."

WALK IN WISDOM

15 See then that you walk circumspectly, not as fools but as wise,

16 redeeming the time, because the days are evil.

17 Therefore do not be unwise, but understand what the will of the Lord is.

18 And do not be drunk with wine, in which is dissipation; but be filled with the Spirit,

19 speaking to one another in psalms and hymns and spiritual songs, singing and making melody in your heart to the Lord,

20 giving thanks always for all things to God the Father in the name of our Lord Jesus Christ,

21 submitting to one another in the fear of God.[a]

MARRIAGE—CHRIST AND THE CHURCH

22 Wives, submit to your own husbands, as to the Lord.

23 For the husband is head of the wife, as also Christ is head of the church; and He is the Savior of the body.

24 Therefore, just as the church is subject to Christ, so *let* the wives *be* to their own husbands in everything.

25 Husbands, love your wives, just as Christ also loved the church and gave Himself for her,

26 that He might sanctify and cleanse her with the washing of water by the word,

27 that He might present her to Himself a glorious church, not having spot or wrinkle or any such thing, but that she should be holy and without blemish.

28 So husbands ought to love their own wives as their own bodies; he who loves his wife loves himself.

29 For no one ever hated his own flesh, but nourishes and cherishes it, just as the Lord *does* the church.

30 For we are members of His body,[a] of His flesh and of His bones.

5:5 [a]NU-Text reads *For know this.*   5:9 [a]NU-Text reads *light.*   5:21 [a]NU-Text reads *Christ.*
5:30 [a]NU-Text omits the rest of this verse.

HUSBANDS, LOVE YOUR WIVES, JUST AS CHRIST ALSO LOVED THE CHURCH AND GAVE HIMSELF FOR HER! Ephesians 5:25

I Love You!

Do you like to hear father say, "I love you" to mother? Does it make you feel happy? Would you rather hear father say mean things to her?

1. What do you think this man is saying to his wife? Do you think that makes her happy? Why?
2. Why should it make children happy when their father says "I love you" to their mother?
3. Don't forget to say "I love you" to your parents, too. Will you do it today?
4. How much should a husband love his wife? What does Ephesians 5:25 say? What does this mean?

For more on *Favorite Family Verses* turn to page 1803
For more on *Love* turn to page 1896

DOING SERVICE, AS TO THE LORD, AND NOT TO MEN. Ephesians 6:7

Serving One Another

Jesus said we should serve one another. This little boy is washing a friend's feet. That's what Jesus did at the Last Supper, didn't He? This is a way of saying, "I love you. I want to do something special for you."

1. How is this boy serving his friend?
2. What are some things you can do to serve your parents? What are some things you can do to serve others?
3. What are some things you can do to serve Jesus? Will you?

For more on *Favorite Family Verses* turn to page 1805

For more on *Serving* turn to page 35

31 *"For this reason a man shall leave his father and mother and be joined to his wife, and the two shall become one flesh."*a

32 This is a great mystery, but I speak concerning Christ and the church.

33 Nevertheless let each one of you in particular so love his own wife as himself, and let the wife *see* that she respects *her* husband.

CHILDREN AND PARENTS

6 Children, obey your parents in the Lord, for this is right.

2 *"Honor your father and mother,"* which is the first commandment with promise:

3 *"that it may be well with you and you may live long on the earth."*a

4 And you, fathers, do not provoke your children to wrath, but bring them up in the training and admonition of the Lord.

BONDSERVANTS AND MASTERS

5 Bondservants, be obedient to those who are your masters according to the flesh, with fear and trembling, in sincerity of heart, as to Christ;

6 not with eyeservice, as menpleasers, but as bondservants of Christ, doing the will of God from the heart,

7 with goodwill doing service, as to the Lord, and not to men,

8 knowing that whatever good anyone does, he will receive the same from the Lord, whether *he is* a slave or free.

9 And you, masters, do the same things to them, giving up threatening, knowing that your own Master alsoa is in heaven, and there is no partiality with Him.

THE WHOLE ARMOR OF GOD

10 Finally, my brethren, be strong in the Lord and in the power of His might.

11 Put on the whole armor of God, that you may be able to stand against the wiles of the devil.

12 For we do not wrestle against flesh and blood, but against principalities, against powers, against the rulers of the darkness of this age,a against spiritual *hosts* of wickedness in the heavenly *places*.

13 Therefore take up the whole armor of God, that you may be able to withstand in the evil day, and having done all, to stand.

14 Stand therefore, having girded your waist with truth, having put on the breastplate of righteousness,

15 and having shod your feet with the preparation of the gospel of peace;

16 above all, taking the shield of faith with which you will be able to quench all the fiery darts of the wicked one.

17 And take the helmet of salvation, and the sword of the Spirit, which is the word of God;

18 praying always with all prayer and supplication in the Spirit, being watchful to this end with all perseverance and supplication for all the saints—

19 and for me, that utterance may be given to me, that I may open my mouth boldly to make known the mystery of the gospel,

20 for which I am an ambassador in chains; that in it I may speak boldly, as I ought to speak.

5:31 aGenesis 2:24   6:3 aDeuteronomy 5:16
6:9 aNU-Text reads *He who is both their Master and yours.*   6:12 aNU-Text reads *rulers of this darkness.*

Favorite Family Verses

PUT ON THE WHOLE ARMOR OF GOD, THAT YOU MAY BE ABLE TO STAND AGAINST THE WILES OF THE DEVIL. Ephesians 6:11

God's Armor

Have you ever seen a picture of a knight in armor? What was he wearing? If you read Ephesians 6:11–18 you will learn more about a knight's armor. But the armor described here is God's armor, not a knight's armor. Look up this Scripture and talk about each piece.

1. With God's armor, what should you put around your waist? Do you sometimes tell a lie? God's Word, the Bible, is true. Everything in it is true, the truth.
2. With which pieces of armor does God compare righteousness, peace, faith, salvation, and the Word of God? Why should you want each one of these? What will you do with each one?
3. Don't try to fight the devil all by yourself. Ask God to help you.

For more on *Favorite Family Verses* turn to page 1811
For more on *Temptation* turn to page 1836

A GRACIOUS GREETING

21 But that you also may know my affairs *and* how I am doing, Tych′i-cus, a beloved brother and faithful minister in the Lord, will make all things known to you;
22 whom I have sent to you for this very purpose, that you may know our affairs, and *that* he may comfort your hearts.
23 Peace to the brethren, and love with faith, from God the Father and the Lord Jesus Christ.
24 Grace *be* with all those who love our Lord Jesus Christ in sincerity. Amen.

PHILIPPIANS

GREETING

PAUL and Timothy, bondservants of Jesus Christ,

To all the saints in Christ Jesus who are in Phi·lip′pi, with the bishops*a* and deacons:

2 Grace to you and peace from God our Father and the Lord Jesus Christ.

THANKFULNESS AND PRAYER

3 I thank my God upon every remembrance of you,
4 always in every prayer of mine making request for you all with joy,
5 for your fellowship in the gospel from the first day until now,
6 being confident of this very thing, that He who has begun a good work in you will complete *it* until the day of Jesus Christ;
7 just as it is right for me to think this of you all, because I have you in my heart, inasmuch as both in my chains and in the defense and confirmation of the gospel, you all are partakers with me of grace.
8 For God is my witness, how greatly I long for you all with the affection of Jesus Christ.
9 And this I pray, that your love may abound still more and more in knowledge and all discernment,
10 that you may approve the things that are excellent, that you may be sincere and without offense till the day of Christ,
11 being filled with the fruits of righteousness which *are* by Jesus Christ, to the glory and praise of God.

CHRIST IS PREACHED

12 But I want you to know, brethren, that the things *which happened* to me have actually turned out for the furtherance of the gospel,
13 so that it has become evident to the whole palace guard, and to all the rest, that my chains are in Christ;
14 and most of the brethren in the Lord, having become confident by my chains, are much more bold to speak the word without fear.
15 Some indeed preach Christ even from envy and strife, and some also from goodwill:
16 The former*a* preach Christ from selfish ambition, not sincerely, supposing to add affliction to my chains;
17 but the latter out of love, knowing that I am appointed for the defense of the gospel.
18 What then? Only *that* in every way, whether in pretense or in truth, Christ is preached; and in this I rejoice, yes, and will rejoice.

TO LIVE IS CHRIST

19 For I know that this will turn out for my deliverance through your prayer and the supply of the Spirit of Jesus Christ,
20 according to my earnest expectation and hope that in nothing I shall be ashamed, but with all boldness, as always, so now also Christ will be magnified in my body, whether by life or by death.
21 For to me, to live *is* Christ, and to die *is* gain.

1:1 *a*Literally *overseers*   1:16 *a*NU-Text reverses the contents of verses 16 and 17.

A TRUNK FULL OF YESTERDAY Philippians 1:3, 4

Do you have an old trunk in your attic with memories in it? Some people do. To go through that old trunk is to relive good days of yesterday. Memories are like going back and reliving those good days.

1. When you see a photo of someone you love, do you thank God for that person?
2. When you see a memory in an old trunk, do you thank God for the person in that memory?
3. Read Philippians 1:3, 4. What does that say? Do you?

For more on *Family Memories* turn to page 232
For more on *Family* turn to page 1818

22 But if *I* live on in the flesh, this *will mean* fruit from *my* labor; yet what I shall choose I cannot tell.
23 For*a* I am hard-pressed between the two, having a desire to depart and be with Christ, *which is* far better.
24 Nevertheless to remain in the flesh *is* more needful for you.
25 And being confident of this, I know that I shall remain and continue with you all for your progress and joy of faith,
26 that your rejoicing for me may be more abundant in Jesus Christ by my coming to you again.

STRIVING AND SUFFERING FOR CHRIST

27 Only let your conduct be worthy of the gospel of Christ, so that whether I come and see you or am absent, I may hear of your affairs, that you stand fast in one spirit, with one mind striving together for the faith of the gospel,
28 and not in any way terrified by your adversaries, which is to them a proof of perdition, but to you of salvation,*a* and that from God.
29 For to you it has been granted on behalf of Christ, not only to believe in Him, but also to suffer for His sake,
30 having the same conflict which you saw in me and now hear *is* in me.

UNITY THROUGH HUMILITY

2 Therefore if *there is* any consolation in Christ, if any comfort of love, if any fellowship of the Spirit, if any affection and mercy,
2 fulfill my joy by being like-minded, having the same love, *being* of one accord, of one mind.
3 *Let* nothing *be done* through selfish ambition or conceit, but in lowliness of mind let each esteem others better than himself.
4 Let each of you look out not only for his own interests, but also for the interests of others.

1:23 *a*NU-Text and M-Text read *But*.
1:28 *a*NU-Text reads *of your salvation*.

HONORING Philippians 1:20

Taking Care of My Body

You and I only get one body. There is no spare body in the closet. When this one is gone, it is gone. So God expects us to take care of the body He gave us. He expects us to honor Him with the body He gave us. But how can we do that?

1. Read the last part of Philippians 1:20, "Christ will be magnified in my body, whether by life or by death." How can we honor Christ (or magnify Him) with our bodies?
2. When we eat too much and let our bodies get out of shape, are we honoring Christ? When we drink the wrong things and hurt our bodies, are we honoring Christ? If we put unhealthy things into our bodies, things that will hurt us, are we honoring Christ?
3. How can you honor Christ with your body? Talk about this as a family.

For more on *Values* turn to page 1816
For more on *Responsibility* turn to page 1828

THE HUMBLED AND EXALTED CHRIST

5 Let this mind be in you which was also in Christ Jesus,
6 who, being in the form of God, did not consider it robbery to be equal with God,
7 but made Himself of no reputation, taking the form of a bondservant, *and* coming in the likeness of men.
8 And being found in appearance as a man, He humbled Himself and became obedient to *the point of* death, even the death of the cross.
9 Therefore God also has highly exalted Him and given Him the name which is above every name,
10 that at the name of Jesus every knee should bow, of those in heaven, and of those on earth, and of those under the earth,
11 and *that* every tongue should con-

fess that Jesus Christ *is* Lord, to the glory of God the Father.

LIGHT BEARERS

12 Therefore, my beloved, as you have always obeyed, not as in my presence only, but now much more in my absence, work out your own salvation with fear and trembling;
13 for it is God who works in you both to will and to do for *His* good pleasure.
14 Do all things without complaining and disputing,
15 that you may become blameless and harmless, children of God without fault in the midst of a crooked and perverse generation, among whom you shine as lights in the world,
16 holding fast the word of life, so that I may rejoice in the day of Christ

that I have not run in vain or labored in vain.

17 Yes, and if I am being poured out *as a drink offering* on the sacrifice and service of your faith, I am glad and rejoice with you all.

18 For the same reason you also be glad and rejoice with me.

TIMOTHY COMMENDED

19 But I trust in the Lord Jesus to send Timothy to you shortly, that I also may be encouraged when I know your state.

20 For I have no one like-minded, who will sincerely care for your state.

21 For all seek their own, not the things which are of Christ Jesus.

22 But you know his proven character, that as a son with *his* father he served with me in the gospel.

23 Therefore I hope to send him at once, as soon as I see how it goes with me.

24 But I trust in the Lord that I myself shall also come shortly.

EPAPHRODITUS PRAISED

25 Yet I considered it necessary to send to you E·paph·ro·dī′tus, my brother, fellow worker, and fellow soldier, but your messenger and the one who ministered to my need;

26 since he was longing for you all, and was distressed because you had heard that he was sick.

27 For indeed he was sick almost unto death; but God had mercy on him, and not only on him but on me also, lest I should have sorrow upon sorrow.

28 Therefore I sent him the more eagerly, that when you see him again you may rejoice, and I may be less sorrowful.

29 Receive him therefore in the Lord with all gladness, and hold such men in esteem;

30 because for the work of Christ he came close to death, not regarding his life, to supply what was lacking in your service toward me.

ALL FOR CHRIST

3 Finally, my brethren, rejoice in the Lord. For me to write the same things to you *is* not tedious, but for you *it is* safe.

2 Beware of dogs, beware of evil workers, beware of the mutilation!

3 For we are the circumcision, who worship God in the Spirit,*a* rejoice in Christ Jesus, and have no confidence in the flesh,

4 though I also might have confidence in the flesh. If anyone else thinks he may have confidence in the flesh, I more so:

5 circumcised the eighth day, of the stock of Israel, *of* the tribe of Benjamin, a Hebrew of the Hebrews; concerning the law, a Phar′i·see;

6 concerning zeal, persecuting the church; concerning the righteousness which is in the law, blameless.

7 But what things were gain to me, these I have counted loss for Christ.

8 Yet indeed I also count all things loss for the excellence of the knowledge of Christ Jesus my Lord, for whom I have suffered the loss of all things, and count them as rubbish, that I may gain Christ

9 and be found in Him, not having my own righteousness, which *is* from the law, but that which *is* through faith in Christ, the righteousness which is from God by faith;

10 that I may know Him and the power of His resurrection, and the

3:3 *a*NU-Text and M-Text read *who worship in the Spirit of God.*

fellowship of His sufferings, being conformed to His death,

11 if, by any means, I may attain to the resurrection from the dead.

PRESSING TOWARD THE GOAL

12 Not that I have already attained, or am already perfected; but I press on, that I may lay hold of that for which Christ Jesus has also laid hold of me.
13 Brethren, I do not count myself to have apprehended; but one thing *I do,* forgetting those things which are behind and reaching forward to those things which are ahead,
14 I press toward the goal for the prize of the upward call of God in Christ Jesus.
15 Therefore let us, as many as are mature, have this mind; and if in anything you think otherwise, God will reveal even this to you.
16 Nevertheless, to *the degree* that we have already attained, let us walk by the same rule,*a* let us be of the same mind.

OUR CITIZENSHIP IN HEAVEN

17 Brethren, join in following my example, and note those who so walk, as you have us for a pattern.
18 For many walk, of whom I have told you often, and now tell you even weeping, *that they are* the enemies of the cross of Christ:
19 whose end *is* destruction, whose god *is their* belly, and *whose* glory *is* in their shame—who set their mind on earthly things.
20 For our citizenship is in heaven, from which we also eagerly wait for the Savior, the Lord Jesus Christ,
21 who will transform our lowly body that it may be conformed to His glorious body, according to the working by which He is able even to subdue all things to Himself.

4 Therefore, my beloved and longed-for brethren, my joy and crown, so stand fast in the Lord, beloved.

BE UNITED, JOYFUL, AND IN PRAYER

2 I implore Eū·ō′di·a and I implore Syn′ty·chē to be of the same mind in the Lord.
3 And*a* I urge you also, true companion, help these women who labored with me in the gospel, with Clem′ent also, and the rest of my fellow workers, whose names *are* in the Book of Life.
4 Rejoice in the Lord always. Again I will say, rejoice!
5 Let your gentleness be known to all men. The Lord *is* at hand.
6 Be anxious for nothing, but in everything by prayer and supplication, with thanksgiving, let your requests be made known to God;
7 and the peace of God, which surpasses all understanding, will guard your hearts and minds through Christ Jesus.

MEDITATE ON THESE THINGS

8 Finally, brethren, whatever things are true, whatever things *are* noble, whatever things *are* just, whatever things *are* pure, whatever things *are* lovely, whatever things *are* of good report, if *there is* any virtue and if *there is* anything praiseworthy—meditate on these things.
9 The things which you learned and received and heard and saw in me, these do, and the God of peace will be with you.

3:16 *a*NU-Text omits *rule* and the rest of the verse.
4:3 *a*NU-Text and M-Text read *Yes.*

REJOICE IN THE LORD ALWAYS. AGAIN I WILL SAY, REJOICE!
Philippians 4:4

Rejoice!

Something must be special! Do you see the angel rejoicing? We don't know if an angel can blow a trumpet. But if it could, it would. Something wonderful has happened. What do you think it is?

1. Philippians 4:4 tells us that we should rejoice always in the Lord. That means we should be joyful because of who the Lord is and what He has done for us. Are you joyful today? Say so! Rejoice!

2. What would cause angels to rejoice? Look up Luke 15:10. The angels in heaven have joy when something special happens. What? Do you rejoice also when that happens?

For more on *Favorite Family Verses* turn to page 1841
For more on *Praise* turn to page 893

PHILIPPIAN GENEROSITY

10 But I rejoiced in the Lord greatly that now at last your care for me has flourished again; though you surely did care, but you lacked opportunity.

11 Not that I speak in regard to need, for I have learned in whatever state I am, to be content:

12 I know how to be abased, and I know how to abound. Everywhere and in all things I have learned both to be full and to be hungry, both to abound and to suffer need.

13 I can do all things through Christ[a] who strengthens me.

14 Nevertheless you have done well that you shared in my distress.

15 Now you Phi·lip′pi·ans know also that in the beginning of the gospel, when I departed from Mac·e·dō′ni·a, no church shared with me concerning giving and receiving but you only.

16 For even in Thes·sa·lo·nī′ca you sent *aid* once and again for my necessities.

17 Not that I seek the gift, but I seek the fruit that abounds to your account.

18 Indeed I have all and abound. I am full, having received from E·paph·ro·dī′tus the things *sent* from you, a sweet-smelling aroma, an acceptable sacrifice, well pleasing to God.

19 And my God shall supply all your need according to His riches in glory by Christ Jesus.

20 Now to our God and Father *be* glory forever and ever. Amen.

GREETING AND BLESSING

21 Greet every saint in Christ Jesus. The brethren who are with me greet you.

22 All the saints greet you, but especially those who are of Caesar's household.

23 The grace of our Lord Jesus Christ be with you all.[a] Amen.

4:13 [a]NU-Text reads *Him who.*   4:23 [a]NU-Text reads *your spirit.*

COLOSSIANS

GREETING

PAUL, an apostle of Jesus Christ by the will of God, and Timothy our brother,

2 To the saints and faithful brethren in Christ *who are* in Colos'sē:

Grace to you and peace from God our Father and the Lord Jesus Christ.*a*

THEIR FAITH IN CHRIST

3 We give thanks to the God and Father of our Lord Jesus Christ, praying always for you,
4 since we heard of your faith in Christ Jesus and of your love for all the saints;
5 because of the hope which is laid up for you in heaven, of which you heard before in the word of the truth of the gospel,
6 which has come to you, as *it has* also in all the world, and is bringing forth fruit,*a* as *it is* also among you since the day you heard and knew the grace of God in truth;
7 as you also learned from Ep'aphras, our dear fellow servant, who is a faithful minister of Christ on your behalf,
8 who also declared to us your love in the Spirit.

PREEMINENCE OF CHRIST

9 For this reason we also, since the day we heard it, do not cease to pray for you, and to ask that you may be filled with the knowledge of His will in all wisdom and spiritual understanding;

10 that you may walk worthy of the Lord, fully pleasing *Him,* being fruitful in every good work and increasing in the knowledge of God;
11 strengthened with all might, according to His glorious power, for all patience and longsuffering with joy;
12 giving thanks to the Father who has qualified us to be partakers of the inheritance of the saints in the light.
13 He has delivered us from the power of darkness and conveyed *us* into the kingdom of the Son of His love,
14 in whom we have redemption through His blood,*a* the forgiveness of sins.
15 He is the image of the invisible God, the firstborn over all creation.
16 For by Him all things were created that are in heaven and that are on earth, visible and invisible, whether thrones or dominions or principalities or powers. All things were created through Him and for Him.
17 And He is before all things, and in Him all things consist.
18 And He is the head of the body, the church, who is the beginning, the firstborn from the dead, that in all things He may have the preeminence.

RECONCILED IN CHRIST

19 For it pleased *the Father that* in Him all the fullness should dwell,
20 and by Him to reconcile all things to Himself, by Him, whether things on earth or things in heaven, having

---

1:2 *a*NU-Text omits *and the Lord Jesus Christ.*
1:6 *a*NU-Text and M-Text add *and growing.*
1:14 *a*NU-Text and M-Text omit *through His blood.*

made peace through the blood of His cross.

21 And you, who once were alienated and enemies in your mind by wicked works, yet now He has reconciled

22 in the body of His flesh through death, to present you holy, and blameless, and above reproach in His sight—

23 if indeed you continue in the faith, grounded and steadfast, and are not moved away from the hope of the gospel which you heard, which was preached to every creature under heaven, of which I, Paul, became a minister.

SACRIFICIAL SERVICE FOR CHRIST

24 I now rejoice in my sufferings for you, and fill up in my flesh what is lacking in the afflictions of Christ, for the sake of His body, which is the church,

25 of which I became a minister according to the stewardship from God which was given to me for you, to fulfill the word of God,

26 the mystery which has been hidden from ages and from generations, but now has been revealed to His saints.

27 To them God willed to make known what are the riches of the glory of this mystery among the Gentiles: which[a] is Christ in you, the hope of glory.

28 Him we preach, warning every man and teaching every man in all wisdom, that we may present every man perfect in Christ Jesus.

29 To this *end* I also labor, striving according to His working which works in me mightily.

NOT PHILOSOPHY BUT CHRIST

2 For I want you to know what a great conflict I have for you and those in Lā·o·di·cē′a, and *for* as many as have not seen my face in the flesh,

2 that their hearts may be encouraged, being knit together in love, and *attaining* to all riches of the full assurance of understanding, to the knowledge of the mystery of God, both of the Father and[a] of Christ,

3 in whom are hidden all the treasures of wisdom and knowledge.

4 Now this I say lest anyone should deceive you with persuasive words.

5 For though I am absent in the flesh, yet I am with you in spirit, rejoicing to see your *good* order and the steadfastness of your faith in Christ.

6 As you therefore have received Christ Jesus the Lord, so walk in Him,

7 rooted and built up in Him and established in the faith, as you have been taught, abounding in it[a] with thanksgiving.

8 Beware lest anyone cheat you through philosophy and empty deceit, according to the tradition of men, according to the basic principles of the world, and not according to Christ.

9 For in Him dwells all the fullness of the Godhead bodily;

10 and you are complete in Him, who is the head of all principality and power.

NOT LEGALISM BUT CHRIST

11 In Him you were also circumcised with the circumcision made without hands, by putting off the body of the sins[a] of the flesh, by the circumcision of Christ,

12 buried with Him in baptism, in which you also were raised with *Him* through faith in the working of God, who raised Him from the dead.

13 And you, being dead in your tres-

1:27 [a]M-Text reads *who*.   2:2 [a]NU-Text omits *both of the Father and.*   2:7 [a]NU-Text omits *in it.*   2:11 [a]NU-Text omits *of the sins.*

passes and the uncircumcision of your flesh, He has made alive together with Him, having forgiven you all trespasses,

14 having wiped out the handwriting of requirements that was against us, which was contrary to us. And He has taken it out of the way, having nailed it to the cross.

15 Having disarmed principalities and powers, He made a public spectacle of them, triumphing over them in it.

16 So let no one judge you in food or in drink, or regarding a festival or a new moon or sabbaths,

17 which are a shadow of things to come, but the substance is of Christ.

18 Let no one cheat you of your reward, taking delight in *false* humility and worship of angels, intruding into those things which he has not*a* seen, vainly puffed up by his fleshly mind,

19 and not holding fast to the Head, from whom all the body, nourished and knit together by joints and ligaments, grows with the increase *that is* from God.

20 Therefore,*a* if you died with Christ from the basic principles of the world, why, as *though* living in the world, do you subject yourselves to regulations—

21 "Do not touch, do not taste, do not handle,"

22 which all concern things which perish with the using—according to the commandments and doctrines of men?

23 These things indeed have an appearance of wisdom in self-imposed religion, *false* humility, and neglect of the body, *but are* of no value against the indulgence of the flesh.

Not Carnality but Christ

3 If then you were raised with Christ, seek those things which are above, where Christ is, sitting at the right hand of God.

2 Set your mind on things above, not on things on the earth.

3 For you died, and your life is hidden with Christ in God.

4 When Christ *who is* our life appears, then you also will appear with Him in glory.

5 Therefore put to death your members which are on the earth: fornication, uncleanness, passion, evil desire, and covetousness, which is idolatry.

6 Because of these things the wrath of God is coming upon the sons of disobedience,

7 in which you yourselves once walked when you lived in them.

8 But now you yourselves are to put off all these: anger, wrath, malice, blasphemy, filthy language out of your mouth.

9 Do not lie to one another, since you have put off the old man with his deeds,

10 and have put on the new *man* who is renewed in knowledge according to the image of Him who created him,

11 where there is neither Greek nor Jew, circumcised nor uncircumcised, barbarian, Scyth′i·an, slave *nor* free, but Christ *is* all and in all.

Character of the New Man

12 Therefore, as *the* elect of God, holy and beloved, put on tender mercies, kindness, humility, meekness, longsuffering;

13 bearing with one another, and forgiving one another, if anyone has a complaint against another; even as Christ forgave you, so you also *must do.*

2:18 *a*NU-Text omits *not.*   2:20 *a*NU-Text and M-Text omit *Therefore.*

Values

FORGIVENESS Colossians 3:13

Forgiving One Another

These two boys have been fighting. Nobody knows why they were
fighting. They aren't even sure now. But they are not fighting now. They are
singing a song about Jesus at church. The words of the song are about loving
each other. What do you think they should do about their fight now?

1. What do you think these boys will say to each other when they think
   about the song? What should they say? Should they ask each other to
   forgive?
2. Have you fought or argued or quarreled with someone lately? The
   Bible says you and your friend should forgive each other.
3. Read Colossians 3:13. What does it tell you about forgiving?

For more on *Values* turn to page 1824
For more on *Forgiveness* turn to page 1883

14 But above all these things put on love, which is the bond of perfection.
15 And let the peace of God rule in your hearts, to which also you were called in one body; and be thankful.
16 Let the word of Christ dwell in you richly in all wisdom, teaching and admonishing one another in psalms and hymns and spiritual songs, singing with grace in your hearts to the Lord.
17 And *whatever* you do in word or deed, *do* all in the name of the Lord Jesus, giving thanks to God the Father through Him.

THE CHRISTIAN HOME

18 Wives, submit to your own husbands, as is fitting in the Lord.
19 Husbands, love your wives and do not be bitter toward them.
20 Children, obey your parents in all things, for this is well pleasing to the Lord.
21 Fathers, do not provoke your children, lest they become discouraged.
22 Bondservants, obey in all things your masters according to the flesh, not with eyeservice, as men-pleasers, but in sincerity of heart, fearing God.
23 And whatever you do, do it heartily, as to the Lord and not to men,
24 knowing that from the Lord you will receive the reward of the inheritance; for[a] you serve the Lord Christ.
25 But he who does wrong will be repaid for what he has done, and there is no partiality.

4 Masters, give your bondservants what is just and fair, knowing that you also have a Master in heaven.

CHRISTIAN GRACES

2 Continue earnestly in prayer, being vigilant in it with thanksgiving;

3 meanwhile praying also for us, that God would open to us a door for the word, to speak the mystery of Christ, for which I am also in chains,
4 that I may make it manifest, as I ought to speak.
5 Walk in wisdom toward those *who are* outside, redeeming the time.
6 *Let* your speech always *be* with grace, seasoned with salt, that you may know how you ought to answer each one.

FINAL GREETINGS

7 Tych′i·cus, a beloved brother, faithful minister, and fellow servant in the Lord, will tell you all the news about me.
8 I am sending him to you for this very purpose, that he[a] may know your circumstances and comfort your hearts,
9 with Ō·nes′i·mus, a faithful and beloved brother, who is *one* of you. They will make known to you all things which *are happening* here.
10 Ar·is·tar′chus my fellow prisoner greets you, with Mark the cousin of Bar′na·bas (about whom you received instructions: if he comes to you, welcome him),
11 and Jesus who is called Jus′tus. These *are my* only fellow workers for the kingdom of God who are of the circumcision; they have proved to be a comfort to me.
12 Ep′a·phras, who is *one* of you, a bondservant of Christ, greets you, always laboring fervently for you in prayers, that you may stand perfect and complete[a] in all the will of God.
13 For I bear him witness that he has a great zeal[a] for you, and those

---

3:24 [a]NU-Text omits *for.*   4:8 [a]NU-Text reads *you may know our circumstances and he may.*
4:12 [a]NU-Text reads *fully assured.*   4:13 [a]NU-Text reads *concern.*

What Should I Do?

A HAPPY HOME STARTS WITH A HAPPY COUPLE Colossians 3:19

Here's a happy couple. They were just married. The husband loves his wife. The wife loves her husband. Do you think they will have a happy marriage? Do you think they will have a happy home?

1. Read Colossians 3:19. Should a husband love his wife? Should a wife love her husband? Why is that so important?
2. Are you glad when you know that mother and father love each other? Does it make you sad if they quarrel?
3. Do you help to make your home happy? How? What else could you do to make your home happy?

For more on *What Should I Do?* turn to page 1823
For more on *Family* turn to page 1823

who are in Lā·o·di·cē'a, and those in Hī·er·ap'o·lis.

14 Luke the beloved physician and Dē'mas greet you.

15 Greet the brethren who are in Lā-o·di·cē'a, and Nym'phas and the church that *is* in his*a* house.

CLOSING EXHORTATIONS AND BLESSING

16 Now when this epistle is read among you, see that it is read also in the church of the Lā·o·di·cē'ans, and that you likewise read the epistle from Lā·o·di·cē'a.

17 And say to Ar·chip'pus, "Take heed to the ministry which you have received in the Lord, that you may fulfill it."

18 This salutation by my own hand—Paul. Remember my chains. Grace *be* with you. Amen.

4:15 *a*NU-Text reads *Nympha . . . her house.*

The First Epistle of Paul the Apostle to the
THESSALONIANS

GREETING

PAUL, Sil·vā′nus, and Timothy,

To the church of the Thes·sa·lō′ni·ans in God the Father and the Lord Jesus Christ:

Grace to you and peace from God our Father and the Lord Jesus Christ.*a*

THEIR GOOD EXAMPLE

2 We give thanks to God always for you all, making mention of you in our prayers,
3 remembering without ceasing your work of faith, labor of love, and patience of hope in our Lord Jesus Christ in the sight of our God and Father,
4 knowing, beloved brethren, your election by God.
5 For our gospel did not come to you in word only, but also in power, and in the Holy Spirit and in much assurance, as you know what kind of men we were among you for your sake.
6 And you became followers of us and of the Lord, having received the word in much affliction, with joy of the Holy Spirit,
7 so that you became examples to all in Mac·e·dō′ni·a and A·chā′i·a who believe.
8 For from you the word of the Lord has sounded forth, not only in Mac·e·dō′ni·a and A·chā′i·a, but also in every place. Your faith toward God has gone out, so that we do not need to say anything.
9 For they themselves declare concerning us what manner of entry we had to you, and how you turned to God from idols to serve the living and true God,
10 and to wait for His Son from heaven, whom He raised from the dead, *even* Jesus who delivers us from the wrath to come.

PAUL'S CONDUCT

2 For you yourselves know, brethren, that our coming to you was not in vain.
2 But even*a* after we had suffered before and were spitefully treated at Phi·lip′pī, as you know, we were bold in our God to speak to you the gospel of God in much conflict.
3 For our exhortation *did* not *come* from error or uncleanness, nor *was it* in deceit.
4 But as we have been approved by God to be entrusted with the gospel, even so we speak, not as pleasing men, but God who tests our hearts.
5 For neither at any time did we use flattering words, as you know, nor a cloak for covetousness—God *is* witness.
6 Nor did we seek glory from men, either from you or from others, when we might have made demands as apostles of Christ.
7 But we were gentle among you, just as a nursing *mother* cherishes her own children.
8 So, affectionately longing for you, we were well pleased to impart to you not only the gospel of God, but also our own lives, because you had become dear to us.
9 For you remember, brethren, our labor and toil; for laboring night and day, that we might not be a burden to

---

1:1 *a*NU-Text omits *from God our Father and the Lord Jesus Christ.*   2:2 *a*NU-Text and M-Text omit *even.*

any of you, we preached to you the gospel of God.

10 You *are* witnesses, and God *also,* how devoutly and justly and blamelessly we behaved ourselves among you who believe;

11 as you know how we exhorted, and comforted, and charged[a] every one of you, as a father *does* his own children,

12 that you would walk worthy of God who calls you into His own kingdom and glory.

THEIR CONVERSION

13 For this reason we also thank God without ceasing, because when you received the word of God which you heard from us, you welcomed *it* not *as* the word of men, but as it is in truth, the word of God, which also effectively works in you who believe.

14 For you, brethren, became imitators of the churches of God which are in Judea in Christ Jesus. For you also suffered the same things from your own countrymen, just as they *did* from the Judeans,

15 who killed both the Lord Jesus and their own prophets, and have persecuted us; and they do not please God and are contrary to all men,

16 forbidding us to speak to the Gentiles that they may be saved, so as always to fill up *the measure of* their sins; but wrath has come upon them to the uttermost.

LONGING TO SEE THEM

17 But we, brethren, having been taken away from you for a short time in presence, not in heart, endeavored more eagerly to see your face with great desire.

18 Therefore we wanted to come to you—even I, Paul, time and again—but Satan hindered us.

19 For what *is* our hope, or joy, or crown of rejoicing? *Is it* not even you in the presence of our Lord Jesus Christ at His coming?

20 For you are our glory and joy.

CONCERN FOR THEIR FAITH

3 Therefore, when we could no longer endure it, we thought it good to be left in Athens alone,

2 and sent Timothy, our brother and minister of God, and our fellow laborer in the gospel of Christ, to establish you and encourage you concerning your faith,

3 that no one should be shaken by these afflictions; for you yourselves know that we are appointed to this.

4 For, in fact, we told you before when we were with you that we would suffer tribulation, just as it happened, and you know.

5 For this reason, when I could no longer endure it, I sent to know your faith, lest by some means the tempter had tempted you, and our labor might be in vain.

ENCOURAGED BY TIMOTHY

6 But now that Timothy has come to us from you, and brought us good news of your faith and love, and that you always have good remembrance of us, greatly desiring to see us, as we also *to see* you—

7 therefore, brethren, in all our affliction and distress we were comforted concerning you by your faith.

8 For now we live, if you stand fast in the Lord.

9 For what thanks can we render to God for you, for all the joy with which we rejoice for your sake before our God,

2:11 [a]NU-Text and M-Text read *implored.*

10 night and day praying exceedingly that we may see your face and perfect what is lacking in your faith?

PRAYER FOR THE CHURCH

11 Now may our God and Father Himself, and our Lord Jesus Christ, direct our way to you.

12 And may the Lord make you increase and abound in love to one another and to all, just as we *do* to you,

13 so that He may establish your hearts blameless in holiness before our God and Father at the coming of our Lord Jesus Christ with all His saints.

PLEA FOR PURITY

4 Finally then, brethren, we urge and exhort in the Lord Jesus that you should abound more and more, just as you received from us how you ought to walk and to please God;

2 for you know what commandments we gave you through the Lord Jesus.

3 For this is the will of God, your sanctification: that you should abstain from sexual immorality;

4 that each of you should know how to possess his own vessel in sanctification and honor,

5 not in passion of lust, like the Gentiles who do not know God;

6 that no one should take advantage of and defraud his brother in this matter, because the Lord *is* the avenger of all such, as we also forewarned you and testified.

7 For God did not call us to uncleanness, but in holiness.

8 Therefore he who rejects *this* does not reject man, but God, who has also given*a* us His Holy Spirit.

A BROTHERLY AND ORDERLY LIFE

9 But concerning brotherly love you have no need that I should write to you, for you yourselves are taught by God to love one another;

10 and indeed you do so toward all the brethren who are in all Mac·e·dō′-ni·a. But we urge you, brethren, that you increase more and more;

11 that you also aspire to lead a quiet life, to mind your own business, and to work with your own hands, as we commanded you,

12 that you may walk properly toward those who are outside, and *that* you may lack nothing.

THE COMFORT OF CHRIST'S COMING

13 But I do not want you to be ignorant, brethren, concerning those who have fallen asleep, lest you sorrow as others who have no hope.

14 For if we believe that Jesus died and rose again, even so God will bring with Him those who sleep in Jesus.*a*

15 For this we say to you by the word of the Lord, that we who are alive *and* remain until the coming of the Lord will by no means precede those who are asleep.

16 For the Lord Himself will descend from heaven with a shout, with the voice of an archangel, and with the trumpet of God. And the dead in Christ will rise first.

17 Then we who are alive *and* remain shall be caught up together with them in the clouds to meet the Lord in the air. And thus we shall always be with the Lord.

18 Therefore comfort one another with these words.

4:8 *a*NU-Text reads *who also gives.*   4:14 *a*Or *those who through Jesus sleep*

WHAT ABOUT THE FAMILY BEYOND YOUR FAMILY? 1 Thessalonians 4:9

Someone in your family gets married. Your sister or your brother marries. Or someone else in your family marries. That person marries another person, who also has a family. Now your family has a new family—new brothers, sisters, uncles, aunts, cousins, mother, father, grandparents or other relatives. You can love your new family. Or you can argue and fight with them. Which will it be?

1. Has someone in your family married this past year? What new family members did you get?
2. Do you like these new family members? How do you show them that you like them?
3. Read 1 Thessalonians 4:9. If we should love other Christians like this, how about other family members? Should we love them even more?

For more on *What Should I Do?* turn to page 1825
For more on *Family* turn to page 1824

Values

COOPERATION 1 Thessalonians 5:11–15

1 + 1 Sometimes = 1

We have always been taught that $1 + 1 = 2$. Right? Usually it does. One apple plus one apple equals two apples. One puppy with another puppy equals two puppies. But suppose there is one special job to do. Two people work together on it. The *two* people do *one* job *three* times as fast and as well as *one* person could. Ask mother and father about marriage. Two people working together get much more done than two people pulling in opposite directions. It's like two people riding one bike. One decides to put on the brakes while the other pedals. What will happen? One decides to go in one direction while the other wants to go in the other direction. What happens? Together, one cooperating with another one can do one job in a very special way. So $1 + 1$ can $= 1$, can't it?

1. Think of some situations where two together can do much more than two pulling in opposite directions or working against each other. That's called *cooperation*.
2. Read 1 Thessalonians 5:11–15. What does this say about togetherness or cooperation? What happens then?
3. The next time two family members want to go in different directions, remember the two people on the bike!

For more on *Values* turn to page 1828
For more on *Family* turn to page 1846

WHAT DO YOU DO WHEN YOU MEET A NEW FRIEND?
1 Thessalonians 5:15

What do you do when you meet a new friend? What do you say? Are you friendly? Will your new friend keep on being a new friend if you aren't friendly? Are you kind to your new friend? Will your new friend keep on being a friend if you aren't kind?

1. Read 1 Thessalonians 5:15. What does this say about being kind to others? Do you want friends who are kind or unkind to you?
2. What kind of person do you want a friend to be to you? Are you that kind of person to others?

For more on *What Should I Do?* turn to page 1826
For more on *Friendship* turn to page 435

THE DAY OF THE LORD

5 But concerning the times and the seasons, brethren, you have no need that I should write to you.

2 For you yourselves know perfectly that the day of the Lord so comes as a thief in the night.

3 For when they say, "Peace and safety!" then sudden destruction comes upon them, as labor pains upon a pregnant woman. And they shall not escape.

4 But you, brethren, are not in darkness, so that this Day should overtake you as a thief.

5 You are all sons of light and sons of the day. We are not of the night nor of darkness.

6 Therefore let us not sleep, as others *do,* but let us watch and be sober.

7 For those who sleep, sleep at night, and those who get drunk are drunk at night.

8 But let us who are of the day be sober, putting on the breastplate of faith and love, and *as* a helmet the hope of salvation.

9 For God did not appoint us to wrath, but to obtain salvation through our Lord Jesus Christ,

10 who died for us, that whether we wake or sleep, we should live together with Him.

11 Therefore comfort each other and edify one another, just as you also are doing.

VARIOUS EXHORTATIONS

12 And we urge you, brethren, to recognize those who labor among you, and are over you in the Lord and admonish you,

13 and to esteem them very highly in love for their work's sake. Be at peace among yourselves.

14 Now we exhort you, brethren, warn those who are unruly, comfort the fainthearted, uphold the weak, be patient with all.

15 See that no one renders evil for evil to anyone, but always pursue what is good both for yourselves and for all.

16 Rejoice always,

17 pray without ceasing,

What Should I Do?

WHEN MY MASTERPIECE BECOMES A MESS 1 Thessalonians 5:18

You spend all day making something special, or doing something special. Then suddenly something happens. Your masterpiece becomes a mess. Now what should you do?

1. You've worked so hard to make something special. This was going to be your masterpiece. But now it's a mess. What will you do? What should you do?
2. Is it better to complain, grumble, gripe, or blame God, or is it better to thank God for the fun of making your masterpiece? Should you praise God that *you* are OK? Should you praise God that things aren't worse? What should you do?
3. Read 1 Thessalonians 5:18. What does this verse say you should do? What is God saying here?

For more on *What Should I Do?* turn to page 1846
For more on *Facing Trials* turn to page 372

18 in everything give thanks; for this is the will of God in Christ Jesus for you.
19 Do not quench the Spirit.
20 Do not despise prophecies.
21 Test all things; hold fast what is good.
22 Abstain from every form of evil.

BLESSING AND ADMONITION

23 Now may the God of peace Himself sanctify you completely; and may your whole spirit, soul, and body be preserved blameless at the coming of our Lord Jesus Christ.
24 He who calls you *is* faithful, who also will do *it*.
25 Brethren, pray for us.
26 Greet all the brethren with a holy kiss.
27 I charge you by the Lord that this epistle be read to all the holy[a] brethren.
28 The grace of our Lord Jesus Christ *be* with you. Amen.

5:27 [a]NU-Text omits *holy*.

THESSALONIANS

GREETING

PAUL, Sil·vā′nus, and Timothy,

To the church of the Thes·sa·lō′-ni·ans in God our Father and the Lord Jesus Christ:

2 Grace to you and peace from God our Father and the Lord Jesus Christ.

GOD'S FINAL JUDGMENT AND GLORY

3 We are bound to thank God always for you, brethren, as it is fitting, because your faith grows exceedingly, and the love of every one of you all abounds toward each other,

4 so that we ourselves boast of you among the churches of God for your patience and faith in all your persecutions and tribulations that you endure,

5 *which is* manifest evidence of the righteous judgment of God, that you may be counted worthy of the kingdom of God, for which you also suffer;

6 since *it is* a righteous thing with God to repay with tribulation those who trouble you,

7 and to *give* you who are troubled rest with us when the Lord Jesus is revealed from heaven with His mighty angels,

8 in flaming fire taking vengeance on those who do not know God, and on those who do not obey the gospel of our Lord Jesus Christ.

9 These shall be punished with everlasting destruction from the presence of the Lord and from the glory of His power,

10 when He comes, in that Day, to be glorified in His saints and to be admired among all those who believe,a because our testimony among you was believed.

11 Therefore we also pray always for you that our God would count you worthy of *this* calling, and fulfill all the good pleasure of *His* goodness and the work of faith with power,

12 that the name of our Lord Jesus Christ may be glorified in you, and you in Him, according to the grace of our God and the Lord Jesus Christ.

THE GREAT APOSTASY

2 Now, brethren, concerning the coming of our Lord Jesus Christ and our gathering together to Him, we ask you,

2 not to be soon shaken in mind or troubled, either by spirit or by word or by letter, as if from us, as though the day of Christa had come.

3 Let no one deceive you by any means; for *that Day will not come* unless the falling away comes first, and the man of sina is revealed, the son of perdition,

4 who opposes and exalts himself above all that is called God or that is worshiped, so that he sits as Goda in the temple of God, showing himself that he is God.

5 Do you not remember that when I was still with you I told you these things?

6 And now you know what is restraining, that he may be revealed in his own time.

7 For the mystery of lawlessness is

1:10 aNU-Text and M-Text read *have believed.*
2:2 aNU-Text reads *the Lord.*   2:3 aNU-Text reads *lawlessness.*   2:4 aNU-Text omits *as God.*

AMBITION 2 Thessalonians 3:10

Congratulations! You Did It!

You went to school. And you finished all your work with good grades. Congratulations! You did it! Or you started to build something. You could have quit, but you didn't. Congratulations! You did it! You finished what you started. Or you started some other project and finished it with success. You did it! Congratulations!

1. Why is it important to finish work that we start? Why not quit when we want to?
2. Why should we do our work well? Why not do it sloppily?
3. Why should we work hard? Why not be lazy?
4. Read Ecclesiastes 9:10. What does this say? Now read Philippians 1:6. What does this say? One more. Read 2 Thessalonians 3:10. What does this say?

For more on *Values* turn to page 1843
For more on *Responsibility* turn to page 1843

already at work; only He*a* who now restrains *will do so* until He*b* is taken out of the way.

8 And then the lawless one will be revealed, whom the Lord will consume with the breath of His mouth and destroy with the brightness of His coming.

9 The coming of the *lawless one* is according to the working of Satan, with all power, signs, and lying wonders,

10 and with all unrighteous deception among those who perish, because they did not receive the love of the truth, that they might be saved.

11 And for this reason God will send them strong delusion, that they should believe the lie,

12 that they all may be condemned who did not believe the truth but had pleasure in unrighteousness.

STAND FAST

13 But we are bound to give thanks to God always for you, brethren beloved by the Lord, because God from the beginning chose you for salvation through sanctification by the Spirit and belief in the truth,

14 to which He called you by our gospel, for the obtaining of the glory of our Lord Jesus Christ.

15 Therefore, brethren, stand fast and hold the traditions which you were taught, whether by word or our epistle.

16 Now may our Lord Jesus Christ Himself, and our God and Father, who has loved us and given *us* everlasting consolation and good hope by grace,

17 comfort your hearts and establish you in every good word and work.

PRAY FOR US

3 Finally, brethren, pray for us, that the word of the Lord may run

swiftly and be glorified, just as *it is* with you,

2 and that we may be delivered from unreasonable and wicked men; for not all have faith.

3 But the Lord is faithful, who will establish you and guard *you* from the evil one.

4 And we have confidence in the Lord concerning you, both that you do and will do the things we command you.

5 Now may the Lord direct your hearts into the love of God and into the patience of Christ.

WARNING AGAINST IDLENESS

6 But we command you, brethren, in the name of our Lord Jesus Christ, that you withdraw from every brother who walks disorderly and not according to the tradition which he*a* received from us.

7 For you yourselves know how you ought to follow us, for we were not disorderly among you;

8 nor did we eat anyone's bread free of charge, but worked with labor and toil night and day, that we might not be a burden to any of you,

9 not because we do not have authority, but to make ourselves an example of how you should follow us.

10 For even when we were with you, we commanded you this: If anyone will not work, neither shall he eat.

11 For we hear that there are some who walk among you in a disorderly manner, not working at all, but are busybodies.

12 Now those who are such we command and exhort through our Lord

2:7 *a*Or *he* *b*Or *he*   3:6 *a*NU-Text and M-Text read *they.*

DO YOU FIGHT LIKE CATS AND DOGS? 2 Thessalonians 3:16

Does mother or father ever say to you and your brother or sister, "You fight like cats and dogs"? Are they saying, "You fight too much or you fight too loud or too long or too nasty or too something with your brother or sister"? What are they saying?

1. Do you ever fight or argue or quarrel with your brother or sister? Why?
2. What good thing do you do by fighting or arguing? Anything? Is there any good that comes from that?
3. Read 2 Thessalonians 3:16. Where does peace come from? Who gives it to us?
4. Why should brothers and sisters be family friends?

For more on *Family Friends* turn to page 109
For more on *Peacemaking* turn to page 356

Jesus Christ that they work in quietness and eat their own bread.

13 But *as for* you, brethren, do not grow weary *in* doing good.

14 And if anyone does not obey our word in this epistle, note that person and do not keep company with him, that he may be ashamed.

15 Yet do not count *him* as an enemy, but admonish *him* as a brother.

BENEDICTION

16 Now may the Lord of peace Himself give you peace always in every way. The Lord *be* with you all.

17 The salutation of Paul with my own hand, which is a sign in every epistle; so I write.

18 The grace of our Lord Jesus Christ *be* with you all. Amen.

TIMOTHY

GREETING

PAUL, an apostle of Jesus Christ, by the commandment of God our Savior and the Lord Jesus Christ, our hope,

2 To Timothy, a true son in the faith:

Grace, mercy, *and* peace from God our Father and Jesus Christ our Lord.

NO OTHER DOCTRINE

3 As I urged you when I went into Mac·e·dō′ni·a—remain in Eph′e·sus that you may charge some that they teach no other doctrine,

4 nor give heed to fables and endless genealogies, which cause disputes rather than godly edification which is in faith.

5 Now the purpose of the commandment is love from a pure heart, *from* a good conscience, and *from* sincere faith,

6 from which some, having strayed, have turned aside to idle talk,

7 desiring to be teachers of the law, understanding neither what they say nor the things which they affirm.

8 But we know that the law *is* good if one uses it lawfully,

9 knowing this: that the law is not made for a righteous person, but for *the* lawless and insubordinate, for *the* ungodly and for sinners, for *the* unholy and profane, for murderers of fathers and murderers of mothers, for manslayers,

10 for fornicators, for sodomites, for kidnappers, for liars, for perjurers, and if there is any other thing that is contrary to sound doctrine,

11 according to the glorious gospel of the blessed God which was committed to my trust.

GLORY TO GOD FOR HIS GRACE

12 And I thank Christ Jesus our Lord who has enabled me, because He counted me faithful, putting *me* into the ministry,

13 although I was formerly a blasphemer, a persecutor, and an insolent man; but I obtained mercy because I did *it* ignorantly in unbelief.

14 And the grace of our Lord was exceedingly abundant, with faith and love which are in Christ Jesus.

15 This *is* a faithful saying and worthy of all acceptance, that Christ Jesus came into the world to save sinners, of whom I am chief.

16 However, for this reason I obtained mercy, that in me first Jesus Christ might show all longsuffering, as a pattern to those who are going to believe on Him for everlasting life.

17 Now to the King eternal, immortal, invisible, to God who alone is wise,*a* be honor and glory forever and ever. Amen.

FIGHT THE GOOD FIGHT

18 This charge I commit to you, son Timothy, according to the prophecies previously made concerning you, that by them you may wage the good warfare,

19 having faith and a good conscience, which some having rejected, concerning the faith have suffered shipwreck,

20 of whom are Hȳ·me·naē′us and

1:17 *a*NU-Text reads *to the only God.*

Alexander, whom I delivered to Satan that they may learn not to blaspheme.

PRAY FOR ALL MEN

2 Therefore I exhort first of all that supplications, prayers, intercessions, *and* giving of thanks be made for all men,

2 for kings and all who are in authority, that we may lead a quiet and peaceable life in all godliness and reverence.

3 For this *is* good and acceptable in the sight of God our Savior,

4 who desires all men to be saved and to come to the knowledge of the truth.

5 For *there is* one God and one Mediator between God and men, *the* Man Christ Jesus,

6 who gave Himself a ransom for all, to be testified in due time,

7 for which I was appointed a preacher and an apostle—I am speaking the truth in Christ*a and* not lying—a teacher of the Gentiles in faith and truth.

MEN AND WOMEN IN THE CHURCH

8 I desire therefore that the men pray everywhere, lifting up holy hands, without wrath and doubting;

9 in like manner also, that the women adorn themselves in modest apparel, with propriety and moderation, not with braided hair or gold or pearls or costly clothing,

10 but, which is proper for women professing godliness, with good works.

11 Let a woman learn in silence with all submission.

12 And I do not permit a woman to teach or to have authority over a man, but to be in silence.

13 For Adam was formed first, then Eve.

14 And Adam was not deceived, but the woman being deceived, fell into transgression.

15 Nevertheless she will be saved in childbearing if they continue in faith, love, and holiness, with self-control.

QUALIFICATIONS OF OVERSEERS

3 This *is* a faithful saying: If a man desires the position of a bishop,*a he desires a good work.

2 A bishop then must be blameless, the husband of one wife, temperate, sober-minded, of good behavior, hospitable, able to teach;

3 not given to wine, not violent, not greedy for money,*a but gentle, not quarrelsome, not covetous;

4 one who rules his own house well, having *his* children in submission with all reverence

5 (for if a man does not know how to rule his own house, how will he take care of the church of God?);

6 not a novice, lest being puffed up with pride he fall into the *same* condemnation as the devil.

7 Moreover he must have a good testimony among those who are outside, lest he fall into reproach and the snare of the devil.

QUALIFICATIONS OF DEACONS

8 Likewise deacons *must be* reverent, not double-tongued, not given to much wine, not greedy for money,

9 holding the mystery of the faith with a pure conscience.

10 But let these also first be tested; then let them serve as deacons, being *found* blameless.

2:7 *a*NU-Text omits *in Christ.*   3:1 *a*Literally overseer   3:3 *a*NU-Text omits *not greedy for money.*

11 Likewise, *their* wives *must be* reverent, not slanderers, temperate, faithful in all things.

12 Let deacons be the husbands of one wife, ruling *their* children and their own houses well.

13 For those who have served well as deacons obtain for themselves a good standing and great boldness in the faith which is in Christ Jesus.

THE GREAT MYSTERY

14 These things I write to you, though I hope to come to you shortly;

15 but if I am delayed, *I write* so that you may know how you ought to conduct yourself in the house of God, which is the church of the living God, the pillar and ground of the truth.

16 And without controversy great is the mystery of godliness:

God*a* was manifested in the flesh,
Justified in the Spirit,
Seen by angels,
Preached among the Gentiles,
Believed on in the world,
Received up in glory.

THE GREAT APOSTASY

4 Now the Spirit expressly says that in latter times some will depart from the faith, giving heed to deceiving spirits and doctrines of demons,

2 speaking lies in hypocrisy, having their own conscience seared with a hot iron,

3 forbidding to marry, *and commanding* to abstain from foods which God created to be received with thanksgiving by those who believe and know the truth.

4 For every creature of God *is* good, and nothing is to be refused if it is received with thanksgiving;

5 for it is sanctified by the word of God and prayer.

A GOOD SERVANT OF JESUS CHRIST

6 If you instruct the brethren in these things, you will be a good minister of Jesus Christ, nourished in the words of faith and of the good doctrine which you have carefully followed.

7 But reject profane and old wives' fables, and exercise yourself toward godliness.

8 For bodily exercise profits a little, but godliness is profitable for all things, having promise of the life that now is and of that which is to come.

9 This *is* a faithful saying and worthy of all acceptance.

10 For to this *end* we both labor and suffer reproach,*a* because we trust in the living God, who is *the* Savior of all men, especially of those who believe.

11 These things command and teach.

TAKE HEED TO YOUR MINISTRY

12 Let no one despise your youth, but be an example to the believers in word, in conduct, in love, in spirit,*a* in faith, in purity.

13 Till I come, give attention to reading, to exhortation, to doctrine.

14 Do not neglect the gift that is in you, which was given to you by prophecy with the laying on of the hands of the eldership.

15 Meditate on these things; give yourself entirely to them, that your progress may be evident to all.

16 Take heed to yourself and to the doctrine. Continue in them, for in do-

3:16 *a*NU-Text reads *Who.*   4:10 *a*NU-Text reads *we labor and strive.*   4:12 *a*NU-Text omits *in spirit.*

ing this you will save both yourself and those who hear you.

TREATMENT OF CHURCH MEMBERS

5 Do not rebuke an older man, but exhort *him* as a father, younger men as brothers,
2 older women as mothers, younger women as sisters, with all purity.

HONOR TRUE WIDOWS

3 Honor widows who are really widows.
4 But if any widow has children or grandchildren, let them first learn to show piety at home and to repay their parents; for this is good and*a* acceptable before God.
5 Now she who is really a widow, and left alone, trusts in God and continues in supplications and prayers night and day.
6 But she who lives in pleasure is dead while she lives.
7 And these things command, that they may be blameless.
8 But if anyone does not provide for his own, and especially for those of his household, he has denied the faith and is worse than an unbeliever.
9 Do not let a widow under sixty years old be taken into the number, *and not unless* she has been the wife of one man,
10 well reported for good works: if she has brought up children, if she has lodged strangers, if she has washed the saints' feet, if she has relieved the afflicted, if she has diligently followed every good work.
11 But refuse *the* younger widows; for when they have begun to grow wanton against Christ, they desire to marry,

12 having condemnation because they have cast off their first faith.
13 And besides they learn *to be* idle, wandering about from house to house, and not only idle but also gossips and busybodies, saying things which they ought not.
14 Therefore I desire that *the* younger *widows* marry, bear children, manage the house, give no opportunity to the adversary to speak reproachfully.
15 For some have already turned aside after Satan.
16 If any believing man or*a* woman has widows, let them relieve them, and do not let the church be burdened, that it may relieve those who are really widows.

HONOR THE ELDERS

17 Let the elders who rule well be counted worthy of double honor, especially those who labor in the word and doctrine.
18 For the Scripture says, *"You shall not muzzle an ox while it treads out the grain,"a* and, "The laborer *is* worthy of his wages."*b*
19 Do not receive an accusation against an elder except from two or three witnesses.
20 Those who are sinning rebuke in the presence of all, that the rest also may fear.
21 I charge *you* before God and the Lord Jesus Christ and the elect angels that you observe these things without prejudice, doing nothing with partiality.
22 Do not lay hands on anyone hastily, nor share in other people's sins; keep yourself pure.
23 No longer drink only water, but

5:4 *a*NU-Text and M-Text omit *good and.*
5:16 *a*NU-Text omits *man or.*
5:18 *a*Deuteronomy 25:4 *b*Luke 10:7

FAITH 1 Timothy 6:12

How Shall We Fight for the Lord?

Someone says, "Fight for the Lord." Should you pick up a gun and shoot with it? Should you put on boxing gloves and punch someone for the Lord? How do you fight for the Lord?

1. Read the first phrase of 1 Timothy 6:12, "Fight the good fight of faith." What do you think that means?
2. This verse tells us that we should fight with *faith,* not with a gun or boxing gloves. Faith is what we believe and we learn that from God's Word. Learning and living God's Word helps us fight against the enemies—Satan and his evil followers.

For more on *Favorite Bible Words* turn to page 1858
For more on *Temptation* turn to page 1863

use a little wine for your stomach's sake and your frequent infirmities.
24 Some men's sins are clearly evident, preceding *them* to judgment, but those of some *men* follow later.
25 Likewise, the good works *of some* are clearly evident, and those that are otherwise cannot be hidden.

HONOR MASTERS

6 Let as many bondservants as are under the yoke count their own masters worthy of all honor, so that the name of God and *His* doctrine may not be blasphemed.
2 And those who have believing masters, let them not despise *them* because they are brethren, but rather serve *them* because those who are benefited are believers and beloved. Teach and exhort these things.

ERROR AND GREED

3 If anyone teaches otherwise and does not consent to wholesome words, *even* the words of our Lord Jesus Christ, and to the doctrine which accords with godliness,
4 he is proud, knowing nothing, but is obsessed with disputes and arguments over words, from which come envy, strife, reviling, evil suspicions,
5 useless wranglings*a* of men of corrupt minds and destitute of the truth, who suppose that godliness is a *means of* gain. From such withdraw yourself.*b*
6 Now godliness with contentment is great gain.
7 For we brought nothing into *this* world, *and it is* certain*a* we can carry nothing out.
8 And having food and clothing, with these we shall be content.
9 But those who desire to be rich fall into temptation and a snare, and *into* many foolish and harmful lusts which drown men in destruction and perdition.
10 For the love of money is a root of all *kinds of* evil, for which some have

6:5 *a*NU-Text and M-Text read *constant friction.*
*b*NU-Text omits this sentence.   6:7 *a*NU-Text omits *and it is certain.*

ABOUT GOD'S PROVISION 1 Timothy 6:17

Thank You, God, for a Warm House

You would get quite cold if you could never heat your house, wouldn't you? So where do you get the heat for your house? This boy is enjoying a wood fire in the stove. Someone cut a tree and split the wood. Now the wood heats his house. Some of our houses are heated with oil or gas. Some are heated with electricity. But God made the oil. He made the gas. And He made the power from which electricity came. Thank You, God for a warm house. You really do provide for me.

1. What does God provide for you? Can you think of five things?
2. Have you said "thank You" to God lately? Would you like to do that now? Read 1 Timothy 6:17 first.

WOOD BOX

For more on *What the Bible Says* turn to page 1863
For more on *God's Care* turn to page 1885

strayed from the faith in their greediness, and pierced themselves through with many sorrows.

THE GOOD CONFESSION

11 But you, O man of God, flee these things and pursue righteousness, godliness, faith, love, patience, gentleness.

12 Fight the good fight of faith, lay hold on eternal life, to which you were also called and have confessed the good confession in the presence of many witnesses.

13 I urge you in the sight of God who gives life to all things, and *before* Christ Jesus who witnessed the good confession before Pon'ti·us Pilate,

14 that you keep *this* commandment without spot, blameless until our Lord Jesus Christ's appearing,

15 which He will manifest in His own time, *He who is* the blessed and only Potentate, the King of kings and Lord of lords,

16 who alone has immortality, dwelling in unapproachable light, whom no man has seen or can see, to whom *be* honor and everlasting power. Amen.

INSTRUCTIONS TO THE RICH

17 Command those who are rich in this present age not to be haughty, nor to trust in uncertain riches but in the living God, who gives us richly all things to enjoy.

18 *Let them* do good, that they be rich in good works, ready to give, willing to share,

19 storing up for themselves a good foundation for the time to come, that they may lay hold on eternal life.

GUARD THE FAITH

20 O Timothy! Guard what was committed to your trust, avoiding the profane *and* idle babblings and contradictions of what is falsely called knowledge—

21 by professing it some have strayed concerning the faith. Grace *be* with you. Amen.

GREETING

PAUL, an apostle of Jesus Christ[a] by the will of God, according to the promise of life which is in Christ Jesus,

2 To Timothy, a beloved son:

Grace, mercy, *and* peace from God the Father and Christ Jesus our Lord.

TIMOTHY'S FAITH AND HERITAGE

3 I thank God, whom I serve with a pure conscience, as *my* forefathers *did,* as without ceasing I remember you in my prayers night and day,
4 greatly desiring to see you, being mindful of your tears, that I may be filled with joy,
5 when I call to remembrance the genuine faith that is in you, which dwelt first in your grandmother Lō′is and your mother Eū′nice, and I am persuaded is in you also.
6 Therefore I remind you to stir up the gift of God which is in you through the laying on of my hands.
7 For God has not given us a spirit of fear, but of power and of love and of a sound mind.

NOT ASHAMED OF THE GOSPEL

8 Therefore do not be ashamed of the testimony of our Lord, nor of me His prisoner, but share with me in the sufferings for the gospel according to the power of God,
9 who has saved us and called *us* with a holy calling, not according to our works, but according to His own purpose and grace which was given

to us in Christ Jesus before time began,
10 but has now been revealed by the appearing of our Savior Jesus Christ, *who* has abolished death and brought life and immortality to light through the gospel,
11 to which I was appointed a preacher, an apostle, and a teacher of the Gentiles.[a]
12 For this reason I also suffer these things; nevertheless I am not ashamed, for I know whom I have believed and am persuaded that He is able to keep what I have committed to Him until that Day.

BE LOYAL TO THE FAITH

13 Hold fast the pattern of sound words which you have heard from me, in faith and love which are in Christ Jesus.
14 That good thing which was committed to you, keep by the Holy Spirit who dwells in us.
15 This you know, that all those in Asia have turned away from me, among whom are Phȳ′gel·lus and Her·mog′e·nēs.
16 The Lord grant mercy to the household of On·e·siph′o·rus, for he often refreshed me, and was not ashamed of my chain;
17 but when he arrived in Rome, he sought me out very zealously and found *me.*
18 The Lord grant to him that he may find mercy from the Lord in that Day—and you know very well how many ways he ministered *to me*[a] at Eph′e·sus.

1:1 [a]NU-Text and M-Text read *Christ Jesus.*
1:11 [a]NU-Text omits *of the Gentiles.*   1:18 [a]*To me* is from the Vulgate and a few Greek manuscripts.

BE STRONG IN GRACE

2 You therefore, my son, be strong in the grace that is in Christ Jesus.

2 And the things that you have heard from me among many witnesses, commit these to faithful men who will be able to teach others also.

3 You therefore must endure*a* hardship as a good soldier of Jesus Christ.

4 No one engaged in warfare entangles himself with the affairs of *this* life, that he may please him who enlisted him as a soldier.

5 And also if anyone competes in athletics, he is not crowned unless he competes according to the rules.

6 The hardworking farmer must be first to partake of the crops.

7 Consider what I say, and may*a* the Lord give you understanding in all things.

8 Remember that Jesus Christ, of the seed of David, was raised from the dead according to my gospel,

9 for which I suffer trouble as an evildoer, *even* to the point of chains; but the word of God is not chained.

10 Therefore I endure all things for the sake of the elect, that they also may obtain the salvation which is in Christ Jesus with eternal glory.

11 *This is* a faithful saying:

For if we died with *Him,*
We shall also live with *Him.*
12 If we endure,
We shall also reign with *Him.*
If we deny *Him,*
He also will deny us.
13 If we are faithless,
He remains faithful;
He cannot deny Himself.

APPROVED AND DISAPPROVED WORKERS

14 Remind *them* of these things, charging *them* before the Lord not to strive about words to no profit, to the ruin of the hearers.

15 Be diligent to present yourself approved to God, a worker who does not need to be ashamed, rightly dividing the word of truth.

16 But shun profane *and* idle babblings, for they will increase to more ungodliness.

17 And their message will spread like cancer. Hȳ·me·naē′us and Phi·lē′tus are of this sort,

18 who have strayed concerning the truth, saying that the resurrection is already past; and they overthrow the faith of some.

19 Nevertheless the solid foundation of God stands, having this seal: "The Lord knows those who are His," and, "Let everyone who names the name of Christ*a* depart from iniquity."

20 But in a great house there are not only vessels of gold and silver, but also of wood and clay, some for honor and some for dishonor.

21 Therefore if anyone cleanses himself from the latter, he will be a vessel for honor, sanctified and useful for the Master, prepared for every good work.

22 Flee also youthful lusts; but pursue righteousness, faith, love, peace with those who call on the Lord out of a pure heart.

23 But avoid foolish and ignorant disputes, knowing that they generate strife.

24 And a servant of the Lord must not quarrel but be gentle to all, able to teach, patient,

25 in humility correcting those who are in opposition, if God perhaps will grant them repentance, so that they may know the truth,

26 and *that* they may come to their

2:3 *a*NU-Text reads *You must share.*
2:7 *a*NU-Text reads *the Lord will give you.*
2:19 *a*NU-Text and M-Text read *the Lord.*

ALL WHO DESIRE TO LIVE GODLY IN CHRIST JESUS WILL SUFFER PERSECUTION. 2 Timothy 3:12

Any Rotten Eggs Lately?

A boy has been preaching. He has been telling people about Jesus. He told them that he loves Jesus and they should love Him too. But guess what has happened. Someone didn't like what he said. Someone doesn't love Jesus. Someone doesn't want to love Jesus. The boy is persecuted. That means he has bad things happening to him because he loves Jesus.

1. Why would someone throw rotten eggs at this boy? What did he say that someone didn't like?
2. Do your friends know that you love Jesus and want them to love Him too? Do any of them say mean things about you because of this? These mean things aren't rotten eggs, but they are like rotten eggs, aren't they?
3. Should you stop loving Jesus because a friend doesn't love Him? Should you stop telling others about Jesus because someone says something mean? Why not?

For more on *Favorite Family Verses* turn to page 1867
For more on *Dedication* turn to page 1893

senses *and escape* the snare of the devil, having been taken captive by him to *do* his will.

PERILOUS TIMES AND PERILOUS MEN

3 But know this, that in the last days perilous times will come:

2 For men will be lovers of themselves, lovers of money, boasters, proud, blasphemers, disobedient to parents, unthankful, unholy,

3 unloving, unforgiving, slanderers, without self-control, brutal, despisers of good,

4 traitors, headstrong, haughty, lovers of pleasure rather than lovers of God,

5 having a form of godliness but denying its power. And from such people turn away!

6 For of this sort are those who creep into households and make captives of gullible women loaded down with sins, led away by various lusts,

7 always learning and never able to come to the knowledge of the truth.

8 Now as Jan'nēs and Jam'brēs resisted Moses, so do these also resist the truth: men of corrupt minds, disapproved concerning the faith;

9 but they will progress no further, for their folly will be manifest to all, as theirs also was.

THE MAN OF GOD AND THE WORD OF GOD

10 But you have carefully followed my doctrine, manner of life, purpose, faith, longsuffering, love, perseverance,

11 persecutions, afflictions, which

happened to me at An′ti·och, at I̅·co̅′-ni·um, at Lys′tra—what persecutions I endured. And out of *them* all the Lord delivered me.

12 Yes, and all who desire to live godly in Christ Jesus will suffer persecution.

13 But evil men and impostors will grow worse and worse, deceiving and being deceived.

14 But you must continue in the things which you have learned and been assured of, knowing from whom you have learned *them,*

15 and that from childhood you have known the Holy Scriptures, which are able to make you wise for salvation through faith which is in Christ Jesus.

16 All Scripture *is* given by inspiration of God, and *is* profitable for doctrine, for reproof, for correction, for instruction in righteousness,

17 that the man of God may be complete, thoroughly equipped for every good work.

PREACH THE WORD

4 I charge *you* therefore before God and the Lord Jesus Christ, who will judge the living and the dead at*a* His appearing and His kingdom:

2 Preach the word! Be ready in season *and* out of season. Convince, rebuke, exhort, with all longsuffering and teaching.

3 For the time will come when they will not endure sound doctrine, but according to their own desires, *because* they have itching ears, they will heap up for themselves teachers;

4 and they will turn *their* ears away from the truth, and be turned aside to fables.

5 But you be watchful in all things, endure afflictions, do the work of an evangelist, fulfill your ministry.

PAUL'S VALEDICTORY

6 For I am already being poured out as a drink offering, and the time of my departure is at hand.

7 I have fought the good fight, I have finished the race, I have kept the faith.

8 Finally, there is laid up for me the crown of righteousness, which the Lord, the righteous Judge, will give to me on that Day, and not to me only but also to all who have loved His appearing.

THE ABANDONED APOSTLE

9 Be diligent to come to me quickly;

10 for De̅′mas has forsaken me, having loved this present world, and has departed for Thes·sa·lo·ni̅′ca—Crescens for Galatia, Titus for Dal·ma̅′tia.

11 Only Luke is with me. Get Mark and bring him with you, for he is useful to me for ministry.

12 And Tych′i·cus I have sent to Eph′e·sus.

13 Bring the cloak that I left with Car′pus at Tro̅′as when you come—and the books, especially the parchments.

14 Alexander the coppersmith did me much harm. May the Lord repay him according to his works.

15 You also must beware of him, for he has greatly resisted our words.

16 At my first defense no one stood with me, but all forsook me. May it not be charged against them.

THE LORD IS FAITHFUL

17 But the Lord stood with me and strengthened me, so that the message might be preached fully through

4:1 *a*NU-Text omits *therefore* and reads *and by* for *at.*

PERSEVERANCE 2 Timothy 4:7, 8

Don't Stop! Don't Quit! Keep Going!

This boy tried something. But it didn't work well at first. It didn't work well the first three times! But he kept on trying. Now it works! Another boy ran a race. But he got tired. He wanted to quit. But he didn't. He kept going. He even won the race.

1. Do you think this boy wanted to quit? He didn't. He wasn't a quitter.
2. Do you ever want to quit? When? Why?
3. If something is worth doing, keep at it. Don't quit. Read 2 Timothy 4:7, 8. What does this say to you? Why doesn't the Lord want you to be a quitter in your work for Him?

For more on *Values* turn to page 1861
For more on *Responsibility* turn to page 157

me, and *that* all the Gentiles might hear. Also I was delivered out of the mouth of the lion.

18 And the Lord will deliver me from every evil work and preserve *me* for His heavenly kingdom. To Him *be* glory forever and ever. Amen!

COME BEFORE WINTER

19 Greet Pris′ca and A·qui′la, and the household of On·e·siph′o·rus.

20 Ē·ras′tus stayed in Corinth, but Troph′i·mus I have left in Mī·lē′tus sick.

21 Do your utmost to come before winter. Eū·bū′lus greets you, as well as Pū′dens, Lī′nus, Clau′di·a, and all the brethren.

FAREWELL

22 The Lord Jesus Christ*a* be with your spirit. Grace be with you. Amen.

4:22 *a*NU-Text omits *Jesus Christ*.

TITUS

GREETING

PAUL, a bondservant of God and an apostle of Jesus Christ, according to the faith of God's elect and the acknowledgment of the truth which accords with godliness,
2 in hope of eternal life which God, who cannot lie, promised before time began,
3 but has in due time manifested His word through preaching, which was committed to me according to the commandment of God our Savior;

4 To Titus, a true son in *our* common faith:

Grace, mercy, *and* peace from God the Father and the Lord Jesus Christ^a our Savior.

QUALIFIED ELDERS

5 For this reason I left you in Crēte, that you should set in order the things that are lacking, and appoint elders in every city as I commanded you—
6 if a man is blameless, the husband of one wife, having faithful children not accused of dissipation or insubordination.
7 For a bishop^a must be blameless, as a steward of God, not self-willed, not quick-tempered, not given to wine, not violent, not greedy for money,
8 but hospitable, a lover of what is good, sober-minded, just, holy, self-controlled,
9 holding fast the faithful word as he has been taught, that he may be able, by sound doctrine, both to ex-

hort and convict those who contradict.

THE ELDERS' TASK

10 For there are many insubordinate, both idle talkers and deceivers, especially those of the circumcision,
11 whose mouths must be stopped, who subvert whole households, teaching things which they ought not, for the sake of dishonest gain.
12 One of them, a prophet of their own, said, "Crē'tans *are* always liars, evil beasts, lazy gluttons."
13 This testimony is true. Therefore rebuke them sharply, that they may be sound in the faith,
14 not giving heed to Jewish fables and commandments of men who turn from the truth.
15 To the pure all things are pure, but to those who are defiled and unbelieving nothing is pure; but even their mind and conscience are defiled.
16 They profess to know God, but in works they deny Him, being abominable, disobedient, and disqualified for every good work.

QUALITIES OF A SOUND CHURCH

2 But as for you, speak the things which are proper for sound doctrine:
2 that the older men be sober, reverent, temperate, sound in faith, in love, in patience;
3 the older women likewise, that they be reverent in behavior, not slanderers, not given to much wine, teachers of good things—
4 that they admonish the young

1:4 ^aNU-Text reads *and Christ Jesus.*
1:7 ^aLiterally *overseer*

SHOULD I BEHAVE BETTER WHEN A STRANGER IS WITH ME?
Titus 2:1–8

A stranger comes into your home. Do you behave better? Do you say nicer things when a stranger is there than when the stranger leaves? Do you quarrel less with a stranger in the house? Do you say better words to a stranger than to your family? Why?

1. Why do some behave better when a stranger is there? Should they?
2. How should we behave with our family? Why?
3. Read Titus 2:1–8. When should we behave this way? Why should we behave as well when we are with our family as with strangers? Do you?

For more on *What Should I Do?* turn to page 1876
For more on *Family* turn to page 277

women to love their husbands, to love their children,

5 to be discreet, chaste, homemakers, good, obedient to their own husbands, that the word of God may not be blasphemed.

6 Likewise, exhort the young men to be sober-minded,

7 in all things showing yourself *to be* a pattern of good works; in doctrine *showing* integrity, reverence, incorruptibility,*a*

8 sound speech that cannot be condemned, that one who is an opponent may be ashamed, having nothing evil to say of you.*a*

9 *Exhort* bondservants to be obedient to their own masters, to be well pleasing in all *things,* not answering back,

10 not pilfering, but showing all good fidelity, that they may adorn the doctrine of God our Savior in all things.

TRAINED BY SAVING GRACE

11 For the grace of God that brings salvation has appeared to all men,

12 teaching us that, denying ungodliness and worldly lusts, we should live soberly, righteously, and godly in the present age,

13 looking for the blessed hope and glorious appearing of our great God and Savior Jesus Christ,

14 who gave Himself for us, that He might redeem us from every lawless deed and purify for Himself *His* own special people, zealous for good works.

15 Speak these things, exhort, and rebuke with all authority. Let no one despise you.

GRACES OF THE HEIRS OF GRACE

3 Remind them to be subject to rulers and authorities, to obey, to be ready for every good work,

2 to speak evil of no one, to be peaceable, gentle, showing all humility to all men.

3 For we ourselves were also once foolish, disobedient, deceived, serving various lusts and pleasures, living in malice and envy, hateful and hating one another.

4 But when the kindness and the love of God our Savior toward man appeared,

5 not by works of righteousness which we have done, but according to His mercy He saved us, through the washing of regeneration and renewing of the Holy Spirit,

6 whom He poured out on us abundantly through Jesus Christ our Savior,

7 that having been justified by His grace we should become heirs according to the hope of eternal life.

8 This is a faithful saying, and these things I want you to affirm constantly, that those who have believed in God should be careful to maintain good works. These things are good and profitable to men.

AVOID DISSENSION

9 But avoid foolish disputes, genealogies, contentions, and strivings about the law; for they are unprofitable and useless.

10 Reject a divisive man after the first and second admonition,

11 knowing that such a person is warped and sinning, being self-condemned.

FINAL MESSAGES

12 When I send Ar′te·mas to you, or Tych′i·cus, be diligent to come to me

2:7 *a*NU-Text omits *incorruptibility.*
2:8 *a*NU-Text and M-Text read *us.*

at Ni·cop'o·lis, for I have decided to spend the winter there.

13 Send Zē'nas the lawyer and A·pol'los on their journey with haste, that they may lack nothing.

14 And let our *people* also learn to maintain good works, to *meet* urgent needs, that they may not be unfruitful.

FAREWELL

15 All who *are* with me greet you. Greet those who love us in the faith. Grace *be* with you all. Amen.

The Epistle of Paul the Apostle to
PHILEMON

GREETING

PAUL, a prisoner of Christ Jesus, and Timothy *our* brother,

To Phī·lē'mon our beloved *friend* and fellow laborer,
2 to the beloved*a* Ap'phi·a, Ar·chip'-pus our fellow soldier, and to the church in your house:

3 Grace to you and peace from God our Father and the Lord Jesus Christ.

PHILEMON'S LOVE AND FAITH

4 I thank my God, making mention of you always in my prayers,
5 hearing of your love and faith which you have toward the Lord Jesus and toward all the saints,
6 that the sharing of your faith may become effective by the acknowledgment of every good thing which is in you*a* in Christ Jesus.
7 For we have*a* great joy*b* and consolation in your love, because the hearts of the saints have been refreshed by you, brother.

THE PLEA FOR ONESIMUS

8 Therefore, though I might be very bold in Christ to command you what is fitting,
9 *yet* for love's sake I rather appeal *to you*—being such a one as Paul, the aged, and now also a prisoner of Jesus Christ—
10 I appeal to you for my son Ō·nes'-i·mus, whom I have begotten *while* in my chains,

11 who once was unprofitable to you, but now is profitable to you and to me.
12 I am sending him back.*a* You therefore receive him, that is, my own heart,
13 whom I wished to keep with me, that on your behalf he might minister to me in my chains for the gospel.
14 But without your consent I wanted to do nothing, that your good deed might not be by compulsion, as it were, but voluntary.
15 For perhaps he departed for a while for this *purpose,* that you might receive him forever,
16 no longer as a slave but more than a slave—a beloved brother, especially to me but how much more to you, both in the flesh and in the Lord.

PHILEMON'S OBEDIENCE ENCOURAGED

17 If then you count me as a partner, receive him as *you would* me.
18 But if he has wronged you or owes anything, put that on my account.
19 I, Paul, am writing with my own hand. I will repay—not to mention to you that you owe me even your own self besides.
20 Yes, brother, let me have joy from you in the Lord; refresh my heart in the Lord.

2 *a*NU-Text reads *to our sister Apphia.*
6 *a*NU-Text and M-Text read *us.*   7 *a*NU-Text reads *had.* *b*M-Text reads *thanksgiving.*
12 *a*NU-Text reads *back to you in person, that is, my own heart.*

21 Having confidence in your obedience, I write to you, knowing that you will do even more than I say.
22 But, meanwhile, also prepare a guest room for me, for I trust that through your prayers I shall be granted to you.

FAREWELL

23 Ep'a·phras, my fellow prisoner in Christ Jesus, greets you,
24 *as do* Mark, Ar·is·tar'chus, Dē'mas, Luke, my fellow laborers.
25 The grace of our Lord Jesus Christ *be* with your spirit. Amen.

The Epistle to the
HEBREWS

GOD'S SUPREME REVELATION

GOD, who at various times and in various ways spoke in time past to the fathers by the prophets,
2 has in these last days spoken to us by *His* Son, whom He has appointed heir of all things, through whom also He made the worlds;
3 who being the brightness of *His* glory and the express image of His person, and upholding all things by the word of His power, when He had by Himself[a] purged our[b] sins, sat down at the right hand of the Majesty on high,
4 having become so much better than the angels, as He has by inheritance obtained a more excellent name than they.

THE SON EXALTED ABOVE ANGELS

5 For to which of the angels did He ever say:

> "You are My Son,
> Today I have begotten You"?[a]

And again:

> "I will be to Him a Father,
> And He shall be to Me a Son"?[b]

6 But when He again brings the firstborn into the world, He says:

> "Let all the angels of God worship Him."[a]

7 And of the angels He says:

> "Who makes His angels spirits
> And His ministers a flame of fire."[a]

8 But to the Son *He says:*

> "Your throne, O God, is forever
>   and ever;
> A scepter of righteousness is the
>   scepter of Your kingdom.
9 You have loved righteousness and
>   hated lawlessness;
> Therefore God, Your God, has
>   anointed You
> With the oil of gladness more
>   than Your companions."[a]

10 And:

> "You, LORD, in the beginning laid
>   the foundation of the earth,
> And the heavens are the work of
>   Your hands.
11 They will perish, but You remain;
> And they will all grow old like a
>   garment;
12 Like a cloak You will fold them
>   up,
> And they will be changed.
> But You are the same,
> And Your years will not fail."[a]

13 But to which of the angels has He ever said:

> "Sit at My right hand,
> Till I make Your enemies Your
>   footstool"?[a]

14 Are they not all ministering spirits sent forth to minister for those who will inherit salvation?

1:3 [a]NU-Text omits *by Himself.* [b]NU-Text omits *our.* 1:5 [a]Psalm 2:7 [b]2 Samuel 7:14
1:6 [a]Deuteronomy 32:43 (Septuagint, Dead Sea Scrolls); Psalm 97:7 1:7 [a]Psalm 104:4
1:9 [a]Psalm 45:6, 7 1:12 [a]Psalm 102:25–27
1:13 [a]Psalm 110:1

Do Not Neglect Salvation

2 Therefore we must give the more earnest heed to the things we have heard, lest we drift away.
2 For if the word spoken through angels proved steadfast, and every transgression and disobedience received a just reward,
3 how shall we escape if we neglect so great a salvation, which at the first began to be spoken by the Lord, and was confirmed to us by those who heard *Him,*
4 God also bearing witness both with signs and wonders, with various miracles, and gifts of the Holy Spirit, according to His own will?

The Son Made Lower
than Angels

5 For He has not put the world to come, of which we speak, in subjection to angels.
6 But one testified in a certain place, saying:

"*What is man that You are mindful of him,
Or the son of man that You take care of him?*
7 *You have made him a little lower than the angels;
You have crowned him with glory and honor,a*
And set him over the works of Your hands.
8 *You have put all things in subjection under his feet."a*

For in that He put all in subjection under him, He left nothing *that is* not put under him. But now we do not yet see all things put under him.
9 But we see Jesus, who was made a little lower than the angels, for the suffering of death crowned with glory and honor, that He, by the grace of God, might taste death for everyone.

Bringing Many Sons to Glory

10 For it was fitting for Him, for whom *are* all things and by whom *are* all things, in bringing many sons to glory, to make the captain of their salvation perfect through sufferings.
11 For both He who sanctifies and those who are being sanctified *are* all of one, for which reason He is not ashamed to call them brethren,

Praises

Hebrews 2:12

Where do you praise God? Must you be in a quiet place, away from your friends? Or will you praise Him when others are near? Will you praise Him when your friends are there? Will you say good things about God when those near you don't believe in Him? Do you praise Him "in the midst of the assembly"?

12 saying:

"*I will declare Your name to My brethren;
In the midst of the assembly I will sing praise to You."a*

13 And again:

"*I will put My trust in Him."a*

And again:

"*Here am I and the children whom God has given Me."b*

2:7 aNU-Text and M-Text omit the rest of verse 7.
2:8 aPsalm 8:4–6   2:12 aPsalm 22:22
2:13 a2 Samuel 22:3; Isaiah 8:17   bIsaiah 8:18

14 Inasmuch then as the children have partaken of flesh and blood, He Himself likewise shared in the same, that through death He might destroy him who had the power of death, that is, the devil,
15 and release those who through fear of death were all their lifetime subject to bondage.
16 For indeed He does not give aid to angels, but He does give aid to the seed of Abraham.
17 Therefore, in all things He had to be made like *His* brethren, that He might be a merciful and faithful High Priest in things *pertaining* to God, to make propitiation for the sins of the people.
18 For in that He Himself has suffered, being tempted, He is able to aid those who are tempted.

THE SON WAS FAITHFUL

3 Therefore, holy brethren, partakers of the heavenly calling, consider the Apostle and High Priest of our confession, Christ Jesus,
2 who was faithful to Him who appointed Him, as Moses also *was faithful* in all His house.
3 For this One has been counted worthy of more glory than Moses, inasmuch as He who built the house has more honor than the house.
4 For every house is built by someone, but He who built all things *is* God.
5 And Moses indeed *was* faithful in all His house as a servant, for a testimony of those things which would be spoken *afterward*,
6 but Christ as a Son over His own house, whose house we are if we hold fast the confidence and the rejoicing of the hope firm to the end.*a*

BE FAITHFUL

7 Therefore, as the Holy Spirit says:

"Today, if you will hear His voice,
8 Do not harden your hearts as in the rebellion,
In the day of trial in the wilderness,
9 Where your fathers tested Me, tried Me,
And saw My works forty years.
10 Therefore I was angry with that generation,
And said, 'They always go astray in their heart,
And they have not known My ways.'
11 So I swore in My wrath,
'They shall not enter My rest.' "*a*

12 Beware, brethren, lest there be in any of you an evil heart of unbelief in departing from the living God;
13 but exhort one another daily, while it is called *"Today,"* lest any of you be hardened through the deceitfulness of sin.
14 For we have become partakers of Christ if we hold the beginning of our confidence steadfast to the end,
15 while it is said:

"Today, if you will hear His voice,
Do not harden your hearts as in the rebellion."*a*

FAILURE OF THE WILDERNESS WANDERERS

16 For who, having heard, rebelled? Indeed, *was it* not all who came out of Egypt, *led* by Moses?
17 Now with whom was He angry forty years? *Was it* not with those

3:6 *a*NU-Text omits *firm to the end.*
3:11 *a*Psalm 95:7–11   3:15 *a*Psalm 95:7, 8

who sinned, whose corpses fell in the wilderness?

18 And to whom did He swear that they would not enter His rest, but to those who did not obey?

19 So we see that they could not enter in because of unbelief.

THE PROMISE OF REST

4 Therefore, since a promise remains of entering His rest, let us fear lest any of you seem to have come short of it.

2 For indeed the gospel was preached to us as well as to them; but the word which they heard did not profit them,*a* not being mixed with faith in those who heard *it.*

3 For we who have believed do enter that rest, as He has said:

"So I swore in My wrath,
'They shall not enter My rest,' "*a*

although the works were finished from the foundation of the world.

4 For He has spoken in a certain place of the seventh *day* in this way: "And God rested on the seventh day from all His works";*a*

5 and again in this *place:* "They shall not enter My rest."*a*

6 Since therefore it remains that some *must* enter it, and those to whom it was first preached did not enter because of disobedience,

7 again He designates a certain day, saying in David, *"Today,"* after such a long time, as it has been said:

"Today, if you will hear His voice,
Do not harden your hearts."*a*

8 For if Joshua had given them rest, then He would not afterward have spoken of another day.

9 There remains therefore a rest for the people of God.

10 For he who has entered His rest has himself also ceased from his works as God *did* from His.

THE WORD DISCOVERS OUR CONDITION

11 Let us therefore be diligent to enter that rest, lest anyone fall according to the same example of disobedience.

12 For the word of God *is* living and powerful, and sharper than any two-edged sword, piercing even to the division of soul and spirit, and of joints and marrow, and is a discerner of the thoughts and intents of the heart.

13 And there is no creature hidden from His sight, but all things *are* naked and open to the eyes of Him to whom we *must give* account.

OUR COMPASSIONATE HIGH PRIEST

14 Seeing then that we have a great High Priest who has passed through the heavens, Jesus the Son of God, let us hold fast *our* confession.

15 For we do not have a High Priest who cannot sympathize with our weaknesses, but was in all *points* tempted as *we are, yet* without sin.

16 Let us therefore come boldly to the throne of grace, that we may obtain mercy and find grace to help in time of need.

QUALIFICATIONS FOR HIGH PRIESTHOOD

5 For every high priest taken from among men is appointed for men in

---

4:2 *a*NU-Text and M-Text read *profit them, since they were not united by faith with those who heeded it.*   4:3 *a*Psalm 95:11   4:4 *a*Genesis 2:2
4:5 *a*Psalm 95:11   4:7 *a*Psalm 95:7, 8

things *pertaining* to God, that he may offer both gifts and sacrifices for sins.

2 He can have compassion on those who are ignorant and going astray, since he himself is also subject to weakness.

3 Because of this he is required as for the people, so also for himself, to offer *sacrifices* for sins.

4 And no man takes this honor to himself, but he who is called by God, just as Aaron *was*.

A PRIEST FOREVER

5 So also Christ did not glorify Himself to become High Priest, *but it* was He who said to Him:

*"You are My Son,
Today I have begotten You."*[a]

6 As *He* also *says* in another *place*:

*"You are a priest forever
According to the order of
Mel·chiz'e·dek";*[a]

7 who, in the days of His flesh, when He had offered up prayers and supplications, with vehement cries and tears to Him who was able to save Him from death, and was heard because of His godly fear,

8 though He was a Son, *yet* He learned obedience by the things which He suffered.

9 And having been perfected, He became the author of eternal salvation to all who obey Him,

10 called by God as High Priest *"according to the order of Mel·chiz'e·dek,"*

11 of whom we have much to say, and hard to explain, since you have become dull of hearing.

SPIRITUAL IMMATURITY

12 For though by this time you ought to be teachers, you need *someone* to teach you again the first principles of the oracles of God; and you have come to need milk and not solid food.

13 For everyone who partakes *only* of milk *is* unskilled in the word of righteousness, for he is a babe.

14 But solid food belongs to those who are of full age, *that is,* those who by reason of use have their senses exercised to discern both good and evil.

THE PERIL OF NOT PROGRESSING

6 Therefore, leaving the discussion of the elementary *principles* of Christ, let us go on to perfection, not laying again the foundation of repentance from dead works and of faith toward God,

2 of the doctrine of baptisms, of laying on of hands, of resurrection of the dead, and of eternal judgment.

3 And this we will[a] do if God permits.

4 For *it is* impossible for those who were once enlightened, and have tasted the heavenly gift, and have become partakers of the Holy Spirit,

5 and have tasted the good word of God and the powers of the age to come,

6 if they fall away,[a] to renew them again to repentance, since they crucify again for themselves the Son of God, and put *Him* to an open shame.

7 For the earth which drinks in the rain that often comes upon it, and bears herbs useful for those by whom it is cultivated, receives blessing from God;

8 but if it bears thorns and briers, *it*

5:5 [a]Psalm 2:7   5:6 [a]Psalm 110:4
6:3 [a]M-Text reads *let us do.*   6:6 [a]Or *and have fallen away*

is rejected and near to being cursed, whose end is to be burned.

A BETTER ESTIMATE

9 But, beloved, we are confident of better things concerning you, yes, things that accompany salvation, though we speak in this manner.
10 For God is not unjust to forget your work and labor of[a] love which you have shown toward His name, in that you have ministered to the saints, and do minister.
11 And we desire that each one of you show the same diligence to the full assurance of hope until the end,
12 that you do not become sluggish, but imitate those who through faith and patience inherit the promises.

GOD'S INFALLIBLE PURPOSE IN CHRIST

13 For when God made a promise to Abraham, because He could swear by no one greater, He swore by Himself,
14 saying, *"Surely blessing I will bless you, and multiplying I will multiply you."*[a]
15 And so, after he had patiently endured, he obtained the promise.
16 For men indeed swear by the greater, and an oath for confirmation is for them an end of all dispute.
17 Thus God, determining to show more abundantly to the heirs of promise the immutability of His counsel, confirmed it by an oath,
18 that by two immutable things, in which it is impossible for God to lie, we might[a] have strong consolation, who have fled for refuge to lay hold of the hope set before us.
19 This *hope* we have as an anchor of the soul, both sure and steadfast, and which enters the Presence *behind* the veil,

20 where the forerunner has entered for us, *even* Jesus, having become High Priest forever according to the order of Mel·chiz′e·dek.

THE KING OF RIGHTEOUSNESS

7 For this Mel·chiz′e·dek, king of Sā′lem, priest of the Most High God, who met Abraham returning from the slaughter of the kings and blessed him,
2 to whom also Abraham gave a tenth part of all, first being translated "king of righteousness," and then also king of Sā′lem, meaning "king of peace,"
3 without father, without mother, without genealogy, having neither beginning of days nor end of life, but made like the Son of God, remains a priest continually.
4 Now consider how great this man *was,* to whom even the patriarch Abraham gave a tenth of the spoils.
5 And indeed those who are of the sons of Levi, who receive the priesthood, have a commandment to receive tithes from the people according to the law, that is, from their brethren, though they have come from the loins of Abraham;
6 but he whose genealogy is not derived from them received tithes from Abraham and blessed him who had the promises.
7 Now beyond all contradiction the lesser is blessed by the better.
8 Here mortal men receive tithes, but there he *receives them,* of whom it is witnessed that he lives.
9 Even Levi, who receives tithes, paid tithes through Abraham, so to speak,
10 for he was still in the loins of his father when Mel·chiz′e·dek met him.

6:10 [a]NU-Text omits *labor of.*   6:14 [a]Genesis 22:17   6:18 [a]M-Text omits *might.*

NEED FOR A NEW PRIESTHOOD

11 Therefore, if perfection were through the Le·vit'i·cal priesthood (for under it the people received the law), what further need *was there* that another priest should rise according to the order of Mel·chiz'e·dek, and not be called according to the order of Aaron?
12 For the priesthood being changed, of necessity there is also a change of the law.
13 For He of whom these things are spoken belongs to another tribe, from which no man has officiated at the altar.
14 For *it is* evident that our Lord arose from Judah, of which tribe Moses spoke nothing concerning priesthood.a
15 And it is yet far more evident if, in the likeness of Mel·chiz'e·dek, there arises another priest
16 who has come, not according to the law of a fleshly commandment, but according to the power of an endless life.
17 For He testifies:a

> "You are a priest forever
> According to the order of
> Mel·chiz'e·dek."b

18 For on the one hand there is an annulling of the former commandment because of its weakness and unprofitableness,
19 for the law made nothing perfect; on the other hand, *there is the* bringing in of a better hope, through which we draw near to God.

GREATNESS OF THE NEW PRIEST

20 And inasmuch as *He was* not *made priest* without an oath
21 (for they have become priests without an oath, but He with an oath by Him who said to Him:

> "The LORD has sworn
> And will not relent,
> 'You are a priest forevera
> According to the order of
> Mel·chiz'e·dek' "),b

22 by so much more Jesus has become a surety of a better covenant.
23 Also there were many priests, because they were prevented by death from continuing.
24 But He, because He continues forever, has an unchangeable priesthood.
25 Therefore He is also able to save to the uttermost those who come to God through Him, since He always lives to make intercession for them.
26 For such a High Priest was fitting for us, *who is* holy, harmless, undefiled, separate from sinners, and has become higher than the heavens;
27 who does not need daily, as those high priests, to offer up sacrifices, first for His own sins and then for the people's, for this He did once for all when He offered up Himself.
28 For the law appoints as high priests men who have weakness, but the word of the oath, which came after the law, *appoints* the Son who has been perfected forever.

THE NEW PRIESTLY SERVICE

8 Now *this is* the main point of the things we are saying: We have such a High Priest, who is seated at the right hand of the throne of the Majesty in the heavens,
2 a Minister of the sanctuary and of the true tabernacle which the Lord erected, and not man.
3 For every high priest is appointed to offer both gifts and sacrifices.

7:14 aNU-Text reads *priests*.   7:17 aNU-Text reads *it is testified*. bPsalm 110:4   7:21 aNU-Text ends the quotation here. bPsalm 110:4

FOR Hebrews 7:25–27

A Singing Telegram

The doorbell rings. A young man from the telegraph company is there. He begins to sing, "Happy birthday to you." But he doesn't even know you. Then he says, "This is from Danny." Danny lives far away. He wanted to sing happy birthday to you, but he couldn't. So he paid the telegraph company to send this young man in his place. That's the way it was with Jesus. We couldn't die on the cross for our sins. So Jesus went to the cross in our place.

1. What is the telegraph man doing for Danny? Why isn't Danny doing it?
2. Why didn't you die on the cross for your sins? Since you couldn't do it, who did?
3. Have you accepted Jesus as your Savior? Have you let Him take away your sins?

For more on *Favorite Bible Words* turn to page 1871
For more on *Salvation* turn to page 1929

Therefore *it is* necessary that this One also have something to offer.

4 For if He were on earth, He would not be a priest, since there are priests who offer the gifts according to the law;

5 who serve the copy and shadow of the heavenly things, as Moses was divinely instructed when he was about to make the tabernacle. For He said, *"See that you make all things according to the pattern shown you on the mountain."*[a]

6 But now He has obtained a more excellent ministry, inasmuch as He is also Mediator of a better covenant, which was established on better promises.

A NEW COVENANT

7 For if that first *covenant* had been faultless, then no place would have been sought for a second.

8 Because finding fault with them, He says: *"Behold, the days are coming, says the LORD, when I will make a new covenant with the house of Israel and with the house of Judah—*

9 *"not according to the covenant that I made with their fathers in the day when I took them by the hand to lead them out of the land of Egypt; because they did not continue in My covenant, and I disregarded them, says the LORD.*

10 *"For this is the covenant that I will make with the house of Israel after those days, says the LORD: I will put My laws in their mind and write them on their hearts; and I will be their God, and they shall be My people.*

11 *"None of them shall teach his neighbor, and none his brother, saying, 'Know the LORD,' for all shall know Me, from the least of them to the greatest of them.*

8:5 [a]Exodus 25:40

12 *"For I will be merciful to their un-righteousness, and their sins and their lawless deeds*a *I will remember no more."*b
13 In that He says, *"A new cov-enant,"* He has made the first obso-lete. Now what is becoming obsolete and growing old is ready to vanish away.

THE EARTHLY SANCTUARY

9 Then indeed, even the first *covenant* had ordinances of divine service and the earthly sanctuary.
2 For a tabernacle was prepared: the first *part,* in which *was* the lamp-stand, the table, and the showbread, which is called the sanctuary;
3 and behind the second veil, the part of the tabernacle which is called the Holiest of All,
4 which had the golden censer and the ark of the covenant overlaid on all sides with gold, in which *were* the golden pot that had the manna, Aar-on's rod that budded, and the tablets of the covenant;
5 and above it were the cherubim of glory overshadowing the mercy seat. Of these things we cannot now speak in detail.

LIMITATIONS OF THE EARTHLY SERVICE

6 Now when these things had been thus prepared, the priests always went into the first part of the taber-nacle, performing *the services.*
7 But into the second part the high priest *went* alone once a year, not without blood, which he offered for himself and *for* the people's sins *com-mitted* in ignorance;
8 the Holy Spirit indicating this, that the way into the Holiest of All was not yet made manifest while the first tabernacle was still standing.

9 It *was* symbolic for the present time in which both gifts and sacri-fices are offered which cannot make him who performed the service per-fect in regard to the conscience—
10 *concerned* only with foods and drinks, various washings, and fleshly ordinances imposed until the time of reformation.

THE HEAVENLY SANCTUARY

11 But Christ came *as* High Priest of the good things to come,a with the greater and more perfect tabernacle not made with hands, that is, not of this creation.
12 Not with the blood of goats and calves, but with His own blood He en-tered the Most Holy Place once for all, having obtained eternal redemp-tion.
13 For if the blood of bulls and goats and the ashes of a heifer, sprinkling the unclean, sanctifies for the purify-ing of the flesh,
14 how much more shall the blood of Christ, who through the eternal Spirit offered Himself without spot to God, cleanse your conscience from dead works to serve the living God?
15 And for this reason He is the Me-diator of the new covenant, by means of death, for the redemption of the transgressions under the first cov-enant, that those who are called may receive the promise of the eternal in-heritance.

THE MEDIATOR'S DEATH NECESSARY

16 For where there *is* a testament, there must also of necessity be the death of the testator.
17 For a testament *is* in force after

8:12 aNU-Text omits *and their lawless deeds.*
bJeremiah 31:31–34 9:11 aNU-Text reads *that have come.*

men are dead, since it has no power at all while the testator lives.

18 Therefore not even the first *covenant* was dedicated without blood. 19 For when Moses had spoken every precept to all the people according to the law, he took the blood of calves and goats, with water, scarlet wool, and hyssop, and sprinkled both the book itself and all the people, 20 saying, *"This is the blood of the covenant which God has commanded you."*a 21 Then likewise he sprinkled with blood both the tabernacle and all the vessels of the ministry. 22 And according to the law almost all things are purified with blood, and without shedding of blood there is no remission.

GREATNESS OF CHRIST'S SACRIFICE

23 Therefore *it was* necessary that the copies of the things in the heavens should be purified with these, but the heavenly things themselves with better sacrifices than these. 24 For Christ has not entered the holy places made with hands, *which are* copies of the true, but into heaven itself, now to appear in the presence of God for us; 25 not that He should offer Himself often, as the high priest enters the Most Holy Place every year with blood of another— 26 He then would have had to suffer often since the foundation of the world; but now, once at the end of the ages, He has appeared to put away sin by the sacrifice of Himself. 27 And as it is appointed for men to die once, but after this the judgment, 28 so Christ was offered once to bear the sins of many. To those who eagerly wait for Him He will appear a second time, apart from sin, for salvation.

ANIMAL SACRIFICES INSUFFICIENT

10 For the law, having a shadow of the good things to come, *and* not the very image of the things, can never with these same sacrifices, which they offer continually year by year, make those who approach perfect. 2 For then would they not have ceased to be offered? For the worshipers, once purified, would have had no more consciousness of sins. 3 But in those *sacrifices there is* a reminder of sins every year. 4 For *it is* not possible that the blood of bulls and goats could take away sins.

CHRIST'S DEATH FULFILLS GOD'S WILL

5 Therefore, when He came into the world, He said:

"Sacrifice and offering You did not desire,
But a body You have prepared for Me.
6 *In burnt offerings and sacrifices for sin*
You had no pleasure.
7 *Then I said, 'Behold, I have come—*
In the volume of the book it is written of Me—
*To do Your will, O God.' "*a

8 Previously saying, *"Sacrifice and offering, burnt offerings, and offerings for sin You did not desire, nor had pleasure in them"* (which are offered according to the law), 9 then He said, *"Behold, I have come to do Your will, O God."*a He

9:20 aExodus 24:8   10:7 aPsalm 40:6–8
10:9 aNU-Text and M-Text omit *O God*.

GOODNESS Hebrews 10:24

You Little Angel

Does mother or father ever say, "You little angel" to you? Is that when you are being a good boy or girl? Would they ever say that to you when you are being naughty?

1. Why do people think you are like a little angel when you're good? Why would they never think you are like a little angel when you're naughty?
2. We should try to be good, shouldn't we? But should we also try to help others be good? Read Hebrews 10:24. What have you done to friends or family to "stir up love and good works"? What would you like to do today to "stir up love and good works" in friends or family? Will you?

For more on *Values* turn to page 1869
For more on *Godliness* turn to page 1881

takes away the first that He may establish the second.

10 By that will we have been sanctified through the offering of the body of Jesus Christ once *for all*.

CHRIST'S DEATH PERFECTS THE SANCTIFIED

11 And every priest stands ministering daily and offering repeatedly the same sacrifices, which can never take away sins.

12 But this Man, after He had offered one sacrifice for sins forever, sat down at the right hand of God,

13 from that time waiting till His enemies are made His footstool.

14 For by one offering He has perfected forever those who are being sanctified.

15 But the Holy Spirit also witnesses to us; for after He had said before,

16 *"This is the covenant that I will make with them after those days, says the LORD: I will put My laws into their hearts, and in their minds I will write them,"a*

17 *then He adds, "Their sins and their lawless deeds I will remember no more."a*

18 Now where there is remission of these, *there is* no longer an offering for sin.

HOLD FAST YOUR CONFESSION

19 Therefore, brethren, having boldness to enter the Holiest by the blood of Jesus,

20 by a new and living way which He consecrated for us, through the veil, that is, His flesh,

21 and *having* a High Priest over the house of God,

22 let us draw near with a true heart in full assurance of faith, having our hearts sprinkled from an evil conscience and our bodies washed with pure water.

23 Let us hold fast the confession of *our* hope without wavering, for He who promised *is* faithful.

24 And let us consider one another in order to stir up love and good works,

25 not forsaking the assembling of ourselves together, as *is* the manner of some, but exhorting *one another,* and so much the more as you see the Day approaching.

THE JUST LIVE BY FAITH

26 For if we sin willfully after we have received the knowledge of the truth, there no longer remains a sacrifice for sins,

27 but a certain fearful expectation of judgment, and fiery indignation which will devour the adversaries.

28 Anyone who has rejected Moses' law dies without mercy on the testimony of two or three witnesses.

29 Of how much worse punishment, do you suppose, will he be thought worthy who has trampled the Son of God underfoot, counted the blood of the covenant by which he was sanctified a common thing, and insulted the Spirit of grace?

30 For we know Him who said, *"Vengeance is Mine, I will repay,"a* says the Lord.b And again, *"The LORD will judge His people."c*

31 It is a fearful thing to fall into the hands of the living God.

32 But recall the former days in which, after you were illuminated, you endured a great struggle with sufferings:

33 partly while you were made a spectacle both by reproaches and tribulations, and partly while you be-

10:16 aJeremiah 31:33   10:17 aJeremiah 31:34
10:30 aDeuteronomy 32:35   bNU-Text omits *says the Lord.* cDeuteronomy 32:36

ABOUT GOD'S PUNISHMENT Hebrews 10:30

Don't Try to Be God

Do you ever try to be God? Do you ever make plans to punish someone for his or her sins? Someone does something wrong. God is in the business of rewarding or punishing people for the way they live. But you want to do it. Should you?

1. Read Romans 12:19. What does God say about your avenging or punishing of others for their sins? Read Hebrews 10:30. Who does He say should do it?
2. What will you remember the next time you want to be God?

For more on *What the Bible Says* turn to page 2
For more on *Temptation* turn to page 44

came companions of those who were so treated;

34 for you had compassion on me[a] in my chains, and joyfully accepted the plundering of your goods, knowing that you have a better and an enduring possession for yourselves in heaven.[b]

35 Therefore do not cast away your confidence, which has great reward.

36 For you have need of endurance, so that after you have done the will of God, you may receive the promise:

37 *"For yet a little while,*
     And He[a] who is coming will come
         and will not tarry.
38 *Now the[a] just shall live by faith;*
     But if anyone draws back,
     My soul has no pleasure in him."[b]

39 But we are not of those who draw back to perdition, but of those who believe to the saving of the soul.

BY FAITH WE UNDERSTAND

11 Now faith is the substance of things hoped for, the evidence of things not seen.

2 For by it the elders obtained a *good* testimony.

3 By faith we understand that the worlds were framed by the word of God, so that the things which are seen were not made of things which are visible.

FAITH AT THE DAWN OF HISTORY

4 By faith Abel offered to God a more excellent sacrifice than Cain, through which he obtained witness that he was righteous, God testifying of his gifts; and through it he being dead still speaks.

5 By faith E'noch was taken away so that he did not see death, *"and was not found, because God had taken him";[a]* for before he was taken he had this testimony, that he pleased God.

6 But without faith *it is* impossible to please *Him,* for he who comes to God must believe that He is, and *that*

10:34 [a]NU-Text reads *the prisoners* instead of *me in my chains.* [b]NU-Text omits *in heaven.*
10:37 [a]Or *that which*   10:38 [a]NU-Text reads *My just one.* [b]Habakkuk 2:3, 4   11:5 [a]Genesis 5:24

He is a rewarder of those who diligently seek Him.

7 By faith Noah, being divinely warned of things not yet seen, moved with godly fear, prepared an ark for the saving of his household, by which he condemned the world and became heir of the righteousness which is according to faith.

FAITHFUL ABRAHAM

8 By faith Abraham obeyed when he was called to go out to the place which he would receive as an inheritance. And he went out, not knowing where he was going.

9 By faith he dwelt in the land of promise as in a foreign country, dwelling in tents with Isaac and Jacob, the heirs with him of the same promise;

10 for he waited for the city which has foundations, whose builder and maker is God.

11 By faith Sarah herself also received strength to conceive seed, and she bore a child[a] when she was past the age, because she judged Him faithful who had promised.

12 Therefore from one man, and him as good as dead, were born as many as the stars of the sky in multitude—innumerable as the sand which is by the seashore.

THE HEAVENLY HOPE

13 These all died in faith, not having received the promises, but having seen them afar off were assured of them,[a] embraced them and confessed that they were strangers and pilgrims on the earth.

14 For those who say such things declare plainly that they seek a homeland.

15 And truly if they had called to mind that country from which they had come out, they would have had opportunity to return.

16 But now they desire a better, that is, a heavenly country. Therefore God is not ashamed to be called their God, for He has prepared a city for them.

THE FAITH OF THE PATRIARCHS

17 By faith Abraham, when he was tested, offered up Isaac, and he who had received the promises offered up his only begotten son,

18 of whom it was said, "In Isaac your seed shall be called,"[a]

19 concluding that God was able to raise him up, even from the dead, from which he also received him in a figurative sense.

20 By faith Isaac blessed Jacob and Esau concerning things to come.

21 By faith Jacob, when he was dying, blessed each of the sons of Joseph, and worshiped, leaning on the top of his staff.

22 By faith Joseph, when he was dying, made mention of the departure of the children of Israel, and gave instructions concerning his bones.

THE FAITH OF MOSES

23 By faith Moses, when he was born, was hidden three months by his parents, because they saw he was a beautiful child; and they were not afraid of the king's command.

24 By faith Moses, when he became of age, refused to be called the son of Pharaoh's daughter,

25 choosing rather to suffer affliction with the people of God than to enjoy the passing pleasures of sin,

26 esteeming the reproach of Christ

11:11 [a]NU-Text omits she bore a child.
11:13 [a]NU-Text and M-Text omit were assured of them.   11:18 [a]Genesis 21:12

greater riches than the treasures in*a* Egypt; for he looked to the reward.
27 By faith he forsook Egypt, not fearing the wrath of the king; for he endured as seeing Him who is invisible.
28 By faith he kept the Passover and the sprinkling of blood, lest he who destroyed the firstborn should touch them.
29 By faith they passed through the Red Sea as by dry *land, whereas* the Egyptians, attempting *to do* so, were drowned.

By Faith They Overcame

30 By faith the walls of Jericho fell down after they were encircled for seven days.
31 By faith the harlot Rā′hab did not perish with those who did not believe, when she had received the spies with peace.
32 And what more shall I say? For the time would fail me to tell of Gideon and Bar′ak and Samson and Jeph′thah, also *of* David and Samuel and the prophets:
33 who through faith subdued kingdoms, worked righteousness, obtained promises, stopped the mouths of lions,
34 quenched the violence of fire, escaped the edge of the sword, out of weakness were made strong, became valiant in battle, turned to flight the armies of the aliens.
35 Women received their dead raised to life again. Others were tortured, not accepting deliverance, that they might obtain a better resurrection.
36 Still others had trial of mockings and scourgings, yes, and of chains and imprisonment.
37 They were stoned, they were sawn in two, were tempted,*a* were slain with the sword. They wandered about in sheepskins and goatskins,

being destitute, afflicted, tormented—
38 of whom the world was not worthy. They wandered in deserts and mountains, *in* dens and caves of the earth.
39 And all these, having obtained a good testimony through faith, did not receive the promise,
40 God having provided something better for us, that they should not be made perfect apart from us.

The Race of Faith

12 Therefore we also, since we are surrounded by so great a cloud of witnesses, let us lay aside every weight, and the sin which so easily ensnares *us,* and let us run with endurance the race that is set before us,
2 looking unto Jesus, the author and finisher of *our* faith, who for the joy that was set before Him endured the cross, despising the shame, and has sat down at the right hand of the throne of God.

The Discipline of God

3 For consider Him who endured such hostility from sinners against Himself, lest you become weary and discouraged in your souls.
4 You have not yet resisted to bloodshed, striving against sin.
5 And you have forgotten the exhortation which speaks to you as to sons:

"*My son, do not despise the
    chastening of the LORD,
Nor be discouraged when you are
    rebuked by Him;*
6 *For whom the LORD loves He
    chastens,*

11:26 *a*NU-Text and M-Text read *of.*
11:37 *a*NU-Text omits *were tempted.*

And scourges every son whom He receives."a

7 If*a* you endure chastening, God deals with you as with sons; for what son is there whom a father does not chasten?

8 But if you are without chastening, of which all have become partakers, then you are illegitimate and not sons.

9 Furthermore, we have had human fathers who corrected *us,* and we paid *them* respect. Shall we not much more readily be in subjection to the Father of spirits and live?

10 For they indeed for a few days chastened *us* as seemed *best* to them, but He for *our* profit, that *we* may be partakers of His holiness.

11 Now no chastening seems to be joyful for the present, but painful; nevertheless, afterward it yields the peaceable fruit of righteousness to those who have been trained by it.

RENEW YOUR SPIRITUAL VITALITY

12 Therefore strengthen the hands which hang down, and the feeble knees,

13 and make straight paths for your feet, so that what is lame may not be *dislocated,* but rather be healed.

14 Pursue peace with all *people,* and holiness, without which no one will see the Lord:

15 looking carefully lest anyone fall short of the grace of God; lest any root of bitterness springing up cause trouble, and by this many become defiled;

16 lest there *be* any fornicator or profane person like Esau, who for one morsel of food sold his birthright.

17 For you know that afterward, when he wanted to inherit the blessing, he was rejected, for he found no place for repentance, though he sought it diligently with tears.

THE GLORIOUS COMPANY

18 For you have not come to the mountain that*a* may be touched and that burned with fire, and to blackness and darkness*b* and tempest,

19 and the sound of a trumpet and the voice of words, so that those who heard *it* begged that the word should not be spoken to them anymore.

20 (For they could not endure what was commanded: *"And if so much as a beast touches the mountain, it shall be stoneda or shot with an arrow."b*

21 And so terrifying was the sight *that* Moses said, *"I am exceedingly afraid and trembling."a*)

22 But you have come to Mount Zion and to the city of the living God, the heavenly Jerusalem, to an innumerable company of angels,

23 to the general assembly and church of the firstborn *who are* registered in heaven, to God the Judge of all, to the spirits of just men made perfect,

24 to Jesus the Mediator of the new covenant, and to the blood of sprinkling that speaks better things than *that of* Abel.

HEAR THE HEAVENLY VOICE

25 See that you do not refuse Him who speaks. For if they did not escape who refused Him who spoke on earth, much more *shall we not escape* if we turn away from Him who *speaks* from heaven,

12:6 *a*Proverbs 3:11, 12   12:7 *a*NU-Text and M-Text read *It is for discipline that you endure; God . . . .*   12:18 *a*NU-Text reads *to that which.* *b*NU-Text reads *gloom.*   12:20 *a*NU-Text and M-Text omit the rest of this verse. *b*Exodus 19:12, 13   12:21 *a*Deuteronomy 9:19

I WILL NEVER LEAVE YOU NOR FORSAKE YOU. Hebrews 13:5

I Will Not Leave You

Sometimes it's nice to be alone for a little while. But no one wants to be alone forever. Arlene needs a friend. Arlene's friend needs a friend. We all need friends and family. And we all need the Lord with us, don't we?

1. How would you feel if your friends deserted you?
2. How would you feel if your friends and family deserted you?
3. How would you feel if your friends and family and God deserted you? God said, "I will never leave you nor forsake you." Will you say "thank You, God" now?

For more on *Favorite Family Verses* turn to page 1872
For more on *God's Promises* turn to page 16

26 whose voice then shook the earth; but now He has promised, saying, *"Yet once more I shakeª not only the earth, but also heaven."ᵇ*

27 Now this, *"Yet once more,"* indicates the removal of those things that are being shaken, as of things that are made, that the things which cannot be shaken may remain.

28 Therefore, since we are receiving a kingdom which cannot be shaken, let us have grace, by which we mayª serve God acceptably with reverence and godly fear.

29 For our God *is* a consuming fire.

CONCLUDING MORAL DIRECTIONS

13 Let brotherly love continue.

2 Do not forget to entertain strangers, for by so *doing* some have unwittingly entertained angels.

3 Remember the prisoners as if chained with them—those who are mistreated—since you yourselves are in the body also.

4 Marriage *is* honorable among all, and the bed undefiled; but fornicators and adulterers God will judge.

5 *Let your* conduct *be* without covetousness; *be* content with such things as you have. For He Himself has said, *"I will never leave you nor forsake you."ª*

6 So we may boldly say:

*"The LORD is my helper;
I will not fear.
What can man do to me?"ª*

CONCLUDING RELIGIOUS DIRECTIONS

7 Remember those who rule over you, who have spoken the word of God to you, whose faith follow, considering the outcome of *their* conduct.

8 Jesus Christ *is* the same yesterday, today, and forever.

9 Do not be carried aboutª with various and strange doctrines. For *it is* good that the heart be established by grace, not with foods which have not profited those who have been occupied with them.

10 We have an altar from which those who serve the tabernacle have no right to eat.

11 For the bodies of those animals, whose blood is brought into the sanctuary by the high priest for sin, are burned outside the camp.

12 Therefore Jesus also, that He might sanctify the people with His own blood, suffered outside the gate.

13 Therefore let us go forth to Him, outside the camp, bearing His reproach.

14 For here we have no continuing city, but we seek the one to come.

15 Therefore by Him let us continually offer the sacrifice of praise to God, that is, the fruit of *our* lips, giving thanks to His name.

16 But do not forget to do good and to share, for with such sacrifices God is well pleased.

17 Obey those who rule over you, and be submissive, for they watch out for your souls, as those who must give account. Let them do so with joy and not with grief, for that would be unprofitable for you.

PRAYER REQUESTED

18 Pray for us; for we are confident that we have a good conscience, in all things desiring to live honorably.

19 But I especially urge *you* to do

12:26 ªNU-Text reads *will shake.* ᵇHaggai 2:6
12:28 ªM-Text omits *may.* 13:5 ªDeuteronomy 31:6, 8; Joshua 1:5 13:6 ªPsalm 118:6
13:9 ªNU-Text and M-Text read *away.*

SHARING Hebrews 13:16

May I Share Something with You?

Do you like to share good things with others? If you have two sandwiches and a friend has none, do you share? If you hear of someone who needs food or clothing, do you want to share? When it's playtime, do you like to share your toys with brother or sister or friend? Gift-giving time is sharing time, isn't it? When you give a birthday or Christmas gift, you share with someone. More than sharing your gift, you are sharing your love. Do you like that?

1. What have you shared today? Do you like to share?
2. What do you share when you give a gift? What do you share more than the gift itself?
3. Read Hebrews 13:16. What does this say to you?
4. What can you share with Jesus? Would you like to do that?

For more on *ßValues* turn to page 1881
For more on *Sharing* turn to page 883

this, that I may be restored to you the sooner.

BENEDICTION, FINAL EXHORTATION, FAREWELL

20 Now may the God of peace who brought up our Lord Jesus from the dead, that great Shepherd of the sheep, through the blood of the everlasting covenant,
21 make you complete in every good work to do His will, working in you[a] what is well pleasing in His sight,

through Jesus Christ, to whom *be* glory forever and ever. Amen.
22 And I appeal to you, brethren, bear with the word of exhortation, for I have written to you in few words.
23 Know that *our* brother Timothy has been set free, with whom I shall see you if he comes shortly.
24 Greet all those who rule over you, and all the saints. Those from Italy greet you.
25 Grace *be* with you all. Amen.

13:21 [a]NU-Text and M-Text read *us.*

The Epistle of
JAMES

GREETING TO THE TWELVE TRIBES

JAMES, a bondservant of God and of the Lord Jesus Christ,

To the twelve tribes which are scattered abroad:

Greetings.

PROFITING FROM TRIALS

2 My brethren, count it all joy when you fall into various trials,
3 knowing that the testing of your faith produces patience.
4 But let patience have *its* perfect work, that you may be perfect and complete, lacking nothing.
5 If any of you lacks wisdom, let him ask of God, who gives to all liberally and without reproach, and it will be given to him.
6 But let him ask in faith, with no doubting, for he who doubts is like a wave of the sea driven and tossed by the wind.
7 For let not that man suppose that he will receive anything from the Lord;
8 *he is* a double-minded man, unstable in all his ways.

THE PERSPECTIVE OF
RICH AND POOR

9 Let the lowly brother glory in his exaltation,
10 but the rich in his humiliation, because as a flower of the field he will pass away.
11 For no sooner has the sun risen with a burning heat than it withers the grass; its flower falls, and its beautiful appearance perishes. So the rich man also will fade away in his pursuits.

LOVING GOD UNDER TRIALS

12 Blessed *is* the man who endures temptation; for when he has been approved, he will receive the crown of life which the Lord has promised to those who love Him.
13 Let no one say when he is tempted, "I am tempted by God"; for God cannot be tempted by evil, nor does He Himself tempt anyone.
14 But each one is tempted when he is drawn away by his own desires and enticed.
15 Then, when desire has conceived, it gives birth to sin; and sin, when it is full-grown, brings forth death.
16 Do not be deceived, my beloved brethren.
17 Every good gift and every perfect gift is from above, and comes down from the Father of lights, with whom there is no variation or shadow of turning.
18 Of His own will He brought us forth by the word of truth, that we might be a kind of firstfruits of His creatures.

QUALITIES NEEDED IN TRIALS

19 So then,*a* my beloved brethren, let every man be swift to hear, slow to speak, slow to wrath;
20 for the wrath of man does not produce the righteousness of God.

DOERS—NOT HEARERS ONLY

21 Therefore lay aside all filthiness and overflow of wickedness, and re-

1:19 *a*NU-Text reads *Know this* or *This you know.*

PRAYER James 1:6

When You Pray for Rain, Do You Bring an Umbrella?

You need rain, so you get together to pray for rain. Should you bring an umbrella to your prayer meeting?

1. Read James 1:6. What does this tell you about praying? It is enough to pray? Should you do something more? What?
2. Should you believe your prayers will be answered? Why?

For more on *Favorite Bible Words* turn to page 1890
For more on *Prayer* turn to page 1876

ceive with meekness the implanted word, which is able to save your souls.

22 But be doers of the word, and not hearers only, deceiving yourselves.
23 For if anyone is a hearer of the word and not a doer, he is like a man observing his natural face in a mirror;
24 for he observes himself, goes away, and immediately forgets what kind of man he was.
25 But he who looks into the perfect law of liberty and continues *in it,* and is not a forgetful hearer but a doer of the work, this one will be blessed in what he does.
26 If anyone among you[a] thinks he is religious, and does not bridle his tongue but deceives his own heart, this one's religion *is* useless.
27 Pure and undefiled religion before God and the Father is this: to visit orphans and widows in their trouble, *and* to keep oneself unspotted from the world.

BEWARE OF PERSONAL FAVORITISM

2 My brethren, do not hold the faith of our Lord Jesus Christ, *the Lord* of glory, with partiality.

2 For if there should come into your assembly a man with gold rings, in fine apparel, and there should also come in a poor man in filthy clothes,
3 and you pay attention to the one wearing the fine clothes and say to him, "You sit here in a good place," and say to the poor man, "You stand there," or, "Sit here at my footstool,"
4 have you not shown partiality among yourselves, and become judges with evil thoughts?
5 Listen, my beloved brethren: Has God not chosen the poor of this world *to be* rich in faith and heirs of the kingdom which He promised to those who love Him?
6 But you have dishonored the poor man. Do not the rich oppress you and drag you into the courts?
7 Do they not blaspheme that noble name by which you are called?
8 If you really fulfill *the* royal law according to the Scripture, *"You shall love your neighbor as yourself,"*[a] you do well;
9 but if you show partiality, you commit sin, and are convicted by the law as transgressors.

1:26 [a]NU-Text omits *among you.*
2:8 [a]Leviticus 19:18

BUT BE DOERS OF THE WORD, AND NOT HEARERS ONLY, DECEIVING YOURSELVES. James 1:22

Listen to God's Word and Do What It Says

Do you see what this Bible-time person is doing? He is writing something on a scroll. A scroll is like our books today. It was a long piece of animal skin or paper made from strips of plants. People wrote on scrolls. When they were not using them, they rolled the scrolls on a piece of wood. Much of our New Testament was written on scrolls. God told people what to write and they wrote it down. So what should we do with it? James 1:22 says we should do two things: (1) listen to it, and (2) do what it says. Do you think that's a good idea?

1. Do you read often from the Bible? Does someone read it to you? Do you listen to what God says? Listen carefully. You will learn what He wants you to do.

2. When you hear what God says in His Word, what do you do about it? Will you obey Him? Think of one Bible verse. Try today to do what it says.

For more on *Favorite Family Verses* turn to page 1883
For more on *Bible* turn to page 271

10 For whoever shall keep the whole law, and yet stumble in one *point,* he is guilty of all.

11 For He who said, *"Do not commit adultery,"a* also said, *"Do not murder."b* Now if you do not commit adultery, but you do murder, you have become a transgressor of the law.

12 So speak and so do as those who will be judged by the law of liberty.

13 For judgment is without mercy to the one who has shown no mercy. Mercy triumphs over judgment.

FAITH WITHOUT WORKS IS DEAD

14 What *does it* profit, my brethren, if someone says he has faith but does not have works? Can faith save him?

15 If a brother or sister is naked and destitute of daily food,

16 and one of you says to them, "Depart in peace, be warmed and filled," but you do not give them the things which are needed for the body, what *does it* profit?

17 Thus also faith by itself, if it does not have works, is dead.

18 But someone will say, "You have faith, and I have works." Show me your faith without youra works, and I will show you my faith by myb works.

19 You believe that there is one God. You do well. Even the demons believe—and tremble!

20 But do you want to know, O foolish man, that faith without works is dead?a

21 Was not Abraham our father justified by works when he offered Isaac his son on the altar?

22 Do you see that faith was working together with his works, and by works faith was made perfect?

23 And the Scripture was fulfilled which says, *"Abraham believed God, and it was accounted to him for righ-teousness."a* And he was called the friend of God.

24 You see then that a man is justified by works, and not by faith only.

25 Likewise, was not Rā′hab the harlot also justified by works when she received the messengers and sent *them* out another way?

26 For as the body without the spirit is dead, so faith without works is dead also.

THE UNTAMABLE TONGUE

3 My brethren, let not many of you become teachers, knowing that we shall receive a stricter judgment.

2 For we all stumble in many things. If anyone does not stumble in word, he *is* a perfect man, able also to bridle the whole body.

3 Indeed,a we put bits in horses' mouths that they may obey us, and we turn their whole body.

4 Look also at ships: although they are so large and are driven by fierce winds, they are turned by a very small rudder wherever the pilot desires.

5 Even so the tongue is a little member and boasts great things. See how great a forest a little fire kindles!

6 And the tongue *is* a fire, a world of iniquity. The tongue is so set among our members that it defiles the whole body, and sets on fire the course of nature; and it is set on fire by hell.

7 For every kind of beast and bird, of reptile and creature of the sea, is tamed and has been tamed by mankind.

8 But no man can tame the tongue.

2:11 aExodus 20:14; Deuteronomy 5:18   bExodus 20:13; Deuteronomy 5:17   2:18 aNU-Text omits *your.*   bNU-Text omits *my.*   2:20 aNU-Text reads *useless.*   2:23 aGenesis 15:6   3:3 aNU-Text reads *Now if.*

It is an unruly evil, full of deadly poison.

9 With it we bless our God and Father, and with it we curse men, who have been made in the similitude of God.

10 Out of the same mouth proceed blessing and cursing. My brethren, these things ought not to be so.

11 Does a spring send forth fresh *water* and bitter from the same opening?

12 Can a fig tree, my brethren, bear olives, or a grapevine bear figs? Thus no spring yields both salt water and fresh.*a*

HEAVENLY VERSUS DEMONIC WISDOM

13 Who *is* wise and understanding among you? Let him show by good conduct *that* his works *are done* in the meekness of wisdom.

14 But if you have bitter envy and self-seeking in your hearts, do not boast and lie against the truth.

15 This wisdom does not descend from above, but *is* earthly, sensual, demonic.

16 For where envy and self-seeking *exist,* confusion and every evil thing *are* there.

17 But the wisdom that is from above is first pure, then peaceable, gentle, willing to yield, full of mercy and good fruits, without partiality and without hypocrisy.

18 Now the fruit of righteousness is sown in peace by those who make peace.

PRIDE PROMOTES STRIFE

4 Where do wars and fights *come* from among you? Do *they* not *come* from your *desires for* pleasure that war in your members?

2 You lust and do not have. You murder and covet and cannot obtain. You fight and war. Yet*a* you do not have because you do not ask.

3 You ask and do not receive, because you ask amiss, that you may spend *it* on your pleasures.

4 Adulterers and*a* adulteresses! Do you not know that friendship with the world is enmity with God? Whoever therefore wants to be a friend of the world makes himself an enemy of God.

5 Or do you think that the Scripture says in vain, "The Spirit who dwells in us yearns jealously"?

6 But He gives more grace. Therefore He says:

> *"God resists the proud,*
> *But gives grace to the humble."a*

HUMILITY CURES WORLDLINESS

7 Therefore submit to God. Resist the devil and he will flee from you.

8 Draw near to God and He will draw near to you. Cleanse *your* hands, *you* sinners; and purify *your* hearts, *you* double-minded.

9 Lament and mourn and weep! Let your laughter be turned to mourning and *your* joy to gloom.

10 Humble yourselves in the sight of the Lord, and He will lift you up.

DO NOT JUDGE A BROTHER

11 Do not speak evil of one another, brethren. He who speaks evil of a brother and judges his brother, speaks evil of the law and judges the law. But if you judge the law, you are not a doer of the law but a judge.

3:12 *a*NU-Text reads *Neither can a salty spring produce fresh water.*   4:2 *a*NU-Text and M-Text omit *Yet.*   4:4 *a*NU-Text omits *Adulterers and.*
4:6 *a*Proverbs 3:34

12 There is one Lawgiver,*a* who is able to save and to destroy. Who*b* are you to judge another?*c*

Do Not Boast About Tomorrow

13 Come now, you who say, "Today or tomorrow we will*a* go to such and such a city, spend a year there, buy and sell, and make a profit";
14 whereas you do not know what *will happen* tomorrow. For what *is* your life? It is even a vapor that appears for a little time and then vanishes away.
15 Instead you *ought* to say, "If the Lord wills, we shall live and do this or that."
16 But now you boast in your arrogance. All such boasting is evil.
17 Therefore, to him who knows to do good and does not do *it*, to him it is sin.

Rich Oppressors Will Be Judged

5 Come now, *you* rich, weep and howl for your miseries that are coming upon *you!*
2 Your riches are corrupted, and your garments are moth-eaten.
3 Your gold and silver are corroded, and their corrosion will be a witness against you and will eat your flesh like fire. You have heaped up treasure in the last days.
4 Indeed the wages of the laborers who mowed your fields, which you kept back by fraud, cry out; and the cries of the reapers have reached the ears of the Lord of Sab′a·ōth.*a*
5 You have lived on the earth in pleasure and luxury; you have fattened your hearts as*a* in a day of slaughter.
6 You have condemned, you have murdered the just; he does not resist you.

Be Patient and Persevering

7 Therefore be patient, brethren, until the coming of the Lord. See *how* the farmer waits for the precious fruit of the earth, waiting patiently for it until it receives the early and latter rain.
8 You also be patient. Establish your hearts, for the coming of the Lord is at hand.
9 Do not grumble against one another, brethren, lest you be condemned.*a* Behold, the Judge is standing at the door!
10 My brethren, take the prophets, who spoke in the name of the Lord, as an example of suffering and patience.
11 Indeed we count them blessed who endure. You have heard of the perseverance of Job and seen the end *intended by* the Lord—that the Lord is very compassionate and merciful.
12 But above all, my brethren, do not swear, either by heaven or by earth or with any other oath. But let your "Yes" be "Yes," and *your* "No," "No," lest you fall into judgment.*a*

Meeting Specific Needs

13 Is anyone among you suffering? Let him pray. Is anyone cheerful? Let him sing psalms.
14 Is anyone among you sick? Let him call for the elders of the church, and let them pray over him, anointing him with oil in the name of the Lord.
15 And the prayer of faith will save

4:12 *a*NU-Text adds *and Judge.* *b*NU-Text and M-Text read *But who.* *c*NU-Text reads *a neighbor.*
4:13 *a*M-Text reads *let us.*   5:4 *a*Literally, in Hebrew, *Hosts*   5:5 *a*NU-Text omits *as.*
5:9 *a*NU-Text and M-Text read *judged.*
5:12 *a*M-Text reads *hypocrisy.*

DRESSED UP LIKE A FAIRY PRINCESS James 5:13

You know what to do when things go wrong, don't you? Most people pray. They ask God for help. They beg God to take care of them or help them get well. But what do you do when everything seems wonderful? What do you do about God when you feel like you're a fairy princess or prince charming and the world lays its best gifts at your feet?

1. Read James 5:13. What should you do when things are tough? Do you? What should you do when things are wonderful? Do you?
2. Think of some tough times you have had lately. Did you pray? Think of some wonderful times you had lately. Did you sing praises to God?
3. Will you remember to praise God the next time things are wonderful? Thank Him for all the good things that happen to you.

For more on *What Should I Do?* turn to page 1880
For more on *Prayer* turn to page 1914

the sick, and the Lord will raise him up. And if he has committed sins, he will be forgiven.

16 Confess *your* trespasses*a* to one another, and pray for one another, that you may be healed. The effective, fervent prayer of a righteous man avails much.

17 E·li'jah was a man with a nature like ours, and he prayed earnestly that it would not rain; and it did not rain on the land for three years and six months.

18 And he prayed again, and the heaven gave rain, and the earth produced its fruit.

BRING BACK THE ERRING ONE

19 Brethren, if anyone among you wanders from the truth, and someone turns him back,

20 let him know that he who turns a sinner from the error of his way will save a soul*a* from death and cover a multitude of sins.

5:16 *a*NU-Text reads *Therefore confess your sins.*
5:20 *a*NU-Text reads *his soul.*

The First Epistle of

PETER

GREETING TO THE ELECT PILGRIMS

PETER, an apostle of Jesus Christ,

To the pilgrims of the Dispersion in Pon′tus, Galatia, Cap·pa·dō′ci·a, Asia, and Bi·thyn′i·a,
2 elect according to the foreknowledge of God the Father, in sanctification of the Spirit, for obedience and sprinkling of the blood of Jesus Christ:

Grace to you and peace be multiplied.

A HEAVENLY INHERITANCE

3 Blessed *be* the God and Father of our Lord Jesus Christ, who according to His abundant mercy has begotten us again to a living hope through the resurrection of Jesus Christ from the dead,
4 to an inheritance incorruptible and undefiled and that does not fade away, reserved in heaven for you,
5 who are kept by the power of God through faith for salvation ready to be revealed in the last time.
6 In this you greatly rejoice, though now for a little while, if need be, you have been grieved by various trials,
7 that the genuineness of your faith, *being* much more precious than gold that perishes, though it is tested by fire, may be found to praise, honor, and glory at the revelation of Jesus Christ,
8 whom having not seen*a* you love. Though now you do not see *Him,* yet believing, you rejoice with joy inexpressible and full of glory,
9 receiving the end of your faith—the salvation of *your* souls.
10 Of this salvation the prophets have inquired and searched carefully, who prophesied of the grace *that would come* to you,
11 searching what, or what manner of time, the Spirit of Christ who was in them was indicating when He testified beforehand the sufferings of Christ and the glories that would follow.
12 To them it was revealed that, not to themselves, but to us*a* they were ministering the things which now have been reported to you through those who have preached the gospel to you by the Holy Spirit sent from heaven—things which angels desire to look into.

LIVING BEFORE GOD OUR FATHER

13 Therefore gird up the loins of your mind, be sober, and rest *your* hope fully upon the grace that is to be brought to you at the revelation of Jesus Christ;
14 as obedient children, not conforming yourselves to the former lusts, *as* in your ignorance;
15 but as He who called you *is* holy, you also be holy in all *your* conduct,
16 because it is written, *"Be holy, for I am holy."a*
17 And if you call on the Father, who without partiality judges according to each one's work, conduct yourselves throughout the time of your stay *here* in fear;
18 knowing that you were not redeemed with corruptible things, *like* silver or gold, from your aimless conduct *received* by tradition from your fathers,
19 but with the precious blood of

1:8 *a*M-Text reads *known.*   1:12 *a*NU-Text and M-Text read *you.*   1:16 *a*Leviticus 11:44, 45; 19:2; 20:7

Christ, as of a lamb without blemish and without spot.

20 He indeed was foreordained before the foundation of the world, but was manifest in these last times for you

21 who through Him believe in God, who raised Him from the dead and gave Him glory, so that your faith and hope are in God.

THE ENDURING WORD

22 Since you have purified your souls in obeying the truth through the Spirit*a* in sincere love of the brethren, love one another fervently with a pure heart,

23 having been born again, not of corruptible seed but incorruptible, through the word of God which lives and abides forever,*a*

24 because

"All flesh is as grass,
And all the glory of man*a* as the
    flower of the grass.
The grass withers,
And its flower falls away,

25 But the word of the LORD endures
    forever."*a*

Now this is the word which by the gospel was preached to you.

2 Therefore, laying aside all malice, all deceit, hypocrisy, envy, and all evil speaking,

2 as newborn babes, desire the pure milk of the word, that you may grow thereby,*a*

3 if indeed you have tasted that the Lord *is* gracious.

THE CHOSEN STONE AND HIS CHOSEN PEOPLE

4 Coming to Him *as to* a living stone, rejected indeed by men, but chosen by God *and* precious,

5 you also, as living stones, are being built up a spiritual house, a holy priesthood, to offer up spiritual sacrifices acceptable to God through Jesus Christ.

6 Therefore it is also contained in the Scripture,

"Behold, I lay in Zion
A chief cornerstone, elect,
    precious,
And he who believes on Him will
    by no means be put to shame."*a*

7 Therefore, to you who believe, *He is* precious; but to those who are disobedient,*a*

"The stone which the builders
    rejected
Has become the chief
    cornerstone,"*b*

8 and

"A stone of stumbling
And a rock of offense."*a*

They stumble, being disobedient to the word, to which they also were appointed.

9 But you *are* a chosen generation, a royal priesthood, a holy nation, His own special people, that you may proclaim the praises of Him who called you out of darkness into His marvelous light;

10 who once *were* not a people but *are* now the people of God, who had not obtained mercy but now have obtained mercy.

1:22 *a*NU-Text omits *through the Spirit.*
1:23 *a*NU-Text omits *forever.*   1:24 *a*NU-Text reads *all its glory.*   1:25 *a*Isaiah 40:6–8
2:2 *a*NU-Text adds *up to salvation.*   2:6 *a*Isaiah 28:16   2:7 *a*NU-Text reads *to those who disbelieve.*   *b*Psalm 118:22   2:8 *a*Isaiah 8:14

What Should I Do?

WHAT DO YOU THINK ABOUT YOURSELF? 1 Peter 2:9

Do you think you're the greatest? Or do you think you're the worst? Do you love yourself too much? Or do you hate yourself? Are you proud of yourself, so proud that you don't even need God? Or do you think you're just a nobody, someone even mother can't love? What do you think of yourself? What *should* you think of yourself?

1. The Bible says we should not have too much pride. Read Romans 12:3. What does it say about pride?
2. But the Bible also tells us how much God loves us. Read John 3:16. How much does God think you are worth? Read also Matthew 10:31. How much are you worth in God's eyes. Now read 1 Peter 3:3, 4, where God speaks of true beauty, which is "very precious in the sight of God."
3. Read also 1 Peter 2:9. What does it say?
4. Keep a good balance. We are precious in God's sight. But we must not be proud and haughty.

For more on *What Should I Do?* turn to page 6
For more on *Humility* turn to page 824

LIVING BEFORE THE WORLD

11 Beloved, I beg *you* as sojourners and pilgrims, abstain from fleshly lusts which war against the soul,
12 having your conduct honorable among the Gentiles, that when they speak against you as evildoers, they may, by *your* good works which they observe, glorify God in the day of visitation.

SUBMISSION TO GOVERNMENT

13 Therefore submit yourselves to every ordinance of man for the Lord's sake, whether to the king as supreme,
14 or to governors, as to those who are sent by him for the punishment of evildoers and *for the* praise of those who do good.
15 For this is the will of God, that by doing good you may put to silence the ignorance of foolish men—
16 as free, yet not using liberty as a cloak for vice, but as bondservants of God.
17 Honor all *people*. Love the brotherhood. Fear God. Honor the king.

SUBMISSION TO MASTERS

18 Servants, *be* submissive to *your* masters with all fear, not only to the good and gentle, but also to the harsh.
19 For this *is* commendable, if because of conscience toward God one endures grief, suffering wrongfully.
20 For what credit *is it* if, when you are beaten for your faults, you take it patiently? But when you do good and suffer, if you take it patiently, this *is* commendable before God.

FAMILY 1 Peter 3:3, 4

What Is a Beautiful Woman?

Is a beautiful woman one who has the most makeup and the prettiest dresses? Is a beautiful woman one who has the best hair arrangement? What is a beautiful woman?

1. Read 1 Peter 3:3, 4. What does this say about true beauty?
2. Could this also be said about a handsome man?
3. A beautiful woman or a handsome man is a beautiful *person,* the real person, the real you. And what is more beautiful than godliness?

For more on *Values* turn to page 1884
For more on *Godliness* turn to page 1010

21 For to this you were called, because Christ also suffered for us,*a* leaving us*b* an example, that you should follow His steps:

22 *"Who committed no sin,*
　　Nor was deceit found in His
　　　　mouth";a

23 who, when He was reviled, did not revile in return; when He suffered, He did not threaten, but committed *Himself* to Him who judges righteously;
24 who Himself bore our sins in His own body on the tree, that we, having died to sins, might live for righteousness—by whose stripes you were healed.
25 For you were like sheep going astray, but have now returned to the Shepherd and Overseer*a* of your souls.

SUBMISSION TO HUSBANDS

3 Wives, likewise, *be* submissive to your own husbands, that even if some do not obey the word, they, without a word, may be won by the conduct of their wives,
2 when they observe your chaste conduct *accompanied* by fear.
3 Do not let your adornment be *merely* outward—arranging the hair, wearing gold, or putting on *fine* apparel—
4 rather *let it be* the hidden person of the heart, with the incorruptible *beauty* of a gentle and quiet spirit, which is very precious in the sight of God.
5 For in this manner, in former times, the holy women who trusted in God also adorned themselves, being submissive to their own husbands,
6 as Sarah obeyed Abraham, calling him lord, whose daughters you are if you do good and are not afraid with any terror.

A WORD TO HUSBANDS

7 Husbands, likewise, dwell with *them* with understanding, giving honor to the wife, as to the weaker vessel, and as *being* heirs together of the grace of life, that your prayers may not be hindered.

CALLED TO BLESSING

8 Finally, all *of you be* of one mind, having compassion for one another; love as brothers, *be* tenderhearted, *be* courteous;*a*
9 not returning evil for evil or reviling for reviling, but on the contrary blessing, knowing that you were called to this, that you may inherit a blessing.
10 For

"He who would love life
　And see good days,
　Let him refrain his tongue from
　　evil,
　And his lips from speaking deceit.
11 Let him turn away from evil and
　　do good;
　Let him seek peace and pursue it.
12 For the eyes of the LORD are on
　　the righteous,
　And His ears are open to their
　　prayers;
　But the face of the LORD is
　　against those who do evil."*a*

SUFFERING FOR RIGHT AND WRONG

13 And who *is* he who will harm you if you become followers of what is good?
14 But even if you should suffer for righteousness' sake, *you are* blessed. *"And do not be afraid of their threats, nor be troubled."a*

2:21 *a*NU-Text reads *you.*　*b*NU-Text and M-Text read *you.*　2:22 *a*Isaiah 53:9　2:25 *a*Greek *Episkopos*　3:8 *a*NU-Text reads *humble.*　3:12 *a*Psalm 34:12–16　3:14 *a*Isaiah 8:12

NOT RETURNING EVIL FOR EVIL. 1 PETER 3:9

Should I Get Even?

Someone teases you. What should you do? Should you try to get even or do something kind for that person? Someone hurts you. What should you do? Should you try to get even or do something kind for that person? Someone says something mean about you, or to you. Should you try to get even or do something kind for that person?

1. What *do* you do when someone does something bad to you? Do you try to get even? Are you repaying evil for evil when you try to get even?

2. What *should* you do when someone does something bad to you? Should you try to get even? Should you repay evil with evil, or with good? What do you think?

For more on *Favorite Family Verses* turn to page 1885
For more on *Forgiveness* turn to page 55

15 But sanctify the Lord God*a* in your hearts, and always *be* ready to *give* a defense to everyone who asks you a reason for the hope that is in you, with meekness and fear;
16 having a good conscience, that when they defame you as evildoers, those who revile your good conduct in Christ may be ashamed.
17 For *it is* better, if it is the will of God, to suffer for doing good than for doing evil.

CHRIST'S SUFFERING AND OURS

18 For Christ also suffered once for sins, the just for the unjust, that He might bring us*a* to God, being put to death in the flesh but made alive by the Spirit,
19 by whom also He went and preached to the spirits in prison,
20 who formerly were disobedient, when once the Divine longsuffering waited*a* in the days of Noah, while *the* ark was being prepared, in which

a few, that is, eight souls, were saved through water.
21 There is also an antitype which now saves us—baptism (not the removal of the filth of the flesh, but the answer of a good conscience toward God), through the resurrection of Jesus Christ,
22 who has gone into heaven and is at the right hand of God, angels and authorities and powers having been made subject to Him.

4 Therefore, since Christ suffered for us*a* in the flesh, arm yourselves also with the same mind, for he who has suffered in the flesh has ceased from sin,
2 that he no longer should live the rest of *his* time in the flesh for the lusts of men, but for the will of God.

3:15 *a*NU-Text reads *Christ as Lord.*
3:18 *a*NU-Text and M-Text read *you.*
3:20 *a*NU-Text and M-Text read *when the longsuffering of God waited patiently.* 4:1 *a*NU-Text omits *for us.*

GIVING 1 Peter 4:10

What Is Your Gift from God? How Are You Using It for God?

Are you a good musician? Do you use your musical gifts for God? Are you a good artist? Do you use your artistic gifts for God? Are you a plumber, or carpenter, or barber, or cook, or leader, or administrator, or finance expert? Do you use those special gifts for God? Should you?

1. Read 1 Peter 4:10. What does this say about using the gifts God gives you?
2. Why should we not try to use gifts that we don't have? What would happen then?
3. Have you thanked God for the special gifts He has given you? What are those gifts? How will you use them for Him?

For more on *Values* turn to page 1896
For more on *Giving* turn to page 232

3 For we *have spent* enough of our past lifetime*a* in doing the will of the Gentiles—when we walked in lewdness, lusts, drunkenness, revelries, drinking parties, and abominable idolatries.

4 In regard to these, they think it strange that you do not run with *them* in the same flood of dissipation, speaking evil of *you*.

5 They will give an account to Him who is ready to judge the living and the dead.

6 For this reason the gospel was preached also to those who are dead, that they might be judged according to men in the flesh, but live according to God in the spirit.

SERVING FOR GOD'S GLORY

7 But the end of all things is at hand; therefore be serious and watchful in your prayers.

8 And above all things have fervent love for one another, for *"love will cover a multitude of sins."a*

9 *Be* hospitable to one another without grumbling.

10 As each one has received a gift, minister it to one another, as good stewards of the manifold grace of God.

11 If anyone speaks, *let him speak* as the oracles of God. If anyone ministers, *let him do it* as with the ability which God supplies, that in all things God may be glorified through Jesus Christ, to whom belong the glory and the dominion forever and ever. Amen.

SUFFERING FOR GOD'S GLORY

12 Beloved, do not think it strange concerning the fiery trial which is to try you, as though some strange thing happened to you;

13 but rejoice to the extent that you partake of Christ's sufferings, that when His glory is revealed, you may also be glad with exceeding joy.

14 If you are reproached for the

4:3 *a*NU-Text reads *time.*   4:8 *a*Proverbs 10:12

CASTING ALL YOUR CARE UPON HIM, FOR HE CARES FOR YOU.
1 Peter 5:7

He Cares for You

Do you have a pet? What kind of a pet do you have? Do you play with it? Do you take care of it and feed it? Could it be said that your pet "casts all its care on you, for you care for it"? That's the way God takes care of us. If we have cares, we may cast them on Him. He cares for us!

1. Do you think your pet is worried that you will not take care of it? Or does your pet trust you completely to take care of it?
2. Should you be worried that God will not take care of you? Or should you trust God completely to take care of you?

For more on *Favorite Family Verses* turn to page 1893
For more on *God's Care* turn to page 1903

name of Christ, blessed *are you,* for the Spirit of glory and of God rests upon you.*a* On their part He is blasphemed, but on your part He is glorified.

15 But let none of you suffer as a murderer, a thief, an evildoer, or as a busybody in other people's matters.

16 Yet if *anyone suffers* as a Christian, let him not be ashamed, but let him glorify God in this matter.*a*

17 For the time *has come* for judgment to begin at the house of God; and if *it begins* with us first, what will *be* the end of those who do not obey the gospel of God?

18 Now

> "If the righteous one is scarcely saved,
> Where will the ungodly and the sinner appear?"*a*

19 Therefore let those who suffer according to the will of God commit their souls *to Him* in doing good, as to a faithful Creator.

SHEPHERD THE FLOCK

5 The elders who are among you I exhort, I who am a fellow elder and a witness of the sufferings of Christ, and also a partaker of the glory that will be revealed:

2 Shepherd the flock of God which is among you, serving as overseers, not by compulsion but willingly,*a* not for dishonest gain but eagerly;

3 nor as being lords over those entrusted to you, but being examples to the flock;

4 and when the Chief Shepherd appears, you will receive the crown of glory that does not fade away.

SUBMIT TO GOD, RESIST THE DEVIL

5 Likewise you younger people, submit yourselves to *your* elders. Yes,

all of *you* be submissive to one another, and be clothed with humility, for

> "God resists the proud,
> But gives grace to the humble."*a*

6 Therefore humble yourselves under the mighty hand of God, that He may exalt you in due time,

7 casting all your care upon Him, for He cares for you.

8 Be sober, be vigilant; because*a* your adversary the devil walks about like a roaring lion, seeking whom he may devour.

9 Resist him, steadfast in the faith, knowing that the same sufferings are experienced by your brotherhood in the world.

10 But may*a* the God of all grace, who called us*b* to His eternal glory by Christ Jesus, after you have suffered a while, perfect, establish, strengthen, and settle *you.*

11 To Him *be* the glory and the dominion forever and ever. Amen.

FAREWELL AND PEACE

12 By Sil·vā'nus, our faithful brother as I consider him, I have written to you briefly, exhorting and testifying that this is the true grace of God in which you stand.

13 She who is in Babylon, elect together with *you,* greets you; and *so does* Mark my son.

14 Greet one another with a kiss of love. Peace to you all who are in Christ Jesus. Amen.

4:14 *a*NU-Text omits the rest of this verse.
4:16 *a*NU-Text reads *name.*   4:18 *a*Proverbs 11:31   5:2 *a*NU-Text adds *according to God.*
5:5 *a*Proverbs 3:34   5:8 *a*NU-Text and M-Text omit *because.*   5:10 *a*NU-Text reads *But the God of all grace . . . will perfect, establish, strengthen, and settle you.*   *b*NU-Text and M-Text read *you.*

The Second Epistle of
PETER

GREETING THE FAITHFUL

SIMON Peter, a bondservant and apostle of Jesus Christ,

To those who have obtained like precious faith with us by the righteousness of our God and Savior Jesus Christ:

2 Grace and peace be multiplied to you in the knowledge of God and of Jesus our Lord,
3 as His divine power has given to us all things that *pertain* to life and godliness, through the knowledge of Him who called us by glory and virtue,
4 by which have been given to us exceedingly great and precious promises, that through these you may be partakers of the divine nature, having escaped the corruption *that is* in the world through lust.

FRUITFUL GROWTH IN THE FAITH

5 But also for this very reason, giving all diligence, add to your faith virtue, to virtue knowledge,
6 to knowledge self-control, to self-control perseverance, to perseverance godliness,
7 to godliness brotherly kindness, and to brotherly kindness love.
8 For if these things are yours and abound, *you will be* neither barren nor unfruitful in the knowledge of our Lord Jesus Christ.
9 For he who lacks these things is shortsighted, even to blindness, and has forgotten that he was cleansed from his old sins.
10 Therefore, brethren, be even more diligent to make your call and elec-

tion sure, for if you do these things you will never stumble;
11 for so an entrance will be supplied to you abundantly into the everlasting kingdom of our Lord and Savior Jesus Christ.

PETER'S APPROACHING DEATH

12 For this reason I will not be negligent to remind you always of these things, though you know and are established in the present truth.
13 Yes, I think it is right, as long as I am in this tent, to stir you up by reminding *you,*
14 knowing that shortly I *must* put off my tent, just as our Lord Jesus Christ showed me.
15 Moreover I will be careful to ensure that you always have a reminder of these things after my decease.

THE TRUSTWORTHY PROPHETIC WORD

16 For we did not follow cunningly devised fables when we made known to you the power and coming of our Lord Jesus Christ, but were eyewitnesses of His majesty.
17 For He received from God the Father honor and glory when such a voice came to Him from the Excellent Glory: "This is My beloved Son, in whom I am well pleased."
18 And we heard this voice which came from heaven when we were with Him on the holy mountain.
19 And so we have the prophetic word confirmed,*a* which you do well

1:19 *a*Or *We also have the more sure prophetic word.*

to heed as a light that shines in a dark place, until the day dawns and the morning star rises in your hearts;

20 knowing this first, that no prophecy of Scripture is of any private interpretation,a

21 for prophecy never came by the will of man, but holy men of Goda spoke *as they were* moved by the Holy Spirit.

DESTRUCTIVE DOCTRINES

2 But there were also false prophets among the people, even as there will be false teachers among you, who will secretly bring in destructive heresies, even denying the Lord who bought them, *and* bring on themselves swift destruction.

2 And many will follow their destructive ways, because of whom the way of truth will be blasphemed.

3 By covetousness they will exploit you with deceptive words; for a long time their judgment has not been idle, and their destruction doesa not slumber.

DOOM OF FALSE TEACHERS

4 For if God did not spare the angels who sinned, but cast *them* down to hell and delivered *them* into chains of darkness, to be reserved for judgment;

5 and did not spare the ancient world, but saved Noah, *one of* eight *people,* a preacher of righteousness, bringing in the flood on the world of the ungodly;

6 and turning the cities of Sod'om and Go·mor'rah into ashes, condemned *them* to destruction, making *them* an example to those who afterward would live ungodly;

7 and delivered righteous Lot, *who* was oppressed by the filthy conduct of the wicked

8 (for that righteous man, dwelling among them, tormented *his* righteous soul from day to day by seeing and hearing *their* lawless deeds)—

9 *then* the Lord knows how to deliver the godly out of temptations and to reserve the unjust under punishment for the day of judgment,

10 and especially those who walk according to the flesh in the lust of uncleanness and despise authority. *They are* presumptuous, self-willed. They are not afraid to speak evil of dignitaries,

11 whereas angels, who are greater in power and might, do not bring a reviling accusation against them before the Lord.

DEPRAVITY OF FALSE TEACHERS

12 But these, like natural brute beasts made to be caught and destroyed, speak evil of the things they do not understand, and will utterly perish in their own corruption,

13 *and* will receive the wages of unrighteousness, *as* those who count it pleasure to carouse in the daytime. *They are* spots and blemishes, carousing in their own deceptions while they feast with you,

14 having eyes full of adultery and that cannot cease from sin, enticing unstable souls. *They have* a heart trained in covetous practices, *and are* accursed children.

15 They have forsaken the right way and gone astray, following the way of Bā'laam the *son* of Bē'or, who loved the wages of unrighteousness;

16 but he was rebuked for his iniquity: a dumb donkey speaking with a

---

1:20 aOr *origin spoke from God.*　　1:21 aNU-Text reads *but men* 2:3 aM-Text reads *will not.*

man's voice restrained the madness of the prophet.

17 These are wells without water, clouds*a* carried by a tempest, for whom is reserved the blackness of darkness forever.*b*

DECEPTIONS OF FALSE TEACHERS

18 For when they speak great swelling *words* of emptiness, they allure through the lusts of the flesh, through lewdness, the ones who have actually escaped*a* from those who live in error.

19 While they promise them liberty, they themselves are slaves of corruption; for by whom a person is overcome, by him also he is brought into bondage.

20 For if, after they have escaped the pollutions of the world through the knowledge of the Lord and Savior Jesus Christ, they are again entangled in them and overcome, the latter end is worse for them than the beginning.

21 For it would have been better for them not to have known the way of righteousness, than having known *it,* to turn from the holy commandment delivered to them.

22 But it has happened to them according to the true proverb: *"A dog returns to his own vomit,"a* and, *"a sow, having washed, to her wallowing in the mire."*

GOD'S PROMISE IS NOT SLACK

3 Beloved, I now write to you this second epistle (in *both of* which I stir up your pure minds by way of reminder),

2 that you may be mindful of the words which were spoken before by the holy prophets, and of the commandment of us,*a* the apostles of the Lord and Savior,

3 knowing this first: that scoffers will come in the last days, walking according to their own lusts,

4 and saying, "Where is the promise of His coming? For since the fathers fell asleep, all things continue as *they were* from the beginning of creation."

5 For this they willfully forget: that by the word of God the heavens were of old, and the earth standing out of water and in the water,

6 by which the world *that* then existed perished, being flooded with water.

7 But the heavens and the earth *which* are now preserved by the same word, are reserved for fire until the day of judgment and perdition of ungodly men.

8 But, beloved, do not forget this one thing, that with the Lord one day *is* as a thousand years, and a thousand years as one day.

9 The Lord is not slack concerning *His* promise, as some count slackness, but is longsuffering toward us,*a* not willing that any should perish but that all should come to repentance.

THE DAY OF THE LORD

10 But the day of the Lord will come as a thief in the night, in which the heavens will pass away with a great noise, and the elements will melt with fervent heat; both the earth and the works that are in it will be burned up.*a*

11 Therefore, since all these things will be dissolved, what manner *of persons* ought you to be in holy conduct and godliness,

2:17 *a*NU-Text reads *and mists.* *b*NU-Text omits *forever.*   2:18 *a*NU-Text *are barely escaping.*   2:22 *a*Proverbs 26:11   3:2 *a*NU-Text and M-Text read *commandment of the apostles of your Lord and Savior* or *commandment of your apostles of the Lord and Savior.*   3:9 *a*NU-Text reads *you.*   3:10 *a*NU-Text reads *laid bare* (literally *found*).

GROWING 2 Peter 3:18

How Does God Want Us to Grow?

Each year you grow a little taller. You weigh a little more. Your hands and feet are a little bigger. But there is an even more important way to grow. What is it?

1. Read 2 Peter 3:18. What does it say about growing?
2. Why is growing spiritually more important than growing physically?
3. Why does God want you to grow in His ways? How do you help yourself grow the way God wants?

For more on *Favorite Bible Words* turn to page 1909
For more on *Obeying* turn to page 138

12 looking for and hastening the coming of the day of God, because of which the heavens will be dissolved, being on fire, and the elements will melt with fervent heat?
13 Nevertheless we, according to His promise, look for new heavens and a new earth in which righteousness dwells.

BE STEADFAST

14 Therefore, beloved, looking forward to these things, be diligent to be found by Him in peace, without spot and blameless;
15 and consider *that* the longsuffering of our Lord *is* salvation—as also our beloved brother Paul, according

to the wisdom given to him, has written to you,
16 as also in all his epistles, speaking in them of these things, in which are some things hard to understand, which untaught and unstable *people* twist to their own destruction, as *they do* also the rest of the Scriptures.
17 You therefore, beloved, since you know *this* beforehand, beware lest you also fall from your own steadfastness, being led away with the error of the wicked;
18 but grow in the grace and knowledge of our Lord and Savior Jesus Christ. To Him *be* the glory both now and forever. Amen.

The First Epistle of
JOHN

WHAT WAS HEARD, SEEN, AND TOUCHED

THAT which was from the beginning, which we have heard, which we have seen with our eyes, which we have looked upon, and our hands have handled, concerning the Word of life—
2 the life was manifested, and we have seen, and bear witness, and declare to you that eternal life which was with the Father and was manifested to us—
3 that which we have seen and heard we declare to you, that you also may have fellowship with us; and truly our fellowship is with the Father and with His Son Jesus Christ.
4 And these things we write to you that your*a* joy may be full.

FELLOWSHIP WITH HIM AND ONE ANOTHER

5 This is the message which we have heard from Him and declare to you, that God is light and in Him is no darkness at all.
6 If we say that we have fellowship with Him, and walk in darkness, we lie and do not practice the truth.
7 But if we walk in the light as He is in the light, we have fellowship with one another, and the blood of Jesus Christ His Son cleanses us from all sin.
8 If we say that we have no sin, we deceive ourselves, and the truth is not in us.
9 If we confess our sins, He is faithful and just to forgive us *our* sins and to cleanse us from all unrighteousness.
10 If we say that we have not sinned,

we make Him a liar, and His word is not in us.

2 My little children, these things I write to you, so that you may not sin. And if anyone sins, we have an Advocate with the Father, Jesus Christ the righteous.
2 And He Himself is the propitiation for our sins, and not for ours only but also for the whole world.

THE TEST OF KNOWING HIM

3 Now by this we know that we know Him, if we keep His commandments.
4 He who says, "I know Him," and does not keep His commandments, is a liar, and the truth is not in him.
5 But whoever keeps His word, truly the love of God is perfected in him. By this we know that we are in Him.
6 He who says he abides in Him ought himself also to walk just as He walked.
7 Brethren,*a* I write no new commandment to you, but an old commandment which you have had from the beginning. The old commandment is the word which you heard from the beginning.*b*
8 Again, a new commandment I write to you, which thing is true in Him and in you, because the darkness is passing away, and the true light is already shining.
9 He who says he is in the light, and hates his brother, is in darkness until now.
10 He who loves his brother abides

1:4 *a*NU-Text and M-Text read *our*.   2:7 *a*NU-Text reads *Beloved*.   *b*NU-Text omits *from the beginning*.

DO NOT LOVE THE WORLD OR THE THINGS IN THE WORLD. IF ANYONE LOVES THE WORLD, THE LOVE OF THE FATHER IS NOT IN HIM. 1 John 2:15

Torn Between Two Loves

Todd's mother made the nicest dinner and he would love to eat it. But his doggie ate it! Todd loves what his mother made for him. He also loves his doggie. He is torn between two loves. That's the way it is when we love material things in this world and we also love God and His wonderful home in heaven. We are torn between two loves. What shall we do?

1. Read 1 John 2:15 again. You may want to memorize it. When we love worldly things so much we neglect God, we have misplaced our love. God says, "Don't do it."
2. But can we enjoy things? Can I enjoy my toys, my home, our family car? Of course. We can delight in them and what they do for us. But to love them with love that we should reserve for God is a no-no.

For more on *Favorite Family Verses* turn to page 1903
For more on *Dedication* turn to page 995

in the light, and there is no cause for stumbling in him.

11 But he who hates his brother is in darkness and walks in darkness, and does not know where he is going, because the darkness has blinded his eyes.

THEIR SPIRITUAL STATE

12 I write to you, little children,
Because your sins are forgiven
you for His name's sake.
13 I write to you, fathers,
Because you have known Him
who is from the beginning.
I write to you, young men,
Because you have overcome the
wicked one.
I write to you, little children,
Because you have known the
Father.
14 I have written to you, fathers,
Because you have known Him
who is from the beginning.

I have written to you, young men,
Because you are strong, and the
word of God abides in you,
And you have overcome the
wicked one.

DO NOT LOVE THE WORLD

15 Do not love the world or the things in the world. If anyone loves the world, the love of the Father is not in him.
16 For all that *is* in the world—the lust of the flesh, the lust of the eyes, and the pride of life—is not of the Father but is of the world.
17 And the world is passing away, and the lust of it; but he who does the will of God abides forever.

DECEPTIONS OF THE LAST HOUR

18 Little children, it is the last hour; and as you have heard that the[a]

2:18 [a]NU-Text omits *the*.

Antichrist is coming, even now many antichrists have come, by which we know that it is the last hour.

19 They went out from us, but they were not of us; for if they had been of us, they would have continued with us; but *they went out* that they might be made manifest, that none of them were of us.

20 But you have an anointing from the Holy One, and you know all things.*a*

21 I have not written to you because you do not know the truth, but because you know it, and that no lie is of the truth.

22 Who is a liar but he who denies that Jesus is the Christ? He is antichrist who denies the Father and the Son.

23 Whoever denies the Son does not have the Father either; he who acknowledges the Son has the Father also.

LET TRUTH ABIDE IN YOU

24 Therefore let that abide in you which you heard from the beginning. If what you heard from the beginning abides in you, you also will abide in the Son and in the Father.

25 And this is the promise that He has promised us—eternal life.

26 These things I have written to you concerning those who *try to* deceive you.

27 But the anointing which you have received from Him abides in you, and you do not need that anyone teach you; but as the same anointing teaches you concerning all things, and is true, and is not a lie, and just as it has taught you, you will*a* abide in Him.

THE CHILDREN OF GOD

28 And now, little children, abide in Him, that when*a* He appears, we may have confidence and not be ashamed before Him at His coming.

29 If you know that He is righteous, you know that everyone who practices righteousness is born of Him.

3 Behold what manner of love the Father has bestowed on us, that we should be called children of God!*a* Therefore the world does not know us,*b* because it did not know Him.

2 Beloved, now we are children of God; and it has not yet been revealed what we shall be, but we know that when He is revealed, we shall be like Him, for we shall see Him as He is.

3 And everyone who has this hope in Him purifies himself, just as He is pure.

SIN AND THE CHILD OF GOD

4 Whoever commits sin also commits lawlessness, and sin is lawlessness.

5 And you know that He was manifested to take away our sins, and in Him there is no sin.

6 Whoever abides in Him does not sin. Whoever sins has neither seen Him nor known Him.

7 Little children, let no one deceive you. He who practices righteousness is righteous, just as He is righteous.

8 He who sins is of the devil, for the devil has sinned from the beginning. For this purpose the Son of God was manifested, that He might destroy the works of the devil.

9 Whoever has been born of God does not sin, for His seed remains in him; and he cannot sin, because he has been born of God.

2:20 *a*NU-Text reads *you all know.*   2:27 *a*NU-Text reads *you abide.*   2:28 *a*NU-Text reads *if.* 3:1 *a*NU-Text adds *And we are.*   *b*M-Text reads *you.*

THE IMPERATIVE OF LOVE

10 In this the children of God and the children of the devil are manifest: Whoever does not practice righteousness is not of God, nor *is* he who does not love his brother.

11 For this is the message that you heard from the beginning, that we should love one another,

12 not as Cain *who* was of the wicked one and murdered his brother. And why did he murder him? Because his works were evil and his brother's righteous.

13 Do not marvel, my brethren, if the world hates you.

14 We know that we have passed from death to life, because we love the brethren. He who does not love *his* brother*a* abides in death.

15 Whoever hates his brother is a murderer, and you know that no murderer has eternal life abiding in him.

THE OUTWORKING OF LOVE

16 By this we know love, because He laid down His life for us. And we also ought to lay down *our* lives for the brethren.

17 But whoever has this world's goods, and sees his brother in need, and shuts up his heart from him, how does the love of God abide in him?

18 My little children, let us not love in word or in tongue, but in deed and in truth.

19 And by this we know*a* that we are of the truth, and shall assure our hearts before Him.

20 For if our heart condemns us, God is greater than our heart, and knows all things.

21 Beloved, if our heart does not condemn us, we have confidence toward God.

22 And whatever we ask we receive from Him, because we keep His commandments and do those things that are pleasing in His sight.

23 And this is His commandment: that we should believe on the name of His Son Jesus Christ and love one another, as He gave us*a* commandment.

THE SPIRIT OF TRUTH AND THE SPIRIT OF ERROR

24 Now he who keeps His commandments abides in Him, and He in him. And by this we know that He abides in us, by the Spirit whom He has given us.

4 Beloved, do not believe every spirit, but test the spirits, whether they are of God; because many false prophets have gone out into the world.

2 By this you know the Spirit of God: Every spirit that confesses that Jesus Christ has come in the flesh is of God,

3 and every spirit that does not confess that*a* Jesus Christ has come in the flesh is not of God. And this is the *spirit* of the Antichrist, which you have heard was coming, and is now already in the world.

4 You are of God, little children, and have overcome them, because He who is in you is greater than he who is in the world.

5 They are of the world. Therefore they speak *as* of the world, and the world hears them.

6 We are of God. He who knows God hears us; he who is not of God does not hear us. By this we know the spirit of truth and the spirit of error.

3:14 *a*NU-Text omits *his brother.*   3:19 *a*NU-Text reads *we shall know.*   3:23 *a*M-Text omits *us.*   4:3 *a*NU-Text omits *that* and *Christ has come in the flesh.*

LOVE 1 John 4:7

A Hundred Ways to Say I Love You

This lady is doing something special. You can see how much work it is to make that quilt. The little hearts say, "I love you." The lady's work says, "I love you." The lady will probably say "I love you" when she gives this quilt to her friend. There are at least a hundred ways to say "I love you."

1. Read 1 John 4:7. Why should we love each other? Who loved us first?
2. Think of three ways to say "I love you" to your parents. Will you say them today?
3. Think of three other ways to say "I love You" to God. Will you say them today also?

For more on *Values* turn to page 1897
For more on *Love* turn to page 1897

Values

LOVE 1 John 4:10–19

What Do We Say on Valentine's Day?

What do we say on Valentine's Day? Do we say, "I hate you"? That wouldn't be a very good valentine, would it? Do we say, "I don't like you"? That wouldn't be a very good valentine either. Do we say, "I love you"? Now that would make a good valentine, wouldn't it?

1. Valentine's Day is a day to say, "I love you." But is that the only day of the year we should say that? Which other days are good days to say, "I love you"?
2. Do you love your parents? Have you said, "I love you" to them today? Would you like to do that now? Do you love Jesus? Have you said, "I love You" to Him today? Would you like to do that now?
3. Read 1 John 4:10–19. Is this something like a valentine from God to us? What does it say about God's love? What does it say about our love for God?

For more on *Values* turn to page 35
For more on *Love* turn to page 180

KNOWING GOD THROUGH LOVE

7 Beloved, let us love one another, for love is of God; and everyone who loves is born of God and knows God. 8 He who does not love does not know God, for God is love. 9 In this the love of God was manifested toward us, that God has sent His only begotten Son into the world, that we might live through Him. 10 In this is love, not that we loved God, but that He loved us and sent His Son *to be* the propitiation for our sins. 11 Beloved, if God so loved us, we also ought to love one another.

SEEING GOD THROUGH LOVE

12 No one has seen God at any time. If we love one another, God abides in us, and His love has been perfected in us.

13 By this we know that we abide in Him, and He in us, because He has given us of His Spirit. 14 And we have seen and testify that the Father has sent the Son *as* Savior of the world. 15 Whoever confesses that Jesus is the Son of God, God abides in him, and he in God. 16 And we have known and believed the love that God has for us. God is love, and he who abides in love abides in God, and God in him.

THE CONSUMMATION OF LOVE

17 Love has been perfected among us in this: that we may have boldness in the day of judgment; because as He is, so are we in this world. 18 There is no fear in love; but perfect love casts out fear, because fear involves torment. But he who fears has not been made perfect in love.

19 We love Him*a* because He first loved us.

OBEDIENCE BY FAITH

20 If someone says, "I love God," and hates his brother, he is a liar; for he who does not love his brother whom he has seen, how can*a* he love God whom he has not seen?

21 And this commandment we have from Him: that he who loves God *must* love his brother also.

5 Whoever believes that Jesus is the Christ is born of God, and everyone who loves Him who begot also loves him who is begotten of Him.

2 By this we know that we love the children of God, when we love God and keep His commandments.

3 For this is the love of God, that we keep His commandments. And His commandments are not burdensome.

4 For whatever is born of God overcomes the world. And this is the victory that has overcome the world— our*a* faith.

5 Who is he who overcomes the world, but he who believes that Jesus is the Son of God?

THE CERTAINTY OF GOD'S WITNESS

6 This is He who came by water and blood—Jesus Christ; not only by water, but by water and blood. And it is the Spirit who bears witness, because the Spirit is truth.

7 For there are three that bear witness in heaven: the Father, the Word, and the Holy Spirit; and these three are one.

8 And there are three that bear witness on earth:*a* the Spirit, the water, and the blood; and these three agree as one.

9 If we receive the witness of men, the witness of God is greater; for this is the witness of God which*a* He has testified of His Son.

10 He who believes in the Son of God has the witness in himself; he who does not believe God has made Him a liar, because he has not believed the testimony that God has given of His Son.

11 And this is the testimony: that God has given us eternal life, and this life is in His Son.

12 He who has the Son has life; he who does not have the Son of God does not have life.

13 These things I have written to you who believe in the name of the Son of God, that you may know that you have eternal life,*a* and that you may *continue to* believe in the name of the Son of God.

CONFIDENCE AND COMPASSION IN PRAYER

14 Now this is the confidence that we have in Him, that if we ask anything according to His will, He hears us.

15 And if we know that He hears us, whatever we ask, we know that we have the petitions that we have asked of Him.

16 If anyone sees his brother sinning a sin *which does* not *lead* to death, he will ask, and He will give him life for those who commit sin not *leading* to death. There is sin *leading* to death. I do not say that he should pray about that.

17 All unrighteousness is sin, and there is sin not *leading* to death.

4:19 *a*NU-Text omits *Him.*   4:20 *a*NU-Text reads *he cannot.*   5:4 *a*M-Text reads *your.*
5:8 *a*NU-Text and M-Text omit the words from *in heaven* (verse 7) through *on earth* (verse 8). Only four or five very late manuscripts contain these words in Greek.   5:9 *a*NU-Text reads *God, that.*
5:13 *a*NU-Text omits the rest of this verse.

KNOWING THE TRUE—REJECTING THE FALSE

18 We know that whoever is born of God does not sin; but he who has been born of God keeps himself,*a* and the wicked one does not touch him.

19 We know that we are of God, and the whole world lies *under the sway of* the wicked one.

20 And we know that the Son of God has come and has given us an understanding, that we may know Him who is true; and we are in Him who is true, in His Son Jesus Christ. This is the true God and eternal life.

21 Little children, keep yourselves from idols. Amen.

5:18 *a*NU-Text reads *him.*

JOHN

GREETING THE ELECT LADY

THE Elder,

To the elect lady and her children, whom I love in truth, and not only I, but also all those who have known the truth,

2 because of the truth which abides in us and will be with us forever:

3 Grace, mercy, *and* peace will be with you*a* from God the Father and from the Lord Jesus Christ, the Son of the Father, in truth and love.

WALK IN CHRIST'S COMMANDMENTS

4 I rejoiced greatly that I have found *some* of your children walking in truth, as we received commandment from the Father.

5 And now I plead with you, lady, not as though I wrote a new commandment to you, but that which we have had from the beginning: that we love one another.

6 This is love, that we walk according to His commandments. This is the commandment, that as you have heard from the beginning, you should walk in it.

BEWARE OF ANTICHRIST DECEIVERS

7 For many deceivers have gone out into the world who do not confess Jesus Christ *as* coming in the flesh. This is a deceiver and an antichrist.

8 Look to yourselves, that we*a* do not lose those things we worked for, but *that* we*b* may receive a full reward.

9 Whoever transgresses*a* and does not abide in the doctrine of Christ does not have God. He who abides in the doctrine of Christ has both the Father and the Son.

10 If anyone comes to you and does not bring this doctrine, do not receive him into your house nor greet him;

11 for he who greets him shares in his evil deeds.

JOHN'S FAREWELL GREETING

12 Having many things to write to you, I did not wish *to do so* with paper and ink; but I hope to come to you and speak face to face, that our joy may be full.

13 The children of your elect sister greet you. Amen.

3 *a*NU-Text and M-Text read *us.*   8 *a*NU-Text
reads *you.* *b*NU-Text reads *you.*   9 *a*NU-Text
reads *goes ahead.*

The Third Epistle of
JOHN

GREETING TO GAIUS

THE Elder,

To the beloved Gāʹiʹus, whom I love in truth:

2 Beloved, I pray that you may prosper in all things and be in health, just as your soul prospers.
3 For I rejoiced greatly when brethren came and testified of the truth *that is* in you, just as you walk in the truth.
4 I have no greater joy than to hear that my children walk in truth.*a*

GAIUS COMMENDED
FOR GENEROSITY

5 Beloved, you do faithfully whatever you do for the brethren and*a* for strangers,
6 who have borne witness of your love before the church. *If* you send them forward on their journey in a manner worthy of God, you will do well,
7 because they went forth for His name's sake, taking nothing from the Gentiles.
8 We therefore ought to receive*a* such, that we may become fellow workers for the truth.

DIOTREPHES AND DEMETRIUS

9 I wrote to the church, but Dīʹotʹ-rē·phēs, who loves to have the preeminence among them, does not receive us.
10 Therefore, if I come, I will call to mind his deeds which he does, prating against us with malicious words. And not content with that, he himself does not receive the brethren, and forbids those who wish to, putting *them* out of the church.
11 Beloved, do not imitate what is evil, but what is good. He who does good is of God, but*a* he who does evil has not seen God.
12 De·mēʹtri·us has a *good* testimony from all, and from the truth itself. And we also bear witness, and you know that our testimony is true.

FAREWELL GREETING

13 I had many things to write, but I do not wish to write to you with pen and ink;
14 but I hope to see you shortly, and we shall speak face to face. Peace to you. Our friends greet you. Greet the friends by name.

4 *a*NU-Text reads *the truth*.   5 *a*NU-Text adds *especially*.   8 *a*NU-Text reads *support*.
11 *a*NU-Text and M-Text omit *but*.

The Epistle of
JUDE

GREETING TO THE CALLED

JUDE, a bondservant of Jesus Christ, and brother of James,

To those who are called, sanctified[a] by God the Father, and preserved in Jesus Christ:

2 Mercy, peace, and love be multiplied to you.

CONTEND FOR THE FAITH

3 Beloved, while I was very diligent to write to you concerning our common salvation, I found it necessary to write to you exhorting you to contend earnestly for the faith which was once for all delivered to the saints.
4 For certain men have crept in unnoticed, who long ago were marked out for this condemnation, ungodly men, who turn the grace of our God into lewdness and deny the only Lord God[a] and our Lord Jesus Christ.

OLD AND NEW APOSTATES

5 But I want to remind you, though you once knew this, that the Lord, having saved the people out of the land of Egypt, afterward destroyed those who did not believe.
6 And the angels who did not keep their proper domain, but left their own abode, He has reserved in everlasting chains under darkness for the judgment of the great day;
7 as Sod'om and Go·mor'rah, and the cities around them in a similar manner to these, having given themselves over to sexual immorality and gone after strange flesh, are set forth as an example, suffering the vengeance of eternal fire.

8 Likewise also these dreamers defile the flesh, reject authority, and speak evil of dignitaries.
9 Yet Michael the archangel, in contending with the devil, when he disputed about the body of Moses, dared not bring against him a reviling accusation, but said, "The Lord rebuke you!"
10 But these speak evil of whatever they do not know; and whatever they know naturally, like brute beasts, in these things they corrupt themselves.
11 Woe to them! For they have gone in the way of Cain, have run greedily in the error of Ba'laam for profit, and perished in the rebellion of Ko'rah.

APOSTATES DEPRAVED AND DOOMED

12 These are spots in your love feasts, while they feast with you without fear, serving only themselves. They are clouds without water, carried about[a] by the winds; late autumn trees without fruit, twice dead, pulled up by the roots;
13 raging waves of the sea, foaming up their own shame; wandering stars for whom is reserved the blackness of darkness forever.
14 Now E'noch, the seventh from Adam, prophesied about these men also, saying, "Behold, the Lord comes with ten thousands of His saints,
15 "to execute judgment on all, to convict all who are ungodly among them of all their ungodly deeds which they have committed in an ungodly way, and of all the harsh things which ungodly sinners have spoken against Him."

---

1 [a]NU-Text reads beloved.   4 [a]NU-Text omits God.   12 [a]NU-Text and M-Text read along.

NOW TO HIM WHO IS ABLE TO KEEP YOU FROM STUMBLING, / AND TO PRESENT YOU FAULTLESS / BEFORE THE PRESENCE OF HIS GLORY WITH EXCEEDING JOY. Jude 24

What If I Fall?

Are you ever afraid of making a mistake? Are you afraid of stumbling or falling before others? Are you afraid of being ashamed of something you do? Are you afraid others will make fun of you for something you do wrong? What should you do?

1. Who can keep you from stumbling or falling or making yourself look foolish? Read Jude 24. What does it say?
2. Not only will the Lord keep you from falling, what else does this verse say He will do? Why is that so important?

For more on *Favorite Family Verses* turn to page 1913
For more on *God's Care* turn to page 1913

Apostates Predicted

16 These are grumblers, complainers, walking according to their own lusts; and they mouth great swelling *words,* flattering people to gain advantage.

17 But you, beloved, remember the words which were spoken before by the apostles of our Lord Jesus Christ:

18 how they told you that there would be mockers in the last time who would walk according to their own ungodly lusts.

19 These are sensual persons, who cause divisions, not having the Spirit.

Maintain Your Life with God

20 But you, beloved, building yourselves up on your most holy faith, praying in the Holy Spirit,

21 keep yourselves in the love of God, looking for the mercy of our Lord Jesus Christ unto eternal life.

22 And on some have compassion, making a distinction;*a*

23 but others save with fear, pulling *them* out of the fire,*a* hating even the garment defiled by the flesh.

Glory to God

24 Now to Him who is able to keep you*a* from stumbling,
And to present *you* faultless
Before the presence of His glory with exceeding joy,

25 To God our Savior,*a*
Who alone is wise,*b*
Be glory and majesty,
Dominion and power,*c*
Both now and forever.
Amen.

22 *a*NU-Text reads *who are doubting* (or *making distinctions*).   23 *a*NU-Text adds *and on some have mercy with fear* and omits *with fear* in first clause.   24 *a*M-Text reads *them.*   25 *a*NU-Text reads *To the only God our Savior.*   *b*NU-Text omits *Who . . . is wise* and adds *Through Jesus Christ our Lord.*   *c*NU-Text adds *Before all time.*

THE REVELATION
of Jesus Christ

INTRODUCTION AND BENEDICTION

THE Revelation of Jesus Christ, which God gave Him to show His servants—things which must shortly take place. And He sent and signified *it* by His angel to His servant John,

2 who bore witness to the word of God, and to the testimony of Jesus Christ, to all things that he saw.

3 Blessed *is* he who reads and those who hear the words of this prophecy, and keep those things which are written in it; for the time *is* near.

GREETING THE SEVEN CHURCHES

4 John, to the seven churches which are in Asia:

Grace to you and peace from Him who is and who was and who is to come, and from the seven Spirits who are before His throne,

5 and from Jesus Christ, the faithful witness, the firstborn from the dead, and the ruler over the kings of the earth. To Him who loved us and washed*a* us from our sins in His own blood,

6 and has made us kings*a* and priests to His God and Father, to Him *be* glory and dominion forever and ever. Amen.

7 Behold, He is coming with clouds, and every eye will see Him, even they who pierced Him. And all the tribes of the earth will mourn because of Him. Even so, Amen.

8 "I am the Alpha and the Omega, *the* Beginning and *the* End,"*a* says the Lord,*b* "who is and who was and who is to come, the Almighty."

VISION OF THE SON OF MAN

9 I, John, both*a* your brother and companion in the tribulation and kingdom and patience of Jesus Christ, was on the island that is called Pat'mos for the word of God and for the testimony of Jesus Christ.

10 I was in the Spirit on the Lord's Day, and I heard behind me a loud voice, as of a trumpet,

11 saying, "I am the Alpha and the Omega, the First and the Last," and,*a* "What you see, write in a book and send *it* to the seven churches which are in Asia:*b* to Eph'e·sus, to Smyrna, to Per'ga·mos, to Thy̆·a·tī'ra, to Sar'dis, to Philadelphia, and to Lā·o·di·cē'a."

12 Then I turned to see the voice that spoke with me. And having turned I saw seven golden lampstands,

13 and in the midst of the seven lampstands *One* like the Son of Man, clothed with a garment down to the feet and girded about the chest with a golden band.

14 His head and hair *were* white like wool, as white as snow, and His eyes like a flame of fire;

15 His feet *were* like fine brass, as if refined in a furnace, and His voice as the sound of many waters;

16 He had in His right hand seven stars, out of His mouth went a sharp two-edged sword, and His countenance *was* like the sun shining in its strength.

1:5 *a*NU-Text reads *loves us and freed;* M-Text reads *loves us and washed.*   1:6 *a*NU-Text and M-Text read *a kingdom.*   1:8 *a*NU-Text and M-Text omit *the Beginning and the End.*   *b*NU-Text and M-Text add *God.*   1:9 *a*NU-Text and M-Text omit *both.*   1:11 *a*NU-Text and M-Text omit *I am* through third *and.*   *b*NU-Text and M-Text omit *which are in Asia.*

17 And when I saw Him, I fell at His feet as dead. But He laid His right hand on me, saying to me,*a* "Do not be afraid; I am the First and the Last.

18 "I *am* He who lives, and was dead, and behold, I am alive forevermore. Amen. And I have the keys of Hā′dēs and of Death.

19 "Write*a* the things which you have seen, and the things which are, and the things which will take place after this.

20 "The mystery of the seven stars which you saw in My right hand, and the seven golden lampstands: The seven stars are the angels of the seven churches, and the seven lampstands which you saw*a* are the seven churches.

THE LOVELESS CHURCH

2 "To the angel of the church of Eph′e·sus write,

'These things says He who holds the seven stars in His right hand, who walks in the midst of the seven golden lampstands:

2 "I know your works, your labor, your patience, and that you cannot bear those who are evil. And you have tested those who say they are apostles and are not, and have found them liars;

3 "and you have persevered and have patience, and have labored for My name's sake and have not become weary.

4 "Nevertheless I have *this* against you, that you have left your first love.

5 "Remember therefore from where you have fallen; repent and do the first works, or else I will come to you quickly and remove your lampstand from its place—unless you repent.

6 "But this you have, that you hate the deeds of the Nic·ō·lā′i·tans, which I also hate.

7 "He who has an ear, let him hear what the Spirit says to the churches. To him who overcomes I will give to eat from the tree of life, which is in the midst of the Paradise of God." '

THE PERSECUTED CHURCH

8 "And to the angel of the church in Smyrna write,

'These things says the First and the Last, who was dead, and came to life:

9 "I know your works, tribulation, and poverty (but you are rich); and *I know* the blasphemy of those who say they are Jews and are not, but *are* a synagogue of Satan.

10 "Do not fear any of those things which you are about to suffer. Indeed, the devil is about to throw *some* of you into prison, that you may be tested, and you will have tribulation ten days. Be faithful until death, and I will give you the crown of life.

11 "He who has an ear, let him hear what the Spirit says to the churches. He who overcomes shall not be hurt by the second death." '

THE COMPROMISING CHURCH

12 "And to the angel of the church in Per′ga·mos write,

'These things says He who has the sharp two-edged sword:

13 "I know your works, and where you dwell, where Satan's throne *is*. And you hold fast to My name, and did not deny My faith even in the days in which An′ti·pas *was* My faithful martyr, who was killed among you, where Satan dwells.

1:17 *a*NU-Text and M-Text omit *to me.*
1:19 *a*NU-Text and M-Text read *Therefore, write.*
1:20 *a*NU-Text and M-Text omit *which you saw.*

14 "But I have a few things against you, because you have there those who hold the doctrine of Bā′laam, who taught Bā′lak to put a stumbling block before the children of Israel, to eat things sacrificed to idols, and to commit sexual immorality.

15 "Thus you also have those who hold the doctrine of the Nic·ō·lā′i-tans, which thing I hate.a

16 "Repent, or else I will come to you quickly and will fight against them with the sword of My mouth.

17 "He who has an ear, let him hear what the Spirit says to the churches. To him who overcomes I will give some of the hidden manna to eat. And I will give him a white stone, and on the stone a new name written which no one knows except him who receives it." '

THE CORRUPT CHURCH

18 "And to the angel of the church in Thȳ·a·tī′ra write,

'These things says the Son of God, who has eyes like a flame of fire, and His feet like fine brass:

19 "I know your works, love, service, faith,a and your patience; and as for your works, the last are more than the first.

20 "Nevertheless I have a few things against you, because you allowa that womanb Jez′e·bel, who calls herself a prophetess, to teach and seducec My servants to commit sexual immorality and eat things sacrificed to idols.

21 "And I gave her time to repent of her sexual immorality, and she did not repent.a

22 "Indeed I will cast her into a sickbed, and those who commit adultery with her into great tribulation, unless they repent of theira deeds.

23 "I will kill her children with death, and all the churches shall know that I am He who searches the minds and hearts. And I will give to each one of you according to your works.

24 "Now to you I say, anda to the rest in Thȳ·a·tī′ra, as many as do not have this doctrine, who have not known the depths of Satan, as they say, I willb put on you no other burden.

25 "But hold fast what you have till I come.

26 "And he who overcomes, and keeps My works until the end, to him I will give power over the nations—

27 'He shall rule them with a rod of iron;
They shall be dashed to pieces like the potter's vessels'a—

as I also have received from My Father;

28 "and I will give him the morning star.

29 "He who has an ear, let him hear what the Spirit says to the churches." '

THE DEAD CHURCH

3 "And to the angel of the church in Sar′dis write,

'These things says He who has the seven Spirits of God and the seven stars: "I know your works, that you have a name that you are alive, but you are dead.

2 "Be watchful, and strengthen the things which remain, that are ready to die, for I have not found your works perfect before God.a

2:15 aNU-Text and M-Text read likewise for which thing I hate. 2:19 aNU-Text and M-Text read faith, service. 2:20 aNU-Text and M-Text read I have against you that you tolerate. bM-Text reads your wife Jezebel. cNU-Text and M-Text read and teaches and seduces. 2:21 aNU-Text and M-Text read time to repent, and she does not want to repent of her sexual immorality. 2:22 aNU-Text and M-Text read her. 2:24 aNU-Text and M-Text omit and. bNU-Text and M-Text omit will. 2:27 aPsalm 2:9 3:2 aNU-Text and M-Text read My God.

3 "Remember therefore how you have received and heard; hold fast and repent. Therefore if you will not watch, I will come upon you as a thief, and you will not know what hour I will come upon you.

4 "You*a* have a few names even in Sar′dis who have not defiled their garments; and they shall walk with Me in white, for they are worthy.

5 "He who overcomes shall be clothed in white garments, and I will not blot out his name from the Book of Life; but I will confess his name before My Father and before His angels.

6 "He who has an ear, let him hear what the Spirit says to the churches."'

THE FAITHFUL CHURCH

7 "And to the angel of the church in Philadelphia write,

'These things says He who is holy, He who is true, *"He who has the key of David, He who opens and no one shuts, and shuts and no one opens"*:*a*

8 "I know your works. See, I have set before you an open door, and no one can shut it;*a* for you have a little strength, have kept My word, and have not denied My name.

9 "Indeed I will make *those* of the synagogue of Satan, who say they are Jews and are not, but lie—indeed I will make them come and worship before your feet, and to know that I have loved you.

10 "Because you have kept My command to persevere, I also will keep you from the hour of trial which shall come upon the whole world, to test those who dwell on the earth.

11 "Behold,*a* I am coming quickly! Hold fast what you have, that no one may take your crown.

12 "He who overcomes, I will make him a pillar in the temple of My God, and he shall go out no more. I will write on him the name of My God and the name of the city of My God, the New Jerusalem, which comes down out of heaven from My God. And *I will write on him* My new name.

13 "He who has an ear, let him hear what the Spirit says to the churches."'

THE LUKEWARM CHURCH

14 "And to the angel of the church of the Lā·o·di·cē′ans*a* write,

'These things says the Amen, the Faithful and True Witness, the Beginning of the creation of God:

15 "I know your works, that you are neither cold nor hot. I could wish you were cold or hot.

16 "So then, because you are lukewarm, and neither cold nor hot,*a* I will vomit you out of My mouth.

17 "Because you say, 'I am rich, have become wealthy, and have need of nothing'—and do not know that you are wretched, miserable, poor, blind, and naked—

18 "I counsel you to buy from Me gold refined in the fire, that you may be rich; and white garments, that you may be clothed, *that* the shame of your nakedness may not be revealed; and anoint your eyes with eye salve, that you may see.

19 "As many as I love, I rebuke and chasten. Therefore be zealous and repent.

20 "Behold, I stand at the door and knock. If anyone hears My voice and opens the door, I will come in to him and dine with him, and he with Me.

3:4 *a*NU-Text and M-Text read *Nevertheless you have a few names in Sardis.*   3:7 *a*Isaiah 22:22
3:8 *a*NU-Text and M-Text read *which no one can shut.*   3:11 *a*NU-Text and M-Text omit *Behold.*
3:14 *a*NU-Text and M-Text read *in Laodicea.*
3:16 *a*NU-Text and M-Text read *hot nor cold.*

CREATE Revelation 4:11

Who Made That Mouse?

Maybe you have looked at a tiny mouse and asked, "Who made that mouse?" Or, "who made my puppy or kitty?" Perhaps you have wondered, "Who made my mother or father?" "Who made me?" Who did?

1. Read Revelation 4:11. Who did make everything that is made? The Bible uses the word *create,* which means "make from nothing."
2. Can you create a mouse? Can you create a kitty or puppy or a mother or father? Can you make *anything* from nothing? Who can?
3. Have you thanked God today for creating you? Have you thanked Him for creating our wonderful world? Why not do that now?

For more on *Favorite Bible Words* turn to page 1914
For more on *God's Creation* turn to page 769

21 "To him who overcomes I will grant to sit with Me on My throne, as I also overcame and sat down with My Father on His throne.

22 "He who has an ear, let him hear what the Spirit says to the churches."'"

THE THRONE ROOM OF HEAVEN

4 After these things I looked, and behold, a door *standing* open in heaven. And the first voice which I heard *was* like a trumpet speaking with me, saying, "Come up here, and I will show you things which must take place after this."

2 Immediately I was in the Spirit; and behold, a throne set in heaven, and *One* sat on the throne.

3 And He who sat there was^a like a jasper and a sardius stone in appearance; and *there was* a rainbow around the throne, in appearance like an emerald.

4 Around the throne *were* twenty-four thrones, and on the thrones I saw twenty-four elders sitting, clothed in white robes; and they had crowns^a of gold on their heads.

5 And from the throne proceeded lightnings, thunderings, and voices.^a Seven lamps of fire *were* burning before the throne, which are the^b seven Spirits of God.

6 Before the throne *there was*^a a sea of glass, like crystal. And in the midst of the throne, and around the throne, *were* four living creatures full of eyes in front and in back.

7 The first living creature *was* like a lion, the second living creature like a calf, the third living creature had a face like a man, and the fourth living creature *was* like a flying eagle.

8 *The* four living creatures, each having six wings, were full of eyes around and within. And they do not rest day or night, saying:

4:3 ^aM-Text omits *And He who sat there was* (which makes the description in verse 3 modify the throne rather than God). 4:4 ^aNU-Text and M-Text read *robes, with crowns.* 4:5 ^aNU-Text and M-Text read *voices, and thunderings.* ^bM-Text omits *the.* 4:6 ^aNU-Text and M-Text add *something like.*

"Holy, holy, holy,*a*
Lord God Almighty,
Who was and is and is to come!"

9 Whenever the living creatures give glory and honor and thanks to Him who sits on the throne, who lives forever and ever,

10 the twenty-four elders fall down before Him who sits on the throne and worship Him who lives forever and ever, and cast their crowns before the throne, saying:

11 "You are worthy, O Lord,*a*
To receive glory and honor and power;
For You created all things,
And by Your will they exist*b* and were created."

THE LAMB TAKES THE SCROLL

5 And I saw in the right *hand* of Him who sat on the throne a scroll written inside and on the back, sealed with seven seals.

2 Then I saw a strong angel proclaiming with a loud voice, "Who is worthy to open the scroll and to loose its seals?"

3 And no one in heaven or on the earth or under the earth was able to open the scroll, or to look at it.

4 So I wept much, because no one was found worthy to open and read*a* the scroll, or to look at it.

5 But one of the elders said to me, "Do not weep. Behold, the Lion of the tribe of Judah, the Root of David, has prevailed to open the scroll and to loose*a* its seven seals."

6 And I looked, and behold,*a* in the midst of the throne and of the four living creatures, and in the midst of the elders, stood a Lamb as though it had been slain, having seven horns and seven eyes, which are the seven

Spirits of God sent out into all the earth.

7 Then He came and took the scroll out of the right hand of Him who sat on the throne.

WORTHY IS THE LAMB

8 Now when He had taken the scroll, the four living creatures and the twenty-four elders fell down before the Lamb, each having a harp, and golden bowls full of incense, which are the prayers of the saints.

9 And they sang a new song, saying:

"You are worthy to take the scroll,
And to open its seals;
For You were slain,
And have redeemed us to God by Your blood
Out of every tribe and tongue and people and nation,

10 And have made us*a* kings*b* and priests to our God;
And we*c* shall reign on the earth."

11 Then I looked, and I heard the voice of many angels around the throne, the living creatures, and the elders; and the number of them was ten thousand times ten thousand, and thousands of thousands,

12 saying with a loud voice:

"Worthy is the Lamb who was slain
To receive power and riches and wisdom,
And strength and honor and glory and blessing!"

4:8 *a*M-Text has *holy* nine times.   4:11 *a*NU-Text and M-Text read *our Lord and God*.   *b*NU-Text and M-Text read *existed*.   5:4 *a*NU-Text and M-Text omit *and read*.   5:5 *a*NU-Text and M-Text omit *to loose*.   5:6 *a*NU-Text and M-Text read *I saw in the midst . . . a Lamb standing*. 5:10 *a*NU-Text and M-Text read *them*.   *b*NU-Text reads *a kingdom*.   *c*NU-Text and M-Text read *they*.

13 And every creature which is in heaven and on the earth and under the earth and such as are in the sea, and all that are in them, I heard saying:

"Blessing and honor and glory and power
Be to Him who sits on the throne,
And to the Lamb, forever and ever!"*a*

14 Then the four living creatures said, "Amen!" And the twenty-four*a* elders fell down and worshiped Him who lives forever and ever.*b*

FIRST SEAL: THE CONQUEROR

6 Now I saw when the Lamb opened one of the seals;*a* and I heard one of the four living creatures saying with a voice like thunder, "Come and see."
2 And I looked, and behold, a white horse. He who sat on it had a bow; and a crown was given to him, and he went out conquering and to conquer.

SECOND SEAL: CONFLICT ON EARTH

3 When He opened the second seal, I heard the second living creature saying, "Come and see."*a*
4 Another horse, fiery red, went out. And it was granted to the one who sat on it to take peace from the earth, and that *people* should kill one another; and there was given to him a great sword.

THIRD SEAL: SCARCITY ON EARTH

5 When He opened the third seal, I heard the third living creature say, "Come and see." So I looked, and behold, a black horse, and he who sat on it had a pair of scales in his hand.

6 And I heard a voice in the midst of the four living creatures saying, "A quart*a* of wheat for a denarius,*b* and three quarts of barley for a denarius; and do not harm the oil and the wine."

FOURTH SEAL: WIDESPREAD DEATH ON EARTH

7 When He opened the fourth seal, I heard the voice of the fourth living creature saying, "Come and see."
8 So I looked, and behold, a pale horse. And the name of him who sat on it was Death, and Hā′dēs followed with him. And power was given to them over a fourth of the earth, to kill with sword, with hunger, with death, and by the beasts of the earth.

FIFTH SEAL: THE CRY OF THE MARTYRS

9 When He opened the fifth seal, I saw under the altar the souls of those who had been slain for the word of God and for the testimony which they held.
10 And they cried with a loud voice, saying, "How long, O Lord, holy and true, until You judge and avenge our blood on those who dwell on the earth?"
11 Then a white robe was given to each of them; and it was said to them that they should rest a little while longer, until both *the number of* their fellow servants and their brethren, who would be killed as they *were,* was completed.

5:13 *a*M-Text adds *Amen.*   5:14 *a*NU-Text and M-Text omit *twenty-four.* *b*NU-Text and M-Text omit *Him who lives forever and ever.*   6:1 *a*NU-Text and M-Text read *seven seals.*   6:3 *a*NU-Text and M-Text omit *and see.*   6:6 *a*Greek *choinix;* that is, approximately one quart *b*This was approximately one day's wage for a worker.

SIXTH SEAL: COSMIC DISTURBANCES

12 I looked when He opened the sixth seal, and behold,*a* there was a great earthquake; and the sun became black as sackcloth of hair, and the moon*b* became like blood.
13 And the stars of heaven fell to the earth, as a fig tree drops its late figs when it is shaken by a mighty wind.
14 Then the sky receded as a scroll when it is rolled up, and every mountain and island was moved out of its place.
15 And the kings of the earth, the great men, the rich men, the commanders,*a* the mighty men, every slave and every free man, hid themselves in the caves and in the rocks of the mountains,
16 and said to the mountains and rocks, "Fall on us and hide us from the face of Him who sits on the throne and from the wrath of the Lamb!
17 "For the great day of His wrath has come, and who is able to stand?"

THE SEALED OF ISRAEL

7 After these things I saw four angels standing at the four corners of the earth, holding the four winds of the earth, that the wind should not blow on the earth, on the sea, or on any tree.
2 Then I saw another angel ascending from the east, having the seal of the living God. And he cried with a loud voice to the four angels to whom it was granted to harm the earth and the sea,
3 saying, "Do not harm the earth, the sea, or the trees till we have sealed the servants of our God on their foreheads."
4 And I heard the number of those who were sealed. One hundred *and*

forty-four thousand of all the tribes of the children of Israel *were* sealed:

5 of the tribe of Judah
twelve thousand *were* sealed;*a*
of the tribe of Reuben
twelve thousand *were* sealed;
of the tribe of Gad
twelve thousand *were* sealed;
6 of the tribe of Ash′er
twelve thousand *were* sealed;
of the tribe of Naph′ta·li
twelve thousand *were* sealed;
of the tribe of Ma·nas′seh
twelve thousand *were* sealed;
7 of the tribe of Sim′e·on
twelve thousand *were* sealed;
of the tribe of Levi
twelve thousand *were* sealed;
of the tribe of Is′sa·char
twelve thousand *were* sealed;
8 of the tribe of Zeb′u·lun
twelve thousand *were* sealed;
of the tribe of Joseph
twelve thousand *were* sealed;
of the tribe of Benjamin
twelve thousand *were* sealed.

A MULTITUDE FROM THE GREAT TRIBULATION

9 After these things I looked, and behold, a great multitude which no one could number, of all nations, tribes, peoples, and tongues, standing before the throne and before the Lamb, clothed with white robes, with palm branches in their hands,
10 and crying out with a loud voice, saying, "Salvation *belongs* to our God who sits on the throne, and to the Lamb!"
11 All the angels stood around the

6:12 *a*NU-Text and M-Text omit *behold.* *b*NU-Text and M-Text read *the whole moon.* 6:15 *a*NU-Text and M-Text read *the commanders, the rich men.* 7:5 *a*In NU-Text and M-Text *were sealed* is stated only in verses 5a and 8c; the words are understood in the remainder of the passage.

AND GOD WILL WIPE AWAY EVERY TEAR FROM THEIR EYES.
Revelation 7:17

Who Will Wipe Our Tears Away?

Did you ever cry? What for? Did you cut your finger? Did someone say something unkind to you? Did someone bully you? Were you sad or lonely?

1. Who wipes your tears and hugs you when you cry? Does mother or father do this? Does a brother or sister do this? Does a friend do this? God is always there to wipe your tears away.
2. When we go to heaven, God wipes *all* of our tears away. We will never cry again. We will never need to. Doesn't that sound wonderful?
3. Would you like to thank God for being our most wonderful tear wiper of all?

For more on *Favorite Family Verses* turn to page 1929
For more on *God's Care* turn to page 2

throne and the elders and the four living creatures, and fell on their faces before the throne and worshiped God,
12 saying:

"Amen! Blessing and glory and
wisdom,
Thanksgiving and honor and
power and might,
Be to our God forever and ever.
Amen."

13 Then one of the elders answered, saying to me, "Who are these arrayed in white robes, and where did they come from?"
14 And I said to him, "Sir,*a* you know." So he said to me, "These are the ones who come out of the great tribulation, and washed their robes and made them white in the blood of the Lamb.
15 "Therefore they are before the throne of God, and serve Him day and night in His temple. And He who sits on the throne will dwell among them.

16 "They shall neither hunger anymore nor thirst anymore; the sun shall not strike them, nor any heat;
17 "for the Lamb who is in the midst of the throne will shepherd them and lead them to living fountains of waters.*a* And God will wipe away every tear from their eyes."

SEVENTH SEAL: PRELUDE TO THE SEVEN TRUMPETS

8 When He opened the seventh seal, there was silence in heaven for about half an hour.
2 And I saw the seven angels who stand before God, and to them were given seven trumpets.
3 Then another angel, having a golden censer, came and stood at the altar. He was given much incense, that he should offer *it* with the prayers of all the saints upon the

---

7:14 *a*NU-Text and M-Text read *My lord.*
7:17 *a*NU-Text and M-Text read *to fountains of the waters of life.*

golden altar which was before the throne.

4 And the smoke of the incense, with the prayers of the saints, ascended before God from the angel's hand.

5 Then the angel took the censer, filled it with fire from the altar, and threw *it* to the earth. And there were noises, thunderings, lightnings, and an earthquake.

6 So the seven angels who had the seven trumpets prepared themselves to sound.

FIRST TRUMPET: VEGETATION STRUCK

7 The first angel sounded: And hail and fire followed, mingled with blood, and they were thrown to the earth.*a* And a third of the trees were burned up, and all green grass was burned up.

SECOND TRUMPET: THE SEAS STRUCK

8 Then the second angel sounded: And *something* like a great mountain burning with fire was thrown into the sea, and a third of the sea became blood.

9 And a third of the living creatures in the sea died, and a third of the ships were destroyed.

THIRD TRUMPET: THE WATERS STRUCK

10 Then the third angel sounded: And a great star fell from heaven, burning like a torch, and it fell on a third of the rivers and on the springs of water.

11 The name of the star is Wormwood. A third of the waters became wormwood, and many men died from the water, because it was made bitter.

FOURTH TRUMPET: THE HEAVENS STRUCK

12 Then the fourth angel sounded: And a third of the sun was struck, a third of the moon, and a third of the stars, so that a third of them were darkened. A third of the day did not shine, and likewise the night.

13 And I looked, and I heard an angel*a* flying through the midst of heaven, saying with a loud voice, "Woe, woe, woe to the inhabitants of the earth, because of the remaining blasts of the trumpet of the three angels who are about to sound!"

FIFTH TRUMPET: THE LOCUSTS FROM THE BOTTOMLESS PIT

9 Then the fifth angel sounded: And I saw a star fallen from heaven to the earth. To him was given the key to the bottomless pit.

2 And he opened the bottomless pit, and smoke arose out of the pit like the smoke of a great furnace. So the sun and the air were darkened because of the smoke of the pit.

3 Then out of the smoke locusts came upon the earth. And to them was given power, as the scorpions of the earth have power.

4 They were commanded not to harm the grass of the earth, or any green thing, or any tree, but only those men who do not have the seal of God on their foreheads.

5 And they were not given *authority* to kill them, but to torment them *for* five months. Their torment *was* like the torment of a scorpion when it strikes a man.

8:7 *a*NU-Text and M-Text add *and a third of the earth was burned up.* 8:13 *a*NU-Text and M-Text read *eagle.*

6 In those days men will seek death and will not find it; they will desire to die, and death will flee from them.

7 The shape of the locusts was like horses prepared for battle. On their heads were crowns of something like gold, and their faces *were* like the faces of men.

8 They had hair like women's hair, and their teeth were like lions' *teeth.*

9 And they had breastplates like breastplates of iron, and the sound of their wings *was* like the sound of chariots with many horses running into battle.

10 They had tails like scorpions, and there were stings in their tails. Their power *was* to hurt men five months.

11 And they had as king over them the angel of the bottomless pit, whose name in Hebrew *is* A·bad′don, but in Greek he has the name A·pol′lyon.

12 One woe is past. Behold, still two more woes are coming after these things.

SIXTH TRUMPET: THE ANGELS FROM THE EUPHRATES

13 Then the sixth angel sounded: And I heard a voice from the four horns of the golden altar which is before God,

14 saying to the sixth angel who had the trumpet, "Release the four angels who are bound at the great river Eū·phrā′tēs."

15 So the four angels, who had been prepared for the hour and day and month and year, were released to kill a third of mankind.

16 Now the number of the army of the horsemen *was* two hundred million; I heard the number of them.

17 And thus I saw the horses in the vision: those who sat on them had breastplates of fiery red, hyacinth blue, and sulfur yellow; and the heads of the horses *were* like the heads of lions; and out of their mouths came fire, smoke, and brimstone.

18 By these three *plagues* a third of mankind was killed—by the fire and the smoke and the brimstone which came out of their mouths.

19 For their power[a] is in their mouth and in their tails; for their tails *are* like serpents, having heads; and with them they do harm.

20 But the rest of mankind, who were not killed by these plagues, did not repent of the works of their hands, that they should not worship demons, and idols of gold, silver, brass, stone, and wood, which can neither see nor hear nor walk.

21 And they did not repent of their murders or their sorceries[a] or their sexual immorality or their thefts.

THE MIGHTY ANGEL WITH THE LITTLE BOOK

10 I saw still another mighty angel coming down from heaven, clothed with a cloud. And a rainbow *was* on his head, his face *was* like the sun, and his feet like pillars of fire.

2 He had a little book open in his hand. And he set his right foot on the sea and *his* left *foot* on the land,

3 and cried with a loud voice, as *when* a lion roars. When he cried out, seven thunders uttered their voices.

4 Now when the seven thunders uttered their voices,[a] I was about to write; but I heard a voice from heaven saying to me,[b] "Seal up the things which the seven thunders uttered, and do not write them."

5 The angel whom I saw standing

9:19 [a]NU-Text and M-Text read *the power of the horses.*　　9:21 [a]NU-Text and M-Text read *drugs.* 10:4 [a]NU-Text and M-Text read *sounded.* [b]NU-Text and M-Text omit *to me.*

on the sea and on the land raised up his hand[a] to heaven

6 and swore by Him who lives forever and ever, who created heaven and the things that are in it, the earth and the things that are in it, and the sea and the things that are in it, that there should be delay no longer,

7 but in the days of the sounding of the seventh angel, when he is about to sound, the mystery of God would be finished, as He declared to His servants the prophets.

JOHN EATS THE LITTLE BOOK

8 Then the voice which I heard from heaven spoke to me again and said, "Go, take the little book which is open in the hand of the angel who stands on the sea and on the earth."

9 So I went to the angel and said to him, "Give me the little book." And he said to me, "Take and eat it; and it will make your stomach bitter, but it will be as sweet as honey in your mouth."

10 Then I took the little book out of the angel's hand and ate it, and it was as sweet as honey in my mouth. But when I had eaten it, my stomach became bitter.

11 And he[a] said to me, "You must prophesy again about many peoples, nations, tongues, and kings."

THE TWO WITNESSES

11 Then I was given a reed like a measuring rod. And the angel stood,[a] saying, "Rise and measure the temple of God, the altar, and those who worship there.

2 "But leave out the court which is outside the temple, and do not measure it, for it has been given to the Gentiles. And they will tread the holy city underfoot *for* forty-two months.

3 "And I will give *power* to my two witnesses, and they will prophesy one thousand two hundred and sixty days, clothed in sackcloth."

4 These are the two olive trees and the two lampstands standing before the God[a] of the earth.

5 And if anyone wants to harm them, fire proceeds from their mouth and devours their enemies. And if anyone wants to harm them, he must be killed in this manner.

6 These have power to shut heaven, so that no rain falls in the days of their prophecy; and they have power over waters to turn them to blood, and to strike the earth with all plagues, as often as they desire.

THE WITNESSES KILLED

7 When they finish their testimony, the beast that ascends out of the bottomless pit will make war against them, overcome them, and kill them.

8 And their dead bodies *will lie* in the street of the great city which spiritually is called Sod'om and Egypt, where also our[a] Lord was crucified.

9 Then *those* from the peoples, tribes, tongues, and nations will see their dead bodies three-and-a-half days, and not allow[a] their dead bodies to be put into graves.

10 And those who dwell on the earth will rejoice over them, make merry, and send gifts to one another, because these two prophets tormented those who dwell on the earth.

10:5 [a]NU-Text and M-Text read *right hand.*
10:11 [a]NU-Text and M-Text read *they.*
11:1 [a]NU-Text and M-Text omit *And the angel stood.*   11:4 [a]NU-Text and M-Text read *Lord.*
11:8 [a]NU-Text and M-Text read *their.*
11:9 [a]NU-Text and M-Text read *nations see . . . and will not allow.*

THE WITNESSES RESURRECTED

11 Now after the three-and-a-half days the breath of life from God entered them, and they stood on their feet, and great fear fell on those who saw them.

12 And they[a] heard a loud voice from heaven saying to them, "Come up here." And they ascended to heaven in a cloud, and their enemies saw them.

13 In the same hour there was a great earthquake, and a tenth of the city fell. In the earthquake seven thousand people were killed, and the rest were afraid and gave glory to the God of heaven.

14 The second woe is past. Behold, the third woe is coming quickly.

SEVENTH TRUMPET: THE KINGDOM PROCLAIMED

15 Then the seventh angel sounded: And there were loud voices in heaven, saying, "The kingdoms[a] of this world have become *the kingdoms* of our Lord and of His Christ, and He shall reign forever and ever!"

16 And the twenty-four elders who sat before God on their thrones fell on their faces and worshiped God,

17 saying:

"We give You thanks, O Lord God Almighty,
The One who is and who was and who is to come,[a]
Because You have taken Your great power and reigned.

18 The nations were angry, and Your wrath has come,
And the time of the dead, that they should be judged,
And that You should reward Your servants the prophets and the saints,

And those who fear Your name, small and great,
And should destroy those who destroy the earth."

19 Then the temple of God was opened in heaven, and the ark of His covenant[a] was seen in His temple. And there were lightnings, noises, thunderings, an earthquake, and great hail.

THE WOMAN, THE CHILD, AND THE DRAGON

12 Now a great sign appeared in heaven: a woman clothed with the sun, with the moon under her feet, and on her head a garland of twelve stars.

2 Then being with child, she cried out in labor and in pain to give birth.

3 And another sign appeared in heaven: behold, a great, fiery red dragon having seven heads and ten horns, and seven diadems on his heads.

4 His tail drew a third of the stars of heaven and threw them to the earth. And the dragon stood before the woman who was ready to give birth, to devour her Child as soon as it was born.

5 She bore a male Child who was to rule all nations with a rod of iron. And her Child was caught up to God and His throne.

6 Then the woman fled into the wilderness, where she has a place prepared by God, that they should feed her there one thousand two hundred and sixty days.

11:12 [a]M-Text reads *I*.   11:15 [a]NU-Text and M-Text read *kingdom . . . has become*.
11:17 [a]NU-Text and M-Text omit *and who is to come*.   11:19 [a]M-Text reads *the covenant of the Lord*.

SATAN THROWN OUT OF HEAVEN

7 And war broke out in heaven: Michael and his angels fought with the dragon; and the dragon and his angels fought,
8 but they did not prevail, nor was a place found for them*a* in heaven any longer.
9 So the great dragon was cast out, that serpent of old, called the Devil and Satan, who deceives the whole world; he was cast to the earth, and his angels were cast out with him.
10 Then I heard a loud voice saying in heaven, "Now salvation, and strength, and the kingdom of our God, and the power of His Christ have come, for the accuser of our brethren, who accused them before our God day and night, has been cast down.
11 "And they overcame him by the blood of the Lamb and by the word of their testimony, and they did not love their lives to the death.
12 "Therefore rejoice, O heavens, and you who dwell in them! Woe to the inhabitants of the earth and the sea! For the devil has come down to you, having great wrath, because he knows that he has a short time."

THE WOMAN PERSECUTED

13 Now when the dragon saw that he had been cast to the earth, he persecuted the woman who gave birth to the male *Child.*
14 But the woman was given two wings of a great eagle, that she might fly into the wilderness to her place, where she is nourished for a time and times and half a time, from the presence of the serpent.
15 So the serpent spewed water out of his mouth like a flood after the woman, that he might cause her to be carried away by the flood.

16 But the earth helped the woman, and the earth opened its mouth and swallowed up the flood which the dragon had spewed out of his mouth.
17 And the dragon was enraged with the woman, and he went to make war with the rest of her offspring, who keep the commandments of God and have the testimony of Jesus Christ.*a*

THE BEAST FROM THE SEA

13 Then I*a* stood on the sand of the sea. And I saw a beast rising up out of the sea, having seven heads and ten horns,*b* and on his horns ten crowns, and on his heads a blasphemous name.
2 Now the beast which I saw was like a leopard, his feet were like *the feet of* a bear, and his mouth like the mouth of a lion. The dragon gave him his power, his throne, and great authority.
3 And *I saw* one of his heads as if it had been mortally wounded, and his deadly wound was healed. And all the world marveled and followed the beast.
4 So they worshiped the dragon who gave authority to the beast; and they worshiped the beast, saying, "Who *is* like the beast? Who is able to make war with him?"
5 And he was given a mouth speaking great things and blasphemies, and he was given authority to continue*a* for forty-two months.
6 Then he opened his mouth in blasphemy against God, to blaspheme His name, His tabernacle, and those who dwell in heaven.
7 It was granted to him to make war with the saints and to overcome

---

12:8 *a*M-Text reads *him.*   12:17 *a*NU-Text and M-Text omit *Christ.*   13:1 *a*NU-Text reads *he.* *b*NU-Text and M-Text read *ten horns and seven heads.*   13:5 *a*M-Text reads *make war.*

them. And authority was given him over every tribe,*a* tongue, and nation.

8 All who dwell on the earth will worship him, whose names have not been written in the Book of Life of the Lamb slain from the foundation of the world.

9 If anyone has an ear, let him hear.

10 He who leads into captivity shall go into captivity; he who kills with the sword must be killed with the sword. Here is the patience and the faith of the saints.

THE BEAST FROM THE EARTH

11 Then I saw another beast coming up out of the earth, and he had two horns like a lamb and spoke like a dragon.

12 And he exercises all the authority of the first beast in his presence, and causes the earth and those who dwell in it to worship the first beast, whose deadly wound was healed.

13 He performs great signs, so that he even makes fire come down from heaven on the earth in the sight of men.

14 And he deceives those*a* who dwell on the earth by those signs which he was granted to do in the sight of the beast, telling those who dwell on the earth to make an image to the beast who was wounded by the sword and lived.

15 He was granted *power* to give breath to the image of the beast, that the image of the beast should both speak and cause as many as would not worship the image of the beast to be killed.

16 He causes all, both small and great, rich and poor, free and slave, to receive a mark on their right hand or on their foreheads,

17 and that no one may buy or sell except one who has the mark or*a* the name of the beast, or the number of his name.

18 Here is wisdom. Let him who has understanding calculate the number of the beast, for it is the number of a man: His number *is* 666.

THE LAMB AND THE 144,000

14 Then I looked, and behold, a*a* Lamb standing on Mount Zion, and with Him one hundred *and* forty-four thousand, having*b* His Father's name written on their foreheads.

2 And I heard a voice from heaven, like the voice of many waters, and like the voice of loud thunder. And I heard the sound of harpists playing their harps.

3 They sang as it were a new song before the throne, before the four living creatures, and the elders; and no one could learn that song except the hundred *and* forty-four thousand who were redeemed from the earth.

4 These are the ones who were not defiled with women, for they are virgins. These are the ones who follow the Lamb wherever He goes. These were redeemed*a* from *among* men, *being* firstfruits to God and to the Lamb.

5 And in their mouth was found no deceit,*a* for they are without fault before the throne of God.*b*

THE PROCLAMATIONS OF THREE ANGELS

6 Then I saw another angel flying in the midst of heaven, having the

13:7 *a*NU-Text and M-Text add *and people.*
13:14 *a*M-Text reads *my own people.*
13:17 *a*NU-Text and M-Text omit *or.*
14:1 *a*NU-Text and M-Text read *the.* *b*NU-Text and M-Text add *His name and.* 14:4 *a*M-Text adds *by Jesus.* 14:5 *a*NU-Text and M-Text read *falsehood.* *b*NU-Text and M-Text omit *before the throne of God.*

everlasting gospel to preach to those who dwell on the earth—to every nation, tribe, tongue, and people—

7 saying with a loud voice, "Fear God and give glory to Him, for the hour of His judgment has come; and worship Him who made heaven and earth, the sea and springs of water."

8 And another angel followed, saying, "Babylon*a* is fallen, is fallen, that great city, because she has made all nations drink of the wine of the wrath of her fornication."

9 Then a third angel followed them, saying with a loud voice, "If anyone worships the beast and his image, and receives *his* mark on his forehead or on his hand,

10 "he himself shall also drink of the wine of the wrath of God, which is poured out full strength into the cup of His indignation. He shall be tormented with fire and brimstone in the presence of the holy angels and in the presence of the Lamb.

11 "And the smoke of their torment ascends forever and ever; and they have no rest day or night, who worship the beast and his image, and whoever receives the mark of his name."

12 Here is the patience of the saints; here *are* those*a* who keep the commandments of God and the faith of Jesus.

13 Then I heard a voice from heaven saying to me,*a* "Write: 'Blessed *are* the dead who die in the Lord from now on.'" "Yes," says the Spirit, "that they may rest from their labors, and their works follow them."

REAPING THE EARTH'S HARVEST

14 Then I looked, and behold, a white cloud, and on the cloud sat *One* like the Son of Man, having on His head a golden crown, and in His hand a sharp sickle.

15 And another angel came out of the temple, crying with a loud voice to Him who sat on the cloud, "Thrust in Your sickle and reap, for the time has come for You*a* to reap, for the harvest of the earth is ripe."

16 So He who sat on the cloud thrust in His sickle on the earth, and the earth was reaped.

REAPING THE GRAPES OF WRATH

17 Then another angel came out of the temple which is in heaven, he also having a sharp sickle.

18 And another angel came out from the altar, who had power over fire, and he cried with a loud cry to him who had the sharp sickle, saying, "Thrust in your sharp sickle and gather the clusters of the vine of the earth, for her grapes are fully ripe."

19 So the angel thrust his sickle into the earth and gathered the vine of the earth, and threw *it* into the great winepress of the wrath of God.

20 And the winepress was trampled outside the city, and blood came out of the winepress, up to the horses' bridles, for one thousand six hundred furlongs.

PRELUDE TO THE BOWL JUDGMENTS

15 Then I saw another sign in heaven, great and marvelous: seven angels having the seven last plagues, for in them the wrath of God is complete.

2 And I saw *something* like a sea of glass mingled with fire, and those who have the victory over the beast, over his image and over his mark*a*

14:8 *a*NU-Text reads *Babylon the great is fallen, is fallen, which has made;* M-Text reads *Babylon the great is fallen. She has made.* 14:12 *a*NU-Text and M-Text omit *here are those.* 14:13 *a*NU-Text and M-Text omit *to me.* 14:15 *a*NU-Text and M-Text omit *for You.* 15:2 *a*NU-Text and M-Text omit *over his mark.*

and over the number of his name, standing on the sea of glass, having harps of God.

3 They sing the song of Moses, the servant of God, and the song of the Lamb, saying:

"Great and marvelous *are* Your
    works,
Lord God Almighty!
Just and true *are* Your ways,
O King of the saints!a

4 Who shall not fear You, O Lord,
    and glorify Your name?
For *You* alone *are* holy.
For all nations shall come and
    worship before You,
For Your judgments have been
    manifested."

5 After these things I looked, and behold,a the temple of the tabernacle of the testimony in heaven was opened.
6 And out of the temple came the seven angels having the seven plagues, clothed in pure bright linen, and having their chests girded with golden bands.
7 Then one of the four living creatures gave to the seven angels seven golden bowls full of the wrath of God who lives forever and ever.
8 The temple was filled with smoke from the glory of God and from His power, and no one was able to enter the temple till the seven plagues of the seven angels were completed.

16 Then I heard a loud voice from the temple saying to the seven angels, "Go and pour out the bowlsa of the wrath of God on the earth."

FIRST BOWL: LOATHSOME SORES

2 So the first went and poured out his bowl upon the earth, and a foul and loathsome sore came upon the men who had the mark of the beast and those who worshiped his image.

SECOND BOWL: THE SEA TURNS TO BLOOD

3 Then the second angel poured out his bowl on the sea, and it became blood as of a dead *man;* and every living creature in the sea died.

THIRD BOWL: THE WATERS TURN TO BLOOD

4 Then the third angel poured out his bowl on the rivers and springs of water, and they became blood.
5 And I heard the angel of the waters saying:

"You are righteous, O Lord,a
The One who is and who was and
    who is to be,b
Because You have judged these
    things.
6 For they have shed the blood of
    saints and prophets,
And You have given them blood to
    drink.
Fora it is their just due."

7 And I heard another froma the altar saying, "Even so, Lord God Almighty, true and righteous *are* Your judgments."

FOURTH BOWL: MEN ARE SCORCHED

8 Then the fourth angel poured out his bowl on the sun, and power was given to him to scorch men with fire.

15:3 aNU-Text and M-Text read *nations.*
15:5 aNU-Text and M-Text omit *behold.*
16:1 aNU-Text and M-Text read *seven bowls.*
16:5 aNU-Text and M-Text omit *O Lord.*   bNU-Text and M-Text read *who was, the Holy One.*
16:6 aNU-Text and M-Text omit *For.*
16:7 aNU-Text and M-Text omit *another from.*

9 And men were scorched with great heat, and they blasphemed the name of God who has power over these plagues; and they did not repent and give Him glory.

FIFTH BOWL: DARKNESS AND PAIN

10 Then the fifth angel poured out his bowl on the throne of the beast, and his kingdom became full of darkness; and they gnawed their tongues because of the pain.
11 They blasphemed the God of heaven because of their pains and their sores, and did not repent of their deeds.

SIXTH BOWL: EUPHRATES DRIED UP

12 Then the sixth angel poured out his bowl on the great river Eū·phrā′tēs, and its water was dried up, so that the way of the kings from the east might be prepared.
13 And I saw three unclean spirits like frogs *coming* out of the mouth of the dragon, out of the mouth of the beast, and out of the mouth of the false prophet.
14 For they are spirits of demons, performing signs, *which* go out to the kings of the earth and*a* of the whole world, to gather them to the battle of that great day of God Almighty.
15 "Behold, I am coming as a thief. Blessed *is* he who watches, and keeps his garments, lest he walk naked and they see his shame."
16 And they gathered them together to the place called in Hebrew, Ar·ma·ged′don.*a*

SEVENTH BOWL: THE EARTH UTTERLY SHAKEN

17 Then the seventh angel poured out his bowl into the air, and a loud voice came out of the temple of heaven, from the throne, saying, "It is done!"
18 And there were noises and thunderings and lightnings; and there was a great earthquake, such a mighty and great earthquake as had not occurred since men were on the earth.
19 Now the great city was divided into three parts, and the cities of the nations fell. And great Babylon was remembered before God, to give her the cup of the wine of the fierceness of His wrath.
20 Then every island fled away, and the mountains were not found.
21 And great hail from heaven fell upon men, *each hailstone* about the weight of a talent. Men blasphemed God because of the plague of the hail, since that plague was exceedingly great.

THE SCARLET WOMAN AND THE SCARLET BEAST

17 Then one of the seven angels who had the seven bowls came and talked with me, saying to me,*a* "Come, I will show you the judgment of the great harlot who sits on many waters,
2 "with whom the kings of the earth committed fornication, and the inhabitants of the earth were made drunk with the wine of her fornication."
3 So he carried me away in the Spirit into the wilderness. And I saw a woman sitting on a scarlet beast *which was* full of names of blasphemy, having seven heads and ten horns.
4 The woman was arrayed in purple and scarlet, and adorned with

16:14 *a*NU-Text and M-Text omit *of the earth and.*
16:16 *a*M-Text reads *Megiddo.*   17:1 *a*NU-Text and M-Text omit *to me.*

gold and precious stones and pearls, having in her hand a golden cup full of abominations and the filthiness of her fornication.*a*

5 And on her forehead a name *was* written:

MYSTERY, BABYLON THE GREAT,
THE MOTHER OF HARLOTS
AND OF THE ABOMINATIONS
OF THE EARTH.

6 I saw the woman, drunk with the blood of the saints and with the blood of the martyrs of Jesus. And when I saw her, I marveled with great amazement.

THE MEANING OF THE WOMAN AND THE BEAST

7 But the angel said to me, "Why did you marvel? I will tell you the mystery of the woman and of the beast that carries her, which has the seven heads and the ten horns.

8 "The beast that you saw was, and is not, and will ascend out of the bottomless pit and go to perdition. And those who dwell on the earth will marvel, whose names are not written in the Book of Life from the foundation of the world, when they see the beast that was, and is not, and yet is.*a*

9 "Here *is* the mind which has wisdom: The seven heads are seven mountains on which the woman sits.

10 "There are also seven kings. Five have fallen, one is, *and* the other has not yet come. And when he comes, he must continue a short time.

11 "The beast that was, and is not, is himself also the eighth, and is of the seven, and is going to perdition.

12 "The ten horns which you saw are ten kings who have received no kingdom as yet, but they receive authority for one hour as kings with the beast.

13 "These are of one mind, and they will give their power and authority to the beast.

14 "These will make war with the Lamb, and the Lamb will overcome them, for He is Lord of lords and King of kings; and those *who are* with Him *are* called, chosen, and faithful."

15 Then he said to me, "The waters which you saw, where the harlot sits, are peoples, multitudes, nations, and tongues.

16 "And the ten horns which you saw on*a* the beast, these will hate the harlot, make her desolate and naked, eat her flesh and burn her with fire.

17 "For God has put it into their hearts to fulfill His purpose, to be of one mind, and to give their kingdom to the beast, until the words of God are fulfilled.

18 "And the woman whom you saw is that great city which reigns over the kings of the earth."

THE FALL OF BABYLON THE GREAT

18 After these things I saw another angel coming down from heaven, having great authority, and the earth was illuminated with his glory.

2 And he cried mightily*a* with a loud voice, saying, "Babylon the great is fallen, is fallen, and has become a dwelling place of demons, a prison for every foul spirit, and a cage for every unclean and hated bird!

3 "For all the nations have drunk of the wine of the wrath of her fornication, the kings of the earth have committed fornication with her, and the

---

17:4 *a*M-Text reads *the filthiness of the fornication of the earth.*   17:8 *a*NU-Text and M-Text read *and shall be present.*   17:16 *a*NU-Text and M-Text read *saw, and the beast.*   18:2 *a*NU-Text and M-Text omit *mightily.*

merchants of the earth have become rich through the abundance of her luxury."

4   And I heard another voice from heaven saying, "Come out of her, my people, lest you share in her sins, and lest you receive of her plagues.

5   "For her sins have reached*a* to heaven, and God has remembered her iniquities.

6   "Render to her just as she rendered to you,*a* and repay her double according to her works; in the cup which she has mixed, mix double for her.

7   "In the measure that she glorified herself and lived luxuriously, in the same measure give her torment and sorrow; for she says in her heart, 'I sit *as* queen, and am no widow, and will not see sorrow.'

8   "Therefore her plagues will come in one day—death and mourning and famine. And she will be utterly burned with fire, for strong *is* the Lord God who judges*a* her.

THE WORLD MOURNS BABYLON'S FALL

9   "The kings of the earth who committed fornication and lived luxuriously with her will weep and lament for her, when they see the smoke of her burning,

10   "standing at a distance for fear of her torment, saying, 'Alas, alas, that great city Babylon, that mighty city! For in one hour your judgment has come.'

11   "And the merchants of the earth will weep and mourn over her, for no one buys their merchandise anymore:

12   "merchandise of gold and silver, precious stones and pearls, fine linen and purple, silk and scarlet, every kind of citron wood, every kind of object of ivory, every kind of object of most precious wood, bronze, iron, and marble;

13   "and cinnamon and incense, fragrant oil and frankincense, wine and oil, fine flour and wheat, cattle and sheep, horses and chariots, and bodies and souls of men.

14   "The fruit that your soul longed for has gone from you, and all the things which are rich and splendid have gone from you,*a* and you shall find them no more at all.

15   "The merchants of these things, who became rich by her, will stand at a distance for fear of her torment, weeping and wailing,

16   "and saying, 'Alas, alas, that great city that was clothed in fine linen, purple, and scarlet, and adorned with gold and precious stones and pearls!

17   'For in one hour such great riches came to nothing.' Every shipmaster, all who travel by ship, sailors, and as many as trade on the sea, stood at a distance

18   "and cried out when they saw the smoke of her burning, saying, 'What *is* like this great city?'

19   "They threw dust on their heads and cried out, weeping and wailing, and saying, 'Alas, alas, that great city, in which all who had ships on the sea became rich by her wealth! For in one hour she is made desolate.'

20   "Rejoice over her, O heaven, and *you* holy apostles*a* and prophets, for God has avenged you on her!"

FINALITY OF BABYLON'S FALL

21   Then a mighty angel took up a stone like a great millstone and

18:5 *a*NU-Text and M-Text read *have been heaped up.*   18:6 *a*NU-Text and M-Text omit *to you.*
18:8 *a*NU-Text and M-Text read *has judged.*
18:14 *a*NU-Text and M-Text read *been lost to you.*
18:20 *a*NU-Text and M-Text read *saints and apostles.*

threw *it* into the sea, saying, "Thus with violence the great city Babylon shall be thrown down, and shall not be found anymore.

22 "The sound of harpists, musicians, flutists, and trumpeters shall not be heard in you anymore. No craftsman of any craft shall be found in you anymore, and the sound of a millstone shall not be heard in you anymore.

23 "The light of a lamp shall not shine in you anymore, and the voice of bridegroom and bride shall not be heard in you anymore. For your merchants were the great men of the earth, for by your sorcery all the nations were deceived.

24 "And in her was found the blood of prophets and saints, and of all who were slain on the earth."

HEAVEN EXULTS OVER BABYLON

19 After these things I heard[a] a loud voice of a great multitude in heaven, saying, "Alleluia! Salvation and glory and honor and power *belong* to the Lord[b] our God!

2 "For true and righteous *are* His judgments, because He has judged the great harlot who corrupted the earth with her fornication; and He has avenged on her the blood of His servants *shed* by her."

3 Again they said, "Alleluia! Her smoke rises up forever and ever!"

4 And the twenty-four elders and the four living creatures fell down and worshiped God who sat on the throne, saying, "Amen! Alleluia!"

5 Then a voice came from the throne, saying, "Praise our God, all you His servants and those who fear Him, both[a] small and great!"

6 And I heard, as it were, the voice of a great multitude, as the sound of many waters and as the sound of mighty thunderings, saying, "Alleluia! For the[a] Lord God Omnipotent reigns!

7 "Let us be glad and rejoice and give Him glory, for the marriage of the Lamb has come, and His wife has made herself ready."

8 And to her it was granted to be arrayed in fine linen, clean and bright, for the fine linen is the righteous acts of the saints.

9 Then he said to me, "Write: 'Blessed *are* those who are called to the marriage supper of the Lamb!'" And he said to me, "These are the true sayings of God."

10 And I fell at his feet to worship him. But he said to me, "See *that you do* not *do that!* I am your fellow servant, and of your brethren who have the testimony of Jesus. Worship God! For the testimony of Jesus is the spirit of prophecy."

CHRIST ON A WHITE HORSE

11 Now I saw heaven opened, and behold, a white horse. And He who sat on him *was* called Faithful and True, and in righteousness He judges and makes war.

12 His eyes *were* like a flame of fire, and on His head *were* many crowns. He had[a] a name written that no one knew except Himself.

13 He *was* clothed with a robe dipped in blood, and His name is called The Word of God.

14 And the armies in heaven, clothed in fine linen, white and clean,[a] followed Him on white horses.

15 Now out of His mouth goes a sharp[a] sword, that with it He should

19:1 [a]NU-Text and M-Text add *something like.* [b]NU-Text and M-Text omit *the Lord.* 19:5 [a]NU-Text and M-Text omit *both.* 19:6 [a]NU-Text and M-Text read *our.* 19:12 [a]M-Text adds *names written, and.* 19:14 [a]NU-Text and M-Text read *pure white linen.* 19:15 [a]M-Text adds *two-edged.*

strike the nations. And He Himself will rule them with a rod of iron. He Himself treads the winepress of the fierceness and wrath of Almighty God.

16 And He has on *His* robe and on His thigh a name written:

KING OF KINGS AND LORD
OF LORDS.

THE BEAST AND HIS
ARMIES DEFEATED

17 Then I saw an angel standing in the sun; and he cried with a loud voice, saying to all the birds that fly in the midst of heaven, "Come and gather together for the supper of the great God,*a*
18 "that you may eat the flesh of kings, the flesh of captains, the flesh of mighty men, the flesh of horses and of those who sit on them, and the flesh of all *people,* free*a* and slave, both small and great."
19 And I saw the beast, the kings of the earth, and their armies, gathered together to make war against Him who sat on the horse and against His army.
20 Then the beast was captured, and with him the false prophet who worked signs in his presence, by which he deceived those who received the mark of the beast and those who worshiped his image. These two were cast alive into the lake of fire burning with brimstone.
21 And the rest were killed with the sword which proceeded from the mouth of Him who sat on the horse. And all the birds were filled with their flesh.

SATAN BOUND 1000 YEARS

20 Then I saw an angel coming down from heaven, having the key to the bottomless pit and a great chain in his hand.
2 He laid hold of the dragon, that serpent of old, who is *the* Devil and Satan, and bound him for a thousand years;
3 and he cast him into the bottomless pit, and shut him up, and set a seal on him, so that he should deceive the nations no more till the thousand years were finished. But after these things he must be released for a little while.

THE SAINTS REIGN WITH CHRIST
1000 YEARS

4 And I saw thrones, and they sat on them, and judgment was committed to them. Then *I saw* the souls of those who had been beheaded for their witness to Jesus and for the word of God, who had not worshiped the beast or his image, and had not received *his* mark on their foreheads or on their hands. And they lived and reigned with Christ for a*a* thousand years.
5 But the rest of the dead did not live again until the thousand years were finished. This *is* the first resurrection.
6 Blessed and holy *is* he who has part in the first resurrection. Over such the second death has no power, but they shall be priests of God and of Christ, and shall reign with Him a thousand years.

SATANIC REBELLION CRUSHED

7 Now when the thousand years have expired, Satan will be released from his prison
8 and will go out to deceive the nations which are in the four corners of

19:17 *a*NU-Text and M-Text read *the great supper of God.* 19:18 *a*NU-Text and M-Text read *both free.* 20:4 *a*M-Text reads *the.*

the earth, Gog and Mā′gog, to gather them together to battle, whose number *is* as the sand of the sea.

9 They went up on the breadth of the earth and surrounded the camp of the saints and the beloved city. And fire came down from God out of heaven and devoured them.

10 The devil, who deceived them, was cast into the lake of fire and brimstone where*a* the beast and the false prophet *are*. And they will be tormented day and night forever and ever.

THE GREAT WHITE THRONE JUDGMENT

11 Then I saw a great white throne and Him who sat on it, from whose face the earth and the heaven fled away. And there was found no place for them.

12 And I saw the dead, small and great, standing before God,*a* and books were opened. And another book was opened, which is *the Book* of Life. And the dead were judged according to their works, by the things which were written in the books.

13 The sea gave up the dead who were in it, and Death and Hā′dēs delivered up the dead who were in them. And they were judged, each one according to his works.

14 Then Death and Hā′dēs were cast into the lake of fire. This is the second death.*a*

15 And anyone not found written in the Book of Life was cast into the lake of fire.

ALL THINGS MADE NEW

21 Now I saw a new heaven and a new earth, for the first heaven and the first earth had passed away. Also there was no more sea.

2 Then I, John,*a* saw the holy city,

New Jerusalem, coming down out of heaven from God, prepared as a bride adorned for her husband.

3 And I heard a loud voice from heaven saying, "Behold, the tabernacle of God *is* with men, and He will dwell with them, and they shall be His people. God Himself will be with them *and be* their God.

4 "And God will wipe away every tear from their eyes; there shall be no more death, nor sorrow, nor crying. There shall be no more pain, for the former things have passed away."

5 Then He who sat on the throne said, "Behold, I make all things new." And He said to me,*a* "Write, for these words are true and faithful."

6 And He said to me, "It is done!*a* I am the Alpha and the Omega, the Beginning and the End. I will give of the fountain of the water of life freely to him who thirsts.

7 "He who overcomes shall inherit all things,*a* and I will be his God and he shall be My son.

8 "But the cowardly, unbelieving,*a* abominable, murderers, sexually immoral, sorcerers, idolaters, and all liars shall have their part in the lake which burns with fire and brimstone, which is the second death."

THE NEW JERUSALEM

9 Then one of the seven angels who had the seven bowls filled with the seven last plagues came to me*a* and talked with me, saying, "Come, I will show you the bride, the Lamb's wife."*b*

20:10 *a*NU-Text and M-Text add *also.*
20:12 *a*NU-Text and M-Text read *the throne.*
20:14 *a*NU-Text and M-Text add *the lake of fire.*
21:2 *a*NU-Text and M-Text omit *John.*
21:5 *a*NU-Text and M-Text omit *to me.*
21:6 *a*M-Text omits *It is done.*   21:7 *a*M-Text reads *overcomes, I shall give him these things.*
21:8 *a*M-Text adds *and sinners.*   21:9 *a*NU-Text and M-Text omit *to me.*   *b*M-Text reads *I will show you the woman, the Lamb's bride.*

AND GOD WILL WIPE AWAY EVERY TEAR FROM THEIR EYES; THERE SHALL BE NO MORE DEATH, NOR SORROW, NOR CRYING. THERE SHALL BE NO MORE PAIN. Revelation 21:4

No Hospitals or Funeral Homes in Heaven

We couldn't do without hospitals here, could we? That's because there is so much sickness. We couldn't do without funeral homes here, either. That's because each of us will die someday, and we need someone to prepare us to be buried. But there isn't a hospital or funeral home in heaven. That's because there is no sickness, sorrow, tears, crying, pain, or death. What a wonderful home! Wouldn't you like to go there to live forever? Read Revelation 21:4 or memorize it.

1. Have you ever been a patient in a hospital? You were glad to have a hospital in your area, weren't you? Sick people appreciate a hospital. But why will there be no hospitals in heaven?
2. Have you visited a funeral home? Why? Who died? But why will there be no funeral homes in heaven?
3. Have you asked Jesus to be your Savior so that you may live forever in His home in heaven? Would you like to ask Him now?

For more on *Favorite Family Verses* turn to page 14
For more on *Salvation* turn to page 1168

10 And he carried me away in the Spirit to a great and high mountain, and showed me the great city, the holy^a Jerusalem, descending out of heaven from God,

11 having the glory of God. Her light *was* like a most precious stone, like a jasper stone, clear as crystal.

12 Also she had a great and high wall with twelve gates, and twelve angels at the gates, and names written on them, which are *the names* of the twelve tribes of the children of Israel:

13 three gates on the east, three gates on the north, three gates on the south, and three gates on the west.

14 Now the wall of the city had twelve foundations, and on them were the names^a of the twelve apostles of the Lamb.

15 And he who talked with me had a gold reed to measure the city, its gates, and its wall.

16 The city is laid out as a square; its length is as great as its breadth. And he measured the city with the reed: twelve thousand furlongs. Its length, breadth, and height are equal.

17 Then he measured its wall: one hundred *and* forty-four cubits, *according* to the measure of a man, that is, of an angel.

18 The construction of its wall was *of* jasper; and the city *was* pure gold, like clear glass.

19 The foundations of the wall of the city *were* adorned with all kinds of precious stones: the first foundation *was* jasper, the second sapphire, the third chalcedony, the fourth emerald,

20 the fifth sardonyx, the sixth sardius, the seventh chrysolite, the eighth beryl, the ninth topaz, the tenth chrysoprase, the eleventh jacinth, and the twelfth amethyst.

21 The twelve gates *were* twelve pearls: each individual gate was of one pearl. And the street of the city *was* pure gold, like transparent glass.

THE GLORY OF THE NEW JERUSALEM

22 But I saw no temple in it, for the Lord God Almighty and the Lamb are its temple.

23 The city had no need of the sun or of the moon to shine in it,^a for the glory^b of God illuminated it. The Lamb *is* its light.

24 And the nations of those who are saved^a shall walk in its light, and the kings of the earth bring their glory and honor into it.^b

25 Its gates shall not be shut at all by day (there shall be no night there).

26 And they shall bring the glory and the honor of the nations into it.^a

27 But there shall by no means enter it anything that defiles, or causes^a an abomination or a lie, but only those who are written in the Lamb's Book of Life.

THE RIVER OF LIFE

22 And he showed me a pure^a river of water of life, clear as crystal, proceeding from the throne of God and of the Lamb.

2 In the middle of its street, and on either side of the river, *was* the tree of life, which bore twelve fruits, each *tree* yielding its fruit every month. The leaves of the tree *were* for the healing of the nations.

3 And there shall be no more curse, but the throne of God and of the

---

21:10 ^aNU-Text and M-Text omit *the great* and read *the holy city, Jerusalem.*   21:14 ^aNU-Text and M-Text read *twelve names.*   21:23 ^aNU-Text and M-Text omit *in it.*   ^bM-Text reads *the very glory.*   21:24 ^aNU-Text and M-Text omit *of those who are saved.*   ^bM-Text reads *the glory and honor of the nations to Him.*   21:26 ^aM-Text adds *that they may enter in.*   21:27 ^aNU-Text and M-Text read *anything profane, nor one who causes.*   22:1 ^aNU-Text and M-Text omit *pure.*

Lamb shall be in it, and His servants shall serve Him.

4 They shall see His face, and His name *shall be* on their foreheads.

5 There shall be no night there: They need no lamp nor light of the sun, for the Lord God gives them light. And they shall reign forever and ever.

THE TIME IS NEAR

6 Then he said to me, "These words *are* faithful and true." And the Lord God of the holy*a* prophets sent His angel to show His servants the things which must shortly take place.

7 "Behold, I am coming quickly! Blessed *is* he who keeps the words of the prophecy of this book."

8 Now I, John, saw and heard*a* these things. And when I heard and saw, I fell down to worship before the feet of the angel who showed me these things.

9 Then he said to me, "See *that you do* not *do that.* For*a* I am your fellow servant, and of your brethren the prophets, and of those who keep the words of this book. Worship God."

10 And he said to me, "Do not seal the words of the prophecy of this book, for the time is at hand.

11 "He who is unjust, let him be unjust still; he who is filthy, let him be filthy still; he who is righteous, let him be righteous*a* still; he who is holy, let him be holy still."

JESUS TESTIFIES TO THE CHURCHES

12 "And behold, I am coming quickly, and My reward *is* with Me, to give to every one according to his work.

13 "I am the Alpha and the Omega, *the* Beginning and *the* End, the First and the Last."*a*

14 Blessed *are* those who do His commandments,*a* that they may have

the right to the tree of life, and may enter through the gates into the city.

15 But*a* outside *are* dogs and sorcerers and sexually immoral and murderers and idolaters, and whoever loves and practices a lie.

16 "I, Jesus, have sent My angel to testify to you these things in the churches. I am the Root and the Offspring of David, the Bright and Morning Star."

17 And the Spirit and the bride say, "Come!" And let him who hears say, "Come!" And let him who thirsts come. Whoever desires, let him take the water of life freely.

A WARNING

18 For*a* I testify to everyone who hears the words of the prophecy of this book: If anyone adds to these things, God will add*b* to him the plagues that are written in this book;

19 and if anyone takes away from the words of the book of this prophecy, God shall take away*a* his part from the Book*b* of Life, from the holy city, and *from* the things which are written in this book.

I AM COMING QUICKLY

20 He who testifies to these things says, "Surely I am coming quickly." Amen. Even so, come, Lord Jesus!

21 The grace of our Lord Jesus Christ *be* with you all.*a* Amen.

22:6 *a*NU-Text and M-Text read *spirits of the prophets.* 22:8 *a*NU-Text and M-Text read *am the one who heard and saw.* 22:9 *a*NU-Text and M-Text omit *For.* 22:11 *a*NU-Text and M-Text read *do right.* 22:13 *a*NU-Text and M-Text read *the First and the Last, the Beginning and the End.* 22:14 *a*NU-Text reads *wash their robes.* 22:15 *a*NU-Text and M-Text omit *But.* 22:18 *a*NU-Text and M-Text omit *For.* *b*M-Text reads *may God add.* 22:19 *a*M-Text reads *may God take away.* *b*NU-Text and M-Text read *tree of life.* 22:21 *a*NU-Text reads *with all;* M-Text reads *with all the saints.*

MORE HELPS FOR STUDY

The Parables of Jesus Christ

The Miracles of Jesus Christ

Monies, Weights, and Measures

Harmony of the Gospels

THE PARABLES OF JESUS CHRIST

Parable	Matthew	Mark	Luke
1. Lamp Under a Basket	5:14–16	4:21, 22	8:16, 17 11:33–36
2. A Wise Man Builds on Rock and a Foolish Man Builds on Sand	7:24–27		6:47–49
3. Unshrunk (New) Cloth on an Old Garment	9:16	2:21	5:36
4. New Wine in Old Wineskins	9:17	2:22	5:37, 38
5. The Sower	13:3–23	4:2–20	8:4–15
6. The Tares (Weeds)	13:24–30		
7. The Mustard Seed	13:31, 32	4:30–32	13:18, 19
8. The Leaven	13:33		13:20, 21
9. The Hidden Treasure	13:44		
10. The Pearl of Great Price	13:45, 46		
11. The Dragnet	13:47–50		
12. The Lost Sheep	18:12–14		15:3–7
13. The Unforgiving Servant	18:23–35		
14. The Workers in the Vineyard	20:1–16		
15. The Two Sons	21:28–32		
16. The Wicked Vinedressers	21:33–45	12:1–12	20:9–19
17. The Wedding Feast	22:2–14		
18. The Fig Tree	24:32–44	13:28–32	21:29–33
19. The Wise and Foolish Virgins	25:1–13		
20. The Talents	25:14–30		
21. The Growing Seed		4:26–29	
22. The Absent Householder		13:33–37	
23. The Creditor and Two Debtors			7:41–43
24. The Good Samaritan			10:30–37
25. A Friend in Need			11:5–13
26. The Rich Fool			12:16–21
27. The Faithful Servant and the Evil Servant			12:35–40
28. Faithful and Wise Steward			12:42–48
29. The Barren Fig Tree			13:6–9
30. The Great Supper			14:16–24
31. Building a Tower and a King Making War			14:25–35
32. The Lost Coin			15:8–10
33. The Lost Son			15:11–32
34. The Unjust Steward			16:1–13
35. The Rich Man and Lazarus			16:19–31
36. Unprofitable Servants			17:7–10
37. The Persistent Widow			18:1–8
38. The Pharisee and the Tax Collector			18:9–14
39. The Minas (Pounds)			19:11–27

THE MIRACLES OF JESUS CHRIST

Miracle	Matthew	Mark	Luke	John
1. Cleansing a Leper	8:2	1:40	5:12	
2. Healing a Centurion's Servant (of paralysis)	8:5		7:1	
3. Healing Peter's Mother-in-law	8:14	1:30	4:38	
4. Healing the Sick at Evening	8:16	1:32	4:40	
5. Stilling the Storm	8:23	4:35	8:22	
6. Demons Entering a Herd of Swine	8:28	5:1	8:26	
7. Healing a Paralytic	9:2	2:3	5:18	
8. Raising the Ruler's Daughter	9:18, 23	5:22, 35	8:40, 49	
9. Healing the Hemorrhaging Woman	9:20	5:25	8:43	
10. Healing Two Blind Men	9:27			
11. Curing a Demon-possessed, Mute Man	9:32			
12. Healing a Man's Withered Hand	12:9	3:1	6:6	
13. Curing a Demon-possessed, Blind and Mute Man	12:22		11:14	
14. Feeding the Five Thousand	14:13	6:30	9:10	6:1
15. Walking on the Sea	14:25	6:48		6:19
16. Healing the Gentile Woman's Daughter	15:21	7:24		
17. Feeding the Four Thousand	15:32	8:1		
18. Healing the Epileptic Boy	17:14	9:17	9:38	
19. Temple Tax in the Fish's Mouth	17:24			
20. Healing Two Blind Men	20:30	10:46	18:35	
21. Withering the Fig Tree	21:18	11:12		
22. Casting Out an Unclean Spirit		1:23	4:33	
23. Healing a Deaf Mute		7:31		
24. Healing a Blind Paralytic at Bethsaida		8:22		
25. Escape from the Hostile Multitude			4:30	
26. Draught of Fish			5:1	
27. Raising of a Widow's Son at Nain			7:11	
28. Healing the Infirm, Bent Woman			13:11	
29. Healing the Man with Dropsy			14:1	
30. Cleansing the Ten Lepers			17:11	
31. Restoring a Servant's Ear			22:51	
32. Turning Water into Wine				2:1
33. Healing the Nobleman's Son (of fever)				4:46
34. Healing an Infirm Man at Bethesda				5:1
35. Healing the Man Born Blind				9:1
36. Raising of Lazarus				11:43
37. Second Draught of Fish				21:1

MONIES, WEIGHTS, AND MEASURES

The Hebrews probably first used coins in the Persian period (500–350 B.C.). However, minting began around 700 B.C. in other nations. Prior to this, precious metals were weighted, not counted as money.

Some units appear as both measures of money and measures of weights. This comes from naming the coins after their weight. For example, the shekel was a weight long before it became the name of a coin.

It is helpful to relate biblical monies to current values. But we cannot make exact equivalents. The fluctuating value of money's purchasing power is difficult to determine in our own day. It is even harder to evaluate currencies used two- to three-thousand years ago.

Therefore, it is best to choose a value meaningful over time, such as a common laborer's daily wage. One day's wage corresponds to the ancient Jewish system (a silver shekel is four day's wages) as well as to the Greek and Roman systems (the drachma and the denarius were each coins representing a day's wage).

The monies chart below takes a current day's wage as thirty-two dollars. Though there are differences of economies and standards of living, this measure will help us apply meaningful values to the monetary units in the chart and in the biblical text.

Monies			
Unit	*Monetary Value*	*Equivalents*	*Translations*
Jewish Weights			
Talent	gold—$5,760,000[1] Silver—$384,000	3,000 shekels; 6,000 bekas	talent
Shekel	gold—$1,920 silver—$128	4 days' wages; 2 bekas; 20 gerahs	shekel
Beka	gold—$960 silver—$64	1/2 shekel; 10 gerahs	bekah
Gerah	gold—$96 silver—$6.40	1/20 shekel	gerah
Persian Coins			
Daric	gold—$1,280[2] silver—$64	2 days' wages; 1/2 Jewish silver shekel	drachma
Greek Coins			
Tetradrachma (Stater)	$128	4 drachmas	piece of money
Didrachma	$64	2 drachmas	tribute
Drachma	$32	1 day's wage	piece of silver
Lepton	$.25	1/2 of a Roman kodrantes	mite
Roman Coins			
Aureus	$800	25 denarii	
Denarius	$32	1 day's wage	denarius
Assarius	$2	1/16 of a denarius	copper coin
Kodrantes	$.50	1/4 of an assarius	penny, quadrans
[1] Value of gold is fifteen times the value of silver. [2] Value of gold is twenty times the value of silver.			

Weights

Unit	Weight	Equivalents	Translations
Jewish Weights			
Talent	c. 75 pounds for common talent, c. 150 pounds for royal talent	60 minas; 3,000 shekels	talent
Mina	1.25 pounds	50 shekels	mina
Shekel	c. .4 ounce (11.4 grams) for common shekel c. .8 ounce for royal shekel	2 bekas; 20 gerahs	shekel
Beka	c. .2 ounce (5.7 grams)	¹/₂ shekel; 10 gerahs	half a shekel
Gerah	c. .02 ounce (.57 grams)	¹/₂₀ shekel	gerah
Roman Weight			
Litra	12 ounces		pound

Measures of Length

Unit	Length	Equivalents	Translations
Day's journey	c. 20 miles		day's journey
Roman mile	4,854 feet	8 stadia	mile
Sabbath day's journey	3,637 feet	6 stadia	Sabbath day's journey
Stadion	606 feet	¹/₈ Roman mile	furlong
Rod	9 feet (10.5 feet in Ezekiel)	3 paces; 6 cubits	measuring reed, reed
Fathom	6 feet	4 cubits	fathom
Pace	3 feet	¹/₃ rod; 2 cubits	pace
Cubit	18 inches	¹/₂ pace; 2 spans	cubit
Span	9 inches	¹/₂ cubit; 3 hand-breadths	span
Handbreadth	3 inches	¹/₃ span; 4 fingers	handbreadth
Finger	.75 inches	¹/₄ handbreadth	finger

Dry Measures

Unit	Weight	Equivalents	Translations
Homer	6.52 bushels	10 ephahs	homer
Kor	6.52 bushels	1 homer; 10 ephahs	kor, measure
Lethech	3.26 bushels	¹/₂ kor	half homer
Ephah	.65 bushel, 20.8 quarts	¹/₁₀ homer	ephah
Modius	7.68 quarts		basket
Seah	7 quarts	¹/₃ ephah	measure
Omer	2.08 quarts	¹/₁₀ ephah; 1⁴/₅ kab	omer
Kab	1.16 quarts	4 logs	kab
Choenix	1 quart		measure
Xestes	1¹/₆ pints		pot
Log	.58 pint	¹/₄ kab	log

Liquid Measures

Unit	Weight	Equivalents	Translations
Kor	60 gallons	10 baths	kor
Metretes	10.2 gallons		gallons
Bath	6 gallons	6 hins	measure, bath
Hin	1 gallon	2 kabs	hin
Kab	2 quarts	4 logs	kab
Log	1 pint	1/4 kab	log

HARMONY OF THE GOSPELS

Date	Event	Location	Matthew	Mark	Luke	John
INTRODUCTIONS TO JESUS CHRIST						
	(1) Luke's Introduction				1:1–4	
	(2) Pre-fleshly state of Christ					1:1–18
	(3) Genealogy of Jesus Christ		1:1–17		3:23–38	
BIRTH, INFANCY, AND ADOLESCENCE OF JESUS AND JOHN THE BAPTIST						
7 B.C.	(1) Announcement of Birth of John	Jerusalem (Temple)			1:5–25	
7 or 6 B.C.	(2) Announcement of Birth of Jesus to the Virgin	Nazareth			1:26–38	
c. 5 B.C.	(3) Song of Elizabeth to Mary	{ Hill Country { of Judea			1:39–45	
	(4) Mary's Song of Praise				1:46–56	
5 B.C.	(5) Birth, Infancy, and Purpose for Future of John the Baptist	Judea			1:57–80	
	(6) Announcement of Jesus' Birth to Joseph	Nazareth	1:18–25			
5–4 B.C.	(7) Birth of Jesus Christ	Bethlehem	1:24, 25		2:1–7	
	(8) Proclamation by the Angels	{ Near { Bethlehem			2:8–14	
	(9) The Visit of Homage by Shepherds	Bethlehem			2:15–20	
	(10) Jesus' Circumcision	Bethlehem			2:21	
4 B.C.	(11) First Temple Visit with Acknowledgments by Simeon and Anna	Jerusalem			2:22–38	
	(12) Visit of the Wise Men	{ Jerusalem & { Bethlehem	2:1–12			
	(13) Flight into Egypt and Massacre of Innocents	{ Bethlehem, { Jerusalem & { Egypt	2:13–18			
	(14) From Egypt to Nazareth with Jesus		2:19–23		2:39	
Afterward A.D. 7–8	(15) Childhood of Jesus	Nazareth			2:40, 51	
	(16) Jesus, 12 Years Old, Visits the Temple	Jerusalem			2:41–50	
Afterward	(17) 18-Year Account of Jesus' Adolescence and Adulthood	Nazareth			2:51, 52	
TRUTHS ABOUT JOHN THE BAPTIST						
C. A.D. 25–27	(1) John's Ministry Begins	Judean Wilderness	3:1	1:1–4	3:1, 2	1:19–28
	(2) Man and Message		3:2–12	1:2–8	3:3–14	
	(3) His Picture of Jesus		3:11, 12	1:7, 8	3:15–18	1:26, 27
	(4) His Courage		14:4–12		3:19, 20	
BEGINNING OF JESUS' MINISTRY						
C. A.D. 27	(1) Jesus Baptized	Jordan River	3:13–17	1:9–11	3:21–23	1:29–34
	(2) Jesus Tempted	Wilderness	4:1–11	1:12, 13	4:1–13	
	(3) Calls First Disciples	Beyond Jordan				1:35–51
	(4) The First Miracle	Cana in Galilee				2:1–11
	(5) First Stay in Capernaum	(Capernaum is "His" city)				2:12
A.D. 27	(6) First Cleansing of the Temple	Jerusalem				2:13–22
	(7) Received at Jerusalem	Judea				2:23–25

Date	Event	Location	Matthew	Mark	Luke	John
A.D. 27	(8) Teaches Nicodemus about Second Birth	Judea				3:1–21
	(9) Co-Ministry with John	Judea				3:22–30
	(10) Leaves for Galilee	Judea	4:12	1:14	4:14	4:1–4
	(11) Samaritan Woman at Jacob's Well	Samaria				4:5–42
	(12) Returns to Galilee			1:15	4:15	4:43–45

THE GALILEAN MINISTRY OF JESUS

Date	Event	Location	Matthew	Mark	Luke	John
A.D. 27–29						
A.D. 27	(1) Healing of the Noble-man's Son	Cana				4:46–54
	(2) Rejected at Nazareth	Nazareth			4:16–30	
	(3) Moved to Capernaum	Capernaum	4:13–17			
	(4) Four Become Fishers of Men	Sea of Galilee	4:18–22	1:16–20	5:1–11	
	(5) Demoniac Healed on the Sabbath Day	Capernaum		1:21–28	4:31–37	
	(6) Peter's Mother-in-Law Cured, Plus Others	Capernaum	8:14–17	1:29–34	4:38–41	
C. A.D. 27	(7) First Preaching Tour of Galilee	Galilee	4:23–25	1:35–39	4:42–44	
	(8) Leper Healed and Response Recorded	Galilee	8:1–4	1:40–45	5:12–16	
	(9) Paralytic Healed	Capernaum	9:1–8	2:1–12	5:17–26	
	(10) Matthew's Call and Reception Held	Capernaum	9:9–13	2:13–17	5:27–32	
	(11) Disciples Defended via a Parable	Capernaum	9:14–17	2:18–22	5:33–39	
A.D. 28	(12) Goes to Jerusalem for Second Passover; Heals Lame Man	Jerusalem				5:1–47
	(13) Plucked Grain Precipitates Sabbath Controversy	En Route to Galilee	12:1–8	2:23–28	6:1–5	
	(14) Withered Hand Healed Causes Another Sabbath Controversy	Galilee	12:9–14	3:1–6	6:6–11	
	(15) Multitudes Healed	Sea of Galilee	12:15–21	3:7–12	6:17–19	
	(16) Twelve Apostles Selected After a Night of Prayer	{Near {Capernaum		3:13–19	6:12–16	
	(17) Sermon on the Mt.	{Near {Capernaum	5:1—7:29		6:20–49	
	(18) Centurion's Servant Healed	Capernaum	8:5–13		7:1–10	
	(19) Raises Widow's Son from Dead	Nain			7:11–17	
	(20) Jesus Allays John's Doubts	Galilee	11:2–19		7:18–35	
	(21) Woes Upon the Privileged		11:20–30			
	(22) A Sinful Woman Anoints Jesus	Simon's House, Capernaum			7:36–50	
	(23) Another Tour of Galilee	Galilee			8:1–3	
	(24) Jesus Accused of Blasphemy	Capernaum	12:22–37	3:20–30	11:14–23	
	(25) Jesus' Answer to a Demand for a Sign	Capernaum	12:38–45		{11:24–26, { 29–36	
	(26) Mother, Brothers Seek Audience	Capernaum	12:46–50	3:31–35	8:19–21	

Date	Event	Location	Matthew	Mark	Luke	John
A.D. 28	(27) Famous Parables of Sower, Seed, Tares, Mustard Seed, Leaven, Treasure, Pearl, Dragnet, Lamp Told	By Sea of Galilee	13:1–52	4:1–34	8:4–18	
	(28) Sea Made Serene	Sea of Galilee	8:23–27	4:35–41	8:22–25	
	(29) Gadarene Demoniac Healed	{ E. Shore of Galilee	8:28–34	5:1–20	8:26–39	
	(30) Jairus' Daughter Raised and Woman with Hemorrhage Healed		9:18–26	5:21–43	8:40–56	
	(31) Two Blind Men's Sight Restored		9:27–31			
	(32) Mute Demoniac Healed		9:32–34			
	(33) Nazareth's Second Rejection of Christ	Nazareth	13:53–58	6:1–6		
	(34) Twelve Sent Out		9:35—11:1	6:7–13	9:1–6	
	(35) Fearful Herod Beheads John	Galilee	14:1–12	6:14–29	9:7–9	
Spring A.D. 29	(36) Return of 12, Jesus Withdraws, 5000 Fed	{ Near Bethsaida	14:13–21	6:30–44	9:10–17	6:1–14
	(37) Walks on the Water	Sea of Galilee	14:22–33	6:45–52		6:15–21
	(38) Sick of Gennesaret Healed	Gennesaret	14:34–36	6:53–56		
	(39) Peak of Popularity Passes in Galilee	Capernaum				{ 6:22–71 7:1
A.D. 29	(40) Traditions Attacked		15:1–20	7:1–23		
	(41) Aborted Retirement in Phoenicia: Syro-Phoenician Healed	Phoenicia	15:21–28	7:24–30		
	(42) Afflicted Healed	Decapolis	15:29–31	7:31–37		
	(43) 4000 Fed	Decapolis	15:32–39	8:1–9		
	(44) Pharisees Increase Attack	Magdala	16:1–4	8:10–13		
	(45) Disciples' Careless-ness Condemned; Blind Man Healed		16:5–12	8:14–26		
	(46) Peter Confesses Jesus Is the Christ	{ Near Caesarea Philippi	16:13–20	8:27–30	9:18–21	
	(47) Jesus Foretells His Death	{ Caesarea Philippi	16:21–26	8:31–38	9:22–25	
	(48) Kingdom Promised		16:27, 28	9:1	9:26, 27	
	(49) The Transfiguration	{ Mountain Unnamed	17:1–13	9:2–13	9:28–36	
	(50) Epileptic Healed	{ Mt. of Trans-figuration	17:14–21	9:14–29	9:37–42	
	(51) Again Tells of Death, Resurrection	Galilee	17:22, 23	9:30–32	9:43–45	
	(52) Taxes Paid	Capernaum	17:24–27			
	(53) Disciples Contend About Greatness; Jesus Defines; also Patience, Loyalty, Forgiveness	Capernaum	18:1–35	9:33–50	9:46–62	
	(54) Jesus Rejects Brothers' Advice	Galilee				7:2–9
c. Sept. A.D. 29	(55) Galilee Departure and Samaritan Rejection		19:1		9:51–56	7:10
	(56) Cost of Discipleship		8:18–22		9:57–62	

LAST JUDEAN AND PEREAN MINISTRY OF JESUS

Date	Event	Location	Matthew	Mark	Luke	John
A.D. 29–30						
Oct. A.D.29	(1) Feast of Tabernacles	Jerusalem				7:2, 10–52
	(2) Forgiveness of Adulteress	Jerusalem				{ 7:53— 8:11

Date	Event	Location	Matthew	Mark	Luke	John
A.D. 29	(3) Christ—the Light of the World	Jerusalem				8:12–20
	(4) Pharisees Can't Meet the Prophecy Thus Try to Destroy the Prophet	{Jerusalem—Temple				8:21–59
	(5) Man Born Blind Healed; Following Consequences	Jerusalem				9:1–41
	(6) Parable of the Good Shepherd	Jerusalem				10:1–21
	(7) The Service of the Seventy	{Probably Judea				10:1–24
	(8) Lawyer Hears the Story of the Good Samaritan	Judea (?)			10:25–37	
	(9) The Hospitality of Martha and Mary	Bethany			10:38–42	
	(10) Another Lesson on Prayer	Judea (?)			11:1–13	
	(11) Accused of Connection with Beelzebub				11:14–36	
	(12) Judgment Against Lawyers and Pharisees				11:37–54	
	(13) Jesus Deals with Hypocrisy, Covetousness, Worry, and Alertness				12:1–59	
	(14) Repent or Perish				13:1–5	
	(15) Barren Fig Tree				13:6–9	
	(16) Crippled Woman Healed on Sabbath				13:10–17	
	(17) Parables of Mustard Seed and Leaven	{Probably Perea			13:18–21	
Winter A.D. 29	(18) Feast of Dedication	Jerusalem				10:22–39
	(19) Withdrawal Beyond Jordan					10:40–42
	(20) Begins Teaching Return to Jerusalem with Special Words About Herod	Perea			13:22–35	
	(21) Meal with a Pharisee Ruler Occasions Healing Man with Dropsy; Parables of Ox, Best Places, and Great Supper				14:1–24	
	(22) Demands of Discipleship	Perea			14:25–35	
	(23) Parables of Lost Sheep, Coin, Son				15:1–32	
	(24) Parables of Unjust Steward, Rich Man and Lazarus				16:1–31	
	(25) Lessons on Service, Faith, Influence				17:1–10	
	(26) Resurrection of Lazarus	{Perea to Bethany				11:1–44
	(27) Reaction to It: Withdrawal of Jesus					11:45–54
A.D. 30	(28) Begins Last Journey to Jerusalem via Samaria & Galilee	{Samaria, Galilee			17:11	
	(29) Heals Ten Lepers				17:12–19	
	(30) Lessons on the Coming Kingdom				17:20–37	
	(31) Parables: Persistent Widow, Pharisee and Tax Collector				18:1–14	
	(32) Doctrine on Divorce		19:1–12	10:1–12		

Date	Event	Location	Matthew	Mark	Luke	John
A.D. 30	(33) Jesus Blesses Children: Objections	Perea	19:13–15	10:13–16	18:15–17	
	(34) Rich Young Ruler	Perea	19:16–30	10:17–31	18:18–30	
	(35) Laborers of the 11th Hour		20:1–16			
	(36) Foretells Death and Resurrection	{Near {Jordan	20:17–19	10:32–34	18:31–34	
	(37) Ambition of James and John		20:20–28	10:35–45		
	(38) Blind Bartimaeus Healed	Jericho		10:46–52	18:35–43	
	(39) Interview with Zacchaeus	Jericho			19:1–10	
	(40) Parable: the Minas	Jericho			19:11–27	
	(41) Returns to Home of Mary and Martha	Bethany				{11:55— { 12:1
	(42) Plot to Kill Lazarus	Bethany				12:9–11

JESUS' FINAL WEEK OF WORK AT JERUSALEM

Date	Event	Location	Matthew	Mark	Luke	John
Spring **A.D. 30**						
Sunday	(1) Triumphal Entry	Bethany, Jerusalem, Bethany	21:1–9	11:1–11	19:28–44	12:12–19
Monday	(2) Fig Tree Cursed and Temple Cleansed	{Bethany to {Jerusalem	21:10–19	11:12–18	19:45–48	
	(3) The Attraction of Sacrifice	Jerusalem				12:20–50
Tuesday	(4) Withered Fig Tree Testifies	{Bethany to {Jerusalem	21:20–22	11:19–26		
	(5) Sanhedrin Challenges Jesus. Answered by Parables: Two Sons, Wicked Vinedressers and Marriage Feast	Jerusalem	{21:23— { 22:14	{11:27— { 12:12	20:1–19	
	(6) Tribute to Caesar	Jerusalem	22:15–22	12:13–17	20:20–26	
	(7) Sadducees Question the Resurrection	Jerusalem	22:23–33	12:18–27	20:27–40	
	(8) Pharisees Question Commandments	Jerusalem	22:34–40	12:28–34		
	(9) Jesus and David	Jerusalem	22:41–46	12:35–37	20:41–44	
	(10) Jesus' Last Sermon	Jerusalem	23:1–39	12:38–40	20:45–47	
	(11) Widow's Mite	Jerusalem		12:41–44	21:1–4	
	(12) Jesus Tells of the Future	Mt. Olives	24:1–51	13:1–37	21:5–36	
	(13) Parables: Ten Virgins, Talents, The Day of Judgment	Mt. Olives	25:1–46			
	(14) Jesus Tells Date of Crucifixion		26:1–5	14:1, 2	22:1, 2	
	(15) Anointing by Mary at Simon's Feast	Bethany	26:6–13	14:3–9		12:2–8
	(16) Judas Contracts the Betrayal		26:14–16	14:10, 11	22:3–6	
Thursday	(17) Preparation for the Passover	Jerusalem	26:17–19	14:12–16	22:7–13	
Thursday **P.M.**	(18) Passover Eaten, Jealousy Rebuked	Jerusalem	26:20	14:17	{22:14–16, { 24–30	
	(19) Feet Washed	Upper Room				13:1–20
	(20) Judas Revealed, Defects	Upper Room	26:21–25	14:18–21	22:21–23	13:21–30
	(21) Jesus Warns About Further Desertion; Cries of Loyalty	Upper Room	26:31–35	14:27–31	22:31–38	13:31–38
	(22) Institution of the Lord's Supper	Upper Room	26:26–29	14:22–25	22:17–20	

Date	Event	Location	Matthew	Mark	Luke	John
Thursday P.M.	(23) Last Speech to the Apostles and Intercessory Prayer	Jerusalem				{ 14:1— 17:26
Thursday-Friday	(24) The Grief of Gethsemane	Mt. of Olives	{ 26:30, 36–46	{ 14:26, 32–42	22:39–46	18:1
Friday	(25) Betrayal, Arrest, Desertion	Gethsemane	26:47–56	14:43–52	22:47–53	18:2–12
	(26) First Examined by Annas	Jerusalem				{ 18:12–14, 19–23
	(27) Trial by Caiaphas and Council; Following Indignities	Jerusalem	{ 26:57, 59–68	{ 14:53, 55–65	{ 22:54, 63–65	18:24
	(28) Peter's Triple Denial	Jerusalem	{ 26:58, 69–75	{ 14:54, 66–72	22:54–62	{ 18:15–18, 25–27
	(29) Condemnation by the Council	Jerusalem	27:1	15:1	22:66–71	
	(30) Suicide of Judas	Jerusalem	27:3–10			
	(31) First Appearance Before Pilate	Jerusalem	{ 27:2, 11–14	15:1–5	23:1–7	18:28–38
	(32) Jesus Before Herod	Jerusalem			23:6–12	
	(33) Second Appearance Before Pilate	Jerusalem	27:15–26	15:6–15	23:13–25	{ 18:39— 19:16
	(34) Mockery by Roman Soldiers	Jerusalem	27:27–30	15:16–19		
	(35) Led to Golgotha	Jerusalem	27:31–34	15:20–23	23:26–33	19:16, 17
	(36) 6 Events of First 3 Hours on Cross	Calvary	27:35–44	15:24–32	23:33–43	19:18–27
	(37) Last 3 Hours on Cross	Calvary	27:45–50	15:33–37	23:44–46	19:28–30
	(38) Events Attending Jesus' Death		27:51–56	15:38–41	{ 23:45, 47–49	
	(39) Burial of Jesus	Jerusalem	27:57–60	15:42–46	23:50–54	19:31–42
Friday-Saturday	(40) Tomb Sealed	Jerusalem	27:61–66		23:55, 56	
	(41) Women Watch	Jerusalem		15:47		

THE RESURRECTION THROUGH THE ASCENSION

Date	Event	Location	Matthew	Mark	Luke	John
A.D. 30						
Dawn of First Day (Sunday, "Lord's Day")	(1) Women Visit the Tomb	Near Jerusalem	28:1–10	16:1–8	24:1–11	
	(2) Peter and John See the Empty Tomb				24:12	20:1–10
	(3) Jesus' Appearance to Mary Magdalene	Jerusalem		16:9–11		20:11–18
	(4) Jesus' Appearance to the Other Women	Jerusalem	28:9, 10			
	(5) Guards' Report of the Resurrection		28:11–15			
Sunday Afternoon	(6) Jesus' Appearance to Two Disciples on Way to Emmaus			16:12, 13	24:13–35	
Late Sunday	(7) Jesus' Appearance to Ten Disciples Without Thomas	Jerusalem			24:36–43	20:19–25
One Week Later	(8) Appearance to Disciples with Thomas	Jerusalem				20:26–31
During 40 Days until Ascension	(9) Jesus' Appearance to Seven Disciples by Sea of Galilee	Galilee				21:1–25
	(10) Great Commission		28:16–20	16:14–18	24:44–49	
	(11) The Ascension	Mt. Olivet		16:19, 20	24:50–53	